A DICTIONARY OF MODERN WRITTEN ARABIC

HANS WEHR

A DICTIONARY OF MODERN WRITTEN ARABIC

EDITED BY

J MILTON COWAN

THIRD EDITION

Spoken Language Services, Inc.

Library of Congress Cataloging in Publication Data

Wehr, Hans (Date)
A dictionary of modern written Arabic.

"An enlarged and improved version of 'Arabisches Wörterbuch für die Schriftsprache der Gegenwart' and includes the contents of the 'Supplement zum Arabischen Wörterbuch für die Schriftsprache der Gegenwart.' "
1. Arabic language--Dictionaries--English.
I. Cowan, J Milton. II. Title.
[PJ6640.W43 1976] 492'.7'321 75-24236
ISBN 0-87950-001-8

Spoken Language Services, Inc.
P.O. Box 783
Ithaca, New York 14850

Preface

Shortly after the publication of Professor Hans Wehr's *Arabisches Wörterbuch für die Schriftsprache der Gegenwart* in 1952, the Committee on Language Programs of the American Council of Learned Societies recognized its excellence and began to explore means of providing an up-to-date English edition. Professor Wehr and I readily reached agreement on a plan to translate, edit, and enlarge the dictionary. This task was considerably lightened and hastened by generous financial support from the American Council of Learned Societies, the Arabian American Oil Company, and Cornell University.

This dictionary will be welcome not only to English and American users, but to orientalists throughout the world who are more at home with English than with German. It is more accurate and much more comprehensive than the original version, which was produced under extremely unfavorable conditions in Germany during the late war years and the early postwar period.

Ithaca, New York J. MILTON COWAN
November 1960

Preface to The Pocket-Book Edition

In order to meet the enormous increase of interest in Arabic brought about by political, economic and social developments of the past decade, we have now published our 3rd Revised Edition of *A Dictionary of Modern Written Arabic* in this handy, comprehensive and unabridged version.

Münster HANS WEHR
Ithaca, New York J. MILTON COWAN
February 1976

Introduction

This dictionary presents the vocabulary and phraseology of modern written Arabic. It is based on the form of the language which, throughout the Arab world from Iraq to Morocco, is found in the prose of books, newspapers, periodicals, and letters. This form is also employed in formal public address, over radio and television, and in religious ceremonial. The dictionary will be most useful to those working with writings that have appeared since the turn of the century.

The morphology and syntax of written Arabic are essentially the same in all Arab countries. Vocabulary differences are limited mainly to the domain of specialized vocabulary. Thus the written language continues, as it has done throughout centuries of the past, to ensure the linguistic unity of the Arab world. It provides a medium of communication over the vast geographical area whose numerous and widely diverse local dialects it transcends. Indeed, it gives the Arab people of many countries a sense of identity and an awareness of their common cultural heritage.

Two powerful and conflicting forces have affected the development of the modern Arabic lexicon. A reform movement originating toward the end of the last century in Syria and Lebanon has reawakened and popularized the old conviction of educated Arabs that the ancient *ʿarabīya* of pre-Islamic times, which became the classical form of the language in the early centuries of Islam, is better and more correct than any later form. Proponents of this puristic doctrine have held that new vocabulary must be derived exclusively in accordance with ancient models or by semantic extension of older forms. They have insisted on the replacement of all foreign loanwords with purely Arabic forms and expressions. The purists have had considerable influence on the development of modern literary Arabic although there has been widespread protest against their extreme point of view. At the same time and under the increasing influence of Western civilization, Arab writers and journalists have had to deal with a host of new concepts and ideas previously alien to the Arab way of life. As actual usage demonstrates, the purists have been unable to cope with the sheer bulk of new linguistic material which has had to be incorporated into the language to make it current with advances in world knowledge. The result is seen in the tendency of many writers, especially in the fields of science and technology, simply to adopt foreign words from the European languages. Many common, everyday expressions from the various colloquial dialects have also found their way into written expression.

From its inception, this dictionary has been compiled on scientific descriptive principles. It contains only words and expressions which were found in context during the course of wide reading in literature of every kind or which, on the basis of other evidence, can be shown to be unquestionably a part of the present-day vocabulary. It is a faithful record of the language as attested by usage rather than a normative presentation of what theoretically ought to occur. Consequently, it not only lists classical words and phrases of elegant rhetorical style side by side with new coinages that conform to the demands of the purists, but it also contains neologisms, loan translations, foreign loans, and colloquialisms which may not be to the linguistic taste of many educated Arabs. But since they occur in the corpus of materials on which the dictionary is based, they are included here.

A number of special problems confront the lexicographer dealing with present-day Arabic. Since for many fields of knowledge, especially those which have developed outside the Arab world, no generally accepted terminology has yet emerged, it is evident that a practical dictionary can only approximate the degree of completeness found in comparable dictionaries of Western languages. Local terminology, especially for many public institutions, offices, titles, and administrative affairs, has developed in the several Arab countries. Although the dictionary is based mainly on usage in the countries bordering on the eastern Mediterranean, local official and administrative terms have been included for all Arab countries, but not with equal thoroughness. Colloquialisms and dialect expressions that have gained currency in written form also vary from country to country. Certainly no attempt at completeness can be made here, and the user working with materials having a marked regional flavor will be well advised to refer to an appropriate dialect dictionary or glossary. As a rule, items derived from local dialects or limited to local use have been so designated with appropriate abbreviations.

A normalized journalistic style has evolved for factual reporting of news or discussion of matters of political and topical interest over the radio and in the press. This style, which often betrays Western influences, is remarkably uniform throughout the Arab world. It reaches large sections of the population daily and constitutes to them almost the only stylistic norm. Its vocabulary is relatively small and fairly standardized, hence easily covered in a dictionary.

The vocabulary of scientific and technological writings, on the other hand, is by no means standardized. The impact of Western civilization has confronted the Arab world with the serious linguistic problem of expressing a vast and ever-increasing number of new concepts for which no words in Arabic exist. The creation of a scientific and technological terminology is still a major intellectual challenge. Reluctance to borrow wholesale from European languages has spurred efforts to coin terms according to productive Arabic patterns. In recent decades innumerable such words have been suggested in various periodicals and in special publications. Relatively few of these have gained acceptance in common usage. Specialists in all fields keep coining new terms that are either not understood by other specialists in the same field or are rejected in favor of other, equally short-lived, private fabrications.

The Academy of the Arabic Language in Cairo especially, the Damascus Academy, and, to a lesser extent, the Iraqi Academy have produced and continue to publish vast numbers of technical terms for almost all fields of knowledge. The academies have, however, greatly underestimated the difficulties of artificial regulation of a language. The problem lies not so much in inventing terms as it does in assuring that they gain acceptance. In some instances neologisms have quickly become part of the stock of the language; among these, fortunately, are a large number of the terms proposed by academies or by professional specialists. However, in many fields, such as modern linguistics, existential philosophy, or nuclear physics, it is still not possible for professional people from the different Arab states to discuss details of their discipline in Arabic. The situation is further complicated by the fact that the purists and the academies demand the translation into Arabic even of those Greek and Latin technical terms which make possible international understanding among specialists. Thus while considerable progress has been made in recent decades toward the standardization of Arabic terminology, several technical terms which all fit one definition may still be current, or a given scientific term may have different meanings for different experts.

Those technical terms which appear with considerable frequency in published works, or which are familiar to specialists in various fields and are considered by them to be standardized terminology, presented no particular problem. Nevertheless it has not always been possible to ascertain the terms in general acceptance with the experts of merely one country, let alone those of all. Doubtful cases are entered and marked with a special symbol. A descriptive dictionary such as this has no room for the innumerable academic coinages which experience has shown are by no means assured of adoption. Only those that are attested in the literature have been included.

Classicisms are a further special problem. Arab authors, steeped in classical tradition, can and do frequently draw upon words which were already archaic in the Middle Ages. The use of classical patterns is by no means limited to belles-lettres. Archaisms may crop up in the middle of a spirited newspaper article. Wherever an aesthetic or rhetorical effect is intended, wherever the language aims more at expressiveness than at imparting information, authors tend to weave in ancient Arabic and classical idioms. They are artistic and stylistic devices of the first order. They awaken in the reader images from memorized passages of ancient literature and contribute to his aesthetic enjoyment. Quotations from the Koran or from classical literature, whose origins and connotations may well elude the Western reader, are readily recognized by Arabs who have had a traditional education and who have memorized a wealth of ancient sources. In former years many writers strove to display their erudition by citing lexical rarities culled from ancient dictionaries and collections of synonyms. As often as not the author had to explain such *nawādir* in footnotes, since nobody else would understand them. This pedantic mannerism is going out of fashion and there is a trend in more recent literature toward smoothness and readability in style. Nevertheless it is clear from the foregoing that it is not possible to make a sharp distinction between living and obsolete usage. All archaic words found in the source material have, therefore, been included in this dictionary, even though it is sometimes evident that they no longer form a part of the living lexicon and are used only by a small group of well-read literary connoisseurs. Such included forms are but a small sample of what the user is likely to encounter in the writings of a few modern authors; the impossibility of including the entire ancient vocabulary is obvious. The user who encounters an old Arabic word which he does not understand will have to consult a lexicon of the *ʿarabīya*. Finally, some modern authors will occasionally take great liberties with older words, so that even highly educated Arabs are unable to understand the sense of certain passages. Items of this kind have not been entered. They would contribute nothing to a dictionary whose scope did not permit inclusion of source references.

The vocabulary of modern Arabic, then, is by no means standardized, its scope in times difficult to delimit. These results emerge from the very character of modern Arabic — a written language, powerfully influenced by traditional norms, which nevertheless is required to express a multitude of new foreign concepts, not for one country only, but for many distributed over a vast geographical area. Arabic phonology, morphology, and syntax have remained relatively unchanged from earliest times, as has much of the vocabulary. Here traditional adherence to ancient linguistic norms and to the models of classical literature, especially the Koran, has had the effect of preserving the language intact over the centuries. But as vocabulary and phraseology must adapt to the new and ever-changing requirements of external circumstances, these are more prone to change. Strictly speaking, every epoch of Arab history has had its own peculiar vocabulary, which should be set forth in a separate dictionary. But as we have seen, the vocabulary of modern Arabic confronts the lexicographer who aims at completeness with more than a fair share of problems and difficulties.

In the presentation of the entries in the dictionary, homonymous roots are given separately in only a few especially clear instances. The arrangement of word entries under a given root does not necessarily imply etymological relationship. Consistent separation of such roots was dispensed with because the user of a practical dictionary of modern Arabic will not generally be concerned with Semitic etymology. In conformity with the practice customary in bilingual dictionaries of modern European languages, where the material is treated in purely synchronic fashion, the origin of older loanwords and foreign terms is not indicated. For recent loans, however, the source and the foreign word are usually given. Personal names are generally omitted, but large numbers of geographical names are included; the *nisba* adjectives of these can be formed at will, hence are not entered unless some peculiarity such as a broken plural is involved. In transliteration, while the ending of *nisba* adjectives regularly appears as *-ī* (e.g., *janūbī, dirāsī, makkī*), the same ending is shown as *-īy* for nominal forms of roots with a weak third radical, i.e., where the third radical is contained in the ending (e.g., *qaṣīy, ṣabīy, maḥmīy, mabnīy*). This distinction, not present in Arabic script, may prove valuable to the user of the dictionary. Because of a distinction which retains importance in quantitative metrics, the third person singular masculine suffix is transcribed with a long vowel (*-hū, -hī*) following short syllables and with a short vowel (*-hu, -hi*) after long syllables. In any bilingual dictionary, the listing of isolated words with one or more isolated translations is, strictly speaking, an inadmissible abstraction. In order to provide the syntactical information to be expected in a dictionary of this size, a liberal selection of idiomatic phrases and sentences illustrating usage has been added. Symbols showing the accusative and prepositional government of verbs are also supplied. Synonyms and translations have been included in large numbers in order to delineate as accurately as possible the semantic ranges within which a given entry can be used.

The material for the dictionary was gathered in several stages. The major portion was collected between 1940 and 1944 with the co-operation of several German orientalists. The entire work was set in type, but only one set of galleys survived the war. The author resumed the collection of material in the years 1946 through 1948 and added a considerable number of entries. The German edition of the dictionary, *Arabisches Wörterbuch für die Schriftsprache der Gegenwart*, which appeared in 1952, was based on a corpus of approximately 45,000 slips containing citations from Arabic sources. The primary source materials consisted of selected works by Ṭāhā Ḥusain, Muḥammad Ḥusain Haikal, Taufīq al-Ḥakīm, Maḥmūd Taimūr, al-Manfalūṭī, Jubrān Kalīl Jubrān, and Amīn ar-Raiḥānī. Further, numerous Egyptian newspapers and periodicals, the Egyptian state almanac, *taqwīm miṣr*, for 1935 and its Iraqi counterpart, *dalīl al-ʿirāq*, for 1937, as well as a number of specialized Egyptian handbooks were thoroughly sifted. The secondary sources used in preparation of the German edition were the first edition of Léon Bercher's *Lexique arabe-français* (1938), which provides material from the Tunisian press in the form of a supplement to J. B. Belot's *Vocabulaire arabe-français*, G. S. Colin's *Pour lire la presse arabe* (1937), the third edition of E. A. Elias' comprehensive *Modern Dictionary Arabic-English* (1929), and the glossary of the modern Arabic chrestomathy by C. V. Odé-Vassilieva (1929). Items in the secondary sources for which there were attestations in the primary sources were, of course, included. All other items in the secondary sources were carefully worked over, in part with the help of Dr. Tahir Khemiri. Words known to him, or already included in older dictionaries, were incorporated. Apart from the primary and secondary sources, the author had, of course, to consult a number of reference works in European languages, encyclopedias, lexicons, glossaries, technical dictionaries, and specialized literature on the most diverse subjects in order to ascertain the correct translation of many technical terms. For older Arabic forms, the available indices and collections of Arabic terminology in the fields of religion (both Islam and Eastern Church), jurisprudence, philosophy, Arabic grammar, botany, and others were very helpful. These collections were, however, not simply accepted and incorporated en bloc into the dictionary, but used only to sharpen the definition of terms in the modern meanings actually attested in the primary source materials.

After publication of the German edition the author continued collecting and presented new material, together with corrections of the main work, in *Supplement zum arabischen Wörterbuch für die Schriftsprache der Gegenwart*, which appeared in 1959. The *Supplement* contains the results of extensive collection from the writings of ʿAbdassalām al-ʿUjailī, Mīkā'īl Nuʿaima, and Karam Malḥam Karam, from newspapers and periodicals of all Arab countries, as well as from Syrian and Lebanese textbooks and specialized literature. In the postwar years several lexicographical works dealing with modern Arabic became available to the author: the second edition of Bercher (1944), the fourth edition of Elias (1947), D. Neustadt and P. Schusser's Arabic-Hebrew dictionary, *Millōn ʿArabī-ʿIbrī* (1947), Charles Pellat's *L'arabe vivant* (1952), and C. K. Baranov's comprehensive Arabic-Russian dictionary, *Arabsko-Russkiy Slovar* (1957). In preparing the *Supplement*, the author compared these with his own work but was reluctant to incorporate items which he could not find attested in context, and which would merely increase the number of entries derived from secondary sources.

The author is indebted to Dr. Andreas Jacobi and Mr. Heinrich Becker who, until they were called up for military service in 1943, rendered valuable assistance in collecting and collating the vast materials of the German edition and in preparing the manuscript. A considerable amount of material was contributed by a number of Arabists. The author wishes to express his gratitude for such contributions to Prof. Werner Caskel, Dr. Hans Kindermann, Dr. Hedwig Klein, Dr. Kurt Munzel, Prof. Annemarie Schimmel, Dr. Richard Schmidt, and especially to Prof. Wolfram von Soden, who contributed a large amount of excellent material. I am deeply grateful to Dr. Munzel, who contributed many entries from newspapers of the postwar period and likewise to his colleague Dr. Muḥammad Safṭī. I appreciate having been able to discuss many difficult items with them. The assistance of Dr. Tahir Khemiri was especially useful. He contributed 1,500 very valuable items and, until 1944, his advice to the author during the collection and sifting of material shed light upon many dubious cases. Prof. Anton Spitaler likewise provided valuable observations and greatly appreciated advice. Contributions to the *Supplement* were supplied by Dr. Eberhard Kuhnt, Dr. Götz Schregle, and Mr. Karl Stowasser. Moreover, in the course of two visits to a number of Arab countries, many Arab contributors, students, scholars, writers, and professional people too numerous to mention generously provided useful information and counsel. Here, as in the prefaces to the German edition of the dictionary and the *Supplement*, the author wishes to express his sincere thanks to all those who have contributed to the success of this undertaking.

This English edition includes all the material contained in the German edition of the dictionary and in the *Supplement*, as well as a number of additions and corrections the need for which became obvious only after the publication of the *Supplement*. Additions have been inserted in the proof almost up to the present time. It was therefore possible to include a number of contributions made by Dr. Walter Jesser in Alexandria. The number of cross-references has been considerably increased. A new type font was introduced for the Arabic. The second edition of Webster's New International Dictionary was used as a standard reference for spelling and for certain definitions. On the suggestion of the editor, three changes were made in the system of transliteration used in the German edition, namely, *j* for ج, *ḵ* for خ, and *ḡ* for غ. Also, following his preference, proper names were transliterated without capital letters, since there is no capitalization in Arabic script. The author followed a suggestion made by Prof. Charles A. Ferguson in his review of the dictionary (Language 30: 174, 1954) to transcribe feminine endings of roots having a weak third radical (اة-) with the pausal form *-āh* instead of *-āt*. Also following Dr. Ferguson's advice, the author has transcribed many more foreign words than in the German edition. The letters *e*, *ē*, *ə*, *o*, *ō*, *g*, *v*, and *p*, which have no counterpart in classical Arabic, have been added. The system of transcription for Arabic words throughout the dictionary is simply a transliteration of the Arabic script. For foreign words and Arabic dialect words, however, the usual transliteration of the Arabic is inadequate to indicate the pronunciation. In order to avoid discrepancy between spelling and pronunciation, the author, in his German edition, would often refrain from giving any transcription at all, but merely enter the foreign word as a rough guide to pronunciation. In the present edition practically all foreign words have been transcribed (e.g., *diblōmāsī*, *helikoptar*, *vīzā*, *vētō*) with the help of the added letters. Arab students at the University of Münster were consulted for the approximately correct pronunciation. Nevertheless, in many instances the foreign source word is also entered because pronunciation varies considerably from speaker to speaker, depending on the dialect and the degree of assimilation. One other deviation from a strict transliteration of the Arabic was made for certain foreign words in order to provide a closer approximation to the usual pronunciation. In writing European words with Arabic letters, ا, و, ى are, contrary to regular practice in Arabic, frequently used to indicate short vowels. Where this is the case, we have transcribed accordingly (e.g., اوتوماتيكى *otomātīkī*, دانمارك *danmark*).

Finally, the author wishes to express his sincere gratitude to the editor, Prof. J Milton Cowan, thanks to whose initiative and energy this English edition can now be presented to the public. His generous expenditure of time and effort on this project has been greatly appreciated by all involved. To Theodora Ronayne, who performed the exacting task of preparing a meticulously accurate typescript, thereby considerably lightening our labors, we are indeed grateful. Professor Cowan joins me in recording our special thanks to Mr. Karl Stowasser, whose quite remarkable command of the three languages involved and whose unusual abilities as a lexicographer proved indispensable. He has devoted his untiring efforts to this enterprise for the past four years, co-ordinating the work of editor and author across the Atlantic. The bulk of the translation was completed in 1957–1958, while he was in Ithaca. During the past two years in Münster he has completed the incorporation of the *Supplement* into the body of the dictionary and assisted the author in seeing the work through the press.

* * *

The following paragraphs describe the arrangement of entries and explain the use of symbols and abbreviations:

Arabic words are arranged according to Arabic roots. Foreign words are listed in straight alphabetical order by the letters of the word (cf. باريس *bāris* Paris, كادر *kādir* cadre). Arabicized loanwords, if they clearly fit under the roots, are entered both ways, often with the root entry giving a reference to the alphabetical listing (cf. قانون *qānūn* law, نيزك *naizak* spear).

Two or more homonymous roots may be entered as separate items, including foreign words treated as Arabic forms (e.g., كريم *karīm* under the Arabic root ¹كرم and ²كريم, the French word *crème*; cf. also the consonant combination *k-r-k*). In order to indicate to the reader that the same order of letters occurs more than once and that he should not confine his search to the first listing, each entry is preceded by a small raised numeral (cf. برد, مر).

Under a given root the sequence of entries is as follows. The verb in the perfect of the base stem, if it exists, comes first with the transliteration indicating the voweling. It is followed by the vowel of the imperfect and, in parentheses, the verbal nouns or *maṣādir*. Then come the derived stems, indicated by boldface Roman numerals II through X. For Arab users unaccustomed to this designation generally used by Western orientalists, the corresponding stem forms are: II فعل *fa''ala*, III فاعل *fā'ala*, IV افعل *af'ala*, V تفعل *tafa''ala*, VI تفاعل *tafā'ala*, VII انفعل *infa'ala*, VIII افتعل *ifta'ala*, IX افعل *if'alla*, X استفعل *istaf'ala*. Wherever there is any irregularity, for the rare stems XI through XV, and for the derived stems of quadriliteral verbs the Arabic form is entered and transliterated (cf. محو VII, وحد VIII, حدب XII, سلطح III). Then come nominal forms arranged according to their length. Verbal nouns of the stems II through X and all active and passive participles follow at the end. The latter are listed as separate items only when their meaning is not immediately obvious from the verb, particularly where a substantival or adjectival translation is possible (cf. حاجب *ḥājib* under حجب, ساحل *sāḥil* under سحل). The sequence under a given root is not determined by historical considerations. Thus, a verb derived from a foreign word is placed at the head of the entire section (cf. اقلم *aqlama*, ²ترك II).

Essentially synonymous definitions are separated by commas. A semicolon marks the beginning of a definition in a different semantic range.

The syntactic markings accompanying the definitions of a verb are ه for the accusative of a person, ه for the accusative of a thing, ها for the feminine of animate beings, هم for a group of persons. It should be noted that the Arabic included in parentheses is to be read from right to left even if separated by the word "or" (cf. رضى, بوح). Verb objects in English are expressed by s.o. (someone) and s.th. (something), the reflexive by o.s. (oneself).

A dash occurring within a section indicates that the following form of a plural or of a verbal noun, or in some instances the introduction of a new voweling of the main entry, holds for all following meanings in the section even if these are not synonymous and are separated by semicolons. This dash invalidates all previously given verbal nouns, imperfect vowels, plurals, and other data qualifying the main entry. It indicates that all following definitions apply only to this latest sub-entry (cf. خفق *ḵafaqa*, عدل *'adala*).

In the transcription, which indicates the voweling of the unpointed Arabic, nouns are given in pausal form without *tanwīn*. Only nouns derived from verbs with a weak third radical are transcribed with nunnation (e.g., قاض *qāḍin*, مقتضى *muqtaḍan*, مأتى *ma'tan* in contrast with بشرى *bušrā*).

A raised ² following the transcription of a noun indicates that it is a diptote. This indication is often omitted from Western geographical terms and other recent non-Arabic proper names because the inflected ending is practically never pronounced and the marking would have only theoretical value (cf. استوكهولم *istokholm*, ابريل *abrīl*).

The symbol ○ precedes newly coined technical terms, chiefly in the fields of technology, which were repeatedly found in context but whose general acceptance among specialists could not be established with certainty (cf. تلفاز *tilfāz* television set, حدس *ḥads* intuition, محر *miḥarr* heating installation).

The symbol □ precedes those dialect words for which the Arabic spelling suggests a colloquial pronunciation (cf. حداف *ḥaddāf*, ²حدق II).

Dialect words are marked with abbreviations in lower-case letters (e.g., *syr.*, *leb.*, *saud.-ar.*, etc.). These are also used to indicate words which were found only in the sources of a particular area. This does not necessarily mean that a word or meaning is confined to that area (cf. جارور *jārūr*, بصة *baṣṣa*, شيلمان *šilmān*).

The same abbreviations, but with capital letters, mark entries as the generally accepted technical terms or the official designations for public offices, institutions, administrative departments, and the like, of the country in question (cf. مجلس *majlis*, محكمة *maḥkama*).

The abbreviation *Isl. Law* marks the traditional terminology of Islamic *fiqh* (cf. حدث *ḥadaṯ*, لعان *li'ān*, متعة *mut'a*), as distinguished from the technical terms of modern jurisprudence which are characterized by the abbreviation *jur.* (cf. عمدى *'amdī*, تلبس *talabbus*). For other abbreviated labels see List of Abbreviations below.

Elatives of the form *af'alu* are translated throughout with the English comparative because this most often fits the meaning. The reader should bear in mind, however, that in certain contexts they will best be rendered either with the positive or the superlative.

The heavy vertical stroke | terminates the definitions under an entry. It is followed by phrases, idioms, and sentences which illustrate the phraseological and syntactic use of that entry. These did not have to be transcribed in full because it has been necessary to assume an elementary knowledge of Arabic morphology and syntax on the part of the user, without which it is not possible to use a dictionary arranged according to roots. Consequently, no transcription is given after the vertical stroke for:

1 the entry itself, but it is abbreviated wherever it is part of a genitive compound (e.g., *ṣ. al-ma'ālī* under *ṣāḥib*, *ḥusn al-u.* under *uḥdūṯa*);

2 nouns whose Arabic spelling is relatively unambiguous (e.g., دار, آثار, ساعة, فائدة);

3 words known from elementary grammar, such as pronouns, negations, and prepositions the third person perfect of the verb type *fa'ala*, occasionally also the definite article;

4 frequent nominal types, such as:

a) the verbal nouns (*maṣādir*) of the derived stems II and VII—X:
تفعيل *taf'īl*, انفعال *infi'āl*, افتعال *ifti'āl*, افعلال *if'ilāl*, استفعال *istif'āl*;

b) the active and passive participles of the basic verb stem:
فاعل *fā'il*, فاعلة *fā'ila*, and مفعول *maf'ūl*, مفعولة *maf'ūla*;

c) the nominal types فعيل *fa'īl*, فعيلة *fa'īla*, فعال *fi'āl*, and فعول *fu'ūl* (also as a plural); فعالة *fi'āla* and فعولة *fu'ūla* as well as افعل *af'al*;

d) the plural forms افعال *af'āl*, افعلاء *af'ilā'*, فعالل *fa'ālil*, افاعل *afā'il*, مفاعل *mafā'il*, فعائل *fa'ā'il*, فعاعل *fa'ā'il*, فعاليل *fa'ālīl*, افاعيل *afā'īl*, تفاعيل *tafā'īl*, مفاعيل *mafā'īl*, فعاللة *fa'ālila*.

All other possible vowelings are transcribed (e.g., *if'āl*, *fa''āl*, *fu'ail*, *fa'ūl*, *af'ul*, *fā'al*). Words with weak radicals belonging in the form types listed above are also transcribed wherever any uncertainty about the form might arise (cf. راغ *rāğin* under رغو, زيت الخروع under زيت *zait*, المسجد الاقصى under مسجد *masjid*).

In transcription, two nouns forming a genitive compound are treated as a unit. They are transcribed as noun — definite article — noun, with the entry word abbreviated (cf. under صاحب *sāḥib*, شبه *šibh*). In a noun compound where the second noun is in apposition or attributive, it alone is transcribed (cf. under إبرة *ibra*, جلد *jild*). In this manner the difference between the two constructions is brought out clearly without resorting to transliteration of the *iʿrāb* endings. A feminine noun ending in *-a*, as first member of a genitive compound, is also abbreviated, and the construct ending *-t* is to be read even though it is not expressed in the transcription.

In view of the great variety and intricacy of the material presented, it is inevitable that inconsistencies will appear and that similar examples will be treated here and there in a different manner. For such incongruities and for certain redundancies, we must ask the user's indulgence.

Münster HANS WEHR

November 1960

* * *

List of Abbreviations

abstr.	abstract	cf.	compare
acc.	accusative	*chem.*	chemistry
A.D.	anno Domini	*Chr.*	Christian
adj.	adjective	coll.	collective
adm.	administration	*colloq.*	colloquial
adv.	adverb	*com.*	commerce
A.H.	year of the Hegira	conj.	conjunction
Alg.	Algeria	*constr.-eng.*	construction engineering
alg.	Algerian	*Copt.*	Coptic
a.m.	ante meridiem	*cosm.*	cosmetics
anat.	anatomy	*dam.*	Damascene
approx.	approximately	def.	definite
arch.	architecture	dem.	demonstrative
archeol.	archeology	*dial.*	dialectal
arith.	arithmetic	dimin.	diminutive
astron.	astronomy	*dipl.*	diplomacy
athlet.	athletics	do.	ditto
biol.	biology	E	east, eastern
bot.	botany	*econ.*	economy
Brit.	British	*Eg.*	Egypt
ca.	circa, about	*eg.*	Egyptian
caus.	causative	e.g.	for example

el.	electricity	*med.*	medicine
ellipt.	elliptical	*mil.*	military
Engl.	English	*min.*	mineralogy
esp.	especially	*Mor.*	Morocco
ethnol.	ethnology	*mor.*	Moroccan
f.	feminine	*mus.*	music
fem.	feminine	*myst.*	mysticism
fig.	figuratively	N	north, northern
fin.	finance	n.	noun, nomen
foll.	following	*N.Afr.*	North Africa
Fr.	French	NE	northeast, northeastern
G.	German	*naut.*	nautics
G.B.	Great Britain	neg.	negation
genit.	genitive	nom.	nominative
geogr.	geography	n. un.	nomen unitatis
geom.	geometry	n. vic.	nomen vicis
Gr.	Greek	NW	northwest, northwestern
gram.	grammar	obl.	obliquus
Hebr.	Hebrew	*opt.*	optics
ḥij.	Hejazi	o.s.	oneself
hort.	horticulture	Ott.	Ottoman
i.e.	that is	*Pal.*	Palestine
imp.	imperative	*pal.*	Palestinian
imperf.	imperfect	*parl.*	parliamentary language
indef.	indefinite	part.	particle
interj.	interjection	pass.	passive
Intern. Law	International Law	*path.*	pathology
intr.	intransitive	perf.	perfect
Ir.	Iraq	Pers.	Persian
ir.	Iraqi	pers.	person, personal
Isl.	Islam, Islamic	*pharm.*	pharmacy
It.	Italian	*philos.*	philosophy
Jord.	Jordan Kingdom	*phon.*	phonetics
journ.	journalism	*phot.*	photography
Jud.	Judaism	*phys.*	physics
jur.	jurisprudence	*physiol.*	physiology
Leb.	Lebanon	pl.	plural
leb.	Lebanese	pl. comm.	pluralis communis
lex.	lexicography	p.m.	post meridiem
lit.	literally	*poet.*	poetry
m.	masculine	*pol.*	politics
magn.	magnetism	prep.	preposition
Mağr.	Maghrib	pron.	pronoun
mağr.	Maghribi	*psych.*	psychology
masc.	masculine	q.v.	which see
math.	mathematics	refl.	reflexive

rel.	relative
relig.	religion
rhet.	rhetoric
S	south, southern
Saudi Ar.	Saudi Arabia
saud.-ar.	Saudi-Arabian
SE	southeast, southeastern
sing.	singular
s.o.	someone
Span.	Spanish
specif.	specifically
s.th.	something
styl.	stylistics
subj.	subjunctive
subst.	substantive
surg.	surgery
SW	southwest, southwestern
Syr.	Syria
syr.	Syrian
techn.	technology
tel.	telephone
temp.	temporal
theat.	theatrical art
theol.	theology
trans.	transitive
Tun.	Tunisia
tun.	Tunisian
Turk.	Turkish
typ.	typography
U.A.R.	United Arab Republic
uninfl.	uninflected
verb.	verbal
W	west, western
Yem.	Yemen
yem.	Yemenite usage
zool.	zoology

ا

ا *a* particle introducing direct and indirect questions; ام — ا *a — am* in alternative questions; ام — ا سواء *sawā'un a — am* no matter whether — or; او *a-wa* particle indicating or implying doubt: or? perhaps? اوتشك في ذلك (*tašukku*) you wouldn't doubt it, would you? do you perhaps doubt it? or do you doubt it? الا *a-lā* and اما *a-mā* intensifying interjections introducing sentences: verily, truly, indeed, oh yes, etc., الا فانظروا (*fa-nẓurū*) oh, do look! why, look! اما انه (*innahū*) why, he is ...!

[1]آب *āb*[2] August (month; *Syr., Leb., Jord., Ir.*)

[2]اب see ابو

[3]اب *abba u* to long, yearn (الى وطنه *ilā waṭanihī* for one's homeland)

[4]ابيب look up alphabetically

اباتى (It. *abate*) *abātī* abbot (*Chr.*)

ابالة *ibāla, ibbāla* bundle, bale

يا ابت see ابو

ابجد *abjad* alphabet

ابجدى *abjadī* alphabetic(al); ابجديات elementary facts, simple truths | الحروف الابجدية the letters of the alphabet, the alphabet

ابد *abada i* (ابود *ubūd*) to stay, linger (ب at a place); — *i u* to roam in a state of wildness, run wild, be shy, shy away, run away (animal, game) II to make lasting or permanent, perpetuate, eternize (ه s.th.) V to be perpetuated, become lasting or permanent; to return to a state of wildness

ابد *abad* pl. آباد *ābād* endless, eternal duration, eternity; ابدا *abadan* always, forever; ever, (with neg.) never (in the future), not at all, on no account; (alone, without negation) never! not at all! by no means! | ابد الدهر and على الابد ,الى الابد *abada d-dahri* forever; ابد الابدين *abada l-abadīn* and الى ابد الابدين *ilā abadi l-a.* forever and ever

ابدى *abadī* everlasting, eternal, endless

الابدى *al-abadī* eternity

ابدية *abadīya* infinite duration, endless time, eternity

آبد *ābid* wild, untamed

آبدة *ābida* pl. اوابد *awābid*[2] unusual thing, prodigious event | اوابد الدنيا *a. ad-dunyā* the Wonders of the World

مؤبد *mu'abbad* eternal, endless, everlasting | سجن مؤبد (*sijn*) life imprisonment

[1]ابر *abara i u* (*abr*) to prick, sting II to pollinate (ه a palm tree)

ابرة *ibra* pl. ابر *ibar* needle, pin; indicator (of an instrument); shot, injection (*med.*); sting, prick | حقنه ابرة *ḥaqanahū ibratan* to give s.o. an injection; ابرة الراعى *i. ar-rā'ī* geranium (*bot.*); ابرة مغناطيسية (*magnāṭīsīya*) magnetic needle; شغل الابرة *šugl al-i.* needlework

مئبر *mi'bar* needlecase; pack needle

[2]آبار *ābār* see بئر

ابرشية *abrašīya* and ابروشية *abrūšīya* pl. *-āt* diocese, bishopric (*Chr.*); parish (*Chr.*)

ابراميس ,ابرميس *abramīs*, bream (*zool.*)

ابريز *ibrīz* pure gold

ابريسم *ibrīsam, ibrīsim* silk

ابريق *ibrīq* pl. اباريق *abārīq*[2] pitcher, jug

ابريل *abrīl* April

ابزن *abzan* pl. ابازن *abāzin*[2] washbowl

ابزيم *ibzīm* pl. ابازيم *abāzīm*[2] buckle, clasp

ابض *ubḍ* pl. آباض *ābāḍ* and مأبض *ma'biḍ* pl. مآبض *ma'ābiḍ*[2] hollow of the knee, popliteal space

ابط V to take or carry under one's arm (ه s.th.); to put one's arm (ه, ه around s.o., around s.th.), hold in one's arm (ه, ه s.o., s.th.)

ابط *ibṭ* pl. آباط *ābāṭ* m. and f. armpit

ابق *abaqa* i (اباق *ibāq*) to escape, run away (a slave from his master)

ابق *abaq* a kind of hemp

آبق *ābiq* pl. اباق *ubbāq* runaway, escaped; a fugitive

ابل[1] *ibil* (coll.) camels

ابالة[2] *ibāla, ibbāla* bundle, bale

ابليز *iblīz* alluvial deposits (of the Nile)

ابليس *iblīs*[2] pl. ابالسة *abālisa* devil, Satan

ابن[1] II to celebrate, praise, eulogize (ه a deceased person), deliver a funeral oration (ه in praise of s.o.)

ابنة *ubna* passive pederasty

ابان *ibbān* time; ابان *ibbāna* during, فى ابان at the time of, during

تأبين *ta'bīn* commemoration (of a deceased person) | حفلة التأبين *ḥaflat at-t.* commemorative celebration (in honor of a deceased person)

مأبون *ma'būn* catamite; weakling, mollycoddle, sissy; scoundrel

ابن[2] see بن[1]

ابنوس *abnūs* ebony

ابه *abaha* and *abiha* a (*abh*) to pay attention (ل, also ب to), heed (ل, also ب s.th.), take notice (ل, also ب of) | امر لا يؤبه له (*yu'bahu*) an insignificant, unimportant matter V to display proud, haughty manners; to turn away, keep one's distance, remain aloof (عن from), look down (عن upon), think o.s. far above (عن s.o or s.th.)

ابهة *ubbaha* splendor, pomp, ostentation, pageantry; pride

اب *ab* pl. آباء *ābā'* father (also *eccl.*); ancestor, forefather; يا ابت *yā abati* O my father! الابوان *al-abawān* the parents, father and mother; ابونا *abūnā* reverend father, form of address and title of a priest (*Chr*). | ابا عن جد *aban 'an jaddin* handed down from father to son, as s.th. inherited from forefathers; ابو سعن *abū su'n* marabou; ابو النوم *abū n-naum* poppy; ابو الهول *abū l-haul* the Sphinx; ابو اليقظان *abū l-yaqẓān* rooster, cock

ابوة *ubūwa* fatherhood, paternity

ابوى *abawī* paternal, fatherly

ابونيت ebonite

ابونيه (Fr. *abonné*) *abūnēh* pl. *-āt* subscription; subscription card (e.g., for public conveyances, a concert season, etc.)

ابى *abā* a (اباء *ibā'*, اباءة *ibā'a*) to refuse, decline; to turn down, reject, scorn, disdain (ه s.th.); to deny (على ه s.o. s.th.) | ابى الا ان يفعله (*illā an yaf'alahū*) he insisted on doing it; ابى الله الا ان God willed that . . . V to refuse, decline

اباء *ibā'*, اباءة *ibā'a* rejection; dislike, distaste, aversion, disdain; pride

ابى *abīy* disdainful, scornful; proud, lofty, lofty-minded

آب *ābin* pl. اباة *ubāh* reserved, standoffish; unwilling, reluctant, grudging

ابيب *abīb* the eleventh month of the Coptic calendar

ابيقورى *abīqūrī* Epicurean

ابيقورية *abīqūrīya* Epicureanism

اترج *utrujj* and اترنج *utrunj* citron (Citrus medica; *bot.*)

آتشجى (Turk. *ateşçi*) *ātešgī* fireman, stoker

مأتم *ma'tam* pl. مآتم *ma'ātim*[2] obsequies, funeral ceremony

[1]اتان *atān* pl. آتن *ātun*, اتن *utun*, *utn* female donkey, she-ass

[2]اتون *atūn*, *attūn* pl. اتن *utun*, اتاتين *atātīn*[2] kiln, furnace, oven

اتاوة *itāwa* pl. اتاوى *atāwā* duty, tax, tribute

اتوبيس (Fr.) *otobīs* autobus, bus

اتوماتيكى (Fr.) *otomātīkī* automatic

اتومبيل and اتوموبيل (Fr.) *otomobīl* automobile

اتى *atā i* (اتيان *ityān*, اتى *aty*, مأتاة *ma'tāh* to come (ه or الى to; على over s.o.), arrive (ه or الى at); اتى ب to bring, bring forward, produce, advance, accomplish or achieve s.th.; اتى ه ب to bring, give or offer s.o. s.th.; to do, perform (ه a deed), carry out, execute (ه e.g., movements); to commit, perpetrate (ه a sin, a crime); to mention (على s.th.); to finish off (على s.th., also s.o.); to finish, complete, carry through, dispose, settle, wind up, conclude, terminate, bring to a close (على s.th.); to destroy, annihilate, eradicate, wipe out (على s.th.); to eliminate, carry away, sweep away (على s.th.), do away (على with); to use up, exhaust (also a subject), present exhaustively, in great detail (على s.th.), elaborate (على on s.th.) | كما يأتى as follows; اتى على آخره (*āḵirihī*) to complete, finish s.th.; to spend or use up the last of s.th.; اتى على الاخضر واليابس to destroy everything, wreak havoc; اتى البيوت من ابوابها (*buyūta*) to tackle s.th. in the right way, knock on the right door; يؤتى من قبل *yu'tā min qibali* is undermined, weakened, ruined by III to offer, furnish, give, afford (ه ب to s.o. s.th.), provide, supply (ه ب s.o. with); to be propitious, be favorable (ه for s.o.), favor (ه s.o.); to turn out well (ه for s.o.), be in favor (ه of); to suit, befit, become (ه s.o.), be appropriate (ه for s.o.); to agree (ه with s.o.; food) | آتاه كل شىء (*kullu šai'in*) everything was in his favor, turned out well for him, came his way IV to bring (ه ه s.o. s.th.); to give (ه ه s.o. s.th.); to grant (ه ه to s.o. s.th.), bestow (ه ه upon s.o. s.th.) | آتى الزكاة (*zakāta*) to give alms V to originate, stem, derive, spring, arise, result (عن from); to end (عن with), result (عن in); to get (الى to), arrive (الى at); to be easy to do, be feasible without difficulty, be attainable, go well, progress; to go about s.th. (فى) gently, cautiously X to ask to come, induce to come (ه s.o.)

مأتى *ma'tan* pl. مآت *ma'ātin* place where s.th. comes from; place at which one arrives; access; pl. مآت place of origin; origin, source, provenance; place where one has been or to which one has come; place where s.th. starts, where s.th. ends

آت *ātin* coming, next; following | الاسبوع الآتى (*usbū'*) the coming week, next week; كالآتى as follows

مواتٍ *mu'ātin*, *muwātin* favorable, propitious, opportune, convenient, suitable

اث *aṯṯa u i a* (اثاثة *aṯāṯa*) to be luxuriant, grow profusely (hair, plants) II to fix up, prepare (ه s.th.); to furnish (ه an apartment) V to be or become rich, wealthy, to prosper; to be furnished

اثاث *aṯāṯ* furniture, furnishings (of an apartment, of a room)

تأثيث *ta'ṯīṯ* furnishing

اث *aṯṯ*, اثيث *aṯīṯ* abundant, luxuriant, profusely growing (hair, plants)

[1]اثر *aṯara u i* (*aṯr*, اثارة *aṯāra*) to transmit, pass along, report, relate (ه s.th., عن from, or based on the authority of, s.o.) II to

affect, influence (في or على s.o., s.th.), act (في or على upon), produce an effect, make an impression, have influence (في or على on); to induce (*phys.*) **IV** to prefer (ه على s.th. to), like (ه s.th.) more (على than); to have a predilection, a liking (ه for), like (ه s.th.), be fond (ه of); to choose, deem wise or advisable (ان to do s.th.); to adore (ه, ه s.o., s.th.) | آثر نفسه بالخير (*nafsahū bi-l-kair*) to wish o.s. well, hope for the best for o.s. **V** to be impressed, be influenced; to let o.s. be impressed, be impressible; to be moved, be touched (ب or ل by, also من); to be excited, be stimulated; to be affected (ب by, said of materials, e.g., iron by acid); to be induced (*phys.*); to follow in s.o.'s (ه) tracks, follow s.o.'s example, emulate (ه s.o.); to pursue, follow up (ه a question, a problem); to perceive, feel (ه s.th.) **X** to claim a monopoly; to possess alone, with the exclusion of others, monopolize (ب s.th.); to appropriate (ب s.th.), take exclusive possession (ب of); to preoccupy (ه s.th.), engross (ه the attention) | استأثر الله به the Lord has taken him unto Himself

اثر *aṯar* pl. آثار *āṯār* track, trace, vestige; sign, mark; touch; impression, effect, action, influence (في on); tradition (relating the deeds and utterances of Mohammed and his Companions); work (of art, esp. of literature); ancient monument; آثار antiquities; remnants, vestiges; (religious) relics | علم الآثار *ʿilm al-ā.* archeology; دار الآثار museum of antiquities; لا اثر له (*aṯara*) ineffective, ineffectual; باثر رجعى (*rajʿī*) with retroactive force (*jur.*); اصبح اثرا بعد عين *aṣbaḥa aṯaran baʿda ʿainin* to be destroyed, be wiped out, leave nothing but memory behind; اعاده اثرا بعد عين (*aʿādahū*) to destroy s.th. completely; على اثره, في اثره (also *fī iṯrihī*) on his (its) track, at his heels, after him; immediately afterwards, presently, thereupon; على الاثر immediately afterwards, presently

اثر *iṯra* (prep.) immediately after, right after

اثرى *aṯarī* archeologic(al); archeologist (also آثارى *āṯārī*); old, ancient, antique | عالم اثرى archeologist; لغة اثرية (*luġa*) dead language

اثر *aṯir* egoistic, selfish

اثرة *aṯara* selfishness, egoism

اثير *aṯīr* favored, preferred (عند by s.o.), in favor (عند with s.o.); select, exquisite, noble; see also alphabetically

اثارة *aṯāra* remainder, remnant; faint trace, vestige

مأثرة *maʾṯara, maʾṯura* pl. مآثر *maʾāṯir*[2] exploit, feat, glorious deed

تأثير *taʾṯīr* action, effect, influence, impression (في, على on); effectiveness, efficacy; induction (*phys.*)

تأثيرى *taʾṯīrī* produced by induction, inductive, inductional, induced (*phys.*)

ايثار *īṯār* preference; altruism; predilection; love, affection

تأثر *taʾaṯṯur* being influenced; agitation, emotion, feeling; excitability, sensitivity; (pl. *-āt*) feeling, sensation, perception | سريع التأثر easily impressed, impressible, sensitive

تأثرى *taʾaṯṯurī*: المذهب التأثرى (*maḏhab*) the impressionistic movement

تأثرية *taʾaṯṯurīya* impressionism

استئثار *istiʾṯār* arrogation of a monopoly; monopolization; presumption, presumptuousness; exclusive power

مأثور *maʾṯūr* transmitted, handed down | قول مأثور (*qaul*) and كلمة مأثورة (*kalima*) proverb

مؤثر *muʾaṯṯir* affecting, acting upon; effective; impressive; moving, touching, pathetic; (pl. *-āt*) influencing factor, influence

اثير[2] look up alphabetically

اثفية *uṯfīya* pl. اثاف *aṯāfin* trivet, tripod (in ancient times: any one of the three stones supporting a cooking pot near the fire) | ثالثة الاثافى that which rounds out a number, caps s.th., puts the lid on s.th., the crowning touch

اثل *aṯala i* to consolidate, strengthen **II** to become rich **V** to be consolidated, be strengthened; to become rich

اثل *aṯl* pl. اثول *uṯūl* (coll.; n. un. ة, pl. *aṯalāt*) tamarisk (*bot.*)

اثيل *aṯīl* and مؤثل *mu'aṯṯal* deep-rooted; of noble origin, highborn

اثم *aṯima a* (*iṯm*, *aṯam*, مأثم *ma'ṯam*) to sin, err, slip **V** to eschew sin, shun evil; to restrain o.s., hold back

اثم *iṯm* pl. آثام *āṯām* sin, offense, misdeed, crime

مأثم *ma'ṯam* pl. مآثم *ma'āṯim*[2] sin, offense, misdeed, crime

تأثيم *ta'ṯīm* sin, offense, misdeed, crime

آثم *āṯim* pl. اثمة *aṯama* and اثيم *aṯīm* pl. اثماء *uṯamā'*[2] sinful, criminal, wicked, evil; sinner

اثمد *iṯmid* antimony

اثير *aṯīr* ether

اثينا *aṯīnā* Athens

اثيوبيا *aṯyūbiyā* Ethiopia

اثيوبى *aṯyūbī* Ethiopian; (pl. *-ūn*) an Ethiopian | البلاد الاثيوبية Ethiopia

اج *ajja u i* (اجيج *ajīj*) to burn, blaze, flame (fire) **II** to light, kindle, start (ه a fire) **V** = **I**

ماء اجاج *mā' ujāj* bitter, salty water

اجاج *ajjāj* burning, blazing, hot

متأجج *muta'ajjij* burning, blazing, flaming

اجبية *ajabīya* horologium (*Copt.-Chr.*)

[1]اجر *ajara u* (*ajr*) to reward, recompense, remunerate (ه s.o.) **II** to let for rent, let out, hire out, rent, lease (ه s.th.); (with *nafsahū*) to hire o.s. out **IV** to let for rent, let out, hire out, rent, lease (ه s.th.); to rent, hire, lease, hold under a lease (ه s.th.), take a lease (ه on); to hire, engage, take on (ه s.o.), engage the services (ه of s.o.) **X** to rent, hire, lease, hold under a lease (ه s.th.), take a lease (ه on); to charter (ه a vessel); to hire, engage, take on (ه s.o.), engage the services (ه of s.o.)

اجر *ajr* pl. اجور *ujūr* wages, pay, honorarium, recompense, emolument, remuneration; price, rate, fee | اجور السفر *u. as-safar* fares

اجرة *ujra* hire, rent, rental; price, rate, fee; fixed rate, (official) charge; postage | اجرة البريد postage; اجرة النقل *u. an-naql* transport charges, freight(age), carriage, cartage

اجير *ajīr* pl. اجراء *ujarā'*[2] hireling; workman, laborer, day laborer; employee

اجيرة *ajīra* working woman, factory girl, female laborer; woman employee

تأجير *ta'jīr* letting, leasing, hiring out, letting on lease; lease | مشروع التأجير والاعارة (*i'āra*) Lend-Lease Act

ايجار *ījār* pl. *-āt* rent; letting, leasing, hiring out, letting on lease | للايجار for rent, to let

اجارة *ijāra* pl. *-āt* rent; letting, leasing, hiring out, letting on lease

استئجار *isti'jār* rent, lease, tenure

مأجور *ma'jūr* paid, salaried, on the payroll, gainfully employed; employee; mercenary, venal, hired, bribed

مؤجر *mu'ajjir* pl. *-ūn* landlord, lessor

مستأجر *musta'jir* leaseholder, lessee, tenant; employer

آجر[2] *ājurr* (n. un. ة) baked brick

اجزاجى see جزء

اجزاخانة see جزء

اجاص *ijjāṣ* pear

اجل *ajila a* (*ajal*) to hesitate, tarry, linger II to delay, postpone, put off, defer, adjourn (ه s.th. الى till) V to be postponed, be deferred, be adjourned (الى till, to) X to request postponement (ه of s.th.); to seek to delay (ه s.th.)

اجل *ajal* yes, indeed! certainly! by all means!

لأجل *li-ajli* or من اجل *min ajli* because of, on account of, for the sake of; for | لاجل ان in order that, that, so that; من اجل هذا therefore, for that reason, on this account

اجل *ajal* pl. آجال *ājāl* appointed time, date, deadline; instant of death; respite, delay | بالاجل on credit (*com.*); قصير الاجل short-term, short-time; short-lived; الى اجل غير مسمى (*ġairi musamman*) for an indefinite period, sine die, until further notice

تأجيل *ta'jīl* delay, postponement, adjournment, deferment, respite; appointment of a time or date

آجل *ājil* delayed, protracted; deferred; later, future (as opposed to عاجل) | عاجلا او آجلا *'ājilan au ājilan*, فى عاجله او آجله sooner or later, now or later on; فى العاجل والآجل now and in the future

الآجلة *al-ājila* the life to come, the hereafter

مؤجل *mu'ajjal* delayed, late, postponed, deferred; fixed in time, deadlined

اجمة *ajama*, coll. اجم *ajam* pl. *-āt*, اجم *ujum*, آجام *ājām* thicket, jungle, forest; reeds, canebrake

اجمية *ajamīya* malaria | بعوضة الاجمية *ba'ūḍat al-a.* anopheles

آجن *ājin* brackish (water)

اجندة *ajanda* notebook

اح *aḫḫa u* (*aḫḫ*) to cough

احد II to make into one, unite, unify (ه s.th.) VIII اتحد *ittaḥada* see وحد

احد *aḥad*, f. احدى *iḥdā* one; somebody, someone, anybody, anyone (esp. in negative sentences and questions); الاحد the One (God); Sunday | احدهم *aḥaduhum* every one of them; يوم الاحد *yaum al-a.* Sunday; احد السعف *a. as-sa'af* Palm Sunday; احد العنصرة *a. al-'anṣara* Whitsunday; آحاد الالوف *āḥād al-ulūf* a few thousand (2—9000; as distinguished from مئات الالوف and عشرات الالوف)

احدى *aḥadī* dominical, Sunday (adj.)

احدية *aḥadīya* unity, oneness

الآحاد *al-āḥād* the units (*math.*)

احن[1] *aḥina a* (*aḥan*) to hate (على s.o.)

احنة *iḥna* pl. احن *iḥan* old feud, deep-rooted hatred

آحين[2] see اوح

اخ see اخو

اخت see اخو

اخذ *aḵaḏa u* (*aḵḏ*) to take (ه s.th. من from or out of); to take (ه s.th.) along; to get, receive, obtain (ه s.th. من from); to take up, seize (ه s.th.); to grab (ب s.o., s.th.), take hold of (ب); to perceive, notice (ه s.o., said of the eye); to gather, understand, infer, deduce (ه s.th. من from), read (ه s.th.) between the lines (من of); to grip, captivate, thrill, spellbind (ب s.o.); to take up, acquire, make one's own (ب s.th., e.g., a method); to keep, adhere (ب to), observe, take over, adopt, embrace, follow, copy, imitate (ب s.th.); to accept (ب s.th.); to take, lead (ب الى s.o. to); to admonish, urge, drive (ب ه

s.o. to do s.th.); to enjoin, impose (ه ب on s.o. s.th.); to take away (ه على from s.o. s.th.), strip, deprive (ه على s.o. of), cut off, bar (ه على s.o. from); to reproach, blame (ه على s.o. for); to hold against s.o. (على) that ... (ان), fix the blame (على on s.o., ان for the fact that); to obligate (ب على s.o. to); to learn (على or عن from s.o., ه s.th.), acquire knowledge (على or عن from s.o.), اخذ العلم عنه (*'ilm*) to study under s.o.; to begin, start (في or ب with s.th. or s.th., with foll. imperf.: to do s.th.), prepare, set out, be about (في or ب to do s.th.) | اخذ اهبته (*uhbatahū*) to make preparations, prepare o.s., get ready; اخذ مأخذ فلان (*ma'kad*) to adopt the same course as s.o. else, follow s.o.'s example; اخذ منه مأخذا to seize s.o., take possession of s.o. (a sensation, or the like); اخذ مجراه (*majrāhu*) to take its course; اخذ مجلسه (*majlisahū*) to take one's seat, sit down; اخذ حذره (*ḥiḏrahū*) to be on one's guard; اخذه بالحسنى (*ḥusnā*) to be friendly, be nice to s.o.; اخذ بخاطره (*bi-ḵāṭirihī*) to show o.s. complaisant toward s.o., try to please s.o.; اخذه بذنبه (*bi-ḏanbihī*) to punish s.o. for his offense; اخذ رأيه (*ra'yahū*) to ask s.o.'s opinion, consult s.o.; اخذ الرأى عليه (*ukiḏa r-ra'yu*) the matter was put to a vote; اخذ باسباب (*bi-asbābi*) to embrace, adopt s.th., e.g., اخذ باسباب الحضارة الاوربية (*ḥaḍāra*) to adopt European culture; اخذه بالشدة (*šidda*) to deal with s.o. severely, give s.o. a rough time; اخذ عليه طريقه to obstruct s.o.'s way, hinder s.o. from moving on; اخذه على عاتقه to shoulder s.th., take s.th. upon o.s.; اخذ العدة ل (*'udda*) to prepare, set out, get ready to do s.th.; اخذ عليه عهدا (*'ahdan*) to put s.o. under an obligation, impose a commitment on s.o.; اخذ على (حين) غرة *ukiḏa 'alā (ḥīni) ġirratin* to be taken by surprise, be caught unawares; اخذ بالمقابلة (*muqābala*) to repay like for like; شيء ياخذ القلوب s.th. which captivates the heart, a fascinating, thrilling thing; اخذنا المطر (*maṭaru*) we got caught in the rain; اخذ بناصره (*bi-nāṣirihī*) to help s.o., stand by s.o., take care of s.o., look after s.o.; اخذ نفسه (*nafasahū*) to draw breath; اخذ عليه انفاسه to take s.o.'s breath away; اخذه النوم (*naum*) sleep overwhelmed him; اخذ بيده (*bi-yadihī*) to help s.o., stand by s.o. **II** to lay under a spell, enchant, bewitch (ه s.o.) **III** to censure, blame (ه على, ب s.o. for s.th.); to punish (ه على, ب s.o. for); to hold s.th. (على) against s.o. (ه), resent (على s.th. ه in s.o.) | لا تؤاخذنى! *lā tu'āḵiḏnī* pardon me! forgive me! no offense, I hope! **VIII** اتخذ *ittaḵaḏa* to take (ه s.th.); to take on, assume (ه s.th.); to take up, occupy (ه s.th.); to pass, adopt (ه e.g., a resolution); to take, single out, have in mind (هه, ه ه s.o. or s.th. as); to make use (ه of s.th.), use (ه s.th.); to imitate, affect (ه e.g., s.o.'s manner of speaking); to make (ه من s.th. out of s.o. or s.th.) | اتخذ شكلا (*šaklan*) to take on a form or shape; اتخذ موقفا (*mauqifan*) to take an attitude, assume a position; اتخذ التدابير اللازمة to take the necessary measures; اتخذ قرارا (*qarāran*) to pass or adopt a resolution; اتخذ المواقع الجديدة to take up new positions (troops)

اخذ *aḵḏ* acceptance, reception; seizure; taking out, taking away, removal, etc. | اخذ الرأى *a. ar-ra'y* voting, vote; اخذ ورد (*wa-radd*) discussion, debate, dispute, argument; شيء لا يقبل اخذا ولا ردا (*yaqbalu*) an indisputable matter; اخذ وعطاء (*wa-'aṭā'*) give-and-take; traffic, trade; dealings, relations (esp. business, commercial); discussion, debate; fight, battle

اخذة *ukḏa* spell, charm

اخيذ *aḵīḏ* prisoner of war

اخيذة *aḵīḏa* booty, spoils

اخاذ *aḵḵāḏ* captivating, fascinating, thrilling

مأخذ *ma'kad* pl. مآخذ *ma'ākid*² place from which one takes s.th., source; ○ wall socket, outlet (*el.*); adoption, borrowing, loan; manner of acting, mode of procedure, approach; pl. مآخذ source references, bibliography (in books); reprehensible points, faults, flaws, defects, shortcomings | المأخذ الاقرب the simplest, easiest approach; قريب المأخذ easy to handle or to use; see also *akada* (middle of paragraph)

مؤاخذة *mu'ākada* objection, exception; censure, blame | لا مؤاخذة ! (*mu'ākadata*) pardon me! no offense, I hope!

مأخوذ *ma'kūd* taken, seized; taken by surprise, caught, trapped; surprised; taken (ب with), fascinated (ب by); مأخوذ به in force, valid

مأخوذات *ma'kūdāt* receipts, takings, returns (*com.*)

اخر II to delay, put off, defer, postpone, adjourn (ه s.th.); to hinder, impede, obstruct, hold up (ه s.o., ه s.th.), slow down, retard (ه s.th.); to draw out, delay (عن ه s.th. beyond its appointed time); to put back (ه, ه s.o., s.th.), shelve (ه s.th.); to set back (ه a watch, a clock); to suspend, discharge, dismiss, remove (ه s.o. from an office) V to be late; to be delayed, fall or lag behind (عن), tarry, linger, hesitate; to default (عن on), be behindhand, be in arrears (عن with), be behind (عن in); to hesitate (عن with); to be suspended (from service), be discharged, be dismissed | لم يتاخر بعد ذلك من ان after that, he did not hesitate long before he ..., presently, he ...

آخر *ākir* pl. *-ūn*, *-āt*, اواخر *awākir*² last, ultimate, utmost, extreme; end, close, conclusion; foot, bottom (of a paper); الآخر and الآخرة the hereafter | الدار الآخرة the abode in the hereafter, the everlasting abode; الى آخره *ilā ākirihī* and so forth, et cetera; آخر الامر *ākira l-amri* eventually, finally, in the end, after all; آخر الدهر *ākira d-dahri* forever; آخر الزمان *ā. az-zamān* time at which the Day of Judgment is to be expected, the end of the world; عن آخره to the last, down to the grass roots, entirely, completely, e.g., دمر عن آخره (*dummira*) to be completely destroyed, be wiped off the map; من آخره from behind, from the rear; ما له آخر endless, infinite; فى آخر الآخر after all, last of all; اواخر الشهر *a. aš-šahr* the end of the month, the last ten days of the month; اخيرا وليس آخرا last but not least

الآخرة *al-ākira* the hereafter

آخر *ākar*², f. اخرى *ukrā*, pl. comm. اخر *ukar*² (and آخرون *ākarūn* or اخريات *ukrayāt* respectively) another, one more, the other | مرة اخرى (*marratan*) once more; هو الآخر, هى الاخرى he also, she also, he in turn, she in turn, انا الآخر I also; ان كانت الاخرى (*in kānat*) otherwise; من آن الى آخر from time to time; من سنة الى اخرى (*sana*) from year to year; بين فترة واخرى (*fatra*) once in a while, from time to time; آونة — اخرى (*āwinatan*) sometimes — sometimes, at times — at times

الاخرى *al-ukrā* the hereafter

اخروى *ukrawī* of or relating to the life to come or the hereafter

اخير *akīr* last; latest; rearmost; the second of two; اخيرا eventually, finally, in the end, after all, at last; recently, lately, the other day; الاول — الاخير the former — the latter | اخيرا وليس آخرا last but not least

مئخار *mi'kār* palm which retains its fruit into the winter

تأخير *ta'kīr* delay, deferment, postponement; obstruction, retardation; putting back, temporary shelving

تأخر *ta'akkur* delay, lag, retardation; hesitation, tarrying, lingering; slowness, tardiness; backwardness, underdevelopment (of a country)

مؤخر *mu'akkar* rear part, tail, end; stern (of a ship); remainder, balance (of a sum, to be paid later); مؤخرا *mu'akkaran* recently, lately, the other day; at last, finally, eventually

مؤخرة *mu'akkara* rear, rear guard (of an army); rear positions or lines (*mil.*); stern (of a ship)

متأخر *muta'akkir* delayed, belated, late; occurring later (عن than); behind, behindhand, in arrears; backward, underdeveloped; lagging, staying behind; defaulter; المتأخرون the later, or modern, authors, writers, or the like (as opposed to المتقدمون); المتأخرات arrears, balance of a sum remaining due after previous payment | البلدان المتأخرة (*buldān*) the underdeveloped countries

اخطبوط *uktubūt* octopus

اخو III to fraternize, associate as brothers (ه with s.o.) V to act or show o.s. as a brother or friend VI to fraternize, associate as brothers

اخ *ak* pl. اخوة *ikwa*, اخوان *ikwān* brother; fellow man, neighbor; friend; pl. اخوان specif., brethren or members of an order; الاخوان religious brotherhood of the Wahabi sect, militant in character, established by Ibn Sa'ūd in 1910 | يا اخى my dear friend! اخو ثقة *akū tiqa* trustworthy, reliable; اخ شقيق brother through both father and mother, brother-german

اخت *ukt* pl. اخوات *akawāt* sister; (*gram.*) cognate; counterpart | اختها the other (of two), its mate, its counterpart (after a fem. noun)

خوى *kuwaiy* little brother

اخوى *akawī* brotherly, fraternal

اخوية *akawīya* brotherhood (as a religious association)

اخاء *ikā'*, اخوة *ukūwa* brotherhood, brotherliness, fraternity

اخاوة *ikāwa* fraternization, fraternity, brotherliness

تآخ *ta'ākin* fraternization

اخور *akūr* barn, stable

اد ***adda u i*** to befall, afflict (ه s.o.)

امر اد *amr idd* a terrible, evil, horrible thing

ادب ***aduba u*** (*adab*) to be well-bred, well-mannered, cultured, urbane, have refined tastes; — *adaba i* (*adb*) to invite (to a party or banquet, ه s.o.), entertain (ه s.o.) | ادب مأدبة (*ma'duba*) to arrange a banquet, give a formal dinner **II** to refine, educate (ه s.o.); to discipline, punish, chastise (ه s.o.) **IV** to invite as a guest (ه s.o.) **V** to receive a fine education; to be well-bred, well-educated, cultured, have refined tastes; to show o.s. polite, courteous, civil, urbane; to educate o.s., refine one's tastes (ب by, through); to let o.s. be guided (ب by) | تأدب بأدبه (*bi-adabihi*) to follow s.o.'s moral example

ادب *adab* pl. آداب *ādāb* culture, refinement; good breeding, good manners, social graces, decorum, decency, propriety, seemliness; humanity, humaneness; the humanities; belles-lettres | بيت الادب toilet, water closet; قليل الادب and عديم الادب ill-mannered, ill-bred, impolite, uncivil; الادب العامى (*'āmmī*) popular literature; رجال الادب literati, men of letters; كلية الآداب *kullīyat al-ā.* (= faculté des lettres) college of arts; آداب rules, rules of conduct, e.g., آداب السلوك rules of decorum, etiquette; الآداب decency, morals

ادبى *adabī* moral, ethic(al); literary | واجب ادبى moral obligation; ادبيا وماديا

adabīyan wa-māddīyan morally and physically; الفلسفة الادبية (*falsafa*) ethics, moral science

ادبيات ***adabīyāt*** literature, belles-lettres

ادبخانة ***adabkāna*** pl. *-āt* toilet, water closet

اديب ***adīb*** pl. ادباء ***udabā'***[2] cultured, refined, educated; well-bred, well-mannered, civil, urbane; a man of culture and refined tastes; man of letters, writer, author

اديبة ***adība*** authoress, writer

مأدبة ***ma'duba*** pl. مآدب ***ma'ādib***[2] banquet, formal dinner

تأديب ***ta'dīb*** education; discipline; punishment, chastisement; disciplinary punishment | مجلس التأديب ***majlis at-t.*** disciplinary board

تأديبي ***ta'dībī*** disciplinary; punitive, retaliatory | قضية تأديبية (*qaḍīya*) disciplinary action

تأدب ***ta'addub*** good breeding, good manners, civility, politeness, courteousness, tact

آدب ***ādib*** host

مؤدب ***mu'addib*** pl. *-ūn* educator; teacher in a Koranic school (*Tun.*); — ***mu'addab*** well-bred, well-mannered, civil, urbane

ادرة ***udra*** scrotal hernia

ادرنة ***adirna***[2] Edirne, Adrianople (city in NW Turkey)

الادرياتيك (Fr. *adriatique*) ***al-adriyatīk*** and بحر الادرياتيك ***baḥr al-a.*** the Adriatic Sea

[1]ادم ***adama*** *i* (*adm*) to take some additional food (ه with the bread), enrich (ه the bread) with some extra food or condiment

ادام ***idām*** anything eaten with bread; shortening, fatty ingredient

[2]ادم, ادمة ***adam, adama*** skin

اديم ***adīm*** skin; surface; tanned skin, leather | اديم الارض ***a. al-arḍ*** the surface of the earth

ادام ***addām*** tanner

[3]آدم ***ādam***[2] Adam | ابن آدم human being

آدمى ***ādamī*** human; humane; poor, inferior, meager; (pl. *-ūn*, اوادم ***awādim***[2]) human being

آدمية ***ādamīya*** humaneness, humanity; humanism

اداة ***adāh*** pl. ادوات ***adawāt*** tool; instrument; utensil, implement, device, appliance; apparatus; (*gram.*) particle | اداة الحكم ***a. al-ḥukm*** machinery of government; اداة التعريف definite article (*gram.*); اداة تنفيذية (*tanfīḏīya*) executive agency; pl. materials, equipment, gear, ادوات حربية (*ḥarbīya*) war material; ادوات احتياطية (*iḥtiyāṭīya*) stand-by equipment (*techn.*); ادوات منزلية (*manzilīya*) household utensils, household effects

الادون ***al-adōn*** (Hebr.) the Lord; Mr. ... (*Isr.*)

ادى **II** to convey, take, bring, lead, steer, channel (ه, ه or ب s.o., s.th., الى to), see that s.o. or s.th. (ه, ه or ب) gets to (الى); to bring about, cause, effect, produce (الى s.th.); to lead, contribute, be conducive (الى to a result); to amount, come practically (الى to); to tend (الى to), aim (الى at); to carry out, execute, discharge (ه s.th.); to perform (ه a ritual, etc.); to do (واجبه *wājibahū* one's duty); to fulfill (وظيفة a function, رسالة a mission); to accomplish (مأمورية a task); to take (يمينا an oath; امتحانا an examination); to render (خدمة ***kidmatan*** a service, ل or الى to s.o.; ه e.g., a meaning, a musical composition, etc.) | ادى السلام (*salām*) to greet, salute **V** to lead, be conducive, contribute (الى to results); to be carried out, be performed, be accomplished; to arrive (الى at), be lead (الى to) **X** to demand, claim (ه ه from s.o. s.th.)

اداء *adā'* pl. *-āt* (as verbal noun of II) rendering (of a service); pursuit, performance, execution, discharge (of a duty), realization, effectuation, accomplishment (of a task); rendition, reading (e.g., of a musical composition); fulfillment; payment | حسن الاداء *ḥusn al-a.* good rendition (of a work of art, of a musical composition)

تأدية *ta'diya* rendering (of a service); pursuit, performance, execution, discharge (of a duty), realization, effectuation; accomplishment (of a task); fulfillment; payment

مؤدى *mu'addan* assignment, task, function; sense, meaning, signification, import, underlying idea

اذ *iḏ* 1. (introducing a verbal clause) (and) then; اذ ذاك *iḏ ḏāka* (also written اذاك) then, at that time, at the same time, in doing so; 2. (conj.; temp. and caus.) as, when; since, as, the more so as, because; اذ ان *iḏ anna* since, as, in view of the fact that; for, because

[1]اذا *iḏā* 1. (introducing a nominal clause the subject of which may be expressed by ب with foll. genit.) and then, and all of a sudden; (with noun in nominative case or with ب) there was ..., and all of a sudden there was ...; 2. (conj.) when; if, whenever; whether, if (introducing indirect questions); اذا ما when, whenever; الا اذا (*illā*) unless, if not; except when

[2]اذا (اذن) *iḏan* then, therefore, in that case, hence, consequently

آذار *āḏār*[2] March (month; *Syr., Leb., Jord., Ir.*)

[1]اذن *aḏina a* to listen (الى to s.o.); to allow, permit (ل ه s.o. s.th.); to hear, learn (ب of s.th.), be informed (ب about) **II** to call (ب to), esp. to call to prayer (بالصلاة); to crow (rooster) **IV** to announce, make known (ب s.th., ب ه to s.o. s.th.), inform, notify (ه s.o.); to call to prayer; to call upon s.o. (ه), urge, admonish, exhort (ه s.o.) to do s.th. (ب); to herald (ب or ه s.th.); to foreshadow (ب s.th.); to be on the verge (ان of doing s.th.) | آذن بالسقوط (بالزوال) (*zawāl*) to show signs of the imminent downfall (end); آذن الليل بانتصاف (*lailu bi-ntiṣāf*) it was close to midnight **V** to herald, announce (ب s.th.) **X** to ask permission (في to do s.th., rarely ب); to ask permission to enter (على s.o.'s house), have o.s. announced (على to s.o.); to take leave (من of s.o.), say good-by (من to)

اذن *iḏn* permission, authorization; باذن الله if God choose, God willing; (pl. اذون *uḏūn*, اذونات *uḏūnāt*) (postal) order | اذن البريد pl. اذونات البريد postal money order; اذن البوسته do.

اذن *uḏun*, *uḏn* f., pl. آذان *āḏān* ear; handle (of a cup) | التهاب الاذن الوسطى (*wusṭā*) middle-ear infection, otitis media (*med.*)

اذان *aḏān* call to prayer

اذينة *uḏaina* little ear; ear lobe

مأذنة *ma'ḏana*, مئذنة *mi'ḏana* pl. مآذن *ma'āḏin*[2] minaret

ايذان *īḏān* declaration, proclamation, announcement (ب of s.th.) | ايذانا بانتهاء الحديث indicating that the conversation is (was) ended

مأذون *ma'ḏūn* authorized; slave with limited legal rights (*Isl. Law*); = مأذون شرعى (*šar'ī*) official authorized by the cadi to perform civil marriages (*Isl. Law*)

مأذونية *ma'ḏūnīya* leave, furlough (*mil. Syr.*); license, franchise (*Syr.*)

مؤذن *mu'aḏḏin* muezzin, announcer of the hour of prayer

اذن **iḏan** see ²اذا

اذى **aḏiya a** to suffer damage, be harmed **IV** to harm, hurt, wrong (ه s.o.); to molest, annoy, irritate, trouble (ه s.o.) | لا يؤذى *lā yu'ḏī* innocuous, harmless, inoffensive **V** to suffer damage, be wronged; to feel offended, be hurt

اذى *aḏan*, اذاة *aḏāh*, اذية *aḏīya* damage, harm; injury; trouble, annoyance, grievance, wrong, offense, insult

اذاية *iḏāya* damage, harm, harmfulness, noxiousness

ايذاء *īḏā'* harm, damage, prejudice; offense, hurt; grievance, nuisance

مؤذ *mu'ḏin* hurtful, harmful, injurious, detrimental, prejudicial; annoying, irksome, troublesome; painful, hurting, offensive, insulting

اراتيقى ***arāṭīqī*** and اراتيكى pl. اراتقة ***arāṭiqa*** a heretic (*Chr.*)

آرامى *ārāmī* Aramaean; Aramaic

ارب *ariba a* (*arab*) to be skillful, proficient (ب in s.th.); — *araba i* to tighten (ه a knot) **III** to try to outwit (ه s.o.)

ارب *arab* pl. آراب *ārāb* wish (فى for), desire, need (فى of s.th.); purpose, aim, goal, end

ارب ***irb*** pl. آراب *ārāb* limb | مزقه اربا اربا (*mazzaqahū*) to tear s.th. to pieces or to shreds

اربة ***irba*** skill, resourcefulness, cleverness, smartness

اربة ***urba*** pl. ارب ***urab*** knot, bow

اريب *arīb* skillful, resourceful, clever, intelligent

مأرب *ma'rab* pl. مآرب *ma'ārib*² wish, desire; object of desire, purpose, aim, goal, end

اربيل *arbīl*² Erbil (the ancient Arbela, city in N Iraq)

ارتوازى ***artuwāzī*** artesian (well)

¹ارث **II** to sow dissension (بين between, among)

²ارث ***irṯ*** inheritance, heritage; estate (of inheritance)

ارثوذكسى ***urṯūḏuksī*** orthodox; الارثوذكسية the Orthodox Church

الروم الارثوذكس ***ar-rūm al-urṯūḏuks*** the Greek Orthodox Church

ارج ***arija a*** (***araj***, أريج ***arīj***) to be fragrant **V** do.

ارج ***araj*** fragrance, sweet smell

ارج ***arij*** fragrant, sweet-smelling

اريج ***arīj*** fragrance, sweet smell

ارجح **II** ***ta'arjaḥa*** to rock, swing

متأرجح ***muta'arjiḥ*** fluctuating

الارجنتين ***al-arjantīn*** Argentina

ارجوان ***urjuwān*** purple

ارجوانى ***urjuwānī*** purple(-colored)

ارجوز popular spelling (*eg.*) of قره جوز ***'ara-gōz*** (q.v.); Punch (in a Punch and Judy show)

ارخ **II** to date (ه a letter, and the like, ب with a date); to write the history of s.th. (ه)

تاريخ ***ta'rīḵ*** dating (of a letter, etc.); ***tārīḵ*** pl. تواريخ ***tawārīḵ²*** date; time; history; chronicle, annals | تاريخ الحياة ***t. al-ḥayāh*** biography; curriculum vitae; تاريخ عام (*'āmm*) world history; علماء التاريخ the historians

تاريخى ***tārīḵī*** historic(al)

مؤرخ ***mu'arriḵ*** pl. *-ūn* historiographer, historian, chronicler, annalist; — ***mu'arraḵ*** dated

ارخبيل ***arḵabīl*** archipelago

ارخن (ἄρχων) pl. اراخنة ***arāḵina*** archon, pl. notables (*Chr.-Copt.*)

اردب *irdabb* (now usually pronounced *ardabb*) pl. ارادب *arādib*[2] ardeb, a dry measure (*Eg.*; = 198 l)

اردبة *irdabba* cesspool

الاردن *al-urdunn* Jordan (river and country)

اردنى *urdunnī* Jordanian | المملكة الاردنية الهاشمية *al-mamlaka al-u. al-hāšimīya* the Hashemite Kingdom of Jordan (official designation)

اردواز (Fr. *ardoise*) *arduwāz* slate

[1]ارز *arz* (n. un. ة) cedar

[2]ارز *aruzz* rice

ارس *arasa i* (*ars*) to till the land

اريس *irrīs* and *arīs* peasant, farmer

ارستقراطى *aristuqrāṭī* aristocratic; aristocrat

ارستقراطية *aristuqrāṭīya* aristocracy

ارسطو *arisṭū* Aristotle

ارش *arš* indemnity, amercement, fine, penalty; blood money (for the shedding of blood; *Isl. Law*)

ارشى ابسقوبس (Gr. ἀρχιεπίσκοπος) archbishop

ارشيدوق (Fr. *archiduc*) archduke, ارشيدوقة archduchess

ارض *arḍ* f., pl. اراض *arāḍin*, ارضون *araḍūn* earth; land, country, region, area; terrain, ground, soil | الارض السفلى (*suflā*) the nether world; الارض المقدسة (*muqaddasa*) the Holy Land, Palestine

ارضى *arḍī* terrestrial, of the earth; soil-, land- (in compounds); situated on or near the ground, ground (adj.); earthly; underground, subterranean

ارضى شوكى *arḍī šaukī* artichoke

ارض *araḍ* (coll.; n. un. ة) termite; woodworm

ارضية *arḍīya* pl. *-āt* floor; ground (also, e.g., of a printed fabric, of a painting); ground floor, first floor (*tun.*); storage, warehouse charges

ارضروم *arḍurūm*[2] Erzurum (city in NE Turkey)

ارطة (also اورطة) *urṭa* pl. ارط *uraṭ* (اورط) battalion (formerly, *Eg.*; *mil.*)

ارطقة *arṭaqa* pl. *-āt* heresy (*Chr.*)

تاريخ see ريخ

ارغن *urġun* pl. اراغن *arāġin*[2] organ (mus. instr.)

ارغول *urġūl, arġūl* a wind instrument (related to the clarinet, consisting of two pipes of unequal length)

ارق *ariqa a* to find no sleep II to make sleepless (ه s.o.), prevent s.o. (ه) from sleeping

ارق *araq* sleeplessness, insomnia

اريكة *arīka* pl. ارائك *arāʼik*[2] couch, sofa; throne

اركيلة *argīla* pl. اراكيل *arāgīl*[2] (*syr.*) water pipe, narghile

ارلندى *irlandı* Irish

[1]ارم *arama i* to bite

ارم *urram* molar teeth | حرق الارم (*ḥarraqa*) to gnash one's teeth (in anger)

ارومة *arūma, urūma* root, origin; stump of a tree

مئرم *miʼram* root (of a tooth)

[2]آرام *ārām* (= ارآم pl. of رئم *riʼm*) white antelopes

الارمن *al-arman* the Armenians

ارمنى *armanī* Armenian (adj. and n.)

ارمينيا *armēniyā* Armenia

الارناوط *al-arnāuṭ* the Albanians

ارناوطى *arnāuṭī* Albanian

ارنب *arnab* f., pl. ارانب *arānib*[2] hare; rabbit | ارنب هندى (*hindī*) guinea pig

ارنبة *arnaba* female hare, doe | ارنبة الانف *a. al-anf* tip of the nose; nose, muzzle (of an animal)

ارنيك (Turk. *örnek*) *urnīk* pl. ارانيك *arānīk*[2] pattern, model; form, blank

اروبا *urubbā* Europe

اروبى *urubbī* European (adj. and n.)

[1]ارى *ary* honey

[2]آرى *ārī* Aryan

آرية *ārīya* Aryanism

اريحا *arīḥā* Jericho

از *azza u i* (ازيز *azīz*) to simmer; to hum, buzz; to whiz, hiss; to fizzle; to wheeze

ازيز *azīz* hum(ming), buzz(ing); whizzing, whizz, whistle (e.g., of bullets)

[1]ازب *azaba i* (*azb*) to flow, run (water)

مئزاب *mi'zāb* pl. مآزيب *ma'āzīb*[2] and ميزاب *mīzāb* pl. ميازيب *mayāzīb*[2] drain; gutter, eaves trough

[2]ازب *izb* dumpy, pudgy, stocky; small man

الازبك *al-uzbak* the Uzbeks

ازر *azara i* (*azr*) to surround (ه s.th.) **II** to clothe (ه s.o. with an ازار *izār* q.v.); to cover, wrap up (ه s.o., ه s.th.); to strengthen, brace (ه s.o., ه s.th.) **III** to help (ه s.o.); to support, back up, strengthen (ه s.o.) **V** and **VIII** to put on an *izār* (see below), wrap o.s. in an *izār* **VI** to help each other; to rally, unite, join forces

ازر *azr* strength | شد ازره *šadda azrahū* or شد من ازره (*min azrihī*) to help, support, encourage s.o., back s.o. up; *šadda azruhū* to be energetic, vigorous, lusty, courageous

ازار *izār* m. and f., pl. ازر *uzur* loincloth; wrap, shawl; wrapper, covering, cover

مئزر *mi'zar* pl. مآزر *ma'āzir*[2] apron; wrapper, covering, cover

مؤازرة *mu'āzara* support, aid, assistance, backing

تآزر *ta'āzur* mutual assistance

ازف *azifa a* (*azaf*, ازوف *uzūf*) to come, approach, draw near (a time)

ازق *azaqa i* (*azq*) to be narrow **V** do.

مأزق *ma'ziq* pl. مآزق *ma'āziq*[2] narrow passageway, narrow pass, strait, bottleneck; predicament, fix, dilemma, critical situation, also مأزق حرج (*ḥarij*)

ازل *azal* pl. آزال *āzāl* eternity (without beginning), sempiternity

ازلى *azalī* eternal, sempiternal

ازلية *azalīya* sempiternity, eternity

ازم **V** to be or become critical, come to a head (situation, relations)

ازمة *azma* pl. *azamāt* emergency; crisis | ازمة وزارية (*wizārīya*) cabinet crisis

تأزم *ta'azzum*: تأزم الحالة *t. al-ḥāla* critical development, aggravation of the situation

مأزوم *ma'zūm* victim of a crisis

ازمير *izmīr*[2] Izmir (formerly Smyrna, seaport in W Turkey)

ازميل *izmīl* pl. ازاميل *azāmīl*[2] chisel

ازوت (Engl.) *azōt* azote, nitrogen

ازوتى *azōtī* nitrogenous

ازى **III** to be opposite s.th. (ه), face (ه s.o., ه s.th.)

ازاء *izā'a* (prep.) opposite, face to face with, facing; in front of; in the face of (e.g., of a situation); as compared with; بازاء *bi-izā'i* opposite, face to face with, facing; in front of; على ازاء *'alā izā'i* in the face of (e.g., of a situation)

آس[1] *ās* myrtle

آس[2] pl. *-āt* ace (playing card)

اسّ[3] II to found, establish, set up (ه s.th.), lay the foundation (ه for) V to be founded, be established, be set up

اس *uss* foundation, basis; exponent of a power (*math.*)

اساس *asās* pl. اسس *usus* foundation (also, of a building), fundament, groundwork, ground, basis; keynote, tonic (*mus.*) | على اساس (with foll. genit.) on the basis of, on the strength of, on account of, according to; لا اساس له من الصحة (*asāsa, ṣiḥḥa*) completely unfounded (news, rumor)

اساسى *asāsī* fundamental, basic; elementary; essential; principal, chief, main | حجر اساسى (*ḥajar*) cornerstone, foundation stone

اساسيات *asāsīyāt* fundamentals, principles

تأسيس *ta'sīs* founding, foundation, establishment, setting up, institution; grounding, laying of the substructure (*arch.*); pl. *-āt* facilities, utilities; institutions

تأسيسى *ta'sīsī* founding; foundational, fundamental | مجلس تأسيسى (*majlis*) constituent assembly

مؤسس *mu'assis* founder

مؤسسة *mu'assasa* pl. *-āt* foundation, establishment; firm (*com.*); institution; organization

الاسبان *al-asbān, al-isbān* the Spaniards

اسبانى *isbānī* Spanish; (pl. *-ūn*) Spaniard

اسبانخ *isbānak* spinach

اسبانيا *isbāniyā* Spain

اسبداج *isbidāj* and اسبيداج *isbīdāj* white lead, ceruse

اسبرتو (It. *spirito*) *isbirto* alcohol

اسبليطة *isbalīṭa* epaulet

است see ست[1]

استاتيكى *istātīkī* static (*el.*)

استاد (Fr. *stade*) *istād* stadium

استاذ *ustāḏ* pl. اساتذة *asātiḏa* master; teacher; professor (academic title); form of address to intellectuals (lawyers, journalists, officials, writers and poets); ledger (*com.*) | الاستاذ الاعظم (*a'ẓam*) Grand Master (of a lodge); الاستاذ الاكبر title of the Rector of Al Azhar University; استاذ كرسى (*kursī*; *Eg.*) and استاذ بكرسى (*Syr.*) full professor; استاذ بلا كرسى (*Syr.*) associate professor; استاذ غير متفرغ (*mutafarriğ*; *Eg.*) part-time professor (holding an office outside the university); استاذ مساعد (*musā'id*) assistant professor (*Eg.*; *Syr.*); استاذ زائر (*Eg.*; *Syr.*) visiting professor; هم اساتذة فى الجدل (*jadal*) they are masters of disputation

استاذية *ustāḏiya* mastership; professorship, professorate

استانبول *istanbūl*[2] Istanbul, Constantinople

استانبولى *istanbūlī* of Istanbul

الآستانة *al-āsitāna*, الاستانة *al-astāna, al-istāna* Constantinople, Istanbul

استبرق *istabraq* brocade

استراتيجى *istrātījī* strategic

استرالى *usturālī* Australian

استراليا *usturāliyā* Australia

استرلينى *istarlīnī* sterling | جنيه استرلينى pound sterling; منطقة الاسترلينى *minṭaqat al-i.* sterling area

استمارة see امر

استوبة (It. *stoppa*) tow, oakum; cotton waste

استوديو (It.-Engl. *studio*) *istūdiyō* pl. استوديوهات *istūdiyōhāt* studio; atelier

استوكهولم *istokholm* Stockholm

استونيا (Engl.) *istōniyā* Estonia

استياتيت *istiyātīt* steatite, soapstone (*min.*)

اسوج look up alphabetically

اسد X to display the courage of a lion (على against)

اسد *asad* pl. اسد *usud, usd,* اسود *usūd,* آساد *āsād* lion; Leo (*astron.*) | داء الاسد leontiasis (*med.*)

[1]اسر *asara i* (*asr*) to bind, fetter, shackle, chain (ه s.o.); to capture, take prisoner (ه s.o.); to captivate, fascinate, hold spellbound (ه s.o.), absorb, arrest (ه the attention) X to surrender, give o.s. up as prisoner

اسر *asr* (leather) strap, thong; capture; captivity | شدة الاسر *šiddat al-a.* vigor, energy

اسرة *usra* pl. اسر *usar, -āt* family; dynasty; clan, kinsfolk, relatives; — *asirra* see سرير

بأسره *bi-asrihī* entirely, completely, altogether, جاءوا بأسرهم all of them came, they came one and all

اسار *isār* (leather) strap, thong; captivity; captivation, enthrallment | وقع فى اساره to be subjected to s.th., fall into the clutches of s.th.

اسير *asīr* pl. اسراء *usarā'*[2], اسرى *asrā,* اسارى *asārā* prisoner, captive, prisoner of war

اسيرة *asīra* pl. *-āt* female prisoner, slave girl

آسر *āsir* winning, captivating, fascinating; captor

مأسور *ma'sūr* captivated, fascinated, enthralled (ب by)

[2]اسرة *asirra* see سرير

[3]ماسورة look up alphabetically

اسرائيل *isrā'īl*[2] Israel | بنو اسرائيل *banū i.* the Israelites; دولة اسرائيل *daulat i.* the State of Israel

اسرائيلى *isrā'īlī* Israelitish; Israelite; Israeli (adj. and n.); اسرائيليات Judaica

اسرافيل *isrāfīl*[2] Israfil, the angel who will sound the trumpet on the Day of Resurrection

اسرب *usrub* lead (metal)

اسطانبول *isṭanbūl*[2] Istanbul, Constantinople

اسطبل *isṭabl* pl. *-āt* stable, barn

اسطبة (It. *stoppa*) *usṭubba* tow, oakum

اسطرلاب *asṭurlāb* astrolabe

اسطقس *isṭaqis* pl. *-āt* element

اسطوانة *usṭuwāna* pl. *-āt* column (*arch.*); cylinder (*math.*; of an engine); phonograph record; — pl. اساطين *asāṭīn*[2] high-ranking, prominent personalities; stars, celebrities, authorities, masters (e.g., of art: اساطين الفن *a. al-fann*)

اسطوانى *usṭuwānī* cylindric(al)

اسطورة *usṭūra* pl. اساطير *asāṭīr*[2] legend, fable, tale, myth, saga

اسطورى *usṭūrī* fabulous, mythical, legendary

اسطول *usṭūl* pl. اساطيل *asāṭīl*[2] fleet; squadron

□ اسطى *usṭā* (colloq. for استاذ) pl. اسطوات *usṭawāt* master; foreman, overseer; also form of address to those in lower callings, e.g., to a cab driver, coachman, etc.

اسف *asifa a* (*asaf*) to regret (على or ل s.th.), feel sorry (على for), be sad (على about) V do.

اسف *asaf* grief, sorrow, chagrin, regret | وا اسفاه! *wā asafāh!* oh, what a pity! it's too bad! ويا للاسف *wa-yā lal-asafi* (or only للاسف) unfortunately; مع الاسف and بكل اسف *bi-kulli asafin* do.

اسف *asif* and اسيف *asīf* regretful, sorry, sad, grieved, distressed

تأسف *ta'assuf* regret

آسف *āsif* regretful, sorry, sad | تركته غير آسف (*ġaira āsifin*) I left him without regret, I was only too glad to leave him

مأسوف عليه *ma'sūf ʿalaihi* mourned (esp. of a dead person, = the late lamented)

مؤسف *mu'sif* distressing, sad, regrettable

متأسف *muta'assif* sad, sorry, regretful; متأسف! sorry!

اسفاناخ *isfānāḵ* and اسفانخ *isfānaḵ* spinach | اسفاناخ رومى (*rūmī*) garden orach (Atriplex hortensis, *bot.*)

اسفلت *asfalt* asphalt

اسفنج *isfanj, isfunj* sponge

اسفنجى *isfanjī* spongy; porous

اسفندان *isfindān* maple (*bot.*)

اسفيداج *isfīdāj* white lead, ceruse

اسفين *isfīn* pl. اسافين *asāfīn*² wedge

اسقربوطى *isqarbūṭī*: مرض اسقربوطى (*maraḍ*) scurvy (*med.*)

اسقف *usquf* pl. اساقفة *asāqifa*, اساقف *asāqif*² bishop | رئيس الاساقفة archbishop

اسقفى *usqufī* episcopal

اسقفية *usqufīya* episcopate, bishopric

اسقمرى *usqumrī, isqumrī* mackerel (*zool.*)

اسقيل *isqīl* an Oriental variety of sea onion (Scilla)

اسكتش (Engl.) *isketš* sketch

اسكتلندا *iskotlandā* Scotland

اسكتلندى *iskotlandī* Scottish, Scotch

اسكلة *iskila* pl. اساكل *asākil*² seaport, commercial center (in the East)

اسكملة *iskamla* stool, footstool

اسكندرونة *iskandarūna*² Iskenderon (formerly Alexandretta, seaport in S Turkey)

الاسكندرية *al-iskandarīya* Alexandria (city in N Egypt)

اسكنديناڤيا *iskandīnāfiyā* Scandinavia

اسل II to sharpen, point, taper (ه s.th.)

اسل *asal* (coll.) rush (*bot.*)

اسلة *asala* pl. -*āt* thorn, spike, prong; point (also, e.g., of a pen = nib); tip of the tongue

الحروف الاسلية *al-ḥurūf al-asalīya* the letters ز, س and ص

اسيل *asīl* smooth | خد اسيل (*ḵadd*) smooth cheek

اسالة *asāla* eliptic, oval form

مؤسل *mu'assal* pointed, tapered

اسلامبولى (variant of استانبولى) *islāmbūlī* of Istanbul

اسلانده *islanda* Iceland

اسم see ¹سم

اسمانجونى *asmānjūnī* sky-blue, azure, cerulean

اسمره *asmara* Asmara (capital of Eritrea)

اسمنت *asmant, ismant* cement

اسمنتى *asmantī* cement (adj.)

اسن *asana i u* and *asina a* to become brackish (water)

آسن *āsin* brackish

اسو and اسا (اسى) *asā u* (*asw*, اسا *asan*) to nurse, treat (ه a wound); to make peace (بين between, among); — اسى *asiya* (اسى,

اسا *asan*) to be sad, grieved, distressed **II** to console, comfort (ه s.o.); to nurse (ه a patient) **III** to share (one's wordly possessions, ه with s.o.), be charitable (ه to s.o.); to assist, support (ه s.o.); to console, comfort (ه s.o.); to treat, cure (ه s.th., medically) **V** to be consoled, find solace **VI** to share the worldly possessions; to assist one another, give mutual assistance

اسى *asan* grief, sorrow, distress

اسوة *uswa, iswa* example, model, pattern | اسوة ب *uswatan bi* following the model or pattern of, along the lines of; in the same manner as, just as, like

مأساة *ma'sāh* pl. مآس *ma'āsin* tragedy, drama

تأسية *ta'siya* consolation, comfort

مواساة *muwāsāh* (for *mu'āsāh*) consolation; charity, beneficence

اسوار **iswār**, *uswār* pl. أساور *asāwir*², اساورة *asāwira* bracelet, bangle

اسوان *aswān*² Aswan (city in S Egypt)

اسوج *asūj* Sweden

اسوجى *asūjī* Swedish

اسو see اسى

آسيا *āsiyā* Asia | آسيا الصغرى (*ṣuġrā*) Asia Minor

آسيوى *āsiyawī* Asiatic, Asian (adj. and n.)

اسيوط *asyūṭ*² Asyût (city in central Egypt)

اشب **V** to be mixed, heterogeneous, motley (a crowd)

اشابة *ušāba* pl. اشائب *ašā'ib*² mixed, motley crowd

اشبيلية *išbīliya*² Seville (city in SW Spain)

اشبين *išbīn* pl. اشابين see شبن

اشر *ašara u* (*ašr*) to saw (ه s.th.); — *i* to file, sharpen with a file (ه s.th.) **II** to mark, indicate, state, enter, record (ه s.th.); to grant a visa; to provide with a visa (على s.th.)

اشر *ašar* liveliness, high spirits, exuberance; wildness; insolence, impertinence

اشر *ašir* lively, sprightly, in high spirits, exuberant; wild; insolent, impertinent, arrogant

مئشار *mi'šār* pl. مواشير *mawāšīr*² saw

تأشير *ta'šīr* issuance of an official endorsement; official endorsement; visa

تأشيرة *ta'šīra* pl. *-āt* visa | تأشيرة مرور *t. murūr* or تأشيرة اجتياز transit visa

مؤشر *mu'aššir* indicator, needle (of a measuring instrument)

مؤشر *mu'aššar* jagged, serrated; marked, designated (ب by, with)

اشفى *išfā* pl. اشاف *ašāfin* awl, punch

اشنان *ušnān* potash; saltwort (Salsola kali; *bot.*)

اشنة *ušna* moss

اشور *ašūr* Assyria

اشورى *ašūrī* Assyrian (adj. and n.)

اصيص *aṣīṣ* pl. اصص *uṣuṣ* flowerpot

اصد **II** to close, shut (a door, etc.)

اصر *iṣr* pl. آصار *āṣār* covenant, compact, contract; load, encumbrance, burden; sin; pl. آصار bonds, ties

آصرة *āṣira* pl. اواصر *awāṣir*² bond, tie (fig., e.g., اواصر الولاء *a. al-walā'* bonds of friendship); obligation, commitment

اصطبل *iṣṭabl* pl. *-āt* stable, barn

اصفهان *iṣfahān*² Isfahan (city in W central Iran)

اصل *aṣula u* (اصالة *aṣāla*) to be or become firmly rooted; to be firmly established; to be of noble origin **II** to found (ه s.th.), give s.th. (ه) a firm foundation, establish the foundation or origin of (ه) **V** to be or become firmly rooted, deep-rooted, ingrained; to take root, be or become firmly established; to derive one's origin (من from) **X** to uproot, root out, extirpate, exterminate, annihilate (ه s.th.); to remove (ه an organ by a surgical operation) | استأصل شأفته (*ša'fatahū*) to eradicate s.th., eliminate s.th. radically

اصل *aṣl* pl. اصول *uṣūl* root; trunk (of a tree); origin, source; cause, reason; descent, lineage, stock (esp., one of a noble character); foundation, fundament, basis; the original (e.g., of a book); — pl. اصول *uṣūl* principles, fundamentals, rudiments, elements (e.g., of a science); rules; basic rules, principles, axioms; real estate, landed property; assets (*fin.*); — اصلا *aṣlan* originally, primarily; (with neg.) by no means, not at all, not in the least | فى الاصل originally, at first; اصول الفقه *u. al-fiqh* the 4 foundations of Islamic jurisprudence, i.e., Koran, Sunna, *qiyās* (analogy) and *ijmā'* (consensus); اصول وخصوم assets and liabilities; اصول مضاعفة (*muḍā'afa*) double-entry bookkeeping; حسب الاصول (*ḥasaba*) properly, in conformity with regulations

اصلى *aṣlī* original, primary, primal, initial; genuine, authentic, pure; basic, fundamental, principal, chief, main | الثمن الاصلى (*ṯaman*) cost price; الجهات الاصلية (*jihāt*) the cardinal points (of the compass); عدد اصلى (*'adad*) cardinal number; عضو اصلى (*'uḍw*) regular member

اصولى *uṣūlī* in accordance with the rules, conforming to prevailing principles; traditional, usual; legist

اصيل *aṣīl* pl. اصلاء *uṣalā'*[2] of pure, noble origin; original, authentic, genuine; pure; proper, actual; firm, solid; sound, reasonable, sensible; of strong, unswerving character, steadfast; deep-rooted; native, indigenous | الاصل الاصيل the actual reason; اصيل الرأى of sound, unerring judgment

اصيل *aṣīl* pl. آصال *āṣāl*, اصائل *aṣā'il*[2] time before sunset, late afternoon

اصالة *aṣāla* firmness, steadfastness, strength of character; nobility of descent, purity of origin; *aṣālatan* immediately, directly, personally | اصالة الرأى *a. ar-ra'y* clarity and firmness of judgment; judiciousness; بالاصالة عن نفسه spontaneously, of one's own accord, in one's own name, personally, privately (as opposed to بالنيابة عن غيره); اصالة ونيابة *aṣālatan wa-niyābatan* directly and indirectly

تأصيلة *ta'ṣīla* pedigree, genealogy

تأصل *ta'aṣṣul* deep-rootedness

استئصال *isti'ṣāl* extirpation, extermination, (radical) elimination; removal b surgery

متأصل *muta'aṣṣil* deep-rooted, deep-seated; chronic (illness)

اطيط *aṭīṭ* the moaning bray of a camel

اطر[1] *aṭara i u* (*aṭr*) and **II** to bend, curve (ه s.th.)

اطار *iṭār* pl. *-āt*, اطر *uṭur* frame (also, of eyeglasses); tire (of a wheel); hoop (of a barrel, etc.)

اطارة *iṭāra* rim, felly (of a wheel)

اطارى *iṭārī* framelike, hoop-shaped

اطرية[2] see طرى

اطرغلة *uṭrugulla* a variety of pigeon

اطرون *aṭrūn* = نطرون

الاطلنطيق, الاطلانتيك *al-aṭlantik, al-aṭlanṭīq* the Atlantic

اطلانطى *aṭlanṭiqī* and اطلانطى *aṭlanṭī* Atlantic

اطلس *aṭlas*[2] satin; (pl. اطالس *aṭālis*[2]) atlas, volume of geographical maps

اطلسى *aṭlasī* Atlantic

اطلنطى *aṭlanṭī* Atlantic | الحلف الاطلنطى (*ḥilf*) the Atlantic Pact

اطوم *aṭūm* sea turtle

اغا *aġā*, آغا *āġā* pl. اغوات *aġawāt* aga, lord, master, sir; eunuch, harem chamberlain

الاغريق *al-iġrīq*, الاغارقة *al-aġāriqa* the Greeks

اغريقى *iġrīqī* Greek, Grecian (adj. and n.)

اغسطس *aġusṭus* August (month)

افّ V to grumble, mutter in complaint (من about)

اف *uff* dirt (in the ears or under the nails), earwax, cerumen

اف *uff* interj. expressing anger or displeasure

افف *afaf* displeasure; grumbling, grumble

تأفف *ta'affuf* displeasure; grumbling, grumble

الافرنج *al-ifranj* the Franks, the Europeans | بلاد الافرنج Europe

افرنجى *ifranjī* European

افرنسى *ifransī* French; الافرنسية the French language; الافرنسيون the French

افريز *ifrīz* pl. افاريز *afārīz*[2] frieze; edge; curb; sidewalk | افريز المحطة *i. al-maḥaṭṭa* platform (of a railroad station); افريز الحائط molding (*arch.*)

افريقا *afrīqā* f. and افريقيا *ifrīqiyā*, now usually pronounced *afrīqiyā* f. Africa | افريقيا الشمالية (*šamālīya*) North Africa

افريقى *ifrīqī*, now usually pronounced *afrīqī* African; (pl. *-ūn*, افارقة *afāriqa*) an African

آفرين *āfirīn* bravo! well done!

افسنتين *ifsantīn*, *ifsintīn* wormwood, absinthe (Artemisia absinthium; *bot.*)

افشين *ifšīn* pl. افاشين *afāšīn*[2] litany (*Chr.*)

الافغان *al-afġān* the Afghans; Afghanistan

افغانستان *afġānistān* Afghanistan

افغانى *afġānī* Afghan (adj. and n.)

افق *ufq*, *ufuq* pl. آفاق *āfāq* horizon; range of vision, field of vision; pl. distant lands, faraway countries, remote regions; provinces, interior of the country (as distinguished from the capital) | آفاق الارض *ā. al-arḍ* the remotest parts of the earth; آفاق البلاد *ā. al-bilād* the outlying portions of the country; شذاذ الآفاق *šuḏḏāḏ al-ā.* foreigners, travelers

افقى *ufqī* horizontal

آفاقى *āfāqī* coming from a distant country or region

افاق *affāq* wandering, roving, roaming; tramp, vagabond

افك *afaka i* (*afk*) and *afika a* (*ifk*, *afk*, *afak*, افوك *ufūk*) to lie, tell a lie

افك *ifk* and افيكة *afīka* pl. افائك *afā'ik*[2] lie, untruth, falsehood

افاك *affāk* liar, lying

افل *afala u i* (افول *ufūl*) to go down, set (stars)

افول *ufūl* setting (of stars)

آفل *āfil* transitory, passing

افلاطون *aflāṭūn*[2] Plato

افن *afan* stupidity

افين *afīn* and مأفون *ma'fūn* stupid, foolish, fatuous; fool

افندى *afandī* pl. *-īya* gentleman (when referring to non-Europeans wearing Western clothes and the tarboosh); (after the name) a title of respect (*eg.*); !افندم *afandim!* Sir! (*eg.*) *afandim?* (I beg your) pardon? What did you say?

افوكاتو (It. *avvocato*) *avokātō* advocate, lawyer, attorney | الافوكاتو العمومى representative of the attorney general (= Fr. *avocat général*)

افيون *afyūn* opium | روح الافيون *rūḥ al-a.* laudanum

اقة *uqqa* pl. *-āt* oka, a weight, in Eg. = 1.248 kg, in Syr. = 1.282 kg

مؤقت see وقت

اقحوان *uqḥuwān* pl. اقاحى *aqāḥīy* daisy

اقرباذين *aqrabādīn* composite medicament | علم الاقرباذين *ʿilm al-a.* pharmaceutics, pharmacology

اقرباذينى *aqrabādīnī* pharmaceutic(al)

اقط *aqiṭ* cottage cheese

اقليد *iqlīd* look up alphabetically

اقلم *aqlama* to acclimate, acclimatize, adapt, adjust II *taʾaqlama* to acclimatize (o.s.)

اقليم *iqlīm* pl. اقاليم *aqālīm*² climate; area, region; province, district; administrative district (*Eg.*; = مديرية); الاقاليم country, provinces (as distinguished from the city)

اقليمى *iqlīmī* climatic; regional, local; territorial | المياه الاقليمية (*miyāh*) territorial waters

اقليد *iqlīd* pl. اقاليد *aqālīd*² key

اقليدس *iqlīdis*² Euclid

اقنوم *uqnūm* pl. اقانيم *aqānīm*² hypostasis, divine person within the Trinity (*Chr.*); constitutive element

اقونة (Gr. εἰκών) *iqūna* icon (*Chr.*)

اقيانوسية *uqyānūsīya* Oceania

اكادى *akkādī* Akkadian

اكاديمية *akādīmīya* academy

اكتوبر *oktōbir* October

اكد II to assure (ه ل s.o. of, ان that); to give assurance (ه ل to s.o. of); to confirm (ه s.th., a view) V to be or become convinced, convince o.s. (من of s.th.); to reassure o.s., make sure (من of s.th.); to be sure (من of); to be urgent, imperative, requisite

تأكيد *taʾkīd* pl. *-āt* assurance; confirmation; emphasis; بالتأكيد most certainly! of course!

تأكد *taʾakkud* assurance, reassurance

اكيد *akīd* certain, sure; firm (resolve); definite (desire); urgent, imperative (need); اكيدا *akīdan* certainly! surely!

مؤكد *muʾakkad* certain, definite, sure; confirmed

متأكد *mutaʾakkid* convinced (من of)

اكر[1] *akara i* (*akr*) to plow, till, cultivate (ه the land)

اكار *akkār* pl. *-ūn*, اكرة *akara* plowman

اكرة[2] *ukra* pl. اكر *ukar* ball (for playing)

اكزيما *ekzēmā* eczema (*med.*)

اشعة اكس *ašiʿʿat iks* X-rays

اكسترا extra

اكسجين *oksižēn* oxygen

اكسد *aksada* to oxidize, cause to rust II *taʾaksada* to oxidize, rust, become rusty

اكسيد *uksīd* pl. اكاسيد *akāsīd*² oxide

اكسفورد Oxford

اكسيجين *oksižēn* oxygen

اكسير *iksīr* elixir

اكف *akuff* see كف

اكل *akala u* (*akl*, مأكل *maʾkal*) to eat (ه s.th.); to eat up, consume, swallow, devour, destroy (ه s.th.); to eat, gnaw (ه at), eat away, corrode, erode (ه s.th.); to spend unlawfully (ه s.th.), enrich o.s., feather one's nest (ه with) | اكل عليه الدهر وشرب (*dahru, šariba*) to be old and worn out, be timeworn; اكل الربا (*ribā*) to take usurious interest; يعلم من اين تؤكل الكتف *ya'lamu min aina tu'kalu l-katif* he knows how to tackle the matter properly; اكله جلده (*jilduhū*) his skin itched; اكل فى صحن (*ṣaḥn*) to eat off a plate; اكل حقه (*ḥaqqahū*) to encroach upon s.o.'s rights **II** and **IV** to give s.o. (ه) s.th. (ه) to eat, feed (ه ه s.o. s.th.) **III** to eat, dine (ه with s.o.) **V** to be devoured, be consumed; to be eaten away, corrode, undergo corrosion; to become old, worn, timeworn, full of cracks; to be destroyed by corrosion **VI** = **V**

اكل ***akl*** food; meal, repast; fodder, feed | غرفة الاكل *ġurfat al-a.* dining room; (*eg.*) اكل البحر *a. al-baḥr* land washed away by the sea or the Nile (as opposed to طرح البحر)

اكل ***ukul, ukl*** food; fruit | آتى اكله to bear fruit

اكلة ***akla*** pl. *akalāt* meal, repast; — *ukla* bite, morsel

اكال ***ukāl*** O prurigo, itch eruption (*med.*)

اكال ***akkāl***, اكيل ***akīl***, اكول ***akūl*** voracious, gluttonous; hearty eater, gourmand, glutton

مأكل ***ma'kal*** pl. مآكل *ma'ākil*[2] food, eats

تأكل ***ta'akkul*** wear; corrosion; erosion (*geol.*)

تآكل ***ta'ākul*** wear; corrosion; erosion (*geol.*)

ائتكال ***i'tikāl*** erosion (*geol.*)

آكل ***ākil*** eater

آكلة ***ākila*** gangrenous sore

مأكول ***ma'kūl*** eatable, edible; pl. مأكولات food, foodstuffs, eatables, edibles

مؤاكل ***mu'ākil*** table companion

متأكل ***muta'akkil*** and متآكل ***muta'ākil*** corroded; eroded; worn, timeworn; full of cracks; rusty, rust-eaten

اكليروس ***iklīrūs*** clergy (*Chr.*)

اكليروسية ***iklīrūsīya*** clericalism

اكليركى ***iklīrikī*** cleric(al)

اكلينيكى ***iklīnīkī*** clinical

اكمة ***akama*** pl. *-āt*, اكام *ikām*, اكم *ukum*, آكام *ākām* (coll. اكم *akam*) hill; reef; heap, pile | وراء الاكمة ما وراءها (*warā'a*) something's fishy! there is more to it than meets the eye

ال ***ill*** pact, covenant; blood relationship, consanguinity

الا[1] ***a-lā*** and اما *a-mā* see ا *a*

الا[2] ***alā*** see الو[1]

الا[3] ***allā*** (= ان لا *an lā*) lest, that ... not, in order that ... not, so as not to

الا[4] ***illā*** (= ان لا *in lā*) unless, if not; except, save; (after negation:) only, but, not until | الا ان *illā anna* except that ..., yet, however, nevertheless (also introducing main clauses); الا اذا *illā iḏā* unless, if not; except when; والا *wa-illā* (and if not =) otherwise, or else; الا وهو *illā wa-huwa* (with a preceding negation) unless he ..., except that he ...; وما هى الا ان *wa-mā hiya illā an* (with following verb in perf.) it was not long until ...; presently, forthwith; وما هى الا ان ... حتى *wa-mā hiya illā an ... ḥattā* no sooner had he ... than ..., e.g., فما هى الا ان هم حتى فعل (*hamma*) he had no sooner made his plan than he carried it out

الاسكا ***alaskā*** Alaska

الاى ***alāy*** and آلاى *ālāy* pl. *-āt* regiment

الب[1] *alaba u i* (*alb*) to gather, join forces, rally II to incite (على ه s.o. against) V to rally, band together, plot, conspire (على against)

جبال الالب[2] *jibāl al-alb* the Alps

الالبان *al-albān* the Albanians

البانيا *albāniyā* Albania

الخ abbreviation of الى آخره *ilā āḵirihī* and so on, etc.

الذى *allaḏī*, f. التى *allatī*, pl. m. الذين *allaḏīna* f. اللاتى *allātī*, اللواتى *allawātī*, اللائى *allā'ī* (relative pronoun) he who, that which; who, which, that | بعد اللتيا والتى *ba'da l-lutayyā wa-llatī* after lengthy discussions, after much ado

الزاس (Fr. *Alsace*) *alzās*[2] Alsace (region of NE France)

الس II to belittle, disparage (على s.o.)

الف[1] *alf* pl. الوف *ulūf*, آلاف *ālāf* thousand; millennium | الوف مؤلفة (*mu'allafa*) or آلاف مؤلفة thousands and thousands; عشرات الالوف *'ašarāt al-u.* tens of thousands; مئات الالوف *mi'āt al-u.* hundreds of thousands

الفى *alfī*: عيد الفى (*'īd*) millennial celebration, millenary

الف[2] *alif* name of the letter ا | من الفه الى يائه from beginning to end, from A to Z; يعرف الفه وياءه (*wa-yā'ahū*) he knows it from A to Z; الف باء ABC

الف[3] *alifa a* (*alf*) to be acquainted, familiar, conversant (ه with s.th.); to be on intimate terms (ه with s.o.); to be or get accustomed, used, habituated (ه to); to like (ه s.th.), be fond of (ه); to become tame II to accustom, habituate (ه ه s.o. to s.th.); to tame, domesticate (ه an animal); to form (ه e.g., a committee, a government); to unite, join, combine, put together (بين different things); to compile, compose, write (ه a book) V to be composed, be made up, consist (من of); to be united, be combined VI to be attuned to each other, be in tune, be in harmony; to harmonize (مع with) VIII to be united, be linked, be connected; to be on familiar, intimate terms (ب with); to form a coalition (*pol.*); to fit, suit (مع s.th.), go well, agree, harmonize (مع with); to be well-ordered, neat, tidy X to seek the intimacy, court the friendship (ه of s.o.)

الف *ilf* pl. الاف *ullāf* intimate; close friend, intimate, confidant; lover

الفة *ulfa* familiarity, intimacy; friendship, love, affection; union, concord, harmony, congeniality

اليف *alīf* familiar, intimate; tame, domesticated (animal); friendly, amicable, genial; (pl. الائف *alā'if*[2]) intimate, close friend, associate, companion

الوف *alūf* familiar, intimate; tame, domesticated (animal); attached, devoted, faithful

مألف *ma'laf* object of familiarity

تأليف *ta'līf* formation (e.g., of a government); union, junction, combination (بين of separate things); literary work; composition, compilation, writing (of a book, of an article); (pl. تآليف *ta'ālīf*[2], تواليف) work, book, publication

تآلف *ta'āluf* harmony; familiarity, intimacy, mutual affection; comradeship, camaraderie

ائتلاف *i'tilāf* concord, harmony; agreement (مع with); union; coalition, entente (*pol.*)

ائتلافى *i'tilāfī* coalition- (in compounds) | وزارة ائتلافية coalition cabinet

مألوف *ma'lūf* familiar, accustomed; usual, customary; custom, usage

مؤلف *mu'allif* pl. *-ūn* author, writer; — *mu'allaf* composed, consisting, made up (من of); written, compiled; (pl. *-āt*) book, publication; see also [1]الف *alf*

متآلف *muta'ālif* harmonious

الق *alaqa i* (*alq*) to shine, radiate, flash, glitter, glisten **V** and **VIII** do.

الق *alaq* brightness, brilliance

الاق *allāq* bright, shining, brilliant, radiant; glittering, flashing, sparkling

تألق *ta'alluq* glow, radiance, effulgence

متألق *muta'alliq* bright, shining, brilliant, radiant

الكترونى *elektrōnī* electronic | عقل الكترونى (*'aql*) electronic computer

[1]الم *alima a* (*alam*) to be in pain, feel pain; to suffer (ب from s.th.) **II** and **IV** to cause pain or suffering (ه to s.o.), pain, ache, hurt (ه s.o.) **V** = **I**; to complain

الم *alam* pl. آلام *ālām* pain, ache, suffering, agony | آلام نفسانية (*nafsānīya*) mental agony; اسبوع الآلام *usbū' al-ā.* Passion Week (*Chr.*)

اليم *alīm* aching, sore; sad, grievous, painful, excruciating; hurting

تألم *ta'allum* sensation of pain, pain, ache

مؤلم *mu'lim* aching, painful; sad, grievous, distressing

متألم *muta'allim* aching, painful; in pain, suffering, deeply afflicted; tormented

[2]الام *ilā-ma* see ال

الماس *almās* (*al* sometimes interpreted as definite article) diamond

الالمان *al-almān* the Germans

الماني *almānī* German; (pl. *-ūn*, المان *almān*) a German

المانيا *almāniyā* Germany

المانية *almānīya* German character or characteristics, Germanity

اله **II** to deify (ه s.o.), make a god of s.o. (ه) **V** to become a deity, a godhead; to deify o.s.

اله, الاه *ilāh* pl. آلهة *āliha* god, deity, godhead

الاهة *ilāha* pl. *-āt* goddess

الهى, الاهى *ilāhī* divine, of God; theological; الالاهيات *al-ilāhīyāt* theological, spiritual concerns | علم الالاهيات *'ilm al-i.* theology

الله *allāh* Allah, God (as the One and Only) | لله درك *li-llāhi darruka* exclamation of admiration and praise, see در

اللهم *allāhumma* O God! | اللهم الا (*illā*) unless, were it not that, except that, or at best (after a negative statement); اللهم اذا (*idā*) at least if or when; if only; اللهم نعم (*na'am*) by God, yes! most certainly!

الوهية *ulūhīya* divine power, divinity

تأليه *ta'līh* deification, apotheosis

آله *ālih* (pagan) god

آلهة *āliha* pl. *-āt* goddess

آلهى *ālihī* divine

متأله *muta'allih* divine, heavenly

اللاهوت etc., see لاهوت

[1]الا (الو) *alā u* to neglect or fail to do, not to do (فى s.th.), desist, refrain (فى from s.th.) | لا يألو جهدا فى (*jahdan*) he will go to any length, he spares no effort, goes out of his way for **IV** to swear | آلى على نفسه ان he promised himself that he …

ايلاء *īlā'* oath

[2]آلو (Fr. *hallo*) hello!

الومنيا *alūminyā* and الومنيوم *alūminyom* aluminum

¹الى *ilā* (prep.) to, toward; up to, as far as; till, until; الى ان (conj.) until | الى آخره (*āḵirihī*) and so forth, et cetera; الى ذلك besides, moreover, furthermore, in addition to that; الى غد till tomorrow! الى اللقاء (*liqā'*) good-by! الام *ilāma* (= الى ما) up to where? how far? الى متى till when? how long? اليك عنى (*'annī*) get away from me! away with you! الى جانب ذلك (*jānibi ḏ.*) besides, moreover, in addition to that; هذا الى ان moreover, furthermore; الى غير ذلك (*ḡairi ḏ.*) and the like; وما اليه and the like, et cetera; ومن اليه (اليهم) (*wa-man*) and other people like that; اليك (addressing the reader) now here you have ...; here is (are) ...; following is (are) ..., e.g., والى القارئ ما in the following, the reader will find what ...; اسلوب عبرانى الى العربية (*uslūb 'ibrānī*) a style of Hebrew approximating Arabic; لا الى هذا ولا الى ذاك neither this way nor that way, belonging to neither group; الامر اليك it's up to you, the decision is yours

²آلاء *ālā'* (pl. of الى *ilan*) benefits, blessings

³الية *alya, ilya* pl. *alayāt* fat tail (of a sheep); buttock

الياذة *iliyāḏa* Iliad

¹ام *am* or? (introducing the second member of an alternative question)

²امة *ama* pl. اماء *imā'*, اموات *amawāt* bondmaid, slave girl

³ام *amma u* (*amm*) to go, betake o.s., repair (ه to a place), go to see (ه s.o.); — (امامة *imāma*) to lead the way, lead by one's example (ه s.o.); to lead (ه s.o.) in prayer; — (امومة *umūma*) to be or become a mother II to nationalize (ه s.th.) V to go, betake o.s., repair (ه to a place), go to see (ه s.o.) VIII to follow the example (ب of s.o.)

ام *umm* pl. امهات *ummahāt* mother; source, origin; basis, foundation; original, original version (of a book); the gist, essence of s.th.; pl. امهات matrix (*typ.*) | ام الحبر *u. al-ḥibr* cuttlefish, squid; ام الحسن *u. al-ḥasan* (*maḡr.*) nightingale; ام الخلول *u. al-ḵulūl* river mussel (*zool.*); ام درمان *u. durmān* Omdurman (city in central Sudan, opposite Khartoum); ام الراس *u. ar-ra's* skull, brain; cerebral membrane, meninges; ام اربع واربعين *u. arba' wa-arba'īn* centipede; ام شملة *u. šamla(ta)* this world, the worldly pleasures; بام العين *bi-u. il-'ain* or بام عينه with one's own eyes; ام القرآن and ام الكتاب the first sura of the Koran; ام القرى *u. al-qurā* Mecca; ام الكتاب also: the original text of the Book from which Koranic revelation derives; the uncontested portions of the Koran; ام الوطن *u. al-waṭan* capital, metropolis; امهات الحوادث the most important events; امهات الحروف matrix (*typ.*); امهات المسائل the main problems; امهات الفضائل the principal virtues

امة *umma* pl. امم *umam* nation, people; generation | امة محمد Mohammed's community, the Mohammedans; الامم المتحدة (*muttaḥida*) the United Nations

امى *ummī* maternal, motherly; illiterate uneducated; (pl. *-un*) an illiterate

امية *ummīya* ignorance; illiteracy; see also under ²اموى

اممى *umamī* international

امومة *umūma* motherhood; motherliness, maternity

امام *amāma* (prep.) in front of; in the presence of | الى الامام (*amāmi*) to the front, forward, onward, ahead; لم يكن امامه الا ان (*illā an*) he had no other alternative but to ...; وقف امامه (*waqafa*) to oppose, resist, stop, check s.th.

امامى *amāmī* front, fore-, anterior, forward, foremost | نقطة امامية (*nuqṭa*) outpost

امام *imām* pl. ائمة *a'imma* imam, prayer leader; leader; master; plumb line

امامة *imāma* imamah, function or office of the prayer leader; imamate; leading position; precedence

تأميم *ta'mīm* pl. *-āt* nationalization

¹اما *a-mā* see ا *a*

²اما *ammā* (with foll. ف *fa*) as to, as for, as far as ... is concerned; but; yet, however, on the other hand | اما بعد (*ba'du*) (a formular phrase linking introduction and actual subject of a book or letter, approx.:) now then ..., now to our topic: ...

³اما *immā* if; واما — اما be it — or, either — or (also او — اما)

امبراطور *imbarāṭūr* emperor

امبراطورى *imbarāṭūrī* imperialist(ic)

امبراطورية *imbarāṭūrīya* empire, imperium; imperialism

امبير *ambīr* pl. امابير *amābīr*² ampere (*el.*)

امبيق *imbīq* = انبيق

امت *amt* crookedness, curvedness, curvation, curvature; weakness

امد *amad* pl. آماد *āmād* end, terminus, extremity; period, stretch or span of time, time; distance | منذ امد بعيد for a long time (past); قصير الامد short-dated; of short duration, short-lived; short-term

امر *amara u* (*amr*) to order, command. bid, instruct (ه s.o. ب to do s.th.), commission, charge, entrust (ه s.o. ب with s.th. or to do s.th.); — *amara, amura u* (امارة *imāra*) to become an emir **II** to invest with authority, make an emir (ه s.o., على over) **III** to ask s.o.'s (ه) advice, consult (ه s.o.) **V** to come to power; to set o.s. up as lord and master; to behave like an emir; to assume an imperious attitude; to be imperious, domineering **VI** to take counsel, deliberate together, confer, consult with each other; to plot, conspire (على against) **VIII** to deliberate, take counsel (ب about); to conspire, plot, hatch a plot (ب against s.o.) | ائتمر بامره to carry out s.o.'s orders

امر *amr* 1. pl. اوامر *awāmir*² order, command, instruction (ب to do s.th.); ordinance, decree; power, authority; (*gram.*) imperative | امر عال (*'ālin*) royal decree (formerly, *Eg.*); امر على (*'alīy*) decree, edict of the Bey (formerly, *Tun.*); امر قانونى ordinance having the force of law (*Tun.*); الامر والنهى (*wa-n-nahy*) pl. الاوامر والنواهى (lit.: command and interdiction, i.e.) sovereign power; full power(s), supreme authority; امر توريد (delivery) order (*com.*); تحت أمرك at your disposal, at your service. — 2. pl. امور *umūr* matter, affair, concern, business | امر واقع (accomplished) fact; امر معروف common knowledge; فى اول الامر at first, in the beginning; لامر ما (*amrin*) for some reason or other; اليس الامر كذلك isn't it so? اما والامر كذلك (*ammā wa-l-amru*) things being as they are, there will, no doubt, ...; مهما يكن من امر (*min amrin*) whatever may happen; however things may be; هو بين امرين he has two possibilities (or alternatives); الامر الذى which (introducing a relative clause the antecedent of which is another clause); قضى امره *quḍiya amruhū* it's all over with him; in the latter and similar phrases, امره is a frequent paraphrase of "he"

امر *immar* simple-minded, stupid

امرة *imra* power, influence, authority, command | تحت امرته under his command

امارة *amāra* pl. *-āt*, امائر *amā'ir*² sign, token, indication, symptom, mark, characteristic

امارة *imāra* position or rank of an emir; princely bearing or manners; principality, emirate; authority, power | امارة البحر *i. al-baḥr* office or jurisdiction of an admiral, admiralty; امارات ساحل عمان (*i. s. ʿumān*) Trucial Oman

امير *amīr* pl. امراء *umarā'*[2] commander; prince, emir; title of princes of a ruling house; tribal chief | امير الاى (*alāy*) commander of a regiment (formerly, *Eg.*; approx.: colonel; as a naval rank, approx.: captain); امير الامراء approx.: major general (*Tun.*); امير البحار (*Eg.* 1939) approx.: admiral, كبير امراء البحار (*Eg.* 1939) approx.: fleet admiral; امير البحر *a. al-baḥr* admiral (when referring to a non-Arab officer of this rank; *Eg.* 1939 approx.: vice admiral); امير البحر الاكبر or امير البحار الاعظم fleet admiral (when referring to a non-Arab officer of this rank); امير اللواء *a. al-liwā'* (*Ir.*, since 1933) brigadier; امير لواء العسة *a. l. al-ʿassa* commandant of the Bey's palace guard (formerly, *Tun.*); امير المؤمنين *a. al-mu'minīn* Commander of the Faithful, Caliph

اميرة *amīra* pl. *-āt* princess

اميرى *amīrī* (and □ ميرى *mīrī*) government(al), state-owned, state, public | ارض اميرى (*arḍ*) government land (*Syr.*); المطبعة الاميرية government press

امار *ammār* constantly urging, always demanding (ب to do s.th.); inciting, instigating | النفس الامارة بالسوء (*nafs, sū'*) the baser self (of man) that incites to evil

تأمور *ta'mūr* soul, mind, spirit; pericardium (*anat.*) | التهاب التأمور pericarditis (*med.*)

مؤامرة *mu'āmara* pl. *-āt* deliberation, counsel, conference; plot, conspiracy

تأمر *ta'ammur* imperiousness, domineeringness; imperious deportment, overbearing manners

تآمر *ta'āmur* joint consultation, counsel, deliberation, conference; plot, conspiracy

ائتمار *i'timār* deliberation, counsel, conference; plot, conspiracy

استئمارة *isti'māra* (frequently written استمارة) form, blank

آمر *āmir* commander; lord, master; orderer, purchaser, customer, client | الآمر الناهى absolute master, vested with unlimited authority

مأمور *ma'mūr* commissioned, charged; commissioner; civil officer, official, esp., one in executive capacity; the head of a *markaz* and *qism* (*Eg.*) | مأمور البوليس commissioner of police; مأمور التفليسة (*taflīsa*) receiver (in bankruptcy; *jur.*); مأمور الحركة *m. al-ḥaraka* traffic manager (railroad); مأمور التصفية *m. at-taṣfiya* receiver (in equity, in bankruptcy; *jur.*)

مأمورية *ma'mūrīya* pl. *-āt* order, instruction; errand; task, assignment, mission; commission; commissioner's office, administrative branch of a government agency, e.g., مأمورية قضائية (*qaḍā'īya*) judicial commission charged with jurisdiction in outlying communities (*Eg.*)

متآمرون *muta'āmirūn* conspirators, plotters

مؤتمرون *mu'tamirūn* conspirators, plotters; members of a congress, convention, or conference, conferees

مؤتمر *mu'tamar* pl. *-āt* conference; convention, congress | مؤتمر الصلح *m. aṣ-ṣulḥ* peace conference

امرك II *ta'amraka* to become Americanized, adopt the American way of life, imitate the Americans

تأمرك *ta'amruk* Americanization

امرلس *amarillis* amaryllis (*bot.*)

امريكا *amrīkā* (formerly, also امريقا) America | امريكا الجنوبية (*janūbīya*) South America

امريكى *amrīkī* American; (pl. *-ūn*) an American

الامريكان *al-amrīkān* the Americans

امريكانى *amrīkānī* American; (pl. *-ūn*) an American

امس *amsu* (but acc. امسا *amsan*) the day past, yesterday; the immediate past, recent time; — *amsi* (adv.) yesterday; recently, lately, not long ago | بالامس *bi-l-amsi* yesterday; not long ago; امس الاول *amsi l-awwal* two days ago, the day before yesterday

امسية *umsīya* pl. *-āt*, اماسى *amāsīy* evening

امستردام *amstirdām* Amsterdam

امشير *amšīr* the sixth month of the Coptic calendar

امع *imma'* and امعة *imma'a* characterless person; opportunist, timeserver

امل *amala u* (*amal*) to hope (ه or ب for), entertain hopes (ه or ب of) II to hope; to expect (ه من s.th. of s.o.); to raise hopes (ه in s.o.), hold out hopes (ه for s.o.), give (ه s.o.) reason to hope or expect | امله خيرا (*kairan*) to let s.o. hope for the best V to look attentively (ه, فى at), regard, contemplate (ه, فى s.th.); to meditate; to consider, think over, ponder (ه, فى s.th.), reflect (ه, فى on)

امل *amal* pl. آمال *āmāl* hope, expectation (فى of s.th., also ب) | امل كاذب fallacious hope

مأمل *ma'mal* pl. مآمل *ma'āmil*[2] hope

تأمل *ta'ammul* pl. *-āt* consideration; contemplation; pl. تأملات meditations

آمل *āmil* hopeful

مؤمل *mu'ammil* hopeful

مأمول *ma'mūl* hoped for, expected

متأمل *muta'ammil* contemplative, meditative, reflective; pensive, wistful, musing

امن *amuna u* (امانة *amāna*) to be faithful, reliable, trustworthy; — *amina a* (*amn*, امان *amān*) to be safe, feel safe (من or ه from) II to reassure (ه s.o.), set s.o.'s (ه) mind at rest; to assure, ensure, safeguard, guarantee, warrant, bear out, confirm, corroborate (على, ه s.th.); to insure (ضد الحريق against fire); to entrust (ه to s.o., على s.th.); to say "amen" (على to s.th.) IV to believe (ب in) VIII to trust (ه s.o.), have confidence, have faith (ه in); to entrust (على ه s.o. with, to s.o. s.th.) X = VIII; to ask for protection, for a promise of security, for indemnity (ه s.o.)

امن *amn* safety; peace, security, protection | الامن العام (*'āmm*) public safety; رجال الامن the police

امان *amān* security, safety; peace; shelter, protection; clemency, quarter (*mil.*); safeguarding, assurance of protection; indemnity, immunity from punishment | فى امان الله (a valedictory phrase) in God's protection!

امين *amīn* pl. امناء *umanā'*[2] reliable, trustworthy, loyal, faithful, upright, honest; safe, secure; authorized representative or agent; trustee; guarantor (على of); chief, head; superintendent, curator, custodian, guardian, keeper; chamberlain; master of a guild (*Tun.*); (*mil.*) approx.: quartermaster-sergeant (*Eg.* 1939) | الامين الاول (*awwal*) Lord Chamberlain (formerly, at the Eg. Court); كبير الامناء approx.: Chief Master of Ceremonies (ibid.); امين المخزن *a. al-makzan* warehouse superintendent; stock clerk; امين سر الدولة *a. sirr ad-daula* and امين السر *a. as-sirr* permanent secretary of state (*Syr.*); امين الصندوق *a. aṣ-ṣundūq* and امين المال treasurer; cashier; امين العاصمة mayor (esp. *Ir.*); امين عام (*'āmm*) secretary general; امين المكتب *a. al-maktab* (formerly) a subaltern rank in the Eg. navy (1939)

آمين *āmīn* amen!

امانة *amāna* reliability, trustworthiness; loyalty, faithfulness, fidelity, fealty; integrity, honesty; confidence, trust, good faith; deposition in trust; trusteeship; (pl. *-āt*) s.th. deposited in trust, a deposit, trust, charge; secretariat | امانة الصندوق *a. aṣ-ṣundūq* treasury department; امانة عامة (*'āmma*) secretariat general; مخزن الامانات *makzan al-a.* baggage checkroom

مأمن *ma'man* place of safety, safe place

تأمين *ta'mīn* securing, protection; assurance; safeguarding; reassurance; ensuring; guaranty, warranty; security, surety; insurance | تأمين اجتماعى (*ijtimā'ī*) social security; تأمين ضد الحريق (*ḍidda*) fire insurance; تأمين على الحياة (*ḥayāh*) life insurance

ايمان *īmān* faith, belief (ب in)

ائتمان *i'timān* trust, confidence; credit

استئمان *isti'mān* trust, confidence

آمن *āmin* peaceful

مأمون *ma'mūn* reliable, trustworthy

مؤمن عليه *mu'amman 'alaihi* insured

مؤمن *mu'min* believing, faithful; believer

مؤتمن *mu'taman* entrusted (على with); confidant; sequestrator (*jur.*)

امنيبوس *omnibus* omnibus, bus

[1]اموى *amawī* of or like a bondmaid or handmaid

[2]اموى *umawī* Ommiad (adj.)

بنو امية *banū umayya* the Ommiads

اميبا *amībā* amoebae

اميرال *amīrāl* admiral

اميركه, اميركا *amērikā*, *amērika* America

اميرالية *amīrālīya* admiralty

[1]ان *an* (conj.) that; — *in* 1. (conj.) if; وان *wa-in* although, even though, even if; ان — وان be it — or (be it); الا *illā* (= ان لا) look up alphabetically 2. (particle) not, esp. in the phrase ان هو الا *in huwa illā* (f. ان هى الا) it is nothing but, it is no more than

[2]ان *anna* (conj.) that; بما انه *bi-mā annahū* since he (it), because he (it); على انه *'alā annahū* while he (it), whereas he (it); introducing a main clause: however, yet; وذلك انه that is to say, namely, to wit; — *inna* (intensifying particle introducing a nominal clause) verily, truly (in most cases not translated in English)

انما *innamā* but, but then; yet, however; rather, on the contrary

[3]ان *anna i* (انين *anīn*, تأنان *ta'nān*) to groan, moan (من at)

انة *anna* pl. *-āt* moan, groan | انات وآهات wails and laments

انين *anīn* plaintive sound, wail; groan, moan(ing)

انا *anā* I

انانى *anānī* egotistic; egoistic(al), selfish

انانية *anānīya* egoism, selfishness

الاناضول *al-anāḍūl* Anatolia

اناناس *anānās* pineapple

انب II to blame, censure, reprehend, upbraid (ه s.o.)

تأنيب *ta'nīb* blame, censure, rebuke

انبا (pronounced *ambā*) Abba, a high ecclesiastic title of the Coptic Church, preceding the names of metropolitans, bishops, patriarchs, and saints (< Ἀββᾶ)

انبار *anbār* pl. انابر *anābir*[2], انابير *anābīr*[2] warehouse, storehouse, storeroom

انباشی (Turk. *onbaşı*) *onbaši* a mil. rank: corporal (formerly, *Eg.*); وكيل انباشی approx.: private first class (*Eg.*)

انبوب, انبوبة see نب

انبيق *inbīq* alembic

انت *anta*, f. *anti* thou, you (2nd pers. sing.); pl. m. انتم *antum*, f. انتن *antunna* you (2nd pers. pl. and polite form of address); dual انتما *antumā* both of you

انتذا *anta-ḏā* it's you!

انتيكخانة *antīkḵāna* museum

انتيكة *antīka* pl. *-āt* (*eg.*) old, old-fashioned, outmoded

انتيمون *antīmūn* antimony

انث ***anuṯa u*** **(انوثة** ***unūṯa*****) to be or become feminine, womanly, womanish, effeminate II to make feminine; to effeminate, make effeminate; to put into the feminine form (*gram.*) V to become feminine (also *gram.*)**

انثى ***unṯā*** **pl.** اناث ***ināṯ***, اناثى ***anāṯā*** **feminine; female; a female (of animals);** الانثيان ***al-unṯayān*** **the testicles**

انثوى ***unṯawī*** **womanly, female, women's (in compounds)**; effeminate, womanish

انوثة ***unūṯa*** femininity, womanliness

تأنيث ***ta'nīṯ*** the feminine, feminine form (*gram.*)

مؤنث ***mu'annaṯ*** (*gram.*) feminine (adj.)

انثروبولوجيا ***anṯrōbōlōjiyā*** anthropology

انجاص ***injāṣ*** (*syr.*) pear

انجلترا (It. *Inghilterra*) *ingilterā* England

الانجليز ***al-ingəlīz*** the English

انجليزى ***ingəlīzī*** English; Englishman

انجيل ***injīl*** pl. اناجيل ***anājīl***[2] gospel

انجيلى ***injīlī*** evangelical; evangelist

انجيلية ***injīlīya*** evangelical creed

الاندلس *al-andalus* Spain

اندونيسيا *indūnīsiyā* Indonesia

انس *anisa a* and *anusa u* (*uns*) to be companionable, sociable, nice, friendly, genial; انس به to like s.o.'s company, like to be together with s.o.; to be or get on intimate terms (ب or الى with s.o.); to be used, accustomed, habituated (الى to); to perceive, notice, find (ه a quality, من, فى in s.o.); to sense, feel, make out, recognize (ه s.th., فى in, at) | انس لحديثه (*li-ḥadīṯihī*) to like to listen to s.o. **II** to put at ease; to tame **III** to be friendly, nice (ه to s.o.); to entertain, amuse (ه s.o.) **IV** to keep s.o. (ه) company; to entertain, delight, amuse (ه s.o.); to perceive, discern, make out (with the eyes; ه s.th.); to sense (ه s.th.); to find, see, notice, observe, e.g., آنس فيه الكفاية he saw that he was duly qualified, that he was a capable man **V** to become incarnate (Son of God) **X** to be sociable, companionable; to get on familiar terms, become intimate; to become tame; to be friendly, nice, kind (ه to s.o.); to accommodate o.s., accustom o.s., settle down; to be familiar, familiarize o.s., acquaint o.s. (ب or الى with); to inform o.s., gather information (ب about); to take into consideration, take into account, bring into play (ب s.th.), draw upon s.th. (ب); to listen (ل to s.th.), heed (ب an opinion)

انس *uns* sociability; intimacy, familiarity, friendly atmosphere

انسى *unsī*: كعب انسى (*ka'b*) talus, inner anklebone (*anat.*)

انس *ins* (coll.) man, mankind, human race

انسى *insī* human; human being

ناس *nās* (coll.) and اناس *unās* people

ناسوت *nāsūt* mankind, humanity

اناسى *anāsīy* (pl.) people, human beings, humans

انيس *anīs* close, intimate; close friend; friendly, kind, affable, civil, polite, courteous

انسان *insān* man, human being | انسان العين *i. al-'ain* pupil (of the eye)

انسانة *insāna* woman

انسانى *insānī* human; humane; humanitarian, philanthropist

انسانية *insānīya* humanity, humaneness; politeness, civility; mankind, the human race

مؤانسة *mu'ānasa* intimacy, familiarity, friendliness, geniality, cordiality; sociability; conviviality

ايناس *īnās* exhilaration; friendliness, geniality; familiarity, intimacy, cordiality; sociability

تأنس *ta'annus* incarnation (*Chr.*)

ائتناس *i'tinās* social life, sociability

آنسة *ānisa* pl. *-āt*, اوانس *awānis*[2] young lady, miss

مأنوس *ma'nūs* familiar, accustomed

مستأنس *musta'nis* tame

انش (Engl.) *inš* inch

انشوجة (It. *acciuga*) *anšūga* (*eg.*) anchovy

انطاكية *anṭākiya*[2] Antioch (ancient city in Syria; now Antakya, in S Turkey)

انطولوجى *onṭōlōjī* ontologic(al) (*philos.*)

انف **anifa** *a* (*anaf*) to disdain, scorn (من s.th., ان to do s.th.); to reject haughtily (ه s.th.) X to resume, renew, recommence (ه s.th.); (*jur.*) to appeal (ه a sentence)

انف *anf* pl. آناف *ānāf*, انوف *unūf* nose; spur (of a mountain); pride | رغم انفه *raḡma anfihī* in defiance of him, to spite him; كسر انفه (*anfahū*) to humiliate s.o., put s.o.'s nose out of joint; شامخ الانف stuck-up, haughty, proud

انفى *anfī* nasal

انفة *anafa* pride; rejection; disdain (من of s.th.)

انوف *anūf* proud, haughty, stuck-up, supercilious, disdainful

استئناف *isti'nāf* fresh start, recommencement, renewal, resumption, reopening (also, of a legal case); appeal (*jur.*) | قدم استئنافا (*qaddama*) to appeal, make an appeal (*jur.*)

استئنافى *isti'nāfī* of appeal, appellate; استئنافيا *isti'nāfīyan* by appeal

آنف *ānif* preceding, above | آنف الذكر (*ḏikr*) preceding, above, above-mentioned; آنفا *ānifan* previously, above, in the foregoing

مؤتنف *mu'tanaf* primordial, virginal state; beginning

انفرس (Fr. *Anvers*) *anvers* Antwerp (city in N Belgium)

انفلونزا *influwanzā* influenza, grippe

انق **aniqa** *a* to be neat, trim, smart, spruce, comely, pretty; to be happy (ب about), be delighted (ب by) IV to please (ه s.o.) | يؤنقه الشىء (*šai'u*) he likes the thing V to apply o.s. eagerly and meticulously (فى to); to be meticulous, fastidious, finical; to be chic, elegant

اناقة *anāqa* elegance

انيق *anīq* neat, trim, spruce, comely, pretty; elegant, chic

انوق *anūq* Egyptian vulture (Neophron percnopterus) | اعز من بيض الانوق *a'azz*[2] *min baiḍi l-a.* (lit.: rarer than the eggs of a vulture, i.e.) approx.: scarcer than hens' teeth (proverbially for s.th. rare)

تأنق *ta'annuq* elegance

مؤنق *mu'niq*, مونق *mūniq* pretty, comely, winsome, nice, pleasing

متأنق *muta'anniq* chic, elegant

انقره *anqara* Ankara

انقليس *anqalīs* eel

آنك *ānuk* lead (metal)

انكشارى *inkišārī* pl. *-īya* Janizary

انكلترا ,انكلترة (It. *Inghilterra*) *ingilterā, ingiltera* England

الانكلوسكسون *al-anglosaksūn* the Anglo-Saxons

الانكلوسكسونية *al-anglosaksūnīya* Anglo-Saxondom

الانكليز *al-inglīz* the English

انكليزى *inglīzī* English; Englishman

انكليس *ankalīs* eel

الانام *al-anām* and الآنام (coll.) mankind, the human race

انموذج *unmūḏaj* model, pattern; type, example; sample, specimen

انمون *anamūn* anemone (*bot.*)

[1]انى *anā i* to mature, become ripe; to draw near, approach, come (esp. time) | انى له ان it is (high) time that he; esp. in negative statements: الم يأن *a-lam ya'ni?* isn't it about time ...? **V** to act slowly, proceed unhurriedly, bide one's time, be patient **X** to take one's time, hesitate (فى in, with); to wait

انى *anan* pl. آناء *ānā'* (span of) time, period | فى آناء الليل (*laili*) all night long; آناء الليل واطراف النهار *ānā'a l-laili wa-aṭrāfa n-nahār* by day and by night

اناة *anāh* deliberateness; perseverance, patience | طول الاناة *ṭūl al-a.* long-suffering, great patience; طويل الاناة long-suffering (adj.)

اناء *inā'* pl. آنية *āniya*, اوان *awānin* vessel, container, receptacle | آنية الطعام *ā. aṭ-ṭa'ām* table utensils, dishes; mess kit

تأن *ta'annin* slowness, deliberateness

متأن *muta'annin* slow, unhurried, deliberate

[2]انى *annā* (interrog. part.) where ... from? why is it that ...? why? where? (place and direction); how? wherever; however | ... وأنى له الا (*allā*) and why shouldn't he ...?

انيسون, آنيسون *anīsūn*, aniseed

انيميا *anīmiyā* anemia | ○ انيميا خبيثة pernicious anemia (*med.*)

آه *āhi!* آها *āhan!* (interj.) oh!

اهب **II** to prepare, make ready, equip (ه, ه ل s.o., s.th. for) **V** to be ready, be prepared; to prepare o.s., get ready; to equip o.s., be equipped (ل for)

اهبة *uhba* pl. اهب *uhab* preparation, preparedness, readiness, alertness; equipment, outfit, gear | اهبة الحرب *u. al-ḥarb* military equipment; على اهبة الرحيل ready to set out; على اهبة الاستعداد fully prepared; on the alert (*mil.*); اخذ اهبته to make one's preparations, get ready

اهاب *ihāb* skin, hide

تأهب *ta'ahhub* preparedness, readiness; (pl. *-āt*) preparation

متأهب *muta'ahhib* ready, prepared

اهل *ahala u i* (اهول *uhūl*) to take a wife, get married; — *ahila a* to be on familiar terms (ب with); — pass. *uhila* to be inhabited, be populated (region, place) **II** to make fit or suited, to fit, qualify (ه ,ه ل s.o., s.th. for); to make possible (ه ل for s.o. s.th.), enable (ه ل s.o. to do s.th.), make accessible (ه ل to s.o. s.th.); to welcome (ب s.o.) **V** to be or become fit, suited, qualified (ل for s.th.); to take a wife; to marry, get married X to deserve, merit (ه s.th.), be worthy (ه of)

اهل *ahl* pl. *-ūn*, اهال *ahālin* relatives, folks, family; kin, kinsfolk; wife; (with foll. genit.) people, members, followers, adherents, possessors, etc.; inhabitants; deserving, worthy (ل of s.th.); fit, suited, qualified (ل for); pl. الاهالى, الاهلون the natives, the native population | اهل البيت *a. al-bait* members (of the house, i.e.) of the family; the Prophet's family; أهل الدار the people living in the house; اهل الحرفة *a. al-ḥirfa* people of the trade; اهل الحلف *a. al-ḥilf* people pledged by oath, members of a sworn confederacy; اهل الخبرة *a. al-ḵibra* people of experience, experts; اهل السفسطة *a. as-safsaṭa* Sophists; اهل السنة *a. us-sunna* the adherents of the Sunna, the Sunnis; اهل المدر والوبر *a. al-madar wa-l-wabar* the resident population and the nomads; اهل الوجاهة *a. al-wajāha* people of rank and high social standing; اهلا وسهلا *ahlan wa-sahlan* welcome! اهلا بك *ahlan bika* welcome to you! له فى دارنا اهل وسهل he is a welcome guest in our house

اهلى *ahlī* domestic, family (adj.); native, resident; indigenous; home, national | بنك اهلى national bank (*Eg.*); حرب اهلية (*ḥarb*) civil war; محكمة اهلية (*maḥkama*) indigenous court (*Eg.*); القضاء الاهلى (*qaḍā'*) jurisdiction of indigenous courts; الانتاج الاهلى (*intāj*) domestic production; وقف اهلى (*waqf*) family wakf

اهلية *ahlīya* aptitude, fitness, suitableness, competence; qualification | الاهلية القانونية the civil rights; كامل الاهلية legally competent; عديم الاهلية legally incompetent, under tutelage

آهل *āhil* and مأهول *ma'hūl* inhabited, populated (region, place)

مؤهلات *mu'ahhilāt* qualifications, abilities, aptitudes

متأهل *muta'ahhil* married

مستأهل *musta'hil* worthy, deserving, meriting; entitled

اهليلج *ihlīlaj* myrobalan, emblic (fruit of Phyllanthus emblica L.; *bot.*); ellipse (*geom.*)

اهليلجى *ihlīlajī* elliptic(al)

او *au* or; (with foll. subj.) unless, except that

(اوب)[1] آب *āba u* (*aub*, اوبة *auba*, اياب *iyāb*) to return; آب ب to catch, contract, suffer, incur s.th., be in for s.th., be left with, get one's share of

من كل اوب *min kulli aubin* from all sides or directions; من كل اوب وصوب (*wa-ṣaubin*) do.

اوبة *auba* return

اياب *iyāb* return | ذهابا وايابا *ḏahāban wa-iyāban* there and back; back and forth, up and down

مآب *ma'āb* place to which one returns; (used as verbal noun:) return | ذهوب ومآب coming and going

آب[2] look up alphabetically

اوبرا and اوپرا (It. *opera*) *ōpərā* opera; opera house

اوبريت (Fr.) *ōpərēt* operetta

اوت (Fr. *août*) August (month; *maḡr.*)

اوتوبيس (Fr. *autobus*) *otobīs* autobus, bus

اوتوجراف (Fr.) *otograf* pl. *-āt* autograph

اوتوقراطى *otūqrāṭī* autocratic

اوتوماتيكى (Fr.) *otomātīkī* automatic

اوتوموبيل (Fr.) *otombīl* automobile

اوتيل (Fr.) *ōtēl* pl. *-āt* hotel

اوج *auj* highest point, acme, pinnacle; culmination, climax; apogee (*astron.*); peak (fig.; of power, of fame)

آح *āḥ* albumen, eggwhite

○ آحين *āḥīn* albumin

(اود) آد *āda* u (*aud*) to bend, flex, curve, crook (ه s.th.); to burden, oppress, weigh down (ه s.o.); — اود *awida* a (*awad*) to bend; to be bent V to bend; to bow

اودة *auda* burden, load

اود *awad*: قام بأوده to provide for s.o.'s needs, stand by s.o. in time of need; اقام اوده (*awadahū*) do.; to support s.o., furnish s.o. with the means of subsistence

اوار *uwār* heat, blaze; thirst

اوربا *urubbā* Europe

اوربى *urubbī* European

اورشليم *ūrušalīm*[2] Jerusalem

اورطة (= ارطة) *urṭa* pl. ارط *uraṭ* battalion (formerly, *Eg.*; *mil.*)

اورغواى *uruğuwāy* Uruguay

اوركسترا (It.) *orkestrā* orchestra

اورنك (Turk. *örnek*) *urnīk* pl. ارانيك *arānīk*[2] sample, specimen; model, pattern; form, blank

اوروبا *urubbā*, آوروپا Europe

اوروبى *urubbī* European

اوروجواى *ūrūguwāy* Uruguay

اوز II (*eg.*) to ridicule (على s.o.), make fun of s.o. (على)

اوز *iwazz* (coll.; n. un.) goose, geese

آس *ās* myrtle; see also alphabetically

اوستراليا *usturāliyā* Australia

اوستريا (It.) *austriyā* Austria

اوسلو Oslo

اوسطى *ūstā* see اسطى

اوشية *ūšīya* pl. اواش *awāšin* prayer, oration (*Copt.-Chr.*)

آفة *āfa* pl. *-āt* harm, hurt, damage, ruin, bane, evil; epidemic, plague; plant epidemic

مؤوف *ma'ūf* stricken by an epidemic

اوفرول (Engl.) *ovirōl* overalls

[1](اوق) آق *āqa* u to bring s.o. (على) bad luck, cause discomfort or hardship (على to) II to burden (ه s.o.) with s.th. unpleasant, troublesome or difficult

[2]اوقة see اقة

[3]اويقات *uwaiqāt* (dimin. of اوقات) short times; good times

اوقيانوس, اوقيانس *oqiyānus*, *oqiyānūs* ocean

اوقية *ūqīya* pl. *-āt* ounce, a weight of varying magnitude (Eg.: 37.44 g; Aleppo 320 g; Jerusalem 240 g; Beirut 213.3 g)

اوكازيون (Fr. *occasion*) *okazyōn* clearing sale, special sale

اوكرانيا *ukrāniyā* Ukraine

اوكسجين (Fr. *oxygène*) *oksižēn* oxygen

(اول) آل *āla* u (*aul*, مآل *ma'āl*) to return, revert (الى to); to go back, be attributed, be attributable (الى to), spring, derive (الى from); to lead, conduce, tend (الى to), result eventually (الى in); to come or go eventually (الى to s.o.), pass into the hands of (الى) | آل الامر الى the long and the short of it was that ...; آل به المطاف الى (*maṭāfu*) he eventually got to the point where ... II to interpret, explain (ه s.th.)

آل *āl* family, relatives, kinsfolk, clan; companions, partisans, people; mirage, fata morgana

آلة *āla* pl. *-āt* instrument, utensil; tool; apparatus; device, implement, appliance; machine | آلات الحس *ā. al-ḥiss* sensory organs; آلة بخارية (*buḵārīya*) steam engine; آلة الجر *ā. al-jarr* tractor; آلة جهنمية (*jahannamīya*) infernal machine; آلة حربية (*ḥarbīya*) instrument of war; آلة التحريك

motor, engine; آلة حاسبة calculating machine; آلة الحياكة *ā. al-ḥiyāka* power loom; آلة الخياطة sewing machine; آلة راديو radio; آلة رافعة hoisting machine, crane, derrick; pump; آلة مسخنة and آلة التسخين (*musakkina*) heater; آلة التصوير (photographic) camera; آلة الطباعة printing press; آلة الغسل *ā. al-ġasl* washing machine; آلة التفريخ incubator; آلة الاستقبال receiver, receiving set (*radio*); آلة مقطرة (*muqaṭṭira*) distilling apparatus, still; آلة كاتبة and آلة الكتابة typewriter; آلة لعب القمار *ā. laʿb al-qimār* slot machine; آلة موسيقية (*mūsīqīya*) musical instrument; آلة التنبيه alarm; siren; horn (of an automobile); آلة صماء (*ṣammā'*) (fig.) tool, creature, puppet

آلى *ālī* mechanic(al); mechanized; motorized; instrumental; organic | محراث آلى (*miḥrāṯ*) motor plow; القوات الآلية (*qūwāt*) motorized troops; حركة آلية (*ḥaraka*) a mechanical movement

آلية *ālīya* mechanics

آلاتى *ālātī* pl. آلاتية *ālātīya* (*eg.*) musician; singer

اول *awwal*², f. اولى *ūlā*, pl. m. *-ūn*, اوائل *awā'il*² first; foremost, most important, principal, chief, main; first part, beginning; (with def. article also) earlier, previous, former; see also under ول | الانسان الاول (*insān*) primitive man; طبيب اول physician-in-chief; الاولون, الاوائل the forebears, forefathers, ancestors; اوائل الشهر *a. aš-šahr* the first ten days of a month, beginning of a month; لاول مرة *li-awwali marratin* or للمرة الاولى for the first time; من اوائله ,من اوله since its beginnings, from the very beginning; من اوله الى آخره (*āḵirihī*) from beginning to end, from A to Z; اول الامر *awwala l-amri* at first, in the beginning; الاول فالاول each time the first available; اول ما (*awwala*) the moment when, just when; at the very outset of; اكثر من الاول (*akṯara*) more than before

اولا *awwalan* first, firstly, in the first place; at first, in the beginning | اولا بأول and اولا فأولا by and by, gradually, one after the other, one by one; اولا واخيرا and اولا وآخرا (*āḵiran*) first and last, altogether, simply and solely, merely

اولى *awwalī* prime, primary, primordial, original, initial, first; elemental, fundamental, basic, principal, chief, main; elementary; primitive, pristine, primeval | مدرسة اولية (*madrasa*) elementary school, grade school; مواد اولية (*mawādd*) raw materials; عدد اولى (*ʿadad*) prime number; فاتورة اولية (*fātūra*) pro forma invoice

اولية *awwalīya* pl. *-āt* fundamental truth, axiom; primary constituent, essential component, element; precedence; priority

ايل *ayyil, iyyal, uyyal* pl. ايائل *ayā'il*² stag

ايالة *iyāla* pl. *āt* province; regency

ايلولة *ailūla* title deed (*jur.*)

مآل *ma'āl* end; outcome, final issue, upshot; result, consequence | فى الحال وفى المآل at present and in the future

تأويل *ta'wīl* pl. *-āt* interpretation, explanation

اولاء *ulā'i*, اولئك ,اولائك *ulā'ika* these; those, pl. of the demonstr. pron. ذا and ذلك

اولمبى *olimbī* Olympic | الالعاب الاولمبية the Olympic games

اولمبياد *olimbiyād* Olympiad

اولو *ulū* (pl. of ذو) owners, possessors, people (with foll. genit.: of) | اولو الأمر *u. l-amr* rulers, powerful leaders; اولو الحل والعقد *u. l-ḥall wa-l-ʿaqd* (lit.: masters of solving and binding) do.; اولو الشأن *u. š-ša'n* the responsible people

اوام[1] *uwām* thirst

اوم[2] ohm (*el.*)

اومنيبوس *omnībūs* omnibus, bus

[1]آن *ān* time; الآن *al-āna* now | فى آن and فى آن واحد at the same time, simultaneously; من آن الى آخر (*ākara*) from time to time; ما بين آن وآخر (*wa-ākara*) and آنا بعد آن sometimes, at times, now and then, once in a while; آنا فآنا gradually, by and by, little by little; آنا — وآونة (*āwinatan*) sometimes — sometimes, at times — at times; قبل الآن *qabla l-āna* before, previously, formerly; للآن *li-l-āna* and حتى الآن *ḥattā l-āna* until now, hitherto, so far; بعد الآن *ba'da l-āna* from now on, henceforth, in the future; من الآن فصاعدا *min al-āna fa-ṣā'idan* do.

آنئذ *āna'iḏin* that day, at that time, then

آنذاك *ānaḏāka* that day, at that time, then

اون *aun* calmness, serenity, gentleness

اوان *awān* pl. آونة *āwina* time | قبل اوانه prematurely; فى اوانه at the right time, timely, seasonably, فى غير اوانه at the wrong time, untimely, unseasonably; بين الآونة from time to time; بين الآونة والآخرى (*ukrā*) and آونة بعد اخرى (*āwinatan, ukrā*) at times, sometimes; آونة — واخرى sometimes — sometimes, at times — at times; فات الاوان (*fāta*) it is too late; آن الاوان (*āna*) the time has come, it is time (ل for, to do s.th.)

[2]ايوان look up alphabetically

اونباشى *onbaši* corporal, see انباشى

(اوه) آه *āha u* and II to moan, sigh V to moan, sigh; to sigh with admiration (ل over), exclaim "ah!"

اوه *awwah* (interj.) oh!

آه *āhi*, آها *āhan*, اواه *uwwāhi* oh!

آهة *āha* pl. *-āt* sigh, moan; pl. آهات sighs of admiration; rapturous exclamations

تأوه *ta'awwuh* moaning, sighing; admiring exclamation; plaintive sound, wail

اوى *awā i* to seek refuge, seek shelter (الى at a place); to go (الى to bed); to betake o.s., repair (الى to a place); to shelter, house, put up, lodge, accommodate, receive as a guest (ه, ه s.o., s.th.) II to shelter, lodge, put up, accommodate, receive as a guest (ه s.o.) IV to seek shelter (الى at a place), to retire (الى to a place); to betake o.s., repair (الى to a place); to shelter, house, put up, lodge, accommodate (ه s.o.)

ايواء *īwā'* accommodation, lodging, housing, sheltering

مأوى *ma'wan* pl. مآو *ma'āwin* place of refuge, retreat, shelter; abode; resting place; dwelling, habitation | مأوى ليلى (*lailī*) shelter for the night; doss house

ابن آوى *ibn āwā* pl. بنات آوى *banāt ā.* jackal

[1]آية *āya*, coll. آى *āy*, pl. *-āt* sign, token, mark; miracle; wonder, marvel, prodigy; model, exemplar, paragon, masterpiece (فى of, e.g., of organization, etc.); Koranic verse, آى الذكر الحكيم (*āy aḏ-ḏikr*) the verses of the Koran; passage (in a book), utterance, saying, word; آيات (with foll. genit.) most solemn assurances (of love, of gratitude)

[2]اى *ay* that is (to say), i.e.; namely, to wit

[3]اى *ī* yes (with foll. والله yes, indeed! yes, by God!)

[4]اى *ayy*, f. اية *ayya* (with foll. genit. or suffix) which? what? what kind of? whoever, whosoever; any, every, no matter what...; (with neg.) no; ايما *ayyumā* whatever, whatsoever | ايا كان, اية كانت *ayyan kāna, ayyatan kānat* whoever he (or she) is, no matter who he (or she) is; اى من كان *ayyu man kāna* whoever it may be, whosoever; على اى حال (*ayyi ḥālin*) in any case, at any

rate, at all events, by all means; ای واحد ayyu wāḥidin any one; ان له شأنا ای شأن inna lahū ša'nan ayya ša'nin it is of the greatest importance (lit.: it is of importance, and of what importance!); اعجب به ايما اعجاب u'jiba bihī ayyamā i'jābin how much he admired him! he admired him greatly; اقبل عليه ايما اقبال aqbala 'alaihi ayyamā iqbālin he showed the greatest interest in it

ايا iyyā with nominal suffix to express the accusative | اياك ان take care not to ..., be careful not to ...; اياك و , اياك من beware of ...! واياك (dial. wayyāk), واياه (wayyāh) with you, with him

ايار see اير [2]

ايد II to back, support (ه s.o., ه a claim, an aspiration, etc.); to confirm, corroborate, endorse (ه news, a judgment, etc.) V = pass. of II

تأييد ta'yīd corroboration, confirmation, endorsement, backing, support

ايدروجين (Fr. hydrogène) idrožēn hydrogen

قنبلة ايدروجينية (qunbula) hydrogen bomb

[1]اير air pl. ايور uyūr penis

[2]ايار ayyār[2] May (Syr., Leb., Ir., Jord.)

ايران īrān Iran, Persia

ايرانى īrānī Iranian, Persian; (pl. -ūn) a Persian, an Iranian

ايرلندا irlandā Ireland

ايرلندى irlandī Irish; (pl. -ūn) Irishman

ايريال (Engl.) ēriyāl aerial, antenna

ايزيس īzīs Isis

ايس ayisa a (اياس iyās) to despair (من of s.th.)

اياس iyās despair

ايشرب (Fr. écharpe) sash

آض (ايض) āḍa i to return, revert (الى to s.th.); to become (الى s.th.)

ايضا aiḍan also, too, as well, likewise, equally; again; in addition, besides, moreover

ايطاليا iṭāliyā Italy

ايطالى iṭālī Italian; (pl. -ūn) an Italian

ايقونة (Gr. εἰκών) īqūna and ايقونية īqūniya pl. -āt icon (Chr.)

ايك aik (coll.; n. un. ة) thicket, jungle

[1]ايل and ايالة see اول

[2]ايلول ailūl[2] September (Syr., Leb., Ir., Jord.)

[3]ايلولة ailūla title deed (jur.)

آم (ايم) āma i: آم من زوجه (zaujatihī) to lose one's wife, become or be a widower, آمت من زوجها (zaujihā) to lose one's husband, become or be a widow

ايمة aima, ايوم uyūm and تأيم ta'ayyum widowhood

ايم ayyim pl. ايائم ayā'im[2], ايامى ayāmā widower, widow

ايوم aiwam[2] see يوم

ايما ayyumā see [4]اى ayy

[1](اين) آن āna i to come, approach, draw near (time) | آن الاوان (awān) the time has come: آن له ان it's time for him to ...

آن see اون

اين aina where? (= at or to what place?) | من اين min aina where ... from? الى اين where? (= to what place?) اين نحن من how far we still are from ..., worlds separate us from ... (fig.); اين هذا من ذاك what is this compared with that!

الاين *al-ainu* the where; space (*philos.*)

اينما *ainamā* wherever

ايان *ayyāna* when? (conj.) when

2اين II to ionize (ه s.th.) V to be ionized (*el.*)

ايون *iyōn* pl. *-āt* ion

تأيين *ta'yīn* ionization

متأين *muta'ayyin* ionized

ايه *īhi, īha, īhin* (interj.) well! now then! all right!

ايها *ayyuhā,* with fem. also ايتها *ayyatuhā* (vocative particle) O ...!

ايوب *ayyūb*[2] Job

الايوبيون *al-ayyūbiyūn* the Ayubites

ايوم *aiwam*[2] see يوم

1ايون see 2اين

2ايوان *īwān* pl. *-āt* recess-like sitting room with a raised floor, usually opening on the main room or courtyard through an arcade; estrade

ب

1ب abbreviation of باب chapter

2ب *bi* (prep.) in, at, on (place and time); with (indicating connection, association, attendance); with, through, by means of (designating instrumentality or agency, also with pass. = by); for (= at the price of); by (= to the amount of); by (introducing an oath) | بالليل *bi-l-lail* at (by) night, بالنهار *bi-n-nahār* during the daytime, by day; شمالا بشرق *šamālan bi-šarqin* northeast; فبها ونعمت *fa-bihā wa-ni'mat* in that case it's all right; ليس بي ان it is not my intention to ...; هذا بذاك *hāḏā bi-ḏāka* now we are even, we are quits; قبل مجيئه بساعة (*majī'ihi*) an hour before his arrival; ب "with" frequently gives causative meaning to a verb, e.g., نهض بشيء (lit.: to rise with s.th., i.e.) to boost, further, promote s.th.; بلغ به الى to cause s.o. to arrive at, lead s.o. to; for its use as copula after negations, etc., see grammar; بلا *bi-lā* without; بما ان *bi-mā anna* in view of the fact that; since, as, inasmuch as, because; بما فيه *bi-mā fīhi* including

باء *bā'* name of the letter ب

بابا *bābā* pl. بابوات *bābawāt,* باباوات pope; papa, father, daddy

بابوى *bābawī,* باباوى papal

بابوية *bābawīya* papacy

1بأبأ *ba'ba'a* to say "papa" (child)

2بؤبؤ *bu'bu'* root, source, origin; core, heart, inmost part; pupil of the eye, also بؤبؤ العين *b. al-'ain*

بابل *bābil*[2] Babel, Babylon

بابلى *bābilī* Babylonian

بابه *bābih* the second month of the Coptic calendar

بابوج *bābūj* pl. بوابيج *bawābīj*[2] slipper

بابور *bābūr* pl. *-āt,* بوابير *bawābīr*[2] (= وابور) locomotive, engine; steamship, steamer

بابونج *bābūnaj* camomile (*bot.*)

باتستة *bātista* batiste

باثولوجى *bāṯōlōjī* pathologic(al)

باثولوجيا *bāṯōlōjiyā* pathology

باذنجان *bāḏinjān* and بيذنجان *baiḏinjān* (coll.; n. un. ة) pl. *-āt* eggplant, aubergine

[1]بار *bār* pl. *-āt* bar; taproom

[2]بأر *ba'ara a* to dig a well

بئر *bi'r* f., pl. آبار *ābār*, بئار *bi'ār* well, spring

بؤرة *bu'ra* pl. بؤر *bu'ar* center, seat (fig.); site; pit; abyss

باراشوت (Fr. *parachute*) *bārāšūt* parachute

باراغواى *bārāğuwāy* Paraguay

باربونى see بربونى

باركيه (Fr.) *barkēh* parquet, parquetry floor

بارناج see برناج

بارة *bāra* pl. *-āt* para (coin)

بارود *bārūd* saltpeter; gunpowder

بارودة *bārūda* pl. بواريد *bawārīd*² rifle, carbine

باريس *bārīs*² Paris

باريسى *bārīsī* Parisian

باز *bāz* pl. بيزان *bīzān* and بأز *ba'z* pl. بؤوز *bu'ūz*, بئزان *bi'zān* falcon

بازار *bāzār* pl. *-āt* bazaar

بازلت *bāzalt* basalt

بازوبند *bāzūband* bracelet

بؤس *ba'usa u* (بأس *ba's*) to be strong, brave, intrepid; — بئس *ba'isa a* (بؤس *bu's*) to be miserable, wretched VI to feign misery or distress VIII to be sad, worried, grieved

بئس الرجل *bi'sa r-rajulu* what an evil man!

بأس *ba's* strength, fortitude, courage, intrepidity (as verbal noun of بؤس *ba'usa*); harm, hurt, injury, impairment, detriment, wrong | شديد البأس courageous, brave, intrepid; لا بأس به (*ba'sa*) there is no objection to it; unobjectionable; not bad, rather important, considerable, e.g., كيات لا بأس بها (*kammīyāt*) considerable quantities; لا بأس (*ba'sa*) never mind! it doesn't matter! it's all right! لا بأس ان it doesn't matter that ...; اى بأس؟ *ayyu ba'sin?* what does it matter? what of it? ليس عليه بأس من (*ba'sun*) he will be none the worse for ...; لا بأس عليك (*ba'sa*) it won't do you any harm! don't worry! don't be afraid

بنات بئس *banātu bi's* calamities, adversities, misfortunes

بؤس *bu's*, بأساء *ba'sā'*², بؤوس *bu'ūs* and بؤسى *bu'sā* pl. ابؤس *ab'us* misery, wretchedness, suffering, distress

بئيس *ba'īs* pl. بؤساء *bu'asā'*² miserable, wretched

بائس *bā'is* miserable, wretched

باستيل (Fr.) *bastēl* pastel

باسيل *bāsīl* bacilli

باش *bāš* senior, chief (in compounds)

باشجاويش *bāščāwīš* and باشچاويش approx.: master sergeant (formerly, *Eg.*)

باشحكيم *bāšḥakīm* physician-in-chief

باشريس *bāšrayyis* a naval rank, approx.: petty officer 3rd class (*Eg.*)

باشكاتب *bāškātib* chief clerk

باشمفتى *bāšmuftī* chief mufti (*Tun.*)

باشمفتش *bāšmufattiš* chief inspector

باشمهندس *bāšmuhandis* chief engineer

باشا *bāšā* pl. باشوات *bāšawāt* (باشاوات) pasha

باشق *bāšaq*, *bāšiq* pl. بواشق *bawāšiq*² sparrow hawk

الباشقرد *al-bāšqird* the Bashkirs

باشكير see بشكير

باص (Engl.) *bāṣ* pl. *-āt* bus, autobus

باطون *bāṭūn* concrete, béton

باغة *bāġa* celluloid; tortoise shell

الباكستان *al-bākistān* Pakistan

باكستانى *bākistānī* Pakistani (adj. and n.)

[1]بال *bāl* whale (*zool.*)

[2]بالة *bāla* pl. *-āt* bundle, bale

بالطو *balṭō* pl. بالطوات *balṭowāt*, بلاطى *balāṭī* overcoat; paletot

بالو (It. *ballo*) ball, dance

بالون *bālūn* balloon

جزر الباليار *juzur al-bāliyār* the Balearic Islands

باليه (Fr.) *bālēh* ballet

باميا and بامية *bāmiya* gumbo, okra (Ḥibiscus esculentus L., *bot.*, a popular vegetable in Egypt)

بان see بون

شاشة بانورامية *šāša bānōrāmīya* (= Fr. *écran panoramique*) cinemascope screen

بؤونة *ba'ūna* the tenth month of the Coptic calendar

باى *bāy*, f. باية *bāya* pl. *-āt* formerly, in Tunisia, a title after the names of the members of the Bey's family

دار الباى *dār al-bāy* (formerly) the Tunisian government

ببر *babr* pl. ببور *bubūr* tiger

ببغاء *babġā'*[2] (and *babbaġā'*[2]) pl. ببغاوات *babġāwāt* parrot

بت *batta u i* (*batt*) to cut off, sever (ه s.th.); to complete, finish, achieve, accomplish, carry out (ه s.th.); to fix, settle, determine (ه s.th.), decide (ه s.th., فى on s.th.) II to adjudge, adjudicate, award (ه s.th.) VII to be cut off; to be finished, be done; to be decided | قد انبت الامر بينه وبينهم it's all over between him and them, they are through with each other

بت *batt* settlement, decision; بتا *battan* definitely, once and for all

بتة *batta* pl. *-āt* adjudication, award; final decision; البتة *al-battata* and بتة *battatan* definitely, positively, decidedly, esp. with negations: absolutely not, definitely not

بتى *battī* definite, definitive

بتية *battīya, bittīya* pl. بتاتى *batātīy* barrel; tub

بتاتا *batātan* decidedly, definitely, positively, categorically, unquestionably, absolutely

تبتيت *tabtīt* adjudication, award

بات *bātt* definite, definitive | منع بات (*man'*) categorical interdiction

[1]بتر *batara u* (*batr*) to cut off, sever (ه s.th.); to amputate (ه s.th.); to mutilate, render fragmentarily (ه a text) VII to be cut off, be severed, be amputated

بتر *batr* cutting off, severance, separation; amputation

ابتر *abtar*[2] curtailed, docked, clipped, trimmed; imperfect, defective, incomplete; without offspring

بتار *battār* cutting, sharp

باتر *bātir* cutting, sharp

مبتور *mabtūr* broken, abrupt, unconnected; fragmentary, incomplete

[2]بتراء *bitrā'*[2], *batrā'*[2] Petra (ancient city of Edomites and Nabataeans; ruins now in SW Jordan)

بترك *batrak* patriarch

بترول *batrūl, bitrōl* petroleum

ابتع *abta'*[2] an assonant intensifier of اجمع *ajma'*[2] all, altogether, whole, entire

باتع *bāti'* strong; full, whole, entire

بتك II to cut off (ه s.th.)

بتل[1] *batala i u* (*batl*) and II to cut off, sever (ه s.th.); to make final, close, settle, make conclusive, clinch (ه s.th.) V to retire from the world and devote one's life to God (الى الله); to be pious, chaste and self-denying; to live in chastity VII to be cut off, be curtailed, be docked

بتول *batūl* virgin; البتول the Virgin Mary

بتولى *batūlī* virginal

بتولية *batūlīya* virginity

متبتل *mutabattil* an ascetic, a recluse; a pious, godly man

بتولا[2] *batūlā* birch tree

بث *baṯṯa u* (*baṯṯ*) to spread, unroll, unfold (ه s.th., e.g., a rug); to scatter, disperse (ه s.th.); to disseminate, propagate, spread (ه s.th., e.g., a spirit, an ideology, a doctrine); to sprinkle (ه ه s.th. on); to let s.o. (ه, also ل) in on s.th. (ه, esp. on a secret); to broadcast, transmit by radio | بث العيون to peer around; بث الالغام to plant, or lay, mines IV to let (ه s.o.) in on a secret (ه) VII to be spread; to be scattered

بث *baṯṯ* spreading, dissemination, propagation; grief, sorrow

بثر *baṯara i* (*baṯira a*) and V to break out with pimples or pustules (skin)

بثر *baṯr* pl. بثور *buṯūr* (n. un. بثرة *baṯra* pl. *baṯarāt*) pimples, pustules

بثر *baṯir*, بثير *baṯīr* pustulate, pimpled

بثق *baṯaqa i u* (with النهر *an-nahra*) to open flood gates so that the river will overflow its banks VII to break forth, burst out, well out, pour out, gush out; to emanate, proceed, spring (من or عن from)

انبثاق *inbiṯāq* outpouring, effusion, outpour, outburst; emanation

بجح *bajiḥa a* (*bajaḥ*) to rejoice (ب at) V to vaunt, flaunt (ب s.th.), boast, brag (ب of)

تبجح *tabajjuḥ* bragging, braggery

متبجح *mutabajjiḥ* braggart

بجدة *bajda*, *bujda* root, source, heart, essence, basis | بجدة الامر the heart of the matter, the actual state of affairs, the true facts; هو ابن بجدتها (*ibn bujdatihā*) he knows the job from the ground up, he is the right man for it

ابجر *abjar*[2] obese, corpulent

بجس *bajasa u i* (*bajs*) and II to open a passage (for the water), cause (the water) to flow V and VII to flow freely, pour forth copiously, gush out

بجس *bajs*, بجيس *bajīs* flowing freely, streaming

بجع *baja'* (n. un. ة) pelican

بجل II to honor, revere, venerate, treat with deference (ه s.o.), show respect (ه to s.o.); to give precedence (ه على or ه to s.o. or s.th. over) V to be honored, be revered, be venerated

بجل *bajal* syphilis (*ir.*)

تبجيل *tabjīl* veneration, reverence; deference, respect

مبجل *mubajjal* revered, respected; venerable

بجم *bajama i* (*bajm*, بجوم *bujūm*) to be speechless, dumfounded

بجن II to clinch (ه a nail)

بح *baḥḥa a* (*baḥḥ*, بحح *baḥaḥ*, بحوح *buḥūḥ*, بحاح *baḥāḥ*, بحوحة *buḥūḥa*, بحاحة *baḥāḥa*) to be or become hoarse, be raucous, husky, harsh (voice) II and IV to make hoarse (ه s.o.)

بحة *buḥḥa* hoarseness

ابح *abaḥḥ*[2] hoarse

مبحوح *mabḥūḥ* hoarse

بحبح II *tabaḥbaḥa* to be prosperous, live in easy circumstances; to enjoy o.s., have a good time

بحبوح *baḥbūḥ* gay, merry

بحبوحة *buḥbūḥa* middle; life of ease and comfort, prosperity, affluence | في بحبوحة من amidst

مبحبح *mubaḥbaḥ* well-to-do, prosperous; enjoying an easy, comfortable life

بحت *baḥt* pure, unmixed, sheer; exclusive, also بحت الامر; بحتا *baḥtan* merely, solely, purely, exclusively, nothing but ...

بحتر *buḥtur* stocky, pudgy, thickset

بحترى *buḥturī* stocky, pudgy, thickset

بحث *baḥaṯa a* (*baḥṯ*) to look, search (ه or عن for s.th.), seek (ه or عن s.th.); to do research; to investigate, examine, study, explore (ه or عن s.th., less frequently with في or على), look into (ه or عن); to discuss (ه a subject, a question) III to discuss (ه with s.o., في a question) VI to have a discussion, discuss together; to confer, have a talk (مع with s.o., في about)

بحث *baḥṯ* pl. بحوث *buḥūṯ*, بحوثات, ابحاث *abḥāṯ* search (عن for), quest (عن of); examination, study; research; investigation, exploration; discussion; treatise; (pl. ابحاث) study, scientific report (في on)

بحاث *baḥḥāṯ* pl. *-ūn* scholar, research worker

بحاثة *baḥḥāṯa* eminent scholar

مبحث *mabḥaṯ* pl. مباحث *mabāḥiṯ*² subject, theme, field of investigation or discussion, object of research; research, study, examination; investigation

مباحثة *mubāḥaṯa* pl. *-āt* negotiation, parley, conference, talk, discussion

باحث *bāḥiṯ* pl. *-ūn* and بحاث *buḥḥāṯ* scholar, research worker; examiner, investigator

بحثر *baḥṯara* to disperse, scatter (ه s.th.); to waste, squander, dissipate (ه s.th.) II *tabaḥṯara* pass. of I

بحثرة *baḥṯara* waste, dissipation

مبحثر *mubaḥṯir* squanderer, wastrel, spendthrift

¹بحر *baḥira a* to be startled, be bewildered (with fright)

²بحر II to travel by sea, make a voyage IV do.; to embark, go on board; to put to sea, set sail, sail, depart (ship); to go downstream, be sea-bound (ship on the Nile) V to penetrate deeply, delve (في into); to study thoroughly (في a subject) X = V

بحر *baḥr* pl. بحار *biḥār*, بحور *buḥūr*, ابحار *abḥār*, ابحر *abḥur* sea; large river; a noble, or great, man (whose magnanimity or knowledge is comparable to the vastness of the sea); meter (*poet.*) | في بحر in the course of, during, في بحر سنتين (*sanatain*) in the course of two years, within two years; البحر الابيض المتوسط (*abyaḍ, mutawassiṭ*) the Mediterranean (sometimes shortened to البحر الابيض); بحر البلطيق *b. al-balṭīq* the Baltic Sea; بحر الجنوب *b. al-janūb* the South Seas; البحر الاحمر the Red Sea (also بحر القلزم *b. al-qulzum*); بحر الخزر *b. al-ḵazar* the Caspian Sea (also البحر الكسبيانى); بحر الروم *b. ar-rūm* the Mediterranean; البحر الاسود (*aswad*) the Black Sea; بحر الظلمات *b. aẓ-ẓulumāt* the Atlantic; بحر لوط *b. lūṭ* and البحر الميت (*mayyit*) the Dead Sea; بحر النيل (*eg.*) the Nile

البحرين *al-baḥrain* the Bahrein Islands

بحرانى *baḥrānī* of the Bahrein Islands; البحارنة *al-baḥārina* the inhabitants of the Bahrein Islands

بحرى *baḥrī* sea (adj.), marine; maritime; nautical; naval; navigational; (in Eg.) northern, *baḥrīya* (with foll. genit.) north of; (pl. *-ūn*, ة) sailor, seaman, mariner | بحرى ماهر approx.: seaman apprentice (*Eg.*); القوات البحرية (*qūwāt*) the naval forces; نباتات بحرية (*nabātāt*) marine flora, water plants

بحرية *baḥrīya* navy

بحرة *baḥra* pond, pool

بحار *baḥḥār* pl. *-ūn*, بحارة *baḥḥāra* seaman, mariner, sailor; pl. بحارة crew (of a ship, of an airplane)

بحيرة *buḥaira* pl. *-āt*, بحائر *baḥā'ir*² lake; (*tun.*) vegetable garden, truck garden

بحران *buḥrān* crisis (of an illness); climax, culmination (also, e.g., of ecstasy)

تبحر *tabaḥḥur* deep penetration, delving (ق into a subject), thorough study (ق of)

متبحر *mutabaḥḥir* thoroughly familiar (ق with); profound, erudite, searching, penetrating

بحلق *baḥlaqa*: بحلق عينيه (*'ainaihi*) to stare, gaze (ق at)

¹بخ بخ *bak̲ bak̲* excellent! well done! bravo!

²بخ *bak̲k̲a u* (*bak̲k̲*) to snore; to spout, spurt, squirt (ه s.th.); to sprinkle, splatter (ه ب s.th. with)

بخاخة *bak̲k̲āk̲a* nozzle

بخيخة (*eg.*) *buk̲k̲ēk̲a* squirt, syringe

مبخة *mibak̲k̲a* nozzle

بخت *bak̲t* luck; a kind of lottery | قليل البخت unlucky; سوء البخت bad luck

بخيت *bak̲īt* lucky, fortunate

مبخوت *mabk̲ūt* lucky, fortunate

بخَتر II *tabak̲tara* to strut, prance

بخر II to vaporize, evaporate (ه s.th.); to fumigate (ه s.th.); to disinfect (ه s.th.); to perfume with incense, expose to aromatic smoke (ه s.th.) V to evaporate (water); to volatilize, turn into smoke or haze; to perfume o.s., or be perfumed, with incense

بخار *buk̲ār* pl. *-āt*, ابخرة *abk̲ira* vapor, fume; steam

بخارى *buk̲ārī* steam (adj.), steam-driven

بخور *bak̲ūr* incense; frankincense | بخور مريم *b. maryam* cyclamen (*bot.*)

ابخر *abk̲ar*² suffering from halitosis

مبخرة *mibk̲ara* pl. مباخر *mabāk̲ir*² (also *-āt*) censer; thurible; fumigator

تبخير *tabk̲īr* fumigation

تبخر *tabak̲k̲ur* evaporation, vaporization

باخرة *bāk̲ira* pl. بواخر *bawāk̲ir*² steamer, steamship

بويخرة *buwaik̲ira* small steamboat

بخس *bak̲asa a* (*bak̲s*) to decrease, diminish, reduce (ه s.th.); to lessen (e.g., قيمته *qīmatahū* the value of s.th.); to disregard, neglect, fail to heed (ه s.th.)

بخس *bak̲s* too little, too low; very low (price)

باخس *bāk̲is* small, little, trifling, unimportant

بخشيش *bak̲šīš* pl. بخاشيش *bak̲āšīš*² tip, gratuity

بخع *bak̲a'a a* (*bak̲'*) with نفسه: to kill o.s. (with grief, anger, rage)

ابخق *abk̲aq*², f. بخقاء *bak̲qā'*² one-eyed

بخل *bak̲ila a* (*bak̲al*), *bak̲ula u* (*buk̲l*) to be niggardly, be stingy (ب with s.th., عن or على with regard to s.o.), scrimp (عن, على s.o., ب for), stint (ب in, عن or على s.o.), withhold (عن, على from s.o., ب s.th.) VI to give reluctantly, grudgingly (عن, على to s.o., ب s.th.)

بخل *buk̲l* avarice, cupidity, greed

بخيل *bakīl* pl. بخلاء *bukalā'*[2] avaricious, greedy; miser, skinflint

مبخلة *mabkala* cause of avarice, that which arouses avarice or greed

بخنق *buknuq* pl. بخانق *bakāniq*[2] kerchief, veil (to cover the head)

بد *badda u* (*badd*) to distribute, spread, disperse II to divide, distribute, spread, scatter, disperse (ه s.th.); to remove, eliminate (ه s.th.); to waste, squander, fritter away, dissipate (ه s.th.) V pass. of II; X to be independent, proceed independently (ب in, e.g., in one's opinion, i.e., to be opinionated, obstinate, headstrong); to possess alone, monopolize (ب s.th.); to take possession (ب of s.o.), seize, grip, overwhelm, overcome (ب s.o.; said of a feeling, of an impulse); to dispose arbitrarily, highhandedly (ب of s.th.); to rule despotically, tyrannically, autocratically (ب over)

بد *budd* way out, escape | اذا لم يكن بد من ان (*buddun*) if it is inevitable that ...; لا بد (*budda*) definitely, certainly, inevitably, without fail; by all means; لا بد من it is necessary, inescapable, unavoidable, inevitable, لا بد له منه he simply must do it, he can't get around it; من كل بد *min kulli buddin* in any case, at any rate

اباديد *abādīd*[2] (pl.) scattered

تبديد *tabdīd* scattering, dispersal, dispersion; removal, elimination; waste, dissipation

استبداد *istibdād* arbitrariness, highhandedness; despotism; autocracy; absolutism

استبدادى *istibdādī* arbitrary, highhanded, autocratic, despotic; استبداديات *istibdādīyāt* arbitrary acts

مبدد *mubaddid* scatterer, disperser; squanderer, wastrel, spendthrift

مستبد *mustabidd* arbitrary, highhanded, autocratic, tyrannical, despotic; autocrat, tyrant, despot | مستبد برأيه (*bi-ra'yihī*) opinionated, obstinate, headstrong

بدأ *bada'a a* (بدء *bad'*) to begin, start (ب or في with s.th., ه s.th.; ه with s.o.; with foll. imperf.: to do s.th. or doing s.th. respectively); to set in, begin, start, arise, spring up, crop up II to put (ه s.th., على before s.th. else), give precedence or priority (ه to s.th., على over s.th. else) III to begin, start (ب s.th., ه with regard to s.o.), make the first step, take the initiative or lead (ب in s.th., ه toward s.o.), e.g., باداه بالكلام (*kalām*) to accost s.o., speak first to s.o. IV to do or produce first (ه s.th.), bring out (ه s.th. new) | ما يبدئ وما يعيد *mā yubdi'u wa-mā yu'īdu* he can't think of a blessed thing to say; يبدئ ويعيد he says or does everything conceivable VIII to begin, start (ب with s.th.)

بدء *bad'* beginning, start | منذ البدء from the (very) beginning; فعله عودا وبدءا (*'audan wa-bad'an*) or عوده على بدئه (*'audahū 'alā bad'ihī*) or عودا الى بدء (*ilā bad'in*) he did it all over again, he began anew

بدأة *bad'a*, بديئة *badī'a*, بداية *bidāya* beginning, start | في بداية الامر in the beginning, at first

بداءة *badā'a* beginning, start; first step, first instance | بداءة بدء *badā'ata bad'in* right at the outset, at the very beginning

بدائى *budā'ī* primitive

مبدأ *mabda'* pl. مبادئ *mabādi'*[2] beginning, start, starting point; basis, foundation; principle; invention; pl. principles, convictions (of a person); ideology; rudiments, fundamental concepts, elements | كتب المبادئ *kutub al-m.* elementary books

مبدئى *mabda'ī* original, initial; fundamental, basic; مبدئيا *mabda'īyan* originally; in principle

ابتداء *ibtidā'* beginning, start; novitiate (*Chr.*) | ابتداء من *ibtidā'an min* from, beginning ..., as of (with foll. date)

ابتدائى *ibtidā'ī* initial; preparatory, elementary, primary; of first instance (*jur.*); original, primitive | محكمة ابتدائية (*maḥkama*) court of first instance; التعليم الابتدائى elementary education; مدرسة ابتدائية (*madrasa*) lower grades of a high school, approx.: junior high school (as distinguished from ثانوية); شهادة ابتدائية (*šahāda*) approx.: junior high school graduation certificate

بادئ *bādi'* beginning, starting | بادئ الامر *bādi'a l-amr* and فى بادئ الامر in the beginning, at first; فى بادئ الرأى right away, without thinking twice, unhesitatingly; بادئ ذى بدء *bādi'a ḏī bad'in* above all, first of all, in the first place, primarily; البادئ ذكره *al-bādi'u ḏikruhū* (the person or thing) mentioned at the outset, the first-mentioned

مبتدئ *mubtadi'* beginning; beginner; novice (*Chr.*)

مبتدأ *mubtada'* beginning, start; (*gram.*) subject of a nominal clause

بدر[1] **badara** *u* to come unexpectedly, by surprise; to escape (من s.o.; e.g., words in excitement) **III** to come to s.o.'s (ه) mind, occur to s.o. (ه) all of a sudden, strike s.o. (idea, notion); to embark, enter (الى upon s.th.) or set out (الى to do s.th.) without delay; to rush, hurry (الى to s.o., to a place); to hurry up (ب with s.th.), بادر الى with foll. verbal noun: to do s.th. promptly, without delay, hasten to do s.th.; to fall upon s.o (ه) with (ب), accost, assail, surprise (ه ب s.o. with s.th.; e.g., بادره بكلام غليظ to snap rudely at s.o.); to react, respond (الى to s.th.) | بادر الى انجاز الوعد (*injāzi l-wa'd*) to set out to fulfill a promise **VI** تبادر الى الذهن (*ḏihn*) to suggest itself strongly, be obvious; to appear at first glance as if (أن); تبادر الى ذهنى أن (*ḏihnī*) it occurred to me all of a sudden that ...; تبادر الى الفهم (*fahm*) to be immediately understood **VIII** to hurry, rush, hasten (ه to); to get ahead of s.o. (ه), anticipate, forestall (ه s.o.) | ابتدرها قائلا before she could say a word he exclaimed ...

بدر *badr* pl. بدور *budūr* full moon

بدرة *badra* pl. *badarāt*, بدار *bidār* huge amount of money (formerly = 10,000 dirhams) | بدرات الاموال enormous sums of money

بدار *badāri* hurry! quick!

مبادرة *mubādara* undertaking, enterprise

بادرة *bādira* pl. بوادر *bawādir*[2] herald, harbinger, precursor, forerunner, first indication, sign; unforeseen act; stirring, impulse, fit (e.g., of rage); blunder, mistake; بوادر stirrings, impulses | بادرة خير *b. ḵairin* a good, or generous, impulse

بيدر[2] **baidar** pl. بيادر *bayādir*[2] threshing floor

بدروم and بدرون (Turk. *bodrum*) **badrūm, badrūn** pl. *-āt* basement

بدع **bada'a** *a* (*bad'*) to introduce, originate, start, do for the first time (ه s.th.), be the first to do s.th. (ه); to devise, contrive, invent (ه s.th.) **II** to accuse of heresy (ه s.o.) **IV** = **I**; to create (ه s.th.); to achieve unique, excellent results (فى in); to be amazing, outstanding (فى in s.th.) **VIII** to invent, contrive, devise, think up (ه s.th.) **X** to regard as novel, as unprecedented (ه s.th.)

بدع *bad'* innovation, novelty; creation | بدعا وعودا *bad'an wa-'audan* repeatedly

بدع *bid'* pl. ابداع *abdā'* innovator; new, original; unprecedented, novel | لا بدع *lā bid'a* no wonder! لا بدع ان *lā bid'a an* no wonder that ...; بدع من s.th. else than; unlike, different from

بدعة *bid'a* pl. بدع *bida'* innovation, novelty; heretical doctrine, heresy; pl. creations (of fashion, of art) | اهل البدع *ahl al-b.* heretics

بديع *badī'*, بدع *bud'* unprecedented, marvelous, wonderful, amazing, admirable, singular, unique; creator | علم البديع *'ilm al-b.* the art or science of metaphors and (in general) of good style

بديعة *badī'a* pl. بدائع *badā'i'*[2] an astonishing, amazing thing, a marvel, a wonder; original creation

بديعى *badī'ī* rhetorical

ابدع *abda'*[2] more amazing, more exceptional; of even greater originality

ابداع *ibdā'* creation, fashioning, shaping; a marvelous, unique achievement; uniqueness, singularity, originality; creative ability

○ابداعى *ibdā'ī* romantic (*lit.*)

○ابداعية *ibdā'īya* romanticism (*lit.*)

مبدع *mubdi'* producing, creating; creative; creator; exceptional, unique, outstanding (in an achievement, esp. of an artist)

مبتدع *mubtadi'* innovator; creator; heretic

بيدق look up alphabetically

بدل *badala u* to replace (ب ه s.th. by), exchange (ب ه s.th. for) **II** to change, alter (ه ه s.th. to), convert (ه ه s.th. into); to substitute (ه for s.th., ب or من s.th.), exchange, give in exchange (ه s.th., ب or من for); to change (ه s.th.) **III** to exchange (ه ه with s.o. s.th.) **IV** to replace (ب ه s.th. by), exchange (ب ه for s.th. s.th. else); to compensate (ه ب ه s.o. for s.th. with s.th. else), give s.o. (ه) s.th. (ه) in exchange for (ب) **V** to change; to be exchanged **VI** to exchange (ه s.th., also words, views, greetings) **X** to exchange, receive in exchange, trade, barter (ه ب and ب ه s.th. for); to replace (ه ب and ب ه s.th. by), substitute (ه ب and ب ه for s.th. s.th. else)

بدل *badal* pl. ابدال *abdāl* substitute, alternate, replacement; equivalent, compensation, setoff; reimbursement, recompense, allowance; price, rate; (*gram.*) appositional substantive standing for another substantive | بدل الجراية *b. al-jirāya* allowance for food; بدل السفرية *b. as-safarīya* travel allowance; بدل الاشتراك subscription rate; بدل التمثيل expense account, expense allowance

بدل *badala* (prep.) instead of, in place of, in lieu of

بدلا من *badalan min* in place of, instead of, in lieu of

بدلة *badla* pl. *badalāt*, بدل *bidal* suit (of clothes); costume | بدلة الحمام *b. al-ḥammām* bathing suit; بدلة رسمية (*rasmīya*) uniform; بدلة تشريفاتية (*tašrīfātīya*) full-dress uniform

بدلية *badalīya* compensation, smart money

بدال *badāla* (prep.) instead of, بدال ما (conj.) instead of (being, doing, etc.)

بديل *badīl* pl. بدلاء *budalā'*[2] substitute, alternate (عن or من for); stand-in, double (*theat.*); (f. ة) serving as a replacement or substitute | مفرزة بديلة (*mafraza*) reserve detachment (*mil.*)

بدال *baddāl* grocer; money-changer

بدالة *baddāla* culvert; pipeline; telephone exchange, central

□ مبادل *mabādil*[2] see بذل

تبديل *tabdīl* change, alteration

مبادلة *mubādala* pl. *-āt* exchange | مبادلات تجارية (*tijārīya*) commercial exchange, trade relations

ابدال *ibdāl* exchange, interchange, replacement (ب by), substitution (ب of); change; phonetic change

تبدل *tabaddul* change, shift, turn; transformation; transmutation, conversion

تبادل *tabādul* (mutual) exchange | تبادل السلام *t. as-salām* exchange of greetings; تبادل الخواطر thought transference, telepathy

استبدال *istibdāl* exchange, replacement, substitution

مبدل *mubdil*: مبدل الاسطوانات *m. al-usṭuwūnāt* automatic record changer

متبادل *mutabādal* mutual, reciprocal

بدن **baduna** *u* and *badana u* to be fat, corpulent

بدن *badan* pl. ابدان *abdān*, ابدن *abdun* body, trunk, torso

بدنى *badanī* bodily, corporal, physical, somatic

بدانة *badāna* corpulence, obesity

بدين *badīn* pl. بدن *budun* stout, corpulent, fat, obese

بدونة *budūna* corpulence, obesity

بادن *bādin* pl. بدن *budn* stout, corpulent, fat, obese

بده **badaha** *a* to come, descend suddenly (ه upon s.o.), befall unexpectedly (ه s.o.); to surprise (ه s.o.) with s.th. (ب) III to appear suddenly, unexpectedly (ه ب before s.o. with s.th.) VIII to extemporize, improvise, do offhand, on the spur of the moment (ه s.th.)

بداهة *badāha* spontaneity, spontaneous occurrence, impulse; simple, natural way, naturalness, matter-of-factness; بداهة *badāhatan* and بالبداهة all by itself, spontaneously

بديهة *badīha* s.th. sudden or unexpected; improvisation; impulse, inspiration, spontaneous intuition; intuitive understanding or insight, empathy, instinctive grasp, perceptive faculty | على البديهة all by itself, spontaneously; offhand; حاضر البديهة quick-witted, quick at repartee; بديهة حاضرة presence of mind

بديهى *badīhī* and بدهى *badahī* intuitive; self-evident; a priori (adj.)

بديهية *badīhīya* pl. *-āt* an axiom, a fundamental or self-evident truth; truism, commonplace, platitude

بدائه *badā'ih*[2] fundamental or self-evident truths

(بدو) بدا **badā** *u* to appear, show, become evident, clear, plain or manifest, come to light; to be obvious; to seem good, acceptable, proper (ل to s.o.) III to show, display, evince, manifest, reveal, declare openly | بادى بالعداوة (*'adāwa*) to show open hostility IV to disclose, reveal, manifest, show, display, evince (ه s.th.); to demonstrate, bring out, bring to light, make visible (ه s.th.); to express, utter, voice (ه s.th.) | ابدى رأيه فى (*ra'yahū*) to express one's opinion about; ابدى رغبة (*raḡbatan*) to express a wish or desire V = I; to live in the desert VI to pose as a Bedouin

بدو *badw* desert; nomads, Bedouins

بدوى *badawī* Bedouin, nomadic; rural (as distinguished from urban); a Bedouin

بدوية *badawīya* pl. *-āt* Bedouin woman, Bedouin girl

بداة *badāh* pl. بدوات *badawāt* whim, caprice; ill-humor

بداوة *badāwa* and *bidāwa* desert life, Bedouin life; Bedouinism, nomadism

بيداء *baidā'*[2] desert, steppe, wilderness, wild

ابداء *ibdā'* expression, manifestation, declaration

باد *bādin* apparent, evident, obvious, plain, visible; inhabiting the desert; pl. بداة *budāh* Bedouins

بادية *bādiya* desert, semidesert, steppe; peasantry; (pl. بواد *bawādin*) nomads, Bedouins

بداية *bidāya* = بداءة

بذ *baḏḏa u* (*baḏḏ*) to get the better of (ه), beat, surpass (ه s.o.)

بذ *baḏḏ* and باذ *bāḏḏ* slovenly, untidy, shabby, filthy, squalid

بذاذة *baḏāḏa* slovenliness, untidiness, shabbiness, dirtiness, filth

بذأ *baḏa'a a* to revile, abuse (على s.o.), rail (على at s.o.); — بذئ *baḏi'a a*, بذؤ *baḏu'a u* to be obscene, bawdy

بذىء *baḏī'* disgusting, loathsome, nauseous, foul, dirty, obscene, bawdy, ribald

بذاء *baḏā'* and بذاءة *baḏā'a* obscenity, ribaldry, foulness (of language); disgust, loathing, aversion, contempt

بذخ *baḏaka a* to be haughty, proud

بذخ *baḏak* luxury, pomp, splendor; haughtiness, pride

باذخ *bāḏik* pl. بواذخ *bawāḏik*[2] high, lofty; proud, haughty

بذر *baḏara u* (*baḏr*) to sow, disseminate (ه s.th., seed, also fig. = to spread) II to waste, squander, dissipate (ه s.th.)

بذر *baḏr* pl. بذور *buḏūr*, بذار *biḏār* seeds, seed; seedling; pl. بذور pips, pits, stones (of fruit)

بذرة *baḏra* (n. un.) a seed, a grain; pip, pit, stone (of fruit); germ; (fig.) germ cell (of a development, and the like)

بذار *biḏār* seedtime

تبذير *tabḏīr* waste, squandering, dissipation

مبذر *mubaḏḏir* squanderer, wastrel, spendthrift

بيذق look up alphabetically

بذل *baḏala i u* (*baḏl*) to give or spend freely, generously (ه s.th.); to sacrifice (ه s.th.); to expend (ه s.th.); to offer, grant (ه s.th.) | بذل جهده (*jahdahū*) to take pains; بذل مجهودا do.; بذل كل مساعدة (*kulla musā'adatin*) to grant every assistance; بذل المساعى to make efforts; بذل الطاعة ل to obey s.o., defer to s.o.; بذل كل غال (*kulla ḡālin*) and بذل الغالى والرخيص فى سبيل to spare no effort, go to any length, give everything, pay any price for or in order to; بذل ماء وجهه (*mā'a wajhihī*) to sacrifice one's honor; بذل نفسه دون فلان (or عن فلان) to sacrifice o.s. for s.o.; بذل وسعه (*wus'ahū*) to do one's utmost, do one's best V to fritter away one's fortune, be over-generous; to prostitute o.s. (woman); to display common, vulgar manners VIII to wear out in common service, make trite, vulgar, commonplace, to hackney (ه s.th.); to abuse (ه s.th.); to express o.s. in a vulgar manner, use vulgar language; ابتذل نفسه to degrade o.s., demean o.s., sacrifice one's dignity

بذل *baḏl* giving, spending; sacrifice, surrender, abandonment; expenditure; offering, granting

بذلة *baḏla* suit (of clothes)

مبذل *mibḏal* pl. مباذل *mabāḏil*[2] slipper; pl. مباذل casual clothing worn around home | فلان فى مباذله so-and-so in his private life

ابتذال *ibtiḏāl* triteness, commonness, commonplaceness; banality; debasement, degradation

باذل *bāḏil* spender

متبذل *mutabaddil* vulgar, common

مبتذل *mubtadal* trite, hackneyed, banal, common, vulgar; everyday, commonplace (adj.)

¹بر **barra** (1st pers. perf. *barirtu, barartu*) *a i* (*birr*) to be reverent, dutiful, devoted; to be kind (ه or ب to s.o.); to be charitable, beneficent, do good (ب to s.o.); to obey (ه s.o., esp. God); to treat with reverence, to honor (ب or ه the parents); to be honest, truthful; to be true, valid (sworn statement); to keep (ب a promise, an oath) **II** to warrant, justify, vindicate; to acquit, absolve, exonerate, exculpate, clear (ه, ه s.o., s.th.) | برر وجهه ب (*wajhahū*) to justify o.s. by **IV** to carry out, fulfill (ه s.th., a promise, an oath) **V** to justify o.s.; to be justified

بر *birr* reverence, piety; righteousness, probity; godliness, devoutness; kindness; charitable gift

بر *barr* and بار *bārr* pl. ابرار *abrār* and بررة *barara* reverent, dutiful (ب toward), devoted (ب to); pious, godly, upright, righteous; kind

مبرة *mabarra* pl. *-āt* and مبار *mabārr*² good deed, act of charity, benefaction; philanthropic organization; charitable institution, home or hospital set up with private funds

تبرير *tabrīr* justification, vindication

بار *bārr* reverent, faithful and devoted; see also under بر *barr* above

مبرور *mabrūr* (accepted into the grace of the Lord, i.e.) blessed (said of a deceased person)

مبرر *mubarrir* pl. *-āt* justification; excuse | لا مبرر له (*mubarrira*) unjustifiable

²بر *barr* land (as opposed to sea), terra firma, mainland; open country; برا *barran* out, outside | برا وبحرا *barran wa-baḥran* by land and sea

برى *barrī* terrestrial, land (adj.); wild (of plants and animals) | سيارة برية مائية (*sayyāra, mā'iya*) amphibious vehicle

برية *barrīya* pl. برارى *barārīy* open country; steppe, desert; see also ¹برأ

برانى *barrānī* outside, outer, exterior, external; foreign, alien

³بر *burr* wheat

¹برأ **bara'a** *a* (برء *bar'*) to create (ه s.th., said of God)

برء *bar'* creation

برية *barīya* pl. *-āt*, برايا *barāyā* creation (= that which is created); creature; see also ²بر

البارئ *al-bāri'* the Creator (God)

²برئ **bari'a** *a* (براءة *barā'a*) to be or become free, be cleared (من from, esp. from guilt, blame, etc., الى toward s.o.); to recover (من from an illness) **II** to free, clear, acquit, absolve, exculpate (ه s.o., من from suspicion, blame, guilt) | برأ ساحة الرجل (*sāḥata r-rajul*) he acquitted the man **IV** to acquit, absolve, discharge, exculpate (ه s.o.); to cause to recover, cure, heal (ه s.o.) | ابرأ ذمته (*dimmatahū*) to clear s.o. or o.s. from guilt, exonerate s.o. or o.s. **V** to clear o.s. (من from suspicion, from a charge), free o.s. (من from responsibility, etc.), rid o.s. (من of); to declare o.s. innocent, wash one's hands (من of); to be acquitted **X** to restore to health, cure, heal (ه s.o.); to free o.s. (من from), rid o.s. (من of)

برء *bur'* and بروء *burū'* convalescence, recovery

برئ *barī'* pl. ابرياء *abriyā'*², براء *burā'*, *birā'* free, exempt (من from), devoid (من of); guiltless, innocent; guileless, harmless; healthy, sound

براء *barā'* free, exempt (من from) | ذمته براء من (*ḏimmatuhū*) he is innocent of ...

براءة *barā'a* being free; disavowal, withdrawal; innocence, guiltlessness; naiveté, guilelessness, artlessness; (pl. *-āt*) license, diploma, patent | براءة اختراع patent on an invention; براءة التنفيذ exequatur (a written authorization of a consular officer, issued by the government to which he is accredited); براءة الثقة *b. aṯ-ṯiqa* (*Tun.*) credentials (*dipl.*); على براءة harmless; without guilt, innocent

تبرئة *tabri'a* freeing, exemption; acquittal, absolution, discharge, exoneration

مبارأة *mubāra'a* mubarat, divorce by mutual consent of husband and wife, either of them waiving all claims by way of compensation (*Isl. Law*)

ابراء *ibrā'* acquittal, absolution, release; release of a debtor from his liabilities, remission of debt (*Isl. Law*)

استبراء *istibrā'* : استبراء الحمل *ist. al-ḥamal* the ceremony of selecting and purifying the Host before Mass (*Copt.-Chr.*)

براجواى *baraguwāy* Paraguay

البرازيل *al-bərāzil* Brazil

براسيرى (Fr. *brasserie*) *brāserī* beer parlor, taproom

براغ Prague

برافان (Fr. *paravent*) *baravān* folding screen

براهما *bərahmā* Brahma

بربة *birba* and بربى *birbā* pl. برابى *barābī* ancient Egyptian temple, temple ruins dating back to ancient Egypt (*eg.*); labyrinth, maze

بربخ *barbaḵ* pl. برابخ *barābiḵ*[2] water pipe, drain, culvert, sewer pipe

بربر *barbara* to babble noisily (e.g., a large crowd), jabber, mutter, prattle

البربر *al-barbar* the Berbers

بربرى *barbarī* Berber (adj.); barbaric, uncivilized; — (pl. برابرة *barābira*) a Berber; a barbarian

بربرية *barbarīya* barbar(ian)ism, barbarity, savagery, cruelty

متبربر *mutabarbir* barbaric, uncivilized

بربيس look up alphabetically

بربيش *barbīš* (*syr.*) tube (of a narghile, of an enema, etc.)

بربط *barbaṭa* to splash, paddle, dabble (in water)

بربونى (It. *barbone*) *barbūnī*, also بربون red mullet (Mullus barbatus; *zool.*)

بربى see بربة

بربيس *barbīs* barbel (*zool.*)

برتغال *burtuġāl* Portugal

برتغالى *burtuġālī* Portuguese

برتقال *burtuqāl*, برتقان *burtuqān* orange

برتقالى *burtuqālī*, برتقانى *burtuqānī* orange, orange-colored

برثن *burṯun* pl. براثن *barāṯin*[2] claw, talon

[1]برج V to display, show, play up her charms (woman); to adorn herself, make herself pretty (woman)

[2]برج *burj* pl. بروج *burūj*, ابراج *abrāj* tower; castle; sign of the zodiac | برج الحمام *b. al-ḥamām* pigeon house, dovecot; برج المياه *b. al-miyāh* water tower

[3]بارجة *bārija* pl. بوارج *bawārij*[2] warship, battleship; barge

[1]لعب البرجاس *la'b al-birjās* a kind of equestrian contest, joust, tournament

[2]البرجيس *al-birjīs* Jupiter (*astron.*)

برجل *barjal* pl. براجل *barājil*[2] compass, (pair of) dividers

برجمة *burjuma* pl. براجم *barājim*[2] knuckle, finger joint

برح **bariḥa** *a* (براح *barāḥ*) to leave (ه or من a place, الى for), depart (ه from, الى on one's way to); with neg.: to continue to be (= زال) | ما برح في he is still in ...; ما برح غنيا (*ġanīyan*) he is still rich; برح الخفاء (*kafā'*) the matter has come out, has become generally known; غدا وبرح to come and go **II** to beset, harass, trouble, molest (ب s.o.) **III** to leave (ه a place, الى for), depart (ه from, الى on one's way to)

براح *barāḥ* departure; cessation, stop; a wide, empty tract of land, vast expanse, vastness; براحا *barāḥan* openly and plainly, patently

تباريح *tabārīḥ*[2] agonies, torments (e.g., of longing, of passion)

مبارحة *mubāraḥa* departure

بارح *bāriḥ* (showing the left side, i.e.) ill-boding, inauspicious, ominous (as opposed to سانح); البارح *al-bāriḥa* yesterday

البارحة *al-bāriḥata* yesterday | الليلة البارحة (*lailata*) last night; اول البارحة *awwala l-b.* the day before yesterday, two days ago

مبرح *mubarriḥ* violent, intense, excruciating, agonizing (esp., of pains)

مبرح به *mubarraḥ bihī* stricken, afflicted, tormented

[1]برد **barada** *u* to be or become cold; to cool, cool off (also fig.); to feel cold; to cool, chill (ه s.th.); to soothe, alleviate (ه pain); — *baruda u* to be or become cold **II** to make cold (ه s.th.); to refrigerate (ه s.th.); to cool, chill (ه s.th., also fig.); to soothe, alleviate (ه pain) **V** to refresh o.s., cool o.s. off; to be soothed, be alleviated **VIII** to become cold, cool off

برد *bard* coldness, chilliness, coolness; cooling; alleviation; cold, catarrh

برد *barad* hail, بردة *barada* (n. un.) hailstone

برود *barūd* collyrium

برود *burūd* coldness, coolness, chilliness; emotional coldness, frigidity

برودة *burūda* coldness, coolness, chilliness; emotional coldness, frigidity | برودة الدم *b. ad-dam* cold-bloodedness

بردية *bardīya* ague, feverish chill; see also below

برداء *buradā'*[2] ague, feverish chill

برادة *barrāda* cold-storage plant; refrigerator, icebox

تبريد *tabrīd* cooling, chilling; cold storage, refrigeration; alleviation, mitigation | جهاز التبريد *jahāz at-t.* cold-storage plant, refrigerator; غرفة التبريد *ġurfat at-t.* cold-storage room

بارد *bārid* cold; cool, chilly; easy; weak; stupid, inane, silly, dull; dunce, blockhead | الحرب الباردة (*ḥarb*) the cold war; غنيمة باردة an easy prey; عيش بارد (*'aiš*) an easy life; حجة باردة (*ḥujja*) a weak argument; تبغ بارد (*tibġ*) light, mild tobacco

مبرد *mubarrid* cooling, refreshing; pl. *-āt* refreshments (beverages, etc.)

مبرد *mubarrad* cooled, chilled

[2]برد **barada** *u* to file (ه a piece of metal, etc.)

براد *barrād* fitter (of machinery)

برادة *birāda* fitter's trade or work

برادة *burāda* iron filings

مبرد *mibrad* pl. مبارد *mabārid*[2] file, rasp

[3]برد **burd** pl. ابراد *abrād* garment

بردة *burda* Mohammed's outer garment

برداية *burdāya* curtain, drape

[4]برد IV to send by mail, to mail (ه a letter)

بريد *barīd* post, mail | البريد الجوى (*jawwī*) air mail

بريدى *barīdī* postal; messenger, courier; mailman

[5]بارود look up alphabetically

[6]بردى *bardī, burdī* papyrus (*bot.*)

بردية *bardīya* pl. *-āt* papyrus | علم البرديات *'ilm al-b.* papyrology

برداق *bardāq* pl. براديق *barādīq*[2] jug, pitcher

لعب البردج *la'b al-b.* bridge (game)

بردخ *bardaka* to polish, burnish (ه s.th.)

□ برذعة = بردعة

برتقان = بردقان

بردقوش *bardaqūš* (= مردقوش) marjoram

بردورة (Fr. *bordure*) *bardūra* curbstone, curb

برذعة *barda'a* pl. براذع *barādi'*[2] saddle, packsaddle (for donkeys and camels)

براذعى *barādi'ī* maker of donkey saddles, saddler

برذون *birdaun* pl. براذين *barādīn*[2] work horse, jade, nag

[1]برز *baraza u* to come out, show, appear, come into view, emerge; to jut out, protrude, stand out, be prominent (also fig.); to surpass, excel (على s.o.) **II** to cause to come out, bring out, expose, show, set off, accentuate (ه s.th.); to excel, surpass (على في s.o. in), stand out (في for), distinguish o.s. (في by) **III** to meet in combat or duel (ه s.o.); to compete in a contest (ه with s.o.) **IV** to cause to come out, bring out, expose, make manifest (ه s.th.); to publish, bring out (ه a book, etc.); to present, show (ه e.g., an identity card) **V** to evacuate the bowels **VI** to vie, contend

بروز *burūz* prominence, projection, protrusion

براز *birāz* excrement, feces; competition, contest, match (in sports); duel

بريزة *buraiza* (*birēza; eg.*) ten-piaster coin

ابرز *abraz*[2] more marked, more distinctive; more prominent

مبارزة *mubāraza* competition, contest, match, esp. in sports; duel; fencing

ابراز *ibrāz* bringing out, displaying, setting off, accentuation; production; presentation

بارز *bāriz* protruding, projecting, salient; raised, embossed, in relief; marked, distinct, conspicuous; prominent (personality)

مبرز *mubarriz* surpassing (على s.o.), superior (على to s.o.); winner, victor (in contest)

مبارز *mubāriz* competitor, contender; combatant, fighter; fencer

[2]بريز (Fr. *prise*) *brīz* pl. *-āt* (plug) socket, wall plug, outlet (*syr.*); بريزة *barīza* pl. برائز *barā'iz*[2] do. (*eg.*)

[3]ابريز look up alphabetically

[4]برزان *barazān* trumpet

برزخ *barzak* pl. برازخ *barāzik*[2] interval, gap, break, partition, bar, obstruction; isthmus

برزوق *burzūq* sidewalk

[1]برسام *birsām* pleurisy

[2]ابريسم look up alphabetically

[3]برسيم *birsīm* clover, specif., berseem, Egyptian clover (Trifolium alexandrinum L.; *bot.*)

[1]برش *burš* pl. ابراش *abrāš* mat

ابرش *abraš*[2] spotted, speckled

ابرشية² look up alphabetically

برشت *birišt*: بيض برشت (*baiḍ*) soft-boiled eggs

برشلونه *baršilōna* Barcelona (seaport in NE Spain)

برشم *baršama* to stare, gaze (الى at s.th.); to rivet (ه s.th.)

برشمة *baršama* riveting

برشام *buršām* and برشان (n. un. ة) pl. *-āt* wafer; Host (*Chr.*)

برشامة *buršāma* rivet

برشامجى *buršāmjī* riveter

برشمجية *buršamjīya* riveting

برص¹ *bariṣa a* (*baraṣ*) to be a leper

برص *burṣ* wall gecko (Tarentola mauritanica, *zool.*)

برص *baraṣ* leprosy

ابرص *abraṣ*² leprous; leper | سام ابرص *sāmm a.* wall gecko

برصة² *burṣa* stock exchange

برض *baraḍa u* (بروض *burūḍ*) to germinate, sprout (plant)

برطوز *barṭūz*: برطوز البحرية *b. al-baḥrīya* forecastle, crew quarters (on a merchant vessel)

برطع *barṭaʿa* (برطعة *barṭaʿa*) to gallop

برطل *barṭala* (برطلة *barṭala*) to bribe (ه s.o.) II *tabarṭala* to take bribes, be venal

برطيل *birṭīl* pl. براطيل *barāṭīl*² bribe

برطم¹ *barṭama* to rave, talk irrationally

برطوم *burṭūm*, *barṭūm* trunk of an elephant

برطمان² *barṭamān* pl. *-āt* (*syr.*, *eg.*) tall earthen or glass vessel (for preserves, oil, etc.)

برع *baraʿa a* to surpass, excel (ه s.o.); (also *baruʿa u*) to distinguish o.s., be skillful, proficient **V** to contribute, give, donate (ب s.th.); to undertake (voluntarily, ب s.th.), volunteer (ب for), be prepared, willing (ب to do s.th.); to be ready, be on hand (ب with)

براعة *barāʿa* skill, proficiency; efficiency, capability, capacity

بروعة *burūʿa* superior skill, outstanding proficiency

تبرع *tabarruʿ* pl. *-āt* gift, donation; contribution

بارع *bāriʿ* skilled, skillful, proficient, capable, efficient; brilliant, outstanding (work of art)

برعم *barʿama* to bud, burgeon, sprout

برعم *burʿum* pl. براعم *barāʿim*² and برعوم *burʿūm* pl. براعيم *barāʿīm*² bud, burgeon; blossom, flower

برغوث *burğūṯ* pl. براغيث *barāğīṯ*² flea; pl. براغيث (*syr.*) small silver coins | برغوث البحر *b. al-baḥr* shrimp (*zool.*)

برغش *barğaš* (coll.; n. un. ة) gnat(s), midge(s)

برغل *burğul* cooked, parched and crushed wheat, served together with other food (*eg.*, *syr.*)

برغى (Turk. بورغى *burğų*) *burğī* pl. براغى *barāğī* screw

برفير *birfīr* pl. برافير *barāfīr*² purple

بروقة look up alphabetically

برق¹ *baraqa u* to shine, glitter, sparkle, flash | برقت السماء (*samāʾu*) there was lightning **IV** = **I**; to emit bolts of lightning (cloud); to flash up, light up; to brighten (face); to cable, wire, telegraph (الى to)

برق *barq* pl. بروق *burūq* lightning; flash of lightning; telegraph | برق خلب (*ḵullab*) lightning without a downpour, used fig., e.g., of s.o. given to making promises without ever living up to them

برقى *barqī* telegraphic, telegraph- (in compounds)

برقية *barqīya* pl. *-āt* telegram, wire, cable

بريق *barīq* pl. برائق *barā'iq*[2] glitter, shine, gloss, luster | ذو بريق معدنى (*ma'dinī*) lustered, coated with metallic luster

براق *burāq* Alborak, name of the creature on which Mohammed made his ascension to the seven heavens (معراج)

براق *barrāq* shining, lustrous, sparkling, flashing, glittering, twinkling

مبرق *mabraq* glitter, flash | فى مبرق الصبح *fī m. iṣ-ṣubḥ* with the first rays of the morning sun

بارق *bāriq*: بارق الامل *b. al-amal* glimpse of hope

بارقة *bāriqa* pl. بوارق *bawāriq*[2] gleam, twinkle

مبرق *mubriq*: مبرق كاتب teletype

[2]البرقة *al-barqa* Cyrenaica (region of E Libya)

[3]ابريق look up alphabetically

[4]استبرق look up alphabetically

برقش *barqaša* (برقشة *barqaša*) to variegate, paint or daub with many colors (ه s.th.); to embellish (ه s.th.; قوله one's speech) II *tabarqaša* reflex. and pass. of I

برقش *birqiš* finch

برقشة *barqaša* colorful medley, variety, variegation

مبرقش *mubarqaš* colorful, variegated, many-colored

برقع *barqa'a* to veil, drape (ه, ه s.o., s.th.) II *tabarqa'a* to put on a veil, veil o.s.

برقع *burqu'* pl. براقع *barāqi'*[2] veil (worn by women; long, leaving the eyes exposed)

برقوق *barqūq* (coll.; n. un. ة) plum

[1]برك *baraka* u to kneel down II and IV to make (ه the camel) kneel down II to invoke a blessing (على or فى on s.th., ل on s.o.) III to bless (فى or ه s.o., also ل or على), invoke a blessing on; to give one's blessing (ه to s.th.), sanction (ه s.th.) V to be blessed (ب by); to enjoy (ب s.th.), find pleasure, delight (ب in); to ask s.o.'s (ب) blessing VI to be blessed, be praised; ... تبارك *tabāraka* ... God bless ...! X to be blessed

بركة *birka* pl. برك *birak* pond, small lake; puddle, pool | بركة السباحة *b. as-sibāḥa* swimming pool

بركة *baraka* pl. *-āt* blessing, benediction | قلة البركة *qillat al-b.* misfortune, bad luck

ابرك *abrak*[2] more blessed

تبريك *tabrīk* pl. *-āt* good wish; blessing, benediction

مبارك *mubārak* blessed, fortunate, lucky

[2]براريك *barārīk*[2] (*mor.*) barracks

بركار *birkār* compass, (pair of) dividers

بركان *burkān* pl. براكين *barākīn*[2] volcano

بركانى *burkānī* volcanic

برلمان *barlamān* parliament

برلمانى *barlamānī* parliamentary

برلمانية *barlamānīya* parliamentarianism

برلنتى (It. *brillante*) *brillantī* brilliant, diamond

برلين *barlīn* Berlin

[1]برم *barima* a (*baram*) to be or become weary, tired (ب of), be fed up, be bored (ب with), find annoying, wearisome (ب s.th.) V to feel annoyed (ب by), be displeased (ب with); to be fed up (ب with), be sick and tired (ب of, also من); to be impatient, discontented, dissatisfied; to grieve, be pained

برم *barim* weary, tired (ب of), disgusted (ب at, with); dissatisfied, discontented

تبرم *tabarrum* weariness, boredom, disgust; discontent, dissatisfaction; uneasiness, discomfort, annoyance

متبرم *mutabarrim* cross, peevish, vexed, annoyed

[2]برم *barama u* (*barm*) to twist, twine (ه a rope); to shape (ه s.th.) round and long; to roll up (ه the sleeves); to settle, establish, confirm (ه s.th.) **IV** to twist, twine (ه a rope); to settle, establish, confirm (ه s.th.); to conclude (ه a pact); to confirm (ه a judicial judgment); to ratify (ه a treaty, a bill) **VII** to be settled, be established, be confirmed; to be twisted, be twined

برامة *barrāma* pl. *-āt* drilling machine

بريم *barīm* rope, string, cord, twine

بريمة *barrīma* pl. *-āt* drill, borer, gimlet, auger, bit; ○ corkscrew

○ بريمية *barrīmīya* spirochete

ابرام *ibrām* settlement, establishment; confirmation; conclusion (of a pact, etc.); ratification | محكمة النقض والابرام *maḥkamat an-naqḍ wa-l-i.* Court of Cassation (*Eg.*)

مبروم *mabrūm*: ○ سلك مبروم (*silk*) wire rope, cable

مبرم *mubram* firm, strong; irrevocable, definitely established; confirmed, ratified | قضاء مبرم (*qaḍā'*) inescapable fate; بصورة مبرمة irrevocably

[3]برمة *burma* pl. برم *buram*, برام *birām* earthenware pot

برما *burmā* Burma

برمائى *barmā'ī* amphibious | دبابة برمائية (*dabbāba*) amphibious tank (*mil.*)

○ برمائية *barmā'īya* amphibian

برماننت (Engl.) *barmānant* permanent wave | برماننت على البارد cold wave (in hair)

برمق *barmaq* pl. برامق *barāmiq*[2] baluster; spike (of a wheel)

برمهات *baramhāt* the seventh month of the Coptic calendar

برمنكهام Birmingham

برموده *barmūda* the eighth month of the Coptic calendar

برميل *barmīl* pl. براميل *barāmīl*[2] barrel; keg, cask; tun

برنية *barnīya* pl. برانى *barānīy* clay vessel

برنامج *barnāmaj* pl. برامج *barāmij*[2] program, plan, schedule; roster, list, index; curriculum

برنجك *burunjuk* gauze, crepe

[1]برنس *burnus* pl. برانس *barānis*[2] (also برنوس *barnūs*, *burnūs* pl. برانيس *barānīs*[2]) burnoose, hooded cloak; casula, chasuble (of Coptic priests) | برنس الحمام *b. al-ḥammām* bathrobe

برانسى *barānisī* pl. *-īya* maker of burnooses

[2]جبال البرانس *jibāl al-barānis* the Pyrenees

[3]برنس *brins* prince

برنسيسة *brinsēsa* princess

برنط II *tabarnaṭa* to wear a hat

برنيطة *burnaiṭa* pl. *-āt*, برانيط *barānīṭ*[2] (European) hat (men's and women's); lamp shade

برهة *burha* pl. *burahāt*, بره *burah* a while, a time; short time; instant, moment; برهة *burhatan* a little while | بعد برهتين (after two moments =) in a short time

□ برهم *barham* (*syr.*) = مرهم *marham*

برهمن *barahman* pl. براهمة *barāhima* Brahman

برهمية *barahmīya* Brahmanism

برهن *barhana* to prove, demonstrate (على or عن s.th.)

برهان *burhān* pl. براهين *barāhīn*² proof

برهنة *barhana* proving, demonstration

بروة *barwa* waste, scrap

بروتستانتى *brotostantī* Protestant; (pl. *-ūn*) a Protestant

بروتستانتية *brotostantīya* Protestantism

بروتستو (It. *protesto*) *brotostō* protest (of a bill of exchange)

بروتوكول *brotokōl* protocol

بروتون *brōtōn* proton

بروجرام *brogrām* program

بروجى *burūjī* pl. *-īya* trumpeter, bugler

بروز *barwaza* to frame

برواز *barwāz, birwāz* pl. براويز *barāwīz*² frame

بروسيا (It. *Prussia*) *burūsiyā* Prussia

بروسى *burūsī* Prussian

بروفة and بروڤة (It. *prova*) *brōva, brōfa* pl. *-āt* test, experiment; proof sheet; rehearsal

برونز (Fr.) *bronz* bronze

برونزى *bronzī* bronze, bronzy | العصر البرونزى (*ʿaṣr*) the Bronze Age

¹برى *barā i* (*bary*) to trim, shape (ه s.th.), nib (ه a pen), sharpen (ه a pencil); to scratch off, scrape off (ه s.th.); to exhaust, tire out, wear out, emaciate, enervate (ه s.o.), sap the strength of (ه) **III** to vie, compete (ه with s.o.), try to outstrip (ه s.o.) **VI** to vie, compete, contend, be rivals; to meet in a contest, try each other's strength (esp. in games and sports) **VII** to be trimmed, be nibbed, be sharpened; to defy, oppose (ل s.o.); to undertake, take in hand (ل s.th.), set out to do s.th. (ل), enter, embark (ل upon); to break forth (من from); to get going; to break out, let fly, explode (with words, esp. in anger or excitement)

برى *baran* dust, earth

براية *barrāya*, براية الاقلام *b. al-aqlām* pencil sharpener

مبراة *mibrāh* pocketknife

مباراة *mubārāh* pl. مباريات *mubārayāt* contest, tournament, match (in games and sports); competition, rivalry

بار: اعط القوس باريها *aʿṭi l-qausa bāriyahā* give the bow to him who knows how to shape it, i.e., always ask an expert

متبار *mutabārin* participant in a contest, contestant, contender; competitor, rival

²برية see ¹برأ and ²بر

بريطانيا *bariṭāniyā, biriṭāniyā* Britain, بريطانيا العظمى (*uẓmā*) Great Britain

بريطانى *bariṭānī, biriṭānī* British; Britannic

¹بز *bazza u* (*bazz*) to take away, steal, wrest, snatch (ه ه from s.o. s.th.), rob, strip (ه ه s.o. of s.th.); to defeat, beat, outstrip, excel (ه s.o.), triumph, be victorious (ه over) **VIII** to take away, steal, pilfer (ه s.th.); to take away, snatch (ه money, من from s.o.); to rob, fleece (ه s.o.) | ابتز اموال الناس to lift money out of people's pockets, relieve people of their money

ابتزاز *ibtizāz* theft, robbery; fleecing, robbing (of s.o.)

²بز *bazza u* to bud, burgeon

بز *buzz, bizz* pl. بزاز *bizāz*, ابزاز *abzāz* nipple, mammilla (of the female breast); teat, female breast

[3]بز bazz pl. بزوز buzūz linen; cloth, dry goods

بزة bizza clothing, clothes, attire; uniform | بزة رسمية (rasmīya) uniform

بزاز bazzāz draper, cloth merchant

بزازة bizāza cloth trade

بزبوز bazbūz pl. بزابيز bazābīz[2] nozzle, spout

بزر bazara i (bazr) to sow

بزر bizr pl. بزور buzūr seed(s); pl. ابزار abzār and ابازير abāzīr[2] spice

بزرة bizra (n. un.) seed; kernel, pip, pit, stone (of fruit); germ

بزار bazzār seedsman

بزيرة buzaira pl. -āt spore (bot.)

بزغ bazaġa u to break forth, come out, to dawn (day); to rise (sun)

بزوغ buzūġ appearance, emergence; rise (of the sun)

بزق bazaqa u (bazq) to spit

بزاق buzāq spit, spittle, saliva

بزاقة bazzāqa snail; cobra

مبزقة mibzaqa pl. مبازق mabāziq[2] spittoon, cuspidor

[1]بزل bazala u (bazl) to split (ه s.th.); to pierce (ه s.th.), make a hole (ه in); to tap, broach (ه s.th.; a cask); to puncture, tap (ه s.o.; med.); to clear, filter (ه a liquid)

بزل bazl puncture, tapping, paracentesis (med.)

بزال buzāl bung (of a cask)

مبزل mibzal pl. مبازل mabāzil[2] spile, spigot, tap; cock, faucet

[2]بزلة (It. piselli) bizilla and بزلا green peas

ابزيم ibzīm pl. ابازيم abāzīm[2] buckle, clasp

بزموت bizmūt bismuth

بزنطى bizanṭī Byzantine

باز bāzin pl. بزاة buzāh, بواز bawāzin, بيزان bīzān falcon

بس bass and بسة bassa pl. بساس bisās cat

بسأ basa'a a (بسء bas') to treat amicably (ب s.o.); to be intimate, be on familiar terms (ب with)

بسارابيا besārābiyā Bessarabia

بسباس basbās, بسباسة basbāsa (eg.) mace (bot.); (maġr.) fennel

بسبوسة basbūsa (eg.) pastry made of flour, melted butter, sugar and oil

بستيلية (Fr.) bastīliya pastilles, lozenges

[1]بستان bustān pl. بساتين basātīn[2] garden

بستانى bustānī gardener; garden (adj.); horticultural

بستنة bastana gardening, horticulture

[2]بستون (Fr. piston) bistōn, بستن (Engl.) bistan pl. بساتن basātin[2] piston

[3]بستونى (It. bastone) bastūnī spades (suit of playing cards)

بسخة baska Easter; Passion Week (Chr.)

بسر basara u (بسور busūr) to scowl, frown; — basara u (basr) and VIII to begin too early (ه with), take premature action, be rash (ه in s.th.)

بسر busr (n. un. ة) pl. بسار bisār unripe dates

باسور bāsūr pl. بواسير bawāsīr[2] hemorrhoids

بسط basaṭa u (basṭ) to spread, spread out (ه s.th.); to level, flatten (ه s.th.); to enlarge, expand (ه s.th.); to stretch out, extend (ه s.th.); to unfold, unroll (ه s.th.); to grant, offer, present (ه s.th.); to submit, state, set forth, expound, explain (ه s.th., ل or على to s.o.); to flog (ه s.o.; Nejd); to please, delight (ه s.o.) | بسط ذراعيه (dirā'aihi) to spread one's arms;

بسط يد المساعدة ل (*yada l-musā'ada*) to extend a helping hand to s.o.; بسط المائدة to lay the table; — *basuṭa u* (بساطة *basāṭa*) to be simple, openhearted, frank, candid II to spread, spread out, extend, expand (ه s.th.); to level, flatten (ه s.th.); to simplify, make simple (ه s.th.) III to set forth, state, expound, explain; to be sincere (ه ب with s.o. about or in s.th.), confess frankly (ه ب to s.o. s.th.) V to be spread, be unrolled, be spread out, be extended; to speak at great length (في about), enlarge (في on), treat exhaustively, expound in detail (في a theme); to be friendly, communicative, sociable, behave unceremoniously, be completely at ease | تبسط في الحديث to talk freely, without formality VII to spread, extend, expand (intr.); to be glad, be delighted, be or become happy

بسط *basṭ* extension, spreading, unrolling, unfolding; presentation, statement, explanation, exposition; cheering, delighting, delectation; amusement; (*Eg.*) numerator (of a fraction) | بسط اليد *b. al-yad* avarice, greed, cupidity

بسطة *basṭa* extension, extent, expanse; size, magnitude; skill, capability, abilities; excess, abundance; (pl. *-āt*) statement, exposition, presentation; — (pl. بساط *bisāṭ*) landing (of a staircase); estrade, dais, platform (*eg.*)

بساط *bisāṭ* pl. *-āt*, ابسطة *absiṭa*, بسط *busuṭ* carpet, rug | بساط الرحمة *b. ar-raḥma* winding sheet, shroud; طرح (or وضع) مسألة على بساط البحث (*mas'alatan, baḥṭ*) to raise a question, bring a question on the carpet, also على بساط المناقشة (*b. il-munāqaša*) for discussion; طوى البساط بما فيه to bring the matter to an end, settle it once and for all

بسيط *basīṭ* pl. بسطاء *busaṭā'*² simple; plain, uncomplicated; slight, little, modest, inconsiderable, trivial, trifling; البسيط name of a poetical meter; pl. بسطاء simple souls, ingenuous people | بسيط اليدين *b. al-yadain* (pl. بسط *busuṭ*) generous, openhanded

البسيطة *al-basīṭa* the earth, the world

بسائط *basā'iṭ*² elements; simple remedies, medicinal plants; basic facts

بساطة *basāṭa* simplicity, plainness

○ ابسوطة *ubsūṭa* pl. اباسيط *abāsīṭ*² rim, felly (of a wheel)

ابسط *absaṭ*² simpler; wider, more extensive

تبسيط *tabsīṭ* simplification

انبساط *inbisāṭ* (n. vic. ة) extensity, extensiveness, extension; expansion, expanse; joy, delight, happiness, gaiety, cheerfulness

عضلة باسطة *'aḍala bāsiṭa* extensor (*anat.*)

مبسوط *mabsūṭ* extended, outstretched; spread out; extensive, large, sizeable; detailed, elaborate (book); cheerful, happy, gay; feeling well, in good health; (*tun.*) well-to-do

منبسط *munbasiṭ* extending, spreading; gay, happy, cheerful; level surface

بسطرمة (Turk.) *basṭurma* a kind of jerked, salted meat (*eg.*)

البسفور *al-busfūr* the Bosporus

بسق *basaqa u* (بسوق *busūq*) to be high, tall, lofty, towering; to excel, surpass (ه or على s.o.)

باسق *bāsiq* high, tall, lofty, towering

مبسق *mubsiq* high, tall, lofty, towering

بسكليت (Fr. *bicyclette*) *biskilēt*, *baskilēt* bicycle

بسكوت (It. *biscotto*) *baskūt* biscuit

بسكويت *baskawīt* biscuit

¹بسل *basula u* (بسالة *basāla*) to be brave, fearless, intrepid V to scowl, glower X to be reckless, defy death

بسالة *basāla* courage, intrepidity

استبسال *istibsāl* death defiance

باسل *bāsil* pl. بسلاء *busalā'*[2], بواسل *bawāsil*[2] brave, fearless, intrepid

مستبسل *mustabsil* death-defying, heroic

بسلة[2] *bisilla* peas

بسم *basama i* (*basm*), V and VIII to smile

بسمة *basma* pl. *basamāt* smile

بسام *bassām* smiling

مبسم *mabsim* pl. مباسم *mabāsim*[2] mouth; mouthpiece, holder (for cigars, cigarettes, etc.)

ابتسام *ibtisām* and (n. vic.) ابتسامة pl. *-āt* smile

بسمل *basmala* to utter the invocation بسم الله الرحمن الرحيم "In the name of God, the Benificent, the Merciful"

بسملة *basmala* utterance of the above invocation; the invocation itself

بسينة *busaina* kitty

بسيكولوجى *psikolōjī* psychologic(al)

بش *bašša a* (*bašš*, بشاشة *bašāša*) to display a friendly, cheerful, happy mien; to smile; to be friendly (ل to s.o.), give s.o. (ل) a smile

بشوش *bašūš*, بشاش *baššāš* smiling, friendly, cheerful

بشاشة *bašāša* smile; happy mien

باش *bāšš* smiling, happy; friendly, kind

بشت *bušt* (*Nejd, Baḥr., Ir.*) a kind of cloak, = عباءة *'abā'a*

بشتة *bišta* (*eg.*) woolen cloak worn by Egyptian peasants

[1]بشر *bašara i, bašira a* to rejoice, be delighted, be happy (ب at s.th.) II to announce (as good news; ب ه to s.o. s.th.); to bring news (ب ه to s.o. of s.th.); to spread, propagate, preach (ب s.th.; a religion, a doctrine) | بشر نفسه ب (*nafsahū*) to indulge in the happy hope that ... IV to rejoice (at good news) X to rejoice, be delighted, be happy (ب at s.th., esp. at good news), welcome (ب s.th.); to take as a good omen (ب s.th.) | استبشر به خيرا (*kairan*) to regard s.th. as auspicious

بشر *bišr* joy

بشر *bušr* glad tidings

بشرى *bušrā* glad tidings, good news

بشارة *bišāra* pl. *-āt*, بشائر *bašā'ir*[2] good news, glad tidings; annunciation, prophecy; gospel; بشائر good omens, propitious signs | عيد البشارة *'īd al-b.* the Annunciation, the Day of Our Lady (*Chr.*)

بشير *bašīr* pl. بشراء *bušarā'*[2] bringer of glad tidings, messenger, herald, harbinger, forerunner, precursor; evangelist (*Chr.*)

تبشير *tabšīr* announcement (of glad tidings); preaching of the Gospel; evangelization, missionary activity

تبشيرى *tabšīrī* missionary

تباشير *tabāšīr*[2] foretokens, prognostics, omens, first signs or indications, heralds (fig.); beginnings, dawn | تباشير الفجر *t. al-fajr* the first shimmer of aurora, the first glimpse of dawn

مبشر *mubaššir* pl. *-ūn* announcer, messenger (of glad tidings); evangelist (*Chr.*); preacher; missionary (*Chr.*)

مستبشر *mustabšir* happy, cheerful

[2]بشر *bašara u* to peel (ه s.th.); to scrape off, shave off, scratch off (ه s.th.); to grate, shred (ه s.th.) III to touch (ه s.th.), be in direct contact (ه with s.th.); to have sexual intercourse (ه with s.o.); to attend, apply o.s. (ه or ب to s.th.), take up, take in hand, pursue, practice, carry out (ه s.th., a job, a task, etc.)

بشر **bašar** man, human being; men, mankind

بشرى **bašarī** human; human being; epidermal, skin (adj.) | طبيب بشرى dermatologist

بشرة **bašara** outer skin, epidermis, cuticle; skin; complexion

بشرية **bašarīya** mankind, human race

مبشرة **mibšara** pl. مباشر **mabāšir**[2] scraper, grater

مباشرة **mubāšara** pursuit, practice; direct, physical cause (*Isl. Law*); **mubāšaratan** immediately, directly

مبشور **mabšūr**: جبنة مبشورة (*jubna*) shredded cheese

مباشر **mubāšir** pl. *-ūn* direct, immediate; practitioner, pursuer, operator; director; ○ manager (*Eg.*); court usher (*Syr.*); (*mil.*) approx.: staff sergeant (*Eg.* 1939) | غير مباشر indirect; اصابات مباشرة (*iṣābāt*) direct hits

بشروش **bašarūš** flamingo

بشع **baši'a** *a* (بشاعة **bašā'a**) to be ugly, loathsome **II** to make ugly, disfigure, distort (ه s.th.); to disparage, run down (ه s.th.) **X** to regard as ugly, find ugly or repugnant (ه s.th.)

بشع **baši'** ugly; offensive, disgusting, distasteful, repugnant; unpleasant

بشيع **bašī'** ugly; offensive, disgusting, distasteful, repugnant; unpleasant

بشاعة **bašā'a** ugliness

ابشع **abša'**[2] uglier; more repulsive

[1]باشق look up alphabetically

[2]بشقه (*eg.*; Turk. *başka*; invar.) different

بشك **VIII** to lie, prevaricate

بشاك **baššāk** liar

ابتشاك **ibtišāk** lie, deceit, trickery

[1]بشكور **baškūr** pl. بشاكير **bašākīr**[2] poker, fire iron

[2]بشكير **baškīr** pl. بشاكير **bašākīr**[2] towel

بشلة (It.) **bišilla** pl. *-āt* bacillus

بشم **bašima** *a* (**bašam**) to feel nauseated, be disgusted (من by s.th.), be fed up (من with) **IV** to nauseate, sicken, disgust (ه s.o.)

بشم **bašam** surfeit, satiety, loathing, disgust

بشمار **bašmār** (*tun.*) lacework, trimmings

بشامرى **bašāmirī** (*tun.*) laceworker, lacemaker

بشمق **bašmaq** slipper (worn by *fuqahā'* and women)

بشنة **bašna** (*maġr.*) sorghum, millet

بشنس **bašans** the ninth month of the Coptic calendar

بشنوقة **bašnūqa** pl. بشانيق **bašānīq**[2] kerchief tied under the chin (*pal.*)

بشنين **bašnīn** lotus

بص **baṣṣa** *i* (**baṣṣ**, بصيص **baṣīṣ**) to glow, sparkle, glitter, shine; — (*eg.*) *u* to look

بصة **baṣṣa** embers

بصيص **baṣīṣ** glow, shine; glimpse, ray (e.g., of hope); lustrous, shining

بصاص **baṣṣāṣ** lustrous, shining; (*eg.*) spy, detective

بصبص **baṣbaṣa** (بصبصة **baṣbaṣa**) to wag (بذنبه *bi-ḏanabihī* its tail); (*eg.*) to ogle, make sheep's eyes, cast amorous glances

بصخة **baṣḵa** see بسخة

[1]بصر **baṣura** *u*, **baṣira** *a* (**baṣar**) to look, see; to realize, understand, comprehend, grasp (ب s.th.) **II** to make (ه s.o.) see, understand or realize (ه or ب s.th.), make (ه s.o.) aware (ه or ب of s.th.); to en-

lighten (ه ه or ب ه s.o. on or as to s.th.); to tell, inform (ه ه or ب ه s.o. about) IV to see (ه, ه s.o., s.th.); to make out, behold, perceive, discern, notice (ه, ه s.o., s.th.), set eyes on (ه, ه), catch sight of (ه, ه); to recognize (ه, ه s.o., s.th.); to reflect (ب on), ponder (ب s.th.) V to look (ه at), regard (ه s.th.); to reflect (فى on s.th.), ponder (فى s.th.) X to have the faculty of visual perception, be able to see; to be endowed with reason, be rational, reasonable, intelligent; to reflect (فى on s.th.), ponder (فى s.th.)

بصر **baṣar** pl. ابصار **abṣār** vision, eyesight; glance, look; insight; sight, discernment, perception | قصير البصر short-sighted, myopic; لمح البصر *lamḥ al-b.* glance of the eye; فى لمح البصر, كلمح البصر, فى اقل من لمح البصر, دون لمح البصر (*dūna*), (*aqalla*) in the twinkling of an eye, in a moment, in a flash, instantly; على مدى البصر (*madā*) within sight; له بصر ب he is knowledgeable in, he is familiar with

بصرى **baṣarī** optic(al), visual, ocular

بصريات **baṣrīyāt** optics

بصارة **baṣāra** perception, discernment; perspicacity, acuteness of the mind, sharp-wittedness

بصير **baṣīr** pl. بصراء **buṣarā'**[2] endowed with eyesight; acutely aware (ب of), having insight (ب into); possessing knowledge or understanding (ب of), discerning, discriminating, versed, knowledgeable, proficient (ب in), acquainted (ب with s.th.)

بصيرة **baṣīra** pl. بصائر **baṣā'ir**[2] (keen) insight, penetration, discernment, understanding, (power of) mental perception, mental vision | عن بصيرة deliberately, knowingly; كان على بصيرة من to have insight into s.th., be informed about s.th.; نافذ البصيرة discerning, clear-sighted, perspicacious, sharp-witted; نفاذ البصيرة *nafāḏ al.-b.* sharp discernment, perspicacity

ابصر **abṣar**[2] more discerning

تبصرة **tabṣira** enlightenment; instruction, information

تبصر **tabaṣṣur** reflection, consideration; penetration, clear-sightedness, perspicacity

باصرة **bāṣira** pl. بواصر **bawāṣir**[2] eye

البصرة **al-baṣra** Basra (port in S Iraq)

بصق **baṣaqa** *u* to spit (على on s.o.)

بصقة **baṣqa** (n. vic.) expectoration; (expectorated) spit, spittle, saliva

بصاق **buṣāq** spit, spittle, saliva

مبصقة **mibṣaqa** spittoon, cuspidor

بصل **baṣal** (coll.; n. un. ة) onion(s); bulb(s) | بصل الفار *b. al-fa'r* sea onion (Scilla verna)

بصلى **baṣalī** bulbous

بصيلة **buṣaila** pl. *-āt*, بصيلة الشعر *b. aš-ša'r* bulb of the hair (*anat.*)

بصم **baṣama** *u* (**baṣm**) to print, imprint (ه s.th.); to stamp (ه s.th.); to make, or leave, an imprint (ه on)

بصمة **baṣma** pl. **baṣamāt** imprint, impression | بصمة الختم *b. al-ḵatm* stamp imprint, stamp; بصمة الاصابع fingerprint

بصوة **baṣwa** embers

بض **baḍḍ** tender-skinned

بضع **baḍa'a** *a* (**baḍ'**) to cut, slash or slit open (ه s.th.); to cut up, carve up, dissect, anatomize (s.th.); to amputate (*surg.*) II to cut up, carve up, dissect, anatomize III to sleep (ها with a woman) IV to invest capital (ه) profitably in a commercial enterprise V pass. of II; to trade; to shop, make purchases X to trade

بضع *baḍʿ* amputation

بضع *biḍʿ* (commonly, with genit. pl. of f. nouns, بضعة with genit. pl. of m. nouns; in classical Arabic بضع with both genders) some, a few, several

بضعة *biḍʿa* pl. بضع *biḍaʿ* piece (of meat); meat; see also *biḍʿ* above

بضع *buḍʿ* vulva

بضاعة *biḍāʿa* pl. بضائع *baḍāʾiʿ²* goods, merchandise, wares, commodities; that which s.o. has to offer, which he has to show, with which he is endowed (also attributes, qualities) | قطار البضاعة freight train; اخرج ما عنده من بضاعة he said what he had intended to say

مبضع *mibḍaʿ* pl. مباضع *mabāḍiʿ²* dissecting knife, scalpel

ابضاع *ibḍāʿ* mandate for the management of affairs (*Isl. Law*); partnership in a limited company, capital investment

مبضع *mubḍiʿ* pl. *-ūn* limited partner (*com.*)

مستبضع *mustabḍiʿ* manager, managing agent (*Isl. Law*)

بط **baṭṭ** (n. un. ة) duck; بطة *baṭṭa* leather flask | بطة الساق calf (of the leg)

بطؤ **baṭuʾa** *u* (بطء *buṭʾ*, بطاء *biṭāʾ*, بطاءة *baṭāʾa*) to be slow; to be slowgoing, slow-footed, slow-paced; to tarry, linger, wait, hesitate **II** to retard, slow down, delay, hold up (ب على s.o. in s.th.) **IV** to slow down, decelerate, retard, delay, hold up (ه s.th.); to be slow, go or drive slowly, slow down; to be late (عن for s.th., in meeting s.o.), keep s.o. (عن) waiting **V** to be slow, tardy (في in) **VI** to be slow, leisurely, unhurried; to go, drive, act or proceed slowly, leisurely; to be slowgoing, slow-footed, slow-paced; to slow down **X** to find slow (ه, ه s.o., s.th.); to have to wait a long time (ه for s.o.), be kept waiting (ه by s.o.)

بطء *buṭʾ* slowness, tardiness | ببطء slowly, leisurely, unhurriedly

بطیء *baṭīʾ* pl. بطاء *biṭāʾ* slow, unhurried; slowgoing, slow-footed, slow-paced; tardy, late; sluggish, lazy; slow, gradual, imperceptible | ○ بطیء التردد *b. at-taraddud* of low frequency (*el.*)

ابطأ *abṭaʾ²* slower | ابطأ من غراب نوح (*ġurābi nūḥ*) tardier than Noah's raven, i.e., slower than a ten years' itch (proverbially of s.o. who is very tardy)

ابطاء *ibṭāʾ* slowing down, retardation, deceleration, reduction of speed; tarrying, delay; slowness | دون ابطاء without delay

تباطؤ *tabāṭuʾ* slowness; slowing down, retardation

بطارية **baṭṭārīya** pl. *-āt* battery (*el.* and *mil.*)

بطاطا **baṭāṭā**, بطاطة *baṭāṭa* sweet potato, yam

بطاطس **baṭāṭis** potatoes

بطاقة see بطق

بطبط **baṭbaṭa** (بطبطة *baṭbaṭa*) to quack (duck)

بطح **baṭaḥa** *a* (*baṭḥ*) to prostrate, lay low, fell, throw to the ground, throw down (ه, ه s.o., s.th.) **V** and **VII** to be prostrated, be laid low; to lie prostrate, sprawl, stretch out; to extend, stretch; to lie

ابطح *abṭaḥ²* flat, level; (pl. اباطح *abāṭiḥ²*) basin-shaped valley, wide bed of a wadi

بطحاء *baṭḥāʾ²* pl. بطاح *biṭāḥ*, بطحاوات *baṭḥāwāt* basin-shaped valley; plain, level land, flatland, open country; (*tun.*) public square

بطيحة *baṭīḥa* pl. بطائح *baṭāʾiḥ²* wide bed of a stream or wadi; a stagnant, shallow and broad body of water

منبطح *munbaṭiḥ* prostrate; flat, level; level land, plain

بطيخ *biṭṭīḵ, baṭṭīḵ* (n. un. ة) melon, watermelon; *baṭṭīḵ* hub (of a wheel; *syr.*)

مبطخة *mabṭaḵa* melon patch

[1]بطر *baṭira a* (*baṭar*) to be wild, wanton, reckless; to be proud, vain; to be discontented (ه with s.th.); to disregard (ه s.th.) IV to make reckless

بطر *baṭar* wantonness, cockiness, arrogance, hubris, pride, vanity

اباطرة *abāṭira* (pl.) bons vivants, playboys, epicures

[2]البطراء *al-baṭrā'* Petra (ancient city of Edomites and Nabataeans; ruins now in SW Jordan)

بطرخ *baṭraḵ* pl. بطارخ *baṭāriḵ*[2] roe (of fish)

بطرس *buṭrus* Peter

بطرشيل *baṭrašīl* and بطرشين *baṭrašīn* stole (*Chr.*)

بطريق *biṭrīq* pl. بطارقة *baṭāriqa*, بطاريق *baṭārīq*[2] patrician; Romaean general; penguin (*zool.*)

بطرك *baṭrak*, بطريك *baṭrīk*, بطريرك *baṭriyark* pl. بطاركة *baṭārika* Patriarch (as an ecclesiastic title, *Chr.*)

بطركية *baṭrakīya*, بطريركية *baṭriyarkīya* patriarchate (*Chr.*)

بطش *baṭaša i u* (*baṭš*) to attack with violence; to bear down on, fall upon s.o. (ب or فى); to knock out (ه s.o.); to hit, strike (ب s.th.), land with a thud (ب on)

بطش *baṭš* strength, power, force, violence; courage, valor, bravery; oppression, tyranny

بطشة *baṭša* impact

بطاقة *biṭāqa* pl. *-āt*, بطائق *baṭā'iq*[2] slip (of paper), tag; card, calling card; ticket; label | بطاقة الزيارة calling card; بطاقة شخصية (*šaḵṣīya*) and بطاقة التعريف identity card; بطاقة المواد الغذائية *b. al-mawādd al-ġiḏā'īya*, بطاقة التموين food ration card; بطاقة المايدة *b. al-mu'āyada* greeting card

[1]بطل *baṭala u* (*buṭl*, بطلان *buṭlān*) to be or become null, void, invalid, false, untenable, vain, futile, worthless; to be abolished, fall into disuse, become obsolete; to cease, stop, be discontinued; to be inactive, be out of work II to thwart, foil, frustrate, make ineffective, counteract, neutralize, nullify, invalidate (ه s.th.); to abolish, cancel, annul, suppress (ه s.th.) IV = II; to talk idly, prattle; to paralyze, immobilize, hold down, pin down (ه the opponent)

بطل *buṭl* nullity; uselessness, futility, vanity; falsity, falseness, untruth

بطالة *biṭāla* and *baṭāla* idleness, inactivity; free time, time off, holidays, vacations; unemployment

بطال *baṭṭāl* pl. *ūn* idle, inactive, unemployed, out of work

بطلان *buṭlān* nullity; uselessness, futility, vanity; falsity, untruth; invalidity

ابطال *ibṭāl* thwarting, frustration, invalidation; ruin, destruction; abolition, cancellation

باطل *bāṭil* nugatory, vain, futile; false, untrue; absurd, groundless, baseless; worthless; invalid, null, void; deception, lie, falsehood; بالباطل and باطلا *bāṭilan* falsely; futilely, in vain; pl. اباطيل *abāṭīl*[2] vanities, trivialities, trifles, flimflam, idle talk, prattle

مبطل *mubṭil* prattler, windbag; liar

مبطل *mubṭal* nugatory, futile, vain

متبطل *mutabaṭṭil* unemployed

[2]بطل *baṭula u* (بطالة *baṭāla*, بطولة *buṭūla*) to be brave, be heroic, be a hero

بطل *baṭal* pl. ابطال *abṭāl* brave, heroic; hero; champion, pioneer; hero, protagonist (of a narrative, etc.), lead, star (of a play); champion (*athlet.*) | بطل العالم *b. al-ʿālam* world champion

بطلة *baṭala* heroine (of a narrative), female lead, star (of a play); woman champion (*athlet.*)

بطالة *baṭāla* bravery, valor, heroism

بطولة *buṭūla* bravery, valor, heroism; leading role, starring role (theater, film); championship (*athlet.*) | البطولة العالمية (*ʿālamīya*) and بطولة العالم *b. al-ʿālam* world championship (*athlet.*); دور البطولة the part or role of the hero, leading role

بطالسة *baṭālisa* Ptolemies

بطم *buṭm, buṭum* terebinth (*bot.*)

[1]بطن *baṭana u* (*baṭn,* بطون *buṭūn*) to be hidden, concealed, to hide; — *baṭuna u* (بطانة *baṭāna*) to be paunchy **II** to line (ه a garment, ب ه s.th. with); to cover the inside (ب ه of s.th. with), hang, face, fill (ب ه s.th. with) **IV** to hide, conceal, harbor (ه s.th.) **V** to be lined, have a lining (garment); to penetrate, delve (ه into), become absorbed, engrossed (ه in) **X** to penetrate, delve (ه into), become absorbed, engrossed (ه in); to try to fathom (ه s.th.); to fathom (ه s.th.), get to the bottom of (ه); to have profound knowledge (ه of s.th.), know thoroughly, know inside out (ه s.th.)

بطن *baṭn* pl. بطون *buṭūn,* ابطن *abṭun* belly, stomach, abdomen; womb; interior, inside, inner portion; depth | بطن القدم *b. al-qadam* sole of the foot; بطن الكف *b. al-kaff* palm of the hand; رقص البطن and رقص البطون *raqṣ al-b.* belly dance; فى بطن (*baṭni*) in, within, in the midst of; فى بطون inside, within, in; ولدت بطنا واحدا (*waladat* she gave birth only once; بطنا لظهر (*li-ẓahrin*) upside down

بطنى *baṭnī* ventral, abdominal

بطن *baṭin* paunchy

بطنة *biṭna* gluttony; overeating, indigestion

بطان *biṭān* pl. ابطنة *abṭina* girth (of a camel)

بطانة *biṭāna* pl. بطائن *baṭāʾin*[2] inside, inner side; lining (of a garment); retinue, suite, entourage | فى بطانة among, amidst; within

بطين *baṭīn* pl. بطان *biṭān* and مبطان *mibṭān* paunchy, fat, corpulent, stout; gluttonous

بطين *buṭain* ventricle (of the heart; *anat.*)

بطانية *baṭṭānīya* pl. *-āt,* بطاطين *baṭāṭīn*[2] cover; blanket; quilt

باطن *bāṭin* pl. بواطن *bawāṭin*[2] inner, interior, inward, inmost, intrinsic; hidden, secret; الباطنة coastal plain of E Oman; باطنا *bāṭinan* inwardly, secretly | باطن الكف *b. al-kaff* palm of the hand; باطن القدم *b. al-qadam* sole of the foot; فى باطن الامر at bottom, after all, really; بواطن الامر the factors, circumstances or reasons at the bottom of s.th.; بواطن الارض *b. al-arḍ* the secret depths of the earth

باطنى *bāṭinī* internal | مرض باطنى (*maraḍ*) internal disease; الطب الباطنى (*ṭibb*) internal medicine

الباطنية *al-bāṭinīya* name of a school of thought in Islam, characterized by divining a hidden, secret meaning in the revealed texts

مبطون *mabṭūn* affected with a gastric or intestinal ailment

مبطن *mubaṭṭan* lined; filled (ب with)

[2]بطن **II** (*tun.*) to full (ه s.th.)

باطان (Span. *batán*) *bāṭān* fulling mill

باطية *bāṭiya* pl. بواط *bawāṭin* pitcher, jug

بظ *baẓẓa u* to spout, gush out, well out

بظر *baẓr* pl. بظور *buẓūr* clitoris (*anat.*)

بعبع *buʿbuʿ* pl. بعابع *baʿābiʿ*[2] bugaboo, bogey

بعث *baʿaṯa a* (*baʿṯ*) to send, send out, dispatch (ه ,ه s.o. or s.th. to); to forward (ب or ه s.th. to); to delegate (ه or ب الى s.o. to); to emit (ب or ه s.th.); to evoke, arouse, call forth, awaken (ه s.th.); to stir up, provoke, bring on (ه s.th.); to revive, resuscitate (ه s.th.); to resurrect (ه s.o., من الموت from death); to incite, induce (على to s.th.), instigate (على s.th.); to cause (على s.th.; e.g., astonishment) | بعث اليه هزة الخوف (*hazzat al-ḵauf*) to scare the wits out of s.o.; بعث روح الحياة فى (*rūḥa l-ḥayāh*) to breathe life into s.th. or s.o., revive s.th. **VII** to be sent out, be emitted, be dispatched, be delegated; to be triggered, be caused, be provoked; to be resurrected (من الموت from death); to originate (من in), come (من from), be caused (من by); to emanate (fragrance); to arise, spring, proceed, develop (من from), grow out of (من); to set out to do s.th. (with foll. imperf.) **VIII** to send, dispatch (ه s.o.)

بعث *baʿṯ* sending out, emission, dispatching, delegation, etc.; resurrection; pl. بعوث *buʿūṯ* delegations, deputations | حزب البعث *ḥizb al-b.* approx.: Renaissance Party, a political party with strong socialist tendencies; يوم البعث Day of Resurrection (from the dead)

بعثة *baʿṯa* pl. *baʿaṯāt* delegation, deputation, mission; expedition; student exchange; group of exchange students; revival, rebirth, renaissance, rise | بعثة عسكرية (*ʿaskarīya*) military mission; بعثة دبلوماسية diplomatic mission; بعثة اثرية (*aṯarīya*) archaeological expedition; رئيس البعثة *raʾīs al-b.* chief of mission (*dipl.*)

باعوث *bāʿūṯ* Easter (*Chr.*)

مبعث *mabʿaṯ* sending, forwarding, dispatch; emission; awakening, arousal; — (pl. مباعث *mabāʿiṯ*[2]) cause; factor

باعث *bāʿiṯ* pl. بواعث *bawāʿiṯ*[2] incentive, inducement, motive, spur, reason, cause, occasion

مبعوث *mabʿūṯ* dispatched, delegated; envoy, delegate; representative, deputy (in the Ottoman Empire)

منبعث *munbaʿaṯ* source, point of origin

بعثر *baʿṯara* (بعثرة *baʿṯara*) to scatter, strew around, fling about (ه s.th.); to disarrange, throw into disorder (ه s.th.); to squander, waste, dissipate (ه s.th.) **II** *tabaʿṯara* pass.

مبعثر *mubaʿṯar* scattered, widespread

بعج *baʿaja a* (*baʿj*) to slit open (ه the belly); to groove, dent, notch (ه s.th.) **VII** to have indentations or notches; to be bruised, dented, bumpy; to get battered

منبعج *munbaʿij* notched, indented

بعد *baʿuda u* (*buʿd*) to be distant, far away, far off; to keep away, keep one's distance (عن from); to go far beyond (عن), exceed by far (عن s.th.); to be remote, improbable, unlikely | بعد به عن he kept him away from; لا يبعد ان it is not unlikely that ... **II** to remove (ه s.o.); to banish, exile, expatriate (ه s.o.) **III** to cause a separation (بين between) | باعد بين فلان وبين الشيء to prevent s.o. from attaining s.th.; باعد بين اجفانه (*ajfānihī*) to stare wide-eyed **IV** to remove (ه s.th.); to take away (ه s.th.); to eliminate (ه s.th.), do away with (ه); to send away, dismiss (ه s.o.); to expatriate, banish, exile (ه s.o.); to exclude, make unlikely, improbable, impossible (ه s.th.); to go or move far away; to go very far (فى in or with s.th.) **VI** to be separated, lie apart, lie at some distance from one another; to separate, part company, become estranged; to move away, go away, withdraw, depart (عن from); to keep away, keep one's distance (عن from); to quit, leave, avoid (عن s.th.); to follow in regular intervals VIII to move or go away; to keep away, withdraw (عن from); to quit, leave, avoid (عن s.th.); to leave out of consideration, disregard (عن s.th.) X to single out, set aside (ه s.th.); to think remote, farfetched (ه s.th.); to regard as unlikely (ه s.th.); to disqualify (ه s.o.)

بعد *bu'd* remoteness, farness; (pl. ابعاد *ab'ād*) distance; dimension; interval (*mus.*) | على بعد and على البعد in the distance, far off; على بعد مئة متر at a distance of 100 meters; عن بعد and من بعد from a distance, from afar; ذو ثلاثة ابعاد three-dimensional; قياس الابعاد *qiyās al-a.* linear measure; بعد الهمة *b. al-himma* high aspirations, loftiness of purpose; بعد الشقة *b. aš-šiqqa* wide interval, wide gap; بعد الصيت *b. aṣ-ṣīt* renown, fame, celebrity; بعد الصوت *b. aṣ-ṣaut* do.; بعد النظر *b. an-naẓar* far-sightedness, foresight; بعدا ل *bu'dan li* away with ...!

بعد *ba'du* then, thereupon; afterwards, later, after that, in the following; still, yet | فيما بعد afterwards, later; اما بعد see اما[1]; هو بعد صغير he is only a small boy, he is still young; لم يأت بعد (*ya'ti*) he hasn't come yet

بعد *ba'da* (prep.) after; in addition to, beside; aside from | بعد كونه ... (*kaunihī*) aside from the fact that he is ...; بعد ذلك afterwards, after that, later (on); besides, moreover; بعد ذاك besides, moreover; بعد ان *ba'da an* (conj.) after; بعد اذ (*iḏ*), بعد ما and من بعد ما (*ba'di*) do.; سفه ما بعده سفه (*safahun*) the height of stupidity

بعدئذ *ba'da'iḏin* then, thereafter, thereupon, after that, afterwards

بعيد *ba'īd* pl. بعداء *bu'adā'*[2], بعد *bu'ud*, بعدان *bu'dān*, بعاد *bi'ād* distant, far away, far (عن from); remote, outlying, out-of-the-way; far-reaching, extensive; far-fetched, improbable, unlikely; unusual, strange, odd, queer; incompatible, inconsistent (عن with) | من بعيد from afar, from a distance; منذ عهد بعيد (*'ahd*) a long time ago; بعيد الاثر *b. al-aṯar* of far-reaching consequence; بعيد التاريخ remote in time, going way back in history, ancient; بعيد الشأو *b. aš-ša'w* high-minded, bold; بعيد الشقة *b. aš-šiqqa* far apart; بعيد الغور *b. al-ġaur* deep; unfathomable; بعيد المدى *b. al-madā* long-distance, long-range; extensive, far-reaching; بعيد النظر *b. an-naẓar* farsighted; farseeing; بعيد المنال *b. al-manāl* hardly attainable, hard to get at; ذهب بعيدا to go far away, go to distant lands; تطلع الى بعيد to look off into the distance

بعيد *bu'aida* (prep.) shortly after, soon after

ابعد *ab'ad*[2] pl. اباعد *abā'id*[2] farther, remoter, more distant; more extensive; less likely, more improbable; pl. اباعد *abā'id*[2] very distant relatives | الشرق الابعد (*šarq*) the Far East; الابعد the absent one (used as a polite periphrasis for s.o. who is being criticized or blamed for s.th.; also when referring to the 1st and 2nd persons)

ابعادية *ab'ādīya* pl. *-āt* country estate

تبعيد *tab'īd* banishment

بعاد *bi'ād* distance

مباعدة *mubā'ada* sowing of dissension, estrangement, alienation

ابعاد *ib'ād* removal, separation, isolation; elimination; expatriation, banishment, deportation

تباعد *tabā'ud* interdistance; mutual estrangement

مبعد *mub'ad* deported; deportee

متباعد *mutabā'id* separate | فى فترات متباعدة (*fatarāt*) in wide intervals; فى فترات متباعدة من الزمن (*zaman*) at infrequent intervals, from time to time

مستبعد *mustab'ad* improbable, unlikely

بعر[1] *ba'r, ba'ar* droppings, dung (of animals)

بعير[2] *ba'īr* pl. ابعرة *ab'ira,* بعران *bu'rān,* اباعر *abā'ir*[2], بعارين *ba'ārīn*[2] camel

بعزق *ba'zaqa* (بعزقة *ba'zaqa*) to scatter, dissipate, squander, waste (ه s.th.)

مبعزق *muba'ziq* squanderer, spendthrift, wastrel

بعض II to divide into parts or portions (ه s.th.) V to be divided, be divisible

بعض *ba'ḍ* part, portion; one; some, a few; a little of, some of | بعض العلماء *b. al-'ulamā'* one (or some) of the scholars; رفعنا بعضهم فوق بعض (*rafa'nā*) we have exalted some of them above the others; البعض — البعض الآخر some — some, a few — others; بعضهم بعضا one another, each other, mutually, reciprocally; بعضه فى بعض one in the other, within one another; بعض الشىء *ba'ḍa š-šai'* to some extent, somewhat, a little, rather; ماثله بعض المماثلة (*ba'ḍa l-m.*) he resembled him somewhat, to some extent; منذ قرن وبعض قرن (*qarn*) for the last hundred years and more

بعوض *ba'ūḍ* (n. un. ة) gnats, mosquitoes

تبعيض *tab'īḍ* division, partition, portioning

بعكوكة *bu'kūka* club, society

بعل *ba'l* the god Baal; land or plants thriving on natural water supply; — (pl. بعول *bu'ūl,* بعولة *bu'ūla*) lord; husband

بعلة *ba'la* wife

بعلى *ba'lī* unirrigated (land, plants)

بعلبك *ba'labakk*[2] Baalbek (ancient Heliopolis, village in E Lebanon)

بغت *baġata a* (*baġt,* بغتة *baġta*) to come unexpectedly, descend unawares (ه upon s.o.) III do.; to surprise (ه s.o.) VII to be taken by surprise; to be taken aback, be aghast, be nonplused

بغتة *baġta* surprising event, surprise; *baġtatan,* على بغتة *'alā baġtatin* all of a sudden, suddenly, surprisingly

مباغتة *mubāġata* sudden arrival, surprising incident or event, surprise; sudden attack, raid

بغاث *buġāṯ* pl. بغثان *biġṯān* small birds

بغادة see بوغادة

بغدد II *tabaġdada* to swagger, throw one's weight around, be fresh (properly, to behave like one from Baghdad)

بغداد *baġdād*[2] Baghdad

بغدادى *baġdādī* pl. *-ūn,* بغاددة *baġādida* a native of Baghdad

بغش[1] *buġiša u*: بغشت السماء (*samā'u*) there was a light shower

بغشة *baġša* light rain shower

بغشة[2] *buġša* = بقشة

بغاشة[3] (*eg.*) *buġāša* stuffed pastry made of flour, eggs and butter

بغض *baġiḍa a, baġuḍa u* (*buġḍ,* بغاضة *baġāḍa*) to be hated, hateful, odious II to make (ه s.o.) hateful (الى to s.o.) III to loathe, detest, hate (ه s.o.) IV to loathe, detest, hate (ه s.o.) VI to hate each other

بغض *buġḍ,* بغضة *biġḍa* and بغضاء *baġḍā'*[2] hatred, hate

بغيض *baġīḍ* hateful, odious (الى to s.o.), loathsome, abominable

تباغض *tabāġuḍ* mutual hatred

مبغوض *mabġūḍ* detested, hateful, odious

مبغض *mubġiḍ* pl. *-ūn* hater; — *mubġaḍ* detested, hateful, odious

بغل *baġl* pl. بغال *biġāl,* ابغال *abġāl* mule; بغلة *baġla* pl. *baġalāt* female mule | بغال القنطرة *b. al-qanṭara* the piers of the bridge

بغال *baġġāl* pl. *-ūn* mule driver, muleteer

بغى *baġā* i (بغاء *buġā'*) to seek, desire, covet, seek to attain (ه s.th.), wish for s.th. (ه); — (*baġy*) to wrong, treat unjustly (على s.o.); to oppress (على s.o.), commit outrage (على upon); to whore, fornicate **VII** ينبغى it is desirable, necessary; it is proper, appropriate, seemly; it ought to be, should be; with له: it behooves him, with عليه: he must, he should, he ought to **VIII** to seek, desire (ه s.th.), aspire (ه to s.th.), strive (ه for)

بغى *baġy* infringement, outrage, injustice, wrong

بغى *baġīy* pl. بغايا *baġāyā* whore, prostitute

بغية *buġya* object of desire; wish, desire; *buġyata* (prep.) with the aim of, for the purpose of

بغاء *biġā'* prostitution

بغاء *buġā'* wish(ing), desire, endeavor, effort

مبغى *mabġan* pl. مباغ *mabāġin* brothel

مباغ *mabāġin* coveted things, desiderata, wishes, desires

ابتغاء *ibtiġā'* desire, wish; *ibtiġā'a* (prep.) for the purpose of

باغ *bāġin* pl. بغاة *buġāh* desiring, coveting, striving; committing outrages, oppressive, unjust; oppressor, tyrant

مبتغى *mubtaġan* aspired goal; aspiration, desire, endeavor, effort

بفتة *bafta* calico, Indian cotton cloth

بفتيك *biftēk* beefsteak

¹بق *baqq* (n. un. ة) bedbug, chinch | شجرة البق elm (*bot.*)

²بق *baqqa* u (*baqq*) to give off in abundance

بقاق *baqqāq* garrulous, loquacious; chatterbox, prattler

بقبق *baqbaqa* (بقبقة *baqbaqa*) to gurgle, bubble, splutter, purl (water); to chatter, prattle

بقباق *baqbāq* garrulous, loquacious; chatterbox, prattler

بقبوقة *baqbūqa* blister (of the skin)

بقجة *buqja* pl. بقج *buqaj* bundle, pack, package

بقدونس *baqdūnis, baqdūnas* parsley

بقر *baqara* u to split open, rip open, cut open (ه s.th.) **IV** do.

بقر *baqar* (coll.) bovines, cattle; n. un. بقرة *baqara* pl. *-āt* cow

بقرى *baqarī* bovine, cattle-, cow- (in compounds)

بقار *baqqār* pl. ة cowhand, cowboy

بقس *baqs* box, boxwood (*bot.*)

بقسمات *buqsumāt* rusk, zwieback; biscuit

بقشة *buqša* Yemenite copper coin

بقشيش *baqšīš* pl. بقاشيش *baqāšīš*² present of money; tip, gratuity, baksheesh

بقع **II** to spot, stain, smudge (ه s.th.) **V** to become stained, get smudged; to be spotted, stained

بقعة *buqʻa* pl. بقع *buqaʻ*, بقاع *biqāʻ* spot, blot, smudge, stain; place, spot, site; plot, patch, lot

ابقع *abqaʻ*² spotted, speckled

باقعة *bāqiʻa* pl. بواقع *bawāqiʻ*² sly dog, shrewd fellow

بقل *baqala* u (*baql*) to sprout (plant)

بقل *baql* (coll.; n. un. ة) pl. بقول *buqūl*, ابقال *abqāl* herbs, potherbs, greens, herbaceous plants; specif., legumes | الفصيلة البقلية the Leguminosae; البقلة الباردة hyacinth bean (Dolichos lablab L.); البقلة الحمقاء (*ḥamqā'*) purslane (*bot.*); البقلة الذهبية (*ḏahabīya*) garden orach (*bot.*); بقلة الخطاطيف celandine (*bot.*); بقلة الملك *b. al-malik* common fumitory (*bot.*)

بقال *baqqāl* pl. *-ūn*, بقالة *baqqāla* greengrocer; grocer

بقالة *biqāla* the grocery business

بقلاوة *baqlāwa*, بقلاوا a kind of Turkish delight, pastry made of puff paste with honey and almonds or pistachios

بقم *baqqam* brazilwood

بقى *baqiya a* (بقاء *baqā'*) to remain, stay, continue to be (على in a state or condition); to keep up, maintain (على a state or condition); to be left behind, be left over; to last, continue, go on; (with foll. imperf. or part.) to continue to do s.th., keep doing s.th.; to become | لم يبق طفلا (*yabqa ṭiflan*) he is no longer a child **II** to leave, leave over, leave behind (ه s.th.) **IV** to make (ه s.o.) stay; to retain, leave unchanged, leave as it is, preserve, maintain, keep up (ه s.th.); to leave, leave over, leave behind (ه s.th., ه s.o.); to leave untouched, save, spare (على s.o., s.th., e.g., s.o.'s life) **V** to remain, stay, continue to be (على in a state or condition); to be left, be left over **X** to make stay, ask to stay, hold back, detain (ه s.o.); to spare, save, protect (ه s.o., ه s.th.); to preserve (ه s.th.); to retain, keep (ه s.th.); to store, put away (ه s.th.)

بقية *baqīya* pl. بقايا *baqāyā* remainder, rest; remnant, residue | بقية الدول *b. ad-duwal* the remaining countries, the rest of the countries; البقية الباقية (*bāqiya*) the last remnant

بقاء *baqā'* remaining, staying, lingering, abiding; continuation, continuance, duration; survival, continuation of existence after life; immortality, eternal life; existence; permanence | دار البقاء the hereafter

ابقى *abqā* more lasting, more durable, more permanent; better preserving; conducive to longer wear, better protecting

ابقاء *ibqā'* continuation, retention; maintenance, conservation, preservation | ابقاء الحالة على ما كانت عليه maintenance of the status quo

استبقاء *istibqā'* continuation, retention; maintenance, conservation, preservation

باق *bāqin* staying; remaining; left; remainder (*arith.*); lasting, continuing, permanent, unending; surviving; living on; everlasting, eternal (God) | الباقيات الصالحات the good works

متبق *mutabaqqin* residue, remnant, remainder, rest

بك *bē* (Eg. pronunciation) pl. بكوات *bakawāt*, بهوات *bahawāt* bey (title of courtesy; cf. بيك)

بكوية *bekawıya* rank of a bey

بكئ *bakī'* pl. بكاء *bikā'* having or giving little, sparing (e.g., of words)

بكاسين *bikāsīn* bécassine, snipe (*zool.*)

بكالوريا (Fr. *baccalauréat*) *bakālōriyā* baccalaureate, bachelor's degree

بكالوريوس *bakālōriyūs* bachelor (academic degree)

بكباشى (Turk. *binbaşı*) *bimbāšī*, *bikbāšī* major (*mil*; formerly, *Eg.*)

بكت **II** to censure, blame (ه s.o.)

تبكيت *tabkīt* blame, reproach | تبكيت الضمير remorse

بكتيرى *baktērī* bacterial, caused by bacteria

بكتيريا *baktēriyā* bacteria

بكر *bakara u* to set out early in the morning, get up early; to come early (الى to), be early (الى at) **II** do.; بكر فى and بكر ب with foll. verbal noun: to do s.th. early, prematurely, ahead of its time **III** to be ahead of s.o. (ه), anticipate, forestall (ه s.o.) **IV** = **I**; **VIII** to be the first to take (ه s.th.), be the first to embark (ه

on s.th.); to deflower (ها a girl); to invent (▲ s.th.); to create, originate, start (▲ s.th.)

بكر ***bakr*** pl. ابكر ***abkur***, بكران ***bukrān*** young camel

بكر ***bikr*** pl. ابكار ***abkār*** first-born, eldest; firstling; unprecedented, novel, new; virgin; virginal

بكرى ***bikrī*** first-born, first

بكرية ***bikrīya*** primogeniture

بكرة ***bakra*** and ***bakara*** pl. بكر ***bakar***, *-āt* reel; pulley (*mech.*); spool, coil; winch, windlass | خيط بكرة *ḵaiṭ b.* thread

بكرة ***bakra***: على بكرة ابيهم *ʿalā bakrati abīhim*, عن بكرة ابيهم and عن بكرتهم all without exception, all of them, all together; خرجت الجماهير عن بكرتها the crowd went forth as one man

بكرة ***bukra*** pl. بكر ***bukar*** early morning; ***bukratan*** early in the morning; tomorrow; on the following day, next day

بكير ***bakīr*** coming early; early, premature; precocious

بكور ***bakūr*** and باكور ***bākūr*** coming early; early, premature; precocious

بكور ***bukūr*** earliness, prematureness, premature arrival | بكورى فى العود (*ʿaud*) my early return

بكارة ***bakāra*** virginity

بكارة ***bakkāra*** pulley (*mech.*) | بكارة مركبة (*murakkaba*) set of pulleys, block and tackle

بكورة ***bukūra*** and بكورية ***bukūrīya*** primogeniture

باكورة ***bākūra*** pl. بواكير ***bawākīr***[2] firstlings; first results, first fruits; beginning, rise, dawn; (with foll. genit.) initial, early, first; pl. بواكير first signs or indications; initial symptoms; heralds, harbingers (fig.) | باكورة الفواكه early fruit; كان باكورة اعماله the first thing he did was...

ابكر ***abkar***[2] rising earlier

مبكار ***mibkār*** precocious

ابتكار ***ibtikār*** pl. *-āt* novelty, innovation; creation; invention; origination, first production; initiative; creativity, originality; pl. ابتكارات specif., creations of fashion, fashion designs

باكر ***bākir*** early; premature; باكرا ***bākiran*** in the morning; early (adv.) | فى الصباح الباكر (*ṣabāḥ*) early in the morning; الى باكر till tomorrow

باكرة ***bākira*** pl. بواكر ***bawākir***[2] firstlings, first produce, early fruits, early vegetables; pl. first indications or symptoms, heralds, harbingers

مبكر ***mubakkir*** doing early; early; مبكرا ***mubakkiran*** early in the morning, early

مبتكر ***mubtakir*** creator; creative; inventor; — ***mubtakar*** newly created, novel, new, original; (pl. *-āt*) creation, specif., fashion creation, invention | ثوب مبتكر (*ṯaub*) original design, model, dress creation

بكرج ***bakraj*** pl. بكارج ***bakārij***[2] kettle, coffee pot

بقسمات, بكسماط, بكسماد see بقسماط

بكل II to buckle, buckle up, button up (▲ s.th.); to fold, cross (▲ the arms)

بكلة ***bukla*** pl. بكل ***bukal***, *-āt* buckle

بكلاه (It. *baccalà*) ***bakalāh*** codfish

بكلوريوس ***bakalōriyūs*** bachelor (academic degree)

بكم ***bakima*** *a* to be dumb; — ***bakuma*** *u* to be silent, hold one's tongue IV to silence (• s.o.) V to become silent; to become dumb

بكم ***bakam*** dumbness

ابكم ***abkam***[2], f. بكماء ***bakmāʾ***[2], pl. بكم ***bukm*** dumb

بكوات and بكوية see بك

بكى *bakā i* (بكاء *bukā'*, بكى *bukan*) **to cry, weep (على over); to bemoan, lament, bewail (ه s.o.), mourn (ه for) II and IV to make (ه s.o.) cry X to move (ه s.o.) to tears, make (ه s.o.) cry**

بكاء *bakkā'* **given to weeping frequently, tearful, lachrymose**

حائط المبكى *ḥā'iṭ al-mabkā* **the Wailing Wall (in Jerusalem)**

باكية *bākiya* **pl.** بواك *bawākin* **wailing-woman, hired mourner; (*eg.*) arch, arcade**

باك *bākin* **pl.** بكاة *bukāh* **weeping, crying; weeper, wailer, mourner**

مبك *mubkin, mubakkin* **causing tears, tearful; sad, lamentable, deplorable**

بكين *bikīn* **Peking**

[1]بل *bal* **(also with foll.** و *wa-*) **nay, — rather...; (and) even; but, however, yet**

[2]بل *balla u* (*ball*) **to moisten, wet, make wet (ه s.th., ه s.o.); —** *balla i* **to recover (من مرض from an illness) II to moisten, wet, make wet (ه s.th., ه s.o.) IV to recover (من مرض from an illness) V and VIII to be moistened, be wetted; to become wet**

بل *ball* **moistening, wetting; moisture**

بل *bill* **recovery, convalescence, recuperation**

بلة *billa* **moisture, humidity |** ما زاد الطين بلة *mā zāda ṭ-ṭīna billatan* **what made things even worse ...**

بلل *balal* **moisture, humidity; moistness, dampness, wetness**

بليل *balīl* **a moist, cool wind**

بليلة *balīla* (*eg.*) **dish made of stewed maize and sugar**

ابلال *iblāl* **recovery, convalescence, recuperation**

تبلل *taballul* **moistness, dampness, humidity**

مبلول *mablūl*, مبلل *muballal*, مبتل *mubtall* **moist, damp, wet**

[3]بلى *billī* **(from Fr.** *bille*): كرسى بلى (*kursī*) **ball bearing**

بلا see [2]ب

بلاتين, پلاتين *blātīn, plātīn* **platinum**

بلاج **(Fr.** *plage*) *blāž* **beach**

بلاجرا *balagrā* **pellagra**

بلارج *balāraj* **stork**

بلاستيك **(Fr.** *plastique*) *blāstīk* **plastic**

بلاط see بلط

بلاك **(Engl.** *plug*) **spark plug (*ir.*)**

بلان, بلانة see بلن

بلبط *balbaṭa* **to gurgle**

[1]بلبل *balbala* **to disquiet, make uneasy or restive, stir up, rouse, disturb, trouble, confuse (ه s.o., ه s.th.) II** *tabalbala* **to feel uneasy, be anxious; to be or become confused, get all mixed up**

بلبلة *balbala* **pl.** بلابل *balābil*[2] **anxiety, uneasiness, concern; confusion, muddle, jumble, chaos**

بلبال *balbāl* **anxiety, uneasiness, concern**

بلابل *balābil*[2] **anxieties, apprehensions**

تبلبل *tabalbul* **muddle, confusion |** تبلبل الالسنة *t. al-alsina* **confusion of tongues (at the tower of Babel)**

[2]بلبل *bulbul* **pl.** بلابل *balābil*[2] **nightingale**

بلج *balaja u* (بلوج *bulūj*) to shine; to dawn (morning, aurora); — *balija a* (*balaj*) to be happy, be glad (ب about), be delighted (ب at) IV to shine (sun) V and VII = *balaja*

ابلج *ablaj*[2] gay, serene, bright, clear, fair, nice, beautiful

انبلاج الفجر *inbilāj al-fajr* daybreak

بلجيكا *beljīkā* Belgium

بلجيكى *beljīkī* Belgian (adj. and n.)

بلح *balaḥ* (coll.; n. un. ة) dates (*bot.*)

بلد *baluda u* (بلادة *balāda*) to be stupid, idiotic, dull-witted **II** to acclimatize, habituate (ه s.th., to a country or region) **V** pass. of **II**; to become stupid, besotted, lapse into a state of idiocy; to show o.s. from the stupid side **VI** to feign stupidity

بلد *balad* m. and f., pl. بلاد *bilād* country; town, city; place, community, village; بلاد country; بلدان *buldān* countries | بلاد الحبش *b. al-ḥabaš* Ethiopia; بلاد الصين *b. aṣ-ṣīn* China; بلاد الهند *b. al-hind* India

بلدة *balda* town, city; place, community, village; rural community; township

بلدى *baladī* native, indigenous, home (as opposed to foreign, alien); (fellow) citizen, compatriot, countryman; a native; communal, municipal | مجلس بلدى (*majlis*) city council, local council

بلدية *baladīya* pl. *-āt* township, community, rural community; ward, district (of a city); municipality, municipal council, local authority

بليد *balīd* and ابلد *ablad*[2] stupid, doltish, dull-witted, idiotic

بلادة *balāda* stupidity, silliness

تبلد *taballud* idiocy, dullness, obtuseness, apathy

متبلد *mutaballid* besotted, dull, stupid

ابليز look up alphabetically

ابليس pl. ابالسة look up alphabetically

بلسان *balasān* balsam, balm; balsam tree; black elder (*bot.*)

بلسم *balsam* pl. بلاسم *balāsim*[2] balsam, balm

بلسمى *balsamī* balsamic, balmy

بلشف *balšafa* to Bolshevize **II** *tabalšafa* to be Bolshevized

بلشفة *balšafa* Bolshevization

بلشفى *bulšifī* pl. بلاشفة *balāšifa* Bolshevist(ic); Bolshevik, Bolshevist

بلشفية *bulšifīya* Bolshevism

بلشون *balašūn* heron (*zool.*)

[1]بلص *balaṣa u* (*balṣ*) and **II** to extort, wring forcibly (ه من from s.o. s.th.); to blackmail (ه s.o.)

بلص *balṣ* extortion, blackmail; forcible imposition of taxes

[2]بلاص *ballāṣ* pl. بلاليص *balālīṣ*[2] (*eg.*) earthenware jar

[1]بلط **II** to pave (ه s.th., with flagstones or tiles)

بلاط *balāṭ* pavement, tiled floor; floor tiles; palace; pl. ابلطة *abliṭa* floor tiles | البلاط الملكى (*malakī*) the royal court; حداد البلاط *ḥidād al-b.* court mourning

بلاطة *balāṭa* floor tile; flagstone, slabstone; paving stone

تبليط *tablīṭ* paving, tile-laying

مبلط *muballaṭ* paved, tiled

[2]بلوط *ballūṭ* oak; acorn

[3]بلطة *balṭa* pl. *-āt*, بلط *bulaṭ* ax

بلطجى *balṭajī* pl. *-īya* engineer, sapper, pioneer (*mil.*); gangster; procurer, panderer, pimp; sponger, hanger-on, parasite

[4]بلطة *balaṭa* balata gum

[5]بلطو (Fr. *paletot*) *balṭō* pl. *-āt*, بلاطى *balāṭī* paletot, overcoat

[6]بلطى *bulṭī* bolti (Tilapia nilotica), a food fish of the Nile

البلطيق *al-baltīq* the Baltic countries | بحر البلطيق *baḥr al-b.* the Baltic Sea

بالوظة *bālūẓa* hand press; (*eg.*) a kind of cream made of cornstarch, lemon juice and honey, or the like

بلع *bala'a* and *bali'a a* (*bal'*) to swallow, swallow up (ه s.th.); to gulp down (ه s.th.); to put up (ه with s.th.), swallow, stomach, brook (ه s.th.) | بلع ريقه (*rīqahū*) lit.: to swallow one's saliva, i.e., to catch one's breath, take a little rest, have a break; to restrain o.s., hold back (said of one in a rage) **II** and **IV** to make (ه s.o.) swallow (ه s.th.) | بلعه ريقه (*rīqahā*) to grant s.o. a short rest **VIII** = **I**

بلعة *bal'a* large bite, big gulp

بلاعة *ballā'a*, بلوعة *ballū'a* pl. *-āt*, بلاليع *balālī'*[2] sink, drain

بالوعة *bālū'a* pl. *-āt*, بواليع *bawālī'*[2] sewer, sink, drain

بلعم *bul'um* pl. بلاعم *balā'im*[2] and بلعوم *bul'ūm* pl. بلاعيم *balā'īm*[2] pharynx (*anat.*); بلعوم gullet, esophagus (*anat.*)

[1]بلغ *balaḡa u* (بلوغ *bulūḡ*) to reach (ه s.o., ه s.th.), get (ه, ه to), arrive (ه at); to come, amount (ه to), be worth (ه so and so much); to come to s.o.'s (ه) ears; to attain puberty (boy); to ripen, mature (fruit, or the like); to come of age; to exhaust, wear out (من s.o.); to act (من upon s.o.), have its effect (من on), affect (من s.o.); to go far (فى, من in s.th.), attain a high degree (فى, من of s.th.) | بلغ به الى to make s.o. or s.th. get to or arrive at, lead or take s.o. or s.th. to, get s.o. or s.th. to the point where, بلغ به الترنح ان (*tarannuḥ*) he began to reel so violently that...; بلغ الامر مبلغ الجد (*mablaḡa l-jidd*) the matter became serious; بلغ السيل الزبى *b. s-sailu z-zubā* the matter reached a climax, things came to a head; بلغ مبلغ الرجال (*mablaḡa r-rijāl*) to be sexually mature, attain manhood, come of age; بلغ اشده (*ašuddahū*) to attain full maturity, come of age; to reach its climax; بلغ فى الشيء مبلغا (من الشيء or) (*mablaḡan*) to attain a high degree of s.th.; حين بلغت بذكرياتى هذا المبلغ (*ḥīna, ḏikrayātī, mablaḡa*) when I had come to this point in my reminiscences; بلغ منه كل مبلغ (*kulla mablaḡin*) to work havoc on s.o.; بلغ منتهاه (*muntahāhu*) to reach its climax, come to a head **II** to make (ه s.o.) reach or attain (ه s.th.); to take, bring (ه الى s.th. to s.o.), see that s.th. (ه) gets (الى to); to convey, transmit, impart, communicate, report (ه ه to s.o. s.th.); to inform, notify (ه ه s.o. of s.th.), tell, let know (ه ه s.o. about); to report (عن about), give an account of (عن); to inform (عن against s.o.), report, denounce (عن s.o.) | بلغ رسالة to fulfill a mission; بلغه سلامى *balliḡhu salāmī* give him my best regards! **III** to exaggerate (فى in s.th.); to overdo, do too long (فى s.th.); to go to greatest lengths, do one's utmost (فى in) **IV** to make (ه, ه s.o., s.th.) reach or attain (الى s.th.); to make (ه s.th.) amount (الى to), raise (ه an amount, a salary, الى to); to inform, notify (ب or عن ه s.o. of s.th.), tell, let know (ب or عن ه s.o. about); to announce, state, disclose (ه s.th.); to inform (عن against s.o.), report, denounce (عن s.o.) | ابلغ البوليس ب to report s.th. to the police **V** to content o.s., be content (ب with); to eke out an existence; to still one's hunger (ب with), eat (ب s.th.); to be delivered, be transmitted

سمعا لا بلغا *sam'an lā balḡan!* may it be heard but not fulfilled, i.e., God forbid! (used at the mention of s.th. unpleasant)

بلغة *bulḡa* and بلاغ *balāḡ* sufficiency, competency, adequacy (see also [2]بلغة below)

بلاغ *balāḡ* pl. *-āt* communication, information, message, report; announcement, proclamation; communiqué; statement; notification (of the police) | بلاغ اخير ultimatum

بليغ **balīğ** pl. بلغاء **bulağā'**[2] eloquent; intense, lasting, deep, profound (e.g., an impression); serious, grave (e.g., an injury)

بلوغ **bulūğ** reaching, attainment, arrival (at); maturity, legal majority

بلاغة **balāğa** eloquence; art of good style, art of composition; literature | علم البلاغة *'ilm al-b.* rhetoric

ابلغ **ablağ**[2] intenser, deeper, more lasting; more serious, graver

مبلغ **mablağ** pl. مبالغ *mabāliğ*[2] amount, sum of money; extent, scope, range; (see also examples under بلغ I) | مبلغ اسمى (*ismī*) nominal par; المبالغ المودعة (*mūda'a*) the deposits (at a bank); ليتبين مبلغ قولى من الجد (*li-yatabayyana, qaulī, jidd*) in order to find, out to what extent my words were meant seriously

تبليغ **tablīğ** pl. *-āt* conveyance, transmission, delivery (الى to s.o.); information (عن about); report, notification (عن of); communication, announcement, notice | كتاب التبليغ credentials

مبالغة **mubālağa** pl. *-āt* exaggeration

ابلاغ **iblāğ** conveyance, transmission

بالغ **bāliğ** extensive, far-reaching; considerable; serious (wound), deep, profound, violent, vehement (feelings), strong, intense; mature; of age, legally major

مبلغ **muballiğ** bearer (of news), messenger; informer, denouncer; detective

[2]بلغة **bulğa, balğa** pl. *-āt*, *bulağ* slipper of yellow leather

بلغاريا **bulğāriyā** Bulgaria

بلغارى **bulğārī** Bulgarian (adj. and n.)

بلغم **balğam** phlegm; (pl. بلاغم *balāğim*[2]) expectoration, sputum

بلغمى **balğamī** phlegmatic; phlegmy, mucous

بلف **balafa** *i* (*balf*) to bluff **II** do.

بلف **balf**, بلفة **balfa** bluff

ابلق **ablaq**[2] piebald

بلقيس **bilqīs**[2] Muslim name of the Queen of Sheba

البلقان **al-balqān** the Balkans

بلقانى **balqānī** Balkan

بلقع **balqa'** and بلقعة **balqa'a** pl. بلاقع **balāqi'**[2] wasteland

بلك see بلوك

بلكون **balkōn** balcony

[1]بلم **balam** anchovy

[2]بلم **balam** pl. ابلام **ablām** sailing barge (*ir.*)

[3]بلم **IV** to be silent, hold one's tongue

بلان **ballān** bathhouse attendant; name of a plant growing near stagnant waters

بلانة **ballāna** female bathhouse attendant; lady's maid

بلنسية **balansiya**[2] Valencia (region and city in E Spain)

بلين pl. بلالين look up alphabetically

بله **baliha** *a* to be stupid, simple-minded **VI** to feign foolishness, pretend to be stupid **X** to deem (ه s.o.) stupid or simple-minded

بله **balah** and بلاهة **balāha** stupidity, foolishness, simple-mindedness; idiocy, imbecility | بلاهة مبكرة (*mubakkira*) dementia praecox

بله **balha** let alone, not to speak of, not to mention

ابله **ablah**[2] stupid, doltish, dull-witted; idiotic

بلهارسيا *bilharsiyā* bilharziasis, schistosomiasis (*med.*)

بلهنية *bulahniya* abundance, wealth, variety (of earthly possessions)

بلهوان[1] see بهلوان.

□ بلهون[2] *bulhōn* pl. بلاهين *balāhīn*[2] (= ابو الهول; *eg.*) sphinx

بلو (and بلى) بلا *balā u* (*balw*, بلاء *balā'*) to test, try, put to the test (ه s.o., ه s.th.); to know from long experience (ه s.th.); to afflict (ه s.o.); — بلى *baliya a* (بلى *bilan*, بلاء *balā'*) to be or become old, worn, shabby (clothes); to dwindle away, vanish; to deteriorate, decline, become decrepit; to disintegrate (a corpse), decay, rot, spoil **III** to care, be concerned (ب or ه, ه about), be mindful (ب or ه, ه of s.o., of s.th.); to pay attention (ب or ه to), mind, heed, take into consideration, take into account (ب or ه s.th.); to take notice (ب of) | ما ابالى *mā ubālī*, لا ابالى I don't care! I don't mind! it's all right with me! لا يبالى (as a relat. clause) unconcerned, heedless, careless, reckless **IV** to try, test, put to the test (ه s.o.); to make experienced, harden, inure (ه s.o.; said of trials, experiences); to work havoc (ه on s.th.); to wear out (ه s.th.) | ابلى بلاء حسنا (*balā'an ḥasanan*) to stand the test; to prove o.s. brave (in war) **VIII** to try, tempt, put to the test (ه s.o.); to afflict (ب ه s.o. with), visit (ب ه on s.o. s.th.); pass. *ubtuliya* to become or be afflicted (ب with, by), suffer (ب from)

بلى *bilan* decline, deterioration; decay, putrefaction, decomposition; worn condition; wear; shabbiness

بلى *balīy* worn, old, shabby, threadbare; decrepit, dilapidated, decaying, decomposed, rotten

بلية *balīya* pl. بلايا *balāyā* trial, tribulation, visitation, affliction, distress, misfortune, calamity

بلاء *balā'* trial, tribulation, visitation, affliction, distress, misfortune; scourge, plague; creditable performance, bravery, gallantry, heroic action | بلاء حسن (*ḥasan*) favor, blessing, grace (of God); good performance

بلوى *balwā* trial; tribulation, visitation, affliction, distress, misfortune, calamity; necessity, need | عمت البلوى به (*'ammat*) it has become a general necessity

مبالاة *mubālāh* consideration, regard, heed, attention | لامبالاة *lā-mubālāh* indifference, unconcern, carelessness

ابتلاء *ibtilā'* trial, tribulation, affliction, visitation

بال *bālin* old, worn, worn out; shabby, threadbare, ragged, tattered; decrepit, dilapidated; decayed, rotten; obsolete, antiquated

مبال *mubālin* observant, heedful, mindful (ب of) | غير مبال ب heedless of

مبتلى *mubtalan* (less correctly مبتل *mubtalin*) afflicted (ب with, by), suffering (ب from)

بلور **II** *tabalwara* to crystalize; to be crystalized; to be covered with crystals

بلور *ballūr*, *billaur* pl. *-āt* crystal; crystal glass, flint glass, glass | ○ بلور صخرى (*ṣakrī*) rock crystal, transparent quartz

بلورة *billaura* (n. un.) pl. *-āt* crystal; crystal glass, flint glass, glass; tube (*radio*); crystal, quartz plate (of a detector; *radio*); (*syr.*, pronounced *ballōra*) negative (*phot.*)

بلورى *ballūrī*, *billaurī* crystalline; crystal (adj.)

بلورية *ballūrīya*, *billaurīya* pl. *-āt* lense (*opt.*)

مبلور *mubalwar*: فواكه مبلورة candied fruits

بلوز, بلوزة (Fr. *blouse*) *bəlūz, bəlūza* pl. *-āt* blouse

بلوك (Turk. *bölük*) *bulūk* pl. *-āt* company (*mil.; Eg.*) | بلوك امين *b. amīn* (*mil.*) approx.: quartermaster sergeant (formerly, *Eg.*)

بلون *ballūn* balloon

[1]بلى *balā* yes, yes indeed, certainly, surely

[2]بلى *baliya* etc., see بلو

بلياتشو (It. *pagliaccio*) *palyatšō* clown, buffoon

بلياردو (It. *bigliardo*) *bilyardō* billiards

بليسيه *bilīsēh* plissé, pleating

[1]بلين *ballīn* pl. بلالين *balālīn*[2] pallium, liturgical vestment of a bishop worn over the chasuble (*Chr.*); monk's robe (*Copt.-Chr.*)

[2]بليون *balyūn* pl. بلايين *balāyīn*[2] (U.S.) billion, (G.B.) milliard; (U.S.) trillion, (G.B.) billion

بم *bamm* lowest string of a musical instrument

بمباغ *bumbāğ*, بمباغة *bumbāğa* bow tie

بمباى *bombāy* Bombay

بامية look up alphabetically

[1]بن V تبنى *tabannā* to adopt as son (ه s.o.); to adopt, embrace (ه s.th.)

ابن *ibn* pl. ابناء *abnā'*, بنون *banūn* son; descendant, scion; offspring, son (of a nation or people) | ابن آدم pl. بنو آدم (son of Adam) man, human being; ابن آوى *ibn āwā* jackal; ابن البلد *ibn al-balad* local inhabitant, native; ابناء البلاد natives, native population; ابن الحرب *ibn al-ḥarb* warrior, soldier; warlike, bellicose; ابن السبيل wayfarer, wanderer; ابن خمسين سنة 50 years old; ابن ساعته *ibn sā'atihī* temporal, transient, passing; ابن صلبه *ibn ṣulbihī* his own son; ابن عرس *ibn 'irs* weasel; بنو ماء السماء *banū mā' as-samā'* the Arabs; بنى سويف Beni Suef (city in Egypt, S of Cairo)

ابنة *ibna* and بنت *bint* pl. بنات *banāt* daughter; بنت girl | ابنة العم *i. al-'amm* (female) cousin; periphrastically for wife: ابنة عمك your wife; بنت الفكر *b. al-fikr* pl. بنات الافكار thought, idea; بنات الارض *b. al-arḍ* insects and worms; بنات بئس *b. bi's* calamities, afflictions; بنات الدهر *b. ad-dahr* do.; بنت الشفة *b. aš-šafa* word; بنات الصدر *b. aṣ-ṣadr* worries, fears, anxieties; بنات وردان *b. wardāna* earthworms, rainworms

بنى *bunaiya* my little son

بنوة *bunūwa* sonship, filiation

بنوى *banawī* filial

تبن *tabannin* adoption (also fig., e.g.. of ideas, principles, etc.)

[2]بن *bunn* coffee beans, coffee

بنى *bunnī* coffee-colored, brown

[3]بنان *banān* finger tips | يشار عليه ببنان (*yušāru*) lit.: he is pointed at with fingers, i.e., he is a famous man; انا طوع بنانك *anā ṭau'a banānika* I am at your disposal, I am at your service

بنادورة *banādōra* (*syr.;* from It. *pomodoro*) tomato(es)

بنارس *banāris*[2] Banaras or Benares (the Holy City of the Hindus, in N India)

بنباشى see بكباشى

بنت see [1]بن

بنتو *bintū* napoleon, louis d'or (gold coin of 20 francs)

بنج II to dope, narcoticize (with *banj*; ه s.o.); to anesthetize (ه s.o.)

بنج *banj* henbane (Hyoscyamus niger; *bot.*); an anesthetic, a narcotic

البنجاب *al-banjāb* the Punjab (region, NW Indian subcontinent)

بنجر *banjar* red beet (*eg.*)

بند *band* pl. بنود *bunūd* article, clause, paragraph (of a law, contract, etc.); banner; large body of troops

[1]بندر *bandar* pl. بنادر *banādir*[2] seaport; commercial center; district capital (*Eg.*); بنادر see also under بندرة below | بندر عباس *b. 'abbās* Bandar Abbas (seaport in S Iran)

[2]بندورة look up alphabetically

بندق *bunduq* (coll.; n. un. ة) pl. بنادق *banādiq*[2] hazelnut(s), filberts; hazel, hazel tree; بندقة hazelnut, filbert; bullet

بندقى *bunduqī* Venetian sequin

بندقية *bunduqīya* pl. بنادق *banādiq*[2] rifle, gun | بندقية رش *b. rašš* shotgun

البندقية *al-bunduqīya* Venice

بندقانى *bunduqānī* pl. -*ūn*, بنادقة *banādiqa* a Venitian

بندوق *bundūq* pl. بناديق *banādīq*[2] bastard

بندورة *banadōra* (*syr.*; from It. *pomodoro*) tomatoes

احمر بندورى *aḥmar*[2] *banadōrī* tomato-red

بندول (Fr. *pendule*) *bandūl* pendulum

بنديرة (Span. *bandera*) *bandēra* pl. بنادر *banādir*[2] pennon, flag, banner

بنور *bannūr* (= بلور *ballūr*) glass

بنزهير *banzahīr* bezoar, bezoar stone

بنزين *banzīn*, *benzīn* gasoline, benzine

بنس (Engl.) pence

بنسلين *benisilīn* penicillin

بنسيه (Fr. *pensée*) *bansēh* pansy (*bot.*)

بنسيون *bansiyōn* pl. -*āt* boardinghouse; boarding school

بنصر *binṣir* f., pl. بناصر *banāṣir*[2] ring finger

بنط *bunṭ* pl. بنوط *bunūṭ* point (stock market)

بنطلون *banṭalūn* (from It. *pantaloni*) pl. -*āt* trousers, pants

بنغازى *banǧāzī* Bengasi (city in NE Libya, capital of Cyrenaica)

البنغال *al-banǧāl* Bengal (region, NE Indian subcontinent)

بنفسج *banafsaj* (coll.; n. un. ة) violet (*bot.*)

بنفسجى *banafsajī* violetlike, violetish; violet (adj.) | فوق البنفسجى or وراء البنفسجى ultraviolet

بنفش *banfaš*, *banafš* amethyst (*min.*)

بنقة *binaqa* and بنيقة *banīqa* gore, gusset (of a shirt or garment)

[1]بنك *bunk* root, core, heart, best part | بنك العمر *b. al-'umr* the prime of life, the best years

[2]بنك *bank* pl. بنوك *bunūk* bank, banking house | بنك التسليف credit bank; بنك التوفير deposit bank; بنك الدم *b. ad-dam* blood bank; البنك الدولى (*daulī*) the World Bank

[3]مبنك *mubannak* stranded

[4]محنك مبنك *muḥannak mubannak* shrewd, sly, astute

بنكنوت (Engl.) *banknōt* banknote

بنوة and بنوى see [1]بن

بنوار (Fr. *baignoire*) *banwār* baignoire, theater box of the lowest tier

[1]بنى *banā* i (بناء *binā'*, بنيان *bunyān*) and VIII to build, erect, construct, set up (ه s.th.); to build, establish, rest (ه على s.th. on); to consummate the marriage (عليها and بها with a woman); pass. *buniya*, *ubtuniya* to be based, be built, rest (على on) | بنى كلمة على (*kalimatan*) to give a word an indeclinable ending in (a certain vowel or a vowelless consonant; *gram.*) V see [1]بن

بناء *binā'* building, construction, erection, setting up; structure (also, e.g., of an organism), setup, make-up; (pl. ابنية *abniya*) building, structure, edifice | اعادة البناء *iʿādat al-b.* reconstruction; البناء الحر (*ḥurr*) Freemasonry; بناء على *bināʾan ʿalā* according to, in accordance with, on the basis of, by virtue of, on the strength of; بناء على هذا accordingly, thus

بنائى *bināʾī* constructional, building (used attributively); architectural; structural

بنية *binya, bunya* pl. بنى *binan, bunan* structure, setup, make-up; *binya* build, frame, physique, physical constitution | ضعيف البنية of delicate constitution; صحيح البنية and سليم البنية of sound constitution, healthy; قوى البنية *qawīy al-b.* husky, sturdy

بناء *bannāʾ* pl. *-ūn* builder; mason; constructive | بناء حر (*ḥurr*) Freemason

بناية *bināya* pl. *-āt* building, structure, edifice

بنيان *bunyān* building, construction, erection, setting up; building, structure, edifice; physique, stature

مبنى *mabnan* pl. مبان *mabānin* building, construction, erection, setting up; building, structure, edifice; form; foundation, fundament, basis | الرأى والمبنى (*raʾy*) content and form

تبن *tabannin* see [1]بن

بان *bānin* pl. بناة *bunāh* builder

مبنى *mabnīy* built, set up, erected; founded, based, resting (على on); fixed, established; indeclinable; ending indeclinably (على in; *gram.*)

[2]پنى (Engl.) penny

بنيو (It. *bagno*) *banyō* bath, bathtub

بهت *bahita a, bahuta u* and pass. *buhita* (*baht*) to be astonished, amazed, bewildered, startled, perplexed, flabbergasted, speechless; — *bahita* to be or become pale, fade (color); — *bahata a* to astonish, amaze, bewilder, startle, stagger, flabbergast (ه s.o.); (بهتان *buhtān*) to slander, defame (ه s.o.) **III** to come or descend unexpectedly (ه upon s.o.); to startle, stagger, flabbergast (ه s.o.) **IV** to surprise, astonish, amaze (ه s.o.) **VII** = **I**

بهت *buht* and بهتان *buhtān* slander, false accusation; lie, untruth

بهتة *bahta* perplexity, amazement, bewilderment, stupefaction

باهت *bāhit* pale, pallid, faded (color); perplexed, aghast

مبهوت *mabhūt* perplexed, astonished, amazed, startled, flabbergasted, aghast

بهج *bahija a* to be glad, be happy (ب about), be delighted (ب at); — *bahuja u* to be beautiful, look wonderful **IV** to gladden, delight, make happy (ه s.o.) **VIII** to be glad, be happy (ب about), be delighted (ب at)

بهجة *bahja* splendor, magnificence, beauty, resplendence; joy, delight | بهجة الانظار delight of the eyes, welcome sight

بهج *bahij*, بهيج *bahīj* magnificent, splendid, beautiful; happy, joyous; delightful

مبهجة *mabhaja* a moment of happiness and joy

مباهج *mabāhij*[2] joys, delights; pleasures, amusements, diversions; splendid things; splendor, pomp, magnificence

ابتهاج *ibtihāj* joy, rejoicing, delight (ب at)

مبهج *mubhij* pleasant, charming, delightful

مبتهج *mubtahij* happy, glad, delighted

بهدل *bahdala* to insult (ه s.o.); to treat contemptuously, meanly (ه s.o.); to expose (ه s.o.) to ridicule, make a laughingstock (ه of s.o.) **II** *tabahdala* pass. of **I**

بهدلة *bahdala* insult, affront, abuse, outrage; meanness; triteness, insipidity

مبهدل *mubahdal* maltreated, oppressed, miserable

بهر **bahara** *a* (*bahr*) and **IV** to glitter, shine; to dazzle, overwhelm (ه s.o., ه s.o.'s eyes) | شئ يبهر الابصار a dazzling, overwhelming thing; — pass. *buhira* to be out of breath, to pant **VII** to be dazzled, blinded; to be smitten with blindness; to be out of breath **VIII** to flaunt, parade, show off, present in a dazzling light (ب s.th.)

بهر *bahr* deception, dazzlement (ب by)

بهر *buhr* difficult respiration, labored breathing

بهرة *bahra* (n. vic.) being dazzled, dazzlement

بهرة *buhra* middle, center | ... فى بهرة amidst

ابهر *abhar*[2] more brilliant, more magnificent

ابهر *abhar*[2] aorta (*anat.*)

بهار *bahār* pl. *-āt* spice

ابتهار *ibtihār* dazzling display, show (ب of s.th.)

باهر *bāhir* dazzling, brilliant, splendid

مبهور *mabhūr* breathless, out of breath, panting

بهرج **bahraja** (بهرجة *bahraja*) to adorn, deck out, dress up showily; to give a deceptive brightness (ه to); to glamorize (ه s.th.); to reject as false (ه a witness); to fake, counterfeit (ه s.th.) **II** *tabahraja* to adorn o.s., spruce o.s. up, dress up; to be fake

بهرج *bahraj* false, spurious, fake, sham, worthless, bad; counterfeit money; tinsel, frippery, cheap finery; trash, cheap stuff

بهرجة *bahraja* empty show, hollow pomp

بهرجان *bahrajān* tinsel, frippery

مبهرج *mubahraj* showy, tawdry, gaudy, ornate, ostentatious; trashy, rubbishy, cheap, inartistic

بهريز **bahrīz** (*eg.*) a soup

بهظ **bahaẓa** *a* (*bahẓ*) to oppress, weigh down (ه s.o.; a load, work), weigh heavily (ه on s.o.) **IV** do.

باهظ *bāhiẓ* heavy, oppressive, trying; excessive, exorbitant, enormous; expensive, costly

بهق **bahaq** a kind of lichen (*bot.*); herpetic eruption, tetter; vitiligo alba, a mild form of leprosy (*med.*)

بهل **bahala** *a* (*bahl*) to curse (ه s.o.) **V** and **VI** to curse one another **VIII** to supplicate, pray humbly (to God)

ابهل *abhal* savin (Juniperus sabina; *bot.*)

ابتهال *ibtihāl* supplication, prayer

باهل *bāhil* pl. بهل *buhl, buhhal* free, independent

بهلول **buhlūl, bahlūl** pl. بهاليل *buhālīl*[2] buffoon, jester, clown, fool

بهلوان **bahlawān** pl. *-āt, -īya* acrobat, tumbler, equilibrist, ropedancer, tightrope walker

بهلوانى *bahlawānī* acrobatic | حركات بهلوانية (*ḥarakāt*) acrobatics; antics, capers of a tumbler; طيران بهلوانى (*ṭayarān*) aerial acrobatics, stunt flying

بهم **IV** to make obscure, dubious, unintelligible (ه s.th.) **V** and **X** to be obscure, ambiguous, unintelligible (على to s.o.)

بهمة *bahma* lamb, sheep

بهيم *bahīm* pl. بهم *buhum* jet-black

بهيمة *bahīma* pl. بهائم *bahā'im*[2] beast, animal, quadruped; pl. livestock, cattle, (large) domestic animals

بهيمى *bahīmī* animal, bestial, brutish

بهيمية *bahīmiya* brutishness, bestiality, brutality

ابهام *ibhām* obscurity; vagueness, ambiguity

ابهام *ibhām* pl. اباهيم *abāhīm*[2] thumb; big toe

باهم *bāhim* big toe

مبهم *mubham* obscure, dark, cryptic, doubtful, vague, ambiguous | عدد مبهم (*'adad*) abstract number (*math.*); ○ العصب المبهم (*'aṣab*) the vagus (*anat.*); الاسم المبهم (*ism*) the demonstrative pronoun (*gram.*)

بها[1] (بهو) *bahā u*, *bahuwa u* and بهى *bahiya a* (بهاء *bahā'*) to be beautiful **III** to vie, compete (ب ه with s.o. in s.th.); to pride o.s. (ب on), be proud (ب of), boast (ب of, ه ب to s.o. of s.th.) **VI** to compete with one another; to be proud (ب of), pride o.s. (ب on)

بهو *bahw* pl. ابهاء *abhā'* hall; parlor, drawing room, reception hall

بهى *bahīy* beautiful, magnificent, splendid; brilliant, radiant, shining

بهاء *bahā'* beauty, magnificence, splendor; brilliancy

بهائى *bahā'ī* Bahai (adj.); (pl. *-ūn*) an adherent of the Bahai sect, a Bahai

ابهى *abhā* more splendid, more brilliant

مباهاة *mubāhāh* and تباه *tabāhin* pride, vainglory, boastfulness

بهوات[2] see بك

(بوء) باء *bā'a u* to come again, return; to come back (ب with s.th.), bring back, yield, bring in (ب s.th.) | باء بالخيبة or بالفشل (*kaiba*, *fašal*) to fail **II** to provide accommodations (ل and ه for s.o., ه at a place), put up (ل or ه s.o., ه at) | بوأ مكانا (*makānan*) to take a place, settle down, live or stay at a place **IV** to provide accommodations (ه for s.o., ه at a place); to settle down, reside, live (ب at a place) **V** to settle down (ه at a place), occupy (مركزا *markazan* a place), hold (مقاما *maqāman* a position) | تبوأ مكانا (*makānan*) to gain ground, become generally accepted; تبوأ العرش (*'arš*) to ascend the throne; تبوأ الحكم (*ḥukm*) to come to power, take over power

بيئة *bī'a* pl. *-āt* (usually pronounced *bai'a*) pl. *-āt* residence, domicile, seat; situation; surroundings, environment, milieu; home, habitat

مباءة *mabā'a* place to which s.th. comes; abode, dwelling, habitation

تبوء *tabawwu'*: تبوء العرش *t. al-'arš* accession to the throne

بوب **II** to divide into chapters or sections (ه s.th.); to arrange in groups, arrange systematically, class, classify (ه s.th.)

باب *bāb* pl. ابواب *abwāb*, بيبان *bībān* door; gate; opening, gateway; entrance; chapter, section, column, rubric; group, class, category; field, domain (fig.) | الباب العالى the Sublime Porte; باب المندب *b. al-mandab* Bab el Mandeb (strait between SW Arabia and Africa; *geogr.*); على الابواب near, imminent; فتح بابا جديدا to open up a new way, a new possibility; فتح باب *futiḥa bābu* ... was (were) begun, ... got under way; قفل باب الشىء (*qafala*) to put an end to s.th., terminate, close s.th.; من باب الفضل (*b. il-faḍl*) as a favor; من باب اولى (*aulā*) with all the more reason, the more so; فى هذا الباب about this matter, about this; من باب الضرورة ان (*b. iḍ-ḍarūra*) it is necessary that ...; ليس هذا من باب الصدفة (*b. is-ṣudfa*) that's no coincidence; دخل فى باب or كان من باب (with foll. genit.) to belong to, fall under; فريد فى بابه unique of its kind; طلع على باب الله to pursue one's livelihood, earn one's bread

بابة *bāba* pl. *-āt* kind, sort, class, category

بواب *bawwāb* pl. *-ūn* doorman, gatekeeper

بوابة *biwāba* office of gatekeeper

بوابة *bawwāba* pl. *-āt* (large) gate, portal | بوابة القنطرة *b. al-qanṭara* lock gate

تبويب *tabwīb* division into chapters, sectioning, classification, systematic arrangement, grouping

مبوب *mubawwab* arranged in groups, classed, classified

بوبلين **boblīn** poplin

بوبينة (Fr. *bobine*) *bobīna* spool, reel

بويت *buwait* see بيت

بوتاس, بوتاسا (It. *potassa*) *būtāsā, būtās* potash

بوتقة *būtaqa* (usually pronounced *bautaqa*) crucible, melting pot | فى بوتقة الزمان (*zamān*) in the melting pot of time

بوجيه (Fr. *bougie*) *bužīh* pl. *-āt* spark plug (*eg.*)

باح (بوح) *bāḥa u* (*bauḥ*) to become known, be revealed, be divulged, leak out (secret); to reveal, disclose, divulge (ه or ب s.th., a secret; الى and ل to s.o.) **IV** to disclose, reveal (ه or ب s.th., ل to s.o.); to release, abandon, make public property, declare ownerless (ه s.th.); to permit, allow, leave (ه s.th., ل to s.o.); to justify, warrant (ه s.th.) **X** to reveal (ه s.th.); to regard as public property, as ownerless, as fair game; to deem permissible, lawful (ه s.th.); to hurt (حرمته *ḥurmatahū* s.o.'s honor); to take possession (ه of), appropriate, take as booty (ه s.th.); to seize, confiscate (ه s.th.) | استباح دمه (*damahū*) to proscribe, outlaw s.o.

بوح *bauḥ* divulgence, disclosure (of a secret); confession

بوح *būḥ* wide, open space; courtyard; hall

باحة *bāḥa* pl. *-āt* wide, open space; open place, square, plaza; courtyard; hall

اباحة *ibāḥa* divulgence, disclosure (of a secret); permission, authorization; licentiousness

اباحى *ibāḥī* licentious, unrestrained, uninhibited; anarchist; freethinker

اباحية *ibāḥīya* freethinking, libertinism; anarchism

استباحة *istibāḥa* appropriation, capture, seizure; spoliation, confiscation

مباح *mubāḥ* permitted, allowed, permissible; legal, lawful, licit, legitimate; open to everyone, permitted for all, free; ownerless (*Isl. Law*); indifferent (said of actions for which neither reward nor punishment is to be expected, but which are permissible, pl. مباحات indifferent, permissible actions, *Isl. Law*)

باخ (بوخ) *bāḵa u* to abate, subside, let up, decrease; to die, go out (fire); to fade, bleach; to spoil, rot (e.g., meat) **II** to spoil (ه s.th.)

بواخ *buwāḵ* evaporation, exhalation, vapor, steam

تبويخ *tabwīḵ*: تبويخ النكتة *t. an-nukta* the spoiling of the point of a story

□ بايخ *bāyiḵ* spoiled, bad; vapid, insipid, stale (also, e.g., of a joke)

بوخارست *būḵārest* Bucharest

بودرة (Fr. *poudre*) *būdra* powder

بودقة *būdaqa* pl. بوادق *bawādiq*² crucible, melting pot

بوذا *būḏā* Buddha

بوذى *būḏī* Buddhistic; Buddhist

بوذية *būḏiya* Buddhism

بار (بور) *bāra u* (*baur*, بوار *bawār*) to perish; to lie fallow, be uncultivated (land); to be futile, unsuccessful, unprofitable, lead to nothing (work); to be unsalable, be dead stock (merchandise) | بارت البنت (*bint*) the girl could not get a husband **II** to let lie fallow (ه land); to make unprofitable, useless (ه s.th.) **IV** to destroy

بور **būr** uncultivated, fallow | ارض بور (*arḍ*), pl. اراض بور (*arāḍin*) fallow land, wasteland

بوار **bawār** perdition, ruin | دار البوار hell

بائر **bā'ir** uncultivated, fallow (land)

بورانى **būrānī** (*eg.*) a vegetable stew

بور سعيد **būr sa'īd** Port Said (seaport in NE Egypt)

بور سودان **būr sūdān** Port Sudan (seaport in NE Sudan)

بورتوريكو **burturīkū** Puerto Rico

بورتوغال **burtuḡāl** Portugal

بورصة **burṣa** pl. **-āt** stock exchange

بور فؤاد **būr fu'ād** Port Fuad (seaport in NE Egypt, opposite Port Said)

بورق **bauraq** borax

بورما **burmā** Burma

1بورى (Turk. **boru**) **būrī** trumpet, bugle

بوروجى **būrūjī** pl. **-īya** trumpeter, bugler

2بورى **būrī** (pl. بوارى **bawārī**) striped mullet (Mugil cephalus; *zool.*)

3بوريه (Fr.) **būrēh** purée

1بوز **II** to pout, sulk, look glum, sullen

بوز **būz** pl. ابواز **abwāz** muzzle, snout

تبويزة **tabwīza** sullen mien

مبوز **mubawwiz** sullen, glum

2بوز **būz**, بوزة **būza** ice cream

3بوزة **būza** a beerlike beverage

4باز **bāz** pl. ابواز **abwāz**, بيزان **bīzān** falcon

1بوس **būs** bus

2(بوس) باس **bāsa** *u* (**baus**) to kiss (ه s.o.)

بوسة **bausa**, **būsa** kiss

بوستو (It. *busto*) **bustū** corset

بوسطة, بوستة (It. *posta*) **busṭa**, **busta** post, mail

البوسفور **al-busfūr** the Bosporus

(بوش) باش **bāša** *u* (**bauš**) to be boisterous, shout, roar (crowd) **II** do.

بوش **bauš** pl. اوباش **aubāš** (for ابواش) mob, rabble

1بوص **būṣ** (coll.; n. un. ة) reed

بوصة **būṣa** pl. **-āt** inch

2بوص **būṣ** pl. ابواص **abwāṣ** linen or silk fabric

بوصلة (It. *bussola*) **boṣla** compass

بوطة **būṭa** crucible, melting pot

بوظة **būẓa** a beerlike beverage

1بوع **bū'** metatarsal bone (*anat.*) | لا يعرف الكوع من البوع he wouldn't know his knee from his elbow (proverbially, of a stupid person)

2باع **bā'** pl. ابواع **abwā'** the span of the outspread arms, fathom; in Eg. today = 4 *ḏirā' mi'mārīya* = 3 m | طويل الباع mighty, powerful; capable, able; knowledgeable; generous, liberal; قصير الباع powerless, helpless, impotent, weak, incapable; niggardly, stingy; قصور الباع impotence, weakness; incapability (عن of); بالباع والذراع with might and main

1بوغ **II** to surprise

2باغة **bāḡa** celluloid; tortoise shell

بوغادة **būḡāda** and بوغاضة **būḡāḍa** potash, lye

بوغاز *būġāz* pl. بواغيز *bawāġīz*[2] strait(s); harbor | بوغاز الدردنيل the Dardanelles

بوفيه (Fr. *buffet*) *būfēh* buffet; bar; sideboard

بوق II to blow the trumpet

بوق *būq* pl. *-āt*, ابواق *abwāq* trumpet, bugle; fanfare; horn (of an automobile, of a gramophone); acoustic signaling device; megaphone; mouthpiece, spokesman; duplicity, treachery, betrayal | بوق الصوت *b. aṣ-ṣaut* or بوق الراديو loudspeaker (*radio*); ○ بوق رحمى (*raḥimī*) oviduct, Fallopian tube (*anat.*)

بواق *bauwāq* trumpeter, bugler

باقة *bāqa* bundle; bunch of flowers, nosegay, bouquet

بائقة *bā'iqa* pl. بوائق *bawā'iq*[2] misfortune, calamity

بوقال *būqāl*, بوقالة *būqāla* pl. بواقيل *bawāqīl*[2] vessel without handles, mug

بوكسفورد *boksəford* patrol wagon, paddy wagon, Black Maria

بوكسكاف (Engl.) *boksəkāf* box calf

[1]بال (بول) *bāla u* (*baul*) and V to make water, urinate IV to be diuretic X to cause to urinate

بول *baul* pl. ابوال *abwāl* urine | مرض البول السكرى *maraḍ al-b. as-sukkarī* diabetes

بولى *baulī* uric, urinary, urinous | المسالك البولية the urinary passages; الامراض البولية diseases of the kidney and urinary bladder; تسمم بولى (*tasammum*) uremia (*med.*)

بيلة *bīla*: ○ بيلة آحينية (*āḥinīya*) albuminuria; ○ بيلة دموية (*damawīya*) hematuria (*med.*)

بوالة *bauwāla* public lavatory

مبولة *mabwala* pl. مباول *mabāwil*[2] urinal; a diuretic; — *mibwala* chamber pot; toilet, water closet

استبوال *istibwāl*: ○ استبوال الدم *ist. ad-dam* uremia (*med.*)

[2]بال *bāl* state, condition; heart, mind; notice, regard, attention | ذو بال significant, notable, considerable, important, serious, grave; فراغ البال *farāġ al-b.* leisure; مشغول البال anxious, uneasy, concerned, worried; طويل البال long-suffering, patient; ما باله ... (with verb) why is it that he (it) ...? why ...? ما بالك how about you? what do you think? خلا باله *ḵalā bāluhū* his mind is at rest, he has no worries; خطر بباله it occurred to him, it came to his mind; اعطى (القى، جعل) باله الى (ل) (*a'ṭā, alqā, ja'ala*) to turn one's mind to, give one's attention to, pay attention to, take into account, be mindful of, bear in mind, heed s.th.; لم يلق لقولى بالا *lam yulqi li-qaulī bālan* he didn't pay any attention to what I said; لا يقل عنه بالا (*yaqillu*) no less significant than this

[3]بول *būl* postage stamp

[4]بال *bāl* whale (*zool.*)

[5]بالة look up alphabetically

□ بولاد *būlād* (= فولاذ) steel

بوليسة see بولصة

بولاق *būlāq*[2] a district of Cairo

بولندة *bōlanda* Poland

بولندى *bōlandī* Polish; (pl. *-ūn*) Pole

بولو *bōlō* polo

بولونيا (It. *Polonia*) *būlūniyā* Poland

بولونى *būlūnī* Polish; Pole

[1]بوليس (Fr. *police*) *būlīs* police | بوليس الآداب vice squad; البوليس الجنائى (*jinā'ī*) criminal police; البوليس الحربى (*ḥarbī*) military police; البوليس السرى (*sirrī*) secret police; بوليس المرور traffic police

رواية بوليسية *riwāya būlīsiya* detective story

²بوليسة and بوليصة (Fr. *police*) *būlīsa, būlīṣa* pl. بوالص *bawāliṣ*², بوالس *bawālis*² certificate of insurance, policy | بوليسة الشحن *b. aš-šaḥn* bill of lading

بوليفيا *būlīfiyā* Bolivia

بوليفى *būlīfī* Bolivian

○داء البولينا *dā' al-baulīnā* uremia

بوم *būm* (coll.; n. un. ة) pl. ابوام *abwām* owl

¹بون *baun, būn* interval, distance; difference

²بان (coll.; n. un. ة) ben tree (Moringa; *bot.*); horse-radish tree (Moringa oleifera; *bot.*); Egyptian willow (Salix aegyptiaca L.; *bot.*)

بونس‌ايرس Buenos Aires

بونى (Engl.) *bōnī* pl. بوانى *bawānī* pony

باه *bāh* coitus; sexual potency; sexuality

بوهيميا (Engl.) *bōhīmiyā* Bohemia

بوهيمى *bōhēmī* Bohemian (adj. and n.)

بوهيمية *bōhēmīya* Bohemianism, Bohemian life

بؤونة *ba'ūna* the tenth month of the Coptic year

بوية (Turk. *boya*) *bōya* paint; shoe polish

بوياجى, بويجى (*eg.*) *boyagī* house painter, painter; shoeshine, bootblack

بية *bayya* = باية look up alphabetically

بيئة see بوء

بيادة *biyāda* infantry (*Eg.*)

بيادى *biyādī* infantryman, foot soldier

بيان, بيانة, بيانو *biyān, biyāna, biyānō* pl. بيانات *biyānāt* piano

¹بيب *bīb* pipe, tube; feed pipe, spout (of a reservoir or tank)

²بيبة *bība* (Western) smoking pipe

بات (بيت) *bāta i* (مبيت *mabīt*) to pass or spend the night; to stay overnight; to become; to be (فى in a situation); with foll. imperf.: to get into a situation, get to the point where; to continue to do s.th., go on or keep doing s.th., stick to s.th. **II** to brood (by night; ه about s.th.); to contrive, hatch (ه an evil plan, ل against s.o.), plot (ل against s.o.); to put up for the night (ه s.o.) | بيت فى الصف (*ṣaff*; *eg.*) to flunk, fail promotion (pupil) **IV** to put up for the night (ه s.o.)

بيت *bait* pl. بيوت *buyūt*, بيوتات *buyūtāt* house, building; tent (of nomads); room; apartment, flat; (garden) bed; family; case, box, covering, sheath; pl. بيوتات large, respectable houses; respectable families; (pl. ابيات *abyāt*) verse | بيت الابرة *b. al-ibra* (navigator's) compass; اهل البيت *ahl al-b.* family, specif., the family of the Prophet; اهل البيوتات people from good, respectable families; بيوتات تجارية (*tijārīya*) commercial houses; البيت الحرام (*ḥarām*) the Kaaba; بيت الخلاء *b. al-ḵalā'* and بيت الادب *b. al-adab* toilet, water closet; بيت الداء origin or seat of the disease; بيت ريفى (*rīfī*) country house; بيت القصيدة and بيت القصيد (the essential, principal verse of the kasida, i.e.) the quintessence; the gist, the essentials, the hit of s.th.; s.th. that stands out from the rest, the right thing; بيت لحم *baitalaḥm*² Bethlehem; البيت المالك the ruling house; بيت المال treasure house; fisc, treasury, exchequer (*Isl. Law*); (*Tun.*) administration of vacant Muslim estates

بيتى *baitī* domestic, private, home, of the house, house- (in compounds); domesticated (animals); homemade

بويت *buwait* pl. *-āt* small house; small tent

بيات *bayyāt* pl. *-ūn* and بياتة *bayyāta* boarder (student); (pl. *-ūn*) pupil of a boarding school (*tun.*)

بيوت *bayyūt* stale, old

مبيت *mabīt* overnight stop, overnight stay; shelter for the night

بائت *bā'it* stale, old; (*eg.*) not promoted, في الصف (*ṣaff*) in school

مبيت *mubayyit* plotter, schemer, intrigant

بيجاما *bījāmā* and بيجامة *bījāma* pajama

باد (بيد)[1] *bāda* *i* to perish, die, pass away, become extinct **IV** to destroy, exterminate, extirpate (ه, ه s.o., s.th.)

بيد ان *baida anna* although, whereas; (esp., introducing a sentence:) yet, however, but, ... though

بيداء *baidā'*[2] pl. بيد *bīd*, بيداوات *baidāwāt* desert, steppe, wilderness

ابادة *ibāda* annihilation, extermination, eradication, extirpation

بائد *bā'id* passing, transitory, temporal; past, bygone

مبيد *mubīd* destructive, annihilative; (pl. *-āt*) means of extermination | مبيدات حشرية (*ḥašarīya*) insecticides

بيادة[2] look up alphabetically

بيدر *baidar* pl. بيادر *bayādir*[2] threshing floor

بيدق *baidaq* (and بيذق) pl. بيادق *bayādiq*[2] pawn (in chess)

بيذنجان see باذنجان alphabetically

□[1] بيارة *bayyāra* pl. *-āt* (*pal.*) irrigation wheel; plantation

بيرة ,بيرا[2] (It. *birra*) *bīrā, bīra* beer | مصنع البيرا *maṣna' al-b.* brewery

بيرق *bairaq* pl. بيارق *bayāriq*[2] flag, banner, standard

بيرقدار *bairaqdār* color-bearer, standard-bearer

جبال البيرنيه (Fr. *Pyrénées*) *jibāl al-bīrinēh* the Pyrenees

بيرو[1] *bērū* Peru

بيرو[2] (Fr. *bureau*) *bīrō* pl. *-āt* office, bureau

بيروت *bairūt*[2] Beirut (capital of Lebanon)

بيروتى *bairūtī* pl. بوارتة *bawārita*, بيارتة *bayārita* a native or inhabitant of Beirut

بيروقراطى *bīruqrāṭī* bureaucratic

بيروقراطية *bīruqrāṭīya* bureaucracy; red tape

بيزنطيا *bīzanṭiyā* Byzantium

بيزنطى *bīzanṭī* Byzantine

بيسون *bīsōn* bison

باض (بيض) *bāḍa* *i* to lay eggs (also ه); to stay, settle down, be or become resident (ب at a place) | باض بالمكان وفرخ (*wa-farraka*) to be born and grow up in a place; to establish itself and spread (plague) **II** to make white, paint white, whitewash, whiten (ه s.th.); to bleach, blanch (ه s.th., textiles, laundry, rice, etc.); to tin, tinplate (ه s.th.); to make a fair copy (ه of s.th.) | بيض وجهه (*wajhahū*) to make s.o. appear blameless, in a favorable light, to whitewash, exculpate, vindicate, justify s.o., play s.o. up, make much of s.o.; to honor s.o., show honor to s.o.; بيض الله وجهه may God make him happy! لا يبيض من صحيفته this doesn't show him in a favorable light **V** pass. of **II**; **IX** to be or become white

بيض *baiḍ* pl. بيوض *buyūḍ* eggs

بيضة *baiḍa* (n. un.) pl. *-āt* egg; testicle; helmet; main part, substance, essence | بيضة الديك *b. ad-dīk* (the egg of a rooster i.e.) an impossible or extraordinary thing; بيضة البلد *b. al-balad* a man held in high esteem in his community; في بيضة النهار (*b. in-nahār*) in broad daylight; بيضة الصيف *b. aṣ-ṣaif* the hottest part of the summer; بيضة الاسلام the territory or pale of Islam; الدفاع عن بيضة الدين ,عن

بيضة الوطن (*b. id-dīn, b. il-waṭan*) defense of the faith, of the country; بيضة الخدر *b. al-ḵidr* a woman secluded from the outside world, a chaste, respectable woman

بيضى *baiḍī*, بيضوى *baiḍawī* and بيضاوى *baiḍāwī* egg-shaped, oviform, oval, ovate

بييضة *buyaiḍa* and بويضة *buwaiḍa* pl. *-āt* small egg, ovule; ovum

بياض *bayāḍ* white, whiteness; whitewash; — (pl. *-āt*) barren, desolate, uncultivated land, wasteland; gap, blank space (in a manuscript); blank; leucoma (*med.*); linen, pl. بياضات linen goods, linens; (*syr.*) milk, butter, and eggs | بياض البيض *b. al-baiḍ* white of egg, albumen; بياض العين *b. al-ʿain* the white of the eye; بياض النهار *b. an-nahār* daylight, (acc.) by day, during the daytime; بياض يومه وسواد ليله *bayāḍa yaumihī wa-sawāda lailihī* by day and by night; بياض الوجه *b. al-wajh* fine character, good reputation; سمك بياض *samak b.* a Nile fish (*eg.*); على بياض blank, free from writing, printing or marks, uninscribed; لبس (or ارتدى) البياض (*labisa, irtadā*) to dress in white

بيوض *bayūḍ* pl. بيض *buyuḍ, bīḍ* (egg-) laying

ابيض *abyaḍ*², f. بيضاء *baiḍā'*², pl. بيض *bīḍ* white; bright; clean, shiny, polished; blameless, noble, sincere (character); empty, blank (sheet of paper); pl. البيضان *al-bīḍān* the white race; الابيض white of egg, albumen | ارض بيضاء (*arḍ*) barren, uncultivated land, wasteland; ثورة بيضاء (*ṯaura*) peaceful, bloodless revolution; الخيط الابيض (*ḵaiṭ*) first light of dawn; الذهب الابيض (*ḏahab*) platinum; بالسلاح الابيض with cold steel; صحيفته بيضاء (*ṣaḥīfatuhū*) his reputation is good; he has noble deeds to his credit, he has a noble character; صحف بيضاء (*ṣuḥuf*) noble, glorious deeds; اكذوبة بيضاء (*ukḏūba*) white lie, fib; ليلة بيضاء (*laila*) a sleepless night, a night spent awake; الموت الابيض (*maut*) natural death; يد بيضاء (*yad*) beneficent hand, benefaction

مبيض *mabīḍ, mibyaḍ* ovary (*anat.*)

تبييضة *tabyīḍa* fair copy

○ ابيضاض *ibyiḍāḍ* leukemia (*med.*)

بائض *bā'iḍ* pl. بوائض *bawā'iḍ*² (egg-) laying

مبيض *mubayyiḍ* pl. *-ūn* whitewasher; bleacher; tinner; copyist, transcriber (of fair copy)

مبيضة *mubayyaḍa* fair copy

بيطر *baiṭara* to practice veterinary science; to shoe (ه a horse)

بيطار *baiṭār* pl. بياطرة *bayāṭira* veterinarian; farrier

بيطرى *baiṭarī* veterinary | الطب البيطرى (*ṭibb*) veterinary medicine; طبيب بيطرى veterinarian

بيطرة *baiṭara* veterinary science; farriery

¹(بيع) باع *bā'a i* (*baiʿ*, مبيع *mabīʿ*) to sell (ه s.th., ه or ل to s.o., ب for a price) III to make a contract (ه with s.o.); to pay homage (ه to s.o.); to acknowledge as sovereign or leader (ه s.o.), pledge allegiance (ه to) IV to offer for sale (ه s.th.) VI to agree on the terms of a sale, conclude a bargain VII to be sold, be for sale VIII to buy, purchase (ه من s.th. from s.o. and ه ه from s.o. s.th.) | لا ابتاع منه ولا ابيعه (*abtāʿu, abīʿuhū*) I don't trust him

بيع *baiʿ* pl. بيوع *buyūʿ*, بيوعات *buyūʿāt* sale | للبيع for sale; بيوع (or بيوعات) جبرية (*jabrīya*) forced sales, compulsory sale by auction; بيع بالجملة (*jumla*) wholesale sale; بيع بالخيار (*ḵiyār*) optional sale (*Isl. Law*); بيع لآخر راغب (*li-āḵiri rāġibin*) sale to the highest bidder; بيع العينة *b. al-ʿīna* credit operation (*Isl. Law*)

بيعة *baiʿa* agreement, arrangement; business deal, commercial transaction, bargain; sale; purchase; homage | على البيعة into the bargain

بياع *bayyāʿ* salesman, merchant, dealer, commission agent, middleman

مبيع *mabīʿ* sale, pl. *-āt* sales (esp. on the stock market)

مبايعة *mubāyaʿa* pl. *-āt* conclusion of contract; homage; pledge of allegiance; transaction

ابتياع *ibtiyāʿ* purchase

بائع *bāʾiʿ* pl. باعة *bāʿa* seller, vendor; dealer, merchant; salesman

بائعة *bāʾiʿa* saleswoman

مبيع *mabīʿ* and مباع *mubāʿ* sold

مبتاع *mubtāʿ* buyer, purchaser

²بيعة *bīʿa* pl. *-āt*, بيع *biyaʿ* (*Chr.*) church; synagogue

بيك *bē* (*eg.*), *bēy*, *bēk* pl. بيكوات *begawat* (*syr.*) bey (title of courtesy); cf. بك

بيكوية *bēkawīya* rank of bey

بيكار *bīkār* compass, (pair of) dividers

بكباشى see بيكباشى

بيكه (Fr.) *bīkeh* piqué (fabric)

¹بيل (Fr. *bille*) *bīl* ball | كرسى بيل *kursī b.* ball bearing

²بيلة *bīla* see بول

بيلسان *bailasān* black elder (*bot.*)

بيلهارسيا *bilharsiyā* bilharziasis, schistosomiasis (*med.*)

بيليه (Fr. *bille*) *bīlya* pl. *-āt* little ball, marble

بيمارستان *bīmāristān* hospital; lunatic asylum

¹(بين) بان *bāna i* (بيان *bayān*) to be or become plain, evident, come out, come to light; to be clear (ل to s.o.); (بين *bain*, بينونة *bainūna*) to part, be separated (من from) II to make clear, plain, visible, evident (ه s.th.); to announce (ه s.th.); to state (ه s.th.); to show, demonstrate (ه s.th.); to explain, expound, elucidate (ه s.th.), throw light (ه on) III to part, go away (ه from), leave (ه s.o.); to differ, be different (ه, ه from), be unlike s.th. (ه); to contradict (ه s.th.), be contrary (ه to); to conflict, be at variance, be inconsistent (ه with s.th.) IV to explain, expound, elucidate (ل ه s.th. to s.o.); to separate, sift, distinguish (من ه s.th. from); to be clear, plain, evident V to be or become clear, intelligible (ل to s.o.); to turn out, prove in the end, appear, become evident; to follow (من from), be explained (من by); to be clearly distinguished (من from); to seek to ascertain (ه s.th.), try to get at the facts (ه of); to eye or examine critically, scrutinize (ه, ه s.o., s.th.); to look, peer (ه at); to see through s.th. (ه), see clearly, perceive, notice, discover, find out (ه s.th.); to distinguish (من ه s.th. from) VI to differ, be different, be opposed, be contrary; to vary greatly, differ widely; to vary, differ, fluctuate (بين between two amounts or limits) X to be or become clear, plain, evident; to see, know, perceive, notice (ه s.th.); pass. *ustubīna* to follow clearly, be clearly seen (من from)

بين *bain* separation, division; interval; difference | ذات البين enmity, disunion, discord; فى البين in the meantime, meanwhile

بين *baina* (prep.) or فيما بين *fī-mā b.* between; among, amidst | بين — و either — or, partly — partly, e.g., كان القوم بين صامت ومتكلم (*ṣāmitin wa-mutakallimin*) the crowd was divided among those who were silent and those who talked; بين يديه (*yadaihi*) in front of him, before him, in his presence; with him, on him, in his possession, e.g., لا سلاح بين يديه (*silāḥa*) he hasn't got a weapon on him, he is unarmed; فيما بين ذلك meanwhile, in the meantime; فيما بينى وبين نفسى in my heart, at heart, inwardly; بين ذراعيه in his arms; من بينهم *min bainihim* from among them, from their midst; بين بين something between, a cross, a mixture, a combination; neither good nor bad, medium, tolerable; شيء بين بين something between, a cross, a mixture, a combination; بين وقت وآخر (*waqt, āḵar*), بين فترة واخرى (*fatra, uḵrā*) at times, from time to time

مابين *mā-bain* look up alphabetically

بينا *bainā*, بينما *bainamā* (conj.) while; whereas

بين *bayyin* clear, plain, evident, obvious, patent; (pl. ابيناء *abyināʼ*²) eloquent

بيان *bayān* pl. *-āt* clearness, plainness, patency, obviousness; statement, declaration, announcement; manifestation; explanation, elucidation, illustration; information, news; (official) report, (official) statement; enumeration, index, list; eloquence; البيان the Koran; see also alphabetically | بيان الحقيقة correction (*journ.*); غنى عن البيان (*ğanīy*) self-explanatory, self-evident; علم البيان *ʻilm al-b.* rhetoric; عطف البيان *ʻaṭf al-b.* explicative apposition (*gram.*)

بيانى *bayānī* explanatory, illustrative; rhetorical

بينة *bayyina* pl. *-āt* clear proof, indisputable evidence; evidence (*Isl. Law*); a document serving as evidence | بينة ظرفية (*ẓarfīya*) circumstantial evidence; كان على بينة من as has been proved; على بينة من to be fully aware of; to be well-informed, well-posted, up-to-date about

ابين *abyan*² clearer, more distinct, more obvious

تبيان *tibyān* exposition, demonstration, explanation, illustration

تبيين *tabyīn* and ابانة *ibāna* exposition, demonstration, explanation, illustration

تباين *tabāyun* difference, unlikeness, dissimilarity, disparity

تباينى *tabāyunī* different, differing, conflicting

بائن *bāʼin* clear, plain, evident, obvious, patent; final, irrevocable (divorce; *Isl. Law*); of great length | بائن الطول *b. aṭ-ṭūl* towering, of unusual height (person)

بائنة *bāʼina* bride's dowry

مبيونة *mabyūna* distance

مبين *mubīn* clear, plain, evident, obvious, patent | الكتاب المبين the Koran

متباين *mutabāyin* dissimilar, unlike, differential, differing, varying

بيانة ,بيان² look up alphabetically

بكباشى see بينباشى

بنتو see بينتو

بيه *bēh* = بك

بيوريه¹ (Engl.) *biyūrēh* purée

بيوريه² (Fr. *pyorrhée*) *biyōrēh* pyorrhea (*med.*)

ت

ت¹ abbreviation of تلفون telephone

ت² *ta* (particle introducing oaths) by, تالله *ta-llāhi* by God!

تاء *tā'* name of the letter ت

تابوت *tābūt* pl. توابيت *tawābīt*² box, case, chest, coffer; casket, coffin, sarcophagus |

تابوت العهد *t. al-ʿahd* ark of the covenant; تابوت رفع المياه *t. rafʿ al-miyāh* Archimedean screw; تابوت الساقية *t. as-sāqiya* scoop wheel, Persian wheel

تابيوكا *tābiyōkā* tapioca

تأتأ *taʼtaʼa* to stammer (with fright)

تاج see توج

تؤدة see وأد

تأر[1] IV اتأر البصر (*baṣara*) to stare (ه or الى at s.o.)

تارة[2] see تور

تازة *tāza* (= طازة) fresh, tender, new

تاك *tāka* fem. of the demonstrative pronoun ذاك *ḏāka* (dual nom. تانك *tānika*, genit., acc. تينك *tainika*)

توأم, توم *tauʼam*, f. ة, pl. توائم *tawāʼim*[2] twin

التاميز *at-tāmīz* the Thames

تاى *tāy* (*tun.*, *alg.*) tea | تاى احمر black tea

تايور *tāyōr* and تاير *tāyēr* (Fr. *tailleur*) pl. *-āt* ladies' tailored suit, tailleur

تب *tabba* i (*tabb*, تبب *tabab*, تباب *tabāb*) to perish, be destroyed **X** to stabilize, be stabilized, be or become stable; to be settled, established, well-ordered, regular, normal; to progress well | استتب له الامر everything went well with him

تبا له *tabban lahū!* may evil befall him! may he perish!

استتباب *istitbāb* normalcy, regularity, orderliness, order; stability; favorable course or development

التبت *at-tibt* Tibet

تبر *tabara* i (*tabr*) to destroy, annihilate (ه s.th.)

تبر *tibr* raw metal; gold dust, gold nuggets; ore

تبار *tabār* ruin, destruction

تبرية *tibrīya* dandruff

تبريز *tabrīz*[2] Tabriz (city in NW Iran, capital of Azerbaijan province)

تبع *tabiʿa* a (*tabaʿ*, تباعة *tabāʿa*) to follow, succeed (ه s.o., ه s.th.), come after s.o. or s.th. (ه, ه); to trail, track (ه, ه s.o., s.th.), go after s.o. or s.th. (ه, ه); to walk behind s.o. (ه); to pursue (ه s.th.); to keep, adhere, stick (ه to s.th.), observe (ه s.th.); to follow, take (ه a road), enter upon (ه a road or course); to comply (ه with s.th.); to belong, pertain (ه to); to be subordinate, be attached (ه to s.o.), be under s.o.'s (ه) authority or command, be under s.o. (ه) | تبع الدروس (*durūsa*) to attend classes regularly **III** to follow (ه, ه s.o., s.th.; also — to keep one's mind or eyes on, e.g., on a development); to agree, concur (ه with s.o., على in s.th.), be in agreement or conformity (ه, على with); to pursue, chase, follow up (ه s.o., ه s.th.); to continue (ه s.th.; سيره *sairahū* on one's way), go on (ه with or in) **IV** to cause to succeed or follow (in time, rank, etc.); to place (ه s.o.) under s.o.'s (ه) authority or command, subordinate (ه ه to s.o. s.o., ه ه to s.th. s.th.) **V** to follow (ه s.th., esp. fig.: a topic, a development, the news, etc., = to watch, study); to pursue, trail, track (ه, ه s.o., s.th.); to trace (ه s.th.); to be subordinate (ه, ه to), be attached (ه to s.o.) **VI** to follow in succession, be successive or consecutive, come or happen successively; to form an uninterrupted sequence **VIII** to follow, succeed (ه s.o., ه s.th.), come after (ه, ه); to make (ه s.th.) be succeeded or followed (ب by s.th. else); to prosecute (ه s.o.), take legal action (ه against); to follow, obey, heed, observe, bear in mind (ه s.th.); to pursue (ه s.th.); to examine, investigate, study (ه s.th.); pass. *uttubi'a* to have or find followers, adherents (على for s.th., e.g., for an idea) | اتبع سياسة (*siyāsatan*) to pursue a policy; اتبع يمينه (*yamīnahū*) to keep (to the) right X to make (ه s.o.) follow, ask (ه s.o.) to follow; to seduce (ه s.o.); to have as its consequence, engender, entail (ه s.th.); to subordinate to o.s., make subservient to o.s. (ه s.th.)

تبع *taba'* succession; subordinateness, dependency; following, followers; subordinate, subservient (ل to s.th.); بالتبع successively, consecutively; تبعا ل *taba'an li* according to, in accordance with, pursuant to, in observance of; due to, in consequence of, as the result of; — (pl. اتباع *atbā'*) follower, companion, adherent, partisan; subject, national, citizen; appertaining, appurtenant, pertinent, incident

تبعى *taba'ī*: عقوبة تبعية (*'uqūba*) incidental punishment (*jur.*)

تبعة *tabi'a* pl. *-āt* consequence; responsibility, responsibleness | ألقى التبعة على (*alqā*) to make s.o. or s.th. responsible

تبيع *tabī'* pl. تباع *tibā'* following attached, attending, adjunct; — (pl. تبائع *tabā'i'²*) follower, adherent, partisan; aide, help, assistant, attendant, servant

تبعية *taba'īya* pl. *-āt* subordination, subjection; subordinateness, dependency; citizenship, nationality; بالتبعية subsequently, afterwards; consequently, hence, therefore, accordingly

تباعا *tibā'an* in succession, successively, consecutively, one after the other, one by one

متابعة *mutāba'a* following, pursuing, pursuit, prosecution; continuation

اتباع *itbā'* (*gram.*) intensification by repeating a word with its initial consonant changed, such as *kaṭīr baṭīr*

تتبع *tatabbu'* following (esp. fig., of an argument, of a development, see V above); pursuit; prosecution; succession, course | التتبع التاريخى the course of history; تتبعات عدلية (*'adlīya*) legal action, prosecution

تتابع *tatābu'* succession; relay (*athlet.*); بالتتابع consecutively, successively, in succession; serially, in serialized form

اتباع *ittibā'* following; pursuit (e.g., of a policy); adherence (to), compliance (with), observance (of); اتباعا ل *ittibā'an li* according to, in accordance or conformity with, pursuant to, in observance of

○ اتباعى *ittibā'ī* classical

○ اتباعية *ittibā'īya* classicism

تابع *tābi'* pl. تبعة *taba'a*, تباع *tubbā'* following, succeeding, subsequent; subsidiary, dependent; minor, secondary; subordinate (ل to s.o.), under s.o. (ل); belonging (ل to); subject to s.o.'s (ل) authority or competence; adherent (ل to), following (ل s.o. or s.th.); — (pl. اتباع *atbā'*) adherent, follower, partisan; subject, citizen, national; subordinate, servant; factotum; (pl. توابع) appositive (*gram.*); appendix, addendum, supplement; ○ function (*math.*) | الدول التابعة (*duwal*) the satellite countries

تابعة *tābi'a* pl. توابع *tawābi'²* female attendant, woman servant; a female demon who accompanies women; appurtenance, dependency; consequence, effect, result; responsibility; pl. توابع dependencies, dependent territories; ○ satellites (*pol.*), = الدول التوابع (*duwal*) the satellite countries

تابعية *tābi'īya* nationality, citizenship

متبوع *matbū'* followed, succeeded (ب by); one to whom service or obedience is rendered, a leader, a principal (as distinguished from تابع subordinate)

متابع *mutatābi'* successive, consecutive

متبع *muttaba'* observed, adhered to, complied with (e.g., regulation, custom); followed, traveled (road, course)

تبغ *tibḡ* pl. تبوغ *tubūḡ* tobacco

تبل *tabala* i to consume, waste, make sick (ه s.o.; said of love) II, III and توبل *taubala* to spice, season (ه s.th.)

تابل *tābal, tābil* pl. توابل *tawābil*² coriander (*bot.*); spice, condiment, seasoning

تبولة *tabbūla* (*syr., leb.*) a kind of salad made of bulgur, parsley, mint, onion, lemon juice, spices, and oil

متبول *matbūl* (love-)sick, weak, ravaged, consumed

متبل *mutabbal* spiced, seasoned, flavored; (*syr., leb.*) stuffed with a mixture of rice, chopped meat and various spices, e.g., باذنجان متبل (*bāḏinjān*) stuffed eggplant

تبلوه (Fr. *tableau*) *tablōh* pl. *-āt* a painting

تبن *tibn* straw

تبنى *tibnī* straw-colored, flaxen

تبان *tabbān* straw vendor

درب التبانة *darb at-tabbāna* the Milky Way

متبن *matban* pl. متابن *matābin*² strawstack

تبيوكا *tabiyōkā* tapioca

¹التتر *at-tatar* and التتار *at-tatār* the Tatars

تترى *tatarī* Tatarian; Tatar

²تترى *tatrā* (from وتر) one after the other, successively, in succession

تتك *titik* trigger

تتن *tutun* tobacco

تتنوس *tetanūs* tetanus (*med.*)

تجر *tajara* u and VIII to trade, do business; to deal (في or ب in s.th.) III do. (ه with s.o.)

تجارة *tijāra* commerce; traffic, trade; merchandise

تجارى *tijārī* commercial, mercantile, trade, trading, business (used attributively); commercialized | بيت تجارى (*bait*) commercial house, business house; الحركة التجارية (*ḥaraka*) trade, traffic; شركة تجارية (*širka*) trading company; اتفاق تجارى (*ittifāq*) trade agreement

متجر *matjar* pl. متاجر *matājir*² business, transaction, dealing; merchandise; store, shop

متجرى *matjarī* commercial, trade, trading, business (used attributively)

اتجار *ittijār* trade, business (ب in s.th.)

تاجر *tājir* pl. تجار *tujjār*, *tijār* merchant, trader, businessman, dealer, tradesman | تاجر الجملة *t. al-jumla* wholesale dealer; تاجر التجزئة *t. at-tajzi'a* and تاجر القطاعى *t. al-qiṭā'ī* retailer

بضاعة تاجرة *biḍā'a tājira* salable, marketable merchandise

تجاه *tujāha* (prep.) in front of, opposite, face to face with, facing

تحت *taḥta* (prep.) under; below, beneath, underneath | تحت التجربة (*tajriba*) on probation; in an experimental state; تحت التحضير in preparation; تحت الحفظ (*ḥifẓ*) in custody, under guard; تحت السداد (*sadād*), تحت التسديد due, outstanding, unsettled, unpaid (*com.*); تحت السلاح under arms; تحت سمعهم (*sam'ihim*) in their hearing, for them to hear; تحت التسوية (*taswiya*) outstanding, unpaid, unsettled (*com.*); تحت اشراف (*išrāfi*) under the patronage or superintendence of; تحت الشعور subconscious; تحت تصرفه (*taṣarrufihī*) at his disposal; تحت الطبع (*ṭab'*) in press; تحت عنوان (*'unwāni*) under the title of; تحت اعيننا (*a'yuninā*) before our eyes; تحت التمرين in training; تحت اليد (*yad*) in hand, at hand, available, handy; تحت يده in his power; من تحت *min taḥti* from under, from beneath; under

تحت *taḥtu* (adv.) below, beneath, underneath

تحتانى *taḥtānī* lower, under- (in compounds) | ملابس تحتانية underwear

تحف IV to present (ه ب or ه ه s.o. with s.th.)

تحفة *tuḥfa* pl. تحف *tuḥaf* gift, present; gem (fig.), curiosity, rarity, article of virtu, objet d'art; work of art | تحفة فنية (*fannīya*) unique work of art

متحف *matḥaf* pl. متاحف *matāḥif*² museum | متحف الشمع *m. aš-šam'* waxworks

تخ *takka u* to become sour, ferment (dough)

¹تخت *takt* pl. تخوت *tukūt* bed, couch; bench; seat; sofa; chest, case, box, coffer, cabinet; wardrobe; platform, dais; band, orchestra | تخت الملك *t. al-mulk* throne; royal residence, capital; تخت المملكة *t. al-mamlaka* capital (of a country)

تخت روان, تختروان *taktaruwān, taktarawān* mule-borne litter

²تختة *takta* board; desk; blackboard

تختخ *taktaka* to rot, decay

¹تخم *takima a* to suffer from indigestion, feel sick from overeating IV to surfeit, satiate (ه s.o.); to give (ه s.o.) indigestion, make sick (ه s.o.); to overstuff, cloy (ه the stomach) VIII = I

تخمة *tukama, tukma* pl. تخم *tukam, -āt* indigestion, dyspepsia

متخوم *matkūm* suffering from indigestion, dyspeptic

²تخم *takama i* to fix the limits of (ه), delimit, limit, confine, bound (ه s.th.) III to border (ه on), be adjacent (ه to s.th.)

تخم *takm, tukm* pl. تخوم *tukūm* boundary, border, borderline, limit

متاخم *mutākim* neighboring, adjacent

تدرج *tadruj*², تدرجة *tadruja* pheasant

تدمر *tadmur*², usually pronounced *tudmur*² Palmyra (ancient city of Syria, now a small village)

تدمرى *tadmurī*, usually pronounced *tudmurī* anyone | لا تدمرى nobody, not a living soul

ترابيزة (*eg.*; *tarābēza*) pl. *-āt* table

تراخوما *trākōmā* trachoma (*med.*)

تراس (Fr. *terrasse*) *terās* terrace

ترام, تراموای *trām, tramwāy* tramway

ترب *tariba a* to be or become dusty, covered with dust II and IV to cover with dust or earth (ه s.o., ه s.th.) III to be s.o.'s (ه) mate or comrade, be of the same age (ه as s.o.) V to be dusty, be covered with dust

ترب *tirb* pl. اتراب *atrāb* person of the same age, contemporary, mate, companion, comrade

ترب *tarib* dusty, dust-covered

تربة *turba* pl. ترب *turab* dust; earth, dirt; ground (also fig.); soil; grave, tomb; graveyard, cemetery, burial ground

تربى *turabī* pl. *-īya* (*eg.*) gravedigger

تراب *turāb* pl. اتربة *atriba*, تربان *tirbān* dust, earth, dirt; ground, soil

ترابى *turābī* dusty; dustlike, powdery; earthlike, earthy; dust-colored, gray

○ ترابة *turāba* cement

تريبة *tarība* pl. ترائب *tarā'ib*² chest, thorax

متربة *matraba* poverty, misery, destitution; (pl. متارب *matārib*²) dirt quarry

مترب *mutrib* dusty, dust-covered

ترbس tarbasa (= دربس) to bolt (ه a door)

ترباس tirbās pl. ترابيس tarābīs², ترابس tarābis² bolt, latch (of a door or window)

تربنتين tarbantīn turpentine

تربيزة (eg.) tarabēza table

تربين turbīn pl. -āt turbine

تراث see ورث

ترتر tirtir gold and silver spangles (eg.)

ترجم tarjama to translate (ه s.th. عن from one language الى to another); to interpret (ه s.th.); to treat (ه of s.th.) by way of explanation, expound (ه s.th.); to write a biography (ل of s.o., also ه)

ترجمة tarjama pl. تراجم tarājim² translation; interpretation; biography (also ترجمة الحياة); introduction, preface, foreword (of a book) | الترجمة السبعينية (sabʿīnīya) the Septuagint

ترجمان turjumān pl. تراجمة tarājima, تراجيم tarājīm² translator, interpreter

مترجم mutarjim translator, interpreter; biographer

مترجم mutarjam translated | مترجم على الفلم (film) synchronized (film)

ترح tariḥa a (taraḥ) and V to grieve, be sad II and IV to grieve, distress (ه s.o.)

ترح taraḥ pl. اتراح atrāḥ grief, distress, sadness

ترزى tarzī pl. ترزية tarzīya (eg.) tailor

ترزية tarzīya tailoring

ترس¹ look up alphabetically

ترس² II to provide with a shield or armor

ترس turs pl. اتراس atrās, تروس turūs shield; disk of the sun; — tirs pl. turūs cogwheel, gear | صندوق التروس ṣundūq at-t. gearbox, transmission; سمك الترس samak at-turs turbot (zool.)

مترس matras, mitras pl. متارس matāris² and مترس mitrās pl. متاريس matārīs² bolt, door latch; rampart, bulwark, barricade; esp. pl. متاريس barricades

ترسانة tarsāna, ترسخانة tarskāna arsenal; shipyard, dockyard

ترسكل (Fr. tricycle) tricycle

ترسينة (It. terrazzino) tarasīna balcony

ترع tariʿa a to be or become full (vessel) IV to fill (ه s.th., esp. a vessel)

ترعة turʿa pl. ترع turaʿ, -āt canal; artificial waterway | ترعة الايراد t. al-īrād feeder, irrigation canal; ترعة التصريف drainage canal (Eg.); الترعة الشريفة the Residence of the Sultan of Morocco

ترغل, ترغلة turġul, turġulla turtledove

ترف tarifa a to live in opulence, in luxury IV to effeminate (ه s.o.); to provide with opulent means, surround with luxury (ه s.o.) V = I

ترف taraf and ترفة turfa luxury, opulence, affluence; effemination

ترف tarif opulent, sumptuous, luxurious

مترف mutraf living in ease and luxury; sumptuous, luxurious; luxuriously adorned, ornate, overdecorated (ب with)

ترفاس tirfās (maġr.) truffle (bot.)

ترفل tarfala to strut

ترقوة tarquwa pl. تراق tarāqin collarbone, clavicle (anat.)

ترك¹ taraka u (tark) to let be, leave, relinquish, renounce, give up, forswear (ه s.th.); to desist, refrain, abstain (ه from s.th.); to leave, quit (ه s.o., ه a place); to leave out, omit, drop, neglect, pass over, skip (ه s.th.); to leave (ل or الى ه s.th. to); to leave behind, leave, bequeath, make over (ه s.th., ل to s.o.; as a legacy) |

ترکه يفعل to let s.o. do s.th.; ترك مكانا الى to leave one place for (another); ترکه فى ذمته (fī dimmatihī) to leave s.th. in s.o.'s care, leave s.th. to s.o.; ترکه على حاله to leave s.th. or s.o. unchanged, leave s.th. or s.o. alone; ترکه وشأنه (wa-ša'nahū) to leave s.o. alone, leave s.o. to his own devices III to leave (ه s.o.); to leave alone (ه s.o.); to leave off hostilities (ه against s.o.)

ترك **tark** omission, neglect; relinquishment, abandonment; leaving, leaving behind

تركة **tarika** pl. -āt (also **tirka**) heritage, legacy, bequest

تريكة **tarīka** pl. ترائك **tarā'ik**[2] old maid, spinster

متاركة **mutāraka** truce

متروك **matrūk** pl. -āt heritage, legacy

[2]ترك II to Turkify, Turkicize (ه s.o.) X to become a Turk, become Turkified, adopt Turkish manners and customs

الترك **at-turk** and الاتراك **al-atrāk** the Turks

تركى **turkī** Turkish; Turk; التركية **at-turkīya** theTurkish language

تركيا **turkiyā** Turkey

تتريك **tatrīk** Turkification

تركستان **turkistān**[2] Turkistan

التركمان **at-turkumān** the Turkmen

ترمبيط **turumbēṭ** (syr.) pl. -āt (Western) drum; ترمبيطة **turumbēṭa** (eg.) pl. -āt do.; specif., bass drum

ترمبطجى **turumbaṭgī** (eg.) drummer; bandsman (mil.)

ترمس **turmus**, ترموس **turmūs** lupine (bot.)

ترمومتر **termūmitr** thermometer

ترنج **turunj** see اترج, اترنج

تره **tariha** a to concern o.s. with trifles

ترهة **turraha** pl. -āt sham, mockery, farce; lie, humbug, hoax

ترواده (Fr. Troade) **tirwāda** Troy

تروب (Engl. troop) squad, platoon; squadron | تروب سوارى (sawārī) cavalry squadron (Eg.)

ترومبيتجى = ترمبطجى see under ترمبيط above

ترياق **tiryāq** theriaca; antidote

تريكو (Fr.) tricot

تسعة **tis'a** (f. تسع **tis'**) nine

تسعة عشر **tis'ata 'ašara**, f. تسع عشرة **tis'a 'ašrata** nineteen

تسع **tus'** pl. اتساع **atsā'** one ninth, the ninth part

تسعون **tis'ūn** ninety

التاسع **at-tāsi'** the ninth

تشرين **tišrīn**[2] **al-awwal** October, تشرين الثانى **t. aṯ-ṯānī** November (Syr., Ir., Leb., Jord.)

تشيكوسلوفاكيا **tšekoslovākiyā** Czechoslovakia

تشيلى **tšili** Chile

تطوان **tiṭwān**[2] Tetuán (city in N Morocco)

تع abbreviation of تعالى, see علو

تعب **ta'iba** a (ta'ab) to work hard, toil, slave, drudge, wear o.s. out; to be or become tired, weary (من of s.th.) IV to trouble, inconvenience (ه s.o.); to irk, bother, weary, tire, fatigue (ه s.o.)

تعب **ta'ab** pl. اتعاب **at'āb** trouble, exertion, labor, toil, drudgery; burden, nuisance, inconvenience, discomfort, difficulty, hardship; tiredness, weariness, fatigue; pl. اتعاب fees, honorarium

تعب **ta'ib** and تعبان **ta'bān** tired, weary, exhausted

متاعب *matā'ib*² troubles, pains, efforts; discomforts, inconveniences, difficulties, troubles; complaints, ailments, ills (attending disease); hardships, strains

متعب *mut'ib* troublesome, inconvenient, toilsome, laborious; burdensome, irksome, annoying; wearisome, tiresome, tiring; tedious, dull, boring

متعب *mut'ab* tired, weary

تعتع *ta'ta'a* to stammer; to shake (ه s.o.); اتعتع *itta'ta'a* to move, stir

تعز *ta'izz*² Taizz (city in S Yemen, seat of government)

تعس *ta'asa a*, *ta'isa a* to fall, perish; to become wretched, miserable; *ta'asa* and **IV** to make unhappy or miserable, ruin (ه s.o.)

تعس *ta's* and تعاسة *ta'āsa* wretchedness, misery

تعس *ta'is* and تعيس *ta'īs* pl. تعساء *tu'asā'*² wretched, miserable, unfortunate, unhappy

متعوس *mat'ūs* pl. متاعيس *matā'īs*² wretched, miserable, unfortunate, unhappy

تف *taffa* to spit **II** to say "phew"

تف *tuff* dirt under the fingernails; تفا لك *tuffan laka* phew! fie on you!

○ تفافة *taffāfa* spittoon, cuspidor

تفتا *tafettā*, تفتاه taffeta

تفاح *tuffāḥ* (coll.; n. un. ة) apple(s)

تفكة *tufka* pl. تفك *tufak* (*ir.*) gun, rifle

تفل *tafala u i* (*tafl*) to spit

تفل *tufl* and تفال *tufāl* spit, spittle, saliva

تفل *tafil* ill-smelling, malodorous

متفلة *mitfala* spittoon, cuspidor

تفه *tafiha a* (*tafah*, تفاهة *tafāha*, تفوه *tufūh*) to be little, paltry, insignificant; to be flat, tasteless, vapid, insipid

تفه *tafah* and تفوه *tufūh* paltriness, triviality, insignificance

تفاهة *tafāha* paltriness, triviality, insignificance; flatness, vapidity, insipidity, tastelessness; inanity, stupidity, silliness

تفه *tafih* and تافه *tāfih* little, paltry, trivial, trifling, insignificant; worthless; commonplace, common, mediocre; flat, tasteless, vapid, insipid; trite, banal

تافهة *tāfiha* pl. توافه *tawāfih*² worthless thing; triviality, trifle

تقاوى see قوى

تقلية see قلى

تقن **IV** to perfect, bring to perfection (ه s.th.); to master, know well (ه s.th., e.g., a language), be proficient, skillful, well-versed (ه in s.th.)

تقن *tiqn* skillful, adroit

تقانة *taqana* firmness, solidity; perfection

اتقن *atqan*² more perfect, more thorough

اتقان *itqān* perfection; thoroughness, exactitude, precision; thorough skill, proficiency; mastery, command (e.g., of a special field, of a language) | فى غاية الاتقان to greatest perfection; of excellent workmanship

متقن *mutqan* perfect; exact, precise

تقى *taqā i* to fear (esp. God) **VIII** see وقى

تقى *taqīy* pl. اتقياء *atqiyā'*² God-fearing, godly, devout, pious

اتقى *atqā* more pious

تقى *tuqan* and تقوى *taqwā* godliness, devoutness, piety

¹تك *takka u* to trample down, trample underfoot, crush (ه s.th.); to intoxicate (ه s.o.; wine)

²تكة *tikka* pl. تكك *tikak* waistband (in the upper seam of the trousers)

³تك *takka* to tick (clock)

تكة *tikka* pl. *-āt* ticking, ticktock (of a clock), ticking noise

⁴تكية look up alphabetically

تكوت *tukūt* pl. of Engl. *ticket*

¹تكتك *taktaka* to trample down, trample underfoot (ه s.th.)

²تكتك *taktaka* to bubble, simmer (boiling mass)

³تكتك *taktaka* to tick (clock)

تكتكة *taktaka* ticking, ticktock (of a clock), ticking noise

⁴تكتيك *taktīk* tactics

تكية *takīya* pl. تكايا *takāyā* monastery (of a Muslim order); hospice; home, asylum (for the invalided or needy)

¹تل *tall* pl. تلال *tilāl*, اتلال *atlāl*, تلول *tulūl* hill, elevation | تل ابيب *t. abīb* Tel Aviv (city in W Israel)

²تل *tull* tulle

تلاتل *talātil*² hardships, troubles, adversities

تليد *talīd*, تالد *tālid*, تلاد *tilād* inherited, time-honored, old (possession, property)

تلسكوب *tiliskūb* telescope

تلع IV to stretch one's neck; to crane (ه the neck)

تلعة *tal'a* pl. تلاع *tilā'* hill, hillside, mountainside; (torrential) stream

تليع *talī'* long, outstretched, extended; high, tall

تلغراف *tiliğrāf*, *taliğrāf* pl. *-āt* telegraph; telegram, wire, cable | ارسل تلغرافا الى to send a wire to

تلغرافى *tiliğrāfī*, *taliğrāfī* elegraphic

تلف *talifa a* (*talaf*) to be annihilated, be destroyed; to be or become damaged or spoiled, be ruined, break, get broken, go to pieces II to ruin (ه s.th.); to wear out, "finish" (ه s.o.) IV to destroy, annihilate (ه s.th.); to ruin, damage, spoil, break (ه s.th.); to waste (ه s.th.)

تلف *talaf* ruin, destruction; ruination, damage, injury, harm; loss; waste

تلفان *talfān* spoiled; useless, worthless, good-for-nothing

متلف *matlaf*, متلفة *matlafa* pl. متالف *matālif*² desert

متلاف *mitlāf* wastrel; ruinous, harmful, injurious

اتلاف *itlāf* pl. *-āt* annihilation, destruction; damage, injury, harm

تالف *tālif* ruined, damaged, broken; spoiled, bad

متلوف *matlūf* and متلف *mutlaf* ruined, damaged, broken; spoiled, bad

متلف *mutlif* annihilator, destroyer; injurer; damaging, ruinous, harmful, injurious, noxious

تلفز *talfaza* to televise, transmit by television

تلفزة *talfaza* television

اذاعة تلفزية *iḏā'a talfazīya* television broadcast, telecast

○ تلفاز *tilfāz* television set

تلفزيون (Fr. *télévision*) *tilivisyōn* television

تلفن *talfana* to telephone

تلفون *tilifūn* and تليفون *talīfūn* pl. *-āt* telephone

تلقاء see لقى

تلك *tilka* fem. of the demonstrative pronoun ذلك

تلم *talam* pl. اتلام *atlām* (plow) furrow

تلمذ *talmaḏa* to take on as, or have for, a pupil or apprentice (ه s.o.); to be or become a pupil or apprentice (ل of s.o., also (على), receive one's schooling or training (على, ل from) II *tatalmaḏa* to be or become a pupil or apprentice (ل or على يده of s.o.), work as an apprentice (ل or على يده under s.o.)

تلمذة *talmaḏa* school days, college years; apprenticeship; (time of) probation

تلماذ *tilmāḏ* learning, erudition

تلميذ *tilmīḏ* pl. تلاميذ *talāmīḏ*², تلامذة *talāmiḏa* pupil, student, apprentice; probationer; trainee; disciple | تلميذ بحرى (*baḥrī*) approx.: chief warrant W-3 (naval rank; *Eg.*); تلميذ سفرى (*safarī*) approx.: chief warrant W-4 (naval rank; *Eg.*)

تلميذة *tilmīḏa* pl. *-āt* girl student

تلمسان *tilimsān*² Tlemcen (city in NW Algeria)

تلمود *talmūd* Talmud

تله *taliha a* (*talah*) to be astonished, amazed, perplexed, at a loss

تاله *tālih* and متله *mutallah* at a loss, bewildered, perplexed | تاله العقل *t. al-ʿaql* absent-minded, distracted

تلا (تلو) *talā u* (تلو *tulūw*) to follow, succeed; to ensue; — (تلاوة *tilāwa*) to read, read out loud (ه s.th., على to s.o.); to recite (ه s.th.) VI to follow one another, be successive

تلو *tilwa* (prep.) after, upon | ارسل كتابا تلو كتاب to send letter after letter

تلاوة *tilāwa* reading; public reading; recital, recitation

تال *tālin* following, succeeding, subsequent, next; بالتالى *bi-t-tālī* then, later, subsequently; consequently, hence, therefore, accordingly

متتال *mutatālin* successive, consecutive

تل *tallī* (*tun.*) tulle

تليباثى *tilībāṯī* telepathy; telepathic

تليس *tallīs*, *tillīs* pl. تلاليس *talālīs*² sack

تليفزيون (Fr. *télévision*) *tilīvisyōn* television

تليفون pl. *-āt talīfūn* telephone

تليفونى *talīfūnī* telephonic, telephone- (in compounds)

تم *tamma i* to be or become complete, completed, finished, done; to be performed, be accomplished (ل by s.o.); to come to an end, be or become terminated; to come about, be brought about, be effected, be achieved, come to pass, come off, happen, take place, be or become a fact; to be on hand, be there, present itself; to persist (على in); to continue (على s.th. or to do s.th.) II and IV to complete, finish, wind up, conclude, terminate (ه s.th.); to make complete, supplement, round out, fill up (ه s.th.); to carry out, execute, perform, accomplish, achieve (ه s.th.) X to be complete, completed, finished

تمام *tamām* completeness, wholeness, entirety, perfection; full, whole, entire, complete, perfect; separate, independent; تماما *tamāman* completely, entirely, wholly, perfectly, fully, quite; precisely, exactly | بدر تمام (*badr*) and قمر تمام (*qamar*) full moon; فى تمام الساعة السادسة at 6 o'clock sharp; بتمام معنى الكلمة (*maʿnā l-kalima*) in the full sense of the word; بالتمام entirely, completely

تميمة *tamīma* pl. تمائم *tamāʾim*² amulet

اتم *atamm*² more complete, more perfect

تتمة *tatimma* completion; supplementation; supplement

تتميم *tatmīm* completion; perfection; consummation, execution, fulfillment, realization, effectuation, accomplishment

اتمام *itmām* completion; perfection; termination, conclusion; consummation, execution, fulfillment, realization, effectuation, accomplishment

استتمام *istitmām* termination, conclusion

تام *tāmm* complete, perfect, entire; consummate; of full value, sterling, genuine

تمباك *tumbāk* Persian tobacco (esp. for the narghile)

تمتم *tamtama* to stammer, mumble, mutter; to recite under one's breath (ب s.th.)

تمر *tamr* (coll.; n. un. ة, pl. *tamarāt*, تمور *tumūr*) dates, esp. dried ones | تمر هندى (*hindī*) tamarind (*bot.*)

تمرجى (*eg. tamargī*), تومرجى ,تيمارجى ,تمورجى pl. *-ya* male nurse, hospital attendant; تمرجية pl. *-āt* female nurse

تموز look up alphabetically

تمساح *timsāḥ* pl. تماسيح *tamāsīḥ*[2] crocodile

تمغة *tamğa* stamp; stamp mark | ورق تمغة *waraq t.* stamped paper

تمن *tumman* rice

تموز *tammūz*[2] July (*Syr.*, *Ir.*, *Leb.*, *Jord.*)

تن[1] *tunn* tuna (*zool.*)

تنين[2] *tinnīn* pl. تنانين *tanānīn*[2] sea monster; Draco (*astron.*); waterspout (*meteor.*); see also alphabetically

تانئ *tāni'* pl. تناء *tunnā'* resident

تنباك *tunbāk* (pronounced *tumbāk*) and تنبك *tumbak* Persian tobacco (esp. for the narghile)

تنبال *tinbāl* pl. تنابيل *tanābīl*[2] short, of small stature

تنبر (Fr. *timbre*) *tambar* pl. تنابر *tanābir*[2] stamp (*magr.*)

متنبر *mutambar* stamped (*magr.*)

تنبل (Turk. *tembel*) *tambal* pl. تنابلة *tanābila* lazy

تنجستين (Fr. *tungstène*) *tongəstēn* tungsten

تندة (It. *tenda*) *tanda* awning; roofing, sun roof

تنور *tannūr* pl. تنانير *tanānīr*[2] a kind of baking oven, a pit, usually clay-lined, for baking bread

تنورة *tannūra* (*syr.*, *leb.*) (lady's) skirt

تنس tennis

تنك[1] *tanak* tin plate

تنكجى *tanakjī* tinsmith, whitesmith

تنكة *tanaka* pl. *-āt* tin container, can, pot; jerry can

تانك[2] *tānika* see تاك alphabetically

تنيس tennis

تنين *tannīn* tannin, tannic acid

تهته *tahtaha* to stammer, stutter

تهمة[1] *tuhma* pl. تهم *tuham* accusation, charge; suspicion; insinuation

تهامة[2] *tihāma*[2] Tihama, coastal plain along the southwestern and southern shores of the Arabian Peninsula

توا *tawwan* right away, at once, immediately; just (now), this very minute | للتو *li-t-tawwi* at once, right away, also with pers. suffixes: لتوى *li-tawwī*, لتوها *li-tawwihā* (I have, she has) just ...; at once, presently, immediately

تواليت (Fr. *toilette*) *tuwālēt* toilette

توأم see تأم

(توب) تاب *tāba u* (توب *taub*, توبة *tauba*, متاب *matāb*) to repent, be penitent, do penance; with عن: to turn from (sin), be converted from, renounce, forswear s.th.; (said of God) to restore to His grace, forgive (على s.o.) | تاب الى الله to turn to God in repentance **II** to induce to repentance or penitence, make repent (ه s.o.) **X** to call on s.o. (ه) to repent

توبة *tauba* repentance, penitence, contrition; penance

توّاب *tawwāb* doing penance; repentant, penitent, contrite; forgiving, merciful (God)

تائب *tā'ib* repentant, penitent, contrite

توبل see تبل

توبوغرافيا *tobоğrāfiyā* topography

توت[1] *tūt* mulberry tree; mulberry | توت ارضى (*arḍī*) and توت افرنجى (*ifranjī*) strawberry; توت شوكى (*šaukī*) and توت العليق *t. al-'ullaiq* raspberry

توت[2] *tūt* the first month of the Coptic calendar

توتيا *tūtiyā*, توتياء *tūtiyā'*, توتية *tūtiya* zinc

توج II to crown (ه s.o.; also fig. ه ب s.th. with) V to be crowned

تاج *tāj* pl. تيجان *tījān* crown; miter (of a bishop) | تاج العمود *t. al-'amūd* capital (of a column or pilaster); تاج الكرة *t. al-kura* calotte

تويج *tuwaij* little crown, coronet

تتويج *tatwīj* crowning, coronation

توجو *tōgo* and توجولند *tōgōland* (Eg. spelling) Togo (region in W Africa)

(توح) تاح see تيح

تارة *tāratan* once; sometimes, at times | تارة — اخرى (*tauran*), تارة — طورا ,تارة — تارة (*ukrā*) sometimes — sometimes, at times — at other times

توراة *taurāh* Torah, Pentateuch; Old Testament

توربيد, تورپيد *turpīd*, *turbīd* torpedo (submarine missile)

توربين *turbīn* pl. *-āt* turbine

تورتة *torta* pl. *-āt* pie, tart

(توق) تاق *tāqa u* (*tauq*, توقان *tawaqān*) to long, yearn, wish (الى for), hanker (الى after), desire, crave, covet (الى s.th.), strive (الى for), aspire (الى to)

توق *tauq*, توقان *tawaqān* longing, yearning, craving, desire

تواق *tawwāq* longing, yearning, eager (الى for), craving (الى s.th.)

تائق *tā'iq* longing, yearning, eager (الى for), craving (الى s.th.)

توكة امامية (*tōka amāmīya; eg.*) belt buckle (*mil.*)

تول *tūl* tulle

تومرجى see تمرجى

تون *tūn* and تونة *tūna* tuna (*zool.*)

تونج (Turk. *tunç*) *tunj* bronze

تونس *tūnus*[2], *tūnis*[2] Tunis

تونسى *tūnisī* pl. *-ūn*, توانسة *tawānisa* Tunisian (adj. and n.)

تونية *tūniya* pl. توانى *tawānī* alb of priests and deacons (*Chr.*)

(توه) تاه *tāha u* and II = (تيه) تاه *tāha i* and II

توهة *tūha* daughter

تياترو (It. *teatro*) *tiyātrō* theater

تيتل *taital* pl. تياتل see ثيتل □

تيتانوس *titānūs* tetanus (*med.*)

(تيح) تاح *tāḥa i* to be destined, be foreordained (by fate, by God; ل to s.o.); to be granted, be given (ل to s.o.) IV to destine, foreordain (ه ل to s.o. s.th.); to grant, afford, offer (ه ل s.o. s.th.); pass. *utīḥa* to be destined, be foreordained, be granted, be given (ل to s.o.) | اتيح له التوفيق (*utīḥa*) he met with success, he was successful; اتيح له الفرصة (*furṣa*) he was given the opportunity, he had the chance

تيار *tayyār* pl. *-āt* flow, stream, course, current, flood; fall (of a stream); movement, tendency, trend; draft (of air); (*el.*) current | تيار مباشر ○ (*mubāšir*) and تيار مستمر (*mustamirr*) direct current; ○ تيار متناوب (*mutanāwib*) and ○ تيار متغير (*mutağayyir*) alternating current; ○ تيار متذبذب (*mutaḏabḏib*) oscillating current (*el.*); ○ تيار نابض (*nābiḍ*) pulsating current;

○ تيار سريع التردد (*sarī' at-taraddud*) high-frequency current; ○ تيار بطيء التردد (*baṭī' at-taraddud*) low-frequency current; ○ تيار عالى الجهد (*'ālī l-jahd*) high-tension current; ○ تيار واطئ الجهد (*wāṭi' al-jahd*) low-tension current; ○ تيار ذاتى (*ḏātī*) self-induced current

○ متار *matār* (*syr.*) dynamo, generator

تيزه (Turk. *teyze*) *tēza* maternal aunt

تيس *tais* pl. اتياس *atyās*, تيوس *tuyūs* billy goat

اتيس *atyas*[2] foolish, crazy

الحمى التيفودية *al-ḥummā t-tīfūdīya* typhoid fever

تيفوس *tīfūs* typhus

تيك *tīka* fem. of the demonstrative pronoun ذاك *ḏāka*

[1]تيل II (from Turk. *tel*) to cable, wire, telegraph (*syr.*)

[2]تيل *tīl* hemp; linen

[3]تيلة *tīla* fiber, staple

[1](تيم) تام *tāma i* (*taim*) to become enslaved, enthralled by love; to enslave, make blindly subservient (ه s.o.; through love) II to enslave, enthral (love; ه s.o.); to make blindly subservient, drive out of his mind, infatuate (ه s.o.; love)

متيم *mutayyam* enslaved, enthralled (by love), infatuated

[2]تيماء *taimā'*[2] Taima (oasis in NW Arabia)

تمرجى see تيمارجى

تين *tīn* (coll.; n. un. ة) fig | تين شوكى (*šaukī*) fruit of the Indian fig (Opuntia ficus-indica Haw.)

تينك *tainika* see تاك alphabetically

(تيه) تاه *tāha i* to get lost, wander about, lose one's way, go astray; to stray, wander (thoughts); to escape (من s.o.), slip (من s.o.'s memory); to perish, be destroyed, be lost; to be perplexed, startled, astonished; to be haughty; to swagger, boast, brag (على to s.o.) | تيه على وجهه ابتسامة a smile flits over his face II to mislead, lead astray (ه s.o.); to distract, divert (ه s.o.); to confuse, confound, bewilder (ه s.o.) IV = II

تيه *tīh* desert, trackless wilderness; maze, labyrinth; haughtiness, pride

تياه *tayyāh* straying, stray, wandering; haughty

تيهان *taihān*[2] straying, stray, wandering; perplexed, at a loss, bewildered; proud, haughty

تيهاء *taihā'*[2] and متاهة *matāha* a trackless, desolate region; متاهة maze, labyrinth

تائه *tā'ih* straying, stray, wandering, roving, errant; lost in thought, distracted, absent-minded; lost, forlorn; infinite; haughty

تيوليب (Engl.) tulip

ث

ث abbreviation of ثانية second (time unit)

ثاء *ṯā'* name of the letter ث

ثئب *ṯa'iba a* (ثأب *ṯa'b*) and VI to yawn

ثؤباء *ṯu'abā'*[2] yawning, yawn; fatigue, weariness

ثأر *ṯa'ara a* (*ṯa'r*) to avenge the blood of (ه or ب), take blood revenge (ه or ب for s.o. killed), take vengeance, avenge o.s. (ب ه on s.o. for, also من or ل for) **IV** and **VIII** اثأر *itta'ara* to get one's revenge, be avenged

ثأر *ta'r* pl. *-āt*, اثآر *at'ār*, آثار *āṯār* revenge, vengeance, blood revenge; retaliation, reprisal | اخذ بالثأر or اخذ ثأره to take revenge, avenge o.s.; مباراة الثأر *mubārāt at-t.* return match (sports)

ثائر *ṯā'ir* avenger

ثؤلول *ṯu'lūl* and ثؤلولة *ṯu'lūla* pl. ثآليل *ṯa'ālīl*² wart

ثأى *ṯa'ā* scars

ثبت *ṯabata u* (ثبات *ṯabāt*, ثبوت *ṯubūt*) to stand firm, be fixed, stationary, immovable, unshakable, firm, strong, stable; to hold out, hold one's ground (ل against s.o. or s.th.), be firm, remain firm (ل toward s.o. or s.th.), withstand, resist, defy (ل s.o. or s.th.); to be established, be proven (fact); to remain, stay (ب at a place); to maintain (على s.th.), keep, stick, adhere (على to s.th.), abide or stand by s.th. (على; e.g., by an agreement); to insist (على on) | ثبت فى وجهه (*fī wajhihī*) to hold one's own against s.o., assert o.s. against s.o. **II** to fasten, make fast, fix (ه s.th.); to consolidate, strengthen (ه s.th.); to stabilize (ه s.th.); to confirm, corroborate, substantiate (ه s.th.); to appoint permanently (ه s.o.; to an office); to prove, establish (ه s.th.), demonstrate, show (بأن that); to prove guilty, convict (على a defendant); to confirm (*Chr.*) | ثبت بصره به (*baṣarahū*) to fix one's eyes on, gaze at; ثبت قدميه (*qadamaihi*) to gain a foothold **IV** to establish, determine (ه s.th.); to assert as valid or authentic, affirm (ه s.th.); to confirm, corroborate, substantiate (ه s.th.); to prove (ه على s.th. to s.o.; ل to s.o., ان that); to demonstrate, show (ه s.th.); to furnish competent evidence (ه for); to bear witness, attest (ه to); to acknowledge (ه s.th., e.g., a qualification, a quality, ل in s.o.), concede (ه ل s.th. to s.o.); to prove guilty, convict (على a defendant); to enter, record, register, list (ه فى s.th. in a book, in a roster, etc.) | اثبته فى الورق (*waraq*) to put s.th. down in writing, get s.th. on paper; اثبت الشخص (*šaḵṣa*) to determine s.o.'s identity, identify s.o.; اثبت شخصيته (*šaḵṣīyatahū*) to identify o.s., prove one's identity **V** to ascertain, verify (فى s.th., هل if), make sure (فى of s.th., هل if); to consider carefully (فى s.th.), proceed with caution (فى in) **X** to show o.s. steadfast, persevering; to seek to verify (ه s.th.), try to make sure (ه of), seek confirmation of or reassurance with regard to (ه); to ascertain, verify (ه s.th.), make sure (ه of s.th.); to find right, proven or true, see confirmed (ه s.th.); to regard as authentic (ه s.th.)

ثبت *ṯabt* firm, fixed, established; steadfast, unflinching; brave

ثبت *ṯabat* reliable, trustworthy, credible

ثبت *ṯabat* pl. اثبات *aṯbāt* list, index, roster

ثبات *ṯabāt* firmness; steadiness, constancy, permanence, stability; certainty, sureness; perseverance, persistence, endurance; continuance, maintenance, retention (على of s.th.), adherence (على to)

ثبوت *ṯubūt* constancy, immutability, steadiness; permanence, durability; certainty, sureness | ثبوت الشهر *ṯ. aš-šahr* the official determination of the beginning of a lunar month

اثبت *aṯbat*² more reliable, firmer, steadier, etc.

تثبيت *taṯbīt* consolidation, strengthening; stabilization; confirmation; corroboration, substantiation | سر التثبيت *sirr at-t.* the Sacrament of Confirmation (*Chr.*)

اثبات *iṯbāt* establishment; assertion; confirmation; affirmation, attestation; demonstration; proof, evidence; registration, entering, listing, recording; documentation, authentication, verification | شاهد اثبات witness for the prosecution; عبء الاثبات *'ib' al-i.* burden of proof (*jur.*)

اثباتى *iṯbātī* affirmative, confirmatory, corroborative, positive

تثبت *taṯabbut* ascertainment; verification, examination, check; careful, cautious procedure, circumspection; interment (of the remains of a saint; *Chr.*)

ثابت *ṯābit* firm, fixed, established; stationary, immovable; steady, invariable, constant, stable; permanent, lasting, durable, enduring; confirmed, proven; a constant | ثابت الجأش *ṯ. al-ja'š* undismayed, fearless, staunch, steadfast; ثابت العزم *ṯ. al-'azm* firmly resolved, determined; املاك ثابتة and اموال ثابتة immovable property, real estate, realty; ○ ثابت الاتجاه *ṯ. al-ittijāh* unidirectional, rectified (*el.*)

ثابتة *ṯābita* pl. ثوابت *ṯawābit*² fixed star

مثبوت *maṯbūt* established, confirmed; certain, sure, positive, assured; proven

ثبر *ṯabara* *u* to destroy, ruin (ه s.o.); (ثبور *ṯubūr*) to perish III to apply o.s. with zeal and perseverance (على to s.th.), persevere, persist (على in)

ثبور *ṯubūr* ruin, destruction | نادى (دعا or) بالويل والثبور *nādā* (*da'ā*) *bi-l-wail wa-ṯ-ṯ.* to wail, burst into loud laments

مثابرة *muṯābara* persistence, perseverance, endurance; diligence, assiduity

ثبط *ṯabaṭa* *u* and II to hold back, keep, prevent (ه عن s.o. from doing s.th.); to hinder, handicap, impede, slow down, set back (ه, ه s.o., s.th.); to bring about the failure (ه of s.th.), frustrate (ه s.th.)

ثبنة *ṯubna* pl. ثبن *ṯuban* lap, fold of a garment (used as a receptacle)

ثبان *ṯibān* = ثبنة *ṯubna*

ثيتل look up alphabetically

ثج *ṯajja* *u* to flow copiously

ثجاج *ṯajjāj* copiously flowing, streaming

ثخن *ṯakuna* *u* to be or become thick, thicken; to be firm, solid, compact IV to wear out, exhaust, weaken (ه s.o.) | اثخنه ضربا (*ḍarban*) to wallop s.o., give s.o. a sound thrashing; اثخن فى العدو (*'adūw*) to massacre the enemy; اثخنه بالجراح to weaken s.o. by inflicting wounds

ثخن *ṯikan*, ثخانة *ṯakāna*, ثخونة *ṯukūna* thickness, density; consistency; compactness

ثخين *ṯakīn* pl. ثخناء *ṯukanā'*² thick; dense

ثدى *ṯady* and *ṯadan* m. and f., pl. اثداء *aṯdā'* female breast; udder

ثر *ṯarr* abounding in water | ثرة من الدمع (*dam'*) tear-wet, tear-blurred (eye)

ثرب *ṯaraba* *i* (*ṯarb*) and II to blame, censure (ه and على s.o.)

تثريب *taṯrīb* blame, censure, reproof

ثرثر *ṯarṯara* (ثرثرة *ṯarṯara*) to chatter, prattle

ثرثار *ṯarṯār* prattler, chatterbox; ثرثارة *ṯarṯāra* do. (fem.)

ثرثرة *ṯarṯara* chatter, prattle

ثرد *ṯarada* *u* to crumble and sop (ه bread)

ثريد *ṯarīd* a dish of sopped bread, meat and broth

مثرد *miṯrad* bowl

ثرم *ṯarama* *i* (*ṯarm*) to knock s.o.'s (ه) tooth out; — *ṯarima* *a* (*ṯaram*) to have a gap between two teeth

ثرى (ثرو and ثرى) *ṯariya* *a* to become wealthy IV to become or be rich, wealthy (ب or من through s.th.); to make rich, enrich (ه s.o.)

ثرى *ṯaran* moist earth; ground, soil | اين الثرى من الثريا *aina ṯ-ṯ. min aṯ-ṯurayyā* (proverbially of things of disproportionate value) what has the ground to do with the Pleiades? طيب الله ثراه (*ṭayyaba*) approx.: may God rest him in peace!

ثرى *ṯarīy* pl. اثرياء *aṯriyā'*[2] wealthy, rich | ثرى الحرب *ṯ. al-ḥarb* war profiteer, nouveau riche

ثريات *ṯarīyāt* plantations

ثروة *ṯarwa* and ثراء *ṯarā'* fortune, wealth, riches | اهل الثروة *ahl aṯ-ṯ.* the rich, the wealthy; ثروة قومية (*qaumīya*) national wealth; ثروة مائية (*mā'īya*) abundance of water, abundant supply of water (of a region)

ثريا *ṯurayyā* Pleiades; (also ثرية) pl. ثريات *ṯurayyāt* chandelier

مثر *muṯrin* wealthy, rich

ثعبان *ṯu'bān* pl. ثعابين *ṯa'ābīn*[2] snake | ثعبان الماء *ṯ. al-mā'* eel

ثعبانى *ṯu'bānī* snaky, snakelike, serpentine; eely

مثعب *maṯ'ab* pl. مثاعب *maṯā'ib*[2] drain

ثعالة *ṯu'āla* fox

ثعلب *ṯa'lab* pl. ثعالب *ṯa'ālib*[2] fox | داء الثعلب alopecia (*med.*), loss of hair

ثعلبي *ṯa'labī* foxy, foxlike

ثعلبة *ṯa'laba* vixen; ○ tetter (*med.*)

ثغر *ṯaġr* pl. ثغور *ṯuġūr* front tooth; mouth; port, harbor, inlet, bay; seaport

ثغرة *ṯuġra* pl. ثغر *ṯuġar* breach, crevasse, crack, rift, crevice; opening, gap; cavity, hollow; narrow mountain trail

ثغام *ṯaġām* white, whiteness

ثاغم *ṯāġim* white (adj.)

ثغا (ثغو) *ṯaġā u* (ثغاء *ṯuġā'*) to bleat (sheep)

ثغاء *ṯuġā'* bleating, bleat

ثاغ *ṯāġin* bleating | ما له ثاغية ولا راغية (*rāġiya*) he has absolutely nothing, he is deprived of all resources, prop.: he has neither a bleating (sheep) nor a braying (camel)

ثفر *ṯafar* pl. اثفار *aṯfār* crupper (of the saddle)

ثفل *ṯufl* dregs, lees, sediment; residues

ثفن III to associate (ه with s.o.), frequent s.o.'s (ه) company; to pursue, practice (ه s.th.)

ثفنة *ṯafina* pl. *-āt*, ثفن *ṯifan* callus, callosity

اثفية look up alphabetically

ثقة see وثق

ثقب *ṯaqaba u* (*ṯaqb*) to bore, or drill, a hole (ه in s.th.), pierce, puncture, perforate (ه s.th.) II do. II and IV to light, kindle (ه s.th.) V and VII to be pierced, be punctured, be perforated

ثقب *ṯaqb* piercing, boring, puncture, perforation; (also *ṯuqb* pl. ثقوب *ṯuqūb*, اثقاب *aṯqāb*) hole, puncture, borehole, drill hole

ثقبة *ṯuqba* pl. ثقب *ṯuqab* hole

ثقاب and عود الثقاب *'ūd aṯ-ṯiqāb* matchstick; matches

ثقوب *ṯuqūb* keenness, acuteness (of the mind)

مثقب *miṯqab* pl. مثاقب *maṯāqib*[2] borer, drill, gimlet, auger, brace and bit, wimble, perforator; drilling machine

اثقاب *iṯqāb* kindling, lighting

ثاقب *ṯāqib* penetrating, piercing, sharp (mind, eyes) | ثاقب النظر *ṯ. an-naẓar* perspicacity; sharp-eyed; ثاقب الفكر *ṯ. al-fikr* sagacity, acumen, mental acuteness; shrewd, sagacious, sharp-witted

ثاقبات *ṯāqibāt* borers (*zool.*)

ثقف *ṯaqifa a* (*ṯaqf*) to find, meet (ه s.o.); — *ṯaqifa a* and *ṯaqufa u* to be skillful, smart, clever II to make straight, straighten (ه s.th.); to correct, set right, straighten out (ه s.th.); to train, form, teach, educate (ه s.o.); to arrest (ه s.o.); to seize, confiscate (ه s.th.) III to fence (ه with s.o.) V to be trained, be educated

ثقافة *ṯaqāfa* culture, refinement; education; (pl. -*āt*) culture, civilization

ثقافي *ṯaqāfī* educational; intellectual; cultural | ملحق ثقاف (*mulḥaq*) cultural attaché

تثقيف *taṯqīf* cultivation of the mind; training, education; instruction

مثاقفة *muṯāqafa* fencing, art or sport of fencing, swordplay, swordsmanship

تثقف *taṯaqquf* culturedness, culture, refinement, education

مثقف *muṯaqqaf* educated; trained; cultured

ثقل *ṯaqula u* (*ṯiql*, ثقالة *ṯaqāla*) to be heavy; with ب: to load or burden s.th., make s.th. heavy; to be hard to bear (على for s.o.), weigh heavily (على on), be burdensome, cumbersome, oppressive (على to s.o.); to be heavy-handed, sluggish, doltish, dull-witted; to be too dull, too sluggish (عن for s.th., to do s.th.), not to bother (عن about) II to make heavy, weight (ه s.th.); to burden, encumber (على s.o., ه with s.th.), overburden (على s.o.), overtax s.o.'s (على) strength, ask too much (على of s.o.); to trouble, inconvenience, bother (ب s.o., ب with s.th.), pester, molest (على s.o.) and ثقل كاهله and اثقل كاهله (*kāhilahū*) to burden s.o. or s.th.; ثقل كاهل المزان to burden the budget IV to burden (ه s.o., ه s.th.); to oppress, distress (ه s.o.), weigh heavily (ه on); to be hard to bear (ه for s.o.) | اثقل كاهله (*kāhilahū*) see II; VI to become or be heavy; to be troublesome, burdensome

(على to s.o.), trouble, oppress (على s.o.); to be sluggish, doltish, slow; to be in a bad mood, be sullen, grumpy; to find burdensome and turn away (عن from s.th.); not to bother (عن about); to be too dull, too sluggish (عن for s.th., to do s.th.) X to find heavy, hard, burdensome, troublesome (ه s.th.), find annoying (ه, ه s.o., s.th.) | استثقل ظله (*ẓillahū*) to find s.o. unbearable, dislike s.o.

ثقل *ṯiql* pl. اثقال *aṯqāl* weight; burden, load; gravity; heaviness | رفع الاثقال *raf' al-a.* weight lifting (*athlet.*); الثقل النوعى (*nau'ī*) specific gravity

ثقل *ṯiqal* heaviness; sluggishness, dullness

ثقل *ṯaqal* pl. اثقال *aṯqāl* load, baggage

الثقلان *aṯ-ṯaqalān* the humans and the jinn

ثقلة *ṯaqla* trouble, inconvenience, discomfort

ثقالة *ṯaqāla* heaviness; sluggishness, doltishness; dullness

ثقيل *ṯaqīl* pl. ثقلاء *ṯuqalā'²*, ثقال *ṯiqāl* heavy; weighty, momentous, grave, serious, important; burdensome, troublesome, cumbersome, oppressive; unpleasant, disagreeable, distasteful (person) | ثقيل الدم *ṯ. ad-dam* insufferable, unpleasant, disagreeable (person); ثقيل الروح *ṯ. ar-rūḥ* doltish, dull (person); a bore; ثقيل الظل *ṯ. aẓ-ẓill* disagreeable, insufferable (person); ثقيل الفهم *ṯ. al-fahm* slow of understanding, slow-witted; ثقيل السمع *ṯ. as-sam'* hard of hearing; صناعة ثقيلة (*ṣinā'a*) heavy industry; ماء ثقيل heavy water (*phys.*)

اثقل *aṯqal²* heavier; more oppressive

مثقال *miṯqāl* pl. مثاقيل *maṯāqīl²* weight (also s.th. placed as an equipoise on the scales of a balance); miskal, a weight (in Egypt = 24 قراط = 4.68 g) | مثقال ذرة *m.*

ḏarra the weight of a dust speck, i.e., a tiny amount; a little bit; مثقال من a little of, a little bit of

تثقيل *taṯqīl* weighting, burdening; molestation

تثاقل *taṯāqul* sluggishness, dullness

مثقل *muṯaqqal* and *muṯqal* burdened, encumbered; overloaded; weighted (ب with s.th.); oppressed (ب by); heavy

متثاقل *mutaṯāqil* sluggish, dull; sullen, grumpy

ثكل **ṯakila** *a* (*ṯakal*) to lose a child (ه), also: to be bereaved of a loved one (ه) by death **IV** اثكل الام ولدها *aṯkala l-umma waladahā* to bereave a mother of her son

ثكل *ṯakal* state of one who has lost a friend or relative; mourning over the loss of a loved one

ثكلان *ṯaklān*(²) bereaved of a child

ثكلى *ṯaklā* bereaved of a child (mother)

ثاكلة *ṯākila* pl. ثواكل *ṯawākil*² bereaved of a child (mother)

ثكنة **ṯukna** pl. ثكن *ṯukan*, *-āt* barracks (*mil.*)

ثل **ṯalla** *u* (ثلل *ṯalal*) to tear down, destroy, overthrow, subvert (ه s.th., esp. عرشا *'aršan* to topple a throne) **VII** to be subverted, overthrown (throne)

ثلة *ṯulla* pl. ثلل *ṯulal* troop, band, party, group (of people); military detachment

ثلب **ṯalaba** *i* (*ṯalb*) to criticize, run down (ه s.o.); to slander, defame (ه s.o.)

ثلب *ṯalb* slander, defamation

مثلبة *maṯlaba* pl. مثالب *maṯālib*² shortcoming, defect, blemish, stain, disgrace

ثالب *ṯālib* slanderous, defamatory; slanderer

ثلث **II** to triple, make threefold (ه s.th.); to do three times (ه s.th.)

ثلث *ṯulṯ* pl. اثلاث *aṯlāṯ* one third; *ṯuluṯ* a sprawling, decorative calligraphic style

ثلاثة *ṯalāṯa* (f. ثلاث *ṯalāṯ*) three; ثلاثا *ṯalāṯan* three times, thrice

ثلاثى *ṯalāṯī* tertiary; Tertiary (*geol.*) | ما قبل الثلاثى pre-Tertiary

ثلاثة عشر *ṯalāṯata 'ašara*, f. ثلاث عشرة *ṯalāṯa 'ašrata* thirteen

الثالث *aṯ-ṯāliṯ* the third; ثالثا *ṯāliṯan* thirdly; ثالثة 1/60 of a second

ثلاثون *ṯalāṯūn* thirty

الثلاثاء *aṯ-ṯalāṯā'* and يوم الثلاثاء *yaum aṯ-ṯ.* Tuesday

ثلاث *ṯulāṯ*² and مثلث *maṯlaṯ*² three at a time

ثلاثى *ṯulāṯī* tripartite, consisting of three, (*gram.*) triliteral, consisting of three radicals; tri-; trio (*mus.*) | ثلاثى الزوايا *ṯ. z-zawāyā* triangular; ثلاثى الورقات *ṯ. l wa raqāt* trifoliate

ثالوث *ṯālūṯ* Trinity (*Chr.*); trinity, triad; triplet | زهرة الثالوث *zahrat aṯ-ṯ.* pansy (*bot.*)

تثليث *taṯlīṯ* doctrine of the Trinity; Trinity (*Chr.*)

تثليثى *taṯlīṯī* trigonometric(al)

مثلث *muṯallaṯ* tripled, triple, threefold; having three diacritical dots (letter); triangular; (pl. *-āt*) triangle (*geom.*) | العلم المثلث (*'alam*) الراية المثلثة الالوان (*rāya*), and المثلث the tricolor; المثلث الحاد (*ḥādd*) acute-angled triangle; مثلث الزوايا *m. az-zawāyā* triangular; المثلث المتساوى الساقين (*mutasāwī s-sāqain*) isosceles triangle; المثلث المتساوى الاضلاع equilateral triangle; المثلث القائم right-angled triangle

المثلثات *al-muṯallaṯāt* and حساب المثلثات *ḥisāb al-m.* trigonometry

ثلج **ṯalaja** *u*: ثلجت السماء (*samā'u*) it snowed, was snowing; — *ṯalija* *a* to be delighted, be gladdened (soul, heart; ب by) **II** to cool with ice (ه s.th.); to freeze, turn into ice (ه s.th.) **IV** اثلجت السماء it snowed, was snowing; to cool, moisten (ه s.th.) | اثلج صدره (*ṣadrahū*) to delight, please, gratify s.o. **V** to become icy, turn into ice, congeal; to freeze

ثلج *ṯalj* pl. ثلوج *ṯulūj* snow; ice; artificial ice | ندفة الثلج *nudfat aṯ-ṯ.* snowflake

ثلجى *ṯaljī* snowy, snow- (in compounds); icy, glacial, ice- (in compounds)

ثلج *ṯalij* icy

ثلاج *ṯallāj* pl. *-ūn* ice vendor

ثلاجة *ṯallāja* pl *-āt* iceberg, ice floe; refrigerator, icebox

مثلجة *maṯlaja* pl. مثالج *maṯālij*[2] icebox, refrigerator; cold-storage plant

مثلوج *maṯlūj* snow-covered; iced, icy; مثلوجات frozen food; iced beverages

مثلج *muṯallaj* iced; icy, ice-cold

ثلم **ṯalama** *i* (*ṯalm*) to blunt, make jagged (ه s.th.), break the edge of (ه); to make a breach, gap or opening (ه in a wall); to defile, sully (ه reputation, honor); — *ṯalima a* to be or become jagged, dull, blunt **II** to blunt (ه s.th.) **V** to become blunt **VII** to be defiled, be discredited (reputation)

ثلم *ṯalm* nick, notch; breach, opening, gap; crack, fissure, rift | ثلم الصيت *ṯ. aṣ-ṣīt* defamation

ثلمة *ṯulma* pl. ثلم *ṯulam* = *ṯalm* | سد ثلمة *sadda ṯulmatan* to fill a gap; ثلمة لا تسد (*tusaddu*) a gap that cannot be closed, an irreparable loss

ثالم *ṯālim* dull, blunt

مثلوم *maṯlūm* defiled, sullied (reputation, honor)

متثلم *mutaṯallim* blunted, blunt; cracking (voice)

منثلم الصيت *munṯalim aṣ-ṣīt* of ill repute, of dubious reputation

ثم **ṯamma** there | من ثم *min ṯamma* hence, therefore, for that reason

ثم *ṯumma* then, thereupon; furthermore, moreover; and again, and once more (emphatically in repetition) | كلا ثم كلا (*kallā*) no and a hundred times no! من ثم *min ṯumma* then, thereupon

ثمة *ṯammata* (ثمت) there; there is | ليس ثمة there isn't

ثمام *ṯumām* a grass | على طرف الثمام (*ṭarafi ṯ-ṯ.*) within easy reach, handy; جعله على طرف الثمام he made it readily understandable, he presented it plausibly for all

اثمد look up alphabetically

ثمر **ṯamara** *u* to bear fruit **IV** do. **X** to profit, benefit (ه from); to exploit, utilize (ه s.th.); to invest profitably (ه money)

ثمر *ṯamar* pl. ثمار *ṯimār*, اثمار *aṯmār* fruits, fruit (coll.); result, effect, fruit, fruitage; yield, profit, benefit, gain

ثمرة *ṯamara* (n. un. of *ṯamar*) pl. *-āt* fruit; result, effect; yield, profit, benefit, gain

استثمار *istiṯmār* exploitation (also *pol.-econ.*), utilization, profitable use

مثمر *muṯmir* fruitful, productive, profitable, lucrative

مستثمر *mustaṯmir* pl. *-ūn* exploiter (*pol.-econ.*); beneficiary

ثمل **ṯamila** *a* (*ṯamal*) to become drunk **IV** to make drunk, intoxicate (ه s.o.)

ثمل *ṯamal* intoxication, drunkenness

ثملة *ṯamala* drunken fit, drunkenness

ثمل *ṯamil* intoxicated, drunk(en)

ثمالة *ṯumāla* residue, remnant, dregs (of a liquid), heeltap (of wine); scum, foam, froth

[1]ثمن II to appraise, assess, estimate (ه s.th.), determine the price or value (ه of s.th.); to price (ه s.th.) | لا يثمن *lā yuṯammanu* invaluable, inestimable, priceless

ثمن *ṯaman* pl. اثمان *aṯmān*, اثمنة *aṯmina* price, cost; value | الثمن الاصلى (*aṣlī*) cost price; الثمن الاساسى (*asāsī*) par, nominal value

ثمين *ṯamīn* costly, precious, valuable

اثمن *aṯman*[2] costlier, more precious, more valuable

تثمين *taṯmīn* estimation, appraisal, assessment, valuation, rating

مثمون *maṯmūn* object of value

مثمن *muṯammin* estimator, appraiser | خبير مثمن assessor

مثمن *muṯamman* prized, valued, valuable, precious

مثمن *muṯmin* costly, precious, valuable

مثمن *muṯman* object of value

[2]ثمانية *ṯamāniya* (f. ثمان *ṯamānin*) eight

ثمانية عشر *ṯamāniyata ʿašara*, f. ثمانى عشرة *ṯamāniya ʿašrata* eighteen

ثمن *ṯumn* pl. اثمان *aṯmān* one-eighth

ثمنة *ṯumna* pl. *-āt* a dry measure (*Eg.* = $^1/_8$ قدح = .258 l; *Pal.* = ca. 2.25 l)

ثمانون *ṯamānūn* eighty

الثامن *aṯ-ṯāmin* the eighth

مثمن *muṯamman* eightfold; octagonal

ثنة *ṯunna* pl. ثنن *ṯunan* fetlock

ثندوة *ṯundu'a*, *ṯunduwa* pl. ثناد *ṯanādin* breast (of the male)

ثنى *ṯanā* i (*ṯany*) to double, double up, fold, fold up, fold under (ه s.th.); to bend, flex (ه s.th.); to turn away, dissuade, keep, prevent, divert (عن ه s.o. from) | ثنى عنان فرسه (*ʿināna farasihī*) he galloped off II to double, make double (ه s.th.); to do twice, repeat (ه s.th.); to pleat, plait (ه s.th.); to form the dual (ه of a word); to provide with two diacritical dots (ه a letter) IV to commend, praise, laud, extol (على s.th., s.o.), speak appreciatively (على of) | اثنى عليه عاطر الثناء (*ʿāṭira ṯ-ṯanā'*) to speak in the most laudatory terms of s.o. V to double, become double; to be doubled; to be repeated; to bend, fold; to be bent, be folded, be folded up or under; to walk with a swinging gait VII to bend, bend up, down or over, lean, incline, bow; to fold, be foldable, be folded back; to turn away (عن from), give up, renounce (عن s.th.); to turn, face (الى toward); to apply o.s., turn (الى to s.th.); (with foll. imperf.) to set out, prepare (to do s.th.) X to except, exclude (من ه or ه s th. or s.o. from), make an exception (ه of s.th.)

ثنى *ṯany* bending; folding; turning away, dissuasion, keeping, prevention

ثنى *ṯiny* pl. اثناء *aṯnā'* fold, pleat, plait, crease (in cloth); bend, twist | ثنيا بعد ثنى *ṯinyan baʿda ṯinyin* from time to time

اثناء *aṯnā'a* (prep.) during; in the course of | فى اثناء *fī aṯnā'i* do.; فى اثناء ذلك, فى تلك الاثناء, فى هذه الاثناء in the meantime, during all this time, meanwhile

ثنية *ṯanya* pl. *ṯanayāt* fold, pleat, plait, crease (in cloth)

ثنية *ṯaniya* pl. ثنايا *ṯanāyā* middle incisor; narrow pass; mountain trail | فى ثنايا in, inside, among, between, frequently only a fuller, rhetorically more elegant expression for "in", e.g., فى ثنايا نفسه in his heart, inwardly, فى ثنايا الكتب in the books; بين ثنايا in, inside, among, between; طلاع الثنايا *ṭallāʿ aṯ-ṯ.* one with high-flung aspirations

ثناء *ṯanā'* commendation, praise, eulogy; appreciation

ثناء *ṯunā'*[2] and مثنى *maṯnā* two at a time

ثنوى *ṯanawī* dualist

ثنوية *ṯanawīya* dualism

ثنائى *ṯanā'ī* laudatory, eulogistic

ثنائى *ṯunā'ī* twofold, double, dual, binary, bi-; biradical (*gram.*); duet, duo (*mus.*) | محرك ثنائى المشوار (*muḥarrik ṯ. l-mišwār*) two-cycle engine

○ ثنائية *ṯunā'īya* dualism; duet, duo (*mus.*)

اثنان *iṯnāni*, f. اثنتان *iṯnatāni* two

اثنا عشر *iṯnā 'ašara*, f. اثنتا عشرة *iṯnatā 'ašrata* twelve

يوم الاثنين *yaum al-iṯnain* and الاثنين Monday

الثانى *aṯ-ṯānī* the second; the next; ثانيا *ṯāniyan* and ثانية *ṯāniyatan* secondly; for the second time, once more, again | ثانى اثنين *ṯ. ṯnain* the second of a pair, pendant, companion piece, match

ثانية *ṯāniya* pl. ثوان *ṯawānin* second (time unit)

ثانوى *ṯānawī* secondary; minor | امور ثانوية matters of secondary importance, minor matters; مدرسة ثانوية secondary school; تسويغ ثانوى subletting

تثنية *taṯniya* repetition; plaiting, pleating; doubling, gemination; (*gram.*) dual; second sequel (e.g., of a collection of short stories); commendation, praise, eulogy | تثنية الاشتراع Deuteronomy

انثناء *inṯinā'* bending, flection; flexibility, foldability | قابل للانثناء foldable, folding

انثناءة *inṯinā'a* pl. *-āt* (n. vic.) bend, flexure, curve

استثناء *istiṯnā'* exception, exclusion | باستثناء with the exception of, except; بدون استثناء without exception

استثنائى *istiṯnā'ī* exceptional; استثنائيا *istiṯnā'īyan* as an exception | احوال استثنائية emergencies; جلسة استثنائية (*jalsa*) emergency session

مثنى *maṯnīy* folded; plaited, pleated; doubled

مثنى *muṯannan* double, twofold; in the dual (*gram.*)

مستثنى *mustaṯnan* excepted, excluded (من from)

ثوة *ṯūwa* see ثوى

ثاب (ثوب)[1] *ṯāba u* to return, come back (also, e.g., a state or condition, الى or ل to s.o.); with ب: to return s.th. (الى to s.o.) | ثاب الى نفسه to regain consciousness, come to; ثاب اليه رشده (*rušduhū*) to recover one's senses II to reward (ه s.o.; said of God) IV to repay, requite (ه ه s.th. with); to reward (ه على s.o. for) X to seek reward

ثوب *ṯaub* pl. ثياب *ṯiyāb*, اثواب *aṯwāb* garment, dress; cloth, material; (fig.) garb, outward appearance, guise, cloak, mask; pl. ثياب clothes, clothing, apparel | ثياب السهرة *ṯ. as-sahra* formal dress, evening clothes; فى ثوب بسيط in plain, homely form; طاهر الثياب of flawless character, irreproachable

ثواب *ṯawāb* requital, recompense, reward (for good deeds); (*Isl. Law*) merit, credit (arising from a pious deed)

مثوبة *maṯwaba* requital, recompense, reward (bestowed by God for good deeds)

مثاب *maṯāb* and مثابة *maṯāba* place to which one returns; meeting place; rendezvous; resort, refuge

مثابة *maṯāba* (with foll. genit.) place or time at which s.th. appears or recurs;

manner, mode, fashion; see also preceding entry | بمثابة (with foll. genit.) like, as; tantamount to, equivalent to, having the same function as

تثاوب[2] = تثاءب (ثئب VI) to yawn

(ثور) ثار *ṯāra* u to stir, be stirred up, be aroused, be excited; to swirl up, rise (dust); to arise (question, problem; a difficulty, في وجهه *fī wajhihī* before s.o.); to be triggered, be unleashed, break out; to revolt, rebel, rise (على against); to rage, storm | ثار ثائره (*ṯā'iruhū*) to fly into a rage, become furious, flare up **IV** to agitate, excite (ه s.o., ه s.th.); to stimulate (ه s.o., ه s.th.); to irritate (ه s.o., ه s.th.); to arouse, stir up, kindle, excite (ه s.th., e.g., feelings), cause, provoke, awaken (ه s.th.); to raise, pose, bring up (مسألة *mas'alatan* a question, a problem) | اثار ثائرته (*ṯā'iratahū*) to infuriate s.o., excite s.o. **X** to excite, stir up, kindle (ه s.th., esp. passions); to rouse (ه s.th.); to arouse, awaken (ه s.th., esp. feelings); to elicit, evoke (ه wails, outcries, من from s.o.); to incite, set (ه على s.o. against) | استثار غضبه (*ġaḍabahū*) to infuriate s.o., make s.o. angry

ثور *ṯaur* pl. ثيران *ṯīrān* bull, steer; ox; Taurus (*astron.*) | شوربة ذيل الثور *šōrabat ḏail aṯ-ṯ.* oxtail soup

ثورة *ṯaura* excitement, agitation; outbreak, outburst, fit (of fury, of despair, etc.); eruption (of a volcano); (pl. *-āt*) upheaval, uprising, insurrection, riot, rebellion, revolt, revolution | ثورة اهلية (*ahlīya*) internal strife, civil war

ثوري *ṯaurī* revolutionary (adj. and n.)

ثوروي *ṯaurawī* revolutionary (adj. and n.)

ثوران *ṯawarān* agitation, excitation, flare-up, eruption, outbreak, outburst; dust whirl

مثار *maṯār* incentive, stimulus, motive, spur, occasion, cause | مثار الجدل *m. al-jadal* and مثار النزاع object of controversy, point of contention

اثارة *iṯāra* excitation, stirring up, kindling; agitation, incitement; provocation, (a)rousing, awakening; irritation, stimulation

ثائر *ṯā'ir* excited, agitated, raving, furious, mad; rebellious; fury, rage (in the idiomatic phrase ثار ثائره see above); (pl. ثوار *ṯuwwār*) insurgent, rebel, revolutionary

ثائرة *ṯā'ira* pl. ثوائر *ṯawā'ir*[2] tumult; excitement, agitation; fury, rage

مثير *muṯīr* exciting; provocative; stimulative, irritative; excitant, irritant, stimulant; instigator; germ, agent; pl. مثيرات stimulants

ثوريوم *ṯōriyūm* thorium (*chem.*)

ثول **VII** to swarm, crowd, throng (على around s.o.); to come over s.o. (على)

ثول *ṯaul* and ثول النحل *ṯ. an-naḥl* swarm of bees

ثوم *ṯūm* (coll.; n. un. ة) garlic

ثوى *ṯawā* i (ثواء *ṯawā'*, ثوي *ṯuwīy*, مثوى *maṯwan*) to stay, live (ب at a place); to settle down (ب at a place); pass. *ṯuwiya* to be buried **IV** to stay, live; to lodge, put up as a guest (ه s.o.)

ثوي *ṯawīy* guestroom

ثوة *ṯūwa* pl. ثوى *ṯuwan* signpost, roadsign

مثوى *maṯwan* pl. مثاو *maṯāwin* abode, habitation, dwelling; place of rest

ثيب *ṯayyib* pl. *-āt* a deflowered but unmarried woman, widow, divorcée

ثيتل *ṯaital* pl. ثياتل *ṯayātil*[2] a variety of wild goat (Capra jaela)

ج

جاثليق *jāṯalīq* = جثليق

جؤجؤ *ju'ju'* pl. جآجئ *ja'āji'*[2] breast; prow, bow (of a ship)

جأر *ja'ara a* (*ja'r*, جؤار *ju'ār*) to low, moo; to supplicate, pray fervently (الى to God)

جأر *ja'r* and جؤار *ju'ār* lowing, mooing (of cattle)

[1]جاز *gāz* pl. *-āt* (Eg. spelling) gas

[2]جاز *jāz* jazz

جازون (Fr. *gazon*, Eg. spelling) *gāzōn* lawn

جأش *ja'aša a* (*ja'š*) to be agitated, be convulsed (with pain or fright)

جأش *ja'š* emotional agitation; heart, soul | ربط جأشه *rabaṭa ja'šahū* to remain calm, composed, self-possessed; رابط الجأش or ثابت الجأش calm, composed, cool, self-possessed, undismayed; بجأش رابط with unswerving courage, unflinchingly

جاكتة, جاكته and جاكيته *žakēta* jacket, coat

جالون *galōn* gallon

جالبرى (Eg. spelling) *galērī* gallery (*theat.*)

جام *jām* pl. *-āt* cup; drinking vessel; bowl

جامكية *jāmakīya* pl. *-āt*, جوامك *jawāmik*[2] pay

جاموس *jāmūs* pl. جواميس *jawāmīs*[2] buffalo

جاموسة *jāmūsa* buffalo cow

جانرك (pronounced *žānəreg*, from Turk. *caneriği*; coll.; n. un. *žānərgēye*) a variety of small green plum with several stones (*syr.*)

جاه *jāh* rank, standing, dignity, honor, glory, fame

جاوه *jāwa* Java

جاوى *jāwī* Javanese; benzoin; (pl. *-ūn*) a Javanese

جاودار *jāwadār* rye

جاويش *čāwīš* sergeant = شاوش, شاويش

[1]جب *jubb* pl. اجباب *ajbāb*, جباب *jibāb* well, cistern; pit

[2]جبة *jubba* pl. جبب *jubab*, جباب *jibāb*, جبائب *jabā'ib*[2] jubbah, a long outer garment, open in front, with wide sleeves

جبح *jabḥ* pl. اجبح *ajbuḥ*, جباح *jibāḥ*, اجباح *ajbāḥ* beehive

جبخانة *jabḵāna*, *jabaḵāna* powder magazine; ammunition; artillery depot

جبر *jabara u* (*jabr*, جبور *jubūr*) to set (ه broken bones); to restore, bring back to normal (ه s.th.); to help back on his feet, help up (ه s.o.; e.g., one fallen into poverty); to force, compel (ه على s.o. to do s.th.) | جبر خاطره (*ḵāṭirahū*) to console, comfort, gratify, oblige s.o.; to treat (s.o.) in a conciliatory or kindly manner **II** to set (ه broken bones) **III** to treat with kindness, with friendliness (ه s.o.), be nice (ه to s.o.) **IV** to force, compel (ه على s.o. to do s.th.); to hold sway (على over) **V** to show o.s. proud, haughty; to act strong, throw one's weight around; to show o.s. strong or powerful, demonstrate one's strength or power; to be set (broken bones) | تجبر الله بابنك (*bi-bnika*) God has demonstrated His power on your son, i.e., He has taken him unto Himself **VII** to be mended, repaired, restored

جبر *jabr* setting (of broken bones); force, compulsion; coercion, duress; power, might; (predestined, inescapable) decree of fate; جبرا *jabran* forcibly, by force | علم الجبر *'ilm al-j.* algebra; يوم جبر البحر *yaum j. al-baḥr* a local holiday of Cairo (the day on which, in former times, the water of the Nile was channeled into the now-abandoned *ḵalīj*, or City Canal, thus marking the beginning of the irrigation season)

جبرى *jabrī* algebraic; compulsory, forced; — *jabarī* an adherent of the doctrine of predestination and the inescapability of fate; fatalist

جبرية *jabarīya* an Islamic school of thought teaching the inescapability of fate; fatalism

جبار *jabbār* pl. *-ūn*, جبابر *jabābir*², جبابرة *jabābira* giant; colossus; tyrant, oppressor; almighty, omnipotent (God); gigantic, giant, colossal, huge; Orion (*astron.*) | جبار الخطوة *j. al-ḵuṭwa* striding powerfully, taking huge strides

جبارة *jibāra* (art of) bonesetting

جبيرة *jabīra* and جبارة *jibāra* pl. جبائر *jabā'ir*² splint (*surg.*)

جبروت *jabarūt* omnipotence; power, might; tyranny

جبرياء *jibriyā'*² pride, haughtiness

○ تجبير *tajbīr*, تجبير العظام orthopedics

اجبار *ijbār* compulsion, coercion

اجبارى *ijbārī* forced, forcible, compulsory, obligatory | التجنيد الاجبارى compulsory recruitment; military conscription

جابر *jābir* and مجبر *mujabbir* bonesetter

مجبور *majbūr* and مجبر *mujbar* forced, compelled

جبرئيل *jabra'īl*², جبريل *jibrīl*² Gabriel

¹جبس II to plaster, coat, patch, or fix with plaster (ه s.th.); to put in a cast, set in plaster (ه s.th.)

جبس *jibs* gypsum; plaster of Paris

جباسة *jabbāsa* gypsum quarry; plaster kiln

²جبس *jabas* (coll.; n. un. ة; *syr.*) watermelon(s)

¹جبل *jabala u i* (*jabl*) to mold, form, shape, fashion (ه s.th.); to knead (ه s.th.); to create (ه على s.o. with a natural disposition or propensity for); pass. جبل على (*jubila*) to be born for, be naturally disposed to, have a propensity for

جبلة *jibla*, *jibilla* pl. *-āt* natural disposition, nature, temper

²جبل *jabal* pl. جبال *jibāl*, اجبال *ajbāl* mountain; mountains, mountain range | جبال الالب *j. al-alb* the Alps; جبال الاوراس the Aurès Mountains (in E Algeria); جبل جليد iceberg; جبل سينا *j. sīnā* Mount Sinai; جبل طارق Gibraltar; جبل نار volcano

جبلى *jabalī* mountainous, hilly, mountain (adj.); montane; (pl. *-ūn*) highlander, mountaineer

جبلاوى *gabalāwī* (*eg.*) highlander, mountaineer

جبلاية *gabalāya* pl. *-āt* (*eg.*) grotto, cave

جبن *jabuna u* (*jubn*, جبانة *jabāna*) to be a coward, be fearful; to be too much of a coward (عن to do s.th.), shrink (عن from s.th.) II to cause to curdle (ه milk); to make into cheese (ه s.th.); to curdle; to accuse of cowardice, call a coward (ه s.o.) V to curdle (milk), turn into cheese

جبن *jubn* and جبانة *jabāna* cowardice

جبن *jubn* and جبنة *jubna* cheese

جبان *jabān* pl. جبناء *jubanā'*² coward; cowardly

جبان *jabbān* cheese merchant

جبين *jabīn* pl. جبن *jubun*, اجبنة *ajbina*, اجبن *ajbun* forehead, brow; façade, front; face | من جبينى *min jabīnī* I alone; على جبين السماء in the sky

جبينى *jabīnī* frontal

اجبن *ajban*[2] more cowardly

جبّانة *jabbāna* pl. *-āt* cemetery

تجبين *tajbīn* cheese making, processing into cheese

[1]جبه *jabaha* a to meet, face, confront (ه s.o.) III to face, confront, oppose, defy (ه s.o., ء s.th.), show a bold front (ه to); to face (ء a problem, a difficulty)

جبهة *jabha* pl. جباه *jibāh*, جبهات *jabahāt* forehead, brow; front, face, façade; front-line, battle front

مجابهة *mujābaha* facing, confrontation, opposition

جبخانة see جبه خانة[2]

جبى *jabā* i (جباية *jibāya*) to collect, raise, levy (ء taxes, duties) II to prostrate o.s. (in prayer) VIII to pick, choose, elect (ء s.th., ه s.o.)

جباية *jibāya* raising, levying (of taxes); (pl. *-āt*) tax, duty, impost

جبائى *jibā'ī* tax- (in compounds); fiscal

مجبى *majban* pl. مجاب *majābin* tax, impost

جاب *jābin* pl. جباة *jubāh* tax collector, revenue officer, collector; (bus, etc.) conductor (*ir.*)

جابية *jābiya* pl. جواب *jawābin* pool, basin

جتا *jatā* (abbreviation of جيب التّام) cosine (*math.*)

جثّ *jatta* u (*jatt*) and VIII to tear out, uproot (ء a tree, also fig.)

جثّة *jutta* pl. جثث *jutat*, اجثاث *ajtāt* body; corpse, cadaver; carcass

مجتثّ *mujtatt* uprooted (also fig.)

جثل *jatl* thick, dense (esp. hair)

جثليق *jitlīq* pl. جثالقة *jatāliqa* catholicos, primate of the Armenian Church

جثم *jatama* u i (*jatm*, جثوم *jutūm*) to alight, sit, perch (bird); to crouch, cower; to fall or lie prone, lie face down; to beset, oppress (على s.th.)

جثمة *jatma* (n. vic.) motionless sitting or lying

جثام *jutām* and جاثوم *jātūm* nightmare, incubus

جثمان *jutmān* pl. *-āt* body, mortal frame

جثمانى *jutmānī* bodily, physical, corporeal

جاثم *jātim* pl. جثّم *juttam* squatting, crouching; perching; prostrate, prone

(جثو) جثا *jatā* u (*jutūw*) to kneel, rest on the knees; to bend the knee, genuflect; to fall on one's knees

جثوّ *jutūw* kneeling position

جثوة *jutwa* rock pile, mound; sepulchral mound, tumulus

مجثى *majtan* hassock

جاث *jātin* kneeling; الجاثى Hercules (*astron.*)

جحد *jaḥada* a (*jaḥd*, جحود *juḥūd*) to negate (ء s.th.); to disclaim, disavow, disown, deny (ء s.th.); to refuse, reject, repudiate (ء s.th.); to renounce, forswear, adjure (ء a belief); to deny (ء ه s.o. his right) | جحد جميله (*jamīlahū*) to be ungrateful to s.o.

جحد *jaḥd* denial; repudiation, disavowal, rejection, disclaimer; unbelief (*rel.*)

جحود *juḥūd* denial; evasion, dodging, shirking (of a moral obligation); ingratitude; repudiation, disavowal, rejection, disclaimer; unbelief (*rel.*)

جاحد *jāḥid* denier; infidel, unbeliever

جحر VII to hide in its hole or den (animal)

جحر *juḥr* pl. اجحار *ajḥār*, جحور *juḥūr* hole, den, lair, burrow (of animals)

جحش *jaḥš* pl. جحاش *jiḥāš*, جحشان *jiḥšān*, اجحاش *ajḥāš* young donkey; (pl. جحوش *juḥūš*) trestle, horse

جحشة *jaḥša* young female donkey

جحظ *jaḥaẓa a* (جحوظ *juḥūẓ*) to bulge, protrude (eyeball)

جحوظ العين *juḥūẓ al-ʿain* exophthalmic goiter, abnormal protrusion of the eyeball

جحف *jaḥafa a* (*jaḥf*) to peel off, scrape off (ه s.th.); to sweep away (ه s.th.); to have a bias (مع for), side (مع with s.o.) **IV** to harm, hurt, injure, prejudice (ب s.o., s.th.); to ruin, destroy (ب s.o., s.th.); to wrong (ب s.o.)

اجحاف *ijḥāf* injustice, wrong; bias, prejudice

مجحف *mujḥif* unjust, unfair; biased, prejudiced

جحفل *jaḥfal* pl. جحافل *jaḥāfil*² multitude, legion, host, large army; army corps (*Syr.*); eminent man

جحيم *jaḥīm* f. (also m.) fire, hellfire, hell

جحيمى *jaḥīmī* hellish, infernal

جخ *jakka* (*eg.*) to lord it, give o.s. airs; to boast, brag; (*syr.*) to dress up (slightly ironical)

جخاخ *jakkāk* boaster, braggart

¹جد *jadd* pl. جدود *judūd*, اجداد *ajdād* grandfather; ancestor, forefather | الجد الاعلى (*aʿlā*) ancestor

جدة *jadda* pl. *-āt* grandmother

²جد *jadda i* to be new; to be a recent development, have happened lately, have recently become a fact; to be added, crop up or enter as a new factor (circumstances, costs); to appear for the first time (also, e.g., on the stage); to be or become serious, grave; to be weighty, significant, important; to take (فى s.th.) seriously; to strive earnestly (فى for), go out of one's way (فى to do s.th.), make every effort (فى in); to be serious, be in earnest (فى about), mean business; to hurry (فى one's step) **II** to renew (ه s.th.); to make anew, remake (ه s.th.); to modernize (ه s.th.); to restore, renovate, remodel, refit, recondition, refurbish (ه s.th.); to be an innovator, a reformer; to feature s.th. new or novel, produce s.th. new; to rejuvenate, regenerate, revive, freshen up (ه s.th.); to renew, extend (ه a permit); to begin anew, repeat (ه s.th.), make a new start (ه in s.th.); to try again (حظه *ḥaẓẓahū* one's luck) **IV** to strive, endeavor, take pains; to apply o.s. earnestly and assiduously (فى to), be bent, be intent (فى on s.th.); to hurry (فى one's step); to renew, make new (ه s.th.) **V** to become new, be renewed; to revive **X** to be new, be added or enter as a new factor, come newly into existence; to make new, renew (ه s.th.)

جد *jadd* pl. جدود *judūd* good luck, good fortune

جد *jidd* seriousness, earnestness; diligence, assiduity, eagerness; جدا *jiddan* very, much | بجد and من جد earnestly, seriously; جد باهظ *jiddu bāhiẓin* very high (price); جد عظيم *j. ʿaẓīmin* very great; يختلفون جد الاختلاف (*jidda l-iktilāf*) they differ widely; وقف على ساق الجد ل (*sāqi l-j.*) to apply o.s. with diligence to, take pains in, make every effort to

جدى *jiddī* serious; earnest; جديا *jiddīyan* in earnest, earnestly, seriously

جدية *jiddīya* earnestness; seriousness, gravity (of a situation)

جدة *jidda* newness, recency, novelty; modernness, modernity; ○ rebirth, renaissance

جدة *judda*² Jidda (seaport in W Saudi Arabia, on Red Sea)

جديد *jadīd* pl. جدد *judud, judad* new, recent; renewed; modern; novel, unprecedented | الجديدان *al-jadīdān* day and night; من جديد anew, again; (*eg.*) جديد لنج *gadīd lang* brand-new

اجد *ajadd*² more serious, more intent; newer, more recent

تجديد *tajdīd* renewal (also, e.g., of a permit); creation of s.th. new, origination; new presentation, new production (*theat.*); innovation; reorganization, reform; modernization; renovation, restoration, remodeling, refitting, reconditioning, refurbishing; rejuvenation, regeneration; pl. *-āt* innovations; new achievements

تجدد *tajaddud* renewal, regeneration, revival

جاد *jādd* in earnest, earnest; serious (as opposed to comic, funny)

جادة *jādda* pl. *-āt*, جواد *jawādd*² main street; street

مجدود *majdūd* fortunate, lucky

مجدد *mujaddid* renewer; innovator; reformer

مجدد *mujaddad* renewed, extended; remodeled, reconditioned, renovated, restored; rejuvenated, regenerated; new, recent, young

مجد *mujidd* painstaking, diligent, assiduous

مستجد *mustajidd* new, recent; incipient

جدب *jaduba u* (جدوبة *judūba*) to be or become dry, arid (soil) IV to suffer from drought, poverty or dearth; to be barren, sterile; to come to nothing, go up in smoke, fall flat, fizzle out; (*syr.*) to explode in the barrel (shell; *mil.*)

جدب *jadb* drought, barrenness, sterility; sterile, barren

جديب *jadīb* and اجدب *ajdab*², f. جدباء *jadbā'*² barren, sterile

مجدب *mujdib* barren, sterile; desolate, arid; unproductive, unprofitable

جدث *jadaṯ* pl. اجداث *ajdāṯ* grave, tomb

جدجد *judjud* pl. جداجد *jadājid*² cricket (*zool.*)

¹جدر *jadura u* (جدارة *jadāra*) to be fit, suitable, proper, appropriate (ب for s.o., for s.th.); to befit, behoove (ب s.o., s.th.); to be worthy (ب of), deserve (ب s.th.) | يجدر ذكره (*ḏikruhū*) and يجدر بالذكر it is worth mentioning

جدر *jadr* wall

جدير *jadīr* pl. *-ūn*, جدراء *judarā'*² worthy, deserving (ب of s.th.); becoming, befitting (ب s.th.); proper, suited, suitable, fit (ب for), appropriate (ب to) | جدير بالذكر (*ḏikr*) worth mentioning

اجدر *ajdar*² worthier; more appropriate; better suited, more suitable

جدارة *jadāra* worthiness; fitness, suitability, aptitude, qualification; appropriateness

جدار *jidār* pl. جدر *judur*, جدران *judrān* wall

جدارى *jidārī* mural, wall (adj.)

²جدر *judira* (pass.) and II to have smallpox

جدرى *judarī, jadarī* smallpox

مجدور *majdūr* and مجدر *mujaddar* infected with smallpox; pock-marked

مجدرة *mujaddara* dish made of rice or (in Syr.) of bulgur with lentils, onions and oil (*eg., syr.*)

¹جدع *jada'a a* (*jad'*) to cut off, amputate (ه s.th., esp. some part of the body)

بجدع الانف *bi-jad'i l-anf* (prop., at the cost of having the nose cut off) at any price, regardless of the sacrifice involved

اجدع *ajda'*² mutilated (by having the nose, or the like, cut off)

²□ جدع *gada'* (= جذع *jada'*) pl. جدعان *gid'ān* (*eg.*) young man young fellow; he-man

¹جدف II to curse, blaspheme (على s.o., esp. God)

تجديف *tajdīf* imprecation, blasphemy

²جدف *jadafa* *i* and II to row (ه a boat)

مجداف *mijdāf* pl. مجاديف *majādīf*² oar

¹جدل *jadala* *u* *i* (*jadl*) to twist tight, tighten, stretch (ه a rope); to braid, plait (ه s.th., the hair, etc.) II to braid, plait, (ه s.th.) III to quarrel, wrangle, bicker (ه with s.o.); to argue, debate (ه with s.o.); to dispute, contest (في s.th.) VI to quarrel, have an argument; to carry on a dispute

جدل *jadal* quarrel, argument; debate, dispute, discussion, controversy | فرض جدلا *farada jadalan* to assume for the sake of argument, propose as a basis for discussion

جدلى *jadalī* controversial; disputatious; a disputant

جدال *jaddāl* and مجدال *mijdāl* disputatious, argumentative; *mijdal* see also below

جديلة *jadīla* pl. جدائل *jadā'il*² braid, plait; tress

مجدال *mijdāl* pl. مجاديل *majādīl*² flagstone, ashlar; see also above under *jaddāl*

جدال *jidāl* and مجادلة *mujādala* pl. *-āt* quarrel, argument; dispute, discussion, debate | لا يقبل الجدال (*yaqbalu*) incontestable, indisputable; لا جدال *lā jidāla* and بلا جدال *bi-lā j.* incontestably, indisputably

مجدول *majdūl* tightly twisted; braided, plaited; interwoven, intertwined (tress of hair); slender and trim, shapely (e.g., leg)

مجادل *mujādil* disputant, opponent in dispute

²جدول *jadwal* pl. جداول *jadāwil*² creek, brook, little stream; column; list, roster; index; chart, table, schedule | جدول دراسى (*dirāsī*) curriculum; جدول البورصة stock list, خارج جدول البورصة (*kārija*) not quoted (stock exchange); جدول الاعمال agenda; working plan

جدا (جدو) *jadā* *u* to give a present (على to s.o.) IV to give as a present (على ب s.o. s.th.), present (على ب s.o. with); to be of use, be useful, profitable | اجدى نفعا (*naf'an*) to be useful; هذا لا يجديك that won't help you, that will be of no use (to you); ما يجدى عنك هذا .do; لا يجدى فتيلا (*fatīlan*) = لا يغنى فتيلا, see فتيل X to beg for alms; to implore, beg (ه ه s.o. for s.th.), plead (ه for s.th.)

جداء *juda'* advantage, gain (عن for s.o.)

جدوى *jadwā* gift, present; advantage, benefit, gain | بلا جدوى (*bi-lā*) and فى غير جدوى (*gairi*) of no avail, useless, futile, in vain

اجدى *ajdā* more useful, more advantageous

جدى *jady* pl. جداء *jidā'*, جديان *jidyān* kid, young billy goat; Capricorn (*astron.*); الجدى the North Star

جذ *jadda* *u* (*jadd*) to cut off, clip (ه s.th.)

جذاذة *judāda* pl. *-āt* slip of paper; pl. جذاذات small pieces, shreds, scraps, clippings

جذب *jadaba* *i* (*jadb*) to pull, draw (ه s.th.); to attract (ه s.th.); to pull out, draw out, whip out (ه s.th.), draw (ه a weapon, or the like); to appeal, prove attractive (ه to s.o.), attract, captivate, charm, allure (ه s.o.), win (ه s.o.) over (اليه to one's side) III to contend (ه with s.o.) at pulling, tugging, etc. (ه s.th.) | جاذبه الحبل

(*ḥabla*) to vie with s.o.; (to be able) to compete with s.o., measure up to s.o., be a match for s.o.; جاذبه الكلام or جاذبه اطراف الحديث or حديثا (*aṭrāfa l-ḥ.*) he engaged him in conversation, involved him in a discussion; جاذبه اطراف الحضارة (*aṭrāfa l-ḥaḍāra*) to vie with s.o. in culture **VI** to pull back and forth (ه s.o.); to contend (ه, ه for); to attract each other | تجاذبوا اطراف الحديث (*aṭrāfa l-ḥ.*) they were deep in conversation, they were talking together **VII** to be attracted; to be drawn, gravitate (الى toward, to) **VIII** to attract (ه s.o., ه s.th., اليه to o.s.; also *magn.*); to allure, entice (ه s.o.); to win (ه s.o.) over (اليه to one's side); to draw, inhale (ه puffs from a cigarette, etc.)

جذب *jaḏb* attraction; gravitation; appeal, lure, enticement, captivation | اخذ جذبا to wrest away, take away by force; الجذب الجنسى (*jinsī*) sex appeal

جذاب *jaḏḏāb* attractive; magnetic (fig.); suction, suctorial; winning, fetching, engaging; charming, enticing, captivating, gripping

اجذب *ajḏab*² more attractive, more captivating

انجذاب *injiḏāb* attraction, inclination, proneness, tendency

اجتذاب *ijtiḏāb* attraction; enticement, lure

جاذب *jāḏib* attractive; magnetic (fig.); winning, fetching, engaging; charming, enticing, captivating, gripping

جاذبية *jāḏibīya* gravitation; attraction; attractiveness; charm, fascination; magnetism (fig.); lure, enticement | ○ جاذبية الثقل *j. aṯ-ṯiql* gravitational force; جاذبية مغنطيسية (*maḡnaṭīsīya*) magnetism; جاذبية الجنس *j. al-jins* sex appeal

مجذوب *majḏūb* attracted; possessed, maniacal, insane; (pl. مجاذيب *majāḏīb*²) maniac, lunatic, madman, idiot | مستشفى المجاذيب *mustašfā l-m.* mental hospital

متجاذب *mutajāḏib* mutually attractive; belonging together, inseparable

منجذب *munjaḏib* attracted; inclined, tending (الى to)

جذر **jaḏara** u (*jaḏr*) to uproot, tear out by the roots (ه s.th.) **II** do.; to extract the root (ه of a number; *math.*); to take root

جذر *jiḏr*, *jaḏr* pl. جذور *juḏūr* root (also *math.*); stem, base, lower end; (pl. اجذار *ajḏār*) stub (of a receipt book, or the like) | جذر تربيعى (*tarbīʿī*) square root (*math.*)

جذرى *jiḏrī* radical, root (adj.)

تجذير *tajḏīr* evolution, root extraction (*math.*)

جذع **jaḏaʿ** pl. جذعان *juḏʿān* young man, young fellow (cf. □ جدع *gadaʿ*); new, incipient | عادت الحرب جذعة (*ḥarbu, jaḏaʿatan*) the war broke out again, started all over again; اعاد الامر جذعا (*l-amra*) he reopened the whole affair, he reverted to the earlier status

جذع *jiḏʿ* pl. اجذاع *ajḏāʿ*, جذوع *juḏūʿ* stem, trunk; stump, tree stump; torso

جذعى *jiḏʿī* truncal

جذف **II** to row (ه a boat)

مجذاف *mijḏāf* pl. مجاذيف *majāḏīf*² oar

جذل **jaḏila** a (*jaḏal*) to be happy, gay, exuberant, rejoice **IV** to make happy, gladden, cheer (ه s.o.)

جذل *jiḏl* pl. اجذال *ajḏāl*, جذول *juḏūl* stump (of a tree)

جذيل *juḏail* wooden post on which camels rub themselves

جذل *jaḏal* gaiety, hilarity, exuberance, happiness

جذل *jaḏil* pl. جذلان *juḏlān* gay, hilarious, cheerful, in high spirits, exuberant, happy

جذلان *jadlān*[2] gay, hilarious, cheerful, in high spirits, exuberant, happy

جذم *jaḏama i* (*jaḏm*) to cut off, chop off (ه s.th., esp. a part of the body); to remove, take out, excise (ه e.g., the tonsils, the appendix; *surg.*); pass. *juḏima* to be afflicted with leprosy

جذم *jiḏm* pl. جذوم *juḏūm*, اجذام *ajḏām* root

جذام *juḏām* leprosy

جذامة *juḏāma* stubble

اجذم *ajḏam*[2] pl. جذمى *jaḏmā* mutilated (from having an arm, a hand, etc., cut off); leprous; leper

مجذوم *majḏūm* leprous; leper

جذمور *judmūr* stump

جذوة *jaḏwa, jiḏwa, juḏwa* pl. جذى *jiḏan, juḏan*, جذاء *jiḏā'* firebrand; burning log

جر *jarra u* (*jarr*) to draw, pull (ه s.th.); to drag, tug, haul (ه s.th.); to tow (ه s.th.); to trail (ه s.th.); to drag along (ه s.o., ه s.th.); to draw (ه على s.th. on s.o.), bring (ه s.th.) down (على upon s.o.); to lead (الى to), bring on, cause (الى s.th.); to entail (ه e.g., some evil, على for s.o.); (*gram.*) to pronounce the final consonant with *i*, put (a word) into the genitive | جر جريرة (*jarīratan*) to commit an outrage, a crime (على against s.o.); جر قيودا (*quyūdan*) to be in shackles, go shackled; جر النار الى قرصه (*qurṣihī*) to secure advantages for o.s., feather one's nest; لا يجر لسانه بكلمة (*lisānahū bi-kalima*) he won't let a word escape his lips **IV** to ruminate **VII** passive of **I**; to be driven; to be swept along, drift, float | انجر الى الوراء (*warā'i*) to withdraw, fall back, give way **VIII** to ruminate | اجتر آلامه (*ālāmahū*) to mull over one's grief

جر *jarr* pull(ing), drawing, draft; traction; drag(ging), tugging, towage, hauling; bringing on, causing; genitive | حرف الجر *ḥarf al-j.* (*gram.*) preposition; وهلم جرا *wa-halumma jarran* and so forth

جرة *jarra* pl. جرار *jirār* (earthenware) jar

جرة *jarra, jurra* trail, track; rut (left by a wagon) | بجرة قلم *bi-j. qalam* with one stroke of the pen

جرة *jirra* cud (of a ruminant)

من جرى *min jarrā* because of | من جراك because of you, on your account, for your sake

من جراء *min jarrā'i* because of, due to | من جراء أن because

جرار *jarrār* huge, tremendous (army); potter; (pl. *-āt*) tractor; tugboat, steam tug, towing launch

جارور *jārūr* pl. جوارير *jawārīr*[2] (*syr.*) drawer (of a desk, etc.)

جارورة *jārūra* (*leb.*) rake (tool)

جريرة *jarīra* pl. جرائر *jarā'ir*[2] guilt; offense, outrage, crime | من جريرة *min jarīrati* because of, on account of

جرارة *jarrāra* pl. *-āt* a variety of scorpion; tractor

مجر *mijarr* trace, tug (of a harness)

مجرة *majarra* galaxy

انجرارية *ingirārīya* (*eg.*) towage charges for watercraft

مجرور *majrūr* drawn, dragged, towed, etc.; word governed by a preposition, word in the genitive form; (pl. مجارير *magārīr*[2]) drain, sewer (*eg.*); مجارير sewers, sewage system (*eg.*)

مجتر *mujtarr* ruminant (adj. and n.)

جرؤ *jaru'a u* (جرأة *jur'a*, جراءة *jarā'a*) to dare, venture, risk, hazard (على s.th.), take the risk (على of, ان of doing s.th.), have the courage (على for s.th.) II to encourage (على ▪ s.o. to s.th.) V to dare, venture, risk, hazard (على s.th.) VIII to be venturesome, be daring; to become bold, make bold (على with s.o.); to venture (على s.th. or upon s.th.), have the audacity (على to do s.th.)

جرىء *jarī'* pl. اجرياء *ajriyā'*[2] bold, courageous (ب, على in s.th.); forward, immodest, insolent; daring, reckless, foolhardy

جرأة *jur'a* and جراءة *jarā'a* courage, boldness, daring; forwardness, insolence

مجترئ *mujtari'* bold, forward

جراج (Fr.) *garāž* pl. *-āt* garage (*eg.*)

جرام *grām* gram (*eg.*)

جرانيت *granīt* granite (*eg.*)

جرانيتي *granītī* granitic (*eg.*)

[1]جرب *jariba a* (*jarab*) to be mangy; (*eg.*) to fade (color) II to test (▲ s.th.); to try, try out, essay (▲ s.th.); to sample (▲ s.th.); to rehearse, practice (▲ s.th.); to attempt (▲ s.th.); to put to the test, try, tempt (▪ s.o.) | جرب نفسه في to try one's hand at; جرب الايام (*ayyāma*) to gather experience

جرب *jarab* mange; itch, scabies

جرب *jarib* mangy; scabby

اجرب *ajrab*[2], f. جرباء *jarbā'*[2], pl. جرب *jurb* and جربان *jarbān*[2] mangy; scabby

جراب *jirāb* pl. اجربة *ajriba*, جرب *jurub* sack, bag, traveling bag; knapsack; scrotum; covering, case; sheath, scabbard (for the sword)

جراب *jurāb* pl. *-āt* stocking, sock

جريب *jarīb* a patch of arable land

تجربة *tajriba* pl. تجارب *tajārib*[2] trial, test; tryout; attempt; practice, rehearsal; scientific test, experiment; probation; trial, tribulation; temptation; experience, practice; proof sheet, galley proof, also تجربة مطبعية (*maṭba'īya*)

تجريب *tajrīb* trial, test(ing); trial, tribulation; temptation

تجريبي *tajrībī* trial, test (adj.); experimental; based on experience, empirical | علم النفس التجريبي (*'ilm an-nafs*) experimental psychology

○ تجريبية *tajrībīya* empiricism (*philos.*)

مجرب *mujarrib* experimental; tester; examiner; tempter

مجرب *mujarrab* tried, tested; proven or established by experience, time-tested, time-tried; experienced, practiced, seasoned; man of experience

[2]جورب look up alphabetically

جربذة *jarbaḏa* = جربزة

جربز *jurbuz* pl. جرابزة *jarābiza* impostor, confidence man, swindler

جربزة *jarbaza* (also جربذة) deception, swindle

جربوع *jarbū'* (= يربوع) pl. جرابيع *jarābī'*[2] jerboa (*zool.*)

جربندية *jarabandīya* (and جرابندية) knapsack, rucksack

جرثوم *jurṯūm*, جرثومة *jurṯūma* pl. جراثيم *jarāṯīm*[2] root; origin; germ; microbe, bacillus, bacterium | تحت الجرثوم *taḥt al-j.* inframicrobe

جرج look up alphabetically

جرجر *jarjara* (جرجرة *jarjara*) to gargle; to jerk or pull back and forth; to trail, drag (▲ s.th.); to tow away (▲ s.th.) | جرجر خطاه (*kuṭāhu*) to drag one's feet, shuffle along II *tajarjara* pass. and refl. of I

جرجرة *jarjara* gargling; rumbling noise; rumble, clatter (of a wagon)

جرجر *jirjir* (large, thick) beans

جرجير *jirjīr* watercress (*eg.*, *syr.*)

جرح *jaraḥa a* (*jarḥ*) to wound (• s.o.); to injure, hurt (• s.o.; also fig., the feelings) **II** to invalidate (▲ testimony), challenge, declare unreliable (• a witness), take formal exception (•, ▲ to) **VIII** to commit (▲ an outrage, a crime) | اجترح السيآت (*sayyi'āt*) to do evil things

جرح *jurḥ* pl. جراح *jirāḥ*, جروح *jurūḥ*, جروحات *jurūḥāt*, اجراح *ajrāḥ* wound, injury, lesion

جراح *jarrāḥ* pl. *-ūn* surgeon | جراح الاسنان dental surgeon

جراحة *jirāḥa* surgery

جراحى *jirāḥī* surgical | عملية جراحية (*'amalīya*) surgical operation

جريح *jarīḥ* pl. جرحى *jarḥā* wounded, injured, hurt

تجريح *tajrīḥ* surgery; defamation, disparagement

جارح *jāriḥ* injuring; wounding, stinging, painful, hurting; rapacious (beast), predatory

جارحة *jāriḥa* pl. جوارح *jawāriḥ*[2] predatory animal or bird | جوارح الطير *j. aṭ-ṭair* predatory birds

جوارح *jawāriḥ*[2] limbs, extremities (of the body) | بكل جوارحه with might and main, with all his strength

مجروح *majrūḥ* pl. مجاريح *majārīḥ*[2] wounded, injured, hurt

جرد *jarada u* (*jard*) to peel, pare (▲ s.th.); to remove the shell, peel, rind or husk (▲ of s.th.); to denude, divest, strip, bare (▲ s.th.); (*com.*) to take stock; to make an inventory (البضائع of goods on hand) **II** to peel, pare (▲ s.th.); to remove the shell, peel, rind or husk (▲ of s.th.); to denude, divest, strip, dispossess, deprive (من ▲ or • s.o. or s.th. of); to withhold (من • from s.o. s.th.); to draw, unsheathe (السيف the sword); to unleash (على ▲ s.th. against s.o.); to send, dispatch (▲ a military detachment, troops, ضد or على against s.o.); to free (من ▲ or • s.o. or s.th. from); to isolate (▲ s.th.); to abstract (▲ s.th.); to divest (من • s.o. of his citizenship, of a rank, of a vested right, etc.) | جرده من السلاح to disarm s.o.; جرد نفسه من to free o.s. from, rid o.s. of, give up s.th. **V** pass. of **II**; to strip o.s., rid o.s., get rid (من or عن of), free o.s. (من or عن from); to be free (من or عن from, ل for a task); to devote o.s. exclusively (ل to s.th.); to give up, renounce (من or عن s.th.); to isolate o.s.; to be absolute

جرد *jard* bare, threadbare, shabby, worn; (*com.*) inventory; stocktaking

جرد *jarid* without vegetation, barren, bleak, stark (landscape)

اجرد *ajrad*[2], f. جرداء *jardā'*[2], pl. جرد *jurd* desolate, bleak, without vegetation; hairless, bald; threadbare, shabby, worn (garment); open, unprotected (border)

جراد *jarād* (coll.; n. un. ة) locust(s) | جراد رحال (*raḥḥāl*) migratory locust(s); جراد البحر *j. al-baḥr* langouste, sea crayfish; بجرادها *bi-jarādihā* in its entirety

جريد *jarīd* palm branches stripped of their leaves; jereed, a blunt javelin used in equestrian games

جريدة *jarīda* pl. جرائد *jarā'id*[2] (n. un. of جريد) palm-leaf stalk; list, register, roster, index; newspaper | جريدة يومية (*yaumīya*) daily newspaper; جرائد المساء *j. al-masā'* the evening papers; الجريدة الناطقة and الجريدة السينمائية the newsreel

اجرودى *ajrūdī* (*syr.*) beardless, hairless

مجرد *mijrad* pl. مجارد *majārid*[2] scraper

تجريد *tajrīd* peeling, paring; disrobement, stripping; denudation; deprivation; divestment; disarmament; dispatching (of troops); freeing; isolation; abstraction | تجريد من السلاح disarmament

تجريدة *tajrīda* pl. *-āt*, تجاريد *tajārīd*[2] military detachment, expeditionary force

تجرد *tajarrud* freedom (من or عن from); isolatedness, isolation; independence, impartiality; absoluteness; abstractness, abstraction

مجرد *mujarrad* denuded, bare, naked; freed, free (من or عن from); pure, mere, nothing more than; sole; very, absolute; abstract; selfless, disinterested; 1st stem of the verb (*gram.*) | (with foll. noun in genitive = mere, sheer, nothing but:) مجرد لهو *mujarradu lahwin* mere play, just fun; بالعين المجردة with the naked eye; بمجرد ما *bi-mujarradi mā* as soon as, at the very moment when

جردل *jardal* pl. جرادل *jarādil*[2] bucket, pail

جرذ *jurad* pl. جرذان *jirdān*, *jurdān* large rat

جرذون *jirdaun* pl. جراذين *jarādīn*[2] large rat

[1]جرس *jarasa* i (*jars*) to ring, toll, knell, (re)sound **II** to make experienced, inure by severe trials, sorely try (ه s.o.; time, events); to compromise, disgrace, discredit, expose, bring into disrepute (ب s.o.)

جرس *jars*, *jirs* sound, tone

جرس *jaras* pl. اجراس *ajrās* bell

جرسة *jursa* defamation, public exposure; scandal, disgrace

[2]جرسایة *jirsāya*, جرسية *jirsiya* pl. *-āt* jersey, woolen sweater; جرسى jersey cloth

جرش *jaraša* u (*jarš*) to crush (ه s.th.); to grate, bruise, grind (ه s.th.)

جرش *jarš* a grating, scraping noise

جريش *jariš* crushed, bruised, coarsely ground; crushed grain; grits

جاروشة *jārūša* pl. جواريش *jawāriš*[2] quern, hand mill (for grinding grain)

جرض *jariḍa* a (*jaraḍ*): جرض بريقه (*bi-rīqihī*) he choked on his saliva, could not swallow his saliva (because of excitement, alarm, or grief), he was very upset, in a state of great agitation, deeply moved; — *jaraḍa* u (*jarḍ*) to choke, suffocate (ه s.o.) **IV** اجرضه بريقه (cf. I) to alarm s.o., fill s.o. with apprehension

جريض *jarīḍ*: حال الجريض دون القريض *ḥāla l-j. dūna l-qarīḍ* (proverb; lit.: choking prevented poetry, i.e.) in the face of death one does not think of rhyming (among other interpretations)

جرع *jaraʿa* a (*jarʿ*) and *jariʿa* a (*jaraʿ*) to swallow, gulp, devour (ه s.th.); to pour down, toss down (ه a drink) **II** to make (ه s.o.) swallow (ه s.th.); to gulp down **V** to drink (ه s.th.) **VIII** to swallow, gulp down (ه s.th.)

جرعة *jurʿa*, *jarʿa* pl. جرع *juraʿ*, *-āt* gulp, mouthful, draught; potion, dose (*med.*)

جرف *jarafa* u (*jarf*) and **VIII** to sweep away (ه s.th.); to wash away (ه s.th.); to shovel away (ه s.th.); to remove (ه s.th.); to tear away, carry off (ه s.th.); to carry along (ه or ه s.o. or s.th.) **VII** to be swept away, be carried away

جرف *jurf*, *juruf* pl. جروف *jurūf*, اجراف *ajrāf* undercut bank or shore; cliff, steep slope, precipice; bluff (along a river or coast) | جرف جليدى (*jalīdī*) avalanche

جرافة *jarrāfa* pl. *-āt*, جراريف *jarārīf*[2] rake; harrow

مجرف *majraf* pl. مجارف *majārif*[2] torrent, strong current

مجرفة *mijrafa* shovel, scoop; (*syr.*) mattock; trowel

مجراف *mijrāf* pl. مجاريف *majārīf*[2] shovel, scoop

جارف *jārif* torrential (stream, mountain creek); stormy, violent (emotions, passions)

الجركس *al-jarkas* the Circassians

جركسى *jarkasī* pl. جراكسة *jarākisa* Circassian (adj. and n.)

جرم *jarama* **i** (*jarm*) to bone (اللحم *al-laḥma* the meat); — to commit an offense, a crime, an outrage (على or الى against s.o.), sin (على or الى against s.o.), injure, harm, wrong (على or الى s.o.) **II** to incriminate, charge with a crime (ه s.o.; *syr.*) **IV** to commit a crime, to sin (على or الى against s.o.), do wrong (على or الى to s.o.), harm, wrong (على or الى s.o.) **VIII** = **IV**

جرم *garm* pl. جروم *gurūm* (*eg.*) long, flat-bottomed barge, lighter (*naut.*)

جرم *jirm* pl. اجرام *ajrām*, جرم *jurum* body; mass, bulk, volume (of a body) | الاجرام الفلكية (*falakīya*) the celestial bodies

جرم *jurm* pl. اجرام *ajrām*, جروم *jurūm* offense, crime, sin

لا جرم *lā jarama* surely, certainly, of course

جريم *jarīm* hulking, bulky, huge, voluminous, of great size

جريمة *jarīma* pl. جرائم *jarā'im*² crime; offense; sin | جريمة كبرى (or عظمى) (*kubrā*, *'uẓmā*) capital offense; قانون الجرائم penal code

اجرام *ijrām* crime; culpability, delinquency

اجرامى *ijrāmī* criminal

لحم مجروم *laḥm majrūm* fillet (meat)

سنة مجرمة *sana mujarrama* an entire year

مجرم *mujrim* criminal; (pl. *-ūn*) a criminal; evildoer, culprit, delinquent | مجرم عائد recidivous criminal

جرامز *jarāmiz*² and جراميز *jarāmīz*² limbs, legs | ضم جراميزه (*ḍamma*) he beat it, he made off

الجرمان *al-jarmān* the Germanic tribes, the Teutons

جرمانى *jarmānī* Germanic, Teutonic

¹جرن *jurn* pl. اجران *ajrān* (stone) basin; mortar; (*eg.*) threshing floor, barn | جرن المعمودية *j. al-ma'mūdīya* baptismal font

²جران *jirān* the front part of a camel's neck | ضرب بجرانه to become established, take root; القى عليه جرانه (*alqā, jirānahū*) to apply o.s. to s.th. and adjust to it, accustom o.s. to s.th.

جرنال *žurnāl* (*eg.* also *gurnāl*) pl. جرانيل *žarānīl*² (*eg.*, *garānīl*²) journal, newspaper, periodical

جرانيت *granīt* granite

جرانيتى *granītī* granitic

جرو *jarw* (*jirw*, *jurw*) pl. اجر *ajrin*, جراء *jirā'*, اجراء *ajrā'*, اجرية *ajriya* puppy, whelp, cub (of a dog or beast of prey)

جروسة *grōsa* gross (= 12 dozen)

جرى *jarā* **i** (*jary*) to flow, stream (water); to run; to hurry, rush; to blow (wind); to take place, come to pass, happen, occur; to be under way, be in progress, be going on (work); to befall (ل s.o.), happen (ل to); to be in circulation, circulate, be current; to wend one's way (الى to), head (الى for); to proceed (على in accordance with); to follow (مع s.th.), yield, give way (مع to, e.g., to a desire); to entail (ب s.th.); (with وراء) to run or be after s.th., seek to get s.th. | جرى له حديث مع he had a talk with; جرى مجراه (*majrāhu*) to take the same course as, be analogous to, follow the same way as, proceed or act in the same manner as; جرى منه الشيء مجرى الدم (*minhu š-šai'u majrā d-dam*) it had become second nature to him; جرى على الالسن (*alsun*) to circulate, make the rounds (rumor);

جرى على كل لسان to be on everyone's lips; جرى على قلمه (*qalamihī*) to come to s.o.'s pen (e.g., a poem); جرى على خطة (*kiṭṭa*) to follow a plan; ما يجرى عليه العمل (*'amalu*) the way things are handled, what is customary practice; جرى به العمل to be in force, be valid, be commonly observed (law, custom); جرت العادة ب to be customary, be common practice, be a common phenomenon, have gained vogue; جرى بالعادة على to do s.th. customarily, be in the habit of doing s.th.; جرت بذلك عادتهم that was their habit **II** to cause to run | جرى ريقه (*rīqahū*) to make s.o.'s mouth water **III** to concur, agree, be in agreement (ه with s.o., فى in s.th.); to keep pace, keep up (ه with s.o.; also intellectually); to be able to follow (ه s.o.); to go (along) (ه with); to adapt o.s., adjust, conform (ه to), be guided (ه by) **IV** to cause to flow, make flow (ه s.th.); to cause to run, set running (ه, ه s.o., s.th.); to make (ه s.th.) take place or happen, bring about (ه s.th.); to carry out, execute, enforce, put into effect, apply (ه s.th., e.g., rules, regulations); to carry out, perform (ه an action); to set going, set in motion (ه a project), launch (ه an undertaking); to channel (على or ل ه s.th. to), bestow, settle (على or ل ه s.th. upon s.o.); to impose, inflict (على ه s.th., a penalty, on s.o.) | اجرى تجربة (*tajribatan*) to carry out an experiment; اجرى تحقيقا to conduct an investigation; اجرى له اعانة (*i'ānatan*) to grant s.o. a subsidy; اجراه مجرى (*majrā*, with foll. genitive) to treat s.th. in the same manner as, put s.th. on equal footing with

جرى *jary* course | جريا على *jaryan 'alā* in accordance with, according to

من جراك *min jarāka* and من جرائك *min jarā'ika* because of you, on your account, for your sake

جراء *jarrā'* runner, racer

جراية *jirāya* pl. *-āt* daily (food) rations; pay, salary | عيش جراية *'ēš girāya* (*eg.*) coarse bread

جريان *jarayān* flow, flux; course; stream

مجرى *majran* pl. مجار *majārin* watercourse, stream, rivulet, gully; torrent or flood of water; pipeline; canal, channel; drain, sewer, pl. sewers, sewage system; power line (*el.*); current (*el.*); current (of a stream); guide rail (*techn.*); course (of events), progress, passage | مجرى البول *m. l-baul* urethra (*anat.*); مجارى التنفس *m. t-tanaffus* respiratory tract (*anat.*); مجرى الهواء *m. l-hawā'* air stream, current of air, draft; اخذ مجراه to take its course; see also جرى I and IV

ماجريات *mājarayāt*, *mājariyāt* (pl. of ما جرى) (course of) events, happenings

مجاراة *mujārāh* keeping up (with foll. genitive: with); conformity (with foll. genitive: with) | مجاراة ل *mujārātan li* in conformity with, in accordance with, according to

اجراء *ijrā'* pl. *-āt* performance (of an action); execution; enforcement; pl. measures, steps, proceedings | اتخذ اجراءات (*ittakaḍa*) to take measures; اجراءات قانونية (*qānūnīya*) legal steps, proceedings at law

جار *jārin* flowing, streaming, running; circulating; current, present | الشهر الجارى (*šahr*) the current month

جارية *jāriya* pl. *-āt*, جوار *jawārin* girl; slave girl; maid, servant; ship, vessel

جز *jazza u* (*jazz*) to cut off, clip (ه s.th.); to shear, shear off (ه s.th.; esp. the wool of sheep)

جزة *jizza* pl. جزز *jizaz*, جزائز *jazā'iz²* shorn wool, fleece, clip

جزازة *juzāza* pl. *-āt* slip of paper; label, tag

جزاز *jazzāz* pl. *-ūn* shearer, woolshearer

مجز *mijazz* woolshears

جزأ *jaza'a a* and VIII to be content, content o.s. (ب with) II to divide, part, separate, break up, cut up, partition (ه s.th.) V to divide, break up, be or become divided; to be separated, be detached, be partitioned off; to be divisible, separable (عن from)

جزء *juz'* pl. اجزاء *ajzā'* part, portion; constituent, component; fraction; division; section; the 30th part of the Koran (= 2 *ḥizb*)

جزئى *juz'ī* partial; minor, trivial, insignificant, unimportant; (*jur.*) minor, petty; جزئيا *juz'īyan* partly; جزئيات *juz'īyāt* details, particulars; trivialities; subordinate parts; divisions, sections (e.g., of a court of justice) | مواد جزئية (*mawādd*) petty cases (*jur.*); جنح جزئية (*junaḥ*) summary delicts (*jur.*); محاكم جزئية courts of summary justice; نيابة جزئية (*niyāba*) parquet of a summary court; حادثة جزئية minor incident; تسوية جزئية (*taswiya*) part payment; الجزئيات والكليات (*kullīyāt*) the particular and general aspects, the minor and the major issues

جزىء *juzai'* pl. *-āt* molecule

اجزائى *ajzā'ī* pl. *-ūn* pharmacist, druggist

اجزاجى *ajzājī* pl. *-īya* pharmacist, druggist

اجزائية *ajzā'īya* and اجزاخانة *ajzāḵāna* pl. *-āt* pharmacy, drugstore

تجزئة *tajzi'a* division; partition; separation; dissociation; breakdown (into classes, categories, etc.); fragmentation | قابل للتجزئة divisible; قابلية التجزئة divisibility; تاجر التجزئة retailer, retail merchant

جزدان *juzdān, jizdān* pl. *-āt* wallet; change purse

[1]جزر *jazara u* (*jazr*) to slaughter; to kill, butcher (ه an animal); — *i u* (*jazr*) to sink, fall, drop, ebb (water)

جزر *jazr* slaughter; butchering; ebb (of the sea)

جزرة *jazra* blood sacrifice

جزور *jazūr* pl. جزر *juzur* slaughter camel

جزار *jazzār* pl. ة, *-ūn* butcher

جزيرة *jazīra* pl. جزائر *jazā'ir*[2], جزر *juzur* island | شبه جزيرة *šibhu j.* peninsula; الجزيرة Al Jazira, (Northwest) Mesopotamia; الجزائر Algeria; Algiers; جزيرة العرب *j. al-'arab* Arabia, the Arabian Peninsula; الجزائر الخالدات (*ḵālidāt*) the Canary Islands; الجزيرة الخضراء (*ḵaḍrā'*) Algeciras (seaport in SW Spain)

جزرى *jazarī* insular; (pl. *-ūn*) islander

جزائرى *jazā'irī* pl. *-ūn* Algerian (adj. and n.); islander

مجزر *majzir* pl. مجازر *majāzir*[2] slaughterhouse, abattoir, butchery

مجزرة *majzara* pl. مجازر *majāzir*[2] butchery; massacre, carnage

[2]جزر *jazar* (coll.; n. un. ة) carrot(s)

جزع *jazi'a a* (*jaza'*, جزوع *juzū'*) to be or become anxious, worried, concerned; to be sad, unhappy (من about); to feel regret (على for s.o.), pity (على s.o.); to mourn (على for s.o.) V to break apart, break, snap

جزع *jaz'* onyx

جزع *juz'* axle; shaft (*techn.*)

جزع *jaza'* anxiety, uneasiness, apprehension, concern; anguish, fear; sadness

جزع *jazi'* restless, impatient; anxious, worried, uneasy, apprehensive

جزوع *jazū'* and جازع *jāzi'* restless; impatient; anxious, worried, uneasy, apprehensive

مجزع *mujazza'* marbled, veined; variegated, dappled

جزف III to act at random, blindly, indiscriminately, take a chance; to speculate (*fin.*); to speak vaguely, in general terms; to risk, stake (ب s.th.) | جازف بنفسه to risk one's life; جازف به فى to plunge s.o. into (some adventure)

جزاف *juzāf* purchase of a certain amount of things (*Isl. Law*); جزافا *juzāfan* at random, haphazardly

مجازفة *mujāzafa* rashness, recklessness, foolhardiness; risk, hazard; adventure, venture

مجازف *mujāzif* rash, reckless, foolhardy; adventurous; venturesome

[1]جزل *jazula u* to be considerable, abundant, plentiful IV اجزل له العطاء (*'aṭā'a*) to give generously, openhandedly, liberally to s.o. VIII to write shorthand

جزل *jazl* and جزيل *jazīl* pl. جزال *jizāl* abundant, plentiful, ample, much; pure, lucid, eloquent (style) | جزل الرأى of sound, unerring judgment; شكره شكرا جزيلا *šakarahū šukran jazīlan* he thanked him profusely; شكرا جزيلا many thanks!

جزلة *jizla* piece, slice

جزالة *jazāla* profusion, abundance; (*rhet.*) purity (of style)

مجتزل *mujtazil* stenographer

[2]جوزل look up alphabetically

[3]جزلان *juzlān* = جزدان

[1]جزم *jazama i* (*jazm*) to cut off, cut short, clip (ه s.th.); to judge; to decide, settle (ه s.th.); to be positive (ب about), be absolutely certain (ب of s.th.); to assert authoritatively (ب s.th.); to make up one's mind, decide, resolve (على to do s.th.); to impose, make incumbent (ه على s.th. on s.o.); (*gram.*) to pronounce the final consonant (of a word) without a vowel; to put (ه a verb) into the apocopate form or the imperative

جزم *jazm* cutting off, clipping; decision; resolution, resolve; apodictic judgment; (*gram.*) apocopate form | علامة الجزم *'alāmat al-j.* = *jazma*

جزمة *jazma* diacritical mark (°) indicating vowellessness of a final consonant

جازم *jāzim* decisive; peremptory, definite, definitive, final; firmly convinced, absolutely certain (ب of s.th.); (pl. جوازم *jawāzim*[2]) governing the apocopate form (*gram.*)

مجزوم *majzūm* cut off, cut short, clipped; decided, settled; (*gram.*) vowelless (final consonant); in the apocopate form

منجزم *munjazim* (*gram.*) in the apocopate form

[2]جزمة *jazma* pl. *-āt*, جزم *jizam* (pair of) shoes, (pair of) boots | جزمة برباط (*bi-ribāṭ*) laced boots; جزمة لماعة (*lammā'a*) patent-leather shoes

جزمجى *gazmagī* (*eg.*) and جزماتى *gizamātī* (*eg.*), *jazmātī* (*syr.*) pl. *-īya* shoemaker

جزى *jazā i* (جزاء *jazā'*) to requite, recompense (ه s.o., ب or على for), repay (ه to s.o., ب or على s.th.); to reward (ه s.o., ب or على for); to punish (ه s.o., ب or على for); to satisfy (ه s.o.), give satisfaction (ه to s.o.); to compensate, make up (ب ه for s.th. with or by); to compensate, offset (عن s.th.) | جزاك الله خيرا (*ḵairan*) may God bless you for it! جزاه جزاء سنمار (*jazā'a sinimmāra*) he returned to him good for evil III to repay, requite (ب ه s.th. with, ب ه s.o. for), recompense (ب ه s.o. for); to reward (على or ب ه s.o. for); to punish (على or ب ه s.o. for) | جازاهم خيرا (*ḵairan*) he invoked God's reward upon them IV to suffice (ه s.o.), do for s.o. (ه); to take the place, serve instead (عن of), replace (عن s.th.)

جزاء *jazā'* requital, repayment; recompense, return; compensation, setoff;

amends, reparation; punishment, penalty | جزاء نقدى (*naqdī*) fine

جزائى *jazā'ī* penal

جزية *jizya* pl. جزى *jizan*, جزاء *jizā'* tax; tribute; head tax on free non-Muslims under Muslim rule

تجزية *tajziya* reward

مجازاة *mujāzāh* requital, repayment; punishment

جس **jassa** *u* (*jass*, مجسة *majassa*) to touch, feel, handle (ه s.th.); to palpate, examine by touch (ه s.th.); to test, sound, probe (ه s.th.); to try to gain information (ه about), try to find out (ه s.th.); to spy out (ه s.th.) | جس نبضه (*nabḍahū*) to feel s.o.'s pulse, (fig.) جس نبض الشيء to probe, sound out, try to find out s.th. **V** to try to gain information (ه about), try to find out (ه s.th.); to reconnoiter, scout, explore (ه s.th.); to be a spy, engage in espionage; to spy, pry, snoop (على on s.o.) | تجسس له اخبارا (*akbāran*) to gather information for s.o., spy for s.o. **VIII** to touch, feel, handle (ه s.th.); to spy out (ه s.th.)

جس *jass*: طرى الجس *ṭarīy al-j.* delicate to the touch, having a tender surface, fresh

جاسوس *jāsūs* pl. جواسيس *jawāsīs*[2] spy

جاسوسة *jāsūsa* woman spy

جاسوسى *jāsūsī* of espionage, spy- (in compounds)

جاسوسية *jāsūsīya* spying, espionage

جوسسة *jausasa* spying, espionage

مجس *majass* spot which one touches or feels; sense of touch | خشن المجس *kašin al-m.* coarse to the touch, having a rough surface

مجس *mijass* probe (*med.*)

تجسس *tajassus* spying, espionage

جاسى *jāsi'* hard, rough, rugged

جسد **II** to make corporeal, invest with a body, embody, incarnate (ه s.th.), give concrete form (ه to s.th.); to render or represent in corporeal form (ه s.th.) **V** to become corporeal, assume concrete form, materialize; to become incarnate (*Chr.*); to become three-dimensional

جسد *jasad* pl. اجساد *ajsād* body | عيد الجسد *'īd al-j.* and خميس الجسد Corpus Christi Day (*Chr.*)

جسدى *jasadī* bodily, fleshly, carnal

جسدانى *jusdānī* bodily

تجسد *tajassud* materialization; incarnation (*Chr.*)

مجسد *mujassad* embodied, corporified

متجسد *mutajassid* corporeal; incarnate (*Chr.*),

جسر **jasara** *u* to span, cross, traverse (ه s.th.); (جسارة *jasāra*, جسور *jusūr*) to venture, risk (على s.th.), have the courage (على to do s.th.) **II** to build a dam or dike; to embolden, encourage (ه s.o., على to do s.th.) **VI** to dare, venture, risk (على s.th.), have the audacity (على to do s.th.); to be bold, forward, insolent, impudent (على with s.o.) **VIII** to span, cross, traverse (ه s.th.)

جسر *jisr* pl. اجسر *ajsur*, جسور *jusūr* bridge; dam, dike, embankment, levee; — (pl. جسورة *jusūra*) beam, girder; axle, axletree | جسر متحرك (*mutaḥarrik*) movable bridge; جسر معلق (*mu'allaq*) suspension bridge; جسر عائم pontoon bridge, floating bridge

جسور *jasūr* bold, daring; forward, insolent, impudent

جسارة *jasāra* boldness, recklessness, intrepidity; forwardness, insolence

تجاسر *tajāsur* boldness, recklessness, intrepidity; forwardness, insolence

متجاسر *mutajāsir* bold, daring; forward, insolent, impudent

جسطن see جصطن

جسم jasuma u (جسامة jasāma) to be great, big, large, bulky, huge, immense II to make corporeal, invest with a body (ه s.th.), give (ه s.th.) shape or form; to materialize (ه s.th.); to cause to stand out, bring out (ه s.th.); to enlarge, magnify (ه s.th.; e.g., microscope); to make big, bulky, huge (ه s.th.); to play up, exaggerate (ه s.th.) V to become corporeal, become embodied; to materialize; to assume a form, take shape, become tangible or concrete; to be materialized; to become big, large, huge, increase in volume, grow in size

جسم jism pl. اجسام ajsām, جسوم jusūm body (also ○ of an automobile); substance, matter; mass; form, shape

جسمى jismī bodily, physical; substantial, material

جسيم jasīm pl. جسام jisām great, big, large; voluminous, bulky, huge; vast, immense; stout, corpulent; weighty, most significant, momentous, prodigious

جسيم jusaim pl. -āt particle (phys.); corpuscle (biol.)

اجسم ajsam² more voluminous, larger; stouter, more corpulent

جسامة jasāma size, volume; stoutness, corpulence

جسمان jusmān body, mass

جسمانى jusmānī bodily, physical, corporal | التأديب الجسمانى corporal punishment

تجسيم tajsīm embodiment; relief; enlargement, magnification, magnifying power

مجسم mujassam bodily, corporeal; (math.) body; three-dimensional; tangible, material, concrete; raised, relieflike, standing out in relief (e.g., خريطة مجسمة relief map); relief; enlarged, magnified | فلم مجسم (film) three-dimensional (stereoscopic) film, 3-D motion picture

جسمانية jasmānīya² Gethsemane

جسا (جسو) jasā u to become hard, solid

جش jašša u (jašš) to grind, crush, bruise, grate (ه s.th.)

جشة jušša hoarseness, huskiness, raucity (of the voice)

جشيش jašīš ground, grated, crushed

اجش ajašš², f. جشاء jaššā'² hoarse, husky, raucous (voice)

جشأ II and V to belch, burp

جشاء jušā' and جشأة juš'a belch(ing), burp(ing)

جشار jušār livestock

جشع jaši'a a (jaša') and V to be covetous, greedy

جشع jaša' greed, avidity, inordinate desire

جشع jaši' greedy, covetous

جشم jašima a (jašm, جشامة jašāma) to take upon o.s. (ه some hardship) II to make (ه s.o.) suffer or undergo (ه s.th.); to impose (ه ه on s.o. s.th. difficult), burden (ه ه s.o. with s.th.) V to take upon o.s., suffer, undergo (ه s.th., e.g., hardships)

جشنى (eg., cf. ششنى šišnī) sample, specimen; sampling

جص II to plaster, whitewash (ه s.th.)

جص jiṣṣ gypsum; plaster of Paris

جصطن II tajaṣṭana to lounge, stretch lazily, loll

جعة ji'a beer

جعب II to corrugate (ه s.th.)

جعبة ja'ba pl. جعاب ji'āb quiver; tube, pipe; gun barrel; ○ cartridge pouch (Syr.) | جعبة اخبار j. akbār town gossip (person)

جعجع *jaʿjaʿa* (جعجعة *jaʿjaʿa*) to clamor, roar, shout; to clatter, clap; to bluster, explode in anger

جعجعة *jaʿjaʿa* hubbub, rumpus, clamor, roar; creak, clapping noise (of a mill wheel); bluster

جعجاع *jaʿjāʿ* clamorous, boisterous, noisy; bawler, loud-mouthed person

جعد *jaʿuda u* (جعودة *juʿūda*, جعادة *jaʿāda*) and **V** to become curly, frizzed, kinky, curl (hair); to be wavy; to be creased; to be wrinkled **II** to curl, frizz (▲ s.th.; the hair); to wave (▲ s.th.; the hair); to crease, pleat, plait (▲ cloth); to wrinkle (▲ the skin)

جعد *jaʿd* (or جعد اليد *j. al-yad*, جعد الكف *j. al-kaff*) stingy, niggardly, tightfisted

جعدة *jaʿda* curl, lock, ringlet

جعدى *jaʿdī* and اجعد *ajʿad*² curly

جعيدى *gəʿēdī* (*eg.*) bum, loafer, good-for-nothing

تجاعيد *tajāʿīd*² wrinkles, lines (of the face)

تجعدات *tajaʿʿudāt* wrinkles

مجعد *mujaʿʿad* curled, frizzed; wavy; furrowed, creased; wrinkled

متجعد *mutajaʿʿid* curled, frizzed; wavy; furrowed, creased; wrinkled

جعدنة *jaʿdana* idle talk, gossip (*leb.*)

جعر *jaʿara a* (*jaʿr*) to drop its manure (animal)

ابو جعران *abū jiʿrān*² scarabaeus; dung beetle

جعفر *jaʿfar* little river, creek

جعل *jaʿala a* (*jaʿl*) to make (▲ s.th.); to put, place, lay (▲ s.th.); to create (▲ s.th.); to effect, bring about (▲ s.th.); to make (▲ ▲ s.th. a rule, a principle, or the like, • • s.o., e.g., leader, king, etc.), appoint (• • s.o. to an office, rank, or the like); to fix, set (▲ ▲ a sum, a price, at); to think, deem, believe (ب • or • • s.o. to be ..., ▲ ▲ s.th. to be ...), take (ب • or • • s.o. for, ▲ ▲ s.th. for); to represent (▲ s.th., فى صورة as, or in the form of, s.th. else); to appoint, settle (ل ▲ s.th. for s.o., in s.o.'s favor); to give, grant, concede (ل ▲ s.th., an advantage, to s.o.), put s.o. (ل) in the way of s.th. (▲); to attribute (▲ ل to s.o. s.th.), maintain that s.th. (▲) belongs to s.o. (ل); to entrust (الى ▲ s.th. to s.o.); to put, get (• s.o., ▲ s.th., into a specific state or condition); (with foll. imperf.) to begin to, set out to | جعله يفعل to induce s.o. to do; to make s.o. do s.th. (in a narrative); جعله بمنزلة (*bi-manzilati*) to place s.o. on equal footing with; جعله فى متناول يده (*fī mutanāwali yadihī*) to bring or put s.th. within s.o.'s reach **III** to seek to bribe, try to win (ب • s.o. with s.th.)

جعل *juʿl* pl. اجعال *ajʿāl* pay, wages; piece wages; reward, prize

جعلى *juʿlī*: اتفاق جعلى (*ittifāq*) piecework contract

جعل *juʿal* pl. جعلان *jiʿlān* dung beetle; scarabaeus

جعالة *jiʿāla, jaʿāla, juʿāla* pl. جعائل *jaʿāʾil*² pay, wages; allowance; reward, prize; bribe

جغرافيا *juḡrāfiyā* and جغرافية *juḡrāfīya* geography | جغرافية طبيعية (*ṭabīʿīya*) physical geography

جغرافى *juḡrāfī* geographical; geographer

جف *jaffa* (1st pers. perf. *jafaftu*) *i* (جفاف *jafāf*, جفوف *jufūf*) to dry, become dry; to dry out **II** to dry, make dry (▲ s.th.)

جفاف *jafāf* dryness; desiccation; drying up; dullness

تجفاف *tijfāf* pl. تجافيف *tajāfīf*² protective armor

تجفيف *tajfīf* drying; desiccation; dehydration; drainage

جاف *jāff* dry | قلم حبر جاف (*qalam ḥibr*) ball-point pen

مجفف *mujaffaf* dried, desiccated, dehydrated; مجففات dehydrated foods

جفاء *jufā'* useless, vain, futile | ذهب جفاء *ḏahaba jufā'an* to be in vain, be of no avail, pass uselessly

جفت *jift*, چفت *čift* (pronounced *šift*; *eg.*) pincers, tweezers; metal clamp | جفت شريان *j. šaryān* arterial clamps

چفتشى (pronounced *šiftiši*; *eg.*) filigree

جفتلك *jiftlik* farm, country estate; government land (*Pal.*)

جفر *jafr*, علم الجفر *'ilm al-j.* divination, fortunetelling

جفرة *jufra* pl. جفر *jufar* pit, hole

جفل *jafala i u* (*jafl*, جفول *jufūl*) and **IV** to start, jump with fright; to shy (horse) **II** to start, rouse (ه s.th., ه s.o.); to scare away (ه s.o.)

جفل *jafl* and جفول *jufūl* fright, alarm; shying

چفلك (pronounced *šiflik*; *eg.*) = جفتلك

جفن *jafn* pl. جفون *jufūn*, اجفان *ajfān* eyelid

جفنة *jafna* pl. جفان *jifān*, جفنات *jafanāt* bowl; grapevine

(جفو) جفا *jafā u* (*jafw*, جفاء *jafā'*) to be rough, coarse; to treat (ه s.o.) roughly, harshly; to turn away (ه from), shun, avoid, flee (ه s.o.) **III** to treat (ه s.o.) roughly, rudely, harshly; to be cruel (ه to s.o.); to be cross (ه with s.o.); to elude, flee (ه s.o.; slumber); to offend (ه against good taste, one's sense of honor, or the like) **VI** to withdraw (عن from), shun, avoid (ه s.o.); to loathe (عن s.o., s.th.), have an aversion (عن to); to display rude manners, act the ruffian

جفو *jafw* roughness, harshness

جفوة *jafwa* roughness; estrangement, alienation; disagreement, dissension, quarrel

جفاء *jafā'* roughness, harshness; sternness; antipathy, aversion, distaste, loathing; estrangement, alienation

اجفى *ajfā* refraining even more (ل from), more averse (ل to s.th.)

جاف *jāfin* pl. جفاة *jufāh* harsh, rough, coarse; brutish, uncouth, rude

جاكتة look up alphabetically

جكر **III** (*syr.*) to tease (ه s.o.)

[1]جل *jalla i* (جلال *jalāl*) to be great, lofty, exalted, illustrious, sublime; to be too great (عن for), be beyond s.th. (عن), be far above s.th. (عن) | جل عن الحصر (*'an il-ḥaṣr*) to be innumerable **II** to honor, dignify, exalt (ه s.o.); to cover (ه s.th., esp. the ground, as snow, plants, etc.); to envelop, wrap, drape, clothe; to border, edge (ه s.th., ب with) **IV** to honor, dignify, revere, venerate, esteem highly, exalt (ه s.o.); to deem too high, too exalted (عن for s.th.), consider far beyond s.th. (عن) **VI** to deem o.s. far above s.th. (عن) **X** to be great, exalted, sublime

جل *jall* great, outstanding; bulky

جل *jull* major portion, bulk, majority, main part | جله *julluhū* most of it; جل الامة *j. al-umma* the majority of the people; جل ما فيه its main contents; وجل ما يقال انه (*jullu*) that much, at least, can be said that ...

جلل *jalal* important, significant, momentous, weighty

جلى *jullā* pl. جلل *julal* matter of great importance, momentous undertaking, great feat, exploit

جلة *julla*, *jilla* droppings, dung (of animals); *julla* pl. جلل *julal* (cannon) ball; bomb

جلة *julla* attire, clothing | الحلة الحبروية (الكهنوتية) (*ḥabrawīya, kahnūtīya*) episcopal (sacerdotal) vestments (*Chr.*)

جليل *jalīl* pl. اجلاء *ajillā'*, اجلة *ajilla*, جلائل *jalā'il*² great, important, significant, weighty, momentous; lofty, exalted, sublime; revered, honorable, venerable; glorious, splendid

جلال *jalāl* loftiness, sublimity, augustness; splendor, glory

جلالة *jalāla* loftiness, sublimity, augustness; majesty | صاحب (صاحبة) الجلالة His (Her) Majesty, جلالة الملك *j. al-malik* His Majesty, the King

اجل *ajall*² greater; more sublime; more splendid

مجلة *majalla* pl. *-āt* periodical; review, magazine | مجلة اسبوعية (*usbū'īya*) weekly magazine; مجلة شهرية (*šahrīya*) monthly publication; مجلة خاصة ب (*kāṣṣa*) professional journal for ...; مجلة الاحكام lawbook, code; مجلة القوانين do.

تجلة *tajilla* and اجلال *ijlāl* honor, distinction; esteem, deference, respect; reverence

جل² *jull* rose

جلاب *julāb, jullāb* rose water; julep

جلاتين (Fr. *gélatine*) *želātīn* jelly

جلاسيه (Fr. *glacé*) *glasēh* (*eg.*) kid leather

جلب¹ *jalaba i u* (*jalb*) to attract (ه s.th.); to fetch, get, bring (ه s.th., ل to s.o.); to import (ه goods); to bring about (ه a state, condition); to bring (ه harm, shame, etc., على upon s.o.); to gain, win, obtain (ه s.th.); to earn (ه s.th.); (جلوب *julūb*) to scar over, heal (wound) **II** to shout, clamor; to be noisy, boisterous **IV** to earn, gain, acquire (ه s.th.); = **II**; **VII** pass. of I **VIII** to procure, bring, fetch, get (ه s.th.); to draw (ه on s.th.); to import (ه goods) **X** to import (ه goods); to fetch, summon, call in (ه s.o.); to attract, draw (ه, ه s.o., s.th.); to seek to attract or win (ه, ه s.o., s.th.); to get, procure (ه s.th.)

جلب *jalb* bringing, fetching; procurement; acquisition; importation, import; causation, bringing on, bringing about

جلب *jalab* imported; foreign

جلب *jalab* and جلبة *jalaba* clamor; uproar, tumult, turmoil

جلبة *julba* scar

جليب *jalīb* imported, foreign; (pl. جلبى *jalbā*, جلباء *julabā'*²) foreign slave

جلاب *jallāb* attractive, captivating; importer, trader; see also alphabetically | جلاب العبيد slave trader

جلابية *gallābīya* (*eg.*) pl. *-āt*, جلاليب *galālīb*² galabia, a loose, shirtlike garment, the common dress of the male population in Egypt

جلباب see below under جلبب

اجلب *ajlab*² more attractive, more captivating

مجلبة *majlaba* pl. مجالب *majālib*² causative factor, motive, reason, cause, occasion

استجلاب *istijlāb* procurement, acquisition; importation, import; supply; attraction | استجلاب السائحين promotion of tourist traffic

جالب *jālib* causative factor, motive, reason, cause, occasion

جلاب² *julāb, jullāb* rose water; julep

جلبا³ *jalabā* jalap (*bot.*)

جلبب **II** *tajalbaba* to clothe o.s. (ب with), be clothed, be clad (ب in a garment, also fig.)

جلباب *jilbāb* pl. جلابيب *jalābīb*² garment, dress, gown; woman's dress

جلبان *julubbān* chickling vetch, grass pea (Lathyrus sativus)

[1]جلجل *jaljala* to reverberate; to resound, ring out; to rattle; to shake (ه s.th.)

جلجل *juljul* pl. جلاجل *jalājil*[2] (little) bell, sleigh bell; cowbell; jingle

جلجلة *jaljala* sound of a bell; loud, shrill sound

مجلجل *mujaljil* shrill, piercing; ringing, resounding, reverberant

[2]جلجلة *juljula*, جبل الجلجلة *jabal al-j.* Golgotha

[3]جلجلان *juljulān, jiljilān* sesame

جلح *jaliḥa a* (*jalaḥ*) to be or become bald

اجلح *ajlaḥ*[2], f. جلحاء *jalḥā'*[2], pl. جلح *julḥ* bald-headed, bald

جلخ *jalaka a* and II to sharpen (ه s.th.); to whet, hone (ه a knife), strop (ه a razor); to stretch, extend, roll out (ه metal)

جلخ *jalk* grindstone, whetstone, hone

جلد *jalada i* (*jald*) to whip, flog, lash (ه s.o.); — *jalida a* to be frozen, freeze; — *jaluda u* to be tough, hardy, undismayed, steadfast, patient II to bind (ه a book); (to cause) to freeze (ه s.th.) III to fight (ه s.o.) IV to freeze; to be frozen, be covered with ice V to take heart; to show o.s. tough, hardy, robust; to resign o.s. to patience; to bear, suffer VI to engage in a sword fight

جلد *jald* flogging; — (pl. اجلاد *ajlād*) staunch, steadfast; strong, sturdy

جلد *jild* pl. جلود *julūd*, اجلاد *ajlād* skin, hide; leather | جلد سختيان (*suktiyān*) morocco; جلد لماع (*lammā'*) patent leather

جلدة *jilda* skin, hide; piece of leather; race | ابن جلدتنا *ibn jildatinā* our countryman, our fellow tribesman, pl. بنو جلدتنا *banū j.*

جلدى *jildī* dermal, cutaneous, skin (adj.) | امراض جلدية skin diseases

جليدة *julaida* pl. *-āt* membrane, pellicle; ○ film (*phot.*)

جلد *jalad* endurance; suffering; patience; firmament

جلدة *jalda* lash, stroke with a whip

جليد *jalīd* pl. جلداء *juladā'*[2] staunch, steadfast; strong, sturdy

جليد *jalīd* ice | جبل جليد *jabal j.* iceberg; قطعة من الجليد (*qiṭ'a*) ice floe

جليدى *jalīdī* icy, ice-covered, glacial, ice (adj.); snow-covered | العصر الجليدى (*'aṣr*) the Ice Age

جلود *jalūd* long-suffering, patient

جلاد *jallād* pl. *-ūn* leather merchant; executioner, hangman

جلادة *jalāda* and جلودة *julūda* endurance, patience

مجلدة *mijlada* whip, lash, scourge

تجليد *tajlīd* freezing; bookbinding

جلاد *jilād* fight, battle (against)

تجلد *tajallud* endurance, patience

مجلد *mujallid*: مجلد الكتب *m. al-kutub* bookbinder

مجلد *mujallad* frozen, icy, ice-covered; bound (book); (pl. *-āt*) volume (book)

مجالد *mujālid* pl. *-ūn* gladiator

متجلد *mutajallid* patient

جلوز *jillauz* (coll.; n. un. ة) hazelnut; hazel

جلس *jalasa i* (جلوس *julūs*) to sit down (الى with s.o., at a table, etc., على on a chair); to sit (الى with s.o., at a table, على on a chair) | جلس الى الرسام (*rassām*) to sit for a painter III to sit (ه with s.o., next to s.o., in s.o.'s company); to keep s.o. (ه) company IV to ask to sit down, make sit down, seat (ه s.o.)

جلسة *jalsa* pl. *-āt* seat (in an auditorium); session (of parliament, of a committee, of a court, etc.); party, gathering, meeting | عقد جلسة *'aqada jalsatan* to convene a session; جلسة عامة (*'āmma*) plenary session

جلسة *jilsa* manner of sitting

جليس *jalīs* pl. جلساء *julasā'*[2] participant in a social gathering; table companion; one with whom one sits together; جليسه the man who was at the party with him

جليسة *jalīsa* lady companion; fem. of جليس

جلوس *julūs* sitting; sitting down; accession to the throne; pl. of جالس *jālis* sitting

مجلس *majlis* pl. مجالس *majālis*[2] seat; session room, conference room; party, gathering, meeting; social gathering; session, sitting; council meeting; council; concilium; collegium, college; board, committee, commission; administrative board; court, tribunal | فى مجلسه in s.o.'s presence, in s.o.'s company; مجلس التأديب and مجلس تأديبى disciplinary board; مجلس تأسيسى constituent assembly; مجلس آفاق regional court (*tribunal régional; Tun.*); مجلس الامة *m. al-umma* parliament (*Ir.*); مجلس الامن *m. al-amn* the Security Council; مجلس البلدية *m. al-baladīya* and مجلس بلدى (*baladī*) local council, municipal council; مجلس الحرب *m. al-ḥarb* war council; مجلس حسبى (*ḥasbī*) probate court (for Muslims; *Eg.*); مجلس مختلط (*muktaliṭ*) mixed court (*eg.*); مجلس الدفاع defense council; مجلس الادارة *m. al-idāra* administrative board, committee of management, directorate; board of directors (of a corporation or bank); مجلس المديرية *m. al-mudīrīya* provincial council, provincial parliament (*Eg.*); مجلس الدولة *m. ad-daula* Supreme Administrative Court (*Eg.*); مجلس روحى (*rūḥī*) religious court, clerical court (of the Coptic Church); مجلس شورى الدولة *m. šūrā d-daula* council of state; مجلس الشيوخ council of elders; senate (*Eg.*); مجلس عدلى (*'adlī*) court, tribunal (*Syr.*); مجلس عرفى (or عسكرى) (*'urfī, 'askarī*) court-martial; مجلس عصبة الامم *m. 'uṣbat al-umam* Council of the League of Nations; مجلس العموم the House of Commons; مجلس الاعيان *m. al-a'yān* senate (*Ir., Jord.*); مجلس الاقتراع draft board, recruiting commission (*mil.*); مجلس قروى (*qarawī*) local council; مجلس اقتصادى (*iqtiṣādī*) economic council; مجلس قومى (*qaumī*) national assembly; مجلس قيادة الثورة *m. qiyādat aṯ-ṯaura* Supreme Revolutionary Tribunal (*Eg.*); المجلس الكبير and المجلس الاكبر (*akbar*) the Grand Council (= *le Grand Conseil*; *Tun.*); مجلس اللوردين the House of Lords; مجلس النواب *m. an-nuwwāb* lower house, chamber of deputies; مجلس نيابى (*niyābī*) parliament; مجلس الجهة *m. al-jiha* approx.: provincial council (= *conseil de région*; *Tun.*); مجلس الوزراء *m. al-wuzarā'* cabinet, council of ministers

مجالسة *mujālasa* social intercourse

جالس *jālis* pl. جلوس *julūs*, جلاس *jullās* sitting; pl. جلاس participants in a social gathering

جلط *jalaṭa* i (*jalṭ*) to chafe, gall, abrade (ه the skin); to shave (الرأس *ar-ra'sa* the head)

جلطة *julṭa* lump, clot | جلطة دموية (*damawīya*) blood clot, thrombus

جلف *jilf* pl. اجلاف *ajlāf* boorish, rude, uncivil

جلفط *jalfaṭa* (جلفطة *jalfaṭa*) to calk (ه a ship)

جلفن *galfana* (*eg.*) to galvanize

جلفنة *galfana* galvanization

مجلفن *mugalfan* galvanized

جلاقة *jalāqa*: جلاقة قروية (*qarawīya*) yokel, bumpkin

جلم *jalama* i (*jalm*) to clip, shear off (ه s.th.)

جلم *jalam* pl. اجلام *ajlām* shears

ابو جلمبو *abū galambū* (*eg.*) a variety of crab

جلمد II *tajalmada* to be petrified

جلمد *jalmad* pl. جلامد *jalāmid*[2] and جلمود *julmūd* pl. جلاميد *jalāmīd*[2] rock, bolder

جلنار *jullanār* pomegranate blossom

جلا (جلو and جلى) *jalā u* to clean, polish (ه s.th.); to clear (ه the view); to make clear, make plain, clarify, clear up (ه s.th.), throw light on (ه); to reveal, unveil, disclose (ه s.th.); to dislodge, oust, remove (عن ه or ه s.o. or s.th. from); to shine, be brilliant, distinguish o.s. (فى in s.th.); to be or become clear, evident, manifest; to pull out, move out (عن of a place), go away, depart (عن from a place), leave, quit, evacuate (عن a place); — جلى *jalā i* to polish, burnish (ه s.th.) **II** to reveal, disclose, bring to light (عن or ه s.th.); to show, represent (ه s.o., ه s.th.); **IV** to remove, dislodge, oust, drive away (ه, ه s.o., s.th.); to evacuate (ه s.o., عن from); to move away, go away (عن from a place), leave (عن a place) **V** to become clear, evident, manifest; to reveal itself, be revealed; to appear, show, come to light, come out, manifest itself; to be manifested, be expressed, find expression **VII** to be clean or cleaned, be polished, be burnished; to be removed, be dislodged, be ousted; to move away (عن from a place), vacate, evacuate (عن a place); to be dispelled, vanish, go away, pass (crisis, difficulty, etc.); to disappear; to reveal itself, be revealed, be disclosed; to be unveiled (bride); to become manifest, manifest itself; to become clear or plain; to clear up and reveal (عن s.th.); to lead, come (عن to), end (عن in); to result (عن in) | ما ينجلى عنه الامر the outcome of the matter, what will come of it **VIII** to reveal, disclose (ه s.th.); to regard (ه s.th.), look at (ه) **X** to seek to clarify (ه s.th.); to clarify, clear up (ه s.th.), throw light (ه on); to uncover, unearth, bring to light, find out, discover, detect (ه s.th.)

ابن جلا *ibn jalā* a famous, well-known man, a celebrity

جلى *jalīy* clear, plain, evident, patent, manifest, obvious, conspicuous; جليا *jalīyan* obviously, evidently

جلية *jalīya* pl. جلايا *jalāyā* sure thing, plain fact | جلية الامر *jalīyat al-amr* the true state of the affair

اجلى *ajlā* clearer, more obvious, more distinct

جلوة *jilwa* unveiling (of the bride) | ليلة الجلوة *lailat al-j.* wedding night

جلاء *jalā'* clarification, elucidation; clarity, clearness, plainness, distinctness; departure, (e)migration (عن from); evacuation (عن of an area; *mil.*); بجلاء clearly, plainly

جليان *jalayān* vision, revelation, apocalypse (*Chr.*)

مجال *majālin* (pl. of مجلى *majlan*) manifestations

تجلية *tajliya*: تجلية الاهية (*ilāhīya*) divine revelation; theophany (*Chr.*)

تجل *tajallin* revelation, manifestation; Transfiguration (of Christ) | عيد التجلى *'īd at-t.* Transfiguration Day (*Chr.*)

اجتلاء *ijtilā'* contemplation

استجلاء *istijlā'* clarification, elucidation

جالية *jāliya* pl. *-āt*, جوال *jawālin* colony (of foreigners); colony of emigrants

المجلى *al-mujallī* the winner (in a race)

متجل *mutajallin* obvious, evident, manifest, patent

جلون *galōn* pl. *-āt* gallon (*eg.*)

مجلون *mugalwan* galvanized (*eg.*)

جلى *jullā* see [1]جل

جليوتين gilyotīn guillotine (eg.)

[1]ج م abbreviation of جنيه مصرى Egyptian pound

[2]جم jamma i u (jamm) to gather: to collect one's thoughts, concentrate; to rest **II** and **V** to grow luxuriantly (plants) **X** to gather; to collect one's thoughts, concentrate; to rest, relax, seek recreation (من from); to be covered with luxuriant vegetation (ground)

جم jamm abundant, plentiful; much, a great deal of; many, numerous; manifold, multiple; crowd, group of people | جم الاثر j. al-aṯar effective, efficacious; احبه حبا جما (aḥabbahū ḥubban) to be more than fond of; فوائد جمة numerous advantages, ample benefits; جم غفير large crowd, throng

جمام jamām rest, relaxation, recreation, gathering of new strength

مجم majamm place where s.th. gathers or flows together | مجم هذا الرأى ومستجمعه (mustajmaʿuhū) what this opinion amounts to

تجميم tagmīm (eg.) bobbed hairdo (of women)

استجمام istijmām collectedness; concentration; attentiveness, attentive reverence; rest, relaxation, recreation

جمباز, جمبازى, جنباز, جنبازى see

جمبرى (from It. gambero) gambarī, جمرى gammarī (eg.) shrimp (zool.)

[1]جمجم jamjama (جمجمة jamjama), جمجم الكلام (kalāma) and **II** tajamjama to articulate indistinctly, stammer; to express o.s. poorly, speak incoherently; to mumble

[2]جمجمة jumjuma pl. جماجم jamājim[2] skull, cranium

جمجمى jumjumī cranial

جمح jamaḥa a (jamḥ, جماح jimāḥ, جموح jumūḥ) to bolt (horse); to be refractory, unruly, recalcitrant; to be defiant; to be capricious, whimsical, to run out on her husband, run away from home (wife)

جماح jimāḥ recalcitrance, defiance; willfulness

جموح jumūḥ recalcitrance, defiance; willfulness

جموح jamūḥ headstrong, defiant, unruly, ungovernable

جامح jāmiḥ headstrong, defiant, unruly; indomitable, untamable

[1]جمد jamada u, jamuda u (jamd, جمود jumūd) to freeze; to congeal, harden, stiffen, be or become hard or solid, solidify; to coagulate, clot (blood); to be rigid, inflexible (in one's thinking); to stagnate; to be apathetic, indolent, dull, indifferent | جمدت نفسه على to be indifferent toward, put up with, acquiesce in; جمدت يده (yaduhū) to be niggardly, tightfisted **II** to freeze, frost, congeal (ه s.th.); to solidify, coagulate, harden, stiffen (ه s.th.); to curdle (ه s.th.); to freeze (ه assets) **V** to freeze, become frozen, turn into ice, freeze up, become icebound; to freeze to death; to congeal; to solidify; to harden, set (e.g., cement); to coagulate, clot (blood) **VII** to freeze up, become icebound; to freeze, become frozen, turn to ice

جمد jamd freezing; congelation, solidification, coagulation | درجة الجمد darajat al-j. freezing point

جمد jamad ice

جماد jamād pl. -āt a solid; inorganic body; mineral; inanimate body, inanimate being; ○ neuter (gram.)

جمود jumūd frozen state; solid, compact state, compactness, solidity; rigor, rigidity, stiffness; inorganic state; hardening, induration; hardness, inflexibility; deadlock, standstill; inertia, inaction, inactivity; lethargy, apathy, passivity, indifference

جمودة *jumūda* solidity, hardness

تجميد *tajmīd* solidification, hardening; consolidation; reinforcement (of a foundation) | تجميد الاموال *t. al-amwāl* freezing of assets

تجمد *tajammud* freezing; frost; congelation; solidification; coagulation

انجماد *injimād* freezing up or over, icing up; ice formation

جامد *jāmid* hard, solid; stiff; rigid; motionless; inanimate, inorganic; (*gram.*) defective; dry, dull (book, and the like); impervious to progress or innovation, ossified, ultraconservative; pl. جوامد *jawāmid*² inanimate things, inorganic matter, minerals

متجمد *mutajammid* frozen, icy; stiff, congealed; coagulated

منجمد *munjamid* frozen, icy, ice (adj.); arctic | المحيط المنجمد (*muḥīṭ*) the Arctic Ocean

²جمادى *jumādā* name of the fifth and sixth months of the Muslim year (جمادى الاولى *j. l-ūlā* Jumada I and جمادى الآخرة *j. l-āḵira* Jumada II)

¹جمر II to roast (ه meat) VIII to burn incense

جمر *jamr* embers, live coal | كان على احر من الجمر (*aḥarra*) to be on tenterhooks; to be in greatest suspense, be dying with curiosity

جمرة *jamra* (n. un. of جمر) live coal; firebrand, smoldering embers; rankling resentment; (pl. *-āt*) carbuncle (*med.*) | ○ الجمرة الخبيثة anthrax

جمار *jummār* palm pith, palm core (edible tuber growing at the upper end of the palm trunk)

مجمرة *mijmara* pl. مجامر *majāmir*² brazier; censer

²جمرى see جمرى

جمرك (*eg.*) *gumruk* pl. جمارك *gamārik*² customs; customhouse | رسم الجمرك *rasm al-g.* customs duty, tariff

جمركى *gumrukī* customs, tariff (used attributively) | اتحاد جمركى (*ittiḥād*) customs union

مجمرك *mugamrak* duty paid

جميز *jummaiz* (coll.; n. un. ة) sycamore (Ficus sycomorus; *bot.*)

جاموس look up alphabetically

جمش *jamaša i u* (*jamš*) to unhair (ه s.th.) II to make love, caress, pet

جمع *jama'a a* (*jam'*) to gather (ه s.th.); to collect (ه e.g., money); to unite, combine, bring together (parts into a whole); to put together, join (ه things); to set, compose (ه type; *typ.*); to compile (ه a book); to summarize, sum up (ه s.th.); to rally, round up (هم people); to pile up, amass, accumulate (ه s.th.); to assemble (هم several persons); to convoke, convene, call (ه a meeting); to add (ه numbers), add up (ه a column); (*gram.*) to make plural, pluralize (ه a word); to unite, link, bring together (بين several things or persons); to combine (بين — و e.g., both strength and courage); to contain, hold, comprise (ه s.th.) | جمع اطراف الشيء (*aṭrāfa*) to summarize, sum up s.th.; to give a survey of s.th.; جمع البراعة من اطرافها (*barā'ata*) to be very efficient, do an excellent job, do superlatively good work; جمع شمل القطيع (*šamla l-q.*) to round up the herd; يجمع الكتاب بين صفحاتها (*ṣafaḥātihā*) the book contains, lists ...; يجمع بيت على بيوت (*yujma'u*) the plural of *bait* is *buyūt* II to pile up, amass, accumulate (ه s.th.); to rally, round up (ه s.th., هم s.o.); to assemble (ه the parts of a machine) III to have sexual intercourse (ها with a woman) IV to agree (على on s.th., to do s.th.); to be agreed (على on); to decide unanimously (على on), resolve (على to do s.th.) | اجمعوا امرهم (*amrahum*) they came to terms, they made a joint decision V to gather; to assemble, congregate; to rally, band together, flock together (people); to pile up; to accumulate; to gather into a mass, agglomerate; to cluster; to coagulate VIII to be close together; to come together, meet, join; to unite, combine (ب with); to assemble, meet, convene (an organization, a committee, etc.); to be or get together, have a meeting, interview or conference, hold talks (ب, مع with s.o.), meet (ب, مع s.o.); to concur (على in), agree, be agreed (على on s.th.) X to gather, collect (ه s.th.; also قواه *quwāhu* one's strength, افكاره *afkārahū* one's thoughts); to summarize, sum up (ه s.th.); to possess, combine (ه s.th.)

جمع *jam'* gathering; collection; combination; connection, coupling, joining; accumulation; (*arith.*) addition; union, merger, aggregation, integration (بين of); holding together (بين of divergent, separate things); (pl. جموع *jumū'*) gathering, crowd, throng; gang, troop; (*gram.*) plural | جمع الشمل *j. aš-šaml* union, integration; جمع التكسير the broken (= internal) plural, الجمع السالم the regular (= external) plural; اسم الجمع *ism al-j.* collective noun (*gram.*); جمع اليد *j. al-yad* fist

جمع *jum'*, جمع الكف *j. al-kaff*, جمع اليد *j. al-yad* fist, clenched hand | بجمع يديه with clenched fists

جمعة *jum'a* pl. جمع *juma'*, *-āt* week; Friday | يوم الجمعة *yaum al-j.* Friday; جمعة الآلام Passion Week; الجمعة العظيمة and يوم الجمعة الحزينة Good Friday (*Chr.*)

جمعية *jam'īya* pl. *-āt* club, association, society; corporation, organization; assembly | جمعية الامم *j. al-umam* League of Nations; جمعية خيرية (*ḵairīya*) charitable organization; جمعية الاسعاف *j. al-is'āf* approx.: civil ambulance service; جمعية تشريعية (*tašrī'īya*) legislative assembly; جمعية عمومية (*'umūmīya*) and جمعية عامة (*'āmma*) general assembly; general meeting; plenum, plenary session; جمعية تعاونية (*ta'āwunīya*) cooperative

جميع *jamī'* (with foll. genitive) total; whole, entire; all; entirety; e.g., جميع الناس all men, all mankind; الجميع all people, everybody; the public at large; جميعا *jamī'an* in a body, altogether, one and all, all of them; entirely, wholly, totally

اجمع *ajma'*[2] pl. *-ūn*, f. جمعاء *jam'ā'*[2], pl. جمع *juma'*[2] entire, whole, all | العالم الاسلامى اجمع (*ajma'a*) the entire Islamic world; الدار جمعاء (*jam'ā'a*) the whole house; باجمعه *bi-ajma'ihī* in its entirety, to its full extent, completely, altogether; جاؤوا باجمعهم all of them came

جماع *jummā'* aggregate; total, total amount

○ جماع كهربائى *jammā' kahrabā'ī* storage battery

جماعة *jamā'a* pl. *-āt* group (of people); band, gang, party, troop; community; squad (military unit; *Eg.* 1939) | جماعات وافرادا *jamā'ātin wa-afrādan* in groups and individually

جماعى *jamā'ī* collective (as opposed to فردى *fardī* individual)

مجمع *majma'* pl. مجامع *majāmi'*[2] place where two or more things meet, place or point of union, junction; meeting, congregation, convention, assembly; (also مجمع علمى *m. 'ilmī*) academy (scientific); college (e.g., of ecclesiastical dignitaries); synod | مجمع بلدى (*baladī*) provincial synod (*Chr.*); مجمع اكليريكى (*iklīrīkī*) clerical synod (of the Coptic Church); اخذ بمجامع القلوب to win or captivate the hearts;

بمجامع عينيه *bi-m. ʿainaihi* (to look at s.o.) with complete concentration, intently

مجمعى *majmaʿī* academy member, academician

تجميع *tajmīʿ* assembly, assemblage (of the parts of machinery)

جماع *jimāʿ* sexual intercourse; s.th. comprising or involving another thing or a number of things | الخمر جماع الاثم *al-ḵamr j. al-iṯm* wine involves sin, wine is the vessel of sin

اجماع *ijmāʿ* agreement, unanimity (also اجماع الرأى); unanimous resolution (على to do s.th.); (*Isl. Law*) consensus (of the authorities in a legal question; one of the four *uṣūl* of Islamic Law) | بالاجماع unanimously

اجماعى *ijmāʿī* based on general agreement, unanimous; collective, universal

تجمع *tajammuʿ* pl. *-āt* coming together, meeting; gathering; troop concentration; crowd, throng, mob; agglomeration; ○ agglutination (*chem.-med.*)

اجتماع *ijtimāʿ* pl. *-āt* meeting (ب with s.o.; of a corporate body; of parliament); get-together, gathering, assembly; reunion; rally; convention; conjunction, constellation (*astron.*); confluence (of rivers); life in a social group, community life, social life; الاجتماع human society | اجتماع الطرق *ijtimāʿ aṭ-ṭuruq* crossroads, intersection, junction; علم الاجتماع *ʿilm al-ijt.* sociology; علماء الاجتماع sociologists

اجتماعى *ijtimāʿī* community, group (used attributively); social; socialist(ic); sociological | وزارة الشئون الاجتماعية ministry for social affairs; الحالة الاجتماعية personal status; الخدمة الاجتماعية (*ḵidma*) social service, social work; المساواة الاجتماعية (*musāwāh*) social equality; الهيئة الاجتماعية (*haiʾa*) human society

اجتماعية *ijtimāʿīya* socialism

جامع *jāmiʿ* comprehensive, extensive, broad, general, universal; collector; compiler (of a book); compositor, typesetter; (pl. جوامع *jawāmiʿ*[2]) mosque | مسجد جامع (*masjid*) great, central mosque where the public prayer is performed on Fridays

جامعة *jāmiʿa* pl. *-āt* league, union, association; community; federation; religious community, communion; commonness, community of interests or purpose; university | ○ جامعة الكهرباء *j. al-kahrabāʾ* storage battery, accumulator; جامعة الامم *j. al-umam* League of Nations; الجامعة الاسلامية (*islāmīya*) Pan-Islamism; الجامعة العربية (*ʿarabīya*) and جامعة الدول العربية (*duwal*) the Arab League; جامعة شعبية (*šaʿbīya*) university extension, adult education courses, evening courses

جامعى *jāmiʿī* academic, collegiate, university (adj.); university graduate

مجموع *majmūʿ* collected, gathered; totality, whole; total, sum (*arith.*) | الحروف المجموعة matter (*typ.*); مجموع اراضى القطر *m. arāḍī l-quṭr* the total area of the country; مجموع طوله *m. ṭūlihī* its total length; المجموع العصبى (*ʿaṣabī*) the nervous system

مجموعة *majmūʿa* pl. *-āt*, مجاميع *majāmīʿ*[2] collection (e.g., of works of art, of stamps, etc., also of stories); compilation, list; group (also, e.g., of trees, of islands, etc.); series (e.g., of articles in a newspaper); ○ battery (*el.*); alliance, league, bloc (e.g., of states); collective, collectivistic organization; aggregate; complex, block (of buildings); system; bulletin, periodical | المجموعة الشمسية (*šamsīya*) the solar system; مجموعة صناعية (*ṣināʿīya*) syndicate

مجمع *mujammiʿ* collector (*techn.*); ○ storage battery, accumulator

مجمع عليه *mujmaʿ ʿalaihi* (that which is) agreed upon, unanimous

مجتمع *mujtama'* pl. *-āt* gathering place, place of assembly; meeting place, rendezvous; assembly, gathering, meeting; society; human society, community, commune, collective

جمكية = جامكية look up alphabetically

[1]جمل *jamala u* (*jaml*) to sum up, summarize (ه s.th.); — *jamula u* (جمال *jamāl*) to be beautiful; to be handsome, pretty, comely, graceful; to be proper, suitable, appropriate (ب for s.o.), befit (ب s.o.) II to make beautiful, beautify, embellish, adorn (ه, ه s.o., s.th.) III to be polite, courteous, amiable (ه to s.o.) IV to sum, total, add (ه s.th.); to treat as a whole, mention collectively (ه s.th.); to sum up, summarize (ه s.th.); to act well, decently, be nice V to make o.s. pretty, adorn o.s. VI to be courteous, be friendly to one another

جملة *jumla* pl. جمل *jumal* totality, sum, whole; group, troop, body; crowd; wholesale; (*gram.*) sentence, clause; جملة *jumlatan* completely, wholly, on the whole, altogether, in general, at all | جملة واحدة *jumlatan wāḥidatan* all at once, at one swoop; جملة الكائنات everything in existence; كان من جملة اصحابه he was one of his companions, he belonged to his companions; قال فى جملة ما قاله (*jumlati*) among other things, he said ...; وجملة القول ان *wa-jumlatu l-qauli anna* or وجملة الامر ان in short ..., to sum up ..., briefly stated ...; على الجملة in short, in a word; بالجملة wholly, on the whole, altogether, in general, at all; by wholesale (*com.*); جملة الاجرة المستحقة *j. al-ujra al-mustaḥiqqa* gross wages; تاجر الجملة wholesaler, wholesale dealer; سعر الجملة *si'r al-j.* wholesale price; جملة اسمية (*ismīya*) nominal clause; جملة فعلية (*fi'līya*) verbal clause; جملة اخبارية (*ikbārīya*) or جملة خبرية (*kabarīya*) declarative sentence (or clause); جملة انشائية (*inšā'iya*) exclamatory sentence; جملة حالية (*ḥālīya*) circumstantial clause; جملة شرطية (*šarṭīya*) conditional clause; جملة معترضة (*mu'tariḍa*) parenthetical clause

حساب الجمل *ḥisāb al-jummal* (or *jumal*) use of the letters of the alphabet according to their numerical value

جمال *jamāl* beauty | ○ علم الجمال *'ilm al-j.* aesthetics

جميل *jamīl* beautiful, graceful, lovely, comely, pretty, handsome; friendly act, favor, service, good turn; courtesy | معرفة الجميل, اعتراف بالجميل *ma'rifat al-j.* and عرفان بالجميل (*'irfān*) gratitude; نكران الجميل *nukrān al-j.* ingratitude; ناكر الجميل ungrateful; حفظ له جميلا (*ḥafiẓa*) to keep s.o. in fond remembrance, remember s.o. with gratitude

اجمل *ajmal*[2] more beautiful

تجميل *tajmīl* beautification, embellishment; cosmetics

مجاملة *mujāmala* pl. *-āt* (act of) courtesy; civility, amiability; flattery; مجاملة *mujāmalatan* amicably, in a friendly way | زيارة مجاملة *ziyārat m.* courtesy call; قواعد المجاملات etiquette

اجمال *ijmāl* summation, summing up; summarization; اجمالا *ijmālan* on the whole, in general, generally speaking, as a general principle | اجمالا لذلك اقول to sum up, I (would) say ...; فى اجماله in its entirety, as a whole; بالاجمال and على الاجمال in general, on the whole, altogether; بوجه الاجمال *bi-wajhi l-i.* = اجمالا

اجمالى *ijmālī* comprehensive, summary, general, over-all, total, collective | تقرير اجمالى over-all report; غرامة اجمالية (*ġarāma*) collective penalty; نظرة اجمالية (*naẓra*) general view

مجمل *mujmil* pl. *-ūn* wholesaler, wholesale dealer

مجمل *mujmal* summary, résumé, synopsis, compendium; general concept; sum, total | بالمجمل by wholesale

[2]جمل *jamal* pl. جمال *jimāl*, اجمال *ajmāl* camel | جمل اليهود *j. al-yahūd* chameleon

جمال *jammāl* pl. *-ūn* camel driver

جمان *jumān* (coll.; n. un. ة) pearls

جمهر *jamhara* to gather, collect (ه, ه s.th., s.o.); to assemble (ه s.o.) **II** *tajamhara* to gather, flock together (crowd)

جمهرة *jamhara* multitude, crowd, throng; the great mass, the populace

جمهور *jumhūr* pl. جماهير *jamāhīr*[2] multitude; crowd, throng; general public, public; الجماهير the masses, the people

جمهورى *jumhūrī* republican (adj. and n.)

جمهورية *jumhūrīya* pl. *-āt* republic | الجمهورية العربية المتحدة (*ʿarabīya, muttaḥida*) the United Arab Republic; الجمهورية الاتحادية الالمانية (*ittiḥādīya*) the Federal Republic of Germany; الجمهورية الديموقراطية الالمانية (*dīmūqrāṭīya*) the German Democratic Republic

تجمهر *tajamhur* gathering (of people); crowd

جن *janna u* (*jann*, جنون *junūn*) to cover, hide, conceal, veil (ه, على s.th.); to descend, fall, be or become dark (night); pass. *junna*: to be or become possessed, insane, mad, crazy | جن جنونه (*junūnuhū*) to get madly excited, become frantic **II** to craze, make crazy, drive insane, madden, enrage, infuriate (ه s.o.) **IV** to cover, veil, hide, conceal (ه s.th.); = **II**; **V** to go mad, become crazy **X** to be covered, veiled, concealed; to regard (ه s.o.) as crazy, think (ه s.o.) mad

جن *jinn* (coll.) jinn, demons (invisible beings, either harmful or helpful, that interfere with the lives of mortals)

جنى *jinnī* demonic; jinni, demon

جنية *jinnīya* female demon

جنة *janna* pl. *-āt*, جنان *jinān* garden; paradise | جنات النعيم paradise; ساكن الجنان inhabitant of paradise, deceased person, one of blessed memory

جنينة *junaina* pl. *-āt*, جنائن *janāʾin*[2] little garden; garden

جنائنى *janāʾinī* gardener

جنة *jinna* possession, obsession; mania, madness, insanity

جنة *junna* pl. جنن *junan* protection, shelter, shield

جنان *janān* pl. اجنان *ajnān* heart, soul

جنان *jannān* gardener

جنين *janīn* pl. اجنة *ajinna*, اجنن *ajnun* embryo, fetus; germ (in a seed, etc.)

جنون *junūn* possession, obsession; mania, madness, insanity, dementia; foolishness, folly; frenzy, rage, fury; ecstasy, rapture | الجنون فنون *al-j. funūn* madness has many varieties, manifests itself in many ways

جنونى *junūnī* crazy, insane, mad; frantic, frenzied

مجن *mijann* pl. مجان *majānn*[2] shield

مجنة *majanna* madness, insanity

جان *jānn* jinn, demons

مجنون *majnūn* pl. مجانين *majānīn*[2] possessed, obsessed; insane, mad; madman, maniac, lunatic; crazy, cracked; crackpot; foolish; fool

جنب *janaba u* to avert, ward off (ه ه from s.o. s.th.) **II** to keep away, avert, ward off (ه ه from s.o. s.th.), keep s.o. (ه) out of the way of (ه), spare (ه ه s.o. s.th.) **III** to be or walk by s.o.'s (ه) side; to run alongside of (ه), run parallel to (ه), skirt, flank (ه s.th.); to avoid (ه s.th.) **V** to avoid (ه s.th., ه s.o.); to keep away (ه, ه from), steer clear, get out of the way (ه, ه of) **VI** and **VIII** = **V**; **VIII** to be at the side of (ه), run side by side with (ه), run alongside of (ه), skirt, flank (ه s.th.)

جنب *janb* pl. جنوب *junūb*, اجناب *ajnāb* side; *janba* (prep.) beside, next to, near, at | جنبا الى جنب (also جنبا لجنب) side by side; بين جنبيه (*janbaihi*) inside (it), within; ما بين جنبيه (*baina janbaihi*) what it contains, comprises, its contents; على جنب aside, apart; ذات الجنب pleurisy

جنبة *janba* pl. *janabāt* side; region, area | فى جنباته in it, within, inside; ضمه بين جنباته (*ḍammahū*) to comprise, hold, contain s.th.; جنبات الغرفة *j. al-ḡurfa* the whole room; بين جنبات الغرفة in (the middle of) the room; زاخر الجنبات crammed, chock-full, brimful, filled to overflowing or bursting

جنبى *janbī* lateral, side (adj.)

جنب *junub* in a state of major ritual impurity; not belonging to the tribe, not a kinsman | الجار الجنب the neighbor not belonging to the family

جناب *janāb* (title of respect) approx.: Right Honorable; جنابكم Your Honor; you (polite form)

جنابة *janāba* major ritual impurity (*Isl. Law*)

جناب *junāb* (= ذات الجنب) pleurisy

جنوب *janūb* south; جنوبا *janūban* southward, to the south

جنوبى *janūbī* southern | جنوبى افريقيا South Africa

جانب *jānib* pl. جوانب *jawānib*² side; lateral portion; sidepiece; flank; wing; face (*geom.*); part, portion, partial amount; partial view, section (من of a scene, picture or panorama); quantity, amount; a certain number (من of), a few, some | من جانبه on his part; من جانب — من جانب آخر on the one hand — on the other hand; الى جانبه to him, to his address; at his (its) side, next to him (it); بجانبه beside him (it), next to him (it); الى جانب and بجانب side by side with; in addition to; apart from, aside from; وضعه جانبا to put s.th. aside; ودعه جانبا to leave s.th. aside, omit s.th.; فى جانب in comparison with, as compared with, as against; regarding, with regard to; ما بين جوانبهم their hearts; جانبا الفم *jānibā l-fam* the corners of the mouth; جانب من a considerable, or certain, degree of; a considerable amount of, a good deal of; جانب كبير من a great deal of, a large portion of; هو على جانب كبير من he is very ...; كان على جانب عظيم من الكرم (*karam*) to be very generous; على جانب عظيم من الاهمية (*ahammīya*) of great importance; على اعظم جانب من الخطورة *ʿalā aʿẓami jānibin min al-kuṭūra* of utmost importance, of greatest significance; فى كل جانب everywhere, on all sides; خفض له جانبه (*kafaḍa, jānibahū*) to show o.s. condescending, affable or gracious to s.o.; to meet s.o. on fair terms; امن جانبه *amina jānibahū* to be safe from s.o.; لم اعره جانب اهتمام (*uʿirhu*) I paid not the least attention to him; خاف (رهب, هاب) جانبه (*jānibahū*) to fear s.o., be afraid of s.o.; ملك الجانب *milk al-j.* crown lands; جانب الميرى *j. al-mīrī* (*eg.*) fisc, treasury; لين الجانب *layyin al-j.* gentle; docile, tractable, compliant; لين الجانب *līn al-j.* gentleness; رحب الجوانب *raḥb al-j.* roomy; spacious, unconfined; رقيق الجانب friendly, amiable, gentle; مرهوب الجانب feared, dreaded; عزيز الجانب powerful, mighty, strong; عزة الجانب *ʿizzat al-j.* power; مهيب الجانب *mahīb al-j.* dreaded, respected; فى جوانب الدار about the house, all over the house; often فى جوانبه = فيه

جانبى *jānibī* lateral, side, by- (in compounds)

اجنبى *ajnabī* foreign, alien; (pl. *-ūn*, اجانب *ajānib*²) foreigner, alien | البلاد الاجنبية the foreign countries, the outside world; فرقة الاجانب *firqat al-ajānib* the Foreign Legion

جنابية *gannābīya* pl. *-āt* (*eg.*) curb; embankment, levee; side channel, lateral (following a road or railroad tracks); bypass (of a lock or sluice)

تجنب *tajannub* avoidance

اجتناب *ijtināb* avoidance

مجنبة *mujanniba* flank, wing (of an army)

جنبرى see جبرى

جنباز *junbāz*, جباز calisthenics; gymnastics; athletics

جنبازى *junbāzī* (جبازى) calisthenic(al), gymnastic | الالعاب الجبازية gymnastic exercises, physical exercises

جنح *janaḥa a* (جنوح *junūḥ*) to incline, be inclined, tend (ل or الى to); to lean (ل or الى to or toward); to turn, go over (الى to), join (الى s.th.), associate o.s. (الى with); to strand (على or الى on a coast; ship); to diverge, deviate, depart (عن from); to turn away (عن from), break (عن with) **II** to provide (ه s.th.) with wings, lend wings (ه to s.th.) **IV** to incline, be inclined, tend (ل or الى to); to lean (ل or الى to or toward); to turn (ل or الى to s.th.); to strand (ship)

جنح *jinḥ* side

جنح *junḥ, jinḥ* darkness, gloom | فى جنح الليل (*j. il-lail*) in the dark of night, under cover of night; بين جنحى الكرى (*junḥay il-karā*) lit.: between the two halves of slumber, i.e., at night when everyone's asleep

جنحة *junḥa* pl. جنح *junaḥ* misdemeanor (*jur.*, less than a felony, جناية, and more than an infraction, مخالفة)

جناح *janāḥ* pl. اجنحة *ajniḥa*, اجنح *ajnuḥ* wing (of a bird, of an airplane, of a building, of an army); side; flank | انا فى جناحه I am under his protection; على جناح الاثير over the ether, by radio; على جناح السرعة (*j. is-surʿa*) with winged haste

جناح *junāḥ* misdemeanor (*jur.*); sin | لا جناح عليه ان (*junāḥa*) it won't be held against him if he ...; it won't do any harm if he ...

اجنح *ajnaḥ*² more inclined (الى to)

جنوح *janūḥ* inclined (الى to s.th.)

جنوح *junūḥ* inclination, leaning, bent, tendency (الى to)

جانح *jāniḥ* side, flank, wing

جانحة *jāniḥa* pl. جوانح *jawāniḥ*² rib; pl. also bosom, heart, soul | بين جوانحى in my bosom, at heart; طفرت جوانحها (*ṭafarat*) she became happily excited, she trembled with joy

مجنح *mujannaḥ* winged

جند **II** to draft, conscript, enlist, recruit (ه s.o.; *mil.*); to mobilize (ه an army, على against) **V** to be drafted, be conscripted, be enlisted (for military service)

جند *jund* m. and f., pl. جنود *junūd*, اجناد *ajnād* soldiers; army | جند الخلاص *j. al-ḵalāṣ* Salvation Army

جندى *jundī* pl. جنود *junūd* soldier, private | جندى اول (*awwal*) private first class (*Ir., Syr.*); جندى مستجد (*mustajidd*) recruit (*Ir., Syr.*); الجندى المجهول the Unknown Soldier

جندية *jundīya* military affairs; the army, the military; military service

تجنيد *tajnīd* draft, enlistment (*mil.*); recruitment; mobilization | التجنيد الاجبارى (*ijbārī*) military conscription

تجند *tajannud* military service

مجند *mujannad* recruit

جندارى *gindārī* standard-bearer, cornet (*Eg.*)

جندب *jundub* pl. جنادب *janādib*² grasshopper

جندر[1] *gandara* (*eg.*) to mangle (ه laundry)

جندرة *gandara* mangling (of laundry); press; ○ rotary press (*typ.*)

جنداري[2] look up alphabetically

جندرمة *žandarma* gendarmery

جندرمى *žandarmī* gendarme

جندفلى *gandufli* (*eg.*) oysters

[1]جندل *jandala* to throw to the ground, bring down, fell (ه s.o.)

جندل *jandal* pl. جنادل *janādil*[2] stone; pl. جنادل cataract, waterfall (*eg.*)

[2]جندول *gundūl* (*eg.*) pl. جناديل *ganādīl*[2] gondola

جنرال *jenərāl, ginrāl* (*eg.*) general (military rank)

جنز II to say the burial prayers, conduct the funeral service (ه for the deceased; *Chr.*)

جنازة *jināza, janāza* pl. *-āt* جنائز *janā'iz*[2] bier; funeral procession

جناز *junnāz* pl. جنانيز *janānīz*[2] requiem, funeral rites, obsequies; funeral procession

جنزبيل *janzabīl* (= زنجبيل) ginger

[1]جنزر *janzara* (= زنجر) to be or become covered with verdigris

جنزار *jinzār* (= زنجار) verdigris

[2]جنزير *jinzīr* (= زنجير) pl. جنازير *janāzīr*[2] chain; track (of a caterpillar, of a tank, etc.); a linear measure (= 5 *qaṣaba* = 17.75 m; also = 20 m; *Eg.*) | طارة جنزير *ṭārat j.* track sprocket, sprocket wheel

مجنزر *mujanzar* track-laying (vehicle)

جنس II to make alike, make similar (ه s.th.); to assimilate, naturalize (ه s.o.); to class, classify, sort, categorize (ه s.th.) III to be akin, be related, similar (ه, ه to), be of the same kind or nature (ه as s.o., ه as s.th.), be like s.o. or s.th. (ه, ه), resemble (ه s.o., ه s.th.) V to have o.s. naturalized, acquire the citizenship (ب); to be naturalized VI to be akin, related, of the same kind or nature, homogeneous

جنس *jins* pl. اجناس *ajnās* kind, sort, variety, species, class, genus; category; sex (male, female); gender (*gram.*); race; nation | اسم الجنس *ism al-j.* (*gram.*) generic noun, collective noun of nonpersonal things (which form a n. un. in ة); الجنس البشرى (*al-jins al-bašarī*) the human race; ابناء جنسنا *abnā' jinsinā* our fellow tribesmen; هو مصرى الجنس he is Egyptian by nationality; الجنس اللطيف the fair sex, الجنس الخشن the strong sex

جنسى *jinsī* generic; sexual; racial

لاجنسى *lā-jinsī* asexual, sexless

جنسية *jinsīya* pl. *-āt* nationality, citizenship

تجنيس *tajnīs* naturalization; paronomasia (*rhet.*)

جناس *jinās* (*rhet.*) assonance, pun, paronomasia

مجانسة *mujānasa* relatedness, kinship, affinity; similarity, likeness, resemblance

تجنس *tajannus* acquisition of citizenship, naturalization

تجانس *tajānus* homogeneity, homogeneousness, likeness, similarity, resemblance

مجانس *mujānis* similar, like, related; homogeneous

متجنس *mutajannis* naturalized

متجانس *mutajānis* akin, related, of the same kind or nature, homogeneous

جنطيانا (Lat. *Gentiana*) gentian (*eg.*)

[1]جنف VI to deviate (عن from); to incline, be inclined (الى or ل to s.th.)

[2]جنيف look up alphabetically

جنفاص *junfāṣ*, جنفيص *junfaiṣ* sackcloth, sacking

جنك *junk* pl. جنوك *junūk* harp

جنوا *janowā* Genoa (seaport in NW Italy)

جنى *janā* i (*jany*) to pick, gather, harvest, reap (ه s.th., also the fruits of one's work); to pocket, rake in, collect (ه s.th.); to derive (ه profit, من from); to secure, realize (ه profits, an advantage); to incur (ه evil, harm, punishment); to cause, provoke, bring about (ه s.th.); — (جناية *jināya*) to commit a crime, an outrage (على on); to offend, sin (على against); to commit, perpetrate (جناية, ذنبا *ḏanban* a crime, an offense; على, less frequently الى, on or against); to inflict (ه some evil, على on s.o.); to harm (على s.o., s.th.) V to incriminate, accuse, charge with a crime (على s.o.), lay the blame (على on s.o.), blame (على s.o.); to act meanly VIII to gather, harvest (ه s.th.)

جنى *jany* harvest; reaping (fig.); — *janan* (coll.) fruits

جناية *jināya* pl. *-āt* perpetration of a crime; felony (*jur.*; in the strictly legal sense, more than a misdemeanor, جنحة, and an infraction, مخالفة), capital offense | محكمة الجنايات *maḥkamat al-j.* criminal court

جنائى *jinā'ī* criminal | محكمة جنائية (*maḥkama*) criminal court; القانون الجنائى criminal law, penal law

مجنى *majnan* pl. مجان *majānin* that which is picked or harvested, a crop; source of profit or advantage

تجن *tajannin* incrimination, accusation (على of s.o.); mean way of acting, low, underhand dealings

جان *jānin* pl. جناة *junāh* perpetrator (of a delict); delinquent, criminal

مجنى عليه *majnīy ʿalaihi* harmed, injured; aggrieved party; victim of a crime

جنيف (Fr. *Genève*) *žənēf* Geneva

جنيه (Engl. *guinea*) *ginēh*, also *gunaih* pl. *-āt* pound (*eg.*) | جنيه انجليزى (استرلينى) pound sterling, English pound; جنيه مصرى Egyptian pound (abbreviation: ج م)

جهة see وجه

جهبذ *jahbaḏ* pl. جهابذة *jahābiḏa* man endowed with a critical mind; great scholar; bright, brilliant, intelligent

جهد *jahada a* (*jahd*) to endeavor, strive, labor, take pains, put o.s. out; to overwork, overtax, fatigue, exhaust (ه s.o.) III to endeavor, strive; to fight (فى سبيل الشىء for s.th.); to wage holy war against the infidels IV to strain, exert (ه s.th.); to tire, wear out, fatigue (ه s.o.), give trouble (ه to) | اجهد نفسه فى (*nafsahū*) to go to great lengths, go out of one's way (فى for or in s.th.); اجهد فكره فى (*fikrahū*) to concentrate on, put one's mind to, apply o.s. to VIII to put o.s. out (فى for s.th.), work hard; (*Isl. Law*) to formulate an independent judgment in a legal or theological question (based on the application of the 4 *uṣūl*; as opposed to *taqlīd*, q.v.)

جهد *jahd* pl. جهود *juhūd* strain; exertion; endeavor, attempt, effort; trouble, pains (فى on behalf or for the sake of s.th.); ○ voltage, tension (*el.*) | جهد جهده *jahada jahdahū*, also عمل (حاول) جهده to do (try) one's utmost, do (try) all in one's power, make every conceivable effort; بجهد جهيد *bi-jahdin jahīdin* with great difficulty, by dint of strenuous efforts; بعد جهد جهيد after a lot of trouble ○ جهد عال (*ʿālin*) high tension (*el.*)

جهد *juhd* strain, exertion; *juhda* (used prepositionally) to the limit of ... | جهد الطاقة *juhda ṭ-ṭāqa* as far as possible, as much as possible; جهد طاقته *j. ṭāqatihī* as much as he can, to the limit of his abilities; جهد امكانه *juhda imkānihī* do.; جهد ما *juhda mā* as much as, to the limits of what ...; جهدى *juhdī* as far as I can

جهيد *jahīd* see جهد *jahd*

جهاد *jihād* fight, battle; jihad, holy war (against the infidels, as a religious duty)

جهادى *jihādī* fighting, military

مجاهدة *mujāhada* fight, battle

اجهاد *ijhād* exertion; overexertion, overstrain(ing)

اجتهاد *ijtihād* effort, exertion, endeavor, pains, trouble; application, industry, diligence; (*Isl. Law*) independent judgment in a legal or theological question, based on the interpretation and application of the 4 *uṣūl*, as opposed to *taqlīd*, q.v.; individual judgment

مجهود *majhūd* pl. *-āt* endeavor, effort, exertion, pains, trouble, work; ○ voltage, tension (*el.*) | بذل مجهوداته to make every effort, go to greatest lengths

مجاهد *mujāhid* pl. *-ūn* fighter, freedom fighter; warrior; sergeant (*Eg.* 1939)

مجهد *mujhid* strenuous, exacting, trying, grueling; — *mujhad* overworked, exhausted

مجتهد *mujtahid* diligent, industrious; (pl. *-ūn*) mujtahid, a legist formulating independent decisions in legal or theological matters, based on the interpretation and application of the four *uṣūl*, as opposed to *muqallid*, q.v.

جهر *jahara a* (*jahr*, جهار *jihār*) to be brought to light, come out, show, appear; — to declare publicly, announce (ه or ب s.th.); to avow in public, proclaim (ب s.th.); to raise (ه the voice); — *jahura u* (جهارة *jahāra*) to be loud, be clearly audible (voice) III to declare or say openly, voice, utter, express frankly (ب s.th.)

جهر *jahr* and جهار *jihār* publicness, publicity, notoriety; جهرا *jahran* and جهارا *jihāran* publicly, in public

جهرة *jahratan* openly, overtly, frankly, publicly

جهرى *jahrī* notorious, well-known, public

جهير *jahīr* loud (voice, shout)

اجهر *ajhar*[2] day-blind

اجهر *ajhar*[2] (elative) louder, more audible

جهورى *jahwarī* loud (voice)

مجهر *mijhar* loud-voiced

مجهر *mijhar* pl. مجاهر *majāhir*[2] microscope

مجهرى *mijharī* microscopic(al)

مجهار *mijhār* loud-voiced; ○ loudspeaker

مجاهرة *mujāhara* frankness, candor (of one's words)

جهز *jahaza a* to finish off (على a wounded man), deliver the coup de grâce to (على) II to make ready, prepare (ه s.th.); to arrange (ه s.th.); to provide, supply (ه s.th.); to equip, fit out, furnish, supply, provide (ب ه or ه s.th. or s.o. with) IV to finish off (على a wounded man), deliver the coup de grâce to (على); to finish, ruin (على s.o.) V to be equipped, furnished, supplied, provided; to equip o.s.; to prepare o.s., get ready; to be ready, be prepared

جهاز *jahāz* (also pronounced *jihāz*) pl. *-āt*, اجهزة *ajhiza* equipment, appliances, outfit, gear, rig; trousseau; contrivance, gadget; implement, appliance, utensil; installation, apparatus (*techn.*); system, apparatus (*anat.*) | جهاز لاسلكى (*lā-silkī*) wireless set, radio; جهاز راديو radio (receiving set); ○ جهاز مستقبل (*mustaqbil*), ○ جهاز الاستقبال, ○ جهاز الالتقاط receiver, receiving set (*radio*); جهاز مذيع (*mudī'*), ○ جهاز الارسال *j. al-irsāl* transmitter (*radio*); جهاز تليفزيونى television set; جهاز الحفر *j. al-ḥafr* drilling rig; oil derrick; جهاز دورى (*daurī*) circulatory system (*anat.*); جهاز قياس or جهاز لتسجيل الاهتزازات الارضية الهزات الارضية (*hazzāt, arḍīya*) seismograph; جهاز سرى (*sirrī*) secret organization, underground organization; جهاز الاستماع sound locator; الجهاز العصبى (*'aṣabī*) the nervous system; جهاز الهضم *j. al-haḍm* digestive apparatus

تجهيز *tajhīz* equipment, furnishment; preparation; pl. تجهيزات equipment, gear

تجهيزى *tajhīzī* preparatory; (of a school) preparing for college

جاهز *jāhiz* ready, prepared; ready-made; equipped | البسة (ملبوسات or) جاهزة (*albisa*) ready-made clothes

مجهز *mujahhaz* equipped, provided, furnished, supplied (ب with); armed (ب with guns; of a ship, tank, etc.)

جهش IV to sob, break into sobs | اجهش بالبكاء (*bukā'*) to be on the verge of tears, struggle with tears; to break into tears

جهشة *jahša* (n. vic.) pl. *-āt* sob; outburst of tears

اجهاش *ijhāš* outburst of tears

جهض IV to bear young ones, litter; to have a miscarriage (woman) | اجهضت نفسها (*nafsahā*) she induced an abortion

جهض *jihḍ* miscarried fetus

جهيض *jahīḍ* miscarried fetus

اجهاض *ijhāḍ* miscarriage, abortion; induced abortion

جهل *jahila a* (*jahl*, جهالة *jahāla*) to be ignorant; not to know (ب or ه s.th., how to do s.th.); to be irrational, foolish; to behave foolishly (على toward) VI to ignore (ه s.th.); to refuse to have anything to do (ه with), shut one's eyes (ه to), disregard (ه a fact); to affect ignorance, pretend to know nothing X to consider ignorant or stupid (ه s.o.)

جهل *jahl* and جهالة *jahāla* ignorance; folly, foolishness, stupidity | عن جهل out of ignorance

جهول *jahūl* ignorant; foolish, stupid

مجهل *majhal* pl. مجاهل *majāhil*² unknown region, unexplored territory | مجاهل افريقيا unknown Africa

تجهيل *tajhīl* stultification

تجاهل *tajāhul* ignoring, disregard(ing)

جاهل *jāhil* pl. جهلة *jahala*, جهل *juhhal*, جهال *juhhāl*, جهلاء *juhalā'*² not knowing (ب s.th., how to do s.th.); ignorant, uneducated, illiterate; foolish; fool

جاهلى *jāhilī* pagan, of or pertaining to pre-Islamic times

جاهلية *jāhilīya* state of ignorance; pre-Islamic paganism, pre-Islamic times

مجهول *majhūl* unknown; anonymous (also مجهول الاسم *m. al-ism*); pl. مجاهيل *majāhīl*² unknown things | صيغة المجهول *ṣīgat al-m.* passive (*gram.*)

مجهولية *majhūlīya* being unknown, unknown nature

جهم *jahuma u* (جهامة *jahāma*, جهومة *juhūma*) to frown, glower V to frown, scowl, glower; to regard with displeasure (ه, ه or ل s.o. or s.th.), frown (ه or ل on); to eye gloomily, coolly, grimly (ه, ه or ل s.o., s.th.); to become sullen, gloomy (face)

جهم *jahm* sullen, glum, morose, gloomy (face)

جهام *jahām* clouds

جهامة *jahāma* and جهومة *juhūma* grim look, sullen expression; gloominess; brooding silence

جهنم *jahannam*² (f.) hell

جهنمى *jahannamī* hellish, infernal

جو *jaww* pl. اجواء *ajwā'*, جواء *jiwā'* (pl. frequently with singular meaning) air; atmosphere (also fig.); sky; weather; sphere, milieu, environment; جوا *jawwan* by air; by telegraph, telegraphically | بريد الجو air mail; طبقات الجو *ṭabaqāt al-j.* air layers; فى جو ممطر (*mumṭir*) in rainy weather

جوى *jawwī* air, aerial, aero- (in compounds); airy, atmospheric(al); weather (used attributively), meteorologic(al) | الضغط الجوى (*ḍagṭ*) atmospheric pressure; طبقات جوية (*ṭabaqāt*) air layers; اسطول جوى (*usṭūl*) air fleet; غارة جوية air raid; القوات

الجوية (*qūwāt*) air force; الملاحة الجوية aviation; ميناء جوية (*mīnā'*) airport; ارصاد جوية meteorological observations; حجر جوى (*ḥajar*) meteorite

جوا (*colloq.*) *jawwā* (pronounced *gūwa* in Eg.) in it, within; inside

جوانى *jawwānī, juwwānī* inner, inside, interior

جوافة **guwāfa** (*eg.*) guava (fruit); guava shrub

جوال (*eg.*) *guwāl* pl. *-āt* sack

جوانتى (It. *guanti; eg.*) gloves

جوب[1] (Fr. *jupe*) skirt

جوب)[2] جاب (جوب *jāba u* (*jaub*) to travel, wander (ه through), traverse, roam, tour, explore (ه s.th., e.g., foreign lands); to pierce, penetrate (ه s.th.), cut through (ه); to wander, cruise (ه about a place) **III** to answer (ه s.o., على s.th.), reply, respond (ه to s.o., على to s.th.); to comply (ه with), accede (ه to) **IV** to answer (ه or الى s.o., عن or على a question), reply, respond (ه or الى to s.o., على to s.th.); to comply (ه with a request), accede, defer (ه to); to hear (ه s.o.), accede to the request or wishes of (ه); to fulfill, grant (ه a wish); to consent, assent, agree (الى to); to concur (الى in) | اجاب الى طلبه (*ṭalabihī*) to comply with s.o.'s request **VI** to reply to one another; to echo (ه, ب from); to ring out (voices); to be (mutually) corresponding, harmonize; to be favorable, propitious (مع to s.o.; situation) **VII** to scatter, break up, pass over (clouds); to be dispelled, disappear, vanish (worries); to fade (darkness) **X** أستجاب to hear, answer (ه a prayer), grant (ه a request); to comply with the request of (ل), accede or defer to the wishes of (ل); to react (ل to); to respond (ل to, ب with), listen, pay attention (ل to), show interest (ل in); to meet, answer (ل ب s.o. with), reply (ل ب to s.o. with or by doing s.th.); to resound, reverberate, re-echo; to resonate (ل or الى to s.th.), be in resonance with (*phys.*); — استجوب *istajwaba* to interrogate, examine, question (ه s.o.); to hear (ه the defendant or witness); to interpellate (ه s.o.; in parliament)

جوب *jaub* traversing, touring, exploration (of foreign countries); piercing, penetration

جوبة *jauba* pl. *-āt*, جوب *juwab* opening, gap; hole, pit

جواب *jawāb* pl. اجوبة *ajwiba* answer, reply; octave (to a given tone; *mus.*); (*eg.*; pronounced *gawāb* pl. *-āt*) letter, message | جواب الشرط *j. aš-šarṭ* main clause (conclusion) of a conditional sentence, apodosis

جوابى *jawābī* answering (used attributively)

جواب *jawwāb* traverser (of foreign countries), traveler, explorer

اجابة *ijāba* answer(ing), reply(ing), response, respondence; compliance; fulfillment, granting (of a request); accession; consent, assent | اجابة لطلبكم *ijābatan li-ṭalabikum* in compliance with your request; in answer to your request

تجاوب *tajāwub* agreement, conformity; harmony

استجابة *istijāba* hearing, answering (of a prayer); granting, fulfillment (of a request); resonance, consonance (*phys.*) | استجابة ل *istijābatan li* in compliance with, in answer to, in deference to

استجواب *istijwāb* pl. *-āt* interrogation, questioning; hearing; interview; interpellation (in parliament)

متجاوب *mutajāwib* harmonious

مستجيب *mustajīb* hearing, answering, granting; reverberant, resonant, resonating; responsive, susceptible, impressible

جوت (Engl.) *jūt* jute

(جوح) جاح *jāḥa u* and IV to annihilate, destroy, ruin; to flood, inundate (ه the land) VIII do.; to carry away, sweep away (ه s.o., ه s.th.; storm); to put down, subdue, quell (ه s.th., e.g., a riot)

اجاحة *ijāḥa* destruction, annihilation; crop damage; crop failure, bad harvest

اجتياح *ijtiyāḥ* destruction, annihilation; subdual, suppression

جائح *jā'iḥ* crushing, devastating; disastrous

جائحة *jā'iḥa* pl. جوائح *jawā'iḥ*[2] calamity, disaster, ruin; epidemic; crop damage

جوخ *jūḵ* pl. اجواخ *ajwāḵ* broadcloth

(جود) جاد *jāda u* (جودة *jūda*) to be or become good, become better, improve; — (*jūd*) to grant generously (ب s.th.), be so generous as to do s.th. (ب with verbal noun); to be liberal, openhanded (ب with s.th., على toward s.o.), bestow liberally (ب s.th., على upon s.o.), grant, give lavishly (ب of s.th., على to s.o.), shower (على ب s.o. with); to donate (ب a sum of money, etc.) | جاد بنفسه to sacrifice o.s.; to give up the ghost; جادت عيناه بالدمع (*'aināhu bi-d-dam'*) tears welled from his eyes; جادت السماء (heavens granted rain) it rained II to do well (ه s.th.); to make better, improve, better, ameliorate (ه s.th.); to recite (the Koran; cf. تجويد) IV to do well, do excellently (ه s.th.); to master (ه s.th.), be skilled, proficient (ه in), be an expert (ه at), be conversant (ه with an art or field of knowledge); to accomplish or say good, excellent things; to achieve excellent results; to be excellent, outstanding, distinguish o.s. (e.g., as a poet) | اجاد لغة (*luġatan*) to master a language; اجاد العزف على البيانو (*'azfa*) to play the piano well X to think (ه s.th.) good or excellent, approve of (ه); to consider (ه s.th.) suitable for or appropriate to (ل)

جود *jūd* openhandedness, liberality, generosity

جود *jaud* heavy rains

جادة see under ²جد

جودة *jūda* goodness, excellence

جيد *jayyid* pl. جياد *jiyād* good, perfect, faultless; outstanding, excellent, first-rate; good (as an examination grade); جيدا *jayyidan* well, excellently; thoroughly | جيد جدا (*jiddan*) very good (also as an examination grade)

اجود *ajwad*[2] better

جواد *jawād* pl. اجواد *ajwād*, اجاود *ajāwid*[2], اجاويد *ajāwīd*[2], جود *jūd* openhanded, liberal, generous, magnanimous; *jawād* pl. جياد *jiyād*, اجياد *ajyād*, اجاويد *ajāwīd*[2] race horse, racer; charger | ابن الاجواد noble man

تجويد *tajwīd* art of reciting the Koran, Koran reading (in accordance with established rules of pronunciation and intonation)

مجيد *mujīd* adept, efficient, proficient

جودار *jaudār* see جاودار (alphabetically)

(جور) جار *jāra u* (*jaur*) to deviate, stray (عن from); to commit an outrage (على on), bear down (على upon), wrong, persecute, oppress, tyrannize (على s.o.); to encroach, make inroads (على on another's territory) III to be the neighbor of s.o. (ه), live next door to (ه); to be adjacent, be next (ه to s.th.), adjoin (ه s.th.); to be in the immediate vicinity of (ه, ه), be close to (ه, ه); to border (ه on) IV to grant asylum or a sanctuary (ه to s.o.); to protect (ه s.o., من from), take (ه s.o.) under one's wing; to stand by s.o. (ه), aid (ه s.o.) VI to be neighbors; to be adjacent; to have a common border X to seek protection, seek refuge (ب with s.o., من from s.th.), appeal for aid (ه to s.o., من against s.th.)

جور *jaur* injustice; oppression, tyranny; outrage

جار *jār* pl. جيران *jīrān* neighbor; refugee; protégé, charge

جارة *jāra* pl. *-āt* neighboress

جيرة *jīra* neighborhood

جورة *jūra* pl. جور *juwar* pit, hole

جورى see alphabetically

جوار *jiwār* neighborhood, proximity; بجوار in the neighborhood of, in the vicinity of, near, close to

مجاورة *mujāwara* neighborhood, proximity

جائر *jā'ir* pl. جورة *jawara*, جارة *jāra* unjust, unfair; tyrannical, despotic; tyrant, oppressor, despot

مجاور *mujāwir* neighboring, adjacent; near, close by; (pl. *-ūn*) student (esp. of Al Azhar University; living in the vicinity of the Mosque)

مجير *mujīr* protector

متجاور *mutajāwir* having a common border; adjoining, adjacent, contiguous

جورب *jaurab* pl. جوارب *jawārib*[2] stocking; sock

جورجيا *jorjiyā* Georgia (republic of the U.S.S.R.)

[1]جورى *jūrī* damask rose (Rosa damascena, *bot.*); crimson

[2]جورى (Engl.) *jūrī* jury

[1]جاز (جوز) *jāza u* (جواز *jawāz*, مجاز *majāz*) to pass, come, travel (ه through); to pass (ه an examination, a test); to be allowed, permitted, permissible; to be possible, conceivable; to work, succeed (عليه with s.o.; deceit, artifice) | جازت عليه الحيلة (*ḥīla*) the trick worked with him, he fell for the trick **II** to permit, allow (ه s.th.); to approve (ه of), sanction, warrant, authorize (ه s.th.) **III** to pass (ه s.th. or by s.th.), go or walk past s.th. (ه); to go beyond s.th. (ه), overstep, cross, leave behind (ه s.th.), also, e.g., جاوز الثلاثين من العمر (*'umr*) he is past thirty; to exceed, surpass (ه s.th.); to pass over s.th. (عن), disregard (عن s.th.), pay no attention (عن to); to let (عن s.th.) go unpunished; to give up, forgo, relinquish (عن s.th.) **IV** to traverse, cross (ه s.th., الى on the way to); to permit, allow (ه ل to s.o. s.th.); to authorize (ه ل s.o. to do s.th., also ه ه); to license (ه s.th.); to approve, confirm, endorse (ه a decision, a judgment); to approve (ه of s.th.), sanction (ه s.th.) **V** to tolerate, suffer, bear **VI** to pass (ه s.th. or by s.th.), go or walk past s.th. (ه); to go beyond s.th. (ه), overstep, cross, leave behind (ه s.th.); to exceed, surpass (ه s.th., also على), to go too far, overstep all bounds, encroach, make inroads; to pass over s.th. (عن), disregard (عن s.th.), pay no attention (عن to); to give up, forgo, relinquish (ه s.th.); to refrain (عن from) **VIII** to pass, run, go (ه through), cut across (ه); to cross (ه a border, a street, a mountain range); to traverse (ه a country or sea); to cover (ه a distance); to pass (ه through the mind; said of ideas, thoughts); to go (ه through hard times or a crisis); to surmount, overcome (ه a crisis) **X** to deem permissible (ه s.th.); to ask permission

جوز *jauz* pl. اجواز *ajwāz* heart, center (of a desert, of a large area, etc.) | فى اجواز amid, in the middle of, in; فى اجواز الفضاء (*faḍā'*) in space

جواز *jawāz* permissibility, admissibility; lawfulness, legality; permission, (official) permit, license, authorization; possibility, conceivability; passing (of an examination) | جواز السفر *j. as-safar* (pl. *-āt*) (traveling) passport

مجاز *majāz* crossing; passage; corridor (*pol.-geogr.*); metaphor, figurative expression (*rhet.*) | مجازا *majāzan*, على سبيل المجاز figuratively, metaphorically

مجازى *majāzī* figurative, metaphorical

اجازة *ijāza* pl. *-āt* permission, authorization; approval; license; = Fr. *licence* as an academic degree; permit; vacation, leave (of absence) | اجازة الحصر *i. al-ḥaṣr* grant of patent, issue of letters patent; patent; اجازة قنصلية (*qunṣulīya*) exequatur of a consul (*dipl.*); اجازة مرضية (*maraḍīya*) sick leave; الاجازات المدرسية (*madrasīya*) school vacation; غائب بالاجازة on leave, on vacation

مجاوزة *mujāwaza* and تجاوز *tajāwuz* crossing; exceeding; overdraft, overdrawing (of an account); disregard (عن for); relinquishment (عن of s.th.)

اجتياز *ijtiyāz* traversing, crossing; passage; transit; covering (of a distance); passing (of an examination); surmounting (of difficulties)

جائز *jā'iz* permitted, lawful, legal; conceivable, thinkable

جائزة *jā'iza* pl. جوائز *jawā'iz*[2] prize, reward, premium | جائزة دراسية (*dirāsīya*) stipend, scholarship

مجاز *mujāz* licensed; licentiate (as an academic title, = Fr. *licencié*; e.g., مجاز فى العلوم *licencié ès sciences*)

[2]□ جوز = زوج II to give in marriage

□ جوز *jauz* pl. اجواز *ajwāz* = زوج couple

□ مجوز (*syr.*; pronounced *məžwez*, < مزوج *muzwaj*) wind instrument with a double pipe, corresponding to the Egyptian *zummāra*)

[3]الجوزاء *al-jauzā'* Gemini (*astron.*)

[4]جوز *jauz* (coll.; n. un. ة, pl. *-āt*) walnut | جوز الطيب *j. aṭ-ṭīb* nutmeg; جوز القئ *j. al-qai'* nux vomica; جوز الهند *j. al-hind*, جوز هندى (*hindī*) coconut; جوز القز *j. alqazz* cocoon, chrysalis of the silkworm

جوزة *gōza* (*eg.*) narghile

جوزى *jauzī* nut (used attributively and in compounds); nut-brown, hazel

[5]جاز look up alphabetically

جوزل *jauzal* pl. جوازل *jawāzil*[2] young pigeon

جاس (جوس) *jāsa* *u* to peer around, pry around, look around (خلال *kilāla* in); to search, investigate, explore (ه s.th.) VIII to search, investigate, explore (ه s.th.)

جوسق *jausaq* pl. جواسق *jawāsiq*[2] palace; manor, villa

جويطة *gawīṭa* pl. جوائط *gawā'iṭ*[2] (*eg.*) dowel, peg

جاع (جوع) *jā'a* *u* to be hungry; to starve II to cause (ه s.o.) to starve, starve out, famish (ه s.o.) IV do.

جوع *jū'* hunger, starvation | مات جوعا to starve to death

جوعان *jau'ān*[2], f. جوعى *jau'ā*, pl. جياع *jiyā'* hungry, starved, famished

مجاعة *majā'a* pl. *-āt* famine

جائع *jā'i'* pl. جياع *jiyā'*, جوع *juwwa'* hungry, starved, famished

تجويع *tajwī'* starving out

اجاعة *ijā'a* starving out

جوف II to make hollow, hollow out (ه s.th.)

جوف *jauf* pl. اجواف *ajwāf* hollow, cavity; depression; interior, inside, center, heart; belly, abdomen; north (*maġr.*) | فى جوف inside, in the interior of, in the middle of; فى جوف الليل (*j. il-lail*) or جوف الليل (*jaufa*) in the middle of the night

جوفى *jaufī* inner, interior, inside; subterranean, underground, subsurface (of geological strata); northern (*maġr.*) | مياه جوفية ground water

اجوف *ajwaf*[2], f. جوفاء *jaufā'*[2], pl. جوف *jūf* hollow; empty; vain, futile, inane, pointless, senseless

تجويف *tajwīf* pl. تجاويف *tajāwīf*[2] hollow, cavity

مجوف *mujawwaf* hollowed out, hollow

جوق *jauq* pl. اجواق *ajwāq* and جوقة *jauqa* pl. *-āt* troop, group; theatrical troupe, operatic company; choir (*mus.*); orchestra, band (also جوقة موسيقية) | مدير الجوق *mudīr al-j.* conductor, bandleader, choir leader; جوقة الشرف *j. aš-šaraf* Legion of Honor

[1]جول) جال (جول) *jāla u* (*jaul*, جولة *jaula*, تجوال *tajwāl*, جولان *jawalān*) to roam, rove, wander about; to move freely, be at home (فى in a field of learning), occupy o.s. (فى with); to be circulated, go the rounds; to pass (فى, ب through the mind) | جال برأسه to preoccupy s.o., engross s.o.'s attention, ما يجول فى خاطره (بخاطره) what he is preoccupied with, what is on his mind; جال الدمع فى عينيه (*dam'*, *'ainaihi*) his eyes swam in tears; جالت يده فى (*yaduhū*) he laid his hands on, he committed defalcations of IV to circulate, pass around (ه s.th.) | اجال الرأى فى (*ra'ya*) to weigh s.th. thoroughly, ponder s.th.; اجال النظر (*naẓara*) to let one's eyes wander about; to look around V to roam, rove, wander about, move around; to patrol, go the rounds; to cruise; to tour, travel from place to place, travel about

جولة *jaula* pl. *-āt* circuit, round; patrol; excursion, outing; tour; (round) trip; voyage, run (of a steamer); (round-trip) flight (of an airplane); round (in sports)

جوال *jawwāl* wandering, migrant, itinerant, roving; cruising; traveling; ambulant; traveler, tourist; see also alphabetically | رام جوال *rāmin jawwāl* pl. رماة جوالة *rumāh jawwāla* rifleman (*mil.*; *Syr.*)

جوالة *jawwāla* one given to roaming or traveling; wanderer, wayfarer; ○ motorcycle; cruiser

تجوال *tajwāl* migration, wandering, roving, traveling; nomadic life, nomadism

جولان *jawalān* migration, wandering, roving, traveling; nomadic life, nomadism | جولان اليد *j. al-yad* embezzlement, defalcation

مجال *majāl* pl. *-āt* room, space (ل for s.th.); field, domain, sphere; scope, extent; reach; range; elbowroom, free scope; play, clearance; field (*magn.*) | ما ترك مجالا للشك (*šakk*) to admit of no doubt; لا مجال للطعن فيه (*majāla, ṭa'n*) (it is) incontestable; فى هذا المجال in this connection; ودع المجال امامه فسيحا (*amāmahū*) to give s.o. a free hand, wide scope of action; مجال حيوى (*ḥayawī*) lebensraum; مجال العمل *m. al-'amal* field of activity; مجال مغنطيسى (*maḡnaṭīsī*) magnetic field; شدة المجال *šiddat al-m.* field intensity (*magn.*)

تجول *tajawwul* roaming, roving, wandering, migration; going out, moving about; patrol, round; (round) trip, tour; traveling | منع التجول *man' at-t.* curfew

بائع جائل *bā'i' jā'il* pl. باعة جائلون peddler, hawker

متجول *mutajawwil* wandering, migrant, roaming, roving, itinerant; ambulant; traveling; traveler | وكيل متجول traveling salesman; بياع متجول (*bayyā'*) peddler, hawker; قسيس متجول (*qissīs*) itinerant preacher

[2]جوال look up alphabetically

جولف *golf* golf (*eg.*)

جام look up alphabetically

جون *jūn* pl اجوان *ajwān* gulf, inlet, bay

جونيلة, جونلا, جونلة (It. *gonnella*) *gonella* pl. *-āt* (woman's) skirt (*eg.*)

جاء look up alphabetically

جوهر II *tajauhara* to become substance

جوهر *jauhar* pl. جواهر *jawāhir*[2] intrinsic, essential nature, essence; content, substance (as opposed to form; *philos.*); matter, substance; atom; jewel, gem; pl. jewelry | الزيف والجوهر (*zaif*) the spurious and the genuine

جوهرة *jauhara* jewel, gem

جوهرى *jauharī* substantial; intrinsic, essential, inherent; fundamental, main, chief, principal; material; jeweler

جوهرجى *jauharjī* jeweler

مجوهرات *mujauharāt* (*eg.*) jewelry, trinkets; jewels, gems

[1]جوى *jawiya a* (*jawan*) to be passionately stirred by love or grief

جوى *jawan* ardent love, passion

[2]جاوى look up alphabetically

جاودار = جويدار look up alphabetically

(جىء) جاء *jā'a* يجىء *yajī'u* (مجىء *majī'*) to come (ه, ‍ه to); to get (‍ه to), reach (‍ه a place); to arrive; to bring (ب s.th.; ب ه to s.o. s.th.); to bring forth, produce (ب s.th.); to set forth (ب s.th.); to do, perform; to commit, perpetrate (‍ه s.th.); to occur, be mentioned, be said (فى in an article, document or book); (with foll. imperf.) to be about or set out to do s.th. | جاء فى جريدة الاهرام ان the newspaper "Al Ahram" reports that ...; جاء من باريس ان a report from Paris says that ...; جاءت نتائجه مطابقة ل (*muṭābiqatan*) its results coincided with ...

جيئة *jī'a, jai'a* coming, arrival | جيئة وذهاب (*ḏahāb*) coming and going, ذهب جيئة وذهابا to pace the floor, walk up and down

مجىء *majī'* coming, arrival, advent

الجائيات *al-jā'iyāt* the things to come

[1]جيب *jaib* pl. جيوب *juyūb* breast, bosom, heart; sine (*math.*); hole, hollow, cavity, excavation; pocket; purse | الجيب الخاص (*kāṣṣ*) the privy purse; تمام الجيب *tamām al-j.*, جيب التمام cosine (*math.*); ساعة الجيب pocket watch; مصروف الجيب pocket money; الجيوب الانفية (*anfīya*) the nasal sinuses (*anat.*); جيوب المقاومة *j. al-muqāwama* pockets of resistance (*mil.*)

جيبى *jaibī* pocket (adj.)

[2]جيپ *jīp*, جيب *jīb* and سيارة جيب *sayyārat j.* jeep

چيت (*ir.*) *čīt* a colorful cotton fabric, chintz

[1]جيد *jīd* pl. اجياد *ajyād*, جيود *juyūd* neck

[2]جيد *jayyid* see جود

[3]جياد, اجياد see جواد *jawād*

[1]جير *jairi* surely, truly, verily

[2]جير *jīr* lime

جيرى *jīrī* calcareous, lime (adj.)

جيار *jayyār* unslaked lime

جيارة *jayyāra* limekiln

[3]جير II to endorse (*fin.*)

جيرو (It. *giro*) endorsement (*fin.*)

[4]جيرة, جيران see جور

جيزة *gīza* Giza (city in N Egypt); a brand of Egyptian cotton

(جيش) جاش *jāša i* (جيشان *jayašān*) to be excited, be agitated; to rage, storm; to boil, simmer II to levy troops, mobilize an army X to raise, mobilize (‍ه an army, also, e.g., انصارا *anṣāran* followers)

جيش *jaiš* pl. جيوش *juyūš* army, troops, armed forces | جيش الاحتلال occupation forces; جيش احتياطى army reserve; جيش مرابط (*murābiṭ*) territorial army; جيش الانقاذ *j. al-inqāḏ* Salvation Army; جيش المساء *al-masā'* dusk, evening twilight

جياش *jayyāš* agitated, impassioned; excited, boiling up; ebullient; pleasurably excited, happily stimulated

جيشان *jayašān* excitement, agitation; raging

(جيف) جاف *jāfa i*, II and V to be putrid, stink (decaying cadaver)

جيفة *jīfa* pl. جيف *jiyaf*, اجياف *ajyāf* corpse, cadaver

چيكى *čīkī* Czech

جيل *jīl* pl. اجيال *ajyāl* people, nation, tribe; generation; century; epoch, era

جيلاتى (It. *gelati*) *jēlātī* ice cream

جيم *jīm* name of the letter ج

جين (Fr. *gaine*) corselet, sheath corset (*eg.*)

جيوغرافيا *jiyoḡrāfiyā* geography | الجيوغرافيا البشرية (*bašarīya*) anthropogeography

جيوفيزيا *jiyofiziyā* geophysics

جيوفيزيائى *jiyofiziyā'ī* geophysical | السنة الجيوفيزيائية (*sana*) the geophysical year

جيوفيزيقى *jiyofīzīqī* geophysical

جيولوجيا *jiyolōjiyā* geology

جيولوجى *jiyolōjī* geologic(al)

ح

حاء *ḥā'* name of the letter ح

حاخام *ḥāḵām* rabbi | الحاخام الاكبر the chief rabbi

حوول see حول

حامى *ḥāmī* Hamitic

حان and حانة see حين

حانبة (pronounced *ḥamba*) pl. حوانب *ḥawānib*[2] (formerly *Tun.*) hamba, palace gendarme of the Bey of Tunis

حانوت see حنو

[1]حب *ḥabba i* (*ḥubb*) to love, like II to evoke (الى in s.o.) love or a liking (ه, ‍ه for s.th. or s.o.), make (الى s.o.) love or like (ه, ‍ه s.th. or s.o.); to endear (‍ه الى s.th. to s.o.), make (‍ه s.th.) dear, lovable, attractive (الى for s.o.), make (‍ه s.th.) palatable, acceptable (الى to s.o.); to urge (‍ه الى s.th. on s.o.), suggest (‍ه الى s.th. to s.o.) IV (حب *ḥubb*, محبة *maḥabba*) to love, like (‍ه, ه s.o., s.th.); to wish, want, or like, to do s.th. (ان) | احب ان *uḥibbu an* I should like to . . .; احب له ان to like about s.o. that he . . .; لا يحب الخير له (*ḵaira*) he doesn't want him to be happy, he grudges him everything V to show love, reveal one's affections (الى to s.o.); to endear o.s. (الى to s.o.), make o.s. popular, ingratiate o.s. (الى with s.o.); to court, woo (الى a woman) VI to love one another X to like (‍ه s.th.); to deem (‍ه s.th.) desirable, recommendable; to prefer (‍ه على s.th. to s.th. else)

حب *ḥubb* love; affection, attachment | حب الذات *ḥ. aḏ-ḏāt* self-love, amour-propre; حب الاستطلاع curiosity, inquisitiveness; حب الوطن *ḥ. al-waṭan* patriotism; حبا ل (*ḥubban*) out of love o. affection for, out of friendship for; حبا فى in the desire to . . .

حبى *ḥubbī* friendly, amicable, loving; حبيا *ḥubbiyan* in an amicable manner, amicably; by fair means (*jur.*)

حب *ḥibb* pl. احباب *aḥbāb* darling, dear, dearest (one)

حباب *ḥabāb* aim, goal, end

حبيب *ḥabīb* pl. احباء *aḥibbā'*[2], احبة *aḥibba*, احباب *aḥbāb* beloved, sweetheart, lover; darling; dear one, friend; dear (الى to s.o.); popular; الاحباب the beloved ones, the dear ones

حبيبة *ḥabība* pl. حبائب *ḥabā'ib*[2] sweetheart, darling, beloved woman

احب *aḥabb*[2] dearer, more desirable, preferable (الى to s.o.)

حبذا *ḥabbaḏā* (with foll. nominative) how nice, how lovely is ...! how good, excellent, perfect is ...! | حبذا لو how nice it would be if ...; حبذا الحال لو فعل *ḥ. l-ḥālu lau fa'ala* it would be nice, or he would do well, if he did it; يا حبذا الحال (*ḥālu*) that's just wonderful!

محبة *maḥabba* love; affection, attachment | محبة الوطن *m. al-waṭan* patriotism

تحبب *taḥabbub* courtship, wooing

تحابب *taḥābub* mutual love, concord, harmony

محبوب *maḥbūb* beloved; dear; lovable, desirable; popular; favorite; beloved one, lover; (pl. محابيب *maḥābīb*[2]) gold piece, sequin (in Ottoman times; *eg.*)

محبوبة *maḥbūba* sweetheart, darling, beloved woman

محبب *muḥabbab* agreeable, pleasant, desirable, lovable, dear (الى to s.o.); nice, likable

محب *muḥibb* pl. *-ūn* loving; lover; fancier, amateur, fan; friend | محب للناس philanthropic(al), affable; محبنا العزيز our dear friend; محبو الآثار friends of archeology; محب لذاته (*li-ḏātihī*) egoist

متحاب *mutaḥābb* loving one another, concordant

مستحب *mustaḥabb* (re)commendable, desirable (said of acts whose neglect is not punished by God, but whose performance is rewarded; *Isl. Law*); well-liked, popular

[2]حب **II** to produce seed, go to seed (plant); to bear seed (grain); to granulate, become granulated; to granulate (ه s.th.) **IV** to produce seed

حب *ḥabb* (coll.; n. un. ة) grains; seed; — pl. حبوب *ḥubūb* grain, cereals, corn; seed(s); grains, kernels; granules; pellets; pills, pastilles; berries; acne, pustules, pimples | حب العزيز chufa (Cyperus esculentus L.; *bot.*); حب الفقد *ḥ. al-faqad* chaste tree (Vitex agnus castus L.; *bot.*); حب الملوك croton seeds (seeds of Croton tiglium; *bot.*); (*magr.*) cherries; حب الهال *ḥ. al-hāl* and حب الهان (حبهان) *ḥ. al-hān* cardamom (Amomum cardamomum L.; *bot.*); حب الغمام *ḥ. al-ğamām* hail, hailstones

حبة *ḥabba* (n. un.; see also حب *ḥabb*) pl. *-āt* grain, granule; seed; kernel; pill, pastille; berry; pustule, pimple; triviality, trifle; a square measure (*Eg.*; = 58.345 m²); pl. حبات beads (of the rosary) | حبة شعير *ḥ. ša'īr* a linear measure (*Eg.*; = 0.205 cm); حبة حلوة (*ḥulwa*) aniseed; حبة سوداء (*ṣaudā'*[2]) black caraway (Nigella sativa L.; *bot.*); حبات الرمال grains of sand; حبة العين *ḥ. al-'ain* eyeball; pupil (of the eye); حبة القلب *ḥ. al-qalb* dearest one, beloved, darling

حبب *ḥabab* blister

حبيبة *ḥubaiba* pl. *-āt* little grain, small kernel; small pimple or pustule

حبيبي *ḥubaibī* granular, granulated | الرمد الحبيبي (*ramad*) trachoma (*med.*)

حبحب *ḥabḥab* (coll.) watermelon (*ḥij.*)

حباحب *ḥubāḥib* firefly, glowworm

حبذ **II** to approve, think well (ه of s.th.), commend (ه s.th.); to applaud, acclaim, cheer (ه s.o., ه s.th.)

حبذا see [1]حب

تحبيذ *taḥbīḏ* approval; acclamation, acclaim, applause, cheering

حبر **ḥabara** *u* (*ḥabr*) to gladden, make happy, delight (ه s.o.); — *ḥabira a* (حبور *ḥubūr*) to be glad, happy **II** to embellish, refine, make workmanlike (ه s.th.); to compose (ه s.th.) in elegant style; to write, compose (ه s.th.)

حبر *ḥibr* ink | ام الحبر *umm al-ḥ.* squid, cuttlefish; حبر على ورق (*waraq*) mere ink on paper, of no effect (e.g., an agreement, a treaty)

حبر *ḥabr, ḥibr* pl. احبار *aḥbār* a non-Muslim religious authority, learned man, scribe; bishop; rabbi | الحبر الاعظم the Pope; سفر الاحبار *sifr al-a.* Leviticus (Old Test.)

حبرى *ḥabrī* pontifical | قداس حبرى (*quddās*) pontifical mass (*Chr.*)

حبرية *ḥabrīya* office or dignity of a bishop, bishopric, pontificate

حبرة *ḥabara, ḥibara* pl. *-āt* silken shawl or wrap (worn in public by ladies)

حبار *ḥabār, ḥibār* pl. *-āt* mark, trace (esp. of blows), welt, wale

حبور *ḥubūr* joy

حبارى *ḥubārā* pl. حباريات *ḥubārayāt* bustard (*zool.*)

يحبور *yaḥbūr* bustard chick (*zool.*)

محبرة *miḥbara, maḥbara* pl. محابر *maḥābir*[2] inkwell

حبس **ḥabasa** *i* (*ḥabs*) to obstruct, shut off, confine (ه, ه s.o., s.th.), block, bar, hold back, check (ه s.th. عن from; also tears, laughter, etc.); to withhold (ه عن from s.o. s.th.); to hold in custody, detain (ه s.o.); to apprehend, arrest, jail, imprison (ه s.o.); to keep, keep back, put aside, put away (ه على s.th. for); to tie up, invest inalienably (ه capital) | حبس نفسه على (*nafsahū*) to devote o.s. entirely to . . .; حبس يده عن (*yadahū*) to take (s.th.) out from under s.o.'s power; حبس عليه انفاسه (*anfāsahū*) to make s.o. catch his breath, take s.o.'s breath away; حبس مع الشغل *ḥubisa maʿa š-šuğl* he was committed to prison under hard labor **II** to tie up inalienably (ه funds, على for, esp. for a pious purpose), make a religious bequest (ه, for the benefit of على) **VII** to be held back, be held up, stop, be interrupted, intermit; to restrain o.s., hold back **VIII** to block, obstruct, bar, confine (ه, ه s.o., s.th.); to detain, hold in custody (ه, ه s.o., s.th.); to hold back, retain, suppress (ه, ه s.o., s.th.); to be detained, held up; to be impeded, held back; to falter, break, fail (voice), stop (breath)

حبس *ḥabs* (act of) holding or keeping back, obstruction, check, repression; blocking off, barring, confinement; damming up, staving off; safekeeping, custody, retention; imprisonment, arrest, detention, jailing; (pl. حبوس *ḥubūs*) prison, jail | حبس احتياطى (*iḥtiyāṭī*) detention (pending investigation); حبس انفرادى (*infirādī*) solitary confinement; حبس شديد penal servitude

حبس *ḥibs* pl. احباس *aḥbās* dam, weir, barrage

حبس *ḥubs, ḥubus* pl. احباس *aḥbās* (*Tun., Alg., Mor.* = *waqf*) inalienable property the yield of which is devoted to pious purposes, religious bequest, (*Fr. jur.*) "habous" | حبس عام (*ʿāmm*) public habous, حبس خاص (*ḵāṣṣ*) private habous; كان حبسا على (= كان وقفا على) to be entirely dependent on . . .

حبسة *ḥubsa* speech defect, impediment of speech

حبيس *ḥabīs* blocked-off, shut-off, barred, confined, locked-up; secluded; bated (breath); choking (voice); (pl. حبساء *ḥubasāʾ*[2]) hermit

محبس *maḥbas, maḥbis* pl. محابس *maḥābis*[2] place where s.th. is confined or locked up; jail, prison; (prison) cell

محبس *miḥbas* device for shutting off or blocking off

محبسة *maḥbasa* hermitage

انحباس *inḥibās* seclusion, confinement; stoppage, interruption; cessation

احتباس *iḥtibās* retention, restraint; inhibition, impediment, obstruction, stoppage | احتباس البول *iḥtibās el-baul* suppression of urine, ischuria

محبوس *maḥbūs* shut-off (from the outside world), isolated, secluded, confined, locked-up; imprisoned, captive; tied-up (funds); (pl. محابيس *maḥābīs*[2]) prisoner, prison inmate, convict

محبس *muḥabbis* donor of a habous (see حبس *ḥubs*)

المحبس عليه *al-muḥabbas ʿalaihi* beneficiary of a habous (see حبس *ḥubs*)

منحبس *munḥabis* secluded, shut-off

الحبش *al-ḥabaš* Abyssinia, Ethiopia; (pl. الاحباش *al-aḥbāš*) the Abyssinians, Ethiopians

الحبشة *al-ḥabaša* (and بلاد الحبشة) Abyssinia, Ethiopia

حبشى *ḥabašī* pl. احباش *aḥbāš* Abyssinian, Ethiopian

حبط *ḥabaṭa i* (حبوط *ḥubūṭ*) and *ḥabiṭa a* to come to nothing, fail, miscarry, go wrong; to be futile, be of no avail, be lost IV to frustrate, thwart, foil, defeat (ه s.th., على ه in s.th. s.o.; negotiations, efforts, an attempt, etc.)

حبط *ḥabaṭ* scar of a wound, wale, welt

حبوط *ḥubūṭ* futility, failure

احباط *iḥbāṭ* frustration, thwarting, foiling

حبق *ḥabaq* basil (*bot.*); (*eg.*) a variety of speedwell (Veronica anagallis aquatica L.)

حبك *ḥabaka i u* (*ḥabk*) to weave well and tight (ه s.th.); to braid, plait (ه s.th.); to twist, twine, tighten (ه s.th.); to knit (ه s.th.); to devise, contrive (ه a plan, a plot) II to twist, twine, tighten (ه s.th.); to fasten (ه s.th.)

حبكة *ḥabka* fabric, tissue; texture, structure

حبك *ḥubuk*: حبك النجوم *h. an-nujūm* the orbits of the celestial bodies

حباكة *ḥibāka* weaver's trade, weaving

محبوك *maḥbūk* tightly woven; tight, taut; sturdy, strong, robust, husky

محتبك *muḥtabik* interwoven, intersecting

حبل[1] VIII to ensnare, catch in a snare (ه, ه s.o., s.th.)

حبل *ḥabl* pl. حبال *ḥibāl*, احبل *aḥbul*, حبول *ḥubūl*, احبال *aḥbāl* rope, cable, hawser; cord, string, thread; (pl. حبال *ḥibāl*) beam, ray (e.g., of the sun, of light), jet (e.g., of water); vein; sinew, tendon | حبل الوريد jugular vein; الحبل السرى (*surrī*) umbilical cord; الحبل الشوكى (*šaukī*) spine; حبال صوتية (*ṣautīya*) vocal cords; حبل المساكين ivy (*bot.*); حبال الماء jets of water; القى (اطلق) الحبل على الغارب *alqā* (*aṭlaqa*) *l-ḥabla ʿalā l-ḡārib* to let things go, slacken the reins, give a free hand, impose no restraint; ارتخاء الحبل slackening of the reins, yielding; relenting; اضطرب حبله *iḍṭaraba ḥabluhū* to get into a state of disorder, of disorganization, of disintegration, get out of control; لعب على الحبلين (*laʿiba, ḥablain*) to play a double game, work both sides of the street

احبولة *uḥbūla* pl. احابيل *aḥābīl*[2] snare, net; rope with a noose; pl. احابيل tricks, wiles, artifices, stratagems (in order to get s.th.)

حبالة *ḥibāla* pl. حبائل *ḥabāʾil*[2] snare, net

حابل *ḥābil*: اختلط الحابل بالنابل (*iḵtalaṭa*) everything became confused, got into a state of utter confusion; حابلهم ونابلهم all together, all in a medley

²حبل *ḥabila a* (*ḥabal*) to be or become pregnant, conceive **II** and **IV** to make pregnant (ها a woman)

حبل *ḥabal* conception; pregnancy

حبلى *ḥublā* pl. حبالى *ḥabālā* and حبلانة *ḥablāna* pregnant

حبن *ḥaban* dropsy

حبهان (حب الهان *ḥabb al-hān*) cardamom (Amomum cardamomum L.; *bot.*)

حبا (حبو) *ḥabā u* (*ḥabw*) to crawl, creep; to present (ه ه s.o. with s.th.), give, award (ه ه to s.o. s.th.) **III** to be obliging (ه to s.o.), show one's good will (ه toward s.o.); to favor (ه s.o.); to side (ه with s.o.), be partial (ه to s.o.); to show respect, deference (ه to s.o.) **VIII** to sit with one's legs drawn up and wrapped in one's garment

حبوة *ḥibwa, ḥubwa, ḥabwa* gift, present

حباء *ḥibā'* gift, present

محاباة *muḥābāh* obligingness, complaisance, courtesy; favor(ing), favoritism, partiality

حت *ḥatta u* (*ḥatt*) to rub off, scrape off, scratch off (ه s.th.)

حتة *ḥitta* pl. حتت *ḥitat* (*eg.*) piece, bit, morsel

حتى *ḥattā* (prep.) until, till, up to, as far as; (conj.; with perf.) until, so that; (with subj.) until, that, so that, in order that; — (particle) even, eventually even; and even; حتى لو even if; (with preceding negation) not even, and be it only ...

حتات *ḥutāt* scraps; morsels, crumbs

تحات *taḥātt* corrosion

حتد *ḥatida a* (*ḥatad*) to be of pure origin

محتد *maḥtid* descent, origin, lineage

حترة *ḥutra* small piece, bit, trifle

حتار *ḥitār* pl. حتر *ḥutur* border, edge, fringe, surroundings, vicinity

حتف *ḥatf* pl. حتوف *ḥutūf* death | يبحث عن (يسعى الى) حتفه بظلفه *yabḥaṯu ʿan* (*yasʿā ilā*) *ḥatfihī bi-ẓilfihī* he brings about his own destruction, digs his own grave; مات حتف انفه *māta ḥatfa anfihī* he died a natural death

حتم *ḥatama i* (*ḥatm*) to decree, make necessary, prescribe (على ه s.th. for s.o.), make (ه s.th.) a duty, a necessity (على for s.o.); to impose, enjoin (على ه s.th. upon s.o.); to decide, determine definitely (ب s.th.) **II** to decree, make necessary, prescribe (على ه s.th. for s.o.), make (ه s.th.) a duty, a necessity (على for s.o.) **V** to be necessary; to be s.o.'s (على) duty, be incumbent (على upon s.o.)

حتم *ḥatm* pl. حتوم *ḥutūm* imposition, injunction; final decision, resolution, determination; حتما *ḥatman* decidedly, definitely, necessarily, inevitably

حتمى *ḥatmī* decided, definite, final, conclusive, definitive, unalterable, irrevocable, inevitable

حتمية *ḥatmīya* decidedness, definiteness, definitiveness, determinateness, unalterableness; necessity

لاحتمية *lā-ḥatmīya* indeterminism (*philos.*)

محتوم *maḥtūm* imposed, enjoined, obligatory; determined, definitive, determinate, unalterable, inevitable; destined, predestined, ordained (fate)

محتم *muḥattam* imposed, enjoined, obligatory; determined, definitive, determinate, unalterable, inevitable; destined, predestined, ordained (fate)

متحتم *mutaḥattim* absolutely necessary; imperative (duty)

حتى see حت

¹حث *ḥaṯṯa u* (*ḥaṯṯ*) to urge, incite, prompt, goad, spur on, egg on, prod, provoke,

impel (ه s.o., على to do s.th.) | حث خطاه (*kuṭāhu*) to quicken one's pace, hurry (الى to a place); حث الطريق (*ṭarīqa*) to hurry, hasten; حث قدميه (*qadamaihi*) to quicken one's pace, break into a run **VIII** and **X** = **I**

حثيث *ḥaṯīṯ* fast, rapid, quick

○ حاثّة *ḥāṯṯa* hormone

²حثّى *ḥiṯṯī* Hittite (n. and adj.)

حثالة *ḥuṯāla* dregs, lees, sediment; scum (fig.); offal, discard, scraps | حثالة الحرير silk combings

(حثو) حثا *ḥaṯā u* (*ḥaṯw*) to strew, scatter, spread, disperse (ه s.th.)

حج *ḥajja u* to overcome, defeat (ه s.o., with arguments, with evidence), confute (ه s.o.); to convince (ه s.o.); — (*ḥajj*) to make the pilgrimage (to Mecca), perform the hadj **III** to dispute, debate, argue, reason (ه with s.o.) **VI** to argue against each other, carry on a dispute, to debate; to take counsel **VIII** to advance (ب s.th.) as an argument, plea, excuse, or pretext; to allege in support or vindication, plead (ب s.th.); to vindicate, justify (ل s.th.); to protest, remonstrate (على against), object, raise objections (على to)

حج *ḥajj* and حجة *ḥijja* pl. *-āt*, حجج *ḥijaj* pilgrimage; hadj, the official Muslim pilgrimage to Mecca | ذو الحجة *ḏū l-ḥijja* Zu'lhijjah, the last month of the Islamic calendar

حجة *ḥujja* pl. حجج *ḥujaj* argument; pretense, pretext, plea; proof, evidence; document, writ, deed, record; authoritative source, competent authority | بحجة ان under the pretense that . . ., on the plea . . ., on the pretext of . . .

حجاج *ḥajāj* pl. احجة *aḥijja* circumorbital ring (*anat.*)

محج *maḥajj* destination (of a journey)

محجة *maḥajja* pl. محاج *maḥājj*² destination of a pilgrimage, object of pilgrimage, shrine; destination (of a journey); goal; road; way; procedure, method | محجة الصواب *m. aṣ-ṣawāb* the Right Way, the Straight Path; محجة الحديد railroad

حجاج *ḥijāj* argument, dispute, debate

تحجج *taḥajjuj* argumentation, pleading, offering of a pretext, pretense, excuse

احتجاج *iḥtijāj* pl. *-āt* argumentation; pretext, excuse, plea, pretense; protest, remonstrance (على against), objection, exception (على to)

حاج *ḥājj* pl. حجاج *ḥujjāj*, حجيج *ḥajīj* pilgrim; hadji, Mecca pilgrim, honorific title of one who has performed the pilgrimage to Mecca

حجب *ḥajaba u* (*ḥajb*) to veil, cover, screen, shelter, seclude (ه على s.th. from); to hide, obscure (ه عن s.th. from s.th. else, e.g., from sight); to eclipse, outshine, overshadow (ه s.o.); to make imperceptible, invisible (ه عن s.th. to); to conceal (ه عن s.th. from s.o.); to make or form a separation (بين — وبين between — and) **II** to veil, hide, conceal; to hide from sight, keep in seclusion (ها a woman); to disguise, mask (ه ب s.th. with) **V** to conceal o.s., hide (عن from), flee from sight, veil o.s. **VII** to veil o.s., conceal o.s.; to be covered up, become hidden, be obscured **VIII** to vanish, become invisible, disappear from sight; to veil o.s., conceal o.s., hide; to become hidden, be concealed (عن from); to withdraw; to elude perception; to cease or interrupt publication (newspaper, periodical)

حجب *ḥajb* seclusion; screening off; keeping away, keeping off

حجاب *ḥijāb* pl. حجب *ḥujub*, احجبة *aḥjiba* cover, wrap, drape; curtain; woman's veil; screen, partition, folding screen; barrier, bar; diaphragm (also الحجاب الحاجز; *anat.*); amulet

حجابة *ḥijāba* office of gatekeeper

احتجاب *iḥtijāb* concealment, hiddenness, seclusion; veiledness, veiling, purdah

حاجب *ḥājib* concealing, screening, protecting; (pl. حجاب *ḥujjāb*, حجبة *ḥajaba*) doorman, gatekeeper; chamberlain; orderly (*Syr.*, *mil.*); (pl. حواجب *ḥawājib*[2]) eyebrow | حاجب الهواء *ḥ. al-hawā'* airtight, hermetic

محجوب *maḥjūb* concealed, hidden, veiled

[1]حجر *ḥajara u* (*ḥajr*, *ḥijr*, *ḥujr*, حجران *ḥijrān*, *ḥujrān*) to deny access (على to s.o.); to stop, detain, hinder (على or ه s.o.); to forbid, interdict (على ه s.th. to s.o.), prohibit (على s.o.) from doing s.th. (ه); to place (على s.o.) under guardianship, declare (على s.o.) legally incompetent

حجر *ḥajr* restriction, curb(ing), check(ing), obstruction, impeding, limitation, curtailing (على of s.th.); barring, closing, debarment, preclusion; detention; blocking, confinement, containment, suppression (as a protective measure); interdiction, prohibition, ban; revocation, or limitation, of s.o.'s (على) legal competence | حجر صحى (*ṣiḥḥī*) quarantine

حجر *ḥijr* forbidden, interdicted, prohibited; lap; (pl. احجار *aḥjār*, حجور *ḥujūr*, حجورة *ḥujūra*) mare

حجرة *ḥujra* pl. *ḥujarāt*, حجر *ḥujar* room; cell; (railroad) compartment; chamber | حجرة الانتظار waiting room; حجرة النوم *ḥ. an-naum* bedroom; الحجرة الفلاحية (*fallāḥiya*) chamber of agriculture

محجر *maḥjar* pl. محاجر *maḥājir*[2] military hospital, infirmary; prison, jail, dungeon | محجر صحى (*ṣiḥḥī*) quarantine, quarantine station

محجر *maḥjir*, *miḥjar*, *maḥjar* pl. محاجر *maḥājir*[2] (= محجر العين *m. al-'ain*) eye socket; see also below

تحجير *taḥjīr* interdiction, prohibition, ban; see also below

محجور *maḥjūr* pl. محاجير *maḥājīr*[2] (and محجور عليه) one placed under guardianship; minor; ward, charge

[2]حجر II to petrify, turn into stone (ه s.th.); to make hard as stone (ه s.th.) V to turn to stone, petrify, become petrified

حجر *ḥajar* pl. احجار *aḥjār*, حجارة *ḥijāra*, حجار *ḥijār* stone; weight (placed as an equipoise on the scale of a balance) | الحجر الاساسى (*asāsī*) the foundation stone, cornerstone, وضع الحجر الاساسى (*waḍ'*) laying of the cornerstone; حجر البلاط *ḥ. al-balāṭ* flagstone, paving stone; حجر جهنم *ḥ. jahannam* lunar caustic, silver nitrate; حجر الجير *ḥ. al-jīr* limestone; حجر السماق or الحجر السماق (*summāqī*) porphyry; الحجر الاسود (*aswad*) the Black Stone (of the Kaaba); حجر الشادنة hematite (*min.*); حجر العثرة *ḥ. al-'aṯra* stumbling block; حجر الفلاسفة philosopher's stone; ○ حجر القمر *ḥ. al-qamar* selenite; حجر كريم and حجر ثمين precious stone, gem; طبع على الحجر (*ṭab'*) lithograph; طباعة الحجر lithography

حجرى *ḥajarī* stony, stone (adj.) | العصر الحجرى (*'aṣr*) the Stone Age; العصر الحجرى الحديث the Neolithic period; العصر الحجرى القديم the Paleolithic period

حجر *ḥajir* stony, petrified

حجار *ḥajjār* stone mason, stone cutter

محجر *maḥjir* pl. محاجر *maḥājir*[2] (stone) quarry

تحجير *taḥjīr* petrification; stone quarrying

تحجر *taḥajjur* petrification

متحجر *mutaḥajjir* petrified

مستحجر *mustaḥjir* petrified

حجز *ḥajaza u i* (*ḥajz*) to hold back, restrain, hinder, prevent (ه عن s.th. from); to keep away (ه عن s.th. from); to block (off), close, bar; to isolate, insulate, confine, seclude; to make inaccessible; to set apart; to separate (بين two things); to arrest, detain; to seize, sequester, impound (على or ه s.th., e.g., s.o.'s property, salary); to confiscate, safeguard (ه s.th.); to reserve (ه s.th.); to make a reservation (ه for a theater seat, a steamer cabin, a ticket, etc.) **VIII** to retain for o.s., reserve to o.s. (ه s.th.)

حجز *ḥajz* curbing, prevention, restraint; seclusion, confinement, containment, isolation, insulation, separation; arrest, detention, seizure, confiscation, sequestration (على of s.th.); reservation (of seats) | حجز الحرية *ḥ. al-ḥurrīya* deprivation of liberty, unlawful detention, duress (*jur.*); القى الحجز على (*alqā*) to confiscate s.th.

الحجاز *al-ḥijāz* Hejaz, region in W Arabia, on the Red Sea coast

حجازى *ḥijāzī* of or pertaining to Hejaz; (pl. *-ūn*) an inhabitant of Hejaz

حاجز *ḥājiz* and حاجزة pl. حواجز *ḥawājiz*[2] obstacle, hindrance, impediment, obstruction; partition, screen, dividing wall; block, blockade, road block; fence, gate, railing, balustrade; hurdle; bar, barrier; barricade | الحجاب الحاجز diaphragm (*anat.*); ○ حاجز الامواج breakwater; الحواجز القمرقية (الجمركية) (*qumruqīya, gumrukīya*) customs barriers; ○ حاجزة الصواعق lightning rod

○ موظف حاجز *muwaẓẓaf ḥājiz* approx.: bailiff

محاجفة[1] *muḥājafa* singlestick fencing

احجاف[2] *iḥjāf* = اجحاف

حجل *ḥajala u i* (*ḥajl*, حجلان *ḥajalān*) to hop, leap; to skip, gambol

حجل *ḥajl*, *ḥijl* pl. حجول *ḥujūl*, احجال *aḥjāl* anklet

حجل *ḥajal* (coll.; n. un. ة) pl. حجلان *ḥijlān*, حجلى *ḥijlā* partridge; mountain partridge, mountain quail

حجلة *ḥajala* pl. حجال *ḥijāl* curtained canopy, or alcove, for the bride | ربات الحجال *rabbāt al-ḥ.* the ladies

لعبة الحجلة *la'bat al-ḥajla* hopscotch

محجل *muḥajjal* wearing anklets (woman); white-footed (horse); bright, brilliant, radiant; unique, singular, esp. in the phrase اغر محجل (*aḡarr*[2])

حجم *ḥajama u* (*ḥajm*) to cup (ه s.o.; *med.*) **IV** to recoil, shrink, flinch (عن from); to desist, abstain, refrain (عن from), forbear (عن s.th.); to withdraw, retreat

حجم *ḥajm* pl. حجوم *ḥujūm*, احجام *aḥjām* bulk, size, volume; caliber (of a cannon) | كبير الحجم bulky, sizable, massive

حجام *ḥajjām* cupper

حجامة *ḥijāma* cupping, scarification, art of cupping

محجم *miḥjam*, محجمة *miḥjama* pl. محاجم *maḥājim*[2] cupping glass

احجام *iḥjām* desistance, abstention; restraint, aloofness, reserve

حجن *ḥajana i* (*ḥajn*) to bend, curve, crook (ه s.th.) **VIII** to snatch up, grab (ه s.th.), take hold (ه of s.th.)

احجن *aḥjan*[2] curved, crooked, bent

محجن *miḥjan* pl. محاجن *maḥājin*[2] staff or stick with a crooked end, crosier; hook

(حجو) حجا به خيرا *ḥajā bihī kairan* to think well of s.o., have a good opinion of s.o. **III** to propose a riddle (ه to s.o.); to speak in riddles, be enigmatic

حجا, حجى *ḥijan* pl. احجاء *aḥjā'* intellect, brains, understanding, discernment, acumen, sagacity, wit, intelligence

حجى *ḥajīy* appropriate, suitable, proper (ب for)

احجى *aḥjā* more appropriate, more suitable, more proper, more correct, better

احجية *uḥjīya* pl. احاجى *aḥājīy*, احاج *aḥājin* riddle, puzzle, enigma

خام *ḥakām* = حاخام (look up alphabetically)

حد *ḥadda u* (*ḥadd*) to sharpen, hone (ه a knife); to delimit, delineate, demarcate, mark off, stake off (ه land, من from); to set bounds (ه to s.th.), limit, restrict, confine (ه s.th.); to impede, hinder, curb, check (من or ه s.th.); — *i* (حدة *ḥidda*) to become furious, angry (على at): — *i u* (حداد *ḥidād*) to wear mourning, mourn (على the deceased) **II** to sharpen, hone (ه a knife); to forge (ه s.th.; *syr.*); to delimit, demarcate (ه s.th.); to set bounds (ه to s.th.), circumscribe, mark off, delineate sharply; to limit, restrict, confine (من or ه s.th.); to determine, appoint, assign, schedule, lay down, set down, establish (ه s.th.); to fix (ه e.g., prices); to define (ه s.th.) | حدد بصره (*baṣarahū*) to dart sharp glances; to scrutinize (فى s.th.), look sharply (فى at s.th.) **III** to oppose (ه, ه s.o., s.th.), act contrary (ه, ه to s.o., to s.th.), contravene, counteract, violate (ه s.th.) **IV** to sharpen, make sharp (ه s.th.) | احد النظر الى (*naẓar*) to look sharply at, stare at; احد بصره (*baṣarahū*) to dart sharp glances; to scrutinize (فى s.th.), look sharply (فى at s.th.); احد من بصره (*baṣarihī*) to glance sharply; — to put on garments of mourning **V** to be delimited, be delineated, be bounded, be circumscribed; to be determined, be established, be set down, be scheduled, be fixed; to be defined, be definable **VIII** to be or become angry; to become infuriated, be furious (على at), be exasperated (على with); to be agitated, be upset, be in a state of commotion

حد *ḥadd* pl. حدود *ḥudūd* (cutting) edge (of a knife, of a sword); edge, border, brink, brim, verge; border (of a country), boundary, borderline; limit (fig.), the utmost, extremity, termination, end, terminal point, terminus; a (certain) measure, extent, or degree (attained); (*math.*) member (of an equation), term (of a fraction, of a proportion); divine ordinance, divine statute; legal punishment (*Isl. Law*) | لحد *li-ḥaddi* or الى حد until, till, up to, to the extent of, الى حد الآن, لحد الآن *li-ḥ. l-āna* up to now, so far; الى حد ما (*ḥaddin*) to a certain degree, to a certain extent; الى حد بعيد, الى حد كبير to a considerable extent or degree, considerably, extensively; الى اى حد (*ayyi ḥaddin*) how far, to what degree or extent; لا حد له (*ḥadda*) boundless, infinite, unbounded, unlimited; بلا حد *bi-lā ḥaddin*, الى غير حد *ilā ḡairi ḥaddin* boundless, unlimited, without limits; على حد سواء *ʿalā ḥaddin sawāʾin*, على حد سوى *ʿalā ḥ. siwan* in the same manner; equally, likewise; على حد (*ḥaddi*) according to, commensurate with; فى حد ذاته *fī ḥaddi ḏātihī* and بحد ذاته in itself, as such; الحد الاعلى (*aʿlā*), الحد الاقصى (*aqṣā*) the maximum; الحد الادنى (*adnā*) the minimum; حد عمرى (*ʿumrī*) age limit; ذو حدين *ḏū ḥaddain* two-edged; فى حدود (*ḥudūdi*) within, within the framework of; بلغ اقصى حدوده (*aqṣā ḥudūdihī*) to attain its highest degree; حدود الله the bounds or restrictions that God has placed on man's freedom of action

حدة *ḥidda* sharpness, keenness; pitch (of a tone); distinctiveness, markedness; vehemence, violence, impetuosity; fury, rage, wrath, ire, anger; excitability, irascibility, passionateness

حدة *ḥida* see وحد

حدد *ḥadad* forbidden

حداد *ḥidād* (act of) mourning (على over) | ثوب الحداد *ṯaub al-ḥ.* garments of mourning; حداد البلاط *ḥ. al-balāṭ* court mourning

حديد *ḥadīd* iron; pl. حدائد *ḥadā'id*² iron parts (of a structure); forgings, hardware, ironware | حديد خام crude iron, pig iron, iron ore; ○ حديد مطاوع (*muṭāwi'*) wrought iron; حديد غفل (*ġufl*) unprocessed iron, pig iron; حديد ظهر الحديد *ẓahr al-ḥ.*, حديد الظهر cast iron; سكة الحديد *sikkat al-ḥ.* railroad; ضرب فى حديد بارد see ضرب

حديد *ḥadīd* pl. حداد *ḥidād*, احداء *aḥiddā'*², احدة *aḥidda* sharp (knife, eye, tongue, etc.), keen (mind)

احد *aḥadd*² sharper, keener; more vehement, more violent

حديدة *ḥadīda* pl. حدائد *ḥadā'id*² piece of iron; object or tool made of iron | حديدة الحرث *ḥ. al-ḥarṯ* plowshare; على الحديدة (*eg.*) in financial straits, pinched for money

حديدى *ḥadīdī* iron (adj.) | سكة حديدية (*sikka*) railroad

الحديدة *al-ḥudaida* Hodeida (seaport in W Yemen)

حداد *ḥaddād* ironsmith, blacksmith

حدادة *ḥidāda* smithcraft, art of smithing

تحديد *taḥdīd* pl. -*āt* limitation, delimitation; delineation, demarcation; restriction, curb, confinement; determination, fixation, appointment; definition | على التحديد and على وجه التحديد (*wajhi t-t.*) to be exact . . ., strictly speaking . . .

حاد *ḥādd* sharp (also, fig., of a glance), keen (mind); high-pitched (tone); vehement, fiery, impetuous; fierce; vivid; acute (illness) | حاد المزاج *ḥ. al-mizāj*, حاد الطبع *ḥ. aṭ-ṭab'* hot-blooded, hot-headed, hot-tempered, irascible; زاوية حادة (*zāwiya*) acute angle; تحت الحاد subacute

محدود *maḥdūd* bounded, bordered (ب by); circumscribed, confined; limited (= small, e.g., number, knowledge, etc.); delimited, determinate, fixed, definite, definitive | محدود المعنى *m. al-ma'nā* unambiguous; محدود الضمان *m. aḍ-ḍamān* of limited liability; شركة محدودة (المسئولية) (*širka*) limited company, corporation

محدد *muḥaddad* sharpened, sharp; determined, fixed, appointed, destined (ل for); strictly delimited, clearly defined

محتد *muḥtadd* angry, furious, exasperated

حدأة *ḥid'a*, pl. حدأ *ḥida'*, حداء *ḥidā'*, حدآن *ḥid'ān* kite (*zool.*)

حدأة *ḥada'a* pl. حداء *ḥidā'* double-bladed axe

حدب *ḥadiba a* (*ḥadab*) to be convex, dome-shaped, cambered, bent outward; to be hunchbacked; to be nice, kind, friendly (على or ب to s.o.), be solicitous (على or ب about s.o.), care (على or ب for s.o.), take care (على or ب of s.o.) **II** to make convex, emboss, camber, vault, curve, crook, bend (ه s.th.) **V** and **XII** احدودب *iḥdaudaba* to be crooked, vaulted, cambered, embossed, convex

حدب *ḥadab* affection, fondness, love; kindliness; solicitude, care; (pl. حداب *ḥidāb*, احداب *aḥdāb*) elevation of the ground | من كل حدب وصوب (*wa-ṣaubin*) or من كل صوب وحدب from all sides, from all directions, from everywhere; فى كل صوب وحدب everywhere, in every quarter, on all sides

حدب *ḥadib* curved, cambered, vaulted, convex; hunchbacked; kindly, friendly

حدبة *ḥadaba* hunchback, hump; camber, vaulting, curvature

احدب *aḥdab*², f. حدباء *ḥadbā'*², pl. حدب *ḥudb* hunchbacked, humped; — (elative) kindlier, friendlier

محدب *muḥaddab* embossed; cambered, convex

حدث *ḥadaṯa u* (حدوث *ḥudūṯ*) to happen, occur, take place, come to pass; — *ḥaduṯa u* (حداثة *ḥadāṯa*) to be new, recent; to be young **II** to tell, relate, report (ه to s.o., ب or ه s.th., في, عن about); to speak, talk (ه to s.o., عن or في about, of) | حدثه قلبه *ḥaddaṯahū qalbuhū* and حدثته نفسه *ḥaddaṯathu nafsuhū* his heart, his innermost feeling told him (ب s.th.); حدث نفسه ب (*nafsahū*) to talk o.s. into (s.th.), try to believe s.th. or see s.th. (as factual); to resolve, make up one's mind to do s.th.; حدث نفسه ان he said to himself, told himself that ... **III** to speak, talk (عن or في ه to s.o. about s.th.); to discuss (عن or في ه with s.o. s.th.), converse (عن or في ه with s.o. about); to negotiate, confer (ه with s.o.); to address, accost (ه s.o.); to call up (ه s.o., by telephone) **IV** to bring forth, produce, create, originate (ه s.th.); to found, establish (ه s.th.); to bring about, cause, occasion, provoke, effect (ه s.th.); to drop excrement | احدث حدثا (*ḥadaṯan*) to bring about s.th.; to cause or do s.th., esp., s.th. evil, do mischief **V** to speak, talk (الى to s.o., ب ,عن or في about or of s.th.), converse, chat (الى or مع with s.o., ب ,عن or في about s.th.) **VI** to talk with one another, converse, have a conversation **X** to renew (ه s.th.); to buy new (ه s.th.); to introduce, start, invent, originate, create (ه s.th.); to find or deem (ه s.o.) to be young

حدث *ḥadaṯ* pl. احداث *aḥdāṯ* a new, unprecedented thing, a novelty, innovation; event, incident, occurrence, happening; phenomenon; evil symptom; misdeed; misfortune; ritual impurity (*Isl. Law*); excrement, feces; (pl. احداث ,حدثان *ḥudṯān*) young man, youth; احداث juveniles

حديث *ḥadīṯ* pl. حداث *ḥidāṯ*, حدثاء *ḥudaṯā'*[2] new, novel, recent, late; modern; حديثا *ḥadīṯan* recently, lately | حديث البناء *ḥ. al-binā'* new-built, recently built; حديث السن *ḥ. as-sinn* young; حديث العهد *ḥ. al-'ahd* of recent date, recent, new, young; حديث عهد ب ,حديث العهد ب (*ḥ. 'ahdin*) having adopted or acquired (s.th.) recently; not long accustomed to (s.th.), inexperienced at (s.th.), new at (s.th.), newly, e.g., حديث العهد بالولادة (*bi-l-wilāda*) newborn, حديث العهد بالزواج (*bi-z-zawāj*) newly wed; كان حديث العهد بأوربا he had not known Europe until recently

حديث *ḥadīṯ* pl. احاديث *aḥādīṯ*[2], حدثان *ḥidṯān* speech; chat, chitchat, small talk; conversation, talk, discussion; interview; prattle, gossip; report, account, tale, narrative; Prophetic tradition, Hadith, narrative relating deeds and utterances of the Prophet and his Companions | حديث خرافة *ḥ. ḫurāfa* fabulous story, silly talk; حديث قدسى (*qudsī*) Muslim tradition in which God Himself speaks, as opposed to حديث نبوى (*nabawī*) an ordinary Prophetic tradition; حديث النفس *ḥ. an-nafs* s.th. one talks o.s. into; premonition

حدوث *ḥudūṯ* setting in (of a state or condition), occurrence, incidence (of a phenomenon); occurrence, incident, happening

حداثة *ḥadāṯa* newness, recency, novelty; youth, youthfulness

احدث *aḥdaṯ*[2] newer, more recent

حدثان الدهر *ḥidṯān* (or *ḥadaṯān*) *ad-dahr* misfortune, adversities, reverses

احدوثة *uḥdūṯa* pl. احاديث *aḥādīṯ*[2] speech; discussion, talk, conversation; chatter; fabling, fibbing; topic, subject of a conversation; gossip, rumor (about a person) | حسن الاحدوثة *ḥusn al-u.* praise (of s.o.); سوء الاحدوثة *sū' al-u.* slander, defamation

محادثة *muḥādaṯa* pl. *-āt* discourse, conversation, discussion, talk, parley

احداث *iḥdāṯ* production, creation, invention, origination; causation, effectuation

احداثيات *iḥdāṯīyāt* (pl.) co-ordinates (*math.*) | احداثيات عمودية (*'amūdīya*) ordinates; احداثيات افقية (*ufqīya*) abscissas (*math.*)

استحداث *istiḥdāṯ* invention, creation, production, origination

حادث *ḥādiṯ* occurring, happening, taking place; new, recent; fresh; — (pl. حوادث *ḥawādiṯ*[2], also *-āt*) occurrence, incident, event, happening; episode; case (*jur.*); accident, mishap | حادث تزوير a case of forgery; مكان الحادث *makān al-ḥ.* site of action, scene of the crime, locus delicti

حادثة *ḥādiṯa* pl. حوادث *ḥawādiṯ*[2] occurrence, event, happening; plot (of a play); incident, episode; accident, mishap | حادثة المرور *ḥ. al-murūr* traffic accident

محدث *muḥaddiṯ* pl. *-ūn* speaker, talker; spokesman; conversation partner, interlocutor; relator, narrator; a transmitter of Prophetic traditions, traditionary, representative of the science or study of Hadith (see above); ○ phonograph, gramophone

محدث *muḥdaṯ* new, novel, recent, late; modern; upstart, nouveau riche; المحدثون the Moderns

متحدث *mutaḥaddiṯ* spokesman, speaker

مستحدث *mustaḥdaṯ* new, novel; — (pl. *-āt*) novelty, innovation; recent invention, modern product; neologism

حدج *ḥadaja* *i* and II to stare, look sharply (ه, ه at s.o., at s.th., often with ببصره *bi-baṣarihī* or بنظره *bi-naẓarihī*)

حدج *ḥidj* pl. حدوج *ḥudūj*, احداج *aḥdāj* load, burden, encumbrance

ابو حديج *abū ḥudaij* stork

حداجة *ḥidāja* pl. حدائج *ḥadā'ij*[2] camel saddle

حدر *ḥadara*, *ḥadura* *u* (*ḥadr*, حدارة *ḥadāra*) to be thick; — *ḥadara* *u* *i* (*ḥadr*, حدور *ḥudūr*) to bring down, lower (ه s.th.); to cause (ه s.th.) to descend; to drop (ه s.th.); to shed (ه tears); حدر حدرا (*ḥadran*) to rattle off, express quickly (an utterance, a thought); — (*ḥadr*) to come down, step down, descend; to glide down, swoop II to drop (ه s.th.); to lower, incline, dip (ه s.th.) V to descend gradually; to glide down; to come down, descend; to flow down (tears); to derive, stem, originate (من from) VII to come or go down, descend; to glide down, sink down; to be in decline, be on the downgrade, to decline, wane; to flow down (tears); to slope down, slant down, be inclined (terrain); to come (الى to a place), arrive (الى at)

حدر *ḥadr* rapid recitation of the Koran (a terminus technicus of *tajwīd*)

حدور *ḥadūr* slope, downgrade, declivity, declivitous terrain

تحدر *taḥaddur* descent, slant, slope, inclination, incline, declivity

انحدار *inḥidār* slant, dip, pitch, inclination, descent, slope; declivity; fall (of a river); decline, waning; ruin, decay, decadence

حادر *ḥādir* thick

متحدر *mutaḥaddir* descending, slanting, sloping downward

منحدر *munḥadir* descending; lowered, dipped; slanting, sloping, declivitous (terrain); declining, waning, being on the downgrade, in a state of decadence or decline; run-down, seedy, down-at-the-heels, down-and-out

منحدر *munḥadar* pl. *-āt* depression; slope, talus, incline, descent, declivity; fall (of a river)

حدس *ḥadasa* *i* *u* (*ḥads*) to surmise, guess, conjecture (ه s.th.)

حدس *ḥads* surmise, guess, conjecture; ○ intuition

☐ حداف *ḥaddāf* (حذاف >), حداف الماكوك (*syr.*) shuttle (weaving)

☐ طارة حدافة *ṭāra ḥaddāfa* (*syr.*) flywheel

[1]حدق *ḥadaqa i* (*ḥadq*) to surround, encircle, encompass (ب s.o., s.th.); (with بعينه *bi-'ainihī*) to look, glance (ه at s.o.) II to look, glance, gaze, stare (الى or فى at, also ب) | حدق النظر فى (*naẓara*) to fix one's glance on ... IV to surround, encircle, encompass, enclose (ب s.o., s.th.); to look, glance (فى, الى or ب at) | احدق النظر فى (*naẓara*) to fix one's glance on ...

حدقة *ḥadaqa* pl. *-āt*, حدق *ḥadaq*, حداق *ḥidāq*, احداق *aḥdāq* pupil (of the eye); pl. احداق glances

حديقة *ḥadīqa* pl. حدائق *ḥadā'iq*[2] garden | حديقة الحيوانات *ḥ. al-ḥayawānāt* zoological garden, zoo

احداق *iḥdāq* encirclement, encompassment (ب of)

خطر محدق *kaṭar muḥdiq* imminent danger

[2]☐ حدق II (= حذق) to make acid, sour, tart, or sharp (ه s.th.)

☐ حادق *ḥādiq* (= حاذق) sour, tart, acid, sharp (taste)

حدل *ḥadala i* to flatten, level, even, roll (ه s.th.); (*ḥadl*, حدول *ḥudūl*) to treat unjustly (على s.o.)

محدلة *miḥdala* pl. محادل *maḥādil*[2] roller, steamroller

حدم VIII to burn, glow, blaze; to burn up, be consumed by fire; to flare up, break out (fight); to be furious, burn with wrath (على at, over), also احتدم غيظا (*ġaiẓan*)

احتدام *iḥtidām* paroxysm

محتدم *muḥtadim* furious, infuriated, enraged

حدة *ḥida* see وحد

[1]☐ حدوة *ḥidwa* horseshoe

[2]حدا (حدو and حدى) *ḥadā u* (*ḥadw*, حداء *ḥudā'*, *ḥidā'*) to urge forward by singing (ه camels); to urge, spur on, egg on, prompt, instigate, induce, move (ب or ه s.o., الى to s.th., to do s.th.); حدا ب to instigate s.th.; to sway, rock, roll (rider, camel); to swing along, rock along (in riding) | حدا بهم الحديث الى their conversation led them to ...; غرض تحدى اليه الركائب (*ġaraḍun tuḥdā*) a goal much sought after or worth striving for V to compete, vie (ه with s.o.); to challenge, provoke (ه, ه s.o., s.th.); to defy, oppose, resist, withstand (ه, ه s.o., s.th.), stand up (ه, ه against s.o., against s.th.); to incite, stimulate, arouse, animate, sharpen (ه s.th.; ذكاءه *ḏakā'ahū* s.o.'s intellect); to intend (ه s.th., to do s.th.), be bent (ه on doing s.th.)

حداء *ḥudā'* animating singsong, chanting of the caravan leader

حداء *ḥaddā'* camel driver, cameleer

احدوة *uḥdūwa*, احدية *uḥdīya* song of the camel drivers

تحد *taḥaddin* pl. تحديات *taḥaddiyāt* challenge, provocation

حاد *ḥādin* pl. حداة *ḥudāh* caravan leader (who urges the camels forward by singing); camel driver, cameleer; leader

متحد *mutaḥaddin* challenger, provoker

[1]حدى *ḥadiya a* to remain, stay (ب at a place), stick (ب to a place)

[2]حادى عشر see احد

[3]☐ حداية *ḥidāya*, *ḥiddāya* = حدأة *ḥid'a*

حذر *ḥaḏira a* (*ḥiḏr*, *ḥaḏar*) to be cautious, wary, to beware (من or ه, ه of s.o., of s.th.), be on one's guard (من or ه, ه against) II to warn, caution (ه من s.o. of or about), put (ه s.o.) on his guard (من against) III to watch out, be careful; to be on one's guard (ه against), be wary (ه of s.o.) V to beware, be wary (من of) VIII = I

حذر *ḥiḏr* and *ḥaḏar* caution, watchfulness, alertness, wariness, circumspection; precaution | اخذ حذره (*ḥaḏarahū*) to be on one's guard; على حذر *ʿalā ḥaḏarin* cautiously, warily; on one's guard (من against)

حذر *ḥaḏir* cautious, wary

حذار *ḥaḏāri* beware (ان of doing . . ., من of s.th.)! watch out (من for)! be careful (من of)!

تحذير *taḥḏīr* warning, cautioning (من of, against)

محاذرة *muḥāḏara* caution, precaution, precautionary measure

محذور *maḥḏūr* that of which one should beware, against which one should guard; object of caution; — (pl. *-āt*) danger, peril; trouble, difficulty, misfortune

حذف **ḥaḏafa** *i* (*ḥaḏf*) to shorten, clip, curtail (ه or من s.th.); to take s.th. away, cut s.th. off, clip s.th. off (من from s.th.), reduce (من s.th.), strike or cross s.th. (من off s.th.); to cancel, strike out, delete, drop, leave out, omit, suppress (ه s.th.); (*gram.*) to elide, apocopate, drop by aphaeresis; to deduct, subtract (ه s.th.); to throw (ه ب at s.o. s.th.), pelt (ه ب s.o. with s.th.); to cast away, throw away, discard (ب s.th.) II to clip, trim (ه s.th.); to give (ه s.th.) shape, to trim, clip, or cut (ه s.th.) into proper shape

حذف *ḥaḏf* shortening, curtailing, cutting off, trimming, etc.; canceling, cancellation, striking off, crossing off, deletion; omission, dropping, suppression; (*gram.*) elision, ellipsis, apocopation

حذافير **ḥaḏāfīr²**: اخذه بحذافيره he took all of it, he took it lock, stock and barrel

حذق **ḥaḏiqa** *a*, **ḥaḏaqa** *i* (*ḥiḏq*, حذاقة *ḥaḏāqa*) to be skilled, skillful, well-versed, proficient (ه or فى in s.th.), master (ه s.th.); — *ḥaḏaqa u* (حذوق *ḥuḏūq*) to turn sour (milk) V to feign skillfulness, proficiency, cleverness or smartness

حذق *ḥiḏq* and حذاقة *ḥaḏāqa* skill, dexterity, proficiency; smartness, cleverness, intelligence; perspicacity, sagacity, acumen

حاذق *ḥāḏiq* pl. حذاق *ḥuḏḏāq* skillful, skilled, proficient; well-versed, clever, smart, intelligent; sour

حذلق II *taḥaḏlaqa* to pretend to be clever or skillfull, feign skill or knowledge; to be pedantic

حذلقة *ḥaḏlaqa* skillfulness, dexterity

حذا (حذو) **ḥaḏā** *u*: حذا حذوه (*ḥaḏwahū*) to imitate s.o., take after s.o., follow s.o.'s example III to be opposite s.th. (ه), face, parallel (ه s.th.), run parallel (ه to) VI to be opposite each other, be parallel VIII to imitate, copy (ب or على s.o., s.th., also ه s.th.), take or follow (ب or على s.o., s.th., also ه s.th.) as an example or model; to be shod; to wear (ه s.th.) as footgear

حذو *ḥaḏwa* (prep.) opposite, face to face with | حذوك النعل بالنعل *ḥaḏwaka n-naʿla bi-n-naʿl* in a completely identical manner, to a T, like two peas in a pod

حذاء *ḥiḏāʾ* pl. احذية *aḥḏiya* shoe; sandal | صانع الاحذية shoemaker

حذاء *ḥiḏāʾa* (prep.) and بحذاء *bi-ḥiḏāʾi* opposite, face to face with

حذاء *ḥaḏḏāʾ* shoemaker, cobbler

على (فى) محاذاة *ʿalā* (*fī*) *muḥāḏāti* along, alongside of, parallel to

احتذاء *iḥtiḏāʾ* imitation, copying

محاذ *muḥāḏin* opposite, facing

حر **ḥarra** *u* *i* (*ḥarr*, حرارة *ḥarāra*) to be hot II to liberate (ه s.o.); to free, set free, release (ه s.o.); to emancipate (ه s.o.); to consecrate (ه s.o.) to the service of God; to clarify, clear up, make clear (ه s.th.); to formulate precisely, phrase accurately, define exactly, pinpoint (ه s.th.); to revise (ه a book); to edit, redact (ه a book, a periodical); to write, pen, indite, compose, compile (ه s.th.) **V** to become free; to be freed, be liberated (من from); to be emancipated **VIII** to be kindled, be heated, flare up

حر *ḥarr* heat, warmth

حر *ḥurr* pl. m. احرار *aḥrār*, pl. f. حرائر *ḥarā'ir*[2] noble, free-born; genuine (jewels, etc.), pure, unadulterated; free; living in freedom; freeman; independent; free, unrestrained; liberal (*pol.*; الاحرار the Liberals); frank, candid, open (على toward s.o.); free, available, uninvested (money) | الاحتياطى الحر (*iḥtiyāṭī*) free reserves, unencumbered reserves; من حر ماله *min ḥurri mālihī* with his own cash, with funds at his disposal

حرة *ḥarra* pl. *-āt* stony area; volcanic country, lava field

حرية *ḥurrīya* pl. *-āt* freedom, liberty; independence, unrestraint, license (e.g., poetic) | حرية العبادة *ḥ. al-'ibāda* freedom of worship; حرية الفكر *ḥ. al-fikr* freedom of thought; حرية الكلام *ḥ.al-kalām* freedom of speech; حرية النشر (or الصحافة) *ḥ. an-našr* (*aṣ-ṣiḥāfa*) liberty of the press

حرير *ḥarīr* silk; pl. حرائر *ḥarā'ir*[2] (حراير) silken wares, silks | حرير صخرى (*ṣakrī*) asbestos; حرير صناعى rayon

حريرى *ḥarīrī* silken, silky, of silk

حرائرى *ḥarā'irī* silken, silk- (in compounds), of silk; silk weaver

حرار *ḥarrār* silk weaver

حرارة *ḥarāra* heat; warmth; fever heat, fever; temperature; ardor, fervor (of emotion), passion; eagerness, enthusiasm, zeal; vehemence, violence, intensity; burning (of the skin)

حريرة *ḥuraira* pl. *-āt* calorie

حرارى *ḥarārī* thermal, thermic, thermo-, heat (used attributively); caloric | وحدة حرارية (*waḥda*) calorie

○ حرارية *ḥarārīya* pl. *-āt* calorie

حرور *ḥarūr* f., pl. حرائر *ḥarā'ir*[2] hot wind

حران *ḥarrān*[2], f. حرى *ḥarrā*, pl. حرار *ḥirār*, حرارى *ḥarārā* thirsty; passionate, fervent, hot (fig.) | زفرة حرى (*zafra*) a fervent sigh; دموع حرى hot tears

احر *aḥarr*[2] hotter, warmer | على احر من الجمر (*jamr*) on pins and needles, on tenterhooks, in greatest suspense or excitement

○ محر *miḥarr* heating system, heating installation

تحرير *taḥrīr* liberation; release; emancipation; record(ing), writing; editing, redaction; editorship (of a newspaper, a periodical); (pl. *-āt*, تحارير *taḥārīr*[2]) piece of writing, record, brief, document | رئيس التحرير editor-in-chief; ادارة التحرير board of editors, editorial staff

تحريرى *taḥrīrī* liberational; emancipational; liberal; recorded in writing, written, in writing

حار *ḥārr* hot; warm; ardent, glowing, fervent, passionate

محرور *maḥrūr* hot-tempered, hot-headed, fiery, passionate, furious

محرر *muḥarrir* pl. *-ūn* liberator, emancipator; writer, clerk; editor (of a newspaper, of a periodical)

محرر *muḥarrar* consecrated to God; set down in writing, recorded in writing, written; booked; pl. محررات bookings, entries

متحرر *mutaḥarrir* emancipated; an advocate of emancipation

حرب *ḥariba a* (*ḥarab*) to be furious, enraged, angry III to fight, combat (ه s.o.), battle, wage war (ه against s.o.) VI to fight (one another), be engaged in war VIII = VI

حرب *ḥarb* f., pl. حروب *ḥurūb* war, warfare; fight, combat, battle; enemy, enemies (على or ل of s.o.) | حرب اهلية (*ahlīya*) civil war; حرب صحافية (*ṣiḥāfīya*) press feud; الحروب الصليبية (*ṣalībīya*) the Crusades; الحرب العظمى (*'uẓmā*), الحرب العالمية (*'ālamīya*), الحرب العامة (*'āmma*) World War I; كشفت الحرب عن ساقها *kašafat il-ḥarbu 'an sāqihā* and قامت الحرب على ساق *qāmat il-ḥ. 'alā sāqin* war flared up, fierce fighting broke out

حربى *ḥarbī* warlike, bellicose, belligerent, martial, war (adj.), military; (pl. *-ūn*) warrior, soldier, military man | البوليس الحربى (*būlīs*) military police

حربة *ḥarba* pl. حراب *ḥirāb* lance, spear; spearhead; bayonet, sidearm

حرباء *ḥirbā'* pl. حرابى *ḥarābīy* chameleon (*zool.*)

وا حرباه *wā ḥarabāh!* (exclamation of lament) alas! goodness no! oh my!

محراب *miḥrāb* pl. محاريب *maḥārīb*[2] a recess in a mosque indicating the direction of prayer, prayer niche, mihrab

محاربة *muḥāraba* struggle, combat, fight, battle; warfare

احتراب *iḥtirāb* mutual struggle

محارب *muḥārib* warring, belligerent; warrior, combatant, fighter; corporal (*Eg.* 1939)

المتحاربون *al-mutaḥāribūn* the belligerents, the warring parties

حربوشة *ḥarbūša* pl. حرابش *ḥarābiš*[2] (*tun.*) pastille, pill

حرث *ḥarata i u* (*ḥart*) to plow (ه the soil); to cultivate, till (ه the ground)

حرث *ḥart* plowing, tilling, tillage, cultivation of the soil; arable land, tilth; plantation, culture

حرثة *ḥarta* (n. un.) arable land, tilth

حراثة *ḥirāta* cultivation of the soil, farming, agriculture

حراث *ḥarrāt* plowman

محراث *miḥrāt* pl. محاريث *maḥārīt*[2] plow

حارث *ḥārit* pl. حراث *ḥurrāt* plowman | ابو الحارث *abū l-ḥ.* lion

حرج *ḥarija a* (*ḥaraj*) to be close, tight, narrow; to be straitened, be confined, get into a strait, be cornered, be hard pressed; to be oppressed, be anguished (heart); to be forbidden (على to s.o.) II to narrow, tighten, straiten (ه s.th.); to complicate (ه s.th.), make (ه s.th.) difficult; to forbid (ه على s.th. to s.o.); to persist (فى in s.th.) IV to narrow, straiten, confine, cramp, hamper, impede, restrict (ه s.th.); to complicate, make difficult, aggravate, jeopardize (ه a situation, s.o.'s position); to embarrass (ه s.o.); to coerce, constrain, press (ه الى s.o. to); to forbid (ه على s.th. to s.o.) V to refrain from sin or evildoing; to abstain, refrain (من from), avoid (من s.th.); to be cornered, be forced to the wall; to become or be oppressed, anguished, distressed; to become critical, become complicated or difficult, be aggravated (situation), be jeopardized (s.o.'s position) | تحرج صدره من (ب) (*ṣadruhū*) to feel depressed by, feel annoyed at; تحرج به الناس this made things difficult for people

حرج *ḥaraj* closeness, tightness, narrowness; confinement, straitness, constriction, crampedness; restriction, impediment; oppression, distress, anguish; difficulty; critical situation; prohibition, interdiction; s.th. forbidden, s.th. interdicted, sin | لا حرج (*ḥaraja*) there is no objection; لا حرج عليك nothing stands in your way, you are at liberty

حرج *ḥaraj* (coll.; n. un. ة) pl. *-āt*, حراج *ḥirāj*, احراج *aḥrāj* thicket; dense forest; woodland, timberland

حرج *ḥarij* narrow, close, tight, confined, straitened; oppressed, hard pressed, harassed; critical (situation, position)

احرج *aḥraj*[2] narrower, closer, tighter, more straitened; more critical

حراج *ḥarāg* (*eg.*) auction

حراجة *ḥarāja* seriousness, gravity, difficulty, complicatedness (of a situation)

تحريج *taḥrīj* forestation, afforestation

تحرج *taḥarruj* restraint, reserve, aloofness; timidity, diffidence, faint-heartedness; critical complication, gravity, difficulty (of a situation)

محرجات *muḥarrijāt*: محرجات الايمان *m. al-aimān* binding, committing, or solemn, oaths

محرج *muḥrij* disconcerting, embarrassing

متحرج *mutaḥarrij*: متحرج الصدر *m. aṣ-ṣadr* annoyed, vexed, anguished, oppressed

حرد *ḥarida a* (*ḥarad*) to be annoyed, disgruntled, angry, furious (على at, with)

حارد *ḥārid*, حرد *ḥarid* and حردان *ḥardān* annoyed, disgruntled, angry, furious

حردون *ḥirdaun* pl. حراذين *ḥarādīn*[2] lizard

حرز *ḥaraza u* (*ḥarz*) to keep, guard, protect, preserve (ه s.th.), take care (ه of); — *ḥaruza u* (حرازة *ḥarāza*) to be strong be strongly fortified, be impregnable IV to keep, preserve, guard (ه s.th.); to obtain, attain, achieve, win (ه s.th.) | احرز نصرا (انتصارا) (*naṣran*) to win a victory; احرز قصب السبق (*qaṣaba s-sabq*) to come through with flying colors, carry the day, score a great success V to be wary (من of), be on one's guard (من against) VIII to be wary (من of), guard, be on one's guard (من against), be careful, take heed, take precautions

حرز *ḥirz* pl. احراز *aḥrāz* fortified place; refuge, sanctuary, retreat; custody; (pl. احراز, حروز *ḥurūz*) amulet

حريز *ḥarīz* strongly fortified, guarded; inaccessible, impregnable

احراز *iḥrāz* acquisition, acquirement, obtainment, attainment, achievement, winning, gaining

احتراز *iḥtirāz* pl. *-āt* caution, wariness, prudence, circumspection; reservation, reserve | بكامل الاحتراز with all reservation

○ حارزة *ḥāriza* fuse (*el.*)

محرز *muḥriz* obtainer, acquirer, winner, gainer; possessor, holder (على of s.th.)

حرس *ḥarasa u* (*ḥars*, حراسة *ḥirāsa*) to guard, watch, control (ه, ه s.th., s.o.); to oversee, supervise, superintend (ه, ه s.th., s.o.); to secure, protect, safeguard, preserve, keep (ه, ه s.th., s.o.); to watch (على over) V and VIII to beware, be wary (من of), guard, be on one's guard (من against)

حرس *ḥaras* watch; guard, escort; bodyguard | الحرس السيار (*sayyār*) militia, "garde mobile" (*Syr.*) | حرس الشرف *ḥ. aš-šaraf* honor guard; الحرس الملكى (*malakī*) the royal guard (formerly *Ir.*, *Eg.*); الحرس الملوكى (*mulūkī*) (formerly) bodyguard of the Bey (*Tun.*); الحرس الوطنى (*waṭanī*) the National Guard

حراسة *ḥirāsa* guarding, watching, control; watch, guard, guard duty; supervision, superintendence; guardianship, tutelage, custody, care, protection; safe conduct, escort; administration; administration of an estate (*jur.*); sequester | حراسة السواحل coast guard

احتراس *iḥtirās* caution, wariness, prudence; (pl. *-āt*) precaution, precautionary measure | احتراسا من for protection from or against

حارس *ḥāris* pl. حرسة *ḥarasa*, حراس *ḥurrās* vigilant, watchful; watchman; sentry, sentinel, guard; overseer, supervisor, superintendent; administrator; guardian, custodian, keeper, protector, tutelary (in compounds) | حارس التركة *ḥ. at-tirka* administrator of an estate; حارس الخواتم keeper of the seal; حارس المرمى *ḥ. al-marmā* goal keeper; حارس قضائى (*qaḍā'ī*) sequestrator, receiver (in bankruptcy, in equity); ملاك حارس (*mal'ak*) guardian angel (*Chr.*); حارس الليل *ḥ. al-lail* night watchman

محروس *maḥrūs* guarded, safeguarded, secured; protected (by God; esp. used as an epithet after the names of cities); المحروسون the children, the family

محترس *muḥtaris* cautious, wary, careful

حرش **ḥaraša** *i* (*ḥarš*) to scratch (ه, ه s.o., s.th.) **II** to instigate, prod, incite, provoke, incense (ه s.o.); to set (بين people against each other), sow discord, dissension (بين among) **V** to pick a quarrel, start a brawl (ب with s.o.), provoke (ب s.o.)

حرش *ḥirš*, *ḥurš* pl. احراش *aḥrāš*, حروش *ḥurūš* forest, wood(s)

حرش *ḥariš* and احرش *aḥraš*[2] rough, coarse, scabrous

حرش *ḥaraš*, حرشة *ḥurša*, حراشة *ḥarāša* roughness, coarseness, scabrousness

تحريش *taḥrīš* instigation, prodding, incitement, provocation, agitation, incensement

تحرش *taḥarruš* provocation, importunity, obtrusion, meddling, uncalled-for interference

حرشف *ḥaršaf* pl. حراشف *ḥarāšif*[2] scales (of fish)

حرص **ḥaraṣa** *i* and **ḥariṣa** *a* (*ḥirṣ*) to desire, want, covet (على s.th.); to be intent, be bent (على on); to strive (على for), aspire (على to)

حرص *ḥirṣ* greed, avidity, cupidity, covetousness; desire; aspiration, endeavor, wish (على for); avarice | حرصا على in the desire for . . ., in the endeavor to . . .; حرصا على الارواح danger! (on warning signs)

حريص *ḥarīṣ* pl. حراص *ḥirāṣ*, حرصاء *ḥuraṣā'*[2] covetous, greedy, avid, eager (على for); bent (على on), desirous (على of)

احرص *aḥraṣ*[2] more covetous, greedier

حرض **II** to goad, prod, spur on, egg on, incite, rouse, provoke (على ه s.o. to s.th. or to do s.th.); to instigate, abet, stir up, agitate (على ه s.o. to or against); ○ to induce (*el.*)

تحريض *taḥrīḍ* incitement, provocation; instigation, abetment, agitation (على to); inflammatory propaganda (على against s.o.); ○ induction (*el.*) | ○ تحريض ذاتى self-induction (*el.*)

تحريضى *taḥrīḍī* inciting, instigative, agitative, inflammatory; provocative

حارض *ḥāriḍ* bad, wicked, evil

محرض *muḥarriḍ* pl. *-ūn* inciter, baiter; instigator, abettor; demagogue, rabble rouser; agitator, provocator; ○ inductor (*el.*)

متحرض *mutaḥarriḍ* ○ induced (*el.*)

حرف **II** to slant, incline, make oblique (ه s.th.); to bend off, up, down or back, turn up, down or back, deflect (ه s.th.); to distort, corrupt, twist, pervert, misconstrue, falsify (ه s.th.) | حرفه عن موضعه (*'an mauḍi'ihī*) to distort the sense of s.th., rob s.th. of its true meaning **V** to turn off, branch off, take a turning; to deviate, depart, digress (عن from); to avoid (عن s.th.); to be or become bent off, distorted, corrupted, perverted **VII** to turn off, branch off, take a turning; to deviate, depart, digress, turn away (عن from); to slope down, slant, be inclined (terrain); to turn (الى to, toward); to be twisted, be distorted; to be oblique, slanting; to be cocked, rakish (headgear); with ب: to make s.th. appear oblique, slanted, or distorted; to be corrupted, perverted | انحرف به عن to dissuade s.o. from; انحرف مزاجه (*mizājuhū*) to be indisposed, be ill **VIII** to do (ه s.th.) professionally, practice (ه s.th.) as a profession; to strive for success

حرف *ḥarf* pl. حرف *ḥiraf* (cutting) edge (of a knife, of a sword); sharp edge; border, edge, rim, brink, verge; — (pl. حروف *ḥurūf*, احرف *aḥruf*) letter; consonant; particle (*gram.*); type (*typ.*) | على حرف irresolute, wavering, on the fence; الفاظه بحروفها *alfāẓuhū bi-ḥurūfihā* his words literally; بالحرف or بالحرف الواحد literally, verbatim, to the letter; حرفا بحرف *ḥarfan bi-ḥarfin* literally, word for word; وقع بالاحرف الاولى (*waqqa'a, ūlā*) to initial (e.g., معاهدة *mu'āhadatan* a treaty); الحروف الابجدية (*abjadīya*) the alphabetic letters, the alphabet; حروف مجموعة matter (*typ.*); الحروف الشمسية (*šamsīya*) the sun letters (i.e., sibilants, dentals, *r*, *l*, *n* to which the *l* of the article assimilates), الحروف القمرية (*qamarīya*) the moon letters (to which the *l* of the article does not assimilate); حرف الجر *ḥ. al-jarr* preposition (*gram.*); حرف الخفض *ḥ. al-ḵafḍ* do.; حرف التعريف article (*gram.*); حرف العطف *ḥ. al-'aṭf* coordinating conjunction (*gram.*); حرف الاستفهام interrogative particle (*gram.*); حرف القسم *ḥ. al-qasam* particle introducing oaths (*gram.*)

حرفى *ḥarfī* literal

حرف *ḥurf* common garden pepper cress (Lepidium sativum L.; *bot.*)

حرفة *ḥirfa* pl. حرف *ḥiraf* profession, occupation, vocation, business, craft, trade

حريف *ḥarīf* pl. حرفاء *ḥurafā'*[2] customer, patron, client (*tun.*)

حريف *ḥirrīf* pungent, acrid (taste); حريفات spicy food, delicacies

حرافة *ḥarāfa* pungency, acridity (taste)

تحريف *taḥrīf* pl. *-āt* alteration, change; distortion; perversion, corruption, esp. phonetic corruption of a word

انحراف *inḥirāf* pl. *-āt* deviation, digression; obliqueness, obliquity, inclination, slant; declination (*astron.*); ailment, indisposition, also انحراف المزاج

احتراف *iḥtirāf* professional pursuit (of a trade, etc.)

محرف *muḥarraf* corrupted (word)

منحرف *munḥarif* oblique; slanted, slanting, sloping, inclined; distorted, perverted, corrupted, twisted; deviating, divergent; trapezium (*geom.*)

محترف *muḥtarif* one gainfully employed (ب in), person doing s.th. (ب) professionally; professional, a pro (sports); professional (adj.), e.g., صحافى محترف (*ṣiḥāfī*) professional journalist; climber, careerist

○ محترف *muḥtaraf* pl. *-āt* studio, atelier

حرق **ḥaraqa** *i* (*ḥarq*) to burn (ه s.th.); to burn, hurt, sting, smart | حرق قلبه (*qalbahū*), pl. حرق قلوبهم (*qulūbahum*) to vex, exasperate s.o.; — *u* (*ḥarq*) to rub together (ه s.th.) **II** to burn (ه s.th.); حرق اسنانه (*asnānahū*) to gnash one's teeth **IV** to burn (ه s.th.); to destroy by fire (ه s.th.); to singe, scorch, parch (ه s.th.); to scald (ه s.th.); to kindle, ignite, set on fire (ه s.th.) | احرق فحمة ليله فى (*faḥmata lailihi*) to spend the night doing (s.th.), burn the midnight oil over ... **V** to burn, be aflame, burn up, take fire, be consumed by fire, be burned; to be consumed (by an emotion), pine away (ه with), be pained (ه by), eat one's heart out | تحرق شوقا (*šauqan*) to be overcome with longing or nostalgia **VIII** to burn, be aflame, burn up, take fire, be consumed by fire, be burned

حرق *ḥarq* burning, incineration, combustion; kindling, igniting, setting afire; arson, incendiarism; pl. حروق *ḥurūq* burns (*med.*)

حرق *ḥaraq* fire, conflagration

حرقة *ḥurqa, ḥarqa* burning, incineration, combustion; stinging, smarting, burning (as a physical sensation); torture, torment, agony, pain, ordeal

حراق *ḥurāq, ḥurrāq* tinder

حراق *ḥarrāq* burning, aflame, afire; hot

حريق *ḥarīq* and حريقة pl. حرائق *ḥarā'iq*[2] fire; conflagration

○ حراقة *ḥarrāqa* torpedo

حرقان *ḥaraqān* burning, stinging, smarting (as a painful sensation; e.g., of the feet)

○ محرق *maḥraq* pl. محارق *maḥāriq*[2] focus (*phys.*)

تحاريق *taḥārīq*[2] (*Eg.*) season of the Nile's lowest water level, hottest season of the year

احراق *iḥrāq* burning, incineration, combustion

تحرق *taḥarruq* burning, combustion; burning desire (الى for)

احتراق *iḥtirāq* burning, combustion; fire, conflagration | ○ غرفة الاحتراق *ġurfat al-i.* combustion chamber (*techn.*); قابل الاحتراق *qābil al-i.* combustible

حارق *ḥāriq* arsonist, incendiary

محروق *maḥrūq* burned, charred, scorched, parched; reddish, bronze-colored; pl. محروقات *maḥrūqāt* fuel | فخار محروق (*fakkār*) fired clay

محرق *muḥriq*: قنبلة محرقة (*qunbula*) incendiary bomb

○ محرق *muḥraq* crematory

محرقة *muḥraqa* burnt sacrifice

حرقدة *ḥarqada* pl. حراقد *ḥarāqid*[2] Adam's apple

حرقفة *ḥarqafa* pl. حراقف *ḥarāqif*[2] protruding part of the hipbone

حرك **II** to move, set in motion, drive, propel, operate (ه s.th.); to march, move (ه troops); to stir (ه s.th.); to start, get started, get underway (ه s.th.); to agitate, excite, stimulate (ه s.th.); to incite, instigate, goad, prod, provoke, actuate, urge (على ه s.o. to do s.th.); to awaken, arouse, foment, stir up (ه s.th.); to vowel, vowelize (*gram.*, ه a consonant) | حرك مشاعره (*mašā'irahū*) to grip, excite, thrill s.o.; حرك العواطف to affect the feelings, be touching, moving, pathetic; لا يحرك ساكنا (*sākinan*) he doesn't budge, he doesn't bend his little finger, he remains immobile, apathetic; حرك ساكنه (*sākinahū*) to rouse s.o., put s.o. in a state of excitement, commotion or agitation **V** to move, be in motion, stir, budge; to start moving, get moving; to start out, get underway (traveler); to depart, leave (train); to put out, to sail (fleet); to be set in motion, be driven, be operated; to be agitated, be excited, be stimulated; to be awakened, be roused, be fomented, be provoked, be caused

حرك *ḥarik* lively, active, brisk, agile, nimble

حركة *ḥaraka* pl. *-āt* movement, motion; commotion; physical exercise; stirring, impulse; proceeding, procedure, policy; action, undertaking, enterprise; military operation; continuation, progress; traffic (rail, shipping, street); movement (as a social phenomenon); vowel (*gram.*) | فى حركاته وسكناته (*sakanātihī*) in all his doings; in every situation; حركة المرور (through) traffic; حركة المراكب shipping traffic; حركة البضائع exchange of goods; حركة الاموال turnover (*com.*); الحركة النسوية (*niswīya*) feminist movement; خفيف الحركة nimble, lithe, light, quick, agile, adroit; ثقيل الحركة slow in motion, heavy-handed, clumsy, sluggish, lumbering, inert, indolent

O حركى *ḥarakī* kinetic (*phys.*)

حراك *ḥarāk* movement, motion

محرك *maḥrak* path, trajectory (of a projectile)

محراك *miḥrāk* poker, fire iron

تحريكى *taḥrīkī* dynamic

تحرّك *taḥarruk* pl. *-āt* movement, motion; forward motion; start; departure; sailing (of a fleet)

حارك *ḥārik* withers

محرك *muḥarrik* mover, stirrer; rouser, inciter, fomenter, awakener, agent; instigator; — (*-āt*) motive, springs, incentive, spur, motivating circumstance, causative factor; motor, engine (*techn.*)

متحرك *mutaḥarrik* moving, movable, mobile; pronounced with following vowel, voweled, vowelized (consonant; *gram.*) | صور متحركة (*ṣuwar*) movies, motion pictures

حركث *ḥarkaṯa* (and حركش *ḥarkaša*) to stir up, agitate, excite, thrill

حرم *ḥaruma u, ḥarima a* to be forbidden, prohibited, interdicted, unlawful, unpermitted (على to s.o.); — *ḥarama i* (*ḥirm, ḥirmān* حرمان) to deprive, bereave, dispossess, divest (ه ه or من ه s.o. of s.th.), take away, withdraw, withhold (ه ه or من ه or من ه from s.o. s.th.), deny, refuse (ه ه or من ه or من ه to s.o. s.th.); to exclude, debar, preclude, cut off (ه ه or من ه s.o. from s.th.); to excommunicate (ه s.o.; *Chr.*) II to declare (ه s.th.) sacred, sacrosanct, inviolable, or taboo, to taboo (ه s.th.); to declare (ه s.th.) unlawful, not permissible, forbid, interdict, proscribe (ه s.th., على to s.o.); to render (ه s.o.) immune or proof (من against), immunize (من ه s.o. against) | حرمه على نفسه to deny o.s. s.th., abstain, refrain from s.th. IV to excommunicate (ه s.o.; *Chr.*); to enter into the state of ritual consecration (esp., of a Mecca pilgrim; see احرام *iḥrām*) V to be forbidden, interdicted, prohibited; to be holy, sacred, sacrosanct, inviolable VIII to honor, revere, venerate, esteem, respect (ه, ه s.o., s.th.) | احترم نفسه to be self-respecting X to deem (ه s.th.) sacrosanct, sacred, holy, inviolable; to deem (ه s.th.) unlawful or unpermissible

حرم *ḥirm* excommunication (*Chr.*)

حرم *ḥaram* pl. احرام *aḥrām* forbidden, prohibited, interdicted; taboo; holy, sacred, sacrosanct; s.th. sacred, sacred object; sacred possession; wife; sanctum, sanctuary, sacred precinct; الحرمان the two Holy Places, Mecca and Medina | ثالث الحرمين *ṯāliṯ al-ḥaramain* the third Holy Place, i.e., Jerusalem

حرمة *ḥurma* pl. *-āt, ḥurumāt, ḥuramāt* holiness, sacredness, sanctity, sacrosanctity, inviolability; reverence, veneration, esteem, deference, respect; that which is holy, sacred, sacrosanct, inviolable, or taboo; — (pl. حرم *ḥuram*) woman, lady; wife

حرام *ḥarām* pl. حرم *ḥurum* forbidden, interdicted, prohibited, unlawful; s.th. forbidden, offense, sin; inviolable, taboo; sacred, sacrosanct; cursed, accursed | ابن حرام *ibn ḥ.* illegitimate son, bastard;

الاراضى الحرام no man's land; neutral territory; البيت الحرام (*bait*) the Kaaba; الشهر الحرام (*šahr*) the Holy Month Muharram; المسجد الحرام (*masjid*) the Holy Mosque in Mecca; حرام عليك you mustn't do (say) that! بالحرام illicitly, illegally, unlawfully

حرام **ḥirām** pl. *-āt,* احرمة *aḥrima* a woolen blanket (worn as a garment around head and body)

حريم **ḥarīm** pl. حرم *ḥurum* a sacred, inviolable place, sanctum, sanctuary, sacred precinct; harem; female members of the family, women; wife

حريمى **ḥarīmī** women's (in compounds), for women

حروم **ḥurūm** pl. *-āt* excommunication (*Chr.*)

حرامى **ḥarāmī** pl. *-iya* thief, robber, bandit

حرمان **ḥirmān** deprivation, bereavement, dispossession (of s.o., من of s.th.); debarment, exclusion, preclusion (من from); excommunication (*Chr.*); privation | حرمان الارث *ḥ. al-irṯ* exclusion from inheritance, disinheritance (*Isl. Law*)

محرم **maḥram** pl. محارم *maḥārim*² s.th. forbidden, inviolable, taboo, sacrosanct, holy, or sacred; unmarriageable, being in a degree of consanguinity precluding marriage (*Isl. Law*)

محرمة **maḥrama** pl. محارم *maḥārim*² handkerchief

تحريم **taḥrīm** forbiddance, interdiction, prohibition, ban

احرام **iḥrām** state of ritual consecration of the Mecca pilgrim (during which the pilgrim, wearing two seamless woolen or linen sheets, usually white, neither combs nor shaves, and observes sexual continence); garments of the Mecca pilgrim

احترام **iḥtirām** pl. *-āt* deference, respect, regard, esteem, reverence; honoring (e.g., of a privilege); pl. honors, respects, tributes

محروم **maḥrūm** deprived, bereaved, bereft (من of); excluded, precluded, debarred (من from); suffering privation (as opposed to مرزوق); excommunicated (*Chr.*)

محرم **muḥarram** forbidden, interdicted; Muharram, name of the first Islamic month; محرم الحرام *m. al-ḥarām* honorific name of this month

محرم **muḥrim** Mecca pilgrim who has entered the state of ritual consecration (see احرام *iḥrām*)

محترم **muḥtaram** honored, revered, venerated, esteemed, respected; (in the salutation of letters:) my dear . . .; venerable, reverend; notable, remarkable, considerable

حرمل *ḥarmal* African rue (Peganum harmala L.; *bot.*)

حرملة **ḥarmala** pl. حرامل *ḥarāmil*² a loose wrap worn over the shoulders (garment of the dervishes)

حرن *ḥarana, ḥaruna u* (حران *ḥirān, ḥurān*) to be obstinate, stubborn, headstrong

حرون **ḥarūn** pl. حرن *ḥurun* obstinate, stubborn, refractory, reluctant, resistant

حارون **ḥārūn** brazier

حروة *ḥarwa* burning; wrath, rage; acridity, pungency (of taste); pungent, disagreeable odor

حرى V to seek, pursue (ه s.th.), strive (ه for), aspire (ه to); to examine, investigate (ه s.th.); to inquire (عن or ه into), make inquiries (عن or ه about); to be intent (ه on s.th.), take care (ه of s.th.), attend (ه to s.th., also فى), look (ه after s.th., also فى); to see to it (ان that)

بالحرى *bi-l-ḥarā* **hardly, barely**

حرى *ḥarīy* pl. احرياء *aḥriyā'*[2] **adequate, appropriate, suitable (ب for), worthy (ب of s.th.) | حرى بالذكر (*ḏikr*) worth mentioning, considerable; حرى بالتصديق credible, believable; او بالحرى or to be exact, or rather**

احرى *aḥrā* **more adequate, more proper, more appropriate | او بالاحرى or to tell the truth, or more explicitly, or put more exactly, or rather**

تحر *taḥarrin* pl. تحريات *taḥarriyāt* **inquiry; investigation | شرطة التحرى** *šurṭat at-t.* **or** مصلحة التحرى *maṣlaḥat at-t.* **secret police**

حز *ḥazza u* (*ḥazz*) **to notch, nick, incise, indent (ف s.th.), make an incision, cut (ف into s.th.) II and VIII = I**

حز *ḥazz* pl. حزوز *ḥuzūz* **incision, notch, nick, the right time, the nick of time**

حزة *ḥazza* **incision, notch, nick; time; the right time, the nick of time; predicament, plight**

حزاز *ḥazāz* **head scurf, ringworm; tetter, eruption (*med.*)**

حزازة *ḥazāza* **rancor, hatred, hate**

محز *maḥazz* **notch, nick | اصاب المحز to find the right solution, hit the nail on the head, hit the mark, strike home**

حزب *ḥazaba u* (*ḥazb*) to befall (ه s.o.), happen, occur (ه to s.o.) | حزب الامر the matter became serious **II** to rally (ه s.o.); to form or found a party **III** to side, take sides (ه with), be an adherent (ه of s.o.) **V** to take sides; to form a party, make common cause, join forces

حزب *ḥizb* pl. احزاب *aḥzāb* group, troop, band, gang; party (*pol.*); the 60th part of the Koran | هو من احزابه he belongs to his clique, he is of the same breed

حزبى *ḥizbī* party (adj.), factional

حزبية *ḥizbīya* **party activities; partisanship, partiality; factionalism**

حيزبون *ḥaizabūn* **old hag**

تحزب *taḥazzub* **factiousness; factionalism**

حازب *ḥāzib*: حزبه حازب *ḥazabahū ḥ.* **he met with a mishap**

متحزب *mutaḥazzib* **partial, biased; partisan**

[1]حزر *ḥazara i u* (*ḥazr*, محزرة *maḥzara*) **to estimate, assess, appraise (ه s.th.); to make a rough estimate (ه of s.th.), guess (ه s.th.)**

حزر *ḥazr* **estimation, assessment, appraisal; conjecture, guess, surmise**

حزورة *ḥazzūra* **riddle, puzzle**

محزرة *maḥzara* **estimation, assessment, appraisal; conjecture, guess, surmise**

[2]حزيران *ḥazīrān*[2] **June (*Syr., Leb., Ir., Jord.*)**

حزقانى *ḥuzuqqānī* **choleric**

حزوقة *ḥazūqa*, حازوقة *ḥāzūqa* **hiccups**

حزم *ḥazama i* (*ḥazm*) **to tie up, bundle, wrap up, pack, do up in a package or bundle (ه s.th.); to girth (ه an animal); to make fast, fasten, tie (ه s.th.) | حزم امره (*amrahū*) to take matters firmly in hand; — *ḥazuma u* (*ḥazm*, حزامة *ḥazāma*, حزومة *ḥuzūma*) to be resolute, firm, stouthearted, intrepid II to gird (ه s.o.) V and VIII to be girded; to gird o.s., put on a belt**

حزم *ḥazm* **packing, packaging, wrapping; determination, resoluteness, firmness, energy; judiciousness, discretion, prudence**

حزمة *ḥuzma* pl. حزم *ḥuzam* **s.th. wrapped up or tied up; bundle, fagot, fascine; beam of rays, radiation beam (*phys.*); bunch (of herbs, etc.); sheaf; package, parcel**

حزام *ḥizām* pl. *-āt*, احزمة *aḥzima*, حزم *ḥuzum* **belt, girth; girdle; cummerbund,** waistband (worn over the caftan to fasten it); sword belt | حزام الامن *ḥ. al-amn* safety belt

احزم *aḥzam*[2] more resolute; more judicious

حازم *ḥāzim* pl. حزمة *ḥazama* and حزيم *ḥazīm* pl. حزماء *ḥuzamā'*[2] resolute, energetic; judicious, discreet, prudent

حزن **ḥazana** *u* to make sad, sadden, grieve (ه s.o.); — *ḥazina a* (*ḥuzn, ḥazan*) to be sad, grieved (ل or على at or because of); to grieve, mourn (على over) II and IV to make sad, sadden, grieve (ه s. o.)

حزن *ḥuzn* pl. احزان *aḥzān* sadness, grief, sorrow, affliction

حزن *ḥazn* pl. حزون *ḥuzūn* rough, rugged, hard ground

حزن *ḥazin* sad, mournful, grieved

حزين *ḥazīn* pl. حزناء *ḥuzanā'*[2], حزان *ḥizān*, حزانى *ḥazānā* sad; mourning (for a deceased person); sorrowing, mournful, grieved | الجمعة الحزينة (*jum'a*) Good Friday (*Chr.*)

حزنان *ḥaznān*[2] very sad, very grieved, worried; in mourning

□ حزايني *ḥazāyinī* (حزائني *ḥazā'inī*) sad, mournful, melancholic; mourning- (in compounds), mortuary, funereal | قماش حزايني (*qumāš*) cloth for mourning garments

تحزن *taḥazzun* sadness; behavior of a mourner

محزون *maḥzūn* grieved, grief-stricken, pained, sad, saddened

محزن *muḥzin* grievous, saddening; sad; melancholic; tragic; محزنات *muḥzināt* grievous things | قصة تمثيلية محزنة (*qiṣṣa tamṯīlīya*) and رواية محزنة (*riwāya*) tragedy (*theat.*)

حس **ḥassa** (1st pers. perf. *ḥasastu*) *u* (*ḥass*) to curry, currycomb (ه an animal); to feel, sense (ه s.th.); — *ḥassa* (1st pers. perf. *ḥasastu*) *i*, (1st pers. perf. *ḥasistu*) *a* to feel sorry, feel sympathy or compassion (ل for), sympathize (ل with) II to grope, feel IV to perceive, sense, experience (ه or ب s.th.); to feel (ه or ب s.th.); to notice (ه or ب s.th.); to hear (ه a sound, a noise, etc.); to take notice (ه of s.o.) V to grope, probe (ه for s.th.), finger, handle, touch (ه s.th.), run the hand (ه over s.th.); to grope about, feel around; to seek information, make inquiries (من about); to sense, experience, perceive (ه, ب s.th.); to feel (ب s.th.); to be affected, be deeply touched (ب by s.th.)

حس *ḥass* sensation, perception, feeling, sentiment

حس *ḥiss* sensory perception, sensation; feeling, sentiment; sense; voice; sound; noise

حسى *ḥissī* sensory; sensuous; perceptible; palpable | ○ المذهب الحسى (*maḏhab*) sensationalism, sensualism

حسيات *ḥissīyāt* sensations

حسيس *ḥasīs* faint noise

حساس *ḥassās* sensitive; sensible; readily affected, susceptible; sensual (pleasure)

حساسة *ḥassāsa* sensory organ

حساسى *ḥassāsī* allergic | امراض حساسية allergic diseases, allergies (*med.*)

حساسية *ḥassāsīya* sensitivity (also *techn.*); sensibility; faculty of sensory perception; susceptibility; sensuality | مرض الحساسية *maraḍ al-ḥ.* allergy (*med.*)

محسة *miḥassa* currycomb

احساس *iḥsās* pl. *-āt*, احاسيس *aḥāsīs*[2] feel, feeling; sensation, sense (ب of s.th.); perception (ب of s.th.); sensitivity; pl. احساسات feelings, sentiments | ○ احساس بالنور sensitivity to light; ○ شديد الاحساس

highly sensitive; احساس مشترك (*muštarak*) feeling of harmony, concord, unanimity; قلة الاحساس *qillat al-i.* insensitivity, dullness, obtuseness

○ الطائفة الاحساسية *aṭ-ṭā'ifa al-iḥsāsīya* the impressionists

حاسة *ḥāssa* pl. حواس *ḥawāss*² sensation; sense | الحواس الخمس the five senses

محسوس *maḥsūs* felt; sensed; perceptible, noticeable, palpable, tangible; appreciable, considerable (e.g., loss); المحسوس that which is perceptible through the senses; appearance, evidence; المحسوسات things perceptible through the senses

حسب *ḥasaba u* (*ḥasb*, حساب *ḥisāb*, حسبان *ḥisbān*, *ḥusbān*) to compute, reckon, calculate, to count; to charge, debit (على ه s.th. to s.o., to s.o.'s account); to credit (ل ه s.th. to s.o., to s.o.'s account) | حسب حسابه (*ḥisābahū*) to take s.th. or s.o. into account or into consideration, reckon with s.th. or s.o., count on s.th. or s.o.; حسب حسابا ل (*ḥisāban*) do.; to attach importance to s.o. or s.th.; حسب الف حساب ل (*alfa*) to have a thousand apprehensions about...; — *ḥasiba a i* (حسبان *ḥisbān*, محسبة *maḥsaba*, *maḥsiba*) to regard (ه ه s.o. as), consider, deem (ه ه s.o. to be . . .); to think, believe, suppose, assume; to consider, regard (من ه s.o. as belonging to), count (من ه s.o. among); to see (ه في in s.o. s.th.); — *ḥasuba u* (*ḥasab*, حسابة *ḥasāba*) to be of noble origin, be highborn; to be highly esteemed, be valued **III** to settle an account, get even (ه with s.o.); to call (ه s.o.) to account, ask (ه s.o.) for an accounting; to hold (ه s. o.) responsible, make (ه s.o.) answerable | حاسب على نفسه to be careful, be on one's guard **V** to be careful, be on one's guard; to take precautions; to seek to know, try to find out (ه s.th.) **VI** to settle a mutual account **VIII** to debit or credit; to take into account, take into consideration (ب or ه s.th.); to reckon (ب or ه with); (to anticipate a reward in the hereafter by adding a pious deed to one's account with God — such as resigning in God's will at the death of a relative; hence:) احتسب ولدا (*waladan*) to give a son, be bereaved of a son; احتسب عند الله الشيء to sacrifice s.th. in anticipation of God's reward in the hereafter; to charge (على ه s.th. for); to think, believe, suppose; to take (ه ه s.o. for or to be . . .); to be content, content o.s. (ب with); to disapprove (على ه of s.th. in s.o.), take exception (على ه to s.th. in s.o.), reject (على ه s.th. in s.o.); to call (على s.o.) to account, ask (على s.o.) for an accounting

حسب *ḥasb* reckoning, computing, calculation; thinking, opinion, view; sufficiency | حسبك (or بحسبك) درهم *ḥasbuka* (*bi-ḥasbika*) *dirhamun* one dirham is enough for you; حسبك ان it suffices to say that . . .; you know enough when you hear that . . .; you need only . . .; بحسبك مقنعا ان (*muqniʿan*) it will be enough to convince you if . . .; وحسبك بهذا كله شرا (*bi-hāḏā kullihī šarran*) but enough of all these negative aspects! فحسب *fa-ḥasb* and that's all, and no more, only (interchangeable with فقط)

حسبي *ḥasbī*: مجلس حسبي (*majlis*) pl. مجالس حسبية guardianship court, probate court (*Eg.*)

حسب *ḥasab* pl. احساب *aḥsāb* measure, extent, degree, quantity, amount; value; esteem, high regard enjoyed by s.o.; noble descent; *ḥasaba* (prep.), بحسب *bi-ḥasabi* and على حسب *ʿalā ḥasabi* according to, in accordance with, commensurate with, depending on

حسبما *ḥasabamā* (conj.) according to what . . ., as, depending on how . . . | حسبما اتفق (*ttafaqa*) as chance will have it

حسبة *ḥisba* arithmetical problem, sum

حسيب *ḥasīb* pl. حسباء *ḥusabā'*[2] respected, esteemed; noble, of noble birth, highborn

حسبان *ḥusbān* calculation, reckoning, accounting; computation | كان فى الحسبان to be taken into account, be taken into consideration; to be expected, be anticipated; كان فى الحسبان ان it was expected that . . .; حسبانى ان I expect that . . .

حساب *ḥisāb* arithmetic, reckoning, calculus; computation; calculation, estimation, appraisal; accounting, settlement; consideration, considerateness; caution;—(pl. *-āt*) bill, invoice; statement of costs; (bank) account; pl. حسابات bookkeeping | حساب الجمل *ḥ. al-jummal* (*al-jumal*) use of the alphabetic letters according to their numerical value; علم الحساب *'ilm al-ḥ.* arithmetic; حساب التفاضل *ḥ. at-tafāḍul* differential calculus; حساب التكامل *ḥ. at-takāmul* integral calculus; كان فى حسابه he reckoned with it, he expected it, he was prepared for it; عمل حسابا له to take s.o. or s.th. into consideration; to reckon with s.o. or s.th.; الحساب الختامى (*kitāmī*) and حساب نهائى (*nihā'ī*) final statement of account, final accounting; دعاه الى الحساب (*da'āhu*) he called him to account; يوم الحساب *yaum al-ḥ.* the Day of Reckoning, Judgment Day; اقام حسابا ل to render account to s.o.; بلا حساب without limit or bounds, to excess, to an unlimited extent; من غير حساب blindly, without forethought, at random; لحساب فلان to s.o.'s credit, to s.o.'s advantage; على حساب فلان to s.o.'s debit, at s.o.'s expense, to s.o.'s disadvantage; لقى سوء الحساب *laqiya sū'a l-ḥ.* he got a raw deal, he was in for it; حساب جار (*jārin*) current account; حسابات صندوق التوفير *ḥ. ṣundūq at-t.* savings-bank accounts; حساب موقوف blocked account; حسابات دوبيه double-entry bookkeeping; الحساب الشرقى (*šarqī*) the Julian calendar; الحساب الغربى (*ġarbī*) the Gregorian calendar

حسابى *ḥisābī* arithmetical, mathematical, computational

محاسبة *muḥāsaba* pl. *-āt* accounting; clearing (*com.*); bookkeeping; request for accounting; examination of conscience (*theol.*) | قسم المحاسبة *qism al-m.* accounting department, comptroller's office; clearing house

احتساب *iḥtisāb* computation; calculation, consideration, reflection; debiting; crediting; valuation; contentedness, satisfaction

حاسب *ḥāsib* counter, reckoner, arithmetician, calculator, computer

محسوب *maḥsūb* pl. *-ūn*, محاسيب *maḥāsīb*[2] protégé, pet, favorite; obedient, subservient (على to s.o.)

محسوبية *maḥsūbīya* esteem enjoyed by s.o., position of distinction; patronage, favored position, favoritism

محاسب *muḥāsib*, محاسبجى *muḥāsibgī* (*eg.*) accountant, bookkeeper; comptroller, auditor

محتسب *muḥtasab* that for which one can expect reward in the hereafter (e.g., suffering, loss, etc.)

حسد **ḥasada** *u* (*ḥasad*) to envy, grudge (ه s.o., على or ه s.th.), be envious (ه of s.o., على or ه because of s.th.) **VI** to envy each other

حسد *ḥasad* envy

حسود *ḥasūd* pl. حسد *ḥusud* envious

تحاسد *taḥāsud* mutual envy

حاسد *ḥāsid* pl. حساد *ḥussād*, حسدة *ḥasada* envious; envier, grudger

محسود *maḥsūd* envied; smitten by the evil eye

حسر **ḥasara** *u i* (*ḥasr*) to pull away or off, remove (ه عن s.th., a cover, a veil, from); to uncover, lay bare, unveil (عن s.th.); —(حسور *ḥusūr*) to become dim (sight); — *ḥasira a* (*ḥasar*, حسرة *ḥasra*) to regret (على s.th.), be grieved, be pained (على by s.th.); to sigh (على over s.th.); — *ḥasara i*, *ḥasira a* (*ḥasar*) to become tired, fatigued II to fatigue, tire, weaken, sap (ه s.o.); to grieve, sadden (ه s.o.), cause pain or grief (ه to s.o.); to remove (ه a cover, عن from), lay bare, unveil (عن s.th.) V to be distressed, be pained, be grieved (على by); to sigh (على over) VII to be pulled away or off, be removed (عن from); to be rolled up, be turned back (sleeve, عن from the arm); to disappear suddenly (عن from)

حسر *ḥasar* fatigue, debility, weakness | حسر البصر *ḥ. al-baṣar* nearsightedness, myopia

حسر *ḥasir* grieved, sad; fatigued, languid, weary, tired

حسرة *ḥasra* pl. *ḥasarāt* grief, sorrow, pain, distress, affliction; sigh | يا للحسرة *yā la-l-ḥasrati* alas! unfortunately! يا حسرتى *yā ḥasratī* and وا حسرتاه *wā ḥasratāh* what a pity! too bad!

حسير *ḥasīr* pl. حسرى *ḥasrā* tired, weary, fatigued, exhausted; dim, dull (eye), nearsighted | حسير البصر *ḥ. al-baṣar* nearsighted, myopic

حسور *ḥusūr* nearsightedness, myopia

حسران *ḥasrān* regretful, sorry, sad, distressed, grieved

تحسر *taḥassur* sighing; regret

حاسر *ḥāsir* pl. حواسر *ḥawāsir*[2] bared, denuded | حاسر البصر *ḥ. al-baṣar* nearsighted, myopic; حاسر الرأس *ḥ. ar-ra's* bareheaded, hatless

حسك *ḥasak* (coll.; n. un. ة) thorns, spines; spikes, pricks; fishbones; awns, beard (*bot.*); name of several prickly herbs, esp. of the genus Tribulus

حسكى *ḥasakī* thorny, prickly, spiny

حسم *ḥasama i* (*ḥasm*) to cut, sever, cut off (ه s.th.); to finish, complete, terminate (ه s.th.); to decide (ه a question); to settle (ه an argument); to deduct, discount (ه an amount from a sum of money) VII to be severed, be cut off; to be finished, be completed, be terminated; to be settled (argument)

حسم *ḥasm* finishing, completion, termination; decision; settling, settlement (of an argument); discontinuance, shutdown, closing down; deduction, discounting (of an amount)

حسام *ḥusām* sword, sword edge

حسوم *ḥusūm* fatal, trying, grueling (pl.; days, nights, also years)

حاسم *ḥāsim* decisive; final, peremptory, conclusive, definite, definitive

حسن *ḥasuna u* (*ḥusn*) to be handsome, beautiful, lovely, nice, fine, good; to be expedient, advisable, suitable, proper, fitting; to be in a proper state, be in a desirable condition | ان حسن لديك *in ḥ. ladaika* if you like it, if it seems all right to you; يحسن بك ان it is to your advantage that you . . .; you ought to . . .; حسن استعداده ل he was all willing to . . . II to beautify, embellish (ه s.th.); to adorn, decorate (ه s.th.); to improve, put into better form, ameliorate, better (ه s.th.); to make a better presentation (ه of s.th.); to present in a favorable light, depict as nice or desirable (ه ل s.th. to s.o.); to sugar-coat, make more palatable (ه s.th. unpleasant, s.th. disadvantageous) III to treat (ه s.o.) with kindliness IV to do right, act well; to do (ه s.th.) well, expertly, nicely; to know (ه how to do s.th.), be able (ه to do s.th.); to master (ه s.th.), have command (ه of s.th.), be proficient (ه in s.th.; a language, an art, a handicraft, etc.), be conversant (ه with s.th.); to do good, be charitable; to do favors, do good (الى or ب to s.o.), do (الى or ب s.o.) a good turn, be nice, friendly (الى or ب to s.o.); to give alms, give charity (الى to s.o.) | ما احسنه *mā aḥsanahū* how good he is! how handsome he is! احسنت *aḥsanta* well done! bravo! احسن الالمانية (*almānīya*) to master the German language, know German well; احسن التسديد to aim well or accurately; احسن مشورته (*mašūratahū*) to give good advice; احسن الظن ب (*ẓanna*) to have a good opinion of ..., judge s.th. favorably; احسن معاملته (*mu'āmalatahū*) to treat s.o. well **V** to become nicer, more handsome, more beautiful; to improve, ameliorate, get better **X** to deem (ه s.th.) nice, etc., or good; to regard (ه s.th.) as right, advisable or appropriate; to approve (ه of s.th.), sanction, condone (ه s.th.); to come to like, to appreciate (ه s.th.), find pleasure (ه in s.th.); also = **IV**: استحسن الانجليزية (*ingilīzīya*) to know English well; pass. *ustuḥsina* to be good, commendable, advisable

حسن *ḥusn* beauty, handsomeness, prettiness, loveliness; excellence, superiority, perfection | لحسن الحظ *li-ḥ. il-ḥaẓẓ* fortunately; حسن السلوك good manners, good behavior; good conduct; حسن السير والسلوك (*ḥ. as-sair*) an irreproachable life; حسن التصرف *ḥ. at-taṣarruf* discretion, individual judgment; حسن الظن *ḥ. aẓ-ẓann* good opinion, favorable judgment; حسن التعبير euphemism; حسن القصد (النية) *ḥ. al-qaṣd* (*an-nīya*) good intention, good will, good faith; حسن يوسف *ḥ. yūsuf* beauty spot, patch; ست الحسن *sitt al-ḥusn* a kind of bindweed (Convolvulus cairicus L.; *bot.*); deadly nightshade, belladonna

حسن *ḥasan* pl. حسان *ḥisān* beautiful, handsome, lovely; pretty, nice; good, agreeable; excellent, superior, exquisite; حسنا *ḥasanan* well, splendidly, excellently, beautifully; الحسان the ladies; — high sandhill

الحسنيون *al-ḥasaniyūn* the Hasanides, the descendants of Ḥasan, son of 'Alī and Fāṭima

احسن *aḥsan*[2] pl. احاسن *aḥāsin*[2] better; nicer, lovelier, more beautiful; more excellent, more splendid, more admirable | هو احسن حالا منهم he is better off than they are; بالتى هى احسن (*bi-llatī*) in a friendly manner, amicably, with kindness

حسناء *ḥasnā'*[2] pl. حسان *ḥisān* (of a woman) beautiful, a beauty, a belle

الحسنى *al-ḥusnā* pl. *-āt* (f. of الاحسن *al-aḥsan*) the best outcome, the happy ending; fair means, amicable manner | بالحسنى amicably, by fair means, in a friendly manner; الاسماء الحسنى (*asmā'*) the 99 attributes of God

حسنة *ḥasana* pl. *-āt* good deed, benefaction; charity, alms; pl. حسنات advantages, merits

حسون *ḥassūn* pl. حساسين *ḥasāsīn*[2] goldfinch

محسنة *maḥsana* s.th. nice, s.th. good; advantage; pl. محاسن *maḥāsin*[2] beauties, charms, attractions, merits, advantages, good qualities

تحسين *taḥsīn* beautification, embellishment; improvement, amelioration, betterment; processing, refining, finishing; (pl. تحاسين *taḥāsīn*[2]) ornament, decoration | تحسين النسل *t. an-nasl* eugenics ○

محاسنة *muḥāsana* friendly treatment, kindliness, amicability

احسان *iḥsān* beneficence, charity, almsgiving, performance of good deeds

تحسن *taḥassun* improvement, amelioration | فى التحسن on the way to recovery

استحسان *istiḥsān* approval, consent; acclaim; discretion; application of discretion in a legal decision (*Isl. Law*)

محسن *muḥassin* embellisher, beautifier, improver; pl. محسنات *muḥassināt* cosmetics

محسن *muḥsin* beneficent, charitable

مستحسن *mustaḥsan* approved, commendable; pleasant, agreeable

(حسو) حسا *ḥasā u* (*ḥasw*), **V** and **VIII** to drink, sip (▲ s.th.)

حسو *ḥasw* and حساء *ḥasā'* soup, broth

حسوة *ḥaswa* pl. *ḥasawāt* a sip

حسوة *ḥuswa* pl. *ḥusuwāt, ḥusawāt,* احسية *aḥsiya* a sip, small quantity of liquid; soup, broth; bouillon

حش *ḥašša u* (*ḥašš*) to mow, cut (▲ s.th.) **II** to smoke hashish

حشيش *ḥašīš* (coll.) pl. حشائش *ḥašā'iš*² herbs, grasses; weeds; hay; hemp (Cannabis sativa L.; *bot.*), hashish, cannabis; stillborn child | حشيش الدينار *ḥ. ad-dīnār* hops

حشيشة *ḥašīša* (n. un.) herb

حشاش *ḥaššāš* pl. *-ūn* smoker or chewer of hashish, hashish addict

حشاش *ḥušāš*, حشاشة *ḥušāša* last breath, last spark of life

حشيشى *ḥašīšī* (*eg.*) sap-green, reseda-colored

محش *miḥašš*, محشة *miḥašša* pl. محاش *maḥāšš*² sickle, scythe; fire iron, poker

محشة *miḥašša* pl. *-āt* (*eg.*) tool for weeding, weeder

محشش *maḥšaš*, محشش خانة *m.-ḵāna* hashish den

محششة *maḥšaša* pl. محاشش *maḥāšiš*² hashish den

حشد *ḥašada i u* (*ḥašd*) to gather, concentrate, mass (• esp. troops), call up, mobilize (▲ an army); to pile up, store up, accumulate (▲ s.th., الى at a place) **II** to amass, accumulate (▲ s.th.), mass, concentrate (• esp. troops) **V** and **VIII** to rally, come together, assemble, gather, crowd together, throng together; to be concentrated, be massed (troops); to fall into line (troops)

حشد *ḥašd* pl. حشود *ḥušūd* assembling, rallying; gathering, assembly, crowd, throng; concentration, massing (esp. of troops); mobilization, calling up (of an army)

تحشد *taḥaššud* pl. *-āt* concentration (of troops)

احتشاد *iḥtišād* pl. *-āt* gathering, crowd; concentration (of troops)

حاشد *ḥāšid* numerous (of an assembly), crowded (of a public demonstration)

○ حاشدة *ḥāšida* battery (*el.*)

حشر *ḥašara i u* (*ḥašr*) to gather, assemble, rally (• people); to cram, crowd, pack, jam (together); to squeeze, press, force, stuff, tuck (▲ s.th. في or بين into)

يوم الحشر *yaum al-ḥašr* the day of congregation (of the dead), the Day of Resurrection

حشرة *ḥašara* pl. *-āt* insect; pl. vermin, insect pests | علم الحشرات *'ilm al-ḥ.* entomology

حشرى *ḥašarī* insectile, insectival, insect- (in compounds); entomologic(al)

حشرج *ḥašraja* and **II** *taḥašraja* to rattle in the throat

حشرجة *ḥašraja* rattling, rattle in the throat

حشف **V** to be dressed shabbily, dress slovenly

حشف *ḥašaf* dates of inferior quality

حشفة *ḥašafa* glans (penis; *anat.*)

حشك *ḥašaka i* (*ḥašk*) to cram, jam, squeeze, stuff (▲ s.th. في into)

حشم *ḥašama i* (*ḥašm*) to shame, put to shame (• s.o.) **II** and **IV** do. **V** and **VIII** to be ashamed to face s.o. (من or عن); to be reticent, modest, shy, bashful, diffident

حشم *ḥašam* servants, retinue, entourage, suite

حشمة *ḥišma* shame, bashfulness, timidity, diffidence; modesty; decency, decorum

حشيم *ḥašīm* pl. حشماء *ḥušamā'*[2] modest, timid, bashful, shy, diffident

محاشم *maḥāšim*[2] pubes, genitals

تحشم *taḥaššum* and احتشام *iḥtišām* shame, shyness, modesty, reticence, decency, decorum

محتشم *muḥtašim* shy, bashful; modest, reticent, decent, decorous

(حشو) حشا *ḥašā u* (*ḥašw*) to stuff, fill, dress (ب ه s.th. with; esp. fowl, etc.); to fill in (ه s.th.); to load (ه a firearm; ه ه s.th. with, e.g., a camera); to fill (ه a tooth); to insert (ه s.th.) II to interpolate (ه s.th.); to insert (ه s.th.); to provide (ه s.th.) with a margin; to hem (ه a dress); to supply (ه a book) with marginal notes or glosses III to except, exclude (من ه s.o. from) V to keep away, stand aloof, abstain (من from), avoid, shun (من s.th.), beware (من of), be on one's guard (من against) VI to keep away, abstain (عن or من from), beware (ه or عن or من of), avoid, shun (ه or عن or من s.th.)

حشو *ḥašw* that with which s.th. is stuffed or filled; dressing, stuffing (of fowl, etc.); filling (of teeth); insertion; (*gram.*) parenthesis; interpolation

حشوة *ḥašwa* pl. *-āt* filling, stuffing (cushion, cookery, etc.); load (of a cartridge), charge (of a mine); panel, inlay, inserted piece (in paneling, in a door)

حشا *ḥašan* pl. احشاء *aḥšā'* bowels, intestines; interior, inside | فى احشاء in the interior of, within, in

حشى *ḥašan* = حشا *ḥašan*

حشية *ḥašīya* pl. *-āt*, حشايا *ḥašāyā* cushion, pillow; mattress

حاشا, حاشى *ḥāšā* (with genit., acc. or ل) except, save | حاشا لله, حاشى لله God forbid! حاشا لك ان far be it from you that you...; حاشا لك, حاشا لله = (*ḥāša*) حاش لك, حاش لله

تحشية *taḥšiya* insertion; interpolation

تحاش *taḥāšin* avoidance

حاشية *ḥāšiya* pl. حواش *ḥawāšin* border; seam, hem; edge; margin (of a book); marginal gloss; marginal notes; commentary on certain words and passages of a book, supercommentary; footnote; postscript; retinue, entourage, suite, servants; dependents; pl. حواش critical apparatus | رقيق الحاشية and رقيق الحواشى nice, polite, courteous, gracious, amiable, kindly, friendly; رقة الحاشية *riqqat al-ḥ.* niceness, amiability, graciousness

محشو *maḥšūw* filled, dressed; stuffed; loaded (firearm); pl. محشوات *maḥšūwāt* filled, or stuffed, dishes

محشى *maḥšīy* filled, stuffed (esp. food); s.th. filled or stuffed

حص *ḥaṣṣa u* to fall as a share (ه to s.o.) III to share (ه ه s.th. with s.o.) IV to allot s.o. (ه) his share

حص *ḥuṣṣ* saffron

حصة *ḥiṣṣa* pl. حصص *ḥiṣaṣ* share, portion, allotment; share (*fin.*); contingent, quota; span of time; lesson, class period | حصة فى الربح *ḥ. fī r-rabḥ* dividend (*fin.*); ○ حصة التأسيس founders' share; ○ نظام الحصص quota system, apportionment; فى حصة وجيزة in a short time

تحصيص *taḥṣīṣ* quota system, apportionment

محاصة *muḥāṣṣa* allotment; sharing (with s.o.), partaking, participation

حصالبان see حصى

حصب *ḥaṣaba i u* to cover or strew with pebbles or gravel (ه ground); to macadamize (ه ground), metal (ه a road); — *ḥaṣiba a* and pass. *ḥuṣiba* to have the measles II to cover or strew with pebbles or gravel (ه ground); to macadamize (ه ground), metal (ه a road)

حصب *ḥaṣab* road metal, crushed rock, ballast

حصباء *ḥaṣbā'*[2] (coll.) pebbles; gravel

حصبة *ḥaṣba* measles (*med.*)

حاصبة *ḥāṣiba* storm, hurricane

حصحص *ḥaṣḥaṣa* to be or become clear, plain, manifest; to come to light (truth)

حصد *ḥaṣada i u* (*ḥaṣd*, حصاد *ḥaṣād*, *ḥiṣād*) to harvest, reap (ه s.th.); to mow (ه s.th.) **IV, VIII** and **X** to be ripe

حصد *ḥaṣd* and حصاد *ḥiṣād* harvesting, reaping, harvest; حصاد harvest time

حصيد *ḥaṣīd*, حصيدة *ḥaṣīda* pl. حصائد *ḥaṣā'id*[2] crop, harvest yield | قائم وحصيد everything without exception

حصاد *ḥaṣṣād* reaper; harvester

محصد *miḥṣad* pl. محاصد *maḥāṣid*[2] sickle

○ حصادة *ḥaṣṣāda* and ○ محصدة *miḥṣada* mowing machine, mower | ○ حصادة دراسة (*darrāsa*) combine

حاصد *ḥāṣid* reaper

○ حاصدة *ḥāṣida* mowing machine, mower

محصود *maḥṣūd* harvested, reaped, mown

محصد *muḥṣid* and مستحصد *mustaḥṣid* ripe

حصر *ḥaṣara i u* (*ḥaṣr*) to surround, encircle, encompass, ring (ه s.th.); to enclose (ه s.th.); to parenthesize (ه a word); to blockade (ه, ه s.o., s.th.); to besiege, beleaguer (ه, ه s.o., s.th.); to detain, deter, restrain, contain, hold back (ه s.o.); to limit, restrict (ه في or ب s.th. to); to condense, reduce in scope (ه s.th.); to narrow down, confine (ه في s.th. to, also a suspicion to s.o.); to bring together, compile, arrange (ه في s.th. under a rubric); to enter (ه في s.th. in a list); to put together, set up, list, enumerate (ه s.th.); to comprise, contain, include, involve (ه s.th.); — *ḥaṣira a* (*ḥaṣar*) to be in a fix, be in a dilemma **III** to encircle, surround (ه, ه s.o., s.th.); to shut off, seclude (ه, ه s.o., s.th.); to block (ه s.th.); to beleaguer, besiege (ه, ه s.o., s. th.); to blockade (ه, ه s.o., s.th.); to detain, deter, restrain (ه s.o.) **VII** to be straitened, confined, narrowed in; to be or become restricted, limited (ب or في to); to limit o.s. (ب or في to); to be condensed (في to), be concentrated (في in); to be or become united (e.g., تحت حكمه under s.o.'s rule); to be reducible (في to), be expressible (في in terms of), consist (في in)

حصر *ḥaṣr* encirclement, encompassment, enclosure, corralling; parenthesizing; blocking, blockading, beleaguering, siege; detention, determent; restraint, retention, containment, check; limitation, restriction, confinement; narrowing; gathering, collecting (of s.th. scattered), compilation; enumeration, listing, counting, computing; centralization, concentration; (tobacco) monopoly | بالحصر strictly speaking; على سبيل الحصر exhaustively; حصر التموين *ḥ. at-tamwīn* rationing; علامة الحصر *'alāmat al-ḥ.* parentheses, brackets (*typ.*); لا يدخل تحت الحصر (*yadḵulu*) or لا حصر له (*ḥaṣra*) boundless, infinite, immeasurable, innumerable; يفوق الحصر *yafūqu l-ḥaṣra* do.; ○ اجازة الحصر *ijāzat al-ḥ.* patent on an invention; ادارة حصر التبغ والتنباك *idārat ḥ. at-tibḡ wa-t-tumbāk* Government Tobacco Monopoly (*Syr.*)

حصر *ḥuṣr* retention (of urine); constipation

حصر *ḥaṣar* dyslogia, inability to express o.s. effectively

حصير *ḥaṣīr* pl. حصر *ḥuṣur* mat

حصيرة *ḥaṣīra* pl. حصائر *ḥaṣā'ir*[2] mat

حصار *ḥiṣār* block, blockage, barrier; blockade; siege

محاصرة *muḥāṣara* block, blockage, barrier; blockade; siege

انحصار *inḥiṣār* restrictedness, limitation, confinement; (tobacco) monopoly

محصور *maḥṣūr* blocked, blockaded; beleaguered, besieged; limited, restricted, confined (في to); narrow

حصرم **ḥiṣrim** (coll.; n. un. ة) unripe and sour grapes (*syr.*)

حصف **ḥaṣufa** *u* (حصافة *ḥaṣāfa*) to have sound judgment, be judicious, discriminating

حصف *ḥaṣif* endowed with sound judgment, judicious, discriminating

حصيف *ḥaṣīf* endowed with sound judgment, judicious, discriminating

حصافة *ḥaṣāfa* sound judgment, judiciousness

حصل **ḥaṣala** *u* (حصول *ḥuṣūl*) to set in; to be there, be existent, extant; to arise, come about; to result, come out; to happen, occur, transpire, come to pass, take place; to happen, occur (ل to s.o.), come (ل upon s.o.), befall, overtake (ل s.o.); to originate, emanate, derive, stem (من from), be caused, be produced (من by); to attain, obtain, get, receive, achieve (على s.th.), win (على s.o. or s.th.); to come into possession (على of s.th.); to seek (على a permit), apply (على for a permit); to collect, recover (على a debt), call in (على funds); to receive, take in (على s.th.) II to cause s.th. (ه) to happen or set in; to attain, obtain (ه s.th.); to acquire (ه s.th., also knowledge); to infer, deduce (ه s.th.); to collect (ه a fee, fare, etc.), levy (ه taxes, fees, etc.), call in (ه money); to summarize, sum up (ه s.th.) V to result (من from), come out (sum); to be obtained, be attained; to be raised, be levied, be required, be demanded; to be taken in, come in (fees, taxes, funds); to be collected (taxes); to procure for o.s., get (على s.th.); to attain, receive, obtain (على s.th.); to acquire (على s.th.); to collect (على fees) X to procure for o.s., get (على s.th.); to attain, receive, obtain (على s.th.); to acquire (على s.th.)

حصول *ḥuṣūl* setting in, occurrence, incidence, happening (of an event or process); obtainment, attainment (على of s.th.); achievement (على of s.th.); acquisition (على of s.th.)

حصيلة *ḥaṣīla* pl. حصائل *ḥaṣā'il*[2] rest, remainder; amount collected, proceeds, returns; revenue, receipts, yield, income, takings

حوصل, حوصلة and حويصلة look up alphabetically

حصالة *ḥaṣṣāla* collection box, alms box

محصل *maḥṣal* result, outcome, upshot, issue

تحصيل *taḥṣīl* pl. *-āt* attainment, obtainment, gain; acquisition (also of knowledge); learning, studying, scientific studies; collection, raising, levy(ing), calling in (of funds, taxes); income, revenue, receipts, returns, proceeds; résumé, summary, gist (of a speech or opinion); من تحصيل الحاصل ان يقال in summary, it may be said . . .

تحصيلجي *taḥṣilgi* (*eg.*) = محصل *muḥaṣṣil*

حاصل *ḥāṣil* pl. حواصل *ḥawāṣil*[2] setting in, occurring, taking place, happening; result, outcome, sum, total, product (also *math.*); revenues, receipts, proceeds, gain; income, returns; crop, harvest; warehouse, storehouse, granary, depot, magazine; main content, purport, gist, essence, substance (of a speech); الحاصل briefly, in short; pl. حاصلات product(s), yield, produce, production (*econ.*)

محصول *maḥṣūl* pl. *-āt*, محاصيل *maḥāṣīl*[2] result, outcome, issue; yield, gain; product, produce; crop, harvest; production

محصل *muḥaṣṣil* collector; tax collector; cashier; (bus, streetcar) conductor

متحصل *mutaḥaṣṣil* yield, revenue, proceeds, receipts, returns (من from)

حصن **ḥaṣuna** *u* (حصانة *ḥaṣāna*) to be inaccessible, be well fortified; to be chaste (woman) II to make inaccessible (ه s.th.); to strengthen (ه s.th.); to fortify, entrench (ه s.th.); to immunize, make proof (ضد *ḍidda* against) IV to make inaccessible (ه s.th.); to fortify, entrench (ه s.th.); to be chaste, pure (woman); to remain chaste, be of unblemished reputation (woman) V to strengthen one's position, protect o.s.; to be fortified; to be secure, be protected

حصن *ḥiṣn* pl. حصون *ḥuṣūn* fortress, fort, castle, citadel, stronghold; fortification, entrenchment; protection | حصن طائر Flying Fortress

حصان *ḥiṣān* pl. حصن *ḥuṣun*, احصنة *aḥṣina* horse; stallion | حصان البحر *ḥ. al-baḥr* hippopotamus; حصان بخارى (*bukārī*) iron horse; قوة حصان *qūwat ḥ.*, or حصان alone, horse power

حصين *ḥaṣīn* inaccessible, strong, fortified, firm, secure(d), protected; immune, proof, invulnerable (ضد *ḍidda* against) | الحصن الحصين (*ḥiṣn*) stronghold (fig.; e.g., of radicalism)

ابو الحصين *abū l-ḥuṣain* fox

حصانة *ḥaṣāna* strength, ruggedness, forbiddingness, impregnability, inaccessibility; shelteredness, chastity (of a woman); invulnerability, inviolability; immunity (of deputies, diplomats; against illness)

تحصين *taḥṣīn* pl. *-āt* fortification, entrenchment; strengthening, cementing, solidification; immunization

احصان *iḥṣān* blamelessness, unblemished reputation, integrity (*Isl. Law*)

تحصن *taḥaṣṣun* securing, safeguarding, protection, protectedness

محصن *muḥaṣṣan* fortified; entrenched; immune, proof (ضد *ḍidda* against)

محصنة *muḥṣina*, *muḥṣana* sheltered, well-protected, chaste; of unblemished reputation (woman; *Isl. Law*)

حصى IV to count, enumerate (ه s.th.); to calculate, compute (ه s.th. من from); to debit, charge (ه على s.th. to s.o.'s account), hold (ه s.th. على against s.o.) | لا يحصى (*yuḥṣā*) innumerable

حصى *ḥaṣan* (coll.) pebbles, little stones

حصاة *ḥaṣāh*, حصوة *ḥaṣwa* pl. حصيات *ḥaṣayāt* little stone; pebble; calculus, stone (*med.*) | حصاة بولية (*baulīya*) cystic calculus; حصاة صفراوية (*ṣafrāwīya*) gallstone, biliary calculus

حصى لبان *ḥaṣā lubān*, حصالبان rosemary (*bot.*)

حصوى *ḥaṣawī* stony, pebbly, gravelly

احصاء *iḥṣā'* pl. *-āt* count, counting; enumeration; calculation, computation; statistics | احصاء السكان *i. as-sukkān* census

احصائى *iḥṣā'ī* statistic(al); (pl. *-ūn*) statistician

احصائية *iḥṣā'īya* pl. *-āt* statistics

حض **ḥaḍḍa** *u* (*ḥaḍḍ*) and II to spur on, incite (ه s.o., على to), goad, prod (ه s.o., على to do s.th.)

حض *ḥaḍḍ* incitement, inducement, prodding, prompting, instigation

حضيض *ḥaḍīḍ* pl. حضض *ḥuḍuḍ*, احضة *aḥiḍḍa* foot of a mountain; lowland; perigee (*astron.*); depth; state of decay | نزل الى الحضيض to sink low (fig.); دكه الى الحضيض (*dakkahū*) to ruin s.th. completely, run s.th. into the ground

حضر **ḥaḍara** *u* (حضور *ḥuḍūr*) to be present (ه at), be in the presence (ه of s.o.); to attend (ه s.th.); to be present (ه in s.o.'s mind), be readily recalled (ه by s.o.); to take part, participate (مجلسا *majlisan* in a meeting); to come, get (الى or ه, ه to s.o., to a place), arrive (الى or ه at a place); to visit (ه a place), attend (ه a public event), go (ه to a performance, etc.); to appear (امام before a judge, etc., الى in, at), show up (الى in, at); to betake o.s., go (من الى from... to); (حضارة *ḥaḍāra*) to be settled, sedentary (in a civilized region, as opposed to nomadic existence) **II** to ready, make ready, prepare (ه s.th., also, e.g., a medicine = to compound), make, produce, manufacture (ه s.th.); to study, prepare (ه a lesson); to fetch, get, bring (ه s.o., ه s.th.), procure, supply (ه s.th.); to settle (ه s.o.), make s.o. (ه) sedentary; to civilize (ه s.o., ه s.th.) **III** to give a lecture, present s.th. in a lecture (ه to s.o.); to lecture, give a course of lectures **IV** to fetch, get, bring (ه, ه s.o., s.th.), procure, supply (ه s.th.); to take (ه s.o., ه s.th., الى to a place) | احضره معه to have s.th. with one, bring s.th. along **V** to prepare o.s., ready o.s., get ready (ل for); to be ready, prepared; to become settled, be sedentary in a civilized region; to be civilized, be in a state of civilization; to become urbanized, become a town dweller **VIII** to come (ه to s.o.), be in the presence (ه of s.o.); to live in a civilized region; pass. *uḥtuḍira* to die **X** to have s.th. (ه) brought, to call, send (ه, ه for s.o., for s.th.), have s.o. (ه) come; to summon (ه s.o.); to fetch, procure, supply, get, bring (ه s.th.); to conjure, call up, evoke (ه a spirit); to visualize, envision, call to mind (ه s.th.); to carry with o.s., bring along (ه s.th.); to prepare (ه, e.g., a medicinal preparation)

حضر *ḥaḍar* a civilized region with towns and villages and a settled population (as opposed to desert, steppe); settled population, town dwellers (as opposed to nomads)

حضرى *ḥaḍarī* settled, sedentary, resident, not nomadic, non-Bedouin, like urbanites; civilized; urban; town dweller

حضرة *ḥaḍra* presence | فى حضرة in the presence of...; الحضرة العلية (*ʿalīya*) His Highness (formerly, title of the Bey of Tunis); حضرتكم a respectful form of address, esp. in letters; حضرة الدكتور cf. Fr. *Monsieur le docteur*

حضور *ḥuḍūr* presence; visit, participation, attendance; (as one pl. of حاضر) those present | بحضوره in his presence; حضور الحفلة *ḥ. al-ḥafla* attendance of the celebration; حضور الذهن *ḥ. aḏ-ḏihn* presence of mind; ورقة حضور *waraqat ḥ.* summons (*jur.*)

حضورى *ḥuḍūrī*: احكام حضورية (*aḥkām*) judgments delivered in the presence of the litigant parties after oral proceedings (*jur.*); حضوريا *ḥuḍūrīyan* contradictorily (*jur.*)

حضارة *ḥaḍāra* civilization; culture; settledness, sedentariness

حضيرة *ḥaḍīra* pl. حضائر *ḥaḍāʾir*[2] a small group of 6 to 12 people (specif., the smallest unit of boy scouts = patrol); section, squad (*mil.*; *Syr.*)

محضر *maḥḍar* presence; attendance, coming, appearance (of s.o.); assembly, meeting, gathering, convention; (pl. محاضر *maḥāḍir*[2]) minutes, official report, procès-verbal, record of the factual findings | محضر الجرد *m. al-jard* inventory list; بمحضر منه *bi-maḥḍarin minhu* in s.o.'s presence

تحضير *taḥḍīr* preparing, readying, making ready; (pl. *-āt*) preparation (ل for; also e.g., for an examination); making, preparation, cooking (of food, etc.), production, manufacture

تحضيرى *taḥḍīrī* preparatory, preparative | المدارس التحضيرية للمعلمين (*muʿallimīn*)

preparatory institutes for teachers, teachers' colleges (*Eg.*)

محاضرة *muḥāḍara* pl. *-āt* lecture

احضار *iḥḍār* procurement, supply, fetching, bringing

تحضر *taḥaḍḍur* civilized way of life

احتضار *iḥtiḍār* demise, death

استحضار *istiḥḍār* making, production, manufacture; preparation; summoning | استحضار الارواح *istiḥḍār al-arwāḥ* evocation of spirits, spiritism

حاضر *ḥāḍir* pl. حضر *ḥuḍḍar*, حضور *ḥuḍūr* present; attending; الحاضر the present (time); prepared (ل for); ready; (pl. حضار *ḥuḍḍār*, حضرة *ḥaḍara*) settled, sedentary, resident, village or town dweller, not nomadic | فى الوقت or فى الحاضر الحاضر at present, now; حاضر الفكر *ḥ. al-fikr* quick-witted, quick at repartee; نقد حاضر (*naqd*) cash, ready money

حاضرة *ḥāḍira* pl. حواضر *ḥawāḍir*[2] capital city, metropolis; city (as a center of civilization)

محضور *maḥḍūr* possessed, haunted or inhabited by a jinni; demoniac

محضر *muḥaḍḍir* maker, producer, manufacturer; dissector (*med.*)

محاضر *muḥāḍir* lecturer, speaker

محضر *muḥḍir* court usher

متحضر *mutaḥaḍḍir* civilized

محتضر *muḥtaḍar* dying, in the throes of death, on the brink of death; a dying person; haunted or inhabited by a jinni; demoniac

مستحضر *mustaḥḍar* pl. *-āt* preparation (*chem.*, *pharm.*) | مستحضر دوائى (*dawā'ī*) medicinal preparation

حضرموت *ḥaḍramaut*[2] Hadhramaut

حضرمى *ḥaḍramī* pl. حضارم *ḥaḍārim*[2] man from Hadhramaut; Hadhramautian (adj.)

حضن *ḥaḍana* u (*ḥaḍn*, حضانة *ḥiḍāna*) to clasp in one's arms, embrace, hug (ه s.o.); to nurse, bring up, raise (ه a child); (*ḥaḍn*, حضان *ḥiḍān*, حضانة *ḥiḍāna*, حضون *ḥuḍūn*) to hatch, brood, incubate (ه an egg; of a bird) VI to embrace one another, cling to one another, nestle against each other VIII to clasp in one's arms, embrace, hug (ه, ه s.o., s.th.); to harbor in one's bosom (ه feeling); to hatch, concoct, contrive (ه s.th.); to bring up, raise (ه a child)

حضن *ḥiḍn* pl. احضان *aḥḍān* breast, bosom (between the outstretched arms); armful, that which can be carried in one's arms | قبله بالحضن (*qabilahū*) he received him with open arms; بين احضان and فى احضان amid, among; with, in the presence of (s.o.); فى احضان الصحراء (*ṣaḥrā'*) in the heart (or folds) of the desert; اخذتنى بين احضانها she took me in her arms

حضانة *ḥiḍāna*, *ḥaḍāna* raising, bringing up, nursing (of a child); hatching (of an egg), incubation | دار الحضانة children's home, day nursery, crèche

حضين *ḥaḍīn* embraced, hugged, resting in s.o.'s arms

محضن *maḥḍan* pl. محاضن *maḥāḍin*[2] children's home, day nursery, crèche

احتضان *iḥtiḍān* embrace, hug(ging), accolade

حاضنة *ḥāḍina* pl. حواضن *ḥawāḍin*[2] nursemaid, dry nurse

محتضن *muḥtaḍin* embracing, hugging; tender, affectionate

حط *ḥaṭṭa* u (*ḥaṭṭ*) to put, place, put down, set down (ه s.th.); to take down (ه a load, burden); to lower, decrease, diminish, reduce (ه or من s.th.); to depreciate (من قدره *min qadrihī* or من قيمته *min qīmatihī* the value of s.th.) | حط الرحال (*riḥāla*) to halt, make a stop, dismount, encamp (while traveling on horseback, camelback, etc.); — *u* (*ḥaṭṭ*, حطوط *ḥuṭūṭ*) to sink, descend, go down; to alight (bird); to land (airplane); to drop (price) II to put down, set down, take off, unload (ه a load) VII to sink, descend, go down; to decrease, diminish; to decline, decay, wane VIII to put down, set down, take down (ه s.th.)

حط *ḥaṭṭ* (act of) putting or setting down; depreciation, belittling, derogation, disparagement (من of s.th.); reduction, diminution, decrease (من of s.th.)

حطة *ḥiṭṭa* alleviation, relief, mitigation; abasement, debasement, demotion, degradation (in rank, dignity, prestige); humiliation, insult, indignity

احط *aḥaṭṭ*[2] lower

حطيطة *ḥaṭīṭa* price reduction

محط *maḥaṭṭ* place at which s.th. is put down or deposited; stopping place, stop; pause, fermata, hold, concluding strain, cadence (*mus.*) | محط الآمال object of hope, that on which one's hopes are pinned; كان محط الانظار to attract the glances, draw attention to o.s.; محط الكلام *m. al-kalām* sense, or meaning, of one's words

محطة *maḥaṭṭa* pl. *-āt* stopping place, stop (also of public conveyances); station, post; railroad station; broadcasting station, radio station | محطة تحويل التيار *m. taḥwīl at-tayyār* transformer station; محطة الاذاعة (اللاسلكية) *m. al-iḏā'a (al-lā-silkīya)* broadcasting station, radio station; transmitter (station); محطة رئيسية (*ra'īsīya*) (railroad) main station; ○ محطة الاشارات *m. al-išārāt* signal post; ○ محطة الارسال *m. al-irsāl* transmitter (station; *radio*); محطة للارصاد الجوية (*li-l-arṣād al-jawwīya*) meteorological station, weather station; محطة الصرف *m. aṣ-ṣarf* (*Eg.*) pump station (for drainage); power plant; ○ محطة الاستقبال receiving station (*radio*); ○ محطة لاسلكية قصيرة الامواج (*lā-silkīya qaṣīrat al-amwāj*) short-wave transmitter station; محطة توليد الكهرباء *m. taulīd al-kahrabā'* and محطة كهربائية power plant

انحطاط *inḥiṭāṭ* decline, fall, decay, decadence; inferiority | احساس الانحطاط *iḥsās al-inḥ.* sense of inferiority

انحطاطي *inḥiṭāṭī* postclassical writer

منحط *munḥaṭṭ* low, base, low-level, low-grade; fallen, degraded (woman); mean, vile, vulgar; inferior

حطب **ḥaṭaba** *i* to gather firewood | حطب في حبله (*fī ḥablihī*) to support s.o., stand by s.o., back s.o. up VIII to gather firewood

حطب *ḥaṭab* pl. احطاب *aḥṭāb* firewood

حطاب *ḥaṭṭāb* wood gatherer; woodcutter, lumberjack; vendor of firewood

تحطيب *taḥṭīb* singlestick fencing (a popular game, esp. in rural areas; *eg.*)

حاطب *ḥāṭib* wood gatherer; woodcutter, lumberjack; vendor of firewood | كحاطب ليل *ka-ḥāṭibi lailin* lit.: like one who gathers wood at night, i.e., blindly, at random, heedlessly (said of s.o. who does not realize, or think about, what he is doing)

حطم **ḥaṭama** *i* (*ḥaṭm*) to break, shatter, smash, wreck, demolish (ه s.th.) II = I; V to break, go to pieces; to be broken, be smashed, be shattered; to crash (e.g., airplane, structure, etc.); to be wrecked (ship) VII = V

حطمة *ḥiṭma* pl. حطم *ḥiṭam* particle, small piece, shred, bit, morsel; s.th. broken

حطام *ḥuṭām* debris, rubble; fragments, shards, broken pieces; wreckage, wreck (of a ship) | حطام الدنيا *ḥ. ad-dunyā* the ephemeral things of this world, the vanities of the world

حطيم *ḥaṭīm* smashed, shattered, wrecked

تحطيم *taḥṭīm* smashing, shattering, wrecking, breaking, demolition, destruction, disruption | ○ سفينة تحطيم الجليد icebreaker (*naut.*)

تحطم *taḥaṭṭum* crumbling, disintegration; crash (of an airplane); collapse, breakdown

حاطمة *ḥāṭima*: ○ حاطمة الجليد icebreaker (*naut.*)

محطم *muḥaṭṭim* crashing, thundering, roaring (of an explosion, etc.) — *muḥaṭṭam* broken (language)

محطمة *muḥaṭṭima*: محطمة ثلجية (*taljīya*) icebreaker (*naut.*)

حظ *ḥaẓẓa a* (*ḥaẓẓ*) to be lucky, fortunate IV = I

حظ *ḥaẓẓ* pl. حظوظ *ḥuẓūẓ* part, portion, share, allotment; lot, fate, destiny; good luck, good fortune; affluence, wealth, fortune; prosperity; pleasure | ذو حظ من endowed with; لحسن الحظ *li-ḥusni l-ḥ.* and من حسن الحظ fortunately, luckily; سوء الحظ *sū' al-ḥ.* bad luck, misfortune; سيء الحظ *sayyi' al-ḥ.* unlucky, unfortunate; لسوء الحظ unfortunately; من حسن حظي luckily for me, fortunately; كان من حسن حظه ان he was lucky in that he . . .; ليس احسن منها حظا he is no better off than she is

حظيظ *ḥaẓīẓ* lucky, fortunate

محظوظ *maḥẓūẓ* lucky, fortunate; content(ed), happy, glad

حظر *ḥaẓara u* (*ḥaẓr*) to fence in, hedge in (ه s.th.); to forbid (ه على to s.o. s.th.), prohibit (ه على s.o. from doing s.th.)

حظر *ḥaẓr* forbiddance, interdiction, prohibition, ban; embargo

حظار *ḥiẓār*, *ḥaẓār* wall, partition, screen; fence, palisade, railing

حظيرة *ḥaẓīra* pl. حظائر *ḥaẓā'ir*[2] enclosure, railing, fence, palisade, hedge; compound, yard, pound, pinfold; corral, pen, paddock, coop; hangar, shed; field, domain, realm (fig.) | في حظيرة (with foll. genit.) inside of, within; جذبه الى حظيرته (*jaḏabahū*) to bring s.o. under one's influence; حظائر الطائرات aircraft hangars; حظيرة القدس *ḥ. al-quds* Paradise

محظور *maḥẓūr* interdicted, prohibited, forbidden (على to s.o.); embargoed; pl. محظورات forbidden things, restrictions

حظى (حظو and حظى) *ḥaẓiya a* (حظوة *ḥuẓwa*, *ḥiẓwa*) to enjoy the favor or good graces of s.o. (عند), be in s.o.'s (عند) favor or good graces; to acquire, obtain, attain, gain, win (ب s.th.)

حظوة *ḥuẓwa*, *ḥiẓwa* favored position. role of favorite; precedence; favor, grace; good will, benevolence; prestige, credit, standing, respect, esteem | نال حظوة عند (لدى) to find favor with s.o.

حظية *ḥaẓīya* pl. حظايا *ḥaẓāyā* paramour, mistress, concubine

محظية *maḥẓīya* pl. *-āt* paramour, mistress, concubine

حف *ḥaffa u* (*ḥaff*) to surround (ب ه, ه s.o., s.th. with, also ب and حول s.o., s.th.), enclose, encompass, border (ب, ه s.th.); to depilate (ه a part of the body), unhair (ه the skin); to trim, clip (ه the beard); to chafe, rub off, abrade (ه s.th.) | تحف به العيون he is the object of admiring glances, he is the center of attention, all eyes are upon him; — *i* (حفيف *ḥafīf*) to rustle II and VIII to surround, (ب ,حول, ه, ه s.o., s.th.), enclose, encompass, border (ب ,حول, ه s.th.)

حفاف *ḥifāf* side

حفيف *ḥafīf* rustle, rustling

محفة *miḥaffa* (also *maḥaffa*) pl. *-āt* litter, stretcher; roller stretcher; sedan

حاف *ḥāff*: خبز حاف (*ḵubz*) plain bread (without anything to go with it; *eg.*)

حافة *ḥāffa* pl. *-āt* enclosure, edge, margin; brim of a vessel; border, brink, verge; fringe, hem | على حافة الخراب *'alā ḥ. il-ḳarāb* on the brink of ruin

حفيد *ḥafīd* pl. احفاد *aḥfād*, حفدة *ḥafada* grandson; descendant, offspring, scion

حفيدة *ḥafīda* granddaughter

حفر *ḥafara i* (*ḥafr*) to dig (ه s.th.); to drill (for oil); to excavate (*archeol.*); to carve (ه s.th.); to engrave, etch (ه metal) | حفر خنادق to dig trenches; حفر حفرة (*ḥufratan*) to prepare a pitfall, prepare an ambush **VII** pass. of **I**; **VIII** to dig

حفر *ḥafr* digging, earthwork, excavation (also *archeol.*); unearthing; drilling (for oil); carving, inscribing (e.g., of letters); engraving, etching; graphic arts (etching, wood engraving); scurvy (*syr.*) | جهاز الحفر *jahāz al-ḥ.* oil rig; oil derrick

حفرة *ḥufra* pl. حفر *ḥufar* pit; hollow, cavity, excavation; hole

حفرية *ḥafrīya* digging, excavation; ○ gravure; pl. حفريات excavations (*archeol.*)

حفار *ḥaffār* digger; engraver; driller; stone mason | حفار القبور gravedigger

حفير *ḥafīr* dug, dug out, excavated, unearthed

حفيرة *ḥafīra* pl. حفائر *ḥafā'ir*² s.th. excavated or unearthed; pl. excavations (*archeol.*)

احفور *uḥfūr* pl. احافير *aḥāfīr*² s.th. excavated; fossil; pl. excavations (*archeol.*)

محفر *miḥfar* pl. محافر *maḥāfir*² spade

حافر *ḥāfir* pl. حوافر *ḥawāfir*² hoof | وقع الحافر على الحافر to coincide, happen to correspond exactly; على الحافر on the spot, right away, at once

حافرى *ḥāfirī* ungular, ungulate

حافرة *ḥāfira* original condition, beginning | عند الحافرة on the spot, right away, at once; رجع الى حافرته to revert to its original state or origin

محفور *maḥfūr* dug; inscribed, engraved; carved

حفز *ḥafaza i* (*ḥafz*) to pierce, stab (ه s.o., ب with the spear); to incite, instigate, urge, prompt, induce (ه s.o. الى or على to s.th.) **V** to prepare o.s., get ready, be ready, be about to do s.th. (ل or الى), set out to do s.th. (ل or الى); to get ready to jump, make a running start; to listen, pay attention **VIII** to be about to do s.th., be ready (ل for)

تحفز *taḥaffuz* preparedness, readiness; vim, dash, verve, sweep, élan

حافز *ḥāfiz* pl. حوافز *ḥawāfiz*² spur, drive (على to do s.th.), incentive (على to), initiative

متحفز *mutaḥaffiz* ready, prepared (ل for)

حفظ *ḥafiẓa a* (*ḥifẓ*) to preserve (ه s.th.); to protect, guard, defend (ه s.o.); to observe, bear in mind (ه s.th.), comply (ه with s.th.), be mindful, be heedful (ه of s.th.); to keep up, maintain, sustain, retain, uphold (ه s.th.); to hold, have in safekeeping (ه s.th.), take care (ه of s.th.); to keep, put away, save, store (ه s.th); to conserve, preserve (ه s.th.); to retain in one's memory, remember, know by heart (ه s.th.); to memorize, learn by heart, commit to memory (ه s.th., esp. the Koran); to reserve (ه لنفسه for o.s. s.th.); to stay, discontinue, suspend (التحقيق a judicial investigation; *jur.*) | حفظه الله may God protect him! حفظ بالبريد to hold in care of general delivery (ه s.th.); يحفظ فى البوسطة (*yuḥfaẓu*) in care of general delivery, poste restante; حفظ الوفاء ل (*wafā'a*) to be loyal to s.o., keep faith with s.o. **II** to have s.o. (ه) memorize (ه s.th.) **III** to preserve, keep up, maintain, uphold, sustain (على s.th.);

to supervise, control (على s.th.), watch (على over s.th.); to watch out (على for), take care, be heedful, be mindful (على of), look (على after), attend, pay attention (على to); to keep, follow, observe, bear in mind (على s.th.), comply (على with), conform (على to); to protect, guard, defend (ه and على, also عن s.th.) **IV** to vex, annoy, gall, irritate, hurt, offend (ه s.o.) **V** to keep up, maintain, preserve (ب s.th.); to observe, keep in mind (ب s.th.), be mindful, be heedful, take care (ب of s.th.), be concerned (ب with); to be cautious, be wary, be on one's guard; to be reserved, aloof; to have reservations **VIII** to maintain, uphold (ب or ه s.th., e.g., بحقوقه one's rights); to keep up, maintain, retain (ب or ه s.th., e.g., a posture, a characteristic); to take care, take over custody (ب of s.o.), protect, guard (ب s.o.); to defend (against encroachment), hold, maintain (ب a possession); to preserve, sustain, continue, keep up (ب s.th.); to hold, possess (ب s.th.); to put away, hold, have in safekeeping (ب s.th.), take care (ب of s.th.); to keep, retain (ب s.th.); احتفظ لنفسه to keep for o.s., appropriate, reserve for o.s. (ب or ه s.th.), take complete possession (ه of) **X** to ask s.o. (ه) to guard or protect (ه or على s.th.); to entrust (على or ه ه to s.o. s.th.), commit s.th. (على or ه) to the charge of s.o. (ه)

حفظ *ḥifẓ* preservation; maintenance, sustentation, conservation, upholding; protection, defense, guarding; custody, safekeeping, keeping, storage; retention; observance, compliance (with); memorizing, memorization; memory; (*jur.*) discontinuance, stay, suspension (of legal action, of a judicial investigation) | حفظ الآثار preservation of ancient monuments (*Eg.*); حفظ الصحة *ḥ. aṣ-ṣiḥḥa* hygiene, sanitation; رجال الحفظ police

حفظة *ḥifẓa* anger, indignation, resentment, rancor

حفاظ *ḥifāẓ* pl. *-āt* dressing, ligature, bandage | حفاظ الحيض *ḥ. al-ḥaiḍ* sanitary napkin

حفيظ *ḥafīẓ* attentive, heedful, mindful; preserving, keeping, guarding (على s.th.)

حفيظة *ḥafīẓa* pl. حفائظ *ḥafā'iẓ*[2] grudge, resentment, rancor

محفظة *maḥfaẓa, miḥfaẓa* pl. *-āt*, محافظ *maḥāfiẓ*[2] folder, bag, satchel, briefcase dispatch case, portfolio; wallet, pocketbook

محفظة *miḥfaẓa* capsule

تحفيظ *taḥfīẓ* memorization drill, inculcation (esp. of the Koran)

حفاظ *ḥifāẓ* defense, protection, guarding (esp. of cherished, sacred things); preservation, maintenance (على of interests); keeping, upholding (of loyalty), adherence (to a commitment)

محافظة *muḥāfaẓa* guarding; safeguarding; preservation; protection, defense; conservation, sustaining, upholding; retention, maintenance (على of s.th.) conservativism (*pol.*), conservative attitude; following, observance (على of s.th.), compliance (على with s.th.), adherence (على to); guarding (من against misfortune), saving (من from misadventure); garrison (*mil.*); (pl. *-āt*) governorate (one of five administrative divisions of Egypt, in addition to 14 *mudīrīyāt*); office of the *muḥāfiẓ* (head of a governorate); province, any one of the larger administrative districts (*Syr.*) | المحافظة على النفس self-preservation; مذهب المحافظة *maḏhab al-m.* conservative movement, conservativism, Toryism

تحفظ *taḥaffuẓ* caution, wariness, restraint, reticence, reserve, aloofness; —

(pl. -*āt*) precaution, precautionary measure; reservation, limiting condition, conditional stipulation, proviso | مع التحفظ with full reservation

تحفظى *taḥaffuẓī* precautionary, preventive | اجراءات تحفظية (*ijrā'āt*) precautionary measures; صلح تحفظى (*ṣulḥ*) settlement before action, preventive settlement (*jur.*)

احتفاظ *iḥtifāẓ* guarding, safeguarding; preservation; retention, maintenance, continuation, conservation, defense, protection, vindication, sustaining, upholding; keeping, holding, safekeeping, custody (ب of s.th.)

حافظ *ḥāfiẓ* keeper, guarder, guardian, custodian, caretaker; (pl. حفاظ *ḥuffāẓ*, حفظة *ḥafaẓa*) one who knows the Koran by heart (formerly an honorific epithet)

حافظة *ḥāfiẓa* memory; — (pl. حوافظ *ḥawāfiẓ*[2]) wallet, pocketbook; money order (*Eg.*)

محفوظ *maḥfūẓ* kept, held in safekeeping, deposited, guarded, preserved; memorized, committed to memory, etc.; conserved, preserved (food); reserved; ensured, secured, safeguarded; — pl. محفوظات canned goods, conserves; archives; memorized material, what s.o. knows by heart | دار المحفوظات المصرية the Egyptian Public Record Office; مأكولات محفوظة conserves, canned goods; جميع الحقوق محفوظة all rights reserved

محافظ *muḥāfiẓ* supervisory, controlling; observing (على s.th.), complying (على with), etc.; conservative (*pol.*), المحافظون the Conservatives, the Tories; keeper, guarder, guardian, custodian, caretaker, supervisor, superintendent; mayor; governor (*Eg.*: title of the chief officer of a governorate; *Syr.*: chief officer of a province); director general, president (= *Brit.* governor)

متحفظ *mutaḥaffiẓ* vigilant, alert, wary, cautious; reticent, reserved, aloof; staid, sedate

مستحفظ *mustaḥfaẓ* pl. -*āt* reserve (*mil.*)

حفل **ḥafala** *i* (*ḥafl*) to gather, assemble, congregate; to flow copiously; to be replete, teem, superabound (ب with); to pay attention, attend, give one's mind (ب or ل to s.th.), concern o.s. (ب with), make much (ب of), set great store (ب by) | لا حفل به (*ḥafla*) indifferent, of no consequence **II** to adorn, decorate, ornament (ب ه s.th. with) **VIII** to gather, rally, throng together; to celebrate (ب s.th., s.o.); to concern o.s. (ب or ل with), attend, pay attention, give one's mind (ب or ل to s.th.); to honor, welcome, receive kindly (ب s.o.)

حفل *ḥafl* gathering, meeting, assembling; assembly, congregation, throng, crowd; performance, show, public event; celebration; feast, festival

حفلة *ḥafla* pl. -*āt* assembly, gathering, meeting, congregation; party; (social or public) event; show, performance (theater, cinema); concert; festivity, ceremony, festival, festive event, celebration | حفلة التأبين commemoration, commemorative ceremony for a deceased person; الحفلة الاولى (*ūlā*) premiere; حفلة حافلة numerous assembly; حفلة خيرية (*ḵairīya*) charity performance, charity event; حفلة الدفن *ḥ. ad-dafn* funeral ceremony, obsequies; حفلة دينية (*dīnīya*) religious ceremony, Divine Service; حفلة ساهرة and حفلة سمر *ḥ. samar* evening party, soirée; حفلة سينمائية motion-picture show; حفلة الشاى tea party; حفلة العرس *ḥ. al-'urs* wedding; حفلة الاستقبال (public) reception; حفلة موسيقية concert

حفيل *ḥafīl* eager, assiduous, diligent

محفل *maḥfil* pl. محافل *maḥāfil*[2] assembly, congregation, meeting, gathering; party;

body, collective whole; circle, quarter | محفل ماسونى Masonic lodge; المحافل الرسمية (السياسية) (*rasmīya, siyāsīya*) the official (political) circles or quarters

احتفال *iḥtifāl* pl. *-āt* celebration, ceremony, festival, festivities

حافل *ḥāfil* pl. حفل *ḥuffal*, حوافل *ḥawāfil*² full (ب of), filled, replete (ب with); abundant, copious, lavish; much frequented, well attended (by visitors, participants, etc.), numerous (of attendance); solemn, ceremonial, festive

حافلة *ḥāfila* pl. *-āt*, حوافل *ḥawāfil*² ○ autobus

محتفل *muḥtafil*: المحتفلون the participants in a festive event, the celebrators

محتفل *muḥtafal* assembly place, gathering place; party; محتفل به celebrated

حفن *ḥafana u* to scoop up with both hands (ه s.th.); to give a little (ل to s.o.)

حفنة *ḥafna* pl. *ḥafanāt* handful

حفو)¹ and حفى) حفى *ḥafiya a* (حفاوة *ḥafāwa*) to receive kindly and hospitably, to welcome, receive with honors, honor (ب s.o.) V to behave with affection, be affectionate (ب toward) VIII do.; to celebrate (ب an occasion, a festival)

حفى *ḥafīy* welcoming, receiving kindly, greeting (ب s.o., s.th.)

حفاوة *ḥafāwa* friendly reception, welcoming, welcome, salutation (ب of s.o.)

احتفاء *iḥtifā'* reception, welcome, salutation (ب of s.o.); celebration, festivity

حفى² *ḥafiya a* (حفاء *ḥafā'*) to go barefoot; to have sore feet

حاف *ḥāfin* pl. حفاة *ḥufāh* barefoot(ed)

حق *ḥaqqa i u* to be true, turn out to be true, be confirmed; to be right, correct; (also pass. *ḥuqqa*) to be necessary, obligatory, requisite, imperative (على for s.o.), be incumbent (على upon s.o.); to be adequate, suitable, fitting, appropriate (على for s.o.); to be due (ل s.o.); يحق له he is entitled to it, he has a right to it; حق عليه he deserved it (punishment); — *u* to ascertain (ه s.th.), make sure, be sure (ه of s.th.); to recognize, identify (ه s.o.) II to make s.th. (ه) come true; to realize (ه s.th., e.g., a hope), carry out (ه e.g., a wish), carry into effect, fulfill, put into action, consummate, effect, actualize (ه s.th.); to implement (ه e.g., an agreement); to produce, bring on, yield (ه results); to determine, ascertain, find out, pinpoint, identify (ه s.th.); to prove s.th. (ه) to be true, verify, establish, substantiate (ه s.th.); to confirm, assert, aver, avouch, affirm (ه s.th.); to be exact, painstaking, meticulous, careful (ه in doing s.th.), e.g., حقق النظر (*naẓara*) to look closely; to study, examine, investigate, explore (ه s.th.), look, inquire (ه into s.th.); to verify, check (ه or فى s.th.); to investigate (فى s.th.; police); to make an official inquiry (ه into s.th.), institute an investigation (ه of or into; court; *jur.*); to interrogate (مع s.o.), conduct a hearing (مع of s.o.; *jur.*) III to contend for a right (ه with s.o.), contest or litigate a right (ه against s.o.) IV to tell the truth; to be right (فى in s.th.); to enforce (ه s.th., e.g., a legal claim) V to prove true, turn out to be true, be confirmed, prove to be correct; to materialize, become a fact; to be realized, be effected, come into effect; to be examined, be explored; to ascertain (ه s.th., also من), make sure, reassure o.s., gain proof, convince o.s., be convinced, be sure, be certain (ه of s.th.); to check, verify (ه or من s.th.); to be serious (ب about s.th.) X to be entitled, have a claim (ه to s.th.); to claim (ه s.th.), lay claim (ه to); to deserve, merit (ه s.th.), be worthy (ه of); to require, demand, necessitate, make requisite (ه s.th.); to fall due, become payable (sum of money), mature, become due (note); to be due (ل s.o.) | يستحق الذكر (*ḏikra*) worth mentioning, noteworthy; لا يستحق عليه الرسم (*rasmu*) not subject to a fee, free of charge

حق *ḥaqq* truth; correctness, rightness; rightful possession, property; one's due; duty; proper manner; true, authentic, real; right, fair and reasonable; correct, sound, valid; الحق an attribute of God; (pl. حقوق *ḥuqūq*) right, title, claim, legal claim (فى to); الحقوق law, jurisprudence, legal science; حقا *ḥaqqan* really, in reality, in effect, actually, in fact, indeed, truly, in truth; justly, rightly, by rights | احقا ذلك؟ is that (really) so? really? بحق justly, rightly, by rights; بالحق truly, in reality, actually; properly, appropriately, in a suitable manner; بحق *bi-ḥaqqi* and فى حق as to ..., as for ..., with respect to, concerning, regarding; هو على حق he is in the right; الحق معك you are right; الحق عليك you are wrong; هو حق عليك it is your duty; هذا حق عليكم you owe this to me; عرفانا لحقها عليه (*'irfānan*) in recognition of what he owed her; من حقه he is entitled to it, it is his due; كان من حقه ان he should have ..., he ought to have ...; له الحق فى he is entitled to ...; والحق يقال (*yuqāl*) one may say, it must be admitted, it's only fair to say, say what you will ..., ... though (as a parenthetical phrase); عرف حق المعرفة (*ḥaqqa l-ma'rifa*) to know exactly, know for certain, know very well, also علم حق العلم (*ḥaqqa l-'ilm*); فهم حق الفهم *fahima ḥaqqa l-fahm* to understand precisely, comprehend thoroughly, be fully aware; السعادة الحقة (*sa'āda*) true happiness; كلية الحقوق *kulliyat al-ḥ.* law school, faculty of law

حق *ḥuqq* hollow, cavity; socket of a joint (*anat.*); also = حقة *ḥuqqa*

حقة *ḥuqqa* pl. حقق *ḥuqaq*, حقاق *ḥiqāq*, احقاق *aḥqāq* small box, case, pot or jar; receptacle, container; — (pl. *-āt*, حقق *ḥuqaq*) a weight (*Syr.*, *Pal.*) = اقة *uqqa*; حقة استانبولية = 1.280 kg (*Ir.*)

احق *aḥaqq*[2] worthier, more deserving (ب of s.th.); more entitled (ب to s.th.)

حقيق *ḥaqīq* pl. احقاء *aḥiqqā'*[2] worthy, deserving (ب of s.th.), fit, competent, qualified; entitled (ب to)

حقيقة *ḥaqīqa* pl. حقائق *ḥaqā'iq*[2] truth, reality (also *philos.*); fact; the true state of affairs, the facts; true nature, essence; real meaning, true sense; *ḥaqīqatan* really, in reality, in effect, actually, in fact, indeed, truly, in truth | رأيته على حقيقته I saw its true nature, as it really is; فى حقيقة الامر in reality, really, actually; ليس له حقيقة it does not really exist, it is not real

حقيقى *ḥaqīqī* real, true; actual; proper, intrinsic, essential; genuine; authentic; positive

حقوقى *ḥuqūqī* juristic(al); (pl. *-ūn*) jurist, jurisprudent, lawyer

احقية *aḥaqqīya* legal claim, title, right

حقانى *ḥaqqānī* correct, right, proper, sound, valid, legitimate, legal

حقانية *ḥaqqānīya* justice, law | وزارة الحقانية Ministry of Justice (formerly *Eg.*)

تحقيق *taḥqīq* realization, actualization, effectuation, implementation; fulfillment (of a claim, of a wish, etc.); achievement, accomplishment, execution; ascertainment, determination, identification, verification; substantiation; assertion, affirmation, confirmation; pinpointing, precise determination; exactness, accurateness, precision; (= تحقيق النطق *t. an-nuṭq*) precise pronunciation; — (pl. *-āt*) verification, check, checkup, investigation; official or judicial inquiry, inquest | التحقيق ان it is a matter of fact that ..., it is certain that ...; على التحقيق properly speaking, strictly speaking, actually; exactly, precisely; positively, definitely; عند التحقيق properly speaking, strictly speaking, actually; تحقيق الشخصية *t. aš-šakṣīya* identification (of a person), proof of identity; شهادة تحقيق الشخصية *šahādat t. aš-šakṣīya* identity card; قلم تحقيق الشخصية *qalam t. aš-š.* bureau of identification; تحقيق الذاتية *t.. aḏ-ḏātīya* identification; قاضي التحقيق examining magistrate; تحقيق الارباح realization of profits (stock market)

احقاق *iḥqāq*: احقاقا للحق *iḥqāqan li-l-ḥaqq* (so) that truth may prevail

تحقق *taḥaqquq* ascertainment, making sure; conviction, certainty, certitude; verification, check, checkup

استحقاق *istiḥqāq* pl. *-āt* worthiness, deservingness, merit; one's due or desert; maturity, payability, falling due (of a sum of money); re-claiming or calling in of s.th. due, demand of a right; vindication (*Isl. Law*), replevin, detinue | عن استحقاق deservedly, justly, by rights; بدون استحقاق undeservedly; تاريخ الاستحقاق date of maturity (e.g., of a bond); الاستحقاق اللبنانى (*lubnānī*) name of a Lebanese order

محقوق *maḥqūq* worthy, deserving (ب, ل of), fit, competent, qualifying (ب, ل for); wrong, at fault, on the wrong track

محقق *muḥaqqiq* investigator; inquirer; examining magistrate

محقق *muḥaqqaq* sure, certain, beyond doubt, unquestionable, indubitable; assured, established, accepted, recognized | من المحقق ان it is certain that ..., it is a fact that ...

محق *muḥiqq* telling the truth, in the right, being right

متحقق *mutaḥaqqiq* convinced, sure, certain, positive

مستحق *mustaḥiqq* entitled; claiming; beneficiary (of a wakf); deserving, worthy | مستحق الدفع *m. ad-daf'* due, payable (sum)

حقب VIII to put into one's bag, to bag (ه s.th.)

حقب *ḥuqb* pl. احقاب *aḥqāb*, حقاب *ḥiqāb* long stretch of time, long period

حقبة *ḥiqba* pl. حقب *ḥiqab* long time, stretch of time; period, age | حقبة من الزمان *ḥiqbatan min az-zamān* for quite a time, for some time

حقب *ḥaqab* pl. احقاب *aḥqāb* a kind of ornamental belt

حقاب *ḥiqāb* pl. حقب *ḥuqub* a kind of ornamental belt

حقيبة *ḥaqība* pl. حقائب *ḥaqā'ib*[2] valise, suitcase, traveling bag; leather bag | حقيبة دبلوماسية diplomatic pouch; حقيبة النقود portemonnaie, change purse; حقيبة اليد *ḥ. al-yad* ladies' purse, handbag

حقد *ḥaqida a*, *ḥaqada i* (*ḥaqd*, *ḥiqd*) to harbor feelings of hatred (على against) IV to incite to hatred or resentment, embitter, envenom (ه s.o.) V = I; VI to hate one another

حقد *ḥiqd* pl. احقاد *aḥqād*, حقود *ḥuqūd* hatred, malice, spite, resentment, rancor

حقيدة *ḥaqīda* pl. حقائد *ḥaqā'id*[2] hatred, malice, spite, resentment, rancor

حقود *ḥaqūd* full of hatred, spiteful, resentful, malicious, malevolent, rancorous

حاقد *ḥāqid* full of hatred, spiteful, resentful, malicious, malevolent, rancorous; pl. حقدة *ḥaqada* malevolent people

حقر *ḥaqara i* (*ḥaqr*) to despise, scorn, disdain (ه s.o., ه s.th.); to look down (ه, ه on), have a low opinion (ه, ه of); — *ḥaqura u* to be low, base, contemptible, despicable; to be despised, degraded, humiliated **II** to disparage, decry, depreciate (ه s.o.), detract, derogate (ه from s.o.); to degrade, debase, humble, humiliate; to regard with contempt, despise, scorn, disdain (ه s.o., ه s.th.) **VIII** to despise, scorn, disdain (ه s.o., ه s.th.), look down (ه, ه on) **X** to regard as contemptible or despicable, disdain, despise (ه s.o., ه s.th.), look down (ه, ه on)

حقير *ḥaqīr* pl. حقراء *ḥuqarā'*[2] low, base, mean, vulgar, vile; little, small, paltry, inconsiderable, poor, wretched, miserable; despised; despicable, contemptible

احقر *aḥqar*[2] lower, baser, more contemptible

حقارة *ḥaqāra* lowness, vulgarity, baseness, vileness, meanness; smallness, paltriness, insignificance, poorness, wretchedness, miserableness; despicability, contemptibleness; ignominy, infamy

تحقير *taḥqīr* contempt, disdain, scorn; degradation, humiliation, abasement

احتقار *iḥtiqār* contempt, disdain, scorn | نظر اليه بعين الاحتقار (*bi-'aini l-iḥt.*) to regard s.o. with contempt, look down one's nose at s.o.

محتقر *muḥtaqar* despised; contemptible, despicable

حقل *ḥaql* pl. حقول *ḥuqūl* field (also fig. = domain); column | حقول البترول oil fields; حقل الزيت *ḥ. az-zait*, حقل النفط *ḥ. an-nafṭ* oil field; oil area; حقول التجارب experimental fields; حقل كهربائى (*kahrabā'ī*) electric field

حقلى *ḥaqlī* field- (in compounds)

محاقلة *muḥāqala* sale of grain while still in growth, dealing in grain futures (*Isl. Law*)

حقن *ḥaqana* i u (*ḥaqn*) to hold back, withhold, keep back, detain, retain (ه s.th.); to suppress, repress, restrain (ه s.th.); to keep to o.s. (السر *as-sirra* the secret); to spare (دمه *damahū* s.o.'s blood or life); to give (ه s.o.) an injection (*med.*) **VIII** to become congested (esp. blood); to suffer from strangury; to take an enema, a clyster; to be injected | احتقن وجهه (*wajhuhū*) his face was flushed, his face turned red

حقن *ḥaqn* retention, withholding; sparing; injecting, injection (*med.*) | حقنا لدمائهم *ḥaqnan li-dimā'ihim* in order to spare their blood; حقن فى الوريد intravenous injection (*med.*)

حقنة *ḥuqna* pl. حقن *ḥuqan* injection (*med.*); hypodermic; clyster; enema

محقنة *miḥqana* pl. محاقن *maḥāqin*[2] syringe (*med.*)

احتقان *iḥtiqān* congestion | احتقان الدم *iḥt. ad-dam* vascular congestion

محتقن *muḥtaqan* reddened by blood congestion, flushed, red (face)

حقو *ḥaqw* pl. حقاء *ḥiqā'*, احقاء *aḥqā'* loin, groin | شدد حقويه *šaddada ḥaqwaihi* to gird one's loins

حك[1] *ḥakka* u (*ḥakk*) to rub, chafe; to scrape; to scratch; to rub off, scrape off, scratch off, abrade (ه s.th.) | حك فى صدره (*ṣadrihī*) it impressed him, affected him, touched s.th. inside him **IV** to itch **V** to rub o.s., scrape, chafe (ب against); to pick a quarrel (ب with s.o.) **VI** to rub or scrape against each other **VIII** to rub o.s., scrape, chafe (ب against); to be in contact, in touch (ب with) | احتك فى صدره (*ṣadrihī*) it impressed him, affected him, touched s.th. inside him

حك *ḥakk* rubbing, chafing; friction; scratching

حكة *ḥikka* itching; scabies, itch (*med.*)

حكاك *ḥakkāk* lapidary

محك *miḥakk* touchstone; test | ثبت على محك النظر *ṯabata 'alā m. in-naẓar* to stand a critical test

محكة *miḥakka* currycomb

تحاك *taḥākk* (reciprocal) friction

احتكاك *iḥtikāk* pl. *-āt* (reciprocal) friction; close touch or contact; friction (fig., = dissension, controversy) | من غير احتكاك *min ġairi ḥt.* frictionless

محكك *muḥakkak* chafed, worn away

²حكة *ḥukka* (*tun.*, = *ḥuqqa*) pl. حكك *ḥukak* small box, case, pot or jar

حكر VIII to buy up, hoard and withhold, corner (ه a commodity); to monopolize (ه a commercial article); to have exclusive possession (ه of s.th.), hold a monopoly (ه over s.th.)

حكر *ḥikr, ḥukr* and اجرة الحكر *ujrat al-ḥ.* ground rent, quitrent

حكر *ḥakar, ḥukar* hoarded

حكرة *ḥukra* hoarding (of goods); monopoly

حاكورة *ḥākūra* small vegetable garden

احتكار *iḥtikār* pl. *-āt* cornering, buying up; monopoly; preferential position; supremacy, hegemony | احتكار تجارة البن *iḥt. t. al-bunn* coffee-trade monopoly; احتكار السكر *iḥt. as-sukkar* sugar monopoly

احتكارى *iḥtikārī* rapacious, grasping, greedy

حكم *ḥakama u* (*ḥukm*) to pass judgment, express an opinion (على, فى on s.th.), judge (على s.th., ب by, from); to decide, give a decision, pass a verdict, pass sentence (على on); to sentence (على s.o., ب to a penalty; said of the judge), impose, inflict (ب a penalty) on s.o. (على); to pronounce a verdict or judgment, deliver judgment, rule (ل in s.o.'s favor); to adjudicate, adjudge, award (ب ل to s.o. s.th.); to take (ب s.th.) as a standard or norm; to have judicial power, have jurisdiction, have authority (على and ه over), govern, rule, dominate, control (على or ه s.o.); to order, command (ب s.th.); to bridle, check, curb (ه, ه s.th., s.o.) | حكم عليه بالاعدام (*ḥukima, i'dām*) he was sentenced to death; حكم بادانته (*bi-idānatihī*) to convict s.o., find s.o. guilty (*jur.*); حكم ببراءته (*bi-barā'atihī*) to acquit s.o. (*jur.*) II to appoint (ه s.o.) as ruler; to choose (ه s.o.) as arbitrator, make (ه s.o.) the judge (فى over or in s.th., بين between) III to prosecute (ه s.o.); to arraign, bring to trial, hale into court (ه s.o.); to interrogate, hear (ه s.o.) IV to make (ه s.th.) firm, strong, sturdy, solid; to fortify (ه s.th.); to strengthen, consolidate (ه s.th.); to do well, do expertly, master (ه field, work), be proficient (ه in) | احكم امره (*amrahū*) to do s.th. thoroughly, carefully, properly; احكم قفل الباب (*qafla l-bāb*) to lock the door firmly; احكم لغة (*luġatan*) to master a language V to have one's own way (فى in), proceed (فى with) at random, at will, handle (فى s.th.) arbitrarily; to pass arbitrary judgment (فى on); to make o.s. the judge (على of), pass judgment (على on); to decide (ب on); to rule, reign, hold sway (فى over); to dominate, control (فى s.th.), be in control, be in command (فى of) VI to bring one another before the judge (الى الحاكم); to appeal (الى to) for a legal decision; to be interrogated, be heard (in court) VIII to have one's own way (فى in), proceed (فى with, in s.th.) at will, at random, handle (فى s.th.) arbitrarily, judge arbitrarily; to rule, reign, hold sway (على, فى over); to be in control, be in possession (على of); to appeal (الى to) for a legal decision, seek a decision (الى from), have s.o. (الى) decide X to be strong, sturdy, solid, firm; to become stronger, be strengthened, be consolidated; to take root, be or become deep-rooted, deep-seated, ingrained, inveterate, marked, pronounced (feeling, trait)

حكم *ḥukm* pl. احكام *aḥkām* judgment, valuation, opinion; decision; (legal) judgment, verdict, sentence; condemnation, conviction; administration of justice; jurisdiction; legal consequence of the facts of a case (*Isl. Law*); regulation, rule, provision, order, ordinance, decree; judiciousness, wisdom; judgeship; command, authority, control, dominion, power; government, regime; pl. احكام statutes, by-laws, regulations, rules, provisions, stipulations, principles, precepts; حكما *ḥukman* virtually; legally | بحكم *bi-ḥukmi* by virtue of, on the strength of, pursuant to; by force of; فى حكم as good as, all but, e.g., هو فى حكم العدم (*fī ḥukmi l-ʿadam*) it is as good as nothing, it is practically nonexistent; اصبح فى حكم المقرر *aṣbaḥa fī ḥukmi l-muqarrar* it is all but decided; كان فى حكم الشىء also: to be subject to s.th.; نزل على حكمه to give in, yield to s.o.; حكم البراءة *ḥ. al-barāʾa* acquittal; حكم حضورى (*ḥuḍūrī*) judgment delivered in the presence of the litigant parties, after oral proceedings (*jur.*); الحكم بالاعدام (*iʿdām*) death sentence; حكم غيابى (*ğiyābī*) judgment by default (*jur.*); الحكم الذاتى (*ḏātī*) self-determination, autonomy (*pol.*); الحكم الجمهورى (*jumhūrī*) the republican form of government, the republican regime; الحكم المطلق (*muṭlaq*) the absolute, i.e., authoritarian, regime; الحكم النيابى (*niyābī*) the parliamentary regime, parliamentarianism; لجنة الحكم *lajnat al-ḥ.* board of examiners, review board; الاحكام العرفية (*ʿurfīya*) martial law; احكام انتقالية (*intiqālīya*) provisional regulations (*jur.*); احكام ختامية (*ḵitāmīya*) final regulations (*jur.*); احكام خاصة (*ḵāṣṣa*) special regulations; لكل سن حكمه (*sinn*) every age has its own set of rules, must be judged by its own standards; للضرورة احكام (*li-ḍ-ḍarūra*) necessity has its (own) rules, (approx.: necessity knows no law)

حكمى *ḥukmī* legal

حكمدار (*eg.*; pronounced *ḥikimdār*) commandant; chief of police

حكمدارية (*eg.*; pronounced *ḥikimdārīya*) commandant's office

حكم *ḥakam* pl. حكام *ḥukkām* arbitrator, arbiter; umpire, referee

حكمة *ḥikma* pl. حكم *ḥikam* wisdom; sagacity; philosophy; maxim; rationale, underlying reason | لحكمة (with foll. genit.) on account of, because of

حكمى *ḥikmī* gnomic, aphoristic, expressing maxims | الشعر الحكمى (*šiʿr*) gnomic poetry

حكمة *ḥakama* pl. *-āt* bit (of a horse's bridle)

حكيم *ḥakīm* pl. حكماء *ḥukamāʾ*[2] wise, judicious; wise man, sage; philosopher; physician, doctor

حكيمباشى *ḥakīmbāšī* senior physician, chief surgeon

حكومة *ḥukūma* pl. *-āt* government

حكومى *ḥukūmī* of government, governmental; official; state-owned, state-controlled, of the state, state- (in compounds)

احكم *aḥkam*[2] wiser

محكمة *maḥkama* pl. محاكم *maḥākim*[2] court, tribunal | محكمة الاستئناف *m. al-istiʾnāf* court of appeal, appellate court; محكمة اهلية (*ahlīya*) indigenous court (*Eg.*; jurisdiction limited to Egyptian nationals); محكمة ابتدائية (*ibtidāʾīya*) court of first instance; محكمة ابتدائية كلية (*kullīya*) civil court with jurisdiction in cases of major importance, at the same time appellate instance of محاكم جزئية (*Eg.*);

محكمة جزئية (*juz'īya*) in Eg., lowest court of both محاكم اهلية (approx.: district courts) and of محاكم شرعية canonical courts (with jurisdiction in marital and family matters); summary court; محكمة الجنايات *m. al-jināyāt* criminal court; محاكم الاحوال الشخصية (*šakṣīya*) courts dealing with vital statistics; محكمة مختلطة (*muk-taliṭa*) mixed court (with jurisdiction over residents of foreign nationality); محكمة شرعية (*šar'īya*) canonical court (administering justice on the basis of the Sharia), court dealing with family matters of Muslims; محكمة مركزية (*mar-kazīya*) county court, dealing with minor offenses, esp. misdemeanors (*Eg.*); محكمة القضاء الادارى *m. al-qaḍā' al-idārī* administrative court; محكمة النقض والابرام *m. an-naqḍ wa-l-ibrām* Court of Cassation, the highest court of appeal in Egypt; محكمة التمييز Court of Cassation (*Syr., Leb.* = محكمة النقض والابرام in Eg.); ساحات المحاكم tribunals

تحكيم *taḥkīm* appointment of an arbitrator; arbitration; arbitral decision, award; pl. تحكيمات fortifications | تحكيم الحال starting from the present state of a court's findings (*Isl. Law*); هيئة التحكيم *hai'at at-t.* board of arbitration; jury, committee of judges, committee of umpires (in sports), committee of referees (in mil. maneuvers); لجنة تحكيمية (*lajna*) do.

محاكمة *muḥākama* judicial proceeding; trial, hearing (in court); legal prosecution

احكام *iḥkām* perfection; accuracy, exactness, exactitude, precision; exact performance, precise execution | بالاحكام accurately, exactly, precisely; بالغ فى الاحكام of highest perfection

تحكم *taḥakkum* arbitrariness, arbitrary powers or action; despotism; domination, dominion, rule, sway, power; control (فى of, over)

تحكمى *taḥakkumī* arbitrary; despotic

استحكام *istiḥkām* intensification, increase, strengthening; consolidation, stabilization; fortification; pl. استحكامات fortifications

حاكم *ḥākim* ruling, governing; decisive; — (pl. *-ūn*, حكام *ḥukkām*) ruler, sovereign; governor; judge | حاكم بامره (*bi-amrihī*) autocratic; autocrat, dictator; حاكم عام (*'āmm*) governor general; حاكم المباراة *ḥ. al-mubārāh* umpire, referee (*athlet.*); حاكم الصلح *ḥ. aṣ-ṣulḥ* (*Syr.*) justice of the peace; حاكم الناحية *ḥ. an-nāḥiya* (*Tun.*) district magistrate

حاكمية *ḥākimīya* domination, dominion, rule, sovereignty; judgeship, judicature, jurisdiction (*ir.*)

محكوم عليه *maḥkūm 'alaihi* sentenced (ب to) | المحكوم عليهم بالاعدام (*i'dām*) those sentenced to death; محكوم عليه بالفشل (*fašal*) doomed to fail

محكم *muḥakkam* pl. *-ūn* arbitrator, arbiter; umpire, referee (فى in, over)

محكم *muḥkam* strengthened, reinforced; firm, solid, sturdy; tight, taut; perfect, masterly, masterful; well-aimed (blow, hit); accurate, precise, exact | محكم التدبير well-planned, well-contrived

مستحكم *mustaḥkam* reinforced, fortified; strengthened, consolidated, strong; inveterate, deep-seated, deep-rooted, ingrained (custom, trait, etc.); pl. مستحكمات defenses, fortifications

حكم see حكمدارية, حكمدار

حكى *ḥakā* i (حكاية *ḥikāya*) to tell, relate (ه s.th.), report, give an account (ه of); to speak, talk (*syr., leb.*); to imitate, copy (ه s.th.); to resemble (ه, ه s.o., s.th.) III to imitate, copy (ه s.th.), assimilate o.s. (ه to); to be similar (ه to), be like s.th. (ه), resemble (ه s.th.), be attuned, adjusted, adapted (ه to), be in harmony (ه with)

حكاية *ḥikāya* pl. *-āt* story, tale, narrative, account; (*gram.*) literal quotation (of the words of others)

محاكاة *muḥākāh* imitation; similarity, resemblance; harmony

حاك *ḥākin* narrator, storyteller; phonograph; ○ loudspeaker, radio

محكى *maḥkīy* imitated, imitation (adj.)

حكيمباشى see حكم

[1]حل *ḥalla u* (*ḥall*) to untie (ه a knot), unbind, unfasten, unravel, undo (ه s.th.); to solve (ه a problem, a puzzle); to decipher, decode (ه s.th.); to dissolve in water (ه s.th.; *chem.*); to resolve (ه s.th. into its components), analyze (ه s.th.); to melt (ه s.th.); to decompose, disintegrate (ه s.th.); to disband, break up, dissolve (ه an organization or party, parliament); to open, unpack (ه a package, and the like); to loosen, relax (ه s.th.); to release, set free, let go (ه s.th., ه s.o.); to clear, exonerate, exculpate (من ه s.o. from), absolve (ه s.o., من from his sins; *Chr.*); pass. *ḥulla* to be free; to be relaxed; — *i u* (حلول *ḥulūl*) to dismount, alight, stop, halt; to settle down, stay (ب at a place, also فى and ه; على with s.o., at s.o.'s house), come (for a visit, على to); to take up residence (ه in a place or country); to descend, come down; to descend (على upon s.o.; wrath); to overcome, overwhelm (على s.o.; sleep); to befall (ب and على s.o.; punishment, suffering), occur, happen (ب to s.o.); to become incarnate (فى in s.o.; God); to set in, arrive, begin (time, season); — *i* to pass into solution, dissolve; to fade (color); — *i* (*ḥill*) to be allowed, permitted, permissible, lawful; to be due, payable (debt) | حل فى منصب (*manṣib*) to take over or hold an office; حل محله (*maḥallahū*) to be in the right place; حل محل الشىء ,حل محل فلان (*maḥalla*) to take the place of s.o. or s.th., replace, supersede s.o. or s.th., substitute for s.o. or s.th.; حلت فى قلبه محلا (*qalbihī*) she held a place in his heart; حل محل التقدير لديه (*maḥalla t-taqdīri ladaihi*) to enjoy s.o.'s high esteem; حل من نفوس القراء محل الاستحسان (*min nufūsi l-qurrā'i maḥalla l-istiḥsān*) to appeal to the readers, meet with the readers' approval **II** to dissolve, resolve (into its component parts), break up, decompose, analyze (ه s.th.); to make a chemical analysis (ه of s.th.); to be dissolvent, act as a solvent (ه on; *med.*); to discharge, absolve, clear, exonerate, exculpate (ه s.o.); (تحلة *taḥilla*) to expiate an oath; to make permissible or lawful, legitimate, sanction, justify, warrant (ه s.th.); to declare permissible or lawful, allow, permit (ه s.th.) **IV** to discharge, release, absolve, disengage (ه من s.o. from); to declare (ه s.th.) lawful, legally permissible, permit, allow (ه s.th.); to cause to set in or occur, bring about, produce, cause to take root, establish, stabilize (ه s.th.); to cause (ه s.th.) to take or occupy the place (ه of), shift, move, translocate (ه ه s.th., e.g., a tribe, to a place); to settle (ه بين s.th. among) | احله محله (*maḥallahū*) to cause s.o. or s.th. to take the place of s.o. or s.th. else, replace s.o. or s.th. by, substitute s.o. or s.th. for, take s.o. or s.th. as substitute for; احل الشىء محل العناية (*maḥalla l-'ināya*) to pay attention to s.th., make s.th. one's concern **V** to dissolve, melt, disintegrate; to disengage o.s., disassociate o.s., extricate o.s., free o.s. (من from) **VII** to be untied (knot); to be solved, be unraveled (problem); to be dissolved, be broken up, be disbanded (also, of an organization, a party, etc.); to dissolve, melt; to become slack, limp, weak, loose, relaxed; to disintegrate; to melt away **VIII** to settle down (ه at a place); to occupy (*mil.*, ه a territory); to assume, take over, occupy, hold, have (ه a place,

a rank, an office) | احتل المكان الاول (*al-makāna l-awwala*) to occupy the foremost place; احتل اعماله (*aʿmālahū*) to take over s.o.'s functions **X** to regard (ه s.th.) as permissible or lawful, think that one may do s.th. (ه); to regard as fair game, as easy prey, seize unlawfully, misappropriate, usurp (ه s.th.)

حل *ḥall* pl. حلول *ḥulūl* untying, unfastening, undoing (of a knot); solution (of a problem, of a puzzle, etc.); unriddling, unraveling, explanation; solution (*chem.*); dissolution, disbandment, breaking up (of an organization, etc.), abolition, cancellation, annulment; release, freeing, liberation; decontrol, release, unblocking (e.g., of a blocked sum); discharge, clearing, exoneration, exculpation; absolution (*Chr.*) | قابل للحل soluble, solvable; ○ الحل الطيفى (*ṭaifī*) spectral analysis; اهل الحل والعقد *ahl al-ḥ. wa-l-ʿaqd* or اهل الحل والربط (*rabṭ*) influential people, those in power; فى حله وترحاله (*tarḥālihī*) in all his doings, in everything he did

حل *ḥill*: كان فى حل من (عن) (*ḥillin*) he was free to ..., he was at liberty to ...; he had free disposal of ...; انت فى حل من you're free to ..., you may readily ...

حلة *ḥalla* pl. حلل *ḥilal* low copper vessel; cooking pot (*eg.*)

حلة *ḥilla* way station, stopping place, stop, stopover; encampment; absolution (*Chr.*); dispensation (*Chr.*)

حلة *ḥulla* pl. حلل *ḥulal* clothing, dress, garb; vestments (ecclesiastic; *Chr.*); (complete) suit of clothes; (Western) suit | حلة رسمية (*rasmīya*) uniform; حلة السهرة *ḥ. as-sahra* formal dress

حلال *ḥalāl* that which is allowed, permitted or permissible; allowed, permitted, permissible, allowable, admissible, lawful, legal, licit, legitimate; lawful possession | ابن حلال *ibn ḥ.* legitimate son; respectable man, decent fellow

حلول *ḥulūl* stopping, putting up, staying; descending, coming on, befalling, overtaking; incarnation; setting in, advent, arrival (of a time, of a deadline), beginning, dawn; substitution (for s.o.)

حليل *ḥalīl* pl. احلاء *aḥillāʾ*[2] husband

حليلة *ḥalīla* pl. حلائل *ḥalāʾil*[2] wife

احليل *iḥlīl* outer opening of the urethra; urethra (*anat.*)

محل *maḥall* pl. *-āt*, محال *maḥāll*[2] place, location, spot, site, locale, locality, center; (place of) residence; business; business house, firm, commercial house; store, shop; object, cause (e.g., of dispute, admiration, etc.); gear (automobile) | حل محله and احله محله see حل **I** and **IV**; فى محله (*maḥallahū*) in his (its) place; فى محله in his (its) place, in his (its) stead, instead of him; كان فى محله to be in the right place; to be appropriate, expedient, advisable; to be justified, warranted; فى غير محله improper, misplaced, unsuitable, ill-suited; out of place; inappropriate, inexpedient, inopportune; صادف محله *ṣādafa maḥallahū* to be convenient, be most opportune; لا محل ل (*maḥalla*) there is no room for ...; it is out of place, quite déplacé; محل العمل *m. al-ʿamal* place of employment; محل الاقامة *m. al-iqāma* (place of) residence, address; محل تجارى (*tijārī*) business house, commercial house; المحلات العمومية والتجارية (*ʿumūmīya, tijārīya*) public utilities and commercial houses; اسم المحل *ism al-m.* firm; محل رهونات *m. ruhūnāt* pawnshop; محلات السياحة *m. as-siyāḥa* travel agencies; محل مرطبات *m. muraṭṭibāt* refreshment parlor; محل اللهو *m. al-lahw* and محل الملاهى *m. al-malāhī* (pl. محال) amusement center; محل نزاع *m. nizāʿ* object of controversy, controversial matter; لا ارى محلا لعجب *lā arā m. li-'ajabin* I don't see any reason for amazement, there is nothing to be astonished about; محل نظر *m. naẓar* s.th. deserving attention, a striking, remarkable thing

محلى *maḥallī* local; native, indigenous; parochial; pl. محليات local news, local page (of a newspaper)

محل *maḥill* due date; date of delivery

محلة *maḥalla* pl. *-āt* way station, stopping place, stop, stopover, encampment; camp; section, part, quarter (of a city) | المحلة الكبرى (*kubrā*) Mahalla el Kubra (city in N Egypt)

تحليل *taḥlīl* dissolution, resolution, breaking up, decomposition, specification, detailing, analyzation; (pl. تحاليل *taḥālīl*[2]) analysis (*chem.*); absolution (*Chr.*) | بالتحليل in detail; معمل تحليل *ma'mal t.* laboratory for chemical analyses; تحليل كهربائى (*kahrabā'ī*) electrolysis; التحليل النفسى (النفسانى) (*nafsī*) psychoanalysis

تحليلى *taḥlīlī* analytic(al)

تحلل *taḥallul* dissolution, breakup; separation, disengagement, disassociation

انحلال *inḥilāl* dissolution, breakup, decomposition; disintegration; decay, putrefaction; slackening, exhaustion, prostration, weakness, impotence

احتلال *iḥtilāl* occupation (*mil.*) | جيوش الاحتلال occupation forces

احتلالى *iḥtilālī* occupying, occupation (used attributively); advocate of foreign occupation

محلول *maḥlūl* solved; dissolved, resolved, broken up; loose; untied, unfastened, unfettered, free, at large; weakened, prostrate, exhausted, languid; solution (liquid; *chem.*) | محلول الشعر *m. aš-ša'r* with loose, disheveled hair

محلل *muḥallil* analyzer

منحل *munḥall* solved; dissolved, resolved, broken up; disbanded; languid, prostrate, weak; permitted, allowed

جيوش محتلة *juyūš muḥtalla* occupation forces

حيلولة[2] see حول

[1]حلب *ḥalaba i u* (*ḥalb*) to milk (ه an animal) | حلب الدهر اشطره *ḥalaba d-dahra ašṭurahū* he has seen good and bad days V to run, drip, trickle, ooze, seep, leak; to water, drool (mouth, with appetite) | تتحلب له الافواه (*afwāh*) making the mouth water, appetizing; تحلب اللعاب فى فمى (*al-lu'ābu fī famī*) my mouth was watering VIII to milk (ه an animal) X do.; to squeeze juice (ه from)

حلب *ḥalb* milking

حلب *ḥalab* milk

حلبة *ḥalba* pl. *ḥalabāt* race track; arena; dance floor; race horses | حلبة الرقص *ḥ. ar-raqṣ* dance floor; انه ليس من تلك الحلبة he is not made for that, he doesn't belong there, it is not in his line; فارس حلبة ب a master of, excelling or outstanding in

حلبة *ḥulba* fenugreek (Trigonella foenum-graecum; *bot.*); tonic, prepared of yellowish grains, for women in childbed (*eg., syr.*)

حليب *ḥalīb* milk | لبن حليب *laban ḥ.* cow's milk (*eg.*)

حلوب *ḥalūb* lactiferous | بقرة حلوب (*baqara*) milk cow; الماشية الحلوب (*māšiya*) dairy cattle

حلاب *ḥallāb* milker

حلابة *ḥallāba* milkmaid, dairymaid; dairywoman; milk cow

محلب *maḥlab* mahaleb (Prunus mahaleb; *bot.*)

حالب *ḥālib* ureter

مستحلب *mustaḥlab* emulsion | مستحلب اللوز *m. al-lauz* almond milk

حلب[2] *ḥalab*[2] Aleppo

حلتيت *ḥiltīt, ḥaltīt* asafetida (Ferula assafoetida; *bot.*)

حلج *ḥalaja i u* (*ḥalj*, حليج *ḥalīj*) to gin (ه cotton)

حلج *ḥalj* ginning (of cotton)

حليج *ḥalīj* ginning (of cotton); ginned (cotton)

حلاجة *ḥilāja* cotton ginner's work or trade

حلاج *ḥallāj* cotton ginner

محلج *miḥlaj*, محلجة *miḥlaja* pl. محالج *maḥālij*[2] cotton gin

محلج *maḥlaj* pl. محالج *maḥālij*[2] cotton ginnery

حلحل *ḥalḥala* to remove, drive away, shove away II *taḥalḥala* to stir from one's place; to move, stir, budge

حلزون *ḥalazūn* snail; spiral

حلزونة *ḥalazūna* (n. un.) snail; spiral

حلزونى *ḥalazūnī* spiral, helical, volute, winding

حلس *ḥalisa a* to remain, stay permanently (ب at a place), stick (ب to a place)

حلس *ḥils* pl. احلاس *aḥlās* (with foll. genit.) one addicted or given to s.th., one adhering to s.th. | احلاس اللهو *a. al-lahw* people given to pleasure and amusement, bons vivants, playboys

حلس *ḥils* pl. احلاس *aḥlās*, حلوس *ḥulūs* saddle blanket

احلس *aḥlas*[2], f. حلساء *ḥalsā'*[2] bay, chestnut (horse)

حلف *ḥalafa i* (*ḥalf, ḥilf*) to swear (بالله by God) | حلف يمينا (*yamīnan*) to take an oath II to make (ه s.o.) swear; to put to oath, swear in (ه s.o.); to adjure, entreat earnestly (ه s.o.) III to enter into a confederation, into an alliance (ه with s.o.), become an ally (ه of s.o.) VI to commit one another by oath (على to do s.th.), join in alliance; to ally, make an alliance (مع with) X to make (ه s.o.) swear, exact an oath (ه from s.o.); to adjure, entreat earnestly (ه s.o.)

حلف *ḥalf, ḥilf* swearing, oath | حلف اليمين taking the oath

حلف *ḥilf* sworn alliance, confederacy, league; federation; (pl. احلاف *aḥlāf*) ally | حلف عسكرى (*'askarī*) military alliance; الحلف الاطلنطى (*aṭlanṭī*) the Atlantic Pact

حليف *ḥalīf* pl. حلفاء *ḥulafā'*[2] confederate; ally; allied | الحلفاء the Allies (*pol.*)

حليفة *ḥalīfa* pl. *-āt* f. of حليف

حلوف *ḥallūf* pl. حلاليف *ḥalālīf*[2] (*maġr., eg.*) wild boar; pig, swine

حلفاء *ḥalfā'* und حلفة *ḥulfa* (*bot.*) alfa, esparto

تحليف *taḥlīf* swearing in | لجنة التحليف *lajnat at-t.* the jury (in court)

محالفة *muḥālafa* alliance

تحالف *taḥāluf* state of alliance; alliance, treaty of alliance

محلف *muḥallaf* sworn, bound by oath; (pl. *-ūn*) juror (in court)

متحالف *mutaḥālif* interallied, allied

حلق *ḥalaqa i* (*ḥalq*) to shave (ه the head, the face); to shave off (ه the beard) II to circle in the air, hover; to fly, soar (bird; airplane; على and فوق over or above s.th.); to round, make round, circular or ring-shaped (ه s.th.); to ring, surround, encircle (على s.o., s.th.); to clothe V to form a circle, sit in a circle; to gather in a circle (على around s.o.)

حلق *ḥalq* shaving, shave; (pl. حلوق *ḥulūq*, احلاق *aḥlāq*) throat, gullet, pharynx

حلق *ḥalqī* guttural, pharyngeal

حلق *ḥalaq* rings, earrings

حلقة *ḥalqa*, *ḥalaqa* pl. حلق *ḥalaq*, حلقات *ḥalaqāt* ring (also earring, etc.); link (of a chain); circle (also of people); group of students studying under a professor, hence: lecture, course (e.g., at Al Azhar University); part of a sequence or series; ringlet; disk; decade; market | حلقة النجاة *ḥ. an-najāh* life buoy, life preserver; حلقة الاتصال *ḥ. al-ittiṣāl* and حلقة الوصل *ḥ. al-waṣl* connecting link (بين between; fig.); الحلقة المفقودة the missing link, the intermediate form; فى الحلقة السادسة من عمره (*'umrihī*) in the sixth decade of his life, in his fifties; حلقة الاسماك fish market; حلقة القطن *ḥ. al-quṭn* cotton market

حلقى *ḥalaqī* annular, ring-shaped, circular

حلاق *ḥallāq* pl. *-ūn* barber | حلاق صحى (*ṣiḥḥī*), حلاق الصحة *ḥ. aṣ-ṣiḥḥa* barber-surgeon

حليق *ḥalīq* shaved, shaven, shorn

حلاقة *ḥilāqa* shaving, shave; barber's trade | صابون الحلاقة *ṣābūn al-ḥ.* shaving soap; صالون الحلاقة barbershop; قاعة الحلاقة *qā'at al-ḥ.* do.; ○ ماكينة الحلاقة and ○ آلة الحلاقة safety razor

محلق *miḥlaq* pl. محالق *maḥāliq*² straight razor

تحليق *taḥlīq* flying, flight (of an aircraft; على and فوق over a country); take-off (of an airplane)

من حالق *min ḥāliq* from above

حلقوم *ḥulqūm* pl. حلاقيم *ḥalāqīm*² throat, gullet | راحة الحلقوم *rāḥat al-ḥ.* a kind of sweet made of cornstarch, sugar, mastic and pistachios (*eg.*)

حلك *ḥalika a* (*ḥalak*) to be pitch-black, deep-black XII احلولك *iḥlaulaka* do.

حلك *ḥalak* intense blackness

حلكة *ḥulka* intense blackness

حلك *ḥalik* pitch-black, deep-black; gloomy, murky

حلوكة *ḥulūka* gloominess, darkness; blackness

حالك *ḥālik* pitch-black, deep-black; gloomy, murky

حلم *ḥalama u* to dream (ب or عن of; فى ان of being, becoming, doing, etc., in the future); to muse, reflect, meditate (ب on s.th.); to attain puberty; — *ḥaluma u* to be gentle, mild-tempered VIII to attain puberty

حلم *ḥulm* pl. احلام *aḥlām* dream; pl. irreality, utopia

حلمى *ḥulmī* dream- (in compounds), of or pertaining to dreams

حلم *ḥulum* sexual maturity, puberty | بلغ الحلم to attain puberty

حلم *ḥilm* pl. حلوم *ḥulūm*, احلام *aḥlām* gentleness, clemency, mildness; forbearance, indulgence; patience; insight, discernment, understanding, intelligence, reason | صغار الاحلام simple-minded people, simple souls

حلم *ḥalam* (coll.; n. un. ة) tick; mite; nipple, teat, mammilla (of the female breast)

حلمى *ḥalamī* parasitic; mammillary, nipple-shaped

حليم *ḥalīm* pl. حلماء *ḥulamā'*² mild, mild-tempered, gentle; patient

حلوم *ḥalūm*, حالوم *ḥālūm* a kind of Egyptian cheese

حالم *ḥālim* pl. -*ūn* dreamer

محتلم *muḥtalim* sexually mature, pubescent, marriageable

حلو (and حلى) *ḥaluwa u*, *ḥaliya a*, حلا *ḥalā u* (حلاوة *ḥalāwa*, حلوان *ḥulwān*) to be sweet; to be pleasant, agreeable (ل to s.o.) | حلا له الشىء he enjoyed the thing; حلا له ان it pleased him that ..., he was delighted that ...; حسبما يحلو له (*ḥasabamā*) at his discretion, as he pleases; — حلى *ḥalā i* to adorn, grace; — حلى *ḥaliya a* to be adorned (ب with) II to sweeten (ه s.th., e.g., a beverage with sugar); to adorn, bedeck, embellish, attire, furnish, provide (ه, ه s.o., s.th., ب with) V to adorn o.s., be adorned, decked out, embellished, graced, endowed, furnished, provided (ب with) X to find sweet or pleasant, like (ه s.th.), be delighted (ه by)

حلا *ḥalan* sweetness, pleasantness

حلو *ḥulw* sweet; pleasant, nice, charming, delightful, pretty | حلو الحديث a gifted raconteur, amusing, entertaining; الغدة الحلوة (*ġudda*) pancreas (*anat.*)

حلى *ḥaly* pl. حلى *ḥulīy* piece of jewelry, trinket

حلية *ḥilya* pl. حلى *ḥilan*, *ḥulan* decoration, embellishment, finery; ornament

حلوى *ḥalwā* pl. حلاوى *ḥalāwā* candy, confection, confectionery, sweetmeats

حلواء *ḥalwā'*[2] candy, confection, confectionery, sweetmeats

حلويات *ḥalwayāt* (and *eg.* *ḥalawīyāt*) sweets (in general); sweet pastry; candies, confectionery, sweetmeats

حلاوة *ḥalāwa* sweetness; candies, confectionery, sweetmeats; grace, gracefulness, charm, refinement, wittiness, wit; present of money; ransom | حلاوة حمصية (*ḥummuṣīya*) a sweet made of roasted chick-peas; حلاوة طحينية (*ṭaḥinīya*) a sweet made of sesame-seed meal; حلاوة لوزية (*lauzīya*) a sweet made of almonds

حلوان *ḥulwān* present of money, gratuity, tip

حلوانى *ḥalwānī* and حلوائى *ḥalwā'ī* confectioner, candy dealer; pastry cook, fancy baker

ما احيلى *mā uḥailā* oh, how sweet is ..., ما احيلاه oh, how sweet he is!

تحلية *taḥliya* decoration, embellishment, ornamentation

محلى *muḥallan* sweetened; decorated, embellished, adorned, ornamented (ب with)

[1]حم *ḥam* pl. احماء *aḥmā'* father-in-law; pl. relatives of the wife by marriage, in-laws of the wife

حماة *ḥamāh* pl. حموات *ḥamawāt* mother-in-law; see also [1]حمى and [2]حمى

[2]حمة *ḥuma* see [2]حمو

[3]حم *ḥamma u* (*ḥamm*) to heat, make hot (ه s.th.); pass. *ḥumma* to be feverish, have a fever | حم له ذلك (*ḥumma*) that was decreed to him, that is his lot, his destiny II to heat, make hot (ه s.th.); to bathe, wash (ه or ه s.o. or s.th.) IV to heat, make hot (ه s.th.) X to bathe, take a bath

حمة *ḥamma* hot spring

حمة *ḥumma* blackness, swarthiness, dark coloration; fever

حمم *ḥumam* (n. un. ة) charcoal; anything charred or carbonized; ashes, cinder; lava

حمى *ḥummā* f., pl. حميات *ḥummayāt* fever, fever heat | الحمى التيفودية and

الحمى التيفية (*tifiya*) typhoid fever, typhus fever; حمى الدق *ḥ. d-diqq* hectic fever; حمى الربع *ḥ. r-ribʿ* quartan fever; الحمى الراجعة relapsing fever; الحمى الصفراء or الحمى الصفراوية (*ṣafrāʾ*, *ṣafrāwīya*) yellow fever; حمى الغب *ḥ. l-ġibb* tertian fever; الحمى الفحمية (*faḥmīya*) anthrax; الحمى القرمزية (*qirmizīya*) scarlet fever; حمى القش *ḥ. l-qašš* hayfever; الحمى القلاعية (*qulāʿīya*) foot and-mouth disease; الحمى المخية الشوكية (*mukkīya, šaukīya*) cerebrospinal meningitis; الحمى المتموجة (*mutamawwija*) undulant fever, Malta fever, brucellosis; الحمى النفاسية (*nifāsīya*) puerperal fever, childbed fever; O الحمى النمشية (*namašiya*) spotted fever

حمى **ḥummī** feverish, febrile, fever- (in compounds)

حمام **ḥamām** (coll.; n. un. ة) pl. *-āt*, حمائم *ḥamāʾim*[2] dove, pigeon | حمام الزاجل carrier pigeon; ساق الحمام bugloss, oxtongue (Anchusa officinalis; *bot.*)

حمام **ḥimām** (fate of) death

حمام **ḥammām** pl. *-āt* bath; swimming pool; spa, watering place | حمام شمس *ḥ. šams* sunbath; حمامات بحرية (*baḥrīya*) seaside resorts

حميم **ḥamīm** pl. احماء *aḥimmāʾ*[2] close friend; close, intimate; — hot water

احم **aḥamm**[2], f. حماء *ḥammāʾ*[2], pl. حم *ḥumm* black

محم **miḥamm** hot-water kettle, caldron, boiler

استحمام **istiḥmām** bathing, bath

محموم **maḥmūm** feverish, having a fever; frantic, hectic

[1]حمأ **ḥamaʾa** *a* to clean out, dredge (ه a well)

حمأ **ḥamaʾ**, حمأة **ḥamʾa** mud, mire, sludge

[2]حمى **ḥamiʾa** to be or become angry, furious, mad (على at s.o.)

حمحم **ḥamḥama** (حمحمة *ḥamḥama*) to neigh, whinny (horse)

حمحمة **ḥamḥama** neigh(ing), whinnying, whinnies

حمحم **ḥimḥim** oxtongue, bugloss (Anchusa officinalis; *bot.*)

حمد **ḥamida** *a* (*ḥamd*) to praise, commend, laud, extol (على ه s.o. for, ه s.th.) II to praise highly (ه s.o.)

حمد **ḥamd** commendation, praise, laudation | الحمد لله *al-ḥamdu lillāh* thank God! praise be to God! praised be the Lord!

حميد **ḥamīd** praiseworthy, laudable, commendable; benign, harmless (disease)

حمود **ḥamūd** praiseworthy, laudable, commendable, praised

احمد **aḥmad**[2] more laudable, more commendable

الشريعة الاحمدية *aš-šarīʿa al-aḥmadīya* Mohammedan Law

محمدة **maḥmada** pl. محامد *maḥāmid*[2] commendable act; pl. محامد praises, encomiums

محمود **maḥmūd** praised; commendable, laudable, praiseworthy

محمد **muḥammad** praised; commendable, laudable

محمدى **muḥammadī** pertaining or attributable to Mohammed

حمدل **ḥamdala** to pronounce the formula الحمد لله "Praise be to God!"

حمدلة **ḥamdala** the formula الحمد لله (see above)

حمر II to redden, color or dye red (ه s.th.); to roast (ه s.th.); to fry (ه s.th.); to brown (ه flour in preparing a roux) IX to turn red, take on a reddish color, redden, blush

حمر *ḥumar* asphalt

حمرى *ḥumarī* asphaltic, asphalt, tar, tarry

حمرة *ḥumra* redness, red color(ation), red; rouge (*cosm.*); brick dust, brick rubble; erysipelas, St. Anthony's fire (*med.*)

حمار *ḥimār* pl. حمير *ḥamīr*, حمر *ḥumur*, احمرة *aḥmira* donkey, ass | حمار الوحش *ḥ. al-waḥš* and حمار وحشى (*waḥšī*) wild ass, onager; سم الحمار *samm al-ḥ.* oleander (Nerium oleander; *bot.*)

حمارة *ḥimāra* pl. حمائر *ḥamā'ir*² she-ass, female donkey

حمور *ḥumūr* red, red color(ation), redness

حميرة *ḥumaira* redstart (*zool.*)

حمار *ḥammār* pl. ة donkey driver

احمر *aḥmar*², f. حمراء *ḥamrā'*², pl. حمر *ḥumr* red, red-colored, ruddy; rosy, pink | دون الاحمر, تحت الاحمر infrared; البحر الاحمر the Red Sea; الصليب الاحمر the Red Cross; الموت الاحمر (*maut*) violent death; الهوى الاحمر (*hawā*) sexual intercourse; الاحمران ("the two red ones", i.e.) wine and meat; الاسود والاحمر ("the black and the red", i.e.) all mankind; احمر الشفاه lipstick

حمراء *ḥamrā'*² smut, rust (disease affecting cereals); الحمراء Alhambra, the Citadel of Granada

يحمور *yaḥmūr* red; deer, roe, roebuck; wild ass; hemoglobin (*physiol.*)

احمرار *iḥmirār* reddening, blush(ing), redness, red coloration; erythema (*med.*)

محمر *muḥammar* roasted | بطاطس محمرة (*baṭāṭis*) fried potatoes

حمز *ḥamaza i* (*ḥamz*) to bite, or burn, the tongue (taste)

حمس *ḥamisa a* to work with zeal, be zealous, eager, ardent, be or become enthusiastic, get all worked up, get excited, be filled with fanatic enthusiasm V = I; to be overzealous or overenthusiastic (فى in s.th.); to advocate fervently (ل s.th.), throw o.s. wholeheartedly behind s.th. (ل)

حمس *ḥamis* and احمس *aḥmas*² unflinching, staunch, steadfast, ardent, eager, zealous, stout, hearty; fiery, enthusiastic, full of enthusiasm

حماس *ḥamās* and حماسة *ḥamāsa* enthusiasm, fire, ardor, fervor, zeal, fanaticism

حماسي *ḥamāsī* enthusiastic, ardent, fiery, zealous, fanatic; stirring, rousing, thrilling, electrifying

تحمس *taḥammus* unflinching zeal, enthusiasm (ل for), fanaticism

متحمس *mutaḥammis* enthusiastic, ardent, fiery, zealous, fanatic; an ardent follower, a fanatic adherent, a fanatic

حمش *ḥamaša u* to excite, irritate, infuriate, enrage (ه s.o.)

حمشة *ḥamša* catgut (*med.*)

حمص[1] II to roast; to fry, broil (ه s.th.)

حمص *ḥimmiṣ*, *ḥimmaṣ*; (colloq.) *ḥummuṣ* (coll.; n. un. ة) chick-pea

حمص[2] *ḥimṣ*² Homs (the ancient Emesa, city in central Syria)

حمض *ḥamuḍa u* (حموضة *ḥumūḍa*) to be or become sour II to make sour, sour, acidify, acidulate (ه s.th.); to develop (ه a photographic plate, a film; *phot.*); to cause (ه s.th.) to oxidize

حمض *ḥamḍ* pl. احماض *aḥmāḍ* acid (*chem.*) | حمض بولى (*baulī*) uric acid

شجر حمضى *šajar ḥamḍī* citrus trees

حمضية *ḥamḍiya* pl. -*āt* citrus fruit

حموضة *ḥumūḍa* sourness, acidity | مولد الحموضة *muwallid al-ḥ.* oxygen (*chem.*)

حماض *ḥummāḍ*, حميض *ḥummaiḍ* sorrel (*bot.*)

تحميض *taḥmīḍ* souring, acidification; development (*phot.*)

احماض *iḥmāḍ* jocular language, joking remark

حامض *ḥāmiḍ* sour, acid; acidulous; (pl. حوامض *ḥawāmiḍ*²) acid (*chem.*) | حامض الفحم *ḥ. al-faḥm* carbonic acid; حامض كبريتى (*kibrītī*) sulphuric acid

حمق *ḥamiqa a* and *ḥamuqa u* (*ḥumq*, حماقة *ḥamāqa*) to be stupid, silly, foolish, fatuous; to become angry or furious **II** and **IV** to regard (ه s.o.) as a fool, consider (ه s.o.) dumb, stupid, idiotic **VI** pretend to be stupid **VII** to become angry or furious **X** to consider (ه s.o.) dumb, stupid, idiotic

حمق *ḥumq* stupidity, silliness, foolishness, folly

حماقة *ḥamāqa* stupidity, silliness, foolishness, folly; anger, wrath

حماق *ḥumāq*, *ḥamāq* smallpox, variola (*med.*)

احمق *aḥmaq*², f. حمقاء *ḥamqā'*², pl. حمق *ḥum(u)q*, حمقى *ḥamqā*, حماقى *ḥamāqā* dumb, stupid, silly, foolish, fatuous; fool, simpleton, imbecile

حمقان *ḥamqān* dumb, stupid, silly, foolish; angry, furious

حمل *ḥamala i* (*ḥaml*) to carry, bear (ـه s.th.); to lift, pick up (ـه s.th. in order to carry it), load up and take along (ـه s.th.); to hold (ـه s.th., in one's hand); to carry on or with one, take or bring along (ـه s.th.); to transport, carry, convey (ـه s.th.); to bring, take (الى or ل ـه s.th. to s.o.); to take upon o.s. (عن instead of or for s.o., ـه a burden), carry, assume (ـه the burden, عن of s.o. else), relieve (ـه عن s.o. from s.th.), take (ـه a burden, a grievance, etc.) from s.o. (عن); to extend, show, evince, cherish, harbor (ـه a feeling, ل toward s.o.); to become or be pregnant (من by s.o.); to bear fruit (tree); to induce, cause, prompt, get (ه على s.o. to do s.th.), make s.o. (ه) do s.th. (على); to convert, bring around, win over (ه على رأيه s.o. to one's opinion), convince (ه على رأيه s.o. of one's opinion); to attack (على s.o.), also حمل حملة على (*ḥamlatan*) to launch or make an attack on; to know by heart (ـه a book); to relate, refer (ـه على s.th. to), bring (ـه s.th.) to bear (على upon s.th.), link, correlate, bring into relation (ـه s.th., على with); to trace, trace back (ـه على s.th. to); to ascribe, attribute, impute (ـه على s.th. to s.o.); to make (ـه a word) agree grammatically (على with another) | حمل فى نفسه to feel annoyed, be in a melancholy mood, feel blue; حمل على نفسه to pull o.s. together, brace o.s.; حمله على محمل (*maḥmali*) to take s.th. to mean ..., interpret or construe s.th. in the sense of ..., as if it were ...; حمله على غير محمله to misinterpret, misconstrue s.th.; حمله محمل الجد (*maḥmala l-jidd*) to take s.th. seriously, take s.th. at face value **II** to have or make (ه s.o.) carry or bear (ـه s.th.), load, burden, charge, task (ه ,ـه s.o. or s.th. ـه with), impose (ه ـه on s.o. s.th.) **V** to bear, assume, take upon o.s. (ـه s.th., e.g., النفقات *an-nafaqāt* the expenses, المسؤولية *al-mas'ūlīya* the responsibility); to bear up (ـه under), bear, stand, sustain, endure, tolerate, stomach (ـه s.th.); to undergo, suffer (ـه s.th.); to be able to stand (ه s.o.) or put up (ه with s.o.); to set out, get on one's way; to depart **VI** to maltreat, treat unjustly (على s.o.), be prejudiced, be biased, take sides (على against s.o.); to struggle to one's feet, rise with great effort | تحامل على نفسه (nafsihī) to brace o.s.; to pull o.s. together, take heart, pluck up courage VIII to carry, bring (ه s.th.); to carry away, take away, haul off, lug off (ه s.th.); to suffer, undergo, bear, stand, endure, sustain (ه s.th.); to allow, permit, suffer, tolerate, brook, stomach (ه s.th.), acquiesce (ه in), put up, bear (ه with s.th.); to hold (ه s.th.), have capacity (ه for); to imply that s.th. (ه) is possible, permissible, or conceivable; يحتمل *yaḥtamilu* and (pass.) *yuḥtamalu* (it is) bearable, tolerable; (it is) conceivable, possible, probable, likely

حمل *ḥaml* carrying, bearing; inducement, prompting, encouragement (of s.o., على to); delivery; transport, transportation, conveyance; portage, carrying charges; — (pl. احمال *aḥmāl*, حمال *ḥimāl*) foetus; pregnancy | عدم الحمل *'adam al-ḥ.* sterility (of a woman)

حمل *ḥiml*, *ḥaml* pl. احمال *aḥmāl* cargo, load, burden | حمل حى *ḥaml ḥayy* pay load, commercial load, live load; حمل ميت (*mayyit*) dead load; dead weight (*arch.*); حمل موازن (*muwāzin*) counterpoise, counterweight

حمل *ḥamal* pl. حملان *ḥumlān*, احمال *aḥmāl* lamb; (unconsecrated) Host (*Chr.-Copt.*); Aries, Ram (*astron.*)

حملة *ḥamla* pl. *ḥamalāt* attack (على on); offensive; campaign; military expedition; expeditionary force | حملة تأديبية (*ta'dībīya*) punitive expedition; حملة صحافية (*ṣiḥāfīya*) press campaign; حملة استكشافية (*istikšāfīya*) reconnaissance raid (*mil.*); حملة ميكانيكية motorized detachment (*mil.*); حملة انتخابية (*intikābīya*) election campaign

حملى *ḥamalī* pl. *-īya* ambulant water vendor

حميل *ḥamīl* foundling; guarantor, warrantor

حميلة على *ḥamīla 'alā* a burden to, completely dependent upon

حمول *ḥamūl* long-suffering; gentle, mild-tempered

حمال *ḥammāl* pl. *-ūn*, ة porter, carrier

حمالة *ḥimāla* work and trade of a porter or carrier

حمالة *ḥammāla* (carrier) beam, girder, support, base, post, pier, pillar; suspenders | حمالة للصدر (*ṣadr*) brassière

حمولة *ḥumūla* pl. *-āt* load capacity, load limit, capacity; tonnage (of a vessel); portage, freightage, transport charges; (pl. حمائل *ḥamā'il*²) family (*Ir.*)

محمل *maḥmal* see حمل *ḥamala*; also اخذ شيئا على محمل الجد (*m. il-jidd*) to take s.th. seriously

محمل *maḥmil* (colloq. *maḥmal*) pl. محامل *maḥāmil*² camel borne litter, mahmal, a richly decorated litter sent by Islamic rulers to Mecca as an emblem of their independence, at the time of the hadj

تحميل *taḥmīl* burdening; encumbrance; imposition; loading, shipping, shipment

تحميلة *taḥmīla* pl. تحاميل *taḥāmīl*² suppository (*med.*)

تحمل *taḥammul* taking over, assumption (of burdens); bearing, standing, sufferance, endurance; durability; strength, hardiness, sturdiness, solidity (of a material)

تحامل *taḥāmul* prejudice, bias, partiality; intolerance

احتمال *iḥtimāl* bearing, standing, suffering, sufferance, toleration; probability, likelihood, potentiality | صعب الاحتمال (*ṣa'b*) hard to bear, oppressive

حامل *ḥāmil* pl. حملة *ḥamala* porter' carrier; bearer (of a note, of a check, etc.; of an order or decoration); holder (of an identification paper, of a diploma, of a certificate); holding device, holder, clamp, fastener, hold, support (*techn.*); fighter (على against); (pl. حوامل *ḥawāmil*²) pregnant | حامل البريد courier; حملة الاسهم *ḥ. al-ashum* shareholders; حملة الاقلام the publicists, the writers; حامل كلام الله *ḥ. kalām allāh* one who knows the Koran by heart; تيار حامل (*tayyār*) carrier current (*el.*); موجات حاملة (*maujāt*) carrier waves (*el.*)

حاملة *ḥāmila* pl. *-āt* device for carrying, carrier | حاملة خريطة map case; حاملة طائرات *ḥ. ṭā'irāt* aircraft carrier

محمول *maḥmūl* carried, borne; bearable, tolerable; load weight, service weight, cargo; tonnage (of a vessel); predicate, attribute (logic), محمول عليه subject (logic) | مشاة محمولة (*mušāh*) motorized infantry (*mil.*); جنود محمولون جوا (*jawwan*) airborne troops (*mil.*)

محمل *muḥammal* loaded, laden, heavily charged, burdened (ب with), encumbered (ب by)

محتمل *muḥtamal* bearable, tolerable; probable, likely

حملق *ḥamlaqa* (حملقة *ḥamlaqa*) to stare, gaze (في or ب at)

حملايا *ḥimalāyā* Himalaya

¹حمو *ḥamū* (construct state of حم *ḥam*) and حماة *ḥamāh* see ¹حم

²(حمو and حمى) حمى *ḥamiya a* to be or become hot; to glow (metal); to flare up; to fly into a rage, become furious (على at) | حمى الوطيس fierce fighting broke out II to make hot, heat (ه s.th.); to heat to glowing (ه metal); to fire up (ه a stove); to kindle, inflame, stir up, excite (ه s.th.); to bathe (= ³حم II) IV to make hot, heat (ه s.th.)

حمو *ḥamw* heat | حمو النيل *ḥ. an-nīl* prickly heat, heat rash, lichen tropicus (*eg.*)

حمو *ḥumūw* heat

حمة *ḥuma* pl. *-āt*, حمى *ḥuman* sting, stinger (of insects); prick, spine (of plants)

حمى *ḥamīy* hot, glowing; heated, excited

حمى *ḥummā* see ³حم

حمية *ḥamīya* zeal, ardor, fervor; enthusiasm, ardent zeal, fanaticism; violence, vehemence; passion, rage, fury; heat of excitement; temper, temperament | الحمية القومية (*qaumīya*) chauvinism

حميا *ḥumayyā* heat; excitement, agitation; enthusiasm; fire, passion, impetuosity, vehemence; fury, rage; wine

حماوة *ḥamāwa* heat

محمى *maḥman* fire chamber, furnace (of a stove, oven, etc.)

حام *ḥāmin* hot; heated, violent, fierce (e.g., a battle); glowing, passionate, fiery; burning

¹حمى *ḥamā i* (*ḥamy*, حماية *ḥimāya*) to defend, guard (ه, ه s.o., s.th., من against), protect, shelter, shield (ه, ه s.o., s.th. من from); to deny (المريض the patient) harmful food (ه; = to put him on diet); to forbid (ه ان s.o. to do s.th.) III to defend (من s.o. or s.th., also, of a lawyer in court); to shield, protect, support (عن s.o. or s.th.), take up the cause of (عن), stand up for (عن) VI to keep away (ه from), shun, avoid (ه s.th.) VIII to protect o.s. (ه, ه from s.th., from s.o.), defend o.s., cover o.s. (ب with s.th.), seek protection, seek shelter or refuge (ب with s.o., also عند; من from)

حمى *ḥiman* protection; defense; sanctuary

حمية *ḥimya* that which is defended; diet

حماية *ḥimāya* pl. *-āt* protection, patronage, sponsorship, auspices; protectorate (*pol.*)

محاماة *muḥāmāh* defense (*jur.*); legal profession, practicing of law | هيأة المحاماة *hai'at al-m.* the bar

احتماء *iḥtimā'* seeking cover, seeking protection; cover, shelter, protection

حام *ḥāmin* pl. حماة *ḥumāh* protector, defender, guardian; patron | الدولة الحامية (*daula*) protecting power (of a protectorate)

حامية *ḥāmiya* pl. *-āt* patroness, protectress; garrison (*mil.*)

محمى *maḥmīy* protected (ب by); being under a protectorate, having the status of a protectorate | منطقة محمية (*minṭaqa*) protectorate (country)

محمية *maḥmīya* pl. *-āt* protectorate (country; *pol.*)

محام *muḥāmin* pl. محامون *muḥāmūn* defense counsel, counselor-at-law, lawyer, barrister, attorney (at law), advocate

محامية *muḥāmiya* woman lawyer

محتم *muḥtamin* one who seeks protection; protégé; being under a protectorate, having the status of a protectorate

²حماة, حماه *ḥamāh* Hama (city in W Syria)

حن *ḥanna* *i* (حنين *ḥanīn*) to long, yearn, hanker (الى for), crave (الى s.th.); — (حنة *ḥanna*, حنان *ḥanān*) to feel tenderness, affection, sympathy (على for s.o.); to sympathize, commiserate (على with), feel compassion (على for); to pity (على s.o.), have mercy (على on) **II** to move, touch, fill with tenderness, soften, fill with compassion (قلبه *qalbahū* s.o.'s heart); to blossom, flower, be in bloom (tree) **V** to feel sympathy, feel pity, feel compassion (على for s.o.), commiserate (على with s.o.); to be tender, affectionate

حنة *ḥanna* sympathy; commiseration, compassion, pity; favorable aspect, advantage

حنان *ḥanān* sympathy, love, affection, tenderness; commiseration, compassion, pity; حنانيك *ḥanānaika* have pity! have mercy!

حنانة *ḥanāna* compassion, pity, commiseration

حنين *ḥanīn* longing, yearning, hankering, nostalgia, craving, desire

حنون *ḥanūn* affectionate, loving, softhearted, tenderhearted, compassionate, merciful; tender, soft, gentle, kind, moving, touching (voice)

حنان *ḥannān* affectionate, loving, tender; compassionate, sympathetic

تحنان *tiḥnān* attachment, devotion, loyalty

تحنن *taḥannun* tenderness, affection, sympathy

حنا **II** to dye red (ه s.th., with henna)

حناء *ḥinnā'* henna (a reddish-orange cosmetic gained from leaves and stalks of the henna plant) | ابو الحناء *abū l-ḥ.* robin (redbreast); تمر الحناء (colloq. *tamr el-ḥinna*) henna plant (Lawsonia inermis; *bot.*)

حانبة look up alphabetically

حنبلى *ḥanbalī* Hanbalitic, of or pertaining to the *maḏhab* of Aḥmad ibn Ḥanbal; puritanical, strict in religious matters; (pl. حنابلة *ḥanābila*) Hanbalite

حانوت, حانوتى see حنو

حنث *ḥaniṯa* *a* (*ḥinṯ*) with فى يمينه or بيمينه: to break one's oath **V** to practice piety, perform works of devotion; to seek religious purification; to scorn sin, not yield to sin

حنث *ḥinṯ* pl. احناث *aḥnāṯ* perjury; sin

حنجرة *ḥanjara* pl. حناجر *ḥanājir*² larynx, throat

حنجور *ḥunjūr* pl. حناجير *ḥanājīr*² larynx, throat

حنجل *ḥanjala* to prance (horse); to caper, gambol II *taḥanjala* to dance, caper, gambol, frisk

حندس *ḥindis* pl. حنادس *ḥanādis*² dark night

حندقوق *ḥandaqūq* (*bot.*) melilot, (yellow) sweet clover (Melilotus)

حنش *ḥanaš* pl. احناش *aḥnāš* snake

حنط II to embalm (ه a corpse); to stuff (ه a carcass)

حنطة *ḥinṭa* wheat

حناطة *ḥināṭa* embalming

تحنط *taḥannuṭ* mummification

محنط *muḥannaṭ* mummified

عربة الحنطور *ʿarabat al-ḥanṭūr* victoria, light carriage designed for two passengers

حنظل *ḥanẓal* (coll.; n. un. ة) colocynth (Citrullus colocynthis; *bot.*)

حنف *ḥanafa* *i* to turn or bend sideways

حنيف *ḥanīf* pl. حنفاء *ḥunafāʾ*² true believer, orthodox; one who scorns the false creeds surrounding him and professes the true religion; true (religion) | الدين الحنيف (*dīn*) the True (i.e., Islamic) Religion, also الحنيفة السمحاء (*samḥāʾ*)

حنفى *ḥanafī* pagan, heathen, idolater (*Chr.*); Hanafitic (see حنفية); (pl. *-ūn*) Hanafi

حنفية *ḥanafīya* paganism, heathendom (*Chr.*); Hanafitic *maḏhab* (an orthodox school of theology founded by Abu Hanifah); — (pl. *-āt*) faucet, tap; hydrant

الحنيفية *al-ḥanīfīya* the True (i.e., Islamic) Religion

احنف *aḥnaf*² afflicted with a distortion of the foot

حنق *ḥaniqa* *a* (*ḥanaq*) to be furious, mad, angry; to be annoyed, exasperated, peeved, irritated (على or من at, by), be resentful (على or من of) IV to infuriate, enrage, embitter, exasperate, irritate (ه s.o.)

حنق *ḥanaq* fury, rage, ire, wrath, anger, exasperation, resentment, rancor

حنق *ḥaniq* furious, mad, angry; resentful, bitter, embittered, annoyed, exasperated, peeved

حانق *ḥāniq* furious, mad, angry; resentful, bitter, embittered, annoyed, exasperated, peeved | حانق على الحياة (*ḥayāh*) weary of life, dispirited, dejected; حانق على النساء (*nisāʾ*) misogynist

محنق *muḥnaq* infuriated, enraged; embittered, bitter, angry, exasperated, resentful

حنك *ḥanaka* *i* *u*, II and IV to sophisticate, make experienced or worldly-wise through severe trials (said of fate, time, age)

حنك *ḥanak* pl. احناك *aḥnāk* palate

حنكى *ḥanakī* palatal

حنك *ḥunk*, *ḥink* and حنكة *ḥunka* worldly experience, worldly wisdom gained through experience, sophistication

محنك *muḥannak* experienced, worldly wise, sophisticated | محنك مبنك (*mubannak*) shrewd, smart, sharp

(حنو and حنى) حنا *ḥanā* *u* and حنى *ḥanā* *i* to bend, curve, twist, turn; to lean, incline (على or الى toward s.o.); to feel for s.o. (على), sympathize (على with s.o.), commiserate, pity (على s.o.), feel compassion, feel pity (على for s.o.); to bend, bow, flex, curve, crook (ه s.th.) IV to bend, bow, tilt, incline (ه s.th.; e.g., رأسه *raʾsahū* one's head); to sympathize (على

with s.o.), feel compassion, feel pity (على for s.o.), commiserate, pity (على s.o.) **VII** to bend, curve, twist, turn; to be winding, be tortuous, wind, meander (e.g., a road); to turn, deviate, digress (عن from); to bow (ل to s.o.); to lean, incline (على or فوق over s.th., الى toward s.o., toward s.th.); to devote o.s. eagerly (على to s.th.); to contain, harbor (على s.th.) | ان ضلوعى لا تنحنى على ضغن (*ḍulūʿī, ḍiğn*) I harbor no grudge, I feel no resentment

حنو *ḥanw* bending, deflection, flexing, flexure, curving, curvature, twisting, turning

حنو *ḥinw* pl. احناء *aḥnāʾ* bend, bow, turn, twist, curved line, curve, contour; pl. ribs | بين احنائها in her bosom

حنو *ḥunūw* sympathy, compassion, tenderness, affection

حنى *ḥany* bending, deflection, flexing, flexure, curving, curvature, twisting, turning

حنية *ḥanya* bend, turn, curve

حنية *ḥanīya* pl. حنايا *ḥanāyā* arc; camber, curvature | فى حنايا صدره in his bosom; فى حنايا نفسه in his heart, deep inside him

حناية *ḥināya* curving, curvature, twisting, turning, bending

حانوت see below

محنى *maḥnan* pl. محان *maḥānin* curvature, bend, flexure, bow, turn, curve

انحناء *inḥināʾ* bend, deflection, curvature; curve; arc; inclination, tilt; bow, curtsy

انحناءة *inḥināʾa* (n. vic.) bow, curtsy

الحوانى *al-ḥawānī* the longest ribs; (fig.) breast, bosom | بملء حوانيهم *bi-milʾi ḥ.* (they shouted) at the top of their lungs, with all their might

محنى *maḥnīy* bowed, inclined (head); bent, curved, crooked

منحن *munḥanin* bent, curved, crooked, twisted; inclined, bowed

منحنى *munḥanan* pl. منحنيات *munḥanayāt* bend, flexure, deflection, curvature; turn, twist, break, angle; curve (of a road, and *math.*); slope

حانوت *ḥānūt* pl. حوانيت *ḥawānīt*² store, shop; wineshop, tavern

حانوتى *ḥānūtī* pl. *-īya* (*eg.*) corpse washer; undertaker, mortician, grave-digger

حواء *ḥawwāʾ*² Eve

حوب **V** to abstain from sin; to lead a pious life; to refrain, abstain (من from s.th.)

حوبة *ḥauba* sin, offense, misdeed, outrage

حوباء *ḥaubāʾ*² soul

حوت *ḥūt* pl. حيتان *ḥītān*, احوات *aḥwāt* fish; whale; Pisces, Fishes (*astron.*) | حوت سليمان *ḥ. sulaimān* salmon

حوج **IV** *aḥwaja* to have need, stand in need, be in want (الى of s.th.), need, require, want (الى s.th.); to put (ه s.o.) in need of (الى), make necessary (الى ه for s.o. s.th.), require (الى ه of s.o. s.th.), compel, oblige (الى ه s.o. to); to impoverish, reduce to poverty (ه s.o.) | ما احوجه الى (*aḥwajahū*) how much he stands in need of ...! how urgently he needs ...! **VIII** to have need, stand in need, be in want (الى of; also ل), need, want, require (الى s.th., s.o.)

حوج *ḥauj* need, want, lack, deficiency, destitution

حاجة *ḥāja* pl. *-āt* need (الى or ب of); necessity, requirement, prerequisite; natural, bodily need; pressing need, neediness, poverty, indigence, destitution; object of need or desire; desire, wish, request; necessary article, requisite; matter, concern, business, job, work; thing, object; — pl. حوائج *ḥawāʾij*² needs, necessities, necessaries; everyday objects, effects, belongings, possessions, stuff; clothes, clothing | كان فى حاجة الى (ل) to stand in need, be in want of (s.th.), need, require (s.th.); لا حاجة الى (ل) (*ḥājata*) ... is not necessary, not required, there is no need of ...; لا حاجة لى به I don't need it; عند الحاجة if (or when) necessary, if need be, in case of need; فى غير حاجة (*ğairi ḥājatin*) unnecessarily; ما به الحاجة the essentials; محل الحاجة *maḥall al-ḥ.* the essential passage, the gist, the substance, the crux, the interesting part (of an exposition); سد حاجته *sadda ḥājatahū* to meet s.o.'s needs, provide for s.o.'s needs; قضى حاجته *qaḍā ḥājatahū* to fulfill s.o.'s wish; قضى الحاجة to relieve nature

حاجيات *ḥājīyāt* everyday commodities, utensils, utilities, necessaries, necessities

احوج *aḥwaj*² in greater need (الى of s.th.); more necessary

احتياج *iḥtiyāj* want, need, requirement, (pre)requisite, necessity; pl. *-āt* needs, necessities, necessaries

محاويج *maḥāwīj*² (pl. of محوج *muḥwij*) needy, poor, destitute people

محتاج *muḥtāj* in need, in want (الى of s.th.), requiring (الى s.th.); poor, destitute, indigent

حوجلة *ḥaujala* pl. حواجل *ḥawājil*² phial (*chem.*)

حاد (حود) *ḥāda u* (*ḥaud*) to turn aside, turn away (عن from), turn (عن off) **II** to turn off, take a turning

حودة *ḥauda* turn, turning

حاذ (حوذ) *ḥāḏa u* (*ḥauḏ*) to urge on, spur on (ه animals) **IV** do. **X** استحوذ *istaḥwaḏa* to overwhelm, overcome, overpower (على s.o.; esp. emotions), get the better of (على), gain mastery (على over); to seize (على on), take possession (على of), usurp (على s.th.)

حوذى *ḥūḏī* coachman, cabman, driver

حوذية *ḥūḏiya* coachman's work or trade

حار (حور) *ḥāra u* to return (الى to); to recede, decrease, diminish, be reduced (الى to) **II** to change, alter, amend, transform, reorganize, remodel, modify (ه or من s.th.); to roll out (ه dough); to make white, whiten (ه s.th.); to bleach (ه a fabric) **III** to talk, converse, have a conversation (ه with s.o.); to discuss, debate, argue **IV** (with جوابا *jawāban*) to answer, reply (with negations only) **V** to be altered, changed, amended, transformed, reorganized, remodeled, modified **VI** to carry on a discussion

حور *ḥawar* white poplar (also pronounced *ḥaur*); bark-tanned sheepskin, basil; marked contrast between the white of the cornea and the black of the iris

حارة *ḥāra* pl. *-āt* quarter, part, section (of a city); (*Tun.*) ghetto; lane, alley, side street (with occasional pl. حوارى *ḥawārī*) | حارة السد *ḥ. as-sadd* blind alley, dead-end street

احور *aḥwar*², f. حوراء *ḥaurā'*², pl. حور *ḥūr* having eyes with a marked contrast of white and black, (also, said of the eye:) intensely white and deep-black

حوارة *ḥawwāra* (*ḥawāra?*) cretaceous rock; chalk

حوارى *ḥawārī* pl. *-ūn* disciple, apostle (of Jesus Christ); disciple, follower

حوارى *ḥuwwārā* cretaceous rock; chalk

حورية *ḥūrīya* pl. *-āt*, حور *ḥūr* houri, virgin of paradise; nymph; (pl. *-āt*) young locust | حورية الماء water nymph, nixie

حوران *ḥaurān*² the Hauran, a mountainous plateau in SW Syria and N Jordan

محور *miḥwar* pl. محاور *maḥāwir*[2] rolling pin; pivot, core, heart, center; axis; axle, axletree

محار *maḥār* (coll.; n. un. ة) oysters; shellfish, mussels; mother-of-pearl, nacre

محارة *maḥāra* (n. un.) oyster; oyster shell, mussel; trowel

تحوير *taḥwīr* alteration, change, transformation, reorganization, reshuffle, remodeling, modification

حوار *ḥiwār* talk, conversation, dialogue; argument, dispute; text (of a play); script, scenario (of a motion picture)

محاورة *muḥāwara* talk, conversation, dialogue; argument, dispute

تحاور *taḥāwur* discussion

حوز and حيز) حاز *ḥāza u* (*ḥauz*, حيازة *ḥiyāza*) to possess, own, have (ه s.th.); to gain, win, get, receive, obtain, achieve, attain (ه s.th., e.g., success, victory, etc.); to gain possession, gain control (ه of s.th.), seize, monopolize (ه s.th.); — *ḥāza i* (حيز *ḥaiz*) to drive on, urge on (ه camels) **V** *taḥawwaza* and *taḥayyaza* to writhe, twist, coil; — *taḥayyaza* to stay away, keep away, seclude o.s., isolate o.s. (عن from); to be disposed, incline, tend, lean (الى toward); to join (الى s.o. or s.th.); to side (ل, الى with), take sides (ل, الى in favor of) **VII** to isolate o.s., seclude o.s., separate, segregate, disengage o.s., dissociate o.s., stay away, keep away, retire, withdraw (عن or من from); to join (الى s.o. or s.th.); to unite (الى with); to side (الى or ل with), take sides (الى or ل in favor of) **VIII** to possess, own, have (ه s.th.); to take possession (ه of s.th.); to keep, prevent, hinder (ه عن s.o. from)

حوز *ḥauz* possession, holding, tenure; obtainment, attainment, acquisition; taking possession, occupation, occupancy; (*jur.*) tenancy; — (pl. احواز *aḥwāz*) enclosed area, enclosure; precinct(s), boundary, city limits

حوزى *ḥauzī* possessory, tenurial

حوزة *ḥauza* possession, holding, tenure; property; area, territory | فى حوزته or فى حوزة يده *fī ḥ. yadihī* in his possession; الدفاع عن حوزة مصر the defense of Egyptian territory

حيز *ḥayyiz*, *ḥaiz* pl. احياز *aḥyāz* scope, range, reach, extent, compass, confines, field, domain, realm; sphere | لا يدخل فى حيز المعقول (*yadkulu*) it is not within the bounds of reason; برز الى حيز المعقول (to advance to the realm of fact, i.e.) to become a reality; فى حيز الامكان *fī ḥ. il-imkān* within the realm of possibility, quite possible

حيازة *ḥiyāza* possession, holding, tenure; taking possession, occupation, occupancy; acquisition of title, acquisition of the right of possession; obtainment, attainment, acquisition

تحيز *taḥayyuz* partiality; prejudice, bias

انحياز *inḥiyāz* isolation, seclusion, retirement; partiality; prejudice, bias

حائز *ḥā'iz* possessor, holder, tenant

متحيز *mutaḥayyiz* partial, prejudiced, biased

منحاز *munḥāz* secluded, retired, withdrawn, removed (عن from); an outsider, a stranger (عن to)

حوس **VIII** (*eg.*) to be in a quandary, waver, hesitate

[1](حوش) حاش *ḥāša u* (*ḥauš*) to round up, drive into a trap (ه game); to stop, check, prevent, hinder (ه s.th.), stand in the way (ه of); to hold back, stem, stave off (ه s.th.) **II** to gather, collect, amass, accumulate, pile up, hoard (ه s.th.); to save, put by (ه money); to find (ه s.th.)

حوش *ḥauš* pl. احواش *aḥwāš*, حيشان *ḥīšān* enclosure, enclosed area; courtyard

حوش *ḥawaš* mob, rabble, riffraff

حوشى *ḥūši* wild; unusual, odd, queer, strange

اسبوع الحاش *usbū' al-ḥāš* Passion Week (*Chr.*)

حاشا[2], حاشى see حشو, حاش لله *ḥāša lillāh* = حاشى لله

حوص *ḥawaṣ* squinting of the eyes (caused by constant exposure to glaring light)

احوص *aḥwaṣ*,[2] f. حوصاء *ḥauṣā'*[2], pl. حوص *ḥūṣ* having narrow, squinting eyes

حياصة *ḥiyāṣa* girth

حوصل *ḥauṣal*, حوصلة *ḥauṣala* craw (of a bird); bladder; pelican | الحوصلة المرارية (*marārīya*) gall bladder, bile (*anat.*)

حويصل *ḥuwaiṣil* blister, bleb, vesicle; water blister

حويصلة *ḥuwaiṣila* pl. *-āt* blister, bleb, vesicle

حوض *ḥauḍ* pl. احواض *aḥwāḍ*, حياض *ḥiyāḍ*, حيضان *ḥīḍān* basin; water basin; trough, tank, cistern, reservoir, container; basin of a river or sea; pool; (in the Egyptian irrigation system) a patch of land surrounded by dikes, flooded by high water of the Nile; pond; pelvis (*anat.*); (garden) bed; dock; pl. حياض *ḥiyāḍ* (sacred) ground, area, domain (to be protected), sanctum | حوض جاف (*jāff*) dry dock; حوض حمام *ḥ. ḥammām* bathtub; حوض عوام (*'awwām*) floating dock; ذاد عن حياضه to assume the defense of s.o., make o.s. the champion of s.o.; to defend o.s.; ذب عن حياض الدين (*ḏabba*) to defend the faith; احواض الفحم والحديد coal and iron deposits

O حويضة *ḥuwaiḍa* renal pelvis (*anat.*)

حوط) حاط *ḥāṭa u* (*ḥauṭ*, حيطة *ḥīṭa*, حياطة *ḥiyāṭa*) to guard, protect (ه, ه s.o., s.th.), watch (ه, ه over s.o., over s.th.), have the custody (ه, ه of); to attend (ه to), take care (ه of), look after s.th. (ه); to surround, encircle, enclose, encompass (ب s.o., s.th.) II to build a wall (ه around s.th.), wall in (ه s.th.); to encircle, surround (ه s.th.), close in from all sides (ه on s.th.) III to try to outwit, dupe, or outsmart (ه s.o.); to mislead, lead astray, seduce (ه s.o.) IV to surround (ب s.o., s.th., also ه, ه s.o., s.th., ب with); to encompass, enclose, embrace, comprise, contain (ب s.th., also ه); to ring, encircle (ب s.o., s.th., also ه, ه s.o., s.th., ب with s.th.), close in from all sides (ب on); to know thoroughly, comprehend, grasp completely, understand fully (ب s.th.), be familiar, be thoroughly acquainted (ب with) | احاط به علما (*'ilman*) to know s.th. thoroughly, have comprehensive knowledge of s.th.; to take cognizance, take note of s.th.; احاطه علما ب he informed him of ..., he let him know about ...; he brought ... to his notice V to guard, protect (ه, ه s.o., s.th.); to take precautions (ه with regard to), attend (ه to); to be careful, be cautious, be on one's guard VIII to be careful, be cautious, watch out, be on one's guard; to take precautions, make provision (ل for, so as to ensure ...); to surround (ب s.o., s.th.); to guard, protect, preserve (ب على s.th. from), take care (ب of), attend (ب to), look after (ب), see to it (بأن that)

حيطة *ḥīṭa*, *ḥaiṭa*, حوطة *ḥauṭa* cautiousness, caution, provident care, prudence, circumspection | اخذ حيطته (*ḥīṭatahū*) to be on one's guard, take precautions; بلا حيطة thoughtlessly, unthinkingly, inadvertently

حياطة *ḥiyāṭa* guarding, custody, protection, care

تحويط *taḥwīṭ* encirclement

احاطة *iḥāṭa* encirclement, encompassment; comprehension, grasp, understanding, knowledge, cognizance (ب of s.th.), acquaintance, familiarity (ب with); information, communication

تحوط *taḥawwuṭ* provision, care, attention, precaution, prudence; pl. *-āt* precautionary measures, precautions

احتياط *iḥtiyāṭ* caution, cautiousness, prudence, circumspection, carefulness; provision, care, attention, precaution, prevention; pl. *-āt* precautionary measures, precautions | على سبيل الاحتياط as a precaution, out of precaution, to be on the safe side

احتياطى *iḥtiyāṭī* precautionary; prophylactic; preventive; replacement; spare- (in compounds); reserve- (in compounds); stand by; reserve funds, capital reserves (*fin.*); reserve (*mil.*) | حبس احتياطى (*ḥabs*) detention pending investigation; تدابير احتياطية precautionary measures, precautions; قوات احتياطية (*qūwāt*) reserves (*mil.*); مال احتياطى capital reserve, reserve fund; احتياطى الزيت الخام (crude-)oil reserves

حائط *ḥā'iṭ* pl. حيطان *ḥīṭān*, حياط *ḥiyāṭ*, حوائط *ḥawā'iṭ*[2] wall | حائط المبكى *ḥ. al-mabkā* Wailing Wall (in Jerusalem); القى (ضرب) به عرض الحائط *alqā* (*ḍaraba*) *bihī 'urḍa l-ḥā'iṭ* to make little of s.th., scorn, disdain, despise s.th.; to reject s.th., discard s.th., throw s.th. overboard; to ruin, thwart, foil s.th.

حويط *ḥawīṭ* (*eg.*) clever, smart, shrewd

محيط *muḥīṭ* surrounding (ب s.th.); comprehensive; familiar, acquainted (ب with); — (pl. *-āt*) circumference, periphery; extent, range, scope, compass, reach, domain, area; milieu, environment, surroundings; ocean; pl. محيطات surroundings, environment | المحيط الاطلنطى (*aṭlanṭī*) the Atlantic Ocean; المحيط الهادئ (*hādi'*) the Pacific Ocean

محاط *muḥāṭ* surrounded (ب by)

متحوط *mutaḥawwiṭ* cautious, prudent, provident, circumspect, careful, watchful

حوف *ḥauf* edge, rim, brim, brink; border, hem, fringe

حافة *ḥāfa* pl. *-āt*, حواف *ḥawāfin* border, rim, brim, brink, verge; edge; fringe, hem | بين حوافيه within it, in it, therein

(حوق) حاق *ḥāqa u* (*ḥauq*) to surround, enclose, infold, embrace (ب s.o., s.th.) II = I (على s.o., s.th.)

[1]حوقل *ḥauqala* (حوقلة *ḥauqala*) to pronounce the formula: لا حول ولا قوة الا بالله (see حول *ḥaul*)

[2]حوقلة *ḥauqala* pl. حواقل *ḥawāqil*[2] phial (*chem.*), Florence flask

(حوك) حاك *ḥāka u* (*ḥauk*, حياك *ḥiyāk*, حياكة *ḥiyāka*) to weave (ه s.th.); to interweave (ه s.th.); to knit (ه s.th.); to braid, plait (ه s.th.); to contrive, devise, hatch, concoct (ه s.th.; e.g., ruses, intrigues, pretexts), think up, fabricate, create (ه s.th. in one's imagination)

حياكة *ḥiyāka* weaving; knitting; braiding, plaiting

حائك *ḥā'ik* pl. حاكة *ḥāka* weaver; — (*mor.*) an outer garment made of a long piece of white woolen material, covering body and head

(حول and حيل) حال *ḥāla u* to change, undergo a change, be transformed; to shift, turn, pass, grow (الى into s.th., also ه), become (الى s.th.); to deviate, depart (عن from, e.g., a commitment), dodge, evade, fail to meet (عن s.th.); to elapse, pass, go by (time); — (حيلولة *ḥailūla*) to prevent (دون s.th.); to intervene, interfere, interpose, come (بين between) | حال عن عهد (*'ahd*) to withdraw from a contract; حال بين فلان

وبين الامر to make s.th. inaccessible to s.o., impossible for s.o.; to bar or obstruct s.o.'s way to s.th.; to prevent s.o. from s.th., deny s.o. s.th.; حال بين نفسه وبين الاشفاق (*išfāq*) to resist compassion, deny o.s. any sympathy **II** *ḥawwala* to change (الى ه or ه ه s.th. to s.th. else), transform, transmute, convert, turn, make (الى ه or ه ه s.th. into s.th. else); to transplant (ه s.th.); to transfer (ه s.th.); to convert (ه s.th., mathematically); to switch, commutate (ه current; *el.*); to convert, transform (ه current; *el.*); to shunt (ه a railroad car); to switch (ه a railroad track); to remi., send, transmit (ه s.th., e.g., money by mail, الى to s.o.); to pass on, hand on (الى ه s.th. to s.o.); to forward (الى ه s.th. to s.o. or to an address); to endorse (ه a bill of exchange, a promissory note); to direct, turn (ه s.th., also نظرة *naẓratan* a glance, الى to or toward); to divert, distract, keep (عن ه or ه s.o. or s.th. from); to turn away, avert (بصره عن *baṣarahū* one's eyes from); to turn off, switch off, disconnect (ه current; *el.*) | حول الدفة (*daffa*) to turn the helm, change the course **III** *ḥāwala* to try, attempt, endeavor (ه s.th., ان to do s.th.), make an attempt, make an effort (ان to do s.th.); to seek to gain (ه s.th.) by artful means; to deceive by pretenses, make excuses, hedge, dodge **IV** to change (ه ه or الى ه s.th. to), transform, transmute, turn, make (ه ه or الى ه s.th. into); to convert, translate (ه ه or الى ه s.th. into); to transfer (ه s.th.); to remit, send (ه s.th. الى or على to s.o.); to assign (ه, ه s.o., s.th., الى or على to s.o.); to turn over, hand over, pass on (على ه or ه s.o. or s.th. to); to forward (على ه s.th. to); to refer (الى ه s.o. to); to cede, transfer (ه a debt, على to s.o.; *jur.*) | احيل على (الى) المعاش (*uḥīla, ma'āš*) and احيل الى التقاعد (*taqā'ud*) he was pensioned off; احيلت الكمبيالة الى البروتستو the bill was protested (*fin.*) **V** *taḥawwala* to change, undergo a change; to be changed (الى to), be transformed, be transmuted, be converted (الى into), become (الى s.th.), turn, grow (الى into), transform (الى — من or عن from — into), change, develop, evolve (الى — من from — to); to withdraw, go away, leave; to move (الى to a residence); to turn away (من from), turn one's back (عن on); to deviate (عن from); to depart, digress, stray (عن الطريق from the way); to renounce, forgo, relinquish, disclaim (عن s.th.); to proceed slyly or cunningly | تحول كل حيلة to employ every conceivable trick; — *taḥayyala* to employ artful means; to ponder ways and means (ل to an end, in order to attain s.th.) **VI** *taḥāwala* to try, endeavor, take pains (على to do s.th.), strive (على for); — *taḥāyala* and **VIII** to employ artful means, resort to tricks, use stratagems (على against s.o.); to deceive, beguile, dupe, cheat, outwit, outsmart (على s.o.); to be out (على for s.th.) or achieve (على s.th.) by artful means, by tricks **VIII** to work or strive (on one's own resources), make efforts (on one's own) **IX** احول *iḥwalla* to be cross-eyed, to squint **X** to change (الى to, into), turn, be transformed, be converted (الى into); to be transubstantiated (bread and wine, الى into the body and blood of Christ; *Chr.*); to proceed, pass on, shift, switch (الى to s.th. new or s.th. different); to be impossible (على for s.o.); to be inconceivable, absurd, preposterous

حال *ḥāl* m. and f., pl. احوال *aḥwāl* condition, state; situation; position, status; circumstance; case; present, actuality (as opposed to future); circumstantial expression or phrase (*gram.*); pl.: conditions, circumstances; matters, affairs, concerns; cases; *ḥāla* (prep.) during; immediately upon, right after; just at; in case of ..., in the event of ...; حالا

ḥālan presently, immediately, at once, right away, without delay; now, actually, at present | فى الحال and للحال on the spot, at once, immediately; على كل حال (*kulli ḥālin*) and على اى حال (*ayyi ḥ.*) in any case, at any rate, anyhow; يبقى على حاله (*yabqā*) it remains unchanged, just as it is; فى حال من الاحوال in some case or other, anyway, if occasion should arise, possibly; (with neg.) by no means, under no circumstances, not at all, in no way; على حال, بحال, بأى حال *bi-ayyi ḥ.* with neg.: by no means, not at all, in no way; كذلك الحال فى the same goes for ..., it is the same with ..., it is also the case with ...; كما هو الحال فى as is the case with; كيف حالك how are you? شىء بحاله a thing in itself, a separate, independent thing; الاحوال الجوية (*jawwīya*) atmospheric conditions; محاكم الاحوال الشخصية (*šaḵṣīya*) courts dealing with vital statistics; قانون (or نظام) الاحوال الشخصية personal statute; صاحب الحال noun referent of a circumstantial phrase (*gram.*); عرض حال *ʿarḍ ḥ.* application, memorial, petition; لسان الحال, لسان حاله see لسان

حالما *ḥālamā* (conj.) as soon as

حالة *ḥāla* pl. *āt* condition, state; situation; (possible, actual) case; *ḥālata* (prep.) during | حالة ان *ḥālata an* (conj.) whereas; والحالة هذه under these circumstances, such being the case, things being as they are; فى حالة (*ḥālati*) in (the) case of ..., in the event of ..., e.g., فى حالة غيابه (*ḡiyābihī*) in case of his absence, فى حالة الوفاة (*wafāh*) in case of death; فى هذه الحالة in this (that) case; لحالة ان *li-ḥālati an* in case that ..., in the event that ...; فى حالة ما اذا if; كما هى الحالة فى as is the case with ...; حالة اجتماعية (*ijtimāʿīya*) marital status; الحالات الجوية (*jawwīya*) atmospheric conditions; حالة الخطر *ḥ. al-ḵaṭar* stand-by, alert, state of alarm; الحالة الراهنة the status quo; حالة الطوارئ *ḥ. aṭ-ṭawāri'* state of emergency; فى حالة التلبس (*talabbus*) flagrante delicto (*jur.*); الحالة المدنية (*madanīya*) civil status, legal status; سوء الحالة *sū' al-ḥ.* predicament, plight

حالى *ḥālī* present, current, actual, existing; momentary, instantaneous; حاليا *ḥālīyan* at present, actually | صورة حالية (*ṣūra*) snapshot (*phot.*)

حالية *ḥālīya* actuality, topicality, timeliness

حول *ḥaul* pl. احوال *aḥwāl* year; might, power | لا حول ولا قوة الا بالله *lā ḥaula wa-lā qūwata illā bi-llāh* there is no power and no strength save in God; لا حول له ولا حيلة (*wa-lā ḥīlata*) he is completely powerless, he can do nothing, he is at the end of his resources

حول *ḥiwal* change of place, change | لا يبتغون عنه حولا (*yabtaḡūna*) they don't want it otherwise, they ask for it

حول *ḥaula* (prep.) around, about; circa, about, some, approximately, roughly (with following number); about (esp. in news headings, approx. = re, concerning) | من حوله (*ḥaulihī*) (= حوله) around him (or it), about him (or it); من حوليها (*ḥaulaihimā*) around the two of them, about them; from their vicinity, from their surroundings (dual)

حولى *ḥaulī* periodic, temporary, interim; one year old (animal), yearling; young animal; lamb, wether

○ حوليات *ḥaulīyāt* yearbook, annals (= Fr. *annales*, as a scientific publication)

حيل *ḥail* strength, force, power, vigor | على حيله (standing) upright, erect; لا قوة له ولا حيل (*qūwata*) completely helpless and paralyzed

حيلة *ḥīla* pl. حيل *ḥiyal*, احاييل *aḥāyīl*[2] artifice, ruse, stratagem, maneuver, subterfuge, wile, trick; device, shift; a means to accomplish an end; expedient, makeshift, dodge, way-out; legal stratagem (for the purpose of *in fraudem legis agere*) | ما الحيلة what's to be done? لا حيلة لى ف (*ḥīlata*) I have no possibility to ..., I am in no position to ...; ما بيدى حيلة (*bi-yadī*) I can do nothing, I can get nowhere; لم يجد حيلة الا *lam yajid ḥīlatan illā* he couldn't do anything except ..., he had no other choice than ...; اعيته الحيلة (*a'yathu*) he was at a loss, he was at the end of his wits

حيلى *ḥiyalī* cunning, crafty, wily, sly, tricky, foxy

احيل *aḥyal*² craftier, wilier

حول *ḥawal* squinting, strabismus

احول *aḥwal*², f. حولاء *ḥaulā'*², pl. حول *ḥūl* squinting, squint-eyed, cross-eyed, walleyed

حؤول *ḥu'ūl* change, transformation, transmutation; prevention (دون of s.th.)

حوال *ḥiwāl* obstacle; partition, screen

حيال *ḥiyāla* (prep.) in view of ..., with regard to ..., in the face of, opposite, in front of, before

حوالة *ḥawāla* pl. *-āt* assignment, cession (*jur.*); bill of exchange, (promissory) note, check, draft | حوالة البريد, حوالة بريدية money order; حوالة سفر *ḥ. safar* traveler's check

حوالى *ḥawālā* (prep.) around, about; circa, approximately, roughly, about, some (with following number)

حيلولة *ḥailūla* separation, interruption, disruption; prevention (دون of s.th.)

لا محال *lā maḥāla* = لا محالة (see below)

محالة *maḥāla* roller, wheel (of a draw well)

لا محالة منه *lā maḥālata minhu* it is inevitable; there is no doubt about it; (also لا محالة alone) most certainly, positively, absolutely, by all means

تحويل *taḥwīl* transformation, transmutation, conversion (الى into s.th.); change, alteration, modification; transplantation; transposition, reversal, inversion, translocation, dislocation, displacement; transfer, assignment; conversion (e.g., of currency); conversion, transformation (of electric current); ○ transfer (*fin.*; also تحويل الدين *t. ad-dain*); remittance (of money), transmittal, sending, forwarding; bill of exchange, promissory note, draft (*com.*); check; endorsement (*com.*); c.o.d., cash on delivery | قابلية العملة للتحويل الى العملات الاجنبية (*qābilīyat al-'umla, ajnabīya*) convertibility of currency

تحويلة *taḥwīla* pl. تحاويل *taḥāwīl*² branch, offshoot; siding, sidetrack (railroad); side canal (irrigation; *Eg.*); switch (railroad)

محاولة *muḥāwala* pl. *-āt* attempt, try; effort, endeavor; recourse to expedients, shifts, or dodges, dodging, hedging | محاولة على حياته (*ḥayātihī*) attempt on s.o.'s life, murderous assault

احالة *iḥāla* transfer, conveyance, assignment; remittance; forwarding, referring (الى or على to a competent authority); transmission, transmittal; ○ transfer (*fin.*); cession, assignment (*Isl. Law*); absurdity | بالاحالة على with reference to; قاضى الاحالة magistrate sitting at defendant's arraignment, trial judge; احالة الى (على) المعاش (*ma'āš*) and احالة الى التقاعد (*taqā'ud*) pensioning off

تحول *taḥawwul* change, transformation, transmutation; abrupt change, sudden turn, reversal; shift, transition; departure, deviation, digression (عن from); renunciation (عن of) | نقطة التحول *nuqṭat at-t.* turning point

تحيل *taḥayyul* use of tricks, trickery

تحايل *taḥāyul* and احتيال *iḥtiyāl* use of tricks, trickery; cunning, craft, subtlety, artfulness; malice, treachery, perfidy; deception, fraud

تحايلى *taḥāyulī* and احتيالى *iḥtiyālī* fraudulent, e.g., افلاس احتيالى (*iflās*) fraudulent bankruptcy

استحالة *istiḥāla* change, transformation, transmutation, turn, shift, transition; transubstantiation (*Chr.*); impossibility, inconceivability, absurdity, preposterousness

حائل *ḥā'il* pl. حوائل *ḥawā'il*[2] obstacle, obstruction, impediment (دون on the way to s.th., بين — و see حال *ḥāla* I); barrier; partition, screen, folding screen; — (pl. حول *ḥuwwal*) changeable, variable, frequently changing; feeble, languid, wan, pallid

محول *muḥawwil* pl. *-āt* converter, transformer (*el.*); endorser

محولة *muḥawwila* switch (railroad)

محول عليه *muḥawwal ʿalaihi* c.o.d., cash on delivery; محول به collected on delivery

محيل *muḥīl* transferor, assignor (*Isl. Law*)

محال *muḥāl* inconceivable, unthinkable, impossible, absurd, preposterous, unattainable

متحول *mutaḥawwil* changeable, variable, changing | الاعياد المتحولة (*aʿyād*) the movable feasts (*Chr.*)

محتال *muḥtāl* artful, cunning, deceitful, treacherous, perfidious, fraudulent; swindler, cheat, impostor, fraud; crook, scoundrel; assignee (*Isl. Law*) | محتال عليه debtor of a ceded claim, transferee (*Isl. Law*)

مستحيل *mustaḥīl* impossible, absurd, preposterous; مستحيلات impossible things, impossibilities, absurdities

(حوم) حام *ḥāma u* (*ḥaum*, حومان *ḥawamān*) to circle, hover, glide (in the air; of a bird, also of an aircraft); to hover, swarm, buzz (حول and على around) | حامت الشبهة ضده (*šubha, ḍiddahū*) suspicion concentrated on him, he was suspected II to circle in the air; to hover in circles, to circle; to go around, revolve (thoughts and images, in one's head or mind); to browse (فى in a book)

حومة *ḥauma* pl. *-āt* turmoil of battle, thick of the fray; main part, bulk, main body; (*tun.*) quarter, section (of a city)

حان and حانة see حين

حانوت see حنو

حوى *ḥawā i* to gather, collect, unite (ه s.th.); to encompass, embrace, contain, hold, enclose, comprise, include (ه s.th.); to possess, own, have (ه s.th.); to clasp (ه s.th., the hand) V to curl (up), coil (up) VIII to encompass, embrace, contain, hold, enclose, comprise, include (ه or على s.th.); to possess, own, have (ه or على s.th.)

حوية *ḥawīya* convolution, coil, curl, roll; pl. حوايا *ḥawāyā* intestines, bowels, entrails

حواية *ḥawāya* pl. *-āt* (*eg.*) wase, round pad to support a burden on the head or on the back

حاو *ḥāwin* pl. حواة *ḥuwāh* snake charmer; juggler, conjurer, magician

محتويات *muḥtawayāt* content(s) (of a book, of a receptacle) | محتويات النفوس the innermost thoughts, the secrets of the heart

(حيو ,حى) حى *ḥayiya*, حى *ḥayya* يحيا *yaḥyā* (حياة *ḥayāh*) to live; حى *ḥayya* to live to see, experience, witness (ه s.th.), live (ه through a time) | ليحى الملك *li-yaḥya l-malik* long live the king! — حيي *ḥayiya* يحيا *yaḥyā* (حياء *ḥayā'*) to be ashamed (من of, because of) **II** حيا *ḥayyā* to keep (ه s.o.) alive, grant (ه s.o.) a long life; to say to s.o. (ه): حياك الله may God preserve your life!; to greet, salute (ه s.o.) **IV** احيا *aḥyā* to lend life (ه, ه to s.o., to s.th.), enliven, animate, vitalize, endow with life, call into being (ه s.th.), give birth (ه to); to revive, reanimate, revivify (ه s.th.), give new life (ه to); to put on, produce, stage, arrange (ه e.g., a theatrical performance, a celebration, and the like); to celebrate (ه s.th., also a festival) | احيا الذكرى (*dikrā*) to commemorate (a deceased person), observe the anniversary (of s.o.'s death); احيا الليل (*lail*) to burn the midnight oil, احيا الليل صلاة (*ṣalātan*) to spend the night in prayer; احيا السهرة (*sahrata*) to perform in the evening (of an artist); احيا حفلة (*ḥaflatan*) to give a performance; to perform at a celebration (artist); قد احيت الفرقة ثلاث ليال *qad aḥyat il-firqatu ṯalāṯa layālin* the theatrical troupe gave three evening performances **X** استحيا *istaḥyā* to spare s.o.'s (ه) life, let live, keep alive (ه s.o.); استحيا *istaḥyā*, استحى *istaḥā* to be ashamed (ه to face s.o.; من of s.th., because of s.th.); to become or feel embarrassed (من in front of s.o.), be embarrassed (من by); to be bashful, shy, diffident

حى *ḥayy* pl. احياء *aḥyā'* living, live, alive; lively, lusty, animated, active, energetic, unbroken, undaunted, undismayed; living being, organism; tribe, tribal community; block of apartment houses; section, quarter (of a city) | علم الاحياء *'ilm al-aḥyā'* biology; حى العالم *ḥ. al-'ālam* houseleek tree (Sempervivum arboreum L.; *bot.*)

ى *hayya*: حى على الصلاه *ḥayya 'alā ṣ-ṣalāh* come to prayer!

حية *ḥayya* pl. *-āt* snake, serpent, viper

○ احيائى *aḥyā'ī* biologic(al); (pl. *-ūn*) biologist | كيمياء احيائية (*kīmiyā'*) biochemistry

حيي *ḥayīy* bashful, shy, diffident, modest

حياء *ḥayā'* shame, diffidence, bashfulness, timidity; ·hyness | قليل الحياء shameless, impudent; قلة الحياء *qillat al-ḥ.* shamelessness, impudence

حياة *ḥayāh* pl. حيوات *ḥayawāt* life; lifeblood; liveliness, animation | حياة الريف *ḥ. ar-rīf* country life, rural life; الحياة العامة (*'āmma*) public life; الحياة العائلية family life; مستوى الحياة *mustawā l-ḥ.* living standard; ○ علم الحياة *'ilm al-ḥ.* biology

حيوى *ḥayawī* lively, full of life, vital, vigorous; vital, essential to life

حيوية *ḥayawīya* vitality, vigor, vim

حيويات *ḥayawīyāt*: مواد مضادة للحيويات (*mawādd muḍādda*) antibiotics

حيوان *ḥayawān* pl. *-āt* animal, beast; (coll.) animals, living creatures | حيوانات ثديية (*ṯadyīya*) mammals; حيوانات مجترة (*mujtarra*) ruminants; حيوان طفيلى (*ṭufailī*) parasite; علم الحيوان *'ilm al-ḥ.* zoology

حيوانى *ḥayawānī* animal (adj.); zoologic(al)

حيوانية *ḥayawānīya* bestiality; animality, animal nature

حوين *ḥuwayyin* pl. *-āt* minute animal, animalcule

احيى *aḥyā* livelier; more vigorous, more vital

تحية *taḥīya* pl. *-āt*, تحايا *taḥāyā* greeting, salutation; salute; cheer (= wish that God may give s.o. long life) | تحية لذكراه *taḥīyatan li-ḏikrāhu* in order to keep his memory alive, in remembrance of him; التحية العسكرية (*'askarīya*) military salute

احياء *iḥyā'* animation, enlivening; revival, revitalization, revivification; arranging, staging, conducting, putting on, holding (of a celebration) | احياء الذكرى *i. ad-dikrā* commemoration (of a deceased person); احياء لذكرى (*iḥyā'an*) (with foll. gen.) in commemoration of ..., in memoriam ...; احياء الموات *i. al-mawāt* cultivation of virgin land

استحياء *istiḥyā'* shame; diffidence, bashfulness, timidity; shyness

محيا *muḥayyan* face, countenance

الست المستحية *as-sitt al-mustaḥiya* sensitive plant (Mimosa pudica; *bot.*)

حيث[1] *ḥaiṯu* (conj.) where (place and direction); wherever; since, as, due to the fact that; whereas; inasmuch as | حيث ان (*anna*) since, as, because, due to the fact that ...; in that ...; حيث كان wherever it be; in any case, at any rate; الى حيث *ilā ḥaiṯu* where (direction); to where ..., to the place where ...; من حيث *min ḥaiṯu* from where, whence, wherefrom; where (place), whereas; (with foll. nominative) as to, as for, concerning, regarding, with respect to, in view of, because of; من حيث الثقافة *min ḥ. ṯ-ṯaqāfatu* with regard to education, as far as education is concerned; من حيث يدرى ولا يدرى (*yadrī wa-lā yadrī*) whether he knows it or not, knowingly or without his knowledge; من حيث لا (with foll. imperf.) without (being, doing, etc.); من حيث هو as such, in itself, العالم من حيث هو (*'ālam*) the world in itself, the world as such; من حيث ان (*anna*) inasmuch as; in view of the fact that; since, as, due to the fact that; بحيث *bi-ḥaiṯu* inasmuch as; in such a manner that ..., so as to ...; so that ...; such as ...; (he found himself) at a point or degree where, e.g., كانت من البراءة بحيث لا ترى (*barā'a, tarā*) = she was so naive that she couldn't see ...; بحيث لا insofar as ... not, provided that ... not; بحيث ان (*anna*) in such a manner that ..., so as to ..., so that ...

حيثما *ḥaiṯumā* wherever, wheresoever (place); wherever, no matter where ... (direction) | حيثما اتفق (*ittafaqa*) anywhere, wherever it was (or be), haphazardly, at random

حيثية *ḥaiṯīya* pl. *-āt* standpoint; viewpoint, point of view, approach; aspect, respect, regard, consideration; high social standing, social distinction, dignity; pl. also: considerations, legal reasons on which the judgment is based, opinion (*jur.*) | ذوو الحيثيات (البارزة) (*ḏawū*) or اصحاب الحيثيات, اصحاب الحيثية people of (high) social standing, prominent people, people of distinction; من الحيثية الحيوانية (*ḥayawānīya*) from a zoological viewpoint

الحيثيون[2] *al-ḥiṯīyūn* the Hittites

حيد حاد *ḥāda i* (*ḥaid*, حيود *ḥuyūd*, حيدان *ḥayadān*, محيد *maḥīd*) to deviate, swerve, depart, desist (عن from); to leave, quit, give up, abandon, relinquish (عن s.th.); حاد به عن to dissuade or get s.o. away from ...; to incline, tend (نحو, الى to, toward), shade, blend (نحو, الى into) **II** to keep aside, put aside (ه s.th.) **III** to stay away, keep apart (ه, ه from s.o., from s.th.); to avoid, shun (ه, ه s.o., s.th.) **VII** to depart, deviate, digress, swerve (عن from)

حيد *ḥaid*, حيدان *ḥayadān* deviation, digression, departure, swerving, turning aside, turning away

حيدة *ḥaida* deviation, digression, swerving, departure (from a course); neutrality; impartiality | على حيدة aside, apart, to one side

محيد *maḥīd* avoidance (عن of s.th.) | لا محيد عنه (*maḥīda*) it is unavoidable

حياد *ḥiyād* neutrality (*pol.*) | على الحياد neutral; حياد عن الخط (*kaṭṭ*) derailment (railroad)

حيادى *ḥiyādī* neutral (*pol.*)

محايدة *muḥāyada* neutrality (*pol.*)

حائد *ḥā'id* neutral (*pol.*)

محايد *muḥāyid* neutral (*pol.*); المحايدون the neutrals (*pol.*)

متحايد *mutaḥāyid* neutral (*pol.*)

حيدراباد *ḥaidarābād*[2] Hydarabad

(حير) حار *ḥāra* (1st pers. perf. *ḥirtu*) *a* (حيرة *ḥaira*, حيران *ḥayarān*) to become confused; to become or be helpless, be at a loss, know nothing (فى of, about); to waver, hesitate, be unable to choose (بين — وبين between — and) | حار فى امره (*amrihī*) to be confused, baffled, bewildered, dismayed; to be at a loss, be at one's wit's end **II** to confuse, baffle, bewilder, nonplus, embarrass (ه s.o.) **V** to become confused; to be or become dismayed, startled, baffled, perplexed (فى by), be at a loss (فى as to); to waver (uncertainly) (بين between) | تحير فى امره (*amrihī*) to be confused, baffled, bewildered, disconcerted, be at a loss, be at one's wit's end **VIII** = **V**

حير *ḥair* fenced-in garden, enclosure | حير الحيوان *ḥ. al-ḥayawān* zoological garden, zoo

حيرة *ḥaira* confusion, perplexity, bewilderment, embarrassment, helplessness | فى حيرة embarrassed, at a loss, helpless

حيران *ḥairān*[2], f. حيرى *ḥairā*, pl. حيارى *ḥayārā*, *ḥuyārā* confused, perplexed, startled, dismayed, disconcerted, baffled, nonplused, bewildered, appalled, taken aback, stunned; embarrassed, at a loss, at one's wit's end; uncertain, helpless, sheepish (smile, etc.), confused, incoherent (words, and the like)

تحير *taḥayyur* confusion, perplexity, bewilderment, dismay; embarrassment, helplessness

حائر *ḥā'ir* disconcerted, perplexed, startled, dismayed; embarrassed, helpless, at a loss, at one's wit's end; baffled, bewildered, confused, uncertain (فى about); straying, astray | حائر فى امره (*amrihī*) confused, baffled, bewildered, embarrassed, at a loss, helpless

محير *muḥayyar* embarrassed, at a loss, helpless

متحير *mutaḥayyir* and محتار *muḥtār* = حائر

حيز see حوز

حيزبون see حزب

(حيص) حاص *ḥāṣa* *i* (*ḥaiṣ*, حيصة *ḥaiṣa*, محيص *maḥīṣ*) to flee, escape (عن s.th. or from s.th.), run away (عن from), turn one's back (عن on) **VII** do.

حيص *ḥaiṣ*, حيصة *ḥaiṣa* flight, escape

وقع فى حيص بيص *waqa'a fī ḥaiṣa baiṣa* to get into a bad fix, meet with difficulties

حياصة see حوص

محيص *maḥīṣ* flight, escape; place of refuge, retreat, sanctuary | ما عنه محيص it is unavoidable; لم يكن لهم محيص من ان they couldn't but ..., they had no other alternative but to ...

(حيض) حاضت *ḥāḍat* *i* (*ḥaiḍ*, محيض *maḥīḍ*, محاض *maḥāḍ*) and **V** to menstruate, have a monthly period

حيض *ḥaiḍ* (n. un. حيضة) and حياض *ḥiyāḍ* menstruation, monthly period

حائض *ḥā'iḍ* (f.) and حائضة menstruating

حيط ,حياطة ,حيطان ,حياط see حوط

[1](حيف) حاف *ḥāfa* *i* (*ḥaif*) to deal unjustly (على with s.o.), wrong, injure, harm (على s.o.); to restrict, limit, curtail, impair (على s.th.), encroach (على upon) **V** to

impair, injure, prejudice, violate (ه or من s.th.), encroach, infringe (ه or من upon)

حيف *ḥaif* wrong, injustice; harm, damage, prejudice | حيف عليه what a pity! too bad! لا حيف به (*ḥaifa*) it is not out of place, it is quite appropriate

²حيفا *ḥaifā* Haifa (seaport in NW Israel)

(حيق) حاق *ḥāqa* *i* to surround, beset from all sides (ب s.o.); to fall, descend, come (ب upon s.o., punishment), befall, overtake, grip, seize, overcome (ب s.o.), happen, occur (ب to); to penetrate, pierce (فى the body; of a sword); to affect, influence (فى s.o., s.th.) IV to surround, beset from all sides (ب s.o.); to bring down (ب ه upon s.o. s.th.), cause s.th. (ه) to descend (ب upon s.o.)

حيق *ḥaiq* consequence, effect (of a misdeed redounding upon the evildoer)

حيك II to weave

حياكة see حوك

حيك *ḥaik* = حائك; see حوك

¹حيل V, حيلة, احيل, حيال, حيلولة, etc., see حول; احيلى see حلو

²حايل *ḥāyil*² Hail (town and oasis in N Nejd)

(حين) حان *ḥāna* *i* to draw near, approach, come, arrive (time); to happen accidentally | حان الوقت the (right) time has come; now is the time; حان له ان the time has come for him to ...; اما حان لهم ان يفهموا (*a-mā, an yafhamū*) haven't they understood yet ...?; حانت منى التفاتة (*minnī ltifāta*) I happened to turn around (الى to), it just happened that my eyes fell on (الى) II to set a time (ه for s.o.) IV to destroy, wipe out (ه s.o.) V to watch, wait (ه for a time or an opportunity) | تحين الفرصة (*furṣata*) to wait for an opportunity, bide one's time X استحين *istaḥyana* to wait for the right time

حان *ḥān* bar; cabaret

حانة *ḥāna* pl. *-āt* bar, wineshop, wine tavern; pub, tavern, taproom

حين *ḥain* death, destruction

حين *ḥīn* pl. احيان *aḥyān*, احايين *aḥāyīn*² time; propitious time, good time, opportunity; *ḥīna* (prep.) at the time of ..., at, upon; (conj.) at the time when, when; as soon as; حينا *ḥīnan* for some time; once, one day; احيانا *aḥyānan* occasionally, from time to time, sometimes | حينا — حينا sometimes — sometimes, at times — at times; فى الاحايين at times, sometimes, once in a while; فى بعض الاحيان (الاحايين) *fī baʿḍi l-a.* and بعض الاحيان *baʿḍa l-a.* sometimes, occasionally, now and then, once in a while, from time to time, at times; فى اغلب الاحيان *fī aḡlabi l-a.* mostly, most of the time, in most cases; الى حين for some time; meanwhile, for the time being; فى حينه then, at the time, in his (its) time; in due time, at the appointed time; ذا الحين *ḏā l-ḥīna* just now, right now; من ذلك الحين from that time on, from then on; الى ذلك الحين until that time, till then; فى حين (with foll. verb) whereas; فى حين ان and على حين ان (*ḥīni*) at the same time when ..., while; whereas, also without ان, e.g., على حين هم يزعمون *ʿalā ḥīni hum yazʿumūna* whereas they, on the other hand, claim; حينا بعد حين, بين حين وحين, من حين الى حين, بين حين وآخر, من حين لآخر (*li-āḵara*) and (*wa-āḵara*) from time to time, now and then, once in a while

حينئذ *ḥīna'iḏin* at that time, then, that day

حينذاك *ḥīnaḏāka* at that time, then, that day

حينما *ḥīnamā* (conj.) while; when, as

حيوان, حيوى and حيوية see حى

خ

خاء *ḵā'* name of the letter خ

خاتون *ḵātūn* pl. خواتين *ḵawātīn*² lady, socially prominent woman | زهرة الخاتون *zahrat al-ḵ.* little blue flower of the steppe (*syr.*)

خاخام *ḵāḵām* (= حاخام) rabbi

خارصين *ḵāraṣīn* and خارصينى *ḵāraṣīnī* (*eg.*) zinc

خازوق *ḵāzūq* pl. خوازيق *ḵawāzīq*² post, stake, pole; dirty trick | هذا خازوق that's tough luck!

خاقان *ḵāqān* pl. خواقين *ḵawāqīn*² overlord, ruler, sovereign, monarch, emperor

خاكى *ḵākī* earth-colored, khaki

خوولة, خوول see خول

خام *ḵām* raw, unworked, unprocessed; untanned; linen; calico; (pl. *-āt*) raw material; inexperienced, green, untrained, unskilled, artless, uncouth, boorish; pl. خامات raw materials | جلود خام raw leather; خيوط خام raw fibers; زيت خام (*zait*) crude oil; سكر خام (*sukkar*) raw sugar; المواد الخام (*mawādd*) the raw materials

خان *ḵān* pl. *-āt* hostel, caravansary; inn, pub, tavern | الخان الخليلى (*ḵalīlī*) district of Cairo (center of art trade and market activity); خان يونس Khan Yunis (town in Gaza sector)

خانة *ḵāna* pl. *-āt* column (e.g., of a newspaper); square (e.g., on a chessboard)

خب *ḵabba u* (*ḵabb*, خبب *ḵabab*, خبيب *ḵabīb*) to amble (animal); to trot (horse); to jog, saunter (person); to sink (فى in sand); — *u* (*ḵabb*) to surge, heave, be rough (sea) **V** and **VIII** to amble (animal); to trot (horse)

خبب *ḵabab* amble; trot

خب *ḵabb*, *ḵibb* heaving, surging (of the sea), rough sea

خب *ḵabb* impostor, swindler

خبأ *ḵaba'a a* and **II** to hide, conceal (ه s.th.) **V** to hide, conceal o.s.; to be hidden, be concealed **VIII** to hide, conceal o.s.; to disappear; to be hidden, be concealed

خبء *ḵab'*, *ḵib'* that which is hidden, a hidden thing

خبيئة *ḵabī'a* pl. خبايا *ḵabāyā* that which is hidden; a hidden, secret thing; a cache | خبايا الارض *ḵ. l-arḍ* that which is hidden in the earth; natural resources

مخبأ *maḵba'* pl. مخابئ *maḵābi'*² hiding place; hide-out, refuge, haunt, retreat; cellar, shelter, air-raid shelter

خباء *ḵibā'* pl. اخبئة *aḵbi'a*, اخبية *aḵbiya* tent; husk, hull (of grain)

خابئة *ḵābi'a*, خابية *ḵābiya* pl. خوابئ *ḵawābi'*², خواب *ḵawābin* large vessel, cask, jar

مخبآت *muḵabba'āt* hidden, secret things; secrets

مختبئ *muḵtabi'* hidden, concealed

خبت **IV** to be humble (الى before God)

خبث *ḵabuṯa u* (*ḵubṯ*, خباثة *ḵabāṯa*) to be bad, to be wicked, evil, malicious, vicious, malignant **VI** to behave viciously, display malice; to feel awkward, feel embarrassed

خبث *ḵubṯ* badness, wickedness; malignancy (e.g., of a disease); malice, malevolence, viciousness

خبث *ḵabaṯ* refuse, scum, dross, slag

خبيث *ḵabīṯ* pl. خبث *ḵubuṯ*, خبثاء *ḵubaṯā'*[2], اخباث *aḵbāṯ*, خبثة *ḵabaṯa* bad, evil, wicked; malicious, vicious, spiteful; noxious, injurious, harmful; malignant (disease); offensive, repulsive, nauseating, disgusting (odor)

اخبث *aḵbaṯ*[2] worse; more wicked

خباثة *ḵabāṯa* badness, wickedness; malice, malevolence, viciousness, malignancy

خبر *ḵabara u* (*ḵubr*, خبرة *ḵibra*) to try, test (ه s.th.); to experience (ه s.th.); to have tried, have experienced, know by experience (ه s.th.); to get to know thoroughly, know well (ه s.th., ه s.o.); — *ḵabura u* to know thoroughly (ب or ه s.th.), be fully acquainted (ب or ه with s.th.) **II** to notify, advise, apprise, inform, tell (ه s.o., ب of or about) **III** to write (ه to s.o.), address (ه s.o.), turn, appeal (ه to s.o.), contact (ه s.o.) in writing; to negotiate, treat, parley (ه with s.o.) **IV** to notify, inform, apprise, advise (ه ب s.o. of), let know, tell (ه ب s.o. about); to communicate, report, relate (ه ب to s.o. s.th.), tell (ه ب s.o. s.th.) **V** to inquire (ه of s.o.), ask (ه s.o.) **VI** to inform one another, notify one another, keep one another informed; to correspond, write each other; to negotiate, treat, parley (مع with s.o., فى about) **VIII** to explore (ه s.th.), search (ه into), seek information (ه about); to test, examine (ه s.o., ه s.th.); to try, put to the test (ه s.o., ه s.th.); to have tried, have experienced, know by experience (ه s.th.); to know well (ه s.th.) **X** to inquire (ه عن of s.o. about), ask (ه عن s.o. about)

خبر *ḵabar* pl. اخبار *aḵbār* news; information, intelligence; report, communication, message; notification; rumor; story; matter, affair; (*gram.*) predicate of a nominal clause; pl. annals | سأله عن اخباره to inquire of s.o. about s.o. else; دخل فى خبر كان or كان فى خبر كان (*ḵabari kāna*) to belong to the past, be passé, be no longer existent

خبرة *ḵibra*, خبر *ḵubr* experience; knowledge

خبير *ḵabīr* experienced, expert (ب in); familiar, conversant, well-acquainted (ب with), cognizant (ب of); الخبير the Knowing (one of the attributes of God); (pl. خبراء *ḵubarā'*[2]) expert, specialist | خبير الضرائب tax expert, tax adviser

خابور *ḵābūr* pl. خوابير *ḵawābīr*[2] peg; pin; wedge

مخبر *maḵbar* sense, intrinsic significance; (pl. مخابر *maḵābir*[2]) laboratory

مخبار *miḵbar* pl. مخابير *maḵābīr*[2] test tube (*chem.*)

مخابرة *muḵābara* pl. *-āt* correspondence, (esp. written) information (in classified ads: المخابرة ب please write to ..., please contact ...), notice, notification, communication | مخابرة تليفونية telephone call, telephone conversation; مخابرة خارجية (*ḵārijīya*) long-distance call; مخابرة سرية (*sirrīya*) secret communiqué; قلم المخابرات *qalam al-m.* intelligence bureau; المخابرة حضوريا (*ḥuḍūrīyan*) apply in person (in classified ads)

اخبار *iḵbār* notification, information, communication, note, message; report; indirect discourse, oratio obliqua (*gram.*)

اخبارى *iḵbārī* news-, information- (in compounds)

تخابر *taḵābur* negotiation; correspondence

اختبار *iḵtibār* pl. *-āt* exploration, study; examination; test; test item (of an examination); trial, testing; (scientific) investigation, research, experiment; experience, empirical knowledge; practical experience | اختبارات تحريرية (*taḥrīrīya*) written examination items; اختبار ذاتى

(ḏātī) personal experience; على سبيل الاختبار experimentally; تحت الاختبار on probation, on trial; حقول الاختبار experimental fields

اختباري iḵtibārī experimental; experiential; empirical

اختبارية iḵtibārīya empiricism

استخبار istiḵbār pl. -āt inquiry | دائرة الاستخبارات information bureau

مخبر muḵbir pl. -ūn reporter; detective

مختبر muḵtabar pl. -āt laboratory

خبز ḵabaza i (ḵabz) to bake (ه bread) VIII do.

خبز ḵubz pl. اخباز aḵbāz bread

خبزة ḵubza loaf of bread

خباز ḵabbāz pl. -ūn, خبازة baker

خباز ḵubbāz, خبيز ḵubbaiz, خبازى ḵubbāzā mallow (bot.)

خبازة ḵibāza baker's trade, art of baking

مخبز maḵbaz, مخبزة maḵbaza pl. مخابز maḵābiz² bakery

خبص ḵabaṣa i (ḵabṣ) to mix, mingle, intermix (ب ه s.th. with) II to mix, mingle, intermix (ه s.th.); to muddle, jumble, confuse (ه s.th.), make a mess (ه of)

خبيص ḵabīṣ, خبيصة ḵabīṣa medley, mess, mishmash, hodgepodge; خبيصة a jellylike sweet

خباص ḵabbāṣ one who causes confusion, who messes things up; an irresponsible, light-minded person

خبط ḵabaṭa i (ḵabṭ) to beat, strike (ه s.th., against s.th.); to knock, rap (ه on, الباب on the door); to stamp (الارض) the ground; (of animals) | يخبط خبط عشواء (ḵabṭa ʿašwāʾa) he acts haphazardly, he proceeds rashly or at random V to beat, strike, hit (ه s.o.); to bring down, fell, knock out, throw to the ground (ه s.o.); to bump, hit (ه against), collide (ه with), stumble

(ه over); to be lost, wander about, stray; to grope about, fumble about; to struggle, resist; to clatter over the ground, gallop (horse) VIII to bump (against); to struggle, resist; to grope about, fumble about; to be lost, wander around, stray; to stir, bustle

خبطة ḵabṭa blow, stroke; rap, knock; noise, din, uproar

خباط ḵubāṭ insanity, madness, mental disorder

خبل ḵabala u (ḵabl) to confound, confuse, mess up, complicate (ه s.th.); to hinder, impede, handicap, stop, hold back (ه s.o.); to befuddle (ه s.o.), confuse s.o.'s (ه) mind, rob (ه s.o.) of his senses, make (ه s.o.) crazy; — ḵabila a (ḵabal, خبال ḵabāl) to get confused; to be or become mentally disturbed, crazy, insane II to confound, confuse (ه s.th., ه s.o.); to complicate, entangle, mess up, muddle, throw into disorder (ه s.th.); to rob of his senses, drive insane (ه s.o.) VIII to become muddled, disordered (mind)

خبل ḵabl, ḵabal confusion; mental disorder, insanity

خبل ḵabil mad, crazy, insane; feebleminded, dim-witted

اخبل aḵbal² mad, crazy, insane; feebleminded, dim-witted

اختبال iḵtibāl mental disorder

مخبول maḵbūl mad, crazy, idiotic, imbecilic, mentally deranged, insane; muddlehead, dolt, fool

مخبل muḵabbal confused, baffled, perplexed, dismayed; muddled, confused, mixed up

خبا ḵabā u (ḵabw, ḵubūw) to go out, die (fire) (خبو)

خبأ see خباء pl. اخبية and خبايا

خبأ see خواب pl. خابية

خبيارى *kibyārī* caviar

ختر *katara i* (*katr*) to betray (ه s.o.), act perfidiously, disloyally (ه toward s.o.); to deceive, cheat, dupe (ه s.o.)

ختر *katr* disloyalty, breach of confidence, perfidy, treachery, betrayal, deception

ختار *kattār* traitor, disloyal person, cheat, swindler

خاتر *kātir* treacherous, perfidious, disloyal

ختل *katala i u* (*katl*, ختلان *katalān*) to dupe, gull, cheat, double-cross, deceive (ه s.o.) **III** to deceive, cheat, dupe (ه s.o.); to behave hypocritically **VIII** = **I**

ختل *katl* and مخاتلة *mukātala* deception, trickery, double-dealing, duplicity, duping, gulling

مخاتل *mukātil* deceitful, crafty, wily, foxy

ختم *katama i* (*katm*, ختام *kitām*) to seal, provide with a seal or signet (ه s.th.); to stamp, impress with a stamp (ه s.th.); to seal off, close, make impervious or inaccessible (ه s.th.; also على the hearts, said of God); to put one's seal (ه on), conclude, terminate (ه s.th.); to wind up, finish, complete (ه s.th.); to close, heal, cicatrize (wound) **V** to put on or wear a ring (ب) | تختم بالذهب (*dahab*) to wear a golden ring **VIII** to conclude, finish, terminate, wind up (ه s.th.)

ختم *katm* sealing; — (pl. اختام *aktām*, ختوم *kutūm*) seal, signet, seal imprint; stamp, stamp imprint; also = ختمة (see below) | ختم البريد postmark, (postal) cancellation stamp; شمع الختم *šam' al-k.* sealing wax

ختمة *katma* pl. *katamāt* recital of the entire Koran, esp. on festive occasions

خاتم *kātam*, *kātim* pl. خواتم *kawātim*² seal ring, signet ring; ring, finger ring; seal, signet; stamp | خاتم الزواج *k. az-zawāj* wedding ring; خاتم النبيين *k. an-nabīyīn* the Seal (i.e., the last) of the Prophets = Mohammed

خاتام *kātām* pl. خواتيم *kawātīm*² seal ring, signet ring; ring

ختام *kitām* sealing wax; end, close, conclusion, termination | فى الختام at the end, at last, finally, eventually

ختامى *kitāmī* final, concluding | كلمة ختامية (*kalima*) concluding speech

اختتام *iktitām* end, close, conclusion, termination

خاتمة *kātima* pl. خواتم *kawātim*², خواتيم *kawātīm*² end, close, conclusion, termination; epilogue (of a book); خواتيم final stage

مختم *mukattam* ringed, adorned with a ring or rings (hand)

مختتم *muktatam* end, close, conclusion, termination

¹ختن *katana i* (*katn*) to circumcise (ه a boy) **VIII** pass.

ختن *katn* circumcision

ختن *katan* pl. اختان *aktān* son-in-law; bridegroom

ختان *kitān*, ختانة *kitāna* circumcision

²خاتون look up alphabetically

خثر *katara u* and *katira a* to become solid, become thick, solidify, thicken; to be or become viscous, sirupy; to clot, coagulate (liquid); to curdle (milk) **II** and **IV** to thicken, inspissate, condense, coagulate (ه liquid); to curdle (ه milk) **V** = **I**

○ خثرة *katra* thrombosis (*med.*)

خثار *kutār* dregs (of a liquid); scum of the earth, riffraff, mob

خثارة *kutāra* dregs (of a liquid); sediment, lees

تخثر *takaṯṯur* coagulation | ○ تخثر فى المخ (*mukk*) cerebral thrombosis

خاثر *kāṯir* thickened, inspissated, condensed; viscous, ropy, sirupy; curdled, coagulated, clotted; yoghurt, curd

مخثر *mukaṯṯar* thickened, inspissated, condensed; viscous, ropy, sirupy; curdled, coagulated, clotted

خجل *kajila a* (*kajal*) to become embarrassed; to be ashamed (من of s.th. or to face s.o.), be abashed (من by s.th.), feel embarrassed (من about s.th. or in front of s.o.) **II** and **IV** to shame (ه s.o.); to embarrass, abash, put to shame (ه s.o.)

خجل *kajal* shame (من at); bashfulness, diffidence, timidity, shyness; abashment; disgrace, shame, ignominy | يا للخجل (*la-l-k.*) O disgrace! the shame of it!

خجل *kajil* abashed, embarrassed; bashful, diffident, shy, timid; overgrown with luxuriant, profuse vegetation; long and flowing (garment)

خجول *kajūl* abashed, ashamed, shamefaced; shy, bashful, diffident, timid

خجلان *kajlān*[2] abashed, ashamed, shamefaced; shy, bashful, diffident, timid; bewildered with shame, embarrassed

مخجول *makjūl* ashamed, shamefaced

مخجل *mukjil* arousing shame, shameful; shocking, disgraceful, ignominious | الاعضاء المخجلة (*aʿḍāʾ*) the pudenda

خد *kadda u* to furrow, plow (ه the ground) **V** to be furrowed; to become wrinkled (skin)

خد *kadd* pl. خدود *kudūd* cheek; lateral portion, side | صعر خده *ṣaʿʿara kaddahū* to put on a contemptuous mien

خد *kadd* and خدة *kudda* pl. خدد *kudad* furrow, ridge, groove, rut

اخدود *ukdūd* pl. اخاديد *akādīd*[2] furrow, ridge, groove, rut; trench, excavation

مخدة *mikadda* pl. مخاد *makādd*[2] cushion, pillow; seat cushion

خديج *kadīj* premature child

خداج *kidāj* abortion, miscarriage

خدر *kadira a* (*kadar*) to be numb, prickle, tingle (leg, arm); to be or become limp, benumbed, paralyzed; — *kadara u* to confine to women's quarters, keep in seclusion (ها a girl) **II** to numb, benumb, stupefy (ه s.o., ه s.th.); to anesthetize, narcotize, put to sleep (ه s.o., ه s.th.; *med.*); to confine to women's quarters, keep in seclusion (ها a girl) **IV** to make torpid, stupefy, benumb, deprive of sensation, narcotize (ه s.o., ه s.th.) **V** to be numbed, be stunned, be stupefied, be deprived of sensation; to come to rest, calm down

خدر *kidr* pl. خدور *kudūr*, اخدار *akdār*, اخادير *akādīr*[2] curtain, drape; women's quarters of a tent; boudoir, private room (of a lady)

خدر *kadar* and خدرة *kudra* numbness, insensibility (esp. of a limb gone to sleep); daze, torpor, stupor

خدر *kadir* numb (limb); benumbed, torpid, dazed

تخدير *takdīr* anesthetization, narcotization

خادر *kādir* limp, languid; benumbed, torpid, dazed; hidden in his den, lurking (lion)

خادرة *kādira* chrysalis (of a caterpillar; *zool.*)

مخدر *mukaddir* anesthetic, painkilling, tranquilizing; (pl. *-āt*) an anesthetic; a narcotic, drug, dope

مخدر *mukaddar* numb, torpid, insensible; (*eg.*) tipsy, fuddled, drunk

مخدرة *mukaddara* girl kept in seclusion from the outside world

خدش *kadaša i* (*kadš*) to scratch (ه s.th.); to maul, lacerate, tear to pieces (ه s.th.); to violate (ه the rules of decency, s.o.'s honor, and the like); to disturb (ه the peace); to ruin, sully, run down (سمعته *sum'atahū* s.o.'s reputation) **II** to scratch (ه s.th.); to maul, lacerate, tear to pieces (ه s.th.); to violate (ه the rules of decency, s.o.'s honor, etc.); to ruin, sully, run down (سمعته *sum'atahū* s.o.'s reputation)

خدش *kadš* pl. خدوش *kudūš*, اخداش *akdāš* scratch, scratch mark; graze, abrasion

خدع *kada'a a* to cheat (ه s.o., عن out of s.th.); to deceive, mislead, dupe, gull (ه s.o.); pass. *kudi'a* to be mistaken, be wrong (عن about); to fail to see clearly (عن with regard to), get the wrong impression (عن of s.th.) **III** to cheat, dupe, deceive, take in (ه s.o.); to try to deceive or double-cross (ه s.o.) **VII** to let o.s. be deceived, be deceived, deluded, misled (ب by); to be mistaken, be wrong

خدعة *kud'a* pl. خدع *kuda'*, *-āt* deception, cheating, swindle

خدعة *kuda'a* impostor, swindler, cheat, sharper

سوى اخدعه *sawwā akda'ahū* to crush s.o.'s pride, humble s.o.

خديعة *kadī'a* pl. خدائع *kadā'i'*[2] deception, deceit, betrayal, treachery, perfidy, trickery, imposture

خداع *kaddā'* impostor, swindler, sharper, cheat, crook; deceptive, delusive

خيدع *kaida'* fata morgana, mirage

اخاديع *akādī'*[2] swindles, underhand dealings, crooked practices; phantoms, phantasms, delusions

مخدع *mikda'*, *mukda'*, *makda'* pl. مخادع *makādi'*[2] small room, chamber, cabinet; bedchamber

خداع *kidā'* deception, deceit, swindle, imposture, betrayal, treachery, perfidy, trickery, duplicity

خداعى *kidā'ī* deceitful, fraudulent; deceptive, delusive, fallacious

مخادع *mukādi'* swindler, impostor, cheat, sharper, crook

خدل *kadila a* to stiffen, become rigid; to become numb, torpid, limp

خدم *kadama i u* (خدمة *kidma*) to serve, be at service, do service; to have a job; to work; to wait (ه on s.o.); to serve (ه s.o., ه s.th.); to render a service (ه to s.o., ه to s.th.), stand up (ه for s.o.) | خدم الارض to till or cultivate the soil; خدمه خدمات كثيرة (*kidamātin katīratan*) he rendered him many services; خدم ركاب فلان (*rikāba*) to be at s.o.'s beck and call; خدم مصالح فلان (*maṣāliḥa*) to serve s.o.'s interests; خدم القداس (*quddāsa*) to celebrate Mass (*Chr.*) **II** to employ, hire (ه s.o.), engage the services (ه of s.o.); to give work (ه to s.o.), provide work (ه for) **X** to employ, hire, take on (ه s.o., ل for s.th.), engage the services (ل ه of s.o. for s.th.); to put in operation, operate (ه e.g., a public utility); to employ, use (ه s.th., ل for), make use, avail o.s. (ه of s.th., ل for a purpose)

خدم *kadam* servants, attendants

خدمة *kidma* pl. خدم *kidam*, *-āt* a service (rendered); attendance, service; operation; office, employment, occupation, job; work | فى خدمة شىء in the service of s.th.; فى خدمتكم at your service; خدمة للحقيقة (*kidmatan*) in the interest of truth, for the sake of truth; الخدمة العسكرية (*'askarīya*) military service; الخدمة الاجبارية (*ijbārīya*) conscription, compulsory service; الخدمة السرية (*sirrīya*) secret service (*pol.*); خدمة القداس *k. al-quddās* celebration of Mass (*Chr.*)

خدّام *ḵaddām* pl. ة manservant, servant, attendant; woman servant, female domestic servant, maid

خدامة *ḵadāma* attendance, service; employment, occupation, office, job

خدّامة *ḵaddāma* pl. *-āt* woman servant, female domestic servant, maid

تخديم *taḵdīm* work, occupation or duty of an employment agent (مخدّم *muḵaddim* see below) | مكتب التخديم *maktab at-t.* labor office, employment bureau

استخدام *istiḵdām* (putting into) operation; use, utilization; employment, hiring (of an employee); service, occupation, position, job

خادم *ḵādim* pl. خدّام *ḵuddām*, خدمة *ḵadama* domestic servant, help; manservant; woman servant; employee; attendant; waiter; deacon (*Chr.*)

خادمة *ḵādima* woman servant; female domestic servant, maid; woman attendant

خادمية *ḵādimīya* status of a servant

مخدوم *maḵdūm* pl. *-ūn*, مخاديم *maḵādīm*² master, employer

مخدومة *maḵdūma* mistress, lady (of the house), woman employer

مخدومية *maḵdūmīya* status of the master or employer

مخدّم *muḵaddim* pl. *-ūn* employment agent

مستخدم *mustaḵdim* pl. *-ūn* employer; — *mustaḵdam* (colloq. *mustaḵdim*) pl. *-ūn* employee, official

خدن III to befriend (ه s.o.), make friends (ه with s.o.); to associate socially (ه with)

خدن *ḵidn* pl. اخدان *aḵdān* (intimate) friend, companion, confidant

خدين *ḵadīn* (intimate) friend, companion, confidant

خديو *ḵidīw*, خديوى *ḵudaiwī* khedive

خديوى *ḵidīwī* khedivial

خذأ X to submit, subject o.s.

مستخذئ *mustaḵḏi'* submissive, servile, subservient, obedient

خذروف *ḵuḏrūf* pl. خذاريف *ḵaḏārīf*² (spinning) top

خذروفى *ḵuḏrūfī* turbinate, toplike

خذف *ḵaḏafa* i (*ḵaḏf*) to hurl away (ه, ب s.th.)

مخذفة *miḵḏafa* sling, slingshot, catapult

خذل *ḵaḏala* u (*ḵaḏl*, خذلان *ḵiḏlān*) to leave, abandon, forsake, desert, leave in the lurch (ه or عن s.o.); to stay behind; to disappoint; pass. *ḵuḏila* to fail, suffer a setback, meet with disappointment III to leave, abandon, forsake, desert, leave in the lurch (ه s.o.) VI to let up, flag, grow slack, languish, wane, decrease, fade, grow feeble VII to be left in the lurch; to be helpless; to be defeated; to meet with disappointment

خذلان *ḵiḏlān* disappointment

تخاذل *taḵāḏul* fatigue, languor, weakness, feebleness; relaxation, lessening of tension; disagreement, dissent, disunion

انخذال *inḵiḏāl* forsakenness, desertedness, abandonment; defeat

متخاذل *mutaḵāḏil* languid, weak, exhausted, spent, effete

خذو X to submit, subject o.s.

استخذاء *istiḵḏā'* subservience, submissiveness, servility

مستخذ *mustaḵḏin* submissive, servile, subservient, obedient

خر *ḵarra* i u (خرير *ḵarīr*) to murmur, bubble, gurgle, purl (of running water); to ripple, trickle; to snore; — (*ḵarr*, خرور

ḵurūr) to fall, fall down, drop; to sink to the ground, prostrate o.s. | خر على الارض to fall to the ground; خر بين يديه (*baina yadaihi*) he prostrated himself before him; خر تحت قدميه (*taḥta qadamaihi*) he fell at his feet

خرير **ḵarīr** purl, murmur, ripple (of water)

خرئ **ḵari'a** *a* (خرء *ḵar'*) to evacuate the bowels, defecate

خرء **ḵur'** and خراء **ḵarā'** excrement, feces

خراسان **ḵurāsān**[2] Khurasan (province in NE Iran)

[1]خرب **ḵaraba** *i* (*ḵarb*) to destroy, wreck, demolish, shatter, devastate, lay waste (ه s.th.); — **ḵariba** *a* (خراب *ḵarāb*) to be or become destroyed, ruined, waste, go to ruin, fall apart, disintegrate **II** to devastate, lay waste, destroy, wreck, demolish, ruin, lay in ruins (ه s.th.) **IV** = **II**; **V** to be or become destroyed, ruined, waste, go to ruin, fall apart, disintegrate

خرب **ḵarb** destruction, devastation

خرب **ḵurb** hole; eye of a needle; anus

خرب **ḵarib** destroyed, demolished, wrecked, devastated, waste; dilapidated, tumble-down, ramshackle; broken, ruined, out of order

خربة **ḵirba** pl. خرب *ḵirab* (site of) ruins; ruin, disintegrating structure

خربة **ḵarba, ḵurba** irreligion, lawlessness

خربة **ḵurba** pl. خرب *ḵurab* hole; eye of a needle; anus

خربة **ḵariba** (site of) ruins

خراب **ḵarāb** ruin, ruination; state of destruction or dilapidation; desolation; (pl. اخربة *aḵriba*) (site of) ruins

خرابة **ḵarāba** pl. *-āt*, خرائب *ḵarā'ib*[2] disintegrating structure, ruin, ruins

خربان **ḵarbān, ḵirbān** destroyed, wrecked, demolished, devastated, waste; ruined, broken, out of order

تخريب **taḵrīb** pl. *-āt* devastation, destruction, wrecking, demolition; sabotage

عمل تخريبي *'amal taḵrībī* act of sabotage

خارب **ḵārib** annihilator, destroyer

مخرب **muḵarrib** pl. *-ūn* annihilator, destroyer; saboteur

مخرب **muḵrib** annihilator, destroyer

[2]خروب **ḵarrūb** (coll.; n. un. ة) carob, locust; carob bean, locust pod, St.-John's-bread

خروبة **ḵarrūba** pl. *-āt* kharouba, a dry measure (*Eg.*; = $^1/_{16}$ قدح = .129 l)

خربش **ḵarbaša** to scratch; to scrawl, scribble

خربوش **ḵarbūš** pl. خرابيش *ḵarābīš*[2] (*syr.*) tent

○ مخربشات **muḵarbašāt** graffiti

خربط **ḵarbaṭa** to throw into disorder, disarrange, confuse (ه s.th.)

خربق **ḵarbaqa** to perforate, riddle (ه s.th.); to spoil, mar (ه s.th.)

خربق **ḵarbaq** hellebore (*bot.*)

خرت **ḵarata** *u* (*ḵart*) to pierce, bore, perforate (ه s.th.), make a hole (ه in)

خرت **ḵurt, ḵart** pl. اخرات *aḵrāt*, خروت *ḵurūt* hole; bore, drill hole; ring, eye, eyelet

خريت **ḵirrīt** experienced, practiced, skilled; guide

خرتيت **ḵartīt** rhinoceros

خرج **ḵaraja** *u* (خروج *ḵurūj*) to go out, walk out; to come out (من of), emerge (من from); to drive or ride out, go out (in a vehicle); to flow out, exude, effuse; to go away, depart, leave, retire; to protrude, project, stick out; to leave (من s.th.); to dismount, alight, disembark (من from), get out, step out (من of); to emanate, issue, arise, originate, result (من from); to draw away, segregate, separate, secede, dissent (عن from), disagree (عن with); to deviate, depart (عن from an arrangement, from a principle); to be an exception (عن to); to be outside a given subject (عن), go beyond a topic (عن), exceed (عن a topic); to be alien (عن to), be extraneous (عن from), not to belong (عن to), be not included (عن in), have nothing to do with (عن); لا يخرج عن it is limited to ..., it is nothing but ...; to go forth (into battle); to attack (على s.o., s.th.), rise, fight (على against); to rebel, revolt (على against); to violate, break, infringe (على a rule, a regulation); خرج عليه ب to come up to s.o. with ..., confront s.o. with ...; to get out, bring out, take out (ب s.o.); to turn out, oust, dislodge (ب s.o.); to lead away, dissuade (ب عن s.o. from); to find out, discover (ب s.th.) | خرج عن الخط (*kaṭṭ*) to be derailed, run off the track (train) **II** to move out, take out, dislodge (ه s.o., ه s.th.); to turn out, oust, expel, evict, drive out (ه s.o., ه s.th.); to remove, eliminate (ه s.o., ه s.th.); to exclude, except (ه s.th.); to train (ه s.o., في in a skill, and the like); to educate, bring up (ه s.o.); to distill (ه s.th.); to pull out, extract (ه s.th.); to gather, deduce, infer (ه s.th.); to explain, interpret, expound, elucidate (ه s.th.) **IV** to move out, take out, get out, bring out, dislodge (ه s.o., ه s.th.); to unload (ه s.th.), disembark, detrain, etc. (ه s.o., e.g., troops); to turn out, oust (ه s.o.); to emit, send out (ه s.th., e.g., electric waves); to stick out (ه e.g., the tongue); to fish out (ه s.th. from the pocket); to bring out into the open, make public (ه s.th.); to remove, extract (ه s.th.); to eliminate (ه s.th.); to expel, evict, exile, expatriate (ه s.o., من from a country); to dismiss, fire, remove (ه s.o., من from an office); اخرجه من ثروته (*ṯarwatihī*) to rob s.o. of his property, dispossess, expropriate s.o.; to give off, sound, emit (ه s.th., e.g., a tone; said of a musical instrument); to set forth, state, express, utter, voice (ه an opinion); to break (ريحا *rīḥan* wind); to educate, bring up (ه s.o.); to train (ه s.o.); to stage, produce (ه a play; *theat.*); to bring out, make, shoot (رواية *riwāyatan* a film, said of a director); to except, exclude (ه s.th., عن from); to pull out, extract (ه s.th.); to select (ه s.th.) **V** to be educated; to be trained (في in a school, college, also من; في in a field); to graduate (في from a school, from a college, also من) **VI** to part company, separate; to disengage, disassociate, withdraw from one another; to cede, assign, transfer, make over (عن ل s.th. to s.o.) **X** to get out, move out, remove (ه s.th., من from); to take out, draw (ه s.th., من from); to pull out, extract (ه s.th., من from); to mine, extract, recover (ه mineral resources); to win, gain, make (ه a product, من from); to copy, excerpt (ه s.th., من from a book or document); to derive, draw, deduce, figure out, compute (ه من s.th. from); to elicit (ه s.th., e.g., astonishment, من from s.o.); to find out, discover (ه s.th.)

خرج *karj* expenditure, outlay, expense(s), costs; land tax; s.th. appropriate or suitable, that which is s.o.'s due, which s.o. deserves, which s.o. needs; (*eg.*) ration (food); (pl. خروجات *kurūjāt*) trimming; edge, edging, piping; pl. lace; trimmings | هذا خرجك that's what you need, what you deserve; خرج المشنقة *k. al-mašnaqa* one who deserves to be hanged

خرج *kurj* pl. خرجة *kiraja* saddlebag, portmanteau

خرجة *ḵarja* pl. *ḵarajāt* exit, departure; protrusion, protuberance, projection, salient part; (*eg.*) funeral

خراج *ḵarāj* tax; kharaj, land tax (*Isl. Law*)

خراجى *ḵarājī* of or pertaining to land tax; of or pertaining to the taxed and cultivable area

خراج *ḵurāj* (coll.; n. un. ة, pl. *-āt*) skin eruption; tumor, abscess

خروج *ḵurūj* exit; egression, emergence; departure; exodus; emigration; raid, foray, sortie (على against), attack, assault (على on) | خروج عن الخط (*ḵaṭṭ*) derailment (of a train)

خريج *ḵirrīj* pl. *-ūn* graduate (of a school, college, or university) | مؤتمر الخريجين العرب *mu'tamar al-ḵ. al-'arab* Congress of Arab Graduates (a supra-national organization of university graduates advocating a unified Arab world)

مخرج *maḵraj* pl. مخارج *maḵārij*[2] (place of) exit; way out (of a difficult situation), outlet, escape, loophole, shift, dodge, excuse; articulation (of a sound); ○ cathode (*el.*) | علم مخارج الحروف phonetics

تخريج *taḵrīj* education, training (in schools, colleges); raising, upbringing, rearing (of children); extraction; derivation, deduction; interpretation, exegesis

اخراج *iḵrāj* taking out, moving out, removal; unloading, disembarkment, detrainment; emission; moving, carting away, hauling off; evacuation; publication, publicizing, bringing before the public; extraction, removal; elimination; dismissal, removal (from an office); ousting, expulsion, eviction, expatriation, banishment (from a country); excretion (*biol.*); finding out, discovery, figuring out; training, formation, education; direction, production, staging (motion pictures, theater) | تولى الاخراج (*tawallā*) to have the direction (motion pictures, theater); ... من اخراج directed by ... (motion picture)

تخرج *taḵarruj* graduation (from a school or college)

تخارج *taḵāruj* separation, disassociation, disengagement, (mutual) withdrawal

استخراج *istiḵrāj* taking out, moving out, pulling out, removal; withdrawing; extraction, derivation, gaining (of industrial products, etc.), mining, recovery (of mineral resources); preparation of an extract; excerpting, copying; deduction, inference; solution (of a problem)

خارج *ḵārij* outer, outside, outward, exterior; external, foreign; outside, exterior (n.); foreign country or countries; quotient (*arith.*); *ḵārija* (prep.) outside, out of; خارجا *ḵārijan* outside | خارجا عن outside of, apart from; فى الخارج abroad, in foreign countries; outside; الى الخارج abroad, to foreign countries; to the outside, outward, out

الخارجة El Khârga (town in central Egypt, in Khârga oasis)

خارجى *ḵārijī* outer, out- (in compounds), outside, outward, exterior, external; foreign; nonresident | عيادة خارجية (*'iyāda*) policlinic; وزارة الخارجية ministry of foreign (external) affairs, foreign ministry; تلميذ خارجى (*tilmīḏ*) a student not living at a boarding school, a day student

خوارج *ḵawārij*[2] the Khawarij, Kharijites (the oldest religious sect of Islam); dissenters, dissidents, backsliders, rebels

مخرج *muḵrij* pl. *-ūn* (screen or stage) director

مخرج *muḵraj* excerpt, extract (from a book); مخرجات excretions (*biol.*)

متخرج mutaḵarrij pl. -ūn graduate (من or في of a school or college)

مستخرج mustaḵraj pl. -āt extract; excerpt (من from), partial copy (من of)

خرخر ḵarḵara to snore

¹خرد ḵarida a to be a virgin, be untouched, innocent, chaste

خريدة ḵarīda pl. خرائد karā'id², خرد ḵurud virgin; unbored pearl

²خردة ḵurda scrap metal, scrap iron; pl. خردوات ḵurdawāt notions, smallwares; small goods, smalls, miscellaneous small articles; (eg. also) novelties, fancy goods for ladies

خردجي ḵurdajī dealer in miscellaneous smallwares

خردق ḵurdaq, ḵurduq small shot, buckshot

خردل ḵardal (coll.; n. un. ة) mustard seeds; mustard

خرز ḵaraza i u to pierce, bore (ء s.th.)

خرز ḵaraz (coll.; n. un. ة) pearls

مخرز miḵraz pl. مخارز maḵāriz² awl; punch

مخراز miḵrāz awl; punch

¹خرس ḵarisa a (ḵaras) to be dumb, mute; to become silent, keep silent, hold one's tongue IV to silence, reduce to silence, gag (ه s.o.)

خرس ḵaras dumbness, muteness

اخرس aḵras², f. خرساء ḵarsā'², pl. خرس ḵurs, خرسان ḵursān dumb, mute

خرسان ḵarsān² dumb, mute

³خرسان ḵarasān, خرسانة ḵarasāna concrete (béton) | خرسانة مسلحة ○ (musallaḥa) armored (or reinforced) concrete

خرشوف ḵuršūf (coll.; n. un. ة) pl. خراشيف ḵarāšīf² artichoke

خرص ḵaraṣa u (ḵarṣ) to guess, estimate (ه s.th.); to conjecture, surmise (ه s.th.), form conjectures (ه about); to tell an untruth, a falsehood, to lie V to fabricate lies (على against s.o.); to raise false accusations (على against s.o.)

خرص ḵirṣ, ḵurṣ pl. خرصان ḵirṣān, ḵurṣān earring

خراص ḵarrāṣ pl. -ūn liar, slanderer, calumniator

خرط ḵaraṭa u i (ḵarṭ) to pull off, strip (ه leaves from a tree); to turn, lathe, shape with a lathe (ه wood, metal); to exaggerate, boast, brag, lie; — u (eg.) to cut into small pieces; to mince, chop, dice (ه meat, carrots, etc.) II (eg.) to cut into small pieces, mince, chop (ه s.th.) VII to be turned, be lathed, be shaped with a lathe; to join, enter (في سلك في fī silk an organization, a community), affiliate (في, في سلك with an organization, a community); to penetrate (في s.th. or into); to plunge headlong (في into), embark rashly (في upon); to labor, slave, toil | انخرط في البكاء (bukā') to break into tears

خرط ḵarṭ pulling-off (of leaves); دون ذلك خرط القتاد see دون; turning, turnery

خراط ḵarrāṭ pl. -ūn turner, lather; braggart, bluffer, storyteller

خراطة ḵirāṭa turner's trade, turnery, art of turning

خراطة ḵarrāṭa skirt (syr.)

خريطة ḵarīṭa pl. خرائط karā'iṭ², خرط ḵuruṭ map, chart

مخرطة miḵraṭa, maḵraṭa pl. مخارط maḵāriṭ² lathe

خارطة ḵāriṭa pl. -āt map, chart

مخروط maḵrūṭ cone (math.); conic

مخروطي maḵrūṭī conic

خرطوش *kartūš*, خرطوشة *kartūša* pl. خراطيش *karāṭīš*[2] cartridge; lead (of a pencil); cartouche (*arch.*); daybook

خرطال *kartāl* oats

خرطوم *kurṭūm* pl. خراطيم *karāṭīm*[2] proboscis, trunk (of the elephant); hose

الخرطوم *al-karṭūm* Khartoum (capital of the Sudanese Republic)

خراطين *karāṭīn*[2] a kind of earthworm

خراطينى *karāṭīnī* wormlike, vermiform

خرطيط *karṭīṭ* rhinoceros

خرع *karu'a u* (*kur'*, خراعة *karā'a*) and *kari'a a* (*kara'*) to droop, be or become slack, limp, flabby; to be or become languid, soft, spineless, yielding **VII** do. **VIII** to invent, devise, contrive (ه s.th.); to create, originate (ه s.th.)

خرع *kari'* and خريع *karī'* soft, languid, yielding, spineless, devoid of energy, nerveless

خروع *kirwa'* castor-oil plant, palma Christi (Ricinus communis; *bot.*)

اختراع *iktirā'* pl. *-āt* invention

مخترع *muktari'* pl. *-ūn* inventor

مخترع *muktara'* pl. *-āt* invention

خرف *karifa a* (*karaf*) to dote, be senile and feeble-minded; to drivel, talk foolishly

خرف *karaf* feeble-mindedness, dotage, senility; childishness (of an old man)

خرف *karif* and خرفان *karfān* feeble-minded, doting; childish; dotard

خريف *karīf* autumn, fall

خريفى *karīfī* autumnal

خروف *karūf* pl. خراف *kirāf*, اخرفة *akrifa*, خرفان *kirfān* young sheep, lamb, yearling; wether

خرافة *kurāfa* pl. *-āt* superstition; fable, fairy tale

خرافى *kurāfī* fabulous, fictitious, legendary

مخرفة *makrafa* prattle, drivel, twaddle, bosh

تخريف *takrīf* folly, delusion; foolish talk, drivel, twaddle, bosh, buncombe

مخرف *mukarrif* childish, foolish; (pl. *-ūn*) prattler, chatterbox, windbag; charlatan

خرفش *karfaša* to shuffle, mix (ه s.th.)

خرفوشة *karfūša* pl. خرافيش *karāfīš*[2] card of low value, discard (in card playing)

خرق *karaqa i u* (*karq*) to tear, rend, tear apart (ه s.th.); to make a hole (ه in); to perforate, pierce, bore (ه s.th.); to penetrate (ه s.th.), break, pass (ه through s.th.); to traverse, cross, transit (ه s.th., a country); to violate, impair, infringe (ه s.th.), encroach (ه upon); to break (ه a vow, and the like), commit a breach of (ه); to exceed the ordinary, be unusual, extraordinary, unprecedented, unheard-of | خرق العادة to go beyond what is ordinary or customary **IV** to lurk, lie in wait **V** and **VII** to be torn, be rent, be pierced, be broken **VIII** to pierce (ه s.th.); to cut, break, pass (ه through s.th.), penetrate (ه s.th.); to traverse, cross, transit (ه s.th.), travel through s.th. (ه); to exceed (ه e.g., a limit), go beyond s.th. (ه) | اخترق مسامعه (*masāmi'ahū*) to shrill in s.o.'s ears

خرق *karq* tearing, rending, laceration; piercing, boring, perforation; penetration; disruption; breakthrough; traversion, crossing, transit; violation, breach; (pl. خروق *kurūq*) hole, aperture, opening | خرق الامن العام *k. al-amn al-'āmm* violation of public security; خرق العادات offense against common usage, violation of mores; اتسع الخرق على الراقع (*ittasa'a*) the rent is beyond repair

خرق *ḵurq* and خرقة *ḵurqa* awkwardness, clumsiness; stupidity | خرق فى الرأى (*ra'y*) stupidity; folly, madness; من الخرق فى الرأى ان ... it would be very unwise to ...

خرقة *ḵirqa* pl. خرق *ḵiraq* tatter, shred; rag; scrap (of paper); polishing cloth; eraser (cloth)

اخرق *aḵraq*², f. خرقاء *ḵarqā'*², pl. خرق *ḵurq* clumsy, awkward; stupid; irregular; illegal, illicit, unlawful

مخرقة *maḵraqa* trickery, sleight of hand, legerdemain, hocus-pocus, swindle

مخارق *maḵāriq*² a kind of pastry (*tun.*)

اختراق *iḵtirāq* penetration; piercing, disruption; traversion, crossing, transit

خارق *ḵāriq* and خارق العادة (or للعادة) exceeding the customary, unusual, extraordinary, unprecedented, unheard-of; pl. خوارق *ḵawāriq*² preternatural phenomena, miracles; that which transcends the conceivable or the rational | خارق الطبيعة supernatural; خوارق المصادفات *ḵ. al-muṣādafāt* miraculous coincidences

مخترق *muḵtaraq* passage, passageway

خرم *ḵarama i* (*ḵarm*) and II to pierce (ه s.th.), make a hole or holes (ه in); to perforate (ه s.th.) VII to be pierced, be riddled, be torn; to be deranged, unsettled, disorganized; to come to an end, run out, peter out, get lost VIII to destroy, annihilate (ه s.o.); to carry off, carry away (ه s.o., of death); to break (الصفوف the ranks), pass through s.th. (ه)

خرم *ḵarm* pl. خروم *ḵurūm* gap, blank (e.g., in a manuscript, or the like)

خرم *ḵurm* hole | خرم الابرة *ḵ. al-ibra* eye of the needle

خرامة *ḵarrāma* drill, bit, auger, gimlet; punch, perforator

اخرم *aḵram*² having a perforated nasal septum

تخريم *taḵrīm* piercing, boring, drilling; perforation; punching; lacemaking, lacework

تخريمة *taḵrīma* lace, lacework, openwork, filigree

انخرام *inḵirām* state of unsettlement, disturbance, disorganization, derangement | انخرام فى التوازن (*tawāzun*) disturbance of equilibrium

مخروم *maḵrūm* defective, incomplete (e.g., a manuscript)

مخرم *muḵarram* perforated; done in openwork, in filigree

خرماشة *ḵurmāša* pl. *-āt* (*ir.*) harrow

خرنوب *ḵurnūb* carob, locust; carob bean, locust pod, St.-John's-bread

خرنق *ḵirniq* pl. خرانق *ḵarāniq*² young hare, leveret

خروع *ḵirwa'* castor-oil plant, palma Christi (Ricinus communis; *bot.*)

¹خز *ḵazza u* to pierce, transfix (ه s.o.); to stab (ه s.o., ب with) VIII to pierce, transfix (ه s.o., ب with)

²خز *ḵazz* pl. خزوز *ḵuzūz* silk, silk fabric

¹خزر *ḵazara u* to look askance (ه at s.o.), give s.o. (ه) a sidelong glance

²الخزر بحر *baḥr al-ḵazar* the Caspian Sea

خيزران *ḵaizurān* pl. خيازر *ḵayāzir*² cane, reed; rattan; bamboo

خيزرانة *ḵaizurāna* cane, stick

خزع *ḵaza'a a* (*ḵaz'*) to cut, sever (ه s.th.)

خزعبل *ḵuza'bal* idle talk, bosh

خزعبلة *ḵuza'bala* pl. *-āt* idle talk, bosh; joke, jest, hoax; fib, yarn; cock and bull story

خزف *ḵazaf* pottery, earthenware; porcelain, china; ceramics

خزفى *ḵazafī* (made of) porcelain; porcelaneous, porcelain, china (adj.)

خزاف *ḵazzāf* dealer in chinaware; potter

خزافة *ḵizāfa* potter's trade, pottery

1 خزق *ḵazaqa* i to pierce, stab, transfix (ه, ‍ه s.o., s.th.); to drive, ram (ه في الارض s.th. into the ground); to tear, rend, rip apart (ه s.th.) II to tear, rend, rip apart (ه s.th.) V and VII pass of I and II

خزق *ḵazq* rip, rent, tear, hole (in a garment)

خازوق *ḵāzūq* pl. خوازيق *ḵawāzīq*² post, stake, pole; dirty trick | هذا خازوق that's tough luck!

2 خوزق look up alphabetically

خزل *ḵazala* i (*ḵazl*) to cut off, sever (ه s.th.); to hinder, prevent, hold back, restrain, keep (ه s.o., عن from) VIII to cut off, cut short, end abruptly (ه s.th.); to shorten, abridge, abbreviate (ه s.th.); to stand alone (ب with an opinion)

اختزال *iḵtizāl* abridgment, abbreviation; shorthand, stenography

مختزل *muḵtazil* stenographer

خزم *ḵazama* i (*ḵazm*) to string, thread (ه pearls) | خزم انفه (*anfahū*) to pierce the nasal septum (of a camel) and insert the nose ring for the bridle; to make s.o. subservient to one's will

خزام *ḵizām*, خزامة *ḵizāma* pl. خزائم *ḵazā'im*² nose ring

خزامى *ḵuzāmā* lavender (*bot.*)

خزن *ḵazana* u (*ḵazn*) to store, stock, lay up, hoard, amass, accumulate; to keep secret, keep (ه a secret) II and VIII to store, stock, lay up, warehouse (ه s.th.); to store up, accumulate (ه s.th.); to dam (ه s.th.); to put in safekeeping, keep (ه s.th.)

خزن *ḵazn* storing, accumulation, hoarding, amassing; storage, warehousing

خزنة *ḵazna* treasure house; safe, coffer, vault; wardrobe, locker; cupboard

خزانة *ḵizāna* pl. *-āt*, خزائن *ḵazā'in*² treasure house; vault, coffer, safe; treasury, treasury department (of an official agency), any office for the deposit and disbursement of funds; locker, wardrobe, closet; cupboard; library | خزانة الدولة *ḵ. ad-daula* and خزانة عامة (*'āmma*) public treasury, exchequer; خزانة الثلج *ḵ. aṯ-ṯalj* icebox, refrigerator; خزانة الكتب *ḵ. al-kutub* bookcase; library; خزانة خصوصية (*ḵuṣūṣīya*) private library; خزانة الملابس wardrobe, closet, locker

خزينة *ḵazīna* pl. خزائن *ḵazā'in*² treasure house; public treasury, exchequer; treasury, treasury department (of an official agency), any office for the deposit and disbursement of funds; cashier's office; vault, coffer, safe; cashbox, till (of a merchant) | الخزينة الخاصة (*ḵāṣṣa*) (formerly) the Royal Privy Purse (*Ir.*); خزينة الدولة *ḵ. ad-daula* public treasury, exchequer; خزينة نقود راصدة, خزينة راصدة cash register

خزان *ḵazzān* pl. *-āt*, خزازين *ḵazāzīn*² dam; reservoir; basin, sump, pool; storage tank (also for oil); — (pl. *-ūn*) storehouseman, warehouseman

مخزن *maḵzan* pl. مخازن *maḵāzin*² storeroom, storehouse; depository; stockroom, storage room; depot, magazine, warehouse; store, shop, department store; المخزن *al-maḵzan* the Makhzan, the Moroccan government (formerly: governmental finance department; *Mor.*) | مخزن ادوية *m. adwiya* drugstore; مخزن الاصدار *m. al-iṣdār* shipping room (*com.*); مخزن العفش *m. al-'afš* trunk (of an automobile)

مخزنى makzanī being under government control or administration, belonging to the government (*Mor.*) | املاك مخزنية (*amlāk*) government land (*Mor.*)

مخازنى makāzinī pl. -*īya* native gendarme (*Mor.*)

مخازن makāzin²: مخازن الطريق *m. aṭ-ṭarīq* the nearest, shortest way, a short cut

مخزنجى makzanjī storehouseman, warehouseman

خزندار kazandār, kaznadār treasurer

تخزين takzīn storage, storing, warehousing; storing up, accumulation; damming

خازن kāzin pl. خزنة kazana, خزان kuzzān treasurer

مخزون makzūn stored, stored up, deposited, warehoused; (pl. -*āt*) stock, supply, stock in trade

خزى **kaziya** *a* (*kizy, kazan*) to be or become base, vile, despicable, contemptible; (خزاية *kazāya*) to be ashamed (من of); — *kazā i* to disgrace, dishonor, discredit, put to shame (ه s.o.); to shame, abash, embarrass (ه s.o.) **IV** to humiliate, degrade, dishonor (ه s.o.); to shame, put to shame (ه s.o.) **X** to be ashamed

خزى kizy, kazan shame, disgrace, ignominy | يا للخزى! *yā la-l-kazā* what a shame!

خزيان kazyān², f. خزيا kazyā, pl. خزايا kazāyā ashamed, shamefaced, abashed; shameful, disgraceful, scandalous, infamous, base, mean, vile

مخزاة makzāh pl. مخاز makāzin a shameful thing, a disgrace; reason for shame; pl. shameful things, disgraceful acts, infamies

مخزى makzīy ashamed, shamefaced, abashed; embarrassed, confused; المخزى the Devil

مخز mukzin disgraceful, shameful, scandalous, infamous

مخزية mukziya pl. -*āt* disgraceful act, infamy

خس **kassa** (1st pers. perf. *kasistu*) *a* (خسة *kissa*, خساسة *kasāsa*) to be mean, base, vile; to become less, decrease, diminish, depreciate, fall in value; — *kassa u* to lessen, reduce, diminish (ه s.th.) **II** to lessen, reduce, diminish (ه s.th.)

خس kass lettuce (Lactuca sativa; *bot.*)

خسة kassa (n. un.) head of lettuce

خسة kissa and خساسة kasāsa meanness, baseness, vileness

خسيس kasīs pl. اخساء akissā'² mean, base, low, vile, despicable, contemptible, miserable

خسيسة kasīsa pl. خسائس kasā'is² mean trick, infamy

خسأ **kasa'a** *a* (*kas'*) to chase away (ه s.o.); — خسئ *kasi'a a* to be driven away, make off | خسئت *kasi'ta* beat it! scram! اخسأ اليك *iksa' ilaika* do.

اخسأ aksa'² baser, meaner, more despicable; weaker

خاسئ kāsi' spurned, rejected, outcast; low, base, vulgar, despicable, contemptible; disgraceful, shameful, scandalous, infamous; futile, vain (attempt); weak, feeble, languid

خستكة **kastaka** indisposition

مخستك mukastak indisposed, unwell, sickly

خسر **kasira** *a* (*kusr*, خسار *kasār*, خسارة *kasāra*, خسران *kusrān*) to incur a loss, suffer damage; to lose, forfeit (ه s.th.); to go astray, lose one's way, get lost; to perish **II** to cause loss or damage (ه to s.o.); to do harm (ه to s.o.); to destroy, ruin (ه s.o.); to corrupt, deprave (ه s.o.) IV to cause a loss (ه to s.o.); to shorten, cut, reduce (ه s.th.) X to grudge (على or في s.o. ه s.th.), envy s.o. (على or في) the possession of (ه)

خسر *ḵusr* loss, damage

خسران *ḵusrān* loss, damage, forfeiture; decline, deterioration; depravity, profligacy

خسارة *ḵasāra* pl. خسائر *ḵasā'ir*[2] loss, damage; pl. losses, casualties (في in; *mil.*) | يا خسارة what a pity! too bad!

خسران *ḵasrān* (*eg.*) loser; affected by damage or loss

خاسر *ḵāsir* lost, hopeless; involving substantial losses; loser; depraved, corrupted; profligate, disreputable person, scoundrel

مخسر *muḵassir* causing damage, harmful, noxious, injurious, detrimental

خسف **ḵasafa** *i* (*ḵasf*, خسوف *ḵusūf*) to sink, sink down, give way, cave in, disappear, go down; to be eclipsed (moon); — *i* (*ḵasf*) to cause to sink, cause to give way | خسف الله به الارض *ḵ. llāhu bihī l-arḍa* God made him sink into the ground, God made the ground swallow him up VII to sink, sink down, go down

خسف *ḵasf* baseness, ignominy, disgrace, shame; inferiority | سام خسفا *sāma ḵasfan* to humiliate, abase, degrade (ه s.o.)

خسوف *ḵusūf* occultation (*astron.*); lunar eclipse

خش **ḵašša** *i u* (*ḵašš*) to enter (في s.th.)

خشاش *ḵišāš* vermin, insects

خشب II to lignify, become woody or woodlike; to line, face or case with wood, to panel, wainscot (ه s.th.) V to lignify, become woody or woodlike; to become hard, stiff, firm, rigid; to stiffen, freeze (e.g., with panic)

خشب *ḵašab* pl. اخشاب *aḵšāb* wood, lumber, timber | خشب الانبياء *ḵ. al-anbiyā'* guaiacum wood, lignum vitae

خشبة *ḵušubu* pl. *-āt*, اخشاب *aḵšāb* piece of wood; a timber; pale, post; plank, board | خشبة الميت *ḵ. al-mayyit* coffin; خشبة المسرح *ḵ. al-masraḥ* stage (of a theater), على خشبة المسرح on the "boards"

خشبي *ḵašabī* wooden, woody, ligneous, made of wood; timber-, lumber- (in compounds)

خشاب *ḵaššāb* pl. ة lumber merchant

تخشيب *taḵšīb* paneling, wainscoting

تخشيبة *taḵšība* pl. *-āt*, تخاشيب *taḵāšīb*[2] barrack, wooden shed

تخشب *taḵaššub* stiffness, rigor, rigidity; stiffening

متخشب *mutaḵaššib* frozen, rigid; stiff, hard, firm

خشت **ḵušt** pl. خشوت *ḵušūt* javelin

[1]خشخاش **ḵašḵāš** (coll.; n. un. ة) pl. خشاخيش *ḵašāḵīš*[2] poppy

[2]خشخش **ḵašḵaša** to clank, clatter, rattle; to rustle

خشخشة *ḵašḵaša* pl. *-āt* noise; clank, clatter, rattle; rustle, rustling; crash

خشخيشة (= شخشيخة) rattle (toy)

خشارة **ḵušāra** leftover (of a meal); offal, refuse; a discard, a worthless thing

خشع **ḵašaʿa** *a* (خشوع *ḵušūʿ*) to be submissive, be humble; to humble o.s.; to fade (voice) | خشع ببصره (*baṣarihī*) to lower one's eyes II to humble, reduce to submission (ه s.o.) V to display humility; to be humble; to be moved, be touched

خشوع *ḵušūʿ* submissiveness, submission, humility

خاشع *ḵāšiʿ* pl. خشعة *ḵašaʿa* submissive, humble

خشاف‎ ‏<u>k</u>ušāf various fruits, stewed and soaked in sirup or rose water, compote

خشكار‎ ‏<u>k</u>uškār coarsely ground grain, grits

خشكريشة‎ ‏<u>k</u>aškarīša scab, slough, scurf

خشم‎ II to intoxicate, make drunk (ه s.o.)

خشم‎ ‏<u>k</u>ašm nose; mouth; vent, outlet

خيشوم‎ ‏<u>k</u>aišūm pl. خياشيم‎ ‏<u>k</u>ayāšim² nose; gills; also pl. خياشيم‎ nose

خشن‎ ‏<u>k</u>ašuna u (خشونة‎ ‏<u>k</u>ušūna) to be rough, coarse, crude; to be raw, uncut, unpolished II to roughen, coarsen, make crude (ه s.th.) III to be rude, uncivil, boorish (ه to s.o.) V to display rough, rude, or coarse, manners; to be rough, uneven; to lead a rough life XII اخشوشن‎ i<u>k</u>šaušana to be rough, coarse. crude; to lead a rough life

خشن‎ ‏<u>k</u>ašin pl. خشان‎ ‏<u>k</u>išān rough, crude; coarse (as opposed to ناعم‎ nā'im); rude, unpolished, uncouth; tough, harsh (life); hoarse, raucous (voice) | خشن اللمس‎ ‏<u>k</u>. al-lams coarse to the touch, rough, uneven, wrinkled; خشن الخلق‎ ‏<u>k</u>. al-<u>k</u>ulq uncouth, boorish; خشن القشرة‎ ‏<u>k</u>. al-qišra thick-shelled; الجنس الخشن‎ (jins) the strong sex

اخشن‎ a<u>k</u>šan², f. خشناء‎ ‏<u>k</u>ašnā'², pl. خشن‎ ‏<u>k</u>ušn rough, tough, harsh, rude, uncouth

الخشناء‎ al-<u>k</u>ašnā' the vulgar, uneducated people

خشونة‎ ‏<u>k</u>ušūna roughness, coarseness; crudeness; rudeness

خشى‎ ‏<u>k</u>ašiya a (خشية‎ ‏<u>k</u>ašya) to fear, dread (ه s.o., ه s.th., على‎ for s.o. or s.th.), be afraid (ه of) II to frighten, scare, terrify, alarm (ه s.o.) V = I; VIII to be embarrassed; to be ashamed

خشية‎ ‏<u>k</u>ašya fear, anxiety, apprehension | خشية من‎ ‏<u>k</u>ašyatan min for fear of

اخشى‎ a<u>k</u>šā more timorous, more fearful; more to be feared, more frightening

خشيان‎ ‏<u>k</u>ašyān², f. خشيا‎ ‏<u>k</u>ašyā, pl. خشايا‎ ‏<u>k</u>ašāyā timorous, timid, anxious, apprehensive

خاش‎ ‏<u>k</u>āšin timorous, timid, anxious, apprehensive

خص‎ ‏<u>k</u>aṣṣa u to distinguish, favor (especially, before others), single out (ه s.o.), bestow special honors (ه upon s.o., in preference to others); to endow (ب ه s.o. with), confer, bestow (ب ه upon s.o. s.th.); to apportion, allot, assign, accord, give, dedicate, devote (ب ه to s.o. s.th., in preference to others); with لنفسه‎: to take possession (ه of), demand (ه s.th.; also خص به نفسه‎ nafsahū); to be specifically associated (ه with s.o.), be characteristic (ه of s.o.), be peculiar (ه to); to apply in particular (ه to), be especially valid (ه for); to concern, regard (ه s.o., ه s.th.), have special relevance (ه to), bear (ه on) | خصه بعنايته‎ (bi-'ināyatihī) to devote one's attention to s.o., favor s.o. with one's attention; خصه بالذكر‎ (bi-<u>d</u>-<u>d</u>ikr) to make special mention of s.o. or s.th.; واخص منهم‎ (a<u>k</u>uṣṣu) I mention, among them, especially (with foll. acc.); هذا لا يخصني‎ this does not concern me, this is none of my business II to specify, particularize, itemize (ه s.th.); to specialize (ه s.th.), narrow, restrict (ل ه s.th. to); to designate, destine, set aside, earmark, single out (ل ه or ه s.o. or s.th. for a purpose); to devote in particular, dedicate, assign (ل ه s.th. to); to allocate, allot, apportion (ل ه s.th. to); to appropriate (ل ه funds for); to reserve, hold, withhold (ل ه s.th. for); to tie down (ب ه s.o. to a special field) V to specialize (ل in, also ب or ج, in a scientific field); to devote all one's attention (ل to s.th.); to apply o.s. (ل to), go in for s.th. (ل); to be peculiar (ب to); to be chosen, destined, earmarked (ل for) **VIII** to distinguish, favor (ب ه s.o. with), confer distinction (ب ه upon s.o. by); to devote, give, accord, afford (ب ه to s.o. s.th., in preference to others); to dedicate (ب ه to s.o. s.th., e.g., one's services); (with لنفسه) to take exclusive possession (ه of), claim, demand (ه s.th.), lay special claim (ه to; also اختص به نفسه *nafsahū*); to be distinguished, be marked (ب by); to possess alone, in distinction from all others, have above others (ب s.th.), have the advantage over others (ب that); to be peculiar (ب to); to concern, regard (ب s.th.), bear (ب on); to be pertinent, have relevance (ب to), have to do (ب with); to be duly qualified, be competent, have jurisdiction (ب in; e.g., an authority); to have as a special function or task (ب s.th.)

خس *kass* lettuce (*bot.*)

خص *kuṣṣ* pl. خصاص *kiṣāṣ*, اخصاص *akṣāṣ*, خصوص *kuṣūṣ* hut, shack, shanty, hovel

خصة *kaṣṣa* jet of water

خصاص *kaṣāṣ* interstice, interval, crevice, crack, gap

خصاصة *kaṣāṣa* crevice, crack, interval, gap

خصيصة *kaṣīṣa* pl. خصائص *kaṣā'iṣ*² special characteristic or quality, specialty, particularity, peculiarity

خصيصا *kiṣṣīṣan* particularly, especially, specifically

خصوص *kuṣūṣ* specialness; خصوصا *kuṣūṣan* especially, in particular, specifically | من خصوص ,في خصوص and بخصوص (with foll. genit.) as to, concerning, regarding, with respect to, as regards; من هذا الخصوص and بهذا الخصوص in this connection, in this matter, in this respect, about this, concerning this; على الخصوص and على وجه الخصوص (*wajhi l-k.*) especially, particularly, in particular, specifically

خصوصى *kuṣūṣī* special; private, personal

خصاصة *kaṣāṣa* poverty, penury, privation, destitution, want

اخص *akaṣṣ*² more special, more specific | على الاخص especially; في الاخص do.

اخصاء *akiṣṣā'*² intimate friends, confidants

اخصائى *ikṣā'ī* see ²خصى

تخصيص *takṣīṣ* specialization; specification, particularization, itemization; designation, destination (for a purpose); allotment, apportionment, allocation; reservation; (pl. *-āt*) appropriation, financial allocation; credit | على تخصيص and على وجه التخصيص specifically

تخصص *takaṣṣuṣ* specialization (esp., in a scientific field)

اختصاص *iktiṣāṣ* pl. *-āt* jurisdiction, competence; special province or domain, bailiwick (fig.); pl. prerogatives, privileges, monopolies; concessions (*Intern. Law*); ذو (ذات) الاختصاص duly qualified, authorized, responsible, competent; دائرة الاختصاص scope of competence, sphere of authority, jurisdiction, province, domain, field

اختصاصى *iktiṣāṣī* pl. *-ūn* specialist

خاص *kāṣṣ* special, particular; specific, peculiar; relative, relevant, pertinent (ب to), concerning (ب s.th.); earmarked, designated, destined, set aside (ب for); especially valid or true (ب for), especially applicable (ب to), characteristic (ب of); distinguished; private; exclusive, not public | جريدة خاصة ب professional journal for ...; الخاص والعام (*'āmm*) the special and the general; high and low, all people; الطبيب الخاص physician in ordinary

خاصة *ḵāṣṣa* pl. خواص *ḵawāṣṣ*² exclusive property; private possession; specialty, particularity, peculiarity, characteristic, property, attribute; essence, intrinsic nature; leading personalities, people of distinction, الخاصة the upper class, the educated; *ḵāṣṣatan* and بخاصة *bi-ḵāṣṣatin* especially, in particular | فى خاصة انفسهم *fī ḵ. anfusihim* at the bottom of their hearts, deep inside

خاصية *ḵāṣṣiya* pl. *-āt*, خصائص *ḵaṣā'iṣ*² specialty, particularity, characteristic, peculiarity, property, special attribute, feature, trait, qualification; prerogative, privilege; jurisdiction, competence

خويصة *ḵuwaiṣṣa* (dimin. of خاصة *ḵāṣṣa*) one's own business, private affair | يدخل فى حويصة امرى he meddles in my private affairs

مخصوص *maḵṣūṣ* special

مخصص *muḵaṣṣaṣ* chosen, set aside, earmarked, designated, destined (ل for); allotted, apportioned, allocated; — pl. مخصصات (financial) allocations; appropriations, credits; (daily) allowances; (food) rations | مخصصات اضافية (*iḍāfīya*) extra allowances; مخصصات الملك *m. al-malik* civil list

مختص *muḵtaṣṣ* pertaining, pertinent, relevant, relative (ب to); duly qualified, authorized, responsible, competent; special; pl. مختصات *muḵtaṣṣāt* competences | المقامات المختصة the competent authorities; الدوائر المختصة competent (or authoritative) quarters

خصب *ḵaṣaba* i and *ḵaṣiba* a (*ḵiṣb*) to be fertile (soil) II to make fertile (ﻫ s.th.); to fructify, fertilize (ﻫ s.th.) IV = I

خصب *ḵiṣb* fertility; abundance, plenty; superabundance, profusion

خصب *ḵaṣib* and خصيب *ḵaṣīb* fertile, productive, fat

خصوبة *ḵuṣūba* fertility

تخصيب *taḵṣīb* fructification, fertilization

اخصاب *iḵṣāb* fertility

مخصبات *muḵaṣṣibāt* fertilizers

مخصب *muḵṣib* fertile, productive, fat

خصر *ḵaṣira* a (*ḵaṣar*) to become cold; to suffer from the cold III to clasp (ه s.o.) around the waist, put one's arm around s.o.'s (ه) waist VIII to shorten, condense, abridge, epitomize (ﻫ s.th.); to summarize (ﻫ s.th.)

خصر *ḵaṣr* pl. خصور *ḵuṣūr* hip, haunch, waist

مخصرة *miḵṣara* pl. مخاصر *maḵāṣir*² stick, baton, wand; mace, scepter

اختصار *iḵtiṣār* shortening, condensation, abridgment, summarization, epitomizing (of a statement); brevity | بالاختصار and باختصار briefly, in short, in a few words

مختصر *muḵtaṣar* shortened, condensed, abridged; brief, short; concise, terse, succinct; (pl. *-āt*) short excerpt, brief exposition, synopsis, outline, summary, abstract, epitome, compendium

خاصرة *ḵāṣira* pl. خواصر *ḵawāṣir*² hip, haunch, waist | شوكة فى خاصرته (*šauka*) a thorn in his side

خصف *ḵaṣafa* i (*ḵaṣf*) to mend, repair, sew (ﻫ a shoe)

خصفة *ḵaṣfa* pl. خصاف *ḵiṣāf* basket (made of palm leaves)

خصلة *ḵuṣla* pl. خصل *ḵuṣal*, *-āt* tuft; bunch, cluster; lock, wisp (of hair)

خصلة *ḵaṣla* pl. خصال *ḵiṣāl* quality, property, characteristic, peculiarity, trait; (natural) disposition

خصم *ḵaṣama* i to defeat (ه an opponent) in argument; to deduct, subtract (ﻫ s.th., من from); to discount (ﻫ a bill, a note) III to argue, quarrel, dispute (ه with s.o.);

to bring legal action (ه against s.o.), sue (ه s.o.), litigate (ه with); VI to quarrel, argue, have a fight; to go to law, carry on a lawsuit, litigate (مع with s.o.) VII to be deducted, be subtracted VIII to quarrel, argue, have a fight

خصم *ḵaṣm* pl. خصوم *ḵuṣūm*, اخصام *akṣām* adversary, antagonist, opponent; opposing party (in a lawsuit)

خصم *ḵaṣm* deduction; subtraction; rebate; discount; pl. خصوم *ḵuṣūm* liabilities (*fin.*) | سعر الخصم *si'r al-ḵ.* discount rate, bank rate; خصم الكمبيالات *ḵ. al-kambiyālāt* bill discount

خصيم *ḵaṣīm* pl. خصماء *ḵuṣamā'*², خصمان *ḵuṣmān* adversary, antagonist, opponent

خصومة *ḵuṣūma* quarrel, argument, dispute, controversy, feud; lawsuit

خصام *ḵiṣām* quarrel, argument, dispute, controversy, feud; lawsuit

مخاصم *muḵāṣim* adversary, opponent, opposing party (in a lawsuit); antagonist; litigant

¹خصى *ḵaṣā i* (خصاء *ḵiṣā'*) to castrate, emasculate (ه s.o.)

خصى *ḵaṣīy* pl. خصيان *ḵiṣyān*, خصية *ḵiṣya* a castrate, eunuch

خصية *ḵuṣya* pl. خصى *ḵuṣan* testicle

مخصى *maḵṣīy* castrated, emasculated | فرس مخصى (*faras*) gelding

²اخصائى *iḵṣā'ī* pl. *-ūn* specialist; expert (of a specialized field)

خض *ḵaḍḍa* (*ḵaḍḍ*) to jolt, jog (ه s.th.); to shake (ه s.th.); to frighten, scare (ه s.o.)

لبن خض *laban ḵaḍḍ* buttermilk

خضة *ḵaḍḍa* concussion, shock, jolt; fright, terror, fear

خضب *ḵaḍaba i* (*ḵaḍb*) to dye, color, tinge (ه s.th.); — *ḵaḍaba i* and *ḵaḍiba a* (خضوب *ḵuḍūb*) to be or become green (plant) II to color, tinge (ه s.th.); to dye (ه s.th) XII اخضوضب *iḵḍauḍaba* to be or become green (plant)

خضب *ḵuḍb* chlorophyll (*biol.*) ○

خضاب *ḵiḍāb* dye, dyestuff | خضاب ○ الدم *ḵ. ad-dam* hemoglobin (*biol.*)

خضوب *ḵuḍūb* green, greenness, green color

خضيب *ḵaḍīb* dyed

خضخض *ḵaḍḵaḍa* (خضخضة *ḵaḍḵaḍa*) to set in motion, upset, rock, shake (ه s.th.)

خضخضة *ḵaḍḵaḍa* concussion, shock, jolt

خضد *ḵaḍada i* (*ḵaḍd*) to cut off, break off (ه thorns) | خضد شوكته (*šaukatahū*) to tame s.o., hold s.o. in check, curb s.o.'s power

خضر *ḵaḍira a* (*ḵaḍar*) to be green II to make green, dye or color green (ه s.th.) | خضر الارض (*arḍ*) to sow the land, till the earth IX to be or become green XII اخضوضر *iḵḍauḍara* = IX

خضر *ḵaḍir* green, verdant; verdure, greenery; young green crop (of grain)

الخضر *al-ḵaḍir*, *al-ḵiḍr* a well-known legendary figure

خضرة *ḵuḍra* green, greenness, green color; — (pl. خضر *ḵuḍar*) vegetation, verdure, greenery, greens; meadow; خضر vegetables

خضرى *ḵuḍarī* greengrocer

خضار *ḵaḍār* green, greenness, green color; greens, herbs, potherbs

خضير *ḵaḍīr* green

خضارة *ḵuḍāra* greens, herbs, potherbs

خضار *ḵaḍḍār* greengrocer

اخضر *aḵḍar*², f. خضراء *ḵaḍrā'*², pl. خضر *ḵuḍr* green | اتى على الاخضر واليابس (*atā*) to destroy everything, wreak havoc

الخضراء *al-ḵaḍrā'* "the Verdant" (epithet of Tunis); the sky

خضراوات *ḵaḍrāwāt* vegetables; greens, herbs, potherbs

الخضيراء *al-ḵuḍairā'* Paradise

○ يخضور *yaḵḍūr* chlorophyll (*biol.*)

مخضرة *maḵḍara* meadow, lawn, turf, sod, greens, verdant land

مخضرات *muḵaḍḍarāt* vegetables

خضرم *ḵiḍrim* pl. خضارم *ḵaḍārim*² abundant, copious; well-watered, abounding in water; openhanded, generous, liberal, munificent

مخضرم *muḵaḍram* designation of such contemporaries of Mohammed, esp. of poets, whose life span bridges the time of paganism and that of Islam; an old man who has lived through several generations or historical epochs

خضع *ḵaḍa'a a* (خضوع *ḵuḍū'*) to bow, defer, submit, yield, surrender (ل to s.o., to s.th.), humble o.s. (ل before), obey, follow (ل s.o. or s.th.); to be subject (ل and ال to a law, to a power, etc.), be under s.o.'s (ل or ال) control II and IV to humble, subjugate, subdue, make tractable (ه s.o.); to submit, subject, expose (ل ه or ه s.th. or s.o. to s.th.)

خضوع *ḵuḍū'* submission, obedience, humility, subjection

خضوع *ḵaḍū'* pl. خضع *ḵuḍu'* submissive, humble

اخضاع *iḵḍā'* subjugation, subdual; subjection

خاضع *ḵāḍi'* pl. خضع *ḵuḍḍa'*, خضعان *ḵuḍ'ān*, *ḵiḍ'ān* submissive, humble; obedient, pliant, tractable; subject, liable, prone (ل to s.th.)

خضل *ḵaḍila a* to be or become moist II and IV to moisten, wet (ه s.th.) IX = I

خضل *ḵaḍil* moist, wet; juicy, succulent; refreshing, gay, lighthearted

خضم *ḵaḍama i* (*ḵaḍm*) to munch (ه s.th., with a full mouth), bite (ه into s.th.)

خضم *ḵiḍamm* vast (said of the sea); sea, ocean

خط *ḵaṭṭa u* (*ḵaṭṭ*) to draw or trace a line (على on); to draw, trace, sketch, design (ه s.th.); to write, pen (ه s.th.); to carve, engrave, inscribe (ه s.th.); to outline, mark, trace out, prescribe (ه ل for s.o. s.th.) | خط خطا (سطرا) (*ḵaṭṭan, saṭran*) to draw a line; خطه الشيب (*šaibu*) his hair turned gray II to draw lines; to rule (ه s.th.); to furrow, ridge (ه s.th.); to mark with lines or stripes, stripe, streak (ه s.th.); to pencil (ه the eyebrows); to mark, designate, earmark, indicate (ه s.th.): to demarcate, delimit, delineate, stake out, survey (ه land, real estate); to lay out, map out (ه roads) VIII to trace out, mark, outline, prescribe (ه a way); to mark, demarcate, delimit, stake out, delineate (ه s.th.); to map out, plan, project (ه e.g., the construction of a city); to make, design, devise (ه a plan); to plan (ه s.th.), make plans (ه for)

خط *ḵaṭṭ* pl. خطوط *ḵuṭūṭ* line; stroke; stripe, streak; (railroad) line, line of communication; telephone line; frontline (*mil.*); furrow, ridge; handwriting; writing, script; calligraphy, penmanship | ○ خط ارضى (*arḍī*) ground wire (*radio*); ○ الخط الاسفينى (*isfīnī*) cuneiform writing; الخطوط الامامية (*amāmīya*) the foremost lines, battle lines (*mil.*); خط بارز (*bāriz*) relievo script; خط تليفونى telephone line; خطوط جوية (*jawwīya*) airlines; خط حديدى (*ḥadīdī*) and خط سكة الحديد *ḵ. sikkat al-ḥadīd* railroad line, railroad track; خط الزوال *ḵ. az-zawāl* meridian (*astron.*; = خط نصف النهار *ḵ. niṣf an-nahār*); ○ الخط المسمارى (*mismārī*) cuneiform writing; خط الاستواء *ḵ. al-istiwā'* equator; خط الطول *ḵ. aṭ-ṭūl* or خط طولى (*ṭūlī*) circle of longitude, meridian (*geogr.*); خط العرض *ḵ. al-'arḍ* or

خط عرضى (*'arḍī*) parallel (of latitude) (*geogr.*); خط تقسيم المياه *ḵ. taqsīm al-miyāh* divide, watershed; خط القوة الكهربائية *ḵ. al-qūwa al-kahrabā'īya* power lines; خط الهاجرة meridian (*geogr.*); خرج عن الخط to derail, run off the rails (train); على خط مستقيم (*mustaqīm*) straightaway, in a straight line; outright, out and out; على طول الخط (*ṭūl al-ḵ.*) all along the line

خط *ḵuṭṭ* section, district, quarter (of a city)

خطى *ḵaṭṭī* handwritten; linear; spear

خطة *ḵuṭṭa* matter, affair; condition, state; office, function, position

خطة *ḵiṭṭa, ḵuṭṭa* pl. خطط *ḵiṭaṭ, ḵuṭaṭ* a piece of land acquired for the purpose of building a house; a piece of real estate, lot; district; map or plan of a piece of real estate, layout; plan, project, design, intention; line of action, course, policy, rule, precept, guiding principle | خطة العمل *ḵ. al-'amal* operation plan, work plan; طبقا لخطة مرسومة (*ṭibqan*) according to schedule, as scheduled or planned

خطاط *ḵaṭṭāṭ* pl. *-ūn* penman, calligrapher; — tracing lines, leaving a straight trace | فشك خطاط (*fašak*) or قذيفة خطاطة tracer bullet, tracer (*mil.*)

تخطيط *taḵṭīṭ* ruling, drawing of, or marking with, lines; lineation; designation, marking; earmarking; surveying, survey (of land); planning; projecting, mapping out, laying out (of cities, of roads); plan, design

رسم تخطيطى (*rasm*) rough draft, first sketch, design

مخطوط *maḵṭūṭ* handwritten; manuscript

مخطوطة *maḵṭūṭa* pl. *-āt* manuscript

مخطط *muḵaṭṭaṭ* striped, streaked, ruled; furrowed; designated, marked, earmarked; planned, guided, controlled; (pl. *-āt*) sketch, design, plan, layout; map (of a city)

خطئ *ḵaṭi'a a* (خطأ *ḵaṭa'*) to be mistaken; to commit an error, make a mistake; to sin II to charge with an offense, incriminate, declare guilty (ه s.o.); to accuse (ه s.o.) of an error or mistake; to fine (ه s.o.; *tun.*) IV to be mistaken, to err, commit an error, be at fault (فى in); to be wrong (فى about, in); to make a mistake (فى in, with); to miss (ه s.o., e.g., a shot; ه the target); to escape (ه s.o. or s.o.'s notice; a fact) | اخطأ فأله (*fa'luhū*) (his omen was wrong, i.e.) his expectations do not come true, are not fulfilled; that's where he is wrong, that's where he made a mistake! اخطأه الشىء (*šai'u*) (lit.: the thing escaped him, missed him, i.e.) he lacked it; اخطأه التوفيق he failed, was unsuccessful; اخطأ فى استنتاجاته he drew the wrong conclusions; اخطأ بين الشيئين he confused the two things, he mistook one thing for the other

خطء *ḵiṭ'* slip, lapse, fault, offense, sin

خطأ *ḵaṭa'* and خطاء *ḵaṭā'* error; mistake, incorrectness; offense, fault; *ḵaṭa'an* erroneously, by mistake | من الخطأ ان ... it is (would be) wrong to ...; اصلاح الخطأ *iṣlāḥ al-ḵ.* corrigenda, errata, list of corrections; قتل الخطأ *qatl al-ḵ.* accidental homicide (*jur.*)

خطيئة *ḵaṭī'a* pl. *-āt*, خطايا *ḵaṭāyā* mistake, blunder; slip, lapse; fault, offense; crime sin; fine (*tun.*)

خاطئ *ḵāṭi'* wrong, incorrect, erroneous; mistaken, at fault; (pl. خطاة *ḵuṭāh*, actually, pl. of colloq. *ḵāṭī*), f. خاطئة *ḵāṭi'a* pl. خواطئ *ḵawāṭi'*[2] sinner

مخطئ *muḵṭi'* mistaken, at fault, wrong; incorrect, wrong, erroneous

خطب *ḵaṭaba u* (خطبة *ḵuṭba*, خطابة *ḵaṭāba*) to deliver a public address, make a speech; to preach, deliver a sermon (فى الناس and الناس *an-nāsa* to the people); — (*ḵaṭb*,

خطبة *ḵiṭba*) to propose (ها to a girl; said of the man), ask for a girl's hand (ها) in marriage (ل on behalf of s.o.; said of the matchmaker); to give in marriage, betroth, affiance, engage (بنته ل or على one's daughter to s.o.) | خطب ودها (*wuddahā*) and خطب مودتها (*mawaddatahā*) he courted her love **III** to address (ه s.o.), speak, talk, direct one's words (ه to s.o.), turn (ه to s.o., orally or in writing) | خاطبه بالتليفون to telephone s.o., call s.o. up; خاطبه بالكاف (*bi-l-kāf*) to address s.o. on an intimate first-name basis **VI** to talk to one another; to converse, confer, have a talk, carry on a conversation; to write each other, correspond, carry on a correspondence **VIII** to seek a girl's (ها) hand in marriage, ask for a girl's hand

خطب *ḵaṭb* pl. خطوب *ḵuṭūb* matter, affair, concern, business; situation, conditions, circumstances; misadventure, mishap | ما خطبك what do you want? what's the trouble? what's the matter with you? ما خطبه في what concern of his is ...? what has he to do with ...? ما خطب ذلك what's it all about?

خطبة *ḵiṭba* courtship; betrothal, engagement

خطبة *ḵuṭba* pl. خطب *ḵuṭab* public address; speech; lecture, discourse; oration; sermon, specif., Muslim Friday sermon, khutbah | خطبة الافتتاح opening address

خطاب *ḵiṭāb* pl. *-āt*, اخطبة *aḵṭiba* public address, speech; oration; letter, note, message | خطاب ترحيب welcoming address; خطاب العرش *ḵ. al-'arš* speech from the throne; خطاب مستعجل (*musta'jil*) express letter, special-delivery letter; خطاب تقدمة *ḵ.taqdima* letter of introduction; ○ خطابات ذات القيمة المقررة (*ḏāt al-qīma al-muqarrara*) (= lettres avec valeur déclarée) registered, insured letters (*eg.*); فصل الخطاب *faṣl al-ḵ.* (in letters:) conclusion of the formal greetings by the words اما بعد *ammā ba'du*; conclusion, termination, end; decision; unmistakable judgment; بيني وبينك فصل الخطاب we're through with one another once and for all

خطابي *ḵiṭābī* oratorical, rhetorical, speech-, lecturing (in compounds)

خطيب *ḵaṭīb* pl. خطباء *ḵuṭabā'*[2] (public) speaker; orator; lecturer; preacher, khatib; suitor (for the hand of a girl); fiancé

خطيبة *ḵaṭība* fiancée

خطابة *ḵaṭāba* preaching, sermonizing, oratory

خطابة *ḵiṭāba* rhetoric, oratory; speech, lecture, discourse

خطوبة *ḵuṭūba* courtship; betrothal, engagement

مخاطبة *muḵāṭaba* pl. *-āt* address; public address, speech; proclamation; conversation, talk; conference, parley | مخاطبة تليفونية telephone conversation, telephone call

تخاطب *taḵāṭub* conversation; talk, discussion; (inter)communication (also, e.g., telephonic, by radio, etc.) | لغة التخاطب *luḡat at-t.* colloquial language

خاطب *ḵāṭib* pl. خطباء *ḵuṭabā'*[2], خطاب *ḵuṭṭāb* suitor; matchmaker

خاطبة *ḵāṭiba* pl. خطاب *ḵuṭṭāb* woman matchmaker

مخطوبة *maḵṭūba* fiancée

مخاطب *muḵāṭab* addressed, spoken to; (*gram.*) second person

اخطبوط look up alphabetically

خطر *ḵaṭara* i (خطران *ḵaṭarān*) to swing, wave, brandish (ب s.th.); to shake, tremble, vibrate; to walk with a (proud) swinging gait; to strut, parade haughtily; — i u (خطور *ḵuṭūr*) to occur (ل to s.o.), come to s.o.'s (ل) mind | خطر الامر على باله (bālihī) the matter came to his mind, occurred to him, he recalled the matter (also في باله and خطر له خاطر; (على قلبه) or بباله he had an idea; أمر لم يخطر ببال (lam yakṭir bi-bālin) an unexpected matter, s.th. one wouldn't dream of; — ḵaṭura u (خطورة ḵuṭūra) to be weighty; to be important, significant; to be grave, serious, momentous, dangerous, perilous, risky, hazardous III to risk, hazard, stake (ب s.th., بنفسه one's life); to incur the danger, run the risk (ب of), risk (ب s.th.); to bet, wager (ه s.o., على a stake) IV to notify, inform (ه s.o.), let (ه s.o.) know (ب about s.th.); to warn, caution (ه s.o.) V to walk with a lofty, proud gait; to stride, strut (with a swinging gait); to pendulate, oscillate, vibrate VI to make a bet (على against a stake)

خطر ḵaṭar weightiness, momentousness; importance, consequence, significance; seriousness, gravity; — (pl. -āt, اخطار aḵṭār) danger, peril, menace (على to); riskiness, dangerousness; risk; hazard; (pl. خطار ḵiṭār) stake, bet, wager | جليل الخطر of very great importance, momentous; ذو خطر dangerous, perilous; معرض للخطر (muʿarrad) endangered, jeopardized; اشارة الخطر išārat al-ḵ. alarm signal

خطر ḵaṭir dangerous, perilous, risky, hazardous; serious, grave, weighty, important, significant

خطرة ḵaṭra pl. ḵaṭarāt pompous walk, strut; swinging gait; idea, thought, notion

خطار ḵaṭṭār pendulum (phys.)

خطير ḵaṭīr pl. خطر ḵuṭr weighty, momentous; important, significant; grave, serious | خطير الشأن of great importance

خطورة ḵuṭūra weight(iness), importance, moment(ousness); consequence, significance; gravity, seriousness

خطران ḵaṭarān swinging, oscillation, vibration

اخطر aḵṭar² more dangerous, riskier; weightier, of greater consequence; more serious, graver

خطرة look up alphabetically

مخاطر maḵāṭir² dangers, perils

مخاطرة muḵāṭara pl. -āt venture, risk, hazard

اخطار iḵṭār notification, information; warning

خاطر ḵāṭir pl. خواطر ḵawāṭir² idea, thought, notion; mind; desire, inclination, liking | لاجل خاطرك (li-ajli) for your sake; من كل خاطر min kulli ḵāṭirin with all one's heart, most gladly; عن طيبة خاطر ʿan ṭībati ḵāṭirin gladly, with pleasure; of one's own free will, voluntarily; على خاطرك as you like; اخذ بخاطره to afford satisfaction to s.o., to comfort, reassure s.o.; اخذ على خاطره من to feel offended by, take offense at; صدع خاطره ṣaddaʿa ḵāṭirahū to trouble, bother s.o.; طمن الخواطر (ṭammana) to calm the excitement; بخاطره ان (marra) the thought crossed his mind that ...; اكراما خاطرك (ikrāman) for your sake, to please you; سرعة الخاطر surʿat al-ḵ. presence of mind; سريع الخاطر quick-witted

مخاطر muḵāṭir one who risks s.th., who takes a chance; daring, bold, venturesome

مخطر muḵṭir dangerous, perilous, risky, hazardous

خطرف ḵaṭrafa (eg.) to be delirious, to rave, talk irrationally

خطرفة ḵaṭrafa delirium, raving

خطف ḵaṭifa a, ḵaṭafa i (ḵaṭf) to snatch, wrench or wrest away, seize, grab (ه s.th.); to make off (ه with s.th.); to abduct, kidnap (ه s.o.); to dazzle (البصر

al-baṣara the eyes) **V** to carry away, sweep away (ه s.o.) **VI** to snatch or seize (ه s.th.) from one another **VII** to be snatched away, be wrested away; to be carried away, be swept away **VIII** to grab, seize, take forcibly (ه s.th.); to snatch, wrest, wrench (من ه s.th. from s.o.); to abduct, kidnap (ه s.o.); to run away, elope (ها with a woman); to make off (ه with s.th.); to dazzle (البصر al-baṣara the eyes)

خطف ḵaṭf grabbing, forcible seizure, rape; abduction, kidnaping; خطفا ḵaṭfan rapidly, quickly

خطفة ḵaṭfa pl. ḵaṭafāt (n. vic.) a snatching away, a grab; sudden stirring, flash | فى خطفة البرق (bcrq) instantly, in a trice, like a streak of lightning; خطفة من خطفات الشعور an impulse, a sudden emotion

خطاف ḵaṭṭāf rapacious; robber

خطاف ḵuṭṭāf pl. خطاطيف ḵaṭāṭīf² (iron) hook; fishhook; (coll.; n. un. ة) swift, a variety of swallow

خطيف ḵaṭṭīf pl. خطاطيف ḵaṭāṭīf² iron hook

اختطاف iḵtiṭāf grabbing, forcible seizure, rape; abduction, kidnaping

خاطف ḵāṭif pl. خواطف ḵawāṭif² ravenous; rapacious; rapid, prompt; quick, sudden; lightninglike; fleeting; shoṛt, brief | ذئاب خاطفة ravenous wolves; صورة خاطفة (ṣūra) snapshot; حرب خاطفة (ḥarb) blitzkrieg

خطل ḵaṭila a (ḵaṭal) to talk nonsense **IV** do. **V** to strut, walk with a pompous gait; to walk with a proud, swinging gait

خطل ḵaṭal idle talk, prattle

خطل ḵaṭil garrulous, chattering, given to silly talk; stupid, foolish

خطم ḵaṭm nose, snout, muzzle (of an animal); front part (nose and mouth); foremost or

first part; important matter | اطل خطمه (aṭalla) approx.: to manifest its force, set in (e.g., of a disaster)

خطمى ḵiṭmī, ḵaṭmī (coll.; n. un. ة) marsh mallow (Althaea officinalis; bot.)

خطام ḵiṭām pl. خطم ḵuṭum noseband, halter (of a camel)

خطا (خطو) ḵaṭā u (ḵaṭw) to step, pace, walk; to proceed, advance, progress | خطا خطوات واسعة (ḵaṭawātin) to take large strides, also fig. = to make extraordinary progress **II** and **V** to overstep, transgress (ه s.th.); to cross (ه s.th.), go or walk through s.th. (ه); to ford (ه a river); to leave its banks, overflow (river); to cross, traverse (البحار the seas); to omit, disregard, ignore, pass by (ه s o.); to go beyond s.th. (ه); to extend (الى to); to exceed, transcend (ه s.th.); to excel, surpass, outstrip, outdo (ه s.o.); to proceed, pass (ه through s.th., الى to), leave s.th. (ه) behind and turn to s.th. else (الى); to disregard (ه, ه s.o., s.th.) in order to turn one's attention to (الى) | تخطى به الى الامام (ilā l-amāmi) to promote, advance s.th. **VIII** to step, pace, walk; to proceed, advance, progress

خطوة ḵaṭwa pl. ḵaṭawāt and ḵuṭwa pl. ḵuṭwāt, ḵuṭuwāt, خطى ḵuṭan step, pace, stride | سار فى خطاه (ḵuṭāhu) to walk, or follow, in s.o.'s footsteps; تقدم خطوة فخطوة taqaddama ḵuṭwatan fa-ḵuṭwatan to proceed or advance step by step; اتخذ خطوة (ittaḵaḏa) to take a decisive step; خطوتان وقفزة ḵaṭwatān wa-qafza hop, skip and jump (athlet.)

خطية ḵaṭīya (= خطيئة) slip, lapse, transgression, fault, offense, sin

خطاة ḵuṭāh pl. of خاطئ ḵāṭi' sinner

خف ḵaffa i to be light (of weight); to be slight, insignificant; to become lighter, decrease in weight, lose weight; to decrease in intensity, grow lighter (color);

to be nimble, agile, quick; to hasten, hurry, rush (الى to) II to make lighter (ه s.th.), reduce the weight of (ه); to ease, lighten, relieve, soften (ه عن for s.o. s.th. difficult or oppressive, also ه على; من s.th., e.g., s.o.'s situation); to lessen, decrease, reduce, diminish (ه or من s.th.); to mitigate, alleviate, moderate, temper (ه or من s.th.); to thin, dilute (ه e.g., a liquid); (*gram.*) to pronounce (ه a consonant) without *tašdīd* | خفف عنك *ḵaffif ʿanka!* cheer up! be of good cheer! خفف من سرعتك *ḵaffif min surʿatika!* slow down! خفف الآلام عنه to soothe s.o.'s pains V to dress lightly; to disburden, relieve o.s. (of a burden); to rid o.s., free o.s. (من of s.th.); to hurry away (عن from), leave (عن s.th.) in a hurry X to deem (ه s.th.) light; to value lightly, disdain, scorn, despise (ب s.o. or s.th.), look down (ب upon), think nothing (ب of), make light (ب of), set little store (ب by); not to take seriously (ب s.th.), attach no importance (ب to); to carry away, transport (ه s.o., e.g., joy)

خف *ḵuff* pl. خفاف *ḵifāf*, اخفاف *aḵfāf* shoe, slipper; — (pl. اخفاف *aḵfāf*) camel hoof; foot (of the ostrich); sole (of the foot) | رجع بخفي حنين *rajaʿa bi-ḵuffai ḥunain* to return with empty hands, without having achieved one's mission; to accomplish nothing, fail, be unsuccessful

خفة *ḵiffa* lightness (of weight); slightness, insignificance, triviality; sprightliness, buoyancy; agility, nimbleness; inconstancy, fickleness, flightiness, levity, frivolity | خفة الحركة *ḵ. al-ḥaraka*, خفة فى الحركة nimbleness, agility, quickness; خفة الدم *ḵ. ad-dam* amiability, charm; خفة الروح *ḵ. ar-rūḥ* do.; خفة اليد *ḵ. al-yad* manual skill, dexterity, deftness

اخف *aḵaff*[2] lighter; lesser, slighter; weaker | اخف الضررين *a. aḍ-ḍararain* the lesser of two evils

خفاف *ḵafāf*, حجر الخفاف *ḥajar al-ḵ.* pumice, pumice stone

خفان *ḵuffān* pumice, pumice stone

خفيف *ḵafīf* pl. خفاف *ḵifāf*, اخفاف *aḵfāf*, اخفاء *aḵiffā'*[2] light (of weight); slight, little, trivial, insignificant; thin, scanty, sparse; nimble, agile, sprightly, lively; — الخفيف name of a poetic meter | خفيف الحركة *ḵ. al-ḥaraka* easily movable, very mobile; nimble, agile; خفيف الدم *ḵ. ad-dam* amiable, charming; خفيف الروح *ḵ. ar-rūḥ* likable, charming, winning, amiable; gay, in high spirits, cheerful; خفيف الظل *ḵ. aẓ-ẓill* likable, nice (person); خفيف العارضين *ḵ. al-ʿāriḍain* having a thin beard; خفيف العقل *ḵ. al-ʿaql* feeble-minded, dimwitted; خفيف اليد *ḵ. al-yad* nimble-fingered, deft; شاى خفيف weak tea

تخفيف *taḵfīf* lightening, easing; lessening, decrease, diminution; reduction; allaying, mitigation, alleviation, palliation, moderation; commutation (*jur.*); relief; thinning, dilution (e.g., of a liquid) | ظروف التخفيف extenuating circumstances (*jur.*)

استخفاف *istiḵfāf* disdain, scorn, contempt; levity, frivolity

ظروف مخففة *ẓurūf muḵaffifa* extenuating circumstances (*jur.*)

مخفف *muḵaffaf* thin, diluted

خفت *ḵafata u* (خفوت *ḵufūt*) to become inaudible, die down, die away (sound, voice); to become silent, become still III خافت بكلامه, بصوته (*bi-kalāmihī, bi-ṣautihī*) to lower one's voice IV to silence, reduce to silence (ه s.o.) VIII = I

خفوت *ḵufūt* fading (*radio*)

خافت *ḵāfit* dying away, dying down, becoming silent; inaudible; faint, dying, fading, trailing off (sound, voice); soft, subdued (light, color)

مختفت *muḵtafit* soft, low, subdued

خفر *ḵafara u* (*ḵafr*, خفارة *ḵifāra*) to watch (ه, ه s.o., s.th. or over s.o., over s.th.), guard, protect (ه s.o., ه s.th.); — *ḵafira a* (*ḵafar*, خفارة *ḵafāra*) to be timid, shy, bashful II = I *ḵafara* V = I *ḵafira*

خفر *ḵafr* watching, watch, guard(ing)

خفر *ḵafar* guard detachment, guard; escort | خفر السواحل coast guard (*Eg.*)

خفر *ḵafar* timidity, shyness, bashfulness, diffidence

خفر *ḵafir* bashful, diffident, timid, shy, embarrassed, coy

خفير *ḵafīr* pl. خفراء *ḵufarā'*[2] watchman; protector. guardian; guard, sentry, sentinel

خفارة *ḵifāra* watch(ing), guard(ing), protection; guard duty

مخفر *maḵfar* pl. مخافر *maḵāfir*[2] guardhouse, guardroom; guard, control post | مخفر الشرطة *m. aš-šurṭa* police station

خافرة *ḵāfira*: خافرة السواحل *ḵ. as-sawāḥil* coastguard cruiser (*Eg.*)

مخفور *maḵfūr* under escort, escorted; covered, sheltered, protected

خفس *ḵafasa u* (*ḵafs*) to ridicule, scorn (ه s.o.), laugh, mock (ه at); to destroy, demolish, tear down (ه a house)

خفش *ḵafaš* day blindness, hemeralopia

اخفش *aḵfaš*[2], f. خفشاء *ḵafšā'*[2], pl. خفش *ḵufš* day blind, hemeralopic; weak-sighted, afflicted with defective vision

خفاش *ḵuffāš* pl. خفافيش *ḵafāfīš*[2] bat (*zool.*)

خفض *ḵafaḍa i* (*ḵafḍ*) to make lower (ه s.th.); to lower, decrease, reduce, lessen, diminish (ه s.th.); to lower, drop (ه, من s.th., also, e.g., the voice); (*gram.*) to pronounce the final consonant of a word with *i*; to put (ه a word) in the genitive | خفض جناحه ل (*janāḥahū*) to unbend toward s.o., show o.s. open-minded, responsive, accessible to; — *ḵafuḍa u* to be carefree, easy, comfortable (life); to sink, dip, drop, settle, subside; to become low, drop to an undertone (voice) II to lower, decrease, reduce (ه s.th., price) | خفض عليك *ḵaffiḍ ʿalaika!* take it easy! خفض عليك جأشك (*ja'šaka*) cool off! calm down! relax! IV اخفض صوته (*ṣautahū*) he lowered his voice V and VII to sink, dip, drop, settle, subside; to be lowered, be reduced (price); to decrease, grow less; to be diminished

خفض *ḵafḍ* lowering, lessening, decrease, diminution, reduction; subduing, lowering, muffling (of the voice); curtailment, limitation, restriction; ease (of life); (*gram.*) pronunciation of the final consonant with *i* | خفض القيمة *ḵ. al-qīma* devaluation (of a currency); خفض العيش *ḵ. al-ʿaiš* carefree, easy life; هو فى خفض من العيش he lives in ease and comfort; خفض الصوت *ḵ. aṣ-ṣaut* lowering of the voice; حرف الخفض *ḥarf al-ḵ.* preposition (*gram.*)

خفيض *ḵafīḍ* low, soft, subdued (voice)

تخفيض *taḵfīḍ* lowering, cutback, reduction (esp. of prices); diminution, decrease, lessening, curtailment, restriction, limitation

انخفاض *inḵifāḍ* sinking, dropping, subsidence; lowering, reduction; lessening, decrease. diminution, decrement; dropping of the water level, low water | انخفاض جوى (*jawwī*) low-pressure area (*meteor.*)

مخفض *muḵaffaḍ* lowered, reduced, low, moderate (price, rate); lower

منخفض *munḵafiḍ* low (altitude, frequency, price, etc.); soft, low, subdued, muffled (voice) | الاراضى المنخفضة the Netherlands; — *munḵafaḍ* pl. *-āt* low ground; depression (*geogr.*)

خفق **ḵafaqa** *i u* (*ḵafq*, خفقان *ḵafaqān*, خفوق *ḵufūq*) to vibrate; to tremble, shake; to beat, throb, palpitate (heart); to flutter, wave, stream (flag); to flap the wings, flutter (bird); to waver, flicker; — (*ḵafq*) to flash (lightning); to beat, whip (ه s.th.; eggs, cream, etc.); to make the sound of footsteps (shoe); — (خفوق *ḵufūq*) to drop one's head drowsily, nod off, doze off (خفق خفقة *ḵ. ḵafqatan*); — *i* (خفوق *ḵufūq*) to set, go down (celestial body) **II** to roughcast, plaster, stucco (ه a wall) **IV** to flap the wings, flutter (bird); to set, go down (celestial body); to be unsuccessful, go wrong, fail, miscarry, come to nothing, be abortive; to fail, be unsuccessful (في in s.th.)

خفق **ḵafq** throb(bing) palpitation; beating, beat; footfall, footstep, tread (of a boot, of the foot)

خفقة **ḵafqa** pl. *ḵafaqāt* (n. vic.) beat, throb; tap, rap, knock; ticking noise, tick

خفقان **ḵafaqān** palpitation of the heart, heartbeat; throb(bing), beat(ing); fluttering, flutter

خفاق **ḵaffāq** palpitant, throbbing (heart); fluttering, waving, streaming (flag)

○ مخفقة **miḵfaqa** whisk, eggbeater

اخفاق **iḵfāq** failure, fizzle, flop, fiasco

خافق **ḵāfiq** palpitant, throbbing (heart); fluttering, waving, streaming (flag); الخافقان *al-ḵāfiqān* East and West; الخوافق *al-ḵawāfiq* the cardinal points, the four quarters of the world

خافقي **ḵāfiqī** mortar, plaster, roughcast; stucco

خفان see خف

خفي **ḵafiya** *a* to be hidden, be concealed; to be unknown (a fact; على to s.o.); to disappear, hide | لا يخفى أن it is well known that ...; as everybody knows ..., it is obvious that ...; لا يخفى عليك you know very well ..., you are well aware (of it); — *ḵafā i* to hide, conceal (ه s.th.); to keep secret (ه s.th.) **IV** to hide, conceal (ه s.th.); to afford (ه s.o.) a place to hide, shelter, hide (ه s.o.); to keep secret (ه s.th.); to disguise, conceal (ه s.th., على or عن from s.o.) | اخفى الصوت to lower the voice, speak in an undertone **V** to hide, keep o.s. out of view; to disguise o.s. **VIII** to hide, keep o.s. out of view; to disappear, vanish; to be hidden, be unknown; to be lacking, be missing, be absent | اختفى عن الانظار to be hidden or disappear from sight **X** to hide, keep o.s. out of view; to be hidden, be concealed; to be hidden from s.o.'s (عن) view, become invisible (عن to s.o.), disappear from sight

خفي **ḵafīy** hidden, concealed; secret, unknown; unseen, invisible; mysterious | خفي الاسم *ḵ. al-ism* anonymous; ○ انوار خفية (*anwār*) indirect lighting

خفية **ḵufyatan, ḵifyatan** secretly, clandestinely, covertly; خفية عنه without his knowledge

خفية **ḵafīya** pl. خفايا *ḵafāyā* a secret, a secret affair

خفاء **ḵafā'** secrecy, hiddenness | في الخفاء secretly, clandestinely, covertly; لا خفاء في ان (*ḵafā'a*) it is quite evident, it is quite obvious that ...

اخفاء **iḵfā'** hiding, secretion; concealment; lowering of the voice

تخف **taḵaffin** disguise

اختفاء **iḵtifā'** disappearance

خاف **ḵāfin** hidden, concealed; secret, unknown; unseen, invisible

خافية **ḵāfiya** pl. خواف *ḵawāfin* a secret; — pl. الخوافي *al-ḵawāfī* the coverts, the secondaries (of a bird's wing)

مخفي **maḵfīy** hidden, concealed

متخف *mutakaffin* disguised, in disguise

مختف *muktafin* hidden, concealed, clandestine, covert, secret; disappearing, vanishing

مختفى *muktafan* hiding place, hide-out

خاقان look up alphabetically

خل *kalla u* (*kall*) to pierce, transfix (ه s.th.) II to turn sour; to make sour, to sour, acidify (ه s.th.); to pickle, marinate (ه s.th.); to salt, cure with salt or in brine (ه s.th.); to pick (ه the teeth); to run the fingers (ه through s.th.), part, comb (ه the hair, the beard, also with the fingers) III to treat (ه s.o.) as a friend IV to offend (ب against), infringe, transgress (ب s.th.); to violate, break (ب s.th., e.g., a rule, a custom); to fail to fulfill, fail to meet (ب an agreement); to forsake, desert, abandon (ب s.o., s.th.); to disturb, upset, harm, prejudice (ب s.th.) V to be, lie or come between s.th. (ه; also in time), intervene (ه between); to be located or situated, be interposed, be placed (ه between); to permeate, pervade, interpenetrate (ه s.th.), mix, mingle, blend (ه with) VIII to be or become defective; to be in disorder, be faulty, deficient, imperfect; to become disordered; to be upset, be unbalanced; to be disturbed (order, system) | اختلت الشروط the conditions are not fulfilled; اختل توازنه (*tawāzunuhū*) to lose one's balance, become unbalanced; اختل عقله (*'aqluhū*) to be mentally deranged

خل *kall* vinegar

خل *kill, kull* pl. اخلال *aklāl* friend, bosom friend

خلل *kalal* pl. خلال *kilāl* gap, interval, interstice; cleft, crack, rupture, fissure; a defective, unbalanced state, imbalance; defectiveness, imperfection; fault, flaw, defect, shortcoming; disturbance, upset, disorder; damage, injury, harm (that s.th. suffers or suffered); خلال *kilāla* during; between; through | فى خلل *fī kalali* and فى خلال *fī kilāli* during; in the course of, within, in a given period of; فى خلال ذلك meanwhile, in the meantime; من خلال *min kilāli* across, through, right through the middle of; out of, from within; (to judge, reason, draw conclusions, etc.) by, on the basis of, on the strength of, (to recognize) from

خلة *kalla* need, want, lack; — (pl. خلال *kilāl*) property, attribute, peculiarity; characteristic; natural disposition

خلة *kulla* pl. خلل *kulal* friendship

خلال *kilāl* pl. اخلة *akilla* boring or drilling implement; peg, pin; spit, skewer; (also خلالة, pl. *-āt*) toothpick; see also خلل *kalal*

خليل *kalīl* pl. اخلاء *akillā'*[2], خلان *kullān* friend, bosom friend; lover; الخليل Hebron (town in Jordanian Palestine) | خليل الله epithet of Abraham

خليلة *kalīla* pl. *-āt* girl friend, woman friend; sweetheart, paramour

ام الخلول *umm al-kulūl* river mussel (*zool.*)

اخلال *iklāl* pl. *-āt* breach, infraction, violation (of a law, of a treaty, and the like); offense (against), transgression, infringement (of); disturbance (of an order, of a system); impairment, injury, harm (to); average, damage by sea | مع عدم الاخلال ب (*'adami l-i.*) without prejudice to, without detriment to

اختلال *iktilāl* deficiency, defectiveness, imperfection; (a falling into) disrepair, deterioration; faultiness; disturbance (of a system, of a function, of the equilibrium, etc.); disorder, confusion

مخلل *mukallal* pickled; salted; (pl. *-āt*) pickles, pickled vegetables

مخل *mukill* disgraceful, shameful | مخل بالآداب immoral, indecent, improper

خلب **ḵalaba** *i u* (*ḵalb*) to seize with the claws, clutch (ه s.th.), pounce (ه on); — *u* (خلابة *ḵilāba*) to cajole, coax, wheedle (ه s.o.); to inveigle, beguile, bewitch, enchant (ه s.o., عقله *'aqlahū* s.o.'s mind); to charm, fascinate, captivate (ه s.o.) **III** to cajole, wheedle, coax. inveigle, beguile, bewitch, enchant (ه s.o.) **VIII** to seize with the claws, clutch (ه s.th.), pounce (ه on); to cajole, inveigle, beguile, bewitch, enchant (ه s.o.)

خلب **ḵilb** pl. اخلاب *aḵlāb* fingernail, claw, talon

برق خلب *barqun ḵullabun* and *barqu ḵullabin* lightning without a downpour; a disappointing, disillusioning matter; خلب and خلب من برق delusion, illusion

خلبي **ḵullabī**: فشك خلبي (*fašak*) blank cartridges (*Syr.*; *mil.*)

خلاب **ḵallāb** gripping, captivating, fascinating; attractive, engaging, winning; tempting, enticing; fraudulent, deceitful; deceptive, delusive, fallacious

خلابة **ḵilāba** engaging manners, attractiveness, charm

مخلب **miḵlab** pl. مخالب *maḵālib*[2] claw, talon

خالب **ḵālib** = خلاب *ḵallāb*

خلبص **II** *taḵalbaṣa* (*eg.*) to clown

خلبوص **ḵalbūṣ** pl. خلابيص *ḵalābīṣ*[2], خلابصة *ḵalābiṣa* (*eg.*) clown, buffoon, harlequin

خلج **ḵalaja** *i* and **III** to be on s.o.'s (ه) mind, trouble, preoccupy, prepossess (ه s.o., s.o.'s mind; said of worries, doubts, etc.); to pervade, fill (ه s.o.; said of a feeling) | خالج قلبه (*qalbahū*) to be uppermost in s.o.'s heart **V** to be shaken, be convulsed, be rocked **VIII** to quiver, tremble, quake, shake; to twitch (eye, limb, body); to animate, move, stir, inspire, fill, pervade, possess (ه, في the heart; said of a feeling) | اختلج غما (*ḡamman*) to be filled with sorrow, with grief (heart)

خلجة **ḵalja** pl. *ḵalajāt* emotion, sentiment; scruple, qualm, misgiving

خليج **ḵalīj** pl. خلج *ḵuluj*, خلجان *ḵuljan* bay, gulf; canal; الخليج name of Cairo's ancient city canal which was abandoned and leveled at the end of the 19th century | الخليج الفارسي the Persian Gulf

خلاج **ḵilāj** misgiving, doubt, scruple, qualm

اختلاجة **iḵtilāja** (n. vic.) convulsion, jerk, twitch; tremor

خالجة **ḵālija** pl. خوالج *ḵawālij*[2] emotion, sentiment; scruple, qualm; idea

خلخل **ḵalḵala** to shake, convulse, rock (ه s.th.); to rarefy (ه s.th., e.g., air; *chem.-phys.*) **II** *taḵalḵala* to be shaken, be rocked; to come off, become disjointed, become detached; to become loose, work loose, to be or become rarefied (*chem.-phys.*)

خلخل **ḵalḵal** pl. خلاخل *ḵalāḵil*[2] anklet

خلخال **ḵalḵāl** pl. خلاخيل *ḵalāḵīl*[2] anklet

تخلخل **taḵalḵul** rarefication

مخلخل **muḵalḵal** and متخلخل *mutaḵalḵil* rarefied

خلد **ḵalada** *u* (خلود *ḵulūd*) to remain or last forever, be everlasting; to be immortal, deathless, undying; to abide forever (الى or ب in, with); to remain, stay (الى or ب or في at a place) | خلد الى الراحة to rest, relax; خلد الى النوم to lie down to sleep **II** to make eternal or everlasting, perpetuate, eternalize (ه s.th.), make immortal, immortalize (ه s.o.); to make ineffaceable, unforgettable (ه s.th.; a memory); to remain, stay, abide, linger (ب at, in a place); to grow very old, enjoy a long life, be long-lived **IV** to eternize, immortalize, make immortal (ه s.o., ه s.th.); to perpetuate (ه s.th.); to remain, stay, abide, linger (الى or ب at, in a place);

to be disposed, incline, lean, tend (الى to) V to become eternal or immortal, perpetuate o.s.; to be or become long, lasting, perpetual

خلد ḵuld infinite duration, endless time, perpetuity, eternity | دار الخلد Paradise, the hereafter

خلد ḵuld mole (zool.)

خلد ḵalad, pl. اخلاد aḵlād mind, heart, spirit, temper

خلود ḵulūd infinite duration, endless time, perpetuity; eternity; eternal life, immortality; abiding, remaining, staying

تخليد taḵlīd perpetuation, eternization, immortalization

خالد ḵālid everlasting, perpetual, eternal; immortal, deathless, undying; unforgettable, glorious; pl. خوالد ḵawālid² mountains | الجزائر الخالدات the Canary Islands

مخلد muḵlid disposed, inclined, tending (الى to)

خلس ḵalasa i (ḵals) to steal (ه s.th.); to pilfer, filch, swipe, purloin (ه s.th.) III خالس النظر (naẓara) to glance furtively at s.o. VIII to steal, pilfer, filch, swipe (ه s.th.); to get under false pretenses or by crooked means (ه s.th.); to embezzle, misappropriate (ه s.th.); to spend secretly (ه hours) | اختلس الخطى الى (ḵuṭā) to sneak up on s.o.; اختلس النظر الى (ى) to glance furtively at s.o.

خلسة ḵulsatan by stealth, stealthily, surreptitiously, furtively

خلاسي ḵilāsī mulatto, bastard

اختلاس iḵtilās pl. -āt embezzlement, misappropriation, defalcation

مختلس muḵtalis embezzler, defalcator

خلص ḵalaṣa u (خلوص ḵulūṣ) to be pure, unmixed, unadulterated; to belong (ل to s.o.); to get, come (الى to), arrive (الى at);

— (خلاص ḵalāṣ) to be or become free, be freed, be liberated (من from), be cleared, get rid (من of); to be saved, be rescued, escape (من from); to be redeemed, be delivered, attain salvation (Chr.); — (colloq.) to be finished, be done, be through, be over; to be all gone II to clear, purify, refine, purge, rectify (ه s.th.); to clarify (ه a situation); to liberate, free, save, rescue (ه s.o., من from), rid (ه s.o., من of); to redeem, deliver (Chr.); to prepay the postage (على on); to pay duty (على البضائع on merchandise), clear (على goods); to settle (ه a bill); (colloq.) to finish (ه s.th.) | خلص حقه (ḥaqqahū) to restore one's right, secure one's due III to act with integrity, with sincerity (ه toward s.o.), treat (ه s.o.) fair and square; to get even, become quits (ه with s.o.) IV to dedicate (ه ل to s.o. s.th.); to be loyal (ل to s.o.); to be devoted, be faithful (ل to) | اخلص له الحب (ḥubba) to love s.o. dearly; اخلص لله دينه (li-llāhi dīnahū) to worship God faithfully and sincerely V to rid o.s. (من of), free o.s. (من from), get rid (من of); to be freed, be delivered, be saved, be rescued, escape (من from) VI to act with reciprocal integrity and sincerity; to be quits, be even X to extract (ه s.th., من from); to copy, excerpt (ه s.th., من from); to abstract, take, gather, work out (ه s.th., as the quintessence, من of); to deduce, infer, derive (ه s.th., من from); to discover, make out, find out (ه s.th.); to select, choose (ه s.th.); to demand payment of a sum (ه) and get it (من from s.o.) | استخلص فائدة من to derive profit from, profit, benefit from; استخلص منه وعدا (wa'dan) to exact a promise from s.o.

خلاص ḵalāṣ liberation, deliverance, riddance; rescue, salvation (من from); redemption (Chr.); payment, settlement, liquidation (of a bill); receipt; placenta, afterbirth

خلاصة ḵulāṣa pl. -āt excerpt; extract, essence; quintessence, substance, gist (of s.th.); abstract, résumé, summary, epitome; synopsis | خلاصة نهائية (nihāʾīya) summation (jur.); الخلاصة اللاهوتية (al-lāhūtīya) the "summa theologica" (of Thomas Aquinas); خلاصة عطرية (ʿiṭrīya) perfume essence; وبالخلاصة in short, briefly, in a word (introducing a summary of the basic ideas)

خليص ḵalīṣ pl. خلصاء ḵulaṣāʾ² pure, clear, unmixed, unadulterated; sincere, faithful, loyal; loyal adherent

خلوص ḵulūṣ clearness, purity; sincerity, candor, frankness

خلاص ḵallāṣ (maḡr.) tax collector

مخلص maḵlaṣ safe place; refuge, escape, rescue, salvation, deliverance

تخليص taḵlīṣ clearing, purification, refining, rectification; clarification; liberation, extrication, deliverance, rescue, salvation; payment, settlement, liquidation; prepayment of postage (على on); customs clearance, payment of duty على البضائع on merchandise: also تخليص (البضائع)

مخالصة muḵālaṣa pl. -āt receipt

اخلاص iḵlāṣ sincere devotion, loyal attachment, sincere affection; sincerity, frankness, candor; loyalty, faithfulness, fidelity, allegiance (ل to)

تخلص taḵalluṣ freedom, liberation, release, extrication, escape (من from)

استخلاص istiḵlāṣ extraction; excerption; derivation, deduction; selection; collecting (of a sum of money)

خالص ḵāliṣ pl. خلص ḵullaṣ clear; pure, unmixed, unadulterated; sincere, frank, candid, true; free, exempt (من from) | خالص الاجرة ḵ. al-ujra post-free; خالص الرد ḵ. ar-radd prepaid, reply paid for (tele-

gram); خالص من الكرك (gumrug) dutyfree; خالص الضريبة tax-exempt

مخلص muḵalliṣ liberator; Savior, Redeemer (Chr.)

مخلص (عليه) muḵallaṣ (ʿalaihi) postage paid

مخلص muḵliṣ devoted; sincere, frank, candid; loyal; faithful (ل to s.o., to s.th.); purehearted, virtuous, righteous; المخلص (in letters) approx.: yours truly ..., sincerely yours ...

مستخلص mustaḵlaṣ pl. -āt extract, excerpt

خلط ḵalaṭa i (ḵalṭ) to mix, mingle, commingle, blend (ب ﺷ s.th. with); to confuse, confound, mix up (بين two things; و ﺷ s.th. with), mistake (و ﺷ s.th. for) II to mix, mingle, commingle, blend (ﺷ s.th.); to cause confusion III to mix, mingle, blend, merge, fuse (ﺷ with s.th.); to meddle (ﺷ in), interfere (ﺷ with); to mix, associate (ﺷ with s.o.); to have to do (ﺷ with s.o.) | خالط نفسه (nafsahū) to befall, attack s.o. (pain, etc.); خولط فى عقله ḵūliṭa fī ʿaqlihī to be or become disordered in mind VIII to be mixed, mix, mingle, form a mixture or blend; to consist of a heterogeneous mixture, be motley, promiscuous; to associate, be on intimate terms (ب with); to be or become confused, get all mixed up

خلط ḵalṭ mixing, blending; combination; mingling, commingling (ب with); confusing, confounding, mistaking, mix-up, confusion

خلط ḵilṭ pl. اخلاط aḵlāṭ component of a mixture; ingredient; pl. mixture, blend | اخلاط الانسان the four humors of the human body (blood, phlegm, yellow bile, and black bile); اخلاط من الناس common people, populace, rabble, riff-raff, mob; خلط ملط ḵilṭ milṭ, ḵalṭ malṭ motley, pell-mell, promiscuously

خلطة *kalṭa* mixture, blend, medley

خلطة *kulṭa* company; mixture

خلاط *kallāṭ* and خلاطة *kallāṭa* pl. *-āt* mixer, mixing machine

خليط *kalīṭ* mixed, blended; motley, heterogeneous, promiscuous; mixture, blend (من of); medley, hodgepodge; (pl. خلطاء *kulaṭā'*²) associate, companion, comrade

تخليط *taklīṭ* pl. *-āt* insanity; delirium

مخالطة *mukālaṭa* company, intercourse, association

اختلاط *iktilāṭ* (process of) mixing, blending; mingling, commingling; confusion; mental disorder; (social) intercourse, association, dealings (ب with)

مخلوط *maklūṭ* pl. مخاليط *makālīṭ*² mixture, blend; alloy

مخلط *mukallaṭ* confused, disordered

مخالط *mukālaṭ* stricken, afflicted (ب e.g., by a disease)

مختلط *muktaliṭ* mixed | المحاكم المختلطة the mixed courts, see محكمة; تعليم مختلط coeducation

خلع *kala'a a* (*kal'*) to take off, put off, slip off (ه a garment); to doff, take off (طربوشه one's tarboosh); to extract, pull (ه a tooth); to wrench, dislocate, luxate (ه a joint); to depose, remove, dismiss, discharge (ه s.o., من from an office); to renounce, forgo, give up (ه s.th.), withdraw (ه from); to throw off, cast off (عذاره *'iḏārahū* one's restraint, one's inhibitions); to refuse (الطاعة obedience); to disown, repudiate (ابنه one's son); to divorce (ها one's wife) in return for a compensation to be paid by her; to get through, have done (ه with s.th.), be through, have gone through s.th. (ه, e.g., a hard day); to impart (على ه s.th. to); to confer, bestow (على ه s.th. upon s.o.), grant, award (على ه s.th. to s.o.) | خلع ثيابه (*ṯiyābahū*) to undress; خلعه من العرش (*'arš*) to dethrone s.o.; خلع عليه خلعة (*kil'atan*) to bestow a robe of honor upon s.o.; خلع على نفسه حق (*ḥaqqa*) to arrogate to o.s. the right of ...; — *kalu'a u* (خلاعة *kalā'a*) to be dissolute, morally depraved **II** to take away, remove, displace, dislocate (ه s.th.); to knock out of joint, take or break apart (ه s.th.); pass. *kulli'a* to fall to pieces, get out of joint **III** to divorce (ها one's wife, in return for a compensation to be paid by her) **V** to go to pieces, fall apart, break; to become or be luxated, dislocated (joint); to take a vacation in the country (*tun.*) | تخلع فى الشراب (*šarāb*) to be addicted to drinking, drink heavily **VII** to be displaced, be dislocated, be removed; to be divested, be deprived, be stripped (من of s.th.), forfeit, lose (من s.th.) | انخلع قلبه (*qalbuhū*) he was completely taken aback, he was alarmed, startled

خلع *kal'* slipping off, taking off (of clothes); deposition (e.g., of a ruler); dislocation, luxation | خلع الاسنان extraction of teeth

خلع *kul'* khula, divorce at the instance of the wife, who must pay a compensation (*Isl. Law*)

خلعة *kil'a* pl. خلع *kila'* robe of honor

خليع *kalī'* pl. خلعاء *kula'ā'*² deposed, dismissed, discharged (from an office); repudiated, disowned; wanton, dissolute, dissipated, profligate, morally depraved

خلاع *kallā'* wild, unruly, wanton, shameless, impudent

خلاعة *kalā'a* dissoluteness, dissipation, profligacy, wantonness, licentiousness, moral depravity; (*tun.*) recreation in the country, summer vacation

خولع *kaula'* fool, dolt, simpleton

خالع *ḵāli'*: خالع العذار *ḵ. al-'iḏār* unrestrained, uninhibited, wanton; libertine, debauchee, roué, rake

مخلوع *maḵlū'* unrestrained, uninhibited, wanton; wild, unruly; reckless, heedless, irresponsible; crazy, mad

خلف *ḵalafa u* to be the successor (ه of s.o.), succeed (ه s.o.); to follow (ه s.o.), come after s.o. (ه); to take the place of s.o. (ه), substitute (ه for s.o.); to replace (ه s.o., ه s.th.); to lag behind s.o. (عن); to stay behind (عن after s.o.'s departure); to be detained, be held back, be kept away, stay away (عن from) **II** to appoint as successor (ه s.o.); to leave behind, leave (ه, ه s.o., s.th.); to have descendants, have offspring **III** to be contradictory, contrary, opposed (ه to); to conflict, clash, be at variance (ه with); to contradict (ه s.o., ه s.th.); to be different, differ, diverge (ه from), be inconsistent, incompatible, not in keeping, not to harmonize (ه with); to offend (ه against a command, a rule), break, violate, disobey (ه a command, a rule) **IV** to leave (ه offspring, children); to compensate, requite, recompense (على s.o.; said of God); to break, fail to keep (وعده *wa'dahū* one's promise), go back on one's word; to disappoint (الرجاء *ar-rajā'a* the hopes) **V** to stay behind; to lag or fall behind (عن); to stay, stay on, remain; to fail to appear or show up; to play truant; to be absent; to stay away (عن from), not go (عن to), not attend (عن s.th.) | تخلف عن المجىء (*majī'*) to fail to come or arrive; تخلف عن العودة (*'auda*) not to return **VI** to disagree, differ, be at variance; to differ in opinion, be of a different mind **VIII** to differ, be different, vary (عن from); to be varied, varying, variable, various, diverse, dissimilar; to vary (بين between); to disagree, differ in opinion, be at variance, argue, quarrel, dispute (فى about); to come or go frequently (الى to), frequent, patronize (الى a place), visit frequently (الى s.o., s.th.), come and go (الى at), to come, descend (على upon s.o.; said of afflictions), befall, overtake (على s.o.) **X** to appoint as successor or vicar (ه s.o.)

خلف *ḵalf* back, rear, rear part or portion; successors; *ḵalfu* and من خلف *min ḵalfu* (adv.) at the back, in the rear; *ḵalfa* (prep.) behind, after, in the rear of | جرى خلفها he ran after her; من خلف *min ḵalfi* behind, in the rear of; من الخلف from behind, from the rear; الى الخلف to the rear, backward, back; الى خلف الشىء in the wake of s.th.; فى الخلف in the rear; at the back, in the background

خلفى *ḵalfī* rear, hind, hinder, back

خلف *ḵilf* pl. اخلاف *aḵlāf* teat, nipple, mammilla

خلف *ḵulf* dissimilarity, disparity, difference, contrast, variance, discrepancy

خلف *ḵalaf* pl. اخلاف *aḵlāf* substitute; successor; descendant, offspring, scion

خلفة *ḵilfa* dissimilarity, disparity, difference; that which follows s.th. and replaces it (e.g., second growth of plants, day and night, etc.)

خليفة *ḵalīfa* pl. خلفاء *ḵulafā'*[2], خلائف *ḵalā'if*[2] vicar, deputy; successor; caliph; (formerly) senior official of the native administration in Tunis, assigned to a قائد; (formerly) title of the ruler of Spanish Morocco

المنطقة الخليفية *al-minṭaqa al-ḵalīfīya* the Caliphate Zone (formerly, designation of Spanish Morocco)

خلافة *ḵilāfa* vicarship, deputyship; succession; caliphate, office or rule of a caliph; (formerly) administrative department of a خليفة (*Tun.*), see above

مخلاف *miḵlāf* pl. مخاليف *maḵālīf*[2] province (Yemen)

خلاف *ḵilāf* pl. *-āt* difference, disparity, dissimilarity; divergence, deviation; contrast, contrariety, incongruity, contradiction, conflict; disagreement, difference of opinion (على or فى about); dispute, controversy; *ḵilāfa* (prep.) beside, apart from, aside from | خلافه *ḵilāfuhū* (= غيره) other, the like, خلافهم others (than those mentioned), وخلافه and the like (after an enumeration); بخلاف *bi-ḵilāfi* beside, apart from, aside from; contrary to, as opposed to, unlike; خلافا ل *ḵilāfan li* contrary to, against, in contradiction to; على خلاف ذلك unlike that, contrary to that, on the contrary, on the other hand

خلافى *ḵilāfī* controversial, disputed

مخالفة *muḵālafa* pl. *-āt* contrast, contrariety; contradiction, inconsistency; contravention, infringement, violation; misdemeanor (*jur.*; as distinguished from جنحة and جناية); fine (for a misdemeanor)

تخلف *taḵalluf* staying away, nonappearance, nonattendance, nonpresence, absence, truancy (also تخلف عن الحضور); staying behind, staying on; stopover (railroad); backwardness

اختلاف *iḵtilāf* pl. *-āt* difference, dissimilarity, disparity; diversity, variety; variant, variation; difference of opinion, disagreement; controversy | الرعية على اختلاف المذاهب الدينية (*ra'īya, dīnīya*) the subjects of every (= irrespective of their) religious denomination; على اختلاف احزابهم whichever party they may belong to; الفواكه على اختلافها all the different fruits, fruits of every kind

مخلوفة *maḵlūfa* pl. *-āt* camel saddle

مخلف *muḵallaf* left, left behind; left over; pl. مخلفات heritage, legacy, estate; scraps, leftovers

مخالف *muḵālif* divergent, varying, different; inconsistent, incompatible, contradictory, contrasting, conflicting; transgressor (of a command)

متخلف *mutaḵallif* residual; left over; retarded, backward, underdeveloped (mentally, in growth, etc.); pl. *-ūn* one left behind; straggler; pl. متخلفات heritage, legacy, estate; leftovers; scraps, refuse, offal | اتربة متخلفة (*atriba*) waste material, overburden, superstratum (in mining); المياه المتخلفة (*miyāh*) waste water, sewage

مختلف *muḵtalif* different, varying, divergent (من from); varied, various, diverse; having a different opinion, disagreeing (فى or على about)

مختلف فيه (عليه) *muḵtalaf fīhi ('alaihi)* controversial, disputed

خلق *ḵalaqa u* (*ḵalq*) to create, make, originate (ه s.th.); to shape, form, mold (ه s.th.); — *ḵaliqa a* and *ḵaluqa u* to be old, worn, shabby (garment); — *ḵaluqa u* (خلاقة *ḵalāqa*) to be fit, suitable, suited **II** to perfume (ه s.th.) **IV** to wear out (ه s.th.), let (ه s.th.) become old and shabby **V** pass. of **II**; to be molded, be shaped (ب by a model or pattern), change (ب with a model); to become angry **VIII** to invent, contrive, devise (ه s.th.); to fabricate, concoct, think up (ه s.th.); to attribute falsely (ه على to s.o. s.th.)

خلق *ḵalq* creation; making; origination; s.th. which is created, a creation; creatures; people, man, mankind; physical constitution

خلق *ḵulq, ḵuluq* pl. اخلاق *aḵlāq* innate peculiarity; natural disposition, character, temper, nature; — pl. اخلاق *aḵlāq* character (of a person); morals; morality | سوء الخلق *sū' al-ḵ.* ill nature; سيئ الخلق *sayyi' al-ḵ.* ill-natured; سهل الخلق *sahl al-ḵ.* complaisant, obliging; ضيق الخلق *ḍayyiq al-ḵ.* impatient, restless; علم الاخلاق *'ilm al-a.* ethics; moral science, morals;

سمو الاخلاق *sumūw al-a.* nobility of character; مكارم الاخلاق noble manners, high moral standards; شرطة الاخلاق *šurṭat al-a.* vice squad

خلقي *ḵulqī* ethic(al), moral | جرائم خلقية offenses against public morals

خلق *ḵalaq* (m. and f.) pl. خلقان *ḵulqān*, اخلاق *aḵlāq* shabby, threadbare, worn (garment)

خلقة *ḵilqa* pl. خلق *ḵilaq* creation; innate peculiarity of character, natural disposition, nature; constitution; physiognomy; خلقة *ḵilqatan* by nature

خلقي *ḵilqī* natural, native, congenital, innate, inborn, inbred

خلقة *ḵalaqa* rag, tatter

خلاق *ḵalāq* share (of positive qualities, of religion) | لا خلاق له (*ḵalāqa*) disgraceful, ignominious, despicable; a worthless fellow, a good-for-nothing

خليق *ḵalīq* pl. خلقاء *ḵulaqā'* fit, qualified, suitable, appropriate (ل , ب for s.th.; ان to do s.th.); apt (ان to do s.th.); in keeping with (ب), adequate (ب to), worthy (ب of) | نحن خليقون ان it is (would be) only fair that we ..., we should ..., we ought to ...; هو خليق ان he is apt to ..., it is only natural for him that he ...; خليق بهذا ان يكون مؤلما (*mu'liman*) this is apt to be painful, it is only natural that this is painful; نظرة يسيرة خليقة ان تقنعنا بأن (*tuqniʿanā*) no more than a quick glance is apt to convince us that ...

خلوق *ḵalūq* of firm character, steadfast, upright

اخلق *aḵlaq²* more adequate, more appropriate, more natural

خلاق *ḵallāq* Creator, Maker (God)

خليقة *ḵalīqa* the creation, the universe created by God; nature; natural disposition, trait, characteristic; creatures,

created beings; pl. خلائق *ḵalā'iq²* creatures, created beings

اخلاقي *aḵlāqī* moral; ethic(al); ethicist, moral philosopher | جرم اخلاقي (*jurm*) offense against public morals; الفلسفة الاخلاقية (*falsafa*) moral science, moral philosophy; ethics

اخلاقية *aḵlāqīya* morality, moral practice

خلقاني *ḵulqānī* dealer in old clothes

خالق *ḵāliq* creative; Creator, Maker (God)

مخلوق *maḵlūq* created; (pl. -āt, مخاليق *maḵālīq²*) creature, created being

مختلق *muḵtaliq* inventor, fabricator (of untruths)

مختلق *muḵtalaq* fabricated, trumped up, invented, fictitious; apocryphal; pl. -āt lies, falsehoods, fabrications, fictions

خلقين *ḵalqīn* pl. خلاقين *ḵalāqīn²* caldron, boiler, kettle

¹ خلنج *ḵalanj* heath, erica (*bot.*)

² خلنجان *ḵulungān* (*eg.*) (rhizome of) galingale (Polypodium Calaguala Kz.; *bot.*)

خلا *ḵalā u* (خلو *ḵulūw*, خلاء *ḵalā'*) to be empty, vacant; — (*ḵulūw*) to be free (من or عن from); to be devoid (من of s.th.), lack, want (من s.th.), be in need (من of); to be vacant (office); — (خلوة *ḵalwa*) to be alone (مع , الى , ب with s.o., الى also: with or in s.th.); to isolate o.s., seclude o.s.; to withdraw, retire (المداولة *li-l-mudāwala* for deliberation; court, jury); to withdraw for spiritual communion, in order to take counsel (الى with); to devote o.s., apply o.s., give one's attention (ل to s.th.); خلا به to forsake, desert s.o., leave s.o. in the lurch; — to pass (ه s.o.), go by s.o. (ه); to pass, elapse, go by, be bygone, past, over (time) | خلا له الجو (*jauw*) to have free scope, have freedom of action; لا يخلو من جمال (*jamāl*) it is not without a certain beauty; لا يخلو من مبالغة (*mubālaġa*) it is slightly exaggerated; لا يخلو من فائدة it is not quite useless; خلا الى نفسه to be alone with o.s.; to commune with o.s., take counsel with o.s., search one's heart; منذ عشر سنوات خلت *munḏu ʿašri sanawātin ḵalat* for the past ten years **II** to vacate, evacuate (ه s.th.); to leave, leave alone (ه s.o.); to release, let go (ه s.o., ه s.th.); to desist, abstain, refrain (عن from), give up (عن s.th.) | خلى سبيله (*sabīlahū*) to let s.o. off, let s.o. go, release s.o.; خلى بين فلان وبين الشيء to give s.o. a free hand in, let s.o. have his own way with or in, let s.o. alone with; to open the way for s.o. to; خل عنك هذه الميول *ḵalli ʿanka h. l-muyūla* desist from such desires! **IV** to empty, void, drain, deplete (ه من s.th. of); to vacate, leave uninhabited or untenanted (ه a place); to evacuate (ه a city) | اخلى سبيله (*sabīlahū*) to let s.o. off, let s.o. go, release s.o.; اخلى السبيل ل to open the way for ...; اخلى طرفه (*ṭarafahū*) to dismiss, discharge s.o., send s.o. away; to exonerate, exculpate, clear s.o.; اخلى سمعه ل (*samʿahū*) to be all ears for ..., listen intently to ...; اخلى بينه وبين ما يقول to let s.o. say whatever he likes, let s.o. talk freely **V** to give up, relinquish, forgo, abandon (عن or من s.th.), withdraw, resign (عن or من from); to cede, leave, surrender (عن ل s.th. to s.o.); to lay down (عن an office) **VIII** to retire, withdraw, step aside, be alone (ب or مع with)

خلو *ḵilw* free (من from), devoid (من of)

خلو *ḵulūw* emptiness, vacuity; freedom (من from)

خلا *ḵalā* and ما خلا (with foll. acc. or genit.) except, save, with the exception of

خلاء *ḵalā'* emptiness, vacuity; empty space, void, vacancy, vacuum; open country | في الخلاء or تحت الخلاء under the open sky, outdoors, in the open air; بيت الخلاء *bait al-ḵ.* toilet, water closet

خلوة *ḵalwa* pl. *ḵalawāt* privacy, solitude; seclusion, isolation, retirement; place of retirement or seclusion, retreat, recess; secluded room; hermitage; religious assembly hall of the Druses; booth, cabin | على خلوة alone; in retirement, in seclusion; خلوة الحمام *ḵ. al-ḥammām* bathhouse

خلوى *ḵalawī* lonely, solitary, secluded, isolated, outlying; located in the open country, rural, rustic, country | بيت خلوى (*bait*) country house

خلى *ḵalīy* pl. اخلياء *aḵliyā'*[2] free (من from), void, devoid (من of) | خلى البال carefree, easygoing, happy-go-lucky

خلية *ḵalīya* pl. خلايا *ḵalāyā* beehive; cell (*biol.*) | ○ الخلية الحيوية الاولى (*al-ḥayawīya l-ūlā*) protoplasm; من خلايا from within ..., from inside ..., out of ...

مخلاة *miḵlāh* nosebag

تخلية *taḵliya* vacating, evacuation

اخلاء *iḵlā'* emptying, voiding, draining; clearing; vacating, evacuation | اخلاء سبيله *i. sabīlihī* his release

تخل *taḵallin* relinquishment, abandonment, surrender, renunciation, resignation (عن of s.th.)

اختلاء *iḵtilā'* privacy, solitude

خال *ḵālin* empty, void; open, vacant (office, position); free, unrestrained, untrammeled, unencumbered; free (من from), devoid (من of) | in numerous compounds corresponding to Engl. -less or un-, e.g., خال من الفائدة useless, خال من السكان (*sukkān*) uninhabited, untenanted, unoccupied; خالى الدين *ḵālī d-dain* not bound by, without obligation to, free (من from); خالى البال carefree, easygoing, happy-go-lucky; — (pl. خوال *ḵawālin*) past, bygone (time) | القرون الخالية the past centuries; في الايام الخوالي *fī l-ayyāmi l-ḵawālī* in the days past

خم **ḵammu** *u* (*ḵamm*) to sweep (ه a room), — *i u* (*ḵamm*, خموم *ḵumūm*) to exude a rotten, foul smell; to rot, putrify, decay

خم **ḵumm** pl. اخمام *aḵmām* coop, chicken coop, brooder; poultry pen

خمة **ḵamma** putrid smell, stench

خام **ḵāmm** stinking, rotten, putrid, foul-smelling; *ḵām* look up alphabetically

مخم **muḵimm** stinking, rotten, putrid, foul-smelling

خمج **ḵamija** *a* (*ḵamaj*) to spoil, rot, decay

خمد **ḵamada** *u* (خمود *ḵumūd*) to go out, die (fire); to abate, subside, let up, calm down, cease, die down **IV** to extinguish, put out (ه fire); to calm, appease, placate, soothe, lull, still, quiet (ه s.th.), to suppress, quell (ه s.th.); to subdue, soften, deaden, dull (ه s.th.); to stifle, smother, kill (ه s.th.; fig.)

خمود **ḵumūd** extinction; decline, degeneration, deterioration; quietness, stillness, tranquillity, calm; immobility, motionlessness

اخماد **iḵmād** extinction, putting out; calming, soothing, placation, appeasement, lulling, stilling; subduing, softening, dulling; settlement; suppression, quelling (of a riot)

خامد **ḵāmid** dying; abating, subsiding; calm, tranquil, still, quiet

خمر **ḵamara** *u* (*ḵamr*) and **II** to cover, hide, conceal (ه s.th.); to leaven, raise (ه dough); to ferment (ه s.th.), cause fermentation (ه in) **III** to permeate, pervade (ه s.th.), mix, blend (ه with); to possess, seize, overcome (ه s.o., e.g., an idea, a feeling) **IV** to leaven, raise (ه dough); to ferment (ه s.th.), cause fermentation (ه in); to harbor, entertain (ه s.th.); to bear a grudge, feel resentment (ل against s.o.) **V** to ferment, be in a state of fermentation; to rise (dough); to veil the head and face (woman) **VI** to conspire, plot, collude, scheme, intrigue (على against) **VIII** to ferment, be in a state of fermentation; to rise (dough); to become ripe, ripen (also fig.: an idea in s.o.'s mind)

خمر **ḵamr** m. and f., pl. خمور *ḵumūr* wine; pl. alcoholic beverages, liquor

خمرة **ḵamra** wine

خمري **ḵamrī** golden brown, reddish brown, bronze-colored (actually, wine-colored)

خمرية **ḵamrīya** pl. *-āt* wine poem, bacchanalian verse

خمار **ḵimār** pl. اخمرة *aḵmira*, خمر *ḵumur* veil covering head and face of a woman

خمار **ḵumār** aftereffect of intoxication, hang-over

خمير **ḵamīr** leavened (dough); ripe, mature, mellow; leaven; leavened bread

خميرة **ḵamīra** pl. خمائر *ḵamā'ir*² leaven; ferment; barm, yeast; enzyme (*chem.*); (fig.) starter, nucleus, basis (from which s.th. greater develops)

خمار **ḵammār** wine merchant, keeper of a wineshop

خمارة **ḵammāra** wineshop, tavern

خمير **ḵimmīr** winebibber, drunkard, tippler, sot

تخمير **taḵmīr** leavening, raising (of dough); fermenting, fermentation

اختمار **iḵtimār** (process of) fermentation

مخمور **maḵmūr** drunk, intoxicated, inebriated

مختمر **muḵtamir** fermenting, fermented; alcoholic

خمس II to quintuple, make fivefold, multiply by five (ه s.th.); to make pentagonal (ه s.th.); to divide into five parts (ه s.th.)

خمس *ḵums* pl. اخماس *aḵmās* one fifth | ضرب اخماسه فى اسداسه *ḍaraba aḵmāsahū fī asdāsihī* and ضرب اخماسا لاسداس (*li-asdāsin*) to rack one's brain in search of a way out; to be at one's wit's end; to scheme, intrigue

خمسة *ḵamsa* (f. خمس *ḵams*) five

خمسة عشر *ḵamsata ʿašara* (f. خمس عشرة *ḵamsa ʿašrata*) fifteen

خمسون *ḵamsūn* fifty | عيد الخمسين *ʿīd al-ḵ.* Whitsuntide, Pentecost; احد الخمسين *aḥad al-ḵ.* Whitsunday; ايام الخماسين *ayyām al-ḵamāsīn* the period of about 50 days between Easter and Whitsuntide; □ خمسين and خماسين khamsin, a hot southerly wind in Egypt

عيد خمسينى *ʿīd ḵamsīnī* 50th anniversary

خميس *ḵamīs* and يوم الخميس *yaum al-ḵ.* Thursday | خميس الجسد *ḵ. al-jasad* Corpus Christi Day (*Chr.*); خميس الفصح *ḵ. al-fiṣḥ*, خميس الاسرار *ḵ. al-asrār*, and خميس العهد *ḵ. al-ʿahd* Maundy Thursday (*Chr.*)

خماس *ḵammās* pl. خماسة *ḵamāmisa* (*maḡr.*) sharecropper receiving one fifth of the crop as wages

خماسى *ḵumāsī* fivefold, quintuple; consisting of five consonants (*gram.*) | خماسى الزوايا (*zawāyā*) pentagonal, five-cornered

خميسة *ḵumaisa* (*mor.*, pronounced *ḵmīsa*) ornament in the shape of a hand (worn by women and children as a talisman against the evil eye)

الخامس *al-ḵāmis* the fifth

مخمس *muḵammas* pentagonal, five-cornered; pentagon; fivefold, quintuple; ○ pentameter

خمش *ḵamaša i u* (*ḵamš*) and II to scratch (ه e.g., the face, the skin, with the nails)

خمش *ḵamš* pl. خموش *ḵumūš* scratch, scratch mark, scar

خماشة *ḵumāša* pl. -*āt* scratch, scar

خمص *ḵamaṣa u* and *ḵamiṣa a* to be empty, hungry (stomach)

خميص *ḵamīṣ*, خميص البطن *ḵ. al-baṭn*, خميص الحشا *ḵ. al-ḥašā* with an empty stomach, hungry

اخمص القدم *aḵmaṣ al-qadam* pl. اخامص *aḵāmiṣ*[2] hollow of the sole (of the foot) | من الرأس الى اخمص القدم from head to toe

خمع *ḵamaʿa a* (*ḵamʿ*, خموع *ḵumūʿ*) to limp, walk with a limp

خمل *ḵamala u* (خمول *ḵumūl*) to be unknown, obscure, undistinguished; to be weak, languid

خمل *ḵaml* and خملة *ḵamla* nap, the rough, hairy surface of a fabric; fibers

خمل *ḵamil* languid, sluggish, dull, listless

خمول *ḵumūl* obscurity; weakness, lassitude, languor, lethargy; indolence, sluggishness, inactivity; apathy, indifference; sleepiness, drowsiness

خميلة *ḵamīla* pl. خمائل *ḵamāʾil*[2] place with luxuriant tree growth; thicket, brush, scrub

خامل *ḵāmil* unknown, obscure, undistinguished, unimportant, minor; weak, languid, sluggish

مخمل *muḵmal* velvet-like fabric, velvet

مخملى *muḵmalī* velvety | جلد مخملى (*jild*) deerskin, buckskin

خمن II to guess, conjecture, surmise; to make conjectures (ه as to); to assess, appraise, estimate (ه s.th.)

تخمين *taḵmīn* appraisal, assessment, estimation; تخمينا *taḵmīnan* and على تخمين approximately, roughly

مخمن *muḵammin* appraiser, assessor

[1] خن *ḵanna i* (خنين *ḵanīn*) to speak nasally, nasalize; to twang, speak through the nose

خنة *ḵunna* nasal twang

خنين *ḵanīn* twanging, nasal twang

اخن *aḵann*², f. خناء *ḵannā'*² twanging, speaking through the nose

[2] خن *ḵunn* (= خم *ḵumm*) pl. اخنان *aḵnān* coop, chicken coop, brooder

خنث *ḵaniṯa a* to be soft, effeminate **V** to display effeminate manners, become or be effeminate

خنث *ḵaniṯ* oft, effeminate

خنثى *ḵunṯā* pl. خناث *ḵināṯ*, خناثى *ḵunāṯā* hermaphrodite

خنوثة *ḵunūṯa* effeminacy

تخنث *taḵannuṯ* effeminacy

مخنث *muḵannaṯ* bisexual; effeminate; powerless, impotent, weak

خنجر *ḵanjar* pl. خناجر *ḵanājir*² dagger

خنخن *ḵanḵana* to nasalize, speak nasally; to twang, speak through the nose

خندق *ḵandaqa* to dig a ditch or trench (خندقا); to take up positions, prepare for battle

خندق *ḵandaq* pl. خنادق *ḵanādiq*² ditch; trench

خنزوانية *ḵunzuwānīya* megalomania

خنزب *ḵanzab* Satan, Devil

خنزير *ḵinzīr* pl. خنازير *ḵanāzīr*² swine, pig, hog; خنزير برى (*barrī*) wild boar; خنازير scrofula, scrofulosis (*med.*)

خنزيرة *ḵinzīra* sow

خنازيرى *ḵanāzīrī* scrofulous

الخناس *al-ḵannās* epithet of the Devil (properly speaking, he who withdraws when the name of God is mentioned)

خنس اخنس *aḵnas*², f. خنساء *ḵansā'*², pl. *ḵuns* pugnosed

خنشار *ḵinšār* fern (*bot.*)

خنوص *ḵinnauṣ* pl. خنانيص *ḵanānīṣ*² piglet

خنصر *ḵinṣir* pl. خناصر *ḵanāṣir*² little finger | عقد الخنصر (الخناصر) على to give s.th. top-rating because of its excellence, put s.th. above everything else

خنع *ḵanaʿa a* (خنوع *ḵunūʿ*) to yield, surrender, bow, stoop (ل or الى to s.o.), humble o.s., cringe (ل or الى before s.o.)

خنوع *ḵanūʿ* submissive, servile, meek, humble; treacherous, perfidious, disloyal

خنوع *ḵunūʿ* submissiveness, meekness, servility

خنف *ḵanaf* (*eg.*) twanging, nasal twang

خنفر *ḵanfara* to snuffle, snort

خنفس *ḵunfus* and خنفساء *ḵunfusā'* pl. خنافس *ḵanāfis*² dung beetle, scarab

خنق *ḵanaqa u* (*ḵanq*) to choke (ه s.o.); to suffocate, stifle, smother, strangle, throttle, choke to death (ه s.o.); to throttle down (*techn.*; ه s.th.); to slow down, cut, check, suppress (ه s.th.) **III** to quarrel, have a fight (ه with s.o.) **VI** to quarrel, dispute, have a fight (مع with s.o.) **VII** pass. of **I**; **VIII** to be throttled, be suppressed; to be tight, constricted (throat); to be strangled, be choked to death

خنق *ḵanq* strangling, strangulation; throttling, suppression | خنق الانوار *ḵ. al-anwār* dim-out

خنقة اليد *ḵanqat* (*ḵunqat*) *al-yad* wrist

خناق *ḵunāq* suffocation; angina (*med.*); *ḵunāq* and خانوق *ḵānūq* quinsy, diphtheria (*med.*); pl. خوانق *ḵawāniq*² and خوانيق *ḵawānīq*² do.

خناق *ḵannāq* choking, throttling, strangling

مخنق *maḵnaq* neck, throat | اخذه بمخنقه to grab s.o. by the throat, bear down on s.o.; to have power over s.o.

خناق *ḵināq* strangling cord; neck, throat | ضيق الخناق على (*ḍayyaqa*) to tighten the grip around s.o.'s throat, tread on s.o.'s neck, oppress s.o., beset s.o. grievously; اخذ بخناقه to grab s.o. by the throat

خناق *ḵināq* and خناقة *ḵināqa* quarrel, fight, row

اختناق *iḵtināq* suffocation, asphyxiation; constriction; asphyxia (*med.*)

خانق *ḵāniq* choking, strangling; suffocating, asphyxiating, stifling, smothering; throttling, throttle- (in compounds; *techn.*); (pl. خوانق *ḵawāniq*²) choke coil, reactor (*radio*); gorge, ravine, canyon | غاز خانق asphyxiating gas; خانق الذئب *ḵ. aḏ-ḏi'b* wolfsbane, monkshood, aconite (*bot.*)

مخنوق *maḵnūq* strangled; suffocated, stifled, smothered; suppressed, choking (voice, laughter, etc.); constricted; strangulated; throttled

مختنق *muḵtaniq* crammed, jammed, crowded, chock-full (ب with)

(خنو and خنى) خنا *ḵanā u*, خنى *ḵaniya a* (خنى *ḵanan*) to use obscene language **IV** to hit hard, afflict grievously, wear down, ruin, destroy, crush (على s.o., s.th.; said of fate)

خنى *ḵanan* obscene language; s.th. indecent or obscene; prostitution; fornication

خواجة *ḵawāja* pl. *-āt* sir, Mr. (title and form of address, esp., for Christians and Westerners, used with or without the name of the person so addressed)

خوان *ḵuwān*, *ḵiwān* pl. اخونة *aḵwina*, اخاوين *aḵāwīn*² table | خوان الزينة *ḵ. az-zīna* dressing table

خوجة *ḵōga* (*eg.*) teacher, schoolmaster

خوخ **II** (*eg.*) to rot, decay, spoil

خوخ *ḵauḵ* (coll.; n. un. ة) peach (*eg.*); plum (*syr.*)

خوخة *ḵauḵa* pl. خوخ *ḵuwaḵ* skylight, windowlike opening; wicket (of a canal lock, of a gate); (*eg.*) alley connecting two streets

خوذة *ḵūḏa* pl. *-āt*, خوذ *ḵuwaḏ* helmet

¹(خور) خار *ḵāra u* (خوار *ḵuwār*) to low, moo (cattle); — خور *ḵawira a* (خور *ḵawar*) and خار *ḵāra u* to decline in force or vigor; to grow weak, spiritless, languid, to languish, flag; to dwindle, give out (strength)

خور *ḵaur* pl. اخوار *aḵwār*, خيران *ḵīrān* inlet, bay

خور *ḵawar* weakness, fatigue, enervation, languor, lassitude

خوار *ḵuwār* lowing, mooing

خوار *ḵawwār* weak, languid, strengthless

²خورى *ḵūrī* pl. خوارنة *ḵawārina* parson, curate, priest; see also under خير

خورس *ḵūrus* choir (of a church)

خوزق *ḵauzaqa* to impale (ه s.o.); to corner, drive into a corner, get into a bad fix (ه s.o.)

خازوق see خزق

ورق خوشق *waraq ḵaušaq* wrapping paper; blotting paper

¹خوص *ḵūṣ* (coll.; n. un. ة) palm leaves

خوصة *ḵūṣa* (*eg.*) plaitwork of palm leaves (resembling that of Panama hats; used as a tarboosh lining)

خواصة *ḵiwāṣa* art of palm-leaf plaiting

²خوص *ḵawaṣ* and اخوص see حوص

³خويصة see خصّ

¹(خوض) خاض *ḵāḍa u* (*ḵauḍ*, خياض *ḵiyāḍ*) to wade (ه into water); to plunge, dive, rush (ه into s.th.), tackle courageously (ه s.th.), embark boldly (ه on); to penetrate (ه or في into), become absorbed, engrossed (ه or في in); to go into a subject (في), take up (في a subject), deal (في with) | خاض المعركة (*ma'raka*) to rush into battle; خاض غمار الحرب (*ǧimāra l-ḥarb*) to enter the war

خوض *ḵauḍ* plunge, rush (into); entering, entry (into, e.g., into war, into negotiations); penetration; search (في into), examination, discussion, treatment (في of a subject)

مخاضة *maḵāḍa* pl. *-āt*, مخاوض *maḵāwiḍ*² ford

²مخاض see مخض

(خوف) خاف *ḵāfa* (1st pers. perf. *ḵiftu*) *a* (*ḵauf*, مخافة *maḵāfa*, خيفة *ḵīfa*) to be frightened, scared; to be afraid (ه, ه or من of), dread (ه, ه or من s.o. or s.th.); to fear (ه, ه or من s.o., s.th.; على for s.o., for s.th.; ان that) **II** and **IV** to frighten, scare, alarm, fill with fear (ه s.o.) **V** = **I**

خوف *ḵauf* fear, dread (من of); خوفا *ḵaufan* for fear (من of), fearing (على for)

خيفة *ḵīfa* fear, dread (من of)

خواف *ḵawwāf*, خويف *ḵawwīf* fainthearted, fearful, timid, timorous; coward, poltroon

اخوف *aḵwaf*² more timorous; more dreadful, more to be feared

مخافة *maḵāfa* fear, dread | مخافة ان (*maḵāfatan*) for fear that ..., afraid that ...

مخاوف *maḵāwif*² (pl. zu مخافة) fears, apprehensions, anxieties; horrors, dangers, perils

تخويف *taḵwīf* and اخافة *iḵāfa* intimidation, bullying, cowing, frightening, scaring

تخوف *taḵawwuf* fear, dread

خائف *ḵā'if* pl. خوف *ḵuwwaf* fearful, timid, timorous; scared, frightened, alarmed (من by); afraid (من of); anxious (على about), apprehensive (على for)

مخوف *maḵūf* feared, dreaded; dangerous, perilous

مخيف *muḵīf* fear-inspiring, frightful, dreadful, terrible, horrible

خاكى look up alphabetically

خول **II** to grant, accord, give, concede (ه ه to s.o. s.th., also ه ل; esp., the right, the power to do s.th.), bestow, confer (ه ه upon s.o. s.th., also ه ل), vest, endow (ه ه s.o. with s.th., also ه ل)

خال *ḵāl* pl. اخوال *aḵwāl*, خوول *ḵu'ul*, خوولة *ḵu'ūla* (maternal) uncle; — (pl. خيلان *ḵīlān*) mole, birthmark (on the face); ○ patch, beauty spot

خالة *ḵāla* pl. *-āt* (maternal) aunt

خول *ḵawal* chattels, property, esp., that consisting in livestock and slaves; servants; (*eg.*) dancer; effeminate person, sissy

خولى *ḵaulī* supervisor, overseer (of a plantation); gardener

خؤولة *ḵu'ūla* relationship of the maternal uncle

مخول *muḵawwal* authorized (ب to)

خام look up alphabetically

¹(خون) خان *ḵāna u* (*ḵaun*, خيانة *ḵiyāna*) to be disloyal, faithless, false, treacherous, perfidious, act disloyally, treacherously, perfidiously (ه toward s.o.); to betray (ه s.o.); to cheat, dupe, gull, hoodwink (ه s.o.), impose (ه upon), deceive (زوجته one's wife); to fool, deceive, mislead

(ه s.o.; said, e.g., of the memory); to forsake, let down, desert (ه s.o.); to fail (ه s.o.; e.g., the voice, and the like); to fail to keep (ه e.g., a promise), break (عهدا 'ahdan a contract) **II** to regard as or call faithless, false, disloyal, treacherous, dishonest, unreliable (ه s.o.); to distrust, mistrust (ه s.o.) **V** to impair, harm, hurt, prejudice (ه s.th.) **VIII** to dupe, gull, cheat, deceive, double-cross, betray (ه s.o.) **X** استخون istaḵwana to distrust, mistrust (ه s.o.)

خيانة ḵiyāna faithlessness, falseness, disloyalty, treachery, perfidy; breach of faith, betrayal; treason; deception, fooling | خيانة الامانة ḵ. al-amāna breach of faith; خيانة عظمى ('uẓmā) high treason; خيانة الوعود breach of promise

خؤون ḵa'ūn faithless, false, disloyal, traitorous, treacherous, perfidious; unreliable, tricky, deceptive

خوان ḵawwān unreliable, faithless, disloyal, treacherous, perfidious; traitor

خائن ḵā'in pl. خوان ḵuwwān, خونة ḵawana disloyal, faithless, false, unreliable, traitorous, treacherous, perfidious; traitor

خانة and خان² look up alphabetically

خوان³ look up alphabetically

خوى ḵawā i (خواء ḵawā', خوى ḵawan) to be empty, be hungry; — ḵawiya a (خواء ḵawā') to be empty, bare, dreary, desolate, waste

خواء ḵawā' and خوى ḵawan emptiness (of the stomach), hunger

خاو ḵāwin empty, vacant; dreary, waste, desolate | خاو على عروشه ('urūšihī) completely devastated; خاوى الوفاض ḵ. l-wifāḍ (= خالى الوفاض) with an empty pouch, empty-handed, without a catch

خوى⁴ **III** to join (ه s.o.), join the company of (ه), accompany (ه s.o.)

خوى ḵuwaiy little brother

خوة ḵūwa brotherliness, fraternity (= اخوة uḵūwa)

مخاو muḵāwin brotherly, fraternal

خيار ḵiyār (coll.; n.un. ة) cucumber | خيار شنبر ḵ. šanbar (eg.) drumstick tree, purging cassia (Cassia fistula; bot.); خيار قثة ḵ. qašša (eg.) gherkins, pickles

خاب ḵāba i (خيبة ḵaiba) to fail, miscarry, be without success, be unsuccessful; to be frustrated, be dashed, be disappointed (hopes); to go wrong **II** and **IV** to cause to fail; to thwart, frustrate, foil, defeat (ه s.th.); to disappoint, dash (آماله āmālahū s.o.'s hopes) **V** = **I**

خيبة ḵaiba failure, miscarriage, defeat, frustration; fizzle, flop; disappointment | ولد خيبة walad ḵ., f. بنت خيبة bint ḵ. (eg.) a good-for-nothing, a ne'er-do-well

خائب ḵā'ib failing; abortive, unsuccessful; disappointed

خار ḵāra i (خير) to choose, make one's choice; to prefer (على ه s.th. to) **II** to make or let (ه s.o.) choose (بين between, ق from), give (ه s.o.) the alternative, option or choice (بين between, ق in); to prefer (على ه s.th. to) **III** to vie, compete (ه with s.o.); to make or let (ه s.o.) choose, give (ه s.o.) the choice, option or alternative **V** to choose, select, pick (ه, ه s.o., s.th.) **VIII** to choose, make one's choice; to choose, select, elect, pick (ه, ه s.o., s.th.), fix upon s.o. or s.th. (ه, ه); to prefer (على ه s.th. to) | اختار الله الى جواره ... (جى wārihī) approx.: the Lord has taken ... unto Himself **X** to seek or request what is good or best (ه) for o.s. (ه from s.o.); to consult an oracle, cast lots | استخار الله فى to ask God for proper guidance in

خير ḵair pl. خيار ḵiyār, اخيار aḵyār good; excellent, outstanding, superior, admirable; better; best; — (pl. خيور

ḵuyūr) good thing, blessing; wealth, property; — good, benefit, interest, advantage; welfare; charity | خير الناس اخيار الناس,خيار الناس the best of all people; the best people, the pick of the human race; هو خير منك he is better than you; هو خير لك it is better for you; الخير كل الخير the very best; الخير العام (ʿāmm) the commonweal, general welfare; دولة الخير العام welfare state; لخير for the benefit of; لخير انفسهم li-ḵ. anfusihim for their own good; اعمال الخير charitable deeds; صباح الخير ṣabāḥ al-ḵ. and صباحك بالخير good morning! ذكره بالخير (ḏakarahū) to retain a good impression of s.o.; to speak well of s.o.

خيرى **ḵairī** charitable, beneficent, benevolent, philanthropic | جمعية خيرية (jamʿīya) charitable organization

خيرية **ḵairīya** charity, charitableness, benevolence, beneficence

خير **ḵayyir** generous, liberal, openhanded, munificent; charitable, beneficent, benevolent; benign, gracious, kind

خيرة **ḵaira** pl. -āt good deed, good thing; pl. خيرات resources, treasures (e.g., of the earth, of a country), boons, blessings

خيرة **ḵīra** and **ḵiyara** the best, choice, prime, flower, pick, elite

خيرى **ḵīrī** gillyflower (*bot.*)

اخير **aḵyar**², f. خيرى ḵīrā, خورى ḵūrā, pl. اخاير aḵāyir² better, superior

خيار **ḵiyār** choice; option, exercise of the power of choice (*Isl. Law*); refusal, right of withdrawal (*Isl. Law*); the best, choice, prime, flower, pick, elite; see also alphabetically

خيارى **ḵiyārī** optional, facultative; voluntary

اختيار **iḵtiyār** choice; election (also *pol.*; pl. -āt); selection; preference (على to); option; free will (*philos.*); اختيارا iḵtiyāran of one's own accord, spontaneously, voluntarily

اختيارى **iḵtiyārī** voluntary, facultative, elective (studies)

مخير **muḵayyar** having the choice or option

مختار **muḵtār** free to choose, having the choice or option (فى in), volunteering, مختارا muḵtāran (adv.) voluntarily, spontaneously, of one's own accord; choice, select, exquisite; chosen, preferred, favorite; a favorite; مختارات selection, selected writings, anthology; (pl. مخاتير maḵātīr²) village chief, mayor of a village (*Syr., Leb., Ir.*)

خزر see خيزران

خاس **ḵāsa** i (خيس ḵais, خيسان ḵayasān) (خيس) to break (ب an agreement, a promise)

خيش **ḵaiš** sackcloth, sacking, canvas

خيشة **ḵaiša** piece of sackcloth; (pl. -āt, خيش ḵiyaš) sack; straw mattress, pallet; Bedouin tent

خشم see خيشوم

خاط **ḵāṭa** i (ḵaiṭ) (خيط) and II to sew, stitch (ه s.th.)

خيط **ḵaiṭ** pl. خيوط ḵuyūṭ, اخياط aḵyāṭ, خيطان ḵīṭān thread; twine, cord; packthread, string; fiber | خيط امل ḵ. amal a spark of hope, a thread of hope

خيطى **ḵaiṭī** threadlike; fibrous

خياط **ḵiyāṭ** needle

خياطة **ḵiyāṭa** sewing; needlework, tailoring, dressmaking | آلة الخياطة sewing machine

خياط **ḵayyāṭ** pl. -ūn tailor

خياطة **ḵayyāṭa** pl. -āt dressmaker; seamstress

مخيط **miḵyaṭ** needle

خائط **ḵāʾiṭ** tailor

268

¹خال (خيل) ḵāla a to imagine, fancy, think, believe, suppose (ان that); to consider, deem, think (‥ s.o. to be ..., ‥ s.th. to be ...), regard (‥ s.o. as, ‥ s.th. as) II to make (الى s.o.) believe (ان that), suggest (الى to s.o., ‥ s.th.), give s.o. (الى) the impression that (‥) خيل اليه (له) ان (ḵuyyila) he imagined, fancied, thought that ..., it seemed, it appeared to him that ...; على ما خيلت (ḵayyalat; النفس being understood) as the heart dictates, i.e., as chance will have it, at random, unhesitatingly IV to be dubious, doubtful, uncertain, intricate V to imagine, fancy (‥ s.th.); to present itself, reveal itself (ل to s.o.'s mind), become the object of imagination, appear (= II ḵuyyila; ل to s.o.) تخيل فيه الخير (ḵaira) to suspect good qualities in s.o., have an inkling of s.o.'s good qualities, think well of s.o., have a good opinion of s.o. VI to pretend (ب ل to s.o. s.th., that ...), act (ل toward s.o., ب as if); to feel self-important, be conceited; to behave in a pompous manner, swagger, strut about; to conceive eccentric ideas, get all kinds of fantastic notions, have a bee in one's bonnet; to appear dimly, in shadowy outlines; to appear, show (على on), hover (على about; e.g., a smile about s.o.'s lips), flit (على across, e.g., a shadow across s.o.'s face, etc.) VIII to feel self-important, be conceited; to behave in a pompous manner, swagger, strut about

خيال ḵayāl pl. اخيلة aḵyila disembodied spirit, ghost, specter; imagination; phantom, apparition; phantasm, fantasy, chimera, vision; shadow, trace, dim reflection | خيال شك ḵ. šakk slightest doubt; خيال الصحرا ḵ. aṣ-ṣaḥrā' scarecrow; خيال الظل ḵ. aẓ-ẓill shadow play

خيالة ḵayāla pl. -āt ghost, spirit, specter; phantom; phantasm, fantasy, chimera

خيالى ḵayālī imaginary, unreal; ideal, ideational, conceptual; utopian

اخيل aḵyal² more conceited, haughtier, prouder

اخيل aḵyal pl. خيل ḵīl, اخايل aḵāyil² green woodpecker

خيلاء· ḵuyalā'² (f.) conceit, conceitedness, haughtiness, pride; الخيلاء al-ḵuyalā'a haughtily, proudly

خيلولة ḵailūla conceit, conceitedness, snobbery, arrogance, haughtiness

مخيلة maḵīla conceit, conceitedness, snobbery, arrogance, haughtiness; (pl. مخايل maḵāyil²) indication, sign, symptom, characteristic; pl. مخايل visions, mental images, imagery

تخييل taḵyīl play acting | فن التخييل fann at-t. dramatic art

تخيل taḵayyul pl. -āt imagination, phantasy; delusion, hallucination, fancy, whim, fantastic notion

تخيلى taḵayyulī fantastic, fanciful, imaginary

اختيال iḵtiyāl pride; arrogance, haughtiness

مخيلة muḵayyila imagination, phantasy

مخيل muḵīl dubious, doubtful, uncertain, intricate, tangled, confused; confusing, bewildering

مختال muḵtāl conceited, haughty, arrogant

²خيل II to gallop (on horseback)

خيل ḵail (coll.) pl. خيول ḵuyūl horses; horsepower, H.P. | سباق الخيل horse racing, horse race

خيال ḵayyāl pl. ة, -ūn horseman, rider

خيالة ḵayyāla cavalry (Ir.; Eg. 1939)

سرية خيالة sarīya ḵayyāla cavalry squadron (Eg. 1939)

³خال see خول

¹خيم II to pitch one's tent, to camp; to settle down; to stay, linger, rest, lie down, lie (على on, في or ب at a place); (fig.) to reign (e.g., calm, silence, peace, etc.; في or ب at, in), settle (على over) V to pitch one's tent; to camp

خيمة *kaima* pl. *-āt*, خيام *kiyām*, خيم *kiyam* tent; tarpaulin; arbor, bower; pavilion

خيام **kayyām** tentmaker

مخيم ***mukayyam*** pl. -*āt* camping ground, camp, encampment

²خيم **kīm** natural disposition, nature, temper, character; inclination, bent, tendency | اخذ خيمه (*eg.*) to feel s.o.'s pulse, sound s.o. out

³خام look up alphabetically

□ خية ***kayya*** pl. -*āt* noose

د

دأب *da'aba a* (*da'b, da'ab*, دؤوب *du'ūb*) to persist, persevere, be indefatigable, untiring, tireless (في or على in s.th.); to go in for s.th. (على), apply o.s., devote o.s. (على to), practice eagerly (على s.th.)

دأب *da'b* pl. ادؤب *ad'ub* habit

دأب *da'b, da'ab* and دؤوب *du'ūb* persistence, perseverance, tirelessness, indefatigability, assiduity, eagerness

دئب *da'ib* and دائب *dā'ib* addicted, devoted, persistent, assiduous, eager, indefatigable, untiring, tireless (على in)

دءوب *da'ūb* untiring, tireless, indefatigable, persevering, persistent

ادأب *ad'ab*² more persistent, more assiduous

دادة *dāda* governess, dry nurse, nurse

داغ *dāğ* pl. *-āt* brand (made on cattle, etc.)

دال *dāl* name of the letter د

داليا *dāliyā* dahlia(s) (*bot.*)

داما *dāmā* checkers | لوحة الداما *lauḥat ad-d.* checkerboard

دامجانة see دمجانة

دانتيلا (Fr. *dentelle*) *dantilla* lace

دانق *dānaq, dāniq* pl. دوانق *dawāniq*² an ancient coin, = $^1/_6$ dirham; small coin; a square measure (*Eg.*; = 4 *sahm* = 29.17 m²)

دانمارك *danmark* Denmark

دانماركى *danmarkī* Danish

الدانوب *ad-dānūb* the Danube

داية *dāya* pl. *-āt* wet nurse; midwife

دب *dabba i* (*dabb*, دبيب *dabīb*) to creep, crawl (reptile); to proceed, advance, or move slowly; to go on all fours; to enter (في s.th.), come (في into); to steal, creep (في نفسه into s.o.'s heart; of a feeling, e.g., doubt); to spread (في over, in, through), fill, pervade, invade (في s.th.); to gain ground; to gain ascendancy (في in s.o.; of a condition, an idea, a sensation); to stream in, rush in (of sensations, في upon s.o.) | دب فيه دبيب الحياة (*d. al-ḥayāh*) to gain vitality II to sharpen, point, taper (ه s.th.)

دب *dubb* pl. ادباب *adbāb*, دببة *dibaba* bear | الدب الاصغر (*aṣğar*) Little Bear, Ursa Minor (*astron.*); الدب الاكبر (*akbar*) Great Bear, Ursa Major (*astron.*)

دبى *dubbī* ursine

دبة *dabba* sand hill, mound

دبيب *dabīb* creeping, crawling; infiltration; influx, inflow, flow (e.g., of sensations, of life, of vigor); reptile

دباب *dabbāb* creeping, crawling, repent, reptant

دبابة *dabbāba* pl. *-āt* tank, armored car

مدب *madabb*: من مدب النيل الى مصبه (*maṣabbihī*) from the lower Nile to its mouth

دابة *dābba* pl. دواب *dawābb*² animal, beast; riding animal (horse, mule, donkey)

دويبة *duwaibba* tiny animal, animalcule; insect

مدبب *mudabbab* pointed, tapered

دبج II to embellish, decorate, adorn, ornament (ه s.th.); to put in good style, formulate, compose, write down, put down in writing (ه s.th.)

ديباج *dībāj* pl. دبابيج *dabābīj*² silk brocade

ديباجة *dībāja* (n. un. of ديباج) brocade; introductory verses or lines, proem, preamble; face, visage; style, elegance of style; renown, repute, standing, prestige

تدبيج *tadbīj* embellishment, adornment, ornamentation; composition, writing (of a book)

مدبجات *mudabbajāt* embellishments of speech, fine figures of speech

دبدب *dabdaba* to tread, tap

دبدبة *dabdaba* sound of footsteps, footfall, pitapat; pattering or clattering noise; snapping, flapping noise

دبدوبة *dabdūba* pl. دباديب *dabādīb*² point, tip, tapered end

¹دبر *dabara u* (دبور *dubūr*) to turn one's back; to elapse, pass, go by (time) II to make arrangements, make plans (ه for), prepare, plan, organize, design, frame, devise, concert, arrange, get up, bring about (ه s.th.); to hatch (ه a plot, etc.); to contrive, work up (ه a ruse); to direct, conduct, manage, run, engineer, steer, marshal, regulate (ه s.th.), be in charge (ه of); to manage well, economize (ه s.th.) | دبر خطة (*kiṭṭatan*) to devise a plan; دبر الشؤون to conduct the course of business, be in charge IV to turn one's back (عن or على on s.o.); to flee, run away; to escape, dodge; to slip away V to be prepared, planned, organized, managed; to reflect, ponder (فى or ه on); to consider, weigh, contemplate (فى or ه s.th.); to treat or handle with care, with circumspection (فى s.th.) VI to face in opposite directions, stand back to back; to be contrary, opposite, opposed; to be inconsistent, incompatible X to turn the back (ه on s.o.)

دبر *dubr, dubur* pl. ادبار *adbār* rump backside, buttocks, posteriors; rear part, rear, hindpart; back; last part, end, tail | من دبر behind, at the back, in the rear; from behind, from the rear; ولى دبره *wallā duburahū* to turn one's back; to flee, run away

دبرى *dabarī* trailing behind, belated, late

دبرة *dabra* turn (of fate)

دبور *dabūr* west wind

دبور *dabbūr* pl. دبابير *dabābīr*² hornet; wasp

تدبير *tadbīr* pl. *-āt* planning, organization; direction, management, disposal, regulation; economy, economization; — (pl. تدابير *tadābīr*²) measure, move, step | تدبير المنزل *t. al-manzil* housekeeping, household management; تدبير منزلى (*manzilī*) do.; اتخذ التدابير and قام بالتدابير اللازمة

اللازمة (*ittakada*) to take the necessary measures

ادبار *idbār* flight, retreat

تدبر *tadabbur* reflection, meditation (فى on), thinking (فى about); consideration, contemplation (فى of)

تدابر *tadābur* disparity, dissimilarity, contrast

دابر *dābir* past, bygone (time); the ultimate, utmost, extremity, end; root | قطع دابر الشىء (*dābira š-šai'*) to eradicate, root out s.th., suppress s.th. radically; بالامس الدابر (*amsi*) sometime in the past; ذهب كامس الدابر (*ka-amsi d-dābiri*) to vanish into thin air, disappear without leaving a trace (actually: like yesterday gone by)

مدبر *mudabbir* manager, director; ruler, disposer; leader; ringleader | مدبر المكائد schemer, intriguer, intrigant

مدبر *mudbir*: مدبرا ومقبلا *mudbiran wa-muqbilan* from the rear and from in front

[2]دبارة *dubāra* (= دوبارة) packthread, string, twine, cord, rope; thread

[1]دبس *dibs* sirup, molasses, treacle, esp. of grapes

[2]دبوس *dabbūs* pl. دبابيس *dabābis*[2] pin; safety pin | دبوس انكليزى safety pin

دبش *dabaš* junk, rubbish, trash; — *dabš* rubblestone, rubble; crushed rock (used as substratum in macadamizing)

دبغ *dabağa a i u* (*dabğ*) to tan (ه a hide)

دباغة *dibāğa* tanning, tanner's trade

دباغ *dabbāğ* tanner

مدبغة *madbağa* pl. مدابغ *madābiğ*[2] tannery

دبق *dabiqa a* (*dabaq*) to stick, adhere (ب to); to cleave, cling (ب to) **II** to catch with birdlime (ه a bird)

دبق *dibq* birdlime

دبق *dabiq* sticky, gluey, limy

دبك *dabaka u* (*dubk*) to stamp the feet; to dance the *dabka* (see below)

دبكة *dabka* (*syr.*) a group dance in which the dancers, lined up with locked arms or holding hands, stamp out the rhythm and sing

دبلة *dibla* pl. دبل *dibal* ring

دبلوم *diblōm* and دبلومة *diblōma* pl. *-āt* diploma

دبلوماسى *diblōmāsī* diplomatic; diplomat

دبلوماسية *diblōmāsīya* diplomacy

دثر *datara u* (دثور *dutūr*) to fall into oblivion, be forgotten, become obsolete, antiquated, extinct; to be blotted out, wiped out, effaced, obliterated (track by the wind) **II** to cover, envelop (ه s.o.); to destroy, annihilate (ه s.th.) **V** to wrap o.s. (فى in), cover o.s. (فى with) **VII** to be or become wiped out, blotted out, effaced, obliterated; to be old; to be forgotten, have fallen into oblivion, be obsolete **VIII** *iddatara* to wrap o.s. (ب in), cover o.s. (ب with)

دثار *ditār* pl. دثر *dutur* blanket, cover

مدثور *madtūr* past, bygone, ancient (time)

دج *dajja i* (*dajj*, دجيج *dajīj*) to walk slowly **II** دججه بالسلاح to arm s.o. to the teeth

دج *dujj* (*syr.*) thrush (*zool.*)

دجة *dujja* intense darkness, pitch-darkness

دجاج *dajāj* (coll.) chickens; fowl (as a generic designation)

دجاجة *dajāja* (n. un.) hen; chicken | دجاجة الحبش *d. al-ḥabaš* guinea fowl

مدجج بالسلاح *mudajjaj bi-s-silāḥ* heavily armed, bristling with arms

دجر **dajira a** (*dajar*) to be embarrassed, be at a loss

ديجور **daijūr** pl. دياجير *dayājīr*[2] gloom, darkness, dark

ديجورى **daijūrī** dark, gloomy

1 دجل **dajala u** to deceive, dupe, cheat, take in (على s.o.); to be a swindler, a charlatan, a quack **II** to coat, smear (ه s.th.); to gild (ه s.th.); to deceive, dupe, cheat, take in (على s.o.), impose (على on)

دجل **dajl** deceit, trickery, humbug, swindle

دجال **dajjāl** pl. *-ūn*, دجاجلة *dajājila* swindler, cheat, imposter; quack, charlatan (fem. دجالة); Antichrist

تدجيل **tadjīl** imposture, humbug; charlatanry, quackery

2 دجلة **dijla**[2] the Tigris river

دجن **dajana u** (*dajn*, دجون *dujūn*) to be dusky, murky, gloomy (day); — (*dujūn*) to remain, stay; to get used, become accustomed, become habituated; to become tame, be domesticated **II** to tame; to domesticate (ه an animal) | دجنه لخدمة فلان (*li-kidmati f.*) to put s.th. or s.o. to use for s.o., make s.th. or s.o. of service to s.o. **III** to flatter, cajole, coax, wheedle, try to win or entice by gentle courtesy (ه s.o.) **IV** to be murky, gloomy, overcast (day); to be dark (night)

دجنة **dujna**, *dujunna* darkness, gloominess, gloom

ادجن **adjan**[2] dark

داجن **dājin** tame, tamed, domesticated (animal); dark, gloomy | حيوانات داجنة (*ḥayawānāt*) domestic animals

دواجن **dawājin**[2] poultry

دجا (دجو) **dajā u** to be dark, gloomy, dusky; to overshadow, cover, veil, shroud, blanket (ه s.th.), spread (ه over) **III** to play the hypocrite, pose as a friend (ه of s.o.); to cajole, flatter (ه s.o.)

دجى **dujan** gloom, darkness, duskiness

دياجى الليل **dayājī l-lail** dark of night

مداجاة **mudājāh** hypocrisy; flattery, adulation, sycophancy

داج **dājin** dark, gloomy

دحدح **II** *tadaḥdaḥa* to waddle

دحدح **daḥdaḥ** and دحداح *daḥdāḥ* dumpy, squat, stocky

دحر **daḥara a** (*daḥr*, دحور *duḥūr*) to drive away, chase away (ه s.o.); to dislodge, remove (ه s.o.); to defeat (ه an army) **VIII** to be driven away, be routed, be repelled, be thrown back; to be defeated (army); to go under, go to ruin, succumb, break down, collapse

اندحار **indiḥār** banishment, rejection; (pl. *-āt*) defeat (*mil.*); ruin, fall, breakdown, collapse; catastrophe | اندحار الكون *ind. al-kaun* end of the world

مدحور **madḥūr** routed, repelled; expelled, cast out; ostracized, banished

دحرج **daḥraja** to roll (ه s.th.) **II** *tadaḥraja* to roll, roll along; to roll down

داحس **dāḥis** pl. دواحس *dawāḥis* whitlow, felon (*med.*)

دحش **daḥaša a** (*daḥš*) to insert, thrust in, shove in, foist in, smuggle in **VII** to interfere, meddle; to mix

دحض **daḥaḍa a** to be invalid, void, untenable (argument); to disprove, refute, invaliuate (ه an argument) **II** and **IV** to disprove, refute, invalidate (ه an argument)

دحض **daḥḍ** refutation, disproof

دحوض **duḥūḍ** invalidity, shakiness, weakness, refutability (of an argument or a claim)

مدحاض **midḥāḍ**: دعوى مدحاض (*da'wā*) an invalid, unjustified claim

(دحو) دحا *daḥā u* (*daḥw*) to spread out, flatten, level, unroll

○ مدحى *midḥan* pl. مداح *madāḥin* roller, steamroller

ادخر *iddakara*, مدخرة *muddakira* see ذخر

دخس *dukas* dolphin

دخل *dakala u* (دخول *dukūl*) to enter (ه, less frequently فى, also الى, s.th.), go, step, walk, move, come, get (ه, فى, الى into); to penetrate, pierce (ه, فى, الى s.th.); to take possession of s.o. (ه), befall, seize (ه s.o.; e.g., doubt); to take up (خدمة a post), start at a job; to enter s.o.'s (على) room or house, drop in on s.o. (على), come to see s.o. (على); to call on s.o. (على); to consummate the marriage, cohabit, sleep (ب or على with a woman); to come (على over s.o.; e.g., joy); (*gram.*) to be added (على to); to supervene, enter as a new factor, aspect, element, etc. (على upon s.th.), be newly introduced (على into s.th.); to make one's own, acquire (على s.th.); to join, enter (ه or فى e.g., a religious community); to participate, take part (ه in); to set in, begin (time, event); to be included (فى in; also ضمن *ḍimna*), fall, come (فى, ضمن, تحت under), belong, pertain (فى, ضمن, تحت to), be within s.th. (فى, ضمن, تحت); pass.: *dukila* to be sickly, diseased, abnormal | دخل على الامر تعديل (*ta'dīlun*) the matter has undergone modification; دخل الخدمة (*kidma*) to take up one's post, start at a job, report for work; دخل المدرسة (*madrasa*) to enter school; دخل الميناء (*mīnā'*) to enter the harbor, put in; دخل فى الموضوع to come to the point; دخل فى عقله (فى جسمه) *dukila fī 'aqlihī* (*fī jismihī*) to suffer from a mental (physical) disturbance **II** to make or let enter, bring in, let in (ه, ه s.o., s.th.); to enter, insert, include (ه s.th., فى or ه in) **III** to come over s.o. (ه), befall, seize (ه s.o.; e.g., doubt, suspicion, despair) **IV** to make or let enter, bring in, let in, admit, lead in, show in (ه s.o.); to move, take, haul (على or فى ه s.th. into); to incorporate, include, embody, insert (فى or ه ه s.th. in); to cause to set in, bring about, produce, set off, trigger (على ه s.th. in); to introduce (ه s.th., e.g., an innovation, an improvement, على in or on s.th.) | ادخله المدرسة (*madrasa*) to send s.o. to school; ادخل تغييرا على to bring about a change in ...; ادخلت عليه تعديلات (*udkilat*) the matter was subjected to modifications **V** to meddle (فى in), interfere (فى in, with); to interpose, intervene (فى in); to invade (فى s.th.), intrude, obtrude (فى on), disturb (فى s.th.); to interlock, mesh, gear **VI** to meddle (فى in, e.g., فى شؤونه in s.o.'s affairs), butt in (فى الحديث on a conversation); to interfere (فى in, with), interpose, intervene (فى in); to interlock, mesh, gear; to be superimposed; to intergrade, shade, blend (بعضه فى بعض or ببعض one into the other); to come over s.o. (ه), befall, strike, seize (ه s.o.; e.g., doubt, grief)

دخل *dakl* income; revenues, receipts, returns, takings (as opposed to خرج *karj*); interference, intervention; doubt, misgiving | ضريبة الدخل income tax; ليس له أى دخل فيه (*ayyu daklin*) and لا دخل له فى or ب (*dakla*) he should not meddle in ..., he has nothing to do with ..., it is none of his business

دخل *dakal* disturbance, derangement, disorder, imbalance, or defect of the mind; defect, infirmity

دخلة *dikla* intrinsic nature, essence; inner self, innermost, heart, soul (of a person); secret intention | راجع دخلته *rāja'a diklatahū* to commune with o.s., search one's soul

دخلة *dukla*: ليلة الدخلة *lailat ad-d.* wedding night

دخلة *dukkala* a variety of warbler

دخيل *da<u>k</u>īl* inner, inward, internal; inner self, heart, core; — (pl. دخلاء *du<u>k</u>alā'*[2]) extraneous; foreign, alien; exotic; foreigner, alien, stranger; not genuine, false, spurious; newly added (على to); novice; (new) convert; guest; protégé, charge, ward | كلمة دخيلة (*kalima*), لفظ دخيل (*lafẓ*) foreign word or expression; (*syr.-pal.*) دخيلك (*da<u>k</u>īlak*) please, if you please

دخيلة *da<u>k</u>īla* pl. دخائل *da<u>k</u>ā'il*[2] inner self, inmost being, intrinsic nature, essence; heart, soul | فى دخيلة نفسه inwardly, inside, in his heart; دخائل نفوسنا our inmost being; دخائل الامور the underlying nature of things, the factors at the bottom of things; دخائل شؤونه *d. šu'ūnihī* his private affairs, (of a country, etc.) its internal affairs

دخول *du<u>k</u>ūl* entry, entrance, admission; entering, ingress; beginning, setting in; penetration; intrusion, invasion; first coition in marriage (*Isl. Law*) | دخول الحرب *d. al-ḥarb* entry into war

دخولية *du<u>k</u>ūlīya* octroi, city toll

مدخل *mad<u>k</u>al* pl. مداخل *madā<u>k</u>il*[2] entrance; hallway, vestibule, anteroom; entrance hall, lobby, foyer; mouth (of a port, of a canal); ○ anode (*el.*); introduction (to a field of learning); behavior, conduct | مدخل للسيارات (*sayyārāt*) driveway; مدخل لدراسة القانون introduction to the study of law; حسن المدخل *ḥusn al-m.* good manners, good conduct

مداخلة *mudā<u>k</u>ala* interference, intervention; participation, interest (فى in)

ادخال *id<u>k</u>āl* leading in, showing in, bringing in, taking in, hauling in; involvement, implication; insertion, interpolation, incorporation, inclusion; introduction (e.g., of a constitution; of an improvement, على on an apparatus, or the like)

تدخل *tada<u>k</u><u>k</u>ul* entry, entrance; invasion; interference (فى with, in), intervention; intrusion, obtrusion | عدم التدخل *'adam at-t.* noninterference, nonintervention (*pol.*)

تداخل *tadā<u>k</u>ul* interference, intervention; interlock, meshing, gearing; superimposition; intergradation; permeation, pervasion; ○ interference (*phys.*)

داخل *dā<u>k</u>il* belonging, pertaining (فى to), falling (فى under), included (فى in); inner, inward, inside, interior, internal; inside, interior (of s.th.); *dā<u>k</u>ila* (prep.) within, inside, in; داخلا *dā<u>k</u>ilan* inside (adv.) | من الداخل from within; from the inside

داخلة *dā<u>k</u>ila* pl. دواخل *dawā<u>k</u>il*[2] interior, inside, inmost, hidden part; الداخلة the Dakhla oasis (in central Egypt)

داخلى *dā<u>k</u>ilī* inner, inward; internal; interior, inside; domestic, home, inland (as opposed to خارجى *<u>k</u>ārijī* external, foreign; *pol.*); indigenous, native; private; belonging to the house; داخليا *dā<u>k</u>iliyan* inside (adv.) | تلاميذ داخلية boarding students (as opposed to خارجية day students); حرب داخلية (*ḥarb*) civil war; مدرسة داخلية (*madrasa*) boarding school; ملابس داخلية underwear; ملاحة داخلية inland navigation

داخلية *dā<u>k</u>ilīya* interior | داخلية البلاد the interior of the country, the inland; وزارة الداخلية ministry of the interior; وزير الداخلية minister of the interior

مدخول *mad<u>k</u>ūl* sickly, diseased, abnormal; (mentally) disordered; of weak character, spineless; (pl. مداخيل *madā<u>k</u>īl*[2]) revenue, receipts, takings, returns

دخمس **da<u>k</u>masa** (دخمسة *da<u>k</u>masa*) to fool (على s.o.) about one's real intentions, pull the wool over s.o.'s (على) eyes; to cheat; to be sly, crafty, artful

دخمسة *da<u>k</u>masa* deception, fooling, trickery; cunning, craft, slyness

دخن *dakina* a to be smoky; to taste or smell of smoke; — *dakana* a u to smoke, emit smoke (fire) II to fumigate, fume (ه s.th.); to smoke, cure with smoke (ه foodstuffs); to smoke (ه a cigarette, tobacco, a pipe) IV to smoke, emit smoke (fire) V to be smoked, be cured with smoke; to be fumigated

دخن *dukn* pearl millet, dukhn

دخن *dakan* smoke, fume, vapor

دخان *dukān* (*dukkān*) pl. ادخنة *adkina* smoke, fume, vapor; tobacco

دخنة *dukna* smoke color; a kind of incense (Calamus aromaticus)

○ دخينة *dakina* cigarette

دخاخنى *dakākinī* (*eg., tun.*) tobacconist

مدخنة *madkana* pl. مداخن *madākin*[2] chimney, smokestack, funnel

تدخين *tadkīn* fumigation; smoking (e.g., of fish); (tobacco) smoking

داخنة *dākina* pl. دواخن *dawākin*[2] chimney, smokestack, funnel

مدخن *mudakkin* smoker

ديدبان look up alphabetically

ديدن *daidan* habit, practice

ددى III to pamper, spoil (ه a child)

در *darra* i u (*darr*) to flow copiously; to stream, flow, well; to accrue (على to s.o.; profit, wealth); to be abundant, plentiful IV to cause to flow; to bestow lavishly, heap (على ه s.th. upon s.o.), shower, overwhelm (على ه with s.th. s.o.); to yield (ه a profit, على to s.o.) X to stream, flow; to be abundant; to cause or try to bring about the abundant flow of (ه); to cause s.th. (ه) to yield in abundance; to be out for s.th. (ه), seek to gain (ه a profit), try to make (ه a living)

در *darr* milk; achievement, accomplishment | لله دره *li-llāhi darruhū* (literally: his achievement is due to God) how capable, how good, how excellent he is!

در *durr* (coll.) pearls

درة *durra* (n. un.) pl. -*āt*, درر *durar* pearl; — a variety of parrot (Psittacus Alexandri L.)

درى *durrī* glittering, twinkling, brilliant (star)

درة *dirra*, *darra* pl. درر *dirar* teat; udder

مدرار *midrār* showering abundant rain (sky, cloud); spouting, pouring forth, welling out

دار *dārr* flowing copiously; productive, rich, lucrative; profitable

مدر *mudirr*: مدر للبول (*baul*) diuretic(al), pl. مدرات البول diuretics; مدر للعرق (*'araq*) sudorific

درأ *dara'a* (*dar'*) to reject (ه s.th.); to avert, ward off (ه s.th., e.g., خطرا *kaṭaran* a danger, عن from) VI *iddāra'a* to contend (فى for)

دره *dar'* repulsion, prevention, averting; warding off, parrying

دريئة *darī'a* pl. -*āt* target

درابزين *darābazin* railing, parapet, banisters, balustrade

دراج Durrës (It. Durazzo, seaport in W Albania)

دراق *durrāq* (*syr.*) peach

درامى *dərāmī* dramatic

درب *dariba* a (*darab*, دربة *durba*) to be accustomed, be used (ب to), be practiced, trained, skilled (ب in) II to habituate, accustom (ه, ه s.o., s.th., فى or ب or على to); to practice, drill (ه s.o., ب ,فى or على in); to school, train, coach, tutor (ه s.o., فى ,ب or على in) V to be accustomed, be used (على or فى to); to be or become practiced, skilled, trained, drilled, schooled (على or في in); to train (*athlet.*)

درب **darb** pl. دروب *durūb* narrow mountain pass; path, trail, track; road; alley, lane | درب التبانة *d. at-tabbāna* the Milky Way

دربة **durba** habituation, habitude, habit; familiarity (with s.th.), experience; skill, practice

دريبة **darība** court of first instance (*Tun.*)

تدريب **tadrīb** habituation, accustoming; practice; drill; schooling, training, coaching, tutoring | التدريب العسكرى (*ʿaskarī*) military training

مدرب **mudarrib** pl. *-ūn* instructor, drill instructor; trainer, coach (*athlet.*); tamer (of wild animals)

مدرب **mudarrab** experienced; practiced, skilled; trained; schooled

درابزين **darābazīn** and دربزين *darbazīn* railing, parapet, banisters, balustrade

دربس **darbasa** to bolt (ه a door)

درباس **dirbās** pl. درابيس *darābīs*² bolt, doorbolt

دربكة **darabukka** (*eg.*), *dirbakka* (*syr.*) pl. *-āt* darabukka, a conical, one-headed hand drum, open at the small end

دربكة **darbaka** banging or rattling noise, din, uproar, turmoil

درج **daraja** *u* (دروج *durūj*) to go, walk, move' proceed, advance (slowly); to approach gradually, step by step (الى s.th.); to follow a course (على), proceed along the lines of (على), proceed in such and such a manner (على); to go away, leave, depart; to outgrow (من a nest, a habitation); to be past, bygone, over (time); to have passed away, be extinct; to circulate, be in circulation, be current, have currency; to grow up (child); — (*darj*) to roll up, roll together (ه s.th.); to wrap, wind, twist (ه على s.th. around); — *darija a* to rise or advance step by step | درج العرف على *daraja l-ʿurfu ʿalā* it has become the general practice to ... **II** to make (ه s.o.) rise or advance by steps, promote (ه s.o.) by degrees; to move or bring (ه s.th.) gradually closer (الى to); to approximate (ه الى s.th. to); to roll up, fold up (ه s.th.); to circulate, put into circulation (ه s.th.), give currency (ه to s.th.), make (ه s.th.) the general practice; to divide into degrees, steps or grades, graduate, grade, gradate (ه s.th.); to insert, include, enter (ه في s.th. in) **III** to go, keep up (ه with, e.g., with the time, with a fashion) **IV** to insert, include, embody (ه في s.th. in); to incorporate, embody (ه في s.th. in); to enter, register (ه في s.th., e.g., in a list), book (ه s.th.) **V** to progress by steps, advance gradually; to proceed step by step (الى to); to make progress (في in); to graduate, grade, be graded, graduated, gradated **VII** to be inserted, entered, incorporated, embodied, included (في in); to be classified (في in, تحت under) **X** to make (ه s.o.) advance or rise gradually, promote (ه s.o.) by degrees; to lead (ه s.o.) gradually (الى to), bring (ه s.o.) around to (الى, ل); to bait, allure (ه s.o.); to entice, tempt, lure into destruction (ه s.o.)

درج **darj** entry, entering, registering, registration, recording; a rolled or folded paper; roll, scroll | في درج الكتاب in the book; في درج الكلام *fī d. il-kalām* in the course of the talk

درج **durj** pl. ادراج *adrāj* drawer (of a table, desk, etc.); desk (e.g., for pupils in school)

درج **daraj** pl. ادراج *adrāj* way, route, course; flight of steps, stairs, staircase | رجع ادراجه *rajaʿa adrājahū* (also عاد ادراجه) to retrace one's steps, go back the way one came; to go back, turn back; ذهب

ادراج الرياح (*adrāja r-riyāḥ*) to go the ways of the winds, i.e., to pass unnoticed, without leaving a trace; to end in smoke, come to nothing, be futile, be in vain

درجة **daraja** pl. *-āt* step, stair; flight of steps, stairs, staircase; degree, step, tone (of a scale; *mus.*); degree (*math., geogr.*; of temperature); grade, rate; degree, order, rank; class (also, e.g., in trains, of a decoration); phase, state, stage (of a development); mark, grade (in school) | درجة الحرارة *d. al-ḥarāra* (degree of) temperature; الدرجات العليا (*'ulyā*) the maximal temperatures; الدرجات السفلى (*suflā*) the minimal temperatures; درجة الطول *d. aṭ-ṭūl* degree of longitude (*geogr.*); درجة علمية (جامعية) (*'ilmīya, jāmi'īya*) academic degree; درجة العقل *d. al-'aql* level of intelligence, IQ; دفتر الدرجات report card (in school); من (فى) الدرجة الاولى (*ūlā*) first-rate, first-class; ذو درجة of superior quality, high-grade, high-class; لدرجة ان (*li-darajati*) to the extent that ...; to such an extent that ..., so much that ...

دراج **durrāj** pl. دراريج *darārīj*² francolin (*zool.*); see also alphabetically

تدرج **tadruj**², تدرجة **tadruja** pheasant

دراجة **darrāja** pl. *-āt* bicycle | دراجة نارية motorcycle

مدرج **madraj** pl. مدارج *madārij*² way that one follows or pursues; course, route; road, path; starting point, outset, rise, growth, birth, dawn, beginning(s); tarmac, runway (of an airfield); (as also *mudarraj*) amphitheater; (amphitheatered) auditorium or lecture room; grandstand, bleachers | منذ مدرجه since its beginnings; مدرج نشأته *m. naš'atihī* the place where he grew up; سار فى مدارج الرقى (*m. ir-ruqīy*) to travel the road of progress

تدريج **tadrīj** graduation; classification, categorization; gradation | على التدريج, بالتدريج, مع التدريج gradually, by and by, by degrees, by steps, step by step, more and more

تدريجى **tadrījī** gradual, gradatory, progressive; تدريجيا **tadrījīyan** gradually, by and by, by steps, by degrees, in stages

ادراج **idrāj** insertion, interpolation, incorporation; entry, registration, recording (فى in a list)

تدرج **tadarruj** gradual advance or progress; gradation, graduation | بالتدرج gradually, by and by; تدرج ارتقائه *t. irtiqā'ihī* his gradual rise

استدراج **istidrāj** capability of gradually winning s.o. over, persuasiveness, art of persuasion

دارج **dārij** current, prevalent, widespread, popular, common, in vogue, circulating, in circulation | الكلام الدارج (*kalām*) and اللغة الدارجة (*luġa*) the popular language, colloquial language

مدرج **mudarraj** graded, graduated; — (pl. *-āt*) open staircase, open-air stairs, fliers, stoop; grandstand, bleachers; amphitheater; (amphitheatered) auditorium or lecture room

مدرج **mudraj** inserted, interpolated, incorporated; entered, registered; contained, included (فى, ب in), comprised (فى, ب by)

درد **darida** *a* (*darad*) to become toothless, lose one's teeth

ادرد **adrad**² toothless

دردى **durdī** sediment, dregs, lees

دردبيس **dardabīs** ugly old woman, hag

دردرة **dardara** roar, rush (of water); idle talk, prattle, chatter

دردار **dardār** elm (*bot.*)

دردور **durdūr** eddy, whirlpool, vortex

دردشة **dardaša** idle talk, prattle, chatter

[1]درز *daraza* u to sew, stitch

درز *darz* pl. دروز *durūz* seam, hem; suture

[2]درزى *durzī* pl. دروز *durūz* Druse | جبل الدروز *jabal ad-d.* the Jebel ed Druz, the mountainous homeland of the Druses in S Syria

درس *darasa* u (*dars*) to wipe out, blot out, obliterate, efface, extinguish (ه s.th.); to thresh (ه grain); to learn, study (ه s.th., على under s.o.), درس العلم على (*'ilm*) to study under (a teacher, a professor); — u (دروس *durūs*) to be effaced, obliterated, blotted out, extinguished **II** to teach; to instruct (ه s.o., ه in s.th.); **III** to study (ه together with s.o.) **VI** to study (ه s.th.) carefully together **VII** to become or be wiped out, blotted out, effaced, obliterated, extinguished

درس *dars* effacement, obliteration, extinction; — (pl. دروس *durūs*) study, studies; lesson, chapter (of a textbook); class, class hour, period; lecture; lesson (taught by experience, etc.) | القى دروسا عن (*alqā*) to lecture on ...; اعطى دروسا (*a'ṭā*) to give lessons; دروس منزلية (*manzilīya*) homework (of a pupil or student)

دراس *dirās* threshing (of grain)

دراسة *dirāsa* pl. *-āt* studies; study | دراسة عالية (*'āliya*) collegiate studies; دراسة ثانوية (*ṯānawīya*) attendance of a secondary school, secondary education, high-school education; دراسة متوسطة (*mutawassiṭa*) secondary education, high-school education (*Syr.*)

دراسى *dirāsī* of or pertaining to study or studies; scholastic, school; instructional, educational, teaching, tuitional | رسوم دراسية tuition fees; سنة دراسية (*sana*) academic year; scholastic year, school year

دريس *darīs* dried clover

عمال الدريسة *'ummāl ad-darīsa* (*eg.*) railroad section gang, gandy dancers

دراس *darrās* pl. *-ūn* (eager) student

○ دراسة *darrāsa* flail; threshing machine | ○ حصادة دراسة (*ḥaṣṣāda*) combine

درواس *dirwās* mastiff

مدرسة *madrasa* pl. مدارس *madāris*[2] madrasah (a religious boarding school associated with a mosque); school | مدرسة ابتدائية (*ibtidā'īya*) the lower grades of a secondary school, approx. = junior high school; مدرسة اولية (*awwalīya*) elementary school, grade school; مدرسة ثانوية (*ṯānawīya*) secondary school, high school; مدرسة تجارية (*tijārīya*) commercial college or school; مدرسة حربية (*ḥarbīya*) military academy; مدرسة داخلية (*dāḵilīya*) boarding school; مدرسة عالية (عليا) (*'āliya*, *'ulyā*) college; مدرسة الفنون والصنائع school of industrial arts, school of applied art and handicraft; مدرسة كبرى (*kubrā*) college; المدرسة القديمة the old "school" (= intellectual or artistic movement)

مدرسى *madrasī* scholastic, school

تدريس *tadrīs* teaching, instruction, tuition | هيئة التدريس *hai'at at-t.* teaching staff; faculty, professoriate (of an academic institution)

دارس *dāris* pl. دوارس *dawāris*[2] effaced, obliterated; old, dilapidated, crumbling | تجدد دارسه *tajaddada dārisuhū* to rise from one's ashes

مدرس *mudarris* pl. *-ūn* teacher, instructor; lecturer | مدرس مساعد (*musā'id*) assistant professor

درع **II** to arm; to armor, equip with armor (ه s.th.) **V** and **VIII** *iddara'a* to arm o.s., take up arms, put on armor

درع *dir'* m. and f., pl. دروع *durū'*, ادرع *adru'*, ادراع *adrā'* coat of mail, hauberk; (suit of) plate armor; armor plate; armor; armature; (pl. ادراع *adrā'*) chemise

دراعة *darrāʻa* pl. *-āt* armored cruiser

دراعة *durrāʻa* pl. دراريع *darārīʻ*[2] loose outer garment with sleeves, slit in front

دارع *dāriʻ* armored, armor-clad, iron-clad

دارعة *dāriʻa* pl. دوارع *dawāriʻ*[2] armored cruiser

مدرع *mudarraʻ* armored; armadillo (*zool.*) | قوة مدرعة (*qūwa*) tank corps; سيارة مدرعة (*sayyāra*) armored car; مشاة مدرعون (*mušāh*) armored infantry (*mil.*)

مدرعة *mudarraʻa* pl. *-āt* armored cruiser

درف *darf* side, flank, wing; protection

درفة *darfa* pl. درف *diraf* leaf (of a double door or window)

درفيل *darfīl* dolphin

درقة[1] *daraqa* (leather) shield

○ درق *daraq* thyroid gland

درقى *daraqī* shield-shaped; thyroid | الغدة الدرقية (*ḡudda*) thyroid gland

دراق[2] look up alphabetically

درك[1] II to last, continue, keep up (rains) III to reach, get, catch, overtake, outdistance, outrun (ه, ه s.o., s.th.), catch up, come up (ه, ه with); to keep up, continue without interruption (ه s.th.) IV to attain, reach (ه s.th.), arrive (ه at); to get, catch, overtake (ه s.o., ه s.th.), catch up, come up (ه, ه with); to come suddenly, unexpectedly (ه upon s.o.), overtake (ه s.o.; death); to obtain (ه s.th.); to grasp, comprehend (ه s.th.); to perceive, discern, notice (ه s.th.); to realize, understand (ه s.th.), become aware, become conscious (ه of s.th.); to mature, ripen (e.g., a fruit); to attain puberty, reach sexual maturity (boy) V تدركت الشمس الى المغيب (*šams, maḡīb*) the sun prepared to set VI to reach and seize one another; to continue without interruption, go on incessantly; to face, meet, obviate, take steps to prevent (ه s.th.); to put in order, set right, correct (ه s.th.), make amends (ه for), provide compensation or indemnity (ه for a loss, or the like) X to correct, rectify, emend (ه s.th.); to set right, put in order, straighten out (ه s.th.); to make good, repair, redress (ه a damage, a mistake, etc.), make up (ه for); to supplement, supply (ه that which is missing); to anticipate, forestall, obviate (ه an event)

درك *darak* attainment, achievement, accomplishment; overtaking, catching up; police; (pl. ادراك *adrāk*) bottom, lowest level

دركى *darakī* policeman

دركة *daraka* lowest level; pl. *-āt* descending steps (as opposed to درجات; cf. درجات الحياة ودركات الموت *darajāt al-ḥayāh wa-d. al-maut*)

دراك *darrāk* much-accomplishing, efficient, successful

مدارك *madārik*[2] mental faculties, mental powers, intelligence, intellectual capacities, perception, discernment | المدارك الخمس the five senses

دراكا *dirākan* (adv.) constantly, incessantly, without interruption

ادراك *idrāk* reaching, attainment, achievement, accomplishment; realization, perception, discernment, awareness, consciousness (فقد الادراك *faqd al-i.* unconsciousness); comprehension, understanding, grasp; reason, intelligence; sexual maturity, puberty; age of maturity | سن الادراك *sinn al-i.* age of discretion (*Isl. Law*)

تدرك *tadarruk* gradual decline

استدراك *istidrāk* redress, reparation; correction, emendation, rectification

مدرك *mudrik* rational, reasonable, endowed with reason, intelligent; (sexually) mature, pubescent, at the age of puberty

مدركات *mudrakāt* realizations; cognitions; fixed notions, established concepts

درك[2] (Engl.) derrick, derrick crane

درم *darima a* to fall out (teeth) **II** to clip, trim (ه nails)

درن *darina a* (*daran*) to be dirty, filthy **IV** do. **V** to suffer from tuberculosis

درن *daran* pl. ادران *adrān* dirt, filth; tubercles; tuberculosis | درن رئوى (*ri'awī*) pulmonary tuberculosis

درنة *darana* (n. un.) pl. *-āt* tubercle; small tumor, outgrowth, excrescence, tubercule, nodule

درنى *daranī* tubercular, tuberculous

تدرن *tadarrun* tuberculosis | تدرن رئوى (*ri'awī*) and تدرن الرئة *t. ar-ri'a* pulmonary tuberculosis

تدرنى *tadarrunī* tuberculous

متدرن *mutadarrin* affected with tubercles, tuberculated

مدره *midrah* pl. مداره *madārih*[2] spokesman

درهم *dirham* pl. دراهم *darāhim*[2] dirhem, drachma (*Ir.* = coin of 50 فلس); a weight (*Eg.* = $^1/_{12}$ اوقية = ca. 3.12 g); دراهم money, cash

دريهمات *duraihimāt* (dimin. with a derogatory sense; approx.:) pennies

دروة *dirwa* pl. *-āt* (*eg.*) protecting screen or wall; parapet

درواس *dirwās* mastiff

درويش *darwīš* pl. دراويش *darāwīš*[2] dervish

درى[1] *darā i* (دراية *dirāya*) to know (ب or ه s.th. or of s.th.); to be aware, be cognizant (ب or ه of); to understand, comprehend (ب or ه s.th.) | وما يدرى الا و... all of a sudden there was ... **III** to flatter, treat with flattery or gentle courtesy, cajole, coax (ه s.o.); to deceive, fool, mislead (ه s.o.); to dissemble; to conceal, hide, mask, disguise (ه s.th.) **IV** to let (ه s.o.) know (ب s.th. or about s.th.), inform, notify, advise (ب ه s.o. of) | وما ادراك ما ... (*adrāka*), also وما ادراك ب do you realize what ... is? you don't even know what ... means! **VI** to hide, conceal o.s.

دراية *dirāya* knowledge, cognizance, acquaintance

ادرى *adrā* more knowledgeable, better informed, knowing better (ب s.o., s.th.), better acquainted (ب with)

لا ادرى *lā-adrī* a skeptic

مداراة *mudārāh* sociability, affability, companionableness

دار *dārin* knowing, aware, cognizant (ب of s.th.)

مدرى[2] *midran*, مدرة *midra* (= مردى *mirdan*), مدراة *midrāh* pl. مدار *madārin* pole (esp. one for punting boats)

درياق *diryāq* (= ترياق) theriaca; antidote

دزينة (It. *dozzina*) *dazzīna* dozen

دس *dassa u* (*dass*) to put, get, slip, shove, thrust, insert (ه في s.th. into); to bury (ه في s.th. in the ground); to instill, infuse (ه في, ب s.th. in); to administer surreptitiously (السم *as-samma* poison, ل to s.o.); to foist (ه في s.th. into); to smuggle (ه في s.th. into, ه بين s.o. among); to interpolate (ه s.th.); to intrigue, scheme, plot (على, ل against s.o.) | دس الدسائس to engage in secret machinations, intrigue, scheme **II** to put in, get in, slip in, shove in, thrust in, insert (ه s.th.); to hide, conceal (ه s.th.) **V** to engage (secretly, الى in); to be hidden (في in) **VII** to slip (بين between or among, في into), creep, steal, sneak (بين among, في into), infiltrate (في s.th.); to ingratiate o.s., insinuate o.s. (في or الى to s.o., into s.o.'s confidence); to be hidden

دسيسة *dasīsa* pl. دسائس *dasā'is*² intrigue, machination, scheme, plot | دس الدسائس *dass ad-d.* machinations, intrigues, scheming, plotting (ضد against); plot, conspiracy

دساس *dassās* pl. *-ūn* intrigant, intriguer, schemer, plotter, conspirator; sand snake (Eryx jaculus)

¹دست *dast* pl. دسوت *dusūt* place of honor, seat of honor; seat of office; council | دست الحكم *d. al-ḥukm* (a ruler's) throne

²دست *dist* pl. دسوت *dusūt* kettle, boiler, caldron made of copper (*eg., syr.*)

³دستة *dasta* dozen; pack, packet, package

دستور *dustūr* pl. دساتير *dasātīr*² statute; regulations; by-laws; (basic) constitutional law; constitution (*pol.*); — (*colloq.*) *dastūr* permission

دستورى *dustūrī* constitutional | النظام الدستورى constitutional form of government

دستورية *dustūrīya* constitutionality | عدم الدستورية *ʿadam ad-d.* unconstitutionality

دسر *dasara u* (*dasr*) to push, shove, push off (ه s.th.)

○ داسر *dāsir* propeller, airscrew

دسكرة *daskara* pl. دساكر *dasākir*² village

دسم *dasam* fatness (of meat); fat, grease

دسم *dasim* fat; fatty, greasy, grimy, grubby; rich, abundant, substantial; meaty, pithy, full of thoughts (e.g., reading material)

ادسم *adsam*², f. دسماء *dasmā'*², pl. دسم *dusm* very fat; fatty, greasy, grimy, grubby; — richer, more substantial, pithier

دسامة *dasāma* fattiness, greasiness, griminess, grubbiness

دسومة *dusūma* fatness; richness, substantiality

دسام *disām* plug, stopper

ديسم *daisam* amaranth (*bot.*)

دسمبر *disembir, disambir* December

دسو II to introduce, bring in (ه s.th.) V to be hidden, concealed; to penetrate (الى into)

دش (Fr. *douche*) *duš* shower, douche

دشيش *dašīš* and دشيشة a kind of porridge made of crushed wheat and butter

دشت *dašt* junk, trash, rubbish, refuse

دشن II to hand over, present (ه s.th.); to consecrate, dedicate, inaugurate (ه s.th.)

تدشين *tadšīn* consecration, dedication, inauguration | تدشين الكنيسة consecration of the church

دشو V to belch, burp, eruct

دعة *daʿa* see ودع

دع *daʿʿa* to rebuff, turn down (contemptuously, ه the poor, an orphan)

دعب *daʿaba a* (دعابة *duʿāba*) to joke, jest, make fun (ه with s.o.) III to play, toy (ه, ه with s.th., with s.o.); to joke, jest, make fun (ه with s.o.); to give (ه s.o.) a good-natured slap or smack (ب); to flirt (ها with a woman); to dally, philander, play around (ها with a woman); to play (ه about s.o.; e.g., waves); to stroke gently, caress, fondle (ه s.th.); to beguile, tempt, delude (ه s.o.; said of hopes); to play (ه a musical instrument) | داعب البيانو to play on the piano VI to make fun, have fun together, have a good time

دعب *daʿib* joking, jocose, playful, jolly, gay, funny

دعابة *du'āba* pl. *-āt* joking, jesting, fun-making, fun; joke, jest

دعّاب *da''āb* jocose, playful, jolly, gay

مداعبة *mudā'aba* pl. *-āt* play, fun-making, fun; joke, jest; pleasantry; dalliance, flirtation, philandery

داعب *dā'ib* joking, jocose, playful, jolly, gay, funny

مداعب *mudā'ib* joking, jesting

دعبل *di'bil* frog spawn, frog's eggs

مدعبل *muda'bal* indisposed, out of sorts; round, ball-shaped

ادعج *ad'aj*², f. دعجاء *da'jā'*², pl. دعج *du'j* black-eyed; deep-black and large (eye)

دعر *da'ira a* (*da'ar*) to be immoral

دعر *da'ar* immorality, indecency

دعر *da'ir* unchaste, lewd, licentious, dissolute, obscene, bawdy, immoral, indecent

دعارة *da'āra, di'āra* indecency, immorality, licentiousness, debauchery | بيت الدعارة *bait ad-d.* brothel

داعر *dā'ir* pl. دعّار *du''ār* unchaste, lewd, licentious, dissolute, obscene, bawdy, indecent, immoral

دعس *da'asa a* (*da's*) to tread underfoot, trample down, crush (ه s.th.); to knock down, run over (ه s.o.; automobile) **VII** pass. of **I**

دعك *da'aka a* (*da'k*) to rub (ه s.th.); to scrub, scour (ه s.th.); to scrub on a washboard (ه laundry); to crush, squash, mash (ه s.th.); to crumple (ه paper)

دعم *da'ama a* (*da'm*) and **II** to support, hold up (ه s.th.); to prop, shore up, stay, buttress, underpin (ه s.th.); to cement, consolidate, strengthen (ه s.th.) **VIII** ادعم *idda'ama* to be supported; to rest, be based (على on)

دعمة *di'ma* pl. دعم *di'am* support, prop

دعامة *di'āma* pl. *-āt*, دعائم *da'ā'im*² support, prop, stay, shore; pier; buttress; pillar (esp. fig., e.g., دعائم السيادة pillars of authority)

تدعيم *tad'īm* support, strengthening, reinforcement, consolidation, underpinning

دعو and دعى) دعا *da'ā u* (دعاء *du'ā'*) to call (ه s.o.); to summon (ب or ه s.o.), call or send for s.o. (ب or ه); to call up (ه s.o., الى, ل for); to call upon s.o. (ه), appeal to s.o. (ه) for s.th. or to do s.th. (ل, الى), invite, urge (ل, الى ه s.o. to do s.th.); to invite, ask to come (الى ه s.o. to; e.g., to a banquet); to move, induce, prompt (ل, الى ه s.o. to do s.th.), prevail (ل, الى ه on s.o. to do s.th.); to call (ب, ه ه s.o. by a name), name (ب, ه ه s.o. so and so), pass.: دعى *du'iya* to be called, be named; to invoke (الله God = to pray to); to wish (ل s.o.) well, bless (ل s.o.; properly: to invoke God in favor of s.o.), invoke a blessing (ب) upon s.o. (ل), pray (ب for s.th., ل on behalf of s.o.), implore (ل ب for s.o. s.th.); to curse (على s.o.; properly: to invoke God against s.o.), call down evil, invoke evil (على upon s.o.); to propagate, propagandize (ل s.th.), make propaganda, make publicity (ل for); to demand, require (الى s.th.), call for (الى); to call forth, bring about, cause, provoke, occasion (الى s.th.), give rise (الى to) | دعى للاجتماع (*du'iya*) to be summoned, be called into session (parliament); دعى الى حمل السلاح *du'iya ilā ḥamli s-silāḥ* to be called up for military service, be called to the colors; رجل يدعى ... (*yud'ā*) a man called ..., a man by the name of ...; دعا له بطول العمر (*ṭūli l-'umr*) he wished him a long life **III** to challenge (ه s.o.); to pick a quarrel (ه with); to proceed judicially (ه against), prosecute (ه s.o.) **VI** to challenge each other, call each other forth or out, summon each other; to evoke one another (thoughts, reminiscences, sentiments); to be dilapidated, be tumble-down, threaten to fall (walls); to sink, subside, cave in; to fall down, sink to the ground (person); to collapse, break down, decline, degenerate (fig., of a cultural phenomenon); to flock together, rally **VIII** ادعى *idda'ā* to allege, claim, maintain (ه s.th., ان that); to lay claim (ه to s.th.), demand, claim (ه s.th.); to make undue claims (ه to s.th.), arrogate (to o.s.), assume unduly or presumptuously (ه s.th.); to affect, feign, simulate, pretend, purport (ب s.th.); to testify (in court); to accuse (ب or ه على s.o. of), charge (ب or ه على s.o. with), blame (ب or ه على s.o. for), hold s.th. (ب or ه) against s.o. (على) **X** to call or send (ه for s.o.), summon (ه s.o.); to cite, summon for examination or trial (ه s.o.; court, police); to recall (ه s.o., e.g., a diplomatic envoy); to call, appoint (ه s.o., e.g., a professor to a chair); to invoke (ه s.o.); to invite, urge (ه الى s.o. to do s.th.), suggest (ه الى to s.o. s.th. or to do s.th.), call upon s.o. (ه) to do s.th. (الى), appeal (ه الى to s.o. for s.th. or to do s.th.); to call for (ه), require, demand, necessitate, make necessary or requisite (ه s.th.)

دعوة *da'wa* call; appeal; bidding, demand, request; call, convocation, summons (الى to), calling up, summoning; (official) summons, citation; invitation; claim, demand, plea; missionary activity, missionary work (also نشر الدعوة *našr ad-d.*), propaganda; — (pl. دعوات *da'awāt*) invocation, imploration, supplication, prayer; good wish | دعوات صالحات good wishes; دعوة بالشر (*šarr*) imprecation, curse; صاحب الدعوة host

دعوى *da'wā* pl. دعاوى *da'āwā*, دعاو *da'āwin* allegation, pretension; claim; lawsuit, case, action, legal proceedings (*Isl. Law*) | بدعوى ان on the pretext that ...

دعى *da'īy* pl. ادعياء *ad'iyā'*[2] adopted son; bastard; braggart, bigmouth, show-off; pretender; swindler, impostor

دعاء *du'ā'* pl. ادعية *ad'iya* call; invocation of God, supplication, prayer; request, plea; good wish (ل for s.o.); imprecation, curse (على against s.o.)

ادعى *ad'ā* more conducive, more stimulating, of greater incentive (الى, ل to), causing or provoking to a greater extent (الى, ل s.th.)

دعاوة *da'āwa*, *di'āwa* pl. *-āt* propaganda (*pol.*); publicity (ل for)

دعاوى *da'āwī*, *di'āwī* propagandistic

دعاية *di'āya* propaganda (*pol.*)

دعائى *di'ā'ī* propagandistic

مدعاة *mad'āh* determining factor, decisive motive or incentive, cause, occasion

تداع *tadā'in* imminent collapse, impending breakdown; mutual summoning | تداعى المعانى *tadā'ī l-ma'ānī* association of ideas

ادعاء *iddi'ā'* pl. *-āt* claim; arrogation, undue assumption, presumption; allegation; pretension, pretense; accusation, charge; الادعاء the prosecution (in a court of justice)

استدعاء *istid'ā'* summons, summoning; recall, calling back; official summons, citation

داع *dā'in* pl. دعاة *du'āh* one who invites, inviter; propagandist; host; motive, reason, cause | لا داعى (*dā'iya*) it is not necessary, there is no need, there is no cause (ل for)

داعية *dā'iya* one who calls for s.th. (الى), invites to s.th. (الى); propagandist (with foll. genit. or الى: of s.th.), herald;

(pl. دواع *dawāʿin*) motive, reason, cause, occasion; pl. دواع requirements, exigencies | داعية حرب warmonger; لدواع صحية *li-dawāʿin ṣiḥḥīya* for reasons of health; من دواعى سرورى it gives me great pleasure ...

مدعو *madʿūw* one invited, guest; called, named, by the name of

متداع *mutadāʿin* evoking one another, one leading to the other (reminiscences, thoughts); frail, shaky (constitution); dilapidated, tumble-down; ready to fall, threatened with collapse; declining, in a stage of decline, on the downgrade

مدع *muddaʿin* one who makes an allegation or pretension, alleger, pretender; claimer, claimant; plaintiff; prosecutor (*jur.*); arrogant, presumptuous, bumptious | المدعى العمومى (*ʿumūmī*) the public prosecutor; المدعى العام (*ʿāmm*) do. (*Mor.*)

مدعى *muddaʿan* claimed; المدعى عليه the defendant (*jur.*); pl. مدعيات *muddaʿayāt* claims, pretensions

مستدع *mustadʿin* applicant, petitioner

دغدغ *daḡdaḡa* to tickle (ه s.o.); to crush; to chew, munch (ه s.th.)

[1]**دغر** *daḡara a* (*daḡr*, دغرى *daḡrā*) to attack (على s.o.), fall upon s.o. (على)

دغر *daḡr* attack, assault

دغرى *daḡrā* attack, assault

[2]**دغرى** *duḡrī* (*eg., syr.*) direct, straight; straight ahead

دغش IV ادغشت الدنيا *adḡašat id-dunyā* it became dark, twilight fell

دغش *daḡaš* darkness, dusk, twilight

دغيشة *daḡīša* darkness, dusk

دغص *daḡiṣa a* (*daḡaṣ*) to be chock-full, on the point of bursting

داغصة *dāḡiṣa* pl. دواغص *dawāḡiṣ*[2] kneepan, kneecap, patella

دغل *daḡal* pl. ادغال *adḡāl*, دغال *diḡāl* place with luxuriant tree growth; thicket, bush, jungle; — defectiveness, faultiness, corruption

دغل *daḡil* covered with dense undergrowth (place); impenetrable; corrupted

مدغل *mudḡil* covered with dense undergrowth (place); false, perfidious, insidious (in character)

دغم IV and VIII ادغم *iddaḡama* to put (ه فى s.th. into), insert, incorporate, embody (ه فى s.th. in); (*gram.*) to contract (ه فى one letter into another), assimilate (ه فى s.th. to) VII to be incorporated, embodied, merged, amalgamated; to be assimilated, contracted

دف *daffa i* (دفيف *dafīf*) to flap the wings (bird) II to hurry, rush

دف *daff* pl. دفوف *dufūf* side; lateral surface

دف *duff, daff* pl. دفوف *dufūf* tambourine

دفة *daffa* side; leaf (of a double door or window); cover (of a book), الدفتان the two covers of a book; rudder, helm | قائد الدفة or مدير الدفة *mudīr ad-d.* steersman, helmsman; قبض على دفة التنفيذ to take the helm, make o.s. the leader; يد الدفة *yad ad-d.* tiller; من الدفة للشابورة (*eg.*) all together, one and all, all without exception

دفية *diffīya* (*eg.*) loose woolen cloak

دفؤ *dafiʾa a* and دفؤ *dafuʾa u* to be warm; to feel warm II and IV to warm, heat (ه s.th.) V, VIII ادفأ *iddafaʾa* and X to warm o.s.

دفء *difʾ* warmth, warmness, heat

دفئ *dafiʾ* and دفىء *dafīʾ* warm

دفآن *dafʾān*[2], f. دفأى *dafʾā* warm

دفاء *difāʾ* heating

دفاءة *dafāʾa* warmth, warmness, heat

☐ دفاية *daffāya* pl. *-āt* stove

مدفأ *midfa'* and مدفأة *midfa'a* pl. مدافئ *madāfi'*² stove, heating stove

تدفئة *tadfi'a* heating, generation of heat

دفتر *daftar* pl. دفاتر *dafātir*² booklet; notebook, copybook; daybook, journal; ledger (*com.*); roster, register, official register | دفتر حسابى (*ḥisābī*) account book; bankbook, passbook; دفتر الخطابات *d. al-kiṭābāt* letter file, letter book, folder, portfolio; دفتر الشروط publication setting forth the terms of a purchase, the conditions of a lease, the stipulations of a contract, or the like; دفتر الاشتراك subscription booklet; دفتر الصندوق *d. aṣ-ṣundūq* cashbook (*com.*); دفتر المساحة cadastre, land register; دفتر اليومية *d. al-yaumīya* diary, journal; مسك الدفاتر *mask ad-d.* bookkeeping

دفترخانة *daftarkāna* archives, public records office (*Eg.*) | دفترخانة الاملاك العقارية *d. al-amlāk al-'aqārīya* land-registry office (*Tun.*)

دفتيريا *diftēriyā* diphtheria

دفر *dafara* to push, push back (ه s.o.); — *dafira a* (*dafar*) to stink

دفر *dafar* stench

دفر *dafir* stinking, fetid

دفس *dafasa* to hide (ه s.th.); to push

دفع *dafa'a a* (*daf'*) to push; to push away, shove away, push back, drive back, repel, remove, dislodge, drive away (ه ,ه عن s.o., s.th. from); دفعه جانبا (*jāniban*) to push, shove, or elbow, s.o. aside; to rid (عن نفسه o.s., ه of s.th.), get rid of s.th.; to get the better (ه ,ه of s.o., of s.th.), conquer, master control (ه s.o., ه s.th.); to fight (ه ب s.th. with); to reject, repudiate (ه s.th.); to rebut, refute, disprove (ه s.th.); to propel, drive (ه s.th.); to move, cause, urge, impel, egg on, goad (ه or ب s.o., الى or ل to do s.th.), induce, incite, force, compel, oblige (ه or ب s.o., الى or ل to), make s.o. (ب or ه) do s.th. (الى or ل); to hand over, present, turn over (ل or الى ه s.th. to s.o.); to pay (ثمنا *ṯamanan* a price, الى or ل to s.o.) | دفع خطاه الى (*kuṭāhu*) to wend one's way to III to resist, withstand (ه s.o., ه s.th.), offer resistance (ه, ه to); to contradict, oppose (ه s.o., عن so as to make him abstain from s.th.), dissuade (ه s.o., عن from); to suppress (ه s.th.); to defend (عن s.o., s.th.), uphold (عن s.th.); to be entrusted with the defense (عن of s.th., of s.o., also *jur.*) V to dash forward; to dart off, rush off; to pour forth, flow, stream, gush forth (water); to spring up, make itself felt (an idea, a social tendency, and the like) VI to shove or push one another; to push or shove one another away or aside; to push off, shove off (عن from); to issue in intermittent bursts, gush forth intermittently; to burst forth, rush out, sally (من from); to be propelled, be driven forward; to storm forward VII to dart off, rush off; to proceed rashly, blindly, without forethought; to be too impetuous, be too hotheaded; to plunge headlong (فى into s.th.); to rush, dart, make (الى at s.th.), pounce (الى on s.th.); to rush off, hurry off, go quickly (الى to; with foll. imperf.: to do s.th.); to give o.s. (ل to s.o.); to burst forth, gush out, pour forth, spurt, spout, flow, run (من from; water); to let o.s. be carried away or be overcome (وراء by s.th., e.g., وراء شهواته *šahawātihī* by one's bodily appetites, وراء شعوره by one's feelings, وراء العاجلة by worldly things); to proceed, set out, begin (with foll. imperf.: to do s.th.) X to try to ward off or stave off (ه s.th., ب by)

دفع *daf'* pushing back, shoving aside; repulsion, driving away, driving off; dispelling; parrying, warding off, staving off; repulse, rejection, repudiation; rebuttal; handing over, turning in; payment

دفعة *daf'a* (n. vic.) pl. *dafa'āt* shove, push, thrust; impetus, impact, momentum, forceful impulse, drive; ejaculation; payment; deposit; disbursement; pl. issues (stock market)

دفعة *duf'a* pl. *dufu'āt, dufa'āt* that which issues at any one time, a burst, a gush, a spurt, and the like; time, instance | دفعة واحدة (*duf'atan*) all at one time, all at once, in one stroke, in one fell swoop; هذه الدفعة this time; ست دفعات six times; على دفعات متفاوتة (*mutafāwita*) at different times

دفاع *daffā'* propelling, impelling, giving impetus; ○ piston (*techn.*)

مدفع *midfa'* pl. مدافع *madāfi'*[2] gun, cannon | ○ مدافع بعيدة المرى (*ba'īdat al-marmā*) long-range guns; مدفع رشاش (*raššāš*) machine gun; ○ مدافع ضخمة (*ḍakma*) heavy artillery; المدافع المضادة للطائرات (*muḍādda*) or المدافع المقاومة للطائرات (*muqāwima*) anti-aircraft guns; مدفع ثلاثى مضاد للطائرات ○ (*ṯulāṯī, muḍādd*) three-barreled anti-aircraft gun (*mil.*); مدفع هاون *m. hāwun* mortar; ضرب مدفع الظهر *ḍarb m. aẓ-ẓuhr* marking of exact noon by cannon shot

مدفعى *midfa'ī* gun-, cannon-, artillery- (in compounds); artilleryman, gunner, cannoneer

مدفعية *midfa'īya* artillery

دفاع *difā'* protection; defense (عن of s.th., of s.o., also *jur.*) | خط الدفاع *kaṭṭ ad-d.* line of defense; halfbacks (soccer); مجلس الدفاع *majlis ad-d.* defense council; وزارة الدفاع ministry of defense, war ministry; الدفاع الوطنى (*waṭanī*) national defense; الدفاع المضاد للطائرات (*muḍādd*) anti-aircraft defense; دفاع شرعى legitimate self-defense

دفاعى *difā'ī* defensive, protective

مدافعة *mudāfa'a* defense (عن of s.th.)

اندفاع *indifā'* pl. *-āt* rush(ing), plunging, plunge (فى into); outburst, outbreak, eruption; élan, dash, impetuosity, rashness, hotheadedness, fire, exuberance, effusiveness; self-abandon; اندفاعا *indifā'an* spontaneously

اندفاعة *indifā'a* (n. vic.) sudden outburst, outbreak (e.g., of wailing)

دافع *dāfi'* repellent, expellant; driving, pushing, giving impetus, incentive, impellent, propelling, propulsive, etc.; repeller; payer, e.g., دافعو الضرائب the taxpayers; (pl. دوافع *dawāfi'*[2]) incentive, impulse, impetus, spur, motive; بدافع (with foll. genit.) motivated by ..., by reason of ..., on the strength of ...

مدفوعات *madfū'āt* payments

مدافع *mudāfi'* defender (عن of s.o., of s.th.)

دفق *dafaqa u i* (*dafq*) to pour out, pour forth (ه s.th.); — *u* (*dafq*, دفوق *dufūq*) to be shed; to flow, well out, spout, gush forth; to overflow (ه with s.th.) V to pour forth, spout forth, gush forth; to rush in; to break forth, break out, burst out; to go off (shot); to plunge blindly (الى, فى into s.th.); to rush (على against); to crowd (على into) VII = V

دفق *dafq* pouring out, effusion

دفقة *dufqa* pl. *dufuqāt, dufaqāt, dufqāt* = دفعة *duf'a* | دفقة واحدة (*dufqatan*) = دفعة واحدة; دفقات الريح *d. ar-rīḥ* gusts; دفقة من الماء gush of water

دفاق *daffāq* bursting forth, darting out, rushing out

تدفق *tadaffuq* outpour, outflow, issue, effluence, efflux, effusion; influx, run, rush, inrush, inpour; outbreak, outburst; impulsiveness; exuberance, effusiveness

دافق *dāfiq* pl. دوافق *dawāfiq*[2] bursting forth, breaking out, erupting; gushing, torrential

متدفق *mutadaffiq* impulsive; exuberant, effusive

دفلى *diflā* oleander (Nerium oleander L.; *bot.*)

دفن **dafana** *i* (*dafn*) to bury, inter, inhume (ه s.o.); to hide, conceal, keep secret (ه s.th.)

دفن *dafn* burial, interment, inhumation

دفين *dafīn* pl. دفناء *dufanā'*[2] buried, interred; hidden, secret

دفينة *dafīna* pl. دفائن *dafā'in*[2] hidden treasure, treasure-trove

مدفن *madfan*, مدفنة *madfana* pl. مدافن *madāfin*[2] burying place, burial ground, cemetery

دفى see دفاية

دق **daqqa** *i* (دقة *diqqa*) to be thin, fine, fragile, frail; to be little, small, tiny, minute; to be subtle, delicate; to be insignificant, unimportant, trifling, inconsiderable; to be too fine, too subtle (عن for perception); — *u* (*daqq*) to crush, bruise, bray (ه s.th.); to grind, pulverize, powder (ه s.th.); to pound (ه s.th., e.g., meat); to strike (clock); to beat, throb (heart); to hammer, throb (engine); to knock, rap, bang (الباب *al-bāba* on the door); to bump (رأسه بالحائط *ra'sahū bi-l-ḥā'iṭ* one's head against the wall); to drive (ه a nail); to ram in, drive in (*constr. eng.*); to beat, strum, play (على a musical instrument); to type (على on a typewriter); — to sound, resound, ring out (said of musical instruments) | دق الجرس (*jarasa*) to ring the bell; دق جرس الخطر (*j. al-kaṭar*) to sound the alarm; دق الجرس على to call s.o. up, give s.o. a ring; دق الجرس (*jarasu*) the bell rang; دقت الساعة the clock struck **II** to triturate, pulverize, reduce to powder (ه s.th.); to be precise, exact, strict, meticulous, painstaking, proceed with utmost accuracy or care (فى in s.th.); to scrutinize, examine closely, determine exactly (ه s.th.); to do (ه s.th.) carefully, with precision | دقق البحث (*baḥṯa*) to investigate carefully; دقق النظر (*naẓara*) to watch attentively or carefully, scrutinize, examine closely (فى s.th.); دقق الملاحظة (*mulāḥaẓata*) to observe closely **III** to deal scrupulously (ه with s.o.) **IV** to make fine, make thin (ه s.th.) **VII** to be crushed, brayed, pounded; to be broken | اندق عنقه (*'unquhū*) he broke his neck **X** to be or become thin or fine

دق *daqq* crushing, bruising, braying, pounding; pulverization, trituration; grinding (down); beat(ing), throb(bing); bang(ing), knock(ing), rap(ping); tattoo(ing) | دق الجرس *d. al-jaras* peal, ringing, sound of a bell; دق الحنك *d. al-ḥanak* chatter, prattle

دق *diqq* fine, thin; little, small, tiny, minute; delicate, fragile, frail | شجر دق (*šajar*) shrubbery, brush, scrub; حمى الدق *ḥummā d-d.* hectic fever

دقة *daqqa* (n. vic.) pl. *-āt* bang, knock, rap; beat, throb; stroke, striking (of a clock); hammer, hammering sound; thumping, thump | دقات القلب *d. al-qalb* heartbeats; دقة الجرس *d. al-jaras* peal, or ring, of a bell; telephone call, ring

دقة *diqqa* thinness; fineness; smallness, tininess, minuteness; triviality, pettiness, paltriness; subtlety, subtleness, finesse; critical or precarious state, delicate situation; accuracy, exactness, exactitude, precision | بدقة exactly, accurately, precisely, minutely, painstakingly, meticulously, sharply; دقة الشعور acuteness of feeling, sensitivity, sensitiveness, sensibility

دقة *duqqa* pl. دقق *duqaq* fine dust; powder

دقاق *duqāq* crushed, brayed, or pulverized, substance; powder; flour of lupine

دقيق *daqīq* pl. دقاق *diqāq*, ادقة *adiqqa* fine, thin; delicate, frail, fragile; little, small, tiny, puny, minute; subtle;

paltry, petty, trifling, trivial; precise, accurate, exact; painstaking, scrupulous, meticulous; inexorable, relentless, strict, rigorous; delicate (situation), critical, trying, serious, precarious; — flour, meal | دقيق الحساب keeping strict account, strict, relentless, inexorable; دقيق الشعور sensitive; دقيق الصنع *d. aṣ-ṣan'* finely worked, of delicate workmanship; دقيق النظر *d. an-naẓar* clear-sighted, penetrating, discerning, sensitive; ابو دقيق *abū d.* butterfly; الاعضاء الدقيقة (*a'ḍā'*) the genitals

دقيقة *daqīqa* pl. دقائق *daqā'iq*² particle; nicety; intricacy; detail, particular; minute (time unit) | دقائق الامور the niceties, intricacies, or secret implications of things

دقاق *daqqāq* grinder, crusher; flour merchant; frequently or constantly beating, striking, etc.; player of an instrument | ساعة دقاقة repeater (watch)

دقاقة *daqqāqa* knocker, rapper (of a door)

ادق *adaqq*² finer; more delicate; smaller, tinier; more accurate, preciser; stricter

مدق *midaqq* beetle; pounder, pestle; (*eg.*) trail, footpath

مدقة *midaqqa* pl. مداق *madāqq*² pounder, pestle; beetle; clapper, tongue (of a bell)

تدقيق *tadqīq* accuracy, precision, exactness, exactitude | بتدقيق exactly, precisely, accurately, minutely

مدقق *mudaqqiq* exact, accurate (scholar), thorough (investigator), painstaking, meticulous, strict, relentless

مدقق *mudaqqaq* precise, exact (data)

داقرة *dāqira* pl. دواقر *dawāqir*² clay vessel (*tun.*); — stipend for underprivileged students (*tun.*)

دقشوم *daqšūm* (*eg.*) rubblestone, crushed rock; brickbats, gravel

دقع *daqi'a a* (*daqa'*) to grovel, cringe; to be miserable, wretched, humble, abject; to live in poverty IV do.; to make miserable (ه s.o.; poverty)

ادقاع *idqā'* mass poverty

مدقع *mudqi'* miserable, wretched; degrading, abasing (poverty)

دقل *daqal* mast (of a ship); mainmast; (coll.; n. un. ة) a brand of dates of good quality (*magr.*)

¹دك *dakka u* (*dakk*) to make flat, level or even. to smooth, level, ram, stamp, tamp (ه earth, the ground, a road); to press down, weigh down; to beat down; to devastate, demolish, destroy, ruin (ه s.th.) II to mix, mingle (ه s.th.) VII to be crushed; to be leveled

دك *dakk* pl. دكوك *dukūk* level ground; — devastation, demolition, destruction

دكة *dakka* pl. *-āt* rubblestone, crushed rock; ballast

دكة *dikka* pl. دكك *dikak* bench

دكان *dukkān* pl. دكاكين *dakākīn*² bench; store, shop

دكانجى *dukkānji* storekeeper, shopkeeper, retailer

مدك *midakk* pl. *-āt* ramrod; ○ tamper rammer

²دك II to provide (ه trousers) with a waistband (*dikka* or *tikka*)

دكة *dikka* (= تكة *tikka*) waistband (in the upper seam of trousers)

دكتاتورية *diktātūriya* dictatorship

دكتاتورى *diktātūrī* dictatorial

دكتور *duktūr* pl. دكاترة *dakātira* doctor | دكتور فى الحقوق doctor of laws, LL.D.; دكتور فى الطب (*ṭibb*) doctor of medicine, M.D.

دكتوراة *duktūrāh* doctorate, doctorship doctor's degree, title of doctor | الدكتوراة الفخرية (*fakrīya*) honorary doctorate

ذكر *iddakara* see ذكر

دكريتو (It. *decreto*) *dikrītō* pl. دكريتات decree

[1]ادكن *adkan*[2], f. دكناء *daknā'*[2] pl. دكن *dukn* blackish, dark (color)

داكن *dākin* dark, dark-colored | اخضر داكن dark green; اصفر داكن yellowish, of a dingy yellow, mud-colored

[2]دكان see [1]دك

دل *dalla u* (دلالة *dalāla*) to show, demonstrate, point out (على ه to s.o. s.th.); to lead, guide, direct, conduct (ه على or الى s.o. to), show s.o. (ه) the way (على or الى to); to show, indicate, mark (على s.th.); to point (على to s.th.), evince, indicate, denote, imply, bespeak, suggest (على s.th.), be indicative, be suggestive (على of); to furnish evidence (على for s.th.), prove (على s.th.); — (1st pers. perf. *dalaltu*) *i* (دلال *dalāl*) to be coquettish, flirt, dally (of a woman; على with s.o.) **II** to prove (على s.th.), furnish the proof (على for), confirm, corroborate (على ب s.th. with); to sell or put up at auction, auction off (على s.th.); to pamper, coddle, spoil (ه s.o.); to fondle, caress, pet (ه a child) **IV** to make free, take liberties (على with s.o.); to pride o.s. (ب on), be conceited (ب of) **V** to be coquettish, flirt, dally (of a woman; على with s.o.); to be coy, behave affectedly; to take liberties (على with s.o.); to pamper, coddle (على s.o.) **X** to ask to be shown (على s.th.); to seek information, inform o.s. (على about); to obtain information; to be informed (على about); to be guided (ب by), act or proceed in accordance with (ب); to conclude, gather, infer (على s.th., ب or من from), draw conclusions (ب or من from, على with regard to), judge (على s.th., ب or من by)

دل *dall* proper, dignified conduct; coquetry, flirtation

دلة *dalla* pl. دلال *dilāl* pot with long curved spout and handle used for making coffee (among Syrian nomads and in some parts of Saudi Arabia)

دلال *dalāl* coquetry, coquettishness; pampering, coddling, spoiling

دليل *dalīl* pl. ادلة *adilla*, دلائل *dalā'il*[2], ادلاء *adillā'*[2] (the latter of persons) indication (على of); sign, token; symptom; proof, evidence (على of); guide; tourist guide, cicerone; pilot (of a ship, of an airplane); guidebook, guide manual, handbook; directory, telephone directory; railroad guide, timetable; guide rail (*techn.*); roller path (in steel construction) | اقام الدليل على to furnish the proof for, demonstrate, prove s.th.; دليل ظرفى (*ẓarfī*) circumstantial evidence; دليل قاطع cogent proof, conclusive evidence

دلال *dallāl* auctioneer; broker, jobber, middleman, agent, commission merchant; hawker

دلالة *dalāla* pl. *-āt* pointing; guidance; leading, leadership; indication (على of); sign, token; sense, meaning

دلالة *dilāla* auction, public sale; business of a broker or middleman; brokerage commission; trade of a dealer, jobber or agent

دلالة *dallāla* middlewoman, woman broker

ادل *adall*[2] proving more cogently (على s.th.), more indicative or suggestive (على of) | ادل دليل على (*dalīlin*) the surest evidence of, the best proof of

تدليل *tadlīl* reasoning, argumentation, demonstration; proving (على of), furnishing of proof or evidence (على for); corroboration, substantiation, confirmation; pampering, coddling, spoiling; fondling, petting, caressing; pet form (of a name) | اسم التدليل pet name; تدليلا من as a pet form of ...

تدلل *tadallul* coquetry, coquettishness; pampering, coddling, spoiling

استدلال *istidlāl* reasoning, argumentation, demonstration; conclusion, inference, deduction; proof, evidence (على of)

دالة *dālla* familiarity, chumminess; liberty (that one takes with s.o.); audacity, boldness

مدلول *madlūl* proven; (pl. *-āt*) meaning, sense | مدلولات الكلمات *m. al-kalimāt* lexical meanings

مدلل *mudallal* pampered, spoiled (child)

مدل *mudill* presumptuous, arrogant | مدل بنفسه (*bi-nafsihī*) conceited, self-important

[1]دلب *dulb* plane tree, sycamore (*bot.*)

[2]دولاب pl. دواليب look up alphabetically

دلتا Nile Delta, Lower Egypt

دلج IV to set out at nightfall

دلوح *dalūḥ* pl. دلح *duluḥ* moisture-laden cloud

دلدل *daldala* to set into a swinging motion, dangle II *tadaldala* to hang loosely, dangle

دلدل *duldul* and دلدول *duldūl* porcupine (*zool.*)

دلس II to swindle, cheat; to counterfeit, forge, falsify (ه s.th.) III to deceive, defraud (ه s.o.), impose (ه on)

تدليس *tadlīs* deceit, fraud; swindle

تدليسي *tadlīsī* fraudulent

مدلس *mudallas* forged, counterfeit | نقود مدلسة counterfeit money; مفاتيح مدلسة forged keys

دلع *dala'a a* (*dal'*) with لسانه *lisānahū*: to stick out one's tongue; to loll, let the tongue hang out II to pamper, spoil (ه a child); to caress, fondle, pet (ه s.o.) IV شيء يدلع النفس (*eg.*) a nauseating, disgusting thing VII to stick out, be stuck out, hang out, loll (tongue); to dart out, lick out, leap out, flare up (flame), break out (fire); to be pampered, spoiled (child)

دلع *dal'*: اسم الدلع *ism ad-d.* pet name

دلاع *dallā'* (coll.; n. un. ة) watermelon (*maġr.*)

دلغان *dilġān* clay

دلف *dalafa i* (*dalf*, دلوف *dulūf*, دلفان *dalafān*) to walk with short steps, toddle; to go or walk slowly, saunter, stroll (الى to); to advance (على toward); to approach step by step (الى s.o. or s.th.); to penetrate, reach (الى as far as); to grope (الى for, of the hand); to leak, drip, trickle (water)

○ دالف *dālif* pl. دوالف *dawālif*[2] ricochet (*mil.*)

دلفين *dulfīn* pl. دلافين *dalāfīn*[2] dolphin

دلق *dalaqa u* to spill, pour out (ه a liquid) VII to be spilled (liquid)

دلك *dalaka u* (*dalk*) to rub (ه s.th.); to stroke (ه s.th.), pass the hand (ه over s.th.); to knead (العجين the dough); — *u* (دلوك *dulūk*) to set, go down (sun) II to rub (ه s.th., ه s.o.), embrocate (ه s.th.); to knead; to massage (ه s.o.)

دلك *dalk* rubbing; grazing, brushing, touching, touch

دلوك *dalūk* liniment

دلوك *dulūk*, دلوك الشمس *d. aš-šams* sunset

تدليك *tadlīk* embrocation; massage

مدلكة *mudallika* pl. *-āt* masseuse

دله II to rob s.o. (ه) of his senses, drive (ه s.o.) crazy (love) V to go out of one's mind, go crazy (with love) | تدلهت في حبه (*ḥubbihī*) she has fallen in love with him

مدله *mudallah* madly in love

دلهم IV **idlahamma** to be dark, gloomy; to be deep-black

دلهم *dalham* dark, gloomy; deep-black

ادلهمام *idlihmām* a deep black

مدلهم *mudlahimm* dark, gloomy; deep-black

دلو II to let hang, dangle (ه s.th.); to hang, suspend (ه s.th.); to lower (ه s.th.); to drop, let down, let fall down (ه s.th.) IV = II; to cast down (ه glances, ال on s.o.); to let one's glance (بانظاره *bi-anẓārihī*) sweep down; to express, utter, voice (ب s.th., e.g., برأيه *bi-ra'yihī* one's opinion); to deliver, make (بتصريح a statement; *pol.*); to adduce, present, advance, offer (بحجة *bi-ḥujjatin* an argument); to inform, notify, advise (ال ب s.o. of), let (ال s.o.) know (ب about); to offer, present (ال ب to s.o. s.th.); to grant, give (بحديث ل an interview to s.o.); to slander, defame, asperse (في s.o.) | ادلى دلوه بين الدلاء (*dalwahū, dilā'*) or ادلى بدلوه فى الدلاء to make one's contribution (together with others), add one's touch, put in one's two bits' worth V to hang down, be suspended, dangle (من from); to be lowered, be let down; to be or become low; to sink, descend | تدلى للسقوط to threaten to fall down, be ready to fall

دلو *dalw* usually f., pl. ادل *adlin*, دلاء *dilā'*, ادلاء *adlā'* leather bucket; bucket, pail; Aquarius (*astron.*)

دلاية *dallāya* pendant

ادلاء *idlā'* delivery (of a statement); utterance, statement; presentation; granting

دالية *dāliya* pl. دوال *dawālin* water-wheel (for irrigation); trellis, espalier on which grapevines are trained; varix, varicose vein

متدل *mutadallin* pendent, suspended, hanging, dangling; projecting, overhanging, ready to fall down

داليا look up alphabetically

[1]دم *dam* pl. دماء *dimā'* blood; دماء homicide cases (*jur.*) | دم الاخوين *d. al-akawain* dragon's blood (a dark-red, resinous substance derived from the dragon tree, Dracaena draco)

دمى *damī* blood- (in compounds), sanguine

دموى *damawī* blood- (in compounds), sanguine; sanguinary, bloody

[2]دم *damma u* (*damm*) to coat, smear, besmear (ب ه s.th. with); to paint, daub, color, dye, tinge, tint (ب ه s.th. with) II to rub, embrocate, anoint (ب ه s.th. with)

دم *damm* ointment, unguent, salve, liniment, embrocation; paint; pigment, dye, dyestuff; rouge

دمام *dimām* ointment, unguent, salve, liniment, embrocation; paint; pigment, dye, dyestuff; rouge

دميم *damīm* pl. دمام *dimām* ugly; deformed, misshapen | دميم الخلقة *d. al-kilqa* ugly to look at, of repulsive appearance

دمامة *damāma* ugliness; ugly appearance; abominableness, monstrosity

الدمام *ad-dammām* Dammam (seaport in E Saudi Arabia, on the Persian Gulf)

دمث *damuṯa u* (دماثة *damāṯa*) to be gentle, mild (character) II to soften, mellow (ه s.th.)

دمث *damiṯ* pl. دماث *dimāṯ*: دمث الاخلاق gentle, mild-tempered

دماثة *damāṯa* mildness, gentleness, tenderness (of character)

دمج *damaja u* (دموج *dumūj*) to enter (في s.th.), go or come into (في), be inserted, incorporated (في in) II to write shorthand IV to twist tightly, twine firmly (ه s.th.); to enter, insert, include, incorporate, embody (في ه s.th. in); to introduce, interpolate, intercalate (ه في s.th. in); to annex (ه في s.th. to) **VII** to be inserted, be incorporated (في in); to be annexed (في to); to merge (في with), be swallowed up, be absorbed (في by); to be fused, fuse, amalgamate

تدميج *tadmīj* shorthand, stenography

ادماج *idmāj* insertion, incorporation, interpolation; inclusion (في in); assimilation

اندماج *indimāj* incorporation, insertion (في in); amalgamation, merger, merging (في with); absorption (في by); annexation (في to); fusion; assimilation

مدمج *mudmaj* firm, compact

مندمج *mundamij* firm, compact, tight

دمجانة *damajāna* (also داماجانة) pl. *-āt* demijohn, carboy

دمدم *damdama* to mutter, grumble, growl, snarl

دمدمة *damdama* pl. *-āt* growl, snarl; rumbling noise, rumble

[1]دمر *damara u* to perish, be ruined, be destroyed **II** to annihilate, destroy, ruin, demolish, wreck (ه s.th.) **V** to be destroyed, demolished, ruined, wrecked **VII** to be destroyed, be annihilated

دمار *damār* ruin, destruction

تدمير *tadmīr* annihilation, destruction, demolition

اندمار *indimār* utter defeat, rout, destruction, annihilation

مدمرة *mudammira* pl. *-āt* destroyer (*naut.*)

[2]دمور *dammūr* (*eg.*) a coarse calico-like fabric

دمورى *dammūrī* (*eg.*) made of *dammūr* (see above)

[3]دميرة *damīra* (*eg.*) flood season of the Nile

[4]□ لا دومرى *lā dūmarī* (= لا تدمرى) nobody, no one, not a living soul

[5]تدمر *tadmur*², usually pronounced *tudmur*, Palmyra (ancient city in Syria, now a small village)

تدمرى *tadmurī*, usually pronounced *tudmurī*, someone, somebody; لا تدمرى nobody, no one, not a living soul

دمس *damasa u* to hide, conceal, disguise (ه s.th.); to bury (ه في الارض s.o. in the ground) **II** do.

دمس *dims* (*eg.*) cinders, ashes

دماسة *damāsa* darkness

ادماس *admās* (pl.) hovels, shanties, huts

دموس *dammūs* pl. داميس *damāmīs*² cave, cavern

ديماس *daimās, dīmās,* ديموس *daimūs* pl. دياميس *dayāmīs*² dungeon; vault

دامس *dāmis* pitch-dark; dark, gloomy, dusky

فول مدمس *fūl mudammas* stewed beans

دمشق *dimašq*², *dimišq*² Damascus (capital of Syria)

مدمشق *mudamšaq* damascened, damasked; (*syr.*) having adopted a sophisticated style of living (imitating that of Damascus), urbanized

دمع *dama'a a* to water (eye) **IV** to cause to weep, evoke tears, make (the eyes) water

دمع *dam'* pl. دموع *dumū'* tears

دمعة *dam'a* (n. un.) tear, teardrop; (*eg.*) *dim'a* gravy

دمعى *dam'ī*: قنبلة دمعية (*qunbula*) tear-gas bomb

دمعة *dami'a* and دميع *damī'* pl. دمعى *dam'ā*, دمائع *damā'i'*² readily inclined to weep, frequently weeping, tearful, lachrymose (woman)

دموع *damū'* and دماع *dammā'* watering, watery, tearful (eyes)

مدمع *madma'* pl. مدامع *madāmi'*[2] lachrymal canal

[1]دمغ *damağa a* to refute, invalidate (ه a falsehood, an error, a false accusation); to triumph (ه over falsehood; said of truth)

دماغ *dimāğ* pl. ادمغة *admiğa* brain

حجة دامغة *ḥujja dāmiğa* cogent argument; شهادة دامغة (*šahāda*) irrefutable testimony

[2]دمغ *damağa u* (*damğ*) to stamp, provide or mark with a stamp (ه s.th.); to hallmark (ه gold and silver articles); to brand (ه an animal)

دمغ *damğ* stamping | دمغ المصوغات *d. al-maṣūğāt* hallmarking of gold and silver articles

دمغة *damğa* stamp; hallmark (on gold and silver articles) | ورق دمغة *waraq d.* stamped paper

مدموغ *madmūğ* stamped, bearing a stamp

دمقراطى *dimuqrāṭī* democratic; democrat

دمقراطية *dimuqrāṭiya* democracy; democratic attitude or conviction

دمقس *dimaqs* raw silk

دمقسى *dimaqsī* silken, silky

مدموك *madmūk* and مدمك *mudmak* firm, tight, taut

دمل *damala u* (*daml*, دملان *damalān*) to fertilize, manure, dung (ه the soil); — *damila a* (*damal*) to heal, heal up, scar over, cicatrize (wound) **VII** to heal, heal up, scar over, cicatrize (wound); to fester, suppurate (sore)

دمل *dummal* (n. un. ة) pl. دمامل *damāmil*[2], دماميل *damāmīl*[2] abscess, boil, sore, tumor, ulcer; furuncle; bubo, plague boil; inveterate evil

طاعون دملى *ṭā'ūn dummalī* bubonic plague

دملج *dumluj* pl. دمالج *damālij*[2] bracelet, bangle

[1]دمن *damana u* (*damn*) to fertilize, manure, dung (ه the soil) **IV** to give o.s. up, devote o.s., apply o.s. (على or ه to), go in for (على or ه); to be addicted (على e.g., to liquor)

دمن *dimn* (coll.; n. un. ة) pl. دمن *diman* fertilizer, manure, dung

دمنة *dimna* pl. دمن *diman* vestiges or remnants of a dwelling, ruins

دمان *damān* fertilizer, manure, dung

ادمان *idmān* addiction; excess; mania; dipsomania | ادمان المسكرات *i. al-muskirāt* alcoholism

مدمن *mudmin* addicted, given up (على e.g., to wine); an addict (على of)

[2]دمان *dumān* see دومان

دمنهور *damanhūr*[2] Damanhûr (city in N Egypt)

دموى see [1]دم

[1]دمى *damiya a* to bleed **II** and **IV** to cause to bleed

دام *dāmin* bleeding, bloody, gory

مدمى *mudamman*, f. مدماة bloody; blood-red

[2]دمية *dumya* pl. دمى *duman* statue, statuette; image, effigy; dummy; doll

دمياط *dimyāṭ*[2] Damietta (city in N Egypt)

دن *danna u* (*dann*, دنين *danīn*) to buzz, hum (insect); to drone

دن *dann* and دنين *danīn* buzz(ing), hum(ming), droning, drone

دن *dann* pl. دنان *dinān* earthen wine jug

دنأ *dana'a a* and دنؤ *danu'a u* (دنوءة *dunū'a*, دناءة *danā'a*) to be low, mean, base, vile, contemptible, despicable

دنىء *danī'* pl. ادنياء *adniyā'*[2], ادناء *adnā'* low, base, mean, vile, despicable, contemptible; inferior, second-rate, of poor quality

ادنأ *adna'*[2] lower, viler, meaner; more inferior, of poorer quality

دناءة *danā'a* lowness, baseness, meanness, vileness; inferiority

دنتلا, دنتلة (Fr. *dentelle*) *dantilla* lace, lacework

دنجل *dinjil* (*eg.*) pl. دناجل *danājil*[2] axle, axletree

دندرمه (Turk. *dondurma*) *dandurma* ice cream

دنادشة *danādiša* common people, people of no consequence

دندن *dandana* to buzz, hum; to drone; to hum softly, croon (a song); to murmur

دندى *dindī* (*eg.*) turkey

دينار pl. دنانير look up alphabetically

دنس *danisa a* (*danas*) to be soiled, sullied, defiled, polluted **II** to stain, soil, dirty, befoul, sully, pollute, contaminate (ه s.th.); to dishonor, disgrace (ه s.th.); to desecrate (ه s.th.) **V** pass. of **II**

دنس *danas* pl. ادناس *adnās* uncleanness, dirt, filth, squalor; stain, blemish, fault

دنس *danis* pl. ادناس *adnās*, دنساء *dunasā'*[2] unclean, soiled, sullied, foul, polluted, defiled, stained

تدنيس *tadnīs* pollution, defilement, soiling, sullying, contamination; dishonoring, disgracing; desecration, profanation

دنف *danifa a* (*danaf*) to be seriously ill **IV** do.

دنف *danif* pl. ادناف *adnāf* seriously ill

دنف *danaf* long illness; ○ cachexia, marasmus (*med.*)

مدنف *mudnif*, *mudnaf* emaciated, haggard, weak

دانق look up alphabetically

دنقلة *dunqula* Dongola (town in N Sudan, on the Nile)

دنجل = دنكل

دانمرك *danmark*[2] Denmark

(دنو) and (دنى) دنا *danā u* (دنو *dunūw*, دناوة *danāwa*) to be near, be close; to come or go near s.o. or s.th. (من or الى or ل), approach (من, الى, ل s.o., s.th.); to come close, get close (من, الى, ل to), approximate (الى, من, ل s.th.); to draw near, be imminent (time, event); دنا به من to bring s.o. close to ...; — دنى *daniya a* (دنا *danan*, دناية *danāya*) to be low, lowly; to be or become mean, base, vile, despicable, contemptible **II** to bring close (ه s.th., ه s.o., من to), bring, take or move (ه s.th., ه s.o.) near (من), approximate (ه s.th., من to); to apply o.s. (فى to s.th.), busy o.s. (فى with s.th.), delve (فى into); دنى نفسه (*nafsahū*) to lower o.s., abase o.s., humble o.s. **III** to approach (ه s.o., ه s.th.), come or get near s.o. or s.th. (ه, ه), come or get close (ه, ه to); to approximate (ه s.th.); to measure up (ه, ه to) | شىء لا يدانى (*yudānā*) an unequaled thing **IV** to be near, be close; to approach (من or الى or ل s.o. or s.th.), come, go or draw near s.o. or s.th. (من, الى, ل), come close, get close (من, الى, ل to); to bring close (ه s.o., ه s.th., من to), bring, take or move (ه s.o., ه s.th.) near (من), approximate (ه s.th., من to); to lower, drop (ه s.th., e.g., the veil) **V** to approach gradually (الى s.th. or s.o.); to be debased, sink low, sink, decline; to lower o.s., abase o.s., humble o.s. **VI** to come near each other, get close to each other, approach one another; to be close together; to approach, approximate (من s.th.) **VIII** ادنى *iddanā* to be near, be close, come or draw near, approach **X** to wish to be nearer or closer, try to come nearer or closer; to seek to fetch or bring closer (ه s.th., الى to, to o.s.), reach out (ه for s.th.), wish (ه اليه for s.th.)

دنو *dunūw* advent, approach; proximity, nearness, imminence (of an event)

دنى *danīy* pl. ادنياء *adniyā'*[2] near, close; low, lowly; mean, base, vile, despicable, contemptible, inferior, infamous, depraved

دنية *danīya* pl. *-āt*, دنايا *danāyā* a base quality or habit; s.th. disgraceful, infamy, vile action

ادنى *adnā*, f. دنيا *dunyā* pl. m. ادان *adānin*, ادنون *adnauna*, pl. f. دنى *dunan* nearer, closer; situated lower down, nether, lower, inferior; lowlier; smaller, of less significance; more appropriate, better suited, more suitable | الشرق الادنى (*šarq*) the Near East; المغرب الادنى (*mag̱rib*) Algeria; ادنى من حبل الوريد (*ḥabli al-warīd*) very near or close, imminent; الاقارب الادنون the closest relatives; من ادناه الى اقصاه (*aqṣāhu*) from one end to the other; wholly, entirely, completely, altogether; الحد الادنى (*ḥadd*) the minimum; ادناه hereinafter, below (in writings, documents, etc.) e.g., الموقعون ادناه (*muwaqqi'ūn*) those signed below, the undersigned; لا ادنى (with foll. genit.) not the least, not a single, not one

دنيا *dunyā* (f. of ادنى *adnā*) world; earth; this world (as opposed to آخرة); life in this world, worldly existence; worldly, temporal things or possessions; earthly things or concerns | الحياة الدنيا life in this world; ام الدنيا *umm ad-d.* Cairo; اقام الدنيا واقعدها *aqāma d-d. wa-aq'adahā* approx.: to kick up a dust, make a stir, move heaven and earth

دنيوى *dunyawī*, دنياوى *dunyāwī* worldly, mundane, secular; earthly, temporal, transitory, transient

دناوة *danāwa* nearness, closeness, proximity, propinquity; lowness, lowliness; meanness, baseness, vileness

دناية *danāya* lowness, lowliness; meanness, baseness, vileness

تدن *tadannin* sinking, decline; low level, nadir (fig.) | التدنى الاخلاق (*aḵlāqī*) the low level of morality, the moral decline

دان *dānin* low; near, close

متدان *mutadānin* close together

دهر **dahr** pl. دهور *duhūr*, ادهر *adhur* time; long time, age, epoch; lifetime; eternity; fate, destiny | بنات الدهر *banāt ad-d.* blows of fate, trials, afflictions, misfortune; صروف الدهر and تصاريف الدهر vicissitudes of fate, changes of fortune; adversities, adverse circumstances; دهر الداهرين *dahra d-dāhirīn* for all eternity, forever and ever; الى آخر الدهر *ilā āḵiri d-d.* do.; لا ... الدهر كله (*ad-dahra kullahū*) never in all one's life

دهرى *dahrī* an adherent of the *dahrīya*, a materialistic, atheistic doctrine in Islam; atheist, freethinker

دهرى *duhrī* very old, far advanced in years

دهس **dahasa** *a* (= داس) to trample underfoot, trample down, crush (ه s.th.), tread (ه on s.th.); to run over (ه s.o.)

دهش **dahiša** *a* and pass. *duhiša* to be astonished, amazed, surprised (من or ل at); to wonder, marvel (من at); to be baffled, startled, puzzled, perplexed, taken aback (من or ل by) **II** and **IV** to astonish, amaze, surprise, baffle, puzzle, perplex, startle (ه s.o.) **VII** = *dahiša*

دهش *dahaš* perplexity, surprise, consternation, alarm, dismay

دهش *dahiš* astonished, amazed, surprised; baffled, puzzled, nonplused, perplexed, startled, disconcerted, alarmed, upset; dazed, stunned

دهشة *dahša* astonishment, amazement, surprise, wonder; perplexity, consternation, bafflement, bewilderment, dismay, alarm

اندهاش *indihāš* astonishment, amazement; perplexity, consternation, bafflement, bewilderment

مدهش *mudhiš* astonishing, amazing, surprising, marvelous; pl. *-āt* amazing things, marvels, wonders

مدهوش *madhūš* and مندهش *mundahiš* astonished, amazed, surprised; perplexed, baffled, puzzled, nonplused, startled; overwhelmed

دهق[1] *dahaq* stocks (to hold the feet of an offender by way of punishment)

دهاق *dihāq* full (cup), brimful

دهقان[2] *dihqān*, pl. دهاقنة *dahāqina*, دهاقين *dahāqīn*² man of importance, one who plays an important role, leading personality; grandee (in ancient Persia) | دهاقين السياسة *d. as-siyāsa* the political leaders

دهك *dahaka a* (*dahk*) to crush; to mash (ه s.th.)

دهلز II *tadahlaza* to stroll about, walk about (in a hall)

دهليز *dihlīz* pl. دهاليز *dahālīz*² anteroom, vestibule, lobby, foyer; corridor, hallway | ابن الدهليز *ibn ad-d.* pl. ابناء الدهاليز foundling

دهلى *dihlī* Delhi

دهم *dahama a* (*dahm*) and *dahima a* (*daham*) to come or descend (ه upon s.o.) suddenly; to surprise, take unawares, take by surprise (ه s.o.), come unexpectedly (ه to s.o.); to enter suddenly, raid, invade (ه s.th.) **II** to blacken (ه s.th.) **III** to befall, seize, grip, attack (ه s.o.), come over s.o. (ه; e.g., sickness, despair); to surprise, take unawares, catch red-handed (ه s.o.); to attack suddenly (ه s.o.), fall upon s.o. (ه), invade, raid (ه e.g., a house); to overtake (ه s.o.; fate), catch up with (ه) **IX** to be black

دهمة *duhma* blackness

ادهم *adham*², f. دهماء *dahmā'*², pl. دهم *duhm* black, deep-black | داهية دهماء (*dāhiya*) disaster, catastrophe

الدهماء *ad-dahmā'* the masses, the common people, the populace, also دهماء الناس

مداهمة *mudāhama* police raid; house search

مدهم *mudhamm* very dark, pitch-dark

دهن *dahana u* (*dahn*) to oil (ه, ه s.th., s.o., ب with); to anoint (ه, ه s.th., s.o., ب with); to grease, smear (ه, ه s.th., s.o., ب with); to rub, embrocate (ه, ه s.th., s.o., ب with); to paint, daub (ه s.th.); to varnish (ه s.th.) **II** do. **III** to treat with gentleness (ه s.o.); to cajole, flatter (ه s.o.), fawn (ه on s.o.); to cheat, dupe, gull, take in, outsmart (ه s.o.) **V** pass. of **I**

دهن *dahn* oiling, greasing; painting, daubing

دهن *duhn* pl. ادهان *adhān*, دهون *duhūn*, *-āt*, دهان *dihān* oil (edible, lubricating, for the skin); fat, grease

دهنى *duhnī* oily, oil, oleic, oleo- (in compounds); fatty, greasy

دهنيات *duhnīyāt* fats, oils; fatty substances

دهناء *dahnā'*² desert

دهان *dahhān* house painter, painter

دهينة *dahīna* pomade

دهان *dihān* pl. *-āt*, أدهنة *adhina* cosmetic cream, cold cream, salve, ointment, unguent; consecrated oil, anointing oil; paint, varnish; hypocrisy, dissimulation, deceit; — (without pl.) painting, daubing; whitewashing | ورشة للدهان (*warša*) paintshop

مداهنة *mudāhana* flattery, adulation, sycophancy, fawning; hypocrisy, dissimulation; deceit, trickery

مداهن *mudāhin* flatterer, adulator, sycophant; hypocrite

مدهن *mudhin* oily; fatty, greasy

دهور *dahwara* to hurl down (ه s.th.); to tear down, topple, overthrow (ه s.th.) II *tadahwara* pass. of I; to fall, tumble; to slump, sink; to be dragged down, sink to the lowest level

تدهور *tadahwur* fall, downfall; decline, slump

دهى *dahiya a* (دهاء *dahā'*) to be clever, smart, cunning, artful, wily; — *dahā a* to befall, overtake, hit, strike (ه s.o.), come over s.o. (ه; misfortune) II = *dahā* VI to pretend to be smart or cunning

دهاء *dahā'* smartness, slyness, shrewdness, subtlety, cunning, craft

ادهى *adhā* smarter, shrewder; craftier, wilier; more skillful, subtler, more resourceful; worse, more calamitous

داه *dāhin* pl. دهاة *duhāh* smart, sly, shrewd, subtle, cunning, wily, artful; resourceful person

داهية *dāhiya* smart fellow, old fox, sly dog

داهية *dāhiya* pl. دواه *dawāhin* calamity, disaster, catastrophe | داهية دهياء (*dahyā'*) and داهية دهماء (*dahmā'*) disaster, catastrophe; فليذهب فى داهية (*fal-yadhab*) let him go to hell!

داء (دوء) *dā'* pl. ادواء *adwā'* disease, malady | داء الثعلب *d. aṯ-ṯa'lab* alopecia, loss of the hair; ○ داء الرقص *d. ar-raqṣ* St. Vitus's dance; ○ داء الفيل *d. al-fīl* elephantiasis; ○ داء المنطقة *d. al-minṭaqa* shingles, herpes zoster (*med.*)

دواء see دوى

دوب II to wear out, wear off (ه s.th.)

دوبارة *dūbāra* packthread, string, twine, cord, rope; thread

دوبيت *dūbait* a rhymed poem consisting of four hemistichs

دوح VII to spread

دوح *dauḥ* branching trees, branches

دوحة *dauḥa* tall tree with many branches; family tree, genealogical table

داحة *dāḥa* top (child's toy)

داخ (دوخ) *dāḵa u* (*dauḵ*) to conquer, subjugate (ه a country); to resign o.s., humble o.s.; to be or become dizzy, have a feeling of dizziness; to feel ill, be sick, feel nausea II to conquer, subjugate (ه a people); to make submissive, subdue, humble, humiliate, degrade (ه s.o.); to make (ه s.o.) dizzy; to molest, bother, trouble (ه s.o.); to daze, stun (ه s.o.) | دوخ رأسه (*ra'sahū*) to make s.o.'s head go round, make s.o. dizzy

دوخة *dauḵa* vertigo, dizziness; coma; nausea

دائخ *dā'iḵ* dizzy

تدويخ *tadwīḵ* subjugation, conquest

[1]دود II to be or become worm-eaten

دود *dūd* (coll.; n. un. ة) pl. ديدان *dīdān* worm; maggot; larva; caterpillar | دودة الحرير and دودة القز *d. al-qazz* silkworm; دود القرع *d. al-qar'*, دود قرعى (*qar'ī*) ascarids; دود القرمز *d. al-qirmiz* cochineal; دود المش

d. al-mišš cheese maggots; الدودة الوحيدة tapeworm

دودى *dūdī* wormlike, worm-shaped, vermiform

مدود *madūd, mudawwid* wormy, worm-eaten

²□ مدود *midwad* = مذود

(دور) دار *dāra u* (*daur*, دوران *dawarān*) to turn, revolve, rotate, move in a circle (ب, على, حول around s.th. or s.o.), circle (حول, ب, على s.th. or s.o.); to begin to turn or rotate; to circulate; to go round, spread, be current, make the rounds (of rumors, etc.); to run, be in operation (of a machine or engine); to start running, start up (engine); to walk or go about, run around; to roam, rove, move about, wander about, gad about; to make the rounds (على among people), turn successively (على to several people); to turn, turn one's face, wheel around; to veer, shift, change its direction; to change, take a different turn, become different; to turn (على against s.o.); to have to do, deal (حول or على with), treat (حول or على of), refer (حول or على to), bear (حول or على on), concern (حول or على s.th.); to take place, be going on, be in progress, be under way; to be discussed, be talked about (بين among); to circulate, pass around (ب s.th.); to lead, guide or show around (ب s.o.); to let roam, let wander (بنظره, بعينيه *bi-naẓarihī, bi-ʿainaihi* one's eyes, one's glance, فى over) | در *dur!* about face! (command; *mil.*); دار رأسه (*ra'suhū*) to be or become dizzy, giddy; دار مع الفرص (*furaṣ*) to trim sail, adapt o.s. to the situation; دارت رحى الحرب (*raḥā l-ḥarb*) war broke out; المعارك التى دارت رحاها امس the battles that raged yesterday; دار بنفسه (*bi-nafsihī*) it passed through his mind; دار على الالسن (*alsun*) to be much-discussed, be on everyone's lips; دار على الافواه واسلات الاقلام (*afwāh, asalāt al-aqlām*) to be current in both the spoken and written language, be in general use, be generally accepted (e.g., words); دار بلادا واكل اعيادا (*bilādan, aʿyādan*) he had been around in the world and had seen a lot; (*colloq.*) دار باله (*bālahū*) to pay attention (على, الى to), be careful (على, الى with); دارت عليهم الدائرة calamity overtook them **II** to turn in a circle, spin, whirl, rotate, revolve (ب, ه s.th.); to turn, turn around (ب, ه s.th.); to invert, reverse (ب, ه s.th.); to make round, to round (ه s.th.); to circulate, pass around (ه s.th.); to set going, set in motion, start (ه s.th.); to wind (ه a watch, a clock); to look, search (على for s.th.) | دور رأسه (*ra'sahū*) to turn s.o.'s head, persuade s.o., bring s.o. round **III** to go or walk around (ه with s.o.); to try to bring (ه s.o.) round; to ensnare, inveigle (ه s.o.); to try to ensnare (ه s.o.); to try to deceive (ه s.o.); to cheat, trick (على or عن ه s.o. out of s.th.); to get away, escape, dodge, duck out **IV** to turn, revolve, rotate, spin, whirl (ه s.th.); to turn around, turn (ه, ب s.th., رأسه الى one's head toward); to direct (على or الى ه s.th. to, toward), aim (على or الى ه s.th. at); to circulate, pass around (ه s.th.); to set in operation, set going, set in motion (ه a machine, an apparatus); to start, start up (المحرك *al-muḥarrik* the motor); to play, play back (ه e.g., شرائط ناطقة tapes); to act upon s.th. (ه), drive (ه s.th.); to get under way (ه a job, a project); to take up (ه s.th.); to initiate (ه s.th.); to divert, turn away (عن ه, ه s.o., s.th. from); to direct, conduct, steer, manage, head, run (ه s.th.), be in charge (ه of); to revolve in one's mind, think over, ponder (ه s.th., ان that) | ادار بوجهه الى (*bi-wajhihī*) to turn around to s.o., look back at s.o.; ادار رأسه (*ra'sahū*) to turn s.o.'s head, persuade s.o., bring s.o. round; ادار الحديث فى الموضوع to bring conversation around to a topic, broach or discuss a subject V to be or become round; to be circular X do.; to circle, rotate, revolve, spin, turn; to turn (الى to), face (الى s.o.); to turn around; to turn one's head, look back; to circle (حول s.th.), walk around s.th. (حول)

دار *dār* f., pl. دور *dūr*, ديار *diyār*, ديارات *diyārāt*, ديرة *diyara* house; building, structure, edifice; habitation, dwelling, abode; residence, home; seat, side, locality; area, region; land, country (esp. pl. ديار, see below) | دار الآثار museum (of antiquities); دار البريد post office; دار البقاء *d. al-baqā'* the eternal abode, the hereafter; الدار الباقية (*bāqiya*) do.; انتقل للدار الباقية to pass away, die; الدار البيضاء (*baiḍā'*) Casablanca (seaport in W Morocco); the White House (in Washington); دار التجارة commercial house, business house; دار الحرب *d. al-ḥarb* war zone, enemy territory (*Isl. Law*: non-Muslim countries); دار الرياسة seat of the chief executive of a country; دار السعادة *d. as-sa'āda* Constantinople; دار السلطنة *d. as-salṭana* Constantinople (designation before World War I); دار السلام *d. as-salām* paradise, heaven; epithet of Baghdad; Dar es Salaam (seaport and capital of Tanganyika Territory); دور السينما cinemas, movie houses; دار الشرطة *d. aš-šurṭa* police station; دار الصنعة or دار الصناعة arsenal; دار صيني (*ṣīnī*) cinnamon; دار الضرب *d. aḍ-ḍarb* and دار السكة *d. as-sikka* mint (building); الديار العراقية (*'irāqīya*) Iraq; دار العلوم name of a college in Cairo; دار الفناء *d. al-fanā'* (as opposed to دار البقاء see above) the temporal world, this world; دار القضاء *d. al-qaḍā'* court of justice, tribunal; دار الكتب *d. al-kutub* public library; دور اللهو *d. al-lahw* amusement centers; night clubs; دار التمثيل theater, playhouse; دار الملك *d. al-mulk* (royal) residence; الديار المصرية (*miṣrīya*) Egypt; دار الهجرة *d. al-hijra* Medina; دار الايتام *d. al-aitām* orphanage, orphans' home

دارة *dāra* pl. *-āt* halo (of the moon); circle; ○ (*el.*) circuit; ○ villa

داري *dārī* domestic, native

دوري *dūrī* domestic (animal); عصفور دوري (*'uṣfūr*) and دوري house sparrow

دور *daur* pl. ادوار *adwār* round (of a patrol; in sports); role, part (played by s.o. or s.th.); film role, stage role; periodic change, rotation, alternation; crop rotation; period; (one's) turn; phase, stage, step, degree, station; epoch, age, era; fit, attack, paroxysm (of a disease); floor, story; musical composition; number, single performance (within a program) | دور وتسلسل (*wa-tasalsul*) vicious circle, circulus vitiosus; دور نهائي (*nihā'ī*) final round, finals (*athlet.*); دور الانعقاد *d. al-in'iqād* session, term (*parl.*); الدور الاول (*awwal*) or دور البطولة *d. al-buṭūla* leading role, starring role; لعب دورا or قام بدور (*la'iba*) to play a part or role; دور ارضي (*arḍī*) ground floor, first floor; كان دوره it was his turn; الدور له it is his turn; (انا) بدوري I for one, (I) for my part, (هو) بدوره he in turn, (he) for his part; بالدور alternately, by turns

دورة *daura* pl. *-āt* turn, revolution, gyration, rotation; circulation; cycle; circuit; round, patrol; procession (*Chr.*); round trip; tour (in general, of an artist or performer); detour; period (○ also *el.*); session (of parliament); course (of instruction) (*ir., syr.*) | الدورة الدموية (*damawīya*) blood circulation; الدورة الجوية (*jawwīya*) air circulation; دورة اجتياز (تجاوز) الرتبة *d. ijtiyāz* (*tajāwuz*) *ar-rutba* officers' training course (*mil., Syr.*); دورة زراعية (*zirā'īya*) crop rotation; دورة تشريعية (*tašrī'īya*) legislative period; دورة الفلك *d. al-falak* revolution of celestial bodies; دورة التفافية (*iltifāfīya*) flanking maneuver (*mil.*); دورة مالية (*mālīya*) financial period, fiscal year; دورة المياه *d. al-miyāh* lavatory (with running water), toilet, water closet

دورى *daurī* patrolling, patrol- (in compounds); periodic, occurring at regular stated times, recurring, intermittent; circulatory, cyclic, etc., see دور and دورة; series (*athlet.*) | الجهاز الدورى (*jahāz*) the circulatory system

دورية *daurīya* pl. *-āt* patrol, round; patrol, reconnaissance squad | دوريات الاستكشاف reconnaissance squads, patrols

□ داورية *dāwirīya* = دورية *daurīya*

دير *dair* pl. اديار *adyār*, اديرة *adyira*, ديورة *duyūra* monastery, convent, cloister

ديرى *dairī* monastic, monasterial, cloistral

ديرة *dīra* region, area, land, homeland (*bedouin*)

دوار *duwār*, *dawār* vertigo, dizziness, giddiness; seasickness

دوار *dawwār* rapidly or constantly turning, whirling, spinning, rotating, circling, circulating; revolving, rotary, rotatory; whirlpool, eddy, vortex; itinerant, ambulant, roving; (*eg.*) farm building, farm | باب دوار revolving door; بائع دوار peddler, hawker; جهاز حفر دوار (*jahāz ḥafr*) rotary drilling rig; دوار الشمس *d. aš-šams* sunflower

ديار *dayyār* monastic, friar, monk

ديرانى *dairānī* monastic, friar, monk

دوارة *dawwāra* whirlpool, eddy, vortex; compass, pair of dividers (*syr.*) | دوارة الهواء *d. al-hawā'* weather vane ○

ديارى *diyārī* domestic; native

دوران *dawarān* turn(ing), rotation, revolution, gyration; circulation, circling, circuiting; round trip, tour

ادور *adwar*[2] (elative): ادور على الالسن (*alsun*) more talked about, more frequently expressed or discussed

مدار *madār* pl. *-āt* orbit; circling, circuiting, circuit, revolution; axis; pivot; (fig.) that upon which s.th. turns or depends, the central, cardinal, or crucial factor, the pivot; center; subject, topic, theme (of a conversation, of negotiations); scope, range, extent, sphere; tropic (*geogr.*); ○ steering wheel | مدار السرطان *m. as-saraṭān* Tropic of Cancer, مدار الجدى *m. al-jady* Tropic of Capricorn; كان مداره على it (i.e., the dispute, or the like) was about ..., it hinged on ...; على مدار السنة (*m. is-sana*) throughout the year, all year round

تدوير *tadwīr* recitation of the Koran at medium speed (between *tartīl* and *ḥadr*; a technical term of *tajwīd*)

مداورة *mudāwara* pl. *-āt* cheating, humbug, trickery; outwitting; attempted evasion or circumvention, shift, dodge; persuasion, inveigling, ensnaring

ادارة *idāra* turning; turning around or over, reverting, reversion, inversion; starting, setting in operation; operation; drive (*techn.*); direction, management; administration; administrative agency, department, office, bureau | ادارة الامن *i. al-amn* the police; ادارة عرفية (*'urfīya*) military administration; سوء الادارة *sū' al-i.* mismanagement, maladministration; مجلس الادارة *majlis al-i.* board of directors, administrative board, committee of management; مركز الادارة *markaz al-i.* administration center, headquarters

ادارى *idārī* administrative, departmental; administrative officer; manager (*athlet.*); اداريا *idārīyan* through administrative channels, administratively, officially

استدارة *istidāra* roundness, rotundity, circularity

دائر *dā'ir* turning, revolving, spinning; circulating; current (e.g., expression), common; ambulant, itinerant; in progress, under way; working, in operation; running (machine, engine); round

دائرة *dā'ira* pl. دوائر *dawā'ir*² circle (also *math.*); ring; circumference, perimeter, periphery; sphere, scope, range, compass, extent, circuit; field, domain (fig.); official agency, department (esp. *Ir.*, *Syr.*, *Leb.*); office, bureau; department of a court of justice (*Eg.*, *Tun.*); farm, country estate (*eg.*); misfortune, calamity, affliction | في دائرة ... within the framework of ...; على شكل نصف دائرة *'alā šakli niṣfi d.* semicircular; نقطة الدائرة *nuqṭat ad-d.* essential factor, pivot, crucial point, crux; ○ دائرة كهربائية (*kahrabā'īya*) electric circuit; ○ دائرة قصيرة short circuit (*el.*); دائرة المعارف encyclopedia; دوائر الحكومة government circles, الدوائر الرسمية (السياسية, العسكرية) (*rasmīya, siyāsīya, 'askarīya*) official (political, military) circles or quarters (*journ.*); دائرة الاختصاص jurisdiction (of an official agency, esp., of a court of justice); الدائرة السنية (*sanīya*) civil list; دائرة استئنافية (*isti'nāfīya*) appellate court (*Eg.*; *jur.*); دائرة انتخابية (*intikābīya*) electoral district; دارت عليه الدوائر to suffer adversities

دائرى *dā'irī* circular, ring-shaped, annular

مدور *mudawwar* round, circular

مدير *mudīr* head, chief, director; administrator; manager; intendant, superintendent; rector (of a university); mudir, chief officer of a mudiria, approx. = governor (*Eg.*); (pl. مدراء *mudarā'*²) administrative officer at the head of a county (*Syr.*, *Leb.*, *Ir.*, *Saudi Ar.*) | مدير الجوق *m. al-jauq* bandleader, conductor of an orchestra

مديرة *mudīra* directress; administratress

مديرية *mudīriya* direction; administration; management; — (pl. *-āt*) mudiria, province (*Eg.*); approx.: main department of a ministry (*Ir.*)

مستدير *mustadīr* round; circular | مؤتمر المائدة المستديرة (*mu'tamar al-m.*) round-table conference

دورق *dauraq* pl. دوارق *dawāriq*² (*eg.*) bulging vessel with a long, slender neck, carafe

دوزن *dauzana* to tune (a musical instrument); ○ to tune in (*radio*)

دوزان *dūzān* and دوزنة *dauzana* tuning (of a musical instrument); دوزنة ○ tuning (*radio*)

دوزينة (It. *dozzina*) *dōzīna* dozen

داس (دوس) *dāsa* *u* (*daus*, دياس *diyās*) to tread, step (ـه on); to tread (ـه s.th.); to tread down, trample down, trample underfoot, crush (ـه s.th.); to thresh (grain); to treat with disdain, humiliate (ـه s.o.); to run over (ـه s.o.; automobile) VII pass. of I

دوس *daus* treading, trampling, tread, step

ديسة *dīsa* dense forest, jungle, thicket

دواسة *dauwāsa* pedal

مداس *madās* shoe, sandal

مدوس *madūs*, مداس *mudās* trodden, trampled down; crushed; run over

دوسنطاريا *dusinṭāriyā*, دوسنتاريا dysentery

دوسييه (Fr. *dossier*) *dosyē*, دوسيه *dōsē* pl. *-āt* dossier, file

¹دوش (*eg.*) *dawaš* to irritate (ـه s.o.) or drive s.o. crazy by noise

دوشة *dauša* (*eg.*) din, noise, clamor, uproar, hubbub, hullabaloo

²دوش (Fr. *douche*) *dūš* pl. *-āt* shower, douche

دوطة (It. *dote*) *dōṭa* dowry

دوغ II to imprint a mark, to brand

داغ *dāḡ* pl. *-āt* brand (on cattle)

(دوف) داف *dāfa u* (*dauf*) to mix, mingle (ه ب s.th. with); to add, admix (ه في s.th. to)

دوق *dūq* duke

دوقة *dūqa* duchess

دوقي *dūqī* ducal

دوقية *dūqīya* dukedom, duchy

دوك II to chatter, prattle

دوكة *dauka* din, row, hubbub, tumult, confusion

(دول)[1] دال *dāla u* (دولة *daula*) to change periodically, take turns, alternate, rotate; to change, turn (time, fortune) | دالت دولة الاستبداد the time of absolutism is over, belongs to the past; دالت له الدولة fortune has turned in his favor (عليه against him) III to alternate, rotate (ه, ه s.o., s.th.); to cause to succeed by turns or to follow one another (الايام *al-ayyāma* the days; God); to alternate (بين between); to confer, talk (ه with s.o., في about), discuss (ه في with s.o. s.th.) IV to give ascendancy, afford superiority, give the upper hand (ه من to s.o. over); to make victorious, let triumph (ه على s.o. over), grant victory (ه على to s.o. over); to replace (ه ب or من s.th. with), exchange, substitute (ه ب or من for s.th. s.th.) | اديل لبنى العباس من بنى امية *udīla li-banī l-'abbāsi min banī umayyata* the rule passed from the Ommaiads to the Abbasides VI to alternate, take turns (ه with or in s.th., e.g., in some work); to hand each other s.th. (ه), pass s.th. (ه) alternately between themselves; to handle alternately (ه different things), take now this, now that; to exchange (الراى *ar-ra'y* views); to make frequent use (ه of s.th.); to confer, have a discussion, take counsel, deliberate; to parley, negotiate; to circulate, be in circulation, be current, have currency | تداولته الايدى *tadāwalathu l-aidī* it passed from hand to hand, it made the rounds, it circulated; تداولته الالسن (*alsun*) it passed from mouth to mouth, it was the talk of the town, it was on everybody's lips

دولة *daula* pl. دول *duwal* alternation, rotation, change; change of time, turn of fortune; dynasty; state, country; power, empire | صاحب الدولة title of the Prime Minister; دولة رئيس الحكومة *daulat r. al-ḥ.* His Excellency, the Prime Minister; فخامة الدولة *fakāmat ad-d.* title of the President of the Republic (*Syr.*, *Leb.*); الدولة العلية (*'alīya*) name of the ancient Ottoman Empire; الدول الكبرى (or العظمى) (*kubrā, 'uẓmā*) the big powers; دولة منتدبة (*muntadaba*) mandatory power

دولة (*dam.*, pronounced *dōle* = ركوة *rakwa*) metal vessel with long curved handle used for making coffee

دولى *daulī* state (adj.); *duwalī* international

دولية *duwalīya* internationality; internationalism; the International

دويلات *duwailāt* petty states, small countries

دواليك *dawālaika* alternately, by turns; successively, one by one, one after the other | وهكذا دواليك (*wa-hākaḏā*) and so forth, and so on

تدويل *tadwīl* internationalization

مداولة *mudāwala* pl. *-āt* parley, negotiation; deliberation, consultation; discussion; *mudāwalatan* alternately, one after the other, one at a time

تداول *tadāwul* alternation, rotation; circulation, currency; circulation of money | بالتداول alternately, by turns, one by one

متداول *mutadāwal* current, circulating, in circulation; valid; common, in common use, prevailing | الكلام المتداول (*kalām*) the colloquial language

[2]دوال *dawālin* see دلو

دولاب *dūlāb* pl. دواليب *dawālīb*[2] wheel; tire; gearing, gears, wheels, mechanism, machine, machinery, closet, locker, cabinet, cupboard | دولاب للملابس wardrobe

دولار *dōlār* pl. *-āt* dollar

[1](دوم) دام *dāma u* (*daum*, دوام *dawām*) to last, continue, go on; to persevere, persist | ما دام *mā dāma* as long as; (the more so) since, inasmuch as, as, because; while he is ..., when he is ...; ما دام حيا (*ḥayyan*) as long as he is alive; ما دمت معك (*dumtu*) so long as (or while) I am with you **II** to move in a circle, turn, spin, revolve, rotate, gyrate, circle; to turn, revolve, spin, twirl (ه s.th.) **III** to persevere, persist (على in), apply o.s. diligently and steadily (على to), pursue with diligence and perseverance (على s.th.); to continue **IV** to cause to last or continue, perpetuate, make lasting, make permanent (ه s.th.) **X** to make (ه s.th.) last or continue; to continue, go on (ه with s.th.)

دوم *daum* continuance, permanence, duration; دوما *dauman* constantly, at all times, ever, always; — doom palm (*bot.*)

ديمة *dīma* pl. ديم *diyam*, ديوم *duyūm* continuous rain

دوام *dawām* duration, continuance, permanence, perpetuity; uninterrupted succession; endurance, perseverance; abiding, stay (of s.o., في at a place); دواما *dawāman* and على الدوام permanently, perpetually, at all times, ever, always | ساعات الدوام ,اوقات الدوام ,وقت الدوام working hours, office hours (*Ir.*, *Syr.*)

ديمومة *daimūma* = دوام

دوامة *duwwāma* top (child's toy); whirlpool, eddy, vortex

مداومة *mudāwama* perseverance, endurance, persistence; continuance, duration; continuation

دائم *dā'im* lasting, enduring; endless, eternal, perpetual, everlasting; perennial; continued, continuous, continual, incessant, unceasing, constant; permanent, standing, established; durable | دائم التقدم والنمو *d. at-taqaddum wa-n-numūw* in a state of constant progress and growth

دائما *dā'iman* always | دائما ابدا (*abadan*) always and ever

دائمي *dā'imī* = دائم

مدام *mudām* wine

مستديم *mustadīm* constant, continuous, continual, incessant, uninterrupted

[2]دومان *dūmān* rudder, helm

دومانجي *dūmānjī* steersman, helmsman

[1]دون **II** to record, write down, set down, put down in writing (ه s.th.); to enter, list, register, book (ه s.th.); to collect (ه poems) | دون شرطا (*šarṭan*) to stipulate a condition **V** to be recorded, be written down, be put down in writing

ديوان *dīwān* pl. دواوين *dawāwīn*[2] account books of the treasury (in the older Islamic administration); divan, collection of poems written by one author; governmental office, administrative office; chancellery, office, bureau, secretariat; council of state, cabinet; council, consultative assembly, board of advisers, executive committee; government; court of justice, tribunal; hall; davenport, divan; (railway) compartment | لغة الدواوين *luġat ad-d.* official jargon, officialese; ديوان التفتيش inquisitional court; the Inquisition

ديواني *dīwānī* administrative, administrational, official; an Ottoman style of cursive (used by the secretaries of the State Chancellery for treaties, diplomas, firmans, etc.)

تدوين *tadwīn* recording, writing down; entry, listing, booking; registering, registration

مدونة *mudawwana* pl. *-āt* record, note; entry; body of laws; pl. مدونات writings, literature (on a given subject)

دون[2] *dūn* low, lowly; bad, poor, inferior; meager, inadequate | عامله بالدون (*'āmalahū*) he snubbed him

دون *dūna* (prep.) below, beneath, under (in rank, value, etc.); this side of, short of; before; without; more than; with the exclusion of, leaving ... aside, disregarding ...; and not by any means, but not | دون ذلك (with foll. nominative) on the way to that, there is ..., before accomplishing that one must ..., دون ذلك خرط القتاد (*kart al-qatād*) before one can do that, one must strip the tragacanth of its leaves, i.e., accomplish the impossible; بدون, من دون (*dūni*) without; with the exclusion of, excluding; بدون ان and من دون ان without (+ foll. gerund in Engl.); دونك *dūnaka* (with foll. acc.) here you are! take ...! watch out (ه for)! beware (ه of)! هو دونه he is below him, he doesn't measure up to him; كان دونه اهمية (*ahammiyatan*) to be of less importance than ...; اثم دونه كل اثم *iṯmun dūnahū kullu iṯmin* a sin to end all sins; الذين هم دون السن العسكرية (*sinn, 'askariya*) those below the age for military service; دون ما نظر الى (*naẓarin*) regardless of, irrespective of; دون ما فائدة with no benefit at all; completely useless; تخشى ان يسعدن دونها (*takšā an yas'adna*) she is afraid they will be happier than she is; تلك الكتب دون غيرها (*kutub, ġairihā*) those books and no others; انا متعجب من فضلك دون علمك (*muta'ajjib, faḍlika, 'ilmika*) I admire your virtue, but not your knowledge, or, I admire your virtue more than your knowledge; كم الافواه دون التذمر والشكوى (*kamma, taḏammur, šakwā*) he stopped their mouths to keep them from muttering and complaining; اذا كان الغصن دون ما يحتمله (*ġuṣnu, yaḥtamiluhū*) if the branch is not strong enough to carry him; وصل دونهم الى الغاية it was he, not they, who reached the goal; اشاحت بوجهها دونه (*ašāḥat bi-wajhihā*) she averted her face so that he could not see her; حال دون الشيء to prevent s.th.; الاشعة دون الحمراء (*aši''a, ḥamrā'*) the infrared rays; الموجات دون القصيرة (*maujāt*) ultra-short waves (*radio*)

دونم *dūnum* a square measure (*Ir.* = about 2500 m²; *Pal.* = roughly, 900 m²)

دوى[1] *dawā* and II to sound, resound, ring out; to drone; to echo, reverberate III to treat (ه a patient, ه a disease) VI to treat o.s. (with a medicine); to be cured

دوى *dawan* pl. ادواء *adwā'* sickness, illness, disease, malady

دوى *dawīy* sound, noise, ring, clang, roar, thunder, drone; echo, reverberation

دواة *dawāh* (□ دواية *dawāya*) pl. دوى *duwīy*, *diwīy*, دويات *dawayāt* inkwell

دواء *dawā'* pl. ادوية *adwiya* remedy, medicament, medication, medicine, drug

دوائى *dawā'ī* medicinal, medicative, curative

دوه see داه

دواء *diwā'* treatment, therapy (*med.*)

مداواة *mudāwāh* treatment, therapy (*med.*)

تداو *tadāwin* cure

دوى[2] (Fr. *douille*) *dūy* socket (of a light bulb)

ديالوج *diyalōg* (Eg. spelling) pl. *-āt* dialogue

ديباج and ديباجة see دبج

ديوث *dayyūṯ* (□ ديوس) cuckold; procurer, pimp; a variety of warbler (*zool.*)

ديجور see دجر

الديجوليون *ad-dēgōlīyūn* (Eg. spelling) the Gaullists

دياجى see دجو

ديدبان *daidabān, daidubān* pl. *-āt,* ديادبة *dayādiba* guard, sentry; sentinel | ديدبان المراكب ship's pilot

ديدن see ددن

دير, ديرة, اديار, ديار, ديرى اديرة, ديرانى see دور

ديس *dīs* diss (Ampelodesma tenax; *bot.*)

ديم see دسم

ديسة see دوس

ديوس see ديوث

ديسمبر *disembir, disambir* December

ديك *dīk* pl. ديكة *dīka,* ديوك *duyūk,* ادياك *adyāk* cock, rooster | ديك الحبش *d. al-ḥabaš* turkey, turkey cock; ديك رومى (*rūmī*) do.; وزن الديك *wazn ad-d.* bantamweight

السعال الديكى *as-su'āl ad-dīkī* whooping cough

دكتاتورى = ديكتاتورى

ديكور (Fr. *décor*) pl. *-āt* décor, stage decoration

ديماس *daimās, dīmās,* ديموس *daimūs* pl. دياميس *dayāmīs*[2] dungeon, vault

ديمة, ديم, ديمومة see دوم

ديموطيق *dīmūṭīqī* demotic (writing)

ديمقراطى, ديموقراطى *dimuqrāṭī* democratic; democrat

ديمقراطية, ديموقراطية *dimuqrāṭīya* pl. *-āt* democracy; democratic attitude or conviction

[1](دين) دان *dāna i* to borrow, take up a loan; to be a debtor, be indebted; to owe (ل ب s.o. s.th., also, e.g., دان له بالشكر (*šukr*) *d. lahū bi-š-šukr* to owe s.o. one's thanks; ب s.th., e.g., بالحياة *bi-l-ḥayāh* one's life, ل to s.th. or s.o.); to be indebted (ل ب to s.o. for); to be subject, subject o.s., bow, yield, (ل to s.o. or s.th.), be under s.o.'s (ل) power, owe allegiance (ل to s.o.), obey (ل s.o.); to grant a loan, lend money (ه to s.o.); to subject, subjugate (ه s.o.); to requite, repay (ه s.o.); to condemn (ه s.o.), pass judgment (ه on s.o.) **III** to have a debt (ه with s.o.), be indebted (ه to s.o.); to be the creditor (ه of s.o.), have a money claim (ه on s.o.) | داينه بمبلغ خمسة قروش (*bi-mablağ ḵamsat q.*) he had a claim of five piasters on him **IV** to lend money (ه to s.o.); to sell on credit (ه to s.o.); to convict, find guilty, pronounce guilty (ه s.o.) **V** to be indebted, have debts; to subject o.s. (ل to) **VI** تداينوا بدين (*dain*) to contract a mutual loan, borrow money from each other **X** to make or incur debts, take up a loan

دين *dain* pl. ديون *duyūn* debt; pecuniary obligation, liability; obligation (*Isl. Law*); claim (*Isl. Law*), financial claim | بالدين on credit; رب الدين *rabb ad-d.* creditor; ديون الحرب *d. al-ḥarb* war debts; دين مضمون bonded, or funded, debt; دين ممتاز (*mumtāz*) preferred, or privileged, debt; دين موحد (*muwaḥḥad*) consolidated debt; دين مطلق (*muṭlaq*) debt not bound to the physical person of the debtor, but outliving him (*Isl. Law*); دين مستغرق (*mustağriq*) claims against an estate which exceed or equal the assets (*Isl. Law*)

دينونة *dainūna* judgment; Last Judgment

الديان *ad-dayyān* the Judge (attribute of God)

مدينة *madīna* pl. مدائن *madā'in*[2], مدن *mudun* town, city; المدينة Medina (city in W Saudi Arabia); see مدن

ادانة *idāna* verdict of guilty; conviction | صدر الحكم بادانته *ṣadara l-ḥukmu bi-idānatihī* he was convicted

استدانة *istidāna* incurrence of debts

دائن *dā'in* creditor

مديون *madyūn* indebted, in debt; obligated, under obligation

مديونية *madyūnīya* indebtedness, obligation

مدين *madīn* owing; indebted, obligated, under obligation; debtor | مدين بالشكر (*šukr*) owing gratitude, much obliged; كان مدينا ل to be indebted to s.o., stand in s.o.'s debt

مدين *mudīn* moneylender, creditor

مدان *mudān* convicted, found guilty; guilty; judged, condemned

[2](دين) دان *dāna* *i* to profess (ب a religion, a conviction, etc.) | دان بالاسلام to profess Islam; دان بعاداته (*bi-ʿādātihī*) to adhere to one's customs V to profess (ب a religion)

دين *dīn* pl. اديان *adyān* religion, creed, faith, belief | يوم الدين *yaum ad-d.* the Day of Judgment

دينى *dīnī* religious; spiritual | لاديني irreligious; ○ العلم الديني (*ʿilm*) science of religion

دين *dayyin* religious, pious, godly, devout

ديانة *diyāna* pl. *-āt* religion; communion, confession, denomination, sect | صاحب الديانة founder of a religion

ديان *dayyān* pious, godly, devout, religious

تدين *tadayyun* piety, godliness, devoutness, religiousness, religiosity

متدين *mutadayyin* pious, godly, devout, religious

متدينة *mutadayyina* religious community

دينار *dīnār* pl. دنانير *danānīr*[2] dinar, a monetary unit (*Ir.*, *Jord.*); pl. دنانير money

دينارى *dīnārī* diamonds (of a deck of cards)

دينامو *dīnāmō* dynamo, generator

ديناميت *dīnāmīt* dynamite

○ دينم *dainam* pl. ديانم *dayānim*[2] dynamo, generator

دية see ودى

ديوان pl. دواوين and ديوانى see دون[1]

ذ

ذا *ḏā* (demonstr. pron.) pl. اولاء *ulāʾi* this one, this; بذا *bi-ḏā* by this, by this means, thereby; لذا *li-ḏā* therefore; كذا *ka-ḏā* so, thus, in this manner; so and so, so and so much; هكذا *hā-ka-ḏā* so, thus, in this manner; serves as intensifier after interrogative pronouns (roughly corresponding in English to such phrases as: ... on earth, ... then, or the like): ماذا what on earth? لماذا why then? why in heaven's name? — هو ذا *huwa ḏā*, f. هى دى *hiya ḏī* that one; look at that one! why, that is .... now if that isn't ...!; هاءنذا *hāʾana-ḏā* behold, it is I, here I am, pl. ها نحن اولاء *hā naḥnu ulāʾi*; — used as an accusative in the construct state: master, owner, or possessor of, with ذو nominative (q.v.), ذى as genitive; — ذاك *ḏāka*, f. تاك *tāka*, تيك *tika*, pl. اولائك *ulāʾika* this, this one; اذ ذاك (*iḏ*) then, at that time; in those days; — ذلك *ḏālika*, f. تلك *tilka*, pl. اولائك *ulāʾika* that, that one; بذلك *bi-ḏālika* by that, by that means, in that manner; لذلك *li-ḏālika* therefore; بعد ذلك *baʿda ḏālika* after that, upon that, thereafter, thereupon; مع ذلك *maʿa ḏālika* yet, still, nevertheless, for all that; وذلك ان (*anna*) that is (to say), namely, to wit; وذلك لان (*li-anna*) and that is because ..., for the one reason that ...; ذلك بان (*bi-anna*) this is due to the fact that ...; كذلك *kaḏālika* so, thus, in that manner; equally, likewise, in the same manner; — ذلكم *ḏālikum*, f. تلكم *tilkum*, pl. اولائكم *ulā'ikum* that one; — هذا *hāḏā*, f. هذه *hāḏihī*, هذى *hāḏī*, pl. هؤلاء *hā'ulā'i*, dual m. هذان *hāḏāni*, f. هاتان *hātāni* this, this one, see هذا (alphabetically)

ذأب X to be wolflike, be fierce or cruel like a wolf

ذئب *ḏi'b* pl. ذئاب *ḏi'āb*, ذؤبان *ḏu'bān* dieb (Canis anthus), jackal; wolf | مرض الذئب الاحمر *maraḍ aḏ-ḏ. al-aḥmar* name of a noncontagious skin disease

ذؤابة *ḏu'āba* pl. ذوائب *ḏawā'ib*[2] lock, strand (of hair); tuft, wisp

ذات, ذاتى and ذاتية see ذو

ذاك see ذا

ذال *ḏāl* name of the letter ذ

ذب *ḏabba* *u* to drive away, chase away (ه, ه s.o., s.th.); to defend (عن s.o., s.th.)

ذباب *ḏubāb* (coll.; n.un. ة) pl. اذبة *aḏibba*, ذبان *ḏibbān* flies, fly | ذباب قارض gadfly, horsefly

ذبابة *ḏubāba* pl. *-āt* (n. un. of ذباب) fly; tip (of the sword, or the like)

ذبانة *ḏubbāna*, *ḏibbāna* fly; sight, bead (on a firearm)

مذبة *miḏabba* fly whisk, fly swatter

ذبح *ḏabaḥa* *a* (*ḏabḥ*) to kill (by slitting the throat); to slaughter, butcher; to massacre; to murder, slay; to sacrifice, offer up, immolate (ه an animal) **II** to kill, slaughter, butcher, massacre, murder

ذبح *ḏabḥ* slaughtering, slaughter

ذبح *ḏibḥ* sacrificial victim, blood sacrifice

ذبحة *ḏibḥa*, *ḏubḥa* angina (*med.*); diphtheria | الذبحة الصدرية (*ṣadrīya*) angina pectoris (*med.*); ○ الذبحة الفؤادية (*fu'ādīya*) do.

ذباح *ḏabbāḥ* slaughtering, killing, murdering; slaughterer, butcher

ذبيح *ḏabīḥ* slaughtered

ذبيحة *ḏabīḥa* pl. ذبائح *ḏabā'iḥ*[2] slaughter animal; sacrificial victim, blood sacrifice; sacrifice, immolation; offering, oblation

مذبح *maḏbaḥ* pl. مذابح *maḏābiḥ*[2] slaughterhouse; altar (*Chr.*)

مذبحة *maḏbaḥa* massacre, slaughter, carnage, butchery

ذبذب *ḏabḏaba* to set into a swinging motion, swing, dangle (ه s.th.) **II** *taḏabḏaba* to swing, pendulate; to oscillate (*el.*); to be deflected (magnetic needle); to vibrate; to fluctuate; to waver, vacillate, hesitate

ذبذبة *ḏabḏaba* pl. *-āt* pendulous motion, pendulation; oscillation (*el.*); vibration

تذبذب *taḏabḏub* pendulous motion, pendulation, swinging; oscillation (*el.*); deflection (of a magnetic needle)

○ مذبذب *muḏabḏib* oscillator (*el.*)

مذبذب *muḏabḏab* fluctuating, variable; vacillating, wavering, hesitant, unsteady

متذبذب *mutaḏabḏib*: تيار متذبذب (*tayyār*) oscillating current (*el.*)

ذبل *ḏabala*, *ḏabula* *u* (*ḏabl*, ذبول *ḏubūl*) to be wilted, to wilt, wither; to fade; to become dry, dry up; to waste away; to become dull, lose its luster (eye)

ذبل *ḏabl* mother-of-pearl, nacre

ذبالة *ḏubāla* wick

ذابل *ḏābil* pl. ذبل *ḏubul* wilted, withered; dry, dried up; faded (color); languid, dull, lackluster, languishing (glance); feeble, weak, tired

ذحل **ḏaḥl** pl. اذحال aḏḥāl, ذحول ḏuḥūl resentment, rancor, hatred; revengefulness, vindictiveness; blood revenge

ذخر **ḏaḵara** *a* to keep, preserve, store away, put away (ه s.th.); to save, lay by (ه s.th.) VIII ادخر *iddaḵara* to keep, preserve, store away, put away (ه s.th.); to store, accumulate, gather, hoard, amass (ه s.th.); to lay by (ه s.th.); to save (ه s.th., also strength, trouble, etc.) | ادخر حبا ل (*ḥubban*) to harbor love for; لا يدخر جهدا (*juhdan*) he spares no effort

ذخر *ḏuḵr* pl. اذخار *aḏḵār* s.th. stored away, put by, hoarded, or accumulated; stores, supplies; treasure

ذخيرة *ḏaḵīra* pl. ذخائر *ḏaḵā'ir*[2] treasure; stores, supplies; provisions, food; ammunition (*mil.*); (holy) relic

ادخار *iddiḵār* storage; hoarding, amassing, accumulation; storing, gathering; saving

مذخر *muḏaḵḵir* pl. *-ūn* assistant gunner, ammunition passer (*mil., Syr.*)

مذخر *muḏaḵḵar* pl. *-āt* supply

مدخرة *muddaḵira* pl. *-āt* (*Syr.*) storage battery, battery

ذرة[1] **ḏura** see ذرو

ذر[2] **ḏarra** *u* (*ḏarr*) to strew, scatter, spread (ه s.th.); to sprinkle (ه ب on s.th. s.th.) | ذر الرماد فى عينيه (*ar-ramāda fī 'ainaihi*) to throw dust in s.o.'s eyes; — *u* (ذرور *ḏurūr*) to rise, come up, rise resplendent over the horizon (sun) | ذر قرنه (*qarnuhū*) it began to show, it emerged

ذر *ḏarr* strewing, scattering, sprinkling; (coll.) tiny particles, atoms, specks, motes

ذرة *ḏarra* (n. un.) pl. *-āt* atom; tiny particle; speck, mote | مثقال ذرة *miṯqāl ḏ.* the weight of a dust particle, a tiny amount; a little bit; مقدار ذرة *miqdār ḏ.* a tiny amount, a jot, an iota; ذرة من الشك (*šakk*) the least doubt

ذرى *ḏarrī* atomic | قنبلة ذرية (*qunbula*) atomic bomb; النشاط الذرى (*našāṭ*) and طاقة ذرية (*ṭāqa*) atomic energy

ذرور *ḏarūr* powder

ذرورى *ḏarūrī* powdery, powdered, pulverized

ذريرة *ḏarīra* pl. ذرائر *ḏarā'ir*[2] fragrant powder, cosmetic scented powder

ذرى *ḏurrī* of or pertaining to the offspring or progeny

ذرية *ḏurrīya* pl. *-āt*, ذرارى *ḏarārīy* progeny, descendants, children, offspring

يذر[3] *yaḏaru* see (وذر)

ذرب **ḏariba** *a* (*ḏarab*) to be sharp, cutting

ذرب *ḏarab* diarrhea (*med.*)

ذرب *ḏarib* pl. ذرب *ḏurb* sharp, cutting | جرح ذرب (*jurḥ*) a malignant, incurable wound

ذراح **ḏurrāḥ** pl. ذراريح *ḏarārīḥ*[2] Spanish fly, blister beetle (*zool.*)

ذرع **ḏara'a** *a* (*ḏar'*) to measure (ه s.th.); to take the measure or measurements (ه of s.th.); to cover (ه a distance); to cross, traverse (ه a country), travel through (ه); to intercede, intervene, mediate, put in a word (ل for s.o., on behalf of s.o., عند with s.o. else) V to use, employ, apply (بذريعة *bi-ḏarī'a* or بوسيلة *bi-wasīla* a means, an expedient); to use as a pretext, as an excuse (ب s.th.); to use as a means (ب s.th., الى to an end) VII to proceed, advance; to intervene

ذرع *ḏar'* power, ability, capability (ب to do s.th.) | ضاق ذرعا ب and ضاق عنه ذرعا (*ḏar'an*) not to be up to s.th., be unable to do or accomplish s.th.; to be unable to stand or bear s.th., be fed up with, be tired of, feel uneasy about, be oppressed by

ذراع *ḏirāʿ* f. and m., pl. اذرع *aḏruʿ*, ذرعان *ḏurʿān* arm; forearm; connecting rod; cubit, in Syria = .68 m | in Egypt: ذراع بلدى (*baladī*) = .58 m, ذراع استانبولى (*istanbūlī*) = .665 m, ذراع هندازة (*hindāza*) = .656 m, ذراع معمارى (*miʿmārī*) = ca. .75 m, ذراع معمارى مربع (*murabbaʿ*) = .5625 m²; in Iraq: ذراع حلبي (*ḥalabī*) = ca. .68 m, ذراع بغدادى (*baḡdādī*) or ذراع بلدى (*baladī*) = ca. .80 m, ذراع معمارى see above

ذريع *ḏarīʿ* stepping lively, walking briskly; rapid, quick; torrential; rapidly spreading, sweeping (death); devastating; intercessor

ذريعة *ḏarīʿa* pl. ذرائع *ḏarāʾiʿ*², medium, means, expedient; pretext, excuse

ذرف **ḏarafa** *i* (*ḏarf*, ذريف *ḏarīf*, ذروف *ḏurūf*, ذرفان *ḏarafān*) to flow, well forth (tears); to shed (ه tears; said of the eye) **II** to exceed (على an age) **X** to let flow, shed (ه tears)

ذرق **ḏaraqa** *i u* (*ḏarq*) to drop excrement (bird) **IV** do.

ذرق *ḏarq* droppings, excrement (of a bird)

(ذرو and ذرى) ذرا **ḏarā** *u* (*ḏarw*) to disperse, scatter (ه s.th.); to carry off, blow away (ه dust; said of the wind); to winnow, fan (ه grain); — ذرى *ḏarā* *i* (*ḏary*) do. **II** do. **IV** = **I**; to throw down, throw off (ه, ه s.o., s.th.) | اذرت العين الدمع (*damʿa*) the eye shed tears **V** to be winnowed, be fanned; to climb (ه on), scale (ه s.th.); to seek shade or shelter (ب in, at, under); to take refuge (ب with), flee (ب to) **X** to take refuge (ب with), place o.s. under s.o.'s (ب) protection, flee (ب to s.o.)

ذرة *ḏura* durra, a variety of sorghum | ذرة شامى (*eg.*) Indian corn, maize (Zea mays L.); ذرة صفراء (*ṣafrā'*) do. (*syr.*); ذرة عويجة (*eg.*) a variety of millet (Andropogon Sorghum Brot. var. Schweinfurthianus Kcke.); ذرة بيضاء (*baiḍā'*) millet (*syr.*)

ذرى *ḏaran* protection, shelter

ذروة *ḏurwa*, *ḏirwa* pl. ذرى *ḏuran* summit; top; peak; culmination, climax, acme, apex

مذرى *miḏran* and مذراة *miḏrāh* pl. مذار *maḏārin* winnow, winnowing fork

ذعر **ḏaʿara** *a* (*ḏaʿr*) to frighten, scare, alarm, terrify (ه s.o.); pass. *ḏuʿira* to be frightened (ل by), get alarmed (ل at); — *ḏaʿira* *a* (*ḏaʿar*) to be terrified, alarmed, dismayed **IV** to frighten, scare, alarm, terrify (ه s.o.) **V** and **VII** to be frightened, become alarmed

ذعر *ḏuʿr*, fright, terror, alarm, panic

ذعر *ḏaʿar* fright, alarm, dismay, consternation

ذعاف *ḏuʿāf* lethal, deadly, immediately killing (poison) | موت ذعاف (*maut*) a sudden, immediate death

ذعق **ḏaʿaqa** *a* (*ḏaʿq*) to frighten (ه s.o.) by screaming

ذعن **ḏaʿina** *a* (*ḏaʿan*) and **IV** to submit, yield, give in (ل to s.o.), obey (ل s.o., an order, etc.); to concede voluntarily, grant willingly (ل ب to s.o. s.th.)

اذعان *iḏʿān* submissiveness, pliability, compliance, obedience

مذعن *muḏʿin* submissive, pliable, tractable, obedient

مذعان *miḏʿān* pliable, tractable, docile, obedient, obliging, compliant

ذفر **ḏafar** pungent smell, stench

ذقن **ḏaqan**, *ḏiqan* pl. اذقان *aḏqān*, ذقون *ḏuqūn* chin; — *ḏaqn* f., pl. ذقون *ḏuqūn* beard, whiskers | ذقن الشيخ *ḏ. aš-šaiḵ* wormwood, absinthe; خروا لاذقانهم *ḵarrū li-aḏqānihim* they prostrated themselves;

غرق فى العمل حتى الذقن (*ġariqa fī l-'amal*) to be up to one's neck in work, be swamped by work (properly: to drown in work); ضحك على ذقنه (*ḍaḥika*) pl. على ذقونهم (*eg., syr.*) to fool s.o., make fun of s.o., lead s.o. around by the nose (ب with s.th.); to put on an act for s.o.; ضحك فى ذقنه to laugh in s.o.'s face

ذكر **ḏakara** *u* (*ḏikr*, تذكار *taḏkār*) to remember, bear in mind (ه s.th.), think (ه of); to keep in mind (ه s.th.); to recall, recollect (ه s.th.); — (*ḏikr*) to speak, talk (ه of, about); to name, mention, cite, quote (ه s.th.); to state, designate, indicate (ه s.th.); to give (ه e.g., facts, data); to point, refer (ه to s.th.); to report, relate, tell (ل ه s.th. to s.o.) | تقدم يذكر *taqaddumun yuḏkaru* notable progress; لا يذكر (*yuḏkaru*) inconsiderable, not worth mentioning; ذكره بخير (بالخير) (*ḵair*) to have pleasant memories of s.o., hold s.o. in fond remembrance; to speak well of s.o.; ذكره بشر (*šarr*) to have unpleasant memories of s.o.; to speak ill of s.o. **II** to remind (ه ب s.o. of s.th.), point out (ب ه to s.o. s.th.), call s.o.'s (ه) attention (ب to); to make (ه a word) masculine (*gram.*) **III** to parley, negotiate, confer, have a talk, take counsel (ه with s.o.); to memorize, commit to memory, learn, study (ه one's assignment, one s lessons) | ذاكر دروسه (*durūsahū*) to study one's lessons, do one's homework **IV** to remind (ه ه s.o. of s.th.), call (ه s.th.) to s.o.'s (ه) mind **V** to remember, bear in mind (ه s.th.), think (ه of s.th.) **VI** to remind each other (ه of), revive each other's memory of (ه); to confer (together), have a talk, take counsel **VIII** ادكر *iddakara* = **V**; **X** to remember, recall, keep in mind, know by heart (ه s.th.)

ذكر **ḏikr** recollection, remembrance, reminiscence, memory, commemoration; reputation, repute, renown; naming, stating, mention(ing), quoting, citation; report, account, narration, narrative; invocation of God, mention of the Lord's name; (in Sufism) incessant repetition of certain words or formulas in praise of God, often accompanied by music and dancing | على ذكر (with foll. genit.) apropos of, speaking of ...; وعلى ذكر ذلك speaking of that, incidentally, in that connection; الذكر الحكيم the Koran; سالف الذكر above-mentioned, afore-mentioned; سعيد الذكر of blessed memory, deceased, late; اشاد بذكره (*ašāda*) to celebrate, praise, commend s.o. or s.th., speak in glowing terms of s.o. or s.th.; ما زال على ذكر من (*ḏikrin min*) he still remembered ..., he could still recall ...

ذكر **ḏakar** pl. ذكور *ḏukūr*, ذكورة *ḏukūra*, ذكران *ḏukrān* male; (pl. ذكور) penis

ذكرة **ḏukra** reputation, repute, renown

ذكرى **ḏikrā** pl. ذكريات *ḏikrayāt* remembrance, recollection, memory; pl. reminiscences, memoirs

ذكير **ḏakīr** steel

تذكار **taḏkār, tiḏkār** remembrance; reminder, memento; memory, commemoration; souvenir, keepsake; memorial day | تذكار جميع القديسين *t. jamī' al-qiddīsīn* All Saints' Day (*Chr.*)

تذكارى **taḏkārī, tiḏkārī** serving to remind, helping the memory; memorial, commemorative

تذكرة **taḏkira** reminder; memento

تذكرة **taḏkira**, mostly pronounced *taḏkara*, pl. تذاكر *taḏākir*[2] message, note; slip, paper, permit, pass; card; ticket; admission ticket | تذكرة بريد postcard; تذكرة اثبات الشخصية *t. iṯbāt aš-šaḵṣīya* identity card; تذكرة ذهاب واياب *t. ḏahāb wa-iyāb* round-trip ticket; تذكرة الرصيف (*eg.*) platform ticket; تذكرة اشتراك subscriptiou ticket; تذكرة طبية (*ṭibbīya*) medical prescription; تذكرة مرور permit, pass, laissez-passer; passport; تذكرة النفوس

(*Syr.*) identity card (= بطاقة شخصية *Eg.*); تذكرة الانتخاب *t. al-intiḵāb* ballot

تذكرجي *taḏkarjī*, تذكرى *taḏkarī* ticket seller, ticket clerk; (streetcar) conductor

تذكير *taḏkīr* reminding (of s.o., ب of s.th.), reminder, memento; fecundation, pollination (of female blossoms; in pomiculture)

مذاكرة *muḏākara* pl. *-āt* negotiation, consultation, conference; deliberation (of a court; *Syr.*); learning, memorizing, memorization; study

تذكر *taḏakkur* memory, remembrance, recollection

استذكار *istiḏkār* memorizing, memorization, committing to memory

ذاكرة *ḏākira* memory

مذكور *maḏkūr* mentioned; said, abovementioned; celebrated | لم يكن شيئا مذكورا *lam yakun šai'an m.* it was of no importance, it was nothing

مذكر *muḏakkar* masculine (*gram.*)

مذكرة *muḏakkira* pl. *-āt* reminder; note; remark; notebook; memorandum, memorial, aide-mémoire, (diplomatic) note; ordinance, decree; treatise, paper, report (of a learned society, = Fr. *mémoires*); pl. reminiscences, memoirs | مذكرة الاتهام *m. al-ittihām* bill of indictment (*jur.*); مذكرة الجلب *m. al-jalb* writ of habeas corpus; مذكرة شفاهية (*šifāhīya*) verbal note (*dipl.*)

(ذكو and ذكى) ذكا *ḏakā u* (*ḏukūw*, ذكا *ḏakan*, ذكاء *ḏakā'*) to blaze, flare up (fire); to exude a strong odor; — ذكى *ḏakiya* (ذكاء *ḏakā'*) to be sharp-witted, intelligent II and IV to cause to blaze, fan (ه the fire); to kindle (ه s.th.) II to immolate an animal X = *ḏakā*

ذكاء *ḏakā'* acumen, mental acuteness, intelligence, brightness; — *ḏukā'*[2] the sun

ذكى *ḏakīy* pl. اذكياء *aḏkiyā'*[2] intelligent, sharp-witted, clever, bright; redolent, fragrant; tasty, savory, delicious

ذل *ḏalla* *i* (*ḏall*, *ḏull*, ذلالة *ḏalāla*, ذلة *ḏilla*, مذلة *maḏalla*) to be low, lowly, humble, despised, contemptible II to lower, debase, degrade, humiliate, humble (ه, ه s.o., s.th.); to subject, break, subdue, conquer (ه s.o.); to overcome, surmount (ه difficulties, obstacles) IV to lower, debase, degrade, humiliate, humble (ه, ه s.o., s.th.); to subject, break, subdue, conquer (ه, ه s.o., s.th.) V to lower o.s., humble o.s., cringe (الى or ل before s.o.); to be humble, obsequious X to think (ه s.o.) low or despicable; to think little (ه of), disesteem (ه s.o.); to deride, flout, disparage, run down (ه s.o.)

ذل *ḏull* lowness, lowliness, insignificance; ignominy, disgrace, shame, degradation, humiliation; humility, humbleness, meekness, submissiveness

ذلة *ḏilla* lowness, baseness, vileness, depravity; submissiveness, obsequiousness

ذليل *ḏalīl* pl. اذلاء *aḏillā'*[2], اذلة *aḏilla* low, lowly; despised, despicable, contemptible; docile, tractable, pliable; humble, submissive, abject, servile; obsequious, cowering, cringing

ذلول *ḏalūl* pl. ذلل *ḏulul* docile, tractable, gentle (animal); female riding camel

مذلة *maḏalla* humbleness, meekness, submissiveness; humiliation

تذليل *taḏlīl* derogation, degradation, bemeaning; overcoming, conquering, surmounting (of difficulties, of an obstacle, and the like)

اذلال *iḏlāl* degradation, debasement, humiliation

تذلل *taḏallul* self-abasement

ذلذل ḏulḏul pl. ذلاذل ḏalāḏil² lowest, nethermost part of s.th.; train, hem (of a garment) | ذلاذل الناس the mob, the riffraff

اذلف aḏlaf², f. ذلفاء ḏalfā'², pl. ذلف ḏulf having a small and finely chiseled nose

ذلق ḏalq tip, point; tip of the tongue

الحروف الذلق al-ḥurūf aḏ-ḏulq, الحروف الذلقية and الحروف الذولقية (ḏaulaqīya) the liquids *r, l, n* (*phon.*)

ذلق ḏalq, ḏaliq, ذليق ḏulīq eloquent, glib, facile (tongue)

ذلاقة ḏalāqa eloquence, glibness (of the tongue)

ذاك etc., see ذا

ذم ḏamma u (ḏamm, مذمة maḏamma) to blame, find blameworthy, dispraise, criticize (ه s.o.), find fault (ه with s.o.) II to rebuke, censure sharply (ه s.o.)

ذم ḏamm censure, dispraise, derogation, disparagement

ذمة ḏimma pl. ذمم ḏimam protection, care, custody; covenant of protection, compact; responsibility, answerableness; financial obligation, liability, debt; inviolability, security of life and property; safeguard, guarantee, security; conscience | بالذمة؟ honestly? really? seriously? في ذمتي and على ذمتي upon my word, truly; في ذمته ,بذمته in s.o.'s debt, indebted to s.o.; ما بذمته his debt; على ذمته under s.o.'s protection; at s.o.'s disposal; for the benefit of s.o. or s.th., for s.o. or some purpose (allocation of funds); هي على ذمته she is financially dependent on him, he has to support her; اهل الذمة ahl aḏ-ḏ. the free non-Muslim subjects living in Muslim countries who, in return for paying the capital tax, enjoyed protection and safety; طاهر الذمة of pure conscience, upright, honest; برأ ذمته (barra'a) to relieve one's conscience, meet one's obligation

ذمي ḏimmī a zimmi, a free non-Muslim subject living in a Muslim country (see ذمة ḏimma: اهل الذمة)

ذمام ḏimām pl. اذمة aḏimma right, claim, title; protection, custody; security of life and property | في ذمام الليل fī ḏ. al-lail under cover of darkness

ذميم ḏamīm censured; blameworthy, objectionable, reprehensible; ugly, unfair, nasty

ذميمة ḏamīma pl. ذمائم ḏamā'im² blame, censure

مذمة maḏamma pl. -āt blame, censure

مذموم maḏmūm censured; blameworthy, objectionable, reprehensible

ذمر V to grumble, complain (من or على about)

ذمار ḏimār sacred possession, cherished goods; honor

تذمر taḏammur pl. -āt grumbling, complaint, grievance

ذمي ḏamiya a (ذماء ḏamā') to be in the throes of death

ذماء ḏamā' last remnant; last breath of life | ذماء من الحياة (ḥayāh) last breath of life

ذنب IV to do wrong, commit a sin, a crime, an offense; to be guilty, be culpable X to find or declare (ه s.o.) guilty of a sin, of a crime, of an offense

ذنب ḏanb pl. ذنوب ḏunūb offense, sin, crime, misdeed

ذنب ḏanab pl. اذناب aḏnāb tail; end; adherent (*pol.*), follower, henchman

ذنبي ḏanabī caudal, tail- (in compounds); appendaged, appendant, dependent

ذنيب ḏunaib petiole, leafstalk (*bot.*)

مذنب muḏannab comet

مذنب muḏnib culpable, guilty; sinner; evildoer, delinquent, criminal

ذهب *ḏahaba a* (ذهاب *ḏahāb*, مذهب *maḏhab*) to go (الى to); to betake o.s., travel (الى to); to go away, leave, depart; to disappear, vanish, decline, dwindle; to perish, die, be destroyed; with ب: to carry s.th. off, take s.th. away, abduct, steal s.th., sweep s.th. or s.o. away, annihilate, destroy s.th. or s.o.; ذهب به الى to lead or conduct s.o. to, take s.o. along to; to think, believe (الى s.th.), hold the view, be of the opinion (الى that); to escape (عن s.o.; fig.), slip (عن s.o.'s mind), ذهب عنه ان to lose sight of the fact that ..., forget that ...; to ignore, skip, omit (عن s.th.); (with imperf.) to prepare to ..., be about to ... | ذهب وجاء to go back and forth, walk up and down; ذهب الى ابعد من (*ab'ada*) to go beyond ... (fig.); ما يذهب فى نزعته (*naz'atihī*) what follows along these lines; !اين يذهب بك (*yuḏhabu*) the idea of it! you can't mean it! ذهب سدى (*sudan*) to be futile, be in vain, be of no avail; ذهب ادراج الرياح (*adrāja r-riyāḥ*) to go the ways of the winds, i.e., to pass unnoticed, without leaving a trace; to end in smoke, come to nothing, be futile, be in vain; ذهب كامس الدابر (*ka-amsi d-dābir*) to vanish into thin air, disappear without leaving a trace (lit.: like yesterday gone by); ذهب ببهائه (*bi-bahā'ihī*) to take the glamor away from s.th.; ذهب بنفسه (*bi-nafsihī*) to kill s.o. (joy, terror, etc.); ذهب بخياله (*bi-ḵayālihī*) to let one's imagination wander (الى to); ذهب مذهبه (*maḏhabahū*) to embrace s.o.'s *maḏhab* (see below); to follow s.o.'s teaching, make s.o.'s belief one's own, embrace s.o.'s ideas; to adopt s.o.'s policy, proceed exactly like s.o.; ذهب كل مذهب (*kulla maḏhabin*) to do everything conceivable, leave no stone unturned, go to greatest lengths **II** to gild (ه s.th.) **IV** to cause to go away, make disappear, remove, eliminate (ه s.th.); to take away (ه s.th., عن from s.o.)

V تمذهب *tamaḏhaba* (deriv. of مذهب *maḏhab*) to follow, adopt, embrace (ب a teaching, a religion, etc.)

ذهب *ḏahab* (m. and f.) gold; gold piece, gold coin | ○ ذهب ابيض (*abyaḍ*) platinum

ذهبي *ḏahabī* golden, of gold; precious, excellent, apposite (e.g., advice, saying, etc.) | آية ذهبية golden word, maxim, epigram

ذهبية *ḏahabīya* pl. *-āt* dahabeah, a long light-draft houseboat, used on the Nile

ذهاب *ḏahāb* going; passing, passage, falling away, decrease, dwindling, loss, disappearance; leave, departure; trip, journey; outward-bound trip or journey (as opposed to اياب *iyāb* return trip; railroad); opinion, view (الى ان that) | ذهابا وايابا (*iyāban*) there and back; back and forth, up and down; تذكرة ذهاب واياب *taḏkarat ḏ. wa-iyāb* round-trip ticket

ذهوب *ḏuhūb* going | ذهوب ومآب coming and going; فى جيئة وذهوب coming and going, in a state of fluctuation, having its ups and downs

مذهب *maḏhab* pl. مذاهب *maḏāhib*[2] going, leave, departure; way out, escape (عن from); manner followed, adopted procedure or policy, road entered upon; opinion, view, belief; ideology; teaching, doctrine; movement, orientation, trend (also *pol.*); school; mazhab, orthodox rite of *fiqh* (*Isl. Law*); religious creed, faith, denomination | ○ مذهبه فى الحياة (*ḥayāh*) his philosophy of life, his weltanschauung; المذهب المادى (*māddī*) the materialistic ideology, the materialistic approach to life; ذهب مذهبا بعيدا to go very far, be very extensive

مذهبي *maḏhabī* denominational, confessional; sectarian

مذهبية *maḏhabīya* sectarianism

ذاهب *ḏāhib*: ذاهب اللون *ḏ. al-laun* faded, colorless, discolored

مذهوب به *maḏhūb bihī* and مذهوب العقل *m. al-ʿaql* out of one's mind, demented

مذهب *muḏahhab, muḏhab* gilded

ذهل **ḏahala** *a* (*ḏahl*, ذهول *ḏuhūl*) to forget, overlook, omit, neglect, fail to heed (عن s.th.); — *ḏahila a* (ذهول *ḏuhūl*) to be perplexed, alarmed, dismayed, startled, surprised, baffled; to be astonished, be amazed; to frighten, scare, take alarm, flinch; to be absent-minded, be distracted; to be or become distracted (عن from), forget, overlook, fail to heed, neglect (عن s.th.) **IV** to baffle, startle, nonplus (ه s.o.); to distract (ه عن s.o. from), make (ه s.o.) forget (عن s.th.) **VII** = *ḏahila*

ذهول *ḏuhūl* perplexity, consternation, bafflement, daze, stupor; confusion, bewilderment, dismay, alarm, fright; surprise; amazement, astonishment; absent-mindedness, distraction, distractedness (عن from)

ذاهل *ḏāhil* negligent, forgetful, oblivious, distracted, absent-minded; dazed, in a stupor

مذهول *maḏhūl* perplexed, startled, alarmed, dismayed, dazed, confused, baffled, bewildered; distracted, absent-minded

مذهل *muḏhil* startling, baffling, amazing

منذهل *munḏahil* alarmed, dismayed, perplexed, startled, baffled; distracted, absent-minded

ذهن **ḏihn** pl. اذهان *aḏhān* mind; intellect

ذهنى *ḏihnī* mental, intellectual

ذهنية *ḏihnīya* mentality

ذو **ḏū**, genit. ذى *ḏī*, acc. ذا *ḏā*, f. ذات *ḏāt*, pl. m. ذوو *ḏawū*, اولو *ulū*, pl. f. ذوات *ḏawāt* (with foll. genit.) possessor, owner, holder or master of, endowed or provided with, embodying or comprising s.th. | ذو عقل *ḏū ʿaql* endowed with brains, bright, intelligent; ذو مال rich, wealthy; ذو صحة *ḏū ṣiḥḥa* healthy; ذو شأن *ḏū šaʾn* important, significant; ذو القربى *ḏū l-qurbā* relative, kin(sman); غير ذى زرع (*zarʿin*) uncultivated (land); من ذى قبل *min ḏī qablu* than before; من ذى نفسه *min ḏī nafsihī* of one's own accord, spontaneously; ذووه *ḏawūhu* his relatives, his kin, his folks; ذوو المودة والمعرفة *ḏawū l-mawadda wa-l-maʿrifa* friends and acquaintances; ذوو الشبهات *ḏawū š-šubuhāt* dubious persons, people of ill repute; ذوو الشأن *ḏawū š-šaʾn* important, influential people; the competent people (or authorities), those concerned with the matter; اولو الامر *ulū l-amr* rulers, leaders; اولو الحل والعقد *ulū l-ḥall wa-l-ʿaqd* influential people, those in power

ذات *ḏāt* pl. ذوات *ḏawāt* being, essence, nature; self; person, personality; the same, the selfsame; -self; الذوات people of rank, people of distinction, notables; ذاتا *ḏātan* personally | ذات البين *ḏ. al-bain* disagreement, dissension, disunion, discord, enmity; friendship; ذات الجنب *ḏ. al-janb* pleurisy (*med.*); ذات الرئة *ḏ. ar-riʾa* pneumonia; ذات الصدر *ḏ. aṣ-ṣadr* disease of the chest, pectoral ailment; ذات اليد *ḏ. al-yad* wealth, affluence; ذات ايدينا *ḏ. aidīnā* our possessions; ذات اليمين *ḏāta l-yamīni* to the right, ذات الشمال *ḏāta š-šimāli* to the left, ذات اليسار *ḏāta l-yasāri* do.; ذات مرة *ḏāta marratin* once, one time, فى ذات مرة *fī ḏāti marratin* do.; ذات يوم *ḏāta yaumin* one day, فى ذات يوم *fī ḏāti yaumin* do.; فى ذات غد *fī ḏāti ġadin* sometime in the future, before long; ... فى ذات *fī ḏāti* ... (with foll. genit.) as to ..., concerning ..., with reference to ..., re; بالذات *bi-ḏ-ḏāt* none other than ..., ... of all things, ... of all people; personally, in person; انا بالذات I, of all people, ..., none other than I ...; فى لندن بالذات in London, of all places; السعادة بالذات (*sa'āda*) essential happiness, happiness proper; ذات نفسه *ḏāt nafsihī*, ذات انفسهم *ḏ. anfusihim* his self, their selves, his (their) very nature; هو بذاته ,هو ذاته (he) himself; ذات الشىء the same thing; ذات الاشياء the same things; السنة ذاتها (*sana*) the same year; لذاته *li-ḏātihī* by himself (itself); in itself; as such; for his (its) own sake; فى ذاته in itself; فى حد ذاته *fī ḥaddi ḏ.* do.; قائم بذاته self-existent, independent, self-contained, isolated; الثقة بالذات (*tiqa*) self-confidence; حب الذات *ḥubb aḏ-ḏ.* and محبة الذات *maḥabbat aḏ-ḏ.* self-love, selfishness, egoism; الاعتماد على الذات self-confidence, self-reliance; صريح بذاته self-evident, self-explanatory; مناقض ذاته *munāqiḍ ḏātahū* self-contradictory; ابن ذوات *ibn ḏawāt* descended from a good family, highborn

ذاتى *ḏātī* own, proper; self-produced, self-created, spontaneous; personal; self-acting, automatic; subjective (*philos.*); (pl. *-ūn*) subjectivist (*philos.*); ذاتيا *ḏātīyan* of o.s., by o.s.; personally, in person | الحكم الذاتى (*ḥukm*) autonomy

ذاتية *ḏātīya* personality; subjectivism (*philos.*); identity (of a person) | تحقيق الذاتية identification (of a person)

لاذاتية *lā-ḏātīya* impersonality

ذواتى *ḏawātī* high-class, exclusive, luxurious

ذاب[1] see ذوابة

[2]ذاب (ذوب) *ḏāba u* (*ḏaub*, ذوبان *ḏawabān*) to dissolve; to melt; to melt away; to liquefy, deliquesce; to dwindle away, vanish; to pine away, waste away (حسرة واسى *ḥasratan wa-asan* with grief and sorrow) | ذاب حياء (*ḥayā'an*) to die of shame; ذابت اظفاره فى (*aẓfāruhū*) to strive in vain for, make futile efforts in order to II to dissolve, melt, liquefy (ه s.th.) IV to dissolve (also, e.g., tablets in water), liquefy (ه s.th.); to melt (ه s.th.); to smelt (ه metal); to consume, spend, exhaust, use up, sap (ه s.th.) | اذاب جهده (*juhdahū*) to exhaust s.o.'s energy; اذاب عصارة مخه فى (*'uṣārata mukkihī*) to rack one's brain with

ذوب *ḏaub* dissolution; solution (also, as a liquid)

ذوبان *ḏawabān* dissolution, melting, deliquescence, liquefaction | ذوبان الثلج (الثلوج) *ḏ. aṯ-ṯalj* (*aṯ-ṯulūj*) snowbreak, thaw; قابل للذوبان *qābil li-ḏ-ḏ.* meltable, soluble, dissoluble

تذويب *taḏwīb* dissolution, solution, melting, liquefaction

اذابة *iḏāba* dissolution, solution, melting, liquefaction

ذائب *ḏā'ib* dissolved; melted, molten; soluble, dissoluble

ذو and ذوات see ذات

ذاد (ذود) *ḏāda u* (*ḏaud*, ذياد *ḏiyād*) to scatter, drive away, chase away; to remove (ه ,ه عن s.o., s.th. from); to defend, protect (عن s.o., s.th.) | ذاد النوم عن عينيه (*an-nauma 'an 'ainaihi*) to drive or keep the sleep from his eyes

ذود *ḏaud* defense, protection (عن of s.th.)

ذياد *ḏiyād* defense, protection (عن of s.th.)

مذود *miḏwad* pl. مذاود *maḏāwid*[2] manger, crib, feeding trough

ذائد *ḏā'id* pl. ذادة *ḏāda* defender, protector

ذاق (ذوق) *ḏāqa u* (*ḏauq*, ذواق *ḏawāq*, مذاق *maḏāq*) to taste, sample (ه food, etc.); to try, try out, test (ه s.th.); to get a taste

(ه of s.th.), experience, undergo, suffer (ه s.th.), go through s.th. (ه) **IV** to have (ه s.o.) taste or sample (ه s.th.), give (ه ه s.o. s.th.) to taste **V** to taste (ه s.th.) slowly, repeatedly, thoroughly; to get a taste (ه of s.th.); to sense, perceive (ه s.th.); to enjoy thoroughly, savor, relish (ه s.th.); to derive pleasure (من from)

ذوق *ḏauq* pl. اذواق *aḏwāq* gustatory sense; taste (فى for; also, e.g., literary taste); perceptivity, responsiveness (فى for); sensitivity, sensitiveness; savoir-vivre, suavity, urbanity, tact; liking, inclination; taste, flavor (of food, etc.) | الذوق السليم good taste

ذوقى *ḏauqī* of taste, gustative, gustatory

ذواق *ḏawāq* taste

ذواق *ḏawwāq* epicure, connoisseur, gourmet, bon vivant

مذاق *maḏāq* taste

ذائقة *ḏā'iqa* sense of taste

ذوى *ḏawā i* and *ḏawiya a* to wither, wilt, fade; to be withered, be dry **IV** to cause to wilt, to dry

ذاو *ḏāwin* withered, faded, drooping

ذو see ذى

(ذيع) ذاع *ḏā'a i* (ذيوع *ḏuyū'*) to spread, get about, circulate, be spread, be disseminated, be or become widespread; to leak out, become public, become generally known **IV** to spread, spread out, disseminate, propagate (ه or ب s.th.); to make known, announce, make public, publicize, publish (ه or ب s.th.); to promulgate (ه or ب s.th.); to show, manifest, display (ه or ب s.th.), give evidence (ه or ب of); to reveal, disclose, divulge (ه or ب s.th.); to emit (ه electric waves); to broadcast, transmit (ه s.th., على to the public; *radio*) | اذاع بالتلفزة (*talfaza*) to telecast (ه s.th.)

ذيوع *ḏuyū'* widespreadness, commonness; spreading, spread, dispersion, diffusion; circulation (of news)

مذياع *miḏyā'* pl. مذاييع *maḏāyī'*[2] telltale, talebearer, tattler, blabber, indiscret person; radio station, broadcasting station; broadcasting; microphone; ○ radio set

اذاعة *iḏā'a* spreading, dissemination, propagation; announcement, proclamation; publication; revelation, disclosure; playback (of a tape; as opposed to recording); broadcasting, radio; (pl. *-āt*) (radio) broadcast, transmission | اذاعة الاخبار *i. al-aḵbār* newscast, news (*radio*); اذاعة تلفزية (*talfazīya*) television broadcast, telecast; اذاعة لاسلكية (*lā-silkīya*) and اذاعة راديوفونية radio broadcast; broadcasting, radio; اذاعة البوليس police radio; مجلة الاذاعة *majallat al-i.* radio magazine

ذائع *ḏā'i'* widespread, common, general; circulating, in circulation; widely known | ذائع الصيت *ḏ. aṣ-ṣīt* famous, noted, renowned, widely known

مذيع *muḏī'* spreader, disseminator, propagator, proclaimer; broadcasting, transmitting (used attributively); (radio) transmitter; radio announcer

مذيعة *muḏī'a* pl. *-āt* woman announcer (*radio*)

ذيل **II** to furnish (ه s.th., esp. a book) with an appendix, add a supplement (ه to); to provide (ه s.th.) at the end (ب with) **IV** to trample underfoot, degrade, debase (ه s.th.)

ذيل *ḏail* pl. ذيول *ḏuyūl*, اذيال *aḏyāl* the lowest or rearmost part of s.th., lower end; tail; hem, border (of a garment); train (of a skirt); lappet, coat tail; bottom, foot, end (of a page); appendage, appendicle; addenda, supplement, appendix (of a book); retinue, lengthy, extensive; تمسك باذياله *tamassaka bi-aḏyālihī* to cling to s.o.'s coat tails, hold on to s.o.; جر عليه ذيل العفاء (*jarra. ʿafā'*) to wipe out s.th., bring about the doom of s.th., let s.th. sink into oblivion; لاذ باذيال الشىء to resort to s.th.

attendants, suite; dependent; result, consequence | فى ذيله immediately thereafter; طاهر الذيل innocent, blameless, upright, honest; طهارة الذيل *ṭahārat aḏ-ḏ.* innocence, moral integrity, probity, uprightness, honesty; طويل الذيل long,

ر

ر *rā'* name of the letter ر

ر *ri'a* pl. رئون *ri'ūn*, رئات *ri'āt* lung

رئوى *ri'awī* pulmonary, pulmonic, pneumonic, of or pertaining to the lung, lung (used attributively)

رأب *ra'aba a* (*ra'b*) to mend, repair, patch up (ه a rent, and the like); to rectify, put in order, set right (ه s.th.)

رؤبة *ru'ba* patch (for mending a rent)

مرأب *mir'ab* pl. مرائب *marā'ib²* repair shop, garage

رابور (Fr. *rapport*) report

راتينج *rātīnaj* resin

راتينة = رتينة (look up alphabetically)

رؤد *ru'd* soft, tender; *ru'd* and فتاة رؤد (*fatāh*) delicate young girl

رئد *ri'd* pl. ارآد *ar'ād* person of approximately the same age, contemporary

رادار *rādār* radar

راديكالى *radikālī* radical

راديو *rādiyō* radio

راديولوجى *rādiyōlōjī* radiology

راديوم *rādiyūm* radium | ذو راديوم فاعل radioactive

رأرأ *ra'ra'a*: رأرأ بعينيه (*bi-ʿainaihi*) to roll one's eyes

رأس *ra'asa a* (رئاسة *ri'āsa*) to be at the head, be the chairman, be in charge (ه of s.th.); to preside (ه over s.th.); to head, lead, direct, manage, run (ه s.th.); — رؤس *ra'usa u* to be the chief, the leader II to appoint as chief or head, make the director or leader, entrust with the direction, management or chairmanship (ه s.o.) V = *ra'asa* VIII to become or be the chief, head, leader, or director

رأس *ra's* m. and f., pl. رؤوس *ru'ūs*, ارؤس *ar'us* head (also as a numerative of cattle); chief, chieftain, head, leader; upper part, upper end; tip; top, summit, peak; vertex, apex; extremity, end; promontory, headland, cape (*geogr.*); main part; beginning; رأسا *ra'san* directly, straightway; immediately | برأسه sui generis, in a class by itself, independent, self-contained, e.g., علم برأسه (*ʿilm*) a science in itself; رأس برأس (both) alike, one like the other, equally, without distinction; على رأس (with foll. genit.) at the head of; at the end of; at the beginning of, before, prior to; على الرأس والعين (*wa-l-ʿain*) very gladly; just as you wish! at your service! على رؤوس الاشهاد *ʿalā r. il-ašhād* in public, for all the world to see; رأسا على عقب *ra'san ʿalā ʿaqbin* upside down, topsy-turvy, e.g., قلبه رأسا على عقب

(*qalabahū*) to turn s.th. completely upside down, upset s.th. from the bottom up; من الرأس الى القدم (*qadam*) or من الرأس الى اخمص القدم (*akmaṣi l-qadam*) from head to toe; رفع به رأسا to pay attention to s.th.; رأس الآفات the principal evil, the root of all evil; رأس تنورة Ras Tanura (cape, E Saudi Arabia, oil center); رأس ثوم *r. ṯūm* clove of garlic; رأس الجسر *r. al-jisr* bridgehead; رأس حامية (*ḥāmiya*) hothead, hotspur, firebrand; رأس السنة *r. as-sana* New Year; رأس العمود *r. al-ʿamūd* capital (of a column or pilaster); رأس الكتاب letterhead; رأس مال pl. رؤوس اموال capital (*fin.*); مسقط الرأس *masqaṭ, masqiṭ ar-r.* birthplace, home town; سمت الرأس *samt ar-r.* zenith (*astron.*); البلد الرأس (*balad*) the capital city; رؤوس الاصابع tiptoes

رأسى *raʾsī* head (adj.), cephalic; main, chief, principal; perpendicular, vertical

رأسمالى *raʾs-mālī* capitalistic; (pl. *-ūn*) capitalist

رأسمالية *raʾs-mālīya* capitalism

رئيس *raʾīs* pl. رؤساء *ruʾasāʾ*[2] one at the head, or in charge, of; head; chieftain; leader; chief, boss; rais; director; headmaster, principal; chairman; governor; president; manager, superintendent; conductor (*mus.*); superior (as distinguished from مرؤوس subordinate); (*mil.*) captain (*Ir.* 1922, *Leb.*; formerly also *Syr.* and *Eg.*); رئيس اول (*awwal*) military rank between captain and major (= Fr. *capitaine 1ière classe; Ir.* 1922, *Syr.* 1952) | رئيس الاساقفة archbishop; رئيس البلدية *r. al-baladīya* chief of a municipality, mayor; رئيس التحرير editor-in-chief; رئيس اركان الحرب *r. arkān al-ḥarb* chief of general staff; رئيس التشريفات *r. at-tašrīfāt* chief of protocol, master of ceremonies (of the king; formerly *Ir.*); رئيس الشمامسة archdeacon; رئيس عرفاء *r. ʿurafāʾ* (*mil.*) master sergeant (*Ir.*, *Syr.*); رئيس الاقسام *r. al-aqsām* technical director general (of the State Railways; *Eg.*); رئيس النواب *r. an-nuwwāb* president of parliament, speaker of the (lower) house; رئيس هيئة اركان الحرب *r. haiʾat arkān al-ḥarb* chief of general staff; رئيس الوزراء *r. al-wuzarāʾ* and رئيس الوزارة prime minister, premier

رئيسة *raʾīsa* manageress; directress; mother superior

رئيسى *raʾīsī* main, chief, principal, leading | دور رئيسى (*daur*) leading role, leading part; سبب رئيسى (*sabab*) principal cause, main reason; شارع رئيسى main street; الفضائل الرئيسية cardinal virtues (*Chr.*); مقالة رئيسية (*maqāla*) editorial, leading article, leader

□ريس *rayyis* (= رئيس) mate (naval rank; *Eg.*) | ريس ممتاز (*mumtāz*) a naval rank (approx. = petty officer 3rd class; *Eg.* 1939)

رئاسة *riʾāsa*, رياسة *riyāsa* (also رآسة) leadership, leading position; management, direction; chairmanship; presidency, presidentship; supervision, superintendency | رئاسة الوزارة prime ministry, premiership; دار الرياسة presidential palace, seat of the chief executive of a country

ترؤس *taraʾʾus* direction, management; chairmanship

روائس *rawāʾis*[2] cliffs lining river beds (wadis)

مرؤوس *marʾūs* subordinate; (pl. *-ūn*) a subordinate, a subaltern

رأف *raʾafa a* and رؤف *raʾufa u* (رأفة *raʾfa*, رآفة *raʾāfa*) to show mercy (ب on s.o.), have pity (ب with s.o.), be kind, gracious, merciful (ب to s.o.) V do.

رأفة *raʾfa* and رآفة *raʾāfa* mercy, compassion, pity; kindliness, graciousness

رؤوف *raʾūf* merciful, compassionate; kind, benevolent; gracious

ارأف *arʾaf*[2] kindlier, more gracious (ب toward)

رافيا *rāfiyā* raffia, raffia palm

[1]رأم *ra'ama a* (*ra'm*) to repair, mend (ه s.th.)

[2]رئم *ra'ima a* (رئمان *ri'mān*) to love tenderly (ه s.th.), be very fond (ه of); to treat tenderly, fondle, caress (ه s.th.)

رئم *ri'm* pl. ارآم *ar'ām* white antelope, addax

رءوم *ra'ūm* loving, tender (mother to her children)

رام الله *rāmallah* Ramallah (town in W Jordan, N of Jerusalem)

رامية *rāmiya* ramie, a strong, lustrous bast fiber; China jute (*bot.*)

راوند *rāwand* rhubarb

[1]رأى *ra'ā* يرى *yarā* (*ra'y*, رؤية *ru'ya*) to see; to behold, descry, perceive, notice, observe, discern (ه s.th.); to look (ه ه at s.th. as), regard (ه ه s.th. as), consider, deem, think (ه ه s.th. to be ...); to judge; to be of the opinion (ان that), believe, think (ان that); to express one's opinion; to feel (ان that); to deem appropriate, think proper (ه s.th.), decide (ه on s.th., ان to do s.th.); to consider, contemplate | أرأيت *a-ra'aita* tell me! what do you think? رأى رأى العين (*ra'ya l-'ain*) to see with one's own eyes; رأى رؤيا (*ru'yā*) to have a dream; رأى منه العجب (*'ajaba*) to be amazed at s.th.; رأى للشيء فائدة to expect some benefit from s.th.; رأى من واجبه (*min wājibihī*) to regard as one's duty, deem incumbent upon o.s.; رأى له ان to think that it would be in s.o.'s interest to ...; رأى رأيه (*ra'yahū*) to share s.o.'s opinion; pass.: رؤى ان (*ru'iya*) it was decided that ...; رؤى الشيء it was felt proper to do so, it was thought to be the right thing to do III to act ostentatiously, make a show before people, attitudinize; to do eyeservice; to behave hypocritically, act the hypocrite, (dis)simulate, dissemble (ه toward s.o.) IV ارى *arā* to show, demonstrate (ه ه to s.o. s.th.) | يا ترى *yā turā* (in interrogative sentences) what's your opinion? would you say ...? I wonder ..., متى يا ترى I wonder when ..., ترى هل *turā hal* I wonder if ..., would you say that ...? اتراها جاءت؟ (*a-turāhā*) I wonder if she has come, would you say she has come? اترانى اعود؟ would you say I should go back? V to deem, think, believe VI to present o.s. to or come into s.o.'s (ل) view, show o.s. (ل to s.o.); to appear, seem (ل to s.o.); to appear right, seem appropriate (ل to s.o.), be thought proper (ل by s.o.); to see one another; to look at o.s. (in a mirror); to act the hypocrite; to fake, feign, simulate (ب s.th.) VIII to consider, contemplate (ه s.th.); to be of the opinion (ان that), decide (ان that) | ارتأى رأيا (*ra'yan*) to have an opinion; ارتأى رأيه (*ra'yahū*) to share s.o.'s opinion

رأى *ra'y* pl. آراء *ārā'* opinion, view; idea, notion, concept, conception; advice, suggestion, proposal; (*Isl. Law*) subjective opinion, decision based on one's individual judgment (not on Koran and Sunna) | فى رأيي and عند رأيي in my opinion; انا من هذا الرأى I am of this opinion; من رأيه ان he is of the opinion that ...; اخذ الرأى على (*ukida*) it was put to the vote, (the matter) was voted upon; لم يكن عند رأيهم he was not what they had expected; لم يكن له فيه رأى he had no say in the matter; الرأى العام (*'āmm*) public opinion; ذو الرأى pl. ذوو الآراء sensible, judicious; man of good sense and judgment; well-informed, knowledgeable person, one in the know; تبادل الآراء *tabādul al-ā.* exchange of views; صلب الرأى *ṣulb ar-r.* obstinate, stubborn, opinionated; قسم الرأى *qism ar-r.* committee of experts, council on legal and economic matters (attached to the ministries; *Eg.*)

راية *rāya* pl. *-āt* banner, flag

رؤية *ru'ya* seeing, looking, viewing; inspection, examination

رؤيا *ru'yā* pl. رؤى *ru'an* vision; dream | سفر الرؤيا *sifr ar-r.* the Apocalypse (*Chr.*)

مرأى *mar'an* sight, view; vision; apparition | على مرأى من before s.o.'s eyes; على مرأى ومسمع من (*wa-masma'in*) before the eyes and ears of; with full knowledge of

مرآة *mir'āh* pl. مراء *marā'in*, مرايا *marāyā* looking glass, mirror; reflection, reflected image

□ مراية *mirāya* pl. *-āt* looking glass, mirror

رئاء *ri'ā'* and رياء *riyā'* eyeservice; hypocrisy, dissimulation; dissemblance; simulation (ب of s.th.)

مراءاة, مراآة *murā'āh* eyeservice; hypocrisy, dissimulation, dissemblance; simulation (ب of s.th.)

راء *rā'in* viewer, onlooker, spectator, observer

○ رائية *rā'iya* pl. *-āt* view finder (of a camera)

مرئى *mar'īy* seen; visible; المرئيات the visible things, the visible world

مراء *murā'in* pl. مراؤون *murā'ūn* hypocrite

رئة[2] and رئوى see ريه

راى[3] *rāy* an Egyptian variety of salmon

راية[4] see [1]راى

رب *rabba* u (*rabb*, ربابة *ribāba*) to be master, be lord, have possession (ه, ٥ of), control (ه, ٥ s.o., s.th.), have command or authority (ه, ٥ over); — u (*rabb*) and II to raise, bring up (٥ a child) II to deify, idolize (ه, ٥ s.o., s.th.)

رب *rabb* pl. ارباب *arbāb* lord; master; owner, proprietor (*Isl. Law*); (with foll. genit.) one possessed of, endowed with, having to do with, etc.; الرب the Lord (= God) | رب بحرى (*baḥrī*) a naval rank (approx. = seaman; *Eg.*); رب العائلة father of the family, paterfamilias; ارباب السلطان *a. as-sulṭān* the rulers; ارباب المال the capitalists; صعود الرب the Ascension (*Chr.*); ارباب المعاشات *a. al-ma'āšāt* pensioners; ارباب السوابق those previously convicted; ارباب الفنون artists

ربة *rabba* pl. *-āt* mistress; lady | ربة المنزل *r. al-manzil* the lady of the house; ربة البيت *r. al-bait* landlady; ربة شعره *r. ši'rihī* his muse; ربات الحجال *r. al-ḥijāl* the ladies

رب *rubb* pl. رباب *ribāb*, ربوب *rubūb* rob, thickened juice (of fruit); mash, pulp

رب *rubba* (with foll. indet. genit.) many a, e.g., رب رجل (*rajulin*) many a man, رب مرة (*marratin*) many a time

ربما *rubbamā* sometimes; perhaps, maybe, possibly

ربة *rabba, ribba* a kind of skin eruption affecting the head and face

رباب *rabāb*, ربابة *rabāba* rebab or rebec, a stringed instrument of the Arabs resembling the fiddle, with one to three strings (in Eg. usually two-stringed)

ربيب *rabīb* pl. ارباء *aribbā'*[2] foster son, stepson; foster father; confederate, ally

ربيبة *rabība* pl. ربائب *rabā'ib*[2] foster daughter, stepdaughter; foster mother; (woman) ally

ربوبية *rubūbīya* divinity, deity, godship

ربان *rubbān* pl. *-īya*, ربابنة *rabābina* captain, skipper; a naval rank, approx. captain, ربان ثان (*tānin*) approx. = commander (*Eg.* 1939)

ربانى *rabbānī* divine; pertaining to God | الربانيات divine things; الصلاة الربانية (*ṣalāh*) the Lord's Prayer (*Chr.*)

مربة (*eg.*) *mirabba* (= مربى *murabban*) jam, preserved fruit

راب *rābb* stepfather

رابة *rābba* stepmother

ربأ *raba'a a* to hold in esteem, esteem highly (ب s.o.); ربأ به عن to consider s.o. above s.th., above doing s.th., have too high an opinion of s.o. as to suspect him of (doing) s.th. or as to expect him to do s.th.; ربأ بنفسه عن (*bi-nafsihī*) to deem o.s. above s.th., be too proud for, stand aloof from

ربيئة *rabī'a* pl. ربايا *rabāyā* guard

ربت *rabata i* (*rabt*) to pat, caress, stroke (ه s.o.) II do. | ربت على خده (*kaddihī*) to pat s.o.'s cheek; ربت على كتفه (*katifihī*) to pat s.o. on the shoulder; ربت نفسه to be self-satisfied, self-complacent, smug

ربح *rabiḥa a* (*ribḥ, rabaḥ*) to gain (ه من from s.th. s.th.), profit (من from); to win (sports, games) | ما ربحت تجارتهم (*tijāratuhum*) their business was unprofitable II and IV to make (ه s.o.) gain, allow s.o. (ه) a profit

ربح *ribḥ* pl. ارباح *arbāḥ* gain, profit; benefit; interest (on money); pl. proceeds, returns, revenues; ○ dividends | ربح بسيط simple interest, ربح مركب (*murakkab*) compound interest

رباح *rubbāḥ* pl. ربابيح *rabābīḥ*[2] monkey

اربح *arbaḥ*[2] more profitable, more lucrative

مرابحة *murābaḥa* (*Isl. Law*) resale with specification of gain, resale with an advance

رابح *rābiḥ* profiteer, gainer, winner; beneficiary; lucrative, gainful, profitable (business)

مربح *murbiḥ* lucrative, gainful, profitable

ربد V to become clouded, become overcast (sky); to turn ashen, take on a glowering expression (face, with anger) IX to become ashen, assume a glowering expression (face)

مربد *murbadd* clouded; gloomy, morose (face)

ربص *rabaṣa u* (*rabṣ*) to wait, look, watch, be on the lookout (ب for) V to lurk, lie in wait (ل for s.o.), waylay, ambush (ل s.o.); to lay an ambush, move into an ambush; to take up positions (*mil.*); to expect (ه, ب s.th.), wait (ه, ب for s.th.) | تربص الفرصة (*furṣata*) to wait (or look) for an opportunity; تربص به الامر (*amra*) to wait for s.th. to befall s.o. or to happen to s.o., e.g., تربص به الدوائر to wait for s.o. to meet with disaster

تربص *tarabbuṣ* probationary term (*adm.*)

متربص *mutarabbiṣ* candidate, aspirant

ربض *rabaḍa i* (*rabḍ*, ربوض *rubūḍ*) to lie down; to lie, rest (animals; with the chest to the ground); to lurk (ل for s.o.)

ربض *rabaḍ* pl. ارباض *arbāḍ* outskirts, suburb; place where animals lie down to rest

مربض *marbiḍ* pl. مرابض *marābiḍ*[2] place where animals lie down to rest; sheep pen, fold

ربط *rabaṭa u i* (*rabṭ*) to bind, tie up, make fast, moor (ه s.th.); to tie, fasten, attach, hitch (ه الى s.th. to); to connect (ه الى s.th. with); to fix, appoint, determine (ه s.th.); to value, rate, assess (ه s.th.); to add, append, affix (ه الى s.th. to); to insert (ه الى s.th. in); to combine, unite (ه s.th., بين — وبين s.th. with); to ligate (ه s.th.), apply a tourniquet (ه to); to bandage, dress (ه a wound); to bridle, check (ه, على s.th.); to brake (ه a train); to suspend (ه a cleric; *Chr.*) | ربط لسانه (*lisānahū*) to silence s.o.; ربط على قلبه (*qalbihī*) to fortify s.o., give s.o. patience (said of God); ربط جأشه (*ja'šahū*) to keep one's self-control, remain calm, be undismayed;

ربط الطريقة to practice highway robbery III to be lined up, posted, stationed (troops); to line up, take up positions; to be moored (ship); to move into fighting positions | رابط فى قضيته (*qaḍīyatihī*) to defend the cause of, fight for VIII to bind o.s., commit o.s., engage o.s.; to be bound (ب by, also, e.g., by an obligation), be tied (ب to); to be linked, be connected (ب with); to depend (ب on); to unite, join forces

ربط **rabṭ** binding, tying; fastening, joining, attaching, connecting; fixation, determination (of an amount, of a number); valuation, assessment | ربط مالى financial allocation; اهل الحل والربط *ahl al-ḥall wa-r-r.* influential people, those in power; مكان الربط *makān ar-r.* (welded) seam, weld (*techn.*)

ربط **rabaṭ** (*tun.*) section, quarter (of a city), suburb

ربطة **rabṭa** pl. *-āt*, رباط *ribāṭ* ribbon, band, bandage; bundle; parcel, package | ربطة الرقبة *r. ar-raqaba* necktie; ربطة الساق *r. as-sāq* garter; ربطة النقود money purse

رباط **ribāṭ** pl. *-āt*, ربط *rubuṭ*, اربطة *arbiṭa* ribbon, band; ligature, ligament; bandage; dressing (of a wound); bond, fetter, shackle; — suspension (of a cleric; *Chr.*); (pl. *-āt*, ربط *rubuṭ*) inn for travelers, caravansary; hospice (for Sufis or the poor) | رباط الاجربة *r. al-ajriba* garter; رباط الجزمة *r. al-jazma* shoestring; رباط الرقبة *r. ar-raqaba* necktie

رباط **ribāṭ**², رباط الفتح *ribāṭ al-fatḥ* Rabat (capital of Morocco)

رباطة الجأش **ribāṭat al-ja'š** composure, self-control, calmness, intrepidity

مربط **marbiṭ, marbaṭ** pl. مرابط *marābiṭ*² place where animals are tied up

مربط **mirbaṭ** pl. مرابط *marābiṭ*² hawser, mooring cable; rope; ○ terminal (*el.*)

ارتباط **irtibāṭ** connectedness, connection, link; contact, liaison; tie (ب to); obligation, engagement, commitment; bearing (ب on), connection (ب with), relation (ب to); unity; league, confederation | بدون ارتباط *bidūn irt.* not binding, without obligation (*com.*); ضابط ارتباط liaison officer

رابط الجأش **rābiṭ al-ja'š** composed, calm, unruffled, undismayed, fearless

رابطة **rābiṭa** pl. روابط *rawābiṭ*² band; bond, tie; connection, link; confederation, union, league | روابط الصداقة *r. aṣ-ṣadāqa* bonds of friendship; الرابطة الاسلامية (*islāmīya*) the Moslem League

مربوط **marbūṭ** bound; connected; fastened, tied, moored (الى to); fixed, appointed; fixed salary; estimate (of the budget)

مرابط **murābiṭ** posted, stationed; garrisoned (troops); Marabout | الجيش المرابط (*jaiš*) the Territorial Army (*Eg.*)

مرتبط **murtabiṭ** connected, linked (ب with); bound, committed (ب by); depending, conditional (ب on)

ربع **raba'a** *a* to gallop (horse); — to sit; to squat; to stay, live II to quadruple, multiply by four, increase fourfold (ه s.th.); to square (ه a number) V to sit or sit down cross-legged; to sit | تربع على العرش (*'arš*) to mount the throne, sit on the throne

ربع **rab'** pl. ربوع *rubū'*, رباع *ribā'*, ارباع *arbā'*, اربع *arbu'* home, residence, quarters; pl. ربوع region, area, territory, lands; ربع (group of) people | الربع الخالى Rub' al Khali (desert region in S Arabia)

ربع **rib'**: حمى الربع *ḥummā r-rib'* quartan (fever)

ربع **rub'** pl. ارباع *arbā'* quarter, fourth part; roubouh, a dry measure (*Eg.* = 4

قدح = 8.25 l); (*syr.*) 25-piaster piece | ربع سنوى *r. sanawī* quarterly, trimestral

ربعى *rubʿī* quarterly, trimestral

ربعة *rabʿa*: ربعة القوام *r. al-qawām* and ربعة القامة *r. al-qāma* (m. and f.) of medium height, medium-sized

ربعة *rubʿa* robhah, a dry measure (*Eg.*; = 1/4 قدح = 0.516 l)

رباع *rabbāʿ* athlete (boxer, wrestler, weight lifter, etc.)

ربيع *rabīʿ* spring, springtime, vernal season; name of the third and fourth months of the Muslim year (ربيع الاول *r. al-awwali* Rabia I, and ربيع الثانى *r. aṯ-ṯānī* Rabia II); quarter, fourth part

اربعة *arbaʿa* (f. اربع *arbaʿ*) four | ذوات الاربع *ḏawāt al-a.* the quadrupeds

اربعة عشر *arbaʿata ʿašara* (f. اربع عشرة *arbaʿa ʿašrata*) fourteen

اربعون *arbaʿūn* forty; الاربعون a ceremony held on the 40th day after s.o.'s death | عيد الاربعين *ʿīd al-a.* Ascension Day (*Chr.*)

رباعى *rubāʿī* consisting of four, quadripartite, fourfold, quadruple; quadrangular; tetragonal; (*gram.*) consisting of four radical letters, quadriliteral; quartet; (pl. *-āt*) quatrain (*poet.*) | مؤتمر رباعى (*muʾtamar*) four-power conference; رباعى الاضلاع quadrilateral; رباعى الارجل *r. l-arjul* quadruped(al), four-footed; محرك رباعى المشوار *muḥarrik r. l-mišwār* four-cycle engine

الاربعاء *al-arbaʿāʾ*, *al-arbiʿāʾ*, يوم الاربعاء *yaum al-a.* Wednesday

يربوع *yarbūʿ* pl. يرابيع *yarābīʿ*[2] jerboa (Jaculus jaculus; *zool.*)

مربع *marbaʿ* pl. مرابع *marābiʿ*[2] meadow

تربيع *tarbīʿ* lunar quarter; — (pl. ترابيع *tarābīʿ*[2]) quadrangle; square, plaza (surrounded by houses) | تربيع الدائرة quadrature of the circle

تربيعة *tarbīʿa* pl. ترابيع *tarābīʿ*[2] square, quadrangle; square, plaza; square panel; tile, floor tile

تربيعى *tarbīʿī* quadratic, square

الرابع *ar-rābiʿ* the fourth; رابعا *rābiʿan* fourthly, in the fourth place

رابع *rābiʿ* (due to erroneous pointing) = رائع q.v.

مربوع *marbūʿ* of medium height, medium-sized

مربع *murabbaʿ* fourfold, quadruple; quadrangular; tetragonal; square, quadratic; quadrangle; a square; (pl. *-āt*) quadrangular piece; quartet | متر مربع (*mitr*) square meter; مربع الاضلاع quadrilateral (*math.*)

مربعة *murabbaʿa* pl. *-āt* section, district, area

مرابع *murābiʿ* partner in an agricultural enterprise (sharing one quarter of the gains or losses)

جلس متربعا *jalasa mutarabbiʿan* to sit crosslegs

رابغ *rābiḡ* pleasant, comfortable

ربق *ribq* lasso, lariat

ربقة *ribqa*, *rabqa* pl. ربق *ribaq*, رباق *ribāq*, ارباق *arbāq* noose

ربك **rabaka** u (*rabk*) to muddle, entangle, complicate (ه s.th.); to confuse, throw into confusion (ه, ه s.o., s.th.); — *rabika* a (*rabak*) to be in an involved, confused situation VIII to be confused; to become involved (فى in)

ربك *rabak* involved, confused situation

ربك *rabik* confused; in trouble, beset by difficulties

ارتباك *irtibāk* pl. *-āt* entanglement, involvement; snarl, tangle, muddle, mess; confusion; embarrassment; upset (of the stomach)

مربك *murabbik* confusing, bewildering, disconcerting

مرتبك *murtabik* confused, complicated, involved; bewildered, disconcerted, embarrassed; involved (في in)

ربل *rabil* plump, fleshy, fat (person)

ربلي *rablī, rabalī* fleshy

ربلة *rabla* pl. *rabalāt* (mass of) flesh (of the body)

ربيل *rabīl* fleshy, corpulent, fat

ربالة *rabāla* corpulence

ربما see رب

(ربو) ربا *rabā u* (رباء *rabā'*, ربو *rubūw*) to increase; to grow; to grow up; to exceed, (على a number, also عن), be more than (على) | ما يربو على المئة more than a hundred **II** to make or let grow; to raise, rear, bring up (ه s.o.); to educate; to teach, instruct (ه a child); to breed, raise (ه e.g., poultry, cattle); to develop (ه e.g., a method) **III** to practice usury **IV** to make grow, augment, increase (ه s.th.); to exceed (على a number, an age, a measure) **V** to be brought up, be educated; to be bred, be raised

ربو *rabw* dyspnea, asthma

ربوة *rubwa* (*rabwa, ribwa*) pl. ربى *ruban* hill

ربوة *ribwa* pl. *-āt* ten thousand, myriad

ربا *riban* interest; usurious interest; usury

ربوي *ribawī* usurious

رباء *rabā'* surplus, excess; superiority (على over s.o.); favor

تربية *tarbiya* education, upbringing; teaching, instruction; pedagogy; breeding, raising (of animals) | سيئ التربية *sayyi' at-t.* ill-bred; قليل التربية ill-bred, uncivil, ill-mannered; علم التربية *'ilm at-t.* pedagogy, pedagogics; تربية الاطفال baby care; التربية البدنية (*badanīya*) physical education, physical training; تربية الحيوان *t. al-ḥayawān* cattle farming, stockbreeding; تربية الدجاج *t. ad-dajāj* chicken farming, poultry husbandry; تربية السمك *t. as-samak* pisciculture; تربية النباتات *t. an-nabātāt* plant cultivation

تربوي *tarbawī*, تربيوي *tarbiyawī* pedagogic, pedagogical

رابية *rābiya* pl. رواب *rawābin* hill

مرب *murabbin* pl. مربون *murabbūn* educator; pedagogue; breeder (of livestock)

مربية *murabbiya* pl. *-āt* tutoress, governess; dry nurse, nursemaid

مربى *murabban* raised, brought up; educated; well-bred, well-mannered; jam, preserved fruit; pl. مربيات *murabbayāt* preserves

مراب *murābin* usurer

مترب *mutarabbin* well-bred, well-mannered

ربورتاج (Fr. *reportage*) pl. *-āt* reportage, report

ارت *aratt*[2], f. رتاء *rattā'*[2], pl. رت *rutt* afflicted with a speech defect

رتب **II** to array, arrange, dispose (ه s.th. in a regular sequence or order); to decorate, dress (ه a show window); to settle, determine, regulate (ه s.th.); to put into proper order, put together (ه words); to prepare, set aside, earmark (ه s.th.); to fix, appoint (ل ه a salary for s.o.); to make (ه s.th.) result or accrue (على from), derive (على ه s.th. from), make (ه s.th.) the result or consequence of (على) **V** to fall in line; to be arranged, organized or set up (along the lines of); to be set aside, be assigned; to be subordinate (على to s.th.), be the result or consequence (على of), result, follow, derive, spring (على from), be caused (على by) | ترتب بذمته (*bi-ḏimmatihī*) to become the debtor of s.o.

رتبة *rutba* pl. رتب *rutab* degree, grade, level; rank, standing, station; class, quality; (*mil.*) rank; clerical rank, order (of the Christian ministry); religious ceremony (*Chr.*) | كتاب الرتب ritual (of the Roman Catholic Church)

رتابة *ratāba* monotony

رتيب *ratīb* monotonous

رتباء *rutabā'*[2] noncommissioned officers (*Syr.; mil.*)

مرتبة *martaba* pl. مراتب *marātib*[2] step; steplike elevation serving as a seat; mattress; grade, degree, rank, class | فى المرتبة الاول (*ūlā*) first (mortgage)

ترتيب *tartīb* pl. *-āt* order, arrangement, array; sequence, succession; make-up, setup; layout (of a complex, e.g., of houses); organization; preparation, arrangement, provision, measure, step; rite of administering a sacrament (*Chr.*) | بالترتيب one by one, in proper succession; من غير ترتيب disorderly, in confusion

ترتيبى *tartībī* ordinal | عدد ترتيبى (*'adad*) ordinal number

راتب *rātib* monotonous; (pl. رواتب *rawātib*[2]) salary, pay, emolument; pl. رواتب certain supererogatory exercises of devotion

مرتب *murattab* arranged; organized, set up, regulated, etc.; (pl. *-āt*) salary, pay, emolument

رتج *rataja* u (*ratj*) to lock, bar, bolt (ه the door); — *ratija* a (*rataj*) to be tongue-tied, be speechless, falter **IV** pass.: ارتج عليه (*urtija*) words failed him, he was speechless, he didn't know what to say, he was at a loss

رتاج *ritāj* pl. رتج *rutuj*, رتائج *ratā'ij*[2] gate, gateway | محكم الرتاج *muḥkam ar-r.* firmly bolted (gate)

رتينج *ratīnaj* (= راتينج) resin

رتع *rata'a* a (*rat'*, رتوع *rutū'*, رتاع *ritā'*) to pasture, graze; to gormandize, carouse, feast; to revel, indulge freely (فى in) **IV** to pasture, put out to graze (ه cattle)

مرتع *marta'* pl. مراتع *marāti'*[2] rich grazing land, pasture; fertile ground (ل for; fig.); breeding ground, hotbed (of vice, of evil, etc.)

رتق *rataqa* u i (*ratq*) to mend, repair, patch up, sew up (ه s.th.)

رتق *ratq* pl. رتوق *rutūq* patching, mending, repair; darn (of a stocking)

[1]رتك *rataka* u i (*ratk, ratak,* رتكان *ratakān*) to run with short steps, trot

[2]مرتك *martak* litharge (*chem.*)

رتل *ratila* a (*ratal*) to be regular, well-ordered, neat, tidy **II** to phrase elegantly (الكلام *al-kalāma* one's words); to psalmodize, recite in a singsong; to sing, chant (ه spiritual songs, hymns; *Chr.*)

رتل *ratl* pl. ارتال *artāl* railroad train | رتل آلى (*ālī*) motorized convoy (*mil.*)

رتيلاء *rutailā'*[2] harvestman (Phalangium), daddy longlegs; tarantula

ترتيل *tartīl* slow recitation of the Koran (a technical term of *tajwīd*); psalmodizing, psalmody, singsong recitation; singing, chanting (of hymns, etc.; *Chr.*); — (pl. تراتيل *tarātīl*[2]) hymn; religious song (*Chr.*)

ترتيلة *tartīla* pl. تراتيل *tarātīl*[2] hymn

مرتل *murattil* church singer; choirboy, chorister (*Chr.*); singer, chanter

رتم *ratama* i (*ratm*) to utter, say (بكلمة *bi-kalima* a word; only with neg.)

رتم *ratam* (coll.; n. un. ة) retem (Retama raetam Webb., Genista raetam Forsk.; *bot.*)

رتمة *ratma* and رتيمة *ratīma* pl. رتائم *ratā'im*[2], رتام *ritām* thread wound around one's finger as a reminder

(رتو) رتا *ratā u* and II رتّى *rattā* to mend, darn (▲ e.g., stockings)

رتوش (Fr. *retouche*) *ritūš* retouch

رتينج *ratīnaj* (= راتينج) resin

رتينة (It. *retina*) *ratīna* pl. رتائن *ratā'in*² incandescent mantle

رث *raṯṯa i* (رثاثة *raṯāṯa*, رثوثة *ruṯūṯa*) to be ragged, tattered, shabby, worn (garment)

رث *raṯṯ* pl. رثاث *riṯāṯ* old, shabby, worn, threadbare | رث الهيئة *r. al-hai'a* of shabby appearance

رثة *riṯṯa* old, outmoded things, worn clothes

رثيث *raṯīṯ* old, shabby, worn, threadbare

رثاثة *raṯāṯa* shabbiness, raggedness

رثوثة *ruṯūṯa* shabbiness, raggedness

رثو (and رثى) رثا *raṯā u* (*raṯw*) to bewail, lament, celebrate in an elegy, in a funeral oration (• a deceased person); — رثى *raṯā i* (*raṯy*, رثاء *riṯā'*, مرثية *marṯiya*, مرثاة *marṯāh*) to bewail, lament, bemoan (• a deceased person); to elegize, celebrate in an elegy, in a funeral oration (• a deceased person); to mourn (ل for, over), deplore (ل s.o. or s.th.); to pity (ل s.o.), feel sorry (ل for) | رثاه بمرثاة to elegize s.o. (a deceased person), bewail and celebrate him in an elegy; شيء يرثى له (*yurṯā*) a deplorable, regrettable thing

رثى *raṯy* bewailing, bemoaning, lamentation

رثاء *riṯā'* bewailing, bemoaning, lamentation; regret; elegiac poetry

رثية *raṯya* pl. *raṯayāt* arthritis, gout

مرثية *marṯiya* and مرثاة *marṯāh* pl. مراث *marāṯin* elegy, dirge, epicedium; pl. مراث funeral orations

رج *rajja u* (*rajj*) to convulse, shake, rock (▲ s.th.); pass. *rujja* to be shaken, tremble, shake, quake VIII to be convulsed, shake, tremble, quake

رج *rajj* shaking, rocking, convulsion

رجة *rajja* convulsion; shock, concussion

رجاج *rajjāj* trembling, quaking, shaking, rocking

ارتجاج *irtijāj* shock, concussion; trembling, tremor | ○ ارتجاج المخ *irt. al-mukk* cerebral concussion (*med.*)

رجأ IV to postpone, adjourn, defer, put off (▲ s.th.)

ارجاء *irjā'* postponement, deferment, adjournment

رجب *rajaba u* and *rajiba a* (*rajab*) to be afraid (من or عن of), be awed (من or عن by)

رجب *rajab* Rajab, the seventh month of the Muslim year

رجح *rajaḥa a i u* (رجوح *rujūḥ*, رجحان *rujḥān*) to incline (scale of a balance); to weigh more, be of greater weight; to preponderate, predominate; to surpass, excel (• s.o.); to be very likely (ان that), رجح عنده ان it appeared to him most likely that ...; — to weigh (▲ بيده s.th. in the hand) II to make (▲ s.th.) outweigh (على s.th. else), give preponderance (▲ to s.th., على over); to think (▲ s.th.) weightier; to prefer (▲ على s.th. to), give (▲ s.th.) preference (على to), favor (▲ على s.th. more than); to think likely or probable (▲ s.th., ان that) V to carry greater weight, be weightier, preponderate; to swing back and forth, pendulate; to rock; to seesaw, teeter VIII to swing back and forth, pendulate; to rock; to seesaw teeter

رجاحة *rajāḥa* forbearance, indulgence leniency; composure, equanimity

رجحان *rujḥān* preponderance, predominance (على over), ascendancy, superiority

ارجح *arjaḥ*[2] superior in weight, preponderant; having more in its favor, more acceptable; preferable; more likely, more probable | الارجح ان it is most likely that ...; probably ...; على الارجح probably, in all probability

ارجحية *arjaḥīya* preponderance, predominance, prevalence

ارجوحة *urjūḥa* pl. اراجيح *arājīḥ*[2] seesaw; swing; cradle

راجح *rājiḥ* superior in weight, preponderant; having more in its favor, more acceptable; preferable; probable, likely

مرجوحة *marjūḥa* pl. مراجيح *marājīḥ*[2] seesaw; swing

مرجح *murajjaḥ* preponderant, predominant; probable, likely

رجرج *rajraja* and II *tarajraja* to tremble, quiver; to sway

رجراج *rajrāj* agitated; trembling, tremulous; swaying; quivering; الرجراج the sea

رجز[1] VIII to compose or declaim poems in the meter *rajaz*; to thunder, roar, surge (sea)

رجز *rujz, rijz* punishment (inflicted by God); dirt, filth

رجز *rajaz* name of a poetical meter

ارجاز *arjāz* verses in the meter *rajaz*; little (work) song

ارجوزة *urjūza* pl. اراجيز *arājīz*[2] poem in the meter *rajaz*

ارجوز[2] look up alphabetically

رجس *rajisa a* (*rajas*) and *rajusa u* (رجاسة *rajāsa*) to be dirty, filthy; to commit a shameful act, do s.th. disgraceful or dirty

رجس *rijs* pl. ارجاس *arjās* dirt, filth; dirty thing or act, atrocity

رجس *rajas* pl. ارجاس *arjās* dirt, filth

رجس *rajis* dirty, filthy

رجاسة *rajāsa* dirt, squalor

رجاس *rajjās* roaring, surging (sea); thundering

رجع *rajaʿa i* (رجوع *rujūʿ*) to come back, come again, return; to recur; to resort, turn (الى to); to recommence, begin again, resume (الى s.th.); to fall back (الى on), go back, revert (الى to); to look up (الى s.th. in a book), consult (الى a book); to go back, be traceable (الى to), be attributable (الى ان to the fact that ...), derive, stem, spring (الى from); رجع به الى to reduce s.th. to (its elements, or the like); to depend (الى on); to be due, belong by right (الى to); to fall under s.o.'s (ل) jurisdiction, be s.o.'s (ل) bailiwick; to desist, refrain (عن from); to withdraw (عن, also فى, e.g., what one has said), revoke, countermand, repeal, cancel (عن or فى, e.g., a decision); to turn against s.o. (على); رجع به على فلان to claim restitution of s.th. from s.o.; to demand, claim (ب s.th., على from s.o.); to entail, involve (ب s.th., a consequence); to have a good effect (فى on), be successful (فى with) | رجع على عقبه (*ʿaqbihī*) pl. رجعوا على اعقابهم (*aʿqābihim*) to retrace one's steps, go back the way one came; رجع الى الصحة (*ṣiḥḥa*) to regain one's health; رجع الى صوابه (*ṣawābihī*) to come to one's senses; رجع الى نفسه to watch o.s., examine o.s.; يرجع ذلك الى ان this is due to the fact that ...; يرجع السبب الى (*sabab*) the reason is to be found in ...; رجعت به الذاكرة الى he recalled, remembered ...; رجع فى كلامه (*kalāmihī*) to go back on one's word II to cause to come back or return; to return, give back; to send back; to turn away (عن ‌ه s.o. from); to sing or chant in a vibrant, quavering tone; to echo, reverberate (ه s.th.) | رجع صداه (*ṣadāhu*) to return the echo of s.th., echo s.th. III to return, come back (ه, ‌ه to); to revert

(ه to); to go over s.th. (ه) again, reiterate, repeat (ه s.th.); to go back, apply for information (ه to), consult (ه a book), look up (ه in a book); to turn (ه to s.o., في in s.th. for advice, etc.), consult, ask (ه s.o.); to refer (ه, ه to); to check, verify, examine critically (ه s.th.); to audit (ه accounts, etc.) | راجعه عقله (*ʻaqluhū*) to come to one's senses; راجع نفسه (*nafsahū*) to try to make up one's mind, reconsider the whole thing, think the matter over; يراجع *yurājaʻ* (in cross references) see ... **IV** to make or let return; to take back, turn back (ه الى s.o. to s.th.); to force (ه s.o.) to turn back; to ascribe, attribute, trace (ه الى s.th. to) **V** to return, come again; to reverberate, echo **VI** to return to one another; to withdraw, retreat, fall back, back off; to retrograde, fall off, diminish, deteriorate; to depart gradually (عن from); to fall behind, lag behind; to change one's mind **X** to demand the return of s.th. (ه), reclaim (ه s.th.); to get back, recover, retrieve, regain (ه s.th.); to take back, withdraw (e.g., وعدا *waʻdan* a promise), revoke, repeal, countermand, cancel (ه s.th., e.g., a decision); to say the words: انا لله وانا اليه راجعون *innā li-llāhi wa-innā ilaihi rājiʻūn* | استرجعه الى حافظته (*ḥāfiẓatihī*) to call s.th. to mind, recall s.th.

رجع *rajʻ* coming back, return; (also رجع الصوت *r. aṣ-ṣaut*, رجع الصدى *r. aṣ-ṣadā*) echo | كرجع البصر *ka-r. il-baṣar* in the twinkling of an eye, in a moment

رجعى *rajʻī* reactionary; retroactive; revocable (*Isl. Law*) | بأثر رجعى (*bi-aṯar*) with retroactive force (*jur.*)

رجعية *rajʻīya* reactionism, reaction

رجعة *rajʻa* return; recurrence; revocation, cancellation; receipt, voucher; — *rajʻa, rijʻa* return to one's wife after divorce, remarriage with one's divorced wife (*Isl. Law*)

رجعى *rujʻā* reactionism, reaction

رجوع *rujūʻ* return; reverting, coming back (الى to); recourse (الى to); traceability (الى to); revocation, withdrawal, retraction (عن of s.th.); resignation, surrender (عن of s.th.); reclamation; recall; restitution, return | برجوع البريد by return mail

رجيع *rajīʻ* excrement

مرجع *marjiʻ* pl. مراجع *marājiʻ*[2] return; authority to which one turns or appeals; place of refuge, retreat; recourse, resort; authority; competent authority, responsible agency; source (esp. scientific), authoritative reference work; resource; source to which s.th. goes back or to which s.th. can be attributed; starting point, origin; recourse (*jur.*) | مرجع النظر *m. an-naẓar* jurisdiction, competence; المرجع اليه he is the one to turn to; المرجع فى ذلك الى I am thereby referring to ...; كان مرجع هذا الشىء الى this was due to ..., was attributable to ...; اليهم مرجع الفضل (*m. ul-faḍl*) the merit is due to them

مرجعية *marjiʻīya* authority

مراجعة *murājaʻa* reiteration, repetition; inspection, study, examination; consultation (of a reference work); request; application, petition (esp. to an authority); application for advice or instructions, etc., consultation (of s.o.); checking, verification, re-examination; auditing, audit (also مراجعة الحساب); revision, correction (of a manuscript)

ارجاع *irjāʻ* return, restitution; refundment; attribution (الى to); reduction (الى to)

تراجع *tarājuʻ* withdrawal, retreat; change of mind; recession, retrogradation

ارتجاع *irtijāʻ* return to an older form or order, reactionism, reaction

ارتجاعى *irtijāʻī* reactionary

استرجاع **istirjā'** reclamation; recovery, retrieval; retraction, withdrawal, revocation

راجع **rāji'** returning, reverting, etc.; due, attributable (الى to); rightfully belonging (الى to s.o.); subject (ل to s.th.); depending (ل on) | الحمى الراجعة (*ḥummā*) relapsing fever

مراجع **murāji'** checker, verifier, examiner; reviser | مراجع الحسابات *m. al-ḥisābāt* auditor, comptroller

رجف **rajafa** *u* (*rajf*, رجفان *rajafān*) to be convulsed, be shaken; to tremble, quake; to shiver, shudder; — to agitate, convulse, shake (ه s.o.) **IV** to make (ه s.o.) tremble or shudder; to convulse, shake, rock (ه s.th.), to spread lies, false rumors; also with ب, e.g., ارجف بافتراءات (*bi-ftirā'āt*) to spread calumnies **VIII** to tremble, quake; to shudder

رجفة **rajfa** (n. vic.) trepidation, tremor; shudder, shiver

رجاف **rajjāf** trembling, quaking; shaken, convulsed

ارجاف **irjāf** pl. اراجيف *arājīf*[2] untrue, disquieting talk, false rumor

رجل **rajila** *a* to go on foot, walk **II** to comb (ه the hair); to let down (ه the hair), let it hang long **V** = **I**; to dismount (من or عن from; rider); to assume masculine manners, behave like a man | ترجل فى طريقه to walk all the way **VIII** to improvise, extemporize, deliver offhand (ه a speech) **X** to become a man, reach the age of manhood, grow up; to act like a man, display masculine manners or qualities

رجل **rijl** f., pl. ارجل *arjul* foot; leg

رجل **rijl** pl. ارجال *arjāl* swarm (esp. of locusts); — common purslane (*Portulaca oleracea* L.; *bot.*)

رجل **rajil** going on foot, pedestrian, walking

رجل **rajul** pl. رجال *rijāl* man; pl. رجالات *rijālāt* great, important men, leading personalities, men of distinction | رجال الدولة *r. ad-daula* statesmen; رجال السند *r. as-sanad* informants, sources of information

رجالى **rijālī** men's, for men (e.g., apparel)

رجولة **rujūla** masculinity, virility, manhood

رجولية **rujūlīya** masculinity, virility, manhood

مرجل **mirjal** pl. مراجل *marājil*[2] cooking kettle, caldron; boiler

ارتجال **irtijāl** improvisation, extemporization, extemporary speech

ارتجالى **irtijālī** extemporary, improvised, impromptu, offhand, unprepared

راجل **rājil** pl. رجل *rajl*, رجالة *rajjāla*, رجال *rujjāl*, رجلان *rujlān* going on foot, walking; pedestrian

مرتجل **murtajal** improvised, extemporaneous, extemporary, impromptu, offhand

[1]رجم **rajama** *u* (*rajm*) to stone (ه s.o.); to curse, damn, abuse, revile (ه s.o.) | رجم بالغيب (*ġaib*) to talk about s.th. of which one knows nothing; to guess, surmise, make conjectures; to predict the future **II** رجم بالغيب do.

رجم **rajm** stoning; (pl. رجوم *rujūm*) missile | رجم بالغيب (*ġaib*) conjecture, guesswork; prophecy

رجم **rujum** shooting stars, meteorites

رجمة **rujma** pl. رجم *rujam*, رجام *rijām* tombstone

رجيم **rajīm** stoned; cursed, damned; see also alphabetically

[2]ترجم, ترجمة look up alphabetically

مرجونة **marjūna** basket

(رجو) رجا **rajā** *u* (رجاء **rajā'**, رجاة **rajāh**, مرجاة **marjāh**) to hope; to hope for s.th. (ه); to expect, anticipate (ه s.th.), look forward (ه to); to wish (ه for s.th., ه ل s.o. s.th., e.g., success); to ask (ه for s.th., من or ه s.o., ان to do s.th.), request (ه s.th., من from s.o., ان that he ...) | رجاه فى الحاح (*ilḥāḥ*) to plead with s.o., implore s.o.; ارجو عدم المؤاخذة (*'adama l-mu'āḵaḏa*) I must ask your indulgence V to hope (ه, ه for); to expect, anticipate (ه, ه s.th., s.o.), look forward (ه to); to request (ه s.o.); to ask (ه s.o.) VIII to hope (ه, ه for); to expect, anticipate (ه, ه s.th., s.o.), look forward (ه to); to dread (ه s.o.)

رجا *rajan* and رجاء *rajā'* pl. ارجاء *arjā'* side, direction; region; — pl. ارجاء *arjā'* vastnesses (of a land), expanses; whole vicinity or area | فى ارجائه about its interior, e.g., فى ارجاء الغرفة (*ḡurfa*) all about the room, فى ارجاء البلاد all over the country, throughout the country; تجاوبت ارجاء الردهة بالتصفيق (*a. ur-radha*) the entire auditorium resounded with applause; شاسع الارجاء and واسع الارجاء vast in extent, vast-dimensioned

رجاء *rajā'* hope (ب, فى and genit.: of); expectation, anticipation; urgent request | على رجاء in the hope of, hoping for; رجاء العلم *rajā' al-'ilm* for your information (on memos, records, etc.); رأس الرجاء الصالح Cape of Good Hope

رجاة *rajāh* hope, expectation, anticipation

رجية *rajīya* s.th. hoped for; hope

مرجاة *marjāh* hope

راج *rājin* hoping, full of hope

مرجو *marjūw* hoped for, expected; requested | المرجو من فضلك ان (*min faḍlika*) approx.: I hope you will be kind enough to ...; المرجو مراعاة ان (*murā'ātu*) please notice that ..., attention is called to the fact that ...

رجى *rajiya* *a* to become silent; to remain silent; pass. رجى عليه (*rujiya*) to be tongue-tied, be unable to utter a sound

رجيم (Fr. *régime*) *rijīm* diet

رحب **raḥiba** *a* (*raḥab*) and **raḥuba** *u* (**ruḥb**, رحابة **raḥāba**) to be wide, spacious, roomy II to welcome (ب s.o., also ب s.th., e.g., news), bid welcome (ب to s.o.); to receive graciously, make welcome (ب s.o.) V to welcome (ب s.o.), bid welcome (ب to)

رحب *raḥb* wide, spacious, roomy; unconfined | رحب الصدر *r. aṣ-ṣadr* generous, magnanimous; broad-minded, open-minded, liberal; frank, candid, open-hearted; carefree; صدر رحب (*raḥb*) generosity, magnanimity; open-mindedness, broad-mindedness, liberality; frankness, candor; رحب الباع generous, open-handed, liberal; رحب الذراع do.

رحب *ruḥb* vastness, wideness, spaciousness, unconfinedness | اتى على الرحب والسعة (*atā, sa'a*) to be welcome; وجد رحبا وسعة (*sa'atan*) to meet with a friendly reception

رحب *raḥab* vastness, wideness, spaciousness, unconfinedness | رحب الصدر *r. aṣ-ṣadr* magnanimity, generosity; lightheartedness

رحبة *raḥba, raḥaba* pl. *-āt* public square (surrounded by buildings); (pl. *raḥabāt* and رحاب *riḥāb*) vastness, expanse | رحاب الكون *riḥāb al-kaun* and رحاب الفضاء *r. al-faḍā'* vastness of outer space

رحيب *raḥīb* = رحب *raḥb*

رحابة *raḥāba* wideness, vastness, spaciousness, unconfinedness | رحابة الصدر *r. aṣ-ṣadr* magnanimity, generosity

مرحبا بك *marḥaban bika* welcome!

ترحاب *tarḥāb* welcome, greeting | قابله بترحاب (*qābalahū*) to receive s.o. with open arms

ترحيب *tarḥīb* welcoming, welcome, greeting

رحرح *raḥraḥa*: رحرح بالكلام (*kalām*) to equivocate, speak ambiguously, beat around the bush

رحرح *ruḥraḥ* and رحراح *raḥraḥ* wide, broad, flat; carefree, pleasant (life)

رحض *raḥaḍa a* (*raḥḍ*) to rinse, wash

مرحاض *mirḥāḍ* pl. مراحيض *marāḥīḍ*[2] lavatory, toilet

رحيق *raḥīq* exquisite wine; nectar

[1]رحل *raḥala a* (رحيل *raḥīl*) to set out; to depart, leave; to move away, emigrate; to start (عن from a place) | رجل يرحل ويقيم (*yuqīm*) a man constantly on the go, a dynamic man II to make (ه s.o.) leave, induce or urge (ه s.o.) to depart; to evacuate (ه الى s.o. to), resettle, relocate (ه الى s.o. in); to deport (ه الى s.o. to); to allow (ه s.o.) to emigrate; to give (ه s.o.) travel clearance; to carry (passengers, e.g., a ship); to transfer (ه s.th.); to transport, convey, forward (ه s.th.); to dispatch, send out (ه s.th.); to carry over, post (ه an item; bookkeeping); to carry forward (ه the balance; bank) V to wander, roam, migrate, lead a nomadic life; to be evacuated VIII to set out, leave, depart; to move away, emigrate | ارتحل الى رحمة ربه (*ilā raḥmati rabbihī*) to pass away, die

رحل *raḥl* pl. رحال *riḥāl* camel saddle; saddlebags; baggage, luggage; pl. stopping place, stop, stopover | شد الرحال (*šadda*) to set out, break camp; ألقى رحاله *alqā riḥālahū* to stop (فى in, at)

رحلة *riḥla* travel, journey; trip, tour; travelogue

رحلة *ruḥla* destination, place for which one is bound

رحيل *raḥīl* departure, setting out; emigration; exodus; demise

رحال *raḥḥāl* pl. رحل *ruḥḥal* roving, roaming, peregrinating, wandering, migratory, nomadic; — (pl. رحالة *raḥḥāla*) great traveler, explorer; nomad | الطيور الرحالة migratory birds; الاعراب (العربان) الرحل (*'urbān*) the nomadic Bedouins

رحالة *raḥḥāla* great traveler, explorer; globetrotter

مرحلة *marḥala* pl. مراحل *marāḥil*[2] a day's journey; leg of a journey; way station; stage, phase | يزيد عليه بمراحل (*yazīdu*) it exceeds it by far; فى مراحل حياتها (*ḥayātihā*) throughout her life, in every stage of her life

ترحال *tarḥāl* departure, setting out | حياة الترحال *ḥayāt at-t.* nomadic life

ترحيل *tarḥīl* emigration, exodus; effectuation of (s.o.'s) departure; deportation; evacuation; resettlement; transfer; moving; transport, transportation; posting (of accounts); carrying forward (*fin.*); dispatch | ترحيل عمال *t. 'ummāl* assignment (or detailing) of workmen

ارتحال *irtiḥāl* departure, setting out; emigration, exodus; demise

راحل *rāḥil* pl. رحل *ruḥḥal* departing, leaving, parting; traveling; (pl. *-ūn*) deceased, late, esp. الفقيد الراحل the deceased

راحلة *rāḥila* pl. رواحل *rawāḥil*[2] female riding camel | شد راحلته (*šadda*) to saddle one's camel, start out on a journey

مرحل *muraḥḥal* pl. *-āt* carry-over | مجموع مرحل balance carried forward (*fin.*)

[2]راحيل *rāḥīl*[2] Rachel

رحم *raḥima a* (رحمة *raḥma*, مرحمة *marḥama*) to have mercy (ه upon s.o.), have compassion (ه for s.o.); to spare, let off (ه s.o.); to be merciful II رحم عليه to say to s.o.: رحمك الله *raḥimaka llāh* may God have mercy upon you; to ask God to have mercy (على upon s.o.), plead for God's mercy (على for what has happened) V = II; VI to show human understanding for one another, love and respect one another X to ask (ه s.o.) to have mercy

رحم *raḥim, riḥm* f., pl. ارحام *arḥām* uterus; womb; relationship, kinship | ذوو الارحام *ḏawū l-a.* relatives on the maternal side

رحمة *raḥma* pity, compassion; human understanding, sympathy, kindness; mercy | كان تحت رحمته to be at s.o.'s mercy; جعله تحت رحمته to leave s.th. or s.o. to s.o.'s mercy; بساط الرحمة pall

رحيم *raḥīm* pl. رحماء *ruḥamā'*[2] and رحوم *raḥūm* merciful, compassionate

الرحمن *ar-raḥmān* the Merciful (i.e., God)

مرحمة *marḥama* pl. مراحم *marāḥim*[2] pity, compassion, sympathy; mercy

ترحيم *tarḥīm*: ترحيم للموتى (*mautā*) pl. تراحيم *tarāḥīm*[2] intercessory prayer for the dead (*Chr.*)

استرحام *istirḥām* plea for mercy

مرحوم *marḥūm* deceased, late, e.g., المرحوم السيد the late Mr. ...

رحى *raḥan* f., pl. ارحاء *arḥā'*, رحى *ruḥiy*, ارحية *arḥiya* quern, hand mill | حجر الرحى *ḥajar ar-r.* millstone; دارت رحى الحرب (القتال) *dārat r. l-ḥarb* the war (fighting) broke out; the war (fighting) was going on

رحوى *raḥawī* rotating, rotatory

رحاى *raḥḥāy* pl. *-ūn* grinder

رخ *rakka u* to mix with water, dilute (ه wine)

رخ *rakk* (n. un. ة) light shower

رخ *rukk* roc, name of a fabulous giant bird; (pl. رخاخ *rikāk*, رخخة *rikaka*) rook, castle (chess)

رخاخ *rakāk* soft (ground); comfortable, pleasant, easy (life)

رخص *rakuṣa u* (*rukṣ*) to be cheap, inexpensive; (رخاصة *rakāṣa*) to be supple, tender, soft **II** to permit, allow (ل s.o. ب or ق s.th.); to authorize, license (ل s.o., ب or ق to do s.th.); to empower (ل s.o.); to reduce the price (ه of s.th.) **IV** to reduce the price (ه of s.th.) **V** to be willing to please, meet on fair terms (مع ق s.o. in), show o.s. ready to compromise (مع with s.o. ق in s.th.); to make concessions (ق or ب in s.th.); to permit o.s. liberties, take liberties (ق in) **X** to find cheap, regard as inexpensive (ه s.th.); to request s.o.'s (ه) permission

رخص *rakṣ* supple, tender, soft

رخص *rukṣ* cheapness, inexpensiveness

رخصة *rukṣa* pl. رخص *rukaṣ* permission; concession, license, franchise; admission; authorization; leave; permit | رخصة قيادة السيارات *r. qiyādat as-sayyārāt* driving permit, operator's license

رخيص *rakīṣ* supple, tender, soft; cheap, inexpensive, low-priced; base, mean, low; trash, trumpery

ترخيص *tarkīṣ* pl. *-āt*, تراخيص *tarākīṣ*[2] granting of permission; permission; authorization; mandate; concession; license; price reduction, price cut

مرتخص *murtakaṣ* low-priced, inexpensive, cheap | كل مرتخص وغال *kullu murtakaṣin wa-ġālin* every conceivable effort, everything (in one's power)

رخم *rakuma u* (رخامة *rakāma*) and *rakama u* to be soft, mellow, gentle, pleasant (voice); رخمت بيضها (على بيضها) *rakamat baiḍahā* (*'alā baiḍihā*) to sit on the eggs (hen) **II** to soften, mellow (ه the voice); to apocopate (ه a word); to tile with marble (ه the floor)

رخم *rakam* (coll.; n. un. ة) Egyptian vulture (Neophron percnopterus; *zool.*)

رخام *rukām* marble

رخامة *rukāma* pl. *-āt* marble slab

رخيم *rakīm* soft, mellow, pleasant, melodious (voice); ○ note lowered by a semitone, flat (*mus.*)

ترخيم *tarḵīm* shortening, apocopation, esp. of a name in the vocative by elision of the final consonant (*gram.*)

رخو and رخى (رخو) **raḵuwa u** and رخى **raḵiya** *a* (رخاوة *raḵāwa*, رخاء *raḵā'*) to be or become loose, slack, relaxed; to slacken, slump, sag, relax; — رخا **raḵā u** (رخاء *raḵā'*): رخا عيشه (*'aišuhū*) to live in easy circumstances, live in opulence **IV** to loosen, slacken (ه s.th.); to relax (ه s.th.); to let go (ه s.th.); to lower, drop, let down (ه s.th.) **VI** to slacken, sag, droop, become limp; to show little energy or zeal, let up, become lax, be remiss (عن in s.th.); to go down, slump (prices); to lag, become dull or listless (stock market); to diminish, flag, wane, ebb, decrease; to desist (عن from); to be lowered, drop, fall (curtain); to be delayed, be retarded **VIII** to slacken, slump, sag, droop, become limp, flaccid, flabby; to become loose, work loose; to soften, become soft; to relax, become relaxed, unbend; to abate, let up; to languish, flag, lose force or vigor **X** = **VIII**

رخو *raḵw, riḵw* loose, slack; limp, flabby, flaccid; indolent, languid; soft; supple

رخاء *raḵā'* ease, comfort, happiness; prosperity; abundance, opulence (of living); welfare; fairness, lowness (of prices)

رخاء *ruḵā'* gentle breeze

رخاوة *raḵāwa* softness; flaccidity, limpness; laxity | رخاوة العود *r. al-'ūd* weakness of character

رخى *raḵīy* feeble, weakened, languid; relaxed, at ease; cozy, comfortable

تراخ *tarāḵin* limpness; slackness; languor, lassitude; abatement, mitigation, letup; relaxation; loosening, looseness

ارتخاء *irtiḵā'* loosening, slackening; looseness, slackness; laxity; abatement, mitigation, letup; ease, relaxedness; relaxation; limpness; languor, lassitude

استرخاء *istirḵā'* = ارتخاء *irtiḵā'*

راخ *rāḵin* sagging, drooping

متراخ *mutarāḵin* limp, flaccid, flabby; drooping; languid; negligent, indolent, slack

رد **radda u** (*radd*) to send back; to bring back, take back (الى ,ه ,ه s.o., s.th. to); to return (الى ه s.th. to its place), put back, lay back (الى ه s.th. in its place); to throw back, repel, drive back, drive away (ه s.o.); to resist, oppose (ه s.o.); to turn down, refuse, decline (ه s.th., e.g., the fulfillment of a wish); to ward off, parry, repel (هجوما *hujūman* an attack); to reject (تهمة *tuhmatan* a suspicion); to hand back, give back, return, restore (ه s.th., الى to s.o.); to return (السلام *as-salāma* the greeting); to reply (على to s.o.), answer (على s.o.); to reflect (ه light); to throw back, echo (ه the voice); to refute, disprove (على s.th.); to hold back, keep, restrain (عن ه s.o. from s.th.); to dissuade (عن ه s.o. from), prevail upon s.o. (ه) not to do s.th. (عن); to trace back, attribute (الى ه s.th. to an origin); to bring, yield (على ه s.th. to s.o.); to reappoint, reinstate (ه ه s.o. as, e.g., حاكما *ḥākiman* as governor) | رد الباب to close the door; رد جوابا (*jawāban*) to answer; ما يرد هذا عليك شيئا this won't help you at all; لا يرد (*yuraddu*) irrefutable; رده على عقبيه (*'aqbaihi*) pl. ردهم على اعقابهم (*a'qābihim*) to drive s.o. back to where he came from; رد عينه عنه (*'ainahū*) he averted his eyes from it **II** to keep away, avert, prevent, stave off (ه s.th.); to repel, throw back (ه ,ه s.o., s.th.); to repeat (constantly, frequently); to break forth, burst (ه into, e.g., into singing), strike up, intone, let ring out (ه a tune, or the like) | ردد الصدى (*ṣadā*) to return the echo; ردد النظر ى (*naẓara*) to look at s.th. again and again;

ردد طرفه بين (*ṭarfahū*) to let one's eyes wander between, look first at one, then at the other **V** to be thrown back, be reflected (voice, echo); to ring out (shouts); to shift repeatedly (wind); to come and go (على at s.o.'s house; rarely الى), frequent, visit frequently (على s.o.'s house, a place; rarely الى); to return, recur; to hesitate, be reluctant (فى in s.th., to do s.th.); to waver, become uncertain, become doubtful (فى in s.th. or as to s.th.) | تردد على الالسنة (*alsina*) to be frequently discussed (question) **VIII** to withdraw, retreat, fall back; to move backward, retrogress; to go back, return, revert (الى to); to fall back (الى on); to go away, absent o.s.; to desist, refrain (عن from), renounce, give up, abandon, quit, leave (عن s.th.); to forsake, desert (عن one's faith, one's principles, etc.), apostatize, fall off (عن from) | ارتد على عقبيه (*ʿaqbaihi*), pl. ارتدوا على أعقابهم (*aʿqābihim*) to withdraw, turn back **X** to reclaim, demand back, call in (ه s.th.), demand the return (ه of s.th.); to bring back, lead back (ه الى s.o. to); to get back (ه s.th.); to retrieve, recover, regain (ه s.th.); to withdraw (e.g., يده *yadahū* one's hand; also fig., e.g., استقالته *istiqālatahū* one's resignation); to withdraw, take out (ه money, from an account, from a bank) | استرد انفاسه (*anfāsahū*) to catch one's breath

رد **radd** pl. ردود **rudūd** return; restoration, restitution; refund, reimbursement; repayment, requital; repulsion; warding off, parrying; denial, refusal; rejection; reply, answer; reflection (e.g., of light); refutation; attribution (الى to) | ر. الفعل r. *al-fiʿl* reaction; رد الاعتبار rehabilitation; ردا على (*raddan*) in reply to ...; اخذ ورد see اخذ *akd*

ردة **radda** ugliness; reverberation, echo; bran

ردة **ridda** apostasy (عن الاسلام from Islam)

ارد **aradd**[2] more useful, more profitable (على to s.o.)

مرد **maradd** fact to which s.th. is attributable, underlying factor or reason; averting, rejection, repulsion; responsory (*Chr.*) | لا مرد له (*maradda*) irresistible; مرده الى (*maradduhū*) it is attributable to ..., one must ascribe it to ...; لا مرد له الا براعته (*maradda, barāʿatuhū*) it can only be attributed to his efficiency; كان على مرد لسانه (*maraddi lisānihī*) to be constantly on s.o.'s lips, be a standing phrase with s.o.

ترداد **tardād** frequent repetition; frequentation

ترديد **tardīd** repetition, reiteration

تردد **taraddud** frequent coming and going, frequentation; frequency (*el.*); hesitation, irresolution, indecision, wavering; reluctance

ارتداد **irtidād** retreat, withdrawal; retrogression; renunciation, desertion; apostasy (عن الاسلام from Islam) | كارتداد الطرف *ka-rtidādi ṭ-ṭarf* in the twinkling of an eye, in a jiffy

استرداد **istirdād** reclamation, claim of restitution, vindication (*Isl. Law*); recovery, retrieval; retraction, withdrawal; refundment, reimbursement; withdrawal, taking out (of money, from an account)

مردود **mardūd** yield, return(s)

مرتد **murtadd** turncoat, renegade, apostate

[1]ردأ **radaʾa** *a* (**radʾ**) to support, prop, shore up (ه a wall)

ردء **ridʾ** pl. ارداء **ardāʾ** support; help, helper

[2]ردؤ **raduʾa** *u* (رداءة **radāʾa**) to be bad **V** to become bad, be spoiled

رديء **radīʾ** pl. ادرياء **ardiyāʾ**[2] bad; mean, base, vile; evil, wicked; vicious, malicious | ردىء السمعة *r. as-sumʿa* of ill repute

أردأ **arda'**[2] worse; more wicked

رداءة **radā'a** badness; wickedness; viciousness, maliciousness

اردب **irdabb** (now commonly pronounced *ardabb*) pl. ارادب *arādib*[2] ardeb, a dry measure (*Eg.*; = 198 l)

اردبة **irdabba** cesspool

ردح **radaḥ** long period of time | ردحا من الدهر *radaḥan min ad-dahr* for a long time

ردس **radasa** *i u* (*rads*) to crush (ه s.th.); to roll smooth, level by rolling (ه ground)

ردع **radaʿa** *a* (*radʿ*) to keep, prevent (عن ه s.o. from) VIII to be kept, be prevented (من from)

رادع **rādiʿ** deterring; (pl. روادع *rawādiʿ*[2]) deterrent; impediment, obstacle, handicap; restriction, limitation, curb, check; inhibition (*psych.*)

ردغة **radġa, radaġa** mud, mire, slush

ردف **radafa** *u* (*radf*) and *radifa* *a* to come next, come immediately after s.o. or s.th. (ه, ه), follow, succeed (ه s.o., ه s.th.) III to ride behind s.o. (ه, on the same animal); to be the substitute (ه of s.o.), replace (ه s.o., ه s.th.); to be synonymous (ه with) IV to seat (ه s.o.) behind one (on an animal); to make (ه s.th.) be followed (ب by s.th. else); to complement, complete (ب ه s.th. with or by) VI to follow one another, come in succession; to pile up in layers, become stratified; to form a single line; to flock, throng (على to); to be synonymous

ردف **ridf** pl. ارداف *ardāf* rear man (riding on the same animal); one who or that which is subsequent, follows, comes next; posteriors, backside, rump; haunches, croup (of an animal); dual: الردفان *ar-ridfān* day and night

رداف **ridāf** croup, rump (of an animal)

رديف **radīf** rear man, one following next in line; redif, reserve (in the army of the former Turkish Empire)

رديفة **radīfa** fem. of رديف

ترادف **tarāduf** succession; synonymity

مرادف **murādif** synonym (of a word); synonymous, consignificant (ل with); corresponding in meaning, analogous

مترادف **mutarādif** synonymous; مترادفات synonyms

ردم **radama** *i u* (*radm*) to fill up with earth (ه pit, pond) II to repair, fix, mend IV not to leave (على s.o.), cling (على to s.o.; said of disease) V to be mended, be repaired; to repair, mend (ه s.th.); to be worn, show signs of wear

ردم **radm** filling up (of swamps, ponds, etc.); rubble, debris; dam

رديم **radīm** worn, shabby, threadbare (garment)

ردن **radana** *i* (*radn*) to spin; to purr (cat); to grumble (على at)

ردن **rudn** pl. اردان *ardān* sleeve

رديني **rudainī** spear (originally epithet for one of superior quality)

مردن **mirdan** pl. مرادن *marādin*[2] spindle

ردنجوت (Fr. *redingote*) **redengōt** frock coat, Prince Albert

ردهة **radha** hall; large room, sitting room, parlor; lobby; entrance hall, vestibule | ردهة الاستقبال reception hall, drawing room, parlor ردهة المحاضرات *r. al-muḥāḍarāt* lecture room

ردى **radiya** *a* (ردى *radan*) to perish, be destroyed II to bring to the ground (ه s.o.), bring about the fall of (ه) IV to bring to the ground (ه s.o.), bring about the fall of (ه); to destroy, ruin (ه s.o.); to fell

(• s.o.); to kill (• s.o.) | ارداه قتيلا (*qatilan*) to fell s.o. with a deadly blow **V** to fall, tumble; to decline, fall off, come down, go from bad to worse; to deteriorate, become worse; to clothe o.s. (ب with), put on (ب a garment) **VIII** to put on (▲ a garment or headgear); to wear (▲ a garment, a headgear), be clothed, be clad (▲ in) | ارتدى ملابسه (*malābisahū*) to put on one's clothes, dress, get dressed

ردى ***radan*** ruin, destruction

رداء ***ridā'*** pl. اردية ***ardiya*** loose outer garment, cloak, robe; (lady's) dress, gown; attire, costume | رداء المساء ***r. al-masā'*** evening gown

مترد ***mutaraddin*** dressed

رذ ***raḏḏa*** *u*: رذت السماء (*samā'*) and **IV** there was a drizzle, it drizzled

رذاذ ***raḏāḏ*** drizzle

رذل ***raḏila*** *a* and ***raḏula*** *u* (رذالة ***raḏāla***) to be low, base, vile, despicable, contemptible; — ***raḏala*** *u* (***raḏl***) to reject, cast off, discard, repudiate, disown (▲, • s.o., s.th.); to despise, disdain, scorn (▲, • s.o., s.th.); to disapprove (▲, • of) **IV** to reject, cast off, discard, repudiate, disown (▲, • s.o., s.th.) **X** to regard as low or despicable (▲, • s.o., s.th.)

رذل ***raḏl*** rejection; repudation; (pl. رذول ***ruḏūl***, ارذال ***arḏāl***) low, base, mean, vile, despicable, contemptible

رذيل ***raḏīl*** pl. رذلاء ***ruḏalā'***[2] low, base, mean, vile, despicable, contemptible, depraved

رذالة ***raḏāla*** lowness, baseness, meanness, vileness, depravity

رذيلة ***raḏīla*** pl. رذائل ***raḏā'il*** vice; depravity

مرذول ***marḏūl*** depraved, despicable, mean, base, vile, evil, wicked

رز ***ruzz*** (= ارز ***aruzz***) rice

[2]رز ***razza*** *u* (***razz***) to insert, drive in (▲ s.th.) **II** to burnish, polish (▲ s.th.) **IV** to telephone

رزة ***razza*** pl. ***-āt*** staple, U bolt; ring screw; joint pin

ارزيز ◯ ***irzīz*** telephone

رزأ ***raza'a*** *a* (رزء ***raz'***) to deprive (ق or ▲ • s.o. of s.th.); pass. رزئ ***ruzi'a*** to incur or suffer loss; to lose (ب s.th.); to be afflicted (ب by)

رزء ***ruz'*** pl. ارزاء ***arzā'*** heavy loss, serious damage; disaster, calamity

رزيئة ***razī'a*** and رزية ***raziya*** pl. رزايا ***razāyā*** heavy loss, serious damage; disaster, calamity

رزب ***razaba*** *u* (***razb***) to keep, stick, cling (▲ to)

مرزبة ***mirzabba*** pl. مرازب ***marāzib***[2] iron rod

مرزاب ***mirzāb*** pl. مرازيب ***marāzīb***[2] waterspout, gargoyle; (roof) gutter

رزح ***razaḥa*** *a* (رزوح ***ruzūḥ***, رزاح ***ruzāḥ***, ***razāḥ***) to succumb, collapse, sink to the ground (under a burden); to descend, hover (e.g., silence) **III** to suffer

مرزغ ***murziġ*** muddy, boggy, miry

رزق ***razaqa*** *u* to provide with the means of subsistence (• s.o.; said of God); to bestow (▲ • upon s.o. s.th., material or spiritual possessions; said of God), endow (▲ • s.o. with); to bless (▲ • s.o. with, esp. مولودا with a child); — pass. ***ruziqa*** to be endowed (▲ with); to live **VIII** to make a living, gain one's livelihood; to live (من on or by s.th.) **X** to seek one's livelihood; to ask for the means of subsistence

رزق ***rizq*** pl. ارزاق ***arzāq*** livelihood, means of living, subsistence; daily bread, nourishment, sustenance; boon, blessing (of God); property, possessions, wealth, fortune; income; pay, wages | ارزاق ناشفة dry rations, emergency rations (*mil.*)

الرزاق *ar-razzāq* the Maintainer, the Provider (one of the 99 attributes of God)

استرزاق *istirzāq* independent livelihood, self-support

مرزوق *marzūq* blessed (by God), fortunate, prosperous, successful

مرتزق *murtaziq* hired, hireling, mercenary, kept

مرتزقة *murtaziqa* kept persons, hangers-on; mercenaries

مرتزق *murtazaq* means of subsistence, livelihood, living

رزم **razama** *i u* (*razm*) to bundle, bale, pack, wrap up (ه s.th.)

رزمة *rizma* pl. رزم *rizam* bundle; bale, pack; parcel, package; ream (of paper)

رزن **razuna** *u* (رزانة *razāna*) to be grave, serious, sedate, staid, calm, composed, self-possessed **V** to display grave or sedate manners, show o.s. calm, composed, self-possessed

رزين *razīn* grave, serious, sedate, staid; composed, calm, self-possessed

رزانة *razāna* gravity, sedateness, staidness; composure, self-possession, poise

رزنامة **ruznāma** see روزنامة

رزية pl. رزايا see رزيئة

رسيس **rasīs** covered with verdigris

رسب **rasaba** *u* (رسوب *rusūb*) to sink to the bottom, settle, subside (esp., in water); to fail, flunk (in an examination) **II** to cause to settle (ه s.th., in a liquid), deposit (ه a sediment); to precipitate (ه s.th.; *chem.*) **V** to settle, subside, be deposited; to precipitate (*chem.*)

رسوب *rusūb* sediment, deposit; lees, dregs, settlings; precipitate (*chem.*); failure (in an examination)

ترسيب *tarsīb* sedimentation; precipitation (*chem.*)

راسب *rāsib* pl. رواسب *rawāsib*[2] sediment, deposit; dregs, lees, settlings; precipitate (*chem.*); residue

رستامية **rustāmīya** cassock (of a priest)

رستق **rastaqa** to tidy, arrange well, put in order (ه s.th.)

روستو ,رستو (It. *arrosto*) **rostō** roast meat

رستوران (Fr. *restaurant*) **restorān** restaurant

مرسح **marsaḥ** (= مسرح) pl. مراسح *marāsiḥ*[2] theater, playhouse; stage; party, social gathering

مرسحى *marsaḥī* social, party (used attributively); formal (dress)

رسخ **rasaḵa** *u* (رسوخ *rusūḵ*) to be firmly established, be deeply rooted (في in s.th.); to be firm, solid, stable; to be conversant, be thoroughly familiar (في with s.th.), be well versed, be at home (في in s.th., in a field); to seep in; to permeate (في a fabric); to become fast (color or dyes in a fabric) **II** and **IV** to make (ه s.th.) take root(s), establish (ه s.th.); to implant (ه s.th.); to secure, make fast, fix firmly, ground (ه s.th.) | ارسخ الشىء فى ذهنه (*ḏihnihī*) to impress or inculcate s.th. upon s.o.

ارسخ *arsaḵ*[2] more firmly established, more deeply rooted | ارسخ قدما (*qadaman*) do.

راسخ *rāsiḵ* firmly established, deep-rooted; grounded, firmly fixed, stable; conversant (في with s.th.), thoroughly versed, completely at home (في in a field)

رسراس **risrās** (*eg.*) glue, adhesive, specif., one for pasting leather, made of a yellow powder

رسغ **rusḡ** pl. ارساغ **arsāḡ**, ارسغ **arsuḡ** wrist

رسف **rasafa u i** to go in shackles; to be bound; to be moored (ship)

رسل **rasila a** (**rasal**) to be long and flowing (hair) **III** to correspond, carry on a correspondence, exchange letters (ه with s.o.); to contact (ه s.o.), get in touch (ه with s.o.) **IV** to send out, dispatch (ب or ه, ه s.o., s.th. الى, also ل, to); to send off, send away (ب or ه, ه s.o., s.th. الى, also ل, to); to send, forward, ship (ب or ه s.th. الى, also ل, to); to send, transmit (*radio*); to release, let go (ه s.th.); to set free (ه s.th.); to discharge (ه s.th.); to pour forth, vent (ه s.th.), give vent (ه to); to utter (ه words); to shed (ه tears); to let (ه the hair) hang down, let it fall (على on) | ارسل فى طلبه (*ṭalabihī*) to send for s.o.; ارسل الكلام ارسالا (*al-kalāma irsālan*) to speak without restraint, talk freely; ارسل نفسه مع طبيعتها (*nafsahū*) to yield to one's natural impulse, do the natural thing; ارسله على سجيته (*sajīyatihī*) to make s.o. feel at home; ارسل نفسه على سجيتها (*nafsahū*) to feel at home, let o.s. go **V** to proceed leisurely, take one's time (فى in s.th.); to hang down, be long and flowing (hair) **VI** to keep up a correspondence, exchange letters; to send to one another, exchange (ب s.th.) **X** to ask (من s.o.) to send (ه s.th.), have s.o. (من) send (ه s.th.); to be relaxed, at ease, free from restraint; to be long and flowing (hair); to be friendly, affable, intimate, chummy (الى with s.o.); to act naturally, without affectation; to let o.s. go; to enlarge (فى الكلام *fī l-kalām* in discourse, i.e., to talk at length); to abandon o.s., give o.s. up (فى to s.th., also مع or الى); to persist (فى in s.th.), keep up (فى s.th.)

رسل **rasl** easy, gentle, leisurely (pace, gait); loose, slack, relaxed; long and flowing (hair)

رسل **risl** moderation | على رسلك ! slowly! gently! take it easy!

رسيل **rasīl** pl. رسلاء **rusalā'**[2] messenger; runner (*mil.*)

رسول **rasūl** pl. رسل **rusul** messenger; emissary; envoy, delegate; apostle (*Chr.*); الرسول or رسول الله the Messenger of God (i.e., Mohammed)

رسولى **rasūlī** apostolic, papal (*Chr.*) | البركة الرسولية (*baraka*) apostolic benediction; السدة الرسولية (*sudda*) the Holy See; قاصد رسولى apostolic delegate

رسالة **risāla** pl. -**āt**, رسائل **rasā'il**[2] consignment, shipment; mail item; (written) communication, (written) report; missive; letter, note; epistle; dispatch; message; treatise; radio message; (pl. -*āt*) mission, calling, vocation | رسالة برقية (*barqīya*) telegram; رسالة غرامية (*ḡarāmīya*) love letter; رسالة مسجلة (*musajjala*) registered letter

رسيلات **rusailāt**: القى الخبر على رسيلاته (*kabara*) he didn't take the matter seriously

○ مرسال **mirsāl**: مرسال نور **m. nūr** pl. -**āt** searchlight

مراسلة **murāsala** exchange of letters, correspondence; note, message, letter, communication; orderly (*mil.*)

ارسال **irsāl** sending, forwarding, shipping, dispatch

ارسالية **irsālīya** pl. -**āt** consignment; mail item; shipment; transport; (*mil.*) expedition; mission

ترسل **tarassul** art of letter writing

استرسال **istirsāl** ease, naturalness, relaxedness; abandon; elaboration, expatiation

مراسل **murāsil** pl. -**ūn** correspondent, reporter (of a newspaper) | مراسل حربى (*harbī*) war correspondent; مراسل خاص (*ḵāṣṣ*)

special correspondent; مراسل رياضى (*riyāḍī*) sports reporter

مرسل *mursil* sender (of a letter); consignor; ○ transmitter (*radio*)

○ مرسلة *mursila* pl. *-āt* transmitter (*radio*)

مرسل *mursal* sent, forwarded; dispatched; delegated; transmitted (*radio*); long and flowing (hair); (pl. *-ūn*) missionary (*Chr.*); incompletely transmitted (of a Prophetic tradition resting on a chain of authorities that goes no further back than the 2nd generation after the Prophet) | مرسل اليه recipient, addressee (of a letter); consignee; كلام مرسل (*kalām*) prose

مرسلية *mursalīya* mission

مسترسل *mustarsil* loose, flowing (hair); friendly, affable; intimate, chummy; devoted, given up (فى or مع to s.th.)

رسم *rasama u* (*rasm*) to draw, trace (ه s.th.); to sketch (ه s.th.); to describe (ه e.g., a circle); to paint (ه s.th.); to record, put down in writing (ه s.th.); to enter, mark, indicate (ه s.th.); to sketch, outline (ه s.th.; fig.); to describe, depict, portray, picture (ه s.th.); to make, work out, conceive (خطة *kiṭṭatan* a plan); to prescribe (ب or ه ل to s.o. s.th.), lay down as a rule (ب or ه ل for s.o. s.th.); to ordain (ه a priest; *Chr.*) | رسم شارة الصليب to make the sign of the cross, cross o.s. (*Chr.*) II to enter, mark, indicate (ه s.th., فى in); to appoint to a public office (ه s.o.; *tun.*) V to follow (ه s.th., esp. s.o.'s footsteps, an example, etc.); to be appointed to a public office (*tun.*) VIII to come out, find visible expression; to be traced, engraved, inscribed, written; to impress itself, leave an impression (على on); to be ordained, be introduced into the office of the ministry (priest; *Chr.*); to make the sign of the cross (*Chr.*)

رسم *rasm* drawing (e.g., as a subject in school); — (pl. رسوم *rusūm*, رسومات *rusūmāt*) a drawing; sketch; graph; picture; photograph; illustration; pattern (e.g., on a fabric); — (pl. رسوم) trace, impression; designation, mark; inscription, legend; record, notes; (official) document, (legal) instrument; writing; design; prescription, regulation; ceremony, form, formality; rate, fee, tax, due | برسم *bi-rasmi* intended for, care of (c/o), for; اخذ الرسم *akḏ ar-r.* taking of a picture; رسم بيانى (*bayānī*) illustrative figure, diagram (in a book); رسم الدخول admission fee; رسم دخولى (*dukūlī*) import duty, tariff; رسم شمسى (*šamsī*) photograph; رسم عمومى layout, ground plan (*arch.*); رسم تفصيلى detail drawing; رسم قلبى (*qalbī*) cardiogram; رسوم قيدية (*qaidīya*) registration fees; رسم الانتاج *r. al-intāj* excise tax; رسم قيمى (*qīmī*) ad valorem duty; رسم هزلى (*hazlī*) caricature, cartoon

رسمى *rasmī* official, formal, conventional; ceremonial; official, officeholder, public servant; رسميا *rasmīyan* officially; رسميات *rasmīyāt* formalities; ceremonies, ceremonial, ritual; rules, regulations | رجال رسمية officials; ملابس رسمية official dress; court dress; ثياب رسمية uniforms; شبه رسمى *šibhu r.* and شبيه بالرسمى semiofficial; نصف رسمى *niṣfu r.* do.; غير رسمى *ġairu r.* unofficial

رسام *rassām* pl. *-ūn* draftsman; painter, artist

رسامة *risāma, rasāma* ordination, consecration (of a priest; *Chr.*)

روسم *rausam* pl. رواسم *rawāsim*² ○ cliché (*Syr.*)

مرسم *marsam* studio (of an artist)

مراسم *marāsim*² ceremonies, ceremonial, ritual; etiquette, protocol (*dipl.*); customs; principles; regulations | مدير ادارة المراسم *mudīr idārat al-m.* and رئيس المراسم

chief of protocol (*dipl.*); مراسم التتويج coronation ceremonies; مراسم التشريفات court etiquette

ترسّم *tarassum* design, planning

ارتسام *irtisām* pl. *-āt* (visible) expression, manifestation (e.g., of a feeling, of an emotion on s.o.'s face)

مرسوم *marsūm* drawn, traced, sketched; painted; recorded in writing, written; designed, planned; decreed, ordered; — (pl. مراسيم *marāsīm*²) decree; act, edict; regulation, ordinance (ب regarding); مراسيم ceremonies, ceremonial, ritual; etiquette; regulations | مرسوم بقانون (*bi-qānūn*) enactment, statute, ordinance (*Eg.*); مرسوم تشريعي (*tašrīʿī*) and مرسوم اشتراعي (*ištirāʿī*; *Pal., Syr.*) do.; مدير المراسيم *mudīr al-m.* chief of protocol (*dipl.*)

□ رسمال *rasmāl* pl. رساميل *rasāmīl*² = رأس مال capital (*fin.*)

رسن *rasan* pl. ارسن *arsun*, ارسان *arsān*, ارسنة *arsina* halter

(رسو) رسا *rasā u* (*rasw*) to be firm, stable, steady; to anchor (على off a coast), cast anchor, land, dock; to ride at anchor (على off a coast, في in a harbor); to disembark, land (ب s.o.; ship); to come or go eventually (على to), land (على with) | رسا عليه المزاد (*mazādu*) it was knocked down to him (at an auction); رست عليه المناقصة (*munāqaṣa*) the commission or contract went to him (after an invitation to submit tenders) **IV** to make fast, fix firmly (ه s.th.); to anchor, place at anchor (ه a ship)

مرسى *marsan* pl. مراس *marāsin* anchorage | مرسى مطروح Mersa Matrûh (village in NW Egypt, on Mediterranean coast)

مرساة *mirsāh* pl. مراس *marāsin* anchor

راس *rāsin* pl. رواس *rawāsin* fixed, stationary, immovable; firm, steady, stable, firmly established; anchored, at anchor; pl. راسيات *rāsiyāt*, رواس *rawāsin* towering, unshakable mountains

رسى (= رسا see above) to anchor

رش *rašša u* (*rašš*) to spatter, splash, spurt (ه a liquid); to spray (ه a liquid); to sprinkle (ه s.th., ب with, على on); to splatter, spatter, bespatter (ه s.th., ب with water, etc.); to water (ه s.th.)

رش *rašš* sprinkling; watering; splattering, spattering; spraying; buckshot | مصلحة الرش والكنس *maṣlaḥat ar-r. wa-l-kans* street-cleaning department; عربة الرش *ʿarabat ar-r.* watering cart, sprinkler; رمى رشا to fire in bursts (*mil.*)

رشة *rašša* light drizzle

رشاش *rašāš* spattered liquid; drizzle, dribble (esp. fig.)

رشاش *raššāš* pl. *-āt* water hose; machine gun | مدفع رشاش (*midfaʿ*) machine gun; مسدس رشاش (*musaddas*) pl. مسدسات رشاشة submachine gun, Tommy gun

رشاشة *raššāša* pl. *-āt* perfume spray, atomizer; ○ watering can; shower, douche (*Mor.*)

○ مرشة *miraašša* watering can

رشح *rašaḥa a* (*rašḥ*) to sweat, perspire; to leak, be leaky (vessel); to filter, strain, percolate (ه a liquid) **II** to raise, rear, bring up (ه a child); to train, prepare (ه s.o.); to nominate, put up as a candidate (ه s.o., ل for, e.g., for an office), (with نفسه *nafsahū*) to be a candidate, apply (ل for an office, etc.); to filter (ه s.th.) **V** to be reared, be brought up; to be suited, qualified, trained (ل for s.th.); to be nominated as a candidate, be a nominee (ل for s.th.); to catch a cold

رشح *rašḥ* secretion (of a fluid); perspiration, sweating; leaking, leakiness; filtering, filtration, percolation; oozing, trickling; cold, catarrh

رشاحة *rušāḥa* transudate, transudation (*med.*)

ترشيح *taršīḥ* training, preparation; nomination (as a candidate, for election); (ترشيح نفسه =) candidacy, candidature; election; concession

ترشح *taraššuḥ* infiltration (*med.*)

ارتشاح *irtišāḥ* infiltration (*med.*)

مرشح *muraššiḥ* pl. *-āt* filter; percolator; filtering installation; purification plant

مرشح *muraššaḥ* pl. *-ūn* candidate, nominee; having a cold

مترشح *mutaraššiḥ* pl. *-ūn* candidate, nominee

رشد **rašada** *u* (*rušd*) to be on the right way, follow the right course, be well guided, not go astray (esp., in religious matters); to have the true faith, be a true believer; to become sensible, become mature, grow up; to come of age **II** to lead the right way, guide well (ه s.o.) **IV** to lead the right way, guide well (ه s.o.); to lead, guide, direct (ه الى s.o. to s.th.), show (ه s.o.) the way (الى to; fig.); to lead s.o. (ه) to the discovery that (الى ان), suggest to s.o. the idea of, make s.o. realize that; to call s.o.'s (ه) attention (الى to s.th.), point out (ه الى to s.o. s.th.); to teach (ه الى s.o. to do s.th.), instruct, direct, guide (ه الى s.o. in); to inform (ه الى s.o. about), acquaint s.o. (ه) with the facts of (الى); to advise, counsel (ه الى s.o. to do s.th.); to inform (الى against s.o.); to come of age **X** to ask (ه or ب s.o.) to show the right way, ask s.o. for guidance or directions; to ask (ه s.o.) for instructions or information; to consult (ه s.o.), ask s.o.'s (ه) advice, seek guidance (ه from s.o.); to be guided (ب by)

رشد *rušd* integrity of (one's) actions, proper, sensible conduct; reason, good sense, senses; consciousness; maturity (of the mind) | سن الرشد *sinn ar-r.* majority, full legal age; بلغ رشده (*rušdahū*) to come of age; ثاب الى رشده to come to one's senses, calm down, sober up; ضاع رشده to go out of one's mind; ذهب برشده to drive s.o. mad (pain)

رشد *rašad* integrity of conduct, straightforwardness, forthrightness

رشاد *rašād* integrity of conduct; reason, good sense, senses; maturity; garden peppergrass (*Lepidium sativum* L.; *bot.*)

رشيد *rašīd* rightly guided, following the right way; having the true faith; reasonable, rational, intelligent, discriminating, discerning; mature; (pl. رشداء *rušadā'*[2]) of full legal age, major; Rosetta (city in N Egypt)

مراشد *marāšid*[2] where the right way leads to; salvation

ترشيد *taršīd* a declaring (s.o.) of age (*jur.*)

ارشاد *iršād* guidance; a conducting, showing the way (الى to); guiding hand; care; spiritual guidance; instruction; direction; directive; information; advising, advice; pl. ارشادات directives, directions, instructions, advice | بارشاده on his instructions, following his direction; وزارة الارشاد القوى *wizārat al-i. al-qaumī* Ministry of National Guidance (*Eg.*)

شعر ارشادى *ši'r iršādī* didactic poetry

راشد *rāšid* following the right way, rightly guided, having the true faith; sensible, reasonable; of full legal age, major | الخلفاء الراشدون (*kulafā'*) the orthodox caliphs (i.e., Abū Bakr, 'Umar, 'Uṯmān, 'Alī)

مرشد *muršid* pl. *-ūn* leader; guide to the right way; adviser; spiritual guide; informer; instructor; (ship) pilot; tourist guide; Grand Master, Master (e.g., of the Moslem Brotherhood)

مرشدة *muršida* woman guide

رشرش *rušruš* pl. رشارش *rašāriš*[2] belt

رشراش *rašrāš* tender (e.g., meat)

رشف *rašafa i u* (*rašf*) and *rašifa a* (*rašaf*), V and VIII to suck, sip (ه s.th.); to drink (ه s.th.); to drink up, drain (ه a vessel)

رشفة *rašfa* (n. un.) pl. *-āt* gulp, sip (of a drink)

رشق *rašaqa u* (*rašq*) to throw (ب ه at s.o. s.th.), pelt, strike, hurt (ه ب s.o. with s.th.): to insert, fasten, fix (ه في s.th. in); — *rašuqa u* (رشاقة *rašāqa*) to be shapely, of graceful stature; to be elegant, graceful, lissome VI to pelt one another, hurt one another

رشيق *rašīq* elegant, graceful (exterior, style); svelte, slender, slim; lissome

رشاقة *rašāqa* elegance, grace, gracefulness; shapeliness, graceful, slender build; nimbleness, agility

رشم *rašama u* (*rašm*) to mark, designate (ه s.th.); to make the sign of the cross; to seal (ه s.th.) | رشم بصليب على to make the sign of the cross over; رشم الصليب to make the sign of the cross (*Chr.*)

رشم *rašm* pl. رشوم *rušūm*, رشومات *rušūmāt* sign of the cross (*Chr.*); anointment (*Copt.-Chr.*)

رشمة *rašma* ornamental halter decorated with silver pendants, or the like; camel halter

راشن *rāšin* tip, baksheesh

(رشو) رشا *rašā u* (*rašw*) to bribe (ه s.o.) VIII to accept a bribe, be corrupt, be venal

رشو *rašw* bribery, corruption

رشوة *rišwa, rušwa, rašwa* pl. رشى ,رشا *rišan, rušan,* (*eg.*) رشاوى *rašāwī* bribe; bribery, corruption, dishonesty

رشاء *rišā'* rope, well rope

ارتشاء *irtišā'* venality, corruptibility; bribery, corruption

رص *raṣṣa u* (*raṣṣ*) to fit tightly together, press together, compress (ه s.th.); to ram, force (ه s.th. into the ground); to pile up, stack up (ه s.th.); to join together, line up, align, arrange side by side (ه s.th.) II to fit tightly together, press together, compress (ه s.th.); to ram home (ه s.th.); to coat or cover with lead (ه s.th.) VI to be pressed together, be packed together; to press together, crowd together; to be or become compact

رصاص *raṣāṣ* lead; bullets | قلم رصاص *qalam r.* pencil

رصاصة *raṣāṣa* (n. un.) pellet; bullet

رصاصى *raṣāṣī* lead, (made) of lead; leady; leaden, lead-colored, dull gray

رصيص *raṣīṣ* compressed, closely packed, jammed together; compact

○تراص *tarāṣṣ* agglutination

رصد *raṣada u* (*raṣd*) to keep one's eyes (ه, ه on); to lie in wait (ه for); to observe (ه s.th.), watch (ه s.th. or over s.th.), control (ه s.th.); to conjure (a demon) | رصد الافلاك to observe the stars, practice astronomy II to provide, set aside, earmark (ه funds); to prepare, keep ready (ه s.th.); to balance (الحساب the account; *com.*) IV to keep ready (ه s.th.); to provide, set aside, earmark (ه ل s.th., esp. funds, for); to procure, get (ه s.th.) V ترصد الافلاك to observe the stars, practice astronomy

رصد *raṣd, raṣad* pl. ارصاد *arṣād* observation | رصد الافلاك *r. al-aflāk* stargazing, astronomy; ارصاد جوية (*jawwīya*) meteorological observation; تقرير الارصاد weather report

رصدخانة *raṣdaḵāna* observatory

رصد *raṣad* pl. ارصاد *arṣād* spy, watcher, watchdog; lookout, observation post; ambush; talisman

رصاد الجو raṣṣād: r. al-jaww meteorologist

رصيد raṣīd pl. ارصدة arṣida stock on hand (of merchandise, of supplies), avaible funds; balance (com.; also = remainder of a sum to be paid later); capital (fin.) | شيك بدون رصيد uncovered check, check without sufficient covering funds

مرصد marṣad pl. مراصد marāṣid² observatory | مرصد جوى (jawwī) meteorological station, weather station

○ مرصد mirṣad telescope

مرصاد mirṣād observation post, lookout; ambush | وقف بالمرصاد to lie in wait; وقف له بالمرصاد and كان منه بالمرصاد to lie in ambush for s.o., waylay s.o.

راصد rāṣid registering; (pl. رصاد ruṣṣād) watcher, watchdog, spy | ○ خزينة راصدة cash register; ○ ميزان راصد (mīzān) self-registering balance

راصدة فلكية rāṣida: (falakīya) telescope

مبلغ مرصود mablaḡ marṣūd security, cover (fin.)

II to inlay, set, stud (ه s.th., ب with gems or gold); to adorn, decorate, ornament (ب ه s.th. with)

رصف raṣafa u (رصف raṣf) to pave, lay with stone (ه s.th.); — raṣufa u (رصانة raṣāfa) to be firmly joined II to lay with flagstones, pave (ه s.th.)

رصف raṣf paving (of roads)

رصيف raṣīf firmly joined, firm, solid, compact; — (pl. ارصفة arṣifa) pavement; sidewalk; quay; wharf, pier; mole, jetty; platform; (pl. رصفاء ruṣafā'²) colleague | رصيف المحطة r. al-maḥaṭṭa (railway) platform; رصيف لاعمال الحفر فى البحر (li-a'māli l-ḥafr fī l-baḥr) offshore drilling platform (for oil drilling); عوايد الرصيف 'awāyid ar-r. quayage, pierage, wharfage

رصيفة raṣīfa pl. -āt woman colleague | رصيفتنا الغراء (ḡarrā') a phrase of courtesy used by one newspaper when referring to another; approx.: our honorable friends

رصانة raṣāfa firmness, compactness

مرصوف marṣūf paved (ب with)

رصن raṣuna u (رصانة raṣāna) to be firm, strong; to be sedate, calm, composed

رصين raṣīn firm, unshakable; sedate, calm, composed

رصانة raṣāna sedateness, composure, calmness, equanimity

رض raḍḍa u (رض raḍḍ) to crush (ه s.th.); to bruise (ه a part of the body)

رض raḍḍ pl. رضوض ruḍūḍ bruise, contusion

رضيض raḍīḍ crushed; bruised

رضاب ruḍāb spittle, saliva

رضخ raḍaḵa a i (رضخ raḍḵ) to break, smash, shatter (ه s.th.); to crack (ه a kernel); — raḍaḵa a (رضخ raḍḵ) to give (ه s.o.) a small, paltry present; — (رضوخ ruḍūḵ) to yield, bow, give in, subordinate o.s., submit (ل to s.o., to s.th.) VIII ارتضخ لكنة (luknatan) to speak Arabic with a foreign accent

رضخ raḍḵ, رضخة raḍḵa a small, paltry gift

رضيخة raḍīḵa a small, paltry gift; tip, baksheesh

رضوخ ruḍūḵ submission, surrender; yielding, compliance; sympathetic understanding (ل of)

مرضاخ mirḍāḵ nutcracker

رضرض raḍraḍa to break into coarse pieces, pound, crush (ه s.th.)

رضراض raḍrāḍ pebbles, gravel

رضع **raḍi'a a** and **raḍa'a i a** (*raḍ'*, رضاع *raḍā'*, رضاعة *raḍā'a*) to suck (ثدى امه *ṯadya ummihī* at its mother's breast) **II** and **IV** to nurse at the breast, suckle, breast-feed (ه a baby)

رضيع **ruḍī'** pl. رضعاء **ruḍa'ā'**[2], رضائع *raḍā'i'*[2] suckling, infant, baby; foster brother

○ رضاعة **raḍḍā'a** pl. *-āt* nursing bottle

رضاع **riḍā'** foster relationship

راضع **rāḍi'** pl. رضع **ruḍḍa'** sucking; suckling, infant, baby; infant (adj.)

مرضع **murḍi'** and مرضعة **murḍi'a** pl. مراضع *marāḍi'*[2] wet nurse; foster mother

رضه abbreviation of رضى الله عنه, see رضى

رضا see رضى *riḍan*

رضى **raḍiya a** (رضى *riḍan*, رضوان *riḍwān*, مرضاة *marḍāh*) to be satisfied, be content (ه, ب or فى with); to consent, agree (ه, ب or فى to); to approve (ه, ب or فى of), accept, sanction (ه, ب or فى s.th.); to accept the fact, resign o.s. to the fact (ان that); to be pleased (ه, على or عن with); to wish, desire (ه s.th., ل for s.o.) | رضى لنفسه ب (*li-nafsihī*) to permit o.s. s.th.; ما رضى لها المذلة (*maḏallata*) he had no desire to humiliate her; رضى او ابى (*au abā*) whether he likes it or not; رضى الله عنه (Isl. eulogy) may God be pleased with him; رضى من الغنيمة بالاياب (*iyāb*) to be content to return without booty, be happy to have saved one's skin **II** to satisfy, gratify, please (ه s.o.); to compensate (ه s.o.) **III** to seek to satisfy, try to please (ه s.o.); to propitiate, conciliate, win (ه s.o.), gain the good will of (ه) **IV** to satisfy, gratify, please (ه s.o.) **V** to seek to satisfy, try to please (ه s.o.); to seek to propitiate (ه s.o.); to conciliate, appease (ه s.o.) **VI** to come to terms **VIII** to be satisfied, content, pleased (ه with); to consent, agree (ه to s.th.); to approve (ه of s.th.), sanction (ه s.th.) **X** to seek to satisfy, try to conciliate, treat in a conciliatory manner (ه s.o.); to conciliate, appease (ه s.o.); to show o.s. obliging, make o.s. popular, ingratiate o.s., try to gain good will or favor

رضا, رضى **riḍan** contentment, contentedness, satisfaction; agreement, consent, assent, acceptance, approval; pleasure, delight; good will, favor | عن رضى readily, gladly; سريع الرضى easy to please, easily reconciled

رضى **raḍīy** pl. ارضياء *arḍiyā'*[2] satisfied, content; pleasant, agreeable | بنفس رضية (*bi-nafs*) gladly

رضوان **riḍwān** consent, assent, agreement, acceptance, approval, sanction; good will, favor; pleasure, delight

مرضاة **marḍāh** a means affording satisfaction or gratification; satisfaction, pleasure

ترضية **tarḍiya** satisfaction, gratification; compensation

رضاء **riḍā'** contentment, contentedness, satisfaction; agreement, consent, assent, acceptance, approval, sanction; propitiation, conciliation

بالمراضاة *bi-l-murāḍāh* by fair means, amicably

ارضاء **irḍā'** satisfaction, gratification; fulfillment (of a claim, of a desire) | صعب الارضاء *ṣa'b al-i.* hard to please, fastidious

تراض **tarāḍin** mutual consent

استرضاء **istirḍā'** conciliatory attitude, conciliatoriness; propitiation, conciliation

استرضائى **istirḍā'ī** conciliatory

راض **rāḍin** pl. رضاة **ruḍāh** satisfied, content; agreeing, consenting; willing, ready; pleasant, agreeable (life)

مرض **murḍin** satisfactory; satisfying; pleasant, pleasing, gratifying; sufficient

رطب **raṭiba** *a* and **raṭuba** *u* (رطوبة *ruṭūba*, رطابة *raṭāba*) to be moist, damp, humid; to be wet **II** to moisten (ه s.th.); to cool, refresh; to soothe, soften, calm (القلب *al-qalba* the heart); to become succulent, mellow, ripen (dates) **IV** to moisten (ه s.th.); to become succulent, mellow, ripen (dates) **V** to be moistened; to be cooled, be refreshed; to be soothed, be softened, be calmed

رطب **raṭb** moist, damp, humid; wet; fresh, cool; juicy, succulent, tender (plant)

رطب **ruṭab** (coll.; n. un. ة) pl. ارطاب *arṭāb*, رطاب *riṭāb* fresh, ripe dates

رطيب **raṭīb** pl. رطاب *riṭāb* moist, damp, humid; fresh, cool; juicy, succulent, tender (plant)

رطوبة **ruṭūba** moisture, dampness, humidity; wetness

راطب **rāṭib** moist, damp, humid; wet

مرطبات **muraṭṭibāt** refreshments, soft drinks

رطل **raṭl** pl. ارطال *arṭāl* rotl, a weight (in Eg. = 449.28 g; in Syr. = 3.202 kg, in Beirut and Aleppo = 2.566 kg)

رطم **raṭama** *u* (*raṭm*) to involve, implicate, drag (ه s.o. into s.th. unpleasant) **VIII** to tumble, fall, plunge (في into); to stick fast, be stuck; to be involved, be entangled (في in s.th.); to run aground, strand (ship); to bump, hit, crash (ب against)

○ مرطم **marṭam** breakwater, mole, jetty

رطن **raṭana** *u* (رطانة *raṭāna*, *riṭāna*) to speak unintelligible language, talk gibberish, jabber

رطانة **raṭāna**, *riṭāna* lingo, gibberish

رطينى **ruṭainā** lingo, gibberish

رعاع **ra'ā'** rabble, mob, riffraff, scum, ragtag; rowdies, hooligans

رعب **ra'aba** *a* (*ru'b*) to be alarmed, terrified; to be afraid, be scared **II** and **IV** to frighten, scare, terrify (ه s.o.) **VIII** to become frightened, become alarmed, be afraid

رعب **ru'b** fright, alarm, dismay

ارعاب **ir'āb** frightening, intimidation

راعب **rā'ib** dreadful, horrifying, terrible

مرعوب **mar'ūb** frightened, terrified, appalled, afraid

مرعب **mur'ib** frightening, terrifying, terrible, horrible, dreadful

رعد **ra'ada** *a u* (*ra'd*) to thunder; to appall (ل s.o. with ب) **IV** to make (ه s.o.) tremble; pass. *ur'ida* to shudder, shiver, tremble (من with, e.g., with fear) **VIII** to tremble

رعد **ra'd** pl. رعود *ru'ūd* thunder

رعدة **ra'da**, *ri'da* tremor; shudder; shiver

رعاد **ra''ād** (coll.; n. un. ة) electric ray (*zool.*)

رعديد **ri'dīd** pl. رعاديد *ra'ādīd*[2] cowardly; coward

رعرع **ra'ra'a** to come into the prime of life (youth) **II** *tara'ra'a* to grow, develop, flourish, thrive

رعرع **ra'ra'**, *ru'ru'* pl. رعارع *ra'āri'*[2] in full bloom

رعراع ايوب **ra'rā' ayyūb** (*eg.*) a variety of fleabane (Pulicaria arabica Coss., Pulicaria inuloides D. C.; *bot.*)

رعش **ra'aša** *a* (*ra'š*) and **ra'iša** *a* (*ra'aš*) to tremble, shake **IV** to make (ه s.o.) tremble; to make (ه s.o.) shiver **VIII** = *ra'aša*

رعشة **ri'ša** tremor | رعشة الحمى *r. al-ḥummā* feverish shiver

ارتعاش **irti'āš** tremor, trembling

رعص **V** and **VIII** to writhe, wind, coil

رعف *ra'afa u a* and *ra'ifa a*: رعف انفه (*anfuhū*) to have a nosebleed

رعاف *ru'āf* and رعيف *ra'īf* nosebleed

راعف *rā'if* tip of the nose

رعلة *ru'la* wreath

رعيل *ra'īl* pl. رعال *ri'āl* squadron of armored, motorized, or cavalry troops (*Syr.*, *Ir.*; *mil.*)

رعام *ru'ām* glanders

رعمسيس *ra'amsīs* Ramses (name of Eg. kings)

رعن *ra'una u* (رعونة *ru'ūna*) to be lightheaded, frivolous; — *ra'ana u* (*ra'n*): رعنته الشمس *ra'anathu š-šams* to have a sunstroke

رعن *ra'n* sunstroke; — (pl. رعان *ri'ān*) mountain peak

ارعن *ar'an*[2] lightheaded, frivolous, flippant, rash, heedless, careless; stupid, silly; thoughtless; unsteady, fickle, volatile

رعونة *ru'ūna* pl. *-āt* levity, frivolity, flippancy; thoughtlessness

(رعو) رعا *ra'ā u* (*ra'w*, رعوة *ra'wa*, *ru'wa*, رعوى *ra'wā*, *ru'wā*) and IX ارعوى *ir'awā* to desist (من or عن from sin, from error), repent, see the light | ارعوى عن غيه (*ġayyihī*) to repent, turn over a new leaf

رعوى *ra'wā*, *ru'wā* repentance, amendment, conversion

رعوى *ra'awī* and رعوية see رعى

رعى *ra'ā a* (*ra'y*, رعاية *ri'āya*, مرعى *mar'an*) to graze; to tend (ه a flock of animals); — (*ra'y*, رعاية *ri'āya*) to guard, protect, take under one's wing (ه s.o.); to care (ه, ه for), take care (ه, ه of); to watch (ه over); to make a point (ه of s.th.), make it one's business; to observe, bear in mind, heed, respect (ه s.th.); to adhere (ه to), comply (ه with), abide (e.g., عهدا *'ahdan* or معاهدة *mu'āhadatan* by a treaty or an agreement, etc.); to take into consideration (ه s.th.), allow (ه for s.th.) III to supervise, watch, control (ه s.th.), keep an eye (ه on); to maintain, keep up, preserve (ه s.th.); to observe, bear in mind, heed, respect (ه s.th.), comply (ه with, e.g., with regulations); to take into consideration, take into account (ه s.th.), allow, make allowance (ه for s.th.); to show deference, regard or respect (ه for s.o.); to make provision, see to it (ان that) | راعى خاطره (*kāṭirahū*) to defer to s.o., respect s.o.'s feelings or wishes IV ارعيته سمعى *ar'aituhū sam'ī* I listened to him; ارعنى سمعك *ar'inī sam'aka* listen to me! ارعى ه نظره (*naẓarahū*) to follow s.th. attentively with one's eyes VIII to graze, pasture (cattle) X to attract (نظره *naẓarahū* s.o.'s eyes, انتباهه *intibāhahū* s.o.'s attention); to observe (ه s.th.)

رعى *ra'y* care, keeping, custody, guardianship; protection; observance (ل of), adherence (ل to, e.g., to agreements) | رعيا لك God be with you!

رعية *ra'īya* pl. رعايا *ra'āyā* herd, flock; parish (*Chr.*); subjects, citizens; a subject, a citizen

رعوى *ra'awī*, رعاوى *ra'āwī* and رعائى *ra'ā'ī* pastoral, bucolic | كنيسة رعوية parish church (*Chr.*); رسالة رعائية pastoral letter (*Chr.*)

رعوية *ra'awīya* citizenship, nationality

مرعى *mar'an* pl. مراع *marā'in* grassland, grazing land; pasture

رعاية *ri'āya* keeping, custody, charge, care; attention, consideration, regard; patronage, auspices, sponsorship, protectorate | تحت رعاية under the auspices of, sponsored by; مركز رعاية الطفل *markaz r. aṭ-ṭifl* health center for children (*Eg.*); شرط معاملة الدول الاكثر رعاية *šarṭ mu'āmalat ad-duwal al-akṯar ri'āyatan* most-favored-nation clause

مرغوب فيه undesirable ;شخص مرغوب فيه (šaḵṣ) persona grata, شخص غير مرغوب فيه persona non grata (dipl.); مرغوب عنه undesirable, unwanted, objectionable, loathsome

مرغبات muraḡḡibāt attractions, lures, advantages

رغث raḡaṯa a (raḡṯ) to suck (ها at the mother's teats; said of animals)

رغوث raḡūṯ unweaned young female animal

رغد raḡuda u (رغادة raḡāda) and raḡida a (raḡad) to be pleasant, comfortable, carefree (life)

رغد raḡd easy, carefree, pleasant, agreeable (life) | عيش رغد (ʿaiš) a life of plenty and opulence

رغيد raḡīd easy, carefree, pleasant, agreeable (life) | عيش رغيد (ʿaiš) a life of plenty and opulence

رغد raḡad comfort, opulence, affluence (of living)

رغادة raḡāda comfort, opulence, affluence (of living)

رغرغ[1] raḡraḡa to live in opulence and luxury

رغرغ[2] □ raḡraḡa (= غرغر ḡarḡara) to gargle

ارغاطة urḡāṭa pl. -āt, اراغيط arāḡīṭ (eg.) windlass, winch; capstan

رغيف raḡīf pl. ارغفة arḡifa, رغفان ruḡfān, رغف ruḡuf flat loaf of bread; roll, bun (syr.)

رغم IV to force, compel, coerce (ه على s.o. to do s.th.)

رغم raḡma (prep.) despite, in spite of | رغم ان although, though; رغماً عن raḡman ʿan in spite of, despite; رغما عن انفه (anfihī) and على الرغم من انفه just to spite him, in defiance of him, against his will; بالرغم من bi-r-raḡmi min and بالرغم عن and على الرغم من despite, in spite of; بالرغم من كل هذا in

مراعاة murāʿāh consideration, regard, deference, respect; compliance (with), observance (e.g., of regulations, of duties, etc.) | مراعاة ل (murāʿātan) in deference to, out of regard for, for the sake of; in observance of; مراعاة لخواطرهم out of deference to them, out of regard for their feelings, wishes, etc.; مع مراعاة هذا taking this into account, bearing this in mind

راع rāʿin pl. رعاة ruʿāh, رعيان ruʿyān, رعاء ruʿāʾ, riʿāʾ shepherd, herdsman; guardian, keeper, protector; patron, sponsor; pastor (Chr.)

مرعى marʿīy observed, complied with

رغب raḡiba a (رغبة raḡba, رغب raḡab) to desire, wish, want, crave, covet (فى s.th.); to ask (من or الى s.o., فى for s.th., ان to do s.th.), request (فى s.th.; من or الى s.o., ان to do s.th.); to prefer (فى على s.th. to, also ب عن s.th. to), like s.th. (فى, also ب) better than (على, also عن); to dislike, detest, loathe (عن s.th.), have a distaste (عن for); to wish (ل ب s.o. s.th.) | لا يرغب فيه (yurḡabu) undesirable II to make (ه s.o.) desirous (فى of), awaken a desire, a wish (ه فى in s.o. for); to interest (ه فى s.o. in s.th.), excite s.o.'s (ه) interest in (فى); to awaken an aversion (ه عن in s.o. to s.th.) IV = II

رغب raḡab: رغبا ورهبا raḡaban wa-rahaban torn between greed and fear

رغبة raḡba pl. raḡabāt, رغاب riḡāb wish, desire, longing, appetite (فى for)

رغيبة raḡība pl. رغائب raḡāʾib[2] object of desire, desideratum; wish, desire

ترغيب tarḡīb awakening of a desire or longing (فى for); incitement to covetousness; invitation, attraction

راغب rāḡib pl. رغبة raḡaba desiring, desirous | لآخر راغب li-āḵiri rāḡibin (sale) to the highest bidder

مرغوب marḡūb: مرغوب فيه coveted, sought after, in demand; desired, desirable; غير

spite of all this; بالرغم منه and على الرغم منه against s.o.'s will; against one's own will, reluctantly, without wanting it; على رغم منى *'alā raǧmin minnī* without my wanting it; بالرغم من ان in spite of the fact that, although; لا ... الا رغما *lā ... illā raǧman* only reluctantly, only with great effort

رغام *raǧām* dust and sand

رغام *ruǧām* mucus

رغامى *ruǧāmā* windpipe, trachea (*anat.*)

مرغمة *marǧama* pl. مراغم *marāǧim*² compulsion, coercion, force; aversion, unwillingness, reluctance, dislike, distaste

ارغام *irǧām* compulsion (على to)

راغم *rāǧim* reluctant, unwilling | وانفه راغم (*anfuhū*) (as a *ḥāl* clause) reluctantly, grudgingly

ارغن look up alphabetically

(رغو) رغا *raǧā u* (*raǧw*) to foam, froth **II** and **IV** do. | ارغى وازبد (*azbada*) to fume with rage

رغوة *raǧwa, ruǧwa* pl. رغاو *raǧāwin* foam, froth, spume; lather; dross, slag

رغوى *raǧwī* foamy, frothy

رغاء *raǧǧā'* windbag (fig., of a person); garrulous; chatterbox, prattler

رغاوة *ruǧāwa* foam, froth, spume

راغ: ما له ثاغية ولا راغية (*ṯāǧiya*) he has absolutely nothing, he is devoid of all resources, prop.: he has neither a bleating (sheep) nor a braying (camel)

رف *raffa i* (*raff*, رفيف *rafīf*) to gleam, shimmer, glisten, glitter; — *u i* (*raff*) to quiver, twitch; to flicker; to flap the wings (bird); to flutter; to wave, stream; to flash, flare for a moment; to appear suddenly; — *u i* to be anxious to please (ل s.o.), serve (ل s.o.) diligently | رف على ذاكرته it flashed through his mind, it occurred to him all of a sudden

رف *raff* flight, covey (of birds)

رف *raff* pl. رفوف *rufūf*, رفاف *rifāf* shelf; rack; ledge | وضعه على الرف to shelve s.th., put s.th. aside

رفاف *raffāf* radiant, flashing, sparkling, glistening

رفأ *rafa'a a* (*raf'*) to mend, repair, patch (ه clothing), sew up, fine-draw (ه a rent), darn (ه socks); to drag (ه a boat) on shore

رفاء *raffā'* darner, fine-drawer

رفاء *rifā'* (marital) harmony, love | بالرفاء والبنين (*banīn*) live in harmony and beget sons! (felicitation to newlyweds)

مرفأ *marfa'* pl. مراف *marāfi'*² landing place, wharf, quay; port, harbor

¹رفت *rafata i u* (*raft*) to break, smash, crush (ه s.th.); to reject, turn down, decline (ه s.th.); to dismiss, discharge (ه s.o. from service)

رفت *raft* dismissal, discharge (from service)

رفات *rufāt* mortal remains, body (of a person)

²رفتية *raftīya* transit duty; clearance certificate, clearance papers (*com.*)

رفث *rafaṯa i u* to behave in an obscene manner

رفث *rafaṯ* obscenity

رفح *rafaḥ* Rafah (town in S Gaza sector)

رفد *rafada i* (*rafd*) to support, aid, help (ه s.o.); to support, uphold, carry (ه s.th.) **IV** to support, aid, help (ه s.o.) **X** to ask (ه s.o.) for support, appeal (ه to s.o.) for help

رفد *rifd* pl. رفود *rufūd*, ارفاد *arfād* present, gift; support

رفادة *rifāda* dressing, bandage (over a wound); saddlecloth, pad

رافد *rāfid* pl. روافد *rawāfid*[2] tributary stream; الرافدان *ar-rāfidān* (Euphrates and Tigris =) Mesopotamia, Iraq

رافدة *rāfida* pl. روافد *rawāfid*[2] support, prop; rafter

رفرف **rafrafa** to flap the wings (bird); to flutter (flag, wings, or the like); to blow (wind); to blindfold (ه the eyes)

رفرف *rafraf* pl. رفارف *rafārif*[2] cushion, pad; eyeshade, visor (of a cap); fender (of an automobile)

رفروف *rafrūf* pl. رفاريف *rafārīf*[2] eye bandage

رفس **rafasa** i u (*rafs*) to kick (ه s.o.)

رفسة *rafsa* (n. vic.) kick

رفاس *raffās* steam launch, steamboat; motor tug; ○ propeller

رفش *rafš* shovel, spade

رفاص *raffāṣ* (= رفاس *raffās*) steam launch, steamboat

رفض **rafaḍa** i u (*rafḍ*) to leave, abandon (ه s.th.); to discard, dismiss (ه s.th.); to reject, turn down, decline, refuse to accept (ه s.th.) **IV** to finish, conclude, terminate **V** to be bigoted, fanatic **IX** to scatter, disperse, break up; to disappear, cease (e.g., pain); to drip (sweat)

رفض *rafḍ* dismissal; rejection, refusal, nonacceptance

رفيض *rafīḍ* abandoned; rejected, dismissed

ترفض *taraffuḍ* bigotry, fanaticism

رافضة *rāfiḍa* pl. روافض *rawāfiḍ*[2] turncoats, renegades, dissenters, defectors; troops having deserted their leader; Rafidites, a Shiitic sect

رافضى *rāfiḍī* pl. ارفاض *arfāḍ* apostate, renegade, turncoat; Rafidite; disloyal, rebellious; bigoted, fanatical

رفع **rafa'a** a (*raf'*) to lift, lift up, raise aloft, heave up, hoist up (ه s.th.); to raise (ه s.th., e.g., one's head, also fig.: e.g., the intellectual level, a price); to raise in esteem (ه s.th.); to make high or higher (ه s.th.); to elevate (ه s.th.); to heighten, exalt, enhance (ه s.th.); to raise, promote (ه ه الى s.o. to the rank of); to fly, let up (ه, e.g., a kite); to hoist, run up (علما *'alaman* or راية *rāyatan* a flag); to take off, doff, tip (قبعته *qubba'atahū* one's hat); to place, fasten or attach (ه s.th.) high above; to erect, set up (ه s.th.); to raise (صوته *ṣautahū* one's voice); to remove, take away (عن or من ه s.th. from); to abolish, eliminate (ه s.th.); to lift (ه s.th., e.g., a ban), put an end (ه to s.th.); to remedy (ه a mistake); to free, relieve (ه عن s.o. of s.th.); to put s.th. (ه) before s.o. (الى), submit (ه الى s.th., e.g., a petition, to), file (ه الى a report, and the like, with a proper authority); to present, dedicate (ه الى s.th. to s.o.); to offer up (ه sacrifices; *Chr.*); to make, deliver (تقريرا a report); to start, initiate (قضية *qaḍīyatan* legal action); to ascribe (ه الى a Prophetic tradition to an authority or source); (*gram.*) to pronounce the final consonant with *u*; to put (ه a word) in the nominative or indicative, respectively; pass. *rufi'a* it appeared, came in sight, became visible (ل before s.o.); رفع عنه *rufi'a 'anhu* he regained consciousness | رفع شيئا فوق شىء to put s.th. before or above s.th. else; رفع به رأسا (*ra'san*) to pay attention to s.th.; رفع من شأنه (*min ša'nihī*) to enhance the importance of s.th.; to speak of s.th. in glowing terms; رفع من مكانته (*makānatihī*) to upgrade s.th.; رفع يديه عنه (*yadaihi*) to desist, refrain from s.th.; رفع الدعوى عليه (*da'wā*) to sue s.o., lodge a complaint against s.o. (امام in a court); رفع به قضية or رفع قضية عليه (*qaḍīyatan*) to bring legal action against s.o., go with s.o. to court; رفع الاستئناف to appeal, make an appeal (امام to a court) II to raise, lift, elevate; to celebrate carnival III to act as defense counsel (عن of s.o.), defend (عن s.o., in court), plead s.o.'s (عن) cause; to summon, hale (الى ه s.o. to court) V to be or deem o.s. above s.th. (عن), be too proud (عن for s.th.), look down (عن upon) | ترفع برأسه to raise or bear one's head high VI to hale one another before the judge (الى الحاكم); to take one's case before the judge (الى الحاكم); to plead (in court) VIII to rise, lift; to go up, ascend; to become higher; to grow, increase, rise; to ring out (tone, voice, tune); to go away, pass away, be eliminated, disappear (عن from) | ارتفع صوته (*ṣautuhū*) to gain prestige

رفع *raf'* lifting, hoisting (also, of a flag); elevation; raise, raising, stepping up (of prices, of temperatures, etc.); setting up; erection; abolition; lift (e.g., of a ban); remedy, elimination, removal; remission (of a tax); submission, filing (e.g., of a report); pronunciation of the final consonant with *u* (*gram.*) | رفع الاثقال weight lifting (*athlet.*)

رفعة *rif'a* height, elevation (e.g., of a structure); high rank or standing | صاحب الرفعة (formerly:) title of the Egyptian Prime Minister, رفعة رئيس الوزراء *rif'at ra'īs al-wuzarā'* His Excellency the Prime Minister

رفاع *rifā'* Shrovetide (*Chr.*)

رفيع *rafī'* high, high-ranking; lofty, exalted, sublime; loud (voice, sound); thin, fine, delicate; exquisite, refined, subtle; artistic | رفيع الشأن *r. aš-ša'n* approx.: exalted; formerly, in Tunisia, title of the members of the Bey's family; صاحب المقام الرفيع (*maqām*) title conferred upon bearers of the order القلادة *al-qilāda*, established by Fu'ād I in 1936; الفنون الرفيعة (= الفنون الجميلة) the fine arts; الرفيع والوضيع high and low (= all)

ارفع *arfa'*[2] higher; loftier, more exalted; finer; more refined, subtler

رفيعة *rafī'a* pl. رفائع *rafā'i'*[2] legal case brought before the competent authorities; a document submitted to a proper authority

مرفع *marfa'* Shrovetide (*Chr.*); carnival, pl. مرافع *marāfi'*[2] do.

مرفعة *mirfa'a* pl. مرافع *marāfi'*[2] hoisting gear, crane

ترفيع *tarfī'* pl. *-āt* promotion (of an official); salary raise (الى to the amount of)

مرافعة *murāfa'a* pl. *-āt* speech for the defense (in court); proceedings at law | يوم المرافعة *yaum al-m.* date fixed for the trial (of a case in court); قانون المرافعات (*Eg.*) and مجلة المرافعات *majallat al-m.* (*Tun.*) code of procedure

ترفع *taraffu'* arrogance, haughtiness, snobbery (عن toward s.th.), disdain, contempt (عن of s.th.)

ارتفاع *irtifā'* rise (e.g., of prices); elevation; increase; height, altitude (e.g., of a mountain, عن سطح البحر *'an saṭḥi l-baḥr* above sea level, etc.) | على ارتفاع ... at an altitude of ...

رافع *rāfi'* bearer | آلة رافعة hoisting gear, lifting apparatus, hoist; windlass, winch; crane; pump; مضخة رافعة (*miḍakka*) suction pump

رافعة *rāfi'a* pl. روافع *rawāfi'*[2] hoisting gear, lifting apparatus, hoist; crane; hoisting installation (mining) | ○ رافعة هوائية (*hawā'īya*) ejector; ○ رافعة الغام *r. alḡām* mine sweeper

مرفوع *marfū'* traceable in ascending order of traditionaries to Mohammed (Prophetic tradition); (*gram.*) in the nominative or indicative, respectively

مرفع *muraffa'*: المرفع شأنه (*ša'nuhū*) = الرفيع الشأن (see رفيع *rafī'*)

مرافع *murāfi'* plaintiff

مترفع *mutaraffi'* haughty, arrogant, snobbish

مرتفع *murtafi'* rising, ascending; high, elevated; resounding, ringing | سكة الحديد المرتفعة (*sikkat al-ḥ.*) elevated railway

مرتفع *murtafa'* height, altitude; elevated place; ○ terrace; pl. *-āt* heights, elevations, hills

رفق **rafaqa** *u* (*rifq*) and *rafiqa a* (*rafaq*) to be kind, friendly, nice (ب to s.o., also على and ل), treat gently (ب s.o.,), be courteous (ب with s.o.) **III** to be a companion, a comrade (ه of s.o.); to keep (ه s.o.) company; to be on intimate terms, be hand in glove, be friends, associate closely (ه with s.o.); to accompany (ه s.o.; also *mus.*); to escort (ه, ه s.o., s.th.) **IV** to be of use, be useful (ه to s.o.), avail, serve, help (ه s.o.); to accompany (ه ب s.th. with); to attach, enclose, add, append (ه ب to s.th. s.th.) **V** to show o.s. kind, display a gentle, friendly attitude (ب toward s.o., also مع), be nice (ب to s.o., also مع); to do gently (ف s.th.), proceed gently (ف in) | ترفق فى سيره (*sairihī*) to walk slowly, stroll, saunter **VI** to travel together **VIII** to profit, benefit, gain (ب from or by), make use, avail o.s., take advantage (ب of), utilize (ب s.th.); to lean one's elbows, rest one's arms (ه on s.th.)

رفق *rifq* friendliness, kindness, gentleness | جمعية الرفق بالحيوان *jam'īyat ar-r. bi-l-ḥayawān* Society for the Prevention of Cruelty to Animals

رفقة *rifqa*, *rufqa* pl. رفاق *rifāq*, رفق *rifaq*, *rufaq*, ارفاق *arfāq* group, troop, body (of people); company | برفقة accompanied by, in the company of

رفيق *rafīq* pl. رفقاء *rufaqā'²*, رفاق *rifāq* companion, attendant; escort; buddy, friend; comrade (in Marxist terminology); associate, partner; accomplice; kind (ب to), mild, gentle, tender | رفيق المدرسة *r. al-madrasa* classmate, schoolmate

رفيقة *rafīqa* pl. *-āt* woman companion; girl friend; sweetheart; mistress, paramour

مرفق *mirfaq*, *marfiq* elbow; — *mirfaq* pl. مرافق *marāfiq²* anything conducive to personal ease and comfort, convenience; appurtenance (of an apartment, of a house; such as kitchen, bathroom, stable, etc.); attainment of civilization, civilizational institution; pl. مرافق attainments of civilization; conveniences; public utilities; installations; facilities | القيام على مرافقهم (*qiyām*) concern for their welfare; مرافق الحياة *m. al-ḥayāh* conveniences, anything conducive to personal ease and comfort; المرافق العامة (*'āmma*) the public utilities; مرافق التكرير refining facilities (oil industry)

مرافقة *murāfaqa* accompaniment; escort; company, association

ارتفاق *irtifāq* utilization, use; usefulness, serviceableness; easement (*jur.*)

مرافق *murāfiq* pl. *-ūn* companion, attendant; escort; accompanist; adjutant, aide (*Ir.*)

مرفق به *murfaq bihī* attached, enclosed; pl. مرفقات enclosures (in a letter, or the like)

مرتفق *murtafaq* that on which one leans or rests; support; toilet, latrine

رفل **rafala** *u* (*rafl*) to trail a garment; to strut, swagger

رفل *rifl* train (of a garment)

رفه **rafuha** *u* (رفاه *rafāh*, رفاهة *rafāha*, رفاهية *rafāhiya*) to be comfortable, pleasant, luxurious (life) **II** to make (ه life) pleasant and comfortable; to afford (ه s.o.) a pleasant, luxurious life; to be a source of ease and comfort, make things easy (على, عن for s.o.), let (على, عن s.o.) live in comfort; to relax (على, عن s.o.), provide recreation (على, عن for); to ease, soften, mitigate (ه عن for s.o. s.th.); to cheer up (عن s.o.), raise the spirits of (عن); to soothe (عن the soul) | رفه عن نفسه to relax, find recreation (ه from work); رفه على نفسه to find recreation

رفه *rifh* and رفاه *rafāh* well-being, welfare; personal ease and comfort; good living, luxury, comforts of life

رفاهة *rafāha*, رفاهية *rafāhiya* comfortable, luxurious life; luxury; comfort, comfortableness, coziness; complete relaxation and ease

ترفيه *tarfīh* creation of ease and luxury; habituation to luxury; providing of comfort and relaxation; recreation; (mental) relaxation | ترفيه العيش *t. al-ʿaiš* good living, comfortable life; قسم الترفيه *qism at-t.* recreation department

(رفو) رفا *rafā u* (*rafw*) to darn, mend (ه s.th.)

رق *raqqa i* (رقة *riqqa*) to be or become thin, delicate, fine; to be tender, soft; to be pure, clear, limpid (water); to soften, relent (ل toward s.o.), have pity, feel compassion, have sympathy (ل for) | رق له قلبه (*qalbuhū*) he took pity on him **II** to make thin, thin out (ه s.th.); to refine, make fine, soft or tender, render delicate (ه s.th.); to polish, smooth, make elegant (ه one's speech); to flatten, roll out (ه esp. metal) **IV** to make thin, fine or tender, render delicate, refine (ه s.th.); to soften (ه the heart) **V** to soften, relent (ل toward s.o.), have pity, have sympathy (ل for), sympathize (ل with) **X** to be thin, fine, delicate; to soften (ه s.th.); to enslave, make a slave (ه s.o.)

رق *raqq* pl. رقوق *ruqūq* turtle

رق *riqq* quality or condition of being a slave, slavery, bondage

رق *raqq, riqq* parchment; *riqq* (*eg.*) tambourine

رقة *riqqa* thinness; slenderness, slimness; fineness, delicateness, delicacy; gentleness, mildness; amiability, graciousness, friendliness | رقة الحاشية *r. al-ḥāšiya* friendliness, courteousness, amiability; رقة الشعور sensitivity, delicacy of feeling, tact; رقة الطبع *r. aṭ-ṭabʿ* kindness, gentleness, mild temper, friendliness; رقة المزاج gentleness, mild temper

رقاق *ruqāq* flat loaf of bread; ○ waffles

رقيق *raqīq* pl. ارقاء *ariqqāʾ*[2], رقاق *riqāq* slave, slaves (sing. and coll.); flat loaf of bread (*nejd*); thin; slender, slim; fine, delicate; soft, tender, gentle; sensitive, tactful, discreet, prudent | تجارة الرقيق slave trade; رقيق الحال poor, needy; رقيق الحاشية (الحواشي) *r. al-ḥāšiya* (*al-ḥawāšī*) friendly, courteous, civil, amiable; رقيق الشعور sensitive; رقيق الطبع *r. aṭ-ṭabʿ* kind, gentle, mild-tempered, friendly; رقيق المزاج gentlehearted

رقيقة *raqīqa* lamina, flake

ارق *araqq*[2] thinner; slimmer; more delicate

مرقاق *mirqāq* rolling pin

مرقوق *marqūq* thin, flaky pastry

رقأ *raqaʾa a* to cease to flow (tears)

رقب *raqaba u* (رقوب *ruqūb*, رقابة *raqāba*) to observe, watch, regard attentively (ه s.th.); to supervise, control (ه s.th.); to wait (ه for), await (ه s.th.); — (رقوب *ruqūb*) to watch (ه over s.th.), guard (ه s.th.); to take into consideration, heed, observe, respect (ه s.th.); to fear (ه God); to be on one's guard, watch out, be careful | لا يرقب فيه الا ولا ذمة (*illan wa-lā ḏimmatan*) to treat s.o. ruthlessly **III** to watch, observe, regard attentively (ه s.o., ه s.th.), keep an eye (ه, ه on); to make out, detect (ه s.th.); to control (ه s.th., e.g., the traffic, the press, s.o.'s doings, etc.), supervise (ه some work), have an eye (ه on, e.g., on s.o.'s dealings); to fear (ه God) | راقب الله فيه (lit.: to fear God with regard to s.o.) to treat s.o. well for fear of God **V** to expect, anticipate, await (ه s.th.), look forward to (ه), wait, look, look out (ه, ه for); to regard (ه s.th.), look (ه at s.th.); to lie in wait (ه for) **VIII** to expect, anticipate (ه s.th.)

رقبة *riqba* observation; control; attention; caution, wariness; vigilance, watchfulness

رقبة *raqaba* pl. *-āt*, رقاب *riqāb* neck; — (pl. رقاب) slave; (*Isl. Law*) person | ○ رقبة جسر *r. jisr* bridgehead; صلب الرقبة *ṣulb ar-r.* stubborn, obstinate, obstreperous; غليظ الرقبة do.; هذا فى رقابهم responsibility for it rests on their shoulders; اخذ بعضهم برقاب بعض *aḵaḏa ba'ḍuhum bi-r. ba'ḍin* to follow in close succession

رقوب *ruqūb* anticipation, expectation

رقيب *raqīb* pl. رقباء *ruqabā'*[2] vigilant, watchful; guardian, keeper, warden; watcher, observer, lookout; spy; overseer, supervisor, inspector; controller, control officer; postal censor; sergeant (*Syr., mil.*) | رقيب اول (*awwal*) approx.: staff sergeant (*Syr., mil.*)

رقبى *ruqbā* donation with the proviso that it shall either revert to the donor after the donee's death or become the property of the donee upon death of the donor (*Isl. Law*)

رقابة *raqāba* supervision, control; censorship (of the press)

رقوبة *raqūba* and راقوبة *rāqūba* (*eg.*) nest egg

مرقب *marqab* and مرقبة *marqaba* lofty observation post, lookout; watchtower; ○ observatory

مرقب *mirqab* telescope

مراقبة *murāqaba* observation; supervision; surveillance; inspection; control; censorship (of the press); mail censorship; superintendency, controllership; zone of inspection

ترقب *taraqqub* expectation, anticipation

ارتقاب *irtiqāb* expectation, anticipation

مراقب *murāqib* pl. *-ūn* observer; overseer, supervisor, inspector; controller, control officer; censor; sergeant major, quartermaster sergeant (*Eg.* 1939) | مراقب تعليم *m. ta'līm* a military rank (approx.: master sergeant; *Eg.* 1939); مراقب تعيين *m. ta'yīn* a military rank (approx.: quartermaster sergeant; *Eg.* 1939); مراقب مدنى (*madanī*) title of a high local official (*Mor., Tun.*); مراقب الخطوط linesman (soccer)

رقد *raqada u* (*raqd*, رقود *ruqūd*, رقاد *ruqād*) to sleep, be asleep; to go to bed; to lie down to rest; to lie; to rest; to abate, subside, let up, calm down (e.g., a storm); to be down, be flagging; to be dull, listless (market) | رقد على البيض (*baiḍ*) to sit on the eggs (hen) **II** to put (ه s.o.) to sleep; to make (ه s.o.) lie down; to put (ه s.o.) to bed; to lay down, stretch out (ه s.o.) **IV** to put to sleep (ه s.o.); to put to bed (ه a child)

رقدة *raqda* sleep; manner of lying, lying position

رقاد *ruqād* sleep; recumbency, recumbent position

رقود *ruqūd* sleep; recumbency, recumbent position; sleeping, asleep (pl. of the active participle)

راقود *rāqūd* pl. رواقيد *rawāqīd*[2] large jug

مرقد *marqad* pl. مراقد *marāqid*[2] bed; couch; resting place; mausoleum

ترقيد *tarqīd* (*eg.*) layerage (*hort.*) | ترقيد البيض *t. al-baiḍ* hatching of the eggs

ترقيدة *tarqīda* (*eg.*) layer (*hort.*)

راقد *rāqid* pl. رقد *ruqqad*, رقود *ruqūd* sleeping, asleep; lying, reclining, recumbent; resting; quiet, dull, listless (market)

مرقد *muraqqid* somniferous, lulling; pl. مرقدات soporifics

رقرق *raqraqa* to mix, dilute (ه wine with water) II *taraqraqa* to overflow (بالدموع with tears; eyes), be bathed (بالدموع in tears); to glitter, glisten, sparkle: to stir gently, breathe (wind)

رقراق *raqrāq* bathed (in tears), moist, misty (eyes); glittering, glistening; radiant, brilliant, resplendent

رقارق *ruqāriq* not deep, shallow (water)

رقش *raqaša u* to variegate, make multicolored (ه s.th.) II do.; to adorn, embellish, decorate (ه s.th.)

ارقش *arqaš*[2] variegated, multicolored, colorful

○ مرقاش *mirqāš* pl. مراقيش *marāqīš*[2] brush (of the painter)

رقص *raqaṣa u* (*raqṣ*) to dance; to prance (horse; على to a tune) | رقص فرحا (*faraḥan*) to dance with joy II to make (ه s.o.) dance; to set (ه s.th.) in a swinging motion; to make (ه the heart) tremble | رقص الحناجر (prop.: to make the throats tremble) to provoke loud laughter III to dance (ها with a girl) IV = II; VI to move; to dance; to prance; to tremble (heart)

رقص *raqṣ* dancing, dance | معلم الرقص *muʿallim ar-r.* dancing instructor

رقصة *raqṣa* (n. vic.) pl. *raqaṣāt* dance

رقاص *raqqāṣ* (professional) dancer; pendulum (*phys.*; also of a timepiece)

رقاصة *raqqāṣa* female dancer; dancing girl, danseuse; ballerina

مرقص *marqaṣ* pl. مراقص *marāqiṣ*[2] dance hall, ballroom; dance, ball

راقص *rāqiṣ* dancer; dance, dancing (used attributively) | حفلة راقصة (*ḥafla*) dance, ball; موسيقى راقصة dance music; ليلة راقصة (*laila*) dancing party

راقصة *rāqiṣa* pl. *-āt* female dancer; ○ kneecap, patella

مراقصة *murāqiṣa* (female) dancing partner

رقط II to speckle, spot (ه s.th.)

ارقط *arqaṭ*[2] speckled, spotted; leopard

رقع *raqaʿa a* (*raqʿ*) to patch (ه a garment); — *raquʿa u* (رقاعة *raqāʿa*) to be stupid II = *raqaʿa*

رقعة *ruqʿa* pl. رقع *ruqaʿ*, رقاع *riqāʿ* patch; piece of cloth; piece of land, terrain or ground; area; lot, plot of land; ground (of a flag); chessboard; slip of paper, piece of paper; note, brief message; ticket; coupon; bond, security; a cursive style of calligraphy

رقيع *raqīʿ* stupid, silly, foolish; impudent, impertinent, shameless; (pl. ارقعة *arqiʿa*) firmament

رقاعة *raqāʿa* stupidity, foolishness, folly

مرقعة *marqaʿa* and مرقعية *marqaʿīya* tatters, rags

ترقيع *tarqīʿ* patching | ترقيع القرنية *t. al-qarnīya* transplantation of the cornea (*med.*)

مرقعات *muraqqaʿāt* fragments

رقم *raqama u* (*raqm*) to write (ه s.th.); to point, provide with points (ه a text); to brand (ه a horse); to imprint (ه a trace, a mark); to mark (ه s.th.); to stripe (ه a fabric); to number (ه s.th.) II to point, provide with points (ه a text); to stripe, streak (ه s.th.); to rule (ه s.th.); to number (ه s.th.)

رقم *raqm* pl. ارقام *arqām* numeral; number, No. | الارقام الهندية (*hindīya*) the numerals of the Arabs; رقم القياس *r. al-qiyās* or رقم قياسى (*qiyāsī*) record (*athlet.*), سجل رقما قياسيا (*sajjala*) to set a record (*athlet.*)

رقيم *raqīm* inscription tablet; letter, message

مرقم *mirqum* pl. مراقم *marāqim*² drawing pencil, crayon; (painter's) brush

ترقيم *tarqīm* pointing; numbering, numeration

مرقوم *marqūm* pl. مراقيم *marāqīm*² striped blanket

رقوص II *taraqwaṣa* (*syr.*) to toss, fling o.s. about

رقى *raqiya a* (*raqy, ruqīy*) to ascend (الى or فى s.th. or to s.th.); to climb, mount, scale (ه s.th.); to rise (in rank), advance, be promoted; to date back, go back (الى to a bygone era); رقى به to lead s.o. up; to further, promote, encourage s.th.; — *raqā i* (رقية *ruqya*) to use magic or incantations (ه on s.o., من against s.th.) II to cause to ascend; to promote (ه s.o.); to raise, further, promote, advance (ه s.th.) V to ascend, rise, advance, progress VIII to ascend, rise; to ascend (ه s.th.; also, e.g., العرش *al-'arša* the throne), climb (ه s.th., on s.th., also العربة *al-'araba* into the carriage); to advance, be promoted (الى منصب *ilā manṣib* to an office); to rise, increase (الى to the number of); to advance, rise, show an upward trend, develop upward; to date back, go back (الى to a given time)

رقى *ruqīy* rise, progress, upward development; الرقى به promotion, encouragement, furtherance of s.th.

رقية *ruqya* pl. رقى *ruqan* spell, charm, magic; incantation

رقاء *raqqā'* magician, sorcerer

ارقى *arqā* higher, superior; more advanced, more progressed

مرقاة *mirqāh* pl. مراق *marāqin* stairs, staircase; ○ elevator, lift

ترقية *tarqiya* raising; — (pl. *-āt*) promotion (in rank); elevation; promotion, furtherance, encouragement, advancement; extension, development, improvement

ترق *taraqqin* pl. *taraqqiyāt* ascension; ascent; advance, advancement; progress, rise, progressive development

ارتقاء *irtiqā'* climbing, mounting; ascension; ascent; progress, rise, progressive development | ارتقاء العرش *irt. al-'arš* accession to the throne

راق *rāqin* ascending, rising; high, high-ranking; superior. high-grade, high-class, of high standard; educated, refined; advanced | الطبقة الراقية (*ṭabaqa*) the upper class

راق *rāqin* pl. رقاة *ruqāh* magician, sorcerer

مرتق *murtaqin* high, superior, advanced (esp. intellectually)

مرتقى *murtaqan* ascent, rise

رك¹ *rakka i* (*rakk*, ركة *rikka*, ركاكة *rakāka*) to be weak, feeble; to be poor, meager, scanty; — *u* (*rakk*): رك الشىء فى عنقه (*fī 'unuqihī*) to saddle s.o. with the responsibility for s.th., thrust s.th. upon s.o.

ركة *rikka* weakness, feebleness

ركيك *rakīk* pl. ركاك *rikāk*, ركيكة *rakaka* weak, feeble; thin; colorless, pallid (e.g., style); scanty, meager, poor, pitiful

ركاك *rukāk* weak, feeble

ركاكة *rakāka* weakness, feebleness; lowliness; inadequacy, poorness; colorlessness, pallor (e.g., of style)

ركة *rukka* distaff | طب الركة *ṭibb ar-r.* (*eg.*) popular treatment of illnesses by means of charms and incantations, practiced by women

ركب *rakiba a* (ركوب *rukūb*) to ride (ه an animal); to mount (ه an animal); to go, travel (ه in a carriage, in an automobile, on a train, on board a ship, etc.), ride (ه in a vehicle, on a bicycle); to get, climb (ه into a carriage, on a bicycle, etc.), board (ه a train, an airplane, a ship, etc.); to pursue (ه s.o.), be after s.o. (ب with s.th.); to engage (ه in), embark (ه on); to commit, perpetrate (ه a sin, a crime); to master (ه s.th.) | ركب البحر (*baḥr*) to travel by sea; ركب الحياة (*ḥayāh*) to master life; ركب الخطر (*ḵaṭar*) to embark on a risky undertaking; ركب خيوله الحربية (*ḵuyūlahū l-ḥarbīya*) to get on one's high horse; ركب ذنب الريح (*ḏanaba r-rīḥ*) to speed along like the wind; ركب رأسه (*ra'sahū*) to act at one's discretion; to act rashly, follow a whim; ركب السيارة (*sayyāra*) to go by car, travel in an automobile; ركب الشطط (*šaṭaṭ*) to commit excesses, go too far; ركب الطيارة (*ṭayyāra*) to fly, go by plane; ركب متن العنف (*matna l-'unf*) to commit acts of violence; ركب مركب الخطل (*markaba l-ḵaṭal*) to make a foolish mistake, commit a folly; to embark on a reckless course, do irresponsible things; ركب مطية الاخفاق (*maṭīyata 'l-ikfāq*) to back the wrong horse, be on the losing side, fail; ركب الاهوال (*ahwāl*) to defy the horrors; ركب الهواء (*hawā'*) to fly, travel by air; ركب هواه (*hawāhu*) to follow one's whim **II** to make (ه s.o.) ride; to put, place, fasten, mount (على ه s.th. on); to fit, mount, insert, set (في ه s.th. in, e.g., a precious stone in a ring); to build in (ه a machine part); to assemble (ه e.g., the parts of an apparatus); to set up (ه a machine); to install (ه s.th.; *techn.*), lay (ه an electric line, and the like); to assemble, put together, fit together (ه s.th.); to make, prepare (ه s.th. out of several components or ingredients); to construct, build (ه e.g., a technical apparatus) **IV** to make (ه s.o.) ride or mount | اركبه رأسه وهواه (*ra'sahū wa-hawāhu*) to let s.o. have his head, let s.o. do as he pleases **V** to be composed, be made up, consist (من of) **VI** to be superimposed one upon another **VIII** to commit, perpetrate (ه a sin, a crime); to pursue, practice (ه s.th.) | ارتكب شططا (*šaṭaṭan*) to overdo s.th., go too far

ركب *rakb* riders, horsemen, cavalcade; caravan; traveling party; retinue, escort; procession, troop (of people)

ركبة *rukba* pl. ركب *rukab*, *-āt* knee | ابو الركب *abū r-rukab* dengue, breakbone fever (*med.*)

ركاب *rikāb* pl. ركب *rukub* stirrup; (pl. *-āt*, ركب *rukub*, ركائب *rakā'ib*²) riding camel, riding animal, mount | حل ركابه بارضنا *ḥalla rikābahū bi-arḍinā* he has arrived on our soil; هو في ركابه he is his loyal follower, he dogs his footsteps; سار في ركابه do.; to cling to s.o.'s heels, be blindly subservient to s.o.

ركوب *rakūb* mount, riding animal

ركوبة *rakūba* pl. ركائب *rakā'ib*² mount, female riding camel

ركوب *rukūb* (horseback, camelback, etc.) riding; traveling (in a vehicle, by sea, by air, etc.); mounting (of a bicycle, of a horse, etc.), boarding (of a train, of a ship, etc.) | ركوب البحر *r. al-baḥr* navigation; ركوب الهواء *r. al-hawā'* flying, aviation

ركاب *rakkāb* one who rides frequently, (professional) horseman or rider, jockey

ركبان *rukbān* retinue, escort | ذكره سار به الركبان (*ḏikruhū*) approx.: his fame has spread far and wide

مركب *markab* pl. مراكب *marākib*² ship, boat, vessel | مركب بخاري (*bukārī*) steamship, steamer; مركب حربي (*harbī*) warship, man-of-war; مركب دوري (*daurī*) patrol boat; مركب شراعي (*širāʿī*) sailing vessel, sailboat; مركب الصيد *m. aṣ-ṣaid* fishing smack, trawler; مركب النقل *m. an-naql* freighter, transport

مركبة *markaba* pl. *-āt* vehicle; carriage, cab

مراكبي *marākibī* pl. *marākibīya* boatman; ferryman

تركيب *tarkīb* pl. *-āt*, تراكيب *tarākīb*² fitting in, insertion, setting; building in; fastening, mounting; assembling, assembly; final assembly; installation (e.g., of a telephone extension); composition; making, preparation (out of several components or ingredients); construction, building (*techn.*); structure; constitution, build, physique; — (pl. تراكيب *tarākīb*²) phrase, idiom; construction (*gram.*)

تركيبي *tarkībī* constructive, constructional

ارتكاب *irtikāb* perpetration (of a sin or crime)

راكب *rākib* riding, on horseback, mounted; riding, traveling (in a vehicle); (pl. ركاب *rukkāb*, ركبان *rukbān*) rider, horseman; (pl. ركاب *rukkāb*) passenger, occupant (of a conveyance) | راكب دراجة *r. darrāja* cyclist

مركوب *markūb* pl. مراكيب *marākīb*² riding animal, mount; (*eg., syr.*) red-leather shoes | ابو مركوب *abū m.* (*eg.*) shoebill (Balaeniceps rex; *zool.*)

مركبات *murakkibāt* components, constituents, elements, ingredients (esp. *chem.*)

مركب *murakkab* mounted, fastened, fixed (على on); fitted, inserted, set (في in); built-in; assembled; made up, composed, consisting (من of); compound, composite; complex; bound, not free; — (pl. *-āt*) composition; a compound (*chem.*); a composite; a complex (*psychol.*); medication, medicament | ربح مركب (*ribḥ*) compound interest; مركب كيميائي (*kīmiyāʾī*) chemical compound; مركب نقص *m. naqṣ* inferiority complex

مرتكب *murtakib* perpetrator (of a crime)

ركد *rakada u* (ركود *rukūd*) to be motionless, still, stagnant

ركود *rukūd* suspension, standstill, stagnation; sluggishness; stillness, tranquillity

راكد *rākid* stagnant; sluggish

ركز *rakaza u i* (*rakz*) to plant or ram in the ground, set up (ه s.th., e.g., a pole); to fix, embed firmly (ه s.th.) **II** to plant or ram in the ground, set up, (ه s.th., e.g., a pole); to position, emplace (ه s.th.); to fix, embed firmly (ه s.th.); to cause to take root, naturalize (ه s.th.); to concentrate (ه s.th., also one's thoughts, في on) **V** to concentrate; تركز *tarakkaz* ready! (starter's command; *athlet.*) **VIII** to be implanted; to settle permanently, stay (في at a place); to lean, support one's weight (على or الى on); to be fastened, be mounted (على on); to be based, rest (على on); to concentrate (في on); to gravitate (في to)

ركز *rikz* sound, tone

ركزة *rakza* pause, rest, break

ركاز *rikāz* pl. اركزة *arkiza*, ركزان *rikzān* precious minerals, buried treasures of the earth

ركيزة *rakīza* pl. ركائز *rakāʾiz*² treasure; support, brace, shore, stanchion; pillar, pier; post, pile; shoring

مركز *markaz* pl. مراكز *marākiz*² foothold; stand, station; place where s.o. is posted or stationed; post; (police, etc.)

station; office, branch office (*com.*); locality where s.th. takes place, scene, site, seat; position (*mil.*); headquarters; main office, central office; central exchange (telephone); center (of a circle and fig.); focus; markaz, an administrative district (subdivision of a *mudīrīya*, *Eg.*); position, situation, office, post; (social, financial, official, etc.) status, standing; power, position (of a country); situation | مركز اساسى (*asāsī*) starting point, basis; مركز البوليس police station; مراكز حيوية (*ḥayawīya*) vital centers; مركز لادارة *m. al-idāra* main office, central office, headquarters; مركز الداء *m. ad-dā'* the seat of the disease; ○ مركز الاذاعة *m. al-iḏā'a* broadcasting station; مركز رئيسى main office, headquarters; مركز الرياسة *m. ar-riyāsa* central command post; مركز رياسة الجيش *m. riyāsat al-jaiš* Supreme Command of the Army (*Eg.*); مركز رعاية الطفل *m. ri'āyat aṭ-ṭifl* health center for children (*Eg.*); مركز السكة الحديدية *m. as-sikka al-ḥadīdīya* railroad junction; مركز الشرطة *m. aš-šurṭa* police station; مركز نيابى (*niyābī*) parliamentary seat, mandate; ○ مركز التوليد power station

مركزى *markazī* central; district (used attributively); لامركزى ○ centrifugal; decentralized (administration)

مركزية *markazīya* centralism; centrality, central position or situation; لامركزية decentralization

تركيز *tarkīz* setting up; installation; implantation, establishment, naturalization; concentration | جهاز التركيز *juhāz at-t.* stabilizer (*techn.*)

تراكز *tarākuz* concentricity

ارتكاز *irtikāz* support

مركز *murakkaz* concentrated, centralized; ○ condensed

متراكز *mutarākiz* concentric

ركس VIII to suffer a setback, be thrown back; to decline, degenerate, be degenerate; to become stunted, atrophy

ركض *rakaḍa u* (*rakḍ*) to race, rush, run; to run away; to gallop (intrans., said of a horse, and trans. ه a horse) III to race (ه s.o.), run a race (ه with) VI to compete in a race; to run fast

ركاض *rakkāḍ* runner, racer

ركوض *rakūḍ* fast-running, swift

ركع *raka'a a* (ركوع *rukū'*) to bend the body, bow (esp. in prayer); to kneel down, drop to one's knees II and IV to make (ه s.o.) kneel down

ركعة *rak'a* pl. *raka'āt* a bending of the torso from an upright position, followed by two prostrations (in Muslim prayer ritual)

راكع *rāki'* pl. ركع *rukka'* bowing to the ground

ركل *rakala u* (*rakl*) to kick (ه s.o., ه s.th.)

ركلة *rakla* (n. vic.) kick

ركم *rakama u* (*rakm*) to pile up, heap up, accumulate, amass (ه s.th.) VI to accumulate, be heaped up; to pile up, gather (clouds) VIII = VI

ركم *rakam* pile, heap

ركام *rukām* pile, heap; lump; cumulus clouds

○ **مركم** *markam* pl. مراكم *marākim*² storage battery

تراكم *tarākum* accumulation

ركن *rakana u* (ركون *rukūn*) and *rakina a* to lean, support one's weight (الى on); to quiet down, become or be calm; to trust (الى in), rely (الى on); to be dependent, have to rely (الى on) | ركن الى الهدوء to remain calm IV to trust (الى s.o.), rely (الى on), place one's confidence (الى in); to resort (الى to) | يركن اليه (*yurkanu*) reliable, dependable, trustworthy VIII to lean, recline, support one's weight (الى or على on)

ركن **rukn** pl. اركان **arkān** support, prop; corner; nook; basis, basic element, first principle; pl. اركان staff (*mil.*); basic elements, chief elements | اركان الحرب *a. al-ḥarb* general staff (*mil.*); اركان الجيش *a. al-jaiš* do.; رئيس اركان الجيش chief of general staff; وثيق الاركان of strong build, sturdy

ركنى **ruknī**: ضربة ركنية (*ḍarba*) corner kick (soccer)

ركين **rakīn** firm, steady, confident, imperturbable; grave, calm, sedate

ركون **rukūn** reliance, confidence, trust

مركن **mirkan** pl. مراكن **marākin**² washtub

مراكنة **murākana** (*tun.*) betrothal, engagement

اركان **irkān** reliance, confidence, trust

ركوة **rakwa** pl. **rakawāt** (*syr.*) small coffee pot of copper, having a long handle

رم **ramma** *u i* (*ramm*, مرمة *maramma*) to repair, overhaul (ه s.th.); — *i* (*ramm*, رمة *rimma*) to decay; to rot II to decay; to rot V to be repaired, undergo repair

رم **ramm** repair

رم **ramm**: رم الاسنان *r. al-asnān* caries (*med.*)

رمة **rimma** cadaver

برمته **bi-rummatihī** whole, complete, entire | سورية برمتها all Syria

رميم **ramīm** decayed, rotten; رمائم *ramā'im*² decaying bones

رمام **rumām** decayed, rotten

مرمة **maramma** pl. *-āt* repair; shipyard (*Tun.*)

ترميم **tarmīm** pl. *-āt* repair, overhauling, restoration

رمث **ramaṯ** pl. ارماث **armāṯ** log raft

رمح **ramaḥa** *a* (*ramḥ*) to pierce, transfix (with a lance; ه s.o.); to gallop (horse)

رمح **rumḥ** pl. رماح **rimāḥ**, ارماح **armāḥ** lance, pike; spear, javelin; pole | رمى الرمح *ramy ar-r.* javelin throwing (*athlet.*)

رماح **rammāḥ** pl. ة lancer; uhlan

السماك الرامح *as-simāk ar-rāmiḥ* Arcturus (*astron.*)

رمد **ramida** *a* (*ramad*) to have sore eyes; to be inflamed (eye) II to burn to ashes, incinerate (ه s.th.) V to burn to ashes, become ashes

رمد **ramad** ophthalmia, inflammation of the eyes; eye disease | رمد حبيبى (*ḥubaibī*) trachoma, granular conjunctivitis; مستشفى الرمد *mustašfā r-r.* eye clinic

رمدى **ramadī** and طبيب رمدى ophthalmologist, oculist

رمد **ramid** sore-eyed

ارمد **armad**² sore-eyed

رماد **ramād** pl. ارمدة **armida** ashes | اربعاء الرماد *arbi'ā' ar-r.* or يوم الرماد *yaum ar-r.* or عيد الرماد *'īd ar-r.* Ash Wednesday (*Chr.*); نفخ فى الرماد (lit.: to blow into cold ashes, i.e.) to engage in futile undertakings, set out on a wild-goose chase

رمادى **ramādī** ashen, ash-colored, ashgray

ترميد **tarmīd** cremation, incineration

رمز **ramaza** *u i* (*ramz*) to make a sign, to wink, nod, motion; to point (الى to), indicate (الى s.th.); to symbolize, represent or express symbolically (الى s.th.); to designate (ب ل or الى s.th. with a distinguishing mark)

رمز **ramz** pl. رموز **rumūz** sign, nod, wink, motion; hint; allusion, intimation; allegory; riddle; symbol, symbolic figure, emblem, character; secret sign, code sign

رمزى *ramzī* symbolic(al); in code, in cipher

رمزيات *ramzīyāt* cipher, code

راموز *rāmūz* pl. رواميز *rawāmīz*² specimen, sample; ○ facsimile

رمس **ramasa** *i u* (*rams*) to bury (ه s.o.); to cover, efface, wipe out (ه tracks) **VIII** ارتمس فى الماء to be immersed in water

رمس *rams* pl. رموس *rumūs*, ارماس *armās* grave, tomb

راموس *rāmūs* grave, tomb

رمش **ramaša** *i u* to take with the fingertips (ه s.th.); to wink, blink

رمش *ramaš* inflammation of the eyelids, conjunctivitis

رمشة *ramša* blink, wink

رمش *rimš* pl. رموش *rumūš* eyelashes

رمص *ramaṣ* white secretion (of the eye)

رمض **VIII** to be consumed by grief and sorrow

رمض *ramaḍ* parchedness, scorchedness (esp. of the ground due to excessive heat)

رمضاء *ramḍā'*² sun-baked ground | استجار من الرمضاء بالنار approx.: to jump out of the frying pan into the fire

رمضان *ramaḍān*² Ramadan, the ninth month of the Muslim calendar

رمق **ramaqa** *u* (*ramq*) to regard (ه, ه s.o., s.th.), glance, look (ه, ه at) **II** to stare, gaze (ه, ه at); to perform (ه work) perfunctorily and negligently, botch (ه a job); to keep (ه s.o.) barely alive **V** to wait (ه for an opportunity, and the like)

رمق *ramaq* pl. ارماق *armāq* (last) spark of life, breath of life | سد رمقه *sadda ramaqahū* to keep s.o. or o.s. barely alive, eke out a living, manage to keep body and soul together; to provide s.o. with a bare existence; to allay s.o.'s hunger; على آخر رمق *'alā ākiri ramaqin* at the point of death; on the verge of exhaustion, on one's last legs

مرموق *marmūq* regarded, looked at; noted, of note; remarkable, notable, significant, important; lofty, proud

ارمك *armak*², f. رمكاء *ramkā'*² ashen, ash-gray

رمكة *ramaka* pl. *-āt*, رماك *rimāk*, ارماك *armāk* mare

رمل **II** to sprinkle with sand (ه s.th., so as to blot it) **IV** to become a widower or a widow **V** = **IV**

رمل *raml* pl. رمال *rimāl* sand | علم الرمل *'ilm ar-r.* or ضرب الرمل *ḍarb ar-r.* geomancy (divination by means of figures or lines in the sand)

رملى *ramlī* sandy, sabulous; sand- (in compounds) | ساعة رملية sandglass, hourglass

رمل *ramal* name of a poetical meter

رمال *rammāl* geomancer

ارمل *armal*² pl. ارامل *arāmil*² widower

ارملة *armala* pl. ارامل *arāmil*², اراملة *arāmila* widow

مرملة *mirmala* sandbox

ترمل *tarammul* widow(er)hood

¹رمان *rummān* (coll.; n. un. ة) pomegranate; رمانة knob, pommel; (pl. *-āt*), رمانة يدوية (*yadawīya*) hand grenade

²ارمن and ارمنى look up alphabetically

¹رمى **ramā** *i* (*ramy*, رماية *rimāya*) to throw, cast (ه, ب s.th.); to fling, hurl (ه, ب s.th.); to toss away, throw down (ه, ب s.th.); to throw aside, toss aside, discard, lay aside (ه, ب s.th.); to shoot, fire; to pelt, hit, bombard (ه ب s.o. with), shoot, fire (ه ب at s.o. with); to charge (ه ب s.o. with), accuse (ه ب s.o. of), blame, re-

proach (ب ه s.o. for); to aim, drive, be aimed (الى at), have in view, purpose, intend (الى s.th.), be out for (الى); with بين: to sow dissension among or between | رماه بطلق نارى (*ṭalaq*) he fired a shot at him; رمى بالغيب (*ḡaib*) to practice divination **VI** to pelt one another; to throw o.s. to the ground, prostrate o.s., fall to the ground; to throw o.s., fling o.s. (على on); to plunge, rush, throw o.s. (في into s.th.); to be vast, extend far into the distance; to come, get (information, report, news; الى to s.o.) | ترامى على قدميه (*qadamaihi*) to throw o.s. at s.o.'s feet; ترامى بين ذراعيه (*ḏirā'aihi*) to throw o.s. into s.o.'s arms; عاطفة ترامى به عهدها (*'ahduhā*) a feeling that he had known long, long ago, a feeling which lay far behind him; ترامى الينا ان we have received word that ... **VIII** to throw o.s. (على on, e.g., on the bed, on or to the ground); to fling o.s., fall (على upon s.o.), throw o.s., plunge (في into s.th.); to have fallen down and lie prostrate; to lie, sprawl (على on) | ارتمى الى الارض to fall to the ground, tumble

رمى ***ramy*** (act or process of) throwing, flinging, shooting, etc. | رمى الحربة *r. al-ḥarba* javelin throwing, رمى القرص *r. al-qurṣ* discus throwing (*athlet.*); اعدام رميا بالرصاص *i'dām ramyan bi-r-raṣāṣ* execution before a firing squad

رمية ***ramya*** (n. vic.) throw, toss, fling; shot | رب رمية من غير رام *rubba ramyatin min ḡairi rāmin* many a shot is without a (skilled) marksman (proverbially, of unexpected or undeserved success)

رمية ***ramīya*** pl. رمايا *ramāyā* game animal (being shot at or already killed)

مرمى ***marman*** pl. مرام *marāmin* aim, end, purpose; goal (*athlet.*); range (of a gun); reach, extent | حارس المرمى goalkeeper; مرمى النظر *m. an-naẓar* range of vision, field of vision

ترام ***tarāmin*** vastness, expanse | ترامى الاطراف vast expanse, vastness

رام ***rāmin*** pl. رماة *rumāh* throwing; thrower, hurler; marksman; rifleman (*Syr., mil.*) | الرامى Sagittarius (*astron.*); سهم الرامى *sahm ar-r.* Sagitta (*astron.*); رامى اللهيب flame thrower

مترام ***mutarāmin*** wide, extensive | مترامى الاطراف vast, huge

رامية² look up alphabetically

رن ***ranna*** *i* (رنين *ranīn*) to cry, wail, lament; to resound; to echo; to ring

رنة ***ranna*** pl. *-āt* scream; sound; reverberation, echo

رنين ***ranīn*** lament, wailing; sound; reverberation, echo; resonance; ring

رنان ***rannān*** and مرنان ***mirnān*** ringing, resounding; resonant; reverberating, echoing

○ رنانة ***rannāna*** tuning fork (*mus.*)

ارنب and ارنبة look up alphabetically

رنح **II** to make dizzy, make stagger, send reeling (ه s.o.); to sway (ه s.th.) | رنح اعطافه (*a'ṭāfahū*) to work up s.o.'s feelings, send s.o. into a frenzy **V** to stagger, reel, totter, sway; to shake, rock | ترنحت اعطافه (*a'ṭāfuhū*) to get into one's stride, become ecstatic, be carried away; to be beside o.s.

مرنحة ***marnaḥa*** prow (of a ship)

رندح ***randaḥa*** to scan (verse)

رنق **II** to cloud, muddy (ه water); to blur, dim (ه the eyes; said of sleep); to halt, stop, stop over, stay; to look, glance (نحو toward or at s.th.) | رنق النظر الى (*naẓara*) to keep looking at, stare at

رنق ***ranq*** turbid, clouded (water)

رونق ***raunaq*** glamor, splendor, beauty

رنم II and V to sing (ب a song); to intone (ب a song); to recite in a singsong voice, chant (ب s.th.)

ترنيمة *tarnīma* pl. ترانيم *tarānīm*² hymn, anthem; song; a kind of chanting recitation; little story recited in a singsong voice; little song

(رنو) رنا *ranā* *u* to gaze, look (الى at s.th.)

رنق II and IV to please, delight (ه s.o.)

رهب *rahiba* *a* (*rahab*, *ruhb*, رهبة *rahba*) to be frightened, be afraid; to fear, dread (ه s.o.) | رهب جانبه see جانب II to frighten, scare, alarm, intimidate (ه s.o.) IV = II; to terrorize (ه s.o.) V to threaten (ه s.o.); to become a monk, enter monastic life (*Chr.*)

رهبة *rahba* fear, fright, alarm, terror; awe

رهبى *rahbā*, *ruhbā* fear

رهبوت *rahbūt* great fear, fright, terror

رهيب *rahīb* dreadful, awful, fearful, terrible; solemn, grave

ترهيب *tarhīb* intimidation

ارهاب *irhāb* intimidation, frightening; threatening; terror, terrorism (*pol.*); sabotage

ارهابى *irhābī* terrorist(ic); sabotage (used attributively); (pl. *-ūn*) terrorist

ترهب *tarahhub* monasticism, monastic life (*Chr.*)

راهب *rāhib* pl. رهبان *ruhbān* monk (*Chr.*)

راهبة *rāhiba* pl. *-āt* nun (*Chr.*)

مرهوب *marhūb* terrible, dreadful

رهبن II *tarahbana* to become a monk, enter monastic life (*Chr.*)

رهبنة *rahbana* and رهبانية *rahbānīya* monasticism; monastic order, congregation (*Chr.*)

رهج *rahj*, *rahaj* dust

رهط *rahaṭa* *a* to gobble, gulp greedily

رهط *rahṭ*, *rahaṭ* pl. ارهاط *arhāṭ*, ارهط *arhuṭ*, اراهط *arāhiṭ*², اراهيط *arāhīṭ*² group (of people), band, troop

رهط *rahṭ* pl. رهاط *rihāṭ* leather loincloth

رهف *rahufa* *u* (رهافة *rahāfa*) to be thin; to be sharp (sword); — *rahafa* *a* (*rahf*) and IV to make thin (ه s.th.); to make sharp, sharpen (ه s.th., esp. fig.) | ارهف الاذن (*uḏn*) to prick up one's ears (لفلان so as to catch the words of s.o.), ارهف السمع ل (الى) (*sam'*) to listen closely to

رهف *rahif* thin

رهيف *rahīf* thin; slender, slim; sharpened, sharp

ارهاف *irhāf* sharpening

مرهف *murhaf* thin, fine; sharpened, sharp | مرهف الحس *m. al-ḥiss* delicate, sensitive

رهق *rahiqa* *a* (*rahaq*) to come over s.o. or s.th. (ه, ه), overtake (ه, ه s.o., s.th.) III to approach (ه an age); to approach the age of sexual maturity; to be adolescent IV to bring down (ه ه upon s.o. s.th.), make (ه s.o.) undergo or suffer (ه s.th.): to oppress, burden, overburden (ه s.o., ب with s.th.), lie heavily, bear down (ه on s.o.) | ارهقه جذبا (*jaḏban*) to tug at s.o. violently or too violently

مراهقة *murāhaqa* puberty

ارهاق *irhāq* pressure, oppression; suppression; heavy load (e.g., of work)

مراهق *murāhiq* adolescent

مرهق *murhiq* oppressive (burden, heat)

رهل *rahila* *a* to be flabby, soft; to be bloated, fat (flesh, body) V do.

رهل *rahil* flaccid, flabby, soft

تَرهل *tarahhul* obesity, fatness

مترهل *mutarahhil* flaccid, flabby, soft; bloated, fat

رهمة *rihma* pl. رهم *riham*, رهام *rihām* drizzle, lasting fine rain

مرهم *marham* pl. مراهم *marāhim*[2] salve, ointment; cream, cold cream; pomade

رهن **rahana** *a* (*rahn*) to pawn, deposit as security (ه s.th., عند or ه with s.o.); to mortgage (ه real estate) III to bet, lay a wager (ه with s.o., على on, that ...) IV to deposit in pledge, give as a security, pawn (ه s.th.) VIII to receive or take in pledge, as a security (ه من s.th. from s.o.); to pawn, deposit in pledge (ه s.th.); to make (ه s.th.) subject (ب to), make (ه s.th.) conditional (ب on); pass.: *urtuhina* to be subject (ب to) | ارتهن نفسه ب (*nafsahu*) to pledge o.s. or dedicate o.s. to the cause of X to demand as a security (ه ه from s.o. s.th.)

رهن *rahn* pawning, mortgaging, pledging; — (pl. رهون *ruhūn*, رهونات *ruhūnāt*, رهان *rihān*) pawn, pledge; security (ب for s.th.); hostage; mortgage, hypothec; رهن ب depending on, conditional on, subject to; — *rahna* (prep.) pending; depending on, conditional on; subject to, liable to | محل رهونات *maḥall r.* pawnshop; رهن اشارته *rahna išāratihī* at s.o.'s beck and call; رهن سيطرته *r. saiṭaratihī* under s.o.'s power or dominion; هذا رهن ذاك this depends on that; المسألة رهن اهتمامه *al-mas'ala r. htimāmihī* the problem is being given every attention by him; اودع السجن رهن التحقيق *ūdi'a s-sijna rahna t-taḥqīq* he was taken into custody pending investigation

رهنية *rahnīya* mortgage (deed)

رهين *rahīn* pawned, mortgaged, pledged, given as security; held in pledge; security (ب for); responsible (ب for); subject (ب to); (prep.) subject to, depending on | كان رهينه (*rahīnahū*) to be under obligation to s.o.; to be dependent on s.o.

رهينة *rahīna* pl. رهائن *rahā'in*[2] pawn, pledge, security; hostage; mortgage, hypothec

رهان *rihān* bet, wager; competition, contest

مراهنة *murāhana* pl. *-āt* bet, wager

راهن *rāhin* pledger, mortgagor; fixed, established, certain; lasting, permanent; current; present, actual | الظروف الراهنة present circumstances; الحالة الراهنة the present condition; the status quo

مرهون *marhūn* pawned, pledged, mortgaged, given as security; subject (ب to) | الامور مرهونة باوقاتها (*bi-auqātihā*) there is a time for everything

مرتهن *murtahin* mortgagee, pledgee, pawnbroker

[1]رها (رهو) **rahā** *u* (*rahw*) to amble

رهو *rahw* quiet, calm, peaceful, tranquil; stillness, calm, peace, tranquillity; (pl. رهاء *rihā'*) crane (*zool.*)

رهوان *rahwān* ambler (horse); palfrey

[2]الرهاء *ar-ruhā'* the city of Urfa (Gr. Edessa)

رهون **rahwana** and II *tarahwana* to amble (horse)

رهوان see رهو

[1]راب (روب) **rāba** *u* (*raub*) to curdle (milk) II and IV to (cause to) curdle (ه milk)

روب *raub* curdled milk, curds

رائب *rā'ib* curdled (milk)

[2]روب (Fr. *robe*) *rōb* pl. ارواب *arwāb* dressing gown

روبابيكيا (It. *roba vecchia*) *rōbabēkiyā*: بائع الروبابيكيا junk dealer

روبصة *raubaṣa* sleepwalking, somnambulism

ترويص *taraubuṣ* sleepwalking, somnambulism

روبل *rūbel* ruble

روبية *rūbīya* pl. *-āt* rupee

روتانية *rūtāniyā* Ruthenia

(روث) راث *rāṯa u* (*rauṯ*) to drop dung

روث *rauṯ* (coll.; n. un. ة) pl. ارواث *arwāṯ* dung, droppings (of horse, camel, and the like)

[1](روج) راج *rāja u* (رواج *rawāj*) to be spread, circulate, be current; to find a good market, sell well, be in demand (merchandise); to be or become brisk, pick up (market); to be at hand, be available (ل for s.o.) **II** to spread (ه rumors, news, etc.), circulate, put into circulation (ه s.th.; currency, rumors, news, etc.); to push the sale (ه of s.th.), open a market (ه for an article); to sell, bring on the market (ه an article); to promote, further (ه, ل s.th.); to make propaganda (ل for), propagate (ل s.th.)

رواج *rawāj* circulation; marketability, salability; sales

اروج *arwaj*[2] more widespread, more common; better selling

ترويج *tarwīj* spreading, propagation, circulation; sale, distribution (of an article of commerce); promotion, furtherance

رائج *rā'ij* circulating, current; universal, widespread, common; salable, marketable, in demand, selling well (merchandise); brisk (business, market)

[2]روج (Fr.) *rūž* rouge

(روح and ريح) راح *rāḥa u* (رواح *rawāḥ*) to go away, leave, go; (with foll. imperf.) to begin, set out to do **II** *rauwaḥa* to fan (air); to refresh, animate, revive (ه the heart, the spirits); — *rayyaḥa* to give (ه s.o.) rest, make (ه s.o.) relax, make (ه s.o.) comfortable, provide rest and recreation (ه for s.o.); to rest (ه e.g., عينيه one's eyes) | روح عن نفسه to find recreation, relax, amuse o.s. **III** to go in the evening (ه to s.o.); to alternate, vary (بين between two things) **IV** اروح *arwaḥa* to stink, smell bad; — اراح *arāḥa* to give (ه s.o.) rest, let (ه s.th.) rest; to deliver, release (ه من s.o. from); to put (ه s.o.) at ease, soothe (ه the heart, or the like); to relieve, free (ه s.o., من of), ease (ه من for s.o. s.th.); to do (ه s.o.) a good turn, gladden (ه ب s.o. with), make (ه s.o.) happy (ب by) | اراح نفسه من (*nafsahū*) to find recreation from, relax from **V** to fan o.s. (بالمروحة *bi-l-mirwaḥa* with the fan) **VI** to fluctuate, alternate, vary (بين between; esp. with two figures following); to intervene, lie (بين between two events) **VIII** to find rest (من from); to rest, relax, find recreation; to be satisfied, be pleased (الى with s.th.), agree, consent (الى to s.th.); to like (ل or الى s.th.), be happy, be glad (ل or الى about s.th.) | ارتاح للمعروف to be happy to be of service, like doing favors **X** استروح *istarwaḥa* to inhale air, breathe; to smell, sniff (ه s.th.); to be refreshed (الى by or with s.th.); — استراح *istarāḥa* to be calm; to become calm; to find rest; to take a rest, have a break; to be refreshed (الى by or with s.th.); to rest, relax (من from); to be delivered, be saved (من from), be relieved (من of); to calm down, relax; to rely (الى on); to be happy, be glad (الى about), be pleased (الى with)

راح *rāḥ* wine

ريح *rīḥ* f. (occasionally m.) pl. رياح *riyāḥ*, ارواح *arwāḥ*, ارياح *aryāḥ* wind; fart; smell, odor | ابو رياح *abū r.* weather vane; scarecrow; سكنت ريحه *sakanat rīḥuhū* to expire, become obsolete, fall into oblivion; هبت ريحه *habbat rīḥuhū* he was in clover, he was in luck's way; ذهب مع الريح to go with the wind, vanish

ريح *rayyiḥ* windy

روح *rūḥ* m. and f., pl. ارواح *arwāḥ* breath of life, soul; spirit (in all senses); gun barrel | روح القدس *r. al-quds (qudus)*, also الروح القدس the Holy Ghost; لا روح فيه (*rūḥa*) spiritless, insipid, inane; خفيف الروح likable, amiable, charming; ثقيل الروح dull, boring, unpleasant (person); طويل الروح long-suffering, patient; حرصا على الارواح (*ḥirṣan*) danger! (on warning signs)

روحى *rūḥī* spirituous; spiritual; pl. *-āt* spiritual things | حالة روحية state (or frame) of mind; مشروبات روحية alcoholic beverages, spirits

روح *rauḥ* refreshment

روحة *rauḥa* pl. *-āt* journey or errand in the evening

راحة *rāḥa* rest, repose; recreation; ease, leisure; vacation; comfort; (pl. *-āt*, راح *rāḥ*) palm of the hand, hand | بالراحة leisurely, gently, slowly, at one's ease; بكل راحة unhurriedly, leisurely; easily, with ease; بيت الراحة *bait ar-r.* water closet, toilet; اسباب الراحة luxury; معدات الراحة *mu'iddāt ar-r.* conveniences; فترة الراحة *fatrat ar-r.* pause, rest, break, recess; راحة الحلقوم *r. al-ḥulqūm* Turkish delight; راحة اليد *r. al-yad* palm of the hand; راحة القدم *r. al-qadam* sole of the foot

ريحة *rīḥa* smell, odor

روحية *rūḥīya* spirituality; mentality, mental attitude, frame of mind

رواح *rawāḥ* departure; going, leaving; return, return trip (as opposed to جيئة); rest, repose | فى غدوه ورواحه (*ġudūwihī*) (lit.: in his coming and going, i.e.) in everything he did

رياح *rayyāḥ* pl. *-āt* (*eg.*) large irrigation canal, main canal (in the Egyptian irrigation system)

اروح *arwaḥ*[2] more calming, more soothing

اريحى *aryaḥī* generous, liberal, open-handed

اريحية *aryaḥīya* generosity, liberality, munificence

ريحان *raiḥān* (coll.) sweet basil (Ocimum basilicum; *bot.*); (pl. رياحين *rayāḥīn*[2]) aromatic plants | قلم الريحان *qalam ar-r.* or القلم الريحانى (*raiḥānī*) a highly decorative style of Arabic calligraphy

روحانى *rūḥānī* spiritual, immaterial; divine, sacred, holy; (pl. *-ūn*) clergyman, minister (*Chr.*)

روحانية *rūḥānīya* spirituality; transfiguration

مراح *marāḥ* place visited in the evening; — *murāḥ*, also *marāḥ* pasture; daytime pasture

مروحة *mirwaḥa* pl. مراوح *marāwiḥ*[2] fan; ventilator; ○ propeller | المروحة الخوص (*kūṣ*) palm-leaf fan; مروحة الخيش *m. al-kaiš* punkah, a canvas-covered frame suspended from the ceiling for fanning a room

○ مرواح *mirwāḥ* fan; ventilator (*mor.*)

مرياح *miryāḥ* causing flatulence (food)

ترويح *tarwīḥ* fanning; ventilation, airing; refreshment; diversion, amusement (also الترويح عن النفس)

ترويحة *tarwīḥa*: ترويحة نفس *t. nafs* walk, stroll

صلاة التراويح *ṣalāt at-tarāwīḥ* prayer performed during the nights of Ramadan

تريح *taryīḥ* (*eg.*) installation; fitting in, insertion

ارتياح *irtiyāḥ* satisfaction, gratification; pleasure; joy, delight

استرواح *istirwāḥ* airing, ventilation; air intake; respiration | استرواح صدرى (*ṣadrī*) pneumothorax (*med.*)

استراحة *istirāḥa* rest, repose, relaxation, recreation; — (pl. -*āt*) intermission, recess, pause, rest, break; public resthouse (for travelers; *Eg.*)

رائح *rā'iḥ*: رائح وغاد (*gādin*) going back and forth, walking up and down

رائحة *rā'iḥa* pl. روائح *rawā'iḥ*[2] odor, smell; fragrance, perfume; pl. روائح perfumes; flavorings (e.g., those used in baking)

مريح *murīḥ* restful, reposeful; calming, soothing; cozy; comfortable; flatulent | كرسى مريح (*kursī*) armchair; club chair, easy chair

مراح *murāḥ* see above under *marāḥ*

مرتاح *murtāḥ* resting, relaxing; relaxed, calm, serene; reassured, satisfied, content; pleased, delighted | مرتاح البال at ease, relaxed, serene, tranquil; مرتاح الضمير of peaceful mind, undisturbed by scruples

مستريح *mustarīḥ* resting, relaxing; relaxed, calm, reassured

مستراح *mustarāḥ* water closet, toilet

[1](رود) راد *rāda* u (*raud*) to walk about, move about, prowl; to look, search (ه for s.th.) III to seek to win (ه على s.o. for s.th.), try to entice or tempt (ه على s.o. to do s.th.); to approach, accost (ه s.o.); to seek to alienate or lure away (ه عن s.o. from); to attempt to seduce (ها a woman) | راوده عن نفسه to seek to tempt s.o. IV to want (ه s.th., ان to do s.th.), wish, have a mind, be willing (ان to do s.th.); to want to have (ه s.th.), desire, covet (ه s.th.), strive (ه for s.th); to be headed, be bound (ه for a place); to intend (ه s.th., ان to do s.th.); to aim (الى or ه من with s.th. at), purpose, have in view (ه من by s.th. s.th.); to drive (الى at s.th., من with s.th.); to be out (الى or ه for), be bent (الى or ه on); to mean (ه s.o., ه s.th., ب by); to have s.o. (ه) in mind with s.th. (ب), aim at s.o. (ه) with s.th. (ب); to have (good or evil) designs (ه) on s.o. (ب), intend or plan to do s.th. (ه) with s.o. (ب); to be on the point (ه or ان of doing s.th.), be about (ه or ان to do s.th.); to urge, induce, prompt (ه على s.o. to do s.th.) | اراد به ان by this he meant that ...; he understood it to mean that ...; اراد به خيرا (*kairan*) to wish s.o. well; اراده على ان to seek to induce s.o. to (do s.th.); اراد العاصمة he was on his way to the capital; اراد نفسه على الشىء (*nafsahū*) he tried to bring himself to do it VIII to repair, betake o.s. (ه to a place); to explore (ه s.th.)

رود *raud* exploration

ريادة *riyāda* exploration

رويدا *ruwaidan* slowly, gently, leisurely | رويدا رويدا gradually, slowly, by and by; رويدك *ruwaidaka* take it easy! slowly!

مرود *mirwad* pl. مراود *marāwid*[2] pencil, little stick (originally for applying kohl to the eyelids)

ارادة *irāda* will, volition; wish; desire; (pl. -*āt*) irade, decree (of a ruler); will power | حسب الارادة (*ḥasaba*) at will

ارادى *irādī* intentional, willful, voluntary

ارتياد *irtiyād* visit (to a place); exploration

رائد *rā'id* pl. رواد *ruwwād* visitor; scout, reconnoiterer; boy scout; explorer; leader; major (*mil.*; *U.A.R.*); precept, guiding principle, rule (of conduct)

مريد *murīd* pl. -*ūn* novice (of a Sufi order); aspirant; adherent, follower, disciple

مراد *murād* wanted, desired, intended; design, purpose, intention

[2]رود see رؤد

رودس *rūdus*[2] Rhodes (chief island of the Dodecanese)

روديسيا *rōdīsiyā* Rhodesia

(روز) راز *rāza u* (*rauz*) to weigh (ه s.th.); to examine (ه s.th.); to consider (ه s.th.)

روزنامة *rūznāma* almanac

[1]□ روس II (from رأس) to point, sharpen (ه s.th.); to taper (ه s.th.); to supply with a heading or title (ه essay, book)

□ ترويسة *tarwīsa* head, heading, title, caption

[2]مرواس *mirwās* race track

مراويس *marāwīs*[2] race horses

[3]الروس *ar-rūs* the Russians

روسى *rūsī* Russian

الروسية *ar-rūsīya* the Russian language

روسيا *rūsiyā* Russia | روسيا البيضاء (*baiḍā'*) Byelorussia

روستو (It. *arrosto*) *rostō*, لحم روستو (*laḥm*) fried meat; roast

روشن *raušan* pl. رواشن *rawāšin*[2] skylight, scuttle

(روض) راض *rāḍa u* (*rauḍ*, رياضة *riyāḍa*) to tame, domesticate (ه an animal); to break in, train (ه an animal); to train, coach (ه s.o.); to pacify, placate (ه s.o.) | راض نفسه to practice (على s.th.), exercise o.s. (على in) II = I; to tame, regulate (ه e.g., a river) III to seek to make tractable, try to bring round (ه s.o.) V to practice, exercise o.s.; — تريض *tarayyaḍa* (denominative of رياضة) to (take a) walk, promenade; to do physical exercise, go in for sports VI to haggle, bargain (with one another, over a price) VIII to practice, exercise o.s.; to train o.s., school o.s. (ب on or by means of); to (take a) walk, promenade X to be or become glad, happy, cheerful

روضة *rauḍa* pl. روض *rauḍ*, *-āt*, رياض *riyaḍ*, ريضان *riḍān* garden; meadow | روضة الاطفال (pl. رياض) kindergarten, nursery school

الرياض *ar-riyāḍ* Riyadh (capital of Saudi Arabia)

رياضة *riyāḍa* pl. *-āt* practice, exercise; physical exercise, gymnastics; sport; walk, promenade; relaxation, rest; spiritual exercise; رياضات religious exercises, devotions (*Chr.*); mathematics | رياضة نفسه *r. nafsihī* walking, promenading; الرياضة البحتة (*baḥta*) pure mathematics; الرياضة التطبيقية (*taṭbīqīya*) applied mathematics; رياضة عقلية (*'aqlīya*) exercise of wits, intellectual games

رياضى *riyāḍī* sportive, sports (adj.); (pl. *-ūn*) sportsman; mathematic(al) | اخبار رياضية sports news; مراسل رياضى (*murāsil*) sports reporter; الالعاب الرياضية sports

رياضيات *riyāḍiyāt* mathematics

ترويض *tarwīḍ* sports

(روع) راع *rā'a u* (*rau'*) to frighten, scare, alarm (ه s.o.); to startle, surprise (ه s.o.); to awaken s.o.'s (ه) admiration, appeal (ه to s.o.), please, delight, thrill (ه s.o.) | ما راعنى الا مجيؤك (*illā majī'uka*) your arrival has been a complete surprise to me II and IV to frighten, scare, alarm, awe (ه s.o.) V and VIII to be frightened, be alarmed (من at, by)

روع *rau'* fright, alarm, dismay, fear; — *rū'* heart, mind, soul | هدئ روعك (*haddi'*) and سكن روعك (*sakkin*) take it easy! relax! الق (ادخل) فى روعه to persuade s.o., make s.o. believe, talk s.o. into believing (ان that), inspire (ه s.th.); خطر بروعه it occurred to him, it came to his mind

روع *rawa'* beauty

روعة *rau'a* fright, alarm, fear; awe; astonishment, surprise; perplexity; charm, beauty, magnificence, splendor

اروع *arwa'*[2] more wonderful, more marvelous; more charming, more delightful; more magnificent; more obvious, clearer

ارتياع *irtiyā'* alarm, dismay, shock

رائع *rā'i'* splendid, admirable, wonderful, marvelous, glorious, magnificent; charming, delightful; awesome, imposing, impressive, thrilling; clear as daylight | فى رائعة النهار *fī r. in-nahār* in broad daylight; فى رائعة شبابه *fī r. šabābihī* in the prime of his years; الحقيقة الرائعة plain truth

رائعة *rā'i'a* pl. روائع *rawā'i'*[2] an imposing thing | روائع الفن *r. al-fann* masterpieces of art

مروّع *murawwi'* terrible, dreadful, frightening

مروّع *murawwa'* frightened, terrified, alarmed

مريع *murī'* dreadful, terrible, horrible

مرتاع *murtā'* frightened, terrified, alarmed

(روغ) راغ *rāġa u* (*rauġ*, روغان *rawaġān*) to turn off, swerve; to dodge, evade (عن, من s.o., s.th.), get out of the way of (من, عن); furtively to turn away; to go away (الى to), depart, leave (الى for) **III** to deal in an underhanded, fraudulent manner (ه with s.o.), double-cross (ه s.o.); to dodge, engage in low trickery, play fast and loose; to fight with unfair means (ه s.o.)

رواغ *rawāġ* dodge, shift, artifice, sly trick

روّاغ *rawwāġ* sly, wily, insidious, crafty

رويغة *ruwaiġa* dodge, shift, artifice, sly trick

اروغ *arwaġ*[2] more cunning, more insidious

روغان *rawaġān* turning off; swerving; dodging, evasion

مراوغة *murāwaġa* sly, underhanded dealings; humbug, trickery; artifice, cunning; pl. *-āt* distortions, prevarications, lies; tricks, wiles

(روق) راق *rāqa u* (روق *rauq*) to be clear, be pure (liquid); to surpass, excel (على s.o., s.th.), prove superior (على to); to please, delight, (ه or ل s.o., also فى عينه *fī 'ainihī* s.o.), give s.o. pleasure, appeal to s.o. (ه, ل, فى عينه) **II** to clarify, purify, filter (ه a liquid) | روق دمه (*damahū*) to refresh s.o. (drink); to pacify, placate s.o., cool s.o. off; روق البضاعة to make a clearance sale **IV** to pour out (ه a liquid); to shed, spill (ه s.th.); to make (ه a liquid) flow | اراق ماء وجهه (*mā'a wajhihī*) to sacrifice one's honor, lose all respect, lose face **V** to have breakfast

راق *rāq* pl. *-āt* layer, stratum

روق *rauq* pl. ارواق *arwāq* portico; horn

روقة *rūqa* beautiful, pretty, handsome (of persons; for both genders, sing. and pl.)

رواق *riwāq*, *ruwāq* pl. اروقة *arwiqa* tent; curtain, screen; flap of the tent for protection against the wind (used by Syrian Bedouins); sun roof of mats over a bazaar (*syr.*); portico; open gallery, colonnade, loggia; porch, veranda (*syr.*); pavilion of an exposition; living quarters, dormitories and workrooms of the students of Al Azhar University in Cairo, divided according to provinces and nationalities | ضرب رواقه to pitch one's tent, take up quarters, settle down

رواقى *riwāqī* stoic(al); (pl. *-ūn*) a stoic; friar; الرواقية *ar-riwāqīya* Stoicism

راووق *rāwūq* filter

ترويق *tarwīq* filtration, clarification, purification

ترويقة *tarwīqa* (*syr.*) breakfast

اراقة *irāqa* pouring out; shedding, spilling | اراقة الدماء bloodshed

رائق *rā'iq* clear, pure

مال الروك *māl ar-rōk* (*eg.*) public property, community property

[1]رول II to slaver, slobber, drool

روال *ruwāl* slaver, slobber

[2]رول (Fr. *rôle*) *rōl* role

[1](روم) رام *rāma* *u* (*raum*, مرام *marām*) to desire, wish, want, covet (ه s.th.), crave (ه for); to wish (ه ل s.o. s.th.); to look (ه for) | على ما يرام (*yurāmu*) as well as one could possibly wish, in excellent order

رام الله *rāmallah* Ramallah (town in W Jordan, N of Jerusalem)

روم *raum* wish, desire

مرام *marām* pl. *-āt* wish, desire, craving, longing; aspiration

[2]الروم *ar-rūm* the Romaeans, the Byzantines; Byzantium; pl. الاروام *al-arwām* (the adherents of) the Greek Orthodox Church | بحر الروم *bahr ar-r.* the Mediterranean

رومى *rūmī* pl. اروام *arwām* Romaean, Byzantine; Greek Orthodox (Church) | ديك رومى (*dīk*) turkey (*eg.*); جبنة رومى (*gibna*) a brand of cheese (*eg.*)

روما *rōmā* and رومة *rōma* Rome

رومية *rūmiya* Rome

الرومان *ar-rūmān* the Romans; the Romanic peoples

رومانى *rūmānī* Roman; Romanian; Romanic

رومانيا *rūmāniyā* Romania

روماتزم (Engl.) *rūmatizm* rheumatism

روند *riwand*, راوند *rāwand* rhubarb

رونق see رنق

[1]روى *rawiya* *a* (رى *rayy*, *riyy*) to drink one's fill, quench one's thirst; to be irrigated; — *rawā* *i* to bring (على or ل s.o.) water, give (ه s.o.) to drink; — *rawā* *i* (رواية *riwāya*) to tell, relate (ل ه s.th. to s.o.), report (ه s.th.), give an account of (ه); to pass on, transmit (عن ه s.th. on the strength of an authoritative source), quote (عن from a source) II to quench s.o.'s (ه) thirst; to water, irrigate (ه s.th.) IV to give (ه s.o.) to drink, quench s.o.'s (ه) thirst; to water (ه flowers, etc.); to moisten, wet (ه s.th.) V to draw, obtain (عن ه s.th. from); to ponder (فى s.th.), reflect (فى on) VIII to quench one's thirst; to be supplied with water for drink, be given to drink; to be watered, be irrigated; to draw (on a source, i.e., to obtain information from it)

رى *riyy* quenching (of thirst); — *riyy*, *rayy* watering, irrigation; moistening, wetting

ريا *rayyan* aroma, fragrance

روى *rawiy* thirst-quenching

روى *rawīy* final letter, rhyming letter (in Arabic verse); rhyme | ذو روى واحد monotonous (song)

رواء *rawā'* fresh (water)

رواء *ruwā'* prettiness, comeliness, pleasing appearance

روية *rawiya* deliberation, reflection, consideration | عن روية deliberately, on purpose, عن غير روية offhand, casually

رواية *riwāya* pl. *-āt* tale, narrative; report, account; story; novel; play, drama; motion picture, film | رواية محزنة (*muḥzina*) tragedy; رواية مسرحية (*masraḥīya*) play, stage play; رواية سينمائية motion picture, film; رواية مضحكة (*muḍḥika*) comedy; رواية غنائية (*ginā'īya*) opera; رواية قصصية (*qiṣaṣīya, qaṣaṣīya*) novel; رواية تمثيلية (*tamṯīlīya*) play, drama; رواية ناطقة sound film; رواية هزلية (*hazlīya*) comedy

روائى *riwā'ī* novelist; dramatist, playwright; author, writer

ريان *rayyān*[2], f. ريا *rayyā*, pl. رواء *riwā'* sated with drink; well-watered, well-irrigated; luxuriant, lush, verdant; full, plump (face); succulent, juicy, fresh, pretty; see also alphabetically

تروية *tarwiya* deliberation, reflection, consideration

إروائى *irwā'ī* irrigational; irrigated

ترو *tarawwin* deliberation, reflection, consideration

راو *rāwin* pl. *rāwiyūn*, رواة *ruwāh* and راوية *rāwiya* pl. روايا *rawāyā* transmitter (esp. of ancient Arabic poetry); relater; narrator, storyteller

مرويات *marwīyāt* tales, stories, reports

راية[2] see راى

رؤياء[3] see رأى

رى[1], ريان, ريا see روى

□ رية[2] *riyya* = رئة *ri'a* (see رأ)

رياء[3] see رأى

ريال *riyāl* pl. *-āt* riyal, a silver coin: in Eg. = 20 *qirš ṣāğ* (piasters); in Ir. = 200 *fals*; ريال ماريا تريزا Maria Theresa dollar

ريان Riyan (town and airport in S Hadhramaut, on Gulf of Aden)

(ريب) راب *rāba i* (*raib*) to disquiet, alarm, fill with suspicion or misgivings (ه s.o., ه about s.th.); to give pause (ه to s.o.), make (ه s.o.) stop and think (ان that), make (ه s.o.) uneasy; to cast a suspicion (ه on s.o.), show (ه s.o.) in a suspicious light; to doubt, question, suspect (ه s.th.) IV to disquiet, alarm, startle, fill with suspicion or misgivings (ه s.o.) V to have doubts or misgivings (ب, فى about), be suspicious (ب or فى of) VIII to be suspicious, smell a rat; to suspect, doubt, question (ب or فى s.o., s.th.), have doubts or misgivings (ب or فى about), waver doubtfully (بين between) X to be in doubt, be skeptical (فى about), be suspicious, have misgivings, entertain doubts

ريب *raib* doubt; suspicion; uncertainty | بلا ريب (*bi-lā*) no doubt, undoubtedly, doubtless; لا ريب فيه (*raiba*) there is no doubt about it; ريب المنون *r. al-manūn* unpredictable turn of fortune, threatening fate; misfortune

ريبة *rība* pl. ريب *riyab* doubt, suspicion, misgiving

ارتياب *irtiyāb* doubt, suspicion, distrust, misgiving

مريب *murīb* arousing suspicion, suspicious

مرتاب *murtāb* doubting, doubtful, skeptical; doubter, skeptic; (به or فيه) مرتاب doubted, questionable, doubtful; suspect, suspicious | مرتاب فى امره (*amrihī*) suspicious, suspect, under suspicion

مستريب *mustarīb* doubtful, in doubt (فى about); suspicious

مستراب (فيه) *mustarāb* (*fīhi*) suspect, suspicious

(ريث) راث *rāṯa i* (*raiṯ*) to hesitate, delay, tarry V to hesitate, tarry, be tardy; to give (ب or فى s.th.) long and thorough consideration; to stop; to stay, linger (فى at a place); to be patient, bide one's time, temporize, wait

ريثما *raiṯamā* (conj.) as long as, while; when; until

ارياح, اريحية, اريغ, ريحان, رياح, ريحة, ريع see روح مرياح

رِيغ (G.) *raik* Reich

□ ريس *rayyis* (= رئيس *ra'īs*) mate (Eg. naval rank) | ريس ممتاز (*mumtāz*) a naval rank (approx.: petty officer 3rd class; *Eg.* 1939)

□ رياسة *riyāsa* (= رئاسة *ri'āsa*) see رأس

رياسى *riyāsī* presidential

(ريش) راش *rāša i* (*raiš*) to provide with feathers, feather (ه s.th.); to feather one's nest, become wealthy II to provide with feathers, feather (ه s.th.); to fledge, grow feathers (bird) V to fledge (bird); to become wealthy

ريش *rīš* (coll.; n. un. ة) pl. رياش *riyāš*, ارياش *aryāš* feathers; feathering, plumage; clothes, attire, exterior; bristles (e.g., of a brush)

ريشة *rīša* (n. un.) pl. *-āt* feather; quill; writing pen (also ريشة الكتابة); brush (of a painter); plectrum; lancet; (*eg.*) reed (of certain wind instruments, e.g., of the oboe; *mus.*) | وزن الريشة *wazn ar-r.* featherweight (*athlet.*)

ريشى *rīšī* feather (adj.), feathery, feathered, plumed, pinnate

رياش *riyāš* household effects; furniture; equipment

روض see رياضيات, رياضى, رياضة, رياض, تريض

(ريع) راع *rā'a i* (*rai'*, ريوع *ruyū'*, رياع *riyā'*, ريعان *raya'ān*) to increase, grow, flourish, thrive II to increase, augment (ه s.th.)

ريع *rai'* pl. ريوع *ruyū'* yield; returns, proceeds, income (accruing from an estate), interest; profit share, royalty; prime, choicest part | ريع الشباب *r. aš-šabāb* the prime of youth

ريعان *rai'ān* prime, choicest part | فى ريعان الشباب *fī r. iš-šabāb* in the prime of youth; فى ريعان النهار *fī r. in-nahār* in broad daylight

ارض مريعة *arḍ marī'a* productive land

□ تاريع *tārī'* (*eg.*) cadastre; (also مساحة التاريع) land survey

رائعة *rā'i'a*: فى رائعة النهار *fī r. in-nahār* in broad daylight (see also روع)

ريف *rīf* pl. ارياف *aryāf* fertile, cultivated land; country (as opposed to city), countryside, rural area; الريف or ريف مصر Lower Egypt; seashore, seacoast; Er Rif (hilly coastal region of NE Morocco)

ريفى *rīfī* rural, rustic, peasant (adj.), country (used attributively); peasant, farmer; provincial, yokel, bumpkin; inhabitant of Er Rif (in Morocco)

(ريق) راق *rāqa i* (ريق *raiq*) to shine, glisten, glow, burn; to flow out, pour forth IV to pour out, shed, spill (see also روق)

ريق *rīq* and ريقة *rīqa* pl. ارياق *aryāq* saliva, spittle | على الريق before breakfast, on an empty stomach; بلع ريقه and ابتلع ريقه (*rīqahū*) (lit.: to swallow one's saliva, i.e.) to catch one's breath, rest a while, take a short break; to hold back, restrain o.s. (of s.o. in a rage); بلعه ريقه (*balla'ahū rīqahū*) to allow s.o. a break, let s.o. catch his breath; اجرى الريق (*ajrā*) to make the saliva flow, i.e., to make the mouth water, stimulate the appetite; لا يجف له ريق (*yajiffu*) he is untiring (in speaking), he talks incessantly

ريق *rayyiq*: فى ريق الشباب *fī r. iš-šabāb* in the full bloom of youth

[1](ريل) رال *rāla i* and II to slobber, slaver, drool

مريلة *maryala* (string) apron

مريول *maryūl* bib

[2]ريال look up alphabetically

[1](ريم) رام *rāma i* (*raim*) to go away, move, budge; to leave (ه a place) | ما رام مكانه

(*makānahū*) not to budge, not to move from the spot **II** to stay, remain (بالمكان at the place); (*eg.*) to bluff (على s.o.)

ريم *rīm* (*eg.*) froth, foam

تريم *taryīm* (*eg.*) swaggering, bluffing, swindle

[2]ريم *rīm* (= رئم) addax, white antelope

[1](رين) ران *rāna i* to take possession (على, ب or ه of s.th.), seize, overcome (على, ب or ه s.o., said of passion); to descend or come upon s.th. (على); to reign, prevail (على in, e.g., silence in a room)

[2]ريان, f. ريا see روى

[3]ريان look up alphabetically

ز

زاء *zā'* name of the letter ز

زاؤوق *zā'ūq* quicksilver, mercury

زئبق *zi'baq* quicksilver, mercury

زاج *zāj* vitriol

زاجورا *zāgōra* Zagora, a brand of Egyptian cotton

زأر *za'ara a i* (*za'r*, زئير *za'īr*) to roar, bellow

زئير *za'īr* roaring, roar, bellowing

زأط *za'aṭa a* (زئاط *zi'āṭ*) to clamor, be vociferous

زاغ *zāğ* pl. زيغان *zīğān* crow

موت زؤام *maut zu'ām* a sudden or violent death

[1]زؤان *zu'ān* darnel (Lolium temulentum; *bot.*)

[2]زان *zān* (*syr.*, *eg.*) beech | ثمر زان *ṯamar z.* beechnuts

زانة *zāna* pl. *-āt* spear; pole | الوثب (القفز) بالزانة *al-waṯb* (*al-qafz*) *bi-z-z.* pole vaulting (*athlet.*)

زاووق *zāwūq* quicksilver, mercury

زاي *zāy* name of the letter ز

زب *zubb* pl. ازباب *azbāb* penis

زبيب *zabīb* (coll.; n. un. ة) dried grapes, raisins; (*eg.*) a strong colorless liquor made of raisins, milky white when diluted with water

ازب *azabb*[2], f. زباء *zabbā'*[2], pl. زب *zubb* hairy, hirsute, shaggy

زبد *zabada u* to churn (ه milk) **II** to foam, froth, cream (milk) **IV** to froth, become foamy, foam (also, with rage)

زبد *zabad* pl. ازباد *azbād* foam, froth; dross | زبد البحر *z. al-baḥr* meerschaum

زبدة *zubda* (fresh) butter (as opposed to سمن *samn*); cream; — (pl. زبد *zubad*) choicest part, prime, cream, flower, elite; extract, quintessence; essence, substance; gist, main point

زبدية *zabdīya* pl. زبادئ *zabādīy* bowl

زباد *zabād* civet | سنور الزباد *sinnūr az-z.* civet cat

زبادى *zabādī* and لبن زبادى (*laban*) curdled milk (*eg.*)

مزبد *mizbad*, مزبدة *mizbada* pl. مزابد *mazābid*[2] churn

زبر *zabara u i* to scold (ه s.o.)

زبر *zubr* penis

زبرة *zubra* pl. زبر *zubar* piece of iron

زبور *zabūr* (Book of) Psalms, Psalter

زبرج *zibrij* ornament, ornamentation, decoration, embellishment

زبرجد *zabarjad* chrysolite (*min.*)

زبط *zabaṭa i* (*zabṭ*) to quack (duck)

زبط *zabaṭ* (*eg.*) mud, mire

زباطة *zubāṭa* (*eg.*) bunch of dates

زوبعة *zauba'a* pl. زوابع *zawābi'*[2] storm, hurricane

زبق *zabaqa u i* (*zabq*) to tear out, pluck out (ه hair) VII to slip in

زبل II to dung, manure

زبل *zibl*, زبلة *zibla* dung, manure

زبال *zabbāl* street sweeper; garbage collector

زبالة *zubāla* refuse, rubbish, garbage, sweepings

مزبلة *mazbala*, *mazbula* pl. مزابل *mazābil*[2] dunghill; garbage can

زبون *zabūn* kicking (camel); hot, fierce, cruel (battle); stupid, foolish; fool; — (pl. زبائن *zabā'in*[2]) customer, client, buyer; guest (of a hotel, and the like) | زبون دائم patron, regular customer

زبون *zubūn* undergarment (*nejd, ir.*)

زبانة *zibāna* clientele, patronage, custom

زبانى *zubānā* pedipalpus or claw of a scorpion, of a crayfish (usually dual: زبانيا العقرب)

زبانية *zabāniya* myrmidons; angels who thrust the damned into Hell

زبية *zubya* pl. زبى *zuban* elevated place above the waterline | بلغ السيل الزبى *balaġa s-sailu z-zubā* the matter reached a climax, things came to a head

زت *zatta* (*syr.*) to throw

زج *zajja* (1st pers. perf. *zajajtu*) *u* (*zajj*) to throw, hurl (ه s.th.); to push, shove, urge, drive (ب or ه, ه s.o. or s.th.); to press, squeeze, force, cram (ب or ه, ه s.o. or s.th., فى into) | زج به فى السجن (*zujja, sijn*) he was thrown into prison II to pencil (الحاجبين *al-ḥājibain* the eyebrows); to glaze, coat with glass (ه s.th.); to enamel (ه s.th.)

زج *zujj* pl. زجاج *zijāj* ferrule; arrowhead; spearhead

ازج *azajj*[2], f. زجاء *zajjā'*[2], pl. زج *zujj* having beautifully arched eyebrows

زجاج *zujāj* glass (as substance)

زجاجة *zujāja* (n. un.) pl. *-āt* piece of glass; (glass) bottle, flask; (drinking) glass, tumbler

زجاجى *zujājī* glass (adj.), glassy, vitreous

زجاج *zajjāj* glazier

مزجج *muzajjaj* glazed, enameled; مزججات and مصنوعات مزججة enameled ware

زجر *zajara u* (*zajr*) to drive back, drive away; to hold back, restrain, prevent (ه عن s.o. from); to rebuke, scold, upbraid (ه s.o.) VII and VIII ازدجر *izdajara* pass. of I

زجر *zajr* forcible prevention; suppression (of customs, abuses, crimes); rebuke, reprimand

زجرى *zajrī* reformatory, penitentiary (adj.) | معهد زجرى (*ma'had*) reformatory, reform school

مزجر *mazjar*: قعد منه مزجر الكلب *qa'ada minhu mazjara l-kalb* to sit at a fitting distance from s.o.

زاجر *zājir* handicap, impediment, obstacle

زاجرة *zājira* pl. زواجر *zawājir*[2] check, curb; restriction, limitation

زجل *zajala u* (*zajl*) to let go, release (ه a carrier pigeon)

زجل *zajal* pl. ازجال *azjāl* popular Arabic poem in strophic form; soft humming sound produced by the jinn at night

زجال *zajjāl* reciter of *azjāl* (see above)

حمام الزاجل *ḥamām az-zājil* carrier pigeon, homing pigeon

زجا (زجو) *zajā u* to drive, urge on (ه, ‌ه s.th., s.o.); to squeeze, press, force, cram (ه, ‌ه s.th., s.o., في into) II to shove, push (ه s.th., ‌ه s.o.); to drive, urge on (ه s.th., ‌ه s.o.); to jostle, crowd, cram, jam (ه, ‌ه s.th., s.o., الى into); to take or bring (forcibly) (ه, ‌ه s.o., s.th. الى into); to make (ه time) pass; to pass, spend (ه time) IV to shove, push (ه s.th., ‌ه s.o.); to drive, urge on (ه s.th., ‌ه s.o.); to jostle, crowd, cram, jam (ه, ‌ه s.th., s.o., الى into); to take or bring (forcibly) (ه, ‌ه s.o., s.th. الى into); to make pass, while away (ه time); to extend (ه ل s.th. to s.o.; greetings, compliments, thanks); to bestow (ه ل s.th. on s.o.; e.g., praise) | ازجى الى الذهن ان (*ḏihn*) to suggest (the idea or assumption) that ...

مزجى *muzjan* little, scanty, paltry, trivial, insignificant

زحر *zaḥara a i* (زحير *zaḥīr*, زحار *zuḥār*) to groan, moan

زحير *zaḥīr* groan, moan(s)

زحار *zuḥār* groan, moan(s); dysentery (*med.*)

زحزح *zaḥzaḥa* (زحزحة *zaḥzaḥa*) to move (ه s.th., from its place); to tear, rip (ه عن s.th. off) II *tazaḥzaḥa* to budge, move (عن away from)

زحف *zaḥafa a* (*zaḥf*) to crawl, creep on the ground; to crawl about; to advance (army); to march, be on the march (على against or toward)

زحف *zaḥf* advance, march (of an army); (pl. زحوف *zuḥūf*) soldiery, army

زحاف *zaḥḥāf* creeping, crawling

زحافة *zaḥḥāfa* pl. *-āt* reptile; implement for leveling the ground, leveler; ski

زاحف *zāḥif* creeping, crawling; pl. زواحف *zawāḥif*[2] reptiles

زحل *zaḥala a* (*zaḥl*, زحول *zuḥūl*) to move away, withdraw, retire (عن from a place) II to remove (ه, ‌ه s.o., s.th.) V = I

زحل *zuḥal*[2] the planet Saturn

زحلق *zaḥlaqa* to roll, slide (ه s.th.) II *tazaḥlaqa* to glide, slide, slip, skid

زحلقة *zaḥlaqa*: ميدان الزحلقة *maidān az-z.* skating rink

تزحلق *tazaḥluq* skating; skiing

زحلاوى *zaḥlāwī* from Zaḥle (Lebanon), made in Zaḥle (e.g., arrack)

زحم *zaḥama a* (*zaḥm*) to push, shove, hustle, jostle, crowd, press, beset (‌ه s.o.) III to push, shove, hustle, jostle, crowd, press, beset (‌ه s.o.); to compete, vie (‌ه with s.o.) VI to press together, crowd together, mill about; to be closely packed (في in); to compete with one another VIII ازدحم *izdaḥama* to be crowded, teem, swarm (ب with); to jostle, crowd together, mill about (e.g., people)

زحمة *zaḥma* crush, jam; crowd, throng

زحام *ziḥām* crush, jam; crowd, throng

مزاحمة *muzāḥama* pl. *-āt* competition; rivalry | لا يقبل المزاحمة (*yaqbalu*) unrivaled, matchless, without competition

تزاحم *tazāḥum* (mutual) competition

ازدحام *izdiḥām* crowd, crush, jam; overcrowdedness

مزاحم *muzāḥim* pl. *-ūn* competitor; rival

مزاحمة *muzāḥima* (female) rival

مزدحم *muzdaḥim* overcrowded, packed, jammed; teeming, swarming, crowded, crammed (ب with); — *muzdaḥam* crowd, crush, jam

زخة zaḵḵa pl. -āt downpour, heavy shower

زخر zaḵara a (zaḵr, زخور zuḵūr) to swell, rise (e.g., river); to be overfull, brimful (ب of); to boast (ب of s.th.), vaunt (ب s.th.) V to swell; to rise; to abound (ب in), be full (ب of)

زاخر zāḵir and زخار zaḵḵār full, brimful, filled to overflowing; abounding in water (seas); excessive, profuse; exuberant (feeling)

زخرف zaḵrafa to adorn, embellish, decorate, ornament (ه s.th.) II tazaḵrafa to adorn o.s.; to be embellished, ornamented

زخرف zuḵruf pl. زخارف zaḵārif² decoration, ornament, embellishment; make-up, getup (e.g., of a book); vain, trifling finery | زخارف لفظية (lafẓīya) flowers of speech, rhetorical flourishes; زخارف الدنيا z. ad-dunyā the vanities of this world

زخرفة zaḵrafa pl. -āt decoration (also stage decoration); ornamentation

زخرفي zuḵrufī ornamental, decorative

مزخرف muzaḵrif interior decorator; -- muzaḵraf embellished, ornamented | الخط الكوفي المزخرف (al-ḵaṭṭ al-kūfī) floriated Kufic writing

زخم zaḵama a (zaḵm) to thrust back (ه s.o.); -- zaḵima a (zaḵam) to stink

زخم zaḵim stinking

ازخم azḵam² stinking

زخة zaḵma plectrum

زخة zaḵama stench

زر zarra u to button, button up (ه s.th.); to screw, contort (عينه ʿainahū one's eye) II to button, button up (ه s.th.)

زر zirr pl. ازرار azrār, زرور zurūr button; push button; knob, pommel; bud (of a plant); tassel (of the tarboosh, etc.)

زرب zariba a to flow (water) II to pen, corral (ه livestock)

زربية zurbīya, zirbīya pl. زرابي zarābīy carpet, rug

زريبة zarība pl. زرائب zarāʾib² zareba, cattle pen, corral, stockade, fold; (cattle) barn; (North Afr.) hut made of branches

زاروب zārūb pl. زواريب zawārīb² a long, narrow lane

مزراب mizrāb pl. مزاريب mazārīb² spout

زربون zarbūl pl. زرابيل zarābīl² and زربون zarbūn pl. زرابين zarābīn² a kind of shoe

زرد zarada u (zard) to choke (ه s.o.), strangle (ه s.o.'s neck); to gulp, swallow, devour (ه s.th.) VIII ازدرد izdarada to swallow (ه s.th.)

زردة zarda sweet dish made of rice and honey

زرد zarad pl. زرود zurūd chain mail, coat of mail | حمار الزرد zebra

زردة zarada chain link

زردية zardīya pliers

مزرد mazrad throat, gullet

زرزر zarzara to chirp

زرزر zurzur and زرزور zurzūr pl. زرازير zarāzir² starling (zool.)

زرزوري zurzūrī gray with white spots (horse)

زرع zaraʿa a (zarʿ) to sow (ه s.th.); to spread, scatter (ه s.th.); to plant, raise, grow (ه plants); to till, cultivate (الارض al-arḍa land); to lay (لغما luǧman a mine) VII pass. of I; VIII ازدرع izdaraʿa to sow

زرع zarʿ sowing; (pl. زروع zurūʿ) seed; young standing crop, green crop; plantation; field(s) | الزرع والضرع (ḍarʿ) agriculture and stock farming

زراعة zirāʿa agriculture; tilling, tillage; cultivation (of land); growing, raising (of crops); farming | زراعة البساتين horticulture

زراعى *zirā'ī* agricultural, agrarian, farm- (in compounds) | ارض زراعية (*arḍ*) arable land; طريق زراعى field path, dirt road

زريعة *zarī'a* that which is sown or planted; crop

زراع *zarrā'* pl. ة, *-ūn* peasant, farmer; planter

مزرع *mazra'* (arable) land

مزرعة *mazra'a* pl. مزارع *mazāri'*[2] field under cultivation; farm; plantation; country estate

مزرعانى *mazra'ānī* farmer

مزارعة *muzāra'a* temporary sharecropping contract (*Isl. Law*)

زارع *zāri'* pl. زراع *zurrā'* seedsman, sower; peasant; farmer; planter

مزروع *mazrū'* cultivated, planted

مزروعة *mazrū'a* pl. *-āt* young standing crop, green crop

مزارع *muzāri'* pl. *-ūn* peasant, farmer; agronomist

زرافة *zarāfa* pl. *-āt* body, group, cluster (of people) | زرافات ووحدانا see واحد

زرافة *zarāfa, zurāfa* pl. زراف *zarāfā, zurāfā,* زرائف *zarā'if*[2] giraffe

[1]زرق *zaraqa u i* (= ذرق) to drop excrement (bird); — *zaraqa u* (*zarq*) to hit, pierce (ه ب s.o. with); to jab, bore (ه, ه into s.o. or s.th.); to throw, hurl (ه s.th.)

زرق *zarq*: زرق الابر *z. al-ibar* injections, injectings

مزراق *mizrāq* pl مزاريق *mazārīq*[2] javelin

[2]زرق *zariqa a* (*zaraq*) and IX to be blue

زرق *zaraq* blue, blueness, blue color; ○ glaucoma (*med.*)

زرقة *zurqa* blue, blueness, blue color; ○ cyanosis

ازرق *azraq*[2], f. زرقاء *zarqā'*[2], pl. زرق *zurq* blue; dark-colored; الزرقاء the blue sky, the blue

ازرقاق *izriqāq* blueness, blue | داء الازرقاق *dā' al-izr.* cyanosis

[3]زورق look up alphabetically

زرقون *zarqūn* a bright red

زركش *zarkaša* to embellish with brocade embroidery; to adorn, embellish, decorate, ornament (ه s.th.)

زركش *zarkaš* brocade, gold and silver embroidery

مزركش *muzarkaš* embellished with brocade embroidery, brocaded; embroidered (ب with silver and gold thread); embroidered; embellished, decorated, ornamented | القلم المزركش (*qalam*) ornamental writing

زرنيخ *zirnīḵ, zarnīḵ* arsenic

زرى *zarā i* (زراية *zirāya*) to rebuke, scold, upbraid (على s.o.), find fault (على ه with s.o. because of s.th.); to revile, disparage (ب or على s.o.), detract (ب or على from) IV to derogate, detract (ب from s.o. or s.th.), belittle, ridicule (ب s.o. or s.th.) V = I; VIII ازدرى *izdarā* to slight (ب or ه, ه s.o., s.th.), make light, think little (ب or ه, ه of), defy (ب or ه e.g., danger) X = VIII

زرى *zarīy* bad, poor, miserable, despicable, contemptible

زراية *zirāya* contempt, disdain; revilement, disparagement

ازراء *izrā'* contempt, disregard

ازدراء *izdirā'* contempt, disdain, scorn

مزرى *muzran* despicable, contemptible

زعبر *za'bara* to deceive, cheat (على s.o.)

زعبوط *za'būṭ* pl. زعابيط *za'ābīṭ*[2] a woolen fabric; woolen garment with a low neckline, worn esp. by the fellahin (*eg.*)

زعتر *za'tar* = سعتر

زعج *za'aja a* and **IV** to disturb (ه s.o.); to trouble, inconvenience, molest, pester, harass (ه s.o.); to disquiet, alarm, make uneasy, upset (ه s.o.); to stir up (ه s.o. من or عن from a place), rouse (ه عن or من s.o. from a state, e.g., from sleep, etc.), drive (ه عن or من s.o. from) **VII** to be stirred up, be roused; to be alarmed (من by or at), feel uneasy (من about s.th.)

زعج *za'aj* uneasiness, unrest

ازعاج *iz'āj* disturbance

انزعاج *inzi'āj* inconvenience, trouble, discomfort; disturbance, confusion

مزعج *muz'ij* annoying, troublesome, irksome, inconvenient, unpleasant; harrying; disquieting; unsettling; pl. مزعجات troubles, discomforts

زعر *za'ir* thin-haired

ازعر *az'ar*², f. زعراء *za'rā'*² thin-haired; tailless

ازعر *az'ar* pl. زعران *zu'rān* (*leb., pal.*) highwayman, brigand; crook, scoundrel

زعارة *za'āra* maliciousness, meanness

زعرور *zu'rūr* pl. زعارير *za'ārīr*² ill-tempered, peevish, testy, irascible; azarole, Neapolitan medlar (Crataegus azarolus; *bot.*)

زعزع *za'za'a* to shake violently, convulse, rock (ه s.th.); to shake, upset (ه e.g., a resolve, a belief, etc.) **II** *taza'za'a* to be convulsed; to work loose, wobble, be loose; to shake, rock, totter | لا يتزعزع unshakable

ريح زعزع *rīḥ za'za'* and ريح زعزعان (*za'za'ān*) violent gale, hurricane

زعزعة *za'za'a* pl. زعازع *za'āzi'*² convulsion, shock, concussion

زعزعان *za'za'ān* see ريح زعزع

زعزوع *za'zū'* lean, skinny, lanky, spindling

مزعزع *muza'za'* convulsed, shocked; upset, disorganized; tottering, shaky, wobbly, unsteady, precarious

متزعزع *mutaza'zi'* unsteady, shaky, wobbly, precarious; tottering, rocking; fickle, uncertain, changeable

زعط *za'aṭa* (*za'ṭ*) to drive away

زعف *za'afa a* (*za'f*) to kill instantly (ه s.o.) **IV** do.

سم زعاف *samm zu'āf* a rapidly killing, deadly poison

زعفران *za'farān* saffron

زعق *za'aqa a* (*za'q*) to cry, yell, shriek, scream

زعق *za'q* clamor, shouting, crying, screaming, yelling

زعقة *za'qa* pl. *za'aqāt* cry, outcry, yell, scream, shriek

زعيق *za'īq* clamor, shouting, crying, screaming, yelling

زعل *za'ila a* (*za'al*) to be bored, be fed up (من with s.th.), be tired (من of); to be annoyed, angry **II** to annoy, vex (ه s.o.) **IV** to trouble, annoy (ه s.o.)

زعل *za'al* displeasure, annoyance, irritation, vexation

زعل *za'il* annoyed, angry, vexed, put out

زعلان *za'lān*² annoyed, angry, vexed, put out

زاعولة *zā'ūla* annoyance, anger, irritation, vexation

زعم *za'ama u* (*za'm*) to maintain, allege, claim, pretend (ان that), declare (ل ان to s.o. that); to believe; to take (ه ه s.o. for or to be ...), regard (ه ه s.o. as); | زعم لنفسه to claim for o.s. (ه s.th.) **V** to set o.s. up as leader; to be the leader (ه of), lead, command (ه a body of soldiers, or the like); to pretend to be the leader, pose as leader, be bossy

زعم *za'm* allegation, claim | فى زعمهم as they claim, as they say

زعيم *za'īm* pl. زعماء *zu'amā'*[2] leader; ringleader; colonel (*Ir.* 1922); brigadier general (*mil.*; formerly *Syr.*); guarantor (ب of)

زعامة *za'āma* leadership; leading position in politics

مزاعم *mazā'im*[2] allegations; claims, pretensions; assumptions, conjectures

مزعوم *maz'ūm* pretended, claimed; alleged, so-called

زعنفة *zi'nifa* pl. زعانف *za'ānif*[2] horde, pack, mob, rabble, riffraff; low base, mean; pl. fins (of fish); flippers (of whale, seal, and the like)

زغب *zağab* down, fluff, fuzz

زغب *zağib* downy, fluffy, fuzzy, covered with fuzz

ازغب *azğab*[2] downy, fluffy, fuzzy, covered with fuzz

زغبر *zağbar* nap (of a fabric) | اخذه بزغبره he took all of it

زغد *zağada a* to nudge, poke (ه s.o.)

زغر *zağara a* (*eg.*) to eye (الى or ل s.th., s.o.), leer (الى or ل at)

زغرد *zağrada* (زغردة *zağrada*) to utter shrill, long-drawn and trilling sounds (as a manifestation of joy by Arab women)

زغاريد *zağārīd*[2] shrill, trilling cries of joy (of women)

زغرط *zağraṭa* = زغرد

زغاريط *zağārīṭ*[2] = زغاريد

زغزغ *zağzağa* to hide, conceal (ه s.th.); (*eg.*) to tickle (ه s.o.)

زغطة *zuğuṭṭa* (*eg.*) hiccup

زغل *zağala a* (*zağl*) to pour out (ه s.th.); to counterfeit (ه e.g., coins), adulterate, debase (ه s.th.)

زغل *zağal* counterfeit money

مزغل *mazğal* pl. مزاغل *mazāğil*[2] loophole, embrasure

زغلل *zağlala* to dazzle (النظر *an-naẓar* the eyes)

زغلول *zuğlūl* pl. زغاليل *zağālīl*[2] baby, infant; *zağlūl* (*eg.*) squab, young pigeon

زف *zaffa* (1st pers. perf. *zafaftu*) *i* (*zaff*, زفوف *zufūf*) to hurry; — *u* (*zaff*, زفاف *zifāf*) to conduct in solemn procession (ها the bride, على or ل or الى to the bridegroom); pass. زفت الى *zuffat ilā* to be married off to, be given in marriage to; to conduct in solemn procession to her new home (ها the bride, also said of the bridegroom); to inform (الى s.o., ه of s.th.), tell (الى ه s.th. to s.o.) | زف البشرى الى (*bušrā*) to bring glad tidings to

زفة *zaffa* procession (of people), wedding procession; — one time; زفة *zaffatan* once (= *marratan*)

زفاف *zifāf* wedding, wedding ceremony | ليلة الزفاف *lailat az-z.* wedding night

زفوف *zafūf* ostrich; fleet, swift (camel)

زفيف *zafīf* sough(ing) (of the wind)

مزفة *mizaffa* bridal sedan

زفت II to smear with pitch, to pitch; to asphalt (ه a road)

زفت *zift* pitch; asphalt | زفت وقطران (*qaṭrān*) (lit.: pitch and tar) unpleasant, annoying, awkward; damned (bad luck)!

○ مزفتة *mizfata* pl. مزافت *mazāfit*[2] asphalting machine

تزفيت *tazfīt* asphalting

[1]زفر *zafara i* (*zafr*, زفير *zafīr*) to sigh deeply, heave deep sighs; to pant, groan, moan;

to blow off, exhaust, puff out (ه air, breath)

زفرة *zafra* pl. *zafarāt* sigh, moan

زفير *zafīr* exhaling, exhalation, expiration; sighing, moaning, moans; see also alphabetically

²زفر II to soil with grease, begrime (ه s.th.)

زفر *zafar* grease, greasy food | ثلاثاء الزفر *ṯalāṯā' az-z.* Mardi Gras, Shrove Tuesday (*Chr.*)

زفر *zafir* greasy; grimy; unclean, dirty, filthy; stinking, rancid, rank

زفزفة *zafzafa* soughing, whistling (of the wind)

زفن *zafana i* to dance, gambol

زفير *zifīr* zephyr cloth

زق *zaqqa u* (*zaqq*) to feed (ه its young ones, of a bird)

زق *ziqq* pl. ازقاق *azqāq*, زقاق *ziqāq*, زقان *zuqqān* skin (as a receptacle)

زقاق *zuqāq* m. and f., pl. ازقة *aziqqa* lane, alley; strait, corridor (*geogr.*)

زقزق *zaqzaqa* (زقزقة *zaqzaqa*) to peep, chirp, cheep; to feed (ه its young ones; of a bird); to dandle, rock in one's arms (ه a child)

زقزاق *zaqzāq* pewit, lapwing

الزقازيق *az-zaqāzīq*² Zagazig (city in N Egypt)

¹زقلة *zuqla* and زقلية *zuqlīya* (*eg.*) club, cudgel, truncheon

²زقيلة *zaqīla* pl. زقائل *zaqā'il*² narrow road, path, trail

زقم *zaqama u* (*zaqm*) to swallow, gulp, gobble (ه food) IV to make (ه s.o.) swallow or gulp down (ه s.th.) VIII ازدقم *izdaqama* = I

زقوم *zaqqūm* zaqqum, an infernal tree with exceedingly bitter fruit, mentioned in the Koran

زقا (زقو) *zaqā u* to cry, crow, peep, cheep

زقاء *zuqā'* crowing (of a rooster)

زكب *zakaba u* (زكوب *zukūb*) to fill up, fill (ه s.th.)

زكيبة *zakība* pl. زكائب *zakā'ib*² (*eg.*) sack, bag, gunny sack

زكرة *zukra* pl. زكر *zukar* small (wine)skin; — a wind instrument resembling the oboe (*tun.*)

زكم pass. *zukima* to catch a cold

زكام *zukām* (common) cold, catarrh

زكمة *zakma* (common) cold, catarrh

زكانة *zakāna* flair; intuition

(زكو and زكى) زكا *zakā u* (زكاء *zakā'*) to thrive; to grow, increase; to be pure in heart, be just, righteous, good; to be fit, suitable (ب for s.o.), befit (ب s.o.); — *zakiya a* to grow, increase II to increase, augment, make grow (ه s.th.); to purify, chasten (ه s.th.); to justify, vindicate (ه s.o.), vouch for, or bear witness to, s.o.'s (ه) integrity, declare (ه s.o.) honest, upright or just, attest the honorable record of s.o. (ه); to attest to the truth, validity or credibility of s.th. (ه); to commend, praise (ه s.o.); to recommend IV to cause to grow; to grow (ه s.th.) V to be purified, be chastened

زكى *zakīy* pl. ازكياء *azkiyā'*² pure; chaste; guiltless, blameless, sinless; (also =ذكى *ḏakīy*, e.g., رائحة زكية)

زكاء *zakā'* growth; (moral) purity, integrity, honesty, righteousness

زكاة (زكوة) *zakāh* pl. زكا *zakan*, زكوات *zakawāt* purity; justness, integrity, honesty; justification, vindication; almsgiving, alms, charity; alms tax (*Isl. Law*) | زكاة الفطر *z. al-fiṭr* obligatory donation of foodstuffs required at the end of Ramadan, the month of fasting

ازكى *azkā* purer; more befitting, more appropriate; better

تزكية *tazkiya* purification, chastening; pronouncement of s.o.'s integrity or credibility; attestation of (a witness') honorable record (*Isl. Law*)

زل **zalla** (1st pers. perf. *zalaltu*) *i* (*zall*) and *zalla* (1st pers. perf. *zaliltu*) *a* (زلل *zalal*) to slip; to make a mistake, commit an error, a slip; to slide off s.o. (عن), fail to affect s.o. (عن; said of evil) **IV** to cause (ه s.o.) to slip; to make (ه s.o.) stumble or trip

زل *zall* a kind of reed (*syr.*)

زلة *zalla* slip, lapse | زلة لسان *z. lisān* slip of the tongue

زلل *zalal* slip, slipping; lapse; mistake, error, oversight

زلال *zulāl* cold water | زلال البيض *z. al-baiḍ* white of egg, albumen

زلالى *zulālī* albuminous; زلاليات *zulālīyāt* proteins | مواد زلالية (*mawādd*²) proteins

زلابية **zalābiya** pl. *-āt* a kind of doughnut cooked in oil and sprinkled with sugar

¹زلج **zalaja** *a* (زلوج *zulūj*) and *zalija a* to slip; to slide along, glide along **V** do. | تزلج على الثلج (*ṯalj*) to skate **VII** = **V**

زلج *zalj* slippery

زليج *zalīj* slippery

مزلج *mizlaj* pl. مزالج *mazālij*² skate

مزلاج *mizlāj* pl. مزاليج *mazālīj*², (sliding) bolt (on a door)

²زليج **zulaij** faïence, ornamental tile

زليجى *zulaijī* faïence, ornamental tile

زلزل **zalzala** to shake, rock, convulse, cause to tremble (ه, ه s.th., s.o.); pass. *zulzila* also: to waver, stumble **II** *tazalzala* to quake (earth)

زلزلة *zalzala* pl. زلازل *zalāzil*² earthquake

زلزال *zalzāl*, *zilzāl* concussion, shock, convulsion; earthquake

زلط **zalaṭa** *u* to swallow, gulp down, gobble (ه s.th.) **II** to strip, undress (ه s.o.) **V** to undress, strip

زلط *zulṭ* nakedness, nudity

زلط *zalaṭ* (coll.; n. un. ة) (*eg.*) gravel, pebbles; road metal, ballast

زلعة **zal'a** pl. زلع *zila'* (*eg.*) a kind of tall clay jar

زلعوم **zal'ūm** pl. زلاعيم *zalā'īm*² gullet, throat

زلف **zalafa** *u* (*zalf*, *zalaf*, زليف *zalīf*) to approach (الى s.o. or s.th.), advance (الى toward), go near **II** to exaggerate, blow up (ه a report, فى in) **IV** to bring near, bring close (ه, ه s.o., s.th.) **V** to flatter (الى s.o.), fawn (الى upon s.o.), curry favor, ingratiate o.s. (الى with s.o., also ل) **VIII** ازدلف *izdalafa* to flatter

زلف *zalaf* servile flattery, sycophancy, toadyism, bootlicking

زلفة *zulfa* and زلفى *zulfā* servile flattery, sycophancy, toadyism, bootlicking

متزلف *mutazallif* sycophant, toady, bootlicker

زلق **zaliqa** *a* (*zalaq*) and *zalaqa* *u* (*zalq*) to glide, slide; to slip **II** to make slippery (ه s.th.): to slip, glide (ه فى s.th. into) **IV** to cause (ه s.o.) to slip | ازلقه ببصره (*bi-baṣarihī*) to look at s.o. sternly or disapprovingly **V** and **VII** to glide, slide; to skid, slither, slide (فى into s.th.); to slip; to ski; to skate | تزلق على الثلج (*ṯalj*) to ski; to skate VII to slip from s.o.'s (عن) hand, from s.th. (عن)

زلق *zaliq* slippery

زلقة *zalqa* (n. vic.) slip, skid, sideslip

زلاقة *zalāqa* slipperiness

زلاقة *zallāqa* pl. -*āt* sleigh, sledge, sled; toboggan; toboggan chute, sledding course; gutter, eaves trough

مزلق *mazlaq* pl. مزالق *mazāliq*² slippery spot; slide, chute; esp. pl. treacherous, perilous ground, pitfalls, dangers, perils

مزلقان *mazlaqān* (dual) (loading) ramp; gradient, ramp, driveway, access road

مزلق *mizlaq* skate; مزلقان a pair of skates | ◯ مزلق ذو عجلات (*'ajalāt*) roller skate

مزلقة *mizlaqa* pl. مزالق *mazāliq*² sleigh, sledge, sled; toboggan

انزلاق *inzilāq* slipping, sliding, skidding; skiing; skating

منزلق *munzaliq*: باب منزلق sliding door

¹زلم *zalam* pl. ازلام *azlām* arrow without head and feathers, used in divination

²زلومة *zullūma, zallūma* pl. زلاليم *zalālīm*² trunk (of an elephant)

زم *zamma u* (*zamm*) to tie up, fasten, tighten (ه s.th.); to truss up (ه s.th.) | زم بأنفه (*bi-anfihī*) to turn up one's nose, be supercilious II to bridle (ه a camel), put the bridle (ه on a camel)

زمام *zimām* pl. ازمة *azimma* camel halter, nose rope of the camel; rein, bridle; halter; day book; register; ground, land | بزمامه under his supervision, under his direction; زمام الامر *z. al-amr* reins of power; قبض على ازمة الامر to hold the reins of power in one's hand, be in control of power, wield power; تولى زمام الحكم *tawallā z. al-ḥukm* to seize the reins of power, assume power

زمت V to be prim, sedate, staid

تزمت *tazammut* primness; gravity, sedateness

متزمت *mutazammit* grave, stern, staid, sedate (character); prim; narrow-minded

زمجر *zamjara* (زمجرة *zamjara*) to scold; to storm, rage, rave

¹زمر *zamara i u* (*zamr*, زمير *zamīr*) to blow, play (a wind instrument) II do.

زمر *zamr* blowing, playing (of a wind instrument)

زمر *zamr* pl. زمور *zumūr* a wind instrument resembling the oboe; horn (of an automobile; *syr.*)

زمرة *zumra* pl. زمر *zumar* troop; group (of people); زمرة دموية blood group

زمار *zammār* player (on a wind instrument), piper

زمارة *zammāra, zummāra* pl. زمامير *zamāmīr*² (*eg.*) a wood-wind instrument consisting of two pipes, related to the clarinet; siren | زمارة الانذار *z. al-inḏār* warning siren

مزمار *mizmār* single-pipe wood-wind instrument resembling the oboe

مزمور *mazmūr* pl. مزامير *mazāmīr*² psalm

²ازمير *izmīr*² Izmir, Smyrna (seaport in W Turkey)

زمرد *zumurrud* emerald

زمردي *zumurrudī* emerald(-colored)

زمزم *zamzama* to rumble, roll (thunder); to murmur

زمزم *zamzam* copious, abundant (esp. water); Zemzem, name of a well in Mecca

زمزمية *zamzamīya* water flask, canteen; ◯ thermos bottle

زمزمة *zamzama* pl. زمازم *zamāzim*² roll of thunder; roar of a lion

زمط *zamaṭa* to escape, slip away

زمع II and IV to determine (على, ه on), decide, resolve, be determined (على, ه to do s.th.)

مزمع *muzmi'* determined, resolved; — *muzma'* and مزمع عليه decided; imminent; forthcoming, prospective | المؤتمر المزمع عقده ... في *al-mu'tamar al-m. 'aqduhū fī* the conference which is to be held on (with following date)

[1]زمل III to keep (ه s.o.) company, be s.o.'s (ه) companion, be a colleague or associate (ه في of s.o. in s.th.); to accompany (ه s.o.) VI to be comrades, be close companions

زملة *zumla* party, company (of people)

زميل *zamīl* pl. زملاء *zumalā'*[2] companion, crony, associate, comrade; colleague; accomplice

زميلة *zamīla* pl. *-āt* (woman) companion; (woman) colleague; sister ship

زمالة *zamāla* comradeship; colleagueship; fellowship | زمالة دراسية (*dirāsīya*) scholarship, stipend (*ir.*)

[2]ازميل *izmīl* pl. ازاميل *azāmīl*[2] chisel

زمن *zamina a* (زمانة *zamāna*) to be chronically ill IV to stay long, remain (ب at a place); to last long; to be chronic (disease)

زمن *zaman* pl. ازمان *azmān* time; period, stretch of time; duration; زمنا *zamanan* for some time

زمنة *zamana* period of time

زمن *zamin*, زمين *zamīn* pl. زمنى *zamnā* chronically ill

زمان *zamān* pl. ازمنة *azmina* time; duration; fortune, fate, destiny | من زمان for some time (past), for quite a while; على الزمان always, ever; اهل زمانه *ahl z.* his contemporaries

زمنى *zamanī* temporal, time (adj.); worldly, earthly; passing, transient, transitory; secular | الغام زمنية mines with time fuse; قنبلة زمنية (*qunbula*) time bomb

زمانى *zamānī* temporal, time; worldly, earthly; passing, transient, transitory; secular

زمنية *zamanīya* and زمانية *zamānīya* period of time, given time

زمانة *zamāna* chronic illness

مزمن *muzmin* lasting, enduring, long-lived; old, deep-seated, inveterate; chronic

زمهر *zamhara* to become red, flushed, bloodshot IV ازمهر *izmaharra* do.

زمهرير *zamharīr* bitter cold, severe frost

زن *zanna u* (*zann*) to buzz, drone (insect)

زن *zann* buzz(ing), drone

زنأ *zana'a* to be limited, be restricted, be confined, be curbed, be suppressed II to restrict, keep within bounds, beset, harry, drive in a corner (على s.o.)

زنبر II *tazanbara* to display proud, haughty manners (على toward s.o.)

زنبور *zunbūr* pl. زنابير *zanābīr*[2] hornet

زنبرك *zanbarak, zunburuk, zunburak* pl. زنابك *zanābik* (metal) spring; spiral spring; cock (of a rifle, etc.)

زنبق *zanbaq* (coll.; n. un. ة) pl. زنابق *zanābiq*[2] lily; iris (*bot.*)

□زنبلك *zanbalik* = زنبرك

زنبيل *zanbīl, zinbīl* pl. زنابيل *zanābīl*[2] basket made of palm leaves

زنتارى *zintārī* dysentery

زنج *zanj, zinj* (coll.) pl. زنوج *zunūj* Negro(es)

زنجى *zanjī, zinjī* Negro (adj. and n.)

زنجبار *zanjabār*[2] Zanzibar (island and seaport off E African coast)

زنجبيل *zanjabīl* ginger

[1]زنجر *zanjara* to flip, snap (with the fingers)

[2]زنجار *zinjār* verdigris

زنجفر *zunjufr, zinjafr* cinnabar

زنجير *zinjīr* pl. زناجير *zanājīr*[2] chain | حساب الزنجير double-entry bookkeeping

زنخ *zanika a* (*zanak*) to turn rancid

زنخ *zanik* rancid, rank

زند *zand* m. and f., pl. زناد *zinād*, زنود *zunūd* stick of a fire drill, a primitive device for kindling fire; by extension, the whole fire drill; — *zand, zind* (pl. زنود *zunūd*) ulna (*anat.*); forearm

زناد *zinād* pl. ازندة *aznida* fire steel; cock, hammer (of a rifle, etc.) | حجر الزناد *ḥajar az-zinād* flint

زندق II *tazandaqa* to be a freethinker, an atheist

زندقة *zandaqa* atheism

زنديق *zindīq* pl. زنادقة *zanādiqa* zendik, unbeliever, freethinker, atheist

زر II: زر اليه بعينه (*bi-ʿainihī*) to glare at s.o.

زنار *zunnār* and زنارة *zunnāra* pl. زنانير *zanānīr*[2] belt, girdle; sash; band or rope worn around the waist; cross stripe, traverse band

زنزانة *zinzāna* pl. *-āt* prison cell (*eg.*)

زنزلخت *zanzalakt* China tree (Melia azedarach; *bot.*)

زنطارية *zinṭārīya* dysentery

زنق *zanaqa i* (*zanq*) to tighten, constrict (ه s.th.); to hobble (ه an animal) II to keep on short rations, scrimp (على s.o.), be stingy, tight-fisted (على toward)

زنقة *zanaqa* (*magr. zanqa*) pl. زنق *zinaq* narrow street, lane, alley, dead-end street

زناق *zināq* neckband, collar

زنك *zink* zinc

زنمردة *zanmarda* virago, termagant

زنيم *zanīm* low, despised, ignoble, mean; bastard; stranger, outsider

زنى *zanā i* (زنى, زنا *zinan*, زناء *zinā'*) to commit adultery, fornicate, whore

زنى *zinan* adultery; fornication

زناء *zinā'* adultery; fornication

زان *zānin* pl. زناة *zunāh* fornicator, adulterer

زانية *zāniya* pl. زوان *zawānin* whore, harlot; adulteress

زهد *zahada a, zahida a* and *zahuda u* (*zuhd*) to abstain (فى from, also عن, ه), renounce, abandon, forsake (فى s.th., also عن, ه), withdraw (فى, ه from), refuse to have anything to do with (ه, فى) | زهد فى الدنيا (*dunyā*) to renounce pleasure in worldly things, become an ascetic, lead a pious, ascetic life II to induce (ه s.o.) to withdraw or abstain (فى from); to spoil s.o.'s (ه) pleasure in (فى), arouse a dislike (فى ه in s.o. for) V to practice asceticism, withdraw from the world X to deem little, insignificant, trifling, small

زهد *zuhd* (voluntary) renunciation (فى of s.th.); indifference (فى to, esp. to worldly things); abstemiousness, abstinence; asceticism | الزهد فى الدنيا (*dunyā*) asceticism

زهيد *zahīd* little, low, moderate (esp. price), insignificant, paltry, trifling, small; a little, a small amount (من of)

زهادة *zahāda* smallness, lowness, moderateness

تزهد *tazahhud* asceticism, life of retirement devoted to the service of God

زاهد *zāhid* pl. زهاد *zuhhād* abstemious, abstinent, continent, self-denying; ascetic

زهر *zahara a* (زهور *zuhūr*) to shine, give light, be radiant **IV** to glow, gleam, glare, shine; to blossom, be in bloom (plant, flower) **VIII** ازدهر *izdahara* to shine brightly, be radiant; to blossom, be in bloom; to flourish, prosper, thrive

زهر *zahr* (coll.; n. un. ة) pl. زهور *zuhūr*, ازهر *azhur*, ازهار *azhār*, ازاهر *azāhir*², ازاهير *azāhīr*² flowers; blossoms; — cast iron (also زهر الحديد) | زهر الثالوث *z. at-tālūt* pansy; زهرالربيع primrose; زهر العسل *z. al-'asal* honeysuckle; زهر اللؤلؤ *z. al-lu'lu'* daisy; ماء الزهر orange-flower water

زهرة *zahra* (n. un.) pl. *-āt* flower, blossom; splendor, beauty

زهرة *zuhra* brilliancy, light, brightness; beauty | زهرة الغسيل bluing

الزهره *az-zuhara* the planet Venus

زهرى *zuharī* syphilis | امراض زهرية venereal diseases

زهرية *zuhrīya* pl. *-āt* flower vase

زهار *zahhār* florist

زهراوى *zahrāwī* gay, merry, cheerful (person)

ازهر *azhar*² shining, luminous, radiant, brilliant; bright; — (elative) more radiant | الازهران sun and moon; جامع الازهر and الجامع الازهر Al Azhar Mosque and University in Cairo

ازهرى *azharī* of or pertaining to Al Azhar; (pl. *-ūn*) Azhar student

مزهر *mizhar* pl. مزاهر *mazāhir*² ancient Arabic variety of the lute; (now pronounced *mazhar*) a kind of tambourine (*eg.*)

مزهرية *mazharīya* flowerpot

تزهير *tazhīr* bloom, florescence

ازهار *izhār* florescence

ازدهار *izdihār* flourishing, florescence, bloom, heyday

زاهر *zāhir* shining, luminous, radiant, brilliant; bright

مزهر *muzhir* blooming, in bloom; shining, luminous, bright

زهف *zahafa a* (زهوف *zuhūf*): زهف الى الموت to be on the verge of death **VIII** ازدهف الى الموت do.

زهق *zahaqa a* (*zahq*, زهوق *zuhūq*) to die, pass away, run out, come to nothing; زهقت نفسه (*nafsuhū*) and زهقت روحه (*rūhuhū*) to give up the ghost, die; to weary, become tired (من of s.th.), be disgusted (من with s.th.) **IV** to bring about the ruin or downfall of s.th. (ه); to destroy, annihilate (ه s.th.); ازهق النفس (الروح) to be disgusting, be revolting

زهوق *zahūq* dying, passing, bound to vanish

زهم *zuhm* offensive smell

زهم *zahim* malodorous, fetid

زهمة *zuhma* offensive smell

زهومة *zuhūma* offensive smell

زها (زهو) *zahā u* (*zahw*) to blossom, flower, be in bloom; to grow, thrive; to shine brightly, be radiant, glow, gleam; to give o.s. airs, be haughty, conceited; to pride o.s. (ب upon, both in a favorable and a pejorative sense); pass. زهى *zuhiya* to be proud, conceited (ب of), pride o.s. (ب on), boast (ب of), vaunt (ب s.th.) **IV** to blossom, flower, be in bloom; to grow, thrive; to give o.s. airs, be conceited, be boastful **VIII** ازدهى *izdahā* and pass. *uzduhiya* to be self-satisfied, complacent, conceited, proud; *izdahā* to shine (ب at, in s.th.), have (ب an accomplishment) to show; to boast (ب of s.th.), vaunt (ب s.th.)

زهو *zahw* and *zuhūw* bloom, florescence; splendor; beauty; pride; haughtiness, arrogance; vanity, a vain or futile thing or things; fun, play, amusement

زهى *zahīy* brilliant, splendid, magnificent, gorgeous, sumptuous

زهاء *zahā'* radiance, brilliancy, splendor

زهاء *zuhā'* number, amount; *zuhā'a* roughly, about, some (with foll. figure)

ازهى *azhā* more flourishing; prouder, more conceited

ازدهاء *izdihā'* bloom, florescence, flourishing; heyday; shining; glittering, splendor, radiance; pride (both in a favorable and a pejorative sense)

زاه *zāhin* shining, brilliant, radiant, resplendent; glowing; splendid, gorgeous, magnificent, gaudy, beautiful

مزهو *mazhūw* proud (ب of); haughty, supercilious, vainglorious; cocky, overbearing

زويعة see زبع

¹زوج **II** to pair, couple (من or ب ه s.th. with), join in pairs or couples (ه s.th.); to double, geminate (ه s.th.); to employ parallelism (*rhet.*); to marry off, give in marriage (ه, ب, ها من a girl to s.o.) **III** to form a pair or couple; to use in parallel construction, join in a pair (بين two words, *rhet.*); to marry, join in wedlock, unite in matrimony (بين — و s.o. with) **V** to get married (ه, على, ب, من with), marry (ه, على, ب, من s.o.) **VI** to intermarry; to pair, come together forming a pair, be in pairs, be double **VIII** ازدوج *izdawaja* to pair, be in pairs, be double, appear twice

زوج *zauj* pl. ازواج *azwāj* one of a pair; husband; wife; mate, partner; couple, pair (also, e.g., of shoes); dual زوجان couple

زوجة *zauja* pl. *-āt* wife

زيجة *zīja* marriage, wedding

زوجي *zaujī* in pairs, paired; double; marital, matrimonial, conjugal; doubles (tennis)

زيجي *zījī* marital, matrimonial, conjugal, connubial

زوجية *zaujīya* pl. *-āt* matrimony, marriage

زواج *zawāj* marriage (من with); wedding; matrimony, wedlock | وحدة الزواج *waḥdat az-z.* monogamy

مزواج *mizwāj* frequently marrying

تزويج *tazwīj* marrying off (of a woman, من to)

زواج *ziwāj* doubling, duplication; parallelism (*rhet.*)

مزاوجة *muzāwaja* pairing, coupling, close union (of two things)

تزوج *tazawwuj* marriage

تزاوج *tazāwuj* intermarriage

ازدواج *izdiwāj* pairedness, doubleness; ○ coupling (*el.*) | ازدواج ضريبي (*ḍarībī*) double taxation

متزوج *mutazawwij* married

مزدوج *muzdawij* double, twofold, two- (e.g., of a railroad: two-track)

²زاج look up alphabetically

زاح (زوح) *zāḥa u* = زاح (زيح) *zāḥa i*

زود **II** to supply with provisions (ه s.o.), provision (ه ه s.o. with); to provide, supply, equip (ب ه, ه s.o., s.th. with); to endow (ب ه s.o. with); to enrich (ب ه s.th. with) **IV** to supply with provisions (ه s.o.) **V** to be supplied (with provisions); to take along provisions (on a journey); to learn (من from s.o.); to provide o.s., supply o.s., equip o.s. (ب with)

زاد *zād* pl. ازواد *azwād*, ازودة *azwida* provisions, supplies, stores

زواد *zawād* provisions

زوادة *zuwwāda* provisions

مزود *mizwad* pl. مزاود *mazāwid*², مزائد *mazā'id*² provision bag, haversack

مزادة *mazāda* provision bag, haversack

تزويد *tazwīd* supply, purveyance (ب of), provision, equipment (ب with); manning (of ships)

زائدة pl. زوائد see زيد

مزود *muzawwid* pl. *-ūn* contractor, supplier, furnisher, purveyor, victualer, caterer

مزود *muzawwad* provided, supplied, furnished (ب with); equipped (ب with); armed (ب with guns); connected (ب with), attended, accompanied (ب by)

(زور) زار *zāra u* (*zaur*, زيارة *ziyāra*) to visit (ه s.o.), call (ه on s.o.), pay a visit (ه to); to afflict (ه s.o.) II to forge, falsify, counterfeit (ه s.th.); to fake, simulate VI to exchange visits IX to turn aside, turn away, dissociate o.s. (عن from); to be averse (عن to s.th.); ازور به to turn s.o. away, alienate s.o. (عن from) X to desire s.o.'s (ه) visit

زور *zaur* upper part of the chest; throat | آلام الزور sore throat

زور *zūr* lie, untruth; falsehood | شهادة الزور *šahādat az-z.* false testimony

زور *zūr* force | بالزور by force, forcibly

زور *zawar* inclination, obliqueness, slant; crookedness; falseness; perfidy, insidiousness; squint

زورة *zaura* (n. vic.) pl. *-āt* visit, call

زيارة *ziyāra* pl. *-āt* visit; call (social, of a doctor)

ازور *azwar*[2], f. زوراء *zaurā'*[2], pl. زور *zūr* inclined, slanting, oblique; crooked, curved; squint-eyed, cross-eyed

مزار *mazār* pl. *-āt* place which one visits; shrine, sanctuary

تزوير *tazwīr* forgery, falsification | تزوير فى السندات (*sanadāt*) falsification of documents

ازورار *izwirār* turning away; averseness, aversion, dislike, distaste

زائر *zā'ir* pl. *-ūn*, زوار *zuwwār*, f. زائرة *zā'ira* pl. *-āt*, زور *zuwwar* visitor, caller, guest

مزور *mazūr* visited

مزور *muzawwar* forged, false, counterfeit; obtained by swindle, faked

زورق *zauraq* pl. زوارق *zawāriq*[2] boat, rowboat, skiff | زورق بخارى (*bukārī*) steam launch; زورق الصيد *z. aṣ-ṣaid* fishing boat; زورق النجاة *z. an-najāh* lifeboat; ○ زورق ناسف torpedo boat

[1](زوغ) زاغ *zāḡa u* (*zauḡ*, زوغان *zawaḡān*) to turn aside, depart, deviate (عن from), swerve; to deviate from truth, to swindle; see also زيغ VI to turn aside, swerve

[2]زاغ look up alphabetically

زوفاء *zūfā'*, زوفى *zūfā* hyssop (*bot.*)

[1]زوق II to adorn, embellish, ornament, decorate (ه s.th.); to picture, visualize (ه a story, in one's imagination)

زواق *zawāq* embellishment, adornment, ornamentation; decoration; finery, attire; face painting, make-up, cosmetics

مزوق *muzawwaq* adorned, embellished, ornamented, decorated; florid, flowery (speech); dressed up, meretricious, showy, gaudy

[2]زاووق, زاؤوق look up alphabetically

زول and (زيل) زال *zāla* (1st pers. perf. *zultu*) (زوال *zawāl*) to go away, withdraw (عن or من from), abandon, leave (عن or من s.o. or s.th.); to disappear, vanish; to abate, calm down, die down, come to an end; to go down, set; — (1st pers. perf. *ziltu*) *a* (*zail*) to cease (with negations only) | of زول: زال منه الغضب (*ḡaḍab*) his wrath abated; زال عن الوجود to cease to exist; — of زيل: with neg. ما زال, لم يزل

(*yazal*), لا يزال equivalent to Engl. "still, yet": ما زلت افعله (*af'aluhū*) I have not ceased to do it, I (am) still do(ing) it; ما زال قائما he is still standing; ما زال فى he has not ceased to be or to remain in, he is still in; لا يزال فى حاجة اليه he is still in need of it, he still needs it; لا يزال على ذكر منه (*dikrin*) he still remembers him **II** زول *zawwala* to remove, eliminate (ه s.th.); — زيل *zayyala* to separate, break up, disperse, scatter (ه s.th.) **III** زاول *zāwala* to pursue (ه s.th.), devote o.s., apply o.s. (ه to); — زايل *zāyala* to separate, part (ه, ه from), leave, quit, abandon (ه, ه s.o., s.th.); to separate (بين s.th.) | زايل الدار to move out of the house, leave the house **IV** to cause to cease or stop, make disappear or vanish (ه s.th.); to remove, eliminate (ه s.th.), put an end (ه to s.th.), do away (ه with s.th.), make a clean sweep (ه of s.th.) **VI** تزايل *tazāyala* to be disjointed, incoherent; to pass away, cease, stop

زول *zaul* pl. ازوال *azwāl* person, body, figure; nightly apparition, specter, ghost, phantom, spirit

زوال *zawāl* end, passage, extinction, disappearance, vanishing, cessation; setting (of the sun); noon | سريع الزوال ephemeral, evanescent, fleeting; بعد الزوال in the afternoon; عند الزوال around noon, by noon; خط الزوال *kaṭṭ az-z.* meridian

زوالى *zawālī*: فى الساعة الرابعة زوالية at four o'clock in the afternoon, at four p. m.

زولية *zūlīya* pl. زوالى *zawālī* (*ir., saud.*) knotted rug

مزولة *mizwala* pl. مزاول *mazāwil*[2] sundial

مزاولة *muzāwala* pursuit (of s.th.), application (to); assiduous study; practice (of some work, of a profession)

ازالة *izāla* removal, elimination

زائل *zā'il* transitory, passing, evanescent, fleeting, ephemeral, short-lived

زولوجيا *zōlōjiyā* zoology

زولوجى *zōlōjī* zoologic(al)

زام (زوم) *zāma u* (*eg.*) to growl, snarl (dog) **II** to mumble, mutter

زوم *zūm* pl. ازوام *azwām* juice, sap

[1]زان, زانة look up alphabetically

[2]زوان *ziwān, zuwān* = زؤان (q.v.)

زوى *zawā i* to contract, wrinkle, knit (ه s.th., e.g., the eyebrows); to remove (ه s.th.); to hide, conceal (ه s.th.) | زوى ما بين عينيه (*'ainaihi*) he knitted his eyebrows, he frowned (in anger, and the like) **II** and **V** to withdraw into a corner, go into seclusion, retire **VII** do.; to keep to o.s., live in seclusion or retirement | انزوى فى جلده (*jildihī*) to crawl inside o.s. (out of shame, and the like)

انزواء *inziwā'* retirement, seclusion, isolation

زاوية *zāwiya* pl. زوايا *zawāyā* corner, nook; angle (*math.*); small mosque, prayer room; (*North Afr.*) a small cupolaed mosque erected over the tomb of a Muslim saint, with teaching facilities and a hospice attached to it, usually the establishment of a religious order | الزاوية الحادة (*hādda*) acute angle; الزاوية الخارجة external angle; متساوى الزوايا *mutasāwī z-z.* equiangular; الزاوية المنفرجة (*munfarija*) obtuse angle; الزاوية القائمة right angle; حجر الزاوية *ḥajar az-z.* cornerstone; من زوايا مختلفة (*muktalifa*) from different angles (i.e., aspects)

منزو *munzawin* seclusive, secluding; retired, secluded; outlying, remote, out-of-the-way; obscure

زى **II** زيا, زيى *zayyā* to dress, clothe, costume (ه ب s.o. in) **V** تزيا, تزيى *tazayyā* to dress, put on a dress or costume; to dress up, smarten o.s. up; to be dressed, be clad (ب in), wear (ب s.th.)

زى *ziyy* pl. ازياء *azyā'* clothing, dress, apparel, attire; ○ uniform; outward appearance, make-up; costume; style of dress, manner of dressing; fashion; exterior, guise, form, shape | على الزى الجديد fashionable, modish, stylish

زيبق *zaibaq* (= زئبق *zi'baq*) quicksilver, mercury

زبت II to oil, lubricate, grease (ه a machine, and the like); to add oil (ه to some food)

زيت *zait* pl. زيوت *zuyūt* oil (edible, fuel, motor oil, etc.) | زيت حار (*ḥārr*) linseed oil; زيت حلو (*ḥulw*) sweet oil, oil free of hydrogen sulfide; زيت الحوت *z. al-ḥūt* cod-liver oil; زيت الخروع *z. al-ḵirwa'* castor oil; زيت السمك *z. as-samak* cod-liver oil; زيت التشحيم lubricating oil; زيت الاستصباح fuel oil; زيت الغاز *z. al-ġāz* kerosene

زيتى *zaitī* oily, oil (adj.), oil-bearing | صورة زيتية or لوحة زيتية (*ṣūra, lauḥa*) oil painting

زيات *zayyāt* oil dealer, oilman

زيتون *zaitūn* (coll.; n. un. ة) olive tree; olive(s) | احد الزيتون *aḥad az-z.* Palm Sunday (*Chr.*); جبل الزيتون *jabal az-z.* Mount of Olives (Jerusalem)

زيتونة *zaitūna* (n. un.) pl. *-āt* olive tree; olive | جامع الزيتونة the Zaitouna Mosque (large mosque and university in Tunis)

زيتونى *zaitūnī* olivaceous, olive-colored, olive-green; (pl. *-ūn*) student of the Great Mosque of Tunis

زيتونية *zaitūnīya*, احد الزيتونية *aḥad az-z.* Palm Sunday (*Copt.-Chr.*)

مزيتة *mazyata* oil can, oiler

مزيت *muzayyat* oiled

[1]زيج *zīj* leveling line (used by masons); ephemeris, astronomical almanac

[2]زيجة *zīja* and زيجى *zījī* see زوج

(زيح) زاح *zāḥa i* (*zaiḥ*, زيوح *zuyūḥ*, زيحان *zayaḥān*) to go away, depart, leave IV to remove, drive away, banish (ه s.th.), do away with (ه); to take away (ه s.th.); to pull away, throw back (ه a curtain, a veil, etc., عن from s.th.) | ازاح اللثام عن to reveal, disclose s.th.; ازاح الستار عن تمثال (*timṯāl*) to unveil a monument VII to go away, depart, leave; to be pulled away, be thrown back (curtain)

زيح *zīḥ* pl. ازياح *azyāḥ* (straight) line

زياح *zayyāḥ* pl. *-āt* religious procession

ازاحة *izāḥa* removal, abolition | ازاحة الستار unveiling (of a monument)

(زيد) زاد *zāda i* (زيادة *ziyāda*) to become greater, become more, grow, increase, be compounded, multiply; to be greater, be more, amount to more (عن or على than), exceed (عن or على s.th., an amount, ب by), go beyond an amount or number (على); to augment, increase, compound (ه s.th.), make (ه s.th.) grow or increase; to step up, raise (من, ه s.th., الى ه s.th. to); to add (على ه s.th. to); to add, make additions (على to), enlarge (على s.th.); to extend, expand, further, advance, promote, intensify (ف or من s.th.); to give more (ه ه to s.o. of s.th.) | لا يزيد على it is no more than ..., it is only ...; زاد قائلا he added (in speech followed by quotation); زد على ذلك ان (*zid*) (prop.: add to it that ...) in addition to that there is ..., what's more, there is ...; furthermore, moreover; زاده علما (*'ilman*) to tell s.o. more about it, supply s.o. with more information II to increase, augment, compound, make grow III to make a higher bid (ه than s.o.), outbid (ه s.o.; at an auction) V to increase; to rise, go up (prices); to make additions, add embellishments of one's own, exaggerate (in telling s.th.); to be long-winded, verbose | تزيد من العلم, من المعرفة (*'ilm, ma'rifa*) to acquire additional knowledge, increase one's knowledge VI to outbid one another; to increase gradually, be growing; to become more intense, intensify; to become more and more, exceed more and more (من s.th.) **VIII** ازداد *izdāda* to grow, be growing, increase, be compounded, multiply | ازداد بكاء (*bukā'an*) he wept more and more **X** to demand more, ask for more, go up with one's demands; to try to achieve more; to aim or work at an increase, expansion or extension (ه of); to ask (ه s.o.) to give more of s.th.

الزيدية *az-zaidīya* a Shiitic group forming an independent commonwealth (Yemen)

الزيود *az-zuyūd* the Zaidites, adherents of the Zaidiya sect

زيادة *ziyāda* increase, increment, accretion, growth; surplus, overplus, excess; increase, augmentation, raising, stepping up; enhancement, elevation, intensification; extra pay, allowance (in addition to the salary); addition; زيادة *ziyādatan* in addition, additionally | زيادة عن (*ziyādatan*) over and above, beyond, in excess of; regardless of; aside from; حمله زيادة عن تحمله *ḥammalahū z. ʿan taḥammulihī* he loaded him with more than he could carry; زيادة على ذلك (*ziyādatan*) moreover, besides; زيادة المواليد excess of births; لزيادة الايضاح (*īḍāḥ*) in order to make it even clearer, for further elucidation

ازيد *azyad*[2] more excessive, higher, greater, bigger

مزاد *mazād* pl. *-āt* auction, public sale

مزيد *mazīd* an exceeding (على of s.th.); excess, superabundance; high degree, large extent; utmost, maximum; (with foll. genit.) excessive, extreme, utmost, highest, greatest, superlative; pass. partic. of **I**: increased, etc.; the derivative stems of the verb (*gram.*) | بمزيد الشكر *bi-m. iš-šukr* with many, many thanks; بمزيد الاسف *bi-m. il-asaf* with the greatest regret; بمزيد الارتياح with extreme satisfaction; ليس له من مزيد it is unsurpassable, it's not to be outdone

مزايدة *muzāyada* pl. *-āt* auction, public sale

تزيد *tazayyud* exaggeration (in reporting), one's own embellishments or additions, fables, yarn

تزايد *tazāyud* (gradual) increase, increment, growth

ازدياد *izdiyād* increase, growth, rise, intensification

استزادة *istizāda* a striving for more; pursuit of an increase, expansion or extension; desire or request for more | لم يبق استزادة لمستزيد (*yabqa, li-mustazīdin*) there is nothing to be added, nothing more need be said about it

زائد *zā'id* increasing, growing; excessive, immoderate; exceeding (عن s.th.), in excess (عن of); additional, extra, supernumerary | زائد عن الحاجة more than necessary, surplus

زائدة *zā'ida* pl. زوائد *zawā'id*[2] appendage, appendix (*anat., zool., bot.*); outgrowth (*med.*) | زائدة معوية (*mi'awīya*) and زائدة دودية (*dūdīya*) vermiform appendix (*anat.*)

مزايد *muzāyid* pl. *-ūn* bidder, outbidder (at an auction)

متزايد *mutazāyid* steadily increasing, swelling

[1]زر **II** (*mor.*) to close (ه a button)

[2]زر *zīr* pl. ازيار *azyār*, زيار *ziyār* (*eg., magr.*) large, almost conical jar, made of porous clay, for storing water

[3]زر *zīr* the highest string of stringed instruments (*mus.*)

زز *zīz* (coll.; n. un. ة) pl. زِزان *zīzān* cicada; chrysalis

زيزفون *zaizafūn* jujube (Zizyphus; *bot.*); linden tree

[1](زيغ) زاغ *zāğa* *i* (*zaiğ*, زيغان *zayağān*) to turn aside; to depart, deviate (عن from); to swerve; to turn away (عن from), turn one's back (عن on); to wander, stray, roam (eyes) IV to cause (ه s.th.) to deviate | ازاغ عنى بصره (*baṣarahū*) he looked past me, he snubbed me

زيغ *zaiğ* and زيغان *zayağān* a turning aside; deviation, departure (عن from) | زيغ وسداد (*sadād*) erring and doing right, wrong and right

زائغ *zā'iğ* deviating, divergent; false, wrong, distorted, perverted | نظرات زائغة (*naẓarāt*) wandering glances

[2]زاغ look up alphabetically

(زيف) زاف *zāfa* *i* (*zaif*) to be false, be spurious II to counterfeit (ه money); to declare (ه s.th.) to be false or spurious

زيف *zaif* falseness; pride; (pl. زيوف *zuyūf*) false, spurious, forged, counterfeit

ازيف *azyaf*[2] falser, more spurious

تزييف *tazyīf* falsification, forgery, counterfeiting

زائف *zā'if* false; forged, counterfeit, spurious | اخبار زائفة false reports; نقود زائفة counterfeit money

مزيف *muzayyif* forger, counterfeiter

مزيف *muzayyaf* forged; counterfeit, false, spurious; pseudo-

[1]زيق II (*eg.*) to creak, screech

[2]زيق *zīq* pl. ازياق *azyāq* collar, neckband; border, hem (of a garment)

(زيل) زال and II, III, VI see زول

[1](زين) *zāna* *i* (*zain*) to decorate, adorn (ه s.th.) II to adorn, decorate, embellish, ornament (ه s.th.); to grace (ه, ه s.o., s.th.); to shave (ه s.o.); زينت نفسها (*nafsahā*) to make herself up (lady); to paint in glowing tones, present in a favorable light, extol (ل, الى ه s.th. to s.o.); to conjure up (ه s.th., ل before s.o.'s eyes), create visions (ه of s.th., ل in s.o.'s mind), lead s.o. (ل) to believe (ان that); to give (ل s.o.) the idea (ان to do s.th.), suggest (ل ان to s.o. to do s.th.) V to be decorated, be adorned; to dress up, smarten o.s. up, spruce up, preen o.s.; to shave, get a shave VIII ازدان *izdāna* to be decorated, be adorned; to be graced

زين *zain* beauty; beautiful, nice, pretty

زينة *zīna* pl. *-āt* embellishment, adornment, ornament, decoration; clothes, attire, finery; toilette | زينة الوجه *z. al-wajh* make-up; بيت الزينة *bait az-z.* beauty shop; اشجار الزينة ornamental trees; نباتات الزينة *nabātāt az-z.* ornamental plants; خوان الزينة *kuwān az-z.* dressing table; غرفة الزينة *ğurfat az-z.* dressing room

زيان *zayān* beautiful

زيان *ziyān* embellishment, adornment, decoration; ornament

زيانة *ziyāna* barber's or hairdresser's trade

تزيين *tazyīn* adorning, decoration, ornamentation; make-believe, sham, pretense

مزين *muzayyin* barber, hairdresser

مزين *muzayyan* decorated, ornamented, adorned (ب with); graced (ب with)

مزدان *muzdān* decorated, ornamented, adorned (ب with); graced (ب with)

[2]زان look up alphabetically

زينكو *zinkō* zinc

س

ـ *sa* shortened form of سوف *saufa* (q.v.)

ساتان *sātān* satin

ساج *sāj* pl. سيجان *sījān* teak, Indian oak

ساجات *sājāt* castanets

سادة *sāda* simple; plain, unicolored, uniform (fabric) | قهوة سادة (*qahwa*) unsweetened coffee

سود[2] see سؤدد

سئر *sa'ira a* to remain, be left

سؤر *su'r* pl. اسآر *as'ār* rest, remainder, remnant, leftover (esp. of food and beverages)

سؤرة *su'ra* rest, remainder, remnant, leftover (esp. of food and beverages); vestige of youthful vigor

سائر *sā'ir* remaining; rest, remainder; (with foll. det. genit.) all

الساسانيون *as-sāsānīyūn* the Sassanidae, a dynasty of Persian kings (226—651 A.D.)

ساغو *sāgō* sago

ساكو *sākō*, ساكوه sack coat, lounge jacket

سأل *sa'ala a* (سؤال *su'āl*, مسألة *mas'ala*, تسآل *tas'āl*) to ask (عن or ه ه s.o. s.th. or about s.th.); to inquire (عن ه of s.o. about); to ask (ه من or ه s.o. for s.th.), request, demand, claim (ه من or ه from s.o. s.th.) | سأله الا *sa'alahū illā* to implore, adjure s.o. that he ...; سأله عن اخباره to ask s.o. about s.o. else; سأله رأيه (*ra'yahū*) to ask s.o.'s opinion, consult s.o.; سأله سؤالا to ask s.o. a question; يسأل (*yus'alu*) he is responsible, answerable (عن for) **III** to ask, question, interrogate (ه s.o.); to call (ه s.o.) to account **IV** اسأله سؤله (*su'lahū*) to fulfill s.o.'s wish, comply with s.o.'s request **V** *tasa''ala* and تسول *tasawwala* to beg **VI** to ask; to ask o.s.; to ask one another; تساءل هل (عن) to ask o.s. whether (about); to inquire (عن about)

سؤل *su'l* demand, request, wish

سؤلة *su'la* demand, request, wish

سؤال *su'āl* pl. اسئلة *as'ila* question (عن about); request (عن for); inquiry (عن about); demand, claim

سآل *sa''āl* given to asking questions, inquisitive, curious

سؤول *sa'ūl* given to asking questions, inquisitive, curious

مسألة (مسئلة) *mas'ala* pl. مسائل *masā'il*[2] question; issue, problem; matter, affair, case; request

مساءلة *musā'ala* questioning, interrogation

تسول *tasawwul* begging, beggary

تساؤل *tasā'ul* (self-directed) question; questioning

سائل *sā'il* pl. *-ūn*, سؤال *su''āl*, سألة *sa'ala* questioner; petitioner; beggar

مسؤول *mas'ūl* responsible, answerable, accountable (عن for)

مسئولية *mas'ūlīya* pl. *-āt* responsibility (عن for)

متسول *mutasawwil* pl. *-ūn* beggar

[1]سام *sām* Shem (eldest son of Noah)

سامى *sāmī* Semitic; (pl. *-ūn*) Semite

اللاسامية *al-lā-sāmīya* anti-Semitism

[2]سئم *sa'ima a* (سأم *sa'm*, سآمة *sa'āma*) to be weary, tired (من or ه of s.th.), be bored, fed up (من or ه with s.th.); to dislike, detest, loathe (ان doing s.th.), have an

aversion (ان to doing s.th.) IV to cause or arouse weariness or boredom (ه in s.o.), weary, bore (ه s.o.)

سئم *sa'im* weary, tired, bored

سؤوم *sa'ūm* disgusted, weary, fed up

سآمة *sa'āma* weariness, disgust, boredom, ennui

سب *sabba u* (*sabb*) to insult, abuse, call names, revile (ه s.o.), rail (ه at); to curse (ه s.o.); to blaspheme, curse, swear II to cause, provoke, arouse, produce, bring about, effect, occasion (ه s.th.), give occasion (ه to s.th.) III to exchange insults or abusive language (ه with s.o.) V to be caused, be produced (عن by), be the consequence or result (عن of), follow, arise, spring, result (عن from); to be the reason or cause, be at the bottom (ب or في of), be to blame (في for), be instrumental (في in); to seek reasons or motives (الى for s.th.); to account, give a reason or explanation (ل for), justify, motivate (الى s.th.); to use (ب s.th.) as a means (الى for); to trade, be in the retail business VI to insult each other, call one another names, rail at each other VIII = VI

سب *sabb* abuse, vituperation, insults, cursing

سبة *sabba* period of time, (long) while

سبة *sibba*: سبة الآلام *s. al-ālām* Passion Week (*Chr.*)

سبة *subba* disgrace, shame, dishonor

سبب *sabab* pl. اسباب *asbāb* rope, tent rope; means for obtaining s.th.; reason, cause, motive, occasion (with foll. genit. or في: of); means of subsistence; (esp. pl.) relations (between people) | سبب اكبر main reason; اسباب الحكم *a. al-ḥukm* opinion (*jur.*); اسباب الراحة luxury; بسبب *bi-sababi* because of, on account of, due to, by; بسبب ذلك because of that, for that reason, therefore; كان السبب فيه (*sababa*) to be the cause of s.th., be to blame for s.th.; يرجع السبب الى (*yarji'u*) the reason is to be found in ...; اخذ باسباب الحضارة الحديثة (*ḥaḍāra*) to adopt modern civilization; وصل اسبابه باسبابه (*asbābahū*) to join forces with s.o.; تقطعت الاسباب بين relations between ... are broken off, they no longer have anything in common; شاطره اسباب المسرة *šāṭarahū asbāba l-masarra* to share s.o.'s joy

سببية *sababīya* causality

سباب *sabbāb* abuser, vituperator, reviler

سبابة *sabbāba* index finger

سبيب *sabīb* pl. سبائب *sabā'ib*[2] strand of hair

مسبة *masabba* pl. -*āt* vilification, abuse, insult

تسبيب *tasbīb* mediate causation (*Isl. Law*)

سباب *sibāb* abuse, vituperation, revilement

مسابة *musābba* abuse, vituperation, revilement

مسبب *musabbib* causer, originator, author; مسببات *musabbibāt* causative factors

مسبب *musabbab* caused (عن by) | السبب والمسبب (*sabab*) cause and effect

متسبب *mutasabbib* causer; cause; retailer, small storekeeper

سبا *sabā* and سبأ *saba'* Sheba | ذهبوا ايدى (ايادى) سبا *ḏ. aidiya* (*ayādiya*) *sabā* they were scattered to the four winds

سبانخ *sabānaḵ, sabāniḵ* spinach

سبايس see سباهى

سبايس *sabāyis* and سباهى *sibāhī* spahis, Algerian native cavalry in the French army

[1]سبت *sabata u* to rest; to keep the Sabbath IV to enter on the Sabbath

السبت *as-sabt* pl. السبوت *as-subūt* Sabbath, Saturday | يوم السبت *yaum as-s.* do.; سبت النور *s. an-nūr* Holy Saturday (*Chr.*)

سبات *subāt* lethargy; slumber, sleep

سباتى *subātī* lethargic | الالتهاب المخى السباتى (*mukkī*) encephalitis lethargica, sleeping sickness (*med.*)

مسبت *musbit* lethargic, inactive, motionless

[2]سبت *sabat* pl. -*āt*, اسبتة *asbita* basket

[3]سبت *sibitt* dill (Anethum graveolens; *bot.*)

سبتمبر *sibtambir* September

سبج *sabaj* jet (*min.*)

سبح *sabaḥa* a (*sabḥ*, سباحة *sibāḥa*) to swim (فى, ب in); to float (fig.); to spread II to praise, glorify (الله *allāha*, لله *li-llāhi* God, by saying سبحان الله *subḥāna llāh* praise the Lord!); to praise, extol (ب s.th.) | سبح بحمده (*ḥamdihī*) to sing s.o.'s praise, glorify s.o.

سبحة *sabḥa* (n. un.) a swim, swimming

سبحة *subḥa* pl. سبحات *subuḥāt*, سبح *subaḥ* beads of the Muslim rosary; Muslim rosary; supererogatory salat (*Isl. Law*)

سبحة *subḥa*, *sabḥa* pl. سبحات *subuḥāt*, *sabaḥāt* majesty (of God) | سبحات وجه الله *subuḥātu wajhi llāh* the sublimity, or the august splendor, of God's countenance; سبحات رفيعة (*sabaḥāt*) lofty heights

سبحان الله *subḥāna llāh* exclamation of surprise, etc. (prop.: praise the Lord! God be praised!); سبحان الله عن God is far above ..., God is beyond ...

سباح *sabbāḥ* swimmer

سبوح *sabūḥ* a good swimmer; swift and smooth-running (lit.: floating; of horses)

سباحة *sibāḥa* (art of) swimming

مسبح *masbaḥ* pl. مسابح *masābiḥ*[2] swimming pool

مسبحة *misbaḥa* pl. مسابح *masābiḥ*[2] rosary

تسبيح *tasbīḥ* pl. -*āt*, تسابيح *tasābīḥ*[2] glorification of God (by exclaiming سبحان الله)

تسبيحة *tasbīḥa* pl. -*āt*, تسابيح *tasābīḥ*[2] glorification of God; hymn, song of praise

تسبحة *tasbiḥa* hymn, song of praise

سابح *sābiḥ* pl. -*ūn*, سباح *subbāḥ*, سبحاء *subaḥā'*[2] swimmer; bather | سابح فى افكاره lost in thought

○ سابحة *sābiḥa* glider, sailplane, cargo glider

سابحات *sābiḥāt* and سوابح *sawābiḥ*[2] floating ones (epithet for race horses)

مسبحة *musabbiḥa* index finger

سبحلة *sabḥala* glorification of God

سبخ *sabaka* u (*sabk*) to be sound asleep II do.; to manure, fertilize (الارض *al-arḍa* the land)

سبخ *sabak* dung, manure, fertilizer | سبخ بلدى (*baladī*) manure

سبخ *sabik* briny (soil)

سبخة *sabaka*, *sabka* pl. سباخ *sibāk* salt marsh, salt swamp | ارض سبخة do.

سباخ *sibāk* pl. اسبخة *asbika* dung, manure, fertilizer | سباخ بلدى (*baladī*) manure

سبيخ *sabīk* pl. سبائخ *sabā'ik*[2] loose (unspun) cotton

تسبيخ *tasbīk* deep, sound sleep; ○ coma, somnolence (*med.*)

سبر *sabara* u i (*sabr*) to examine with a probe, to probe (ه a wound); to measure, sound (ه s.th., e.g., the depth); to fathom, explore, examine (ه s.th.) | سبر اغوار الشىء

to probe the depth of s.th., get to the bottom of s.th., study s.th. thoroughly

سبر **sabr** probing (of a wound); fathoming, exploration, examination

سبار **sibār** pl. سبر **subur** probe (*med.*)

سبورة **sabbūra** slate; blackboard

مسبر **misbar** pl. مسابر **masābir**² probe (*med.*)

مسبار **misbār** pl. مسابير **masābīr**² probe (*med.*)

سبس **sibs** small wind instrument resembling the oboe (*eg.*)

سبسب II **tasabsaba** to be lank (hair); to flow (tears)

سبسب **sabsab** pl. سباسب **sabāsib**² desert, wasteland | قفر سبسب (*qafr*) desert, wasteland, desolate region

سبط **sabuṭa** *u* (سبوطة **subūṭa**, سباطة **sabāṭa**) to be lank (hair)

سبط **sabiṭ, sabṭ, sabaṭ** pl. سباط **sibāṭ** lank (hair) | سبط اليدين **sabṭ** (**sabiṭ**) **al-yadain** liberal, openhanded, generous; سبط القامة **s. al-qāma** shapely, well-built, of graceful stature

سبط **sibṭ** pl. اسباط **asbāṭ** grandson; tribe (of the Israelites)

سباط **sabbāṭ** pl. سبابيط **sabābīṭ**² shoe

سباطة **subāṭa** bunch, cluster (of fruit)

ساباط **sābāṭ** pl. سوابيط **sawābīṭ**² arcade, roofed lane or street; archway

سيباط **sībāṭ** and (*eg.*) سباط **subāṭ** arcade, roofed lane or street; archway

سبع II to make sevenfold (ه s.th.); to divide into seven parts (ه s.th.)

سبع **sab'** pl. اسبع **asbu'**, سبوع **subū'**, سبوعة **subū'a** predatory animal, beast of prey; lion

سبع **sabu'** pl. سباع **sibā'** predatory animal, beast of prey; lion

سبعة **sab'a** (f. سبع **sab'**) seven; سبعة عشر **sab'ata 'ašara** (f. سبع عشرة **sab'a 'ašrata**) seventeen

سبع **sub', subu'** pl. اسباع **asbā'** one-seventh

سباعى **subā'ī** consisting of seven parts; seven-lettered, consisting of seven letters

سبعون **sab'ūn** seventy

سبعونى **sab'ūnī** septuagenarian

الترجمة السبعينية **at-tarjama as-sab'īnīya** the Septuagint

السبوعات (Hebr. **š'bū'ōt**) **as-sabū'āt** Shabuoth, the Feast of Weeks, or Pentecost, of the Jews

اسبوع **usbū'** pl. اسابيع **asābī'**² week | اسبوع الآلام Passion Week (*Chr.*)

اسبوعى **usbū'ī** weekly; اسبوعيا weekly, by the week

اسبوعية **usbū'īya** weekly feature (*radio*)

السابع **as-sābi'** the seventh

سبغ **sabaġa** *u a* (سبوغ **subūġ**) to be long and wide; to abound, be abundant IV to make wide, widen (ه s.th.); to make (ه s.th.) complete; to bestow amply (على upon s.o., ه s.th.), shower (على ه s.o. with); to lend, impart liberally (على ه to s.th. s.th.); to attribute, ascribe (على to s.o., ه qualities) | اسبغ الوضوء to perform the ritual ablution properly (*Isl. Law*)

سابغ **sābiġ** pl. سوابغ **sawābiġ**² long and loose-fitting (garment); full, complete, perfect; excessive, abundant, ample

سبق **sabaqa** *i u* (**sabq**) to be, come, go, get, or act, before or ahead of s.o. or s.th. (ه, ه), precede, antecede (ه, ه s.o., s.th., in place and time), arrive before s.o. (ه) at (الى); to outstrip, outdistance, leave behind (ه, ه s.o., s.th.); to forestall (ه s.th.); to anticipate (ه s.th.); to do or say s.th. (الى) spontaneously before one can be stopped; to turn spontaneously, instinctively, without knowing why (الى to s.th.); to surpass, beat (على or ه s.o.) | سبق له ان فعله (*an fa'alahū*) he had already done it before; سبق له ان قابله (*an qābalahū*) he had met him before (paraphrasing the pluperfect); سبق لنا القول ان (*qaulu*) we have previously (already) said that ...; سبق الحكم عليه ب (*ḥukmu*) he had been previously sentenced to ...; سبق لى it happened to me before, I experienced before (ان that); لم يسبق لى ان I have never before ...; لم يسبق له مثيل (as) there has never been one before, (which is) unprecedented; سبق السيف العذل *s. s-saifu l-'adla* (the sword anticipated censure, i.e.) one has to accept the accomplished fact, there is (was) nothing one can (could) do about it, it is (was) already too late; سبقه لسانه (*lisānuhū*) to burst out impulsively (with an utterance) **II** to cause (ه s.th.) to precede or antecede; to premise (ه s.th.); to do or give (ه s.th.) prematurely **III** to try to get ahead of s.o. (ه); to try to defeat or beat (ه s.o.), seek to get the better of s.o. (ه); to race (ه s.o.), run a race (ه with s.o.); to compete, vie (ه with s.o.) **VI** to try to get ahead of one another, seek to outdo one another, compete, vie; to try to beat one another (الى to) **VIII** = **VI**

سبق **sabq** antecedence; precedence, priority | سبق الاصرار *s. al-iṣrār* premeditation, willfulness (*jur.*); ميزة السبق *mīzat as-s.* initiative; احرز قصب السبق see احرز

سبق **sabaq** pl. اسباق **asbāq** stake (in a race)

سبقة **sabqa**: سبقة القلم *s. al-qalam* slip of the pen, lapsus calami

سبقة **subqa** stake (in a race)

سباق **sabbāq** anticipatory; precursory; triumphant | قطار سباق fast train, express train; — (pl. *-ūn*) precursor; winner in contest; ○ race-car driver

اسبق **asbaq**[2] earlier, antecedent; preceding, previous, prior; former, ex- | المقيم الاسبق (*muqīm*) the ex-resident

اسبقية **asbaqīya** precedence, priority; seniority

سباق **sibāq** race (esp. of horses); contest | سباق تتابع ٤ × ١٠٠ متر (*s. tatābu'*) 4 × 100 m relay race; حصان السباق race horse; حلبة (ميدان) السباق *ḥalbat* (*maidān*) *as-s.* race track; سباق القوارب regatta, boat race; سباق التسلح *s. at-tasalluḥ* arms race

مسابقة **musābaqa** pl. *-āt* race (esp. of horses); contest; competition; emulation

تسابق **tasābuq** emulation; competition

سابق **sābiq** pl. *-ūn*, سباق **subbāq** antecedent, preceding, foregoing, previous, prior; former, ex-; retired, ret.; سابقا *sābiqan* formerly, previously | سابق لأوانه (*li-awānihī*) premature; فى السابق formerly, at one time, once; كالسابق as before; كسابق العادة as it was customary before; as usual; المبلغ السابق صرفه (*mablaġ, ṣarfuhū*) the payment already effected

سابقة **sābiqa** precedence, priority; previous case, precedent; previous, earlier publication of an author; pl. سوابق *sawābiq*[2] antecedents; previous convictions | من اصحاب (or ذوى) السوابق previously convicted; من له سوابق (*man*) (one) previously convicted; recidivous criminal

سابقية **sābiqīya**: سابقية القصد *s. al-qaṣd* premeditation (*jur.*)

غير مسبوق **ġair masbūq** unprecedented

مسبقا **musabbaqan** prematurely, in advance

مسابق **musābiq** pl. *-ūn* competitor; contestant; racer, runner

متسابق **mutasābiq** competitor; contestant

سبك *sabaka i u* (*sabk*) to found, cast (ه metal), smelt (ه ore); to form, shape, mold (ه s.o.); to formulate (ه s.th.); to polish the style (ه of s.th.) **II** to found, cast (ه metal), smelt (ه ore); to braise, stew (ه s.th.) **VII** to be poured into a mold, be cast

سبك *sabk* founding, casting; cast (also fig., = arrangement); formulation (of an expression); shaping, forming (of a person) | صناعة سبك المعادن metallurgic industry; سبك ودقة (*diqqa*) accuracy, precision

سباك *sabbāk* smelter, founder

سباكة *sibāka* founder's trade and activity

سبيكة *sabīka* pl. سبائك *sabā'ik*[2] ingot

مسبك *masbak* pl. مسابك *masābik*[2] foundry

تسبيك *tasbīk* stewing, braising (in a covered dish, with scant moisture)

سبل **II** to dedicate to charitable purposes (ه s.th.) **IV** to let (ه s.th.) hang down; to let fall, drop (ه a curtain, drape, etc., على over); to close, shut (ه the eyes); to shed (ه tears); to ear, form ears

سبل *sabal* (coll.; n. un. ة) ears (of cereals)

سبلة *sabla* manure, dung

سبلة *sabala* pl. سبال *sibāl* mustache

سبيل *sabīl* m. and f., pl. سبل *subul*, اسبلة *asbila* way, road, path; access; means, expedient, possibility (الى to, for); — (pl. اسبلة *asbila*) public fountain; — (pl. سبلان *siblān*) clay pipe bowl, clay pipe (of the Bedouins) | ابن السبيل *ibn as-s.* vagabond, tramp; wayfarer, traveler; فى سبيل for the sake of, for, in behalf of, in the interest of; بسبيل or عن سبيل by means of, through, by; فى سبيل الله for the cause of God, in behalf of God and his religion; على سبيل as, by way of, for: e.g., على سبيل التجربة (*tajriba*) for a try, tentatively, على سبيل الفكاهة (*fukāha*) for fun, ذكر الشىء على سبيل المثال to quote s.th. as an example; خلو see خل سبيله; ضاقت به السبل he was at his wit's end; ليس على فى ذلك سبيل (*laisa 'alayya*) there is nothing to keep me from doing that, I am free to do that, it is no sin if I do that

سابل *sābil*: طريق سابلة a public, much-frequented road

السابلة *as-sābila* the passers-by

مسبول *masbūl* lowered, down (curtain)

الاسبانى, اسبانى look up alphabetically

سبنسة (*eg.*) *sibinsa* pl. *-āt* caboose, brake van; baggage car (railroad)

سبه *sabah* dotage

عقل مسبوه *'aql masbūh* impaired mind (esp. due to old age), feeble-mindedness

سبهللا *sabahlalan* indifferently, aimlessly, haphazardly, at random

سباهلة *sabāhila* people without work, idlers, loafers

سباهى look up alphabetically

سبا look up alphabetically

سبور (Fr. *sport*) *sbōr* sport(s)

سبى *sabā i* (*saby*, سباء *sibā'*) to take prisoner, capture; to lead into captivity (esp. in war); to captivate, fascinate, enchant, charm, beguile, intrigue (ه, ه s.o., s.th.) **VIII** = **I**

سبى *saby* capture; captivity

سبى *sabīy* pl. سبايا *sabāyā* captive, prisoner (of war)

سبية *sabīya* (female) prisoner

سبيداج *sibīdāj* white lead, ceruse

سبيذاج *sibīḏāj* white lead, ceruse

س ت abbreviation of سجل تجارى *sijill tijārī* commercial register

است *ist* buttocks, backside

1ستة *sitta* (f. ست *sitt*) six; ستة عشر *sittata 'ašara* (f. ست عشرة *sitta 'ašrata*) sixteen

*ستون *sittūn* sixty

ستونى *sittūnī* sexagenarian

الساد *as-sādd* the sixth

2□ست *sitt* pl. *-āt* lady | ست الحسن *s. al-ḥusn* a variety of morning-glory (Ipomoea caïrica Webb.; *bot.*); also = belladonna, deadly nightshade (*bot.*)

استاذ pl. اساتذة look up alphabetically

ستر *satara u i* (*satr*) to cover, veil (ه, ه s.o., s.th.); to hide, conceal (ه, ه s.o., s.th., عن from); to disguise (ه عن s.th. from s.o.); to shield, guard, protect (ه s.o., ه s.th., عن against or from); to forgive (ه على s.o. s.th.), overlook, condone s.th. (ه) done by s.o. (على) **II** = **I**; **V** to be covered, be veiled; to cover o.s., hide o.s., be concealed (عن from) **VIII** to cover o.s., hide o.s.; to be veiled, be hidden, be concealed (عن from)

ستر *sitr* pl. ستور *sutūr*, استار *astār* veil; screen; curtain, drape, window curtain; covering; cover (also *mil.*); protection, shelter, guard, shield; pretext, excuse

سترة *sutra* pl. ستر *sutar* jacket; tunic

سترى *sutarī* (*eg.*) clown, buffoon

ستار *sitār* pl. ستر *sutur* veil, screen; covering; curtain, drape; pretext, excuse | الستار الحديدى the Iron Curtain (*pol.*); الستار الفضى (*fiḍḍī*) motion-picture screen; ستار من النار (النيران) barrage (*mil.*); رفع الستار عن الشىء to disclose, unveil s.th. (also a monument); من وراء الستار behind the scenes, backstage (fig.)

الستار *as-sattār* the Veiler, the Coverer (attribute of God)

ستارة *sitāra* pl. ستائر *satā'ir*[2] veil; screen; curtain, drape, window curtain; cover, covering

تستر *tasattur* cover (*mil.*)

○ ساتر *sātir* screen, folding screen

مستور *mastūr* hidden, invisible; masked; chaste; (one) having a blameless record (*Isl. Law*); pl. مساتير *masātīr*[2] hidden, secret things

متستر *mutasattir* ○ anonymous

مستتر *mustatir* hidden, concealed, latent; understood, implied (pronoun)

ستف **II** to stack up, store up, stow (ه goods); to arrange

تستيف *tastīf* stacking, stowing, storage

سته *sath, sith, satah* pl. استاه *astāh* buttocks, backside

سجارة، *sigāra* pl. *-āt*, سجائر *sagā'ir*[2], سجاير *sagāyir*[2] (Eg. spelling) cigarette

اسجح *asjaḥ*[2], f. سجحاء *sajḥā'*[2] well-shaped, shapely, beautiful

سجد *sajada u* (سجود *sujūd*) to bow down, bow in worship; to throw o.s. down, prostrate o.s. (ل before); to worship (لله God)

سجدة *sajda* pl. *sajadāt* prostration in prayer | احد السجدة *aḥad as-s.* Whitsunday (*Chr.*)

سجود *sujūd* prostration, adoration, worship; also pl. of ساجد *sājid* (see below)

سجاد *sajjād* pl. *-ūn* worshiper (of God)

سجادة *sajjāda*, coll. سجاد *sajjād* pl. سجاجيد *sajājīd*[2] prayer rug; rug, carpet | صاحب السجادة and شيخ السجادة title of the leaders of certain dervish orders in their capacity of inheritors of the founder's prayer rug

مسجد *masjid* pl. مساجد *masājid*[2] mosque | مسجد جامع (*jāmi'*) large mosque, mosque where the Friday prayer is conducted; المسجد الحرام (*ḥarām*) the Holy Mosque in Mecca; المسجد الاقصى (*aqṣā*) name of a mosque on Jerusalem's Temple Square;

المسجدان the two Mosques (of Mecca and Medina)

ساجد *sājid* pl. سجد *sujjad*, سجود *sujūd* prostrate in adoration, worshiping

[1]سجر *sajara u* to fire up, heat (ه a stove, an oven, etc.) II to cause to overflow (ه water)

مسجر *musajjar* long and flowing (of hair)

[2]سجارة look up alphabetically

سجس II to upset (ه s.o.)

سجع *saja'a a* (*saj'*) to coo (pigeon); to speak in rhymed prose II to speak in rhymed prose

سجع *saj'* rhymed prose

سجعة *saj'a* a passage of rhymed prose

ساجع *sāji'* composer of rhymed prose

سجف *sajf*, *sijf* pl. اسجاف *asjāf*, سجوف *sujūf* curtain, veil

سجاف *sijāf* pl. سجف *sujuf* curtain, veil

سجق (Turk. *sucuk*) *sujuq* sausage | سجق محمر (*muḥammar*) fried, or grilled, sausage

سجل II to register, enter (ه s.th.), make an entry (ه of s.th.); to note down, record (ه s.th.), make a note of (ه); to have (ه s.th.) recorded, put (ه s.th.) on record, make a deposition or statement for the official records; to document, prove by documentary evidence (ه s.th.); to give evidence (ه of s.th.); to score (ه s.th., e.g., اصابة a hit); to put down, write down, book (على ه s.th. to s.o.'s debit); to record (ه s.th., said of an apparatus; also, e.g., فى الشرائط المسجلة on tape); to capture, catch (ه a scene); to set (ه a record; *athlet.*); to register (ه a letter); to enter (ه s.th.) in the commercial register; to have (ه an invention) patented, secure a patent (ه on) | سجل على نفسه ان to go on record for (doing or being s.th.) III to rival, contend; to dispute, debate (ه with s.o.); to contest (ه s.o.'s right ه to s.th.) | ساجله الحديث (*ḥadīṯa*) to draw s.o. into a conversation, have a talk with s.o.

سجل *sijill* pl. *-āt* scroll; register; list, index; سجلات records, archives | السجل التجارى (*tijārī*) commercial register; السجل الذهبي (*ḏahabī*) Golden Book; سجل الزيارات visitors' book, guest book; سجل التشريفات list of visitors (*dipl.*); سجل (سجلات) الاطيان or السجل العقارى cadastre, land register; (*'aqārī*) do.

تسجيل *tasjīl* pl. *-āt* entering, entry, registration; documentation; authentication; booking; recording; tape-recording; registering (of mail) | تسجيل عقارى (*'aqārī*) entry in the land register; آلة تسجيل الصوت (*t. aṣ-ṣaut*) tape recorder

سجال *sijāl* contest, competition with alternate success | كانت الحرب بينهم سجالا (*ḥarb*) their battle had its ups and downs, they fought each other with alternate success

مساجلة *musājala* pl. *-āt* contest, competition; discussion, talk

مسجل *musajjil* pl. *-ūn* registrar; notary public; (pl. *-āt*) tape recorder | شريط مسجل pl. شرائط مسجلة magnetic tape; مسجل الكلية *m. al-kullīya* secretary of the faculty

مسجل *musajjal* registered, etc. (see II) | رسالة مسجلة registered letter; مراسلات مسجلة (*murāsalāt*) registered mail; اطنان مسجلة register tons; حفلة مسجلة (*ḥafla*) concert of recorded music

سجم *sajama u* (سجوم *sujūm*, سجام *sijām*) to flow, stream, well forth (tears, water); — *sajama u i* (*sajm*, سجوم *sujūm*, سجمان *sajamān*) to pour forth (ه water), shed (ه tears) IV to shed (ه tears) VII to flow, stream, well forth (water); to be fluent, elegant (speech); to be harmonious; to harmonize, be in keeping (مع with)

انسجام *insijām* fluency; harmony; order

منسجم *munsajim* harmonious

سجن **sajana** *u* (*sajn*) to jail, imprison (ه s.o.)

سجن *sajn* detention, imprisonment

سجن *sijn* pl. سجون *sujūn* prison, jail

سجين *sajīn* pl. سجناء *sujanā'*², سجنى *sajnā* imprisoned, jailed, captive; prisoner, prison inmate, convict

سجينة *sajīna* pl. *-āt* female prisoner

سجان *sajjān* jailer, prison guard, warden

مسجون *masjūn* pl. مساجين *masājīn*² imprisoned, jailed, captive; prisoner, prison inmate, convict

سجا (سجو) **sajā** *u* (سجو *sajw*, سجو *sujūw*) to be calm, quiet, tranquil (night, sea) **II** to cover with a winding sheet, to shroud (الميت *al-mayyita* the deceased) **V** to cover o.s. (ب with a garment)

سجية *sajīya* pl. *-āt*, سجايا *sajāyā* nature, natural disposition, temper, character; pl. characteristics, traits | عن سجية of one's own accord, spontaneously

ساج *sājin* quiet, calm, tranquil; dark (night)

مسجى *musajjan* covered with a winding sheet, shrouded (corpse); laid out (corpse)

سح **saḥḥa** *u i* (*saḥḥ*, سحوح *suḥūḥ*) to flow down, flow, run, stream | سحت السماء *saḥḥat is-samā'* it rained cats and dogs

عين سحاحة *'ain saḥḥāḥa* tearful eye

سحب **saḥaba** *a* (*saḥb*) to trail on the ground, drag along (ه s.th.); to withdraw (ه, ه s.o., s.th., also, e.g., a measure, an order, etc.); to pull out (هم troops, عن from); to take away (ه من from s.o. s.th.), strip, dispossess, divest (ه من s.o. of); to draw (ه water); to take out, withdraw (ه money, from an account); to draw (ه a bill of exchange, a lot); to unsheathe, draw (ه a sword); to apply, make applicable (ه على s.th. to; said of a law or statute) | سحب العمل به على (*'amala*) to extend the applicability of s.th. to ... **VII** to drag o.s. along, struggle along; to retreat, withdraw, pull out, fall back (من from); to be drawn out; to be applied (على to; of a law or statute)

سحب *saḥb* withdrawal (of troops, of measures, of rights, of money from an account, etc.); (pl. سحوبات *suḥūbāt*) drawing (in a lottery)

سحاب *saḥāb* (coll.) clouds

سحابة *saḥāba* (n. un.) pl. سحب *suḥub*, سحائب *saḥā'ib*² cloud; (pl. *-āt*) umbrella (*magr.*); سحابة *saḥābata* during, in the course of | سحابة النهار (اليوم) *saḥābata n-nahār* (*l-yaum*) all day long; سرنا سحابة يومنا *sirnā saḥābata yauminā* we have been traveling all day; سحابة اربعة قرون in the course of four centuries

سحابة *suḥāba* film on the eye

سحاب *saḥḥāb* (*Syr., Pal.*) zipper, slide fastener

مسحب *masḥab*: مسحب الهواء *m. al-hawā'* source of the breeze or draft; draft (of air)

انسحاب *insiḥāb* withdrawal, retreat, pulling out, evacuation (esp. *mil.*); resignation; stretching, extension

ساحب *sāḥib* drawer (of a bill of exchange)

المسحوب عليه *al-masḥūb 'alaihi* drawee (of a bill of exchange)

سحت **suḥt**, *suḥut* pl. اسحات *asḥāt* s.th. forbidden or banned; illegal possessions, ill-gotten property

سحتوت **saḥtūt** Eg. square measure of 0.304 m^2 (= $^1/_{24}$ *sahm*); — *suḥtūt* penny

سحج **saḥaja** *a* (*saḥj*) to scrape off, shave off, scratch off, rub off (ه s.th.); to graze, abrade (ه the skin), strip off (ه s.th.) **II** to scrape off, abrade, strip off (ه s.th.)

مسحج *misḥaj* pl. مساحج *masāḥij*² plane (tool)

مسحجة *misḥaja* pl. مساحج *masāḥij*² planing machine, planer

مسحاج *misḥāj* pl. مساحيج *masāḥīj*² plane (tool)

مسحوج *masḥūj* raw, sore (like a skin abrasion)

سحر **saḥara** *a* (*siḥr*) to bewitch, charm, enchant, infatuate, fascinate (▲, ● s.o., s.th.); to wheedle, coax (● s.o.) **II** = **I**; **V** tc have a light meal (shortly before daybreak)

سحر *saḥr*, *suḥr* pl. سحور *suḥūr*, اسحار *asḥār* lungs, pulmonary region of the body

سحر *siḥr* bewitchment, beguilement, enchantment, fascination; — (pl. اسحار *asḥār*, سحور *suḥūr*) sorcery, witchcraft, magic; charm (of a woman)

سحرى *siḥrī* magic(al) | فانوس سحرى (*fānūs*) magic lantern, slide projector

سحر *saḥar* pl. اسحار *asḥār* time before daybreak, early morning, dawn

سحور *saḥūr* last meal before daybreak during the month of Ramadan

سحار *saḥḥār* pl. *-ūn* sorcerer, magician, wizard, charmer

سحارة *saḥḥāra* sorceress, witch

سحارة *saḥḥāra* pl. *-āt* culvert; (pl. سحاحير *saḥāḥīr*²) case, crate, chest, box

مساحر *masāḥir*²: انتفخت مساحره (*intafakat*) his lungs became inflated (out of fear or pride)

ساحر *sāḥir* charming, enchanting; (pl. *-ūn*, سحرة *saḥara*, سحار *suḥḥār*) sorcerer, enchanter, magician, wizard, charmer

ساحرة *sāḥira* pl. *-āt*, سواحر *sawāḥir*² sorceress, witch

سحق **saḥaqa** *a* (*saḥq*) to crush (▲, ● s.o., s.th.); to pound, bruise, powder, pulverize (▲ s.th.); to annihilate, wipe out (▲ s.th., e.g., an army); to wear out (▲ clothing); — *saḥiqa a*, *saḥuqa u* (*suḥq*) to be distant, far away, remote **II** to crush; to annihilate, destroy **V** and **VII** to be crushed, be pounded, be bruised, be pulverized

سحق *saḥq* crushing, bruising, pulverization; (pl. سحوق *suḥūq*) worn garment, rag

سحق *suḥq*, *suḥuq* distance, remoteness; depth, vastness (of an abyss) | سحقا له *suḥqan lahū* away with him! to hell with him!

سحيق *saḥīq* far away, distant, remote; deep, bottomless (abyss, depth)

مساحقة *musāḥaqa* and سحاق *siḥāq* tribady, Lesbianism

انسحاق القلب *insiḥāq al-qalb* contrition, penitence, repentance

ساحق *sāḥiq* crushing; overwhelming (majority)

مسحوق *masḥūq* ground, grated (bread, nutmeg, etc.); (pl. مساحيق *masāḥīq*²) powder | مسحوق الفحم *m. al-faḥm* coal dust

منسحق القلب *munsaḥiq al-qalb* contrite, penitent, repentant

سحل **saḥala** *a* (*saḥl*) to scrape off, shave off, peel (▲ s.th.); to smooth, make smooth (▲ s.th.); to plane (▲ s.th.); to file (▲ s.th.)

سحالة *suḥāla* filings, file dust

سحلية *siḥlīya* pl. سحال *saḥālin* lizard (*eg.*)

مسحل *misḥal* pl. مساحل *masāḥil*² tool for smoothing, plane; file

ساحل *sāḥil* pl. سواحل *sawāḥil*² littoral, coast, seashore; (*Eg.*) river harbor, anchorage (on the Nile) | خفر السواحل *kafar as-s.* coast guard; لا ساحل له (*sāḥila*) shoreless

ساحلى *sāḥilī* coastal, littoral; (pl. سواحلة *sawāḥila*) coastal inhabitant; Swahili

سحلب *saḥlab* salep (dried tuber of various species of Orchis); a sweet drink made of salep

سحم *saḥam* blackness, black color

سحمة *suḥma* blackness, black color

سحام *suḥām* blackness, black color

اسحم *asḥam*², f. سحماء *saḥmā'*², pl. سحم *suḥm* black

سحن *saḥana a* (*saḥn*) to crush, pound, bruise, grind (ه s.th.); to smooth by rubbing (ه s.th.)

سحنة *saḥna* and *saḥana* pl. *saḥanāt*, سحن *suḥan* (external) appearance, look(s); facial expression, air, mien

مسحنة *misḥana* pl. مساحن *masāḥin*² pestle

سحاءة *siḥā'a* pl. سحايا *saḥaya* cerebral membrane, cortex

سحائى *siḥā'ī* meningeal | مرض الالتهاب السحائى (*maraḍ al-ilt.*) meningitis

مسحاة *misḥāh* pl. مساح *masāḥin* iron shovel, spade

سختيان *suḵtiyān*, *siḵtiyān* morocco (leather)

سخر *saḵira a* (*saḵar*, *saḵr*, *suḵur*, *suḵr*, سخرة *suḵra*, مسخر *masḵar*) to laugh, scoff, jeer, sneer (من or ب at), mock, ridicule, deride (من or ب s.o., s.th.), make fun (من or ب of) II to subject, make subservient (ه s.o., ه s.th., ل to or for the purpose of); to make serviceable (ه ل s.th. to), employ, utilize, turn to profitable account (ه ل s.th. for), make use (ه، ه of, ل for); to exploit (ه s.o., ه s.th., ل for) V to reduce to servitude, subjugate (ه s.o.); to scoff, jeer, sneer

سخرة *suḵra* laughingstock, target of ridicule; corvée, statute labor, forced labor | رجال السخرة serfs, bondsmen; اعمال السخرة forced labor, slave labor

سخرى *suḵrī*, *siḵrī* laughingstock, target of ridicule; corvée, statute labor, forced labor

سخرية *suḵrīya* scorn, derision, mockery, irony; laughingstock, object of ridicule

مسخرة *masḵara* pl. *-āt*, مساخر *masāḵir*² object of ridicule, laughingstock; ridiculous, droll, ludicrous; masquerade

تسخير *tasḵīr* subjugation, subjection; exploitation

مسخر *musaḵḵir* oppressor

سخط *saḵiṭa a* (*saḵaṭ*) to be annoyed (على or ه، ه at s.o., at s.th.), be displeased, be angry (على or ه with s.o.), resent (على or ه s.th.) IV to discontent, embitter (ه s.o.); to anger, exasperate, enrage (ه s.o.) V = I

سخط *suḵuṭ*, *suḵṭ*, *saḵaṭ* discontent, annoyance, displeasure, indignation, anger, irritation, exasperation; wrath, bitterness, grudge, resentment

مسخطة *masḵaṭa* pl. مساخط *masāḵiṭ*² object of annoyance, of wrath, of anger

مسخوط *masḵūṭ* loathsome, hated, odious; (pl. مساخيط *masāḵīṭ*²) (*eg.*) idol

تسخط *tasaḵḵuṭ* annoyance, displeasure, anger, wrath

سخف *saḵufa u* (*suḵf*, سخافة *saḵāfa*) to be feeble (wit); to be stupid, foolish

سخف *saḵf*, *suḵf* feeble-mindedness, dimwittedness, imbecility, idiocy; nonsense, foolishness, folly

سخيف *saḵīf* pl. سخاف *siḵāf* stupid, fatuous, simple-minded; absurd, silly, ridiculous, foolish; despicable, inferior; (pl. سخفاء *suḵafā'*²) fool

سخافة *saḵāfa* feeble-mindedness, dimwittedness; (pl. *-āt*) folly, silly thing to do, childish prank

سخائف *saḵā'if*² silly things

سَخْلة saḵla pl. سِخَال siḵāl lamb

سخم II to make black, blacken with soot, besmut (ه s.th.) | سخم بصدره (bi-ṣadrihī) to irritate s.o., make s.o. angry V to hate (على s.o.), harbor resentment (على against s.o.), be angry (على with)

سخم saḵam blackness

سُخْمة suḵma blackness; hatred, resentment, ill will

سخام suḵām soot, smut

سخيمة saḵīma pl. سخائم saḵā'im² hatred, resentment, ill will

سخن saḵuna u, saḵana u and saḵina a (سخونة suḵūna, سخانة saḵāna, سخنة suḵna) to be or become hot or warm; to warm (up); to be feverish II to make hot, to heat, warm (ه s.th.) IV = II

سخن suḵn hot, warm

سخانة saḵāna heat, warmth

سخونة suḵūna heat, warmth

○ سخان saḵḵān, سخان مياه s. miyāh boiler, hot-water tank

○ سخانة saḵḵāna hot-water bottle | سخانة الحمام s. al-ḥammām bath heater, geyser

سخانات saḵḵānāt hot springs

ساخن sāḵin pl. سخان suḵḵān hot, warm

سخا saḵā u, سخی saḵiya a (سخاء saḵā') and سخو saḵuwa u (سخاوة saḵāwa) to be liberal, generous (ب with s.th. toward s.o.); to grant, award (ب s.th., على to s.o.), confer, bestow (ب s.th., على upon s.o.) V to show o.s. generous, display liberality; to endeavor to be liberal or generous VI = V

سخاء saḵā' liberality, munificence, generosity

سخی saḵīy pl. اسخياء asḵiyā'² liberal, openhanded, generous; giving generously (ب s.th.), being lavish (ب with) | سخية

(s.) سخی النفس عن الشیء ample funds; اموال an-nafs) only too glad to relinquish or give up s.th.

سخاوة saḵāwa generosity

سد sadda u (sadd) to plug up, close up, stop up (ه s.th.); to clog, congest (ه s.th.); to bar, obstruct, block up, barricade (ه s.th., ه على to s.o. s.th.); to block, blockade (ه s.th.); to cork, plug, stopper (ه s.th.); to pay, defray, settle, cover (ه s.th., esp. expenses, a claim, debts, etc.); to fulfill, satisfy, meet (a claim, and the like) | سد ثغرة (ṯuḡratan) to fill a gap, close a breach; سد ثلمة (ṯulmatan) to fill a gap; سد خلة (ḵallatan) to remedy a shortcoming; سد حاجته (ḥājatahū) to meet s.o.'s need, provide for s.o.; سد رمقه (ramaqahū) to keep s.o. or o.s. barely alive, eke out an existence; to provide s.o. with a bare existence; to allay s.o.'s hunger; سد مسده (masaddahū) to fill s.o.'s place, replace s.o.; سد مطامعه to satisfy or fulfill s.o.'s claims; سد فراغا (farāḡan) to fill a gap; سد النواقص to remove or remedy deficiencies; — sadda i (سدود sudūd, سداد sadād) to be sound, right, in proper condition; to hit the right thing, say or do the right thing; to be apposite, be to the point II to block, bar, obstruct (ه s.th.); to pay, defray, settle, cover (ه expenses, debts, etc.); to guide (ه s.o. to), show (ه s.o.) the right way (نحو to); to direct (الی ه s.th. to), point, level (الی ه s.th. at); to aim (الی at); to sight, take aim by a sight; to focus (الی on; phot.); to draw a bead (الی or نحو on s.th.) | سدد دینا (dainan) to pay or settle a debt; سدد عجزا ('ajzan) to cover a deficit; سدد خطاه (ḵuṭāhu) to guide s.o.'s steps IV to hit the right thing, say or do the right thing; to be apposite, be to the point V to be guided, be directed, be shown (الی to) VII to be blocked, be obstructed, be plugged up, become or be clogged or congested

سد *sadd* plugging, closing, stopping up; obstruction, barring, barricading; blocking; defrayment (of costs), payment, settlement (of a debt, of expenses); fulfillment, satisfaction (of a claim, etc.); — *sadd, sudd* pl. سدود *sudūd*, أسداد *asdād* obstruction, block, obstacle; barrier; rampart, bank, mound; dike; dam; weir; barrage, river dam; bar, rail; hurdle (*athlet.*); bulwark (fig.) | السد العالى (*'ālī*) the High Dam (near Aswān); سد المناطيد balloon barrage (*mil.*); حارة السد blind alley, dead end

سدة *sadda* block, barrier; obstruction, obstacle; barricade; dam | السدة الشريانية (*širyānīya*) embolism (*med.*)

سدة *sudda* pl. سدد *sudad* gate, door; threshold; seat; couch, divan | السدة الرسولية (البابوية) (*rasūlīya*) the Holy See

سدد *sadad* obstruction, clogging (of a pipe)

سداد *sadād* payment, defrayment, settlement, discharge, liquidation; the proper, right thing to do, the apposite thing to say; appropriateness, appositeness (of a remark), lucky hand (in one's actions) | تحت السداد outstanding, due, unpaid (*com.*); بسداد appropriately, appositely; سداد الرأى *s. ar-ra'y* levelheadedness

سداد *sudād* obstruction in the nose

سداد *sidād* pl. أسدة *asidda* plug, stopper, cork | ○ سداد التوصيل plug (*el.*)

سدادة *sidāda* plug, stopper, cork; ○ sight (of a gun)

سديد *sadīd* hitting the target (arrow, spear); apposite, pat, pertinent, relevant, right, correct (answer, view)

أسد *asadd*[2] more apposite, more relevant

تسديد *tasdīd* payment, defrayment, settlement, discharge, liquidation | تحت التسديد outstanding, due, unpaid (*com.*)

ساد *sādd* obstructive

مسدود *masdūd* closed (circuit; *el.*)

□ سدب (*eg.*; *sadab*) = سذاب *sadāb*

سدر *sadira a* (*sadar*, سدارة *sadāra*) to be dazzled (eye); to be confused, bewildered, startled, dazed; to be deluded

سدر *sidr* (coll.; n. un. ة) pl. سدر *sidar*, *-āt*, سدور *sudūr* a variety of Christ's-thorn (Zizyphus spina Christi; *bot.*); lotus tree | سدرة المنتهى *s. al-muntahā* the lotus tree in the Seventh Heaven; بلغ سدرة المنتهى to attain the highest goal, achieve ultimate results

سدارة *sidāra* pl. سدائر *sadā'ir*[2] an Iraqi headgear, commonly of black velvet; overseas cap

سيدارة *sīdāra* pl. *-āt* = سدارة *sidāra*

سادر *sādir* reckless (فى in s.th.)

سدس II to make sixfold (ه s.th.); to multiply by six (ه s.th.); to make hexagonal, make hexangular (ه s.th.)

سدس *suds, sudus* pl. أسداس *asdās* one-sixth

سداسى *sudāsī* sixfold; consisting of six parts

السادس *as-sādis* the sixth

مسدس *musaddas* hexagonal; hexagon; hexahedral; hexahedron; (pl. *-āt*) revolver, sixshooter | مسدس اشارة *m. išāra* Very pistol

مسدسة *musaddasa* pistol, gun, revolver

سدف *sadaf* pl. أسداف *asdāf* darkness, twilight, dusk

سدفة *sudfa* pl. سدف *sudaf* darkness, twilight, dusk; curtain

سدل *sadala u i* (*sadl*) to let (ه s.th.) hang down or fall down; to let down, drop, lower (ه على s.th. on); pass. *sudila* to hang down (على on) II and IV = I; V to hang down, be lowered, be down **VII** to descend (على on)

سدل *sidl, sudl* pl. سدول *sudūl,* اسدال *asdāl* veil, curtain

سدم **VII** to dry up (spring)

سدم *sadam* sorrow, sadness, affliction, grief

سديم *sadīm* pl. سدم *sudum* mist, haze; nebula (*astron.*)

سديمى *sadīmī* nebular; nebulous

سدانة *sidāna* office of gatekeeper or custodian (of a shrine, specif. of the Kaaba)

سادن *sādin* pl. سدنة *sadana* custodian, gatekeeper of the Kaaba; sexton, sacristan (*Chr.*); keeper, curator; pl. سدنة crew (of a machine gun, of a tank, etc.)

(سدو and سدى) **II** to confer (ه الى a benefit on s.o.) **IV** to confer (ل or ه الى a benefit on s.o.); to render, perform, do (ه s.th.) | اسدى اليه خدمة (*kidma*) to render s.o. a service; اسدى اليه الارشادات (*iršādāt*) to make suggestions to s.o., advise s.o.; اسدى الشكر له (*šukr*) to extend one's thanks to s.o., thank s.o.; اسدى فائدة to be beneficial; اسدى اليه (له or) النصح (*nuṣḥ*) to give s.o. (a word of) advice; اسدى اليه يدا (*yadan*) to do s.o. a favor

سدى *sadan* pl. اسدية *asdiya* warp (of a fabric); a continuous, prevailing characteristic or trait, thread (of a story, of an argument, etc.)

سداة *sadāh* warp (of a fabric); a continuous, prevailing characteristic or trait, thread (of a story, of an argument, etc.)

سدى *sudan* in vain, futilely, to no end, uselessly | ذهب سدى to be in vain, futile, useless

سذاب *sadāb* rue, herb of grace (*bot.*)

سذبى *sadabī* of the rue

سذاجة *sadāja* simplicity; innocence, ingenuousness, naïveté; homeliness, plainness; guilelessness

ساذج *sādaj, sādij* pl. سذج *suddaj* simple; plain, unicolored, uniform (fabric); innocent, ingenuous, naïve; plain, homely; artless, guileless, candid, frank (character); primitive

سر[1] (Pers. *sar* head) formerly in compounds: head, chief; سردار *sirdār* (*Eg.*) supreme commander; commanding general; سرعسكر *sar'askar* general (in the former Ottoman army); سرياوران *saryāwarān* adjutant general

سر[2] *sarra u* (سرور *surūr*, تسرة *tasirra*, مسرة *masarra*) to make happy, gladden, delight, cheer (ه s.o.); pass. *surra* (سرور *surūr*) to be happy, glad, delighted (ل or من or ب at), take pleasure (ل or من or ب in) **II** to make happy, gladden, delight, cheer (ه s.o.) **III** to confide a secret (ه to s.o.) | ساره فى اذنه (*udnihī*) to whisper in s.o.'s ear **IV** to make happy, gladden, delight, cheer (ه s.o.); to keep secret, hide, conceal, disguise (ه s.th.); to tell confidentially, confide (ب or ه الى to s.o. s.th.); to tell under one's breath, whisper (ب or ه الى to s.o. s.th.) | اسر فى اذنه (*udnihī*) to whisper in s.o.'s ear (ه s.th.) **V** تسرى *tasarrā* (and تسرر *tasarrara*) to take (ب or ها a woman) as concubine (سرية *surrīya*) **X** to try to hide; to hide, be hidden (عن from); to take as concubine (ها a woman)

سر *sirr* pl. اسرار *asrār* secret; secret thought; heart, inmost; secrecy; mystery; sacrament (*Chr.*); underlying reason (of s.th.); سرا *sirran* secretly, privately | سرا وعلانية (*'alāniyatan*) secretly and publicly; سر الليل *s. al-lail* watchword, password; اسرار القرآن the secret meaning of the Koran; كاتب السر secretary; كاتم السر do.; كلمة السر *kalimat as-s.* watchword, password; بسركم or فى سركم to your health! cheerio! skoal! فى سره secretly, inwardly, in his heart; اتعب سره *at'aba sirrahū* to trouble, worry, bother, harass s.o.; اجرى سرا *ajrā sirran* to dispense a sacrament (*Chr.*); قدس الله سره *qaddasa llāhu sirrahū* may God hallow his secret! (eulogy after the name of a deceased Muslim saint)

سرى **sirrī** secret; private; confidential; mysterious, cryptic; sacramental (*Chr.*) | الامراض السرية venereal diseases

سرية **sirrīya** secret; secretiveness

سر **surr** pl. اسرة *asirra* umbilical cord

سرة **surra** pl. *-āt*, سرر *surar* navel, umbilicus; center

سرى **surrī** umbilical | الحبل السرى (*ḥabl*) umbilical cord

سرر **surur**, *sirar* umbilical cord

سرر **surur** line of the palm or forehead

سرار **sarār**: سرار الشهر *s. aš-šahr* last night of the lunar month

سرار **sirār** pl. اسرة *asirra*, اسارير *asārīr*[2] line of the palm or forehead; pl. features, facial expression, air, also اسارير الوجه *a. al-wajh*

سرور **surūr** joy, happiness, delight, pleasure; glee, gaiety, hilarity, mirth

سرير **sarīr** pl. اسرة *asirra*, سرر *surur*, سراير *sarāyir*[2] bedstead, bed; throne, elevated seat

سريرة **sarīra** pl. سرائر *sarā'ir*[2] secret; secret thought; mind, heart, soul | صفاء السريرة *ṣafā' as-s.* clearness of conscience; طيب السريرة *ṭayyib as.-s.* guileless, simplehearted,

سراء **sarrā'**[2] happiness, prosperity | فى السراء والضراء (*ḍarrā'*) in good and bad days, for better or for worse

سرية **surrīya** pl. سرارى *sarārīy* concubine

مسرة **masarra** pl. *-āt* joy, happiness, delight, pleasure; glee, gaiety, hilarity, mirth

مسرة **misarra** pl. مسار *masārr*[2] speaking tube; telephone

تسر **tasarrin** concubinage

استسرار **istisrār** concubinage

سار **sārr** gladdening, gratifying, joyous, glad, cheering, delightful

مسرور **masrūr** glad, happy, delighted (ب at), pleased (ب with)

مسر **musirr** gratifying, delightful, pleasant

مستسر **mustasarr** place of concealment

سرادق **surādiq** pl. *-āt* large tent, canopy, pavilion

سراط **sirāṭ** = صراط *ṣirāṭ* way, path, road

سراى **sarāy** palace

سراية **sarāya** pl. *-āt* palace | السراية الصفراء (*ṣafrā'*) insane asylum (*eg.*)

[1]سرب **sariba** *a* (*sarab*) to flow; to run out, leak **II** to send in groups or batches (ه, ه s.o., s.th., الى to) **V** to flow; to run out, flow off, escape; to sneak away, slink away, steal away; to stream, penetrate (الى into), infiltrate (الى s.th.); to creep (فى into); to sneak, slip, steal (الى into, among); to creep along, flow along, glide along; to seep through, leak out (الى to, of a report); to spread, circulate, be passed around (news) **VII** to hide, crawl into its lair (animal)

سرب **sirb** pl. اسراب *asrāb* herd, flock, bevy, covey, swarm; squadron, group, wing, formation, flight (of aircraft); heart, mind | سرب من النحل (*naḥl*) swarm of bees; هادئ السرب calm, composed, confident

سرب **sarab** pl. اسراب *asrāb* burrow, hole, den, lair (of an animal); underground passage; tunnel, conduit

سربة *surba* pl. سرب *surab* herd, flock, bevy, covey, swarm

سراب *sarāb* mirage, fata morgana; phantom; sewage

مسرب *masrab* pl. مسارب *masārib*[2] course (taken by s.th.); river bed; drain, sewer

سارب *sārib* conspicuous, visible

ساربة *sāriba* pl. سوارب *sawārib*[2] reptile

[2]اسرب look up alphabetically

سربل *sarbala* to clothe (ه s.o.) with a *sirbāl* (q.v.); to clothe, dress (ب ه s.o. in or with); to cover, wrap (ه s.th., ب with) II *tasarbala* to put on a *sirbāl* (q.v.); to put on, wear (ه a garment); to be clothed, clad, garbed (ب in, also fig.); to wrap o.s. (ب in); to dress up (ب in)

سربال *sirbāl* pl. سرابيل *sarābīl*[2] shirt; coat of mail; garment

متسربل *mutasarbil*: متسربل بالشباب blessed with youthfulness, evincing youthful freshness

[1]سرج *saraja* to braid, plait (ه the hair) II do.; to baste, tack (ه s.th.); to saddle (ه an animal) IV do.; to light (السراج the lamp)

سرج *sarj* pl. سروج *surūj* saddle

سراج *sirāj* pl. سرج *suruj* lamp, light | سراج الحركة *s. al-ḥaraka* traffic light; سراج الليل *s. al-lail* firefly, glowworm

سراجة *sirāja* saddlery, saddler's trade; glanders

سراج *sarrāj* saddler

سروجي *surūjī* saddler

سروجية *surūjīya* saddlery, saddler's trade

اسروجة *usrūja* lie, falsehood

مسرجة *misraja, masraja* pl. مسارج *masārij*[2] lamp; lampstand

[2]سيرج look up alphabetically

[3]سرجين *sirjīn* dung, manure

سرح *saraḥa a* (سروح *surūḥ*) to move away, go away, leave; to roam freely; to graze freely (cattle); to be distracted (mind); — *sariḥa a* to proceed freely, at will, without restraint | سرح ومرح (*mariḥa*) to do as one likes II to send (ه cattle) to pasture; to send, dispatch (ه s.o.); to let go (ه s.o.); to dismiss (ها a woman by divorce); to grant (ه s.o.) leave, dismiss (ه s.o.); to release from an office, discharge, fire (ه s.o.); to release, set free (ه s.o.); to let (ه the eyes) wander; to demobilize, disband (ه an army); to dispel s.o.'s (عن) worries (also سرح غمومه); to comb (ه the hair) | سرح شعره (*ša'rahū*) to comb one's hair, do one's hair; سرح نظره (*naẓarahū*) to set one's eyes on (الى) VII انسرح يفكر (*yufakkiru*) to be deep in thought, be absent-minded, allow one's thoughts to wander

سراح *sarāḥ* dismissal (of a woman by divorce); release | اطلق سراحه *aṭlaqa sarāḥahū* to release s.o., set s.o. free, set s.o. at liberty; اطلاق سراحه *iṭlāq s.* his release; مطلق السراح *muṭlaq as-s.* free, at large

سريح *sarīḥ* and بائع سريح hawker, peddler

سرحان *sirḥān* wolf

مسرح *masraḥ* pl. مسارح *masāriḥ*[2] pasture; stage, theater; scene | مسرح التمثيل theater

مسرحي *masraḥī* dramatic, theatrical, stage (adj.)

مسرحية *masraḥīya* pl. *-āt* (stage) play

تسريح *tasrīḥ* dismissal; discharge; release; demobilization; (pl. تساريح *tasārīḥ*[2]) permission, authorization

تسريحة *tasrīḥa* pl. *-āt* hairdo, coiffure

سارح *sāriḥ*: سارح مارح grazing freely, roaming freely; free and unrestrained; سارح الفكر *sāriḥ al-fikr* distracted, absent-minded

منسرح *munsariḥ*: المنسرح name of a poetic meter | منسرح الفكر *m. al-fikr* distracted, absent-minded

ساروخ *sārūḵ* pl. سوارخ *sawāriḵ*[2] rocket

سرد *sarada u* (*sard*) to pierce, perforate (ه s.th.); to carry on, continue (ه s.th., e.g., a conversation); to tell off one after another, enumerate (ه facts, events); to present, quote, detail, set forth neatly (ه s.th.) **II** to pierce, perforate (ه s.th.)

سرد *sard* enumeration; mentioning, quoting; neat, detailed presentation; recital, presentation, rendition (of an account, of a narrative, etc.); coherent, logical

سريدة *sarīda*: سريدة المولد *s. al-maulid* discourse dealing with the birth of the Prophet (during celebration of Mohammed's birthday; *tun.*)

○ مسرد *masrad* index (of a book)

سرداب *sirdāb* pl. سرادب *sarādib*[2], سراديب *sarādīb*[2] subterranean vault, cellar; basement, basement flat

سردار *sirdār* (formerly *Eg.*) supreme commander; commanding general

سرادق look up alphabetically

سردوك *sardūk* pl. سراديك *sarādīk*[2] rooster, cock (*magr.*)

سردين *sardīn* (coll.; n. un. ة) sardines

سراس *sirās* and سيراس see سيراس (alphabetically)

سرسام *sirsām* a cerebral disease

[1]سرط *sariṭa a* (*saraṭ*, سرطان *saraṭān*) and *saraṭa u i* to swallow, gulp (ه s.th.) **V** and **VIII** do.

سرطان *saraṭān* pl. *-āt* crayfish; cancer (*med.*); Cancer (*astron.*) | سرطان بحرى (*baḥrī*) lobster

[2]سراط *sirāṭ* = صراط

سرع *saruʿa u* (*siraʿ*, *saraʿ*, سرعة *surʿa*) to be quick, fast, prompt, rapid; to hurry **II** to urge (ه s.o.) to hurry; to urge on (ه an animal); to speed up, accelerate, expedite (ه s.th.) **III** to hurry, hasten, rush, run, dash (الى to); to make a beeline (الى for); to hurry (فى in, with), hasten (فى to do s.th.), do in a hurry (فى s.th.); to rush, plunge with undue haste (فى into) **IV** to be quick, fast, prompt, rapid; to hurry, hasten, rush, run, dash (الى to); to hurry (ب or فى with, in), hasten (ب or فى to do s.th.), do in a hurry (ب or فى s.th.); to accelerate, speed up, expedite (ه s.th.) **V** to hurry, hasten, rush, run, dash (الى to); to hurry (ب or فى with, in), hasten (ب or فى to do s.th.), do in a hurry (ب or فى s.th.); to be hasty, be rash (ب or فى in) **VI** to hurry, hasten, rush, run, dash (الى to)

سرع *surʿ*, *sirʿ* pl. اسراع *asrāʿ* reins

سرعة *surʿa* speed, velocity, pace; fastness, rapidity, quickness, promptness; hurry, haste | سرعة الخاطر presence of mind; سرعة التصديق credulity

سرعان ما *sarʿāna*, *sirʿāna*, *surʿāna mā* (with foll. verb) how quickly ...!; soon, before long, presently, in no time

سريع *sarīʿ* pl. سرعان *surʿān*, سراع *sirāʿ* fast, quick, prompt, rapid, speedy, expeditious, swift, nimble; السريع name of a poetic meter; express train; سريعا *sarīʿan* fast, quickly, rapidly, speedily, promptly | سريع التأثر *s. at-taʾaṯṯur* easy to impress, easily affected, sensitive; سريع الخاطر quick-witted; ○ سريع التردد *s. at-taraddud* high-frequency (*el.*); سريع الزوال *s. az-zawāl* ephemeral, fleeting, transient; سريع التصديق credulous; سريع الطلق (الطلقات) *s. aṭ-ṭalq* quick-firing, rapid-fire; سريع العطب *s. al-ʿaṭab* fragile; سريع التنقل *s. at-tanaqqul* mobile, maneuverable, easily manageable

اسرع *asra'*[2] faster, quicker, more rapid | ما اسرع ان رأيته *mā asra'a an ra'aituhū* before long I saw him, it did not take very long before I saw him

سراعا *sirā'an* quickly, in a hurry

اسراع *isrā'* acceleration, speed-up; hurry

تسرع *tasarru'* hurry, haste; hastiness, rashness, precipitance

متسرع *mutasarri'* quick, fast, prompt, rapid; hasty, rash, precipitate

سرعسكر see سر[1]

سرف IV to exceed all bounds, be immoderate, be extravagant (فى in, at), exaggerate, overdo (فى s.th.); to waste, squander, dissipate, spend lavishly (ه, فى s.th., esp. money)

سرف *saraf* and اسراف *isrāf* intemperance, immoderateness, exaggeration; waste, dissipation, extravagance, prodigality

مسرف *musrif* immoderate, intemperate, excessive; extravagant, wasteful, prodigal

سرق *saraqa* i (*saraq, sariq,* سرقة *saraqa, sariqa,* سرقان *sarqān*) to steal, pilfer, filch (ه من or ه ه from s.o. s.th.); to rob (ه من or ه ه s.o. of s.th.) **II** to accuse of theft, call a thief (ه s.o.) **III** سارق النظر اليه (*naẓara*) or سارقه النظر to steal a glance at s.o., glance furtively at s.o.; سارق النوم (*nauma*) to take a short nap **VII** pass. of **I** **VIII** to steal, filch, pilfer (ه من s.th. from s.o.); to steal (الى into) | استرق السمع (*sam'a*) to eavesdrop; to monitor (radio, telephone, etc.); سارق النظر اليه = استرق النظر اليه; استرق الانفاس to gasp, pant

سرقة *sariqa* stealing, filching, pilfering; robbery; (pl. *-āt*) theft, larceny

سراق *sarrāq* thief

سارق *sāriq* pl. *-ūn,* سرقة *saraqa,* سراق *surrāq,* f. سارقة *sāriqa* pl. سوارق *sawāriq*[2] thief

مسروقات *masrūqāt* stolen goods

منسرق *munsariq*: منسرق القوة *m. al-qūwa* debilitated, exhausted

سرقسطة *saraqusṭa*[2] Zaragoza (city in NE Spain)

سرقين *sirqīn* dung, manure

سرك[1] (Fr. *cirque*) *sirk* circus

سركى[2] (Turk. *sergi*) *sarkī* (*com.*) bill of exchange payable to the bearer

سرم *surm* pl. اسرام *asrām* anus

سرمد *sarmad* endless duration, eternity

سرمدى *sarmadī* eternal, without beginning or end

سرنديب *sarandīb*[2] Ceylon

سرو[1] *sarw* (coll.; n. un. ة) evergreen cypress (Cupressus sempervirens L.; *bot.*)

سرو[2] **II** سرى عنه (or عن قلبه) to rid s.o. of worries, and the like, dispel s.o.'s worries (also ه worries); pass. سرى عنه and سرى عن نفسه (*surriya*) to leave s.o. (grief, sorrow, fear, and the like); to regain one's composure, feel at peace again (after anger, fear or excitement); his anxiety or unrest left him; he found relaxation; he was cheered up, his spirits were raised **VII** انسرى عنه = سرى عنه (*surriya*)

سرى *sarīy* pl. سرواء *surawā'*[2], اسرياء *asriyā'*[2], سراة *sarāh* high-ranking, high; high-minded, noble; distinguished personality, notable; pl. سراة elite, leading class, the upper crust; see سرى[1]

سراة *sarāh* pl. سروات *sarawāt* hill; back; chief, head; see also سرى *sarīy* | سروات القوم *s. al-qaum* the leaders of the people

تسرية *tasriya* pl. *-āt* diversion, amusement, pastime

سروال *sirwāl,* سرويل *sirwīl* pl. سراويل *sarāwīl*[2] trousers, pants; drawers; panties

[1]سرى *sarā i* (سرى *suran*, سريان *sarayān*, مسرى *masran*) to travel by night; to set out, depart by night; to circulate; to flow (electric current); to emanate, go out (من from); to spread; to be valid, have validity, be effective, be in, or come into, force (على for), have or take effect (على on); to apply, be applicable (على to); to penetrate (في s.th.), enter deeply (في into); to pervade (الى نفسه s.o.'s soul, of a feeling) | سرى سراه (*surāhu*) to traverse one's nightly course; سرى مفعوله (*maf'ūluhū*) to be valid, be effective, be in force **IV** to travel by night; to make (ب s.o.) travel by night **V** تسرى see [2]سر *sarra* **V**

سرى *sarīy* pl. اسرية *asriya*, سريان *suryān* little creek, brook; see also under [2]سرو

سرية *sariya* pl. سرايا *sarāyā* (military) detachment, flying column, raiding party; company (*mil.*) | سرية خيالة (*kayyāla*) cavalry squadron, سرية الطائرات squadron of aircraft

سريان *sarayān* spread, diffusion; validity, effectiveness, coming into force

مسرى *masran*: مسرى محمد *masrā muḥammad* the point of departure for Mohammed's midnight journey to the seven heavens, i.e., Jerusalem

اسراء *isrā'* nocturnal journey; الاسراء Mohammed's midnight journey to the seven heavens

سار *sārin* pl. سراة *surāh* traveling by night; night reveler, night hawk; contagious (disease); in force, effective, valid | سارى المفعول in force, effective, valid

سارية *sāriya* a mood or atmosphere which prevails in, or pervades, a room (e.g., سارية من الجهامة an all-pervading gloom); — (pl. *-āt*, سوار *sawārin*) column; shipmast

[2]سراى and سراية look up alphabetically

[3]سريان *suryān* Syrians (coll.) members of the East Syrian Church

سريانى *suryānī* Syriac, Syrian; a member of the East Syrian Church

سرياوران *saryāwarān* (formerly) adjutant general

سيسبان look up alphabetically

[1]اسطبة look up alphabetically

[2]مسطبة *masṭaba*, *misṭaba* pl. مساطب *masāṭib*[2] stone bench (against a wall); mastaba

سطح *saṭaḥa a* (*saṭḥ*) to spread out, spread, unfold, unroll (ه s.th.); to level, even, plane, flatten, make smooth (ه s.th.); to throw to the ground, fell (ه s.o.) **II** to spread out, spread, unfold, unroll (ه s.th.); to level, even, plane, flatten, make smooth (ه s.th.) **V** to be spread out, be unfolded; to be leveled, be evened; to lie down on one's back **VII** to be spread out, be unfolded; to lie flat on one's back, be supine

سطح *saṭḥ* pl. سطوح *suṭūḥ* surface (also *geom.*); plane (*geom.*); (pl. also اسطحة *asṭiḥa*, اسطح *asṭuḥ*) (flat) roof, terrace; deck (of a ship); سطوح *suṭūḥ* (*eg.*, *syr.*) roof terrace | سطح البحر *s. al-baḥr* sea level; سطح مائل inclined plane

سطحى *saṭḥī* external, outer, outward, outside, exterior; flat; superficial; سطحيات *saṭḥīyāt* externals, superficialities

سطحية *saṭḥīya* flatness; superficiality

سطيح *saṭīḥ* flat, spread out, stretched out, supine

مسطاح *misṭāḥ* threshing floor

مسطح *musaṭṭaḥ* even, level, flat; (pl. *-āt*) surface | قدم مسطحة (*qadam*) flat foot

[1]سطر *saṭara u* (*saṭr*) and **II** to rule (ه s.th.), draw lines (ه on a sheet of paper); to write, jot down, record (ه s.th.); to draw up, compose (ه s.th.)

سطر *saṭr*, *saṭar* pl. سطور *suṭūr*, اسطر *asṭur*, اسطار *asṭār* line; row

ساطور *sāṭūr* pl. سواطير *sawāṭīr*[2] cleaver

اسطورة *usṭūra* pl. اساطير *asāṭīr*[2] fable, legend, saga, myth; fabulous story, yarn

اسطورى *usṭūrī* mythical, legendary, fabulous

مسطرة *misṭara* pl. مساطر *masāṭir*[2] ruler; underlines, guideline sheet; see also alphabetically | ○ مسطرة الحساب slide rule

مسطار *misṭār* trowel

مسطرين *masṭarīn* (*eg.*) trowel

تسطير *tasṭīr* writing down, recording

مسطر *musaṭṭar* piece of writing, paper, document

[2]سيطر and derivatives look up alphabetically

سطع *saṭaʻa* a (*saṭʻ*, سطوع *suṭūʻ*) to rise; to spread (dust, fragrance); to shine, be brilliant, be radiant; to be or become manifest, obvious, plain, clear

سطع *saṭʻ* brilliance, radiance, glow; brightness, luminosity

سطع *saṭaʻ* thump, thud, plump

سطوع *suṭūʻ* brilliance, radiance, glow; brightness, luminosity

اسطع *asṭaʻ*[2] more brilliant, brighter; clearer, more obvious

ساطع *sāṭiʻ* pl. سواطع *sawāṭiʻ*[2] radiant, brilliant, shining, luminous, bright; manifest, obvious, clear, plain, patent, evident (proof)

[1]سطل *saṭala* u (*saṭl*) to intoxicate (ه s.o.) VII to become or be intoxicated

سطل *saṭl* pl. اسطال *asṭāl*, سطول *suṭūl* bucket, pail (of wood or metal)

[2]اسطول look up alphabetically

سطام *siṭām* plug, stopper

(سطو) سطا *saṭā* u (*saṭw*, سطوة *saṭwa*) to rush, pounce, jump (ب or على upon), assail, attack (ب or على s.o.); to burglarize (على a place.), break into a place (على)

سطو *saṭw* attack, assault; burglary, housebreaking

سطوة *saṭwa* pl. *saṭawāt* attack, assault; influence, authority; presumption, cockiness, pride; power, strength

اسطوانة look up alphabetically

سعة *saʻa* see وسع

سعتر *saʻtar* (= صعتر) wild thyme (Thymus serpyllum; *bot.*)

سعد *saʻida* a and pass. *suʻida* (*saʻd*, سعادة *saʻāda*) to be happy, lucky, fortunate; pass. سعد ب (*suʻida*) to have the good fortune of receiving or sharing s.th. III to help, aid, assist (ه s.o., فى or على in, with), give s.o. (ه) a hand (فى or على in); to support, back (ه على or فى s.o. in); to contribute, be conducive (على, ل or فى to); to favor, encourage (على or فى s.th.) IV to make happy (ه s.o.); to help (ه s.o.) | اسعده الحظ ب (*ḥaẓẓ*) he had the good fortune to ...

سعد *saʻd* pl. سعود *suʻūd* good luck, good fortune

الهيئة السعدية *al-haiʼa as-saʻdiya* the Saadist union (formerly a political movement in Egypt); السعديون *as-saʻdīyūn* the Saadists, the followers of Saad Zaghlūl (1856—1927)

سعد *suʻd* Cyperus (*bot.*)

سعيد *saʻīd* pl. سعداء *suʻadāʼ*[2] happy (ب about, at); radiant, blissful; lucky, auspicious; felicitous | سعيد الذكر *s. ad-ḏikr* of blessed memory, the late ...

سعادة *saʻāda* happiness; bliss, felicity; good fortune, success, prosperity, welfare; title of a pasha; *saʻādat* ... (with foll. name) title of high officials (*Syr.*,

Leb.) | سعادتكم Your Grace (form of address to a pasha); صاحب السعادة title of a pasha; دار السعادة "House of Bliss", ancient name of Istanbul

سعودى *sa'ūdī* Saudi | المملكة العربية السعودية (*mamlaka*) Saudi Arabia

سعدان *sa'dān* pl. سعادين *sa'ādīn*[2] ape

سعدانة *sa'dāna* pl. *-āt* nipple, teat | سعدانة الباب doorknob

اسعد *as'ad*[2] happier, luckier

مساعدة *musā'ada* pl. *-āt* support, backing, aid, help, assistance; encouragement, promotion

ساعد *sā'id* pl. سواعد *sawā'id*[2] forearm | هو ساعده الايمن (*aiman*) he is his right hand, he is indispensable to him; اشتد ساعده *ištadda sā'iduhū* to become strong, powerful; فت فى ساعده (*fatta*) to weaken s.o.

ساعدة *sā'ida* pl. سواعد *sawā'id*[2] tributary

مسعود *mas'ūd* pl. مساعيد *masā'īd*[2] happy, lucky, fortunate

مساعد *musā'id* helper, help, aide; assistant (adj. and n.); adjutant

مسعد *mus'ad* favored by fortune, fortunate, lucky

سعر **sa'ara** *a* (*sa'r*) to kindle, start (ه a fire, a war); pass. *su'ira* to flare up, run mad **II** to kindle, start (ه a fire, a war); to price (ه s.th.), set a price (ه on s.th.); to quote on the stock market **III** to bargain, haggle over the price (ه with s.o.) **IV** to kindle, light, start (ه fire) **V** to burn, blaze; to flare up (anger) **VII** to become mad, furious **VIII** to burn, flare, blaze; to break out (fighting)

سعر *si'r* pl. اسعار *as'ār* price; rate; exchange rate, quotation (stock market) | سعر الخصم *s. al-ḵaṣm* discount rate, bank rate; سعر التسليف rate of interest; سعر الفائدة rate of interest; سعر القطع *s. al-qaṭ'* discount rate, bank rate; سعر القطعة *s. al-qiṭ'a* price by the piece

سعر *su'r* madness; frenzy; voracity

سعر *su'ur* madness, frenzy

سعار *su'ār* voracity

سعير *sa'īr* pl. سعر *su'ur* blazing flame, fire, blaze; hell, inferno

مسعر *mis'ar* pl. مساعر *masā'ir*[2] poker, fire iron

مسعار *mis'ār* pl. مساعير *masā'īr*[2] poker, fire iron

تسعير *tas'īr* pricing, price fixing

تسعيرة *tas'īra* pricing, price fixing | لجنة التسعيرة *lajnat at-t.* price-fixing commission

تسعرة *tas'ira* quotation (stock exchange)

مسعور *mas'ūr* mad, crazy

سعط **VIII** to snuff (ه tobacco)

سعوط *sa'ūṭ* snuff

مسعط *mis'aṭ* snuffbox

سعف **III** to help, aid, support (ه s.o.) **IV** to comply with s.o.'s (ه) wishes (ب for), humor (ه ب s.o. in), grant (ه ب s.o. s.th.); to help, aid, assist (ه s.o.)

سعف *sa'af* (coll.; n. un. ة) pl. *-āt* palm leaves | احد السعف *aḥad as-s.* Palm Sunday (*Chr.*)

اسعاف *is'āf* pl. *-āt* aid, relief, help, assistance; medical service; الاسعاف first aid | اسعاف العجزة *i. al-'ajaza* care for the aged; جمعية الاسعاف *jam'iyat al-i.* approx.: civil ambulance service; رجال الاسعاف first-aid men, ambulance men; medical orderlies, hospital corpsmen; سيارة الاسعاف *sayyārat al-i.* ambulance

سعل **sa'ala** *u* (سعلة *su'la*, سعال *su'āl*) to cough

سعلة *su'la* cough

سعال *su'āl* cough | السعال الديكى (*dīkī*) whooping cough

سعلى *si'lā* pl. سعليات *si'layāt* female demon

سعلاة *si'lāh* pl. سعال *sa'ālin* female demon

ابو سعن *abū su'n* marabou (*zool.*)

سعى *sa'ā a* (*sa'y*) to move quickly, run, speed; to move across the sky (moon); to head, be headed (الى for), proceed (الى to or toward); to strive (ل or الى for), aspire (ل or الى to); to work (الى, ل or وراء for), endeavor, attempt, make an effort (وراء or الى, ل to get or achieve s.th.); to run after s.th. (وراء), pursue, chase (وراء s.th.); to take steps (فى in a matter) | سعى به الى to lead s.o. or s.th. to ...; سعى فى الارض فسادا (*fi l-arḍi fasādan*) to spread evil, cause universal harm and damage; سعى لحتفه بظلفه (*li-ḥatfihī bi-ẓilfihī*) to bring about one's own destruction, dig one's own grave; سعى فى خراب الشىء (*ḵarābi š-š.*) to work at the ruin of s.th., undermine s.th.; — *sa'ā a* (سعى *sa'y*, سعاية *si'āya*) to slander (ب s.o., عند or الى to s.o.), discredit (عند or الى ب s.o. with) **VI** to run about in confusion

سعى *sa'y* run, course; السعى the ceremony of running seven times between Ṣafā and Marwa (performed during the Pilgrimage); effort, endeavor; livestock

سعاية *si'āya* slander, calumniation

مسعى *mas'an* pl. مساع *masā'in* effort, endeavor

ساع *sā'in* pl. *-ūn*, سعاة *su'āh* messenger; office boy, delivery boy; slanderer, calumniator | ساعى البريد postman, mailman

سغب *saḡiba a* (*saḡab*) to hunger (ل for), be or become hungry

سغب *saḡab* hunger, starvation

سغابة *saḡāba* hunger, starvation

مسغبة *masḡaba* famine

ساغب *sāḡib* hungry, starving

سف **IV** to descend, sink, slip, decline (fig.); to stoop (الى to, fig.) | اسف النظر اليه (*naẓara*) to give s.o. a sharp look **VIII** to eat, swallow (ه s.th. dry, e.g., a medicinal powder)

سفوف *safūf* medicinal powder

اسفاف *isfāf* decline (fig.); triviality

سفتجة *suftaja* pl. سفاتج *safātij*[2] bill of exchange (*com.*)

سفح *safaḥa a* (*safḥ*, سفوح *sufūḥ*) to pour out, spill, shed (ه s.th.) **III** to whore, fornicate (ه with s.o.) **VI** to whore, fornicate

سفح *safḥ* pl. سفوح *sufūḥ* foot (of a mountain); pl. سفوح flat, rocky surface

سفاح *saffāḥ* shedder of blood, killer, murderer

سفاح *sifāḥ* fornication

سفد *safida a* and *safada i* (سفاد *sifād*) to cover, mount (على or ها the female); to cohabit (ها with a woman) **II** to put on a skewer (ه meat) **III** to cover, mount (ها the female); to cohabit (ها with a woman)

سفود *saffūd* pl. سفافيد *safāfīd*[2] skewer, spit

سفر *safara i* (سفور *sufūr*) to remove the veil (عن وجهها *'an wajhihā* from her face), unveil o.s.; — *safara i* (*safr*) to shine, glow (aurora) **II** to unveil, uncover, disclose (ه s.th.); to send on a journey, compel to leave, send away (ه s.o.); to dispatch, send off (ه s.th.); to embark, put on board (ه passengers) **III** to travel, make a trip; to leave, depart, go on a journey **IV** to shine, glow (aurora, s.o.'s face, etc.); to disclose, unveil, uncover (عن s.th.); to yield, achieve, bring (عن s.th.); to end (عن with, in), result (عن in) **VII** to rise, disappear (dust, clouds)

السفر *as-safr* the travelers, the passengers

سفر *sifr* pl. اسفار *asfār* book (esp. one of the Scriptures)

سفر *safar* departure; (pl. اسفار *asfār*) journey, travel, trip, tour

سفرة *safra* pl. *safarāt* journey, travel, trip, tour

سفرية *safarīya* pl. *-āt* journey, travel, trip, tour; departure

سفرة *sufra* pl. سفر *sufar* dining table

سفرجى *sufragī* (*eg.*) pl. سفرجية *sufragīya* waiter, steward

سفير *safīr* pl. سفراء *sufarā'*[2] mediator (between contending parties); ambassador (*dipl.*)

سفور *sufūr* uncovering of the face (of a veiled woman); unveiling

سفارة *sifāra* office or function of a mediator, mediation; embassy (*dipl.*)

مسافر *masāfir*[2] (pl.) part of the face not covered by the veil

سافر *sāfir* unveiled, wearing no veil; barefaced, conspicuous, obvious; (pl. سفرة *safara*) scribe

مسافر *musāfir* pl. *-ūn* traveler; passenger; visiting stranger; guest

سفرجل *safarjal* (coll.; n. un. ة) pl. سفارج *safārij*[2] quince (Cydonia; *bot.*)

سفسطة *safsaṭa* sophistry; pl. سفسطات sophistries, casuistic arguments | اهل السفسطة *ahl as-s.* the Sophists

سفسطى *safsaṭī* sophistic; Sophist

سفسفة *safsafa* pl. سفاسف *safāsif*[2] silly talk, nonsense; poor, inferior stuff

سفساف *safsāf* pl. سفاسف *safāsif*[2] silly, inane, trivial; poor, inferior | سفساف الامور poor, inferior stuff

سفط *safaṭ* pl. اسفاط *asfāṭ* basket; scales (of fish)

سفع *safa'a a* (*saf'*) to scorch, parch, burn (ه s.o., ‸ s.o.'s skin; esp. of a hot wind); to flap the wings, flutter (bird); to strike, hit (ه s.o. with the hand), slap (ه s.o.); to lash (‸ s.th., e.g., of a storm)

سفع *saf'* burned spot

سفعة *suf'a* pl. سفع *sufa'* black stain; dark spot, brown discoloration

اسفع *asfa'*[2], f. سفعاء *saf'ā'*[2] dark-brown

سفق *safaqa u* (*safq*) to shut, bang, slam (‸ the door)

سفك *safaka i u* (*safk*) to shed (‸ blood) VI to murder each other VII to be shed, flow (blood)

سفك *safk*: سفك الدماء *s. ad-dimā'* bloodshed

سفاك *saffāk* shedder of blood; bloodshedding

سفل *safala u* (سفول *sufūl*, سفال *safāl*) and *sufila a* to be low; to be below s.th. (‸); — *safala u* to turn downward; — *safula u* (سفالة *safāla*) and *safala u* (*safl*) to be low, base, despicable V to abase o.s., sink low, go from bad to worse; to act in a base manner

سفل *sufl* lowest part of s.th., bottom

سفلى *suflī* lower, at the bottom; low

سفلة *sifla*: سفلة الناس *s. an-nās* lowly people, riffraff

سفالة *safāla* lowness; lowliness; baseness, ignominy, despicableness

سفالة *sufāla* lowest part

اسفل *asfal*[2], f. سفلى *suflā*, pl. اسافل *asāfil*[2] lower; lowest; lower or lowest part, bottom; اسفل *asfala* (prep.) under, underneath, below | الارض السفلى (*arḍ*) the nether world; رده اسفل سافلين *raddahū asfala sāfilīn* to reduce s.o. to the lowest level or status

سافل *sāfil* pl. سفلة *safala* low; lowly; base, mean, despicable

سفلت *saflata* to cover with asphalt, to asphalt

اسفلت *asfalt* asphalt

سفلقة *saflaqa* sponging

سفلاق *siflāq* sponger

[1]سفن *safan* coarse hide used for polishing; emery paper, sandpaper

[2]سفين *safīn* ships (coll.); ship; see also alphabetically

سفينة *safīna* pl. سفن *sufun*, سفائن *safā'in*[2] ship, vessel, boat; السفينة Argo (*astron.*) | سفينة مدفعية (*midfa'īya*) gunboat; سفينة تعليم and سفينة التدريس training ship

سفان *saffān* shipbuilder, shipwright

سفانة *sifāna* (art or trade of) shipbuilding

[3]اسفين look up alphabetically

سفنج *safanj*, *sifanj* and اسفنج *isfanj* sponge

سفه *safiha a* (*safah*) and *safuha u* (سفاهة *safāha*) to be stupid, silly, foolish; to be impudent, insolent **II** to call (ه, ه s.o., s.th.) stupid or foolish; to declare (ه s.o.) legally incompetent; to depreciate, put down as inferior (ه s.th.) | سفه نفسه to make a fool of o.s.; سفه وجهه (*wajhahū*) to expose s.o., show s.o. up, make a fool of s.o., bring s.o. in discredit, disgrace s.o., dishonor s.o. **VI** to pretend to be stupid or foolish

سفه *safah* foolishness, stupidity, silliness; impudence, shamelessness, insolence

سفيه *safīh* pl. سفهاء *sufahā'*[2], سفاه *sifāh* foolish, stupid, silly; fool; an incompetent (*Isl. Law*); impudent, shameless, insolent; insolent fellow

سفاهة *safāha* foolishness, stupidity, silliness; impudence, shamelessness, insolence

سفى *safā i* (*safy*) to raise and scatter (ه the dust; said of the wind) **IV** do.

سافياء *sāfiyā'*[2] dust

مسفى *masfan* s.th. whirled up; plaything, sport (fig.)

سفين *safīn* wedge

سقارة *sigāra* = سجارة cigarette

سقالة (It. *scala*) *saqāla* scaffold

سقر *saqar*[2] f. hell

سقراط *suqrāṭ*[2] Socrates

سقسقة *saqsaqa* chirping, cheeping, peeping (e.g., of sparrows)

سقط *saqaṭa u* (سقوط *suqūṭ*, مسقط *masqaṭ*) to fall (also = to be killed in action); to fall down, drop; to tumble, trip, slip; to fall out (hair); to sink down (على on, to); to hit, stumble (على upon), come across s.th. (على); to find (على s.th.); to get, come (الى to s.o.), reach (الى s.o.); to decline, sink, drop (standard); to become null and void, be abolished, be canceled; to be dropped, be omitted, drop out; to be missing; to escape (من s.o.), slip (من s.o.'s memory) | ليسقط (فليسقط) *li-yasquṭ* (*fal-yasquṭ*) down with ...! سقط به to drop s.o. or s.th.; سقط اليهم عنه انه they had had word from him that he ...; سقط رأسه فى (*ra'suhū*) he was born in ..., his birthplace was ...; سقط من العضوية (*'uḍwīya*) to be dropped from membership; سقط من عينه (*'ainihī*) to drop in s.o.'s estimation; سقط فى الامتحان to fail an examination, flunk; سقط فى يده *suqiṭa fī yadihī* to stand aghast, be at a loss, be bewildered **IV** to let fall, drop (ه, ه s.o., s.th.); to make (ه s.o.) tumble, cause s.o. (ه) to slip; to overthrow, bring down, topple, fell (ه, ه s.o., s.th.); to fail, flunk (ه s.o. in an examination); to shoot down (ه an aircraft); to deduct, subtract (ه a number); to eliminate (ه

s.th. من from); to have a miscarriage, miscarry; to bring about a miscarriage (woman); to slink (ه its young one; animal) | اسقطه من الجنسية (*jinsīya*) to deprive s.o. of his citizenship; اسقط حقه فى (*ḥaqqahū*) to forfeit one's right in s.th., waive one's claim to s.th.; اسقط دعوى (*daʿwā*) to quash a complaint, nonsuit a case; to withdraw or drop a complaint; اسقط الشعر (*šaʿra*) to cause loss of hair; اسقط فى يده *usqiṭa fī yadihī* = سقط فى يده *suqiṭa fī yadihī*
V to learn gradually, pick up information (ه من about s.th. from); to hunt for scraps | تسقط الاخبار to gather information
VI to fall down, come down, collapse; to fall successively or gradually; to fall out (hair); to come gradually (الى to), arrive one by one (الى at); to roll, drip (من off); to dribble | تساقط على نفسه to break down, collapse; تساقط حطاما (*ḥuṭāman*) to go to ruin, disintegrate

سقط *saqṭ* dew

سقط *siqṭ* miscarried fetus

سقط *saqṭ, siqṭ, suqṭ* sparks flying from a flint

سقط *saqaṭ* pl. اسقاط *asqāṭ* any worthless thing; offal, refuse, rubbish, trash; junk | سقط المتاع *s. al-matāʿ* waste, scrap(s)

سقطى *saqaṭī* junk dealer, ragman

سقطة *saqṭa* pl. *saqaṭāt* fall, tumble, plunge; oversight, slip, error, mistake | سقطات الطباعة misprints, errata

سقوط *suqūṭ* fall, tumble; crash (of an airplane); collapse, breakdown, ruin; decline, downfall, fall; devolution (of a right); slip, lapse | سقوط الشعر *s. aš-šaʿr* loss of hair; سقوط الامطار rainfall

سقيط *saqīṭ* hail

سقاطة *saqqāṭa, (eg.) suqqāṭa* door latch

مسقط *masqaṭ, masqiṭ* pl. مساقط *masāqiṭ*[2] place where a falling object lands; waterfall | مسقط افقى (*ufqī*) ground plan, horizontal section; مسقط رأسى (*raʾsī*) front elevation, vertical section (*arch.*); مسقط الرأس *m. ar-raʾs* birthplace, home

مسقط *masqaṭ*[2] Muscat (seaport and capital of Oman)

اسقاط *isqāṭ* overthrow; shooting down (of an aircraft); miscarriage, abortion; deduction, subtraction; rebate | الاسقاط من الجنسية (*jinsīya*) abrogation of citizenship; gation of citizenship; اسقاط قيمة الفرنك (*qīmat al-f.*) devaluation of the franc

تساقط *tasāquṭ* loss (of hair) | تساقط الثلوج snowfall

ساقط *sāqiṭ* pl. سقاط *suqqāṭ* fallen; base, mean, vile; disreputable, notorious (district); omitted, missing; forgotten

ساقطة *sāqiṭa* scrap; (pl. *-āt*) fallen woman, harlot

سقطراء *suquṭrāʾ*[2] Socotra (island, S of Arabia)

سقع *saqaʿa a* (*saqʿ*) to slap, clap (ه, ه s.o., s.th.)

مسقعة *musaqqaʿa* (*eg.*) dish of eggplant and meat

سقف[1] **II** to provide with a roof or ceiling, roof over (ه s.th.)

سقف *saqf* pl. سقوف *suqūf*, سقف *suquf*, اسقف *asquf* roof; ceiling | سقف الحلق *s. al-ḥalq* palate

سقيفة *saqīfa* pl. سقائف *saqāʾif*[2] roofed passage; roofed gallery; roofing, shelter

تسقيف *tasqīf* roofing

مسقوف *masqūf* roofed, covered (ب with)

اسقف[2] *usquf* pl. اساقفة *asāqifa* look up alphabetically

سقالة look up alphabetically

سقلب *saqlaba* to throw down (ه s.o.)

سقلبى *saqlabī* pl. سقالبة *saqāliba* Slav; Slavic

سقم **saqima** *a* (*saqam*) and *saquma u* (*suqm*, سقام *saqām*) to be or become sick, ill, ailing; to become thin, lean, skinny; to be poor, meager, measly **II** to make sick (ه s.o.) **IV** = **II**

سقم *suqm* pl. اسقام *asqām* illness, sickness; leanness, thinness, skinniness

سقم *saqam* pl. اسقام *asqām* illness; sickness; leanness, thinness, skinniness

سقام *saqām* illness, sickness; leanness, thinness, skinniness

سقيم *saqīm* pl. سقام *siqām*, سقماء *suqamā'*[2] sick, ill, ailing; skinny, lean, emaciated; meager, measly; poor, faulty (language)

مسقام *misqām* seriously suffering; constantly ailing, sickly

سقاوة *siqāwa* glanders

سقى *saqā* *i* (*saqy*) to give (ه ه s.o. s.th.) to drink, make s.o. (ه) drink (ه s.th.); to water (ه cattle, plants); to irrigate (ه s.th.); to dip, scoop, draw (water) | سقى الفولاذ (*fūlāḏa*) to temper steel **III** to give (ه ه s.o. s.th.) to drink; to conclude a lease contract (ه with s.o.; cf. مساقاة) **IV** to give (ه ه s.o. s.th.) to drink, make s.o. (ه) drink (ه s.th.); to water (ه cattle, plants); to irrigate (ه s.th.) **VIII** to ask (من s.o.) for a drink; to draw water (من from); to draw (ه من s.th., e.g., information, knowledge, etc., from), take, borrow, obtain (ه من s.th. from) **X** to ask (من s.o.) for a drink (also ه for s.th.); to pray for rain

سقى *saqy* watering; irrigation

سقاء *siqā'* pl. اسقية *asqiya*, اسقيات *asqiyāt*, اساق *asāqin* waterskin, milkskin

سقاء *saqqā'* pl. *-ūn* water carrier; — pelican (*zool.*)

سقاية *siqāya* irrigation, watering; office of water supplier (spec., the traditional office of one in charge of providing water for Mecca pilgrims); watering place; drinking vessel

مسقى *misqā* pl. مساق *masāqin* (*eg.*) irrigation canal

مساقاة *musāqāh* sharecropping contract over the lease of a plantation, limited to one crop period (*Isl. Law*)

استسقاء *istisqā'* dropsy | صلاة الاستسقاء *ṣalāt al-ist.* prayer for rain

استسقائى *istisqā'ī* dropsical, hydropic

ساق *sāqin* pl. سقاة *suqāh* cupbearer, Ganymede, saki

ساقية *sāqiya* barmaid; — (pl. سواق *sawāqin*) rivulet; irrigation ditch, irrigation canal; water scoop; sakieh, water wheel

سك *sakka* *u* (*sakk*) to lock, bolt (ه the door); to mint, coin (ه money); — *sakka* (1st pers. perf. *sakiktu*) *a* (سكك *sakak*) and **VIII** to be or become deaf

سكة *sikka* pl. سكك *sikak* (minting) die; coin; road; (*eg.*) sidestreet, lane (narrower than شارع *šāri'*) | سكة الحديد and السكة الحديدية railroad; سكة زراعية (*zirā'īya*) field path, dirt road; دار السكة mint

سكان *sukkān* pl. *-āt* rudder

اسك *asakk*[2], f. سكاء *sakkā'*[2], pl. سك *sukk* deaf

مسكوكة *maskūka* pl. *-āt* coin; drain hole (*tun.*) | علم المسكوكات *'ilm al-m.* numismatics

سكارة *sigāra* pl. سكائر *sagā'ir*[2] (Syrian spelling) cigarette

سكارين *sakārin* saccharin

سكب *sakaba* *u* (*sakb*) to pour out, shed, spill (ه s.th.) **VII** to pour forth, be poured out, be shed, be spilled

سكيب *sakib* shed, spilled

مسكب *maskab* pl. مساكب *masākib*[2] melting pot, crucible

مسكوبية *maskūbīya* melting pot, crucible

سكباج *sakbāj* meat cooked in vinegar

سكت *sakata* u (*sakt*, سكوت *sukūt*, سكات *sukāt*) to be silent, say nothing; to become silent, lapse into silence; to be or become quiet, calm down, subside; to pass over s.th. (عن) in silence; not to answer (عن s.o.); pass. *sukita* to have a stroke (*med.*) | سكت عنه الغضب (*ġaḍab*) his anger abated **II** to silence, calm, soothe, pacify (ه, ه s.o., s.th.); to order to be silent, hush up (ه s.o.) **IV** do.; to conceal, refuse to tell (ه s.th.)

سكت *sakt* silence; taciturnity, reticence | على السكت silently, in silence, quietly

سكتة *sakta* silence, quiet; stroke, apoplexy (*med.*) | سكتة قلبية (*qalbīya*) heart failure

سكات *sukāt* silence; taciturnity, reticence

سكوت *sukūt* silence; taciturnity, reticence; see also alphabetically

سكوتى *sukūtī* taciturn, reticent

سكوت *sakūt* taciturn, reticent

سكيت *sikkīt* habitually silent

ساكت *sākit* silent, mum; taciturn, reticent; still, quiet, calm, tranquil; quiescent (letter)

[1]سكر *sakara* u (*sakr*) to shut, close, lock, bolt (ه s.th.) **II** do.

[2]سكر *sakira* a (*sakar*, *sukr*) to be drunk; to get drunk, become intoxicated **IV** to make drunk, intoxicate, inebriate (ه s.o.) **VI** to pretend to be drunk

سكر *sukr* intoxication, inebriety, drunkenness

سكر *sakar* an intoxicant; wine

سكرة *sakra* pl. *sakarāt* inebriety, intoxication, drunkenness | سكرة الموت *s. al-maut* agony of death

سكران *sakrān*[2], f. سكرى *sakrā*, pl. سكارى *sukārā*, *sakārā* drunk, intoxicated; a drunk | سكران طينة (*ṭīna*) (*colloq.*) dead drunk

سكير *sikkīr* drunkard, heavy drinker

مسكر *muskir* pl. *-āt* alcoholic beverage, intoxicating liquor

[3]سكر **II** to sugar, sprinkle with sugar (ه s.th.); to candy, preserve with sugar (ه s.th.)

سكر *sukkar* sugar; pl. سكاكر *sakākir*[2] sweetmeats, confectionery, candies | سكر الثمار fructose, levulose, fruit sugar; سكر الشعير maltose, malt sugar; سكر العنب *s. al-'inab* dextro-glucose, dextrose, grape sugar; سكر القصب *s. al-qaṣab* saccharose, sucrose, cane sugar; سكر اللبن *s. al-laban* lactose, milk sugar; سكر النبات *s. an-nabat* sugar candy, rock candy; قصب السكر *qaṣab as-s.* sugar cane; مرض السكر *maraḍ as-s.* diabetes

سكرى *sukkarī* sugar (adj.), sugary, like sugar, saccharine; سكريات confectionery; sweetmeats, candy | مرض البول السكرى (*maraḍ al-baul*) diabetes

سكرية *sukkarīya* sugar bowl

مسكرات *musakkarāt* confectionery, sweetmeats, candy

[4]سكارة pl. سكائر look up alphabetically

[5]سيكران look up alphabetically

سكرتاه (It. *sicurtà*) *sikurtāh* insurance

سكرتارية (Fr. *secrétariat*) *sekretārīya* secretariat; secretaryship

سكرتو (It. *scarto*) *sikartō* cotton waste

سكرتير (Fr. *secrétaire*) *sekretēr* secretary | سكرتير عام (*'āmm*) secretary-general

سكرتيرية *sekretērīya* secretariat

سكرجة *sukurruja, sukruja* pl. سكارج *sakārīj*[2] bowl; platter, plate

سكروز *sukrōz* saccharose, sucrose

سكرين *sukkarīn* saccharin

سكسك II *tasaksaka* to behave in a servile manner

سكسكة *suksuka* wren (?)

تسكسك *tasaksuk* servility

سكسونى *saksōnī* Saxonian; Saxon

سكسونيا *saksōniyā* Saxonia

سكع V to grope about (الظلمة *az-zulmata* in the dark); to loiter, loaf, hang around; to proceed aimlessly, dawdle, potter | طرده الى حيث التسكع (*haiṯu t-tasakku'u*) to drive s.o. out into the dark, leave s.o. to an uncertain fate

سكاف *sakkāf* shoemaker

سكافة *sikāfa* shoemaker's trade, shoemaking

اسكاف *iskāf* and اسكافى *iskāfī* pl. اساكفة *asākifa* shoemaker

اسكفة *uskuffa* threshold, doorstep; lintel

ساكف *sākif* lintel

اسكلة pl. اساكل look up alphabetically

[1]سكن *sakana u* (سكون *sukūn*) to be or become still, tranquil, peaceful; to calm down, repose, rest; (*gram.*) to be vowelless (consonant, i.e., have no vowel immediately following): to abate, subside, remit, cease (anger, pain, and the like); to pass, go away (عن from s.o., pain), leave (عن s.o., pain); to remain calm, unruffled (الى at, in the face of); to be reassured (ل, الى by); to rely (ل, الى on), trust, have faith (ل, الى in); to feel at home (الى in, at); — *sakana u* (*sakan*, سكنى *suknā*) to live, dwell (ب or فى, ـه in), inhabit (ب or فى, ـه s.th.) II to calm (ـه, ه s.o., s.th.), reassure, appease, placate (ه s.o.), soothe, allay, alleviate (ـه pain, and the like); (*gram.*) to make vowelless (ـه a consonant, i.e., pronounce it without a following vowel) III to live together, share quarters (ه فى with s.o. in) IV to give or allocate living quarters (ه to s.o.); to settle, lodge, put up (ه ـه s.o. in) VI to live together, share quarters

سكن *sakan* means or time for rest; dwelling, abode, habitation; inhabited area, human habitations; ashes

سكنى *sakanī* ashen, ash-gray

فى حركاته وسكناته *fī ḥarakātihī wa-sakanātihī* in all his doings; in every situation

سكنة *sakina* pl. *-āt* residence, home

سكون *sukūn* calm, tranquillity, peace; silence, quiet; (*gram.*) vowellessness of a medial consonant; the graphic symbol of this vowellessness | سكون الطائر seriousness, sedateness, gravity

سكان *sakkān* cutler

سكان *sukkān* pl. *-āt* rudder

سكين *sikkīn* m. and f., pl. سكاكين *sakākīn*[2] knife

سكينة *sakīna* pl. سكائن *sakā'in*[2] immanence of God, presence of God; devout, God-inspired peace of mind; calm, tranquillity, peace

سكينة *sikkīna* knife

سكنى *suknā* living, dwelling; stay, sojourn | محل السكنى *maḥall as-s.* place of residence

سكاكينى *sakākīnī* cutler

مسكن *maskan, maskin* pl. مساكن *masākin*[2] dwelling, abode, habitation; house; home, residence, domicile

تسكين *taskīn* pacification, tranquilization, placation

اسكان *iskān* settling, settlement; allocation of living quarters

ساكن *sākin* pl. *-ūn*, سكنة *sakana*, f. سواكن *sawākin*[2] calm, motionless, still; — vowelless (medial consonant); stagnant, standing (water); ○ static (electricity); (pl. سكان *sukkān*, سكنة *sakana*) dweller, inhabitant, resident, occupant; السكان the population | ساكن الجنان inhabitant of Paradise, deceased person, one of blessed memory; كثير السكان populous; لا يحرك ساكنا (*yuḥarriku*) he doesn't budge, he doesn't bend his little finger, he remains immobile, apathetic; حرك ساكنه (*sākinahū*) to rouse, agitate s.o.

مسكون *maskūn* populated, inhabited; haunted (place); possessed (person) | الدار مسكونة the house is haunted

المسكونة *al-maskūna* the inhabited world, the world

مسكونى *maskūnī* ecumenical (*Chr.*)

مسكن *musakkin* pacifier, soother; (pl. *-āt*) sedative, tranquilizer

مساكن *musākin* pl. *-ūn* fellow citizen, neighbor

[2]مسكنة and مسكين pl. مساكين look up alphabetically

سكنجبين *sakanjabīn* oxymel (*pharm.*)

سكندينافيا *sikandināfiyā* and سكندناوة *sikandināwa* Scandinavia

سكندنافى *sikandināfī* Scandinavian

سكوت (Hebr. *sukkōṯ*): عيد السكوت *ʿīd as-s.* Sukkoth, Feast of Tabernacles (*Jud.*)

سكى *skī* ski

[1]سل *sal* imperative of سأل *sa'ala*

[2]سل *salla u* (*sall*) to pull out, withdraw, or remove gently (ه s.th.); pass. *sulla* to have pulmonary tuberculosis, be consumptive V to steal away, slink away, slip away, escape; to spread, extend, get (الى to), reach (الى s.th.); to slip, slink, sneak, steal (الى into); to betake o.s., go (الى to, with secret designs); to invade, infiltrate, enter (الى s.th.); to penetrate (فى to, as far as) VII to steal away, slink away, slip away, escape; to slip, slink, sneak, steal (الى into); to infiltrate (الى s.th., also *pol.*); to advance singly or in small groups (troops in the field; *mil.*); to have pulmonary tuberculosis, be consumptive VIII to pull out or remove gently (ه s.th.); to withdraw gently (ه s.th., e.g., كفه *kaffahū* one's hand, عن from); to unsheathe, draw (ه the sword); to wrest, snatch (ه من from s.o. s.th.)

سل *sall* basket

سل *sill, sull* consumption, phthisis, tuberculosis | السل التدرنى (*tadarrunī*) tuberculosis; السل الرئوى (*ri'awī*) pulmonary tuberculosis

سلة *salla* pl. سلال *silāl* basket | سلة المهملات *s. al-muhmalāt* wastepaper basket; كرة السلة *kurat as-s.* basketball

سليل *salīl* drawn (sword); descendant, scion, son

سليلة *salīla* pl. سلائل *salā'il*[2] (female) descendant

سلال *sallāl* basketmaker, basket weaver

سلالة *sulāla* pl. *-āt* descendant, scion; progeny, offspring; family; race; strain, stock, provenience (of economic plants)

سلالى *sulālī* family (adj.)

مسلة *misalla* pl. *-āt*, مسال *masāll*[2] large needle, pack needle; obelisk

تسلل *tasallul* infiltration (*pol.*); offside position (in football, hockey, etc.)

انسلال *insilāl* infiltration (*pol.*)

مسلول *maslūl* consumptive, affected with pulmonary tuberculosis

مستلة *mustalla* pl. *-āt* offprint (*ir.*)

سلأ *sala'a a* (*sal'*) to clarify (ه butter)

سلاء *silā'* pl. اسلئة *asli'a* clarified butter

سلاطة *salāṭa* salad

سلافى *sulāvī* Slavic; (pl. *-ūn*) Slav

سلاقون *salāqūn* red lead, minium

سلاق see سلق

سلانيك *salānīk*² Salonica (seaport in NE Greece)

سلب *salaba u* (*salb*) to take away, steal, wrest, snatch (ه من or ه ه from s.o. s.th.), rob, strip, dispossess, deprive (ه من or ه ه s.o. of s.th.); to plunder, rifle, loot (ه s.o., ه s.th.); to strip of arms and clothing (ه a fallen enemy); to withhold (ه ه from s.o. s.th.), deny (ه ه to s.o. s.th.); — *saliba a* (*salab*) to put on or wear mourning, be in mourning **V** to be in mourning **VIII** = *salaba*

سلب *salb* spoliation, plundering, looting, pillage, robbing; negation | علامة السلب *'alāmat as-s.* minus sign (*math.*)

سلبى *salbī* negative (also *el.*); passive | المقاومة السلبية or الدفاع السلبى (*muqāwama*) passive resistance

سلبية *salbīya* negativism, negative attitude

سلب *salab* pl. اسلاب *aslāb* loot, booty, plunder, spoils; hide, shanks and belly of a slaughtered animal; — ropes, hawsers (*eg.*)

سلاب *silāb* pl. سلب *sulub* black clothing, mourning (worn by women)

سلاب *sallāb* robber, plunderer, looter

سليب *salīb* stolen, taken, wrested away

اسلوب *uslūb* pl. اساليب *asālīb*² method, way, procedure; course; manner, mode, fashion; style (esp. literary); stylistic peculiarity (of an author) | اسلوب كتابى (*kitābī*) literary style

استلاب *istilāb* spoliation, plundering, looting, pillage, robbing

سالب *sālib* negative (adj.); (pl. سوالب *sawālib*²) ○ negative (*phot.*)

مسلوب *maslūb* unsuccessful

سلبند *salaband* martingale (of the harness)

سلت *salata i u* to extract, pull out (ه s.th.); to chop off (ه s.th., esp. a part of the body) **VII** to steal away, slip away

سلج *salg* (*eg.*) = سلق

السلاجقة *as-salājiqa* the Seljuks

سلجم *saljam* turnip (Brassica rapa; *bot.*); (*eg.*) rape (Brassica napus; *bot.*)

سلح *salaḥa a* (*salḥ*) to void excrement; to drop dung (bird) **II** to arm (ه ه s.o. with) **V** to arm o.s. **VI** to engage in battle, fight, cross swords

سلح *salḥ* and سلاح *sulāḥ* excrements, dung, droppings

سلاح *silāḥ* pl. اسلحة *asliḥa* arm, weapon; arms, weapons; service (as a branch of the armed forces); armor; steel gripper, steel claw; plowshare | سلاح الطيران *s. aṭ-ṭayarān* air force; سلاح الفرسان *s. al-fursān* cavalry; شاك السلاح *šākk as-s.* bristling with arms, armed to the teeth; سلم سلاحه *sallama silāḥahū* to lay down one's arms, surrender

سلاحدار *silāḥdār* sword-bearer, shield-bearer, squire

سليح *salīḥ* pl. *-ūn* apostle (*Chr.*)

تسليح *taslīḥ* pl. *-āt* arming, equipping; armament, rearmament; armoring, reinforcement (in ferroconcrete construction)

تسلح *tasalluḥ* armament, rearmament | سباق التسلح *sibāq at-t.* arms race

مسلح *musalliḥ* armorer

مسلح *musallaḥ* armed; armored, reinforced (with steel); = Fr. *armé* | القوات

المسلحة (*qūwāt*) the armed forces; اسمنت مسلح (*ismant*) ferroconcrete, reinforced concrete; خرسانة مسلحة (*ḵarsāna*) do.; زجاج مسلح (*zujāj*) wired glass

سلحفاة **sulaḥfāh, silaḥfāh** pl. سلاحف *salāḥif*[2] turtle, tortoise

سلحفائية *sulaḥfā'īya* dawdling, dilatoriness

سلخ **salaḵa** *a u* (*salḵ*) to pull off, strip off (ه s.th.); to skin, flay (ه an animal); to detach (ه عن s.th. from); to end, terminate, conclude, bring to a close (ه a period of time); to spend (ه a period of time, في doing s.th.) **V** to peel (skin, from sunburn) **VII** to be stripped off, be shed (skin, slough); to shed, cast off (من, عن the slough, the skin), strip off, take off (من, عن clothing); to abandon, give up, cast off (ه a trait, a quality); to get detached (من, عن from), come off (من, عن); to withdraw, retire (من from); to pass, end (month)

سلخ *salḵ* detaching; skinning, flaying; snakeskin, slough; end of the month

سلخ *salḵ*: خشب سلخ (*ḵašab*) (barkless) soft wood, alburnum, sapwood

سلاخ *sallāḵ* pl. ة, *-ūn* butcher

سليخ *salīḵ* skinned, flayed; tasteless, insipid (food)

سليخة *salīḵa* Chinese cinnamon tree (Cinnamomum cassia; *bot.*); cinnamon bark, cassia bark

سلخانة *salḵāna* pl. *-āt* slaughterhouse, abattoir

مسلخ *maslaḵ* pl. مسالخ *masāliḵ*[2] slaughterhouse, abattoir

مسلاخ *mislāḵ* snakeskin, slough

منسلخ *munsalaḵ* end of the month

سلس **salisa** *a* (*salas*, سلاسة *salāsa*) to be tractable, docile, compliant, obedient; to be smooth, flowing, fluent (style) **IV** to make tractable, render obedient, subdue (ه, ه s.o., s.th.); to make easy, smooth, fluent (ه s.th.)

سلس *salas* incontinence of urine

سلس *salis* tractable, pliable, docile, compliant, obedient; flexible, smooth, fluent (style) | سلس القياد *s. al-qiyād* tractable, pliable, docile, compliant, obedient

سلاسة *salāsa* tractability, pliability, docility, compliance, obedience (also سلاسة القياد *s. al-qiyād*); smoothness, fluency (of style)

اسلس *aslas*[2] more tractable, more pliable, more obedient; more flexible, smoother, more fluent

سلسبيل **salsabīl**[2] name of a spring in Paradise; spring, well

سلسل **salsala** to link together, concatenate, interlink, interlock, connect, unite (ه s.th. ب with); to chain up, enchain, fetter, shackle (ه s.o.); to pour (الماء في water into) | سلسله الى to trace s.o.'s lineage back to s.o. **II** *tasalsala* to flow down, trickle (in a continuous stream); to drip, dribble, fall in drops (water); to form a chain or series, be continuous; to be interlinked, interlocked, linked together, concatenate

سلسل *salsal* cool fresh water

سلسلة *silsila* pl. سلاسل *salāsil*[2] iron chain; chain (also fig.); series (of essays, articles, etc.) | سلسلة الجبال mountain chain; سلسلة الظهر *s. aẓ-ẓahr* backbone, vertebral column; السلسلة الفقرية (*faqrīya*) do.; سلسلة الاكاذيب fabric of lies; سلسلة النسب *s. an-nasab* lineage, line of ancestors

تسلسل *tasalsul* sequence, succession | بالتسلسل without interruption, successively, consecutively, continuously; نشره بتسلسل to serialize s.th., publish s.th. in serial form

مسلسل *musalsal* chained; continuous (numbering) | رد فعل مسلسل (*raddu fi'lin*) chain reaction (*phys.*); المرأة المسلسلة (*mar'a*) Andromeda (*astron.*)

متسلسل *mutasalsil* continuous (numbering)

[1]سلط II to give (ه s.o.) power or mastery (على over), set up as overlord, establish as ruler (على ه s.o. over); to impose, inflict (على ه a penalty on s.o.); to bring to bear, exert (ه force, pressure, and the like, على on); to load, charge (على ه s.th. with electric current) | سلطوا عليه ايديهم (*aidiyahum*) they laid violent hands on..., dealt high-handedly with ...; سلط عليه الكلاب to set the dogs on s.o. **V** to overcome, surmount (على s.th.); to overpower, overwhelm (على s.o.); to prevail, gain the upperhand (على over), get the better of (على); to be absolute master (على of), rule, reign, hold sway (على over); to control, supervise, command (على s.th.)

سلطة *sulṭa* pl. *-āt*, سلط *sulaṭ* power, might, strength; authority; sway, dominion, influence, sovereign power, jurisdiction; (pl. *-āt*) official agency, authority | السلطة الابوية (*abawīya*) paternal authority; patriarchy; السلطة الروحية (*rūḥīya*) spiritual power; السلطة التشريعية (*tašrī'īya*) legislative power; سلطة عسكرية (*'askarīya*) military authority; السلطة القضائية (*qaḍā'īya*) judicial power; السلطة التنفيذية (*tanfīḏīya*) executive power

سلطة *salṭa* jacket

سليط *salīṭ* strong, solid, firm; glib; impudent, sharp, loose, vicious (tongue)

سلاطة *salāṭa* glibness; impudence, lack of restraint (in one's language); see also alphabetically

تسلط *tasalluṭ* mastery, sway, dominion; rule, influence, authority, supremacy (على over); supervision, control

[2]سلطة *salaṭa* and سلاطة *salāṭa* salad

سلطح III اسلنطح *islanṭaḥa* to be broad, be wide

سلاطح *sulāṭiḥ* wide

سلطن *salṭana* to proclaim sultan, establish as ruler (ه s.o.) **II** تسلطن *tasalṭana* to become sultan or ruler

سلطنة *salṭana* sultanate

سلطان *sulṭān* m. and f. power, might, strength; rule, reign, dominion, sway; authority; mandate, authorization; legitimation (ب for); — (pl. سلاطين *salāṭīn*[2]) sultan; (absolute) ruler | سلطان ابراهيم *s. ibrāhīm* red mullet (Mullus barbatus; *zool.*); ما انزل الله به من سلطان (*anzala llāhu*) (lit.: God has revealed no legitimation for it; with preceding indeterminate noun) vain, unfounded, baseless, arbitrary

سلطانة *sulṭāna* sultana, sultaness

سلطانى *sulṭānī* of the sultan; sovereign, imperial, royal | طريق سلطانى imperial highway

سلطانية *sulṭānīya* soup bowl, tureen; large metal bowl

سلع *sali'a a* (*sala'*) to crack, become cracked **VII** to split, break open, burst

سلع *sal'* pl. سلوع *sulū'* crack, fissure, rift

سلعة *sil'a* pl. سلع *sila'* commodity, commercial article; sebaceous cyst, wen

سلف *salafa u* (*salaf*) to be over, be past, be bygone; to precede, antecede **II** to lend, loan, advance (ه ه to s.o. money) **IV** to make (ه s.th.) precede; to lend, loan, advance (ه ه to s.o. money) | اسلفنا (القول) (*qaul*) we have already said, we have previously stated; كما اسلفنا as we have already said **V** to borrow (من ه s.th. from); to contract a loan **VIII** = **V**

سلف *silf* pl. اسلاف *aslāf* brother-in-law

سلفة *silfa* sister-in-law

سلف *salaf* and pl. اسلاف *aslāf* predecessors; forebears, ancestors, forefathers; سلف advance payment, prepayment; free loan, noninterest-bearing loan; سلفا *salafan* in advance, beforehand, before | السلف الصالح the worthy ancestors, the venerable forefathers

سلفية *salafīya* pl. *-āt* free loan; (cash) advance

السلفية *as-salafīya* an Islamic reform movement in Egypt, founded by Mohammed ʿAbduh (1849—1905)

سلفة *sulfa* pl. سلف *sulaf* loan; (cash) advance; inner lining of shoes, inner sole

سلاف *sulāf* choicest wine (made of the juice flowing from unpressed grapes)

سلافة *sulāfa* = سلاف *sulāf*

سلفاء *sulafā'*[2] predecessors

مسلفة *mislafa* harrow

تسليف *taslīf* credit, advance | سعر التسليف *siʿr at-t.* rate of interest; بنك التسليف credit bank

تسليفة *taslīfa* credit, loan | تسليفة عقارية (*ʿaqārīya*) land credit

سالف *sālif* pl. سلف *salaf*, سلاف *sullāf*, سوالف *sawālif*[2] preceding, foregoing, former, previous, bygone, past; predecessor; سالفا *sālifan* formerly, previously; above (as a reference in books, etc.) | سوالف الاحداث former, or past, events; سالف الذكر *s. aḏ-ḏikr* aforementioned; سالف العروس *s. al-ʿarūs* amaranth (*bot.*); فى سالف الزمان *fī s. iz-zamān* in former times, in the old days

[1]سلفات *sulfāt* sulfate | سلفات النشادر *s. an-nušādir* ammonium sulfate

[2]○ سلفت *salfata* to asphalt (ه s.th.)

○ مسلفت *musalfat* asphalted

سلفيد *sulfīd* sulfide

سلق *salaqa u* (*salq*) to lacerate the skin (ه of s.o.; with a whip); to remove with boiling water (ه s.th.); to boil, cook in boiling water (ه s.th.); to scald (ه plants; said of excessive heat); to hurt (ه s.o., بلسانه *bi-lisānihī* with one's tongue, i.e., give s.o. a tongue-lashing) V to ascend, mount, climb, scale (ه s.th.); to climb up (plant)

سلق *salq* (*eg.*), *silq* a variety of chard, the leaves of which are prepared as a salad or vegetable dish

السلاق *as-sullāq* Ascension of Christ

سلاقة *salāqa* vicious tongue, violent language

سليقة *salīqa* pl. سلائق *salā'iq*[2] dish made of grain cooked with sugar, cinnamon and fennel (*syr.*); inborn disposition, instinct

سلقون *saluqūn* and سلاقون *salaqūn* red lead, minium

سلاق *salāqī* saluki, greyhound, hunting dog

سلوق *salūqī* saluki, greyhound, hunting dog

تسلق *tasalluq* climbing; ascent

مسلوق *maslūq* cooked, boiled (meat, egg, vegetable)

مسلوقة *maslūqa* pl. مساليق *masālīq*[2] bouillon, broth

النباتات المتسلقة *an-nabātāt al-mutasalliqa* climbing plants, creepers

سلك *salaka u* (*salk*, سلوك *sulūk*) to follow (ه a road), travel (ه along a road); to take (ه a road), enter upon a course or road (ه; fig.); to behave, comport o.s. (نحو toward s.o.); to proceed, act; to set foot (ه on), enter (ه a place); — *salaka* (*salk*) to insert (ه s.th. فى in), stick (ه فى s.th. into); to pass (ه thread, فى الابرة through the eye of a needle), thread a needle | سلكه فى السلسلة (*silsila*) to chain s.o. up **II** to clean, clear (ه s.th., esp. pipelines, canals, etc.); to unreel, unwind (ه yarn); to clarify, unravel, disentangle (امرا معقدا *amran muʿaqqadan* a complicated affair) **IV** to insert (ه فى s.th. in), stick (ه فى s.th. into); to pass (ه thread, فى الابرة through the eye of a needle), thread a needle

سلك **silk** pl. اسلاك *aslāk* thread; string (also, of a musical instrument); line; wire; rail (*Mor.*); — organization, body; profession (as a group or career); corps; cadre | سلك الارض *s. al-arḍ* or السلك الارضى (*arḍī*) ground wire; اسلاك بحرية (*baḥrīya*) underwater cable; ○ السلك الحرارى (*ḥarārī*) filament (of a radio tube); ○ السلك المتحكم (*mutaḥakkim*) grid (of a radio tube); (رجال) السلك السياسى (*siyāsī*) diplomatic corps; سلك الشرطة *s. aš-šurṭa* the police; السلك الشائك barbed wire; ○ سلك الانصهار الواقى fuse (*el.*); السلك التعليمى (*taʿlīmī*) the teaching profession, the teachers; سلك القضاء *s. al-qaḍā'* the judiciary, the judicature; ○ السلك المقاوم (*muqāwim*) resistor (*el.*); ○ السلك الهوائى (*hawā'ī*) antenna, aerial; انتظم فى (الى) سلك to be a member of an organization and the like; to join an organization and the like, e.g., الانتظام الى السلك البحرى (*baḥrī*) entrance into the navy (as also انخرط فى سلك)

سلكى **silkī** by wire, wire (adj.)

لاسلكى **lā-silkī** wireless; radio, broadcasting (adj. and n.); radiogram; radio specialist | اشارة لاسلكية (*išāra*) radio message; عامل لاسلكى radio operator

سلكة **silka** pl. سلك *silak* wire; thread; string (also, of a musical instrument)

سلوك **sulūk** behavior, comportment, demeanor, manners; conduct, deportment, attitude | حسن السلوك *ḥusn as-s.* good behavior, good manners; قواعد السلوك or آداب السلوك etiquette

مسلك **maslak** pl. مسالك *masālik*[2] way, road, path; course of action, policy; procedure, method | المسالك البولية (*baulīya*) the urinary passages (*anat.*); مسالك الهواء *m. al-hawā'* the respiratory passages (*anat.*); سلك مسلكا to enter upon a course (fig.)

مسلكى **maslakī** professional, vocational, industrial, trade (adj.)

تسليك **taslīk** cleaning, clearing

سالك **sālik** passable, practicable (road); entered upon (course); clear, open, not blocked, not obstructed (also *anat.*); (pl. *-ūn*) one who follows the spiritual path (esp., *myst.*)

مسلوك **maslūk** passable, practicable (road); entered upon (course)

سلم **salima** *a* (سلامة *salāma*, سلام *salām*) to be safe and sound, unharmed, unimpaired, intact, safe, secure; to be unobjectionable, blameless, faultless; to be certain, established, clearly proven (fact); to be free (من from); to escape (من a danger) **II** to preserve, keep from injury, protect from harm (ه s.o.), save (ه من s.o. from); to hand over intact (ه s.th., ل or الى to s.o.); to hand over, turn over, surrender (ه, ه s.o., s.th., ل or الى to s.o.); to deliver (ه ل or الى to s.o. s.th.); to lay down (ه arms); to surrender, give o.s. up (ل or الى to); to submit, resign o.s. (ل or الى to); to greet, salute (على s.o.); to grant salvation (God to the Prophet); to admit, concede, grant (ب s.th.); to consent (ب to s.th.), approve (ب of s.th.), accept, sanction, condone (ب s.th.) | سلم امره الى الله (*amrahū*) to commit one's cause to God, resign o.s. to the will of God; سلم روحه (*rūḥahū*) to give up the ghost; سلم نفسه الاخير (*nafasahū*) to breathe one's last, be in the throes of death; سلم نفسه للبوليس (*nafsahū*) to give o.s. up to the police; سلم اليه على الحسنى والاساءة (*ḥusnā, isā'a*) to put o.s. at s.o.'s mercy; سلم لى عليه (*sallim*) give him my best regards! remember me to him! صلى الله عليه وسلم (*ṣallā*) God bless him and grant him salvation (eulogy after the name of the Prophet Mohammed) **III** to keep the peace, make one's peace, make up (ه with s.o.) **IV** to forsake, leave, desert, give up, betray (ه s.o.); to let sink, drop (رأسه الى ركبتيه *ra'sahū i. rukbataihi* one's head to one's knees); to hand over, turn over (الى to s.o., ه or ه s.o. or s.th.); to leave, abandon (ه الى s.th. to s.o.); to deliver up, surrender, expose (ه الى s.o. to); to commit o.s., resign o.s. (لله to the will of God, with ellipsis of نفسه or امره); (اسلم alone:) to declare o.s. committed to the will of God, become a Muslim, embrace Islam | اسلم امره الى الله (*amrahū*) to commit one's cause to God, resign o.s. to the will of God; اسلم روحه (الروح) (*rūḥahū*) to give up the ghost **V** to get, obtain (ه s.th.); to receive (ه s.th.); to have (ه s.th.) handed over or delivered; to take over, assume (ه the management of s.th.) | تسلم مقاليد الحكم (*m. al-ḥukm*) to take (the reins of) power **VI** to become reconciled with one another, make peace with one another **VIII** to touch, graze (ه s.th.); to receive, get, obtain (ه s.th.); to take over (ه s.th.), take possession (ه of) **X** to surrender, capitulate; to give way, submit, yield, abandon o.s. (ل or الى to s.th.); to give o.s. over (ل or الى to s.th.; to a man, said of a woman); to lend o.s., be a party (ل or الى to s.th.); to succumb (ل to)

سلم *salm* peace

سلم *silm* m. and f. peace; the religion of Islam | حب السلم *ḥubb as-s.* pacifism

سلمى *silmī* peaceful; pacifist

سلم *salam* forward buying (*Isl. Law*); a variety of acacia

سلم *sullam* pl. سلالم *salālim*², سلاليم *salālīm*² ladder; (flight of) stairs, staircase; stair, step, running board; (*mus.*) scale; means, instrument, tool (fig.) | سلم متحرك (*mutaḥarrik*) escalator

سلمة *sullama* step, stair

سلام *salām* soundness, unimpairedness, intactness, well-being; peace, peacefulness; safety, security; — (pl. *-āt*) greeting, salutation; salute; military salute; national anthem | السلام العام (*'āmm*) general welfare, commonweal; دار السلام Paradise; an epithet of Baghdad; Dar es Salaam (seaport and capital of Tanganyika); مدينة السلام (the City of Peace =) Baghdad; نهر السلام *nahr as-s.* the Tigris; السلام عليكم (*salāmu*), سلام عليكم peace be with you! (a Muslim salutation); عليه السلام upon him be peace (used parenthetically after the names of angels and of pre-Mohammedan prophets); يا سلام exclamation of dismay, esp. after s.th. calamitous has happened: good Lord! good heavens! oh dear! يا سلام على exclamation of amazement or grief about s.th.: there goes (go) ...! what a pity for ...! how nice is (are) ...! بلغ سلامى اليه (*balliġ*) give him my kind regards! remember me to him! والسلام (and) that's all, and let it be done with that; على ... السلام it's all over with ...

سلاملك (Turk. *selamlık*) *salāmlik* selamlik, reception room, sitting room, parlor

سلامة *salāma* blamelessness, flawlessness; unimpaired state, soundness, integrity, intactness; well-being, welfare; safety, security; smooth progress; success | السلامة الاجماعية (*ijmā'īya*) collective security; سلامة الذوق *s. aḏ-ḏauq* good taste; سلامة (املاك) البلاد the integrity of the country; سلامة النية *s. an-nīya* sincerity, guilelessness; بسلامة النية in good faith, bona fide; سلامتك a speedy recovery! مع السلامة (a greeting of farewell, said by the person remaining behind) approx.: good-by! farewell! الحمد لله على السلامة (*ḥamdu*) praised be God for your well-being! (said to the traveler returning from a journey)

سليم **salīm** pl. سلماء **sulamā'**² safe, secure; free (من from); unimpaired, undamaged, unhurt, sound, intact, complete, perfect, whole, integral; faultless, flawless; well; safe and sound; safe; healthy; sane; (euphemistically) seriously injured or damaged, on the verge of ruin | سليم البنية *s. al-bunya* healthy, sound in body; سليم العاقبة benign (disease); سليم العقل *s. al-ʿaql* sane; سليم النية *s. an-nīya*, سليم القلب *s. al-qalb* guileless, sincere, goodnatured; ذوق سليم (*dauq*) good taste

سلامى **sulāmā** pl. سلاميات **sulāmayāt** phalanx, digital bone (of the hand or foot)

سلامية **sulāmīya** pl. *-āt* phalanx, digital bone (of the hand or foot)

اسلم **aslam**² safer; freer; sounder; healthier

سليمان **sulaimān**² Solomon | حوت سليمان *ḥūt s.* salmon

سليمانى **sulaimānī** corrosive sublimate, mercury chloride

تسليم **taslīm** handing over, turning over; presentation; extradition; surrender (of s.th.); delivery (*com.*; of mail); submission, surrender, capitulation; salutation; greeting; concession, admission; assent, consent (ب to), acceptance, approval, condonation, unquestioning recognition (ب of)

مسالمة **musālama** conciliation, pacification

اسلام **islām** submission, resignation, reconciliation (to the will of God); — الاسلام the religion of Islam; the era of Islam; the Muslims

اسلامى **islāmī** Islamic

اسلامية **islāmīya** the idea of Islam, Islamism; status or capacity of a Muslim

اسلامبولى look up alphabetically

تسلم **tasallum** receipt; taking over, assumption; reception

استلام **istilām** receipt; acceptance; taking over, assumption | افادة الاستلام acknowledgment of receipt

استسلام **istislām** surrender, capitulation; submission, resignation, self-surrender

سالم **sālim** safe, secure; free (من from); unimpaired, unblemished, faultless, flawless, undamaged, unhurt, intact, safe and sound, safe; sound, healthy; whole, perfect, complete, integral; regular (verb) | الجمع السالم (*jamʿ*) sound (= external) plural (*gram.*)

مسلم **musallam** unimpaired, intact, unblemished, flawless; (also مسلم به) accepted, uncontested, incontestable, indisputable, incontrovertible

مسالم **musālim** peaceable, peaceful, peaceloving; mild-tempered, lenient, gentle

مسلم **muslim** pl. *-ūn* Muslim

مستلم **mustalim** recipient; consignee

سلندر (Fr. *cylindre*) **silender** pl. *-āt* cylinder (of an automobile, and the like)

(سلو) سلا **salā** *u* (سلو *sulūw*, سلوان *sulwān*) and سلى **saliya** *a* (سلى *sulīy*) to get rid of the memory of (ه, ه or عن), forget (ه, ه or عن s.o., s.th.), think no more (ه, ه or عن of) **II** to make (ه s.o.) forget (عن s.o., s.th.); to comfort, console, solace (ه s.o., عن for the loss of); to cheer up (ه s.o.); to distract, divert (ه عن s.o.'s mind from); to amuse, entertain (ه s.o.); to alleviate, dispel (ه worries, and the like) **IV** = **II** **V** to delight, take pleasure (ب in), have a good time, have fun, amuse o.s. (ب with); to console o.s. (ب عن for s.th.

with), find comfort (عن ب for s.th. in); to seek distraction or diversion (عن ب from s.th. in)

سلوة *salwa, sulwa* solace, consolation, comfort; fun, amusement, entertainment, distraction, diversion; pastime | هو فى سلوة من العيش (*ʿaiš*) he leads a comfortable life

سلوى *salwā* consolation, solace, comfort

سلوى *salwā* (n. un. سلواة) pl. سلاوى *salāwā* quail (*zool.*)

سلوان *sulwān* forgetting, oblivion; consolation, solace, comfort

مسلاة *maslāh* pl. مسال *masālin* object of amusement; amusement, entertainment, fun, distraction, diversion; solace, consolation, comfort

تسلية *tasliya* consolation, amusement, distraction, diversion, fun; pastime, entertainment

مسل *musallin* amusing, entertaining; comforting, consoling; comforter, consoler

سلوفينيا *slovēniyā* Slovenia

□ مسلى *maslī* (*eg.*) = سمن *samn*: cooking butter | مسلى نباتى (*nabātī*) vegetable butter

سلينيوم *silīniyūm* selenium

[1] اسم *ism* pl. اسماء *asmāʾ*, اسام *asāmin* name; appellation; reputation, standing, prestige; (*gram.*) noun; اسما *isman* nominally | اسم التاليف pen name, nom de plume; اسم الكتابة do.; اسم تجارى (*tijārī*) firm name (*com.*); اسم علم *ism ʿalam* proper name; اسم جامد (*gram.*) primary noun (not derived from a verb form); اسم الجمع *ism al-jamʿ* (*gram.*) collective noun (which, though forming no nomen unitatis, has a broken plural); اسم الجنس الجمعى *ism al-jins al-jamʿī* (*gram.*) generic collective noun (which can form a nomen unitatis; e.g., حمام *ḥamām* pigeons); اسم الاشارة *ism al-išāra* (*gram.*) demonstrative pronoun; اسم التصغير (*gram.*) diminutive; اسم العدد *ism al-ʿadad* (*gram.*) numeral; اسم المعنى *ism al-maʿnā* (*gram.*) abstract noun; اسم العين *ism al-ʿain* (*gram.*) concrete noun; اسم التفضيل (*gram.*) elative; اسم الفعل *ism al-fiʿl* (*gram.*) verbal noun, nomen verbi; اسم الفاعل (*gram.*) nomen agentis, active participle; اسم المفعول (*gram.*) nomen patientis, passive participle; اسم المرة *ism al-marra* (*gram.*) nomen vicis; الاسماء الحسنى (*ḥusnā*) the 99 names of God (*Isl.*); باسم فلان in s.o.'s name, on behalf of s.o.; بسم الله in the name of God; تقدم الطلبات باسم رئيس الجمعية (*tuqaddamu ṭ-ṭalabāt*) applications will be addressed to the chairman of the society

اسمى *ismī* in name only, nominal, titular; nominal (*gram.*) | مبلغ اسمى (*mablaḡ*) nominal par; جملة اسمية (*jumla*) nominal clause (*gram.*); قيمة اسمية (*qīma*) nominal value, face value

[2] سم *samma u* (*samm*) to put poison (ه into s.th.); to poison (ه s.o., ه s.th.) II to poison (ه s.th.) V to be poisoned, poison o.s.

سم *samm* pl. سموم *sumūm*, سمام *simām* poison, toxin; venom; opening, hole; eye (of a needle) | السموم البيضاء (*baiḍāʾ*) the white narcotics (such as cocaine, Heroin, etc.)

سموم *samūm* f., pl. سمائم *samāʾim*[2] hot wind, hot sandstorm, simoom

مسام *masāmm*[2], مسامات *masāmmāt* (pl.) pores (of the skin)

مسامى *masāmmī* porous

مسامية *masāmmīya* porousness, porosity

تسمم *tasammum* poisoning, toxication; sepsis | التسمم البولى (*baulī*) uremia; التسمم الدموى (*damawī*) blood poisoning, toxemia

سام *sāmm* poisonous; toxic, toxicant; venomous

مسموم *masmūm* poisoned; poisonous

مسم *musimm* poisonous; venomous; toxic, toxicant

سمانجونى *samānjūnī* sky-blue, azure, cerulean

سمباتوى *simbātawī* sympathetic (*physiol.*)

[1]سمت III to be on the other side of (ه), be opposite s.th. (ه), face s.th. (ه)

سمت *samt* pl. سموت *sumūt* way, road; manner, mode; السمت azimuth (*astron.*) | سمت الرأس *s. ar-ra's* zenith, vertex (*astron.*); سمت الشمس *s. aš-šams* ecliptic (*astron.*); سمت الاعتدال equinoctial colure (*astron.*); سمت القدم *s. al-qadam* nadir (*astron.*); سمت الانقلاب solstitial colure (*astron.*); نظير السمت nadir (*astron.*); اخذ سمته الى to take the road to ...

[2]سمات pl. of سمة, see وسم

سمج *samuja u* to be ugly, disgusting, revolting II to make (ه s.th.) ugly or loathsome

سمج *samj* pl. سماج *simāj* and *samij* pl. سماجى *samājā* ugly, disgusting, loathsome, revolting

سميج *samīj* pl. سماج *simāj*, سماجى *samājā*, سمجاء *sumajā'*[2] ugly, disgusting, loathsome, revolting

سماجة *samāja* ugliness, abominableness, odiousness

سمح *samuḥa u* (*samḥ*, سماح *samāḥ*, سماحة *samāḥa*) to be generous, magnanimous, kind, liberal, openhanded; — *samaḥa a* (سماح *samāḥ*) to grant from a generous heart (ب ل s.o. s.th.); to allow, permit (ان or ب ل s.o. s.th. or to do s.th.); to authorize, empower (ب ل s.o. to do s.th.) | لا سمح الله God forbid! II to act with kindness III to show o.s. tolerant (ه with s.o., فى or ب in), treat kindly, with indulgence (فى or ب ه s.o. in the matter of), forgive (فى or ب ه s.o. s.th.) VI to be indulgent, forbearing, tolerant (مع فى toward s.o. in), show good will (فى in); to be not overparticular (فى in); to practice mutual tolerance X to ask s.o.'s (ه) permission; to ask forgiveness, apologize

سمح *samḥ* magnanimity, generosity; kindness; liberality, munificence

سمح *samḥ* pl. سماح *simāḥ* magnanimous, generous; kind; liberal, openhanded

سماح *samāḥ* magnanimity, generosity; kindness; liberality, munificence; indulgence, forbearance, tolerance, forgiveness, pardon; permission (ب for, to do s.th.)

سماحة *samāḥa* magnanimity; generosity; kindness; liberality, munificence; indulgence, forbearance, tolerance; سماحته His Eminence, سماحة المفتى His Eminence the Mufti (title of a mufti)

سميح *samīḥ* pl. سمحاء *sumaḥā'*[2] generous, magnanimous; kind, forgiving; liberal, openhanded

الحنيفة السمحاء *al-ḥanīfa as-samḥā'* the true and tolerant (religion, i.e., Islam)

مسامحة *musāmaḥa* pardon, forgiveness; (pl. *-āt*) vacation, holidays

تسامح *tasāmuḥ* indulgence, forbearance, leniency, tolerance

مسموح به *masmūḥ bihī* allowed, permitted, permissible, admissible | مسموحات licenses, privileges, prerogatives

متسامح *mutasāmiḥ* indulgent, forbearing (مع toward), tolerant

سمحاق *simḥāq* pl. سماحيق *samāḥīq*[2] periosteum (*anat.*)

[1]سمد *samada u* (سمود *sumūd*) to raise one's head proudly, bear one's head proudly erect (also with الرأس) II to dung, manure, fertilize (الارض the soil)

سماد *samād* pl. اسمدة *asmida* dung, manure, fertilizer | سماد صناعى (*sinā'ī*)

chemical fertilizer; سماد عضوى (*'uḍwī*) organic fertilizer

تسميد *tasmīd* manuring, fertilizing

سامد *sāmid*: سامد الرأس *s. ar-ra's* with head erect

مسمدات *musammidāt* fertilizers

2 □ سميد *samīd* (= سميذ) semolina (*syr.*); a kind of biscuit or rusk, sometimes ring-shaped and sprinkled with sesame seed (*eg.*)

سمدور *sumdūr* pl. سمادير *samādīr*² dizziness, vertigo

سميذ *samīḏ* semolina

1سمر *samura u* (سمرة *sumra*) to be or turn brown; — *samara u* (*samr*, سمور *sumūr*) to chat in the evening or at night; to chat, talk (generally) **II** to nail, fasten with nails (الى ه s.th. to or on); to drive in (المسمار *al-mismār* the nail) **III** to spend the night or evening in pleasant conversation, chat at night or in the evening (ه with s.o.); to converse, talk, chat (ه with s.o.) **V** to be or get nailed down, be fastened with nails; to stand as if pinned to the ground **VI** to spend the night or evening in pleasant conversation, chat with one another at night or in the evening; to converse, talk, chat **IX** = **I** *samura*

سمر *samar* pl. اسمار *asmār* nightly, or evening, chat; conversation, talk, chat; night, darkness

سمرة *sumra* brownness, brown color

سمار *samār* (*eg.*) a variety of rush used for plaiting mats (Juncus spinosus F., *bot.*) | سمار هندى صلب (*hindī ṣulb*) a variety of bamboo

سمير *samīr* companion in nightly entertainment, conversation partner; entertainer (in general, with stories, songs, music, amusing improvisations)

سميرة *samīra* woman partner in nightly or evening conversation; woman entertainer; woman companion (who entertains with lively conversation)

اسمر *asmar*², f. سمراء *samrā'*², pl. سمر *sumr* brown; tawny; pl. f. سمراوات *samrāwāt* brown-skinned women

مسامر *masāmir*² (pl.) evening or nightly entertainments (conversations, also games, vocal recitals, storytelling, etc.)

مسمار *mismār* pl. مسامير *masāmīr*² nail; peg; pin, tack, rivet; corn (on the toes)

الخط المسمارى *al-ḵaṭṭ al-mismārī* cuneiform writing

مسامرة *musāmara* nightly or evening chat; conversation, talk, chat

سامر *sāmir* pl. سمار *summār* companion in nightly entertainment; causeur, conversationalist; entertainer

سوامر *sawāmir*² (pl.) evenings of entertainment, social evenings; evening or nightly entertainments (conversations, also games, vocal recitals, storytelling, etc.)

مسمر *musammar* fastened with nails, nailed on, nailed down; provided, or studded, with nails; hobnailed

مسامر *musāmir* companion in nightly entertainment, conversation partner

2السامرة *as-sāmira* the Samaritans

سامرى *sāmirī* Samaritan; (pl. *-ūn*, سمرة *samara*) a Samaritan

3سمور pl. سمامير look up alphabetically

سمرقند *samarqand*² Samarkand (city in Uzbek S.S.R.)

samsara to act as broker or middleman

سمسرة *samsara* brokerage; caravansary

سمسار *simsār* pl. سماسرة *samāsira*, سماسر *samāsir*², سماسير *samāsīr*² broker, jobber, middleman, agent | سمسار الاسهم *s. al-ashum* stockbroker

سمسيرة *samsīra* (*ir.*) go-between, matchmaker

سمسم *simsim* sesame

سمط *samaṭa* *u* (*samṭ*) to scald (ه s.th.); to prepare (ه s.th.)

سمط *simṭ* pl. سموط *sumūṭ* string, thread (of a pearl necklace)

سماط *simāṭ* pl. *-āt*, سمط *sumuṭ*, اسمطة *asmiṭa* cloth on which food is served; meal, repast

مسمط *masmaṭ* pl. مسامط *masāmiṭ*² scalding house (where the carcasses of slaughtered animals are scalded)

○ مسمط *mismaṭ* pl. مسامط *masāmiṭ*² vine prop

سمع *sami'a* *a* (*sam'*, سماع *samā'*, سماعة *samā'a*, مسمع *masma'*) to hear (ه, ه s.o., s.th.; ب of or about s.th.; ه من s.th. from s.o.); to learn, be told (ه من of or about s.th. from s.o.); to listen, pay attention (الى or ل to s.th.; من to s.o.), hear s.o. (من) out; to learn by hearsay (ب about s.th.); to overhear (ب s.th.); to give ear, lend one's ear (الى or ل to s.o., to s.th.) | لم يسمع به (*yusma'*) unheard-of **II** to make or let (ه s.o.) hear (ه s.th.), give (ه ه s.o. s.th.) to hear; to recite (ه s.th.); to say (ه one's lesson); to dishonor, discredit (ب s.o.) **IV** to make or let (ه s.o.) hear (ه s.th.), give (ه ه s.o. s.th.) to hear; to let (ه s.o.) know (ه s.th. or about s.th.), tell (ه ه s.o. about s.th.) **V** to give ear, listen, lend one's ear (الى, ل to s.o., to s.th.); to eavesdrop, listen (secretly) **VI** تسامع به الناس people heard about him from one another, word about him got around, he became known among people **VIII** to hear, overhear (ه s.th.); to listen, listen closely, give ear, lend one's ear (الى or ل or ه, ه to s.o. or s.th.); to eavesdrop; to auscultate (على s.o.)

سمع *sam'* hearing, sense of hearing, audition; ears; (pl. اسماع *asmā'*) ear | شاهد السمع earwitness; السمع والطاعة *as-sam'u wa-ṭ-ṭā'atu* and سمعا وطاعة *sam'an wa-ṭā'atan* I hear and obey! at your service! very well! تحت سمعهم in their hearing, for them to hear; استرق السمع *istaraqa s-sam'a* to eavesdrop; to monitor, intercept; القى بسمعه اليه (*alqā*) to listen to s.o.; مد سمعه *madda sam'ahū* to prick up one's ears

سمعى *sam'ī* auditory, auditive, hearing (used attributively); acoustic; acoustical; traditional | علم السمعيات *'ilm as-sam'īyāt* acoustics

سمعة *sum'a* reputation (specif., good reputation), credit, standing, name | حسن (or جيد) السمعة (*ḥasan*) reputable, respectable; ردىء (or سيئ) السمعة *radī'* (*sayyi'*) *as-s.* ill-reputed, disreputable

سماع *samā'* hearing, listening, listening in; auditioning, audition; hearing, receiving (e.g., of a verdict); (*gram.* and *lex.*) generally accepted usage

سماعى *samā'ī* acoustic; acoustical; audible; (*gram.* and *lex.*) sanctioned by common usage; derived from tradition, traditional, unwritten (*Isl. Law*)

سماعيات *samā'īyāt* acoustics (*phys.*)

سميع *samī'* pl. سمعاء *sumaʻā'*² hearing, listening; hearer, listener; السميع the All-hearing (one of the 99 attributes of God)

سماعة *sammā'a* pl. *-āt* earphone; earpiece; (telephone) receiver; stethoscope; ear trumpet; knocker, rapper (of a door)

مسمع *masma'* earshot, hearing distance | على مسمع من in the hearing of, within earshot of; على مسمع منه for him to hear, so that he could hear it

مسمع *misma'* pl. مسامع *masāmi'*² ear; ○ stethoscope; (telephone) receiver |

على مسامعهم in their hearing, for them to hear

مسمعة *misma'a* earpiece; (telephone) receiver

سامع *sāmi'* pl. *-ūn* hearer, listener

مسموع *masmū'* audible, perceptible | مسموع الكلمة *m. al-kalima* one whose word carries weight, is paid attention to

مستمع *mustami'* pl. *-ūn* hearer, listener; pl. المستمعون the audience

1 سمق *samaqa u* (سموق *sumūq*) to be high, tall, lofty, tower up

سموق *samūq* very high, towering; tall and lanky

سامق *sāmiq* very high, lofty, towering

2 سماق *summāq* sumac (Rhus; *bot.*); its highly acid seeds which, after being dried and ground, serve, together with thyme, as a condiment

حجر سماقى *ḥajar summāqī* porphyry

سمك II to make thick, thicken (ه s.th.)

سمك *samk* roof, ceiling

سمك *sumk* thickness

سمك *samak* (coll.; n. un. ة) pl. سماك *simāk*, اسماك *asmāk* fish | سمك موسى *s. mūsā* plaice (*zool.*)

سمكة *samaka* (n. un.) a fish; السمكة the Fish, Pisces (*astron.*)

سمكى *samakī* fish-like, fishy, piscine, fish (adj.)

سماك *simāk*: السماكان *as-simākān* Arcturus and Spica Virginis (*astron.*) | السماك الرامح Arcturus (*astron.*); السماك الاعزل (*a'zal*) Spica Virginis (*astron.*); حلق الى السماكين (*ḥallaqa*) to have high-flown aspirations

سماك *sammāk* fishmonger; fisherman, fisher

سميك *samīk* thick

سماكة *samāka* thickness

مسامك *masāmik*² fish stores, sea-food stores

سمكرة *samkara* tinsmith's trade, tinsmithing

سمكرى *samkarī* tinsmith, tinner, white-smith

سمكرية *samkarīya* trade or work of a tinsmith, tinsmithing

سمل *samala u* (*saml*) to gouge, scoop out, tear out (عينه *'ainahū* s.o.'s eye); — *samala u* (سمول *sumūl*, سمولة *sumūla*) to be worn, tattered, in rags (garment) IV to be worn, tattered, in rags (garment) VIII to gouge, scoop out, tear out (عينه *'ainahū* s.o.'s eye)

سمل *samal* pl. اسمال *asmāl* worn garment; tatters, rags; last remainder of a liquid in a vessel | شرب الكأس حتى السمل to drain the cup to the dregs

سمن *samina a* (*siman*, سمانة *samāna*) to be or become fat, corpulent, obese, stout, plump, fleshy, put on weight II and IV to make fat or plump, fatten (ه s.o.)

سمن *samn* pl. سمون *sumūn* clarified butter, cooking butter

سمن *siman* fatness, plumpness, fleshiness, stoutness, corpulence; obesity

سمنة *simna* fatness, plumpness, fleshiness, stoutness, corpulence; obesity

سمن *summun* (coll.; n. un. ة) pl. سمامن *samāmin*² quail (*zool.*)

سمين *samīn* pl. سمان *simān* fat; corpulent, plump, fleshy, stout, obese

سمان *summān* (coll.; n. un. ة) quail (*zool.*)

سمان *sammān* butter merchant

سمانة *samāna*: سمانة الرجل *s. ar-rijl* calf of the leg

سمانى *sumānā* (coll.; n. un. سماناة *sumānāh*) pl. سمانيات *sumānayāt* quail (*zool.*)

مسمن *musamman* fat

سمنتو (Sp. *cemento*) cement

سمنجونى *samanjūnī* and سمانجونى *samānjūnī* sky-blue, azure, cerulean

سمندر *samandar* salamander

سمندل *samandal* salamander

سمهرى *samharī* tall and husky, extremely tall, of giant stature (سمهرى القامة); spear (originally epithet of a strong, tough spear)

سمة *sima* see وسم

سما (سمو) *samā u* (سمو *sumūw*) to be high, elevated, raised, erect, lofty, tall, eminent, prominent; to rise high, tower up; to be above or beyond s.th. or s.o. (عن), rise above, tower above (عن); to be too proud (عن for); to be too high or difficult (عن for s.o.), be or go beyond the understanding of s.o. (عن), exceed s.o.'s (عن) understanding; to rise (الى to, على above or beyond); to be higher (على than); to strive (الى for), aspire (الى to, after) | سما به to lift, raise, elevate, exalt, lead up, bring up s.o. or s.th. (الى to); to buoy s.o. up, boost, encourage s.o. **III** to seek to surpass or excel (ه s.o.); to vie for superiority or glory (ه with s.o.) **IV** to lift, raise, elevate, exalt, lead up, bring up (ه, ه s.o., s.th.) **VI** to vie with one another for glory; to be high, elevated, raised, erect, lofty, tall, eminent, prominent; to rise high, tower up; to be above or beyond s.th. or s.o. (عن), rise above, tower above (عن); to claim to be higher in rank (على than s.o. else), claim to be above s.o. (على); to deem o.s. highly superior

سمو *sumūw* height, altitude; exaltedness, loftiness, eminence, highness | سمو الدوق His Grace the Duke; صاحب السمو الملكى (*malakī*) His Royal Highness; صاحبة السمو الملكى Her Royal Highness; سمو الاخلاق nobility of character

سماء *samā'* m. and f., pl. سماوات (سموات) *samāwāt* heaven, sky; firmament | سماء السماوات the highest heaven

سمائى *samā'ī* heavenly, celestial; sky-blue, azure, cerulean

سماوى *samāwī* heavenly, celestial; sky-blue, azure, cerulean; descended from heaven; open-air, outdoor, (being) under the open sky; divine, pertaining to God and religion

سمى *samīy* high, elevated; exalted, lofty, sublime, august

اسمى *asmā* higher, farther up, above; more exalted, higher (in rank), more eminent, loftier, more sublime

سام *sāmin* pl. سماة *sumāh* high, elevated; exalted, lofty, eminent, sublime, august | امر سام (*amr*) royal decree; المندوب السامى the High Commissioner

سمور *sammūr* pl. سمامير *samāmīr*[2] sable (Martes zibellina; *zool.*)

سمى **II** to name, call, designate, denominate (ه, ه s.o., s.th., ب or ه by or with a name), give a name (ه, ه to s.o., to s.th.); to title, entitle (ه or ب ه s.th. as or with); to nominate, appoint (ل ه s.o. to s.th.); to pronounce the name of God by saying بسم الله | سمى الله عليه (*sammā llāha*) or سمى عليه to invoke God over s.th. by saying بسم الله **IV** to name, call, designate, denominate (ه, ه s.o., s.th., ب or ه by or with a name), give a name (ه, ه to s.o., to s.th.); to title, entitle (ه s.th., ه or ب as or with) **V** to be called, be named | تسمى بزيد he was named Zaid, he called himself Zaid

اسم *ism* see سم[1]

سمى *samīy* namesake

تسمية *tasmiya* pl. *-āt* naming, appellation, designation, name, denomination; nomenclature; = بسملة *basmala* (use of the formula بسم الله)

مسمى *musamman* named, called, by name of; — (pl. مسميات *musammayāt*) designation, appellation, name; sense, meaning (of a word) | الى اجل مسمى (*ajalin*) for a limited period, الى اجل غير مسمى for an indefinite time, sine die, until further notice

[1]سنة *sana* pl. سنون *sinūn*, سنوات *sanawāt* year | سنة محمدية (*muhammadīya*) Mohammedan year; سنة كبيسة leap year; سنة مسيحية (*masīhīya*) year of the Christian era, A.D.; سنة هجرية (*hijrīya*) year of the Muslim era (after the hegira), A.H.; سنة ميلادية (*mīlādīya*) year of the Christian era, A.D.

سنوى *sanawī* annual, yearly; سنويا *sanawīyan* annually, yearly, in one year, per year, per annum

مسانهة *musānahatan* annually, yearly

[2]سنة *sina* see وسن

[3]سن *sanna u* (*sann*) to sharpen, whet, hone, grind (ه s.th.); to mold, shape, form (ه s.th.); to prescribe, introduce, enact, establish (ه a law, a custom) | سن قانونا to enact, or pass, a law **II** to sharpen, whet, hone, grind (ه s.th.); to indent, jag, notch (ه s.th.) **IV** to grow teeth, cut one's teeth, teethe; to grow old, to age; to be advanced in years **VIII** to clean and polish one's teeth with the سواك; to take, follow (ه a course or way); to prescribe, introduce, enact, establish (ه a law, a custom) | استن سنة محمد (*sunnata m.*) to follow the Sunna of Mohammed

سن *sann* prescription, introduction, enactment, issuance (of laws)

سن *sinn* f., pl. اسنان *asnān*, اسنة *asinna*, اسن *asunn* tooth (also, e.g., of a comb, of a saw blade); jag; cog, sprocket, prong; tusk (of an elephant, of a boar, etc.); fang (of a snake, etc.); point, tip (of a nail), nib (of a pen); (pl. اسنان *asnān*) age (of a person); — (*eg.*) coarse flour, seconds | سن الرشد *s. ar-rušd* legal age, majority; سن الفيل *s. al fīl* ivory; صغير السن young; كبير السن old; طعن فى السن to be advanced in years, be aged; تقدمت به السن (*taqaddamat*) to grow older, to age; to be advanced in years

سنة *sunna* pl. سنن *sunan* habitual practice, customary procedure or action, norm, usage sanctioned by **tradition**; السنة or سنة النبى *s. an-nabīy* the Sunna of the Prophet, i.e., his sayings and doings, later established as legally binding precedents (in addition to the Law established by the Koran) | اهل السنة *ahl as-s.* the Sunnites, the orthodox Muslims; سنة الطبيعة law of nature

سنى *sunnī* Sunnitic; (pl. *-ūn*) Sunnite, Sunni

سنن *sanan* customary practice, usage, habit, rule

سنان *sinān* pl. اسنة *asinna* spearhead

سنون *sanūn* tooth powder

اسن *asann*[2] older, farther advanced in years

مسن *misann* pl. *-āt*, مسان *masānn*[2] whetstone, grindstone; razor strop

مسنون *masnūn* prescribed (as Sunna), sanctioned by law and custom; sharpened, whetted, honed; tapered; pointed (e.g., mustache, features); stinking, fetid (mire)

مسنن *musannan* toothed, serrated, dentate, denticulate, indented, jagged; pointed, sharp; sharp-featured (countenance)

مسننة *musannana* pl. *-āt* cogwheel

مسن *musinn* pl. مسان *masānn*[2] old, aged, advanced in years; of legal age, legally major

سنو see سنا

سنارة *sinnāra* pl. سنانير *sanānīr*² fishing tackle; fishhook

سنباذج *sunbāḏaj* grindstone, whetstone; emery

سنبوق *sunbūq* pl. سنابيق *sanābīq*² barge, skiff, boat

¹سنبك *sunbuk* pl. سنابك *sanābik*² toe of the hoof; hoof; awl, punch, borer

²سنبك *sunbuk* pl. سنابك *sanābik*² and سنبوك *sunbūk* pl. سنابيك *sanābīk*² barge, skiff, boat

سنبل *sunbul* (coll.; n. un. ة) pl. *-āt,* سنابل *sanābil*² ear, spike (of grain); السنبلة Virgo (*astron.*) | السنبل الروى (*rūmī*) Celtic spikenard (Nardus celtica; *bot.*); السنبل الهندى (*hindī*) Indian spikenard (Nardostachys jatamansi; *bot.*)

سنبلى *sunbulī* spiciform, spicate, shaped like a spike or ear (*bot.*)

سنبوسك *sanbūsik, sanbūsak* (*syr., ir.*) triangular meat pie with a wavy bread crust

سنت cent

سنتمتر *santimitr* pl. *-āt* centimeter

¹سنجة *sanja* pl. سنج *sinaj,* سنجات *sanajāt* weight (placed as a counterpoise on the scales of a balance)

²سنجة *singa* (from Turk. *süngü*) pl. سنج *sinag* bayonet (*eg.*)

³سناج *sinā́j* soot, smut

سنجاب *sinjāb* gray squirrel; fur of the gray squirrel

سنجابى *sinjābī* ash-colored, ashen, gray

سنجق *sanjaq* pl. سناجق *sanājiq*² standard, flag, banner; sanjak, administrative district and subdivision of a vilayet (in the Ottoman Empire)

سنح *sanaḥa a* (*sunḥ, sunuḥ,* سنوح *sunūḥ*) to occur (ل to s.o.), come to s.o.'s mind (ل, idea, thought); to present itself, offer itself (ل to s.o., esp. an opportunity); to afford (ب ل s.o s.th.); — to dissuade (عن ه s.o. from his opinion), argue or reason (عن ه s.o. out of his opinion)

سانح *sāniḥ* pl. سوانح *sawāniḥ*² turning its right side toward the viewer (game or bird); auspicious, propitious; favorable, good (opportunity); pl. سوانح auspices, good omens, auspicious signs; ideas, thoughts

سانحة *sāniḥa* opportunity

سنخ *sinḵ* pl. اسناخ *asnāḵ,* سنوخ *sunūḵ* root, origin; alveolus, gingival margin of a tooth (*anat.*)

سنخ *sanaḵ* rankness (of oil), fustiness

سنخ *saniḵ* rank, rancid (oil), fusty

سناخة *sanāḵa* rankness (of oil), fustiness

¹سند *sanada u* (سنود *sunūd*) to support o.s., prop o.s., rest (الى on, upon), lean, recline (الى upon, against) **II** to support, stay, prop, lean (ه s.th.) **III** to support, back, assist, help, aid (ه s.o.) **IV** to make (ه s.o.) rest (الى on); to make (ه s.o.) lean or recline (الى against, on); to lean (الى ه s.th. against); to rest, support, prop (الى ه s.th. on); to base, found (الى ه s.th. on); (science of Islamic traditions:) to base a tradition (ه) on s.o. (الى) as its first authority, i.e., to trace back the ascription of a tradition, in ascending order of the traditionaries, to its first authority so as to corroborate its credibility; (*gram.*) to lean a term (ه) upon another (الى) being the subject of the sentence, i.e., to predicate it, make it its predicate; to entrust (ل or الى ه s.th. to s.o.), vest (ل or الى ه s.th. in s.o.); to attribute, ascribe (ه ل or الى to s.o. s.th.); to incriminate, charge (ه الى s.o. with); to lean (الى against, to, on), rest (الى on); to be based, be founded (الى on) | اسند التهمة الى (*tuhma*) to direct one's suspicion on

or toward ...; اسندت التّهمة الى (*usnidat*) suspicion fell on ... VI to support one another, give mutual support; to support o.s., lean, rest; to trust, rely VIII to lean, recline, be recumbent (على, الى against, on); to rest one's arms, one's weight (على, الى on), support one's weight (على, الى by); to be based, be founded (على, الى on); to rely (على, الى on), trust, have confidence (على, الى in); to use as (documentary) basis (على s.th.), rest one's case on (على)

سند *sanad* pl. *-āt*, اسناد *asnād* support, prop, stay, rest, back; backing; (pl. اسناد) ascription (of an Islamic tradition), the (uninterrupted) chain of authorities on which a tradition is based | سندات خشبية (*kašabīya*) wooden struts, wood bracing; — (pl. *-āt*) document, deed, paper, legal instrument; voucher, record; commercial, or negotiable, paper, security, bond, debenture, promissory note, note of hand, debenture bond | سند شحن البضائع *s. šaḥn al-b.* bill of lading; رجال السند informants, authorities, sources

سندان *sandān, sindān* pl. سنادين *sanādīn*[2] anvil

مسند *misnad, masnad* pl. مساند *masānid*[2] support, prop, stay; rest, back (of an armchair); cushion, pillow

اسناد *isnād* pl. اسانيد *asānīd*[2] ascription (of an Islamic tradition), the (uninterrupted) chain of authorities on which a tradition is based; اسانيد (documentary) proof, vouchers, records, documents

استناد *istinād* leaning (الى against or upon); dependence (الى on) | استنادا الى based on, on the basis of, on the strength of

مسند *musnad* pl. مساند *masānid*[2] (science of Islamic traditions:) a tradition the ascription of which is traceable, in (uninterrupted) ascending order of the traditionaries, to its first authority; mesh; المسند predicate (*gram.*); المسند اليه subject (*gram.*)

مستند *mustanid* relying, in reliance (على, الى on), trusting (على, الى to)

مستند *mustanad* reason, cause; motive; — (pl. *-āt*) document, paper, deed, legal instrument; voucher, record; receipt; pl. (documentary) proof, records, data; legal evidence (*jur.*) | دار المستندات archives, office of public records; مستندات الشحن *m. aš-šaḥn* bills of lading

[2]السند *as-sind* region extending along the lower course and delta of the Indus river; the province of Sind, of West Pakistan, with the capital city Karachi; the inhabitants of this region

سندروس *sandarūs* sandarac (a resin obtained from the sandarac tree, Callitris quadrivalvis)

سندس *sundus* silk brocade, sarcenet

سندسى *sundusī* (made) of silk brocade or sarcenet

سندال = سندان (see above)

سنديان *sindiyān* (coll.; n. un. ة) evergreen oak, holm oak (Quercus ilex; *bot.*)

سنديانى *sindiyānī* oaken; like oak, oaky

سنديك (Fr. *syndic*) *sandīk* syndic, agent of a corporation

[1]سنور *sinnaur* pl. سنانير *sanānīr*[2] cat

[2]سنارة *sinnāra* pl. سنانير *sanānīr*[2] fishing tackle, fishhook

السنسكريتية *as-sanskrītīya* Sanskrit

[1]سنط *sanṭ* a variety of sant tree (Acacia nilotica; *bot.*)

[2]سنطة *sanṭa* (*eg.*) wart

سنطور *sanṭūr* dulcimer (= سنطير)

سنطورس *sinṭōros* Centaurus (*astron.*)

سنطير *sinṭīr, sanṭīr* psalter; dulcimer

سنغافورة *singāfūra* Singapore

سنغال *siniġāl* Senegal

سنف *sinf* (coll.; n. un. ة) pod, capsule, hull (*bot.*)

سنفرة *sanfara* emery

سنكرى *sankarī* pl. سناكرة *sanākira* tinsmith, tinsman, tinner, whitesmith

سنكسار *sinaksār* synaxarion, martyrologium (*Chr.*)

سنكه (Turk. *süngü*) *sənge* bayonet (*syr.*)

سنكونا *sinkūnā* cinchona (*bot.*)

سنم V to ascend, mount, scale (ه s.th.) | تسنم ذروة المعالى (*ḏarwata l-ma'ālī*) to attain to greatest honors

سنمة *sanama* height, summit, peak

سنام *sanām* pl. اسنمة *asnima* hump (of the camel)

ماء التسنيم *mā' at-tasnīm* the beverage of the blessed in Paradise

تسنم *tasannum* accession to the throne

مسنم *musannam* convex, vaulted, arched

سنمار[1] *sinimmār*[2]: جزاه جزاء سنمار *jazāhu jazā'a s.* he repaid him as they had repaid S., i.e., he requited evil with good

سنمورة[2] *sanamūra* anchovy; salted and smoked fish

سنه[1] V to become stale, spoil (food)

مسانهة[2] *musānahatan* annually, yearly

سنا[1] *sanā*, سنا مكى *s. makkī*, سنا مكة *s. makka* (*bot.*) senna (tree); senna leaflets (*pharm.*)

[2](سنو and سنى) سنا *sanā u* (سناء *sanā'*) to gleam, shine, glisten, be resplendent, radiate; to flash (lightning) II to facilitate, ease, make easy (ه s.th.) V to be easy, be possible, be feasible (ل for or to s.o.), be rendered possible or feasible (ل for s.o.), be put in s.o.'s (ل) power; to rise, be elevated, be exalted

سنى and سنا *sanan* brilliance, resplendence, splendor; flare, flash, sparkle

سناء *sanā'* brilliance, resplendence, splendor, radiance; flash, flare (of lightning); exaltedness, sublimity, majesty, high rank

سنى *sanīy* high, sublime, exalted, splendid

اسنى *asnā* more shining, more radiant, more brilliant

سانية *sāniya* pl. سوان *sawānin* water scoop

مسناة *musannāh* pl. مسنيات *musannayāt* jetty, dam

سنودس (Gr. σύνοδος) *sinōdos* synod

سنونو *sunūnū* swallow (*zool.*)

سنوى *sanawī* annual, yearly; سنويا *sanawīyan* annually, yearly, per year, per annum

سهب IV to speak at great length, talk in detail (عن about, of), enlarge, elaborate, expatiate, dilate (عن on)

سهب *suhb* pl. سهوب *suhūb* level country; steppe region

اسهاب *ishāb* elaboration, elaborateness, expatiation, long-windedness, prolixity | باسهاب elaborately, in detail, at length, lengthily

مسهب *mushib, mushab* prolix, long-winded, lengthy, detailed, elaborate

سهد *sahida a* (*sahad*) to be sleepless, find no sleep II to make sleepless, keep awake, deprive of sleep (ه s.o.) V = I

سهد *suhd* sleeplessness, insomnia

سهد *suhud* insomniac

سهاد *suhād* sleeplessness, insomnia

ساهد *sāhid* sleepless, awake

سهر **sahira** *a* (*sahar*) to be sleepless, find no sleep, pass the night awake (also with الليل); to stay up at night, spend the night (على in or with some activity); to watch (على over), guard (على s.o.'s interests, etc.), look after (على), attend to (على s.o.'s interests, etc.) | سهر فى حفلة to attend a gathering in the evening or at night **IV** to make sleepless, keep awake (ه s.o.)

سهر *sahar* sleeplessness, insomnia; wakefulness, vigil; watchfulness, vigilance (على over) | طال عنده سهرى I spent a long evening with him

سهرة *sahra* pl. *saharāt* evening; evening party, evening gathering, evening show or performance, soirée | سهرة ليلية (*lailīya*) do.; ثياب (or لباس) السهرة evening dress, formal dress

سهران *sahrān* sleepless, awake, wakeful; watchful, vigilant

سهار *suhār* sleeplessness, insomnia; wakefulness, vigil

سهار *sahhār* one who is habitually up and abroad at night, a nighthawk

○ اسهر *ashar* spermatic duct (*anat.*)

مسهر *mashar* pl. مساهر *masāhir*[2] nightclub

ساهر *sāhir* sleepless, awake, wakeful; watchful, vigilant; evening, night, nocturnal, nightly, taking place by night | حفلة ساهرة (*ḥafla*) evening party, evening gathering, evening show or performance, soirée

سهف **sahifa** *a* (*sahaf*) to be very thirsty

سهاف *suhāf* violent thirst

سهل **sahula** *u* (سهولة *suhūla*) to be smooth, level, even (ground); to be or become easy, facile, convenient (على for) | لا يسهل ان hardly ... **II** to smooth, level, even (ه the ground); to facilitate, make easy, ease (ه ل or على for s.o. s.th.); to provide, furnish, supply (ه ل or على s.o. with facilities); (*gram.*) to read without hamzah (ه a word) **III** to be indulgent, mild, forbearing, obliging (ه toward s.o.), show (ه s.o.) one's good will | ساهل نفسه (*nafsahū*) to take liberties **IV** to purge (*med.*); to relieve (ه the constipated bowels, said of a medicine); pass. *ushila* to be relieved (said of constipated bowels), have a bowel movement, have diarrhea **V** to be or become easy (ل for) **VI** to be indulgent, mild, forbearing, obliging, tolerant (مع toward s.o., also ل); to be negligent, careless (فى in s.th.) **X** to deem easy, think to be easy (ه s.th.)

سهل *sahl* and *sahil* smooth, level, even, soft (ground); easy, facile, convenient (على for s.o.); simple, plain; fluent, flowing, facile (style); — (pl. سهول *suhūl*) level, soft ground; plain | سهل الاستعمال handy, easy to handle or to use, convenient for use; سهل الهضم *s. al-haḍm* easily digestible, light; عملة سهلة (*'umla*) soft currency; كان من السهل عليه to be easy for s.o., come easy to s.o.; اهلا وسهلا see اهل

○ سهلة *sahla* (proof) planer (*typ.*)

سهيل *suhail* Canopus (*astron.*)

سهول *sahūl* purgative, laxative, aperient (adj. and n.)

سهولة *suhūla* easiness, ease, facility, convenience | بسهولة easily, conveniently

اسهل *ashal*[2] smoother, evener, leveler; easier; more convenient

تسهيل *tashīl* pl. *-āt* facilitation

اسهال *ishāl* diarrhea

تساهل *tasāhul* indulgence, mildness, leniency, forbearance, tolerance; carelessness, negligence

مسهل *mushil* purgative, laxative, aperient; (pl. *-āt*) a purgative, a laxative

مسهل *mushal* suffering from diarrhea

متساهل *mutasāhil* indulgent, mild, lenient, forbearing, tolerant

مستسهل *mustashal* easy, facile

سهم *sahama u* (سهوم *suhūm*) to look grave, have a grave expression III to cast, or draw, lots (ه with s.o.); to participate, take part (في in), partake (في of s.th.), share (في s.th.) IV to give a share (ل في to s.o. in), make s.o. (ل) share s.th. (في)

سهم *sahm* pl. سهام *sihām*, اسهم *ashum*, سهوم *suhūm* arrow; dart; — (pl. اسهم *ashum*) portion, share, lot; share (of stock); sahme, a square measure of 7.293 m² (*Eg.*) | سهم نارى rocket; اسهم التأسيس founders' shares, original shares; اسهم القرض *a. al-qarḍ* bonds, government bonds; حملة الاسهم *ḥamalat al-a.* shareholders, stockholders; نفذ السهم the die is cast; ضرب بسهم مصيب في (*muṣībin*) to take an active part in, participate actively in ...; ضرب بسهم ونصيب في (*wa-naṣībin*) do.

سهوم *suhūm* graveness; sadness, mourning

اسهمى *ashumī* share-, stock- (in compounds)

مساهمة *musāhama* participation, taking part (في in), sharing (في of) | شركة المساهمة *širkat al-m.* joint-stock company, corporation

ساهم *sāhim* with earnest mien, grave-faced

مساهم *musāhim* shareholder, stockholder

(سهو) سها *sahā u* (*sahw*, *suhūw*) to be inattentive, absent-minded, distracted; to neglect, omit, forget, overlook (عن s.th.) | سهى عليه *suhiya 'alaihi* to be lost in thought

سهو *sahw* inattentiveness, inattention, inadvertence, absent-mindedness, distractedness; negligence, neglectfulness, forgetfulness | سهوا *sahwan* inattentively, distractedly, absent-mindedly, heedlessly, negligently; inadvertently, by mistake

سهوة *sahwa* a kind of alcove

سهوان *sahwān*² inattentive, heedless, distracted, absent-minded, forgetful

ساه *sāhin* inattentive, absent-minded, negligent, forgetful | ساهيا لاهيا *sāhiyan lāhiyan* amusing o.s. in a carefree manner, completely at ease

¹(سوء) ساء *sā'a u* (سوء *sau'*) to be or become bad, evil, foul, wicked; to become worse, deteriorate (condition); to grieve, sadden, afflict, hurt, vex, torment, trouble, offend, pain, make sorry, displease (ه s.o.) | ساء سبيلا (*sabīlan*) what an evil way (= what an evil practice) this is! ساء به ظنا (*ẓannan*) to think badly of s.o., have a poor opinion of s.o.; ساء طالعه (*ṭāli'uhū*) he was under an evil star, was ill-starred, he was unlucky or unfortunate; يسوءنى *yasū'unī* I am sorry II to do badly, spoil, harm (ه s.th.); to blame, censure (ه على s.o. for s.th.); to disapprove (ه of s.th. على in s.o.), dislike (ه على s.th. in s.o.) IV to do badly, spoil, harm (ه s.th.); to deal badly (الى with s.o.), act meanly or evilly (الى toward s.o.); to do evil (الى to s.o.), wrong (الى s.o.); to harm (الى s.o.), do harm (ل to); to hurt, offend, insult (الى s.o.); to inflict pain (ل on s.o.) | اساء التصرف (*taṣarrufa*) to misbehave, comport o.s. badly; اساء التصرف في to go about ... in an evil manner; اساء الظن به (*ẓanna*) to think badly of s.o., have a poor opinion of s.o.; اساء التعبير to choose a poor expression, express o.s. poorly; اساء استعماله to misuse, abuse s.th.; اساء معاملته (*mu'āmalatahū*) to mistreat s.o., treat s.o. badly; اساء الفهم (*fahma*) to misunderstand VIII to go through rugged times, fall on evil days; to be unpleasantly affected; to be offended,

hurt, annoyed, indignant, upset, angered, displeased (من about, at, by); to be dissatisfied, discontent (من with); to take amiss (من s.th.)

سوء *sū'* pl. اسواء *aswā'* evil, ill; iniquity, injury, offense; calamity, misfortune | سوء البخت *s. al-bakt* misfortune, bad luck; سوء الحظ *s. al-ḥaẓẓ* do.; لسوء الحظ unfortunately; سوء الخلق *s. al-kuluq* ill nature, ill-temperedness; سوء الحال bad conditions; سوء الحالة bad situation, predicament; سوء الادارة *s. al-idāra* maladministration, mismanagement; سوء السلوك bad behavior, misbehavior, misconduct; سوء الظن *s. aẓ-ẓann* poor opinion; سوء العلاقات bad relations; سوء المعاملة *s. al-mu'āmala* mistreatment; سوء الاستعمال abuse, misuse; سوء الفهم *s. al-fahm* misunderstanding; سوء التفاهم *s. at-tafāhum* mutual misunderstanding, disharmony, discord; سوء القصد *s. al-qaṣd* evil intent; سوء النية *s. an-nīya* do.; سوء الهضم *s. al-haḍm* indigestion

سوأة, سوءة *sau'a* pl. *-āt* shame, disgrace; disgraceful act, atrocity; private part, pudendum; pudenda | سوءة لك (*sau'atan*) shame on you!

سيء, سيّئ *sayyi'* bad, evil, ill, foul | سيء الحظ *s. al-ḥaẓẓ* unfortunate; unlucky person; سيء الخلق *s. al-kuluq* ill-natured; سيء التربية *s. at-tarbiya* bad-mannered, badly brought up; سيء السمعة *s. as-sum'a* ill-reputed, disreputable; سيء الطبع *s. aṭ-ṭab'* ill-natured, ill-tempered; سيء الطالع unlucky, unfortunate; unlucky person; من سيء الى اسوأ (*aswa'a*) from bad to worse

سيئة *sayyi'a* pl. *-āt* sin, offense, misdeed; bad side, disadvantage (of s.th.)

مساءة *masā'a* pl. مساوئ *masāwi'*[2] evil deed, vile action; pl. disadvantages, bad sides, drawbacks, shortcomings

اساءة *isā'a* misdeed; offense, affront, insult; sin, offense | اساءة الظن *i. aẓ-ẓann* poor opinion (ب of); اساءة المعاملة *i. al-mu'āmala* mistreatment, etc., see IV above

استياء *istiyā'* dissatisfaction, discontent, indignation, displeasure, annoyance, vexation

مسيء *musī'* displeasing, unpleasant, offensive; harmful, disadvantageous, pernicious; insulting

مستاء *mustā'* offended, displeased, annoyed, vexed, indignant (من about, at, by); dissatisfied, discontent (من with)

سوى see سواء[2]

سوارى *sawārī* horseman, cavalryman, sowar; horsemen, cavalry

سوتيان (Fr. *soutien*) *sūtiyān* pl. *-āt* brassière

سوتيه (Fr. *sauté*) *sōtēh* sautéed

ساج[1] look up alphabetically

سياج[2] see اسوجة

ساح (سوح) *sāḥa* *u* to travel, rove, roam about

ساحة *sāḥa* pl. *-āt*, ساح *sāḥ* courtyard, open square; (open) space; arena; field (fig.) | ساحة الحرب *s. al-ḥarb* theater of war; ساحات المحاكم courts, tribunals; ساحة القتال battle field, war zone; ساحة القضاء *s. al-qaḍā'* tribunal, forum; ساحة الالعاب athletic field, sports field; برأ ساحته *barra'a sāḥatahū* to acquit s.o.

سواح *sawwāḥ* pl. *-ūn* traveler, tourist

سائح *sā'iḥ* pl. *-ūn*, سياح *suyyāḥ*, سواح *suwwāḥ* traveler, tourist; itinerant dervish; anchorite (*Chr.*)

ساخ (سوخ) *sāka* *u* (سوخ *sauk*) to be or become doughy, soft, slippery (esp. ground), yield like mud; to sink (فى الارض in the ground, of the foot) | ساخت روحه (*rūḥuhū*) to become faint, swoon

[1]سود II to make black, blacken (ه s.th.); to draft (ه a letter, etc.), make a rough draft (ه of s.th.); to cover with writing (ه sheets), scribble (ه on sheets) | سود وجهه (*wajhahū*) to expose s.o., show s.o. up, make a fool of s.o., bring s.o. into disrepute, discredit, disgrace, dishonor s.o. IX to be or become black

سواد *sawād* black color, black, blackness; (pl. اسودة *aswida*) black clothing, mourning; arable land, tilth; shape, form; inner part, core; majority; multitude | السواد or سواد العراق the rural area of Iraq; السواد الاعظم the great mass, the great majority, the largest part; سواد الناس the common people, the masses; سواد العين *s. al-ʿain* eyeball; سواد المدينة suburb, outskirts of the city; سواد الليل *s. al-lail* the long, dark night

اسود *aswad*[2], f. سوداء *saudā'*[2], pl. سود *sūd* black; dark-colored; — اسود *aswad*[2] pl. سودان *sūdān* a black, Negro | (بلاد) السودان the Sudan; شتائم سوداء severest reproaches; اسود فاحم coal-black, jetblack

سوداء *saudā'*[2] black bile (one of the four humors of ancient medicine); melancholy, sadness, gloom

سويداء *suwaidā'*[2] black bile (one of the four humors of ancient medicine); melancholy, sadness, gloom; السويداء Suweida (capital of the Jebel ed Druz) | سويداء القلب *s. al-qalb* the deepest folds of the heart, the inmost

سوداوى *saudāwī* melancholic, depressed, dejected

(بلاد) السودان (*bilād*) *as-sūdān* the Sudan

سودانى *sūdānī* Sudanese; (pl. *-ūn*) a Sudanese

تسويد *taswīd* rough draft

مسودة *musawwada, muswadda* draft, rough copy, rough sketch, notes; day-book | مسودة الطبع *m. aṭ-ṭabʿ* proof sheet, galley proof

[2](سود) ساد *sāda u* (سيادة *siyāda*, سؤدد *su'dud, su'dad*) to be or become master, head, chief, chieftain, sovereign, lord, overlord (ه, ه of or over people, of or over s.th.), rule, govern (ه, ه s.o., s.th.), reign (ه, ه over); to prevail (e.g., view), reign (e.g., calm); to be predominant, predominate, have the upperhand (على over) II to make (ه s.o.) master, head, chief, chieftain, sovereign, lord, overlord

سيد *sayyid* pl. اسياد *asyād*, سادة *sāda*, سادات *sādāt* master; gentleman; Mister; Sir; lord, overlord; chief, chieftain; title of Mohammed's direct descendants | سيدى (*sayyidī*, colloq. *sīdī*) honorific before the names of Muslim Saints (esp. *maġr.*); السيد فلان Mr. So-and-So; سيدى فلان (*maġr.*) do.; سيد البحار الاعظم Supreme Commander of the Navy (*Eg.* 1939)

سيدة *sayyida* pl. *-āt* mistress; lady; Mrs. | السيدة عقيلته (*ʿaqīlatuhū*) his wife; السيدة فلانة Mrs. So-and-So

سيادة *siyāda* command, mastery; domination, rule, dominion; supremacy; sovereignty; title and form of address of bishops (*Chr.*); *siyādat* ... (with foll. genit.) nowadays, in Egypt, general title of respect preceding the name, سيادتكم = you, a respectful address introduced after the abolition of titles of rank and social class in Egypt | سيادة المطران *s. al-muṭrān* His Eminence the Metropolitan; سيادة الرئيس approx.: His Excellency the President (*Eg.*); دولة ذات سيادة (*daula*) sovereign state

سؤدد *su'dud, su'dad* dominion, domination, rule, reign, power, sovereignty

سائد *sā'id* prevailing (opinion, feeling, mood, calm, etc.)

[3]السويد, سويدى look up alphabetically

سيادة ⁴ look up alphabetically and under سود²

سودن *saudana* to Sudanize (*Eg.*)

سودنة *saudana* Sudanization (*Eg.*)

سور¹ II to enclose, fence in, wall in, surround with a railing or wall (ه s.th.) III to leap (ه at s.o.), beset, assail, attack, assault (ه s.o.); to befall, overcome, grip (ه s.o., emotion) V to scale (ه a wall, a cliff, etc.)

سور *sūr* pl. اسوار *aswār* wall; enclosure, fence, railing

سورة *sūra* pl. سور *suwar* chapter of the Koran, sura

سورة *saura* vehemence, force, violence; severity (of cold)

سوار² *siwār, suwār* pl. سور *sūr*, اسورة *aswira*, اساور *asāwir*², اساورة *asāwira* bracelet, armlet, bangle; armband; cuff, wristband

سوارى³ look up alphabetically

اسوار⁴ look up alphabetically

سورى⁵ *sūrī* Syrian; (pl. *-ūn*) a Syrian

سوريا⁶ *sūriyā* Syria | سوريا الجنوبية (*janūbiya*) Palestine; سوريا الصغرى (*ṣuğrā*) do.; سوريا الكبرى (*kubrā*) (Greater) Syria

سورية⁷ *sūriya*² = سوريا

(سوس¹) ساس *sāsa u* (سياسة *siyāsa*) to dominate, govern, rule (ه s.o.); to lead, guide, conduct, direct (ه, ه s.o., s.th.); to administer, manage, regulate (ه s.th.); — *sawisa yaswasu* to be or become worm-eaten; to become carious (tooth); to rot, decay (bones) II and V = *sawisa*

سوس *sūs* (coll.; n. un. ة) pl. سيسان *sīsān* woodworm, borer; mothworm

سوس *sūs* licorice (Glycyrrhiza glabra; *bot.*) | عرق سوس *'irq s.* licorice root; رب السوس *rubb as-s.* licorice rob, thickened licorice juice

سياسة *siyāsa* pl. *-āt* administration, management; policy; سياسة *siyāsatan* for reasons of expediency (*Isl. Law*) | السياسة الدولية (*duwaliya*) diplomacy; السياسة العملية (*'amalīya*) practical policy, Realpolitik; ○ سياسة التوسع *s. at-tawassu'* policy of expansion

سياسى *siyāsī* political; diplomatic; — (pl. *-ūn*, ساسة *sāsa*) politician; diplomat, statesman | الدوائر السياسية political circles; السلك السياسى (*silk*) diplomatic corps; علم الاقتصاد السياسى (*'ilm al-iqtiṣād*) political science, political economy

تسوس *tasawwus* (dental) caries

سائس *sā'is* pl. ساسة *sāsa*, سواس *suwwās*, سياس *suyyās* stableman, groom; driver (primarily of animals); manager, leader

السويس² *as-suwēs* Suez (seaport in NE Egypt) | قنال السويس *qanāl as-s.* Suez Canal

سواسية³ see سوى

سوسته *susta* zipper (*eg.*)

سوسن *sausan, sūsan* lily of the valley (*bot.*)

(سوط) ساط *sāṭa u* (*sauṭ*) to whip, flog, lash, scourge (ه s.o.)

سوط *sauṭ* pl. اسواط *aswāṭ*, سياط *siyāṭ* whip, lash, scourge

مسوط *miswaṭ* stick or similar implement used for stirring

ساعة *sā'a* pl. *-āt*, ساع *sā'* (short) time, while; hour; timepiece, clock, watch; الساعة the Hour of Resurrection; *as-sā'ata* now, at present, by this time, at this moment, in this instant; at once, instantly, immediately, just | بين ساعة واخرى (*wa-ukrā*) from hour to hour; حتى الساعة until now; من الساعة from now on, henceforth; من ساعته immediately, presently, instantly, at once; منذ الساعة from now on, henceforth; مات لساعته he died instantly; ساعة الجيب *s. al-jaib* pocket watch; ساعة رملية

(*ramlīya*) hourglass; ساعة شمسية (*šamsīya*) sundial; ابن ساعته *ibn sā'atihī* transitory, ephemeral

ساعتئذ *sā'ata'iḏin* in that hour

ساعاتى *sā'ātī* pl. -*ya* watchmaker

سويعة *suwai'a* pl. -*āt* little hour, little while

(سوغ) ساغ *sāğa u* (*sauğ*, مساغ *masāğ*) to be easy to swallow, go down pleasantly (drink, food); to be permissible, be permitted, allowed (ل to s.o.); to swallow (ه s.th.); to permit, allow, accept, tolerate (ه s.th.), put up (ه with s.th.), swallow, stomach s.th. (ه, fig.) II to make permissible, permit, allow (ه ل to s.o. s.th.), admit (ه s.th.); to justify, warrant (ه ب s.th. with); to lease, let (ه s.th.) IV to wash down, swallow easily (ه s.th.); (fig.:) to take, swallow, stomach (ه s.th.), stand for s.th. (ه), put up with s.th. (ه) V to lease (ه s.th.), take a lease (ه of s.th.) X to regard as easy to swallow, find pleasant (ه s.th.); to taste, enjoy, relish (ه s.th.); to approve (ه of s.th.), admit, grant (ه s.th.), deem (ه s.th.) proper

مساغ *masāğ* easy access; possibility; permission | لم يستطع مساغا ل (*yastaṭi'*) he couldn't put up with ..., couldn't reconcile himself to ..., couldn't swallow ...; لا مساغ للشك (*masāğa, šakk*) one cannot possibly doubt it

تسويغ *taswīğ* hiring out on lease, leasing | قانون القرض والتسويغ (*qarḍ*) Lend-Lease Act (*pol., Tun.*)

سائغ *sā'iğ* easy to swallow; tasty, palatable; permissible, permitted, allowed

مسوغ *musawwiğ* pl. -*āt* justifying factor, justification, good reason

مستساغ *mustasāğ* easy to swallow; tasty, palatable

سوف II to put off (ه s.o.); to postpone, draw out, delay, procrastinate (ه s.th.)

سوف *saufa* (abbreviated form سـ *sa*) particle of future tense, e.g., سوف ترى (*tarā*) you will see

مسافة *masāfa* pl. -*āt*, مساوف *masāwif*² distance, interval, stretch; (*mus.*) interval | على مسافة at some distance

تسويف *taswīf* pl. -*āt* procrastination, postponement, delay, deferment

تسويفى *taswīfī* dilatory, delaying, procrastinating

سوفسطائى *sūfisṭā'ī* sophistic

سوفيات *sufyāt*, سوفييت *sovyēt* Soviet

سوفياتى *sufyātī*, سوفيتى, سوفييتى *sofyētī* soviet (adj.) | الاتحاد السوفياتى (*ittiḥād*) the Soviet Union

(سوق) ساق *sāqa u* (*sauq*, سياقة *siyāqa*, مساق *masāq*) to drive, urge on, herd (ه, ه prisoners, cattle); to draft, conscript (للجندية *li-l-jundīya* for military service); to drive (ه an automobile); to pilot (ه an airplane); to carry along, convey, transport (ه s.th.); to send, dispatch, forward, convey, hand over (ه الى s.th. to s.o.); to utter (ه s.th.); to cite, quote, propound, put forth (ه s.th.) | ساق مساقه (*masāqahū*) to follow the example or path of s.o.; ساق الحديث to carry on the conversation; ساق الحديث اليه to address s.o.; اليك يساق الحديث (*yusāqu*) you are the one that is meant II to market, sell (ه merchandise) III to accompany (ه s.o.); to go along, agree (ه with s.o.) V to trade in the market, sell and buy in the market VI to draw out; to form a sequence, be successive, be continuous, be coherent; to harmonize VII to drift; to be driven; to be carried away, be given over | انساق به الى to carry s.o. away to ..., drive or urge s.o. to ... VIII to drive, urge on, herd (ه cattle)

سوق *sauq* driving (of a car); draft, conscription (للجندية *li-l-jundīya* for military service); mobilization (of troops, also of forces, energies, etc.) | اجازة السوق *ijāzat as-s.* driving license

○ سوقية *sauqīya* strategy

ساق *sāq* f., pl. سوق *sūq*, سيقان *sīqān* shank; thigh; leg (also *geom.*); side (*geom.*); trunk (of a tree); stem, stalk (of plants) | ساق الحمام *s. al-ḥamām* bugloss (Anchusa officinalis; *bot.*); ربطة الساق *rabṭat as-s.* garter; وسام ربطة الساق Order of the Garter; عظم الساق *'aẓm as-s.* shinbone, tibia; متساوى الساقين *mutasāwī s-sāqain* isosceles (*geom.*); قامت الحرب على ساق (*ḥarbu*) the war was or became violent, flared up; war broke out; كشفت الحرب عن ساقها (*kašafat*) do.; كشف الامر عن ساقه the matter became difficult; وقف على ساق الجد ل (*s. il-jidd*) to turn one's zeal to, apply o.s. to, exert o.s., make efforts in order to ...; على قدم وساق (*qadam*) in full swing, carried on most energetically (undertaking, preparations, etc.); ارسل ساقه للريح *arsala sāqahū li-r-rīḥ* to speed along like the wind

ساقة *sāqa* rear guard, arrière-garde

سوق *sūq* mostly f., pl. اسواق *aswāq* bazaar street; market; ○ fair | سوق البر والاحسان *s. al-birr wa-l-iḥsān* charity bazaar; السوق الحرة (*ḥurra*) the free market; سوق الاحسان charity bazaar; سوق خيرية (*ḵairīya*) do.; السوق الاسود (*aswad*) the black market; السوق المشترك (*muštarak*) the Common Market; سوق النقد *s. an-naqd* money market (stock exchange); اسواق المحصولات produce markets; سوق عقود القطن *s. 'uqūd al-quṭn* cotton exchange

سوقة *sūqa* subjects; rabble, mob

سوقى *sūqī* plebeian, common, vulgar

سويق *sawīq* a kind of mush made of wheat or barley (also with sugar and dates)

سويق *suwaiq* and سويقة *suwaiqa* stem, stalk (of plants)

سويقة *suwaiqa* small market

سياق *siyāq* succession, sequence, course, thread (of conversation); context

سواق *sawwāq* pl. *-ūn* driver (of animals); driver, chauffeur; (railroad) engineer

مساق *masāq* trend of things, course, development, or progress, of s.th.; مساقه الى it amounts to ..., comes to ..., winds up in ..., is ultimately aimed at ...; also see ساق *sāqa* above | مساق من الدراسات course of studies; افضى بنا المساق الى we have come to the point where ...

تسويق *taswīq* marketing, sale (of merchandise)

تسويقة *taswīqa* (*eg.*) bargain, advantageous purchase

تساوق *tasāwuq* coherence, interrelation, connection, context; harmony

سائق *sā'iq* driving; driving force; — (pl. *-ūn*, ساقة *sāqa*) driver (of animals); chauffeur, driver; (aircraft) pilot

مسوقر *musauqar* (*tun.*) = مسوكر *musaukar*

(سوك) ساك *sāka u* (*sauk*) to rub, scrub, scour (ه s.th.) II to clean and polish, brush, clean (الاسنان the teeth)

سواك *siwāk* pl. سوك *sūk* a small stick (the tip of which is softened by chewing or beating) used for cleaning and polishing the teeth

مسواك *miswāk* pl. مساويك *masāwīk*[2] = سواك

سوكر *saukara* to insure (ه goods, etc.); to register (ه a letter)

مسوكر *musaukar* insured; registered (letter)

[1]سول II to talk or argue s.o. (ل) into s.th. evil or fateful (ه); to entice, seduce (ل s.o., said of the Devil) | سولت له نفسه (*nafsuhū*) he let himself be seduced (ه to)

[2]تسول *tasawwala* (for تسأل *tasa''ala*) to beg

تسول *tasawwul* begging, beggary

متسول *mutasawwil* pl. -*ūn* beggar

[1](سوم) سام *sāma u* (*saum*) to offer for sale (ه ε commodity); to impose (ه ه upon s.o. a punishment or task), force (ه ه upon s.o. a difficult task); to demand of s.o. (ه) s.th. (ه) beyond his power | سامه خسفا (*kasfan*) to treat s.o. unjustly, wrong s.o.; to humiliate s.o.; — (سيامة *siyāma*) to ordain, consecrate (a priest, a bishop, etc.; *Chr.*) II to impose, force (ه ه upon s.o. a difficult task), coerce (ه ه s.o. to s.th. difficult); to demand of s.o. (ه) s.th. (ه) beyond his power; to assess, estimate (ه the value of an object); to mark, provide with a mark (ه s th.) III to bargain, haggle, chaffer over a price (ه with s.o.); to bargain, haggle (ه ب, على or فى with s.o. over) IV to let (ه cattle) graze freely; to let (ه the eye) wander VI to bargain, haggle (فى over, for) VIII to bargain, haggle, chaffer (ب or فى, على over, for)

مساومة *musāwama* pl. -*āt* bargaining, haggling

سائمة *sā'ima* pl. سوائم *sawā'im*[2] freely grazing livestock

[2]سام, سامى look up alphabetically

[3]مسام, مسامات see [2]سم

سومر *sūmir*[2] Sumer

سومطرة *sūmaṭra* Sumatra

اسوان look up alphabetically

سوهج *sōhag* Sohag (city in central Egypt, on the Nile)

سوى *sawiya a* to be equivalent, be equal (ه to s.th.), equal (ه s.th.) II to even, level, nivellate, flatten, straighten (ه s.th.); to smooth (ه s.th.); to smooth down (ه s.th., e.g., folds, wrinkles; من ثيابه one's clothes); to equalize, make equal (ه ب s.th. to s.th. else), put (ه s.th.) on the same level (ب with s.th.); سوى بينهما to put two persons on an equal footing, treat two persons as equals, reconcile two persons; to make regular, make good (ه s.th.); to cook properly (ه s.th.); to regulate, arrange, make up, smooth over, settle, put in order (ه a dispute, a controversy, etc.) | سوى اخدعه to crush s.o.'s pride III to be equivalent, be equal (ه to s.th.), equal (ه s.th.); to be worth (ه s.th.); to equalize, make equal (ه ب s.th. to s.th. else), put (ه s.th.) on the same level (ب with); to establish equality (بين — وبين between — and); ساوى بينهم to make them equals, equalize them, put them on the same footing; to regulate, arrange, make up, smooth over, settle, put in order (ه a dispute, a controversy, etc.); سوى بينهما = ساوى بينهما (*sawwā*) VI to be equal or similar; to be balanced, keep the balance VIII to be even, regular, equal; to be equivalent (ه to); to be on the same level; to be or become straight, even, level; to stand upright, erect, straight; to straighten up; to sit down (على on), mount (على s.th.); to sit firmly (على on an animal); to be properly cooked, be well done; to ripen, mature, be or become ripe

سوى *siwan, suwan* equality, sameness; (with foll. genit. or suffix) other than, except | على حد سوى (*ḥaddin*) equal(ly), indiscriminate(ly), alike, the same; فضله على سواه *faḍḍalahū 'alā siwāhu* he preferred him to everybody else; ليس , لا — سوى — only, nothing but

سواء *sawā'* equal; equality, sameness; *sawā'a* except | سواء لديه كل شىء (*la-*

daihi) it is all the same to him, he is indifferent to everything; سواء بسواء (sawā'an) equally, indiscriminately, without distinction, together; على السواء likewise, in like manner, equally, evenly, indiscriminately, without distinction; all the same, making no difference; سواء على it doesn't make any difference for ...; سواء — ام (او) (sawā'an) regardless whether — or ..., no matter whether — or ..., be it that ... — or ...; سواء — ام do.; تلاميذ سقراط سواء منهم الاثينيون وغير الاثينيين the disciples of Socrates, both Athenians and non-Athenians; سواء السبيل (المحجة) (maḥajja) the straight, right path

سوى sawīy pl. اسوياء aswiyā'[2] straight; right, correct, proper; unimpaired, intact, sound; straight-bodied, straight-shaped, of regular build or growth; even, regular, well-proportioned, shapely, harmonious; سويا sawīyan in common, jointly, together

سوية sawīya pl. سوايا sawāyā equality; sawīyatan together, jointly

سى siyy (for m. and f.) pl. اسواء aswā' equal, similar, (a)like | هما سيان they are alike, are the same; هما سيان عندى they are both the same to me

لا سيما lā siyyamā especially, in particular, mainly

سواسية sawāsiya (pl.) equal, alike | هم (هن) سواسية they are equals

تسوية taswiya leveling, nivellation; settlement, arrangement, adjustment (of controversies, etc.); equalization; settlement (of a bill) | تحت التسوية outstanding, unsettled, unpaid (com.)

مساواة musāwāh equality, equivalence; equal rights, equality before the law; settlement, composition (com.)

تساو tasāwin equality, equivalence, sameness; equal rights, equality before the law | بالتساوى or على التساوى likewise, in like manner, equally, evenly, regularly

استواء istiwā' straightness; evenness, levelness; equality, regularity, steadiness | خط الاستواء ḵaṭṭ al-ist. equator

استوائى istiwā'ī equatorial, tropical | المناطق or المنطقة الاستوائية (minṭaqa) الاستوائية the tropics

مساو musāwin equal, equivalent, similar

متساو mutasāwin equal, similar, (a)like; even, equable, equally strong; of equal weight, equipoised, equiponderant | متساوى الابعاد equidistant; متساوى الزوايا m.z-zawāyā equiangular (geom.); متساوى الساقين m. s-sāqain isosceles (geom.); متساوى الاضلاع equilateral (geom.)

مستو mustawin straight, upright, erect; even, smooth, regular; well done (cooking); ripe, mature

مستوى mustawan level, niveau, standard | مستوى الماء water level; المستوى العلمى ('ilmī) scientific level; مستوى الحياة m. l-ḥayāh standard of living; فى مستوى (with foll. genit.) on an equal level or footing with ...

السويد (Fr. la Suède) as-suwīd Sweden

سويدى suwīdī Swede; Swedish

السويس as-suwēs Suez (seaport in NE Egypt) | قناة (قنال) السويس (qanāt, qanāl) Suez Canal

سويسرا (It. Svizzera) swiserā Switzerland

سويسرى swiserī Swiss

[1]سية siya pl. -āt curved part of a bow

[2]□ سى sī short form of سيد sayyid, سيدى Mr., Sir (esp. maġr.)

[3]سى siyy, سيان see سوى

سيام siyām Siam, Thailand

سيان siyān cyanogen

(سيب) ساب *sāba i* (*saib*) to flow, stream, run (water); to run along, speed along, glide along, creep along, crawl along; to walk fast, hurry; (*eg.*) to leave, give up, relinquish (ه s.th.); (*eg.*) to neglect (ه, ه s.o., s.th.); (*eg.*) to release, let go, free (ه, ه s.o., s.th.) **II** to leave, give up, relinquish (ه s.th.); to neglect (ه, ه s.o., s.th.); to release, let go, free (ه, ه s.o., s.th.) **VII** to flow, stream, run (water); to pour, flow (ال into), enter (ال s.th.); to peter out, seep away, exhaust itself; to speed along, glide along, run along, crawl or creep (along); to glide, slip (بين between); to walk fast, hurry; with foll. imperf.: to begin at once to do s.th.

انسيابى *insiyābī*, انسيابى الشكل *ins. š-šakl* stream-lined

سائب *sā'ib* forlorn, lost, (a)stray; free, loose, lax, unrestrained

سيبريا *sībīriyā* Siberia

سيج[1] **II** to fence in, hedge in, surround with a hedge (ه s.th.) **V** pass. of **II**

سياج *siyāj* pl. *-āt*, اسوجة *aswija*, اسياج *asyāj* hedge; fencing, fence; enclosure; (fig.) bulwark, shield (of a country, of a nation)

ساج[2] look up alphabetically

سيجار *sigār* cigar (*eg.*)

سيجارة *sigāra* pl. *-āt*, سجاير *sagāyir*[2], سجائر *sagā'ir*[2] cigarette (*eg.*)

(سيح) ساح *sāḥa i* (*saiḥ*, سيحان *sayaḥān*) to flow, run (water); to melt, thaw, dissolve, become liquid (snow, metal); — (*saiḥ*, سياحة *siyāḥa*) to travel, journey; to rove, roam about **II** to make flow, cause to flow (ه a river, etc.); to melt, dissolve, liquefy, smelt, fuse (ه metal, and the like); to melt, clarify (ه butter) **IV** to make flow, cause to flow (ه s.th.) **VII** to spread, pour forth

سياحة *siyāḥa* pl. *-āt* travel; tourism

سياح *sayyāḥ* pl. *-ūn* traveler; tourist

سائح *sā'iḥ* pl. *-ūn*, سياح *suyyāḥ*, *suwwāḥ* traveler; tourist; itinerant dervish; anchorite (*Chr.*)

مسيح *musayyaḥ* fluid, liquid; striped (garment)

[1](سيخ) ساخ *sāḵa i* (سيخ *saiḵ*, سيخان *sayaḵān*) to sink into the ground or mud

سيخ[2] *sīḵ* pl. اسياخ *asyāḵ* spit, skewer; foil, rapier; iron prong or bolt

سيد, سيادة see سود[2]

سيدارة *sīdāra* pl. *-āt* (see سدارة) an Iraqi headgear, commonly of black velvet; overseas cap

(سير) سار *sāra i* (سير *sair*, سيرورة *sairūra*, مسير *masīr*, مسيرة *masīra*, تسيار *tasyār*) to move (on), set out, strike out, start, get going; to move along; to march; to travel, journey; to ride (in a vehicle); to go, go away, leave, depart; to run, operate (بين — و between — and, of a train); to flow (electric current); to run, be in operation, function, work, go (machine); to progress (e.g., work); to make (ال for s.th.), be headed (ال for s.th.), approach (ال s.th.), be directed, be oriented (ال toward s.th.); to circulate, make the rounds, be or become current (proverb); to follow, maintain (سيرا *sairan* a behavior, على s.th.); to behave, conduct o.s.; to proceed, act (على or بمقتضى *bi-muqtaḍā* according to) | سار به to lead s.o., lead s.o. away; سار وراءه to follow, pursue s.o.; سار جيئة وذهابا (*ji'atan wa-ḏahāban*) to walk up and down, go back and forth; سار فى سبيل التحسن (*s. it-taḥassun*) to be on the road to recovery; الخطة التى سار فيها (*ḵiṭṭa*) the course he followed; سار سيرة حسنة

(*sīratan ḥasanatan*) to behave well; سار على قدميه (*qadamaihi*) not to be dead and forgotten, be still much alive, be a tangible reality **II** to set in motion, drive (ه s.th.); to make (ه s.th., e.g., an automobile) go; to start, start up, let run (ه a machine); to go in (ه for a task), run, carry on, ply, practice (ه a trade); to drive (ه a car), pilot, steer (ه s.th.); to send, dispatch, send out (ه, ه s.o., s.th.); to circulate, put in circulation (ه s.th.); to stripe (ه a garment, etc.) **III** to keep up, go along (ه with s.o.); to walk at s.o.'s (ه) side; to pursue (ه s.th.); to show o.s. willing to please (ه s.o.), comply (ه with s.o.'s wish); to be in agreement, be consistent (ه with s.th.); to be familiar, intimate, be hand in glove, get along (ه with s.o.); to adapt o.s. (ه to circumstances, events, etc.) **IV** to set in motion, drive (ه s.th.); to send, dispatch (ه, ه s.o., s.th.)

سير ***sair*** trip, tour, travel, journey, walk, errand, march, procession; movement, motion; departure; course, progress (of an undertaking); procedure, practice, conduct, behavior; (way of) life; observance, pursuance (على of s.th.) | حسن السير والسلوك (*ḥusn as-s.*) blameless life; فى السير وراء غرضه (*ḡaradihī*) in pursuance of his intention

سير ***sair*** pl. سيور ***suyūr*** (leather) belt; girth; drive belt, transmission belt | سير متحرك (*mutaḥarrik*) conveyor belt, assembly line

سيرة ***saira*** gait; course

سيرة ***sīra*** pl. سير ***siyar*** conduct, comportment, demeanor, behavior, way of life; attitude, position, reaction, way of acting; (in sg. or pl.) biography, history; pl. campaigns; السيرة the biography of Mohammed

سيار ***sayyār*** traveling frequently, always on the move, continually moving; itinerant, roving, roaming about; circulating; planet | صحف سيارة (*ṣuḥuf*) or جرائد سيارة daily newspapers, dailies

سيارة ***sayyāra*** pl. ***-āt*** automobile, car | سيارة الاجرة *s. al-ujra* taxi cab; سيارة مدرعة (*mudarra'a*) armored car; سيارة دورية (*daurīya*) patrol car; سيارة الاسعاف *s. al-is'āf* ambulance; سيارة مصفحة (*muṣaffaḥa*) armored car; سيارة النقل *s. an-naql* truck, lorry; سائق السيارة (automobile) driver, chauffeur

مسار ***masār*** pl. ***-āt*** path (of rays, etc.)

مسير ***masīr*** travel, journey, tour; march (*mil.*); departure; distance

مسيرة ***masīra*** travel, journey, tour; departure; distance

تسيير ***tasyīr*** dispatch, sending out; propulsion, drive (*techn.*) | التسيير النفاثى (*naffāṯī*) jet propulsion

مسايرة ***musāyara*** adaptation, adjustment

سائر ***sā'ir*** going, walking, running; walker, wayfarer, wanderer; generally known, current (proverb); see also سئر | خدمة سائرة (*ḵadama*) transient laborers, seasonal laborers (*eg.*)

مسير ***musayyar*** directed, controlled (ب by); guided, remote-controlled; not endowed with free will (*philos.*, as opposed to مخير *muḵayyar*)

سيراس ***sīrās*** (*syr.*) glue made of the yellow powder of a pulverized root, used esp. for pasting leather

سيرافيم ***sīrafīm*** seraphim

سيرج ***sīraj*** sesame oil

سيرك (Fr. *cirque*) ***sirk*** circus

سيسبان ***saisabān*** sesban (an indigenous Egyptian shrub whose leaves have a purgative effect, Sesbania aegyptiaca Pers.; *bot.*)

سيسى *sīsī* pl. سيسيات *sīsīyāt*, سياسى *sayāsī* (*eg.*) pony; young rat

سيطر *saiṭara* to command, dominate, control (على s.th.); to be master or lord (على over s.th.), reign, gain power (على over s.th.); to seize (على s.th.), take hold (على of s.th.) **II** *tasaiṭara* = سيطر

سيطرة *saiṭara* rule, dominion, domination, command, supremacy, power, authority (على over); decisive influence (على on); control (على over)

مسيطر *musaiṭir* ruler, sovereign, overlord

سيف *saif* pl. سيوف *suyūf*, اسياف *asyāf*, اسيف *asyuf* sword; sabre, foil, rapier | سيف الاسلام *s. al-islām* title of princes of the royal house of Yemen

سيف *sīf* pl. اسياف *asyāf* shore, coast

سياف *sayyāf* executioner

مسايفة *musāyafa* fencing (with sabre or foil)

سيكارة = سيقارة

سيكارة *sigāra* pl. سكائر *sagā'ir*[2] cigarette (*syr.*)

سيكران *saikurān, saikarān* henbane (Hyoscyamus niger; *bot.*)

سيكورتاه (It. *sicurtà*) *sikurtāh* insurance | سيكورتاه الحريق (الحياة) (*ḥayāh*) fire (life) insurance

سيكولوجى *sīkolōžī, saikolōjī* psychologic(al)

[1]سال (سيل) *sāla* i (*sail*, سيلان *sayalān*) to flow, stream; to be or become liquid; to melt | سال لعابه على (*lu'ābuhū*) his mouth watered for ... **II** to make flow, cause to stream, liquefy, melt, dissolve (ه s.th.) **IV** = **II**

سيل *sail* pl. سيول *suyūl* flood, inundation; torrent, torrential stream | سيل عرام (*'urām*) huge mass, flood, stream; بلغ السيل الزبى (*zubā*) the matter has reached its climax, has come to a head

سيلة *saila* stream

سيولة *suyūla* liquid state, liquidity, flow(ing)

سيال *sayyāl* streaming, pouring, torrential; fluid, liquid; a liquid; stream; a fluid | قلم سيال (*qalam*) facile pen, fluent style

سيالة *sayyāla* rivulet; pocket

سيلان *sayalān* flowing, flow; running; deliquescence, liquefaction; gonorrhea (*med.*); see also below

مسيل *masīl* pl. مسايل *masāyil*[2] river bed, rivulet

سائل *sā'il* fluid, liquid; (pl. سوائل *sawā'il*[2]) a liquid, a fluid | ○ علم السوائل *'ilm as-s.* hydraulics

سائلية *sā'ilīya* fluidity, liquid state of aggregation (*phys.*)

[2]سيلان *sayalān*[2] Ceylon;

[3]سيلان *sīlān* garnet (precious stone)

[1]سيم *sīma* (pass.) and **VII** to be consecrated, be ordained (*Chr.*)

[2]ولاسيما *wa-lā siyyamā* see سوى

[3]سيماء *sīmā'*[2] see next entry

[4]سيمى *sīmā* (سيما *sīmā*), سيماء *sīmā'*[2], سيمة *sīma* pl. سيم *siyam* mark, sign, characteristic; mien, expression

[5]سيميا *simiyā*, سيمياء *simiyā'*[2] natural magic

سين *sīn* name of the letter س

الاشعة السينية *al-aši''a as-sīnīya* X rays

سينا *sīnā* and سيناء *sīnā'*[2] Sinai

سينما (Fr. *cinéma*) cinema, motion-picture theater | دور السينما *dūr as-s.* motionpicture theaters, movies; سينما صامتة (صامت) silent film; سينما (ناطق) ناطقه or سينما صائتة (صائت) sound film, talkie

سينمائى *sīnemā'ī* cinematographic, cinematic, cinema-, movie- (in compounds); motion-picture actor, film star | رواية سينمائية motion picture, film, movie

سينماتوغراف (Fr. *cinématographe*) *sīnimatuġrāf* cinematograph

سينماسكوب (Fr. *cinémascope*) *sīnimaskūb* cinemascope

سينودس (Gr. *σύνοδος*) *sinōdos* synod

ش

ش abbreviation of شارع *šāri'* street (St.)

شاء *šā'* (coll.; n. un. شاة *šāh*) pl. شواه *šiwāh*, شياه *šiyāh* sheep; ewe

شؤبوب *šu'būb* pl. شآبيب *ša'ābīb*[2] downpour, shower

شادر *šadır* tent; storehouse, warehouse, magazine

شاذروان *šāḏarwān* fountain; a small water-driven gadget adorned with bells, and the like, resembling a mobile

شاروبيم *šārūbīm* cherubim

شاسى *šāsī* chassis

شأفة *ša'fa* root | استأصل شأفته *ista'ṣala ša'fatahū* to extirpate, root out, eradicate s.th., remove s.th. drastically

شاكوش *šākūš* and شكوش *šakūš* pl. شواكيش *šawākīš*[2] hammer | ابو شاكوش hammer-head (shark)

شال *šāl* pl. شيلان *šīlān* shawl

شاليه (Fr. *chalet*) *šālēh* pl. *-āt* hunting cabin, shooting lodge; beach cabin, cabana

شأم VI to perceive an evil omen (من or ب in), regard as an evil portent (من or ب s.th.); to foretell calamity (من or ب from); to be superstitious; to be pessimistic X to perceive an evil omen (ب in), regard as an evil portent (ب s.th.); to foretell calamity (ب from)

الشام *aš-ša'm, aš-šām* the northern region, the North; Syria; Damascus | شاما ويمنا (*yamanan*) northward and southward

شامى *šāmī* Syrian; (pl. *-ūn*, شوام *šuwām*) a Syrian

شآمى *ša'āmī* Syrian (adj. and n.)

شؤم *šu'm* calamity, bad luck, misfortune; evil omen, portent | لا تملأ الدنيا شؤما (*tamla', dunyā*) (don't fill the world with evil omen!) approx.: talk of the devil and he will appear!

اشأم *aš'am*[2], f. شؤمى *šu'mā* inauspicious, ill-omened, ominous, portentous, sinister; calamitous, disastrous; unfortunate, fatal, accursed

تشاؤم *tašā'um* pessimism

مشؤوم *maš'ūm* and مشوم *mašūm* pl. مشائيم *mašā'īm*[2] inauspicious, ill-omened, ominous, sinister; unfortunate, unlucky | عدد مشؤوم (*'adad*) unlucky number

متشائم *mutašā'im* pessimist

شأن *ša'n* pl. شؤون *šu'ūn* matter, affair, concern, business; circumstances, state of affairs, case; nature, character, quality, kind; situation, condition, state; significance; importance, consequence; standing, prestige, rank; cranial suture; pl. شؤون tears; *ša'na* like, as | بشأن *bi-ša'ni* regarding, with regard or respect to, relating to, pertaining to, concerning, as to, about; جل شأنه (*jalla*) the Sublime (of God); وزارة الشؤون الاجتماعية Ministry of Social Affairs; الشؤون الخارجية (*ḵārijīya*) foreign affairs; ذو الشأن, f. ذات الشأن the responsible man, the man in charge, the man directly concerned with the matter; اولو الشأن *ulū š-š.* and ذوو الشأن *ḏawū š-š.* the influential people, the competent people; those concerned with the matter; شؤون الحياة *š. al-ḥayāh* worldly affairs; خطير الشأن of great importance; ذو شأن significant, important; رفيع الشأن high-ranking; (formerly, *Tun.*) title of members of the Bey's family; صاحب الشأن the one concerned; اصحاب الشأن those concerned; the important, influential people; ○ مكلف بالشؤون (*mukallaf*) chargé d'affaires (*dipl.*); ... شأنه فى ذلك شأن الـ (*ša'nuhū ... ša'nu l- ...*) in this matter he fares just as the ..., he is, in this respect, in the same situation as the ...; رجل هذا شأنه (*ša'nuhū*) a man whose situation is this, a man who can be described as ..., a man in this situation; شأنك *ša'naka* or انت وشأنك *anta wa-ša'naka* please yourself! do as you like! شأنك وما تريد (*ša'naka*) do as you please! just as you wish! دعنى وشأنى (*da'nī*) let me alone! تركه وشأنه *tarakahū wa-ša'nahū* to let s.o. alone; to let s.o. go; not to pay any attention to s.o.; هو فى شأن he is concerned with a matter; هذا شأنه that's his affair; ما شأنك what's the matter with you? what do you want? ما شأنك وهذا what have you got to do with this? what business of yours is this? ما شأنه والامر (*amra*) what has he got to do with the matter? ما شأنى فى ذلك what have I got to do with that? what business of mine is that? اى شأن لك فى هذا (*ayyu ša'nin*) what business of yours is this? what's that to you? له شأن فى ذلك he has s.th. to do with this, he has a hand in this; لا شأن له فى ذلك (*ša'na*) he hasn't anything to do with this, he has no part in this; ليس لى شأن فى ذلك I shall have nothing to do with that, that is none of my business, I shan't meddle in that; لا شأن لى به (*ša'na*) I haven't anything to do with it, it's none of my business; لى معه شأن آخر (*āḵar*) I still have a bone to pick with him; ذهب لبعض شأنه (*li-ba'ḍi ša'nihī*) he attended to a task; he went to do s.th.; انصرف الى شأنه (*inṣarafa*) he left to do his work; اصلحت من شأنها (*aṣlaḥat*) she made herself up; اهمل شأنه *ahmala ša'nahū* he neglected him; ذلك شأنه that is his habit; هذا شأنه دائما he is always that way; شأنه فى (*ša'nahū*) as he used to do in ...; ... شأنه مع من ... (*ša'nahū*) as he used to deal with people who ...; كان من شأنه it was his wont, he used to ...; من شأنه ان it is in his (its) nature that ..., he (it) tends to ...; it is his business to ...; ليس من شأنه ان it is not his affair or business to ...; it is inappropriate for him to ...; it does not tend to ..., is not conducive to ...; ان لهذا الرجل شأنا (*rajuli*) there is a man to keep an eye on, this is an important man; there is s.th. about this man! لله فى خلقه شؤون (*ḵalqihī*) God has created all kinds of things (meaning: strange things can happen in this world!)

شانتاج (Fr. *chantage*) *šantāž* blackmail

شاه *šāh* shah; king (chess) | شاه بلوط (*ballūṭ*) chestnut tree (*bot.*); شاه مات checkmate (chess)

شاهانى *šāhānī* the shah's, pertaining to the shah; imperial | ارادة شاهانية decree of the Sultan (in Ottoman times)

شاهين *šāhīn* pl. شواهين *šawāhīn*² shahin, an Indian falcon (*zool.*)

(شأو) شآ *šaʼā* **u** (شأو *šaʼw*) to overtake in running, outrace (ه s.o.)

شأو *šaʼw* highest point, summit, peak; goal, object | بعيد الشأو far-aiming, far-aspiring; very ambitious; بلغ شأوه فى (*šaʼwahū*) to get as far in s.th. as s.o. else, match s.o. in s.th.; بلغ شأوا بعيدا فى الرقى (*ruqīy*) to undergo tremendous progress; بلغ الشأو البعيد to carry off the prize, hit the bull's eye

شاورمة *šāwurma, šāwirma* (also شورمة) charcoal-broiled mutton, cut in thin slices and arranged conically on a vertical skewer (*syr.*)

شاوش *šāwuš* (*tun.*) pl. شوّاش *šuwwāš* sergeant; office boy, handy man; doorman, gatekeeper

شاويش *šāwīš* a military rank, approx.: staff sergeant (*Eg.*) | وكيل شاويش a military rank, approx.: sergeant (*Eg.*)

شاى *šāy* tea

شب *šabba* **i** (شباب *šabāb*, شبيبة *šabība*) to become a youth or young man, to adolesce, grow up; — **i u** (شباب *šibāb*, شبيب *šabīb*) to raise the forelegs as if about to jump; to rear; to prance (horse); — **i** (شبوب *šubūb*) to burn, blaze (fire); to break out (fire, war); — **u** (*šabb, šubūb*) to light, kindle (ه fire) | شبت نيران الحرب (*nīrān al-ḥarb*) war broke out; شب عن الطوق (*ṭauq*) to be over the initial stages, with neg.: to be still in its infancy **II** to rhapsodize about a beloved woman (بها) and one's relationship to her, celebrate her in verse; to flirt (بها with a woman) **V** to rhapsodize about a beloved woman (بها) and one's relationship to her, celebrate her in verse; to compose love sonnets; to take fire, blaze up

شب *šabb* (= شاب *šābb*) youth, young man

شب *šabb* alum

شبة *šabba* (= *šābba*) young woman, girl

شبة *šabba* alum

شبب *šabab* fully grown (steer)

شباب *šabāb* youth, youthfulness; youths, young men, adolescents, juveniles | تجديد الشباب rejuvenation

شبابى *šabābī* youthful, juvenile

شبوب *šubūb* outbreak (of a war)

شبابة *šabbāba* reed flute

شبيبة *šabība* youth, youthfulness; الشبيبة the youth (coll.)

شاب *šābb* pl. شبان *šubbān*, شباب *šabāb* شببة *šababa* youthful, juvenile, young; youth, young man

شابة *šābba* pl. *-āt*, شواب *šawābb*[2], شبائب *šabāʼib*[2] young woman, girl

مشبوب *mašbūb* lighted, kindled, ignited, flaming, burning; beautiful

شبت *šibitt* dill (Anethum graveolens; *bot.*)

[1]شبث *šabiṯa* **a** (*šabaṯ*) and **V** to cling, cleave, hold fast, hang on, attach o.s., adhere (ب to)

شبث *šabaṯ* pl. شبثان *šibṯān* spider

تشبث *tašabbuṯ* tenacity; attachment, adherence, fidelity; stubbornness, obstinacy

متشبث *mutašabbiṯ* tenacious; attached, adherent; stubborn, obstinate

[2]شبث *šibiṯṯ* dill (Anethum graveolens; *bot.*)

شبح *šabaḥ, šabḥ* pl. شبوح *šubūḥ*, اشباح *ašbāḥ* blurred, indistinct shape; apparition; phantom; ghost, specter, spirit; nightmare; figure, person

[1]شبر *šabara* **u i** (*šabr*) to measure (ه s.th.) with the span of the hand **II** do.; to gesticulate, make gestures, to gesture

شبر *šibr* pl. اشبار *ašbār* span of the hand | شبرا فشبرا (*fa-šibran*) inch by inch; شبر

قلده من الارض (*arḍ*) a foot of ground; قلده شبرا بشبر وذراعا بذراع (*qalladahū*) to imitate s.o. or s.th. religiously; to follow s.th. literally

²شبور *šabbūr* pl. -*āt*, شبابير *šabābīr*² trumpet

³شبورة *šabbūra* and شابورة *šābūra* (*eg.*) fog, mist

شبرق *šabraqa* to tear to pieces, to shred (ه s.th.)

شبرقة *šabraqa* pocket money

شبشب *šibšib* pl. شباشب *šabāšib*² slipper

¹شبط *šabaṭa* to cling, cleave, hold on (في to)

²شباط *šubāṭ*⁽²⁾ February (*Syr., Ir., Leb., Jord.*)

³شبوط *šabbūṭ* (*syr.*) large fish found in the Euphrates and Tigris rivers

شبع *šabi'a a* (*šab', šiba'*) to satisfy one's appetite (من or ه with s.th.), eat one's fill (من or ه of s.th.); to be or become sated, satisfied in one's appetite; to be full (من or ه of); to be or become fed up, surfeited (من with), be or become sick and tired (من of), have enough (من of) **II** to sate, satiate, fill (ه ,ه ب s.o., s.th. with); to satisfy, gratify (ه the appetite, one's desires, the senses); to load, charge (ه s.th., ب with electricity) **IV** to sate, satiate, fill (ه ب s.o. with); to satisfy, gratify (ه the appetite, the senses); to saturate (ه s.th., e.g., with a dye); to load, charge (ه s.th., ب with electricity); to go in (ه for s.th.) thoroughly; (*gram.*) to lengthen (ه a vowel) by writing it plene; pass. *ušbi'a* to be replete, full (ب with, of) | اشبع الكلام فيه (*kalāma*) to speak in great detail, at great length about s.th., describe or explain s.th. elaborately; اشبعه ضربا (*ḍarban*) to give s.o. a sound beating **V** to be sated, saturated (ب with); to be filled (ب with), be full (ب of); to be loaded or charged (ب with, *el.*)

شبع *šab'* sufficiency, satiety, satiation, saturation, repletion, fullness

شبع *šib', šiba'* s.th. that fills or satisfies the appetite, fill

شبع *šaba'* saturation (*chem.*)

شبعة *šub'a* a fill

شبعان *šab'ān*², f. شبعى *šab'ā*, pl. شباعى *šabā'ā*, شباع *šibā'* sated, satisfied, full; rich

اشباع *išbā'* satiation, saturation, repletion, filling; satisfaction, gratification

مشبع *mušabba', mušba'* satiated, saturated (ب with); replete, filled (ب with), full (ب of) | مشبع بالكهرباء (*kahrabā'*) electrically charged

¹شبق *šabiqa a* (*šabaq*) to be lewd, lecherous, lustful

شبق *šabaq* lewdness, lechery, licentiousness, lust

شبق *šabiq* lewd, lecherous, lustful, licentious

²شبق *šubuq* chibouk

¹شبك *šabaka i* (*šabk*) to interjoin, intertwine, interlace, interweave, entangle (ه s.th.); to fasten, tighten, attach (ه s.th., ب or في to) **II** to interjoin, intertwine, interlace, interweave, entangle, complicate (بين or ه s.th.); to crochet **V** to be interjoined, intertwined, interlaced, interwoven, entangled; to be or become complicated, involved, intricate, confused **VI** to be intertwined, interlaced, interwoven, entangled; to be intermeshed, be interwoven like a net **VIII** to be or become interjoined, interlaced, interwoven, net-like, reticulate; to be intertwined (branches), be interlocked (hands); to be or become entangled, snarled; to get entangled, involved, ensnared, embroiled, implicated, mixed up (في in); to come to blows or to grips

(ب or مع with s.o.); to be or become complicated, involved, intricate, confused (matter); to join, unite, combine, coalesce, merge, fuse (ب with); to meet (eyes, glances) | اشتبك فى حديث to be drawn into a conversation, become engrossed in a discussion; اشتبك فى حرب (*ḥarb*) to become involved in a war

شبكة *šabaka* pl. شبك *šabak*, شباك *šibāk*, شبوكات *šubūkāt* net; netting, network; snare; — (pl. شباك *šibāk*) ○ grid (*radio*) | شبكة شائكة barbed-wire entanglement, concertina: شبكة لاسلكية (*lā-silkīya*) radio network

شبكى *šabakī* reticulate, reticular, netted, net-like; retinal; of framework

شبكية *šabakīya* retina (*anat.*)

شباك *šubbāk* pl. شبابيك *šabābīk*[2] netting, network; plaitwork; grid, grill; window; wicket (post office, box office, etc.) | شباك العرض *š. al-'arḍ* show window, showcase, glass case

مشبك *mišbak* pl. مشابك *mašābik*[2] hook; clasp, pin; hairpin, bobby pin | مشبك الورق *m. al-waraq* paper clip

تشابك *tašābuk* confusion, intricacy, obscurity, abstruseness

اشتباك *ištibāk* entanglement, involvement (فى in); complication; hand-to-hand fight, scuffle, melee (مع with), clash (ب with) | عدم الاشتباك فى القتال (*'adam al-išt.*) nonintervention in battle

مشبك *mušabbak* plaited, resembling plaitwork; (pl. *-āt*) window (or door) adorned with plaited latticework

مشتبك *muštabik* entangled, involved, complicated, intricate

مشتبك *muštabak* plaitwork; thicket (of branches)

شبك[2] *šubuk* chibouk

شوبك[3] look up alphabetically

شبل IV to take care (على of s.o.), look (على after s.o.), take s.o. (على) in hand

شبل *šibl* pl. اشبال *ašbāl* lion cub

شبين *šabīn*, *šibīn* pl. شباين *šabāyin*[2] godfather, sponsor (*Chr.*); best man, groomsman (*Chr.*)

شبينة *šabīna*, *šibīna* pl. *-āt* godmother, sponsor (*Chr.*); bridesmaid (*Chr.*)

اشبين *išbīn* pl. اشابين *ašābīn*[2] godfather, sponsor (*Chr.*); best man, groomsman (*Chr.*)

اشبينة *išbīna* godmother, sponsor (*Chr.*); bridesmaid (*Chr.*)

شبه II to make equal or similar (ب or ه s.th. to s.th. else); to compare (ب ه s.th. with), liken (ب ه s.th. to); pass. *šubbiha* to be doubtful, dubious, uncertain, obscure (على to s.o.) III to resemble (ه, ه s.o., s.th.), bear a resemblance, be similar (ه, ه to s.o., to s.th.), be like s.o. or s.th. (ه, ه), look (exactly) like s.o. (ه) | وما شابه ذلك and the like IV to resemble (ه, ه s.o., s.th.), bear a resemblance, be similar (ه, ه to s.o., to s.th.), be like s.o. or s.th. (ه, ه); to look (exactly) like s.o. (ه) | وما اشبه ذلك and the like V to compare o.s. (ب with); to imitate, copy (ب s.o., s.th.) VI to resemble one another, be similar to one another; to be equal to one another, be identical; to be ambiguous, unclear VIII to resemble one another, be similar to one another; to be in doubt (فى about), doubt (فى s.th.); to suspect (فى امره or فى s.o., s.th.); to be doubtful, dubious, obscure (على to s.o.) | اشتبه فى الامر the matter appeared doubtful to him

شبه *šibh* pl. اشباه *ašbāh* resemblance, similarity, likeness; image, picture; analogue; similar, (a)like; -like, quasi-, semi- (with foll. genit.) | شبه جزيرة *šibhu jazīratin* peninsula; شبه حربى *š. ḥarbī* semi-military; شبه المنحرف *š. al-munḥarif* trapezoid (*geom.*); شبه رسمى *š. rasmī* semi-official, officious (*dipl.*); شبه الظل *š. aẓ-ẓill* penumbra; شبه قارة subcontinent; شبه المعين *š. al-muʿayyan* rhomboid (*geom.*); اشباهه *ašbāhuhū* the likes of him, his kind; وشبههم and the likes of them, and their sort (of people); فى شبه عزلة تامة (*ʿuzlatin tāmma*) all but completely isolated, as good as completely isolated

شبه *šabah* pl. اشباه *ašbāh* resemblance, similarity, likeness; image, picture; analogue; similar, (a)like; brass

شبهة *šubha* pl. شبهات *šubhāt, šubahāt, šubuhāt* obscurity, vagueness, uncertainty; doubt; suspicion; specious argument, sophism; judicial error (*Isl. Law*) | ذوو الشبهات *ḏawū š-šubuhāt* or اصحاب الشبهات dubious persons, people of ill repute; تحت الشبهة suspicious, suspect

شبهان *šabahān* brass

شبيه *šabīh* pl. شباه *šibāh* similar (ب to), like, resembling (ب s.o., s.th.) | شبيه بالمنحرف (*munḥarif*) trapezoid (*geom.*); شبيه بالرسمى (*rasmī*) semi-official, officious (*dipl.*); شبيه بالمعين (*muʿayyan*) rhomboid (*geom.*)

اشبه *ašbah*[2] more similar, more resembling, more like | هو اشبه ب he resembles ... more than anything else, he is just like ...

مشابه *mašābih*[2] similarities, related traits

تشبيه *tašbīh* comparison; allegory, simile, parable; ascription of human characteristics to God, anthropomorphization (of God, *theol.*)

مشابهة *mušābaha* pl. *-āt* resemblance, similarity, likeness

تشبه *tašabbuh* imitation (ب of)

تشابه *tašābuh* resemblance, similarity, likeness; vagueness, haziness, indistinctness, obscurity

اشتباه *ištibāh* resemblance, similarity, likeness; dubiousness, doubtfulness, obscurity, inscrutability; doubt, misgiving, suspicion

مشبوه *mašbūh* suspicious, suspect; dubious, doubtful; notorious; a suspect

مشابه *mušābih* similar

متشابهات *mutašābihāt* obscure, not clearly intelligible passages in the Koran

مشتبه فى امره (*muštabah*) or مشتبه فيه (*amrihī*) suspicious, suspect; a suspect; مشتبه فيه ب suspected of s.th. | مشتبه فى صنعه (*ṣanʿihī*) of doubtful make

شبا *šaban* tip, point | فل من شباه (*falla*) to weaken s.o.

شباة *šabāh* pl. شبوات *šabawāt* tip, point; sting, prick

شت *šatta i* (*šatt*, شتات *šatāt*, شتيت *šatīt*) to be scattered, be dispersed, be dissolved; — *šatta i* to scatter, disperse, break up (هم a crowd, etc., ه s.th.) | شت شملهم (*šamlahum*) to disperse or break up the gathering of people, dissolve their unity II to disperse, scatter, break up (هم a crowd, etc., ه s.th.) | شتت شملهم (*šamlahum*) = شت شملهم IV = II V to be scattered, be dispersed, be dissolved, scatter, disperse, break up

شت *šatt* pl. اشتات *aštāt* dispersed, separate(d), scattered, dissolved; pl. اشتات manifold, variegated, diverse; scattered fragments, single pieces, sections (من of)

شتات *šatāt* dispersed, separate(d), scattered, dissolved

شتيت *šatīt* pl. شتى *šattā* dispersed, separate(d), scattered, dissolved; pl. شتى diverse, sundry, various, different, manifold, miscellaneous, all kinds of | شتى بينهما what a difference between the two of them! how different they are!

شتان *šattāna*: شتان ما بينهما ,شتان بينهما, شتان بين — و what a difference between ... and ...! how different they are!

تشتيت *taštīt* dispersion, scattering, dissolution; disruption, splitting, splintering

شتّر[1] *šutura i* to cut off, tear off, rip off (ه s.th.); to tear (up) (ه s.th.)

شترات[2] *šitrāt* citrate, salt of citric acid

شتل *šatala i* to plant, transplant (ه a plant)

شتلة *šatla* pl. شتول *šutūl*, شتائل *šatā'il*[2] seedling, set, transplant

مشتل *maštal* pl. مشاتل *mašātil*[2] (plant) nursery, arboretum

شتم *šatama i u* (*šatm*) and III to abuse, revile, vilify, scold (ه s.o.) VI to vilify one another, abuse one another, heap curses upon one another

شتم *šatm* abuse, vilification

شتام *šattām* one who indulges in frequent abuse or vilification; impudent, insolent, impertinent, abusive

شتيم *šatīm* abused, reviled, vilified, insulted

شتيمة *šatīma* pl. شتائم *šatā'im*[2] abuse, vilification, vituperation, insult

مشاتمة *mušātama* vilification, vituperation

شتا (شتو) *šatā u* (*šatw*) to pass the winter, to winter (ب at a place); to hibernate II = I; to rain V to pass the winter, to winter, hibernate (ب at a place)

شتاء *šitā'* pl. اشتية *aštiya*, شتى *šutīy* winter; rains, rainy season

شتوى *šatwī*, *šatawī* wintery, hibernal, winter (adj.)

مشتى *maštan* pl. مشات *mašātin* winter residence, winter quarters; winter resort

شات *šātin* wintery, hibernal

مشتى *mušattan* winter residence, winter quarters; winter resort

شتى *šattā* pl. of شتيت *šatīt* (see شت)

شج *šajja u i* (*šajj*) to break, split, cleave, fracture, bash in (ه s.th., esp. the skull)

شجة *šajja* pl. شجاج *šijāj* head wound which lays open the skull; skull fracture

شجب *šajaba u* (*šajb*) and II to doom to destruction, to ruin, destroy (ه s.o.); to condemn morally, criticize sharply (ه s.th.) IV to afflict, grieve (ه s.o.)

شجب *šajb* destruction, routing, crushing

شجب *šajab* sorrow, grief, worry; distress, affliction

شجاب *šijāb* pl. شجب *šujub* clothes hook (attached to the wall)

مشجب *mišjab* pl. مشاجب *mašājib*[2] clothes hook, clothes rack

شجر *šajara u* (*šajr*) to happen, occur; to break out, develop (unrest) III to quarrel, argue, dispute (مع or ه with s.o.) VI to quarrel, fight, dispute (with one another); to quarrel, argue, fight (مع with) VIII do.

الحروف الشجرية *al-ḥurūf aš-šajrīya* the sounds *j*, *š*, *ḍ* (*phon.*)

شجر *šajar* (coll.; n. un. ة) pl. اشجار *ašjār* trees; shrubs, bushes

شجرة *šajara* pl. *-āt* tree; shrub, bush | شجرة النسب *š. an-nasab* genealogical tree

شجر *šajir* woody, wooded, abounding in trees

شجير *šajīr* pl. شجراء *šujarā'*[2] bad companion, bad company

شجيرة *šujaira* pl. *-āt* shrub, bush

شجار *šijār* (wooden) bar, bolt

اشجر *ašjar*[2], f. شجراء *šajrā'*[2] woody, wooded, abounding in trees

تشجير *tašjīr* afforestation

شجار *šijār* fight, quarrel; dispute, argument; see also above

مشاجرة *mušājara* fight, quarrel; dispute, argument

مشجر *mušajjar* figured with designs of plants, branched (cloth)

مشجر *mušjir* abounding in trees, wooded

2شجران *šajarān* shagreen (leather)

شجع *šaju'a u* (شجاعة *šajā'a*) to be courageous, brave, valiant, bold **II** to encourage, embolden, hearten (ه على s.o. to); to favor, support, back, promote, further (ه, ه s.o., s.th.) **V** to take heart, pluck up courage; to show o.s. courageous; to be encouraged

شجاع *šujā'*, *šijā'* pl. شجعة *šaj'a*, شجعان *šuj'ān* courageous, brave, valiant, bold; hero; الشجاع Hydra (*astron.*)

شجيع *šajī'* pl. m. شجعاء *šuja'ā'*[2], شجعان *šuj'ān*, pl. f. شجائع *šajā'i'*[2], شجاع *šijā'* courageous, brave, valiant, bold, audacious

شجاعة *šajā'a* courage, bravery, valor, valiance, boldness, audacity

اشجع *ašja'*[2], f. شجعاء *šaj'ā'*[2] courageous, brave, valiant, bold, audacious

اشجع *ašja'*, *išja'* pl. اشاجع *ašāji'*[2] (proximal or first) phalanx of the finger

تشجيع *tašjī'* encouragement, heartening, animation (على to); favoring, furtherance, promotion, advancement

مشجع *mušajji'* encourager; promoter, supporter, advocate, proponent

شجن *šajina a* to be sad, grieved, distressed, worried; to coo (pigeon); — *šajana u* (*šajn*, شجون *šujūn*) to sadden, grieve, distress, worry (ه s. o.) **II** and **IV** = *šajana*

شجن *šajan* pl. شجون *šujūn*, اشجان *ašjān* worry, anxiety, apprehension; sorrow, grief, distress, sadness; (pl. *šujūn*) twig, branch | الحديث شجون conversation drifts from one topic to another

(شجو and شجى) شجا *šajā u* (شجو *šajw*) to worry, trouble, grieve, sadden, distress, fill with anxiety (ه s.o.); — شجى *šajiya a* (شجا *šajan*) to be or become worried, troubled, grieved, sad, distressed, anxious, apprehensive **II** to move, touch, grip (ه s.o.) **IV** to grieve, worry, trouble, sadden, fill with anxiety (ه s.o.)

شج *šajin*, f. شجية *šajiya* worried, troubled, grieved, sad, anxious, apprehensive

شجو *šajw* grief, worry, distress, anxiety, apprehension, sadness; fear; affectedness, emotion; wailing, plaintive, moving strain (of a tune, of a song, of an instrument)

شجوى *šajawī* worried, troubled, grieved, distressed, sad

شجا and شجى *šajan* foreign body in the throat which inhibits breathing; شجا affectedness, emotion, being moved, a touching, pathetic mood; also = شجو *šajw*

شجى *šajīy* worried, troubled, grieved, distressed, sad; anxious, apprehensive, fearful; gripping, heart-rending, touching, moving (vocal part, music)

مشج *mušajjin* moving, touching, gripping, pathetic

شح *šaḥḥa* (1st. pers. perf. *šaḥaḥtu*) *u i* (*šuḥḥ*) to be or become stingy, tight-fisted, avaricious, miserly, niggardly; to stint, economize (على or ب with or in s.th., على toward s.o.); to be covetous, greedy (على or ب for); to become short, run out, decrease, dwindle **III** to stint, be niggardly, be sparing; to withhold (ب from s.o., على s.th.)

شح *šuḥḥ* stinginess, avarice, niggardliness; greed, covetousness; scarcity, paucity, sparsity; ebb

شحيح *šaḥīḥ* pl. شحاح *šiḥāḥ*, اشحة *ašiḥḥa*, اشحاء *ašiḥḥā'*[2], pl. f. شحائح *šaḥā'iḥ*[2] stingy, tight-fisted, niggardly, miserly, avaricious (على or ب with, على toward):

short, scarce, meager, sparse; greedy, covetous (على for) | الايام الشحائح (*ayyām*) the rainless days, the dry season

مشاحة *mušāḥḥa*: لا مشاحة فى ذلك (*mušāḥḥata*) that is incontestable; لا مشاحة ان it is incontestable that . . ., indisputably . . .; ولا مشاحة incontestably, indisputably

شحب *šaḥaba u a* (شحوب *šuḥūb*), *šaḥuba u* (شحوبة *šuḥūba*) and pass. *šuḥiba* to be or become pale, wan, sallow, emaciated, lean, haggard; to look ill, sickly

شحوب *šuḥūb* paleness, pallor, wanness, sallowness, emaciation

شاحب *šāḥib* pl. شواحب *šawāḥib*² pale, wan, sallow; emaciated, lean, haggard; dim, pale (e.g., light); dull, faded (color); wan (smile)

□ شحت *šaḥata* (= شحذ) to beg, ask for alms

□ شحات *šaḥḥāt* pl. ة beggar | □ شحات العين *š. al-'ain* sty (*med.*)

شحذ *šaḥaḏa a* (*šaḥḏ*) to whet, sharpen, practice, train, strengthen (ه s.th., also, e.g., the intellect, one's forces); to hone, strop (ه a knife); to beg, ask for alms (ه s.o.)

شحاذ *šaḥḥāḏ* (importunate) beggar | شحاذ العين *š. al-'ain* sty (*med.*)

شحاذة *šiḥāḏa* beggary

مشحذ *mišḥaḏ*, مشحذة *mišḥaḏa* whetstone, hone

شحر II to soot, besmut, blacken with soot (ه s.th.)

شحار *šuḥḥār* soot

مشحر *mašḥar* charcoal kiln, pile

مشحرى *mašḥarī* charcoal burner

شحرور *šuḥrūr* pl. شحارير *šaḥārīr*² thrush, blackbird (*zool.*)

مشحر *mušaḥḥar* sooty

شحط *šaḥaṭa a* (*šaḥṭ*) to be far away, distant, remote; to strike (ه a match); to strand, be stranded, run aground (ship); to ground on a sandbank II to strand, be stranded, run aground (ship); to ground on a sandbank; to strand (ه a ship)

شحطة *šaḥṭa* pl. *-āt* stripe, braid (on a uniform)

شحاطة *šaḥḥāṭa* pl. *-āt* (*syr.*) match, lucifer

شحيطة *šuḥḥaiṭa* (*syr.*) match, lucifer

شاحط *šāḥiṭ* far (away), distant, remote, outlying, out-of-the-way; stranded

شحم *šaḥuma u* (شحامة *šaḥāma*) to be or become fat II to grease, lubricate (ه s.th.)

شحم *šaḥm* pl. شحوم *šuḥūm*, شحومات *šuḥūmāt* fat, suet, grease; axle grease, lubricant; tallow, sebum; lard; pulp (of fruit)

شحمة *šaḥma* (n. un.) a piece of fat, etc. (see شحم) | شحمة الاذن *š. al-uḏun* earlobe; شحمة الارض *š. al-arḍ* truffle; شحمة العين *š. al-'ain* eyeball

شحمى *šaḥmī* fatty, sebaceous, stearic

شحم *šaḥim* pulpy, mushy, pappy (fruit)

شحيم *šaḥīm* fat, fatty

○ مشحمة *mišḥama* pl. مشاحم *mašāḥim*² grease box (of a wheel)

تشحيم *tašḥīm* lubrication, greasing, oiling (of a machine) | زيوت التشحيم lubricating oils, lubricants

تشحم *tašaḥḥum* fatness, obesity

مشحم *mušaḥḥam* fat, fatty, greasy

مشحم *mušḥim* pulpy, mushy, pappy (fruit)

شحن *šaḥana a* (*šaḥn*) to fill up (ه ب s.th. with); to load, freight (ه ب a ship with); to ship, freight, consign (ه goods); to load, charge (ب ه s.th. with, *el.*); to drive away, chase away, repel (ه s.o.) III to hate (ه s.o.); to quarrel, argue, fight (ه with s.o.) IV to fill up (ه ب s.th. with); to load, freight (ه ب s.th. with) VI to hate one another; to quarrel, have a feud

شحن ***šaḥn*** loading, freighting; shipment, freightage; cargo, lading, load, freight | بوليسة الشحن *būlīsat aš-š.* bill of lading; سيارة شحن *sayyārat š.* truck, lorry

شحنة ***šaḥna*** pl. *šaḥanāt* cargo, lading, load, freight; charge (*el.*)

شحنة ***šiḥna*** police, police force

شحناء ***šaḥnā'***[2] grudge, rancor, hatred, enmity

مشاحنة ***mušāḥana*** pl. *-āt* grudge, rancor, hatred, enmity; quarrel, feud, controversy

شاحن ***šāḥin*** loaded, laden, freighted (esp. ship) | ○ شاحن المركم *š. al-markam* battery charger

شاحنة ***šāḥina*** pl. *-āt* truck, lorry; baggage car

مشحون ***mašḥūn*** loaded, laden, freighted (esp. ship); charged (*el.*); pl. مشحونات cargo, lading, load, freight

شحور ***šaḥwara*** to soot, besmut, blacken with soot (ه s.th.)

شحور ***šaḥwar*** blackbird (*zool.*)

شحوار ***šuḥwār*** soot, smut

شخ ***šak̲k̲a*** *u* (*šak̲k̲*) to urinate, piss, make water

شخ ***šak̲k̲*** urine, piss

شخاخ ***šak̲āk̲*** urine, piss

مشخخة ***miška̲ka*** public lavatory

شخب ***šak̲aba*** *u a* (*šak̲b*) to flow, stream, run, pour forth, gush forth

شخبط ***šak̲baṭa*** to scribble, scrawl (in writing)

شختور ***šak̲tūr***, شختورة pl. شخاتير ***šak̲ātīr***[2] large, flat-bottomed (wooden) barge; punt

شخر ***šak̲ara*** *i* (شخير *šak̲īr*) to snore; to snort; to neigh, whinny; to bray (donkey)

شخشخ ***šak̲šak̲a*** to rattle, clatter, clank

شخشيخة (*eg.*) ***šuk̲šēk̲a*** pl. شخاشخ *šak̲āšik̲*[2] rattle (toy); toy, plaything; skylight

شخص ***šak̲aṣa*** *a* (شخوص *šuk̲ūṣ*) to rise, tower up; to become high, lofty; to rise, ascend (star); to appear (ل to s.o.); to stare, gaze (الى at, of the eye), be fixed (الى on, of the glance); to be glazed (eyes of a dying person); to start out, leave, depart (الى to see s.o., for a place), travel, journey (الى to s.o., to a place); to pass (من الى from one state or condition into another) | شخص بصره (*baṣarahū*) or شخص ببصره to fix one's eyes, one's glance (الى on), look fixedly (الى at s.o.), stare, gaze (الى at) II to represent as a person or individual, personify (ه s.th.); to specify (ه s.th.), identify (ه, ه s.o., s.th.); to act, play (ه a part, of the actor); to perform (actor) | شخص مرضا (*maraḍan*) to diagnose a disease IV to send off, send out, dispatch (ه s.o.) V to appear, be revealed, show o.s. (ل to s.o.)

شخص ***šak̲ṣ*** pl. اشخاص *ašk̲āṣ*, شخوص *šuk̲ūṣ* individual, person; figure; character (of a play); someone, somebody

شخصى ***šak̲ṣī*** personal, private, of one's own; شخصيا *šak̲ṣīyan* personally | قانون (نظام or) الاحوال الشخصية personal statute

شخصية ***šak̲ṣīya*** pl. *-āt* individuality, personality (also = personage); distinctive way of life, peculiarity, distinctive character, personal stamp; identity | شخصية اعتبارية (*i'tibārīya*) legal person (*jur.*); تحقيق الشخصية identification of a person; شهادة تحقيق الشخصية *šahādat t. aš-š.* identity card; قلم تحقيق الشخصية *qalam t. aš-š.* bureau of identification

شخصاتى *šakṣātī* (comic) actor, comedian

تشخيص *taškīṣ* personification; exact designation, specification; identification, diagnosis; acting, performance (on stage), play(ing) (of an actor)

تشخيصى *taškīṣī* diagnostic | طبيب تشخيصى diagnostician

شاخص *šāḵiṣ* fixed, glazed (glance); pole, stake (*eg.*)

مشخص *mušakkiṣ* actor, player; representative

مشخصة *mušakkiṣa* pl. *-āt* actress, player; personality

مشخصات *mušakkiṣāt* qualities or factors lending s.th. its distinctive character, peculiarities, characteristics

شخط *šakaṭa* (*eg.*) to shout, bark, bellow (ف at s.o.)

شخلل *šaklala* (*eg.*) to jingle, tinkle; to clatter, rattle (ب with); to coquet, flirt

شخليلة *šaklīla* (*eg.*) jingle, jangle, tinkling

شد *šadda i* (شدة *šidda*) to be or become firm, fast, solid, hard, strong, vigorous, robust, vehement, violent, intense; — *šadda u i* (*šadd*) to make firm, hard, strong, solidify, harden, brace (ه s.th.), strengthen, fortify (ه, ه s.o., s.th.); to tighten, pull taut, draw tight (ه s.th., e.g., the bow); to fasten, tie, bind (ه على or الى s.th. on, to), lash (ه على s.th. on); to saddle (على an animal); to put emphasis (على كلمة *'alā kalimatin* on a word), emphasize, stress (على كلمة a word); to pull, drag (ه من s.o. by the coat); to charge, launch an attack (على against, on), assault, attack (على s.o., s.th.); to press (على s.th. or upon s.th.), exert pressure (على on); to insist (فى on s.th.) | شدما *šadda-mā* and لشد ما (*la-šadda*) (with foll. verb) how much . . .! very often . . .; very much, exceedingly, vehemently, violently; لشد ما كان سرورنا اذ tremendous was our joy when . . .; شد ازره (*azrahū*) or شد من ازره to help, support, encourage, back up s.o.; شد ازره (*azruhū*) to be energetic, vigorous, courageous; شد الزمام to tighten the reins, master the situation; شد من عزائمه to strengthen s.o.'s determination; شد عضده (*'aḍudahū*) to strengthen, support, bolster, assist s.o.; شد على راحلته (he saddled his female riding camel =) he started out on the journey; شد الرحال to start out, depart, leave (الى for); شد وثاقه (*waṯāqahū*) to shackle, fetter s.o.; شد يده على (*yadahū*) to adhere, cling to s.th.; شد على يديه (*yadaihi*) to clasp s.o.'s hands **II** to strengthen, intensify (ه s.th.), make (ه s.th.) strong, hard, harsh, severe; (*gram.*) to intensify, double, geminate (ه a consonant); to exert pressure (على on), press (على upon); to be hard, strict, stern (على فى toward s.o. in); to impress (على ب upon s.o. s.th.) | شدد فى طلبه (*ṭalabihī*) to demand s.th. emphatically or inexorably; شدد من عزيمته (*šuddida*) he was strengthened in his determination **III** to argue, have an argument, an exchange of words (ه with s.o.) **V** to be hard, harsh, strict, severe, stern (على toward); to be or become violent, vehement, intense, strong; to show o.s. stern, harsh, hard, inexorable, be relentless, remain unmoved, unrelenting **VI** to argue with one another **VIII** to be or become hard, harsh, rigorous, intense, forceful, severe, strong, vehement, violent, passionate; to become harder, harsher, more rigorous, more intense, more forceful, severer, stronger, more vehement, more violent, more passionate; to intensify, increase, grow; to become aggravated, more critical; to become tormenting, excruciating, distressing, unbearable (على

for s.o.), take a turn for the worse (disease, على with s.o.); to be advanced (time of the day); to run, race, dash | اشتد ساعده (sāʿiduhū) to become strong, vigorous

شد šadd: شد الحبل š. al-ḥabl tug of war

شدة šadda (n. vic.) strengthening, intensification; stress, emphasis; pulling, dragging, tugging; tightness, tautness; stress, strain; doubling sign over a consonant (gram.) | شدة ورق اللعب š. waraq al-laʿb deck of cards

شدة šidda strength, forcefulness, power, vehemence, violence, intensity, severity, force, high degree; (pl. شدائد šadāʾid²) misfortune, calamity, misery, adversity, distress, hardship, affliction, discomfort

شداد šadād pl. اشدة ašidda riding saddle (of a camel)

شديد šadīd pl. اشداء ašiddāʾ², شداد šidād strong, powerful, forceful, vigorous, stern, severe, rigorous, hard, harsh, violent, vehement, intense; bad, evil, ominous, calamitous, difficult (على for s.o.); with foll. subst. frequently corresponding to Engl. "very", e.g., شديد الاعتناء very attentive, very careful | ارض شديدة (arḍ) solid or firm ground; شديد البأس š. al-baʾs courageous, stouthearted, bold, audacious, brave, valiant; شديد الشكيمة stubborn, obstinate, unbending, unyielding, relentless; شديد اللهجة š. al-lahja strongly worded, vehement in language, sharp in tone; شديد الوطأة š. al-waṭʾa cruel

شديدة šadīda pl. شدائد šadāʾid² misfortune, calamity, misery, adversity, distress, hardship, affliction, discomfort

اشد ašadd² stronger, more intense, severer, harder, worse | used with foll. indeterminate abstract substantives as paraphrase of simple elatives, e.g., اشد سوادا (sawādan) blacker, اشد غضبا (ġaḍaban) more wrathful, angrier; اشد ما يكون extremely, exceedingly, very much, e.g., روحهم اشد ما يكون تعطشا الى العلم (rūḥuhum, taʿaṭṭušan, ʿilm) they are extremely eager for knowledge

اشد ašudd physical maturity, virility | بلغ اشده to attain full maturity, come of legal age; to reach its climax

مشد mišadd pl. -āt corset, stays

تشديد tašdīd intensification, strengthening; (gram.) intensified pronunciation, gemination, doubling (of a consonant); doubling sign over a consonant; pressure (على on)

مشادة mušādda exchange of words, squabble, argument, quarrel, fight, controversy, conflict

اشتداد ištidād aggravation, intensification, increase; deterioration

مشدود mašdūd tense, tight, taut

مشدد mušaddid: ظروف مشددة aggravating circumstances

مشدد mušaddad doubled (letter; gram.); emphatic, intense; severe, stern

متشدد mutašaddid pl. -ūn stern zealot, bigot, proponent of a stern viewpoint

شدخ šadaka a (šadk) to break, shatter, smash, crush (ه s.th.) II do.

شادر šādir pl. شوادر šawādir² tent; storehouse, warehouse, magazine

شادوف šādūf pl. شواديف šawādīf² (eg.) shadoof, counterpoised sweep for raising irrigation water

شدق V to announce (ب s.th.) in a boastful, bragging, loud-mouthed manner, to vaunt (ب s.th.); to chatter, prattle | تشدق بالكلام (kalām) to enunciate overcarefully, speak affectedly; to be agape

شدق šidq pl. اشداق ašdāq corner of the mouth; jawbone | ضحك بملء (ملء) شدقيه

ḍaḥika bi-mil'i (mil'a) šidqaihi to grin from ear to ear

اشدق ***ašdaq***[2], f. شدقاء *šadqā'*[2] having a large mouth, largemouthed

متشدق ***mutašaddiq*** pl. *-ūn* braggart, boaster, bigmouth

شدن ***šadana** u* to be weaned, be on its own feet (young animal)

شادن ***šādin*** pl. شوادن *šawādin*[2] gazelle fawn

شده ***šadaha** a* to confuse, perplex, baffle (ه s.o.)

مشدوه ***mašdūh*** perplexed, appalled, baffled

شدا (شدو) ***šadā** u* (*šadw*) to sing; to chant (ه s.th.); to acquire or have education, become or be educated (في in a field) | شدا شيئا من العربية to know a little Arabic, have a smattering of Arabic

شدو ***šadw*** song, chant

شاد ***šādin*** pl. شادون *šādūn* educated, trained (e.g., في اللغة linguistically) | ليلة شادية *laila šādiya* soiree of vocal music

شادية ***šādiya*** songstress, singer

شدياق ***šidyāq*** pl. شدايقة *šadāyiqa* subdeacon (*Chr.*)

شذ ***šaḏḏa** i u* (*šaḏḏ*, شذوذ *šuḏūḏ*) to segregate, separate, isolate o.s. (عن from), be separated, isolated (عن from), be outside s.th. (عن), elude (عن s.th.); to be alone; to be irregular, deviate, stand out (على or عن from), be an exception (على or عن to); to be wanting, lacking; to decrease, dwindle

شذ ***šaḏḏ*** irregularity, deviation, anomaly, exception (عن to)

شذوذ irregularity, deviation, anomaly, exception (عن to); curiosity, eccentricity, eccentric character

شاذ ***šāḏḏ*** pl. شذاذ *šuḏḏāḏ*, شواذ *šawāḏḏ*[2] isolated, separate(d), detached, alone; irregular, abnormal, anomalous, unusual, extraordinary, exceptional, singular, curious, queer, odd, peculiar, strange, eccentric; noncanonical (version); pl. شواذ exceptions | شاذ الاخلاق of deviant (= inferior) character; شاذ الطبع *š. aṭ-ṭab'*, شاذ الاطوار, الطباع eccentric, extravagant, crazy; شذاذ الآفاق the foreigners, the strangers

شواذات ***šawāḏḏāt*** peculiarities, idiosyncrasies

شذب ***šaḏaba** i u* (*šaḏb*) to cut off, sever (ه s.th.); to trim, clip, prune, lop (ه hedges, trees); to adapt, doctor, modify (ه s.th.) II do.

شذر **V** to be scattered, be dispersed; to scatter, disperse

شذرة ***šaḏra*** pl. *šaḏarāt*, شذور *šuḏūr* particle, bit, tiny piece; fragment, section

تفرقوا شذر مذر *tafarraqū šaḏara maḏara, šiḏara miḏara* they scattered in all directions

شذو ***šaḏw*** fragrance of musk

شذا ***šaḏan*** fragrance, scent, aroma

شذى ***šaḏiy*** fragrant, aromatic

شر ***šarra*** (1st pers. perf. *šarirtu*) *a*, (1st pers. perf. *šarurtu*) *u* (*šarr*, شرة *širra*) to be bad, evil, wicked, vicious, malicious, malignant

شر ***šarr*** pl. شرور *šurūr* evil, ill, mischief; calamity, disaster; iniquity, injustice; harm, damage, injury; wickedness, viciousness, malice; vice, sin; — (pl. اشرار *ašrār*) bad, evil, wicked, vicious, malicious; evildoer, culprit; — *šarr* (as elative) worse, more evil | هزمهم شر هزيمة (*šarra hazīmatin*) he brought utter defeat upon them

شرانى *šarrānī* evil, vicious, malicious

شرة *širra* evil, ill, mischief; calamity, disaster; iniquity, injustice; harm, damage, injury; wickedness, viciousness, malice; vice, sin; vivacity enthusiasm, fire of youth

شرير *šarīr* pl. اشراء *aširrā'*[2] bad, evil, wicked, vicious, malicious

شرير *širrīr* very bad, very evil, very wicked, very vicious, very malicious; scoundrel; الشرير the Evil One (= Satan)

شرر *šarar* (coll.; n. un. ة) sparks

شررى *šararī* spark (used attributively)

شرار *šarār* (coll.; n. un. ة) sparks

شرارة *šarāra* pl. *-āt* spark | شمعة الشرارة *šam'at aš-š.* spark plug; مفتاح الشرارة *miftāḥ aš-š.* ignition key (automobile)

شرارى *šarārī* spark (used attributively)

شرار *šarrār* sparkling, scintillating, emitting sparks

اشرأب *išra'abba* to stretch one's neck in order to see s.th. (ل or الى), crane one's neck for (ل or الى); to carry one's head high (out of vanity); to leer (الى at)

شراب *šurrāb* pl. *-āt* stocking, sock

شراس *širās* glue, paste

[1]شرب *šariba a* (*šurb*, مشرب *mašrab*) to drink (ه s.th.); to sip (ه s.th.) | شرب فى حبه (*ḥubbihī*) to drink s.o.'s health, toast s.o.; شرب الدخان (*dukāna*) to smoke; شرب نخبه (*nakbahū*) to drink s.o.'s health, toast s.o. II to give (ه ه s.o. s.th.) to drink, make or let drink (ه ه s.o. s.th.); to drench, soak, saturate, impregnate (ب ه s.th. with); to inculcate, imbue (ه ه s.o. with s.th.) III to drink in s.o.'s (ه) company, have a drink (ه with s.o.) IV to give (ه ه s.o. s.th.) to drink, make or let drink (ه ه s.o. s.th.); to drench, soak, saturate, impregnate (ب or ه ه s.th. with); to inculcate, imbue (ه ه s.o. with); pass. *ušriba* to be or become full (ه of s.th.), be filled, imbued, infused (ه with s.th.), be dominated, permeated (ه by s.th.) | اشربه ما لم يشرب (*yašrab*) to attribute s.th. wrongly to s.o. V to soak up, absorb, imbibe (ه s.th.); to be permeated, imbued, infused (ه, ب with s.th.); to be full (ب of), be filled, replete (ب with)

شرب *šurb* drinking, drink; absorption

شربة *šarba* drink; sip, draught, swallow; dose, potion (of a medicine); laxative, purgative, aperient

شربة *šurba* drink; sip, draught, swallow; dose, potion (of a medicine)

شراب *šarāb* pl. اشربة *ašriba* beverage, drink; wine; fruit juice, fruit syrup, sherbet | شراب التفاح *š. at-tuffāḥ* apple juice; cider; شراب البرتقال *š. al-burtuqāl* orangeade

شراب *šarrāb* drunkard, heavy drinker

شريب *šarīb* drinkable, potable

شرابة *šarrāba*, *šurrāba* pl. شراريب *šarārīb*[2] tassel, tuft, bob | شرابة الراعى *š. ar-rā'ī* (European) holly (Ilex aquifolium; *bot.*)

شريب *širrīb* drunkard, heavy drinker

مشرب *mašrab* drink (as opposed to food); (pl. مشارب *mašārib*[2]) drinking place, water hole, drinking trough, drinking fountain; restaurant, bar; inclination, taste; movement, school (e.g., in philosophy)

مشربة *mašraba* pl. مشارب *mašārib*[2] drinking place, water hole, drinking trough, drinking fountain

مشربية *mašrabīya*, *mušrabīya* and مشربة *mašraba* moucharaby, projecting oriel window with a wooden latticework enclosure; wooden oriel; attic room;

mašrabīya a kind of drinking vessel; vase, pot for flowers

تشرب *tašarrub* absorption, soaking up, imbibing

شارب *šārib* pl. *-ūn,* شرب *šarb,* شروب *šurūb* drinking; drinker; (pl. شوارب *šawārib*[2]) mustache, frequently dual: شاربان

مشروب *mašrūb* pl. *-āt* drink, beverage | مشروبات روحية (*rūḥīya*) alcoholic beverages, liquors

[2]شربة *šorba* soup

شوربة *šorba* (*eg.*), شوربا *šōrabā* (*syr.*) soup

[3]شراب *šurrāb* pl. *-āt* stocking, sock

شربك *šarbaka* to (en)tangle, snarl (ه s.th.); to complicate (ه s.th.)

شربين *šarbīn* a variety of larch (*bot.*)

[1]شرج *šaraj* pl. اشراج *ašrāj* loop, ring, eyelet; buttonhole; anus

شرجي *šarajī* anal

[2]شيرج look up alphabetically

شرح *šaraḥa a* (*šarḥ*)to cut in slices, slice, cut up (ه s.th.); to cut open, rip open (ه s.th.); to bare, expose, make clearly visible or discernible (ه s.th.); to expound (ه s.th.); to explain, elucidate, illustrate, make plain, set forth, describe, depict (ه s.th.); to comment (ه on), interpret (ه s. th.); to open, lay open (صدره *ṣadrahū* s.o.'s heart, ل to or for the acceptance of) | شرح خاطره (*ḵāṭirahū*) to gladden, delight s.o. **II** to cut in slices, slice, cut up (ه s.th.); to dissect, dismember, anatomize (ه a corpse) **VII** to be opened (heart); to be relaxed; to be glad, happy | انشرح صدره (*ṣadruhū*) and انشرح خاطره (*ḵāṭiruhū*) to be or become glad, happy or delighted, rejoice

شرح *šarḥ* expounding, presentation, explanation, illustration, elucidation, exposition, setting forth; commentation; (pl. شروح *šurūḥ*) commentary

شرحي *šarḥī* explanatory, explicatory, illustrative

شرحة *šarḥa* long, thin slice, rasher

شريحة *šarīḥa* pl. شرائح *šarā'iḥ*[2] long, thin slice (e.g., of fruit, etc.), rasher; girth, cinch; ○ (microscope) slide

○ مشرحة *mašraḥa* operating room; operating table; autopsy room

تشريح *tašrīḥ* dissection; anatomy; autopsy, post-mortem examination | علم التشريح *ʿilm at-t.* anatomy; ○ تشريح المقابلة *t. al-muqābala* comparative anatomy

تشريحي *tašrīḥī* dissecting, anatomizing, dissective, dissectional; anatomic(al)

انشراح *inširāḥ* relaxedness, relaxation; joy, delight, glee, gaiety

شارح *šāriḥ* pl. شراح *šurrāḥ* explainer, expounder, interpreter, commentator, expositor

مشرح *mušarriḥ* anatomist

[1]شرخ *šaraḵa u* (شروخ *šurūḵ*) to become a youth, grow from childhood to maturity

شرخ *šarḵ* prime of youth, spring of life

[2]شرخ *šaraḵa a* (*eg.*) to crack, splinter, become cracked

شرخ *šarḵ* pl. شروخ *šurūḵ* (*eg.*) crack, break, fissure, fracture

شرد *šarada u* (شراد *širād*, شرود *šurūd*) to bolt (horse); to run away, flee, take to flight, take to one's heels, break loose, escape; to roam, rove, wander, stray, go astray; to be distracted (thoughts) | شرد ذهنه (*ḏihnuhū*) to be absent-minded; شرد به الفكر (*fikru*) he became lost in thought **II** to frighten away, chase away, drive away (ه s.o.); to scare (ه s.o.), frighten (ه s.o.) into a panic **IV** to chase away, drive away (• s.o.) V to roam, tramp about, lead a vagabond life

شرود *šarūd* pl. شرد *šurud* running away; straying; astray, deviant, aberrant, strange, peculiar

شرود *šurūd* roaming, straying, wandering | شرود الفكر *š. al-fikr* absent-mindedness, distractedness

شريد *šarīd* fugitive, expatriated, displaced, expelled; loafer, tramp, vagrant, vagabond

تشريد *tašrīd* expulsion, banishment, eviction; vagrancy, vagabondage | حياة التشريد *ḥayāt at-t.* the unsettled life, life of a vagabond

تشرد *tašarrud* vagrancy, vagabondage

شارد *šārid* pl. شرد *šurud*, *šurrad*, شوارد *šawārid*[2] fugitive, straying, astray; intimidated, frightened, helpless, at a loss; a fugitive, runaway, deserter; defector; vagrant, tramp, vagabond | شارد الفكر *š. al-fikr* absent-minded, distracted; شوارد اللغة *š. al-luġa* irregularities of the language, linguistic anomalies; شارد النظر (النظرات) *š. an-naẓar* (*an-naẓarāt*) with a blank stare; gazing into the void

شاردة *šārida* pl. شوارد *šawārid*[2] peculiarity, anomaly, exception | لا تفوته شاردة ولا واردة (*tafūtuhū*) nothing escapes him, he doesn't miss a thing

مشرد *mušarrad* fugitive, refugee, displaced person; neglected, unkempt | مشرد البال confused, disconcerted

متشرد *mutašarrid* pl. *-ūn* homeless person, tramp, vagrant, vagabond; adventurer

شردق II *tašardaqa* to swallow the wrong way; to choke (to death)

شرذم II *tašarḏama* to be jagged, indented

شرذمة *širḏima* pl. شراذم *šarāḏim*[2], شراذيم *šarāḏīm*[2] small group, gang, party, troop; little band

[1]شرس *šarisa a* (*šaras*, شراسة *šarāsa*) to be vicious, malicious, mischievous, ill-tempered, unsociable, quarrelsome, petulant, peevish VI to be cross, quarrel (مع with)

شرس *šaras* = شراسة

شرس *šaris* vicious, malicious, mischievous, ill-tempered, unsociable, quarrelsome, petulant, peevish; wild, ferocious, fierce

شريس *šarīs* = شرس *šaris*

شراسة *šarāsa* wickedness, malice, viciousness, meanness, baseness, villainy; ill-temperedness, unsociableness, querulousness, petulance, peevishness

[2]شراس *širās* glue, paste, see سراس, سيراس

شرسوف *šursūf* pl. شراسيف *šarāsīf*[2] rib cartilage

شراسيفي *šarāsīfī* epigastric, pertaining to the anterior walls of the abdomen

شرش II to take root

شرش *širš* pl. شروش *šurūš* root | شرش اللبن *š. al-laban* whey

شرشور *šuršūr* pl. شراشير *šarāšīr*[2] chaffinch (*zool.*)

شرشير *šaršīr* (*eg.*) wild duck (*zool.*)

شراشر *šarāšir*[2] soul, self, nature (of a person)

شرشف *šaršaf* pl. شراشف *šarāšif*[2] bedsheet

شرط *šaraṭa i u* (*šarṭ*) to tear (• s.th.); to make incisions (• in), scratch, scarify (• s.th.); to slit open, rip open (• s.th.); to impose as a condition, as an obligation (• على on s.o. s.th.), make conditional (• على for s.o. s.th.); to stipulate (• s.th.) II to tear to shreds (• s.th.); to scratch, scarify (• s.th.); to make incisions (• in) III to fix mutual conditions; to make a contract, conclude an agreement; to bet, wager (• with s.o.) V to impose severe conditions or terms | تشرط في عمله (*'amalihī*) to be meticulous in one's work, do one's work painstakingly **VIII** to impose as a condition, as an obligation (ه على on s.o. s.th.); to make conditional (ه على for s.o. s.th.); to stipulate (ه s.th.); pass. *ušturiṭa* to be prerequisite, preconditional (ل for)

شرط *šarṭ* pl. شروط *šurūṭ* incision (in the skin); long cut, rip, slash, slit; condition, precondition; provision, proviso, clause; stipulation (of a contract) | شرطا ان (*šarṭan*), على شرط ان ,بشرط on the condition that . . ., provided that . . .; من دون (بدون) شرط unconditional; بلا شرط أو قيد (*au qaidin*) with no strings attached; unconditional (obedience, surrender, etc.); شرط الخيار proviso of the right of withdrawal (from a contract, a commercial transaction, an obligation, and the like, *Isl. Law*)

شرط *šaraṭ* pl. اشراط *ašrāṭ* sign, portent | اشراط الساعة the portents of the Day of Judgment

شرطى *šarṭī* conditional | جملة شرطية (*jumla*) conditional clause (*gram.*)

شرطية *šarṭīya* contract, agreement

شرطة *šarṭa* pl. شرط *šuraṭ* stroke, line; hyphen; dash

شرطة *šurṭa* police, policemen | دار الشرطة police station; تقرير الشرطة police report

شرطى *šurṭī*, *šuraṭī* pl. *-ūn* policeman, officer

شريط *šarīṭ* pl. شرائط *šarā'iṭ*², اشرطة *ašriṭa* band, ribbon, tape; cord, string; leash, line; thong, strap; braid, galloon, chevron, stripe; ribbon (of an order), medal ribbon, service ribbon; (railway) track, line; film strip; film (also شريط سينمائى); (magnetic) tape | شريط مصغر (*muṣaġġar*) microfilm; شريط القياس tape measure; measuring tape; شريط ناطق pl. شرائط ناطقة sound film; sound track; magnetic tape; شريط النار fuse; دودة الشريط *dūdat aš-š.* tapeworm

شريطة *šarīṭa* condition | على شريطة on the condition that . . .

مشرط *mašraṭ* program

مشرط *mišraṭ* pl. مشارط *mašāriṭ*² lancet, scalpel

تشريط *tašrīṭ* scarification, incision

مشارطة *mušāraṭa* agreement, arrangement

اشتراط *ištirāṭ* pl. *-āt* condition, provision, proviso; stipulation

شرطن *šarṭana* to consecrate, ordain (ه s.o., *Chr.*) **II** to be ordained (*Chr.*)

شرطنة *šarṭana* = شرطونية

شرطونية *šarṭūnīya* ordination of a priest, and any ordination of persons by laying on of hands (*Chr.*); simony (*Copt.-Chr.*)

شرع *šara'a a* (*šar'*, شروع *šurū'*) to go (فى into), enter (فى s.th.); to begin, start, commence (فى or ب with; with foll. imperf.: to do s.th.); to point a weapon (ه) at s.o. (على); to untie, unbind, unlace (ه s.th.); to fix (ه bayonets, على on rifles); — *šara'a a* (*šar'*) to introduce, enact (ه laws), prescribe, give (ه ل to s.o. laws), make laws (ه) for s.o. (ل) | شرع مشروعا to devise a plan **II** to draw a weapon (ه) on s.o. (على); to legislate, make laws **IV** to draw or train a weapon (ه) on s.o. (على) | اشرع عينيه الى (*'ainaihi*) to cast one's eyes on . . ., turn one's glance toward . . .; اشرع قلمه (*qalamahū*) to draw one's pen = to prepare to write **VIII** to introduce, enact (ه laws); to prescribe, give (ه ل to s.o. laws), make laws (ه) for s.o. (ل)

الشرع *aš-šar'* the Revelation, the canonical law of Islam | شرعا وفرعا *šar'an wa-far'an* with full right, with good cause, by rights; هم فى هذا شرع واحد they are alike in this

شرعى *šar'ī* lawful, legitimate, legal, rightful; شرعيا *šar'īyan* lawfully, legitimately, etc. | الطب الشرعى (*ṭibb*) forensic medicine; القضاء الشرعى (*qaḍā'*) jurisdiction based on the Sharia; المحاكم الشرعية the religious courts

شرعية *šar'īya* lawfulness, legality, legitimacy, rightfulness

شرعة *šar'a* string (of a bow, of a musical instrument); thong, strap

شرعة *šir'a* law; الشرعة the Sharia, the revealed, or canonical, law of Islam

شراع *širā'* pl. شرع *šuru'*, اشرعة *ašri'a* sail; tent

شراعى *širā'ī* sailing-, sail- (in compounds), rigged with sails | سفينة شراعية sailship, sailboat; طائرة شراعية glider

شراعة *šarrā'a* peep window, peep hole (in a door)

شروع *šurū'* beginning, start, commencement, inception (فى or ب with); plan, attempt, try (فى for or at s.th.) | الشروع فى سرقة (قتل) (*sariqa, qatl*) attempted theft (murder)

شريعة *šarī'a* pl. شرائع *šarā'i'*² water hole, drinking place; approach to a water hole; law; الشريعة the Sharia, the revealed, or canonical, law of Islam | نهر الشريعة *nahr aš-š.* the river Jordan

مشرعة *mašra'a* pl. مشارع *mašāri'*² water hole, drinking place

تشريع *tašrī'* legislation | سلطة التشريع *sulṭat at-t.* legislative power, legislative, legislature

تشريعى *tašrī'ī* legislative | الجمعية التشريعية (*jam'īya*) the legislative assembly; دورة تشريعية (*daura*) legislative period, session; السلطة التشريعية (*sulṭa*) the legislative power, the legislative, the legislature

تثنية الاشتراع *taṯniyat al-ištirā'* Deuteronomy, fifth Book of Moses

اشتراعى *ištirā'ī* legislative

شارع *šāri'* pl. *-ūn* legislator, lawgiver; (pl. شوارع *šawāri'*²) street | شارع رئيسى (*ra'īsī*) main street, thoroughfare; شارع عام (*'āmm*) public street, thoroughfare

مشروع *mašrū'* legitimate, legal, lawful, rightful, licit; permissible, allowed; (pl. *-āt*, مشاريع *mašārī'*²) plan, project, scheme, design, enterprise, undertaking | مشروع قانون *m. qānūn* bill, draft law

مشروعية *mašrū'īya* legitimacy

مشرع *mušarri'* pl. *-ūn* legislator, lawgiver

متشرع *mutašarri'* legislator, lawgiver; jurist, jurisprudent, legist

مشترع *muštari'* pl. *-ūn* legislator, lawgiver; jurist, jurisprudent, legist

شرف *šarufa u* (*šaraf*, شرافة *šarāfa*) to be highborn, high-bred, noble, illustrious, eminent, distinguished, high-ranking **II** to make noble, eminent, illustrious, ennoble, elevate, exalt, raise to distinction, honor, (ه s.o.), confer honor or distinction (ه upon s.o.); to honor (ه s.o. ب with); to give (ه s.o.) the honor **III** to vie for precedence in honor or nobility (ه with s.o.); to approach (ه s.th.), come within sight (ه of s.th.), be within shooting distance (ه of s.th.); to overlook, command (ه s.th.), look down (ه on s.th.); to supervise, control (ه s.th.), watch (ه over s.th.) **IV** to be high, tall, lofty; to tower, rise (على above); to look down (على on), overlook, overtop (على s.th.); to command (على the vicinity, etc.); to open, face (على on, e.g., a window on the garden); to look down (على upon s.th.); to be a spectator, look on (على at); to supervise, oversee, superintend, control (على s.th.), watch, have the supervision (على over), manage, direct, run (على s.th.), be in charge (على of s.th.); to be near s.th. (على), be close (على to s.th.), be on the point of (على); to be on the verge or brink (على of ruin, etc.) **V** to be honored (ب with), have the honor, give o.s. the honor (ب of), تشرفنا *tašarrafnā* it is (was) an honor to me **X** to look up (الى to), raise one's glance (الى to)

شرف *šaraf* elevated place

شرف *šaraf* high rank, nobility, distinction, eminence, dignity; honor, glory | على شرفه in his honor

شرفى *šarafī* honorary, honor- (in compounds)

شرفة *šurfa* pl. *šur(a)fāt, šurufāt,* شرف *šuraf* balcony; balcony loge, box (theater); battlement

شرافة *širāfa* sherifate, office of sherif (in Mecca)

شرافة *šurrāfa* pl. *-āt* balcony; gallery

شريف *šarīf* pl. شرفاء *šurafā'*[2], اشراف *ašrāf* distinguished, eminent, illustrious, noble, highborn, high-bred; honored, celebrated; sublime, exalted, august; honorable, respectable, honest (trade, profession); sherif, title of the descendants of Mohammed; الشريف in Ottoman times, title of the Governor of Mecca

شريفى *šarīfī* sherifian, of or pertaining to the house of the sherifs

مشرف *mašraf* elevated, commanding site, height; pl. مشارف *mašārif*[2] elevations, heights, hills

تشريفة *tašrīfa* pl. *-āt* honoring, bestowal of honors; pl. *tašrīfāt* ceremonial, etiquette, protocol (*dipl.*) | التشريفات الملكية (*malakīya*) (formerly) bulletin of the receptions, inspections and visits of the King of Egypt; رئيس التشريفات master of ceremonies; كسوة التشريفة *kiswat at-t.* parade uniform; ملابس التشريفة gala dress, gala uniforms; مدير التشريفات *mudīr at-t.* chief of protocol (*dipl.*)

تشريفاتى *tašrīfātī* ceremonial; master of ceremonies; royal steward; chief of protocol | بدلة تشريفاتية (*badla*) parade uniform

مشارفة *mušārafa* supervision, superintendence (على over)

اشراف *išrāf* supervision, superintendence, control (على over); patronage, auspices | تحت اشراف under the auspices of, under the patronage of

شارف *šārif* pl. شوارف *šawārif*[2] old (camel mare)

مشرف *mušrif* supervisor, overseer, superintendent | مشرف على الموت (*maut*) dying, in the throes of death, doomed to death, moribund

مستشرف *mustašraf* terrace

شرق *šaraqa u* (*šarq,* شروق *šurūq*) to rise (sun); to shine, radiate; — *šariqa a* (*šaraq*) to swallow the wrong way, have a fit of choking; to choke (ب on s.th., e.g., بدمعه *bi-dam'ihi* on one's tears); — *šaraqa u* to sip, lap, suck in (ه s.th.) **II** to go east; to cut in strips and dry in the sun, to jerk (ه meat, for conservation); see غرب **IV** to rise (sun); to shine, radiate **V** to become an Oriental **X** to become an Oriental, adopt oriental manners; to study the Orient

شرق *šarq* sunrise, east; the Orient, the East; شرقا *šarqan* eastward | شرق الاردن *š. al-urdunn* (till 1950) Transjordan; الشرق الادنى (*adnā*) the Near East; الشرق الاقصى (*aqṣā*) the Far East; الشرق الاوسط the Middle East

شرقى *šarqī* eastern, easterly; oriental; (pl. *-ūn*) Oriental; الشرقيون the Orientals (of the Christian Church) | شرق اوربا Eastern Europe; امارة شرق الاردن *imārat š. l-urdunn* (official designation till 1950) Transjordan

شراق *širāq* pitchy pine wood, lightwood

شروق *šurūq* rise (of the sun)

شراقى *šarāqī* (*eg.*) unirrigated land not reached by the Nile floods

شراق *šarrāq* suctorial device; part of a suction pump

□ شراقوة *šarāquwa* (pl. of شرقاوى) Levantines (*eg.*)

مشرق *mašriq* pl. مشارق *mašāriq*² place of sunrise, east; place of rise; the Orient, the East; المشرقان East and West | مشارق الارض ومغاربها *m. al-arḍ wa-maḡāribuhā* or المشرقان والمغربان (*maḡribān*) the whole world; فى المغربين وفى المشرقين all over the world

مشرقى *mašriqī* eastern, easterly, oriental; (pl. مشارقة *mašāriqa*) an Oriental; المشرقيات orientalia, oriental studies

تشريق *tašrīq* easternization; development of domestic production (esp. in local industry, with the gradual elimination of Europe), drive for (economic) independence | ايام التشريق *ayyām at-t.* the old name of the three days following the Day of Immolation (10th of Zu'lhijja) during the hadj festival

اشراق *išrāq* radiance; radiation, eradiation, emanation; Illuminism (mysticism deriving from Neoplatonism)

الاشراقيون *al-išrāqiyūn* the Illuminists, adherents of Illuminism

الاستشراق *al-istišrāq* oriental studies

مشرق *mušriq* resplendent, radiant, shining

مستشرق *mustašriq* having oriental manners; (pl. *-ūn*) orientalist

شرقرق *šaraqraq*, شرقراق *šaraqrāq* green woodpecker

شرك *šarika a* (*širk*, شركة *širka*, *šarika*) to share (ه فى with s.o. s.th.), participate (ه فى with s.o. in), be or become partner, participant, associate (ه فى of s.o. in) **III** to share (ه or ه فى with s.o., s.th.), participate (ه or ه فى with s.o. in), be or become partner, participant, associate (ه or ه فى of s.o. in); to associate o.s. (ه with s.o.), enter into partnership (ه with s.o.), form a partnership, join, combine (ه or ه فى with s.o. in); to sympathize (ه with s.o.) | شاركه رأيه (*ra'yahū*) to share s.o.'s opinion **IV** to make (ه s.o.) a partner, participant, associate (فى in), give (ه s.o.) a share (فى in), have (ه s.o.) share (فى in); to tie s.th. (ه) closely to s.th. (ب), associate (ه ب s.th. with s.th.) | اشركه بالله to make s.o. the associate or partner of God (in His creation and rule); اشرك بالله to set up or attribute associates to God, i.e., to be a polytheist, an idolator **VI** to enter into partnership (مع with s.o.); to participate together (فى in), share with one another (فى s.th.) **VIII** to enter into partnership, to coöperate (مع with s.o.); to participate (مع فى with s.o. in), share (مع فى with s.o., s.th.), collaborate, take part (فى in), contribute (فى to); to subscribe (فى to); to partake of the Lord's Supper, communicate (*Copt.-Chr.*)

شرك *širk* polytheism, idolatry | اهل الشرك *ahl aš-š.* the polytheists, the idolators

شرك *šarak* pl. شرك *šuruk*, اشراك *ašrāk*, شراك *širāk* net, snare, gin; trap | نصب له شركا to lay a trap for s.o., trap s.o.

شرك *šuruk* spurious, unsound, phony, false

شركة *širka*, *šarika* partnership; communion (*Chr.*); (pl. *-āt*) association, companionship; company, corporation (*com.*); commercial enterprise (*Isl. Law*); establishment, firm, business | شركة التامين insurance company; شركة تجارية (*tijārīya*) trading company, firm; شركة الاذاعة broadcasting corporation; شركة المساهمة *š. al-musāhama* joint-stock company, corporation; شركة سهامية (*sihāmīya*) do.; شركة الشركات trust (*com.*)

شراك *širāk* pl. شرك *šuruk*, اشرك *ašruk*, اشراك *ašrāk* shoelace

شريك *šarīk* pl. شركاء *šurakā'*[2], اشراك *ašrāk* sharer, participant, partner, copartner; associate, companion, confederate, ally; co-owner, coproprietor (*Isl. Law*); accomplice, accessory (in a crime) | ○ شريك موص (*mūṣin*) silent partner (*com.*)

شريك *šuraik* (*eg.*) sesame cake

شريكة *šarīka* pl. شرائك *šarā'ik*[2] woman partner, woman participant, etc. (see شريك)

تشريك *tašrīk*: سياسة التشريك *siyāsat at-t.* policy of alliances

مشاركة *mušāraka* partnership, copartnership, participation (في in); cooperation, collaboration; communion (*Chr.*); complicity, accessoriness (*jur.*)

اشتراك *ištirāk* partnership, copartnership, coparcenary; participation, sharing, joining, co-operation, collaboration (في in); interference (في in); subscription (في to); jointness, community; communion (*Chr.*); (pl. *-āt*) subscription rate; participation fee | بالاشتراك jointly, in concurrence, together (مع with); اشتراك شهرى (*šahrī*) monthly subscription; monthly fee or contribution

اشتراكى *ištirākī* socialist, socialistic; (pl. *-ūn*) a socialist

اشتراكية *ištirākīya* socialism

مشرك *mušrik* pl. *-ūn* polytheist

مشترك *muštarik* pl. *-ūn* participant; subscriber

مشترك *muštarak* common, joint, combined, concurrent, collective, co- | الامن المشترك (*amn*) collective security; بلاغ مشترك (*balāḡ*) joint communiqué; السوق المشترك (*sūq*) the Common Market; الشعور المشترك community spirit, communality, solidarity; الضمان المشترك (*ḍamān*) collective security

شركسى *šarkasī* Circassian; (pl. شراكسة *šarākisa*) a Circassian

شرم *šarama* i (*šarm*) to split, slit, slash (ه s.th.)

شرم *šarm* pl. شروم *šurūm* cleft, crack, split, rift, slit, slot; small bay, inlet

اشرم *ašram*[2], f. شرماء *šarmā'*[2] having a disfigured nose; harelipped

شرمط *šarmaṭa* (*eg., syr.*) to shred, tear to shreds (ه s.th.)

شرموطة *šarmūṭa* pl. شراميط *šarāmīṭ*[2] rag, shred, tatter; whore, slut, prostitute

شرنقة *šarnaqa* pl. شرانق *šarāniq*[2] cocoon (of the silk worm); chrysalis (of an insect); slough (of a snake), snakeskin; — *šarāniq*[2] hemp (Cannabis sativa; *bot.*); hemp seed

شره *šariha* a (*šarah*) to be greedy (الى or على for food); to eat greedily, gormandize, gluttonize, be gluttonous

شره *šarah* gluttony, gourmandism, ravenousness, voracity; greediness, greed, covetousness, avidity

شره *šarih* greedy (على for food), gluttonous; voracious, ravenous; ravenous eater, glutton; greedy, covetous, avid

شراهة *šarāha* gluttony, gourmandism, ravenousness, voracity; greediness, greed, covetousness, avidity

شرو *šarw*, *širw* honey

شروال *širwāl* pl. شراويل *šarāwīl*[2] trousers, pants; drawers

شرى see شروى, شروة

شرى *šarā* i (*širan*, شراء *širā'*) to sell, vend (ه ب s.th. for a certain price); to buy, purchase (ه s.th.); to bring upon o.s., to ask for (e.g., المتاعب troubles, inconveniences) — *šarā* i (*širan*) to expose (ه s.th.) to the sun for drying **II** to expose (ه s.th.) to the sun for drying **VIII** to buy, purchase (ه s.th.); to buy up, acquire, obtain by commercial transaction (ه s.th.); to sell, vend (ه s.th.) **X** to become worse, worsen, deteriorate

شرى *šary* (coll.; n. un. ة) colocynth

شرى *širan* pl. اشرية *ašriya* purchase, buy(ing), bargain

شرى *šaran* an itching skin eruption

شراء *širā'* purchase, buy(ing) | راغب الشراء eager to buy; ○ المقدرة على الشراء (*maqdura*) or ○ قوة الشراء *qūwat aš-š.* purchasing power

شروة *šarwa* purchase, buy(ing)

شروى *šarwā*: لا يملك شروى نقير *lā yamliku š. naqīrin* he hasn't a red cent to his name, he has alsolutely nothing; لا يجدى شروى نقير (*yujdī*) it is of no use at all

○ الحمى الشروية *al-ḥummā aš-šarawīya* nettle rash, urticaria (*med.*)

شريان *širyān* pl. شرايين *šarāyīn*[2] artery | تصلب الشرايين *taṣallub aš-š.* arteriosclerosis

شرياني *širyānī* arterial | السدة الشريانية (*sudda*) embolism (*med.*)

اشتراء *ištirā'* purchase, buy(ing)

شار *šārin* pl. شراة *šurāh* seller, salesman, vendor; purchaser, buyer, customer; — ○ lightning rod (also شارى الصواعق); الشراة *aš-šurāh* designation of the Khawarij

مشتر *muštarin* purchaser, buyer, customer; seller, vendor

المشترى *al-muštarī* Jupiter (*astron.*)

مشترى *muštaran* pl. مشتريات *muštarayāt* that which is purchased, purchased goods; purchase, buy(ing), acquisition

شزرا *šazran*: نظر اليه شزرا to look askance at s.o.

عين شزراء *'ain šazrā'*[2] an eye looking askance, distrustfully or maligrantly; نظرة شزراء (*naẓra*) distrustful, suspicious glance

شست (Fr. *chiste*) slate (*min.*)

شاسع *šāsi'* far (away), distant, remote; wide, large, great (distance); huge, vast, enormous (difference)

شَشخان *šašaḵān* rifled (gunbarrel)

اسلحة الششخانة *asliḥat aš-š.* firearms

مششخن *mušaškan* rifled (gunbarrel)

[1]شَشم *šišm* seed of the Cassia absus (*bot.*), used as eye powder

[2]ششمة *šašma, šišma* toilet, lavatory, privy

ششنى *šišnī* sample, specimen; sampling

ششنجى (*eg.*) *šišnagī* assayer (of precious metals)

شص *šiṣṣ* pl. شصوص *šuṣūṣ* fishhook

شصرة *šaṣara* a kind of gazelle

شط *šaṭṭa* i u (شطط *šaṭaṭ*) to go to extremes, go too far, exceed the proper bounds, be excessive (في in, with); to deviate (عن from), digress, stray (عن الموضوع from the topic) **VIII** to go to extremes, go too far, exceed the proper bounds, be excessive (في in, with)

شط *šaṭṭ* pl. شطوط *šuṭūṭ* bank, shore, coast, seashore, beach, strand | شط العرب *š. al-'arab* Shatt-al-Arab, river in SE Iraq formed by the Tigris and Euphrates rivers; the region traversed by this river on the Persian Gulf

شطة *šaṭṭa* a variety of pepper (Capsicum conicum Mey.; *bot.*)

شطط *šaṭaṭ* that which is excessive or exceeds the proper bounds, excess; inroad, encroachment, infringement

شطيطة *šaṭīṭa* a variety of pepper (Capsicum conicum Mey.; *bot.*)

مشط *mušiṭṭ* excessive

شاطئ *šāṭi'* pl. شواطئ *šawāṭi'*[2], شطآن *šuṭ'ān* shore, coast, seacoast, beach, strand

شطب *šaṭaba* u (*šaṭb*) to cut into slices or strips (ه s.th.); to strike out, cross out, scratch out, write off (على or ه s.th.); to erase, efface (على or ه s.th., e.g., a word, a sentence); to cancel, release (على or ه a mortgage); to drop, nonsuit (دعوى *da'wā* a case) II to make an incision, a longitudinal cut, a slit, a slash (في in s.th.); to strike out, cross out, scratch out, write off (على or ه s.th.); to erase, efface (على or ه s.th., e.g., a word, a sentence); to cancel, release, (على or ه a mortgage), to book, enter, post (ه an item, an account); to finish off, terminate, wind up (على s.th.)

شطب *šaṭb* cut, slash; incision, scratch; crossing out, striking out, writing off; erasure, effacement; annulment, cancellation

شطب *šaṭb* pl. شطوب *šuṭūb* tall, strapping, sturdy, husky

تشطيب *tašṭīb*: تشطيب الحساب posting of an account (to the ledger); ساعة التشطيب curfew

شطح *šaṭaḥa* a (*šaṭḥ*) to roam, rove, stray

شطحة *šaṭḥa* pl. *šaṭaḥāt* escapade

شطر *šaṭara* u (*šaṭr*) to halve, divide into two (equal) parts, bisect, cut through (ه s.th.); to cut off, sever (ه s.th.); — شطر بصره (*baṣaruhū*) u (شطور *šuṭūr*) to be squint-eyed; — *šaṭara* u (شطور *šuṭūr*, شطورة *šuṭūra*, شطارة *šaṭāra*) to withdraw, separate, disassociate o.s. (عن from); — *šaṭara* u, *šaṭura* u (شطارة *šaṭāra*) to be sly, cunning, artful, shrewd; to be clever, smart, bright, skillful, adroit II to halve, divide into two (equal) parts, to bisect, cut through (ه s.th.) III to halve, share by halves, share equally (ه ه with s.o., s.th.), go halves (ه with s.o.); to participate, take part (ه in s.th.), share (ه s.th.) | شاطره آراءه, فرحه (*ārā'ahū*, *faraḥahū*) to share s.o.'s views, s.o.'s joy V to manifest slyness, cleverness, smartness, adroitness, skill VII to divide, split (ه into, intrans.)

شطر *šaṭr* partition, division, separation, halving, bisecting; — (pl. شطور *šuṭūr*, اشطر *ašṭur*) a half, moiety; hemistich; portion, share, lot; direction; *šaṭra* in the direction of . . ., toward | قصد شطره to move toward s.o., walk up to s.o.; ولى انظاره شطره (*wallā anẓārahū*) to direct one's glances toward s.o.; ولى وجهه شطره (*wajhahū*) to turn one's face toward s.th.

شطرة *šiṭra* side, half

شطارة *šaṭāra* slyness, cunningness, shrewdness, adroitness, skill, cleverness, smartness

شطيرة *šaṭīra* sandwich; schnitzel, steak

مشاطرة *mušāṭara* participation, sharing

انشطار *inšiṭār* fission, splitting, cleavage, division, separation

شاطر *šāṭir* pl. شطار *šuṭṭār* sly, cunning, shrewd; scoundrel, villain; clever, smart, bright, adroit, skillful

شطرنج *šiṭranj*, *šaṭranj* chess | لوحة الشطرنج *lauḥat aš-š.* chessboard

شطف *šaṭafa* u (*šaṭf*) to rinse (under flowing water), clean with water, wash (ه s.th.)

شطفة *šuṭfa* piece, chunk, lump; (pl. شطف *šuṭaf*) flint (of a gunlock, *eg.*)

شطفة *šiṭfa* splinter, chip, sliver

¹شطن *šaṭana* u (*šaṭn*) to fasten, attach, tie, bind (ه ب s.th. with a rope)

²شيطان and تشيطن see شيطن (alphabetically)

شظف *šaẓafa* u (*šaẓf*) to castrate

شظف *šaẓaf* pl. شظاف *šiẓāf* discomfort, hardship, difficulty; ruggedness of life | اقام على شظف العيش (*š. il-ʿaiš*) to lead a life of hardships

شظف *šaẓif* hard, harsh, rough, rugged, austere (life, character)

شظى *šaẓiya* a (*šaẓan*) to be splintered, be shattered, splinter, shiver V do.

شظية *šaẓiya* pl. شظى *šaẓīy*, شظايا *šaẓāyā* splinter, sliver, chip; shinbone; bone

شع *šaʿʿa* i (*šaʿʿ*, شعاع *šiʿāʿ*) to disperse, scatter, diffuse, spread; to beam, radiate, flash up IV to emit, spread, diffuse (ه s.th.); to eradiate (ه s.th.); to emit rays or beams, radiate, beam V to emit rays or beams, radiate, beam, eradiate

شع *šuʿʿ* rays, beams; spokes

شعاع *šaʿāʿ* distracted, confused, bewildered, perplexed | طار فؤاده (روحه) شعاعا his mind became confused, bewildered or perplexed

شعاع *šuʿāʿ* (coll.; n. un. ة) pl. اشعة *ašiʿʿa* rays, beams; spokes; horizontal wooden crosspieces (on a door or window) | الاشعة فوق البنفسجية (*banafsajīya*) the ultra-violet rays; الاشعة التى تحت الاحمر the infra-red rays; صورة اشعة X-ray photograph, roentgenogram; ○ فاعلية الاشعة radioactivity

اشعاع *išʿāʿ* pl. *-āt* radiation, eradiation

اشعاعى *išʿāʿī* radiative, radiational | ذو نشاط اشعاعى (*našāṭ*) radioactive ○

تشعع *tašaʿʿuʿ* radiation, eradiation | التشعع الحرارى (*ḥarārī*) radiation of heat; التشعع الشمسى (*šamsī*) solar radiation

مشع *mušiʿʿ* radiating, radiant; emitting rays, radiative; ○ radioactive

○ مشعة *mušiʿʿa* radiator

شعب *šaʿaba* a (*šaʿb*) to gather, assemble, rally (هم people, ه s.th.); to disperse, scatter (هم people, ه s.th.) II to form branches, to branch; to branch (out), ramify, divide into branches or subdivisions (ه s.th.) V to branch (out), ramify; to be subdivided, form subdivisions; to diverge, move in different directions, part company, separate, split, break up, become disunited, disorganized, disrupted; to branch off (عن from); to result (عن from) VIII to branch out, ramify; to branch off

شعب *šaʿb* pl. شعوب *šuʿūb* people, folk; nation; tribe, race

شعبى *šaʿbī* national, people's; popular, folksy, folk- (in compounds) | الجبهة الشعبية (*jabha*) popular front; ديموقراطية شعبية people's democracy (in Marxist terminology)

شعبية *šaʿbīya* popularity

شعوبى *šuʿūbī* adherent of the شعوبية, see below

الشعوبية *aš-šuʿūbīya* a movement within the early Islamic commonwealth of nations which refused to recognize the privileged position of the Arabs

شعب *šiʿb* pl. شعاب *šiʿāb* mountain path, mountain trail; gorge, ravine, canyon; gulf, abyss; reef

شعبة *šiʿba* reef

شعبة *šuʿba* pl. شعب *šuʿab*, شعاب *šiʿāb* branch, bough, limb, ramification; shoot, twig, sprig, spray; prong, tine; (sub-) division, section, department, branch, cell; field of study, discipline (e.g., at a university); part, portion; (pl. شعب *šuʿab*) bronchus | التهاب الشعب bronchitis (*med.*)

شعبي *šu'abī* bronchial

شعيب *ša'īb* disrupted, disorganized, disunited, scattered, dispersed

شعبان *ša'bān*[2] Shaban, name of the eighth month of the Mohammedan year

اشعب *aš'ab*[2] name of a legendary miser, hence, said of s.o. extremely niggardly: اطمع من اشعب greedier than Aš'ab

اشعبي *aš'abī* extremely miserly, avaricious, or greedy; (pl. *-ūn*) skinflint, miser, niggard | طمع اشعبي (*ṭama'*) insatiable greed

تشعب *taša''ub* ramification, branching, branching off; disruption, split(ting), disunion

انشعاب *inši'āb* ramification, branching, branching off; disruption, split(ting), disunion

متشعب *mutaša''ib* ramified, branching; manifold, diverse; many-sided, versatile (متشعب الجنبات *m. al-janabāt*)

شعبذ **ša'baḏa** to practice jugglery, legerdemain, sleight of hand, or magic

شعبذة *ša'baḏa* jugglery, legerdemain, sleight of hand, magic

شعث **ša'iṯa** *a* (*ša'aṯ*) to be or become disheveled, unkempt, matted (hair) **II** to dishevel, ruffle (ه the hair) **V** to become disheveled, ruffled (hair); to disintegrate, fall apart, decay (of buildings)

شعث *ša'aṯ*: لم شعثه *lamma ša'aṯahū* to straighten out the muddled affairs of s.o., help s.o. to get back on his feet; to struggle back to one's feet, "pick up", recover

شعث *ša'iṯ* matted, disheveled, unkempt (hair); having matted, unkempt hair

اشعث *aš'aṯ*[2], f. شعثاء *ša'ṯā'*[2] matted, disheveled, unkempt (hair); having matted, unkempt hair

شعوذ look up alphabetically

شعر **ša'ara** *u* (شعور *šu'ūr*) to know (ب s.th., ان that), have knowledge, be cognizant (ب of); to come to know, realize, notice (ب s.th., ان that); to perceive, feel, sense (ب s.th., ان that), be conscious, be aware (ب of s.th.); — (*ši'r*) to make or compose poetry, poetize, versify | لم يشعر الا بـ . . . (*illā bi-*), . . . لم يشعر الا و (*illā wa-*) and . . . ما شعر الا و . . . ,ما شعر الا بـ before he even realized it, there was all of a sudden . . .; then, all of a sudden, there was . . ., it happened that . . . **IV** to let (ه s.o.) know (ب or ه s.th., of or about s.th.), notify, inform (ب or ه ه s.o. of or about), give notice or information (ه to s.o., ب or ه of or about), impart (ه to s.o., ب or ه s.th.) **X** to feel, sense, notice, perceive, realize (ب, ه s.th.), be conscious, be aware (ه of); to be filled (ه with a feeling)

شعر *ša'r*, *ša'ar* (coll.; n. un. ة) pl. اشعار *aš'ār*, شعور *šu'ūr*, شعار *ši'ār* hair; bristles; fur, pelt

شعرة *ša'ra* (n. un.) pl. *-āt* a hair | لا . . . قدر شعرة (*qadra š.*) not by a hair's breadth

شعري *ša'rī*, *ša'arī* hairy, hirsute, hair (adj.)

شعرية *ša'rīya* pl. *-āt* wire grille, wire netting, lattice work; ○ (without pl.) capillarity | شعرية الشباك *š. aš-šubbāk* (latticed) window shade, jalousie

شعرية *ši'rīya* vermicelli

شعراني *ša'rānī* hairy, hirsute, shaggy

شعر *ši'r* knowledge | ليت شعري *laita ši'rī* I wish I knew . . .! would that I knew . . .! — (pl. اشعار *aš'ār*) poetry; poem

شعري *ši'rī* poetic(al)

شعرى *ša'rā* pl. شعارى *ša'ārā* scrub country

الشعرى *aš-šiʿrā* Sirius, Dog Star (*astron.*)

شعار *šiʿār* pl. شعر *šuʿur*, اشعرة *ašʿira* password, watchword; slogan; motto, device; mark, token, sign; signal; distinguishing mark or feature, characteristic, emblem, badge | شعار تجارى (*tijārī*) trade mark

شعير *šaʿīr* (coll.) barley; (n. un. ة) barleycorn | شعير لؤلؤى (*luʾluʾī*) pearl barley; شعيرة الجفن *š. al-jafn* sty (*med.*)

○ شعيرة *šaʿīra* bead (of a gun sight, *mil.*; *Syr.*)

شعيرات دموية *šuʿairāt damawīya* blood capillaries (*biol.*)

شعيرية *šaʿīrīya* vermicelli

شعور *šuʿūr* knowledge, cognizance; consciousness, awareness; perception, discernment; perceptive faculty; sensation; sentiment; feeling; perceptiveness, sensitivity, sensibility; mood | على غير شعور منه (*ġairi šuʿūrin*) without his being aware of it; غاب عن الشعور to lose consciousness; فاقد الشعور unconscious, insensible; الشعور بالنفس (*nafs*) self-consciousness; الشعور بالذات do.; دقة الشعور *diqqat aš-š.* sensitivity, sensibility; الشعور المشترك (*muštarak*) community spirit, communality, solidarity; عدم الشعور unfeeling, insensitive

شعورى *šuʿūrī* conscious; emotional | لا شعورى unconscious, subconscious

شعارى *šaʿārā* (pl.) goats

شعيرة *šaʿīra* pl. شعائر *šaʿāʾir*[2] religious ceremony, rite, cultic practice; pl. also: places of worship, cultic shrines

اشعر *ašʿar*[2] hairy, hirsute, long-haired, shaggy

شعرور *šuʿrūr* poetaster, versifier, rhymester

شويعر *šuwaiʿir* poetaster, versifier, rhymester

مشعر *mašʿar* pl. مشاعر *mašāʿir*[2] cultic shrine for ceremonies of the hadj; sensory organ; pl. senses, feelings, sensations | المشعر الحرام (*ḥarām*) the hadj station of Muzdalifa east of Mecca

اشعار *išʿār* pl. *-āt* notification, information (ب of, about), notice

شاعر *šāʿir* knowing (by instinctive perception), endowed with deeper insight, with intuition; (pl. شعراء *šuʿarāʾ*[2]) poet

شاعرية *šāʿirīya* pl. *-āt* poetry; poetical work, poetization; poetical talent; poetship

شواعر *šawāʿir*[2] attacks, diatribes, invectives, calumnies, defamations

مشعور *mašʿūr* split, cracked; mad, crazy, idiotic

مشعرانى *mušʿirānī* hairy, hirsute, shaggy

شعشع *šaʿšaʿa* to mix with water, dilute (ه a beverage); to shine, beam, radiate, glitter

مشعشع *mušaʿšaʿ* half drunk, tipsy, fuddled

شعط *šaʿaṭa a* to scorch, sear, singe

شعفة *šaʿfa* pl. شعاف *šiʿāf* summit, top, peak

شعل *šaʿala a* (*šaʿl*), II and IV to light, kindle, ignite, inflame, set on fire (ه s.th.), set fire (ه to s.th.); to set ablaze, fan (ه s.th.) VIII to catch fire, start burning, ignite, burn, flame, blaze, flare up, break out (fire) | اشتعل غضبا (*ġaḍaban*) to be flaming with rage; اشتعل رأسه شيبا (*šaiban*) his hair was, or turned, white

شعلة *šuʿla* pl. شعل *šuʿal* fire, blaze, flame; torch

مشعل *mašʿal*, مشعلة *mašʿala* pl. مشاعل *mašāʿil*[2] torch

مشعال *mišʿāl* torch

مشاعلي **mašā'ilī** pl. مشاعلية **mašā'iliya** torch bearer; hangman, executioner

اشعال **iš'āl** lighting, kindling, ignition, setting on fire, fanning

اشتعال **išti'āl** ignition, inflammation, combustion, burning

مشتعل **mušta'il** burning, ablaze, on fire

شعنينة **ša'nīna** pl. شعانين **ša'ānīn**[2] palm branch | احد (عيد) الشعانين **aḥad ('īd) aš-š.** Palm Sunday (*Chr.*)

شعواء **ša'wā'**[2] (used attributively with غارة **ġāra**, حرب **ḥarb**, حملة **ḥamla**, and the like) large-scale, devastating everything (over a wide area)

شعوذ **ša'waḏa** to practice jugglery, legerdemain, sleight of hand, or magic arts

شعوذة **ša'waḏa** pl. **-āt** jugglery, legerdemain, sleight of hand; magic, magic arts; humbug, swindle, tricks

مشعوذ **muša'wiḏ** juggler, conjurer, magician, practitioner of legerdemain; swindler, trickster (f. مشعوذة)

شغب **šaġaba, šaġiba a** (**šaġb, šaġab**) to disturb the peace, make trouble, stir up riots, cause an uproar, riot; to provoke discord, dissension, or controversy (among ب, على, ه) **III** to make trouble, disturb the peace; to rebel (على against), mutiny

شغب **šaġab, šaġb** unrest, trouble, disturbance, discord, dissension; riot, commotion, uproar, strife, tumult; brawl, fight, broil, fracas; row, wrangle, contention, quarrel, controversy

شغاب **šaġġāb** troublemaker, agitator, subverter

شغوب **šaġūb** causing much noise and unrest, riotous, turbulent, troublous

مشاغب **mašāġib**[2] troubles, disorders, disturbances

مشاغبة **mušāġaba** pl. **-āt** disorder, disturbance, trouble, riot, uproar; rebellion (على against); discord, dissension, row, wrangle, quarrel, controversy

مشاغب **mušāġib** pl. **-ūn** troublemaker, agitator, subverter, rioter, mischief-maker

شغر **šaġara u** (شغور **šuġūr**) to be devoid of fortifications, be unprotected (country); to be free, vacant, unoccupied, open (seat, position)

شغور **šuġūr** vacancy (of a position)

شاغر **šāġir** empty and unprotected (of a country); free, vacant, unoccupied, open (seat, position); شواغر **šawāġir**[2] vacancies

شغف **šaġafa a** (**šaġf**) (to hit, or affect, the pericardium, i.e.) to infatuate, enamor, fill with ardent passion (ه s.o.); pass. شغف به (حبا) **šuġifa bihī** (**ḥubban**) to love s.o. or s.th. passionately, be madly in love with s.o., be infatuated with or enamored of s.o., be extremely fond of s.th. **VII** انشغف به = **šuġifa bihī**

شغف **šaġaf** pericardium; passionate love, passion, sensual desire; infatuation, enamoredness, amorousness; ardent zeal, craze, love, passion

شغف **šaġif** madly in love, infatuated (ب with), enamored (ب of), fascinated (ب by)

شغاف **šaġāf** pericardium

شغوف **šaġūf** obsessed with fervent affection (ب for); madly in love, infatuated (ب with), enamored (ب of)

مشغوف **mašġūf** passionately fond (ب of), madly in love, infatuated (ب with), enamored (ب of), fascinated (ب by)

شغل **šaġala a** (**šaġl, šuġl**) to occupy, busy (ه ب s.o. with); to preoccupy (ه s.o.), keep (ه s.o.) busy, give (ه s.o.) trouble;

to distract, divert, alienate (عن • s.o. from s.th.); to occupy, fill, hold, have (▲ office, seat, position); to take up, fill (▲ s.th.), engage, engross (▲ the attention); to engage, tie down (▲ forces of the opponent); — pass. **šuğila** to occupy o.s., busy o.s., be busy (ب with), be engaged in; to be taken up, occupied (ب by, e.g., ground by buildings); شغل به عن to be distracted by s.th. from | شغل نفسه ب to occupy o.s., busy o.s. with, work at, attend to; شغل البال to disquiet, discomfit, make uneasy, trouble, disturb; شغل الوقت ل (*waqt*) to devote time to **II** to busy, occupy (• s.o.), engage, engross (▲ s.th.); to employ (• s.o.), provide employment (• for s.o.); to put (• s.o.) to work, make (▲ a machine) work, put in operation, make run, start (▲ a machine); to make, produce, manufacture, fabricate (▲ s.th.); to invest (▲ money) **III** to hold in play, keep occupied, divert (• s.o.); to distract (• s.o.) **IV** to occupy, busy, employ (• s.o.); to occupy, hold, fill, have (▲ an office, a position); to fill, take up (▲ s.th.), engage, engross (▲ the attention); to cover (ب ▲ a space with a building or buildings), occupy, take up, fill (ب ▲ a space with); to take, take up, require (▲ time); to engage, tie down (▲ forces of the opponent); to distract, divert, alienate, entice away (عن • s.o. from) | اشغل البال to disquiet, discomfit, make uneasy, trouble, disturb, preoccupy **VI** to occupy o.s., busy o.s., be occupied or busy, be preoccupied (ب with), be engaged (ب in), attend, devote o.s. (ب to s.th.); to pretend to be busy **VII** to occupy o.s., busy o.s., be occupied or busy, be preoccupied (ب with); to be concerned (ب about) **VIII** to busy o.s., occupy o.s., be occupied or busy (ب or فى with), be engaged (ب or فى in), attend, devote o.s. (ب or فى to s.th.); to work; to study (على under or with); to work, run, operate, be in operation, be in motion (machine, and the like) | اشتغل قلبه (*qalbuhū*) to be uneasy, apprehensive, worried; اشتغل به عن to be distracted by s.th. from

شغل **šuğl** occupancy, filling, taking up; detention, prevention, distraction (عن from); — (pl. اشغال **ašğāl**, شغول **šuğūl**) occupation, activity; work, job; business, concern | شغل شاغل that which is uppermost in one's mind, chief or foremost concern; s.th. which preoccupies s.o.'s mind or distracts s.o. (عن from); اشغال شاقة (*šāqqa*) hard labor; اشغال عامة (*ʿāmma*) or اشغال عمومية (*ʿumūmīya*) public works; شغل يدوى (*yadawī*) handwork; manual labor; شغل يد *š. yad* (*colloq.*, used appositionally) handmade; فى شغل preoccupied (من with), concerned (من about); فى شغل ب busy, occupied with; كان فى شغل عن to be too busy or preoccupied (ب with) to be able to attend to s.th.; الزم شغلك *ilzam šuğlaka* mind your own business!

شغال **šağğāl** very busy; hard-working, industrious, diligent, laborious, active; being in operation, running (of a machine); (pl. *-ūn*) worker, workman, laborer

شغيل **šağğīl** pl. ة (*syr.*) worker, workman, laborer, (lowly) employee

شاغول **šāğūl** mainsheet (of a sailing vessel)

مشغل **mašğal** pl. مشاغل **mašāğil**[2] workshop; workhouse

مشغلة **mašğala** pl. مشاغل **mašāğil**[2] occupation, avocation, activity, business, concern, work, job; effort, exertion; diversion, distraction, preoccupation, disturbance

تشغيل **tašğīl** employment, occupation; providing of employment, provision of work; hiring (of s.o., as a worker); opening, starting, putting into operation;

production, manufacture, making; investment (of money)

انشغال *inšiġāl* (state of) being busy or occupied; occupation, activity; overcharge, overwork; apprehension, concern, anxiety

اشتغال *ištiġāl* (state of) being busy or occupied; work, occupation (ب or ف with, at); syntactical regimen, government (of a word by another; *gram.*)

شاغل *šāġil* pl. شواغل *šawāġil*[2] that which preoccupies s.o., engrosses s.o.'s attention, takes up s.o.'s time; occupation, activity; object of concern or worry; pl. شواغل distractions, preoccupations | وجد شاغلا عنه فى he found distraction from it in . . .; هو فى الف شاغل عن (*alfi šāġilin*) he had a thousand other things to think of than . . .; كان اكبر شاغل له (*akbara šāġilin*) it was his greatest worry

مشغول *mašġūl* busy, occupied (ب with); distracted, diverted (عن from); occupied, taken (seat, space); busy, occupied (telephone line, and the like); worked on, processed | مشغول البال anxious, apprehensive, concerned, worried; المشغولات الذهبية والفضية (*ḏahabīya, fiḍḍīya*) gold and silver work

مشغولية *mašġūlīya* anxiety, apprehension, concern

مشغل *mušaġġal* employee, worker

مشتغل *muštaġil* busy, occupied (ب or ف with); in operation, running (of a machine)

شفة *šafa* pl. شفاه *šifāh*, شفوات *šafawāt* lip; rim, edge | الشفة العليا (*'ulyā*) upper lip, الشفة السفلى (*suflā*) lower lip; شفة الارنب *š. al-arnab* harelip; بنت شفة *bint š.* word

شفه see مشافهة and شفهى, شفاها, شفاهى

شفو see شفوى

[1]شفائف *šafā'if*[2], شفايف *šafāyif*[2] lips

[2]شف *šaffa i* (شفوف *šufūf*, شفيف *šafīf*, شفف *šafaf*) to be thin, flimsy; to be transparent, diaphanous, translucid, pellucid; to let (عن s.th.) shimmer through, reveal, disclose, betray (عن s.th.) VIII to drink up, drain, empty (ه s.th.); to eat up, devour (ه s.th.) X to look (ه through s.th., e.g., through a piece of fabric in order to ascertain its quality); to have a glimpse (ه of s.th.), hope (ه for s.th.); to try to see (ه through s.th.), seek to penetrate (ه s.th.); to perceive, discern, make out (ه s.th.); to shimmer (من through s.th.), show (من through s.th.); to manifest itself, become tangible, perceptible, noticeable

شف *šaff*, *šiff* pl. شفوف *šufūf* diaphanous fabric, gauze

شفف *šafaf* transparency, translucence, diaphaneity

شفيف *šafīf* thin, flimsy, translucent, transparent, diaphanous

شفوف *šufūf* transparency, translucence, diaphaneity

شفافة *šufāfa* the rest in the glass

شفاف *šaffāf* thin, flimsy, translucent, transparent, diaphanous

شفافية *šaffāfīya* transparency, translucence, diaphaneity

شفت *šift* pl. شفوت *šufūt* (*eg.*) pincers, tweezers

شفتر *šaftara* to pout, sulk

شفتورة *šaftūra* thick lip

شفتشى see جفتجى

شفتلك see جفتلك

[1]شفر *šafr* pl. اشفار *ašfār* palpebral margin from which the eyelashes grow, (outer) edge of the eyelid; edge, rim, border, fringe

شفر *šufr* pl. اشفار *ašfār* palpebral margin from which the eyelashes grow, (outer) edge of the eyelid; edge, rim, border, fringe; — labium (*anat.*)

شفرة *šafra* pl. *šafarāt*, شفار *šifār* large knife; blade (of a sword, of a knife); razor blade; (pl. شفار) brink, edge, verge | على شفرة الهاوية on the brink of the abyss

شفير *šafīr* palpebral margin from which the eyelashes grow; (outer) edge of the eyelids; edge, rim, border, fringe

مشفر *mišfar* pl. مشافر *mašāfir*[2] flew, chap; trunk, snout, proboscis

[2]شفر (Fr. *chiffre*) cipher, code

شفرى *šifrī* ciphered, coded, in code

شفرة *šifra* cipher, code

شفشف *šafšafa* to dry, dry out, parch, drain (ه s.th.)

شفط *šafaṭa* to suck, suck up, absorb; to empty, drain; to sip

شفاطة *šaffāṭa* pl. *-āt* siphon | ○ شفاطة الغبار *š. al-ġubār* vacuum cleaner

شفع *šafaʿa a* (*šafʿ*) to double (ه s.th.); to attach, add, subjoin (ه ب to s.th. s.th.), enclose (ه ب in s.th. s.th.); to give the (right of) pre-emption (ه ب to s.o. on s.th.), grant (ه s.o.) the first refusal (ب of s.th.); — (شفاعة *šafāʿa*) to mediate, use one's good offices, put in a good word, intercede, intervene, plead (ل or فى for or on behalf of s.o., الى with s.o. else) **V** to mediate, use one's good offices, put in a good word, intercede, intervene, plead (ل الى or فى for or on behalf of s.o. with s.o. else)

شفع *šafʿ* pl. اشفاع *ašfāʿ*, شفاع *šifāʿ* either part of a pair; even number

شفع *šafʿ* diplopia, double vision of a single object

شفعى *šafʿī* even (of a number)

شفعة *šufʿa* (right of) pre-emption

شفيع *šafīʿ* pl. شفعاء *šufaʿāʾ*[2] mediator, intercessor, advocate; patron saint (*Chr.*); holder of the right of pre-emption, pre-emptor

شفاعة *šafāʿa* mediation, intercession, advocacy

شافع *šāfiʿ* mediator, intercessor, advocate; holder of the right of pre-emption, pre-emptor

الشافعى *aš-šāfiʿī* founder of one of the four orthodox Islamic schools of theology; شافعى Shafiitic; (pl. *-ūn*, شوافع *šawāfiʿ*[2]) adherent of the Shafiitic school, Shafiite

مشفوع *mašfūʿ* accompanied (ب by), attended, combined (ب with)

شفق **IV** to pity, commiserate (على s.o.), feel pity (على for), sympathize (على with); to be concerned (ان that, على about) worry (ان that, على about), fear (ان that, على for, من s.o., s.th.), be apprehensive, feel anxiety (على about, من as a result of); to shun, shirk (من s.th.), beware (من of), be on one's guard (من against)

شفق *šafaq* evening glow, twilight, dusk | الشفق الجنوبى (*janūbī*) aurora australis; الشفق الشمالى (*šamālī*) aurora borealis; الشفق القطبي (*quṭbī*) polar light; شفق الآلهة Twilight of the Gods

شفقة *šafaqa* compassion, commiseration, pity, sympathy, kind(li)ness, tenderness, affectionateness, solicitude, loving care | عديم الشفقة pitiless, merciless

شفوق *šafūq* compassionate, sympathetic, affectionate, tender, solicitous, kind(ly)

شفيق *šafīq* compassionate, sympathetic, affectionate, tender, solicitous, kind(ly)

اشفاق *išfāq* compassion, pity, sympathy; tenderness, affectionateness; care, solicitude; concern, worry, anxiety, apprehension

شافن *šāfin* proud

شفه III to speak (mouth to mouth) (ه to s.o.)

شفة pl. شفوات, شفاه see ²شف

شفهى *šafahī* lip-, labio- (in compounds), labial; oral; الشفهى the orals (= oral examination); شفهيا *šafahīyan* orally | الحروف الشفهية the labials *b, f, m, w* (*phon.*)

شفاها *šifāhan* orally

شفاهى *šifāhī* oral; الشفاهى the orals (= oral examination); شفاهيا *šifāhīyan* orally

مشافهة *mušāfahatan* orally

شفو IV to be very close (على to s.th.), be on the verge, on the brink of s.th. (على) | اشفى به على حافة اليأس (*ḥāffat al-ya's*) he brought him to the brink of despair

شفا *šafan* pl. اشفاء *ašfā'* edge, rim, border, brink, verge

شفوى *šafawī* lip-, labio- (in compounds), labial; oral; شفويا *šafawīyan* orally | الحروف الشفوية the labials *b, f, m, w* (*phon.*)

مشف *mušfin* moribund, doomed to death

شفى *šafā i* (شفاء *šifā'*) to cure (ه من s.o. of a disease), heal (ه من s.o. of a disease, ه a wound), make (ه s.o.) well, restore (ه s.o.) to health; — pass. *šufiya* to be healed, be cured, be restored to health, recover, convalesce, recuperate; to heal, heal up (wound) | شفى غلته (غليله) (*ğullatahū*) to quench one's thirst, gratify one's desire, satisfy one's thirst for revenge; شفى غيظه من (*ğaizahū*) to vent one's anger on s.o., take it out on s.o. **V** and **VIII** to be cured, be healed, be restored to health (ب by); to take revenge, avenge o.s., satisfy one's thirst for revenge, vent one's anger, take it out (من on) **X** to seek a cure

شفاء *šifā'* cure, healing, restoration, recovery, recuperation, convalescence; satisfaction, gratification; (pl. اشفية *ašfiya*, اشاف *ašāfin*) remedy, medicament, medication, medicine | قابل للشفاء curable

شفائى *šifā'ī* healing, curative, medicative

مشفى *mašfan* pl. مشاف *mašāfin* hospital

تشف *tašaffin* gratification of one's thirst for revenge, satisfaction

استشفاء *istišfā'* seeking of a cure; cure, (course of) treatment

شاف *šāfin* healing, curative, medicative, salutory; satisfactory, clear, unequivocal (of an answer)

مستشفى *mustašfan* pl. مستشفيات *mustašfayāt* hospital; field hospital; sanitorium | مستشفى المجاذيب insane asylum, mental hospital

شق *šaqqa u* (*šaqq*) to split, cleave, part, tear, rend, rip (ه s.th.); to break (ه s.th.); to plow, till, break up (ه the ground); to furrow, traverse, cross (ه s.th.); to pass, go, travel (ه through a region); to break (dawn); — (شقوق *šuqūq*) to break forth, shoot up, sprout (plant), break through, erupt (tooth); — (*šaqq*, مشقة *mašaqqa*) to be heavy, oppressive, burdensome, unbearable (على for s.o.); to grieve, trouble (على s.o.); to molest, harass, inconvenience (على s.o.), be troublesome, cumbersome (على for s.o.); to visit (على s.o.), call (على upon s.o.) | شقت جيبها (*jaibahā*) to tear the front of the garment as a sign of mourning (woman); شق سبيلا to cut, or open, a way for o.s.; شق السكون to break the silence; شق شارعا (طريقا) to build a street (a road); شق طريقه to force one's way, plow ahead; شق طريقا جديدا to open up, or enter upon, a new path (fig.); شق العصا (ʿaṣā) to part from the community, break with the community; شق عصا الطاعة (ʿaṣā ṭ-ṭāʿa) to rebel, revolt, renounce allegiance; شق عصا القوم (ʿaṣā l-qaum) to sow discord among people; ما شق غبارهم (ḡubārahum) he did not reach their mark; لا يشق غباره (yušaqqu ḡubāruhū) he is unsurpassable, he is incomparable, there is no one like him **II** to split (ه s.th.); to tear open, rip open, slit open (ه s.th.) **V** to be split, be cleft; to split, crack, burst; to be cracked **VII** to be split, be cleft; to split, crack, burst; to split off, separate, segregate, secede, break away, withdraw (عن from), break (عن with), renounce (عن s.th.); to become a schismatic (*Chr.*); to break (dawn) | انشقت عصاهم (ʿaṣāhum) they fell out (with one another); انشقت مرارته (*marāratuhū*) he exploded (with anger), he blew his top **VIII** to derive (ه من a word from)

شق *šaqq* pl. شقوق *šuqūq* fissure, crack, chink, crevice, rift, cleft, crevasse, chasm, split, rent, tear, rip, gap, slit, slot; half, moiety; — fission, splitting, cracking, cleavage | شق الذرة *š. aḏ-ḏarra* atomic fission

شق *šiqq* half, side, part, portion; trouble, difficulty, hardship | شق المعارضة *š. al-muʿāraḍa* opposition party; ... لا بشق الا بشق الانفس (*illā bi-šiqqi l-anfus*), بشق النفس only with great effort, with great difficulty, barely

شقة *šaqqa* rift, tear, rip, fissure, crack, split, crevice

شقة *šiqqa* pl. شقق *šiqaq*, شقاق *šiqāq* a half, moiety; piece; splinter; trouble, toil, labor, difficulty, hardship; difficult journey; destination of a journey; distance

شقة *šiqqa*, *šaqqa* pl. شقق *šiqaq* apartment, flat, split-level apartment; compartment (in a train)

شقة *šuqqa* pl. شقق *šuqaq* trouble, toil, labor, difficulty, hardship; difficult journey; destination of a journey; distance | بعد الشقة *buʿd aš-šuqqa* (and *aš-šiqqa*) large or wide distance; بعيد الشقة *b. aš-šuqqa* (and *aš-šiqqa*) far away, distant, remote

شقيق *šaqīq* a half, moiety; (pl. اشقة *ašiqqa*, اشقاء *ašiqqāʾ*[2]) full brother, brother on the paternal and maternal side; (attributively) brother-, sister-; — anemone | القطر الشقيق (*quṭr*) the brother country; الدول الشقيقة (*duwal*) the sister states (esp. with reference to Arab countries)

شقيقة *šaqīqa* pl. *-āt*, شقائق *šaqāʾiq*[2] full sister, sister on the paternal and maternal side; hemicrania, migraine | شقائق النعمان *š. an-nuʿmān* red anemones (*bot.*)

اشق *ašaqq*[2] more troublesome, more tiresome, more difficult, harder

مشقة *mašaqqa* pl. *-āt*, مشاق *mašāqq*[2] trouble, toil, labor, difficulty, hardship

شقاق *šiqāq* disunity, dissension, discord

انشقاق *inšiqāq* separation, segregation, dissociation, split; schism (*Chr.*); dissension, discord, disunion

اشتقاق *ištiqāq* derivation, etymology (of a word)

شاق *šāqq* troublesome, toilsome, wearisome, cumbersome, tiresome, tedious, fatiguing, arduous, onerous, difficult, hard | اشغال شاقة hard labor

مشاق *mušāqq* schismatic (*Chr.*)

مشتق *muštaqq* pl. *-āt* derivative (*gram.*)

شقح **IV** to send far away, remove to a distant place (ه s.o.)

شقذف *šuqḏuf* pl. شقاذف *šaqāḏif*[2] a kind of sedan

شقر *šaqira a* (*šaqar*) and *šaqura u* (شقرة *šuqra*) to be of fair complexion, be light-skinned; to be blond, fair-haired

شقر *šaqar* fair-complexionedness; blondness

شقرة *šuqra* fair-complexionedness; blondness; redness

اشقر *ašqar*², f. شقراء *šaqrā'*², pl. شقر *šuqr* fair-complexioned, light-skinned; blond, fair-haired; reddish

شقرق *šaqraqa* to be gay, cheerful, be exhilarated, amuse o.s.

شقشق *šaqšaqa* to twitter, peep, chirp; to babble (ب s.th.); to peep, break (dawn) | شقشق بالحديث عن to chat, chatter about s.th.

شقشقة *šaqšaqa* pl. *-āt* twitter(ing), peep(ing), chirp(ing); (silly) prattle; pl. شقاشق *šaqāšiq*² rigmarole, rambling talk | شقشقة اللسان (silly) prattle; شقشقة النهار *š. an-nahār* daybreak, peep of dawn

شقشقة *šiqšiqa* pl. شقاشق *šaqāšiq*² faucal bag of the camel

شقف *šaqaf* (coll.; n. un. ة) (pot)sherds

شقافه *šuqāfa* (pot)sherds

[1]شاقل *šāqil* shekel

[3]شاقول *šāqūl* plumbline, plummet

شقلب *šaqlaba* to turn things upside down, upset things II *tašaqlaba* to be upset, be toppled; to turn a somersault

شقلبة *šaqlaba* pl. *-āt* somersault

(شقو and شقى) شقا *šaqā u* (شقو *šaqw*) to make (ه s.o.) unhappy, miserable, wretched, distress (ه s.o.); — شقى *šaqiya a* (شقاء *šaqā'*, شقاوة *šaqāwa*, شقوة *šaqwa*) to be unhappy, miserable, wretched, distressed; to have trouble (ب with, in s.th.) IV to make (ه s.o.) unhappy, miserable, wretched, distress (ه s.o.)

شقاء *šaqā'* and شقا *šaqan* misfortune, distress, misery, wretchedness, pain, suffering; hardship, trouble, toil, drudgery

شقى *šaqīy* pl. اشقياء *ašqiyā'*² unhappy, unlucky, miserable, wretched, distressed; damned; wretch, villain, culprit, criminal, scoundrel, rogue; nasty, naughty, mischievous

شقوة *šaqwa* misfortune, distress, misery

شقاوة *šaqāwa* misfortune, distress, misery; mischief, nastiness, naughtiness

[1]شك *šakka u* (*šakk*) to pierce, transfix (ه s.o. ب with); to impale, spit (ه ب s.th. on); to prick, stab (ه s.th.); to doubt (ب or فى s.o., s.th.); to distrust, suspect, question (ب or فى s.o., s.th.), entertain doubts, have misgivings (ب or فى about s.o., about s.th.); to be skeptical II to make (ه s.o.) doubt (فى s.th.), fill (ه s.o.) with doubt, misgivings, skepticism, suspicion (فى about) V to doubt (ب or فى s.o., s.th.), have doubts (ب or فى about); to be skeptical, have misgivings

شك *šakk* pl. شكوك *šukūk* doubt, uncertainty, suspicion, misgiving | بلا شك (*bi-lā*), لا شك (*šakka*), ولا شك *wa-lā šakka*, من دون شك *min dūni š.* without doubt, doubtless, undoubtedly, indubitably, certainly, positively; لا سبيل الى الشك فيه (*sabīla*) doubtless, indubitable, beyond any doubt; لا يتطرق اليه الشك (*yataṭarraqu*, *šakku*) do.

شكة *šakka* stab, thrust, jab (with the point of a weapon)

تشكك *tašakkuk* doubt; skepticism

شاك *šākk* doubting, in doubt, skeptical | شاك فى السلاح or شاك السلاح armed to the teeth, bristling with arms

مشكوك فيه *maškūk fihi* doubtful, dubious, uncertain; مشكوك فى امره (*amrihi*) suspect(ed)

[2]شكّك *šakkaka* (*eg.*) to sell on credit; to buy on credit; to borrow

شكك *šukuk* (*eg.*) on credit

[3]شك (Fr. *chèque*) pl. شكات check

[1]شكر **šakara** *u* (*šukr*, شكران *šukrān*) to thank (ل or ه s.o., على or ل or ـه for s.th.), be thankful, grateful (ل or ه to s.o., على or ل or ـه for s.th.); to praise, laud, extol (ل or ه s.o.) | يشكر عليه (*yuškaru*) worthy of thanks, deserving acknowledgment, meritorious, praiseworthy **V** to thank (ـه ل s.o. for s.th.), be thankful, grateful (ـه ل to s.o. for s.th.)

شكر *šukr* pl. شكور *šukūr* thankfulness, gratefulness, gratitude; thanks, acknowledgment; praise, laudation | شكرا لك *šukran laka* I thank you! thanks! شكره شكرا جزيلا to express many thanks to s.o.

شكرى *šukrī* of thanks, thanking

شكران *šukrān* thankfulness, gratefulness, gratitude; thanks, acknowledgment; praise, laudation

شكور *šakūr* very thankful

شاكر *šākir* thankful, grateful

مشكور *maškūr* worthy of thanks, deserving acknowledgment, meritorious, praiseworthy

[2]شكارة *šikāra* pl. شكائر *šakā'ir*[2] (*eg.*) sack, gunny sack

[3]شوكران look up alphabetically

[4]شيكران look up alphabetically

شكس **šakusa** *u* (شكاسة *šakāsa*) and **šakisa** *a* (*šakas*) to be malicious, spiteful, querulous, quarrelsome, peevish, petulant, ill-tempered, morose, surly, sullen, sulky, grumpy, unfriendly **III** to pick a quarrel, to quarrel (ه with s.o.) **VI** to quarrel (with one another), be querulous, quarrelsome, petulant; to be incongruous

شكس *šakis* pl. شكس *šuks* malicious, spiteful, querulous, quarrelsome, peevish, petulant, ill-tempered, morose, surly, sullen, sulky, grumpy, unfriendly

شكاسة *šakāsa* malice, spite, querulousness, peevishness, petulance, ill-temperedness, moroseness, surliness, sullenness, sulkiness, grumpiness, unfriendliness; rudeness

مشاكسة *mušākasa* pl. *-āt* quarrel, controversy, dispute, wrangle; plot, conspiracy; moroseness, surliness, grumpiness; petulance, nagging, querulousness

تشاكس *tašākus* incongruity, absurdity

شاكوش and شكوش look up alphabetically

شكل **šakala** *u* (*šakl*) to hobble (ـه بالشكال an animal with the *šikāl*, q.v.); to vowel, point, provide with vowel points (ـه a text); to be dubious, ambiguous, equivocal, vague, obscure, intricate, difficult **II** = **I**; to shape, fashion, form, create, mold, organize, build up (ـه s.th.); to diversify, vary, variegate (ـه s.th.), bring variety (ـه into s.th.) **III** to be similar (ـه, ه to s.o., to s.th.), resemble (ـه, ه s.o., s.th.), be like s.o. or s.th. (ـه, ه) **IV** to be dubious, ambiguous, equivocal, vague, obscure, intricate, difficult (على for s.o.) **V** to be formed, fashioned, shaped, molded, created, organized, built up, take form, take shape; to be variegated, shaded, graded, form various gradations; to materialize, appear in visible form (ل to s.o.) | تشكل بشكله (*bi-šaklihī*) to take on the shape of s.o., assume the form of s.th. **X** to regard as dubious (ـه s.th.); = **IV**

شكل *šakl* pl. اشكال *aškāl*, شكول *šukūl* similarity, resemblance, likeness; outward appearance, figure, form, shape, build; form of perception, perceptual form (as opposed to matter or content; *philos.*);

type, cut, pattern; mode, manner; sort, kind, specimen; شكل vowelization, voweling; شكلا formally, in form | هم واشكالهم they and the likes of them

شكلي **šaklī** formal; pl. شكليات formalities

○ شكلية **šaklīya** formalism

شكل **šikl** coquetry, coquettishness

شكلة **šakila** coquettish woman, coquette, flirt

شكلي **šuklī** quarrelsome, peevish

شكال **šikāl** pl. -*āt*, شكل **šukul** fetter, hobble (for shackling the feet of a riding animal)

تشكيل **taškīl** pl. -*āt* forming, formation, shaping, molding, fashioning, creation, organization, building up; order of march (*mil.*); pl. تشكيلات formations; organizations

تشكيلة **taškīla** assortment, selection, variety; formation

مشاكلة **mušākala** similarity, resemblance, likeness

اشكال **iškāl** dubiosity, ambiguity, obscurity, vagueness

تشاكل **tašākul** similarity, resemblance

شاكلة **šākila** way, manner, mode; (pl. شواكل **šawākil**²) flank, side, groin | على شاكلة in the manner of, of the kind of, like, على شاكلتهم of their kind, like them; كان على شاكلته to be of the same kind, of the same strain as s.th.

مشكل **mušakkal** different, diverse, manifold, miscellaneous, variegated; vowel(iz)ed

مشكل **muškil** turbid, murky (liquid); dubious, ambiguous, equivocal, obscure, vague, hazy; difficult, intricate, involved, problematic; problem, unsolved question, issue; difficulty

مشكلة **muškila** pl. -*āt*, مشاكل **mašākil**² problem, unsolved question, issue; difficulty

شكم **šakama** *u* (*šakm*) to bridle (ه an animal); to bribe (ه s.o.); to silence, gag, muzzle (ه s.o.)

شكيمة **šakīma** pl. شكائم **šakā'im**², شكم **šukum**, شكيم **šakīm** bit, curb, snaffle, bridoon; (pl. شكائم) ○ brake (of a wheel); unruliness, unyieldingness, obstinacy; contempt, disdain, scorn | شديد الشكيمة stubborn, obstinate, unyielding; قوة الشكيمة **qūwat aš-š.** energy; قوى الشكيمة **qawīy aš-š.** energetic, vigorous, active

شكه III to resemble (ه s.th.), be like s.th. (ه)

(شكو) شكا **šakā** *u* (شكو **šakw**, شكوى **šakwā**, شكاة **šakāh**, شكاية **šikāya**, شكية **šakīya**) to complain (من or ه, ه of, about, ل or الى to s.o., من or ه of or about s.th.), make a complaint; to raise or lodge a complaint (من or ه, ه of, about or against s.o., ل or الى with s.o.); to suffer (ه from s.th.) **V** = **I**; **VI** to complain to one another (ه of, about s.th.) **VIII** = **I**

شكوة **šakwa** complaint, grievance; (pl. شكوات **šakawāt**, شكاء **šikā'**) small skin (for water or milk)

شكوى **šakwā** pl. شكاوى **šakāwā** complaint; accusation; suffering, grievance

شكاة **šakāh** complaint; accusation; suffering, grievance

شكاية **šikāya** complaint; accusation; suffering, grievance

شكية **šakīya** complaint; accusation; suffering, grievance

شكاء **šakkā'** given to complaining, querulous

مشكاة **miškāh** pl. مشكاوات **miškāwāt**, مشاك **mašākin** niche (for a lamp); lamp, pendent lamp

شاك *šākin* complainant, plaintiff | شاك السلاح = شاكي السلاح *šākk as-s.*

مشكو (منه) *maškūw* complained of, accused, charged; an accused, defendant

مشتك *muštakin* complainant, plaintiff

مشتكى عليه *muštakan 'alaihi* complained of, accused, charged; an accused, defendant

شكوريا *šikūriyā* chicory

شكولاته *šukūlāta* (*eg.*), *šikōlāta* (*syr.*), chocolate

شاكوش and شكوش see شاكوش (alphabetically)

شل *šalla a* (*šall*, شلل *šalal*) to dry up, wither, become crippled, stunted; to be paralyzed, be lame; — *šalla u* to paralyze (ه s.th.) | شل حركته (*ḥarakatahū*) to overwhelm s.o., bring s.o. down **IV** to cause (ه the hand) to wither; to paralyze (ه s.th.); to neutralize, bring to a standstill (ه s.th.) **VII** to be paralyzed, be lamed

شلة *šalla* destination (of a journey)

شلة *šilla* pl. شلل *šilal* hank, skein (of yarn); coil, spool; party, group

شلل *šalal* paralysis, palsy, paralyzation (also fig.) | شلل الاطفال *š. al-aṭfāl*, الشلل الطفلى (*ṭiflī*) infantile paralysis, poliomyelitis; الشلل الاهتزازى (*ihtizāzī*) paralysis agitans, Parkinson's disease

شلال *šallāl* pl. *-āt* cataract, waterfall, rapids

اشل *ašall*², f. شلاء *šallā'*² withered, stunted (hand); paralyzed, lame; a paralytic

مشلول *mašlūl* paralyzed, lame

شلبى *šalabī* dandyish, foppish; dandy, fop; (*pal.*) nice, handsome, beautiful

¹شلت **II** to kick

²شلتة *šalta* pl. *-āt*, شلت *šilat* mattress

شلح *šalaḥa a* (*šalḥ*) to take off (ثيابه *ṭiyābahū* one's clothes); to shed the cloth (ه), renounce the ministry (monk, priest) **II** to undress, disrobe, strip (ه s.o.); to rob, plunder (ه s.o.)

مشلح *mašlaḥ* pl. مشالح *mašāliḥ* (*syr.*, *nejd.*) long, flowing cloak of wool or camel's hair, also one with gold embroidery

تشليح *tašlīḥ* robbing, plundering, robbery

مشلح *mušallaḥ* dressing room (in a public bath)

شلشل *šalšala* to dribble, trickle

شلفة *šilfa* (razor) blade

¹شلق *šalaqa u* (*šalq*) to split lengthwise (ه s.th.)

شلق bale (e.g., of hay)

²شولقى *šaulaqī* person with a sweet tooth

شليك look up alphabetically

¹شولم look up alphabetically

²شيلم look up alphabetically

شلن (Engl.) *šilin* pl. *-āt* shilling

شلو *šilw* pl. اشلاء *ašlā'* corpse (esp. one in a state of decay); severed member (of the body); part torn off, fragment; remnant; stump of a limb

شليك (Turk. *çilek*) *šilēk* (*eg.*) strawberries

شم *šamma* (1st pers. perf. *šamimtu*) *a* and (1st pers. perf. *šamamtu*) *u* (*šamm*, شميم *šamīm*) to smell, sniff (ه s.th.); to snuff (ه s.th.); to emanate, exude (من from) | شم النسيم or الهواء (*hawā'a*) to get a breath of fresh air, take a walk; — *šamma* (1st pers. perf. *šamimtu*) *a* (شمم *šamam*) to behave proudly or haughtily, be proud, haughty, supercilious **II** to give (ه ه s.o. s.th.) to smell, let (ه s.o.) smell (ه s.th.) **IV** = **II** **V** to savor the smell of s.th. (ه), sniff (ه s.th.) | تشمم الاخبار to nose about for news **VIII** to smell, sniff (ه s.th.); to gather, understand (ه من s.th. from), read (ه من s.th. into)

شم *šamm* smelling; sense of smell, olfaction | شم النسيم Egyptian popular holiday on the Monday following the Greek Coptic Easter at the end of March, in April or in early May

شمة *šamma* pinch (of snuff); smell, odor; slight trace of s.th., whiff

شمى *šammī* olfactory

شمم *šamam* pride, haughtiness, superciliousness

شمام *šammām* pl. *-ūn* (tobacco) snuffer

شمام *šammām* (coll.; n. un. ة) muskmelon, cantaloupe

اشم *ašamm*², f. شماء *šammā'*², pl. شم *šumm* having a sensitive, or good, nose; supercilious, haughty; proud (in a complimentary sense); highborn; most honorable

الاشمام *al-išmām* the pronunciation of *u* with a trace of *i*, as *rüdda* for *rudda*, and vice versa, *qūla* for *qīla* (*gram.*)

شامة *šāmma* sense of smell, olfaction

مشموم *mašmūm* musk

(شماز) اشمأز *išma'azza* to contract, get contracted, shrink; to shrink back, recoil (من from), shudder (من at), abhor, detest (من s.th.), feel disgust (من for), be nauseated (من by)

اشمئزاز *išmi'zāz* shudder; disgust, aversion, repugnance

مشمئز *mušma'izz* disgusted, nauseated' revolted (من by)

شمبانيا (Fr.) *šambanyā* champagne

شمت *šamita* *a* (شمات *šamāt*, شماتة *šamāta*) to rejoice at the misfortune of s.o. (ب), gloat over s.o.'s (ب) mishaps, savor s.o.'s (ب) bad luck **II** to disappoint (ه s.o.) **IV** to cause s.o. (ه) to take malicious pleasure in the mishaps of another (ب)

شمات *šamāt* malicious joy, Schadenfreude

شماتة *šamāta* malicious joy, Schadenfreude, malice

شامت *šāmit* pl. شمات *šummāt*, pl. f. شوامت *šawāmit*² enjoying another's misfortune, malicious, gloating

شمخ *šamaḵa* *a* (*šamḵ*, شموخ *šumūḵ*) to be high, tall, lofty, tower up, loom (mountain, building); to disdain (على s.th.), turn up one's nose (على at s.th.) | شمخ بانفه (or انفه) (*bi-anfihī*, *anfahū*) to be arrogant, haughty, proud, supercilious **VI** to be high, tall, lofty, tower up, loom; to be boastful, put on airs; to be proud, haughty, supercilious

تشامخ *tašāmuḵ* pride, haughtiness, arrogance

شامخ *šāmiḵ* pl. شمخ *šummaḵ*, شوامخ *šawāmiḵ*² high, tall, lofty, towering; proud, haughty, supercilious | شامخ الانف *š. al-anf* proud, haughty, supercilious, arrogant

متشامخ *mutašāmiḵ* high, tall, lofty, towering; proud, haughty, supercilious; towering in lofty heights

مشمخر *mušmaḵirr* lofty, towering (of buildings)

شمر **II** to gather up, lift, roll up, tuck up, turn up (ه a garment); to prepare, get ready | شمر للامر to embark upon s.th., buckle down to s.th.; شمر عن ساعده to bare the upper arm (by rolling up the sleeve), get to work; شمر عن ساعد الجد (*s. al-jidd*) to buckle down to a job, rally all one's forces, put one's shoulder to the wheel **V** to set to work briskly

شمر *šamar* fennel (*bot.*)

شمرة *šumra, šamra* fennel

شمار *šamār* fennel

مشمر *mušammir* busily at work in (an activity)

شمروخ *šumrūk* pl. شماريخ *šamārīk²* stalk with date cluster; date-palm panicle, branch stripped of its leaves; little stick; detonator, primer cap

شماز see اشماز

شمس *šamasa u* (شموس *šumūs*, شماس *šimās*) to be headstrong, balky, restive (of a horse); — *šamasa i u* and *šamisa a* (*šamas*) to be sunny (day) II to expose (ه s.th.) to the sun, lay (ه s.th.) out in the sun to dry; to perform the office of deacon (*Chr.*) IV to be sunny (day) V to bask, sun o.s., lie or sit in the sun

شمس *šams* f., pl. شموس *šumūs* sun | سمت الشمس *samt aš-š.* ecliptic (*astron.*); شروق الشمس sunrise; ضربة الشمس *ḍarbat aš-š.* sunstroke, heat prostration; عباد الشمس *ʿabbād aš-š.* sunflower; غروب الشمس sunset

شمسى *šamsī* sun- (in compounds), solar | الحروف الشمسية (*gram.*) the sun letters (which assimilate the *l* of the article); صورة شمسية (*ṣūra*) photograph, photo; التصوير الشمسى photography

شمسية *šamsīya* pl. *-āt* (*colloq.* شماسى *šamāsī*) sunshade, parasol; umbrella; curtain, screen; stop (of a wind instrument) | شمسية الشباك *š. aš-šubbāk* window curtain, drape; ○ شمسية الطيار *š. aṭ-ṭayyār* parachute

شموس *šamūs* pl. شمس *šumus* headstrong, balky, restive (horse)

شماس *šammās* pl. شمامسة *šamāmisa* deacon of the lower rank of the ministry, nowadays, with unconsecrated persons frequently performing this office, corresponding to the sexton or sacristan (*Chr.*); acolyte and liturgical cantor of Oriental Christian rites (clerics and laymen)

شامس *šāmis* sunny (day)

مشمس *mušmis* sunny (day)

شمشم *šamšama* to sniff (ه s.th.)

شمط *šamiṭa a* (*šamaṭ*) to become gray-haired, turn gray

اشمط *ašmaṭ²*, f. شمطاء *šamṭāʾ²*, pl. شمط *šumṭ*, شمطان *šumṭān* gray-haired

شمع II to rub, or smear, with wax, to wax (ه s.th.) | شمع الفتلة (*fatla*) to slip away, abscond, make off, decamp

شمع *šamʿ, šamaʿ* (coll.; n. un. ة) pl. شموع *šumūʿ* wax; (wax) candles | الشمع الاحمر sealing wax; شمع الختم *š. al-katm* do.; شمع لتلميع الارضية (*li-talmīʿ al-arḍīya*) floor wax

شمعة *šamʿa, šamaʿa* (n. un.) (wax) candle | ○ شمعة الشرارة *š. aš-šarāra* spark plug

شمعى *šamʿī, šamaʿī* waxy, waxen, ceraceous, cero- (in compounds), made of wax

شماع *šammāʿ* chandler, maker or seller of candles

شماعة *šammāʿa* clothes rack, clothes peg, hat rack

مشمع *mušammaʿ* waterproof, impermeable (of a garment); — (pl. *-āt*) waterproof material; impregnated linen; waterproof cover or coating; oilcloth, wax cloth; linoleum | مشمع بتيومين للسقف (*li-s-saqf*) bituminous roof covering, roofing felt, tar paper; معطف مشمع (*miʿṭaf*) raincoat

شمعدان *šamʿadān* pl. *-āt*, شماعد *šamāʿid²*, شماعدين candlestick, candelabrum

يشمق look up alphabetically

[1]شمل šamila a (šamal) and šamala u (šaml, شمول šumūl) to contain, comprise, comprehend, enclose (ه s.th.); to imply, implicate, include (ه s.th.); to touch, affect, fill, overcome, pervade (ه, ه s.o., s.th., of feelings, emotions); to prevail, be general, universal | شمله بعنايته (bi-ʿināyatihī) to bestow one's care on s.o., take s.o. under one's wing **V** تشمل بالشملة to wrap o.s. in the šamla (q.v.) **VIII** = **V**; to wrap o.s. (ه, ب in s.th.); to contain, comprise, comprehend, enclose, enfold, imply, implicate, include (على s.th.) | اشتمله السواد (sawādu) it was completely black

شمل šaml uniting, gathering, concentration; unity, union | جمع الشمل jamʿ aš-š. reunion, reunification; اجتماع الشمل reunion; unity, union; مزق شمله mazzaqa šamlahū to break up, dismember, dismantle, parcel s.th.; to partition s.th., divide s.th. up

شملة šamla pl. šamalāt cloak; turban | ام شملة ummu šamlata the world, the temporal joys

شمائل šamāʾil[2] (pl.) good qualities; character, nature

اشمل ašmal[2] more comprehensive; more general, more universal

شامل šāmil comprehensive, exhaustive; general, universal, complete, total

مشمول mašmūl contained, comprised, included, implied | مشمول برعايته (bi-riʿāyatihī) enjoying the protection or patronage of s.o.; مشمولات الوظيفة the inherent functions of an office

مشتمل muštamil comprising, containing, including (على s.th.)

مشتمل muštamal cottage (for rent)

مشتملات muštamalāt contents

[2]شمال šamāl, šimāl north; north wind; šimāl left hand; left side; left; الشمال the left (pol.); شمال šimāla north of . . .; شمالا šimālan to the left; northward, to the north | شمال شرق (šarqī) northeast; شمال غربى (ḡarbī) northwest; كوكب الشمال kaukab aš-š. polar star; اليد الشمال (yad) the left hand

شمالى šamālī, šimālī northern, northerly, north; situated on the left; الشماليون the leftist parties (pol.) | الشفق الشمالى (šafaq) aurora borealis, northern lights

[3]شملول šumlūl pl. شماليل šamālīl[2] small amount, small quantity; — (eg.) šamlūl brisk, vivid, agile, lively, nimble

[4]مشملة, مشملا look up alphabetically

شمندر šamandar white beet, chard

شمندورة šamandūra buoy

[1]شن šanna u (šann): شن غارة (ḡāratan) to make a raid, an invasion; to make an attack, launch an attack (على against, on) **IV** = **I**

شن šann pl. شنون šunūn (water)skin

مشنة mišanna basket without handles

[2]اشنان look up alphabetically

شنأ šanaʾa a (شنآن šanʾān, šanaʾān) to hate

شنب šanab pl. اشناب ašnāb mustache

شنتيان šintiyān pl. شناتين šanātīn[2] loose trousers resembling pantalets, worn by women

شنج šanija a (šanaj) to contract, shrink; to suffer from convulsions **V** = **I**; to twitch

تشنج tašannuj contraction, shriveling, shrinking (of the skin); convulsive contraction (of a muscle), twitch, jerk, convulsion, spasm, fit, cramp | التشنج الرعشى (raʿšī) clonic spasm; التشنج الكزازى (kuzāzī) tonic spasm

تشنجى tašannujī spastic, spasmodic, cramplike, paroxysmal, convulsive

شنخوبة *šunkūba* pl. شناخيب *šanākīb*[2] large rock, boulder

شنر II to blame, censure, revile, slander, abuse (على s.o.)

شنار *šanār* disgrace, ignominy

شنارق *šanāriq*[2] = شرانق *šarāniq*[2]

شنشنة *šanšana* rustling (of paper); cracking, crackling

شنشنة *šinšina* pl. شناشن *šanāšin*[2] nature, disposition; habit, custom, practice

[1]شنيطة *šunaiṭa* knot; noose, loop

[2]شنطة *šanṭa* pl. شنط *šunaṭ* suitcase; satchel; bag, traveling bag | شنطة اليد *š. al-yad* handbag

شنع *šanuʿa u* (*šanaʿ*, شناعة *šanāʿa*) to be ugly, abominable, repugnant, repulsive, atrocious, hideous, horrid, horrible, disgraceful; — *šanaʿa a* (*šanʿ*) to dishonor, disgrace (ب or ه s.o.) II to calumniate, slander, revile, defame (على s.o.); to pillory, expose, condemn, denounce (على s.o., s.th.)

شنع *šaniʿ* ugly, abominable, repugnant, repulsive, disgusting, atrocious, hideous, horrid, horrible, disgraceful, ignominious

شنعة *šunʿa* ugliness, hideousness, horridness, repulsiveness

شنيع *šaniʿ* ugly, abominable, repugnant, repulsive, disgusting, atrocious, hideous, horrid, horrible, disgraceful, ignominious

شناعة *šanāʿa* ugliness, hideousness, horridness, repulsiveness

اشنع *ašnaʿ*[2], f. شنعاء *šanʿāʾ*[2] ugly, abominable, repugnant, repulsive, disgusting, atrocious, hideous, horrid, horrible, disgraceful, ignominious

شنغوبة *šunġūba* pl. شناغيب *šanāġīb*[2] spicate protuberance; thorn, spike

شنف II شنف الآذان (*ādāna*) to please the ears, to delight (of a voice)

شنف *šanf* pl. شنوف *šunūf* earring

شنق *šanaqa u* (*šanq*) to hang (ه s.th., ه s.o. on the gallows)

شنق *šanq* hanging

شنق *šanaq* rope

مشنقة *mišnaqa* pl. مشانق *mašāniq*[2] gallows, gibbet; scaffold, place of execution (by hanging); *mašnaqa* gallows, gibbet

مشنوق *mašnūq* hanged

شنقب *šunqub* bécassine, snipe (*zool.*)

شنكل *šankala* (*eg.*) to trip (ه s.o.) up; to hook up

شنكل *šankal* pl. شناكل *šanākil*[2] clothes peg; hook

شنهق *šanhaqa* to bray (donkey)

شهب *šahab* gray color, gray

شهبة *šuhba* gray color, gray

شهاب *šihāb* pl. شهب *šuhub*, شهبان *šuhbān* flame, blaze, fire; shooting star, luminous meteor; star

اشهب *ašhab*[2], f. شهباء *šahbāʾ*[2], pl. شهب *šuhb* gray; الشهباء epithet of Aleppo (Syria)

شهد *šahida a* (شهود *šuhūd*) to witness (ه s.th.), be witness (ه of s.th.); to experience personally (ه s.th.), see with one's own eyes (ه s.o. in a situation); to be present (ه at), attend (ه a celebration); to be present at the public appearance of s.o. (ه); to see (ه s.th.); — (شهادة *šahāda*) to testify, bear witness; to attest, confirm, certify (ب s.th., ان that), testify, give testimony, give evidence (على against s.o., to or about s.th., ل in s.o.'s favor); to sign as a witness, to witness (على a document);

to acknowledge, adjudge (ل ب to s.o., s.th.) | شهد بالله to swear by God; شهد قانونيا to notarize III to see (with one's own eyes), view, inspect, watch, observe, witness (ه s.th.) IV to call (ه upon s.o.) as a witness (على for s.th.); pass. *ušhida* to be martyred, die as a martyr X to call (ه or ب upon s.o.) or cite (ه or ب s.o.) as witness (على against or for, فى in); to cite, quote (ب s.th.); to attest (e.g., على معنى كلمة ببيت *'alā ma'nā kalimatin bi-baitin* the meaning of a word by a verse); pass. *ustušhida* to be martyred, die as a martyr

شهد *šahd, šuhd* pl. شهاد *šihād* honey; honeycomb

شهدة *šahda* carbuncle

شهيد *šahīd* pl. شهداء *šuhadā'*² witness; martyr, one killed in battle with the infidels; one killed in action

شهيدة *šahīda* (woman) martyr

شهادة *šahāda* pl. *-āt* testimony, witness, evidence, deposition; statement; certificate, certification, testimonial, affidavit; attestation, attest; credentials, identification; (Muslim) creed (= doctrinal formula); martyrdom | شهادة الاثبات *š. al-iṯbāt* evidence for the prosecution; شهادة حسن السير والسلوك (*š. ḥusn as-sair*) certificate of good conduct; شهادة خلو الطرف عن العمل *š. ḵulūw aṭ-ṭaraf 'an il-'amal* certificate of discharge (from a position); شهادة الدراسة الثانوية (*ṯānawīya*) secondary school diploma; شهادة زور *š. zūr* false testimony; شهادة على شهادة indirect testimony (*Isl. Law*); شهادة العالمية *š. al-'ālimīya* (*Eg.*) diploma of higher learning (highest diploma awarded by Al Azhar University); شهادة عالية (*'āliya*) diploma; شهادة النفى *š. an-nafy* evidence for the defense; شهادة الولادة birth certificate

مشهد *mašhad* pl. مشاهد *mašāhid*² place of assembly, assembly, meeting; place where a martyr or hero died; religious shrine venerated by the people, esp. the tomb of a saint; funeral cortege; procession; view, aspect, spectacle, sight, scenery; place or object of interest; scene (e.g., of a crime, of nature); act, number (as part of a program, e.g., in vaudeville), scene (in theater, as part of a play); aspect | مشهد غنائى (*ginā'ī*) song scene, vocal recital; مشاهد الحياة *m. al-ḥayāh* aspects of life

مشاهدة *mušāhada* seeing, viewing, witnessing, inspection; (pl. *-āt*) view, sight, spectacle; apparition, vision

اشهاد *išhād* pl. *-āt* written certification

استشهاد *istišhād* citation, quotation; death of a martyr; death of a hero, heroic death; martyrdom

شاهد *šāhid* pl. شهود *šuhūd*, شهد *šuhhad* present; — (pl. شهود *šuhūd*, اشهاد *ašhād*) witness (على for); notary public; — (pl. شواهد *šawāhid*²) (piece of) evidence (على for); attestation; quotation serving as textual evidence; testimony; an oblong, upright tombstone | شاهد الاثبات *š. al-iṯbāt* witness for the prosecution; شاهد السمع *š. as-sam'* earwitness; شاهد العين *š. al-'ain*, شاهد عيان *š. 'iyān* شاهد عيانى (*'iyānī*) eyewitness; شاهد النفى *š. an-nafy* witness for the defense; على رؤوس الاشهاد in public, for everyone to see

شاهدة *šāhida* pl. شواهد *šawāhid*² an oblong, upright tombstone; index finger; true copy, copy of a letter, duplicate; الشاهدة the Earth

مشهود *mašhūd* taking place in the presence of spectators or witnesses; happening before a large audience, well-attended; memorable (day, event) | بالجرم المشهود (*jurm*) in the act, redhanded, flagrante delicto | اليوم المشهود (*yaum*) the Day of Resurrection; red-letter day, festive public holiday

مشاهد *mušāhid* pl. *-ūn* spectator, onlooker, observer

مشاهد *mušāhad* visible, perceptible; pl. مشاهدات things seen, sights; visible things

شهر **šahara** *a* (*šahr*) to make well-known, famous, renowned, notorious (ه, ه s.o., s.th.); to spread, make known, divulge, proclaim, announce (ه s.th.); to draw, unsheathe (ه a weapon); pass. *šuhira* to be or become well-known, famed, famous, renowned, notorious (ب by or for s.th. respectively, by or under a name) | شهر الحرب عليه (*ḥarb*) to declare war on s.o.; شهر البندقية (*bunduqīya*) to level a gun (على at s.o.) II to make well-known, famous, renowned, notorious (ه, ه s.o., s.th.); to spread, make known, divulge, proclaim, announce (ه s.th.); to defame, slander, revile publicly, pillory, condemn, denounce (ه s.o.) III to engage or hire (ه s.o.) on a monthly basis, rent (ه s.th.) by the month IV to make known, proclaim, announce, spread, divulge (ه s.th.); to unsheathe, draw (ه a weapon); to sell at auction, also اشهر المزاد (*mazāda*) | اشهر مزاد بيع شىء (*mazāda bai'i š.*) to auction s.th. off, put s.th. up at auction VIII to be or become well-known, famed, famous, renowned, notorious (ب by or for s.th. respectively, by or under a name); to be known (عن of s.o., a trait, and the like); to be widespread, common

شهر *šahr* pl. اشهر *ašhur*, شهور *šuhūr* new moon; month | شهر العسل *š. al-'asal* honeymoon

شهرى *šahrī* monthly, mensal; شهريا *šahrīyan* monthly, per month, by the month | اشتراك شهرى monthly subscription; monthly fee or contribution; نصف شهرى *niṣfu šahrīyin* fortnightly, semimonthly, appearing biweekly

شهرية *šahrīya* monthly salary

شهرة *šuhra* repute, reputation, renown, fame, famousness, celebrity; notoriety; surname (*Syr., Leb.*) | شهرة عالمية (*'ālamīya*) world-wide renown, world-wide fame

شهير *šahīr* widely known, well-known, famous, renowned, celebrated (ب by a name); notorious, ill-reputed

اشهر *ašhar*[2] better known, more widely known

مشاهرة *mušāhara* pl. *-āt* monthly salary; pl. monthly payments, monthly allowances; *mušāharatan* monthly, per month, by the month

اشهار *išhār* announcement, proclamation, declaration; public sales, auction; publicity, advertising | اشهار الافلاس *i. al-iflās* notice of bankruptcy, declaration of insolvency

اشتهار *ištihār* repute, reputation, renown, fame, famousness, celebrity; notoriety

مشهور *mašhūr* pl. مشاهير *mašāhīr*[2] well-known, widely known, renowned, famous, celebrated; notorious, ill-reputed; widespread, common; a famous, celebrated personality, a celebrity; accepted, established, canonical (textual variant, version of the Koran) | على المشهور according to the general belief, as it is (was) generally understood

مشهر *mušahhar* well-known, widely known, renowned, famous, celebrated; notorious, ill-reputed

شهق **šahaqa** *a i* (شهيق *šahīq*) to bray (donkey); — *šahaqa a i* and *šahiqa a* (شهيق *šahīq*, شهاق *šuhāq*, تشهاق *tašhāq*) to inhale; to sigh deeply; to sob, gulp; to moan, groan IV اشهق بالبكاء (*bi-l-bukā'*) to burst into tears, break out into loud weeping

شهقة *šahqa* moan(ing), groan(ing); gulping

شهيق *šahīq* braying, brays (of a donkey); sobbing, sobs; sighing, sighs; inhalation, breathing in

شاهق *šāhiq* pl. شواهق *šawāhiq*[2] high, lofty, towering (building, mountain) | علو شاهق (*'ulūw*) tremendous height

شواهق *šawāhiq*[2] heights

شهل II to accelerate, speed up, expedite (ه s.th.); to remove quickly, hurry off (ه s.o.)

شهل *šahil* nimble, swift, quick

شهلة *šuhla* bluish-black color of the eyes

اشهل *ašhal*[2], f. شهلاء *šahlā'*[2] having bluish-black eyes

شهم *šahm* pl. شهام *šihām* perspicacious, sagacious, astute, clever; bold, audacious; energetic; noble, gallant, decent; gentleman

شهامة *šahāma* perspicacity, sagacity, astuteness, cleverness; audacity, boldness, gallantry, noble-mindedness; energy, vigor, verve; decency, respectability

شاهين pl. شواهين look up alphabetically

(شهو and شهى) شها *šahā u* and شهى *šahiya a* (شهوة *šahwa*) to desire, wish, covet, crave (ه s.th.), long (ه for s.th.) **II** to make covetous, fill with desire, allure, entice (ه s.o.); to arouse greed, desire, appetite (ه in s.o., ه for s.th.); to whet the appetite, be appetizing (food) **V** and **VIII** to be covetous, greedy, to long (ه for s.th.), crave, desire, wish (ه s.th.), feel appetite (ه for s.th.) | شىء لا يشتهى (*yuštahā*) an undesirable thing

شهوة *šahwa* pl. *šahawāt* greed, craving, desire, ardent wish, longing, yearning, eagerness, passion, carnal appetite, lust; appetite

شهوى *šahwī* sensual, sensuous, lustful, instinctual, uninhibited

شهوان *šahwān*[2], f. شهوى *šahwā*, pl. شهاوى *šahāwā* covetous, greedy; lewd, lecherous, lascivious, libidinous, dissolute, debauched

شهوانى *šahwānī* covetous, greedy; lewd, lecherous, lascivious, libidinous, dissolute, debauched; sensual, sensuous, lustful, instinctual, uninhibited

شهى *šahīy* pleasant, agreeable, desirable; appetizing, inviting, tasty

شهية *šahīya* appetite | فاتح الشهية or ما يفتح الشهية (*yaftaḥu*) stimulating the appetite, appetizing; قلة الشهية للطعام *qillat aš-š. li-ṭ-ṭa'ām* want of appetite

تشه *tašahhin* greed, avidity, cupidity, craving, desire

اشتهاء *ištihā'* greed, craving, desire, ardent wish, longing, yearning, eagerness, passion, carnal appetite, lust; appetite

مشه *mušahhin* stimulating the appetite, appetizing; مشهيات appetizers, relishes, hors d'oeuvres

مشته *muštahin* covetous, greedy, avid, craving, desirous, lustful

مشتهى *muštahan* desirable; desired, welcome, agreeable, pleasant; (pl. مشتهيات *muštahayāt*) that which is coveted, object of desire

شاء *šā'* (coll.; n. un. شاة *šāh*) pl. شواه *šiwāh*, شياه *šiyāh* sheep; ewe

شوال *šuwāl, šiwāl* pl. *-āt* (large) sack

[1](شوب) شاب *šāba u* (*šaub*, شياب *šiyāb*) to mix, blend (ه ب s.th. with); to adulterate, vitiate, contaminate, spoil, corrupt, pollute, tarnish, sully, stain, spot (ه s.th.); to mix, blend, intermix (ه with) | لا تشوبه شائبة blameless, flawless, unblemished, immaculate

شوب *šaub* mixture; tarnishing, sullying, roiling, rendering turbid; impairment, blemish, flaw; hot wind

شائبة *šā'iba* pl. شوائب *šawā'ib*[2] dirt, stain, spot, flaw, blemish, defect, fault; suspicion, reason for suspicion, suspicious fact

مشوب *mašūb* mixed; adulterated, vitiated | مشوب بالهموم troubled with worries

[2]شابة look up alphabetically

شوبق *šaubaq* pl. شوابق *šawābiq*[2] rolling pin

شوبك *šaubak* pl. شوابك *šawābik*[2] rolling pin

[1]شوح II (*eg.*) to grill, broil, roast (ه s.th.)

[2]شوح *šūḥ* (coll.; n. un. ة) fir, sapin

[3]شوحة *šūḥa* kite (*zool.*)

[4]مشاحة see شح

شور II to make a sign, beckon, signal, wink, blink (الى to s.o.); to point out (الى s.th.), point (الى at) **III** to ask s.o.'s (ه) advice, seek s.o.'s (ه) advice, consult (ه s.o.); to consult, take counsel (ه with s.o.), شاور نفسه (*nafsahū*) to take counsel with o.s., reflect, bethink o.s. **IV** to make a sign, beckon, signal, wink, blink (ل or الى to s.o.), motion (ل or الى s.o., ب to do s.th.); to ask, invite, urge (الى s.o.); to point, allude (الى to), hint (الى at), indicate, point out (على or الى s.th.), call s.o.'s (ل) attention to (على); to advise (على ب s.o. of s.th., على ان s.o. to do s.th.), suggest (على ب to s.o. s.th., على ان to s.o. to do s.th.), command, order على ب or ان s.o. to do s.th.); to state, indicate (ب s.th.) | ما يشار اليه بالبنان (*yušāru, banān*) that which is pointed at with the finger tips, i.e., s.th. very remarkable, s.th. outstanding; ما اشار بطرف (*bi-ṭarfin*) he did not bat an eye **VI** to take counsel, deliberate, consult (مع ف with s.o. about) **X** to ask for advice (ه s.o.), take counsel (ه with s.o.), consult (ه s.o.)

شارة *šāra* pl. *-āt* sign, token, distinguishing mark, badge; guise, outward appearance | شارة الصليب sign of the cross

شورى *šūrā* consultation, deliberation, taking counsel; counsel; advice | مجلس الشورى *majlis aš-š.* and مجلس شورى الدولة *m. š. d-daula* state council

شورى *šūrī* consultative, advisory

مشوار *mišwār* pl. مشاوير *mašāwīr*[2] errand; ○ stroke (of an internal-combustion engine; *techn.*) | محرك ثنائى المشوار *muḥarrik ṯunā'ī l-m.* two-cycle engine; محرك رباعى المشوار (*rubā'ī l-m.*) four-cycle engine

مشورة *mašwara, mašūra* pl. *-āt* consultation, deliberation, conference; counsel, advice, suggestion

مشاورة *mušāwara* pl. *-āt* consultation, deliberation, conference

اشارة *išāra* pl. *-āt* sign, motion, nod, wink, wave; gesture; signal; indication; allusion, hint, intimation; symbolic expression; (silent) reminder; advice, counsel, suggestion; instruction, order, command | اشارة برقية (*barqīya*) telegram, wire, dispatch, cable(gram); اشارة تلغرافية telegram, wire; اشارة الخطر *i. al-ḵaṭar* air-raid warning, alert; اشارة الصليب sign of the cross (*Chr.*); اشارة ضبط الوقت *i. ḍabṭ al-waqt* (radio) time signal; اشارة لاسلكية (*lā-silkīya*) radio message; محطة الاشارات *maḥaṭṭat al-i.* signal post; اسم الاشارة *ism al-i.* demonstrative pronoun; وحدات الاشارة *waḥadāt al-i.* signal-corps units (*mil.*); رهن اشارته (*rahna*) at s.o.'s beck and call, at s.o.'s disposal

اشارى *išārī* (*mil.*) signalman, member of the signal corps (*Eg.* 1939)

اشارجى *išargī* (*mil.*) signalman, member of the signal corps (*Eg.*)

تشاور *tašāwur* joint consultation, deliberation (مع with)

استشارة *istišāra* pl. *-āt* a seeking of advice, consultation; guidance, advice (one receives)

استشارى *istišārī* consultative, advisory

مشاور *mušāwar* adviser, counselor, consultant

مشير *mušīr* indicative (الى of); adviser, counselor, consultant; field marshal (*Eg.*; *Ir.* 1933); Fleet Admiral (*Eg.* 1939)

المشار اليه *al-mušār ilaihi* the aforementioned, the aforesaid, the said

مستشار *mustašār* adviser, counselor, consultant, councilor; chancellor; approx.: justice (title; *Eg.*) | مستشار السفارة counselor of embassy; مستشار المفوضية *m. al-mufawwaḍīya* counselor of legation

دار المستشارية *dār al-mustašārīya* office of the chancellor, chancellery

¹شورب *šaurab* flycatcher (*zool.*)

²شوربة *šorba* (*eg.*), *šōraba* (*syr.*) and شوربا soup

شورت (Engl.) *šort* short, short feature (motion pictures)

شورمة *šawurma* see شاورمة (alphabetically)

اشوس *ašwas*², f. شوساء *šausā'*², pl. شوس *šūs*, اشاوس *ašāwis*² proud; bold, audacious, daring, venturesome | شوس الحرب *š. al-ḥarb* war heroes

¹شوش II to muddle, confuse, confound, jumble (ه s.th.), disturb (على or ه s.th.), complicate (ه s.th.) V to be confused, confounded, muddled, jumbled, deranged, disturbed; to feel indisposed, be ill

شاش *šāš* muslin; white cloth

شاشة *šāša* white cloth; الشاشة *aš-šāša* and الشاشة البيضاء (*baiḍā'*) (motion picture) screen

شاشية *šāšiya*, *šāšīya* pl. شواشى *šawāšī* a kind of headgear, cap, skullcap

شوش *šūš* Maria Theresa dollar (*Nejd*)

شوشة *šūša* tuft of hair, lock; crest (of birds)

شواش *šawāš* confusion, muddle, (state of) disorder, disturbance, derangement (e.g., of the mind)

شواشى *šawwāšī* pl. شواشية *šawwāšīya* a maker of *šāšiya's* (see above)

تشويش *tašwīš* confusion, confounding, muddling; disturbance, derangement; ailment

مشوش *mušawwaš* muddled, jumbled, befuddled, confused; disturbed, deranged (e.g., of a sensorial function); ailing, ill | مشوش الفكر *m. al-fikr* bewildered, confused, baffled

²شاوش pl. شواش look up alphabetically

³شاويش look up alphabetically

شوشبرك *šušbarak* (*eg.*) small pastry stuffed with meat and served with milk rice

شوط *šauṭ* pl. اشواط *ašwāṭ* race to a goal; state, phase; round, game, half, course (in sports and games); goal, aim | قطع شوطا كبيرا (بعيدا) فى التقدم (الرقى) (*taqaddum*, *ruqīy*) and قطع فى ميدان الرقى اشواطا (*maidāni r-ruqīy*) to make good progress or headway, advance in great strides, do.; قطع اشواطا شاسعة يفوقه اشواطا (*yafūquhū*) he surpasses him by far

شواظ *šuwāẓ* flame; fire, fervor, ardor, passion

¹شوف II to polish (ه s.th.); to adorn, deck out (ها a woman) V to look out expectantly, longingly (الى for), look forward (الى to), expect, anticipate (الى s.th.)

شوف *šauf* harrow

الشوف *aš-šūf* name of an administrative district of Lebanon

شوفة *šaufa* (*colloq.*) sight, spectacle, view

شوفان *šūfān* oats

شاق (شوق) *šāqa u* (*šauq*) to please, delight (ه s.o.), give joy (ه to s.o.); to fill (ه s.o.) with longing, craving, desire, arouse longing, craving, desire (ه in s.o.) **II** to fill (ه s.o.) with longing, craving, desire, arouse longing, craving, desire (ه in s.o.) **V** and **VIII** to long, yearn (الى or ه, ه for), crave, covet, desire ardently (الى or ه s.th.)

شوق *šauq* pl. اشواق *ašwāq* longing, yearning, craving, desire, wish

شيق *šayyiq* longing, yearning, craving, desirous, covetous; brilliant, gorgeous, splendid

تشويق *tašwīq* arousing of desire, of longing; fascination, thrilling, awakening of excitement, of eagerness

تشوق *tašawwuq* longing, yearning, desire, inclination, craving, eagerness

اشتياق *ištiyāq* longing, yearning, desire, inclination, craving, eagerness

شائق *šā'iq* arousing longing, stimulating desire; brilliant, gorgeous, splendid, beautiful

مشوق *mušawwiq* arousing desire or longing; thrilling, exciting, fascinating, absorbing, stimulating, stirring, attractive, interesting; — *mušawwaq* filled with longing (الى for), desirous, covetous (الى of)

مشتاق *muštāq* longing, yearning, craving, desirous, covetous

(شوك) شاك *šāka u* (*šauk*) to sting, prick, hurt, injure, pierce (ه ب s.o. with a thorn, a needle, and the like) **II** to be thorny; to stud (ه s.th.) with thorns or spikes; to sting, prick, hurt, injure, pierce (ه ب s.o. with a thorn, with a needle) **IV** to sting, prick, hurt, injure

شوك *šauk* (coll.; n. un. ة) pl. اشواك *ašwāk* thorns, spikes, pricks, prickles, spines; fishbone; forks | على الشوك on tenterhooks, on pins and needles

شوكة *šauka* (n. un.) thorn, spike, prick, prickle, spine, sting, point; tine, prong; spur (of a rooster); fork; fishbone; furor of fighting, bravura, bravery, valor, verve, dash, élan; might, power

شوكى *šaukī* thorny, spiky, prickly, spiny; spinal | التين الشوكى (*tīn*) fruit of the Indian fig (Opuntia ficus-indica Haw.; *bot.*); الحبل الشوكى (*ḥabl*) spinal cord; الحمى الشوكية المخية (*ḥummā, mukḵīya*) cerebrospinal meningitis (*med.*); العمود الشوكى (*'amūd*) vertebral column, backbone; spine; النخاع الشوكى (*nukā'*) spinal cord

شوك *šawik* thorny, spiky, prickly, spiny

شائك *šā'ik* thorny, spiky, prickly, spiny; delicate, ticklish, critical, difficult | سلك شائك (*silk*) pl. اسلاك شائكة barbed wire

شوكران *šaukarān* poison hemlock (Conium maculatum; *bot.*)

[1](شول) شال *šāla u* (*šaul*) to rise, be raised, elevated; to raise, lift (ه or ب s.th.); to carry (ه or ب s.th.) | شالت نعامته (*na'āmatuhū*) he went away, departed; he died, he is dead **II** to become sparse, scarce, short in supply **III** to attack, assail (ه s.o.) **IV** to raise, lift (ه s.th.); to carry (ه s.th.)

شول *šawil* nimble, adroit, swift, quick, expeditious (at work)

شوال *šawwāl* pl. *-āt* شواويل *šawāwīl*[2], also الشوال Shawwal, name of the tenth month of the Muslim year

مشال *mašāl* carrying, carriage, conveyance, transportation (of loads); porterage, carrying charges

[2]شال pl. شيلان look up alphabetically

[3]شوال look up alphabetically

شولق *šaulaqī* person with a sweet tooth

شولم *šaulam* darnel (Lolium temulentum; *bot.*); a variety of vetch

شأم[1] see مشوم ,شوام .pl شامى ,الشام

شومة[2] *šūma* stick, cudgel

شون II to garner, store (▲ s. th., esp. grain)

شونة *šūna* pl. *-āt*, شون *šuwan* (*eg.*) storehouse, granary, shed, barn

شوندر *šawandar* white beet, chard

شوه[1] *šawiha* a (*šawah*) and شاه *šāha u* (شوه *šauh*) to be or become ugly, misshapen, deformed, defaced, disfigured, distorted, malformed **II** to disfigure, deform, deface, distort, mar, mutilate (• s.o., ▲ s.th., esp. the face); to revile, slander, defame (• s. o.); to jam (اذاعة a broadcast) | شوه وجه الحقيقة (*wajha l-ḥ.*) to distort the truth; شوه وجه وظيفته to disgrace one's profession **V** = **I**

شوه *šawah* ugliness, misshapenness, malformation, deformity, disfigurement, distortion, perversion

اشوه *ašwah*[2], f. شوهاء *šauhā'*[2], pl. شوه *šūh* misshapen, malformed, ugly, disfigured, deformed, disfeatured, defaced; distorted, perverted

تشويه *tašwīh* deformation, disfigurement, defacement, mutilation; defamation; crippledness

تشوه *tašawwuh* ugliness, misshapenness, malformation, deformity, disfigurement, distortion, perversion

شائه *šā'ih* misshapen, malformed, ugly, disfigured, deformed, disfeatured, defaced; distorted, perverted

مشوه *mušawwah* disfigured, defaced, deformed; mutilated, maimed; misshapen, malformed, ugly; distorted, perverted | مشوه الحرب *m. al-ḥarb* disabled (in active service); disabled veteran

شاه[2] look up alphabetically

شاة[3] (n. un.) see شوه

شواه[4] pl. of شاه see شوه

شوى *šawā i* (شى *šayy*) to broil, grill, roast (▲ meat)

شواء *šiwā'*, *šuwā'* broiled, or grilled, meat, and the like | شواء السجق *š. as-sujuq* grilled sausages

شوى *šawīy* broiled, grilled, roasted

شواة *šawāh* pl. شوى *šawan* scalp

شواية *šawwāya* gridiron, grill

مشواة *mišwāh* pl. مشاو *mašāwin* gridiron, grill

شى[1] see شوى

شية[2], شيات see وشى

شيأ) شاء) *šā'a a* (مشيئة *mašī'a*) to want; to wish (▲ s.th., ان that) | ان شاء الله (*in*) God willing; it is to be hoped; I (we) hope so; ما شاء الله whatever (howsoever, how long soever) God intend (used to express an indefinite quantity, amount, number, or period of time); various, sundry, all kinds of, God knows what; also, exclamation of surprise: amazing! that's right! good! bravo! الى ما شاء الله forever and ever, for all time and time to come; لفق ما شاء له التلفيق (*laffaqa, talfīqu*) to fabricate the most outrageous lies

شىء *šai'* pl. اشياء *ašyā'*[2] thing; something; (with neg.) nothing | شىء من ... some, a little, a certain (amount of), a considerable . . .; شىء من النشاط (*našāṭ*) some activity; شىء من القلق (*qalaq*) some uneasiness, some anxiety; بدون شىء من الجهد (*jahd*) without any effort at all; هذا شىء وذاك شىء آخر (*āḵar*) this and that are two entirely different things (or matters); فى الامر شىء there is s.th. wrong, there is a fly in the ointment; بعض الشىء *ba'ḍa š-š.* to a certain extent, a little, somewhat; فى شىء ,بشىء in negative sentences: not in any way; in no way, by no means, not at all, not in the least; على شيء كثير من very, extremely, e.g., على شيء كثير من البساطة (*basāṭa*) very simple; الشيء الكثير the most; اشبه شيء ب (*ašbahu šai'in*) very much like...; شيئا فشيئا or شيئا بعد شيء (*fa-šai'an*) bit by bit, one after the other, by and by, gradually; لا شيء *lā-šai'* a nothing, nil, nonentity; nothing (in sport scoring); اللاشيء the nothing; لا شيء *lā-šai'a* nothing (as object); لا ... غير الشيء اليسير (*ġaira š-šai'i l-yasīr*) only very little; ليس بشيء it is nothing, it is of no consequence; ليس هذا فى شيء من ذلك this has absolutely nothing to do with that

شيئى *šai'ī* objective, factual

لاشيئية *lā-šai'īya* nonexistence, nothingness, nihility, nullity

شيىء *šuyai'* a little thing, trifle

شوية *šuwayya* (*colloq.*) a little, a bit, somewhat

مشيئة *maši'a* volition, will; wish, desire | بمشيئة الله God willing

¹شيب) شاب) *šāba* i (*šaib*, شيبة *šaiba*, مشيب *mašīb*) to become white-haired, gray-haired; to turn white or gray (hair); to grow old, to age; to make white-haired; to bleach (ه s.th.) **II** to make (ه s.o.) white-haired, cause s.o.'s (ه) hair to turn white (grief) **IV** = **II**

شيب *šaib* grayness of the hair, gray or white hair; old age

شيبة *šaiba* a variety of artemisia (Artemisia arborescens L.; *bot.*)

اشيب *ašyab*², f. شيباء *šaibā'*², pl. شيب *šīb* white, gray (hair); white-haired, gray-haired (person); old, aged; old man

مشيب *mašīb* grayness of the hair, gray or white hair; old age

شائب *šā'ib* white, gray (hair); white-haired, gray-haired (person); old, aged; old man

²شابة look up alphabetically

شيت *šīt* pl. شيوتات *šuyūtāt* chintz, printed calico (*eg.*)

¹شيح **II** (*tun.*) to dry, blot (ه s.th.) **IV** to turn away, avert (ب the eyes, one's face, عن from)

شياح *šayyāḥ* blotting paper

²شيح *šīḥ* an oriental variety of wormwood (*bot.*)

شيخ) شاخ) *šāḵa* i (شيخ *šayaḵ*, شيوخة *šuyūḵa*, شيخوخة *šaiḵūḵa*) to age, grow old; to attain a venerable age

شيخ *šaiḵ* pl. شيوخ *šuyūḵ*, اشياخ *ašyāḵ*, مشيخة *mašyaḵa*, مشايخ *mašāyiḵ*², مشائخ *mašā'iḵ*² an elderly, venerable gentleman; old man; elder; chief, chieftain, sheik, patriarch, head (of a tribe); title of the ruler of any one of the sheikdoms along the Persian Gulf; title of native scholars trained in the traditional sciences such as clerical dignitaries, members of a religious order, professors of spiritual institutions of higher learning, etc.; master; master of an order (Sufism); senator (*parl.*) | الشيخ ارز اسمر (*aruzz asmar*), الشيخ ارز ابيض (*abyaḍ*) (*eg.*) popular names for certain rice dishes; شيخ البحر *š. al-baḥr* sea calf (*zool.*); شيخ البلد *š. al-balad* chief of a village, village mayor; شيخ السجادة *š. as-sajjāda* title of the leaders of certain dervish orders in their capacity of inheritors of the founder's prayer rug; شيخ الاسلام *š. al-islām* sheikh ul-Islam, formerly, esp. in medieval Egypt, title of the Grand Mufti, the spiritual head of Islam, later being bestowed more and more exclusively upon the Mufti of Constantinople in the Ottoman Empire; title of the chief mufti in Tunisia; شيخ المدينة inspector of police (*Maġr.*); مشيخة الجامع الاعظم professoriate, or faculty, of the Great Mosque in Tunis; الشيوخ (pl. of majesty) title of a ruler among the inhabitants of Nejd; مجلس الشيوخ *majlis aš-š.* senate

شيخة *šaiḵa* pl. *-āt* an old, or elderly, woman, a matron

شياخة *šiyāḵa* position, or dignity, of a sheik

شيخوخة *šaiḵūḵa* old age, senility

شيخوخى *šaiḵūḵī* senile, characteristic of old age

مشيخة *mašyaḵa* pl. *-āt*, مشايخ *mašāyiḵ*² office, or dignity, of a sheik; sheikdom (in general, specif., any one of the semi-independent territories on the Persian Gulf); an administrative subdivision (*Tun.*); professoriate (e.g., of Al Azhar)

(شيد) شاد *šāda i* (شيد *šaid*) to erect, set up, construct, build (ه an edifice, and the like) II = I; IV = I; به or اشاد بذكره (*bi-dikrihī*) to celebrate, praise, commend s.o. or s.th., speak in glowing terms of s.o. or s.th.

شيد *šīd* plaster (of a wall); plaster of Paris; mortar

تشييد *tašyīd* erection, setting up, construction, building (of an edifice)

اشادة *išāda* praise, commendation, extolment (ب of)

مشيد *mušayyad* high, lofty, imposing (of a structure)

شيراز *šīrāz*² Shiraz (city in SW Iran)

شيرج *šīraj* sesame oil

شيرة *šīra* a refreshment (made of fruit juice)

شيزوفرانيا *šīzofrāniyā* schizophrenia

¹شيش *šīš* foil, rapier; jalousie, Venetian blind | معلم الشيش *mu'allim aš-š.* fencing instructor; لعبة الشيش *la'bat aš-š.* fencing, swordplay

²شيشة *šīša* bottle of the narghile; narghile, hookah

(شيط) شاط *šāṭa i* (شيط *šaiṭ*) to burn (esp. food) II to burn slightly, singe, scorch, sear (ه s.th.) IV = II; V = I; X استشاط غضبا (*ġaḍaban*) to be or become fuming with rage, flare up, fly off the handle

شيطن II *tašaiṭana* to behave like a devil

شيطان *šaiṭān* pl. شياطين *šayāṭīn*² Shaitan, Satan, devil, fiend

شيطانى *šaiṭānī* satanic, devilish, fiendish; demonic, demoniac, hellish, infernal

شيطنة *šaiṭana* devilry, villainy, dirty trick

(شيع) شاع *šā'a i* (شيع *šai'*, شيوع *šuyū'*) to spread, be divulged, become known, become public (news); to spread (out), diffuse (فى over); to fill, pervade, dominate (ه s.o., s.th.; of a feeling); شاع فى to be generally attributable, be generally applicable to s.th.; شاع به to spread, divulge, publicize, circulate s.th.; make s.th. known, bring s.th. to public notice II to see (ه s.o.) off, escort, accompany (ه s.o.); to bid farewell (ه to s.o.); to pay (ه the deceased) the last honors; to send (ه، ه s.o., s.th.); to adhere (ه to a faction) | شيعت الجنازة *šuyyi'at il-janāzatu* the deceased was escorted to his final resting place, the funeral took place III to follow (ه على s.o. in), adapt o.s. (ه على to s.o. in); to conform, fall in (ه على with s.o. in); to side (ه، ه على with s.o., with s.th. in), take sides (ه، ه على for s.o., for s.th. in) IV to spread, divulge, publish, publicize, make known, bring to public notice, circulate (ب or ه s.th.) V to side (ل فى with s.o., with s.th. in), take sides (ل فى for s.o., for s.th. in), join (ل s.o., s.th., a faction), make common cause, hold (ل with s.o.); to become a Shiite; to pretend to be a Shiite VI to come to an agreement (على in, about)

شيعة *šī'a* pl. شيع *šiya'* followers, adherents, disciples, faction, party, sect; الشيعة the faction of Ali, the Shiah, the Shiites (that branch of the Muslims who recognize Ali, the Prophet's son-in-law, as his rightful successor); pl. اشياع *ašyā'* adherents, followers, partisans

شيعى *šī'ī* Shiitic; (pl. *-ūn*) Shiite

شياع *šiyā'* community (of property) (*jur.*)

شيوع *šuyū'* publicity, spread, circulation (of news) | على الشيوع in common, jointly, in joint possession

شيوعى *šuyū'ī* communistic, communist; (pl. *-ūn*) a communist

شيوعية *šuyū'iya* communism

تشييع *tašyī'*: تشييع الجنازة *t. al-janāza* funeral, burial

مشايعة *mušāya'a* partisanship, partiality

اشاعة *išā'a* spreading, publication, circulation (of news); rumor; news, information

○ اشاعية *išā'īya* collectivism (*pol.*)

تشيع *tašayyu'* partisanship, partiality, bias (ل for)

شائع *šā'i'* widespread; (well-)known, public; general, universal; common, joint | الشائع ان it is rumored that ...; شائع الذيوع widely known, widespread, common; شائع الاستعمال in general use, commonly used, generally accepted; ملك شائع (*milk*) joint property

شائعة *šā'i'a* pl. *-āt*, شوائع *šawā'i'*[2] rumor

مشايع *mušāyi'* partial; adherent, partisan

مشاع *mušā'* widespread; (well-)known, public; general, universal; common, joint; joint (or collective) ownership, joint tenancy (*Isl. Law*); public property, public domain

متشيع *mutašayyi'* partial; partisan

مشتاع *muštā'* partner, co-partner, co-owner

شيف II to cut up, chop or slice (a fruit)

اشياف *ašyāf* (pl.) cuts, slices

شيفون *šifūn* chiffon (fabric)

شيق see شوق

[1]شيك (Fr.) *šīk* chic

اشيك *ašyak*[2] very chic

[2]شيك (Fr. *chèque*) *šēk, šīk* pl. *-āt* check | شيك السياحة traveler's check

شيكوريا (It. *cicoria*) *šikōriyā* chicory

شيكولاته *šikōlāta* (*syr.*) chocolate

[1](شيل) شال *šāla i* to carry, convey, transport (a s.th.); to raise, elevate, lift (a s.th.)

شيلة *šaila* pl. *-āt* load, burden

شيالة *šiyāla* carrying, carriage, conveyance, transportation (of loads); porterage, carrying charges

شيال *šayyāl* pl. *-ūn*, شيالة *šayyāla* porter, carrier

شيالة *šayyāla* suspender

مشال *mašāl* carrying, carriage, conveyance, transportation (of loads); porterage, carrying charges

[2]شال pl. شيلان look up alphabetically

شيلم *šailam* darnel (Lolium temulentum; *bot.*); a variety of vetch

شيلمان *šilmān* (coll.; n. un. ة) steel girders (*ir.*)

شيلى *šīlī* Chile

(شيم) شام *šāma i* to look out (a for), be on the lookout, watch; to expect (a s.th.), hope (a for)

شيمة *šīma* pl. شيم *šiyam* nature, temper, disposition, character; habit, custom, practice

شامة *šāma* pl. *-āt*, شام *šām* mole, nevus, birthmark

شيمية *šimiya* pl. شيامى *šayāmī* (*eg.*) vortex, whirlpool, eddy

مشيمة *mašima* pl. مشيم *mašim*, مشايم *mašāyim*[2] placenta

(شين)[1] شان *šāna* i (شين *šain*) to disfigure, disfeature, mar, dishonor, disgrace (ه, ه s.o., s.th.) | شان سمعته (*sum'atahū*) to detract from s.o.'s good reputation II = I

شين *šain* disfigurement, marring, dishonoring, disgracing; disgrace, shame

شائن *šā'in* dishonorable, scandalous, disgraceful

مشين *mušayyin* dishonorable, scandalous, disgraceful

شين[2] *šīn* name of the letter ش

شاى look up alphabetically

شياه pl. of شاء, see شوه

ص

ص abbreviation of صفحة *ṣafḥa* page (of a book)

ص ب abbreviation of صندوق البريد *ṣundūq al-barīd* post-office box, p. o. b.

صؤاب *ṣu'āb* (coll.; n. un. ة) pl. صئبان *ṣi'bān*, صيبان *ṣībān* nit

صابورة see صبر[2]

صابون see صبن

صاج *ṣāj* thin sheet iron; bread tin, baking tin | صاج مضلع (*muḍalla'*) corrugated iron

يا صاح *yā ṣāḥi* = يا صاحبي *yā ṣāḥibī*

صاد *ṣād* name of the letter ص

صاغ *ṣāġ* in order, right, proper, sound, regular, standard; a rank in army and police (intermediate between captain and major); a naval rank intermediate between lieutenant and lieutenant commander (*Eg.*) | عملة صاغ (*'umla*) standard currency; غرش صاغ (*ġirš*) standard piaster

صاغقول اغاسى (Turk. *sağkol ağası*) military rank intermediate between captain and major (*Eg.*)

صالة (It. *sala*) *ṣāla* pl. *-āt* hall, large room

صالون *ṣālūn* salon, parlor, reception room | عربة صالون *'arabat ṣ.* parlor car, club car

صامولة see صمولة *ṣamūla*

صأى *ṣa'ā* a i (صئى *ṣa'īy*) to twitter, chirp (of a bird)

صب *ṣabba* u (*ṣabb*) to pour, pour forth, cast, empty, fill (ه ق s.th. into); to impose, صب عليه بلاء (*balā'an*) a trial upon s.o. | صب الغارة to commit an assault; — i (*ṣabb*) to be poured out, pour forth, shed, flow (ق into); to befall (على s.o.), come upon s.o. (على); — (1st pers. perf. *ṣabibtu*) a (صبابة *ṣabāba*) to love ardently (ال s.o.) V to pour forth, shed, flow; to drip, overflow (ه with), be bathed (ه in); to dissolve, melt, deliquesce | تصبب عرقا (*'araqan*) to be wet with perspiration, break into a sweat VII to be poured out, pour forth, flow, shed, effuse, gush out; to be intent, be bent (على or ال on), be out for (على or ال); to apply o.s. (على or ال to s.th.), study, endeavor (على or ال to be or do s.th.); to be aimed, directed, oriented (على at), bear upon (على)

صب *ṣabb* pouring; casting, founding (of metal); cast; flow, gush; outpour, effusion; ardently in love, enamored

صبب *ṣabab* pl. اصباب *aṣbāb* declivity; slope, incline, hillside

صبيب *ṣabīb* poured out, shed, spilled; blood; sweat, perspiration

صبابة *ṣabāba* ardent love, fervent longing

صبابة *ṣubāba* rest, remainder, remnant

مصب *maṣabb* pl. *-āt*, مصاب *maṣābb*[2] outlet, escape, drain; mouth (of a river, and the like); drainpipe; funnel

مصبوب *maṣbūb* lead (metal); pl. مصبوبات cast-metal goods, foundry products

صبأ[1] *ṣaba'a a* (صبوء *ṣubū'*) to grow (tooth, nail), sprout (plant); — *ṣaba'a a* to turn (الى to, toward)

صابئ[2] *ṣābi'* Sabian; Mandaean, see the following

الصابئة *aṣ-ṣābi'a* the Sabians, designation of two different sects: 1) the Mandaeans, a Judaeo-Christian gnostic, baptist sect in Mesopotamia (Christians of St. John), used in this sense in the Koran. 2) The Sabians of Harrān, a pagan sect extant as late as the 11th century A. D.

صبح *ṣabaḥa a* (*ṣabḥ*) to offer a morning draught (ه to s.o.); — *ṣabuḥa u* (صباحة *ṣabāḥa*) to be beautiful, graceful, handsome, comely, pretty; to beam, be radiant (face) **II** to offer a morning draught (ه to s.o.); to come in the morning (ه to s.o.); to wish a good morning (على or ه to s.o.) **III** يصابحه ويماسيه he attends to it mornings and evenings, he is constantly, incessantly occupied with it **IV** to enter upon morning; to wake up, be awake, be in one's senses; to be or become clear; to become, be, or happen in the morning; to get (في into a situation), reach a state, come to a point where . . .; to become, grow, turn; to be | اصبح الصباح (*ṣabāḥu*) it became morning; اصبح على خير to have a good morning, begin the day happily; تصبح على خير (*tuṣbiḥ*) parting word at night: may you be well tomorrow morning! يفعله اذا اصبح ويفعله اذا امسى (*amsā*) he does it mornings and evenings, he does it all the time, incessantly; اصبح الحق (*ḥaqqu*) truth has come to light; لم يصبح يفعل he no longer did (so); لم يصبح له وجود it no longer existed **VIII** to have a morning draught; to light (ه s.th., e.g., a lamp); to use for lighting (ب s.th.) **X** to begin the day

صبح *ṣubḥ* pl. اصباح *aṣbāḥ* dawn; daybreak; morning; (ellipt. for صلاة الصبح *ṣalāt aṣ-ṣ.*) morning prayer (at dawn)

صبحة *ṣubḥa* early morning; breakfast, morning meal

صباح *ṣabāḥ* morning; صباحا *ṣabāḥan* in the morning | صباح مساء *ṣabāḥa masā'a* in the morning and in the evening, mornings and evenings; صباح اليوم *ṣabāḥa l-yaum* this morning; صباحك بالخير, صباح بالخير (*bi-l-ḵair*) good morning! عم صباحا (*'im*) do.

صباحى *ṣabāḥī* morning (adj.)

صباح *ṣubāḥ* and صبحان *ṣabḥān*[2], f. صبحى *ṣabḥā* pretty, comely, handsome, beautiful, graceful

صبيح *ṣabīḥ* pl. صباح *ṣibāḥ* pretty, comely, handsome, beautiful, graceful

صباحة *ṣabāḥa* beauty, gracefulness, grace

صبيحة *ṣabīḥa* morning

صبوح *ṣabūḥ* morning draught; beautiful as the early day, radiant, bright

مصباح *miṣbāḥ* pl. مصابيح *maṣābīḥ*[2] lamp; light, luminary (also fig.); headlight (of an automobile) | مصباح الاضاءة

incandescent light, light bulb; مصباح كشاف (*kaššāf*) searchlight; مصباح كهربائى (*kahrabā'ī*) electric light, light bulb; مصباح كهربائى يدوى (*yadawī*) electric flashlight

اصباح *iṣbāḥ* morning

استصباح *istiṣbāḥ* illumination, lighting | غاز الاستصباح illuminating gas

مصبح *muṣbaḥ* morning

[1] صبر *ṣabara* **i** (*ṣabr*) to bind, tie, fetter, shackle (ه s.o.); to be patient, be forbearing, have patience, take patience, persevere; to bear calmly, patiently, stoutly, endure (على s.th.); to refrain, abstain, desist (عن from), renounce (عن s.th.); to hold one's own (ل against s.o.), withstand (ل s.o.) **II** to ask (ه s.o.) to be patient; to admonish (ه s.o.) to be patient; to console, comfort, solace (ه the heart); to make (ه s.th.) durable; to conserve (ه s.th.); to preserve, can (ه s.th.) | صبر بطنه (*baṭnahū*; *eg.*) to have a snack **III** to vie in patience (ه with s.o.); to bear stoutly **V** to be patient, be forbearing, have or take patience, persevere **VIII** = **V**

صبر *ṣabr* fettering, shackling; patience, forbearance; composure, equanimity, steadfastness, firmness; self-control, self-command, self-possession; perseverance, endurance, hardiness | قتله صبرا *qatalahū ṣabran* to kill s.o. in captivity; لا صبر لى (*ṣabra*) I cannot bear it! this is unbearable! قلة الصبر *qillat aṣ-ṣ.* impatience; قليل الصبر impatient; قل صبره *qalla ṣabruhū* to be impatient; to lose patience; لم يبق فى قوس صبرى منزع *lam yabqa fī qausi ṣabrī minza'* (there is no arrow left for the bow of my patience, i.e.) my patience is at an end

صبر *ṣabir*, *ṣabr* aloe (*bot.*)

صبرة *ṣabra* severe cold

صبرة *ṣubra* heap, pile; *ṣubratan* summarily, on the whole, in the lump

صبار *ṣabbār* (very) patient, enduring, perseverant, steadfast

صبار *ṣubār*, *ṣubbār* Indian fig (Opuntia ficus-indica; *bot.*)

صبير *ṣubbair* Indian fig (Opuntia ficus-indica; *bot.*)

صبور *ṣabūr* pl. صبر *ṣubur* (very) patient, enduring, perseverant, steadfast

صبارة *ṣabāra* and *ṣabārra* severe cold

تصبيرة *taṣbīra* (*eg.*) light meal in the forenoon, a snack

مصابرة *muṣābara* long-suffering, longanimity, endurance, perseverance, patience, forbearance

اصطبار *iṣṭibār* patience, forbearance, endurance, perseverance

صابر *ṣābir* patient, long-suffering, enduring, perseverant, steadfast

مصبرات *muṣabbarāt* conserves, canned goods

[2] صبر *ṣabbara* to ballast (ه a ship)

صابورة *ṣābūra* ballast of a ship

صبع *ṣaba'a* **a** (*ṣab'*) to point with the finger (على or ب at); to insert one's finger (ها into the hen, so as to ascertain whether she is going to lay an egg)

اصبع *iṣba'* pl. اصابع *aṣābi'²* finger; toe (also اصبع القدم *i. al-qadam*); a linear measure (*Eg.*; = 3.125 cm) | اصابع من البطاطس French fried potatoes; اصبع الاحمر lipstick; اصابع السجق *a. as-sujuq* frankfurters; بصمة الاصابع *baṣmat al-a.* fingerprint; طابع الاصابع do.; له اصبع فى هذا الامر he has a hand in this matter

صباع *ṣubā'* (*eg.*) finger; toe (also صباع القدم *ṣ. al-qadam*)

اصبوع *uṣbū'* pl. اصابيع *aṣābī'²* finger; toe

مصبع *muṣabba'* gridiron, grill

صبغ *ṣabaḡa u i a* (*ṣabḡ, ṣibaḡ*) to dye, stain (ه s.th., e.g., a fabric), color, tint, tinge, paint, daub (ه s.th.); to give s.th. (ه) the air, touch, or appearance (ب of s.th.); to dip, immerse (ه s.th., ق in water); to baptize (ه s.o.) | صبغه صبغة اخرى (*ṣibḡatan ukrā*) to transform, change s.o. **VIII** to be dyed, be or become colored or tinted; to be baptized, receive baptism

صبغ *ṣibḡ* pl. اصباغ *aṣbāḡ* color, dye, dyestuff; pigment; (coat of) paint, varnish; make-up, grease paint, face paint

صبغة *ṣibḡa* color, dye, dyestuff; pigment; tincture (*med.*); coloring, tinge, tint, shade, hue, nuance, touch, air; nature, character; (coat of) paint, varnish; baptism; religion | صبغة الافيون *ṣ. al-afyūn* tincture of opium, laudanum; صبغة اليود *ṣ. al-yūd* tincture of iodine; صبغة محلية (*maḥallīya*) local touch, local color; اخرجه من صبغته (*akrajahū*) to change, disfigure s.o. or s.th.

○ صبغيات *ṣibḡīyāt* chromosomes

صباغ *ṣibāḡ* pl. اصبغة *aṣbiḡa* color, dye, dyestuff; spice, condiment, seasoning, sauce

صباغ *ṣabbāḡ* dyer

صباغة *ṣibāḡa* dyer's trade, art of dyeing or staining

مصبغة *maṣbaḡa* dyehouse, dye works

صابغ *ṣābiḡ* dyer; baptist | يوحنا الصابغ (*yuḥannā*) John the Baptist

مصبوغ *maṣbūḡ* dyed, stained, colored, tinted; having a touch or air (ب of); influenced (ب by); imbued (ب with)

صبن **II** to soap, rub with soap (ه s.th.)

صابون *ṣābūn* soap | حجر الصابون *ḥajar aṣ-ṣ.* soapstone, steatite

صابونة *ṣābūna* (n. un.) a cake of soap

صابونى *ṣābūnī* soapy, soap-like, saponaceous, made of soap

صبان *ṣabbān* soap boiler

مصبنة *maṣbana* soap works

(صبو) صبا *ṣabā u* (*ṣabw, ṣubūw,* صبا *ṣiban,* صباء *ṣabā'*) to be a child, be childish; — (*ṣubūw,* صبوة *ṣabwa*) to bend, incline (الى to), feel sensual desire (الى for); to strive (الى for), aspire (الى to); — صبى *ṣabiya a* (صباء *ṣabā',* صبا *ṣiban*) to behave like a child, act in a childish manner **II** to rejuvenate, render youthful again **V** to behave like a child, act in a childish manner; to incline to youthful pleasures; to rejuvenesce, undergo rejuvenation, regain youth, become young again; to woo, court (ها a woman); to tempt, entice, captivate, charm (ه s.o., ه the heart) **VI** to behave like a child **X** = **VI**

صبا *ṣaban* pl. صبوات *ṣabawāt,* اصباء *aṣbā'* east wind

صبا, صبى *ṣiban* childhood, boyhood, youth; youthfulness; inclination, propensity, bent, longing, desire

صباء *ṣabā'* childhood, boyhood, youth; youthfulness

صبوة *ṣabwa* youthful passion; amorous disposition; sensual desire; childish manners

صبو *ṣubūw* youthful passion; amorous disposition; sensual desire; childish manners

صبوة *ṣubūwa* childhood, boyhood, youth; youthfulness

صبى *ṣabīy* pl. صبية *ṣibya, ṣabya,* صبيان *ṣibyān, ṣubyān,* اصبية *aṣbiya* boy, youth, lad

صبية *ṣabīya* pl. صبايا *ṣabāyā* girl; young girl

صبيانى *ṣibyānī* boyish, childlike; childish, puerile; children's

صاب *ṣābin* youthful, juvenile, thoughtless, rash

صبو see صبي

صح *ṣaḥḥa* *i* (صحة *ṣiḥḥa*, صحاح *ṣaḥāḥ*) to be healthy; to be all right, be in order; to recover, recuperate (من from); to heal (of a wound); to be sound, strong, vigorous, firm, right, correct, faultless, unimpaired, unblemished; to be firm, unshakable (resolution); to be admissible, permissible; to be true, authentic, certain, sure; to prove true, turn out to be true; to hold good, go (على for), apply (على to), be true (على of); to result or follow definitely (عن from); to be a fact, turn out (ل for); to become a fact; to be successful, work out well (ل for s.o.); to fall to s.o. or to s.o.'s share (ل) | صح عزمه or صحت عزيمته على (*'azmuhū*) he was firmly resolved to . . ., his mind was made up to . . .; يصح الاعتماد عليه it may serve as a basis; يصح ان يقال فيه it is rightly said of him . . .; صح فى الاذهان to appear right, adequate, reasonable **II** to restore to health, cure, heal (ه s.o.); to correct, emend, rectify (ه s.th.); to prepare a critical edition (ه of a text); to legalize, authenticate (ه a document), certify, confirm, attest (ه the authenticity of a document), sign (ه a document); to impose one's signature, undersign (*magr.*) **V** to undergo correction, emendation, rectification, be corrected, emended, rectified **X** to regain health; to recover, recuperate (من from)

صحة *ṣiḥḥa* health; hygiene; faultlessness, rightness, soundness, correctness; truth, genuineness, verity, veracity, credibility, authenticity; validity; legal validity, legality | وزارة الصحة العمومية (*'umūmīya*) Ministry of Public Health (*Eg.*)

صحى *ṣiḥḥī* wholesome, salubrious, healthy, healthful (diet, and the like); sanitary; hygienic | المحجر الصحى (*maḥjar*) quarantine

صحيح *ṣaḥīḥ* pl. صحاح *ṣiḥāḥ*, اصحاء *aṣiḥḥā'*[2], اصحة *aṣiḥḥa* healthy, well, sound, healthful; complete, integral, perfect; whole, entire, undivided; right, correct, proper; true, veritable, actual, real; authentic, genuine, truthful, reliable, credible, believable; valid, legally valid, legal, lawful, rightful; strong (*gram.*; of a consonant, a verb) | جمع صحيح (*jam'*) sound plural (ending in ون *-ūn* or ات *-āt*; *gram*); عدد صحيح (*'adad*) whole number, integer (*math.*); ... صحيح انه (*annahū*) true, he was (he is) . . ., he was (he is), it is true, . . .

اصح *aṣaḥḥ*[2] sounder, healthier; more correct, more proper | او على الاصح or more properly speaking

اصحاح *aṣḥāḥ*, *iṣḥāḥ* chapter of the Holy Scriptures (*Chr.*)

مصح *maṣaḥḥ* pl. *-āt* sanatorium; health retreat, sanitarium

مصحة *maṣaḥḥa* that which promotes or is conducive to health; sanatorium

تصحيح *taṣḥīḥ* correction, rectification; emendation, critical revision

مصحح *muṣaḥḥiḥ* ○ vernier (of a range finder) | المصحح اسفله (*asfalahū*) the undersigned

صحب *ṣaḥiba* *a* (صحبة *ṣuḥba*, صحابة *ṣaḥāba*, *ṣiḥāba*) to be or become a companion, an associate, a comrade, a friend (ه of s.o.), make or become friends, be friends (ه with s.o.); to associate, have social intercourse (ه with s.o.); to accompany, escort (ه s.o.); to be closely associated (ه with s.o.) **III** = **I**; to keep (ه s.o.) company **IV** to send along, delegate as companion or escort (ه ه or ه for s.o. s.o. else or s.th.) **VI** to have social intercourse, associate (مع with); to become friends, be friends (مع with) VIII to accompany, escort (ه s.o.); to take (ه s.o.) as companion or escort, have o.s. escorted or accompanied (ه by s.o.); to take along (ه s.th., ه a companion) X to take as companion or escort, take along

صحبة *ṣuḥba* friendship, companionship, comradeship; accompanying, company, escort; association, intercourse; friends, companions, associates, comrades; (*eg.*) nosegay, bunch of flowers; *ṣuḥbata* accompanied by; with | صحبة هذا (*ṣuḥbata*) herein enclosed

الصحابة *aṣ-ṣaḥāba* the Companions of the Prophet Mohammed

صحابي *ṣaḥābī* a Companion of the Prophet Mohammed

مصاحبة *muṣāḥaba* accompanying, company, escort

اصطحاب *iṣṭiḥāb* accompanying, company, escort; association

صاحب *ṣāḥib* pl. اصحاب *aṣḥāb*, صحب *ṣaḥb*, صحابة *ṣaḥāba*, صحبان *ṣuḥbān*, صحبة *ṣuḥba* associate, companion, comrade, friend; adherent, follower; the other (of two); (with foll. genit.) man, owner, possessor, holder, master, lord, commander, representative, author or originator of ...; entrusted with; addicted or given to; يا صاح *yā ṣāḥi* = يا صاحبي *yā ṣāḥibī* | صاحب الامر *ṣ. al-amr* ruler, master, overlord, sovereign; صاحب البواخر shipowner; صاحب الجلالة *ṣ. al-jalāla* His Majesty; صاحب حال the noun to which a circumstantial phrase (*ḥāl*) refers; صاحب الدولة *ṣ. ad-daula* (formerly) title of the Prime Minister (*Eg.*); صاحب الدين *ṣ. ad-dain* creditor; صاحب الرفعة *ṣ. ar-rif'a* (formerly) title of the Prime Minister (*Eg.*); صاحب السجادة *ṣ. as-sajjāda* title of the leaders of certain dervish orders in their capacity of owners of the founder's prayer rug; صاحب السعادة *ṣ. as-sa'āda* title of a pasha; صاحب السماحة *ṣ. as-samāḥa* title of a mufti, approx. "His Eminence"; صاحب السمو الملكى *ṣ as-sumūw al-malakī* His Royal Highness; اصحاب الشأن *a. aš-ša'n* those concerned; the important, influential people; اصحاب الشبهات *a. aš-šubuhāt* dubious persons, people of ill repute; صاحب الطابع (formerly) Keeper of the Seal (of the Bey of Tunisia); صاحب العزة *ṣ. al-'izza* title of a bey; صاحب العظمة *ṣ. al-'aẓama* His Majesty; صاحب المعالى *ṣ al-ma'ālī* title of a cabinet minister; صاحب العمل *ṣ. al-'amal* employer; صاحب الغبطة *ṣ. al-ġibṭa* title of the Coptic Patriarch; صاحب الفضيلة title of Islamic theologians and sheiks, such as Rector and Professors of Al Azhar University; صاحب الفكرة *ṣ. al-fikra* father to the thought, the originator of an idea; صاحب المقام الرفيع (*ṣ. al-maqām*) formerly, title bestowed on bearers of the order القلادة established by Fuad I in 1936

صاحبة *ṣāḥiba* pl. *-āt*, صواحب *ṣawāḥib*², صواحبات *ṣawāḥibāt* fem. of صاحب woman companion, etc. | صاحبة الجلالة *ṣ. al-jalāla* Her Majesty; صاحبة السمو الملكى *ṣ. as-sumūw al-malakī* Her Royal Highness; صاحبة العصمة *ṣ. al-'iṣma* title of a lady of high social standing

صويحب *ṣuwaiḥib* friend (diminutive of صاحب)

صويحبة *ṣuwaiḥiba* pl. *-āt* girl friend (diminutive of صاحبة)

مصحوب *maṣḥūb* accompanied (ب by); attended (ب with); associated (ب with); provided (ب with)

اصحر *aṣḥar*², f. صحراء *ṣaḥrā'*² desertlike; of the color of desert sand; desolate, bleak

صحراء *ṣaḥrā'*² pl. صحار *ṣaḥārin*, صحاري *ṣaḥārā*, صحراوات *ṣaḥrāwāt* desert, steppe

صحراوى *ṣaḥrāwī* desert, desolate, waste | اراض صحراوية (*arāḍin*) desert areas

صحارة *ṣaḥḥāra* pl. صحاحير *ṣaḥāḥīr*² case, chest, crate, box

صحف II to misplace the diacritical marks; to misread, mispronounce, misspell (ه a word); to misrepresent, distort, twist (ه a report, etc.) V to be misread or misspelled (word)

صحفة *ṣaḥfa* pl. صحاف *ṣiḥāf* bowl, dish, platter

صحيفة *ṣuḥaifa* saucer

صحيفة *ṣaḥīfa* pl. صحف *ṣuḥuf*, صحائف *ṣaḥā'if*² leaf (in a book or notebook), page; newspaper, paper, daily, journal; epidermis; surface; exterior | الصحيفة البيضاء (*baiḍā'*) honorable name, honor

صحفى *ṣuḥufī* newspaper-, news-, press- (in compounds), journalistic; (pl. *-ūn*) newspaperman, journalist | مؤتمر صحفى (*mu'tamar*) press conference

صحافة *ṣiḥāfa* journalism, news business; the press

صحافى *ṣiḥāfī* journalistic; journalist, newspaperman, newsman

صحافية *ṣiḥāfīya* woman journalist

مصحف *maṣḥaf*, *muṣḥaf* pl. مصاحف *maṣāḥif*² volume; book; copy of the Koran (مصحف شريف)

تصحيف *taṣḥīf* misplacement of the diacritical marks; misspelling, slip of the pen; (grammatical) mistake; misrepresentation, distortion

صحل *ṣaḥal* raucous voice

¹صحن *ṣaḥn* pl. صحون *ṣuḥūn* bowl, dish; plate; dish, meal, food; yard, courtyard; surface, plane; disk; (pl. اصحنة *aṣḥina*) phonograph record, disc (*tun.*) | صحن الدار courtyard, patio; صحن السجاير ashtray; على صحن الخد (*ṣ. il-ḵadd*) on the (surface of the) cheek

مصحون *maṣḥūn* ground, brayed, pounded, crushed, grated

²صحناة *ṣaḥnāh* sardine

صحو and (صحى) صحا *ṣaḥā u* (*ṣaḥw*) and صحى *ṣaḥiya a* (صحا *ṣaḥan*) to be or become clear, bright, cloudless, serene (day, sky); — (صحو *ṣaḥw*, *ṣuḥūw*) to regain consciousness, come to; to recover (من from intoxication), sober up; to wake up, awake (من from sleep); to become alert (الى to s.th.), become aware (الى of s.th.) II to wake up, awaken, rouse (ه s.o.) IV to be or become clear, bright, cloudless, serene (day, sky); to wake up, awaken, rouse (ه s.o.)

صحو *ṣaḥw* cloudlessness, brightness, serenity (of the weather); clarity, alertness of the mind, consciousness; bright, serene, cloudless, sunny (weather)

صحوة *ṣaḥwa* awakening, recovery of consciousness; state of consciousness

صاح *ṣāḥin* bright, serene, cloudless, clear (weather); — (pl. *-ūn*, صحاة *ṣuḥāh*) awake, wakeful, watchful, alert, vigilant; conscious; sober

صخب *ṣaḵiba a* (*ṣaḵab*) to shout, cry, yell, clamor, roar, bellow; to scold (على s.o., s.th.); to rage, roar, be loud VIII to raise a din, roar simultaneously, be tumultuous, resound in utter confusion, rage

صخب *ṣaḵab* shouting, roar(ing), bellowing, yelling, clamor, din, hubbub; cry, outcry, yell; raging

صخب *ṣaḵib* crying, yelling, noisy, clamoring, vociferous, roaring, raging

صخاب *ṣaḵḵāb* clamorous, boisterous, roaring, bellowing, raging

اصطخاب *iṣṭiḵāb* noise, din, clamor, hubbub, uproar, tumult, turmoil, roar, raging

صاخب *ṣāḵib* loud, noisy, clamorous, boisterous, vociferous, tumultuous, roaring, raging | قوة صاخبة (*qūwa*) power of the voice

مصطخب *muṣṭakab* noise, din, hubbub, tumult, raging, roar(ing)

صخر *ṣakr* (coll.; n. un. ة) pl. صخور *ṣukūr*, صخورة *ṣukūra*, صخرات *ṣakarāt* rocks, solid rock, boulders, rock formations; pl. صخور rock (*geol.*)

صخرة *ṣakra* boulder, rock | قبة الصخرة *qubbat aṣ-ṣ.* the Dome of the Rock, the Mosque of Omar (in Jerusalem)

صخرى *ṣakrī* rocky, stony

صخر *ṣakir* rocky, stony

صد *ṣadda* *u* (*ṣadd*) to turn away, alienate, discourage, divert, deter, restrain, reject, send away (عن ه s.o. from); to dissuade (عن ه s.o. from his desire); to repel, parry, ward off (ه s.th., e.g., an attack); to hinder, prevent (عن ه s.o. from); to impede, hamper, stop, bring to a standstill (ه s.o.); to resist, oppose (ه s.o.) | لا يصد النظر (*naẓara*) it does not offend the eye, it is nice to look at; — *i u* (*ṣadd*, صدود *ṣudūd*) to turn away (عن from), turn one's back (عن on s.o., on s.th.); to stay away, remain aloof (عن from s.th.) **II** to suppurate, maturate, fester **IV** do. **V** to face, confront (ل s.o.)

صد *ṣadd* averting, turning away; checking, stopping; repulsion, rejection; hindering, impeding, obstruction, prevention; resistance, aversion, reluctance

صدد *ṣadad* nearness, proximity; intention, purpose, design, aim; respect, regard, relation, concern, subject, matter; topic (of a discussion); *ṣadada* (prep.) opposite, in front of | على صدد and بصدد opposite, in front of; فى صدد concerning, regarding, re, with respect to; فى هذا الصدد in this respect, with regard to this, with relation to this, on this occasion, in this connection; هو بصدد امر he is currently busy with s.th., he is at present occupied with a matter; نرجع الى ما نحن بصدده (*narjiʿu*) we return to what is our present concern or to what we are just discussing

صديد *ṣadīd* pus, matter

صديدى *ṣadīdī* suppurative, purulent, festering

صدئ *ṣadiʾa* *a* (صدأ *ṣadaʾ*) and صدؤ *ṣaduʾa* *u* (صداءة *ṣadāʾa*) to become or be rusty, rust, oxidize **II** = **I**; to make (ه s.th.) rusty, cause (ه s.th.) to rust, corrode (ه s.th.)

صدأ *ṣadaʾ* rust; oxidation; smut, rust (plant disease)

صداءة *ṣadāʾa* rustiness

صدئ *ṣadiʾ* rusty, rust-covered; dirty, mean, shabby

مصدأ *muṣdaʾ* rusty, rust-covered

صدح *ṣadaḥa* *a* (*ṣadḥ*, صداح *ṣudāḥ*) to chant, sing; to play (ب a song, a tune)

صدح *ṣadaḥ* banner

صدحات *ṣadaḥāt* (musical) strains

○ صادح *ṣādiḥ* note raised a semitone, a sharp (*mus.*)

صدر *ṣadara* *u i* (صدور *ṣudūr*) to go out, step out (عن or من of, from within); to proceed, emanate, arise, originate, stem (عن or من from), have its origin (عن or من in); to come out, be issued, be promulgated (order, ordinance, law); to appear, be published (book); to leave, go out (mail); to go (الى to); to happen, occur, come to pass; pass. *ṣudira* to have a chest complaint | صدر عن الجد (*jidd*) to set about seriously, get to work earnestly; صدر عن ارادته to act on one's own volition **II** to send, send off, dispatch, forward (ه s.th.); to export (ه s.th.); to publish, bring out (ه a book); to preface (ه a book); to introduce, commence (ب ه a book with)

III to seize, impound, confiscate (ه s.th.); to urge, press, oppress (ه s.o.), throw obstacles in s.o.'s (ه) way IV to send, send out, dispatch (ه s.th.); to export (ه s.th.); to issue (ه s.th., e.g., banknotes, bonds), make out (ه s.th., e.g., a passport); to publish, bring out (ه s.th., e.g., a book); to give, issue (ه an order); to pronounce, pass (ه a legal sentence); to utter, express (ه an opinion, a view) V to be sent, be dispatched; to preside (ه over), head (ه a group); to have a front seat (ه at a social gathering); to resist, oppose (ل s.o.), throw obstacles in s.o.'s (ل) way, stand in s.o.'s (ل) way X to bring about, obtain (ه s.th., esp. حكما *ḥukman* a legal judgment or sentence); to issue (مرسوما an ordinance)

صدر *ṣadr* pl. صدور *ṣudūr* chest, breast, bust; bosom, heart; front part, front; part, portion; first hemistich; leader, commander; beginning, start, outset, commencement, inception; early period, beginnings, dawn (fig.) | صدر الدار one who occupies the highest position in the house, who plays first fiddle in the house; صدر رحب (*raḥb*) generosity, magnanimity; open-mindedness, broad-mindedness, liberality, frankness, candor; صدر الاسلام early period of Islam, early Islam; الصدر الاعظم title of the Grand Vizier in the Ottoman Empire; grand vizier (*Mor.*); صدر المكان *ṣ. al-makān* the foremost part of a room; صدر النهار *ṣ. an-nahār* daybreak, beginning of the day; ابو صدر robin (*zool.*); بنات الصدر *banāt aṣ-ṣ.* worries, anxieties, apprehensions; باب الصدر front door; ذات الصدر chest complaint; bottom of the heart, secret thoughts; رحب الصدر *raḥb aṣ-ṣ.* generous, magnanimous; open-minded, broad-minded, liberal; free of misgivings, unhesitating; رحيب الصدر do.; ضيق الصدر *ḍayyiq aṣ-ṣ.* annoyed, angry (ب at); disgruntled, depressed; منقبض الصدر *munqabiḍ aṣ-ṣ.* dejected, low-spirited, crestfallen; مكانة الصدر *makānat aṣ-ṣ.* first place, precedence, priority; صدرا من الزمان ;رحب الصدر = واسع الصدر (*zamān*) quite a stretch of time, for some time; فى الصدر in the foreground; سخم بصدره (*sakkama*) to irritate s.o., make s.o. angry; انشرح صدره *inšaraḥa ṣadruhū* to be gladdened, be pleased, be cheered, be happy, rejoice

صدرى *ṣadrī* pectoral, chest (used attributively) | نزلة صدرية (*nazla*) bronchitis

صدرة *ṣudra* vest, waistcoat; camisole, (under)waist, bodice

صديرى *ṣudairī* and صديرية pl. *-āt* vest, waistcoat; bodice

صدار *ṣidār* vest, waistcoat; (under-) waist, bodice

صدارة *ṣadāra*, *ṣidāra* precedence; presidency, chairmanship; first place, preeminence; grand vizierate, office, chancellery, or position, of the Grand Vizier (*Mor.*)

صدور *ṣudūr* coming out, appearance, publication (e.g., of a book), issuance (e.g., of an ordinance)

مصدر *maṣdar* pl. مصادر *maṣādir*[2] starting point, point of origin; origin, source (fig.); (*gram.*) infinitive, verbal noun; absolute or internal object

تصدير *taṣdīr* sending (off), dispatch, forwarding; exportation, export; preface, foreword (of a book); issuance

مصادرة *muṣādara* seizure, confiscation

اصدار *iṣdār* exportation, export; issue, issuance, bringing out, edition, publication; making out, issuance | مصرف الاصدار *maṣrif al-i.* bank of issue

استصدار *istiṣdār* issue, making out; issuance

صادر *ṣādir* going out, emanating, originating; issued, come out, published, etc.; exportation, export; yield; الصادرات export goods, exports

مصدور *maṣdūr* affected with a pectoral ailment, phthisical, consumptive, tubercular

مصدِّر *muṣaddir* export merchant, exporter

صدع *ṣada'a a* (*ṣad'*) to split, cleave, part, sunder (ه s.th.); to crack, break (ه an object), cause (ه an object) to crack; to break (ه through obstacles), conquer, overcome, surmount (ه obstacles, difficulties) | صدع بالحق (*ḥaqq*) to come out openly with the truth; صدع بأمر (*amr*) to execute an order, comply with an order; pass. *ṣudi'a* to have or get a headache II to cause a headache (ه to s.o.); to molest, harass, trouble (خاطره *kāṭirahū* s.o.); pass. *ṣuddi'a* to have or get a headache V to get split, get cleft, come apart, burst, break, crack; to go to pieces; to reel, waver, be shaken; to separate (عن from), part (عن with) VII to get split, get cleft, come apart, break, crack; to be rudely interrupted; to break, dawn (morning)

صدع *ṣad'* pl. صدوع *ṣudū'* crevice, fissure, crack, break, rift, cleft

صداع *ṣudā'* headache

مصدوع *maṣdū'* having a crack, cracked, broken

صدغ *ṣudḡ* pl. اصداغ *aṣdāḡ* temple (*anat.*); earlock, lovelock (also قصة الصدغ *quṣṣat aṣ-ṣ.*)

صدغى *ṣudḡī* temporal (*anat.*)

صدف *ṣadafa i u* (*ṣadf*, صدوف *ṣudūf*) to turn away (عن from), avoid, shun (عن s.o., s.th.); — *i* (*ṣadf*) to turn (ه s.o.) away (عن from), discourage, restrain, deter (عن ه s.o. from); to happen by chance III to find (ه, ه s.o., s.th.), meet (ه s.o., ه with s.th.); to meet unexpectedly, by chance (ه s.o.), light (ه, ه on), come across s.o. or s.th. (ه, ه), run into s.o. or s.th. (ه, ه), encounter (ه, ه s.o., s.th.); to coincide, be coincident, concur (ه with s.th.); to fall (ه on a given date); to happen by chance, come to pass (ان that) | صادف الاستحسان to meet with approval; صادف محله (*maḥallahū*) to come in handily, be convenient, be opportune V to turn away (عن from), avoid, shun (عن s.o., s.th.) VI to happen by chance, come to pass

صدف *ṣadaf* (coll.; n. un. ة) pl. اصداف *aṣdāf* pearl oyster, sea shell, conch | صدفة الاذن *ṣ. al-uḏun* external ear, auricle, pinna

صدف *ṣadaf*, مرض الصدفية *maraḍ aṣ-ṣadafīya* a noncontagious skin disease, psoriasis (*med.*)

صدفى *ṣadafī* sea-shell, shell (adj.); nacreous, mother-of-pearl (adj.)

صدفة. *ṣudfa* pl. صدف *ṣudaf* chance, haphazard, coincidence, unexpected concurrence; صدفةً *ṣudfatan* by chance, by coincidence, accidentally | بالصدفة or بطريق الصدفة by chance, by coincidence, accidentally; as chance will have it, haphazardly

مصادفة *muṣādafa* pl. *-āt* encounter, meeting; chance, haphazard, coincidence, unexpected concurrence; *muṣādafatan* by chance, by coincidence, accidentally

مصادف *muṣādif* corresponding (ل to), concurrent (ل with a date of another chronological system), coincident (ل with), falling (ل on a given date)

صدق *ṣadaqa u* (*ṣadq*, *ṣidq*) to speak the truth, be sincere; to tell (ه s.o.) the truth (عن about); to prove to be true, turn out to be correct, come true; to be right; to fit exactly (على s.o. or s.th.), apply (على to), hold true (على of) |

وعده or صدق فى وعده (*fī waʿdihī* or *waʿdahū*) to keep, or fulfill, one's promise; صدقه النصيحة (*naṣīḥata*) to advise s.o. sincerely; صدقه الحب (*ḥubba*) to love s.o. sincerely, truly **II** to deem (ه, ه s.o., s.th.) credible, accept (ه s.th.) as true, give credence (ه, ه to s.o., to s.th.), believe, trust (ه, ه s.o., s.th.); to consider or pronounce (ه s.th.) to be true, right, correct or credible; to believe (ب in); to give one's consent, to consent, assent, agree (على to s.th.), approve (على of s.th.), grant, license, sanction, certify, confirm, substantiate, attest, ratify, authenticate, legalize, verify (على s.th.) | لا يصدق (*yuṣaddaqu*) incredible, unbelievable, unreliable, untrustworthy; صدق او كذب *ṣaddiq au kaddib* (as an affirmative parenthesis) believe it or not **III** to treat (ه s.o.) as a friend; to maintain one's friendship (ه with s.o.); to be or become friends (ه with s.o.), befriend (ه s.o.); to give one's consent, to consent, assent, agree (على to s.th.), approve (على of), grant, license, sanction, certify, confirm, substantiate (على s.th.); to legalize, authenticate (على a signature, etc.) **IV** to fix a (bridal) dower (لها for a woman) **V** to give alms (على to s.o.); to give as alms, donate (على to s.o., ب s.th.)

صدق *ṣidq* truth, trueness, truthfulness; sincerity, candor; veracity, correctness (of an allegation); efficiency; صدقا *ṣidqan* truly, really, in truth

صدقة *ṣadaqa* pl. *-āt* alms, charitable gift; almsgiving, charity, voluntary contribution of alms, freewill offering; legally prescribed alms tax (*Isl. Law*) | صدقة الفطر *ṣ. al-fiṭr* almsgiving at the end of Ramadan (*Isl. Law*)

صداق *ṣadāq*, *ṣidāq* pl. صدق *ṣuduq*, اصدقة *aṣdiqa* (bridal) dower; — (pl. اصدقة) marriage contract (*tun.*)

صداقة *ṣadāqa* pl. *-āt* friendship

صديق *ṣadīq* pl. اصدقاء *aṣdiqāʾ*[2], صدقاء *ṣudaqāʾ*[2], صدقان *ṣudqān* friend; friendly, connected by bonds of friendship

صدوق *ṣadūq* veracious, truthful, honest, sincere

صديق *ṣiddīq* strictly veracious, honest, righteous, upright; الصديق epithet of the first Caliph, Abū Bakr

اصدق *aṣdaq*[2] truer, sincerer | اصدق برهان على (*a. burhānin*) the most reliable, or best, proof for . . .; اصدق صديق the most loyal, or best, friend

مصداق *miṣdāq* confirmation, corroboration, substantiation; touchstone, criterion

تصديق *taṣdīq* belief, faith (ب in); consent, assent, agreement (على to), approval, sanctioning, licensing, certification, confirmation, attestation, ratification, verification, authentication, legalization (على of s.th.) | سرعة التصديق *surʿat at-t.* credulity; سريع التصديق credulous

مصادقة *muṣādaqa* consent, assent, agreement (على to), concurrence (على in); approval, sanctioning, certification, confirmation, attestation, ratification (على of s.th.); legalization, authentication (على of a document)

تصادق *taṣāduq* legalization, authentication (على of a document)

صادق *ṣādiq* true, truthful, veracious, sincere, candid; reliable; accurate, true, genuine, faithful, authentic

مصدقة *muṣaddiqa* certificate, certification, attestation

مصدق *muṣaddaq* credible, believable, reliable, trustworthy | غير مصدق incredible; مصدق عليه رسميا (*rasmīyan*) legalized, officially certified

صيدل look up alphabetically

صدم *ṣadama i* (*ṣadm*) to bump, strike, knock, dash, bounce, bang, run (ه, ه against), hit (ه upon); to run (ه into s.o., e.g., an automobile, etc.); to collide, clash (ب with, e.g., train with car) III to bump, strike, knock, dash, bounce, bang, run (ه, ه against s.o. or s.th.); to resist, oppose (ه, ه s.o., s.th.), battle (ه, ه against); to encounter (hostilely), clash; pass. صودم *ṣūdima* to be severely afflicted (ب by) VI to collide (e.g., trains), encounter (armies); to clash, conflict (e.g., different opinions) VIII to collide, clash (ب or مع with); to bump, strike, run (ب against), hit (ب s.th., e.g., a mine); to take offense (ب at, e.g., at mistakes), take exception (ب to); to fail (ب due to), be thwarted (ب by); = VI

صدمة *ṣadma* pl. *ṣadamāt* push, thrust, jolt, shock, blow, stroke; upset, commotion, (psychic) shock; obstacle, difficulty

صدام *ṣidām* collision, clash; breakdown, collapse | صدام وجدانى (*wijdānī*) mental breakdown

مصادمة *muṣādama* pl. *-āt* collision, clash, impact

تصادم *taṣādum* collision, clash; bounce, impact (ب on); upset, commotion, (psychic) shock | طاسة التصادم buffer (railroad)

اصطدام *iṣṭidām* collision, clash; bounce, impact (ب on); upset, commotion, (psychic) shock

صدى *ṣadiya a* (*ṣadan*) to be very thirsty IV to echo, resound, reverberate V to occupy o.s. (ل or الى with); to turn, apply o.s. (ل or الى to s.th.); to undertake (ل or الى s.th.), embark (ل or الى upon); to oppose, resist, counteract, antagonize (ل s.o.), throw obstacles in s.o.'s (ل) way, be in s.o.'s (ل) way

صدى, صدا *ṣadan* pl. اصداء *aṣdā'* echo, reverberation

تصدية *taṣdiya* hand clapping

صر *ṣarra i* (*ṣarr*, صرير *ṣarīr*) to chirp, stridulate (cricket); to creak (door); to squeak, screech; to grate, scratch; to gnash, chatter (teeth); to lace, cord, tie up, truss up, bind (ه s.th.); to shove, put (ه في money into a purse); to prick up (ه or ب one's ears) IV to persist (على in), insist (على on); to make up one's mind, resolve, determine, decide (على to do s.th.); to prick up (ه or ب one's ears)

صرة *ṣurra* pl. صرر *ṣurar* (money) bag, purse; bundle, packet, parcel | الصرة or صرة الحرمين *ṣ. al-ḥaramain* the *ṣurra* for Mecca and Medina, the traditional funds sent by the different Islamic countries (nowadays, e.g., by Egypt and Tunisia) with the hadj caravan to be distributed among the poor of Mecca and Medina; امين الصرة the Trustee of the *ṣurra* (who is responsible for its delivery); صرة النقود cash remittance

صرير *ṣarīr* chirping, stridulation (of crickets); squeaking, screeching

صرار *ṣarrār* or صرار الليل *ṣ. al-lail* cricket (*zool.*)

صريرة *ṣarīra* coins wrapped in a purse

اصرار *iṣrār* persistence, perseverance (على in), insistence (على on) | سبق الاصرار *sabq al-i.* premediation, willfulness (*jur.*)

مصر *muṣirr* persistent, insistent; determined, resolute

الصرب *aṣ-ṣirb* Serbia; the Serbs

صربى *ṣirbī* Serbian

صرح *ṣaruḥa u* (صراحة *ṣarāḥa*, صروحة *ṣurūḥa*) to be or become pure, unadulterated, uncontaminated, clear; — *ṣaraḥa a* (*ṣarḥ*) to make clear, clarify, explicate, explain (ه s.th.) II to explain, explicate, clarify, make clear (ه s.th.); to declare, state, announce (ب s.th.), make a statement (ب about); to speak out frankly, openly, be clear, be explicit (ب, عن about), let (ب, عن s.th.) be known; to allow, permit, grant (ل ب to s.o. s.th.); to license (ب s.th.), give a permit, grant a license (ب for) III to speak frankly, openly; to speak out frankly or openly, be clear, be explicit (ب about), avow (ب s.th.), let (ب s.th.) be known; to declare (ه ان to s.o. that) IV to make clear, clarify, explicate, explain (ه s.th.) VI to become clear, evident, manifest, come to light VII to become evident, manifest, clear

صرح *ṣarḥ* pl. صروح *ṣurūḥ* castle, palace, lofty edifice, imposing structure

صراح *ṣurāḥ* pure, unadulterated, uncontaminated, clear; distinct, plain, obvious, evident, patent, manifest, unambiguous, unequivocal

صريح *ṣarīḥ* pl. صرحاء *ṣuraḥā'*[2], صرائح *ṣarā'iḥ*[2] pure, unadulterated, uncontaminated; clear; distinct, plain, obvious, evident, patent, manifest, unambiguous, unequivocal; open, frank, sincere, candid; free, openhearted

صراحة *ṣarāḥa* clearness, clarity, distinctness, plainness; unambiguousness; openness, frankness, candor, sincerity, openheartedness; *ṣarāḥatan* clearly, plainly, distinctly, patently, unequivocally, unambiguously; openly, frankly, bluntly, straightforward, honestly, openheartedly

اصرح *aṣraḥ*[2] purer, clearer; sincerer

تصريح *taṣrīḥ* pl. *-āt*, تصاريح *taṣārīḥ*[2] (public) statement, declaration; permission, (official) permit, license

[1]صرخ *ṣaraḵa u* (صراخ *ṣurāḵ*, صريخ *ṣarīḵ*) to cry, yell, scream, shriek, shout; to cry for help; to call (ب s.o.); to call out, shout (على to s.o.); to yell, bellow, roar (ق or ق وجهه at s.o.) | صرخ صرخة (*ṣar-ḵatan*) to cry out, let out a cry X to cry for help; to call (ه to s.o.) for help

صرخة *ṣarḵa* pl. *-āt* cry, outcry, yell, scream; call for help

صراخ *ṣurāḵ* crying, yelling; clamor, screaming, screams

صريخ *ṣarīḵ* crying, yelling; clamor, screaming, screams

صراخ *ṣarrāḵ* crier, screamer, bawler; peacock

صاروخ *ṣārūḵ* pl. صواريخ *ṣawārīḵ*[2] rocket; siren (*maḡr.*) | صاروخ عابر ○ القارات intercontinental ballistic missile, ICBM

قنبلة صاروخية *qunbula ṣārūḵīya* rocket bomb, guided missile

صارخ *ṣāriḵ* gaudy, flashy (color); glaring (color, light); crude, gross, coarse; noisy, loud; crier, caller

صرد *ṣard* severe cold (spell)

صراد *ṣurrād* drifting clouds, cirrus

صريد *ṣurraid* drifting clouds, cirrus

صرصر *ṣarṣara* to let out a piercing cry, scream shrilly

ريح صرصر *rīḥ ṣarṣar* violent, cold wind, icy gale

صرصر *ṣurṣur* pl. صراصر *ṣarāṣir*[2] a variety of cockroach (Blatta aegyptiaca; *zool.*); cricket (*zool.*)

صرصور *ṣurṣūr* pl. صراصير *ṣarāṣīr*[2] cricket (*zool.*); cockroach (*syr.*)

صرصار *ṣarṣār* cricket (*zool.*)

صراط *ṣirāṭ* way, path, road

صرع *ṣara'a a* (*ṣar'*, *ṣir'*, مصرع *maṣra'*) to throw down, fell, bring to the ground (ه s.o.); — pass. *ṣuri'a* to be epileptic, have an epileptic fit; to be or go mad

III to wrestle (also as a sport), fight (ه with s.o.) VI to wrestle with one another VII to be or go mad VIII = VI

صرع *ṣar'* epilepsy

صرع *ṣur'* rein

صريع *ṣarī'* pl. صرعى *ṣar'ā* thrown to the ground, felled; epileptic; demented, insane, mad, crazy; (with foll. genit.) succumbing to s.th., fallen victim to s.th., | سقط صريعا to be killed (in battle); صريع الشراب *ṣ. aš-šarāb* addicted to the bottle; صريع الكرى *ṣ. al-karā* overcome by sleep

مصرع *maṣra'* pl. مصارع *maṣāri'*[2] battle-ground; ruin, destruction, perdition, death; fatal accident; vital part of the body (the injury of which can cause death)

مصراع *miṣrā'* pl. مصاريع *maṣārī'*[2] leaf of a door; hemistich | صفائح المصراع door panel; الباب مفتوح على مصراعيه (*miṣrā'aihi*) the door is wide open

صراع *ṣirā'* wrestling, wrestling match; fight, struggle

مصارعة *muṣāra'a* wrestling, wrestling match; fight, struggle

اصطراع *iṣṭirā'* fight, struggle, conflict, controversy

مصروع *maṣrū'* thrown to the ground, felled; epileptic; demented, insane, mad, crazy

مصارع *muṣāri'* wrestler; fighter

صرف *ṣarafa* i (*ṣarf*) to turn; to turn away, avert (عن ,ه ,ه s.o., s.th. from); to dissuade, alienate, keep away (عن ه s.o. from); to divert, distract (عن ه s.o. from); to turn, direct (الى ه s.th., e.g., one's eyes, one's attention, to s.th.); to grant leave, dismiss, send away (ه s.o.); to give s.o. (ه) the brush-off; to spend, expend (على ه money for); to defray the cost (على of s.th.), pay (على for s.th.); to pay out, disburse (ل ه money to); to issue, give out (ه s.th., e.g., tickets), make out (ه s.th., e.g., a permit); to spend, devote (ل or الى or في ه time, effort on); to pass, spend (في ه time at s.th., doing s.th.); to change money (ه); to inflect (ه a word) | صرف النظر عن (*naẓar*) to avert one's glance from, disregard s.th., pay no attention to s.th., leave s.th. out of consideration; — i (صريف *ṣarīf*) to creak, grate II to cause to flow off, draw off (ه water); to drain (ه land); to dispatch, expedite, wind up, liquidate (ه business); to change money (ه); to market, retail, distribute, sell (ه merchandise), dispose (ه of merchandise); to circulate (ه s.th.); to give a free hand (في ه to s.o. in s.th.), let (ه s.o.) dispose freely (في over, in), grant the right of disposal (في ه to s.o. over or in s.th.); to inflect (ه a word), conjugate (ه a verb), decline (ه a noun) V to act independently; to dispose freely, have the right of disposal (في over); to move freely, act without restriction (في in), administer (freely) (في s.th.); to behave, act, conduct o.s., comport o.s.; to exercise sacerdotal functions (*Copt.-Chr.*); to be inflected (*gram.*); to be derived | تصرف تصرفا كيفيا في (*taṣarrufan kaifīyan*) to proceed arbitrarily in or at VII to turn away; to go away, depart (عن from), leave (عن s.th.); to give up, abandon, relinquish, quit (عن s.o., s.th.); to flow off, drain; to pass on, change over, turn one's attention (الى to s.th.); to proceed (الى to some activity or to do s.th.); to apply o.s., devote o.s. (الى to s.th.); to be spent, be expended (money); to be issued, be made out (e.g., ticket); to be fully, i.e., triptotically, inflected | انصرف الى نفسه to withdraw by o.s., isolate o.s.; انصرف يفعل to set about to do s.th., proceed to do s.th.

صرف *ṣarf* averting, turning away; expenditure, expense; spending, use, application (e.g., of time, of effort, etc.); issuance, issue, making out; disbursement; money changing; barter (*Isl. Law*); drainage; inflection (*gram.*); (pl. صروف *ṣurūf*) adversities, misfortunes (also صروف الدهر *ṣ. ad-dahr*) | محطة الصرف *maḥaṭṭat aṣ-ṣ.* (*el.*) power station; drainage station, pumping station; سعر الصرف *si'r aṣ-ṣ.* exchange rate; علم الصرف *'ilm aṣ-ṣ.* morphology (*gram.*); ممنوع من الصرف indeclinable (*gram.*); بصرف النظر عن (*bi-ṣ. in-naẓar*) regardless of, irrespective of, notwithstanding, to say nothing of

صرف *ṣirf* pure, unadulterated, unmixed; mere, sheer, absolute

صرفيات *ṣarfīyāt* payments, disbursements

صريف *ṣarīf* squeak(ing), creak(ing), squeal(ing)

صراف *ṣarrāf* money changer; cashier, teller, treasurer; paymaster; banker

صرافة *ṣarrāfa* (woman) cashier | صرافة التذاكر (woman) ticket agent

صيرف *ṣairaf* pl. صيارف *ṣayārif*[2] money changer; cashier, teller, treasurer

صيرفى *ṣairafī* pl. صيارفة *ṣayārifa* money changer; cashier, teller, treasurer

صريفة *ṣarīfa* pl. صرائف *ṣarā'if*[2] reed-mat hut

مصرف *maṣrif* pl. مصارف *maṣārif*[2] drainage canal, drainage ditch, drain; bank; pay office, teller's window (at a bank)

تصريف *taṣrīf* drawing off (of water), drainage; sale, retail, disposal, distribution; change, alteration; inflection, declension, conjugation | تصاريف الدهر *t. ad-dahr* the vicissitudes of fate; تصريف الشئون settlement, windup, or management, of affairs

تصرف *taṣarruf* pl. *-āt* free disposal (فى over), right of disposal; usufruct; administration; action, way of acting, demeanor, behavior, conduct; outflow, efflux, effluence, output (in terms of the capacity of a pump), discharge, throughput, quantity of water flowing through; pl. تصرفات measures, dispositions, regulations | تصرف منجز (*munjaz*) regulation effective immediately (*Isl. Law*); حسن التصرف *ḥusn at-t.* discretion; مطلق التصرف *muṭlaq at-t.* having unrestricted right of disposal, invested with full power; بتصرف freely; تحت تصرفه at s.o.'s disposal; وضع شيئا تحت تصرفه to put s.th. at s.o.'s disposition; تصرفات الزمن *t. az-zaman* the vicissitudes of time

انصراف *inṣirāf* going away, leave, departure; avertedness, aversion (عن to); abstention (عن from), renunciation (عن of)

مصروف *maṣrūf* devoted, dedicated (الى to s.th.); money spent, expenditure; pl. *-āt*, مصاريف *maṣārīf*[2] expenses, expenditures, costs | مصروف البريد and مصاريف البريد postage; مصروف الجيب *m. al-jaib* pocket money; خالص المصاريف postage free, franked; وفى المصاريف (*wafā*) to cover the costs, defray the expense; مصروف من الخدمة (*kidma*) dismissed, discharged

متصرف *mutaṣarrif* approx.: provincial governor (*Ir.*; administering any one of the 14 *liwā'*, q.v.); former title of a Turkish administrative officer in Arab countries

متصرفية *mutaṣarrifīya* jurisdiction of a *mutaṣarrif* (q.v.), approx.: province; dignity, government, authority, etc., of a *mutaṣarrif*.

منصرف *munṣarif* fully inflected, i.e., triptotical (*gram.*); المنصرف the money spent, expenditures

منصرف *munṣaraf* departure, leave, going away | لا منصرف عنه (*munṣarafa*)

indispensable, inevitable; منصرفهم *munṣarafahum* at their departure, when they left; فى منصرف النهار (*m. in-nahār*) at the parting of day, at day's end

[1]صرم *ṣaruma u* (صرامة *ṣarāma*) to be sharp; to be stern, hard, harsh, severe; — *ṣarama i* (*ṣarm, ṣurm*) to cut, cut off, sever (ه s.th.); to leave, forsake (ه s.o.), separate (ه from s.o.), part (ه with s.o.) **II** to cut, cut off, cut through, sever, separate (ه s.th.) **V** to decrease, wane, dwindle; to elapse, go by, pass; to be past, be bygone, be over (time) **VII** to elapse, go by, pass; to be past. be bygone, be over (time)

صرم *ṣarm* severance, separation

صرمة *ṣirma* pl. صرم *ṣiram* herd of camels

صرامة *ṣarāma* sharpness, keenness; harshness, sternness, severity, rigor, unfriendliness

صريمة *ṣarīma* horse bridle

مصارمة *muṣārama* estrangement, break, antagonism, hostility

صارم *ṣārim* sharp, harsh, hard, severe, stern

منصرم *munṣarim* elapsed, past, bygone (period of time)

[2]صرم *ṣurm* = سرم

[3]صرمة *ṣarma* pl. صرم *ṣuram* (*eg.*) shoe

صرماية *ṣurmāya* pl. *-āt*, صرامى *ṣarāmī* (*syr.*) shoe made of red or yellow leather; shoes

مصر see مصارين

صار *ṣārin* and صارية *ṣāriya* pl. صوار *ṣawārin* mast, pole | صارى العلم *ṣ. l-ʿalam* flagpole

مصطبة *maṣṭaba, miṣṭaba* pl. مصاطب *maṣāṭib*[2] outdoor stone bench (built into the side of a house), mastaba

مصطول *maṣṭūl* fool

صعب *ṣaʿuba u* (صعوبة *ṣuʿūba*) to be hard, difficult (على for); to be embarrassing, shocking, unpleasant (على for, to) **II** to make hard, make difficult (ه ل for s.o. s.th.); to present as difficult (ه ل to s.o. s.th.) **V** to become difficult; to make (ه s.th.) hard or difficult **VI** to be difficult (of a person); to be hard to please **X** to find or consider difficult (ه s.th.)

صعب *ṣaʿb* pl. صعاب *ṣiʿāb* hard, difficult; pl. difficulties | صعب الاحتمال hard to bear, oppressive; صعب الارضاء *ṣ. al-irḍā'* hard to please, fastidious; صعب المراس obstinate, stubborn, self-opinionated, recalcitrant, headstrong; عملة صعبة (*ʿumla*) hard currency

صعوبة *ṣuʿūba* difficulty | صعوبة المراس obstinacy, stubbornness, recalcitrance, refractoriness

مصاعب *maṣāʿib*[2] difficulties

صعتر *ṣaʿtar* wild thyme (Thymus serpyllum; *bot.*)

صعد *ṣaʿida a* (صعود *ṣuʿūd*) to rise, go up; to lift, climb, ascend, slope upward; to mount, scale, ascend, climb (ه s.th.), climb up (ه on s.th.); to take off (airplane); صعد به الى to make s.o. ascend, lead s.o. up to . . . **II** to ascend, mount; to go upstream; to travel to Upper Egypt; to send up (ه s.o.); to cause (ه s.th.) to rise or ascend; to heave (from one's breast), utter (ه sigh, wails, and the like); to cause (ه s.th.) to evaporate, vaporize, volatilize (ه s.th.); to sublimate (ه s.th.; *chem.*) | صعد الزفرات (*zafarāt*) to heave deep sighs **IV** to make (ه s.o.) ascend or advance; to ascend (الى to elevated terrain); to go upstream; to travel up, travel **V** to evaporate, vaporize **VI** to rise, lift, ascend

صعد *ṣuʿd* height, altitude

صعدة *ṣaʿda* pl. *ṣaʿadāt* rise, incline; slope, declivity

صعود *ṣuʿūd* rising, lifting, ascending; take-off (of an airplane); ascent; boom; advance (الى toward) | صعود الرب *ṣ. ar-rabb* and عيد الصعود *ʿīd aṣ-ṣ.* Ascension Day (*Chr.*)

صعود *ṣaʿūd* steep hill

صعيد *ṣaʿīd* pl. صعد *ṣuʿud* highland, upland, plateau; الصعيد and صعيد مصر *ṣ. miṣr* Upper Egypt | فى صعيد واحد on a common basis, on common ground, on equal footing, without distinction, indiscriminately; على صعيد واحد congenial, like-minded, kindred in spirit, agreed

صعيدى *ṣaʿīdī* pl. صعايدة *ṣaʿāyida* Upper Egyptian

صعداء *ṣuʿadāʾ*[2] (deep) sigh | تنفس الصعداء *tanaffasa ṣ-ṣuʿadāʾa* to sigh (deeply), heave a (deep) sigh

مصعد *maṣʿad* pl. مصاعد *maṣāʿid*[2] point of ascent

مصعد *miṣʿad* pl. مصاعد *maṣāʿid*[2] elevator, lift; ○ anode

مصعدة *miṣʿada* elevator, lift

صاعد *ṣāʿid* pl. صواعد *ṣawāʿid*[2] rising, ascending (also, e.g., of vapors) | فصاعدا *fa-ṣāʿidan* and beyond that, and more; من — فصاعدا from — on, from — upward; من الآن فصاعدا (*min al-āna*) from now on, henceforth

متصاعد *mutaṣāʿid* rising, ascending (also, e.g., of vapors)

صعر *ṣaʿira a* (*ṣaʿar*) to be awry (face; with pride) **II** صعر خده (*kaddahū*) to put on a contemptuous mien

صعق *ṣaʿaqa a* (صاعقة *ṣāʿiqa*) to strike s.o. (ه) down with lightning, destroy, hit, slay (ه s.o.; of lightning); to stun, stupefy, make unconscious (ه s.o.); — *ṣaʿiqa a* and pass. *ṣuʿiqa* (*ṣaʿaq*, صعقة *ṣaʿqa*) to be thunderstruck; to lose consciousness | صعق فى مكانه (*makānihī*) to stop dead in one's tracks, stand as if thunderstruck **IV** to strike down, slay, destroy (ه s.o.; of lightning); to stun, stupefy, make unconscious (ه s.o.) **VII** to be struck by lightning

صعق *ṣaʿaq* thunder, peal of thunder

صعق *ṣaʿiq* thunderstruck, dumfounded

صاعقة *ṣāʿiqa* pl. صواعق *ṣawāʿiq*[2] bolt of lightning, thunderbolt

مصعوق *maṣʿūq* struck by lightning; thunderstruck, stupefied, dumfounded; crushed, destroyed

صعلكة *ṣaʿlaka* loitering, loafing

صعلوك *ṣuʿlūk* pl. صعاليك *ṣaʿālīk*[2] utterly destitute; have-not, pauper, poor wretch; beggar; tramp, vagabond, loafer

صغر *ṣaḡura u* (*ṣiḡar*, صغارة *ṣaḡāra*) and *ṣaḡira a* (*ṣaḡar*) to be or become small, little, scanty; to diminish, decrease, wane, dwindle; to be young; to be lowly, submissive, servile, humble; — *ṣaḡara u* (*ṣaḡr*) to be younger (ه ب than s.o. by) | ما صغرنى الا بسنة (*bi sanatin*) he was only one year younger than I **II** to make small(er) or little(r), lessen, minimize, reduce, diminish, decrease (ه s.th.); to belittle, deride, ridicule, debase, bemean (ه, ه s.o., s.th.); to form a diminutive (ه of a noun) **VI** to prove o.s. contemptible, be servile, fawn, cringe, grovel **X** to deem (ه, ه s.o., s.th.) small, little or paltry; to make light (ه, ه of s.o., of s.th.), undervalue (ه, ه s.o., s.th.); to think little (ه, ه of s.o., of s.th.) | استصغر نفسه (*nafsahū*) to feel inferior

صغر *ṣiḡar* smallness, littleness, scantiness, paltriness, paucity, insignificance; youthfulness, juvenility (also صغر السن *ṣ. as-sinn*)

صغرة *ṣiḡra*: هو صغرة ابويه (*ṣ. abawaihi*) he is the youngest of his parents' children

صغير *ṣaḡīr* pl. صغار *ṣiḡār*, صغراء *ṣuḡarā'*[2] small, little; paltry, scanty, insignificant; tiny, minute; young, juvenile, minor; a minor, one under age | صغير السن *ṣ. as-sinn* young; صغير النفس *ṣ. an-nafs* mean-spirited, base, servile, toadying, cringing, groveling صغار الموظفين *ṣ. al-muwaẓẓafīn* small officials, subaltern officials; العيد الصغير (*'īd*) Little Bairam, i.e., the feast of fast breaking on the 1st of Shawwal; كل صغيرة وكبيرة *kullu ṣ. wa-kabīra* every detail

صغيرة *ṣaḡīra* pl. صغائر *ṣaḡā'ir*[2] venial sin (*Isl. Law*); minor mistake; pl. trivialities, trifles

صغارة *ṣaḡāra* littleness, paltriness, scantiness, paucity; lowliness, servility, humility, humbleness

اصغر *aṣḡar*[2], f. صغرى *ṣuḡrā*, pl. m. اصاغر *aṣāḡir*[2] smaller, littler; younger | اصغر الشرين *a. aš-šarrain* the lesser of two evils; آسيا الصغرى Asia Minor; الدول الصغرى (*duwal*) the small countries; سوريا الصغرى (*sūriyā*) Palestine; النهاية الصغرى the minimum

تصغير *taṣḡīr* diminution, lessening, decrease, reduction | اسم التصغير *ism at-t.* diminutive (*gram.*)

اصغار *iṣḡār* disdain, contempt, disregard

تصاغر *taṣāḡur* servility, toadying, cringing, groveling

صاغر *ṣāḡir* low, lowly, despised, contemptible; humiliated, meek, dejected; submissive, servile; subject (ل to s.o.)

مصغر *muṣaḡḡar* reduced, decreased, diminished | في صورة مصغرة (*ṣūra*) on a reduced or small scale, in miniature; فلم مصغر (*film*) microfilm

صغا *ṣaḡā* *u* (صغو *ṣaḡw*, *ṣuḡūw*) and صغى (صغو) to incline, bend, lean (الى to, toward); — صغى *ṣaḡiya* *a* (*ṣaḡan*, *ṣuḡīy*) to incline, bend, lean (الى to, toward); to listen (ل to) IV to listen, pay attention, lend one's ear (ل or الى to s.th., to s.o.), heed (ل or الى s.th.)

صغو *ṣaḡw* and صغا *ṣaḡan* inclination, disposition, tendency; affection, attachment, good will

اصغاء *iṣḡā'* attention, attentiveness

صاغ *ṣāḡin* inclined, disposed; attentive; listener, hearer

مصغ *muṣḡin* attentive; listener, hearer

[1]صفة see وصف

[2]صف *ṣaffa* *u* (*ṣaff*) to set up in a row or line, line up, align, array, arrange, order (ه s.th.); to set, compose (ه type, *typ.*); to range, class, classify (ه مع s.o. among); to cut (ه s.th.) in strips II to set up in a row or line, line up, align, array, arrange, order (ه s.th.); to comb (ه the hair) straight VI to line up, take position in a row or line, stand in a row or line, be lined up, be aligned, be strung in a line VIII = VI; to fall in, stand in formation (of a military detachment) | اصطف الى جانب الطريق to line the road, form a lane (e.g., troops, police, etc.)

صف *ṣaff* aligning or arranging in a line or row; — (pl. صفوف *ṣufūf*) row, line, file, rank, queue; row, or tier, of seats; grade, form (in school); class, course; section, division, group | صف الدم *ṣ. ad-dam* blood group; آلة صف الحروف typesetting machine; ضابط الصف (also صف ضابط pl. صف ضباط) noncommissioned officer; انتظم صفوفا *intaẓama ṣufūfan* to line up in rows or files

صفة *ṣuffa* pl. صفف *ṣufaf* (stone) molding; ledge

صفاف *ṣaffāf* and صفاف الحروف typesetter, compositor

مصف *maṣaff* pl. مصاف *maṣāff*[2] position (of an army); battle line; row, line, file; composing stick (*typ.*) | رفعه الى مصاف (with foll. genit.) to class s.o. with, put s.o. on the same level with

صفح *ṣafaḥa a* (*ṣafḥ*) to broaden, widen, flatten, beat into a leaf, foliate, plate (ه s.th.); to pardon, forgive (عن s.o., s.th.) **II** to broaden, widen, flatten, beat into a leaf, foliate (ه s.th.); to roll out (ه s.th.); to plate, overlay, or cover, with metal plates (ه s.th.); to armor (ه s.th.); to equip, furnish, cover (ه ب s.th. with) **III** to shake hands (ه with s.o.); to greet (ه s.o.); to touch (ه s.th.) lightly or gently, graze (ه s.th.), brush, glide (ه over s.th.), pass, blow (ه over s.th., of the wind, breath, etc.) | صافح سمعه (*sam'ahū*) to reach s.o.'s ear **V** to leaf, thumb (ه a book, etc.); to examine, scrutinize, regard, study (ه s.th.) **VI** to shake hands **X** to ask s.o.'s (ه) forgiveness (ه for), apologize (ه ه to s.o. for)

صفح *ṣafḥ* pardon, forgiveness; (pl. صفاح *ṣifāḥ*) side, surface | ضرب (اضرب) عنه صفحا to turn away from s.o. or s.th., pass over s.o. or s.th., ignore, snub, slight, disregard s.o. or s.th., desist from s.th.

صفحة *ṣafḥa* pl. *ṣafaḥāt* outside, exterior; plane, surface; page; leaf, sheet; phase

صفيح *ṣafīḥ* broad side or surface; sheet iron; tin, tinplate; tin plates, tin sheets

صفيحة *ṣafīḥa* pl. صفائح *ṣafā'iḥ*[2] plate, sheet (of metal), leaf (of wood), slab, flag (of stone), ledger stone (on a tomb); tin plate, tin sheet; can, jerry can | صفائح المصراع *ṣ. al-miṣrā'* door panel; ○ صفائح المقول *ṣ. al-miqwal* phonograph records, gramophone discs

صفوح *ṣafūḥ* forgiving, ready to forgive

صفاح *ṣuffāḥ* pl. *-āt*, صفافيح *ṣafāfīḥ*[2] plate, sheet, leaf; flagstone, stone slab

تصفيح *taṣfīḥ* plating

تصفح *taṣaffuḥ* examination, scrutinization, scrutiny, study

مصفح *muṣaffaḥ* shaped into plates or thin layers, plated, foliated; armored, armor-clad, ironclad, metal-covered | خشب مصفح (*kašab*) plywood; سيارة مصفحة (*sayyāra*) armored car

مصفحة *muṣaffaḥa* pl. *-āt* armored car, armored reconnaissance car (*mil.*)

صفد *ṣafada i* (*ṣafd*) to bind, fetter, shackle (ه s.o.) **II** and **IV** = **I**

صفد *ṣafad* pl. اصفاد *aṣfād* bond, tie, fetter

صفاد *ṣifād* bond, tie, fetter | صفاد اليدين *ṣ. al-yadain* manacle, handcuff

صفر[1] *ṣafara i* (صفير *ṣafīr*) to whistle (bird, person); to hiss (snake); to chirp, stridulate (cricket); to scream (siren) **II** = **I**

صفير *ṣafīr* whistling, whistle, etc. (see above); high, thin tone (e.g., of a flute) | حروف الصفير sibilants; — see also below and alphabetically

صفارة *ṣaffāra* pl. *-āt* whistle; siren | صفارة الامان *ṣ. al-amān* all-clear siren; صفارة الانذار *ṣ. al-indār* warning siren

صفر[2] **II** to dye yellow, make yellow, to yellow (ه s.th.) **IX** to turn yellow, to yellow; to pale, become pale | اصفر وجهه (*wajhuhū*) he grew pale, he turned white

صفر *ṣufr* brass; money

صفر *ṣafar* iaundice

صفرة *ṣufra* yellow color, yellowness, yellow; pallor, paleness (of the face)

صفار *ṣafār* yellow color, s.th. yellow; pallor, paleness | صفار البيضة *ṣ. al-baiḍa* egg yolk

صفار *ṣaffār* pl. ة brass founder

اصفر *aṣfar*², f. صفراء *ṣafrā'*², pl. صفر *ṣufr* yellow; pale, pallid, wan | ضحكة صفراء (*ḍaḥka*) forced, or embarrassed, laugh; نحاس اصفر (*nuḥās*) brass

صفراء *ṣafrā'*² bile, gall

صفير (*eg.*) golden oriole (*zool.*)

صفارية *ṣufārīya* golden oriole (*zool.*)

صفراوى *ṣafrāwī* bilious; choleric | الحمى الصفراوية (*ḥummā*) yellow fever; ضحكة صفراوية (*ḍaḥka*) bitter, or sardonic, laugh (= Fr. *rire jaune*)

اصفرار *iṣfirār* yellowing, yellow; pallor, paleness (of the face)

مصفر *muṣfarr* yellow-colored; pale, pallid, wan

³صفر *ṣafira a* (*ṣafar*, صفور *ṣufūr*) to be empty, be devoid, vacant (من of) | صفرت يده من الشىء (*ṣafirat yaduhū*) to have lost s.th. **II** to empty, void, vacate, evacuate, free (ه s.th.) **IV** = **II**

صفر *ṣafr*, *ṣifr*, *ṣufr*, *ṣafir*, *ṣufur* pl. اصفار *aṣfār* empty, void, devoid, (من of), free (من from) | صفر اليدين *ṣifr al-yadain* empty-handed

صفر *ṣifr* zero, naught; nothing

اصفر *aṣfar*² empty, void

مصفر *muṣfir* empty-handed | مصفر اليد *m. al-yad* with an empty hand; مصفر اليد من كل شىء without any possessions at all, completely destitute

⁴صفر *ṣafar* pl. اصفار *aṣfār* Safar, name of the second month of the Mohammedan year

¹صفصاف *ṣafṣāf* (coll.; n. un. ة) a variety of willow (Salix Safsaf F.; *bot.*)

²صفصف *ṣafṣaf* even, level; waste, desolate, barren, empty | قاع صفصف wasteland, desolate area; جعله قاعا صفصفا to devastate s.th., lay s.th. waste

صفع *ṣafa'a a* (*ṣaf'*) to cuff, buffet, slap lightly (ه s.o.); to slap s.o.'s (ه) face, box s.o.'s (ه) ears; to violate (ه a rule) **VI** to slap one another

صفعة *ṣaf'a* (n. vic.) slap, cuff, smack; blow

صفاع *ṣaffā'* pl. *-ūn* a kind of buffoon

صفق *ṣafaqa i* (*ṣafq*) to slap, smack (ه, ه s.o., s.th.); to set into motion (ه s.th.); to flap, clap; to shut, slam, bang (ه a door); — *ṣafuqa u* (صفاقة *ṣafāqa*) to be thick, heavy, close in texture (cloth) **II** to flap, clap, smack; to clap one's hands (also بيديه), applaud (ل s.o.); to flap (ب the wings)

صفقة *ṣafqa* pl. *ṣafaqāt* handclasp (in concluding a deal); conclusion of a contract (*Isl. Law*); deal, bargain, transaction | صفقة خاسرة poor deal, bad bargain; صفقة رابحة favorable deal, good bargain; صفقة واحدة *ṣafqatan wāḥidatan* all at once, wholly, entirely, altogether; اعطى صفقة (*a'ṭā*), عقد صفقة to conclude a bargain, effect a transaction; عاد (رجع) بصفقة المغبون or) to lose the game, return empty-handed; كانت له الصفقة الخاسرة do.

صفاق *ṣifāq* pl. صفق *ṣufuq* dermis, underskin; peritoneum

صفيق *ṣafīq* pl. صفاق *ṣifāq* thick, heavy, close in texture (cloth) | صفيق الوجه *ṣ. al-wajh* impudent, insolent, brazen

صفاقة *ṣafāqa* impudence, insolence, brazenness

تصفيق *taṣfīq* hand clapping; applause, acclaim | تصفيق الاستحسان applause

صفاكس *ṣafākis*² Sfax (seaport in Tunisia)

[1]صفن *ṣafana* i to stand with one foot (ب) slightly raised; to pore, brood, ponder, reflect, muse

صفن *ṣafan* pl. اصفان *aṣfān* scrotum

[2]صفين *ṣafīn* savin (Juniperus sabina; *bot.*)

(صفو) صفا *ṣafā* u (*ṣafw, ṣufūw*, صفاء *ṣafā'*) to be or become clear, unpolluted, limpid, cloudless, untroubled, serene, undisturbed, pure; صفا ل to apply o.s. to s.th. with clear intent, devote o.s. wholeheartedly to, be completely given to, be solely preoccupied with, be exclusively ready for (heart, mind) **II** to make clear, limpid, pure, clarify, clear, purify (ه s.th.); to settle, straighten out (مسألة *mas'alatan* a question, a problem); to remove the water, pour off the water (ه from s.th., e.g., in cooking; also صفاه من الماء); to rid of moisture, dry out (ه s.th.); to clarify, purify, rectify (ه s.th., من by removing s.th.); to filter, strain (ه s.th.); to settle, pay, liquidate (ه s.th.); to realize (ه assets) **III** to be sincere (ه toward s.o), deal honestly (ه with s.o.) **IV** = **III** (ه or ل); to be no longer in a position (to ...), possess no longer, forfeit; to cease composing poetry (poet) | اصفاه بالشيء to have s.o. in mind for s.th., choose, select, or single out s.o. for s.th., grant s.o. s.th. in preference to others, bestow upon s.o. s.th. (دون فلان which others do not have) **VI** to be sincere toward one another, be honest with one another, be of pure intent toward one another **VIII** to choose, select (ه s.o.) **X** = **VIII**; to deem (ه s.th.) clear or pure | استصفى ماله to realize all one's assets; to confiscate s.o.'s property

صفو *ṣafw* clearness, clarity, limpidity, untroubledness, cloudlessness, serenity, purity, sheerness; happiness, felicity, pleasure, delight; clear, limpid; untroubled, undisturbed, serene, pure, sheer

صفوة *ṣafwa, ṣufwa* the best, or choicest, part, prime, cream, flower, elite, quintessence

صفا *ṣafan* (coll.; n. un. صفاة *ṣafāh* pl. صفوات *ṣafawāt*) stone(s), rock(s)

صفوان *ṣafwān* stones, rocks

صفوة *ṣifwa* sincere friend, best friend, bosom friend

صفاء *ṣafā'* clearness, clarity, limpidity, untroubledness, cloudlessness, serenity, purity, sheerness; happiness, felicity, serenity, gaiety, cheerfulness; sincerity, candor, honesty | ساعات صفاء pleasant time, delightful hours

صفي *ṣafīy* clear, limpid, untroubled, undisturbed, serene, cloudless, pure, sheer; (pl. اصفياء *aṣfiyā'*[2]) sincere friend, best friend, bosom friend

صفية *ṣafīya* pl. صفايا *ṣafāyā* leader's share of the loot; lion's share of the booty

مصفى *maṣfan* refinery

مصفى *miṣfan* sieve

مصفاة *miṣfāh* pl. مصاف *maṣāfin* strainer, colander, filter; strainer cloth; sieve; refinery, purification plant | مصفاة القهوة coffee filter, percolator

تصفية *taṣfiya* pl. *-āt* clarification, clearance, purification (also fig.); filtering, filtration; elimination (also in sports); settlement, straightening out, adjustment; clearing (*com.*); liquidation (*com.*); clearance sale | تصفية الحسابات *t. al-ḥisābāt* settlement of accounts; مأمور التصفية official receiver, receiver in equity

مصافاة *muṣāfāh* cordiality, concord, harmony; good will, sincere attitude or disposition

تصاف *taṣāfin* peaceful settlement, compromise (بين between)

اصطفاء *iṣṭifā'* selection (also *biol.*)

استصفاء *istiṣfā'*: استصفاء الاموال sequestration of property

صاف *ṣāfin* clear, limpid; sheer, pure, straight, unmixed, undiluted, unadulterated; untroubled, undisturbed; serene; pure; net | صافى النية *ṣ. n-nīya* sincere, candid, openhearted; صافى الحمولة net tonnage; صافى الارباح net profit

مصف *muṣaffin* official receiver, receiver in equity; clarifier, clarifying agent

مصفى *muṣaffan* purified, pure, clear, limpid, cloudless

مصطفى *muṣṭafan* chosen, selected; المصطفى epithet of Mohammed

صفير *ṣafīr* sapphire

صقالة (It. *scala*) *ṣaqāla* pl. صقائل *ṣaqā'il*² scaffold; gangway, gangplank

صقب III to approach (ه s.o.), go or come near (ه s.o.); to be neighbors (ه with s.o.), be adjacent (ه to s.th.), adjoin (ه s.th.)

○ مصاقبة *muṣāqaba* affinity

¹صقر *ṣaqr* pl. صقور *ṣuqūr*, اصقر *aṣqur* saker, falcon, hawk

²صاقور *ṣāqūr* stone axe

صقع *ṣaqa'a a* (*ṣaq'*, صقاع *ṣuqā'*) to crow (rooster); pass. *ṣuqi'a* to be covered with hoarfrost (ground) II to be icy, ice-cold, frozen

صقع *ṣuq'* pl. اصقاع *aṣqā'* area, region, country, district, locality, land | الاصقاع المتجمدة الجنوبية (*mutajammida, janūbīya*) the Antarctic

صقعة *ṣaq'a* frost, severe cold

صقيع *ṣaqī'* frost; ice; hoarfrost

اصقع *aṣqa'*² more eloquent

مصقع *miṣqa'* pl. مصاقع *maṣāqi'*² eloquent; loud-voiced, having a stentorian voice

¹صقل *ṣaqala u* (*ṣaql*, صقال *ṣiqāl*) to smooth, polish, burnish, cut (ه s.th.); to refine (ه style, taste, and the like) VII to become smooth

صقل *ṣaql* polishing, burnishing | صقل الاذهان mental training

صقيل *ṣaqīl* polished, burnished; smooth, shiny, glossy

صقال *ṣaqqāl* polisher, smoother

صيقل *ṣaiqal* pl. صياقلة *ṣayāqila* polisher, smoother

مصقلة *miṣqala* pl. مصاقل *maṣāqil*² burnisher (tool)

مصقول *maṣqūl* polished, burnished; cut (glass, and the like); acute, refined (wit)

²صقالة look up alphabetically

صقلب *ṣaqlab* pl. صقالبة *ṣaqāliba* Slav

صقلية *ṣiqillīya*² Sicily

¹صك *ṣakka u* (*ṣakk*) to beat, strike; to shut, lock (ه the door) | صكت به الآذان his ears were tingling or ringing; صك سمعه (*sam'ahū*) to strike s.o.'s ear (noise); to roar in s.o.'s ears VIII to knock together, shake, tremble (knees), chatter (teeth)

²صك *ṣakk* pl. صكوك *ṣukūk*, صكاك *ṣikāk*, اصك *aṣukk* (instrument of) contract (*Isl. Law*); legal instrument, document, deed; check, cheque

¹صلة see وصل

²صل *ṣalla i* (صليل *ṣalīl*) to ring, clink, clank, clatter, rattle

صل *ṣill* pl. اصلال *aṣlāl*, صلال *ṣilāl* a variety of venomous adder, viper

صليل *ṣalīl* rattle, clatter, clash (e.g., of weapons), jingling (of coins)

[1]صلب *ṣaluba u* (صلابة *ṣalāba*) and *ṣaliba a* to be or become hard, firm, solid, stiff, or rigid, solidify, harden, set, stiffen **II** to make hard, firm, solid, stiff, or rigid, harden, solidify, stiffen, indurate (ه, ه s.o., s.th.); to support, prop, shore up (ه s.th.); to harden (ه the heart) **V** = **I**; to show o.s. hard or severe

صلب *ṣulb* hard, firm, solid, stiff, rigid; steel; — (pl. اصلب *aṣlub*, اصلاب *aṣlāb*) spinal column, backbone; loins; — text, body (of a book, and the like) | صلب الرأى *ṣ. ar-ra'y* obstinate, stubborn, headstrong, opinionated; صلب الرقبة *ṣ. ar-raqaba* do.; صلب العود *ṣ. al-'ūd* of robust physique, strongly built, husky, sturdy; stubborn, resistant, unbending, unyielding, relentless; هو ابن صلبه (*ibn ṣulbihī*) and هو من صلبه he is his own son, his offspring; درامة مستخرجة من صلب الحياة (*mustakraja min ṣulbi l-ḥayāh*) a drama taken from real life; فى صلبه at heart, in his innermost

صلبة *ṣulba*: صلبة العين *ṣ. al-'ain* sclera (*anat.*)

صليب *ṣalīb* hard, firm, solid, stiff, rigid

صلابة *ṣalāba* hardness, callousness; hardening, induration; firmness, solidity, stiffness, rigidity; stubbornness, obstinacy, unyieldingness; intolerance | صلابة العود *ṣ. al-'ūd* sternness, severity, hardness, obstinacy, stubbornness, inflexibility, relentlessness

تصلب *taṣallub* hardness, callousness, hardening | تصلب الشرايين *t. aš-šarāyīn* arteriosclerosis

متصلب *mutaṣallib* unyielding, inflexible, relentless, hard

[2]صلب *ṣalaba i* (*ṣalb*) to crucify (ه s.o.) **II** = **I**; to make the sign of the cross (على over); to cross o.s.; to cross, fold (ه one's arms)

صلب *ṣalb* crucifixion

صليب *ṣalīb* pl. صلبان *ṣulbān*, صلب *ṣulub* cross | الصليب الجنوبى (*janūbī*) the Southern Cross (*astron.*); الصليب الاحمر the Red Cross; صليب معقوف swastika; شارة الصليب and اشارة الصليب sign of the cross (*Chr.*); عود الصليب *'ūd aṣ-ṣ.* peony (Paeonia; *bot.*)

صليبي *ṣalībī*: الحروب الصليبية the crusades; الصليبيون the crusaders

صلبوت *ṣalbūt* (representation of the) crucifixion, crucifix

مصلب *muṣallab* crossing, interjunction (of roads)

صلت *ṣaluta u* (صلوتة *ṣulūta*) to be glossy, be smooth and shining **IV** to draw, unsheathe (السيف *as-saifa* the sword); pass. *uṣlita* to be drawn (sword)

[1]صلج *ṣullaj* (coll.; n. un. ة) pl. *-āt* cocoon, chrysalis of the silkworm

[2]صولجان look up alphabetically

صلح *ṣalaḥa u a* (صلاح *ṣalāḥ*, صلوح *ṣulūḥ*, مصلحة *maṣlaḥa*) and *ṣaluḥa u* (صلاح *ṣalāḥ*, صلاحية *ṣalāḥiya*) to be good, right, proper, in order, righteous, pious, godly; to be well, thrive; to be usable, useful, practicable, serviceable, fitting, suitable, or appropriate (ل for), lend itself (ل to), suit, match (ل s.th.), fit (مع s.th. or s.o.), apply (مع to s.o. or s.th.); to be admissible, permissible (مع in, at, with); to be valid, hold true (ل for) **II** to put in order, settle, adjust, restore, restitute (ه s.th.), make amends, compensate (ه for); to mend, improve, ameliorate, fix, repair (ه s.th.) **III** to make peace, become reconciled, make up, reach a compromise or settlement (ه with s.o.); to foster peace (بين between), reconcile (بين people) **IV** to put in order, settle, adjust (من or ه s.th.), overhaul, restore, restitute, rebuild, reconstruct; to make amends, compensate (من or

ه for); to mend, improve, ameliorate, fix, repair (من or ه s.th.); to make suitable or fitting, adjust, modify (ه s.th.); to reform (من or ه s.th.); to remove, remedy (من or ه s.th.); to make arable or cultivable, reclaim, cultivate, till, (ه land); to further, promote, encourage (ه s.o.), make (ه s.o.) thrive or prosper, bring good luck (ه to s.o.); to make peace (بين between), bring together (بين people), bring about an agreement (بين between), conciliate (بين people) **VI** to make peace, make up, become reconciled with one another **VII** to be put in order, be righted, be corrected, be improved, be ameliorated **VIII** = **VI**; to agree (على on), accept, adopt (على s.th.) **X** to deem (ه s.th.) good, proper, suitable, fitting, usable, useful, practicable, or serviceable; to make arable, cultivable, reclaim (ه land)

صلح *ṣulḥ* peace, (re)conciliation, settlement, composition compromise; peace (*pol.*), peacemaking, conclusion of peace | حاكم الصلح (*Syr.*) justice of the peace; قاضى الصلح do.; قضوية الصلح *qaḍawīyat aṣ-ṣ.* jurisdiction of the قاضى الصلح

صلحى *ṣulḥī* of peace, peace (adj.); arbitrative, arbitrational, arbitration- (in compounds) | لجنة صلحية (*lajna*) arbitration committee

صلاح *ṣalāḥ* goodness, properness, rightness; usability, practicability, usefulness; righteousness, probity, piety, godliness

صلاحية *ṣalāḥiya* suitability, fitness, appropriateness, aptness; efficiency; usability, practicability, usefulness, use, worth; serviceability, proper or working condition (e.g., of a machine); competence; validity, applicability; (pl. *-āt*) full or mandatory power, power of attorney, also صلاحية تامة (*tāmma*) | جهات ذات الصلاحية competent authorities; مطلق الصلاحية *muṭlaq aṣ-ṣ.* plenipotentiary (*dipl.*)

صلوحية *ṣulūḥīya* = صلاحية *ṣalāḥiya*

اصلح *aṣlaḥ*[2] better, more proper, more correct; more pious, godlier; fitter, more suitable

مصلحة *maṣlaḥa* pl. مصالح *maṣāliḥ*[2] matter, affair; requirement, exigency; that which is beneficial, helpful, or promoting; advantage, benefit, interest, good, welfare; office, authority, department, governmental agency, administration (chiefly *Eg.*) | مصلحة الآثار المصرية (*miṣrīya*) Administration of Egyptian Antiquities; مصالح الامة *m. al-umma* the welfare of the people; مصلحة البريد postal administration; مصلحة الحدود administrative agency for the territories outside the cultivated area (*Eg.*); المصالح الحكومية (*ḥukūmīya*) the governmental agencies; مصلحة الصحة *m. aṣ-ṣiḥḥa* health office; المصلحة العامة (*ʿāmma*) public welfare, commonweal; فى مصلحة فلان in s.o.'s interest; فى المصلحة والمفسدة (*mafsada*) in good and bad times, for better or for worse; لمصلحة فلان in s.o.'s favor, for the benefit of s.o., to s.o.'s advantage, on behalf of s.o., in s.o.'s interest; خدم مصالح فلان to serve s.o.'s interests

مصلحى *maṣlaḥī* administrational, official, governmental

تصليح *taṣlīḥ* pl. *-āt* restoration, restitution, mending, fixing, overhauling, repair, improvement, amelioration

مصالحة *muṣālaḥa* peace, conciliation; compromise; composition, settlement

اصلاح *iṣlāḥ* pl. *-āt* restoration, restitution, redressing, reparation; improvement, amelioration, betterment, mending, correction; reconstruction; reconditioning, repair; renovation, refurbishing; adjustment, settling, remedying, removal, elimination; restoration of order, establishment of peace, happiness and order; reformation, reform; reclamation, cultivation (of land); (re)conciliation, settlement, compromise, peacemaking (بين between)

اصلاحى **iṣlāḥī** reformatory, reformational, reform- (in compounds); reformer, reformist | معهد اصلاحى (*ma'had*) reformatory, house of correction

اصلاحية **iṣlāḥīya** revisionism, reformism; (pl. *-āt*) reformatory, house of correction

تصالح **taṣāluḥ** (re)conciliation

اصطلاح **iṣṭilāḥ** pl. *-āt* agreement, convention, practice, usage; (colloquial, linguistic) usage; technical term, terminus technicus

اصطلاحى **iṣṭilāḥī** conventional; technical (of a term)

استصلاح **istiṣlāḥ** reclamation, cultivation

صالح **ṣāliḥ** good, right, proper, sound; thorough, substantial, downright, out-and-out, solid; virtuous, pious, devout, godly; usable, useful, practicable, serviceable, fitting, suitable, appropriate (ل for); (pl. صوالح *ṣawāliḥ²*) advantage, benefit, interest, good, welfare | السلف الصالح (*salaf*) the worthy ancestors, the venerable forefathers; صالح السير (*sair*) passable, practicable (road); صالح للعمل (*'amal*) fit for action, ready for use, serviceable, practicable; valid (ل for), applicable (ل to); الصالح العام (*'āmm*) public welfare, commonweal; فى صالح (with foll. genit.) in favor of, for the benefit of, to the advantage of, in the interest of s.o. or s.th.; لصالح do.; كان من صالحه it was in his interest; صوالح شخصية (*šaḵṣīya*) personal interests

الصالحات **aṣ-ṣāliḥāt** the good works, the good deeds

مصالح **muṣāliḥ** peacemaker, conciliator

مصلح **muṣliḥ** peacemaker, conciliator; reformer, reformist; salt

مصطلح **muṣṭalaḥ** and مصطلح عليه generally accepted, universally followed, commonly established, conventional, customary; (pl. *-āt*) technical term, terminus technicus

صلد **ṣalada** (صلادة *ṣalāda*, صلودة *ṣulūda*) to be or become hard, firm, solid, compact (ground) IV = I

صلد **ṣald** pl. اصلاد *aṣlād* hard, firm, solid, dry, barren, arid (ground); rigid, lifeless, inert

صلودة **ṣulūda** hardness, firmness, solidity (of the ground)

صلصة (It. *salsa*) **ṣalṣa** pl. *-āt* and صلص sauce | صلصة مايونيز mayonnaise

صلصل **ṣalṣala** to ring, clink, clank; to clatter, rattle II *taṣalṣala* do.

صلصلة **ṣalṣala** clank(ing), clatter(ing), clash, rattle

صلصال **ṣalṣāl** dry clay, argillaceous earth

مصلطح *muṣalṭaḥ* = مسلطح shallow, shoal, flat

صلع **ṣali'a** *a* (*ṣala'*) to be bald

صلع **ṣala'** baldness

صلعة **ṣul'a**, *ṣala'a* bald pate, bald head

اصلع **aṣla'²**, f. صلعاء *ṣal'ā'²*, pl. صلع *ṣul'*, صلعان *ṣul'ān* bald(-headed)

صلعم abbreviation of the eulogy following the name of the Prophet Mohammed: صلى الله عليه وسلم (*ṣallā, sallam*) God bless him and grant him salvation!

صلف **ṣalifa** *a* (*ṣalaf*) to boast, brag, bluster, swagger V = I

صلف **ṣalaf** vainglory, bragging, boasting, conceit, arrogance, pomposity, self-importance

صلف *ṣalif* pl. صلفاء *ṣulafā'*[2] vainglorious, bragging, boastful, showing off, pompous, blustering, swaggering; braggart, boaster, show-off, swaggerer, fourflusher

تصلف *taṣalluf* vainglory, bragging, boasting, conceit, arrogance, pomposity, self-importance

متصلف *mutaṣallif* vainglorious, bragging, boastful, showing off, pompous, blustering, swaggering

صلو II to perform the salat (صلوة see below), pray, worship | صلى بالناس to lead people in prayer; صلى على to pray for; (of God) to bless s.o.: صلى الله عليه وسلم (*sallam*) God bless him and grant him salvation! (eulogy after the name of the Prophet Mohammed)

صلوة, صلاة *ṣalāh* pl. صلوات *ṣalawāt* salat, the official Islamic prayer ritual; intercession, intercessory prayer, benediction; blessing, grace (of God) | الصلاة الربانية (*rabbānīya*) the Lord's prayer; صلاة التراويح a prayer performed during the nights of Ramadan; صلاة الستار vesper prayer (*Chr.*)

مصل *muṣallin* prayer, worshiper

مصلى *muṣallan* place of prayer, oratory

صلون *ṣalūn* salon, parlor, reception room

صلى *ṣalā i* (*ṣaly*) to roast, broil, fry (ه s.th.); — *ṣaliya a* (*ṣalan, ṣulīy,* صلاء *ṣilā'*) to burn (intr.; ب or ه in); to be exposed to the blaze of (ب or ه) II to warm, heat (ه ب s.th. with or on) IV = II (ه ه s.th. on or with); to make (ه s.o.) burn (ه in, esp. النار in the fire) | اصلاه نارا من الغيرة (*ḡaira*) to make s.o. undergo the most excruciating pangs of jealousy; اصلاه نارا to set s.th. on fire; to fire at s.o. or s.th. (*mil.*) V to warm o.s., seek warmth (ب at, by, بالنار by the fire) VIII = V | لا يصطلى بناره (*yuṣṭalā bi-nārihī*) invincible, a great hero

مصطلى *muṣṭalan* fireplace

صم *ṣamma* (1st pers. perf. *ṣamimtu*) *a* (*ṣamm,* صمم *ṣamam*) to be or become deaf; — *ṣamma* (1st pers. perf. *ṣamamtu*) *u* (*ṣamm*) to close, plug, cork, stopper (ه s.th., e.g., a bottle) II to deafen (ه s.o.); to make up one's mind (على to do s.th.), determine (على upon, to do s.th.), resolve, be determined (على to do s.th.), decide (على on, to do s.th.); to persist (على in); to design (ه s.th.); to plan (ه s.th.), design (ه ل s.th. for) IV to be or become deaf; to deafen (ه s.o.), make (ه s.o.) deaf (ه, عن to s.th.) VI to give a deaf ear (عن to)

صمة *ṣimma* plug, cork, stopper

صمم *ṣamam* deafness | كان فى صمم عن to be deaf to s.th.

صمام *ṣimām* pl. *-āt* plug, cork, stopper; valve; tube (*radio*) | صمام الامان (الامن) *ṣ. al-amān* (*al-amn*) safety valve; ○ صمام التقويم rectifier tube; رفع الصمام عن to let s.th. take its course, give free rein to s.th. (also to a feeling)

○ صمامة *ṣammāma* embolism (*med.*)

صميم *ṣamīm* innermost, heart; core, essence, marrow, pith; true, sincere, genuine | من صميم القلب (*ṣ. il-qalb*) from the bottom of the heart, wholeheartedly, most sincerely; ... فى صميم amid, in; ضربه فى الصميم to affect s.o. to the very core, touch s.o. most deeply

صميمى *ṣamīmī* cordial, hearty

اصم *aṣamm*[2], f. صماء *ṣammā'*[2], pl. صم *ṣumm,* صمان *ṣummān* deaf; hard and solid, massive (rock); الاصم the deaf one, epithet of the month of Rajab | فعل اصم (*fi'l*) triliteral verb with identical second and third radical, verbum mediae geminatae (*gram.*); اصم اصلخ (*aṣlak*) stone-deaf; جذر اصم (*jaḏr*) irrational or surd root (*math.*); آلة صماء willing tool

تصميم *taṣmīm* determination (على for, to do s.th.), resolution, decision; resolute action; tenacious pursuit (of a plan); planning, projecting; design, designing (e.g., of a dress); (pl. *-āt*, تصاميم *taṣāmīm*²) plan; design; sketch | من تصميم فلان designed by so-and-so

مصمم *muṣammim* determined (على to do s.th.) | مصمم الازياء fashion creator, designer

صمت *ṣamata* u (*ṣamt*, صموت *ṣumūt*) to be silent, be taciturn, hold one's tongue, hush up, be or become quiet or still **II** to silence (ه s.o.) **IV** = **II**

صمت *ṣamt* silence | فى صمت silently, quietly

صموت *ṣumūt* silence; pl. of act. participle صامت

صموت *ṣamūt* silent, taciturn

صامت *ṣāmit* pl. صموت *ṣumūt* silent | سينما صامتة silent film

مصمت *muṣmat* uniform (color); plain, unpatterned; blank (wall); uniform in texture, made of a single material; massive, solid, not hollow, compact

صماخ *ṣimāk* pl. اصمخة *aṣmiḵa* auditory meatus

صمد *ṣamada* u (*ṣamd*) to betake o.s., repair, go (ه, ه or ل or الى to, into, toward); to turn, apply o.s. (ه or ل or الى to s.th.); — (صمود *ṣumūd*) to defy, brave, withstand (فى وجهه *fī wajhihī* or ل s.o., s.th.); to stand up (فى وجهه or ل against s.o. or s.th.), resist, oppose (فى وجهه or الى s.o. or s.th.); to hold out (فى وجهه or ل against); — *i* to close, plug, cork, stopper (ه s.th., e.g., a bottle) **II** to betake o.s., repair, go (ه to s.o., ه to, toward); to close, plug, cork, stopper (ه s.th., e.g., a bottle); to save, lay by (money) **III** to come to blows, fight (ه with s.o.)

صمد *ṣamad* lord; eternal, everlasting (epithet of God)

صمدانى *ṣamadānī* eternal, everlasting

صمادة *ṣimāda* (*ir.*) headcloth (worn by men)

صمصم *ṣamṣama* to persist (فى in)

صومعة *ṣauma'a* pl. صوامع *ṣawāmi'*² monk's cell, hermitage; silo (for grain storage); (*mor.*) minaret

صمغ **II** to gum (ه s.th.); to paste, glue (ه s.th.) **IV** to exude gum (tree)

صمغ *ṣamḡ* pl. صموغ *ṣumūḡ* gum; resin | صمغ سائل mucilage; صمغ عربى (*'arabī*) gum arabic; صمغ اللك *ṣ. al-lakk* shellac; صمغ مرن (*marin*) rubber, caoutchouc; صمغ هندى (*hindī*) do.; شجر الصمغ *šajar aṣ-ṣ.* rubber trees

صمغى *ṣamḡī* gummy, gummiferous, gumlike, mucilaginous

تصميغ *taṣmīḡ* gumming; resinification

¹صمل *ṣamala* u (*ṣaml*) to be firm, be hard, hold one's ground, stand firm, hold out, last, endure

صمل *ṣaml* rigidity, stiffness, | صمل جيفى (*jīfī*) rigor mortis

²صمولة *ṣamūla* pl. صوامل *ṣawāmil*², صامولة *ṣāmūla* pl. صواميل *ṣawāmīl*² nut (of a bolt), rivet

صملاخ *ṣimlāk* pl. صماليخ *ṣamālīk*² earwax, cerumen

صمى **IV** to deal (ه s.o.) a fatal blow; to hit (ه, ه s.o., s.th.) fatally | رمى فاصمى *ramā fa-aṣmā* to shoot and hit, shoot dead on the spot

صن *ṣann* basket

صنة *ṣinna* odor emanating from the armpit

صنان *ṣunān* odor emanating from the armpit

صنارة *ṣinnāra* pl. صنانير *ṣanānīr*² hook, fishhook

صنبور *ṣunbūr* pl. صنابير *ṣanābīr*[2] (water) faucet, tap

صنوبر look up alphabetically

صنتيم *ṣantīm* pl. *-āt* centime ($^1/_{100}$ franc)

[1]صنج *ṣanj* pl. صنوج *ṣunūj* cymbal (*mus.*)

[2]صنجة *ṣinja* = [1]سنجة

[3]صناجات *ṣannājāt* castanets

صنجقية *ṣanjaqīya* see سنجق

صنديد *ṣindīd* pl. صناديد *ṣanādīd*[2] leader, notable; brave, valiant

صندوق *ṣundūq*, *ṣandūq* pl. صناديق *ṣanādīq*[2] crate, box; chest; trunk, suitcase; case, cabinet; money box, till, coffer; pay office, treasurer's office; any public institution where funds are deposited and disbursed for a special purpose (e.g., sick fund, health insurance, etc.) | صندوق البريد post-office box; صندوق المكاتيب mailbox; صندوق النقد الدولى *ṣ. an-naqd ad-duwalī* International Monetary Fund; صندوق التوفير savings bank; ابو صندوق (*eg.*) hunchback; امين الصندوق treasurer; دفتر الصندوق *daftar aṣ-ṣ.* cashbook

صندل *ṣandal* sandalwood; sandals; (pl. صنادل *ṣanādil*[2]) (freight) barge; lighter, barge

صنارة look up alphabetically

[1]صنع *ṣana'a a* (*ṣan'*, *ṣun'*, صنيع *ṣanī'*) to do, make (ه s.th.); to arrange, stage, put on (ه s.th.); to produce, build, manufacture, fabricate, design (ه s.th.); to work, treat, process (ه s.th.) | صنع اليه معروفا to do s.o. a favor; صنع معه جميلا do.; صنع به ه to do s.th. to s.o.; صنع به صنيعا قبيحا to do s.o. a dirty trick **II** to industrialize (ه s.th.) **III** to cooperate, go along (ه, ه with); to flatter, cajole (ه s.o.); to bribe (ه s.o. with ب) **V** to pretend, feign, simulate, fake, sham, affect (ه s.th.); to speak or write in an artificial, affected, stilted, or mannered way; to use means for enhancing her beauty (woman) **VIII** to order, commission (ه s.th.); to create (ه s.th.) synthetically; to produce, manufacture, make, fabricate (ه s.th.); to pretend, feign, fake, assume falsely (ه s.th.); to invent (ه s.th.); to make (ه ل s.th. into), take, use (ه ل s.th. for); to commit, bind (ه ل s.o. to) **X** to have (ه s.o.) make (ه s.th.)

صنع *ṣan'*, *ṣun'* production, manufacture, fabrication, making, design, make, workmanship | صنع اليد *ṣ. al-yad* handwork; بديع الصنع *badī' aṣ-ṣan'* of wonderful workmanship

صنعى *ṣan'ī* artifical, synthetic

صنع *ṣun'* benefit, favor

صنعة *ṣan'a* work, workmanship, making, manufacture, fabrication; art; technical skill, artistic skill; work, craft, trade, business, occupation, vocation, profession | صاحب الصنعة artisan, craftsman; expert, specialist

صناع *ṣanā'*: صناع اليد *ṣ. al-yad* skillful, skilled, dexterous, deft

صناعة *ṣinā'a* pl. *-āt*, صنائع *ṣanā'i'*[2] art, skill; occupation, vocation, calling, business, profession; handicraft; trade, craft; industry; pl. branches of industry, industries | صناعة شريفة honorable, respectable trade; ارباب الصناعات the artisans, craftsmen; رجل الصناعة *rajul aṣ-ṣ.* industrialist; اصحاب الصنائع والحرف (*ḥiraf*) artisans and tradesmen

صنائعى *ṣanā'i'ī* artificial, synthetic, imitation; workmanlike, handicraft, trade (adj.); industrial; artisan, craftsman

صناعى *ṣinā'ī* artificial, synthetic, imitation; workmanlike, handicraft, trade (adj.); industrial | سر صناعى (*sirr*) industrial secret; الفن الصناعى (*fann*) applied arts, artistic handicraft

صنيع *ṣanī'* action, acting, doing; act, deed; fact; good deed, benefit, favor; charge, protégé; creature, willing tool; meal, repast, banquet

صنيعة *ṣanī'a* pl. صنائع *ṣanā'i'*[2] action, deed; good deed, good turn, benefit, favor; charge, protégé; creature, willing tool

مصنع *maṣna'* pl. مصانع *maṣāni'*[2] factory, plant, mill, works; establishment, firm; مصانع also: large structures, installations, man-made works | ارباب (اصحاب) المصانع manufacturers, industrialists

مصنعية *maṣna'īya* wages, pay

تصنيع *taṣnī'* industrialization

تصنع *taṣannu'* hypocrisy, dissimulation, dissemblement; affectedness, affectation, mannerism

اصطناع *iṣṭinā'* production, making

اصطناعى *iṣṭinā'ī* artificial, synthetic, imitation

صانع *ṣāni'* pl. صناع *ṣunnā'* maker, producer, manufacturer, creator, artisan, craftsman; worker, workman, laborer; servant

مصنوع *maṣnū'* product, produce; pl. مصنوعات (industrial) products, produce, articles, manufactured goods

متصنع *mutaṣanni'* subtilizing, overrefining; affected, stilted, mannered

مصطنع *muṣṭana'* artificial, synthetic; affected, simulated, imitated, sham, bogus, phony | مفتاح مصطنع (*miftāḥ*) duplicate key, masterkey

صنعاء[2] *ṣan'ā'*[2] San'a (capital of Yemen)

صنف II to sort, assort, classify, categorize (ه s.th.); to compile, compose, write (ه a book)

صنف *ṣanf*, *ṣinf* pl. اصناف *aṣnāf*, صنوف *ṣunūf* kind, sort, specimen; article (*com.*); genus, species, class, category; sex; صنفا in kind (as opposed to: in cash)

تصنيف *taṣnīf* classification, categorization, sorting, assorting; compilation, composition, writing; (pl. تصانيف *taṣānīf*[2]) literary work

تصنيفة *taṣnīfa* assortment, selection

مصنف *muṣannif* author, writer

مصنف *muṣannaf* pl. *-āt* literary work

صنفر *ṣanfara* to rub with sandpaper, to sandpaper, to emery (ه s.th.)

صنفر *ṣanfar* and صنفرة *ṣanfara* emery

صنم *ṣanam* pl. اصنام *aṣnām* idol, image

صنو *ṣinw* pl. صنوان *ṣinwān*, اصناء *aṣnā'* one of two, twin brother

صنوبر *ṣanaubar* stone pine (Pinus pinea; *bot.*) | حب الصنوبر *ḥabb aṣ-ṣ.* pine nut, piñon

صنوبرى *ṣanaubarī* pine (adj.), piny, pinelike; pineal | الغدة الصنوبرية (*ğudda*) pineal gland

صه *ṣah* pst! hush! quiet!

صهب IX and XI *iṣhābba* to be or become reddish, red-brown

اصهب *aṣhab*[2], f. صهباء *ṣahbā'*[2], pl. صهب *ṣuhb* reddish; الصهباء wine

صهد *ṣahada a* (*ṣahd*) to scorch, parch, burn (ه, ه s.o., s.th., esp. of the sun)

صهد *ṣahd* heat

صهيد *ṣahīd* scorching heat, blaze

صهود *ṣuhūd* scorching heat, blaze

صهر *ṣahara a* (*ṣahr*) to melt, fuse, smelt (ه s.th.) III to become related by marriage (ى or ه to s.o.) IV to become related by marriage (الى or ب to s.o.) VI to be related by marriage VII to melt, fuse; to melt away, vanish, break (intr.)

صهر *ṣihr* relationship by marriage; — (pl. اصهار *aṣhār*) husband of one's daughter, son-in-law; husband of one's sister, brother-in-law

صهير *ṣahīr* molten, in fusion

مصاهر *maṣāhir*[2] (pl.) smelting furnaces; blast furnaces

مصهر *miṣhar* pl. *-āt* fuse (*el.*) ○

مصاهرة *muṣāhara* relationship by marriage; ○ affinity

انصهار *inṣihār* melting process | ○ سلك الانصهار الواق *silk al-inṣ. al-wāqī* fuse (*el.*)

صهريج *ṣihrīj*, *ṣahrīj* pl. صهاريج *ṣahārīj*[2] cistern; large (water) container, tank

صهل *ṣahala a i* (صهيل *ṣahīl*) to whinny, neigh (horse)

صهيل *ṣahīl* whinny(ing), neighing

صهوة *ṣahwa* pl. *ṣahawāt*, صهاء *ṣihā'* back (of a horse)

صهيون *ṣahyūn*[2], also *ṣihyaun*[2] Zion

صهيونى *ṣahyūnī*, *ṣihyaunī* Zionistic, Zionist

صهيونية *ṣahyūnīya*, *ṣihyaunīya* Zionism

(صوب)[1] صاب *ṣāba u* (*ṣaub*, صيبوبة *ṣaibūba*) to hit (▲ s.th., the target); to be right, hold true, be to the point, hit the mark, be pertinent, be apposite (opinion) | صاب ام اقلع (*am aqla'a*) by all means, under all circumstances **II** to direct, fix (▲ الى s.th., also, e.g., the glance on, to), aim, point, train (▲ الى s.th. at or on); to agree (• with s.o.), concur (▲, • with s.o., in s.th.), consent, assent (▲ to s.th.), approve (▲ of s.th.), sanction (▲ s.th.) **IV** to hit (▲ a target); to attain, reach, achieve (▲ s.th., e.g., end, purpose); to reach out (▲ for s.th., of the hand); to get, obtain, win, gain (▲ e.g., a fortune), acquire (▲ s.th., e.g., a certain amount of knowledge); to have, eat (▲ a snack); to take (▲ a meal); to befall (• s.o.), fall (• upon s.o.), happen (• to s.o.); to allot (• ب to s.o. s.th.), bestow (• ب upon s.o. s.th.), make (ب s.th.) fall to s.o.'s (•) lot; to cause losses (من to s.o.); to be right, be in the right; to do the right thing, hit the mark; to do right, properly (▲ s.th., expressed by a verbal noun); to say the right word; pass. اصيب *uṣība* to be stricken, attacked, afflicted (ب by a disease, and the like); to be killed | اصاب اصابات (*iṣābāt*) to score, make goals (in sports); اصاب فى عمله (*'amalihī*) to do right, act properly; اصيب بجراح to incur multiple wounds; اصيب بخسارة (*bi-ḵasāratin*) to suffer a loss; اصيب اصابة شديدة (*iṣābatan*) to be hard hit, be grievously afflicted **X** استصوب *istaṣwaba* to approve (▲ of s.th.), sanction (▲ s.th.)

صوب *ṣaub* direction, quarter; that which is right, proper, or correct; *ṣauba* (prep.) in the direction of, toward, to | من كل حدب وصوب (*ḥadabin*) or من كل صوب وحدب or من كل فج وصوب (*fajjin*) from all sides, from all directions, from all quarters, from everywhere; فى كل صوب وحدب every place, everywhere, all over, in all quarters

صيب *ṣayyib* rain cloud

صابة *ṣāba* pl. *-āt* harvest (*tun.*)

صواب *ṣawāb* that which is right, proper, or correct; right, proper, correct; rightness, correctness, properness; reason, intellect, mind, consciousness; صوابا *ṣawāban* rightly, justly | هو على صواب he is right; سلك طريق الصواب والحق (*ḥaqq*) to act in exactly the right manner, pursue the right course; رجع (فاء) الى صوابه to regain one's reason, get back to one's senses, become reasonable again; فقد صوابه, اضاع صوابه to lose one's mind; غاب عن صوابه to lose consciousness; غائب عن صوابه unconscious, senseless

اصوب *aṣwab*² more pertinent, more apropos, more apposite, more proper, more correct

اصوبية *aṣwabīya* advisability, expediency

تصويب *taṣwīb* aiming; turning, pointing; (pl. *-āt*) correction, rectification

اصابة *iṣāba* pl. *-āt* hit; goal, score (in sports); injury, wound; state or process of being afflicted (by a disease), (attack of) illness, sickness; accident | اصابة العمل *i. al-'amal* industrial accident; محل الاصابة *maḥall al-i.* scene of the accident

استصواب *istiṣwāb* approval

صائب *ṣā'ib* pertinent, apropos, apposite, right, correct; suited, appropriate

مصيب *muṣīb* pertinent, apropos, apposite, right, correct; suited, appropriate

مصيبة *muṣība* pl. *-āt*, مصائب *maṣā'ib*² misfortune, calamity, disaster

مصاب *muṣāb* stricken, befallen, attacked, afflicted (ب by); injured, wounded, sick, ill; wounded person, casualty; victim of an accident; misfortune, calamity, disaster | مصاب اليم grievous misfortune, mournful event, death

²صوبة (Turk. *soba*) *ṣōba* stove (*syr.*)

(صوت) صات *ṣāta* *u* *a* (*ṣaut*) to ring, sound, make a noise or sound; to raise one's voice, shout II → I; to vote, cast ballots (at an election)

صوت *ṣaut* pl. اصوات *aṣwāt* sound (also *phon.*); voice; tone, strain; melody, tune; noise; fame, renown; vote; pl. interjections (*gram.*) | بعد الصوت *bu'd aṣ-ṣ.* fame, celebrity; رجع الصوت *raj' aṣ-ṣ.* echo, reverberation; علم الاصوات *'ilm al-a.* phonetics; قوة الصوت *qūwat aṣ-ṣ.* volume, intensity (*radio*); بصوت مسموع audibly; بصوت عال aloud; بصوت واطئ (*wāṭi'*) softly, in a low voice, under one's breath

صوتي *ṣautī* sonant, sound- (in compounds), vocal, sonic, acoustic; resounding, resonant, sonorous; phonetic

صوتيات *ṣautīyāt* phonetics

صوات *ṣuwāt* crying, shouting, clamor

صيت *ṣīt* (good) repute, standing, prestige; fame, renown; celebrity, famousness | بعد الصيت *bu'd aṣ-ṣ.* fame, celebrity; ذائع الصيت famous, celebrated, well-known

صيت *ṣayyit* loud-voiced, having a stentorian voice; ○ loud-speaker (*Syr.*)

○ مصوات *miṣwāt* microphone

تصويت *taṣwīt* voting, vote, casting of ballots, polling (election)

صائت *ṣā'it* sound- (in compounds) | ○ سينما صائتة sound film

مصوت *muṣawwit* voter; entitled to vote, franchised

صاج look up alphabetically

صوح II to dry (ه s.th.)

مصوح *muṣawwaḥ* withered, dried (herb, etc.)

¹(صوخ) صاخ *ṣāḵa* *u* = ساخ *sāḵa* *u*

²صوخ IV to listen, lend one's ear (الى or ل to s.o., to s.th.)

صاد name of the letter ص

صودا soda | صودا كاوية (*kāwiya*) caustic soda, sodium hydroxide; نترات الصودا (*nitrāt*) sodium nitrate

صوديوم (Lat. *sodium*) sodium

¹صور II to form, shape, mold, fashion, create (ه s.th.); to paint, draw, sketch (ه، ه s.o., s.th.); to illustrate (with drawings or pictures, ه s.th.); to make a picture (ه، ه of s.o., of s.th.); to photograph (ه، ه s.o., s.th.); to represent, portray (ه s.th., fig.) | صور له (*ṣuwwira*) it appeared to him, seemed to him

V = pass. of II; to imagine, fancy, conceive (ه s.th.); to think (ه, ه s.o., s.th.) to be s.o. or s.th. (ه, ه); to seem, appear, look (ل to s.o.) | لا يتصوره العقل (ʿaqlu) unimaginable, inconceivable, unthinkable

صور ṣūr horn, bugle; see also below

صورة ṣūra pl. صور ṣuwar form, shape; pictorial representation, illustration; image, likeness, picture; figure, statue; replica; copy, carbon copy, duplicate; manner, mode; ṣūratan formally | صورة جامعة total picture, overall picture; صور متحركة (mutaḥarrika) motion picture, film; دار الصور المتحركة motion-picture theater, cinema; صورة شمسية (šamsīya) photograph; صورة طبق الاصل (ṭibqa l-aṣl) true copy; exact replica (fig.); undistorted picture; صورة مكبرة (mukabbara) enlargement, blowup (phot.); فى صورة آدميين in human shape; بصورة جلية (jalīya) obviously, evidently; بصورة محسوسة perceptibly, tangibly, palpably; بصورة خاصة (ḵāṣṣa) especially, particularly; بصورة عامة (ʿāmma) generally, in general; بصورة مكبرة (mukabbara) increasingly, on a larger scale, to an increasing degree; بصورة ملحوظة noticeably, markedly; على صورة كيميائية (kīmiyāʾīya) chemically, by chemical means; فى صورة ما اذا in case that . . ., if; فى صورة مصغرة (muṣaḡḡara) on a reduced scale, in miniature

صورى ṣūrī, ṣuwarī formal; superficial; false, sham, deceptive, fallacious; artificial, fictitious, seeming, fancied, imaginary

تصوير taṣwīr drawing, sketching; representation, portrayal, depiction; illustration; painting; photography, also التصوير الشمسى (šamsī); take (in motion picture making) | آلة التصوير camera

تصويرة taṣwīra pl. تصاوير taṣāwīr[2] pictorial representation, image, picture, illustration

تصور taṣawwur pl. -āt imagination (also philos.), fancy, fantasy, idea; conception, concept (philos.)

تصورى taṣawwurī existing in imagination only, imaginary, fancied, fictitious | ○ المذهب التصورى (maḏhab) idealism (as a philosophical school)

مصور muṣawwir pl. -ūn former, shaper, fashioner, creator; painter; photographer; cameraman (motion pictures); draftsman, commercial artist, illustrator | مصور الكائنات the Creator of the Universe; المصور الكهربائى للقلب (kahrabāʾī, qalb) electrocardiograph

مصورة muṣawwira camera

مصور muṣawwar illustrated; — (pl. -āt) photographer's studio; motion-picture studio | مصور الجغرافيا m. al-juḡrāfiyā atlas

[2]صور ṣūr[2] Tyre (town in S Lebanon)

[1]صوص ṣūṣ pl. صيصان ṣīṣān young chicken, chick (syr.)

[2]صوصى ṣauṣā (eg.) to peep, cheep, squeak

صوع VII to turn on one's heel; to obey, yield, give in, submit (ل to s.o., to s.th.)

صاع ṣāʿ pl. اصوع aṣwuʿ, اصواع aṣwāʿ, صيعان ṣīʿān saa, a cubic measure of varying magnitude | صاعا بصاع tit for tat; رد له الصاع صاعين (radda, ṣāʿain) or كال له صاعا بصاعين to pay s.o. back twofold, bring double retaliation on s.o.

صاعة ṣāʿa salon, parlor, reception room

[1]صاغ (صوغ) ṣāḡa u (ṣauḡ, صياغة ṣiyāḡa) to form, shape, mold, fashion, create (ه s.th.); to formulate (ه s.th.); to coin (ه a word); to fabricate, invent, make up (ه a lie) | صاغ الذهب والفضة (ḏahab, fiḍḍa) to work in gold and silver, practice the art of goldsmithing

صوغ ṣauḡ forming, shaping, molding, fashioning, creating

صيغة *ṣīḡa* forming, shaping, molding, fashioning, creating; — (pl. صيغ *ṣiyaḡ*) shape, form; external form; wording, text, version (e.g., of a letter, of a treaty); formula (in general, also *math.*, *chem.*); jewelry, gold and silver articles; (*gram.*) form | صيغة الفاعل the active (*gram.*); صيغة المفعول the passive (*gram.*); بصيغة حاسمة in a decided form, in no uncertain terms

صياغة *ṣiyāḡa* composing, drafting, wording, forming, formulation, fashioning, molding, shaping; goldsmithery, goldsmithing

مصاغ *maṣāḡ* jewelry, jewels, gold and silver articles

صائغ *ṣā'iḡ* pl. صياغ *ṣuyyāḡ*, صاغة *ṣāḡa*, صواغ *ṣuwwāḡ* goldsmith, jeweler

مصوغات *maṣūḡāt* gold and silver jewelry, goldsmithery, jewelry

ساغ[2] look up alphabetically

صوف *ṣūf* pl. اصواف *aṣwāf* wool

صوفى *ṣūfī* of wool, woolen; Islamic mystic, Sufi

صوفية *ṣūfīya* Sufi way of life; الصوفية Sufism (Islamic mysticism)

صوفان *ṣūfān* tinder, touchwood, punk

صوفانة *ṣufāna* tinder, touchwood, punk

صواف *ṣawwāf* wool merchant

التصوف *at-taṣawwuf* Sufism (Islamic mysticism), the Sufi way of life; mysticism

المتصوفة *al-mutaṣawwifa* the Sufis, members of Sufi communities, mystics

صوفيا *ṣōfiyā* Sofia (capital of Bulgaria)

[1]صال (صول) *ṣāla u* (*ṣaul*, صولة *ṣaula*, صيال *ṣiyāl*) to spring, jump, leap (على on), attack, assail, assault (على s.o.) **II** to pan, wash out (ه grain, gold) **III** to vie, compete (ه with s.o.)

صولة *ṣaula* pl. *-āt* attack, assault; force; tyranny, despotism, arbitrariness

[2]صول (Turk. *sol*) approx.: sergeant major, technical sergeant (*Eg.*) | صول تعليم approx.: master sergeant; صول تعيين approx.: quartermaster sergeant (*mil.*)

صولجان *ṣaulajān* pl. صوالجة *ṣawālija* staff with a curved end; polo mallet; scepter, mace

صام (صوم) *ṣāma u* (*ṣaum*, صيام *ṣiyām*) to abstain (عن from s.th.); to abstain from food, drink, and sexual intercourse; to fast

صوم *ṣaum* abstention, abstinence, abstemiousness; fasting, fast; الصوم fasting during the month of Ramadan, one of the five principal duties of the Muslim | الصوم الكبير the Great Fast = Lent (*Chr.*); عيد صوم الغفران *'īd ṣ. al-ḡufrān* Yom Kippur, Day of Atonement (*Jud.*)

صيام *ṣiyām* fasting, fast

صيامى *ṣiyāmī* Lenten fare

صائم *ṣā'im* pl. *-ūn*, صوم *ṣuwwam*, صيم *ṣuyyam*, صيام *ṣiyām* fasting (adj.); faster, one who fasts

الصومال *aṣ-ṣomāl* Somaliland

صومالى *ṣomālī* Somali (adj. and n.)

صومعة *ṣauma'a* see صمع

صان (صون) *ṣāna u* (*ṣaun*, صيانة *ṣiyāna*) to preserve, conserve, keep, retain, maintain, sustain, uphold (ه s.th.); to maintain (ه e.g., a machine, an automobile); to protect, guard, safeguard, keep, save (ه, ه عن s.o., s.th. from); to defend (ه, ه عن s.o., s.th. against) **V** to uphold one's honor, live chastely, virtuously (woman); to shut o.s. off, seclude o.s., protect o.s.

صون *ṣaun* preservation, conservation, guarding, keeping; susten(ta)tion, upholding; maintenance, upkeep, care;

protection, safeguard(ing), securing, defense; chastity, respectability | صاحبة الصون honorary title of ladies of high social standing

صوان *ṣiwān, ṣuwān* pl. اصونة *aṣwina* cupboard, case

صوان *ṣawwān* (coll.; n. un. ة) flint; granite

صوانى *ṣawwānī*: ادوات صوانية (*adawāt*) flint implements

صيانة *ṣiyāna* = صون *ṣaun* | ملك الصيانة *malak aṣ-ṣ.* guardian angel (*Chr.*)

صائن *ṣā'in* preserver, sustainer, maintainer, keeper, guardian, protector; protective

مصون *maṣūn* well-protected, well-kept, well-guarded, sheltered; chaste, virtuous (woman); also an epithet for women

صوة *ṣūwa* pl. صوى *ṣuwan* stone landmark, trail mark

صوى *ṣawā i* (*ṣuwīy*) and *ṣawiya a* (*ṣawan*) and II to dry up, wither, wilt; — *ṣawā* to peep, cheep, squeak, chirp, screech

صيت see صوت

(صيح) صاح *ṣāḥa i* (*ṣaiḥ*, صياح *ṣiyāḥ*) to cry, yell, shout; to scream, screech; to crow; to utter, let out (صيحة *ṣaiḥatan* a cry); to call out (ب to s.o.), shout, bellow, bawl (فى or على at s.o.) II to cry out (loud), roar, bellow, bawl VI to shout at one another, call out to one another; to clamor, raise a din

صيح *ṣaiḥ* crying, clamor

صيحة *ṣaiḥa* (n. vic.) pl. *-āt* cry, outcry, shout | صيحة الحرب *ṣ. al-ḥarb* battle cry, war cry; ارسل صيحات (*arsala*) to utter cries; صاح صيحة to utter a cry; على صيحة within shouting distance; ذهب صيحة فى واد (*ṣaiḥatan*) to die unheard (call)

صياح *ṣiyāḥ* crying, clamor, cry, outcry; cry of a bird

صياح *ṣayyāḥ* crier, loud-mouthed person; noisy, clamorous, vociferous, crying

تصايح *taṣāyuḥ* crying, clamor, roar, bellow(ing)

[1](صيد) صاد *ṣāda i* (*ṣaid*) to catch (in a trap), trap (ه game); to hunt (ه game); to hunt down (ه game); to catch (ه fish) V to hunt for prey; to hunt down (ه s.th.); to catch (ه s.th.) VIII = I | اصطاد فى الماء العكر (*'akir*) to fish in troubled waters

صيد *ṣaid* hunting, hunt; angling, fishing (also صيد السمك *ṣ. as-samak*); game, venison, prey, quarry | من صيد خياله (*ṣ. ḵayālihī*) dreamed up by him, a product of his fantasy (of a story)

صياد *ṣayyād* pl. *-ūn* hunter; fisher | صياد السمك *ṣ. as-samak* fisher, fisherman; kingfisher (*zool.*).

صيداء *ṣaidā'*[2] Sidon (city in Lebanon)

مصيدة *miṣyada* pl. مصايد *maṣāyid*[2] trap, snare; net; hunting or fishing implement

مصيدة *maṣyada* pl. مصايد *maṣāyid*[2] fishery, fishing grounds (also مصيدة الاسماك)

[2]صاد *ṣād* name of the letter ص

صيدلة *ṣaidala* apothecary's trade; pharmacy, pharmacology

صيدلى *ṣaidalī* pl. صيادلة *ṣayādila* pharmacist, druggist, apothecary

صيدلانى *ṣaidalānī* pharmacist, druggist, apothecary

صيدلية *ṣaidalīya* pl. *-āt* pharmacy; drugstore

صيدليات *ṣaidalīyāt* drugs, pharmaceutics

(صير) صار *ṣāra i* (*ṣair*, صيرورة *ṣairūra*, مصير *maṣīr*) to become (ه s.th.); (with foll. imperf.) to begin, commence, start to…, come to…, get to…, get into a situation where…, get to the point where…; to set in, occur, happen, come to pass, take place; to fall to s.o.'s (ل) lot, befall (ل s.o.); to betake o.s., come, get (عند or الى to); to arrive (الى at); to end, wind up (الى with). result (الى in); صار به الى to lead, bring s.o. or s.th. to; يصار الى (*yuṣāru*) one proceeds to..., one will eventually..., one will wind up with... **II** to induce (ه s.o.) to become (ه s.th.), make (ه ه s.o. into s.th., out of s.o. s.th.)

صير *ṣīr* crack (of the door); small salted fish

صيرورة *ṣairūra* (act or process of) becoming, development; end, outcome, upshot, result

مصير *maṣīr* development, progress (e.g., of work); — (pl. مصاير *maṣāyir*²) place at which one arrives; end, outcome, upshot, issue, result; fate, destiny, lot; life; see also under مصر | تقرير المصير self-determination (*pol.*); مصير كل حي *m. kulli ḥayyin* the way of all flesh

تصيير *taṣyīr* cession, transfer (*jur.*)

صيصية *ṣīṣiya* pl. صياص *ṣayāṣin* spur of the rooster

صيغة see صوغ

صاف (صيف) *ṣāfa i* (*ṣaif*) to be summery; to spend the summer, estivate (ه or ب in) | صاف الزمان ام شتا (*zamānu am šatā*) at all times, under all circumstances **II, V, VIII = I**

صيف *ṣaif* pl. اصياف *aṣyāf* summer

صيفى *ṣaifī* summery, estival, summer (adj.) | توقيت صيفى daylight-saving time

مصيف *maṣīf* pl. مصايف *maṣāyif*² summer residence, summer resort; rest center, holiday camp

اصطياف *iṣṭiyāf* summering, summer vacationing

صائفة *ṣā'ifa* summer(time)

مصطاف *muṣṭāf* summer resort; (pl. *-ūn*) vacationist, summer visitor

الصين *aṣ-ṣīn* China; the Chinese | بلاد الصين China

صينى *ṣīnī* Chinese (adj. and n.); porcelain, china

صينية *ṣīnīya* (*syr. ṣēnīya, leb. ṣainīya*) pl. صوانى *ṣawānī* a large, round metal plate with raised brim, esp. one made of copper, used as baking tin, serving tray and table top; turntable, also صينية متحركة (*mutaḥarrika*); pl. chinaware, porcelain vessels

صيوان *ṣīwān* pl. *-āt*, صواوين *ṣawāwīn*² (large) tent, pavilion, marquee

ض

ضاد *ḍād* name of the letter ض; a sound peculiar to Arabic, hence: اهل الضاد *ahl aḍ-ḍ.* the Arabic-speaking peoples, the Arabs; ابناء الضاد do.; اقطار الضاد the Arabic-speaking countries; لغة الضاد *luġat aḍ-ḍ.* the Arabic language

ضؤل *ḍa'ula u* (ضآلة *ḍa'āla*, ضؤولة *ḍu'ūla*) to be small, tiny, little, scanty, meager, slight, sparse, feeble, faint, thin; to diminish, dwindle, wane, decline, shrink, decrease **VI = I**

ضآلة *ḍa'āla* (ضئالة *ḍi'āla*) smallness, littleness, tininess; minuteness, scantiness, meagerness, slightness, sparsity, paucity, feebleness, faintness, thinness; waning, dwindling, diminution, decrease; shrinking, shrinkage; small number

ضؤولة *ḍu'ūla* = ضآلة *ḍa'āla*

ضئيل *ḍa'īl* pl. ضئال *ḍi'āl*, ضؤلاء *ḍu'alā'*[2] small, tiny, minute, little, scanty, slight, meager, sparse, feeble, faint, thin

تضاؤل *taḍā'ul* = ضآلة *ḍa'āla*

ضامة *ḍāma* checkers

ضأن *ḍa'n* sheep (coll.)

ضأني *ḍa'nī*, *ḍānī* mutton (meat)

ضائن *ḍā'in* sheep

ضب *ḍabba* *i* (*ḍabb*) to take hold (على of s.th.); to keep under lock, put in safekeeping, guard carefully (على s.th.) **II** = **I**; to bolt (▲ the door) **IV** to be foggy (day)

ضب *ḍabb* pl. ضباب *ḍibāb*, اضب *aḍubb*, ضبان *ḍubbān* lizard

ضب *ḍabb* (*eg.*) front teeth

ضبة *ḍabba* pl. *-āt*, ضباب *ḍibāb* door bolt, latch; wooden lock

ضباب *ḍabāb* fog, mist

ضبر *ḍabara* *u* to gather, collect, assemble

ضبارة *ḍibāra*, *ḍubāra* and اضبارة *iḍbāra* pl. اضابير *aḍābīr*[2] file, dossier

اضبور *uḍbūr* file, dossier

ضبح *ḍabaḥa* *a* (*ḍabḥ*) to blacken (▲ s.th., said of fire); to snort (horse)

ضبط *ḍabaṭa* *i* *u* (*ḍabṭ*) to grab, grasp, seize, catch, apprehend, arrest, detain (▲, ◦ s.o., s.th.), take hold (▲, ◦ of s.o., of s.th.); to keep, hold, retain (▲ s.th.); to tackle resolutely, master, overcome (▲ s.th.), cope (▲ with s.th.); to have (▲ s.th.) under control, have command (▲ over s.th.); to restrain, hold back, keep down, subdue, check, curb, control (▲, ◦ s.o., s.th.); to seize, distrain, impound, confiscate (▲ s.th.); to do (▲ s.th.) accurately, precisely, meticulously, or well; to render precise, define precisely (▲ s.th.); to regulate, adjust (▲ s.th., e.g., *techn.*); to determine precisely (كلمة *kalimatan* the spelling and pronunciation of a word), vowel(ize) (▲ a word); to observe strictly, keep exactly (▲ time); to regulate, settle, put or keep in order (▲ s.th.); to correct (▲ s.th.); to enter, book, record, register (▲ s.th.); to measure off exactly, measure out (▲ s.th.), take exactly the right amount, the right proportion (▲ of) **VII** to be detained, be held back, be held up; to be regulated, be kept in order, be disciplined; to be determined, be established, etc. (pass. of *ḍabaṭa*)

ضبط *ḍabṭ* capture, apprehension, arrest(ing), detention; restraint, suppression, subdual, curb(ing), check(ing); control; seizure, impoundage, distraint, confiscation; accuracy, correctness, exactitude, precision; vowelization; correction, amendment, settlement; regulation, adjustment of an apparatus (*techn.*); (pl. ضبوط *ḍubūṭ*) protocol, minutes, procès-verbal; entering, entry, record, registry; ضبطا *ḍabṭan* accurately, exactly, precisely, punctually | ضبطا = بالضبط *ḍabṭan*; ضبط الاراضى *ḍ. al-arāḍī* cadastral survey; ضبط الحسابات bookkeeping; ضبط الشهوة *ḍ. aš-šahwa* abstemiousness, continence; ضبط الاملاك العقارية (*aqārīya*) cadastral survey; ضبط النفس self-control, self-command; جهاز الضبط *jahāz aḍ-ḍ.* control apparatus, controlling device; عار عن الضبط (*'ārin*) unvowel(iz)ed

ضبطية *ḍabṭīya* police station; police

مضبطة *maḍbaṭa* pl. مضابط *maḍābiṭ*[2] protocol, minutes, procès-verbal

انضباط *inḍibāṭ* discipline | لجنة الانضباط *lajnat al-inḍ.* disciplinary board

ضابط *ḍābiṭ* controlling device, control, governor, regulator (*techn.*); prepositor entrusted with discipline (in Eg. schools); (pl. ضباط *ḍubbāṭ*) officer; (pl. ضوابط *ḍawābiṭ*²) general rule, canon, (moral) precept or order | ضابط آمر senior officer; ضابط مأمور subaltern officer; ضابط الصف *ḍ. aṣ-ṣaff* pl. ضباط الصف noncommissioned officer; ضابط الصوت *ḍ. aṣ-ṣaut* volume control (*radio*); صف ضابط *ṣaff ḍ.* pl. صف ضباط noncommissioned officer; بغير ضابط ولا رادع (*ġair*) completely unrestrained, out of all control

ضابطة *ḍābiṭa* police; (pl. ضوابط *ḍawābiṭ*²) curbing force, order

مضبوط *maḍbūṭ* accurate, exact, correct, right, precise

ضبع **ḍabʿ**, *ḍabuʿ* f., pl. ضباع *ḍibāʿ*, اضبع *aḍbuʿ* hyena

ضبن VIII to take under one's arm

ضبن *ḍibn* armpit

ضج **ḍajja** *i* (*ḍajj*, ضجيج *ḍajīj*) to be noisy, boisterous; to clamor, shout, raise a hue and cry IV = I

ضجة *ḍajja* cry, yell, outcry; clamor, noise, din, row, hubbub, tumult

ضجيج *ḍajīj* cry, yell, outcry; clamor, noise, din, row, hubbub, tumult

ضجوج *ḍajūj* roaring, bellowing, screaming, crying

ضجاج *ḍajjāj* violently roaring, bellowing, screaming, crying, boisterous, uproarious

ضجر **ḍajira** *a* (*ḍajar*) to be angry, annoyed, irritated, exasperated (من or ب at, about); to be dissatisfied, discontent, displeased (من or ب with); to sorrow, be worried, uneasy (من or ب about), be disquieted, grieved, troubled (من or ب by, over) IV to anger, vex, irritate, trouble, torment (ه s.o.), disquiet, discomfit, aggrieve (ه s.o.) V = I

ضجر *ḍajar* annoyance, irritation, vexation, anger; dissatisfaction; discontent, displeasure; sorrow, worry, grief

ضجر *ḍajir* annoyed, irritated, angry, vexed; morose, sullen; dissatisfied, discontent, displeased, uneasy, restless; worried, grieved, troubled

مضجر *muḍjir* annoying, irritating, exasperating, irksome, tedious

متضجر *mutaḍajjir* = ضجر *ḍajir*

ضجع **ḍajaʿa** *a* (*ḍajʿ*, ضجوع *ḍujūʿ*) to lie on one's side, lie down; to lie, recline, be prostrate; to sleep III to lie, have sexual intercourse (ها with a woman) VII = I VIII (اضطجع and اضجع *iḍḍajaʿa*) = I

ضجعة *ḍajʿa* (n. vic.) lying position, lying, recumbency; slumber

ضجعة *ḍujaʿa*, *ḍujʿa* late riser, slugabed, sluggard, lazybones; lazy, sluggish, inert

ضجعى *ḍujʿī* late riser, slugabed, sluggard, lazybones; lazy, sluggish, inert

ضجيع *ḍajīʿ* one sharing the bed; bedfellow; comrade, companion

مضجع *maḍjaʿ* pl. مضاجع *maḍājiʿ*² couch, bed | اخذ مضجعه he lay down (to sleep); اقض مضجعه *aqaḍḍa maḍjaʿahū* or اقض مضجعه or اقلق مضجعه or عليه المضجع (*maḍjaʿahū*) to deprive s.o. of sleep

مضاجع *muḍājiʿ* bedfellow

مضطجع *muḍṭajaʿ* couch, bed

ضحضح **ḍaḥḍaḥa** to vibrate, flicker (mirage); to shatter, break, crush II to vibrate, flicker (mirage)

ضحضاح *ḍaḥḍāḥ* shallow, shoal, flat (water)

ضحك **ḍaḥika** *a* (*ḍaḥk*, *ḍiḥk*, *ḍaḥik*) to laugh (ب or من at, about, over); to jeer, scoff, jibe (ب or على or من at s.o., at s.th.), deride, ridicule, mock, scorn (ب or على or من s.o., s.th.) | ضحك بملء شدقيه (*bi-milʾi* *šidqaihi*) or ضحك ملء شدقيه (*mil'a*) to grin from ear to ear; ضحك عن در منضد (*durrin munaḍḍadin*) (to laugh by showing stringed pearls, i.e., the teeth), to show a toothy smile; to grin from ear to ear; ضحك على ذقنه (*ḏaqanihī*; pl. على ذقونهم) (*eg. syr.*) to fool s.o., make a fool of s.o., pull s.o.'s leg, make fun of s.o., lead s.o. around by the nose (ب with s.th.), put on an act for s.o.; ضحك فى ذقنه (*ḏaqanihī*) to laugh in s.o.'s face **II** to make (ه s.o.) laugh **III** to joke, jest, banter (ه with s.o.) **IV** and **X** to make (ه s.o.) laugh (من about) | ما يضحك الثكلى (*ṯaklā*) (that which makes a woman who has lost her child laugh =) irresistibly comical **VI** to laugh

ضحك **ḍaḥk**, **ḍiḥk**, **ḍaḥik** laugh(ing); laughter

ضحكة **ḍaḥka** (n. vic.) pl. *-āt* laugh

ضحكة **ḍuḥka** object of ridicule, laughingstock

ضحوك **ḍaḥūk** frequently, or constantly, laughing; laugher

ضحاك **ḍaḥḥāk** frequently, or constantly, laughing; laugher; joker, jester, wag, buffoon

اضحوكة **uḍḥūka** pl. اضاحيك **aḍāḥīk**[2] object of ridicule, laughingstock; lark, spree, hoax, practical joke

اضحك **aḍḥak**[2] more ridiculous, more laughable, more ludicrous, funnier, more comical

مضحكة **maḍḥaka** object of ridicule, laughingstock

ضاحك **ḍāḥik** pl. ضواحك **ḍawāḥik**[2] laughing | ضاحك السن *ḍ. as-sinn* cheerful, gay, sunny

مضحك **muḍḥik** ridiculous, laughable, ludicrous, droll, funny, comical; comedian, buffoon, jester | قصة تمثيلية مضحكة (*qiṣṣa tamṯīlīya*) comedy

ضحل **ḍaḥl** shallow, shoal, flat; a shallow, a shoal

(ضحى and ضحو) ضحا **ḍaḥā** *u* (*ḍaḥw*, *ḍuḥūw*) to become visible, appear; — ضحى **ḍaḥiya** *a* (ضحا *ḍaḥan*) to become visible, appear; to be struck by the sun's rays **II** to sacrifice, offer up, immolate (ب s.th.) | ضحى بنفسه to sacrifice o.s.; ضحى بالنفس والنفيس to sacrifice life and property (properly: the soul and that which is precious) **IV** to be, become; with foll. imperf.: to begin, start, commence, or set about to (do s.th.); to come to…, get to…, get to the point where…, get into a situation where…

ضحوة **ḍaḥwa** pl. **ḍaḥawāt** forenoon; morning

ضحى **ḍuḥan** (m. and f.) forenoon | بين عشية وضحاها (*'ašīyatin wa-ḍuḥāhā*) over night, from one day to the next, all of a sudden

ضحية **ḍaḥīya** forenoon; — (pl. ضحايا **ḍaḥāyā**) slaughter animal, blood sacrifice, immolation; victim | ذهب or وقع ضحيته (*ḍaḥīyatahū*) to fall victim to, become a victim of s.th. or s.o.

اضحى **aḍḥan** (coll.; n. un. اضحاة **aḍḥāh**) slaughter animal, blood sacrifice, immolation | عيد الاضحى *'īd al-a.* the Feast of Immolation, or Greater Bairam, on the 10th of Zu'lhijja; يوم الاضحى *yaum al-a.* the Day of Immolation, i.e., the 10th of Zu'lhijja

اضحية **uḍḥīya** pl. اضاحى **aḍāḥīy**[2] slaughter animal, blood sacrifice, immolation

تضحية **taḍḥiya** sacrificing, immolation; (pl. *-āt*) sacrifice

ضاح **ḍāḥin**: ضاح للشمس sunlit

ضاحية **ḍāḥiya** pl. ضواح **ḍawāḥin** surroundings, vicinity, outskirts; suburb

مضحى **muḍaḥḥan** place where one has breakfast

ضخ **ḍak̲k̲a** *u* (*ḍak̲k̲*) to spurt, spout, squirt (ه water)

مضخة **miḍak̲k̲a** pl. *-āt* squirt, spray(er); pump | مضخة جذابة (*jad̲d̲āba*) suction pump; مضخة الحرائق (الحريق) fire engine; مضخة رافعة suction pump

ضخم **ḍak̲uma** *u* (ضخامة *ḍak̲āma*) to be or become big, large, bulky, heavy, gross, voluminous **II** to inflate, blow up (ه s.th.) **V** to swell, become inflated; to expand, distend

ضخم **ḍak̲m** pl. ضخام *ḍik̲ām* big, large, sizable, great (also of a name, of prestige); bulky, gross; heavy, voluminous, huge, vast, ample, colossal; stout, corpulent, plump, buxom; magnificent, splendid, gorgeous, luxurious, pompous | المدفعية الضخمة (*midfaʿīya*) heavy artillery

ضخامة **ḍak̲āma** bigness, largeness, greatness; bulkiness, grossness; heaviness; volume, voluminosity; stoutness, plumpness, corpulence, obesity; pomp, splendor

تضخيم **tadk̲īm** inflating

تضخم **taḍak̲k̲um** inflation; swelling, expansion, dilation, distention; (monetary) inflation, also تضخم مالى (نقدى) (*naqdī*) | تضخم الطحال distention of the spleen (*med.*)

مضخم **muḍak̲k̲im** pl. *-āt* amplifier | مضخم الصوت *m. aṣ-ṣaut* loud-speaker

ضد **III** to be contrary, opposed, contrasting, antagonistic, inverse; to act, set o.s. (ه, ه against), antagonize (ه s.o.), contravene, violate (ه s.th.), be opposed (ه, ه to), be contradictory (ه to s.th.), act contrary to s.o. or s.th. (ه, ه) **VI** to be opposed to each other, be contradictory, contradict one another

ضد **ḍidd** pl. اضداد *aḍdād* an opposite, a contrary, contrast; word with two opposite meanings; adversary, opponent; antitoxin, antidote, anti- (in compounds); ضد **ḍidda** (prep.) against | كان على الضد من ذلك to do or think the opposite, take an opposite stand

ضدية **ḍiddīya** contrariness, oppositeness, opposition; enmity, hostility, animosity

مضادة **muḍādda** contrast, opposite, contradiction

تضاد **taḍādd** contrast, opposite, contradiction

مضاد **muḍādd** opposed, opposite, contrary, counter-, contra-, anti- (in compounds); pl. مضادات antidotes | مضادات للحبل (*ḥabal*) contraceptives; مضادات حشرية (*ḥašarīya*) insecticides; مضادات للفساد (*li-l-fasād*) antiseptics

متضاد **mutaḍādd** contrary, opposite

ضر **ḍarra** *u* (*ḍarr*) to harm, impair, prejudice, damage, hurt, injure (ه, ب s.o., s.th.), do harm, be harmful, noxious or injurious (ه, ه to s.o., to s.th.) **II** to damage, harm, prejudice **III** = **I**; **IV** = **I** (ب or ه, ه); to force, compel, coerce, oblige (ه على s.o. to); to do violence (ه to s.o.), bring pressure to bear (ه on); to add a second wife to one's household **V** to be damaged, harmed, impaired, prejudiced, hurt, or injured; to suffer damage or loss; to complain (من of, about) **VII** to be damaged, harmed, impaired, prejudiced, hurt, or injured; to suffer damage or loss **VIII** to force, compel, coerce, oblige (ه s.o., الى to); — pass. *uḍṭurra* to be forced, compelled, obliged (الى to); to be in an emergency or predicament, be hard pressed; to be in need (الى of s.th.), need, want (الى s.th.)

ضر **ḍurr**, **ḍarr** damage, harm, impairment, prejudice, detriment, injury, hurt; loss, disadvantage

ضر **ḍirr**, **ḍurr** addition of a second wife to one's household

ضرة *ḍarra* pl. *-āt*, ضرائر *ḍarā'ir*[2] wife other than the first of a plural marriage; udder

ضرر *ḍarar* pl. أضرار *aḍrār* harm, damage, detriment; loss, disadvantage | ما الضرر what does it matter? what's the harm of it? اخف الضررين *akaff aḍ-ḍ.* the lesser of the two evils

ضراء *ḍarrā'*[2] distress, adversity | فى السراء والضراء (*sarrā'*) in good and bad days, for better or for worse

ضرير *ḍarīr* blind

ضرورة *ḍarūra* pl. *-āt* necessity, stress, constraint, need; distress, plight, emergency, want, austerity; *ḍarūratan* necessarily | بالضرورة necessarily; عند الضرورة in case of need, if need be, when necessary; للضرورة القصوى (*quṣwā*) in case of dire necessity, if worst comes to worst; للضرورة احكام and الضرورات تبيح المحظورات (*tubīḥu*) necessity knows no laws

ضرورى *ḍarūrī* necessary, imperative, requisite, indispensable, inevitable; pl. ضروريات *ḍarūrīyāt* necessaries, necessities | كان من الضرورى to be necessary; ضروريات الحياة *ḍ. al-ḥayāh* necessities of life; ضروريات الاحوال exigencies, requirements of the situation

مضرة *maḍarra* pl. *-āt*, مضار *maḍārr*[2] harm, damage, detriment, loss, disadvantage (على for)

اضطرار *iḍṭirār* compulsion, coercion; necessity, exigency, requirement; plight, predicament, emergency | عند الاضطرار in case of emergency

اضطرارى *iḍṭirārī* coercive, compulsory, inevitable, necessary, obligatory

ضار *ḍārr* harmful, injurious, detrimental, noxious, disadvantageous

مضر *muḍirr* harmful, injurious, detrimental, noxious, disadvantageous (ب to, for)

مضطر *muḍṭarr* forced, compelled, obliged (الى to); poor, destitute; wanting (الى s.th.), in need (الى of s.th.)

ضرب *ḍaraba* *i* (*ḍarb*) to beat, strike, hit (ه s.o., ه s.th., ب with; ب على with s.th. on; ه على s.o. on); to shoot, fire (ه, ه at s.o., at s.th.), shell, bombard (ه, ه s.o., s.th.); to play (ه, على a musical instrument); to make music; to type (on a typewriter); to sting (scorpion); to separate, part (بين people); to impose (ه على on s.o. s.th.); ضرب عن to turn away from, leave, forsake, abandon, avoid, or shun s.o. or s.th.; — (*ḍarb*, ضربان *ḍarabān*) to pulsate, palpitate, throb, beat (vein, heart); to ache (violently), hurt (wound, tooth); to move, stir; to rove, roam about, travel (فى in, through), loiter, stroll (in streets); to cruise (ship); to migrate (bird); to incline (الى to a color), shade (الى into a color); — (ضراب *ḍirāb*) to cover, mount (ها the camel mare) | ضرب له اجلا (*ajalan*) to fix a date for s.o.; ضرب الارز (*aruzz*) to hull rice; ضرب فى الارض (*arḍ*) to travel; ضرب بوية على (*bōya*) to paint or daub s.th.; ضرب الباب to knock on the door; ضرب الجرس (*jaras*) to ring the bell; ضرب حقنا (*ḥaqnan*) to administer a syringe, give an injection; ضرب خطا (*kaṭṭan*) to draw a line; ضرب اخماسا لاسداس (*li-asdāsin*) and ضرب اخماسه فى اسداسه to brood, rack one's brain in order to find a way out; to be at one's wit's end; to intrigue, scheme; to build air castles; to daydream; ضرب خيمة (*kaimatan*) to pitch a tent; ضرب الرقم القياسى (*raqma, qiyāsīya*) to break a record; ضرب السلام (*salām*) to give a military salute; ضرب ضريبة to impose a tax (على on s.o.); ضرب اطنابه فى (*aṭnābahū*) to take root, prevail (at a place); ضرب اطنابه على to settle down, take up permanent residence in a place; ضرب طوبا (*ṭūban*) to make brick; ضرب عددا فى آخر (*'adadan fī ākara*) to multiply a number by another; ضرب عنقه (*'unuqahū*) to behead, decapitate s.o., have s.o.'s head cut off; ضرب قالبه (*qālabahū*) to imitate s.th.; ضربه كفا (*kaffan*) to slap s.o.'s face; ضرب مثلا ل (*maṯalan*) to apply a proverb to; ضرب له مثلا (*maṯalan*) to give s.o. an example, point out a model for s.o.; ضرب مثلا to give an example; to quote as an example (ب على ه or ل s.th. for); ضرب الامثال to impart words of wisdom, point out morals; ضرب نقودا to mint money; ضرب موعدا (*mau'idan*) to agree on time or place of a meeting, make an appointment; ضرب الى الحمرة (الى الصفرة) (*ḥumra, ṣufra*) to shade into red (into yellow); ضرب به الارض (*arḍ*) to throw s.o. or s.th. to the ground; ضرب فى الخيال (*ḵayāl*) to be in the clouds, be unrealistic; to want the impossible; ضرب برأسه على صدره (*bi-ra'sihī 'alā ṣadrihī*) to let one's head sink to the chest; ضرب بسهم مصيب فى (*bi-sahmin muṣībin*) to take an active part in; ضرب بسهم ونصيب فى (*wa-naṣībin*) to participate in, share s.th.; ضرب فيه بعرق (*bi-'irq*) do.; ضرب به عرض الحائط (*'urḍa l-ḥ.*) not to give a hoot for s.th.; to disdain, despise, reject s.th.; to throw s.th. overboard, jettison s.th.; ضرب بنظره الى (*naẓarihī*) to turn one's glance to; ضرب بوجه صاحبه (*bi-wajhi ṣāḥibihī*) to boomerang, fall back on the originator; ضرب على كلمة (*kalima*) to efface, strike, or erase, a word; ضرب عنه صفحا (*ṣafḥan*) to turn away s.o. or s.th.; to disregard, ignore s.o. or s.th., pay no attention to, pass over s.o. or s.th.; ضرب فى حديد بارد to take futile steps; to beat the air; ضرب لنفسه سبعة ايام (*sab'ata ayyāmin*) he decided to stay seven days; ضرب بينى وبينه الايام (*ayyām*) fate separated me from him, drew us apart II to mix, blend (ه ب s.th. with); to sow dissension, cause trouble (بين among); to quilt (ه a fabric) III to contend, vie, fight (ه with s.o.); to speculate IV to turn away (عن from), leave, abandon, forsake, desert, avoid, shun (عن s.o., s.th.); to remain, stay, abide (فى in) | اضرب جأشا ل (*ja'šan*) to be prepared for s.th., make up one's mind to take s.th. upon o.s.; اضرب صفحا عن (*ṣafḥan*) to desist, abstain from; اضرب (عن العمل) (*'amal*) to stop work, to strike; اضرب عن الطعام (*ṭa'ām*) to go on a hunger strike VI to come to blows, brawl, fight, strike one another; to be divided, differ, conflict, clash, be contradictory (opinions, and the like) VIII to clash, surge, lap (waves); to be set, or get, into a state of unrest, turmoil, excitement, commotion, tumult, agitation, be or become agitated, troubled; to be in a lively stir, move about, bustle, hustle, romp; to sway, reel, waver; to be or become disturbed, unsettled, disorganized, disarranged, disordered, confused, entangled, upset, restless, uneasy, or anxious; to tremble, shake

ضرب **ḍarb** beating, striking, hitting, rapping; shooting, shelling, gunning, bombing, bombardment; multiplication; coining, formation; minting (of money); — (pl. ضروب *ḍurūb*) kind, sort, specimen, species, variety; last foot of the second hemistich; (pl. اضراب *aḍrāb*) similar, like | ضربخانة and دار الضرب (money) mint; ضرب الرمل *ḍ. ar-raml* geomancy; ضرب النار shooting, firing, shelling, gunning, bombardment; وضع السلاح تحت الضرب to level a weapon, hold a weapon ready to fire; هو واضرابه he and the likes of him

ضربة **ḍarba** (n. vic.) pl. *ḍarabāt* blow, knock, punch; thrust, push, jolt, shock; stroke, lash; shot; plague, affliction, trial, tribulation, punishment | ضربة الشمس *ḍ. aš-šams* sunstroke, heatstroke; ضربة قاضية (*qāḍiya*) fatal blow, deathblow (على for); ضربة جزاء *ḍ. jazā'* penalty kick (in soccer)

ضراب *ḍirāb* copulation (of a female animal)

ضريب *ḍarīb* beaten, struck, smitten, hit; similar, like | ضريب للشيخ فلان one of the caliber of Sheik So-and-So

ضريبة *ḍarība* pl. ضرائب *ḍarā'ib*² imposition, impost; levy, tax, duty; character, nature | ضريبة الدخل *ḍ. ad-dakl* income tax; ضريبة كسب العمل *ḍ. kasb al-'amal* wage tax; ضريبة الملاهى *ḍ. al-malāhī* admissions tax, entertainment tax

مضرب *maḍrib* pl. مضارب *maḍārib*² camp site, camp; place, spot, locality; way, path; large tent, marquee | كان مضرب المثل (الامثال) (*m. al-maṯal*) to be proverbial, be exemplary, be unique, be cited as an example; مضارب ارز *m. aruzz* rice-hulling facilities

مضرب *miḍrab* pl. مضارب *maḍārib*² large tent, marquee, pavilion; bat, mallet; racket (tennis, etc.); whisk, beater (e.g., for eggs); swatter, flyswatter; piano

مضراب *miḍrāb* bat, mallet, racket (ball games, tennis)

مضاربة *muḍāraba* pl. *-āt* speculation (stock exchange); silent partnership (*Isl. Law*), limited partnership, partnership in commendam

اضراب *iḍrāb* pl. *-āt* strike

تضارب *taḍārub* opposition, contradiction, inconsistency, discrepancy, incompatibility, conflict, clash (of opinions, and the like)

اضطراب *iḍṭirāb* pl. *-āt* disturbance, disorder, disarray; confusion, muddle, perturbation; disorganization, disruption, upset, derangement; trouble, commotion, unrest, riot (also *pol.*); restlessness, restiveness | اضطرابات عصبية (*'aṣabīya*) nervous disorders

ضوارب *ḍawārib*² pl. of ضارب *ḍārib* beating, striking, etc. | العروق الضوارب the arteries; طير ضوارب (*ṭair*) migratory birds

مضروب *maḍrūb* appointed, agreed upon, fixed, determined (time, date, place); multiplicand (*math.*) | مضروب فيه multiplier (*math.*)

مضربة *muḍarraba* quilt, comforter

مضارب *muḍārib* pl. *-ūn* speculator

متضارب *mutaḍārib* conflicting, irreconcilable, incompatible, divided (opinions, and the like); contradictory, discrepant, inconsistent

مضطرب *muḍṭarib* disturbed, disordered, disarrayed, unsettled; confused, muddled, perturbed; upset, disrupted, disorganized, deranged; uneasy, restive, agitated, excited, anxious; weak, insufficiently supported (tradition)

مضطرب *muḍṭarab* playground (fig.)

ضربخانة see ضرب *ḍarb*

ضرج *ḍaraja u* (*ḍarj*) to spot, stain, befleck, smear (ه s.th. with بالدم blood) II = I V to redden, be or become red

مدرج *muḍarraj*: مضرج اليدين *m. al-yadain* with bloodstained hands; (caught) red-handed, in the act

ضريح *ḍarīḥ* pl. ضرائح *ḍarā'iḥ*², اضرحة *aḍriḥa* grave, tomb; mausoleum

ضرس *ḍarasa i* (*ḍars*) to bite firmly or fiercely (ه s.th.); — *ḍarisa a* (*ḍaras*) to be dull (teeth from acid food and drink) II to make (ه s.o.) tough, battle-hardened; to render dull (الاسنان the teeth by acid food and drink) IV to render dull (الاسنان the teeth by acid food and drink)

ضرس *ḍirs* pl. اضراس *aḍrās*, ضروس *ḍurūs* molar tooth | ضرس العقل *ḍ. al-'aql* wisdom tooth

حرب ضروس *ḥarb ḍarūs* fierce, murderous war

تضاريس *taḍārīs*²: تضاريس الارض *t. al-arḍ* elevations, undulations of the ground; تضاريس الوجه *t. al-wajh* wrinkles of the face

ضرط **ḍaraṭa** *i* (*ḍarṭ*, ضريط *ḍarīṭ*, ضراط *ḍurāṭ*) to break wind

ضرط *ḍarṭ* (n. un. ة) wind, fart

ضراط *ḍurāṭ* wind, fart

ضرع **ḍaraʿa** *a*, *ḍaruʿa* *u* (ضراعة *ḍarāʿa*) and *ḍariʿa* *a* (*ḍaraʿ*) to be humble, submissive (ل toward s.o.), humiliate o.s., abase o.s. (ل before); to implore, beg, beseech, entreat (ل s.o.) **III** to be similar, be equal (ه, ه to s.o., to s.th.), be like s.o. or s.th. (ه, ه), resemble (ه, ه s.o., s.th.) **V** and **VIII** to humiliate o.s., abase o.s. (ل before); to implore, beg, beseech, entreat (ل s.o.)

ضرع *ḍarʿ* pl. ضروع *ḍurūʿ*, ضراع *ḍirāʿ* udder, teat | الزرع والضرع (*zarʿ*) agriculture and stock farming

ضرع *ḍirʿ* like, alike, similar

ضراعة *ḍarāʿa* submissiveness, humbleness; imploring, begging, entreaty, supplication

مضارعة *muḍāraʿa* likeness, similarity, resemblance

تضرع *taḍarruʿ* imploring, begging, entreaty, supplication

ضارع *ḍāriʿ* frail (of a person)

مضارع *muḍāriʿ* like, alike, similar; (*gram.*) imperfect

ضرغم **ḍarġam** pl. ضراغم *ḍarāġim*² lion

ضرغام *ḍirġām* pl. ضراغمة *ḍarāġima* lion

ضرم **ḍarima** *a* (*ḍaram*) to catch fire, be on fire, burn, flare, blaze; to break out, flare up (war) **II** to kindle. light (ه fire) | ضرم النار فى to set s.th. on fire, set fire to s.th. **IV** = **II**; **V** to burn, flare, flame, be ablaze (also of emotions, of passion) **VIII** = **I**

ضرام *ḍirām* burning, blaze, flare; fire, conflagration

اضطرام *iḍṭirām* burning, flare, blaze; fire, conflagration

مضطرم *muḍṭarim* burning, flaming, on fire

ضرو **II** to set (ه ب a dog on game); to provoke (ه s.o.) to a fight (ب with)

ضرو *ḍirw* pl. اضر *aḍrin*, ضراء *ḍirā'* hound, hunting dog

ضراوة *ḍarāwa* greed, voracity

ضار *ḍārin* voracious, ferocious, savage, rapacious; (pl. ضوار *ḍawārin*) beast of prey, predatory animal

ضعضع **ḍaʿḍaʿa** to tear down, demolish, raze, ruin, undermine, weaken (ه s.th.) **II** *taḍaʿḍaʿa* to decline, decay, become dilapitated, perish; to become weak or weaker, wane; to dissolve, fall apart (organization)

ضعضعة *ḍaʿḍaʿa* demolition, razing; sapping, undermining; debility, frailty, feebleness | ضعضعة الكبر *ḍ. al-kibar* senility, dotage

متضعضع *mutaḍaʿḍiʿ* dilapidated, decayed; weakened, debilitated; weak, frail, feeble; submissive, humble

[1]ضعف **ḍaʿufa** *u* (*ḍuʿf*, *ḍaʿf*) to be or become weak, weakly, feeble, frail, delicate, debilitated, impotent, languid, flabby, or slack; to become weaker, wane, decrease, diminish, abate, be attenuated; to be too weak (عن for s.th.) **IV** to weaken, enfeeble, debilitate (من or ه, ه s.o., s.th.) **X** to deem (ه s.o.) weak; to behave arrogantly (ه toward s.o.)

ضعف *ḍuʿf, ḍaʿf* weakness, feebleness, frailty; weakening, enfeeblement, debilitation | ضعف الارادة weakness of will; الضعف العصبي (*ʿaṣabī*) neurasthenia, nervous debility; ضعف التناسل *ḍ. at-tanāsul* sexual impotence

ضعيف *ḍaʿīf* pl. m. ضعفاء *ḍuʿafāʾ*², ضعاف *ḍiʿāf*, ضعفة *ḍaʿafa*, pl. f. ضعائف *ḍaʿāʾif*² weak, feeble; frail, weakly, delicate, debilitated, impotent, languid, flabby, slack; deficient (as a school-report mark) | ضعيف الارادة weak-willed; ضعيف العقل *ḍ. al-ʿaql* dim-witted, feeble-minded; ضعيف القلب *ḍ. al-qalb* weak-spirited, pusillanimous, meek, faint-hearted, despondent, cowardly; هذا الضعيف my own insignificant self, I (as an expression of modesty)

اضعاف *iḍʿāf* weakening, enfeeblement, debilitation; impairment

مستضعف *mustaḍʿaf* deemed weak; weak; oppressed, miserable

ضعف² II to double, redouble (ه s.th.); to multiply, compound (ه s.th.) III do. (من or ه s.th.) VI to be doubled, be compounded, be multiplied

ضعف *ḍiʿf* pl. اضعاف *aḍʿāf* double, that which is twice as much; a multiple, that which is several times as much, (after numerals) -fold; fold of a garment; pl. interstice, space | مئة ضعفه *miʾatu ḍiʿfihī* a hundred times as much, the hundredfold of it; ثلاثة اضعافه *ṯalāṯatu aḍʿāfihī* thrice as much, the threefold of it; اضعاف اضعافه *a. aḍʿāfihī* many times as much, e.g. فاق هذا المبلغ مرتبه اضعاف اضعافه (*mablaḡu murattabahū aḍʿāfa a.*) this amount was many times as much as his salary; اضعافا مضاعفة *aḍʿāfan muḍāʿafatan* many times, a hundredfold

تضاعيف *taḍāʿīf*² contents, text (of a piece of writing); folds; space between the lines; (as an expletive after ف) في تضاعيفه within it, therein contained

مضاعفة *muḍāʿafa* doubling, compounding, multiplying; pl. *-āt* complications (of a disease)

تضاعف *taḍāʿuf* doubling, multiplying

مضعف *muḍaʿʿaf* twofold, double; multiplied, compounded, increased many times

مضاعف *muḍāʿaf* twofold, double; multiplied, compounded, increased many times; see also *ḍiʿf*

ضعة *ḍaʿa, ḍiʿa* see وضع

ضغث *ḍaḡaṯa a* (*ḍaḡṯ*) to confuse, muddle, mix up (ه a story)

ضغث *ḍiḡṯ* pl. اضغاث *aḍḡāṯ* bunch, bouquet; mixture, muddle, jumble, maze | اضغاث الاحلام confused dreams; زاد ضغثا على ابالة (*ibbāla*) to make a thing worse

ضغط *ḍaḡaṭa a* (*ḍaḡṭ*) to press, squeeze (ه, ه s.o., s.th.); to compress (ه air); to exert pressure (على on); to oppress, suppress (على s.o., s.th.), bear down heavily (على upon) VII to be pressed, be squeezed, be compressed

ضغط *ḍaḡṭ* pressure; emphasis, stress; oppression, suppression; voltage, tension (*el.*) | الضغط الجوى (*jawwī*) atmospheric pressure; ضغط الدم *ḍ. ad-dam* and الضغط الدموى (*damawī*) blood pressure; ضغط الهواء *ḍ. al-hawāʾ* air pressure; تحت ضغط الرأى العام (*ḍ. ir-raʾyi l-ʿāmm*) under the pressure of public opinion

ضغطة *ḍaḡṭa* (n. vic.) pressure

○ ضغوطية *ḍuḡūṭīya* (wind) pressure

ضاغوط *ḍāḡūṭ* nightmare

○ مضاغط *maḍāḡiṭ*²: مضاغط هوائية (*hawāʾīya*) compressors

تضاغط *taḍāḡuṭ* compression (*phys.*; as opposed to تخلخل *takalkul*)

انضغاط *inḍiğāṭ* compressibility

ضاغط *ḍāğiṭ*: آلة ضاغطة compressor

مضغوط *maḍğūṭ*: هواء مضغوط (*hawā'*) compressed air

ضغن **ḍağina** *a* (*ḍağan*) to bear a grudge, harbor (secret) hatred (على against), resent (على s.o.) **VI** to harbor a grudge against one another

ضغن *ḍiğn* pl. اضغان *aḍğān* rancor, spite, grudge, malice, malevolence, ill will, (secret) hatred

ضغن *ḍağin* malicious, malevolent, rancorous, spiteful, resentful

ضغينة *ḍağīna* pl. ضغائن *ḍağā'in*² rancor, spite, grudge, malice, malevolence, ill will, (secret) hatred

ضفة **ḍaffa** crowd, throng, jam (of people)

ضفة *ḍiffa, ḍaffa* pl. ضفاف *ḍifāf* bank, shore; coast

ضفف *ḍafaf* poverty, destitution

ضفدع **ḍifdiʻ**, *ḍafdaʻ* pl. ضفادع *ḍafādiʻ*² frog | ○ ضفدع بشرى (*bašarī*) frogman (*mil.*)

ضفر **ḍafara** *i* (*ḍafr*) to braid, plait (ه hair), interweave, interlace, intertwine (ه s.th.); to twine (ه a rope) **II** = **I**; **III** to help, assist, aid (ه s.o.) **VI** to help one another (على to do s.th.); to be tightly interwoven, be tied up, be closely connected (مع with); to be concatenated (evidence)

ضفر *ḍafr* pl. ضفور *ḍufūr* (saddle) girth

ضفار *ḍafār* pl. ضفر *ḍufur* (saddle) girth

ضفيرة *ḍafīra* pl. ضفائر *ḍafā'ir*² plait; braid, tress, pigtail; plaitwork, wickerwork; galloon, lace; strand, hank, skein; plexus (*anat.*)

ضفا (ضفو) **ḍafā** *u* (*ḍafw*) to be abundant, copious; to flow over **IV** to allot generously (ه على s.th. to); to grant, award (ه على s.th. to); to let s.o. or s.th. (على) have (ه s.th.); to fill (ه على s.th. with); to wrap, envelope (على s.th., ه with), spread (ه على s.th. over)

ضفوة *ḍafwa*: ضفوة العيش *ḍ. al-ʻaiš* an easy, comfortable life

ضاف *ḍāfin* abundant, copious, ample; detailed, elaborate, extensive

ضل **ḍalla** *i* (ضلال *ḍalāl*, ضلالة *ḍalāla*) to lose one's way, go astray; to stray (عن or ه from the way); to err | ضل سعيه (*saʻyuhū*) his effort was in vain **II** to mislead, lead astray, misguide (ه s.o.); to delude, deceive (ه s.o.) | ضلل نفسه to delude o.s. **IV** = **II**; to make (ه s.o.) lose his way (ه); to let (ه) s.th. get lost

ضل *ḍull* error

ضلال *ḍalāl* a straying from the right path or from truth; error | ○ ضلال الالوان color blindness, dichromatism

ضلالة *ḍalāla* error

اضلولة *uḍlūla* pl. اضاليل *aḍālīl*² error

مضلة *maḍalla* an occasion, or possibility, of going astray

تضليل *taḍlīl* misleading, misguidance, delusion, deception

اضلال *iḍlāl* misleading, misguidance, delusion, deception

ضال *ḍāll* pl. ضوال *ḍawāll*² straying, roaming, wandering; astray, lost; erroneous, false

ضالة *ḍālla* goal of persistent search, object of a long-cherished wish | ضالة منشودة do.

مضلل *muḍallil* misleading, misguiding, deceptive, delusive, fallacious

مضل *muḍill* misleading, misguiding, deceptive, delusive, fallacious

ضلع **ḍalaʻa** *a* (*ḍalʻ*) with مع: to side with s.o., make common cause with s.o.; — *ḍaluʻa* *u* (ضلاعة *ḍalāʻa*) to be strong, sturdy, robust; — *ḍaliʿa a* (*ḍalaʿ*) to be crooked, bent, curved, to curve **II** to crook, bend, curve (ه s.th.) **V** to be jammed, crammed (من with); to be versed, skilled, proficient, knowledgeable (من in), be conversant, be thoroughly familiar or acquainted (من with), be at home (من in a field of knowledge) **VIII** to be versed, skilled, proficient (ب in), be thoroughly familiar or acquainted, be conversant (ب with); to assume, take over, take upon o.s. (ب s.th., a task, financial expenses, a job, and the like) **X** to be versed, skilled, proficient (من in), be thoroughly familiar or acquainted, be conversant (من with)

ضلع *ḍalʿ* affection, attachment | ضلعه معه he sympathizes with him, he is on his side

ضلع *ḍilʿ*, *ḍilaʿ* pl. ضلوع *ḍulūʿ*, اضلاع *aḍlāʿ*, اضلع *aḍluʿ* rib; cutlet, chop; side (of a triangle); الاضلاع the chest, the breast | ضلع البرميل *ḍ. al-birmīl* barrel stave; متساوى الاضلاع *mutasāwī l-a.* equilateral (*geom.*); كان له ضلع فى الامر he had s.th. to do with the matter, he had a hand in it, he played a role in the affair

ضليع *ḍalīʿ* strong, sturdy; knowledgeable, experienced, skilled

ضلاعة *ḍalāʿa* strength, sturdiness, robustness (of the body)

مضلع *muḍallaʿ* ribbed; polygonal; (pl. *-āt*) polygon | صاج مضلع corrugated iron

متضلع *mutaḍalliʿ* versed, skilled, proficient (من in), thoroughly familiar, conversant (من with); expert (من in)

ضلمه (Turk. *dolma*) *ḍolma* stuffed food (e.g., eggplants stuffed with meat and rice)

ضم *ḍamma u* (*ḍamm*) to bring together, join, draw together, contract (ه s.th.); to add (up), sum up (ه s.th.); to gather, collect, reap, harvest (ه s.th.); to unite, bring together (هم persons); to embrace, hug (ه s.o.); to join, subjoin, annex (ه s.th. to الى), add, attach (ه ,ه s.o., s.th. to الى), unite (ه ,ه s.o., s.th. with الى); to combine (within o.s., ه different things); to close, compress (ه the lips); to grasp, grip, grab, seize (على s.o., s.th.); to get (ه s.o.) into a predicament (said of fate); to pronounce with the vowel *u* (ه a consonant; *gram.*) | ضم الصفوف to close the ranks; ضمه الى صدره (*ṣadrihī*) to press s.o. to one's bosom, embrace s.o.; ضم اليه زوجته (*zaujatahū*) he embraced his wife **VI** to unite, rally, join forces **VII** to close, draw or crowd together, be closely packed; to be joined, united, or combined (الى with), unite, join forces (الى with), to be added, be annexed (الى to); to associate, affiliate (الى with); to enter, join (الى an organization, and the like); to comprise, include, encompass, embrace, contain (على s.th.)

ضم *ḍamm* addition, subjunction; gathering, collecting, rallying, joining, uniting, amalgamation, fusion; admission, enrollment; the vowel *u* (*gram.*)

ضمة *ḍamma* the vowel point for *u*; (pl. *-āt*) embrace, hug

ضميمة *ḍamīma* pl. ضمائم *ḍamāʾim*[2] addition, supplement; increase, raise (of salary)

تضام *taḍāmm*: تضاما مع together with, jointly with

انضمام *inḍimām* annexation (الى to), joining (الى of), union, association, affiliation (الى with); entry, enrollment (الى into an organization, and the like), accession (الى to)

مضموم *maḍmūm* closed, tight, compressed (mouth)

منضم *munḍamm*: نظام منضم close order (*mil.*)

منضمة *munḍamma* accessory, attachment (*techn.*)

اضمحل *iḍmaḥalla* to disappear, vanish, dwindle, fade away, melt away; to decrease, become less

اضمحلال *iḍmiḥlāl* disappearance, vanishing, evanescence; fading

مضمحل *muḍmaḥill* vanishing, evanescent, fading; damped (oscillations, waves; *phys.*)

ضمخ **ḍamaḵa** *u* (*ḍamḵ*) and **II** to oil, anoint, rub, perfume (ه ,ه ب s.o., s.th. with)

ضمد **ḍamada** *u i* (*ḍamd*, ضماد *ḍimād*) and **II** to dress, bandage (ه s.th., esp. a wound)

ضماد *ḍimād* bandaging (of a wound); bandage, band, ligature; carrying on of several love affairs (of a woman)

ضمادة *ḍimāda* dressing (of a wound), bandage

مضمد *muḍammid* (*ir.*) male nurse

مضمدة *muḍammida* ○ compress; (*ir.*) nurse

ضمر **ḍamara**, **ḍamura** *u* (*ḍumr*, ضمور *ḍumūr*) to be or become lean, emaciated, skinny, thin, slim, slender; to contract, shrink **II** to emaciate, make lean, thin, or slender (ه s.th.) **IV** = **II**; to secrete, conceal, hide, keep secret (ه في نفسه s.th. in one's heart), keep (ه s.th.) to o.s. (في نفسه); to harbor, entertain (ه ل a feeling toward, against) | اضمر له الشر (*šarra*) to bear s.o. a grudge, harbor ill will against s.o. **V** to become lean, emaciated **VII** to dry up, wither, wilt, shrivel

ضمر *ḍumr* emaciation; leanness, skinniness, thinness, slenderness, slimness

ضمور *ḍumūr* emaciation; leanness, skinniness, thinness, slenderness, slimness; atrophy (*med.*)

ضمار *ḍimār*: دين ضمار (*dain*) bad debt (i.e., a debt deemed uncollectible)

ضمير *ḍamīr* pl. ضمائر *ḍamā'ir*[2] heart; mind; innermost; conscience; (independent or suffixed) personal pronoun (*gram.*) | تأنيب الضمير compunctions, contrition, repentance; حى الضمير *ḥayy aḍ-ḍ.* conscientious, scrupulous; مرتاح الضمير *murtāḥ aḍ-ḍ.* of peaceful mind; فاقد الضمير unscrupulous

مضمار *miḍmār* pl. مضامير *maḍāmīr*[2] race course, race track; arena; field of activity, field, domain

اضمار *iḍmār* concealment (of a thought), mental reservation; ellipsis (*rhet.*)

ضامر *ḍāmir* lean, skinny, thin; slender, slim, svelte

مضمر *muḍmar* secret, hidden, covert; (independent or suffixed) personal pronoun, also اسم مضمر (*ism*; *gram.*)

ضمن **ḍamina** *a* (ضمان *ḍamān*) to be or become responsible or liable, be guaranty, give security or guaranty, vouch (ب or ه for), warrant, ensure, safeguard, guarantee (ه ل to s.o. s.th.); to insure (ه من s.th. against) | ضمن لنفسه شيئا to be absolutely certain of s.th. **II** to have (ه s.th.) insured (من against); to insert, include, enclose (ه ه s.th. in s.th. else) **V** to comprise, include, comprehend, imply, embrace, contain (ه s.th.) **VI** to be jointly liable, have joint responsibility (ه for s.th.); to be solidary, be in accord, stick together

ضمن *ḍimn* inside, interior; *ḍimna* (prep.) in, within, inside of, among; ضمنا *ḍimnan* (adv.) inclusively, implicitly, tacitly | مفهوم ضمنا tacitly comprised, implicit; من ضمن *min ḍimni* (with foll. genit.) included in, implied in, belonging to, falling under; من ضمنهم among them; مباشرة وضمنا (*mubāšaratan*) directly and indirectly

ضمنى *ḍimnī* included, implied; hidden, implicit, tacit

ضمان[4] *ḍamān* responsibility, guaranty, warrant, surety, security, liability, assurance, safeguard; insurance | ضمان جماعى (*jamāʿī*) collective security; الضمان المشترك (*muštarak*) do.; محدود الضمان of limited liability, Ltd.; شركة الضمان *širkat aḍ-ḍ.* insurance company

ضمين *ḍamīn* pl. ضمناء *ḍumanā'*[2] responsible, answerable, liable (ب for); warrantor, bail(sman), bondsman, surety, guarantor (ب for)

ضمانة *ḍamāna* guaranty, surety, warrant(y), collateral, security, bail

اضمن *aḍman*[2] offering better guaranty

تضامن *taḍāmun* mutuality, reciprocity; joint liability; solidarity | شركة التضامن *širkat at-t.* commercial company of joint liability

ضامن *ḍāmin* responsible, answerable, liable; warrantor, bail(sman), bondsman, surety, guarantor

مضمون *maḍmūn* guaranteed, ensured, warranted; insured (object); (pl. مضامين *maḍāmīn*[2]) content, purport, meaning (of a letter, and the like) | مضمون الوصول registered (letter); دين مضمون (*dain*) bonded, or funded, debt (*fin.*)

مضمن *muḍamman* included, implied

متضامن *mutaḍāmin* mutual, reciprocal; solidary, united in solidarity

ضن *ḍanna* (1st pers. perf. *ḍanintu*) *a* and *ḍanna* (1st pers. perf. *ḍanantu*) *i* (*ḍann*) to keep back (ب s.th.), be sparing or stingy (على ب toward s.o. with), withhold (على ب from s.o. s.th.), (be)grudge (على s.o. ب s.th.) | ما ضن بمشقة على (*bi-mašaqqatin*) to shun no effort for the sake of

ضن *ḍann*: ضنا ب (*ḍannan*) in order to spare s.th., in due consideration of

ضنين *ḍanīn* niggardly, avaricious, stingy; sparing, thrifty, economical, scanty, meager, poor, insufficient

ضنك *ḍanuka u* (*ḍank*, ضناكة *ḍanāka*) to be straitened, cramped, confined (circumstances); to be weak, be exhausted

ضنك *ḍank* poverty, distress, straits | عيش ضنك (*ʿaiš*) a hard, wretched life

مضانك *maḍānik*[2] straits, hardships

مضنك *muḍnik* weak, exhausted

ضنو *ḍanw*, *ḍinw* children

ضنى *ḍaniya a* (*ḍanan*) to become or be lean, emaciated, gaunt, enervated, or worn out; to pine away, be consumed (with grief) **IV** to emaciate, debilitate, weaken, enervate (ه s.o.); to exhaust, wear out (ه s.o.); to undermine, sap (ه the health); to consume (ه s.o.; of anxiety, and the like)

ضن *ḍanin* lean, emaciated, gaunt, languished, wasted, worn out, enervated; exhausted; consumed with grief, careworn

ضنى *ḍanan* weakness, feebleness, debility, exhaustion, emaciation; grief

مضنى *muḍnan* lean, emaciated, gaunt, languished, wasted, worn out, enervated; exhausted; pining away, wasting away

ضهد *ḍahada a* (*ḍahd*) to suppress, oppress, treat unjustly, persecute (ه s.o.) **VIII** = **I**

اضطهاد *iḍṭihād* pl. *-āt* suppression, repression, oppression, maltreatment, persecution, enslavement

مضطهد *muḍṭahid* oppressor, tyrant, persecutor

ضهر *ḍahr* pl. ضهور *ḍuhūr* summit, top (of a mountain)

ضهى **III** to be similar, alike, or corresponding; to resemble (ه s.o., ه s.th.), be like s.o. or s.th. (ه, ه), correspond (ه to s.o., ه to s.th.); to compare (ه ب, على s.th. with; بين — وبين two things); to imitate (ب s.o., s.th.)

ضهى *ḍahan* ○ menopause, climacteric

ضهى *ḍahīy* similar, (a)like, corresponding, analogous

مضاهاة *muḍāhāh* similarity, resemblance, likeness, correspondence, analogy; comparison (على with)

مضاه *muḍāhin* similar, (a)like, corresponding, analogous

(ضوء) ضاء *ḍā'a u* (*ḍau'*) to gleam, beam, radiate, shine **II** to light (ه s.th., a lamp); to illumine, illuminate (ه s.th., e.g., a house) **IV** = **I**; to shed light, cast light (على upon, over); to light, illumine, illuminate (ه s.th.); to enlighten (ه s.th., the mind) **V** = **I**; **X** to be illumined, be lit; to seek light; to seek (to obtain) enlightenment or insight (ب by, through, in, with); to let o.s. be enlightened or guided (ب by)

ضوء *ḍau'* pl. اضواء *aḍwā'* light; brightness, glow | ضوء الشمس *ḍ. aš-šams* sunlight, sunshine; ضوء القمر *ḍ. al-qamar* moonlight; ضوء كاشف searchlight; ضوء النهار *ḍ. an-nahār* daylight; على ضوء (with foll. genit.) in the light of, under the circumstances of, as seen from...; according to

ضوئى *ḍau'ī* luminary, light- (in compounds) | سنة ضوئية (*sana*) light-year

ضياء *ḍiyā'* light, brightness, glow

اضاءة *iḍā'a* lighting; illumination | الاضاءة المقيدة (*muqayyada*) restricted illumination = dim-out; مصباح الاضاءة *miṣbāḥ al-i.* incandescent lamp

مضئ *muḍī'* shining, luminous, bright

ضاد *ḍād* name of the letter ض

(ضور) ضار *ḍāra u* (*ḍaur*) to harm, injure, damage, prejudice (ه, ه s.o., s.th.), inflict damage (ه, ه upon); to suffer violent hunger, starve to death **V** to writhe with pain; to writhe, wince, be convulsed (ه with pain, with hunger)

ضور *ḍaur* violent hunger

ضوضاء *ḍauḍā'* noise, din, uproar

ضوضى *ḍauḍan* noise, din, uproar

(ضوع) ضاع *ḍā'a u* (*ḍau'*) to spread, diffuse, emanate (fragrance); to be fragrant, exhale fragrance **V** = **I**

ضامة look up alphabetically

ضوى *ḍawā i* to resort, have recourse (الى to); — *ḍawiya a* to be lean, thin, spare, slight, scrawny **IV** اضوى to weaken, debilitate (ه, ه s.o., s.th.); to harm, injure, damage, prejudice (ه s.o., ه s.th.) **VII** to join, follow (الى s.o.), attach o.s. (الى to s.o.); to rally, flock (الى around, تحت لوائه around or under s.o.'s banner)

ضاو *ḍāwin* thin, lean, spare, slight, scrawny

(ضير) ضار *ḍāra i* (*ḍair*) to harm, injure, damage, prejudice (ه, ه s.o., s.th.), inflict damage (ه, ه upon)

ضير *ḍair* harm, damage, injury, prejudice; wrong, iniquity, offense

قسمة ضيزى *qisma ḍīzā* unjust division

(ضيع) ضاع *ḍā'a i* (*ḍai'*, ضياع *ḍayā'*) to get lost, be lost (على for s.o.); to lose itself, disappear; to perish **II** and **IV** to ruin, let perish, thwart, frustrate, mar, destroy (ه, ه s.o., s.th.); to lose, forfeit (ه s.th.), be deprived (ه of s.th.); to waste, squander, spend uselessly (ه s.th.); to neglect, omit (ه s.th.); to miss, let go by (ه s.th.), let slip (ه s.th., e.g., an opportunity) | ضيع حقه (*ḥaqqahū*) to forfeit one's right; الصيف ضيعت اللبن *aṣ-ṣaifa ḍayya'ti l-labana* (invar.) approx.: you have let the opportunity go by, you missed your chance; اضاع صوابه (*ṣawābahū*) to lose one's mind; اضاع عليه فرصة (*furṣa*) to make s.o. miss an opportunity; اضاع الوقت (*waqt*) to waste time

ضيع *ḍai'* loss

ضيعة *ḍai'a* pl. ضياع *ḍiyā'* landed estate, country estate, domain; small village, hamlet

ضياع *ḍayā'* loss; ruin, destruction, perdition | ضياع الوقت *d. al-waqt* loss of time

يا ضيعانه *yā ḍi'ānahū* what a loss!

مضياع *miḍyā'* prodigal, squandering, wasteful; squanderer, wastrel, spendthrift

تضييع *taḍyī'* waste, squandering, dissipation; neglect, omission

اضاعة *iḍā'a* waste, squandering, dissipation; neglect, omission | اضاعة الوقت *i. al-waqt* waste of time

ضائع *ḍā'i'* pl. ضيع *ḍuyya'*, ضياع *ḍiyā'* (getting) lost; poor, wretched, miserable

مضيعة *maḍī'a* ruin, destruction, perdition, loss; — *muḍī'a*, مضيعة للوقت (*li-l-waqt*) waste of time, loss of time

مضيع *muḍayyi'* prodigal, squandering, wasteful

(ضيف) ضاف *ḍāfa i* (ضيافة *ḍiyāfa*) to stop or stay as a guest **II** to take in as a guest, receive hospitably, entertain (ه s.o.) **IV** = **II**; to add, subjoin, annex, attach (ه الى s.th. to); to admix (ه الى s.th. to); to connect, bring in relation (ه الى s.th. with); to ascribe, attribute, assign (ه الى s.th. to s.o.) | اضاف اسما الى اسم (*isman*) to annex a noun (the first member of a genitive construction) to another (the second member; *gram.*); اضف الى ذلك ان (*aḍif*) what's more..., moreover..., furthermore... **VII** to be added, be annexed, be subjoined, be attached (الى to) **X** to invite s.o. (ه) to be one's guest

ضيف *ḍaif* pl. ضيوف *ḍuyūf*, اضياف *aḍyāf*, ضيفان *ḍifān* guest; visitor

ضيافة *ḍiyāfa* hospitable reception, entertainment as guest, accomodation; hospitality | انت فى ضيافتى you are my guest

مضياف *miḍyāf* hospitable; hospitable host

مضافة *maḍāfa* hostel, guesthouse, inn

مضيفة *maḍyafa* guest room; guesthouse

اضافة *iḍāfa* addition, apposition; subjunction, annexation, appending, attachment, augmentation, supplementation; assignment, allocation; ascription, attribution (الى to); genitive construction (*gram.*) | اضافة الى اجل (*ajal*) limitation (of a legal transaction; *Isl. Law*); بالاضافة الى in comparison with, in relation to; with respect to, regarding...; with regard to, in consideration of; in addition to, beside; بالاضافة الى ذلك moreover, furthermore, besides

اضافى *iḍāfī* additional, supplementary, auxiliary, contributory, extra; secondary, subsidiary, tributary, accessory, incidental, side-, by- (in compounds); relative (*philos.*)

اضافية *iḍāfīya* relativity (*philos.*)

مضيف *muḍīf* host

مضيفة *muḍīfa* hostess; air hostess, stewardess

مضاف *muḍāf* added, subjoined, adjoined, apposed; construct state (*gram.*) | المضاف اليه the second, or governed, noun of a genitive construction (*gram.*); مضافا الى ذلك moreover, furthermore, besides

(ضيق) ضاق *ḍāqa i* (*ḍaiq*, *ḍīq*) to be or become narrow, straitened, cramped, confined; to become too narrow, too confined (ب for); to be anguished, uneasy, depressed, dejected (ب because of, by, at, about); to become or be tired, weary (ب of s.o., of s.th.) | ضاقت به الارض (*arḍu*) to be at a loss, be at one's wit's end; ضاقت به الحياة (*ḥayātu*) life depressed him, he had a bad time, he was bad off; ضاقت به السبل (subulu) to be at a loss, be at the end of one's tether, be at one's wit's end; ضاق ذرعا ب (ḏar'an) not to be up to s.th., be unable to do or accomplish s.th.; not to be able to stand or bear s.th., be fed up with, be tired of, feel uneasy about, be oppressed by; ضاق عنه ذرعا do.; ضاق صدره (ṣadruhū) to be annoyed, angry; ضاقت يده عن (yaduhū) to be incapable of; to be too poor to... **II** to make narrow or narrower, narrow (down), straiten, cramp, tighten, confine, constrain, restrain, restrict, contract (ه s.th.); to pull tight (ه s.th., e.g., a dress); to harass, oppress, beset, besiege, beleaguer (على s.o.); to keep (على s.o.) short (في in s.th.) | ضيق الحصار to tighten the blockade; ضيق على نفسه to restrain o.s., take restrictions upon o.s. **III** to vex, annoy, anger (ه s.o.); to harass, oppress, beset (ه s.o.); to trouble, bother, inconvenience, disturb, hinder, hamper, impede, affect gravely (ه, ه s.o., s.th.), bear down heavily (ه, ه upon); to cause trouble (ه to s.o.) **VI** to be or become narrow, to narrow; to become annoyed, become irritated; to be angry (من at, about)

ضيق ḍīq narrowness; tightness, closeness; confinement, restriction, limitation, constraint; shortage, scarcity; oppression, anguish; dejectedness, depression, distress; lack, want, paucity, poverty; care, worry, anxiety; anger, annoyance, irritation, exasperation; weariness, ennui | ضيق ذات اليد *ḍ. ḏāt al-yad* poverty, destitution; ضيق المقام *ḍ. al-maqām* crampedness, lack of space; ضيق النطاق do.; small range, limited extent, narrow scope; ضيق اليد *ḍ. al-yad* poverty, destitution

ضيق **ḍayyiq** narrow; tight; cramped; short, scarce; confined, limited, restricted | ضيق الخلق *ḍ. al-ḵuluq* illiberal, ungenerous; impatient, annoyed; ضيق الصدر *ḍ. aṣ-ṣadr* vexed, annoyed (ب over, at, by), angry (ب at, with); upset, depressed, downcast, dejected; ضيق العقل *ḍ. al-'aql* narrow-minded, hidebound, dull-witted; ضيق النطاق small-range; of narrow scope, limited in extent; confined, limited, restricted

ضيقة **ḍaiqa, ḍīqa** straitened circumstances, poverty; anguish

اضيق **aḍyaq²** narrower, tighter

مضيق **maḍīq** pl. مضايق **maḍāyiq²**, مضائق **maḍā'iq²** strait(s); defile, (mountain) pass; narrow(s), stricture

تضييق **taḍyīq** narrowing, tightening; restriction, limitation; oppression | تضييق الحصار tightening of the blockade; تضييق الخناق (tightening of the rope =) strangling, suppression

مضايقة **muḍāyaqa** pl. *-āt* affliction, distress, grievance, embarrassment; obstruction, impediment, disturbance, harassment, molestation; depressing state; anger, annoyance, vexation, irritation; inconvenience, difficulty, trouble, nuisance

ضائقة **ḍā'iqa** pl. ضوائق **ḍawā'iq²** predicament, straits, difficulty; critical situation, crisis | ضائقة العيش *ḍ. al-'aiš* straitened circumstances; ضائقة مالية (*mālīya*) financial straits

مضايق **muḍāyiq** troublesome, irksome, wearisome, disturbing, annoying; nuisance (person)

متضايق **mutaḍāyiq** annoyed, vexed, irritated, exasperated, angry; hard pressed

ضيم[1] ضام **ḍāma** i (*ḍaim*) to wrong, harm (ه s.o.), inflict damage (ه upon s.o.); to treat unjustly (ه s.o.) **X** = **I**

ضيم **ḍaim** pl. ضيوم **ḍuyūm** wrong, inequity, injustice; harm, damage, detriment, injury

ضامة[2] look up alphabetically

ط

ط abbreviation of قيراط *qīrāṭ*

طاء *ṭā'* name of the letter ط

طابة *ṭāba* pl. *-āt* ball

طابور *ṭābūr* pl. طوابير *ṭawābīr*[2] battalion; (*eg.*) line, file, single file (of soldiers, of persons walking one behind the other); queue | الطابور الخامس the fifth column

طابية *ṭābiya* pl. طواب *ṭawābin* fortress, fort; round fortress tower; (*eg.*) rook, castle (chess)

طاجن *ṭājin* pl. طواجن *ṭawājin*[2] frying pan; (*eg.*) shallow earthen pot

طار, طارة see طور

طارمة *ṭārima* pl. *-āt* kiosk, booth, cabin, stall

طازه *ṭāza* fresh, tender, new

طازج *ṭāzaj* fresh, new

[1]طاس and طاسة see طوس

[2]طاؤوس *ṭā'ūs* and طاوس *ṭāwūs* pl. طواويس *ṭawāwīs*[2] peacock

طأطأ *ṭa'ṭa'a* to incline, bend, tilt, bow (رأسه *ra'sahū* one's head; also used without رأسه)

مطأطئ *muṭa'ṭi'* with bowed head

مطأطأ *muṭa'ṭa'*: مطأطأ الرأس *m. ar-ra's* with bowed head

[1]طاق *ṭāq* pl. *-āt*, طيقان *ṭīqān* arch (*arch.*); (pl. *-āt*) layer, stratum

[2]طاقة *ṭāqa* pl. *-āt* window

[3]طاقية *ṭāqīya* pl. □ طواق *ṭawāqī* white cotton skullcap (often worn under the tarboosh; in Eg. = عرقية); fatigue cap (of the Eg. Territorial Army)

طمأن see طأمن

طاولة (It. *tavola*) *ṭāwula* table | لعبة الطاولة *la'bat aṭ-ṭ.* backgammon, tricktrack; تنس الطاولة table tennis

طب *ṭabba u i* (*ṭabb, ṭibb, ṭubb*) to treat medically (ه, ـه s.o., s.th.), give medical treatment (ه, ـه to s.o., to s.th.); to seek to remedy, tackle (ل s.th.) II to treat medically (ه, ـه s.o., s.th.), give medical treatment (ه, ـه to s.o., to s.th.) V to receive, or undergo, medical treatment, submit to medical treatment; to practice medicine, engage in the medical field X to seek medical advice (ـه from s.o.), consult (ـه a doctor)

طب *ṭibb* medical treatment; medicine, medical science | طب الاسنان *ṭ. al-asnān* dentistry, dental science; الطب البيطرى (*baiṭarī*) veterinary science; الطب الشرعى (*šar'ī*) forensic medicine; الطب النفسانى (*nafsānī*) psychiatry; علم الطب *'ilm aṭ-ṭ.* medical science, medicine; كلية الطب *kullīyat aṭ-ṭ.* medical school, medical college, (chiefly G. B.:) faculty of medicine

طبى *ṭibbī* medical, pertaining to the medical profession or science | لائق طبيا (*ṭibbīyan*) physically fit (e.g., for military service)

طبة *ṭabba* pl. *-āt* (*eg.*) cushion, pad; plug, stopper, stopple; bung

طبيب *ṭabīb* pl. اطباء *aṭibbā'*[2], اطبة *aṭibba* physician, doctor | طبيب بيطرى (*baiṭarī*) veterinarian; طبيب خاص (*ḵāṣṣ*) physician in ordinary, private physician (e.g., of a king); طبيب ساحر medicine man, shaman; طبيب الاسنان dental surgeon, dentist; طبيب شرعى (*šar'ī*) medical examiner (*jur.*); طبيب الامراض الجلدية (*jildīya*) dermatologist

طبيبة *ṭabība* female doctor, doctress

طبابة *ṭibāba* medical treatment; medical profession

تطبيب *taṭbīb* healing art, medical practice, medical profession

متطبب *mutaṭabbib* quack, quacksalver

طبخ *ṭabaḵa* u a (*ṭabḵ*) to cook (ه s.th.) VII to be or get cooked

طبخ *ṭabḵ* cooking, cookery; cooked food; ○ celluloid

طبخة *ṭabḵa* (n. un.) (article of cooked) food, meal, dish, course

طباخ *ṭabbāḵ* cook

طبيخ *ṭabīḵ* cooked food, fare

طباخة *ṭibāḵa* culinary art, cookery, cuisine

مطبخ *maṭbaḵ* pl. مطابخ *maṭābiḵ*[2] kitchen; cookshop, eating house, luncheonette

مطبخ *miṭbaḵ* pl. مطابخ *maṭābiḵ*[2] any cooking apparatus (also, e.g., a hot plate), cooking stove, kitchen range, portable range

[1]طبر *ṭabar* hatchet, ax, battle-ax

طبردار *ṭabardār* sapper, pioneer (*mil.*)

[2]طابور look up alphabetically

[3]طبرية *ṭabarīya*[2] Tiberias (city in Palestine, on W shore of Sea of Galilee)

طبشورة *ṭabšūra* (*syr.*) chalk

طباشير *ṭabāšīr*[2] chalk

طباشيرى *ṭabāšīrī* chalky, cretaceous, chalk- (in compounds)

طبطب *ṭabṭaba* to gurgle, purl (water); to pat, stroke, caress (على s.o.)

طبطابة *ṭabṭāba* bat, mallet, racket (for ball games)

طبع *ṭaba'a* a (*ṭab'*) to provide with an imprint, impress or impression (ه or على s.th.); to impress with a stamp, seal or signet (ه or على s.th.), leave or set one's stamp, seal, mark, or impress (على or ه, ه on s.o., on s.th.); to stamp, imprint, impress (على ه s.th. on); to mint, coin (ه money); to print (ه s.th.); pass. *ṭubi'a* to have a natural aptitude or disposition, have a propensity, be disposed by nature (على for) | طبعه بطابعه (*bi-ṭābi'ihi*) to place, set, or leave one's stamp, mark, or impress on s.o. or s.th., impart one's own character to s.o. or s.th.; طبع عليه (*ṭubi'a*) to be innate, inherent in s.o., be native, natural to s.o. II to tame, domesticate, break in, train (ه an animal) V تطبع بطباعه (*bi-ṭibā'ihī*) to take on, assume, or receive s.o.'s peculiar character, bear s.o.'s stamp or impress VII to be stamped, be printed, be imprinted, be impressed; to leave an imprint or impression (فى on); to be disposed by nature (على for)

طبع *ṭab'* printing (of a book), print; (pl. طباع *ṭibā'*) impress, impression, stamp, hallmark, peculiarity, characteristic, nature, character, temper, (natural) disposition | طبع الحجر *ṭ. al-ḥajar* lithography; طبع الحروف typography; تحت الطبع in (the) press, at press (*typ.*); مسودة الطبع *musuwaddat* and *musawwadat aṭ-ṭ.* proof sheet, galley proof (*typ.*); اعادة الطبع *i'ādat aṭ-ṭ.* reprinting reprint; طبعا *ṭab'an* or بالطبع by nature, by natural disposition; naturally! of course! certainly! to be sure! سيئ الطبع *sayyi' aṭ-ṭ.* ill-disposed, ill-natured, evil by nature; شاذ الطبع (الطباع) *šāḏḏ aṭ-ṭ.* eccentric, extravagant

طبعة *ṭab'a* pl. *-āt* printing, print; edition, issue, impression

طباع *ṭabbā'* printer

طباعة *ṭibā'a* art of printing | آلة الطباعة printing press

طباعى *ṭibā'ī* typographic(al)

طبيعة *ṭabīʿa* pl. طبائع *ṭabāʾiʿ*² nature; natural disposition, constitution; peculiarity, individuality, character; regular, normal manner; physics; natural science | بطبيعة الحال by the very nature of the case, as is (was) only natural, ipso facto, naturally, as a matter of course; عالم الطبيعة physicist; natural scientist; علم الطبيعة *ʿilm aṭ-ṭ.* physics; natural science; فلسفة ما وراء (بعد) الطبيعة (*falsafatu*) metaphysics; فوق الطبيعة supernatural; طبائع الاشياء the nature of things, state of affairs

طبيعى *ṭabīʿī* nature's, of nature, nature- (in compounds), natural; inborn, innate, inherent, native; normal, ordinary, usual, regular; physical; physicist; natural scientist; naturalist | عالم طبيعى physicist; natural scientist; الطبيعيات physics; natural science

مطبع *maṭbaʿ* print shop, printing office, printing house, press

مطبعة *maṭbaʿa* pl. مطابع *maṭābiʿ*² print shop, printing office, printing house, press | حرية المطابع *ḥurrīyat al-m.* freedom of the press

مطبعى *maṭbaʿī* printing, printer's (in compounds), typographic(al) | خطأ مطبعى (*kaṭaʾ*) and غلطة مطبعية (*ḡalṭa*) typographical error, misprint, erratum

مطبعجى (*eg.*) *maṭbaʿgī* printer

مطبعة *miṭbaʿa* pl. مطابع *maṭābiʿ*² printing machine, printing press

طابع *ṭābiʿ* printer; — *ṭābaʿ* impress, stamp, mark, character; (pl. طوابع *ṭawābiʿ*²) seal, signet; stamp; imprint, print, impress, impression; (postage, etc.) stamp; tablet, pill | طابع البريد and طابع بريدى postage stamp; طابع تذكارى (*taḏkārī*) commemorative stamp; طابع الاصابع fingerprint; صاحب الطابع keeper of the seal; طبعه بطابعه to place, set, or leave, one's stamp, mark, or impress on s.o. or s.th., impart one's own character to s.o. or s.th.

مطبوع *maṭbūʿ* printed, imprinted; stereotyped; pl. *-āt* printed material, prints; printed matter | مطبوع بطابعه bearing the stamp, mark or impress of s.o. or s.th., being characterized by; مطبوع على do., being by its very nature..., having the innate property of...; مطبوع دورى (*daurī*) a periodical; قانون المطبوعات press law

طبق[1] II to cover, cover up (ه s.th.); to make coincident or congruent, cause to coincide, superpose (بين two figures; *geom.*); to fold (ه s.th., also, e.g., the hands); (*eg.*) to shoe (ه a horse); to apply (ه على s.th. to); to be common, universal, widespread; to spread (also ه throughout s.th.), pervade (ه s.th.); pass. *ṭubbiqa* to be applied, apply, be applicable, be effective, be valid | طبقت شهرته الآفاق (*šuhratuhū*) he (it) enjoyed, or achieved, world-wide fame; طبق صيته الخافقين (*ṣītuhū, kāfiqain*) do., his (its) fame spread throughout the world III to bring to coincidence, make coincident or congruent, cause to coincide (بين — وبين s.th. with), correlate, compare, contrast (بين — وبين s.th. with); to adapt, adjust, tally, trim into shape (ه s.th.); to suit, fit, match (ه, ه s.o., s.th.), go, tally (ه, ه with), adapt o.s., adjust o.s. (ه, ه to s.o., to s.th.); to correspond (ه to s.th.), concur, agree, conform, be in keeping (ه, ه with s.o., with s.th.), fit (ه into s.th.) IV to close, shut (ه s.th., e.g., the eyes, mouth, etc.); to cover, cover up (ه, على s.th., also ه with one's hand على s.th.); to surround, encircle, encompass (على s.o.); to be agreed, agree, come to an agreement (على on, about) | اطبق على يدى (*yadī*) he pressed my hand V to get or be covered or closed VII = V; to be applicable, apply (على to), fit, suit (على s.o., s.th.), hold good (على for), be true (على of); to be in conformity, be consistent, be compatible, be in keeping, conform, agree (على with), correspond (على to s.th.)

طبق *ṭibqa* (prep.) according to, corresponding to, in accordance with, in conformity with | طبقا ل (*ṭibqan*) do.; صورة طبق الاصل (*ṣūra, aṣl*) true copy; exact replica

طبق *ṭabaq* pl. اطباق *aṭbāq* lid, cover; plate; dish, shallow bowl; (round) tray, salver; ash tray; (pl. أطباق, also طباق *ṭibāq*) layer, tier; stratum (of the air); pl. طباق (with foll. genit.) superposed masses, layered formations, piles, large quantities of... | اطباق طائرة flying saucers

يد طبقة *yad ṭabiqa* closed hand

طبقة *ṭabaqa* pl. *-āt* layer; stratum (of earth, air, society, etc.); floor, story (of a building); class, category; generation | ○ الطبقة الطخرورية (*ṭukrūrīya*) stratosphere; الطبقات النجسة (*najisa*) the impure castes, the pariahs; الطبقة المتوسطة (*mutawassiṭa*) the middle class(es); حرب الطبقات *ḥarb aṭ-ṭ.* class struggle; علم طبقات الارض *ʿilm ṭ. al-arḍ* geology; معدود فى الطبقة الثالثة regarded as third-rate

طابق *ṭābaq, ṭābiq* pl. طوابق *ṭawābiq*² large bricks; floor, story (of a building) | الطابق الارضى (*arḍī*) ground floor

طاباق *ṭābāq* pl. طوابيق *ṭawābīq*² large bricks

طباق *ṭibāq* (with foll. genit. or suffix) that which is in agreement, in keeping, or in conformity with..., corresponding, analogous (to s.th.), in accordance (with), conformable (to), consistent (with), compatible (with); antithesis, juxtaposition of contrasting ideas (*rhet.*)

طبيق *ṭabīq* (with foll. genit. or suffix) s.th. in agreement, in keeping, or in conformity with..., corresponding, analogous (to s.th.), in accordance (with), consistent (with), compatible (with)

تطبيق *taṭbīq* adaptation, accommodation, adjustment; application

تطبيقى *taṭbīqī* applied; practical, serving practical ends | علوم تطبيقية applied sciences

مطابقة *muṭābaqa* agreement, conformity, congruity, correspondence

تطابق *taṭābuq* congruence (*geom.*)

مطابق *muṭābiq* corresponding, congruous, conformable, in agreement or conformity (with) | مطابق للحقيقة true, truthful, veracious, agreeing with the facts, true to nature, lifelike

مطبق *muṭbiq* entire, complete, utter, absolute, total; — *muṭbaq* pressed; coated, incrusted (بالذهب with gold); subterranean dungeon, oubliette, underground chamber | الحروف المطبقة (*muṭbaqa*) (*phon.*) the sounds *ṣ, ḍ, ṭ, ẓ*

²طباق *ṭabāq, ṭubāq* (*eg.*) tobacco

¹طبل *ṭabala u* (*ṭabl*) to beat a drum; to drum **II** = **I**; to beat the drum (ل for s.o., i.e., to campaign, make propaganda for s.o.)

طبل *ṭabl* drumming, drumbeat; (pl. طبول *ṭubūl*, اطبال *aṭbāl*) drum; bass drum (of the Western orchestra)

طبلة *ṭabla* drum | طبلة الاذن *ṭ. al-uḏun* eardrum, tympanic membrane

طبلة *ṭabla* pl. *-āt*, طبل *ṭubal* (*eg.*) lock, padlock

طبلى *ṭablī* drum-shaped

طبال *ṭabbāl* pl. *-ūn* drummer

مطبل *muṭabbal* moist, damp (ground)

²طبلة *ṭabla* pl. *-āt* table

طبلية *ṭablīya* pl. *-āt*, □ طبالى *ṭabālī* a low, round table; turntable; tray, wooden salver

¹طبن *ṭabina a* to be bright, intelligent

طبن *ṭabin* bright, intelligent

[2]طابونة *ṭābūna* (طبونة *ṭubūna*) pl. *-āt* a small, jar-shaped oven, sunk in the ground, open on top, used for baking bread; bakery; (*pal., eg.*) (baker's) oven

[3]طبان *ṭabbān* pl. *-āt* (wheel) tire

طبنجة *ṭabanja* pl. *-āt* pistol

طابية *ṭābiya* pl. طواب look up alphabetically

طاجن *ṭāj.n* pl. طواجن *ṭawājin*[2] frying pan; (*eg.*) shallow earthen pot

طحطح *ṭaḥṭaḥa* to break, shatter, smash (ه s.th.)

طحل (*ṭuḥl, ṭaḥl?*) sediment, dregs, lees

طحال *ṭiḥāl* pl. *-āt*, طحل *ṭuḥul* spleen, milt

طحالى *ṭiḥālī* splenic

طحال *ṭuḥāl* inflammation of the spleen, splenitis

مطحول *maṭḥūl* having a diseased spleen, splenetic

طحلب *ṭuḥlub* (coll.; n. un. ة) pl. طحالب *ṭaḥālib*[2] water moss

طحن *ṭaḥana a* (*ṭaḥn*) to grind, mill, bray, pulverize (ه s.th., esp. grain); to crush, ruin, destroy (ه, ه s.o., s.th.); to wear out, wear down (ه s.o.), exact a heavy toll (ه of s.o.; age, years) VI to quarrel, wrangle, be antagonistic, be in conflict (with one another), to conflict

طحن *ṭiḥn* flour, meal

طحين *ṭaḥīn* flour, meal

طحينى *ṭaḥīnī* mealy, farinaceous

طحينية *ṭaḥīnīya* (*eg.*) a sweet made of sesame-seed meal and sugar

طحينة *ṭaḥīna* (*eg., syr.*) a thick sauce made of sesame oil, and served with salads, vegetables, etc.

طحان *ṭaḥḥān* miller

طاحون *ṭāḥūn* and طاحونة *ṭāḥūna* pl. طواحين *ṭawāḥīn*[2] mill, grinder | طاحونة الهواء *ṭ. al-hawā'* windmill

مطحنة *miṭḥana* pl. مطاحن *maṭāḥin*[2] mill, grinder

مطحنة *maṭḥana* pl. مطاحن *maṭāḥin*[2] mill; flour mill

طاحن *ṭāḥin* molar tooth, grinder

طاحنة *ṭāḥina* pl. طواحن *ṭawāḥin*[2] molar tooth, grinder

○ الطبقة الطخرورية *aṭ-ṭabaqa aṭ-ṭukrūrīya* the stratosphere

طر *ṭarra u* (*ṭarr*, طرور *ṭurūr*) to sharpen, hone, whet (ه s.th.); to grow; to sprout, come out (mustache, hair)

طرا *ṭurran* altogether, all without exception, one and all

طرة *ṭurra* pl. طرر *ṭurar* forelock; knotted cloth or kerchief

طرار *ṭarrār* pl. طرارة *ṭarrāra* (*maḡr.*) tambourine player; rogue, scoundrel

طرأ *ṭara'a a* (*ṭar'*, طروء *ṭurū'*) to descend, break in, come (على upon), overtake, befall (على s.o.), happen unexpectedly (على to s.o.); to occur (على or ل to s.o., of an idea) | ماذا طرأ عليه what's got into him all of a sudden? what's the matter with him all of a sudden? طرأت عليه فكرة (*fikratun*) an idea occurred to him, he had an idea; لم يطرأ على الحالة تبدل يذكر (*tabaddulun yudkaru*) (no change worth mentioning came over the situation, i.e.) the situation remained substantially unchanged IV to praise, laud, extol (ه s.o.)

طرىء *ṭarī'* fresh, new

طارئ *ṭāri'* foreign, extraneous, extrinsic, unusual; accidental, incidental, casual, unforeseen, unexpected, contingent; a new factor or development intervening suddenly, a contingent;

unexpected visitor; sudden stirring, sudden impulse (من e.g., of joy)

طارئة *ṭāri'a* pl. طوارئ *ṭawāri'*[2] unforeseen event, unexpected case, a contingent; new factor or development; incident, accident | حالة الطوارئ state of emergency

طرآنى *ṭur'ānī* of unknown origin, wild

طرابلس *ṭarābulus*[2]: طرابلس الشام Tripoli (in Lebanon); طرابلس الغرب *t. al-ḡarb* Tripoli (in Libya)

طرب *ṭariba a* (*ṭarab*) to be moved (with joy or grief); to be delighted, be overjoyed, be transported with joy **II** to delight, fill with delight, enrapture, please, gratify (ه s.o.); to sing, vocalize, chant **IV** to delight, fill with delight, enrapture, please, gratify (ه s.o.); to make music; to sing, vocalize, chant; to play music (ه for s.o.), sing (ه to s.o.)

طرب *ṭarab* pl. اطراب *aṭrāb* joy, pleasure, delight, rapture; amusement, entertainment (with music and the like); music | آلة الطرب musical instrument

طرب *ṭarib* pl. طراب *ṭirāb* moved (with joy or grief), touched, affected; delighted, enraptured, transported, pleased, charmed

طروب *ṭarūb* gay, merry, lively

اطرب *aṭrab*[2] more delightful; making better music, being a better musician; more melodious

اطراب *iṭrāb* delight, delectation, diversion

مطرب *muṭrib* delightful, ravishing, charming, amusing, entertaining; melodious; musician; singer, vocalist, chansonnier

مطربة *muṭriba* singer, songstress, vocalist, chanteuse

طربيزة *ṭarabēza* (*eg.*) table

طرابلس look up alphabetically

طربوش *ṭarbūš* pl. طرابيش *ṭarābīš*[2] tarboosh, fez

طرابيشى *ṭarābīšī* tarboosh merchant

مطربش *muṭarbaš* wearing a tarboosh, tarbooshed

متطربش *mutaṭarbiš* wearing a tarboosh, tarbooshed; hence, in Eg., a member of the white-collar class, of the educated middle class

طرح *ṭaraḥa a* (*ṭarḥ*) to throw, cast, fling, toss (ب على or ه s.th. onto or upon); to throw, toss, or fling away, throw off, discard, dump (ب or ه s.th.); to remove, drive away, expel, reject, disown, repudiate (ب or ه, ه s.o., s.th.); to throw or put (ه على a garment on or over s.o.); to present, submit (ه على s.th. to s.o.); to teach (ه على a tune to s.o.); to cede, surrender, yield (ه ل s.th. to s.o.); to miscarry, have a miscarriage; to deduct, subtract, discount (ه من s.th. from) | طرحه فى المناقصة العامة (*munāqaṣa, 'āmma*) to invite tenders, or bids, publicly for s.th. (e.g., the government for some project); طرح عليه سؤالا (*su'ālan*) to put a question to s.o.; طرح مسألة على بساط البحث (*mas'alatan, b. il-baḥṯ*) to broach or raise a question, present a problem for consideration **II** to cause a miscarriage (ها to a woman); طرح ه اطراحا (*iṭṭirāḥan*) to throw s.th. far away, fling s.th. off or away **III** to exchange (ه ه with s.o. s.th.) | طارحه الكلام (*kalām*) to converse with s.o., have a talk with s.o.; طارحه الحديث to chat with s.o., have a conversation with s.o.; طارحه الاسئلة (*as'ila*) to exchange questions with s.o. **V** to drop, fall, or tumble to the ground **VI** to exchange with one another (ه e.g., thoughts) **VII** to be flung, be tossed, be thrown, be rejected, be expelled, be disowned, be repudiated; to throw o.s. down, prostrate o.s. (e.g., على الارض on the ground); to be thrown down, be dropped **VIII** to throw far away, fling off or away (ه s.th.); to discard, throw away (ه s.th.)

طرح *ṭarḥ* expulsion, rejection, repulsion, banishment, repudiation; miscarriage, abortion; subtraction, deduction, discount | طرح البحر *ṭ. al-baḥr* (*eg.*) alluviation, alluvial deposits

طرح *ṭirḥ* miscarried foetus

طرحة *ṭarḥa* pl. طرح *ṭuraḥ* veil (sometimes embroidered) worn by Arab women as a headcloth; headcloth, head veil

طريح *ṭarīḥ* pl. طرحى *ṭarḥā* thrown down, cast down, dumped; thrown to the ground, felled, prostrate; expelled, banished, rejected, disowned, repudiated | طريح الفراش bedridden, confined to bed

طريحة *ṭarīḥa* assignment, task | شغل بالطريحة (*šuġl*) job work, piecework (*eg.*)

طراحة *ṭarrāḥa* pl. طرارح *ṭarāriḥ*² mattress; hassock, ottoman

اطروحة *uṭrūḥa* dissertation, thesis (*Syr.*)

مطرح *maṭraḥ* pl. مطارح *maṭāriḥ*² place where s.th. is thrown or at which s.th. is discarded, a dump; place, spot, location, locality; seat (in an auditorium)

اطراح *iṭṭirāḥ* rejection, repudiation

مطروح *maṭrūḥ* thrown down, cast down, dumped, thrown off, discarded; lying on the ground, prostrate; subtrahend (*math.*) | المطروح منه minuend (*math.*)

منطرح *munṭariḥ* thrown down, cast down, dumped, thrown off, discarded; expelled, banished, rejected, disowned, repudiated

طرخون *ṭarḵūn* tarragon (Artemisia dracunculus; *bot.*)

طرد *ṭarada* u (*ṭard*) to drive away, chase away, push away, shove away, reject, repel, banish, exile, dismiss, drive out, expel, evict (ه, ه من s.o., s.th. from); to chase, hunt, hound (ه, ه s.o., s.th.) | طرده من منصبه (*manṣibihī*) to relieve s.o. of his office, dismiss s.o. **II** = **I**; **III** to assault, attack (ه, ه s.o.), launch an attack (ه, ه on); to stalk (ه an animal, game); to pursue, follow (ه, ه s.o., s.th.), run after s.o. or s.th. (ه, ه), give chase (ه, ه to) **VIII** to drive away as booty (ه animals); to be consecutive, be continuous, form an uninterrupted sequence, succeed one another continuously; to flow uninterruptedly, carry water perennially (river); to progress or get on at a rapid pace, make good headway (undertaking) **X** to proceed (in one's speech), go on to say, continue (ه s.th., e.g., one's speech); to change, pass on (in speech) (من — ل from — to); to digress (in speaking), make an excursus | استطرد من ذلك الى قوله ان (*qaulihī*) thereupon he proceeded to speak about..., then he broached the subject of..., after that he went on to say that...

طرد *ṭard* driving away, chasing away, repulsion, expulsion, eviction, dismissal, banishment, expatriation; pursuit, chase, hunt; swarm (of bees); (pl. طرود *ṭurūd*) parcel, package | بحث مسألة طردا وعكسا (*mas'alatan ṭardan wa-'aksan*) to study a problem from all sides, in all its aspects

طردى *ṭardī* parcel-, package- (in compounds), like a parcel or package

طردة *ṭarda* (n. vic.) a driving away, chasing away, repulsion, expulsion, eviction, banishment

طريد *ṭarīd* expelled, evicted, ousted, outcast, outlawed, banished, exiled, expatriate(d); fugitive, fleeing, on the run; expellee; outcast, outlaw; الطريدان **aṭ-ṭarīdān** night and day

طريدة **ṭarīda** pl. طرائد **ṭarā'id**[2] game animal, game beast; game

طراد **ṭarrād** cruiser (warship); (*eg.*) dike, embankment, dam, levee (esp. of the Nile)

طرادة **ṭarrāda** cruiser (warship)

طراد **ṭirād** pursuit, chase

مطاردة **muṭārada** repulsion, expulsion, banishment; pursuit, chase; hunt | طائرة المطاردة fighter plane, pursuit plane, interceptor

اطراد **iṭṭirād** uninterrupted or regular sequence, continuity

استطراد **istiṭrād** pl. *-āt* digression, divagation; excursus

مطارد **muṭārid** pursuer; hunter | طائرة مطاردة fighter plane, pursuit plane, interceptor

مطرد **muṭṭarid** incessant, uninterrupted, continuous, continual, unvarying, steady, constant; general | قاعدة مطردة general rule; مطرد النسق **m. an-nasq** uniform (adj.); مطرد النغم **m. an-nağm** monotonous (song)

طرز II to embroider (ه s.th.); to embellish (ه a story); to garnish (ه ب s.th., e.g., a dish with)

طرز **ṭarz** pl. طروز **ṭurūz** type, model, make, brand, sort, kind; fashion, style

طرزى **ṭarzī** fashion- (in compounds)

طراز **ṭirāz** pl. طرز **ṭuruz**, اطرزة **aṭriza** type, model, class, make, brand, sort, kind, variety, species; fashion, style; architectural style; embroidery | من الطراز القديم old-fashioned, outmoded; قديم الطراز do.; مسلح باحدث طراز **musallaḥ bi-aḥdaṯ ṭ.** equipped with the latest arms; من الطراز الاول (*awwal*) first-class, first-rate

تطريز **taṭrīz** embroidering, embroidery

طرس **ṭirs** pl. اطراس **aṭrās**, طروس **ṭurūs** sheet (of paper); paper

[1]طرش **ṭariša** *a* (**ṭaraš**) to be or become deaf; — **ṭaraša** *u* to vomit, throw up, disgorge II to deafen (ه s.o.)

طرش **ṭarš** whitewashing

طرش **ṭarš** pl. طروش **ṭurūš** (*syr.*) herd (of cattle), flock (of sheep)

طرش **ṭaraš** deafness

طرشة **ṭurša** deafness

اطرش **aṭraš**[2], f. طرشاء **ṭaršā'**[2], pl. طرش **ṭurš** deaf | اطرش اسك (*asakk*[2]) stone-deaf

مطرش **muṭarriš** vomitive; emetic

[2]طرشى **ṭuršī** mixed pickles

طرطر **ṭarṭara** to brag, boast, swagger, show off

طرطور **ṭurṭūr** pl. طراطير **ṭarāṭīr**[2] high, conical cap (of dervishes, clowns, etc.)

طرطور **ṭaraṭūr** and طراطور **ṭarāṭūr** (*eg., syr.*) a sort of mayonnaise (made of **ṭaḥīna**, parsley, lemon, oil, milk, garlic and nuts)

طرطش **ṭarṭaša** to splash, bespatter, splatter (ه s.o.); to roughcast (ه a building, a wall)

طرطوفة **ṭarṭūfa** end, tip, point; Jerusalem artichoke (Helianthus tuberosus L.; *bot.*); truffle

طرطير **ṭarṭīr** tartar, wine stone

طرف **ṭarafa** *i* (**ṭarf**) to blink, twinkle, wink, squint (also بعينيه **bi-'ainaihi**); — **ṭarufa** *u* (طرافة **ṭarāfa**) to be newly acquired, be a recent acquisition IV to feature or tell s.th. new or novel, say s.th. new or original, introduce a novel angle or idea; to present (ه s.o. ب with s.th. new or novel), give (ه to s.o. ب s.th. new or novel) V to be on the extreme side, hold an extreme viewpoint or position, go to extremes, be radical, have radical views

طرف *ṭarf* eye; glance, look | ما اشار بطرف (*ašāra*) he didn't bat an eye; من طرف خفى (*ḵafīy*) secretly, furtively, discreetly; كارتداد الطرف *ka-rtidādi ṭ-ṭ.* in the twinkling of an eye, instantly

طرف *ṭaraf* pl. اطراف *aṭrāf* utmost part, outermost point, extremity, end, tip, point, edge, fringe, limit, border; side; region, area, section; طرف من a part of, a bit of, some; party (as, to a dispute, of a contract, etc.); *ṭarafa* (prep.) with, at, on the part or side of; pl. اطراف limbs, extremities; (with foll. genit.) sections of, parts of | طرفى النهار *ṭarafayi n-nahār* in the morning and in the evening, mornings and evenings; كانوا على طرفى نقيض (*ṭarafai naqīḍin*) they were at variance, they carried on a feud; كان واياه على طرفى نقيض (*wa-iyyāhu*) they held diametrically opposed views or positions; اطراف البدن *a. al-badan* the extremities of the body, the limbs; اطراف الاصابع fingertips; على اطراف قدميه (*a. qadamaihi*) on tiptoe; اطراف المدينة *a. al-madīna* the outskirts of the city; الاطراف المتعاقدة (*muta'āqida*) the contracting parties; بطرف with, at, on the part or side of; من طرف on the part of; من طرف الى طرف from one end to the other; احزاب طرف اليمين the right-wing parties; جاذب اطراف الحديث *jāḏaba aṭrāfa l-ḥ.* to talk, converse, have a conversation; جمع البراعة من اطرافها (*barā'ata*) to be a highly efficient man, be highly qualified; جمع اطراف الشىء to give a survey or outline of s.th., summarize, sum up s.th.; قص عليه طرفا (اطرافا) من حياته to tell s.o. an episode (episodes) of one's life

طرفة *ṭarfa*: بطرفة عين *bi-ṭ. 'ainin* and فى طرفة عين in the twinkling of an eye, instantly; ما — طرفة عين (*ṭarfata*) not one moment

طرفة *ṭurfa* pl. طرف *ṭuraf* novelty, rarity, curiosity, curio, rare object, choice item; exquisite present; masterpiece, chef-d'oeuvre; hit, high light, pièce de résistance

طرفاء *ṭarfā'*[2] (coll.; n. un. ة) tamarisk (*bot.*)

طريف *ṭarīf* curious, strange, odd: novel, exquisite, singular, rare, uncommon

طريفة *ṭarīfa* pl. طرائف *ṭarā'if*[2] rare, exquisite thing; uncommon object or piece (e.g., of art); pl. طرائف curiosities, oddities, uncommon qualities

طرافة *ṭarāfa* novelty, uncommonness, peculiarity, oddness, strangeness, curiosity, originality

مطرف *miṭraf*, *muṭraf* shawl

تطرف *taṭarruf* excess, excessiveness, immoderation, extravagance, extremism, extreme standpoint or position, radical attitude, radicalism

طارف *ṭārif* newly acquired

متطرف *mutaṭarrif* utmost, outmost, farthest outward, located at the outermost point; extreme, extremistic; radical; an extremist, a radical | جهة متطرفة (*jiha*) outlying district, outskirt(s)

طرق *ṭaraqa u* (*ṭarq*) to knock, rap, bang (ه at, on, esp. at a door); to hammer, strike with a hammer, forge (ه s.th., esp. metal); to come over s.o. (ه), befall (ب s.o.; of a feeling); to come (ه, ه to, upon; also of events); to reach (ه s.th.), get to s.th. (ه), get as far as s.th. (ه); to come by night | طرق اذنه (*uḏunahū*) to strike s.o.'s ear, reach s.o.'s ear; طرق بباله (*bi-bālihī*) to occur to s.o., come to s.o.'s mind; طرق فى ذهنه (*ḏihnihī*) do.; طرق سمعه (*sam'ahū*) and طرق مسامعه to reach s.o.'s ear, come to s.o.'s knowledge or attention; طرق طريقا to tread, travel, follow, take, or use a road; طرق موضوعا to treat of a subject, discuss a topic; to broach a subject, touch on a theme **II** to hammer, strike with a hammer, forge, extend (ه s.th., esp. metal) **IV** to bow one's head in silence | اطرق رأسه (*ra'sahū*) or برأسه to bow one's head **V** to seek to gain access (الى to); to penetrate (الى s.th. or into s.th.); to get (الى to), reach (الى s.th.), arrive (الى at); (in a speech, and the like) to touch (الى on a subject), go into s.th. (الى), treat of s.th. (الى) | لا يتطرق اليه شك (*šakkun*) not open to doubt, admitting no doubt

طرقة *ṭarqa* (n. vic.) pl. *ṭaraqāt* knock, rap(ping), bang(ing) (e.g., at a door); blow; one time (= مرة), طرقتين *ṭarqatain* twice

طرقة *ṭurqa* way, road; passage, passageway, alleyway, corridor

طريق *ṭarīq* m. and f., pl. طرق *ṭuruq*, طرقات *ṭuruqāt* way; road, highway; trail, track, path; method | طريق الجو *ṭ. al-jaww* air route; طريق البحر *ṭ. al-baḥr* sea route; طريق رئيسى (*ra'īsī*) main road; طريق عام (*'āmm*) public road, highway, thoroughfare; طريق عمومية (*'umūmīya*) do.; عن طريق by way of, via; by means of, through; عن طريق الجو (*ṭ. il-jaww*) by air; من طريق by means of, through; عابر الطريق wanderer, wayfarer; قاطع الطريق pl. قطاع الطرق *quṭṭā' aṭ-ṭ.* highwayman, waylayer, brigand; قطع الطريق to commit highway robbery; كان فى طريقه to have sense, be sensible or normal

طريقة *ṭarīqa* pl. طرائق *ṭarā'iq*[2], طرق *ṭuruq* manner, mode, means; way, method, procedure; system; creed, faith, religion; (pl. *-āt*, طرق *ṭuruq*) religious brotherhood, dervish order | طريقة الاستعمال directions for use

طرقى *ṭuruqī* pl. *-ūn* adherent of a religious brotherhood

مطرق *miṭraq* and مطرقة *miṭraqa* pl. مطارق *maṭāriq*[2] hammer

مطراق *miṭrāq* versatile, many-sided, of varied skills or talents

اطراقة *iṭrāqa* (n. vic.) a bowing of the head

استطراق *istiṭrāq* transit permission, free passage or entry

طارق *ṭāriq* pl. طراق *ṭurrāq* knocking, rapping, banging, striking, beating; nocturnal visitor

طارقة *ṭāriqa* pl. طوارق *ṭawāriq*[2] misfortune, disaster, calamity

مطروق *maṭrūq* much-frequented, much-traveled, well-trodden (road, trail, path) | موضوع مطروق a much-discussed, frequently treated subject

مطرق *muṭriq* and مطرق الرأس with bowed head

طرقع **ṭarqa'a** (*eg.*) to crack (intr., also trans.: ب or ه s.th., e.g., a whip); to crack, crunch (ه s.th.)

طارمة **ṭārima** pl. *-āt* kiosk, booth, cabin, stall

طرمبة **ṭurumba** pl. *-āt* pump

(طرو and طرى) طرو **ṭaruwa** *u*, طرى **ṭariya** *a* (طراوة *ṭarāwa*) to be or become fresh, succulent, moist, tender, soft, mild **II** to make fresh, succulent, moist, tender, soft, mild (ه s.th.); to moisten, wet (ه s.th.); to perfume, scent (ه s.th.) **IV** to praise (highly), extol, laud (ه s.o.), lavish praise (ه on s.o.)

طرى *ṭarīy* fresh, succulent, new; moist; tender, soft, mild

طراوة *ṭarāwa* freshness, succulence, moistness; tenderness, softness, mildness | طراوة الخلق *ṭ. al-ḵulq* gentleness; softness of character

اطرية *iṭriya* vermicelli

اطراء *iṭrā'* (high) commendation, praise, laudation, extolment

طروادة *ṭirwāda*² (from Fr. *Troade*) Troy

طازج *ṭāzaj* look up alphabetically

طزلق (Turk. *tozluk*) *ṭuzluq* pl. طزالق *ṭazāliq*² gaiter(s), legging(s)

طازه *ṭāza* look up alphabetically

طزينة (It. *dozzina*) pl. طزازن *ṭazāzin*² dozen

طست *ṭast, ṭist* pl. طسوت *ṭusūt* basin; washbasin, washbowl

طشت *ṭašt, ṭišt* pl. طشوت *ṭušūt* basin; washbasin, washbowl

طشقند *ṭašqand*² Tashkent (capital of Uzbek S.S.R.)

طصلق *ṭaṣlaqa* (*eg.*) to do inaccurately, perform sloppily, bungle, botch, scamp (ه a job, work)

طصلقة *ṭaṣlaqa* inaccurate, sloppy, or slipshod work

طعم *ṭaʿima a* (*ṭaʿm*) to eat (ه s.th.); to taste (ه s.th.); to relish, enjoy, savor (ه s.th.) **II** to graft, engraft (ه s.th.); to inoculate, vaccinate (ه ب s.o. with); to inlay (ه ب s.th. with, e.g., wood with ivory) **IV** to feed, give to eat (ه ه s.o. s.th.), nourish (ه ه s.o. with), serve food or drink (ه) to s.o. (ه) | اطعمه من جوع (*jūʿ*) to appease s.o.'s hunger **V** to taste (ه s.th.) **X** = **V**; to ask for food

طعم *ṭaʿm* pl. طعوم *ṭuʿūm* taste, flavor, savor; pleasing flavor, relish

طعمية *ṭaʿmīya* (*eg.*) patty made of beans, and seasoned with onion, garlic and parsley

طعم *ṭuʿm* graft, cion; bait, lure, decoy; (pl. طعوم *ṭuʿūm*) vaccine

طعيم *ṭaʿīm* tasty, savory, delicious

طعمة *ṭuʿma* pl. طعم *ṭuʿam* food; bait; quarry, catch, bag | اصبح طعمة النيران *aṣbaḥa ṭuʿmata n-nīrān* to be destroyed by fire; طعمة لمدافع الحرب (*li-madāfiʿi l-ḥarb*) cannon fodder

طعام *ṭaʿām* pl. اطعمة *aṭʿima* food, nourishment, nutriment, fare, diet; meal, repast | اضرب عن الطعام (*aḍraba*) to go on a hunger strike

مطعم *maṭʿam* pl. مطاعم *maṭāʿim*² eating house, restaurant; dining room; mess, messhall (on a ship); food | مطعم الشعب *m. aš-šaʿb* and مطعم شعبي soup kitchen

تطعيم *taṭʿīm* inoculation, vaccination; inlay work | تطعيم القرنية *t. al-qarnīya* transplantation of the cornea (*med.*)

اطعام *iṭʿām* feeding

مطعوم *maṭʿūm* tasted; already known

طعن *ṭaʿana u a* (*ṭaʿn*) to thrust, pierce, transfix (ه, ه ب s.o., s.th. with); to stab (ه s.o.); to defame, discredit, hurt (with words; على or في s.o., s.th.), speak evil (على or في of); to contest, challenge, impeach (في حكم a judgment), appeal (في حكم against a judgment); to refute, disprove (في s.th.); to penetrate, enter (في s.th. or into s.th.) | طعن في السن (*sinn*) to be advanced in years, be old; طعن في قول (*qaul*) to refute a (theological) doctrine **VI** to thrust each other; to attack each other, battle one another

طعن *ṭaʿn* piercing, transfixion; slandering, calumniation, defamation; appeal (في against; *jur.*), challenge, contestation, impeachment (في of; *jur.*); pl. طعون *ṭuʿūn* calumnies, defamations; attacks

طعنة *ṭaʿna* (n. vic.) pl. *ṭaʿanāt* stab, thrust; attack; calumny, defamation, vilification

طاعون *ṭāʿūn* pl. طواعين *ṭawāʿīn*² plague, pestilence | الطاعون الدملي (*dummalī*) bubonic plague; الطاعون البقري (*baqarī*) and طاعون الماشية *ṭ. al-māšiya* rinderpest, cattle plague, steppe murrain

مطاعن *maṭā'in*[2] (pl.) invectives, abuses (فى against s.o.)

طاعن *ṭā'in* and طاعن فى السن (*sinn*) aged, old, advanced in years | رسالة طاعنة lampoon

مطعون *maṭ'ūn* plague-infected, plague-stricken

طغار[1] an Iraqi weight equaling 2000 kg, in Basra 1537 kg

طغراء[2] *ṭuḡrā'*[2] pl. *-āt* tughra, caligraphically intricate signature of the Ottoman Sultan, interwoven with his father's name and his own honorific, customarily used on written decrees, state documents and coins

طغرى *ṭuḡrā* = طغراء *ṭuḡrā'*[2]

طغام *ṭaḡām* common people, populace; lowly, insignificant

طغمة *ṭuḡma*, *ṭuḡma* pl. *-āt* band, troop, group

طغا (طغو and طغى) *ṭaḡā u* and طغى *ṭaḡā a* (*ṭaḡy*) and *ṭaḡiya a* (طغى *ṭaḡan*, طغيان *ṭuḡyān*) to exceed proper bounds, overstep the bounds, be excessive; to be rough, tumultuous, rage (sea); to overflow, leave its banks (river); to flood, overflow, inundate, deluge (على s.th.); to overcome, seize, grip, befall (على s.o.); to be tyrannical or cruel (على against s.o.), tyrannize, oppress, terrorize (على s.o.), ride roughshod (على over s.o.); — طغى *ṭaḡā a* to predominate, prevail, preponderate (على in, at), dominate, outweigh, outbalance (على s.th.), be preponderant (على over, in comparison with s.th.)

طغوان *ṭuḡwān* flood, inundation, deluge

طغيان *ṭuḡyān* flood, inundation, deluge; tyranny, oppression, suppression, repression, terrorization

طاغ *ṭāḡin* pl. طغاة *ṭuḡāh* tyrant, oppressor, despot

طاغية *ṭāḡiya* tyrant, oppressor, despot; bully, brute, gorilla

طاغوت *ṭāḡūt* an idol, a false god; seducer, tempter (to error)

طف II to make deficient or scanty (ه s.th.); to be niggardly, stingy (على toward s.o.), stint (على s.o.)

طفيف *ṭafīf* deficient; small, little, slight, trivial, trifling, insignificant, inconsiderable

تطفيف *taṭfīf* stinting, scrimping, niggardliness, stinginess, parsimony

طفئ *ṭafi'a a* (طفوء *ṭufū'*) to go out, die down, be extinguished (fire, light); to be out, have gone out (fire, lamp) **IV** to put out, extinguish, smother, stifle (ه a fire), turn off, switch off (ه light); to quench (ه fire, thirst), slake (ه thirst, also lime) | اطفأ جذوة يومه واحرق فحمة ليله فى العمل (*jaḏwata yaumihī wa-aḥraqa faḥmata lailihī fī l-'amal*) to work day and night **VII** = طفئ *ṭafi'a*

□ طفاية *ṭaffāya* fire-extinguishing device

مطفأة *miṭfa'a* pl. مطافئ *maṭāfi'*[2] fire-fighting equipment, fire extinguisher, fire engine | رجال المطافئ the fire department, the firemen

اطفاء *iṭfā'* putting out, quenching, extinguishing, extinction, fire fighting | جهاز اطفاء الحريق *jahāz i. al-ḥarīq* fire-fighting equipment رجال الاطفاء the fire department, the firemen; عمليات الاطفاء *'amalīyāt al-i.* fire-fighting operations

اطفائى *iṭfā'ī* fireman

اطفائية *iṭfā'īya* fire department

مطفأ *muṭfa'* extinguished, gone out, out; mat, dull, flat, lusterless

طفح *ṭafaḥa a* (*ṭafḥ*, طفوح *ṭufūḥ*) to flow over, run over, overflow (ب with, also, e.g., the heart with generosity, etc.); to cause to overflow (ب e.g., the milk) II to fill to overflowing, fill to the brim (ه a vessel); to overfill (ه s.th.) IV = II

طفح *ṭafḥ* superabundance, repletion; skin eruption, rash, exanthema (*med.*)

طفحة *ṭafḥa* skin eruption, rash, exanthema (*med.*)

طفحى *ṭafḥī* eruptive, exanthematic (*med.*)

طفوح *ṭufūḥ* superabundance, repletion

طفاحة *ṭufāḥa* skimmings, foam, froth

طفحان *ṭafḥān*[2], f. طفحى *ṭafḥā* flowing over, running over, brimful, replete, overfull, filled to overflowing

مطفحة *miṭfaḥa* skimmer, skimming ladle

طافح *ṭāfiḥ* flowing over, running over, brimful, replete, overfull, filled to overflowing

[1]طفر *ṭafara i* (*ṭafr*) to jump, leap, bounce | طفرت جوانحها approx.: her bosom heaved violently (with joyous agitation)

طفرة *ṭafra* jump, leap, bounce, bound; impulsive motion, impetuosity; upswing, rise, upturn, successful step; *ṭafratan* in one leap

طفران *ṭafrān* pauper, have-not

[2]□ طفر *ṭafar* (= ثفر) crupper (of the saddle)

طفش *ṭafaša i* (*ṭafš*) to run away, flee, escape (*eg.*)

طفق *ṭafiqa a* (*ṭafaq*) with foll. imperf.: to begin, set out to do s.th.; to do s.th. suddenly

طفل II to intrude, obtrude, impose o.s. (على upon); to sponge (على on s.o., على مائدته at s.o.'s table), live at other people's expense V = II; to arrive uninvited or at an inconvenient time, disturb, intrude; to be obtrusive

طفل *ṭafl* tender, soft; potter's clay, argil

طفل *ṭifl* pl. اطفال *aṭfāl* infant, baby, child

طفلة *ṭifla* little girl

طفلى *ṭiflī* child (adj.), baby (adj.), children's, of or pertaining to childhood or infancy; infantile, childlike, childish | الطب الطفلى (*ṭibb*) pediatrics

طفل *ṭafal* infancy, babyhood, early childhood; childhood, childhood stage

طفلة *ṭafla* potter's clay, argil

طفال *ṭufāl* potter's clay; argil; clay, loam

طفالة *ṭafāla* infancy, babyhood, early childhood; childhood, childhood stage; initial stage, beginnings, dawn, early period

طفولة *ṭufūla* infancy, babyhood, early childhood; childhood, childhood stage; children

طفولية *ṭufūlīya* infancy, babyhood, early childhood; childhood, childhood stage

طفولى *ṭufūlī* child (adj.), baby (adj.), children's, of or pertaining to childhood or infancy; infantile, childlike, childish

طفيلى *ṭufailī* uninvited guest, intruder, obtruder, sponger, hanger-on, parasite, sycophant; pl. طفيليات parasites (*med.*, *biol.*) | علم الطفيليات *'ilm aṭ-ṭ.* parasitology

متطفل *mutaṭaffil* parasitic(al); parasite, sponger, uninvited guest

(طفو) طفا *ṭafā u* (طفو *ṭafw*, *ṭufūw*) to float, drift; to emerge, rise to the surface | طفا به الى السطح (*saṭḥ*) to bring s.th. to the surface

طفاوة *ṭufāwa* anything drifting or floating, driftage, floatage, flotsam; halo (around the sun or moon)

طاف *ṭāfin* superficial

طافية *ṭāfiya* floating iceberg

□ طفاية *ṭaffāya* see طفو

طق *ṭaqqa* u (*ṭaqq*) to crack, pop; to clack, smack, flap; to burst, explode

طقس II to introduce into one of the orders of the ministry (*Chr.*) V to perform a rite, follow a ritual

طقس *ṭaqs* weather; climate; — (pl. طقوس *ṭuqūs*) rite, ritual; religious custom; order of the ministry, clerical rank (*Chr.*)

طقسى *ṭaqsī* liturgical; liturgist (*Chr.*); الطقسيات *aṭ-ṭaqsīyāt* the liturgical books (*Chr.*)

طقطق *ṭaqṭaqa* to crack, snap, rattle, clatter, chug, pop, crash; to crackle, (de)crepitate, rustle

طقطوقة *ṭaqṭūqa* crash, bang; clap, thud, crack, pop; (pl. طقاطيق *ṭaqāṭīq*[2]) ditty, gay, popular song

طقم II to harness, bridle (ه a horse)

طقم *ṭaqm* pl. طقوم *ṭuqūm*, طقومة *ṭuqūma*, اطقم *aṭqum* a number of complementary objects or things; series; suit (of clothes); set (of tools, and the like); harness (of a horse); service (e.g., of china, etc.) | طقم الاسنان denture, set of teeth

طاقم *ṭāqim* = *ṭaqm*; crew (of a ship) | طاقم الاسنان denture, set of teeth

طل *ṭalla* u (*ṭall*) to bespray, besprinkle, bedrizzle, bedew (ه s.th., esp. the sky — the earth); — *ṭalla* u to emerge, rise, loom up, come into view, appear, show IV to look down (على upon), tower (على above), command a view of s.th. (على), overlook, survey (على s.th.); to command, dominate, overtop (على s.th., e.g., the surrounding area); (of a room, window, etc.) to open (على upon, to, toward), give (على on), face (على toward); to look out, peek out, peep out (من of s.th.); to appear, show

طل *ṭall* pl. طلال *ṭilāl* dew; fine rain, drizzle

طلل *ṭalal* pl. اطلال *aṭlāl*, طلول *ṭulūl*, used chiefly in the pl.: remains, ruins (of houses); remains, or traces, of an abandoned encampment

مطلول *maṭlūl*: دم مطلول (*dam*) unavenged blood

طلب *ṭalaba* u (*ṭalab*, مطلب *maṭlab*) to look, search (ه, ‍ه for s.o., for s.th.); to set out (ه for a place), get on one's way (ه to), go to see (ه, ‍ه s.o., s.th.); to request (ه s.th.), apply (ه for); to seek, try to obtain, claim (ه من s.th. from), ask, beg (ه من s.o. for); to demand, exact, require (ه الى of s.o. s.th.); to want, wish (ه من s.th. from; الى s.o. ان to do s.th.); to call (الى upon s.o.), appeal (الى to s.o.), invite, request, entreat, beseech (الى s.o.); to order, demand (ه من s.th. from), call (ه for s.th., من from), call in (ه s.th., من from); to be after s.o. or s.th. (ه, ‍ه); to study III to demand back, reclaim (ب or ه ‍ه from s.o. s.th.), call for the return or restitution of s.th. (ب or ه), demand, claim (ب or ه ‍ه from s.o. s.th.); to demand, claim (ب s.th.) V to require, necessitate, make necessary or requisite (ه s.th.) VII pass. of I

طلب *ṭalab* search, quest, pursuit; — (pl. *-āt*) demand, claim, call (for), invitation (to), solicitation, wish, desire, request, entreaty; application, petition; order, commission; demand (*com.*); study | تحت طلبه at s.o.'s disposal; عند الطلب and لدى الطلب on demand, by request, if desired, on application; ○ لحين الطلب *li-ḥīni ṭ-ṭ.* at sight (*com.*); العرض والطلب (*'arḍ*) supply and demand; طلب العلم *ṭ.*

al-'ilm quest of knowledge, craving for knowledge, studiousness; طلب عدم الثقة *ṭ. 'adam aṯ-ṯiqa* motion of "no confidence" (*parl.*)

طلبة *ṭalba* litany, prayer (*Chr.*)

طلبة *ṭaliba, ṭilba* desire, wish, request, demand; application

طلبية *ṭalabīya* pl. *-āt* order, commission (*com.*)

طلاب *ṭallāb* exacting, persistently claiming or demanding

مطلب *maṭlab* search, quest, pursuit; — (pl. مطالب *maṭālib*²) demand, call (for); request, wish; claim; problem, issue; pl. مطالب (claims of the government =) taxes

مطالبة *muṭālaba* demand; call, appeal (with genit. or ب for); claim (with genit. or ب to)

طالب *ṭālib* pl. طلاب *ṭullāb*, طلبة *ṭalaba* seeker, pursuer; claimer, claimant; applicant, petitioner; candidate; student, scholar, also طالب العلم *ṭ. al-'ilm*; pupil; a naval rank, approx.: midshipman (*Eg.* 1939) | طالب ممتاز (*mumtāz*) a naval rank, approx.: ensign (*Eg.* 1939); طلاب الحاجات petitioners; طالب الزواج *ṭ. az-zawāj* suitor

طالبى *ṭālibī* student's, student- (in compounds), of or pertaining to studies or students

مطلوب *maṭlūb* wanted (in classified ads); due, owed (money); unknown (of a quantity; *math.*); (pl. مطاليب *maṭālīb*²) wish, desire; pl. مطلوبات liabilities, debts; pl. مطاليب claims

مطالب *muṭālib* claimer, claimant; — *muṭālab* one of whom s.th. or s.o. (ب) is demanded, one accountable (ب for), held answerable (ب for)

متطلبات *mutaṭallabāt* requirements

طلح **ṭalaḥa** *u* (طلاح *ṭalāḥ*) to be or become bad, evil, wicked, vicious, depraved

طلح *ṭalḥ* (coll.; n. un. ة) pl. طلوح *ṭulūḥ* a variety of acacia (Acacia gummifera); banana tree; banana

طلحية *ṭalḥīya* pl. طلاحى *ṭalāḥīy* sheet of paper

طليحة *ṭalīḥa* (*syr.*) ream of paper

طالح *ṭāliḥ* bad, evil, wicked, vicious, depraved, villainous

¹طلس **ṭalasa** *i* (*ṭals*) to efface, obliterate, blot out (ه s.th., esp. writing)

طلس *ṭals* effacement, obliteration

طلس *ṭils* effaced, obliterated, blotted out (inscription); illegible

²اطلس **aṭlas**² satin; (pl. اطالس *aṭālis*²) atlas, volume of geographical maps

¹طلسانة **ṭalasāna** (*eg.*) coping (*arch.*)

²طيلسان **ṭailasān** pl. طيالسة *ṭayālisa* look up alphabetically

طلسم **ṭilasm, ṭillasm** pl. *-āt*, طلاسم *ṭalāsim*² talisman, a seal, or the like, inscribed with mysterious words or characters; charm, magical combination of words; pl. طلاسم cryptic characters

طلع **ṭala'a** *u* (طلوع *ṭulū'*, مطلع *maṭla'*) to rise, ascend, come up (esp. of celestial bodies); to come into view, appear, show, become visible; to erupt (tooth), come up, sprout, break forth (plant); to go out, get out, come out, emerge (من from); to come suddenly (على upon s.o. or s.th.), overtake (على s.o., s.th.); طلع عليه ب to take or bring to s.o. s.th.; — *ṭala'a a u* (طلوع *ṭulū'*) and *ṭali'a a* to mount, ascend, climb, scale (ه s.th.); to get (ه on top of s.th., aboard s.th., into an automobile, on a train, etc.), board (ه a train, etc.) III to read, peruse (ه s.th.); to study (ه s.th.); to look (ه at s.th.), inspect, view (ه s.th.); to acquaint (ه s.o. ب with), make clear, elucidate, explain, expound, disclose (ب ه to s.o. s.th.), give an insight (ب ه to s.o. into), let s.o. (ه) in on s.th. (ب); to shine (ه on s.th.; of the sun) IV to erupt (tooth), come up, sprout, break forth (plant); to acquaint (على ه s.o. with); to inform (ه s.o. من or على of or about), apprise, notify (عن or على ه s.o. of), let s.o. (ه) know (على s.th. or about s.th.), tell (على ه s.o. about); to demonstrate, point out, disclose, reveal, show (على ه to s.o. s.th.); to give an insight (على ه to s.o. into), let s.o. (ه) in on s.th. (على) V to have an eye on s.th. (الى), wait, look out (الى for); to watch (الى for); to strive, be out (الى for), be bent (الى on); to look (الى at s.o.), regard (الى s.o.); to look attentively or closely, gaze, stare (ب or في at) VIII to look; to see, behold, view (على s.th.); to study, come to know (على s.th.), become acquainted (على with), become aware or cognizant (على of), obtain information (على about), be informed (على of); to inspect, examine (على s.th.), look into s.th. (على); to know (على s.th. or of s.th.), be aware, be cognizant (على of); to be (well) informed (على about), have (inside) information (على of), be (thoroughly) acquainted (على with), be privy (على to), be in on s.th. (على); to find out, discover, detect (على s.th.) X to seek to discover, explore, scout, reconnoiter (ه s.th.); to inquire (ه about s.th.); to arouse curiosity (ه in s.o.) | استطلعه رأيه (*ra'yahū*) to consult s.o., ask s.o.'s advice or opinion; استطلع خبره (*kabarahū*) to seek information about s.o. or s.th.

طلع *ṭal'* (also coll.) spadix or inflorescence of the palm tree; pollen

طلعة *ṭal'a* look(s), appearance, aspect, outward appearance, guise

طلعة *ṭula'a* inquisitive, nosy, curious

طلاع *ṭallā'* striving, aspiring | طلاع الثنايا والانجد (*ṯanāyā, anjud*) efficient, energetic, vigorous; طلاع الى التعرف (*ta'arruf*) curious, eager for news

طلوع *ṭulū'* rising, going up, ascending, ascension; rise (esp. of celestial bodies); appearance; climbing, ascent (of a mountain)

●

طليعة *ṭalī'a* pl. طلائع *ṭalā'i'*[2] front row, foremost rank, vanguard, avant-garde; pl. harbingers, precursors, presages, portents, first indications, symptoms; beginnings | في الطليعة in front, at the head, in the lead

مطلع *maṭla'* pl. مطالع *maṭāli'*[2] rise, time of rising (of celestial bodies); point of ascent; starting point, point of departure; break (e.g., of day), dawn (e.g., of an era); onset, outset, start, beginning; introduction, preface, proem; opening verses (of a poem); prelude; lookout; ladder, steps, stairs

مطالعة *muṭāla'a* reading, perusal, study; (pl. *-āt*) (official) announcement | قاعة المطالعة reading room, study hall

تطلع *taṭallu'* striving, aspiration, endeavor, aim; inquisitiveness, curiosity

اطلاع *iṭṭilā'* pl. *-āt* study, examination, inspection; perusal; information, intelligence, knowledge; notice, cognizance; acquaintance, conversance, familiarity

استطلاع *istiṭlā'* study, research, investigation, probing; scouting, reconnoitering, reconnaissance; exploration; suspense (in anticipation of s.th.) | حب الاستطلاع *ḥubb al-ist.* inquisitiveness, curiosity; حبا في الاستطلاع (*ḥubban*) out of curiosity; طائرة الاستطلاع reconnaissance plane

استطلاعى *istiṭlā'ī* research-, study- (in compounds), explorational, exploratory, fact-finding; scout-, reconnaissance- (in compounds)

طالع *ṭāliʻ* pl. طوالع *ṭawāliʻ*[2] rising, ascending (esp. a celestial body); star of destiny; ascendant, nativity | حسن الطالع *ḥusn aṭ-ṭ.* good fortune, lucky star, good luck; لحسن طالعى luckily for me, fortunately; سيء الطالع *sayyiʼ aṭ-ṭ.* ill-starred, ill-fated, unfortunate, unlucky; hapless person; ساء طالعه (*ṭāliʻuhū*) he fell on evil days, he met with ill fortune

طالعة *ṭāliʻa* outset, beginning, start

مطالع *muṭāliʻ* reader

متطلع *mutaṭalliʻ* curious, eager, waiting (الى for)

مطلع *muṭṭaliʻ* viewer, observer; informed (على about, of), acquainted, familiar (على with), cognizant (على of), privy (على to)

طلق *ṭaluqa u* (طلاقة *ṭalāqa*) to be cheerful, jovial, happy (face, countenance); — *ṭalaqat u, ṭaluqat u* (طلاق *ṭalāq*) to be divorced, get a divorce (said of a woman); — pass. *ṭuliqat* (طلق *ṭalq*) to be in labor **II** to set loose, release, set free, let go (ه, ه s.o., s.th.); to leave, forsake (ه, ه s.o., s.th.); to repudiate, divorce (زوجته *zaujatahū* one's wife); to grant a divorce decree (على against a woman; said of the judge) | طلقت نفسها (*nafsahā*) she dissolved her marriage, got a divorce; طلقت عليه (*ṭulliqat*) she was granted a divorce from him (by judicial decree) **IV** to undo, loose, disengage (ه s.th.); to free, set free (ه, ه s.o., s.th., also *chem.*), release, set at liberty, let go, let off, set loose (ه, ه s.o., s.th.); to send out, dispatch (ه, ه s.o., s.th.); to discharge (ه a firearm), fire (ه s.th., على at), shoot (على at); to utter, emit (ه a sound); to let burst forth (ه laughter); to repudiate, divorce (زوجته *zaujatahū* one's wife); to generalize (ه s.th.); to apply (ه s.th., e.g., an expression, a designation, على to) | اطلق عليه اسم ... (*isma*) to name or call s.th...., designate s.th. as...; يطلق على (*yuṭlaqu*) it has (absolute) validity for..., it applies to...; اطلق الحبل على الغارب (*ḥabla*) to give free rein, impose no restraints, let things take their course; اطلق حربا من عقالها (*ḥarban*) to unleash a war; اطلق الدواء بطنه (*dawāʼu baṭnahū*) the medicine loosened his bowels; اطلق الرصاص على (*raṣāṣa*) to fire, shoot at; اطلق رجليه الى الريح (*rijlaihi, rīḥ*) to run away head over heels, to beat it; اطلق ساقيه للريح (*sāqaihi*) to run away head over heels, dash off like the wind, to bolt; اطلق الارادة to give a free hand (ل to s.o. فى in s.th. or to do s.th.); اطلق سبيله to release s.o., set s.o. free, let s.o. go; اطلق السبيل لعبرته (*li-ʻabratihī*) to let one's tears flow freely; اطلق سراحه (*sarāḥahū*) to set s.o. at liberty, free s.o., release s.o. (from jail or custody); اطلق العنان له to give free rein to s.o. or s.th., give vent to s.th.; اطلق لحيته (*liḥyatahū*) to let one's beard grow; اطلق لسانه فيه اطلاقا شنيعا to indulge in defamatory remarks about s.o., backbite s.o.; اطلق السنتهم ب (*alsinatahum*) to incite s.o., e.g., a crowd, the mob (to boisterous demonstrations, emotional outbursts, and the like); اطلق النفس على سجيتها (*nafsa, sajīyatihā*) he gave free rein to his instincts; اطلق النار على to open fire on, fire or shoot at; اطلق النار فى to set fire to, set s.th. on fire; اطلق يده ب (*yadahū*) to be openhanded with, bestow s.th. lavishly; اطلق يده فى (ل) to give s.o. a free hand (in, to do s.th.), give s.o. unlimited authority for; اطلقوا ايديهم فى البلاد (*aidiyahum*) they did as they pleased with the country, they dealt high, handedly with the country **V** to brighten-beam, be radiant (with joy) | تطلق وجهها بابتسامة (*wajhuhā bi-btisāma*) her face broke into a radiant smile **VII** to be free, be loose, be set free (also *chem.*); to be emitted, emanate; to race along, sweep along, dash along; to hurry, rush (الى to); to be hurled off, be flung away;

to be discharged, be fired (firearm); to explode, go off; to burst forth, burst out, ring out (shouts, voices); to take off, start off, decamp, depart (من from); to start rolling, move off, pull out (train, vehicle); to go on, proceed on one's way; to go away, leave; to go by, pass, elapse (hours, years); to brighten, beam (face); with ب: to utter s.th. (tongue); with foll. imperf.: to set out to do s.th., begin or start with s.th. | يجري انطلق (yajrī) he set out in a hurry; انطلق مسرعا (musriʿan) he went away quickly, rushed away, dashed off; انطلق لسانه على (lisānuhū) to utter words against; انطلق وجهه (wajhuhū) his face brightened, became cheerful X استطلق بطنه (baṭnuhū) he had a bowel movement

طلق ṭalq talc (min.); labor pains, travail; free, open, unconfined, unrestrained, unimpeded, uninhibited; free (من from), rid (من of) | طالق المحيا ṭalq (ṭilq, ṭulq) al-muḥayyā with a happy, cheerful face, bright-faced; طلق الوجه ṭalq (ṭilq, ṭulq) al-wajh do.; طلق اللسان eloquent; في الهواء الطلق (hawāʾ) outdoors, in the open, under the open sky; طلق اليدين f. al-yadain openhanded, liberal, generous

طلق ṭilq permissible, admissible

طلق ṭalaq pl. اطلاق aṭlāq run, race, foot race; (pl. -āt, اطلاق aṭlāq) shot (with a firearm) | سريع الطلق rapid-fire (rifle, gun)

لسان طلق lisān ṭaliq a facile, fluent tongue

طلقة ṭalqa pl. ṭalaqāt divorce | بالثلاثة طلقة (ṭalāta) definite divorce

طلقة ṭalaqa pl. -āt shot | طلقة نارية do

طلاق ṭalāq divorce, talak | طلاق بالثلاثة (ṭalāta) definite divorce; طلاق رجعي (rajʿī) revocable (not definite) divorce; كتاب الطلاق bill of divorce; حلف بالطلاق to swear by all that's holy

طليق ṭalīq pl. طلقاء ṭulaqāʾ² freed, released, set free, free; freedman; الطلقاء name of those Meccans who remained heathen until the surrender of Mecca

طلاقة ṭalāqa ease, relaxedness; unrestraint; cheerfulness | طلاقة اللسان fluency, eloquence; طلاقة الوجه f. al-wajh cheerfulness of the face, gaiety

طليقة ṭalīqa repudiated or divorced woman, divorcee

طلوقة ṭalūqa pl. طلائق ṭalāʾiq² stallion

اطلاق iṭlāq freeing, liberation; setting loose, releasing, release; dispatch(ing); application (على to); generalization; اطلاقا iṭlāqan absolutely | على الاطلاق absolutely, unrestrictedly, without exception, in any respect, under any circumstances; اطلاق الرصاص (i. ar-raṣāṣ) the firing at s.th., the shooting of s.o.; اطلاق السراح i. as-sarāḥ release (of s.o.); اطلاق النار (nīrān) opening of fire, shelling, gunning, cannonade

انطلاق inṭilāq outburst, outbreak, eruption, explosion, release (e.g., of forces, of energies); unrestraint, liberty | نقطة الانطلاق nuqṭat al-inṭ. starting point, point of departure

طالق ṭāliq (of a woman) repudiated, divorced | هي طالق ثلاثا (ṭalāṭan) she is irrevocably divorced

مطلق muṭlaq free; unlimited, unrestricted, absolute; general; مطلقا muṭlaqan absolutely, unrestrictedly, without exception, in any respect, under any circumstances | الدول ذات الحكم المطلق (duwal ḍāt al-ḥukm) the authoritarian states; مطلق السراح m. as-sarāḥ free, at large, at liberty

متطلق mutaṭalliq cheerful, jovial, happy (face)

مطلمة miṭlama rolling pin

طلمبة ṭulumba pl. -at pump

طلمس *ṭalmasa* to frown, scowl, glower, lower

(طلو and طلى) طلى *ṭalā i* (*ṭaly*) to paint, daub (ه ب s.th. with); to coat, overlay, plate (ه ب s.th. with) | طلى ه بالذهب (*ḏahab*) to gild s.th.; طلى ه بالكهرباء (*kahrabā'*) to galvanize, electroplate s.th.; طلى ه بالميناء (*mīnā'*) to enamel s.th. **VII** لم تنطل عليه هذه الحيلة (*ḥīla*) he wouldn't be deceived by this ruse, this trick couldn't fool him

طلاء *ṭilā'* coating, overlaying, plating; coat, covering (e.g., of sugar); (coat of) paint; make-up, face paint | الطلاء بالكهرباء (*kahrabā'*) galvanization, electroplating

طلي *ṭalīy* pleasant, becoming, nice, pretty

طلاوة *ṭalāwa* beauty, gracefulness, grace, elegance

الطليان *aṭ-ṭulyān* the Italians

طليطلة *ṭulaiṭila*[2] Toledo (town in Spain)

طم *ṭamma u* (*ṭamm*, طموم *ṭumūm*) to overflow, flood, inundate, deluge, engulf (ه s.th.) **VII** pass. of **I**

طم *ṭimm* large quantity, huge amount; sea | الطم والرم (*rimm*) tremendous riches

طامة *ṭāmma* pl. *-āt* (overwhelming) calamity, disaster

طماطة *ṭumāṭa* tomato

طماطم *ṭamāṭim*[2] (coll.; n. un. ة) tomatoes

طمأن *ṭam'ana* and طأمن *ṭa'mana* to calm, quiet, pacify, appease, assuage, soothe (ه, ه s.o., s.th.), set s.o.'s mind at rest; to fill s.o. (ه) with confidence (الى in), reassure (ه الى s.o. of or with regard to) **II** تطأمن *taṭa'mana* = طمن **VI**; **IV** اطمأن *iṭma'anna* to remain quietly (في in a place); to come to rest; to be or become still, quiet, calm, tranquil, at ease, composed, or reassured, feel assured, confident, or secure; to be sure, be certain (من or الى of s.th.); to have confidence, to trust (الى in), rely, depend (الى on, upon); to make sure (على of s.th.), reassure o.s. (على of or with regard to); to find reassurance (الى in), derive confidence (الى from)

طمأنينة *ṭuma'nīna* calm, repose, serenity, peace, peacefulness, tranquillity; reassurance, peace of mind, composure, calmness, equanimity; trust, confidence

اطمئنان *iṭmi'nān* calm, repose, serenity, peace, peacefulness, tranquillity; reassurance, peace of mind, composure, calmness, equanimity; trust, confidence

مطمئن *muṭma'inn* (of land) low, lowlying; calm, quiet, at ease, composed, (re)assured, tranquil, serene, peaceable, peaceful, safe, secure; sure, certain; trusting, confident, of good hope

طمث *ṭamaṯa u* and *ṭamiṯa a* (*ṭamṯ*) to menstruate; — *ṭamaṯa u i* (*ṭamṯ*) to deflower (ها a girl)

طمث *ṭamṯ* menstruation; menses, menstrual discharge

طمح *ṭamaḥa a* (طموح *ṭumūḥ*) to turn, be directed (الى to, toward; of the eye, of glances); to aspire (الى to, after), be bent (الى on), strive, crave, long, yearn (الى for), covet (الى s.th.); to take away, remove (ب s.th.)

طموح *ṭumūḥ* striving, endeavor, aspiration, desire, craving, coveting, longing, yearning; ambition; high aspirations, loftiness of purpose

طموح *ṭamūḥ* high-aiming, high-aspiring, ambitious; craving, covetous, desirous, avid, eager

طماح *ṭammāḥ* high-aiming, high-aspiring, ambitious; craving, covetous, desirous, avid, eager

مطمح *maṭmaḥ* pl. مطامح *maṭāmiḥ*[2] object of one's longing or striving, (aspired) goal, aim, ambition, burning desire

طامح *ṭāmiḥ* high-aiming, high-aspiring; longing, yearning, craving, covetous, avid, eager

[1]طمر **ṭamara u i** (*ṭamr*) to bury, inter, cover with earth (ه s.th., esp. a corpse); — *ṭamara i* to cover up (ه a thing), fill up (ه a well)

طمر *ṭimr* pl. اطمار *aṭmār* old, tattered garment, rags, tatters

طمر *ṭimirr* fiery steed, race horse

مطمر *miṭmar* plumb line

مطمور *maṭmūr* subterranean, underground | ○ علم المطمورات *'ilm al-maṭmūrāt* paleontology

مطمورة *maṭmūra* pl. مطامير *maṭāmīr*[2] subterranean storehouse for grain, underground granary, mattamore

[2]طمر **II** (*eg.*) to curry(comb), rub down (ه a horse)

طمار *ṭumār* (*eg.*) currycomb

[3]طومار *ṭūmār* pl. طوامير *ṭawāmīr*[2] look up alphabetically

طمس **ṭamasa u i** (*ṭams*, طموس *ṭumūs*) to be effaced, be obliterated, be erased, be wiped out, be blotted out, be destroyed, be eradicated; to lose animation, become lusterless (eye, glance); — *ṭamasa i* (*ṭams*) to efface, obliterate, erase, expunge, blot out, wipe out, destroy, eradicate (على or ه s.th.) **VII** to be effaced, be obliterated, be wiped out, be blotted out, become extinct

طمس *ṭams* effacement, obliteration

انطماس *inṭimās* incomprehensibleness, abstruseness

طامس *ṭāmis* extinct, dead; blurred, indistinct; incomprehensible, abstruse, recondite, obscure

طماطة *ṭumāṭa* tomato

طماطم *ṭamāṭim*[2] (coll.; n. un. ة) tomatoes

طمطمانى *ṭumṭumānī* barbarous, barbaric, uneducated (esp. speech, pronunciation)

طمع **ṭami'a a** (*ṭama'*) to covet, desire (ب or فى s.th.), wish, crave, strive (ب or فى for), aspire (ب or فى to, after); to expect (ب s.th., من from); to hope (فى for); to be ambitious; — *ṭamu'a u* (طماعة *ṭamā'a*) to be covetous, avid, greedy, avaricious **II** to make (ه s.o.) desirous (فى of), fill (ه s.o.) with greed (فى for); to allure, tempt, entice (ه s.o.); to give (ه s.o.) hope (فى of), hold out hopes (ه to s.o., فى of s.th.), embolden (ه s.o.), encourage (ه فى s.o. to do s.th.) **IV** = **II**

طمع *ṭama'* pl. اطماع *aṭmā'* greed, greediness, avidity, covetousness; ambitious desire, ambition; object of desire

طماع *ṭammā'* avid, greedy, covetous, desirous; avaricious, grasping

طماعية *ṭamā'iya* avidity, greed; cupidity, avarice

مطمع *maṭma'* pl. مطامع *maṭāmi'*[2] coveted object; covetousness, craving, desire; hope, expectation; pl. ambitious designs, ambitions, schemes, aspirations, desires

مطمعة *maṭma'a* lure, enticement, temptation

مطماع *miṭmā'* filled with greed; obsessed by ambition, overambitious

طمن **II** to quiet, calm, appease, pacify, allay, assuage, soothe (ه, ه s.o., s.th.); see also طأمن *ṭa'mana* under طمأن **VI** to be low; to become low, sink, subside; to calm down, be or become quiet, calm, still, to abate; to be bent over, to stoop

طمان *ṭamān* calm, quiet, repose, peace, peacefulness, serenity, tranquillity; reassurance, ease, calmness, peace of mind, composure, equanimity; trust, confidence

تطمين *taṭmīn* appeasement, mollification, calming, assuaging, soothing

متطامن *mutaṭāmin* low

طمى (طمو and طمى) طما *ṭamā u* (طمو *ṭumūw*), *ṭamā i* (*ṭamy*) to flow over

طمى *ṭumy* (*eg., syr.*) alluvial mud, silt, alluvium

طن[1] *ṭunn* pl. اطنان *aṭnān* ton | طن مسجل (*musajjal*) register ton

طن[2] *ṭanna i* (طنين *ṭanīn*) to ring, sound, peal, jingle, tinkle (bell); to hum, buzz, drone (insect); to ring (ears) **II** = **I**

طنين *ṭanīn* ring(ing), peal, jingle, tinkle, tinkling (of a bell); buzz(ing), hum(ming), drone (of an insect); ringing (of the ears)

طنان *ṭannān* ringing, sounding, pealing, jingling, tinkling; resounding, reverberating, echoing; humming, buzzing, droning; whistle, buzzer (of a kettle); famous, renowned, celebrated

طنب **II** to remain, abide, stay to live, settle down (ب in, at a place) **IV** to be excessive (في in), overdo, exaggerate (في s.th.); to brag

طنب *ṭunub* pl. اطناب *aṭnāb* tent rope; sinew, tendon | شد اطنابه (*šadda*) to stay, sojourn, reside; ضرب اطنابه على to settle down, take up permanent residence in a place; ضرب اطنابه في to take root, prevail (at a place)

اطناب *iṭnāb* exaggeration; fussiness, circumstantiality, prolixity, lengthiness, verbosity

طنبور *ṭunbūr* pl. طنابير *ṭanābīr*[2] a long-necked, stringed instrument resembling the mandolin; a device used to raise water for irrigation, Archimedean screw; drum, cylinder (*techn.*)

طنبورى *ṭunbūrī* player of the طنبور

طنبوشة *ṭanbūša* pl. *-āt* paddle box (of a paddle steamer)

طنجة *ṭanja*[2] Tangier

طنجى *ṭanjī* from Tangier; native of Tangier, Tangerine

طنجرة *ṭanjara* pl. طناجر *ṭanājir*[2] (copper) casserole, saucepan, skillet

طنطا *ṭanṭā* Tanta (city in N Egypt)

طنطن *ṭanṭana* to ring, sound, peal, jingle, tinkle (bell); to hum, buzz, drone (insect); to clang, boom, roar, rumble; to blare out (ب s.th.)

طنطنة *ṭanṭana* ring(ing), peal, jingle, tinkle, tinkling (of a bell); hum(ming), buzz(ing), drone (of an insect); clangor, boom, roar

طنف *ṭunuf* (*ṭanaf, ṭunf*) pl. طنوف *ṭunūf*, اطناف *aṭnāf* top, summit, peak (of a mountain); ledge, molding, eaves

طنفسة *ṭinfisa, ṭanfasa, ṭunfusa* pl. طنافس *ṭanāfis*[2] velvet-like carpet, mockado carpet

طه a group of letters opening the 20th sura; *Ṭāhā* a Muslim masculine proper name

طهر *ṭahara, ṭahura u* (*ṭuhr*, طهارة *ṭahāra*) to be clean, pure; — *ṭaharat, ṭahurat* (of a woman) to be clean (as opposed to menstruating) **II** to clean, cleanse, deterge, expurgate, purge, purify, chasten (ه, ه s.o., s.th.); to disinfect, sterilize (ه s.th.); to dredge (ه e.g., a canal); to circumcise (ه s.o.) **III** to circumcise (ه s.o.) **V** to clean o.s., cleanse o.s., perform an ablution

طهر *ṭuhr* cleanness, purity; chastity

طهور *ṭahūr* circumcision; cleansing, purging, detergent; clean, pure

طهارة *ṭahāra* cleanness, cleanliness, purity; cultic purity (*Isl. Law*); chastity; holiness, sanctity, saintliness; circumcision | طهارة الذيل *ṭ. aḏ-ḏail* innocence; probity, uprightness, integrity, honesty

مطهر *maṭhar* purgatory (*Chr.*)

مطهرة *maṭhara* pl. مطاهر *maṭāhir*[2] washroom, lavatory, toilet

تطهير *taṭhīr* cleaning, cleansing, purging, expurgation, purification; disinfection; purgation, use of aperients; dredging; circumcision

تطهيرى *taṭhīrī* cleaning, cleansing, detergent

طاهر *ṭāhir* pl. اطهار *aṭhār* clean, pure; chaste, modest, virtuous | طاهر الذمة *ṭ. aḏ-ḏimma* upright, righteous, honest; طاهر الذيل *ṭ. aḏ-ḏail* innocent, pure, unblemished, blameless, upright, righteous, honest

مطهر *muṭahhir* pl. *-āt* a detergent (esp. antiseptic); an antiseptic, a disinfectant

مطهر *muṭahhar* pure, immaculate

طهران *ṭihrān*[2] Teheran (capital of Iran)

طهق V to despise, detest, abhor, loathe (من s.th.)

مطهم *muṭahham* of perfect beauty (esp. as an epithet of noble horses)

طهو and طهى) طها *ṭahā u* and يطهى *yaṭhā* (طهو *ṭahw*, طهى *ṭuhīy*, *ṭahy*, طهاية *ṭahāya*) to cook (ه s.th.); to stew (ه s.th.); to braise (ه s.th.); to broil, fry (ه s.th.); to bake (ه s.th.)

طهى *ṭuhan* cooked dish, cooked meal

طهاية *ṭihāya* cook's trade

مطهى *maṭhan* kitchen

طاه *ṭāhin* pl. طهاة *ṭuhāh* cook

طواشى *ṭawāšī* pl. طواشية *ṭawāšiya* eunuch

طواية *ṭawwāya* frying pan

[1]طابة *ṭāba* look up alphabetically

[2]طوب II to beatify (ه s.o.; *Chr.*)

طوبى *ṭūbā* blessedness, beatitude; Beatitude (title of honor of a patriarch; *Chr.*)

تطويب *taṭwīb* beatification (*Chr.*)

[3]طوب *ṭūb* (coll.; n. un. ة) brick(s) | طوب احمر (*aḥmar*) baked brick(s); طوب مفرغ (*mufarraḡ*) hollow tile(s), air brick(s); طوب نى (*nayy*) unburned, sun-dried brick(s)

طواب *ṭawwāb* brick burner, brickmaker, tilemaker

طوبجى *ṭōbjī*, (*eg.*) *ṭobgī* pl. *-īya* artillerist, artilleryman

طوبجية *ṭōbjīya* artillery

طوبه *ṭūba* the fifth month of the Coptic calendar

طاح (طوح) *ṭāḥa u* (*ṭauḥ*) to perish, die; to lose one's way, go astray, stray, wander about; to fall; to throw, cast, fling, hurl, toss, carry away, sweep away (ب s.o., s.th.) II to cause to or let perish (ه or ب s.o.); to endanger, expose to peril (ه or ب s.o.); to throw away, toss away, hurl away (ب s.th.); to throw, cast, hurl, toss, fling (ب ال s.o. into); to carry away, transport (ب ال s.o. to, into); to move, induce, tempt (ه s.o., ال to s.th., to do s.th.) | طرحت به الطوائح fate dealt him severe blows IV to drop, discard (ه, ه s.o., s.th.), shed (ه s.th.); to let s.th. (ب) be swept away; to carry away, tear away, rip away (ب s.th.); to chop off (ه s.th., esp. the head) V to fall, drop, be thrown, be tossed; to stray, wander about; to sway, reel, stagger

طوائح *ṭawā'iḥ*[2] adversities, blows of fate

مطوحة *muṭawwiḥa* pl. *-āt* adventure

طود VII to rise in the air, soar up

طود *ṭaud* pl. اطواد *aṭwād* (high, towering) mountain

منطاد *munṭād* pl. مناطيد *manāṭīd*² balloon, blimp; zeppelin, dirigible | منطاد مقيد (*muqayyad*) captive balloon, kite balloon; ○ منطاد هوائى ثابت (*hawā'ī*) barrage balloon

¹طور II to develop, further, advance, promote (ه s.th.) V to develop, evolve; to change; to race (motor)

طور *ṭaur* pl. اطوار *aṭwār* one time (= Fr. *fois*); state, condition; limit, bound; stage, degree; phase (also *phys.*, esp. *el.*) | طورا بعد طور time and again, again and again; طورا — طورا or حينا — طورا sometimes — sometimes, at times — at times; خرج عن طوره to lose one's self-control, become upset; اخرجه عن طوره (*akrajahū*) to upset, discompose, disconcert s.o.; غريب الاطوار of odd behavior, eccentric

طور *ṭūr* pl. اطوار *aṭwār* mountain | طور سيناء *ṭ. sīnā'* and طور سينا *ṭ. sīnā* Mount Sinai

طورى *ṭūrī* wild

طوار *ṭawār* sidewalk

طورانى *ṭūrānī* wild; Turanian

تطور *taṭawwur* pl. *-āt* development; evolution; pl. *-āt* stages of development, evolutionary phases, developments | قابل التطور developable, capable of development or evolution

تطورى *taṭawwurī* evolutional, evolutionary | نظرية تطورية (*naẓarīya*) theory of evolution, evolutionism

²طار *ṭār* (= اطار *iṭār*), طارة *ṭāra* hoop, ring; tire; frame; wheel, tambourine

³اطار *iṭār* see اطر

⁴طورية *ṭūrīya* look up alphabetically

طوربيد *ṭurbīd* pl. *-āt*, طرابيد *ṭarābīd*² torpedo

طورية *ṭūrīya* (*eg.*) pl. □ طوارى *ṭawārī* hoe, mattock

طوزلق (Turk. *tozluk*) gaiter(s), legging(s)

طوس II to adorn, decorate, deck out (ه, ه s.o., s.th.)

طاس *ṭās* pl. *-āt* round, shallow drinking cup made of metal, drinking vessel; finger bowl

طاسة *ṭāsa* pl. *-āt* round, shallow drinking cup made of metal, drinking vessel | طاسة التحمير frying pan; ○ طاسة التصادم *ṭ. at-taṣādum* buffer (railroad)

طاووس *ṭāwūs* pl. طواويس *ṭawāwīs*² peacock

مطوس *muṭawwas* ornate, ostentatiously made-up

طوش II to castrate, emasculate (ه s.o.)

طواشى *ṭawāšī* pl. طواشية *ṭawāšiya* eunuch

طاع (طوع) *ṭā'a u* (*ṭau'*) to obey (ل or ه s.o.), be obedient (ل or ه to s.o.) II to render obedient, bring into subjection, subdue, subject, subjugate (ه s.o.) | طوعت له نفسه (*nafsuhū*) (lit.: his soul permitted him, made it easy or feasible for him, i.e.) he allowed himself to do s.th. (ه), he had no qualms about doing s.th. (ه), he did not hesitate to do s.th. (ه) III to comply with or accede to s.o.'s (ه) wishes (على or فى in, with regard to), yield, submit, be obedient (ه to s.o., على or فى in), obey (ه s.o., على or فى in); to be at s.o.'s (ه) command (of a faculty, skill, etc.); to consent, assent (فى to s.th.) IV to obey, follow (ه, ه s.o., s.th.), be obedient, submit, yield (ه, ه to s.o., to s.th.), comply (ه, ه with s.o.'s wishes, with s.th.), accede (ه, ه to s.o.'s wishes, to s.th.) V to do voluntarily (ل or ب or ه s.th.), volunteer (ل or ب or ه for, in, to do s.th.); to enlist, volunteer (*mil.*) | تطوع خيرا (*kairan*) to perform a good deed voluntarily VII to obey, follow (ل s.o., s.th.), be obedient, submit, yield, accede (ل to), comply (ل with) X to be able (ه to do s.th.), be in a position to do, to get, to carry out, or to take upon o.s. (ه s.th.), be capable (ه of s.th., ان of doing s.th.)

طوع *ṭau'* obedience; voluntariness, spontaneity (in connection with a legally relevant action, esp. a delict; *Isl. Law*); (for m. and f.) obedient, compliant, submissive; طوعا *ṭau'an* voluntarily, of one's own free will, of one's own accord | طوعا او كرها (*karhan*) willingly or unwillingly, willy-nilly, whether I (you, etc.) will it or not; طوع العنان tractable, docile, amenable; طوع يده *ṭau'a yadihī* under s.o.'s thumb, at s.o.'s beck and call; هو طوع ايدينا (*ṭau'a aidīnā*) he is at our beck and call, he is in our power; طوع امرك *ṭau'a amrika* at your disposal

طوعيا *ṭau'īyan* voluntarily, of one's own free will, of one's own accord

طيع *ṭayyi'* obedient, compliant, submissive

طاعة *ṭā'a* obedience, compliance, submissiveness; (pl. *-āt*) pious deed (*Isl. Law*) | بيت الطاعة *bait aṭ-ṭ.* the husband's house to which a woman, in case of unlawful desertion, must return (*Isl. Law*); السمع والطاعة *as-sam'u wa-ṭ-ṭā'atu* I hear and obey! at your service! very well! سمعا وطاعة *sam'an wa-ṭā'atan* do.

طواعية *ṭawā'iya* obedience | عن طواعية voluntarily, of one's own free will, of one's own accord

مطواع *miṭwā'* obedient. compliant

تطويع *taṭwī'* diploma of the Great Mosque of Tunis

اطاعة *iṭā'a* obedience

تطوع *taṭawwu'* voluntariness; volunteering; voluntary service (في in a branch of the armed forces); service as an unsalaried trainee, voluntary traineeship

استطاعة *istiṭā'a* ability, capability, faculty; possibility

طائع *ṭā'i'* obedient, compliant, submissive | طائعا او كارها willingly or unwillingly, whether I (you, etc.) will it or not

مطوع *muṭawwa'* pl. *-ūn* holder of the diploma issued by the Great Mosque of Tunis; — *muṭṭawwi'* volunteer (also *mil.*); unsalaried trainee

مطاوع *muṭāwi'* obedient, compliant, submissive; yielding, pliable, pliant; المطاوع the reflexive, frequently = the passive (*gram.*) | حديد مطاوع mild steel

مطيع *muṭī'* obedient, compliant

متطوع *mutaṭawwi'* pl. ة volunteer (also *mil.*); unsalaried trainee

مستطاع *mustaṭā'* possible, feasible | قدر المستطاع *qadra l-m.* as far as possible, as far as it is feasible; بقدر (على قدر) المستطاع do.

(طوف) طاف *ṭāfa u* (*ṭauf*, طواف *ṭawāf*, طوفان *ṭawafān*) to go about, walk about, ride about, travel about, move about, rove about, wander about, run around (ه in s.th.), tour (ه s.th.); to go, walk, ride, run (ب, حول around s.th.), circumambulate (ب, حول s.th.); to make the rounds, walk around (على among people); to circle, circuit, compass (ب, حول s.th.); to roam, rove, range (ب s.th.); to show around, guide (بـ s.o.); to familiarize o.s., acquaint o.s. (ب with); to become acquainted (ب with s.o., with s.th.), come to know (ب s.o., s.th.); — (*ṭauf*) to appear to s.o. (ب) in his sleep; to come (على upon s.o.), afflict (على s.o.); to overflow, leave its banks (river); to swim, float, drift **II** to go about, walk about, stroll about, ride about, travel about (في in), tour (في s.th.); to go or walk around s.th. (ب), circle, circumambulate (ب s.th.); to show around, guide (ب or ه s.o.); to let (ب s.th.) roam (ه s.th.), let (ب s.th.) make the rounds

(ب in), let one's eyes (ب) wander; to perform the circumambulation of the Kaaba (*ṭawāf*) **IV** to surround, encompass, encircle, circumscribe (ب s.th.) **V** to move about, rove, roam, wander, walk about

طوف **ṭauf** round, circuit, beat; low wall, enclosure; (pl. اطواف *aṭwāf*) patrol; raft made of inflated waterskins tied together

طواف **ṭawāf** round, circuit, beat; round trip, round-trip excursion; round-trip flight; circumambulation of the Kaaba (as part of the Islamic pilgrimage ceremonies)

طواف **ṭauwāf** ambulant, itinerant, migrant, roving, wandering; going the rounds, making the circuit, walking the beat; (pl. ة) mounted rural mail carrier (*Eg.*) | محطات الطوافة *maḥaṭṭāt aṭ-ṭ.* (*Eg.*) circuit stations which have the mail delivered by mounted rural mail carriers

طوافة **ṭauwāfa** pl. *-āt* patrol boat, coastal patrol vessel (employed by the Egyptian Coast Guard)

طوفان **ṭūfān** flood, inundation, deluge

مطاف **maṭāf** riding about, traveling, touring; round trip | آل (انتهى) به المطاف الى to end with, wind up with, arrive eventually at; خاتمة المطاف the end of the matter, the final issue, the upshot of it

تطواف **taṭwāf** traveling, touring, wandering, itineration, roving life

طائف **ṭā'if** ambulant, itinerant, migrant, roving, wandering; one going the rounds or making the circuit or walking the beat; one performing the *ṭawāf* | طاف به طائف he had a sudden impulse or urge; طاف عليه طائف من القدر القاسى (*qadar*) tragedy befell him, he met with a harsh fate

الطائف **aṭ-ṭā'if** Taif (town in S Hejaz)

طائفة **ṭā'ifa** pl. طوائف *ṭawā'if*[2] part, portion; number; troop, band, group; swarm, drove, bevy, covey; people; class; sect, denomination; confession, communion; party, faction; religious minority | ○ الطائفة الاحساسية (*iḥsāsīya*) the impressionists; ملوك الطوائف princelings, petty kings

طائفى **ṭā'ifī** factional, sectarian, denominational, confessional

طائفية **ṭā'ifīya** sectarianism, denominationalism; confessionalism

مطوف **muṭauwif** pl. *-ūn* pilgrims' guide in Mecca

(طوق) طاق **ṭāqa** *u* (*ṭauq*) to be able, be in a position (ه to do s.th.), be capable (ه of, of doing s.th.); to be able to bear or stand (ه s.th.), bear, stand, sustain, endure (ه s.th.) **II** to put a collar or necklace (طوقا *ṭauqan*) around s.o.'s (ه) neck; to hoop (ه s.th., e.g., a barrel); to surround, clasp, enwrap, ring, encompass (ب ه, ه s.o., s.th. with), encircle (ه, ه s.o., s.th.), form or throw a circle or cordon (ه, ه around s.o., around s.th.), enclose (ه s.th.); to play (ه about, e.g., a smile about the lips), flit (ه across s.th.) | طوقه بذراعيه (*bi-ḏirā'aihi*) to take s.o. in one's arms, embrace, hug, clasp s.o.; طوق عنقه ب (*'unuqahū*) to present s.o. with, bestow upon s.o. s.th. **IV** = **I** (على, ه s.th., to do s.th., of s.th. or of doing s.th.); to master (ه a method) | لم يطق صبرا *lam yuṭiq ṣabran* he could not stand or bear it, he could not control himself; شىء لا يطاق (*yuṭāqu*) s.th. unbearable, s.th. intolerable

طوق **ṭauq** ability, faculty, power, strength, potency, capability, aptitude, capacity; endurance; — (pl. اطواق *aṭwāq*) necklace; neckband, ruff, collar; hoop, circle | طوق للنجاة (*najāh*) life buoy; اخرجه الحزن عن طوقه (*akrajahū l-ḥuznu*) grief drove him out of his mind

طوقى *ṭauqī* collar-like, loop-shaped, ring-shaped, annular

طاق *ṭāq* pl. *-āt*, طيقان *ṭīqān* arch (*arch.*); (pl. *-āt*) stratum, layer

طاقة *ṭāqa* pl. *-āt* window

طاقة *ṭāqa* pl. *-āt* ability, faculty, capability, aptitude, capacity, power, strength, potency; energy (*phys.*, etc.); capacity (of a technical apparatus); bunch, bouquet (of flowers) | فى الطاقة (with foll. *maṣdar*) it is possible to . . .; قدر الطاقة *qadra ṭ-ṭ.* as far as possible, in the best way possible; على قدر طاقته according to his capability; طاقة مدخرة (*muddakara*) accumulated energy; potential (*phys.*); الطاقة الذرية (*ḏarrīya*) atomic energy, atomic power; طاقة انتاجيه (*intājīya*) productive power, productional capacity, output capacity

طاقية look up alphabetically

تطويق *taṭwīq* pl. *-āt* encirclement, encompassment, enclosure, surrounding, ringing

اطاقة *iṭāqa* ability, faculty, aptitude, power, capability, capacity

مطوق *muṭawwaq* ringdove

مطاق *muṭāq* bearable, endurable, tolerable

طوكيو *ṭōkiyō* Tokyo

[1]طال (طول) *ṭāla u* (*ṭūl*) to be or become long; to last long; to lengthen, grow longer, extend, be protracted, become drawn out; to surpass, excel (على or ه s.o.) | طال به الزمن حتى (*zamanu*) it took a long time before he . . .; يطول بى هذا this will (would) take me too long; طال الزمان او قصر (*zamānu, qaṣura*) sooner or later, before long **II** to make long or longer, lengthen, elongate, stretch out, prolong, extend, protract (ه s.th.); to be very elaborate, very detailed, very exhaustive, long-winded, prolix; to grant a delay or respite (ل to s.o.) | طول باله عليه (*bālahū*) to be patient with **III** to keep putting off (ه ف s.o. in or with s.th.); to vie for power, greatness or stature, contend, compete (ه with s.o.), rival, emulate (ه s.o.) **IV** to make long or longer, lengthen, elongate, stretch out, extend, prolong, protract, draw out (ه or من s.th.); to take too long, find no end | اطال عليه to keep s.o. waiting a long time; اطال لسانه (*lisānahū*) to speak in a forward manner, be pert, saucy, insolent in speech; اطال النظر اليه (*naẓara*) he kept staring at him; اطال الوقوف he stayed a long time **VI** to become long, be lengthened, be extended, be prolonged; to stretch up, stretch o.s.; to stretch (الى for), crane one's neck (الى at); to attack (على s.o.); to become insolent, get fresh (على with s.o.); to be insolent enough, have the cheek (ل to do s.th.); to dare do s.th. (ب), presume (ب s.th.), pretend (ب to s.th.); to arrogate to o.s. (الى a rank) | تطاول برأسه (*bi-ra'sihī*) to bear one's head high (with pride) **X** to be or become long; to be or become overbearing, presumptuous, display an arrogant behavior (على toward)

طالما *ṭālamā* and لطالما *la-ṭālamā* how often! often, frequently (with foll. verbal clause) | طالما ان (*anna*) while, as, the more so as

طول *ṭaul* might, power | صاحب الحول والطول (*ṣ. al-ḥaul*) the Almighty

طول *ṭūl* pl. اطوال *aṭwāl* length; size, height, tallness | طول الاناة *ṭ. al-anāh* long-suffering, longanimity, forbearance, patience; طول النظر *ṭ. an-naẓar* far-sightedness, hyperopia; خط الطول *kaṭṭ aṭ-ṭ.* geographical longitude, degree of longitude, meridian; بالطول and طولا lengthwise, longitudinally; طول *ṭūla* (prep.) during, throughout, . . . long, e.g., طول هذه المدة (*mudda*) during this period, during all this time, طول النهار (*nahār*) all day (long); طول ما as long as; على طول (with foll. genit.) along, alongside of; على طول (*eg.*) straight ahead; straightway, directly; at last, finally, after all; فى طول البلاد وعرضها (*wa-'arḍihā*) throughout the country, all over the country; انا فى طولك (*eg.*) have mercy on me!

طولى *ṭūlī* of length, linear, longitudinal | خط طولى (*ḵaṭṭ*) geographical longitude, degree of longitude, meridian

طول *ṭuwwal* a long-legged waterfowl

طوال *ṭawāla, ṭiwāla* (prep.) during, throughout; along, alongside of

طويل *ṭawīl* pl. طوال *ṭiwāl* long; large, big, tall; high; الطويل name of a poetical meter; طويلا *ṭawīlan* long (adv.), a long time | طويل الاجل *ṭ. al-ajal* long-term, long-dated; طويل الاناة *ṭ. al-anāh* long-suffering forbearing, patient; طويل الباع mighty, powerful; capable, efficient; generous, liberal, openhanded; طويل الروح *ṭ. ar-rūh* long-suffering, forbearing, patient; طويل القامة tall; طويل اللسان insolent, impertinent, pert, saucy

طوال *ṭuwāl* long

طوالة *ṭuwāla* pl. *-āt* stable

طيلة *ṭīlata* (prep.) during, throughout, . . . long

طولانى *ṭūlānī* measured lengthwise, longitudinal

اطول *aṭwal*², f. طولى *ṭūlā* longer, larger, bigger, taller; extremely tall, very long

تطويل *taṭwīl* lengthening, elongation, stretching, extension, prolongation, protraction; elaborateness, exhaustiveness, prolixity, long-windedness

اطالة *iṭāla* lengthening, elongation, stretching, extension, prolongation, protraction; elaborateness, exhaustiveness, prolixity, long-windedness

استطالة *istiṭāla* overbearing attitude, haughtiness, presumptuousness, arrogance

طائل *ṭā'il* long; huge, immense, ample, enormous (of funds); use, avail; might, power, force | طائل الصولة *ṭ. aṣ-ṣaula* mighty, powerful, forceful; دون طائل and لا طائل تحته (فيه) (*ṭā'ila*) of no use, of no avail, useless, unavailing, futile; ما فاز بطائل to accomplish nothing, be unsuccessful, fail

طائلة *ṭā'ila* might, power, force; vengeance, revenge, retribution, retaliation | وقع تحت طائلة القانون to be subject to punishment by law; تحت طائلة الموت (*ṭ. il-maut*) under penalty of death

مطول *muṭawwal* elaborate, detailed, exhaustive, circumstantial

متطاول *mutaṭāwil* long-extended, long-stretched, long-protacted, prolonged, lengthy

مستطيل *mustaṭīl* long, oblong, elongate(d), long-stretched; protracted, prolonged, long drawn out; a rectangle, an oblong; a saucy, presumptuous person

طاولة² look up alphabetically

طولكرم Tulkarm (town in NW Jordan)

طومار *ṭūmār* pl. طوامير *ṭawāmīr*² roll, scroll

نهر الطونة *nahr aṭ-ṭūna* the Danube river

طونولاطة (It. *tonnellata*) *ṭonolāṭa* ton

طوى *ṭawā* i (طى *ṭayy*) to fold, fold up, fold in, fold over, fold under, roll up (ه s.th.); to shut, close (ه a book); to keep secret, secrete, conceal, hide (ه s.th.); to harbor, hold, contain (ه s.th.); to swallow up, envelop, wrap up, enwrap

(ه s.o.; of the dark of night); to settle finally, bury (ه the past), have done with s.th. in the past (ه); to cross, traverse (ه s.th., esp. a country); to cover quickly (ه the way, the distance, الى to); to spend, pass (ه a period of time); to possess o.s., take possession (ه of), appropriate (ه s.th.); pass. طوى على *ṭuwiya ʿalā* (= to be folded around or over, i.e.) to bear (within itself), harbor, contain, involve s.th. | طوى الارض طيا (*l-arḍa ṭayyan*) to rush through a country; طوى بساطه (*bisāṭahū*) to be finished, be done, come to an end, finish; طوى البساط بما فيه to settle an affair once and for all, wind up an affair; طوى جوانحه على (*jawāniḥahū*) to harbor s.th., conceal s.th. in one's heart; طوى كشحه (كشحا) على (*kašḥahū, kašḥan*) and طوى صدره على (*ṣadrahū*) to harbor or lock (a secret) in one's bosom, keep s.th. secret, secrete, conceal, hide s.th.; طوى صفحته (*ṣafḥatahū*) to have done with s.th., be through with s.th., give up, abandon s.th.; طوى الطريق الى to hurry or rush to; طوى الماضى طى السجل للكاتب (*l-māḍiya ṭayya s-sijilli*) to break with the past, let bygones be bygones; — طوى *ṭawiya a* (طوى *ṭawan*) to be hungry, suffer hunger, starve **IV** = *ṭawiya* **V** to coil (snake) **VII** to be folded, be folded up, in, over, or under, be rolled up, be turned (over) (page, leaf), be shut (book, etc.); to go by, pass, elapse (time); to disappear, vanish; to be covered (distance); to be hidden, be concealed (تحت under), be enveloped, be wrapped (تحت in); to contain, comprise, encompass, comprehend, embrace, involve, include (على s.th.); to harbor, nurse, bear (ه feelings, esp. hatred, love) | انطوى على نفسه to withdraw within o.s., be self-centered, be introverted

طى *ṭayy* concealment, hiding; (pl. أطواء *aṭwāʾ*) fold, pleat | طيه *ṭayyahū* and طى هذا (*ṭayya*) herein enclosed, herewith (in a letter); فى طى الغيب (*ṭ. il-ġaib*) secretly, covertly; تحت (فى) طى الكتمان (*ṭ. il-kitmān*) under the seal of secrecy; فى اطواء (with foll. genit.) in

طية *ṭayya* pl. *-āt* fold, pleat | حمل بين طياته to involve, comprise, contain

طية *ṭīya* intention, design | مضى (ذهب) لطيته he went to his destination; he left in order to do what he had in mind; he went his way

طوى *ṭawan* hunger; mat | على الطوى on an empty stomach, without having eaten

طوية *ṭawīya* pl. طوايا *ṭawāyā* fold, pleat; innermost thoughts, real conviction, true mind; intention, design; conscience | سليم الطوية guileless, artless; فى طوايا (with foll. genit.) inside, within, in, amid

طواية *ṭawwāya* pl. *-āt* frying pan

مطوى *maṭwan* pl. مطاو *maṭāwin* pocket knife, penknife; pl. folds, pleats | فى مطاوى (with foll. genit.) inside, within, in, amid; فى مطاويه inwardly, at heart, in his bosom

مطواة *miṭwāh* pocket knife, penknife

انطواء *inṭiwāʾ* introversion (*psych.*) | الانطواء على النفس (*nafs*) do.

انطوائى *inṭiwāʾī* introverted (*psych.*)

طاو *ṭāwin* starved | طاوى البطن *ṭ. l-baṭn* starved, lean, emaciated

مطوى *maṭwīy* folded up, infolded, rolled up, etc.; مطوى على bearing (within itself), harboring, containing, involving s.th. | مطوى الضلوع على harboring s.th. in one's bosom

منطو *munṭawin*: منطو على نفسه self-absorbed, low-spirited, depressed

[1]طيب طاب *ṭāba i* (طيب *ṭīb*, طيبة *ṭība*) to be good, pleasant, agreeable; to be or become

delightful, delicious; to please (ل s.o.), be to s.o.'s (ل) liking; to be or become ripe, to ripen; to regain health, recover, recuperate, convalesce | طابت ليلتكم (*lailatukum*) may your night be pleasant! good night! طابت نفسه (*nafsuhū*) he was gay, cheerful, cheery, in good spirits, he felt happy; طاب نفسا عن (*nafsan*) to give up s.th. gladly, renounce s.th. willingly; طابت نفسه اليه (*nafsuhū*) he had a liking for it, it was to his taste **II** to make (ه s.th.) good, pleasant, agreeable, delightful, delicious, or sweet, to sweeten (ه s.th.); to scent, perfume (ه, ه s.o., s.th.); to spice, season (ه food), mull (ه wine); to sanitate, improve (ه air, drinking water); to heal, cure (ه s.o.); to massage (ه s.o.) | طيب خاطره to mollify, soothe, placate, conciliate s.o., set s.o.'s mind at rest; طيب الله ثراه (*ṯarāhu*) may God make his earth light (a eulogy added after mentioning the name of a pious deceased) **III** to joke, jest, banter, make fun (ه with s.o.) **IV** to make (ه s.th.) good, pleasant, agreeable, delightful, delicious, or sweet, to sweeten (ه s.th.) **V** to perfume o.s. **X** استطاب and استطيب *istaṭyaba* to find or deem (ه s.th.) good, pleasant, agreeable, delightful, delicious, sweet; to like (ه s.th.), be fond (ه of)

طيب *ṭīb* goodness; (pl. طيوب *ṭuyūb*) scent, perfume | طيب العرق *ṭ. al-ʿirq* noble birth, noble descent; جوز الطيب *jauz aṭ-ṭ.* nutmeg

طيب *ṭayyib* good; pleasant, agreeable; delicious; gay; well-disposed, friendly, kindly; well, in good health | طيب الخلق *ṭ. al-ḵulq* good-natured, genial; طيب الرائحة sweet-smelling, fragrant, sweet-scented; طيب العرق *ṭ. al-ʿirq* highborn, of noble descent; طيب النفس *ṭ. an-nafs* gay, cheerful, cheery, in high spirits

طيبات *ṭayyibāt* nice, pleasant things; gustatory delights, pleasures of the table

طيبة *ṭība* goodness; good nature, geniality | عن طيبة خاطر gladly, most willingly, with pleasure

طوبى *ṭūbā* blessedness, beatitude; Beatitude (title of honor of a patriarch; *Chr.*)

طياب *ṭayāb*, *ṭiyāb* (*eg.*) north wind

طياب *ṭayyāb* pl. *-ūn* masseur

اطيب *aṭyab*[2] better; — pl. اطايب *aṭāyib*[2] the best parts (of s.th.); pleasures, comforts, amenities; delicacies, dainties

مطايب *maṭāyib*[2] comforts, amenities (e.g., of life)

مطايبة *muṭāyaba* pl. *-āt* banter, joke, jest, teasing remark

طائب *ṭā'ib* unobjectionable (ل for; *Isl. Law*)

مطيب *muṭayyab* bouquet, bunch (of flowers)

[2]طيبة *ṭība*[2] Thebes

طاح (طيح) *ṭāḥa* *i* (*ṭaiḥ*) to perish, die **II** to lose (ه s.th.)

طار (طير) *ṭāra* *i* (طيران *ṭayarān*) to fly; to fly away, fly off, take to the wing; to hasten, hurry, rush, fly (الى to); to be in a state of commotion, be jubilant, exult, rejoice; طار ب to snatch away, carry away, carry off (s.o., s.th.) | طار بخياله الى (*bi-ḵayālihī*) to let one's imagination wander to; طار له صيت فى الناس (*ṣīt*) his fame spread among people, he became well-known; طار طائره (*ṭā'iruhū*) to become angry, blow one's top; طار عقله (*ʿaqluhū*) to lose one's mind, go crazy; طار فؤاده (روحه) شعاعا (*fu'āduhū, rūḥuhū šaʿāʿan*) his mind became confused, he became all mixed up; طار فرحا (*faraḥan*) to be beside o.s. with joy, be overjoyed; طار بلبه (*bi-lubbihī*) to drive s.o. out of his mind; طار بصوابه (*bi-ṣawābihī*) to make s.o. unconscious **II** to make or let fly (ه, ه s.o., s.th.), to fly, send up (ه s.th., e.g., a balloon, a kite); to pass on promptly, dispatch posthaste, forward without delay, rush, shoot (ه الى s.th. to, esp. a report, a message); to knock out (ه s.th., e.g., an eye, a tooth) | طير رأسه (*ra'sahū*) to chop off s.o.'s head, behead s.o. **IV** to make or let fly (ه, ه s.o., s.th.), to fly (ه s.th.); to blow away (ه s.th.; of the wind); to make (ه s.th.) disappear at once, dispel (ه s.th.) **V** to see an evil omen (من or ب in) **VI** to be scattered, be dispersed, scatter, disperse, spread, diffuse; to be exuded, rise (fragrance); to fly apart, fly about, fly in all directions (esp. sparks); to vanish, disappear, be dispelled **X** to make fly, cause to fly (ه s.th.); to knock (ه s.th.) out of s.o.'s hand; to alarm or upset seriously (ه s.o.), agitate, excite (ه, ه s.o., s.th.); = **VI**; pass. استطير *ustuṭīra* to be terrified | استطير عقله (*'aqluhū*) to go out of one's mind (with astonishment or fright)

طير *ṭair* (coll. and n. un.) pl. طيور *ṭuyūr*, اطيار *aṭyār* birds, bird; augury, omen; طيور poultry; fowl | طيور جارحة predatory birds, birds of prey; علم الطيور *'ilm aṭ-ṭ.* ornithology; كأن على رؤوسهم الطير (*ka'anna, ṭaira*) motionless or silent with awe

طيرة *ṭaira* commotion, agitation (of anger, wrath); flight; female bird

طيرة *ṭīra, ṭiyara* evil omen, portent, foreboding

طيار *ṭayyār* flying; evanescent, fleeting; volatile (liquid); floating, wafting, hovering; (pl. *-ūn*) flyer, aviator, pilot | زيوت طيارة volatile oils; طيار اول (*awwal*) a military rank, approx.: first lieutenant of the Air Force (*Eg.* 1939); طيار ثان (*ṯānin*) approx.: second lieutenant of the Air Force (*Eg.* 1939)

طيارة *ṭayyāra* pl. *-āt* aviatrix, woman pilot; airplane, aircraft; kite (toy) | طيارة رياضية (*riyāḍīya*) sport plane; طيارة قذافة (*qaḏḏāfa*) bomber; طيارة مائية seaplane

طيران *ṭayarān* flying, flight; aviation, aeronautics | طيران بهلوانى (*bahlawānī*) stunt flying; طيران شراعي (*širā'ī*) glider flying, gliding; خطوط الطيران airlines; سلاح الطيران air force; وزير الطيران minister of aviation

مطار *maṭār* pl. *-āt* airfield, airport | ○ مطار عائم aircraft carrier

مطارة *maṭāra* airfield, airport

مطير *maṭīr* airfield, airport

تطير *taṭayyur* pessimism

طائر *ṭā'ir* flying; flyer, aviator, pilot; (pl. *-āt*, طير *ṭair*) bird; omen, presage | سكون الطائر graveness, sedateness; على الطائر الميمون (*maimūn*) good luck! Godspeed! (said to s.o. setting out on a journey); طار طائره (*ṭā'iruhū*) to become angry, blow one's top

طائرة *ṭā'ira* pl. *-āt* airplane, aircraft | على متن الطائرة (*matni ṭ-ṭ.*) aboard the airplane; by (air)plane (e.g., traveling); طائرة بحرية (*baḥrīya*) seaplane; ○ طائرة دورية (*daurīya*) (short-range) reconnaissance plane, observation plane; طائرة شراعية (*širā'īya*) sailplane, glider; طائرة المطاردة *ṭ. al-muṭārada* fighter, pursuit plane, interceptor; طائرة عمودية (*'amūdīya*) helicopter; طائرة القتال light bomber, combat plane; طائرة المقاتلة *ṭ. al-muqātala* do.; ○ طائرة انقضاضية or ○ طائرة الانقضاض dive bomber; طائرة مائية seaplane; طائرة نفاثة (*naffāṯa*) jet plane; طائرة النقل *ṭ. an-naql* transport (plane); ○ حاملة الطائرات and ○ ناقلة الطائرات aircraft carrier

متطير *mutaṭayyir* pessimist

مستطير *mustaṭīr* imminent, impending, threatening (of disaster); scattered, dispersed; spread out, spread all over, scattered about; widespread; pessimist

طيش طاش *ṭāša i* (*ṭaiš*, طيشان *ṭayašān*) to be inconstant, changeable, fickle, lightheaded, thoughtless, heedless, frivolous, reckless, undecided, confused, helpless, aimless, desultory; to miss the mark (of an arrow, also عن الغرض); to stray (عن from the target), miss (عن a spot, e.g., said of the hand) | طاش سهمه (*sahmuhū*) to be on the wrong track, bark up the wrong tree, be unsuccessful, fail; طاش صوابه (*ṣawābuhū*) to lose one's head

طيش *ṭaiš* inconstancy, fickleness; recklessness, heedlessness, rashness; thoughtlessness; lightheadedness, levity, frivolity

طيشان *ṭayašān* inconstancy, fickleness; recklessness, heedlessness, rashness; thoughtlessness; lightheadedness, levity, frivolity

طياشة *ṭiyāša* inconstancy, fickleness; recklessness, heedlessness, rashness; thoughtlessness; lightheadedness, levity, frivolity

طائش *ṭā'iš* inconstant, changeable, fickle; lightheaded, frivolous; thoughtless, heedless, reckless; undecided, confused, perplexed, helpless; aimless, desultory, purposeless

طاف *ṭāfa* i (طيف *ṭaif*) to appear to s.o. (ب) in his sleep (of a specter)

طيف *ṭaif* pl. اطياف *aṭyāf*, طيوف *ṭuyūf* fantasy, phantasm; vision, apparition; phantom, specter, ghost; spectrum (*phys.*)

طيفى *ṭaifī* spectral, spectroscopic

مطياف *miṭyāf* spectroscope | مطياف مصور (*muṣawwir*) spectrograph

طيلة see طول

طيلسان *ṭailasān* pl. طيالسة *ṭayālisa* a shawl-like garment worn over head and shoulders

طين II to daub or coat with clay (▲ s.th.)

طين *ṭīn* pl. اطيان *aṭyān* clay, potter's clay, argil; soil; basis, foundation | الطين الخزفى (*ḵazafī*) kaolin, porcelain clay; زاد فى الطين بلة *zāda ṭ-ṭīna ballatan*, زاد الطين بلة to make things worse, aggravate or complicate the situation

طينة *ṭīna* clay, potter's clay, argil; stuff, material, substance (of which s.th. is made); kind, specific character, disposition, constitution, nature

طيان *ṭayyān* mortar carrier, hod carrier

طيون *ṭayyūn* Linula viscosa (*bot.*)

ظ

ظاء *ẓā'* name of the letter ظ

ظئر *ẓi'r* wet nurse

ظبى *ẓaby* pl. ظباء *ẓibā'* gazelle (Gazella dorcas)

ظبية *ẓabya* pl. *ẓabayāt* female gazelle

ظر *ẓirr* sharp-edged stone, flint

ظربان *ẓaribān*, *ẓirbān* pl. ظرابين *ẓarābīn*², ظرابى *ẓarābīy* polecat, fitchew

ظرف *ẓarufa* u (*ẓarf*, ظرافة *ẓarāfa*) to be charming, chic, nice, elegant, neat; to be witty, full of esprit II to adorn, embellish, polish (▲, ◦ s.o., s.th.), impart charm (▲, ◦ to s.o., to s.th.); to put (▲ s.th.) into an envelope, cover or wrap, to envelop, wrap up, cover (▲ s.th.) V to affect charm or elegance, display affectedness; to show o.s. elegant, witty, full of esprit VI = V; X to deem or find (▲, ◦ s.o., s.th.) elegant, charming, adroit, witty, etc.

ظرف *ẓarf* elegance, gracefulness, grace, charm; cleverness, resourcefulness; wittiness, esprit; — (pl. ظروف *ẓurūf*) vessel, receptacle, container; covering, wrap, cover; (letter) envelope; capsule, case; (*gram.*) adverb denoting place or time; pl. ظروف circumstances, conditions | بظرف or فى ظرف within, in a (given) period of; ظروف مخففة (*mukaffifa*) and ظروف التخفيف extenuating circumstances; ظروف مشددة (*mušaddida*) aggravating circumstances; بحسب الظروف *bi-ḥasabi ẓ-ẓ.* according to circumstances, depending on the circumstances

ظرفى *ẓarfī* adverbial | بينة ظرفية (*bayyina*) or دليل ظرفى circumstantial evidence

ظريف *ẓarīf* pl. ظرفاء *ẓurafā'*², f. ظرائف *ẓarā'if*² elegant, graceful, charming; full of esprit, witty, nice, fine

ظرافة *ẓarāfa* elegance, gracefulness, grace, charm; esprit, wittiness

تظريف *taẓrīf* wittiness, brilliant and witty manner

تظرف *taẓarruf* gracefulness, grace, elegance, charm, wittiness, esprit

مظروف *maẓrūf* pl. مظاريف *maẓārīf*² envelope

متظرف *mutaẓarrif* élégant, dandy, fop

مستظرف *mustaẓraf* elegant | اصناف مستظرفة luxury articles, fancy goods

ظعن **ẓa'ana** *a* (*ẓa'n*) to move away, leave, depart

ظعن *ẓa'n* departure, start, journey, trek (esp. of a caravan)

ظعينة *ẓa'īna* pl. ظعن *ẓu'un*, اظعان *aẓ'ān* camel-borne sedan chair for women; a woman in such a sedan

ظاعن *ẓā'in* ephemeral, transient, transitory

ظفر **ẓafira** *a* (*ẓafar*) to be successful, succeed, be victorious, be triumphant; to gain a victory (على or ب over), conquer, vanquish, defeat, overcome, surmount, overwhelm (على or ب s.o., s.th.), get the better (على or ب of s.o., of s.th.); to seize (على or ب s.o., s.th.), take possession (على or ب of s.o., of s.th.); to get, obtain, attain, achieve, gain, win (على or ب s.th.) **II** to grant victory (على or ب ه to s.o. over), make (ه s.o.) triumph, render (ه s.o.) victorious (على or ب over) **IV** = **II**; **VI** to ally, enter into an alliance or confederacy, join forces (على against)

ظفر *ẓufur*, *ẓufr*, *ẓifr* pl. اظفار *aẓfār*, اظافر *aẓāfir*², اظافير *aẓāfīr*² nail, fingernail; toenail; claw, talon | من (منذ or) نعومة اظفاره from (the days of) his earliest youth, since his earliest youth or adolescence; ناعم الظفر youthful, of tender age

ظفر *ẓafar* victory, triumph

ظفر *ẓafir* victorious, successful, triumphant; (pl. ظفران) young man, youth (*hij.*)

اظفور *uẓfūr* pl. اظافير *aẓāfīr*² nail, fingernail, toenail; claw, talon

ظافر *ẓāfir* victorious, triumphant; successful; victor, conqueror

مظفر *muẓaffar* victorious, successful, triumphant

ظل **ẓalla** (1st pers. perf. *ẓaliltu*) *a* (*ẓall*, ظلول *ẓulūl*) to be; to become, turn into, grow into; (with foll. imperf., participle or على:) to continue to do s.th., go on doing s.th., persevere in doing s.th., stick to s.th., remain, persist in, e.g., ظل يسكن البيت (*yaskunu l-baita*) he continued to live in the house; ظل صامتا he remained silent, persisted in his silence; ظل على موقف (*mauqif*) to persist in a standpoint or attitude **II** to shade, overshadow (ه, ه s.o., s.th.), cast a shadow (ه, ه over s.o., over s.th.); to screen, shelter, protect (ه, ه s.o., s.th.); to preserve, guard, maintain, keep up

(ه s.th.) IV = II; V to be shaded (ب by), sit in the shadow (ب of) X = V; to protect o.s. from the sun (ب by or through s.th.), hide in the shadow (ب of s.th.), seek the shadow (ب of s.th.); to place o.s. under the protection or patronage of s.o. (ب), seek shelter or refuge with s.o. (ب), be under the patronage or protection of s.o. (ب)

ظل *ẓill* pl. ظلال *ẓilāl*, ظلول *ẓulūl*, اظلال *aẓlāl* shadow, shade, umbra; shelter, protection, patronage; shading, hue; slightest indication, semblance, trace, glimpse (of s.th.); tangent (*geom.*) | في ظل (with foll. genit.) under the protection or patronage of, under the auspices of: under the sovereignty of; تحت ظل under the protection or patronage of, under the auspices of; ثقيل الظل insufferable, repugnant (of a person); خفيف الظل likable, nice (of a person); استثقل ظله (*istaṯqala*) to dislike s.o., find s.o. insufferable, unbearable, a bore; تقلص ظله (or قلص) *taqallaṣa ẓilluhū* his prestige or authority faded, diminished; it decreased, diminished, dwindled away, waned

ظلة *ẓulla* pl. ظلل *ẓulal* awning, marquee, canopy, sheltering hut or tent, shelter; shack, shanty; kiosk, stall; beach chair

ظليل *ẓalīl* shady, shaded, umbrageous

مظلة *miẓalla, maẓalla* pl. *-āt*, مظال *maẓāll*² umbrella, parasol, sunshade; lamp shade; awning; ○ veranda, porch | عيد المظلة *ʿīd al-m.* Feast of Tabernacles, Sukkoth (*Jud.*); مظلة واقية (*wāqiya*) parachute; مظلة هابطة do.; جندى المظلة *jundī al-m.* pl. (جنود المظلات) paratrooper

مظلى *miẓallī* pl. *-ūn* paratrooper; pl. paratroops, airborne troops

مظلل *muẓallil* shady, shadowy, umbrageous, shading, causing shadow

مظل *muẓill* shady, shadowy, umbrageous, shading, causing shadow

ظلع *ẓalaʿa a* (*ẓalʿ*) to limp, walk with a limp, walk lamely

ظالع *ẓāliʿ* lame

ظلف *ẓilf* pl. ظلوف *ẓulūf*, اظلاف *aẓlāf* cloven hoof

ظلم *ẓalama i* (*ẓalm, ẓulm*) to do wrong or evil; to wrong, treat unjustly, ill-treat, oppress, beset, harm, suppress, tyrannize (ه s.o.), commit outrage (ه upon s.o.); to act the tyrant, act tyrannically (ه toward or against s.o.); — *ẓalima a* and IV to be or grow dark, dusky, gloomy, murky, tenebrous, darken, darkle V to complain (من of, about) VII and VIII اظلم *iẓẓalama* to suffer injustice, be wronged

ظلم *ẓulm* wrong; iniquity; injustice, inequity, unfairness; oppression, repression, suppression, tyranny; ظلما *ẓulman* unjustly, wrongfully

ظلمة *ẓulma* pl. *-āt, ẓulumāt, ẓulamāt*, ظلم *ẓulam* darkness, duskiness, gloom, murkiness | بحر الظلمات *baḥr az-ẓ.* the Atlantic Ocean

ظلماء *ẓalmā*'² darkness | ليلة ظلماء (*laila*) pitch-dark night

ظلام *ẓalām* darkness, duskiness, gloom, murkiness

ظلام *ẓallām* evildoer, villain, malefactor, rogue, scoundrel, tyrant, oppressor

ظليم *ẓalīm* pl. ظلمان *ẓilmān* male ostrich

ظلامة *ẓulāma* pl. *-āt* misdeed, wrong, iniquity, injustice, outrage

اظلم *aẓlam*² darker, duskier, gloomier, murkier; a viler, more infamous, more heinous villain

مظلمة *maẓlima* pl. مظالم *maẓālim*² misdeed, wrong, iniquity, act of injustice, outrage

اظلام *iẓlām* darkness, gloom

ظالم *ẓālim* pl. *-ūn*, ظلام *ẓullām*, ظلمة *ẓalama* unjust, unfair, iniquitous, tyrannical, oppressing; tyrant, oppressor; offender, transgressor, sinner

مظلوم *maẓlūm* wronged, ill-treated, unjustly treated, tyrannized

مظلم *muẓlim* dark, dusky, gloomy, tenebrous, murky

ظمئ *ẓami'a a* (ظمأ *ẓama'*, ظماء *ẓamā'*, ظماءة *ẓamā'a*) to thirst, be thirsty **II** to make (ه s.o.) thirst

ظمء *ẓim'*, ظمأ *ẓama'* and ظماء *ẓamā'* thirst

ظمآن *ẓam'ān*², f. ظمأى *ẓam'ā* thirsty

ظامئ *ẓāmi'* thirsty

ظن *ẓanna* (1st pers. perf. *ẓanantu*) *u* (*ẓann*) to think, believe, assume, presume, suppose (ه s.th.); to hold, think, deem, consider (ه or ه ه s.o. to be s.o. or s.th.; ه ه s.th. to be s.th.); to suspect (ب or ه s.o.) | ظنه يفعل to think s.o. capable of doing s.th., believe of s.o. that he would do s.th.; لا اظن احدا ينكر (*aḥadan yunkiru*) I don't think that anyone can deny; لا اظنك تخالفنى (*tuk̲ālifunī*) I don't believe that you can contradict me; ظن فيه القدرة على (*qudrata*) he considered him capable of...; ظن به الظنون (*ẓunūna*) to think ill of s.o., have a low opinion of s.o.; ظن به الغباء (*ḡabā'a*) to suspect s.o. of stupidity **IV** to suspect (ه s.o.) **V** to surmise, form conjectures

ظن *ẓann* pl. ظنون *ẓunūn* opinion, idea, assumption, view, belief, supposition; doubt, uncertainty | حسن الظن *ḥusn aẓ-ẓ.* good opinion; سوء الظن *sū' aẓ-ẓ.* low opinion, distrust; فى اغلب الظن or فى اكثر الظن most probably, most likely; اكثر الظن ان it is very likely that ...; ظنا منه ان (*ẓannan*) since he believed that...; ما ظنك ب (*ẓannuka*) what is one to think of...; حسن ظنه به (*ḥasuna ẓannuhū*) to have a good opinion of s.o., think well of s.o.; احسن الظن ب (*aḥsana ẓ-ẓanna*) do.; ساء به ظنا to have a low opinion of s.o., think ill of s.o.; اساء الظن ب (*asā'a*) do.

ظنى *ẓannī* resting on mere assumption, presumptive, supposed, hypothetical

ظنة *ẓinna* pl. ظنن *ẓinan* suspicion, misgiving

ظنين *ẓanīn* suspicious, suspect(ed); unreliable, untrustworthy (على with regard to); a suspect

ظنون *ẓanūn* suspicious, distrustful

مظنة *maẓinna* pl. مظان *maẓānn*² time or place where one expects s.th.; (with foll. genit. or suffix) place where s.th. or s.o. is presumably to be found, its most likely location, the most likely place for it (or him) to be; suspicion, misgiving | التمسته فى مظانه I looked for him where I expected to find him, where he presumably was; فى غير مظانه in places where he couldn't possibly be

مظنون *maẓnūn* supposed, presumed, assumed; suspicious, suspect(ed)

ظنبوب *ẓunbūb* pl. ظنابيب *ẓanābīb*² shinbone

ظهر *ẓahara a* (ظهور *ẓuhūr*) to be or become visible, perceptible, distinct, manifest, clear, apparent, evident, obvious (ل to s.o.), come to light, appear, manifest itself, come into view, show, emerge, crop up; to appear, seem (ل to s.o.); to break out (disease); to come out; to appear, be published (book, periodical); to arise, result (من from); to ascend, climb, mount (ه s.th.); to gain the upperhand, to triumph (على over), get the better (على of), overcome, overwhelm, conquer, vanquish (على s.o.); to get (على s.th.) into one's power; to gain or have knowledge (على of), come to know (على s.th.), become acquainted (على with); to know (على s.th.); to learn, receive information (على about); to be cognizant (على of); to learn (على s.th.) **II** to endorse (ه a bill of exchange) **III** to help, assist, aid, support (ه s.o.) **IV** to make visible, make apparent, show, demonstrate, present, produce, bring to light, expose, disclose, divulge, reveal, manifest, announce, proclaim, make known, expound, set forth (ه s.th.); to develop (ه film; *phot.*); to grant victory (ه على to s.o. over), render victorious (ه على s.o. over); to acquaint (ه على s.o. with s.th.), initiate (ه على s.o. into s.th.), give knowledge or information (ه على to s.o. about), inform, enlighten (ه على s.o. about), explain (ه على to s.o. s.th.); to let (ه s.o.) in on s.th. (على), make (ه s.o.) realize (على s.th.); to show, reveal (ه على to s.o. s.th.); to articulate fully **VI** to manifest, display, show outwardly, exhibit, parade (ب s.th.); to feign, affect, pretend, simulate (ب s.th.), act as if, make out as if (ب); to demonstrate, make a public demonstration; to help one another, make common cause (على against) **X** to show, demonstrate, expose (ه s.th.); to memorize, learn by heart (ه s.th.); to know by heart (ه s.th.); to seek help, assistance, or support (ب with), appeal for help, for assistance (ب to s.o.); to overcome, surmount, conquer, vanquish (على s.o., s.th.), have or gain the upperhand (على over), get the better (على of)

ظهر *ẓahr* cast iron | ظهر الحديد and حديد ظهر see زهر الظهر

ظهر *ẓahr* pl. ظهور *ẓuhūr*, اظهر *aẓhur* back; rear, rear part, rear side, reverse; flyleaf; deck (of a steamer); upper part, top, surface; ظهورات *ẓuhūrāt* (as a genit.; *eg.*) pro tempore, provisional, temporary | سلسلة الظهر *silsilat aẓ-ẓ.* spine, vertebral column; ظهرا لبطن *ẓahran li-baṭnin* upside down, topsy-turvy; ظهرا على عقب (*ʿaqib*) from the ground up, radically, entirely, completely; بظهر الغيب *bi-ẓ. il-ḡaib* behind s.o.'s back, insidiously, treacherously; secretly, stealthily, clandestinely; بين اظهرهم in their midst, among them; من بين اظهرنا from our midst, from among us; على ظهر on (e.g., on the ground, on the water, etc.), على ظهر الباخرة on board the steamer; عن ظهر القلب (*ẓ. il-qalb*), عن ظهر قلب (*ẓ. qalbin*) or عن ظهر الغيب (*ẓ. il-ḡaib*) by heart; مستخدم ظهورات (*mustakdam*) temporary employee

ظهر *ẓuhr* pl. اظهار *aẓhār* noon, midday; (f.) midday prayer (*Isl. Law*) | بعد الظهر in the afternoon, p.m.; قبل الظهر in the forenoon, a.m.

ظهرى *ẓihrī*: نبذه (طرحه) ظهريا to pay no attention to s.th., not to care about s.th., disregard s.th.

ظهير *ẓahīr* helper, assistant, aid, supporter; partisan, backer; back (in soccer); (*mor.*) decree, edict, ordinance

ظهور *ẓuhūr* appearance; visibility, conspicuousness; pomp, splendor, show, ostentation, window-dressing | حب الظهور *ḥubb aẓ-ẓ.* ostentatiousness, love of pomp; عيد الظهور *ʿīd aẓ-ẓ.* Epiphany (*Chr.*)

الظهران *aẓ-ẓahrān* Dhahran (town in extensive oil region of E Saudi Arabia)

بين ظهرانيهم *baina ẓahrānaihim* in their midst, among them

ظهارة *ẓihāra* outside, right side (of a garment); blanket (e.g., of a mule)

ظهيرة *ẓahīra* noon, midday, midday heat

اظهر *aẓhar*[2] more distinct, more manifest, clearer

مظهر *maẓhar* pl. مظاهر *maẓāhir*[2] (external) appearance, external make-up, guise; outward bearing, comportment, conduct, behavior; exterior, look(s), sight, view; semblance, aspect; bearer or object of a phenomenon, object in which s.th.

manifests itself; phenomenon; symptom (*med.*); pl. manifestations, expressions | مظاهر الحياة *m. al-ḥayāh* manifestations of life (*biol.*); فى المظهر externally, in outward appearance, outwardly

تظهير *taẓhīr* endorsement, transfer by endorsement (of a bill of exchange; *com.*)

ظهار *ẓihār* pre-Islamic form of divorce, consisting in the words of repudiation: you are to me like my mother's back (انت على كظهر امى *anti ʿalayya ka-ẓahri ummī*)

مظاهرة *muẓāhara* assistance, support, backing; (pl. *-āt*) (public) demonstration, rally

اظهار *iẓhār* presentation, exposition, demonstration, exhibition, disclosure, exposure, revelation, announcement, declaration, manifestation, display; developing (*phot.*)

تظاهر *taẓāhur* dissimulation, feigning, pretending, pretension; hypocrisy, dissemblance; (pl. *-āt*) (public) demonstration, rally

ظاهر *ẓāhir* (of God) mastering, knowing (على s.th.); visible, perceptible, distinct, manifest, obvious, conspicuous, clear, patent, evident, apparent; external, exterior, outward; seeming, presumed, ostensible, alleged; outside, exterior, surface; outskirts, periphery (of a city); (*gram.*) substantive; (pl. ظواهر *ẓawāhir*²) external sense, literal meaning (specif., of Koran and Prophetic Tradition); ظاهرا *ẓāhiran* externally, outwardly; seemingly, presumedly, ostensibly, allegedly | ظاهر اللفظ *ẓ. al-lafẓ* the literal meaning of an expression; الظاهر ان it seems, it appears that...; حسب الظاهر *ḥasaba ẓ-ẓ.* in outward appearance, externally, outwardly; فى الظاهر apparently, obviously, evidently; فى الظاهر and فى ظاهر الامر (*ẓ. il-amr*) seen outwardly, externally; outwardly; من الظاهر from outside

ظاهرى *ẓāhirī* outer, outside, external, exterior, outward; superficial; Zahiritic, interpreting the Koran according to its literal meaning

ظاهرة *ẓāhira* pl. ظواهر *ẓawāhir*² phenomenon, outward sign or token, external symptom or indication | ظواهر الحياة *ẓ. al-ḥayāh* biological phenomena (*biol.*); علم الظواهر الجوية *ʿilm aẓ-ẓ. al-ǧawwīya* meteorology; ستّر الظواهر (*ẓawāhira*) to keep up appearances

متظاهر *mutaẓāhir* pl. *-ūn* demonstrator

ظاء *ẓāʾ* name of the letter ظ

ع

عب *ʿabba u* (*ʿabb*) to drink in large draughts, gulp down (ه s.th.); to pour down, toss down (ه a drink); to lap up, drink avidly (ه s.th.)

عب *ʿubb, ʿibb* breast pocket

عباب *ʿubāb* f. torrents, floods; waves, billows

يعبوب *yaʿbūb* torrential river

عبأ *ʿabaʾa a* with negation; ما عبأ ب not to care about, not to give a hoot for, pay no attention to, attach no importance to, not to insist on | لا يعبأ به (*yuʿbaʾu*) unimportant, insignificant; غير عابئ indifferent, unconcerned II to prepare, arrange (ه s.th.); to array, set up (ه s.th.); to mobilize, call up (جيشا *jaišan* an army); to fill, pack (ب ه s.th. with);

to load, charge (ب ه s.th. with); to draw off, decant (في ه s.th. into), bottle (ه s.th.)

عبء *'ib'* pl. اعباء *a'bā'* load, burden (على on), encumbrance (على to) | عبء الاثبات *'i. al-iṯbāt* burden of proof (*jur.*); نهض or قام بالاعباء كلها to take all burdens upon o.s., carry all burdens

عباء *'abā'* pl. اعبئة *a'bi'a* aba, cloak-like woolen wrap (occasionally striped)

عباءة *'abā'a* pl. *-āt* aba, a cloak-like, woolen wrap (occasionally striped)

تعبئة *ta'bi'a* mobilization; drafting, conscription; filling, drawing off, bottling

عابئ *'ābi'* see under verb **I**

عبث *'abiṯa a* (*'abaṯ*) to fool around, indulge in horseplay, commit a folly; to play, joke, jest (ب with); to toy, play a frivolous game (ب with), mock (ب s.o., s.th.); to play (absent-mindedly), fidget, fuss, dawdle, fiddle (ب with s.th., e.g., while talking); to handle, manipulate (ب s.th.), tinker (ب with); to abuse (ب s.th.); to commit an offense (ب against), violate (ب s.th.), infringe, encroach (ب upon); to impair, injure (ب s.th.) **III** to amuse o.s., make fun, play around, banter, dally (ه with s.o.), tease (ه s.o.), play a trick, prank or joke (ه on s.o.)

عبث *'abaṯ* (frivolous) play; pastime, amusement; joke, jest; mockery; عبثا *'abaṯan* in vain, futilely, to no avail, uselessly, fruitlessly | من العبث ان it is foolish and useless to...; ولكن عبثا استطاع ان يجيبه (*istaṭā'a, yujībahū*) but he couldn't give him an answer

معابثة *mu'ābaṯa* pl. *-āt* teasing, joke or prank played on s.o.; funmaking, jesting, banter, raillery

عابث *'ābiṯ* joking, jocular; mocking, scornful; frivolous; wanton, wicked, outrageous; offender, transgressor, evildoer, sinner

عبد[1] *'abada u* (عبادة *'ibāda*, عبودة *'ubūda*, عبودية *'ubūdīya*) to serve, worship (ه a god), adore, venerate (ه s.o., a god or human being), idolize, deify (ه s.o.) **II** to enslave, enthrall, subjugate, subject (ه s.o.); to improve, develop, make serviceable, make passable for traffic (ه a road) **V** to devote o.s. to the service of God **X** to enslave, enthrall, subjugate (ه s.o.)

عبد *'abd* pl. عبيد *'abīd*, عبدان *'ubdān*, *'ibdān* slave, serf; bondsman, servant; — (pl. عباد *'ibād*) servant (of God), human being, man; العباد humanity, mankind | العبد لله = I (form of modesty); العبد الضعيف do.

عبدلاوى, عبد اللاوى *'abdallāwī* (*eg.*) a variety of melon

عبدة *'abda* pl. *-āt* woman slave, slave girl, bondwoman

عباد *'abbād*: عباد الشمس and عبادة الشمس *'a. aš-šams* sunflower (Helianthus annuus L.)

عبادة *'ibāda* worship, adoration, veneration; devotional service, divine service (*Chr.*); pl. *-āt* acts of devotion, religious observances (*Isl. Law*)

عبودة *'ubūda* humble veneration, homage, adoration, worship; slavery, serfdom; servitude, bondage

عبودية *'ubūdīya* humble veneration, homage, adoration, worship; slavery, serfdom; servitude, bondage

معبد *ma'bad* pl. معابد *ma'ābid*[2] place of worship; house of God, temple

تعبيد *ta'bīd* enslavement, enthrallment, subjugation, subjection; paving, pavement | تعبيد الطرق *t. aṭ-ṭuruq* road construction

تعبد *ta'abbud* piety, devoutness, devotion, worship; hagiolatry, worship or cult of saints (*Chr.*)

استعباد *isti'bād* enslavement, enthrallment, subjugation

عابد *'ābid* pl. *-ūn*, عباد *'ubbād*, عبدة *'abada* worshiper, adorer

معبود *ma'būd* worshiped, adored; deity, godhead; idol

معبودة *ma'būda* ladylove, adored woman

معبد *mu'abbad* passable, smooth, improved (road)

متعبد *muta'abbid* pious, devout; pious worshiper (*Chr.*)

عبدان *'abadān*[2] Abadan (island and town in W Iran, oil center)

عبر *'abara u* (*'abr*, عبور *'ubūr*) to cross, traverse (ه s.th.); to ford (ه s.th.), wade (ه through s.th.); to swim (ه s.th. or across s.th.); to pass (ه over s.th.); to ferry (ه a river, and the like); عبر به to carry s.o. across or over s.th.; to pass, elapse (time), fade, dwindle; to pass away, die, depart; — *'abira a* (*'abar*) to shed tears II to interpret (ه a dream); to state clearly, declare, assert, utter, express, voice (عن s.th.), give expression (عن to a feeling); to designate (عن ب s.th. with or by); to determine the weight of a coin (ه), weigh (ه a coin) VIII to be taught a lesson, be warned; to learn a lesson, take warning, to learn, take an example (ب from); to consider, weigh, take into account or consideration (ه s.th.), allow, make allowances (ه for s.th.); to acknowledge a quality (ه) in s.o. (ل); to deem, regard, take (ه ه, ه s.o., s.th. as), look (ه ه, ه at s.th. as); to esteem, honor, revere, value, respect, hold in esteem (ه s.o.), have regard (ه for s.o.) X to shed tears, weep

عبر *'abr* crossing, traversing, transit; passage; fording; *'abra* (prep.) across, over; beyond, on the other side of

عبور *'ubūr* crossing, traversing, transit; passage; fording

عبير *'abīr* fragrance, scent, perfume, aroma; bouquet (of wine)

عبرى *'ibrī* Hebrew, Hebraic; (pl. *-ūn*) a Hebrew; العبرى or العبرية Hebrew, the Hebrew language

عبرة *'abra* pl. *'abarāt*, عبر *'ibar* tear

عبرة *'ibra* pl. عبر *'ibar* admonition, monition, warning; (warning or deterring) example, lesson; advice, rule, precept (to be followed); consideration befitting s.th.; that which has to be considered, be taken into consideration or account, that which is of consequence, of importance, s.th. decisive or consequential | موطن العبرة *mauṭin al 'i.* the salient point, the crucial point; لا عبرة به (*'ibrata*) it deserves no attention, it is of no consequence; العبرة ب or ى the crucial factor(s) is (are)..., decisive is (are)...; لا عبرة لمن (*li-man*) it is of no consequence if s.o. ...

عبارة *'ibāra* pl. *-āt* explanation, interpretation; mode of expression, diction; word; sentence, clause, phrase, idiom, expression | بعبارة اخرى (*ukrā*) in other words, expressed otherwise; عبارة فعبارة *'ibāratan fa-'ibāratan* sentence by sentence, word by word; عبارة عن consisting in; tantamount to, equivalent to, meaning...

عبرانى *'ibrānī* Hebrew, Hebraic; a Hebrew; العبرانى or العبرانية Hebrew, the Hebrew language

معبر *ma'bar* pl. معابر *ma'ābir*[2] crossing point, crossing, traverse, passage(way); ford; pass, pass road, defile; ○ lobby

معبر *mi'bar* pl. معابر *ma'ābir*[2] medium for crossing, ferry, ferryboat; bridge

تعبير *ta'bīr* interpretation (of a dream); assertion, declaration, expression, utterance (عن of a feeling); (pl. *-āt*) expression (in general, also artistic); (pl. تعابير *ta'ābīr*²) (linguistic) expression, phrase, term | بتعبير آخر (*ākar*) in other words, expressed otherwise

تعبيرى *ta'bīrī* expressional, expressive, emotive

اعتبار *i'tibār* respect, regard, deference, esteem; (pl. *-āt*) consideration, regard; reflection, contemplation; approach, outlook, point of view, view | اعتبارا ل (or ب) (*i'tibāran*) with respect to, with regard to, in consideration of, considering..., in view of (s.th.); اعتبارا من from, as of, beginning..., starting with..., effective from... (with foll. indication of time); باعتبار الشىء with respect to, with regard to, in consideration of, considering..., in view of (s.th.); باعتبار ان *bi-'tibāri an* considering (the fact) that..., with regard to the fact that..., in view of the fact that...; provided that..., with the proviso that...; باعتباره as, in terms of, in the capacity of, e.g., وزير الخارجية باعتباره اقدم الوزراء (*aqdama l-wuzarā'i*) the Foreign Minister in his capacity of senior-ranking minister; بهذا الاعتبار from this standpoint, from this viewpoint; على اعتبار ان considering (the fact) that..., with regard to the fact that..., in view of the fact that...; on the assumption that...; على هذا الاعتبار from this standpoint, from this viewpoint; فى كل اعتبار in every respect; اعتبارا او حقيقة (*ḥaqīqatan*) from a subjective point of view or in reality

اعتبارى *i'tibārī* based on a subjective approach or outlook; relative | شخصية اعتبارية (*šakṣīya*) legal person (*jur.*)

عابر *'ābir* passing; crossing, traversing, etc. (see I); fleeting (smile); transient, transitory, ephemeral; bygone, past, elapsed (time); (pl. *-ūn*) passer-by | ○ صاروخ عابر القارات intercontinental ballistic missile, ICBM

معبر *mu'abbir* interpreter (عن of feelings); expressive, significant | رقص معبر (*raqṣ*) interpretative dancing

□ عبرود (*ḥij.*) musket, gun

عبس *'abasa* i (*'abs*, عبوس *'ubūs*) to frown, knit one's brows; to glower, lower, scowl, look sternly | عبس فى وجهه to give s.o. an angry look, scowl at s.o. II = I

عبوس *'abūs* frowning, scowling; gloomy, dismal, melancholy; stern, austere; ominous

عبوس *'ubūs* gloominess, gloom, dreariness; sternness, austerity, severity, gravity

عبوسة *'ubūsa* frown, scowl; glower, gloomy look, a gloomy, morose, sullen or stern mien

عباسى *'abbāsī* Abbaside; (pl. *-ūn*) an Abbaside

عابس *'ābis* frowning, scowling; gloomy, morose, sullen; austere, stern, severe

عبيط *'abīṭ* pl. عبطاء *'ubaṭā'*² stupid, imbecile, idiotic, silly, foolish

اعتباطا *i'tibāṭan* at random, haphazardly, arbitrarily

عبق *'abiqa* a (*'abaq*) to cling (ب to), linger (ب on, of a scent); to be fragrant, exhale fragrance; to be filled, be redolent (ب with a scent, etc.)

عبق *'abiq* fragrant, redolent, exhaling fragrance

عبقة *'abqa* pressure (on the chest), feeling of suffocation

عابق *'ābiq* fragrant, redolent, exhaling fragrance

عبقر *'abqar* legendary place inhabited by jinn; fairyland, wonderland

عبقرى *'abqarī* multicolored, colorful carpet; ingenious, genial; (pl. *-ūn*, عباقرة *'abāqira*) ingenious person, genius

عبقرية *'abqarīya* ingenuity, genius

عبك *'abak* camlet (woolen fabric)

عبل *'abl* pl. عبال *'ibāl* plump, well rounded, chubby, fat (e.g., arms)

عبال *'abāl* (coll.; n. un. ة) a variety of wild rose, eglantine

اعبل *a'bal* granite

عبو II = عبأ II; to fill, pack (ه ب s.th. with); to load, charge (ه ب s.th. with)

عبوة *'ubūwa* pl. *-āt* package, pack (of an article, of a commodity); container with its contents

عباية *'abāya* = عباءة *'abā'a* q. v.

عتب *'ataba i u* (*'atb*, معتب *ma'tab*) to blame, censure, reprove, scold (على s.o.); — عتب بابه *'ataba bābahū* to cross the threshold of s.o. II to hesitate, be slow, be tardy III to blame, censure, reprove, scold (ه على s.o. for)

عتب *'atb* censure, blame, rebuke, reproof, reprimand

عتبة *'ataba* pl. عتب *'atab*, اعتاب *a'tāb* doorstep, threshold; (door) lintel, also العتبة العليا (*'ulyā*); step, stair | الاعتاب السنية (*sanīya*) (formerly:) His Highness the Bey (*Tun.*); رفعه لاعتاب الملك *rafa'ahū li-a. il-malik* to present s.th. (e.g., a gift) most obediently to the king

عتاب *'itāb* censure, blame, rebuke, reproof, reprimand

معاتبة *mu'ātaba* censure, blame, rebuke, reproof, reprimand

عتد *'atuda u* (عتاد *'atād*) to be ready, be prepared IV to prepare, ready, make ready (ه s.th.)

عتاد *'atād* pl. اعتد *a'tud*, اعتدة *a'tida* equipment; (war) material, matériel, ammunition | عتاد حربى (*ḥarbī*) war material, matériel, ammunition

عتيد *'atīd* ready, prepared; future, forthcoming; venerable; solemn

□ معتر *mu'attar* (< معثر) slovenly, sloppy; stupid; unfortunate

عتق *'atuqa u* (عتاقة *'atāqa*) and *'ataqa i* (*'atq*, *'itq*) to grow old, age; to mature, mellow (wine); — *'ataqa i* to be emancipated, be free (slave) IV to free, set free, release, emancipate, manumit (ه s.o., esp. a slave) VII to free o.s., rid o.s. (من of)

عتق *'itq* age, vintage (esp. of wine); liberty (as opposed to slavery); emancipation, freeing, manumission (of a slave)

عتيق *'atīq* old, ancient, antique; matured, mellowed, aged (wine); of ancient tradition, long-standing; antiquated, outmoded, obsolete; free, emancipated (slave); noble | عتيق الطراز old-fashioned

عتاقة *'atāqa* age, vintage (esp. of wine)

اعتاق *i'tāq* freeing, liberation, manumission (of a slave)

عاتق *'ātiq* pl. عواتق *'awātiq*[2] shoulder | اخذه على عاتقه (*akadahū*) to take s.th. upon o.s., take over, assume s.th; الق المسؤولية على عاتقه (*alqā l-mas'ūliyata*) to place the responsibility on s.o.; وقع على عاتق فلان to be at s.o.'s expense, fall to s.o.

معتق *mu'attaq* mellowed, matured (wine); old, ancient

معتق *mu'tiq* emancipator, liberator, manumitter (of slaves)

عتك *'ataka i* to attack

عاتك *'ātik* clear, pure, limpid (esp. wine)

عتل *ʻatala u i* (*ʻatl*) to carry (ه s.th.)

عتال *ʻattāl* porter, carrier

عتلة *ʻatala* pl. عتل *ʻatal* crowbar

عتالة *ʻitāla* porter's or carrier's trade; porterage

عتم *ʻatama i* (*ʻatm*) to hesitate **II** to darken, obscure, cloud, black out (ه s.th.); to hesitate (esp. with neg.) | لم, لا يعتّم ان ,يعتّم ان , ما عتّم ان it does not (did not) take long until..., before long..., presently... **IV** to hesitate, waver

عتم *ʻutm* (coll.; n. un. ة) wild olive tree

عتمة *ʻatma* dark, gloom, darkness

عتمة *ʻatama* first third of the night

عتامة *ʻatāma* opacity, opaqueness; (pl. *-āt*) darkness

تعتيم *taʻtīm* darkening, obscuring, clouding

معتم *muʻtim* dark

عته pass. *ʻutiha* (*ʻuth*, *ʻatah*, عتاهة *ʻatāha*) to be or become idiotic, imbecile, dimwitted, feeble-minded, demented, insane, mad, crazy

عته *ʻuth*, *ʻatah* idiocy, imbecility dimwittedness, feeble-mindedness

عتاهة *ʻatāha* idiocy, imbecility, dimwittedness, feeble-mindedness

معتوه *maʻtūh* pl. معاتيه *maʻātīh*[2] idiotic, insane, mad, crazy; idiot, lunatic, imbecile, demented person, insane person

(عتو and عتى) عتا *ʻatā u* (عتو *ʻutūw*, عتى *ʻutīy*, *ʻitīy*) to be insolent, refractory, recalcitrant, unruly; to be violent, fierce, strong, wild, furious, raging (e.g., storms) **V** do.

عتو *ʻutūw* presumption, haughtiness, insolence, impertinence, arrogance; recalcitrance, unruliness, wildness, ferocity

عتى *ʻutīy* presumption, haughtiness, insolence, impertinence, arrogance; recalcitrance, unruliness, wildness, ferocity | بلغ من العمر عتيا (*ʻumr*) to attain great age; to be far advanced in years

عتى *ʻatīy* pl. اعتاء *aʻtāʼ* haughty, impertinent, insolent; recalcitrant, refractory, unruly, intractable, wild

عات *ʻātin* pl. عتاة *ʻutāh* presumptuous, impudent, impertinent, insolent, arrogant; violent, fierce, strong, wild, furious, raging (storm)

عث *ʻuṯṯ* (coll.; n. un. ة) pl. عثث *ʻuṯaṯ* moth worm, moth larva; moth

معثوث *maʻṯūṯ* moth-ridden, full of moths, moth-eaten

عثر *ʻaṯara u i* (*ʻaṯr*, عثير *ʻaṯīr*, عثار *ʻiṯār*) to stumble, trip; عثّر به to trip s.o., make s.o. stumble, make s.o. fall, fell s.o., topple s.o.; — *ʻaṯara u* (عثور *ʻuṯūr*) to come (ب or على across), hit, light, strike, stumble (ب or على upon), find, discover, detect (ب or على s.o., s.th.) **II** to cause (ه s.o.) to stumble, trip (ه s.o.), make (ه s.o.) fall, topple (ه s.o.) **IV** = **II**; to acquaint (ه على s.o. with s.th.); to lead (ه على s.o. to s.th.) **V** to stumble, trip; to stutter, stammer, speak brokenly | تعثّر باذيال الخيبة (*bi-aḏyāli l-ḵaiba*) to fail, meet with failure

عثرة *ʻaṯra* pl. *ʻaṯarāt* stumbling, tripping; false step, slip, fall | حجر عثرة *ḥajar ʻa.* stumbling block; وقف عثرة فى سبيله (*ʻaṯratan*) to be a stumbling block for s.o., obstruct s.o.'s way

عثور *ʻuṯūr* discovery, detection (على of)

عثير *ʻiṯyar* dust, fine sand

عاثور *ʻāṯūr* pl. عواثير *ʻawāṯīr*[2] pitfall; difficulty

متعثر *mutaʻaṯṯir* stumbling, tripping; speaking (a foreign language) brokenly; broken (of a foreign language)

عثمانى *ʻuṯmānī* Ottoman; (adj. and n.)

عثنون *'uṯnūn* pl. عثانين *'aṯānīn*² beard

(عثو and عثى) عثا *'aṯā u* (عثو *'uṯūw*), عثى *'aṯā a i* (*'uṯīy, 'iṯīy*) to act wickedly, do harm, cause mischief

عج *'ajja i* (*'ajj*, عجيج *'ajīj*) to cry, yell, roar; to cry out for help (الى to); to rage, roar; to thunder, resound (ب with); to swarm, teem (ب with) II to raise, swirl up (الغبار *al-ġubāra* the dust; of the wind)

عج *'ajj* crying, yelling; clamor, roar

عجة *'ujja* omelet

عجيج *'ajīj* crying, yelling; clamor, roar

عجاج *'ajāj* (swirling) dust; smoke

عجاجة *'ajāja* pl. *-āt* cloud of dust; billow of smoke

عجاج *'ajjāj* crying, yelling, clamoring, roaring, boisterous, vociferous; raging (esp. sea)

عجب *'ajiba a* (*'ajab*) to wonder, marvel, be astonished, be amazed (من or ل at, over) II to strike with wonder or astonishment, amaze, astonish, surprise (ه s.o.) IV = II; to please, delight (ه s.o.), appeal (ه to s.o.); — pass. IV *u'jiba* to admire (ب s.o., s.th.), have a high opinion (ب of); to be proud (ب of), be vain (ب about), glory (ب in) | اعجب بنفسه (*u'jiba*) to be conceited, be vain V to wonder, marvel, be astonished, be amazed (من at, over) X = V

عجب *'ujb* pride (ب of, in), vanity (ب in), conceit

عجب *'ajab* astonishment, amazement; (pl. اعجاب *a'jāb*) wonder, marvel; عجبا *'ajaban* how strange! how odd! how astonishing! how remarkable! يا للعجب *yā la-l-'ajab* oh, how wonderful! لا عجب (*'ajaba*) no wonder! امر عجب *amrun 'ajabun* a wonderful, marvelous thing; عجب عجاب (*'ujāb*) most prodigious happening, wonder of wonders

عجاب *'ujāb* wonderful, wondrous, marvelous, astonishing, amazing; see *'ajab*

عجيب *'ajīb* wonderful, wondrous, marvelous, admirable; astonishing, amazing, remarkable, strange, odd

عجيبة *'ajība* pl. عجائب *'ajā'ib*² wondrous thing, unheard-of thing, prodigy, marvel, miracle, wonder; pl. remarkable things, curiosities, oddities | من عجائب الامر ان the remarkable thing about the matter is that...

اعجب *a'jab*² more wonderful, more marvelous; more astonishing, more remarkable

اعجوبة *u'jūba* pl. اعاجيب *a'ājīb*² wondrous thing; unheard-of thing, prodigy, marvel, miracle, wonder

تعجيب *ta'jīb* arousing of admiration (من for s.th.), boosting (من of s.th.), publicity (من for s.th.)

اعجاب *i'jāb* admiration (ب for); pleasure, satisfaction, delight (ب in); acclaim; pride; self-complacency, conceit

تعجب *ta'ajjub* astonishment, amazement

استعجاب *isti'jāb* astonishment, amazement

معجب *mu'jib* causing admiration, admirable

معجب *mu'jab* admirer (ب of s.o., of s.th.); proud (ب of), vain (ب about) | معجب بنفسه (*bi-nafsihī*) conceited, vain

متعجب *muta'ajjib* amazed, astonished

عجر *'ajar* outgrowth, protuberance, excrescence, projection

عجر *'agr* (*eg.*) green, unripe

عجرة *'ujra* pl. عجر *'ujar* knot, knob, hump, protuberance, excrescence | عجره وبجره *'ujaruhū wa-bujaruhū* his (its) obvious and hidden shortcomings, all his (its) faults

عجور *ʿaggūr* (coll.; n. un. ة) a variety of green melon (*eg.*)

عجرف II *taʿajrafa* to be presumptuous, arrogant, haughty

عجرفة *ʿajrafa* presumption, arrogance, haughtiness

عجز *ʿajaza* **i** (*ʿajz*) and *ʿajiza* **a** to be weak, lack strength, be incapable (عن of), be unable (عن to do s.th.); — *ʿajaza* **u** (عجوز *ʿujūz*) and *ʿajuza* **u** to age, grow old (woman) | ما عجز عن ان (*ʿajaza, ʿajiza*) not to fail to… **II** to weaken, debilitate, disable, incapacitate, hamstring, cripple, paralyze (ه s.o.) **IV** to weaken, debilitate, disable, incapacitate, hamstring, cripple, paralyze (ه s.o.); to be impossible (ه for s.o.); to speak in an inimitable, or wonderful, manner | اعجزه عن الدب والمشى (*dabb, mašy*) to paralyze s.o.'s every move; اعجزه عن الفهم (*fahm*) to make comprehension impossible for s.o. **X** to deem (ه s.o.) incapable (عن of)

عجز *ʿajz* weakness, incapacity, disability, failure, impotence (عن for, to do s.th.); deficit

عجز *ʿajuz, ʿajz* pl. اعجاز *aʿjāz* backside, rump, posteriors | اعجاز النخل *a. an-nakl* stumps of palm trees; رد العجز على الصدر (*ṣadr*) to bring the rear to the fore, i.e., to reverse conditions, make up for a deficiency

عجوز *ʿujūz* old age

عجوز *ʿajūz* pl. عجائز *ʿajāʾiz*[2], عجز *ʿujuz* old woman; old man; old, advanced in years

عجيزة *ʿajīza* posteriors, buttocks (of a woman)

اعجاز *iʿjāz* inimitability, wondrous nature (of the Koran)

عاجز *ʿājiz* pl. عواجز *ʿawājiz*[2] weak, feeble, powerless, impotent; incapable (عن of), unable (عن to do s.th.); — (pl. عجزة *ʿajaza*) physically weak; physically disabled; decrepit | اسعاف العجزة *isʿāf al-ʿa.* care for the aged

معجز *muʿjiz* miracle (esp. one performed by a prophet)

معجزة *muʿjiza* pl. *-āt* miracle (esp. one performed by a prophet)

عجعج *ʿajʿaja* to bellow, bawl, roar

عجعجة *ʿajʿaja* clamor, roar, bellowing

عجف اعجف *aʿjaf*[2], f. عجفاء *ʿajfāʾ*[2] pl. عجاف *ʿijāf* slender, slim, svelte; lean, emaciated

عجل *ʿajila* **a** (*ʿajal*, عجلة *ʿajala*) to hurry, hasten, speed, rush, be in a hurry; to rush, hasten, hurry, come quickly (الى to) **II** to hurry, hasten, speed, rush, be in a hurry; to bring about quickly, hasten on (ب s.th.), bring or take quickly (ب ل s.th. to); to hurry, rush, urge, impel, drive (ه s.o.), expedite, speed up, accelerate (ه s.th.); to pay in advance; to pay spot cash (ه ل to s.o. for) **III** to hurry in order to catch up (ه, ه with s.o., with s.th.), rush, hurry (ه, ه after s.o., after s.th.); to catch up (ه with s.o.), overtake (ه s.o.; esp. death), descend swiftly (ه, ه upon); to anticipate, forestall (ب ه s.o. in or with) **IV** to hurry, rush, urge, impel, drive (ه s.o.) | اعجله الوقت عن (*waqtu*) the time was too short for him to… **V** to hurry, hasten, speed, rush, be in a hurry; to seek to get ahead in a hurry; to hurry, rush, urge (ه الى s.o. to); to anticipate, forestall (ه, ه s.o., s.th.); to be ahead (ه of s.th.), precede (ه e.g., events); to receive at once, without delay (ه a sum), receive spot cash | تعجله الجواب (*jawāba*) to demand a quick reply from s.o. **X** to hurry, hasten, rush, speed, be in a hurry; to wish to expedite (ه s.th.); to hurry, rush, urge, impel, drive (ه s.o.), expedite, speed up, accelerate (ه s.th.)

عجل *ʿijl* pl. عجول *ʿujūl*, عجلة *ʿijala* calf | عجل البحر *ʿi. al-baḥr* sea calf, seal

عجل *ʿajal* hurry, haste | على عجل in a hurry, hurriedly, speedily, quickly, fast, rapidly

عجل *ʿajil* quick, fast, swift, speedy, rapid

عجلة *ʿajala* hurry, haste; precipitance, precipitation

عجلة *ʿajala* pl. *-āt* wheel; bicycle | ○ عجلة سيارة (*sayyāra*) motorcycle; عجلة القيادة steering wheel; ○ عجلة نارية (*nārīya*) motorcycle

عجيل *ʿajīl* pl. عجال *ʿijāl* quick, fast, swift, speedy, rapid

عجول *ʿajūl* pl. عجل *ʿujul* quick, fast, swift, speedy, rapid; hasty, precipitate, rash

عجالة *ʿujāla* work quickly thrown together, hastily prepared work, rush job; ○ sketch (*lit.*); quickly compiled report

عجلان *ʿajlān*², f. عجلى *ʿajlā*, pl. عجالى *ʿajālā*, عجال *ʿijal* quick, fast, swift, speedy, hurried, rapid, hasty, cursory

اعجل *aʿjal*², f. عجلى *ʿujlā*, pl. عجل *ʿujl* quicker, faster; hastier; more cursory

تعجيل *taʿjīl* speeding-up, expediting, acceleration

استعجال *istiʿjāl* hurry, haste; precipitance, precipitation | على وجه الاستعجال (*wajhi l-ist.*) expeditiously, speedily

استعجالى *istiʿjālī* speedy, expeditious; temporary, provisional

عاجل *ʿājil* pertaining to this world, worldly; temporal; immediate; عاجلا *ʿājilan* soon, presently, before long; at once, immediately, instantly | حكم عاجل (*ḥukm*) summary judgment (*jur.*); عاجلا او آجلا sooner or later; فى العاجل والآجل now and in the future; فى عاجله او آجله sooner or later; فى القريب العاجل in the immediate future

عاجلة *ʿājila* fast train, express train; العاجلة life in this world, temporal existence

معجل *muʿajjal* urgent, pressing; premature | معجل الرسم *m. ar-rasm* prepaid, postpaid (mail item); حكم بالنفاذ المعجل (*ḥukm, nafāḏ*) summary judgment, sentence by summary proceedings (*jur.*)

دفع معجلا *dafaʿa muʿajjalan* to pay in advance

متعجل *mutaʿajjil* hasty, rash, precipitate

مستعجل *mustaʿjil* hurried, in a hurry

مستعجل *mustaʿjal* expeditious, speedy; urgent, pressing; precipitate, premature | قاضى الامور المستعجلة magistrate of summary justice

عجم *ʿajama u* (*ʿajm*) to try, test, put to the test (ه s.o.) | عجم عوده (*ʿūdahū*) to try, test s.o., put s.o. to the test IV to provide (ه a letter) with a diacritical point (with diacritical points) VII to be obscure, incomprehensible, unintelligible (على to s.o.; language) X to become un-Arabic

عجم *ʿajam* (coll.) barbarians, non-Arabs; Persians; بلاد العجم or العجم Persia

عجم *ʿajam* (coll.; n. un. ة) stone, kernel, pit, pip, seed (of fruit)

عجمى *ʿajamī* pl. اعجام *aʿjām* barbarian, non-Arab; Persian (adj. and n.)

عجمة *ʿujma* barbarism, incorrectness (in speaking Arabic)

عجماء *ʿajmāʾ*² pl. عجماوات *ʿajmāwāt* (dumb) beast

اعجم *aʿjam*², f. عجماء *ʿajmāʾ*², pl. اعاجم *aʿājim*² speaking incorrect Arabic; dumb, speechless; barbarian, non-Arab, foreigner, alien; a Persian

اعجمى a'jamī non-Arabic; non-Arab, foreigner, alien; a Persian

معجم mu'jam incomprehensible, unintelligible, obscure (language, speech); dotted, provided with a diacritical point (letter); (pl. معاجم ma'ājim²) dictionary, lexicon | حروف المعجم the letters of the alphabet

عجن 'ajana i u ('ajn) to knead (ه s.th.); to soak (ه s.th.) | لت وعجن فى مسألة (latta, mas'ala) to bring up a problem time and again, harp on a question

عجان 'ijān perineum (anat.)

عجان 'ajjān, f. ة dough kneader

عجين 'ajīn dough, batter, paste; pastes (such as noodles, vermicelli, spaghetti, etc.)

عجينة 'ajīna a piece of dough; dough; soft mass, soggy mixture; pl. عجائن 'ajā'in² plastics

عجينى 'ajīnī doughy, doughlike, pasty, paste-like

معجن mi'jan pl. معاجن ma'ājin² kneading trough; kneading machine

معجون ma'jūn pl. معاجين ma'ājīn² paste, cream (cosmet.); putty; electuary; majoon (confection made of hemp leaves, henbane, datura seeds, poppy seeds, honey and ghee, producing effects similar to those of hashish and opium) | معجون الاسنان tooth paste

معجنات mu'ajjanāt (pot) pies, pasties

عجوة 'ajwa pressed dates | اقراص عجوة a pastry made of rich dough with almonds and date paste (syr.)

عد 'adda u ('add) to count, number, reckon (ه s.th., ه من s.o. among); to enumerate (ه s.th.); to compute, calculate (ه s.th.); to regard (ه ه, ه s.o., s.th. as), look (ه ه, ه at s.o., at s.th. as), consider, think, deem (ه ه, ه s.o., s.th. to be s.th.); — pass. 'udda to be considered, go (ه as s.th.), pass (ه for s.th.); to amount (ب to) | عد الانفاس عليه (to count s.o.'s breathing =) to watch closely over s.o., keep a sharp eye on s.o., watch s.o.'s every move; عد ه على to put down, or charge, s.th. to s.o.'s disadvantage; لا يعد (yu'addu) numberless, countless, innumerable **II** to count off, enumerate (ه s.th.); to make numerous, multiply, compound (ه s.th.) | عدد الميت (mayyita) to enumerate the merits of a dead person, eulogize s.o. **IV** to prepare (ل ه, ه s.o., s.th. for); to ready, make ready, get ready (ل ه, ه s.o., s.th. for); to prepare, finish, fit, fix up, adapt, adjust, dress, arrange, dispose, set up, make (ل ه s.th. for), draw up, draft, work out (ه e.g., a report); to prepare (ه one's lesson) | اعد عدته ل ('uddatahū) to make one's preparations for, prepare o.s. for **V** to be or become numerous, be manifold, be multifarious, be multiple; to multiply, increase in number, proliferate, be compounded **VIII** to regard (ه ه, ه s.o., s.th. as), look (ه ه, ه at s.o., at s.th. as), consider, think, deem (ه ه, ه s.o., s.th. to be s.th.); to reckon (ب with), rely (ب upon); to put down (ه, ب s.th., ل to s.o.'s credit, على to s.o.'s disadvantage); to hold (على ب against s.o. s.th.), take exception (على ب to s.o. because of s.th.); to provide o.s., equip o.s. (ب with); (of a woman) to observe the iddat, or legally prescribed period of waiting, before contracting a new marriage **X** to get ready, ready o.s.; to stand prepared, keep in readiness, stand by; to prepare o.s.; to be ready, willing, prepared (ل for, to do s.th.)

عد 'add counting, count; enumeration, listing; computation, calculation

عدة 'udda readiness, preparedness; — (pl. عدد 'udad) equipment, outfit; implement, instrument, tool; gadget, device, appliance, contrivance; rigging, tackle, sails; harness (of a horse) | اخذ اعد عدته ل or (*a'adda*) to make one's preparations for, prepare o.s. for; اخذ عدة الشيء to make preparations for s.th.; عدة الساعة clockwork, watchwork

عدة *'idda* number; (attributively:) several, numerous, many, e.g., رجال عدة (*'iddatun*) many men, عدة مرات *'iddata marrātin* several times; iddat, legally prescribed period of waiting during which a woman may not remarry after being widowed or divorced (*Isl. Law*)

عدد *'adad* pl. اعداد *a'dād* number, numeral; figure, digit, cipher; quantity; number, issue (of a newspaper) | عدد خاص (*ḵāṣṣ*) special number, special issue (e.g., of a periodical)

عددى *'adadī* numerical, numeral, relative to a number or numbers

عديد *'adīd* (with foll. genit.) counted among or with; numerous; number; large quantity; equal | عدد عديد (*'adad*) enormous quantity, great multitude; هذا عديد ذاك this equals that

عداد *'addād* pl. *-āt* counter, meter (for electricity, gas, etc.)

معداد *mi'dād* pl. معاديد *ma'ādīd*² abacus

تعداد *ta'dād* counting, count; enumeration, listing; computation, calculation | تعداد الانفس *t. al-anfus* census

عداد *'idād* number, quantity | لا عداد له (*'idāda*) innumerable, countless; فى عداد among, e.g., هو فى عدادهم he is counted among them, he is one of them

اعداد *i'dād* preparation, readying, arranging, setting up, making, drawing up, drafting

اعدادى *i'dādī* preparatory | شهادة اعدادية (*šahāda*) certificate granted after completing four years of secondary school (*eg.*)

تعدد *ta'addud* variety, diversity, multiplicity, plurality, great number, multitude | تعدد الآلهة polytheism; تعدد الزوجات *t. az-zaujāt* polygamy

اعتداد *i'tidād* confidence, reliance, trust (ب in) | الاعتداد بنفسه (*bi-nafsihī*) self-confidence, self-reliance

استعداد *isti'dād* readiness, willingness, preparedness; (pl. *-āt*) inclination, tendency, disposition, propensity; predisposition (ل for a disease), susceptibility (ل to a disease); pl. conveniences, amenities, comfort | كان على استعداد ل to be prepared, be set for...; to be ready, willing, inclined, in a position to...

استعدادى *isti'dādī* preparatory

معدود *ma'dūd* countable, numerable, calculable; limited in number, little, few, a few, some

معددة *mu'addida* (hired) female mourner

معد *mu'add* destined, intended (ل for); ready, prepared (ل for, to do s.th.), willing (ل to do s.th.)

معدات *mu'addāt* equipment, material, matériel, gear; appliances, devices, implements, gadgets | معدات حربية (عسكرية) (*ḥarbīya, 'askarīya*) war material; معدات الحريق *m. al-ḥarīq* fire-fighting equipment

متعدد *muta'addid* manifold, multiple, plural, numerous, varied, variegated, various, diverse, different; multi-, many-, poly- (in compounds) | متعدد الخلايا *m. al-ḵalāyā* multicellular (*biol.*); متعدد النواحى *m. an-nawāḥī* multifarious, variegated, varied, manifold

مستعد *musta'idd* prepared, ready (ل for); inclined, in a position (ل to, to do s.th.); predisposed (ل for), susceptible (ل to, esp. to a disease)

عدس *'adas* (coll.; n. un. ة) lentil(s)

عدسة *'adasa* pl. *-āt* lens; magnifying glass; object lens, objective

عدسى *'adasī* lenticular

عدل *'adala i* (*'adl*, عدالة *'adāla*) to act justly, equitably, with fairness | عدل بينهم to treat everyone with indiscriminate justice, not to discriminate between them; — *'adala i* to be equal (ـه, ه to s.o., to s.th.), be equivalent (ـه to s.th.), be on a par (ـه, ه with), be the equal (ه of s.o.), equal, match (ـه, ه s.o., s.th.), counterbalance, outweigh (ـه s.th.); to make equal, equalize, level (ه ب s.o. with another), place (ه s.o.) on the same level or footing (ب with another); — *'adala i* (عدول *'udūl*) to deviate, swerve, deflect, turn away (عن الى from — toward); to digress, depart, refrain, desist, abstain, avert o.s., turn away (عن from), leave off, relinquish, abandon, renounce, disclaim, give up, forego, waive, drop (عن s.th.) | عدل به عن to make s.o. desist, abstain or turn away from; عدل ببصره الى (*bi-baṣarihī*) to let one's eyes stray to or toward; — *'adula u* (عدالة *'adāla*) to be just, fair, equitable **II** to straighten, make or put straight, set in order, array (ـه s.th.); to balance, right, rectify, put in order, straighten out, fix, settle, adjust (ـه s.th.); to make (ـه s.th.) just; to adapt (ـه s.th.); to change, alter, commute, amend, modify, improve (ـه s.th.); to modulate (ـه current, waves; *el.*) **III** to be equal (ـه, ه to s.o., to s.th.), be equivalent (ـه to s.th.), be on a par (ـه, ه with), be the equal (ه of s.o.), equal, match (ـه, ه s.o., s.th.), counterbalance, outweigh (ـه s.th.); to equate, treat as equal (بين — وبين two persons or things) **IV** to straighten, make or put straight (ـه s.th.) **V** to be changed, be altered, be commuted, be modified, undergo modification, change or alteration **VI** to be in a state of equilibrium, be balanced; to be equal, be on a par; to offset one another, strike a balance **VIII** to straighten (up), tense; to draw o.s. up, sit straight, sit up; to be straight, even, balanced; to be moderate, be temperate

عدل *'adl* straightness, straightforwardness; justice, impartiality; fairness, equitableness, probity, honesty, uprightness; equitable composition, just compromise; — (pl. عدول *'udūl*) just, equitable, fair, upright, honest; person of good reputation, person with an honorable record (*Isl. Law*); juristic adjunct assigned to a cadi (*Magr.*); عدلا *'adlan* equitably, fairly, justly | وزير العدل minister of justice

عدلى *'adlī* forensic, legal, judicial, juridical, juristic

عدل *'idl* equal, tantamount, corresponding; — (pl. اعدال *a'dāl*, عدول *'udūl*) either of the two balanced halves of a load carried by a beast of burden; sack, bag

عديل *'adīl* equal, like, tantamount, corresponding; (with foll. genit.) equal (to s.o.), on a par (with s.o.); (*eg.*; pl. عدائل *'adā'il*) brother-in-law (husband of one's sister)

عدول *'udūl* refraining, abstention, desistance (عن from), forgoing, renunciation, resignation, abandonment, relinquishment (عن of s.th.)

عدالة *'adāla* justice, fairness, impartiality; probity, integrity, honesty, equitableness; decency, proper conduct; honorable record (*Isl. Law*)

عدلية *'adliya* justice, administration of justice, jurisprudence | وزير العدلية minister of justice

اعدل *a'dal*[2] more regular, more uniform; more balanced; juster, fairer, more equitable; more upright, more honest, more righteous

تعديل *ta'dīl* straightening, straightening out, settling, setting right; — (pl. *-āt*) change, alteration, commutation, amendment, modification; settlement, adjustment, regulation; improvement; reshuffle (of the cabinet); modulation (*el.*) | تعديل وزارى (*wizārī*) cabinet reshuffle

معادلة *mu'ādala* assimilation, approximation, adjustment, equalization, leveling, balancing, equilibration; balance, equilibrium; equality; equivalence; evenness, proportion, proportionateness, proportionality; equation (*math.*)

تعادل *ta'ādul* balance, equilibrium; equality; equivalence; evenness, proportion, proportionateness, proportionality; draw, tie (in sports) | تعادل الاصوات tie vote, equal number of votes

اعتدال *i'tidāl* straightness, erectness, tenseness; evenness, symmetry, proportion (e.g., of stature, of growth); moderateness, moderation, temperance, temperateness; equinox | سمت الاعتدال *samt al-i.* equinoctial colure (*astron.*)

اعتدالى *i'tidālī* equinoctial

عادل *'ādil* just, fair, equitable; upright, honest, straightforward, righteous

معدل *mu'addal* average; average amount or sum | معدل السرعة *m. as-sur'a* average speed; بمعدل as an average, on the average

معادل *mu'ādil* equal, of equal status, having equal rights

متعادل *muta'ādil* balanced, neutral

معتدل *mu'tadil* straight, even, proportionate, symmetrical, harmonious; moderate, temperate; mild, clement (weather) | المنطقة المعتدلة (*minṭaqa*) the Temperate Zone

عدم *'adima a* (*'udm, 'adam*) to be deprived, be devoid, be in want, be deficient (ه of s.th.); to lack, not to have (ه s.th.); to lose, miss (ه, ه s.o., s.th.); — pass. *'udima* to be lacking, be missing, be absent, be nonexistent; to be lost, be gone, have disappeared; to disappear, vanish **IV** to cause (ه s.o.) to miss or lack (ه s.th.); to deprive (ه ه s.o. of s.th.); to destroy, annihilate, wipe out (ه, ه s.o., s.th.); to execute (ه s.o.); to be or become poor, be reduced to poverty, become impoverished **VII** = pass. I

عدم *'adam* non-being, nonexistence; nothing, nothingness, nihility; lack, want, absence; loss, privation; (with foll. genit.) non-, un-, in-, dis-; (pl. اعدام *a'dām*) nonentity, nullity, banality, trifle | عدم الاهتمام inattention, indifference; عدم الاختصاص noncompetency; عدم الوجود non-being, nonexistence

عدمى *'adamī* nihilist

عدمية *'adamīya* non-being, nonexistence; nihilism

عديم *'adīm* not having, lacking, wanting; deprived (of); devoid (of), without, -less, in-, un- (with foll. genit.) | عديم الحياة *'a. al-ḥayāh* inanimate, lifeless; عديم النظير unequaled, incomparable, unique

اعدام *i'dām* destruction, annihilation; execution | الحكم بالاعدام (*ḥukm*) death sentence

اعدامية *i'dāmīya* headcloth without *iqāl* (as a sign of mourning)

انعدام *in'idām* absence, lack, nonexistence

عادم *'ādim* pl. عوادم *'awādim*[2] nonexistent, lost; unrestorable, irreclaimable; waste- (in compounds); pl. waste, refuse, scraps | المياه العادمة sewage, sullage, waste water; عوادم الاقطان cotton waste; انبوبة العوادم *unbūbat al-'a.* exhaust pipe (automobile)

معدوم *ma'dūm* nonexistent, wanting, lacking, absent; missing; lost; gone, vanished

معدم *mu'dim* poor, destitute; impoverished

عدن *ʿadn* Eden, Paradise; *ʿadan*² Aden (city in southern Arabia)

معدن *maʿdin* pl. معادن *maʿādin*² mine; lode; metal; mineral; treasure-trove, bonanza (fig.); (place of) origin, source | علم المعادن *ʿilm al-m.* mineralogy; امتحن معدنه to probe into s.o.'s very nature

معدن *maʿdan* (*eg.*; *syr. maʿdin*) very good! bravo! well done!

معدنى *maʿdinī* metallic, mineral; المعدنيات mineralogy | ماء معدنى mineral water

تعدين *taʿdīn* mining of metals and minerals; mining, mining industry

معدن *muʿaddin* miner

عدنان *ʿadnān*² legendary ancestor of the North Arabs

(عدو) عدا *ʿadā u* (*ʿadw*) to run, speed, gallop, dash, race; to pass (ه, ه or عن s.o., s.th.), go past s.o. or s.th. (ه, ه or عن); to give up, abandon, leave (ه, ه or عن s.o., s.th.); to pass over, bypass, omit (ه s.o.), not to bother (ه ب s.o. with), exempt, except (ه ب s.o. from); to cross, overstep, exceed, transcend (ه s.th.), go beyond s.th. (ه); to exceed the proper bounds; to infect (الى s.o.); — *u* (عدو *ʿadw*, *ʿudūw*, عداء *ʿadāʾ*, عدوان *ʿudwān*, *ʿidwān*) to engage in aggressive, hostile action, commit an aggression, a hostile act (على against); to act unjustly (على toward), wrong (على s.o.); to assail, assault, attack, raid (على s.o., s.th.); — *u* (عدو *ʿadw*) to handicap, hamper, impede, obstruct (ه عن s.o. in); to prevent, hinder (ه عن s.o. from) | عدا طوره (*ṭaurahū*) to transcend one's bounds or limits; لا يعدو ان يفعله not to fail to do s.th.; to do s.th. inevitably; ... لا يعدو ان يكون it is no more than..., it is only or merely... **II** to cause to cross, overstep, exceed or transcend; to ferry (ه s.o., over a river); (*gram.*) to make transitive (ه a verb); to give up, abandon, leave (ه, ه or عن s.o., s.th.); to cross (ه s.th., e.g., a river) **III** to treat as an enemy (ه s.o.), show enmity (ه toward s.o.), be at war, feud (ه with s.o.); to fall out (ه with s.o.), contract the enmity (ه of s.o.); to act hostilely (ه toward s.o.); to counteract, disobey (ه, ه s.o., s.th.), act in opposition (ه, ه to), contravene, infringe (ه s.th.) **IV** to infect (ه s.o., من with a disease) **V** to cross, overstep (ه s.th.); to traverse (ه s.th.); to exceed, transcend, surpass (ه s.th.), go beyond s.th. (ه); to go beyond s.th. (ه) and turn one's attention to s.th. else (الى), not to be limited to s.th. (ه) but also to comprise (الى s.th. else), extend beyond s.th. (ه) to s.th. else (الى); to overtake, pass, outstrip, outdistance, leave behind (ه s.th.); to overcome, surmount (ه s.th., e.g., a crisis); to pass on, shift, spread (الى to); to transgress, infract, violate, break (ه s.th., e.g., laws); to engage in brutal, hostile action, commit agression, a hostile act (على against); to act unjustly (على toward s.o.); to assail, assault, attack, raid (على s.o., s.th.); to infringe, encroach, make inroads (على upon) | تعدى عليه بالضرب (*ḍarb*) to come to blows with s.o., lay hands upon s.o. **VI** to harbor mutual enmity, be hostile to one another, be enemies **VII** to be infected (ب with a disease), catch an infection (من by, from) **VIII** to cross, overstep (ه s.th.); to exceed, transcend, surpass (ه s.th.), go beyond s.th. (ه); to act outrageously, brutally, unlawfully (على against); to commit excesses (على against); to engage in aggressive, brutal, hostile action (على against), commit an aggression, a hostile act (على against); to act unjustly (على toward); to violate (على a woman); to assail, assault, attack, raid (على s.o., s.th.), infringe, encroach, make inroads (على upon), make an attempt on s.o.'s (على) life **X** to appeal for assistance (ه

to s.o. على against); to stir up, rouse, incite (على ه s.o. against)

عدا *'adā,* ما عدا or فيا عدا *fi-mā 'adā* (with foll. acc. or genit.) except, save, with the exception of, excepting ...; فيا عدا ذلك besides

عدو *'adw* running, run, race (also in sports)

عدوة *'udwa* side, slope (of a valley), bank, embankment (of a river), shore

عدو *'adūw* pl. اعداء *a'dā',* عدى *'idan, 'udan,* عداة *'udāh,* اعاد *a'ādin,* f. عدوة *'adūwa* enemy | عدو لدود (لديد, الد) *(ladūd, aladd²)* foe, archenemy

عدوة *'adūwa* fem. of عدو *'adūw*

عدى *'adīy* acting hostilely, aggressive

عداء *'adā'* enmity, hostility, antagonism, animosity; aggression

عدائى *'adā'ī* hostile, inimical, antagonistic, aggressive

عداء *'addā'* runner, racer

اعدى *a'dā*: اعدى الاعداء *a. l-a'dā'* the worst of enemies

عدوى *'adwā* infection, contagion; — *'udwā* hostile action

عداوة *'adāwa* pl. *-āt* enmity, hostility, antagonism, animosity

عدواء *'udawā'²* hindrance, handicap, impediment; inconvenience, nuisance, discomfiture | ذو عدواء rough, rugged, uneven; adverse, discomfiting, inconvenient; bad, poor (mount)

عدوان *'udwān, 'idwān* enmity, hostility, hostile action, aggression

عدوانى *'udwānī*: سياسة عدوانية policy of aggression

معدى *ma'dan* escape, way out, avoidance | لا معدى عنه *(ma'dā)* inevitable, unavoidable, inescapable

معدية *ma'diya* pl. معاد *ma'ādin* ferry, ferryboat

تعدية *ta'diya* ferrying, ferry service; conversion into the transitive form *(gram.)*

تعد *ta'addin* crossing, overstepping, exceeding, transcending; overtaking, passing (e.g., of an automobile); — (pl. تعديات *ta'addiyāt*) infraction, violation, breach (e.g., of laws), transgression, encroachment, inroad (على on), infringement of the law; offense against law, tort, delict *(Isl. Law)*; attack, assault; aggression

اعتداء *i'tidā'* pl. *-āt* attack, assault, raid, inroad (على on), attempt (على on s.o.'s life), criminal attack (على on); outrage (على upon); aggression (على against; esp. *pol.*) | معاهدة (اتفاق) عدم الاعتداء *mu'āhadat (ittifāq) 'adam al-i't.* pact of nonaggression

عاد *'ādin* pl. عواد *'awādin* aggressive, attacking, assailing, raiding; (pl. عداة *'udāh*) enemy | عوادى الوحوش beasts of prey, predatory animals

عادية *'ādiya* pl. *-āt,* عواد *'awādin* wrong, offense, misdeed, outrage; adversity, misfortune, reverse; obstacle, impediment, obstruction; pl. vicissitudes | عدت عليهم عواد *('adat)* fate dealt them heavy blows, they fell on evil days

معاد *mu'ādin* hostile, inimical, antagonistic

معد *mu'din* contagious, infectious | امراض معدية contagious diseases

متعد *muta'addin* transitive *(gram.)*; aggressor, assailant

معتد *mu'tadin* pl. *-ūn* assailant, assassin; aggressor *(pol.)*

عذب *'aḏuba u* (عذوبة *'uḏūba*) to be sweet, pleasant, agreeable; — *'aḏaba i* to hinder, handicap, impede, obstruct (ه s.o.) II to afflict, pain, torment, try, agonize, torture, rack (ه s.o.); to punish, chastise, castigate (ه s.o.) V to be punished, suffer punishment; to feel pain, suffer; to torment o.s., be in agony, be harassed X to find (ه s.th.) sweet, pleasant, or agreeable; to think (ه s.th.) beautiful, nice

عذب *'aḏb* pl. عذاب *'iḏāb* sweet; pleasant, agreeable | مياه عذبة fresh water; عذب الحديث entertaining, amusing, companionable, personable

عذاب *'aḏāb* pl. *-āt*, اعذبة *a'ḏiba* pain, torment, suffering, agony, torture; punishment, chastisement, castigation

عذوبة *'uḏūba* sweetness

اعذب *a'ḏab*² sweeter, more pleasant, more agreeable

تعذيب *ta'ḏīb* affliction, tormenting, agonizing, torture, torturing; punishment, chastisement, castigation

عذر *'aḏara* *i* (*'uḏr*, معذرة *ma'ḏira*) to excuse, absolve from guilt (ه s.o.), forgive (ه s.o. ه or في or عن s.th.) | لم يعذرني he wouldn't let me give any excuses, he wouldn't take no for an answer, he kept insisting; — *'aḏara* *i* (*'aḏr*) to circumcise (ه s.o.) IV = I; to have an excuse | اعذر من انذر (*man anḏara*) he who warns is excused V to be difficult, impossible, impracticable, unfeasible (على for) VIII to excuse o.s., apologize (ل or الى to s.o. for من s.th.); to give or advance (ب s.th.) as an excuse (عن or من for), plead s.th. (ب) in defense of (عن or من) X to wish to be excused; to make an apology, excuse o.s., apologize

عذر *'uḏr* pl. اعذار *a'ḏār* excuse | ابو عذر *abū 'u.* (with foll. genit.) responsible for, answerable for; هو ابو عذر هذا التطور (*taṭawwur*) he is the originator of this development

عذرة *'uḏra* virginity, virginhood; name of an Arab tribe | ابو عذرة = ابو عذر see above

عذرى *'uḏrī* belonging to the tribe of *'uḏra* (see above)

الهوى العذرى (*hawā*) platonic love

عذار *'iḏār* pl. عذر *'uḏur* cheek; fluff, first growth of beard (on the cheeks); cheekpiece (of a horse's harness) | خلع عذاره to throw off all restraint, drop all pretenses of shame; خالع العذار unrestrained, wanton, uninhibited

عذراء *'aḏrā'*² pl. عذارى *'aḏārā* virgin; العذراء Virgo (*astron.*); the Virgin Mary (*Chr.*) | فتاة عذراء (*fatāh*) maiden, virgin

معذرة *ma'ḏira* pl. معاذر *ma'āḏir*² excuse, forgiveness, pardon

معذار *mi'ḏār* pl. معاذر *ma'āḏir*² excuse, plea

تعذر *ta'aḏḏur* difficulty, impossibility, impracticability, unfeasibility

اعتذار *i'tiḏār* apology, excuse, plea

معذور *ma'ḏūr* excused, justified, warranted; excusable

متعذر *muta'aḏḏir* difficult, impossible, impracticable, unfeasible

عذق *'iḏq* pl. اعذاق *a'ḏāq* bunch, cluster (of dates, of grapes)

عذل *'aḏala* *u* (*'aḏl*) to blame, censure, reprove, rebuke, reproach (ه s.o.) II = I

عذل *'aḏl* blame, censure, reproof, reproach

عذول *'aḏūl* stern censurer, rebuker, severe critic

عاذل *'āḏil* pl. عذال *'uḏḏāl*, f. عاذلة *'āḏila* pl. عواذل *'awāḏil*² censurer, reprover, critic

عذو) and عذى) عذا *'aḏā* *u* and عذى *'aḏiya* *a* to be healthy (country, city; due to its climate, air, etc.)

عر *'arra* u to be a shame, be a disgrace (ه, ه for s.o., for s.th.); to bring shame or disgrace (ه, ه upon s.o., upon s.th.), disgrace, dishonor (ه, ه s.o., s.th.)

عرة *'urra* scabies, mange; dung; a disgraceful, shameful thing

عرر *'arar* scabies, mange

معرة *ma'arra* shame, disgrace, ignominy; stain, blemish, stigma

معتر *mu'tarr* miserable, wretched; scoundrel, rogue

عرب **II** to Arabicize, make Arabic (ه, ه s.o., s.th.); to translate into Arabic (ه s.th.); to express, voice, state clearly, declare (عن s.th.); to give earnest money, give a handsel, make a down payment **IV** to Arabicize, make Arabic (ه, ه s.o., s.th.), give an Arabic form (ه to s.th.); to make plain or clear, state clearly, declare (عن or ه s.th.), express (unmistakably), utter, voice, proclaim, make known, manifest, give to understand (عن s.th., esp. a sentiment), give expression (عن to s.th., esp. to a sentiment); (*gram.*) to use desinential inflection, pronounce the *i'rāb* **V** to assimilate o.s. to the Arabs, become an Arab, adopt the customs of the Arabs **X** = **V**

عرب *'arab* (coll.) pl. عروب *'urūb*, اعرب *a'rub*, عربان *'urbān*, اعراب *a'rāb* Arabs; true Arabs, Arabs of the desert, Bedouins

عربى *'arabī* Arab, Arabic, Arabian; truly Arabic; an Arab; العربية the *'Arabīya*, the language of the ancient Arabs; classical, or literary, Arabic

عربة *'araba* a swift river; (pl. *-āt*) carriage, vehicle, wagon, cart; (railroad) car, coach; araba, coach | عربة الاجرة *'a. al-ujra* cab, hack, hackney; عربة الاكل *'a. al-akl* dining car, diner; عربة رش *'a. rašš* water wagon, sprinkling wagon; عربة الركوب cab, hack, hackney; عربة الشحن *'a. aš-šaḥn* wagon, lorry; freight car; عربة مطعم (*maṭ'am*) dining car, diner; عربة الاطفال baby carriage; عربة النقل *'a. an-naql* wagon, lorry, van; freight car; عربة النوم *'a. an-naum* sleeping car, sleeper; عربة يد *'a. yad* handcart, pushcart; wheelbarrow

عربية *'arabīya* pl. *-āt* carriage, vehicle; araba, coach; see عربى

عربجى *'arbajī* pl. *-iya* coachman, cabman

عربخانة *'arbaḵāna* car shed, coach house

عراب *'arrāb* godfather, sponsor

عرابة *'arrāba* godmother, sponsor

اعرابى *a'rābī* pl. اعراب *a'rāb* an Arab of the desert, a Bedouin

عروبة *'urūba* Arabism, Arabdom, the Arab idea, the Arab character

تعريب *ta'rīb* Arabicizing, Arabization; translation into Arabic; incorporation (of loanwords) into Arabic

اعراب *i'rāb* manifestation, declaration, proclamation, pronouncement, utterance; expression (عن of a sentiment); desinential inflection (*gram.*)

معرب *mu'arrib* translator into Arabic

معرب *mu'arrab* Arabicized; translated into Arabic

معرب *mu'rab* desinentially inflective (*gram.*)

مستعرب *musta'rib* Arabist

عربد *'arbada* to be quarrelsome, be contentious, pick quarrels; to be noisy, boisterous, riotous, raise a din

عربدة *'arbada* quarrelsomeness, contentiousness; noise, din, uproar, riot

عربيد *'irbīd* quarrelsome, contentious; noisy, boisterous, riotous

معربد *mu'arbid* quarrelsome, contentious; noisy, boisterous, riotous

عربس *'arbasa* to upset, disturb, confuse (ه s.o.)

عربن *'arbana* to give earnest money, give a handsel, make a down payment (ه to s.o.)

عربون *'urbūn*, *'arabūn* pl. عرابين *'arābīn*[2] handsel, earnest money, down payment; pledge, pawn, gage

عرج *'araja* u (عروج *'urūj*) to ascend, mount, rise; — *'arija* a (*'araj*) to be lame, walk lamely, limp, hobble II to turn (على to, toward); to stop, halt, stop over (على in, at); to turn (عن off s.th.), swerve (عن from); to lame, cripple, paralyze (ه s.o.); to zigzag, make zigzag (ه s.th.) IV to lame, cripple, paralyze (ه s.o.) V to zigzag, follow a zigzag course VII to incline, lean, bend, curve; to be or become crooked, curved, bent, sinuous, winding

عرج *'araj* lameness

اعرج *a'raj*[2], f. عرجاء *'arjā'*[2], pl. عرج *'urj*, عرجان *'urjān* lame, limping; — jack (in a deck of cards)

معرج *ma'raj* pl. معارج *ma'ārij*[2] place of ascent; (route of) ascent

معرج *mi'raj* pl. معارج *ma'ārij*[2] ladder, stairs

معراج *mi'rāj* pl. معاريج *ma'ārīj*[2] ladder, stairs; المعراج the midnight journey to the seven heavens (made by Mohammed on the 27th of Rajab, from Jerusalem) | ليلة المعراج *lailat al-m.* the night of Mohammed's ascension to the seven heavens

تعاريج *ta'ārīj*[2] (pl.) curves, curvatures, bends, turns, twists, windings, sinuosities; wavy lines, serpentines

تعرج *ta'arruj* zigzag (course)

متعرج *muta'arrij* winding, twisting, tortuous, sinuous; zigzag

منعرج *mun'arij* crooked, curved, bent, winding, twisting, tortuous, sinuous

منعرج *mun'araj* pl. -*āt* bend, turn, curve, twist, angle (of roads, etc.)

عرزال *'irzāl* hut or shack of the rural warden (usually in a tree or on top of a roof)

عرس II (*nejd.*) to marry (ه ب s.o. to) IV to arrange a wedding feast

عرس *'urs*, *'urus* pl. اعراس *a'rās*, عرسات *'urusāt* marriage; wedding, wedding feast

عرس *'irs* pl. أعراس *a'rās* husband; wife | ابن عرس *ibn 'irs* pl. بنات عرس *banāt 'irs* weasel (*zool.*)

عرسة *'irsa* weasel

عروس *'arūs* pl. عرس *'urus* bridegroom; f. (pl. عرائس *'arā'is*[2]) bride; doll; العروسان *al-'arūsān* bride and groom, the newlyweds | عرائس النيل *'a. an-nīl* lotus

عروسة *'arūsa* pl. عرائس *'arā'is*[2] bride; doll, baby doll | عروسة البرقع *'a. al-burqu'* metal tubes ornamenting the veil of Muslim women

عريس *'arīs* bridegroom

عريس *'irrīs* lair of a lion, lion's den

عرش *'araša* i u to erect a trellis (ه for grapevines), train on a trellis or espalier, to trellis, to espalier (ه vines) II to roof over (ه s.th.)

عرش *'arš* pl. عروش *'urūš*, اعراش *a'rāš* throne; tribe (*maġr.*)

عريش *'arīš* pl. عرش *'uruš*, عرائش *'arā'iš*[2] arbor, bower; hut made of twigs; booth, shack, shanty; trellis (for grapevines); shaft, carriage pole

العريش El Arish (town in N Egypt, on Mediterranean)

تعريشة *ta'rīša* pl. تعاريش *ta'ārīš*[2] trellis, lattice-work; arbor, bower

عرص *'ariṣa* a (*'araṣ*) to be lively, gay, merry

عرصة *'arṣa* pl. *'araṣāt*, اعراص *a'rāṣ* vacant lot; courtyard, court of a house

معرص *mu'arraṣ* pimp, procurer; cuckold

[1]عرض *ʿaruḍa* u to be or become wide, broad, to widen, broaden; — *ʿaraḍa* i (*ʿarḍ*) to become visible, appear (ل to s.o.); to get in s.o.'s (ل) way; to happen (ل to s.o.), befall (ل s.o.); to occur (ل to s.o.), come to s.o.'s (ل) mind; to turn (ل to s.o., to s.th.); to take care (ل of), concern o.s. (ل with), turn one's attention, put one's mind, apply o.s., attend (ل to), go in (ل for), go into s.th. (ل), enter, embark (ل upon), take up, treat (ل s.th.), deal (ل with); to show, demonstrate, present, set forth, display, exhibit, lay open, submit, turn in (ه على s.th. to s.o.), lay, put (ه على s.th. before s.o.); to show (ه e.g., a film), stage (ه e.g., a play); to offer, suggest, propose (ه على s.th. to s.o.); to subject (ه على s.th. to a critical examination, and the like); to inspect (ه s.th.); to review (ه troops), pass in review (ه s.th., also before one's mental eye); pass. *ʿuriḍa* to be or go mad, insane | عرض له عارض an obstacle arose in his path; عرض له خاطر a thought occured to him, he had an idea **II** to make wide or broad, widen, broaden, extend (ه s.th.); to expose (ل ه, ه s.o., s.th. to s.th., esp. to risk; ل ه s.th. to the sun); to intimate, insinuate (ل or ب s.th.), allude (ل or ب to), hint (ل or ب at) | عرضه للنور to hold s.th. against the light **III** to offer resistance (ه, ه to s.o., to s.th.), resist (ه, ه s.o., s.th.), work against s.o. or s.th. (ه, ه); to contradict, oppose (ه, ه s.o., s.th.), raise objections, protest, remonstrate (ه, ه against s.o., against s.th.); to be against s.o. or s.th. (ه, ه); to avoid, shun (ه, ه s.o., s.th.); to compare (ه ب s.th. with) **IV** to turn away, avert o.s. (عن from), avoid, shun (عن s.o., s.th.), shirk (عن s.th.), give up, abandon, relinquish, discard, renounce, disclaim (عن s.th.); not to mention (عن s.th.); اعرض عن الى to turn away from s.th. and to s.th. else **V** to resist, oppose (ل s.o., s.th.), stand up (ل against), raise objections, object (ل to); to face (ل s.th., e.g., a problem); to interfere (ل with), meddle (ل in); to put one's mind, turn one's attention (ل to), go into s.th. (ل, e.g., a topic); to undertake (ل s.th.), embark (ل upon s.th.); to expose o.s., be exposed, be subjected (ل to s.th.); to run the risk (ل of), risk (ل doing or being s.th.); to dare, venture, risk (ل s.th.) **VI** to oppose one another; to be contradictory, conflict, be incompatible (مع with) **VIII** to betake o.s., go, present o.s. (ه to s.o.); to raise an objection, make objections, object (على to), veto (على s.th.), remonstrate, protest (على against); to resist, oppose (على s.o., s.th.); to stand up (ل or ه, ه against s.o., against s.th.), stand in, or obstruct, the way of s.o. or s.th. (ل or ه, ه); to hinder impede, obstruct (ل s.o.); to happen (ه to s.o.), befall (ه s.o.) | اعترض سبيله to block s.o.'s way **X** to ask to be shown (ه s.o., ه s.th.); to pass in review (ه s.th., esp. in one's imagination, before one's mental eye), call up, conjure up, call to one's mind, picture to o.s., visualize (ه s.th.); to weigh, consider, examine (ه s.th.); to inspect, review (ه troops); to expound, set forth (ه s.th.); to proceed ruthlessly; to massacre without much ado (هم the enemy)

عرض *ʿarḍ* pl. عروض *ʿurūḍ* breadth; width; presentation, demonstration, staging, show(ing), performance; display, exposition, exhibition; submission, filing (e.g., of an application); proposition, proposal, offer, tender; parade; review (*mil.*); merchandise, goods | بالعرض across, crosswise, in breadth; العرض والطلب (*ṭalab*) supply and demand; عرض الازياء *ʿa. al-azyā'* fashion show; عرض حال *ʿa. ḥāl* or عرضحال pl. عرضحالات *ʿarḍuḥālāt* application, petition, memorial; خط (درجة) العرض *katt* (*darajat*) *al-ʿa.* degree of latitude; شباك العرض *šubbāk al-ʿa.* show window; يوم العرض *yaum al-ʿa.* the Day of Judgment, Doomsday

عرضى *ʿarḍī* cross- (in compounds), transverse, horizontal | خط عرضى (*ḵaṭṭ*) latitudinal degree, geographical latitude

عرض *ʿirḍ* pl. اعراض *aʿrāḍ* honor, good repute; dignity | انا فى عرضك I rely on your generosity, have mercy upon me!

عرض *ʿurḍ* side; middle | فى عرض البحر (*ʿu. il-baḥr*) at sea, on the high seas; الق (ضرب) به عرض الحائط to undervalue, scorn, disdain, despise, reject s.th.; to ruin, thwart, foil s.th.; to throw s.th. overboard, jettison s.th.; نظر اليه عن عرض (*ʿan ʿurḍin*) he looked askance at him, he gave him a slanting glance (contemptuously); فى عرض الناس amid the crowd of people; هو من عرض الناس he belongs to the common people

عرضانى *ʿarḍānī* transversal, transverse, latitudinal; measured crosswise

عرض *ʿaraḍ* pl. اعراض *aʿrāḍ* accident (*philos.*); contingent, nonessential characteristic; s.th. nonessential, a contingent, s.th. accidental; symptom, manifestation of disease; عرضا *ʿaraḍan*, بالعرض incidentally, by chance

عرضى *ʿaraḍī* accidental (*philos.*), nonessential, unessential; incidental, accidental, contingent, fortuitous, casual; عرضيات *ʿaraḍīyāt* unessential incidents, unessentials; accidentals | خطيئة عرضية venial sin (*Chr.*)

عرضة *ʿurḍa* target; (object of) intention, intent, design; object (ل of); exposed, subject(ed), liable (ل to s.th.); (with foll. genit.) suitable for, fitting for, appropriate for

عروض *ʿarūḍ* prosody; (pl. اعاريض *aʿārīḍ*²) last foot of the first hemistich | علم العروض *ʿilm al-ʿa.* metrics, prosody

عروضى *ʿarūḍī* prosodic(al), metrical

عريض *ʿarīḍ* pl. عراض *ʿirāḍ* broad, wide; extensive, vast

عريضة *ʿarīḍa* pl. عرائض *ʿarāʾiḍ*² petition, application, memorial

معرض *maʿriḍ* pl. معارض *maʿāriḍ*² place where s.th. is exhibited or displayed; showroom, stage; exposition, exhibition; show; fair (*com.*); (with foll. genit.) time, occasion for s.th. | فى معرض (with foll. genit.) in the form of ..., in ... manner; on the occasion of, at the occurrence or appearance of; ... لسنا الآن فى معرض (*lasnā*) with foll. verbal noun: this is not the place for us to ...; لسنا فى معرض الكلام عن let us not speak of ... now, this is not the place to speak of ...; معرض الازياء *m. al-azyāʾ* fashion show; معرض الصحف *m. aṣ-ṣuḥuf* press review

معرض *miʿraḍ* wedding gown

معراض *miʿrāḍ*: قال فى معراض كلامه (*m. kalāmihī*) to mention casually, say among other things

تعريض *taʿrīḍ* intimation, allusion, hint, indication

معارضة *muʿāraḍa* opposition (esp. *pol.*); resistance, contradiction, remonstrance, objection, exception, protest; ○ resistance (*el.*)

اعراض *iʿrāḍ* shunning, avoidance, evasion; reluctance | فى اعراض reluctantly

تعارض *taʿāruḍ* conflict, clash, antagonism, contradiction, contrariety

اعتراض *iʿtirāḍ* pl. *-āt* resistance, opposition, objection, exception, counterargument, counterassertion, counterblast, riposte, rebuttal, rejoinder, expostulation, remonstrance, protest; (right of) veto (*Isl. Law*) | حق الاعتراض *ḥaqq al-iʿt.* (right of) veto (*pol.*)

استعراض *istiʿrāḍ* examination, survey; parade, review; revue, musical show

استعراضى *istiʿrāḍī* revue-, show- (in compounds), revue-like | فرقة استعراضية (*firqa*) show troupe; revue troupe; فلم استعراضى film musical

عارض *ʿāriḍ* pl. *-ūn* exhibitor (e.g., at a fair); demonstrator; — (pl. عوارض *ʿawāriḍ*²) obstacle, impediment, obstruction; temporary disturbance, anomalous condition (physically); attack, fit, spell; s.th. accidental, s.th. nonessential, an accident; side of the face; — العارضان the cheeks | خفيف العارضين *ḵ. al-ʿāriḍain* having a sparse beard; فى عارض الطريق in the middle of the road

عارضة *ʿāriḍa* pl. *-āt* woman demonstrator, woman exhibitor; — (pl. عوارض *ʿawāriḍ*²) side of the face; doorpost, jamb; crossbeam, transom; joist, girder; purlin; ○ anode (*el.*) | قوة العارضة *qūwat al-ʿā.* eloquence; عارضة الازياء mannequin

عارضى *ʿāriḍī* accidental, casual, occasional

معروض *maʿrūḍ* pl. معاريض *maʿārīḍ*² exposition, report; memorial, petition, application; — pl. *-āt* propositions, proposals, offers, tenders; exhibits, exhibited articles

معارض *muʿāriḍ* adversary, opponent, antagonist, opposer; contradicter

معترض *muʿtariḍ* running or lying across, transversal, transverse; adversary, opponent, antagonist, opposer; contradicter; resistance (*el.*) | جملة معترضة (*jumla*) parenthetical clause, parenthesis

²عرضى *ʿurḍī* (from Turk. *ordu*) military encampment, army camp

عرف *ʿarafa* *i* (معرفة *maʿrifa*, عرفان *ʿirfān*) to know (ه, ٥ s.o., s.th.); to recognize, perceive (ه, ٥ s.o., s.th.); to be cognizant, be aware (ه of s.th.), be acquainted (ه with s.th.); to discover, experience, find out (ه s.th.); to recognize, acknowledge (ب s.th., ه s.th. as being right; ه ه s.th. as); to concede, acknowledge (ل ه s.th. to s.o.), allow (ل ه for s.th. in s.o.); to approve (ه of); to distinguish, differentiate (ه, ٥ من s.o., s.th. from); pass. *ʿurifa* to be known (ب as, by the name of) | عرف حق المعرفة (*ḥaqqa l-m.*) to know for sure, be sure (of), be positive (about); عرفت له الجميل she was grateful to him, she appreciated his service, she gratefully acknowledged his service **II** to announce (ه ٥ to s.o. s.th.), inform, advise, apprise (ه ٥ s.o. of), acquaint (ه ٥ s.o. with s.th.); to introduce (الى or ب ٥ s.o. to s.o. else), have (٥ s.o.) meet (الى or ب s.o. else), present (ب ٥ s.o. to s.o. else); to define (ه s.th.); to determine, specify, characterize, explain (ه s.th.); (*gram.*) to make definite (ه a noun); (*Chr.*) to confess (٥ a penitent), hear the confession (٥ of s.o.) **V** to become acquainted (ب or الى, also على with s.o.), meet (ب or الى s.o.), make the acquaintance of s.o. (ب or الى); to make o.s. known, disclose one's identity, reveal o.s. (الى to s.o.); to acquaint o.s., familiarize o.s. (على or الى with), get to know (على or الى s.th.); to sound, explore (ه s.th.); to trace, discover, uncover (ه s.th.); (*gram.*) to be or become definite (noun) **VI** to become acquainted with one another, become mutually acquainted, get to know each other; to become acquainted (ب with); to come to know (ه s.th.), learn (ه about) **VIII** to confess, admit, acknowledge, own, avow (ه s.th.); to recognize (ب s.o., s.th.), grant recognition (ب to s.o., to s.th.); to concede, acknowledge (ل ب s.th. to s.o.); to make a confession, to confess (*Chr.*) | اعترف بالجميل to be grateful **X** to discern, recognize (ه s.th.)

عرف *ʿarf* fragrance, perfume, scent, aroma

عرف *'urf* beneficence, kindness; custom, usage, practice, convention, tradition, habit; legal practice; custom, customary law (*jur.*); (pl. اعراف *a'rāf*) crest, comb (of a rooster), mane (of a horse) | فى عرفه as was his wont, according to his habit; in his opinion; العرف السياسى (*siyāsī*) protocol

عرفى *'urfī* traditional, conventional, usual, common, customary, habitual; pertaining to secular legal practice (as opposed to *šar'ī*); private, unofficial (as opposed to *rasmī*) | الحكم العرفى (*ḥukm*) martial law; الاحكام العرفية do.; محكمة عرفية (*maḥkama*) court-martial

عريف *'arīf* pl. عرفاء *'urafā'*[2] knowing (ب s.th.), cognizant, aware (ب of s.th.); expert, authority, specialist; teaching assistant, monitor (an older pupil assisting the teacher of a Koran school); sergeant (*Ir.*); corporal (*U.A.R*); رئيس العرفاء a military rank, approx.: master sergeant (*Ir., Syr.*); نائب عريف approx.: corporal (*Ir.*); (pl. عرفان *'irfān*) teacher, esp. a teacher and precentor of congregational singing (*Copt.-Chr.*)

عراف *'arrāf* diviner, fortuneteller

عرافة *'arrāfa* pl. *-āt* (woman) fortuneteller

عرافة *'irāfa* fortuneteller's trade; fortunetelling, divination

عرفات *'arafāt* Arafat, name of a mountain and adjacent plain, located four hours' distance east of Mecca, where the Mecca pilgrims spend the 9th day of Zu'lhijja

عرفان *'irfān* cognition, knowledge, perception; recognition, acknowledgment | عرفان الجميل gratitude, thankfulness; عرفان الفضل *'i. al-faḍl* do.

اعرف *a'raf*[2] knowing better (ب s.th.), more cognizant, more knowledgeable (ب of), better acquainted, more conversant (ب with), more expert, more versed (ب in); a better connoisseur (ب of); (f. عرفاء *'arfā'*[2]) having a crest or mane, crested, maned

معرفة *ma'rifa* pl. معارف *ma'ārif*[2] knowledge, learning, lore, information, skill, know-how; cognition, intellection, perception, experience, realization; gnosis; acquaintance, cognizance, conversance, versedness; an acquainted person, an acquaintance, a friend; (*gram.*) definite noun; pl. المعارف cultural affairs, education | بمعرفة by, through (after the passive); مع المعرفة knowingly, deliberately (*jur.*); وزير المعارف العمومية (*'umūmīya*) minister of education; لم يكن معرفة فى قومه (*qaumihī*) he was unknown among his people

معارف *ma'ārif*[2] face, countenance, features

تعريف *ta'rīf* pl. *-āt*, تعاريف *ta'ārīf*[2] announcement, notification, communication, information; instruction, direction; (social) introduction; definition, determination, identification, specification, characterization; a rendering definite (*gram.*) | اداة التعريف *adāt at-t.* (*gram.*) the definite article; بطاقة التعريف identity card

تعريفة *ta'rīfa* notification, information, apprising; — (pl. *-āt*, تعاريف *ta'ārīf*[2]) tariff; price list

تعرف *ta'arruf* acquaintance (ب or الى with); exploration, study; cognition, knowledge, perception, realization

اعتراف *i'tirāf* recognition, acceptance; acknowledgment, avowal, admission, confession; (*Chr.*) confession | اعترافا ب in recognition of; الاعتراف بالجميل (*bi-l-jamīl*) gratitude, thankfulness; ابو الاعتراف *abū l-i't.* father-confessor, confessor (*Chr.*); سر الاعتراف *sirr al-i't.* sacrament of penance (*Chr.*); معلم الاعتراف *mu'allim al-iʿt.* father-confessor, confessor (*Chr.*); من الاعتراف ان it must be admitted that ..., admittedly ...

عارف *ʿārif* acquainted, conversant, familiar (ب with); connoisseur, expert; master (*tun.*)

عارفة *ʿārifa* (*syr.*) sage, wise man (of a village or tribe)

معروف *maʿrūf* known, well-known; universally accepted, generally recognized; conventional; that which is good, beneficial, or fitting, good, benefit; fairness, equity, equitableness; kindness, friendliness, amicability; beneficence; favor rendered, courtesy, mark of friendship; active voice (*gram.*) | بالمعروف or بمعروف in (all) fairness, with appropriate courtesy, in a friendly manner, amicably; ناكر المعروف ungrateful; المعروف أن it is (well-) known that ..., as is well-known ...; it is commonly held that ..., it is generally understood that ...

متعارف *mutaʿāraf* or متعارف عليه common, usual, customary; commonplace, trivial, trite, hackneyed, banal

معترف *muʿtarif* confessor (in the hierarchy of saints; *Chr.*)

معترف به *muʿtaraf bihī* recognized, accepted, admitted, granted, approved-of, licensed, authorized

عرق *ʿariqa a* (*ʿaraq*) to sweat, perspire **II** to make or let (ه s.o.) sweat, promote perspiration; to add water (ه to a drink), dilute (ه a drink); to take root, strike roots; to be deeply rooted; to vein, marble (ه s.th.) **IV** to take root, strike roots **V** = **IV**

عرق *ʿirq* pl. عروق *ʿurūq* root; stem (of a plant, of a leaf); vein (*bot.*, *anat.*); hereditary disposition; race, stock, descent | عرق الذهب *ʿi. aḏ-ḏahab* ipecac, ipecacuanha (*bot.*); عرق سوس *ʿi. sūs* licorice root; عرق النسا *ʿi. an-nasā* sciatica (*med.*); طيب العرق *ṭīb al-ʿi.* noble descent; طيب العرق *ṭayyib al-ʿi.* of noble descent, high born; العرق دساس (*dussās*) blood will tell, what is bred in the bone will come out in the flesh; ضرب فيه بعرق to have a share in s.th., participate in s.th.

عرق *ʿaraq* sweat, perspiration; arrack, a strong colorless liquor made of raisins, milky white when diluted with water (esp. *syr.*; = *eg. zabīb*) | عرق القربة *ʿa. al-qirba* pains, toil, exertion; عرق زحلاوى (*zaḥlāwī*) a well-known brand of arrack made in Zahlé (Lebanon)

عرقة *ʿaraqa* transom between two layers of stone or brick

عرقية *ʿaraqīya* (*eg.*) white cotton skullcap (often worn under the tarboosh)

عراقة *ʿarāqa* deep-rootedness; ancient ancestral line, old family | عراقة فى النسب (*nasab*) noble descent

عراقية *ʿarrāqīya* (*eg.*) white cotton skullcap (often worn under the tarboosh)

عريق *ʿarīq* deep-rooted | عريق فى القدم (*qidam*) ancient; centuried, centuries-old; من عائلة عريقة from an old, respectable family; عريق النسب *ʿa. an-nasab* of noble descent, highborn

العراق *al-ʿirāq* Iraq; العراقان *al-ʿirāqān* Basra and Kufa

عراقى *ʿirāqī* Iraqi, Iraqian; (pl. *-ūn*) an Iraqi

اعرق *aʿraq*² more deep-rooted

معروق *maʿrūq* gaunt, emaciated, lean (face, hand, etc.)

معرق *muʿarriq* sudorific, promoting perspiration

معرق *muʿarraq* veined; *muʿriq* firmly rooted | معرق فى القدم (*muʿriq, qidam*) very old, ancient, centuried, centuries-old

عرقب *ʿarqaba* to hamstring (ه an animal)

عرقوب *ʿurqūb* pl. عراقيب *ʿarāqīb*² Achilles' tendon; hamstring; *ʿurqūb* name of a famed liar | اكذب من عرقوب a greater liar than ʿUrqūb

عرقوبى *ʿurqūbī* false, deceitful (promise)

عرقل *ʿarqala* to render difficult, complicate, handicap, hinder, hamper, encumber, impede, obstruct, delay (ه, ه s.o., s.th.), throw obstacles in the way of s.o. or s.th. (ه, ه); (*tun.*) to seize, confiscate, impound (ه s.th.) **II** *taʿarqala* to be aggravated, rendered difficult, be or become complicated, be hindered, hampered, encumbered, impeded, obstructed, handicapped, delayed

عرقلة *ʿarqala* impeding, hindering, encumbering; — (pl. عراقيل *ʿarāqīl*²) encumbrance, impediment, hindrance; obstacle, difficulty, handicap

عرك *ʿaraka u* (*ʿark*) to rub (ه s.th.); to turn, adjust (ه the knobs of a radio, and the like); to play havoc (ه with), damage severely (ه s.th.); — *ʿarika a* to be strong in battle, be a tough fighter **III** to fight, struggle, contend (ه with s.o.) **VI** to engage in a fight, fight one another **VIII** = **VI**

عرك *ʿark* experience (gained through suffering)

عركة *ʿarka* fight, struggle, battle, combat

عريكة *ʿarīka* disposition, frame of mind, temper, nature

معركة *maʿraka, maʿruka* pl. معارك *maʿārik*² battlefield; battle

عراك *ʿirāk* struggle, fight, strife, battle, combat

معاركة *muʿāraka* struggle, fight, strife, battle, combat

معترك *muʿtarak* fighting ground, battle ground

عرم **II** to heap up, pile up, stack (ه s.th.) **VIII** to be vicious; to be stubborn, obstinate, headstrong

عرم *ʿarim* vicious; strong, violent, vehement, powerful, terrific; dam, dike | جيش عرم (*jaiš*) numerous, huge army

عرام *ʿurām* viciousness (of character); violence, vehemence | سيل عرام (*sail*) huge quantity, tremendous flood

عرمة *ʿurma* pl. عرم *ʿuram* heap, pile, bulk, mass, large amount, multitude

عرمة *ʿarama* pl. عرم *ʿaram* heap, pile, bulk, mass, large amount, multitude

عارم *ʿārim* vicious; tempestuous, violent, vehement, strong; tremendous, enormous, huge

عرمرم *ʿaramram* strong, violent, vehement | جيش عرمرم (*jaiš*) a numerous, huge army

عرين *ʿarīn* pl. عرن *ʿurun* thicket; lair of a lion, lion's den

عرينة *ʿarīna* pl. عرائن *ʿarāʾin*² lair of a wild animal

عرنين *ʿirnīn* pl. عرانين *ʿarānīn*² upper part of the nose, bridge of the nose

عرناس *ʿirnās* pl. عرانيس *ʿarānīs*² distaff | عرناس ذرة *ʿi. dura* corncob (*syr.*)

(عرو) عرا *ʿarā u* (*ʿarw*) and **VIII** to befall, grip, seize, strike, afflict (ه s.o.), come, descend (ه upon s.o.), happen (ه to s.o.); to take possession (ه of s.o.)

عروة *ʿurwa* pl. عرى *ʿuran* buttonhole; loop, noose, coil; ear, handle (of a jug, and the like); tie, bond, e.g., عرى الصداقة *ʿu. ṣ-ṣadāqa* bonds of friendship; support, prop, stay | العروة الوثقى (*wuṯqā*) the firm, reliable grip or hold, the firm tie

عرى *ʿariya a* (*ʿury*, عرية *ʿurya*) to be naked, nude; to be free, be bare (عن of) | عرى عن ثيابه (من or) to take off one's clothes, strip (naked), undress, have no clothes on; عرى عن كل اساس (*asās*) to be completely unfounded, be without any foundation II to disrobe, unclothe, undress (ه s.o.); to bare, denude, lay bare, uncover (ه s.th.); to strip (ه من ثيابه s.o. of his clothes); to deprive, divest, strip (ه من s.o. of s.th.)

عرى *'ury* nakedness, nudity; unsaddled (horse)

عرية *'urya* nakedness, nudity

عراء *'arā'* nakedness, nudity; bareness; open space, open country | فى العراء in the open air, under the open sky, outside, outdoors; مسرح فى العراء (*masraḥ*) open-air theater

عريان *'uryān* pl. عرايا *'arāyā* naked, nude, undressed, bare | عريان ملط (*malṭ*) stark-naked (*eg.*)

○ عريانية *'uryānīya* nudism

المعارى *al-ma'ārī* the uncovered parts of the body (hands, feet, face)

عار *'ārin* pl. عراة *'urāh* naked, nude, undressed, bare; free, devoid, destitute, bare, deprived, stripped, denuded (من or عن of s.th.); blank, bare (e.g., a room), stark (e.g., a narrative) | عارى الاقدام barefoot(ed), unshod

عز *'azza* i (*'izz*, عزة *'izza*, عزازة *'azāza*) to be or become strong, powerful, respected; to be or become rare, scarce, be scarcely to be found; to be or become dear, cherished, precious (على to s.o.); عز عليه ان he is sorry that...; to be hard, difficult (على for s.o.); to hurt, pain (على s.o.), be painful (على for s.o.), be hard (على on s.o.) II to make strong, strengthen, reinforce, fortify, corroborate, confirm, solidify, invigorate, harden, advance, support (ه, ه s.o., s.th.); to consolidate (ه s.th.); to honor (ه s.o.); to raise in esteem, elevate, exalt (ه s.o.); to make dear, endear (ه s.o.) | عزز جانبه to strengthen, reinforce, fortify, solidify, consolidate s.th., make s.th. strong, powerful, mighty IV to make strong, strengthen, fortify, reinforce, invigorate, harden, steel (ه, ه s.o., s th.); to love (ه, ه s.o., s.th.); to honor (ه, ه s.o., s.th.); to esteem, value, prize (ه, ه s.o., s.th.); to make dear, endear (ه, ه s.o., s.th.) V to be or become strong, powerful, mighty, forceful, strengthened, fortified, reinforced, invigorated, hardened, solidified, consolidated; to be proud, boast (ب of), pride o.s., glory, exult (ب in) VIII to feel strong or powerful (ب due to, because of); to be proud, boast (ب of), pride o.s., glory, exult (ب in); to arrogate to o.s. (ب s.th.) X to overwhelm, overcome (على s.o.); to become powerful, mighty, respected, honored, be exalted; to make or hold dear, value highly, esteem (ه s.o.)

عز *'izz* might, power, standing, weight; strength, force; honor, glory, high rank, fame, celebrity, renown | عزها Her Highness (title); فى عز شبابه (*šabābihī*) in the prime of his youth

عزة *'izza* might, power, standing, weight; strength, force; honor, glory, high rank, fame, celebrity, renown; pride | عزة الجانب power, might; العزة القومية (*qaumīya*) national pride; عزة النفس *'i. an-nafs* sense of honor, self-respect, self-esteem; صاحب العزة title of a bey

عزيز *'azīz* pl. اعزاء *a'izzā'*[2], اعزة *a'izza* mighty, powerful, respected, distinguished, notable; strong; noble, esteemed, venerable, august; honorable; rare, scarce, scarcely to be found; difficult, hard (على for); precious, costly, valuable; dear, beloved (على to), cherished, valued (على by); friend; ruler, overlord | عزيزى my dear! (esp. as a salutation in letters); عزيز الجانب mighty, powerful, strong

اعز *aʿazz*[2] mightier, more powerful; stronger; dearer, more beloved; العزى *al-ʿuzzā* a goddess of the pagan Arabs

معزة *maʿazza* esteem, regard, affection, love

تعزيز *taʿzīz* pl. *-āt* strengthening, consolidation, support, backing

اعزاز *iʿzāz* strengthening, fortification, reinforcement, consolidation; love, affection, esteem, regard

اعتزاز *iʿtizāz* pride (ب in)

معتز *muʿtazz* proud; mighty, powerful

عزب **ʿazaba** *i u* (عزوب *ʿuzūb*) to be far, be distant (عن from); to slip, escape (عن s.o.'s mind) | عزب عن الاذهان to be forgotten, sink into oblivion; — *ʿazaba u* (عزبة *ʿuzba*, عزوبة *ʿuzūba*) to be single, unmarried

عزب *ʿazab* pl. عزاب *ʿuzzāb*, اعزاب *aʿzāb* celibate, single, unmarried; bachelor

عزبة *ʿizba* pl. عزب *ʿizab* (*eg.*) country estate, farm; rural settlement

عزبة *ʿuzba* celibacy; bachelorhood

عزوبة *ʿuzūba* celibacy; bachelorhood

اعزب *aʿzab*[2] celibate, single, unmarried; bachelor

معزب *muʿazzab* sheik, emir (Nejd)

عزر **ʿazar** *i* (*ʿazr*) to censure, rebuke, reprove, reprimand (ه s.o.); to refuse to have anything to do with s.o.; — *ʿazara i* to curb, restrain, subdue (ه s.o.'s pride, and the like) **II** to censure, rebuke, reprove, reprimand (ه s.o.); to refuse to have anything to do with s.o.

عزر *ʿazr* censure, blame, rebuke, reproof, reprimand

تعزير *taʿzīr* censure, blame, rebuke, reproof, reprimand; chastisement, castigation

اعتزار *iʿtizār* self-discipline

عزرائيل *ʿizrāʾīl*[2] Azrael, the angel of death

عزف **ʿazafa** *i* (*ʿazf*) to play (على on a musical instrument, ه tunes); to play (ل to or for s.o.), make music (ل for s.o.); — *i u* (*ʿazf*, عزوف *ʿuzūf*) to turn away (عن from s.th.), become averse (عن to s.th.), avoid, shun (عن s.th.), abstain, refrain (ان from doing s.th.)

عزوف *ʿazūf* disinclined, averse (عن to s.th.)

معزف *miʿzaf* pl. معازف *maʿāzif*[2] stringed instrument; ○ piano

عازف *ʿāzif* player, (musical) performer

معزوفة *maʿzūfa* pl. *-āt* piece of music, performance, recital (on an instrument)

عزق **ʿazaqa** *i* (*ʿazq*) to hoe, dig up, break up, loosen (الارض *al-arḍa* the soil)

معزقة *miʿzaqa* pl. معازق *maʿāziq*[2] hoe, mattock

عزل **ʿazala** *i* (*ʿazl*) to remove, set aside, isolate, separate, segregate, detach, cut off (عن ,ه ,ه s.o., s.th. from); to depose (ه s.o.), release, dismiss, discharge (ه s.o. عن منصبه *ʿan manṣibihī* of his office) **IV** اعزل منصبه (*manṣibahū*) to give up one's position, resign **VII** to be or become isolated, cut off, separated, segregated, detached (عن from) **VIII** to keep away, stand aloof, leave, withdraw; to retire, seclude o.s., segregate, secede, detach o.s., dissociate o.s., separate o.s., isolate o.s. (عن or ه ,ه from s.o., from s.th.), part (عن or ه ,ه with s.o., with s.th.); to be or get deposed | اعتزل الخدمة (*ḵidmata*), اعتزل العمل (*ʿamala*) to retire from service, from work, go into retirement

عزل *ʿazl* removal, dissociation, detachment, setting aside, isolation (also, e.g., in case of contagious disease), cutting-off, segregation, separation; deposition, discharge, dismissal | حائط عزل الحرق (*ḥarq*)

fire wall; غير قابل للعزل irremovable, appointed for life tenure (judge)

عزل *ʿazal* unarmedness, defenselessness

عزل *ʿuzul* unarmed, defenseless

عزلة *ʿuzla* retirement, seclusion, retreat, privacy; segregation, separation, detachedness; insulation, insularity, isolatedness; isolation; solitude | في عزلة عن secluded, segregated, cut off, detached, separated, insulated, isolated from

عزلة *ʿizla* pl. عزل *ʿizal* subdistrict of a *nāḥiya* (Yemen)

عزال *ʿizāl* (*eg.*) furniture, household effects, movable goods, luggage

اعزل *aʿzal*², f. عزلاء *ʿazlā'*², pl. عزل *ʿuzl* unarmed, defenseless | السماك الاعزل star α in the constellation Virgo, Spica Virginis (*astron.*)

معزل *maʿzil* pl. معازل *maʿāzil*² place of retirement, house of retreat; seclusion, segregation, isolation; isolation ward (in a hospital) | بمعزل عن separated, detached, apart, secluded, segregated, isolated from

انعزال *inʿizāl* detachedness, seclusion, segregation, insularity, insulation; isolation

انعزالية *inʿizālīya* isolationism

اعتزال *iʿtizāl* retirement, seclusion, retreat, privacy | اعتزال الخدمة *iʿt. al-kidma* retirement from service

○ عازل *ʿāzil* insulator (*el.*)

○ عازلة *ʿāzila* pl. -*āt*, عوازل *ʿawāzil*² insulator, nonconductor (*el.*)

معزول *maʿzūl* far, distant, remote (عن from); isolated, insulated

منعزل *munʿazil* isolated, single, solitary, sporadic

المعتزلة *al-muʿtazila* name of a theological school which introduced speculative dogmatism into Islam

معتزل *muʿtazal* pl. -*āt* (place of) solitude, (place of) retirement

عزم *ʿazama* *i* (*ʿazm*, عزيمة *ʿazīma*) to decide, resolve (على on s.th.); to make up one's mind, determine, be determined, be resolved (على to do s.th.), be bent (على on s.th.); to adjure (على s.o.); to invite (ه s.o. ان or على to or to do s.th.) **II** to enchant, spellbind (على s.o., s.th., by magic rites) **VIII** to decide, resolve (على or ه on s.th.), make up one's mind, determine, be determined, be resolved (على or ه to do s.th.), be bent (على or ه on s.th.)

عزم *ʿazm* determination, firm will, firm intention, decision, resolution; energy

عزمة *ʿazma* decision, resolution; strict order (ب to do s.th.)

عزوم *ʿazūm* determined, resolved, resolute

عزومة *ʿuzūma* invitation; banquet

عزيمة *ʿazīma* determination, firm will, firm intention; (pl. عزائم *ʿazā'im*²) resolution (على to do s.th.), decision; incantation; spell

عازم *ʿāzim* determined, resolved (على to do s.th.)

معتزم *muʿtazim* determined, resolved (على to do s.th.)

عزا (عزو and عزى) *ʿazā* *u* (*ʿazw*) and عزى *ʿazā* *i* (*ʿazy*) to trace (back) (ل or الى ه s.th. to an origin), ascribe, attribute, impute, owe (ل or الى ه s.th. to s.o., to s.th.); to charge, incriminate (ل or الى ه with s.th. s.o. or s.th.), blame (الى ه for s.th. s.o. or s.th.), lay the blame (الى ه for s.th. on s.o., on s.th.); — عزى *ʿaziya* *a* (عزاء *ʿazā'*) and عزا *ʿazā* *u* (عزاء *ʿazā'*) to take patience, console o.s. **II** to persuade (ه s.o.) to bear with equanimity (في or عن s.th., the death of s.o. or the loss of s.th.), comfort, console (ه عن s.o. over), give comfort, express one's sympathy, offer one's condolences (ه to s.o.) **V** to take patience; to console o.s. (عن for) **VII** to console o.s. (ب with), find solace (ب in) **VIII** to trace (back) one's descent (الى to)

عزو *'azw* tracing back, ascription, attribution; imputation, accusation

عزوة *'izwa*: حسن العزوة *ḥasan al-'i.* of good ancestry, of good stock

عزاء *'azā'* composure, equanimity; comfort, consolation, solace; ceremony of mourning

تعزية *ta'ziya* pl. تعاز *ta'āzin* consolation, solace, comfort; condolence | رفع تعزيته to express one's sympathy, offer one's condolences; قدم التعازى (*qaddama*) do.

معز *mu'azzin* comforter, consoler, condoler

عس *'assa u* (*'ass*) to make the rounds by night, patrol by night

عسس *'asas* patrol (as a body of men)

عسة *'assa* guard | العسة المصونة (*maṣūna*) (formerly:) the bodyguard of the Bey of Tunisia

عسيب *'asīb* tail bone (of the horse); (pl. عسب *'usub*) a palm branch stripped of its leaves

يعسوب *ya'sūb* pl. يعاسيب *ya'āsīb*² male bee, drone; notable, chief, leader

عوسج *'ausaj* boxthorn (Lycium europaeum L. and Lycium arabicum Schwf.; *bot.*)

عسجد *'asjad* gold

عسجدى *'asjadī* golden

معسجد *mu'asjad* gilded

عسر *'asura u* (*'usr, 'usur*) and *'asira a* (*'asar*) to be difficult, hard, trying, adverse (على for s.o.); — *'asara i u* (*'asr*) to press, urge (على ه s.o. to); to force, compel, coerce (على ه s.o. to) **II** to make difficult or hard (ه s.th.); to act hostilely (على toward s.o.); to oppress, distress (على s.o.), bear down hard (على on s.o.) **III** to treat (ه s.o.) roughly or harshly **IV** to be in distress, be in a fix, in a predicament; to become impoverished, be reduced to poverty, be up against it, be in financial straits, live in straitened circumstances **V** to be difficult, hard, trying, adverse (على for s.o.) **VI** = **V**; **X** = **V**; to find (ه s.th.) difficult, hard, trying, or adverse

عسر *'usr, 'usur* difficulty, trying or distressful situation, predicament, plight, fix, pinch, press, straits, straightened circumstances, distress, poverty, destitution

عسر *'asir* hard, difficult; trying, distressing, adverse

عسرة *'usra* = عسر *'usr*

عسير *'asīr* difficult, hard, harsh, rough; Asir (mountainous district in SW Arabia, between Hejaz and Yemen)

اعسر *a'sar*² left-handed; harder, more difficult

معسرة *ma'sara* = عسر *'usr*

اعسار *i'sār* poverty; financial straits, insolvency

تعسر *ta'assur* difficulty

معسور *ma'sūr* (living) in straitened circumstances

معسر *mu'sir* (living) in straitened circumstances; poor, impoverished

متعسر *muta'assir* hard, difficult, trying, distressing, adverse

عسعس *'as'asa* to darken, grow dark

عسف *'asafa i* (*'asf*) to act recklessly or thoughtlessly (فى in s.th.), do (فى s.th.) rashly; to treat unjustly, oppress, tyrannize (ه s.o.) **II** to overburden, overtask, overtax (ه s.o.) IV = II; V to do (ه s.th.) at random, haphazardly, dispose arbitrarily (في of); to deviate, stray (عن from) VIII to do (ه s.th.) at random, haphazardly; to deviate, stray (عن from); to go astray; to force, compel, coerce (ه ب s.o. to)

عسف *'asf* injustice, oppression, tyranny

عسوف *'asūf* oppressor, despot, tyrant

عساف *'assāf* oppressor, despot, tyrant

تعسف *ta'assuf* arbitrariness; an arbitrary, liberal, inaccurate manner of using the language; aberration; deviation

تعسفى *ta'assufī* arbitrary; despotic, tyrannical

اعتساف *i'tisāf* straying, aberration, deviation; coercion, compulsion, force

عسقلان *'asqalān*[2] Ashkelon (seaport in SW Palestine)

عسكر *'askar* pl. عساكر *'asākir*[2] army, host, troops | عساكر ضابطية (*ḍābiṭīya*) constabulary, police troops

عسكرى *'askarī* military, army- (in compounds); pl. العسكريون the military; — (pl. عساكر *'asākir*[2]) soldier; private (*mil.*); policeman; pl. enlisted men, ranks

عسكرية *'askarīya* military service; militarism; soldiership, soldiery, soldierliness

معسكر *mu'askar* pl. *-āt* military encampment, army camp; camp | معسكر الاعتقال concentration camp

عسل II to prepare or mix with honey (ه s.th.); to sweeten, make sweet or pleasant (ه s.th.)

عسل *'asal* pl. اعسال *a'sāl*, عسول *'usūl* honey | عسل سكر *'a. sukkar* molasses, treacle; عسل اسود do.; شهر العسل *šahr al-'a.* honeymoon

عسلى *'asalī* honey-colored, amber, brownish

عسال *'assāl* gatherer of honey; beekeeper, apiculturist

عسالة *'assāla* beehive

عيسلان *'aisalān* hyacinth (*bot.*)

معسلة *ma'sala* beehive

تعسيلة *ta'sīla* (*eg.*) nap, doze

معسول *ma'sūl* prepared with honey; honeyed, honeysweet

معسل *mu'assal*: دخان معسل (*dukān*) a mild-tasting tobacco, due to its preparation with molasses, glycerine, fragrant oils or essences

عسلج *'usluj* pl. عسالج *'asālij*[2] tender sprig, small twig, shoot

عسلوج *'uslūj* pl. عساليج *'asālīj*[2] tender sprig, small twig, shoot

[1]عسى *'asā* with foll. ان *an* and subjunctive: it might be, it could be that..., possibly..., maybe..., perhaps... | ما عسى ان يكون what might be...?! ماذا عسى ان افعل what should I do? ما عسى ينفع هذا (*yanfa'u*) of what use could this possibly be? ماذا عساه يقول what could he possibly say?

عسى *'asīy* appropriate, proper, fitting (with personal construction) | هو عسى ب, هم عسيون ب (or ان) it befits him (them) to ... or that he (they) ..., it is proper for him (for them) to ... or that he (they) ...

[2]عاس *'āsin* dry, withered, wilted

عش II to build a nest, to nest; to take root, become established, settle in VIII to build a nest, to nest

عش *'ušš* pl. عشاش *'išāš*, اعشاش *a'šāš*, عششة *'išaša* nest

عشة *'ušša*, *'išša* pl. عشش *'ušaš*, *'išaš* hut, shanty, shack, hovel; arbor, bower

عشب *'ašiba a, 'ašuba u* to be grassy, grass-covered (ground) **II** do.

عشب *'ušb* (coll.; n. un. ة) pl. اعشاب *a'šāb* (green) grass, herbage, plants; pasture

عشبة *'ušba* plant, herb

عشبى *'ušbī* herbaceous, herbal, vegetable, vegetal, plant- (in compounds) | مجموعة عشبية herbarium

عشب *'ašib* grassy, abundant in grass

عشابة *'ašāba* luxuriant vegetation

معشب *mu'šib* grassy, abundant in grass

عشتروت *'aštarūt*² Astarte

عشر *'ašara u* to collect the tithe (ه from s.o., ه of s.th.) **II** = **I**; to divide into tenths **III** to be on intimate terms, associate (closely) (ه with s.o.) **VI** to be on intimate terms, associate with one another, live together

عشر *'ušr* pl. اعشار *a'šār*, عشور *'ušūr* one tenth, tenth part; tithe | عشر معشار *'u. mi'šār* one hundredth

عشرى *'ušrī* decimal (adj.)

اعشارى *a'šārī* decimal (adj.)

عشرة *'išra* (intimate) association, intimacy, companionship, relations, (social) intercourse, company; conjugal community, community of husband and wife

عشرة *'ašara* (f. عشر *'ašr*) ten; العشر the first ten days of Muharram

ثلاثة عشر *ṯalāṯata 'ašara* (f. ثلاث عشرة *ṯalāṯa 'ašrata*) thirteen

عشرات *'ašarāt* some tens, tens (of); decades; (with foll. genit.) dozens of..., scores of ...

عشار *'išār* (*eg.*) with young, pregnant (animal)

عشار *'aššār* collector of the tithe

عشير *'ašīr* pl. عشراء *'ušarā'*² companion, fellow, associate, friend, comrade

عشيرة *'ašīra* pl. عشائر *'ašā'ir*² clan, kinsfolk, closest relatives; tribe; pl. العشائر (*syr.*) the Bedouins | حرس العشائر *ḥaras al-'a.* Bedouin police (responsible for surveillance of the nomads)

عشائرى *'ašā'irī* (*syr.*) Bedouin (adj.) | العرف العشائرى (*'urf*) the customary law of the Bedouins

عاشوراء *'āšūrā'*², عشوراء *'ašūrā'*², يوم عاشوراء *yaum 'ā.*, ليلة عاشوراء *lailat 'ā.* Ashura, name of a voluntary fast day on the tenth day of Muharram; day of mourning sacred to the Shiites, the anniversary of Husain's martyrdom at Kerbela (10th of Muharram A. H. 60)

عشرون *'išrūn* twenty

معشر *ma'šar* pl. معاشر *ma'āšir*² assemblage, community, company, society, group, troop; kinsfolk | يا معشر الشباب *yā ma'šara š-šabāb* oh ye young men!

معشار *mi'šār* one tenth, tenth part

معاشرة *mu'āšara* (intimate) association, intimacy, social relations, social intercourse; company, society, companionship; community, jointness

معاشر *mu'āšir* companion, fellow, associate, friend, comrade

عشق *'ašiqa a* (*'išq*) to love passionately (ه, ه s.o., s.th.), be passionately in love (ه, ه with s.o., with s.th.) **II** to fit tightly together, interjoin closely, dovetail (ه s.th.); to couple, connect (ه s.th.; *techn.*) **V** to court, woo (ها a woman), make love (ها to a woman)

عشق *'išq* love, ardor of love, passion

عشيق *'ašīq* lover, sweetheart (m.)

عشيقة *'ašīqa* beloved, sweetheart (f.)

عشيق *'iššīq* lover

تعشيق *taʿšīq* tight interjunction, dovetailing; coupling (*techn.*)

عاشق *ʿāšiq* pl. *-ūn*, عشاق *ʿuššāq* lover; fancier, fan, -phile (in compounds); — (pl. عواشق *ʿawāšiq*²) knucklebone; (game of) knucklebones

معشوق *maʿšūq* lover, sweetheart (m.)

معشوقة *maʿšūqa* beloved, sweetheart (f.)

عشو and عشا (عشى) *ʿašā u* (*ʿašw*) and عشى *ʿašiya a* (عشا *ʿašan*) to be dim-sighted; to be night-blind **II** to make dim-sighted, make night-blind (ه s.o.); to give a dinner (ه for s.o.) **IV** to make dim-sighted (ه s.o., ه the eyes) **V** to have dinner (or supper), to dine, to sup

عشا *ʿašan* dim-sightedness; night-blindness, nyctalopia

عشى *ʿašīy* evening

عشاء *ʿašāʾ* pl. اعشية *aʿšiya* dinner, supper | العشاء السرى (*sirrī*) the Lord's supper, the Eucharist (*Chr.*)

عشاء *ʿišāʾ* evening; (f.) evening prayer (*Isl. Law*)

عشوة *ʿašwa* darkness, dark, gloom; dinner, supper

عشاوة *ʿašāwa* dim-sightedness; night-blindness, nyctalopia

عشية *ʿašīya* pl. *-āt*, عشايا *ʿašāyā* (late) evening | عشية امس *ʿašīyata amsi* last night, yesterday in the evening; بين عشية وضحاها (*ḍuḥāhā*) from one day to the other, overnight, all of a sudden

عشواء *ʿašwāʾ*² darkness, dark, gloom; also see اعشى *aʿšā*

اعشى *aʿšā*, f. عشواء *ʿašwāʾ*² dim-sighted; night-blind, nyctalopic; blind, aimless, haphazard, desultory, senseless | يخبط خبط عشواء *yakbiṭu kabṭa ʿašwāʾa* he acts blindly, thoughtlessly, at random, haphazardly

عص *ʿaṣṣa a* (*ʿaṣṣ*, عصص *ʿaṣaṣ*) to be or become hard, harden

عصعص *ʿuṣaṣ, ʿuṣuṣ* coccyx

عصب *ʿaṣaba i* (*ʿaṣb*) to wind, fold, tie, bind, wrap (على ه s.th. around or about s.th.); to bind up, bandage (ه s.th.); to fold (ه s.th.); to wrap (ه the head) with a brow band, sash, or turban | عصب الريق فاه (*rīqu fāhu*) the saliva dried in his mouth, clogged his mouth **II** to wind around, fold around, tie around, wrap around (ه s.th.); to bind up, bandage (ه s.th.); to wrap (ه the head) with a brow band, sash, or turban **V** to wind the turban round one's head, put on the turban; to apply a bandage, bandage o.s.; to take sides, to side (مع ,ل with; على against); to cling obdurately or fanatically (ل to); to be fanatic, bigoted, be a fanatic, a zealot; to form a league, clique, group, team, gang, or coalition, gang up, team up; to plot, conspire, collude, connive (على against) **VIII** to form a league, clique, group, team, gang, or coalition, gang up, team up; to go on strike, to strike

عصب *ʿaṣab* pl. اعصاب *aʿṣāb* nerve; sinew

عصبى *ʿaṣabī* sinewy, nerved, nervy; nervous, neural, nerve-, neuro-, neur- (in compounds); nervous, high-strung | عصبى المزاج nervous, high-strung; الجهاز العصبى (*jahāz*) the nervous system; حالة عصبية nervousness, nervosity; الضعف العصبى (*ḍuʿf*) neurasthenia

عصبية *ʿaṣabīya* nervousness, nervosity; — (pl. *-āt*) zealous partisanship, bigotry, fanaticism; party spirit, team spirit, esprit de corps; tribal solidarity, racialism, clannishness, tribalism. national consciousness, nationalism

عصبة *ʿaṣba* pl. عصب *ʿuṣab* (*eg.*) a black headcloth with red or yellow border

عصبة *ʿaṣaba* pl. *-āt* and *ʿuṣba* pl. عصب *ʿuṣab* union, league, federation, association; group, troop, band, gang, clique; *aṣaba* paternal relations, relationship, agnates | عصبة الامم *ʿuṣbat al-umam* the League of Nations

عصيب *ʿaṣīb* hot, crucial, critical (time, stage)

عصاب *ʿiṣāb* band, ligature, dressing, bandage

عصابة *ʿiṣāba* pl. عصائب *ʿaṣā'ib*² band, ligature, dressing, bandage; headcloth, headband, fillet; brow band, frontlet; — (pl. *-āt*) union, league, federation, association; group, troop, band, gang | عصابات الخطف *ʿi. al-ḵaṭf* bands of robbers; حرب العصابات *ḥarb al-ʿi.* guerilla war(fare)

تعصب *taʿaṣṣub* fanaticism, ardent zeal, bigotry, fanatical enthusiasm; party spirit, partisanship; clannishness, racialism, race consciousness, tribalism

اعتصاب *iʿtiṣāb* pl. *-āt* strike

متعصب *mutaʿaṣṣib* fanatically enthusiastic (ل for); enthusiast, fanatic, bigot, zealot

عصيدة *ʿaṣīda* a thick paste made of flour and clarified butter

عصر *ʿaṣara* *i* (*ʿaṣr*) to press (out), squeeze (out) (ه s.th., e.g., grapes, olives, etc.); to wring (ه s.th., esp. wet clothes); to compress (ه s.th.) **III** to be a contemporary (ه of s.o.); to be contemporaneous, coeval, or concomitant (ه with) **V** to be pressed (out), be squeezed (out) **VII** = **V** **VIII** to press (out), squeeze (out) (ه s.th., e.g., grapes, olives, etc.) | اعتصر جبينه (*jabīnahū*) to knit one's brows (pensively)

عصر *ʿaṣr* (act of) pressing (out), squeezing (out); (act of) wringing (out); (pl. اعصر *aʿṣur*, عصور *ʿuṣūr*, اعصار *aʿṣār*) age, era, time; period; epoch; afternoon; (f.) afternoon prayer (*Isl. Law*) | العصر الحجرى (*ḥajarī*) the Stone Age; العصر الحاضر the present (time), our time; فى كل عصر ومصر (*wa-maṣrin*) always and everywhere, at any time and any place

عصرى *ʿaṣrī* modern, recent, present, actual, contemporary; (pl. *-ūn*) a contemporary

عصرية *ʿaṣriya* modernism

عصير *ʿaṣīr* that which is pressed or squeezed out, (squeezed-out) juice, extract (also fig.); the best, the pick, the prime of s.th.

عصيرة *ʿaṣīra* (squeezed-out) juice

عصار *ʿuṣār* juice, sap

عصارة *ʿuṣāra* pl. *-āt* juice, sap (also *physiol.*)

عصارة *ʿaṣṣāra* pl. *-āt* press, squeezer; oil press; cane press (also عصارة القصب *ʿa. al-qaṣab*); wringer

عصارى يوم *ʿaṣāriya yaumin* one afternoon

اعصار *iʿṣār* pl. اعاصير *aʿāṣīr*² whirlwind, tornado, cyclone, hurricane | ○ ضد الاعصار *ḍidd al-i.* anticyclone

معصرة *miʿṣara* pl. معاصر *maʿāṣir*² press, squeezer; oil press; cane press

معصرى *maʿṣarī* (*tun.*) a brand of lamp oil

معاصر *muʿāṣir* contemporary, contemporaneous; a contemporary

عصعص *ʿuṣʿuṣ*, *ʿaṣʿaṣ* pl. عصاعص *ʿaṣāʿiṣ*² coccyx

عصف *ʿaṣafa* *i* (*ʿaṣf*, عصوف *ʿuṣūf*) to storm, rage, blow violently (wind); عصف به to blow s.th. away, carry s.th. away (wind); to shake s.o. thoroughly, through and through

عصف *ʿaṣf* storming, blowing; stalk and leaves of grain

عصفة *'aṣfa* (n. vic.) gust of wind, blast

عصافة *'uṣāfa* chaff; straw

عاصف *'āṣif* blowing violently | ريح عاصف (*rīḥ*) or ريح عاصفة violent wind, gale

عاصفة *'āṣifa* pl. عواصف *'awāṣif*² violent wind, gale, tempest, storm, hurricane

¹عصفر *'uṣfur* safflower (Carthamus tinctorius; *bot.*); the red dyestuff prepared from its flower heads

معصفر *mu'aṣfar* dyed with *'uṣfur*

²عصفور *'uṣfūr* pl. عصافير *'aṣāfīr*² sparrow; any small bird | عصفور الجنة *'u. al-janna* swallow; عصفور دورى (*dūrī*) house sparrow; عصفور مغن (*muğannin*) warbler; عصفور كنارى (*kanārī*) canary; ضرب (اصاب) عصفورين بحجر (واحد) (*aṣāba, 'uṣfūraini bi-ḥajarin*) to kill two birds with one stone; عصفور فى اليد خير من الف على الشجرة (*kairun min alfin, šajara*) a bird in the hand is worth two in the bush (proverb)

عصفورة *'uṣfūra* female sparrow; dowel, pin, peg

عصفورية *'uṣfūrīya* (*syr.*) insane asylum, madhouse

عصل *'aṣala u* (*'aṣl*) to bend, twist, warp (ه s.th.); — *'aṣila a* (*'aṣal*) to be twisted; to warp (wood)

عصم *'aṣama i* (*'aṣm*) to hold back, restrain, curb, check, prevent, hinder (ه, ه s.o., s.th.); to preserve, guard, safeguard, protect, defend (ه, ه s.o., s.th.); to immunize, render immune (ه s.o., *med.*) **VIII** to cling, keep, adhere (ب to); to seek shelter or refuge (ب with, in), take refuge, resort (ب to); to keep up, maintain, guard, preserve (ب s.th., e.g., بالصمت *bi-ṣ-ṣamt* silence, برباطة الجأش *bi-r. il-ja'š* equanimity) **X** = **VIII**; to resist (a temptation)

عصمة *'uṣma* necklace

عصمة *'iṣma* hindering, hindrance, prevention, obviation; preservation, guarding, safeguarding; defense; protection; chastity, purity, modesty, virtuousness; impeccance, sinlessness, infallibility | صاحبة العصمة title of ladies of high social standing; عصمة النكاح the bond of marriage; فى عصمة فلان under s.o.'s custody, protection, or power; married to s.o.; جعلت عصمتها فى يدها *ja'alat 'iṣmatahā fī yadihā* she made herself independent; she became or remained independent; فك عصمتها من زوجها *fakka 'iṣmatahā min zaujihā* to revoke the husband's matrimonial authority over his wife (*jur.*)

عصام *'iṣām* pl. اعصمة *a'ṣima*, عصم *'uṣum*, عصام *'iṣām* strap, thong

عصامى *'iṣāmī* noble, eminent, distinguished (due to one's own merits, as opposed to عظامى *'iẓāmī*); self-made; (pl. *-ūn*) self-made man

عصامية *'iṣāmīya* self-made success

اعصم *a'ṣam*², f. عصماء *'aṣmā'*², pl. عصم *'uṣm* having a white foot (animal); excellent, valuable, precious | اندر من الغراب الاعصم (*ğurāb*) rarer than a white-footed crow (proverbially of s.th. rare)

معصم *mi'ṣam* pl. معاصم *ma'āṣim*² wrist

○ معصم *ma'ṣam* pl. معاصم *ma'āṣim*² traffic island, safety isle

اعتصام *i'tiṣām* clinging, adherence (ب to), maintenance, preservation, guarding, safeguarding

عاصم *'āṣim* protector, guardian

عاصمة *'āṣima* pl. عواصم *'awāṣim*² capital city, metropolis

معصوم *ma'ṣūm* inviolable, sacrosanct, protected by the laws of vendetta (*Isl. Law*); infallible, sinless, impeccant, impeccable | معصوم من الزلل (*zalal*) infallible

(عصو) عصا *'aṣan* (f.) pl. عصى *'uṣīy, 'iṣīy*, اعص *a'ṣin* staff, rod; wand; stick;

walking stick, cane; scepter, mace; (field marshal's) baton | عصا المارشالية *'a. l-mārišālīya* field marshal's baton; لعب العصا *la'b al-'a.* (*eg.* = تحطيب) singlestick fencing (a popular game, esp. in rural areas); شق العصا (*šaqqa*) to dissent, secede from the community; شق عصا الطاعة to rebel, revolt, renounce allegiance; شق عصا القوم (*'aṣā l-qaum*) to sow dissension among the people; انشقت عصاهم (*inšaqqat*) they fell out (with one another), broke with one another

عصاة *'aṣāh* staff, rod; wand; stick

□ عصاية *'aṣāya* staff, rod; wand; stick; walking stick, cane

عصية *'uṣayya* little stick, little rod; ○ bacillus

عصى *'aṣā i* (*'aṣy*, معصية *ma'ṣiya*, عصيان *'iṣyān*) to disobey, resist, oppose, defy (ه ، s.o. in s.th.), refuse, or renounce, one's obedience (ه ، to s.o. in s.th.), rebel, revolt (ه against s.o.) **III** = **I**; **V** to be or become difficult, intricate, or involved (affair) **VI** to be difficult, hard, inaccessible, or impossible (على for s.o.); to refuse (عن to do s.th.) **VIII** = **V** **X** to resist, oppose, withstand, defy (على s.o., s.th.), revolt, rebel (على against s.o.); to be recalcitrant, insubordinate, rebellious; to be difficult, hard (على for s.o.); to be malignant, insidious, incurable (disease); to elude, escape, defy (عن s.th.), be beyond s.th. (عن); (of an instrument, machine, etc.) to fail, break down (على on s.o.), refuse to work (على for s.o.), fail to operate

عصى *'aṣīy* pl. *-ūn*, اعصياء *a'ṣiyā'*[2] rebel; intractable, refractory, recalcitrant | عصى النطق *'aṣīy an-nuṭq* unable to speak, incapable of speech

عصيان *'iṣyān* disobedience, insubordination, refractoriness; insurrection, revolt, rebellion, sedition

معصية *ma'ṣiya* disobedience, insubordination, refractoriness; insurrection, sedition, revolt, rebellion; (pl. معاص *ma'āṣin*) sin

استعصاء *isti'ṣā'* refractoriness, recalcitrance, obstinacy; impenetrability, unfathomableness; difficulty; malignancy, virulence, insidiousness; mechanical failure, breakdown, malfunction; jam, misfire (of a firearm)

عاص *'āṣin* pl. عصاة *'uṣāh* disobedient, insubordinate, rebellious, mutinous, riotous, seditious, subversive; rebel, insurgent; sinning, sinful

متعص *muta'aṣṣin* difficult, intricate, implicated, involved, delicate; incurable, irremediable

مستعص *musta'ṣin* difficult, intricate, implicated, involved, delicate; incurable, irremediable

عض *'aḍḍa* (1st pers. perf. *'aḍiḍtu*) *a* (*'aḍḍ*, عضيض *'aḍīḍ*) to grab with the teeth, bite (ب or على or ه ، s.o., s.th.); to bite into s.th. (ه); to hold on, cling, cleave (ب to); to torment (ه s.o., e.g., hunger) | عضه الزمان (*zamānu*) or عضه الدهر بنابه *'aḍḍahū d-dahru bi-nābihī* time, or fate, gave him a raw deal, heaped trials and tribulations upon him, he suffered reverses **II** to bite fiercely or frequently (ه ، s.o., s.th.)

عض *'iḍḍ* small prickly shrubs, brambles

عضة *'aḍḍa* a bite

عضاض *'aḍḍāḍ* (given to) biting, snappish, mordacious

عضوض *'aḍūḍ* (given to) biting, snappish, mordacious

عضب *'aḍb* sharp, caustic, acid (tongue)

عضد *'aḍada u* (*'aḍd*) to help, aid, assist, support, back (ه ، s.o., s.th.), stand up (ه for s.o.), advocate (ه s.th.) **II** and

III = I; VI to help, assist, or support one another, give mutual help, assistance, or support; to work hand in hand, cooperate

عضد *ʿaḍd* help, aid, assistance, support, backing; helper, aide, assistant, supporter, backer

عضد *ʿaḍud* (m. and f.) pl. اعضاد *aʿḍād* upper arm; strength, power, vigor, force | شد عضده (*ʿaḍudahū*) to aid, assist s.o., stand by s.o.; هو عضده المتين he is an indispensable aid to him

تعضيد *taʿḍīd* help, aid, assistance, support, backing

معاضدة *muʿāḍada* help, aid, assistance, support, backing

تعاضد *taʿāḍud* mutual aid, mutual assistance, cooperation

تعاضدى *taʿāḍudī* cooperative (adj.)

معضد *muʿaḍḍid* helper, aide, assistant, supporter, backer

عضل *ʿaḍila a* (*ʿaḍal*) to be or become muscular; — *ʿaḍala u i* (*ʿaḍl*) to prevent (ها a woman) from marrying IV to be or become difficult, problematic, puzzling, enigmatic, or mysterious (ب or ه for s.o.) | اعضل الداء الاطباء (*aṭibbāʾa*) the disease defied all medical skill, gave the physicians a headache, posed a puzzling problem for the doctors V تعضل الداء الاطباء = اعضل الداء الاطباء

عضل *ʿaḍil* muscular, brawny

عضلة *ʿaḍala* pl. *-āt*, عضل *ʿaḍal* muscle | عضلة باسطة extensor; عضلة قابضة flexor

عضلى *ʿaḍalī* muscle-, musculo-, muscul- (in compounds), muscular

عضال *ʿuḍāl* inveterate, chronic, incurable (disease)

معضل *muʿḍil* difficult, problematic, puzzling, enigmatic, mysterious

معضلة *muʿḍila* pl. *-āt*, معاضل *maʿāḍil*² difficulty, problem, dilemma, puzzle, enigma

عضاه *ʿiḍāh* fair-sized thorny shrubs

عضو *ʿuḍw* pl. اعضاء *aʿḍāʾ* member, limb, organ (of the body); member (of an organization) | عضو اصلى (*aṣlī*) regular member; عضو التأنيث pistil (*bot.*); عضو احتياطى (*iḥtiyāṭī*) substitute member, alternate member; عضو التذكير stamen (*bot.*); عضو فخرى (*fakrī*) honorary member; اعضاء التناسل *a. at-tanāsul* and الاعضاء الدقيقة the sexual organs, the genitals; الدول الاعضاء (*duwal*) the member states; علم وظائف الاعضاء *ʿilm w. al-a.* physiology

عضوات *ʿuḍuwāt* female members

عضوى *ʿuḍwī* organic; لاعضوى or غير عضوى inorganic | كتلة عضوية (*kutla*) organism

عضوية *ʿuḍwīya* pl. *-āt* membership; organism

عطب *ʿaṭiba a* (*ʿaṭab*) to perish, be destroyed, be ruined II to ruin, destroy, wreck, damage, injure, impair, mar, spoil (ه s.th.); to spice, mull (ه s.th.); to brew, mix (ه a drink) IV to ruin, destroy, wreck, damage, injure, impair, mar, spoil (ه, ه s.o., s.th.) V to be damaged VIII = I

عطب *ʿaṭab* perdition; wreck (e.g., of ships); destruction, ruin; damage, injury

تعطيب *taʿṭīb* damaging, ruin(ing), wreck, destruction

تعطب *taʿaṭṭub* a suffering of damage, impairment, ruin

عطر II to perfume, scent (ه, ه s.o., s.th.) V to perfume o.s.

عطر *ʿiṭr* pl. عطور *ʿuṭūr*, عطورات *ʿuṭūrāt* perfume, scent; essence | عطر الورد *ʿi. al-ward* attar of roses, rose oil

عطر *ʿaṭir* sweet-smelling, fragrant, aromatic | سمعة عطرة (*sumʿa*) brilliant or excellent reputation

عطرى *ʿiṭrī* sweet-smelling, fragrant, aromatic

عطرية *ʿiṭrīya* pl. *-āt* aromatic, perfume, scent

عطار *ʿaṭṭār* perfumer, perfume vendor; druggist

عطارة *ʿiṭāra* drug business; perfumeries; drugs

عاطر *ʿāṭir* sweet-smelling, fragrant, aromatic | اثنى عليه عاطر الثناء *aṯnā ʿalaihi ʿāṭira ṯ-ṯanāʾ* to extol s.o. to the skies

معطر *muʿaṭṭar* perfumed, scented

عطارد *ʿuṭārid*² (the planet) Mercury

عطس *ʿaṭasa i u* (*ʿaṭs*, عطاس *ʿuṭās*) to sneeze II to cause (ه s.o.) to sneeze

عطسة *ʿaṭsa* (n. vic.) a sneeze

عطاس *ʿuṭās* sneezing, sneezes

عاطوس *ʿāṭūs* snuff (tobacco)

معطس *maʿṭis* pl. معاطس *maʿāṭis*² nose

عطش *ʿaṭiša a* (*ʿaṭaš*) to be thirsty, to thirst; to long, languish, thirst (الى for) II to make thirsty, cause to thirst (ه, ه s.o., s.th.) IV = II; V to thirst, languish, long, yearn (الى for)

عطش *ʿaṭaš* thirst

عطش *ʿaṭiš* thirsty; dry, parched (soil)

عطشان *ʿaṭšān*², f. عطشى *ʿaṭšā*, pl. عطاش *ʿiṭāš* thirsty; covetous, desirous (الى of), languishing, yearning, craving (الى for)

عاطش *ʿāṭiš* thirsty; covetous, desirous (الى of), languishing, yearning, craving (الى for)

متعطش *mutaʿaṭṭiš* thirsty; covetous, desirous (الى of), languishing, yearning, craving (الى for)

عطشجى *ʿaṭašjī* pl. عطشجية *ʿaṭašjīya* stoker, fireman

عطعط *ʿaṭʿaṭa* to clamor, yell; to be uproarious, very noisy

عطف *ʿaṭafa i* (*ʿaṭf*) to bend, incline, bow (ه s.th.); to incline, lean (الى toward, to); to be favorably disposed (على toward s.o.), be attached (على to s.o.), harbor affection (على for), be fond (على of s.o.), have or feel compassion, sympathize (على with s.o.), feel (على for s.o.); to turn away (عن from); عطف به to incline, dispose s.o. (على toward), awaken affection or sympathy (على for) or interest (على in s.th.); عطف به على to make s.o. appreciate s.th., bring s.th. close to s.o.'s heart; عطف به عن to dissuade, alienate s.o. from II to fold, double, fold up (ه s.th.); to make (ه s.o.) favorably disposed; to soften s.o.'s (ه) heart, move s.o.; to awaken affection, sympathy, tenderness (ه in s.o., على for); to fill with affection, love, etc. (ه s.o., ه s.o.'s heart, على or نحو for) V to be favorably disposed (على toward s.o.), be attached (على to s.o.), be fond (على of s.o.), have or feel compassion, sympathize (على with s.o.), feel (على for s.o.); to deign (ب to do s.th.) | تعطف بالعطاف to put on a coat, wrap o.s. in a coat or cloak VI to harbor mutual affection, be attached to one another VII to be bent, inclined, crooked, or curved; to bend, curve; to bow, make a bow; to turn off (الى toward, to), turn, swing (الى into a road, etc.); to be favorably disposed (الى, على toward), be attached (الى, على to), be fond (الى, على of), have or feel compassion, sympathize (الى, على with), feel (الى, على for s.o.); to turn away, turn around VIII تعطف = اعتطف بالعطاف بالعطاف X to ask for, or seek, s.o.'s (ه) compassion or sympathy; to entreat, beseech, implore (ه s.o.); to affect winning or conciliatory manners, display affection; to seek to conciliate, propitiate, or win over (خاطره *ḵāṭirahū* or ه s.o.); to seek to be friends (ه with s.o.); to try to attract or win (ه s.th.)

عطف *'aṭf* bend(ing), inclination, curving, curvature; corner; sympathy (على with), affection, attachment, liking (على for) | اداة (حرف) العطف *adāt (ḥarf) al-'a.* conjunction (*gram.*); عطف البيان *'a. al-bayān* explicative apposition (*gram.*)

عطف *'iṭf* pl. اعطاف *a'ṭāf* side (of the body) | لين الاعطاف *layyin al-a.* tractable, docile, pliant; ترنحت الاعطاف (*tarannaḥat*) they were carried away, became ecstatic; ضم بين اعطافه to combine, encompass, comprise s.th.

عطفة *'uṭfa* turn, turning, twist, curve, bend; (pl. *-āt*, عطف *'uṭaf*) blind alley, dead end (*eg.*)

عطاف *'iṭāf* pl. عطف *'uṭuf*, اعطفة *a'ṭifa* coat, cloak

عطوف *'aṭūf* compassionate, sympathetic, affectionate, loving, tender, kind

عطوفة *'uṭūfa* affection, attachment, benevolence, good will; (as an honorific title before the name = صاحب العطوفة) His Grace

معطف *mi'ṭaf* pl. معاطف *ma'āṭif*[2] coat, overcoat; smock, frock | معطف مشمع (*mušamma'*) (impregnated) raincoat; معطف فرو *m. farw* fur coat

انعطاف *in'iṭāf* inclination, bend(ing), curving, curvature; sympathy, compassion; liking, attachment, affection

استعطاف *isti'ṭāf* imploring, entreaty, earnest supplication; tender affection; conciliatory attitude

عاطف *'āṭif* compassionate, sympathetic, affectionate, loving, tender, kind | حرف عاطف (*ḥarf*) conjunction (*gram.*)

عاطفة *'āṭifa* pl. عواطف *'awāṭif*[2] amorous affection; affectionate benevolence, solicitude, sympathy, compassion, affection, attachment, liking, kind(li)ness; feeling, sentiment

عاطفى *'āṭifī* sentimental; emotional; emotive, feeling; tender, affectionate, loving

عاطفية *'āṭifīya* sentimentality; emotionalism, emotionality

منعطف *mun'aṭaf* pl. *-āt* (road) turn, curve; turn, turning, winding, tortuosity, twist, bend; lane, alley, narrow street

مستعطف *musta'ṭif* imploring, beseeching, supplicatory; tender, affectionate

عطل *'aṭila a* (*'aṭal*) to be destitute, be devoid (من of s.th.), lack (من s.th.); to be idle, not to work, rest; to be without work, be unemployed **II** to leave without care, to neglect (ه, ه s.o., s.th.); to leave without work, leave idle (ه ه s.o. s.th.); to hinder, hamper, impede, obstruct (ه s.th.); to interrupt, suspend, defer, discontinue, stop (ه s.th., esp. some activity); to ban temporarily, suspend (ه s.th., esp. publication of a newspaper); to damage (gravely), destroy, ruin, wreck, paralyze, neutralize, put out of service or commission, lay up, put out of action, make inoperative (ه s.th.); to stop, shut off (ه s.th., e.g., a motor); to shut down, keep closed (ه s.th., e.g., an office) **V** to remain without work or employment; to be or become unemployed (also تعطل عن العمل); to be or become idle, inactive; to be hindered, hampered, impeded, obstructed, delayed, suspended, deferred, or interrupted; to stop, stall (motor, machine); to fail (apparatus); to be (gravely) damaged, be or be put out of action or commission; to be shut down, be or remain closed; to be no longer valid, be ineffective (statutes)

عطل *'uṭl* destitute, devoid (من of s.th.); impairedness, defectiveness, (gravely) damaged state; damage, loss

عطل *ʿaṭal* unemployment

عطلة *ʿuṭla* unemployment, also عطلة عن الشغل (*šuġl*); leisure, holidays, vacation(s), recess; (pl. *-āt*, عطل *ʿuṭal*) holiday, off day, free day | عطلة رسمية (*rasmīya*) official, or legal, holiday; ايام العطلات الرسمية (*ayyām al-ʿu.*) official, or legal, holidays; عطلة الاسبوع *ʿu. al-usbūʿ* weekend; عطلة قضائية (*qaḍāʾīya*) court recess (*jur.*); عطلة نهاية الاسبوع *ʿu. nihāyat al-usbūʿ* weekend

عطالة *ʿaṭāla* unemployment

تعطيل *taʿṭīl* hindering, obstruction, hampering; discontinuance, interruption, deferment, suspension (of some activity); temporary ban, suspension (of a newspaper); impairment, damaging, destruction, ruining, wrecking, injury; paralyzation, neutralization, stoppage (e.g., of traffic); stopping, shutting-off (of a motor); shutdown, closure (of an office); a theological concept denying God all attributes (as opposed to تشبيه *tašbīh*; *theol.*) | تعطيل حركة المرور *t. ḥarakat al-murūr* traffic congestion

تعطل *taʿaṭṭul* unemployment; inactivity, idleness; (mechanical) failure, breakdown; standstill | تعطل عن العمل (*ʿamal*) unemployment

عاطل *ʿāṭil* destitute, devoid (من of s.th.); inactive, idle, out of work, jobless, unemployed; an unemployed person; useless | عضو عاطل (*ʿuḍw*) functionless organ (*biol.*)

عواطل *ʿawāṭil*² vacations, holidays

معطل *muʿaṭṭil* one who denies God all attributes (*theol.*)

معطل *muʿaṭṭal* inactive, idle, out of work, jobless, unemployed; inoperative, out of action, service, or commission, shut-down; stopped, shut-off (motor); closed (office)

عطن *ʿaṭana* *i u* (*ʿaṭn*) to soak (الجلد *al-jilda* the skin or hide so as to remove the hair, in tanning); to macerate (الكتان *al-kattāna* the flax); — *ʿaṭina a* (*ʿaṭan*) to rot, decay, putrefy (skin, hide, in tanning) **II** = **I** *ʿaṭana*

عطن *ʿaṭan* resting place of camels near a waterhole | ضيق العطن *ḍayyiq al-ʿa.* narrow-minded, parochial; رحب العطن *raḥb al-ʿa.* broad-minded

عطن *ʿaṭin* putrid, rotten, stinking

عطين *ʿaṭīn* putrid, rotten, stinking

عطان *ʿiṭān* tanbark

عطو **III** to give (ه ٥ to s.o. s.th.) **IV** to give (ه ل or ٥ to s.o. s.th.); to present, hand over, offer (ه ٥ to s.o. s.th.); to grant, award, accord (ه ٥ to s.o. s.th.); to present (ه ٥ s.o. with s.th.), bestow (ه ٥ upon s.o. s.th.); pass. *uʿṭiya* to get, obtain, receive (ه s.th.) | اعطى دروسا to give lessons; اعطى اقواله (*aqwālahū*) to give evidence, give one's testimony (*jur.*); اعطى له الكلمة (*kalimata*) to allow s.o. to speak; اعطاه بيده (*bi-yadihī*) to surrender or submit to s.o. **V** to ask for charity, ask for alms (٥ s.o.); to beg **VI** to take (ه s.th.); to swallow, take (ه a medicine); to take over, assume, undertake, take upon o.s. (ه a task); to occupy o.s., be occupied or busy (ه with s.th.), be engaged (ه in s.th.), pursue, practice (ه an activity) **X** = **V**.

عطا *ʿaṭan* gift, present

عطاء *ʿaṭāʾ* pl. اعطية *aʿṭiya* gift, present; (pl. *-āt*) offer, tender | قدم عطاء (*qaddama*) to make an offer or tender

عطية *ʿaṭīya* pl. عطايا *ʿaṭāyā* gift, present

معاطاة *muʿāṭāh* exercise, practice, pursuit (of an activity)

اعطاء *iʿṭāʾ* donation; presentation, grant(ing), award(ing)

تعاط *taʿāṭin* pursuit, practice (of an activity)

استعطاء *isti'ṭā'* begging, mendicity

معط *mu'ṭin* giver, donor

معطى *mu'ṭan* given; (pl. *-āt*) given quantity (*math.*)

مستعط *musta'ṭin* beggar

عظل III عاظل الكلام (*kalāma*) to be repetitious in one's speech, use tautologisms, repeat o.s. in speaking

عظم *'aẓuma u* (*'iẓam*, عظامة *'aẓāma*) to be or become great, big, large, grand, grandiose, magnificent, imposing, powerful, or mighty; to be huge, vast, enormous, tremendous, immense, stupendous; to be hard, distressing, painful, agonizing, or oppressive (على for s.o.) **II** to make, or cause to become, great(er), big(ger), large(r), (more) grandiose, (more) imposing, (more) magnificent, mighty or mightier, (more) powerful (ه, ه s.o., s.th.), enhance the greatness, grandeur, magnificence, power, or might (ه, ه of s.o., of s.th.); to enlarge, enhance, magnify (ه s.th.); to aggrandize, glorify, extol, exalt (ه, ه s.o., s.th.) **IV** = **II**; to attach great importance (ه to s.th.); to regard (ه s.th.) as huge, vast, tremendous, enormous, immense, or stupendous; to find (ه s.th.) hard, distressing, or oppressive **V** to be proud (ب of s.th.); to boast (ب of), vaunt, flaunt (ب s.th.); to be arrogant, presumptuous, haughty **VI** to be proud, arrogant, presumptuous, haughty, supercilious; to be great, grand, grandiose, imposing, huge, prodigious; to equal in weight, significance or importance (ه s.th.); to be weighty, grave, serious, portentous (ه for s.o.) | لا يتعاظمه شأن العدو (*ša'nu l-'adūw*) the enemy's importance does not unduly impress him **X** to be proud, arrogant, presumptuous, haughty, supercilious; to regard as great, significant, or important (ه s.th.)

عظم *'aẓm* pl. اعظم *a'ẓum*, عظام *'iẓām* bone | عظم الساق shinbone; مسحوق العظام bone meal; لين العظام *līn al-'i.* softening of the bones, osteomalacia

عظمى *'aẓmī* bone-, osteo- (in compounds) osseous, bony

عظم *'iẓam*, *'uẓm* greatness, magnitude, grandeur, power, might; significance, importance

عظمة *'aẓma* piece of bone; bone

عظمة *'aẓama* majesty; pride, arrogance, haughtiness; exaltedness, sublimity, augustness | صاحب العظمة His Majesty; His Highness; عظمة السلطان *'a. as-sulṭān* His Highness, the Sultan

عظموت *'aẓamūt* greatness, magnitude, grandeur, power, might

عظيم *'aẓīm* pl. عظماء *'uẓamā'*², عظام *'iẓām*, عظائم *'aẓā'im*² great, big, large; strong, powerful, mighty; significant, important; grand, grandiose, imposing, stately, magnificent; lofty, exalted, august, sublime, splendid, gorgeous, glorious, superb; huge, vast, prodigious, enormous, tremendous, immense, stupendous; hard, distressing, gruesome, trying, oppressive | فرصة عظيمة (*furṣa*) golden opportunity; عظائم الامور great or terrible things; العظماء والكبراء (*kubarā'*) the great of the world

عظيمة *'aẓīma* pl. عظائم *'aẓā'im*² a prodigious, terrible thing; great misfortune, calamity, disaster

عظامى *'iẓāmī* of noble descent, highborn, aristocratic, noble, blue-blooded, of or pertaining to nobility; aristocrat, nobleman

اعظم *a'ẓam*², f. عظمى *'uẓmā*, pl. اعاظم *a'āẓim*² greater, bigger; more significant, more important; greatest, major, supreme; most significant, paramount | اعاظم رجال مصر *a. r. miṣr* the most outstanding men of Cairo; جريمة عظمى capital crime; الحرب العظمى (*ḥarb*) World War I; السواد الاعظم (*sawād*) the great mass, the great majority, the major portion (of the people); الصدر الاعظم (*ṣadr*) (formerly:) title of the Grand Vizier of the Ottoman Empire (Ott.-Turk.: *ṣadr-i aʿẓam*)

تعظيم *taʿẓīm* aggrandizement, glorification, exaltation; military salute

معظم *muʿaẓẓam* glorified, exalted, revered, venerated; sublime, august (esp. of rulers); splendid, gorgeous, glorious, magnificent, resplendent; bony; ossified

معظم *muʿẓam* most of (them), the majority, major part or portion (of), main part; maximum | في معظمه mostly, for the most part, largely

متعاظم *mutaʿāẓim* proud, arrogant, presumptuous, haughty, supercilious

عظة *ʿiẓa* see وعظ

عف *ʿaffa i* (عفة *ʿiffa*, عفاف *ʿafāf*) to refrain, abstain (عن from s.th. forbidden or indecent); to be abstinent, continent, virtuous, chaste, modest, decent, pure **V** = **I**; to shrink (عن from), be shy (عن of), be ashamed

عف *ʿaff* chaste, modest, virtuous, pure; decent; honest, upright, righteous

عفة *ʿiffa* abstinence, continence, virtuousness, virtue, chastity, decency; purity; modesty; integrity, probity, honesty, uprightness, righteousness

عفاف *ʿafāf* = عفة *ʿiffa*

عفيف *ʿafīf* pl. اعفاء *aʿiffāʾ*², اعفة *aʿiffa* chaste, modest, virtuous, pure; decent; honest, upright, righteous

اعف *aʿaff*² chaster, more virtuous; more decent, of greater integrity

تعفف *taʿaffuf* abstinence, continence, chastity, modesty; restraint

متعفف *mutaʿaffif* chaste, modest virtuous, pure; decent; honest, upright righteous

عفر *ʿafara i* (*ʿafr*) to cover with dust, to soil, begrime (also بالتراب *bi-t-turāb*; ه, ه s.o., s.th.) **II** = **I**; to dust, sprinkle with dust or powder (ه s.th.); to glean

عفر *ʿafar* pl. اعفار *aʿfār* dust

عفار *ʿufār* (*eg.*) dust

○ عفارة *ʿaffāra* pl. *-āt* spray, atomizer

اعفر *aʿfar*², f. عفراء *ʿafrāʾ*² dust-colored, earth-colored

يعفور *yaʿfūr* pl. يعافير *yaʿāfīr*² earth-colored gazelle

تعفير *taʿfīr* (act of) dusting, sprinkling with dust or powder

عفرت **II** *taʿafrata* to behave like a demon or devil

عفريت *ʿifrīt* pl. عفاريت *ʿafārīt*² malicious, mischievous; sly, cunning, crafty, wily; afreet, demon, imp, devil; (*eg.*) naughty child | ولد عفريت (*walad*) mischievous child, good-for-nothing, ne'er-do-well (*eg.*)

عفريتة *ʿafrīta* (lifting) jack (*eg.*)

عفرتة *ʿafrata* devilry; dirty trick

عفارم *ʿafārim* (*eg.*) bravo! well done!

عفش *ʿafaša i* (*ʿafš*) to gather, collect, heap up, amass (ه s.th.)

عفش *ʿafš* refuse, rubbish, trash, junk; luggage, baggage; household effects, furniture

عفاشة *ʿufāša*: عفاشة من الناس worthless people

عفص *ʿafṣ* galls, gallnuts, oak apples

عفص *ʿafiṣ* sharp, pungent, acrid, astringent and bitter (of taste)

عفوصة *ʿufūṣa* sharpness, pungency, acridity, astringence (of taste)

عفن *ʿafina a* (*ʿafan*, عفونة *ʿufūna*) to rot, decay, putrefy, spoil; to be rotten, decayed, putrid spoiled; to be or become moldy, musty, mildewy, decomposed **V** = **I**

عفن *ʿafan* rottenness, putridity, decay, spoiledness

عفن *ʿafin* rotten, putrid, decayed, decomposed, spoiled, moldy, musty, mildewy; septic | الحمى العفنة (*ḥummā*) putrid fever

عفونة *ʿufūna* rottenness, putridity, decay, spoiledness

تعفن *taʿaffun* rottenness, putridity, decay, spoiledness

معفن *muʿaffan* rotten, putrid, decayed decomposed, spoiled, moldy, musty mildewy; septic

متعفن *mutaʿaffin* rotten, putrid, decayed, decomposed, spoiled, moldy, musty, mildewy; septic

(عفو) عفا *ʿafā u* (*ʿafw*, عفاء *ʿafāʾ*) to be or become effaced, obliterated, wiped out, eliminated; — *ʿafā u* (*ʿafw*) to efface, obliterate, wipe out, eliminate (عن or ه s.th.); to forgive (عن s.o.); to excuse, free, relieve, exempt (ل عن s.o. from s.th.); to desist, abstain, refrain (عن from) **II** to efface, obliterate, wipe out, eliminate (على or ه s.th.) **III** and **IV** to restore to health, heal, cure (ه s.o.); to guard (عن or من ه s.o. against), protect, save (عن or من ه s.o. from); to free, release, relieve, exempt, except (ه, ه s.o., s.th. عن or من from), excuse, dispense (عن or من ه s.o. from s.th.) **IV** to dismiss, discharge, fire, depose (ه s.o.) **VI** to recuperate, recover, regain health **VIII** to call on s.o. (ه) in order to obtain s.th. **X** to ask s.o.'s (ه) pardon, ask for a reprieve (ه s.o.); to request (ه of s.o.) exemption (من from s.th.); to tender one's resignation (من from an office); to resign (من from an office)

عفو *ʿafw* effacement, obliteration, elimination; pardon, forgiveness; waiver of punishment (*Isl. Law*); amnesty (عن for); boon, kindness, favor; surplus; عفوا *ʿafwan* I beg your pardon! excuse me! (in reply to "thank you") you're welcome! don't mention it!; of one's own accord, by o.s., spontaneously; casually; without design, in passing, incidentally | عفو عام (شامل) (*ʿāmm*) amnesty (عن for); حق العفو عن العقوبة (*ḥaqq al-ʿa.*, *ʿuqūba*) right of granting pardon (*jur.*); عفو الخاطر *ʿafwa l-ḵāṭir* spontaneously, unhesitatingly, casually

عفو *ʿafw* pl. عفاء *ʿifāʾ* young donkey

عفوى *ʿafwī* spontaneous

عفى *ʿafīy* (*eg.*) strong, vigorous, husky, robust

عفاء *ʿafāʾ* effacement, obliteration, extinction, ruin, fall; dust | ادركه العفاء *adrakahū l-ʿafāʾu* to fall into disuse, pass out of use; عليه العفاء it's all over with him, he is done for

معافاة *muʿāfāh* exemption, excuse, dispensation

اعفاء *iʿfāʾ* exemption (from a fee, and the like), excuse, dispensation; remission (of punishment); discharge, dismissal (from an office)

استعفاء *istiʿfāʾ* request for pardon; excuse, apology; resignation (من from an office)

عاف *ʿāfin* effaced, obliterated, wiped out, eliminated

عافية *ʿāfiya* (good) health, well-being; vigor, vitality

معاف *muʿāfan* exempt(ed), free, excused, dispensed (من from); healthy

عق *ʿaqqa u* (*ʿaqq*) to cleave, split, rip, rend (ه s.th.); — *ʿaqqa u* (عقوق *ʿuqūq*) to be disobedient, disrespectful, undutiful, refractory, recalcitrant (اباه *abāhu* or والده *wālidahū* toward his father, of a child)

عق *ʿaqq* disobedient, disrespectful, undutiful, refractory, recalcitrant (child)

عقيق *ʿaqīq* (coll.; n. un. ة) pl. عقائق *ʿaqāʾiq*² carnelian; (pl. أعقة *aʿiqqa*) canyon, gorge, ravine

عقيق *ʿaqīqī* carnelian-red

عقوق *ʿuqūq* disobedience, unruliness, refractoriness, recalcitrance (of a child)

اعق *aʿaqq*² more irreverent, more disrespectful, naughtier | ما اعقك (*aʿaqqaka*) how irreverent you are!

عاق *ʿāqq* disobedient, disrespectful, undutiful, refractory, recalcitrant (child)

عقب *ʿaqaba u* (*ʿaqb*) to follow (ه, ه s.o., s.th. or after s.o., after s.th.), succeed (ه, ه s.o., s.th.); to come after, ensue; to continue **II** to follow (ه, ه s.o., s.th. or after s.o., after s.th.), succeed (ه, ه s.o., s.th.); to pursue, follow, trail (ه, ه s.o., s.th.); to expose, compromise, show up (على s.o.); to revise, correct, rectify, amend; to review critically, criticize (على s.th.), comment (على on s.th.) | عقب آثاره to tread in s.o.'s footsteps **III** to alternate, take turns (ه with s.o.); to punish (على or ب ه s.o. for) **IV** to follow (ه ه s.o., s.th. or after s.o., after s.th.), succeed (ه, ه s.o., s.th.); to come after, ensue; to have for son (ه s.o.), be the father (ه of a son); to have as offspring, have sired (ه s.o.); to revert from evil to good, mend one's ways, reform; to end well, succeed **V** to pursue, follow, trail (ه, ه s.o., s.th.) **VI** to be successive or consecutive, succeed one another, follow one after the other; to dart one by one (على upon), launch successive attacks, act successively, embark successively (على upon)

عقب *ʿaqib*, *ʿaqb* pl. اعقاب *aʿqāb* heel; last part of s.th., end; that which follows subsequently or ensues, subsequence (with foll. genit.); grandson; offspring, progeny: *ʿaqiba* (prep.) immediately after, subsequent to | جاء عقبه (*ʿaqibahū*) or جاء فى عقبه ,جاء بعقبه he came closely after him; على عقب *ʿalā ʿaqibi* immediately after...; رجع (عاد) على عقبيه (*ʿaqibaihi*) pl. رجعوا (عادوا) على اعقابهم to retrace one's steps, turn back; رده على عقبيه (*raddahū*) pl. ردهم على اعقابهم to drive s.o. back to where he came from; ارتد على عقبيه (*irtadda*) pl. ارتدوا على اعقابهم to withdraw, retreat; رأسا على عقب (*raʾsan*) head over heels, topsy-turvy, upside down; from the ground up, radically; ظهرا على عقب (*ẓahran*) do.; فى اعقاب الشهر (*a. iš-šahr*) at the end of the month; اعقاب الصلوات *a. aṣ-ṣalawāt* (supererogatory) prayers performed after the prescribed salat; فى اعقاب الليلة at daybreak, immediately after night was over

عقب *ʿuqb* pl. اعقاب *aʿqāb* end, outcome, upshot; issue, effect, result, consequence; rest, remnant, remainder; (cigarette, etc.) end, butt, stub (of a pencil, of a candle, of a check, etc.); counterfoil

عقبة *ʿaqaba* pl. عقاب *ʿiqāb* steep road or track, steep incline; pass, mountain road; العقبة or قلعة العقبة *qalʿat al-ʿa.* Aqaba (seaport in SW Jordan); (pl. *-āt*, عقاب *ʿiqāb*) obstacle; difficulty | وقف عقبة دون (*ʿaqabatan*) to stand in the way of s.th., obstruct s.th.

عقيب *ʿaqīb* one who, or that which, succeeds or is subsequent; following, subsequent | عقيب ذلك (*ʿaqība*) thereafter, afterwards, subsequently

عقاب *ʿuqāb* (usually f.) pl. اعقب *aʿqub*, عقبان *ʿiqbān* eagle; العقاب Aquila (*astron.*)

عقابى *ʿuqābī* eagle- (in compounds), aquiline

عقيب *ʿuqayyib* a small eagle, eaglet

عقوبة *ʿuqūba* pl. *-āt* punishment, penalty; pl. punitive measures, sanctions | عقوبات اقتصادية (*iqtiṣādīya*) economic sanctions; قانون العقوبات penal code

عقوبى *ʿuqūbī* penal, punitive

عقبى *ʿuqbā* end, outcome, upshot; issue, effect, result, consequence

يعقوب *yaʿqūb*² Jacob, James; *yaʿqūb* (pl. يعاقيب *yaʿāqīb*²) male mountain quail (*zool.*) | لحاجة فى نفس يعقوب *li-ḥājatin fī nafsi y.* for some unknown reason, from secret motives

يعقوبى *yaʿqūbī* pl. يعاقبة *yaʿāqiba* a Jacobite, an adherent of Jacob Baradai; Jacobite (adj.; *Chr.*)

تعقيب *taʿqīb* pl. *-āt* pursuit, chase; investigation; comment(ing); appeal (of a sentence, *jur.*) | دائرة التعقيب court of review, appellate court (*Tun.*)

معاقبة *muʿāqaba* infliction of punishment, punishment; pl. معاقبات sanctions (*pol.*)

عقاب *ʿiqāb* infliction of punishment, punishment; penalty

عقابى *ʿiqābī* penal, punitive

تعقب *taʿaqqub* pl. *-āt* pursuit, chase; investigation

تعاقب *taʿāqub* succession | على تعاقب العصور in the course of centuries

عاقب *ʿāqib*: على العاقب successively

عاقبة *ʿāqiba* pl. عواقب *ʿawāqib*² end, outcome, upshot; issue, effect, result, consequence | سليم العاقبة benign (disease)

معاقب *muʿāqib* alternate; punisher

متعاقب *mutaʿāqib* successive, consecutive, uninterrupted, continuous

عقد *ʿaqada i* (*ʿaqd*) to knit, knot, tie (ه s.th.); to fasten with a knot (ه s.th.); to put together, join, fold, lock (ه one's hands, and the like); to contract (ه the brows, and the like); to fix (ه one's eyes, ب on); to arch, vault (ه a structure); to hold, convene, convoke, summon, call (ه s.th., e.g., a session, a meeting); to conclude (ه a contract), effect (ه a transaction, a sale); to contract (ه a loan) | عقد املا على (*ʿaqada amalan*) to pin, or set, one's hope(s) on...; عقد جبهته (*jabhatahū*) to knit, or wrinkle, one's brows, frown; عقد محادثة (*muḥādatatan*) to strike up a conversation; عقد خطبتها على (*ʿuqida kiṭbatuhā*) she became engaged to...; عقد الخنصر (الخناصر) على (*kinṣir, kanāṣir*) to give s.th. top-rating because of its excellence, put s.th. above everything else; عقد زواجا (*zawājan*) to contract a marriage; عقد العزم (العزيمة) على (*ʿazma*) to make up one's mind to do s.th., be (firmly) determined to do s.th.; عقد لسانه to silence s.o.; عقد لواء الشيء to found, start, originate, launch, produce, kindle, provoke s.th.; السفينة المعقود لها لواء القيادة (*liwāʾu l-q.*) the flagship; البارجة المعقود لواؤها للاميرال (*liwāʾuhā li-l-amīrāl*) the admiral's flagship; عقد ناصيته (*nāṣiyatahū*) = عقد جبهته; عقد نطاقا (*niṭāqan*) to form a cordon (حوله around s.o.); عقد النية على (*nīyata*) to resolve, make up one's mind to do s.th., decide on s.th.; عقد له لواء المجد (النصر) *ʿuqida lahū liwāʾu l-majd* (*n-naṣr*) approx.: he was awarded the laurel of fame (of victory); عقد على المرأة (*ʿalā l-marʾa*) to marry a woman **II** to knit (tightly), knot, tie (ه s.th.); to pile up, mass together (ه e.g., clouds), cluster (ه e.g., vapors, steam); to complicate, make difficult, intricate, or tangled (ه s.th.) **II** and **IV** to congeal, coagulate, clot, thicken, inspissate (ه s.th., esp. by boiling) **V** to be knit (together), knotted, tied with knots; to be or become intricate or complicated; to congeal, coagulate, clot, thicken; to gather (of clouds, etc.) | تعقد لسانه (*lisānuhū*) to express o.s. with difficulty, speak laboringly; to be unable to speak, be tongue-tied **VI** to be interknit, interknotted, interjoined, interlinked; to make a contract; to reach agreement, come to mutual agreement (على on, about) **VII** to be knit (together), knotted, tied with knots, entangled; to contract, become contracted (e.g., brows); to be inhibited (tongue); to congeal, coagulate, clot, thicken; to be concluded (contract), be effected (sale); to convene, assemble, meet (a committee, a conference, and the like) | الاجماع منعقد على ان (*ijmā'*) there is general conviction that ...; لم ينعقد له زهر ولا ثمر (*zahr, ṯamar*) to remain without blossom and fruit, be without any effect and consequence **VIII** to believe (firmly) (ه s.th., ب in)

عقد *'aqd* knitting, knotting, tying; joining, junction, locking; holding, summoning, convocation (of a session, of a meeting); conclusion (of a contract, of a sale); contraction (of a loan, and the like); — (pl. عقود *'uqūd*) contract, agreement, arrangement; legal act, legal transaction; document, deed; vault, arch; group of ten, half-score; decade, decennium | عقد الفى (*alfī*) millennium; عقد الزواج *a. az-zawāj* contraction of marriage, marriage; marriage certificate; عقد القران contraction of marriage, marriage; عقد الملكية *'a. al-milkīya* title deed; انفرط عقدهم (*infaraṭa*) they broke up, they went their own ways

عقد *'iqd* pl. عقود *'uqūd* chaplet, necklace | واسطة العقد center, focus, highlight, chief attraction, pièce de résistance

عقدة *'uqda* pl. عقد *'uqad* knot (also = nautical mile); inch; joint (*anat.*); splice; knot, knur, knob, swelling, nodule, node, protuberance, excrescence, outgrowth; compact, covenant, contract; problem, difficulty; puzzle, riddle; complex (*psychol.*)

عقاد *'aqqād* a producer and seller of cords, braiding and tassels, maker of trimmings

عقادة *'iqāda* manufacture of trimmings, braiding, etc.

عقيد *'aqīd* pl. عقداء *'uqadā'*[2] contracting party, contractant, contractor; a military rank, approx. lieutenant colonel (*Ir.*); colonel (*mil., U.A.R.*)

عقيدة *'aqīda* pl. عقائد *'aqā'id*[2] article of faith, tenet, doctrine; dogma; creed, faith, belief; conviction; ○ ideology | عقيدة خرافية (*kurāfīya*) superstition; فى عقيدتى according to my conviction, as I believe

عقائدى *'aqā'idī* ○ ideological

اعقد *a'qad*[2] (elative) knottier, more knotted; more complicated, more difficult; — *a'qad*[2], f. عقداء *'aqdā'*[2] knotty, knotted, gnarled | عصا عقداء (*'aṣan*) knotty stick, brier cane

معقد *ma'qid* pl. معاقد *ma'āqid*[2] place where s.th. is knotted or tied in a knot or knots; point where s.th. joins or meets, a junction, a juncture, a joint, a seam | معقد آماله the object on which s.o. pins his hopes; لا ياخذ الكرى بمعقد جفنه (*karā bi-m. jafnihī*) no slumber closed his lids

تعقيد *ta'qīd* complication, entanglement, involvement; complicatedness, intricacy, complexity, tangledness; pl. *-āt* intricate, complicated problems

تعقد *ta'aqqud* complicatedness, complexity, intricacy

انعقاد *in'iqād* meeting, convening, session (of a committee, and the like) | دور الانعقاد *daur al-in.* session, term (*parl.*)

اعتقاد *i'tiqād* (firm) belief, faith, trust, confidence, conviction; — (pl. *-āt*) (religious) creed, faith; article of faith; principle of faith, tenet; doctrine; dogma

اعتقادى *i'tiqādī* dogmatic; (pl. *-ūn*) dogmatist | المذهب الاعتقادى (*maḏhab*) dogmatism

عاقد *'āqid* legally competent to contract (*Isl. Law*)

معقود *ma'qūd* knit, knotted, etc., see عقد I; (of milk) curdled | معقود اللسان tongue-tied, incapable of speech | كان الامل معقودا ان (*amalu*) it was hoped that...

معقد *mu'aqqad* knotted, knotty, gnarled; complicated, intricate, entangled, snarled, involved, difficult

معاقد *mu'āqid* contracting party, contractant, contractor

متعاقد *muta'āqid*: المتعاقدان the two contracting parties

معتقد *mu'taqad* believed; المعتقد ان it is believed that ..., it is held that ...; — (pl. *-āt*) article of faith, principle of faith, tenet; doctrine; dogma; creed, faith; conviction, belief, view, opinion

عقر *'aqara i* (*'aqr*) to wound (ه, ه s.o., s.th.); — *'aqura u* and *'aqara i* (*'uqr, 'aqr,* عقارة *'aqāra*) to be barren, sterile; to be childless **III** to be addicted, be given (ه to s.th., e.g., to drinking) **IV** to stun, stupefy (ه s.o.)

عقر *'uqr, 'aqr* barrenness, sterility; middle, center | فى عقر الدار within the house itself (not outside the house); فى عقر داره in his own house; فى عقر ديارهم within the country; in their own country, on their own ground

عقر *'uqr* indemnity for illicit sexual intercourse with a woman slave (*Isl. Law*); childless man

عقار *'aqār* pl. *-āt* immovable property, immovables, real property, real estate, realty; piece of real estate, landed property

عقار *'uqār* residue

عقارى *'aqārī* of or pertaining to immovable property, immovables, landed property, or real estate; consisting in immovable property, immovables, landed property, or real estate; landed | بنك عقارى real-estate bank, land-mortgage bank; رهن عقارى (*rahn*) mortgage on landed property, landed security; القسم العقارى (*qism*) real-estate administration (*Tun.*); ملك عقارى (*milk*) landed property

عقور *'aqūr* mordacious, rapacious, voracious (animal)

عقار *'aqqār* pl. عقاقير *'aqāqīr*[2] drug; medicament, remedy

عقارة *'aqāra* barrenness, sterility

عقيرة *'aqīra* voice

عاقر *'āqir* (f.) barren, sterile (woman)

عقرب *'aqrab* pl. عقارب *'aqārib*[2] scorpion; sting, prick; hand (of a watch or clock); lock, curl; العقرب Scorpio (*astron.*)

معقرب *mu'aqrab* crooked, curved, curled

عقص *'aqaṣa i* (*'aqṣ*) to braid, plait (ه the hair)

عقيصة *'aqīṣa* pl. عقائص *'aqā'iṣ*[2], عقاص *'iqāṣ* braid, plait (of hair), lock

عقعق *'aq'aq* pl. عقاعق *'aqā'iq*[2] magpie (*zool.*)

عقف *'aqafa i* (*'aqf*) to crook, hook, bend sharply (ه s.th.) **II** = **I**

عقفة *'uqfa* pl. *-āt* loop, ring, eyelet (to hold a button, the cords of the *'iqāl*, and the like)

اعقف *a'qaf*[2], f. عقفاء *'aqfā'*[2] crooked, bent, hooked

○ معقف *ma'qif* square bracket

معقوف *ma'qūf* crooked, bent, hooked; bent at the ends, handlebar-shaped (mustache); dual معقوفان square brackets (*typ.*) | الصليب المعقوف the swastika

منعقف *mun'aqif* square bracket | بين منعقفين in square brackets

عقل *ʿaqala* ɪ (*ʿaql*) to hobble with the *ʿiqāl* (عقال q.v.; البعير *al-baʿīra* the camel); to intern, confine, detain, arrest, put under arrest (ه s.o.); to throw (ه s.o.) in wrestling; to pay blood money or wergild (ه ل for the slain to s.o.); to be endowed with (the faculty of) reason, be reasonable, have intelligence; to be in one's senses, be conscious; to realize, comprehend, understand (ه s.th.) | عقل لسانه (*lisānahū*) to tongue-tie s.o., make s.o. speechless **II** to make (ه s.o.) reasonable or sensible, bring (ه s.o.) to reason **V** to be or become reasonable, sensible, rational, intelligent, judicious, prudent, wise; to comprehend, grasp (ه s.th.) **VIII** to arrest, put under arrest, apprehend, detain (ه s.o.); to intern (ه s.o.); to seize, impound (ه s.th.)

عقل *ʿaql* blood money, bloodwite, wergild; (pl. عقول *ʿuqūl*) sense, sentience, reason, understanding, comprehension, discernment, insight, rationality, mind, intellect, intelligence | مختل العقل *muktall al-ʿa.* mentally deranged, demented, insane, mad; سليم (صحيح) العقل sane; ○ العقل الباطن (or اللاشعورى, or غير الواعى) (*lā-šuʿūrī, ġairu l-wāʿī*) the unconscious, the subliminal; ○ العقل الشعورى (or الواعى, or الظاهر) (*šuʿūrī*) the subconscious, the coconscious; ○ العقل المميز (*mumayyiz*) the conscious; ○ عقل الكترونى electronic computer

عقلى *ʿaqlī* reasonable, rational; ratiocinative; mental; intellectual; (pl. *-ūn*) rationalist; an intellectual; العقليات *al-ʿaqlīyāt* the mental world | المذهب العقلى (*madhab*) rationalism; الامراض العقلية mental diseases

عقلية *ʿaqlīya* mentality, mental attitude

عقلة *ʿuqla* pl. عقل *ʿuqal* knot, knob, node (e.g., of a reed, cane, etc.); joint, articulation; knuckle; layer (*hort.*); trapeze

عقال *ʿiqāl* pl. عقل *ʿuqul* cord used for hobbling the feet of a camel; a headband made of camel's hair, holding the *kūfīya* in place | اطلق حربا من عقالها (*aṭlaqa ḥarban*) to unleash or start a war

عقول *ʿaqūl* understanding, reasonable, sensible, discerning, intelligent; costive medicine; (and عاقول *ʿāqūl*) a low spiny shrub of the steppes of North Africa and Western Asia (camel's-thorn, Alhagi maurorum; Alhagi manniferum Desv.; *bot.*)

عقيلة *ʿaqīla* pl. عقائل *ʿaqāʾil*[2] the best, the pick; wife, spouse | السيدة عقيلته (*sayyida*) his wife; عقائل الصفات *ʿa. aṣ-ṣifāt* the very best qualities

اعقل *aʿqal*[2] brighter, smarter, more intelligent

معقل *maʿqil* pl. معاقل *maʿāqil*[2] refuge, sanctuary; stronghold, fortress, fort; ○ pillbox, bunker, dugout (*mil.*); fortified position

معقلة *maʿqula* pl. معاقل *maʿāqil*[2] blood money, wergild

تعقل *taʿaqqul* understanding, discernment, prudence, judiciousness, wisdom | بتعقل sensibly, intelligently

اعتقال *iʿtiqāl* pl. *-āt* arrest, detention, internment; cramp, spasm | معسكر الاعتقال *muʿaskar al-iʿt.* concentration camp

عاقل *ʿāqil* pl. *-ūn*, عقلاء *ʿuqalāʾ*[2], عقال *ʿuqqāl* understanding, reasonable, sensible, rational, discerning, intelligent, prudent, judicious, wise; in full possession of one's mental faculties, compos mentis, sane in mind

عاقلة *ʿāqila* a clan committed by unwritten law of the Bedouins to pay the bloodwite for each of its members

معقول *maʿqūl* reasonable, sensible, intelligible, comprehensible, understandable, plausible, logical; rational; apprehensive faculty, comprehension, intellect, discernment, judiciousness, judgment; common sense | غير معقول unintelligible, incomprehensible, nonsensical, incongruous, preposterous, absurd

معقولية *ma'qūlīya* comprehensibility, intelligibility; logical, rational, or reasonable character, logicality, rationality, reasonableness

معتقل *mu'taqal* pl. *-āt* concentration camp; prison camp; internment camp, detention camp

عقم *'aqama u* and *'aquma u* (*'aqm*; *'uqm*) to be barren, sterile (womb, woman); — *'aqama i* (*'aqm*) to render barren (ه the womb) **II** to render sterile or barren, sterilize (ه, ه s.o., s.th.); to degerminate (ه s.th.); to pasteurize (ه s.th.); to disinfect (ه s.th.) **V** to be rendered barren, be sterilized

عقم *'aqm*, *'uqm*, *'aqam* barrenness, sterility

عقمة *'uqma* barrenness, sterility

عقيم *'aqīm* pl. عقم *'uqum*, عقام *'iqām* barren; sterile; useless, unavailing, futile, fruitless, ineffectual, ineffective, unproductive (e.g., work, attempt)

تعقيم *ta'qīm* sterilization, degermination, pasteurization; disinfection

○ معقم *mu'aqqim* disinfector, disinfecting apparatus

معقم *mu'aqqam* sterilized, pasteurized, disinfected, degerminated

عك *'akka i* (*'akk*) to be sultry, muggy (day)

عك *'akk* sultry, muggy, sweltering

عكة *'akka²*, عكاء *'akkā'²* and عكا *'akkā* Acre (seaport in Palestine)

عكيك *'akīk* sultry, muggy, sweltering (day)

عكر *'akira a* (*'akar*) to be or become turbid, muddy, roily **II** to render turbid, to roil, to muddy (ه or على s.th.); to disturb, trouble (ه or على s.th.) | عكر الصفو (*ṣafwa*) to destroy the untroubled state, disturb the order; عكر صفوه (*ṣafwahū*) and عكر عليه الصفو (*ṣafwa*) to kill s.o.'s good spirits, spoil s.o.'s good humor **V** to become turbid, become muddy; to deteriorate, be aggravated, become worse (situation)

عكر *'akar* turbidity, muddiness; sediment, dregs, lees

عكر *'akir* turbid, muddy, roily; troubled, disturbed

عكارة *'akāra*, *'ikāra* (*eg.*) sediment, dregs, lees

تعكير *ta'kīr* (act of) rendering turbid, roiling, muddying; disturbance, troubling, derangement

معكر *mu'akkar* turbid, sedimentous, roiled, muddy; disturbed, troubled

عكز **V** to lean (على on a staff)

عكاز *'ukkāz*, عكازة *'ukkāza* pl. *-āt*, عكاكيز *'akākīz²* staff, stick; crutch

عكس *'akasa i* (*'aks*) to reverse, invert (ه s.th.); to reflect, throw back, cast back, mirror (ه s.th.) **III** to counteract, oppose, contradict (ه, ه s.o., s.th.), thwart (ه s.th.); to disturb, trouble (ه, ه s.o., s.th.); to molest, vex, tease, harass (ه s.o.) **VI** to be reversed, be inverted; to be thrown back, be cast back, be reflected, be mirrored **VII** to be reversed, be inverted; to turn back (على against); to redound (على to, on); to be thrown back, be cast back (على or عن by), be reflected, be mirrored (على or عن by, in)

عكس *'aks* reversal, reversion, inversion; reflection; opposite, contrast, contrary, reverse | عكس ذلك *'aksa d.* and على عكس ذلك in contrast with that, contrary to that; كان على العكس من to be in contrast to, be in opposition to; بالعكس on the contrary, conversely; والعكس and vice versa; بحث المسألة طردا وعكسا بالعكس

(*mas'alata ṭardan*) he studied the problem from all sides or in all its aspects

عكسى *'aksī* contrary, opposite, contrasting, antithetical, adverse

عكيس *'akīs* layer, shoot, cion (*hort.*)

معاكسة *mu'ākasa* pl. *-āt* disturbance; molestation, pestering, harassment; struggle, fight, battle | معاكسة الحالة الجوية (*jawwīya*) inclemency of the weather

انعكاس *in'ikās* reflection; (pl. *-āt*) reflex

انعكاسى *in'ikāsī* reflectional, reflexive, reflex (adj.) | حركة انعكاسية (*ḥaraka*) reflex action, reflex (*physiol.*)

عاكس *'ākis* screen, lamp shade; reflector

عاكسة *'ākisa* reflector; eye shade; lamp shade

معاكس *mu'ākis* counter-, contra-, anti- | هجمة معاكسة (*hajma*) counterattack

متعاكس *muta'ākis* contrasting, opposite, opposed, conflicting

منعكس *mun'akis* reflected | صورة منعكسة (*ṣūra*) mirror image, reflected image, reflection, reflex; افعال منعكسة reflex actions

عكاشة *'akāša* awkwardness, clumsiness

عكاشة *'ukāša*, *'ukkāša* spider; spider web, cobweb

عكف *'akafa u i* (عكوف *'ukūf*) to adhere, cling, stick, keep (على to); to give o.s. over, apply o.s., devote o.s., be addicted (على to s.th.), indulge (على in s.th.), be obsessed (على by), be bent, be intent (على on s.th.); to be busily engaged (على in), busy o.s. (على with); to remain uninterruptedly (فى in); to seclude o.s., isolate o.s. (فى in, at a place), withdraw, retire (فى into, to a place); — *'akafa u i* (*'akf*) to hold back, restrain, keep (ه عن s.o. from) **II** to hold back, restrain, keep (ه عن s.o. from) **V** to remain uninterruptedly (ه in); to seclude o.s., isolate o.s. (فى in, at a place; عن from), withdraw, retire (فى into, to a place; عن from); to live in seclusion, in retirement (عن from) **VIII** = **V**; to devote o.s., apply o.s. assiduously (الى to s.th.), busy o.s. (ل with)

عاكف *'ākif* pl. *-ūn*, عكوف *'ukūf*, عكف *'ukkaf* given, addicted (على to s.th.); obsessed (على by), bent, intent (على on); busily engaged (على in), busy (على with)

عكم *'akama i* (*'akm*) to bundle up, pack, tie in a cloth, and the like (ه s.th.)

عل[1] *'alu* see علو

عل[2] *'alla*, لعل *la'alla* (particle; with accusative noun immediately following) perhaps, maybe | من يدرى لعل (*man yadrī*) who knows if ...

عل[3] *'alla i* and pass. *'ulla* to be or fall ill **II** to occupy, busy, keep busy, entertain, distract (ه ب s.o. with); to justify, motivate, explain (ه ب s.th. with) | علل نفسه (or النفس) ب to indulge in the hope that ..., entertain or cherish the hope of or that ..., be given to the illusion that ...; علل نفسه بآمال to indulge in hopes; to entertain vain hopes; علل الآمال ب to cherish the hope of ...; علله بالوعود to put s.o. off with promises **V** to occupy o.s., busy o.s., amuse o.s., distract o.s., divert o.s. (ب with); to make an excuse, offer a pretext; to offer or use as an excuse, as a pretext (ب s.th.); to use as an expedient, as a makeshift (ب s.th.) | تعلل بعلة (*bi-'illatin*) to make a pretext, plead s.th. as an excuse **VIII** to be or fall ill; to be weak, defective; to make an excuse, offer a pretext; to adduce, give, offer (ب a reason or excuse, على for s.th.); to pretend, purport, allege, feign, dissimulate, offer as a pretext or excuse (ب s.th.)

علة *ʿilla* pl. *-āt*, علل *ʿilal* illness, sickness, disease, malady; deficiency, defect, weakness; weakness, defectiveness (of a letter or word; *gram.*); metrical variation or irregularity (prosody); — (pl. علل *ʿilal*) cause, reason, occasion; excuse, pretense, pretext, plea | حروف العلة the weak letters (ا, و, ى; *gram.*); على علاته in spite of his weaknesses, such as he is; العلة والمعلول cause and effect; علة العلل فى the principal cause of ..., the deeper reason underlying ...

علة *ʿalla* pl. *-āt* concubine | بنو العلات *banū l-ʿa.* sons of a man by different mothers

عليل *ʿalīl* pl. اعلاء *aʿillāʾ*[2] sick, ill, ailing; sick person, patient; soft, gentle, mild, pleasant

علية *ʿillīya* causality

علية *ʿilya*, *ʿullīya* and عليون *ʿillīyūn* see علو

علالة *ʿulāla* comfort, consolation; remainder, remnant, rest

تعليل *taʿlīl* pl. *-āt* entertainment, diversion, distraction; argumentation, justification, motivation, explanation

تعلة *taʿilla* pl. *-āt* pretext, pretense, excuse; makeshift, expedient, substitute, surrogate

اعتلال *iʿtilāl* illness, sickness, disease, malady; weakness, defectiveness

معلول *maʿlūl* ill, sick, ailing; effect | العلة والمعلول (*ʿilla*) cause and effect; اتخذ المعلول علة *ittakada l-maʿlūla ʿillatan* to mistake cause and effect

معل *muʿall* ill, sick, ailing

معتل *muʿtall* ill, sick, ailing; weak (letter; *gram.*); defective (word; *gram.*)

علب **II** to can, tin, preserve in cans (ه s.th.)

علبة *ʿulba* pl. علب *ʿulab*, علاب *ʿilāb* box, case; can, tin; etui

علج **III** to treat (ه s.o., a patient; ه a disease, also a subject); to occupy o.s., concern o.s., have to do, deal (ه, ه with s.o., with s.th.), attend, turn (ه, ه to s.o., to s.th.); to cultivate (ه s.th., e.g., a literary genre); to take up (ه s.th.), go in (ه for s.th.), apply o.s. (ه to s.th.); to take upon o.s. (ه s.th.), undergo (ه s.th.); to work (ه s.th. or on s.th.), process, treat, manipulate, handle (ه s.th.); to endeavor, take pains, try hard (ان or ه to do s.th.); to palpate, paw, finger, touch (ه s.o.), fumble around (ه on s.o.); to influence (ه s.o.), work (ه upon s.o. by arguments or persuasions), prevail (ه on s.o.) | عالج الرمق الاخير (*ramaqa*) to be on the verge of death, be dying; عالجه بطعنة (*bi-ṭaʿnatin*) to land a stab on s.o., stab s.o. **VI** to be under medical treatment, receive or undergo medical treatment **VIII** to wrestle, struggle, fight (with one another); to be in violent commotion or agitation, heave, surge, tremble

علج *ʿilj* pl. علوج *ʿulūj* infidel; uncouth fellow, lout

معالجة *muʿālaja* treatment (of a patient, also of a subject); nursing (of a patient); cultivation (of an art); manipulation, handling, processing, treatment (of a material, etc.)

علاج *ʿilāj* medical treatment; remedy; cure, therapy

علاجى *ʿilājī* curative, therapeutic

تعالج *taʿāluj* medical treatment (which one undergoes)

علف *ʿalafa* i (*ʿalf*) to feed, fodder (ه livestock)

علف *ʿalaf* pl. اعلاف *aʿlāf*, علاف *ʿilāf*, علوفة *ʿulūfa* fodder, forage, provender

علاف *ʿallāf* pl. ة seller of provender

علوفة *ʿalūfa* pl. علائف *ʿalāʾif*[2] stall-fed animal; — (pl. علف *ʿuluf*) fodder, forage, provender

معلف *mi'laf* pl. معالف *ma'ālif*² manger, trough

معلوف *ma'lūf* stall-fed, fattened (animal)

علق **'aliqa** *a* (*'alaq*) to hang, be suspended, dangle; to stick, cling, cleave, adhere (ب to); to catch (ب on, فى in), get caught or stuck (ب on, فى in); to be attached, affixed, subjoined (ب to s.th.); — (علوق *'ulūq*, علاقة *'alāqa*) to keep (ب to s.o.), be attached, be devoted (ب to s.o.), be fond (ب of s.o.); (with foll. imperf.) to begin, commence to . . ., start doing s.th.; — *'aliqat* (علوق *'ulūq*) to become pregnant, conceive (woman) **II** to hang, suspend (على or ب ه s.th. on), attach, hitch, fasten, affix, tie (ه s.th. على or ب to); to leave undecided, keep pending, keep in abeyance (ه s.th.); to make dependent or conditional (ه s.th. ب or على on); to comment (على on s.th.), annotate, gloss, furnish with notes or a commentary (على s.th.), remark, state (على with regard to); to make notes (ه of s.th.), jot down (ه s.th.) | علق الآمال على to set one's hopes on; علق اهمية (خطورة) على (*ahammīyatan*) to attach importance to s.th. **IV** to hang, suspend (ه ب s.th. on), attach, hitch, fasten, affix, tie (ه ب s.th. to); to apply leeches **V** to hang, be suspended, dangle (ب from); to cling, cleave, adhere (ب to); to keep, stick, hang on (ب to); to be attached, be devoted (ب to), be fond (ب of s.o.); to depend, be dependent or conditional (على or ب on); to refer, pertain, belong, be related (ب to), be connected, have to do (ب with), concern (ب s.th.) | تعلق بحبه (*bi-ḥubbihī*) to be fond of s.o., be affectionately attached to s.o.; فيما يتعلق ب with regard to, as to, regarding, concerning

علق *'ilq*, *'alq* pl. اعلاق *a'lāq* precious thing, object of value

علق *'alaq* (coll.; n. un. ة) pl. *-āt* medicinal leech; leech; (coagulated) blood, blood clot

علقة *'alqa* (*eg.*) beating; bastinado; a thrashing, spanking

عليق *'alīq* pl. علائق *'alā'iq*² fodder, forage, provender

عليق *'ullaiq* twining and creeping plants or shrubs (of various kinds); the lesser bindweed (Convolvulus arvensis; *bot.*); common English blackberry, bramble (Rubus fruticosus; *bot.*); blackberry; raspberry

عليقة *'ullaiqa*: عليقة موسى *'u. mūsā* the Burning Bush

علاق *'allāq* coat hanger

علاقة *'alāqa* attachment, devotion, affection, bond; (pl. *-āt*, علائق *'alā'iq*²) relation, affiliation, association, contact, bond, connection (ب with) | العلاقات العامة public relations; ذو علاقة ب connected with, related to; السلطات ذات العلاقة (*sulṭāt*) the competent authorities; قطع العلاقات (العلائق) *qaṭ' al-'a.* severance of relations; توتر العلاقات (العلائق) *tawattur al-'a.* tenseness of relations, tension in the relations

علاقة *'ilāqa* pl. علائق *'alā'iq*² a strap, and the like, for suspending s.th.

علاقة *'allāqa* coat hanger

اعلق *a'laq*²: اعلق بالذهن (*ḏihn*) that to which the mind is more inclined

معلاق *mi'lāq* pl. معاليق *ma'ālīq*² pluck (of an animal)

تعليق *ta'līq* hanging, suspending; temporary stay, remission or abrogation, suspension; the oblique, "hanging" ductus (in Arabic calligraphy); (pl. *-āt*, تعاليق *ta'ālīq*²) commentary, comment(s), explanatory remarks; suspended lamp | تعليق الطلاق *t. aṭ-ṭalāq* conditional repudiation, conditional pronunciation of the talak (*Isl. Law*); تعليق على الانباء (*anbā'*) news commentary (radio)

تعليقة *taʿlīqa* pl. *-āt*, تعاليق *taʿālīq*[2] marginal note, annotation, note, gloss, scholium

تعلق *taʿalluq* attachment, devotion (ب to), affection (ب for); linkage, connection, relationship (ب with)

معلق *muʿalliq* commentator (radio, press)

معلق *muʿallaq* suspended, hanging; in suspense, in abeyance, pending, undecided; hinging (ب on); depending, dependent, conditional (ب or على on), conditioned (ب or على by) | جسر معلق (*jisr*) suspension bridge; حساب معلق suspense account; قاطرات معلقة suspension railways; مسائل معلقة pending questions; رغبته معلقة ب (*raġbatuhū*) his desire is directed toward ...

معلقة *muʿallaqa* pl. *-āt* placard, poster, bill; المعلقات the oldest collection of complete ancient Arabic kasidas

متعلق *mutaʿalliq* attached, devoted (ب to); connected (ب with), related, pertaining (ب to), concerning (ب s.o. or s.th.) | متعلق بحبه (*bi-ḥubbihī*) affectionately attached to s.o.; من متعلقاته depending on s.o. or s.th., pertaining to s.o.'s authority

علقم *ʿalqam* pl. علاقم *ʿalāqim*[2] colocynth (*bot.*) | ذاق العلقم to taste bitterness, suffer annoyance, vexation, chicanery or torments (من from)

علك *ʿalaka u i* (*ʿalk*) to chew, champ (ه s.th., esp. اللجام the bit, of a horse)

علك *ʿilk* mastic

علم *ʿalima a* (*ʿilm*) to know (ب or ه, ه s.o., s.th.), have knowledge, be cognizant, be aware (ب or ه of s.th.), be informed (ب or ه about or of s.th.), be familiar, be acquainted (ب or ه with s.th.); to perceive, discern (ب or ه s.th.), find out (ب or ه about s.th., من from), learn, come to know (ب or ه s.th. or about s.th., من from); to distinguish, differentiate (ه من s.th. from) II to teach (ه ب or ه ه s.o. s.th.), instruct, brief (ه ب or ه ه s.o. in s.th.); to train, school, educate (ه s.o.); to designate, mark, earmark, provide with a distinctive mark (على s.th.); to put a mark (على on) IV to let (ه s.o.) know (ب or ه s.th. or about s.th.), tell (ب or ه ه s.o. about), notify, advise, apprise, inform (ه ب or ه ه s.o. of or about s.th.), acquaint (ه ب or ه ه s.o. with) V to learn, study (ه s.th.); to know (ه s.th.) X to inquire (ه عن or ه ه of s.o. about), ask, query (ه عن or ه ه s.o. about), inform o.s. (ه عن or ه ه through s.o. about), gather information (ه عن or ه ه from s.o. about)

علم *ʿilm* knowledge, learning, lore; cognizance, acquaintance; information; cognition, intellection, perception, knowledge; (pl. علوم *ʿulūm*) science; pl. العلوم the (natural) sciences | علما وعملا *ʿilman wa-ʿamalan* theoretically and practically; ليكن فى علمه (*li-yakun*) be it known to him, may he know, for his information; كان على علم تام ب (*tāmm*) to know s.th. inside out, be thoroughly familiar with s.th.; to have full cognizance of s.th.; علم الجراثيم bacteriology; علم الاجتماع sociology; علم الحساب arithmetic; علم الحياة *ʿi. al-ḥayāh* biology; علم الاحياء do., علم الحيوان *ʿi. al-ḥayawān* zoology; علم الاخلاق ethics; علم الذرات *ʿi. aḏ-ḏarrāt* nuclear physics; علم التربية *ʿi. at-tarbiya* pedagogy; علم الصحة *ʿi. aṣ-ṣiḥḥa* hygiene; علم الاصوات phonetics; علم المعادن *ʿi. al-maʿādin* mineralogy; علم اللغة *ʿi. al-luġa* lexicography; علم النباتات *ʿi. an-nabātāt* botany; علم النفس *ʿi. an-nafs* psychology; علم وظائف الاعضاء *ʿi. w. al-aʿḍāʾ* physiology; طالب علم *ṭālib ʿilm* student; كلية العلوم *kullīyat al-ʿu.* the Faculty of Science of the Egyptian University

علمى *ʿilmī* scientific; erudite (book); learned (society)

علم *ʿalam* pl. اعلام *aʿlām* sign, token, mark, badge, distinguishing mark, characteristic; harelip; road sign, signpost, guidepost; flag, banner; a distinguished, outstanding man; an eminent personality, an authority, a star, a luminary; proper name (*gram.*) اشهر من نار على علم very famous; اسم علم *ismun ʿalamun* or *ismu ʿalamin* pl. اسماء الاعلام proper name (*gram.*); علم الوصول receipt

عالم *ʿālam* pl. *-ūn*, عوالم *ʿawālim²* world; universe, cosmos; العالمان *al-ʿālamān* the two worlds = Europe and America; عالمون *ʿālamūn* inhabitants of the world, specif. human beings | عالم الحيوان *ʿā. al-ḥayawān* the animal kingdom; عالم المعادن *ʿā. al-maʿādin* the mineral kingdom; عالم النبات *ʿā. an-nabāt* the vegetable kingdom; عالم الوجود this world, this life

عالمى *ʿālamī* worldly, secular, world (adj.); international; world-wide, world-famous, enjoying world-wide renown

عالمية *ʿālamīya* internationality; *ʿālimīya* see after *ʿālim*

علمانى *ʿalmānī*, عالمانى laic, lay; (pl. *-ūn*) layman (in distinction from the clergy)

عليم *ʿalīm* pl. علماء *ʿulamāʾ²* knowing; cognizant, informed; learned, erudite; العليم the Omniscient (one of the attributes of God)

علام *ʿallām* knowing thoroughly (with foll. genit.: s.th.), completely familiar (with)

علام *ʿalāma* see على *ʿalā* (prep.) under علو

علامة *ʿallāma* most erudite, very learned

علامة *ʿalāma* pl. *-āt*, علائم *ʿalāʾim²* mark, sign, token; badge, emblem; distinguishing mark, characteristic; indication, symptom | علامة هذا (*ʿalāmata*) in token of that, as a sign of that; علامة تجارية (*tijārīya*) trade-mark; علامة الرتبة *ʿa. ar-rutba* insignia of rank; ○ علامة التأثر *ʿa. at-taʾaṯṯur* and علامة التعجب *ʿa. at-taʿajjub* exclamation point; علامة الاستفهام question mark; ○ علامة التنصيص quotation mark

عيلم *ʿailam* tender; (pl. عيالم *ʿayālim²*) well with abundant water; sea

اعلومة *uʿlūma* pl. اعاليم *aʿālīm²* road sign, signpost, guidepost

تعلامة *tiʿlāma* most erudite, very learned

معلم *maʿlam* pl. معالم *maʿālim²* place, abode, locality, spot; track, trace; landmark, mark, distinguishing mark, characteristic; road sign, signpost, guidepost; peculiarity, particularity; pl. sights, curiosities; characteristic traits; outlines, contours (e.g., of the body), lineaments, features (of the face)

معلمة *maʿlama* pl. *-āt* encyclopedia

تعليم *taʿlīm* pl. *-āt*, تعاليم *taʿālīm²* information, advice, instruction, direction; teaching, instruction; training, schooling, education; apprenticeship; pl. تعليمات instructions, directions, directives; information, announcements | تعليم مختلط (*mukṭaliṭ*) coeducation; تعليم عال (*ʿālin*) higher education, academic studies; مراقب تعليم *murāqib t.* a military rank, approx.: master sergeant (*Eg.* 1939); صول تعليم *ṣol t.* do. (*Eg.*); ○ فن التعليم *fann at-t.* pedagogy, pedagogics

تعليمى *taʿlīmī* instructional, educational

اعلام *iʿlām* notification, advice; information; notice

تعلم *taʿallum* learning, studying, study; education

استعلام *istiʿlām* inquiry (عن about); (pl. *-āt*) information | مكتب الاستعلامات *maktab al-ist.* information office, information desk; news agency, press agency, wire service

عالم *ʿālim* knowing; familiar, acquainted (ب with), cognizant (ب of); expert, connoisseur, professional; (pl.

علماء *ʿulamā'*[2]) learned, erudite; scholar, savant, scientist | عالم طبيعى (*ṭabīʿī*) physicist, natural scientist; العلماء المختصون (*muktaṣṣūn*) the specialists, the experts

عالمة *ʿālima* woman of learning, woman scholar; (*eg.*) singer, chanteuse

عالمية *ʿālimīya* learnedness, scholarliness, erudition, rank or dignity of a *ʿālim*; rank of scholarship, conferred by diploma, of the Great Mosque in Tunis and of Al Azhar in Cairo

اعلم *aʿlam*[2] having more knowledge; more learned | الله اعلم God knows best

معلوم *maʿlūm* known; fixed, determined, given; of course! certainly! sure! no doubt! (as an affirmative reply); known quantity (*math.*); المعلوم the active voice (*gram.*); — (pl. معاليم *maʿālīm*[2]) fixed sum, fixed rate (money); fixed income; tax, duty, fee; sum, amount, cost(s) | معلوم الحيوانات *m. al-ḥayawānāt* impost on livestock (*Tun.*); — pl. معلومات *maʿlūmāt* knowledge, lore, learning, perceptions, discoveries, findings; known facts; information, data; news, tidings

معلم *muʿallim* pl. *-ūn* teacher, instructor; master (of a trade, etc.) | معلم الاعتراف father-confessor, confessor

معلمة *muʿallima* pl. *-āt* woman teacher, woman instructor

معلم *muʿallam* taught, instructed, trained, schooled; معلم عليه designated, marked | معلم عليه بالاحمر marked with red pencil

متعلم *mutaʿallim* apprentice; educated; an educated person

علن *ʿalana u*, *ʿaluna u* (علانية *ʿalāniya*) to be or become known, manifest, evident **III** to indicate, make known, reveal, disclose (ه ب to s.o. s.th.) **IV** to manifest, reveal, make known (ه s.th.); to make public, publicize, publish, disclose, declare, announce, proclaim, promulgate (ه s.th.); to state frankly (ه الى to s.o. s.th.); to announce (ان that); to issue a summons (الى to s.o.); to give notice (عن of); to advertise (عن s.th., e.g., the rent or sale of s.th. in a newspaper); to give evidence (عن of), indicate, show, betray, bespeak (عن s.th.) | اعلن الحرب عليه (*ḥarba*) to declare war on s.o. **VIII = I; X = I;** to seek to bring out or to disclose (ه s.th.); to bring to light (ه s.th.)

علنا *ʿalanan* openly, overtly, publicly, in public

علنى *ʿalanī* open, overt, public

علن *ʿalin* open, overt, public; evident, patent

علانية *ʿalāniya* openness, overtness, publicness, publicity (as opposed to secrecy); *ʿalāniyatan* openly, overtly, publicly, patently, in public

اعلان *iʿlān* pl. *-āt* publication, promulgation; revelation, manifestation; proclamation; declaration, statement, pronouncement; announcement, notice; advertising, publicity (عن for); advertisement, ad; poster, bill, placard | اعلان حضور *i. ḥuḍūr* summons; اعلان الحرب *i. al-ḥarb* declaration of war; اعلان عدم الثقة *i. ʿadam aṯ-ṯiqa* vote of "no confidence"; اعلانات مبوبة (*mubawwaba*) classified ads; اعلانات ضوئية (*ḍauʾīya*) electric signs, sky signs

معلن *muʿlin* announcer, master of ceremonies (e.g., in a cabaret)

معلن *muʿlan*: معلن اليه summoned (before a court)

علو (علا and علي) علا *ʿalā u* (*ʿulūw*) to be high, elevated, rise high, loom, tower up; to rise, ascend; to ring out (voice); to heave (chest); to be higher or taller (عن or ه, ه than s.o., than s.th.), (over)top (عن or ه, ه s.o., s.th.), tower (عن or ه, ه over s.o., over s.th.), be located or situated higher (عن or ه than s.th.); to be attached, fixed or fastened above or on top of s.th.(ه); to rise (عن or ه above s.th.); to exceed, excel, surpass (ه, ه or عن s.o., s.th.); to be too high (ه, ه or عن for s.o., for s.th.); to overcome, overwhelm (على or ه s.o.), get the better of s.o. (ه); to turn upward; to ascend, mount, climb, scale (ه s.th.); to overspread, cover (ه s.th.), come, descend (ه, ه upon s.o., upon s.th.), befall, seize (ه, ه s.o., s.th.) | علا به to raise s.th. or s.o.; to exalt, extol s.o.; علت به السن (*sinnu*) he had attained great age, he was an old man; علا صوته ب (*ṣautuhū*) his voice rang out with ..., he exclaimed ... aloud; — علي *ʿaliya a* (علاء *ʿalāʾ*) to be high, elevated; to excel, stand out, surpass; — على *ʿalā i* (*ʿaly*) to climb (السطح *as-saṭḥa* to the roof) | علا الاداة الصدأ (*adāta, ṣadaʾu*) rust has covered the tool; علت وجهه صفرة الاموات *ʿalat wajhahū ṣufratu l-a.* deathly pallor suffused his face; علته السآمة *ʿalathu s-saʾāma* he was overcome by fatigue; علت شفتيه رغوة *ʿalat šafataihi raḡwa* foam appeared on his lips **II** to raise, raise aloft, lift, hoist, lift up, elevate, uplift, exalt (ه, ه s.o., s.th.) **IV** = **II** | اعلى شأنه (*šaʾnahū*) to play up, stress, emphasize s.th., put emphasis on s.th.; to further, promote, advance s.th.; to raise s.o.'s prestige **V** to rise, become high **VI** to rise, lift, ascend, rise aloft; to resound, ring out; to be high, exalted, sublime (esp. of God); to deem o.s. above s.o. or s.th. (على), look down (على on s.o., on s.th.); to stay away (عن from); تعال *taʿāla* come (here)! come on! let's go! forward! **VIII** to rise, lift, ascend, rise aloft; to rise high, tower up; to mount, ascend, climb, scale (ه s.th.); to step (up) (ه on s.th.); to be enthroned, be perched (ه on s.th.); to tower (ه above s.th.); to ascend the throne; to accede to a high office **X** to rise, tower (على above); to master (على s.th.); to take possession (على of s.th.), appropriate (على s.th.)

عل *ʿalu*: من عل *min ʿalu* from above

علو *ʿulūw* height, tallness, elevation, altitude; greatness, grandeur, highness, exaltedness, sublimity | علو الصوت *ʿu. aṣ-ṣaut* sound volume, sound intensity; علو الكعب *ʿu. al-kaʿb* high, outstanding position

علوى *ʿulwī* upper; heavenly, divine | ارادة علوية (*irāda*) supreme will, divine decree

علوى *ʿalawī* upper; heavenly, celestial; Alawi (adj. and n.); pl. العلويون the Alawis (official name of the Nusairis inhabiting the coastal district of Latakia in NW Syria)

علا *ʿulan* height, tallness, elevation, altitude; highness, exaltedness, augustness, sublimity; high rank

على *ʿalā* (prep.) on, upon, on top of, above, over (place, rank); at, on, by; in, in the state of, in the manner of, in possession of; to, toward, for; in addition to; to the debit of, to the disadvantage of; against, in spite of, despite; on the basis of, on the strength of, by virtue of, due to, upon; by, through; according to, in accordance with, pursuant to; to (one's taste, one's mind, one's liking, etc.); during; (as to syntactical regimen see under respective verb) | من على from above ..., from upon ..., from the top of ...; على ان (*an, anna*) on the condition that ..., provided that ...; although, though, albeit; على ان (*anna*) (introducing a main clause) however, but, on the other hand, nevertheless, yet, still, ... though; على انه (in the subjective notion or view that ..., i.e.) as, e.g.: جنى ثمرات الارض على انها نعمة الآلهة

janā ṯamarāti l-arḍi ʿalā annahā niʿmatu l-āliha he reaped the fruits of the earth (accepting them) as a boon bestowed by the grace of the gods; على ظهر الخيل (*ẓahri l-ḵail*) on horseback; على ظهر الباخرة aboard the steamer; السلام عليكم (*salāmu*) may peace be upon you! على الرأس و العين *ʿalā r-raʾs wa-l-ʿain* very gladly! with pleasure! على رؤوس الاشهاد publicly, for everyone to see; جلس على النار he was sitting by the fire; على يمينه (*yamīnihī*) to (at) his right; على كل حال (*kulli*) or على كل (*kullin*) in any case, at any rate; على الخصوص especially, particularly, specifically; على الاطلاق (*iṭlāq*) absolutely, unrestrictedly, without exception, in any respect, under any circumstances; على التقريب approximately, almost, nearly, about, circa; على التوالى (*tawālī*) continuously, incessantly, in uninterrupted succession; على ضوء (*ḍauʾi*) or على نور (*nūri*) in the light of ...; كان على حق (*ḥaqqin*) or كان على الحق to be on the right way, have hit on the right thing, be right; كان على الباطل or كان على خطأ (*ḵaṭaʾin*) to be on the wrong way, be wrong, be mistaken; هو على احسن ما يرام (*aḥsani, yurāmu*) he is as well as you can possibly wish (for him); هو على شىء من ... he has certain ...; هو على شىء من الذكاء (*ḏakāʾ*) he has a good deal of intelligence; ليس هذا على شىء there is nothing in it, it's worthless; ليس من هذا كله على شىء all this is unfamiliar to him; he doesn't understand a thing about it; كان على دين المسيح (*dīni l-m.*) to belong to the Christian religion, be a Christian; كان على علم ب (*ʿilmin*) to be informed about, be acquainted with ...; كان على انتظاره to wait for s.o. or s.th.; على غير شىء for no reason; على بصيرة من الامر in cognizance of the matter, knowing the matter; على غير معرفة منه (*maʿrifatin*) without his knowing about it, without his knowledge, unwittingly; عليك ب (ـه, ه or) take ...! help yourself to ...! make use of ...! عليك بالصبر (*bi-ṣ-ṣabr*) you must have patience! علينا به he is the one we must have! على به (*ʿalayya*) bring, give him (or it) to me! I must have him (or it)! عليه ان it is incumbent on him to ..., it's his duty to ...; he must ..., he will have to ...; لا عليك don't worry! لا عليه never mind! it's nothing! no harm done! (indicating forgiveness, indulgence); ما علينا what of it? what does it matter? let's forget it! ما عليك من don't worry about ..., don't mind ..., don't give ... a thought; ما عليه ان he doesn't care if ...; it's of little importance to him that ...; على حسابه (*ḥisābihī*) at his expense; عليه دين (*dain*) he is in debt(s); هو على سنه قوى (*sinnihī qawīy*) he bears his years well; علام *ʿalāma* wherefore? what for? why? استيقظ على الاذان *istaiqaẓa ʿalā l-aḏān* he awoke over the call to prayer, he was awakened by the azan; قيل على لسانه ما (*qīla, lisānihī*) he was supposed to have said things which ..., statements were ascribed to him which ...; على يده (*yadihī*) through him, by him, at his hand; على ذلك in this manner, thus; accordingly, hence; على ما يقال (*yuqālu*) as they say, as it is said; على حسب *ʿalā ḥasabi* (prep.) according to, in accordance with, commensurate with, depending on; على طوع منها (*ṭauʿin*) with her obeying, without opposition on her part; على عادته according to his habit, as was his wont, as he used to do; على حين غفلة (*ḥīni ḡaflatin*) suddenly, all of a sudden, unawares, unexpectedly; على عهد (*ʿahdi*) at the time of

على *ʿalīy* high, tall, elevated; exalted, sublime, lofty, august, excellent; العلى the Most High, the Supreme (one of the attributes of God) | الدولة العلية (*daula*) name of the old Ottoman Empire

علية *ʿilya* (pl. of على *ʿalīy*): علية الناس, علية القوم upper class, people of distinction, prominent people

علية *'ullīya, 'illīya* pl. علالى *'alālīy* upper room, upstairs room

عليون *'illīyūn* the uppermost heaven; loftiest heights

علاء *'alā'* high rank, high standing, nobility

علاة *'alāh* pl. علا *'alan* anvil

علياء *'alyā'*[2] loftiness, exaltedness, sublimity, augustness; lofty height; heaven(s) | اهل العلياء *ahl al-'a.* people of highest social standing

علاوة *'ilāwa* addition; increase, raise, extra allowance, subsidy | علاوة على (*'ilāwatan*) in addition to

علاية *'alāya* height, loftiness

اعلى *a'lā*, f. عليا *'ulyā*, pl. على *'ulan*, اعال *a'ālin* higher, highest; upper, uppermost; اعال *a'ālin* the highest portion of s.th.; heights, peaks (fig.) | اعلاه *a'lāhu* further up, above; مذكور اعلاه above-mentioned; مؤتمر (منعقد) على اعلى مستوى (*mu'tamar mun'aqid, mustawan*) top-level conference; باعلى صوت *bi-a'lā ṣautin* very loud, at the top of one's voice; سفينة اعالى البحار seagoing vessel; اعالى النيل *a. n-nīl* the upper course of the Nile

معال *ma'ālin* (pl.): معالى الامور noble things; صاحب المعالى or معاليه *ma'ālīhi* His Excellency, معالى الوزير His Excellency the Minister (title of cabinet ministers)

تعلية *ta'liya* elevation, enhancement, uplift, exaltation; raising (e.g., of the voice)

اعلاء *i'lā'* elevation, enhancement, uplift, exaltation; raising, lifting | اعلاء شأن الشيء *i. ša'ni š.* boosting, furtherance, promotion, or advancement of s.th.

اعتلاء *i'tilā'* ascension (e.g., to the throne); accession to office (e.g., of a cabinet minister)

استعلاء *isti'lā'* superiority

عال *'ālin* high, tall, elevated; loud, strong (voice); higher (as opposed to elementary); lofty, exalted, sublime, high-ranking, of high standing; excellent, first-class, first-rate, outstanding, of top quality (commodity) | الباب العالى the Sublime Porte; ضغط عال (*ḍaġṭ*) high voltage, high tension (*el.*); تواتر عال (*tawātur*) high frequency (*el.*); عاليه *'āliyahū* above, above-mentioned (in letters; esp. in official and business style); مذكور بعاليه (*bi-'ālīhi*) above-mentioned; (*eg.*) عال العال *'āl al-'āl* excellent, first-rate, top-quality, A-1 (merchandise)

متعال *muta'ālin* high, elevated, lofty, exalted; resounding, ringing; المتعالى the Most High, the Supreme Being (one of the attributes of God)

عنون = علون

عنوان = علوان

على see علو, علاية, علياء, عليون, علية

[1]عم abbreviation of the formula عليه السلام (*salāmu*) may peace be upon him!

[2]عم *'amma* = عما (< عن ما),

[3]عم *'amma u* (عموم *umūm*) to be or become general, universal, common, prevalent, comprehensive, all-embracing, to spread, prevail; — *'amma u* to comprise, include, embrace, encompass, pervade (ه s.th.), extend, stretch, be spread, be diffused, be prevailing (ه all over s.th.) عمت البلوى به (*balwā*) it has become a general necessity **II** to generalize (ه s.th.); to spread universally, universalize, popularize, democratize (ه s.th.); to make (ه s.th.) universally accessible, open (ه s.th.) to the public at large; to introduce (ه s.th.) universally; to attire (ه s.o.) with a turban **V** to put on or wear a turban **VIII** = **V**

عم *'amm* pl. عموم *'umūm*, اعمام *a'mām* father's brother, paternal uncle | ابن العم

ibn al-ʿamm cousin on the father's side; بنت العم *bint al-ʿamm* female cousin on the father's side

عمة *ʿamma* pl. *-āt* paternal aunt

عمة *ʿimma* turban

عميم *ʿamīm* general, universal, common, prevalent; all-comprehensive

عموم *ʿumūm* generality, universality, prevalence; whole, total, totality, aggregate; العموم the (general) public, the public at large; عموما *ʿumūman* in general, generally | عموما — خصوصا in general — in particular; على العموم in general, generally; بوجه العموم *bi-wajhi l-ʿu.* generally speaking, in general; فى عموم القطر (*ʿu. il-quṭr*) throughout the country; مجلس العموم *majlis al-ʿu.* the House of Commons, the Lower House; *ʿumūm* frequently replaces عمومى *ʿumūmī* in compound terms of administrative language, e.g.: جامعة عموم العمال *j. ʿu. al-ʿummāl* general federation of labor; ادارة عموم الجمارك General Administration of Customs and Tariffs (*Eg.*); ديوان عموم المصلحة (*dīwān ʿu. al-maṣlaḥa*) administration headquarters, chief administration office; ديوان عموم المالية *d. ʿu. al-mālīya* General Administration of Finances (*Eg.*); تفتيش عموم الرى *t. ʿu. ar-riyy* General Inspectorate of Irrigation (*Eg.*); مفتش عموم النيل الجنوبى *mufattiš u. an-nīl al-janūbī* Inspector General for the Southern Nile (*Eg.*)

عمومى *ʿumūmī* public; universal; general; common; state, civil, public | جمعية عمومية (*jamʿīya*) plenary session; general assembly; دار الكتب العمومية (*dār al-kutub*) public library; اشغال عمومية public works; الصندوق العمومى (*ṣundūq*) public treasure

عمومة *ʿumūma* uncleship, unclehood; pl. of عم *ʿamm*

عمامة *ʿimāma* pl. عمائم *ʿamāʾim*[2] turban

تعميم *taʿmīm* generalization, universalization, general propagation or diffusion, popularization, democratization; vulgarization

عام *ʿāmm* public; universal, prevalent; general; common | الامن العام (*amn*) public security; مدير عام (*mudīr*) director general, general manager; الرأى العام (*raʾy*) public opinion; الصالح العام or المصلحة العامة (*maṣlaḥa*) public welfare, the commonweal; الخاص والعام (*ḵāṣṣ*) high and low, all men, all, everybody (also العام والخاص)

عامة *ʿāmma* generality; commonalty; the masses, the people; عامة *ʿāmmatan* in general; generally; commonly, altogether, in the aggregate, collectively | خاصة — عامة (*ḵāṣṣatan*) in particular — in general; عامة الناس the common people, the masses, the populace; الخاصة والعامة (*ḵāṣṣa*) high and low, all men, all, everybody

العوام *al-ʿawāmm* (pl. of عامة *ʿāmma*) the common people, the populace; the laity (*Chr.*)

عامى *ʿāmmī* common, vulgar, plebeian, ordinary, popular; ordinary person, man in the street; العامية *al-ʿāmmīya* popular language, colloquial language

معمم *muʿammam* wearing a turban, turbaned

عماه *ʿammā* = عن ما

عمد *ʿamada* i (*ʿamd*) to support, prop, shore, buttress (ه s.th.); to intend, purpose (ل or الى or ه s.th.); to betake o.s., repair, go (ل or الى or ه to); to approach, undertake (ل or الى s.th.), go, set (ل or الى about s.th.), proceed, apply o.s., turn, attend (ل or الى to), embark (ل or الى upon); to take up (الى s.th.); to be intent (الى on s.th.); — *ʿamada* i to baptize, christen (ه s.o.) II to baptize, christen (ه s.o.) IV to support, prop, shore, buttress (ه

s.th.); to baptize, christen (ه s.o.) **V** to intend, purpose, do intentionally, do on purpose (ه s.th.); to approach (ه s.th.) with a definite aim in mind; to single out (ه s.o.), aim (ه, ه at); to be baptized, be christened | ما تعمدها باهانة (*ihāna*) he was not out to insult her, he had no intention of offending her **VIII** = **V**; to lean (على against), support one's weight (على on); to rely, depend (ه, ه or على on s.o., on s.th.); to use as a basis (ه or على s.th.); to employ, use, apply (ه s.th., e.g., a new method); to confirm (ه s.th.); to sanction, authorize (ه s.th.); to loan, give on credit (ه ل to s.o. a sum)

عمد *ʿamd* intention, intent, design, purpose; premeditation, willfulness (*jur.*); عمدا *ʿamdan* intentionally, deliberately, on purpose; willfully, premeditatedly (*jur.*) | شبه العمد *šibh al-ʿa.* quasi-deliberate intent (*Isl. Law*)

عمدى *ʿamdī* intentional, deliberate; premeditated, willful (*jur.*)

عمدة *ʿumda* support, prop, shore; main subject, main issue, basic issue (e.g., of a controversy); (pl. عمد *ʿumad*) chief of a village, chief magistrate of a small community (*eg.*); mayor

عماد *ʿimād* pl. عمد *ʿamad* support, prop, stay (also fig.); bracket, buttress, post, pole, pillar; — *ʿimād* baptism

عميد *ʿamīd* pl. عمداء *ʿumadāʾ*[2] support; head, chief; dean (of a faculty); principal, headmaster, director (of a secondary school); doyen, dean (as, of a diplomatic corps); high commissioner (also العميد السامى), resident general; military ranks, approx. major (*Eg.* 1939), approx. lieutenant commander (*Eg.* 1939), approx. (commanding) general (*Ir.*), lieutenant colonel (*U.A.R.*) | عميد ثان (*tānin*) a military rank intermediate between those of major and captain, Brit.: adjutant-major (*Eg.* 1939); a naval rank intermediate between those of lieutenant commander and lieutenant (*Eg.* 1939)

عميدة *ʿamīda* principal, headmistress, directress (of a secondary school for girls)

عمود *ʿamūd* pl. اعمدة *aʿmida*, عمد *ʿumud* flagpole, shaft (of a standard); pale, post, prop, shore, pier, buttress; lamppost; (telephone, telegraph) pole; column, pillar, pilaster; stem (of a glass); — (pl. اعمدة) column (of a newspaper); ○ element, cell (*el.*) | العمود الشوكى (*šaukī*) the vertebral column, the spine; العمود الفقرى (*faqrī*) do.; ○ عمود كهربائى (*kahrabāʾī*) electrode

عامود *ʿāmūd* pl. عواميد *ʿawāmīd*[2] = عمود *ʿamūd* | ○ عامود القيادة steering column, steering mechanism (of an automobile)

عمودى *ʿamūdī* columnar, pillar-shaped; vertical, perpendicular, upright | طائرة عمودية helicopter

يوحنا المعمدان *yūḥannā l-maʿmadān* John the Baptist

تعميد *taʿmīd* baptism

تعمد *taʿammud* intention, intent, design; resolution, determination, purpose; تعمدا *taʿammudan* and بتعمد intentionally, deliberately, willfully, on purpose, premeditatedly

تعمدى *taʿammudī* intentional, deliberate, premeditated, willful

اعتماد *iʿtimād* reliance, dependence (على on), confidence, trust (على in); confirmation; sanction, approbation, authorization; accreditation (of diplomats); (pl. *-āt*) credit, loan | الاعتماد على النفس (*nafs*) self-confidence, self-reliance; كتب الاعتماد *kutub al-iʿt.* or اوراق الاعتماد *aurāq al-iʿt.* credentials (of diplomats); اعتماد اضافى (*iḍāfī*) supplementary loan

معمودية *maʿmūdīya* baptism; baptismal font

معمد *muʿammad* baptizee, one receiving baptism

متعمد *mutaʿammid* deliberate, premeditated, willful; intentional

معتمد *muʿtamad* reliable, dependable; object of reliance, support; sanctioned, approved, authorized; accredited; commissioner, authorized agent, proxy, envoy, representative; commissary, commissar | المعتمد السامى (*sāmī*) the High Commissioner; معتمد قنصلى (*qunṣulī*) consular agent (*dipl.*)

معتمدية *muʿtamadīya* legation (*dipl.*)

عمر *ʿamara u i* (*ʿamr, ʿumr*) to live long, be longevous; — *u i, ʿamura u* (عمارة *ʿamāra*) to thrive, prosper, flourish, flower, bloom; to be or become inhabited, peopled, populated, civilized, cultivated; to be full, filled, filled up; — *ʿamara u* to fill with life, cause to thrive, make prosperous; to inhabit (ه s.th.), live, dwell (ه in s.th.); to fill, pervade (جوانحه s.o.'s heart), reign (جوانحه in s.o.'s heart); to build, erect, construct, raise, rebuild, reconstruct, restore (ه s.th.) **II** to let (ه s.o.) live, preserve (ه s.o.) alive; to prolong s.o.'s (ه) life, grant long life (ه to s.o.; of God); to populate, people (ه s.th.); to build, erect, construct, raise, rebuild, reconstruct, restore, repair, overhaul, refurbish, recondition (ه a building); to provide, furnish, supply, fill (ه ب s.th. with, e.g., the lamp with oil, the censer with charcoal, the goblet with wine); to load (ه a gun); to fill (ه a pipe); to fill in (ه a form, a blank; *tun.*) | عمر وقته (*waqtahū*) to take up, or claim, s.o.'s time **IV** to populate, people (ه s.th.); to perform the *ʿumra* (q.v.) **VIII** to visit (ه, ه s.o., s.th.); to perform the *ʿumra* (q.v.) **X** to settle (ه ق s.o. in); to settle, colonize (ه s.th.); to turn (ه a country) into a colony

عمر *ʿumr* (*ʿamr* in oaths) pl. اعمار *aʿmār* life, duration of life, life span, lifetime; age (of a person) | لعمرى *la-ʿamrī* upon my life! لعمر الله *la-ʿamru llāhi* by the everlasting existence of God! by the Eternal God! ذات العمرين *ḏāt al-ʿumrain* amphibian (n.); عمره عشرين سنة (*ʿišrīna sanatan*) he is twenty years old

عمرة *ʿamra* headgear (e.g., turban); (*eg.*) repair, repair work

عمرة *ʿumra* pilgrimage to Mecca (the so-called "minor hadj" which, unlike the hadj proper, need not be performed at a particular time of the year and whose performance involves fewer ceremonies)

عمرى *ʿumrā* donation for life (*Isl. Law*)

عمارة *ʿamāra* (naval) fleet

عمارة *ʿimāra* pl. *-āt*, عمائر *ʿamāʾir*[2] building, edifice, structure; real estate, tract lot; العمارة or فن العمارة *fann al-ʿi.* or هندسة العمارة *handasat al-ʿi.* architecture, art of building

عمران *ʿumrān* inhabitedness, activity, bustling life, thriving, flourishing, prosperity (as opposed to خراب *ḵarāb*); populousness and prosperity (of a country); culture, civilization; building, edifice, structure

عمرانى *ʿumrānī* cultural, civilizational; serving, or pertaining to, cultural development

عمارية *ʿammārīya* camel-borne sedan and the virgin riding in it into battle

اعمر *aʿmar*[2] more inhabited, more populated, more populous; more cultivated, more civilized; more flourishing, more thriving

معمار *miʿmār* builder, architect; mason

معمارى *mi'mārī* architectonic, architectural; — (pl. *-iya*) builder, architect; mason | مهندس معمارى (*muhandis*) builder, architect; الفن المعمارى (*fann*) art of building, architecture

تعمير *ta'mīr* building, construction, erection; restoration, repair, overhauling, refurbishing, reconditioning; filling, filling-up

تعميرة *ta'mīra* filling, filling-up

استعمار *isti'mār* colonizing, colonization, foundation of colonies; imperialistic exploitation; imperialism, colonialism

استعمارى *isti'mārī* colonial; colonizer; imperialistic

استعمارية *isti'mārīya* imperialism, colonialism

عامر *'āmir* inhabited; peopled, populated, populous; full, filled, filled up; jammed, crowded, filled to capacity (ب with); amply provided, splendidly furnished; civilized; cultivated (land); flourishing, thriving, prosperous; العامر is a frequent epithet of castles, palaces, etc., of ruling houses | عامر بالامل (*amal*) full of hope; عامر الجيب *'ā. al-jaib* with a full pocket; عامر الذمة ل (*'ā. aḏ-ḏimma*) obliged to s.o., committed to s.o.; عامر النفس ب (*'ā. an-nafs*) obsessed by, possessed by; ام عامر *umm 'āmir* hyena (*zool.*); نهود عامرة voluptuous bosoms

معمور *ma'mūr* inhabited, populated, populous; المعمور or المعمورة the (inhabited) world | فى كل انحاء المعمور (المعمورة) all over the world, throughout the world

معمر *mu'ammir* pl. *-ūn* colonist

معمر *mu'ammar* pl. *-ūn* senior (in sports)

مستعمر *musta'mir* colonial, imperialistic; settler, colonist; foreign conqueror, invader; imperialist

مستعمرة *musta'mara* pl. *-āt* colony, settlement | ○ مستعمرة مستقلة (*mustaqilla*) dominion

اعمش *a'maš*[2] affected with an eye disease, blear-eyed

عماص *'umāṣ* (*eg.*) mucous discharge of the eye, rheum

عمق *'amuqa u* (*'umq*, عماقة *'amāqa*) to be or become deep, profound II to deepen, make deep or deeper (ه s.th.) IV = II V to penetrate deeply, go deeply (ه or فى into s.th.), become absorbed (ه or فى in)

عمق *'amq*, *'umq* pl. اعماق *a'māq* depth, profoundness, profundity; bottom | من اعماق قلبه (*a. qalbihī*) from the bottom of his heart, from the depth of his soul; من اعماق النفس (*a. in-nafs*) do.

عميق *'amīq* deep (also of feelings), profound

عمل *'amila a* (*'amal*) to do, act, operate, be active, work (also: فى in a field); to make, produce, manufacture, fabricate, perform, carry out, execute (ه s.th.); to act (ب according to, in accordance with, on the strength of, on the basis of); to operate, put into operation, set going (ب s.th.); to plan, contrive, seek to accomplish, practice, pursue (على s.th.), aim, work away (ل or على at), be out, strive (ل or على for), apply o.s. (على to), take pains, endeavor, exert o.s. (على to do s.th.), be active (على in the service of s.th.); to process, work, treat (فى s.th.); to act (فى upon s.th.), affect (فى s.th.); (*gram.*) to govern (فى a syntactical member) | يعمل به (*yu'malu*) it is valid, is effective, is in force (e.g., an ordinance); عمل ترتيبات to make arrangements or preparatious; عمل اعماله (*a'mālahū*) to behave, or act, like s.o.; لا به يعمل ولا عليه يعول (*yu'malu, yu'awwalu*) null and void II to appoint as vicegerent or governor (على ه s.o. over, of); to fester, suppurate, be purulent (wound)

III to apply (ب ه toward s.o. s.th.); to treat (ب ه s.o. in a manner), proceed, deal (ب ه with s.o. in a manner); to trade, do business (ه with s.o.) | عامله بالمثل (bi-l-miṯl) to repay s.o. like for like, treat s.o. in like manner IV to make (ه s.th.) work, put to work, operate, put into operation, bring to bear, employ, use (ه s.th.); اعمل ه فى or ب to putter, or tinker, with s.th. about s.th. else, work with s.th. on s.th. else | اعمل الفكر (fikra) to busy the mind, think, reflect, ponder, muse; اعمل السيف فى رقابهم (saifa) he caused a massacre among them, had them massacred V to go to a lot of trouble, take great pains, spend much effort VI to trade, do business (with one another); to trade, do business (مع with) VIII to work, be active, operate X to apply (ه s.th.), use, employ (ه, ه s.o., s.th.); to put into operation, operate, run (ه s.th.); to place s.o. (ه) at the head of s.th. (على), install, instate (على ه s.o. over) | استعمل معه وسائل القسوة (wasā'ila l-qaswa) he brought severe measures to bear upon him

عمل *'amal* doing, acting, action, activity; work, labor; course of action, way of acting, practice; achievement, accomplishment; activity (على for), work (على in the service of s.th.); making, production, manufacture, fabrication; performance, execution; make, workmanship; practical work, practice; — (pl. اعمال *a'māl*) act, action; operation (*mil.*); work, job, chore, labor; deed, feat, achievement, exploit; occupation, business; trade, craft, handicraft; vicegerency, province, district; administrative district (e.g., *Eg.*, *Tun.*); العمل ب validity, effectiveness of s.th. (e.g., of an ordinance, and the like) | اجراء العمل ب (*ijrā' al-'a.*) enforcement, implementation of s.th.; ما العمل الآن what's to be done now? what's there to be done? what can you do? عملا ب (*'amalan*) in execution of, in pursuance of, according to, pursuant to, as stipulated by; اعمال حربية (*ḥarbīya*) belligerent, or warlike, acts, military operations; الاعمال الاربعة (*arba'a*) the first four rules of arithmetic; اعمال منزلية (*manzilīya*) household chores, household work; اعمال يدوية (*yadawīya*) handiwork(s), manual work; صاحب العمل employer

عملى *'amalī* work-, working- (in compounds); serving practical purposes, practical; applied; عمليا *'amalīyan* practically, in practice | الحياة العملية practical life, workaday life, professional life; المذهب العملى (*maḏhab*) pragmatism; السياسة العملية practical policy, "Realpolitik"

عملية *'amalīya* pl. *-āt* work, job; action, activity; making, manufacture, fabrication, production; procedure, method, technique; operation (as an action done as part of practical work; *med.*; *mil.*); process | عملية قيصرية (*qaiṣarīya*) Caesarean section

عملة *'amla* evil deed | بعملته in the very act, red-handedly, flagrante delicto

عملة *'umla* wages, pay; currency; current money, currency in circulation; money | عملة زائفة counterfeit money; عملة سهلة (*sahla*) soft currency; عملة صعبة (*ṣa'ba*) hard currency; مزيف العملة *muzayyif al-'u.* counterfeiter; تهريب العملة currency smuggling

عميل *'amīl* pl. عملاء *'umalā'*[2] (business) representative; agent (also *pol.*); commission merchant (*com.*); customer, patron; patient; client

عميلة *'amīla* woman customer, woman client

○ عميلة *'umaila* pl. *-āt* erg (unit of energy or work; *phys.*)

عمالة *'amāla* pl. *-āt* wages, pay; brokerage, commission; department, district, province; (*Alg.*) prefecture, administrative district

عمولة *'umūla* brokerage, commission

عمّالى *'ummālī* labor, workers' (in compounds) | صحيفة عمالية labor organ, labor (news)paper

معمل *ma'mal* pl. معامل *ma'āmil*² factory, mill; workshop, plant, works, establishment; institute; laboratory; pl. معامل industrial plant | معمل البحث *m. al-baḥt* research institute; معمل التكرير refinery; معمل اللبن *m. al-laban* dairy

معاملة *mu'āmala* pl. *-āt* treatment; procedure; social intercourse, social life, association (with one another); behavior, conduct (toward others); business; transaction; (esp. in pl.) mutual relations, business relations; pl. معاملات handling (of freight, luggage, etc.) | المعاملة بالمثل (*mitl*) reciprocity (in international trade); شرط معاملة الدول الاكثر رعاية *šarṭu m. id-duwali l-akṯari ri'āyatan* most-favored-nation clause (*dipl.*)

تعمل *ta'ammul* affectedness, affectation, finicality, mannerism

تعامل *ta'āmul* commercial intercourse, trade relations, trade, dealings, transactions; business, transactions (stock exchange); (pl. *-āt*) ○ reaction (*chem.*)

استعمال *isti'māl* application, use, employment; utilization, exploitation: operation, handling (e.g., of a machine) | سهل الاستعمال *sahl al-ist.* easy to handle; سوء الاستعمال *sū' al-ist.* abuse, misuse; شائع الاستعمال in general use, commonly used, generally accepted; اساء استعماله *asā'a sti'mālahū* to abuse, misuse, misemploy s.th.

عامل *'āmil* active; effective; — (pl. عوامل *'awāmil*²) factor, constituent, element, (causative) agent, motive power; word governing another in syntactical regimen, regent (*gram.*); — (pl. عمال *'ummāl*) maker, producer, manufacturer; doer, perpetrator, author; worker, workman, workingman, laborer; wage earner, employee; governor, vicegerent, lieutenant; administrative officer at the head of a *'amal* (*Tun.*); (*Alg.*) district president, prefect (of a *'amāla*) | الجيش العامل (*jaiš*) the regular, or active, army; تحت عامل الغضب (*'ā. il-ğaḍab*) in wrathful agitation, infuriated; حزب العمال *ḥizb al-'u.* labor party (specif., the Brit. Labour Party); عضو عامل (*'uḍw*) active member

معمول به *ma'mūl bihī* in force, effective, valid; in use, applied

المعاميل *al-ma'āmīl* the coffee implements (*bedouin*)

معامل *mu'āmil* ○ coefficient (*math.*)

مستعمل *musta'mil* user

مستعمل *musta'mal* employed, used (also = not new, secondhand); in use, applied

عملاق *'imlāq* pl. عمالقة *'amāliqa* Amalekite; gigantic, giant, huge; a giant | عمالقة البحار huge ocean liners

¹عمّن *'amman* = عن من *'an man*

²عمان *'umān*² Oman, sultanate in SE Arabia

عمانى *'umānī* Omani, Oman (adj.)

³عمّان *'ammān*² Amman (the ancient Philadelphia, capital city of the Hashemite Kingdom of Jordan)

عمه *'amiha a* (*'amah*) to wander about, stray, rove; to stray (عن from)

عمى *'amiya a* (*'aman*) to be or become blind, lose one's eyesight; to be blind (عن to s.th.); to be obscure (على to s.o.) II to blind, render blind (ه s.o.); to blindfold (ه s.o.); to obscure, render cryptic, enigmatic or mysterious, mystify (ه s.th.) IV to blind, render blind (ه s.o.); to blindfold (ه s.o.); to make (ه s.o.) blind (عن to a fact) V to be or become blind, lose one's eyesight **VI** to shut one's eyes (عن on s.th.), pretend not to see (عن s.th.); to be blind (عن to)

عمى *ʿaman* blindness

عمية *ʿamīya* ignorance, folly

عماء *ʿamāʾ* heavy clouds

عماية *ʿamāya* ignorance, folly

اعمى *aʿmā*, f. عمياء *ʿamyāʾ*², pl. عمى *ʿumy* or عميان *ʿumyān* blind

معماة *maʿmāh* pl. معام *maʿāmin* roadless desert, roadless area

تعام *taʿāmin* blindness, (state of) delusion

معمى *muʿamman* pl. معميات *muʿammayāt* riddle, puzzle

¹عن *ʿan* (prep.) off, away from; from (designating the source); out of (a feeling); about, on (a topic); according to, as attested or declared by, from what ... says, on the authority of; on the basis of, on the strength of; for, in defense of; as a substitute for; (as to syntactical regimen see under respective verb) | عن يمينه (*yamīnihī*) to (or at) his or its right, at (or on) his or its right side, to the right of him or it; على ارتفاع الف قدم عن سطح البحر (*alfi qadamin, saṭhi l-baḥr*) 1000 feet above sea level; عن طريق (*ṭarīqi*) by way of, via; by means of, through; اليك عنى *ilaika ʿannī* away from me! عن امره (*amrihī*) by s.o.'s order(s), at s.o.'s instigation, on s.o.'s initiative; عن بصيرة consciously, fully aware of the situation; عن حسن نية (*ḥusni nīya*) in good faith, bona fide; عن حق (*ḥaqq*) justly, rightly, by rights; عن خوف (*ḵauf*) for fear; عن علم ,عن دراية (*ʿilm*) on the basis of sound knowledge, in full cognizance of the situation; عن سرور gladly, happily, joyfully; عن قناعة وجدانية (*qanāʿatin wijdānīya*) out of absolute inner conviction; عن قليل or عما قليل ,عما قريب or عن قريب (*ʿammā*) shortly, presently, after a (little) while, soon; عن وساطة فلان through the good offices of ...; يوما عن يوم (*yauman*) day after day, from day to day; قتلوا عن آخرهم (*qutilū*) they were killed to the last man; مات عن ثمانين سنة (*ṯamānīna sanatan*) he died at the age of eighty; مات عن تركة كبيرة (*tarika*) he died leaving a large fortune

²عن *ʿanna i u* (*ʿann*, عنن *ʿanan*) to present itself, offer itself (ل to s.o.); to take shape, to form, arise, spring up (ل in s.o.'s mind), suggest itself (ل to s.o.; of an opinion); to appear (ل to, before) | عن له ان it occured to him that ...

عنة *ʿunna* impotence (of the male)

عنان *ʿanān* (coll.; n. un. ة) clouds

عنان *ʿinān* pl. اعنة *aʿinna* rein(s); bridle | اطلق له العنان (*aṭlaqa, ʿināna*) to give free rein to s.o. or s.th., give vent to s.th.; جرت الامور فى اعنتها (*jarat, aʿinnatihā*) things took a normal course, developed as scheduled

عنين *ʿinnīn* impotent (male)

عنب *ʿinab* (coll.; n. un. ة) pl. اعناب *aʿnāb* grape(s) | عنب الذئب *ʿi. aḏ-ḏiʾb* black nightshade (Solanum nigrum; *bot.*)

عناب *ʿunnāb* (coll.; n. un. ة) jujube (Zizyphus vulgaris Lam.; *bot.*); (its fruit) jujube

¹عنبر *ʿanbar* ambergris; (pl. عنابر *ʿanābir*²) sperm whale, cachalot (*zool.*)

عنبرى *ʿanbarī* perfumed with ambergris; liqueur (also نبيذ عنبرى); a variety of pigeon

عنبرة الشتاء *ʿanbarat aš-šitāʾ* the severity of winter

²عنبر *ʿanbar* pl. عنابر *ʿanābir*² storehouse, magazine, depot, warehouse; factory hall; hold (of a ship); ward, section (of a hospital); quarters (of a ship's crew); barrack(s)

عنت *ʿanita a* (*ʿanat*) to fall on evil days, come to grief, meet with hardship, be in distress, suffer adversity; to commit a sin, specif., commit fornication **II** to force s.o. (ه) to perform a difficult task **IV** to distress, afflict, harass (ه s.o.), bring hardship (ه upon s.o.); to treat s.o. (ه) harshly, deal with s.o. (ه) roughly **V** to cause vexation, annoyance or distress (ه to s.o.), bring trouble (ه upon s.o.), harass, press, molest (ه s.o.); to seek to confuse s.o. (ه) with questions; to pick a quarrel, be out for a fight (مع with s.o.); to stickle, be pigheaded, insist stubbornly

عنت *ʿanat* distress, affliction, hardship, misery, adversity; pains, trouble, inconvenience; constraint, coercion

اعنات *iʿnāt* torment, harassment, molestation, chicanery, constraint, coercion

تعنت *taʿannut* obstinacy, obduracy, pigheadedness, stubborn zeal, stickling

متعنت *mutaʿannit* obstinate, obdurate, pigheaded, stubborn

عنتر *ʿantara* to display heroism

عنتر *ʿantar* Antar (the hero of a well-known romance of chivalry)

عنترى *ʿantarī* pl. *-iya* popular reciter of the Antar romance

عنترى *ʿantarī* pl. عناترة *ʿanātira* brassière; bodice, corsage

عنترية *ʿantariya* Antar, the romance of Antar, cycle of stories relating the deeds of Antar

عنجهية *ʿunjuhīya* haughtiness, self-importance, pride

عند *ʿanada u i* (عنود *ʿunūd*), *ʿanida a* (*ʿanad*) and *ʿanuda u* to swerve, deviate, diverge, depart (عن from); to resist stubbornly; to be headstrong, obstinate, stubborn **III** to resist or oppose (ه s.o., doggedly), offer (stubborn) resistance (ه to s.o.) **X** to cling stubbornly (ه to s.th.)

عند *ʿinda* (prep.) at, near, by, with, on (of place, time and possession); upon; in the opinion of, in the view of; من عند *min ʿindi* from; from the home of; away from; من عنده in his turn, for his part; اضاف شيئا من عنده he added s.th. of his own; عندها then, at that moment, with these words; على عندى (*ʿindī*) against me; عند البيت (*bait*) near the house, at the house; عند التحقيق to be exact ..., strictly speaking ...; عند طلوع الشمس (*ṭ. iš-šams*) at sunrise; عندى دينار واحد (*ʿindī dīnār*) I have only one dinar (with me); عند ذلك then, thereupon, at that moment; ملوك الارض عند الله تراب (*m. ul-arḍ, turāb*) the kings of this world are mere dust in comparison with God; عندى in my opinion, as I think; ما عندك what do you think? what is your opinion? لم يكن عند رأيهم (*yakun, ra'yihim*) he was not what they had expected; كان عند حسن ظنه (*ḥusni ẓannihī*) to meet, or be up to, s.o.'s high expectation; كان عند حسن الظن به (*ḥusni ẓ-ẓanni*) to have a good opinion of s.o.; كان عند نصحه (*nuṣḥihī*) to follow s.o.'s advice

عندما *ʿindamā* as soon as, whenever; when, as

من عندياته *min ʿindīyātihī* sprung from his own mind, his own brain child; of one's own accord, on one's own initiative

عندئذ *ʿinda'iḏin* then, at that time; at that moment, thereupon, then; with that, thereby

عنيد *ʿanīd* pl. عند *ʿunud* resisting stubbornly (ل s.o., s.th.); stubborn, obstinate, obdurate, pigheaded, headstrong, opinionated, willful, pertinacious

عناد *ʿinād* resistance, opposition; stubbornness, obstinacy, obduracy, pigheadedness, headstrongness, opinionatedness, willfulness, pertinacity

معاندة *muʿānada* resistance, opposition; stubbornness, obstinacy, obduracy, pigheadedness, headstrongness, opinionatedness, willfulness, pertinacity

معاند *muʿānid* resisting stubbornly (ل s.o., s.th.); stubborn, obstinate, obdurate, pigheaded, headstrong, opinionated, willful, pertinacious

عندلة *ʿandala* song of the nightingale

عندليب *ʿandalīb* pl. عنادل *ʿanādil*[2] nightingale

عندم *ʿandam* brazilwood, sapanwood (used for dyeing); red dyestuff

عندمى *ʿandamī* deep-red

عنز *ʿanz* pl. اعنز *aʿnuz*, عنوز *ʿunūz*, عناز *ʿināz* goat

عنزة *ʿanza* (n. un.) pl. *-āt* goat

عنزة *ʿanaza* a short spear, iron-tipped at its lower end

عانس *ʿānis* pl. عوانس *ʿawānis*[2] spinster, old maid

عنصر *ʿunṣur* pl. عناصر *ʿanāṣir*[2] origin; race, stock, breed; ethnic element; element (*chem.*, *pol.*); component, constituent, ingredient; pl. also: nationalities

عنصرى *ʿunṣurī* race, racial; ethnic; elemental, of or pertaining to the elements | التباغض العنصرى (*tabāğuḍ*) or الاحقاد العنصرية race hatred; المسألة العنصرية (*mas'ala*) the nationality problem, the problem of ethnic minorities

عنصرية *ʿunṣurīya* race, nationality; racial theory

العنصرة *al-ʿanṣara* Whitsuntide; Whitsunday, Pentecost (*Chr.*) | عيد العنصرة *ʿīd al-ʿa.* Whitsuntide, Pentecost (*Chr.*); Shabuoth, Feast of Weeks, Pentecost (*Jud.*)

عنصل *ʿunṣul* pl. عناصل *ʿanāṣil*[2] squill, sea onion

عنعنات *ʿanʿanāt* (pl.) traditions

معنعن *muʿanʿan* transmitted, handed down

عنف II to treat severely, harshly, with rigor (ب or على or ه s.o.), deal with s.o. (ب or على or ه) roughly; to reprimand, rebuke, censure sharply, berate, chide, scold (ب or ه s.o.) IV to treat severely, harshly, with rigor (ه s.o.), deal with s.o. (ه) roughly

عنف *ʿunf*, *ʿanf* sternness, severity, rigor; harshness; bluntness, gruffness; ruggedness, roughness; violence, vehemence; fierceness, bitterness, embitterment, toughness; use of force

عنيف *ʿanīf* stern, severe, drastic, rigorous; harsh, hard; ungentle, rough, rude; blunt, gruff; rugged, rough; violent, vehement; fierce, embittered, tough; strenuous, exacting, difficult (e.g., reading)

عنفوان *ʿunfuwān* vigor, prime, bloom | فى عنفوان شبابه (*ʿu. šabābihi*) in the prime of his youth

اعنف *aʿnaf*[2] sterner, severer, harsher, harder, fiercer

تعنيف *taʿnīf* stern censure, reprimand, rebuke

عنق II to grab by the neck, to collar (ه s.o.) III to embrace, hug (ه s.o.); to associate closely (ه with), attach o.s. closely (ه to) VI to embrace each other VIII to embrace, hug (ه s.o.); to adopt, embrace (ه s.th., esp. a religion or doctrine), be converted (ه to s.th.), take up (ه s.th.); to combine (ه with s.th.; *chem.*); to embrace each other

عنق *ʿunuq*, *ʿunq* pl. اعناق *aʿnāq* neck, nape

عناق *ʿanāq* pl. اعنق *aʿnuq*, عنوق *ʿunūq* she-kid, young she-goat | عناق الارض *ʿa. al-arḍ* caracal, desert lynx (Lynx caracal; *zool.*)

عنقاء *ʿanqāʾ*[2] a legendary bird, griffon

عناق *ʿināq* embrace, hug, accolade

معانقة *muʿānaqa* embrace, hug, accolade

اعتناق *iʿtināq* embracement (of a religion or doctrine), adoption, acceptance (of a doctrine)

عنقود *ʿunqūd* pl. عناقيد *ʿanāqīd*[2] cluster, bunch; bunch of grapes

عنقاش *ʿinqāš* peddler, hawker

عنكبوت *ʿankabūt* pl. عناكب *ʿanākib*[2] spider | بيت (نسيج) العنكبوت *bait al-ʿa.* cobweb, spider web

عنا (عنو) *ʿanā u* (*ʿunūw*) to be humble, submissive, subservient, servile (ل toward, before), be obedient, yield, submit (ل to s.o.), obey (ل s.o.); — *u* (عنوة *ʿanwa*) to take by force (ه s.th.); — *u* to be on s.o.'s (ه) mind, disquiet, discomfort, worry, preoccupy (ه s.o.); to concern, affect, regard, interest (ه s.o.)

عنوة *ʿanwa* force, compulsion; forcibleness, violence; *ʿanwatan* forcibly, by force

معنوى see عنى

عان *ʿānin* humble, subservient, submissive, servile, obedient; captive; miserable, distressed, in trouble

عنون *ʿanwana* to furnish with an address or title, entitle, address (ه s.th.)

عنوان *ʿunwān* pl. عناوين *ʿanāwīn*[2] address; title, heading; model, epitome; sign, token | عنوانا ل or على in token of s.th., as a sign of s.th.

معنون *muʿanwan* addressed (الى to), inscribed; entitled (ب as)

عنى *ʿanā i* (عناية *ʿināya*) to be on s.o.'s (ه) mind; to disquiet, discomfort, worry, preoccupy (ه s.o.); to concern, affect, regard, interest (ه s.o.); — *ʿaniya a* (عناء *ʿanāʾ*) to be worried, concerned, anxious; to toil, labor, drudge; — *ʿanā i* (*ʿany*) to have in mind (ه s.th.), mean (ه, ه s.o., s.th. by); يعنى *yaʿnī* or اعنى *aʿnī* that is, i.e.; — pass. *ʿuniya* (عناية *ʿināya*) to worry, be concerned (ب about), take an interest (ب in); to take care (ب of), see (ب to) **II** to torment, agonize, distress, harass (ه s.o.) **III** to be preoccupied (ه with s.th.); to take pains (ه with s.th., in doing s.th.), spend effort (ه on s.th.); to see to it, make efforts, bear in mind, make sure (ان that); to undergo, incur, endure, suffer, sustain, bear (ه s.th.); to suffer (ه from), be afflicted (ه with) **V** to toil, labor, drudge **VIII** to be solicitous (ب about, for, of), go to trouble (ب for), be concerned, anxious (ب about), feel concern (ب for); to take care (ب of), care, provide (ب for), look (ب after), see (ب to), tend (ب s.th.), put one's mind, devote one's attention (ب to); to attend (ب to), nurse (ب s.o., s.th., e.g., a patient)

عناء *ʿanāʾ* pains, trouble, toil, hardship, difficulty, distress

عناية *ʿināya* concern; care, solicitude, providence (ب for); care(fulness), painstaking, meticulousness (ب in); heed, notice, regard, attention (ب to); interest (ب in) | العناية الالهية (*ilāhīya*) divine providence; عناية طبية (*ṭibbīya*) medical care

معنى *maʿnan* pl. معان *maʿānin* sense, meaning, signification, import; concept, notion, idea, thought; thematic purport (e.g., of a work of art, as distinguished from its form); a rhetorical, figurative, or allegorical expression; المعانى the good qualities (of a person) | اسم معنى *ism m.* abstract noun (*gram.*); علم المعانى *ʿilm al-m.* rhetoric; ذو معنى significant, meaningful, telling, telltale; بكل معنى الكلمة *bi-kulli m. l-kalima* in the full sense of the word; لا معنى له

(*maʿnā*) meaningless, without meaning; وما فى معناه and the like; نظرات كلها معان (*naẓarāt kulluhā*) telling glances, glances full of meaning

معنوى *maʿnawī* relating to the sense or import (of a word or expression; as opposed to لفظى *lafẓī*); semantic, significative, of or pertaining to meaning; ideal, ideational, ideative; abstract; mental; spiritual (as opposed to material) | شخص معنوى (*šakṣ*) artificial, conventional, or juristic, person, a body corporate as a subject of rights and duties

معنويات *maʿnawīyāt* ideal, immaterial things; morale, spirit (of an army)

معاناة *muʿānāh* effort(s)

تعن *taʿannin* pains, trouble, toil, drudgery

اعتناء *iʿtināʾ* providing, solicitude, concern (ب for), attendance (ب to), maintenance, nursing, cultivation (ب of), care (ب of, for), carefulness, painstaking (ب in); attention (ب to), interest (ب in)

عان *ʿānin* miserable, distressed, in trouble

معنى *maʿnīy* concerned, affected; interested (ب in)

معنى *muʿannan* (*syr.*) unmetrical poem with end rhyme

معتن *muʿtanin* concerned, solicitous, careful, heedful, mindful, thoughtful, attentive

عهد *ʿahida a* (*ʿahd*) to know (ه, ه s.o., s.th.; ه s.th., e.g., a quality, a trait, ب of s.o.), be acquainted, familiar (ه, ه with); to observe closely, heed (ه s.th.), adhere (ه to s.th.); to attend (ه to), look after s.th. (ه); to delegate, entrust, assign, commit (الى ب to s.o., s.th.), vest (الى ب in s.o. s.th.), commission, charge, authorize, empower, entrust (الى ب s.o. with, or s.o. with the task of ...); to impose, enjoin (الى ب on s.o. s.th., or on s.o. the obligation to ...), obligate, commit (الى ب s.o. to do s.th.) | فيما اعهد (*aʿhadu*) to my knowledge, as far as I know; عهد وعده (*waʿdahū*) to fulfill, or keep, one's promise **III** to make a contract, compact, or covenant (ه على with s.o. concerning); to promise (ه على to s.o. s.th., also ب s.th.); to engage, undertake, bind o.s., pledge o.s., commit o.s., obligate o.s. (ه على to s.o. to do s.th.) **V** to advocate, support (ه s.th.), stand up (ه for s.th.); to observe, heed, keep in mind (ه s.th.), pay attention, see, attend (ه to s.th.), take care (ه of s.th.); to care (ه for s.th.), maintain, keep up, service (ه s.th.); to be liable for the maintenance or upkeep (ه of s.th.); to assume, take upon o.s. (ب s.th.); to engage, undertake, bind o.s., pledge o.s., commit o.s., obligate o.s. (ل ب to s.o. to do s.th., also على ان to do s.th.); to promise (ل ب to s.o. s.th.) **X** to exact a written pledge or commitment (من from s.o.); to have s.o. (من) sign a contract

عهد *ʿahd* knowledge; acquaintance, contact (ب with); the well-known, familiar nature (of s.o.); close observance, strict adherence (to), keeping, fulfillment (of a promise); delegation, assignment, committing (ب الى of s.th. to s.o.), vesting (الى ب in s.o. of s.th.), commissioning, charging, entrusting (الى ب of s.o. with s.th.); commission; — (pl. عهود *ʿuhūd*) commitment, obligation, liability; responsibility; pledge, vow; promise; oath; contract, compact, covenant, pact, treaty, agreement; time, epoch, era | بعد العهد *buʿd al-ʿa.* the fact that s.th. is long past, that s.th. belongs to the remote past; حديث العهد recent, late, new, young; قريب العهد do.; حديث العهد ب or حديث عهد ب (*ḥ. ʿahdin*) having adopted or acquired (s.th.) recently; not long accustomed to (s.th.), inexperienced at (s.th.), new at (s.th.), newly, e.g., حديث عهد بعرس (*bi-ʿursin*) newly wed, حديث العهد بالولادة newborn; كان حديث عهد بأوربا he had not known Europe until recently; قديم العهد of an early date, long past, long-standing; قديم العهد ب of long experience in, long acquainted with; قريب عهد ب (*q. ʿahdin*), قريب العهد ب = حديث عهد ب, قريب عهد بالفطام; حديث العهد ب (*fiṭām*) just weaned, newly weaned; من عهد قريب for a short time (past), of late; recent, late; recently, lately, the other day; منذ عهد بعيد a long time ago; لا عهد له ب (*ʿahda*) not to know s.th.; not having experienced s.th., being unacquainted with ...; عهدنا بهذه المسألة (*ʿahdunā, masʾala*) our long-standing knowledge of this question; اخذ عهدا عليه to exact a promise from s.o., pledge s.o.; قطع عهدا to conclude a treaty, make a contract; to make a promise; قطع على نفسه عهدا to assume an obligation, commit o.s., obligate o.s., pledge o.s.; to vow, make a vow (ب to do s.th.); عهد الامان *ʿa. al-amān* (formerly:) an order bestowed by the Bey of Tunis; عهد الامان المرصع (*muraṣṣaʿ*) a higher class of the afore-mentioned order; العهد الجديد the New Testament; العهد القديم the Old Testament; ولى العهد *walīy al-ʿa.* heir-apparent, crown prince; على عهده at or in his time; فى عهد فلان during s.o.'s lifetime; in s.o.'s epoch; عهده his familiar nature or manner, his nature as it had always been known; ظل كعهده (*ẓalla*) he remained as he had always been, as everybody used to know him; عهدهم به the nature or manner that they know (knew) of him (or of it), that they are (were) used to; كعهدهم به such as they used to know him; ما زلت انت كعهدى بك you are still the same! ما زال على عهده to be unchanged, be as always; طال به العهد (*ʿahdu*) to last, or have lasted, a long time

عهدة *ʿuhda* contractual obligation (*Isl. Law*); responsibility; charge, custody, guardianship; guaranty | فى عهدته in his care, custody, or charge, entrusted to him; عهدته عليه (*ʿuhdatuhū*) he is responsible for it

عهيد *ʿahīd* ally, confederate

معهد *maʿhad* pl. معاهد *maʿāhid²* place, locality (which one had known before or which one revisits); public institute or institution; (scientific) institute; seminar | معاهد الذكريات *m. aḏ-ḏikrayāt* places fraught with memories; معهد اصلاحى (*iṣlāḥī*) reformatory

معاهدة *muʿāhada* pl. *-āt* agreement, arrangement, accord; alliance, treaty, pact | معاهدة السلام (الصلح) *m. as-salām* (*aṣ-ṣulḥ*) peace treaty; معاهدة عدم الاعتداء *m. ʿadam al-iʿtidāʾ* nonaggression pact

تعهد *taʿahhud* advocacy, support; care; charge, custody, guardianship, tutelage (with foll. genit.: over); care, maintenance, servicing, upkeep; assumption, undertaking (ب of s.th.); (pl. *-āt*) promise, pledge, commitment, engagement, obligation, liability, contractual duty

معهود *maʿhūd* well-known; المعهود the said ..., the ... in question

متعهد *mutaʿahhid* pl. *-ūn* contractor, entrepreneur; concessionaire | متعهد فنى (*fannī*) impresario

متعاهد *mutaʿāhid*: المتعاهدان the two contracting parties

عهر *ʿahara a* (*ʿahr, ʿihr*) and *ʿahira a* (*ʿahar*) to commit adultery, whore (اليها with a woman) III = I (ها with a woman)

عهر *ʿihr* adultery, fornication, whoredom; prostitution

عهر *ʿahr* adulterer, whoremonger, fornicator

عهارة *ʿahāra* adultery, fornication, whoredom; prostitution

عاهر *'āhir* committing adultery, fornicating, whoring; (pl. عهار *'uhhār*) adulterer, fornicator, whoremonger; — (pl. عواهر *'awāhir*[2]) adulteress; whore, harlot, prostitute

عاهرة *'āhira* pl. *-āt*, عواهر *'awāhir*[2] adulteress; whore, harlot, prostitute

عاهل *'āhil* pl. عواهل *'awāhil*[2] sovereign, prince, ruler, monarch

عهن *'ihn* (colored) wool

عواهن *'awāhin*[2] (pl. of عاهن *'āhin*) limbs, extremities (of the body); palm branches | القى (رمى) الكلام على عواهنه (*alqā, kalāma*) to talk without restraint, ramble

عوج *'awija a* (*'awaj*) to be crooked, curved, twisted, tortuous, bent, bowed, stooping; to bend, twist, curve; — عاج *'āja u* to turn off the road (while traveling); to stop (over), put up (على at, in) II to bend, crook, curve, twist (ه s.th.) V and IX = I

عوج *'iwaj, 'awaj* crookedness, twistedness, curvature, bend(ing), tortuosity; unevenness; deviation (from that which is right)

عاج *'āj* ivory

عاجى *'ājī* ivory (adj.)

اعوج *a'waj*[2], f. عوجاء *'aujā'*[2], pl. عوج *'ūj* crooked, curved, bent, twisted, tortuous, sinuous; stooping, bowed; wry; odd, queer

اعوجاج *i'wijāj* crookedness, twistedness, curvature, bend(ing), tortuosity; unevenness; deviation (from that which is right); crooked ways

معوجة *mu'awwaja* pl. *-āt* retort (*chem.*)

معوج *mu'wajj* crooked, curved, bent, twisted, tortuous, sinuous; stooping, bowed; wry; odd, queer

(عود) عاد *'āda u* (*'aud*, عودة *'auda*, معاد *ma'ād*) to return, come back (ل or الى to); to flow back; to go back, be traceable, be attributable (الى to); to revert, redound, accrue (على to); to refer, relate (على to); to be due, go back (الى to); to fall to s.o.'s (الى) lot or share, fall in s.o.'s (الى) bailiwick; to belong, (ap)pertain, be proper (الى or ل to); to give up, abandon, relinquish (عن s.th.), withdraw, resign (عن from); عاد ب to return with = to lead back, bring back, take back, return, reduce, revert s.o. or s.th. (الى to); عاد عليه ب to bring about, entail s.th. for s.o., result in s.th. for s.o., yield, bring in, return s.th. to s.o.; (with predicate adjective or noun in acc.) to become, grow (into), turn into; (with foll. imperf. or الى) to resume, renew (an activity); (with neg. and foll. imperf.) to do s.th. no more or no longer; (with foll. finite verb) to do s.th. again or anew; — *u* (عيادة *'iyāda*) to visit (ه a patient), have under treatment (ه s.o.; of a physician) | عاد الى نفسه to regain consciousness, come to; to take counsel with o.s., hold self-communion, examine o.s. introspectively, search one's soul; عادت المياه الى مجاريها (*majārīhā*) the situation returned to normal; عاد الى رأس امره (*ra'si amrihī*) to start s.th. all over again; عاد ادراجه (*adrājahū*) to retrace one's steps; to turn back, go back; عاد على عقبيه (*'aqbaihi*), pl. عادوا على اعقابهم (*a'qābihim*) do.; لم اعد استطيع صبرا *lam a'ud astaṭī'u ṣabran* I could not stand it any longer; لم يعد له طاقة به (*ya'ud, ṭāqatun*) he no longer had any power over it; لم يعد اليه سبيل there is no longer any possibility for it; عاد يقول he continued (after a pause in his speech) II to accustom, habituate, condition, inure, season (على or ه ه s.o. to s.th.), make s.o. (ه) get used (على or ه to s.th.) III to return (ه, ه to s.o., to s.th.); to revert, come back, turn again, apply o.s. anew (ه to s.th.), take up again, resume (ه

s.th.); to befall again, seize again (ه s.o.), come again (ه over s.o.) **IV** to cause to return, bring back, take back (الى ه, ه s.o., s.th. to); to return, give back, send back (الى ه, ه s.o., s.th. to s.o.); to put back, lay back (ه s.th., الى محله *ilā maḥallihī* in its place); to repeat (على ه s.th., i.e., words, to s.o.); to reiterate, repeat, do again or anew, renew, resume (ه s.th.); to re-establish, restore, repair (ه s.th.); to restore (ه ه s.th. to), make s.th. (ه) once more (ه s.th.); to reinstate, reinstall (ه s.o.) | اعاد بناء مسجد (*binā'a masjidin*) to rebuild a mosque; اعاد ذكريات (*ḏikrayātin*) to revive, or reawaken, memories; اعاد طبع الكتاب (*ṭab'a l-k.*) to reprint a book; يعيد القول ويبدأه (*yu'īdu, yabda'uhū*) he keeps talking of it, he continues to bring up the subject; اعاد النظر فى (*naẓara*) to re-examine, reinvestigate, reconsider, check, verify, revise s.th., go over s.th. or into s.th. again; اعاد النظر فى الدعوى (*da'wā*) to retry the case (*jur.*) **V** to get used, be accustomed, habituate o.s. (على or ه to s.th.), make a habit (على or ه of s.th.), be used to doing, be wont to do (على or ه s.th.) **VIII** = **V**; **X** to recall, call back (ه, ه s.o., s.th.); to reclaim, demand back (من ه s.th. from); to regain, recover, recuperate, reconquer, fetch back, get back, retrieve (ه s.th.); to recall, recollect, call back to one's mind (ه s.th.); to ask s.o. (ه) to repeat (ه s.th.)

عود *'ūd* pl. اعواد *a'wād*, عيدان *'īdān* wood; stick, rod, poie; branch, twig, switch; stem, stalk; cane, reed; aloes (wood); lute (musical instrument); body, build, physique; strength, force, intensity; pl. اعواد full intensity (e.g., of a disease) | عود الثقاب matchstick, match; عود الصليب peony (Paeonia; *bot.*); عود الكبريت *'ūd al-kibrīt* matchstick, match; رخاوة العود *rakāwat al-'ūd* weakness of character; صلب العود *ṣulb al-'ūd* of robust physique, strongly built, husky, sturdy; stubborn, resistant, unbending, unyielding, relentless; صلابة العود *ṣalābat al-'ūd* sternness, severity, hardness, obstinacy, stubbornness, inflexibility, relentlessness; لدن العود *ladn al-'ūd* lissome, lithe, of elastic physique; ثقف عوده (*ṯaqqafa*) to train, educate s.o.; عجم عوده (*'ūdahū*) to test s.o., put s.o. to the test; كسر عوده (*'ūdahū*) to break s.o.'s power of resistance, crush s.o.'s spirit

عود *'aud* return; reversion; recurrence; recidivism (*jur.*); repetition, reiteration | فعله عودا وبدءا *fa'alahū 'audan wa-bad'an* or فعله عوده على بدئه (*'audahū*) or فعله عودا الى بدء he did or started it all over again

عودة *'auda* return | بعودة البريد by return mail; الى غير عودة never to return again, gone forever; good riddance! farewell forever!

عادة *'āda* pl. *-āt*, عوائد *'awā'id*[2] habit, wont, custom, usage, practice; *'ādatan* usually, customarily, ordinarily, habitually; pl. عوائد taxes, duties; charges, fees, rates | فوق العادة extraordinary, unusual, uncommon; special, extraordinary, emergency (e.g., meeting); على عادته according to his habit, as was his wont, as he used to do; كسابق العادة *ka-sābiqi l-'ā.* as was formerly customary, as usual; جرت العادة ب (*jarat il-'ādatu*) to be customary, usual, common or current, prevail, be a common phenomenon, be the vogue, have become common practice; جرت بذلك عادتهم that was their habit, that's what they used to do; العادة السرية (*sirrīya*) onanism, masturbation; عوائد الجمرك *'a. al-gumruk* customs duties; عوائد مبان *'a. mabānin* house taxes; عوائد الاملاك taxes on real estate

عادى *'ādī* customary, usual, common, ordinary, normal, regular; undistinguished, run-of-the-mill; ordinary, regular (e.g., meeting, as opposed to extraordinary, special, emergency); simple, plain, ordinary (man); old, ancient, antique; عاديات *ʿādīyāt* antiques, antiquities

عياد *ʿiyād* repetition, reiteration, recurrence

عيادة *ʿiyāda* visit (with a patient), doctor's call (on a patient); — (pl. *-āt*) clinic; office (of a physician), consultation room (of a physician) | عيادة خارجية (*kārijīya*) policlinic; outpatient clinic

عوادة *ʿawwāda* pl. *-āt* woman lutist

معاد *maʿād* return; place to which one returns; (place of) destination; المعاد the hereafter, the life to come | المبدأ والمعاد (*mabda'*) the crux (of a matter), the all-important factor (of s.th.)

تعويد *taʿwīd* accustoming, habituation, conditioning, inurement (على to)

اعادة *iʿāda* giving back, handing back, sending back, return(ing); reinstatement, reinstallment; repetition, reiteration; resumption; re-establishment, restoration, repair | اعادة البناء reconstruction; اعادة الحقوق rehabilitation; اعادة التسلح *i. at-tasalluḥ* rearmament; اعادة الشؤون على ما كانت عليه restoration of the status quo ante; اعادة التكوين re-formation; اعادة النظر ف (*i. an-naẓar*) re-examination, reinvestigation, reconsideration, revision of s.th.; اعادة النظر فى دعوى (*daʿwā*) retrial of a case (*jur.*); اعادة التنظيم reorganization

تعود *taʿawwud* contraction of a habit, habituation

اعتياد *iʿtiyād* contraction of a habit, habituation

اعتيادى *iʿtiyādī* ordinary, common; usual, customary, habitual; normal, regular; plain, simple, ordinary (man)

استعادة *istiʿāda* reconquest, recovery, recuperation, regaining, reclamation, retrieval

عائد *ʿā'id* returning, reverting, recurrent; accruing (profit, merit); belonging, (ap)pertaining, proper (ل or ال to s.o., to s.th.); (pl. *-ūn*) returning emigrant, re-emigrant; (pl. عواد *ʿuwwād*) visitor (to a sick person); pl. عائدات revenues | عائد الارباح net profit, net gain

عائدة *ʿā'ida* pl. عوائد *ʿawā'id*[2] benefit, profit, advantage, gain (على for s.o.)

عائدية *ʿā'idīya* a belonging (to), a being part (of), membership

معود *muʿawwad* used, accustomed, habituated, conditioned, inured, seasoned (على to); wont (على to do s.th.), being in the habit (على of doing s.th.)

معيد *muʿīd* pl. *-ūn* repetitor, tutor, coach; assistant conducting drill sessions (university)

معاد *muʿād*: معاد تصديره (*taṣdīruhū*) forwarded (mail)

متعود *mutaʿawwid* used, accustomed, habituated, conditioned, inured, seasoned (على to); wont (على to do s.th.), being in the habit (على of doing s.th.)

معتاد *muʿtād* used, accustomed, habituated, conditioned, inured, seasoned (على to); wont (على to do s.th.), being in the habit (على of doing s.th.); usual, customary, normal | كالمعتاد as usual; معتاد الجرائم habitual criminal

(عوذ) عاذ *ʿāḏa u* (*ʿauḏ*, عياذ *ʿiyāḏ*, معاذ *maʿāḏ*) to seek the protection (ب من of s.o. from or against), take refuge (ب من with s.o. from) | اعوذ بالله *aʿūḏu bi-llāh* God forbid! God save me from that! **II** to protect (ه من s.o. from or against, by placing him under the wing ب of s.o. else); to pronounce a charm or incantation (ه over s.o.); to fortify (ه s.o.) with a charm, incantation or amulet **IV** = **II**; to place s.o. (ه) under God's protection, pray to God that he guard s.o. (ه) against s.th.

V = I; X = I; to protect o.s., make o.s. proof (ب by means of)

عوذ *ʿauḏ* (act of) taking refuge

عوذ *ʿawaḏ* refuge, place of refuge, retreat, asylum, sanctuary

عوذة *ʿūḏa* pl. عوذ *ʿuwaḏ* amulet, talisman; charm, spell, incantation

عياذ *ʿiyāḏ* (act or instance of) taking refuge | عياذ الله *ʿiyāḏa llāh* or العياذ بالله (*ʿiyāḏa*) God forbid! God save (protect) me (us) from that!

معاذ *maʿāḏ* (act or instance of) taking refuge; refuge, place of refuge, retreat, asylum, sanctuary | معاذ الله *maʿāḏa llāh(i)* God forbid! God save (protect) me (us) from that!

تعويذ *taʿwīḏ* pl. تعاويذ *taʿāwīḏ*[2] amulet, talisman; charm, spell, incantation

[1]عور *ʿawira a* (*ʿawar*) to lose an eye, be or become one-eyed **II** to deprive of one eye, make blind in one eye (ه s.o.); to damage, mar, spoil (ه s.th.); to gauge (ه measures, weights), test the accuracy (ه of measures, of weights) **IV** to lend, loan (ه ه to s.o. s.th.) **VI** to alternate, take turns (ه in s.th.), do by turns, take alternately (ه s.th.); to seize, grip, befall, overcome (alternately, successively) (ه s.o., ه s.th.) **VIII** اعتور *iʿtawara* to befall, affect (alternately, successively) (ه s.o.), come (alternately, successively) (ه over s.o.); to shape, mold, form (ه s.th., said of heterogeneous influences or factors); to stand in the way of (ه), hinder (ه s.th.) **X** to borrow (ه من s.th. from)

عورة *ʿaura* defectiveness, faultiness, deficiency, imperfection; — (pl. *-āt*) pudendum, genitals; weakness, weak spot

عوار *ʿawār*, *ʿiwār* fault, blemish, defect, flaw, imperfection

عوار *ʿuwwār* a variety of swallow

عيرة *ʿīra* (*eg.*) false, artificial (teeth, hair)

اعور *aʿwar*[2], f. عوراء *ʿaurāʾ*[2], pl. عور *ʿūr* one-eyed | المعى الاعور (*maʿy*) caecum, blind gut

اعارة *iʿāra* lending

اعارى *iʿārī*: مكتبة اعارية (*maktaba*) lending library, circulating library

تعاور *taʿāwur* alternation, variation, fluctuation

استعارة *istiʿāra* borrowing; metaphor

استعارى *istiʿārī* metaphorical, figurative

عارية *ʿāriya* or *ʿārīya* pl. عوار *ʿawārin* s.th. borrowed, borrowing; loan

معير *muʿīr* lender

معار *muʿār* lent, loaned

مستعير *mustaʿīr* borrower

مستعار *mustaʿār* borrowed; used metaphorically or figuratively; false, artificial (e.g., hair) | اسم مستعار (*ism*) pseudonym; وجوه مستعارة masked faces; hypocrites

[2]عار *ʿārin* see عرى

عوز *ʿawiza a* (*ʿawaz*) to be or become poor, needy, destitute; — عاز *ʿāza u* (*ʿauz*) to need, require (ه s.th.), be in want or need (ه of s.th.) **IV** اعوز *aʿwaza* to be or become poor, needy, destitute | اعوزه الشىء (*šaiʾu*) he lacked the thing, he needed it, he was in want of it

عوز *ʿawaz* lack, need, want, necessity, exigency; poverty, neediness, destitution, indigence, penury

عوز *ʿawiz* poor, needy, destitute, necessitous, indigent

عازة *ʿāza* lack, need, want, necessity, exigency; poverty, poorness

اعوز *aʿwaz*[2] poor, needy, destitute, indigent, necessitous

اعاوز *aʿāwīz²* (pl.) poor

اعواز *iʿwāz* lack, need, want, necessity, exigency; poverty, neediness, destitution, indigence, penury

عائز *ʿāʾiz* poor, needy, destitute, indigent, necessitous

معوز *muʿwiz, muʿwaz* poor, needy, destitute, indigent, necessitous; (pl. *-ūn*) pauper, poor man

عوسج *ʿausaj* boxthorn (Lycium europaeum L. and Lycium arabicum Schwf.; *bot.*)

عوص *ʿawiṣa a* (عوص *ʿawaṣ*, عياص *ʿiyāṣ*) to be difficult, abstruse, recondite, be difficult to comprehend **VIII** = **I**

عويص *ʿawīṣ* difficult, difficult to comprehend, abstruse, recondite, obscure

اعتياص *iʿtiyāṣ* difficulty

(عوض) عاض *ʿāḍa u* (*ʿauḍ, ʿiwaḍ*, عياض *ʿiyāḍ*) to give in exchange, pay as a price (ه to s.o. ه s.th. عن or من for); to replace (ه, ه s.o., s.th. عن or من with or by), substitute (عن or من ه, ه for s.o., for s.th. s.o. or s.th. else), compensate, indemnify, requite, recompense (عن or من ه s.o. for); to replace (ه ه to s.o. s.th.; ب ه s.th. by or with); to make up to s.o. (على) for a loss, or the like (ه) **II** = **I** | لا يعوض (*yuʿawwaḍu*) irreplaceable, irreparable **III** = **I**; **IV** = **I** **V** to take or receive as substitute (ه s.th.), use as a substitute (من ه s.th. for); to seek compensation (ب in, by, من for), take as compensation (ب s.th., من for), gain a setoff (من against) **VIII** to take or receive as substitute or compensation (من or عن ه s.th. for) **X** to take as a substitute (ب عن s.th. for), exchange (عن ب s.th. for), replace (عن ب s.o., s.th. with or by), substitute (عن ب for s.o., for s.th. s.o. or s.th. else), exchange (عن ب s.th. with s.th. else); to receive compensation (من for), gain a setoff (من against), be compensated, be recompensed, be indemnified (عن ب for s.th. by or with)

عوض *ʿiwaḍ* substitute, compensation, recompense, indemnity; consideration, return, equivalent (*Isl. Law*); *ʿiwaḍa* (prep.) and عوضا عن (من) (*ʿiwaḍan*) as a substitute for, in replacement of, in exchange or return for, in compensation for, instead of, in lieu of

تعويض *taʿwīḍ* replacement, substitution; compensation, indemnification, reparation (عن for), reimbursement, restitution, settlement (عن of); (pl. *-āt*) return, consideration, equivalent, substitute; recompense, compensation, satisfaction, setoff, amends, indemnity, damages, reparation; compensation (*psych.*); pl. reparations (as war indemnity)

تعويضى *taʿwīḍī* substitutional, compensational, compensatory, reparative

معاوضة *muʿāwaḍa* pl. *-āt* a commutative contract on the basis of "do ut des" (*Isl. Law*)

استعاضة *istiʿāḍa* replacement (عن ب of s.th. by or with), substitution (ب عن of s.th. for); exchange (عن ب of s.th. for)

(عوق) عاق *ʿāqa u* (*ʿauq*) to hinder, prevent, detain, restrain, withhold, hold back (عن ه s.o. from); to impede, hamper, defer, delay, retard, put off (ه, ه s.o., s.th.) **II** and **IV** = **I**; **V** to be hindered, be prevented, be detained, be restrained, be withheld (عن from); to be impeded, be delayed, be retarded, be deferred **VIII** = **I**

عوق *ʿauq* hindering, detaining, restraining, check(ing); impeding, stopping, delay(ing), retardation, deferment

اعاقة *iʿāqa* hindering, detaining, restraining, check(ing); impeding, stopping, delay(ing), retardation, deferment

عائق *'ā'iq* hindrance, obstacle, impediment; (*eg.*; pl. عياق *'uyyāq*) dandy, fop

عائقة *'ā'iqa* pl. عوائق *'awā'iq*² hindrance, obstacle, impediment, obstruction, barrier

(عول) عال *'āla u* (*'aul*) to deviate from the right course; to oppress, distress (ه s.o.), weigh heavily (ه upon s.o.); عال صبره (*ṣabruhū*) and عيل صبره (*'īla*) to lose patience; — *'āla u* (*'aul*, عيالة *'iyāla*) to support, sustain, have to feed (ه s.o., esp. members of the family), have to provide for s.o.'s (ه) sustenance, be responsible for s.o.'s (ه) support; to supply with sustenance (ه s.o.), provide (ه for s.o.); to have a numerous family **II** to lament, wail, howl, cry; to yelp, yip (dog); to rely, depend (على on); to resolve, decide (على upon), intend, purpose, make up one's mind (على to do s.th.) | لا به يعمل ولا عليه يعول (*yu'malu, yu'awwalu*) null and void **IV** اعول *a'wala* to lament, wail, howl, cry; — اعال *a'āla* to support, sustain, have to feed (ه s.o., esp. family members), have to provide for s.o.'s (ه) sustenance, be responsible for s.o.'s (ه) support; to supply with sustenance (ه s.o.), provide (ه for s.o.); to have a numerous family

عول *'aul* lament, wailing, howling, crying; support, sustenance of the family; helper

عول *'iwal* reliance, dependence; trust; confidence

عيل *'ayyil* family (depending on one's support), household; (*eg.*) baby, little child; pl. عيال *'iyāl*, عالة *'āla* dependents | عيال على and عالة على (for sg. and pl.) living at the expense of ...; entirely dependent on ...; being a burden on (s.o.)

عالة *'āla* rooflike shelter from the rain; see *ayyil*

عويل *'awīl* lament, wailing, howling, crying; (*eg.*) sponger, hanger-on, parasite

معول *mi'wal* pl. معاول *ma'āwil*² pickax, pick, mattock; (*eg.*) hoe; that which serves for undermining or destruction, (negative) element | معاول هدامة (*haddāma*) destructive elements; معاول الافساد والتقويض (*m. al-ifsād*) destructive and subversive elements

اعالة *i'āla* sustenance, support, provision

عائل *'ā'il* sustainer, breadwinner, family provider

عائلة *'ā'ila* pl. *-āt*, عوائل *'awā'il*² family, household

عائلى *'ā'ilī* family (adj.), domestic

معول *mu'awwil* determined, resolved (على on); — *mu'awwal* object of trust; reliance, dependence | ليس عليه معول (*mu'awwal*) he (it) is not reliable, one cannot rely on him (on it)

معيل *mu'īl* sustainer, breadwinner, family provider

¹(عوم) عام *'āma u* (*'aum*) to swim; to float **II** to launch, float, set afloat (ه a ship): (*eg*.) to flood (ه s.th.)

عوم *'aum* swimming, natation

عام *'ām* pl. اعوام *a'wām* year

عامئذ *'āma'iḏin* in that year

عوام *'awwām* good swimmer | ○ حوض عوام (*ḥauḍ*) floating dock

عوامة *'awwāma* pl. *-āt* buoy; raft; pontoon; float (of a bait line, of an oil lamp, etc.)

عائم *'ā'im* swimming, floating, natant | ○ جسر عائم (*jisr*) floating bridge, pontoon bridge; ○ رافعة عائمة floating crane

²عامة *'āmma* and عوام *'awāmm*² see ³عم *'amma*

عون III to help (فى ه s.o. in or with; على ه s.o. to s.th.), aid, assist (فى ه s.o. in or with), support (فى ه s.o. in) IV = III; to free, liberate, rid, relieve (من ه s.o. of) VI to help, assist, or support one another; to cooperate X to ask, or call for, s.o.'s (ب or ه) help (على against), turn to s.o. (ب or ه) for help (على against), seek help (ب or ه from s.o. in s.th., على against), resort, have recourse (ب or ه، ه to s.o., to s.th.); to make use (ب or ه of s.th., على in or for)

عون ʿaun help, aid, assistance, succor, relief, support, backing; — (pl. أعوان aʿwān) helper, aide, assistant; servant; bodyguard; minor official (Tun.); court usher (Tun.) | أعوان المطافئ firemen

عونة ʿauna forced labor, conscript labor, corvée

عانة ʿāna pubic region, pubes

عوان ʿawān middle-aged; intermediate, intermediary (بين between) | حرب عوان (ḥarb) an intermittent, endless war

عين عوينات see

معوان miʿwān pl. معاوين maʿāwīn² one who helps frequently, a reliable stand-by; helper; resource, resort, help; aid

معونة maʿūna help, aid, assistance, succor, relief, support, backing | مد يد المعونة madda yada l-m. to extend one's help (ل to)

معاونة muʿāwana help, aid, assistance, succor, relief, support, backing | معاونة ذاتية (ḏātīya) self-help

إعانة iʿāna help, aid, assistance, succor, relief, support, backing; — (pl. -āt) subvention; subsidy, contribution, allowance, aid (in money)

تعاون taʿāwun cooperation | شركة التعاون širkat at-t. cooperative society, cooperative

تعاونى taʿāwunī cooperative (adj.) | جمعية تعاونية (jamʿīya) cooperative society, cooperative; هيئة تعاونية (haiʾa) cooperative corporation, cooperative

تعاونية taʿāwunīya cooperative spirit, community spirit, cooperation

استعانة istiʿāna (act or instance of) seeking help (ب with, from, in), resorting (ب to); making use, utilization, use (ب of s.th.)

معاون muʿāwin helper, supporter, standby; aide; assistant; adjutant, aide-decamp; police officer heading a city precinct (ir.)

معاونية muʿāwinīya police station (ir.)

معين muʿīn pl. -ūn helper, supporter, stand-by; aide; assistant

عاهة ʿāha pl. -āt disease, malady, infirmity, frailty, decrepitude; bodily defect; physical disablement; blight, blast, mildew, and the like (عوه)

معوه maʿūh blighted, blasted, affected by mildew, and the like

معيوه maʿyūh blighted, blasted, affected by mildew, and the like

عوى ʿawā i (عواء ʿuwāʾ) to howl (dog, wolf, jackal); to squeak, whine, yelp III to howl (ه at s.o.) X to make (ه s.o.) howl

عواء ʿuwāʾ howling, howls

عواء ʿawwāʾ Boötes (astron.)

معاوية muʿāwiya bitch (in heat) that howls at the dogs

عى ʿayya, عيى ʿayiya, imperf. يعى yaʿay-yu, يعيا yaʿyā (عى ʿiyy) not to find the right way or the right method; to be incapable (عن or ب of), lack the strength or power (عن or ب for); to be unable to express o.s., stammer, stutter, falter, speak haltingly; to be or fall ill | يعيا بامره (عى) ʿayya, عى ʿayiya, imperf. يعى ya-

(*bi-amrihī*) he is at his wit's end, is in utter despair, despairs of himself **IV** to be or become tired, weary, fatigued, feeble, faint, weak; to tire, weary, fatigue, exhaust (ه s.o.); to render incapable, incapacitate, disable (ه s.o.); to thwart all efforts (ه of s.o.); to defy (ه s.o., s.o.'s efforts); to fail, break down, malfunction, not to work (ه despite s.o.'s skill) | اعيا الداء الاطباء (*dā'u, aṭibbā'a*) the disease defied all medical skill, defeated the physicians, thwarted all efforts of the doctors; اعيته الحيلة (*ḥīla*) he didn't know what to do, he was at the limit of his resources, he knew no way out, he was at the end of his tether, he was at his wit's end

عى *'iyy* stammer, faltering, incapability of expressing o.s.; fatigue, weariness, exhaustion

عى *'ayy* pl. اعياء *a'yā'* incapable, unable, impotent, powerless, weak, sapless, feeble, exhausted; incapable of expressing o.s.

عياء *'ayā'* incapability, inability; weakness, feebleness, faintness, fatigue; (incurable, grave) disease (also داء عياء)

عيان *'ayyān* incapable, unable; tired, weary, fatigued; (*eg.*) sick, ill

اعياء *i'yā'* weariness, fatigue; exhaustion, weakness, saplessness, lack of strength; impotence, helplessness, powerlessness

معى *mu'yin* tired, weary, fatigued, exhausted, debilitated, feeble, faint

(عيب) عاب *'āba i* (*'aib*) to be defective, faulty, blemished, deficient; to be full of faults, defects or deficiencies; to render faulty or defective, mar, disfigure, spoil (ه s.th.); to find fault (ه, ه with s.o., with s.th.), take exception (ه, ه to s.o., to s.th.), accuse (ه s.o.) of a fault or vice; to dishonor, disgrace (ه, ه s.o., s.th.); to blame, censure, denounce, decry, reprove (ه على s.o. for) **II** to render faulty or defective (ه s.th.); to spoil, mar, disfigure (ه s.th.); to find fault (ه, ه with s.o., with s.th.), take exception (ه, ه to s.o., to s.th.), accuse (ه s.o.) of a fault or vice; to blame, censure, denounce, decry, reprove, reprimand, reproach, chide (ه s.o.)

عيب *'aib* pl. عيوب *'uyūb* fault, defect, blemish, flaw, shortcoming, imperfection; vice, failing, weakness, foible; shame, disgrace | عيب جسمى (*jismī*) physical defect; (*eg.*) عيب عليك shame on you! you ought to be ashamed!

عيبة *'aiba* pl. *-āt*, عيب *'iyab*, عياب *'iyāb* leather bag, leather suitcase; fault, defect, blemish, blot, disgrace

معاب *ma'āb* pl. معايب *ma'āyib*[2] fault, defect, blemish, flaw, shortcoming, imperfection; vice, failing, weakness, foible, blot, shame, disgrace

معابة *ma'āba* pl. معايب *ma'āyib*[2] fault, defect, blemish, flaw, shortcoming, imperfection; vice, failing, weakness, foible, blot, shame, disgrace

معيب *ma'īb* defective, deficient, faulty, blemished, unsound; shameful, disgraceful

معيوب *ma'yūb* defective, deficient, faulty, blemished, unsound; shameful, disgraceful

معيب *mu'ayyib* censurer, faultfinder, critic

(عيث) عاث *'āṯa i* (*'aiṯ*) to create disaster, cause havoc, rage, ravage (فى in, among) عاث فسادا فى (*fasādan*) do.; عاث فى ماله to squander, or dissipate, one's fortune **II** to fumble, grope about in the dark

عيد **II** to celebrate, or observe, a feast; to felicitate (على s.o.) on the occasion of a feast, wish (على s.o.) a merry feast **III** to felicitate (على s.o.) on the occasion of a feast, wish (على s.o.) a merry feast

عيد *'īd* pl. اعياد *a'yād* feast, feast day, festival, holiday | عيد الرسل *'īd ar-rusul* Day of St. Peter and Paul (*Chr.*); عيد الصعود Ascension Day (*Chr.*); العيد الصغير the Minor Feast = عيد الفطر (q.v.); عيد الاضحى *'īd al-aḍḥā* the Feast of Immolation, or Greater Bairam, on the 10th of Zu'lhijja; عيد الفطر *'īd al-fiṭr* the Feast of Breaking the Ramadan Fast, or Lesser Bairam, on the 1st of Shawwal; العيد الكبير the Major Feast = عيد الاضحى the Feast of Immolation, or Greater Bairam; عيد القيامة Easter (*Chr.*); عيد الكسوة *'īd al-kiswa* (*Eg.*) the Festival of the Kiswa, celebrated in the month of Shawwal on the occasion of the ceremonial transport of the Kiswa (q.v.) from Cairo to Mecca; عيد كل القديسين (*qiddīsīn*) All Saints' Day (*Chr.*); عيد الميلاد *'īd al-mīlād* Christmas (*Chr.*)

عيدية *'īdīya* gift, present given on the occasion of a feast; New Year's present

معايدة *mu'āyada* cocelebration, exchange of felicitations; (pl. *-āt*) congratulatory call on feast days

¹(عير) عار *'āra i* (*'air*) to wander, stray, roam, rove II to reproach, upbraid, blame, rebuke, condemn (على or ب or ه ، s.o. for); to abuse, insult, revile (، s.o.), rail (، at s.o.) III to gauge (ه measures, weights), test the accuracy (ه of measures, of weights) VI to revile each other

عار *'ār* pl. اعيار *a'yār* shame, disgrace, dishonor, ignominy (على for)

عير *'air* pl. اعيار *a'yār* wild ass, onager

عير *'īr* pl. عيرات *'iyarāt* caravan | لا فى العير ولا فى النفير neither here nor there; in no way, in no manner; unimportant, of no consequence

عيار *'iyār* pl. *-āt* standard measure, standard, gauge (of measures and weights); fineness (of gold and silver articles), standard (of gold and silver coins); caliber; (pl. *-āt*, اعيرة *a'yira*) (rifle) shot (also عيار نارى *'i. nārī*)

عيار *'ayyār* pl. *-ūn* loafer, scoundrel, bum; vagabond, vagrant; (pl. *-āt*) crane (machine)

معيار *mi'yār* measuring, mensuration, gauging, measurement, measure; — (pl. معايير *ma'āyīr*²) standard measure, standard, gauge (of measures and weights); standard; norm | معيار العيش *m. al-'aiš* living standard; معيار الذهب *m. aḏ-ḏahab* gold standard

معاير *ma'āyir*² (pl.) faults, vices, infamies, abominations

معايرة *mu'āyara*: معايرة الموازين والمكاييل verification of weights and measures of capacity (by the bureau of standards)

²عيرة *'īra* see عور

اعيس *a'yas*², f. عيساء *'aisā'*², pl. عيس *'īs* of a dirty white color, yellowish white (camel); عيس *'īs* camels of good stock, breeding camels

عيسلان *'aisalān* hyacinth (*bot.*)

عيسى *'īsā* Jesus

عيسوى *'īsawī* Christian

(عيش) عاش *'āša i* (*'aiš*, عيشة *'īša*, معيش *ma'īš*, معيشة *ma'īša*, معاش *ma'āš*) to live, be alive | عاش الملك and ليعش الملك *li-ya'iš il-malik* long live the king! عاش حياته (*ḥayātahū*) to enjoy one's life, make much of one's life II to keep alive, make or let live (، s.o.); to feed, support, sustain (، s.o.), provide (، for s.o.) III to live together (، with s.o.) IV = II; V to eke out a living, just manage to make both ends meet; to earn one's bread, make a living (ب with); to live, subsist (من on, by) **VI** to live together **VIII** do.

عيش *'aiš* life, way of living, way (or mode) of life; livelihood, subsistence, living; (chiefly *eg.*) bread | مستوى العيش *mustawā l-'aiš* living standard; عيش غراب (*eg.*) *'ēš ğurāb* mushrooms

عيشة *'īša* sort of life, way (or mode) of living, way of life, life

عياش *'ayyāš* (*eg.*) bread seller

معاش *ma'āš* life, manner (or style) of living; livelihood, subsistence, living; means of subsistence; income; (pl. *-āt*) retirement pay, pension; benefits or allowances from a public-welfare fund | ذو المعاش pensioner; ارباب المعاشات pensioners; احيل الى (على) المعاش (*uḥila*) to be pensioned off, be retired, be superannuated

معيشة *ma'īša* pl. معايش *ma'āyiš*[2] life, way of living, way (or mode) of life; form of life; livelihood, subsistence, living; household | معيشة الريف *m. ar-rīf* rural life, life in the country

معيشى *ma'īšī* of or pertaining to the way of living | الحالة المعيشية living standard

معايشة *mu'āyaša* coexistence (*pol.*)

اعاشة *i'āša* sustenance, nourishment, food | بطاقة الاعاشة food ration card

تعايش *ta'āyuš* coexistence (*pol.*)

عائش *'ā'iš* living, alive; well off, well-to-do, prosperous

عيط **II** to yell, scream, cry out; to shout, call (على for), call out (على to s.o.), hail (على s.o.); to weep, cry

عياط *'iyāṭ* yelling, screaming, shouting; clamor

(عيف) عاف *'āfa a i* (*aif*, عياف *'iyāf*, عيفان *'ayafān*) to loathe (ه s.th.), have an aversion (ه to s.th.), feel disgust (ه at s.th.)

عيف *'aif* disgust, loathing, horror, aversion

عياف *'ayyāf* augur prognosticating by the flight of birds

عيوف *'ayūf* proud, disdainful

عيفان *'ayafān* disgust, loathing, horror, aversion

عيوق *'ayyūq* Capella (*astron.*); foppish, dandyish; dandy, fop

(عيل) عال *'āla i* (عيلة *'aila*) to be or become poor, be reduced to poverty, become impoverished **II** and **IV** اعيل *a'yala* to have a numerous family

عيل *'ayyil*, عيال *'iyāl*, عالة *'āla* and عائلة *'ā'ila* see عول

عائل *'ā'il* poor, needy, indigent, destitute (also see عول)

معيل *mu'īl*, *mu'ayyal* father of a family; provider for a large family

عيلم *'ailam* see علم

عين **II** to individualize, particularize, specify, itemize, designate, mark (ه s.th.); to fix, determine, appoint, assign, schedule, lay down, set down, prescribe, define, stipulate (ه s.th.); to nominate, appoint, assign (ف or ه ه s.o. as or to an office), designate, destine, set aside, earmark, single out (ه ه s.th. for); to allot, apportion, assign (ل ه s.th. to s.o.), allocate, appropriate (ل ه funds to s.o.); to fix one's eyes (على on), be bent (على on), be out (على for) | عين سببا (*sababan*) to give a reason **III** to view, eye, see with one's own eyes, examine, inspect (ه, ه s.o., s.th.), survey (ه s.th.) **V** to see (ه, ه s.o., s.th.); to be destined, set aside, earmarked; to be appointed, assigned, nominated; to be specifically imposed (على on s.o.), be incumbent (على

upon s.o.), be obligatory (على for s.o.), be s.o.'s (على) duty

عين *ʿain* f., pl. عيون *ʿuyūn*, اعين *aʿyun* eye; evil eye; spring, source, fountainhead (of water); scout, reconnoiterer; hole; mesh; flower, choice, prime (of s.th.); — (pl. اعيان *aʿyān*) an eminent, important man, used esp. in pl.: people of distinction, important people, leading personalities, leaders, notables, prominent persons; substance, essence; self, individuality; — chattel, object of material value, (corporeal or personal) property, personalty, capital asset (*Isl. Law*); — ready money, cash; name of the letter ع | عين السمكة *ʿa. as-samaka* corn (on the toes); عين شمس *ʿa. šams* Heliopolis; سواد العين *sawād al-ʿa.* eyeball; شاهد عين eyewitness; طرفة — عين (لحظة) ما (*ṭarfata, laḥẓata*) not one moment; اسم العين *ism al-ʿa.* concrete noun (*gram.*); مجلس الاعيان *majlis al-a.* senate (*Ir.*); فرض عين *farḍ ʿa.* individual duty (*Isl. Law*); بام عينه *bi-ummi ʿainihī* with one's own eyes; بعيني رأسه *bi-ʿainai raʾsihī* do.; بعينه *bi-ʿainihī* in person, personally; exactly the same, the very same thing; هو بعينه none other than he, precisely this one; هو هو بعينه it's none other than he; هو شخص بعينه (*šaḵṣun*) he is a real person, a man who actually exists; للسبب عينه *li-s-sababi ʿainihī* for the same reason; على العين والرأس very gladly! with pleasure! رأى رأى العين *raʾā raʾya l-ʿain* to find out, or see, with one's own eyes; اعاده اثرا بعد عين (*aʿādahū aṯaran*) to ruin s.th. completely; ملأ عينه (*ʿainahū*) to satisfy s.o.; to please s.o.; نزل من عيني I lost all respect for him; نظر اليه بعين الاحتقار to look at s.o. contemptuously; وقعت العين على العين (*waqaʿat*) fighting broke out; عيون الشعر *ʿuyūn aš-šiʿr* gems of poetry, choicest works of poetry

عيني *ʿainī* ocular, eye- (in compounds); real; corporeal, material (*jur.*), consisting in goods of material value, in produce or commodities, in kind

عينية *ʿainīya* identity; ○ (pl. *-āt*) eyepiece, ocular (*opt.*)

عين *ʿayyin* easily crying, tearful, crybabyish

عينة *ʿayyina* pl. *-āt* sample, specimen

عيني *ayyinī* serving as a sample

عوينات *ʿuwaināt* eyeglasses, spectacles; pince-nez

معين *maʿīn* spring, source (of water)

تعيين *taʿyīn* specification, particularization, itemization, designation; fixation, determination, appointment, assignment, scheduling; nomination, appointment; stipulation; allotment, apportionment, assignment, allocation, appropriation; (pl. *-āt*) ration, food | مراقب تعيين *murāqib t.* a military rank, approx.: quartermaster staff sergeant (*Eg.* 1939); صول تعيين *sol t.* do. (*Eg.*)

معاينة *muʿāyana* view(ing), examination, survey(ing); inspection; surveillance, supervision, control; observation

عيان *ʿiyān* (eye)witnessing, seeing (with one's own eyes), view(ing); clear, evident, plain, manifest | شاهد العيان eyewitness; بدا للعيان to come to light, come in sight, be before one's eye

عياني *ʿiyānī*: شاهد عياني eyewitness

معين *muʿayyan* fixed, determined, designated, assigned, scheduled, prescribed, stipulated; nominated, appointed; rhombus; (pl. *-āt*) fixed sum or amount (of money), rate, e.g., معين الكراء rental, rent | شبه المعين *šibh al-m.* or شبيه بالمعين rhomboid

معاين *muʿāyin* spectator, onlooker, viewer

غ

غابانى *ġābānī* cashmere, a soft twilled fabric

غار *ġār* see غور

غاز *ġāz* pl. *-āt* gas; petroleum, oil (*maġr.*) | الغازات السامة (*sāmma*) the poison gases

غازى *ġāzī* gaseous, gaslike | مياه غازية carbonated water, mineral water

غازوزة (It. *gasosa*) *ġāzūza* soda water

[1]غال *ġāl* pl. *-āt* padlock

[2]الغال *al-ġāl* Gaul (country)

غالى *ġālī* Gallic; (pl. *-ūn*) a Gaul

غانة *ġāna*[2], غانا Ghana

[1]غب to attack every other day (على, ه s.o., of fever)

غب *ġibb* end, outcome, upshot, issue, effect, result, consequence; *ġibba* (prep.) after | زاره غبا *zārahū ġibban* to visit s.o. at intervals; حمى الغب *ḥummā l-ġ.* tertian fever

غبب *ġabab* pl. اغباب *aġbāb* dewlap (of bovines), wattle

مغبة *maġabba* pl. *-āt* end, outcome, upshot, issue, effect, result, consequence

[2]غب *ġabba u* (= عب *'abba u*) to gulp down, pour down, toss down, drink avidly (ه s.th.)

غبة *ġubba* swallow, gulp, draught

غبر *ġabara u* (غبور *ġubūr*) to go by, elapse, pass; to be past, elapsed, bygone **II** to soil, or cover, with dust (ه, ه s.o., s.th.); to raise dust | غبر فى وجهه (*wajhihī*) to surpass, outstrip, outdo s.o., be superior to s.o. **IV** = **II**; **V** to be dust-covered, be or become dusty **IX** to be dust-colored

غبر *ġabir* recrudescent, reopening (wound)

غبرة *ġubra* dust color

غبرة *ġabara* dust

غبار *ġubār* dust; (pl. اغبرة *aġbira*) dust cloud | لا غبار عليه (*ġubāra*) clear, plain, distinct; unobjectionable, incontestable; blameless, irreproachable, faultless, impeccable (morally); ما شق غباره *mā šaqqa ġubārahū* he never quite attained his (another's) eminence, he did not measure up to him; لا يشق غباره *lā yušaqqu ġubāruhū* or لا يشق له غبار (*yušaqqu*) he is unsurpassable, he is unequaled; unsurpassable, unequaled, unrivaled, peerless, incomparable; جرى فى غباره (*jarā*) to follow s.o. loyally

اغبر *aġbar*[2], f. غبراء *ġabrā'*[2], pl. غبر *ġubr* dust-colored; dust-covered, dusty; الاغبر the earth, the ground; الغبراء the Earth

اغبرار *iġbirār* grudge, rancor, resentment (على toward)

غابر *ġābir* pl. غوابر *ġawābir*[2] bygone, past, elapsed; the past | الازمان الغابرة or القديم الغابر old times, ancient times

غبش *ġabaš* pl. اغباش *aġbāš* darkness, dark, duskiness; the twilight before sunrise, last shadows of the night

غبش *ġabiš* dark (night); opaque, not transparent

غبشة *ġubša* twilight (of dawn)

اغبش *aġbaš*[2], f. غبشاء *ġabšā'*[2], pl. غبش *ġubš* dark (night); opaque, not transparent

غباشة *ġabāša* weakness of the eyes, asthenopia

غبط *ġabaṭa* **i** (*ġabṭ*) **to envy (على ه s.o. s.th. or for s.th.); pass. *ġubiṭa* to be happy II to make (ه s.o.) envious; to deem (ه s.o.) fortunate, call (ه s.o.) happy VIII to be** glad, be delighted, rejoice, exult, be jubilant (ب at, about), be elated (ب by); to be happy (ب about); to be pleased, be satisfied (ب with)

غبطة *ğibṭa* state of happiness, happiness, exultation, delight, rapture, bliss, felicity; beatitude; title of the Patriarch (*Copt.-Chr.*) | صاحب الغبطة do.; كان محل غبطة (*maḥalla ğ.*) to be in an enviable position

اغتباط *iğtibāṭ* joy, delight, rejoicing, exultation, triumph, jubilation; happiness, contentedness, satisfaction, gratification, pleasure

مغبوط *mağbūṭ* in an enviable position, happy, lucky, fortunate; blessed, beatified, canonized (*Chr.*)

مغتبط *muğtabiṭ* glad, happy, delighted (ب at), pleased, satisfied (ب with), gratified (ب by)

غبن[1] **ğabana** *i* (*ğabn*) to cheat, dupe, gull, defraud, overreach (ه في s.o. in), impose (ه في upon s.o. in)

غبن *ğabn*, *ğubn* pl. غبون *ğubūn* fraud, deceit, imposture, swindle; defraudation, cheating, duping; damage, wrong, prejudice | غبن فاحش criminal fraud (*Isl. Law*)

غبن *ğaban* stupidity

تغابن *tağābun* mutual cheating | يوم التغابن *yaum at-t.* the Day of Resurrection

مغبون *mağbūn* deceived, defrauded, cheated, gulled, duped; prejudiced, wronged, injured | عاد or رجع بصفقة المغبون (*bi-ṣafqati l-m.*) to return empty-handed; to lose the game

غبانى[2] **ğabānī** and غابانى *ğābānī* cashmere, a soft twilled fabric

(غبو and غبى) **ğabiya** *a* (غباوة *ğabāwa*) not to comprehend (عن or ه s.th.), have no knowledge, be ignorant (عن or ه of s.th.); to be unknown, unfamiliar (على to s.o.) **VI** to be unaware (عن of s.th.)

غبى *ğabīy* pl. اغبياء *ağbiyā'*[2] unwise, unjudicious, ignorant, foolish, stupid; dolt, numbskull, ignoramus

غباء *ğabā'* ignorance, foolishness, stupidity

غباوة *ğabāwa* ignorance, foolishness, stupidity

غبوة *ğabwa* riddle, puzzle

اغبى *ağbā* stupider, more foolish, more simple-minded

غت **ğatta** *u* (*ğatt*) to press, choke, throttle (ه s.o.); to dip, plunge, immerse (ه, ه في s.o., s.th. in) | غت الضحك (*ḍaḥika*) to suppress one's laughter, bite one's lip

غث **ğaṯṯa** *i a* (غثاثة *ğaṯāṯa*, غثوثة *ğuṯūṯa*) to be or become lean, meager; — *ğaṯṯa* *i* (*ğaṯṯ*, غثيث *ğaṯīṯ*) to fester, suppurate, discharge pus (wound)

غث *ğaṯṯ* lean, thin, scrawny; meager, scanty, poor, wretched

غثيث *ğaṯīṯ* lean, thin, scrawny; pus, matter

غثاثة *ğaṯāṯa* leanness, thinness, scrawniness

غثى **ğaṯā** *i* to confuse, muddle, jumble, garble (ه s.th.); — غثت نفسه *ğaṯat nafsuhū* (*ğaṯy*, غثيان *ğaṯayān*) and غثيت نفسه (*ğaṯiyat*) to feel like vomiting, feel sick, be indisposed

غثى *ğaṯy* nausea, qualmishness, sickness; indisposition

غثيان *ğaṯayān* nausea, qualmishness, sickness; indisposition

غثاء *ğuṯā'* scum

غجر **II** (*eg.*) to scold, use abusive language, curse, swear

غجرى *ğajarī* pl. غجر *ğajar* gipsy

تغجير *tağjīr* scolding, cursing, abusive language

غد see غدو

غدد **ǧadad** cattle epidemic

غدة **ǧudda** pl. غدد **ǧudad** gland | الغدة الدرقية (*daraqīya*) thyroid gland; غدة صماء (*ṣammā'*) endocrine (or ductless) gland; الغدة الصنوبرية (*ṣanaubarīya*) pineal gland; الغدة النكفية (*nakfīya*) parotid gland

غددى **ǧudadī** glandular

غدر **ǧadara** *i u* (*ǧadr*) to act treacherously, perfidiously (ب or ب or ه toward s.o.), doublecross, deceive, betray, delude (ب or ه s.o.) **III** to leave (ه, ه s.o., s.th.; الى ه a place for), depart (الى ه from a place to)

غدر **ǧadr** perfidy, breach of faith, betrayal, treason, treachery

غدير **ǧadīr** pl. غدر **ǧudur**, غدران **ǧudrān** pond, pool, puddle; stream, brook, creek, river

غديرة **ǧadīra** pl. غدائر **ǧadā'ir**[2] queue, pigtail, braid, plait, tress (of hair)

غدار **ǧaddār** perfidious, disloyal, treacherous, traitorous; false, faithless, deceitful

غدارة **ǧaddāra** pl. *-āt* pistol | غدارة سريعة الطلق (*s. aṭ-ṭalq*) submachine gun, Tommy gun

غادر **ǧādir** perfidious, disloyal, treacherous; false, faithless, deceitful

غدفة **ǧudfa** pl. غدف **ǧudaf** headcloth, kerchief

غداف **ǧudāf** raven

غدق **ǧadiqa** *a* (*ǧadaq*) to be copious, be heavy, pour down (rain) **IV** = **I**; to give bountifully (على to s.o.), shower, load (على ه s.o. with s.th.), bestow liberally (على ه upon s.o. s.th.)

غدق **ǧadiq** copious, abundant (water, rain)

مغدق **muǧdiq** copious, abundant (water, rain)

غدن **XII** **iǧdaudana** to grow long and luxuriantly (hair)

غدن **ǧadan** languor, lassitude, flaccidity, limpness

غدنة **ǧudna** languor, lassitude, flaccidity, limpness

غدان **ǧidān** clothes peg

مغدودن **muǧdaudin** luxuriant, flowing, long (hair)

(غدو) غدا **ǧadā** *u* (*ǧudūw*, *ǧadw*, غدوة *ǧadwa*) to go (away), leave, come, do, or be, early in the morning; to run; to become (ه s.th.), grow, turn (ه into), come to be (ه s.th.) | غدا وراح (*wa-rāḥa*) to go back and forth, walk to and fro; to come and go; — غدى **ǧadiya** *a* (غدا *ǧadan*) to breakfast, have breakfast **II** to give breakfast (ه to s.o.); to give lunch (ه to s.o.) **III** to go early in the morning (ه to s.o.) | يراوحها ويغاديها *yurāwiḥuhā wa-yuǧādīhā* he calls on her time and again or constantly **V** to breakfast, have breakfast; to lunch, have lunch

غد **ǧad** the morrow, the following day; غدا **ǧadan** tomorrow; on a future day, sometime in the future | من غد, فى غد on the following day, tomorrow; فى الغد do.; on a future day, sometime in the future; بعد غد day after tomorrow; فى ذات غد see ذات

غداء **ǧadā'** pl. اغدية **aǧdiya** breakfast; lunch

غداة **ǧadāh** pl. غدوات **ǧadawāt** early morning; الغداة *al-ǧadāta* this morning

غدوة **ǧudwa** pl. غدى **ǧudan** early morning

غدوة **ǧadwa** pl. *ǧadawāt* lunch; morning errand; غدواته وروحاته (*rauḥātuhū*) all his goings, his coming and going

مغدى **maǧdan** place to which one goes in the morning | مغدى ومراح (*wa-marāḥ*) an ever frequented place, an aspired goal

غذ *ğadda* i (*ğadd*) to fester, suppurate (wound) IV do.; to hasten, speed, make forced marches | اغذ (فى) السير (*sair*) to run fast, hasten, hurry, speed

غذا (غذو) *ğadā* u (*ğadw*) to feed (ه ب s.o. s.th.), nourish, nurture (ه ب s.o. with) II to feed (ه ب s.o. s.th.), nourish, nurture (ه ب s.o. with); to provide, supply, furnish, sustain (ه ب ,ه s.o., s.th. with), feed, charge. replenish (ه ب s.th. with) V to be fed (ب s.th.), be nourished, be nurtured (ب with); to feed, live (ب on); to be supplied, be provided, be furnished, be fed (ب with, e.g., with electric power) VIII to be fed, be nourished, be nurtured

غذو *ğadw* feeding, nourishment, alimentation, nutrition, nurture

غذاء *ğidā'* pl. اغذية *ağdiya* nourishment, nutriment, nutrition, nurture, food; pl. foodstuffs, victuals, food

غذائى *ğidā'ī* alimental, alimentary, nutritional, nutritious, nutritive | مواد غذائية (*mawādd*) foodstuffs, victuals, food, nutritive substances

تغذية *tağdiya* feeding (also *techn.*), nourishment, alimentation, nutrition, provisioning, supply, input, charging (e.g., of an electric battery)

غر *ğarra* u (غرور *ğurūr*) to mislead, deceive, beguile (ب s.o.); to delude, gull, dazzle, blind (ه s.o.) II to deceive, beguile (ب s.o.); to delude, gull, dazzle, blind (ب s.o.); to entice, allure, tempt, seduce (ب s.o.); to expose to danger, endanger, imperil (ب s.o., s.th.), risk, jeopardize, hazard (ب s.th.) | غرر بنفسه to expose o.s. to danger, risk one's life VIII to be dazzled, blinded, fooled, deluded, misled, let o.s. be deceived (ب by), be mistaken (ب in, about); to be or become overweening or conceited X to come unexpectedly (ه to s.o.), surprise (ه s.o.)

غر *ğarr* (cutting) edge of a sword

غر *ğirr* pl. اغرار *ağrār* inexperienced, gullible, new, green; a greenhorn; inattentive, inadvertent, heedless

غرة *ğurra* pl. غرر *ğurar* white spot on a horse's face, blaze; the best, the finest, the prime (of s.th.); highlight | غرة الشهر *ğ. aš-šahr* the first day of the month; فى غرة العام at the beginning of the year

غرة *ğirra* inadvertency, heedlessness, inattentiveness, inattention; unguarded moment, moment of inadvertence | على غرة or على حين غرة (*ḥīni ğ.*) unexpectedly, unawares, inadvertently, surprisingly; اخذ على (حين) غرة (*ukida*) to be surprised, be taken by surprise, be caught unawares

غرر *ğarar* risk, hazard, jeopardy, danger, peril

غرور *ğurūr* deception; delusion, illusion; conceit, overweeningness, snobbery; vanities, trifles, banalities; danger, peril | الغرور بنفسه self-deception, self-delusion

غرور *ğarūr* deceptive, delusive, fallacious, illusory

غرير *ğarīr* deceived, misled, tempted; (pl. also اغراء *ağirrā'*[2], اغرة *ağirra*) inexperienced, naive, ingenuous, gullible

غرار *ğirār* (cutting) edge of a sword; غرارا *ğirāran* in a hurry, hastily | على غرار in a hurry, hastily; ... على (من) غرار like ..., similar to ..., in the manner of ..., after the pattern of ...; على هذا الغرار in this manner; على غرار واحد after one pattern, in the same manner, likewise, alike

غرار *ğarrār* deceptive, delusive, fallacious

غرارة *ğarāra* inconsiderateness, thoughtlessness, heedlessness | على غرارة in the manner of ..., after the pattern of ...

غرارة *ğirāra* pl. غرائر *ğarā'ir*² sack (for straw or grain)

اغر *ağarr*², f. غراء *ğarrā'*², pl. غر *ğurr* having a blaze (horse); beautiful, handsome; magnanimous, generous; noble; esteemed, honorable (esp. as a complimentary epithet following the name of a newspaper) | اغر محجل (*muḥajjal*) unique, singular

مغرور *mağrūr* deceived, fooled, misled, tempted; deluded, dazzled, blind; vain, conceited, overweening, snobbish

غرام *ğrām* pl. *-āt* gram(me)

غرب *ğaraba u* (*ğarb*) to go away, depart, absent o.s., withdraw (عن from), leave (عن s.o., s.th.); — *ğaraba u* (غروب *ğurūb*) to set (sun, etc.); — *ğaruba u* (غرابة *ğarāba*) to be a stranger; to be strange, odd, queer, obscure, abstruse, difficult to comprehend | لا يغرب عنك ان you will not have failed to notice that ..., you are, no doubt, aware (of the fact) that ..., you know very well that ... **II** to go away, leave, depart, absent o.s.; to go westward; to expel from the homeland, banish, exile, expatriate (ه s.o.) | غرب وشرق (*wa-šarraqa*) to get around in the world, see the world **IV** to say or do a strange or amazing thing; to exceed the proper bounds (فى in), overdo, exaggerate (فى s.th.) | اغرب فى الضحك (*ḍaḥik*) to laugh noisily or heartily, guffaw **V** to go to a foreign country, emigrate; to be (far) away from one's homeland; to become an occidental, become Westernized, be Europeanized; to assimilate o.s. to the Western way of life **VIII** to go to a foreign country, emigrate; to be (far) away from one's homeland **X** to find (ه s.th.) strange, odd, queer, unusual; to deem (ه s.th.) absurd, preposterous, grotesque; to disapprove (ه of s.th.); to become an occidental, become Westernized, be Europeanized; to assimilate o.s. to the Western way of life | استغرب فى الضحك (*ḍaḥik*) to laugh noisily or heartily, guffaw

غرب *ğarb* west; occident; vehemence, violence, impetuosity, tempestuousness; الغرب the West, the Occident; غربا *ğarban* westward, toward the west | فل غربه *falla ğarbahū* to subdue s.o., put a damper on s.o.; غربا بجنوب *ğarban bi-janūbin* southwestward, toward the southwest

غربى *ğarbī* western, westerly; occidental, Western; European; an Occidental, a Westerner; الغربيون *al-ğarbīyūn* the Western Church (*Chr.*)

غربة *ğurba* absence from the homeland; separation from one's native country, banishment, exile; life, or place, away from home

غراب *ğurāb* pl. غربان *ğirbān*, اغرب *ağrub*, اغربة *ağriba* crow; raven; — occiput; blade (esp. of a hatchet)

غريب *ğarīb* pl. غرباء *ğurabā'*² strange, foreign, alien, extraneous (على or عن to s.o.); strange, odd, queer, quaint, unusual, extraordinary, curious, remarkable, peculiar; amazing, astonishing, baffling, startling, wondrous, marvelous; grotesque; difficult to understand, abstruse, obscure (language); remote, outlandish, rare, uncommon (word); (pl. also اغراب *ağrāb*) stranger, foreigner, alien; pl. اغراب those living abroad, those away from home, emigrés | غريب الاطوار whimsical, capricious, eccentric, cranky; مادة غريبة (*mādda*) foreign body, extraneous substance

غريبة *ğarība* pl. غرائب *ğarā'ib*² peculiarity; a strange, striking thing, oddity, curiosity, marvel, prodigy, wonder

غروب *ğurūb* setting (of the sun, of a star)

غرابة *ğarāba* strangeness, curiousness; oddness, queerness, singularity, peculiarity

اغرب *aḡrab*[2] stranger, more alien; odder, queerer, more unusual

مغرب *maḡrib* pl. مغارب *maḡārib*[2] place or time of sunset; west, occident; (f.) prayer at sunset (*Isl. Law.*); المغرب Maghrib, northwest Africa | مغرب الشمس *m. aš-šams* time of sunset, sunset; بلاد المغرب Maghrib, northwest Africa; مشارق الارض ومغاربها (*m. al-arḍ*) the entire world; المشرقان والمغربان *al-mašriqān wa-l-m.* do.; فى المغربين وفى المشرقين all over the world, throughout the world

مغربى *maḡribī* North African, Maghribi; (pl. مغاربة *maḡāriba*) a North African, a Maghribi

مغربة look up alphabetically

تغريب *taḡrīb* banishment, expatriation

تغرب *taḡarrub* separation from one's native country; emigration; Europeanism, Occidentalism, Westernism

اغتراب *iḡtirāb* separation from one's native country; emigration; Europeanism, Occidentalism, Westernism

استغراب *istiḡrāb* wonder, surprise, astonishment, amazement, perplexity

غارب *ḡārib* pl. غوارب *ḡawārib*[2] withers (of the camel, of the horse); pl. wave crests | ترك (or القى) حبله على غاربه (*alqā ḥablahū*) to give free rein to s.o. or to s.th.

مغرب *muḡarrab* expatriated, exiled, banished; expatriate, exile

مغترب *muḡtarib* stranger, foreigner, alien; living away from home

مستغرب *mustaḡrib* Europeanized, Westernized

مستغرب *mustaḡrab* strange, odd, queer, quaint, unusual, extraordinary, curious, peculiar

غربل **ḡarbala** (غربلة *ḡarbala*) to sieve, sift, riddle (ه s.th.)

غربال *ḡirbāl* pl. غرابيل *ḡarābīl*[2] sieve

غرابلى *ḡarābilī* pl. *-ūn*, غرابلية *ḡarābilīya* sieve maker, sieve merchant

غرد **ḡarida** *a* (*ḡarad*) to sing, twitter (bird), warble II and V = I

غرد *ḡarad* singing, song, twitter(ing), warbling (of a bird)

غرد *ḡurd* pl. غرود *ḡurūd* dune, shifting dune

غريد *ḡirrīd* singing, twittering, warbling (bird)

اغرودة *uḡrūda* pl. اغاريد *aḡārīd*[2] twittering, warbling, song (of birds)

تغريد *taḡrīd* singing, song, twitter(ing), warbling

مغرد *muḡarrid* singing, twittering, warbling (bird) | طائر مغرد songbird

غرز **ḡaraza** *i* (*ḡarz*) to prick (ه ب s.th. with, e.g., with a needle); to thrush, plunge, insert, stick, stab, ram, push, bore (ه فى s.th. into); to plant, implant (ه فى s.th. in) II to thrust, plunge, insert, stick, stab, ram, push, bore (ه فى s.th. into) IV = II; V to penetrate deeply (فى into), pierce (فى s.th.); to be inserted, be stuck (فى into) VII to bore, penetrate (فى into), pierce (فى s.th.); to sink (فى into) VIII to penetrate deeply (فى into), pierce (فى s.th.); to be inserted, be stuck (فى into) | اغترز السير (*saira*) (he put his foot in the stirrup, ready to depart=) his departure was imminent

غرز *ḡarz* leather stirrup

غرزة *ḡurza* pl. غرز *ḡuraz* stitch

غريزة *ḡarīza* pl. غرائز *ḡarā'iz*[2] nature, natural disposition; natural impulse, instinct

غريزى *ḡarīzī* natural, native, innate, inborn; instinctive

مغرز *maḡraz* pl. مغارز *maḡāriz*[2] (*eg.*) prank, practical joke

غرس *ğarasa* *i* (*ğars*) to plant, implant (ه في s.th. in); to place, put, set, infix, interpose, interpolate, insert (ه في s.th. into) **IV** to plant, implant (ه s.th.) **VII** to be planted, be implanted; to sink in

غرس *ğars* planted; (pl. اغراس *ağrās*, غراس *ğirās*) plant, layer, cion, nursery plant, seedling

غرس *ğirs* pl. اغراس *ağrās* plant, layer, cion, nursery plant, seedling

غرسة *ğarsa* plant

غراس *ğirās* plant; planting time

غراسة *ğirāsa* cultivation, growing, raising | غراسة الزيتون (الزياتين) *ğ. az-zaitūn* olive growing; غراسة العنب *ğ. al-ʿinab* wine growing; viticulture

غريسة *ğarīsa* pl. غرائس *ğarāʾis*², غراس *ğirās* nursery plant, layer, cion, seedling

مغرس *mağris* pl. مغارس *mağāris*² place where s.th. is infixed, interposed or inserted; nursery, plantation, bed

مغارسة *muğārasa* pl. *-āt* a contract for the lease of an orchard providing that the lessee, who undertakes to cultivate the orchard, will become owner of one half of it after the orchard has yielded profit (*Tun.*)

مغارسى *muğārisī* pl. *-ūn* one who concludes a *muğārasa* (q.v.) (*Tun.*)

غرش *ğirš*, *ğurš* pl. غروش *ğurūš* piaster | غرش صاغ standard piaster

غرض **IV** اغرض الغرض (*ğaraḍa*) to attain the goal **V** to take sides, be partial, have a predilection, have a bias (ل for)

غرض *ğaraḍ* pl. اغراض *ağrāḍ* target, aim, goal, objective, object; intention, design, purpose; object of desire; (personal, selfish) interest; inclination, tendency, propensity; bias, prejudice; pl. اغراض (*syr.*) articles of everyday use, things, objects, stuff, odds and ends

غرضى *ğaraḍī* tendency- (in compounds), marked by directional, or purposive, presentation

غريض *ğarīḍ* pl. اغاريض *ağārīḍ*² fresh, tender

تغرض *tağarruḍ* prejudice, bias; tendentious attitude

مغرض *muğriḍ* partial, biased, tendentious; — (pl. *-ūn*) partial person; biased person; person guided by personal interests

غرغر *ğarğara* (غرغرة *ğarğara*) to gargle; to gurgle; to simmer, bubble (pot) **II** *tağarğara* to gargle; to gurgle | تغرغرت عينه بالدمع (*ʿainuhū bi-d-damʿ*) his eyes were bathed in tears

غرغر *ğirğir* (coll.; n. un. ة) guinea fowl

غرغرة *ğarğara* gargling, gargle, gurgle

غرف *ğarafa* *i* *u* (*ğarf*) to ladle, spoon, scoop (ه s.th.); to ladle (ه food) from a cooking pot, and the like, (into a bowl) for serving; to serve (ه a meal) **VIII** to ladle, scoop (ه من s.th. from or out of)

غرفة *ğurfa* pl. غراف *ğirāf* the amount of water scooped up with one hand; handful; — (pl. *-āt*, غرف *ğuraf*) upstairs room, room on an upper floor; room; chamber (= room; as a public body of administration, etc.); cabinet; compartment, ward | غرفة الاكل *ğ. al-akl* dining room; غرفة التجارة or الغرفة التجارية chamber of commerce; غرفة السفرة *ğ. as-sufra* dining room; غرفة القيادة bridge (*naut.*); غرفة النوم *ğ. an-naum* bedroom

غراف *ğarrāf* pl. غراريف *ğarārīf*² (*syr.*) a water wheel turned by oxen or horses and used for raising irrigation water from a river onto the fields

مغرفة *miğrafa* pl. مغارف *mağārif*² large spoon, ladle, scoop

غرق *ğariqa a* (*ğaraq*) to plunge, dive, become immersed, immerge, become submersed, submerge, sink, founder (ف in); to go under, be drowned (ف in); to be immersed, be engrossed, be absorbed (ف in); to be wholly engaged, be lost (ف in), be completely taken up (ف with) **II** to plunge, dip, immerse, submerse (ه, ه s.o., s.th.); to sink, founder (ه s.th.), drown (ه, ه s.o., s.th.); to inundate, flood (ه s.th.; السوق the market ب with) **IV** = **II**; to exceed the proper bounds (ف in); to exaggerate, overdo (ف s.th.); to be excessive (ف in s.th.), carry (ف s.th.) to excess | اغرق فى الضحك (*ḍaḥik*) to laugh noisily or heartily, guffaw **V** to be sunk, be foundered **X** to sink (ف into sleep, and the like), be immersed (ف in); to absorb, engross, engage wholly, claim completely, fill, take up, occupy (ه, ه s.o., s.th.); to take, last (ه a certain time) | استغرق فى الضحك (*ḍaḥik*) to laugh noisily or heartily, guffaw **XII** اغرورقت عيناه بالدموع (*iğrauraqat ʿaināhu*) his eyes were bathed in tears

غريق *ğariq* pl. غرقى *ğarqā* drowned; a drowned person; immersed, engrossed, absorbed (ف in)

غرقان *ğarqān* drowned

تغريق *tağrīq* drowning; sinking, foundering, scuttling (of a ship); inundation, flooding

اغراق *iğrāq* drowning; sinking, foundering, scuttling (of a ship); inundation, flooding; exaggeration; excessiveness, exorbitance, immoderation, extravagance; hyperbole (*rhet.*)

غارق *ğāriq* sunk, drowned; immersed, engrossed, absorbed (ف in) | غارق فى الدهشة (*dahša*) completely taken aback, deeply shocked, utterly dismayed

مغرق *muğriq* immersed, engrossed, absorbed (ف in)

مستغرق *mustağriq* immersed, engrossed, absorbed (ف in)

غرلة *ğurla* pl. غرل *ğural* foreskin, prepuce

غرم *ğarima a* (*ğurm*, غرامة *ğarāma*, مغرم *mağram*) to pay (ه a fine, and the like); to suffer loss **II** to fine (ه s.o.), impose a fine (ه on s.o.) **IV** = **II**; pass. *uğrima* to be very fond, be enamored (ب of), be in love, be infatuated (ب with) **V** to be fined, be mulcted

غرم *ğurm* damage, loss

غرام *ğarām* infatuation (ب with), love (ب of), passion, ardent desire (ب for); penalty, mulct, fine; see also alphabetically

غرامى *ğarāmī* passionate, impassioned, erotic, amorous, amatory, love (used attributively); غراميات *ğarāmīyāt* amours, romances, love affairs, amorous adventures | رسالة غرامية love letter

غريم *ğarīm* pl. غرماء *ğuramā'*[2] debtor; creditor; opponent, adversary, antagonist, rival; insulter

غريمة *ğarīma* woman opponent, female antagonist, rival

غرامة *ğarāma* pl. *-āt* fine, mulct; indemnity, compensation, damages; reparation, amends, penalty

مغرم *mağram* pl. مغارم *mağārim*[2] damages, loss; debt; liability, financial obligation; fine

مغرم *muğram* enamored (ب of), in love, infatuated (ب with)

غرين *ğarīn* (alluvial) mud

غرناطة *ğarnāṭa*[2] Granada (city in S Spain)

غرنوق *ğurnūq* pl. غرانيق *ğarānīq*[2] crane (*zool.*)

غرنيق *ğirnīq* pl. غرانيق *ğarānīq*[2] crane (*zool.*)

(غرو) غرا *ḡarā u* (*ḡarw*) to glue, fix with glue (ه s.th.) II = I; IV to make (ه s.o.) covetous (ب for), prod, spur on, goad, egg on, incite, induce, instigate, abet, urge, impel (ب ه s.o. to do s.th.); to entice, allure, tempt, seduce (ب ه s.o. to); to set (ب ه s.o. on), sick (ب ه a dog, etc., on game); to bring about, cause, produce, provoke (ه s.th.); pass. *uḡriya* to desire ardently, love (ب s.th.), be attached (ب to s.th.) | اغرى العداوة بين (*ʻadāwata*) to cause or excite enmity among ...

لا غرو *lā ḡarwa* no wonder! it is small wonder

غرا *ḡaran* glue

غراء *ḡirā'* glue

غرائى *ḡirā'ī* gluey, glutinous

غروى *ḡirawī* gluey, glutinous, sticky, ropy, viscous; colloidal (*chem.*)

لا غروى *lā ḡarwā* no wonder! it is small wonder

غراية *ḡarrāya* pl. *-āt* (*eg.*) glue pot

مغراة *miḡrāh* glue pot

اغراء *iḡrā'* incitement, instigation, inducement, spur, goad, impetus; incentive, stimulus; enticement, allurement, temptation, seduction

مغر *muḡrin* enticing, alluring, tempting; inciter, instigator, abettor; tempter, seducer

مغريات *muḡriyāt* lures, temptations

[1]غز IV to be thorny, prickly; to prick

[2]غزة *ḡazza*[2] Gaza (seaport in S Palestine)

غزى *ḡazzī* gauze

[1]غزر *ḡazura u* (*ḡazr*, غزارة *ḡazāra*) to be plentiful, copious, abundant

غزر *ḡazr* abundance, copiousness, profusion, plenty, large quantity, lavish supply

غزير *ḡazīr* pl. غزار *ḡizār* much, plentiful, copious, abundant, ample; densely growing, luxuriantly growing; rich (ب in) | غزير المادة *ḡ. al-mādda* well-informed, learned, well-read; غزير المواد *ḡ. al-mawādd* offering a wealth of information (book)

غزارة *ḡazāra* abundance, copiousness, profusion, plenty, large quantity, lavish supply

[2]غزارى *ḡazārī* a variety of pigeon

غزل *ḡazala i* (*ḡazl*) to spin (ه s.th.); — *ḡazila a* (*ḡazal*) to display amorous behavior (ب toward a woman), make love (ب to a woman), court, woo (ب a woman), flirt (ب with a woman); to eulogize in verses (ب a woman) III to speak words of love, make love (ها to a woman), court, woo (ها a woman), flirt, dally, philander (ها with a woman) V to court, woo (ب a woman), make love (ب to a woman), flirt, dally (ب with a woman), make eyes (ب at a woman); to celebrate in love poems (ب a woman, also ف s.o.); to extol, laud, eulogize (ب s.th.) VI to flirt (with one another) VIII to spin (ه s.th.)

غزل *ḡazl* spinning; (pl. غزول *ḡuzūl*) spun thread, yarn | مصنع الغزل *maṣnaʻ al-ḡ.* spinning mill

غزل *ḡazal* flirt, flirtation, dalliance, dallying; love; words of love, cooing of lovers; love poetry, erotic poetry

غزلى *ḡazalī* amorous, amatory, erotic, love (used attributively)

غزال *ḡazāl* pl. غزلة *ḡizla*, غزلان *ḡizlān* gazelle

غزال *ḡazzāl* spinner (of yarn)

غزالة *ḡazāla* female gazelle, doe; (rising) sun, disk of the sun; pommel of the camel saddle

غزالة *ḡazzāla* spider

مغزل *maḡzil* pl. مغازل *maḡāzil*² spinning mill

مغزل *miḡzal, muḡzal* pl. مغازل *maḡāzil*² spindle | ابو مغازل *abū m.* (*eg.*) stork

مغازلة *muḡāzala* pl. *-āt* flirt, flirtation, dalliance, dallying

تغزل *taḡazzul* flirt, flirtation, dalliance, dallying

غزو غزا *ḡazā u* (*ḡazw*) to strive (ه for), aspire (ه to); to mean, intend (ه s.th.); — *ḡazā u* (*ḡazw*, غزوان *ḡazawān*) to carry out a military expedition, make a raid, foray, or incursion, commit aggression (ه, ه against s.o., against s.th.), attack, assault (ه, ه s.o., s.th.), raid, invade (ه s.th.); to conquer (ه s.th., ه s.o.); to overcome (ه, ه s.o., s.th.) | غزا السوق (*sūq*) to flood the market (*com.*)

غزو *ḡazw* assault, raid, incursion, inroad, invasion, attack, aggression; conquest

غزوة *ḡazwa* pl. *ḡazawāt* military expedition, foray; raid, incursion, inroad, invasion, attack, aggression; conquest; campaign of conquest

غزاة *ḡazāh* pl. غزوات *ḡazawāt* military expedition, foray; raid, incursion, inroad, invasion, attack, aggression; conquest; campaign of conquest

مغزى *maḡzan* pl. مغاز *maḡāzin* sense, meaning, signification, import; moral (of a story); motto; importance, significance, moment, consequence | مغزى دقيق subtle meaning; ذو مغزى *ḏū m.* significant

مغزاة *maḡzāh* pl. مغاز *maḡāzin* military expedition, foray, raid; المغازى the military campaigns of the Prophet

غاز *ḡāzin* pl. غزاة *ḡuzāh* one who carries out a military expedition or a foray; raider, invader, aggressor, conqueror; الغازى *al-ḡāzī* the war lord, warrior champion, ghazi

غازية *ḡāziya* pl. غواز *ḡawāzin* woman dancer, danseuse

غس *ḡuss* (sing. and pl.) worthless

غسق *ḡasaq* dusk, twilight before nightfall; dark of night

غسل *ḡasala i* (*ḡasl*) to wash (ه, ه ب s.o., s.th. with), launder (ه ب s.th. with); to cleanse, clean (ه s.th., e.g., the teeth); to purge, cleanse, clear, wash (ه s.th., من of); to wash (ه against s.th.) **II** to wash thoroughly (ه , ه s.o., s.th.) **VIII** to wash (o.s.); to take a bath, bathe; to perform the major ritual ablution (i.e., a washing of the whole body; *Isl. Law*)

غسل *ḡusl* pl. اغسال *aḡsāl* washing, ablution; the major ritual ablution, i.e., a washing of the whole body (*Isl. Law*); wash water

غسل *ḡisl* wash water

غسلة *ḡasla* pl. *ḡasalāt* (n. vic.) a wash, an ablution

غسيل *ḡasīl* washed; (dirty or washed) clothes, washing

غسول *ḡasūl* wash water; washing agent, detergent

غاسول *ḡāsūl* soap; lye

غسال *ḡassāl* washer, washerman, laundryman

غسالة *ḡassāla* pl. *-āt* washerwoman, laundress; washing machine

غسالة *ḡusāla* dirty wash water, slops

مغسل *maḡsil, maḡsal* pl. مغاسل *maḡāsil*² washing facility, washroom, lavatory; washhouse

مغسل *miḡsal* washbasin, washbowl, washdish, washtub

مغسلة *maḡsala* pl. مغاسل *maḡāsil*² washstand

مغتسل *muḡtasal* washroom, lavatory

غش *ğašša u* (*ğašš*) to act dishonestly (ه toward s.o.); to deceive, fool, mislead, cheat, gull, dupe (ه s.o.); to debase, vitiate, adulterate (ه s.th., esp. foodstuffs) **II** to act dishonestly (ه toward s.o.); to deceive, fool, mislead, cheat, gull, dupe (ه s.o.) **VII** and **VIII** to be deceived, be fooled, be cheated, be duped; to let o.s. be deceived **X** to regard (ه s.o.) as dishonest or as a fraud; to suspect (ه s.o.) of fraud or deception

غش *ğašš* adulteration, corruption, debasement; fraud, deceit

غش *ğišš* faithlessness, disloyalty, perfidy; deception, deceit; fraud, imposture, swindle

غشاش *ğaššāš* fraud, cheat, swindler, impostor; deceptive, delusive, false

مغشوش *mağšūš* deceived, fooled, cheated, duped; adulterated, corrupted, debased

غشم *ğašama i* (*ğašm*) to treat unjustly or tyrannically, to wrong, oppress (ه s.o.); to act unjustly or tyrannically (ه toward s.o.); to act thoughtlessly, haphazardly (ه in s.th.) **VI** to feign ignorance or inexperience **X** to regard (ه s.o.) as dumb, stupid, ignorant, or inexperienced

غشم *ğašm* oppression, repression, ill-treatment

غشوم *ğašūm* unjust, unfair, iniquitous, tyrannical; oppressor, tyrant | القوة الغشوم brute force

غشيم *ğašīm* pl. غشماء *ğušamā'*[2] inexperienced, ignorant, foolish, dumb, stupid; new (at an office), green, a greenhorn; raw, boorish, uneducated; unskilled, untrained, clumsy, awkward, gauche; raw, crude, unprocessed, unworked

غشومة *ğušūma* inexperience, foolishness

غاشم *ğāšim* unjust, unfair, iniquitous, tyrannical; oppressor, tyrant; scum, dross | قوة غاشمة (*qūwa*) brute force

غشو (and غشى) غشا *ğašā u* (*ğašw*) to come (ه to s.o.; ه to a place); — غشى *ğašiya a* (غشاوة *ğašāwa*) to cover, wrap up, envelop, conceal, veil (ه، ه s.o., s.th.); to come, descend (ه upon s.o.), overcome, overwhelm (ه s.o.); to be dark (night); — *ğašiya a* (غشيان *ğašayān*, *ğišyān*) to come (to s.o.; ه to a place); to go to see, visit (ه s.o., ه s.th.), call (ه on s.o.); to sleep (ها with a woman); to cover (ها the female animal); to commit, perpetrate (ه e.g., an outrage); to yield, give in (ه to a craving); — pass. غشى عليه (*ğušiya*) (غشى *ğašy*, *ğušy*) to lose consciousness, faint, swoon **II** to cover, wrap up, envelop, veil (ه، ه s.o., s.th.); to spread a cover or wrap (ه، ه over s.o., over s.th.); to overlay, coat, plate (ه s.th.) **IV** to be dark (night); to spread a cover or wrap (على، ه over) **V** to cover o.s. (ب with), wrap o.s. (ب in) **X** استغشى ثيابه (*tiyābahū*) to hide one's head in one's clothes so as not to see or hear

غشى *ğašy*, *ğušy* unconsciousness, fainting, swoon(ing)

غشية *ğašya* fainting spell, swoon, faint

غشوة *ğašwa* veil, wrap, cover, covering

غشاء *ğišā'* pl. اغشية *ağšiya* cover, covering, wrap, wrapper, wrapping, envelope; coating, coat, plating; integument; film, pellicle; membrane; valve | الغشاء الانفى (*anfī*) nasal mucosa; غشاء البكارة *ğ. al-bakāra* hymen, virginal membrane; الغشاء المخاطى (*mukāṭī*) mucous membrane, mucosa

غشائى *ğišā'ī*: الخناق الغشائى (*kunāq*) diphtheria (*med.*)

غشاوة *ğišāwa*, *ğašāwa* veil, wrap, cover, covering

غشيان *ğašayān*, *ğišyān* unconsciousness, faint(ing), swoon(ing)

مغشى *mağšan* place at which one arrives, object of a visit

غاشية *ġāšiya* pl. غواش *ġawāšin* pericardium; misfortune, calamity, disaster; faint, swoon; insensibility, stupor; servants, attendants, retinue, suite

غص *ġaṣṣa* (1st pers. perf. *ġaṣiṣtu*) *a* (غصص *ġaṣaṣ*) to be choked; to choke (ب on, esp. on some food); to be overcrowded, congested, jammed, packed, crammed (ب with) | غص بهم المكان (*makānu*) the place was overcrowded **IV** to choke (ه s.o.) **VIII** to be overcrowded, congested, jammed, packed, crammed

غصة *ġuṣṣa* pl. *-āt*, غصص *ġuṣaṣ* that which causes choking, a lump in the throat; mortal distress, torment, agony, ordeal; choking sound, suppressed moan | غصة الموت *ġ. al-maut* agony of death

غاص *ġāṣṣ* replete, crowded, jammed, packed, crammed (ب with)

غصب *ġaṣaba* *i* (*ġaṣb*) to take away by force or illegally, extort (ه s.th., ه, من, على from s.o.), rob (ه s.th.; ه ه or من or على s.o. of s.th.), seize unlawfully, usurp (ه s.th.), take illegal possession (ه of s.th.); to force, compel, coerce (ه s.o., على to); to abduct, carry off (ها a woman); to rape, ravish, violate (ها a woman); to conquer, subdue (على s.o.) **VIII** = **I** | اغتصب ابواب البلاد to force one's entry into a country

غصب *ġaṣb* forcible, illegal seizure, extortion; usurpation, unlawful arbitrariness (*Isl. Law*); force, compulsion, coercion, constraint | غصبا *ġaṣban* and بالغصب forcibly, by force; غصبا عنه against his will, in defiance of him

اغتصاب *iġtiṣāb* forcible, illegal seizure, extortion, robbery; illegal appropriation, usurpation; ravishment, violation, rape (of a woman); force, compulsion, coercion, constraint

غاصب *ġāṣib* pl. *-ūn*, غصاب *ġuṣṣāb* usurper

مغصوب *maġṣūb* acquired by unlawful arbitrariness, extorted, usurped; forced, compelled, coerced, constrained

مغتصب *muġtaṣib* violent, outrageous, brutal; usurper

غصن **II** and **IV** to put forth branches, to branch (tree)

غصن *ġuṣn* pl. غصون *ġuṣūn*, اغصان *aġṣān*, twig, bough, limb, branch

غصنة *ġuṣna* twig, shoot, cion, sprout

غض *ġaḍḍa* (1st pers. perf. *ġaḍaḍtu*) *i* and (1st pers. perf. *ġaḍiḍtu*) *a* (غضوضة *ġuḍūḍa*, غضاضة *ġaḍāḍa*) to be or become fresh, succulent, tender (esp. a plant); — *ġaḍḍa u* (*ġaḍḍ*, غضاضة *ġaḍāḍa*) to cast down, lower (من or ه one's eyes, one's glance, out of modesty, and the like); to lower, lessen, diminish (من the value, the prestige of s.o. or s.th.), detract, derogate (من from s.o., from s.th.) | غض طرفه (*ṭarfahū*) to lower one's eyes; غض النظر (*naẓara*) or الطرف عنه to overlook, let pass, disregard s.th., pass over s.th., wink at s.th., pay no attention to s.th., have no objection to s.th.

غض *ġaḍḍ* aversion (of the glance) | غض النظر (الطرف) عنه *ġ. an-naẓar* (*aṭ-ṭarf*) overlooking of s.th.; disregarding of s.th.; بغض النظر عن aside from ..., not to speak of ..., let alone ..., regardless of ..., irrespective of ..., notwithstanding ...

غض *ġaḍḍ* fresh, succulent, juicy, tender; lush, luxuriant (plant)

غضة *ġuḍḍa* shortcoming, deficiency, fault, defect

غضيض *ġaḍīḍ* fresh, succulent, juicy, tender

غضاضة *ġaḍāḍa* freshness, succulence, juiciness, tenderness; shortcoming, deficiency, fault, defect; blot, stain, disgrace, shame | ما وجد غضاضة في to take no offense at ..., have no objection to ...

غضوضة ġuḍūḍa freshness, succulence, juiciness, tenderness

غضب ġaḍiba a (ġaḍab) to be or become angry, cross, mad, vexed, irritated, exasperated, furious, to fret (من or على at s.th., with s.o.); to stand up (ل for), defend (ل s.th.) **III** to be cross, be on bad terms (ه with s.o.) **IV** to annoy, exasperate, anger, make angry, enrage, infuriate (ه s.o.); to vex, irrigate, gall, provoke (ه s.o.) **V** = **I**

غضب ġaḍab wrath, rage, fury; anger, exasperation, indignation; غضبا ل (ġaḍaban) for the protection of

غضب ġaḍib wrathful, angry, exasperated, irate, furious, infuriated, enraged; vexed, annoyed, irritated, galled

غضبة ġaḍba fit of rage, angry outburst, tantrum

غضوب ġaḍūb irascible, choleric, irritable

غضابى ġuḍābī irascible, choleric, irritable; sullen, morose

غضبان ġaḍbān[2], f. غضبى ġaḍbā, pl. غضاب ġiḍāb, غضابى ġaḍābā, ġuḍābā wrathful, angry, exasperated, irate, furious, infuriated, enraged

اغضاب iġḍāb exasperation, infuriation; vexation, irritation, annoying; provocation

غاضب ġāḍib wrathful, angry, exasperated, irate, furious, infuriated, enraged; vexed, annoyed, irritated, galled

مغضوب maġḍūb: مغضوب عليه object of anger

غضر ġaḍara i (ġaḍr) to turn away (عن from); to turn (على against s.o. or to s.o.); — ġaḍira a (ġaḍar) to be or become rich, abundant, lavish, opulent, lush, luxuriant

غضر ġaḍir abundant, lavish, opulent, lush, luxuriant

غضير ġaḍīr fresh, green (plant)

غضارة ġaḍāra freshness; affluence, prosperity, opulence

غضروف ġuḍrūf pl. غضاريف ġaḍārīf[2] cartilage, gristle

غضن **II** to wrinkle, pucker, shrivel, fold, crease (ه s.th.) **III** to wink amorously (ها at a woman) **V** to wrinkle, shrivel, form creases or corrugations; to be or become wrinkled, creased, folded, corrugated

غضن ġaḍn, ġaḍan pl. غضون ġuḍūn wrinkle, fold, crease, corrugation; (only sg.) trouble, toil, labor, hardship, difficulty | في غضون ... in the course of, during, within; في غضون ذلك meanwhile, in the meantime

غضنفر ġaḍanfar lion

(غضو) **IV** to close one's eyes (also with عينه ʻainahū); to overlook, disregard, avoid seeing, condone (عن, ه s.th.), let (عن, ه s.th.) pass, shut one's eyes (عن, ه to s.th.), take no notice (عن, ه of s.th.); to be lenient (عن with), have indulgence, show forbearance (عن for), wink, connive (عن at) **VI** to pretend not to notice; to disregard (عن s.th.); اغضى عنه = تغاضى عنه

غضا (غضى) ġaḍan: على احر من جمر الغضى (aḥarra, jamri l-ġ.) lit: in a hotter spot than the live embers of ġaḍā (i.e., a variety of euphorbia), i.e., on pins and needles, in an unbearable situation

اغضاء iġḍā' overlooking, connivance, condonation, disregard; indulgence, forbearance

تغاض taġāḍin overlooking, connivance, condonation, disregard; indulgence, forbearance

غط *ġaṭṭa u* (*ġaṭṭ*) to immerse, dip, plunge (في ه, ه s.o., s.th. in); — *ġaṭṭa i* (غطيط *ġaṭīṭ*) to snore IV to immerse, dip, plunge (في ه, ه s.o., s.th. in) VII to be immersed, be dipped, be plunged (في in)

غطيط *ġaṭīṭ* snoring, snore

غطيطة *ġuṭaiṭa* fog, mist

غطرة *ġuṭra* designation of the *kūfīya*, or headcloth worn under the *'iqāl*, in Nejd and Bahrein

غطرس *ġaṭrasa* to be haughty, arrogant, supercilious, overbearing, snobbish, conceited, overweening, self-important II *taġaṭrasa* do. | تغطرس في مشيته (*mišyatihī*) to display a haughty bearing, swagger, strut

غطرسة *ġaṭrasa* haughtiness, superciliousness, arrogance, insolence, impudence, snobbishness, conceitedness, self-importance

غطريس *ġiṭrīs* pl. غطاريس *ġaṭārīs*² haughty, supercilious, arrogant, overbearing, snobbish, conceited, overweening, self-important

متغطرس *mutaġaṭris* haughty, supercilious, arrogant, overbearing, snobbish, conceited, overweening, self-important

غطريف *ġiṭrīf* pl. غطاريف *ġaṭārīf*², غطارف *ġaṭārif*², غطارفة *ġaṭārifa* potentate; a noble, great, famous man

غطس *ġaṭasa i* (*ġaṭs*) to dip, plunge, immerse, submerse (في ه, ه s.o., s.th. into water); to dive, plunge, become immersed, sink, submerge (في in water) II to dip, plunge, immerse, submerse (في ه, ه s.o., s.th. into water); (*Chr.*) to baptize (ه s.o.) V to dive; to bathe (في in)

غطس *ġaṭs* dipping, plunging, immersion; diving; sinking (trans. and intr.); submersion

غطاس *ġiṭās* baptism (*Chr.*); الغطاس Epiphany (*Chr.*)

غطاس *ġaṭṭās* diver (man or bird)

مغطس *maġṭis* (*miġṭas*) pl. مغاطس *maġāṭis*² bathtub; plunge bath | عيد المغطس *'īd al-m.* Epiphany (*Chr.*)

تغطيس *taġṭīs* dipping, plunging, immersion; submersion; baptism (*Chr.*)

غاطس *ġāṭis* draft (of a ship)

غطش *ġaṭaša i* (*ġaṭš*) to be or become dark (night); — *ġaṭiša a* (*ġaṭaš*) to become dim (eye); to be dim-sighted V to be dim, dim-sighted (eye)

غطش *ġaṭaš* dim-sightedness

غطم *ġiṭamm* huge, vast (ocean)

(غطو) غطا *ġaṭā u* (*ġaṭw*) to cover, cover up (ه s.th.) II to cover, wrap, envelop, conceal (ب ه, ه s.o., s.th. with); to slip (ب ه over s.th. s.th. else), cover (ب ه s.th. with); to cover (ه s.th., e.g., expenses, the goal in sports); to outshine, eclipse, obscure (على s.o., s.th.); to drown (على s.th., of voices, etc.); to be stronger, be more decisive (على than) V to be covered, wrapped, enveloped, concealed (ب with, by); to cover o.s. (ب with), wrap o.s., veil o.s., conceal o.s. (ب in) VIII = V

غطاء *ġiṭā'* pl. اغطية *aġṭiya* cover, covering, integument, wrap, wrapper, wrapping, envelope; covering (= clothing); lid | غطاء الرأس headgear

تغطية *taġṭiya* cover(ing) (of expenses, of currency, of the goal in sports); cover of notes in circulation, backing of notes, note coverage

غف *ġaffa i* (*eg.*) to take unawares; to grab, grasp, seize (على s.o.)

¹غفر *ġafara i* (*ġafr*, مغفرة *maġfira*, غفران *ġufrān*) to forgive (ل ه s.o. s.th.), grant pardon (ل ه to s.o. for s.th.), remit (ه s.th.) | لا يغفر (*yuġfaru*) unpardonable, irremissible, inexcusable VIII to forgive

(ه ل s.o. s.th.), grant pardon (ه ل to s.o. for), remit (ه s.th.) | لا يغتفر (yuġtafaru) unpardonable, irremissible, inexcusable X to ask s.o.'s (ه) pardon (ل or من or ه for an offense), ask (ه s.o.) to forgive (ل or من or ه an offense), apologize (ه to s.o., ل or من or ه for) | استغفر الله I ask God's forgiveness! a formular phrase used on various occasions, esp. when modestly declining compliments and amiabilities, approx.: please don't (say so)! not at all!

غفر ġafr pardon, forgiveness; غفرا ġafran pardon me! I beg your pardon!

غفور ġafūr readily inclined to pardon, much-forgiving (esp. of God)

غفار ġaffār readily inclined to pardon, much-forgiving (esp. of God)

غفران ġufrān pardon, forgiveness, remission | عيد صوم الغفران ʿīd ṣaum al-ġ. or عيد الغفران Day of Atonement, Yom Kippur (*Jud.*)

مغفرة maġfira pardon, forgiveness, remission

مغفور maġfūr: المغفور له (he who has been forgiven), the deceased, the late ...

²غفر II to guard (على s.o., s.th.), watch (على over s.o., over s.th.)

غفرة ġufra cover; lid

غفير ġafīr numerous (crowd), abundant (quantity), large (number); (pl. غفراء ġufarā'²) guard, sentinel; watchman | جم (جمع) غفير (jamm, jamʿ) large number or quantity, large gathering of people

غفارة ġifāra pl. غفائر ġafā'ir² kerchief for covering the head, headcloth

غفارة ġaffāra cope (*Chr.*)

مغفر miġfar pl. مغافر maġāfir² helmet

غفقة ġafqa light slumber

غفل ġafala u (غفلة ġafla, غفول ġufūl) to neglect, not to heed, disregard, ignore (عن s.th.), be forgetful, be heedless, be unmindful (عن of), pay no attention (عن to) II to make (ه s.o.) negligent, careless, heedless, or inattentive III to use, or take advantage of, s.o.'s (ه) negligence, inadvertence, inattention, heedlessness, or carelessness; to surprise, take by surprise, take unawares (ه s.o.) IV to neglect, not to heed, disregard, ignore (ه s.th.), be forgetful, be heedless, be unmindful (ه of s.th.), pay no attention (ه to s.th.); to pass (ه over s.th.), slight, leave out, omit, skip (ه s.th.); to leave unspecified (ه s.th.) V = III; VI to feign inattention, inadvertence, negligence, or carelessness; to pretend to be, or make as if, inattentive, inadvertent, negligent, or careless; to neglect, disregard, ignore, slight (ه, ه s.o., s.th.), pay no attention (عن to), be uninterested (عن in), be indifferent (عن to) X = III; to regard (ه s.o.) as stupid, as a fool; to make a fool of s.o. (ه), pull s.o.'s (ه) leg

غفل ġufl careless, heedless, unmindful, inadvertent; undesignated, unmarked; without name, anonymous; not provided (من with), devoid (من of) | غفل من التأريخ undated, without date, bearing no date; غفل من الامضاء (التوقيع) (imḍā') without signature, unsigned, anonymous; حديد غفل unprocessed iron, pig iron, crude iron

غفل ġafal negligence, inadvertence, inattention, heedlessness, carelessness

غفلة ġafla negligence, inadvertence, inattention, heedlessness, carelessness; indifference; foolishness; stupidity | موت الغفلة maut al-ġ. sudden death; على غفلة and على حين غفلة (ḥīni ġ.) suddenly, all of a sudden, unawares, inadvertently, unexpectedly, surprisingly

غفلان ġaflān⁽²⁾ negligent, neglectful, careless, heedless, inadvertent, inattentive; drowsy, sleepy

تغفيل taġfīl stultification

اغفال *iğfāl* neglect, disregard, ignoring, nonobservance, slight(ing); omission, skipping

تغافل *taġāful* neglect

غافل *ġāfil* pl. *-ūn*, غفول *ġufūl*, غفل *ġuffal* negligent, neglectful, careless, heedless, inadvertent, unaware, inattentive

مغفل *muġaffal* apathetic, indifferent, inattentive; gullible, easily duped, a sucker; simple-minded, artless; simpleton

مغفل *muġfal* anonymous | شركة مغفلة (= Fr. *société anonyme*) joint-stock corporation

متغفل *mutaġaffil* dunce, dolt, numskull

غفا *ġafā u* (*ġafw*, *ġufūw*) to slumber, doze, take a nap; to doze off, nod off, fall asleep; — *ġafiya a* (غفية *ġafya*) do. **IV** do. (غفو and غفى)

غفوة *ġafwa* pl. *-āt* slumber, nap, doze, cat nap

اغفاءة *iġfā'a* slumber, nap, doze, cat nap

غل *ġalla u* (*ġall*) to insert, put, stick, enter (ه في s.th. in(to) or between); to penetrate, enter (ه s.th. or into s.th.); to apply an iron collar or manacles (ه on s.o.), handcuff, shackle, fetter (ه s.o.); to produce, yield, yield crops (land) | غل يده الى عنقه (*yadahū*, *'unuqihī*) (lit.: to fetter one's hand to one's neck, i.e.) not to spend or give away anything, be niggardly; — *ġalla i* (*ġill*) to be filled with hatred or rancor (breast); — pass. *ġulla* (*ġull*, غلة *ġulla*) to suffer violent thirst, burn with thirst **II** to apply an iron collar or manacles (ه on s.o.), handcuff, shackle, fetter (ه s.o.) **IV** to produce, yield, yield crops (land); to yield (ه على to s.o. s.th.) **V** to enter, penetrate (في s.th. or into s.th.) **VII** = **V** **X** to rake in, gain, win, obtain, reap (ه s.th.); to realize, or make, a profit (ه on s.th.), receive the proceeds (ه of s.th., esp. of land, and the like), turn to (good) account, invest profitably, utilize (ه s.th.); to profit (ه by s.o., ه by s.th.), derive advantage or profit (ه, ه from), make capital (ه out of s.th.), capitalize (ه on s.th.); to take advantage (ه, ه of), exploit (ه, ه s.o., s.th.)

غل *ġill* rancor, hatred, spite, malice

غل *ġull* burning thirst; (pl. اغلال *aġlāl*) iron collar; manacles, handcuffs; pl. chains, shackles, fetters

غلة *ġulla* burning thirst

غلة *ġalla* pl. *-āt*, غلال *ġilāl* yield, produce, crops; proceeds, revenue, returns (esp. of farming); grain, cereals; corn; fruits

غليل *ġalīl* burning thirst; thirst for revenge; rancor, ill will; ardent desire; (pl. غلال *ġilāl*) exhausted with thirst, very thirsty

غلالة *ġilāla* pl. غلائل *ġalā'il*[2] a fine, diaphanous cape, mantilla, veil; shirtlike garment, gown | غلالة النوم *ġ. an-naum* nightshirt, nightgown

استغلال *istiġlāl* utilization; development, working (of a mine, and the like), exploitation (of a mine; also = selfish utilization, sweating); usufruct; abuse

استغلالى *istiġlālī* serving exploitation, exploitative

مغلول *maġlūl* fettered, shackled; exhausted with thirst, very thirsty | مغلول اليد *m. al-yad* inactive, idle

مغل *muġill* productive, fruitful, fertile (land, soil)

مستغل *mustaġill* exploiter, utilizer, usufructuary, beneficiary

مستغل *mustaġall* pl. *-āt* that which yields crops, proceeds, or profit; yield, produce, proceeds; profit

غلب *ḡalaba* **i** (*ḡalb*, غلبة *ḡalaba*) to subdue, conquer, vanquish, defeat, beat, lick (على or ه, ه s.o., s.th.), get the better (على or ه, ه of s.o., of s.th.), be victorious, triumph, gain ascendancy, get the upperhand, achieve supremacy (على or ه, ه over s.o., over s.th.); to master, surmount, overcome (على or ه s.th.); to seize (على or ه s.th.), take possession (على or ه of s.th.), lay hold (على or ه on s.th.); to overpower, overcome, overwhelm (على or ه s.o.); to snatch, wrench, wrest (ه على from s.o. s.th.), rob, plunder (ه على s.o. of s.th.); to prevail, (pre)dominate, be preponderant (على in s.th.); to be probable, be likely | غلب على الظن (*ẓann*) to be probable, be likely; تغلب عليه الصحة or الجدة (*ṣiḥḥatu, jiddatu*) (to be) fairly, almost correct or new; تغلب عليه الكآبة (*ka'ābatu*) he is in low spirits most of the time, melancholy prevails in him; يغلب عليه الكرم (*karamu*) his predominant, or foremost, quality is generosity **II** to make (ه s.o.) get the upperhand (على over), make (ه s.o.) triumph (على over); to put (ه على s.th. above or before) **III** to try to defeat (ه s.o.); to fight, combat (ه, ه s.o., s.th.), struggle, wrestle (ه, ه with; المصاعب with difficulties); to befall, overcome (ه s.o.; e.g., sleep) **V** to triumph, gain the mastery (على over), overcome, surmount, master (على s.th.), cope (على with), break (على a resistance); to outweigh (على s.th.) | تغلب عليه النعاس (*nu'āsu*) he was overcome by drowsiness **VI** to wrestle with one another, struggle

غلب *ḡalab* (act of) conquering, defeating, surmounting, overcoming

غلبة *ḡalaba* victory; (*eg.*) idle talk, chatter, prattle

غلباوى *ḡalabāwī* (*eg.*) garrulous, voluble, talkative; chatterbox, prattler, windbag

غلاب *ḡallāb* victorious, triumphant, conquering

اغلب *aḡlab*[2] (elative, with def. article or foll. genit.) the greater portion, the majority, most (of) | فى الاغلب in most cases; mostly, in general, generally; فى الاغلب والأعم (*wa-l-a'amm*) do.; فى اغلب الظن (*a. iẓ-ẓann*) most likely, most probably, in all probability; اغلب امره *aḡlaba amrihī* and اغلب الامر in most cases, mostly; most likely, most probably, in all probability

اغلبية *aḡlabīya* majority, greater portion | اغلبية خاصة (*ḵāṣṣa*) qualified majority; اغلبية مطلقة (*muṭlaqa*) absolute majority (*pol.*)

غلاب *ḡilāb* combat(ing), fight; struggle, strife, contest

مغالبة *muḡālaba* combat(ing), fight; struggle, strife, contest

تغلب *taḡallub* surmounting, overcoming, mastery (على of s.th.)

غالب *ḡālib* (pre)dominant; (with foll. genit. or suffix) most of, the greater portion of, the majority of; (pl. غلبة *ḡalaba*) victor | غالبا *ḡāliban* and فى الغالب mostly, in most cases, for the most part, largely; in general, generally; most likely, most probably; والغالب ان and the rule is that ..., as a rule ...

غالبية *ḡālibīya* majority, greater portion

مغلوب *maḡlūb* defeated, vanquished; beaten; recessive (*biol.*) | مغلوب على امره (*amrihī*) helpless

مغلب *muḡallab* defeated, overwhelmed, overcome

غلس *ḡalas* darkness of night (esp. that preceding daybreak)

غلصمة *ḡalṣama* pl. غلاصم *ḡalāṣim*[2] epiglottis

غلط *ḡaliṭa* **a** (*ḡalaṭ*) to make, or commit, a mistake, commit an error, err, be mistaken **II** to accuse (ه s.o.) of a mistake or error, put s.o. (ه) in the wrong; to make (ه s.o.) commit a mistake or error

III to seek to involve (ه s.o.) in errors or mistakes; to deceive, beguile, cheat, swindle (ه s.o.) **IV** to make (ه s.o.) commit a mistake or error **VI** to mislead one another, cheat one another

غلط *ġalaṭ* pl. اغلاط *aġlāṭ* error, mistake, blunder; incorrect, wrong | غلط الحس *ġ. al-ḥiss* deception of the senses, illusion; فى الامر غلط (*amr*) there is a but in the case, there is a hitch somewhere

غلطة *ġalṭa* pl. *ġalaṭāt*, اغلاط *aġlāṭ* error, mistake, blunder | غلطة مطبعية (*maṭba'iya*) misprint, erratum

غلطان *ġalṭān*² one who commits a mistake or error; mistaken, erring, wrong

اغلوطة *uġlūṭa* pl. *-āt*, اغاليط *aġālīṭ*² captious question

مغلطة *maġlaṭa* pl. مغالط *maġāliṭ*² captious question

مغالطة *muġālaṭa* pl. *-āt* cheating, deceit; swindle, fraud; falsification, distortion; fallacy, sophism

غلظ *ġaluẓa u* and *ġalaẓa i* (*ġilaẓ*, غلظة *ġilẓa*, غلاظة *ġilāẓa*) to be or become thick, gross, coarse, crude, rude, rough, rugged; to become viscous, viscid, tough, sirupy (of a liquid, mush); to treat (على s.o.) harshly, ruthlessly **II** to make (ه s.th.) thick, gross, big, coarse, crude, rude, rough, or rugged; to thicken, coarsen (ه s.th.) | غلظ اليمين to swear a sacred oath **IV** اغلظ له القول or فى القول (*qaula, fī l-qauli*) to bark at s.o. rudely, use rude language toward s.o., speak rudely, impolitely with s.o. **X** to become thick, gross, big, coarse, crude, rude, rough, rugged; to find (ه s.th.) thick, coarse, crude, rude, rough, rugged

غلظ *ġilaẓ* thickness, grossness; coarseness, crudeness, roughness, ruggedness; harshness, ruthlessness, rudeness, impoliteness, boorishness

غلظة *ġilẓa* thickness, grossness; coarseness, crudeness, roughness, ruggedness; harshness, ruthlessness, rudeness, impoliteness, boorishness

غليظ *ġalīẓ* pl. غلاظ *ġilāẓ* thick (e.g., curtain, fabric); fat and uncouth, hulking, burly, gross (person, body); viscous, viscid, sirupy (liquid); solid, stringy, tough (food); coarse, crude (fabric, words, person); rough, rugged (ground); harsh, callous, rude, churlish, inconsiderate, boorish; inviolable, sacred (alliance, oath) | غليظ الرقبة *ġ. ar-raqaba* stiff-necked, obdurate, obstinate, stubborn; المعى الغليظ (*mi'ā*) the large intestine (*anat.*); يمين غليظة binding, sacred oath

غلاظة *ġilāẓa* thickness, grossness; coarseness, crudeness, roughness, ruggedness

اغلظ *aġlaẓ*² thicker, grosser; coarser, cruder, rougher; ruder, more impolite

مغلظ *muġallaẓ*: يمين مغلظة binding, sacred oath

غلغل *ġalġala* to penetrate (فى s.th. or into s.th.); to enter (فى s.th. or into s.th.); to plunge, become immersed, submerge (فى in) **II** *taġalġala* to set in, descend, fall (night); to penetrate (فى s.th. or into s.th.); to enter (فى s.th. or into s.th.); to plunge, become immersed, submerge (فى in); to be crammed (فى into), be deeply embedded, be ensconced (فى in); to interfere, meddle

متغلغل *mutaġalġil* deeply embedded (فى in); extensive, widely extended, far-reaching (connections)

غلف **II** to put or wrap (ه s.th.) in a cover, wrap, envelope, or case; to wrap, envelop (ه s.th.); to cover (ه ب s.th. with)

غلفة *ġulfa* foreskin, prepuce

غلاف *ġilāf* pl. غلف *ġuluf* cover, covering, wrap, wrapper, wrapping, jacket (of a book); case, box; envelope

اغلف *aḡlaf*², f. غلفاء *ḡalfā'*², pl. غلف *ḡulf* uncircumcised; rude, uncivilized

مغلف *muḡallaf* uncircumcised; (pl. *-āt*) cover, covering, wrap, wrapper, wrapping, envelope (of a letter)

غلق *ḡalaqa i* (*ḡalq*) to close, shut (ه s.th., a door); to lock, bolt (ه s.th., a door); — *ḡaliqa a* (*ḡalaq*): غلق الرهن (*rahnu*) the pledge was forfeited as the pledger was unable to redeem it **II** to close, shut (ه s.th., a door); to lock, bolt (ه s.th., a door) **IV** = **II**; to declare a pledge (رهنا *rahnan*) to be forfeited, foreclose (رهنا a mortgage); pass. *uḡliqa* to be obscure, dark, ambigous, dubious, incomprehensible (على to s.o.) **VII** to be closed, shut, locked, or bolted; to be incomprehensible **X** to be obscure, dark, ambiguous, incomprehensible; to be difficult, intricate, complicated | استغلق عليه الكلام (*kalāmu*) he was unable to speak, he was struck dumb, he was speechless

غلق *ḡalaq* pl. اغلاق *aḡlāq* lock, padlock

غلق *ḡaliq* obscure, dark, ambiguous, dubious, abstruse, recondite, difficult to comprehend

غلاقة *ḡilāqa* unpaid balance

مغلاق *miḡlāq* pl. مغاليق *maḡālīq*² lock; padlock; breech (of a firearm); any closing or fastening mechanism, as, a latch, a catch, a clasp, a cap, a cover, a lid, a cutoff, etc.

اغلاق *iḡlāq* closing, shutting, locking, bolting, shutting-off, barring; foreclosure (of a mortgage)

انغلاق *inḡilāq* obscurity, abstruseness, incomprehensibility

مغلق *muḡlaq* closed, shut; locked, bolted; obscure, dark, ambiguous, dubious, abstruse, recondite, difficult to comprehend

مستغلق *mustaḡliq* obscure, dark, cryptic, ambiguous, equivocal

غلم *ḡalima a* (*ḡalam*, غلمة *ḡulma*) to be excited by lust, be seized by sensuous desire **VIII** = **I**

غلم *ḡalim* excited by lust, seized by sensuous desire, wanton, lewd, lascivious, lustful; in heat, rutted

غلمة *ḡulma* lust, carnal appetite, sensuous desire; heat, rut

غلام *ḡulām* pl. غلمان *ḡilmān*, غلمة *ḡilma* boy, youth, lad; slave; servant, waiter

غلامية *ḡulāmīya* youth, youthfulness

غيلم *ḡailam* male tortoise

غلومة *ḡulūma* youth, youthfulness

غلا (غلو) *ḡalā u* (*ḡulūw*) to exceed the proper bounds, be excessive, go too far (في in), overdo, exaggerate (في s.th.); — *ḡalā u* (غلاء *ḡalā'*) to be high, be stiff (price); to become expensive, undergo a price raise (merchandise); to be expensive, be high priced **II** to raise the price of s.th. (ه) **III** to exceed the proper bounds, be excessive, go too far (في in), overdo, exaggerate (في s.th.); to demand too high a price, charge too much (ب for); to put great store (ب by s.th.), ascribe great value (ب to s.th.), rate highly (ب s.th.) **IV** = **II**; to declare (ه s.th.) to be dear or precious, appreciate, value, prize, treasure, cherish (ه s.th.); to laud, extol, praise highly (ه s.th.) **VI** to exceed the proper bounds, be excessive, go too far (في in); to overdo, exaggerate (في, ب s.th.) **X** to find (ه s.th.) expensive or costly

غلو *ḡulūw* exceeding of proper bounds, excess, extravagance; exaggeration

غلاء *ḡalā'* high cost, high level of prices, rise in prices; high price

غلواء *ḡulawā'*², *ḡulwā'*² exceeding of proper bounds, excess, extravagance | خفف من غلوائه (*ḵaffafa*) to dampen s.o.'s ardor, curb s.o.'s enthusiasm

اغلى *aḡlā* more expensive; more valuable, more costly

مغالاة *muḡālāh* exceeding of proper bounds, excess, extravagance; exaggeration

اغلاء *iḡlā'* laudation, extolment, high praise; admiration

غال *ḡālin* expensive, high priced; valuable, costly; dear, beloved; — (pl. غلاة *ḡulāh*) adherent of an extreme sect; extremist, radical; fanatic adherent, fanatic

غلى *ḡalā i* (*ḡaly*, غليان *ḡalayān*) to boil, bubble up; to ferment (alcoholic beverage) II to make (ه s.th.) boil; to boil (ه s.th.) IV = II

غلى *ḡaly* boiling, ebullition

غليان *ḡalayān* boiling, ebullition

غليون *ḡalyūn* pl. غلايين *ḡalāyīn*² water pipe, narghile, hubble-bubble; smoking pipe, tobacco pipe; see also below

غلاية *ḡallāya* pl. *-āt* boiler, kettle, caldron | آلة غلاية steam boiler

غالية *ḡāliya* a perfume made of musk and ambergris (Galia moschata)

مغلى *maḡlīy* broth; decoction (*pharm.*)

غليون *ḡalyūn* pl. غلايين *ḡalāyīn*², غلاوين *ḡalawīn*² galleon; see also غلى

غم *ḡamma u* (*ḡamm*) to cover, veil, conceal (ه s.th.); to fill (ه s.o.) with sadness, pain, or grief, to pain, grieve, distress (ه s.o.); pass. *ḡumma* to be obscure, incomprehensible (على to s.o.) II to cover, veil, conceal (ه s.th.) IV to be overcast (sky); to fill (ه s.o.) with sadness, pain, or grief, to pain, grieve, distress (ه s.o.) VII to be distressed, be worried, be sad, grieve, pine, worry VIII = VII

غم *ḡamm* pl. غموم *ḡumūm* grief, affliction, sorrow, distress, sadness, worry, anxiety

غمة *ḡumma* grief, affliction, sorrow, distress, sadness, anxiety

غمام *ḡamām* (coll.; n. un. ة) pl. غمائم *ḡamā'im*² clouds | حب الغمام *ḥabb al-ḡ.* hail

غمامة *ḡimāma* pl. غمائم *ḡamā'im*² blinder, blinker (for horses, etc.); muzzle (for animals)

اغم *aḡamm*², f. غماء *ḡammā'*² covered with dense hair, hairy, hirsute, shaggy; thick, dense (clouds)

غام *ḡāmm* grievous, distressing, sorrowful, sad, painful; sultry, muggy (day, night)

مغموم *maḡmūm* grieved, distressed, afflicted, worried, sad

مغتم *muḡtamm* grieved, distressed, afflicted, worried, sad

غمد *ḡamada i u* (*ḡamd*) to sheathe, put into the scabbard (ه the sword); to plunge, thrust (ه the sword into s.o.'s breast); to encompass, shelter, protect, cover (ه s.o., برحمته *bi-raḥmatihī* with His grace; of God) II to conceal s.o.'s (ه) offenses or shortcomings IV to sheathe, put into the scabbard (ه the sword) V to encompass, shelter, protect, cover (ه s.o., برحمته *bi-raḥmatihī* with His grace, of God)

غمد *ḡimd* pl. اغماد *aḡmād*, غمود *ḡumūd* sheath, scabbard

غمر *ḡamura u* (غمارة *ḡamāra*, غمورة *ḡumūra*) to be plentiful, copious, abundant, abound (water); to overflow (intr.); — *ḡamara u* (*ḡamr*) to flood, inundate (ه s.th., ب ه s.th. with), overflow (ه s.th.); to douse, cover (ه s.th., ب with a liquid), pour a liquid (ب) over s.th. (ه); to lay, soak (ه في s.th. in a liquid); to immerse, steep, submerge, place, embed (ه في, ه s.o. s.th. in(to); esp. fig.: in(to) an environment, an atmosphere); to cover, bury (ه, ٥ s.o., s.th.); to bestow liberally, lavish, heap, load (ب ٥ upon s.o. s.th.), shower (ب ٥ s.o. with); to fill, pervade (٥ s.o., ه the heart; of feelings) **III** to plunge (blindly), throw o.s. (headlong) (في or ه into); to venture; to risk (ب s.th.) | غامر بنفسه to engage in daring adventures, risk one's life **VIII** to cover, bury, engulf, swallow (ه s.th.)

غمر *ǧamr* flooding, overflowing, submersion, inundation; (pl. غمار *ǧimār*, غمور *ǧumūr*) deluge, flood (also fig.); all-engulfing, flooding, overflowing (water); of overflowing liberality, lavishly openhanded, generous; — *ǧamr* and *ǧumr* (pl. اغمار *aǧmār*) inexperienced, green, gullible, simple, ingenuous

غمرة *ǧamra* pl. *ǧamarāt*, غمار *ǧimār* deluge, flood, inundation; (emotional) exuberance; pl. غمار flood (fig., e.g., of events); adversities, hardships, ups and downs (of life, of battle, etc.); abundance, profusion (e.g., of knowledge) | غمرات الموت *ǧ. al-maut* mortal throes

غمر *ǧumr* pl. اغمار *aǧmār* armfull

غمار *ǧimār* risk, hazard

مغامرة *muǧāmara* pl. *-āt* a hazardous, or foolhardy, undertaking; adventure; risk, hazard

غامر *ǧāmir* overflowing, all-engulfing, all-encompassing; plentiful, copious, abundant; desolate, waste, empty (land)

مغمور *maǧmūr* obscure, unknown

مغامر *muǧāmir* reckless, foolhardy; adventurer

غمز *ǧamaza* **i** (*ǧamz*) to feel, touch, palpate (ه, ٥ ب s.o., s.th. with); to make a sign, to signal (ب ٥ to s.o. with); to beckon with one's eyes, wink (٥ at s.o.); to twinkle, blink (ب with one's eyes); to slander, calumniate (على or ب s.o.) | غمز الجرس (*jarasa*) to press the bell button, ring the bell; غمز قناته (*qanātahū*) to sound s.o. out, probe into s.o., feel s.o.'s pulse **VI** to signal to one another, wink at one another **VIII** to detract (ه from s.th.), belittle, decry, disparage (ه s.th.)

غمزة *ǧamza* pl. *-āt* sign, signal, hint, wink (with the eye), twinkle; taunt, gibe

غمازة *ǧammāza* dimple

غميزة *ǧamīza* failing, fault, shortcoming, blemish (of character)

مغمز *maǧmaz* pl. مغامز *maǧāmiz*² failing, fault, shortcoming, blemish (of character); weakness, weak spot, s.th. which arouses doubt, invites comment, taunts, and the like

غمس *ǧamasa* **i** (*ǧams*) to dip, plunge, steep, immerse, submerse, sink (في ه, ٥ s.o., s.th. in) **II** = **I**; **VII** to be dipped, be plunged, become immersed, be submersed, be sunk; to plunge, throw o.s. (في into) **VIII** = **VII**

غموس *ǧamūs* ominous, calamitous, disastrous

مغموس *maǧmūs* immersed (ب or في in)

غمص *ǧamaṣa* **i** (*ǧamṣ*) to esteem lightly, belittle, undervalue, despise, hold in contempt (ه, ٥ s.o., s.th.)

اغمص *aǧmaṣ*² blear-eyed

غمض *ǧamuḍa* **u** and *ǧamaḍa* **u** (غموض *ǧumūḍ*) to be hidden, be concealed, hide; to close (eye); to be obscure, dark, abstruse, recondite, difficult to comprehend **II** to make (ه s.th.) obscure, abstruse, recondite, difficult to comprehend; to close, shut (عينيه عن *ʿainaihi* one's eyes to, over, toward, or in the face of); to sleep, be asleep | غمض جفونه على القذى (*jufūnahū, qaḏā*) see قذى **IV** to blur, dim (عينيه عن *ʿainaihi* s.o.'s eye for), make s.o. blind to; to close, shut (عينيه عن one's eyes to, over, على toward, in the face of); to pretend not to see (عن s.th.), feign blindness (عن to), overlook (عن s.th.), wink, connive (عن at); to bear, stand, tolerate (على, عن s.th.) | اغمض من عينيه (*'ainaihi*) to close one's eyes, refuse to see **VII** to close, be closed (eye) **VIII** do.; to sleep, be asleep

غمض *ğumḍ* sleep

غمضة *ğamḍa* twinkle, blink, wink | في غمضة عين in a moment, in a jiffy

غماض *ğimāḍ* twinkle, blink, wink

غموض *ğumūḍ* obscureness, obscurity, ambiguity, abstruseness, reconditeness, mystery, inscrutability; inexplicability, lack of clarity, vagueness, uncertainty, incertitude

غموضة *ğumūḍa* obscureness, obscurity, abstruseness, reconditeness

اغمض *ağmaḍ*² obscurer, more cryptic

غامض *ğāmiḍ* pl. غوامض *ğawāmiḍ*² hidden, concealed; obscure, dark, ambiguous, abstruse, recondite, difficult to comprehend; inscrutable, cryptic(al), mysterious, enigmatic(al)

غامضة *ğāmiḍa* pl. *-āt*, غوامض *ğawāmiḍ*² unsolved problem, riddle, enigma, mystery | غوامض افكاره s.o.'s innermost thoughts

غمط *ğamaṭa* *i* and *ğamiṭa* *a* (*ğamṭ*) to despise, hold in contempt, esteem lightly, belittle, undervalue (ه s.o.); to be ungrateful (ه for s.th.) | غمطه حقه (*ḥaqqahū*) to encroach upon s.o.'s rights, refuse to recognize s.o.'s rights

غمغم *ğamğama* to mumble, mutter

غمغمة *ğamğama* pl. غماغم *ğamāğim*² cry, battle cry

غمق *ğamiqa* *a* (*ğamaq*), *ğamaqa* *u* and *ğamuqa* *u* to be damp, moist, wet

غامق *ğāmiq*² dark (color)

غملج *ğamlaj* fickle, inconstant, unstable

غملاج *ğimlāj* fickle, inconstant, unstable

غمى *ğamā* *i* (*ğamy*) to provide with a roof, to roof (ه a house); pass.: غمى عليه (*ğumiya*) to swoon, faint, lose consciousness **II** to blindfold **IV** pass. اغمى عليه (*uğmiya*) to swoon, faint, lose consciousness

غمى *ğamy* swoon, faint, unconsciousness

اغماء *iğmā'* swoon, faint, unconsciousness

□ استغماية (*eg.*; pronounced *istuğummāya*): لعبة الاستغماية *la'bat al-ist.* blindman's buff

مغمى عليه *mağmīy*, *muğman 'alaihi* in a swoon, unconscious

غن *ğanna* (1st pers. perf. *ğanintu*) *a* (*ğann*, غنة *ğunna*) to speak through the nose, speak with a nasal twang, nasalize

غن *ğann* nasal pronunciation, nasalization

غنة *ğunna* nasal pronunciation, nasalization; (pl. *-āt*) nasal sound, twang; sound (also, e.g., of complaint, of regret)

اغن *ağann*², f. غناء *ğannā'*² nasal; melodious, pleasant, sonorous (voice); luxuriant, lush, gorgeous (of a garden)

غنج *ğanija* *a* (*ğunj*) to coquet, flirt, play the coquette (woman) **V** do.

غنج *ğunj* coquetry, flirtation, dalliance, coquettish behavior

غنجة *ğanija* coquettish, flirtatious (woman); a coquette

مغناج *miğnāj* coquettish, flirtatious

غندر **II** *tağandara* to play the dandy, act like a fop

غندر *ğundur* fat, plump, chubby

غندور *ğandūr* pl. غنادرة *ğanādira* (*eg.*) dandy, fop

غندقجى (*eg.*) *ğundaqǧī* armorer, gunsmith

غنغرينا *ğanğarīnā* gangrene (*med.*)

غنم *ğanima a* (*ğunm, ğanm, ğanam,* غنيمة *ğanīma*) to gain booty; to take as (war) booty, capture, gain, obtain (ه s.th.); to pillage, plunder, sack, loot **II** to give (in a disinterested manner) (ه ه to s.o. s.th.), bestow (ه ه on s.o. s.th.), grant (ه ه s.o. s.th.) **IV** to give as booty (ه ه to s.o. s.th.) **VIII** to take as (war) booty, capture (ه s.th.) | اغتنم الفرصة (*furṣata*) to seize, or take, the opportunity, avail o.s. of the opportunity **X** استغنم الفرصة = اغتنم الفرصة

غنم *ğunm* spoils, booty, loot, prey; gain, profit, advantage, benefit

غنم *ğanam* (coll.) pl. اغنام *ağnām* sheep (and goats), small cattle

غنام *ğannām* shepherd

غنيمة *ğanīma* pl. غنائم *ğanā'im*² spoils, booty, loot, prey | غنيمة باردة easy prey; راض من الغنيمة بالاياب (*rāḍin, iyāb*) (content with returning without booty, i.e.) glad to have saved one's skin; اقتنع من الغنيمة بالاياب (*iqtana'a*) to have to return empty-handed, with nothing accomplished

مغنم *mağnam* pl. مغانم *mağānim*² spoils, booty, loot, prey; gain, profit, advantage, benefit

غانم *ğānim* successful | عاد سالما غانما (*sāliman ğāniman*) approx.: he returned safe and sound

غنى *ğaniya a* (*ğinan,* غناء *ğanā'*) to be free from want, be rich, wealthy; not to need, be able to spare (عن s.o., s.th.), be able to dispense (عن with), manage, be able to do (عن without), have no need (عن for), be in no need (عن of) **II** to sing (ب or ه s.th., ه ه to s.o. s.th.), chant (ب or ه s.th.); to sing the praises (ب of s.o.), eulogize, extol (ب s.o.) **IV** to make free from want, make rich, enrich (ه s.o.); to suffice (عن or ه s.o. or for s.o.), be sufficient, be enough, be adequate, do (عن or ه for s.o.), be of use, be of help (عن or ه to s.o.), avail, profit, benefit, help (عن or ه s.o.); to satisfy, content (عن s.o.); to be a substitute or setoff (عن to s.o.), make dispensable or superfluous (عن ه for s.o. s.th.); to make up (عن for s.th.), be a substitute (عن for s.th.); to dispense, free, relieve (عن ه s.o. of s.th.), spare, save (عن ه s.o. s.th.); to protect, guard, help (عن ه s.o. against) | ما اغنى (عنه) شيئا to be of no use, be of no avail (to s.o.); لا يغنى فتيلا (*yuğnī*) it is of no use at all (عن to s.o.), it doesn't help (عن s.o.) a bit, it isn't worth a farthing **V** to sing, chant (ب s.th.); to sing the praises (ه or ب of s.o., of s.th.); to eulogize, praise, extol (ب s.o.) **VIII** to become rich, gain riches (ب by) **X** to become rich; not to need, be able to spare (عن s.o., s.th.), be able to dispense (عن with), manage, be able to do (عن without), have no need (عن for), be in no need (عن of); to get by, do, manage, be satisfied (ب with) | لا يستغنى عنه (*yustağnā*) indispensable

غنى *ğinan* wealth, affluence, riches | لا غنى عنه indispensable (ل for); ما له عنه غنى he cannot dispense with it, he cannot do without it; هو فى غنى عنه he can dispense with it, he does not need it; كان فى غنى عنه to forgo, renounce s.th., dispense with s.th., be in no need of s.th., not to need s.th., need not do s.th.

غنية *ğunya, ğinya*: ما له عنه غنية = ما له عنه غنى (*ğinan*)

غنى *ğanīy* pl. اغنياء *ağniyā'*² rich (ب in), wealthy, prosperous, well-to-do | غنى الحرب *ğ. al-ḥarb* war profiteer; غنى عن البيان (*bayān*) self-evident, self-explanatory; it is self-evident, it goes without saying (ان that)

غناء *ġanā'* wealth, affluence, riches; sufficiency, adequacy; ability, capability; use, avail, usefulness, utility (عن for) | لا غناء فيه (*ġanā'a*) useless; it is insufficient, inadequate, not enough, it is no good, it is to little avail, it is of little use; له غناء عنه (*ġanā'un*), هو فى غناء عنه he can dispense with it, he does not need it

غناء *ġinā'* singing, song

غنائى *ġinā'ī* singing-, song- (in compounds), vocal | حفلة غنائية (*ḥafla*) song recital, concert of vocal music

غناء *ġannā'*[2] see غن

اغنية *uġnīya* (*iġnīya*), *uġniya* (*iġniya*) pl. *-āt*, اغان *aġānin* song, melody, tune, lay

مغنى *maġnan* pl. مغان *maġānin* habitation; (*eg.*) villa

غانية *ġāniya* pl. *-āt*, غوان *ġawānin* pretty girl, beautiful woman, belle, beauty

مغن *muġannin* (male) singer, vocalist, chanter

مغنية *muġanniya* (female) singer, vocalist, songstress, chanteuse

غيهب *ġaihab* pl. غياهب *ġayāhib*[2] darkness, dark, duskiness; gloom

غوث IV to help, succor (ه s.o.), go to the aid (ه of s.o.) X to appeal for help (ه or ب to s.o., على against), seek the aid (ه or ب of s.o., على against); to call for help

غوث *ġauṯ* call for help; help, aid, succor

غياث *ġiyāṯ* help, aid, succor

اغاثة *iġāṯa* help, aid, succor | وكالة اغاثة اللاجئين (التابعة للامم المتحدة) (*li-l-umami l-muttaḥida*) United Nations Relief and Works Agency, UNRWA

استغاثة *istiġāṯa* appeal for aid; call for help

مغيث *muġīṯ* helper

غار (غور) *ġāra u* (*ġaur*) to penetrate deeply (فى into); — *ġāra u a* (*ġaur*) to fall in, sink in, become hollow (eyes, and the like); to seep away, ooze away (water); to dry up (spring) II to fall in, sink in, become hollow (eyes, and the like); to seep away, ooze away (water) IV to travel in the lowlands; to make a predatory incursion, make a foray (على into s.o.'s territory); to raid, invade (على a country); to attack (على s.c., s.th.); to commit aggression (على against a nation)

غور *ġaur* pl. اغوار *aġwār* bottom; declivity, depression; depth (also fig.); الغور designation of that part of the Syrian Graben which constitutes the Jordan valley | بعيد الغور deep; profound, unfathomable

غار *ġār* pl. اغوار *aġwār*, غيران *ġīrān* cave, cavern; — (coll.; n. un. ة) laurel tree, bay

غارة *ġāra* pl. *-āt* predatory incursion, raid, invasion, inroad, foray; attack (على on); a certain gait of camels | غارة جوية (*jawwīya*) air raid; غارات متواصلة or متوالية (*mutawāṣila, mutawāliya*) rolling attacks, attacks in waves; شن غارة على (*šanna*) to attack s.o. or s.th., launch an attack on

مغار *maġār* cave, cavern; grotto

مغارة *maġāra* pl. *-āt*, مغاور *maġāwir*[2], مغاير *maġāyir*[2] cave, cavern; grotto

مغوار *miġwār* pl. مغاوير *maġāwīr*[2] fleet, swift-running (horse); making raids or attacks, raiding, aggressive; bold, daring, audacious; pl. مغاوير commandos, shock troops (*Syr., mil.*)

اغارة *iġāra* pl. *-āt* attack (على on)

غائر *ġā'ir* low-lying; sunk, hollow (of the eyes)

مغير *muġīr* assailant, raider, aggressor

غوريلا *ġurillā* gorilla

غاز, غازى look up alphabetically

غويشة (eg.) ǧuwēša pl. -āt, غوايش ǧawāyiš² glass bracelet, bangle

(غوص) غاص ǧāṣa u (ǧauṣ, مغاص maǧāṣ, غياص ǧiyāṣ, غياصة ǧiyāṣa) to plunge (فى into), become immersed, submerge (فى in), dive (فى into; على for); to practice pearl-fishery II to make (ه s.o.) dive (فى into), plunge, immerse, submerse (ه فى s.o. in)

غويص ǧawīṣ deep

غواص ǧawwāṣ pl. -ūn diver; pearl diver

غواصة ǧawwāṣa pl. -āt submarine

مغاص maǧāṣ diving place | مغاص اللؤلؤ m. al-lu'lu' pearl diving, pearl-fishery

غوط¹ II to deepen, make deeper (ه a well) V to evacuate the bowels, relieve nature

غوط ǧauṭ pl. غوط ǧūṭ, اغواط aǧwāṭ, غياط ǧiyāṭ, غيطان ǧīṭān cavity, hollow, depression

الغوطة al-ǧūṭa name of the fertile oasis on the south side of Damascus

غويط ǧawīṭ deep

غائط ǧā'iṭ human excrements, feces

غوطى² ǧūṭī Gothic

غاغة ǧāǧa mob, rabble, riffraff; noise, clamor, din, tumult

غوغاء ǧauǧā'² mob, rabble, riffraff; noise, clamor, din, tumult

(غول) غال ǧāla u (ǧaul) to take (away) unawares, snatch, seize, grab (ه, ه s.o., s.th.); to destroy (ه s.o.) VIII = I; to assassinate, murder (ه s.o.)

غال ǧāl pl. -āt (syr.) padlock

غول ǧūl usually fem., pl. اغوال aǧwāl, غيلان ǧīlān ghoul, a desert demon appearing in ever varying shapes; demon, jinni, goblin, sprite; ogre, cannibal; — calamity, disaster

غيلة ǧīla assassination | قتله غيلة (ǧīlatan) to assassinate s.o.

اغتيال iǧtiyāl pl. -āt murder(ing), assassination

غائلة ǧā'ila pl. غوائل ǧawā'il² calamity, disaster; ruin, havoc, danger

غوى ǧawā i (غى ǧayy, غواية ǧawāya) to stray from the right way, go astray, err (in one's actions); to misguide, mislead, lead astray (ه s.o.), seduce, tempt, entice, lure, induce (ه ب s.o. to do s.th.); — ǧawiya a to covet, desire, like II to misguide, mislead, lead astray, tempt, seduce, entice, lure, allure (ه s.o.) IV = II X to misguide, mislead, lead astray (ه s.o.); to tempt, seduce, entice, lure, bait, ensnare, beguile, win (ه ب s.o. with)

غى ǧayy trespassing, transgression, offense, error, sin; seduction, temptation, enticement, allurement

غية ǧayya, ǧīya pl. -āt error, sin; taste, inclination, liking

غواية ǧawāya error, sin; seduction, temptation, enticement, allurement

اغوية uǧwīya pl. اغاوى aǧāwīy pitfall, trap

اغواء iǧwā' seduction, temptation, enticement, allurement

غاو ǧāwin tempter, seducer, enticer, allurer; (pl. غواة ǧuwāh) amateur, fan, lover, dilettante, dabbler

مغواة muǧawwāh pl. مغويات muǧawwayāt pitfall, trap

غيى II to hoist (ه a flag)

غاية ǧāya pl. -āt extreme limit; utmost degree, the outmost, extremity; aim, goal, end, objective, intention, intent, design, purpose; destination (of a journey) | لغاية (with foll. genit.) as far as, up to, to the extent of, until, till; للغاية extremely, very (much); كان غاية فى الجهال

(*ġāyatan, jamāl*) to be of extraordinary beauty; الغاية تبرر الواسطة (*tubarriru l-wāsiṭata*) the end justifies the means; انطلق لغايته to head or set out for one's destination

غوى and see غية and غى

○ غائية *ġā'īya* finality (*philos.*)

(غيب) غاب *ġāba* **i** (*ġaib*, غيبة *ġaiba*, غياب *ġiyāb*, غيبوبة *ġaibūba*, مغيب *maġīb*) to be or remain absent, be or stay away; to absent o.s., withdraw (عن from), leave (عن s.o., s.th.); to vanish (عن from s.o.'s sight, from s.o., from s.th.); to disappear, be swallowed up (فى in); to hide, be hidden, be concealed (عن from); — (مغيب *maġīb*) to set, go down (sun, and the like) | غاب الشىء عن باله the matter has slipped from his memory, he has forgotten the matter; غاب عن صوابه (*ṣawābihī*) to lose consciousness, faint, swoon, become unconscious; غاب عن الوجود do.; لا تغيب عنه الشمس (*šamsu*) it is not veiled in darkness **II** to lead away, take away, carry away, remove (ه, ‍ه s.o., s.th.); to cause (ه, ‍ه s.o., s.th.) to disappear; to hide, conceal (ه, ‍ه عن s.o., s.th. from); to make (‍ه s.o.) forget everything, make (‍ه s.o.) oblivious of everything | غيبه عن الوجود it drove him out of his mind; غيبه الثرى (*ṯarā*) the earth covered, or buried, him **V** to be absent, be away, stay away (عن from s.o., from s.th.); to be not present, be not there; to play truant, play hooky (عن from school) **VIII** to slander, calumniate (‍ه s.o.) **X** to use s.o.'s (‍ه) absence for maligning him, backbite (‍ه s.o.); to slander, calumniate (‍ه s.o.)

غيب *ġaib* absence; hidden, concealed, invisible; — (pl. غيوب *ġuyūb*) that which is hidden, the invisible; that which is transcendental, the supernatural; divine secret | غيبا *ġaiban* or عن ظهر الغيب (*ẓahri l-ġ.*) by heart, from memory; علام الغيوب *'allām al-ġ.* he who thoroughly knows the invisible, or transcendental, things = God; عالم الغيب *'ālam al-ġ.* the invisible world; بظهر الغيب *bi-ẓahri l-ġ.* behind s.o.'s back, insidiously, treacherously; نظر بعين الغيب الى (*bi-'aini l-ġ.*) to foresee, foreknow, divine s.th.

غيبى *ġaibī* secret, hidden, invisible

غابة *ġāba* pl. *-āt*, غاب *ġāb* (coll.) low ground, depression, hollow; forest, wood, copse, thicket; jungle; reed | الغاب الهندى (*hindī*) bamboo

غيبة *ġaiba* absence; concealment, invisibility

غيبة *ġība* slander, calumniation, calumny

غياب *ġiyāb* absence, being away; setting (of the sun)

غيابى *ġiyābī*: حكم غيابى (*ḥukm*) judgment by default (*jur.*); غيابيا *ġiyābīyan* in absence, in absentia (*jur.*)

غيابة *ġayāba* pl. *-āt* bottom, depth (of a well, of a dungeon, of a ditch, and the like)

غيبوبة *ġaibūba* swoon, faint, unconsciousness; trance, daze, stupor

مغيب *maġīb* absence; setting (of the sun)

تغيب *taġayyub* absence, nonattendance, being away, staying away, truancy

اغتياب *iġtiyāb* slander, calumniation, defamation; gossip about (genit.)

غائب *ġā'ib* pl. *-ūn*, غيب *ġuyyab*, غياب *ġuyyāb* absent, not present, not there; hidden, concealed, unseen, invisible; third person (*gram.*)

مغيبات *muġayyibāt* narcotics, stupefacients, anesthetics

مغيب *muġayyab* hidden, concealed, invisible; pl. المغيبات *al-muġayyabāt* the hidden, transcendental things, the divine secrets

مغيب *muğīb* and مغيبة woman whose husband is absent, grass widow

متغيب *mutağayyib* absent (عن from)

مغتاب *muğtāb* slanderer, calumniator

غيتو ghetto

(غيث) غاث *ğāṯa i* (*ğaiṯ*) to water with rain (ه s.th.), send rain (ه, ه upon s.o., upon s.th., of God)

غيث *ğaiṯ* pl. غيوث *ğuyūṯ*, اغياث *ağyāṯ* (abundant) rain

غيد **VI** to walk with a graceful, swinging gait

غيد *ğayad* delicacy, slender shapeliness, tenderness, softness (of a woman)

غادة *ğāda* pl. *-āt* young girl, young lady

اغيد *ağyad*², غيداء *ğaidā'*², غيد *ğīd* young and delicate; الغيد the young ladies

(غير) غار *ğāra a* (غيرة *ğaira*) to be jealous (من of); to display zeal, vie (على for); to be solicitous (على about, for); to guard or protect jealously (على من s.o., s.th. from) **II** to alter, modify, make different (من or ه s.th.), change (ه s.th.) **III** to be dissimilar, be different, differ; to be in contrast (ه, ه to), be unlike s.o. or s.th. (ه, ه); to change (ه e.g., a garment); to interchange, exchange (بين between); to haggle, bargain, chaffer (ه with s.o.); to vie, compete (ه with s.o.) **IV** to make jealous (ه s.o.) **V** to be altered, be modified, be changed, change, alter, vary, undergo an alteration or change **VI** to differ, be different, be heterogeneous

غير *ğair* other than (with dependent genit.), different from, unlike, no, not, non-, un-, in-, dis-; (prep.) *ğaira* except, save, but | الغير the others, fellow men, neighbors; وغير ذلك, وغيره and the like, and so forth, and so on, et cetera; and others, and other things, et alii, et alia; لا غير and ليس غير (*ğairu*) (and) that's all, nothing else, no more, nothing but, only, merely, solely; غير ان *ğaira anna* except that..., however, but, yet, ...though; غير واحد *ğairu wāḥidin* more than one, several; غير مرة *ğaira marratin* more than once, quite often, frequently; بغير *bi-ğairi* or من غير *min ğairi* without; في غير (ما) *fī ğairi* (*mā*) without (generally followed by abstract noun), في غير ترو (*tarawwin*) without thinking, unhesitatingly; في غير ما تهيب (*tahayyubin*) without fear; على غير معرفة منه (*ma'rifatin*) or من غير علم منه (*'ilmin*) without his knowing or having known it, without his knowledge, unwittingly

غيرى *ğairī* altruist

غيرية *ğairīya* altruism

غير *ğiyar*, غير الدهر *ğ. ad-dahr* vicissitudes of fate

غيرة *ğaira* jealousy; zeal, fervor, earnest concern, vigilant care, solicitude (على for); sense of honor, self-respect

غيور *ğayūr* pl. غير *ğuyur* (very) jealous; zealous, fervid, eager (على in, in the pursuit of), keen, eagerly intent (على on), earnestly concerned (على with), enthusiastic (على for)

غيران *ğairān*², f. غيرى *ğairā*, pl. غيارى *ğayārā* = غيور

تغيير *tağyīr* pl. *-āt* changing, alteration, modification, variation; change, replacement, relief

تغييرة *tağyīra* pl. تغايير *tağāyīr*² exchange, interchange, change, replacement; lending of books and manuscripts sheet by sheet (one *malzama* after the other; *eg.*)

غيار *ğiyār* exchange, interchange, change, replacement; (pl. *-āt*) dressing, bandage (of a wound) | قطع الغيار *qiṭa' al-ğ.* spare parts

تغير *taǧayyur* pl. *-āt* alteration, variation, change

مغاير *muǧāyir*: مغاير للآداب indecent, immoral

متغير *mutaǧayyir* changeable, variable. liable to change or alteration | تيار متغير (*tayyār*) alternating current (*el.*)

(غيض) غاض *ǧāḍa* *i* (*ǧaiḍ*, مغاض *maǧāḍ*) to decrease, diminish, recede, become less, dwindle away | غاض لونه (*launuhū*) his face lost all color, he turned pale

غيض *ǧaiḍ* prematurely born fetus

غيضة *ǧaiḍa* pl. *-āt*, غياض *ǧiyāḍ*, اغياض *aǧyāḍ* thicket, jungle

غيط *ǧaiṭ* pl. غيطان *ǧīṭān* field

(غيظ) غاظ *ǧāẓa* *i* (*ǧaiẓ*) to anger, enrage, infuriate, irritate, exasperate, vex, gall (ه s.o.) II and IV = I; V to become furious, become angry (من with s.o., at s.th.) VII and VIII = V

غيظ *ǧaiẓ* wrath, anger, ire, exasperation, fury, rage

اغتياظ *iǧtiyāẓ* wrath, anger, ire, exasperation, fury, rage

منغاظ *munǧāẓ* angry, irate, furious, enraged

مغتاظ *muǧtāẓ* angry, irate, furious, enraged

[1]غيل *ǧīl* pl. اغيال *aǧyāl* thicket

غال *ǧāl* pl. *-āt* (*syr.*) padlock

[2]غيلة *ǧīla* and غيلان *ǧīlān* see غول

(غيم) غام *ǧāma* *i* (*ǧaim*) to become cloudy, become overcast (sky); to become fogged, become blurred II do.; to form clouds; to billow, float, waft (smoke) IV *aǧāma* and *aǧyama* = I

غيم *ǧaim* (coll.; n. un. ة) pl. غيوم *ǧuyūm* غيام *ǧiyām* clouds; mist, fog

غائم *ǧā'im* clouded, overcast; cloudy

متغيم *mutaǧayyim* clouded, overcast

[1]غين *ǧain* pl. *-āt*, غيون *ǧuyūn*, اغيان *aǧyān* name of the letter غ

غينة *ǧaina* dimple on the cheek

[2]غيني *ǧīnī*: خنزير غيني (*kinzīr*) guinea pig

غينيا *ǧīniyā* Guinea | غينيا الجديدة *Ǧīniyā l-jadīda* New Guinea

غيهب see غهب

ف

[1]ف abbreviation of فدان *faddān* (a square measure)

[2]ف *fa* (conj.) then, and then; and so, thus, hence, therefore; but then, then however; for, because; (with subjunctive:) so that | يوما فيوما (*yauman*) day after day, day by day; شيئا فشيئا (*šai'an*) gradually, step by step; امر فقتلوه (*fa-qatalūhu*) he ordered him to be killed

فان *fa'inna* (with foll. suffix or noun in acc.) for, because

فاء *fā'* name of the letter ف

فابريقة *fābrīqa* and فابريكة pl. *-āt*, فبارك *fabārik*[2] factory, plant

فأت VIII to tell lies (على about); to take violent measures (على against); to violate (على a duty, etc.); pass. افتئت *uftu'ita* to die suddenly | افتأت برأيه (*bi-ra'yihī*) to act on one's own judgment

افتئات *ifti'āt* oppression, violence

فاتورة (It. *fattura*) *fātūra* pl. فواتير *fawātīr*[2] invoice, bill

الفاتيكان *al-fatikān, al-vatikān* the Vatican

فؤاد *fu'ād* pl. افئدة *af'ida* heart

فؤادية *fu'ādīya* "Fuad cap", summer field-cap of the Egyptian Air Force (1939)

فأر *fa'r* (coll.; n. un. ة) pl. فئران *fi'rān* mouse; rat

فار *fār* (coll.; n. un. ة) pl. فيران *fīrān* mouse; rat

فارة *fāra* (= فأرة *fa'ra*) mouse; (pl. *-āt*) plane (tool)

فارس *fāris*[2] Persia, also بلاد فارس

فارسى *fārisī* Persian; a Persian

فاروز *fārūz* turquoise

فازلين *fazlīn, vazlīn* vaseline

فأس *fa's* f., pl. فؤوس *fu'ūs*, افؤس *af'us* ax, hatchet; hoe

[1]فاس *fās* = فأس *fa's*

[1]فاس *fās*[2] Fez or Fès (city in Morocco)

فاشستى *fāšistī* fascist(ic); a fascist

فاشستية *fāšistīya* fascism

فاشى *fāšī* fascist(ic); a fascist

فاشية *fāšīya* fascism

فاشيستى *fāšistī* fascist(ic); a fascist

فاصوليا *fāṣūliyā* (*eg.-syr.*) common European bean (Phaseolus vulgaris L.; *bot.*)

فأفأ *fa'fa'a* to stammer, stutter

فاكون (Fr. *wagon*) *fākōn* pl. فواكين *fawākīn*[2] (railroad) car, coach

فأل VI to regard as a good omen, as an auspicious beginning (ب s.th.); to be optimistic

فأل *fa'l* pl. فؤول *fu'ūl*, افؤل *af'ul* good omen, favorable auspice; optimistic outlook, hope; omen, auspice, sign | قرأ الفأل to tell fortunes, predict the future

تفاؤل *tafā'ul* optimism

متفائل *mutafā'il* optimistic; optimist

فالس (Fr. *valse*) *vals* waltz

فالوذج *fālūḏaj* a sweet made of flour and honey

فالوذجى *fālūḏajī* soft and flabby, like *fālūḏaj*

فئام *fi'ām* group (of people)

فأن *fa-inna* see [2]ف *fa*

فانلة *fanella* and فانلا pl. *-āt* flannel; undershirt; pl. فانلات *fanellāt* underwear, underclothing

فانوس *fānūs* pl. فوانيس *fawānīs*[2] lantern | فانوس سحرى (*siḥrī*) laterna magica, magic lantern; (slide) projector

فئة *fi'a* pl. *-āt* group, class; troop, band, party; platoon (of light arms; *Syr., mil.*); rate (of taxation), (tax) bracket; tax, rate, fee; price

فاوريقة *fāwarīqa* pl. فواريق *fawārīq*[2] factory plant

□ فايظ *fāyiẓ* (= فائض) see فيظ

فبراير *fabrāyir* February

فبارك *fabārik*[2] (pl.) factories, plants

فت *fatta u* (*fatt*) to weaken, undermine, sap (فى s.th.) | فت فى عضده or فى ساعده (*'aḍudihī*) to weaken s.o., sap s.o.'s strength, discourage, enervate s.o. **II** to crumble, fritter (ه s.th.); to divide into small fragments (ه s.th.) | يفتت القلب (الاكباد) (*qalba*) heartbreaking, heart-rending **V** to crumble, disintegrate, break up into fragments **VII** = **V**

فتة *fatta* a kind of bread soup

فتات *futāt* crumbs, morsels

فتيت *fatīt* crumbs, crumbled bread

فتيتة *fatīta* a kind of bread soup

فتأ *fata'a a* and فتئ *fati'a a* (with negation) not to cease to be (ه s.th.); فتئ *fati'a a* (فتء *fat'*) to desist, refrain (عن from), cease (عن doing s.th.), stop (عن s.th., doing s.th.) | ما فتئ يفعل not to cease doing, do incessantly

فتح *fataḥa a* (*fatḥ*) to open (ه s.th.); to turn on (ه a faucet); to switch on, turn on (ه an apparatus); to dig (ه a canal); to build (ه a road); to open, preface, introduce, begin (ه s.th.); to conquer, capture (ه s.th.); to reveal, disclose (ه على to s.o. s.th.); to grant victory or success (ه على to s.o. over or in s.th.; of God), give into s.o.'s (على) power (ه s.th.; of God); to open the gates (of profit) (على to s.o.; of God); to infuse, imbue, inspire, endow (ب or ه على s.o. with; of God); (*gram.*) to pronounce with the vowel *a* (ه a consonant) | فتح البخت (*bakta*) to tell fortunes; فتح عينيه على آخرهما (*'ainaihi*) to open one's eyes wide, stare wide-eyed; فتح الشهية (*šahīyata*) to stimulate the appetite **II** to open (ه s.th.); (of a flower) to open **III** to address first (ه s.o.), speak first (ه to s.o.); to open the conversation or talk (ه في with s.o. about); to disclose (ه or ب ه to s.o. s.th.), let s.o. (ه) in on s.th. (ه or ب) **V** to open, open up, unfold (intr.); to be opened (عن so that s.th. becomes perceptible); to be open, be responsive (heart) **VII** to open, open up, unfold (intr.); to be opened **VIII** to open, inaugurate (ه s.th.); to introduce, preface, begin (ه ب s.th. with); to conquer, capture (ه s.th.) **X** to begin, start, commence (ه s.th.); to seek the assistance of God (على against), implore God for victory (على over)

فتح *fatḥ* opening; introduction, commencement, beginning | فتح الاعتماد opening of a credit, presentation of a letter of credit; — (pl. فتوح *futūḥ*, فتوحات *futūḥāt*) conquest; victory, triumph; pl. فتوحات alms; donations, contributions (for a *zāwiya*; *Tun.*)

فتحة *fatḥa* the vowel point *a* (*gram.*)

فتحة *futḥa* pl. فتح *futaḥ*, *-āt* opening, aperture, breach, gap, hole; sluice

فتاح *fattāḥ* opener (of the gates of profit, of sustenance; one of the attributes of God)

فتاحة *fattāḥa* pl. *-āt* can opener

مفتاح *miftāḥ* pl. مفاتيح *mafātīḥ*[2] key (to a door, of a keyboard, esp. that of a piano); switch (*el.*, railroad); lever, pedal (of a vehicle); knob (on a radio); stop (of a wind instrument); valve (of a trumpet); peg, pin (of a stringed instrument)

مفتاحجى *miftāḥjī* (railroad) switchman

مفاتحة *mufātaḥa* opening of a conversation

افتتاح *iftitāḥ* opening, inauguration; introduction, beginning | ليلة الافتتاح *lailat al-ift.* première, opening night

افتتاحى *iftitāḥī* opening, introductory, preliminary, prefatory, proemial; inaugurational | مبلغ افتتاحى (*mablaḡ*) opening bid, lowest bid (at auctions); فصل (or مقال) افتتاحى (*faṣl*, *maqāl*) and مقالة افتتاحية (*maqāla*) editorial, leading article, leader; ليلة افتتاحية (*laila*) première, opening night

افتتاحية *iftitāḥiya* editorial, leading article, leader; overture (*mus.*)

استفتاح *istiftāḥ* start, beginning, commencement, inception, incipience; earnest money, handsel

فاتح *fātiḥ* opener; beginner; conqueror, victor; light (color) | فاتح البخت *f. al-bakt* fortuneteller; أزرق فاتح light-blue

فاتحة *fātiḥa* pl. فواتح *fawātiḥ*[2] start, opening, beginning, commencement, inception, incipience; introduction, preface, preamble, proem | فاتحة الكتاب or الفاتحة name of the first sura

مفتوح *maftūḥ* opened, open | الباب مفتوح على مصراعيه (*miṣrā'aihi*) the door is wide open

مفتح *mufattiḥ* appetizing; (pl. *-āt*) apéritif

مفتتح *muftataḥ* start, beginning, commencement, inception, opening, inauguration

[1]فتر *fatara u* (فتور *futūr*) to abate, subside; to become listless, become languid, languish, flag, slacken; to cool off, become tepid, become lukewarm (water); to slacken, flag, become lax, become remiss, let up (عن in) **II** to cause (ه s.th.) to subside, abate, allay, mitigate, ease, soothe (ه s.th.); to make languid, make listless, exhaust, slacken. weaken, sap, enfeeble (ه, ه s.o., s.th.); to make tepid (ه water) **IV** to make languid, make listless, exhaust, slacken, weaken, sap, enfeeble (ه, ه s.o., s.th.) **V** to become listless, become languid, languish, flag, slacken; to become tepid, become lukewarm (water)

فتر *fitr* pl. افتار *aftār* small span (the space between the end of the thumb and the end of the index finger when extended); corner

فترة *fatra* lassitude, languor, listlessness, slackness, weakness, feebleness, debility; tepidity, indifference, coolness (of a feeling); — (pl. *fatarāt*) interval of time, intermission, pause; period, spell, while | فترة الانتقال transition period; بين فترة واخرى (*wa-uḵrā*) now and then, from time to time; فى الفترة بعد الفترة at certain intervals, now and then, off and on, once in a while

فتور *futūr* lassitude, languor, listlessness, slackness, laxity, slackening, flagging; tepidity

فاتر *fātir* languid, weak, feeble, listless, slack, loose, flabby; dull, listless, stagnant (stock exchange); tepid, lukewarm

متفتر *mutafattir* intermittent

[2]فاتورة pl. فواتير look up alphabetically

فتش **II** to examine (thoroughly), scrutinize, search, investigate, explore (ه s.th.); to look, search (ه into s.th.); to inquire (عن about, after), look, search (عن for); to supervise, superintend, control, inspect (على or ه, ه s.o., s.th.); to be in charge, exercise supervision, control, or inspection (على of)

فتاش *fattāš* thorough examiner, investigator, explorer, researcher

تفتيش *taftīš* pl. تفاتيش *tafātīš*[2] examination, scrutiny, searching, search; investigation; inquiry, research, exploration; supervision, superintendence, control, charge; inspection; survey, review; controlling body, board of control; inquisition; circle of irrigation, irrigation district, also تفتيش الرى *t. ar-rīy* (*Eg.*) | تفتيش جوى (*jawwī*) aerial inspection

تفتيشى *taftīšī* investigational, investigatory, examining, examinatory

مفتش *mufattiš* inspector, supervisor | مفتش بيطرى (*baiṭarī*) veterinary inspector (*Eg.*); مفتش الرى *m. ar-rīy* irrigation inspector (*Eg.*)

مفتشية *mufattišīya* inspectorate

فتفت *fatfata* to speak secretly (الى to); to fritter, crumble (ه s.th., esp. bread)

فتفوتة *fatfūta* pl. فتافيت *fatāfīt*[2] crumb, morsel (esp. of bread)

فتق *fataqa u* (*fatq*) to undo the sewing (ه of s.th., e.g., of a garment), unsew, unstitch, rip, rip open, tear apart, rend, slash, slit open (ه s.th.) | فتق الذهن (*ḏihna*) to make s.o. see his way clear, cause s.o. to see things in their true light; الضرورة تفتق الحيلة (*ḥīlata*) necessity is the mother of invention; فتقت له حيلة *futiqat lahū ḥīlatun* a ruse came to his mind **II** to unsew, unstitch, rip, tear, etc. (= **I**; ه s.th.) **V** to be unsewn, be unstitched (e.g., a garment), be ripped open, be torn apart, be rent, be slashed, be slit open; to bring forth, produce (عن s.th.); to hatch, contrive, devise (عن s.th., fig., of the mind) **VII** to be unsewn, be unstitched (e.g., a garment), be ripped open, be torn apart, be rent, be slashed, be slit open; to bring forth, produce (عن s.th.)

فتق *fatq* pl. فتوق *futūq* rip, rent, tear, cleft, crack, fissure, slit, slash; hole (e.g., in a stocking); hernia, rupture (*med.*) | مصاب بالفتق (*muṣāb*) afflicted with hernia; person suffering from hernia

فتاق *fitāq* hernia, rupture (*med.*)

فتيق *fatīq* unstitched, ripped, ripped open, slit, rent, torn; sharp

مفتوق *maftūq* unstitched, ripped, ripped open, slit, rent, torn; afflicted with hernia

فتك **fataka** *u* *i* (*fatk*) to assassinate, murder, slay, kill (ب s.o.), destroy, annihilate (ب s.th.); to attack suddenly, assault (ب s.o.) | فتك بهٗ فتكا ذريعا (*fatkan ḏarīʿan*) to cut off, destroy, wipe out, eradicate, extirpate, exterminate s.o.; to decimate, thin the ranks of ... (esp., said of a disease)

فتك *fatk* assassination, murder; destruction, annihilation

فتكة *fatka* pl. *-āt* devastation, ravage, havoc

فتاك *fattāk* deadly, lethal, murderous; of disastrous effect, wreaking havoc (ب on)

افتك *aftak*[2] deadlier, more destructive

فاتك *fātik* pl. فتاك *futtāk* assassin, murderer, killer

فتل **fatala** *i* (*fatl*) to twist together, twine, entwine, plait, throw (ه s.th.); to spin (ه s.th.) **II** to twist, twine, wreathe, wind, weave, plait (ه s.th.); to splice (ه a rope) **V** to be twisted, be twined, be plaited, be woven, be wound **VII** = **V**; to turn on one's heel and leave, turn away (من from) | انفتل من الباب to slip out the door

فتلة *fatla* (n. vic.) twist(ing), twining, plaiting; (*eg.*; pl. فتل *fital*) thread | شمع الفتلة (*šammaʿa*) to make off, make a getaway, beat it

فتيل *fatīl* twisted, twined, entwined, plaited, wreathed, wound, woven, coiled; — (pl. *-āt*, فتائل *fatāʾil*[2]) wick; gauze tampon; fuse, slow match, match cord | لا يغنى فتيلا (*yuğnī*) it is of no use at all (من to s.o.), it won't help him (عنه) a bit, it isn't worth a farthing; لا يجدى فتيلا (*yujdī*) = لا يغنى فتيلا

فتيلة *fatīla* pl. *-āt*, فتائل *fatāʾil*[2] wick; ○ filament of a light bulb

فتال *fattāl* ropemaker, cordmaker

مفتول *maftūl* strapping, sturdy, husky; (watch) tower (Nejd) | مفتول الساعد muscular, brawny, strong, husky, burly

فتن **fatana** *i* (*fatn*, فتون *futūn*) to turn away (ه s.o. from من); to subject to temptations or trials, seduce, tempt, entice, allure, beguile (ه s.o.); to enamor, charm, enchant, captivate, enthrall, enrapture, fascinate, infatuate (ه s.o.); — *fatana* *i* (*fatn*) to torture, torment (ه s.o.); to denounce (على s.o.), inform (على against s.o.); pass. *futina* to be charmed, be enraptured, be infatuated (ب by), be enamored (ب of), be in love (ب with); to be crazy (ب over), be like mad (ب

after) IV to enamor, charm, enchant, captivate, enthrall, enrapture, fascinate, infatuate (ه s.o.) VIII to subject to temptations (ه s.o.); to be charmed, be tempted, be infatuated; act. *iftatana* and pass. *uftutina*: to be subjected to temptations, be lead from the right course; pass. *uftutina* = *futina*

فتنة ***fitna*** pl. فتن ***fitan*** temptation, trial; charm, charmingness, attractiveness; enchantment, captivation, fascination, enticement, temptation; infatuation; intrigue; sedition, riot, discord, dissension, civil strife

فتان ***fattān*** fascinating, captivating, enchanting, charming; tempter, seducer; denunciator, informer, slanderer

افتن ***aftan***² more charming, more attractive, more delightful

مفاتن ***mafātin***² charming qualities; charms; magic powers

فاتن ***fātin*** pl. فواتن ***fawātin***² tempting, alluring, seductive, fascinating, captivating, enchanting, charming; tempter, seducer

مفتون ***maftūn*** fascinated, captivated, infatuated, enraptured, charmed (ب by); enamored (ب of), in love (ب with); madman, maniac

(فتو and فتى (فتى ***fatiya*** *a* (فتاء ***fatā'***) to be youthful, young, adolescent IV to give a formal legal opinion (ه في to s.o. in or regarding; *Isl. Law*); to furnish (ه s.o.) with information (في about), expound, set forth (ه في to s.o. s.th.); to deliver an opinion (في about), decide by a legal opinion (ب for or in favor of s.th.), state as a (legal) opinion (بان that) X to ask (ه s.o.) for a formal legal opinion (في in or regarding; *Isl. Law*); to ask (ه s.o.) for a formal opinion (في about), request information (ه في of s.o. about), seek s.o.'s (ه) counsel (في in, about), consult (ه في s.o. in, about), ask s.o.'s (ه) opinion (في about)

فتى ***fatan*** pl. فتيان ***fityān***, فتية ***fitya*** youth, adolescent, juvenile, young man; slave; hero; pl. young people, adolescents, juveniles

فتاة ***fatāh*** pl. فتيات ***fatayāt*** young woman, (young) girl

فتاء ***fatā'*** youth, adolescence

فتى ***fatīy*** youthful, juvenile, adolescent, young

فتية ***fatīya*** youthfulness, juvenility

فتوى ***fatwā*** pl. فتاو ***fatāwin***, فتاوى ***fatāwā*** futwa, formal legal opinion (*Isl. Law*)

فتيا ***futyā*** formal legal opinion (*Isl. Law*)

فتوة ***futūwa*** youth, adolescence; the totality of the noble, chivalrous qualities of a man, noble manliness, magnanimity, generosity, nobleheartedness, chivalry; designation of Islamic brotherhoods of the Middle Ages, governed by chivalrous precepts; name of several youth organizations in Arabic countries; (*eg.*; pl. *-āt*) bully, brawler, rowdy, tough; racketeer (*eg.*)

افتاء ***iftā'*** deliverance of formal legal opinions (*Isl. Law*); office of mufti (*Isl. Law*); deliverance of formal opinions, advising, advice, counseling

استفتاء ***istiftā'*** request for a formal legal opinion (*Isl. Law*); consulting, consultation; referendum, plebiscite, also استفتاء الشعب *ist. aš-ša'b* and استفتاء شعبي (*ša'bī*)

مفت ***muftin*** pl. *-ūn* deliverer of formal legal opinions (*Isl. Law*); official expounder of Islamic law, mufti | مفتى الديار المصرية (*miṣrīya*) Grand Mufti of Egypt; سماحة المفتى *samāḥat al-m.* (title of a mufti) His Eminence the Mufti

فثأ ***faṯa'a*** *a* (فثء ***faṯ'***) to quench, still (ه s.th., hunger, thirst, also fig.)

فج *fajja u* (*fajj*): فج رجليه (*rijlaihi*) to straddle IV to stride, hurry

فج *fajj* pl. فجاج *fijāj* way, road between two mountains | من كل فج عميق or من كل فج وصوب (*wa-ṣaubin*) from all sides, from all directions, from everywhere

فج *fijj* unripe, green (fruit); blunt, rude (speech)

فجأ *faja'a* and فجئ *faji'a a* (فجء *faj'*, فجأة *faj'a*, فجاءة *fujā'a*) and III to come suddenly, descend unexpectedly (ه upon s.o.), confront (ه s.o.) suddenly or unexpectedly, take (ه s.o.) by surprise, surprise (ه ب s.o. with), attack, assail (ه s.o.)

فجأة *faj'atan* suddenly, unexpectedly, inadvertently, unawares

فجاءة *fujā'atan* suddenly, unexpectedly, inadvertently, unawares

فجائى *fujā'ī* sudden, unexpected, surprising

مفاجأة *mufāja'a* pl. مفاجآت *mufāja'āt* surprise

فاجئ *fāji'* sudden, unexpected, surprising

مفاجئ *mufāji'* sudden, unexpected, surprising; pl. مفاجئات surprising events, surprises

فجر *fajara u* (*fajr*) to cleave, break up, dig up (ه e.g., the ground); — (فجور *fujūr*) to act immorally, sin, live licentiously, lead a dissolute life, indulge in debauchery; to commit adultery II to create an outlet or passage (ه for water, and the like), let (ه water, and the like) flow or pour forth; to split, cleave (ه s.th.); to explode (ه s.th.) IV to commit adultery V to gush out, spurt forth, break forth, break out, erupt, burst out VII = V; to go off, discharge, burst; to burst forth; to explode, detonate; to overflow (ب with); to descend suddenly, break in, rush in, swoop down (على upon)

فجر *fajr* dawn, daybreak, morning twilight; dawn (fig.), beginning, outset, start; (f.) morning prayer (*Isl. Law*)

فجور *fujūr* immorality, iniquity, depravation, dissolution, debauchery, licentiousness, profligacy, dissolute life, fornication, whoredom

تفجر *tafajjur* outbreak, outburst, eruption

انفجار *infijār* pl. *-āt* outbreak, outburst, eruption; explosion, detonation | مواد الانفجار *mawādd al-inf.* explosives

انفجارى *infijārī* explosive, blasting (adj.)

فاجر *fājir* pl. فجار *fujjār*, فجرة *fajara* libertine, profligate, debauchee, roué, rake; adulterer; liar; insolent, impudent, shameless, brazen

فاجرة *fājira* pl. فواجر *fawājir*[2] adulteress; whore, harlot

متفجر *mutafajjir* explosive, blasting (adj.)

منفجر *munfajir* explosive, blasting (adj.)

فجع *faja'a a* (*faj'*) to inflict suffering and grief (ه upon s.o.), afflict, distress (ه s.o.); to make miserable (ه s.o., ب by bereaving him of s.o.) | فجع بولده *fuji'a bi-waladihī* he was stricken by the death of his son II to torment, torture, distress, grieve (ه, ه s.o., s.th.) V to be or become painfully affected, be mentally distressed

فجعة *faj'a* gluttony

فجاعة *fajā'a* gluttony

فجوع *fajū'* painful, grievous, trying, distressing

فجيعة *fajī'a* pl. فجائع *fajā'i'*[2] misfortune, calamity, disaster

فجعان *faj'ān* voracious, insatiable; glutton, ravenous eater

تفجع *tafajju'* agony, mental distress, affliction, suffering, grief

فاجع *fāji'* painful, grievous, trying, distressing

فاجعة *fāji'a* pl. فواجع *fawāji'*[2] misfortune, disaster, calamity; catastrophe; drama, tragedy

مفجعات *mufajji'āt* horrors, terrors

تفجعن *tafaj'ana* to eat greedily, ravenously, be gluttonous

فجعنة *faj'ana* gluttony

فجفج *fajfaj* garrulous, loquacious; thoughtless chatterer, windbag; braggart, boaster, swaggerer

فجفاج *fajfāj* garrulous, loquacious; thoughtless chatterer, windbag; braggart, boaster, swaggerer

فجل *fujl* (coll.; n. un. ة) pl. فجول *fujūl* radish (Raphanus sativus L.; *bot.*)

(فجو) فجا *fajā u* (*fajw*) to open (ه a door)

فجوة *fajwa* pl. *fajawāt*, فجاء *fijā'* opening, aperture, breach, gap, interstice; (horizontal) tombstone

فح *faḥḥa u i* (*faḥḥ*, فحيح *faḥīḥ*) to hiss (snake), whistle (storm)

فحش *faḥuša u* (*fuḥš*) to be monstrous; to be excessive, exorbitant; to be detestable, abominable, atrocious, obscene, indecent, foul, shameless, impudent **IV** to use obscene language; to commit atrocities **VI** = **I** and **IV**

فحش *fuḥš* monstrosity; abominableness, atrocity; obscenity, indecency; obscene language

فحشاء *faḥšā'*[2] monstrosity, abomination, atrocity, vile deed, crime; adultery, fornication, whoredom

فحاش *faḥḥāš* obscene, lewd, shameless in speech or action | تأليف فحاش pornography

تفاحش *tafāḥuš* monstrosity, abominableness

فاحش *fāḥiš* monstrous; immoderate, excessive, exorbitant; absurd, preposterous, nonsensical; detestable, loathsome, abominable, atrocious, repugnant, disgusting; dirty, foul, vile, indecent, obscene; shameless, impudent

فاحشة *fāḥiša* harlot, whore, prostitute; — (pl. فواحش *fawāḥiš*[2]) monstrosity, abomination, atrocity, vile deed, crime; adultery, fornication, whoredom

مفحشة *mufḥiša* harlot, whore

فحص *faḥaṣa a* (*faḥṣ*) to scratch up (ه the ground); to examine (ه s.o., also medically, ه s.th.), test (ه, ه s.o., s.th.), investigate (ه s.th.), scrutinize (ه, ه s.o., s.th.); to search (عن for), inquire (عن about, into s.th.), seek information (عن about) **V** to search (عن for), inquire (عن about, into s.th.), seek information (عن about); to examine (ه s.th., ه s.o., medically)

فحص *faḥṣ* pl. فحوص *fuḥūṣ* test; examination (in general, school, medical); (medical) checkup; investigation, scrutiny; search, inquiry

افحوص *ufḥūṣ* pl. افاحيص *afāḥīṣ*[2] dugout hollow in the ground in which a bird lays its eggs, nesting place, breeding place

فحل **X** to become dreadful, terrible, momentous, serious, difficult (على for s.o.; affair), to get out of control, become excessive, become irreparable (damage)

فحل *faḥl* pl. فحول *fuḥūl*, فحولة *fuḥūla* male (of large animals), stallion; outstanding personality, luminary, star,

master; a paragon (of) | الشعراء الفحول
(šu'arā') the master poets

فحولة fuḥūla excellence, perfection

استفحال istifḥāl dreadfulness, terribleness; gravity, seriousness; difficulty

مستفحل mustafḥil dreadful, terrible; grave, serious; difficult; overwhelming, overpowering, rampant, spreading dangerously

فحم faḥuma u (فحوم fuḥūm, فحومة fuḥūma) to be or become black; — faḥama a (faḥm) to be dumfounded, nonplused, unable to answer II to blacken (with charcoal), make black (ه، ه s.o., s.th.); to char, carbonize, reduce to charcoal (ه s.th.) IV to dumfound, nonplus, strike dumb (ه s.o.); to silence (ه s.o.) with arguments; to put (ه s.o.) off brusquely, give s.o. (ه) the brush-off

فحم faḥm (coll.; n. un. ة) charcoal(s); coal(s); pl. فحومات fuḥūmāt coals, brands of coal | فحم حجري (ḥajarī) soft coal, bituminous coal; فحم حطب f. ḥaṭab charcoal; فحم قوالب briquettes; فحم كوك (kōk) coke

فحمة faḥma pl. فحمات faḥamāt lump of coal | فحمة الليل f. al-lail deep-black night; — (pl. فحام fiḥām, فحوم fuḥūm) blackness

فحمي faḥmī black, coal-black

فحيم faḥīm black

فحام faḥḥām coal merchant, coal dealer; collier, miner

فاحم or اسود فاحم fāḥim black | فاحم السواد f. as-sawād coal-black, pitch-black, jet-black

فحوى faḥwā or فحواء faḥwā'² sense, meaning, signification, import; purport, tenor (of a letter, of a speech, etc.)

فخ faḵḵ pl. فخاخ fiḵāḵ, فخوخ fuḵūḵ trap, snare

فخت faḵata a (faḵt) to perforate, pierce (ه s.th.)

فخذ faḵiḏ, faḵḏ, fiḵḏ f., pl. افخاذ afḵāḏ thigh; leg (of mutton, etc.); (m.) subdivision of a tribe

فخذة faḵḏa leg (of mutton, etc.)

فخذي faḵiḏī, faḵḏī femoral

فخر faḵara a (faḵr, faḵar, فخار faḵār) to glory (ب in), boast (ب of s.th.), brag (ب of), vaunt (ب s.th.); to pride o.s. (ب upon), be proud (ب of); — faḵira a (faḵar) to despise, disdain III to vie in glory (ه with s.o.); to be proud (ب of), pride o.s. (ب upon), boast (ب ه before s.o. of) V to be proud, haughty VI and VIII = I faḵara X to find (ه s.th.) excellent

فخر faḵr glory, pride; honor; vainglorious poetry (as a literary genre) | غير فخر ولا wa-lā ġaira faḵrin or فخرا faḵra I say this without boasting

فخري faḵrī honorary, honoris causa

فخرة fuḵra glory, pride

فخار faḵār glory, pride

فخور faḵūr vainglorious, boastful, bragging; proud (ب of)

فخير faḵīr boasting, bragging, swaggering, boastful

فخار faḵḵār (fired) clay; earthenware, crockery, pottery

فخاري faḵḵārī potter's, earthen; potter

فاخورة fāḵūra pottery, earthenware manufactory

فاخوري fāḵūrī potter

افخر afḵar² more splendid, more magnificent

مفخرة mafḵara pl. مفاخر mafāḵir² object of pride, s.th. to boast of; glorious deed, exploit, feat; glorious trait or quality

مفاخرة *mufāḵara* boasting, bragging, vainglory, pride

تفاخر *tafāḵur* boasting, bragging, vainglory

افتخار *iftiḵār* pride, vainglory, boasting, bragging

فاخر *fāḵir* proud, vainglorious, boastful, bragging; outstanding, excellent, first-rate, perfect, splendid, superb, glorious, magnificent; sumptuous, de luxe

مفاخر *mufāḵir* boastful, vainglorious, proud

مفتخر *muftaḵir* proud, vainglorious, boastful, bragging; outstanding, excellent, first-rate, perfect, splendid, superb, glorious, magnificent; sumptuous, de luxe

فخفخ **faḵfaḵa** to be boastful, vainglorious; to boast, brag

فخفخة *faḵfaḵa* ostentation, showiness, pageantry, pomp

فخم **faḵuma** *u* (فخامة *faḵāma*) to be stately, imposing, splendid, magnificent, grand II to intensify (ه s.th.); to honor, treat with respect (ه s.o.), show deference (ه to); to pronounce emphatically, make emphatic (ه a consonant)

فخم *faḵm* stately, imposing, splendid, superb, magnificent, grand, grandiose

فخامة *faḵāma* stateliness, imposingness, imposing appearance; splendor, magnificence, eminence, high rank; title of the head of a nonmonarchic state; title of honor given to high-ranking foreign dignitaries, approx.: Highness, Excellency, = صاحب الفخامة | فخامة الدولة *f. ad-daula* title of the President of the Republic (*Syr.*, *Leb.*); فخامة رئيس الدولة do. (*Syr.*, *Leb.*); فخامة الرئيس *f. ar-ra'īs* title of a foreign head of state, approx.: His Excellency, the President; فخامة المعتمد السامى *f. al-mu'tamad as-sāmī* His Excellency, the High Commissioner

تفخيم *tafḵīm* emphatic or velarized pronunciation of a consonant (*phon.*) | آلة التفخيم amplifier (*radio*)

مفخم *mufaḵḵam* honored | الحروف المفخمة the emphatics (*phon.*)

فدح **fadaḥa** *a* (*fadḥ*) to oppress, burden (ه s.o.), weigh (ه upon s.o.) X to regard (ه s.th.) as a heavy burden, as painful

فداحة *fadāḥa* oppressiveness, burdensomeness

افدح *afdaḥ*[2] more oppressive, more burdensome, more serious, heavier

فادح *fādiḥ* burdensome, oppressive; grave, serious (mistake), heavy (loss), bad (physical defect)

فادحة *fādiḥa* pl. فوادح *fawādiḥ*[2] misfortune, calamity

فدخ **fadaḵa** *a* (*fadḵ*) to break, smash (ه s.th.)

فدر **fadar** pl. فدور *fudūr* chamois

فدفد **fadfad** pl. فدافد *fadāfid*[2] wasteland, tract of desert land, desert

فدم **fadama** *i* to seal (ه the mouth, an aperture)

فدم *fadm* pl. فدام *fidām* clumsy in speech; heavy-witted, sluggish, dull, stupid

فدن II to fatten, stall-feed (ه s.th.)

فدان *faddān* pl. فدادين *fadādīn*[2] yoke of oxen; (pl. افدنة *afdina*) feddan, a square measure (*Eg.* = 4200.833 m²)

فادن *fādin* pl. فوادن *fawādin*[2] plummet, plumb bob

فدى **fadā** *i* (*fidan*, فداء *fidā'*) to redeem, ransom (ب ,ه ,ه s.o., s.th. with or by); to sacrifice (ب ه for s.o. s.th.) III to sacrifice, offer up (ب s.th.) VI to beware (من of), guard (من against), get away, keep away (من or ه from); to get rid (من or ه of); to prevent, obviate, avert, avoid (من or ه s.th.) **VIII** = **I**; to obtain (ه s.th.) by sacrificing s.th. else (ب); to redeem o.s.. ransom o.s. (ب with or by); to free o.s. (من from) | افتداه بالنفس to sacrifice o.s. for s.o. or s.th., risk life and property for s.o. or s.th.

فدى *fidan, fadan* redemption, ransoming; ransom; sacrifice (with foll. genit.: for s.th., to save or liberate s.o. or s.th.) | جعلت فداك (*ju'iltu*) (lit.: may I be made your ransom, i.e.) oh, could I but sacrifice myself for you! مات فدى للوطن (*waṭan*) he died for his country

فدية *fidya* pl. فديات *fidayāt*, فدى *fidan* ransom; redemption (from the omission of certain religious duties, by a material donation or a ritual act; *Isl. Law*)

فداء *fidā'* redemption, ransoming; ransom; price (one has to pay for s.th.), sacrifice (one makes for s.th.) | جعل كل شيء فداءه (*fidā'ahū*) he sacrificed or gave up everything for it

فدائى *fidā'ī* one who sacrifices himself (esp., for his country); esp. pl. فدائيون fighters who risk their lives recklessly, soldiers prepared to sacrifice their lives; fedayeen, commandos, shock troops (*Eg.*)

فدائية *fidā'īya* spirit of self-sacrifice

مفاداة *mufādāh* sacrifice

فاد *fādin* redeemer

مفدى *mafdīy* (prop., object of self-sacrifice) following the name of a king, also after وطن *waṭan*, عرش *'arš*, and the like, approx.: dearly beloved, dear

فذ *fadd* pl. افذاذ *afdād*, فذوذ *fudūd* alone, only, sole, single; singular, unique; uncommon, unusual, infrequent; pl. افذاذ extraordinary people

فذلكة *fadlaka* brief summary, résumé, survey, outline, abstract, epitome

فر *farra* *i* (*farr*, فرار *firār*, مفر *mafarr*) to flee, run away, run off, escape (من from) | فر هاربا (*hāriban*) to flee, take to one's heels **IV** to put (ه s.o.) to flight **VIII** to open up or part (عن so that s.th. becomes visible); to bare, show (عن the teeth when smiling), reveal (عن s.th.); to shimmer, gleam

فرار *firār* flight

فرار *furār*: عينه فراره *'ainuhū furāruhū* (*firāruhū*) his outward appearance bespeaks his inner worth; you need only look at him to know what to think of him

فرار *farrār* fugitive, runaway, escaped; a fugitive, a runaway; deserter, defector; quicksilver, mercury

فررة *furrēra* teetotum (*eg.*)

مفر *mafarr* flight, escape | لا مفر منه (*mafarra*) unavoidable, inevitable

فار *fārr* pl. *-ūn*, فارة *fārra* fugitive, fleeing; a fugitive

فرأ *fara'* pl. افراء *afrā'* wild ass, onager

فراء *farā'* wild ass, onager | كل الصيد فى جوف الفراء *kullu ṣ-ṣaidi fī jaufi l-f.* there are all kinds of game in the belly of the wild ass (proverbially of s.o. or s.th. that combines all good qualities and advantages and makes everything else dispensable)

فراك (Fr. *frac*) *firāk, frāk* pl. *-āt* swallow-tailed coat, full dress, tails

فراولة *faraula* (from It. *fragola*) strawberry (*eg.*)

الفرات *al-furāt* the Euphrates; فرات sweet (water)

فرتيكة *furtīka* clasp, buckle (*eg.*)

فرج *faraja* *i* (*farj*) and **II** to open, part, separate, cleave, split, gap, breach (ه s.th.), make an opening, gap or breach (ه in); to dispel, drive away (ه s.th., e.g., grief, worries); to comfort, solace, relieve (عن s.o.) **II** to show (ه على to s.o. s.th.) **IV** to leave (عن a place); to free, liberate, set free (عن s.o.), release (عن s.o., s.th.) **V** to be opened, be separated, be cleft, be split; to part, divide, move apart (e.g., a crowd so as to let s.o. pass); to be dispelled (grief, sorrow); to derive comfort (في or على from the sight of), take pleasure, delight (في or على in looking at); to regard, view, observe, watch, inspect (على s.o., s.th.), look (على at s.o., at s.th.) **VII** to be opened, be separated, be cleft, be split; to open or part widely, widen, diverge, split open, gape, yawn; to open (عن so that s.th. becomes visible); to show, reveal (عن s.th.); to relax, become relaxed (features; crisis); to be dispelled, be driven away (grief, sorrow); to become gay

فرج *farj* pl. فروج *furūj* opening, aperture, gap, breach; pudendum of the female, vulva

فرج *faraj* freedom from grief or sorrow, release from suffering; joy; relaxation; relief, ease, repose, pleasure, comfort; happy ending

فرجة *furja* state of happiness (esp. after suffering); pleasure, delight; — (pl. فرج) opening, aperture, gap, breach, hole; onlooking, watching, inspection, viewing; sight, spectacle

فروج *farrūj* (coll.; n. un. ة) pl. فراريج *farārīj*[2] chick, young chicken, pullet

فرارجى (*eg.*) *farargī* seller of chicken, poulterer

مفرج *mafraj* pl. مفارج *mafārij*[2] relief, relaxation; denouement, happy ending

افراج *ifrāj* freeing, liberation; release (عن of s.o., of s.th.), unblocking (عن e.g., of assets), decontrol (عن e.g., of rationed foodstuffs, etc.)

تفرج *tafarruj* inspection, viewing, regarding; watching, observation

انفراج *infirāj* relaxedness, relaxation

متفرج *mutafarrij* pl. *-ūn* viewer, watcher, observer, spectator, onlooker

منفرج *munfarij* opened wide, wide-open; relaxed; gay, merry | زاوية منفرجة (*zāwiya*) obtuse angle (*geom.*)

فرجار *firjār* compass, dividers

فرجون *firjaun* currycomb, brush

فرح *fariḥa* *a* (*faraḥ*) to be glad, happy delighted, rejoice (ل, ب at), be gay, merry, cheerful (ل, ب about, over) **II** to gladden, delight, cheer, exhilarate, make merry, happy, gay (ه s.o.)

فرح *faraḥ* joy, gladness, glee, gaiety, hilarity, mirth, exhilaration, merriment, happiness; wedding; pl. افراح *afrāḥ* feast of rejoicing, celebration, festival, festivity; wedding (feast) | ردهة الافراح *radhat al-a.* banquet hall, ballroom

فرحة *farḥa* joy

فرح *fariḥ* merry, gay, cheerful, joyful, glad, delighted, happy

فرحان *farḥān*[2] merry, gay, cheerful, joyful, glad, delighted, happy

مفارح *mafāriḥ*[2] feasts of rejoicing, joyous events

تفريح *tafrīḥ* exhilaration, amusement

فارح *fāriḥ* merry, gay, cheerful, joyful, glad, delighted, happy

مفرح *mufriḥ* gladdening, cheering, exhilarating, joyous, delightful

فرخ II to have young ones (bird); to hatch (said of eggs); to hatch, incubate (ه s.th.); to germinate, sprout, put out new shoots (of a tree); to spread, gain ground **IV** to have young ones (bird); to hatch (said of eggs); to hatch, incubate (ه s.th.); to germinate, sprout, put out new shoots (of a tree) | افرخ روعه (*rau'uhū*) fear left him

فرخ *farḵ* pl. افراخ *afrāḵ* فروخ *furūḵ*, فراخ *firāḵ*, فرخان *firḵān* young bird; shoot, spout (of a plant, of a tree) | فرخ ورق *f. waraq* (*eg.*) sheet of paper

فرخة *farḵa* pl. فراخ *firāḵ* young female bird; hen | فرخة رومى (*rūmī*) (*eg.*) turkey hen

فراخ *firāḵ* (pl. of فرخة) poultry, domestic fowls

تفريخ *tafrīḵ* hatching, incubation | آلة التفريخ incubator

فرد[1] *farada* and *faruda* *u* (فرود *furūd*) to be single, be alone; to be singular, be unique; — *farada* *u* (فرود *furūd*) to withdraw, retire, segregate (عن from); — *farada* *i* (*eg.*) to spread, spread out, extend, stretch (ه s.th.); to unfold (ه s.th.) **IV** to set aside, separate, segregate, isolate (ه, ه s.o., s.th.); to single out, assign especially (ه ب or ل s.th. for), devote (ه ب or ل s.th. to s.th. else) **V** to be alone; to do alone, perform singlehandedly (ب s.th.); to possess alone (ب s.th.); to be matchless, be unique **VII** = **V**; to stand alone, be without parallel (ب or فى with or in s.th.); to withdraw, segregate, walk away (عن from); to be isolated (عن from) **X** to find (ه, ه s.o., s.th.) singular, unique or isolated; to isolate (ه s.th., *chem.*)

فرد *fard* pl. افراد *afrād*, فرادى *furādā* alone, single; sole, only; solitary, lone, lonely; singular, unique, matchless, unrivaled, peerless, incomparable; one, a single one, a single thing, a single person, individual; odd, uneven (number); الفرد epithet of the month of Rajab; (pl. فراد *firād*) one, one of a couple, one of a pair; (pl. فرود *furūd*, فرودة *furūda*) pistol; — singular (*gram.*) | فردا فردا (*fardan*) singly, separately, one by one, one at a time, one after the other

فردة *farda* one part, one half, one of a pair

فردى *fardī* single, solitary; single- (in compounds); pertaining to a single person; one-man (in compounds); solo (adj.); singles (tennis); individual, personal; individualist; odd, uneven (number)

فردية *fardīya* individuality, individualism

فريد *farīd* alone, lone, lonely, solitary; singular, unique, matchless, peerless, unrivaled, incomparable; (with foll. genit.) especially endowed with | فريد فى بابه unique of its kind

فريدة *farīda* pl. فرائد *farā'id*[2] precious pearl, precious gem, solitaire; (*eg.*) quire (of paper)

فرادا *furādan* singly, separately, one by one, one at a time, one after the other

فرادى *furādā* singly, separately, one by one, one at a time, one after the other

تفريدى *tafrīdī* detailed, itemized

انفراد *infirād* solitude, loneness, loneliness; isolation, seclusion | على انفراد alone, apart, isolatedly, in solitude, in seclusion; singly, by o.s.; confidentially; الانفراد بالسلطة (*sulṭa*) autocracy

انفرادى *infirādī* individual; individualistic; autocratic; isolationistic, tending to isolation

مفرد *mufrad* single, solitary, lone, detached, isolated; (*gram.*) simple, consisting of only one word (expression); being in the singular; singular (*gram.*); (pl. *-āt*) vocable, word; pl. words, terms, names, expressions (of a scientific field); details | مفردات خاصة (*ḵāṣṣa*) technical terms, terminology; بمفرده by o.s., alone, apart, singly, isolatedly, in solitude, in seclusion, solitarily; بالمفردات in detail; by retail

منفرد *munfarid* isolated, detached, separated; lone, solitary, alone; solo (adj.; also *mus.*)

[2] □ فردة *firda* (< فرضة *furḍa*) pl. فرد *firad* tax, head tax, poll tax

الفردوس *al-firdaus* f., pl. فراديس *farādīs*[2] Paradise

فردوسى *firdausī* paradisiacal, heavenly

[1] فرز **faraza** *i* (*farz*) and **IV** to set apart, separate, detach, isolate (ه s.th.); to secrete, excrete, discharge (ه s.th.; *physiol.*); to sort, sift, classify (ه s.th.); to examine (ه s.th.), screen (ه, ه s.o., s.th.), muster (ه s.o.); to select, pick out (ه s.th.); to distinguish, discriminate, differentiate (ه من s.th. from)

فرز *farz* separation, detachment, isolation; secretion, excretion, discharge; sorting, sifting; mustering, muster, screening, examination; selection, selecting | فرز عسكرى (*'askarī*) pre-induction examination (*mil.*)

فرازة *farrāza*: ○ فرازة آلية (*ālīya*) seed separator, seed-screening apparatus

مفرزة *mafraza* pl. مفارز *mafāriz*[2] group, detachment, party, troop, band

افراز *ifrāz* pl. *-āt* secretion, excretion, exudation, discharge, expectoration (*physiol.*) | قسمة افراز *qismat i.* partition in kind (*Isl. Law*)

○ فارزة *fāriza* comma

مفرزات *mufrazāt* secretions, excretions, exudations (*physiol.*) | المفرزات الداخلية (*dāḵilīya*) internal secretions, endocrines

[2] فريز pl. افرزة = افريز

[3] فيروز, فاروز and فيروزج look up alphabetically

[4] افريز pl. افاريز look up alphabetically

فرزن **II** *tafarzana* to queen, become a queen (of a pawn; in chess)

فرزان *firzān* pl. فرازين *farāzīn*[2] queen (in chess)

[1] فرس **farasa** *i* (*fars*) to kill, tear (ه its prey, of a predatory animal) **V** to regard searchingly, eye, scrutinize (ه, ه or فى s.o., s.th.), look firmly (ه, ه or فى at s.o., at s.th.); to recognize, detect (ه a quality, فى in s.o.) **VIII** = **I**; to ravish, rape (ها a woman)

فرس *faras* m. and f., pl. افراس *afrās* horse, mare; knight (chess) | فرس البحر *f. al-baḥr* hippopotamus; فرس الرهان race horse; الفرس الاعظم Pegasus (*astron.*)

فراسة *farāsa* horsemanship, equitation

فراسة *firāsa* perspicacity, acumen, discernment, discrimination, minute observation; keen eye (esp. for traits of character); intuitive knowledge of human nature | علم الفراسة *'ilm al-f.* physiognomy; فراسة اليد *f. al-yad* chiromancy, palmistry

فريسة *farīsa* pl. فرائس *farā'is*[2] prey (of a wild animal)

فريسى *farrīsī*, فرسى Pharisee

فروسة *furūsa* horsemanship, equitation; chivalry, knighthood

فروسية *furūsīya* horsemanship, equitation; chivalry, knighthood; heroism, valor

فارس *fāris* pl. فرسان *fursān*, فوارس *fawāris*[2] horseman, rider; knight, cavalier;

hero; pl. cavalry | لست من فرسان ذلك الميدان (*lastu, maidān*) I am unfamiliar with this field, I am not competent in this field

فارسة *fārisa* pl. *-āt* horsewoman; mounted female warrior, Amazon

مفترس *muftaris* rapacious, ravenous (animal) | حيوان مفترس (*ḥayawān*) predatory animal, beast of prey

²الفرس *al-furs* the Persians; Persia, also بلاد الفرس

فارس *fāris*², also بلاد فارس Persia

فارسى *fārisī* Persian (adj. and n.)

فرساى *virsāy* Versailles

فرسخ *farsak* pl. فراسخ *farāsik*² a measure of length, parasang

فرسوفيا *varsōviyā* Warsaw (capital of Poland)

¹فرش *faraša u* (*farš*, فراش *firāš*) to spread, spread out (ه s.th.); — *faraša u i* (*farš*) to pave, cover (ه the ground, floor, path, room, etc., ب with) II to cover (ه the floor, etc., ب with); to furnish, provide with furniture (ه s.th.); to tile, pave (ه s.th.) VIII to spread, spread out (ه s.th.); to lie down, stretch out, sprawl (ه on s.th.); to sleep (ها with a woman) | افترش لسانه (*lisānahū*) to give one's tongue free rein

فرش *farš* pl. فروش *furūš* furnishing; furniture, household effects; mat, rug, carpet; anything spread on the ground as bedding; foundation (*arch.*)

فرشة *farša* bed; mattress

فراش *farāš* wheel (of a mill); (coll.; n. un. ة) moths; butterflies

فراشة *farāša* (n. un.) moth; butterfly; flighty, fickle person

فراش *firāš* pl. فرش *furuš*, افرشة *afriša* cushion, pillow; blanket, cover, spread; mattress; bed

فراش *farrāš* one who spreads the carpets; servant, attendant; house servant, valet; office boy, errand boy

مفرش *mifraš* pl. مفارش *mafāriš*² tablecloth, table cover, cover (in general); bedspread, counterpane

مفرشة *mifraša* pl. مفارش *mafāriš*² saddle blanket

مفروش *mafrūš* covered (ب with); furnished; مفروشات *mafrūšāt* furniture, household effects

²فرش II to brush (ه s.th.)

فرشة *furša* pl. فرش *furaš* brush; paintbrush | فرشة البودرة powder puff; فرشة اسنان *f. asnān* toothbrush

فرشاة *furšāh* brush; paintbrush

فرشاية *furšāya* (*syr.*) brush

فرشح *faršaḥa* (فرشحة *faršaḥa*) to straddle, stand with one's legs apart

فرشخ *faršaka* = فرشح *faršaḥa*

فرشينة (It. *forcina*) *furšīna* pl. *-āt* hairpin

فرص II to make holidays

فرصة *furṣa* pl. فرص *furaṣ* opportunity, chance, auspicious moment; holidays, vacation | فرصة من الزمن (*furṣatan, zaman*) for a short time, briefly; انتهز الفرصة (*intahaza*) to seize the opportunity, avail o.s. or take advantage of the opportunity

فريصة *farīṣa* pl. فرائص *farā'iṣ*² flesh or muscle beneath the shoulder-blades | ارتعدت فرائصه or فريصته (*irta'adat*) violent fear or excitement seized him

مفرص *mufarriṣ* holiday-maker, vacationist, tourist

فرصاد *firṣād* mulberry; mulberry tree

فرض *faraḍa i* (*farḍ*) to decide, determine; to decree, order, ordain (ه s.th.); to appoint, assign, apportion, allocate (ه ل to s.o. s.th., money, and the like); to impose, enjoin, make incumbent (ه على upon s.o. s.th.), prescribe (ه على to s.o. s.th.); to impose (الحصار a blockade, على on); to assume, presume, suppose, presuppose, postulate (ه s.th., ان that) | فرض ارادته عليه (irādatahū) to force one's will on s.o. II to notch (ه s.th.), make incisions (ه in s.th.) VIII to impose, enjoin, make incumbent (ه على upon s.o. s.th.), prescribe (ه على to s.o. s.th.); to decree, order (ه s.th.); to assume, suppose (ه s.th., ان that)

فرض *farḍ* pl. فروض *furūḍ* notch, incision; duty, precept, injunction, order, decree, ordinance, command; religious duty (*Isl. Law*); statutory portion, lawful share (*Isl. Law*); assumption, supposition, presupposition, premise, postulate, hypothesis | فروض التحية *f. at-taḥīya* prescribed forms of salutations; فرض عين *f. ʿain* individual duty (*Isl. Law*); فرض كفاية collective duty (*Isl. Law*); على فرض on the premise of ...; على فرض ان on the assumption that ..., with the understanding that .... supposing that ...

فرضى *farḍī* hypothetic(al), suppositional, conjectural, assumed without proof

فرضية *farḍīya* hypothesis

فرضة *furḍa* pl. فرض *furaḍ* notch, incision; opening, gap, crevice, crack; seaport, river harbor, small port town

فريضة *farīḍa* pl. فرائض *farāʾiḍ*[2] religious duty (*Isl. Law*); divine precept, ordinance of God (*Isl. Law*); obligatory prayer (*Isl. Law*); pl. distributive shares in estate (*Isl. Law*) | فريضة الجمعة *f. al-jumʿa* the obligatory divine service on Friday (*Isl. Law*); ذوو الفرائض *ḏawū l-f.* the "Koranic heirs", i.e., those entitled to a statutory portion in estate according to sura IV, 12ff. (*Isl. Law*); علم الفرائض *ʿilm al-f.* law of descent and distribution

افتراض *iftirāḍ* assumption, supposition, presupposition, premise, postulate, hypothesis

افتراضى *iftirāḍī* hypothetic(al)

فارض *fāriḍ* old, advanced in years

مفروض *mafrūḍ* supposed, assumed, premised; pl. مفروضات duties, obligations

فرط **faraṭa** *u* to precede (ه s.o.); to escape inadvertently, slip (من s.o.'s tongue; of words); to escape (من s.o.), get lost (من on s.o.); to happen (inadvertently) (من to s.o., faux pas, etc.); to neglect (فى s.th.), be lax, be remiss (فى with regard to); to strip off (ه fruits) | فرط منه الشىء (*šaiʾu*) he missed the thing, lost it II to leave, abandon, forsake, give up (ه s.o., فى or ه s.th.), renounce, waive (فى or ه s.th.); to separate (ه or عن from), part (ه or عن with); to neglect (فى s.th.), be lax, be remiss (فى with regard to); to exceed the proper bounds, go too far, be excessive (فى in), exaggerate, overdo (فى s.th.); to waste, squander (فى s.th.) IV to exceed the proper bounds, go too far, be excessive (فى in), exaggerate, overdo, abuse (فى s.th.) VII to be stripped off, be loosened, become detached (من from); to be dissolved, dissolve, break up | انفرط عقدهم (*ʿaqduhum*) they broke up, they parted company, they dissolved

فرط *farṭ* excess, immoderation, exaggeration; (with foll. abstract noun) hyper- (in compounds)

فرط *faraṭ* (*eg.*) interest (on money, capital, etc.)

فراطة *furāṭa* small change, coins

تفريط *tafrīṭ* negligence, neglect

افراط *ifrāṭ* excess, immoderation, exaggeration

فارط *fāriṭ* elapsed, bygone, past, last, e.g., يوم الاحد الفارط (*yauma l-aḥad*) last Sunday

مفرط *mufarriṭ* prodigal, wasteful, squandering; wastrel, spendthrift, prodigal, squanderer

مفرط *mufriṭ* exaggerated, excessive

فرطح **farṭaḥa** to make broad, broaden, flatten (ه s.th.)

مفرطح **mufarṭaḥ** broad; flattened, flat, oblate; fat and flabby, bloated

فرع **fara'a** *a* (*far'*, فروع *furū'*) to surpass, outstrip (ه s.o.); to excel (ه s.o.) **II** to put forth branches, to branch; to derive, deduce (ه من s.th. from) **V** to branch out, ramify, become ramified, spread in all directions; to divide, fork, bifurcate (road, pipeline); to branch off **VIII** to deflower

فرع *far'* pl. فروع *furū'*, افرع *afru'* twig, branch, bough, limb, (also coll.) branches, twigs; derivative; section, subdivision; branch office, subsidiary establishment, branch; branch line, feeder line; branch wire, feed wire (*el.*) | علم الفروع or الفروع *'ilm al-f.* the doctrine of the branches, i.e., applied *fiqh*, applied ethics (consisting in the systematic elaboration of canonical law in Islam); شرعا وفرعا *šar'an wa-far'an* with full right, with good cause, justly

فرعى *far'ī* branch, subsidiary, tributary, sub-, side (in compounds); subdivisional; secondary

افرع *afra'*[2], f. فرعاء *far'ā'*[2] tall, slender

تفرع *tafarru'* many-sidedness, versatility; (pl. *-āt*) ramification; pl. secondary things, concomitant circumstances, minor factors

فارع *fāri'* tall, lofty, towering; high-grown, slender, slim; beautiful, handsome, pretty | فارع الطول *f. aṭ-ṭūl* tall, high-grown; فارع القامة tall and slender

مفرع *mufarra'* ramified, branching

متفرعات *mutafarri'āt* secondary things, concomitant circumstances, minor factors

فرعون **fir'aun**[2] pl. فراعنة *farā'ina* Pharaoh

فرغ **faraḡa** *u* and **fariḡa** *a* (فروغ *furūḡ*, فراغ *farāḡ*) to be empty, be void; to be vacant; to be exhausted, be used up; to be rid (من of s.o.), be done, be finished (من with); to finish, terminate, conclude, close, wind up, finish off, settle, complete, bring to an end (من s.th.); to devote o.s., apply o.s., attend, tend (الى or ل to s.o., to s.th.), occupy o.s. (الى or ل with) | فرغ الى نفسه to collect one's thoughts **II** to empty, void, vacate, evacuate, discharge (ه s.th.); to unload (ه a cargo); to pour out (ه s.th.) **IV** to empty, void, vacate, evacuate (ه s.th.); to pour out (ه على s.th. over, فى into); to unload (ه s.th., e.g., from a ship) | افرغه فى قالب (*qālab*) to mold s.th. (fig.); افرغ جهده (or مجهوده) (*jahdahū*) to exert o.s. to the utmost, make every effort (فى in), do one's best **V** to be free from work, be unoccupied, be idle, have leisure; to be free, disengage o.s. (الى or ل for some work), occupy o.s. exclusively (الى or ل with), devote o.s., apply o.s., attend (الى or ل to) **X** to empty (ه a bowl, and the like); to vomit | استفرغ مجهوده to exert o.s. to the utmost, make every effort (فى in), apply every ounce of strength (فى to), do one's best

فرغ *fariḡ* empty, void; vacant

فراغ *farāḡ* void, vacuity, vacancy, vacuum, empty space; gap; space (ل for s.o., for s.th.); cession (of things which are not transferable as a property, but transferable as a possession; *Isl. Law*); leisure, sparetime

فراغى *farāḡī* vacuum (adj.)

فروغ *furūḡ* emptiness, voidness, vacuity; vacancy, unoccupiedness; termination, expiration, exhaustion | فروغ الصبر *f. aṣ-ṣabr* impatience

افرغ *afraḡ*[2] emptier

تفريغ *tafrīḡ* emptying, vacating, evac uation; discharge; unloading (of a cargo)

افراغ *ifrāḡ* emptying, vacating, evacuation; pouring out

استفراغ *istifrāḡ* emptying, voiding, vacating, evacuation; vomiting

فارغ *fāriḡ* pl. فراغ *furrāḡ* empty, void; vacant; unoccupied, not busy, idle, leisurely; inane, vacuous, idle, useless; — tare (*com.*) | بالفارغ in the void (of the target) = in the bull's-eye; بفارغ الصبر *bi-f. iṣ-ṣabr* impatiently

مفروغ منه *mafrūḡ minhu* finished, settled (question, problem, and the like); exhausted (topic, and the like)

مفرغ *mufarriḡ* emptying; creating a vacuum | ○ آلة مفرغة vacuum pump

مفرغ *mufarraḡ* emptied, vacated, exhausted of air, vacuum (adj.); hollow

مفرغ *mufraḡ* cast (in a mold) | حلقة مفرغة (*ḥalqa*) seamless ring; vicious circle, circulus vitiosus

[1]فرفر *farfara* to shake itself (of animals, esp. of a bird)

فرفر *furfur* small bird

فرفور *furfūr* small bird

[2]فرفوری *farfūrī* = فغفوری fine porcelain

[3]فرفير *firfīr* purple, purpure

فرفش *farfaša*: فرفش نفسه (*eg.*) to recover, pick up, revive

فرفشة *farfaša* (*eg.*) ease, comfort, convenience, leisure

فرفير *firfīr* purple, purpure

[1]فرق *faraqa u* (*farq*, فرقان *furqān*) to separate, part, divide, sever, sunder (ه s.th.); to make a distinction (بين between), distinguish, differentiate, discriminate (بين between); — (*farq*) to part (ه the hair); — *fariqa a* (*faraq*) to be terrified, be dismayed; to be afraid (من of) II to separate, part, divide, sever, sunder (ه s.th.); to strew about, scatter, disperse (ه s.th.); to make a distinction (بين between), distinguish, differentiate (بين between; عن ه s.o. from); to distribute (ه على or في s.th. to, among); to frighten, scare, daunt, terrify, horrify (ه s.o.) | فرق تسد *farriq tasud* divide and rule! divide et impera! III to separate o.s., disengage o.s., withdraw, depart (ه, ه from s.o., from s.th.), part (ه, ه with s.o., with s.th.), leave, quit (ه, ه s.o., s.th.) V to be or become separated, split, disunited, divided, scattered, dispersed, separate, part, divide, scatter, disperse, dissolve, break up VII to be or become separated, disunited, divided, separate o.s., disengage o.s. (عن from), part (عن with) VIII = V | افترق طرائق قددا (*ṭarā'iqa qidadan*) to split into many parts or groups, become divided

فرق *farq* separation, severance, sunderance, division, partition; differentiation, distinction, discrimination; parting (of the hair); — (pl. فروق *furūq*) difference, dissimilarity, distinction; small change, coins; pl. cases similar with regard to facts, yet different as to their legal implications (*Isl. Law*)

فرق *firq* part, portion, division, section, unit; band, company, party, detachment, troop, group; herd, flock

فرق *faraq* fear, fright, terror

فرق *fariq* fearful, timid, timorous, cowardly, craven

فرقة *firqa* pl. فرق *firaq* part, portion, division, section, unit; band, company, party, detachment, troop, group; class; grade, class (in school); pupils or students of a course; troupe, ensemble; team, crew; division (*mil.*); sect | الفرقة الأجنبية (*ajnabīya*) the Foreign Legion; الفرقة الخامسة the fifth column; فرقة مصفحة (*muṣaffaḥa*) armored division; فرقة المطافئ

(الاطفاء or) *f. al-maṭāfi'* (or *al-iṭfā'*) fire department, fire brigade; فرقة الاعدام *f. al-i'dām* firing squad; فرقة استعراضية (*isti'rāḍīya*) show troupe, revue troupe; فرقة موسيقية (*mūsīqīya*) orchestra; فرقة موسيقى *f. mūsīqā* (military) band

فرقة *furqa* separatedness, separation, disunion

فريق *farīq* pl. فروق *furūq*, افرقة *afriqa*, افرقاء *afriqā'*[2] band, company, troop, detachment, unit; party; faction; team (sports); — a military and naval rank, approx.: lieutenant general (*Eg.*), vice admiral (*Eg.*) | فريق اول (*awwal*) lieutenant general (*Ir.*); فريق ثان (*ṯānin*) major general (*Ir.*)

فروق *farūq* very fearful, timid, timorous, cowardly, craven; — Constantinople

فاروق *fārūq* very timorous; الفاروق he who distinguishes truth from falsehood (epithet of the 2nd Caliph, Omar)

فاروقية *fārūqīya* "Faruk cap", winter field cap of the Egyptian Air Force (1939)

فرقان *furqān* proof, evidence; الفرقان the Koran

مفرق *mafraq*, *mafriq* pl. مفارق *mafāriq*[2] crossing, intersection, bifurcation, forking, fork, junction, interjunction; road fork, highway intersection, crossroads, also مفرق الطرق *m. aṭ-ṭuruq*; المفرق *al-mafraq* or قلعة المفرق *qal'at al-m.* Mafrak (city in N Jordan) | مفرق الشعر *mafriq aš-ša'r* parting (of the hair)

تفريق *tafrīq* separation, severance, sunderance, partition, division; dispersion, dispersal, scattering; differentiation, distinction, discrimination; distribution; pl. تفاريق *tafārīq*[2] single, separate parts, detached sections | بالتفريق in detail; in portions; by retail (*com.*)

تفرقة *tafriqa* separation, severance, sunderance, partition, division; dispersion, dispersal, scattering; differentiation, distinction, discrimination; distribution | بالتفرقة in detail; in portions; by retail (*com.*)

مفارقة *mufāraqa* separation, parting, farewell, leave-taking, departure; difference, dissimilarity, distinction

فراق *firāq* separation, parting, farewell, leave-taking, departure; difference, dissimilarity, distinction

تفرق *tafarruq* separation, disunion, division; dispersing, dispersal, scattering; deployment (in the field; *mil.*)

افتراق *iftirāq* separation, disunion, division

فارق *fāriq* distinguishing, differential, distinctive, discriminative, separative; (pl. فوارق *fawāriq*[2]) a separating or distinctive factor; distinctive characteristic, criterion; difference, distinction, dissimilarity, disparity | مع بعد الفارق (*bu'di l-f.*) in spite of the great difference

مفرق *mufarriq* distributor, retailer; mailman, postman

مفرق *mufarraq* retail (adj.) | تاجر المفرق retail merchant, retailer; بالمفرق by retail

متفرق *mutafarriq* dispersed, scattered; sporadic; متفرقات miscellany, sundries (*com.*). miscellaneous items

مفترق *muftaraq* crossing, intersection, bifurcation, forking, fork, junction, interjunction; road fork, highway intersection, crossroads, also مفترق الطرق *m. aṭ-ṭuruq*

فاوريقة[2] pl. فواريق look up alphabetically

افريقيا[3] look up alphabetically

افريقى[4] pl. افارقة look up alphabetically

فرقد *farqad* calf; الفرقدان two bright stars of Ursa Minor (β and γ)

فرقع *farqa'a* (فرقعة *farqa'a*) to pop, crack, burst, explode II *tafarqa'a* = I

فرقعة *farqa'a* crack, pop, report (of a firearm); explosion, blast

مفرقع *mufarqi'* explosive, blasting (adj.); pl. مفرقعات explosives; firecrackers, fireworks

فرقلة *farqilla* (*eg.*) pl. *-āt* whip with a leather thong, used in driving animals

[1]فرك *faraka u* (*fark*) to rub (ه s.th.) II = I V to be rubbed VII = V

فريك *farīk* rubbed; cooked green wheat

○ مفراك *mifrāk* twirling stick

[2]فراك look up alphabetically

فركش *farkaša* (*eg.*) to disarrange, dishevel, tangle (ه s.th.), tousle, muss, tear (hair)

[1]فرم *farama i* (*farm*) to cut into small pieces (ه meat, tobacco), mince, chop, hash (ه meat) II = I

مفرمة *miframa* meat grinder; mincer, mincing machine

مفروم *mafrūm*: دخان مفروم (*dukān*) finely cut tobacco; لحم مفروم (*laḥm*) chopped meat, hashed meat

[2]فرمة (It. *forma*) *furma* pl. فرم *furam* mold

فرمان *faramān* pl. *-āt*, فرامين *farāmīn*[2] firman; decree, edict; (letter of) safe-conduct, laisser-passer (formerly, in the Ottoman Empire)

فرمبواز (Fr. *framboise*) *frambuwāz* raspberry

فرمسون (*eg.*) *firmasōn* (from Fr. *franc-maçon*) Freemason

فرملة *farmala* pl. فرامل *farāmil*[2] brake (of a wheel, etc.)

فرملجى (*eg.*) *farmalgī* pl. *-īya* brakeman

فرموزا *farmōza, formōza* Formosa

فرن *furn* pl. افران *afrān* oven, baking oven

فران *farrān* baker

فرنج II *tafarnaja* to become Europeanized, adopt European manners, imitate the Europeans

الافرنج *al-ifranj* the Europeans | بلاد الافرنج Europe

افرنجى *ifranjī* European; الافرنجى syphilis

فرنجة *firanja*[2] Land of the Franks, Europe

تفرنج *tafarnuj* Europeanization, imitation of the Europeans

متفرنج *mutafarnij* Europeanized

[1]فرند *firind* a sword of exquisite workmanship

[2]فرنده *faranda, varanda* pl. *-āt* veranda, porch

فرنس *farnasa* (فرنسة *farnasa*) to make French, Frenchify, imbue with French culture (ه s.th.) II *tafarnasa* to become a Frenchman; to imitate the French

فرنسا *faransā* (also فرنسة) France

فرنسى *faransī* French; (pl. *-ūn*) Frenchman

فرنساوى *faransāwī* (also فرنسوى) French

الفرنسيس *al-faransīs* the French

الفرنسيسكان *al-faransiskān* the Franciscans

فرنك (Fr. *franc*) *firank* and فرنكة pl. *-āt* franc

فره *farih* lively, agile, nimble

فراهة *farāha* liveliness, agility, nimbleness, swiftness (of an animal); sturdiness

فاره *fārih* lively, agile, nimble, swift (animal); comely, pretty; sturdy; big

فرو *farw* (coll.; n. un. ة) pl. فراء *firā'* furriery, fur(s), skin(s), pelt(s), peltry

فروة *farwa* (n. un.) fur, pelt; skin, hide | فروة الرأس scalp; ابو فروة *abū f.* (*eg.*) chestnut

فراء *farrā'* furrier

فرى *farā* **i** (*fary*) to split lengthwise, cut lengthwise (ه s.th.); (*eg.*) to mince, chop (ه s.th.); to invent lyingly, fabricate, trump up (ه على s.th. against) | فرى كذبا (*kidban*) to fabricate, or invent, a lie (على against) **II** to split lengthwise, cut lengthwise (ه s.th.) **IV** = **II**; **VIII** to invent lyingly, fabricate, trump up (ه على s.th. against); to slander, libel, calumniate (على s.o.)

فرية *firya* pl. فرى *firan* lie, falsehood, falsity; slander, calumny

فرى *farīy*: اتى (or جاء) شيئا فريا to do s.th. unheard-of, do an unprecedented thing

مفراة *mifrāh* (*eg.*) (= مفرمة) meat grinder; mincer, mincing machine

افتراء *iftirā'* lie, falsehood, falsity; slander, calumny

مفتر *muftarin* slanderer, calumniator

مفتريات *muftarayāt* lies, falsities; calumnies

فريز *farīz* pl. افرزة *afriza* = افريز *ifrīz* (look up alphabetically)

فز *fazza* **i** (*fazz*) to jump up, start, bolt; to be or become frightened, terrified, dismayed, startled; to frighten, alarm, startle (ه, ه s.o., s.th.), scare away (ه, ه عن s.o., s.th. from) **IV** to frighten, alarm, startle (ه, ه s.o., s.th.), scare away (ه, ه عن s.o., s.th. from) **V** to become restless, restive, uneasy **X** to fill with unrest or excitement, rouse, agitate, excite, stir up, instigate, incite, egg on, inflame, whip up (ه s.o.), provoke (ه an incident); to startle (ه عن s.o. out of); to stir up, arouse (ه من s.o. from)

فزة *fazza* start, jump, bolt, dart

استفزاز *istifzāz* pl. *-āt* instigation, agitation, incitement, provocation

استفزازى *istifzāzī* agitative, instigative, inflammatory, rabble-rousing, provocative, incendiary

فزر *fazara* **u** (*fazr*) to tear, rent, burst (ه s.th.) **V** to be torn, be rent, split open, burst **VII** = **V**

فزارة *fazāra* female leopard

فزورة *fazzūra* pl. فوازير *fawāzīr*[2] (*eg.*) riddle, puzzle

فزع *fazi'a* **a** (*faza'*) and *faza'a* **a** (*faz'*, *fiz'*) to be afraid, be scared (من of), be alarmed, frightened, terrified (ل or من by); — *fazi'a* **a** to take refuge, flee (الى to), seek asylum (الى with) **II** to strike (ه s.o.) with fear; to frighten, scare, alarm, terrify, dismay, startle (ه s.o.) **IV** to frighten, startle, terrify, scare (ه s.o.) **V** to be terrified, startled, dismayed; to be frightened | تفزع من نومه (*naumihī*) to be roused from one's sleep

فزع *faza'* pl. افزاع *afzā'* fear, fright, terror, alarm, dismay, anxiety, consternation, panic

فزع *fazi'* frightened, terrified, scared, alarmed, startled, dismayed, fearful, timorous

فزعان *faz'ān* frightened, terrified, scared, alarmed, startled, dismayed, fearful, timorous

فزاعة *fazzā'a* one who inspires fear; scarecrow

مفزع *mafza'* place of refuge, retreat, sanctuary

مفزعة *mafza'a* place of refuge, retreat, sanctuary; scarecrow

مفزع *mufzi'* terrible, dreadful, alarming

مفزع *mufza'* frightened, terrified, alarmed, startled

فستان *fustān* pl. فساتين *fasātīn*[2] (woman's) dress, gown, frock

فستق *fustuq*, *fustaq* pistachio (*bot.*)

فسح *fasuḥa* **u** (فسحة *fusḥa*, فساحة *fasāḥa*) to be or become wide, spacious, roomy; —

fasaḥa a (*fasḥ*) to make room, clear a space (ه, في in, ل for) **II** to make wide, make spacious, widen, broaden, extend, expand (ه s.th.); to make room, clear a space (ل for) | فسح مجالا له (*majālan*) to make room for s.o., or s.th., give s.o. or s.th. free play or free scope; to open up an opportunity for s.o.; فسح له الطريق to open or pave the way for s.o. or s.th. **IV** to make room, clear a space (ل for); to clear, open up (ه s.th., ل for) **V** to be or become wide, spacious, roomy; to walk, take a walk **VII** to be or become wide, spacious, roomy; to extend, expand, dilate; to be free, be ample (time) | انفسحت لى الاوقات I had plenty of time

فسحة *fusḥa* wideness, ampleness, spaciousness, roominess; extensive possibilities, ample opportunities, wide scope for action; (time) margin, enough time (ل for); — (pl. فسح *fusaḥ*, *-āt*) free, open, or empty, space; holidays, vacation; walk, promenade, stroll, ride, drive, outing, excursion | ما زال فى الوقت فسحة (*waqt*) there is still time

فسحة *fasaḥa* pl. *-āt* (*eg.*) anteroom, vestibule, hallway, entrance hall; (*eg.*, also *syr.*) open space between houses; courtyard

فسيح *fasīḥ* pl. فساح *fisāḥ* wide, ample, spacious, roomy, broad

انفساح *infisāḥ* wideness, ampleness; extension, expansion, dilation

منفسح *munfasaḥ* wideness, ampleness; plane, surface

فسخ *fasaḵa a* (*fasḵ*) to dislocate, disjoint, luxate, put out of joint (ه a limb); to sever, sunder, tear (ه s.th.); (*jur.*) to cancel, abolish, rescind, revoke, abrogate, annul, nullify, invalidate, dissolve, void, vacate (ه s.th.); — *fasiḵa a* (*fasaḵ*) to lose color; to fade (color) **II** to tear to pieces, tear apart, lacerate, mangle (ه s.th.); (*eg.*) to salt (ه fish) **V** to break up into fragments, fall apart, disintegrate **VII** (*jur.*) to be canceled, abolished, rescinded, revoked, abrogated, annulled, nullified, invalidated, dissolved, voided, vacated

فسخ *fasḵ* (*jur.*) cancellation, abolishment, abolition, rescission, revocation, abrogation, annulment, nullification, invalidation, dissolving, voiding, vacating

فسخى *fasḵī* abolitionary, revocatory, abrogative, nullifying

فسخة *fasḵa* (wood) splinter, chip, sliver

فسيخ *fasīḵ* (*eg.*) small salted fish

متفسخ *mutafassiḵ* degenerate(d)

فسد *fasada u i* (فساد *fasād*, فسود *fusūd*) to be or become bad, rotten, decayed, putrid, be spoiled; to be or become vicious, wicked, vile, corrupt, depraved, be marred, impaired, corrupted, perverted, vitiated; to be empty, vain, idle, unsound, false, wrong **II** to spoil, deprave, ruin, corrupt, demoralize (ه, ه s.o., s.th.); to degrade, abase, sully, tarnish, defile (ه, ه s.o., s.th.) **IV** to spoil (ه, ه s.o., s.th.; ه s.th. على of s.o., e.g., s.o.'s plans, etc.), deprave, corrupt, pervert, demoralize (ه, ه s.o., s.th.); to mar, distort, devaluate, depreciate, denigrate, degrade (ه s.th., على for s.o.); to weaken, sap, undermine, upset, ruin, destroy, foil, thwart, frustrate (ه s.th.); to alienate, estrange (ه على s.o. from another; ه على s.o. from s.th.), entice away (على s.o., ه from s.th.); to sow, or stir up, dissension (بين among); to act evilly, wickedly; to cause mischief | افسد عليه امره (*amrahū*) to play s.o. a dirty trick **VII** = **I**

فساد *fasād* rottenness, spoiledness, corruption, decay, decomposition, putrefaction, putridity; depravity, wickedness, viciousness, iniquity, immorality; weakness; pervertedness, wrongness; incorrectness, imperfection (of a legal transaction; *Isl. Law*)

مفسدة *mafsada* pl. مفاسد *mafāsid*[2] cause of corruption or evil; scandalous deed, heinous act; pl. مفاسد dirty tricks, malicious acts, chicaneries | فى المصلحة والمفسدة (*maṣlaḥa*) in good and bad times, for better or for worse

افساد *ifsād* thwarting, undermining, sabotaging

فاسد *fāsid* pl. فسدى *fasdā* bad, foul, rotten, spoiled, decayed, decomposed, putrid; depraved, corrupt, vicious, wicked, immoral; empty, vain, idle, unsound, false, wrong; imperfect (legal transaction; *Isl. Law*) | دور فاسد (*daur*) vicious circle, circulus vitiosus

فسر II to explain, expound, explicate, elucidate, interpret (ه s.th.), comment (ه on) V to be explained, interpreted, etc. (see II); to have an explanation (ب in), be explainable (ب with, by) X to ask (ه s.o.) for an explanation (عن of), inquire (ه عن of s.o. about), ask (ه عن s.o. about); to seek an explanation (عن for)

تفسير *tafsīr* pl. تفاسير *tafāsīr*[2] explanation, exposition, elucidation, explication, interpretation; commentary (esp. one on the Koran)

تفسيرى *tafsīrī* explanatory, explicatory, illustrative

تفسرة *tafsira* urine specimen (of a patient, for diagnosis)

استفسار *istifsār* pl. *-āt* inquiry, question (عن about)

مفسر *mufassir* commentator

فسطاط *fusṭāṭ, fisṭāṭ* pl. فساطيط *fasāṭīṭ*[2] (large) tent made of haircloth; tent, pavilion, canopy; الفسطاط *al-fusṭāṭ* ancient Islamic city south of present-day Cairo

فسطان *fusṭān* pl. فساطين *fasāṭīn*[2] see فستان

فسفات *fusfāt* phosphate

فسفر *fasfara* and II *tafasfara* to phosphoresce

فسفور *fusfūr* phosphorus

فسفس *fasfas* (coll.; n. un. ة) pl. فسافس *fasāfis*[2] bedbug

فسفوسة *fasfūsa* pl. فسافيس *fasāfīs*[2] pustule, pimple

فسيفساء *fusaifisā'*[2] mosaic, mosaic work

[1]فسق *fasaqa u i* (*fisq*, فسوق *fusūq*) and *fasuqa u* to stray from the right course; to stray, deviate (عن from); to act unlawfully, sinfully, immorally, lead a dissolute life; to fornicate (ب with) II (*Isl. Law*) to declare (ه s.o.) to be a *fāsiq* (q.v.)

فسق *fisq* sinfulness, viciousness, moral depravity, dissolute life | دور الفسق *dūr al-f.* brothels

فسوق *fusūq* outrage, iniquity

مفسقة *mafsaqa* pl. مفاسق *mafāsiq*[2] brothel

فاسق *fāsiq* pl. فساق *fussāq*, فسقة *fasaqa* godless, sinful, dissolute, wanton, licentious, profligate, vicious, iniquitous, nefarious; trespasser, offender, sinner; fornicator, adulterer; a person not meeting the legal requirements of righteousness (*Isl. Law*)

[2]فسقية *fasqīya, fisqīya* pl. *-āt*, فساقى *fasāqīy* fountain; well

[1]فسل *fasl* pl. فسول *fusūl* low, lowly, ignoble; despicable; false, deceitful

فسولة *fusūla* lowliness; weakness

فسيلة *fasīla* pl. فسيل *fasīl*, فسائل *fasā'il*[2] palm seedling, palm shoot

[2]فسوليه *fasūliya* = فصوليا

فسلجة *faslaja* physiology

فسلجى *faslajī* physiologic(al)

(فسو) فسا *fasā u* (*fasw*, فساء *fusā'*) to break wind noiselessly

فاسياء *fāsiyā'*[2] dung beetle

فسوليه *fasūliya* = فصوليا

فسيولوجيا *fisiyōlōjiyā* physiology

فسيولوجى *fisiyōlōjī* physiologic(al); physiologist

فش *fašša u* (*fašš*) to cause (ه a swelling, and the like) to subside; to go down, subside (swelling) | فش خلقه (or غله) فى (*kulqahū*, *gillahū*) (*eg.*) to vent one's anger on . . . **VII** to go down, subside (swelling, and the like)

فشة *fišša* pl. فشش *fišaš* (*eg.*, *syr.*) lung, lights (of animals)

فاشى and فاشية look up alphabetically

فشخ *fašaka a* (*fašk*) to straddle; to stride, take large steps

فشخة *faška* pl. *-āt* stride, large step

فشر *fašara u* to brag, boast, swagger

فشر *fašr* bragging, swagger, vain boasting

فشار *fušār* bragging, swagger, vain boasting

فشار *fišār* (*eg.*) popcorn

فشار *faššār* braggart, swaggerer, vain boaster

فشفاش *fašfāš* (*eg.*) lung, lights (of animals)

فشك *fašak* (coll.; n. un. ة) cartridges | فشك خلبى (*kullabī*) blank cartridges (*Syr.*); فشك دخانى (*dukānī*) smoke cartridges (*Syr.*)

فشل *fašila a* (*fašal*) to lose courage, be or become cowardly or faint-hearted, lose heart, despair; to be disappointed; to fail, be unsuccessful (فى in); to miscarry, go wrong, fail **II** and **IV** to thwart, foil, frustrate (ه s.th.) **V** to fail, be unsuccessful

فشل *fašal* disappointment, failure, flop, fiasco

فشل *fašl*, *fašil* weak, faint-hearted, cowardly, craven

فاشل *fāšil* failing, unsuccessful, futile, doomed to failure; no good, worthless

(فشو) فشا *fašā u* (فشو *fašw*, *fušūw*, فشى *fušīy*) to spread, spread about, diffuse, gain ground, make the rounds, circulate; to be revealed, be disclosed, be divulged **IV** to spread, disseminate, put in circulation (ه s.th.); to reveal, disclose, divulge (ه or ب s.th.) **V** to spread, spread about, gain ground, rage (e.g., a disease)

تفش *tafaššin* spreading, spread, outbreak

فص **II** (*eg.*) to remove the outer shell (ه of s.th.)

فص *faṣṣ* pl. فصوص *fuṣūṣ* stone of a ring; clove (of garlic); segment (of an orange); lobe (*anat.*, *bot.*); joint; essence | فص ملح *f. milḥ* (*eg.*) lump of salt; بنصه وفصه (*naṣṣihī*) in the very words, ipsissimis verbis, literally, precisely

فصح[1] *faṣuḥa u* (فصاحة *faṣāḥa*) to be eloquent **II** to bring (ه the language) into literary form, make (ه the language) correct Arabic, purify (ه the language) **IV** to express o.s. in flawless literary Arabic; to speak clearly, distinctly, intelligibly; to give expression (عن to), express, state clearly, declare outright, make plain (عن s.th.), speak openly, frankly (عن about); to orient, inform (ل عن s.o. about); to become clear, plain, distinct **V** to affect eloquence, affect mastery of the language **VI** = **V**

فصيح *faṣīḥ* pl. فصحاء *fuṣaḥā'*[2], فصاح *fiṣāḥ*, فصح *fuṣuḥ* pure, good Arabic (language), literary; skillful in using the correct literary language; clear, plain, distinct, intelligible (language, speech); fluent, eloquent

فصاحة *faṣāḥa* purity of the language; fluency, eloquence

افصح *afṣaḥ*², f. فصحى *fuṣḥā* of purer language; more eloquent | العربية (اللغة or) الفصحى (*'arabīya, luġa*) classical Arabic; الفصحى do.

افصاح *ifṣāḥ* flawless literary Arabic style; frank statement, open word (عن about), open declaration (عن of)

مفصح *mufṣiḥ* clear, plain, distinct, intelligible; cloudless, sunny, bright (day)

²فصح IV to celebrate Easter (*Chr.*); to celebrate Passover (*Jud.*)

فصح *fiṣḥ, faṣḥ* pl. فصوح *fuṣūḥ* Easter (*Chr.*); Pesach, Passover (*Jud.*)

فصد *faṣada* i (*faṣd*, فصاد *fiṣād*) to open a vein; to bleed (ه s.o.), perform a venesection (ه on) V to drip (e.g., the face, عرقا *'araqan* with perspiration) VII to be bled, undergo a venesection; to bleed (nose)

فصد *faṣd* opening of a vein, bloodletting, venesection, phlebotomy

فصاد *fiṣād* opening of a vein, bloodletting, venesection, phlebotomy

فصادة *fiṣāda* pl. فصائد *faṣā'id*² bloodletting, venesection, phlebotomy | ابو فصادة *abū f.* (*eg.*) wagtail (*zool.*)

مفصد *mifṣad*, pl. مفاصد *mafāṣid*² lancet

فصفات *fuṣfāt* phosphate

فصفور *fuṣfūr* phosphorus

فصفورى *fuṣfūrī* phosphoric, phosphorous | ضياء فصفورى phosphorescence

فصل *faṣala* i (*faṣl*) to separate, part, divide, disjoin, divorce, cut off, detach, set apart, segregate (ه, ه عن s.o., s.th. from); to separate (بين two things or persons); to isolate (ه s.th.); to cut, sever, sunder, interrupt (ه s.th.); to discharge, dismiss, fire, sack, expel (ه عن or من s.o. from an office), relieve, divest (ه عن or من s.o. of an office), cashier (ه s.o.); to decide (ه a controversy, and the like), make a decision, render judgment (ف in, about, with respect to); to fix the price (ه for s.th.); — (فصال *fiṣāl*) to wean (ه عن الرضاع the infant from sucking); — *faṣala* u (فصول *fuṣūl*) to go away, depart, move away (عن or من from), leave (عن or من a place), pull out (عن or من of a place) II to divide into particular sections, arrange in sections, group, classify, categorize (ه s.th.); to present in logical order, set forth in detail, detail, particularize (ه s.th.); to make (ه s.th.) clear, plain, distinct; to make to measure, cut out (ه a garment) III to separate o.s., dissociate o.s., be separated (ه from s.o.), part company (ه with); to haggle, bargain (ه على with s.o. for) VII to separate o.s., disengage o.s., disssociate o.s., segregate, secede (عن from); to be separated, disjoined, detached, removed, set aside, cut off (عن from), be interrupted; to be discharged, dismissed, fired, sacked, cashiered; to retire, resign (من or عن from an office), be relieved, be divested (من or عن of an office); to quit, leave (من or عن a political party, and the like)

فصل *faṣl* parting, disjunction, detachment. severance, sunderance, cutting off; separation; division, partition; discharge, dismissal (من or عن from an office); decision, (rendering of) judgment; — (pl. فصول *fuṣūl*) section, part; chapter; act (of a play); movement (of a symphony, etc.); article (in a newspaper); class, grade (school); season | فصل الخطاب (in letters:) conclusion of the formal greetings by the words أما بعد

ammā ba'du; conclusion, termination; decision; unmistakable judgment; بينى وبينك فصل الخطاب we're through with one another once and for all; فصل التمثيل (theater) season; القول الفصل (*qaul*) the last word, the final decision; يوم الفصل *yaum al-f.* Day of Judgment, Doomsday

○ فصلة *faṣla* comma | ○ فصلة منقوطة semicolon

فصلة *fiṣla* offprint, reprint

فصيل *faṣīl* pl. فصال *fiṣāl*, فصلان *fuṣlān* young (weaned) camel

فصيلة *faṣīla* pl. فصائل *faṣā'il*² genus, species, family (*bot.*, and the like); detachment, squad; group, cell (*pol.*); platoon, squadron (of heavy arms; *mil.*) | فصيلة دم *f. dam* blood group; فصيلة الاعدام *f. al-i'dām* firing squad, execution squad; فصيلة الاستكشاف reconnaissance squad, patrol

فيصل *faiṣal* decisive criterion; arbitrator, arbiter

فيصلية *faiṣalīya* "Faisal cap", Iraqi field cap (formerly, *Ir.*)

مفصل *mafṣil* pl. مفاصل *mafāṣil*² joint, articulation

مفصلى *mafṣilī* articular

تفصيل *tafṣīl* detailed statement, elaborate or minute exposition, particularization, detailing; elaborateness, minuteness, completeness of detail; cutting out, cut (of a garment); (pl. *-āt*, تفاصيل *tafāṣīl*²) detail, particular | تفصيلا *tafṣīlan* and بالتفصيل in detail, elaborately, minutely, circumstantially; من تفصيل ... (with foll. genit.) made to measure by ...; tailored by ...; ثياب التفصيل tailor-made clothes; محبوك التفصيل well-fitting (garment)

تفصيلى *tafṣīlī* detailed, minute, particular, elaborate; analytic(al); تفصيليا *tafṣīlīyan* separately, singly, one at a time | المساحة التفصيلية land survey

انفصال *infiṣāl* separation; disengagement, dissociation, withdrawal; secession; interruption | ○ حرب الانفصال *ḥarb al-inf.* the American Civil War; انصار الانفصال separatists

انفصالى *infiṣālī* separatistic; (pl. *-ūn*) separatist

انفصالية *infiṣālīya* separatism

فاصل *fāṣil* separatory, separating, parting, dividing; isolating, insulating; decisive, crucial; conclusive; separation, partition, division, interruption | بلا فاصل without interruption, uninterrupted, unbroken; فاصل الحرارة *f. al-ḥarāra* heat-insulating (*phys.*); مباراة فاصلة (*mubārāh*) finals, final match (sports); خط فاصل (*ḵaṭṭ*) demarcation line

فاصلة *fāṣila* pl. فواصل *fawāṣil*² partition, division; interstice, interspace, interval; ○ comma; ○ dash (punctuation mark); end, rhyme of a Koranic verse

مفصل *mufaṣṣal* set forth or described minutely, elaborately or in great detail, detailed, minute, elaborate, circumstantial; tailor-made, custom-made; مفصلا *mufaṣṣalan* in detail, minutely, elaborately, circumstantially

مفصلة *mufaṣṣala* pl. *-āt* hinge

منفصل *munfaṣil* separate, detached

فصم *faṣama* i (*faṣm*) to cause (ه s.th.) to crack, crack (ه s.th.); to split, cleave (ه s.th.); pass. *fuṣima* to be destroyed (house) VII to have a crack, be cracked; to be split, be cleft

فصم *faṣm* pl. فصومات *fuṣūmāt* recess, niche, chamfer (in walls; *arch.*)

انفصام *infiṣām* split; ○ schizophrenia

فصوليا *faṣūliyā* (or فصولية) the common European bean (Phaseolus vulgaris L.; *bot.*)

فصى V to free o.s., rid o.s. (من of), shake off (من s.th.)

فض *faḍḍa* (1st pers. perf. *faḍaḍtu*) *u* (*faḍḍ*) to break (open), pry open, force open, undo (ه s.th., e.g., a seal); to break, snap (ه s.th.); to scatter, disperse, break up, rout (ه s.th.); to perforate, pierce (ه a pearl); to conclude, close (ه a session, and the like); to dissolve (ه parliament); to settle (ه a conflict, and the like); to shed (ه tears) | فض بكارتها (*bakāratahā*) to deflower a girl; لا فض فوك *lā fuḍḍa fūka* how well you have spoken! II to plate or coat with silver, to silver (ه s.th.) VII to be opened, be broken, be undone (e.g., a seal); to be scattered, be dispersed, be routed; to scatter, disperse, disband, break up, dissolve; to be concluded, be closed (session, and the like) VIII to deflower (ها a girl)

فض *faḍḍ* opening, breaking, undoing (e.g., of a seal); dispersion, scattering, breaking up, routing; settlement, settling (of a dispute); conclusion, closure (e.g., of a session) | فض البكارة *f. al-bakāra* defloration

فضة *fiḍḍa* silver

فضى *fiḍḍī* silver, silvery, argentic, argentous, made of silver, like silver; فضيات *fiḍḍīyāt* silverware | الجمهورية الفضية (*jumhūrīya*) Argentina; الستار الفضى the motion-picture screen, the silver screen

مفض *mifaḍḍ* implement for opening or breaking open | مفض الخطابات letter opener

انفضاض *infiḍāḍ* dissolution, breaking up, dispersal; end, close, conclusion, closure (e.g., of a session)

افتضاض *iftiḍāḍ* defloration

فضح *faḍaḥa a* (*faḍḥ*) to disclose or uncover s.o.'s (ه) faults or offenses, expose, show up, compromise, shame, disgrace, dishonor (ه s.o.); to outshine, eclipse (ه s.th., e.g., the moon the stars); to ravish, violate, rape (ها a woman); to disclose, reveal, show, bring to light, divulge, betray (ه s.th.) VII to be exposed, be compromised, be disgraced, be dishonored VIII to become public, become known, come to light | افتضح امره (*amruhū*) he was exposed

فضح *faḍḥ* exposure, humiliation, mortification, debasement, degradation, disgracing, dishonoring

فضيح *faḍīḥ* covered with shame, exposed, compromised, humiliated, shamed, disgraced, dishonored; disgraceful, shameful, infamous, ignominious

فضيحة *faḍīḥa* exposure, humiliation, mortification, debasement, degradation, disgracing, dishonoring; — (pl. فضائح *faḍā'iḥ*²) disgraceful, or scandalous, act or thing; infamy, ignominy; shame, disgrace, scandal

فضاح *faḍḍāḥ* divulging secrets, unearthing shameful things

افتضاح *iftiḍāḥ* disgracefulness, ignominy, infamy

فاضح *fāḍiḥ* disgraceful, shameful, infamous, ignominious, dishonorable, discrediting, scandalous

مفضوح *mafḍūḥ* covered with shame, exposed, compromised, humiliated, shamed, disgraced, dishonored; disgraceful, shameful, infamous, ignominious

فضفاض *faḍfāḍ* wide, loose, flowing (garment); ample, abundant; plump, corpulent (girl); pompous, high-sounding, bombastic (speech)

فضل *faḍala u* and *faḍila a* (*faḍl*) to be surplus, be in excess, be left (over), remain; — *faḍala u* (*faḍl*) to excel, surpass (على or ه, ه s.o., s.th.); to be excellent, superior, exquisite, good, be better, be more adequate II to prefer (ه ,ه على s.o., s.th. to s.o., to s.th.), like better (ه ,ه s.o., s.th., على than); to give preference (ه ,ه على to s.o., to s.th. over), set s.o. or s.th. (ه ,ه) before or above (على) III to contend for precedence or superiority (ه with s.o.) | فاضل بين شيئين to compare two things in order to determine which deserves preference IV to confer a benefit (على upon s.o.), do (على s.o.) a favor, oblige (على s.o.); to present, honor (على ب s.o. with), bestow, confer (على ب upon s.o. s.th.), grant, award (على ب to s.o. s.th.) V = IV; to have the kindness (ب of doing or to do s.th.; or ف fa with finite verb), be so kind (ب as to do s.th.; or ف with finite verb), deign, condescend, be graciously disposed (ب to do s.th.; or ف with finite verb); (imperative) *tafaḍḍal* please! if you please; to put on house clothes, be dressed for around the house

فضل *faḍl* pl. فضول *fuḍūl* surplus, overplus, excess, superfluity, overflow; leftover, remainder, remnant, rest; matter of secondary importance, subordinate matter; — pl. فضول that which is superfluous, redundant or in excess, a surplus, overplus, superfluity; waste, refuse; droppings, excrements; — superiority (على over); precedence, priority (على over), preference (على to); grace, favor (على to, toward); kindness, graciousness, amiability; erudition, culture, refinement; — (pl. افضال *afḍāl*) merit, desert (فى on behalf of, with respect to), credit (for, in), service(s) (على to); benefit, favor, gift, present | فضلا عن (*faḍlan*) beside, aside from..., not to speak of ..., let alone ..., to say nothing of ...; فضلا عن ذلك besides, moreover, furthermore; بفضل thanks to, owing to, due to; من فضلك please! if you please; يرجع الفضل فى ذلك اليه (*yarji'u*) or الفضل فى ذلك عائد عليه the merit thereby is his due, he deserves all the credit for it; ليس بالفضول ان it is not superfluous that ...; فضول الاحاديث futile talk, idle words; من فضول الكلام ان (*f. il-kalām*) it would be needless talk to ..., it would be a waste of words if ...

فضلة *faḍla* pl. *faḍalāt* remnant, remainder, residue, leftover, rest, surplus, overplus; waste, scrap, discard, offal, waste product; pl. excretions (*physiol.*), excrements

فضول *fuḍūl* curiosity, inquisitiveness, officiousness, meddling

فضولى *fuḍūlī* inquisitive, curious; busybody, officious, meddlesome; prattler, chatterer; manager without commission, uncommissioned agent (*Isl. Law*)

فضولية *fuḍūlīya* inquisitiveness, curiosity; obtrusiveness, importunity, officiousness, indiscreetness

فضيل *faḍīl* pl. فضلاء *fuḍalā'*[2] outstanding, eminent, very good, first-rate, excellent; distinguished, deserving; learned, erudite

فضالة *fuḍāla* pl. *-āt* remnant, remainder, residue, leftover, rest, surplus, overplus; offal, refuse, scum

فضيلة *faḍīla* pl. فضائل *faḍā'il*[2] moral excellence, excellent quality, virtue; merit, advantage, excellence, exquisiteness | صاحب الفضيلة title of Islamic scholars (as, for instance, Rector and sheiks of Al Azhar University), also preceding the title of sheik: فضيلة الشيخ

افضل *afḍal*[2], f. فضلى *fuḍlā*, pl. m. *-ūn*, افاضل *afāḍil*[2], f. فضليات *fuḍlayāt* better, best; more excellent, preferable, etc.; افاضل (very) excellent, learned men; فضليات السيدات *f. as-sayyidāt* the worthy (or esteemed) ladies

افضلية *afḍalīya* precedence, priority (على over), preference (على to, over); predilection

مفضل *mifḍal* pre-eminent, most outstanding, most excellent, very generous, very liberal

مفضلة *mifḍala* pl. مفاضل *mafāḍil*² house dress, everyday dress

مفضال *mifḍāl* pre-eminent, most outstanding, most excellent; very generous, very liberal

تفضيل *tafḍīl* preference, preferment, favoring; esteem, high estimation | اسم التفضيل *ism at-t.* noun of preference = elative (*af'al*²; *gram.*)

مفاضلة *mufāḍala* comparison, weighing

تفضل *tafaḍḍul* deigning, condescension, complaisance, courteousness, courtesy, favor, grace | لبسة التفضل *libsat at-t.* careless manner of dressing for around the house

تفاضل *tafāḍul* rivalry for precedence; quantitative disparity (of two services rendered; *Isl. Law*) | ○ حساب التفاضل differential calculus

○ تفاضلى *tafāḍulī* differential (adj.)

فاضل *fāḍil* remaining, leftover, left, surplus, exceeding, in excess; (pl. فواضل *fawāḍil*²) remainder, remnant, residue, rest, leftover, surplus, overplus, excess; — (pl. *-ūn*, فضلاء *fuḍalā'*²) outstanding, eminent, very good, first-rate, superior, excellent, distinguished, deserving; learned; man of culture and refinement

مفضل *mufaḍḍal* preferable, preferred

(فضو and فضى) فضا *faḍā u* (فضو *fuḍūw*, فضاء *faḍā'*) to be or become spacious, wide, large (space); to be empty, void, vacant **II** to empty, void, vacate (ه s.th.) **IV** to come, attain (الى to), arrive (الى at), reach (الى s.o., s.th.); to lead (ب الى s.o. to; الى to, e.g., to results); to inform, notify (الى ب s.o. of), announce (الى ب to s.o. s.th.) **V** to have free time, have leisure (ل for)

فضاء *faḍā'* vast and unlimited space, empty space; space (*phys.*); cosmic space; sky; vast expanse, vastness, void | سفينة الفضاء spaceship; رمى به فى الفضاء to throw s.th. in the air; — (pl. افضية *afḍiya*) open area, open tract of land, open country

فضائى *faḍā'ī*: سفينة فضائية spaceship

فاض *fāḍin* empty, vacated, vacant; unoccupied, not busy, at leisure, free (of commitments)

فطح *faṭaḥa a* (*faṭḥ*) and **II** to spread out, make broad and flat, flatten (ه s.th.)

افطح *afṭaḥ*² and مفطح *mufaṭṭaḥ* broad-headed, broad-nosed

فطاحل *faṭāḥil*² (pl. of فطحل *fiṭaḥl*) important, outstanding, leading men or personalities, luminaries, celebrities, stars | زمن الفطحل *zaman al-fiṭaḥl* primeval times, preadamic period

فطر *faṭara u* (*faṭr*) to split, cleave, break apart (ه s.th.); — (فطور *fuṭūr*) to break the fast, eat and drink after a fast; to breakfast, have breakfast; — (*faṭr*) to make, create, bring into being, bring forth (ه s.th.; of God); to endow (ه على s.o. with; of God); pass. *fuṭira* to have a natural disposition (على for); فطر على (*fuṭira*) ... is native of him, ... is in his nature **IV** to break the fast, eat and drink after a fast; to breakfast, have breakfast **V** to be split, be cleft, be broken **VII** = **V**; انفطر بالبكاء (*bi-l-bukā'*) to break into tears

فطر *faṭr* pl. فطور *fuṭūr* crack, fissure, rift, cleavage, rupture

فطر *fiṭr* fast breaking | صدقة الفطر *ṣadaqat al-f.* almsgiving at the end of Ramadan (*Isl. Law*); عيد الفطر *'īd al-f.* Feast of Breaking the Ramadan Fast, or Lesser Bairam, celebrated on the 1st of Shawwal

فطر *fuṭr* (coll.; n. un.) fungi, mushrooms

فطرى *fuṭrī* fungal, fungus, fungi-, myco- (in compounds); فطريات *fuṭrīyāt* parasitic fungi; mushrooms; fungal cultures | المرض الفطرى (*maraḍ*) mycosis

فطرة *fiṭra* creation; (pl. فطر *fiṭar*) nature, (natural) disposition, constitution, temperament, innate character, instinct; *fiṭratan* by nature

فطرى *fiṭrī* natural; instinctive, native, inborn, innate | الانسان الفطرى (*insān*) natural man; الديانات الفطرية natural religions

فطور *faṭūr* breakfast

فطير *faṭīr* unleavened; immature, unbaked; fresh, new, newly made; unleavened bread

فطيرة *faṭīra* (coll. فطير *faṭīr*) pl. فطائر *faṭā'ir*² (unleavened) bread; pastry made of water, flour and shortening (sometimes with sugar added); a cake-like white bread (made with eggs and butter; *eg.*)

فطايرى *faṭāyirī* pl. فطايرية *faṭāyirīya* (*tun.*) maker or seller of *faṭīra* (see above)

فطاطرى *faṭāṭirī* pl. فطاطرية *faṭāṭirīya* (*eg.*) maker or seller of *faṭīra* (see above)

افطار *ifṭār* fast breaking; breakfast; first meal after sunset during Ramadan

الفاطر *al-fāṭir* the Creator (= God)

فطس **faṭasa** *i* (فطوس *fuṭūs*) to die **II** to kill (ه s.o.); to suffocate, strangle, choke to death (ه s.o.) **VII** to become flattened (nose)

فطيس *faṭīs* suffocated, stifled

فطيسة *faṭīsa* pl. فطائس *faṭā'is*² corpse, body; carrion, carcass

افطس *afṭas*² flat-nosed, snub-nosed

فطم **faṭama** *i* (*faṭm*) to wean (ه s.o.; an infant or a young animal) **VII** to be weaned; to abstain (عن from)

فطام *fiṭām* weaning, ablactation

فطيم *faṭīm* pl. فطم *fuṭum* weaned

فاطمى *fāṭimī* Fatimid (adj. and n.); الفاطميون the Fatimids

فطن **faṭina** *a*, **faṭana** *u* and **faṭuna** *u* (فطنة *fiṭna*) to be or become clever, smart, discerning, sagacious, perspicacious, bright, intelligent; to notice, realize, comprehend, understand (ب or ل or الى s.th.); to be or become aware (ب or ل or الى of); to think (الى of s.th.) **II** to make intelligent (ه s.o.); to make (ه s.o.) realize or understand (ب, ل, الى s.th.), explain (ب, ل, الى ه to s.o. s.th.); to remind (ب, ل, الى ه s.o. of) **V** to comprehend, understand (ل s.th.)

فطن *faṭin* clever, smart, astute, sagacious, perspicacious, bright, intelligent

فطنة *fiṭna* pl. فطن *fiṭan* cleverness, astuteness, sagacity, perspicacity, acumen, intelligence

فطين *faṭīn* pl. فطناء *fuṭanā'*² clever, smart, bright, intelligent

فطانة *faṭāna* cleverness, smartness

تفطن *tafaṭṭun* intelligence; intellection

فظ **faẓẓ** pl. افظاظ *afẓāẓ* crude, rude, coarse, blunt, gruff, impolite, uncivil, uncouth, boorish, uneducated; — walrus

فظاظة *faẓāẓa* crudeness, rudeness, coarseness, bluntness, gruffness, impoliteness, uncouthness, boorishness

فظع **faẓu'a** *u* (فظاعة *faẓā'a*) to be or become abominable, detestable, hideous, ugly, repulsive, disgusting, shocking, odious, heinous, atrocious, horrid, horrible **X** to find (ه s.th.) abominable, detestable, etc. (see **I**); to call abominable, revolting, shocking (ه s.th.)

فظيع *faẓī'* abominable, detestable, hideous, ugly, repulsive, disgusting, shocking, odious, heinous, atrocious, horrid, horrible

فظيع *faẓī'* abominable, detestable, hideous, ugly, repulsive, disgusting, shocking, odious, heinous, atrocious, horrid, horrible

فظاعة *faẓā'a* pl. فظائع *faẓā'i'*[2] abominableness, hideousness, ugliness, repulsiveness, odiousness, heinousness, atrocity, horridness, horror; pl. atrocities

مفظع *mufẓi'* abominable, detestable, hideous, ugly, repulsive, disgusting, shocking, odious, heinous, atrocious, horrid, horrible

فعل *fa'ala a* (*fa'l, fi'l*) to do (ه s.th.); to act; to perform some activity; to have an influence or effect (في or ب on), affect (في or ب s.o., s.th.); to do (ب to s.o. ه s.th.; في ه s.th. with) | فعل فيه فعلا كريها (*fi'lan*) to have an unpleasant effect on s.o. **II** to scan (ه a verse) **VI** to interact, interplay; (*chem.*) to enter into combination, form a compound; to combine (مع with) **VII** to be done; to be or become influenced or affected (ل by), be under the influence of s.o. or s.th. (ل); to be agitated, excited, upset **VIII** to concoct, invent, fabricate (كذبا على *kidban* a lie against); to falsify, forge (ه s.th., e.g., a handwriting); to invent (ه s.th.)

فعل *fi'l* activity, doing, work, action, performance; function; — (pl. افعال *af'āl*, فعال *fi'āl*) deed, act, action; effect, impact; — (pl. افعال *af'āl*) verb (*gram.*); pl. افاعيل *afā'īl*[2] great deeds, exploits, feats; machinations | فعلا *fi'lan* or بالفعل indeed, in effect, actually, really, practically; بفعل out of, because of, due to

فعلى *fi'lī* actual, factual, real; effective, efficacious, efficient; practical; de facto; verbal (*gram.*)

فعلة *fa'la* pl. *-āt* deed, act, action

فعال *fa''āl* effective, efficacious, efficient

فعالية *fa''āliya* effectiveness, efficacy, efficiency; activity

افعل *af'al*[2] more effective, more efficacious

تفعيل *taf'īl* pl. تفاعيل *tafā'īl*[2] foot of a verse; (*poet.*) meter

تفاعل *tafā'ul* pl. *-āt* interaction, interplay; formation of a chemical compound, chemical process, chemical reaction

انفعال *infi'āl* (state of) being affected, acted upon, or influenced, passivity; stimulation, irritation (*biol.*); (pl. *-āt*) agitation, excitement, excitation, commotion

انفعالى *infi'ālī* excitable, irritable, susceptible (*biol.*); caused by affect, affective (*philos.*)

انفعالية *infi'ālīya* excitability, irritability (*biol.*)

فاعل *fā'il* effective; efficacious, efficient; (pl. *-ūn*) doer, actor, perpetrator; (pl. فعلة *fa'ala*) worker, workman, laborer; — active subject of a verbal clause (*gram.*) | اسم الفاعل *ism al-f.* nomen agentis, active participle (*gram.*); ذو راديوم فاعل radioactive

فاعلية *fā'ilīya* effectiveness, efficacy; activity

مفعول *maf'ūl* object (*gram.*); مفعول به do.; — (pl. مفاعيل *mafā'īl*[2]) effect, impression, impact; effectiveness, validity | اسم المفعول *ism al-m.* nomen patientis, passive participle (*gram.*); سرى مفعوله *sarā maf'ūluhū* to be or become effective, be valid (على for); سارى المفعول *sārī l-m.* valid (e.g., an identity card); مفعول رجعى (*raj'ī*) retroactive force, retroactivity

منفعل *munfa'il* excited, agitated, upset; irritable

مفتعل *mufta'al* artificial, fabricated, forged, falsified, false, spurious

فعم IV to cram, jam, pack, fill to overflowing, fill up (ه s.th. with ب)

مفعم *muf'am* brimful, chock-full, filled to capacity or overflowing, replete, overfull, filled entirely, crammed, jampacked (ب with)

افعى *af'an* f., pl. افاع *afā'in* adder, viper, asp

افعوان *uf'uwān* adder, viper, asp

فغر *fağara a u* (*fağr*) to open (ه the mouth) wide, gape VII to open wide, be agape (mouth)

فغرة *fuğra* pl. فغر *fuğar* mouth of a valley

فغفورى *fağfūrī* fine porcelain

فاغية *fāğiya* henna blossom

فقأ *faqa'a a* (فقء *faq'*) to knock out, gouge out (ه an eye); to lance, open (ه an abscess, and the like) | فقأ عينه (*'ainahū*) to deal s.o. (an opponent, an enemy) a heavy blow, ruin s.o. V to burst, explode, pop

فقحة *faqḥa* pl. فقاح *fiqāḥ* anus, anal orifice

فقد *faqada i* (*faqd*, فقدان *fiqdān*, *fuqdān*) to fail to find (ه, ه s.o., s.th.); to lose (ه, ه s.o., s.th.); to have lost, miss (ه, ه s.o., s.th.); not to have (ه s.th.), be bereaved (ه of s.o.), be deprived, bereft, destitute (ه of s.th.); to mislay, have mislaid (ه s.th.); to miss (ه an opportunity, and the like) | فقد صوابه (*ṣawābahū*) to go out of one's mind IV to cause (ه s.o.) to lose or miss or forfeit (ه s.th.); to bereave, deprive, dispossess, rob (ه ه s.o. of s.th.) V to seek (ه s.th.), look, search (ه for s.th.); to examine, study, survey, inspect, check, investigate (ه s.th.); to visit (ه s.th.), review, inspect (ه troops, and the like) VIII = V; to miss (ه, ه s.o., s.th.) X to miss (ه, ه s.o., s.th.)

فقد *faqd* loss; bereavement

فقيد *faqīd* lost, missing; dead, deceased; deceased person | فقيد العلم *f. al-'ilm* one whose death is deplored by science; الفقيد الراحل the deceased

فقدان *fiqdān*, *fuqdān* loss; bereavement | فقدان الصواب *f. aṣ-ṣawāb* folly, madness; فقدان الذاكرة loss of memory, amnesia

تفقد *tafaqqud* pl. *-āt* examination, study, survey, inspection, check, investigation; review, inspection (e.g., of troops); visit

افتقاد *iftiqād* examination, study, survey, inspection, check, investigation; review, inspection (e.g., of troops); visit

فاقد *fāqid* devoid, destitute, bereft, deprived (of s.th.; with foll. genitive), bereaved (of s.o.; with foll. genitive); -less, un-, in-; loser | فاقد الشعور unconscious; insensible, senseless; فاقد الضمير unconscionable, unscrupulous, unhesitating; فاقدو التهذيب people without education, unmannered people

مفقود *mafqūd* lost, missing, nonexistent, absent, lacking, wanting; missing person

متفقد *mutafaqqid* controller, inspector

فقر *faqara u i* (*faqr*) to pierce, bore, perforate (ه s.th.); — *faqura u* (فقارة *faqāra*) to be or become poor, needy II to pierce, bore, perforate (ه s.th.) IV to make poor, impoverish (ه, ه s.o., s.th.), reduce (ه s.o.) to poverty; to put (ه s.o.) in need (الى of s.th.) VIII to become poor; to need (الى s.o., s.th.), lack, require (الى s.th.), be in need, be in want (الى of s.o., of s.th.)

فقر *faqr* poverty; need, lack, want

فقرة *fiqra* pl. *fiqrāt*, *fiqarāt*, فقر *fiqar* vertebra; section, paragraph, passage, article

فقرى *fiqrī* spinal, vertebral | السلسلة الفقرية (*silsila*) or العمود الفقرى (*'amūd*) spine, vertebral column; حيوانات فقرية (*ḥayawānāt*) vertebrates

فقار *faqār* (coll.; n. un. ة) vertebra; *faqār* spine, vertebral column

فقارى *faqārī* spinal, vertebral | السلسلة الفقارية (*silsila*) spine, vertebral column

فقير *faqīr* pl. فقراء *fuqarā'*[2] poor, poverty-stricken; poor man, pauper; mendicant dervish, Sufi mendicant

افتقار *iftiqār* need, requirement, want, lack (الى of)

فقوس *faqqūs* a kind of large cucumber (= فقوص)

مفقس *mifqas* pl. مفاقس *mafāqis*[2] incubator

فقش *faqaša* *i* (*faqš*) to break, crush (ه s.th.)

فقش *faqš*: لوز فقش (*lauz*) thin-shelled almonds

فقص II to hatch, incubate (ه an egg; of a bird)

فقوص *faqqūṣ* (coll.; n. un. ة) a kind of large cucumber

تفقيص *tafqīṣ* hatching, incubation | آلة التفقيص or آلة لتفقيص البيض (*t. il-baiḍ*) incubator

فقط II: فقط الحساب *faqqaṭa l-ḥisāba* to write the word فقط *faqaṭ* "only" after the total on an invoice so as to prevent fraudulent additions; to spell out the figures of an invoice

فقط *faqaṭ* only, no more (postpositive); altogether, total (after figures)

فقع *faqa'a* *a* to burst, pop, explode II to crack, snap, pop VII = *faqa'a*

فقاعة *fuqqā'a* pl. فقاقيع *faqāqī'*[2] bubble

فاقع *fāqi'* bright yellow; bright, intense, brilliant, vivid (color)

فاقعة *fāqi'a* pl. فواقع *fawāqi'*[2] blister, vesicle; pustule

فقم *faqima* *a* (*faqam*, *faqm*, فقوم *fuqūm*), *faquma* *u* (فقامة *faqāma*) and VI to be or become grave, serious, critical, dangerous, increase dangerously, become aggravated, reach alarming proportions, come to a head

فقم *fuqqam*, *fuqm* (coll.; n. un. ة) seal (*zool.*)

تفاقم *tafāqum* aggravation, increasing gravity

فقنس *fuqnus* phoenix

فقه *faqiha* *a* (*fiqh*) to understand, comprehend (ه s.th.); — *faqiha* *a* (*fiqh*) and *faquha* *u* (فقاهة *faqāha*) to have knowledge, esp., have legal knowledge II to teach (ه s.o.), instruct (ه في s.o. in) IV to teach (ه ه s.o. s.th.), instruct (ه ه s.o. in s.th.) V to understand, comprehend (ه s.th.); to study the *fiqh* (q.v.); to apply o.s. to the acquisition of knowledge (في in), study (في s.th.), devote one's studies to (في), work at or on s.th. (في); to gain information, get a clear picture, obtain a clear idea

فقه *fiqh* understanding, comprehension; knowledge; الفقه jurisprudence in Islam, fiqh | فقه اللغة *f. al-luġa* (indigenous, Arabic) philology

فقهى *fiqhī* juristic(al); relating to jurisprudence in Islam

فقيه *faqīh* pl. فقهاء *fuqahā'*[2] legist, jurisprudent (and theologian), expert of *fiqh* (q.v.); — (popular usage; *eg.*, pronounced *fiqī*) reciter of the Koran; elementary-school teacher

فك *fakka* (1st pers. perf. *fakaktu*) *u* (*fakk*) to separate, disjoin, disconnect, sever, sunder (ه s.th.); to break (open) (ه s.th., e.g., a seal); to open (ه s.th., e.g., the hand); to dislocate, disjoint (ه s.th., e.g., a bone); to take apart, disassemble, dismount, take to pieces, disintegrate, break up, decompose, dismember, fragmentize (ه s.th.); to dismantle, tear down (ه s.th.); to untie, unbind, unfasten, undo (ه s.th.); to detach, disengage, take off (ه من s.th. from); to unbutton (ه s.th.); to unscrew (ه s.th.); to lift, raise (الحجز *al-ḥajza* the confiscation, عن of s.th.); to solve (ه s.th., e.g., a problem); (*eg.*) to change (ه money); — *fakka* (1st pers. perf. *fakaktu*) *u* (*fakk*, فكاك *fikāk, fakāk*) to ransom, redeem, buy off, liberate, emancipate, release, set free (ه s.o.); — *fakka u* (*fakk*, فكوك *fukūk*) to redeem (ه s.th., e.g., a pledge) **II** to loosen, unfasten (ه s.th.); to take to pieces, take apart, disassemble, dismount (ه s.th.); to disrupt, shatter, fragmentize (ه s.th.) **V** to be taken apart, be disassembled, be dismounted; to be disrupted, be shattered, be fragmentized; to break apart (e.g., a ship); to split, fissure, fission, break up, dissolve, disintegrate, come apart **VII** to be separated, be disjoined, be disconnected, be loosened, be unfastened, be undone, be untied, be unbound, be unbuttoned, be unscrewed; to separate o.s., detach o.s., disengage o.s. (من from), rid o.s. (من of) | لم ينفك (with foll. imperf. or predicative acc.) not to stop doing, keep doing **VIII** to redeem (ه s.th., e.g., a pledge); to dissolve, break up, separate, disintegrate, destroy (ه s.th.); to snatch away (ه من s.th. from s.o.)

فك *fakk* redemption (of a pledge); (pl. فكوك *fukūk*) jawbone, jaw | الفك الاسفل the lower jaw, mandible; الفك الاعلى (*a'lā*) the upper jaw, maxilla

فكة *fakka* small change, coins

فكاك *fikāk, fakāk* disengagement; redemption, liberation, emancipation, release; ransom

مفك *mifakk* pl. *-āt* screw driver

تفكيك *tafkīk* fragmentation, dismemberment, decomposition | ○ تفكيك الذرة *t. aḏ-ḏarra* nuclear fission

تفكك *tafakkuk* fragmentation, breakup, dissolution, disruption, rupture, disunion, split; disintegration, decomposition

انفكاك *infikāk* disengagement

افتكاك *iftikāk* redemption (of a pledge)

مفكوك *mafkūk* loose

مفكك *mufakkak* disconnected, disjointed, incoherent (words, phrases)

فكر *fakara u i* (*fakr*) to reflect, meditate, cogitate, ponder, muse, speculate (في on), revolve in one's mind, think over, contemplate, consider (في s.th.); to think (في of, also ب) **II** = **I**; to remind (في or ب ه s.o. of) **IV** = **I**; **V** to reflect, meditate, cogitate, ponder, muse, speculate (في on), revolve in one's mind, think over, contemplate, consider (في s.th.); to think (في of) **VIII** = **V**; to remember, recall, recollect (ه, ه s.o., s.th.)

فكر *fikr* pl. افكار *afkār* thinking, cogitation, reflection, meditation, speculation, contemplation, consideration; thought, idea, notion, concept; opinion, view | شارد الفكر absent-minded, distracted; مشوش الفكر *mušawwaš al-f.* confused, bewildered, perplexed, dismayed, embarrassed

فكرة *fikra* pl. فكر *fikar* thought, idea, notion, concept; qualm, scruple, demur, hesitation | صاحب الفكرة (father to the thought =) the originator, author; على فكرة (*eg.*) incidentally ..., by the way ..., speaking of ..., apropos (of) ...

فكرى *fikrī* ideational, ideative, speculative, mental; intellectual

فكير *fikkīr* pensive, meditative, cogitative, thoughtful

تفكير *tafkīr* thinking, cogitation, meditation, reflection; speculation, contemplation, consideration; thought

تفكر *tafakkur* thinking, cogitation, meditation, reflection; speculation, contemplation, consideration

مفكر *mufakkir* thinking, reflecting, meditating, pondering, musing; pensive, meditative, cogitative; thinker

مفكرة *mufakkira* notebook | مفكرة يومية (*yaumīya*) diary, journal

مفكرات *mufakkarāt* thoughts, considerations

فكش *fakaša u* to sprain VII to be sprained

فكه *fakiha a* (*fakah*, فكاهة *fakāha*) to be or become gay, merry, cheerful, sportive, jocular, humorous II to amuse (ه s.o.) with jokes III to joke, jest, make fun (ه with), banter (ه s.o.) V to amuse o.s., have fun (ب with), be amused (ب by); to joke, make fun

فكه *fakih* gay, merry, gleeful, jolly, cheerful, sportive, fun-loving, jocular, humorous; amusing (thing)

فكاهة *fukāha* joking, jesting, funmaking; humor

فكاهى *fukāhī* humorous, humoristic; humorist

افكوهة *ufkūha* joking, jesting, funmaking; humor; pl. افاكيه *afākīh*² jokes, jests, pranks, antics

تفكهة *tafkiha* amusement, exhilaration, delectation

مفاكهة *mufākaha* bantering talk, joking, kidding

تفكه *tafakkuh* delight, enjoyment, amusement, diversion; humorous talk, joking, banter

فاكه *fākih* gay, merry, gleeful, jolly, funny; humorous

فاكهة *fākiha* (coll.) pl. فواكه *fawākih*² fruit(s)

فاكهانى *fākihānī* fruit seller, fruit dealer

¹فل *falla u* (*fall*) to dent, notch, blunt (ه s.th., e.g., a sword); to break (ه s.th.); — *falla* to flee, run away | فل غربه (*ğarbahū*), فل من حدته (*ḥiddatihī*) and فل حديده to weaken s.o.; to dampen, subdue s.o.; فل من شباه (*šabāhu*) to weaken s.o. II to dent, notch, blunt (ه s.th., e.g., a sword)

فل *fall* pl. فلول *fulūl* dent, notch, jag; — *fall* (for sg. and pl.) pl. فلول *fulūl*, افلال *aflāl*, فلال *fullāl* defeated, vanquished; scattered remnants of an army

مفلول *maflūl* dented, jagged, notched, blunt

²فل *fill, full* (*eg.*) Arabian jasmine (Jasminum sambac L.; *bot.*)

³فل *fall, fill* cork

⁴فلة *villa* pl. *-āt* villa, country house

فلمنكى see فلامنكى

فلت *falata i* (*falt*) to escape (من s.o., s.th.; from), slip away, get away (من from s.o., from s.th.); to be freed, be set free, be released, be liberated, be set at liberty; to let (ه, ه s.o., s.th.) escape or slip away or get away, let loose, free, release, liberate, set free, set at liberty (ه, ه s.o., s.th.) IV = I; V to escape (من s.o., s.th.; from), slip away, get away (من from s.o., from s.th.); to free o.s., extricate o.s. (من from); to be freed, be set free, be released, be liberated, be set at liberty VII to escape (من s.o., s.th.; from), slip away, get away (من from s.o., from s.th.); to free o.s., extricate o.s. (من from); to be finished (من with); to be freed, be set free, be released, be liberated, be set at liberty

فلت *falat* escape

فلتة *falta* pl. *falatāt* unexpected event, unexpected turn; extravagance; slip, oversight, error, lapse; *faltatan* suddenly, unexpectedly

فلاتى *falātī* pl. فلاتية *falātīya* (*eg.*) licentious, wanton, dissolute, debauched; debauchee, libertine, roué, rake; good-for-nothing, ne'er-do-well

افلات *iflāt* escape

انفلات *infilāt* escape

فالت *fālit* escaped, free, at liberty, at large; escapee; (pl. فلتاء *fulatā'*[2]) licentious, wanton, dissolute, debauched; debauchee, libertine, roué, rake; good-for-nothing, ne'er-do-well

[1]فلج *falaja u i* (*falj*) to split, cleave (ه s.th.); pass. *fulija* to be semiparalyzed **II** to split, cleave (ه s.th.) **VII** to be semiparalyzed

فلج *falj* pl. فلوج *fulūj* crack, split, crevice, fissure, cleft, rift

فالج *fālij* semiparalysis, hemiplegia

مفلوج *maflūj* semiparalyzed, hemiplegic

[2]فيلج pl. فيالج look up alphabetically

□ فلجان *filjān* = فنجان *finjān*

فلح *falaḥa a* (*falḥ*) to split, cleave (ه s.th.); to plow, till, cultivate (الارض *al-arḍa* the land) | ان الحديد بالحديد يفلح (*yuflaḥu*) lit.: iron is cleft with iron, i.e., approx.: rudeness must be met with rudeness **IV** and **X** to thrive, prosper, become happy; to have luck or success, be lucky, be successful (فى in, with)

فلاح *falāḥ* thriving, prosperity; salvation; welfare; success

فلاحة *filāḥa* cultivation, tillage; agriculture, farming, husbandry

فلاح *fallāḥ* pl. *-ūn*, فلاحة *fallāḥa* tiller of the soil, husbandman; peasant, farmer, fellah

فلاحة *fallāḥa* pl. *-āt* peasant woman; peasant girl

فلاحى *fallāḥī* peasant's, farmer's, farming, country, rural, rustic, agricultural

فالح *fāliḥ* lucky, fortunate, successful

مفلح *mufliḥ* lucky, fortunate, successful; one who prospers, one who is well off

[1]فلذة *filḏa* pl. *filaḏāt*, فلذ *filaḏ*, افلاذ *aflāḏ* a piece (of meat) | فلذة كبده *f. kabidihī* his own blood, his own child; افلاذ الارض *a. al-arḍ* the hidden treasures of the earth

[2]فولاذ and فولاذى look up alphabetically

فلور look up alphabetically

فلز *filizz, filazz* pl. *-āt* (nonprecious) metal

فلس **II** to declare (ه s.o.) bankrupt or insolvent **IV** to be or become bankrupt or insolvent, to fail; to be ruined

فلس *fals* (*colloq.* pronounced *fils*) pl. فلوس *fulūs* fels, a small coin, in Iraq and Jordan = $^1/_{1000}$ of a dinar; pl. فلوس (*eg.*) money; scales (of a fish)

تفليس *taflīs* (n. vic. ة) declaration of bankruptcy; (pl. تفاليس *tafālīs*[2]) bankruptcy, insolvency, failure | مأمور التفليسة receiver (in bankruptcy; *Eg.*)

افلاس *iflās* bankruptcy, insolvency, failure

مفلس *muflis* pl. مفاليس *mafālīs*[2] bankrupt, insolvent

فلسطين *filasṭīn*[2] Palestine

فلسطينى *filasṭīnī* Palestinian; (pl. *-ūn*) a Palestinian

فلسف *falsafa* to philosophize **II** *tafalsafa* do.; to pretend to be a philosopher

فلسفة *falsafa* philosophy

فلسفى *falsafī* philosophic(al)

فيلسوف *failasūf* pl. فلاسفة *falāsifa* philosopher

مفلسف *mufalsif* pl. *-ūn* philosopher

متفلسف *mutafalsif* philosophaster, philosophist

فلط *volṭ* pl. افلاط *avlāṭ* volt (*el.*)

فلطح *falṭaḥa* to make broad, broaden, flatten (ه s.th.)

فلطاح *filṭāḥ* broad, flattened, flat

مفلطح *mufalṭaḥ* broad, flattened, flat

فلع *fala'a a* (*fal'*) to split, cleave, rend, tear asunder (ه s.th.) II do.

فلع *fal'*, *fil'* pl. فلوع *fulū'* crack, split, crevice, fissure, cleft, rift

فلفل *falfala* to pepper (ه s.th.)

فلفل *fulful*, *filfil* (coll.; n. un. ة) pepper; n. un. فلفلة peppercorn | فلفل اخضر (*akḍar*) green peppers; دارفلفل *dārafilfil* (*eg.*) a variety of pepper (Piper Chaba Hout.; *bot.*)

فلفلى *fulfulī*, *filfilī* pepperlike, peppery, pepperish

مفلفل *mufalfal* peppered

فلق *falaqa i* (*falq*) to split, cleave, rive, sunder, tear asunder (ه s.th.); to cause (ه dawn) to break, dispel the shadows of night (of God) II to split, cleave, rive, sunder, tear asunder (ه s.th.) V to be split, be cleft, be torn apart; to split, cleave, crack, fissure, be or become cracked, be full of cracks or fissures VII = V; to burst; to break (dawn); (*eg.*) *infaliq* go hang yourself! go to hell!

فلق *falq* pl. فلوق *fulūq* crack, split, crevice, fissure, cleft, rift

فلق *falaq* daybreak, dawn

فلقة *filqa* pl. فلق *filaq* one half (of a split thing)

فلقة *falaqa* a device for holding the legs of the delinquent during the bastinado

فلاق *fallāq* pl. ة bandit, highwayman, highway robber

فيلق *failaq* pl. فيالق *fayāliq*[2] a large military unit; army corps; corps

[1]فلك **II to have round breasts (girl); (*syr.*) to predict the future, prophesy**

فلك ***falak*** **pl.** افلاك ***aflāk*** **celestial sphere; celestial body, star; circuit, orbit (of celestial bodies) |** علم الفلك ***'ilm al-f.*** **astronomy; astrology**

فلك ***fulk*** **(m. and f.) ship, (also coll.) ships; (Noah's) Ark**

فلكى ***falakī*** **astronomic(al); astrologic(al) (pl. *-ūn*,** فلكية ***falakīya*****) astronomer, astrologer |** عالم فلكى **do.**

مفلوك ***maflūk*** **ill-starred, unlucky, unfortunate**

مفلك ***mufallik*** **girl with round breasts**

[2]فلوكة ***falūka*** **pl.** فلائك ***falā'ik***[2] **sloop, felucca; boat**

فلائكى ***falā'ikī*** **(**فلايكى**) boatman**

فلكن ***falkana*** **to vulcanize (ه s.th.)**

فلم ***film*** **pl.** افلام ***aflām*** **film; motion picture |** فلم مجسم **(*mujassam*) 3 D film;** فلم ملون **(*mulawwan*) color film;** فلم ناطق **sound film**

فلمندى ***falamandī*** **Flemish; Fleming**

فلمنكى ***falamankī*** **Dutch, Hollandish, Netherlander**

[1]فلان ***fulān*****, f.** فلانة ***fulāna***[2] **(substituting for an unnamed or unspecified person or thing) so-and-so**

فلانى ***fulānī*** **adjective of the above |** فى الساعة الفلانية **at such and such an hour**

[2]فلين **look up alphabetically**

فلندرة ***falandra*** **Flanders**

فلنكة ***falanka*** **pl. *-āt* (railroad) tie, sleeper (*eg.*)**

فلو ***filw*** **pl.** افلاء ***aflā'*****;** فلو ***falūw*****, *fulūw*** **pl.** افلاء ***aflā'*****,** فلاوى ***falāwā*** **colt, foal**

فلا *falan* (coll.; n. un. فلاة *falāh*) pl. فلوات *falawāt*, افلاء *aflā'* waterless desert; open country; open space

المفالى *al-mafālī* the pastures, the grazing grounds

فلور *flūr* fluorine (*chem.*)

○ مفلور *mufalwir* fluorescent

[1] فلى *falā i* (*faly*) to delouse, search for lice (ه s.th.); to examine, scrutinize, investigate (ه s.th.) II to delouse, search for lice, rid of lice (ه s.th.) V to louse o.s.

فالية *fāliya* spotted dung beetle; touch-hole (of old-time firearms)

[2] فليا *fulayyā* = فلية (see below)

الفليبين *al-filībīn* the Philippine Islands

فلين *fallīn* and فلينة *fallīna* cork

فلية, فليه *fulayya* (*eg.*) pennyroyal (Mentha pulegium L.; *bot.*)

فليون *falyūn* godchild (*Chr.*)

فم *fam* (construct state also فو *fū*) pl. افواه *afwāh*; (*eg.*) *fumm* pl. افمام *afmām* mouth; muzzle; orifice, aperture, hole, vent; mouth, embouchure (of a river), head (of a canal, etc.); mouthpiece (esp., of a cigarette, of a pipe, etc.); cigarette holder | فم الحوت *fam al-ḥūt* star α in the constellation Piscis Australis, Fomalhaut; آلات الفم wind instruments

فن II to diversify, vary, variegate (ه s.th.), bring variety or diversity (ه into s.th.); to mix, mingle, jumble (ه s.th.) V to be or become manifold, multifarious, varied, variegated, diverse, many-sided, versatile; to use different kinds; to be a specialist, an expert, a master (فى in a field), master (فى s.th.) VIII = V

فن *fann* pl. فنون *funūn*, افنان *afnān*, افانين *afānīn*[2] kind, specimen, variety; pl. افانين various sides (of s.th.), diversity | افانين من all kinds of, sundry, various; الجنون فنون (*junūn*) insanity has many varieties, manifests itself in many ways; — (pl. فنون *funūn*) scientific discipline, field of work, special field, specialty; art | الفن الحربى (*ḥarbī*) art of war, strategy; ○ الفنون or الفنون الرفيعة or الفنون الجميلة المستظرفة (*mustaẓrafa*) the fine arts; فن المكتبات *f. al-maktabāt* library science; الفن الصحفى (*ṣuḥufī*) science of journalism; journalism

فنى *fannī* specialist(ic); expert, professional; technical; artistic(al); tactical, strategic(al); technician; artist

فنية *fannīya* artistry

فنن *fanan* pl. افنان *afnān* branch, twig (of a tree, of a shrub)

فنان *fannān* pl. *-ūn* artist | ○ عامل فنان pl. عمال فنانون (*'ummāl*) artistic handicraftsman, commercial artist

فنانة *fannāna* woman artist

افنون *ufnūn* pl. افانين *afānīn*[2] branch, twig (of a tree)

تفنن *tafannun* diversity, variety, multiplicity, multifariousness; many-sidedness, versatility (فى in); varied activity, activity in various fields; mastery; skillful, workmanlike or chic manner

افتنان *iftinān* diversity, variety, multiplicity, multifariousness; many-sidedness, versatility (فى in); varied activity, activity in various fields; mastery

متفنن *mutafannin* many-sided, versatile

مفتن *muftann* masterful, expert, mastering one's field

فنار *fanār* pl. *-āt* lighthouse

فنجال *finjāl* pl. فناجيل *fanājīl*[2] = فنجان

فنجان *finjān* and فنجانة *finjāna* pl. فناجين *fanājīn*[2] cup; coffee cup | جعل زوبعة فى فنجان

(*zauba'atan*) to cause a tempest in a teapot

فنجر *fanjara*: فنجر عينيه (*'ainaihi*) to stare, glare (فى at s.o., at s.th.)

فنخ *fanaka* a to squeeze (ه s.th.); to invalidate, nullify, void (ه s.th.); to break (ه a contract, an agreement)

فند II to call (ه s.o.) a liar, prove (ه s.o.) wrong, disprove, confute, refute, rebut (ه, ه s.o., s.th.); to classify, specify (ه s.th., e.g., the items of an invoice); to detail, particularize, itemize (ه s.th.) IV to prove (ه s.o.) wrong; to disprove, confute, refute, rebut (ه, ه s.o., s.th.)

فندق *funduq* pl. فنادق *fanādiq*[2] hotel, inn

فنار pl. *-āt* look up alphabetically

فانوس pl. فوانيس look up alphabetically

فنط II to detail, particularize, itemize, enumerate item by item (ه s.th.)

فنطاس *fintās* pl. فناطيس *fanātīs*[2] water tank, reservoir, cistern; large container

فنطيس *fintīs* pl. فناطيس *fanātīs*[2] broad-nosed

فنطيسة *fintīsa* pl. فناطيس *fanātīs*[2] snout (of swine)

فنغراف *funuğrāf* pl. *-āt* phonograph

فنق V to live in ease and affluence

[1]فنك *fanak* fennec (*zool.*)

[2]فنيك look up alphabetically

فنلندا *finlandā* Finland

فنلندى *finlandī* Finnish; Finn

فنى *faniya* a (فناء *fanā'*) to pass away, perish, cease to exist, come to nought; to come to an end, cease, wane, dwindle, evanesce, vanish; to be extinguished, become extinct; to be exhausted, be consumed, be spent; to undergo obliteration of the self; to become totally absorbed (فى by) | لا يفنى imperishable, inexhaustible IV to annihilate, bring to nought, ruin, destroy (ه, ه s.o., s.th.); to exhaust, consume, wear out, spend (ه, ه s.o., s.th.); to cause (ه s.th.) to become absorbed or consumed (ه by) VI to annihilate each other; to be consumed (فى by), lose o.s. (فى in), identify o.s. completely (فى with); to dedicate o.s. with heart and soul, give o.s. over wholeheartedly (فى to some activity)

فناء *fanā'* passing away, cessation of being; perdition, ruin, destruction, annihilation; evanescence, vanishing, termination, extinction; exhaustion; nonbeing, nonexistence, nonentity; extinction of individual consciousness, recedence of the ego, obliteration of the self (*myst.*)

فناء *fina'* pl. افنية *afniya* courtyard; open space in front or at either side of a house; open hall | رحابة الفناء *rahābat al-f.* hospitable reception, generous entertainment; سار يخطو فى فناء الغرفة (*yakṭū, f. il-ğurfa*) he walked about the room

افناء *ifnā'* annihilation, ruination, ruin, destruction

تفان *tafānin* mutual annihilation; self-denial, self-sacrifice (in an activity)

فان *fānin* evanescent, transitory, transient, ephemeral, vain; exhausted; far advanced in years, very old

فنيق *finīqī* Phoenician

فنيقية *finīqīya*[2] and فنيقيا *finīqiyā* Phoenicia

فنيك (Fr. *phénique*) *finīk* phenol, carbolic acid, also حامض الفنيك

فهاهة *fahāha* weakness, impotence

فهد *fahd* pl. فهود *fuhūd*, افهد *afhud* lynx (also the term for cheetah and panther)

فهرس **fahrasa** (فهرسة *fahrasa*) to compile an index (كتابا for a book), to index (كتابا a book)

فهرس **fihris** and فهرست **fihrist** pl. فهارس *fahāris*² table of contents, index; catalogue; list

فهم **fahima** a (*fahm, faham*) to understand, comprehend, realize (ه s.th.); to note (ه s.th.), take note, take cognizance (ه of s.th.); to hear, learn (ه من of s.th. from), be informed (ه من of s.th. by); فهم عنه to understand s.o., understand what s.o. says or means | يفهم ان (*yufhamu*) it is reported, it is said that ..., we understand that ... **II** to make (ه s.o.) understand or see (ه s.th.), instruct (ه ه s.o. in s.th.), give (ه ه s.o. s.th.) to understand **IV** = **II**; **V** to try to understand or comprehend (ه s.th.); to understand gradually, come to understand (ه s.th.); to penetrate, fathom (ه s.th.); to understand, comprehend (ه s.th.) **VI** to understand one another; to communicate with each other; to reach an understanding, come to an agreement, come to terms (مع with, على in, about); to be comprehended, be understood **VIII** to understand, comprehend (ه s.th.) **X** to inquire (عن or ه ه of s.o. about s.th.), ask (عن or ه ه s.o. s.th. or about s.th.)

فهم **fahm** pl. افهام *afhām* understanding; comprehension, grasp; perceptive faculty, perceptivity; brains, intellect; discernment, acumen, penetration, insight, intelligence | سوء الفهم *sū' al-f.* misapprehension, misunderstanding

فهم **fahim** quick-witted, of acute discernment

فهيم **fahīm** pl. فهماء *fuhamā'*² discerning, judicious, sensible, intelligent

فهامة **fahhāma** very understanding, extremely sympathetic

تفهيم **tafhīm** instruction, orientation

تفهم **tafahhum** gradual understanding; understanding, comprehension, grasping, grasp

تفاهم **tafāhum** mutual understanding, mutual agreement, concurrence, accord; understanding (مع with, على on, about); agreement, arrangement (مع with) | سوء التفاهم *sū' at-t.* (mutual) misunderstanding, discord, disharmony, dissension

استفهام **istifhām** inquiry (عن about; also على); question | علامة الاستفهام *'alāmat al-ist.* question mark

استفهامى **istifhāmī** interrogative (*gram.*)

مفهوم **mafhūm** understood; comprehensible, intelligible, understandable; known; sense, meaning, signification; (pl. مفاهيم *mafāhīm*²) notion, concept | بالمفهوم in the literal sense, literally; unequivocally, unambiguously, clearly; المفهوم ان it is said, it is reported that ...

فو **fū** see فم *fam*

فوال (Fr.) **fuwāl** voile (dress material)

فوة **fūwa** (*eg.*) madder (Rubia tinctorum L.; *bot.*)

(فوت) فات **fāta** u (*faut*, فوات *fawāt*) to pass away, vanish; to be over, be past; to go by s.o. (ه), pass s.o. (ه); to escape, elude (ه s.o.), slip away; to abandon, give up, leave behind, relinquish (ه s.th.); to anticipate, forestall (ه s.o.); to exceed, surpass (ه ب s.o. by) | فات الوقت (*waqt*) it is (too) late; فاته ان it escaped him that ...; he omitted, neglected, failed, or forgot to ...; he failed to see that ..., he overlooked the fact that ...; لم يفته ان (*yafuthu*) he did not fail to ..., he did not neglect to ...; فاتته الفرصة *fātathu l-furṣatu* he missed the opportunity; فاته القطار he missed the train **II** to make (ه s.th.) escape (على s.o.); to cause (على s.o.) to miss (ه s.th.); to let (ه s.o.) pass; to alienate, sell (ه s.th., *tun.*) **IV** to make

(ه s.th.) escape (ه s.o.); to make (ه s.o.) miss (ه s.th.) **VI** to differ, be different, be dissimilar **VIII** to offend against s.th. (على), act contrary to (على), belie, betray (على s.th.)

فوت *faut* escape; — (pl. افوات *afwāt*) distance, interval; difference

فوات *fawāt* passing, lapse | فوات الأجل *f. al-ajal* the passing of the appointed time, expiration of the deadline; الفوات بالمدة (*bi-l-mudda*) superannuation; بعد فوات الوقت (الأوان) (*f. il-waqt, il-awān*) too late; قبل فوات الوقت (or الأوان) before it is too late

فويت *fuwait* (m. and f.) one following his, or her, own opinion only, acting in his, or her, way only

تفويت *tafwīt* pl. *-āt* alienation, transfer, sale (*tun.*)

تفاوت *tafāwut* difference, dissimilarity, disparity, contrast; disharmony

افتيات *iftiyāt* treason (على to), betrayal (على of), offense (على against)

فائت *fā'it* past, elapsed (time); passing; transitory, transient; passerby

متفاوت *mutafāwit* different

فوتوغرافيا (It. *fotografia*) *fotūğrāfiyā* photography

فوتوغرافى *fotūğrāfī* photographic; photographer

فوتيه (Fr. *fauteuil*) *fūtēh* pl. *-āt* armchair, fauteuil

فوج *fauj* pl. افواج *afwāj* group, crowd, troop, band; detachment; party; shift (in a mine); battalion (*Ir.* till 1922; *Syr.*, *Leb.*); regiment (*Ir.* since 1922); افواجا *afwājan* in droves, in crowds | تبدل الفوج *tabaddul al-f.* change of shift

(فوح) فاح *fāḥa u* (*fauḥ*, فوحان *fawaḥān*) to diffuse an aroma, exhale a pleasant odor, be fragrant; to spread, diffuse, emanate (fragrance) | فاح منه شذا القداسة (*šaḏā l-qadāsa*) he was reputed to be a holy man

فوحة *fauḥa* fragrant emanation, breath of fragrance

فواح *fawwāḥ* exhaling, diffusing (fragrance)

فود *faud* pl. افواد *afwād* temple; hair around the temples

[1](فور) فار *fāra u* (*faur*, فوران *fawarān*) to boil, simmer, bubble; to boil over (also fig.); to effervesce, fizz; to flare up, burst into passion; to gush forth, well forth, gush up, shoot up (water from the ground) **II** to make (ه s.th.) boil (also fig., e.g., the blood); to excite, stir up (ه s.th.) **IV** to make (ه s.th.) boil

فور *faur* boiling, simmering, bubbling, ebullition, etc. (see **I**); فورا *fauran* at once, right away, instantly, forthwith, on the spot, without delay, promptly, immediately, directly; فور *faura* (prep.) immediately after | من فوره or من الفور (من فورها etc.) or على الفور at once, right away, instantly, forthwith, on the spot, without delay, promptly, immediately, directly

فورى *faurī* prompt, instantaneous, instant, immediate, direct

فورة *faura* flare-up, outburst, tantrum

فوار *fawwār* boiling up, ebullient; effervescent, fizzing; bubbling (spring, etc.); foaming, frothy; hot-headed, irascible

فوارة *fawwāra* spring, fountain, jet d'eau

فوران *fawarān* boiling, simmering, bubbling, ebullition; flare-up, outburst

فائرة *fā'ira* uproar, riot; commotion, agitation, excitement

[2]فار pl. فيران and فارة look up alphabetically

فورشة = فرشة *furša*

فورشينة (It. *forcina*) *furšīna* hairpin

فوريقة = فاوريقة look up alphabetically

فاز (فوز) *fāza u* (*fauz*) to be successful, be victorious, triumph; to attain, achieve, accomplish, obtain, gain, win (ب s.th.); to defeat, beat (على an opponent, ب with; sports, etc.); to escape (من s.th.) | ما فاز بطائل (*bi-ṭā'ilin*) to fail, be unsuccessful, accomplish nothing **II** to cross the desert, travel through or in the desert

فوز *fauz* success, triumph, victory; obtainment, attainment, achievement, accomplishment; escape

مفازة *mafāza* pl. *-āt*, مفاوز *mafāwiz*[2] desert

فائز *fā'iz* successful, victorious, triumphant; victor, winner

فائزة *fā'iza* victress, winner

فاس *fās* = فأس *fa's*

فوسفات *fusfāt* phosphate

فاشى and فاشية look up alphabetically

فوصفور *fuṣfūr* phosphorus

فوض **II** to entrust, consign, commit (ه ل or الى to s.o. s.th.); to entrust, charge (ه ل or الى s.o. with), commission s.o. (ل or الى) to do s.th. (ه); to authorize, empower, delegate (ل or الى s.o.), give full power (ل or الى to s.o.) **III** to negotiate (ه s.th.), treat, parley, confer (فى on, about, ه, مع with) **VI** to negotiate or treat or parley with one another, confer (فى on, about); to negotiate (فى s.th.), treat, parley, confer (فى on, about; مع with)

فوضى *fauḍā* disorder, disarray, confusion, tohubohu, chaos; anarchy

فوضوى *fauḍawī* anarchic; chaotic

فوضوية *fauḍawīya* anarchism

تفويض *tafwīḍ* entrustment, commitment, consignment, commission(ing), charging; authorization, empowerment, delegation of authority; authority, warrant, authorization, mandate, mandatory power, procuration, proxy, power of attorney | تفويض مطلق (or تام) (*muṭlaq, tāmm*) general power of attorney, unlimited authority; وثيقة التفويض warrant of attorney

مفاوضة *mufāwaḍa* pl. *-āt* negotiation, parley, talk, conference; partnership (*Isl. Law*) | فتح باب المفاوضات to open negotiations

مفوض *mufawwaḍ* authorized agent, deputy, proxy, mandatory; commissioner | وزير مفوض minister plenipotentiary (*dipl.*); المفوض السامى (*sāmī*) the High Commissioner (formerly in *Syr.*)

مفوضية *mufawwaḍīya* pl. *-āt* legation (*dipl.*); commissariat | المفوضية العليا (*'ulyā*) the High Commissariat (formerly in *Syr.*); مستشار المفوضية *mustašār al-m.* counselor of legation (*dipl.*)

فوطة *fūṭa* pl. فوط *fuwaṭ* apron, pinafore; napkin, serviette; towel

فوعة *fau'a*: فوعة الشباب *fau'at aš-šabāb* prime of youth

فوف *fūf* pellicle, membrane

فوفة *fūfa* pellicle, membrane

مفوف *mufawwaf*: ثوب مفوف (*ṯaub*) white-striped garment

فاق (فوق) *fāqa u* (*fauq*, فواق *fawāq*) to surpass, excel, overtop (ه, ه s.o., s.th.), tower (ه, ه above); to be superior (ه to s.o.); to outweigh, outbalance; to transcend, exceed (ه s.th.); — to remember (على s.th.) | فاق بنفسه (فووق *fuwūq*, فواق *fuwāq*) to give up the ghost, expire, die **II** to direct, level (ه الى a weapon at), aim (ه الى s.th. at);

to (a)waken, wake up, revive, restore to consciousness (ه s.o.); to clear, sober (ه the head); to remind (ه s.o.) **IV** to recover, recuperate, convalesce (من from), regain health; to wake up, awake; to get up (من النوم *min an-naum* from sleep); to be awake; to come to, regain consciousness (من after, e.g., after a swoon, after a state of intoxication); to awaken, arouse, stir up (ه من s.o. from) **V** to be superior (على to), surpass, excel, overtop (على s.o., s.th.), tower (على above); to do excellent work, show outstanding skill (ب in, with); to pass an examination with distinction (ق in a course) **X** to recover, recuperate, convalesce (من from), regain health; to wake up, awaken; to get up (من النوم *min an-naum* from sleep); to be awake; to come to, regain consciousness (من after, e.g., after a swoon, after a state of intoxication)

فوق *fauqu* (adv.) up, upstairs, on top, above; *fauqa* (prep.) above, over; on, on top of; beyond, more than | فوق الحد *f. al-ḥadd* boundless, unlimited, infinite, excessive, exaggerated; فوق ذلك moreover, besides, furthermore, in addition to that, beyond that; فوق البنفسجى (*banafsajī*) ultraviolet; فوق الطبيعة supernatural; فوق العادة extraordinary, unusual, exceptional; special, emergency (e.g., meeting); فوق انه in addition to the fact that it ..., beyond its being ...; فا فوقه and upward, and more (than that); من فوقه *min fauqihī* above it: from above it, from atop it

فوقانى *fauqānī* located higher or above, higher, upper

فاقة *fāqa* poverty, want, neediness, indigence

فواق *fuwāq* hiccup(s); gasping of a dying person, death rattle

افاويق *afāwīq*² (pl. of فيقة *fīqa*) milk (gathering in the udder between two milkings); (fig.) boons, kindnesses, benefactions | ارضعنى افاويق بره *arḍaʿanī a. birrihī* he showered me with kindnesses

افاقة *ifāqa* recovery, recuperation, convalescence; awakening; revival, restoration to consciousnese

تفوق *tafawwuq* superiority; preponderance, predominance, ascendancy, supremacy; above-average performance, talent | تشجيع التفوق promotion of young talent

فائق *fāʾiq* superior; surpassing, excellent, exquisite, first-rate; outstanding, remarkable, striking; pre-eminent; exceeding, extraordinary; going far beyond (a restriction, etc.); awake, waking, wakeful

مفيق *mufīq* awake, waking, wakeful

متفوق *mutafawwiq* superior; surpassing, excellent, exquisite, first-rate, outstanding, remarkable, striking; pre-eminent; victor

مستفيق *mustafīq* awake, waking, wakeful

فول *fūl* (coll.; n. un. ة) pl. *-āt* bean(s); broad bean(s), horse bean(s) | فول مدمس (*eg., mədammis*) cooked broad beans with oil (national dish in Egypt); فول سودانى (*sūdānī*) peanut(s)

فوال *fawwāl* seller of beans

فولاذ *fūlāḏ* steel

فولاذى *fūlāḏī* and فلاذى *fulāḏī* steel (adj.), of steel, made of steel; steely, steel-like, steel-hard

فولت *volt* volt (*el.*)

فوم *fūm* = ثوم *ṯūm*

فونوغراف *funuğrāf* pl. *-āt* phonograph

فاه (فوه) *fāha u* (*fauh*) to pronounce, utter, voice, say (ب s.th.) **V** = **I**

افواه *afwāh* pl. of فم *fam*; — افواه *afwāh*, افاويه *afāwīh*² aromatics, spices

فوة *fūwa* (*eg.*) madder (Rubia tinctorum L.; *bot.*)

فوهة *fūha* pl. *-āt*. افواه *afwāh*, فوائه *fawā'ih*[2] mouth; opening, aperture, orifice, hole, vent; muzzle; crater; abyss, gulf, chasm; hydrant (*syr.*)

افوه *afwah*[2] broad-mouthed

مفوه *mufawwah* eloquent

فى *fī* (prep.) in; at; on; near, by; within, during; among, in the company of, with; about, on; concerning, regarding, with reference to, with regard or respect to, as to; dealing with, treating of, consisting in (in book titles); for the sake of, on behalf of, because of, for; according to; in proportion to; (as to syntactical regimen see under the respective verb) | هل لك فى ... do you feel like ...? would you like to ...? do you want to ...? خمسة فى ثلاثة five times three; خمسة امتار فى عشرة five meters by ten (width and length); كذب فى كذب (*kiḏb*) lie after lie; كلام فى كلام (*kalām*) just so many words, idle talk; نحن اقارب فى اقارب our social relations are those of kinsfolk; فيما مضى *fīmā maḍā* or فيما مضى من الزمان (*zamān*) in the past; formerly, before; فيما يلى (*yalī*) and فيما بعد (*ba'du*) in the following, in what follows, below; فيما اعتقد (*a'taqidu*) as I believe; فيما بينهم among themselves, among them; تبسم فى خبث *tabassama fī ḵubṯ* he smiled maliciously

فيما *fīmā* (conj.) while; in that, as | فيما اذا in case that ..., if

[1](فيأ) فاء *fā'a i* (فىء *fai'*) to return; to shift from west to east (shadow) II to afford shadow, be shady (tree) IV to give as booty (ه على to s.o. s.th.); to give, afford, grant, award (ه على to s.o. s.th.), bestow (ه على upon s.o. s.th.) V to shade o.s. (فى or ه with s.th.), seek shade (فى or ه under s.th.)

فىء *fai'* pl. افياء *afyā'*, فيوء *fuyū'* (afternoon) shadow

[2]فئة *fi'a* see [2]فى

فيتامين *fītāmīn* pl. *-āt* vitamin

فيتنام *viyetnām* Vietnam

فيتو *vītō, vētō* veto (*pol.*) | حق الفيتو *ḥaqq al-v.* veto power (*pol.*)

فيتون *faitūn* phaeton (light four-wheeled carriage)

افيح *afyaḥ*[2], f. فيحاء *faiḥā'*[2] fragrant, redolent, aromatic, sweet-smelling; wide, vast, extensive; الفيحاء epithet of Damascus

فياح *fayyāḥ* heavy-scented, strong-smelling

(فيد) IV to benefit, help, avail (ه s.o.), be of use, of help, bring advantages (ه to s.o.), be useful, helpful, beneficial, profitable, advantageous (ه for s.o.); to teach (ه ه s.o. s.th.); to notify, advise (ب or ه ه s.o. of), acquaint (ب or ه ه s.o. with s.th.), inform (ب or ه ه s.o. of, about), let (ه s.o.) know (ب or ه about); to report (ب or ه s.th., also, e.g., to the police; بان or ان that); to acquire, gain, win (ه s.th.); to derive benefit, profit, or advantage (من from), profit, benefit (من by), turn (من s.th.) to account or advantage; (*gram.*) to convey a complete, self-contained meaning X to acquire, gain, win (ه s.th.); to learn, be told, be informed (ه about); to derive benefit, profit, or advantage (ب or من from), profit, benefit (ب or من by), turn (ب or من s.th.) to account or advantage; to utilize, turn to profitable use, use (ب or من s.th.), make use (ب or من of s.th.); to gather, conclude, deduce, infer (من from)

افيد *afyad*[2] more useful; more profitable

افادة *ifāda* utility, usefulness, benefit, advantage; (pl. *-āt*) notice, notification, communication, information, message;

testimony, deposition (in court) | افادة الاستلام acknowledgment of receipt

استفادة *istifāda* utilization, use

فائدة *fā'ida* pl. فوائد *fawā'id*[2] utility, avail, benefit, advantage; gain, profit; interest (on money); useful lesson, moral; use (e.g., of a medicine)

مفيد *mufīd* useful, beneficial, advantageous; favorable, profitable; instructive

مفاد *mufād* contents, substance, purport, meaning (e.g., of an article) | اشاعة مفادها ان *išā'atun mufāduhā an* a rumor to the effect that ...

فيدرالى *fīdirālī* federalistic | دولة فيدرالية (*daula*) federal state

فيروز *fairūz* and فيروزج *fīrūzaj* turquoise

فيروس *vairus* pl. *-āt* virus

ڤيزا ,فيزا (Engl.) *vīzā* visa

فيزياء *fīziyā'* physics

فيزيائى *fīziyā'ī* physical

فيسيولوجيا *fīsiyōlōjiyā* physiology

فيش[1] (Fr. *fiche*) *fīš* pl. *-āt* (electric) plug (*syr.*)

فياش[2] *fayyāš* braggart, show-off, self-inflated person

فيصل *faiṣal* see فصل

(فيض) فاض *fāḍa* *i* (*faiḍ*, فيضان *fayaḍān*) to overflow, flow over, run over; to inundate, flood, deluge (على s.th.); to flow, stream, pour forth, issue, emanate; to abound, superabound, be abundant, plentiful, superabundant; — (*faiḍ*) to spread (of news); — (*faiḍ*, فيوض *fuyūḍ*): فاضت روحه or نفسه (*rūḥuhū, nafsuhū*) to give up the ghost IV to pour forth; to fill (ه s.th.) to overflowing; to pour, pour out, pour forth (ه على s.th. over), shed (ه s.th., esp. tears); to be prolix, long-winded, verbose (فى in one's speech); to abandon o.s. without restraint (فى to s.th.); to speak or report extensively, in detail, at great length (ب about), dwell (ب on), describe in detail (ب على to s.o. s.th.); to pronounce distinctly (ب a word) X to pour forth, spread (على over), flood (على s.th.); to spread (of news); to be superabundant, be too much; to be elaborate, complete in detail, exhaustive, thorough

فيض *faiḍ* flood, inundation, deluge; emanation; superabundance, plenty, copiousness, abundance; (pl. فيوض *fuyūḍ*) stream

فياض *fayyāḍ* overflowing, effusive, exuberant; elaborate, exhaustive (speech); munificent, bountiful, liberal, generous | فياض الخاطر brilliant, overflowing with ideas

فيضان *fayaḍān* flood, inundation, deluge | فيضان النيل the annual inundation of the Nile

مفيض *mafīḍ* outlet, vent, drain; escape, way out | ليس لنا منه مفيض we cannot help doing it, we cannot but do it; لا يجد مفيضا من (*yajidu*) he must by all means ...; لا يجد مفيضا الى الكلام he can't find an opportunity to speak freely

افاضة *ifāḍa* elaborateness, detailedness, exhaustiveness

استفاضة *istifāḍa* (super)abundance, plenty, profusion

فائض *fā'iḍ* abundant, copious, plentiful, profuse, superabundant; surplus; (pl. فوائض *fawā'iḍ*[2]) interest (on money)

مستفيض *mustafīḍ* elaborate, detailed, extensive, exhaustive, thorough

□ فايظ (< فائض see above) *fāyiẓ* usury (*eg.*)

فايظجى *fāyiẓgī* usurer (*eg.*)

فيفاء *faifā'*[2] pl. فياف *fayāfin* desert

فيكونت (Fr. *vicomte*) *vikōnt* and (Engl.) *vaikaunt* viscount

[1](فيل) فال *fāla i* (فيولة *fuyūla*, فيلولة *failūla*) to be erroneous (view)

[2]فيل *fīl* pl. فيلة *fiyala*, فيول *fuyūl*, افيال *afyāl* elephant; bishop (chess) | سن الفيل *sinn al-f.* ivory

فيلا *villā* pl. فيلات villa, country house

ديدان الفيلاريا *dīdān al-fīlāriyā* filaria (*zool.*)

الفيلبين *al-fīlibīn* the Philippines

فيلج *failaj*, فيلجة *failaja* pl. فيالج *fayālij*[2] cocoon of the silkworm

فيلسوف *failasūf* pl. فلاسفة *falāsifa* philosopher

فيلق *failaq* pl. فيالق *fayāliq*[2] large military unit; army corps; corps

فيلم = فلم *film* film

فيلولوجيا *filōlōjiyā* philology

فيم *fīma* = فيما *fī-mā* why? wherefore?

فيما *fīmā* see في

فينة *faina* pl. *-āt* time, point of time, instant, moment | الفينة بعد الفينة (*al-fainata*), الفينة بعد الاخرى *al-fainata ba'da l-ukrā*, فى الفينة بعد الفينة, بين الفينة والفينة from time to time, now and then, once in a while, at times, sometimes

فينان *fainān* having beautiful, luxuriant hair; luxuriant, long, flowing (hair)

فيينا, فينا (It. *Vienna*) *fiyennā*, *viyēnā* Vienna

فينوس *fīnūs* Venus

فينيسيا *fīnīsiyā* Venice

فينيق *fīnīqī* Phoenician; (pl. *-ūn*) a Phoenician

فيهق II *tafaihaqa* to be prolix, long-winded, circumstantial

فيهقة *faihaqa* prolixity, long-windedness

الفيوم *al-fayyūm* El Faiyûm (town in N Egypt)

ق

ق abbreviation of دقيقة *daqīqa* minute

قادس *qādis*[2] Cádiz (seaport in SW Spain)

قادوس *qādūs* pl. قواديس *qawādīs*[2] water-wheel bucket, scoop (used in irrigation; *Eg.*)

قازوزة (It. *gasosa*) *gāzūza* soda water (*saud.-ar.*)

قاشانى *qāšānī* faïence; porcelain, china

قاف *qāf* name of the letter ق | جبل القاف *jabal al-q.* in Islamic cosmology, name of the mountains surrounding the terrestrial world

[1]قاقلة *qāqulla* cardamom (*bot.*)

[2]قاقلى *qāqullā* a variety of saltwort (Salsola fruticosa; *bot.*)

قاقم *qāqum* ermine

قالب *qālab*, *qālib* pl. قوالب *qawālib*[2] form; mold; cake pan; model; matrix; last, boot tree, shoe tree | قالب جبن (*jubn*) a (chunk or loaf of) cheese; قالب سكر (*sukkar*) sugar loaf; قالب صابون (*ṣābūn*) a cake or bar of soap; قلبا وقالبا (*qalban*) with heart and soul; inwardly and outwardly

قالوش (Fr. *galoche*) *galōš* pl. *-āt* galosh, overshoe

قاموس *qāmūs* pl. قواميس *qawāmīs*[2] ocean; dictionary, lexicon

قان احمر *aḥmar*[2] *qān*(*in*) blood-red, deep-red

قانئ *qāni'* blood-red, deep-red (= قان *qānin*)

قانون *qānūn* pl. قوانين *qawānīn*[2] canon; established principle, basic rule, axiom, norm, regulation, rule, ordinance, prescript, precept, statute; law; code; tax, impost; (*Tun.*) tax on olives and dates; a stringed musical instrument resembling the zither, with a shallow, trapezoidal sound box, set horizontally before the performer | القانون الاساسى (*asāsī*) basic constitutional law; statutes; قانون التأسيس statutes, constitution; القانون الجنائى (*jinā'ī*) criminal law; penal law; قانون الاحوال الشخصية (*šaḵṣīya*) personal statute; القانون الدستورى (*dustūrī*) constitutional law; القانون الدولى (*duwalī*) international law; قانون المرافعات *q. al-murāfa'āt* code of procedure (*jur.*; *Eg.*); قانون اصول المحاكمات الحقوقية do. (*Syr.*); قانون السلك الادارى *q. as-silk al-idārī* administrative law; قانون كيماوى (*kīmāwī*) chemical formula; القانون المدنى (*madanī*) civil law

قانونى *qānūnī* canonical; legal, statutory; lawful, legitimate, licit, accordant with law or regulations, valid, regular; legist, jurisprudent, jurist | صيدلى قانونى (*ṣaidalī*) certified and licensed pharmacist; غير قانونى *ḡair q.* illegal

قانونية *qānūnīya* legality, lawfulness

قاورمة *qāwirma* (*eg.*) mutton or beef cut in small pieces and braised with squash (*qar'*) or onions and tomatoes

قاوق *qāwuq* and قاووق *qāwūq* pl. قواويق *qawāwīq*[2] a kind of high headgear made of felt

قاوون *qāwūn* melon

قايش *qāyiš* pl. قوايش *qawāyiš*[2] leather thong, strap, belt, girth; strop

[1]قب *qabba u* (*qabb*) to chop off, cut off (ه s.th., e.g., the hand); to straighten up, draw o.s. up, become erect; to rise, ascend; to stand on end, bristle (hair)

قب *qabb* pl. اقب *aqubb* hub, nave (of a wheel); lever, beam (of a balance)

قبة *qubba* pl. قباب *qibāb*, قبب *qubab* cupola, dome; cupolaed structure, dome-shaped edifice; domed shrine, memorial shrine, kubba (esp., of a saint) | قبة الجرس *q. al-jaras* belfry, bell tower; قبة الاسلام *q. al-islām* epithet of the city of Basra

مقبب *muqabbab* cupolaed, domed, spanned by a cupola or dome; convex

[2]قبة *qabba* pl. *-āt* collar (of a garment)

قبج *qabj*, *qabaj* (coll.; n. un. ة) pl. قباج *qibāj* a kind of partridge

قبح *qabuḥa u* (*qubḥ*, *qabḥ*, قباحة *qabāḥa*) to be ugly, repulsive, repugnant, disgusting (physically or morally); to be ignominious, infamous, shameful, disgraceful, foul, vile, base, mean **II** to make ugly, repulsive, or repugnant, disfigure (ه s.o., ه s.th.); to denounce s.o.'s action (عليه فعله *'a. fi'lahū*) as ugly, ignominious, infamous, shameful, or disgraceful; to censure, rebuke (عليه فعله s.o. for his action) **X** to find (ه, ه s.o., s.th.) ugly, repugnant, or repulsive, find (ه s.th.) ignominious, infamous, shameful, disgraceful, foul, vile, base, or mean; to disapprove (ه of s.th.), dislike (ه s.th.)

قبح *qubḥ*, *qabḥ* ugliness; ignominy, infamy, shamefulness | قبحا له shame on him!

قبيح *qabīḥ* pl. قباح *qibāḥ*, قباحى *qabāḥā*, قبحى *qabḥā* ugly, repulsive, repugnant, disgusting (physically or morally); ignominious, infamous, shameful, disgraceful, foul, vile, base, mean; impudent, shameless, insolent, impertinent

قبيحة *qabīḥa* pl. قبائح *qabā'iḥ*[2], قباح *qibāḥ* abomination, shameful deed, dirty trick, low act

قباحة *qabāḥa* ugliness; ignominy, infamy, shamefulness

اقبح *aqbaḥ*² uglier; more infamous; fouler, viler

مقابح *maqābiḥ*² ugly traits, repulsive qualities

¹قبار *qubbār, qabbār* capers (*bot.*)

²قبر *qabara u i* (*qabr*, مقبر *maqbar*) to bury, inter, entomb (ه, ه s.o., s.th.)

قبر *qabr* pl. قبور *qubūr* grave, tomb, sepulcher

مقبر *maqbar* pl. مقابر *maqābir*² tomb, burying place, burial ground; cemetery, graveyard

مقبرة *maqbura, maqbara* pl. مقابر *maqābir*² tomb, burying place, burial ground; cemetery, graveyard

مقبرى *maqburī, maqbarī* caretaker of a cemetery; gravedigger

³قبر *qubbar* (coll.; n. un. ة) lark (*zool.*)

قبرص *qubruṣ*² and قبرس *qubrus*² Cyprus

قبرصى *qubruṣī* Cyprian, Cypriote (adj. and n.); القبارصة *al-qabāriṣa* the Cypriotes

قبس *qabasa i* (*qabs*) to derive, acquire, loan, borrow, adopt, take over (ه من s.th. from) VIII to take, or seek to take, fire (من from, also نارا من); to acquire or seek to acquire knowledge (من from, also علما من); to learn (ه s.th.); to loan, borrow, adopt, take over (عن or من ه s.th. from)

قبس *qabas* firebrand; live coal

قبسة *qabsa* firebrand

قابوس *qābūs* nightmare

اقتباس *iqtibās* learning, acquisition (of knowledge); loaning, loan, borrowing (fig.); adoption, taking over, acceptance, adaptation (of a literary text or passage); quotation, citation (of another's literary work or ideas)

مقتبسات *muqtabasāt* loans, borrowings (fig.)

قبص *qabaṣa i* (*qabṣ*) to take up with finger and thumb (ه s.th.), take a pinch (ه of s.th.)

قبصة *qabṣa, qubṣa* as much as may be taken between the finger and the thumb, a pinch

قبض *qabaḍa i* (*qabḍ*) to seize, take, grab, grasp, grip, clasp, clutch (على or ب or ه, ه s.o., s.th.), take hold, take possession (على or ب or ه, ه of); to hold (على, ب ه, ه s.o., s.th.); to apprehend, arrest (على s.o.); to receive, collect (ه s.th., e.g., money); to contract, constringe (ه s.th.); to constipate (البطن *al-baṭna* the bowels); to oppress, deject, dishearten, dispirit, depress (ه s.o.); pass. *qubiḍa* or قبضت روحه *qubiḍat rūḥuhū* to die | قبضه الله or قبض الله روحه (*rūḥahū*) God made him die; قبض يده عن (*yadahū*) to keep o.s. from seizing s.o. or s.th.; to be ungenerous, be stingy toward; قبض الصدر (or النفس) (*ṣadr, nafs*) to oppress, deject, dishearten, dispirit, depress II to contract, constringe (ه s.th.); to give (ه s.th.) into s.o.'s (ه) possession; to pay (ه a price) | قبض الصدر (or النفس) (*ṣadr, nafs*) to oppress, deject, dishearten, dispirit, depress V to contract, become contracted; to shrink, shrivel; to be constipated (bowels) VII = V; to be received; to shut o.s. off (عن from, to), close one's mind (عن to); to be dejected, depressed, dispirited, ill at ease, also انقبض صدره (*ṣadruhū*)

قبض *qabḍ* gripping, grasping, seizing, seizure, holding; taking possession, appropriation; apprehension, arrest (على of s.o.); receiving, receipt (esp., of money); contraction, constriction, constipation | القبض والدفع (*daf'*) revenues and expenditures; القى القبض عليه (*alqā l-qabḍa*) to arrest s.o.

قبضة *qabḍa* pl. *qabaḍāt* seizure; grip, hold, clasp, grasp; handful; (*Eg.*) a linear measure of 12.5 cm; — (pl. قباض *qibāḍ*) handle, haft, hilt | قبضة اليد *q. al-yad* fist; فى قبضته in s.o.'s possession, in s.o.'s hands, in s.o.'s power; فى قبضة يده do.; وقع فى قبضته to fall into s.o.'s hands

قبضة *qubḍa* pl. قبض *qubaḍ* handful

قباضة *qibāḍa* raising, collecting, levying (of funds, of taxes)

قبضاى *qabaḍāy* pl. *-āt* (*syr., leb.*) strongarm (esp. one serving as bodyguard for politicians and prominent personalities); tough, bully

مقبض *maqbiḍ, miqbaḍ* pl. مقابض *maqābiḍ*[2] handle, haft, hilt

مقبض *miqbaḍ* pl. مقابض *maqābiḍ*[2] handle, knob, grip (also, e.g., of a walking stick)

تقابض *taqābuḍ* (*Isl. Law*) a reciprocal taking possession (of a commodity and its monetary equivalent by buyer and seller respectively)

انقباض *inqibāḍ* contraction, shriveling, shrinking, shrinkage; constipation (of the bowels); oppression, anguish, anxiety, dejectedness, depression, low spirits, gloom, also انقباض الصدر *inq. aṣ-ṣadr*

قابض *qābiḍ* constipating, costive (*med.*); grievous, distressing, embarrassing; receiver, recipient; gripper, clamp, claw, catcher, tongs, holder (*techn.*); (pl. *-ūn*, قباض *qubbāḍ*) (tax) collector | عضلة قابضة (*ʿaḍala*) flexor; قابض على الامر (*amr*) ruler, potentate

مقبوض *maqbūḍ*: مقبوض عليه person under arrest; (pl. *-āt*, مقابيض *maqābīḍ*[2]) revenue (*fin.*)

منقبض *munqabiḍ* oppressed, worried, dispirited, disheartened, downcast, dejected, depressed, ill at ease | منقبض الصدر (or النفس) *m. aṣ-ṣadr* (or *an-nafs*) do.

[1]قبط II قبط وجهه (*wajhahū*) to knit the brows, frown, scowl, glower

[2]القبط *al-qibṭ, al-qubṭ* pl. الاقباط *al-aqbāṭ* the Copts

قبطى *qibṭī, qubṭī*: Coptic; Copt

[3]قبطان *qubṭān* pl. قباطين *qabāṭīn*[2], قباطنة *qabāṭina* captain (of a ship and, in *Tun.*, as a military rank = Fr. *capitaine*)

قبع *qabaʿa a* (قبوع *qubūʿ*) to retract the head (hedgehog); to crouch, squat, sit; — (*qabʿ*, قباع *qibāʿ*, *qubāʿ*) to grunt (hog); to trumpet (elephant); — (*qabʿ*) to drink in hasty gulps (*eg.*)

قبعة *qubbaʿa* pl. *-āt* hat; cap; (*syr.*) small felt cap

مقبع *muqabbaʿ* wearing a hat, hatted

قبقب *qabqaba* to swell, bulge

قبقاب *qabqāb* pl. قباقيب *qabāqīb*[2] wooden clog, patten | قبقاب الانزلاق skate

قباقيبي *qabāqībī*: مسمار قباقيبي (*mismār*) small nail, blue tack (*eg.*)

قبل *qabila a* (قبول *qabūl, qubūl*) to accept (ب or ه, ه s.o., s.th.); to receive (kindly, hospitably) (ه s.o.), give (ه, ه s.o., s.th.) a friendly reception, receive (ه s.th.) favorably, approve (ه, ه of s.o., of s.th.); to acquiesce (ه in s.th.), put up (ه with s.th.), agree, consent, assent (ه to, also ب); to admit (ه, ه فى s.o., s.th. to); to obey (من s.o.), yield, give in (من to s.o.), submit to s.o.'s (من) command; — *qabila a* and *qabala u i* (قبالة *qabāla*) to guarantee, vouch, be surety (ب for) | قبل الذهاب معى (*ḏahāba*) he was willing to go with me; *qabila* with acc. of a *maṣdar* frequently corresponds to an English adjective in -able, -ible, -ive, -al, e.g., داء يقبل الشفاء (*šifāʾa*) a curable disease, بضائع تقبل الالتهاب (highly) combustible merchandise; اثمان لا تقبل المزاحمة (*muzāḥamata*) prices that are beyond competition; قبل شكا (*šakkan*) to admit doubt
II to kiss (ه, ه s.o., s.th.); (*eg.*) to go

south(ward) III to be or stand exactly opposite s.o. or s.th. (ه, ه), be face to face (ه, ه with); to confront, face, counter (ه s.o.; ه ب s.th. with, e.g., a situation with caution); to meet (ه s.o.; ه ب s.th., e.g., a danger, with, by); to encounter (ه s.o.), run across s.o. (ه); to visit (ه s.o.), call on s.o. (ه); to meet, get together, have a talk or interview (ه with s.o.); to interview (ه s.o.); to receive (in audience) (ه s.o.), grant an audience (ه to s.o.); to receive (ه ب, ه s.o., s.th. with, e.g., a news with joy); to repay, return, requite (ه ب s.th. with); to compare, collate (ه ب or على s.th. with) | قابله على الرحب والسعة (rahb, sa'a) to welcome s.o. or s.th.; قابله بالمثل (bi-l-mitl) to return like for like IV to turn forward; to draw near, come close to s.o. or to a place (على), approach (على s.o., a place); to advance (على to, toward); to turn (على to, toward); to embark, enter (على upon s.th.), engage (على in); to give one's attention, devote o.s. (على to s.o., to s.th.), dedicate o.s., apply o.s., attend (على to s.th.), occupy o.s. (على with); to take an interest, become or be interested (على in); to go, come (الى to); to be abundant (crop); (with foll. imperf.) to begin to do | اقبل عليه الدهر (dahru) or اقبلت عليه الدنيا (dunyā) luck is on his side, fortune smiles on him V to accept, receive (ه s.th.); to hear, grant (دعاءه du'ā'ahū s.o.'s prayer; of God) VI to be opposite each other, face each other; to meet (e.g., two persons); to get together, have a meeting, meet (مع with); to be compared, be collated VIII to receive (ه, ه s.o., s.th.); to apply o.s. gladly and willingly (ه to s.th.) X to turn one's face (ه, ه to s.o., toward s.th.); to go to meet, to meet (ه s.o.); to face, confront, meet (ه, ه s.o., s.th.); to take upon o.s., assume (ه s.th.); to receive (ه a visitor, a guest; ه s.th., e.g., a radio broadcast)

قبل *qablu* (adv.) or من قبل *min qablu* and قبلا *qablan* previously, formerly, earlier, before; من ذى قبل (*qablu*), عن ذى قبل (after a comparative) ... than before; — *qabla* (prep.) before, prior to | قبل كل شىء *qabla kulli šai'in* first of all, above all; من قبل *min qabli* before, prior to; قبل ان (conj.) before

قبلئذ *qabla'idin* previously, formerly, once, in former times

قبيل *qubaila* (prep.) shortly before, prior to; قبيل ان (conj.) shortly before

قبل *qubl, qubul* fore part, front part, front, face | من قبل (*qubulin*) in front; from the front, from in front

قبل *qibal* power, ability; — *qibala* (prep.) in the presence of, before, near; in the direction of, toward | لا قبل له به (*qibala*) he has no power over it, it is not in his power; he is incapable of accomplishing it; من قبل *min qibali* on the part of, from, by; من قبل نفسه by himself (or itself), of his (or its) own accord; لى قبله دين *lī qibalahū dain* he owes me a debt, he is indebted to me

قبلة *qubla* pl. *qublāt, qubulāt,* قبل *qubal* kiss

قبلة *qibla* kiblah, direction to which Muslims turn in praying (toward the Kaaba); recess in a mosque indicating the direction of the Kaaba, prayer niche | اولى القبلتين *ūlā l-qiblatain* the first of the two kiblahs, i.e., Jerusalem; قبلة الانظار *q. al-anzār* focus of attention, target of all eyes, ideal, goal sought after and aspired to; قبلة الاهتمام object of widespread interest, focus of attention

قبلى *qiblī* southern, south | الوجه القبلى (*wajh*) Upper Egypt

قبول *qabūl, qubūl* (friendly) reception; welcome; acceptance; concurrence, consent, assent, approval, admission, admittance; with foll. *maṣdar* corresponding to English abstract nouns in -ability, -ibility, -ivity, -ality, e.g., عدم قبول التفرقة *'adam q. at-tafriqa* indivisibility

قبيل *qabīl* guarantor, bail(sman), surety; kind, specimen, species, sort; tribe | من هذا القبيل of this kind, like this, such; in this respect; من قبيل الايضاح (*q. il-īḍāḥ*) by way of illustration, as an explanation; من كل قبيل ودبير (*dabīr*) of every origin (whatsoever); ليس من هذا الامر فى قبيل ولا دبير he is not in the least involved in this affair, he has absolutely nothing to do with this affair

قبيلة *qabīla* pl. قبائل *qabā'il*² tribe

قبلى *qabalī* tribal

قبالة *qabāla* bail, guaranty, suretyship, liability, responsibility; contract, agreement

قبالة *qibāla* midwifery, obstetrics

قبالة *qubālata* (prep.) opposite, face to face with, vis-à-vis, in front of

تقبيل *taqbīl* kissing

قبال *qibāla* (prep.) opposite, face to face with, vis-à-vis, in front of

مقابلة *muqābala* encounter; meeting; conversation, talk, discussion; interview; audience, reception; comparison, collation | مقابلة ذلك *muqābalata ḏ.* or فى مقابلة ذلك in return for that, in exchange for that, in compensation for that, as an equivalent for that, for that, therefor; تشريح المقابلة comparative anatomy; المقابلة بالمثل (*bi-l-miṯl*) requital; retaliation, reprisal; اخذ بالمقابلة to return like for like

اقبال *iqbāl* drawing near, advance, approach; coming, arrival, advent; turning, application, attention, response, responsiveness (على to), concern (على for), interest (على in), demand; good fortune, prosperity, welfare | اقبالا وادبارا *iqbālan wa-idbāran* back and forth, to and fro, up and down

تقبل *taqabbul* receptivity, susceptibility, sensibility

اقتبال *iqtibāl* reception

استقبال *istiqbāl* pl. -*āt* reception; opposition (*astron.*); full moon (as an astronomical aspect); the future; استقبالا *istiqbālan* in the future | آلة الاستقبال receiving set, receiver; غرفة الاستقبال *ġurfat al-ist.* reception room, parlor; كان فى استقباله he was present to greet him, he had come to meet him, he received him

قابل *qābil* obstetrician, accoucheur; coming, next (e.g., month); subject, liable, susceptible, disposed (لـ to s.th.); ○ receiver (*radio*); with foll. لـ and *maṣdar* corresponding to English adjectives in -able, -ible, -ive, -al, e.g., قابل للموت (*li-l-maut*) mortal; قابل للشفاء curable; قابل للالتهاب (highly) combustible, inflammable; قابل للتوصيل conductive (*el.*); غير قابل سرجع irrevocable; يكون جواز السفر قابلا للتجديد اربع مرات (*jawāz as-safar, arba'a marrātin*) the passport can be renewed four times

قابلة *qābila* pl. -*āt*, قوابل *qawābil*² midwife, accoucheuse; — (pl. قوابل *qawābil*²) receptacle, container; — pl. قوابل beginnings

قابلية *qābilīya* faculty, power, capacity, capability, ability; aptitude, fitness; tendency, disposition, liability, susceptibility, sensibility, receptivity (لـ to); appetite | قابلية للتوصيل conductivity (*el.*); قابلية القسمة *q. al-qisma* divisibility; cf. قابل

مقبول *maqbūl* acceptable, reasonable; satisfactory (as an examination grade; *Eg.*); pleasing, obliging, complaisant, amiable; well-liked, likable, popular, welcome

مقبلات *muqabbilāt* appetizers, hors d'oeuvres

مقابل *muqābil* facing, opposite; counter- (in compounds); equivalent, wages, remuneration, recompense | مقابل ذلك (*muqābila*) or فى مقابل ذلك accordingly, in accordance with that, in return for that, in exchange for that, in compensation for that, as an equivalent for that, for that, therefor; مقابل تقديم الكوبون upon presentation of the coupon; مائة سفينة مقابل خمسين فى العام السابق (*mi'at safīna m. kamsīn*) 100 ships as compared with 50 the previous year; من غير مقابل or بدون مقابل without compensation, for nothing, gratis

مقبل *muqbil* coming, next (e.g., month, year)

مقتبل *muqtabal*: فى مقتبل العمر *fī m. il-'umr* in the prime of life; مقتبل الليل (*muqtabala l-lail*) at the beginning of the night, early at night

مستقبل *mustaqbil* receiving set, receiver (*radio*)

مستقبل *mustaqbal* front part, front, face; future (adj.); the future

قبن II to weigh (with a steelyard) (ه s.th.)

قبان *qabbān* steelyard; scale beam; platform scale, weighbridge

[1]قباء *qabā'* pl. اقبية *aqbiya* an outer garment with full-length sleeves

[2]قبا (قبو) *qabā u* to vault, arch, camber, curve, bend (ه s.th.)

قبو *qabw* pl. اقبية *aqbiya* vault; vaulted roof; cellar; tunnel, gallery, drift, adit (mining); ○ prompt box | قبو الوقاية من ○ الغارات الجوية (*jawwīya*) air-raid shelter

قبوة *qabwa* vault

قباء *qibā'* interval, interspace, distance

قبودان *qabūdān* captain

قت *qatta u* (*qatt*) to render falsely, misrepresent, depreciate, belittle, minimize (ه s.th.); to lie VIII to uproot, root out, extirpate (ه, ه s.o., s.th.)

قتات *qattāt* slanderer, calumniator

قتب *qatab* pl. اقتاب *aqtāb* (*eg.*) hunch, hump

مقوتب *muqautab* hunchbacked

قتاد *qatād* tragacanth (Astragalus; *bot.*) | جلس على قتاد he was sitting on a bed of thorns

قتر *qatara u i* (*qatr*, قتور *qutūr*) and II to be stingy, tightfisted, niggardly, parsimonious (على toward s.o.), keep (على s.o.) short, stint (على s.o.) IV do.; to live in straitened circumstances, be or become poor

قتر *qatr* stinginess, niggardliness, parsimony (على toward)

قترة *qatara* dust

قتار *qutār* aroma, smell (of s.th. fried or cooked)

تقتير *taqtīr* stinginess, niggardliness, parsimony (على toward)

قاتر *qātir* stingy, tightfisted, miserly, niggardly, parsimonious (على toward)

مقتر *muqattir*, *muqtir* stingy, tightfisted, miserly, niggardly, parsimonious (على toward)

قتل *qatala u* (*qatl*) to kill, slay, murder, assassinate (ه s.o.); to mitigate, alleviate (ه s.th., e.g., البرد *al-barda* the cold, الجوع *al-jū'a* the hunger); to mix, dilute (ه ب s.th. with, e.g., wine with water); to know, master (ه s.th., e.g., a skill) | قتله خبرا (*kubran*, *'ilman*) or (علما or) قتله درسا وبحثا (*darsan wa-baḥtan*) to know or master s.th. (e.g., a skill, a field of study) thoroughly; قتل الموضوع بحثا (*baḥtan*) to study a topic most thoroughly, treat a subject exhaustively; قتل الدهر خبرة (*dahra kibratan*) to have long experience with life, be worldly wise II to kill, massacre (هم people), cause carnage (هم among people) III to combat, battle (ه s.o.), fight (ه s.o., with s.o., or against s.o.) | قاتله الله lit.: may God fight him! i.e., approx.: damned bastard! **VI** and **VIII** to fight with one another, combat each other **X** to risk one's life, defy death

قتل *qatl* killing; manslaughter, homicide; murder, assassination | قتل بسبب (*bi-sababin*) indirect killing (*Isl. Law*); قتل الخطأ *q. al-ḵaṭa'* accidental homicide (*jur.*); القتل العمد (*'amd*) or القتل العمدى (*'amdī*) or القتل عمدا (*'amdan*) or القتل العمد مع سبق الاصرار (*sabqi l-iṣrār*) premeditated murder

قتل *qitl* pl. اقتال *aqtāl* enemy, foe, adversary, opponent

قتيل *qatīl* pl. قتلى *qatlā* killed; killed in battle, fallen; one killed in battle, casualty | قتيل الحرب *q. al-ḥarb* man killed in war

قتال *qattāl* murderous, deadly, lethal

اقتل *aqtal*² deadlier, more lethal in effect

مقتل *maqtal* murder, death; murderous battle; (pl. مقاتل *maqātil*²) vital part of the body (the injury of which will bring about death), mortal spot, mortal organ; Achilles' heel, vulnerable spot | ضربه فى مقاتله (*ḍarabahū*) or اصاب منه المقتل (*aṣāba*) he hit him at his most vulnerable spot

مقتلة *maqtala* pl. *-āt* butchery, slaughter, carnage, massacre

تقتيل butchery, slaughter, carnage, massacre

قتال *qitāl* fight, struggle, contention (against); combat, strife, battle | ساحة القتال battlefield

مقاتلة *muqātala* fight, struggle, contention (against); combat, strife

تقاتل *taqātul* mutual struggle

قاتل *qātil* killing, murdering; deadly, lethal, mortal, fatal; (pl. قتال *quttāl*, قتلة *qatala*) killer, manslayer; murderer, assassin

قاتلات *qātilāt* lethal agents (ل against)

مقتل *muqattal* experienced, practiced, tried, tested

مقاتل *muqātil* fighter, combatant, warrior; fighting, combat-, battle- (in compounds)

مقاتلة *muqātila* (coll.) combatants, warriors, fighting forces

مقاتلة *muqātila* pl. *-āt* combat plane, light bomber

مقتتل *muqtatal* battlefield, battleground

مستقتل *mustaqtil* death-defying, heroic

قتم *qatama u* (قتوم *qutūm*) to rise (dust) **IX** to be dark(-colored), blackish

قتمة *qutma, qatama* dark or blackish color, darkness, gloom

قتام *qatām* dark or blackish color, darkness, gloom

اقتم *aqtam*² dark colored, blackish, dark

قاتم *qātim* pl. قواتم *qawātim*² black, dark | اسود قاتم pitch-black

¹قث *qaṯṯa u* (*qaṯṯ*) and **VIII** to pull out, tear out, uproot (ه s.th.)

²قثاء *qiṯṯā', quṯṯā'* (coll.; n. un. ة) cucumber

قثاطير *qaṯāṭīr*² catheter

○ قثطرة *qaṯṭara* catheter

¹قح *qaḥḥa* to cough

²قح *quḥḥ* pl. اقحاح *aqḥāḥ* pure, sheer, unmixed, unadulterated; genuine

قحبة *qaḥba* pl. قحاب *qiḥāb* whore, harlot, prostitute

قحط *qaḥaṭa a* (*qaḥṭ*, قحوط *quḥūṭ*) and *qaḥiṭa a* (*qaḥaṭ*) to be withheld, fail to set in (rains); active and pass. *quḥiṭa* to be rainless (year) **II** to pollinate (النخلة *an-naḵlata* the palm tree); (*eg.*) to scratch off, scrape off (ه s.th.) **IV** to be rainless (year)

قحط *qaḥṭ* want of rain, rainlessness; drought, dryness; famine; dearth, lack, want, scarcity

قحطان *qaḥṭān*[2] legendary ancestor of the South Arabians

قحف *qaḥafa a* (*qaḥf*) to swallow, gulp down (ه s.th.); to sweep away, carry away (ه s.th.; of a river) **VIII = I**

قحف *qiḥf* pl. قحوف *quḥūf*, اقحاف *aqḥāf*, قحفة *qiḥafa* skull; cranium, brainpan

قحاف *quḥāf* torrential (river)

قحل *qaḥila a* (*qaḥal*) and pass. *quḥila* to be or become dry or arid, dry up, wither

قحل *qaḥal* dryness, aridity

قحل *qaḥil* dry, arid

قحولة *quḥūla* dryness, aridity

قحلاء *qaḥlā'*[2] f. dry

قاحل *qāḥil* dry, arid

قحم **IV** to push, drag (في ه s.o. into s.th.), involve (في ه s.o. in); to introduce forcibly, cram (في ه s.th. into) | اقحم نفسه بينهم (*nafsahū*) he squeezed himself between them **VIII** to plunge, rush, hurtle (ه into s.th.); to break (ه into s.th.), intrude, invade (ه s.th.); to burst (ه into a room); to jump, leap, dive (ه into s.th.); to rush, dart (ه at); to storm, take by storm (ه s.th.); to embark boldly (ه upon s.th.); to defy (ه danger, hardships, etc.)

قحمة *quḥma* pl. قحم *quḥam* danger one rushes into, hazardous undertaking

مقحام *miqḥām* pl. مقاحيم *maqāḥīm*[2] one who plunges heedlessly into danger, reckless, daring, foolhardy

اقحام *iqḥām* dragging in, implicating, involvement

اقتحام *iqtiḥām* breaking in, inrush, irruption, intrusion, obtrusion; inroad, invasion, incursion; storming, capture by storm

اقحوان *uqḥuwān* pl. اقاح *aqāḥin*, اقاحى *aqāḥīy* camomile (*bot.*); daisy (*bot.*)

[1]قد *qad* (particle) with foll. perf. indicates the termination of an action; sometimes corresponding to English "already"; with foll. imperf.: sometimes, at times; perhaps, or English "may", "might"

[2]قد *qadda u* (*qadd*) to cut lengthwise, cut into strips (ه s.th.); to cut off (ه s.th.); to chop off (ه s.th.); to cut out, carve out (ه s.th.) | قد قلبه من حجر *qudda qalbuhū min ḥajarin* to have a heart of stone **II = I**; to cut into strips and dry (ه s.th., e.g., meat, fruits), to jerk (ه meat) **VII** to split, burst (also, e.g., with laughter) **VIII = I**

قد *qidd* pl. اقد *aqudd* strip (of leather), strap, thong

قدة *qidda* pl. قدد *qidad* rail; ruler | تفرقوا طرائق قددا *tafarraqū ṭarā'iqa qidadan* to split into many parts or groups, break up, dissolve

قديد *qadīd* meat cut into strips and dried, jerked meat

قد *qadd* pl. قدود *qudūd* shape, build, frame, physique, stature, height, figure; (*eg.*) size, bulk, volume, quantity | على قده of the same size, of equal size, just as (large)

قدح *qadaḥa a* (*qadḥ*) to bore, pierce (في s.th.); to slander, defame, malign, vilify (في s.o.); to rebuke, censure, blame (في s.o.); to reprove, reproach, chide (في s.o.); to reject as objectionable (في a witness, a testimony); to impair, depreciate, belittle, lessen, diminish, degrade (ب or في s.th.), detract (ب or في from); to violate, infringe (في s.th.), offend (في

against); to strike fire (with a flint) (also with النار *an-nāra*) | قدح زناد الفكر (*z. al-fikr*) to ponder, think hard, rack one's brain; قدح فكره (*fikrahū*) to think hard; قدح شررا (*šararan*) to strike or emit sparks **VIII** to strike fire (with a flint), also اقتدح النار; to weigh, consider (ه s.th.)

قدح *qadḥ* slander, calumniation, calumny, defamation, vilification, aspersion; censure, rebuke, reproof, reproach; depreciation, detraction (ب or فى from), impairment

قدح *qidḥ*, pl. قداح *qidāḥ*, اقدح *aqduḥ*, اقداح *aqdāḥ*, اقاديح *aqādīḥ*[2] arrow shaft; arrow; divining arrow, arrow used for oracles | القدح المعلى (*mu'allā*) the seventh of the divining arrows used in the ancient Arabian game of *maisir*, i.e., the best of them which won seven shares of the slaughtered camel, hence: له القدح المعلى فى to be the principal agent in, have a major impact on, exert decisive influence on, be of crucial importance for

قدح *qadaḥ* pl. اقداح *aqdāḥ* drinking bowl; (drinking) cup; goblet; glass, tumbler; tea glass; keddah, a dry measure (*Eg.* = $^1/_{96}$ اردب *ardabb* = 2.062 l)

قداح *qaddāḥ* and قداحة *qaddāḥa* pl. *-āt* flint; fire steel, fire iron (for striking sparks from flint); flint and steel; lighter (e.g., for cigarettes)

مقدحة *miqdaḥa* fire steel, fire iron (for striking sparks from flint)

قدر *qadara* *u* *i* (*qadr*) to decree, ordain, decide (ه s.th.; of God) — *qadara* *i* (قدرة *qudra*, مقدرة *maqdura*, *maqdara*, *maqdira*) and *qadira* *a* (*qadar*) to possess strength, power, or ability; to have power (على over s.th.), be master (على of s.th.), be equal (على to s.th.), be up to s.th. (على); to have the possibility to do (على s.th.), be in a position to do s.th. (ان or على), be able to do s.th. (ان or على), be capable (ان or على of) **II** to appoint, assign, determine, ordain, decree (ه s.th., على for s.o.; of God); to predetermine, foreordain, (pre)destine (ه s.th.; of God); to appraise (ه s.th.; with respect to its worth and amount), assess, estimate, calculate, tax, evaluate, value, rate (ه ب s.th. at); to anticipate, foresee (ه s.th.); to surmise, guess, presume, suppose, believe, think, be of the opinion (ان that); to esteem highly, value, treasure, prize, cherish (ه s.o., ه s.th., ه ل s.th. in s.o., because of s.th. s.o.); to appreciate (ه s.th.); to enable (ه على s.o. to do s.th.), put (ه s.o.) in a position (على to do s.th.); (*gram.*) to imply in an expression (ل or ه) another (ب or ه) as virtually existing | لا قدر الله (which) God forbid! قدر فكان (*quddira*) the inevitable happened! قدره حق قدره (*ḥaqqa qadrihī*) to attach the proper value to s.o. or s.th., fully appreciate the value of s.o. or s.th.; لا يقدر *lā yuqaddaru* inestimable, invaluable, immeasurable, immense, huge, enormous, tremendous **IV** to enable (ه على s.o. to do s.th.), put (ه s.o.) in a position (على to do s.th.) **V** to be appointed, assigned, determined, ordained, destined, fated, decreed **VIII**=**I** *qadara* *i* **X** to ask (ه God) for strength or ability

قدر *qadr*, pl. اقدار *aqdār* extent, scope, quantity, amount, scale, rate, measure, number; sum, amount; degree, grade; worth, value, standing, rank; divine decree | ليلة القدر *lailat al-q.* the night in which, according to sura 97, the Koran was revealed, celebrated during the night between the 26th and 27th of Ramadan; قدر من a certain extent of, a certain degree of; قدر *qadra*, بقدر *bi-qadri*, على قدر commensurate with, corresponding to, according to, in proportion to; بقدر ما *bi-qadri mā* in the same measure as, to the same extent as, as much as, as large as; على قدر ما *'alā qadrin mā* to a certain extent, relatively; قدر المستطاع *qadra l-mustaṭā'*, على قدر المستطاع ,بقدر المستطاع, قدر الطاقة *qadra ṭ-ṭ.*, قدر الامكان *qadra l-imkān*, بقدر الامكان and على قدر الامكان as far as possible, as much as possible, in the best way possible, to the best of one's abilities; اغلبية قدرها مائة صوت *aḡlabīya qadruhā mi'atu ṣautin* a majority of a hundred votes; ذوو قدر *ḏawū q.* people of distinction, important people

قدر *qadar* pl. اقدار *aqdār* divine foreordainment, predestination; fate, destiny, lot | مذهب القدر *maḏhab al-q.* fatalism; القضاء والقدر (*qaḍā'*) fate and divine decree; قضاء وقدرا *qaḍā'an wa-qadaran* or بالقضاء والقدر by fate and divine decree; جاء على قدر he arrived just at the right time

القدرية *al-qadarīya* a theological school of early Islam asserting man's free will

قدر *qidr* m. and f., pl. قدور *qudūr* cooking pot, kettle, pot

قدرة *qidra* cooking pot, kettle, pot

قدرة *qadara* small bottle, flask

قدرة *qudra* faculty (على of), power, strength (على for), potency; capacity, ability, capability, aptitude; omnipotence (of God) | ○ القدرة على العمل (*'amal*) power, capacity (*techn., phys.*); ○ القدرة على الانتقاء selectivity (*radio*)

قدير *qadīr* possessing power or strength, powerful, potent; having mastery (على over s.th.), capable (على of s.th.); omnipotent, almighty, all-powerful (God)

اقدر *aqdar*[2] mightier, more powerful; more capable (على of), abler (على to do s.th.)

مقدرة *maqdura, maqdara, maqdira* faculty (على of), power, strength (على for), potency; capacity, ability, capability, aptitude | ○ المقدرة الحربية (*ḥarbīya*) military resources, military potential

مقدار *miqdār* pl. مقادير *maqādīr*[2] measure; extent in space and time; scope, extent, scale, rate, range; quantity; amount | مقدار ادنى (*adnā*) a minimum; مقدار اقصى (*aqṣā*) a maximum; بمقدار ما *bi-miqdāri mā* to the same extent or degree as ..., as much as ...; بهذا المقدار to such an extent or degree, so much; بمقدار to a certain extent or degree, somewhat, a little

تقدير *taqdīr* pl. *-āt*, تقادير *taqādīr*[2] estimation, appraisal, assessment, taxation, rating; calculation, estimate, valuation; appreciation; esteem; assumption, surmise, supposition, proposition; implication of a missing syntactical part (*gram.*); (pl. *-āt*) grading, evaluation (of achievement; school, university); تقديرا *taqdīran* by implication, implicitly, virtually | تقديرا لهذا in appreciation of this; على اقل تقدير *'alā aqalli t.* at least; على اكثر تقدير at most; عن مبلغ تقديرى *'an mablaḡi taqdīrī* as far as I can judge for myself

اقتدار *iqtidār* might, power, strength, potency; ability, capability, faculty, capacity, efficiency, aptitude

قادر *qādir* possessing power or strength, powerful, potent; having mastery (على over s.th.), being equal (على to s.th.); capable (على of s.th.), able (على to do s.th.); efficient, capable, talented

مقدور *maqdūr* decreed (على against, by fate); (pl. مقادير *maqādīr*[2]) destiny, fate; (pl. *-āt*) faculty, capability, ability; potential, resources | فى مقدوره ان to be able to ..., be capable of ..., be in a position to ..., have the possibility to ...

مقدر *muqaddir* estimator, appraiser, assessor, taxer

مقدر *muqaddar* decreed, foreordained, predestined; implied, implicit, virtual; مقدرات fates, destinies; estimates, preliminary calculations

مقتدر *muqtadir* possessing power or strength, powerful, potent; having mastery (على over s.th.), being equal (على to s.th.); able (على to do s.th.), capable (على of); efficient capable, talented

[1]قدس *qadusa u* (*quds, qudus*) to be holy, be pure II to hallow, sanctify (ه, ه s.o., s.th.); to dedicate, consecrate (ه s.th.); to declare to be holy, glorify (الله God); to hold sacred, venerate, revere, reverence, worship (ه, ه s.o., s.th.); (*Chr.*) to canonize (ه s.o.); (*Chr.*) to say Mass, celebrate | قدس الله سره (*sirrahū*) may God sanctify his secret! (eulogy used when mentioning the name of a deceased Muslim saint) V to be hallowed, be sacred or sanctified

قدس *quds, qudus* holiness, sacredness, sanctity; (pl. اقداس *aqdās*) sanctuary, shrine; القدس *al-quds* Jerusalem | قدس الاقداس the holy of holies (*Chr., Jud.*); الروح القدس, روح القدس (*ar-*)*rūḥ al-qudus* the Holy Ghost (*Chr.*)

قدسى *qudsī* holy, sacred; saintly; saint

قدسية *qudsīya* holiness, sacredness, sanctity; saintliness

قداس *quddās* pl. *-āt,* قداديس *qadādīs*[2] Mass (*Chr.*)

قداسة *qadāsa* holiness, sacredness, sanctity; saintliness | قداسة البابا His Holiness the Pope

قدوس *qaddūs, quddūs* most holy; القدوس the Most Holy, the All-Holy (God)

قديس *qiddīs* pl. *-ūn* holy, saintly; Christian saint | عيد كل القديسين *ʿīd kull al-q.* All Saints' Day (*Chr.*)

اقدس *aqdas*[2] more hallowed, more sacred, holier

بيت المقدس *bait al-maqdis* Jerusalem

تقديس *taqdīs* sanctification, hallowing; dedication, consecretion; celebration (*Chr.*); Consecration (as part of the Roman Catholic Mass; *Chr.*); reverence, veneration, worship

مقدس *muqaddis* reverent, reverential, venerative

مقدس *muqaddas* hallowed, sanctified, dedicated, consecrated; holy, sacred; pl. *-āt* sacred things, sacrosanct things | الارض (البلاد) المقدسة (*arḍ*) the Holy Land, Palestine; البيت المقدس (*bait*) Jerusalem; الكتاب المقدس the Holy Scriptures, the Holy Bible (*Chr.*)

متقدس *mutaqaddis* hallowed, sanctified, dedicated, consecrated; holy, sacred

[2]قادس *qādis*[2] Cádiz (seaport in SW Spain)

[3]قادوس pl. قواديس look up alphabetically

قدم *qadama u* (*qadm,* قدوم *qudūm*) to precede (ه s.o.); — *qadima a* (قدوم *qudum,* قدمان *qidmān,* مقدم *maqdam*) to arrive (ه at a place); to come; to get (الى or على or ه to s.o.; ه to a place), reach (الى or على, ه s.o.; ه a place); to have the audacity to do s.th. (على); — *qaduma u* (*qidam*) to be old, be ancient II to make or let (ه, ه s.o., s.th.) precede, go before, or lead the way; to send forward, send ahead, send off, dispatch, send on in advance (ه, ه s.o., s.th.); to set forth beforehand, premise (ل ه s.th. as introductory to s.th., e.g., a preface to a book); to place (ه, ه s.o., s.th.) at the head; to set forward, set ahead (ه a clock); to do earlier, do beforehand, do before s.th. else (ه s.th.); to give precedence (على ه, ه to s.o., to s.th. before), give priority (على ه to s.th. over); to prefer (على ه, ه s.o., s.th. to s.o. or s.th. else), give preference (على ه, ه to s.o., to s.th. over); (*Tun.*) to appoint as legal guardian (على ه s.o. for); to prepare, ready, keep ready, provide, set aside, earmark (ل ه s.th. for); to provide, make provisions (ل for); to offer, proffer, tender, extend, present, produce, exhibit, display (ه s.th., الى or ل to s.o.); to hand over, deliver (ه s.th., الى or ل to s.o.); to submit, refer (ه s.th., الى or ل to s.o.), lay s.th. (ه) before s.o. (الى or ل); to give as a present (ه s.th., الى or ل to s.o.), offer up, present (الى or ل ه, ه s.o., s.th. to s.o., to s.th.); to dedicate (الى or ل ه s.th., e.g., a book, to s.o.); to file, turn in (ه s.th., e.g., a report), send in, submit (ه s.th., e.g., an application, الى or ل to), lodge (ه e.g., a complaint, الى or ل before); to give (ه an answer); to take (ه an examination); to bring s.o. (ه) before a proper authority, esp., before a tribunal (امام or الى), arraign s.o.; to introduce, present (ل or الى ه s.o. to s.o. else), make (ه s.o.) acquainted (ل or الى with s.o. else); (intr.) to precede; to be fast (clock) | قدمه بين يديه (*baina yadaihi*) to send s.th. ahead of s.th. else, let s.th. precede s.th. else; قدم له الثمن (*ṯamana*) to pay the price to s.o. in advance, advance the price to s.o.; قدم خدمة (*ḵidmatan*) to render a service; قدم خطوة (*ḵuṭwatan*) to make a step forward; قدم الشكر له (*šukra*) to extend one's thanks to s.o., thank s.o.; قدم نفسه الى البوليس to give o.s. up to the police; ما قدمت وما اخرت (*aḵḵartu*) what I have ever committed; ما قدمت يداك (*yadāka*) what you have committed or perpetrated; يقدم رجلا ويؤخر اخرى *yuqaddimu rijlan wa-yu'aḵḵiru uḵrā* to hesitate, waver, be undecided; فرق شهور لا تقدم ولا تؤخر *farqu šuhūrin lā tuqaddimu wa-lā tu'aḵḵiru* a difference of a few months which is of no consequence **IV** to be bold, audacious, daring; to make bold, have the audacity to do s.th. (على); to venture, risk, undertake, tackle (على s.th.), set about s.th. (على); to brave (على s.th.), embark boldly (على upon), dare to engage (على in), venture upon s.th. (على); to attack (على s.o., s.th.) **V** to precede (عن or على or ه, ه s.o., s.th., in space and time), go before s.o. or s.th. (عن, على, ه, ه); to head (على or هم a group of people), be at the head (على or هم of a group of people); to belong to an earlier, older time; to go forward, move (forward), proceed (نحو toward), advance-march (نحو against, toward); to progress, make progress; to come on, come closer, move nearer (الى to); to approach (الى s.o. or s.th.), accost (الى s.o.); to step up (الى to); to present o.s. (بين يديه or الى to), step before (بين يديه or الى); ○ to meet, face (ل or الى an opposing team, in sports); to turn, apply (ل ب or الى to s.o. with a request); to submit (ل or الى to s.o. ب s.th., e.g., a request); to order, direct, commission (الى ب s.o. to do, to bring, etc., s.th.) | تقدم به to further, advance, promote, improve s.th.; تقدمت به السن (*sinnu*) to get older, be advanced in years; كما تقدم as already mentioned; غفر الله له ما تقدم من ذنبه وما تأخر (*ḏanbihī, ta'aḵḵara*) God has forgiven all his sins; وقت بغداد متقدم ساعتين عن وقت اوربا الوسطى *waqtu baġdāda mutaqaddimun sā'ataini 'an waqti urubbā l-wusṭā* Baghdad time is two hours ahead of Central European time; تقدم نحوه (*naḥwahū*) to step up to s.o.; تقدم منه to approach s.o., head for s.o.; تقدم للامتحان to submit o.s. to an examination **VI** to become antiquated, grow obsolete, get out of date, become old, age | تقادم الزمن (*zamanu*) much time has gone by (since); تقادم عهده (*'ahduhū*) it happened long ago, it belongs to the past, it is of early date **X** to ask (ه s.o.) to come, send (ه for s.o.), summon (ه s.o.)

قدم *qidm* time long since past, old times; قدما *qidman* in old(en) times, in former times, once, of old, of yore

قدم *qidam* time long since past, old times; remote antiquity, time immemorial; oldness; ancientness; infinite pre-existence, sempiternity, timelessness (of God); seniority | منذ القدم from times of old, by long tradition, of long standing; قدم عهده ب (*qidamu ʿahdihī*) his long-standing familiarity with

قدم **qadam** (usually f.) pl. اقدام **aqdām** foot (also as a measure of length); step | قدم مكعبة (*mukaʿʿaba*) cubic foot; سمت القدم *samt al-q.* nadir (*astron.*); اصبع القدم *iṣbaʿ al-q.* toe; على قدميه (*qadamaihi*) on foot (of several: على الاقدام); على اطراف قدميه on tiptoe; على قدم الحذر (*q. al-ḥaḏar*) anxious, timid, fearful; على قدم الاهبة والاستعداد (*q. il-uhba*) in a state of extreme alertness; جرى (قام) على قدم وساق (*wa-sāqin*) to become fully effective, be in full progress, be in full swing; ليس له قدم فى he has no part in ..., he is not involved in ...

قدم **qudum**: مضى (سار) قدما (*quduman*) to go straight ahead or forward

قديم **qadīm** pl. قدماء **qudamāʾ**², قدامى **qudāmā**, قدائم **qadāʾim**² old, ancient; antique; existing from time immemorial, eternally pre-existent, sempiternal; القديم the Infinitely Pre-existent, the Sempiternal, the Eternal (as an attribute of God) | قديما *qadīman* or فى القديم in old(en) times, in ancient times, in former times, once, of old, of yore; من قديم or منذ القديم from times of old, by long tradition, of long standing; قديم العهد ب (*q. al-ʿahd*) of long familiarity or acquaintance with, long familiar or acquainted with; of long-standing experience in, long-experienced in, (being) a long-time holder of; دراسات قديمة classical studies

قدوم **qudūm** coming, advent, arrival

قدوم **qadūm** pl. قدم **qudum** bold, audacious, daring, intrepid, undaunted, courageous, brave, valiant

قدوم **qadūm**, **qaddūm** pl. قدائم **qadāʾim**², قدم **qudum** adz

قدام **quddām** fore part, front part; **quddāma** (prep.) in front of

قيدوم **qaidūm** prow, bow of a ship

اقدم **aqdam**² older, more ancient; الاقدمون the ancients

اقدمية **aqdamīya** seniority

مقدم **maqdam** coming, advent; arrival

مقدام **miqdām** bold, audacious, daring, intrepid, undaunted, courageous, brave, valiant; a military rank, approx.: staff sergeant (*Eg.* 1939)

تقديم **taqdīm** sending forward, sending off, dispatching, etc., see II; presentation; submission, turning in, filing; offering up, oblation; dedication; offer, proffer, tender, bid; memorial; (pl. تقاديم **taqādīm**²) officially established guardianship (*Tun.*)

تقدمة **taqdima** offer, proffer, tender, bid; dedication; (social) introduction, presentation; offering up, oblation, offertory (*Chr.*); (pl. *-āt*, تقادم **taqādim**²) present, gift

اقدام **iqdām** boldness, audacity, daring, intrepidity, fearlessness, undauntedness, stoutheartedness, pluck, courage, enterprise, initiative

تقدم **taqaddum** precedence, priority; (ad)vantage, lead; advance, drive, push; advancement, progression, progress

تقدمى **taqaddumī** progressive, progressionist

تقادم **taqādum**: تقادم العهد (الزمن) *t. al-ʿahd* (*az-zaman*) progression or lapse of time; مع تقادم الزمن in the course of time

قادم **qādim** pl. *-ūn*, قدوم **qudūm**, قدام **quddām** one arriving, arriver, arrival, newcomer; — coming, next (e.g., year, month, and the like)

مقدم **muqaddim** offerer, tenderer, presenter, giver, donor | مقدم الطلب *m. aṭ-ṭalab* applicant

مقدم muqaddam put before s.th. (على),
prefixed, prefaced (على to s.th.), anteced-
ing, preceding (على s.th.); front, face; fore
part, front part; prow, bow (of a ship);
○ nose (of an airplane, and the like);
antecedent of a proportion (math.);
overseer, supervisor; foreman; a military
rank, approx.: major (Ir., U.A.R.); lieutenant colonel (formerly Syr.); officially
appointed legal guardian (Tun.); admin-
istrator or trustee of a wakf estate
(Tun.); مقدم عليه a legal minor placed
under officially established guardianship
(Tun.); مقدما muqaddaman in advance,
beforehand

مقدمة muqaddima, muqaddama pl. -āt
fore part, front part; front, face; prow,
bow (of a ship); foreground; foremost
rank or line, forefront, head, lead;
advance guard, vanguard, van; foreword,
preface, introduction, prologue, proem,
preamble; prelude; premise

متقدم mutaqaddim preceding, antecedent; moving forward, advancing; well-
advanced; (being) in front, ahead, in the
fore part; foremost; aforesaid, before-
mentioned; advanced; senior (athlet.) |
المتقدم ذكره (ḏikruhū) the aforesaid, the
before-mentioned; متقدم فى السن or (فى العمر)
(sinn, 'umr) advanced in age, well along
in years, old; متقدم على ابانه (ibbānihī)
premature, precipitate, untimely; المتقدمون
والمتأخرون (wa-l-muta'akkirūn) the earlier
and the later = all

قدا qadā u (qadw) and قدى (قدى and قدو)
qadiya a قدى qadan, قداوة qadāwa) to
be tasty, savory (food) VIII to imitate,
copy (ب s.o., s.th.), emulate (ب s.o.),
follow s.o.'s (ب) model or example, be
guided (ب by)

قدوة qudwa, qidwa model, pattern,
example, exemplar

قدى qadiy tasty, savory, palatable
(food)

اقتداء iqtidā' imitation, emulation; اقتداء
ب iqtidā'an bi following the model or
example of

قذة quḏḏa pl. قذذ quḏaḏ, قذاذ qiḏāḏ feather of
an arrow | حذو القذة بالقذة (ḥaḏwa) exactly
identical, deceptively alike

قذر qaḏira a (qaḏar) and qaḏura u (قذارة
qaḏāra) to be or become dirty, unclean,
filthy II to make dirty, soil, sully,
contaminate, pollute, defile (ه، s.o.,
s.th.) X to find or deem (ه، s.o., s.th.)
dirty, unclean, impure, filthy, squalid

قذر qaḏar uncleanliness, impurity;
(pl. اقذار aqḏār) dirt, filth, squalor

قذر qaḏir, qaḏr dirty, unclean, impure,
filthy, squalid

قذور qaḏūr dainty, fastidious, squeamish

قذارة qaḏāra dirtiness, uncleanliness,
impurity, filthiness, squalidness

قاذورة qāḏūra pl. -āt dirt, filth, squalor;
rubbish, garbage; (moral) defilement

مقاذر maqāḏir² dirty things, dirt, filth

قذع qaḏa'a a (qaḏ') to defame, malign,
vilify (ه s.o.), backbite, wag an evil
tongue, make slanderous remarks

قذف qaḏafa i (qaḏf) to throw, cast (ب or
ه s.th.); to throw away, discard (ب or
ه s.th.); to fling, hurl, toss (ب or ه s.th.);
to hurl down, toss down (ب or ه، ه s.o.,
s.th.); to push, shove (ب or ه، ه s.o.,
s.th.); to row, oar (ب or ه s.th.); to
eject, emit, discharge (ب or ه s.th.); to
expel (ب or ه، ه s.o., s.th.); to evict, oust
(ب or ه s.o.); to drop (ب s.th.); to pelt
(ب، ه s.o. with); to defame, slander,
calumniate (ه s.o.); to accuse (ب ه s.o.
of), charge (ب ه s.o. with); to vomit |
قذف بالقنابل to bomb s.th., strafe s.th.
with bombs; قذف عليه الشتائم to hurl
abusive language at s.o. II to row, oar

VI to pelt one another (ب with); to throw to each other, throw back and forth (ه s.th.); to shove around, push around (ه or ب s.o.) | تقاذفت به الامواج (amwāju) to be tossed about by the waves VII to be thrown, be cast, be flung, be hurled, be tossed, be flung off

قذف qaḏf defamation; calumny, slander, false accusation (esp., of fornication; Isl. Law); rowing, oaring | القذف بالقنابل bombing, bombardment; طائرة قذف القنابل bomber

قذفى qaḏfī slanderous, libelous, defamatory

قذاف qaḏḏāf: طيارة قذافة (ṭayyāra) bomber

قذيفة qaḏīfa pl. قذائف qaḏā'if² projectile; bomb; shell; fuse, detonator | قذيفة نسافة (nassāfa) torpedo; قذيفة يدوية (yadawīya) hand grenade

مقذف miqḏaf pl. مقاذف maqāḏif² oar, paddle

مقذاف miqḏāf pl. مقاذيف maqāḏīf² oar, paddle

تقذيف taqḏīf rowing, oaring

قاذفة qāḏifa: قاذفات القنابل pl. قاذفة القنابل bomber; قاذفة اللهب q. al-lahab or قاذفة النار flame thrower

مقذوف maqḏūf pl. مقاذيف maqāḏīf² and مقذوفة maqḏūfa pl. -āt missile; projectile

قذال qaḏāl pl. قذل quḏul, اقذلة aqḏila occiput

قذى IV: اقذى عينه ('ainahū) to vex, annoy, gall s.o., cause s.o. worry

قذى qaḏan (coll.; n. un. قذاة qaḏāh) s.th. that gets in one's eye or into a beverage, a floating impurity, mote, speck; foreign body in the eye | قذى فى عينه ('ainihī) an odious thing, approx.: an eyesore, a thorn in the flesh; اغضى على القذى (aḡḍā) to bear annoyance patiently, grin and bear it, swallow the bitter pill; غمض جفونه على القذى (ḡammaḍa jufūnahū) do.

قذى qiḏan pl. اقذاء aqḏā' fine dust; pl. اقذاء particles floating in the air

قر qarra (1st pers. perf. qarartu) i, (1st pers. perf. qarirtu) a (قرار qarār) to settle down, establish o.s., become settled or sedentary, take up one's residence, rest, abide, dwell, live, reside, remain, stay, linger (ب or فى in, at a place) | قر الرأى على (ra'yu) it was decided to ..., the decision was reached to ..., a resolution was passed on s.th. or to the effect that; قر رأيه على (ra'yuhū) to resolve, determine on s.th., make up one's mind to (do s.th.), decide, make a decision for or on or to do s.th.; لا يقر له حال to be flighty, be of unstable temperament; لا يقر له قرار (qarār) to be restless, restive, uneasy, wavering, undecided; — qarra a i (qarr) to be cold, chilly, cool | قر عينا ('ainan) to be of good cheer; قرت عينه ('ainuhū) to be glad, be delighted (ب at) II to settle, make sedentary (ه فى s.o. in, at a place), establish (ه فى s.th. in); to fix, settle, appoint, assign, schedule, determine, stipulate, regulate (ه s.th.); to decide (ه s.th.); to determine, resolve, decide (ه on s.th.); to confirm, establish, affirm, aver (ه s.th.); to report, relate, tell (ه s.th.); to make a report, give a paper (عن on); to make a statement; to force s.o. (ه) to confess or acknowledge s.th. (على or ب), make s.o. (ه) confess or acknowledge s.th. (على or ب) IV to settle, make sedentary (ه فى s.o. in, at a place), establish (ه فى s.th. in); to safeguard (ه s.th.); to have (ه s.o.) sit down, seat (ه s.o., فى in, in a seat); to set up, institute (ه s.th.); to found, establish (ه s.th.); to install, instate (ه فى s.o. in an office); to confirm, establish, affirm, aver (ه s.th.); to agree, consent (ب or ه to); to acknowledge, own (ب or ه s.th.); to confess, avow, admit (ب s.th.), own (ب to s.th.); to concede, grant (ه or ب ل to s.o. s.th.) | اقر عينه (*'ainahū*) (to cool s.o.'s eye =) to gladden, delight s.o. **V** to be fixed, be settled, be appointed, be scheduled, be determined, be regulated, be stipulated, be decided; to resolve itself (situation) **X** to settle down, establish o.s., become settled or sedentary, take up one's residence (ب or فى in, at a place); to come to rest (ب or فى in, at a place); to rest, abide, dwell, live, reside, remain, stay, linger (ب or فى in, at a place, الى with s.o.); to be firmly embedded, get stuck, get lodged (فى in); to be firm, solid, enduring, durable, lasting, stable; to become stabilized, stabilize, be consolidated (situation, conditions); ultimately to attain (على a state or condition), finally find a firm position (على in); to become finally (على s.th.), ultimately turn into s.th. (على); to be established, settled, fixed; to be stationary | استقر خاطره على (*kāṭiruhū*) his mind dwelled on ...; استقر الرأى على (*ra'yu*) it was decided to ..., the decision was reached to ...; a resolution was passed on s.th. or to the effect that; استقر رأيه على (*ra'yuhū*) to resolve, determine on s.th., make up one's mind to (do s.th.), decide, make a decision for or on or to do s.th.; استقر له الامور his situation had stabilized; لا يستقر له قرار (*qarārun*) to be restless, restive, uneasy, wavering, undecided; لم نستقر بعد على حال (*ba'du*) we haven't yet arrived at a lasting solution, we haven't yet attained a definitive position; استقر على امره he finally became ..., he ended up as ...; استقر فى نفسه to be a positive fact with s.o., be beyond doubt for s.o.; استقر به المقام (or المكان) (*muqāmu, makānu*) to settle down permanently; to sit down; not to move from one's seat; استقر به المجلس (*majlisu*) to sit down, get seated, take a seat; استقر به الحال to be firmly established, be settled; to be in a secure position

قر *qarr* cold, chilly, cool

قر *qurr* cold, coldness, chilliness, coolness

قرة *qirra* cold, coldness, chilliness, coolness

قرة العين *qurrat al-'ain* consolation for the eye, delight of the eye; joy, pleasure, delight; darling; (*bot.*) cress

قرار *qarār* sedentariness, settledness, stationariness, sedentation; fixedness, fixity; firmness, solidity; steadiness, constancy, continuance, permanency, stability; repose, rest, stillness; duration; abode, dwelling, habitation; residence; resting place; bottom (e.g., of a receptacle); depth (of the sea); (pl. *-āt*) decision, resolution | لا قرار له (*lā qarāra*) inconstant, changeable, unstable; bottomless, unfathomable, immeasurable; دار القرار the hereafter, the world to come; ○ قرار الموجة *q. al-mauja* wave trough (*techn.*); قرارات التعديل modifying regulations

قرارة *qarāra* bottom; low ground, depression, depth | فى قرارة النفس (*q. in-nafs*) in the depth of the heart

قرير *qarīr*: قرير العين *q. al-'ain* happy, gratified, delighted, glad

قارورة *qārūra* pl. قوارير *qawārīr*[2] long-necked bottle

مقر *maqarr* pl. مقار *maqārr*[2] abode, dwelling, habitation; residence; storage place; seat, center; site, place; station; position (at sea) | مقر العمل *m. al-'amal* place of employment; مقر القيادة headquarters; مقر الوظيفة official seat, seat of office

تقرير *taqrīr* establishment, settlement; fixation; appointment, assignment, regulation, arrangement, stipulation; determination; decision; (pl. تقارير *taqārīr*[2]) report, account | تقرير المصير self-determination (*pol.*); حق الشعوب فى تقرير مصيرها (*ḥaqq aš-š.*) the right of peoples to self-determination; تقرير الحالة الجوية

(*ǧawwīya*) weather report; تقرير الشرطة *t. aš-šurṭa* police report

اقرار *iqrār* settling, settlement (of nomads); setting up, institution, establishment; foundation; installation, instatement; delivery of a confirmation or assurance; confirmation, affirmation, averment; assurance; acknowledgment; confession, avowal, admission

استقرار *istiqrār* sedentariness, settledness, stationariness, sedentation; remaining, abiding, lingering, stay, sojourn; settling, settlement, establishment; steadiness, constancy, continuance, permanency; strengthening, consolidation, stabilization, stability; repose, rest, stillness

قار *qārr* sedentary, settled, resident; standing, permanent; fixed, stationary; cold, chilly, cool | الاداءات (غير) القارة (*adā'āt*) (in)direct taxes (*magr.*); لجنة قارة (*lajna*) permanent committee, standing committee

قارة *qārra* pl. *-āt* continent, mainland

مقرر *muqarrir* pl. *-ūn* reporter (in general and of a newspaper)

مقرر *muqarrar* established, settled; fixed, determined, decided, appointed, assigned, scheduled, regulated, stipulated, decreed; (pl. *-āt*) curriculum; مقررات decisions | مقرر الميزانية *m. al-mīzānīya* the proposed budget; حقيقة مقررة accomplished fact; اموال مقررة direct taxes

مستقر *mustaqirr* sedentary, settled, resident; firmly established, deep-seated, deep-rooted; fixed, immobile, stationary; firm, solid, enduring, durable, lasting, stable

مستقر *mustaqarr* abode, dwelling, habitation; residence; seat; resting place

قرأ *qara'a a* (قراءة *qirā'a*) to declaim, recite (ه s.th., esp. the Koran; ه على to s.o. s.th.); to read (ه s.th.; ه ل or على s.o. s.th.); to peruse (ه s.th.); to study (ه على under s.o. s.th.) | قرأ عليه السلام (*salāma*) to greet, salute s.o.; to extend greetings to s.o.; قرأ حسابه ل to reckon with s.th., take s.th. into account; قرأ له الف حساب (*alfa ḥ.*) to have a thousand apprehensions about s.th. **IV** to make or have (ه s.o.) read (ه s.th.); to teach (ه s.o.) the art of reciting (ه s.th.); to teach (ه s.o.) how to read (ه s.th.) | اقرأه السلام (*salāma*) to extend greetings to s.o. **X** to ask s.o.(ه) to recite or read; to investigate, examine, explore (ه s.th.), search (ه into s.th.); to study thoroughly (ه s.th.)

قرء *qur'* pl. قروء *qurū'* menses, menstruation

قراءة *qirā'a* pl. *-āt* recitation, recital (esp. of the Koran); reading (also, e.g., of measuring instruments; *parl.*); manner of recitation, punctuation and vocalization of the Koranic text | قراءة الكف *q. al-kaff* chiromancy, palmistry

القرآن *al-qur'ān* the Koran

قرآنى *qur'ānī* Koranic, of or pertaining to the Koran

استقراء *istiqrā'* pl. *-āt* investigation, examination, exploration; see also under قرو

استقرائى *istiqrā'ī* see under قرو

قارئ *qāri'* pl. *-ūn*, قراء *qurrā'* reciter (esp. of the Koran); reader | قارئ الكف *q. al-kaff* chiromancer, palmist

مقروء *maqrū'* read (past part.); legible, readable; worth reading

مقرئ *muqri'* reciter of the Koran

قراج *garāž* pl. *-āt* (Saudi Arabian spelling) garage

[1]**قرب** *qaruba u* (*qurb*, مقربة *maqraba*) to be near (الى or من to s.o., to s.th.); to come near, get close (الى or من to s.o., to s.th.), close in (الى or من on s.o., on s.th.), approach

(الى or من s.o., s.th.); to approximate (الى or من s.th.); — *qariba a* to be near (ه, ه to s.o., to s.th.); to come near, get close (ه, ه to s.o., to s.th.), close in (ه, ه on s.o., on s.th.), approach (ه, ه s.o., s.th.); to approximate (ه s.th.); to draw near, be coming on, approach | ما يقرب من (*yaqrubu*) (with foll. figure) approximately, about, some, circa **II** to cause or allow (ه, ه s.o., s.th.) to come near or get close (الى or من to s.th.), make or let (ه, ه s.o., s.th.) approach (الى or من s.th.), bring close (ه, ه s.o., s.th.; الى or من to s.th.), advance, move (ه, ه s.o., s.th.; الى or من toward s.th.), approximate (ه s.th.; الى or من to); to bring home (ه من or الى to s.o. s.th., e.g., an idea); to take as associate or companion (ه من s.o. for o.s.); to bring closer to comprehension, reveal more fully (ه s.th.), clarify the concept, facilitate the understanding (ه of s.th.); to offer up, present (ه ل to God as sacrifice); (*Chr.*) to administer Communion (ه to s.o.); to sheathe, put into the scabbard (ه the sword) | قرب بينهم to bring people closer together, make peace among people, reconcile people **III** to be near (ه, ه to s.o., to s.th.); to come near, come close, get close (ه, ه to s.o., to s.th.), close in (ه, ه on s.o., on s.th.), approach (ه, ه s.o., s.th.); to approximate (ه s.th.); to be almost equivalent (ه with s.th.), amount to almost the same thing (ه as s.th.); to be on the point (ان of doing s.th.), be about (ان to do s.th.); to bring (close) together (بين — و different things) **V** to approach (من or الى s.o., s.th.), come or get near s.o., near s.th. (من or الى), come close, get close (من or الى to s.o.), gain access (من or الى to s.o.); to seek to gain s.o.'s (الى) favor, curry favor (الى with s.o.); (*Chr.*) to receive Communion **VI** to be or come near each other, approach one another, approximate each other **VIII** to approach (من s.o., s.th.), come, advance, or get near s.o. or s.th. (من), come close, get close (من to) **X** to find near, regard as near (ه s.th.)

قرب *qurb* nearness, closeness, proximity, vicinity; *qurba* (prep.) in the vicinity of, near, toward | قرب الظهر *qurba ẓ-ẓuhr* toward noon; بالقرب من or بقرب in the vicinity of, near, close to; عن قرب from a short distance, from close up

قربة *qirba* pl. *-āt*, قرب *qirab* waterskin; — (pl. قرب *qirab*) bagpipe

قربى *qurbā* relation, relationship, kinship | ذو القربى pl. ذوو القربى *ḏawū l-q.* relative, relation

قريب *qarīb* near (in place and time), nearby, close at hand; in the neighborhood or vicinity (الى or من of s.o., of s.th.), close (الى or من to s.o., to s.th.), adjacent (الى or من to s.th.); easily understood, simple; (pl. اقرباء *aqribā'*[2]) relative, relation; قريبا *qarīban* soon, before long, shortly, in the near future; recently, lately, not long ago, the other day | من قريب and عما قريب (*'ammā q.*) soon, before long, shortly, in the near future; لا — من قريب او بعيد not — in the least, not by a far cry; فى القريب العاجل in the immediate future; قريب من الحسن (*ḥasan*) fair, fairly good (as a school-report grade); قريب العهد *q. al-'ahd* recent, new, young; من عهد قريب since recently, of late, of a recent date; recently, lately, not long ago, the other day; قريب العهد ب having adopted or acquired s.th. very recently; not long familiar or acquainted with s.th., inexperienced at s.th., a novice in s.th.; قريب التناول *q. at-tanāwul* easy to understand

قراب *qirāb* pl. قرب *qurub*, اقربة *aqriba* sheath, scabbard (of a sword); receptacle, container, case, etui, covering

قرابة *qarāba* relation, relationship, kinship

قرابة *qurāba*: قرابة ثلاثة اعوام *qurābata ṯalāṯati aʿwām* almost three years

قربان *qurbān* pl. قرابين *qarābīn*² sacrifice, offering, immolation, oblation; Mass (*Chr.*); Eucharist (*Chr.*) | قربان الشكر *q. aš-šukr* thank offering; عيد القربان *ʿīd al-q.* Corpus Christi (*Chr.*); تناول القربان (*tanāwala*) to receive Communion (*Chr.*); قدم القربان عن or رفع القربان على (*qaddama*) to read Mass for s.o. (*Chr.*)

قربانة *qurbāna* Host; Communion (*Chr.*)

اقرب *aqrab*² nearer, nearest, next; more probable, more likely; probable, likely; pl. اقربون *aqrabūn*, اقارب *aqārib*² relations, relatives | اقرب الى الفهم (*fahm*) easier to understand, more comprehensible; هو اقرب الى الصحة (or الصواب) (*ṣiḥḥa*, *ṣawāb*) it is quite probable, it is fairly correct, it is rather exact, it comes fairly close to the truth; فى اقرب وقت (ممكن) *fī aqrabi waqtin* (*mumkinin*) or باقرب ما يمكن (*yumkinu*) as soon as possible, in the shortest time possible

مقرب *maqrab* pl. مقارب *maqārib*² nearest or shortest way, short cut

مقربة *maqraba*, *maqruba* nearness, closeness, proximity, vicinity; (pl. مقارب *maqārib*²) nearest or shortest way, short cut | على مقربة nearby, close at hand; على مقربة من in the vicinity of, near, close to

تقريب *taqrīb* approximation | تقريبا *taqrīban*, بالتقريب, بوجه التقريب *bi-wajhi t-t.* or على التقريب approximately, almost, nearly, roughly, about; محسوس تقريبا just barely perceptible

تقريبى *taqrībī* approximate, approximative

تقرب *taqarrub* approach; approximation (من to)

تقارب *taqārub* mutual approach; mutual approximation; rapprochement

اقتراب *iqtirāb* approach; approximation

مقرب *muqarrab* pl. -*ūn* close companion, favorite, protégé, intimate

مقارب *muqārib* approximate, approximative, estimated; mediocre, medium, of medium quality

متقارب *mutaqārib* close together, following in close intervals, consecutive, successive, subsequent, المتقارب name of a poetical meter

²قارب *qārib* pl. قوارب *qawārib*² boat, skiff | قارب الزبدة *q. az-zubda* (*eg.*) sauceboat for melted butter; قارب مسلح (*musallaḥ*) gunboat; قارب النجاة *q. an-najāh* lifeboat; قارب التنقيب عن الالغام mine sweeper; قارب نارى motorboat

قواربى *qawāribī* boatman

قربوس *qarabūs* (*qarbūs*) pl. قرابيس *qarābīs*² saddlebow

قربينة *qarabīna* pl. -*āt* carbine

قرح *qaraḥa a* (*qarḥ*) to wound (ه s.o.); — *qariḥa a* (*qaraḥ*) to ulcerate, fester; to be covered with ulcers, be ulcerous **II** to wound (ه s.o.) **V** to ulcerate, fester; to be covered with ulcers, be ulcerous **VIII** to invent, originate, think up (ه s.th.); to improvise, extemporize, deliver offhand (ه a speech); to demand in a brash or imperious manner (ه or ب على of s.o. s.th.); to propose, suggest (ه على to s.o. s.th.)

قرح *qarḥ* pl. قروح *qurūḥ* wound; ulcer, sore

قرح *qariḥ* covered with ulcers, ulcerous, ulcerated; ulcerating, festering

قرحة *qarḥa* pl. قرح *qiraḥ* ulcer, sore; abscess, boil | القرحة الرخوة (*rakwa*) soft chancre, chancroid (*med.*)

قراح *qarāḥ* pure, limpid, clear (esp. water)

قريح *qarīḥ* pure, limpid, clear (esp. water)

قريحة *qarīḥa* pl. قرائح *qarā'iḥ*[2] natural disposition, innate disposition, bent; genius, talent, gift, faculty

تقرح *taqarruḥ* ulceration

اقتراح *iqtirāḥ* invention, improvisation; (pl. *-āt*) proposition, proposal, suggestion; motion

مقرح *muqarraḥ* covered with ulcers, ulcerous, ulcerated

متقرح *mutaqarriḥ* covered with ulcers, ulcerous, ulcerated; ulcerating, festering

مقترح *muqtaraḥ* pl. *-āt* proposition, proposal, suggestion; motion

قرد **qird** pl. قردة *qirada*, قرود *qurūd* ape, monkey

قرد *qurd* (coll.; n. un. ة) tick (*zool.*)

قراد *qurād* (coll.; n. un. ة) pl. قردان *qirdān* tick, ticks (*zool.*) | ابو قردان *abū q.* (*eg.*) white egret (*zool.*)

مقرود *maqrūd* exhausted

قريدس **quraidis** (*syr.*) shrimp (*zool.*)

قرس **qarisa** *a* (*qaras*) to be severe, fierce, biting, grim (the cold) **II** to freeze, make torpid, (be)numb, nip (ه, ه s.o., s.th.; of the cold)

قارس *qāris* severe, fierce, biting, grim (of the cold); very cold, bitterly cold, freezing, frozen

قرش **qaraša** *i u* (*qarš*) to gnash, grind (one's teeth); to nibble, crunch, chew (ه s.th.); — *qaraša i* (*qarš*), **II** and **VIII** to earn money, make a living (لعياله *li-'iyālihī* for one's family)

قرش *qirš* shark (*zool.*); (pl. قروش *qurūš*) piaster | قرش صاغ (*eg.*, = 1/100 Eg. pound) standard piaster; قرش تعريفة (*eg.*, = 1/2 قرش صاغ) little piaster

قريش *quraiš* Koreish, name of an Arab tribe in ancient Mecca

قرشي *qurašī* of, pertaining to, or belonging to the Koreish tribe; Koreishite

قريش *qarīš*, قريشة *qarīša* sour cheese

مقرش *muqriš* rich, well-to-do, prosperous, wealthy, moneyed

قرص **qaraṣa** *u* (*qarṣ*) to pinch, nip, tweak (ه, ه s.o., s.th.); to scratch (ه, ه s.o., s.th.); to bite, sting (ه s.o.; of a gnat, flea, and the like) | قرصه بلسانه (*bi-lisānihī*) to hurt s.o. with words **II** to pinch or nip sharply, tweak (ه, ه s.o., s.th.); to scratch all over (ه, ه s.o., s.th.); to shape into round, flat loaves (العجين the dough)

قرص *qurṣ* pl. اقراص *aqrāṣ* round, flat loaf of bread; (flat, circular) plate, disk, discus; phonograph record, disc; sheave, pulley (*mech.*); tablet, pastille, lozenge, troche | قرص الارقام dial (of a telephone); اقراص عجوة *a. 'ajwa* a pastry made of rich dough with almonds and date paste (*syr.*); قرص عسل *q. 'asal* honeycomb; جلب النار لقرصه (*nāra*) approx.: to feather one's nest, have an eye out for one's own interest, know on which side one's bread is buttered

قرصي *qurṣī*: قرصى الشكل *q. aš-šakl* disklike, disk-shaped, discoid, discous

قرصة *qurṣa* pl. قرص *quraṣ* round, flat loaf of bread

قرصة *qarṣa* pl. *qaraṣāt* pinch, nip, tweak; bite, sting (of a gnat, flea, and the like); crowbar, pinch bar, handspike, lever

قريص *qurraiṣ* stinging nettle (Urtica urens L.; *bot.*)

قراصة *qarrāṣa* pincers, nippers

قراصية *qarāṣiya* (*syr.*) small, black plums; (*eg.*) prunes

قارص *qāriṣ* biting; stinging; painful, nipping, tormenting (e.g., cold) | قوارص الكلمات *q. al-kalimāt* biting words

قرصنة *qarṣana* piracy, robbery on the high seas, freebooting

قرصان *qurṣān* pl. قراصن *qarāṣin*², قراصين *qarāṣīn*² corsair, pirate, freebooter

قرض *qaraḍa* i (*qarḍ*) to cut, sever, cut off, clip (▲ s.th.); to gnaw (▲ s.th. or on s.th.), nibble (▲ s.th. or at s.th.), bite, champ (▲ s.th.), eat (▲ into s.th.), corrode (▲ s.th.) | قرض رباطه (*ribāṭahū*) to die; قرض الشعر (*ši'ra*) to write poetry, make verses II = I; IV to loan, lend, or advance, money (• to s.o.); to lend (▲ • to s.o. s.th.) VI تقارضوا الثناء (*ṯanā'a*) they competed in the recital of eulogies VII to die out; to become extinct; to perish VIII to raise a loan (من with), borrow (من from) X to ask for a loan (من s.o.)

قرض *qarḍ* (*qirḍ*) pl. قروض *qurūḍ* loan | قرض حسن (*ḥasan*) interest-free loan with unstipulated due date; قرض مالى (*mālī*) (monetary) loan; اسهم القرض *ashum al-q.* bonds

قريض *qarīḍ* poetry

قراضة *qurāḍa* pl. *-āt* chips, shreds, parings, shavings, scraps; iron filings

قراضة *qarrāḍa* clothes moth

مقراض *miqraḍ* pl. مقاريض *maqārīḍ*² scissors

انقراض *inqirāḍ* dying out, gradual disappearance; extinction

اقتراض *iqtirāḍ* loan

استقراض *istiqrāḍ* raising of a loan; loan

القوارض *al-qawāriḍ* the rodents

مقرض *muqriḍ* pl. *-ūn* moneylender; lender

منقرض *munqariḍ* extinct, exterminated, perished

[1]قرط *qaraṭa* u (*qarṭ*) to cut into small pieces, chop, mince (▲ s.th.) II do.; to snuff, trim (▲ a candle, a wick); to squeeze (على s.th.); (*eg.*) to urge, ply (على s.o.); to be stern, be strict (على with s.o.); to beset, harass, press hard (على s.o.); to give little (على to s.o.), be illiberal, be stingy (على with s.o.), scrimp (على s.o.)

قرط *qurṭ* pl. اقراط *aqrāṭ*, قراط *qirāṭ*, قروط *qurūṭ* earring; eardrop, pendant for the ear

تقريطة *taqrīṭa* pl. تقاريط *taqārīṭ*² wrapper worn by women (*tun.*)

[2]قيراط pl. قراريط look up alphabetically

قرطجنة see قرطاجنة

قرطاس *qirṭās*, pl. قراطيس *qarāṭīs*² paper; sheet of paper; paper bag

قرطبة *qurṭuba*² Cordova (city in Spain)

قرطجنة *qarṭajanna*², قرطاجنة Carthage

قرطس *qarṭas* paper; sheet of paper

قرطم *qarṭama* to cut off, clip (▲ s.th.)

قرطم *qirṭim*, *qurṭum* safflower (Carthamus tinctorius; *bot.*)

قرطمان *qurṭumān* oats

قرظ II to praise, commend, laud, extol, acclaim (• s.o.); to eulogize (▲ s.th.), lavish praise (▲ on)

قرظ *qaraẓ* pods of a species of sant tree (Acacia nilotica; *bot.*)

قريظ *qarīẓ* eulogy, encomium, panegyric

تقريظ *taqrīẓ* pl. *-āt*, تقاريظ *taqārīẓ*² eulogy, encomium, panegyric

قرع *qara'a* a (*qar'*) to knock, rap (▲ at s.th.); to hit, bump (▲ s.th. or against s.th.); to strike, beat, thump (▲ against s.th.; ▲, • ب s.o., s.th. with; ب على with s.th. on or s.th. else); to thrash, spank (• ب s.o. with); to clink, touch (▲ glasses); to ring, sound (ه s.th.); — *qari'a* (*qara'*) to be or become bald(headed); to be empty, bare, stark (place) | قرع الجرس (*jarasa*) to ring the bell; قرع سمعه (*sam'ahū*) to reach s.o.'s ear; قرع سنه (*sinnahū*) to gnash one's teeth; قرع سن (على or) ل الندم (*sinna n-nadam*) to repent s.th.; قرعه ضميره (*ḍamīruhū*) his conscience tormented or smote him, he had a guilty conscience, he felt grave compunctions; قرع الكأس (*ka'sa*) to touch glasses, drink to s.o.'s (ل) health **II** to scold, chide, upbraid (ه s.o.), snap (ه at s.o.); to rebuke, blame, censure (ه s.o.) **III** to fight, come to blows (ه with s.o.); to battle, fight (ه s.o.); to contend by force of arms (ه عن with s.o. for s.th.); to cast or draw lots (ه with s.o.) **VI** to bump against each other, clash; to cast lots among each other (على for) **VIII** to cast lots among each other (على for); to vote, take a vote (على on); to draw lots (ه for s.o.), choose by lot (ه s.o.); to muster, recruit (ه s.o.; *mil.*); to elect (ه, ه s.o., s.th.)

قرع *qar'* knock(ing), rap(ping), beating, striking, thumping; ring(ing)

قرع *qar'* (coll.; n. un. ة) gourd, pumpkin | قرع ضروف (*eg.*) bottle gourd, calabash (Lagenaria vulgaris Ser.; *bot.*); قرع كوسى *q. kūsā* (*eg., syr.*) zucchini (*bot.*)

قرع *qara'* baldness, baldheadedness; emptiness, bareness, starkness

قرعة *qar'a* (n. vic.) knock, rap, blow, stroke, thump; — (n. un.) gourd, pumpkin; skull, head

قرعى *qar'ī* gourd-, pumpkin- (in compounds), cucurbitaceous

قرعة *qur'a* pl. قرع *qura'* lot; ballot; lot-casting; (*mil.*) conscription, recruitment (by lot), balloting | قرعة عسكرية (*'askarīya*) enlistment, draft, recruitment (*mil.*); انفار القرعة drafted recruits

قراع *qurā'*, القراع مرض *maraḍ al-qurā'* a skin disease, ringworm (*med.*)

قريع *qarī'* exquisite, select | قريع الدهر *q. ad-dahr* the greatest hero of his time

اقرع *aqra'*[2] bald; baldheaded; empty, bare, stark; scabby, scurfy

مقرعة *miqra'a* pl. مقارع *maqāri'*[2] knocker, rapper (of a door); whip, switch; cudgel, club

تقريع *taqrī'* chiding, scolding, reproof, rebuke, censure

مقارعة *muqāra'a* fight, struggle (with genit. = against)

اقتراع *iqtirā'* pl. *-āt* balloting, recruitment, draft (*mil.*); vote (على on); election

قارعة *qāri'a* pl. قوارع *qawāri'*[2] (sudden) misfortune, calamity; adversity; القارعة the hour of the Last Judgment | قارعة الطريق middle of the road, roadway; road, highway; على قارعة الطرق (*ṭuruq*) on the open road

قرف **qarafa** *i* (*qarf*) to peel, pare, bark, derind (ه s.th.); — *qarifa a* (*qaraf*) to loathe (ه s.th.), feel disgust (ه for), be nauseated (ه by) **II** to peel, pare, bark, derind (ه s.th.); to be loathsome, arouse disgust **III** to let o.s. be tempted (ه to a sin), yield (ه to a desire) **VIII** to commit, perpetrate (ه a crime)

قرف *qaraf* loathing, disgust, detestation

قرفة *qirfa* pl. قرف *qiraf* rind, bark, skin, crust; scab, scurf; cinnamon

قرافة *qarāfa* (*eg.*) cemetery, specif., graveyard below the Mokattam Hills near Cairo

قريفة *qarīfa* ill humor, ill temper

قرفان *qarfān* (*eg.*) disgusted, nauseated, sick and tired

اقتراف *iqtirāf* commission, perpetration (of a crime)

مقرف *muqrif* loathsome, disgusting, nauseating, repulsive, detestable

مقترف *muqtarif* perpetrator (of a crime)

قرفص *qarfaṣa* to squat on the ground (with thighs against the stomach and arms enfolding the legs)

قرفصاء *qurfuṣā'*[2] squatting, squatting position | جلس (قعد or) القرفصاء (*qurfuṣā'a*) to squat on one's heels

قرفال *qarfāl* (coll.; n. un. ة) vetch

قرق *qaraqa u* (*qarq*) to cluck (hen)

قرقذان *qarqaḏān* squirrel

قرقر *qarqara* (قرقرة *qarqara*) to roll; to rumble (stomach); to bray (camel); to coo (pigeon); to purr (cat)

قرقرة *qarqara* pl. قراقر *qarāqir*[2] rumbling noise (in the stomach); gurgle; braying (of a camel); cooing (of a pigeon); purr(ing) (of a cat)

قرقوش *qarqūš* pl. قراقيش *qarāqīš*[2] cartilage

قرقوشة *qarqūša* pl. قراقيش *qarāqīš*[2] (*eg.*) a kind of crisp cookies

مقرقش *muqarqaš* (*eg.*) crisp(ed)

قرقض *qarqaḍa* (*eg.*) to gnaw, bite (ه on s.th.) | قرقض عل اسنانه to gnash one's teeth

قرقع *qarqa'a* to be noisy, boisterous; to creak, grate; to crack, pop | قرقع ضاحكا (بالضحك or) (*ḍaḥk*) to burst into loud laughter, laugh noisily, guffaw; قرقع بسوطه (*bi-sauṭihī*) to crack the whip

قرقعة *qarqa'a* uproar, din, noise; creaking, creaks, grating; crack(ing), pop(ping); rumble, rumbling

قرقوز *qaraqōz* (from Turk. *karagöz*) chief character of the Turkish shadow play

قرقول see قره قول

[1]قرم *qarama i* (*qarm*) to gnaw (ه on s.th.), nibble (ه at s.th.)

قرم *qarm* pl. قروم *qurūm* studhorse; lord, master

قرام *qirām* blanket, carpet, curtain

مقرم *miqram* pl. مقارم *maqārim*[2] bedcover, bedspread

[2]قرمة *qurma* pl. قرم *quram* (*eg.*) tree stump; log, block of wood; chopping block

[3]القرم *al-qirim* und القريم *al-qirīm* the Crimea

قرمد *qarmada* to plaster, coat with plaster (ه s.th.); to tile, cover with tile (ه s.th.)

قرمد *qarmad* (coll.) plaster; plaster of Paris

قرميد *qirmīd* (coll.; n. un. ة) pl. قراميد *qarāmīd*[2] (fired) brick, roof tile; plaster of Paris

قرمز *qirmiz* kermes (the dried bodies of the female kermes insect, coccus ilicis, which yield a red dyestuff)

قرمزى *qirmizī* crimson, carmine; scarlet | الحمى القرمزية (*ḥummā*) scarlet fever (*med.*)

قرمش *qarmaša* (*eg.*) to eat s.th. dry (ه), crunch, nibble

مقرمش *muqarmaš* dry, crisp

[1]قرمطى *qarmaṭī* Karmathian (adj. and n.); pl. قرامطة *qarāmiṭa* Karmathians

[2]قرموط *qarmūṭ* pl. قراميط *qarāmīṭ*[2] a variety of sheatfish (*zool.*; *Eg.*)

قرن *qarana i* (*qarn*) to connect, link, join, unite, combine, associate (ه ب or الى s.th. with); to add (ه الى s.th. to); to couple, yoke together, hitch together, put together, bind together (ه s.th.) **III** to unite, join forces, associate (ه with s.o.); to be simultaneous, go hand in hand (ه with s.th.); to compare (ه ,ه ب or بين — وبين s.o., s.th. with; بين شيئين two things with one another), draw a parallel (بين — وبين between — and; بين شيئين between two things) **IV** to combine, interrelate (بين شيئين two things) **VIII** to be connected, be linked, be joined, be united, be combined, be associated (ب with); to combine, associate, unite (ب with); to get married, be married (ب to), marry (ب s.o.); to be coupled, be interconnected, be yoked together, be tied together, be bound together; to become interlinked, become concatenate **X** to ripen, suppurate, come to a head (of a furuncle)

قرن ***qarn*** pl. قرون ***qurūn*** horn (of an animal; as a wind instrument); feeler, tentacle, antenna; top, summit, peak (of a mountain); the first visible part of the rising sun; capsule, pod (*bot.*); century | ام القرن ***umm al-q.*** rhinoceros; وحيد القرن do.; ذو القرنين ***ḏū l-qarnain*** the two-horned (an epithet given to Alexander the Great); قرن البحر ***q. al-baḥr*** coral; قرن سمعى (*sam'ī*) ear trumpet (= Fr. *cornet acoustique*); القرون الوسطى (*wusṭā*) the Middle Ages

قرنى ***qarnī*** horny, corneous, of horn, hornlike; leguminous, pertaining to, or of the nature of, legumes; centennial, centenary

قرنية ***qarnīya*** cornea (*anat.*)

قرن ***qirn*** pl. اقران ***aqrān*** (matched) opponent in battle; an equal, a peer, a match; companion, mate, fellow, associate; equal, like

قرنة ***qurna*** pl. قرن ***quran***, قرانى ***qarānī*** salient angle, nook, corner

قرين ***qarīn*** pl. قرناء ***quranā'***[2] connected, joined, linked, combined, united, associated, affiliated; companion, mate, fellow, associate, comrade; husband, spouse, consort; *qarīna* (prep.) in connection with, in conjunction with, upon, at | منقطع القرين ***munqaṭi' al-q.*** matchless, peerless, unrivaled, incomparable, unique, singular

قرينة ***qarīna*** pl. ***-āt*** wife, spouse, consort; female demon haunting women, specif., a childbed demon; eclampsia (*med.*); — (pl. قرائن ***qarā'in***[2]) connection, conjunction, union, relation, affiliation, association, linkage; (semantic or syntactical) coherence, context; evidence, indication, indicium | السيدة قرينته (*sayyida*) his wife (formal style); قرائن الاحوال the concatenation of circumstances, the indicia, factual evidence; ضم قرينة الى قرينة (*ḍamm*) combination

اقرن ***aqran***[2], f. قرناء ***qarnā'***[2] horned, horny; one with eyebrows grown together | حية قرناء (*ḥayya*) cerastes, horned viper

قران ***qirān*** close union, close connection; conjunction (*astron.*); marriage, wedding

مقارنة ***muqārana*** pl. ***-āt*** comparison | مقارنة اللغات ***m. al-luġāt*** comparative linguistics

اقتران ***iqtirān*** connection, conjunction, union, association, affiliation; link, connectedness, simultaneous interaction; conjunction (*astron.*); new moon (as an astronomical aspect); marriage, wedding

مقرون ***maqrūn*** connected, joined, linked, combined, united, associated, affiliated (ب with) | مقرون الحاجبين ***m. al-ḥājibain*** having joined eyebrows

مقارن ***muqārin*** comparative (science)

قرنبيط ***qarnabīṭ*** cauliflower

قرنفل ***qaranful*** carnation; clove

قره‌جوز (Eg. spelling; pronounced *'aragōz*) Karagöz, chief character of the shadow play; Punch

قره‌قول ***qaraqōl*** pl. ***-āt*** police station; guard (military, police) | قره‌قول الشرف ***q. aš-šaraf*** guard of honor

قرو V to follow up, investigate (ه s.th.), inquire (ه into); to check, verify (ه s.th.) X to follow (ه s.th.); to pursue (ه s.th., e.g., a problem); to examine, study, investigate (ه s.th.); to explore (ه s.th.)

قرو *qarw* pl. قرو *qurūw* watering trough | خشب قرو *kašab q.* oak (wood)

استقراء *istiqrā'* induction (*philos.*); see also under قرأ

استقرائى *istiqrā'ī* inductive (*philos.*)

قرواطيا *qaruwāṭiyā* Croatia

قرواطى *qaruwāṭī* Croatian

قروى see قرى

قرى *qarā i* (قرى *qiran*) to receive hospitably, entertain (ه s.o.) VIII = I

قرى *qiran* hospitable reception, entertainment (of a guest); meal served to a guest

قرية *qarya* pl. قرى *quran* village; hamlet; small town; rural community; القريتان *al-qaryatān* Mecca and Taif; Mecca and Medina | ام القرى *umm al-qurā* Mecca

قروى *qarawī* village-, country- (in compounds), rustic, rural; peasant (adj.); (pl. قرويون *qarawiyūn*) villager, rustic, countryman, inhabitant of the country; from Kairouan, Kairouan (adj.), an inhabitant of Kairouan; a member of al Qarawiya College in Fès (Morocco) | جامع القرويين mosque and college in Fès (Morocco); وزارة الشؤون البلدية والقروية (*baladīya*) Ministry of Municipal and Rural Affairs (*Eg.*)

قروية *qarawīya* countrywoman, peasant woman

قرية *qarīya* pl. قرايا *qarāyā* yard (*naut.*)

مقرى *miqran* very hospitable

مقراء *miqrā'* very hospitable

قار *qārin* villager

قريدس *quraidis* (*syr.*) shrimp (*zool.*)

قز *qazza* (1st pers. perf. *qazaztu*) *u* to loathe, detest (عن or ه, ه s.o., s.th.) II to vitrify (ه s.th.); to glaze (ه s.th.) V to feel disgust (عن or من at), be nauseated (عن or من by), loathe, detest, abhor (عن or من s.o., s.th.), have an aversion (عن or من to)

قز *qazz* pl. قزوز *quzūz* silk; raw silk

قزاز *qizāz* (*eg.*) glass

قزاز *qazzāz* silk merchant

قزازة *qizāza* pl. *-āt*, قزائز *qazā'iz*[2] (*eg.*) bottle

قازوزة look up alphabetically

تقزز *taqazzuz* loathing, disgust, detestation, abhorrence, aversion

قزان (Turk. *kazan*) *qazān* pl. *-āt* kettle, large boiler

قزح II to embellish (ه one's speech)

قوس قزح *qausu quzaḥin* or *qausu quzaḥa* rainbow

قزحية *quzaḥīya* iris (*anat.*)

قزع *qaza'* (coll.; n. un. ة) wind-driven, tattered clouds, scud; tuft of hair

قزعة (*eg.*) *quz'a* dwarf, midget, pygmy

قزيعة *qazī'a* tuft of hair

قزقز *qazqaza* (*eg.*) to crack (ه nuts, shells)

قزل *qazal* limp(ing)

قزم *qazam* pl. اقزام *aqzām* dwarf, midget, pygmy; Lilliputian; little fellow, shrimp, hop-o'-my-thumb, whippersnapper

قزموغرافيا *quzmūğrāfiyā* cosmography

قزموغرافى *quzmūğrāfī* cosmographic(al)

قزان look up alphabetically

بحر قزوين *baḥr qazwīn* Caspian Sea

قس **qaṣṣa** u (qaṣṣ) to seek, pursue (ه s.th.), strive (ه for), aspire (ه to) V do.

قس **qass, qiss** pl. قسوس **qusūs**, قسس **qusus** priest, presbyter, clergyman, minister, parson, vicar, curate, pastor (Chr.); — **qass** (= قص) sternum, breastbone

قساس **qassās** slanderer

قسيس **qissīs** pl. -ūn, قساوسة **qasāwisa**, قسان **qussān**, اقسة **aqissa**, (Copt.-Chr.) قساء **qussā'** priest, presbyter, clergyman, minister, parson, vicar, curate, pastor (Chr.)

قسوسة **qusūsa** ministry, priesthood, presbyterate (Chr.)

رسامة قسوسية **risāma qusūsīya** ordination (of a priest; Chr.)

قسر **qasara** i (qasr) to force, compel, coerce, constrain (ه على s.o. to do s.th.); to conquer, subdue, subjugate (ه, ه s.o., s.th.) **VIII** = **I**

قسر **qasr** force, compulsion, coercion, constraint; قسرا **qasran** compulsorily, forcibly, by force; of necessity, necessarily, inevitably, perforce

اقتسار **iqtisār** conquest, subdual, subjugation

قسط **II** to distribute (ه s.th.); to pay in installments (ه s.th.) **IV** to act justly, in fairness, equitably

قسط **qisṭ** justice, fairness, equity, equitableness, fair-mindedness, rightness, correctness; (for sg. and pl.) just, fair, equitable, fair-minded, right, correct; — (pl. اقساط **aqsāṭ**) part; share, allotment; portion; installment; quantity, amount, measure, extent | على اقساط by installments, gradually; كان على قسط كبير من to possess s.th. (a quality, a characteristic) to a large extent, have a great deal of ...

قسط **qasaṭ** stiffness of a joint, ankylosis (med.)

اقسط **aqsaṭ**[2] juster, fairer; more correct

تقسيط **taqsīṭ** payment in installments | بالتقسيط in installments, gradually

مقسط **muqsiṭ** acting justly or with fairness, doing right; just, fair

قسطر **qaṣṭara** to test the genuineness (ه of coins)

قسطاس **qusṭās, qisṭās** pl. قساطيس **qasāṭīs**[2] balance, scales

[1]قسطل **qasṭal** pl. قساطل **qasāṭil**[2] water pipe, water main

[2]قسطل **qasṭal** (eg.) chestnut

[3]بلاد القساطلة **bilād al-qasāṭila** Castile, Spain

القسطنطينية **al-qusṭanṭīnīya** Constantinople

قسم **qasama** i (qasm) to divide, part, split (ه s.th.); to distribute, deal out, parcel out (ه على s.th. to, among), divide (ه على s.th. among); to let s.o. (ل) share (ف s.th.), give s.o. (ل) a share of s.th. (ف), allot (ل ف to s.o. s.th.); to divide, subdivide, partition, portion, break up (ه الى s.th. into), arrange, classify (ه الى s.th. in); to partition, to compartment (ه s.th.); to assign, apportion, decree, destine, foreordain (ه على or ل to s.o. s.th.; of God or of fate); to divide (ه على a number by another) **II** to divide, part, split (ه s.th.); to distribute, deal out, parcel out, divide (ه بين s.th. among); to divide, subdivide, partition, portion, break up (ه s.th., ه or الى into), section (ه s.th.), arrange, classify (ه s.th., ه or الى in); to partition, to compartment (ه s.th.); (Chr.) to consecrate, ordain (ه s.o.); to exorcise a devil or demon (على from s.o., by adjuration) **III** to share (ه ه with s.o. s.th.); to bind o.s. by oath (ه على to s.o. to do s.th.) **IV** to take an oath, swear (ب by; ل على to s.o. s.th.; على ان to do s.th.) | اقسم عليه الا فعله (illā fa'alahū) to adjure or entreat s.o. to do s.th.; اقسموا جهد ايمانهم (jahda aimānihim) they swore by all that is right and holy, they swore the most solemn oaths; اقسم بمقدساته (*muqaddasātihī*) to swear by all that's holy **V** to be divided, be parted, be split; to be distributed, be parceled out; to share (ه, ‍ه a possession), divide among themselves (ه s.o., ‍ه s.th.); to scatter, disperse (‍ه s.th.); to drive away, dispel (‍ه s.th.); to beset grievously, harass or torment jointly (ه s.o.) | تقسموه ضربا وجيعا (*ḍarban*) they took turns in dealing him painful blows, they gave him a severe beating **VI** to divide or distribute among themselves (‍ه s.th.); to beset, harass, torment (ه s.o.; thoughts, worries, etc.) **VII** to be divided, be parted, be split; to be distributed, be dispersed, be separated; to be divided, be subdivided, be portioned, be broken up (الى into) **VIII** to divide or distribute among themselves (‍ه s.th.) **X** to seek an oracle from the deity, cast lots

قسم **qism** pl. اقسام *aqsām* part, share, allotment; portion; division, compartment; section; department; group, class; district, precinct; police precinct, police station (*Eg.*); administrative subdivision of a *muḥāfaẓa* (*Eg.*); subcommittee; kind, sort, specimen, species

قسمة **qisma** dividing, division, distribution, allotment, apportionment; (*math.*) division (على by); (pl. قسم *qisam*) part, portion, share, allotment; lot, destiny, fate (foreordained by God)

قسم **qasam** pl. اقسام *aqsām* oath; قسما *qasaman* I swear! قسما ب I swear by ...!

قسمات **qasamāt, qasimāt** features, lineaments (of the face)

قسام **qasām** and قسامة **qasāma** beauty, elegance

قسيم **qasīm** pl. قسماء *qusamā'*[2], اقسماء *aqsimā'*[2] sharer, partner, copartner, participant; — (pl. اقسماء *aqsimā'*[2]) part, portion, share, allotment; counterpart

قسيمة **qasīma** pl. قسائم *qasā'im*[2] coupon; receipt

تقسيم **taqsīm** exorcism; (pl. *-āt*) dividing, division, partition, parting, splitting, sectioning, portioning; distribution, allotment, apportionment; dealing out; division, subdivision, partition(ment); pl. تقاسيم *taqāsīm*[2] structure, build, proportions (e.g., of the body); — solo recital (*mus.*)

تقسيمة **taqsīma** pl. تقاسيم *taqāsīm*[2] short solo piece for an instrument (*mus.*)

مقاسمة **muqāsama** partnership, participation, sharing

انقسام **inqisām** division, split, disruption, breakup; schism

اقتسام **iqtisām** dividing, division, distribution (among themselves)

قاسم **qāsim** divider; distributor; divisor, denominator (*math.*)

مقسوم **maqsūm** dividend (*math.*); مقسوم عليه divisor (*math.*)

مقسم **muqassim** divider; distributor

مقاسم **muqāsim** sharer, partner, copartner, participant

قسنطينة **qusanṭīna**[2] Constantine (city in NE Algeria)

(قسو) قسا **qasā** u (قسوة *qaswa*, قساوة *qasāwa*) to be harsh, stern, cruel, merciless, remorseless (على toward s.o.); to handle roughly, treat harshly, severely, cruelly, without mercy (على s.o.) **II** to harden, indurate, render obdurate or impenitent (‍ه the heart) **III** to undergo, suffer, endure, sustain, bear, stand (‍ه s.th.), bear up (‍ه against s.th.) **IV** = **II**

قسو **qasw** hardness, harshness, grimness, sternness, severity, rigor, austerity

قسوة **qaswa** hardness, harshness, grimness, sternness, severity, rigor, austerity; cruelty, mercilessness, remorselessness

قساوة *qasāwa* hardness, harshness, grimness, sternness, severity, rigor, austerity; cruelty, mercilessness, remorselessness

قسى *qasīy* hard, solid, firm

اقسى *aqsā* harder, harsher, sterner, severer; more cruel; more difficult

مقاساة *muqāsāh* undergoing, suffering, enduring, sustaining, bearing, standing

قاس *qāsin* pl. قساة *qusāh* hard, harsh, grim, stern, severe, austere, rough; cruel, inexorable, relentless, merciless, remorseless; difficult

قسى[1] *qasīy* see قسو

قسى[2] *qusīy, qisīy* pl. of قوس *qaus*

قش *qašša i u* (*qašš*) to collect, gather (up), pick up (ه s.th.); to pick up from here and there (ه s.th.); to become dry, dry up, shrivel up, wither (esp., of a plant) II to take of this and that

قش *qašš* straw | قش الحديد steel wool; حمى القش *ḥummā l-q.* hay fever

قشة *qašša* (n. un.) a straw | قشة ثقاب match, matchstick; خيار قشة (*eg.*) gherkins

قشيش *qašīš* sweepings, rubbish, garbage, trash, refuse; offal, waste, scrap

مقشة *miqašša* (*eg.*) broom, besom

قشب *qišb, qašab* pl. اقشاب *aqšāb* poison

قشيب *qašīb* pl. قشب *qušub* new; clean; polished, burnished

قشد *qašada u* (*qašd*) to skim, take off (ه the cream)

قشدة *qišda* cream

قشر *qašara i u* (*qašr*) to peel, pare, shell, derind, bark, skin, scale, shave off, husk, shuck (ه s.th.) II = I; V to be peeled, be pared, be shelled, be derinded, be barked, be skinned, be scaled, be shaved off, be husked, be shucked; to come off in scales, scale off, flake off, peel off (skin; coating) VII = V

قشر *qišr* pl. قشور *qušūr* cover(ing), integument, envelope; shell; peel; rind, bark; skin, crust; scab; scurf; hull, husk, shuck; scales (of fish); slough (of a snake); pl. قشور trash, garbage, refuse; trivialities, banalities; externals, superficialities, formalities; dandruff | قشر الرأس *q. ar-ra'๋s* dandruff

قشرة *qišra* peel, rind (e.g., of a fruit), shell (of an egg, of a nut); bark; skin; crust; scab; scurf; hull, husk, shuck; scale; slough (of a snake)

قشرى *qišrī* scaly, scurfy, scabrous, squamous; crustaceous | الاكزيما القشرية psoriasis (*med.*); ○ الحيوانات القشرية (*ḥayawānāt*) crustaceans

تقشير *taqšīr* peeling, paring, shelling; derinding, barking; skinning; scaling; shaving off, scraping off; husking, shucking

قشط *qašaṭa i* (*qašṭ*) to take off, strip (off), remove (ه عن s.th. from); to skim (ه cream); to scratch off, scrape off, abrade (ه s.th.) II to take off (ه s.th.); to strip off (ه s.th.); to rob (ه ,ه s.o., s.th.), plunder, strip of his belongings (ه s.o.)

قشطة (*eg.*) *qišṭa*, (*syr.*) *qašṭa* cream; (*eg.*) sweetsop (Annona squamosa L.; *bot.*), custard apple

قشاط *qišāṭ* (leather) strap, thong; whiplash; drive belt, transmission belt

قشاط *qušāṭ* (*eg.*) pl. *-āt* jetton, chip, counter; piece, man (checkers, backgammon)

○ مقشط *miqšaṭ* pl. مقاشط *maqāšiṭ*[2] eraser, erasing knife

○ مقشطة *miqšaṭa* pl. مقاشط *maqāšiṭ*[2] milling machine, miller

قشع *qaša'a a* (*qaš'*) to scatter, disperse, drive away, chase away (ه, ه s.o., s.th.), dispel (ه s.th.) **IV** to scatter, disperse, drive away, chase away (ه, ه s.o., s.th.), dispel (ه s.th.); to scatter, disperse, break up (crowd), lift, dissolve (clouds, darkness) **V** and **VII** to be scattered, be dispersed, be driven away, be chased away; to scatter, disperse, break up (crowd), lift, dissolve (clouds, darkness)

(قشعر) **IV** اقشعر *iqša'arra* to shudder, shiver, tremble, quake, shake, have goose flesh (with cold, with fright) | شيء تقشعر منه الجلود (الابدان or) *šai'un taqša'irru minhu l-julūdu* a bloodcurdling thing, a horrible, ghastly thing

قشعريرة *quša'rīra* shudder, tremor, trembling, shakes; shiver(ing); ague

قشعم *qaš'am* pl. قشاعم *qašā'im*² lion | ام قشعم *umm q.* hyena; calamity, disaster

قشف *qašifa a* (*qašaf*) and *qašufa u* (قشافة *qašāfa*) to live in squalor and misery; to have a dirty skin; to pay no attention to cleanliness **II** (*eg.*) to become rough and chapped, to chap (hands) **V** = **I**; to lead an ascetic life, mortify the bodily appetites; (*eg.*) to become rough and chapped, to chap (skin)

قشفة *qišfa* (*eg.*) pl. قشف *qišaf* crust (of bread)

تقشف *taqaššuf* asceticism, mortification of the flesh; simple, primitive way of life

متقشف *mutaqaššif* ascetic(al): (*eg.*) roughened, chapped (hands); المتقشفة *al-mutaqaššifa* the ascetics

قشقش *qašqaša* to cure (ه من s.o. of scabies, of smallpox); to sweep out, sweep away (ه s.th.)

¹قشل *qašila* (*qašal*) (*eg.*) to be poor, penniless, without means

²قشلة (Turk. *kışla*) *qašla* pl. قشل *qišal* (military) barracks (*syr.*); hospital (*eg.*)

قشلاق (Turk. *kışlak*) *qušlāq* pl. *-āt* (military) barracks

قشمش *qismiš* a variety of currants (= seedless raisins)

قاشانى look up alphabetically

قص *qaṣṣa u* (*qaṣṣ*) to cut, cut off, clip (ه s.th.); to shear, shear off (ه s.th.); to trim, curtail, dock, crop, lop (ه s.th.); — (*qaṣṣ*, قصص *qaṣaṣ*): قص أثره (*aṯarahū*) to follow s.o.'s tracks, track s.o.; — (قصص *qaṣaṣ*) to relate, narrate, tell (ه على to s.o. s.th.) **II** to cut off, shear off, clip, curtail, dock, trim, crop, lop (ه s.th.) **III** to retaliate (ه upon s.o.), return like for like (ه to s.o.); to avenge o.s., revenge o.s., take vengeance (ه on s.o.); to punish, castigate, chastise (ه s.o.); (*com.*) to settle accounts (ه with s.o.); to be quits, be even (ه with s.o.) **V** تقصص أثره (*aṯarahū*) to follow s.o.'s tracks, track s.o. **VIII** = **V**; to tell accurately, relate exactly (ه s.th.); to retaliate (من upon s.o.), return like for like (من to s.o.); to avenge o.s., revenge o.s., take vengeance (من on s.o.); to punish, castigate, chastise (من s.o.)

قص *qaṣṣ* clippings, cuttings, chips, snips, shreds, scraps; sternum, breastbone

قصة *quṣṣa* pl. قصص *quṣaṣ*, قصاص *qiṣāṣ* forelock; lock of hair

قصة *qiṣṣa* manner of cutting; cut; (pl. قصص *qiṣaṣ*) narrative, tale, story | قصة هذا الشيء ان the matter is so that ..., the thing is best described by saying that ...

قصص *qaṣaṣ* clippings, cuttings, chips, snips, shreds; narrative, tale, story

قصصى *qiṣaṣī*, *qaṣaṣī* narrative, epic(al); (pl. قصصيون) storyteller, writer of fiction, novelist, romancer | الشعر القصصى (*ši'r*) epic poetry

قصاصة *quṣāṣa* (coll. قصاص *quṣāṣ* and قصاصة *quṣāṣa*) pl. *-āt* cutting, chip, snip, shred; scrap (of paper); slip (of paper); (newspaper) clipping

قصاص *qaṣṣāṣ* shearer; tracker, tracer of tracks; writer of fiction, novelist, romancer

اقصوصة *uqṣūṣa* pl. اقاصيص *aqāṣīṣ*[2] narrative, tale, novella, novel; short story

مقص *miqaṣṣ* pl. مقاص *maqāṣṣ*[2] (pair of) scissors, (pair of) shears; (*syr.*) springs (of an automobile, of a coach) | ابو مقص *abū m.* earwig; skimmer, scissorbill (Rhynchops; *zool.*)

قصاص *qiṣāṣ* requital, reprisal, retaliation; punishment, castigation, chastisement; accounting, clearing, settlement of accounts

مقاصة *muqāṣṣa* accounting, clearing, settlement of accounts; balancing, adjustment, setoff; compensation (*com.*) | غرفة المقاصة *ḡurfat al-m.* clearing house (*fin.*)

مقصوص *maqṣūṣ* pl. مقاصيص *maqaṣīṣ*[2] (*eg.*) lovelock, earlock

مقصوصة *maqṣūṣa* skimming ladle, skimmer

قصاج *quṣāj* pl. *-āt* pliers, pincers, nippers

قصب *qaṣaba i* (*qaṣb*) to cut up, carve up (ه a slaughtered animal) **II** to curl (ه the hair); to brocade, embroider with gold and silver thread (ه s.th.)

قصب *qaṣab* (coll.) cane(s), reed(s); sugar cane; stalks (of cereal grasses); gold and silver thread, gold and silver embroidery; brocade | قصب الذهب *q. aḏ-ḏahab* gold brocade; قصب السكر *q. as-sukkar* sugar cane; القصب الهندى (*hindī*) bamboo; احرز قصب السبق (والغلب) *aḥraza qaṣaba s-sabq* (*wa-l-ḡalb*) to come through with flying colors, carry the day, score a great success

قصبة *qaṣaba* (n. un.) pl. *-āt* cane, reed; pipe, tube; pipestem, pipe tube; writing pen; windpipe, trachea; shaft (of a well); a wind instrument resembling the reed pipe; kassabah, a linear measure (*Eg.* = 3.55 m); citadel; capital city, metropolis | قصبة الرئة *q. ar-ri'a* windpipe, trachea; قصبة المرىء *q. al-marī'* gullet, esophagus

قصابة *qiṣāba* butcher's trade, butchery

قصيبة *quṣaiba* (*tun.*) oats

قصاب *qaṣṣāb* butcher, slaughterer; (*eg.*) land surveyor

قصابة *quṣṣāba* (reed) pipe

مقصب *muqaṣṣab* embroidered with gold and silver thread, brocaded, trimmed with brocade

قصاج look up alphabetically

قصد *qaṣada i* (*qaṣd*) to go or proceed straightaway (الى or ه, ه to s.o., to s.th.), make a beeline (الى or ه, ه for), walk up to s.o. or s.th. (الى or ه, ه); to go to see (الى, ه s.o.), call (الى, ه on s.o.); to betake o.s., repair, go (الى, ه to a place; الى, ه to s.o.), be headed, be bound (الى, ه for a place); to seek, pursue (الى, ه s.th.), strive (الى, ه for), aspire (الى, ه to), intend, have in mind (الى, ه s.th.; ه ب or من s.th. with s.th. else); to aim (الى, ه at s.th.); to have in view, contemplate, consider, purpose (ه s.th.); to mean, try to say (ه ب or من by s.th. s.th.); to adopt a middle course (فى in, at); to be economical, frugal, thrifty, provident; to economize, save | قصد قصده (*qaṣdahū*) to walk up to s.o., go toward s.o.; to follow, imitate s.o. **IV** to induce to go (الى to s.o., to a place; ه s.o.); to compose kasidas **V** to be broken, break; (*eg.*) to be angry (ه with s.o.), be mad (ه at s.o.) **VII** to be broken, break **VIII** to adopt a middle course (فى in, at; بين between); to assume a mediatory position (بين between), act as mediator; to be economical, frugal, thrifty, provident, economize (ﻓﻰ with); to save (ه money, etc.); to compose kasidas

قصد *qaṣd* endeavor, aspiration, intention, intent; design, purpose, resolution; object, goal, aim, end; frugality; thrift, economy | قصدا *qaṣdan*, عن قصد intentionally, purposely, advisedly, on purpose; deliberately; عن غير قصد unintentionally, inadvertently; حسن القصد *ḥusn al-q.* good intention; سوء القصد *sū' al-q.* evil intention هو قصدك (*qaṣdaka, qaṣduka*) he is in front of you, before you, opposite you

قصدى *qaṣdī* intentional; intended

قصاد *quṣād* (prep.) in front of, before, opposite (*eg.*)

قصيد *qaṣīd* aspired, desired, aimed at, intended; faultless, without defects (of a poem); also = قصيدة | بيت القصيد *bait al-q.* (the essential, principal verse of the kasida, i.e.) the main point, the principal part, the essence, the core, the gist, the best, the hit, the climax of s.th., that which stands out from the rest, the right thing

قصيدة *qaṣīda* pl. قصائد *qaṣā'id*² kasida, an ancient Arabic poem having, as a rule, a rigid tripartite structure | بيت القصيدة = بيت القصيد, see under قصيد

اقصد *aqṣad*² directer, directest

مقصد *maqṣid* pl. مقاصد *maqāṣid*² (place of) destination; intention, intent; design, purpose, resolution; object, goal, aim, end; sense, meaning, import, purport, significance | سيئ المقاصد *sayyi' al-m.* malevolent, malicious

اقتصاد *iqtiṣād* saving, economization, retrenchment; thriftiness, thrift, providence; economy | علم الاقتصاد *'ilm al-iqt.*, (علم) الاقتصاد السياسى (*siyāsī*) economics, political economy; اقتصادا فى الوقت *iqtiṣādan fī l-waqt* in order to save time

اقتصادى *iqtiṣādī* economical; saving, thrifty, provident; economic; economist, political economist; الاقتصاديات the economy

قاصد *qāṣid* direct, straight (way); easy, smooth, pleasant, short (of travel) | قاصد رسولى (*rasūlī*) (pl. قصاد *quṣṣād*) apostolic delegate

قصادة رسولية *qiṣāda rasūlīya* papal legation

مقصود *maqṣūd* aimed at, intended; intentional, designed, deliberate; meant

قصدير *qaṣdīr* tin

قصر[1] *qaṣura u* (*qiṣar, qaṣr,* قصارة *qaṣāra*) to be or become short, too short, or shorter; to be insufficient, be inadequate; — *qaṣara u* (قصور *quṣūr*) to miss, fail to reach (عن s.th., e.g., a target), fall short (عن of); to be incapable (عن of), be unable (عن to do s.th.), fail to reach, attain, accomplish, or achieve (عن s.th.); not to be equal (عن to s.th.), not to be up to s.th. (عن), be unable to cope with s.th. (عن); to desist, cease, refrain, abstain (عن from); — *qaṣara i u* (*qaṣr*) to make short or shorter, shorten, cut short, curtail, abridge, reduce, lessen (ه s.th.); — *qaṣara u* (*qaṣr*) to hold back, restrain, check, curb (ه ,ه s.o., s.th.); to keep under supervision or control (ه ,ه s.o., s.th.); to lock up (ه ,ه s.o., s.th.); to limit, restrict, confine (على ه ,ه s.o., s.th. to); — *qaṣara u* (*qaṣr,* قصارة *qiṣāra*) to full, whiten, bleach, blanch (ه s.th.) II to make short or shorter, shorten, cut short, curtail, abridge, reduce, lessen (ه s.th.); to miss, fail to reach (عن s.th., e.g., a target), fall short (عن of); to be incapable (عن of), be unable (عن to do s.th.); to fail to accomplish, achieve, reach, or attain (عن s.th.); not to be equal (عن to s.th.), not to be up to s.th. (عن), be unable to cope with s.th. (عن); to be inadequate, insufficient, inferior; to be remiss (في in, at, in some work), be derelict (في to), fall behind, lag behind (في in); to be negligent, careless; to be lax, negligent, neglectful (في in), neglect (في s.th.); to desist, cease, refrain, abstain (عن from) | لم يقصر في he spared no pains or expense in or with ..., he left nothing undone to ..., he did not fail to ... IV to make short or shorter, shorten, cut short, curtail, abridge, reduce, lessen (ه s.th.); to desist, cease, refrain, abstain (عن from) VI to contract, shrink, dwindle, become smaller; to be incapable (عن of); to desist, cease (عن from); to refrain, abstain (عن from) VIII to limit o.s., restrict o.s., confine o.s., be limited, restricted, or confined (على to); to content o.s., be content (على with) X to find short, regard as deficient or inadequate (ه s.th.)

قصر *qaṣr* shortness, brevity; smallness; incapability, inability; insufficiency, inadequacy; laxity, slackness, negligence, neglectfulness; indolence, inertness, laziness; shortening, curtailment, abridgment, reduction, diminution; limitation, restriction, confinement (على to); the utmost that is in s.o.'s power, e.g., قصرك ان تفعل هذا (*qaṣruka*) the most you can hope to accomplish is to do this; you must limit yourself to doing this

قصر *qaṣr* pl. قصور *quṣūr* castle; palace; palais | قصر العدلية *q. al-'adlīya* (*Mor.*) palace of justice, courthouse

قصرية *qaṣrīya* pl. قصار *qaṣārin* pot; flowerpot; chamber pot

قصر *qiṣar* shortness, brevity; smallness | قصر النظر *q. an-naẓar* nearsightedness, shortsightedness

قصر *qaṣar* slackness, laxity, negligence, neglectfulness; indolence, inertness, laziness

قصار *qaṣār, quṣār*: قصارك ان تفعل هذا = قصاراك ان تفعل هذا (see قصارى)

قصار *qaṣṣār* fuller, bleacher

قصور *quṣūr* incapability, inability; insufficiency, inadequacy; deficiency, shortcoming, lack; reduction, diminution, decrease; slackness, laxity, negligence, neglectfulness; indolence, inertness, laziness; legal minority, nonage | قصور الباع powerlessness, impotence, helplessness, weakness, incapability, inability (عن of, to do s.th.)

قصير *qaṣīr* pl. قصار *qiṣār* short; small, short (of stature), low | قصير الاجل *q. al-ajal* short-term(ed), short-dated, short-lived; قصير الباع powerless, impotent, helpless, weak, incapable, unable; parsimonious, niggardly; قصير اليد *q. al-yad* do.

قصارة *qiṣāra* trade of the fuller or bleacher

قصارى *quṣārā* the utmost, the limit (o) s.o.'s power) | قصاراك ان تفعل هذا (*quṣārāka*) the most you can accomplish is to do this; you must limit yourself to doing this; بذل قصارى الجهد or بذل قصاراه (*q. l-jahd*) to exert every conceivable effort (ل to, in order to; ب on, for), go to great lengths, go out of one's way, do one's best, do all in one's power, leave no stone unturned (ل to, in order to); قصارى الامر *q. l-amr*, قصارى القول *q. l-qaul* in short, in brief, to make a long story short

اقصر *aqṣar*[2] shorter

الاقصر *al-aqṣur* Luxor (town in Upper Egypt)

تقصير *taqṣīr* shortening, curtailment, abridgment, reduction, diminution, limitation, restriction, confinement; incapability, incapacity, inability; insufficiency, inadequacy, inferiority; neglect, dereliction (في of), remissness (في in); slackness, laxity, negligence, neglectfulness; defect, fault, failing, deficiency, shortcoming

قاصر *qāṣir* incapable (عن of), unable (عن to do s.th.); limited, restricted, confined (على to); reserved (على for); intransitive (*gram.*); (pl. *-ūn*, قصر *quṣṣar*) legally minor, under age; a legal minor | قاصرة الطرف *q. aṭ-ṭarf* (of a woman) chaste-eyed, chaste, demure, modest; قاصر اليد *q. al-yad* powerless, impotent, helpless, weak, incapable, unable; parsimonious, niggardly

مقصور *maqṣūr* confined (على to); restricted, limited | مقصورة الطرف *m. aṭ-ṭarf* (woman) chaste-eyed, chaste, demure, modest; الف مقصورة (*alif*) the alif that can be shortened, i.e., final ى, pronounced *-ā* (e.g., رمى *ramā*) and ا, without following hamza (*gram.*)

مقصورة *maqṣūra* pl. *-āt*, مقاصير *maqāṣīr*[2] palace; cabinet, closet; compartment; box or stall in a mosque near the mihrab, reserved for the ruler; (theater, cinema) box, loge; the detached portion of a mosque set aside for the communal prayer, and frequently enclosing the tomb of the patron saint; (prisoner's) dock; chapel (in a church)

مقصر *muqaṣṣir* slack, negligent, neglectful

مقتصر *muqtaṣir* limited, restricted, confined (على to)

مقتصر *muqtaṣar* short, brief, concise, terse, succinct, summary

قيصر[2] look up alphabetically

قصع *qaṣaʿa a* (*qaṣʿ*) to drink in avid gulps, gulp down, pour down, toss down (ه water); to slake, quench (ه the thirst); to grind, crush, bruise, squash, mash (ه (s.th.)

قصعة *qaṣʿa* pl. *qaṣaʿāt*, قصع *qiṣaʿ*, قصاع *qiṣāʿ* large bowl (made of wood or copper); (*ir.*) kettle

قصف *qaṣafa i* (*qaṣf*) to break, shatter, smash (ه s.th.); to beset, harass, press hard, oppress (ه s.o.), bear down (ه upon s.o.); to bomb (ه s.th.); to thunder, roar (esp., of cannon); to roll, rumble, grumble, peal (of thunder); — *u* (*qaṣf*, قصوف *quṣūf*) to feast, revel, carouse; to lead a life of opulence; — *qaṣifa a* (*qaṣaf*) to break; to be frail, delicate, brittle, fragile V and VII to be broken, break, snap

قصف *qaṣf* thunder, roar (e.g., of cannon); revelry, carousal

قصف *qaṣif* frail, delicate, brittle, fragile; broken

قصيف *qaṣīf* frail, delicate, brittle, fragile; broken

قصوف *quṣūf* revelry, carousal

مقصف *maqṣaf* pl. مقاصف *maqāṣif*[2] refreshment room; post exchange, canteen; casino; bar; buffet, refreshment counter

قصقص *qaṣqaṣa* to break, shatter (ه s.th.); (*eg.*) to snip off the ends (ه of s.th.), clip, trim, crop (ه s.th.)

قصل *qaṣala i* (*qaṣl*) to cut off, mow (off) (ه s.th.) VIII to cut off (ه s.th.)

قصل *qaṣal* chaff, husks, shucks, awns (of grain); (n. un. ة) stalks

قصال *qaṣṣāl* sharp, cutting, sharp-pointed

قصيل *qaṣīl* (*eg.*) winter barley

مقصل *miqṣal* sharp, cutting, sharp-pointed

○ مقصلة *miqṣala* pl. *-āt*, مقاصل *maqāṣil*[2] guillotine

قاصل *qāṣil* sharp, cutting

قصم *qaṣama i* (*qaṣm*) to break, shatter (ه s.th.) | قصم ظهره (*ẓahrahū*) (to break s.o.'s back =) to be a mortal blow to s.o. V to be broken, break, snap VII = V

قصم *qaṣim* easily broken, brittle, fragile

قصيم *qaṣīm* easily broken, brittle, fragile

قاصم *qāṣim* pl. قواصم *qawāṣim*² breaking | قاصمة الظهر *qāṣimat aẓ-ẓahr* mortal blow, catastrophe, disaster; ضربات قواصم (*ḍarabāt*) mortal blows, crushing blows

قصا (قصو and قصى) قصا *qaṣā u* (قصو *qaṣw*, *quṣūw*, قصاء *qaṣā'*) and قصى *qaṣiya a* (قصى ,قصا *qaṣan*) to be far away, be far removed, be at a great distance (عن from), be remote, distant; to go far away (عن from) IV to take far away, send far away (عن ه, ه s.o., s.th. from); to remove (عن ه s.o. from); to drive away (عن ه s.o. from); to drag away (عن ه s.o. from); to dismiss (ه s.o., عن الخدمة from a job); to reach the utmost limit (ه of s.th.) | لا يقصيه البصر *lā yuqṣīhi l-baṣaru* out of sight, not within view, invisible V to go far away (عن from); to penetrate deeply, inquire (ه into a problem, and the like), examine, study, investigate (ه s.th.), go to the root (ه of s.th.); to follow out, follow to a conclusion (ه s.th.); to examine, feel out, palpate (ه s.th.) X to penetrate deeply, inquire (ه into a problem, and the like), examine, study, investigate (ه s.th.), go to the root (ه of s.th.); to inquire, make inquiries (عن about)

قصا *qaṣan* and قصاء *qaṣā'* distance, remoteness

قصى *qaṣīy* pl. اقصاء *aqṣā'* far (away), distant, remote

اقصى *aqṣā*, f. قصوى *quṣwā*, pl. اقاص *aqāṣin* more distant, remoter, farther (away); most distant, remotest, farthest; utmost, extreme, ultimate; maximal, maximum; the farthermost part; the utmost, extreme, extremity; end | المسجد الاقصى (*masjid*) name of a mosque on the Temple Square in Jerusalem; الشرق الاقصى (*šarq*) the Far East; المغرب الاقصى (*maḡrib*) (the extreme west =) Morocco; الغاية القصوى من the utmost degree of, the maximum of; اقاصى الارض *aqāṣī l-arḍ* the remotest parts of the earth, the ends of the world; عند الضرورة القصوى (*ḍarūra*) in case of dire necessity, when worst comes to worst; الى اقصى حد *ilā aqṣā ḥaddin* to the extreme limit, to the utmost; as far as possible; من ادناه الى اقصاه or من اقصاه الى اقصاه (*adnāhu*) from one end to the other, throughout, everything without exception

تقص *taqaṣṣin* thorough examination, close study, minute investigation

استقصاء *istiqṣā'* thorough examination, close study, minute investigation; inquiry (عن about)

قاص *qāṣin* pl. قاصون *qāṣūn*, اقصاء *aqṣā'* distant, remote, far (away) | القاصى والدانى (lit.: the distant one and the near one =) everybody, all people; فى القاصية والدانية near and far

قض *qaḍḍa u* (*qaḍḍ*) to pierce, bore, perforate (ه s.th.); to break into pieces, crush, bray, bruise, pulverize (ه s.th.); to tear down, demolish (ه a wall); to pull out, tear out (ه a peg or stake); — *a* (قضض *qaḍaḍ*) to be rough, crude, hard (bed) IV to be rough, crude, hard (bed); to make rough, crude or hard (ه the bed) | اقض عليه المضجع (*maḍja'ahū*) or اقض مضجعه to rob s.o.'s sleep VII to swoop down, pounce down, dive down, descend; to strike (على s.th.; of lightning); to pounce, fall, rush, hurl o.s. (على upon), storm, rush (على against), charge, attack, assail (على s.o.); to be broken, cracked, threaten to collapse; to fall, tumble

قض *qaḍḍ* (coll.) pebbles; gravel | جاء القوم قضهم _ *jā'a l-qaumu qaḍḍuhum* (*qaḍḍahum*) all the people came

قضة *qiḍḍa* pebbles; gravel

قضيض qaḍīḍ pebbles; gravel | جاء القوم (qaum) all the people (or) قضيضهم (قضيضهم came

انقضاض inqiḍāḍ swooping down, pouncing down, dive, downrush; onrush, onslaught, storm, assault | مدفع الانقضاض midfaʿ al-inq. (pl. مدافع madāfiʿ) self-propelled assault gun (mil.); طائرة الانقضاض dive bomber

طائرة منقضة ṭāʾira munqaḍḍa dive bomber

قضب qaḍaba i (qaḍb) to cut off (ﻫ s.th.); to lop, prune, trim (ﻫ trees) II = I; VIII = I; to abridge (ﻫ s.th.), give a condensed extract, make a digest (ﻫ of s.th.); to extemporize, improvise (ﻫ s.th.), quote extempore (ﻫ verses, and the like), deliver offhand (ﻫ a speech)

قضب qaḍb edible herbs

قضيب qaḍīb pl. قضبان quḍbān cut-off branch, twig, switch; stick, rod, staff, wand; bar (of a grate); male organ of generation, penis, phallus; rail (railroad); guide, guide rail, guideway (techn.)

قضابة quḍāba that which is lopped or cut off; lops, prunings, trimmings (of trees)

مقضب miqḍab pruning hook; pruning shears, pruning knife

اقتضاب iqtiḍāb abridgment; digest; extract; conciseness, terseness, brevity; improvisation

مقتضب muqtaḍab short, brief, concise, terse; improvised, extemporaneous, offhand, unprepared; المقتضب name of a poetic meter; pl. مقتضبات short news items, news in brief (journ.)

قضع qaḍʿ gripes, colic

قضاع quḍāʿ gripes, colic

قضف qaḍufa u to be or become slender, slim, thin, narrow

قضم qaḍima a and qaḍama i (qaḍm) to gnaw (ﻫ s.th., on s.th.); to nibble (ﻫ s.th., at s.th.)

قضامة (pronounced qḍāme; syr.) roasted and salted chick-peas; assorted nuts, peanuts, pistachios, etc.; birdseed

الحيوانات القاضمة al-ḥayawānāt al-qāḍima the rodents

قضى qaḍā i (قضاء qaḍāʾ) to settle (ﻫ s.th.); to finish, terminate, conclude, end, close, wind up, complete, consummate, accomplish, achieve (ﻫ s.th.); to carry out, execute, perform, effectuate (ﻫ s.th.); to fulfill (ﻫ a request), comply (ﻫ with); to do, perform (ﻫ one's duty); to gratify (ﻫ a wish), provide (ﻫ for a need), satisfy, meet, answer, discharge (ﻫ a demand, a claim); to pay, settle (ﻫ a debt); to spend, pass (ﻫ time); to die (= قضى اجله); to fix, appoint, determine, decree, decide, rule (ب s.th., بأن that); (of God) to foreordain, predestine; to judge, act as judge, decide judicially (بين between two litigants); to pass or pronounce judgment (ل in favor of s.o.; على against s.o.); to sentence, condemn (ب على s.o. to), impose, inflict (ب على upon s.o. a penalty); to impose or enjoin as a duty (ب على upon s.o. s.th.); to make necessary or requisite (ب على for s.o. s.th.), require s.o. (على) to do s.th. (ب), compel, force (على s.o. ب to do s.th.); to demand, require, necessitate (ب s.th.), call for s.th. (ب); to root out, extirpate, annihilate, exterminate (على s.o., s.th.); to kill, do in (على s.o.), do away (على with s.o., with s.th.), put an end (على to s.th.); to thwart, foil, frustrate (على s.th.) | قضى اجله (ajalahū) to pass away, die; قضى العجب من (ʿajaba) to be full of amazement at, be very astonished at; قضى نحبه (naḥbahū) to fulfill one's vow; to pass away, die; قضى وطره (waṭarahū) to attain one's aim or end, see one's wish fulfilled; قضى الامر

quḍiya l-amru the matter is decided and done with, the die is cast; قضى امره *quḍiya amruhū* and قضى عليه *quḍiya ʿalaihi* it's all over with him, he's a goner **II** to carry out, execute, perform, effectuate (ه s.th.) **III** to summon before a judge, bring before a court of justice, arraign (ه s.o.); to prosecute, sue (ه s.o.), take legal action, bring suit (ه against s.o.); to demand (ه ب from s.o. payment of s.th.), call in (ه ب from s.o. s.th.) **V** to be finished, completed; to pass, go by, elapse, expire, run out (time) **VI** to litigate, carry on a lawsuit; to demand (ه s.th.; ه من or ه from s.o. payment of s.th.; from s.o. s.th.), call in (ه s.th., من or ه from s.o.), claim (ه على for s.th. remuneration), lay claim (ه to s.th.); to get, receive (ه ه from s.o. s.th., also ه من s.th. from, esp. money owed, emolument) **VII** to be completed, be finished, be done, be terminated, be concluded, come to an end, cease, stop; to pass, go by, elapse, expire, run out (time); to have expired, have elapsed, be over, be past (time) **VIII** to demand, claim, exact, require (ه ه from s.o. s.th.); to make necessary, make requisite, necessitate, require (ه s.th.) **X** to demand, claim, exact, require (ه ه from s.o. s.th.)

قضى *qaḍan* judgment, sentence, (judicial) decision, (court) ruling

قضاء *qaḍāʾ* settling, finishing, ending, closing, termination, conclusion, windup, completion, accomplishment; carrying out, execution, performance, effectuation; fulfillment, satisfaction, gratification (of a wish, of a desire); provision (for a need); compliance (with a request); payment, settlement, discharge (of a debt); passing, spending (of a period of time); divine decree, destiny, fate; judgment, sentence, (judicial) decision, (court) ruling, ordinance; administration of the law, judiciary, jurisprudence, justice; law; jurisdiction; office of judge, judgeship, judicature; judging, rendering of judgment; sentencing, condemnation (على of s.o.); extermination, annihilation, extirpation (على of s.o., of s.th.), killing (على of s.o.), thwarting, foiling frustration (على of s.th.); — (pl. اقضية *aqḍiya*) district, province (*Syr., Ir., Leb., Saudi Ar., Yemen*) | قضاء الله death; القضاء الشرعى (*šarʿī*) jurisdiction based on the Sharia; canonical law, Sharia law; دار القضاء court of justice, tribunal; محكمة القضاء الادارى *maḥkamat al-q. al-idārī* administrative court; القضاء والقدر (*wa-l-qadar*) fate and divine decree; بالقضاء والقدر (or قضاء وقدرا *qaḍāʾan wa-qadaran*) by fate and divine decree; قضى القضاء (*quḍiya*) the divine decree was fulfilled, i.e., death came with God's will

قضائى *qaḍāʾī* judicial, judicatory; forensic, legal, judiciary, pertaining to courts of justice | حارس قضائى pl. حراس قضائيون (*ḥurrās*) legally appointed trustee or administrator, receiver in bankruptcy, liquidator, sequestrator

قضوية الصلح *qaḍawīyat aṣ-ṣulḥ* jurisdiction of a justice of the peace

قضية *qaḍiya* pl. قضايا *qaḍāyā* lawsuit; litigation, judicial contest; action at law, suit; (legal) case, cause, legal affair; matter, affair; question, problem, issue; theorem, proposition (*math.*)

مقاضاة *muqāḍāh* trial, hearing

انقضاء *inqiḍāʾ* passing, elapsing, termination, expiry, expiration, end (of a period of time); extinction (of an obligation)

اقتضاء *iqtiḍāʾ* necessity, need, exigency, requirement | عند الاقتضاء in case of need, if need be, when necessary

قاض *qāḍin* decisive, conclusive; deadly, lethal; (pl. قضاة *quḍāh*) judge, magistrate, justice, cadi; pl. قواض *qawāḍin* requirements, exigencies | سم قاض (*samm*) deadly poison; ضربة قاضية (*ḍarba*) decisive blow (على against); knockout (boxing); mortal or crushing blow, deathblow (على to); رأى من قواضى الذمة ان (*q. ḏ-ḏimma*) to regard it as one's duty to …; قاضى البحث *q. l-baḥṯ* (*Tun.*) examining magistrate; قاضى التحقيق (*Eg.*) examining magistrate; قاضى الاحالة *q. l-iḥāla* (*Eg.*) magistrate sitting at defendant's arraignment, trial judge; قاضى الصلح *q. ṣ-ṣulḥ* justice of the peace

مقضى *maqḍīy* settled, finished, done, completed, accomplished, etc. | الامر المقضى accomplished fact, fait accompli

متقاض *mutaqāḍin* pl. متقاضون *mutaqāḍūn* litigant; المتقاضيان *al-mutaqāḍiyān* the two litigants

متقاضى *mutaqāḍan* subject to legal prosecution

مقتضى *muqtaḍan* required, necessary, requisite; (pl. مقتضيات *muqtaḍayāt*) requirement, exigency, necessity, need | بمقتضى *bi-muqtaḍā* (prep.) according to, in accordance with, in conformity with, pursuant to, under; عند مقتضيات الاحوال should the circumstances require it

[1]قط *qaṭṭu* (chiefly with the past tense in negative sentences) ever, (neg.:) never

[2]قط *qaṭṭa* u (*qaṭṭ*) to carve (ه s.th.); to cut, trim, clip, pare (ه s.th.); to mend the point (ه of a pen), nib, sharpen (ه a pen) II to carve, turn (ه wood) VIII to sharpen, nib (ه a pen)

قط *qaṭṭ* short and curly (hair)

قطاط *qaṭṭāṭ* turner

[3]قط *qiṭṭ* pl. قطط *qiṭaṭ*, قطاط *qiṭāṭ*, قططة *qiṭaṭa* male cat, tomcat | قط الزباد *q. az-zabād* civet cat

قطة *qiṭṭa* female cat

قطيطة *quṭaiṭa* kitten

قطب *qaṭaba* i (*qaṭb*) to gather, collect (ه s.th.); — (*qaṭb*, قطوب *quṭūb*) to contract the eyebrows (also قطب حاجبيه *q. ḥājibaihi*), knit the brows, frown, scowl, glower | قطب جبينه (*jabīnahū*) to frown II to scowl, glower; to knit the brows, frown; (*eg.*) to sew together (ه s.th.) V to become gloomy (countenance) X ○ to polarize (ه s.th.; *phys.*)

قطب *quṭb* pl. اقطاب *aqṭāb* axis, axle; pole (*astron.*, *geogr.*, *el.*); pivot; leader; authority, leading personality, celebrity (chiefly used in the pl.) | قطب الرحى *q. ar-raḥā* pivot (of s.th.; fig.); القطب الجنوبى (*janūbī*) the South Pole; القطب الشمالى (*šamālī*) the North Pole; قطب سالب negative pole; cathode, قطب موجب (*mūjab*) positive pole, anode

قطبى *quṭbī* polar | ○ الشفق القطبى (*šafaq*) polar light

قطبة *quṭba* (*eg.*) stitch (in sewing)

قطوب *qaṭūb* frowning, scowling, glowering

○ استقطاب *istiqṭāb* polarization (*phys.*)

قاطبة *qāṭibatan* all together, all without exception, one and all

قطر *qaṭara* u (*qaṭr*, قطران *qaṭarān*) to fall or flow in drops, drip, dribble, trickle II (*qaṭr*) to let fall or flow in drops, drip, drop, dribble, infuse in drops or driblets (ه s.th.); to filter, filtrate (ه s.th.); to refine (ه s.th.); to distill (ه s.th.); to line up camels (ه) in single file and connect them with halters, form a train of camels; to couple (ه vehicles); to tow, tug (ه a ship) V to fall or flow in drops, drip, dribble, trickle; to soak, percolate (الى into), trickle (الى in) VI to come in successive groups, to crowd, throng, flock (الى or على to s.o., to a place) X to drip, drop, dribble (ه s.th.); to distill, extract by distillation (ه s.th.)

قطر *qaṭr* dripping, dribbling, dribble, trickling, trickle; (coll.; n. un. ة) pl. قطار *qiṭār* drops, driblets; rain; — sirup

قطر *qaṭr* pl. قطورات *quṭūrāt* (*eg.*) (railroad) train

قطرجى (*eg.*) *qaṭargī* pl. *-īya* shunter, switchman (railroad)

قطر *quṭr* pl. اقطار *aqṭār* region, quarter; district, section; tract of land; zone; country, land; diameter (of a circle); diagonal; caliber, bore (of a tube) | القطر المصرى (*miṣrī*) Egypt; نصف قطر الدائرة *niṣf q. ad-d.* radius (of the circle); اربعة اقطار الدنيا *arba'at a. ad-dunyā* the four quarters of the world; الروعة التى تأخذنى من جميع اقطارى (*rau'a*) the rapture which holds me completely enthralled, which pervades my heart through and through

قطرى *quṭrī* regional; diametral, diametrical

قطر *qaṭar*² Qatar (sheikdom in eastern Arabia)

قطر *quṭr*, *quṭur* agalloch, aloeswood

قطرة *qaṭra* (n. un. of قطر *qaṭr*) pl. *qaṭarāt* drop (also as a medicine)

قطيرة *quṭaira* pl. *-āt* droplet, driblet

قطار *qiṭār* pl. *-āt*, قطر *quṭur*, قطرات *quṭurāt* train of camels; (railroad) train; railroad; single file (of soldiers; *Eg.*, *mil.*) | قطار البضاعة freight train, goods train; قطار حديدى (*ḥadīdī*) railroad train; قطار خاص (خصوص or خصوصى) (*kāṣṣ*, *kuṣūṣī*) special train; قطار الركاب *q. ar-rukkāb* passenger train; قطار سباق (*sabbāq*) fast train, express train; قطار سريع express train; قطار وقاف (*waqqāf*) local train

قطارة *qaṭṭāra* dropping tube, pipette, dropper

قطران *qaṭrān* (*qiṭrān*, *qaṭirān*) tar

مقطر *miqṭar* pl. مقاطر *maqāṭir*² censer

مقطرة *miqṭara* pl. مقاطر *maqāṭir*² censer; stocks (device for punishment)

تقطير *taqṭīr* filtering, filtration; refining; distilling, distillation

استقطار *istiqṭār* distilling, distillation

قاطرة *qāṭira* pl. *-āt* locomotive; rail car, diesel

مقطورات *maqṭūrāt* trailers, truck trailers

مقطرات *muqaṭṭarāt* spirituous liquors, spirits

قطرميز *qaṭramīz* (large) glass bottle or jar

قطرن *qaṭrana* to tar, smear or coat with tar (ه s.th.)

قطران *qaṭrān* (*qiṭrān*, *qaṭirān*) tar

قطع *qaṭa'a a* (*qaṭ'*) to cut (ه s.th.); to cut off (ه s.th.); to chop off, lop off (ه s.th.); to amputate (ه s.th.); to cut through, cut in two, divide (ه s.th.); to tear apart, disrupt, sunder, disjoin, separate (ه s.th.); to fell (ه a tree); to break off, sever (ه s.th., e.g., relations); to break off one's friendship, break (ه with s.o.); to cut, snub (ه s.o.); to interrupt (ه, ه s.o., s.th.); to cut short, interrupt, silence (ه s.o.); to turn off, switch off, disconnect (ه electric current); to prevent, hinder (ه عن s.o. from); to forbid (ه عن to s.o. s.th.), prohibit (ه عن s.o. from doing s.th.); to deprive (ه عن s.o. of); (*Chr.*) to excommunicate (ه s.o.); to have a profound effect, have a considerable impact, be impressive (spiritually); to make a profound impression (فى on), impress greatly, affect deeply (فى s.o.); to ford (ه a river), cross (ه a river, an ocean), traverse (ه a country), pass through or across s.th. (ه); to cover (ه a distance); to survive (ه s.th., e.g., a danger), surmount, overcome (ه s.th., e.g., a difficulty), get over s.th. (ه); to spend, pass, while away (ه فى time with); to use up, consume (ه food); to decide (ه or ب s.th.); to say with certainty, assert, declare positively (ب s.th.), affirm confidently, aver (بأن that); to prove (بأن that); pass. *quṭiʻa* to break, break apart, be or get broken, be or become interrupted; to snap (rope, string of a musical instrument) | قطع الامل (الرجاء) (*amal, rajā'*) to give up hope, to despair; قطع الثمن (*ṯaman*) to fix the price, agree on the price; قطع تذكرة (بطاقة) (*taḏkiratan*) to buy a ticket; قطع عليه حديثه (*ḥadīṯahū*) to interrupt s.o., cut s.o. short, cut in on s.o.'s talk; قطع دورا (*dauran*) to pass through a phase or period, go through a stage; قطع برأى (*bi-ra'yin*) to express a firm opinion; to decide in favor of an opinion; قطع برأيه (*bi-ra'yihī*) to be guided in one's decisions by s.o., proceed in accordance with s.o.'s opinion or decision; قطع الرحم (*raḥim*) to sever the bonds of kinship, break with one's relatives; to violate the rules of consanguinity; قطع اشواطا (*ašwāṭan*) to make progress; قطع شوطا كبيرا (بعيدا) (or) فى التقدم (or الرق) (*šauṭan, taqaddum, ruqīy*) and قطع فى ميدان الرق اشواطا (*maidāni r-r.*) to make great progress, make great headway; قطع عليه الطريق to cut off s.o.'s way, intercept s.o.; to engage in highway robbery; to waylay s.o., commit highway robbery on s.o.; لا يقطع عقله (*'aqlahū*) it won't get into his head, he can't understand or believe it; قطع عهدا (*'ahdan*) to make a contract; to make a promise, vow, or pledge (ل to s.o.); قطع الوعد and قطع على نفسه عهدا ب (*'ahdan*) على نفسه ب (*wa'da*) to vow s.th., pledge o.s. or bind o.s. to do s.th.; قطع الكمبيالة to discount the bill of exchange; قطع لسانه (*lisānahū*) to silence s.o., seal s.o.'s lips, gag s.o.; قطع الوقت (*waqt*) to while away the time, kill time **II** to cut into pieces, cut up, dismember (ه s.th.); to carve (ه meat); to tear apart, rend, rip apart, gash, slash, lacerate (ه s.th.); to cut seriously, gash deeply (ه one's hand); to interrupt; to scan (ه a verse) | يقطع القلب (*qalba*) heart-rending **III** to dissociate, separate o.s. (ه from), part company, break off one's friendship, break (ه with s.o.); to cut, snub (ه s.o.); to be on bad terms (ه with s.o.); to boycott (ه, ه s.o., s.th.); to interrupt (ه, ه s.o., s.th.); to cut s.o. (ه) short, cut in on s.o.'s (ه) talk, also قاطعه الحديث **IV** to make or let s.o. (ه) cut or cut off (ه s.th.); to make or let s.o. (ه) cross or ford (ه a river); to bestow as a fief (ه ه on s.o. s.th.); to grant, assign, allot (ه ه to s.o. s.th.); to separate o.s., dissociate o.s. (ه from s.o.), part company (ه with s.o.); to break off one's friendship (عن with s.o.); to break (عن with s.o.) **V** to be cut off, be severed, be disrupted, be interrupted, be disconnected; to snap; to be cut up, be chopped up, be hacked to pieces, be dismembered; to be intermittent, flow discontinuously (electric current); to be disjointed, be jerky (words, style); to knock o.s. out (e.g., with eagerness) | تقطعت به الحبال (*ḥibālu*) to be at the end of one's resources, be utterly helpless; تقطعت به الاسباب (*asbābu*) to be at one's wit's end, be at the end of one's tether; هدف تتقطع دونه الاعناق (*hadafun, dūnahū*) lit.: a goal on the way to which throats are slit, i.e., one which remains unattainable **VI** to separate, part company, go apart; to get separated from each other; to break off mutual relations, snub each other; to intersect (lines, roads, etc.; مع s.th.), cut across, cross (of a line or road, مع another) **VII** to be cut off, be or get separated (عن or من from); to be chopped off, be lopped off, be cut through, be sundered, be severed, be torn apart, be disrupted, be broken, be broken off; to be interrupted, be disconnected, be cut off, be shut off (also, e.g., electric current), be blocked, be stopped; to break, break apart, tear, snap (intr., e.g., a rope, a string); to cease, end, come to an end, run out, expire; to stop, come to a halt, come to a standstill, be suspended, be discontinued; to stop, cease (عن s.th.; doing s.th.); to leave off (عن s.th.), desist, abstain, refrain (عن from); to suspend, discontinue, stay (عن s.th.); to withdraw, stay away, hold aloof (عن from); to devote o.s., dedicate o.s., give one's attention, apply o.s. (ل or الى to); to concentrate (ل or الى on); to occupy o.s. exclusively (ل or الى with), give all one's time (ل or الى to) **VIII** to take a part, a little (من of s.th.); to take, borrow, cull, glean (ه من s.th. from, e.g., a story from a book); to tear out, take out, remove (ه e.g., a page, من from a book or notebook); to tear off, rip off, detach (ه e.g., a coupon); to appropriate, acquire (ه s.th.); to possess o.s., take possession (ه of), seize (ه on) **X** to request as a fief (ه ه of s.o. s.th.); (*eg.*) to deduct (ه an amount)

قطع *qaṭʿ* cutting off; chopping off, detruncation; amputation; cutting, scission, section; disruption, sunderance, disjunction, disconnection, separation; felling (of a tree); severance, rupture, breakoff (e.g., of relations); stoppage, blockage, embargo, ban, blackout, suspension; interruption, discontinuation; disconnection, turning off, switching off (of electric current); prevention, hindrance (عن from); deprivation; excommunication (*Chr.*); fording (of a river); crossing (of an ocean); traversion (of a country); covering (of a distance); spending, passing (of a span of time); consumption; deduction, rebate, discount; (pl. اقطاع *aqṭāʿ*) format, size (of a book); (pl. قطوع *quṭūʿ*) section (*geom.*); قطعا *qaṭʿan* decidedly, definitely, positively, for certain; with neg.: absolutely not, not at all, by no means, not in the least | قطع الحسابات settlement of accounts; قطع الطريق highway robbery, brigandage; قطع الطريق على forcible prevention of s.th., radical stop to s.th.; قطع الماهية *q. al-māhīya* salary cut, wage deduction; سعر (or معدل) القطع *siʿr* (or *muʿaddal*) *al-q.* discount rate, bank rate; قطع الربع *q. ar-rubʿ* (*ar-rubuʿ*) quarto format; قطع كتب الجيب *q. kutub al-jaib* pocket size (book); قطع مخروط *q. makrūṭin*, قطع مخروطى (*makrūṭī*) conic section (*geom.*); قطع زائد hyperbola (*geom.*); قطع مكافئ (*mukāfi'*) parabola (*geom.*); قطع ناقص ellipse (*geom.*); قطعا للوقت *qaṭʿan li-l-waqt* as a pastime, just to kill time; بقطع النظر عن (*bi-q. in-naẓari*) irrespective of, regardless of, without regard to; aside from, apart from; همزة القطع disjunctive hamza (*gram.*)

قطعى *qaṭʿī* decided, definite, positive; final, definitive; قطعيا *qaṭʿīyan* decidedly, definitely, emphatically, categorically

قطعية *qaṭʿīya* certainty, definiteness, positiveness

قطعة *qiṭʿa* pl. قطع *qiṭaʿ* piece, fragment, lump, chunk; part, portion; section, division; segment (*geom.*); coin; naval unit; unit (*mil.*) | قطعة الدائرة or القطعة الدائرية segment of a circle (*geom.*); ○ قطعة التركيب part (of a machine, of an apparatus); ○ قطعة الازدواج coupling element (*el.*); قطعة مسرحية (*masraḥīya*) (stage) play; قطعة غنائية (*ġināʾīya*) vocal piece, vocal composition; قطعة غيار or قطعه التغيير spare part; قطعة فنية (*fannīya*) work of art; القطعة الكروية (*kurawīya*) spherical segment (*geom.*); قطعة تمثيلية (*tamṯīlīya*) (stage) play; قطعة موسيقية piece of music, musical composition; قطعة مالية (*mālīya*) coin; العمل بالقطع (*ʿamal*) piecework, job work, taskwork

قطعة *quṭʿa* pl. *quṭuʿāt*, قطع *quṭaʿ* a piece cut off, a cut; stump; plot of land, patch of land, lot

قطعة *qaṭaʿa* pl. *-āt*, قطع *qaṭaʿ* stump

قطاع *qiṭā'*, *quṭā'* pl. *-āt* section; sector (*geom.*) | قطاع عرضى (*'arḍī*) cross section; قطاعات من الانسجة (*ansija*) tissue sections (*biol.*); القطاع الدائرى (*dā'iri*) sector of a circle (*geom.*); القطاع الكروى (*kurawī*) spherical sector (*geom.*)

قطاع *qaṭṭā'* (stone-, wood-) cutter

بالقطاعى *bi-l-qaṭṭā'ī* by retail, retail (adj.)

قطيع *qaṭī'* pl. قطاع *qiṭā'*, قطعان *quṭ'ān*, اقطاع *aqṭā'* troop or group (of animals), drove, flock, herd

قطيعة *qaṭī'a* rupture of relations, break, breach, rift, alienation, estrangement, separation; enmity among relatives (short for قطيعة الرحم *q. ar-raḥim*); (pl. قطائع *qaṭā'i'*[2]) fief, fee, feudal estate, land granted by feudal tenure

اقطع *aqṭa'*[2] more convincing, more conclusive (evidence); (f. قطعاء *qaṭ'ā'*[2]) amputee; one-armed; dumb, mute

مقطع *maqṭa'* pl. مقاطع *maqāṭi'*[2] crossing point, crossing, traverse, passage; ford; (point of) intersection; cross section; section, division; syllable; musical phrase; quarry; group of animals, drove | مقطع الرأى *m. ar-ra'y* decision, judgment

مقطع *miqṭa'* pl. مقاطع *maqāṭi'*[2] cutting instrument | مقطع السيجار cigar cutter; مقطع الورق *m. al-waraq* paper knife; paper cutter

تقطيع *taqṭī'* fragmentation, dismemberment, cutting up, division, partitioning; interruption, disruption, discontinuation; gripes, colic; (pl. تقاطيع *taqāṭī'*[2]) stature, figure; shape, form; pl. parts, portions, sections, members | تقاطيع الوجه *t. al-wajh* features, lineaments of the face

مقاطعة *muqāṭa'a* separation; break (with s.o.); indifference, unfeelingness, unlovingness; boycott; interruption; (pl. *-āt*) area, region, section, district, province

اقطاع *iqṭā'* and اقطاعة *iqṭā'a* pl. *-āt* fief, fee, feudal estate, land granted by feudal tenure | ذو الاقطاع liege lord, feudal lord

اقطاعى *iqṭā'ī* liege, feudatory, feudal; (pl. *-ūn*) liege lord, feudal lord

اقطاعية *iqṭā'īya* feudalism; الاقطاعية the feudal system

تقطع *taqaṭṭu'* pl. *-āt* interruptedness, interruption

تقاطع *taqāṭu'* severance of mutual relations; crossing; intersection, junction

انقطاع *inqiṭā'* separation, disjunction, severance; break, breach, rift, rupture, breakoff; interruption, disruption, discontinuance; cessation, stop, termination, expiration, extinction; stoppage, shutdown, blockage, suspension; end, close, conclusion; absence, withdrawal, aloofness (عن from) | انقطاع التيار *inq. at-tayyār* power shutdown (*el.*); بدون انقطاع or من غير انقطاع incessantly, constantly, continually, without interruption

انقطاعية *inqiṭā'īya* separatism

استقطاع *istiqṭā'* pl. *-āt* cut, deduction (e.g., from salary)

قاطع *qāṭi'* cutting; sharp; convincing, cogent, irrefutable, conclusive, decisive (e.g., evidence); decided, definite, positive, unmistakable, unequivocal; final, definitive; sour (milk); secant (*geom.*); (pl. قواطع *qawāṭi'*[2]) partition, screen | قاطع الطريق pl. قطاع الطرق *quṭṭā' aṭ-ṭuruq* (or قطع الطرق *quṭṭa' aṭ-ṭ.*) highway robber, holdup man, waylayer, brigand; بصفة قاطعة (*bi-ṣifatin*) unmistakably; سن قاطعة (*sinn*) incisor; طير قواطع *ṭairun qawāṭi'u* migratory birds; قاطع التذاكر ticket seller, conductor (streetcar, bus, etc.)

○ قاطعة *qāṭi'a* interrupter, circuit breaker (*el.*)

مقطوع *maqṭūʿ* cut off, severed, chopped off, etc.; مقطوع به decided, finished, settled, done with (matter, affair); (pl. مقاطيع *maqāṭīʿ*²) short poem | مقطوع النظير matchless, peerless, unrivaled, unequaled

مقطوعة *maqṭūʿa* pl. *-āt*, مقاطيع *maqāṭīʿ*² piece (of music) | مقطوعة موسيقية piece of music, musical composition

مقطوعية *maqṭūʿīya* share, portion, allotment; consumption | بالمقطوعية (*eg.*) in the lump, for a lump sum

مقطع *muqaṭṭaʿ* torn, shredded

مقطع *muqṭiʿ* liege lord; — *muqṭaʿ* liege man, feudatory, feudal tenant, vassal

متقطع *mutaqaṭṭiʿ* cut off, torn, ruptured, disrupted, interrupted; discontinuous, flowing intermittently (electric current); in stages (movement); staccato (voice); incoherent, disjointed (words) | تيار متقطع (*tayyār*) alternating current

منقطع *munqaṭiʿ* cut off; severed, disjoined, separate(d), detached; chopped off, detruncated; cut, cut in two, sundered, torn, ruptured, disrupted; broken; broken off; interrupted, discontinued, stopped, blocked; disconnected, turned off, switched off (electric current); halting, discontinuous, intermittent, fitful; outlying, remote, out-of-the-way (region); devoted, dedicated (ل or الى to), set aside exclusively, solely destined (ل or الى for) | منقطع النظير and منقطع القرين unmatched, matchless, peerless, unrivaled, unequaled, incomparable, singular, unique; غير منقطع incessant, unceasing, continual, uninterrupted

مستقطع *mustaqṭaʿ* cut, deduction (from salary)

قطف *qaṭafa i* (*qaṭf*, قطوف *quṭūf*) to pick (ه flowers, fruit); to gather, harvest (ه fruit); to pluck off, pull off, tear off (ه s.th., e.g., leaves); (*eg.*) to skim (ه a liquid from the surface); — (*qaṭf*) to scratch, scratch up (ه s.o.) **II** = **I** **VIII** to pick (ه flowers, fruit); to gather, harvest (ه fruit); to pluck off (ه s.th.); to select, choose, pick out (ه من s.th. from among)

قطف *qaṭf* (act or instance of) picking, etc.; (pl. قطوف *quṭūf*) scratch

قطف *qiṭf* picked fruit

قطاف *qiṭāf* picking, gathering, harvest (of fruit); picking season, vintage, harvest time

دانى القطوف *dānī l-quṭūf* within reach, at hand; easy to apply, easy to use, handy

قطوف *qaṭūf* pl. قطف *quṭuf* short-stepped, slow

قطيفة *qaṭīfa* velvet; plush

قطائف *qaṭāʾif*², قطايف *qaṭāyif*² (pl.) small, triangular doughnuts fried in melted butter and served with honey

مقطف *miqṭaf* pl. مقاطف *maqāṭif*² implement for picking fruit, fruit picker; vine knife

مقطف *maqṭaf* pl. مقاطف *maqāṭif*² basket

اقتطاف *iqtiṭāf* picking, gathering, etc.; selection, choice, pick

مقتطف *muqtaṭaf* pl. *-āt* selected or select piece; selection

قطقوطة *qaṭqūṭa* young girl

قطل *qaṭala u i* (*qaṭl*) to cut off (ه s.th.) **II** = **I**

قطيلة *qaṭīla* towel; floor rag

قطم *qaṭama i* (*qaṭm*) to cut off (ه s.th.); to break off (ه s.th.)

قطمة *qaṭma* piece; bite, morsel

المقطم *al-muqaṭṭam* a range of hills east of Cairo

قطمير *qiṭmīr* pellicle enveloping a date pit | لا يملك قطميرا (*yamliku*) he doesn't own a thing, he hasn't a red cent to his name

قطن[1] **qaṭana** *u* (قطون *quṭūn*) to live, dwell, reside (فى or ب or ه in a place); to inhabit (فى or ب or ه a place) **II** to make live, settle (ه ب s.o. in)

قطن *qaṭan* small of the back

قطن *quṭn, quṭun* pl. اقطان *aqṭān* cotton | قطن خام raw cotton, cotton wool, unginned cotton; قطن سكارتو (It. *scarto*) (*eg.*) cotton waste; قطن طبي (*ṭibbī*) absorbent cotton; قطن ملتهب (*multahib*) guncotton; ○ حطب القطن *ḥaṭab al-q.* excelsior; محلج القطن *miḥlaj al-q.* cotton gin

قطنى *quṭnī* cotton (adj.)

قطنية *quṭnīya, qiṭnīya* pl. قطانى *qaṭānīy* pulse, legumes (peas, beans, lentils)

قطانية *quṭānīya, qiṭānīya* Indian corn, maize (*tun.*)

قطان *qaṭṭān* cotton manufacturer, cotton merchant

يقطين *yaqṭīn* (coll.; n. un. ة) a variety of squash

مقطنة *maqṭana* cotton plantation

قاطن *qāṭin* pl. قطان *quṭṭān* resident, domiciled; inhabitant, dweller

قيطان[2] *qīṭān* pl. قياطين *qayāṭīn*[2] cord, braid, lace

قطا *qaṭan* (coll.; n. un. قطاة *qaṭāh*) sand grouse (Pterocles)

قعد **qaʿada** *u* (قعود *quʿūd*) to sit down, take a seat; to sit, be sitting; to remain seated; to remain, stay, abide; to lie in wait (ل for s.o.), waylay (ل s.o.); to desist, abstain, refrain (عن from), renounce, waive (عن s.th.) | قعد به to make s.o. sit down, make s.o. sit, seat s.o., induce s.o. to stay; to hamper, handicap, hamstring, disable, paralyze s.o.; قعدت به ركبتاه (*rukbatāhu*) his knees buckled under him; قعد به عن to hold back, restrain, discourage, or prevent s.o. from; قعد عن الذهاب (*ḏahāb*) he decided not to go; قام وقعد to be in a state of great anxiety, be seriously upset, be very agitated; to be very alarmed (ل by) **IV** to make (ه s.o.) sit down; to make (ه s.o.) sit; to cause or induce (ه s.o.) to stay; to seat (ه s.o.); to hold back, restrain, discourage, prevent (ه عن s.o. from); to decrease, diminish, reduce (من s.th.); pass. *uqʿida* to be lame, be crippled | اقامه واقعده (*aqāmahū*) to upset s.o. seriously, throw s.o. in a state of violent emotion; اقعد من همته (*himmatihī*) to dampen s.o.'s zeal **V** not to desire (عن s.th.), not to be out for s.th. (عن); to desist, abstain, refrain (عن from) **VI** = **V**; to remain aloof, refrain, forbear, withdraw (عن from); to be pensioned off, retire **VIII** to take or use as a seat (ه s.th.); to sit down (ه on s.th.); to be, remain (ه in a state or condition)

قعد *qaʿad* slackers, shirkers of military service in times of war; also, designation of the Khawarij

قعدة *qaʿda* sitting; backside, seat, buttocks, posteriors; space occupied while sitting, seating space | ذو القعدة name of the eleventh month of the Muslim year

قعدة *qiʿda* manner of sitting, seat, pose, posture; space occupied while sitting, seating space

قعدة *quʿada* constantly or frequently sitting, sedentary; glued to the seat, not budging, seated firmly; lazy, inert, indolent

قعدى *quʿdī* constantly or frequently sitting, sedentary; glued to the seat, not budging, firmly seated; lazy, inert, indolent

قعود *qaʿūd* pl. اقعدة *aqʿida*, قعد *quʿud*, قعدان *qiʿdān*, قعائد *qaʿāʾid*[2] young camel

قعود *qu'ūd* sitting; desistance, abstention, refraining (عن from); renunciation, abandonment, waiver (عن of)

قعيد *qa'īd* companion; one with whom one sits together; keeper, guardian, supervisor, superintendent; crippled, disabled, infirm | قعيد المنزل *q. al-manzil* confined to one's house or to one's quarters

قعيدة *qa'īda* pl. قعائد *qa'ā'id²* woman companion; wife, spouse

مقعد *maq'ad* pl. مقاعد *maqā'id²* s.th. to sit on, space to sit in; seat (in general, in a theater, in parliament, etc.); chair; bench; sofa, settee; box, driver's seat (of a carriage or coach) | مقعد طويل chaise longue; مقعد مريح (*murīḥ*) easy chair, armchair

مقعدة *maq'ada* pl. مقاعد *maqā'id²* backside, seat, buttocks, posteriors

تقاعد *taqā'ud* restraint, reticence, aloofness, reserve; retirement | معاش التقاعد *ma'āš at-t.* retiring allowance, superannuation, pension; احيل الى التقاعد (*uḥīla*) to be pensioned off, be superannuated, be retired

قاعد *qā'id* pl. قعود *qu'ūd*, قعاد *qu''ād*, sitting, seated; inactive, idle, lazy, also قاعد عن العمل (*'amal*); قاعدون *qā'idūn* slackers, shirkers of military service in times of war; — قاعد *qā'id* pl. قواعد *qawā'id²* woman who, because of her age, has ceased to bear children

قاعدة *qā'ida* pl. قواعد *qawā'id²* foundation, groundwork; basis; fundament; base (*geom.*; *mil.*); support, base, socle, foot, pedestal; ○ chassis, undercarriage; precept, rule, principle, maxim; formula; method, manner, mode; model, pattern | قاعدة الاسطول *q. al-usṭūl* or قاعدة بحرية (*baḥriya*) naval base; قاعدة البلاد capital of the country; قاعدة جوية (*jawwiya*) airbase; قاعدة حربية (*ḥarbiya*) base of operation; قاعدة الملك *q. al-mulk* seat of government; مساحة القاعدة *misāḥat al-q.* base, basal surface

مقعد *muq'ad* brought to a standstill, stopped, arrested; lame, crippled, disabled, infirm; an invalid

متقاعد *mutaqā'id* retired; pensioner

قعر *qa'ura u* (قعارة *qa'āra*) to be deep, hollowed out **II** to make deep or deeper, deepen (ه s.th.); to hollow out, make hollow, excavate (ه s.th.); to cry, shout, scream | قعر فى كلامه (*kalāmihī*) to speak gutturally **IV** to make deep or deeper, deepen (ه a well) **V** to be depressed, sunk, low, deep, hollowed out, dished, concave; to descend to the bottom

قعر *qa'r* pl. قعور *qu'ūr* bottom; depth; keel (of a ship); pit, hole, hollow, cavity, depression | من القعر صاعدا (*ṣā'idan*) from the ground up

قعرة *qa'ra* pit, hole, hollow, cavity, depression

قعور *qa'ūr* deep

قعير *qa'īr* deep

مقعر *muqa''ar* depressed, sunk, low, deep; hollow, dished, concave; curved; obscure (language)

قعس *qa'isa a* (*qa'as*) to have a protruding chest and hollow back, be pigeon-breasted **VI** to remain aloof, keep away, stay away, desist, refrain (عن from); to hesitate, waver, be reluctant (عن to do s.th.); to fail, neglect (عن to do s.th.); to be uninterested (عن in) **XIV** اقعنسس *iq'ansasa* = I

اقعس *aq'as²* having a protruding chest and hollow back, pigeon-breasted | عز اقعس (*'izz*) firmly established power

تقاعس *taqā'us* negligence

متقاعس *mutaqā'is* hesitant, wavering, reluctant; negligent, careless, sloppy, listless, idle

قعقع **qaʿqaʿa** (قعقعة qaʿqaʿa) to clatter; to rattle; to clank

قعقع **qaʿqaʿ, quʿquʿ** magpie

قعقعة **qaʿqaʿa** clatter; rattle; clank, clang; noise, din; pl. قعاقع qaʿāqiʿ² high-sounding words

قف **qaffa** u (قفوف qufūf) to be dry, withered, shriveled; to dry up, wither, shrivel; to contract, shrink; to bristle, stand on end (hair)

قفة **quffa** pl. قفف qufaf large basket; (Mesopotamian) round boat, gufa (*ir.*)

قفة **quffa, qaffa** feverish shiver, ague fit

قفر **qafara** u (qafr): قفر أثره (aṯarahū) to follow s.o.'s tracks, track s.o. **IV** to be or become empty, bleak, desolate, deserted, depopulated, uninhabited, devastated, waste; to be destitute, be devoid (من of); to ravage, lay waste, devastate, desolate, depopulate (ه s.th.); to abandon, leave in a state of desolation (ه houses, a city); to gnaw off, pick (ه a bone) **VIII** to follow s.o.'s (ه) tracks, track (ه s.o.)

قفر **qafr** pl. قفار qifār desert, wasteland, desolate region; empty, bleak, forsaken, forlorn, deserted, lifeless, uninhabited, depopulated, devastated, desolate, waste; destitute, devoid (من of) | (قفار or) ارض قفر (arḍ) wasteland; خبز قفر (ḵubz) plain bread, dry bread

قفرة **qafra** pl. qafarāt desert, wasteland, desolate region

خبز قفار **ḵubzun qafārun** plain bread, dry bread

قفير **qafīr** pl. قفران qufrān beehive

بادية قفراء **bādiya qafrāʾ²** arid desert

اقفار **iqfār** emptiness, bleakness, desolateness, desolation; ravage, devastation, depopulation

مقفر **muqfir** empty, bleak, forsaken, forlorn, deserted, lifeless, uninhabited, depopulated, devastated, desolate, waste; destitute, devoid (من of)

قفز **qafaza** i (qafz, قفزان qafazān) to jump, leap, spring, hurdle, bound; to jump up, leap in the air; to jump off, take off **V** to put on or wear gloves

قفز **qafz** jumping (also *athlet.*) | القفز على الحبل (ḥabl) skipping the rope; القفز بالزانة pole vaulting; قفز طويل broad jump; قفز عال (ʿālin) high jump

قفزة **qafza** pl. qafazāt jump, leap, spring, bound

قفاز **quffāz** pl. -āt, قفافيز qafāfīz² glove; a pair of gloves

قفيز **qafīz** pl. اقفزة aqfiza cafiz, a dry measure, ca. 496-640 l, = 16 whibas (*Tun.*)

مقفز **maqfiz** springboard

قفش **qafaša** i u (qafš) to gather, collect (ه s.th.); (*eg.*) to catch, seize, grasp, grab; to find out, discover (ه s.th.)

قفش **qafš** prattle, chatter

قفشات **qafašāt** (pl.) jokes

قفص **qafaṣ** pl. اقفاص aqfāṣ cage; birdcage; pen, coop, wired enclosure; basket (made of palm fronds); thorax, chest; (prisoner's) dock (= قفص الاتهام q. al-ittihām)

تقفيصة **taqfīṣa** poultry coop

قفطان **quftān** pl. قفاطين qafāṭīn² caftan, a long-sleeved outer garment, open in front and fastened by a *ḥizām*

القفقاس **al-qafqās** the Caucasus

قفع **qafiʿa** a (qafaʿ) to contract; to shrink; to shrivel, become wrinkled **II** to shrivel (ه the fingers; of the cold) **V** = **I**

قفع **qafʿ** testudo

قفقف **qafqafa** (قفقفة *qafqafa*) and **II** *taqafqafa* to shiver with cold

قفل **qafala u i** (قفول *qufūl*) to come home, come back, return; — *i* (*qafl*) to shut, close (ه s.th.); to latch, lock, shut up, bolt (ه s.th.); to accumulate, amass, hoard (ه s.th.) **II** and **IV** to padlock (ه s.th.); to shut, close (ه s.th.); to switch off, shut off, turn off (ه s.th.); to cut off, stop (ه the supply of), block, bar, close (ه s.th.); to latch, lock, shut up, bolt (ه s.th.)

قفل **qufl** pl. اقفال *aqfāl*, قفول *qufūl* padlock; lock, latch; bolt; ○ lock (of a canal)

قفال **qaffāl** locksmith

اقفال **iqfāl** shutting, closing, closure; shutting up; locking, bolting; stoppage, blocking, blockage, barring, obstruction

قافل **qāfil** pl. قافلة *qāfila*, قفال *quffāl* home-coming, returning; homecomer, repatriate

قافلة **qāfila** pl. قوافل *qawāfil*[2] caravan; column; convoy | قافلة (تجارية) بحرية (*tijārīya, baḥrīya*) or قافلة السفن *q. as-sufun* naval convoy

(قفو) قفا **qafā u** (*qafw*) to follow (أثره *aṯarahū* s.o.'s tracks) **II** to send (ب or ه ه s.o. after s.o. else); to rhyme, put into rhyme **VIII** اقتفى أثره (*aṯarahū*) to follow s.o.'s tracks, track s.o.; to follow up, pursue s.o. (*mil.*); to follow in s.o.'s tracks, follow s.o.'s example, imitate s.o.

قفا **qafan** m. and f., pl. اقفية *aqfiya*, اقف *aqfin*, اقفاء *aqfā'*, قفي *qufīy*, *qifīy* nape; occiput, back of the head; back; reverse; wrong side (of a fabric)

قفاء **qafā'** nape; occiput, back of the head

اقتفاء **iqtifā'** following (of s.o.'s tracks), tracking; imitation

قافية **qāfiya** pl. قواف *qawāfin* rhyme; (*eg.*) play on words, pun, double-entendre; nape

قيقب look up alphabetically

قاقلة, قاقلى and قاقم look up alphabetically

قل **qalla i** (*qill*, *qull*, قلة *qilla*) to be or become little, small, few (in number or quantity), trifling, insignificant, inconsiderable, scant, scanty, sparse, spare, meager; to be rare, scarce; to be of rare occurrence, happen seldom; to decrease, diminish, wane, grow less; to be or become less, littler, smaller, fewer (in number or quantity), more trifling, less significant, less considerable, scanter, scantier, sparser (عن than); to be second, be inferior (عن to s.o.) — (*qall*) to pick up, raise, lift (عن ه, ه s.o., s.th. from the ground); to carry (ه s.th.) | الا ما قل وندر (*illā, wa-nadara*) but for a few exceptions, with a few exceptions only; قل صبره (*ṣabruhū*) to be impatient lose one's patience **II** to make little or less, diminish, lessen, decrease, reduce, do seldom or less frequently (ه or من s.th.) **IV** = **II**; to do or give little (من in or of); to pick up, raise, lift (عن ه, ه s.o., s.th. from the ground); to be able to carry (ه, ه s.o., s.th.); to carry, transport, convey (ه s.o., ه s.th.) **VI** to think little (ه of), scorn, disdain, despise (ه s.th.) **X** to find (ه s.th.) little, small, inconsiderable, insignificant, trifling; to esteem lightly, undervalue, despise (ه, ه s.o., s.th.); to make light (ه, ه of), set little store (ه, ه by), care little (ه, ه for); to pick up, raise, lift (ه, ه s.o., s.th.); to carry, transport, convey (ه, ه s.o., s.th.); to board (ه s.th., e.g., a ship, a carriage, or the like); to rise; to be independent; to possess alone (ب s.th.) | استقل بحمل (*bi-ḥimlin*) to assume a burden; استقل بصنعه (*bi-ṣan'ihī*) he alone made it, he was the only one who made it; استقل بنفسه

(*bi-nafsihi*) to be entirely self-reliant, be left to one's own devices; to be independent, manage without others, get along by oneself; استقل بمهمة (بواجب) (*bi-muhimmatin, bi-wājibin*) to assume a task (or duty)

قلما *qallamā* (conj.) seldom, rarely; scarcely, barely, hardly

قل *qill, qull* littleness, smallness, fewness; insignificance, inconsiderableness, triviality, paucity, paltriness, scarceness, sparseness, scantiness, insufficiency; a little, a small number, a small quantity, a modicum; — *qill* tremor

قلة *qalla* recovery, recuperation; restoration of prosperity

قلة *qulla* highest point; top, summit; apex; vertex; (cannon) ball; (pl. قلل *qulal*) jug, pitcher

قلة *qilla* pl. قلل *qilal* littleness, fewness; smallness, inconsiderableness, insignificance, triviality; paucity, paltriness, scantiness, sparseness; scarceness, rareness, rarity; minority; lack, want, deficiency, insufficiency, scarcity | قلة الاحساس *q. al-iḥsās* insensitivity, obtuseness; قلة الحياء *q. al-ḥayā'* shamelessness, impudence, insolence, impertinence; قلة الصبر *q. aṣ-ṣabr* impatience; قلة الوجود scantiness, scarcity; rareness, rarity; جمع القلة *jam' al-q.* (*gram.*) plural of paucity (for persons or things whose number is between three and ten)

بقليته *bi-qillīyatihī* completely, wholly, entirely | رحلوا بقليتهم (*raḥalū*) they set out all together or with bag and baggage

قليل *qalīl* pl. اقلاء *aqillā'*², قلائل *qalā'il*², قلال *qilāl* little; few; insignificant, inconsiderable, trifling; small (in number or quantity), scant, scanty, spare, sparse, meager, insufficient; scarce, rare; a small number, a small quantity, a modicum, a little (من of); قليلا *qalīlan* a little, somewhat; seldom, rarely | قليلا ما seldom, rarely; قليلا قليلا by and by, slowly, gradually; الكل الا قليلا *al-kull illā q.* almost everything, nearly all; بعد قليل a little later, some time later on, shortly afterward; shortly, before long; عن قليل or عما قليل (*'ammā*) soon, before long, shortly; ليس منه لا بقليل ولا بكثير to have absolutely nothing to do with s.th.; قليل الادب *q. al-adab* uncivil, impolite, rude, uncouth; قليل الحياء *q. al-ḥayā'* shameless, brazen, impudent, insolent, impertinent; قليل الارتفاع low; قليل الصبر *q. aṣ-ṣabr* impatient; قليل الوجود scanty, scarce; rare

اقل *aqall*² less; fewer; smaller; rarer; الاقل the least, the minimum | على الاقل or بالاقل at the very least; at least; على اقل تقدير (at the lowest estimate) = على الاقل; لا اقل من ان (*aqalla*) the least one can do is to ...; I (you, etc.) could at least ...; اقل من القليل quite insignificant, all but negligible; واقل من هذا وذلك ان let alone that ..., not to mention that ..., to say nothing of . . .

اقلية *aqallīya* smaller number, numerical inferiority; (pl. *-āt*) minority

تقليل *taqlīl* decrease, diminution, reduction

اقلال *iqlāl* decrease, diminution, reduction

استقلال *istiqlāl* independence

استقلالى *istiqlālī* of or pertaining to independence, independence (used attributively); proponent of independence

مقل *muqill* propertyless, unpropertied, without means, poor, destitute

مستقل *mustaqill* independent; autonomous; separate, distinct, particular

قلاووظ, قلاووز (Turk. *kılavuz*) *qalāwūẓ* ship's pilot; screw

قلاية *qallāya* pl. *-āt*, قلالى *qalālīy* (monastic) cell; residence of the Coptic Patriarch (*Chr.*)

قلب *qalaba* i (*qalb*) to turn around, turn about, turn up(ward), upturn (ه s.th.); to turn, turn over (ه s.th.); to turn face up or face down (ه s.th.); to turn inside out or outside in (ه s.th.); to turn upside down (ه s.th.); to tip, tilt over, topple over (ه s.th.); to invert, reverse (ه s.th.); to overturn, upset, topple (ه s.th.); to capsize (ه s.th.); to roll over (ه s.th.); to subvert, overthrow (ه a government); to change, alter, turn, transform, convert, transmute (ه s.th., ه ه s.th. to or into s.th.); to transpose (ه s.th.); to exchange (ه ه s.th. for s.th.) | قلبه رأسا (*ra'san*) to turn s.th. upside down; قلب له ظهر المجن (*ẓahra l-mijann*) to show s.o. the back of the shield, i.e., to give s.o. the cold shoulder, become hostile to s.o. **II** to turn, turn around, turn about, turn up(ward), upturn, turn over (ه s.th.); to turn face up or face down (ه s.th.); to turn inside out or outside in (ه s.th.); to turn upside down (ه s.th.); to tip, tilt over, topple over (ه s.th.); to invert, reverse (ه s.th.); to overturn, upset, overthrow, topple (ه s.th.); to capsize (ه s.th.); to roll over (ه s.th.); to turn, turn over (ه pages); to rummage, ransack, rake (ه s.th.); to roll (ه s.th.); to stir (ه s.th.); to examine, study, scrutinize, investigate (ه, ه s.o., s.th.); to change, alter, turn, transform, convert, transmute (ه s.th., ه ه s.th. to or into s.th.) | قلبه بين يديه (*yadaihi*) to turn s.th. around in one's hands, fidget with s.th.; قلبه بعقله (*bi-'aqlihī*) to turn s.th. over in one's mind, reflect on s.th., ponder s.th., brood over s.th.; قلبه ظهرا لبطن (*ẓahran li-baṭnin*) to turn s.th. completely upside down, turn s.th. topsy-turvy, turn s.th. over and over; قلب كفيه (*kaffaihi*) to repent, be grieved; to be embarrassed; قلب فيه البصر (*baṣara*) or قلب فيه النظر (*naẓara*) to scrutinize, eye, regard s.th. **V** to be turned around, be turned over, be reversed, be inverted; to be overturned, get knocked over (e.g., a glass); to toss and turn, toss about; to writhe, twist, squirm, wriggle; to be changed, be altered, change; to fluctuate (prices); to be changeable, variable, inconstant, fickle (في in s.th.); to move (about), live, be at home (في in); to dispose (في of), have at one's disposal (في s.th.) | تقلب في وظائف عديدة (*waẓā'ifa 'adīdatin*) he held numerous offices; تقلب في أعطاف النعيم or) تقلب في النعمة (*ni'ma*), العيش الناعم (*a. il-'aiš*) to lead a life of ease and comfort, live in prosperity; تقلب على رمضاء البؤس (*ramḍā'i l-bu's*) to live in utmost misery **VII** to be turned, be turned around, be turned about, be turned up(ward), be upturned, be turned over; to be reversed, be inverted; to be turned inside out or outside in; to be turned upside down, be toppled, get knocked over; to be overturned, be upset, be overthrown; to be rolled over; to overturn, somersault; to capsize; to be changed, be altered, be transformed, be converted, be transmuted; to change, turn (ه or الى into s.th.), become (ه or الى s.th.); to turn (على against; الى to); to return; (with foll. imperf.) to proceed suddenly to do s.th., shift instantly to s.th., change over to s.th. | انقلب ظهرا لبطن (*ẓahran li-baṭnin*) to be turned topsy-turvy; to be completely devastated; انقلب الى الهجوم to take the offensive

قلب *qalb* reversal, inversion; overturn, upheaval; conversion, transformation, transmutation; transposition (of letters), metathesis (*gram.*); perversion, change, alteration; overthrow (of a government)

قلب *qalb* pl. قلوب *qulūb* heart; middle, center; core, gist, essence; marrow, medulla, pith; the best or choicest part; mind, soul, spirit | قلب الاسد *q. al-asad* Regulus (star *a* in the constellation Leo;

astron.); قلب الهجوم center forward (soccer); سويداء القلب *suwaidā' al-q.* the innermost of the heart, the bottom of the heart; ضعيف القلب fainthearted, pusillanimous, recreant, cowardly; قاسي القلب *qāsī l-q.* hardhearted, callous, pitiless, merciless, cruel; قساوة القلب *qasāwat al-q.* hardheartedness, callousness, pitilessness, cruelty; انقباض القلب dejectedness, despondency, dispiritedness, depression; عن ظهر القلب (*ẓahri l-q.*) by heart; من صميم القلب from the bottom of the heart, most sincerely; من كل قلبه with all his heart; قلبا وقالبا *qalban wa-qālaban* with heart and soul; inwardly and outwardly; قلوبات (السكر) *qulūbāt (as-sukkar)* small candies, lozenges

قلبي *qalbī* of or pertaining to the heart, heart- (in compounds), cardiac, cardiacal; cordial, hearty, warm, sincere; قلبيا *qalbiyan* cordially, heartily, warmly, sincerely

قلب *qulb, qalb, qilb* palm pith, palm core (edible tuber growing at the upper end of the palm trunk); *qulb* bracelet, bangle

قلبة *qalba* (*eg.*) lapel; (pl. *-āt*) a measure of capacity (*Tun.*; = 20 l)

قلب *qullab* tending to change; agile, adaptable, resourceful; versatile, many-sided, of varied skills or talents

قالب *qālab, qālib* pl. قوالب *qawālib²* form; mold; cake pan; model; matrix; last, boot tree, shoe tree | قالب جبن *q. jubn* a chunk or loaf of cheese; قالب سكر *q. sukkar* sugar loaf; قالب صابون *q. ṣābūn* a cake or bar of soap; قلبا وقالبا (*qalban*) with heart and soul; inwardly and outwardly

قليب *qalīb* m. and f., pl. اقلبة *aqliba*, قلب *qulub*, قلبان *qulbān* well

قلوب *qalūb* tending to change; agile, adaptable, resourceful; versatile, many-sided

قلاب *qallāb* changeable, variable, unsteady, inconstant, fickle, wavering, vacillating; reversible, tiltable; dumper; tip wagon, skip | عربة قلابة (*'araba*) tipcart; قلاب خلاط (*kallāṭ*) rotary mixer

قلابة *qallāba* agitator, stirring machine

مقلب *maqlab* pl. مقالب *maqālib²* (*eg.*) refuse dump, dump pile, dump; intrigue, scheme, plot; April fool's joke

مقلب *miqlab* pl. مقالب *maqālib²* hoe

تقليب *taqlīb*: عند تقليب النظر *'inda t. in-naẓar* on closer inspection or examination, when examined more closely

تقلب *taqallub* pl. *-āt* alteration, transformation, change; variation; fluctuation (of prices); changeableness, variableness, unsteadiness, inconstancy, fickleness; pl. vicissitudes, ups and downs | تقلب جوي (*jawwī*) change of weather; سريع التقلب very changeable, very fickle, capricious

انقلاب *inqilāb* upheaval; revolution, overthrow, bouleversement; alteration, transformation, change; solstice | دائرة الانقلاب tropic (*geogr.*)

مقلوب *maqlūb* turned over, turned upside down, turned about, inverted, inverse, reverse(d), etc.; infolded (hem, seam); reciprocal (*math.*) | بالمقلوب topsy-turvy; upside down; wrong side out; the other way round, reversely, conversely, vice versa

متقلب *mutaqallib*, also متقلب الاطوار (الاحوال or) wavering, vacillating, changeable, variable, inconstant, unsteady, fickle, capricious

منقلب *munqalab* (place of overthrow, i.e.) the hereafter, the end one meets in death, the way of all flesh, final destiny; tropic | منقلب شتوي (*šatawī*) Tropic of Capricorn; منقلب صيفي (*saifī*) Tropic of Cancer

قلبق *qalbaq* a tall, usually cylindrical, fur cap

[1]قلح *qalaḥ* yellowness of the teeth

قلاح *qulāḥ* yellowness of the teeth

[2]قولحة *qaulaḥa* pl. قوالح *qawāliḥ*[2] (*eg.*) cob (of corn, and the like)

[1]قلد **II** to adorn with a necklace (ها a woman); to gird (ه ه s.o. with); to invest (ه ه s.o. with an office), appoint (ه ه s.o. to an office), award (ه ه to s.o. a decoration, an order), confer (ه ه upon s.o. a rank); to grant (ه ه to s.o. a favor); to entrust (ه ه s.o. with the rule or government of s.th.), give (ه s.o.) authority or power (ه over s.th.); to follow blindly another's (ه) opinion; to copy, ape, imitate (ه s.o.); to forge, counterfeit (ه s.th.) **V** to put on or wear a necklace, adorn o.s. with a necklace; to gird o.s. (ه with), put on (ه s.th.); to take upon o.s., assume (ه s.th.); to take over (ه s.th., esp. power, control, government)

قلادة *qilāda* pl. قلائد *qalā'id*[2] necklace; pl. قلائد exquisite poems

مقلد *miqlad* pl. مقالد *maqālid*[2] key

مقلاد *miqlād* pl. مقاليد *maqālīd*[2] key | مقاليد الامور key positions, power; مقاليد الحكم *m. al-ḥukm* the reins of government or power; تسلم مقاليد الحكم (*tasallama*) to take over (the reins of) government, seize power; القى اليه مقاليد الامور (*alqā*) to entrust s.o. with the management, put s.o. in charge

تقليد *taqlīd* pl. تقاليد *taqālīd*[2] imitation; copying; blind, unquestioning adoption (of concepts or ideas); uncritical faith (e.g., in a source's authoritativeness); adoption of the legal decision of a *maḏhab* (*Isl. Law*); pl. tradition; convention, custom, usage

تقليدى *taqlīdī* traditional, customary, conventional; based on uncritical faith (e.g., in a source's authoritativeness)

مقلد *muqallad* imitated, imitation, forged, counterfeit(ed), fake, sham, spurious, false; tradition-bound

[2]اقليد *iqlīd* pl. اقاليد *aqālīd*[2] key

بحر القلزم *baḥr al-qulzum* the Red Sea

[1]قلس *qalasa* *i* (*qals*) to belch, burp, eruct **II** to bow (ل to s.o.); (*eg.*) to make fun (على of), poke fun (على at), ridicule (على s.o., s.th.)

[2]قلس **II** to put a cap (قلنسوة *qalansuwa*, q.v., ه on s.o.'s head)

[3]قلس *qals* pl. قلوس *qulūs* hawser, cable, rope

[1]قلش **II** to molt

تقليش *taqlīš* molting, molt

[2]قالوش (Fr. *galoche*) *galōš* pl. *-āt* galosh, overshoe

قلشين *qalšīn* pl. قلاشين *qalāšīn*[2] puttee

قلص *qalaṣa* *i* (قلوص *qulūṣ*) to contract; to shrink (laundered garment); to decrease, diminish; to dwindle, fade, wane, decline; to become shorter, recede (shadow) | قلص ظله (*ẓilluhū*) his prestige declined; it decreased, dwindled, faded **II** to contract, draw together (ه s.th.); to tuck up, roll up (ه s.th.) **V** = **I**; قلص ظله = تقلص ظله

اقلص *aqlaṣ*[2] shorter

تقلص *taqalluṣ* contraction, shrinking, shrinkage

قليط *qillīṭ* scrotal hernia

قيليط *qīlīṭ* afflicted with scrotal hernia

قلع *qala'a* *a* (*qal'*) to pluck out, tear out, pull out, weed out, uproot (ه s.th.); to root out, exterminate, extirpate (ه s.th.); to take off (ه clothes) | قلعه من جذوره to pull out s.th. with the roots **II** to pluck out, tear out, pull out, weed out, uproot (ه s.th.); to root out, exterminate, extirpate (ه s.th.) **IV** to set sail, prepare to sail, get under sail; to sail, put to sea, depart (ship); to take off (airplane); to desist, abstain, refrain (عن from); leave off, abandon, give up, renounce, relinquish (عن s.th.) **VIII** to pluck out, tear out, pull out, weed out, uproot (ه s.th.); to root out, exterminate, extirpate (ه s.th.)

قلع *qil'* pl. قلوع *qulū'*, قلاع *qilā'* sail (of a ship)

قلعة *qal'a* pl. قلاع *qilā'*, قلوع *qulū'* fortress, stronghold, fort; citadel

قلاع *qulā'* thrush, canker of the mouth, ulcerative stomatitis, stomacace (*med.*)

قلاعى *qulā'ī*: الحمى القلاعية (*ḥummā*) foot-and-mouth disease

مقلع *maqla'* pl. مقالع *maqāli'*[2] stone quarry

مقلاع *miqlā'* pl. مقاليع *maqālī'*[2] slingshot, sling; catapult

اقلاع *iqlā'* sailing, departure (of a ship); take-off (of an airplane)

قلعط *qal'aṭa* to soil, sully, smirch (ه s.th.)

قلعوط *qul'ūṭ* a heretic

[1]قلف *qalafa* *i* (*qalf*) to bark (ه a tree), strip the bark (ه from a tree); — *u* (*qalf*): قلف قلفته (*qulfatahū*) to circumcise s.o.

قلف *qilf* bark, rind (of a tree)

قلفة *qulfa* pl. قلف *qulaf* foreskin, prepuce

قلافة *qulāfa* bark, rind (of a tree)

اقلف *aqlaf*[2] uncircumcised

[2]قلف **II** to calk (ه a ship)

قلافة *qilāfa* calking

[3]قلفة *qalfa* pl. *-āt* (*tun.*) foreman; workman, manual laborer

قلفط *qalfaṭa* to calk (ه a ship); (*eg.*) to do sloppy work, scamp, bungle

قلفون *qalafūn* and قلفونيه *qalafūniya* rosin, colophony

قلق *qaliqa* *a* (*qalaq*) to totter, be unsteady; to be or become uneasy, disquieted, apprehensive, anxious, excited, agitated, upset, perturbed, troubled, disturbed; to be restless, be sleepless, pass a sleepless night, find no sleep **IV** to trouble, worry, alarm, disturb, upset, disconcert, disquiet, discompose, discomfit, discomfort, make uneasy or anxious (ه, ه s.o., s.th.); to make restless, fill with uneasiness or anxiety, perturb, agitate, excite (ه s.o.); to rob s.o. (ه) of his rest

قلق *qalaq* unrest, uneasiness, disquiet, alarm; agitation, excitement, perturbation; stir, sensation; anxiety, apprehensiveness, apprehension, fear, worry, concern; restlessness; sleeplessness; impatience

قلق *qaliq* uneasy, disquieted; apprehensive, worried, concerned, anxious; agitated, excited, perturbed, upset; disturbed, troubled; restless; sleepless; impatient

قلوق *qalūq* (*eg.*) restless

اقلاق *iqlāq* disquieting, troubling, perturbation; disturbance

مقلق *muqliq* intrigant, schemer, troublemaker

قلقاس *qulqās* (coll.; n. un. ة) pl. *-āt* a variety of taro or elephant's ear (Colocasia antiquorum; *bot.*)

قلقل *qalqala* to move, commove, shake, convulse, unsettle (ه, ه s.o., s.th.); to disturb, trouble, harass (ه, ه s.o.; s.th.); to disquiet, alarm, excite, agitate (ه, ه s.o., s.th.); to stir up, incite to rebellion (ه s.o.); to pronounce accurately (the ق) **II** *taqalqala* to be or get in a state of commotion, be shaken, be convulsed, be unsettled, be disturbed, be troubled, be disquieted, be alarmed, be excited, be agitated; to be stirred up, be incited to rebellion, be incensed, be rebellious; to move, budge (من from one's place), stir; to be shaky, precarious, insecure (situation)

قلقلة *qalqala* pl. قلاقل *qalāqil*² unrest, excitement, agitation, commotion; shock, convulsion, concussion; disturbance

قلقيلة (*eg.*) *qulqēla* pl. *-āt* clod, lump of earth

مقلقل *muqalqal* in a state of commotion, agitated, shaken, unsettled, etc.; unstable, inconstant, unsteady

¹قلم *qalama* *i* (*qalm*) to cut, clip, pare (ه nails, etc.), prune, trim, lop (ه trees, etc.) II do. | قلم اظافر خصمه (*aẓāfira ḵaṣmihī*) to neutralize, disarm one's opponent

قلم *qalam* pl. اقلام *aqlām* reed pen; pen; writing, script, calligraphic style, ductus; handwriting; style; office, bureau, agency, department; window, counter; item, entry (*com.*); (*eg.*) stripe, streak, line; (*eg.*) slap in the face | بقلمه *bi-qalamihī* written by him; قلم الحبر *q. al-ḥibr* fountain pen; قلم حبر جاف (*jāff*) and قلم حبر ناشف ball-point pen; قلم التحرير editor's office, editing room; قلم الحركة *q. al-ḥaraka* traffic bureau; قلم الحسابات *q. al-ḥisābāt* accounting department; قلم الادارة *q. al-idāra* administration office, head office; قلم الرصاص *q. ar-raṣāṣ* pencil; قلم السياحة travel agency; قلم الاستعلامات information bureau; قلم المطبوعات press and information office; قلم القيودات bureau of vital statistics, (G.B.) (general) register office; قلم الكتاب *q. al-kuttāb* clerical office; ○ قلم الكوبية *q. al-kōbiya* indelible pencil, copying pencil; قلم المرور (*Eg.*) Traffic Control Board

قلامة *qulāma* pl. *-āt* clippings, cuttings, parings, shavings; nail cuttings

مقلمة *miqlama* pl. *-āt* pen case

تقليم *taqlīm* clipping, trimming, paring; pruning, lopping (of trees) | تقليم الاظافر manicure

مقلم *muqallam* clipped, trimmed, pruned; (*eg.*) striped, streaked | مقلم الظفر *m. aẓ-ẓufr* powerless, helpless, weak

²اقلم *aqlama* to acclimate, acclimatize, adapt, adjust II *t.* *aqlama* to acclimatize (o.s.)

اقليم *iqlīm* pl. اقاليم *aqālīm*² area, region; province; administrative district (*Eg.* = مديرية); الاقاليم the country, countryside, provinces (as opposed to the city)

اقليمى *iqlīmī* climatic; regional, local; territorial | المياه الاقليمية (*miyāh*) territorial waters, coastal waters

قلندار *qalandār* wandering dervish, calender

قلنس II *taqalnasa* to wear a cap

قلنسوة *qalansuwa* and قلنسية *qulansiya* pl. قلانس *qalānis*², قلانيس *qalānīs*² tall headgear, tiara, cidaris; hood, cowl, capuche; cap

(قلو and قلى) قلا *qalā* *u* (*qalw*) and قلى *qalā* *i* (*qaly*) to fry, bake, roast (ه s.th.); — قلا *qalā* *u* (قلا *qilan*, قلاء *qalā'*), قلى *qalā* *i* and قلى *qaliya* *a* (قلى *qilan*, قلاء *qalā'*, مقلية *maqliya*) to hate, loathe, detest (ه s.o.)

قلو *qilw*, قلى *qilan*, *qily* alkali, base, lye (*chem.*)

قلوى *qilwī* alkaline, basic; القلويات *al-qilwīyāt* the bases (*chem.*)

قلاية *qallāya* frying vessel, cooking vessel; see also below

مقلى *miqlan* and مقلاة *miqlāh* pl. مقال *maqālin* frying pan

تقلية *taqliya* (*eg.*) sauce made of garlic, coriander and melted butter and served as a condiment

قلوز *qalwaza* to wind (the turban)

قلاووز see under قلوظ

قلوظ *qalwaẓa* to join with screws, screw together

قلاووظ (also قلاووز) *qalāwūẓ* ship's pilot; screw

[1]قلاية *qallāya* (monk's) cell; residence of the Coptic Patriarch

[2]قلية *qillīya* (monk's) cell

قم *qamma u* (*qamm*) to sweep (ه s.th.)

قمة *qimma* pl. قمم *qimam* top, summit, peak, acme, apex | قمة الرأس *q. ar-ra's* crown of the head; ○ قمة الموجة *q. al-mauja* wave peak (*el.*); هو حسن القمة (*ḥasan al-q.*) he is well-built; من قمة الرأس الى اخمص القدم (*akmaṣi l-qadam*) or من القمة الى الاخمص from head to toe

قمامة *qumāma* sweepings, rubbish, refuse, garbage | صندوق القمامة *ṣundūq al-q.* garbage bin

قمائم *qamā'im*² sweepings, rubbish

مقمة *miqamma* pl. مقام *maqāmm*² broom

قمؤ *qamu'a u* (قماءة *qamā'a*) to be little, lowly, despised, despicable; to feel inferior, feel worthless

قمیء *qamī'* lowly, little, small; insignificant, of little value

قماءة *qamā'a* lowliness, littleness, smallness; insignificance, puniness, inferiority, despicability

قمح II to give a portion only, pay an installment (ه to s.o.) IV to put forth ears, ear, ripen (grain) | اقمح بانفه (*bi-anfihī*) to be proud, bear one's head high

قمح *qamḥ* wheat

قمحى *qamḥī* wheat-colored, wheaten

قمحة *qamḥa* pl. *-āt* wheat kernel; grain (in Eg. = .04875 g = 1/4 قيراط)

شهرا قماح *šahrā qumāḥ* (*qimāḥ*) the two coldest months of winter

قماح *qammāḥ* grain merchant, corn chandler

[1]قمر *qamara i* (*qamr*) to gamble; — *i u* to defeat in gambling (ه s.o.); pass. *qumira* to lose in gambling; — *qamira a* (*qamr*) to be or become snow-blind II to toast (ه bread) III to gamble (ه with s.o.); to stake, risk, hazard (ب s.th.); to bet, speculate (على on) | قامر على الجواد الخاسر (*jawād*) to bet on the wrong horse IV to be moonlit (night) VI to gamble with one another

قمر *qamar* snow blindness; — (pl. اقمار *aqmār*) moon; satellite (*astron.*); القمران *al-qamarān* sun and moon | قمر الدين *q. ad-dīn* a kind of jelly made from apricots finely ground and dried in the sun; قمر كاذب paraselene, mock moon (*astron.*); حجر القمر *ḥajar al-q.* selenite (*min.*)

قمرة *qamara* (n. un.) pl. *-āt* crescent (as an emblem on a uniform); (*eg.*) moonlight; (*eg.*) skylight; see also below

قمرى *qamarī* of or pertaining to the moon, moon-shaped, moonlike, lunar | الاشهر القمرية (*ašhur*) the lunar months; الحروف القمرية the moon letters (*gram.*)

قمرى *qumrī* (coll.; n. un. ة) pl. قمارى *qamārīy* a variety of turtledove

ليلة قمرة *laila qamira* moonlit night

قمرية *qamarīya* pl. *-āt* (*eg.*) skylight, small window

قمراء *qamrā'*² moonlight

قمير *qamīr* pl. اقمار *aqmār* fellow gambler, gambling partner, gambler

اقمر *aqmar*², f. قمراء *qamrā'*² moonlit (night); moon-white, bright, whitish

مقمر *maqmar* and مقمرة *maqmara* pl. مقامر *maqāmir*² gambling house, gambling hell

قمار *qimār* gambling; bet, wager | آلة لعب القمار *ālat la'b al-q.* slot machine

مقامرة *muqāmara* gambling

مقمر *muqammir*, مقمر كهربائى (*kahrabā'ī*) toaster

مقمر *muqammar* (*eg.*) toast, toasted bread

مقامر *muqāmir* gambler

مقمر *muqmir* moonlit (night)

قمرة[2] (It. *camera*) *qamara, qamra* pl. *-āt* berth, bunk, cabin, stateroom

قمرق *gumrug* pl. قمارق *gamārig*[2] customs (*tun.*)

قمز *qamaza u i* (*qamz*) to take with the fingertips (ه s.th.)

قمس *qamasa u i* (*qams*) to dip, immerse, soak, steep (ه في s.th. in)

قاموس *qāmūs* pl. قواميس *qawāmīs*[2] ocean; dictionary, lexicon

قومس *qaumas* pl. قوامس *qawāmis*[2] depths of the sea; pl. mishaps, misfortunes, adversities

قمش[1] *qamaša u i* (*qamš*) to pick up, gather up, collect (ه rubbish) II do.

قماش *qumāš* rubbish, garbage, refuse, offal, trash, junk; (pl. اقمشة *aqmiša*) fabric, material, cloth | قماش البيت *q. al-bait* household effects, furniture; قماش الناس the scum of the earth, riffraff

قماش *qammāš* draper, cloth merchant

قمشة[2] *qamša* (*eg.*) strap, thong; leather whip, cowhide

قمص[1] *qamaṣa u i* (*qamṣ*, قماص *qumāṣ, qimāṣ*) to gallop; to spring, jump, leap, bound; to kick II do.

قمص *qamṣ* gallop

قمص[2] II to clothe with a shirt (ه s.o.) V to put on or wear a shirt; to be clothed, be vested (ه with), dress, attire o.s., wrap o.s. (ه in), cloak o.s. (ه in the mantle of; fig.); to transmigrate, pass into another body (spirit), materialize (ه in another body)

قميص *qamīṣ* pl. قمص *qumuṣ*, اقمصة *aqmiṣa*, قمصان *qumṣān* shirt; dress, gown; covering, cover, case, wrap, envelope, jacket; (*Chr.*) alb, surplice, rochet; incarnation | قميص افرنجى (*ifranjī*) day shirt, upper shirt; قميص النوم *q. an-naum* nightgown

تقميص *taqmīṣ* and تقمص *taqammuṣ* transmigration of souls, metempsychosis

قمص[3] *qummuṣ* pl. قمامصة *qamāmiṣa* archpriest, hegumen (*Copt.-Chr.*)

قمط *qamaṭa u i* (*qamṭ*) to swaddle (ه a baby); to fetter, shackle (ه s.o.); to dress, bandage (ه a wound) II do.

قمط *qimṭ* pl. اقماط *aqmāṭ* rope, fetter

قمطة *qamṭa* a kind of kerchief (*eg.*)

قماط *qimāṭ* pl. *-āt*, قمط *qumuṭ*, اقمطة *aqmiṭa* swaddle, diaper

قمطر *qimaṭr, qimṭar* pl. قماطر *qamāṭir*[2] receptacle for storing books; satchel

قمع *qama'a a* (*qam'*) to tame, curb, bridle, restrain, check, suppress, repress, subdue (ه, ه s.o., s.th.); to hinder, prevent (ه عن s.o. from) II (*eg.*) to cut off the upper end (ه of an okra) IV = I

قمع *qam'* repression, suppression, curbing, prevention; taming, subdual, quelling, subjection

قمع *qam', qim', qima'* pl. اقماع *aqmā'* funnel; — (pl. قموع *qumū'*) stem (of a fruit); pericarp | قمع الخياط *q. al-ḵayyāṭ* thimble; قمع السيكارة cigar butt

قمقم *qamqama* and II تقمقم *taqamqama* to complain, grumble, mutter

قمقم *qumqum* and قمقمة *qumquma* pl. قماقم *qamāqim*[2] a bulgy, long-necked bottle

قمل **qamila** *a* (*qamal*) to be lice-infested, teem with lice V do.

قمل *qaml* (coll.; n. un. ة) louse

قمل *qamil* lousy, lice-infested

مقمل *muqammal* lice-infested

[1]قمن V to intend, purpose, propose (ه to do s.th.)

قمن *qamin* worthy, deserving (ب of s.th.)

قمين *qamīn* worthy (ب of), adequate (ب to), in keeping with (ب); fit(ting), appropriate, suitable (ب for), capable (ب of)

مقمن *maqman* adequate (ل to), appropriate, suited, suitable, fit (ل for)

[2]قمين *qamīn* and قمينة *qamīna* pl. *-āt* kiln, furnace

[1]قن *qunn* pl. قنان *qinān* chicken coop, chicken house

قن *qinn* pl. اقنان *aqnān*, اقنة *aqinna* slave, serf

قنة *qinna* galbanum (*bot.*)

قنة *qunna* pl. *-āt*, قنن *qunan*, قنان *qinān*, قنون *qunūn* mountaintop, summit, peak

قنونة *qunūna* slavery, serfdom

قنينة *qinnīna* pl. قنان *qanānin* bottle, glass bottle; flask, flacon, vial

[2]قن II to make laws, legislate; to determine, fix (ه s.th.)

قانون *qānūn* pl. قوانين *qawānīn*[2] canon; established principle, basic rule, axiom, norm, regulation, rule, ordinance, prescript, precept, statute; law; code; tax, impost; (*Tun.*) tax on olives and dates; a stringed musical instrument resembling the zither, with a shallow, trapezoidal sound box, set horizontally before the performer | القانون الاساسى (*asāsī*) basic constitutional law; statutes; قانون التأسيس statutes, constitution; القانون الجنائى (*jinā'ī*) criminal law, penal law; قانون الاحوال الشخصية (*šaḵṣīya*) personal statute; القانون الدستورى (*dustūrī*) constitutional law; القانون الدولى (*duwalī*) international law; قانون المرافعات *q. al-murāfa'āt* code of procedure (*jur.*; *Eg.*); قانون اصول المحاكمات الحقوقية do. (*Syr.*); قانون السلك الادارى *q. as-silk al-idārī* administrative law; قانون كيماوى (*kīmāwī*) chemical formula; القانون المدنى (*madanī*) civil law

قانونى *qānūnī* canonical; legal, statutory; lawful, legitimate, licit, accordant with law or regulations, valid, regular; legist, jurisprudent, jurist | صيدلى قانونى (*ṣaidalī*) certified and licensed pharmacist; غير قانونى illegal

قانونية *qānūnīya* legality, lawfulness

تقنين *taqnīn* legislation, lawmaking; codification (*jur.*); regulation by law; rationing

مقنن *muqannin* legislative, lawmaking; lawgiver, lawmaker, legislator

مقنن *muqannan* determined, fixed

قانئ *qāni'* blood-red, deep-red

قنال *qanāl* canal | قنال السويس the Suez Canal

قنب *qanb* pl. قنوب *qunūb* calyx

قنب *qunnab*, *qinnab* hemp (Cannabis indica; *bot.*) | خيط القنب *ḵaiṭ al-q.* hemp rope, string, cord, twine, packthread

قنبى *qinnabī* hempen, hemp (adj.)

مقنب *miqnab* pl. مقانب *maqānib*[2] troop of horsemen

[1]قنبار *qunbār* (*ir.*) bast rug, bast runner

[2]قنبر *qunbur* (coll.; n. un. ة) pl. قنابر *qanābir*[2] lark (*zool.*)

[3]قنبرة *qunbura* pl. قنابر *qanābir*[2] bomb

[4]قنبور *qunbūr* hump, hunch | ابو قنبور *abū qunbūr* hunchback

قنباز *qunbāz* pl. قنابيز *qanābīz*[2] (*syr.*) a long, sleeved garment worn by men, open in front and fastened with a belt

[1]قنبل *qanbal* and قنبلة *qanbala* pl. قنابل *qanābil*[2] troop of horsemen; troop, group, band

[2]قنبل *qanbala* to bomb (ه s.th.)

قنبلة *qunbula* pl. قنابل *qanābil*[2] bomb, bomb shell; grenade, shell | قنبلة حارقة incendiary bomb; قنبلة ذرية (*ḏarrīya*) atomic bomb, A bomb; قنبلة غازية (*ḡāzīya*) gas bomb, gas shell; قنبلة مائية (*mā'iya*) depth charge; قنبلة محرقة (*muḥriqa*) incendiary bomb; قنبلة منفجرة (*munfajira*) high-explosive bomb; قنبلة هيدروجينية (*haidrōjīnīya*) hydrogen bomb, H bomb; قنبلة اليد *q. al-yad* or قنبلة يدوية (*yadawīya*) hand grenade

طائرة مقنبلة *ṭā'ira muqanbila* bomber; مقنبلات bombers

قنبيط *qunnabīṭ* cauliflower

قنت *qanata u* (قنوت *qunūt*) to be obedient, submissive, humble

قنوت *qunūt* obedience to God, humility before God, devoutness, piety

قنجة *qanja* pl. *-āt*, قناج *qināj* Nile boat

قند *qand* pl. قنود *qunūd* hard crystalline mass formed by evaporating or boiling cane sugar, candy

مقنود *maqnūd* and مقند *muqannad* sweetened with *qand*

قندز *qunduz* and قندس *qundus* beaver

قندق *qandaq* pl. قنادق *qanādiq*[2] gunstock, rifle butt

قندلفت *qandalaft* pl. *-īya* sexton, sacristan (*Chr.*)

قندول *qandūl* aspalathus (*bot.*)

قنديل *qindīl* pl. قناديل *qanādīl*[2] lamp; candlestick; candelabrum

قنزعة *qunzuʿa*, *qanzaʿa*, *qinziʿa* pl. قنازع *qanāziʿ*[2] tuft of hair; cock's comb, crest of a rooster

قنص *qanaṣa i* (*qanṣ*) and VIII to hunt, shoot, bag (ه s.th.); to hunt up (ه s.th.), get hold (ه of s.th.); to make use, take advantage, avail o.s. (الظروف of the circumstances, الفرصة *al-furṣa* of the opportunity, and the like)

قنص *qanṣ* hunting, shooting, hunt

قنص *qanaṣ* quarry, bag, game

قنيص *qanīṣ* game, quarry, bag, catch; hunter

قناص *qannāṣ* pl. قناصة *qannāṣa* hunter

قانص *qāniṣ* pl. قناص *qunnāṣ* hunter

قانصة *qāniṣa* pl. قوانص *qawāniṣ*[2] gizzard

○ قانصة *qāniṣa* pl. *-āt* tank destroyer (*Syr.*; *mil.*)

مقنوص *maqnūṣ* quarry, bag, catch

قنصل *qunṣul* pl. قناصل *qanāṣil*[2] consul | نائب قنصل and وكيل القنصل vice-consul; قنصل عام (*ʿāmm*) consul general

قنصلى *qunṣulī* consular

قنصلية *qunṣulīya* pl. *-āt* consulate | قنصلية عامة (*ʿāmma*) consulate general

قنصلاتو *qunṣulātō* consulate

قنط *qaniṭa a* (*qanaṭ*), *qanaṭa u i* (قنوط *qunūṭ*) and *qanuṭa u* (قناطة *qanāṭa*) to despair, despond, become disheartened, be without hope, lose all courage **II** to drive to despair, dishearten, discourage (ه s.o.) **IV** do.

قنط *qanaṭ* and قنوط *qunūṭ* despair, despondency, desperateness, hopelessness

قنط *qaniṭ* and قنوط *qanūṭ* despairing, desperate, despondent, disheartened, discouraged

قانط *qāniṭ* despairing, desperate, despondent, disheartened, discouraged

[1]قنطر *qanṭara* to arch, span, vault (ه s.th.)

قنطرة *qanṭara* pl. قناطر *qanāṭir*[2] arched bridge, stone bridge; vault, arch; archway, arcade; arches, viaduct, aqueduct (esp. pl.); dam, weir | قنطرة موازنة regulator, regulating device (at a canal, esp. in the Egyptian irrigation system); القناطر الخيرية (*ḵairīya*) the Barrages, at the entrance of the Nile delta, about 15 miles north of Cairo

مقنطر *muqanṭar* vaulted, arched, arcaded

قنطر *qanṭara* to possess tremendous riches

قنطار *qinṭār* pl. قناطير *qanāṭīr*[2] kantar, a varying weight of 100 رطل *raṭl* (in Eg. = 44.93 kg, in Tunisia = 53.9 kg, in Syria = 256.4 kg) | قناطير مقنطرة (*muqanṭara*) accumulated riches; tremendous sums

قنطاريون *qinṭārīyūn* centaury (Erythrea centauricum; *bot.*)

قنطرمة *qanṭarma* pl. *-āt* snaffle, bridoon

قنع *qaniʿa a* (*qanaʿ*, قنعان *qunʿān*, قناعة *qanāʿa*) to content o.s., be content, be satisfied (ب with); to be convinced **II** to mask (ه the face); to veil (ه the face, ها a woman), to satisfy, content (ه s.o.), give satisfaction (ه to); to convince (ه ب s.o. of); to persuade (ه s.o.) **IV** to content, satisfy (ه s.o.), give satisfaction (ه to); to convince (ه s.o.); to induce, persuade (ه ب s.o. to do s.th.), prevail (ه ب upon s.o. to do s.th.) **V** to mask or conceal one's face; to veil one's face, be veiled, wear a veil **VIII** to content o.s., be content (ب with); to be convinced (ب of)

قنع *qinʿ* pl. اقناع *aqnāʿ* arms, weapons, armor

قنع *qanaʿ* contentment, content, contentedness; frugality, moderation, temperance, abstemiousness

قناعة *qanāʿa* satisfaction; contentment, content, contentedness; frugality, temperance, moderation

قنع *qaniʿ* satisfied, content, contented; temperate, moderate, abstemious

قناع *qināʿ* pl. قنع *qunuʿ* arms, weapons, armor; — (pl. اقنعة *aqniʿa*, also قناعات *qināʿāt*) veil, head veil, mask; pericardium | قناع واق (*wāqin*) gas mask

قنوع *qanūʿ* pl. قنع *qunuʿ* satisfied, content (ب with); frugal, modest, temperate

مقنع *maqnaʿ* sufficiency | فى ذلك مقنع له that is enough for him, he may content himself with that

اقناع *iqnāʿ* satisfying, satisfaction, contenting (of s.o.); persuasion; convincing, convincement, conviction

تقنع *taqannuʿ* mummery, masquerade

اقتناع *iqtināʿ* satisfaction, contentment, content, contentedness; conviction (= convincedness)

قانع *qāniʿ* satisfied, content (ب with)

مقنع *muqannaʿ* veiled; masked

مقتنع *muqtaniʿ* satisfied, content (ب with); convinced

قنفذ *qunfuḏ* pl. قنافذ *qanāfiḏ*[2] hedgehog | قنفذ البحر *q. al-baḥr* or قنفذ بحرى (*baḥrī*) sea urchin (Echinus; *zool.*); porcupine fish (Diodon; *zool.*)

قنقر *qanqar* kangaroo

قنال look up alphabetically

[1]قنم *qanima a* (*qanam*) to be or become rancid, rank

قنومة *qannūma* sacred fish (Mormyrus oxyrhynchus)

[2]اقنوم *uqnūm* pl. اقانيم *aqānīm*[2] hypostasis, person of the Trinity (*Chr.*); basic element, substance, subsistent principle

قنو (and قنى) قنا **qanā u** (قنو *qanw, qunūw,* قنوة *qunwa,* قنوان *qunwān*) to acquire, appropriate, make one's own (ه s.th.); to possess, own, have (ه s.th.); — قنى *qanā i* (*qany,* قنيان *qunyān*) to acquire, gain (ه s.th.); — قنى *qaniya a* (قنا *qanan*) to be hooked, aquiline (nose) **II** to dig (a canal) **VIII** to acquire (ه s.th.); to get, procure, purchase (ه s.th.)

قنو *qunw, qinw* pl. اقناء *aqnā',* قنوان *qunwān, qinwān,* قنيان *qunyān, qinyān* bunch of dates

قنوة *qunwa, qinwa* appropriation, acquisition; property in livestock, wealth, fortune, possessions, property

قنية *qunya, qinya* acquisition, property

قناة *qanāh* pl. قنى *qanan, qunīy,* قناء *qinā',* قنوات *qanawāt,* قنيات *qanayāt* spear, (bamboo) lance; shaft; tube, duct, pipe; — (pl. اقنية *aqniya,* قنوات *qanawāt*) canal; stream, waterway | قناة دمعية (*dam'īya*) lachrymal canal; قناة العلم *q. al-'alam* flagpole; لانت قناته *lānat qanātuhū* to soften, relent; to yield, give in

قناية *qanāya* pl. *-āt* small stream, rivulet, runnel, canal

○ قنية *qunayya* cannula

اقنى *aqnā* bent, curved, crooked, hooked

اقتناء *iqtinā'* purchase, acquisition

قان *qānin* pl. قانية *qāniya* possessor, owner; see also alphabetically

مقتنى *muqtanan* pl. مقتنيات *muqtanayāt* thing acquired, acquisition

قهر *qahara a* (*qahr*) to subject, subjugate, conquer, vanquish, defeat (ه, ه s.o., s.th.); to subdue, overpower, overwhelm, overcome (ه, ه s.o., s.th.); to force, compel, coerce (على ه s.o. to)

قهر *qahr* vanquishing, subdual, subjection, subjugation; compulsion, coercion, force; (*eg.*) annoyance, trouble, sorrow, grief; قهرا *qahran* forcibly, by force; perforce, of necessity

قهرة *quhra* compulsion, coercion, constraint, force

قهرى *qahrī* compelling, conpulsory, mandatory, coercive; forcible, forced | ابتسامة قهرية forced smile; سبب قهرى (*sabab*) compelling reason

قاهر *qāhir* forcible, cogent, overpowering, irresistible; vanquisher, conqueror, victor; القاهر the planet Mars

مصر القاهرة *miṣr al-qāhira* or القاهرة *al-qāhira* Cairo

قاهرى *qāhirī* Cairene; (pl. *-ūn*) a Cairene

قهار *qahhār* conquering, vanquishing; القهار the Subduer, the Almighty (God)

قهرمان *qahramān* pl. قهارمة *qahārima* steward, butler, household manager

قهرمانة *qahramāna* (woman) housekeeper

قهقر *qahqara* to move backward, go back, fall back, retreat, withdraw; to fall behind, lag behind; to recede, retrogress, retrograde, decline, degenerate, deteriorate **II** *taqahqara* do.

قهقرة *qahqara* backward movement, recedence, recession, retrogression, fallback, retreat; decline, retrogradation, degeneration

قهقرى *qahqarā* backward movement, recedence, recession, retrogression, fall-back, retreat; decline, retrogradation, degeneration | عاد القهقرى to fall back, retreat, withdraw

تقهقر *taqahqur* regress, recession, recedence, retrogression, lag, fallback, retreat

قهقه *qahqaha* to laugh boisterously, guffaw

قهقهة *qahqaha* loud burst of laughter, guffaw, horselaugh

قهوة **qahwa** coffee; (pl. *qahawāt* and □ قهاوى *qahāwī*) café, coffeehouse | قهوة سادة coffee without sugar

قهواتى *qahwātī*, *qahawātī* pl. *-īya* (*syr.*) coffeehouse owner

قهوجى *qahwajī* coffeehouse owner; coffee cook

مقهى *maqhan* and مقهاة *maqhāh* pl. مقاه *maqāhin* café, coffeehouse

مقهاية *maqhāya* (*yem.*) café, coffeehouse

قهى **qahiya** *a*: قهى من الطعام (*ṭa'ām*) and IV اقهى من الطعام to have little appetite

قاه *qāhin* supplied with provisions

(قوب) قاب **qāba** *u* (*qaub*) to dig; to dig up, burrow, excavate, hollow out (ه the ground) II do. V to break open, burst open (egg)

قاب *qāb* small distance, short span (between the middle and the end of a bow) | على قاب قوسين (*q. qausain*) quite near, very close; imminent; على قاب لمحة (*q. lamḥa*) in a moment

قوب *qūb* pl. اقواب *aqwāb* young bird, chick

قوباء *qūbā'*, *quwabā'*[2] and قوبة *qūba*, *quwaba* pl. قوب *quwab* tetter (*med.*)

(قوت) قات **qāta** *u* (*qaut*, *qūt*, قياتة *qiyāta*) to feed, nourish, subsist, sustain, support (ه s.o.), provide for the support (ه of) II and IV do. V to be fed, be supported; to feed, live (ب on s.th.); to eat (ب s.th.) VIII do.; to take in or absorb as nourishment (ه s.th.)

قات *qāt* kat (Catha edulis Forskål; *bot.*); the leaves of this shrub which act as an excitant when chewed | قات الرعيان *q. ar-ru'yān* a variety of lettuce (Lactuca inermis Forsk.; *bot.*)

قوت *qūt* pl. اقوات *aqwāt* nutriment, aliment, nourishment, food, viands | مواد القوت *mawādd al-q.* foodstuffs

تقوت *taqawwut* nutrition, alimentation

المقيت *al-muqīt* the Feeder, the Nourisher (God)

(قوح) قاح **qāḥa** *u* (*qauḥ*) to fester, suppurate, swell (wound); to sweep (ه the house) II to sweep (ه the house) III to quarrel, pick a quarrel V to fester, suppurate, swell

قاحة *qāḥa* pl. قوح *qūḥ* courtyard

(قود) قاد **qāda** *u* (*qaud*, قياد *qiyād*, قيادة *qiyāda*, مقادة *maqāda*) to lead, lead by a halter (ه s.th.); to conduct, guide, engineer, steer (ه s.th.); to drive, steer (ه e.g., an automobile), pilot (ه an airplane); to pander, pimp IV to cause (ه s.o.) to retaliate VII to be led, be guided; to follow, obey (ل s.o.), yield, submit (ل to s.o.) VIII to lead; to be led X to retaliate

قود *qaud* leadership; pandering, pimping

قود *qawad* retaliation

قواد *qawwād* pander, pimp, procurer

قؤود *qa'ūd* tractable, docile, amenable, manageable; trained (horse)

اقود *aqwad*[2] tractable, docile, amenable, manageable

قياد *qiyād* leadership, guidance; leading rope, halter | سلس القياد *salis al-q.* tractable, docile, amenable, manageable, pliant; صعب القياد *ṣa'b al-q.* intractable, unruly, ungovernable

قيادة *qiyāda* leadership, guidance; driving, steering, steerage (of a vehicle); command | القيادة العليا (or العامة) (*'ulyā*, *'āmma*) supreme command; عجلة القيادة *'ajalat al-q.* steering wheel (of an automobile)

مقود *miqwad* pl. مقاود *maqāwid*[2] leading rope, leading rein, halter; steering mechanism; steering wheel

انقياد *inqiyād* obedience, compliance, yielding, submission

قائد *qā'id* pl. قواد *quwwād*, قود *quwwad*, قادة *qāda*, قادات *qādāt* leader; director, manager; head, chief; commander, commandant; high-ranking officer, senior officer; caïd, native governmental officer heading a caïdate in Tunisia; steersman, helmsman | قائد الجيش *q. al-jaiš* commander of an army, general; قائد عام (*ʿāmm*) supreme commander; القائد الاعلى (*aʿlā*) commander-in-chief of the Eg. navy; قائد عام الاساطيل الجوية (*ʿāmm, jawwīya*) lieutenant general of the Air Force (*Eg.* 1939); قائد الاساطيل الجوية (*jawwīya*) major general of the Air Force (*Eg.* 1939); قائد اسطول جوى *q. usṭūl jawwī* colonel of the Air Force (*Eg.* 1939); قائد لواء جوى lieutenant colonel of the Air Force (*Eg.* 1939); قائد فرقة جوية *q. firqa jawwīya* major of the Air Force (*Eg.* 1939); قائد جناح *q. janāḥ* wing commander (*Eg.* 1939); قائد سرب *q. sirb* captain of the Air Force (*Eg.* 1939); قادة الفكر *q. al-fikr* leading thinkers

قور II to make a round hole (ه in s.th.); to gouge, scoop out, hollow out (ه s.th.); to cut out in a round form, cut round (ه s.th.) V to coil (snake) VIII اقتار and اقتور *iqtawara* = II

قار *qār* pitch; tar

قارة *qāra* pl. *-āt*, قور *qūr*, قيران *qīrān* hill; see also *qārra* under قر

مقورة *miqwara* gouge

تقوير *taqwīr* gouging, hollowing out

تقويرة *taqwīra* neckline (of a garment)

مقور *muqawwar* cut out in a round form; gouged, hollowed out, scooped out; chiseled out; low-cut, low-necked, décolleté (dress)

قورمة *qawurma* (*eg.*) mutton or beef cut in small pieces and braised with squash (*qarʿ*) or onions and tomatoes

قوس *qawisa a* (*qawas*) to be bent, curved, crooked II = I; to bend, curve, crook (ه s.th.); to shoot V = I; to bend

قوس *qaus* m. and f., pl. اقواس *aqwās*, قسى *qusīy*, *qisīy* bow, longbow; arc (*geom.*); arch, vault (*arch.*; of a bridge); violin bow, fiddlestick; semicircular table; قوسان parentheses (punctuation marks); القوس Sagitta, the Archer (sign of the zodiac) | بين قوسين (*qausain*) in parentheses; قوس قزح *q. quzaḥa* rainbow; قوس الندف *q. an-nadf* teasing bow (for combing or carding cotton); قوس النصر *q. an-naṣr* triumphal arch; لم يبق فى قوس صبرى منزع *lam yabqa fī q. ṣabrī minzaʿ* my patience is at an end (lit.: there is no arrow left for the bow of my patience)

قواس *qawwās* bowmaker; bowman, archer; kavass, consular guard

قويسة *quwaisa* sage (*bot.*)

مقوس *muqawwas* bent, crooked, curved, arched

قوش *qūš* pl. اقواش *aqwāš* crupper (of the saddle or harness); strap, girth

قاووش *qāwūš* pl. قواويش *qawāwīš*[2] prison cell

□ قواص *qawwāṣ* see قواس *qawwās*

(قوض) قاض *qāḍa u* (*qauḍ*) to demolish, tear down, wreck, raze (ه a building), strike (ه a tent) II do.; to break off (ه s.th.); to smash (ه s.th.) V to be demolished, undergo demolition; to collapse, fall in, cave in; to break up, scatter, disperse (crowd); to desist (عن from), give in, give way (عن to)

تقويض *taqwīḍ* wrecking, demolition; destruction, annihilation

مقاوضة *muqāwaḍa* barter, exchange, interchange

قوط[1] *qauṭ* pl. اقواط *aqwāṭ* flock of sheep

[2]القوط *al-qūṭ* the Goths

قوطى *qūṭī* Gothic

[3]قوطة *qauṭa* small basket for fruit; date basket

[4]قوطة *qūṭa* (*eg.*) tomatoes

(قوع) قاع *qā'* pl. قيعان *qī'ān*, اقوع *aqwu'*, اقواع *aqwā'* plain, lowland; bottom, lowest part; wave trough (*phys.*); floor (of a mine); gulf, abyss | قاع النهر *q. an-nahr* river bed; بلاد القاع the Netherlands

قاعة *qā'a* pl. *-āt* paved courtyard; entrance hall, vestibule, corridor; hall; sizable room | قاعة المحاضرات *q. al-muḥāḍarāt* lecture hall, auditorium (of a university); قاعة التدريس lecture room, classroom; قاعة الطعام *q. aṭ-ṭa'ām* dining room; messhall; قاعة العرش *q. al-'arš* throne room; قاعة المطالعة *q. al-muṭāla'a* reading room, study hall; قاعة الافراح banquet hall, ballroom

[1](قوق) قاق *qāqa u* (*qauq*) to cackle, cluck (hen) **II** do.

قاق *qāq* pl. قيقان *qīqān* (*syr.*) raven | قاق الماء cormorant (*zool.*)

ام قويق *umm quwaiq* (*eg.*) owl (*zool.*)

[2]قاوق and قاووق pl. قواويق look up alphabetically

القوقاز *al-qauqāz* and القوقاس *al-qauqās* the Caucasus

القوقازيون *al-qauqāzīyūn* the Caucasians

قوقع *qauqa'* seashell

قوقعة *qauqa'a* pl. قواقع *qawāqi'*[2] snail

[1](قول) قال *qāla u* (قول *qaul*) to speak, say, tell (ه s.th., ل to s.o.; عن ,فى ه s.th. about or of), utter, voice (ه s.th.); to speak (عن of), deal (عن with), treat (عن of); to state, maintain, assert, propound, teach, profess, advocate, defend (ب s.th.); to support, hold (ب a view), stand up (ب for), be the proponent (ب of a doctrine or dogma); to allege (ب s.th.); with على: to speak against s.o., speak ill of s.o., tell lies about s.o. | قال برأسه (*bi-ra'sihī*) to motion with the head, signal, beckon; قيل فى المثل *qīla fī l-maṯal* the proverb says; ولا يقال ان (*inna*) one cannot say that ..., let no one say that ...; او قل *au qul* or, or rather, or say even ...; وقل مثل هذه فى (*wa-qul miṯla*) or وكذلك قل فى or وقل مثله فى the same must be said about ..., the same can be said of ..., the same applies to ... **III** to confer, parley, treat, negotiate (ه with s.o.); to dispute, wrangle, argue; to haggle, bargain (ه with s.o., about the price); to make a contract; to conclude a bargain, make a deal (ه with s.o.) **V** to fabricate lies, spread rumors (على about s.o.); to pretend, allege, purport (ه s.th.) | تقول الاقاويل (*aqāwīla*) to talk foolishly **X** ○ to render (voice by radio)

قال وقيل *qāl wa-qīl* and قيل وقال *qīl wa-qāl* long palaver; idle talk, prattle, gossip

قالة *qāla* speech, talk | سوء القالة *sū' al-q.* malicious gossip, backbiting, defamation

قول *qaul* pl. اقوال *aqwāl*, اقاويل *aqāwīl*[2] word, speech, saying, utterance, remark; statement, declaration; report, account; doctrine, teaching; pl. اقوال also: testimony (in court); اقاويل sayings, locutions; proverbs | قولا وعملا *qaulan wa-'amalan* or بالقول والفعل (*fi'l*) by word and deed; اقوال الشهود testimonies, depositions, evidence; اعطى قوله *a'ṭā qaulahū* to make one's bid (at an auction)

قولة *qaula* (n. vic.) utterance, remark, word; pronoucement, dictum

قولة *quwala* garrulous, voluble, loquacious, talkative, communicative

قوال *qawwāl* garrulous, voluble, loquacious, talkative, communicative; itinerant singer and musician

مقول *miqwal* pl. مقاول *maqāwil*[2] phonograph, gramophone, talking machine

مقال *maqāl* speech; proposition, contention, teaching, doctrine; article; treatise; piece of writing

مقالة *maqāla* pl. *-āt* article; essay; treatise; piece of writing | مقالة افتتاحية (*iftitāḥīya*) editorial, leading article

مقاولة *muqāwala* talk, conversation, parley, conference; dispute; contract; settlement, arrangement, agreement; bargain, deal, transaction, undertaking | بالمقاولة by the job, by the contract, by piece (work)

تقول *taqawwul* pl. *-āt* talk, rumor, gossip

قائل *qā'il* pl. قول *quwwal* saying, telling; teller, narrator; advocate, proponent (ب of s.th.)

مقول *maqūl* pl. *-āt* that which is said, utterance, saying; word(s), speech | المقولات العشر (*'ašr*) the ten categories (*philos.*)

مقاول *muqāwil* contractor; building contractor

قول[2] (Turk. *kol*) *qōl* wing of an army, army corps; قول اغاسى (Turk. *kol ağası*) a military rank intermediate between those of captain and major, adjutant major (*Eg.*)

قولحة *qaulaḥa* pl. قوالح *qawāliḥ*[2] (*eg.*) cob (of corn, and the like)

قولنج *qaulanj* colic

قولون *qolōn* colon (*anat.*)

(قوم) قام *qāma u* (قومة *qauma*, قيام *qiyām*) to get up; to stand up, stand erect; to rise (also fig.: voices, noise, wind); قام عليه to rise or turn against s.o., revolt or rebel against s.o., attack s.o.; قام له to rise in honor of s.o.; to rise from the dead, be resurrected; to ascend; to set out, start out; to depart, leave (train); to betake o.s., go (الى to); to stand; to remain standing; to be, exist, be existent; to be located, be situated, lie; to consist (ب in); to rest, be based, be founded (على on, also ب), be built (على on); to have for its (main) theme (على a problem; of a book, and the like); to begin (يفعل to do s.th.), start (يفعل doing s.th.); to make s.th. (ب) one's business, concern o.s. (ب with), undertake, take upon o.s., perform, do, carry out, execute, accomplish, practice, exercise (ب s.th.); to stand up (ب for), support, advocate, endorse (ب s.th.); to be in charge (على of), manage, run, tend, guard, keep up, preserve (على s.th.); to take care (على of), attend (على to), watch (على over), look after s.th. (على); to cost, be worth (ب so and so much) | قام البرهان على (*burhān*) proof had been furnished for; قام باعباء الحكم (*bi-a'bā'i l-ḥukm*) to assume the burdens of government, take over power; قام باوده (*bi-awadihī*) to provide for s.o.'s needs, stand by s.o. in time of need; قام بدور (*bi-daurin*) to play a part; قام بشأنه (*bi-ša'nihī*) to take care of s.o., look after s.o., take s.o. under one's wing; قام بالمصاريف to defray the costs, pay the expenses; قام بالواجب عليه to do one's duty; قام بوعده (*bi-wa'dihī*) to keep one's word; قامت الحرب على ساق (*ḥarb*) the war was or became violent, flared up; war broke out; قام الحق (*ḥaqq*) truth became or was manifest; قامت الصلاة (*ṣalāh*) the time of prayer has come; قام على قدم وساق (*qadamin wa-sāqin*) to become fully effective, be in full progress, be in full swing; قاموا قومة رجل واحد (*qaumata rajulin*) they rose to a man; لم تقم له قائمة بعد *lam taqum lahū qā'imatun ba'du* he was no longer able to put up any resistance, he was as good as finished; لا تقوم الاعداء قائمة there is no resistance against the enemies; قامت قيامته (qiyāmatuhū) to get excited, get angry, become furious; all hell broke loose in it; قامت قيامته ل (من) to be upset, be shocked, be violently agitated by s.th.; قام في وجهه (wajhihī) to resist, oppose, defy s.o.; قام مقامه (maqāmahū) to replace s.o., substitute for s.o., deputize for s.o., take s.o.'s place; to serve as or instead of s.th., take the place of s.th., replace s.th.; قام منه مقامه to take the place of s.o. with s.o.; قام وقعد (wa-qaʿada) to be in a state of great anxiety, be seriously upset, be very agitated; to be very alarmed (ل by s.th.); لا قام ولا قعد not to be lasting and durable II to set upright, lift up, raise (ه s.th.); to create, shape, form, arrange, set up (ه s.th.); to straighten, make or put straight (ه s.th.); to arrange well, do properly (ه s.th.); to put in order, fix, set going (ه s.th.); to right, put to rights, rectify, correct, reform, amend (ه s.th.); ○ to rectify (el.); to estimate, assess, appraise, value, rate (ب s.th. at) | لا يقوم بثمن lā yuqawwamu bi-ṯamanin inestimable, invaluable, priceless III to resist, oppose (ه s.o.); to fight, combat (ه s.th.); to raise objections, take issue, contend, argue (في o with s.o. because of s.th.); to withstand (o s.o.), hold out, hold one's own (ه against), be on a par (o with s.o.), equal, match (o s.o.), measure up (ه to s.o.) | لا يقاوم lā yuqāwamu irresistible IV to straighten, straighten out, make right or correct, put in order (ه s.th.); to make (o s.o.) rise; to resurrect, raise from the dead (o s.o.); to lift up, elevate (ه s.th.); to set up, raise, erect (ه s.th.); to start, originate, found, call into being (ه s.th.); to fix, determine (ه s.th.); to appoint, nominate, install (ه s.o. as); اقامه على to put s.o. in charge of s.th., commission s.o. with the management of s.th.; to agitate, rouse, excite (ه s.th.);

to make brisk, enliven, animate (ه the market); to hold (ه a meeting, a ceremony, etc.), celebrate (ه a festival), put on, stage, organize (ه a celebration, a pageant, etc.), give (ه a reception); to occupy o.s. constantly (ل with); to abide, stay, remain, dwell, reside, live (ب in); to dwell (على on), persist (على in), keep, stick (على to) | اقام اوده (awadahū) to provide for s.o.'s needs, stand by s.o. in time of need; to support s.o., furnish s.o. with the means of subsistence; اقام البرهان الجلي على (burhāna l-jaliya) to furnish the unmistakable proof for ..., clearly prove s.th.; اقام الحجة (ḥujjata) to protest, lodge a protest; اقام حسابا ل (ḥisāban) to render account to s.o.; to give one's mind to s.o. or s.th., make s.o. or s.th. one's concern; اقام الدليل على ان to prove that ...; اقام الشعائر الدينية (dīnīya) to perform the liturgical rites; اقام الصلاة (ṣalāta) to perform the ritual prayer; اقام العدل (ʿadla) to administer justice, handle the law; اقام القداس على (quddāsa) to read the Mass for s.o.; اقام قضية (or دعوى) على (qaḍiyatan, daʿwā) to take legal action against s.o., sue s.o.; اقام له وزنا (waznan) to set great store by s.th., attach importance to s.th., make much of s.th.; لا يقام له وزن (yuqāmu, wuzn) to be negligible, be of no consequence; اقام مباراة (mubārātan) to stage a contest; اقامه مقامه (maqāmahū) to make s.o. take the place of s.o. else, make s.o. replace s.o. else, substitute s.o. for s.o. else; اقام نفسه مقام الحامي (nafsahū maqāma l-ḥāmī) to pose as the protector; اقامه واقعده (wa-aqʿadahū) to upset s.o. seriously, throw s.o. in a state of violent emotion; اقام الدنيا واقعدها (dunyā wa-aqʿadahā) to move heaven and earth; to make a stir, create a sensation; لا يقيم له قيامة (qiyāmatan) he forestalls any resistance on his part X to rise, get up, stand up; to straighten up, draw o.s. up; to stand upright, stand erect; to be or become straight; to be right, correct, sound, proper, in order; to keep, stick (في to s.th.) | استقام له الكلام في (*kalāmu*) he said the right thing about ..., he talked sense about ...

قوم *qaum* pl. اقوام *aqwām* fellow tribesmen, kinsfolk, kin, kindred; tribe, race, people, nation; people | عالم الاقوام ethnographer, ethnologist; سيقول قوم ان (*inna*) people will say ...

قومة *qauma* rising; uprising, revolt

قومى *qaumī* national; ethnic, racial; قوميات national traits; (pl. *-īya*) "goumier", member of the native cavalry troops recruited from the local tribes in French North Africa

قومية *qaumīya* nationalism; nationality

قامة *qāma* stature, figure, build, frame (of a person); fathom (measure of length = 6 feet); stand, support, tripod

قيم *qayyim* valuable, precious; straight, right; caretaker, curator, custodian, superintendent; القيمة *al-qayyima* the true faith | كتب قيمة (*kutub*) valuable books

قيمة *qīma* pl. قيم *qiyam* value, worth; size of an amount, amount, quantity; price | ذو قيمة valuable; لا قيمة له (*qīmata*) worthless

قيمى *qīmī* relating to the value, by the standard of value, according to the value; nonfungible (*Isl. Law*) | مال قيمى nonfungible things, nonfungibles (*Isl. Law*)

قوام *qawām* upright posture, erect bearing; straightness; stature, physique, build, frame; figure, body (of a person); rightness, properness, proper condition, normal state; strength, vigor, stamina; firmness, consistency; support, stay, prop; livelihood, living

قوام *qiwām* support, stay, prop; basis, foundation; stock, supply; sustenance, subsistence, livelihood | قوام اهله *q. ahlihī* the provider, or supporter, of his family

قوام *qawwām* manager, director, superintendent, caretaker, keeper, custodian, guardian (على of s.th.)

قوامة *qiwāma* guardianship

قويم *qawīm* pl. قيام *qiyām* straight, upright, erect; correct, right, proper, sound, authentic; true (religion); firm, solid

قيام *qiyām* rising, getting up; standing; existence; outbreak (e.g., of a revolt); setting out, leaving, departure (also, esp., of trains); performance, execution, carrying out, consummation, discharge, accomplishment, undertaking (ب of s.th.); support, stay, prop; sustenance, subsistence, livelihood | الى قيام الساعة till doomsday, forever and ever, in perpetuity, for all time to come; قيام اهله *q. ahlihī* the provider, or supporter, of his family; القيام بالعمل (*'amal*) performance; working, functioning

قيامة *qiyāma* resurrection; tumult, turmoil, upheaval, revolution, overthrow; guardianship | عيد القيامة *'īd al-q.* Easter; يوم القيامة *yaum al-q.* the day of resurrection, the day of final judgment; قامت قيامته (*qiyāmatuhū*) to get excited, get angry, become furious; all hell broke loose in it; قامت قيامته ل (عن) to be upset, be shocked, be violently agitated by s.th.

القيوم *al-qayyūm* the Everlasting, the Eternal (God)

اقوم *aqwam*[2] straighter; more correct, sounder; more adequate, more appropriate

مقوم *miqwam* plowtail, plow handle

مقام *maqām* pl. *-āt* site, location, position; place, spot, point, locality; situation; station; standing, position, rank, dignity; tomb of a saint, sacred place; key, tonality, mode (*mus.*) | في هذا المقام on this occasion; مقام ابراهيم small building near the Kaaba in Mecca (housing a stone with Abraham's footprints); مقام الحديث topic of the conversation; المقامات السياسية (الرسمية) (*siyāsīya, rasmīya*) the political (official) agencies; مقام الكسر *m. al-kasr* denominator of a fraction; صاحب المقام الرفيع title conferred upon the holder of the order of "Collier Fouad I", established by Fuad I in 1936; كان عندي في مقام والدي (*m. wālidī*) he assumed the responsibility of fatherhood for me; cf. also *muqām* and under قيم

مقامة *maqāma* pl. *-āt* sitting, session, meeting; a genre of Arabic rhythmic prose

تقويم *taqwīm* pl. تقاويم *taqāwīm*² raising, setting up, erection; appraisal, assessment, estimation, rating, valuation; correction; rectification, amendment, reform, reformation, reorganization, reshaping, modification, adaption; ○ rectification, detection (*el.*, *radio*); land survey, surveying; determination of geographical longitude and latitude; geography; stocktaking; almanac; calendar; chronology | التقويم الجريجوري the Gregorian calendar; تقويم زمني (*zamanī*) chronology; علم تقويم البلدان *'ilm t. al-buldān* geography

مقاومة *muqāwama* resistance; opposition; fight, struggle, battle (with foll. genit.: against); ○ resistance (*el.*) | ○ مقاومة جوية (*jawwīya*) antiaircraft defense; مقاومة سلبية (*salbīya*) passive resistance; دون مقاومة without resistance, unresistingly

اقامة *iqāma* raising, lifting up; elevation; setting up; erection; etablishment (of an institute); execution; performance; holding, convocation (e.g., of a meeting), celebration (e.g., of a festival), putting on, staging (e.g., of a pageant, of a celebration); resurrection (of the dead); stay, sojourn; second call to the salat in a mosque, indicating the imminent beginning of the prayer; (*Magr.*) residentship, office of resident | اقامة الشعائر الدينية (*dīnīya*) performance of the religious ceremonies, celebration of the divine service; اقامة العدل *i. al-'adl* administration of justice; محل الاقامة *mahall al-i.* (place of) residence, domicile; address

استقامة *istiqāma* straightness; sincerity, uprightness, rectitude, integrity, probity, honesty; rightness, soundness, correctness

قائم *qā'im* pl. قوم *quwwam*, قيم *quyyam*, قوام *quwwām*, قيام *quyyām* rising, getting up; standing; upright, erect; stand-up; existing, existent; visible, conspicuous; firm, steadfast, staunch, unflinching, unshakable; revolting, rebelling (على against); vertical, perpendicular (على to) | قائم بالاعمال, قائم باعمال المفوضية (*bi-a. al-mufawwadīya*) chargé d'affaires (*dipl.*); قائم الذات, قائم بذاته, قائم برأسه (*bi-ra'sihī*) and قائم بنفسه (*bi-nafsihī*) self-existent, independent; في قائم حياته (*q. hayātihī*) during his lifetime; قائم الزاوية *q. az-zāwiya* rectangular, right-angled; الزاوية القائمة right angle

قائمقام *qā'im-maqām*, *qā'imaqām* administrative officer at the head of a *qadā'*, approx.: district president (*Ir.*, *Syr.*, *Leb.*); lieutenant colonel (*mil.*; *Tun.*, formerly also *Eg.*); commander (naval rank; *Eg.*)

قائمقامية *qā'im-maqāmīya*, *qā'imaqāmīya* administrative district headed by a *qā'im-maqām*, in Iraq = *qadā'*

قائمة *qā'ima* pl. قوائم *qawā'im* leg, foot, paw (of a quadruped); leg, foot (of furniture); pale, stake, post, prop, stanchion, pillar; pommel (of a sword's hilt); stand, base, support; (fig.) main support, pillar; (pl. also *-āt*) list, roster, register, index, table, schedule; catalogue; invoice, bill | قائمة الطعام *q. aṭ-ṭa'ām* menu, bill of fare; see also قوم I

مقوم *muqawwim* estimator, appraiser, assessor; — (pl. *-āt*) formative element, constituent factor; ○ rectifier, detector (*el., radio*); pl. مقومات elements, constituents, components, formative agents, basic factors, fundamentals | مقومات الحياة *m. al-ḥayāh* means of subsistence; earthly possessions; مقومات الجمال *m. al-jamāl* cosmetics; مقومات العمران *m. al-'umrān* cultural factors

مقوم *muqawwam* highly creditable, valuable, valued, treasured, prized; pl. مقومات valuable possessions, valuables; assets, values

مقاوم *muqāwim* resisting, resistent, reluctant, averse, unwilling; opponent, adversary, antagonist

مقيم *muqīm* raising, lifting up, setting up, erecting, etc.; remaining, staying, abiding, lingering; permanent, lasting, enduring; persistent; living, residing, resident, domiciled; resident (*dipl.*) | مقيم بواجباته (*bi-wājibātihī*) dutiful, conscientious, loyal; مقيم عام (*'āmm*) Resident General (*Tun.*)

مقيمي *muqīmī* residential

مقيمية *muqīmīya* residentship, residency

مقام *muqām* raised, set up, erected, etc.; pending (legal action); stay, sojourn; abode, habitat, whereabouts; place of residence; duration of stay; see also under قم

مستقيم *mustaqīm* upright, erect; straight; dead straight, straight as a die; directed straight ahead; correct, right, sound, proper, in order; even, regular, symmetrical, proportionate, harmonious; honest, straightforward, upright, righteous, honorable; (pl. *-āt*) a straight, straight line (*math.*); rectum (*anat.*)

قومسير (Fr. *commissaire*) *qomisēr* commissioner

قومندان (Fr. *commandant*) *qomandān* commander, commandant

قونة *qūna* pl. قون *quwan* icon; image of a saint

قونية *qōniya*[2] Konya (city in Anatolia)

قوه II to shriek, scream, yell, cry, shout

قوى *qawiya a* (قوة *qūwa*) to be or become strong, vigorous, forceful, mighty; to become stronger, increase in power, gain ascendancy; to be able to do s.th. (على in or about s.th.), have influence (على over s.th.); to be able to cope (على with s.th.), be able to manage or tackle (على s.th.); to be superior (على to s.o.); — (قى *qiyy*, قواية *qawāya*) to be depopulated, deserted, forsaken, desolate (place); — (قوى *qawan*) to starve, be starved; to be denied, be withheld (rain) **II** to make strong or vigorous, strengthen, fortify, consolidate, invigorate, brace (ه, ه s.o., s.th.); to encourage, hearten, embolden (ه s.o.); to intensify (ه s.th.) **III** to vie or compete in strength (ه with s.o.); to equal, match (ه s.o.) **IV** to be poor; to be empty, deserted, forsaken, desolate (place) **V** to be or become strong; to intensify, become stronger; to take heart, take courage **VIII** to claim for o.s. (ه s.th.) **X** = **V**

قواء *qawā'*, *qiwā'* and قى *qiyy* desert, wasteland, desolate country

قواء *qawā'* and قوى *qawan* hunger, starvation

قوة *qūwa* pl. *-āt*, قوى *quwan* strength; vigor; potency; power, force; intensity; violence, vehemence; courage, pluck; faculty, ability, capability, aptitude; efficacy, efficiency, potential; ○ (electric) energy, power, capacity, output; armed force, troop; قوات *qūwāt* armed forces, troops | بالقوة forcibly, by force; inherently, virtually (*philos.*); بقوة وجلاء *bi-qūwatin wa-jalā'in* (to speak) loud and distinctly; منسرق القوة *munsariq al-q.* weakened, debilitated, effete, exhausted, spent; قوة احتياطية (*iḥtiyāṭīya*) reserves (*mil.*); قوة الاذاعة *q. al-iḏā'a* transmitting power (*radio*); قوة الارادة *q. al-irāda* will power; قوة الاستمرار inertia; قوة حافظة memory; قوة الحدود frontier guard, border guard; قوة خفيفة light, mobile task force (*mil.*); ○ قوة دافعة كهربائية (*kahrabā'īya*) electromotive force, e.m.f.; قوة دفاعية (*difā'īya*) total defense potential; ○ قوة سطحية (*saṭḥīya*) surface task force (navy); قوة الشراء purchasing power; قوة الصوت *q. aṣ-ṣaut* volume, intensity (*radio*); قوة عاقلة intellectual power, faculty of perception; قوة عراك combat force; القوة على العمل (*'amal*) working power; output capacity; قوة القانون legal force; قوة قاهرة force majeure; قوة مركزية (*markazīya*) central power; ○ قوة مركزية جاذبة centripetal force; ○ قوة مركزية طاردة centrifugal force; قوة مضادة للطائرات (*muḍādda*) antiaircraft defense; قوة معنوية (*ma'nawīya*) moral strength, morale, spirit; قوة النبت *q. an-nabt* germinative faculty; قوة نظامية (*niẓāmīya*) regular army; قوات برية وبحريه وجوية (*barrīya wa-baḥrīya wa-jawwīya*) ground, sea and air forces; العاب القوى athletics, specif., track and field

قوى *qawīy* pl. اقوياء *aqwiyā'*[2] strong; vigorous; potent; mighty, powerful, forceful; intense, violent, vehement; firm, solid, robust, hardy, sturdy | قوى العارضة eloquent, quick-witted

اقوى *aqwā* stronger

تقوية *taqwiya* strengthening; fortification, consolidation; intensification; encouragement

□ تقاوى *taqāwī* (*eg.*) seed (for sowing)

أقواء *iqwā* depopulation; imperfect rhyme (change of the vowel following the rhyme letter)

مقو *muqawwin* strengthening, fortifying, invigorating; corroborant; (pl. مقويات *muqawwiyāt*) a restorative, tonic, cordial, corroborant; ○ amplifier (*radio*)

مقوى *muqawwan* strengthened, reinforced, stiffened, stiff | ورق مقوى (*waraq*) cardboard, pasteboard

قوى *qiyy* see ق

قاء (قئ) *qā'a i* (قئ *qay'*) to vomit **II** to cause (ه s.o.) to vomit (of an emetic) **V** = **I**

قياء *quyā'* vomit, that which is vomited

مقيئ *muqayyi'* pl. مقيئات *muqayyi'āt* a vomitive, an emetic | الجوز المقيئ (*jauz*) nux vomica

قيتار *qītār* pl. قياتير *qayātīr*[2], قيثار *qīṯār* and قيثارة *qīṯāra* pl. قياثير *qayāṯīr*[2] guitar; lyre

قيح (قاح) *qāḥa i* (*qaiḥ*) to suppurate, fester, be purulent **II** and **V** do.

قيح *qaiḥ* pl. قيوح *quyūḥ* pus, matter

تقيح *taqayyuḥ* suppuration, maturation, purulence

متقيح *mutaqayyiḥ* suppurative, festering, purulent

قيد[1] **II** to bind, tie, fetter, shackle (ب ه s.o. with; also fig.; to bind or tie s.o. to); to limit, restrict, confine, qualify (ه s.th.); to impose restrictions (ه, ه on s.o., on s.th.), set bounds (ه, ه to s.o., to s.th.), curb, check (ه, ه s.o., s.th.); to fix, determine, lay down, specify, stipulate (ه s.th.); to write, write down, note down (ه s.th.), make a note, take notes (ه of); to enter, book (ه s.th.); to register, record (ه s.th., also fig., of the eyes); to enroll (ه s.o., in a list or register); to charge (ه على s.th. to s.o.'s account), debit (ه على with s.th. s.o.); to place s.th. (ه) to s.o.'s credit (ل), credit (ه ل with s.th. s.o.) **V** pass. of **II**; to bind o.s., be bound (ب to, by, e.g., by an obligation);

to be limited, restricted; to enroll, have one's name registered

قيد *qaid* pl. قيود *quyūd* (also اقياد *aqyād*) fetter, shackle, chain; bond, tie; strap, thong; recording, record, booking, entering, entry, registering, registration, registry; enrollment (e.g., at matriculation); fixation, determination, specification, stipulation; document; limitation, confinement, restriction, qualification, reservation; condition, proviso; amount, measure, degree; distance | قيد الاسنان gum(s); قيد الانساب genealogical tree, family tree; من غير قيد او رابط without any reservation, without qualification; بلا قيد ولا شرط (*šarṭ*) without any reservation, without qualification; with no strings attached; unconditional; قلم القيودات *qalam al-quyūdāt* bureau of vital statistics, (G.B.) (general) register office; بقيد الحياة *bi-q. il-ḥayāh* or على قيد الحياة (still) alive, living; قيد شعرة *qaida ša'ratin* by a hairbreadth, within a hair's breadth; لا ... قيد انملة *lā ... qaida unmulatin* not one inch, not one iota; على قيد ساعات معدودة (*q. sā'ātin*) within a few hours; على قيد عشرة كيلومترات at a distance of 10 km; عن قيد البصر (*q. il-baṣar*) within sight

قيد *qaida* (prep.) under, subject to, the object of, in the process of, in the stage of | المشروع قيد الدرس (*dars*) the project is being studied, is under consideration; المسألة قيد البحث (*mas'ala, baḥṯ*) the affair is subject to investigation, is being investigated

قيدى *qaidī* booking-, registration- (in compounds), e.g., رسوم قيدية booking fees, registration fees

تقييد *taqyīd* pl. *-āt*, تقاييد *taqāyīd*² fettering, shackling, tying, binding; reservation, qualification; limitation, restriction, confinement, curtailment; entry, registry, registration, booking | تقييد النسل *t. an-nasl* birth control; رسم التقييد *rasm at-t.* registration fee

تقيد *taqayyud* pl. *-āt* a being bound, obligation, tie, bond; restriction, limitation, confinement

مقيد *muqayyad* fettered, shackled, bound, tied, tied down; limited, restricted, confined; booked, registered | غير مقيد unlimited, unrestricted; ملك مقيد (*mulk*) constitutional monarchy

قياد² and قيادة see قود

قير II to tar, pitch (ه s.th.)

قار *qār* and قير *qīr* tar; pitch

قيراط *qīrāṭ* pl. قراريط *qarārīṭ*² inch; a dry measure (*Eg.* = $^1/_{32}$ قدح = 0.064 l); a square measure (*Eg.* = $^1/_{24}$ فدان = 175.035 m²); kerat, a weight (*Eg.* = $^1/_{16}$ درهم = 0.195 g)

قيروان *qairawān* pl. *-āt* caravan

القيروان *al-qairawān* Kairouan (city in NE Tunisia)

(قيس) قاس *qāsa i* (*qais*, قياس *qiyās*) to measure, gauge, measure out (ه s.th.), take the measurements (ه of); to try on (ه a garment); to weigh, judge (ه s.th., ب, على by analogy with s.th. else), draw analogous conclusions (على from s.th., ه for s.th. else); to compare, correlate, bring into relation (على or ب ه s.th. with, also ه الى), proportion (على or ب ه s.th. to, also ه الى) | وقس عليه *wa-qis 'alaihi* and so forth II to measure (ه s.th.) III to compare (بين الشيئين between two things, ه s.th., الى or ب with or to) VIII to measure (ه s.th.); to imitate, follow (ب s.o.), take after s.o. (ب)

قياس *qiyās* pl. *-āt*, اقيسة *aqyisa* measure, measurement, dimension; scale; exemplar, example; reference, relation; record (*athlet.*); comparison; analogy; deduction by analogy | قياسا على ذلك by analogy (with it), analogously (to it); correspondingly; بالقياس الى in comparison with, (as) compared to; in proportion to, in relation with; with reference to, with respect to, with regard to; على القياس by analogy; regular; after the model, accordant with the model; بغير قياس illogical; اخذ قياسه to take s.o.'s measure (tailor); متناسب القياس *mutanāsib al-q.* fitting together, well matched; equal in proportion, commensurate, commensurable; قياس عالمى (*'ālamī*) world record; قياس فاسد wrong inference, false conclusion, fallacy, sophism, paralogism; شريط القياس tape measure, tapeline

قياسى *qiyāsī* accordant with analogy, analogous; consistent with the model, pattern, rule, or norm; comparable, by comparison; logical | رقم قياسى (*raqm*) record (*athlet.*)

قياس *qayyās* land surveyor, geodesist

مقياس *miqyās* pl. مقاييس *maqāyīs*² measure, measurement; amount, quantity, magnitude; measuring instrument, gauge, water gauge, tide gauge; scale (e.g., of a map); standard; standard of judging, criterion; unit of measure; المقياس Nilometer | تحت المقياس substandard; ○ مقياس التيار *m. at-tayyār* ammeter; ○ مقياس الجهد *m. al-jahd* voltmeter; ○ مقياس الحرارة *m. al-ḥarāra* thermometer; ○ مقياس الزلازل *m. az-zalāzil* seismograph, seismometer; ○ مقياس الزوايا *m. az-zawāyā* protractor; ○ مقياس الكهربائية *m. al-kahraba'iya* electrometer; ○ مقياس المطر *m. al-maṭar* rain gauge, pluviometer, ombrometer, ombrograph; ○ مقياس المغنطيسية *m. al-magnaṭīsiya* magnetometer; مقياس التنفس *m. at-tanaffus* spirometer; مقاييس الاطوال measures of length, linear measures; مقاييس المسطحات *m. al-musaṭṭaḥāt* square measures; مقاييس السطوح do.; مقاييس الحجم *m. al-ḥajm* cubic measures; مقاييس الكيل *m. al-kail* measures of capacity, dry measures, liquid measures

مقاس *maqās* pl. *-āt* measuring, mensuration; gauging; measurement, dimension, size; pl. مقاسات dimensions

مقايسة *muqāyasa* measuring, mensuration, gauging; comparison; appraisal, valuation, estimation by analogy; (preliminary) estimate (of costs); relation, rate, rates, proportion; detailed listing, specification; itemized list (of services, quantities, prices)

قيسرى *qaisarī* pl. قياسر *qayāsir*², قياسرة *qayāsira* big, large, huge, enormous

قيسرية *qaisarīya*² Caesarea (ancient seaport in Palestine)

قيسارية *qaisārīya* pl. قياسر *qayāsir*² large block of public buildings with stores, workshops, etc., roofed market place, bazaar; *qaisārīya*² Caesarea (ancient seaport in Palestine)

قايش pl. قوايش look up alphabetically

قيشانى *qīšānī* faïence; porcelain, china

قيصانة *qaiṣāna* sunfish, moonfish

قيصر *qaiṣar* pl. قياصر *qayāṣir*², قياصرة *qayāṣira* Caesar; emperor, kaiser; tsar

قيصرى *qaiṣarī* Caesarean; imperial; tsarist | العملية القيصرية (*'amalīya*) Caesarean section (*med.*)

قيصرية *qaiṣarīya* kaiserdom, Caesarism, imperialism, empire; imperial dignity; tsarism; Caesarean section (*med.*); large block of public buildings with stores, workshops, etc., roofed market place, bazaar; Caesarea (ancient seaport in Palestine)

(قيض) قاض *qāḍa i* (*qaiḍ*) to break, crack, split, cleave, burst open (ه s.th.); to get broken, crack, burst; to exchange (ه من s.th. for) **II** to foreordain, destine (ه ل s.th. to s.o.; of God); to lead, send (ه s.o., ل to s.o.; of God) **III** to exchange, give in exchange (ه ه ب to s.o. s.th. for) **V** and **VII** to burst, crack, get broken, break; to collapse, fall in, cave in, tumble down

قيض *qaiḍ* eggshell; barter, exchange; article of exchange, barter object, equivalent

قياض *qiyāḍ* barter, exchange

مقايضة *muqāyaḍa* barter, exchange; barter trade, bartering; trading, barter (*Isl. Law*); compensation, barter transaction, barter deal

قيطان see قطن

قيطوس *qīṭūs* Cetus (*astron.*)

قيظ *qaiẓ* heat of summer; high summer, midsummer, dog days; lack of rain, drought, aridity | قيظ النهار *q. an-nahār* daytime heat

مقيظ *maqīẓ* summer residence

قائظ *qā'iẓ* scorchingly hot, midsummery, canicular

قيف II to follow (ه s.o.'s tracks); to study, examine, investigate (ه s.th.); to criticize (ه s.th.)

قيافة *qiyāfa* tracking, pursuit (of a track); make-up, guise, costume

قيقب *qaiqab* maple (*bot.*)

[1]قال (قيل) *qāla i* (*qail*, قائلة *qā'ila*, قيلولة *qailūla*, قيل *qīl*) to take a midday nap; to hold siesta **II** do. **IV** to abolish, repeal, annul (ه s.th.); to cancel, abrogate, rescind, revoke (ه s.th., esp. a sale); to depose, dismiss, discharge (ه s.o.; also with من المنصب *min al-manṣib* from his office); to free, release, exempt (ه s.o., من from an obligation) | اقال الله عثرتك (*'aṯrataka*) may God regard your offense as undone; اقاله من عثرته (*'aṯratihī*) to steady one who has stumbled **X** to demand the cancellation, seek the abrogation (ه of a sale); to ask (ه s.o.) for exemption, release, or annulment; to request to be released from office, tender one's resignation, resign (من or عن from an office); to resign one's commission, quit the service; to ask s.o.'s (ه) pardon, apologize (ه to s.o.)

قيل *qail* pl. اقيال *aqyāl* princeling; chief, chieftain

قيلولة *qailūla* siesta; midday nap

مقيل *maqīl* resting place, halting place

اقالة *iqāla* cancellation, abrogation, rescission, revocation (esp. of a sale); abolishment, abolition, repeal, annulment; deposition, dismissal, discharge from an office

استقالة *istiqāla* resignation, withdrawal (from office); retirement

قائلة *qā'ila* midday nap; noon, midday

مستقيل *mustaqīl* resigned from office, retired, discharged

[2]قيلة *qīla*, قيلة مائية (*mā'īya*) hydrocele (*med.*)

قيام, قيمة, قيم and قيوم see قوم

قين *qain* pl. قيون *quyūn* blacksmith

قينة *qaina* pl. *-āt*, قيان *qiyān* songstress, singer; lady's maid

مقينة *muqayyina* lady's maid

ك

ك *ka* (with foll. genit.) as, like; all but, as good as; as, in my (your, etc.) capacity of | كالاول *ka-l-auwali* as before, as at the beginning, as from the outset; كهذا *ka-hāḏā* such, e.g., رجل كهذا *rajulun ka-hāḏā* such a man, a man like this; هم كالمجمعين على ذلك (*ka-l-mujmi'īna*) they are as good as unanimous about it, they are practically agreed on it; انا كمسلم *anā ka-muslimin* I (in my capacity) as a Muslim

كأن *ka anna* (conj. introducing a nominal clause) as if, as though; it is (was) as if | كأني بها *ka-annī bi-hā* (with imperf.) it is like seeing her before me; I am under the impression that she ..., it looks to me as if she ...

كذا *ka-ḏā* so, thus, that way; so and so, such and such, so-and-so much, so-and-so many | كذا وكذا so and so, such and such, so-and-so much, so-and-so many; بمكان كذا وكذا *bi-makāni k.* at such and such a place; عمره كذا سنوات *'umruhū k. sanawāt* his age is so-and-so many years

كذلك *ka-ḏālika* so, like this, thus; equally; likewise

كما *ka-mā* (conj. introducing a verbal clause) as, just as, as also, as on the other hand; (introducing a main clause) equally, likewise, as well | كما ان *ka-mā anna* (introducing a nominal clause) as, just as, quite as, as also, as on the other hand; كما هو such as it is; as things are, such being the matter; كما لو كان حاضرا as if he were present

مدينة الكاب *madīnat al-kāb* Cape Town

كئب *ka'iba a* (كأب *ka'b*, كأبة *ka'ba*, كآبة *ka'āba*) to be dejected, dispirited, downcast, sad (على about, ل because of), be worried (ل by, because of) **IV** to sadden, aggrieve, distress, worry (ه s.o.); to depress, dishearten, discourage (ه s.o.) **VIII** to be dejected, dispirited, downcast, sad (على about, ل because of), be worried (ل by, because of); to be gloomy

كأب *ka'b*, كأبة *ka'ba*, كآبة *ka'āba* and اكتئاب *ikti'āb* sorrow, grief, distress, sadness, dejection, depression, gloom, melancholy

كئب *ka'ib* and كئيب *ka'īb* sad, dispirited, dejected, downcast, depressed, melancholy; gloomy, morose; grave

مكتئب *mukta'ib* sad, dispirited, dejected, downcast, depressed, melancholy; gloomy, morose; grave; dark-colored, blackish, dismal

كابل[1] (Fr. *câble*) *kābil* cable

كابل[2] *kābul*[2] Kabul (capital of Afghanistan)

كابلى *kābulī* Kabuli, of Kabul; (*eg.*) mahogany wood

كابين (Fr. *cabine*) *kābīn* pl. كبائن *kabā'in*[2], كباين *kabāyin*[2] cabin

كاتدرائية *kātidrā'īya* cathedral

كاثوليكى *kāṯūlīkī* Catholic; a Catholic; see also كثلك

كاخية *kāḵiya* pl. كواخ *kawāḵin* butler, steward

كاد[1] *kād* anacardium (*bot.*) | كاد هندى (*hindī*) cashew tree (Anacardium occidentale; *bot.*)

كأد[2] *ka'ada a* to be sad, distressed, worried

كأداء *ka'dā'*[2] sadness, sorrow, distress, grief; fear; dark night | عقبة كأداء (*'aqaba*) insurmountable obstacle

كؤود *ka'ūd*: عقبة كؤود (*'aqaba*) insurmountable obstacle

كادر (Fr. *cadre*) *kādir* cadre (of a military unit, of a governmental agency, of a corporation, etc.), skeleton organization, skeleton unit, skeleton crew (of a naval unit)

كادميوم *kadmiyom* cadmium

كار *kār* pl. *-āt* work, job, occupation, business; calling, ocation, profession, trade | ابن كار *ibn k.* (*eg.*) artisan, craftsman; ارباب الكارات artisans, craftsmen; عداوة الكار *'adāwat al-k.* professional jealousy, trade rivalry

كارتون *kartōn* cardboard, pasteboard; (pl. *-āt*) carton

كاردينال *kardīnāl* pl. كرادلة *karādila* cardinal

كارى = كرى *karrī* curry

كاريكاتورية *karikātūrīya* caricature, cartoon

كاز = غاز *gāz* gas

كازينو *kāzīnō* pl. كازينوهات *kāzīnōhāt* casino

كأس *ka's* f., pl. كؤوس *ku'ūs*, كئاس *ki'ās*, كأسات *ka'sāt* cup; drinking glass, tumbler; goblet; chalice, calix; calyx (*bot.*)

كاساتا *kasātā* cassata (Italian ice cream)

كاغط *kāgiṭ* (*mor.*) paper

كاف *kāf* name of the letter ك

كافور *kāfūr* camphor, camphor tree; (*eg.*) blue gum (Eucalyptus globulus Lab.; *bot.*)

كاكنج *kākinj*, *kākanj* alkekengi, ground cherry (Physalis alkekengi; *bot.*)

كالو (It. *callo*) *kallō* pl. كالوهات corn (on the toes)

كالون *gālōn* gallon; — (*eg.*) *kālūn* and كيلون *kailūn* pl. كوالين *kawālīn*[2] lock (of a door)

كوالينى *kawālīnī* pl. *-ya* locksmith

كامبوديا *kambōdiyā* Cambodia

كامبيو (It. *cambio*) *kambiyō* rate of exchange

كامخ *kāmak*, *kāmik* pl. كوامخ *kawāmik*[2] vinegar sauce, pickle; (mixed) pickles

كاميرا *kāmērā* camera

كاميه *kāmēh* cameo (precious stone)

سوق الكانتو *sūq al-kantō* rag fair, secondhand market

كانتين *kantīn* post exchange, canteen

كاهية *kāhiya* pl. كواه *kawāhin* chief officer of a كهاية *kihāya* (*Tun.*); deputy, vice-, under-, sub- (*Tun.*)

كاوتشق *kautšuq* rubber, caoutchouc

كب *kabba u* (*kabb*) to prostrate, throw prostrate (لوجهه *li-wajhihī* or على وجهه ه s.o.); to overturn, overthrow, topple, upset, capsize, turn upside down, revert, invert (ه s.th.); to pour out, pour away (ه a liquid) **II** to ball, roll or form into a ball, conglomerate (ه s.th.) **IV** to throw down, prostrate, bend down, bow down (ه s.o.); to throw o.s. down, prostrate o.s.; to bend, bow, lean (على over s.th.); to apply o.s. eagerly, devote o.s., dedicate o.s. (على to s.th.) **VII** to fall prostrate (على وجهه); to throw o.s. down, prostrate o.s.; to bend, bow, lean (على over); to apply o.s. eagerly, devote o.s., dedicate o.s. (على to); to nestle (على against); to be reverted, be inverted, be overturned, be upset, be toppled, get knocked over; to be poured away | انكب على قدميه (*qadamaihi*) to throw o.s. at s.o.'s feet, prostrate o.s. before s.o.

كب *kabb* prostration; overthrow, overturn, reversal; bending, tilting, inclination

كبة *kubba* pl. كبب *kubab* ball; clew, hank; ball of thread, hank of yarn; (*syr.*, *ir.*) a kind of meatballs made of bulgur, onions, minced meat and piñons; (*eg.*) bubo, plague boil

كباب *kabāb* fried or broiled meat; cabobs, meat roasted in small pieces on a skewer; a kind of meatballs made of finely chopped meat (*syr.*, *eg.*) | كباب صينى (*ṣīnī*; *eg.*) cubeb (Piper cubeba Tr.; *bot.*)

كبابة *kabāba*, *kubāba* cubeb (Piper cubeba; *bot.*)

كبيبة (*eg.*) *kubēba* a kind of meatballs, hamburgers | كبيبة بطاطس (*eg.*) baked potato dough stuffed with minced meat, meat patties

□ كباية *kubbāya* pl *-āt* drinking glass, tumbler

مكب *mikabb* pl. *-āt*, مكاب *makābb*² ball of thread, hank of yarn; reel of thread, bobbin, spool, reel

اكباب *ikbāb* devotion, dedication (على to s.th.); occupation (على with), pursuit (على of)

انكباب *inkibāb* devotion, dedication (على to s.th.); occupation (على with), pursuit (على of)

مكب *mukibb* devoted, dedicated, addicted, given over (على to), intent (على on), wholeheartedly engaged (على in)

منكب *munkabb* devoted, dedicated, addicted, given over (على to), intent (على on), wholeheartedly engaged (على in)

كباريه (Fr. *cabaret*) *kabārēh* pl. *-āt* cabaret

¹كبت *kabata i* (*kabt*) to put down, crush, suppress, repress, stifle, subdue, restrain, curb (ه s.th.) | كبت غيظه فى جوفه (*ġaiẓahū fī jaufihī*) to suppress one's anger; كبت انفاسه (*anfāsahū*) to get s.o. out of breath

كبت *kabt* suppression, repression

²كبوت *kabbūt* pl. كبابيت *kabābīt*² hood, cowl; hooded mantle; top of a carriage or automobile

كبتولة *kabtūla* lump, chunk; ball; pellet

مكبتل *mukabtal* round

كبتن (Engl.) *kabtan* captain (military rank)

كبح *kabaḥa a* (*kabḥ*) to rein in (ه a horse); to check, curb, control (ه s.th.); to hamper, hinder, prevent, detain, restrain, hold back (ه عن s.o. from) | كبح جماحه (*jimāḥahū*) to curb s.o.'s defiance, repress s.o. or s.th.

كبح *kabḥ* curbing, checking, subdual, restraint, control; suppression, repression; hindering, prevention

○ مكبح *mikbaḥ* brake (of an automobile)

كبد *kabada u i* (*kabd*) to affect severely, afflict gravely, wear out, wear down (ه s.o.; of pain, losses, etc.) II to cause (ه ه to s.o. s.th., esp. losses), inflict (ه ه upon s.o. s.th., esp. losses); to culminate, pass through the meridian (star); to reach its climax III to bear, suffer, endure, undergo, sustain, stand (ه s.th.) V to bear, suffer, endure, undergo, sustain, stand (ه losses, hardships, etc.); to have to take upon o.s. (ه s.th.), be exposed (ه to); to bear, defray (ه costs); to take up the center, step into the middle (ه of a place); to be in the zenith, culminate

كبد *kabid, kabd, kibd* m. and f., pl. اكباد *akbād*, كبود *kubūd* liver; interior, heart; middle, center; — *kabid, kabad* center of the sky, zenith

كباد *kubād* liver ailment

كباد *kabbād, kubbād* name of several citrus plants (Citrus medica Risso, Citrus Bigaradia Duh., also Zollikoferia spinosa B.; *eg.*); *kabbād* (*syr.*) citron (Citrus medica)

¹كبر *kabara u* (*kabr*) to exceed in age (ه ب s.o. by), be older (ه than s.o., ب so-and-so much); — *kabura u* (*kubr, kibar*, كبارة *kabāra*) to be or become great, big, large; to grow, increase, augment, become greater, bigger or larger; to become famous, gain significance, become important; to become too great, too big, too large (عن for s.th.); to disdain (عن s.th.); to become too oppressive, too painful, too distressing, too burdensome; to appear intolerable (على to s.o.); to become too difficult, too hard (على for s.o.), appear insurmountable (على to s.o.) II to make great(er), big(ger), large(r), enlarge, magnify, enhance, aggrandize (ه s.th.); to extend, expand, widen, amplify (ه s.th.); to increase, augment (ه s.th.); to intensify (ه s.th.);

to exaggerate, play up (▲ s.th.); to aggravate, make worse (▲ s.th.); to praise, laud, extol, exalt, glorify, celebrate (• s.o., ▲ s.th.); to exclaim *allāhu akbar* **III** to treat haughtily, with disdain, with contempt (• s.o.); to seek to excel, try to surpass, strive to outdo (• s.o.); to contend, vie, strive, contest (• with s.o.); to oppose, resist, contradict (• s.o.); to renege, renounce (▲ s.th.), offend (▲ against), act contrary (▲ to); to stickle, insist stubbornly on one's opinion **IV** to consider great, deem significant, regard as formidable (▲ s.th.); to praise, laud, extol (• s.o.); to show respect (• to s.o.), be deferential (• toward s.o.); to admire (▲ s.th.) **V** and **VI** to be proud or haughty, give o.s. airs, swagger; to be overweening, overbearing (على toward s.o.) **X** to deem great or important (▲ s.th.); to be proud, haughty, display arrogance (على toward s.o.)

كبر *kibr* bigness, largeness, magnitude; greatness, eminence, grandeur; significance, importance; standing, prestige; nobility; pride, haughtiness, presumption, arrogance

كبر *kubr* greatness, eminence, grandeur; bigness, largeness, magnitude; size, bulk, extent, expanse; power, might; glory, fame, renown, standing, prestige; nobility; main part, bulk

كبر *kibar* bigness, largeness, magnitude; greatness, eminence, grandeur; old age

كبرة *kabra* old age

كبير *kabīr* pl. كبار *kibār*, كبراء *kubarā'*[2] great, big, large, sizable; bulky, voluminous, spacious; extensive, comprehensive; significant, considerable, formidable, huge, vast, enormous; powerful, influential, distinguished, eminent; important; old | كبير امراء البحار *k. umarā' al-b.* Admiral of the Fleet (Eg.); كبيرة الخدم *k. al-kadam* female head of the household staff; كبير الاساقفة *k. al-asāqifa* archbishop; كبير السن *k. as-sinn* old; كبير القضاة *k. al-quḍāh* chief justice, chief magistrate; ابو كبير (*abū*) asafetida, devil's dung (*pharm.*); كل صغيرة وكبيرة every single detail; كبار الضباط *k. aḍ-ḍubbāṭ* senior officers; كبار الموظفين *k. al-muwaẓẓafīn* senior officials; كبار الهيئات *k. al-hai'āt* the leading personalities of public corporations

كبيرة *kabīra* pl. *-āt*, كبائر *kabā'ir*[2], كبر *kubur* great sin, grave offense, atrocious crime

كبار *kubār*, *kubbār* very great, very big, huge

كبرياء *kibriyā'*[2] grandeur, glory, magnificence, majesty; pride, haughtiness, presumption, arrogance

اكبر *akbar*[2] pl. *-ūn*, اكابر *akābir*[2], f. كبرى *kubrā*, pl. كبريات *kubrayāt* greater, bigger, larger; older; senior-ranking | المفتى الاكبر (*muftī*) grand mufti; سوريا الكبرى (*sūriyā*) Greater Syria; اكابر القوم *a. al-qaum* the leaders of the people; الاكابر والاعيان the grandees and notables

تكبير *takbīr* enlargement, increase, augmentation, magnification; enhancement, aggrandizement; intensification, amplification; exaggeration; augmentative (*gram.*); praise, laudation, extolment, exaltation, glorification; the exclamation الله اكبر *allāhu akbar*

مكابرة *mukābara* haughtiness, superciliousness, overweening, overbearingness; self-importance, pomposity; stubbornness, obstinacy, self-will

اكبار *ikbār* admiration; deference, respect, regard, esteem

تكبر *takabbur* and تكابر *takābur* pride, haughtiness, presumption, arrogance

مكبر *mukabbir* pl. *-āt* ○ amplifier (*el.*) | مكبر الصوت *m. aṣ-ṣaut* or مكبر صوتى (*ṣautī*)

loud-speaker (*radio*); نظارة مكبرة (*naẓẓāra*) magnifying glass

مكبرة *mukabbira* pl. *-āt* magnifying glass

مكبر *mukabbar* enlarged, magnified | صورة مكبرة (*ṣūra*) enlargement, blowup (*phot.*); بصورة مكبرة increasingly, on a larger scale, to an increasing degree

مكابر *mukābir* presumptuous, arrogant, supercilious, haughty, overweening; quarrelsome, contentious, cantankerous; self-willed, obstinate, stubborn; stickler

متكبر *mutakabbir* proud, imperious, high-handed, haughty, supercilious, overweening

²كبر *kabar* capers; caper shrub

كبرت *kabrata* to coat with sulfur (ه s.th.); to sulfurize, sulfurate (ه s.th.); to vulcanize (ه s.th.)

كبريت *kibrīt* sulfur; matches | عود كبريت *'ūd k.* matches, a match

كبريتة *kibrīta* match, matchstick

كبريتى *kibrītī* sulfureous, sulfurate, sulfurous, sulfuric | حمام كبريتى (*ḥammām*) sulfur bath; ينبوع كبريتى (*yanbū'*) sulfur spring

كبريتات *kibrītāt* sulfate

كبرى *kubrī* or كوبرى (from Turk. *köprü*) pl. كبارى *kabārī* bridge; deck

كبس *kabasa* *i* (*kabs*) to exert pressure (على on), press (على s.th. or on s.th.), squeeze (على s.th.); to attack, raid, take by surprise (ه a place); to intercalate (السنة بيوم *as-sanata bi-yaumin* a day in a leap year); to preserve (in vinegar, or the like), pickle (ه s.th.); to marinate (ه s.th.); to conserve (ه s.th.) **II** to press or squeeze hard (ه s.th.); to massage (ه s.o.)

كبس *kabs* pressure, squeeze, pressing; raid, attack; preservation (esp. in vinegar), pickling; intercalation (of a day; *astron.*)

كبسة *kabsa* (n. vic.) raid, surprise attack

كباس *kabbās* piston; press; ramrod | ○ موسى كباس (*mūsā*) penknife

كبيس *kabīs* preserved (esp. in vinegar), pickled; pickled food, preserves; intercalary, intercalated, interpolated | سنة كبيسة (*sana*) leap year

كابوس *kābūs* pl. كوابيس *kawābīs*² nightmare, incubus; terrible vision, phantom, bugbear

مكبس *mikbas* pl. مكابس *makābis*² or مكباس *mikbās* pl. مكابيس *makābīs*² press; piston (of a pump); ramrod | مكبس القطن *m. al-quṭn* cotton press; ○ مكبس الخطابات letter press, copying press; ○ مكبس مائى (*mā'ī*) hydraulic press

تكبيس *takbīs* massage

○ آلة كابسة *āla kābisa* compressor

مكبوس *makbūs* raided, attacked; pressed; preserved, pickled; مكبوسات canned goods, conserves

كبسول *kabsūl* or كبسولة *kabsūla* capsule; percussion cap, primer, detonator; snap fastener

كبش *kabaša* *u* (*kabš*) to take a handful (ه of s.th.); to grasp with the hand, clench (ه s.th.)

كبش *kabš* pl. كباش *kibāš*, اكباش *akbāš* ram, male sheep; bellwether; chieftain, chief, head, leader; battering-ram; pile driver; rammer; (pl. كبوش *kubūš*) buttress, pier, stay, prop, support; mulberry | كبش التصادم *k. at-taṣādum* (pl. كبوش) bumper (railroad); كبوش قرنفل *k. qaranful* cloves

كبشة *kabša* a handful; grasp, grip

كبشة *kabša* ladle, scoop

كبشة *kubša* pl. كبش *kubaš* hook, clamp, cramp, brace; clasp, brooch

كبكب *kabkaba* to topple, upset, capsize, overturn, turn upside down, revert, invert (ه s.th.); to spill (ه s.th.)

كبيكج *kabīkaj* Asiatic crowfoot (Ranunculus asiaticus; *bot.*)

[1]كبل *kabala i* (*kabl*) to put in irons, shackle, fetter (ه s.o.); to keep waiting (ه s.o., ه for s.th., esp. for the payment of a debt) **II** to put in irons, shackle, fetter (ه s.o.) **III** to keep waiting (ه s.o., ه for s.th., esp. for the payment of a debt), defer, put off (الدين *ad-daina* the payment of a debt)

كبل *kabl, kibl* pl. كبول *kubūl* leg iron, chain, shackle, fetter

كبولى *kabūlī* and كابولى *kābūlī* pl. كوابيل *kawābīl*[2] bracket, corbel, console (*arch.*); lean-to roof, pent roof, shed roof (*arch.*)

[2]كابل and كابلى look up alphabetically

كابين pl. كباين look up alphabetically

(كبا) كبو *kabā u* (*kabw, kubūw*) to fall forward (لوجهه *li-wajhihī* on one's face); to stumble, trip, slip; — *u* to empty (ه a vessel), pour out the contents (ه of a vessel); to become dim (light); to become dull, fade, lose luster (color); to rise, swirl up (dust) **IV** to fail, fail to produce a spark (lighter) **VII** to fall headlong; to stumble, trip, slip

كبوة *kabwa* (n. vic.) fall, tumble, drop; stumble, trip, slip, false step; dust

كاب *kābin* dull, dim, pale, dead, flat; slack, weak, decrepit; see كاب alphabetically

كباية see كب

كبوت see [2]كبت

كت *katta i* (*katt*) to hum softly

كت *katt* and كتيت *katīt* soft humming

كتالوج *katālōg* pl. *-āt* catalogue

كتب *kataba u* (*katb*, كتبة *kitba*, كتابة *kitāba*) to write, pen, write down, put down in writing, note down, inscribe, enter, record, book, register (ه s.th.); to compose, draw up, indite, draft (ه s.th.); to bequeath, make over by will (ل ه s.th. to s.o.); to prescribe (على ه s.th. to s.o.); to foreordain, destine (ل or على ه s.th. to s.o.; of God); pass. *kutiba* to be fated, be foreordained, be destined (ل to s.o.) | كتب على نفسه ان to be firmly resolved to ..., make it one's duty to ...; كتب عنه to write from s.o.'s dictation; كتب كتابه (*kitābahū*) to draw up the marriage contract for s.o., marry s.o. (على to) **II** to make (ه s.o.) write (ه s.th.); to form or deploy in squadrons (ه troops) **III** to keep up a correspondence, exchange letters, correspond (ه with s.o.) **IV** to dictate (ه ه to s.o. s.th.), make (ه s.o.) write (ه s.th.) **VI** to write to each other, exchange letters, keep up a correspondence **VII** to subscribe **VIII** to write (ه s.th.); to copy (ه s.th.), make a copy (ه of s.th.); to enter one's name; to subscribe (ل for); to contribute, subscribe (ب ل money to); to be entered, be recorded, be registered **X** to ask (ه s.o.) to write (ه s.th.); to dictate (ه ه to s.o. s.th.), make (ه s.o.) write (ه s.th.); to have a copy made (ه by s.o.)

كتاب *kitāb* pl. كتب *kutub* piece of writing, record, paper; letter, note, message; document, deed; contract (esp. marriage contract); book; الكتاب the Koran; the Bible | اهل الكتاب *ahl al-k.* the people of the Book, the adherents of a revealed religion, the kitabis, i.e., Christians and Jews; كتاب الزواج *k. az-zawāj* marriage contract; كتاب الطلاق *k. aṭ-ṭalāq* bill of divorce; كتاب تعليمى (*ta'līmī*) textbook; كتاب الاعتماد credentials (*dipl.*); دار الكتب library

كتبى *kutubī* pl. *-ya* bookseller, bookdealer

كتابخانة *kitābkāna* and كتبخانة *kutubkāna* library; bookstore

كتاب *kuttāb* pl. كتاتيب *katātīb²* kuttab, Koran school (lowest elementary school)

كتيب *kutayyib* booklet

كتابة *kitāba* (act or practice of) writing; art of writing, penmanship; system of writing, script; inscription; writing, legend; placard, poster; piece of writing, record, paper; secretariat; written amulet, charm; pl. كتابات writings, essays; كتابة *kitābatan* in writing | بالكتابة written; بدون كتابة *bi-dūn k.* unwritten, oral; blank; كتابة التاريخ historiography, historical writing; كتابة الدولة *k. ad-daula* (*Maḡr.*) secretariat of state; كتابة عامة (*ʿāmma*) secretariat general; اسم الكتابة *ism al-k.* pen name, nom de plume; آلة الكتابة typewriter; لغة الكتابة *luḡat al-k.* literary language; ورق الكتابة *waraq al-k.* writing paper

كتابى *kitābī* written, in writing; clerical; literary; scriptural, relating to the revealed Scriptures (Koran, Bible); kitabi, adherent of a revealed religion; the written part (of an examination) | اسلوب كتابى (*uslūb*) literary style; غلطة كتابية (*ḡalṭa*) slip of the pen, clerical error; اعمال كتابية clerical work, office work, desk work; الكمال الكتابى (*kamāl*) literary perfection; لغة كتابية (*luḡa*) literary language; موظف كتابى (*muwaẓẓaf*) clerk, clerical worker (of a government office)

كتيبة *katība* pl. كتائب *katāʾib²* squadron; cavalry detachment; (*Eg.* 1939) battalion, (*Ir.* after 1922) regiment, (later) battalion, (*Syr.*) battalion of armored, cavalry, or motorized, units (*mil.*); (piece of) writing, record, paper, document; written amulet

مكتب *maktab* pl. مكاتب *makātib²* office; bureau; business office; study; school, elementary school; department, agency, office; desk | مكتب الاخبار and مكتب الانباء news agency, press agency, wire service; مكتب البريد post office; مكتب البريد الرئيسى (*raʾīsī*) main post office, مكتب البرق *m. al-barq* telegraph office; مكتب التحرير editorial room; مكتب التليفونات telephone central office; مكتب السفريات *m. as-safariyāt* (*syr.*) travel agency; مكتب الصحة *m. aṣ-ṣiḥḥa* board of health; مكتب الاستعلامات information office, information desk; news agency, press agency, wire service

مكتبة *maktaba* pl. -*āt*, مكاتب *makātib²* library; bookstore; desk

○ مكتاب *miktāb* typewriter

مكاتبة *mukātaba* exchange of letters, correspondence

اكتتاب *iktitāb* enrollment, registration, entering (of one's name); — (pl. -*āt*) subscription; contribution (of funds)

استكتاب *istiktāb* dictation

استكتابى *istiktābī*: آلة استكتابية dictaphone

كاتب *kātib* pl. -*ūn*, كتاب *kuttāb*, كتبة *kataba* writer, scribe, scrivener; secretary; clerk typist; office worker, clerical employee; clerk, registrar, actuary, court clerk; notary; writer, author | كاتب الدولة *k. ad-daula* (*Maḡr.*) (under)secretary of state; كاتب السر *k. as-sirr* private secretary; كاتب قصصى (*qiṣaṣī*) writer, novelist; كاتب المحكمة *k. al-maḥkama* court clerk; آلة كاتبة typewriter

كاتبة *kātiba* pl. -*āt* woman secretary; authoress, writer

مكتوب *maktūb* written, written down, recorded; fated, foreordained, destined (ل or على to s.o.); s.th. written, writing; — (pl. مكاتيب *makātīb²*) a writing, message, note; letter

مكاتب *mukātib* correspondent; (newspaper) reporter

مكتتب *muktatib* subscriber

كتابخانة and كتبخانة see كتب

اكتع *akta'*[2] pl. كتع *kut'* having crippled fingers; one-armed

كتف *katafa* i (*katf*) to fetter, shackle (ه s.o., esp. by tying his hands); to tie up, bind (ه s.th.) **II** to tie the hands behind the back; to cross, fold (ه hands, arms behind the back or in front of the chest) **V** and **X** to cross or fold one's arms **VI** to stand shoulder to shoulder; to support one another; to be united in solidarity, stand together

كتف *katif*, *katf*, *kitf* pl. اكتاف *aktāf*, كتفة *kitafa* shoulder; shoulder blade, scapula; mountain slope; ○ end support of a bridge; (pl. اكتاف *aktāf*) buttress, pier | ما هكذا تؤكل الكتف (*tu'kalu*) that's certainly not the way to do it! that's no way to handle it!

كتاف *kitāf* pl. كتف *kutuf* shackle, manacle, handcuff

اكتف *aktaf*[2], f. كتفاء *katfā'*[2], pl. كتف *kutf* broad-shouldered

[1]كتكت *katkat* floss, silk waste

[2]كتكوت *katkūt* pl. كتاكيت *katākīt*[2] chicken, chick

كتل *katala* u (*katl*) and **II** to agglomerate, conglomerate, gather into a compact mass, press into a lump (ه s.th.) **V** to be heaped up, piled up, agglomerated, clustered, clotted, massed, pressed into a compact mass or lump; to agglomerate, cluster, clot, pile up, gather in a mass; to unite in a bloc or group

كتلة *kutla* pl. كتل *kutal* lump, chunk, clod, clot; bulk, mass; cube; block; bloc; beam, joist, transom, lintel, girder | كتل بشرية (*bašarīya*) crowds, throngs, masses; كتلة الجسد *kutlat al-jasad* bulk of the body, frame; كتلة من الاعصاب (*a'ṣāb*) a fearless, husky fellow; الكتلة الوطنية (*waṭanīya*) the National Bloc

مكتل *miktal* pl. مكاتل *makātil*[2] large basket

تكتل *takattul* formation of blocs (*pol.*) | سياسة التكتل policy of blocs (*pol.*)

متكتل *mutakattil* clotted, lumpy, agglomerate, clustered, massed; concentrated, compact; burly, husky, stocky, heavily built (body)

كتم *katama* u (*katm*, كتمان *kitmān*) to hide (ه s.th., عن from s.o.); to conceal, secrete, keep secret (ه s.th., عن from s.o.); to suppress, repress, restrain, check, curb, subdue (ه anger, passion); to hold (ه one's breath); to lower, muffle (ه the voice); to stifle, smother, quench (ه fire) | كتم انفاسه to take s.o.'s breath away, drive s.o. out of his senses **II** to hide, conceal (ه s.th.) **III** to hide, conceal, keep, withhold (ه ه from s.o. s.th.) **V** to keep silent, hold one's tongue, keep mum **VIII** = **II** **X** to ask (ه s.o.) tc keep (ه a secret); to confide (ه ه to s.o. s.th.)

كتم *katm* and كتمان *kitmān* secrecy, concealment, secretion, silence; restraint, control, suppression (esp. of an emotion)

كتيم *katīm* shut tight, hermetically sealed, impenetrable, impermeable, impervious

كتوم *katūm* reticent, reserved, secretive, uncommunicative, taciturn, discreet

كتام *kitām* (*eg.*) constipation

تكتم *takattum* secrecy, secretiveness, reticence, reserve, taciturnity, discretion

اكتتام *iktitām* concealment, secretion, secrecy, silence

كاتم *kātim*: كاتم السر *k. as-sirr* (private) secretary

مكتوم *maktūm* hidden, concealed, kept, preserved (secret); (*eg.*) constipated

[1]كتن *katina a* (*katan*) to be dirty, soiled, smutty, blackened by soot **II** to smut, soil (ه s.th.)

كتن *katan* dirt, smut, soot

[2]كتان *kattān* (*kittān*) flax; linen

كتانى *kattānī* made of linen, linen (adj.)

[3]كتينة (It. *catena*) *katīna* (watch) chain

كث *kaṯṯa i a* (كثث *kaṯaṯ*, كثاثة *kaṯāṯa*, كثوثة *kuṯūṯa*) to be thick or dense (esp. hair)

كثث *kaṯaṯ* thickness, density

كث *kaṯṯ* and كثيث *kaṯīṯ* thick, dense, thick-grown, densely crowded

كثب *kaṯab* nearness, proximity, vicinity | عن كثب من and على كثب من in the vicinity (or neighborhood) of, near; من (عن) كثب from nearby, at a short distance

كثيب *kaṯīb* pl. اكثبة *akṯiba*, كثب *kuṯub*, كثبان *kuṯban* sandhill, dune

كثر *kaṯara u* (*kaṯr*) to outnumber, exceed in number (ه, ه s.o., s.th.) — *kaṯura u* (كثرة *kaṯra*) to be much, many or numerous; to be more (عن than); to happen frequently, occur often; to increase, augment, multiply, grow **II** to increase, augment, compound, multiply (ه s.th.) **III** to outnumber, exceed in number (ه, ه s.o., s.th.); to vie in quantity or number (ه, ه with) **IV** to do much (من in or of s.th.); to give much or frequently (ل من to s.o. of s.th.); to do constantly, always or frequently (من or فى s.th.); to increase, augment (ه s.th.) **VI** to band together, form a gang, rally (على against) **X** = **IV**; to regard as too much, deem excessive, find exorbitant (ه s.th.); to regard as too high, as too troublesome (ه s.th.); to think not worth the trouble (ه s.th., على with regard to s.o.); to begrudge (ه على s.o. s.th.); to demand much, ask for a lot | استكثر بخيره (*bi-ḵairihī*) to thank s.o.

كثر *kuṯr* large quantity, abundance, plenty; major portion, greater part

كثرة *kaṯra* large quantity, great number, multitude, abundance, copiousness, numerousness, frequency, multiplicity, plurality; majority, major portion (من of) | بكثرة plentifully, abundantly, a lot; جمع الكثرة *jam' al-k.* plural of multitude (*gram.*)

كثير *kaṯīr* pl. -*ūn*, كثار *kiṯār* much, many, numerous, abundant, plentiful, copious; frequent; a large portion, a great deal, a great many, a lot; الكثير the most part, most (من of); كثيرا *kaṯīran* very, much, to a large extent; often, frequently | كثيرا ما *kaṯīran mā* often, frequently; بكثير (after a comparative) far, by far; الكثير من, الكثيرون من the majority of, most of; plenty of, a great many, a lot of; كثير على too much for; الشىء الكثير most of it; هذا كثير that's pretty strong! that's laying it on thick! فى احيان كثيرة and فى كثير من الاوقات frequently, often

كثيراء *kaṯīrā'*[2] tragacanth (Astragalus gummifer Lab.; *bot.*); gum obtained from tragacanth

اكثر *akṯar*[2] more; oftener, more frequently; more numerous; longer; most; major portion, greater part, majority; الاكثرون the majority, most of them | اكثر فاكثر more and more; على الاكثر at most; latest; اكثر الامر *akṯara l-amr* at best; اكثر من ذلك besides, moreover

اكثرية *akṯarīya* majority

مكثار *mikṯār* very talkative, garrulous

تكثير *takṯīr* increase, augmentation, multiplication, propagation, ample provision, abundant supply

اكثار *ikṯār* increase, augmentation, multiplication, propagation, ample provision, abundant supply; raising, increase (esp. of the yield)

تكاثر *takāṯur* growth, increase; multiplication, propagation, proliferation

مكثر *mukṯir* rich, well-to-do

متكاثر *mutakāṯir* numerous, extensive; manifold, multifarious, multiple | متكاثر الرقاع *m. ar-riqā'* patched in numerous places

كثف **kaṯufa** *u* (كثافة *kaṯāfa*) to be thick or dense; to thicken, be condensed, become thicker or denser **II** to make thick or dense, thicken, compress, solidify, concentrate (ه s.th.); to inspissate, condense (ه s.th.); ○ (*el.*) to increase the capacity **V** and **VI** to grow denser, become concentrated; to thicken, become viscous; to be condensed

كثيف *kaṯīf* pl. كثاف *kiṯāf* thick; dense; compact; heavy, coarse, crude; viscous, sirupy (e.g., sauce)

كثافة *kaṯāfa* thickness; density; heaviness; solidity, firmness; compactness, fullness, intensity; consistency, degree of density or viscosity; ○ capacity (*el.*) | كثافة السكان *k. as-sukkān* density of population; ○ كثافة الصوت *k. aṣ-ṣaut* sonority, sound intensity

تكثيف *takṯīf* compression, concentration, solidification; condensation

تكاثف *takāṯuf* concentration, consolidation; condensation

مكثف *mukaṯṯif* pl. *-āt* capacitor, condenser | مكثف متغير (*mutaḡayyir*) variable capacitor (*radio*)

مكثف *mukaṯṯaf* condensed

متكاثف *mutakāṯif* massing, concentrating, gathering, piling up; dense

كثلك **II** *takaṯlaka* to become (a) Catholic

كثوليكي *kaṯūlīkī* pl. كثلكة *kaṯlaka* Catholic; a Catholic

الكثلكة *al-kaṯlaka* Catholicism

كثيراء **kaṯīrā'**[2] tragacanth (Astragalus gummifer Lab.; *bot.*); gum obtained from tragacanth

كح **kaḥḥa** *u* to cough

كحة *kuḥḥa* cough

كحت **kaḥata** *a* and **II** (*eg.*) to scrape off, scratch off (ه s.th.)

كحكح **kaḥkaḥa** to cough, cough slightly, hack

كحكحة *kaḥkaḥa* short, dry cough

كحل **kaḥala** *u a* (*kaḥl*) and **II** to rub, paint or smear (with kohl) (ه the eyes) **V** and **VIII** to color (the edges of) the eyelids with kohl | ما اكتحل غماضا (غمضا) (*ḡamāḍan, ḡimāḍan, ḡumḍan*) to find no sleep

كحل *kuḥl* pl. اكحال *akḥāl* antimony; kohl, a preparation of pulverized antimony used for darkening (the edges of) the eyelids; any preparation for coloring the eyelids

كحل *kaḥal* black coloring (of the edges) of the eyelids

كحل *kaḥil* darkened with kohl, dyed black (eyelids)

كحلي *kuḥlī* dark blue, navy blue

كحلة *kuḥla* (*eg.*) pointing, filling or grouting of the joints (of a wall; *masonry*)

اكحل *akḥal*[2], f. كحلاء *kaḥlā'*[2], pl. كحل *kuḥl* black (eye); الاكحل the medial arm vein

كحلاء *kaḥlā'* (*eg.*) a variety of blueweed (Echium cericeum V.; *bot.*)

كحيل *kaḥīl* pl. كحائل *kaḥā'il*[2] black, dyed black, darkened with kohl (eyelid); horse of noblest breed

كحول *kuḥūl* alcohol, spirit

كحولي *kuḥūlī* alcoholic, spirituous

كحيلي *kuḥailī* and كحيلان *kuḥailān* horse of noblest breed

كحال *kiḥāl* antimony powder, eye powder

كحال *kaḥḥāl* eye doctor, oculist (old designation)

مكحل *mikḥal* and مكحال *mikḥāl* kohl stick, pencil for darkening the eyelids

مكحلة *mukḥula* pl. مكاحل *makāḥil*² kohl container, kohl jar; solar quadrant; (*syr.*) rifle, gun

تكحيل *takḥīl* treatment of the eyes with kohl

كاحل *kāḥil* pl. كواحل *kawāḥil*² anklebone

كخية *kiḵya* and كاخية *kāḵiya* pl. كواخ *kawāḵin* butler, steward

كد **kadda** *u* (*kadd*) to work hard, exert o.s., toil, labor, slave; to fatigue, wear out, overwork, exhaust, weary, tire (ه s.o.) **II** to chase away, drive away (ه s.o.) **VIII** and **X** to urge, drive, rush (ه s.o.); to wear out, overwork, exhaust, weary, tire (ه s.o.)

كد *kadd* trouble, pains, labor, toil, hard work

كدود *kadūd* industrious, hard-working, diligent

مكدود *makdūd* worn out, exhausted, overworked

كدح **kadaḥa** *a* (*kadḥ*) to exert o.s., work hard, toil, labor, slave (في in or with s.th.) **VIII** to earn a living (لعياله *li-ʿiyālihī* for one's family)

كدح *kadḥ* exertion, toil, labor, drudgery

كدر¹ **kadura** *u* and **kadira** *a* (*kadar*, كدارة *kadāra*, كدورة *kudūra*, كدور *kudūr*, كدرة *kudra*) to be turbid, roily, muddy, roiled (liquid); — *kadira a* (*kadar*, كدرة *kudra*) to be muddy, cloudy, blackish, dingy, flat, swarthy, grimy (color); (*kadar*, كدورة *kudūra*) to be dreary, unhappy (life); to be angry (على with s.o.) **II** to render turbid, to roil, muddy (ه s.th.), trouble, disturb, spoil, ruffle (ه s.th., على for s.o., e.g., s.o.'s peace of mind); to grieve, worry, trouble, vex, irritate, annoy, molest, disturb, distress (ه s.o.) **V** to be turbid, roily, muddy, roiled, troubled; to be angry, be sore (من at s.th.), feel offended, be annoyed, be displeased (من by s.th.), be peeved (من at, about) **VII** to become turbid, muddy, dull, flat; to swoop down (bird)

كدر *kadar* turbidity, muddiness, cloudiness, opaqueness, roiledness; worry, sorrow, grief, distress, vexation, irritation, annoyance

كدرة *kudra* turbidity, muddiness, cloudiness, roiledness, impurity; dingy color, dinginess

كدرة *kadara* clod of dirt, filth

كدر *kadir* and كدير *kadīr* turbid, muddy, roily, roiled; dull, flat, dingy, grimy (color); worried, troubled, disturbed

اكدر *akdar*², f. كدراء *kadrā'*², pl. كدر *kudr* dingy, swarthy, dark-colored

تكدير *takdīr* roiling, troubling, ruffling; offending, offense, affront, indignity

متكدر *mutakaddir* angry, sore, peeved (من at), annoyed, irritated, offended (من by)

كادر² look up alphabetically

كدس **kadasa** *i* (*kads*) and **II** to pile up, heap up, accumulate, amass (ه s.th.); to cram together, press together, compress (ه s.th.) **V** to be heaped up, be piled up; to pile up, accumulate (intr.); to press together, get crammed up

كدس *kuds* pl. اكداس *akdās* heap, pile; stack (of grain, hay, etc.)

كداس *kuddās* pl. كداديس *kadādīs*² heap, pile; stack (of grain, hay, etc.)

كداسة *kudāsa* heap, pile, stack

تكديس *takdīs* accumulation; stacking

كدش *kadaša i* (*kadš*) to gain, earn

كديش *kadīš* pl. كدش *kudš* cart horse, nag, jade

كدم *kadama u i* (*kadm*) to bite (with the front teeth); to bruise, contuse

كدمة *kadma* pl. *kadamāt* bite; wound caused by a bite; bruise, contusion

كدى *kadā i* (*kady*) to give little, skimp, stint **II** to beg **IV** = **I**

كدية *kudya* begging, mendicity

كذا *ka-ḏā* see ك *ka*

كذب *kaḏaba i* (*kiḏb, kaḏib*, كذبة *kaḏba, kiḏba*) to lie; to deceive, delude, mislead; to tell (ه or على s.o.) a lie, to lie (ه or على to s.o.) **II** to accuse of lying, call a liar (ه s.o.), disbelieve s.o., give the lie to s.o. (ه); to disprove, refute, disown, deny (ب or ه s.th.) | ما كذب ان فعل he did not hesitate to do so **IV** to cause (ه s.o.) to lie; to call a liar, prove a liar (ه s.o.), give the lie (ه to s.o.)

كذب *kiḏb, kaḏib* and كذبة *kaḏba, kiḏba* lie; deceit, falsehood, untruth | كذبة ابريل April fool's joke

كذوب *kaḏūb* liar

كذاب *kaḏḏāb* liar, swindler; lying, untruthful; false, deceitful

اكذوبة *ukḏūba* pl. اكاذيب *akāḏib*[2] lie

اكذب *akḏab*[2] a greater liar, more mendacious, more untruthful, falser | اكذب من مسيلمة (*musailimata*) a greater liar than Musailima (proverbially of a liar)

تكذيب *takḏīb* denial

كاذب *kāḏib* liar; lying, untruthful; false, deceptive, fallacious, delusive, specious, sham, make-believe | امل كاذب (*amal*) fallacious hope; بلاغ كاذب (*balāḡ*) slander, defamation (*jur.*)

مكذوب *makḏūb* false, untrue, fabricated, trumped up

كذلك see ك *ka*

كرة[1] see كرو[2]

كر[2] *karra u* (*karr*, كرور *kurūr*, تكرار *takrār*) to turn around and attack (على s.o., s.th.); to return, come back, recur; to withdraw, retreat, fall back; to attack (على s.o.), bear down (على upon); — *a* (كرير *karīr*) to rattle in the throat **II** to repeat, reiterate, do again, do repeatedly (ه s.th.); to pose over and over again (ه a question, على to s.o.), ask (على s.o.) repeatedly (ه a question); to clarify, filter (ه s.th.); to rectify, purify (ه s.th.); to refine (ه sugar, etc.) **V** to be repeated, be reiterated, recur; to be rectified, be purified, be refined

كر *karr* attack, charge | الكر والفر (*farr*) attack and retreat (in battle); بين كر وفر alternately, intermittently, by fits and starts, by jerks; على كر الدهور and على كر الزمن (*k. iz-zaman*) in the course of time

كرة *karra* attack; return, comeback, recurrence; — (pl. *-āt*) one time (= مرة); a hundred thousand; *karratan* once; sometimes, at times; at a time | كرة اخرى *karratan ukrā* a second time, once more; كرة بعد كرة repeatedly, time and again

كرار look up alphabetically

كرور *kurūr* return, comeback, recurrence; succession, sequence, order

كرير *karīr* rattle in the throat

كرارية *kurrārīya* pl. *-āt* (*eg.*) spool, bobbin, reel

مكر *makarr* pl. *-āt* reel

تكرير *takrīr* repetition, reiteration; clarification, rectification, purification, refinement; refining | معمل تكرير السكر *ma'mal t. as-sukkar* sugar refinery

تكرار *takrār* repetition, reiteration; تكرارا *takrāran* repeatedly, frequently, quite often | مرارا وتكرارا (*mirāran*) repeatedly, time and again

مكرر *mukarrar* repeated, reiterated; following twice (number), bis (after a number); a multiple; rectified, purified, refined | سكر مكرر (*sukkar*) refined sugar; ص ٣٧ مكرر page 37b

متكرر *mutakarrir* recurring, recurrent, reiterated, reiterative; repeated, frequent

كراج *garāž* pl. *-āt* garage (*syr.*)

كرار *karār* pl. *-āt* pantry, storeroom; cellar

كرافتة *karāfatta* necktie, cravat

كراكوفيا *karākōfiyā* Cracow (city in S Poland)

كراميل (Fr. *caramel*) *karāmēl* caramel candy

كرب *karaba u* (*karb*) to oppress, distress, grieve, worry, trouble, fill with concern (ه s.o.); to overburden (ه a beast of burden) **IV** to hurry, hasten, rush **VII** and **VIII** to be worried, grieved, troubled, distressed, anxious, apprehensive, feel concern, be afraid

كرب *karb* pl. كروب *kurūb* worry, sorrow, care, grief; apprehension, concern, anxiety, fear; distress, trouble; pain, torment, torture, agony

كربة *kurba* pl. كرب *kurab* worry, sorrow, care, grief; apprehension, concern, anxiety, fear; distress, trouble; pain, torment, torture, agony

مكروب *makrūb* sad, worried, grieved, sorrowful, distressed; apprehensive, anxious, alarmed, fearful, troubled, scared, confused; see alphabetically

مكترب *muktarib* sad, worried, grieved, sorrowful, distressed; apprehensive, anxious, alarmed, fearful, troubled, scared, confused

²كرب *kreb* crepe | كرب ديشين *k. dīšīn* and كرب شين *k. šīn* crepe de Chine

³كروب *karūb* and كروبي *karūbī* pl. *-ūn*, كاروبيم *kārūbīm* cherub, archangel

كرباج *kurbāj, kirbāj* pl. كرابيج *karābīj*[2] whip, lash, riding whip, kurbash

كرباس *kirbās* pl. كرابيس *karābīs*[2] a white cotton fabric

كربال *kirbāl* pl. كرابيل *karābīl*[2] teasing bow (for combing or carding cotton); coarse sieve

كربلاء *karbalā'*[2] Karbala (holy city of the Shiites in central Iraq)

كربون (Fr. *carbon*) *karbōn* coal | ورق كربون *waraq k.* carbon paper

¹كرات *kurrāt* (*eg.*) = كراث

²اكرت *akrat*[2] curly, kinky (hair)

¹كرتن *kartana* to put under quarantine, to quarantine (على s.o.) **II** *takartana* to be put under quarantine, be quarantined

²كرتون *kartōn* pl. كراتين *karātīn*[2] cardboard, pasteboard; carton

كرث *karaṯa u i* (*karṯ*) to oppress, depress, distress, worry, trouble (ه s.o.); to concern, affect, move (ه s.o.) **IV** do. **VIII** to care (لـ for), heed, bear in mind (لـ s.th.), pay attention (لـ to), take an interest (لـ in)

كريث *karīṯ* oppressed, depressed, distressed, anguished, worried, troubled, vexed, annoyed

كراث *karrāṯ, kurrāṯ* leek (Allium porrum L.; *bot.*)

اكتراث *iktirāṯ* attention, care, heed, notice, concern, interest | قلة الاكتراث *qillat al-ikt.* indifference

كارث *kāriṯ* oppressive, depressing, grievous, painful

كارثة *kāriṯa* pl. كوارث *kawāriṯ*[2] disaster, catastrophe | كارثة الامطار *k. al-amṭār* natural catastrophe, torrential rains

الكرج *al-kurj* the Georgians

كرجي *kurjī* Georgian (adj. and n.)

كرح *kirḥ* pl. اكراح *akrāḥ* monk's cell

كرخانة *karakāna* pl. *-āt*, كراخين *karākīn*[2] workshop, factory; (*eg.*) brothel

كرخانجى *karkānjī* artisan, craftsman

الكرد *al-kurd* the Kurds | بلاد الكرد Kurdistan

كردى *kurdī* Kurdish; (pl. اكراد *akrād*) Kurd | جبل الاكراد *jabal al-a.* the Kurdish mountains, Kurdistan

كردان *kirdān* pl. كرادين *karādīn*[2] necklace

كردس *kardasa* to heap up, pile up (ه s.th.); to crowd together, cram together (ه, ه s.o., s.th.) **II** *takardasa* to be heaped up, be piled up; to flock together, crowd together

كردون (Fr. *cordon*) *kordōn* pl. *-āt* cordon; ribbon, braid, lace, trimming | كردون صحى (*ṣiḥḥī*) sanitary cordon

[1]كرز *karaza* **i** (كروز *kurūz*) to hide, seek refuge (الى with)

[2]كرز *karaza* (*karz*) to preach, spread (بالانجيل *bi-l-injīl* the Gospel)

كرز *karz* and كرازة *karāza* sermon, preaching of the Gospel | الكرازة المرقسية (*marqusīya*) the missionary province of St. Mark, the jurisdiction of the Coptic Patriarchate

تكريز *takrīz* pl. تكاريز *takārīz*[2] consecration, benediction (*Chr.*)

كارز *kāriz* preacher

[3]كرز *karaz* (coll.; n. un. ة) cherry

كرزى *karazī* cherry-red

[1]كرس **II** to lay the foundation (ه of a building) **V** to stick together, cohere

كرسى *kursī* pl. كراسى *karāsīy*, كراس *karāsin* chair; throne, see; seat; professorial chair; base, pedestal, socle; bearing (*techn.*) | كرسى بيل *k. bīl* and كرسى بلى (*billī*) ball bearing; كرسى دائر revolving stool, swivel chair; الكرسى الرسولى (*rasūlī*) the Apostolic See; كرسى طويل chaise longue; deck chair; كرسى الملك *k. l-malik* royal throne; كرسى المملكة *k. l-mamlaka* capital, metropolis; كرسى هزاز (*hazzāz*) rocking chair; أستاذ كرسى *ustād k.* full professor

كراسة *kurrāsa* pl. *-āt*, كراريس *karārīs*[2] quire; booklet; notebook, copy book; sketchbook; brochure; installment, fascicle (of a book)

[2]كرس **II** to consecrate, dedicate, inaugurate, open ceremonially (ه s.th.; *Chr.*); to hallow, sanctify (ه e.g., principles); to dedicate, devote (ه ل s.th. to s.o.)

تكريس *takrīs* consecration, dedication, ceremonial inauguration (*Chr.*); devoting, dedication

مكرس *mukarras* consecrated; dedicated | ماء مكرس holy water (*Chr.*)

كرسوع *kursū'* pl. كراسيع *karāsī'*[2] carpal end of the ulna, carpal bone, wristbone

كرسف *karsafa* to hamstring, hock (ه an animal)

كرسنة *kirsinna, kirsanna* a variety of vetch (*bot.*)

كرش *kariša* **a** (*karaš*) to be wrinkled, shriveled, crumpled, crinkled, puckered; to shrivel, form wrinkles, be drawn into wrinkles **II** to wrinkle one's face, knit one's brows, frown **V** = **I**

كرش *kirš, kariš* f., pl. اكراش *akrāš*, كروش *kurūš* stomach (primarily of ruminants = craw); paunch; belly

كرشة *kirša* (*eg.*) tripe, intestines

كريشة (*eg.*) *krēša* a thin, crinkled fabric; crepe

اكرش *akraš*[2] and مكرش *mukriš* potbellied, paunchy

كرشونى *karšūnī* Karshuni, Arabic written in Syriac characters

كريطة look up alphabetically; كرارطى ,كرارط ibid.

كرع *karaʿa* and *kariʿa* a (*karʿ*, كروع *kurūʿ*) to sip V to wash one's feet, perform the partial ablution of the legs (in preparation for prayer); to belch, burp, eruct

كرعة *karʿa* (n.vic.) sipping, sip, swallow

كراع *kurāʿ* m. and f., pl. اكرع *akruʿ*, اكارع *akāriʿ*[2] foot, trotter (esp. of sheep or oxen); leg; extremity | اكارع الارض *a. al-arḍ* the remotest areas of the earth

تكريعة *takriʿa* belching, eructation

كارع *kāriʿ* pl. كوارع *kawāriʿ*[2] foot, trotter; ankle, anklebone; pl. (*eg.*) dish prepared of sheep's trotters

كرفس *karafs* celery (Apium graveolens L.; *bot.*)

[1]كرك *kurk* (*syr.*) fur

[2]كركة *karaka* distilling apparatus, distilling flask, retort

[3]كركى *kurkī* pl. كراكى *karākīy* crane (*zool.*); (سمك) الكراكى (*samak*) *al-k.* pike (*zool.*)

[4]كراكة *karrāka* pl. *-āt* dredging machine, dredge; penitentiary

[5]كريك look up alphabetically

كركب *karkaba* (*eg.*) to throw into disorder, upset, confuse, disturb (ه s.th.); to make a noise

كركبة *karkaba* disorder, confusion, muddle, jumble

كركدن *karkaddan*, *karkadann* rhinoceros | كركدن بحرى (*baḥrī*) narwhal (*zool.*)

كركر *karkara* to repeat, reiterate, do repeatedly (ه s.th.); to rumble (stomach); to tickle | كركر فى الضحك (*ḍaḥk*) to burst into loud laughter, roar with laughter

كركرة *karkara* loud laughter; rumbling (of the stomach)

كركم *kurkum* (*bot.*) turmeric (Curcuma longa L.; plant and rootstock); curcumin

كركند *karkand* spinel ruby (gem); (*eg.*) lobster (*zool.*)

كركوز *karakūz* shadow play

كركون *karakōn* (*eg.*) police station

[1]كرم *karuma* u (*karam*, كرمة *karama*, كرامة *karāma*) to be noble, high-minded, noblehearted, magnanimous, generous, liberal, munificent; to be precious II to call noble and high-minded (ه s.o.); to honor, revere, venerate, treat with deference (ه s.o.); to exalt (ه على s.o. above another), bestow honor (ه على upon s.o. before others) | كرم الله وجهه (*wajhahū*) may God honor him! III to vie in generosity (ه s.o.); to meet reverentially, with deference, politely (ه s.o.) IV to call noble and high-minded (ه s.o.); to honor (ه s.o.); to treat reverentially, with deference, politely, hospitably (ه s.o.), bestow honors (ه upon s.o.); to prove o.s. to be high-minded and generous; to honor, present (ه ب s.o. with), confer (ه ب upon s.o. s.th.) V to feign generosity; to show one's generous side; to be noble; to be friendly, kind, kindly; to be so kind, have the kindness (ب to do s.th., على with regard to or in behalf of s.o.); to present (على ب s.o. with), graciously bestow (على ب upon s.o. s.th.)

كرم *karm* (coll.) pl. كروم *kurūm* vine, grapes, grapevines; vineyard; garden, orchard | بنت الكرم *bint al-k.* wine

كرمة *karma* grapevine, vine

كرم *karam* noble nature; high-mindedness, noble-mindedness, noblehearted-ness, generosity, magnanimity; kindness, friendliness, amicability; liberality, munificence; كرما *karaman* most kindly, obligingly, out of kindness | كرم الاخلاق noble-mindedness, noble character; كرم المحتد *k. al-maḥtid* noble descent

كرمة لك *kurmatan laka* and كرمانا لك *kurmānan laka* for your sake, as a favor to you, in your honor

كرامة *karāma* nobility; high-mindedness, noble-heartedness; generosity, magnanimity; liberality, munificence; honor, dignity; respect, esteem, standing, prestige; mark of honor, token of esteem, favor; (pl. *-āt*) miracle (worked by a saint) | حبا وكرامة لك (*ḥubban wa-karāmatan*) for your sake and in your honor; most gladly, with the greatest pleasure; صاحب كرامات worker of miracles

كريم *karīm* pl. كرماء *kuramā'*², كرام *kiram* noble; distinguished, high-ranking, eminent; high-minded, noble-minded, noblehearted; generous. liberal, munificent, hospitable, beneficent; benefactor; kind, kindly, friendly, amicable, obliging, gracious; respectable, honorable, decent; precious, valuable, costly; thoroughbred; see also alphabetically; الكريمان the two noble things, namely Holy War and the pilgrimage to Mecca | كريم الاخلاق high-minded, noble-minded, noblehearted, noble; كريم الاصل *k. al-aṣl* of noble descent, highborn, highbred; حجر كريم (*ḥajar*) precious stone, gem; حصان كريم thoroughbred horse; دخل كريم (*dakl*) a decent income; القارئ الكريم the gentle reader; المعادن الكريمة the precious metals; مر مر الكرام see ¹مر *marra*

كريمة *karīma* pl. كرائم *karā'im*² precious thing, object of value, valuable; vital part (of the body; esp. eye); daughter; see also alphabetically; الكريمتان the two eyes | كرائم المال (الاموال) the most prized possession(s)

كرام *karrām* pl. *-ūn* winegrower, vinedresser

اكرم *akram*² pl. اكارم *akārim*² nobler more distinguished; more precious, more valuable; most honorable; very high-minded, very noblehearted, most generous

مكرم *makram* and مكرمة *makrama* pl. مكارم *makārim*² noble trait, excellent quality | مكارم الاخلاق noble characteristics, noble traits of character

مكرمة *makruma* pl. مكارم *makārim*² noble deed

تكريم *takrīm* and تكرمة *takrima* honoring, tribute, honor (bestowed on s.o.) | تكريما له (*takrīman*) in his honor

اكرام *ikrām* honor, respect, deference, tribute; hospitable reception, hospitality; kindness; honorarium | اكراما له (*ikrāman*) in his honor

اكرامية *ikrāmīya* pl. *-āt* honorarium; bonus

مكرم *mukarram* honored, revered, venerated; venerable; المكرمة epithet of Mecca

²كريم and كريمة look up alphabetically

كرمش *karmaša* (*eg.*) to pucker, be drawn into folds; to crinkle, become wrinkled, shrivel II *takarmaša* do.

كرمشة *karmaša* fold, crease, wrinkle, crinkle, pucker; knitting

¹كرمل : الكرمل *al-karmal* Mount Carmel (promontory in N Palestine)

كرملي *karmalī* Carmelite

²كرملا *karamillā* caramel (candy)

³كراميل look up alphabetically

الكرملين *al-kremlīn* the Kremlin

كرنب *kurunb* (coll.) cabbage

كرنبة *kurunba* (n. un.) head of cabbage

كرنتينة *kurantīna* pl. *-āt* quarantine

كرنيش look up alphabetically

كرناف *kurnāf* pl. كرانيف *karānīf*² palm stump

كرنافة *kurnāfa* pl. *-āt* gunstock, rifle butt

¹كرنك (Engl.) *krank* pl. *-āt* crank, crank shaft

²كرنك *karnak* a brand of Egyptian cotton (named after الكرنك, a village near Luxor)

كرنيش and كورنيش (Fr. *corniche*) *korniš* pl. كرانيش *karāniš*² cornice, ledge, molding, shelf; coast road, road skirting the shoreline

كره *kariha a* (*karh, kurh,* كراهة *karāha,* كراهية *karāhiya*) to feel disgust (ه at), be disgusted (ه by); to detest, loathe, abhor, hate (ه s.th.); to dislike (ه s.th.); — *karuha u* (كراهة *karāha*) to be repugnant, offensive, hateful, odious, detestable **II** to make s.o. (على or ه) hate s.th. (ه), arouse aversion (ه الى or ه ه in s.o. to s.th.) **IV** to force, compel, coerce (على ه s.o. to) **V** to have an aversion (ه to), feel disgust (ه for), loathe, detest (ه s.th.) **X** to have an aversion (ه to), feel disgust (ه for), loathe, detest (ه s.th.); to force, compel, coerce (على ه s.o. to)

كره *karh, kurh* hatred, hate; aversion, antipathy, dislike, distaste; detestation, abhorrence, disgust, repugnance, loathing; كرها *karhan, kurhan* and على كره *ʿalā kurhin,* على كره منه unwillingly, reluctantly, grudgingly, forcedly; under compulsion, under duress

كره *karih* loathsome, repugnant, offensive

كريه *karīh* unpleasant, disagreeable, offensive, bad, repugnant, repulsive, loathsome, hateful, detestable, abominable, ugly

كراهة *karāha* hatred, hate; aversion, antipathy, dislike, distaste; abhorrence, detestation, disgust, repugnance, loathing

كراهية *karahiya* aversion, antipathy, dislike, distaste, disgust, repugnance, loathing; incompatibility (as a reason of divorce); baseness, abominableness, reprehensibility (*Isl. Law*) | على كراهية unwillingly, grudgingly, forcedly

كريهة *karīha* pl. كرائه *karā'ih*² adversity; misfortune, calamity

مكره *makrah* loathesome thing, unpleasant situation

مكرهة *makraha, makruha* hatred, hate, detestation, abhorrence

مكاره *makārih*² loathsome things; adversities, calamities

اكراه *ikrāh* compulsion, coercion, constraint, force; use of force | بالاكراه by force

اكراهى *ikrāhī* compulsory, coercive, forced, enforced

تكره *takarruh* aversion, antipathy, dislike, distaste, disgust, repugnance, loathing

كاره *kārih* reluctant, grudging, unwilling, averse

مكروه *makrūh* detested, abhorred, hated, hateful, odious, loathsome, disgusting, distasteful, disagreeable, unpleasant; reprehensible (*Isl. Law*); مكروه and مكروهة *makrūha* inconvenience, discomfort, nuisance, adversity; accident, mishap, misadventure

مكره *mukrah* forced, compelled

متكره *mutakarrih* unwilling, reluctant

¹كرو) and كرى) كرا *karā u* (*karw*) and كرى *karā i* (*kary*) to dig (ه s.th.)

كرو *karw* digging, excavation

²كرة *kura* pl. *-āt,* كرى *kuran* globe, sphere; ball | كرة الارض *k. al-arḍ* and كرة ارضية (*arḍīya*) terrestrial globe, globe; كرة الثلج *k. aṯ-ṯalj* snowball; كرة السلة *k. as-salla* basketball; كرة الطاولة *k. aṭ-ṭāwula* table tennis; كرة القدم *k. al-qadam* football,

soccer; كرة الكواكب celestial sphere; كرات لحم *k. laḥm* small meatballs; كرة الماء water polo; كرة اليد *k. al-yad* (European) handball; نصف الكرة *niṣf al-k.* hemisphere

كرية *kurayya* globule; pellet | الكريات الحمراء (الحمر) (*ḥamrā'*, *ḥumr*) the red corpuscles, erythrocytes

كرى *kurīy* and كروى *kurawī* globular, globate, globose, ball-shaped, ball-like, spherical

كروية *kurawīya* globosity, sphericity, roundness | كروية الارض *k. al-arḍ* the sphericity of the earth

كرواتيا *kuruwātiyā* Croatia

كروان *karawān* and كيروان a variety of plover (Charadrius oedicnemus L.; *zool.*)

كروب *karūb* and كروبى *karūbī* pl. *-ūn*, كروبيم *karūbīm* cherub, archangel

كروسة (It. *carozza*) *karōsa* pl. *-āt* state carriage, coach

كروكى (Fr. *croquis*) *krōkī* pl. كروكيات *krōkiyāt* sketch, draft, croquis

كروم *krōm* chrome, chromium

كرويا *karawyā* caraway (Carum carvi L.; *bot.*)

[1] كرى **kariya** *a* (*karan*) to sleep, be asleep, slumber; — *karā i* (*kary*) to dig (ه e.g., a canal) **III** and **IV** to rent, lease, let, let out, farm out, hire out (ه ه to s.o. s.th.) **V** to sleep, be asleep, slumber **VIII** and **X** to rent, hire (ه s.th.); to lease, take on lease (ه s.th.), take a lease (ه of s.th.); to hire, employ, engage (ه s.o.), engage the labor or services (ه of s.o.)

كرى *karan* sleep, slumber

كراء *kirā'* rent, hire, hiring; lease; rental, hire; wages, pay

اكراء *ikrā'* renting, rent: leasing, letting on lease, farming out

اكتراء *iktirā'* renting, rent; leasing, taking on lease; hiring

مكار *mukārin* pl. *-ūn* hirer (esp. one of horses, donkeys, mules, etc.); donkey driver, muleteer

مكر *mukrin* hirer, lessor; landlord

مكرى *mukran* rented, let, hired out, let on lease

مكتر *muktarin* and مستكر *mustakrin* renter, tenant, lessee | مكتر ثان (*tānin*) subtenant, sublessee

[2] كرى, كرية see [1] كرو

[3] كرى *karrī* curry

كريت *kirīt*, كريد *kirīd* Crete

كريطة (Span. *carreta*) *karrīṭa* pl. كرارط *karāriṭ*[2] (*tun.*) cart, wagon, dray

كرارطى *karāriṭī* carrier, carter, drayman

كريك (Turk. *körek*) *kurēk* pl. *-āt* shovel

[1] كريم (Fr. *crème*) *krēm* cream | كريم الحلاقة *k. al-ḥilāqa* shaving cream

كريمة (It. *crema*; *eg.*) *krēma* cream; a kind of thick sauce (served as a condiment)

كز **kazza** (1st pers. perf. *kazuztu*) *u* (كزازة *kazāza*, كزوزة *kuzūza*) to become dry and tough, dry up, shrivel; to be withered, shriveled, shrunk; to contract, shrink; (*eg.*) to have an aversion (من to), feel disgust (من at), have a distaste (من for); — (*kuzz*) to contract, shrink, narrow (ه s.th.); pass. *kuzza* to have tetanus | كز على اسنانه (*eg.*) to gnash one's teeth

كز *kazz* pl. كز *kuzz* dry, dried up, withered, desiccated; shriveled, shrunk; tough, inflexible, unyielding, rigid, stiff | كز اليدين *k. al-yadain* closefisted, miserly, niggardly

كزز *kazaz* miserliness, niggardliness

كزاز *kuzāz, kuzzāz* tetanus

كزازة *kazāza* dryness; boringness, dullness, tediousness; stinginess, niggardliness; stiffness, rigidity

كزبرة *kuzbara, kuzbura* coriander (Coriandrum sativum L.; *bot.*) | كزبرة الثعلب *k. at-ta'lab* pimpernel; كزبرة خضراء (*kaḍrā'*) chervil; كزبرة الصخر *k. aṣ-ṣakr* haircap moss (Polytrichum communis L.; *bot.*)

كزرونة (*eg.*) *kazarōna* (from It. *casseruola*) casserole, cooking vessel

كسب *kasaba i* (*kasb*) to gain, win, acquire (ه s.th.); to earn (ه s.th.); to profit, win, gain; to gather, acquire (ه knowledge); to obtain, get, attain (ه s.th.) | كسب هتافا ل (*hutāfan*) win acclaim for, be applauded for; ما كسبت يداه (*yadāhu*) what he has earned in the hereafter by his (good and evil) deeds **II** to make or let s.o. (ه) gain, win or obtain (ه s.th.); to let s.o. (ه) share the profit **IV** to make or let s.o. (ه) gain, win or obtain (ه s.th.), secure (ه ه for s.o. s.th.); to impart (ه ه or ه to s.o. or to s.th. s.th., also e.g., to the face a certain expression) | اكسب مناعة ضد (*manā'atan ḍidda*) to make immune to ... **V** to earn (ه s.th.); to acquire, obtain (ه s.th.); to gain, win (ه s.th.) **VIII** do.; to possess, have, own (ه s.th.); to take on (ه a new quality, a color, a different aspect, and the like)

كسب *kasb* acquisition; earnings; gain, profit; winnings; s.th. acquired or gained, acquirement; acquired knowledge, learning

كسب *kusb* and كسبة *kusba* oil cake

مكسب *maksab, maksib* and مكسبة *maksiba* pl. مكاسب *makāsib*[2] gain, profit

تكسب *takassub* earning, gaining; acquisition; earnings; gain, profit

اكتساب *iktisāb* acquisition; gaining, winning | اكتساب بمرور الزمان (*bi-murūri z-zamān*) prescription, usucapion, acquisition of property or rights by uninterrupted possession of them for a certain period (*jur.*)

كاسب *kāsib* winner; earner, provider

مكسب *muksib* profitable, lucrative

كسبرة *kusbara* coriander (*bot.*; = كزبرة, q.v.)

كستاك *kustāk* see كستك

كستبان *kustubān* pl. كساتبين *kasātibīn*[2] thimble

كستك (Turk. *köstek*) *kustak* and كستيك pl. كساتك *kasātik*[2] watch chain

كستليتة (It. *costoletta*) *kustulēta, kustalēta* cutlet, chop

كستنة *kastana* chestnut (*bot.*)

كستنائى *kastanā'ī* maroon, chestnut-colored

كسح *kasaḥa a* (*kasḥ*) to sweep; to clean, clean out, empty; — *kasiḥa a* (*kasaḥ*) to be crippled; to become a cripple **II** (*eg.*) to cripple (ه s.o.); to bend, twist, warp (ه s.th.) **VIII** to sweep away (ه s.th.); to wash away, flush out, remove (ه s.th.); to overrun (ه s.th.); to flood, overflow (ه s.th.), spread, fan out (ه over s.th.); to plunder, pillage, sack (ه a captured town); to snatch up, seize (ه s.th.), take hold (ه of)

كسح *kasḥ* sweeping; cleaning; clearing; emptying (e.g., of a latrine); lameness, paralysis, palsy

كساح *kusāḥ* rachitis, rickets

كساحة *kusāḥa* sweepings; refuse, garbage, rubbish, trash

كسيح *kasīḥ* lame, palsied, paralyzed; crippled

اكسح *aksaḥ*[2] lame, palsied, paralyzed; crippled

مكسحة *miksaḥa* broom

اكتساح *iktisāḥ* a sweeping away, sweep; removal, elimination; flooding, overflowing, submersion, inundation; rape, seizure, usurpation

كاسحة *kāsiḥa*: كاسحة الالغام *k. al-alḡām* mine sweeper

مكسح *mukassaḥ* crippled; cripple; lame person, paralytic

كسد *kasada* and *kasuda* u (كساد *kasād*, كسود *kusūd*) to find no market, not to move, sell badly (merchandise); to be stagnant, dull, listless (business, market) **IV** to be dull, listless (market)

كساد *kasād* unsalableness of merchandise; economic depression, dullness of the market, stagnation of commerce, recession; slump

○ مكاسدة *mukāsada* dumping

كاسد *kāsid* and كسيد *kasīd* selling badly, little in demand (merchandise); stagnant, dull, listless (market)

[1] كسر *kasara* i (*kasr*) to break, shatter, fracture (ه s.th.); to break open, force open, pry open (ه a door, and the like); to break (also fig.: power, resistance); to violate, infringe (ه a legal duty); to destroy, annihilate, rout (ه s.th.); to defeat (ه an army); to fold (ه s.th.); to provide with the vowel *i* (ه a consonant; *gram.*) | كسر خاطره to disappoint, disoblige, offend, affront s.o.; كسرت الريح *kusirat ir-rīḥu* the wind has calmed down; كسر الصمت (*ṣamt*) to break the silence; كسر العطش (*ʿaṭaš*) to quench the thirst; كسره عن مراده (*murādihī*) to dissuade or hinder s.o. from carrying out his intention; كسر عينه (*ʿainahū*) (*eg.*) to shame s.o., put s.o. to shame; كسر قلبه (*qalbahū*) to break s.o.'s heart; to discourage s.o.; كسر من حدته (*ḥiddatihī*) to blunt the edge of s.th., tone down s.th., curb, temper s.th. or s.o. **II** to break into pieces, fragmentize (ه s.th.); to shatter, smash (ه s.th.) **V** to be broken to pieces, be shattered, be fragmentized; to break, be refracted, be diffracted (also light, rays, *phys.*); to be refined, civilized **VII** to get broken; to be defeated, be routed, be broken (force, violence); to break; to be refracted, be diffracted; to abate, subside (e.g., heat), be quenched (thirst) | انكسرت ساقه (*sāquhū*) he broke his leg

كسر *kasr* breaking, fracturing; shattering, fragmentation; — (pl. كسور *kusūr*) break, breach, fracture; crack, rupture; fracture of a bone; (pl. كسور *kusūr*, كسورات) fraction (*arith.*) | كسر عشرى (اعشارى) (*ʿušrī, aʿšārī*) decimal fraction; وكسور *wa-kusūr* (after figures) ... and some, a little over ..., e.g., جنيه وكسور one pound and some, a little over a pound

كسر *kasr, kisr*: كسر البيت *k. al-bait* nook of the house; جثم فى كسر بيته to live in seclusion, stay in one's four walls

كسرة *kasra* defeat, breakdown, collapse; the vowel point for *i*; nook of the house

كسرة *kisra* pl. كسر *kisar*, *-āt* fragment; a small piece; chunk (of bread); slice (of bread)

كسير *kasīr* pl. كسرى *kasrā*, كسارى *kasārā* broken, fractured, shattered; defeated; see also كسرى alphabetically

○ كسارة *kassāra* nutcracker

كسيرة *kusaira* diopter (*phys.*)

مكسر *maksir*: صلب المكسر *ṣulb al-m.* hard to break, robust, sturdy, hardy, firm, strong; طيب المكسر *ṭayyib al-m.* standing the test, proving its value, of excellent quality; لين المكاسر *layyin al-makāsir* soft, gentle

تكسير *taksīr* breaking, fracturing; shattering, fragmentation | جمع التكسير *jamʿ at-t.* broken plural (*gram.*)

تكسر *takassur* a being broken, breaking; refraction, diffraction (*opt.*) | تكسر الاشعة *t. al-aši''a* refraction of rays

انكسار *inkisār* (state or process of) being broken, brokenness, breaking; fracture; breach, rupture; fragility; defeat, rout; brokenness in spirit, brokenheartedness, dejection; contrition; refraction, diffraction (*phys.*) | انكسار القلب *ink. al-qalb* dejectedness, despondency, contrition

كاسر *kāsir* breaking, shattering, etc.; (pl. كواسر *kawāsir*[2]) rapacious, ferocious, savage (predatory animal) | كاسر الحجر *k. al-ḥajar* saxifrage, stonebreak (*bot.*); طير كاسر (*ṭair*) bird of prey; كواسر الطير *k. aṭ-ṭair* predatory birds

مكسور *maksūr* broken, fractured; shattered, fragmented; defeated; unsuccessful, thwarted, frustrated; bankrupt; having a kasra (consonant; *gram.*)

مكسر *mukassar* fragmented, shattered, smashed; broken (also, e.g., language); مكسرات almonds and nuts | جمع مكسر (*jam'*) broken plural (*gram.*)

اكسير *iksīr* elixir

كسرونة *kasarōna* (*eg.*) see كزرونة

كسرى *kisrā* pl. اكاسرة *akāsira*, اكاسر *akāsir*[2] Khosrau; designation of the Persian kings in general

كسع *kasa'a* a to chase away (ه s.o.); to strike, shove, push, kick (ه s.o. from behind) VIII to put its tail (ب) between its legs

كسف *kasafa* i (كسوف *kusūf*) to be or become dark, gloomy; to be eclipsed, pass through an eclipse (sun); — to reprimand, reprove (ه s.o.); to abash, shame, put to shame (ه s.o.) VII to be eclipsed; to be shamed, be ashamed; to blush

كسف *kasf* darkening, occultation, eclipse; dark, darkness, gloominess

كسوف *kusūf* occultation, eclipse, solar eclipse

انكساف *inkisāf* occultation, eclipse, solar eclipse

كاسف *kāsif* dejected, downcast, sad, worried, grieved; gloomy

كسكس *kaskasa* to pound, bray, grind, powder, pulverize; (*eg.*) to retreat, fall back, withdraw

كسكسو *kuskusū* and كسكسى *kuskusī* couscous, a dish prepared of groats and salt water (staple food in northwest Africa)

كسكاس *kuskās*, *kaskās* sieve for preparing couscous

كسل *kasila* a (*kasal*) to be lazy, idle, sluggish, indolent, negligent; to idle, loaf II to make lazy or negligent (ه s.o.) VI = I

كسل *kasal* laziness, sluggishness, idleness, inactivity, loafing, indolence, negligence

كسل *kasil* and كسول *kasūl* lazy, idle

كسلان *kaslān*, f. ة, كسلى *kaslā*, pl. كسالى *kasālā*, *kusālā*, كسلى *kaslā* lazy, sluggish, slothful, indolent, idle, inactive

مكسال *miksāl* lazybones, sluggard, idler, loafer

تكاسل *takāsul* laziness, sluggishness, indolence

متكاسل *mutakāsil* lazy, sluggish, slothful, indolent

كسم *kasama* i (*kasm*) to make a living (على عياله *'alā 'iyālihi* for one's family) II to give form (ه to s.th.), shape, fashion (ه s.th.)

كسم *kasm* cut, style (of a dress); clothing, clothes, costume, fashion; form, shape; manner, mode

كسيم *kasīm* duty, rate, tax

تكسيم *taksīm* forming, shaping, fashioning, molding; ○ milling

مكسم *mukassam* well-shaped, shapely

كسا (كسى and كسو) *kasā u* (*kasw*) to clothe, dress, garb, attire (ه ه s.o. with or in); to hang, drape, face, line, case (ب or ه ه s.th. with), incase (ب or ه ه s.th. in); to cover (ب or ه ه s.th. with), put, slip (ب or ه ه over s.th. s.th.) | كساه صبغة كذا (*ṣibḡata*) to give s.th. the appearance of ..., make s.th. look like ...; — كسى *kasiya a* (كسا *kasan*) to be or get dressed; to dress IV to clothe, dress, garb, attire (ه ه s.o. with or in) V to be dressed, be clothed, be garbed; to clothe o.s., array o.s., attire o.s. (ب with or in); to cover o.s. VIII do.; to burst into leaf (tree)

كسوة *kiswa* pl. كسى *kusan, kisan,* كساو *kasāwin* clothing, clothes, apparel, attire, raiment; dress, garment; suit of clothes; uniform; draping, lining, casing, facing, paneling, wainscoting (e.g., of walls) | الكسوة (الشريفة) the kiswa, the covering of the Kaaba (black, brocaded carpet covering the walls of the Kaaba, made annually in Egypt and transported with the pilgrimage caravan to Mecca); كسوة التشريفة full-dress uniform, gala uniform

كساء *kisā'* pl. اكسية *aksiya* garment; dress

تكسية *taksiya* clothing, dressing; draping, lining, casing, facing, paneling, wainscoting (e.g., of walls); course of stones (of a macadam road)

كش *kašša i* to recoil (من from)

كشة *kušša* lock of hair

كشتبان *kuštubān, kuštibān* pl. كشاتبين *kašātibīn*[2] thimble

كشح *kašaḥa a* (*kašḥ*): كشح له بالعداوة (*bi-l-ʿadāwa*) to harbor enmity toward s.o., hate s.o.; — to disperse, scatter, break up (هم a crowd), send away, dismiss, drive away, chase away (ه s.o.) III كاشحه بالعداوة (*bi-l-ʿadāwa*) to harbor enmity toward s.o., hate s.o. VII to be dispersed, be scattered; to disperse, scatter, break up; to be dispelled

كشح *kašḥ* pl. كشوح *kušūḥ* region of the hip, haunch, flank, side, waist; Venus's-shell, cowrie | طوى كشحه على (*ṭawā kašḥahū*) to keep s.th. to o.s., keep s.th. secret; طوى كشحه (كشحا) عن to turn from s.o., break with s.o.; ولاه كشحه (*wallāhu*) to turn one's back on s.o.

كشاحة *kušāḥa* secret enmity, rancor, grudge, resentment, hate

كاشح *kāšiḥ* secret enemy

كشر *kašara i* (*kašr*) and II to bare one's teeth; to grimace; to grin, smile (الى at s.o.); to scowl, glower, bear a grim expression | كشر عن اسنانه to bare or show one's teeth; كشر عن نابه (انيابه) do.

كشرة *kišra* grimace

تكشيرة *takšīra* (n. vic.) flash of the teeth

هو جارى مكاشرى *huwa jārī mukāširī* he is my nearest neighbor

انكشارى look up alphabetically

كشط *kašaṭa i* (*kašṭ*) to take off (ه a wrapping, a covering); to pull off (ه s.th.); to erase (ه s.th. written); to remove (ه s.th.); to scratch off, scrape off (ه s.th., ب e.g., with a knife so as to clean it)

مكشط *mikšaṭ* erasing knife

كشف *kašafa i* (*kašf*) to pull away, remove, take off, throw open, lift, raise (ه a covering, a curtain, a veil, etc., عن from); to reveal, disclose, uncover, expose, bare (ه or عن s.th.); to clear up (ه or عن s.th.), shed light (ه or عن on); to show, demonstrate (ه or عن s.th.); to open up, lay open, lay bare (ه or عن s.th.); to bring (ه or عن s.th.); to study, scrutinize, investigate, examine (عن s.th.); to examine medically (على s.o.) | كشف القناع عن to unveil, unmask s.o. or s.th.; كشف عليه طبيا (*ṭibbīyan*) to examine s.o. medically; كشفت الحرب عن ساقها (*ḥarbu*) the war was or became violent, flared up; war broke out **III** to disclose, reveal, manifest, demonstrate, show (ه ب to s.o. s.th.), evince (ه ب toward s.o. s.th.); to make known (ه ب or ه ه to s.o. s.th.), inform (ه ب or ه ه s.o. of) | كاشفه بالعداوة (*bi-l-ʿadāwa*) to manifest open hostility toward s.o. **V** to be uncovered, be exposed, be laid open, be bared, be disclosed, be revealed, be brought to light; to come to light, become visible, manifest itself, show; to open, be opened up (عن شىء so as to reveal s.th.) | تكشف الامر عن لا شىء (*amru*) the matter turned out to be of no consequence; تكشف عن منتهى العجز (*muntahā l-ʿajz*) to show o.s. utterly helpless **VII** to be removed, be lifted, be raised (veil); to be uncovered, be disclosed, be revealed, become manifest (ل to s.o.) **VIII** to discover (ه s.th., esp. scientifically); to find out, detect, uncover (ه s.th.) **X** to seek to discover (ه s.th.); to explore (ه s.th.); to investigate (ه s.th.), search, inquire (ه into s.th.); to scout, reconnoiter (*mil.*); to discover (ه s.th., scientifically); to detect, spot, seek out, search out, find out (ه s.th.)

كشف **kašf** uncovering, disclosure; baring, exposure, unveiling; revelation, illumination (*myst.*); investigation, inquiry, search, quest, study, examination, scrutiny; inspection; boy scout movement; — (pl. كشوف *kušūf*, كشوفات *kušūfāt*) report, account; statement, specification, enumeration; table, schedule, chart; list, roster, index, register, inventory; pl. كشوف discoveries | كشف طبى (*ṭibbī*) medical examination; كشف الاقتراع muster roll; كشف الحساب bill, invoice

كشفى **kašfī** of or pertaining to boy scouts | حركة كشفية (*ḥaraka*) boy scout movement

كشاف **kaššāf** pl. كشافة **kaššāfa** discoverer, inventor; explorer, reconnoiterer, scout; boy scout | ○ كشاف كهربائى (*kahrabāʾī*) searchlight; مصباح كشاف (*miṣbāḥ*) and نور كشاف (*nūr*) pl. انوار كشافة do.

كشافة **kišāfa** exploration; reconnaissance, reconnoitering, scouting (*mil.*); boy scout movement, scouting

كشافى **kišāfī** of boy scouts, boy scout (adj.)

كشيف **kašīf** uncovered, open, exposed

اكتشاف **iktišāf** uncovering, disclosure, detection, spotting, location; (pl. *-āt*) (scientific) discovery

استكشاف **istikšāf** uncovering, clarification, elucidation; discovery; close observation; reconnaissance, reconnoitering, scouting (*mil.*) | طائرة الاستكشاف reconnaissance plane; الاستكشاف البعيد المدى (*madā*) long-range reconnaissance

استكشافى **istikšāfī** explorational, exploratory, of discovery, reconnaissance-, scout- (in compounds)

كاشف **kāšif** pl. كشفة **kašafa** uncovering, revealing, etc.; serving exploratory purposes, instrumental in reconnaissance, conducive to discovery, detection or disclosure; examiner, investigator, discoverer; supervisor, inspector; (*Eg.*) head of a *muqāṭaʿa*, district chief (obsolete); detector (*radio*); كاشف and كاشفة reagent (*chem.*) | ضوء كاشف (*ḍauʾ*) pl. اضواء كاشفة and نور كاشف (*nūr*) pl. انوار كاشفة searchlight; ○ زورق كاشف الالغام (*zauraq*) mine-locating craft, mine sweeper; كاشف بلورى (*ballūrī, billaurī*) crystal detector (*radio*); كاشف المحيط *k. al-muḥīṭ* periscope; بان بالكاشف (*bāna*) to manifest itself clearly and unmistakably

مكشوف *makšūf* bared, exposed, uncovered, open, roofless, coverless, unveiled, naked, bare; (*mil.*) open, undefended, devoid of military installations or fortifications; uncovered (*com.*) | مكشوف الرأس *m. ar-ra's* bareheaded, hatless; بالمكشوف or على المكشوف openly, publicly, overtly, for everyone to see

مكتشف *muktašif* discoverer, explorer

مكتشفات *muktašafāt* (scientific) discoveries

كشك[1] *kušk* pl. اكشاك *akšāk* kiosk; summerhouse, pavilion, cabin, log cabin; hut, shed, shanty; (telephone) booth; stall, stand, booth (at a fair, etc.) | كشك الاستحمام bathhouse; beach chair; كشك الاشارات *k. al-išārāt* block station, signal box (railroad); كشك الديدبان *k. ad-daidabān* sentry box; ○ كشك محول (*muhawwil*) transformer house

كشك[2] *kišk* a dough made of bulgur and sour milk, cut into small pieces, dried and used for the preparation of other dishes (so in Egypt; there are several other ways of preparing it) | (*eg.*) كشك الماز *kišk almāz* asparagus

كشكش *kaškaša* to rustle; to flee, run away; (*eg.*) to pleat

كشكش *kaškaš* pl. كشاكش *kašākiš*[2] seam; hem, edge, border

رواية كشكشية *riwāya kiškišiya* burlesque, popular comedy

كشكول *kaškūl* beggar's bag; scrapbook; album

كشمش *kišmiš* a kind of currants

كشمير *kašmīr*[2] Kashmir (region in NE India); *kašmīr* cashmere (a soft, twilled woolen fabric)

كشنى *kušnā* lentil tare, slender vetch (*bot.*)

□ كض (for كظ) V to be replete, overfull, overloaded, overburdened VIII to be overfilled, be replete (ب with s.th.), be chock-full

تكضض *takaḍḍuḍ* overexertion, overstrain, overburdening

كظ *kaẓẓa u* (*kaẓẓ*) to fill, overfill (ه s.th.); to burden, weight, encumber (ه s.th.); to overstuff, surfeit, cloy (ه the stomach) VIII to be crammed full, be jam-packed, be overcrowded (ب with, esp. with people); to sate o.s., eat one's fill; to be overstuffed, be surfeited, be cloyed (ب with); to be abundant, copious, plentiful

كظة *kiẓẓa* gorging, cloying, overstuffing (of the stomach); surfeit

كظيظ *kaẓīẓ* overfilled, overstuffed, cloyed, surfeited

مكتظ *muktaẓẓ* overcrowded (ب with, esp. with people), crammed full, jam-packed (ب with), chock-full (ب of)

كظر *kuẓr* suet

كظم *kaẓama i* (*kaẓm*, كظوم *kuẓūm*) to conceal or suppress (ه one's anger); to be mum, keep silent

كظيم *kaẓīm* filled with anger

كعب *ka'aba u i* (كعوب *ku'ūb*) to be full and round, be swelling (breasts) II to make cubic, to cube (ه s.th.); to dice (ه s.th.)

كعب *ka'b* pl. كعاب *ki'āb*, كعوب *ku'ūb* knot, knob, node (of cane); joint, articulation; ankle, anklebone; heel (of the foot, of a shoe); ferrule; die; cube; high rank, fame, glory, honor | كعب الكتاب (pl. كعوب) spine of a book; ارقى كعبا *arqā ka'ban* abler, more capable, more qualified, more efficient; رجل عالى الكعب *rajul 'ālī l-k.* a distinguished, capable, successful man; علو الكعب *'ulūw al-k.* high rank, outstanding position; ذهب كعبهم their days of glory are past

كعب *ku'b* breasts, bosom

كعبة *ka'ba* pl. *ka'abāt* cube, cubic structure; الكعبة the Kaaba (in Mecca); (fig.) shrine; object of veneration, focus of interest

كعبى *ka'bī* cubic

كعبة *ku'ba* virginity

كعاب *ka'āb* having swelling breasts, buxom (girl)

ابو كعيب *abū ku'aib* (*eg.*) mumps (*med.*)

تكعيب *tak'īb* cubing, dicing; raising to the third power, cubing

تكعيبة *tak'ība* trellis, espalier

تكعيبى *tak'ībī* cubic

كاعب *kā'ib* pl. كواعب *kawā'ib*² well-developed, full and round, swelling (bosom); having swelling breasts, buxom (girl); كواعب buxom girls

مكعب *muka''ab* cube-shaped, cubiform, cubic; (pl. *-āt*) cube | قدم مكعب (*qadam*) cubic foot; متر مكعب (*mitr*) cubic meter

كعبرة *ku'bura* and كعبورة *ku'būra* pl. كعابر *ka'ābir*² knotty excrescence, knot, knob, node; كعبرة radius (*anat.*) | عظم الكعبرة *'aẓm al-k.* radius (*anat.*)

مكعبر *muka'bar* knotty, knobbed, gnarled

كعبل *ka'bala* (*eg.*) to trip up (ه s.o.); to make (ه s.o.) stumble

كعك *ka'k* (coll.; n. un. ة) cake; designation of various kinds of pastry, also of small baked goods; pretzel (*syr.*)

كعم *ka'ama a* (*ka'm*) to muzzle (ه a camel); to gag (ه s.o.); to cap, seal (ه a vessel)

كغم abbreviation of كيلوغرام *kīloḡrām* kilogram

كفّ *kaffa u* (*kaff*) to border, edge, hem (ه a garment); to desist, refrain (عن from), cease, forbear (عن doing s.th.), give up, stop (عن s.th.); to renounce, waive, forgo (عن s.th.), abstain (عن from); to hold back, restrain (ه عن s.o. from); to hinder, prevent (ه عن s.o. from); to avert (عن s.th.); to check, curb, restrict (من s.th.) | كف بصره *kaffa* (and pass. *kuffa*) *baṣaruhū* to become blind **II** to hem (ه a garment) **V** to beg **VII** to desist, refrain, abstain (عن from) **X** to hold out the hand with an imploring gesture, beg, practice begging; to shade one's eyes with the hand; to coil (snake); to surround (ل or حول s.o., s.th.), flock around s.o. or s.th. (ل, حول)

كف *kaff* desistance, refraining (عن from); abstaining, abstention (عن from); cessation, suspension, stop, stoppage, discontinuation (عن of s.th.); — *kaff* f., pl. كفوف *kufūf*, اكف *akuff* palm of the hand; glove; paw, foot, claw (of an animal); slap; scale (of a balance); handful; quire; bar (of chocolate) | كف مريم *k. maryam* (*eg.*) agnus castus, chaste tree (Vitex agnus-castus; *bot.*); rose of Jericho, resurrection plant (Anastatica hierochuntica L.; *bot.*); الكف الجذماء (*jaḏmā'*) star α in the constellation Cetus; الكف الخضيب star β in Cassiopeia; كف الاسد *k. al-asad* lion's-leaf (*bot.*); وضع حياته على كفه (*ḥayātahū*) to risk one's life; استدر الاكف *istadarra l-akuffa* to secure generous contributions

كفة *kiffa, kaffa* pl. كفف *kifaf*, كفاف *kifāf* palm of the hand; scale (of a balance)

كفة *kaffa*: كفة بارود *k. bārūd* (*eg.*) cartridge pouch

كفة *kuffa* pl. كفف *kufaf* edge, seam, hem, border

كفاف *kafāf* sufficiency, sufficient means for a living

كفاف *kifāf* border, edge, fringe, seam, hem

كفافة *kifāfa* hemming; hem

كفيف *kafīf* blind | كفيف البصر *k. al-baṣar* blind

كافة *kāffa* totality, entirety; (with foll. genit.) all; the people, the masses, the populace; *kāffatan* all without exception, one and all; altogether, in the aggregate, collectively

مكفوف *makfūf* pl. مكافيف *makāfīf*[2] blind

كفأ *kafa'a a* (*kaf'*) to turn around, turn over, reverse, invert (ه s.th.); to turn away, turn aside, turn back (من from) **III** to reward (ه s.o.); to requite, return, repay, recompense (ب ه s.th. with); to compensate, make up (ب ه for s.th. with); to be similar, equal (ه to s.th.), equal (ه s.th.), be commensurate (ه with); to measure up, come up (ه to s.th.), compare favorably (ه with) **IV** to turn over, reverse, invert (ه s.th.) **VI** to be equal, be on a par; to (counter)balance each other, be perfectly matched **VII** to be turned away, be turned aside; to be changed, be altered; to recede, change, fade (color); to turn back, withdraw, retreat, fall back, give way; to be inverted, be reversed, be turned around or over; to fall down, tumble, topple

كفء *kaf'*, *kif'*, *kuf'* pl. اكفاء *akfā'*, كفاء *kifā'* equal, alike; adequate, appropriate, suitable, fit (ل for); equal (ل to s.o.), a match (ل for); qualified, capable, able, competent, efficient

كفوء *kufū'*, كفؤ *kufu'* equal, comparable (ل to), a match (ل for)

كفاء *kifā'* an equivalent

كفاء *kafā'* equality; adequacy, adequateness

كفاءة *kafā'a* equality; adequacy, adequateness; comparableness; fitness, suitability, appropriateness; competence, efficiency, ability, capability; pl. كفاءات qualifications, abilities, capabilities

مكافأة *mukāfa'a* pl. *-āt* requital; recompense, remuneration; compensation, indemnification, indemnity; reward; stipend

تكافؤ *takāfu'* mutual correspondence, equivalence; homogeneity, sameness

انكفاء *inkifā'* retreat, withdrawal

مكافئ *mukāfi'* equal, (a)like, of the same kind, homogeneous, corresponding, commensurate, equivalent

متكافئ *mutakāfi'* alike, (mutually) corresponding, commensurate, equivalent, equal

كفت *kafata i* (*kaft*) to restrain, detain, turn away, prevent, hold back (من ه s.o. from) **II** to plate (ب ه s.th. with); to inlay (ه s.th.)

كفت *kift* cooking pot

كفتة *kufta* meat balls, hamburgers, oblong or round | سمك كفتة (*samak*) fried fish cakes; كفتة بطاطس potato dumplings stuffed with meat

تكفيت *takfīt* inlaid work, inlay; plating, platework

مكفت *mukaffat* inlaid; coated, overlaid, plated

كفح *kafaḥa a* (*kafḥ*) to face frankly, confront, encounter or meet face to face (ه s.o.) **III** = **I**; to combat (ه s.o., ه s.th.), fight, battle, struggle, contend (ه against); to defend (عن s.th.), fight (عن for) | كافح اموره (*umūrahū*) to manage one's affairs personally

كفاح *kifāḥ* and مكافحة *mukāfaḥa* opposition, fight, battle, struggle (with genit.: against); contention, strife

[1]كفر *kafara i* (*kafr*) to cover, hide (ه s.th.); — (*kufr*, كفران *kufrān*, كفور *kufūr*) to be irreligious, be an infidel, not to believe (بالله in God); كفر بالله also: to blaspheme God, curse, swear; to re-

nege one's faith, become an infidel; to be ungrateful (ب or ه for a benefit) **II** to cover, hide (ه s.th.); to expiate (عن s.th.); to do penance, atone, make amends (عن ب for s.th. by or with); to grant remission (ه عن to s.o. of his sins); to forgive (عن or ل ه s.th. to s.o.), grant pardon (عن or ل ه for s.th. to s.o.); to make (ه s.o.) an infidel, seduce (ه s.o.) to unbelief; to accuse of infidelity, charge with unbelief (ه s.o.) **IV** to make (ه s.o.) an infidel; to call (ه s.o.) an infidel, accuse (ه s.o.) of infidelity

كفر *kafr* pl. كفور *kufūr* small village, hamlet

كفر *kufr* and كفران *kufrān* unbelief, infidelity | كفر بالله godlessness, atheism; blasphemy, profanity; كفران بالنعمة (*niʿma*) ingratitude, ungratefulness

كفار *kaffār* infidel, unbeliever

كفارة *kaffāra* penance, atonement (عن for a sin), expiation (عن of); reparation, amends; expiatory gifts, expiations (distributed to the poor at a funeral)

تكفير *takfīr* expiation (عن of), atonement, penance (عن for a sin); seduction to infidelity; charge of unbelief

كافر *kāfir* pl. *-ūn*, كفار *kuffār*, كفرة *kafara*, كفار *kifār* irreligious, unbelieving; unbeliever, infidel, atheist; ungrateful | كافر بالنعمة (*niʿma*) ungrateful

كافور[2] look up alphabetically

كفس *kafisa* a (*kafas*) to be bandy-legged **VII** do.

اكفس *akfas*[2], f. كفساء *kafsā'*[2], pl. كفس *kufs* bandy-legged

كفكف *kafkafa* to hold back (ه tears)

كفل *kafala* u (*kafl*, كفالة *kafāla*) to feed, support (ه s.o.), provide (ه for s.o.; عائلة *ʿā'ilatan* for a family); — *kafala* u i, *kafila* u and *kafula* u (*kafl*, كفول *kufūl*, كفالة *kafāla*) to vouch, answer, go bail, be guaranty, be or stand sponsor, be responsible, liable, answerable (ب for); to guarantee, sponsor (ه s.o.); to be legal guardian (ه of s.o.); to secure; to warrant, ensure (ه s.th.); to guarantee (ل ه s.th. to s.o.); ○ to cover, back (currency with gold) **II** to feed, support (ه s.o.), provide (ه for); to admit as security, sponsor or bail (ه s.o.); to name as sponsor, ask to be security or to go bail, appoint as security or bail (ه s.o.) **III** to conclude an agreement, make a contract (ه with s.o.) **IV** to appoint as security, sponsor or bail (ه s.o.), make (ه s.o.) go bail **V** to be security, go bail, vouch, be or become responsible, answerable or liable (ل ب to s.o. for), be sponsor (ل ب of s.o. for s.th.), guarantee (ل ب to s.o. s.th.); to obligate o.s., pledge o.s. (ل ب to s.o. to do s.th.); to undertake, take upon o.s. (ب s.th.) **VI** to vouch for each other, guarantee each other

كفل *kafl* guaranty, warranty

كفل *kafal* pl. اكفال *akfāl*, كفول *kufūl* rump, buttocks; croup of a horse

كفالة *kafāla* bail, guaranty, security, sponsorship; pledge, deposit, surety, collateral | كفالة مالية (*mālīya*) surety, security; bail; caution money; كفالة بالنفس (*nafs*) bail (esp. for due appearance of a person in court; *Isl. Law*); في كفالة فلان under the protection or tutelage of s.o., in s.o.'s custody

كفيل *kafīl* pl. كفلاء *kufalā'*[2] responsible, liable, answerable; bail, bailsman, security, surety, sponsor, bondsman; guarantor (ب of s.th.); vouching (ب for s.th.), guaranteeing (ب s.th.); protector; legal guardian | كفيل بالنفس (*nafs*) bail, bailsman (esp. one guaranteeing the due appearance of a person in court; *Isl. Law*)

تكافل *takāful* mutual or joint responsibility; solidarity; mutual agreement

كافل *kāfil* pl. كفل *kuffal* breadwinner, supporter, provider; bail, bailsman, security, surety, sponsor, bondsman; protector; legal guardian

مكفول (به) *makfūl (bihī)* guaranteed; covered, backed (banknotes in circulation)

كفن *kafana* i (*kafn*) to cover with a winding sheet, to shroud, dress for the grave (ه the deceased) **II** do.; to wrap (ه ب s.th. in), cover (ه ب s.th. with)

كفن *kafn* saltless

كفن *kafan* pl. اكفان *akfān* shroud, winding sheet

كفهر **IV** *ikfaharra* (اكفهرار *ikfihrār*) to be dark, grow dark, darken, be or become gloomy

اكفهرار *ikfihrār* darkness, dark; dusk, gloom, gloominess

مكفهر *mukfahirr* dim, dusky, gloomy; clouded, overcast; grave, sullen, melancholy

كفى *kafā* i (كفاية *kifāya*) to be enough, sufficient (ه for s.o.), suffice (ه s.o.); to meet all requirements; to protect (ه ه s.o. from s.o., ه ه s.o. from s.th.); to save, spare (ه ه s.o. a trouble) | وكفى *wa-kafā* and that's all! enough of that! that's enough! كفى الله عنك may God give satisfaction in your stead, or, may God make up for your shortcoming (said to s.o. making a mistake, or showing himself inadequate); كفى بالله وكيلا (*wakīlan*) God is the best protector; كفى حزنا ان (*ḥazanan*) it is sad enough that ...; كفاه مؤنة كذا (*mu'nata*) to save s.o. the trouble of ... **III** to be sufficient, enough (ه for s.o.), suffice (ه s.o.); to requite, repay, recompense, reward (ه ب s.o. with) **VIII** to be content, content o.s. (ب with s.th.)

كفاية *kifāya* sufficient amount, degree, extent, etc., sufficiency; that which suffices for performing a duty, a task, etc.; capability, capacity, ability, qualification; appropriateness, suitability, fitness; competence, efficiency, skill | بالكفاية sufficiently, enough; كفاية القتال fighting power; عدم الكفاية الجنسية *'adam al-k. al-jinsīya* sexual impotence; فى هذا كفاية enough of that, that's enough

كفى *kafīy* sufficient, enough

مكافاة *mukāfāh* reward; gratification

اكتفاء *iktifā'* contentedness, contentment

كاف *kāfin* pl. كفاة *kufāh* sufficient, enough, adequate; appropriate, suitable, suited, fit; capable, able, qualified, skilled, skillful, competent, efficient

مكتف *muktafin* contented, content

[1]كلا *kilā*, f. كلتا *kiltā*; obl. كلى *kilai*, f. كلتى *kiltai* (with dependent genit. or suffix) both (of); see also alphabetically

[2]كل *kalla* i (*kall*, كلة *killa*, كلال *kalāl*, كلالة *kalāla*, كلول *kulūl*, كلولة *kulūla*) to be or become tired, fatigued, weary, exhausted, weak; to be dim, dull, languid, expressionless (glance, eyes); to become blunt (sword) | لا يكل indefatigable, untiring **II** to crown (ه s.o., also fig. ه s.th.); (*Chr.*) to perform the marriage ceremony (priest); to become dull, obtuse, expressionless (face); to become blunt (sword) | كلل بالنجاح *kullila bi-n-najāḥ* to be crowned by success **IV** to make languid or tired, to weary, tire, fatigue, exhaust, wear out, harass, torment (ه s.o.); to dim (ه the glance) **V** to be crowned; to wear a crown; (*Chr.*) to be married

كل *kall* weariness, tiredness, fatigue, exhaustion; dimness, dullness; dull, dim, feeble (glance, mind)

كلة *killa* pl. *-āt*, كلل *kilal* thin veil, drape, curtain; mosquito net

كلل *kalal*, كلال *kalāl* and كلالة *kalāla* weariness, tiredness, fatigue, exhaustion; dimness, dullness

كليل *kalīl* exhausted, tired, weary, faint, languid; weak, feeble; dull, blunt

اكليل *iklīl* pl. اكاليل *akālīl*[2], اكلة *akilla* crown; diadem; chaplet, wreath, garland, festoon; tonsure (*Chr.*); wedding, marriage ceremony (*Chr.*); umbel (*bot.*) | اكليل الجبل *i. al-jabal* rosemary (*bot.*); اكليل الشوك *i. aš-šauk* crown of thorns; اكليل الملك *i. al-malik* yellow sweet clover, melilot (Melilotus officinalis L.; *bot.*)

تكليل *taklīl* coronation, crowning

كال *kāll* tired, fatigued, faint, languid

مكلل *mukallal* adorned with a wreath, crowned; married (*Chr.*)

كل[3] *kull* totality, entirety; everyone, each one, anyone; (with foll. def. noun) whole, entire, all; (with foll. indef. noun) every; الكل the whole, all, everything | بالكل on the whole, in the aggregate, taken altogether, in bulk; الكل فى الكل everything, all-embracing, all-comprehensive, all-powerful; كل من فلان وفلان وفلان (*kullun min*) A as well as B as well as C; على كل *'alā kullin* in any case, at any rate; كله *kulluhū* he entirely, all of him, it entirely, all of it; كل ذلك *kullu ḏālika* all that; كل البيت *kullu l-baiti* or البيت كله *al-b. kulluhū* the whole house; كل الرجال or الرجال كلهم all men; كل الحقيقة الحقيقة (*kullu l-ḥ.*) the whole truth, nothing but the truth; السر كل السر (*sirr*) a very great secret; الخير كل الخير (*ḵair*) true or complete happiness; كل رجل *kullu rajulin* every man; كل شىء *k. šai'in* every thing, everything, all; كل احد *k. aḥadin* and كل واحد *k. wāḥidin* every (single) one, each one; كل من *kullu man* everyone who, whoever, whosoever; كل ما *kullu mā* all that ..., whatever, whatsoever; كل ما فى الامر ان *k. mā fī l-amri anna* there is no more to it than ..., it's nothing but ...; كل وقت *kulla waqtin* at any time, always; فى كل سبعة ايام *fī kulli sab'ati ayyāmin* in each seven days, every seven days; لكل الف *li-kulli alfin* per (one) thousand

كلما *kullamā* whenever; the more ..., in the same measure as ... | كلما — كلما the more — the more

كلى *kullī* total, entire, all-round, overall, sweeping, comprehensive, complete; absolute, universal

كلية *kullīya* totality, entirety; integrity, wholeness, entireness, completeness; (pl. *-āt*) faculty, school (of a university); college; institute of higher learning, academy, secondary school; كليات the complete works (of an author); الكليات the five logical predicates or general conceptions (*philos.*); *kullīyatan* wholly, entirely, totally, absolutely | بالكلية on the whole, in the aggregate, altogether; لا — بالكلية not at all, absolutely not; بكليته in its entire being, completely, totally, entirely, wholly; كلية التجارة commercial college; كلية حربية (*ḥarbīya*) military academy

كلة[4] *kulla* pl. كلل *kulal* bullet; cannon ball; shell, grenade; a marble

كلا *kallā* not at all, on the contrary; by no means! certainly not! never! no! (see also كل[1]) | كلا ثم كلا (*ṯumma*) a thousand times no! not at all!

كلأ *kala'a a* (كلء *kal'*, كلاء *kilā'*, كلاءة *kilā'a*) to guard, preserve, watch, protect (ه s.o.) VIII to find no sleep (eye)

كلأ *kala'* pl. اكلاء *aklā'* grass, herbage, pasture

كلوء *kalū'*: كلوء العين *k. al-'ain* sleepless, awake

كلاسكى *kilāsikī* classic(al)

كلاكس *kalaks* pl. *-āt* horn of an automobile

كلب *kaliba a* (*kalab*) to be seized by hydrophobia; to become mad, crazy; to covet greedily (على s.th.) **VI** to rage, rave, storm; to fall, pounce, rush in (على upon), assail (على s.o.); to assail each other, rush against each other **X** to be raging, raving, rabid, furious, mad, frenzied, possessed

كلب *kalb* pl. كلاب *kilāb* dog | الكلب الاكبر the constellation Canis Major with its main star Sirius; الكلب الاصغر the constellation Canis Minor with its main star Procyon; كلب البحر *k. al-baḥr* shark; كلب الماء otter; beaver

كلبة *kalba* pl. *-āt* bitch

كلبى *kalbī* canine (adj.)

كلب *kalab* rabies, hydrophobia; burning thirst; greed (على for)

كلب *kalib* affected with rabies, rabid; mad; greedy

كلاب *kullāb* and كلوب *kallūb* pl. كلاليب *kalālīb*[2] hook; cramp

كلابة *kullāba* pl. *-āt* (pair of) pincers, tongs

كليب *kalīb* pl. كلبى *kalbā* affected with rabies, rabid, raging

تكالب *takālub* fierce struggle, dogfight, free-for-all, melee, brawl; avidity, greed

مكلوب *maklūb* rabid, frenzied, crazed, possessed

كلبش *kalabš* manacles, handcuffs

كلت *kalata i* to pour, pour out (ه s.th.)

كلح *kalaḥa a* (كلاح *kulāḥ*, كلوح *kulūḥ*) to frown, scowl, look gloomy **IV** and **V** do.

كلحة *kalaḥa* zone around the mouth, mien, facial expression

كالح *kāliḥ* grave, austere, somber, gloomy; fallow, livid, dull grey; turned colorless, faded

كلخ *kalḵ* giant fennel (Ferula communis L.; Ferula sinaica B.; *bot.*); — (*eg.*) *kalaḵ* ammoniac

الكلدان *al-kaldān* the Chaldeans

كلدانى *kaldānī* Chaldean (adj. and n.); astrologer

كلس[1] **II** to plaster with lime, whitewash (ه s.th.); to calcine, calcify (ه s.th.)

كلس *kils* lime

كلسى *kilsī* calcic, limy, lime- (in compounds) | حجارة كلسية limestone

كلاسة *kallāsa* limekiln

مكلس *mukallas* calcified

كلسة[2] (It. *calza*) *kalsa* pl. *-āt* stocking

كواليس see كوليس

كلسون (Fr. *caleçon*) *kalsūn* pl. *-āt* (pair of men's) drawers

كلسيطة (It. *calzetta*) *kalsīṭa* pl. كلاسط *kalāsiṭ*[2] stocking

كلسيوم *kalsiyom* calcium

كلف *kalifa a* (*kalaf*) to become brownish red (face); to become freckled, be covered with freckles; to like (ب s.th.), be intent, bent, set, keen (ب on), be very attached (ب to s.o. or s.th.), be very fond (ب of s.o. or s.th.); to be in love, fall in love (ب with s.o.) **II** to commission, charge, entrust (ه s.o., ب or ه with), assign (ب or ه ه to s.o. a task, a job); to cost (ه ه s.o. a certain amount) | كلف خاطره (*ḵāṭirahū*) (*eg.*) to take the trouble, go to the trouble, bother; to put s.o. to the trouble, bother s.o.; كلفه شططا (*šaṭaṭan*) to overtask s.o., expect or demand too much of s.o.; كلف نفسه عناء ... (مؤونة ... or مشقة ...)

(*ʿanāʾa, maʾūnata, mašaqqata*) to take the trouble to ..., to bother to ..., go to the trouble of ...; كلفه ثمنا باهظا (*ṯamanan*) to cost s.o. dearly; مهما كلفه الامر (*mahmā, amru*) whatever it may cost him, at any cost **V** to burden o.s., be burdened (ه or ب with s.th.); to take upon o.s. (ه a job, a task, costs, an office, etc.); to take over, defray, have to bear (ه s.th., e.g., expenses); to do reluctantly or unwillingly, do in a studied or affected manner, simulate, feign, affect (ه s.th.); to force o.s. (ه to do s.th.), do s.th. (ه) with difficulty, e.g., تكلف الضحك (*ḍaḥk*) to force a laugh; to be affected, mannered, unnatural, stiff, formal, ceremonious, punctilious, stand on ceremony; to employ (ه e.g., care), spend (على ه an amount for); to cost (على s.o., ه so-and-so much)

كلف *kalaf* (coll.; n. un. ة) freckles | كلف الشمس *k. aš-šams* sunspots

كلف *kalif* very much in love (ب with), very attached (ب to), very fond (ب of)

كلفة *kulfa* pl. كلف *kulaf* discomfort; trouble, inconvenience; nuisance; ceremonial, ceremony, formality, ceremoniousness, affectedness of behavior, affectation, mannerism, pose; costs, expenses, expenditure, outlay; trimmings, fittings, accessories, notions, ornaments (buttons, buckles, clasps, braiding, lace, etc.); lady's maid | الكلف الشمسية (*šamsīya*) the sunspots

كلاف *kallāf* stable hand, hostler, groom

كلافى *kallāfī* hirer of donkeys

اكلف *aklaf*², f. كلفاء *kalfāʾ*², pl. كلف *kulf* brownish red, russet; freckled; spotted

تكليف *taklīf* pl. تكاليف *takālīf*² burdening, bothering, troubling, inconveniencing; commissioning, charging, authorization; commandment (of God); burden, annoyance, nuisance, bother; trouble, inconvenience, discomfort; fuss, ado; formality, ceremonial of courtesy, ceremony; expenses, expenditure, outlay, costs, charges, overhead; prime cost; taxes, imposts, duties; taxation, encumbrance with a tax; legal capacity (*Isl. Law*) | بلا تكليف informal(ly), unceremonious(ly), without (standing on) ceremony; كشف التكليف *kašf at-t.* terrier; تكاليف المعيشة *t. al-maʿīša* cost of living

تكلف *takalluf* constraint, unnaturalness of manner; mannerism, airs, affectation, affected behavior; studied, unnatural manner; dissimulation, hypocrisy

مكلف *mukallaf* commissioned, authorized, charged (ب with); obligated, under obligation, liable (ب to do s.th.), responsible (ب for); bound, obliged (ب to do s.th.); subject to taxation, taxable; taxpayer; obligated to observe the precepts of religion (*Isl. Law*); legally capable, sane in mind, compos mentis (*Isl. Law*) | مكلف بالشؤون chargé d'affaires, diplomatic envoy

مكلفة *mukallafa* pl. *-āt* (*eg.*) terrier

متكلف *mutakallaf* formal, ceremonial, ceremonious; affected, studied, forced, outward, sham, false, artificial | ضحكة متكلفة (*ḍaḥka*) forced laugh

كلك **kalak** pl. *-āt* (*ir.*) raft of inflated skins

كلكتا **kalkattā** Calcutta (city in NE India)

كلاكيع **kalākīʿ**²: كلاكيع العظام *k. al-ʿiẓām* bone fragments

كلكل **kalkala** and **II** *takalkala* to become callous (skin)

كلكل *kalkal* pl. كلاكل *kalākil*² chest, thorax | تحت كلكله, تحت كلاكله under the oppressive burden of s.th.; ناء بكلكله to oppress s.o. gravely, weigh heavily upon s.o.

كلكلة *kalkala* callosity, callus

مكلكل *mukalkal* callous (skin)

كلم **II** to address (ه s.o.), speak, talk (ه to or with s.o.) **III** to speak, talk, converse (ه with s.o.) **V** to speak, talk (مع with or to s.o., عن or على about, of); to utter, express, voice, say (ب or ه s.th.)

كلم *kalm* pl. كلوم *kulūm*, كلام *kilām* wound, cut, slash

كلمة *kalima* pl. *-āt* (coll. كلم *kalim*) word; speech, address; utterance, remark, saying; aphorism, maxim; brief announcement, a few (introductory) words; short treatise; importance, weight, influence, authority, ascendancy, powerful position | كلمة فكلمة *kalimatan fa-kalimatan* word by word, literally; بكلمة اخرى (*uḵrā*) in other words; الق كلمة *alqā kalimatan* to make a speech, give a public address; لى كلمة معك I've got to talk to you; جمعوا كلمتهم على (*jama'ū kalimatahum*) they decided unanimously to . . ., they were unanimous about . . .; اجتمعت كلمتهم *ijtama'at kalimatuhum* they united, joined forces, came to an agreement; اجتمعت كلمتهم على they were agreed that...; توحيد الكلمة or جمع الكلمة *jam' al-k.* union, joining of forces, unanimity; اتحاد الكلمة *ittiḥād al-k.* concord, agreement, harmony; تقسيم الكلمة dissension, variance, disunion; اعلى كلمته (*a'lā*) to raise the prestige of s.o.; علو الكلمة *'ulūw al-k.* and الكلمة العليا (*'ulyā*) supremacy, hegemony; قال كلمته he said what he had to say, he had his say; كلمة الله the word of God, the Holy Scriptures; ○ كلمة المرور password, watchword, parole; الكلمات العشر (*'ašr*) the ten Commandments; كلمة تمهيدية (*tamhīdiya*) preface; كلمة السر *k. as-sirr*, (*ir.*) كلم السر *kalim as-sirr* parole, watchword, countersign

كلام *kalām* talking, speaking; speech; language, mode of espression, style; talk, conversation, discussion; debate, dispute, controversy; words, word, saying, utterance, statement, remark; aphorism, maxim, phrase, idiom, figure of speech; (*gram.*) sentence, clause | بالكلام orally, verbally; فتح فه بالكلام (*famahū*) to open one's mouth in order to say s.th., prepare to say s.th.; كلام فارغ idle talk, prattle, poppycock, bosh, nonsense; طريقة الكلام manner of speaking, diction; علم الكلام *'ilm al-k.* scholastic theology (*Isl.*); كثير الكلام talkative, loquacious, garrulous; لغة الكلام *luġat al-k.* colloquial language, everyday speech

كلامى *kalāmī* of or pertaining to speech or words, speech-, word- (in compounds), verbal; spoken, oral; scholastic, theological | مشادة كلامية (*mušādda*) battle of words, dispute, altercation

كليم *kalīm* pl. كلمى *kalmā* wounded, injured; sore; — (pl. كلماء *kulamā'*[2]) person addressed; speaker, spokesman, mouthpiece | كليم الله epithet of Moses

كليم see also alphabetically

كلمانى *kalmānī*, *kalamānī*, *killimānī* eloquent; fluent speaker

تكلام *tiklām*, *tikillām* and تكلامة *tiklāma*, *tikillāma* eloquent; good talker, conversationalist; talkative, loquacious, garrulous

مكالمة *mukālama* talk, conversation, discussion | مكالمة تليفونية telephone conversation

تكلم *takallum* speaking; talk, conversation; speech

متكلم *mutakallim* speaking (act. part.); speaker, spokesman; first person (*gram.*); Muslim theologian, scholastic

كلما *kullamā* see [3]كل

كالون look up alphabetically

كلية **kulya** and كلوة **kulwa** pl. كلى **kulan**, □ كلاوى **kalāwī** kidney

كلوى **kulwī** of or pertaining to the kidneys, renal, nephric, nephritic, nephro- (in compounds) | التهاب كلوى inflammation of the kidneys, nephritis; مغص كلوى (*maġṣ*) renal colic

كليشيه **kilīšēh** pl. *-āt* cliché

كليم **kilīm** pl. اكلمة **aklima** kilim, carpet, rug (usually long and narrow)

[1]كم **kam** (interrogative and exclamatory particle with foll. noun in acc.) how much? how many? how much! | كم ولدا لك (*waladan*) how many sons do you have? كم مرة (*marratan*) or كم من مرة how many times? how often? how often! كم بالحرى (*ḥarīy*) how much more ...! how much rather ...! بكم for how much? how much (is it)?

[2]كم **kamm** amount, quantity | نظرية الكم *naẓarīyat al-k.* quantum theory (*phys.*)

كمى **kammī** quantitative

كمية **kammīya** pl. *-āt* amount, quantity, magnitude

[3]كم **kamma** *u* (*kamm*) to cover, cover up, conceal, hide, cloak (ه s.th.); to plug up, stop up (ه s.th.); to muzzle (ه s.o.) | كم فمه (*famahū*) to stop s.o.'s mouth, silence s.o. **II** to muzzle (ه s.o.); to muffle s.o.'s (ه) mouth; ○ to spike (ه a cannon); to provide with sleeves (ه a garment) **IV** to provide with sleeves (ه a garment)

كم **kumm** pl. اكمام **akmām**, كمة **kimama** sleeve

كم **kimm** pl. اكمام **akmām**, اكمة **akimma**, كمام **kimām**, اكاميم **akāmīm**[2] calyx (*bot.*); perianth (*bot.*)

كمام **kimām** muzzle

كمامة **kimāma** pl. *-āt*, كمائم **kamā'im**[2] muzzle; cloth for muffling the mouth; mask; ○ gas mask; perianth, calyx

كمء **kam'** pl. اكمؤ **akmu'** truffle; mushroom

كمأة **kam'a** (pl.) truffles

كما **ka-mā** see ك **ka**

كمان **kamān** violin, fiddle

كمانجى **kamānjī** player of a كمنجة (q.v.)

كمب (Engl.) **kamb** camp

كمبيالة (It. *cambiale*) **kambiyāla** pl. *-āt* bill of exchange, draft

كمبريت **kambarīt** batiste, cambric

كمبيو (It. *cambio*) **kambiyō** exchange, money exchange; rate of exchange

كمت **kamata** *u* (*kamt*) to suppress (ه one's anger)

كميت **kumait** (m. and f.) reddish brown, chestnut, bay, maroon

كمثرى **kummaṯrā** (coll.; n. un. كمثراة **kummaṯrāh** pl. كمثريات **kummaṯrayāt**) pear

كمح **kamaḥa** *a* (*kamḥ*) to pull up, rein in (ه an animal) **IV** do.

[1]كمخ **kamaḵa** *a* (*kamḵ*) with بانفه **bi-anfihī**: to turn up one's nose, be haughty **IV** = **I**

كماخ **kumāḵ** pride, haughtiness, overweening, self-conceit

[2]كامخ **kāmaḵ**, **kāmiḵ** pl. كوامخ **kawāmiḵ**[2] vinegar sauce, pickle; (mixed) pickles

[3]كمخا **kamḵā** silk fabric, damask

كمد **kamida** *a* (*kamd*) to be sad, grieved, distressed, heartsick; to be smutty, swarthy, dull, flat (color); to fade, lose color, become discolored **II** to apply a hot compress, a hot pack (ه to a limb) **IV** to sadden, grieve, worry, make heartsick (ه s.o.) **X** to become smutty, swarthy, dull, flat; to darken, become dark (color)

كمد *kamd*, *kamad* and كمدة *kumda* dull, swarthy color; dullness, duskiness, swarthiness; sadness, grief

كمد *kamid* and كميد *kamīd* sad, grieved, worried, heartsick; gloomy, dark

كماد *kimād* and كمادة *kimāda* compress, pack

اكمد *akmad*[2] dark-colored, blackish, swarthy

تكميد *takmīd* application of hot compresses, fomentation

كامد *kāmid* sad, grieved, worried, heartsick; gloomy, dark; swarthy, dark-colored

مكمد *mukammad* and مكمدة *mukammada* pl. *-āt* compress, pack

كمر[1] *kamar* pl. اكمار *akmār* belt

كمرة *kamara* pl. *-āt* beam, girder, specif., iron girder; arm, jib | كمرة حمالة (*ḥammāla*) and كمرة تحميل قضبان الونش (*quḍbān al-winš*) beam, bridge (of a traveling crane)

مكمور[2] *makmūr* (*eg.*) dish of chopped meat and vegetables

كمرك (*syr.*) *gumrug* pl. كمارك *gamārig*[2] customs; customhouse

كمركي *gumrugī* customs-, tariff- (in compounds)

كمسارى *kumsārī* pl. كمسارية *kumsārīya* (*eg.*) (streetcar, railroad, etc.) conductor

كمش *kamaša* *u* (*kamš*) to seize, grasp, grip, clutch (ه s.th.) V to become wrinkled, to wrinkle; to shrink; to contract; to recoil within o.s., cower, quail VII to become wrinkled, to wrinkle; to shrink; to contract; to tighten, become cramped, be convulsed; to recoil within o.s., cower, quail; to withdraw within o.s., become or be preoccupied with o.s., be self-absorbed; to collect one's thoughts, gather one's strength, concentrate (also with على نفسه)

كمشة *kamša* a handful

كمش *kamiš*, كميش *kamīš* adroit, skillful, skilled | كميش الازار *k. al-izār* do.; efficient, active, diligent, industrious

كماشة *kammāša* pl. *-āt* (pair) of pincers

انكماش *inkimāš* absorption, preoccupation, self-absorption

منكمش *munkamiš* shrunk; cramped, clenched, convulsed; absorbed, preoccupied, self-absorbed, introverted

كمع III to sleep (ه with s.o.), embrace (ه s.o.), have sexual intercourse (ه with s.o.)

كميع *kamīʿ* bedfellow

كمل *kamala*, *kamula* *u* and *kamila* *a* (كمال *kamāl*, كمول *kumūl*) to be or become whole, entire, integral, perfect, complete; to be finished, done, completed, accomplished; to be concluded, come to a close II and IV to finish, wind up, conclude, complete, consummate (ه s.th.); to carry out, execute (ه s.th.); to perfect, round out, complement, supplement (ه s.th.) VI and VIII to be perfect, consummate, integral, be or become complete, finished, done, accomplished, concluded; to reach completion, fulfillment or perfection, to mature, ripen; to be perfected X to complete (ه s.th.); to perfect (ه s.th.); to round out, complement, supplement (ه s.th.); to carry out, meet, fulfill (ه s.th., e.g., conditions)

كمال *kamāl* pl. *-āt* perfection; completeness; completion, consummation, conclusion, termination, windup; maturity, ripeness | بكماله in its full scope, completely, entirely, wholly, totally

كمالى *kamālī* luxury, luxurious, de luxe; كماليات luxuries; luxury

كمالة *kamāla* (*colloq.*) that which fills up or completes a weight or number, a complement; addition, supplement

اكمل *akmal*[2] more complete, more perfect | باكله entirely, wholly, totally; لندن باكلها all London

تكميل *takmīl* completion, complementing, perfecting, perfection; conclusion, termination, windup; consummation, execution

تكميلى *takmīlī* completing, complementing, complementary, supplementary | انتخاب تكميلى by-election

تكملة *takmila* supplement, complement

اكمال *ikmāl* completion, complementing, perfecting, perfection; conclusion, termination; windup; consummation, execution

تكامل *takāmul* integration; unification to a perfect whole | ○ حساب التكامل integral calculus

تكاملى *takāmulī* integrative; all-including and unifying to form a perfect whole

اكتمال *iktimāl* completion; maturity, ripeness

استكمال *istikmāl* conclusion, termination, finishing

كامل *kāmil* pl. كملة *kamala* perfect, consummate; genuine, sterling; complete, full, plenary, full-strength; completed, concluded; whole, entire, total, integral; name of a poetic meter; folio format (paper) | بكامله wholly, entirely, totally, altogether, in its entirety; ○ لبن كامل (*laban*) unskimmed, full-bodied milk

متكامل *mutakāmil* perfect; integrative; complete, integral

كمن **kamana** *u* and *kamina a* (كمون *kumūn*) to hide; to be hidden, concealed, latent; to have its secret seat (فى in); to ambush, waylay (ل s.o.) **V** to lie in wait (ل for s.o.), ambush, waylay (ل s.o.) **X** to hide, lie concealed

كمنة *kumna* black cataract (*med.*)

كمان look up alphabetically

كمون *kammūn* cumin (Cuminum cyminum L.; *bot.*) | كمون اسود black caraway, black cumin (Nigella sativa L.; *bot.*); كمون برى (*barrī*) do.; كمون حلو (*ḥulw*) anise, aniseed

كمين *kamīn* pl. كمناء *kumanā'*[2] hidden, lying in ambush; ambush, secret attack | دبر كمينا (*dabbara*) to hatch a plot; نصب له كمينا to set a trap for s.o.

مكمن *makman* pl. مكامن *makāmin*[2] place where s.th. is hidden; ambuscade; ambush, hiding place | هنا مكمن السر *hunā m. as-sirr* that's where the secret lies

كامن *kāmin* hidden, concealed, latent; secret; pl. كوامن *kawāmin*[2] underlying factors, hidden background, latent depths

كمنجا **kamanjā** and كمنجة *kamanja* oriental stringed instrument having one or two strings; (Western) violin, fiddle

كمه **kamah** blindness (from birth)

اكمه *akmah*[2], f. كمهاء *kamhā'*[2], pl. كمه *kumh* blind, born blind

كمى **kamīy** pl. كماة *kumāh*, اكماء *akmā'* armed and ironclad, in full armor; brave, valiant, courageous

كميون (Fr. *camion*) *kamiyōn* pl. *-āt* truck, lorry

كن **kanna** *u* (*kann*, كنون *kunūn*) to hide (ه s.th.); to conceal, cover, cloak (ه s.th.); to shelter, ensconce, contain (ه s.th.); to harbor (ه ل friendship toward); to calm down, subside, abate (wind) **II** to hide, conceal, secrete, keep secret (ه s.th.); to calm, quiet, still, assuage (ه s.th.) **IV** to hide, conceal, secrete, keep secret (ه s.th.) **VIII** to be hidden, be concealed **X** to be hidden, be concealed; to seek shelter; to lie comfortably, nestle, cuddle, snuggle; to calm down

كن *kann, kinn* pl. اكنان *aknān*, اكنة *akinna* place where one is sheltered; cover, shelter, retreat, refuge; nest; home, house, hut; arbor, bower

كنة *kanna* pl. كنائن *kanā'in*[2] daughter-in-law; sister-in-law

كنة *kinna* shelter, cover, covering

كنة *kunna* pl. *-āt*, كنان *kinān* shed roof, pent roof, awning

كنان *kinān* pl. اكنة *akinna* shed roof, pent roof, awning

كنانة *kināna* pl. *-āt*, كنائن *kanā'in*[2] quiver (for arrows) | ارض كنانة *arḍ kināna*, الكنانة Egypt (land of the Kinana tribe)

كانون *kānūn* pl. كوانين *kawānīn*[2] stove

كانون *kānūn*: كانون الاول *k. al-awwal* December (*Syr., Leb., Jord., Ir.*); كانون الثانى *k. aṯ-ṯānī* January (*Syr., Leb., Jord., Ir.*)

كنين *kanīn* hidden, concealed; well-kept

مكنون *maknūn* hidden, concealed; well-kept; hidden content

كنار[1] *kanār* edge, rim, border, fringe, hem, selvage

كنارى[2] *kanārī* canary

كنب[1] *kanab* callosity, callus

كنب *kanib* and مكنب *muknib* callous (skin)

كنبه[2] or كنبيه (Fr. *canapé*) *kanabēh* pl. *-āt* sofa

الكنج *al-kunj* the Congo

كنجرو *kangarū* kangaroo (*eg.*)

كنود[1] *kunūd* ingratitude

كنود *kanūd* ungrateful

كندا[2] *kanadā* Canada

كندى *kanadī* Canadian

كندر[1] *kundur* frankincense

كندرة[2] *kundura* pl. كنادر *kanādir*[2] (*syr.*) (Western-style) shoe

كندش *kunduš* magpie

كنار look up alphabetically

كنز *kanaza i* (*kanz*) to bury (فى الارض in the ground, ▲ a treasure); to pile up, heap up, lay up, accumulate, amass, collect, gather, save, hoard (▲ s.th.) **VIII** to be firm, compact, sturdy, strapping; to accumulate, amass, gather (▲ money, treasures); to hide (▲ money, treasures)

كنز *kanz* pl. كنوز *kunūz* treasure

كنز *kaniz* firm, compact (flesh); sturdy, strapping (body)

اكتناز *iktināz* strong, sturdy build, sturdiness, compactness, stoutness (of the body)

مكتنز *muktaniz* firm, compact (flesh); sturdy (body); compressed, pinched (lips); massive, strong; — *muktanaz* accumulated, amassed; hidden, buried

كنس *kanasa u* (*kans*) to sweep (▲ the house) **II** do.

كنس *kans* sweeping, cleaning

الكنسة *al-kansa* visit of the ulema to the tomb of the Imam al-Shāfi'ī where they sweep away the dust

كناس *kannās* sweeper; street sweeper, street cleaner

كناسة *kunāsa* sweepings, refuse, garbage, offal

كنيس *kanīs* nose bag

كنيس *kanīs* synagogue

كنيسة *kanīsa* pl. كنائس *kanā'is*[2] church (*Chr.*); synagogue, temple (*Jud.*)

كنسى *kanasī* and كنائسى *kanā'isī* ecclesiastic(al); clerical

مكنسة *miknasa* pl. مكانس *makānis*² broom; ○ sweeper, street sweeper (machine) | مكنسة كهربائية (*kahrabā'īya*) vacuum cleaner

مكناس *miknās*², مكناسة *miknāsa*² Meknes (city in N Morocco)

كناش *kunnāš*, كناشة *kunnāša* scrapbook; كناشات fundamentals, principles

كنصول (Fr. *console*) *kunṣōl* pl. *-āt* console

كنعان *kan'ān*² Canaan

كنغر *kanğar* kangaroo

كنف *kanafa u* (*kanf*) to guard, protect (ه s.o.); to fence in, hedge, provide with an enclosure (ه s.th.); to surround (ه s.th., ه s.o.); to help, assist (ه s.o.) III and IV to shelter, protect, help, assist (ه s.o.) VIII to surround (on both sides), enclose, embrace (ه s.th.)

كنف *kanaf* pl. اكناف *aknāf* side, flank; wing; shadow, shelter, pale, fold; bosom | فى كنف under cover of ..., in an atmosphere of ...; فى اكنافه under his protection, under his sponsorship

كنافة *kunāfa*, pl. *-āt* vermicelli baked in sugar, melted butter and honey

كنيف *kanīf* pl. كنف *kunuf* water closet, toilet; public lavatory

مكتنف *muktanaf* surrounded, enclosed (ب by)

كنفاش (Engl.) *kanfāš* canvas

كنكة *kanaka* (= تنكة; *eg.*) pl. *-āt* coffee pot

¹كنكن *kankana* to stay at home; to settle down, make o.s. at home; to nestle, snuggle, cuddle up

²كنكينا *kanakīnā* quinine

كنه VIII to fathom, probe, sound, investigate, explore (ه s.th.), look (ه into s.th.); to get to the bottom (ه of s.th.); to understand thoroughly, grasp in its entirety (ه s.th.) X to seek to explore or find out (ه s.th.); to fathom, discover, find out, grasp, understand (ه s.th.)

كنه *kunh* utmost degree, extreme; core, essence, substance, true nature, essential being | يعرفه كنه المعرفة *ya'rifuhū kunha l-ma'rifa* he understands it most thoroughly, he grasps its very essence

تكهنات *takannuhāt* = تكهنات

اكتناه *iktināh* and استكناه *istiknāh* fathoming, penetration, exploration

كنهور *kanahwar* cumuli

كنو and كنى) كنا (كنى *kanā u* and كنى *kanā i* (كناية *kināya*) to use metonymically (ب عن s.th. for); to allude (ب عن with s.th. to); — كنى *kanā i* (كنية *kunya*) and II to call (ه s.o.) by the surname of (ب) V and VIII to be known by the surname of (ب), call o.s. by the surname of (ب)

كنية *kunya* pl. كنى *kunan* surname, agnomen (consisting of *abū* or *umm* followed by the name of the son)

كناية *kināya* indirect expression, metonymy; allusion; indirect declaration of (legal) intent (*Isl. Law*) | بالكناية indirect, not clear and unequivocal (as opposed to صريح); هو كناية عن it is tantamount to ..., it means ..., it stands for ..., it consists in ...; كناية عن *kināyatan 'an* tantamount to; in lieu of, instead of

مكنى عنه *maknīy 'anhu* metonymically expressed

مكنى *mukannan* surnamed

كهرب *kahraba* to electrify, electrize (ه s.th.); to ionize (ه s.th.) II *takahraba* to be electrified, be electrized, become electric; to be charged with electricity; to be ionized

كهربة *kahraba* electrization, electrification; electricity

كهرب **kahrab** pl. كهارب *kahārib*[2] electron

كهيرب *kuhairib* pl. *-āt* electron

كهيربى *kuhairibī* electronic, electron- (in compounds) | المجهر الكهيربى (*mijhar*) electron microscope

كهاربى *kahāribī* electronic, electron- (in compounds)

كهرباء *kahrabā'* and كهربا *kahrabā* amber; electricity; الكهرباء (*eg.*) the streetcar, the trolley

كهربائى *kahrabā'ī* and كهربى *kahrabī* electric(al); electrician | تيار كهربائى (*tayyār*) electric current; جامعة كهربائى storage battery, secondary battery, accumulator; مصباح كهربائية (*miṣbāḥ*) electric lamp, lightbulb; علاج كهربائى diathermy; عالم كهربائى electrophysicist; مغنطيس كهربائى (*mağnaṭīs*) electromagnet; مغنطيسية كهربائية electromagnetism; نور كهربائى (*nūr*) electric light

كهربائية *kahrabā'īya* and كهربية *kahrabīya* electricity

مكهرب *mukahrab* electrically charged, electrized, electrified; ○ electrically conductive, conducting, ionized; ○ electrically ignited, provided with electric ignition

كهرطيسى *kahraṭīsī* electromagnetic

كهرمان *kahramān* amber

كهف *kahf* pl. كهوف *kuhūf* cave, cavern; depression, hollow, cavity | كهف رئوى (*ri'awī*) pulmonary abscess, vomica (*med.*); اصحاب الكهف the Seven Sleepers

كهل *kahala a* (كهول *kuhūl*), *kahula u* (كهولة *kuhūla*) and VIII to be middle-aged, be at the height of one's life

كهل *kahl* pl. كهل *kuhhal*, كهال *kihāl*, كهول *kuhūl*, كهلان *kuhlān* middle-aged, man of mature age

كهولة *kuhūla* maturity of age

كاهل *kāhil* pl. كواهل *kawāhil*[2] upper part of the back; withers | ثقل كاهله *taqqala kāhilahū* to load, burden, encumber s.o. or s.th., e.g., ثقل كاهل الميزان (*k. al-mīzān*) to burden the budget; تخفيف العبء عن كاهله (*t. al-'ib'*) unburdening, disencumbrance of s.o. or s.th.

كهامة *kahāma* dullness, bluntness; lassitude languor, weakness

[1]كهن *kahana a u* (كهانة *kahāna*) to predict the future, tell the fortune (ل of s.o), prophesy (ل to s.o.) V to predict, foretell, presage, prophesy (ب s.th.)

كهانة *kahāna* prediction; prophecy

كهانة *kihāna* divination, soothsaying, fortunetelling

كهنوت *kahnūt*, *kahanūt* priesthood | رجال الكهنوت the clergy, the ministry

كهنوتى *kahanūtī* priestly, sacerdotal, ministerial, clerical, ecclesiastic(al)

مكهن *makhan* (place of an) oracle

تكهن *takahhun* pl. *-āt* prediction, prophecy; conjecture, surmise

كاهن *kāhin* pl. كهان *kuhhān*, كهنة *kahana* diviner, soothsayer, prognosticator, fortuneteller; priest | رئيس الكهنة and كبير الكهنة high priest

متكهن *mutakahhin* diviner, soothsayer, prognosticator, fortuneteller

[2]كهنة *kuhna* rags, shreds, scrap, junk; ragged, tattered

كهنجى *kuhnajī* ragman, ragpicker

كهاية *kihāya* administrative district in Tunisia

كاهية *kāhiya* pl. كواه *kawāhin* chief officer of a كهاية; deputy, vice-, under-, sub- (*Tun.*)

كوة *kūwa* pl. *-āt*, كوى *kuwan*, كواء *kiwā'* aperture; small window, attic window, skylight; peephole

كواليني *kawālīnī* pl. *-ya* locksmith

كوب *kūb* pl. اكواب *akwāb* drinking glass, tumbler; (*ir.*) cup

كوبة *kūba* drinking glass, tumbler; hearts (in a deck of cards)

كوبرته (It. *coperta*) *kūbarta* deck (of a ship)

كوبرى (Turk. *köprü*) *kubrī* pl. □ كبارى *kabārī* bridge (*eg.*)

كوبنهاج (Fr. *Copenhague*) Copenhagen

كوبنهاجن *kōbinhāgin* Copenhagen

كوبيا (It. *copia*) *kōbiyā* copy | قلم كوبيا *qalam k.* copying pencil, indelible pencil

كوبيل (Engl. *cobble*) cobbled pavement, cobblestones

كوبيه (It. *copia*) *kōbiya* copy

الكويت *al-kuwait* Kuwait

كوتر (Engl. *cutter*) *kōtar* pl. كواتر *kawātir*[2] (*eg.*) cutter, yawl

كوثة *kauṯa* fertility; abundance, profusion

كوثر *kauṯar* much, ample, abundant, plentiful; large quantity; الكوثر *al-kauṯar* name of a river in Paradise

كوثل *kauṯal* stern (of a ship)

مكوجى see [1]كوى

[1]كوخ *kūḵ* pl. اكواخ *akwāḵ* hut

[2]كاخية look up alphabetically

[1]كاد (كود) *kāda* (1st pers. perf. *kidtu*) imperf. يكاد *yakādu* to be on the point (ان of doing s.th.), be about (ان to do s.th.); (with imperf.) it wouldn't have taken much more ..., he (it) all but ...; he (would have) almost ... | كاد يموت he almost died; كدت اذهب *kidtu aḏhabu* I almost went; يكاد يكون فى حكم العدم (*ḥukmi l-ʿadam*) it is almost as good as nonexistent; (with neg. corresponding to Engl. "hardly, scarcely, barely; no sooner ..., as soon as ..."): ما كاد يقوم no sooner had he got up ...; لا تكاد ترى (*tarā*) you will hardly ever see, or, you barely see, or, the moment you see ...; لم يكد يراها *lam yakad yarāhā* no sooner had he seen her, the moment he saw her; ما كاد — حتى and لم يكد — حتى no sooner — than, as soon as he — he ..., the moment he — he ...

كاد *kād*: بالكاد almost, nearly; see also alphabetically

[2]كود II to heap up, pile up (ه s.th.)

كودة *kauda* pl. اكواد *akwād* heap, pile

[3]كودية زار (*eg.*) *kudyit zār* woman leader of the Zar ritual

[1]كور II to roll, roll up, coil, roll into a ball (ه s.th.); to wind (ه the turban); to make round, ball-shaped (ه s.th.); to clench (قبضته *qabḍatahū* one's fist) V to become round, be or become ball shaped, globular, spherical; to curl up (in a lying position); to conglomerate, form or gather into a ball

كور *kūr* pl. اكوار *akwār*, اكور *akwur*, كيران *kīrān* camel saddle; forge; furnace, smelting furnace; bellows

كورة *kūra* pl. كور *kuwar* district, rural district; small town; village; ball (= كرة)

كورى see below, alphabetically

كوارة *kuwāra* pl. كوائر *kawāʾir*[2] beehive

كوروى *kūrawī* ball-shaped, globular, spherical

مكور *mikwar* and مكورة *mikwara* turban

مكور *mukawwar* ball-shaped, globular, round

[2]كار look up alphabetically

بالكورجة *bi-l-kauraja* in the bulk, wholesale, in the lump

كوردون (Fr. *cordon*) *kordōn* pl. *-āt* cordon; ribbon, braid, lace, trimming

كورس (Engl.) *kōras* chorus (also fig.); choir

كورسيه (Fr. *corset*) *korsēh* pl. كورسيهات *korsēhāt* corset

كوريك, كورك (Turk. *kürek*) *kūrēk* forced labor (*eg.*)

كورنيش (Fr. *corniche*) see كرنيش

كوريا *kōriyā* Korea

كورى *kōrī* Korean

كوريك see كريك and كورك

كوز *kūz* pl. اكواز *akwāz*, كيزان *kīzān* small jug of clay or tin; mug, tankard | كوز الذرة *k. aḏ-ḏura* (*eg.*) corncob

1 كوس *kūs* pl. *-āt* small drum

2 كاس *kās* pl. اكواس *akwās* = كأس

3 كويس *kuwayyis* (*eg.*) nice, fine, pretty, comely, handsome, beautiful

اكوس *akwas*² more beautiful, prettier, nicer

كوسا or كوسى *kūsā* (coll.; n.un. كوساة *kūsāh*, □ كوساية *kūsāya*) (*eg., syr.*) zucchini; see also under كيس

كوسج *kausaj* swordfish (Xiphias gladius)

كوشة *kūša* pl. كوش *kuwaš* kiln (specif., limekiln)

كوع *kūʿ* and كاع *kāʿ* pl. اكواع *akwāʿ*, كيعان *kīʿān* projecting carpal end of the radius, wristbone; elbow (*anat.*); *kūʿ* elbow, angle, bend (of a pipe); curve, turn, bend (of a road) | كوع الماسورة kneepiece or elbow of a pipe; لا يعرف الكوع من البوع (*yaʿrifu*) he doesn't know his knee from his elbow (proverbially of a stupid person)

كوف V to band together, throng together, gather in a crowd

الكوفة *al-kūfa* Kufa (town in Iraq)

كوفى *kūfī* Kufic; Kufic writing; الكوفيون the Kufic (school of) grammarians

كوفية *kūfīya* pl. *-āt* kaffiyeh, square kerchief diagonally folded and worn under the *ʿiqāl* as a headdress

كوك (Engl.) *kōk* coke

كوكب *kaukab* pl. كواكب *kawākib*² star (also, fig., of screen, stage, etc.); leucoma, white opacity in the cornea of the eye | كوكب سينمائى (*sīnamāʾī*) film star

كوكبة *kaukaba* star; group, troop, party; (pl. كواكب *kawākib*²) (*Syr.*; *mil.*) squadron (of armored units, of cavalry)

كوكبى *kaukabī* star-shaped, stelliform, starlike, stellular, stellate, stellar; starry, starred; astral

اكوكتيل *koktēl* cocktail

كولان *kaulān*, *kūlān* papyrus (Cyperus papyrus; *bot.*)

كولومبو *kolombō* Colombo (capital of Ceylon)

كولومبيا *kolombiyā* Colombia

كولونيا *kolōniyā* Cologne; Eau de Cologne

كوليرا (Fr. *choléra*) *kōlīrā* cholera

كوليس *kūlīs* pl. كواليس *kawālīs*² side scene, coulisse, backdrop | وراء الكواليس behind the scenes, backstage (also fig.)

كوالين pl. of كالون, which see (alphabetically); كوالينى ibid.

كوم II to heap, pile up, stack up (ه s.th.) V to be piled up; to pile up; to accumulate; to sink to the ground, crumple, collapse in a heap

كوم *kaum* pl. اكوام *akwām*, كيمان *kīmān* heap, pile; hill; pl. كيمان *kīmān* esp. garbage piles, refuse dump

كومة *kauma*, *kūma* pl. *-āt*, كوم *kuwam*, اكوام *akwām* heap, pile; mass | كومة الحطب *k. al-ḥaṭab* pyre, stake

كوماندان *komāndān* commandant, commander

كسارى see كومسارى

كومسيونجى *kūmisyōnjī* commission merchant

كومودينو (It. *commodino*) *komudīnō* bedside table

كوميديا *kōmīdiyā* comedy

[1]كون) كان) *kāna u* (*kaun*, كيان *kiyān*, كينونة *kainūna*) to be; to exist; to happen, occur, take place; with acc. of the predicate: to be s.th.; with foll. perf. denoting the pluperfect; with foll. imperf. expressing duration in the past = Engl. progressive past: was doing (often corresponding to Engl. "used to ...", "would ..."); with ل: to belong to, be one's own (كان له بيت he had or owned a house); with ل and s.th.: to be the right man for, be qualified for; with من: to belong to, pertain to; with على: to be incumbent on, be the duty of; with الى: to be assigned to, be the lot or share of, be left to, be due (s.o.) | ما يكون foll. the elative: على اتم ما يكون (*atammi*) in the most perfect manner conceivable, as perfect(ly) as possible; اقوالهم اقرب ما تكون الى الصواب (*ṣawāb*) what they said came quite close to the truth: لم يكن ل (*lam yakun*) or ما كان ل (with foll. subjunctive) he is (or was) not the right man for, he was not capable of, he was not in a position to ...; it is (or was) not apt to ...; لم يكن ليصعب عليه ان (*li-yaṣʿuba*) it wouldn't have been difficult for him to ..., there was no reason why he couldn't have ...; ما كان منه الا ان (or لم يكن) (*illā an*) he had no other choice but to ..., there was nothing for him to do but to ...; he did no more than ...; ما كان له ان it is (or was) impossible for him to ...; he is (or was) unable to ...; اصبح فى خبر كان *aṣbaḥa fī ḵabari k.* to disappear, become dated, belong to the past; كان وكان a popular form of poem consisting of quatrains II to make, create, produce, originate, bring forth, bring into being, form, shape, fashion (ه s.th.) V to be created, be formed; to come into existence, form, arise, develop; to consist, be composed, be made up (من of), be formed (من by) X to become lowly, humble, miserable; to submit, yield, surrender, humble o.s., abase o.s., eat humble pie; to abandon o.s., give o.s. over (الى to s.th.)

كون *kaun* pl. اكوان *akwān* being, esse; existence; event, occurrence, incident; الكون the existent, the existing, reality; the world; the cosmos, the universe | الكون الاعلى (*aʿlā*) the Supreme Being, God; with foll. genit. or suffix of the logical subject and acc. of the predicate: the fact that s.o. or s.th. is ..., لكونه مجنونا *li-kaunihī majnūnan* because he is mad, مع كونه مجنونا although he is mad

كونى *kaunī* of or relating to the universe or cosmos, universal, cosmic, cosmo- (in compounds) | ◯ الاشعة الكونية (*ašiʿʿa*) cosmic rays; نظام كونى cosmic system

كيان *kiyān* being, esse; existence; essence, substance; nature

اليكون *al-yakūn* the sum total

مكان *makān* pl. امكنة *amkina*, اماكن *amākin*[2] place where one is or stands; place, site, spot, location; passage (in a book); locality, locale; seat, place (e.g., in a railroad compartment); position, standing, rank, dignity; importance, consequence, weight; space (*philos.*); presence; situation, conditions, circumstances; مكان *makāna* in the place of, in lieu of, instead of | لو كنت مكانك *lau kuntu makānaka* if I were in your place, if I were you; مكانه *makānahū* on the spot, at once; مكانك *makānak* stop! فى كل مكان everywhere; اخلى مكانا (*aḵlā*) to make room; احتل مكانا مكينا (*iḥtalla*) to have or hold a strong, powerful position; هو من الشجاعة بمكان (*šajāʿa*) he is extremely brave; ذلك من الاهمية بمكان (ahammīya) that is of considerable importance; هاته النظرية من الضعف بمكان (naẓarīya, ḍuʿf) this theory is rather weak; مكان الشيء من نفسه (nafsihī) the importance of s.th. for s.o., the place that s.th. has in s.o.'s mind; مكان الحادث site of action, scene of the crime, locus delicti; ظرف المكان ẓarf al-m. adverb of place (gram.); اماكن وعرة (waʿra) difficult terrain, rugged country

مكانة makāna pl. -āt place; location, situation; position, office; standing, authority, influence, rank, dignity | مكانة الصدر m. aṣ-ṣadr first place, precedence, priority

مكانى makānī local

مكانية makānīya spatiality (philos.)

تكوين takwīn forming, shaping, formation, creation, origination; (pl. تكاوين takāwīn²) formation (of rock; geol.) | جميل التكوين well-shaped, shapely; سفر التكوين sifr at-t. the Genesis

تكون takawwun genesis, birth, nascency, origin, incipience, rise, development; formation

استكانة istikāna yielding, submission, resignation, passivity

كائن kāʾin being; existing, existent; situated, located; a being, entity, creature, creation; (pl. -āt) thing; s.th. existing, an existent | الكائن المطلق (muṭlaq) the Absolute Being, God; الكائنات the created things, the universe, the world; كائنا من كان (man) whoever it may be; كائنا ما كان be it what it may, whatever it may be

مكون mukawwin creator; — mukawwan made, created; consisting, composed, made up (من of), formed (من by)

مستكين mustakīn humiliated, oppressed, resigned, submissive

²كيوان look up alphabetically

كونتراتو (It. contratto) kontrātō agreement, accord, treaty, contract

كونكرداتو (It. concordato) konkurdātō settlement, composition (between debtor and creditors)

كونياك konyāk cognac

□ مكوه for مكوى see ¹كوى

¹كوى kawā i (كى kayy) to burn (ه s.th.); to sear (ه s.th.); to cauterize, treat with a cautery (ه s.o.; med.); to brand (ه s.o.); to bite, burn (acid); to sting (scorpion); to press, iron (ه laundry, and the like) **VIII** to be burned, be seared; to be cauterized; to be pressed, be ironed; to burn o.s., burn one's skin

كى kayy burning; cauterization, cautery; pressing, ironing | حجر الكى ḥajar al-k. lunar caustic, silver nitrate; ○ الكى الكهربائى (kahrabāʾī) diathermy

كية kayya a burn, a brand

كواء kawwāʾ slanderer, calumniator; ironer, presser

كواية kawwāya ironing woman, ironer

كوية kawīya (syr.) press, crease (in trousers)

مكواة mikwāh and مكوى makwan pl. مكاو makāwin flatiron; hot iron (for cauterizing), cautery (med.) | مكواة الشعر m. aš-šaʿr curling iron

مكوى makwan ironing establishment

□ مكوجى makwajī ironer, presser; laundryman

كاو kāwin caustic

²كوى kuwan see كوة

¹كى kai, لكى li-kai so that, in order that, in order to | كيلا and لكيلا in order not to, lest

كيما *kai-mā*, لكيما *li-kai-mā* that, so that, in order that, in order to

كَيّ [2] *kayy* and كَيّة *kayya* see كوى [1]

كيت [1] *kīt* Indian dress material

كيت وكيت [2] *kaita wa-kaita, kaiti wa-kaiti* so and so, such and such, thus and thus

كيد [1] كاد *kāda* i (*kaid*, مكيدة *makīda*) to deceive, dupe, outwit (ه s.o.); to harm by artful machinations (ل s.o., s.th.), lay snares (ل for s.o.), plot s.o.'s (ل) downfall, conspire (ل against s.o.) **III** to deceive, dupe, outwit (ه s.o.); to seek to double-cross (ه s.o.)

كيد *kaid* pl. كياد *kiyād* ruse, artifice, stratagem; craftiness, slyness, cunning, subtlety; deception, deceit; artful plot; trick, dodge

مكيدة *makīda* pl. مكايد *makāyid*[2] ruse, artifice, trick; smart action, clever approach, shrewd policy; stratagem; plot, conspiracy, machinations, schemes, intrigues

كاد [2] look up alphabetically

كير *kīr* pl. اكيار *akyār*, كيران *kīrān* bellows

كيروسين (Engl.) *kirusīn* kerosene

كيس كاس *kāsa* i (*kais*, كياسة *kiyāsa*) to be smart, clever, intelligent; to be nice, fine, pretty, comely, handsome, attractive, chic **II** to refine, make elegant

كيس *kais* smartness, cleverness, intelligence; subtlety, finesse, gracefulness, elegance

كيس *kīs* m. and f., pl. اكياس *akyās*, كيسة *kiyasa* sack; bag; pouch; purse; Turkish towel | كيس الوسادة pillowcase, pillow slip; كيس الصفراء *k. aṣ-ṣafrā'* gall, bile; على كيسه at his expense

كيس *kayyis* pl. اكياس *akyās*, كيسى *kaisā*, f. كيسة *kayyisa*, pl. كياس *kiyas* sly, smart, astute, shrewd, sagacious; adroit, dexterous, skillful; nice, fine, elegant, stylish, chic, attractive, comely, pretty, handsome

كياسة *kiyāsa* adroitness, dexterity, skill; cleverness, smartness, astuteness, shrewdness, slyness, sagacity, subtlety, finesse; courtesy, civility, politeness; gracefulness, grace; elegance, chic, stylishness

اكيس *akyas*[2], f. كيسى *kīsā* and كوسى *kūsā*, pl. كيس *kīs* smarter, slier; more skillful; more stylish, more chic, nicer

مكيس *mukayyis* and □ مكيساتى *mukayyisātī* (*eg.*) bath attendant, masseur

مكيس *mukayyas* shrewd, subtle, astute, smart, sly

كيف **II** to form, shape, fashion, mold (ه s.th.); to fit, condition, modify, conform, adjust, adapt (ه s.th., نفسه o.s.); to regulate (ه s.th.); to put in high spirits, exhilarate, amuse, delight (ه s.o.); to intoxicate slightly, dope, stupefy (ه s.o.; of a narcotic) **V** to be shaped, be formed; to assume a form, take on a shape; to adapt o.s., adjust o.s., conform; to be in high spirits, be cheerful, gay; to amuse o.s., enjoy o.s., have a good time, have fun; to revel; to be slightly intoxicated, be tipsy, fuddled; to smoke (ه tobacco, etc.)

كيف *kaifa* (interrogative and exclamatory particle) how? how ...! | كيف حالك (*ḥāluka*) how are you? كيف لا و ... why shouldn't it be so since ...! فكيف ب just imagine how much more (or less) ...! and how much more ...! and how much less ...!

كيفما *kaifamā* however, howsoever | كيفما كان الحال whatever the case may be, be that as it may; in any case, at any rate

كيف *kaif* state, condition; mood, humor, state of mind, frame of mind; pleasure, delight, well-being, good humor, high spirits; discretion, option, will; (pl. كيوف *kuyūf*) narcotic, opiate | على كيفك at your discretion, as you please; as you wish, as you like; اصحاب الكيف bons vivants, epicures

كيفى *kaifī* arbitrary, discretionary, optional; qualitative

كيفية *kaifīya* manner, mode, fashion; property, quality; nature, state, condition; particulars, particular circumstances (e.g., of an event) | كيفية العمل *k. al-'amal* operation (e.g., of a machine); كيفية الاستعمال directions for use

تكييف *takyīf* forming, shaping, fashioning; formation; adaptation, adjustment, conditioning, modification; regulation; descriptive designation, qualification; air conditioning, = تكييف الهواء *t. al-hawā'*

تكيف *takayyuf* adaptation, adjustment, conformity

مكيفة *mukayyifa*, مكيفة الهواء *m. al-hawā'* pl. *-āt* air-conditioning installation, air conditioner

مكيفات *mukayyifāt* narcotics, opiates

كيكة[1] *kaika* pl. كياكى *kayākī* egg

كيكة[2] *kīka*, كيكا *kīkā* (*eg.*) hide-and-seek

(كيل) كال *kāla* *i* (*kail*, مكال *makāl*, مكيل *makīl*) to measure (ه s.th.); to weigh (ه s.th.); to compare by measuring (ه ب s.th. with), measure s.th. (ه) by the standard of (ب); to measure out, mete out, allot, apportion (ه ل s.th. to s.o.) | كال له الشتائم to heap abuse on s.o.; كال له اللطمات (*laṭamāt*) to give s.o. a beating, spank, thrash s.o. II to measure (ه s.th.) III to return like for like, repay in kind (ه to s.o.)

كيل *kail* pl. اكيال *akyāl* measure; dry measure for grain; holding capacity

كيلة *kaila* pl. *-āt* kilah, a dry measure (*Eg.* = 16.72 l; *Pal.* = 36 l)

كيلى *kailī* and مكيل *makīl* (volumetrically) measurable, volumetric(al)

كيال *kayyāl* corn measurer; one who metes out, who determines the right measure, master, lord

مكيال *mikyāl* pl. مكاييل *makāyīl*[2] and مكيل *mikyal*, مكيلة *mikyala* pl. مكايل *makāyil*[2] measure; dry measure for grain | الموازين والمكاييل the weights and measures

كيلو *kīlō* and كيلوجرام *kīlogrām* pl. *-āt* kilogram

كيلوسيكل (Fr. *kilocycle*) *kīlōsikl* pl. *-āt* kilocycle (*radio*)

كيلومتر *kīlōmitr* pl. *-āt* kilometer

كيلوواط *kīlōwāṭ* kilowatt

كيلون = كالون, look up alphabetically

كيما *kai-mā* see [1]كى

كيموس *kaimūs* gastric juice

كيمياء *kīmiyā'* chemistry; alchemy | الكيمياء الاحيائية (*aḥyā'īya*) biochemistry; كيمياء التربة *k. at-turba* agricultural chemistry

كيمى *kīmī* chemical

كيميائى *kīmiyā'ī*, كيماوى *kīmāwī* chemical; — (pl. *-ūn*) chemist; alchemist; كيماويات *kīmāwīyāt* chemicals

(كين) كان *kāna* *i* (*kain*) to humble o.s., abase o.s., eat humble pie, submit, resign o.s. X do.

كينا *kīnā* quinine | خشب الكينا *ḵašab al-k.* cinchona, china bark, Peruvian bark

كينين *kīnīn* quinine

كيهك *kiyahk*, *kīhak* the fourth month of the Coptic year

كيوان *kaiwān* the planet Saturn

كيوبيد (Engl.) *kiyūbid* Cupid

ل

لَ[1] *la* (intensifying particle) truly, verily; certainly, surely; frequently after ان *inna*, introducing the predicate: ان ربى لسميع الدعاء *inna rabbī la-samī'u d-du'ā'* truly, my Lord hears the prayer; also as a correlative of لو *lau* and لولا *lau-lā*: لو كنت تفعل هذا لكان انفع (*la-kāna anfa'a*) if you did this it would be more useful; لولا تاب لهلك *lau-lā tāba la-halaka* if he had not repented he would have perished; (particle of oath) لعمرك *la-'amruka* by your life!

لِ[2] *li* 1. (prep.) for; on behalf of, in favor of; to (of the dative); because of; for the sake of; due to, owing to; for, for the purpose of; at the time of, when, as; by (designating the author or originator); occasionally substituting for الى; as to ل paraphrasing the genit. and acc. see grammar | لى عليه مال he owes me money; ما له وما عليه his right and his duty; his credit and his debit, his assets and his liabilities; له أن he has a right to ..., he is entitled to ..., he may ...; it is possible for him to ..., he is able to ..., he can ...; ليس لى ان I have no right to ..., it does not behoove me to ...; لك ذلك or لك هذا you can have that! it's up to you; it's all right with me! all right! O.K.! agreed! ألك فى or هل لك فى would you like ...? do you want...? do you feel like ...? قرأت له كتابا I read a book by him, I read one of his books; لا تدوم له حال (*tadūmu*) no state is of any permanence with him, he is never the same for a very long time; قاموا لمعاونتنا (*li-mu'āwanatinā*) they set out in our support; لسبع ليال خلون من شعبان *li-sab'i layālin kalauna min ša'bāna* when seven nights of Shaban had passed; للمرة الاولى *li-l-marrati l-ūlā* for the first time; لاول وهلة *li-awwali wahlatin* at first sight, at once; اخوه لابيه وامه *akūhu li-abīhi wa-ummihī* his brother on the paternal and maternal side, his brother-german, his full brother 2. (conj. with the subjunctive) that, so that, in order that, in order to; (with apoc.) expressing an order, an invitation: ليكتب *li-yaktub* he shall write, let him write (with preceding و *wa* or ف *fa* contracted to *wal-* ... or *fal-* ... with elision of the *i*)

لاجل *li-ajli* (with foll. genit.) because of, on account of, for

لان *li-an* (conj. with the subjunctive) that, so that, in order that, in order to; (with لا) لئلا *li-allā* in order not to, lest

لان *li-anna* (conj.) on the grounds that; because; for

لذلك *li-ḏālika* therefore, hence, that is why, for that reason

لكى *li-kai* and لكيما *li-kai-mā* (conj. with the subjunctive) that, so that, in order that, in order to

لما *li-mā* (shortened لم *li-ma*) why? wherefore? for what reason? لماذا *li-mā-ḏā* why (on earth)?

لهذا *li-hāḏā* therefore, hence, that is why, for that reason

لا *lā* (particle) not; no! with apoc. expressing negative imperative: لا تقل *lā taqul* don't say! with indef. acc. expressing a general negation; there is not, there is no ..., e.g., لا اله الا الله *lā ilāha illā llāh* there is no god but Allah; لا خير فيه (*kaira*) there is no good in it, it's no good; لا بد منه (*budda*) there is no escape from it, it is inevitable; لا جرم *lā jarama* certainly, surely; لا شك

lā šakka no doubt, doubtless; لا سيما *lā siyyamā* especially, particularly; الا *a-lā* see أ; بلا *bi-lā* without; ولا *wa-lā* (with preceding neg.) nor, ... either; not even, also حتى ولا *ḥattā wa-lā*, e.g., لم يعطني حتى ولا قرشا (*lam yuʿṭinī, qiršan*) he did not give me even a piaster, he did not give me as much as a piaster; لا — ولا neither — nor

لاابالية *lā-ubālīya* indifferent attitude, indifference

لاادرية *lā-adrīya* skepticism; agnosticism

اللاانا *al-lā-anā* the nonego (*philos.*)

لاانانية *lā-anānīya* selflessness, unselfishness

لاجنسية *lā-jinsīya* statelessness, being without nationality

لاديني *lā-dīnī* antireligious, irreligious, without religion

لادينية *lā-dīnīya* irreligion, godlessness

لاسامي *lā-sāmī* anti-Semitic; anti-Semite

لاسامية *lā-sāmīya* anti-Semitism

لاسلكي *lā-silkī* wireless, radio (adj.); radio, broadcasting; radio message | اشارة لاسلكية (*išāra*) radio message

اللاشعور *al-lā-šuʿūr* the unconscious, unconscious mind, unconsciousness

لاشعوري *lā-šuʿūrī* unconscious, unaware

لاشيء *lā-šaiʾ* nothing, nonentity, nil

لاشيئية *lā-šaiʾīya* nonexistence, nothingness; nullity, nihility

لامبالاة *lā-mubālāh* and لامبالية *lā-mubālīya* indifferent attitude, indifference

لامركزية *lā-markazīya* decentralization

لامسؤولية *lā-masʾūlīya* irresponsibility

لانظام *lā-niẓām* lack of system, confusion

اللانهاية *al-lā-nihāya* the infinite

لانهائي *lā-nihāʾī* infinite

اللاتين *al-lātīn* the (ancient) Latins

لاتيني *lātīnī* Latin | الحي اللاتيني (*ḥayy*) the "Quartier latin" (in Paris)

اللاتينية *al-lātīnīya* the Latin language, Latin

لادن *lādan, lādin* laudanum

لازورد *lāzuward, lāzaward* lapis lazuli; azure

لازوردي *lāzuwardī* azure-blue, azure, sky-blue, cerulean

لازوردية *lāzuwardīya* azure, blue of the sky

لاسيه (Fr. *lacet*) *lāsēh* lace, cord

لأك[1] IV to send as a messenger (ه s.o. to الى)

ملأك *malʾak* and ملك *malak* pl. ملائك *malāʾik*[2], ملائكة *malāʾika* angel; messenger, envoy

ملائكي *malāʾikī* angelic(al); heavenly

لاكي[2] look up alphabetically

لاكن *lākin, lākinna* however, yet, but

لألأ *laʾlaʾa* (لألأة *laʾlaʾa*) to shine, flash, glitter, glisten, sparkle, gleam, shimmer, glimmer, beam, radiate; to wag (بذنبه *bi-ḏanabihī* the tail) II *talaʾlaʾa* to shine, glitter, glisten, sparkle, gleam, shimmer, glimmer, beam, radiate

لألأة *laʾlaʾa* shine, glow, brightness, brilliancy, radiance, flash, glitter, twinkle

لألاء *laʾlāʾ* glitter, flash; light, glow, gleam; perfect joy, unruffled gaiety; dealer in pearls

لؤلؤ *luʾluʾ* (coll.; n. un. ة) pl. لآلئ *laʾāliʾ*[2] pearls | زهر اللؤلؤ *zahr al-l.* daisy; عرق اللؤلؤ *ʿirq al-l.* mother-of-pearl, nacre

لؤلؤي *luʾluʾī* pearly; pearl-colored, whitish | شعير لؤلؤي pearl barley

تلألؤ *tala'lu'* shining, radiance, brilliancy

متلألئ *mutala'li'* shimmering, glistening, glittering, flashing, sparkling

لأم *la'ama a* (*la'm*) to dress, bandage (ه a wound); to repair, mend (ه s.th.); to solder, weld; — لؤم *la'uma* (*lu'm*, لآمة *la'āma*, ملأمة *mal'ama*) to be ignoble, lowly (of character and birth); to be base, mean, vile, evil, wicked **III** to agree (ه with s.o.); to suit, fit (garment; ه s.o.); to be adequate, appropriate (ه to s.th.), be suitable, fit, proper, convenient, favorable, propitious (ه for s.th.); to be adapted (ه to), be in harmony (ه with), match (ه s.th.); to agree (climate, food; ه with s.o.), be wholesome (climate, air, food; ه for s.o.); to bring about a reconciliation, make peace (بين between), reconcile (بين — و s.o. with); to make consistent or congruous, reconcile, harmonize, bring into harmony (بين different things) **IV** to act ignobly, behave shabbily **VI** to be mended, be repaired, be corrected; to go well (مع with); to act meanly **VIII** to be mended, be repaired, be corrected; to be joined, be connected, be patched up, be soldered, be welded; to match, fit together, harmonize, be in harmony, agree, go together, be congruous, conformable, consistent; to be tuned or geared to each other (fig.); to unite, combine; to cohere, stick together; to heal, close (wound); to gather, assemble, convene (persons); to meet (committee, congress, council, etc.)

لأم *la'm* dressing, bandaging (of a wound); joining, junction, connection; repair

لؤم *lu'm* ignoble mind, baseness, meanness, vileness, wickedness; niggardliness, miserliness; sordidness; iniquity

لئم *li'm* peace; concord, agreement, union, unity, unanimity; conformity, consistency, harmony

لأمة *la'ma* cuirass, pair of cuirasses

لئيم *la'īm* pl. لئام *li'ām*, لؤماء *lu'amā'*[2], لؤمان *lu'mān* ignoble, lowly, low, base, mean, evil, vile, wicked, depraved; sordid, filthy, dirty; niggardly, miserly

ملاءمة *mulā'ama* adequacy, appropriateness, properness, suitability, fitness; peacemaking, (re)conciliation; concord, union, agreement, harmony

ملائم *mulā'im* adapted, suited, appropriate (ل to), suitable, fit, proper, convenient, favorable, propitious (ل for); agreeing, harmonizing, in conformity, consistent (ل with)

لام *lām* name of the letter ل

لامى *lāmī* lām-shaped, resembling the letter ل

لاما *lāmā* llama (*zool.*)

لانش (Engl.) *lanš* pl. *-āt* launch, motorboat, small steamer

لاهاى *lāhāy* The Hague (city in SW Netherlands)

لاهوت *lāhūt* godhead, deity; divine nature, divinity | علم اللاهوت *'ilm al-l.* theology

لاهوتى *lāhūtī* theological; theologian

اللاهوتية *al-lāhūtīya* theology

لاهور *lāhūr*[2] Lahore (city in W Pakistan)

لأواء *la'wā'*[2] severe distress, hardship

لأى *la'y* slowness, tardiness; tediousness, tiresomeness | بعد لأى after great difficulties, in the end, finally, after all

لائكى (from Fr. *laïque*) *lā'ikī* layman; secular, laic, lay

لائكية *lā'ikīya* laicism

لب *labba* u (*labb*) to remain, abide, stay (ب in a place); — (1st pers. perf. *labibtu*) a (لبب *labab*) and (1st pers. perf. *labubtu*) u (لبابة *labāba*) to be sensible, reasonable, intelligent **II** to kernel, ripen into kernels, produce kernels (grain, nuts) **V** to gird o.s., prepare o.s. (ل for)

لب *lubb* pl. لبوب *lubūb* kernels, core (of fruits); the innermost, marrow, pith; core, gist, essence; prime, best part; — (pl. ألباب *albāb*) heart; mind, intellect, reason, understanding

لبة *labba* pl. *-āt* upper part of the chest; throat of an animal, spot where its throat is slit in slaughtering

لبة *libba* (*eg.*) golden necklace

لبب *labab* pl. ألباب *albāb* upper part of the chest; throat of an animal, spot where its throat is slit in slaughtering; breast collar (of a horse's harness); martingale

لباب *lubāb* marrow, pith, core, quintessence, gist, prime, best part | ○ لباب خشب *l. kašab* cellulose

لبيب *labīb* pl. ألباء *alibbā'*[2] understanding, reasonable, sensible, intelligent

تلبيب *talbīb* pl. تلابيب *talābīb*[2] collar | اخذ بتلابيبه to collar s.o., seize s.o. by the collar

لبؤة *labu'a* pl. *-āt* lioness

لبتة *labta* carp (*zool.*)

لبث *labiṯa* a (*labṯ*, *lubṯ*, *labaṯ*, لباث *lubāṯ*) to hesitate, tarry, linger; to abide, remain, stay (ب in a place); (with imperf.) to persist in an activity, keep doing s.th. | ما لبث (لم يلبث) أن (حتى) it did not take long before he ..., presently he ..., he lost no time in ...; لبث يفعله he did it for a while **V** to hesitate, tarry, linger; to abide, remain, stay

لبث *labṯ*, *lubṯ*, *labaṯ* hesitation, tarrying, delay; stay, sojourn

لبثة *lubṯa* short delay, brief respite; pause; temporary stay or stop, stopover

لبخ *labk*, *labak* (coll.; n. un. ة) a variety of acacia (Mimosa lebbec L.), also lebbek tree (Albizzia lebbek Bth.; *bot.*)

لبخة *labka* pl. *labakāt* cataplasm, poultice; soft mass, mush; emollient plaster, emollient

لبيخ *labīk* fleshy, corpulent

لبد *labada* u (لبود *lubūd*) to stick, adhere, cling (ب to s.th.), get stuck (ب on); to abide, remain, stay (ب in a place) **II** to cause to adhere and mat together, to felt, mat (ه wool); to line with felt (ه s.th.); to beat down, weigh down (ه s.th., e.g., the hail — grass); to full (ه s.th.) **IV** to cling firmly, adhere, stick (ب to s.th.) **V** do.; to stick together; to become felted, matted, entangled, interwoven; to be compressed; to become clouded; to become overcast (بالغيوم with clouds; sky); to become gloomy (face)

لبد *libd* pl. لبود *lubūd*, ألباد *albād* felt | لبود من الغمائم thick masses of clouds

لبد *labad* wool

لبد *labid* coherent; compact

لبد *lubad* the seventh vulture of Luqmān (whose death ended Luqmān's life; metaphor of longevity)

لبدة *libda* pl. لبد *libad* mane (of a lion); (*eg.*) skullcap of felt, worn under or without a tarboosh; felt hat (of the dervishes)

لبدة *lubda* pl. لبد *lubad* matted and pressed wool or hair, felt

لباد *labbād* feltmaker; felt

لبادة *lubbāda* pl. *-āt* horse blanket, saddle blanket; — (pl. لبابيد *labābīd*[2]) felt cap

ملبد *mulabbad*: ملبد بالغيوم (*bi-l-ğuyūm*) overcast, heavily clouded (sky)

متلبد *mutalabbid*: متلبد بالغيوم overcast, heavily clouded (sky)

لبس **labisa** *a* (*lubs*) to put on, wear (ه a dress, garment); to dress (ه in), clothe o.s., garb o.s. (ه in or with) **II** to dress (ه ه s.o. in), clothe, garb, attire (ه ه s.o. with); to cover, envelop, overlay, coat (ه ب s.th. with a layer); to drape, line, face, case (ه ب s.th. with); to inlay (e.g., wood with ivory); to suffuse (ه s.o., e.g., pallor), seize (ه s.o., e.g., a tremor); to make obscure, unclear, abstruse, involved, complicated (ه على s.th. for s.o.); to deceive, dupe (على s.o.) **III** to be on intimate terms, associate closely, hobnob (ه with s.o.); to be in close contact (ه, ه with s.o., with s.th.); to surround (ه s.o.; environment, milieu, conditions) **IV** to dress (ه ه s.o. in), clothe, garb, attire (ه ه s.o. with); to drape, envelop, coat, overlay, cover, face, line, case (ه s.th.) **V** to dress, get dressed (ب in), clothe o.s. (ب in or with); to be dressed, clad, attired; to be covered (ب with), be enveloped, wrapped (ب in); to get involved (ب in s.th.), be drawn (ب into s.th.); to meddle, bother (ب with), go into s.th. (ب); to be obscure, incomprehensible, dubious, equivocal, ambiguous (على for s.o.) **VIII** to be obscure, dubious, equivocal, ambiguous (على for s.o.); to get mixed up (ب with); to mistake (ه s.th., ب for)

لبس *labs*, *lubs* and لبسة *lubsa* tangle, muddle, confusion, intricacy, obscurity, uncertainty, abstruseness, ambiguity | كان فى لبس من امره to be uncertain about s.o.; to have doubts about s.o.

لبس *libs* pl. لبوس *lubūs* clothes, clothing, dress, apparel; costume

لبسة *libsa* manner or style of dressing, costume

لباس *libās* pl. *-āt*, البسة *albisa* clothes, clothing; costume; apparel; garment, robe, dress; (*eg.*, *syr.*) (men's) drawers | لباس الرأس *l. ar-ra's* headdress, headgear; لباس التقوى *l. at-taqwā* decency, modesty; لباس رسمى (*rasmī*) and لباس عسكرى (*'askarī*) uniform; لباس السهرة *l. as-sahra* evening gown, evening clothes, formal dress; لباس وطنى (*waṭanī*) national costume; البسة جاهزة ready-made clothes

لبيس *labīs* worn; worn clothes, second-hand clothes; Nile carp (Cyprinus niloticus; *zool.*)

لبوس *labūs* clothing, clothes; suppository (*med.*) | لبوس رسمى (*rasmī*) uniform

ملبس *malbas* pl. ملابس *malābis*[2] garment, dress, robe, apparel, suit; pl. also: clothing, clothes, costume | ○ ملبس الوقاية protective clothes; ملابس التشريفة dress uniform; ملابس داخلية وخارجية (*dāḵilīya wa-ḵārijīya*) underwear and outer clothes; ملابس رسمية (*rasmīya*) livery, uniform; ○ ملابس الميدان *m. al-maidān* field uniform; محل الملابس *maḥall al-m.* ready-made-clothes store

تلبيس *talbīs* clothing, dressing, garbing; draping, lining, facing, casing; overlaying, coating; wall facing, wall plaster, paneling; inlay work; deception, deceit, fraud

تلبيسة *talbīsa* suppository (*med.*)

ملابسة *mulābasa* intercourse, intimate association, close relations; ملابسات relations, connections; concomitants, accompanying phenomena; surrounding conditions, environment

الباس *ilbās* clothing, dressing, garbing

تلبس *talabbus*: قضايا التلبس *qaḍāyā t-t.* (*jur.*) cases of "flagrante delicto", criminal cases in which the perpetrator was caught in the act

التباس *iltibās* confusion, tangle, intricacy, obscurity, ambiguity, dubiousness, doubt | رفع الالتباس *rafʿ al-ilt.* correction, rectification, clarification; احاط به الالتباس (*aḥāṭa*) to be wrapped in obscurity, be completely ambiguous

ملبوس *malbūs* worn, used (clothes); (*eg.*) possessed, in a state of frenzy or religious ecstasy; pl. ملبوسات articles of clothing, clothes

ملبس *mulabbas* involved, intricate, obscure, dubious; inlaid, coated, incrusted; sugar-coated, candied; (pl. *-āt*) bonbon, candy; dragée

متلبس *mutalabbis*: متلبسا بالجريمة (he was caught, and the like) redhanded, in the act, flagrante delicto

ملتبس *multabis* involved, intricate, ambiguous, equivocal; dubious, doubtful, uncertain, unclear

لبط *labaṭa u* (*labṭ*): لبط به الارض (*arḍa*) to throw s.o. to the ground, fell s.o.; — *i* to kick; to gallop about (animal)

لبق *labuqa u* (لباقة *labāqa*) to be clever, slick, adroit, skilled, skillful, versatile, suave, elegant, have refined manners; — *labiqa a* (*labaq*) do.; to fit, suit, become (clothes; ب s.o.) **II** to fit, adapt, adjust (ه s.th.)

لبق *labaq* cleverness, smartness, slyness, subtlety; skill, adroitness, slickness, ingenuity; seemliness, propriety, decency, decorum

لباقة *labāqa* cleverness, smartness, slyness, subtlety; skill, adroitness, slickness, ingenuity; seemliness, propriety, decency, decorum; elegance, refined manners, suavity, gracefulness

لبق *labiq* clever, smart, sly, subtle; slick, adroit, skilled, skillful, versatile; elegant, suave, of refined manners; fitting, proper, becoming, seemly

لبيق *labīq* clever, smart, sly, subtle; skillful, adroit; elegant, suave, refined

[1]لبك *labaka u* (*labk*) and **II** to mix, mingle, intermix (ه s.th.); to confuse, mix up, muddle, jumble (ه s.th.); — *labika a*, **V** and **VIII** to get confused, be thrown into disorder, be disarranged, become disorganized

لبك *labk* and لبكة *labka* mixture; confusion, muddle, jumble

[2]لبيك see لبى

لبلب *lablaba* to fondle, caress (ب her child; mother)

لبلب *lablab*, *lublub* affectionate, tender

لبلاب *lablāb* English ivy (Hedera helix; *bot.*); (*eg.*) lablab, hyacynth bean (Dolichos lablab; *bot.*)

لبلوب *lablūb* (*eg.*) pl. لباليب *labālīb*[2] young shoot, sprout, vine

لبن **II** to make brick **VIII** to suck milk

لبن *libn*, *labin* (coll.) unburnt brick(s), adobes

لبنة *labina* (n. un.) pl. *-āt* brick, adobe

لبن *laban* pl. البان *albān*, لبان *libān* milk; (*syr.*) leban, coagulated sour milk; pl. البان dairy products, milk products | لبن الخض *l. al-ḵaḍḍ* buttermilk; شرش اللبن *širš al-l.* whey; ○ ميزان اللبن *mīzān al-l.* lactoscope; فرع الالبان *farʿ al-a.* dairy department

لبنى *labanī* lactic, milk (adj.); milky, milklike, lacteous, lacteal

لبنية *labanīya* a dish prepared of milk

لبنات *labanāt* lactate | لبنات الجير *l. al-jīr* calcium lactate

لبان *labān* breast

لبان *lubān* frankincense, olibanum | لبان جاوى (*jāwī*) benzoin; لبان ذكر *l. ḏakar* (*eg.*) olibanum, oriental frankincense (resin of Boswellia carteri; *bot.*); لبان شامى, (*eg.*) a pitchy resin used as a depilatory (resin of Pinus Brutia Ten.); لبان العذراء *l. al-'adrā'* magnesia, Epsom salts, bitter salt

لبان *liban* sucking, nursing; (*eg.*) tow-line

لبان *labbān* brickmaker; milkman

لبانة *lubāna* pl. *-āt,* لبان *lubān* wish, desire, object, aim, goal, end; business, undertaking, enterprise

لبانة *libāna* selling or production of milk products, dairy

لبنة *labina,* لبون *labūn,* لبونة *labūna* pl. لبان *libān,* لبن *lubn, lubun,* لبائن *labā'in*[2] milch, giving milk | حيوان لبون (*ḥayawān*) mammal

لبنى *lubnā* storax tree

لبنان *lubnān*[2] Lebanon

لبنانى *lubnānī* Lebanese; (pl. *-ūn*) a Lebanese

ملبن *malban* a sweet made of corn-starch, sugar, mastic and pistachios

ملبنة *malbana* dairy

لبوة *labwa* pl. *labawāt* lioness

لبى **II** to follow, obey (ه a call, an invitation), respond, accede (ه to), comply (ه with a request), carry out (ه an order) | لبى نداء ربه (*nidā'a rabbihī*) to be called away by the Lord, pass away

لبيك *labbaika* here I am! at your service!

تلبية *talbiya* following, obeying, observance, accedence, response, compliance | تلبية ل (*talbiyatan*) in compliance with; تلبية لدعوته (*li-da'watihī*) upon his invitation

ليبريا *libēriyā* Liberia

لت *latta u* (*latt*) to pound, bray, crush (ه s.th.); to mix with water (ه flour); to knead (ه dough), to roll (ب ه s.th. in), coat (ب ه s.th. with); (*eg.*) to prattle, chatter | لت وعجن فى مسألة (*wa-'ajana, mas'ala*) not to tire of raising a problem anew, discuss a question back and forth

لت *latt* (*eg.*) idle talk, prattle

لتات *lattāt* (*eg.*) prattler, chatterbox, windbag

لتر *litr* pl. *-āt* liter

لتموس (Engl.) *litmūs* litmus

لتوانيا *lituwāniyā* Lithuania

التى *allatī* see الذى (alphabetically)

لثة see لثو

لثغ *laṯiġa a* (*laṯaġ*) to pronounce defectively (esp. the lingual *r*), lisp (ث for س) | لثغ بالسين (*sīn*) to lisp the *s*

لثغة *luṯġa* defective pronunciation, lisping

ألثغ *alṯaġ*[2], f. لثغاء *laṯġā'*[2], pl. لثغ *luṯġ* having a speech defect, lisping

لثم *laṯama i* (*laṯm*) to kiss (ه s.th.); to strike, hit, wound, injure (ه s.th.) **II** to veil (ه the face) with the *liṯām* (q.v.); to veil, cover (ه s.th.) **V** and **VIII** to veil one's face; to cover o.s., wrap o.s. up, muffle o.s.

لثمة *laṯma* kiss

لثام *liṯām* veil (covering the lower part of the face to the eyes); cover, wrapping

ملثم *mulaṯṯam* and متلثم *mutalaṯṯim* veiled

لثة *liṯa* pl. *-āt,* لثى *liṯan* gums

لثوى *liṯawī* gingival, alveolar, of or pertaining to the gums | الحروف اللثوية the interdental sounds ث, ذ and ظ (*phon.*)

لج *lajja* (1st pers. perf. *lajijtu*) *a* and (1st pers. perf. *lajajtu*) *i* (لجج *lajaj,* لجاج *lajāj,* لجاجة *lajāja*) to be stubborn, obstinate, unyielding, relentless; to persist, persevere (فى in); to insist (فى on); to continue (فى s.th.), keep doing s.th. (فى); to importune, pester, trouble, bother, inconvenience (على s.o.); to bear down (ب on s.o.), hit hard, wear out, weaken, exhaust (ب s.o., e.g., battle), torment, harass (ب s.o., e.g., hunger) **III** to argue or dispute obstinately (ه with s.o.) **VIII** to be noisy, uproarious, tumultuous; to roar, storm, rage

لج *lujj* and لجة *lujja* pl. لجج *lujaj*, لجاج *lijāj* depth of the sea; gulf, abyss, chasm, depth

لجي *lujjī* fathomless, of tremendous depth (sea)

لجة *lajja* clamor, din, noise, hubbub

لجاجة *lajāja* stickling, disputatiousness; obstinacy, stubbornness; insistence, persistence

لجوج *lajūj* and لاج *lājj* obstinate, stubborn, unyielding, relentless, insistent, troublesome, importunate, obtrusive, officious

لجأ *laja'a a* (لجء *laj'*, لجوء *lujū'*) and لجئ *laji'a a* (لجأ *laja'*) to take refuge (الى in), resort, have recourse (الى to), fall back (الى on); to seek information (الى from), refer (الى to) **II** to coerce, force, compel (الى ه s.o. to) **IV** do.; to shelter, protect, guard (ه s.o.); to entrust, commit (امره الى *amrahū* one's cause, one's affairs to) **VIII** to flee (الى to), take refuge (الى in), resort, have recourse (الى to)

ملجأ *malja'* pl. ملاجئ *malāji'*[2] (place of) refuge, retreat; shelter; sanctuary, asylum; home; base; pillbox, bunker, dugout | ملجأ الاطفال day nursery, nursery school, children's home; ملجأ الايتام orphanage; ملجأ الشيوخ home for the aged; ملجأ العميان *m. al-'umyān* institution for the blind; ملجأ العجزة *m. al-'ajaza* infirmary; ○ ملجأ مضاد للغارات الجوية (*muḍādd, jawwīya*) air-raid shelter

التجاء *iltijā'* resorting, recourse (الى to), seeking refuge (ب in, with)

لاجئ *lāji'* one seeking refuge; refugee; emigrant; inmate of an asylum

ملتجئ *multaji'* one seeking refuge, a refugee

لجب *lajab* noise, uproar, tumult; huge, boisterous army

لجب *lajib* uproarious, tumultuous, noisy, clamorous

لجلج *lajlaja* and **II** *talajlaja* to repeat words in speaking; to stammer, stutter

لجلجة *lajlaja* stutter; stammering, stammer

لجلاج *lajlāj* stutterer, stammerer

ملجلج *mulajlaj* constantly repeated, reiterated

لجم *lajama u* (*lajm*) to sew (ه s.th.) **II** and **IV** to bridle, rein in (ه a horse); to restrain, curb, hold down, silence (ه s.o.); to put the bridle (ه on s.o.) **VIII** to be bridled, be curbed, be tamed, be harnessed (e.g., energies)

لجام *lijām* pl. الجمة *aljima*, لجم *lujum* bridle, rein

ملجوم *maljūm* and ملجم *muljam* bridled, curbed, harnessed

لجن *lajina a* (*lajan*) to cling, adhere, stick (ب to)

لجنة *lajna* pl. *-āt*, لجان *lijān*, لجن *lijan* board, council, commission, committee | لجنة التحقيق investigating committee; لجنة ادارية (*idārīya*) administrative board, committee of management; لجنة الامتحان board of examiners, examination board; لجنة الانضباط disciplinary board; لجنة تنفيذية (*tanfīḏīya*) executive committee; لجنة صلحية (*sulḥīya*) arbitration committee, board of arbitration; لجنة فرعية (*far'īya*) subcommittee; لجنة قارة (مستديمة) (*qārra, mustadīma*) standing committee, permanent committee; لجنة المراقبة *l. al-murāqaba* board of directors

لجين *lujain* silver

لجينى *lujainī* silvery

لح *laḥḥa* (*laḥḥ*) to be close (relationship) **IV** to implore, beseech, request with urgency; to insist (فى on); to beset, importune, pester, harass (على s.o.); to urge, press (على فى or ب s.o. to do s.th.)

لحح *laḥiḥ* and لاح *lāḥḥ* close, narrow

لحوح *laḥūḥ* obstinate, stubborn, persistent

ملحاح *milḥāḥ* obstinate, stubborn, persistent; importunate, obtrusive

الحاح *ilḥāḥ* urging, pressing, urgency, insistence; emphasis; urgent solicitation, earnest request | بالحاح or فى الحاح insistently, earnestly, urgently

ملح *muliḥḥ* pressing, urgent; persistent; insistent, emphatic; importunate, obtrusive

لاحب *lāḥib* open, passable (road); ○ electrode

لحج *laḥaj*[2] Lahej (sultanate and city in the Aden Protectorate)

لحد *laḥada a* (*laḥd*) to dig a grave; to bury, inter (ه s.o.); to deviate from the right course, digress from the straight path; to abandon one's faith, apostatize, become a heretic; to lean, incline, tend (الى to) **IV** = **I**; **VIII** to deviate, digress; to abandon one's faith, apostatize, become a heretic or unbeliever; to be inclined, lean, incline, tend (الى to)

لحد *laḥd* pl. لحود *luḥūd*, الحاد *alḥād* grave, tomb; (ancient meaning: charnel vault with a niche for the corpse in the lateral wall)

لحاد *laḥḥād* gravedigger

الحاد *ilḥād* apostasy; heterodoxy, heresy

الحادى *ilḥādī* of or pertaining to godlessness

ملحد *mulḥid* heretical, unbelieving; (pl. *-ūn*, ملاحدة *malāḥida*) apostate, renegade; heretic

لحس *laḥasa a* (*laḥs*) to eat away (ه s.th., esp. a moth the wool), devour (ه s.th.); — *laḥisa a* (*laḥs*, لحسة *laḥsa*, *luḥsa*, ملحس *malḥas*) to lick (ه s.th.); to lick up, lap up, lick out (ه s.th.)

ملحوس *malḥūs* licked; (*eg.*) imbecilic

لحظ *laḥaẓa a* (*laḥẓ*, لحظان *laḥaẓān*) to regard, view, eye (ه, ه s.o., s.th.), look (ه, ه at); to notice, see, perceive, observe (ه s.th., ان that) **III** to regard, view, eye (ه, ه s.o., s.th.), look (ه, ه at); to see, behold (ه s.o.), catch sight (ه of); to notice, perceive, observe (ان that, ه s.th.); to remark, say, make the remark (ان that); to consider, bear in mind, observe, heed, take into consideration (ه s.th.); to pay attention (ه to); to supervise, superintend (ه s.th.) | لاحظ عليه شيئا to observe or notice s.th. in s.o.; مما يلاحظ ان *mimmā yulāḥaẓu anna* it will be noticed that ..., obviously ..., evidently ...

لحظ *laḥẓ* pl. الحاظ *alḥāẓ* look, glance

لحظة *laḥẓa* pl. *laḥaẓāt* (quick or casual) look, glance, glimpse; moment, instant | اللحظة الراهنة the present moment, the immediate present; فى لحظة in a moment, instantly; فى هذه اللحظة at that moment; لحظات *laḥaẓātin* for a few moments

لحظتئذ *laḥẓata'iḏin* at that moment

ملاحظة *mulāḥaẓa* pl. *-āt* seeing, noticing, perception; observation; remark, comment, casual statement, note; observance, heed, notice, attention, consideration; supervision, superintendence, surveillance, control | ذو ملاحظة considerable, notable

لاحظة *lāḥiẓa* pl. لواحظ *lawāḥiẓ*[2] eye; look, glance

ملحوظ *malḥūẓ* noted, noteworthy, remarkable

ملحوظة *malḥūẓa* pl. *-āt* observation; remark; note

ملاحظ *mulāḥiẓ* director, superintendent; overseer, supervisor, foreman

ملاحظ *mulāḥaẓ*: والملاحظ ان obviously ..., evidently ...

لحف **laḥafa** *a* (*laḥf*) to cover, wrap (ه s.o.) **IV** do.; to request or demand urgently **V** and **VIII** to wrap o.s. (ب in), cover o.s. (ب with)

لحف *liḥf* foot of a mountain

لحاف *liḥāf* pl. لحف *luḥuf* (also الحفة *alḥifa*) cover, blanket; bedcover, counterpane, coverlet, quilt, comforter; wrap

ملحف *milḥaf* and ملحفة *milḥafa* pl. ملاحف *malāḥif*[2] cover, blanket; wrap

الحاف *ilḥāf* importunity (of a petitioner)

ملتحف *multaḥif* wrapped (ب in), covered (ب with)

لحق **laḥiqa** *a* (*laḥq*, لحاق *laḥāq*) to catch up (ب or ه with s.o.), overtake (ب or ه s.o.); to reach (ه, ب s.th.); to catch, make (ه, ب e.g., a train); to touch (ب s.th.); to cling, adhere, attach o.s., stick, hang on, keep close (ب to s.o.); to join (ب s.o.), come along (ب with s.o.); to follow, succeed (ب s.o.); to unite (ب with); to betake o.s., go (ب to); to enter (بمدرسة *bi-madrasatin* a school; بخدمة *bi-ḵidmatin* a service; لحق بخدمته to take up a position with s.o., enter the services of s.o.); to overcome, befall, affect, afflict (ه s.o.; disease, fear, loss, and the like), come, descend (ه upon s.o.; calamity, etc.); to be incumbent (ه upon s.o.), be imperative (ه for) **III** to follow (ه s.o.); to go after s.o. (ه), trail, pursue, chase (ه s.o.) **IV** to attach, affix, join, subjoin, append, annex, add (ه ب s.th. to), enclose (ه ب s.th. in); to connect (ه ب s.th. with); to increase, augment (ه ب s.th. by); to take in as a member, admit (ه ب s.o. to an organization, and the like), enroll (ه ب s.o. in); to inflict (ه ب upon s.o. or s.th. s.th.), cause (ه ب s.o. or s.th. s.th.; esp. damage); pass. *ulḥiqa* to be admitted (ب to an organization, a society, etc.), become a member (ب of), enter (ب a service) **VI** to follow in close succession; to pursue or chase each other; to blend into a continuous sequence, pass insensibly into each other **VIII** to reach (ب s.th. or s.o.); to catch up (ب with), overtake (ب s.th. or s.o.); to join (ب s.o.), go or come along (ب with); to enter (ب a service, a school, a university), join (ب an army, an organization, etc.), become a member (ب of); to matriculate (ب at a university), enroll (ب in a faculty); to take up (ب a position, a job); to be attached (ب to), be connected, be affiliated (ب with); to be attached, devoted, loyal | التحق بالحكومة to go into government service **X** to annex (ه s.th.)

لحق *laḥaq* pl. الحاق *alḥāq* cultivable alluvial soil left behind by a flood

لحقى *laḥaqī*: مواد لحقية (*mawādd*) detritus (*geol.*), alluvium, alluvial residues

لحاق *liḥāq* accession (ب to), entry, entrance (ب to, into), joining (ب of), enrollment (ب in); membership (ب in)

ملاحقة *mulāḥaqa* pl. *-āt* pursuit, chase; legal prosecution

الحاق *ilḥāq* joining, junction, subjunction, attachment, appending, affixation, affixture, addition, annexation; admission (ب to an organization, and the like), enrollment (ب in an association, and the like); political annexation

التحاق *iltiḥāq* entering (ب of), entry, entrance (ب to office, into a school, etc.);

joining (ب of), affiliation (ب with); accession (ب to).

استلحاق *istilḥāq* annexation; avowal of paternity (*jur.*)

لاحق *lāḥiq* reaching; overtaking; subsequent, following; added, affixed, appended, subjoined, attached, joined, connected | سابقا — لاحقا *sābiqan — lāḥiqan* previously — later on, at first — subsequently

لاحقة *lāḥiqa* pl. لواحق *lawāḥiq*² appendage, appurtenance, adjunct; pl. accessories, appurtenances, adjuncts, dependencies

ملحق *mulḥaq* added, affixed, appended, attached, subjoined (ب to s.th.), enclosed (ب in s.th.); adjoining, adjacent, contiguous; written or printed in the margin, marginal; appertaining, appurtenant, incident, pertinent, accompanying; incorporated, annexed; supplement; — (pl. *-āt*, ملاحق *malāḥiq*²) appendix; addition, addendum, postscript; supplement, extra sheet (of a newspaper, periodical, book); enclosure (in a letter); appendage; pendant, locket; tag, label; trailer (of a truck, etc.); annex, subsidiary building, wing or addition to a building; — (pl. *-ūn*) attaché; assistant; pl. ملحقات also: annexed provinces, dependent territories, dependencies | ملحق بحرى (*baḥrī*) naval attaché; ملحق تجارى (*tijārī*) commercial attaché; ملحق جوى (*jawwī*) air attaché; ملحق عسكرى (*ʿaskarī*) or ملحق حربى (*ḥarbī*) military attaché; ملحق صحفى (*ṣuḥufī*) press attaché; ملحق فخرى (*fak̲rī*) titular attaché

متلاحق *mutalāḥiq* successive, consecutive, uninterrupted, continuous | متلاحق الحركة *m. al-ḥaraka* in continuous motion

لحم **laḥama** *u* (*laḥm*) to mend, patch, weld, solder (up) (ه s.th.); — *laḥima a* to get stuck II to solder (ه s.th.) VI to join in battle, engage in a mutual massacre; to cling together, cleave together, stick together, hang together, cohere; to hold firmly together; to be joined, united VIII to adhere, cleave, stick (ب to); to be in immediate contact (ب with); to cling (ب to), fit closely (ب s.th.); to grapple, fight, struggle (in a clinch or in close combat); to cling together, cleave together, cohere; to stick together; to be interjoined, intermesh, be closely united; to close, heal up, scar over, cicatrize (wound)

لحم *laḥm* pl. لحوم *luḥūm*, لحام *liḥām* flesh; meat | بلحمه وشحمه (*šaḥmihī*) in his real human form; لحما ودما (*daman*) dyed in the wool, inveterate

لحمة *laḥma* (n. un.) a piece of flesh or meat

لحمة *laḥma*, *luḥma* pl. لحم *luḥam* woof, weft (of a fabric); decisive factor, motif; *luḥma* relationship, kinship

لحمية *laḥmīya* conjunctiva

لحم *laḥim* fleshy, corpulent; carnivorous

لحام *liḥām* pl. *-āt* soldering; welding; soldered seam, soldered joint; solder

لحام *laḥḥām* butcher; solderer; welder

لحيم *laḥīm* fleshy

لحامة *laḥāma* fleshiness, corpulence

ملحمة *malḥama* pl. ملاحم *malāḥim*² bloody fight, slaughter, massacre, fierce battle

شعر ملحمى *šiʿr malḥamī* heroic poem

التحام *iltiḥām* close union; cohesion; conjunction, union, connection, coherence; adhesion (*phys.*); grapple, struggle, fight, close combat

ملتحمة *multaḥama* conjunctiva

لحن **laḥana** *a* (*laḥn*, لحون *luḥūn*, لحانة *laḥāna*) to speak ungrammatical Arabic (interspersed with barbarisms); — *laḥina a* to be intelligent II to chant, psalmodize; to intone, strike up a melody; to set to music, compose (ه s.th.)

لحن *laḥn* pl. الحان *alḥān*, لحون *luḥūn* air, tune, melody; grammatical mistake, solecism, barbarism

لحن *laḥin* intelligent, understanding, sensible

تلحين *talḥīn* pl. تلاحين *talāḥīn*[2] musical composition, musical arrangement

تلحينى *talḥīnī* singable

ملحون *malḥūn* incorrect, ungrammatical (language); (*magr.*) poetry in colloquial language

ملحن *mulaḥḥin* composer

(لحو and لحى) لحا *laḥā u* (*laḥw*) and لحى *laḥā a* (*laḥy*) to insult, abuse, revile (ه s.o.) VI to call each other names, heap abuses on each other VIII to grow a beard

لحو *laḥw* and لحى *laḥy* insult, abuse, invective, vilification, defamation

لحى *laḥy*, dual: لحيان *laḥyān*, pl. الح *alḥin*, لحى *luḥīy* jawbone

لحية *liḥya* pl. لحى *luḥan*, *liḥan* beard, whiskers (on cheeks and chin), full beard | اطلق لحيته *aṭlaqa liḥyatahū* to let one's beard grow; لحية التيس *l. at-tais* salsify (Tragopogon porrifolium; *bot.*)

لحية *luḥayya*[2] Luhaiya (town in NW Yemen, on Red Sea)

لحاء *liḥā'* bast

الحى *alḥā* long-bearded

ملتح *multaḥin* bearded, having a beard, e.g., ملتح بلحية سوداء (*bi-liḥya saudā'*) a black-bearded man

لخص II to abridge (ه s.th.); to summarize, sum up, epitomize, condense, compress (ه s.th.); to excerpt (ه s.th.), make an excerpt or extract (ه of); to give the essence of s.th.; to sketch, outline (ه s.th.); pass. يلخص *yulakkaṣu* it can be summed up (في ان to the effect that) V to be summarized, be epitomized, be condensed, be summed up (في in), amount briefly (في to), be in its essence (في s.th.), narrow down (في to)

تلخيص *talkīṣ* abridgement; condensation; summary, résumé; epitome, abstract, synopsis, outline; brief, short report

ملخص *mulakkaṣ* abridged, excerpted, summarized, condensed; (pl. *-āt*) extract, excerpt, essence, gist

لخلخ *laklaka* to shake, shake off (ه s.th.) II *talaklaka* to shake, totter

ملخلخ *mulaklak* shaky, unsteady, tottering

لخمة *lakama*, *lukama* sluggish; gauche, awkward, clumsy

لخن *lakan* putrid stench

الخن *aikan*[2], f. لخناء *laknā'*[2], pl. لخن *lukn* stinking; uncircumcized (as an abusive term)

[1]لدة *lida* see ولد

[2]اللد *al-lidd* Lydda (city and international airport in W Israel)

[3]لد *ladda u* (*ladd*) to dispute violently, have a fierce quarrel (ه with s.o.) II to defame, slander (ب s.o.); to bewilder, perplex, nonplus V to turn helplessly right and left, be bewildered, perplexed, confused; to be headstrong, recalcitrant

لدد *ladad* vehement quarrel, violent dispute

لدود *ladūd*, الد *aladd*[2], f. لداء *laddā'*[2], pl. لد *ludd*, لداد *lidād*, الداء *aliddā'*[2] fierce, grim, dogged, tough | عدو الد (*'adūw*) mortal enemy, archenemy, foe; عدو لدود do.

متلدد *mutaladdid* obstinate, recalcitrant, headstrong, rebellious

لدغ *ladağa* u (*ladğ*) to sting, bite (snake, s.o.); to taunt, hurt, offend (ه s.o.)

لدغة *ladğa* sting; bite

لديغ *ladīğ* pl. لدغاء *ludağā'*[2], لدغى *ladğā* stung; bitten

[1]لدن *laduna* u (لدانة *ladāna*, لدونة *ludūna*) to be soft, supple, pliant, flexible, resilient, elastic II to soften (ه s.th.); to mollify, attenuate, temper, ease, mitigate, alleviate (ه s.th.)

لدن *ladn* pl. لدن *ludn*, لدان *lidān* soft, gentle; pliant, pliable, flexible, supple, resilient, elastic; plastic

لادن *lādan*, *lādin* laudanum

لدانة *ladāna* and لدونة *ludūna* softness, pliability, flexibility, suppleness, plasticity, resilience, elasticity

لدائن *ladā'in*[2] plastics

[2]لدن *ladun* (prep.) at, by, near, close to; in the presence of, in front of, before, with; in possession of; من لدن from, on the part of; since; — (conj.) since, from the moment when; لدن ان do.

لدنى *ladunī* (i.e. من لدن الله) mystic; العلم اللدنى (*'ilm*), العلوم اللدنية knowledge imparted directly by God through mystic intuition (in Sufism)

لدى *ladā* (prep.) at, by (place and time); in the presence of, in front of, before, with | لدى الحاجة in case of need, if necessary; لديه *ladaihi* he has; ما لديك the condition you are in, your state of mind; ليس لدينا غير ما . . . (*ğairu*) we know no more than what ...

لذ *ladda* (1st pers. perf. *ladidtu*) a (لذاذ *ladād*, لذاذة *ladāda*) to be sweet delicious, delightful, pleasant, gratify the senses II and IV to please, gratify, delight (ه s.o.); to give pleasure (ه to s.o.) V and VIII to be pleased, delighted (ب at), delight, revel, take pleasure (ب in), be gratified (ب by); to find (ه s.th.) delicious or pleasant, take delight (ه in), enjoy, savor, relish (ه s.th.) X to find delicious or pleasant (ه s.th.); to find delightful (ه s.th.); to take pleasure (ه in)

لذة *ladda* pl. *-āt* joy, rapture, bliss; pleasure, enjoyment, delectation, delight; sensual delight, lust, voluptuousness

لذيذ *ladīd* pl. لذ *ludd*, لذاذ *lidād* delicious, delightful; pleasant; beautiful, wonderful, splendid, magnificent; sweet

لذاذة *ladāda* pl. لذائذ *ladā'id*[2] sweetness; charm; bliss; rapture; enjoyment, delectation; pleasure, delight

ملذة *maladda* pl. *-āt*, ملاذ *maladd*[2] joy, pleasure, amenity, comfort; delightfulness; enjoyment, delectation; voluptuousness

متلذذ *mutaladdid* epicure

لذع *lada'a* a (*lad'*) to burn (ه s.th.); to brand, cauterize (ه s.o.); to hurt (with words), insult, offend (ه s.o.) V to burn

لذع *lad'* burning, combustion; conflagration, fire | لذع البنادق rifle fire

لذاع *laddā'* burning; very hot, scorching; pungent, acrid, sharp; biting (words)

لوذع *lauda'* and لوذعى *lauda'ī* sagacious, ingenious, witty, quick-witted, quick at repartee

لوذعية *lauda'īya* sagacity, ingenuity, esprit, wit, quick-wittedness, mental alertness

لاذع *lādi'* burning; pungent, acrid, biting; sharp

لاذعة *lādi'a* pl. لواذع *lawādi'*[2] gibe, taunt

اللاذقية *al-lādiqīya* Latakia, the ancient Laodicea (seaport in W Syria)

[1]لذى *ladiya* a (*ladan*) to adhere, cleave (ب to)

[2]الذى look up alphabetically

لز *lazza* (1st pers. perf. *lazaztu*) *u* (*lazz*, لزز *lazaz*, لزاز *lazāz*) to tie (ب ▲ s.th. to), connect or join firmly, unite (ب ▲ s.th. with), make (▲ s.th.) stick (ب to) **II** to connect or join firmly, press together (▲ s.th.); to cram together; to urge, press, coerce (الى • s.o. to) **VI** to be crammed together; to lie close together **V** and **VIII** to be united, joined, connected (ب with); to adhere, cleave, stick (ب to)

لز *lazz* and لزة *lazza* U bolt, staple, cramp

ملزز *mulazzaz* crammed together; closely united; firm, solid, compact

لزب *lazaba u* (لزوب *luzūb*) to be firm, be firmly fixed, hold fast; to adhere, cleave, cling (ب to); to stick (ب to); — *laziba a* (*lazab*) to cohere, cleave together, stick together

لزب *lazib* pl. لزاب *lizāb* little

لزبة *lazba* pl. لزب *lizab* misfortune, calamity

لازب *lāzib* sticking, adhering, clinging; firm, firmly fixed | صار ضربة لازب (*ḍarbata l.*) to become necessary, indispensable; ضرب ضربة لازب (*ḍuriba*) to meet with grave misfortune, be stricken by disaster

لزج *lazija a* (*lazaj*, لزوج *luzūj*) to be sticky, ropy, gluey, viscid; to stick, cling, get stuck (ب to)

لزج *lazij* sticky, gluey, ropy, viscid; adhesive

لزوجة *luzūja* stickiness, glueyness, ropiness, viscidity

لزق *laziqa a* (لزوق *luzūq*) to adhere, cling, cleave, stick (ب to) **II** to affix, post (▲ s.th.); to stick on, paste on (▲ s.th.); to paste together (▲ s.th.); (*eg.*) to palm off, foist (ل ▲ s.th. on s.o.) **IV** to paste on, stick on, affix (▲ s.th.) **VIII** = **I**

لزق *lizq* adjoining, adjacent, contiguous | لزقه *lizqahū* or بلزقه close to his side, close by

لزق *laziq* sticky, gluey

لزقة *lazqa* compress, stupe; plaster

لزاق *lizāq* adhesive, agglutinant, glue, cement, paste

لزوق *lazūq* and لازوق *lāzūq* compress, stupe; plaster, adhesive plaster, court plaster

لزم *lazima a* (لزوم *luzūm*) to cling, adhere, belong (▲ to), attend, accompany (▲ s.th.); to persist, persevere (▲ in), stick, keep (▲ to), keep doing (▲ s.th.); to adhere, be attached, keep close, stick (• to s.o.); to be inseparable (▲, • from s.o., from s.th.); to stay permanently (▲ in); to be necessary; to be requisite, imperative, indispensable (• for s.o.); to be incumbent (• upon s.o.), be s.o.'s (•) duty | لزم داره (فراشه) to stay at home (in bed); لزم الصمت (*ṣamta*) to keep silent, maintain silence **III** to attend, accompany (▲ s.th.); to adhere, stick, keep (▲ to); to pursue or practice incessantly (▲ s.th.); to be constantly with s.o. or in s.o.'s company (•), be constantly around s.o. (•); to be assigned (• to), accompany, attend (• s.o.); to be inseparable (•, ▲ from s.th., from s.o.); to keep doing (▲ s.th.), persist, persevere (▲ in); to work with perseverance, display sustained activity (▲ for) **IV** to force, compel (• ▲ s.o. to); to force, press (• ▲, also ب • upon s.o. s.th.); to enjoin, impose as a duty (• ▲, also ب • on s.o. s.th.), obligate (• ▲, also ب • s.o. to or to do s.th.) | الزمه الحجة (*ḥujja*) to force proof on s.o., force s.o. to accept an argument; الزمه الفراش to confine s.o. to bed, compel s.o. to stay in bed (of. a disease); الزمه المال (or بالمال) to impose the payment of a sum on s.o. **VI** to be attached or devoted to each other, be inseparable **VIII** to adhere, stick, keep, hang on (ه to); to keep doing (ه s.th.), persist, persevere (ه in), keep up, maintain preserve (ه s.th.), abide (ه by); to take upon o.s. (ه s.th.); to make a rule (ه of s.th.), make (ه s.th.) one's duty, impose upon o.s. (ه s.th.); to assume as a duty (ب or ه s.th.); to undertake, obligate o.s., bind o.s., pledge (ب or ه to do s.th.); to be in duty bound, be obligated or under obligation, be or become liable (ب or ه to do s.th.); to be forced, be compelled (ب or ه to do s.th.); to be responsible (ب or ه for); to take over the monopoly (ه of s.th.), monopolize, farm (ه e.g., the levying of taxes) X to deem necessary (ه s.th.); to necessitate, make necessary or requisite (ه s.th.); to require, need (ه s.th.), call (ه for), be in need (ه of s.th.)

لزمة *lazma* pl. *-āt* official concession, license, franchise

لزوم *luzūm* necessity, exigency, requirement; need, want | حسب اللزوم *ḥasaba l-l.* as required, as the occasion demands; عند اللزوم in case of need, when (if) necessary, if need be; بسكويت لزوم السفر بالبحر (*l. as-safar bi-l-baḥr*) biscuit for the voyage

لزام *lizām* necessary, requisite; necessity, duty, obligation | كان لزاما عليه ان to be s.o.'s duty to ..., be necessary for s.o. that he ...

الزم *alzam*² more necessary, most necessary

ملزمة *malzama* pl. ملازم *malāzim*² section, signature (of a book, = 16 octavo sheets)

ملزمة *milzama* pl. ملازم *malāzim*² vise; press

ملازمة *mulāzama* adhesion, clinging, sticking; remaining, staying, dwelling; close attachment; dependence; inseparableness, inherence, intrinsicality; following, pursuit, pursuance; perseverance, assiduity, zeal

الزام *ilzām* coercion, compulsion

الزامى *ilzāmī* forced, compulsory, obligatory, required

التزام *iltizām* pl. *-āt* necessity; duty, obligation, commitment, liability; engagement (*philos.*); contract; farming of taxes, farmage; concession, license, franchise; monopoly; التزاما *iltizāman* by contract, by the job | قام بالتزاماته to meet one's obligations

لازم *lāzim* inherent, intrinsic, inseparable, indissoluble; necessary, requisite, imperative, indispensable, unavoidable, inevitable, inescapable; incumbent, binding, obligatory; intransitive (*gram.*); legally binding, irrevocable (*Isl. Law*) | كاللازم as it must be, comme il faut, properly

لازمة *lāzima* fixed attribute, inherent property; standing phrase (of s.o.)

لوازم *lawāzim*² (pl.) necessary, inseparable attributes or manifestations; necessities, exigencies, requirements; necessaries, requisites; accessories, fixtures

ملزوم *malzūm* obligated, under obligation, liable | ملزوم بالاداء (*adā'*) liable for taxes, taxable

ملزومية *malzūmīya* duty, obligation, commitment, liability

ملازم *mulāzim* tenacious (with foll. genit.: of), clinging, keeping, sticking (with foll. genit.: to); persevering, persisting, remaining, abiding; inseparable; closely connected or attached; attending, accompanying; adhering; adherent, follower, partisan; second lieutenant (*U.A.R., Tun.*) | ملازم اول (*awwal; U.A.R., Leb., Jord., Ir.*) first lieutenant; ملازم ثان (*ṯānin; Leb., Jord., Ir.*, formerly also *Eg., Syr.*) second lieutenant

ملتزم *multazim* engaged, committed, under obligation; holder of a concession or monopoly; tax farmer; concessionaire, concessionary; contractor

ملتزم *multazam* pl. *-āt* requirement

مستلزمات *mustalzamāt* requirements, prerequisites, requisites; necessary or inevitable consequences

لستك *lastik* and لستيك *lastīk* rubber; eraser

لسع **lasa'a** *a* (*las'*) to sting (ه s.o.); to burn (ه s.th., e.g., the mouth); to hurt (with words; ه s.o.)

لسعة *las'a* sting, bite; biting words

لسيع *lasī'* pl. لسعى *las'ā*, لسعاء *lusa'ā'*[2] stung

لاسع *lāsi'* stinging; burning; biting, acrid, pungent, sharp

لسن **lasina** *a* (*lasan*) to be eloquent II to point, taper, sharpen (ه s.th.)

لسن *lasan* eloquence

لسن *lasin* and السن *alsan*[2], f. لسناء *lasnā'*[2], pl. لسن *lusn* eloquent

لسان *lisān* m. and f., pl. السنة *alsina*, السن *alsun* tongue; language; mouthpiece (fig.), organ (esp., of a newspaper; = لسان الحال see below) | على لسانه from his mouth, through him; على لسان الصحف (*l. iṣ-ṣuḥuf*) through the organ of the press; قيل على لسانه ما (*qīla*) things were ascribed to him which ..., he was rumored to have said things which ...; لسان رسمى (*rasmī*) official organ; متحدث بلسان وزارة الخارجية (*mutaḥaddiṯ*) a spokesman of the Foreign Ministry; باللسان or لسانا *lisānan* orally, verbally; دار على السنة الخاص والعام (*a. il-ḵāṣṣ wa-l-'āmm*) to be the talk of the town, be on everyone's lips; لسان الثور *l. aṯ-ṯaur* borage (Borago officinalis; *bot.*); لسان الحال the language which things themselves speak, silent language, mute expression (as distinguished from the spoken word); organ (of a party or political movement; a newspaper); ولسان حاله يقول while he seemed to say ..., with an expression as if he wanted to say. ..; لسان الحمل *l. al-ḥamal* plantain (Plantago major L.; *bot.*); لسان العصفور *l. al-'uṣfūr* common ash (Fraxinus excelsior; *bot.*); لسان القفل *l. al-qufl* bolt of the lock; لسان القوم *l. al-qaum* spokesman (of a crowd); لسان الكلب *l. al-kalb* hound's-tongue (Cynoglossum; *bot.*); (*eg.*) also a variety of scorpion's tail (Scorpiurus muricatus L.; *bot.*), having circinately coiled pods; لسان المفتاح *l. al-miftāḥ* bit of the key; ذو لسانين *ḏū lisānain* double-tongued, deceitful, insincere, two-faced

لسانى *lisānī* oral, verbal

ملسون *malsūn* liar

لشبونة *lišbōna*[2] Lisbon (capital of Portugal)

(لشى*; from *lā šai'a*:) III to suppress, crush, destroy, ruin, annihilate (ه s.th.) VI to be suppressed, be crushed, be destroyed, be annihilated; to come to nothing, be ruined, be frustrated, fail; to disappear, vanish, dwindle, wane, fade

ملاشاة *mulāšāh* annihilation, destruction

تلاش *talāšin* annihilation, ruin, failure, frustration; disappearance, evanescence, vanishing, waning, decline

متلاش *mutalāšin* coming to nothing, dwindling, waning; destructible; evanescent, transient, ephemeral

لص **laṣṣa** *u* (*laṣṣ*) to do stealthily or secretly (ه s.th.); to rob, steal (ه s.th.) V to become a thief; to act stealthily

لص *liṣṣ* pl. لصوص *luṣūṣ*, الصاص *alṣāṣ* thief, robber

لصوصية *luṣūṣīya* thievery, theft, robbery

متلصص *mutalaṣṣiṣ* behaving like a thief, thievish | اتى متلصصا الى (*atā*) to steal to, sneak up to

لصق *laṣiqa a* (*laṣq*, لصوق *luṣūq*) to adhere, cleave, cling, stick (ب to) **II** to paste together, stick together (ه s.th.) **III** to adjoin (ه s.th.), be next (ه to s.th.), be contiguous (with), abut (ه on), touch (ه s.th.); to be in touch, in connection, in contact (ه with s.o.) **IV** to attach, affix, stick, paste, glue (ب ه s.th. to); to connect (ب ه s.th. with), join (ب ه s.th. to); to bring (ه s.th.) close (ب to); to press (ب ه s.th. against) | الصق لوحة (*lauḥa*) to post a placard; الصق به تهمة (*tuhma*) to raise an accusation against s.o. **VI** to cleave together, cling together, cohere, stick together; to agglomerate, conglomerate, cake, frit together; to blend, pass into each other **VIII** = **I**; to hang on (ب to), get stuck (ب to, on); to fit closely (ب s.th.), cling (ب to)

لصق *liṣq* adhering, clinging, cleaving | بلصقه close to him (or it); هو بلصقِى or لصقى he and I are inseparable

لصق *laṣiq* sticky, gluey, glutinous; adhesive, agglutinant; tenacious

لصيق *laṣīq* one who cleaves or clings (ب to); adjoining, adjacent, bordering, neighboring, abutting, contiguous; close-fitting, skintight (dress)

لصوق *laṣūq* plaster

ملاصقة *mulāṣaqa* junction, conjunction, connection, contact, union; adjacency, contiguity; ○ adhesion, cohesion (*phys.*)

الصاق *ilṣāq* poster, bill

تلاصق *talāṣuq* and التصاق *iltiṣāq* cohesion, adhesion; contiguity, contact; coherence

ملاصق *mulāṣiq* adjoining, adjacent, abutting, contiguous, bordering, neighboring, in close contact; companion; neighbor; adherent

ملصق *mulṣaq* attached, affixed; stuck on, pasted on, glued on; fastened; brought close; connected, joined; (pl. *-āt*) poster, bill, placard

متلاصق *mutalāṣiq* cohering, sticking together; blending, passing into each other

ملتصق *multaṣiq* attached, affixed, adhesive, sticking; adjoining, adjacent, bordering, neighboring; contiguous, connected, meeting or touching each other, in contact; in the immediate proximity (ب of), close to (ب)

ملضوم *malḍūm* dense (row), close (rank)

لطخ *laṭaḵa a* (*laṭḵ*) to stain, blot, sully, soil, spatter, splash (ب ه s.th. with) **II** do. **V** to be soiled or stained

لطخة *laṭḵa* pl. *laṭaḵāt* smear, blotch, spot; stain, blemish, blot, disgrace

لطخة *luṭaḵa* pl. *-āt* and لطيخ *liṭṭīḵ* ass. dolt, fool

لطس *laṭasa u* (*laṭs*) to strike, hit (ه s.o.)

ملطاس *milṭās* pl. ملاطيس *malāṭīs*[2] pickax

لطش *laṭaša u* (*laṭš*) to strike, hit (ه s.o.)

لطع *laṭaʿa a* (*laṭʿ*) to strike, hit (ه s.o.); to strike out, erase (ه s.th.)

لطعة *laṭʿa* blot, stain

لطف *laṭafa u* (*luṭf*) to be kind and friendly (ب or ل to, toward s.o.); — *laṭufa u* (لطافة *laṭāfa*) to be thin, fine, delicate, dainty; to be graceful; to be elegant; to be nice, amiable, friendly **II** to make mild, soft, gentle, soften (ه s.th.); to mitigate, alleviate, ease, soothe, allay, palliate, assuage, extenuate (ه s.th.; also من); to moderate, temper, lessen, diminish, reduce (ه s.th.; also من); to tone down (ه s.th.; also من) **III** to treat with kindness, with benevolence (ه s.o.); to be civil and polite (ه to, toward s.o.); to be complaisant, obliging, indulgent, compliant (ه toward s.o.), humor (ه s.o.); to flatter (ه s.o.), fawn (ه upon); to caress, fondle, pet (ه s.o.) | لاطفه على

كتفه (*katifihī*) to pat s.o. on the shoulder **V** to be mitigated, be tempered, be moderated; to be civil and polite, show o.s. friendly and kind, be so kind as to do s.th. (ب); to bestow most kindly, have the kindness to give (ب s.th., also, e.g., advice, على to s.o.); to be tender, affectionate, nice (ب to s.o.); to win (ب s.o.) over by subtle means, by favors, by tricks; to go about s.th. (فى or ب) gently, carefully, with caution; to do secretly, covertly, without being noticed (ب with verbal noun: s.th.) **VI** to show o.s. friendly and kind; to be polite, courteous, civil, nice **X** to find (ه s.th.) pretty, sweet, nice; to like, find pleasant or charming (ه s.th.)

لطف ***luṭf*** pl. الطاف *alṭāf* kindness, benevolence, friendliness; gentleness, mildness; civility, courteousness, politeness; daintiness, cuteness, gracefulness; delicateness, delicate grace (e.g., of the limbs) | بلطف gently, softly

لطافة ***laṭāfa*** thinness, fineness, delicateness; gracefulness, loveliness, charm; kindness, benevolence; friendliness; politeness; esprit, intellectual refinement, sophistication; suavity, urbaneness

لطيف ***laṭīf*** pl. لطاف *liṭāf*, لطفاء *luṭafā'*[2] thin; fine; delicate, dainty; little, small, insignificant; gentle, soft, light, mild; pleasant, agreeable; amiable, friendly, kind, nice; civil, courteous, polite; affable, genial; pretty, charming, lovely, graceful; intellectually refined, full of esprit, brilliant, witty; elegant; اللطيف the Kind (one of the attributes of God) | يا لطيف O my God! good heavens! for goodness sake! الجنس اللطيف (*jins*) the fair sex

لطيفة ***laṭīfa*** pl. لطائف *laṭā'if*[2] witticism, quip; joke, jest; subtlety, nicety | لطائف الحيل *l. al-ḥiyal* subtle tricks; لطائف النكات *l. an-nikāt* nice jokes

الطف ***alṭaf***[2] finer; more delicate; kinder, nicer; more elegant

ملاطفة ***mulāṭafa*** amiable treatment, amiability; civility, courteousness, politeness; friendliness; benevolence, kindness; caress; pl. *-āt* caresses

تلطف ***talaṭṭuf*** friendliness (ب toward s.o.), amiability; favoring, favoritism; civility, courteousness, politeness

ملطفات ***mulaṭṭifāt*** sedatives

لطم ***laṭama*** *i* (*laṭm*) to strike with the hand (ه the face, with despair, in lamentation); to slap (ه s.o.); to jolt; to eject; to bump, strike (ه against s.th.); to hit (ه s.th.) **VI** to exchange blows, fight, brawl, battle (hostile armies); to collide, clash (waves) **VIII** to collide, clash

لطمة ***laṭma*** pl. *laṭamāt* blow; slap, box on the ear; jolt, thrust

لطيم ***laṭīm*** parentless

ملطم ***malṭam*** cheek

ملتطم ***multaṭam*** clash (esp., of waves), tumult, turmoil (of a battle, and the like), melee

لظى ***laẓiya*** *a* (لظى *laẓan*) to burn brightly, flare, flame, blaze, be ablaze; to burn with rage **V** and **VIII** do.

لظى ***laẓan*** blazing fire, blaze, flame

لعب ***la'aba*** and ***la'iba*** *a* (*la'b*) to slaver; to slobber, drool (baby); — ***la'iba*** *a* (*lu'b*, *li'b*, *la'ib*, تلعاب *tal'āb*) to play (ب with s.th.; على an instrument); to toy (ب with); to dally (ب with); to trick, cheat, deceive, dupe (على s.o.) | لعب الاوراق (*aurāqa*) to play cards; لعب دورا (*dauran*) to play a part or role; لعب الموسيقى to make music; لعب بالشطرنج (*šaṭranj*) to play chess; لعبت به الهموم he became the sport of sorrows; لعب فى عقله (*'aqlihī*) to turn s.o.'s head **II** to make (ه s.th.) play, set (ه s.th.) going; to wag (ه the tail) **III** to play (ه with s.o.); to have fun, play around, jest, dally, trifle (ه with s.o.) **IV** to make play, cause to play (ه s.o.) **V** to play, act playfully **VI** to play (ب with s.th.); to make fun (ب of s.o.), mock (ب at s.o.); to pull s.o.'s (ب) leg; to play a trick; to act fraudulently

لعب ***la'b, li'b, la'ib*** pl. العاب ***al'āb*** play; game; joke, jest; fun, amusement, diversion, pastime, sport | لعب القمار gambling, gamble; الالعاب الاولمبية the Olympic Games; العاب رياضية (***riyāḍīya***) athletics, sports; العاب سحرية (***siḥrīya***) legerdemain, sleight of hand, magic; العاب القوى ***a. al-quwā*** athletics, specif., track and field; العاب نارية (***nārīya***) fireworks; ساحة الالعاب athletic field; مدرس الالعاب ***mudarris al-a.*** athletic coach, athletics instructor

لعب ***la'ib*** funny, amusing, merry, gay

لعبة ***la'ba*** (n. un.) game; trick

لعبة ***lu'ba*** pl. لعب ***lu'ab*** plaything, toy; doll; butt for mirth or derision, sport, laughingstock

لعبة ***lu'aba***, لعاب ***la''āb*** and لعيب ***li''ib*** very playful

لعاب ***lu'āb*** saliva, spittle; slaver, drivel | لعاب الشمس ***l. aš-šams*** gossamer, air threads; سال لعابه على his mouth watered for ...

لعابى ***lu'ābī*** salivary; mucous, slimy

لعيبة ***lu'aiba*** pl. ***-āt*** (little) doll

لعوب ***la'ūb*** flighty, coquettish, flirtatious (woman); playful, dallying, trifling

العوبة ***ul'ūba*** pl. الاعيب ***alā'īb***[2] plaything, toy; play, sport, dalliance; fun; prank; trick

ملعب ***mal'ab*** pl. ملاعب ***malā'ib***[2] playground; athletic field, stadium; playhouse, theater; scene; circus ring; pl. ملاعب ***malā'ib***[2] matches, contests, events (in sports)

ملعبة ***mal'aba*** plaything, toy

تلاعب ***talā'ub*** game (e.g., of a speculator, of a gambler), gamble; free play | مجال التلاعب (***majāl***) free play, free scope, elbowroom; latitude, margin; clearance

لاعب ***lā'ib*** playing; player; sportsman; athlete; gymnast | لاعب الجنباز ***l. al-jumbāz*** gymnast, athlete

ملعوب ***mal'ūb*** pl. ملاعيب ***malā'īb***[2] covered with spittle; slobbering, driveling, drooling; prank, trick, ruse, artifice

ملاعب ***mulā'ib*** fellow player; playmate, playfellow; fraudulent

لعثم **II** ***tala'ṯama*** to hesitate; to falter, stutter, stammer

لعثمة ***la'ṯama*** and تلعثم ***tala'ṯum*** hesitation; stuttering, stutter

متلعثم ***mutala'ṯim*** and متلعثم اللسان ***m. al lisān*** stammering, stuttering

لعج ***la'aja a*** (***la'j***) to hurt, be sore, burn **III** to oppress, distress, agonize (ه s.o.)

لعجة ***la'ja*** pain

لاعج ***lā'ij*** pl. لواعج ***lawā'ij***[2] ardent, burning (esp., love); pl. لواعج ardent love, ardor (of love)

العس ***al'as***[2], f. لعساء ***la'sā'***[2] red-lipped

لعق ***la'iqa a*** (***la'q***, لعقة ***la'qa, lu'qa***) to lick (ه s.th.)

لعقة ***lu'qa*** spoonful

لعوق ***la'ūq*** electuary

ملعقة ***mil'aqa*** pl. ملاعق ***malā'iq***[2] spoon | ملعقة شاى teaspoon

لعل[1] ***la'l*** garnet (***min.***)

لعل[2] ***la'alla*** see علّ[2]

لعلع ***la'la'a*** to resound, reverberate, clang, roar, boom **II** ***tala'la'a*** to shimmer, glimmer, gleam, flicker; to be starved;

to be parched with thirst; to be exhausted

لعلع *laʿlaʿ* pl. لعالع *laʿāliʿ*² vibration of fata morgana

لعن *laʿana a* (*laʿn*) to curse, damn, execrate (ه s.o.), utter imprecations (ه against s.o.) III to utter the oath of condemnation (لعان *liʿān*, q.v.) VI to curse each other

لعن *laʿn* cursing, execration, malediction

لعنة *laʿna* pl. *laʿanāt*, لعان *liʿān* curse; execration, imprecation | لعنة الله عليه God's curse upon him!

لعنة *luʿna* damned, cursed, confounded; execrable, abominable

لعان *liʿān* oath of condemnation; sworn allegation of adultery committed by either husband or wife (*Isl. Law*)

لعين *laʿīn* and ملعون *malʿūn* pl. ملاعين *malāʿīn*² cursed; confounded; damned; outcast, execrable; detested, abhorred, abominable; اللعين the Evil One, the Devil

متلاعن *mutalāʿin* cursing each other, hostile, inimical

لعا لك *laʿan laka* call to one who has stumbled: may you rise again!

لغوب *luḡūb*, *laḡūb* exhaustion, lassitude, fatigue, weariness; great pains, trouble, toil

لاغب *lāḡib* pl. لغب *luḡḡab* languid, fatigued, weary, tired

لغد *luḡd* pl. الغاد *alḡād*, لغود *luḡūd* and لغدود *luḡdūd* pl. لغاديد *laḡādīd*² flesh at the throat and under the chin

لغز *laḡaza u* (*laḡz*) to speak in riddles; to equivocate III and IV do.

لغز *luḡz* pl. الغاز *alḡāz* riddle, puzzle; enigma; conundrum; mystery, secret | لغز الكلمات المتقاطعة ○ *l. al-kalimāt al-mutaqāṭiʿa* crossword puzzle

ملغز *mulḡaz* puzzling, enigmatic, cryptic, mysterious; dark, obscure, ambiguous, equivocal

لغط *laḡaṭa a* (*laḡṭ*, لغاط *liḡāṭ*) to be clamorous and noisy; to raise a din; to shout, clamor II and IV do.

لغط *laḡṭ*, *laḡaṭ* pl. الغاط *alḡāṭ* noise, din; clamor, shouting; lamentation (عن over or for s.th.); uproar, turmoil, tumult

لغم¹ *laḡama* to mine, plant with mines (ه s.th.)

لغم *luḡm*, *laḡam* pl. الغام *alḡām* mine

لغم *laḡm* and الغام *ilḡām* mining (e.g., of a harbor, of a road, etc.)

لغم² IV to amalgamate, alloy with mercury

لغام *luḡām* foam, froth

الغام *ilḡām* amalgamation

لغمط *laḡmaṭa* (*eg.*) to smear, sully, soil

(لغو) لغا *laḡā u* (*laḡw*) to speak; to be null; — لغا *laḡā u* (*laḡw*) and لغى *laḡiya a* (لغا *laḡan*, لاغية *lāḡiya*, ملغاة *malḡāh*) to talk nonsense; to make mistakes (in speaking) IV to render ineffectual (ه s.th.); to declare null and void or invalid, invalidate, nullify, annul, abolish, abrogate, eliminate (ه s.th.), do away (ه with s.th.); to cancel (ه a project); to withdraw (ه permission, a motion)

لغو *laḡw* foolish talk; nonsense; null, nugatory, ineffectual; mistake, blunder, ungrammatical language

لغة *luḡa* pl. *-āt* language; dialect; idiom; vernacular; lingo, jargon; word; expression, term; اللغة classical Arabic | لغة اجنبية (*ajnabīya*) foreign language; لغة عامية (*ʿāmmīya*) popular language; لغة الكتابة literary language; لغة المحادثة *l. al-muḥādaṯa* colloquial language; لغة المهنة *l. al-mihna* professional jargon, slang; لغة المولد *l. al-maulid* mother tongue; اهل اللغة *ahl al-l.* philologists, lexicographers; علم اللغة *'ilm al-l.* lexicography, philology, linguistic science, linguistics

لغوة *lağwa* dialect, idiom, vernacular

لغوى *luğawī* linguistic; philologic(al); lexicographic(al); philologist, lexicographer, linguist; لغويات linguistic matters, philologica

الغاء *ilğā'* abolishment, abolition, abrogation, repeal, elimination, cancellation, revocation, rescission; annulment, nullification, quashing; countermand

لاغ *lāğin* abrogated, repealed, annulled, canceled, invalid, ineffective, null and void

لاغية *lāğiya* grammatical mistake, incorrect usage

ملغى *mulğan* abrogated, repealed, annulled, canceled, invalid, void; abolished; expired; suppressed; negligible

لف *laffa u* (*laff*) to wrap up, roll up, fold up (ه s.th.); to wind, coil, spool, reel (ه s.th.); to wind (ه على s.th. on; ه حول s.th. around), twist, wrap, fold (ه حول s.th. around); to envelop (ه في or ب s.th. in or with), cover, swathe, swaddle (ه s.th. ب or في in or with), wrap, infold (ب or ه في s.th. in); to connect (ه ب s.th. with), join, attach (ه ب s.th. to); to grow densely, be overgrown, form a tangled mass; to make a round of calls (على on), visit (على people); (*eg.*) to go around s.th. (ه), go about s.th. (ه) in a roundabout way, make a detour, beat about the bush | لف لفه (*laffahū*) to do just like s.o., be of the same kind as s.o., belong to the same sort as s.o. **II** to wrap up or infold tightly **V** to wrap o.s. up (في in), cover o.s. (في with) **VIII** do.; to wind, twist, coil; to turn, make a turn (automobile, etc.); to intertwine, grow in a tangled mass; to gather, assemble, rally (حول around); to clasp, enclose, encircle, embrace (ب s.th.)

لف ***laff*** winding, coiling; wrapping, enfolding; rolling, folding; (*eg.*) circumambience, circumvention, detour, roundabout way, subterfuge, dodge, excuses; pl. الفاف ***alfāf*** swaddling clothes, diapers | اللف والدوران (***dawarān***) detours and evasions; لف ونشر (***našr***) folding and unfolding; involution and evolution (***rhet.***); من غير لف without much ado, without ceremony

لف ***liff*** pl. الفاف ***alfāf*** densely growing trees; pl. thicket, scrub, undergrowth, brushwood

لفة ***laffa*** pl. ***-āt*** turn, rotation, revolution; coil, twist, convolution, whorl, spire; winding; roll, scroll; pack, packet, package, bundle, bale; turban | لفة بريدية (***barīdīya***) postal package; لفات من الرق (***ruqq***) parchment scrolls

لفافة ***lifāfa*** pl. ***-āt***, لفائف ***lafā'if***² wrapping, covering, cover, envelope; wrapper, wrap; altar cloth, cloth covering the paten and chalice (***Copt.-Chr.***); bandage; swaddling band; puttee; cigarette (also لفافة من التبغ ***l. min at-tibğ***); pl. لفائف (fig.) guise (of s.th.)

لفيف ***lafīf*** gathered, assembled; crowded, thronging; multitude, crowd, swarm, body, cluster, group (من of people); mixed company | لفيف الناس mob, rabble, riffraff; اللفيف الاجنبي (***ajnabī***) the Foreign Legion

لفيفة ***lafīfa*** bundle; package, packet, pack; cigarette

الف ***alaff***², f. لفاء ***laffā'***² stout, plump (figure, body)

ملف ***milaff*** pl. ***-āt*** reel, spool; coil (***el.***); winding; wrapping, covering, casing; blanket, sleeping blanket; cover, wrapper, jacket (of a book, etc.); (letter) envelope; folder, portfolio; letter file;

dossier | ○ ملف التأثير induction coil (*el.*); ○ ملف ابتدائى (*ibtidā'ī*) primary coil (*el.*); ○ ملف خانق choking coil, choke (*el.*)

ملفاف **milfāf** wrapping, covering, cover

تلفيف **talfīf** pl. تلافيف **talāfīf**[2] winding; coil, twist, convolution, whorl, spire; pl. تلافيف expletive after فى, e.g., فى تلافيف سويدائها (*suwaidā'ihā*) in the depth of her heart; فى تلافيف الظلام (*ẓalām*) in the dark; بين تلافيفه in it, inside it, around in it

التفاف **iltifāf** turn; bypassing, outflanking, flank movement, envelopment, surrounding

ملفوف **malfūf** wound, coiled; wrapped up (فى in); rolled up, rolled together, convolute; twisted, wound (على around); fastened, attached (على to); swathed (ب in or with); plump, stout (body); (*syr.*) cabbage

ملتف **multaff** winding, twisting, coiling; wound, coiled; rolled up, rolled together, convolute; spirally wound; intertwined, interwoven, entwined; gathered, assembled, grouped (حول around); clasping, enclosing, embracing, encircling (ب s.th.)

لفت **lafata** i (*laft*) and IV to turn, bend, tilt, incline, direct (ه الى s.th. to or toward), focus (ه الى s.th. on); to turn away, avert (ه عن s.th. from) | لفت نظره الى (*naẓarahū*), الفت نظره الى to turn one's eyes or one's attention to; to direct s.o.'s eyes to, call s.o.'s attention to; لفت النظر to catch the eye, attract attention; to be impressive, stately, imposing; الفت النظر do.; لفت الناس to attract, interest, or captivate people V to turn, turn around, turn one's face (الى to); to look around, glance around; to peer around | تلفت حوله (*ḥaulahū*) to look around, glance around; تلفت يمنة ويسرة (*yamnatan wa-yasratan*) he looked to the right and left VIII to turn, turn around, turn one's face (الى to); to wheel around, turn around; to address o.s. (الى to); to pay attention, attend (الى to), heed, observe, bear in mind, consider, take into account, take into consideration (الى s.th.); to take care (الى of), care (الى for) | التفت حوله (*ḥaulahū*) to look around, glance about X to attract (ه the eyes, attention); to claim, arouse, awaken (ه the interest, the attention, من of s.o.) | استلفت نظره (or انظاره) to arouse or attract s.o.'s attention, catch s.o.'s eye

لفت **lift** turnip (Brassica rapa L.; *bot.*)

لفتة **lafta** (n. un.) turnabout, about-face; (pl. *lafatāt*) turn, turning; gesture; sideglance, glance, a furtive, casual, or quick, look

لفات **lafāt** and لفوت **lafūt** ill-tempered, surly, sullen

الفت **alfat**[2], f. لفتاء **laftā'**[2], pl. لفت **luft** left-handed

التفات **iltifāt** turn, inclination, turning (الى to, toward); attention, notice, heed; regard; consideration; care, solicitude; sudden transition (*styl.*) | بدون الالتفات *bi-dūni l-ilt.* inattentive(ly); بدون الالتفات الى inconsiderate of, without consideration for; عدم الالتفات *'adam al-ilt.* inattention; نظر اليه بعين الالتفات (*bi-'aini l-ilt.*) to give s.th. sympathetic consideration

التفاتة **iltifāta** (n. vic.) a turning (الى to, toward); turn of the face or eyes; sideglance, glance

استلفات **istilfāt** stimulation of attention

لافتة **lāfita** sign (bearing an inscription)

ملفت **mulfit**: ملفت النظر (*naẓar*) attracting attention, striking, conspicuous

ملتفت **multafit** turning around, looking (الى at); regardful; attentive; heedful, careful; considerate

لفح **lafaḥa** a (*lafḥ*, لفحان *lafaḥān*) to burn, scorch, sear (ه, ه s.o., s.th.); — (*lafḥ*) to strike lightly; to touch, brush (ه s.th., e.g., of the breath)

لفحة *lafḥa* pl. *lafaḥāt* fire, heat (esp., of fever)

لفوح *lafūḥ* and لافح *lāfiḥ* pl. لوافح *lawāfiḥ*[2] burning, scorching, searing

لفاح *luffāḥ* mandrake (Mandragora officinarum; *bot.*)

لفظ *lafaẓa i* (*lafẓ*) to emit (ب, ه s.th.); to spit out (ب, ه s.th.); to eject (ب, ه s.th.); to throw (ه s.o.) out (من of); to speak, enunciate, articulate; to pronounce, utter, express, voice, say (ب, ه s.th.) | لفظ النفس الاخير (*nafas*) to breathe one's last, die, expire; to be in the throes of death; لفظ انفاسه (*anfāsahū*) to be in the throes of death, breathe one's last; لفظه لفظ النواة (*lafẓa n-nawāh*) to spit s.th. out like a date pit, brush s.th. aside, reject s.th., dismiss s.th. V to pronounce, enunciate, articulate (ب s.th.)

لفظ *lafẓ* pl. الفاظ *alfāẓ* sound-group, phonetic complex; expression, term; word; wording; formulation; articulation, enunciation, pronunciation; لفظا verbatim, literally | لفظا ومعنى (*ma'nan*) in letter and spirit; اخطأ اللفظ (*akṭa'a*) to mispronounce

لفظى *lafẓī* of or pertaining to words, verbal; literal; pronounced; oral

لفظة *lafẓa* pl. *lafaẓāt* word; utterance, saying

لفيظ *lafīẓ* ejected, emitted; pronounced, uttered

تلفظ *taluffuẓ* pronunciation, enunciation, articulation

ملفوظ *malfūẓ* ejected, emitted; pronounced, uttered

لفع *lafa'a a* (*laf'*): لفع الشيب رأسه *l. š-šaibu ra'sahū* grey hair covered his head II to cover (ه s.th., ب with) | لفع الشيب رأسه *l. š-šaibu ra'sahū* = I; V and VIII to wrap o.s. up (ب in)

ملفع *milfa'* head shawl, muffler

لفق II to invent, fabricate (ه s.th.); to concoct, contrive, devise, think out (ه s.th.); to falsify (ه s.th.); to trump up (ه s.th.); to patch up, piece together (ه ,ب s.th. with)

تلفيق *talfīq* invention, fabrication, concoction, fibbing; falsification

تلفيقة *talfīqa* pl. *-āt* invented story, fib, yarn

ملفق *mulaffaq* invented, fabricated, trumped up, fake, fictitious; concocted, contrived, devised; patched up, pieced together; embellished with lies

لفلف *laflafa* to wrap up, envelop, cover (ه s.th.) II *talaflafa* to wrap o.s. up (ب, فى in)

لفو IV to find (ه, ه s.o., s.th.) VI to put right, to right, repair, correct (ه s.th.); to make good (ه a deficiency), eliminate, remove (ه a danger); to remedy (ه s.th.); to redress (ه a loss, and the like), make up (ه for a loss)

ملافاة *mulāfāh* correction, adjustment, elimination (of a deficiency)

تلاف *talāfin* repair, correction; elimination, removal (of a deficiency, of a danger); remedy; redress, reparation

لقب II to call, surname (ب ه s.o. by an agnomen or title) V to be surnamed (ب by an agnomen or title)

لقب *laqab* pl. القاب *alqāb* agnomen; nickname; title, honorific; last name, surname, family name (as opposed to اسم *ism* given name, first name) | لقب البطولة title of champion (in sports)

ملقب *mulaqqab* surnamed, nicknamed, called (ب by the *laqab* ...)

لقح *laqaḥa a* (*laqḥ*) and **II** to impregnate, fecundate, pollinate (ه s.th.); to graft, bud (ه a tree); to inoculate, vaccinate (ه s.o.) **VI** to cross-pollinate

لقح *laqḥ* impregnation, fecundation, pollination

لقاح *laqāḥ* seed, semen, sperm; pollen; infective agent, virus; vaccine | لقاح الجدرى *l. al-judarī* variolovaccine; ○ لقاح الوقاية serum

تلقيح *talqīḥ* impregnation, fecundation, pollination, grafting, budding; inoculation, vaccination | تلقيح الجدرى *t. al-judarī* vaccination (against smallpox)

دقيق اللواقح *daqīq al-lawāqiḥ* pollen

ملقح *mulaqqaḥ* inoculated, vaccinated

لقس *laqis*. لقس النفس *l. an-nafs* annoyed, cross

لقط *laqaṭa u* (*laqṭ*) to gather, collect, pick up from the ground, glean (ه s.th.) **II** = **I** **V** to gather, glean (ه s.th.); to pick up (ه s.th., also, e.g., with the ear) **VIII** = **I**; to receive (ه radio waves, a radio message; to take (ه a picture; *phot.*) | التقط صورة (*ṣūra*) to make a picture

لقط *laqaṭ* that which is picked up or gathered, leftovers, gleanings

لقطة *luqṭa* that which is picked up or gleaned, gleanings; article or thing found; (lucky) find; (*eg.*) bargain, pickup

لقاط *luqāṭ* and لقاطة *luqāṭa* that which is picked up or gleaned; leftover ears of grain, gleanings; offal, refuse

لقيط *laqīṭ* pl. لقطاء *luqaṭā'*[2] picked up, found; foundling

لقيطة *laqīṭa* (female) foundling

ملقط *milqaṭ* pl. ملاقط *malāqiṭ*[2] (pair of) tongs, pincers; (pair of) tweezers, pincette; (pair of) pliers | ملقط الجنين forceps; ملقط النار fire tongs

التقاط *iltiqāṭ* gathering, collection, gleaning; taking up, picking up; reception (*radio*) | جهاز الالتقاط *jahāz al-ilt.* receiver (*radio*)

لاقط *lāqiṭ* receiving (radio set); gleaner; gatherer | ○ لاقط الصوت *l. aṣ-ṣaut* pickup (of a phonograph); phonograph; ○ لاقطة الالغام mine sweeper

ملتقط *multaqiṭ* finder

لقع *laqaʿa a* (*laqʿ*) to throw away, discard (ه s.th.)

لقف *laqifa a* (*laqf*, لقفان *laqafān*) to seize quickly, grab, snatch (ه s.th.); to catch (ه s.th.); to snatch up, take over (ه عن s.th. from s.o.) **V** and **VIII** do.; to seize (ه on), rob, usurp (ه s.th.)

لقلق *laqlaqa* to clatter (stork); to babble, chatter, prattle

لقلق *laqlaq* and لقلاق *laqlāq* pl. لقالق *laqāliq*[2] stork

لقلقة *laqlaqa* clatter (of a stork); babble, chatter, prattle; (*eg.*) gossip

[1]لقم *laqama u* (*laqm*) to clog up, obstruct, block (ه s.th.); — *laqima a* (*laqm*) to eat, devour, gobble, swallow up (ه s.th.) **II** to feed bit by bit (ه s.o.); to load (ه a weapon; *syr.*) | لقم القهوة (*qahwa*) to stir ground coffee into hot water **IV** to make (ه s.o.) swallow; to feed bit by bit (ه s.o.) **VIII** to devour, swallow up (ه s.th.)

لقمة *luqma* pl. لقم *luqam* bite; bit, mouthful; little piece, morsel | لقمة سائغة titbit, choice morsel; جعله لقمة سائغة ل (*jaʿalahū*) to make s.o. an easy prey of ...; لقمة القاضى pastry of fine flour, fried in oil like doughnuts and sprinkled with sugar or honey

لقيمة *luqaima* pl. *-āt* snack, bit, morsel

ملقم *mulaqqim* pl. *-ūn* (*Syr.*; *mil.*) assistant gunner, loader, cannoneer no. 1

[2]لقمى *laqmī* or لاقمى (*maġr.*) palm wine

[3]لقمان *luqmān*[2] Lokman, a legendary sage and author of numerous fables | بقيت دار لقمان على حالها (*baqiyat*) everything has remained as before

لقن **laqina** *a* (لقانة *laqāna*, لقانية *laqāniya*) to understand, grasp (ه s.th.); to gather, infer, note (ه s.th.) **II** to teach (ه ٥ s.o. s.th.), instruct (ه ٥ s.o. in); to dictate (ه ٥ to s.o. s.th.); to instill, infuse, inculcate, inspire (ه ٥ in s.o. s.th.), insinuate, suggest (ه ٥ to s.o. s.th.); to whisper (ه ٥ to s.o. s.th.), prompt (٥ s.o.) **V** = **I**; to learn, receive, get (ه من s.th. from), be informed (ه من of s.th. by)

لقانة **laqāna** and لقانية **laqāniya** quick understanding, grasp

تلقين **talqīn** instruction, direction; dictation; dictate; inspiration, insinuation, suggestion; suborning of a witness (*Isl. Law*)

ملقن **mulaqqin** prompter; inspirer; a *faqīh* who instructs the deceased at his grave what to tell the two angels of death

لقوة *laqwa* facial paralysis

لقى **laqiya** *a* (لقاء *liqā'*, لقيان *luqyān*, لقى *luqy*, لقية *luqya*, لقى *luqan*) to encounter (ه, ٥ s.o., s.th.), meet (ه, ٥ with s.o., with s.th.); to meet (٥ s.o.); to come across s.o. or s.th. (ه, ٥), light upon s.o. or s.th. (ه, ٥); to find (ه, ٥ s.o., s.th.); to experience, undergo, suffer, endure (ه s.th.), meet with s.th. (ه); to fall to s.o.'s (٥) lot or share **III** to meet, come to meet (٥ s.o.); to encounter (٥ s.o.), have an encounter (٥ with); to come across s.o. or s.th. (ه, ٥), light upon s.o. or s.th. (ه, ٥); to experience, undergo, suffer, endure (ه s.th.), meet (ه with s.th.); to receive, get, obtain, achieve (ه s.th.) | لاقى آذانا صاغية (*ṣāǵiyatan*) to find willing ears **IV** to throw, cast, fling (ه s.th.); to throw off, throw down, drop (ه s.th.); to throw away, discard (ه s.th.); to put or lay (ه s.th.) before s.o. (على), submit (ه على s.th. to s.o.), pose (ه على a question to s.o.); to report (على or ه الى on s.th. to s.o.), set forth (على or ه الى s.th. to s.o.); to recite, play, sing (ه a song, a musical composition); to present (ه s.th., e.g., a broadcast); to give (ه a lecture), hold (ه a class), make, deliver (ه a speech); to extend (ه a greeting, الى to s.o.); to impose, lay (ه على s.th. on s.o.), burden (ه على with s.th. s.o.) | القى باله الى ,القى بالا ل to pay attention to; القى بيانا عن (*bayānan*) to make a statement about or on; القى البيض (*baiḍ*) to lay eggs; القى بزمامه الى (*bi-zimāmihī*) or القى مقاليد امره الى فلان (*m. amrihī*) to lay one's fate in s.o.'s hands, entrust one's fate to s.o.; القى بنفسه فى (*bi-nafsihī*) to throw o.s. into, plunge into; القى بنفسه فى احضانه (*aḥḍānihī*) to throw o.s. into s.o.'s arms; القى بيده الى (*bi-yadihī*) to surrender to s.o., give o.s. up to s.o.; القى الحبل على الغارب (*ḥabl*) to give free rein, give a free hand, impose no restraint; القى خطابا على to make a public address to; القى الدرس (*dars*) to recite the lesson; القى الرعب فى قلبه (*ruʿb, qalbihī*) to strike terror to s.o.'s heart, frighten, alarm s.o.; القى السلاح to lay down one's arms, capitulate, surrender; القى السمع اليه (*samʿ*) to lend one's ear to s.o., listen to s.o.; القوا اليه اسماعهم (*asmāʿahum*) they lent him their ears, they listened to him; القى عليه سؤالا (*su'ālan*) to put a question to s.o., ask s.o. a question; القى على عاتقه شيئا to impose s.th. on s.o., hold s.o. responsible for; القى علوما to teach sciences; القى القبض على (*qabḍ*) to arrest s.o.; القى القنابل على to drop bombs on s.th., bomb s.th.; القى عليه القول (*qaul*) to dictate to s.o.; to direct, instruct s.o., give s.o. instructions; القى عليها كلمة الطلاق (*kalimata ṭ-ṭalāq*) he pronounced the formula of divorce against her; القى محاضرة (*muḥāḍara*) to give a lecture, hold a class; القى المسؤولية عليه

(*mas'ūlīya*) to place the responsibility on s.o., saddle s.o. with the responsibility **V** to receive (ه, ه s.o., s.th.); to take, accept (ه s.th.); to get, obtain (ه s.th.); to learn (ه عن of s.th. from), be informed (ه عن of s.th. by); to learn (على or عن ه s.th. from s.o.), take lessons (عن from s.o.), be taught, be instructed, be coached (عن by s.o.) | تلقى امرا (*amran*) to receive an order, have orders (soldier); تلقّى الاوامر to take orders (*com.*, and the like); تلقاه بالتسليم والقبول (*qabūl*) to agree wholeheartedly to s.th., submit willingly to s.th.; تلقى دروسا فى to take lessons in (some field, art, science, etc.); تلقى العلوم فى الجامعة to study at the university **VI** to meet, join each other, come together, get together **VIII** do.; to encounter, meet (ب s.o.) **X** to throw o.s. down; to lie down, lie

لقى *laqan* pl. القاء *alqā'* offal, discard

لقية *luqya* encounter, meeting; *luqya*, *laqīya* s.th. found, a find

لقيا *luqyā* encounter, meeting

لقاية *liqāya* encounter, meeting; s.th. found, a find

القية *ulqīya* riddle, conundrum

تلقاء *tilqā'a* (prep.) opposite; in front of | من تلقاء نفسه *min tilqā'i nafsihi* or من تلقاء ذاته by o.s., of one's own accord, spontaneously, automatically

تلقائى *tilqā'ī* automatic; spontaneous; تلقائيا spontaneously, automatically

ملقى *malqan* pl. ملاق *malāqin* meeting place, rendezvous; junction, crossing, intersection; road or street intersection, crossroads

لقاء *liqā'* encounter; meeting; get-together; reunion; *liqā'a* (prep.) in exchange for, in return for, for, on | لقاء كفالة (*kafāla*) on bail; الى اللقاء good-by! so long! au revoir!

ملاقاة *mulāqāh* encounter, meeting, get-together, reunion; reception

القاء *ilqā'* throwing, casting, throw, cast, fling; delivery, diction; dictation; recitation, recital | علم الالقاء *'ilm al-i.* elocution

تلق *talaqqin* receipt, reception, acceptance; acquisition (also of a skill, of knowledge, etc.); learning (of an art, skill, etc.); pursuit (of studies) | تلق العلوم فى studies at (e.g., at a university)

تلاق *talāqin* meeting, encounter

التقاء *iltiqā'* meeting, reunion (مع with)

ملق *mulqin*: ملقيات الالغام البحرية *mulqiyāt al-a. al-baḥrīya* mine layers

ملقى *mulqan* thrown, cast, discarded

ملتقى *multaqan* pl. ملتقيات *multaqayāt* meeting place, rendezvous; gathering point, collecting center; intersection, junction, confluence, crossroads | الى الملتقى good-by! so long! au revoir!

¹لك *lakka u* (*lakk*) to hit with the fist, to cuff, buffet, pommel (ه s.o.) **VIII** to be pressed together, thickly set, crammed, jammed, crowded; to crowd together, gather in a mass; to make mistakes or blunders, speak ungrammatically

²لك *lakk* pl. الكاك *alkāk*, لكوك *lukūk* lac, one hundred thousand (specif., 100,000 rupees)

³لك *lukk*, *lakk* resin; lac; sealing wax

لكأ *laka'a a* (لكء *lak'*) to strike, hit; — لكئ *laki'a a* (لكأ *laka'*) to abide, remain, stay (ب at a place) **V** to be tardy, dilatory, slow, to dawdle, tarry, hesitate (فى in s.th.); to loiter, loaf, hang about | تلكأ فى الاداء (*adā'*) to be in default, fail to meet one's financial obligations

لكاء *luka'a* hesitant, tardy, dilatory, sluggish, slow; behindhand, in arrears, defaulting

لكز *lakaza* u (*lakz*) to strike with the fist; to kick (ه s.o.); to thrust (ه s.o.)

لكز *lakiz* miserly, stingy

لكاز *likāz* pin; nail; peg

لكيع *lakī'* pl. لكعاء *luka'ā'*[2] mean, base, ignominious, disgraceful, wicked, depraved; silly, foolish

لكاعة *lakā'a* meanness, baseness, disgracefulness, wickedness, depravity

لكم *lakama* u (*lakm*) to strike with the fist, box, punch III to engage in a fist fight, box (ه with s.o.)

لكمة *lakma* pl. *lakamāt* blow with the fist, punch

ملكمة *milkama* boxing glove

ملاكمة *mulākama* fist fight, boxing match

ملاكم *mulākim* boxer, pugilist, prize fighter

[1]لكن *lakina* a (*lakan*, لكنة *lukna*, لكونة *lukūna*, لكنونة *luknūna*) to speak incorrectly, barbarously; to stammer

لكنة *lukna* stutter, stammer; incorrect usage, ungrammatical language; incorrect pronunciation

لكانة *lakāna*: لكانة فى الكلام (*kalām*) speech defect; faltering way of speaking

الكن *alkan*[2], f. لكناء *laknā'*[2], pl. لكن *lukn* speaking incorrectly; stammering, stuttering

[2]لكن *lakan* pl. الكان *alkān* basin, copper basin

[3]لكن *lākin*, *lākinna* see لاكن

لكى *li-kai*, لكيما *li-kai-mā* see ل *li*

[1]لم *lam* (particle; with foll. apoc.) not | لم يكتب *lam yaktub* he did not write; ألم *a-lam* not ... though? ألم اقل لكم (*aqul*) haven't I told you, though? لم — الا *lam — illā* only, nothing but, just; not till not before

[2]لم *lima* = لما *li-mā*, see ل *li*

[3]لم *lamma* u (*lamm*) to gather, collect, assemble (ه s.th.); to reunite (ه s.th.); to arrange, settle, put in order (ه s.th.); to repair (ه s.th.); pass. *lumma* to suffer from or be stricken by a slight mental derangement | لم شعثه (*ša'aṯahū*) to put s.th. in order again, straighten s.th. out, put s.th. right; to recover, pick up; to help s.o. get back on his feet; لم شمل القطيع (*šamla l-q.*) to round up the herd IV to befall, overcome (fatigue, fear, weakness, adversities, etc.; ب s.o.); to pay (ب s.o.) a short visit, call (ب on s.o.), stop, stay (ب at s.o.'s house); to have sexual intercourse (ب with s.o.); to broach (ب a topic), speak (ب about), discuss (ب s.th.); to give a survey (ب of), outline, state briefly (ب s.th.); to touch briefly (ب on a subject); to be acquainted or familiar (ب with s.th.); to get to know (ب s.th.); to familiarize o.s., acquaint o.s. (ب with s.th.); to commit, perpetrate (ب a crime); to take, consume (ب food, drink) VIII to gather, assemble, rally; to unite; to visit (ه s.o.), call (ه on)

لمة *lamma* pl. لمام *limām* collection; gathering, assembly; visit, call; misfortune, calamity; slight mental derangement, touch of insanity

لمة *limma* pl. لمم *limam* curl, ringlet, lock

لمة *lumma* traveling party; group, troop, body (of people)

لمم *lamam* slight mental derangement

لماما *limāman* occasionally, from time to time, rarely, seldom

لمام *lammām* wild thyme (*bot.*)

المام *ilmām* knowledge, cognizance (ب of s.th.); acquaintance, familiarity, conversance (ب with); (pl. *-āt*) survey, outline, summary, résumé

لامة *lāmma* evil eye

ملموم *malmūm* collected, gathered, assembled; concentrated at one point; slightly insane

ملم *mulimm* completely familiar, conversant (ب with); expert, connoisseur | ملم بالقراءة والكتابة literate

ملمة *mulimma* pl. *-āt* misfortune, calamity, disaster

[1]لما *li-mā* see ل *li*

[2]لما *lammā* (conj.) when, as, after; since, whereas; (particle; with foll. apoc.) not, not yet

لمباجو (Engl.) *lambāgō* lumbago

لمبة *lamba* pl. *-āt* lamp; tube (*radio*)

لمج V to take a snack

لمجة *lumja* appetizer, hors d'oeuvre, relish, snack

لمح *lamaḥa a* (*lamḥ*) to glance (الى or ه at s.o.); to see, sight, behold, notice (ه s.o., ه s.th.); to become aware (ان that); — (*lamḥ*, لمحان *lamaḥān*, تلماح *talmāḥ*) to flash, sparkle, glisten, shimmer **II** to insinuate, intimate, give to understand (الى s.th.), hint (الى at), allude, refer (الى to) **III** to cast a casual or furtive glance (ه at s.o.) **IV** to glance casually or furtively (الى or ه at s.o.)

لمح *lamḥ* quick look, glance; moment, instant | لمح البصر *l. al-baṣar* glance of the eye; دون لمح البصر ,كلمح البصر ,فى لمح البصر, فى اقل من لمح البصر (*aqalla*) like lightning, in a trice, instantly, in no time

لمحة *lamḥa* pl. *lamaḥāt* quick, casual look, glance; wink; glow of light, light, brightness, flash (of lightning) | فيه لمحة من ابيه (*abīhi*) he looks like his father

لماح *lammāḥ* shimmering, gleaming, shining

ملامح *malāmiḥ²* features, lineaments; traits; outward appearance, looks | فيه ملامح من ابيه (*abīhi*) he looks like his father; ملامح وظلال (*ẓilāl*) lights and shades (in painting)

تلميح *talmīḥ* pl. تلاميح *talāmīḥ²* allusion, intimation, insinuation, hint, reference; تلميحا by way of suggestion, indirectly

لمز *lamaza u i* (*lamz*) to give (ه s.o.) a wink; to speak ill (ه of s.o.), carp (ه at s.o.), find fault (ه with s.o.), criticize, blame, censure, backbite, slander, defame (ه s.o.)

لمزة *lumaza* and لماز *lammāz* faultfinder, captious critic, caviler, carper

[1]لمس *lamasa u i* (*lams*) to touch, handle, feel with the hand, finger (ه s.th.), pass one's hand (ه over s.th.); to seek (ه s.th.), look, search, ask (ه for); to perceive, notice (ه s.th., ان that), become aware (ه of s.th., ان that) | لا يلمس (*yulmasu*) intangible, impalpable; لمس الحقائق to take things as they are, face the facts **III** to be in touch or contact (ه, ه with s.o., with s.th.); to touch, feel, finger, palpate (ه, ه s.o., s.th.); to have sexual intercourse (ها with a woman) **V** to feel out, finger, palpate (ه s.th.); to fumble, grope about; to grope, fumble (ه for s.th.); to look, search (ه for); to ask (ه for) **VI** to touch each other, be in mutual contact **VIII** to request (ه من s.th. from s.o., ل for s.o.), ask (ه من for s.th. s.o.), solicit (ه ل s.th. for); to beg (ه for), request urgently (ه s.th.); to seek (ه s.th.), look, search (ه, ه for s.th., for s.o.)

لمس *lams* feeling, groping; touching, touch | حاسة اللمس *ḥāssat al-l.* sense of touch

لمسى *lamsī* tactual, tactile, of or pertaining to the sense of touch

لمسية *lamsīya* (*tun.*) date which has not attained full ripeness

لمسة *lamsa* (n. vic.) touch; (pl. *-āt*) retouch

لميس *lamīs* soft to the touch

ملمس *malmas* pl. ملامس *malāmis*[2] place of touch, spot touched, point of contact; ○ feeler, tentacle (of insects); touch; contact | ناعم الملمس soft to the touch

ملمسى *malmasī* tactual, tactile

ملامسة *mulāmasa* touching, touch, contact; feeling, fingering, palpation; sexual intercourse

تلمس *talammus* search, quest

التماس *iltimās* request, solicitation; application, petition

ملموس *malmūs* touched, felt; palpable, tangible; ملموسات things perceptible to the touch, tangible things

ملتمس *multamas* pl. *-āt* request, petition, application

الماس[2] look up alphabetically

لمص **lamaṣa** *u* (*lamṣ*) to rail (ه at s.o.); to make faces (ه at s.o.)

لمظ **lamaẓa** *u* (*lamẓ*) to lick one's lips; to smack one's lips **V** do. | تلمظ بذكره (*bi-ḏikrihī*) to speak ill of s.o., backbite s.o.

لمع **lama'a** (*lam'*, لمعان *lama'ān*) to gleam, glitter, twinkle, flash, sparkle, glisten, shimmer, shine | لمع بسيفه (*bi-saifihī*) to brandish the sword; لمع بيده (*bi-yadihī*) to wave one's hand; لمع فى رأسه خاطر (*ḵāṭirun*) a thought flashed through his mind **II** to cause (ه s.th.) to shine, gleam, or twinkle; to shine (ه s.th.), give brightness (ه to s.th.); to polish (ه s.th.); to burnish (ه s.th.) **IV** to wave (one's hand); to point out, give to understand, intimate, insinuate (الى s.th.), hint (الى at), allude (الى to) **VIII** to flash, radiate, glow, shine; to sparkle, glitter, gleam

لمع *lam'* and لمعان *lama'ān* luster, sheen, shine; shimmer, gleam, glow, brightness, light

لمعة *lum'a* pl. لمع *luma'*, لماع *limā'* shimmer, gleam, glow, flash, sparkle, glitter, brilliancy, radiance, beam; gloss, luster, burnish, polish; some, a little

لماع *lammā'* bright, brilliant, lustrous, sparkling, flashing, glistening, shining, radiant; ○ glossy, glazed, burnished, polished, satined, calendered (*techn.*) | جلد لماع (*jild*) patent leather

ألمع *alma'*[2] and ألمعى *alma'ī* sagacious, smart, shrewd, clever, bright, intelligent; — ألمع *alma'*[2] more lustrous, shinier

ألمعية *alma'īya* sagacity, smartness, shrewdness, cleverness, brightness, intelligence

تلميع *talmī'* polishing, polish

إلماعة *ilmā'a* allusion, hint

لامع *lāmi'* pl. لوامع *lawāmi'*[2] brilliant, lustrous, shining, gleaming, shimmering

لامعة *lāmi'a* fontanel (*anat.*); (pl. لوامع *lawāmi'*[2]) gloss, shine

متلمع *mutalammi'* radiant, brilliant, shining, lustrous

لملم **lamlama** to gather, gather up (ه s.th.)

ململمة *mulamlima* trunk, proboscis (of the elephant)

لن **lan** (conj.; with foll. subj.) not (referring to the future)

جديد لنج (*eg.*) *gadīd lang* brand-new

لندرة **lundra** London

لندن **landan** London

لنش (Engl.) **lanš** pl. *-āt* launch, small steamer, motorboat

لنينغراد **leninġrād** Leningrad

لهب **lahiba** *a* (*lahb*, *lahab*, لهاب *luhāb*, لهيب *lahīb*, لهبان *lahabān*) to flame, burn, blaze **II** and **IV** to kindle, light, set on fire, ignite, inflame (ه s.th.); to excite, stir up, provoke (ه s.th.) **V** to flame; to be aflame, be ablaze, burn (also fig.: cheek, anger, thirst, etc.) **VIII** = **V**; to catch fire, flare up; to be inflamed (also *med.*)

لهب ***lahab***, لهيب ***lahīb*** and لهاب ***luhāb*** flame, blaze, flare

لهبان ***lahbān***², f. لهبى ***lahbā***, pl. لهاب ***lihāb*** parched with thirst

الهاب ***ilhāb*** kindling, lighting, ignition, inflammation

التهاب ***iltihāb*** burning; inflammation (also *med.*); in compounds corresponding to Engl. "-itis" | التهاب الشعب ***ilt. aš-šu'ab*** bronchitis

التهابى ***iltihābī*** inflammatory; inflammable

ملتهب ***multahib*** burning, flaming, blazing, aflame, ablaze; inflamed; heated, excited, glowing, aglow | قطن ملتهب (*quṭn*) guncotton

لاهوت look up alphabetically

لهث **lahaṯa** *a* (*lahṯ*, لهاث *luhāṯ*) to loll one's tongue with thirst or fatigue; to pant, gasp, be out of breath; to breathe heavily

لهاث ***luhāṯ*** panting, pant, gasp | لهاث الموت ***l. al-maut*** death rattle, agony of death

لهثان ***lahṯān***², f. لهثى ***lahṯā*** panting, gasping, out of breath; thirsty

لهج **lahija** *a* (*lahaj*) to be devoted, dedicated (ب to s.th.), be attached (ب to s.o., to s.th.), be very fond (ب of), be in love (ب with); to be bent, be intent, be keen (ب on), be eager (ب for), be mad (ب about, after); to do (ب s.th.) constantly or fervently | لهج بالثناء عليه (*ṯanā'*) to extol s.o. fervently; لهج بذكره (*bi-ḏikrihī*) to speak constantly of s.o., mention s.o.'s name continually with praise; لهج بشكره (*bi-šukrihī*) to launch forth into profuse thanks or praises; لهج بالضراعة (*ḍarā'a*) to resort to humble pleas **IV** causative: الهج لسانه بالشكر (*lisānahū, šukr*) to elicit profuse thanks from s.o. **XI** الهاج ***ilhājja*** to curdle, coagulate (milk)

لهجة ***lahja*** tip of the tongue; tongue; manner of speaking; tone; dialect, vernacular; language | بلهجة العاتب in a reproachful tone, reproachingly; شديد اللهجة in violent language, sharply worded

لهجة ***luhja*** appetizer, hors d'oeuvre

لهد **lahada** *a* (*lahd*) to overburden, overexert (ه s.o.)

لهذم **lahḏam** sharp, pointed

لهط **lahaṭa** *a* (*lahṭ*) to slap

لهف **lahifa** *a* (*lahaf*) to sigh (على for s.th. lost); to regret, deplore, lament (على s.th.); to grieve (على for), fret, worry (على about) **V** do.; to be eager, yearn (على for, also ل), pant (على after, also ل)

لهف ***lahf*** regret, grief, sorrow | يا لهف ***yā lahfa*** and يا لهفا ***yā lahfā*** oh, what a pity! too bad! alas! يا لهف (with foll. genit. of pers.) oh, how unfortunate he is! يا لهفى عليك (*lahfī*) oh, how sorry I feel for you!

لهفة ***lahfa*** sigh, lament; anxiety, apprehension, concern, worry, sorrow, grief; yearning, longing, hankering, desire, impatience

لهفان ***lahfān***², f. لهفى ***lahfā***, pl. لهافى ***lahāfā***, لهف ***luhuf*** sighing; regretful; sad, sorry, worried, sorrowful, grieved; longing, yearning

لهيف ***lahīf*** pl. لهاف ***lihāf*** regretful, sorry, sad, worried, sorrowful, grieved

لاهف ***lāhif*** worried, troubled, sorrowful, grieved, full of regret

ملهوف ***malhūf*** worried, troubled, depressed; apprehensive, concerned, anxious; covetous, eager (الى or على for), desirous (الى or على of); longing, yearning

متلهف *mutalahhif* yearning, longing, hankering; anxious, eager, impatient

لهق *lahiqa a* to be snow-white

لهلق *lahlaqa* to loll one's tongue with thirst

لهم *lahima a* (*lahm*, *laham*), **V** and **VIII** to devour, gobble, swallow up (ه s.th.); to consume, destroy (ه s.th.; fire) **IV** to make (ه s.o.) swallow (ه s.th.); to inspire (ه ه s.o. with) **X** to ask (ه s.o.) for inspiration or advice; to seek to find out (ه s.th.), try to get (ه s.th.); to pray, turn (ه ه to God for)

لهم *lahim* and لهوم *lahūm* greedy, covetous, voracious, gluttonous

الهام *ilhām* pl. *-āt* inspiration; instinct

ملهم *mulham* inspired

لهو and (لهى) لها *lahā u* (*lahw*) to amuse o.s., distract o.s., divert o.s., pass or kill time (ب with s.th.); to play, toy, dally, trifle; to fritter away, trifle away, prattle away (بوقته *bi-waqtihī* one's time); to enjoy o.s., have fun, have a good time; to delight, take pleasure (الى or ب in); to enjoy, savor, relish (ب s.th.); (لهى *luhīy*, لهيان *lihyān*) to turn one's attention (عن from); to try to forget, forget, give up, renounce (عن s.th.), become oblivious (عن of); — لهى *lahiya a* (لها *lahan*) to like, love (ب s.th.), be very fond (ب of), be in love, be infatuated (ب with), be mad (ب about, after); to turn one's attention (عن from), become oblivious (عن of), forget, give up, renounce (عن s.th.); to pay no attention (عن to), be heedless (عن of) **II** to delight, amuse, divert, distract (ب ه s.o. with), divert s.o.'s (ه) attention (عن from), make (ه s.o.) oblivious (عن of); to keep, divert (عن ه s.o. from), take s.o.'s (ه) mind away (عن from) **III** to approach, be near (ه s.o.) **IV** = **II**; **V** and **VI** to amuse o.s., pass the time (ب with s.th.), take pleasure, delight (ب in); to seek distraction (ب, عن in s.th. from) **VIII** do.: to play, toy, trifle (ب with s.th.)

لهو *lahw* amusement, entertainment, diversion, distraction, pastime, pleasure, sport, fun, play | دور اللهو *dūr al-l.* and اماكن اللهو places of entertainment, amusement centers

لهاة *lahāh* pl. لهوات *lahawāt*, لهيات *lahayāt*, لهى *luhīy*, *lihīy*, لها *lahan*, لهاء *lihā'* uvula

لهوى *lahawī* velar (adj.) | الحرفان اللهويتان *al-ḥarfān al-lahawīyatān* the velars *q* and *k*

ملهاة *malhāh* object of delight; comedy | ملهاة عامية (*'āmmīya*) popular farce

ملهى *malhan* pl. ملاه *malāhin* place of entertainment, amusement center; amusement, entertainment, fun, diversion, distraction | ضريبة الملاهى admissions tax, entertainment tax

ملهى *milhan* pl. ملاه *malāhin* plaything, toy; pl. musical instruments, also آلات الملاهى

تلهية *talhiya* distraction, diversion, amusement

لاه *lāhin* (with عن) heedless, inattentive, inadvertent, oblivious, forgetful

مله *mulhin* amusing, entertaining, diverting, pleasant

لو *lau* (conj.) if (as a rule, introducing hypothetical conditional clauses) | لو ان *lau anna* (introducing nominal clauses) if; لولا *laulā* if not; لولانا if it weren't (hadn't been) for us; فيما لو *fī-mā lau* in case that; ولو *wa-lau* although, though; even if; (optative particle) if only ...! would that ...! I wish ...! لو يعلم I wish he knew! if he only knew!

لوبيا *lūbiyā* bean (*bot.*) | لوبيا بلدى (*baladī*) (*eg.*) cowpea (Vigna sinensis Endl.; *bot.*); لوبيا عافن (*eg.*) hyacinth bean, lablab (Dolichos lablab L.; *bot.*)

لوبيا *lūbiyā* Libya

لوبى *lūbī* Libyan

[1](لوت) لات *lāta*: لات حين مناص *l. ḥīnu manāṣin* it's too late to escape

[2]لوت *lūt* (*eg.*) maigre (Sciaena aquila)

(لوث) لاث *lāṯa u* (*lauṯ*) and **II** to stain, tarnish, soil, sully (ه s.th.); — *lawiṯa a* (*lawaṯ*) to be dilatory, tardy, slow; to hesitate, tarry, linger **V** to be or get stained, blotted. tarnished, soiled, sullied (ب with) **VIII** to be dilatory, tardy, slow; to be obscure, confused, complicated (على for s.o.)

لوثة *lauṯa* stain, blot, spot

لوثة *lūṯa* languor, lassitude, fatigue, faintness; passion, weakness (فى for, also with foll. genit.: for) | فيه (به) لوثة he is a little crazy, he has a bee in his bonnet

ملوث *mulawwaṯ* stained, blotted, tarnished, soiled, sullied, unclean; stricken with cholera, pestilence, etc.

ملتاث *multāṯ* mentally confused

لوج (Fr. *loge*) *lōj* pl. *-āt*, الواج *alwāj* (theater) box, loge; (masonic, etc.) lodge

(لوح) لاح *lāḥa u* (*lauḥ*) to appear, show, loom, emerge, come in sight; to become visible (ل to s.o.); to break, begin to show (dawn); to shine, gleam, glint, flash, shimmer, glimmer, sparkle; to seem, appear; to wither, singe, parch, scorch; to tan (ه s.o.; sun) | يلوح لى ان it seems to me that...; على ما يلوح as it seems, apparently **II** to make a sign, beckon, wave (ل ب or الى to s.o. with); to signal; to allude (ب to), hint (ب at), intimate, insinuate (ل ب to s.o. s.th.), give (ل ب s.o. s.th.) to understand; to flourish, brandish, swing, wave (ب s.th.); to turn grey (ه the head; of old age); to burn, tan (ه s.o.; sun); to plank, lay with planks (ه the floor) | لوح بيديه (*bi-yadaihi*) to wave with the hands **IV** to appear, show, come in sight; to shimmer, glimmer, glint, flash, sparkle; to wave, brandish, flourish, swing (ه s.th.)

لوح *lauḥ* pl. الواح *alwāḥ*, الاويح *alāwīḥ*[2] board, blackboard; slate; tablet; slab; plate, sheet; pane; plank, board; panel; small board, signboard; shoulder blade, scapula | لوح اردواز (*arduwāz*) slab of slate, slate; ○ لوح مجعد (*muja''ad*) corrugated iron; لوح الجليد block of ice; لوح حديد sheet iron; لوح زجاج *l. zujāj* sheet of glass, pane; ○ لوح متحرك (*mutaḥarrik*) springboard (in sports); لوح معدنى (*ma'dinī*) metal plate, metal sheet; لوح النافذة windowpane

لوحة *lauḥa* pl. *-āt*, الواح *alwāḥ* board; blackboard; slate; tablet; slab; plate, sheet; pane; panel; plaque; plane, surface; screen; placard, poster; picture, painting | لوحة الاسم *l. al-ism* doorplate, name plate; لوحة التوزيع switchboard (*el.*, *tel.*); لوحة الداما checkerboard; لوحة زيتية (*zaitīya*) oil painting; لوحة سوداء (*saudā'*) blackboard; bulletin board; لوحة الشطرنج *l. aš-šaṭranj* chessboard; لوحة الكتابة slate; writing tablet; blackboard

لواح *lawwāḥ* withering, singeing, parching, scorching

تلويح *talwīḥ* pl. *-āt* beckoning, waving, flourishing, brandishing; sign, signal, wink, wave; allusion; hint, intimation, insinuation; metonymy; pl. hints, references; remarks, annotations, marginal notes

لائحة *lā'iḥa* pl. *-āt*, لوائح *lawā'iḥ*[2] program, project; bill, motion (esp., in parliament); order, decree, edict; ordinance; regulation, rule; pl. لوائح outward appearance, looks, outward sign |

لائحة القانون, لائحة قانونية bill, draft law; لائحة السفر *l. as-safar* timetable, train schedule, railroad guide; لائحة الطعام *l. aṭ-ṭaʿām* (*syr.*) menu, bill of fare

ملوحة *mulawwiḥa* signal, semaphore (railroad)

ملتاح *multāḥ* sun-tanned, sunburned

(لوذ) *lāḏa u* (*lauḏ*, لواذ *liwāḏ*, *lawāḏ*, *luwāḏ*, لياذ *liyāḏ*) to take refuge, seek shelter (ب with s.o., in s.th.), have recourse, resort (ب to); to keep close (ب to), observe religiously (ب s.th.)

ملاذ *malāḏ* refuge, protection; shelter; asylum, sanctuary; protector

لائذ *lā'iḏ* one seeking shelter or protection, refugee

لوذع and لوذعى see لذع

لور *lūr* lyre

لورد (Engl.) *lord* pl. *-āt* lord

لورى (Engl.) lorry, truck

لوز II to stuff with almonds (▲ s.th.); (*eg.*) to form bolls (cotton)

لوز *lauz* almond(s) (coll.); (*eg.*) patch (on a shoe) | لوز القطن *l. al-quṭn* cotton bolls; دودة اللوز *dūdat al-l.* boll weevil

لوزة *lauza* pl. *-āt* almond; اللوزتان the tonsils (*anat.*) | التهاب اللوزتين *ilt. al-lauzatain* tonsillitis

لوزى *lauzī* almond-shaped, almond (adj.)

(لوس) لاس *lāsa u* (*laus*) to taste

(لوص) *lāṣa u* (*lauṣ*) to peep, peer, pry (through a chink in the door, or the like) III do. (ه for s.o.); to stare, gaze (▲ or الى at s.th.); to look firmly, unflinchingly (▲ or الى at s.th.); to dupe, cheat, deceive (ه s.o.)

ملاوص *mulāwiṣ* sly, cunning, wily

(لوط) لاط *lāṭa u* (*lauṭ*) to stick, cling, adhere (ب to); to coat with clay, to plaster (▲ a wall)

لوط *lūṭ* Lot (Biblical name)

لوطى *lūṭī* sodomite, pederast

لواط *liwāṭ* and لواطة *liwāṭa* sodomy, pederasty

(لوع) لاع *lāʿa u* (*lauʿ*) to be or become restive, impatient; to become ill; to seize vehemently, overwhelm, torment, make sick (ه s.o.; love); to tan (ه s.o.; sun) II to torture, torment, agonize VIII to be burning, inflamed, languishing (with love, longing); to feel burning anxiety (على for s.o.)

لوعة *lauʿa* ardor of love, amorous rapture, lovesickness; pain, grief, anguish, anxiety, torment, torture, agony

التياع *iltiyāʿ* burning, enrapturedness; burning anxiety, anguish; agony, pain, suffering

ملاوع *mulāwiʿ* cunning, artful, wily, crafty, sly

لوغاريتمات *lūġāritmāt* logarithms

[1](لوف) لاف *lāfa u* (*lauf*) to eat, chew (▲ s.th.)

[2]لوف *lūf* luffa, dishcloth gourd (Luffa cylindrica Roem; *bot.*)

ملوق *milwaq* pl. ملاوق *malāwiq*[2] spatula

[1](لوك) لاك *lāka u* (*lauk*) to chew (▲ s.th.); to talk constantly about s.th. (▲); to bring into discredit (سمعته *sumʿatahū* s.o.'s reputation) | لاك الكلام (*kalām*) to be inhibited in one's speech, stammer, express o.s. imperfectly; السؤال الذى تلوكه الالسنة (*alsina*) the question which is on everyone's lips; ما تلوكه الالسن (*alsun*) what people say, what is generally rumored

²لانكي and لانكية look up alphabetically

لوكانده (It. *locanda*) and لوكنده *lōkanda* pl. *-āt* inn; hotel

لولب *laulab* pl. لوالب *lawālib*² screw; spiral; spiral spring, coil spring, extension spring; spring; axle; (fig.) mainspring, pivot point

لولبى *laulabī* screw-shaped; spiral, helical | ○ لولبيات زهرية (*zuharīya*) spirochetes, syphilogenous bacteria; درج لولبى (*daraj*) spiral staircase

¹(لوم) لام *lāma u* (*laum*, ملام *malām*, ملامة *malāma*) to blame, censure, rebuke, chide, scold, reproach (ه s.o. على or فى for) **II** to censure sharply, reprove, reprimand (ه s.o.) **IV** = **I**; **V** to blame o.s.; to tarry, linger, take one's time (فى or على in or with s.th.), procrastinate, temporize, hedge **VI** to blame each other **VIII** to be censured, be blamed **X** to deserve blame, be blameworthy, reprehensible

لوم *laum* and لومة *lauma* censure, rebuke, reproof, blame, reproach

لومة *luwama* and لوام *lawwām* severe censurer, stern critic; censorious

ملام *malām* and ملامة *malāma* pl. ملاوم *malāwim*² censure, rebuke, reproof, blame, reproach

تلويم *talwīm* censure, rebuke, reproof

لائم *lā'im* pl. لوم *luwwam*, لوام *luwwām*, ليم *luyyam* censurer, critic, accuser

لائمة *lā'ima* pl. لوائم *lawā'im*² censure, rebuke, reproof, blame, reproach

ملوم *malūm*, مليم *malīm* and ملام *mulām* censured, blamed; blameworthy, reprehensible

لومانا *lūmān* penitentiary, penal servitude

لومانجى *lūmānjī* convict, inmate of a penitentiary

لون **II** to variegate, dapple, make colorful (ه s.th.); to color, tint, tinge, paint, daub (ه s.th.); to make up, rouge (ه the face, etc.) **V** to be colored or tinted; to color, change color, become discolored; to be colorful, variegated; to be fickle

لون *laun* pl. الوان *alwān* color; coloring, tint, tinge, hue, shade; complexion; kind, sort, specimen, species; dish, course; pl. (with foll. genit.) all kinds of | الوان الاطعمة *a. al-aṭ'ima* all kinds of food; مختلف الالوان *mukhtalif al-a.* variegated, multicolored, motley, varied, various; جلى الوانه *jallā alwānahū* to bring out the different aspects of s.th., point up s.th., make s.th. stand out

لونى *launī* colorful, colored, color- (in compounds), chromatic

تلوين *talwīn* coloring

ملون *mulawwan* colored, tinted, colorful, many-colored, variegated, kaleidoscopic

متلون *mutalawwin* colored, tinted; many-colored, multicolored; iridescent, opalescent, scintillating; changeable, inconstant, unsteady; whimsical, capricious, fickle

لونجى (*eg.*) *lawingī* and لاونجى *lāwingī* attendant, bath attendant

لونجية *lawingīya* housekeeper, woman attendant, servant, housemaid

لوندا (It. *lavanda*) *lawandā* lavender | ماء اللوندا lavender water

لوى *lawā i* (لى *layy*, لوى *luwīy*) to turn (ه s.th.); to crook, curve (ه s.th.); to bend, flex, bend up, down, back or over (ه s.th.); to twist, contort, wrench, warp (ه s.th.); to distort, pervert (ه s.th.); to turn (ه the head), turn away, avert (ه the face); to turn around, turn (على to s.o., to s.th.), face (على s.o., s.th.); to think back (على on), recall (على s.th.); to care, bother (على about), pay attention or heed (على to) | لوى فيه اللسان (*lisāna*) to speak ill of s.o., backbite s.o.; لا يلوى على شيء not to care about anything, be utterly reckless; — (لى *layy*, ليان *layyān*) to conceal, keep secret (ه عن s.th. from s.o.); — *lawiya a* (لوى *lawan*) to be crooked, curved, bent; to writhe, twist; to wind, coil **II** to bend, bow, incline, tilt, twist, wrench, contort, turn, crook, curve (ه s.th.); to pervert, distort, complicate (ه s.th.) **IV** to turn, twist, bend, crook, curve (ب or ه s.th.); to avert (ه عن s.th. from); to wave (بيده *bi-yadihī* one's hand); to hoist (ه a flag); to take away, put away, remove (ب s.th.) | الوى عنان الشيء to avert, prevent, restrain s.th. (عن from), check, curb s.th. **V** to be twisted, winding, tortuous, sinuous, bent, crooked; to be turned, be twisted; to turn, twist, wind, meander, coil; to writhe, wriggle, squirm; to display shrewdness and cunning **VIII** to be curved, crooked, bent; to be turned, be twisted; to twist, warp, get contorted, get bent out of shape; to turn off, turn away; to turn one's back (عن on s.th.); to be or become difficult, involved, intricate, complicated (على for s.o.)

لى *layy* bending, twist(ing), turn(ing) | لى الشيشة (*eg.*) the flexible tube of the narghile; لا يعرف الحى من اللى (*ya'rifu l-ḥayya*) he doesn't know enough to come in out of the rain, he wouldn't know a snake from a garden hose

لية *layya* pl. لوى *liwan* bend, fold, flexure, twist, tortuosity, sinuosity, turn, curve

لوى *lawan* pl. الواء *alwā'* gripes, colic; agony, pain, hardship | قاسى الالواء واللأواء (*la'wā'*) to die a thousand deaths

لوى *liwan* pl. الواء *alwā'*, الوية *alwiya* curvature

لواء *liwā'* pl. الوية *alwiya*, الويات *alwiyāt* banner, flag, standard; brigade (*mil.*; *U.A.R., Leb., Ir.*); major general (*mil.*; *U.A.R.*); rear admiral (*Eg.*); province, district (*Ir.*; the country is subdivided into 14 لواء) | امير اللواء brigadier general (*Ir.*); لواء جوى (*jawwī*) air-force brigade; عقد لواء شيء (*liwā'a š.*) to found, start, originate, produce, cause, arouse, provoke s.th.; البارجة المعقود لواؤها للاميرال . . . (*liwā'uhā*) the admiral's flagship . . ; عقد له لواء المجد (النصر) *'uqida lahū l. ul-majd* (*un-naṣr*) approx.: he was awarded the laurel of fame (of victory)

لواء *lawwā'* wryneck (*zool.*)

ملوى *milwan* pl. ملاو *malāwin* spanner, wrench; ○ peg (of stringed instruments)

التواء *iltiwā'* curvedness, curvature; bend, twist, tortuosity, sinuosity, curve; crookedness, wryness; perverseness, absurdity | التواء الارض *ilt. al-arḍ* uneveness of the terrain

التواءة *iltiwā'a* (n. vic.) pl. -*āt* a bending, flexing, twist (e.g., of the body in dancing)

لاو *lāwin* pl. لواة *luwāh* turning, twisting | غير لاو على reckless of, without regard for

ملوى *malwīy* crooked, curved, bent; twisted, warped, contorted; winding, meandering, tortuous, sinuous; perverted, wrong, absurd

ملتو *multawin* = ملوى

ملتوى *multawan* pl. -*āt* turn (of the road), curve; curvature

لى[1] and لية see لوى

لياء[2] *liyyā'* mackerel shark, porbeagle (*zool.*)

ليبريا *libārya* Liberia

ليبيا *lībiyā* Libya; ليبي *lībī* Libyan

ليت *laita* and يا ليت *yā laita* (particle, with foll. noun in acc. or personal suffix) would God! if only ...! | ليتني مت لاجلك *laitanī muttu li-ajlika* would God I had died for you! ليته كان هنا I wish he were here! if only he were here! يا ليت كان يذهب (*yaḏhabu*) I wish he had gone! ليت شعرى (*šiʿrī*) I wish I knew ...!

ليترجية *līturjīya* pl. *-āt* liturgy

ليتوانيا *lītuwāniyā* Lithuania

ليتوانى *lītuwānī* Lithuanian

ليث *laiṯ* pl. ليوث *luyūṯ* lion

ليذ see لوذ

ليرا *līrā* and ليرة *līra* pl. *-āt* pound (as a monetary unit) | ليرة انكليزية (*ingilīzīya*) pound sterling

[1]ليس *laisa* (without imperf.) not to be (with ب or acc. s.th. or s.o.); not to exist; (= intensified لا) not | ليس الا (*illā*) terminating a sentence: only, and no more, and nothing else; ليس — سوى (*siwā*) nothing but, only, merely; ليس على شيء من الحقيقة there is not a grain of truth in it; ليس — فقط — بل (*faqaṭ, bal*) not only — but also; ليس ل not to have, not to possess; ليس لنا شيء we don't have anything; ليس له ان he has no right to ..., he mustn't ...; ليس من not to belong to ..., have nothing to do with ...; اليس كذلك *a-laisa ka-ḏālik*? isn't it so?; (with ب and participle) to be unable to, لست بفاعل *lastu bi-fāʿilin* I can't do it

[2]ليس *layisa a* (*layas*) to be valiant, brave, courageous

اليس *alyas*[2], f. ليساء *laisāʾ*[2], pl. ليس *līs* valiant, brave, courageous

ليسانس (Fr. *licence*) *līsans* the academic degree of a licentiate

ليف II to rub with palm fibers (ه s.th.) V to form fibers, become fibrous

ليف *līf* (coll.; n. un. ة) pl. الياف *alyāf* fibers, fibrils, bast | ليف هندى (*hindī*) coco fibers, coir; الياف الكتان *a. al-kattān* flax fibers

ليفة *līfa* (n. un.) fiber, fibril; tuft of palm fibers used as a brush | ليفة الاستحام bath sponge, luffa

ليفى *līfī* and ليفانى *līfānī* fibered, fibrous

تليف *talayyuf* fibration, fibrillation; cirrhosis (*med.*)

(ليق) لاق *lāqa i* (*laiq*) to befit, become (ب s.o.), be proper, seemly (ب for s.o.), be suitable (ب to s.o.), be worthy (ب of s.o.); to be suited, appropriate, fit (ب for s.th.); to fit (garment)

ليقة *līqa* pl. ليق *liyaq* tuft of cotton or silk threads which is inserted in an inkwell; putty; clay; mortar

لياقة *liyāqa* propriety, seemliness, suitableness; decorum, decency; capability, skill; efficiency, competence; worthiness, merit, desert; correct behavior, blameless conduct, good manners | مخل باللياقة (*mukill*) improper, unseemly, unbecoming

اليق *alyaq*[2] more suitable, more appropriate, more proper, fitter (ب for)

لائق *lāʾiq* suitable, appropriate, proper, befitting, becoming, seemly; suited, adapted, fit; worthy, deserving

ليل *lail* (usually m.) nighttime, night (as opposed to نهار daytime); pl. □ ليالى *layālī* (*syr.*) a certain vocal style; ليلا *lailan* at night | ليل نهار *laila nahāra* day and night

ليلة *laila* pl. *-āt*, ليال *layālin*, ليائل *layāʾil*[2] night (as opposed to يوم); evening; soirée; الليلة *al-lailata* tonight |

بين ليلة وضحاها (*wa-ḍuḥāhā*) overnight; ليلة امس *lailata amsi* last night; yesterday evening; ليلة خيرية (*kairīya*) charity soirée, benefit performance; ليلة الدخلة *l. ad-dukla* wedding night; ليلة راقصة soirée dansante, evening dance; ليلة زاهرة glamorous evening party; ليلة شادية (*šādiya*) soirée of vocal music; ليلة ليلاء (*lailā'*[2]) dark night; فى ليلة ليلاء in the dark of night, under cover of the night; ليلة القدر *l. al-qadr* or ليلة القضاء *l. al-qaḍā'* the night in which, according to sura 97, the Koran was revealed, celebrated between the 26th and 27th of Ramadan; ليلة المعراج *l. al-mi'rāj* the night of the 27th of Rajab in which the Prophet made his journey through the seven heavens; ليلة نصف الشعبان *l. niṣf aš-ša'bān* the night between the 14th and 15th of Shaban, when, according to popular belief, the heavenly tree of life is shaken, shedding the leaves of those who will die next year; ليلة النقطة *l. an-nuqṭa* the night of June 17th (the 11th day of the Coptic month Ba'ūna) when, according to popular belief, a miraculous drop falls from heaven, thus causing the annual rise of the Nile

ليلتئذ *lailata'iḏin* (in) that night; (on) that evening

ليلى *lailī* nocturnal, nightly; of night, night- (in compounds); evening (adj.)

ليلى *lailā* a woman's name | كل يبكى (يغنى) على ليلاه *kullun yabkī* (*yuġannī*) *'alā lailāhu* everyone sings his own tune, does as he pleases, follows his own fancy; كل يدعى وصلا بليلاه (*yadda'ī waṣlan*) everybody claims to be the chosen one, everyone brags in his own way

ليلاء see ليلة

ليلك (Engl.) *lailak* lilac

ليمان *līmān* pl. *-āt* harbor, port; penitentiary

ليمون *laimūn, līmūn* (n. un. ة) pl. *-āt* lemon | ليمون حامض lime; شراب الليمون *šarāb al-l.* lemonade

[1](لين) لان *lāna i* (*līn*, ليان *luyūn*) to be or become soft, tender, gentle, mild, pliable, flexible, supple; to yield, give way; to soften, relent, calm down; to become milder, friendlier | لا يلين inflexible, unbending; لانت قناته (*qanātuhū*) to show o.s. compliant, yield, relent, give in II and IV to soften, relax (ه s.th.); to placate, soothe, allay, mitigate, assuage, temper, moderate (ه s.th.) III to be gentle, kind, friendly (ه to s.o.); to treat with kindness and leniency (ه s.o.)

لين *līn* softness; tenderness; tender treatment; gentleness; flexibility, pliableness, suppleness; yieldingness, compliance, tractability; pliancy, smoothness; diarrhea | لين العظام softening of the bones, osteomalicia (*med.*); لين القياد tractability, docility; حروف اللين the "soft" letters ا , و , ى

لين *layyin* pl. *-ūn*, الينا. *alyinā'*[2] and *lain* pl. *-ūn* soft; flabby, feeble; tender; gentle; flexible, pliable, yielding; pliant, supple, resilient, elastic, tractable | لين العريكة *l. al-'arīka* mild-mannered, gentle-hearted; لين القياد tractable, manageable, docile, obedient; بطنه لين (*baṭnuhū*) he suffers from diarrhea

ليونة *luyūna* softness; tenderness; gentleness; flexibility, pliability, suppleness | ليونة الجانب sociability, companionableness, compliance, yieldingness, tractability

ملاينة *mulāyana* friendliness, kindness

ملين *mulayyin* softening, emollient; dissolvent, diluent; aperient, cathartic, laxative; ملينات laxatives

[2]ليان see لوى

م

م.م.ش (= شركة مسئولية محدودة) Inc., Ltd.

م *ma* for ما what? after prepositions: الى م *ilā ma* whereto? where? which way? whither? بم *bi-ma* with what? wherewith? لم *li-ma* why? wherefore? حتى م *ḥattā ma* how far? to which point?

ما *mā* 1. (interrogative pronoun) what? | لما *li-mā* why? wherefore? for what reason? ماذا *mā-ḏā* what (on earth)? لماذا *li-mā-ḏā* why (on earth)? ما لك what's the matter with you? what is it? ما لك, ما لى etc., (with foll. verb) why? wherefore? what... for? why should I, should you, etc.? ما انت وذاك *mā anta wa-ḏāka* what's that to you? what has this to do with you? what do you know about that? ما اجمله *mā ajmalahū* how handsome he is! ما افضل عمر *mā afḍala ʿumara*! how excellent Omar is! — 2. (relative pronoun) that which, what; something which; whatever, all that ... | ما شاء الله see شاء; كثيرا ما *katīran mā* not seldom, as often as not, very often; بما فيه *bi-mā fīhi* including..., ... inclusive; ما كان من امضاء المعاهدة (*imḍāʾi l-muʿāhada*) the fact that the agreement has been signed, the agreement having been signed; — 3. (indefinite pronoun) foll. an indefinite noun: some, a certain | لامر ما *li-amrin mā* because of something or other, for some reason or other; يوما ما *yauman mā* some day, sometime in the future; — 4. (negation) not | ما ان (*in*) not (intensified); ما ان — حتى *mā an — ḥattā* no sooner had he ... than ..., he had hardly ... when ...; وما هى الا ان *wa-mā hiya illā an* or وما هو الا ان (with foll. verb in perfect) before long he ..., presently ...; then, thereupon; وما هى الا ان — حتى *wa-mā hiya illā an — ḥattā* no sooner had he ... than ..., he had hardly ... when ...; — 5. (conjunction) as long as | ما دمت حيا *mā dumtu ḥayyan* as long as I live; ما لم *mā lam* so long as ... not, unless; — 6. whenever; as far as, to the extent or degree that | ما واتتنى الفرص (*wātatnī l-furaṣ*) (whenever opportunities came my way, i.e.) whenever I had a chance

مابين *mā-bain* antechamber, anteroom (of the Turkish Sultan); chief chamberlain's office (in Ottoman Turkey)

ماء and مائى see موه

ماتينيه (Fr. *matinée*) *mātīnēh* matinee

ماجريات see جرى

ماجستير *mājistēr* master, schoolmaster

ماخور *mākūr* pl. مواخير *mawākīr*[2] house of ill repute, brothel

مار *mār* Mar, lord (*Chr.*, preceding the names of saints), saint

مارس *mars* March (month)

مارستان *māristān* lunatic asylum

مارش *marš* march (*mus.*)

مارشال *mārišāl* marshal, field marshal | مارشال جوى (*jawwī*) air marshal (formerly, a rank reserved exclusively for the King; *Eg.*)

مارشالية *mārišālīya* marshalcy, rank or position of a marshal

مارك *mark* pl. *-āt* mark (monetary unit)

ماركسى *marksī* Marxist

ماركسية *marksīya* Marxism

ماركة *marka* pl. *-āt* mark, sign, token | ماركة تجارية (*tijārīya*) trade-mark

مارونى *mārūnī* pl. موارنة *mawārina* Maronite (adj. and n.)

مازوت *māzūt* mazut (residue in oil distillation, used as a fuel), heavy oil

ماس *mās* and ماسة *māsa* (for الماس) diamond

ماسى *māsī* diamond (used attributively)

ماسورة *māsūra* pl. مواسير *mawāsīr*[2] pipe, tube; hose; pipestem; water pipe, water main; gun barrel; conduit, conduit pipe; pipeline (esp., for oil)

ماسون (Fr. *maçon*) *māsōn* Freemason

ماسونى *masōnī* freemasonic, masonic

ماسونية *māsōnīya* Freemasonry

ماشك *māšik* pl. مواشك *mawāšik*[2] tongs, fire tongs

مئق *ma'iqa a* (مأق *ma'aq*) to sob

مأق *ma'q* pl. مآق *ma'āqin* inner corner of the eye

مأقة *ma'qa* sobbing, sob

موق *mūq* pl. آماق *āmāq* inner corner of the eye

ماكياج (Fr. *maquillage*) *mākiyāž* face painting, make-up

ماكينة *mākīna* pl. *-āt*, مكائن *makā'in*[2] machine

مالطة *malṭa* Malta

مالطى *malṭī* Maltese (adj. and n.)

مالنخوليا *mālinḵōliyā* or ماليخوليا *māliḵōliyā* melancholia

مأمأ *ma'ma'a* to bleat (sheep)

مأن *ma'ana a* (*ma'n*) to sustain, supply with provisions, provision, victual (ه s.o.)

مأنة *ma'na* pl. *ma'anāt*, مؤون *mu'ūn* navel, umbilicus; umbilical region

مؤنة *mu'na* and مؤونة *ma'ūna* pl. مؤن *mu'an* provisions, food; store, stock; supply; burden, encumbrance, inconvenience; trouble, pains, effort | مؤن حربية (*ḥarbīya*) war material

مئينى see مائة below

مانجو *mangō* mango, mango tree (*bot.*)

مانجوست *mangost* mongoose, ichneumon (*zool.*)

المانش (Fr. *la Manche*) *al-mānš* the English Channel

مانوليا *mānōliyā* magnolia (*bot.*)

مانوى *mānawī* Manichaean

مانوية *mānawīya* Manichaeism, doctrines of Manes

مانيفاتورة *mānīfātūra* manufactured goods, dry goods, textiles

مانيفستو *mānīfistū* manifest, list of a ship's cargo

مانيكان *mānīkān*, (also مانوكان *mānūkān*) pl. *-āt* mannequin, fashion model

ماهية *māhīya* pl. *-āt* quality, quiddity, essence, nature; salary, income; pay (*mil.*)

مايسترو (It. *maestro*) *māyistrō* maestro, conductor

مائة or مئة *mi'a* pl. مئون *mi'ūn*, مئات *mi'āt* hundred | في المئة per cent

مئوى *mi'awī* and مئينى *mi'inī* centesimal, centigrade; percentile, percentual | عيد مئوى (*'īd*) 100th anniversary, centennial; نسبة مئوية or نسبة مئينية (*nisba*) percentage; درجة مئوية (*daraja*) centigrade (thermometer)

[1]مايو *māyū* May

[2]مايو (Fr. *maillot*) *māyō* and مايوه *māyōh* tights

مت *matta u* (*matt*) to spread, extend, stretch (ه s.th.); to seek to establish a link (الى to s.o., ب by marriage), enter into relations (الى with); to be related, become related by marriage (الى to), marry into the family of (الى); to belong (الى to); to be associated, be connected (الى with) | مت بصلة الى (*bi-ṣilatin*) to have close ties with s.o., be related (by marriage) to s.o.; to be connected with s.th., have to do with s.th.; مت له باقرب الصلة (*bi-aqrabi ṣ-ṣila*) to be most intimately connected with s.o.

ماتة *mātta* close ties; family ties, kinship

متح *mataḥa a* (*matḥ*) to draw from a well (ه water)

متر *mitr* pl. امتار *amtār* meter (measure of length)

مترى *mitrī* metric(al)

متراليوز (Fr. *mitrailleuse*) *mitrāliyōz* machine gun

متع *mata'a a* (*mat'*, متعة *mut'a*) to carry away, take away (ب s.th.); — (متوع *mutū'*) to be strong, firm, solid | متع النهار (*nahār*) it was broad daylight, the sun was high **II** to make (ه s.o.) enjoy (ب s.th.); to furnish, equip, supply (ه ب s.o. with); to give as compensation (ه ها to a divorced woman s.th.) | متعه الله God grant him enjoyment throughout his life; متع البصر (*baṣara*) to gratify the eye **IV** to make (ه s.o.) enjoy (ب s.th.); to have the usufruct (ب of s.th.) **V** and **X** to enjoy, savor, relish (ب s.th.)

متعة *mut'a* pl. متع *muta'* enjoyment, pleasure, delight, gratification; recreation; compensation paid to a divorced woman (*Isl. Law*); (also نكاح المتعة) muta, temporary marriage, usufruct marriage contracted for a specified time and exclusively for the purpose of sexual pleasure (*Isl. Law*) | اماكن المتعة recreation centers

متاع *matā'* pl. امتعة *amti'a* enjoyment, pleasure, delight, gratification; object of delight; necessities of life; chattel, possession, property; goods, wares, commodities, merchandise; furniture; implements, utensils, household effects; baggage, luggage, equipment, gear; useful article, article of everyday use; things, objects, stuff, odds and ends | متاع العين *m. al-'ain* delight of the eyes; سقط المتاع *saqaṭ al-m.* scrap, waste, discard, refuse; الامتعة الشخصية (*šakṣīya*) personal belongings; متاع المرأة *m. al-mar'a* cunnus (*anat.*)

امتع *amta'*[2] more enjoyable, more delightful; recreative, recreational

امتاع *imtā'* pleasure, delight, gratification (which s.th. affords)

تمتع *tamattu'* enjoyment | اسهم تمتع *ashum t.* participating certificates, shares entitling the holder to participation in the net profit without the right to vote

استمتاع *istimtā'* enjoyment; love of pleasure, epicureanism

ماتع *māti'* long

ممتع *mumatti'* pleasant, delicious, enjoyable, delightful, gratifying

متمتع *mumatta'* enjoying (ب s.th.), in possession (ب of)

ممتع *mumti'* pleasant, delicious, enjoyable, delightful, gratifying; interesting

متن *matuna u* (متانة *matāna*) to be firm, strong, solid **II** to make firm or strong (ه s.th.); to strengthen, consolidate, fortify (ه s.th.)

متن *matn* pl. متون *mutūn*, متان *mitān* half, or side, of the back; back (esp., of animals, but also fig.); main thing, main part; body (e.g., of a document or journal, aside from footnotes, annotations, etc.), text (of a tradition, as distinguished from the *isnād*; of a book, as distinguished from the commentary; also, in general, linguistic or literary text); middle of the road, roadway, pavement; surface; deck of a ship | على متن ... aboard (a ship or airplane);

على متن البحر (m. il-baḥr) by sea, sea-borne; على متن الهواء (m. il-hawā') through the air, air-borne

متن matn and متين matīn firm, strong, solid

متانة matāna firmness, strength, solidity, hardiness; will power, strength of will, determination, backbone, firmness of character, fortitude; succinctness, conciseness of style

تمتين tamtīn strengthening, consolidation

متى matā 1. (interrogative particle) when? at what time? | الى متى and حتى متى till when? how long? — 2. (conjunction) when, whenever | متى ما whenever

مثاث maṯāṯ cream, cosmetic

مثل maṯala u (مثول muṯūl) to resemble (ه s.o.), be or look like s.o. (ه), bear a likeness (ه to); to imitate, copy (ه s.o.); to compare, liken (ب ه s.o. to); to represent, mean, signify (ه s.th.), stand for (ه); to stand erect (بين يديه baina yadaihi before s.o. in audience), appear before s.o.; to present o.s. to s.o.; to present itself to the eye, be on view; to plant o.s., stand; to step forth, come forward, enter, appear, make one's appearance (esp. of an actor, on the stage) | مثل بين يدى الملك (b. yadayyi l-malik) to have an audience with the king, be received in audience by the king; — u (maṯl) to maim, mutilate (ب s.o.); — u (maṯl, مثلة muṯla) to make an example (ب of s.o.); — maṯula u (مثول muṯūl) to stand, appear (بين يديه baina yadaihi before s.o. in audience) II to make (ه s.th.) like s.th. else (ب), make (ه s.th.) similar, analogous (ب to); to assimilate (biol.); to give or quote as an example (ب ل s.th. of, also ه s.th. على of), exemplify (ب ل with s.th. s.th.), use as a simile (ب ه s.th. for); to compare, liken (ب ه, ه s.o., s.th. to); to punish severely, treat harshly (ب s.o.); to maim, mutilate (ب s.o.); to represent pictorially or graphically, show (ه, ه s.o., s.th.), picture, depict, describe (ه, ه s.o., s.th.); to portray, paint (ه s.o.), sculpture a bust or statue (ه of s.o.); to represent (ه s.o., ه s.th.); to act (on stage or screen), appear as an actor; to play, act (دورا dauran a part or role), star (دورا in a role); to stage, perform (ه a play); to form, constitute (chem.) | مثل به اشنع تمثيل (ašnaʿa t.) to make a dreadful example of s.o., punish s.o. with utmost cruelty III to resemble (ه s.o., ه s.th.), be or look like s.o. or s.th. (ه, ه), be similar, bear a likeness (ه, ه to); to correspond, be analogous (ه, ه to s.o., to s.th.); to compare, liken (ب ه s.o. to) V to make o.s. similar, assimilate o.s. (ب to s.o.); to become similar (ب to), become like s.o. or s.th. (ب), follow (ب s.o., s.th.), take after s.o. or s.th. (ب); to take on the shape of s.o. (ب); to assimilate, absorb (ه s.th.); to do likewise, imitate, copy (ب s.o., s.th.); to imagine, fancy (ب s.th., with ه and verb; s.o. to do s.th.); to get an idea (ه of); to give or quote as an example, use as a simile (ب s.th.); to quote, cite (ب a verse); to present itself, be represented, be visible, find visual expression (في in); to embody, personify, (im)personate, typify (ه s.th.); to stand erect, appear (بين يديه baina yadaihi before s.o.) VI to resemble each other, be alike, go together, agree, match; to recover (من from) | تماثل للشفاء or الى الشفاء (šifā') to be on the way to recovery VIII to take as a model or an example, imitate, copy, follow (ه s.th.); to submit, subject o.s. (ل to s.o., to s.th.); to obey (ه an order)

مثل miṯl pl. امثال amṯāl s.th. similar, s.th. of the same kind; resemblance, similarity, similitude, likeness; image; equivalent;

(with foll. genit. or suffix) s.o. like ..., one like ...; s.th. like ...; مثل *miṯla* (prep.) and كمثل *ka-miṯli* similar to, like, just as; one like; s.th. like; the same as; (just) as much as | هم مثله *hum miṯluhū* they are like him, they are of his kind; بالمثل in the same manner, likewise, equally, also, too; مثل ما *miṯla mā* just as, as well as; بمثل ما *bi-miṯli mā* in the same manner as; اجر المثل *ajr al-m.* adequate payment or wages; عامله بالمثل (*ʿāmalahū*) to repay s.o. like for like, treat s.o. in like manner; مبدأ المعاملة بالمثل (*mabdaʾ al-muʿāmala*) principle of reciprocity; مقابلة المثل بالمثل (*muqābalat al-m.*) retaliation, reprisal; امثاله *amṯāluhū* people like him, people of his kind; امثال ابى بكر people like Abū Bakr; الى ثلاثة امثاله up to three times as much

مثلما *miṯlamā* (conj.) as

مثلى *miṯlī* replaceable; fungible (*Isl. Law*)

مثلى *muṯlā* see امثل *amṯal*

مثل *maṯal* pl. امثال *amṯāl* likeness; metaphor, simile, parable; proverb, adage; example; lesson, similar case; ideal, model; مثلا *maṯalan* for example, for instance, e.g. | مثله كمثل ... he is comparable to ..., he is like ...; مثل اسمى (*asmā*) or مثل اعلى (*aʿlā*) ideal; ضرب الامثال see ضرب; الامثال السائرة proverbs; على رأى المثل (*raʾyi l-m.*) as the proverb says

مثال *miṯāl* pl. امثلة *amṯila*, مثل *muṯul* s.th. equal; s.th. similar; simile, parable, allegory; example; pattern, standard; exemplary punishment; model; image, picture | على مثال ... in the manner of ...; after the pattern or model of ...; مثال اعلى (*aʿlā*) pl. مثل عليا (*ʿulyā*) ideal; مثل عالية (*ʿāliya*) ideals

مثالى *miṯālī* parabolic; allegoric; typical, representative; model; exemplary; ideal | مثالى النزعة *m. n-nazʿa* idealist

مثال *maṯṯāl* pl. *-ūn* sculptor

مثالة *maṯāla* exemplariness, perfection, superiority; (pl. *-āt*, مثائل *maṯāʾil*²) lesson, task, assignment

مثيل *maṯīl* pl. مثل *muṯul* like, similar, analogous; equal, match | مثيله f. مثيلتها of his (its) kind, of her kind; لا مثيل له (*maṯīla*), ليس له مثيل, لم يسبق له مثيل (*yasbiq*) incomparable, matchless, unrivaled, unparalleled

مثول *muṯūl* standing erect; appearance; presentation; audience

امثولة *umṯūla* pl. *-āt*, اماثيل *amāṯīl*² example; deterrent example, warning, lesson; proverb; assignment, lesson

امثل *amṯal*², f. مثلى *muṯlā*, pl. اماثل *amāṯil*² closer to perfection, coming nearer the ideal; ideal; model, exemplary, perfect | السبيل المثلى ل the ideal way to ...

تمثال *timṯāl* pl. تماثيل *tamāṯīl*² sculptured image; statue | تمثال نصفى (*niṣfī*) bust

تمثيل *tamṯīl* pl. تماثيل *tamāṯīl*² quotation of examples, exemplification; likening, comparison; assimilation; portrayal, picturing, depiction, description; representation; diplomatic representation; dramatic representation, acting, playing (of an actor); performance, show; dramatic art; exemplary punishment | تمثيل تجارى (*tijārī*) commercial agency; تمثيل فلان (in motion-picture announcements) starring so-and-so; بدل التمثيل *badal at-t.* allowance for representation, allowance for professional expenditure, expense allowance; دار التمثيل theater, playhouse, opera house; فن التمثيل *fann at-t.* dramatic art, theater; sculpture; على سبيل التمثيل for the purpose of illustration

تمثيلى *tamṯīlī* of or pertaining to the theater or stage, theatrical, histrionic; dramatic | ملعب تمثيلى (*malʿab*) theater, playhouse

تمثيلية *tamṯīlīya*: تمثيلية غنائية (*ḡināʾīya*) opera

مماثلة *mumāṯala* resemblance, similarity, similitude, likeness, correspondence; analogy; exact equivalence (*Isl. Law*)

تمثّل *tamaṯṯul* assimilation (*biol.*)

تماثل *tamāṯul* matching, agreement, correspondence, resemblance, similarity, similitude, likeness; recovery, convalescence

امتثال *imtiṯāl* obedience, compliance, consent

ماثل *māṯil* standing, standing forth; placed, set down; displayed, on display; emerging, arising, cropping up, appearing, presenting itself | ماثل امام عينيه (*amāma ʿainaihi*) present before s.o.'s eyes; ماثل للعيان (*li-l-ʿiyān*) visible, conspicuous, evident, obvious; ماثل فى حضرته (*ḥaḍratihī*) in front of s.o., in s.o.'s presence

ماثلة *māṯila* lamp, chandelier

ممثل *mumaṯṯil* representing, representative, representational; — (pl. *-ūn*) representative (also, e.g., diplomatic), deputy, agent; performer, player, stage player, actor; comedian | ممثل تجارى (*tijārī*) commercial agent

ممثلة *mumaṯṯila* pl. *-āt* actress

ممثلية *mumaṯṯilīya* representation, agency | ممثلية سياسية (*siyāsīya*) diplomatic representation

ممثل *mumaṯṯal* depicted, portrayed; represented; assimilated (*biol.*)

مماثل *mumāṯil* resembling, similar, like, comparable; corresponding, analogous

متماثل *mutamāṯil* resembling each other, similar, of the same kind, homogeneous; mutually corresponding, homologous; identical; assimilating, assimilative

ممتثل *mumtaṯil* obedient, submissive, compliant

مثانة *maṯāna* pl. *-āt* (urinary) bladder

مج **majja** *u* (*majj*) **to spit out, disgorge, eject, emit, discharge (ه s.th.); to reject, dismiss, discard (ه s.th.) II to become ripe, ripen, mellow**

مجاج *mujāj* and مجاجة *mujāja* spittle, saliva; juice

مجد **majada** *u* (*majd*) **and** *majuda* *u* (مجادة *majāda*) **to be glorious, illustrious, exalted II and IV to praise, extol, laud, glorify, celebrate V to be extolled, be glorified, be lauded, be praised; to boast, glory**

مجد *majd* pl. امجاد *amjād* glory; splendor, magnificence, grandeur; nobility, honor, distinction

مجدى *majdī* laudable, praiseworthy, glorious

مجيد *majīd* glorious, illustrious; celebrated, famous; glorified, exalted; praiseworthy, laudable, admirable, excellent, splendid; noble | الكتاب المجيد the Koran

مجيدى *majīdī* medjidie, a Turkish silver coin of 20 piasters coined under Sultan Abdul-Medjid; (of money) Turkish

امجاد *amjād* (pl. of مجيد) people of rank, distinguished people

امجد *amjad*[2] pl. اماجد *amājid*[2] more glorious, more illustrious; more distinguished

تمجيد *tamjīd* praise, glorification, exaltation, idolization

[1]مجر **majara** *u* (*majr*) **to be thirsty, feel thirsty, to thirst**

مجر *majr* numerous (army)

ماجور *mājūr* pl. مواجير *mawājīr*[2] (*eg.*) round earthen trough or tub used for making dough; tall, bulging earthen vessel with a wide mouth

[2]المجر *al-majar* the Hungarians; Hungary

مجرى *majarī* Hungarian

[3]مجر *majar* a small weight = 18 قيراط = 3.51 g (*Eg.*)

ماجريات see جرى

مجريط *majrīṭ*[2] Madrid

مجوس look up alphabetically

مجلة *majla* pl. مجال *mijāl*, (coll.) مجل *majl* blister; see also under جل *jalla*

ماجل *mājil* pl. مواجل *mawājil*[2] (*tun.*) cistern

ممجمج *mumajmaj* indistinct, scribbled, illegible

[1]مجن *majana* *u* (*mujn*, مجون *mujūn*, مجانة *majāna*) to joke, jest; to scoff, mock, jeer **III** to jeer, scoff, gibe (ه s.o.), mock, poke fun (ه at s.o.), joke, jest (ه with s.o.), make fun (ه of s.o.), play wild jokes (ه on s.o.) **V** to make insolent jokes **VI** to mock at each other

مجانة *majāna* buffoonery, clowning; (pl. *-āt*) prank; antic

مجان *majjān* impudent, insolent, unrestrained, wanton, shameless; jester, prankster, wag, buffoon; free, free of charge, gratuitous; مجانا *majjānan* or بالمجان *bi-l-majjān* free of charge, for nothing, gratis

مجانى *majjānī* free, free of charge, gratuitous

مجانية *majjānīya* gratuitousness, exemption from fees, remission of fees

مجون *mujūn* buffoonery, clowning; shamelessness, impudence

مجونى *mujūnī* brazen sarcast, cynic

ماجن *mājin* pl. مجان *mujjān* impudent, shameless, brazen, insolent, saucy; joker, jester, wag, buffoon

[2]ماجن *mājin* pl. مواجن *mawājin*[2] (= ماجل) (*tun.*) cistern

مجنيزيوم *magnīziyom* magnesium

مجوس *majūs* Magi, adherents of Mazdaism

مجوسى *majūsī* Magian; Magus, adherent of Mazdaism

مجوسية *majūsīya* Mazdaism

مح *maḥḥ* worn off, threadbare, shabby

مح *muḥḥ* the best, choicest part, pith, gist, quintessence; egg yolk

محص *maḥaṣa* *a* (*maḥṣ*) to render clear, clarify, purify (ه s.th.) **II** do.; to rectify, put right (ه s.th.); to put to the test (ه s.th.); to test, examine closely (ه s.th.) **IV** to reappear, re-emerge, come out again **V** do.; to be clarified, be purified **VII** to be clarified, be purified

محيص *maḥīṣ* shiny, flashing (sword)

تمحيص *tamḥīṣ* pl. *-āt* clarification; testing, thorough examination

محض *maḥaḍa* *a* (*maḥḍ*) to be sincere (ه ه toward s.o. in), show or manifest sincerely (ه ه to s.o. s.th.; e.g., love, affection); — *maḥuḍa* *u* (محوضة *muḥūḍa*) to be of pure descent; to be pure, genuine, unmixed, unadulterated **IV** to be sincere (ه ه toward s.o. in) **V** to devote o.s. exclusively (ل to s.th.), be solely dedicated (ل to s.th.)

محض *maḥḍ* of pure descent, pureblood; pure, unmixed, unadulterated; genuine; sheer, downright, outright (e.g., lie, nonsense, etc.); محضا *maḥḍan* only, merely, exclusively, solely | بمحض اختياره *bi-maḥḍi kt.* entirely of his own accord; لمحض صالحها *li-maḥḍi ṣāliḥihā* solely in her own interest, only for her own good

امحوضة *umḥūḍa* sincere advice

محق *maḥaqa* *a* (*maḥq*) to efface, blot out, strike out, erase (ه s.th.); to eradicate, exterminate, annihilate, destroy (ه s.th.) **IV** to wane, become invisible (moon); to perish V, VII (انمحق or امحق *immaḥaqa*) and VIII to be or become effaced; to be annihilated, be destroyed, perish

محق *maḥq* effacement, obliteration; eradication, extermination, annihilation, destruction

محاق *maḥāq*, *muḥāq*, *miḥāq* waning of the moon

محك *maḥaka a* (*maḥk*) and *maḥika a* (*maḥak*) to be quarrelsome, contentious, cantankerous, quarrel, wrangle, bicker; to dispute stubbornly III to pick a quarrel, quarrel, wrangle, have an argument (ه with s.o.) IV and V = I

محك *maḥik* quarrelsome, contentious, cantankerous, disputatious, bickering; quarrelsome person, bickerer, wrangler

مماحكة *mumāḥaka* quarrelsomeness, disputatiousness, petulance; quarrel, row, wrangle, dispute; (pl. *-āt*) chicanery; bickering, wrangling

ماحك *māḥik* and مماحك *mumāḥik* quarrelsome, contentious, cantankerous, disputatious; quarrelsome person, bickerer, wrangler

محل *maḥala a*, *maḥila a* (*maḥl*, محول *muḥūl*) and *maḥula u* (محالة *maḥāla*) to be barren (land, year); — *maḥala*, *maḥila a* and *maḥula u* (*maḥl*, محال *miḥāl*) to plot, scheme, intrigue (ب against s.o.) IV to be barren and arid; to render barren (ه the soil); to be overdue, be withheld, fail to set in (rains) V to seek to attain by cunning or through intrigues (ه s.th.), strive cunningly (ه for); to seek a pretext; to propagandize or advertise (ل s.th.) artfully or with unfair means | تمحل العذر (*'uḏr*) to use a pretext, make an excuse

محل *maḥl* barrenness, aridity, drought; dearth, famine; cunning, craft, deceit; (see also under حل *ḥalla*)

محالة *maḥāla* pl. محال *maḥāl* pulley, block and tackle; (see also حول)

محال *miḥāl* slyness, cunning, craft, insidiousness

ماحل *māḥil* barren, sterile; bare, bleak

ممحل *mumḥil* barren, sterile

محن *maḥana a* (*maḥn*) and VIII to try, try out, test, put to the test, subject to a test (ه s.o., ه s.th.); to afflict, subject to a trial or trials (ه s.o.); to examine (ه s.o.)

محنة *miḥna* pl. محن *miḥan* severe trial, ordeal, tribulation; affliction; hardship, distress, suffering, misfortune

امتحان *imtiḥān* pl. *-āt* test, experiment; examination | امتحان الدخول entrance examination; امتحان نهائى (*nihā'ī*) final examination

ممتحن *mumtaḥin* tester; examiner

ممتحن *mumtaḥan* examined; tried, tested; examinee, candidate

محا (محو) *maḥā u* (*maḥw*) to wipe off, rub out, scratch out, erase, strike out (ه s.th.); to efface, obliterate, blot out (ه s.th.); to wipe out, eradicate, exterminate, extinguish (ه s.th.); to eliminate, abolish (ه s.th.) | لا يمحى *lā yumḥā* ineffaceable, indelible II to wipe out, extinguish, exterminate, extirpate (ه s.th.) V, VII (انمحى and امحى *immaḥā*) and VIII to be effaced, obliterated, extinguished, wiped out, exterminated; to disappear, vanish

محو *maḥw* effacement, obliteration, blotting out; erasure, deletion; elimination; abolition, abolishment, annulment

○ ممحاة *mimḥāh* and محاية *maḥḥāya* eraser

امحاء *immiḥā'* extinction, extermination, extirpation

ماحية *māḥiya* eraser

مخ *mukk* pl. مخاخ *mikāk*, مخخة *mikaka* brain; marrow, medulla; core, essence; purest and choicest part

مخى *mukkī* brain- (in compounds), cerebral

المخا *al-mukā* Mocha (seaport in SW Yemen)

[1]مخر *makara a* (*makr*, مخور *mukūr*) to plow; to move, cut, shear, cleave (ه through s.th.); (of a ship) to plow, traverse (ه the sea)

ماخر *mākir* plowing the sea (ship)

ماخرة *mākira* pl. مواخر *mawākir*[2] ship

[2]ماخور *mākūr* pl. مواخير *mawākīr*[2] brothel

مخرق *makraqa* to brag, tell fibs; to swindle, cheat

مخض *makada a u i* (*makd*) to churn (ه milk); to shake violently (ه s.th.); — *makida a* (مخاض *makād*, *mikād*) to be parturient, be in labor V = I *makida*; to bear, produce, bring forth, effect; bring about (عن s.th.); to be churned (milk)

مخاض *makād* labor pains

مخيض *makīd* buttermilk

مخاضة *makkāda* and ممخضة *mimkada* pl. ماخض *mamākid*[2] churn

مخط *makata a u* (*makt*, مخوط *mukūt*) and V to blow one's nose

مخاط *mukāt* nasal mucus, snot | مخاط الشمس *m. aš-šams* and مخاط الشيطان *m. aš-šaiṭān* gossamer

مخاطى *mukāṭī* snotty; mucous; slimy, ropy

مخيط *mukkait* (*eg.*) sebesten (Cordia myxa L.; *bot.*)

مخطر II *tamaktara* to walk with a graceful, swinging gait

[1]مخل *mukl* pl. امخال *amkāl*, مخول *mukūl* lever, pinch bar, crowbar

[2]□ مخلة *mikla* (= مخلاة) pl. مخل *mikal*, مخالى *makālī* nosebag

مخمض *makmada* to rinse the mouth

مد *madda u* (*madd*) to extend, distend, expand, dilate (ه s.th.); to stretch, stretch out (ه s.th.), crane (ه the neck); to draw out, protract (ه s.th.); to spread out (ه s.th.); to lay out (ه s.th.), lay (ه tracks, pipeline); to spread (ه a net); to lengthen, elongate, prolong (ه s.th.); to grant a respite or delay; to rise (flood, river); to help, aid, assist (ه s.o.), support (ه ب s.o. by or with), supply, provide (ه ب s.o. with); to reinforce (ه an army); to fertilize, manure (ه the soil) | مد عمره (*'umrahū*) to prolong s.o.'s life (of God); مد البصر الى (*baṣara*) to turn one's eyes, direct one's glance to; مد جذرا فى الارض (*jidran, ard*) to strike roots (tree); مد الحبالة له to lay a snare for s.o.; مد رجله بقدر كسائه (*rijlahū bi-qadri kisā'ihī*) to cut one's coat according to one's cloth, make the best of it, adjust o.s. to the circumstances; مد رجليه بقدر لحافه (*rijlaihi bi-qadri liḥāfihī*) do.; مد سمعه (*sam'ahū*) to prick up one's ears; مد المائدة to set the table; مد فى المشى (*mašy*) to take long strides; مد المواسير to lay pipe; مد اليه يده (*yadahū*) to extend one's hand to s.o. II to extend, distend, expand, dilate (ه s.th.); to stretch out (ه s.th.); to spread, spread out (ه s.th.); to lengthen, elongate, protract, prolong (ه s.th.); to discharge pus, suppurate, fester III to delay, defer, procrastinate; to put off from day to day (ه s.o.) IV to help, aid, assist (ه s.o.), support (ه ب s.o. with), provide, supply, furnish (ه ,ه ب s.o., s.th. with); to lend, impart (ه ب to s.th. s.th.); to reinforce (ه an army); to postpone, delay, grant a respite; to suppurate, fester | امد باجله (*bi-ajalihī*) to grant s.o. another respite in this life (of God) V to be spread, spread out, extended, stretched out; to extend, stretch, spread;

to lengthen, expand, distend, dilate; to stretch o.s., stretch out, sprawl (on a bed, and the like) **VIII** to be extended, distended, stretched; to be laid (wires, pipeline); to extend or reach (الى to s.th.), stretch, spread (الى to s.th., over a distance); to lengthen, become drawn out, become protracted or prolonged; to be long; to develop, grow (الى into) **X** to take, get, draw, derive, borrow (ه من s.th. from), provide o.s. with (ه); to ask for help (ه s.o.)

مد *madd* pl. مدود *mudūd* extension; distension, dilation, expansion; stretching; spreading; lengthening, elongation, prolongation, protraction; drawing out of the voice over long vowels (in Koran recitation); rising, rise (of water, of the flood); supply (ب with) | مد البصر *m. al-baṣar* range of vision; *maddā l-b.* as far as the eye can see; مد النظر *m. an-naẓar* farsightedness, foresight; حروف المد the "literae productionis" ا و ى (*gram.*)

مدة *madda* sign over alif (آ) denoting initial long *a* (*'ā*)

مد *mudd* pl. امداد *amdād*, مداد *midād* mudd, a dry measure (*Pal.* = 18 l, Tangier = 46.6 l)

مدة *midda* pus, purulent matter

مدة *mudda* pl. مدد *mudad* period (of time), space of time, interval; while; duration; limited or appointed time, term; مدة *muddata* within, in the course of, during | في مدة ... within, in the course of, during; مدة من الزمن (*zaman*) period (of time), space of time, interval, while; *muddatan min az-z.* for a while, for some time

مدد *madad* pl. امداد *amdād* help, aid, assistance, support, backing, reinforcement; pl. resources; auxiliaries

مداد *midād* ink; lamp oil; fertilizer, manure, dung; pattern, style | سجله بمداد الفخر *sajjalahū bi-m. il-fakr* to inscribe s.th. with golden letters; على مداد واحد after the same pattern

مديد *madīd* pl. مدد *mudud* extended, outstretched, stretched, elongated; long, prolonged, protracted; tall, big; slender, high, towering; المديد name of a poetical meter | زمان مديد (*zamān*) or مدة مديدة (*mudda*) long time; عمر مديد (*'umr*) great age; مديد البصر *m. al-baṣar* farsighted, farseeing

مداد *maddād* a creeping plant

امدة *amidda* warp of a fabric

تمديد *tamdīd* pl. *-āt* lengthening, elongation, prolongation, extension

امداد *imdād* help, aid, assistance, support, sustentation, maintenance, provisioning; supply (*mil.*); pl. *-āt* auxiliaries, reinforcements, supplies

تمدد *tamaddud* extension, spreading, expansion; stretching, distention, dilation, dilatation, widening

امتداد *imtidād* stretching, stretch, extension, extensity; extensibility, distensibility; expansibility; widening, distention, dilation, dilatation, lengthening, elongation, prolongation; expanse; length; size, extent, spread, compass, range, scope | على امتداد along, alongside of

استمداد *istimdād* procurement of support, bringing up of reinforcements; supply (*mil.*)

ماد *mādd* stretching, expanding, extending, spreading; trailing, creeping (plant)

مادة *mādda* pl. مواد *mawādd*[2] stuff, matter; material possession; substance; material; component, constituent, ingredient; fundamental constituent, radical, chemical element, base; subject, theme, topic; school subject, field of study; discipline, subject matter, curricular subject; article, paragraph (e.g., of a law, treaty or contract); stipulation, contractual term; pl. material, materials; agents, elements | مادة اصلية (*aṣlīya*) root of a word; مواد اولية (*awwalīya*) primary elements; raw materials; مواد تجارية (*tijārīya*) articles of commerce, commodities; مواد التجميل cosmetics; مواد جنائية (*jināʼīya*) criminal cases (*jur.*); مواد حربية (*ḥarbīya*) war material; مواد خام raw materials; مواد الصباغة dyestuffs, dyes; مواد صلبة (*ṣulba*) solid constituents, solids (e.g., of milk); ○ مواد مصنوعة manufactured goods, ready-made goods; ○ مواد التطبيب medicaments, drugs; مواد الاعاشة *m. al-iʻāša*, مواد المعيش *m. al-maʻīš* foodstuffs, food; مواد غذائية (*ġiḏāʼīya*) foodstuffs, victuals, food, nutritive substances; fodder; مواد اللغة *m. al-luġa* vocabulary of a language; ○ مواد مضادة للحيويات (*muḍādda li-l-ḥayawīyāt* antibiotics; مواد ملتهبة (*multahiba*) combustible materials, inflammable matter; fuel; مواد مدنية (*madanīya*) civil cases (*jur.*); مواد النسيج textiles

مادى *māddī* material; corporeal, physical; materialistic; (pl. *-ūn*) materialist; objective (as opposed to شخصى)

مادية *māddīya* materialism | الماديات والمعنويات (*maʻnawīyāt*) material and ideal things

ممدود *mamdūd* extended; outstretched; elongated; prolonged, protracted, drawn out; extensive, great, large; provided with *madda* (*gram.*)

ممدد *mumaddad* spread, outspread; outstretched; stretched out, sprawling, lying; extended, elongated, long

ممتد *mumtadd* extended, outstretched; spread, outspread, laid out; extending, stretching, spreading; extensive, wide, large, comprehensive

مستمد *mustamadd* taken, derived (من from)

مداليه *madāliya* pl. مداليات *madāliyāt* medal

مداليون *madāliyōn* medallion, locket, pendant

مدح **madaḥa** *a* (*madḥ*, مدحة *midḥa*) to praise, commend, laud, extol (ه s.o.); to eulogize, celebrate in poems (ه s.o.) **II** do. **V** to be commended, be praised, be lauded; to boast (ب of s.th.), glory (ب in), pride o.s. (ب on), be proud (ب of) **VIII** = **I**

مدح *madḥ* commendation, laudation, praise; extolment, glorification; panegyrical literature; acclaim | المدح فى الله the glorification of God

مديح *madīḥ* pl. مدائح *madāʼiḥ*[2] praise, laudation, commendation; panegyrical poem, panegyric; eulogy, encomium, tribute

امدوحة *umdūḥa* pl. اماديح *amādīḥ*[2] praise, laudation, commendation; panegyrical poem; eulogy, encomium, tribute

تمدح *tamadduḥ* extolment, glorification; self-praise, vainglory, ostentation, swaggering

مادح *mādiḥ* and مداح *maddāḥ* panegyrist, encomiast, eulogist

[1]مدر *madar* (coll.; n. un. ة) clods of earth or mud, loam, clay | اهل الوبر والمدر *ahl al-wabar wa-l-m.* the tent-dwellers and the city-dwellers, the nomads and the sedentary population

مدرة *madara* clod of earth or mud; small hump of the ground

[2]مدراء *mudarāʼ*[2] pl. of مدير *mudīr*, see دور

مدراس *madrās*[2] Madras (state and city in S India)

مدريد *madrīd*[2] Madrid

مدلن (Engl.) *midlin* middling, of medium quality (*com.*)

مدن **II** to found or build cities; to civilize, urbanize, humanize, refine **V** تمدن *ta-*

maddana to be or become civilized; تمدين *tamadyana* do.; to enjoy the comforts of civilization, the amenities of life

مدينة *madīna* pl. مدن *mudun*, مدائن *madā'in*² town, city | مدينة النبى *m. an-nabī* or المدينة (usually followed by the epithet المنورة *al-munawwara*) Medina (city in W Saudi Arabia); مدينة السلام *m. as-salām* Baghdad (capital of Iraq); مدينة الكاب Cape Town; المدن الكبرى (*kubrā*) the big cities

مدنى *madanī* urban, urbanized, city-dwelling, town-dwelling; civilized, refined, polished; civilian (as opposed to military), civil, civic; secular; town dweller, townsman, city dweller, urbanite, citizen, civilian; of Medina, Medinan (adj. and n.) | دعوى مدنية (*da'wā*) civil action, civil suit, civil proceeding (*jur.*); الطيران المدنى (*ṭayarān*) civil aeronautics; قانون مدنى civil law

مدنية *madanīya* civilization

تمدين *tamdīn* civilizing, civilization, advancement in social culture, humanization, refining, raising of moral standards

تمدينى *tamdīnī* civilizing, civilizatory, civilizational

تمدن *tamaddun* and تمدين *tamadyun* civilization; refinement of social culture

تمدنى *tamadduni* civilized

متمدن *mutamaddin* civilized; sophisticated, refined, educated

متمدين *mutamadyin* civilized, provided with the comforts of civilization

مدى III to grant a respite or delay (ه to s.o.) IV do. VI to persist, persevere (فى or ب or على in), keep, stick, adhere (فى or ب or على to); to continue (فى s.th.), keep or go on (فى doing s.th.); to go far, go to extremes (فى in); to continue, last, draw out

مدى *madan* extension, expanse, stretch, spread, compass, range, scope, space, latitude, reach; distance, interval, interspace; extent, degree, measure, scale, proportion; utmost point, extreme, limit; space of time, duration, period; (prep.) مدى *madā* for the duration of, during, in a (given) period of, in the course of | مدى البصر *m. l-baṣar* range or field of vision, visual range; مدى الحياة *m. l-ḥayāh* lifetime; for life; المدى الحيوى (*ḥayawī*) lebensraum; مدى الدوران *m. d-dawarān* continually, constantly, perpetually; مدى الصوت *m. ṣ-ṣaut* reach of the voice, calling distance; مدى العمر *m. l-'umr* lifetime; مدى الايام *m. l-ayyām* throughout the days, continually; الى مدى بعيد at a great distance; على مدى عشر امتار (*'ašri a.*) at a distance of 10 meters; بعيد المدى far-reaching; مدفع بعيد المدى (*midfa'*) long-range gun; فى المدى الاخير after all, when all's said and done, in the last analysis

مدية *madya*, *mudya*, *midya* pl. مدى *mudan*, *midan*, مديات *mudyāt*, *mudayāt* butcher's knife; knife

مدوى *madawī*, *mudawī*, *midawī* cutler

تماد *tamādin*: مع طول التمادى ,مع التمادى in the long run

مديل (Fr. *modèle*) *modēl* pl. *-āt* model

مدين II *tamadyana* see مدن

مذ *muḏ* since (= منذ *munḏu*)

مذر *maḏira a* (*maḏar*) to be addle (egg), become rotten II to scatter, disperse, spread or sprinkle about (ه s.th.) V = I

شذر مذر *šaḏara maḏara* scattered here and there

مذر *maḏir* spoiled, rotten, putrid

مذق *maḏaqa u* (*maḏq*) to mix with water, dilute

مذق *maḏq* watered wine

مذيق *madīq* diluted, mixed with water, watered, watery

مذاق *maddāq* and مماذق *mumādiq* insincere, hypocritical

مذل *madila a* (*madl,* مذال *madāl*) to reveal, disclose (ب s.th. secret)

مذهب II *tamadhaba* see ذهب

[1]مر *marra u* (*marr,* مرور *murūr,* ممر *mamarr*) to pass (ب or على s.o., s.th. or by s.o., by s.th.), go, walk, saunter, or stroll by or past (ب, على); to march past s.o. (امام), pass in review (امام before s.o.; *mil.*); to pass, elapse, go by, run out (time); to come, go, walk, or pass along s.th. (ب or على), skirt (ب or على s.th.); to pass, go, walk, move, march, travel (ب or من or على through), cross, traverse (من a place, a country, a room); to flow through, run through; to fly through; to lead, run, out (في through an area; border), pass (في over), cross (في an area); to go or pass (ب through a stage or phase), undergo (ب a state or phase); to cross (على a border, a line, mountains, etc.); to fly (فوق over an area; airplane); to depart, go away, leave; to continue (يفعل to do s.th.), keep, or go on, doing s.th. | مر ذكره (*dikruhū*) it has been discussed, it has been mentioned above; كما مر بنا as it has passed before us, as we have already mentioned; مر بالامتحان to pass the examination; مر بسلام (*bi-salām*) to turn out well, go off without mishap; مر عليه ببصره (*bi-baṣarihī*) to scan s.th., peruse s.th. hastily; مر مر البرق (*marra l-barq*) to pass swiftly, flash past, flit past; مر مر الكرام (*marra l-k.*) to pass as if nothing had happened, brush past; مر به (or عليه) مر الكرام to overlook s.th. generously, pass over s.th. with dignity, treat s.th. with disdain **II** to let pass (ه s.th.); to convey, carry or take through (ه s.th.); to pass (ه the ball, in soccer) | مرر سفينة في القناة (*qanāh*) to pass or take a ship through the canal **IV** to let (ه s.o.) go by or past s.o. or s.th. (ب or على); to let (ه s.o.) pass (ب or على s.th.); to make (ه, ه s.o., s.th.) go through s.th. (ب or على), lead, take or send (ه s.o.) through (ب or على), pass, stick (ب or على ه s.th. through); to insert (ب or على ه s.th. in) | أمر نظره على (*naẓarahū*) to pass one's glance over, let one's eyes wander over **X** to last, endure, continue, go on; to remain, stay; to continue (على or في s.th., يفعل to do s.th.), persist, persevere (على or في in s.th.), keep (على or في to s.th., يفعل doing s.th.), go on (يفعل doing s.th.), stick, adhere (على or في to s.th.)

مر *marr* passing, going by; passage, transit; transition; crossing; progression, process, lapse, course (of time); iron shovel, spade; rope | على مر الزمان (*m. iz-zamān*) in the course of time

مرة *marra* pl. *-āt,* مرار *mirār* time, turn; مرة *marratan* once; مرتين *marrataini* twice; مرات *marrātin* repeatedly; several times, quite often; مرارا *mirāran* several times, more than once, quite often; at times, now and then, occasionally, sometimes | مرة ما *marratan mā* or ذات مرة *dāta marratin* once, one time, one day; مرة اخرى *marratan ukrā* or مرة جديدة (*jadīdatan*) once again, once more, anew; مرة بعد مرة or مرة عن مرة time and again, again and again; المرة تلو المرة (*tilwa*) time after time, time and again; مرة واحدة (*wāḥidatan*) at once, at one time; eventually, finally, at last; اكثر من مرة (*akṯara*) more than once, several times; بالمرة at all, absolutely, entirely; (with neg.) not at all, never, by no means; غير مرة *ġaira marratin* or غيرما مرة repeatedly, several times, more than once; كم مرة *kam marratan* how often? how many times? للمرة السادسة for the sixth time; لآخر مرة *li-ākiri marratin* or للمرة الاخيرة for the last time; لاول مرة *li-awwali marratin* for the first time; مرارا عديدة (*ʿadīdatan*) frequently, often; مرارا

وتكرارا (*wa-takrāran*) time and again, again and again

مرور *murūr* passing; parade, march past (امام); passage, march, journey, or trip through (ب, من, على), transit; flowing through, flow; crossing, traversal; flying over (فوق); uninterrupted sequence; traffic (street, tourist, shipping); progression, process, course, lapse (of time); (*eg.*) inspection | مرور الزمان *m. az-zamān* expiration of the deadline; تذكرة المرور *tadkirat al-m.* permit, pass, laissez-passer; passport; حركة المرور *ḥarakat al-m.* through traffic; شرطة المرور *šurṭat al-m* traffic police, highway patrol; نظام المرور traffic regulations

ممر *mamarr* passing, going by; elapsing; lapse, expiration (of time); transition; crossing; access, approach; (pl. *-āt*) aisle, passage, passageway, corridor; ford; (mountain) pass | ممر سفلي (*suflī*) underpass; على ممر العصور in the course of centuries

امرار *imrār* passing through, insertion

استمرار *istimrār* duration, permanence, continuity, continuance, continuation, continued existence, survival; persistence | باستمرار continually, constantly; دواما واستمرارا (*dawāman*) constantly, continuously, incessantly, without interruption; قوة الاستمرار *qūwat al-ist.* inertia, vis inertiae

مار *mārr* passing; going, walking, riding, etc., past or by; (pl. *-ūn*, مارة *mārra*) passer-by, pedestrian, walker, stroller | المار ذكره (*dikruhū*) the above-mentioned, what has already been discussed

مستمر *mustamirr* lasting, permanent, enduring, constant, continual, uninterrupted, unceasing, incessant; continuous, unbroken | تيار مستمر (*tayyār*) direct current (*el.*); موجات مستمرة (*maujāt*) continuous waves (*phys.*)

مر[2] *marra u a* (مرارة *marāra*) to be or become bitter II to make bitter, embitter (ه s.th.) IV to be or become bitter; to make bitter (ه s.th.) VI to fight, contend, dispute (with each other) X to think bitter, find bitter (ه s.th.)

مر *murr* pl. امرار *amrār* bitter; severe; sharp; painful; bitterness; myrrh | مر الصحارى *m. aṣ-ṣaḥārā* colocynth (*bot.*)

مرة *mirra* pl. مرر *mirar* gall, bile; (pl. امرار *amrār*) strength, power

مرارة *marāra* pl. مرائر *marā'ir*[2] bitterness; gall, gall bladder; innermost, heart | انشقت مرارته غيظا (*inšaqqat, ġaiẓan*) he burst with anger

مرير *marīr* pl. مرائر *marā'ir*[2] strong, firm, stubborn, tenacious, dogged, persistent, deep-seated, deep, profound (esp., of feelings)

مريرة *marīra* pl. مرائر *marā'ir*[2] firmness; determination, resoluteness; vigor, energy, tenacity, doggedness; steadiness, constancy

امر *amarr*[2] firmer, stronger; bitterer | الامران the two bitter things (i.e., poverty and old age); قاسى الامرين *qāsā l-amarrain* to go through the worst, be exposed to greatest hardships

ممرور *mamrūr* bilious; foolish, crazy; fool

مرأ *mara'a*, مرئ *mari'a a* and مرؤ *maru'a u* (مراءة *marā'a*) to be wholesome, healthful, palatable (food); — مرؤ *maru'a u* (مروءة *murū'a*) to be manly; — مرؤ *maru'a u* (مراءة *marā'a*) to be healthy and salubrious (climate) X to find wholesome and tasty (ه food); to enjoy, savor, relish (ه s.th.); to be able to digest (ه s.th.; also fig.); to take to s.th. (ه), take a liking (ب to), derive pleasure (ه from)

امرؤ ,امرأ ,امرء *imra'* and امرؤ *imru'* (with definite article المرء *al-mar'*) a man; person, human being; المرء frequently for Engl. "one", as يظن المرء (*yaẓunnu*) one would think

امرأة *imra'a* (with def. article المرأة *al-mar'a*) pl. see نسو, woman; wife | المرأة المسلسلة (*musalsala*) Andromeda (*astron.*)

مروءة *murū'a* and مروة *murūwa* the ideal of manhood, comprising all knightly virtues, esp., manliness, valor, chivalry, generosity, sense of honor

مرىء *marī'* manly, virile; healthful, salubrious, healthy, wholesome | هنيئا مريئا (*hanī'an*) approx.: may it do you much good! I hope you will enjoy it (i.e., food)!

مرىء *marī'* pl. امرئة *amri'a*, مروء *murū'* esophagus, gullet

مراكش *marrākuš*[2], *marrākiš*[2] Marrakech (city in W Morocco); Morocco

مراكشى *marrākušī*, *marrākišī* Moroccan (adj. and n.)

مرث *maraṯa u* (*marṯ*) to suck, bite (ه one's fingers); to soften, crush, squash, mash (ه s.th.); to macerate, soak (in water; ه s.th.)

[1]مرج *marj* pl. مروج *murūj* grass-covered steppe; pasture land; meadow

هرج ومرج *harj wa-marj* confusion, jumble, tumult, hubbub

مرج *maraj* disorder, confusion, jumble

[2]مرجان *marjān*, *murjān* (coll.; n. un. ة) small pearls; corals | سمك مرجان *samak m.* goldfish

مرجانى *marjānī* coralline, coral, coralli- (in compounds), corallike, coral-red | جزيرة مرجانية atoll; شعاب مرجانية coral reefs

مرجح *marjaḥa* to rock II *tamarjaḥa* to swing back and forth, pendulate, dangle; to be in suspense, be pending, be in abeyance

مرح *mariḥa a* (*maraḥ*) to be gay, merry, cheerful, in high spirits, hilarious, exuberant, lively; to be glad, happy, delighted; to rejoice, exult | سرح ومرح (*sariḥa*) to do as one likes, proceed arbitrarily

مرح *maraḥ* joy, cheerfulness, gaiety, glee, mirth, hilarity, merriment, liveliness

مرح *mariḥ* pl. مرحى *marḥā*, مراحى *marāḥā* joyful, gay, happy, merry, cheerful, lively, romping, hilarious, exuberant

مراح *mirāḥ* jollity, hilarity, exuberance

مريح *mirrīḥ* joyful, gay, happy, merry, cheerful, lively, romping, hilarious, exuberant

مرحى *marḥā* well done! bravo! | مرحى ب bravo to ...

ممراح *mimrāḥ* of cheerful disposition, gay-tempered, blithe; gay, jovial person

مرحب *marḥaba* to welcome (ه s.o.)

مرخ *maraḵa a* (*marḵ*) to oil, anoint, rub, embrocate (ه the body) II do. V to rub one's skin with a liniment, oil o.s., anoint o.s.

مرخ *mariḵ* soft; slack, flabby, flaccid

مروخ *marūḵ* liniment; salve, unguent, ointment

مريخ *mirrīḵ* Mars (*astron.*)

مرد *marada u* (مرود *murūd*) and *maruda u* (مرادة *marāda*, مرودة *murūda*) to be refractory, recalcitrant, rebellious; to revolt, rebel (على against) II to strip (ه a branch) of its leaves; to plaster, mortar, face (ه a building) V to be refractory, recalcitrant; to revolt, rebel (على against); to be insolent, arrogant, overbearing

مردى *murdī* pl. مرادى *marādīy* (punting) pole, boat hook

مراد *marād, marrād* pl. مراريد *marārīd*[2] nape, neck

مريد *marīd* pl. مرداء *muradā'*[2] refractory, recalcitrant, rebellious

تمراد *timrād* pl. تماريد *tamārīd*[2] dovecot

امرد *amrad*[2], f. مرداء *mardā'*[2], pl. مرد *murd* beardless; leafless (tree); dry, withered

تمرد *tamarrud* refractoriness, recalcitrance, disobedience, insubordination; uprising, insurrection, mutiny, revolt, rebellion

مارد *mārid* pl. *-ūn*, مردة *marada*, مراد *murrād* refractory, recalcitrant, defiant; rebel, insurgent; demon, evil spirit, devil; giant

متمرد *mutamarrid* refractory, recalcitrant, disobedient, insubordinate, mutinous, rebellious

مردقوش *mardaqūš* marjoram

مرزبان *marzubān* pl. مرازبة *marāziba* vicegerent, provincial governor, satrap (in ancient Persia)

مرزجوش *marzajūš*, مرزنجوش *marzanjūš* = مردقوش

مرس *marasa u* (*mars*) to soak (in water), macerate (ه s.th.) **III** to exercise, pursue, practice (ه s.th., esp., a profession); (intr.) to practice, have or operate a practice; to carry out, execute (ه an action); to apply o.s. (ه to s.th.), go in for (ه); to try **V** to rub o.s. (ب with, against); to have trouble, be at odds (ب with); to exercise (ب an office), pursue, practice (ب a profession); to work (ب with), be in practical contact, have actually to do (ب with s.th.); to have to cope or struggle (ب with s.th.) **VI** to fight, struggle, contend with each other

مرس *mars* game which is won by getting all the tricks

مرس *maris* pl. امراس *amrās* seasoned, practiced, experienced, veteran

مرسة *marasa* pl. امراس *amrās* rope, cord, line; cable, hawser

مراس *mirās* and مراسة *marāsa* strength, power | سهل المراس *sahl al-m.* tractable, manageable, docile, compliant; شديد المراس or صعب المراس *ṣa'b al-m.* intractable, unruly, refractory; صعوبة المراس intractability, unruliness, refractoriness, recalcitrance

مريسة *marīsa* a kind of beer

مريسى *marīsī* hot south wind (*eg.*)

ممارسة *mumārasa* pursuit, exercise, practicing (of a profession); execution, implementation; practical application; practice; experience, routine; negotiation

تمرس *tamarrus* practicing, practice (ب of an activity, of a profession)

مرسيليا *marsīliyā* Marseille (seaport in SE France)

مرسين *marsīn* myrtle (myrtus; *bot.*)

مرش *maraša u* (*marš*) to scratch (ه s.th.)

مرشال *maršāl* (field) marshal

مرص *murṣ* Morse (code)

مرض *mariḍa a* (*maraḍ*) to be or become sick; to fall ill, be taken ill **II** to make ill or sick (ه s.o.); to nurse, tend (ه a sick person) **IV** to make ill or sick (ه s.o.) **V** to be infirm, ailing, sickly, weak **VI** to feign illness, malinger

مرض *maraḍ* pl. امراض *amrāḍ* disease, malady, ailment; illness, sickness | مرض البياض الدقيقى *m. al-bayāḍ ad-daqīqī* mildew; مرض عصبى (*'aṣabī*) nervous disease, neuropathy; مرض عقلى (*'aqlī*) mental disease; مرض فحمى (*faḥmī*) blight, blast (of grain); مرض فرنجى (*firanjī*) syphilis; مرض معد (*mu'din*) contagious disease; امراض باطنية (*bāṭinīya*) internal diseases; امراض

سرية (*sirrīya*) venereal diseases; امراض صدرية (*ṣadrīya*) diseases of the chest, pulmonary diseases

مرضٍ *murḍin* see رضى

مرضى *maraḍī* relating to disease, morbid, pathological, patho- (in compounds)

مريض *marīḍ* pl. مرضى *marḍā*, مراضى *marāḍā* sick, ill, ailing; diseased; unwell, indisposed; sick person, patient | مريض نفسى (*nafsī*) psychopath

ممراض *mimrāḍ* sickly, in poor health, ailing

تمريض *tamrīḍ* sick-nursing

ممرض *mumarriḍ* (male) sick nurse, hospital attendant; ambulance man, first-aid man; doctor's assistant

ممرضة *mumarriḍa* sick nurse, nurse (f.)

متمرض *mutamarriḍ* sickly, in poor health, ailing

مرط *maraṭa* u (*marṭ*) to tear out, pull out, pluck out (ه hair) II do. V to fall out (hair)

مريط *marīṭ* and امرط *amraṭ*², f. مرطاء *marṭā'*², pl. مرط *murṭ* hairless

مرع *mara'a* a (*mar'*) to rub over, anoint (ه s.th.)

مرع *mar'* pl. امرع *amru'*, امراع *amrā'* pasture

مرعة *mur'a* grease, oil

مريع *marī'* fertile, productive (soil)

ممراع *mimrā'* thriving, flourishing, prosperous (city)

مرغ II to roll (in the dust) (ه s.th.); to rub over (ه s.th.); to rub (ه s.th.) IV to soil, sully, make dirty (ه s.th.) V to roll, wallow (esp., in the dust); to waver irresolutely

مرغرين *margarīn* margarine

مرفين *murfīn* morphine

مرق *maraqa* u (مروق *murūq*) to pierce, penetrate (من s.th. or s.o.; esp., of an arrow), go or pass through (من); to dart, rush, shoot, or fly past, pass swiftly; to hurry away, scamper away; to stray (e.g., of an arrow); to digress, deviate; to renege, renounce (esp. من الدين the true faith) | مرق السهم (*sahmu*) (lit.: the arrow has passed through, i.e.) the matter is finished, done with, settled II to sing

مرق *maraq* and مرقة *maraqa* broth, bouillon; gravy

مروق *murūq* straying, deviation; apostasy, defection, desertion, disloyalty

مروقى *murūqī* (*tun.*) nickname of professional Koran reciters in Tunis; (*tun.*) pallbearer

مارق *māriq* pl. مراق *murrāq*, مرقة *maraqa* straying; apostate, renegade, defector, turncoat, deserter; heretic

ممارق *mumāriq* insolent, impudent

مركز II *tamarkaza* to concentrate (فى on, at, in); to settle, establish o.s., gain a footing, take root; to consolidate one's position; to gravitate (to)

مركز, مركزية etc., see ركز

مركيز look up alphabetically

تمركز *tamarkuz* concentration; consolidation (of a position)

مراكش *marrākuš*², *marrākiš*² Marrakech (city in W Morocco); Morocco

مراكشى *marrākušī*, *marrākišī* Moroccan (adj. and n.)

مركيز *markīz* marquis

مرمتون (Fr. *marmiton*) *marmatōn* and مرمطون pl. *-āt* kitchen boy, scullery boy

¹مرمر *marmara* to be or become bitter; to become angry II *tamarmara* to murmur, mumble; to grumble

[2]مرمر *marmar* marble

مرمرى *marmarī* marble (adj.)

مرمط *marmaṭa* (*eg.*) to spoil, damage (ه s.th.)

مرمتون see مرمطون

مرميس *mirmīs* rhinoceros

[1]مرن *marana u* (مرانة *marāna*, مرون *murūn*, مرونة *murūna*) to be pliant, flexible, ductile, elastic; — (مرون *murūn*, مرانة *marāna*) to be or become accustomed, get used (على to) **II** to train, drill (ه s.o.); to accustom, condition, season, inure (ه على s.o. to), make (ه s.o.) get used (على to) **V** to become accustomed, get used (على to); to exercise, practice (على s.th.), train (على in), be practiced, trained, experienced (على in); to be drilled, drill

مرن *marin* pliant, pliable, flexible, bending; elastic; plastic; supple, limber, lithe; ductile, extensible; yielding, compliant

مرانة *marāna* and مرونة *murūna* pliancy, pliability, flexibility; elasticity; ductility; plasticity; agility, nimbleness; resilience

تمرين *tamrīn* pl. *-āt*, تمارين *tamārīn*[2] exercise, practice, training; military training, drill; practical experience; expertness, skill; preparatory training, (period of) probation, apprenticeship, traineeship | تمرين ابتدائى (*ibtidā'ī*) basic training; تمارين جندية (*jundīya*) or تمرينات عسكرية (*'askarīya*) military exercises, maneuvers; ○ تمرين الزيادة coaching, tutoring; extra drill (*mil.*); تمرينات رياضية (*riyāḍīya*) gymnastic exercises; تحت التمرين undergoing preparatory training, engaged on probation (official, employee)

مران *mirān* expertness, skill; exercise, practice, drill, training; habituation, habit; accustomedness; practical experience; routine

تمرن *tamarrun* exercise, practice, training

ممرن *mumarrin* trainer, coach; instructor; drill sergeant

ممرن *mumarran* practiced, seasoned, experienced, trained, skilled (على in); accustomed, used (على to)

متمرن *mutamarrin* practiced, seasoned, experienced, trained, skilled (على in); accustomed, used (على to); probationer, undergoing probation, probationary

[2]مارونى pl. موارنة look up alphabetically

[1]مرو *marw* Merv (present-day Mary, town in Turkmen S.S.R.)

مروى *marwī*, *marauī* native of Merv

[2]مرو *marw* (coll.; n. un. ة) pebble; flint

[3]مروة see مروة

[1]مرى **III** to wrangle, argue, dispute (ه with s.o.); to resist, oppose (ه s.o.); to contest (فى s.th.) **VIII** to doubt (فى s.th.)

مرية *murya*, *mirya* doubt, quarrel, wrangle, argument, dispute

مراء *mirā'* quarrel, wrangle, argument, dispute; doubt | بلا مراء (*bi-lā*) or لا مراء فيه (*mirā'a*) incontestable, indisputable, unquestionable, undisputed, uncontested; لا مراء فى أن it is an incontrovertible fact that ..., unquestionably ...

[2]مرايا pl. of مرآة see رأى

مريم *maryam*[2] Mary, Maria

مريمية *maryamīya* sage (*bot.*)

مز *mazza u* (*mazz*) to suck

مز *muzz* sourish, acidulous

مزة *mazza* pl. *-āt* and مازة *māzza* (*eg.*) relishes, appetizers (taken with drink)

مزج *mazaja u* (*mazj*, مزاج *mizāj*) to mix, mingle, blend (بين different things, ه ب

s.th. with) III to form a mixture or compound, be mixed, be blended, mix, mingle, blend, combine (ه with s.th.); to adapt o.s. (ه to s.o.), humor (ه s.o.) VI to intermix, intermingle, interblend, be intermixed, be intermingled VIII to be mixed, be mingled, be blended, mix, mingle, blend (ب with)

مزج *mazj* mixing, blending

مزاج *mizāj* pl. امزجة *amzija* mixture, medley, blend; temperament, temper, nature, disposition; frame of mind, mood, humor, vein; physical constitution; condition, (state of) health | مزاج دموى (*damawī*) sanguine temperament; مزاج سوداوى (*saudāwī*) melancholic temperament; مزاج صفراوى (*safrāwī*) choleric (or bilious) temperament; مزاج بلغمى (*balġamī*) phlegmatic temperament; المزاج العام (*ʿāmm*) popular taste; مزاج لطيف delicate nature, weakly constitution; محرور المزاج hot-tempered; منحرف المزاج *munḥarif al-m.* unwell, indisposed, out of sorts; هذا لا يوافق مزاجى (*yuwāfiqu*) this is not to my taste

مزيج *mazīj* compounded, blended (من of); mixture, medley, blend (من of); combination, compound, alloy

تمازج *tamāzuj* intermixing, intermingling, interblending, intermixture

امتزاج *imtizāj* mixture, blend

مزح *mazaḥa a* (*mazḥ*) to joke, jest, make fun III to joke, make fun (ه with s.o.)

مزح *mazḥ*, مزاح *muzāḥ*, *mizāḥ* and مزاحة *muzāḥa* joking, joke, jest, fun

مزاح *mazzāḥ* and مازح *māziḥ* joker, jester, buffoon, wag

مزر *mizr* a kind of beer

مزع *mazaʿa a* (*mazʿ*) to run, bound, tear along, gallop along; to tear apart (ه s.th.); to tear, rip (من ه s.th. off) II to pick, pluck (ه wool or cotton); to tear to pieces (ه s.th.)

مزعة *muzʿa*, *mizʿa* pl. مزع *muzaʿ*, *mizaʿ* piece, bit, bite; flock of wool

مزق *mazaqa i* (*mazq*) to tear, rend, rip apart (ه s.th.) II to tear, rend, rip apart (ه s.th.); to tear up, tear to pieces, shred (ه s.th.) V to get torn, be rent; to be in shreds, get torn to pieces; to burst open, tear, break, snap

مزق *mazq* tearing, tearing up, rending; tear, rent, rupture

مزقة *mizqa* pl. مزق *mizaq* piece torn off, shred

تمزيق *tamzīq* tearing, rending, shredding, fragmentation

مزمز *mazmaza* to sip

مزن *muzn* (coll.; n. un. ة, pl. مزن *muzan*) rain clouds

مزية *mazīya* pl. مزايا *mazāyā* and مازية *māziya* pl. *-āt* advantage; privilege, prerogative; excellence, superiority; merit, virtue

مس *massa a* (*mass*, مسيس *masīs*) to feel, finger, handle, palpate (ه s.o., ه s.th.); to touch (ه s.o., ه s.th.); to violate (ه s.th. sacred), infringe (ه upon); to cohabit (ه with a woman); to hit, befall (ه s.o.; damage, calamity) | مسه بأذى (*bi-aḏan*) or مسه بسوء (*bi-sūʾin*) to harm, wrong, hurt s.o.; مس بسوء الشئ to be injurious, damaging to s.th., hurt, impair, prejudice s.th.; مست الحاجة الى (*ḥājatu*) circumstances require ..., (it) is necessary, urgently needed; مس لغما (*luġman*) to hit a mine III to touch (ه s.o.); to be in touch, be in contact (ه with s.o.) VI to touch each other, be in mutual contact

مس *mass* touching, touch; contact; misfortune, calamity; attack, fit (of a disease); insanity, madness, frenzy, possession | مس الحمى *m. al-ḥummā* attack of fever; اصابه مس من الجنون (*aṣābahū*) he has gone crazy

مسة *massa* (n. vic.) touch

مساس *misās* touching, feeling, handling, fingering, palpation; violation (ب of), infringement, encroachment (ب e.g., upon a right); connection, relation, contact | له مساس ب it is connected with ..., it touches upon ..., it concerns; فيما له مساس ب concerning ..., regarding ...

مسيس *masīs* touching, touch | عند مسيس الحاجة should the necessity arise, if (or when) necessary; هو فى مسيس الحاجة ال he is in urgent need of ...

مماسة *mumāssa* touching, tangency; adjacency, contiguity; contact

تماس *tamāss* (mutual) contact

ماس *māss* tangent; touching (ب s.th., also fig., upon s.th.); adjacent, adjoining, contiguous; urgent, pressing, important | حاجة ماسة urgent need, exigency; الحاجة ماسة اليه it is urgently needed; ماس كهربائى (*kahrabā'ī*) short circuit

ممسوس *mamsūs* touched; palpable, tangible; mentally deranged, insane

مماس *mumāss* tangent (*math.*)

مسترده (It. *mostarda*) *mustarda* mustard

مستكه *mistika* = مصطكاء

مستلة (It. *mastello*) *mastilla* pl. *-āt* tub

[1]مسح *masaḥa* *a* (*masḥ*) to stroke with the hand (ه s.th.); to wipe off, wipe away (ه s.th.); to rub off (ه s.th.); to wash, wash off (ه s.th.); to wipe out, blot out, erase (ه s.th.); to clean, polish (ه s.th.); to smooth, smooth with a plane, to plane (ه s.th.); to rub (ه ب s.o. with); to anoint (ه ب s.o. with); to deprive, dispossess (ه من s.o. of), take away, withdraw (ه من from s.o. s.th.); — (*masḥ*, مساحة *misāḥa*) to survey (ه land, estate, etc.), make a cadastral survey (ه of) II to wipe off (ه s.th.); to rub, anoint (ه s.o.); to cajole, coax, wheedle, persuade (ه s.o.); to Christianize (ه s.o.) III to cajole, coax, wheedle, persuade (ه s.o.) V to wipe o.s., wash o.s.; to provoke (ب s.o.), pick a quarrel (ب with)

مسح *masḥ* wiping, wiping off; cleaning; rubbing, embrocation; anointing, anointment, (extreme) unction; land survey

مسح *misḥ* pl. مسوح *musūḥ* coarse woolen fabric, haircloth, sacking; pl. hair shirt, monastic garb, monk's frock | لبست المسوح *labisat il-musūḥa* to take the veil, become a nun

مسحة *masḥa* (n. vic.) a rubbing, embrocation; anointing, anointment; unction; tinge, shade, air, appearance, veneer (fig.); trace, touch (of s.th.) | مسحة المريض extreme unction; مسح المريض بالمسحة to administer extreme unction to a sick person

مساح *massāḥ* land surveyor; bootblack, shoeblack, shoeshine

مساحة *misāḥa* pl. *-āt* plane, surface; area; acreage; floor space; surface extent; terrain sector (*mil.*); surveying, survey; geodesy; cadastre | مساحة الاراضى *m. al-arāḍī* land surface; area, acreage; مساحة مائية (*ma'īya*) area of water; مصلحة المساحة *maṣlaḥat al-m.* survey department, land registry office

مسيح *masīḥ* pl. مسحاء *musaḥā'*[2], مسحى *masḥā* anointed; wiped, clean, smooth; المسيح the Messiah, Christ

مسيحى *masīḥī* Christian, Messianic; (pl. *-ūn*) a Christian | الدين المسيحى (*dīn*) the Christian faith, Christianity

المسيحية *al-masīḥīya* Christendom; Christianity, the Christian faith

ممسح *mimsaḥ* and ممسحة *mimsaḥa* pl. مماسح *mamāsiḥ*[2] dust cloth, dish rag, floor rag; doormat; scraper

ماسح *māsiḥ* bootblack, shoeblack, shoeshine

ممسوح *mamsūḥ* wiped, wiped off, wiped clean; cleaned; smoothed, planed; polished; smooth; anointed; abraded, worn (coin) | ممسوح من المعنى (*ma'nā*) senseless, meaningless, inane

تمساح *timsāḥ* pl. تماسيح *tamāsīḥ*[2] crocodile (*zool.*)

مسخ *masaka a* (*mask*) to transform (ه من — الى s.o. from — into), transmute, convert (ه s.th.); to falsify, distort (ه s.th.); to mar, spoil (ه s.th.)

مسخ *mask* transformation, metamorphosis; transmutation, conversion; falsification, distortion, misrepresentation; metempsychosis

مسخ *mask*, *misk* pl. مسوخ *musūk* transformed into an animal; misshapen, deformed, disfigured; ugly, misshapen midget; freak, monstrosity; monster

مسخة *muska* (*eg.*) buffoon, harlequin, clown

مسيخ *masīk* transformed; disfigured, defaced, deformed, ugly; tasteless, insipid, stale

ممسوخ *mamsūk* transformed; marred, spoiled; disfigured, defaced, deformed, ugly

مسخر *maskara* to ridicule, mock, deride (ه s.o.) II *tamaskara* to make fun (على of), laugh (على at)

مسد II to massage (اعضاءه *a'ḍā'ahū* s.o.'s limbs)

مسد *masad* (coll.) pl. مساد *misād*, امساد *amsād* palm fibers, raffia

تمسيد *tamsīd* massage

[1]ماسورة look up alphabetically

[2]مسرى *misrā* the 12th month of the Coptic calendar

مسطرة (It. *mostra*) *masṭara* pl. مساطر *masāṭir*[2] sample, specimen; see also سطر

مسقط *masqaṭ*[2] Masqat (seaport and capital of Oman)

[1]مسك *masaka u i* (*mask*) to grab, grasp, clutch, clasp, seize (ب or ه s.th.), take hold (ب or ه of); to hold, hold fast (ب or ه s.th.); to stick, cling, cleave, adhere, hang on (ب to) | مسك الحسابات (*ḥisābāt*) to keep the books, keep the accounts; مسك دفة الامور (*daffata l-u.*) to be at the helm, be in charge; مسك لسانه (*lisānahū*) to keep one's tongue in check II to scent with musk (ه s.th.); to have (ه s.o.) seize or hold IV to seize, grip, grasp, clasp, clutch, hold (ب or ه s.th.); to hold fast, grab (ب or ه, ه s.o., s.th., ه من s.o. by his hair, and the like); to hold back, keep, detain, restrain (ه, ه s.o., s.th., عن from); to withhold, not to expend (ه s.th.); to refrain, abstain, keep, desist (عن from), forbear, cease, stop (عن doing s.th.), keep away, remain aloof (عن from); to keep, retain (ه على نفسه s.th. for o.s.) | امسك عليك (*amsik*) keep ...! امسك نفسه واقفا *wāqifan* to hold o.s. upright; امسك بيده (*bi-yadihī*) to take s.o. by the hand; امسك يده (*yadahū*) to take s.o.'s hand; امسكت عن الصدور to stop publication, fold up (newspaper); امسك لسانه (*lisānahū*) to keep one's tongue in check; امسك البطن (*baṭna*) to constipate (*med.*) V to hold on, hold fast (ب to), clutch (ب s.th.); to stick, cling, cleave (ب to); to hang on (ب to), persist (ب in); to keep, adhere (ب to s.th.); to rise (prices), harden, firm up (quotations) | تمسك بأهدابه (*bi-ahdābihī*) to be most devoted to s.o., be at s.o.'s beck and call, be under s.o.'s thumb; تمسك باهداب الشيء to adhere, cling to s.th.; تمسك برأيه (*bi-ra'yihī*) to stick to one's opinion VI to hold together, be firmly connected, be interlocked; to compose o.s., pull o.s. together; to remain undaunted, remain calm, be

composed; to stay on one's feet; to be in full possession of one's strength; to refrain, abstain, keep (عن from) X to keep, stick, cling, adhere (ب to); to grab, seize (ب s.th.); to refrain, abstain, keep (عن from)

مسك *mask* seizure, grip, hold; detention | مسك الدفاتر bookkeeping; مسك الحسابات *m. al-ḥisābāt* keeping of accounts, accountancy

مسكة *maska* pl. *masakāt* grip, hold

مسك *misk* (m. and f.) musk | مسك الجن *m. al-jinn* a variety of goosefoot (Chenopodium Botrys; *bot.*); مسك الختام *m. al-ḵitām* lit.: the concluding musk (i.e., with which, originally, a letter was finally perfumed), the best following in the end, the crowning touch

مسكة *miska* a little, a touch, a glimpse, a whiff (من of)

مسك *musuk* and مسكة *musaka* grasping, greedy, avaricious

مسكة *muska* pl. مسك *musak* handle; hold; grip; handhold, support | مسكة الامل *m. al-amal* that to which hope clings

مسكة *muska*, *musuka* and مساكة *masāka*, *misāka* avarice

مسكان *muskān* earnest money, pledge

مساك *misāk* dam, weir; hem, border

مسيك *masīk* tenacious; avaricious, miserly; watertight, waterproof

امساك *imsāk* seizure; restraint, detention, check; stop, cessation; abstinence; avarice; constipation (*med.*); time of the day which marks the beginning of the Ramadan fast

امساكية *imsākīya* calendar of fasting during the month of Ramadan

تمسك *tamassuk* adherence; devotedness, devotion, attachment; written commitment, I O U; firming-up, or consolidation, of the market, hardening of quotations | قانون التمسك legal moratorium, moratory law (*jur.*)

تماسك *tamāsuk* holding together, cohesiveness; coherence; cohesion (*phys.*); firmness, solidity; tenacity

استمساك *istimsāk* adherence, loyalty (ب to)

ممسك *mumassak* musky, musk-scented, perfumed

ممسك *mumsik* holding, clutching, grabbing; checking, restraining, withholding; economical, thrifty; grasping, greedy, avaricious

متمسك *mutamassik* holding fast, hanging on, clinging, adhering; tenacious; firm, solid

متماسك *mutamāsik* holding together, coherent, cohesive, hanging together, firmly connected, interlocked; continuous, uninterrupted; firm, solid; tenacious

مستمسك *mustamsik* composed, calm (mind)

مسكاتى[2] *muskātī* muscatel (wine)

مسكن II *tamaskana* to become poor, be reduced to poverty; to pretend to be poor; to feign poverty or humility; to be submissive, servile, slavish, fawning

مسكنة *maskana* poverty, misery; humbleness, humility, submissiveness

مسكين *miskīn* pl. -*ūn*, مساكين *masākīn*[2] poor, miserable; beggar; humble, submissive, servile

مسو II to wish (ه s.o.) a good evening | مساك الله بالخير *massāka llāhu bi-l-ḵair* good evening! III see صبح III; IV to enter into evening; to be or become in the evening; to be, become | يفعله اذا اصبح ويفعله اذا امسى (*aṣbaḥa*) he does so in the morning and in the evening

مساء *masā'* pl. امساء *amsā'*, امسيات *amsiyāt* evening; *masā'an* in the evening | مساء امس *masā'a amsi* yesterday evening, last night; مساء الخير *m. al-kair* or مساؤكم بالخير good evening! صباح مساء *ṣabāḥa masā'a* mornings and evenings, in the morning and in the evening

مسائى *masā'ī* evening (adj.) | الاخبار المسائية the evening news

امسية *umsīya* pl. اماسى *amāsīy* evening

مسورة = ماسورة look up alphabetically

مسى *masā i* (*masy*) to make lean, cause to lose flesh, emaciate (ه livestock; of the heat)

مسيو (Fr. *Monsieur*) *misyū* Mr.; sir

مش *mašša u* (*mašš*) to suck the marrow (ه from a bone); to macerate, soak in water (ه s.th.)

مش *mišš* whey

مشوش *mašūš* napkin

مشيج *mašīj* gamete, germ cell

مشح *mašaḥa a* (*mašḥ*) to administer extreme unction (ه to s.o.)

مشحة *mašḥa* extreme unction

مشط *mašaṭa u i* (*mašṭ*) to comb **II** do. **V** and **VIII** to comb one's hair

مشط *mušṭ* pl. *amšāṭ*, مشاط *mišāṭ* comb; rake; bridge (of stringed instruments); ○ (*mil.*) cartridge clip | مشط الرجل *m. ar-rijl* metatarsus, instep (*anat.*); مشط اليد *m. al-yad* metacarpus (*anat.*)

مشطى *mušṭī* toothed, indented, jagged, dentate; comblike, pectinate

تمشيط *tamšīṭ* combing, carding (of wool)

ماشط *māšiṭ* barber, hairdresser

ماشطة *māšiṭa* lady's maid; (woman) hairdresser

ممشط *mumaššaṭ* combed, carded (wool)

مشق *mašaqa u* (*mašq*) to draw out, stretch, extend (ه s.th.); to comb (ه s.th.); to tear, tear up, shred (ه s.th.); to whip, lash (ه s.o.) **V** to be or get torn or shredded **VIII** to snatch away, whip away (ه من s.th. from s.o.); to draw, unsheathe (ه the sword)

مشق *mašq* pl. امشاق *amšāq* model, pattern (esp., one to be copied in writing)

مشق *mišq* slender, slim, svelte

مشقة *mišqa* pl. مشق *mišaq* flock of wool or cotton; rag, clout, shred; scrap of carding wool; scrap of hemp, oakum

مشيق *mašīq* slender, slim, svelte

مشاق *mušāq* scrap of flax or hemp; oakum, tow

مشاقة *mušāqa* scrap of flax or hemp; oakum, tow | مشاقة حرير floss

امتشاق *imtišāq* slenderness

ممشوق *mamšūq* slender, slim, svelte | ممشوق كالحسام (*ka-l-ḥusām*) slender as a wand

ماشك look up alphabetically

مشلوز *mišlauz* sweet-kerneled apricot

مشمش *mišmiš* (coll.; n. un. ة) apricot; apricot tree | مشمش كلابى (*kilābī*) bitter-kerneled apricot; مشمش لوزى or حموى (*lauzī*, *ḥamawī*) sweet-kerneled apricot

مشملا *mušmullā*, *mišmillā* medlar (*bot.*)

مشملة *mušmula*, *mišmila* medlar (*bot.*)

المشهد *al-mašhad* Meshed (city in NE Iran)

مشى (مشو and مشى) *mašā i* (*mašy*) to go on foot, walk; to go; to pace, stride; to move along, proceed; to march | مشى بالنميمة to scatter slanderous rumors **II** to let or make (ه s.o.) go or walk; to adapt, adjust, fit, accommodate (ه مع s.th. to) **III** to keep pace, keep in step (ه with s.o.); to go along, keep up, keep abreast (ه, ه with s.o., with s.th.), keep to s.o.'s (ه)

side; to be likeminded (ه ف with s.o. in s.th.), be guided by the same considerations or principles (ه ف as s.o. in s.th.), act in unison (ه ف with s.o. in s.th.) IV = II; to have an aperient effect (ه on s.o.; *med.*) V to go on foot, walk; to take a walk, to stroll, promenade; to walk slowly, saunter; to pace, move along, stride along; to keep step, keep up, keep abreast, go along, agree, harmonize, be compatible, be consistent, be in accordance, be in keeping (مع with), fit, suit (مع s.th.), be appropriate, correspond, come up (مع to s.th.); to proceed (على in accordance with a principle or method); to follow, observe (على a principle) | تمشى في اوصاله approx.: to perfuse s.o.'s limbs (of a sensation); تمشى جيئة وذهابا (*ji'atan wa-ḏahāban*) to walk back and forth, pace up and down

مشو *mašw* a laxative, aperient

مشى *mašy* going, walking; walk

مشية *mišya* manner of walking, gait, pace, step, bearing, carriage

مشاء *maššā'* pl. *-ūn* good walker; walker (*athlet.*)

مشاية *maššāya* pl. *-āt* long, narrow carpet, runner; ○ baby walker, gocart; hallway, corridor; footpath, path(way)

ممشى *mamšā* pl. ماش *mamāšin* hallway, corridor, passageway, passage; aisle; footpath, path(way), alley; promenade; crossing, overpass, bridge; bridge of a ship; runner, small rug

تمشيا مع *tamaššiyan ma'a* (or على) in conformity with, in accordance with, according to

ماش *māšin* pl. مشاة *mušāh* going, walking; pedestrian; foot soldier, infantryman; المشاة the infantry; ماشيا *māšiyan* on foot

ماشية *māšiya* pl. مواش *mawāšin* livestock, cattle

مص *maṣṣa* (1st pers. perf. *maṣiṣtu*) *a* and (1st pers. perf. *maṣaṣtu*) *u* (*maṣṣ*) to suck, suck up, soak up, suck in, absorb (ه s.th.); to sip, lap, lap up, lick up (ه s.th.); to suck out (ه s.th.) V to sip gradually, drink in small sips (ه s.th.) VIII to suck, suck up, suck in (ه s.th.); to sip, lap, lap up, lick up (ه s.th.); to soak up, absorb, swallow up (ه s.th.)

مص *maṣṣ* sucking, suction, suck, sucking up, soaking up, soak, soakage, absorption | قصب المص *qaṣab al-m.* sugar cane

مصة *maṣṣa* (n. vic.) sucking, suck, suction; sip

مصاص *maṣṣāṣ* one who sucks, sucker; cupper; bloodsucker, extortioner, usurer

مصاصة *muṣāṣa* that which one sucks, s.th. to suck | مصاصة القصب *m. al-qaṣab* sugar-cane refuse

مصاصة *maṣṣāṣa* screech owl; vampire

مصيص *maṣīṣ* moist, damp (ground)

مصيص *miṣṣīṣ* string, twine, packthread

ممص *mimaṣṣ* suction pipe, sucker; ○ siphon

امتصاص *imtiṣāṣ* sucking, suck, suction; sucking up, soaking up, soak, soakage, absorption | قوة الامتصاص *qūwat al-imt.* suction

ممصوص *mamṣūṣ* soaked up; drained, exhausted; emaciated, very lean, skinny

ممتص *mumtaṣṣ* soaking up, absorbing; absorbent, absorptive

مصر II to found, build, settle, civilize, colonize (ه a place); to Egyptianize, make Egyptian (ه s.th.) V to become a populated, civilized area, become a big city, a metropolis; to Egyptianize, adopt Egyptian ways; to become an Egyptian

مصر *miṣr* pl. امصار *amṣār* big city; metropolis, capital; — *miṣr*², (*colloq.*)

maṣr Egypt; Cairo | مصر القاهرة Cairo; مصر الجديدة Heliopolis (section of modern Cairo)

مصرى *miṣrī* Egyptian; Cairene; (pl. *-ūn*) an Egyptian; a Cairene, a native of Cairo

مصرية *miṣriya* Egyptianism. Egyptian national character; (pl. *-āt*) Egyptian woman or girl

مصير *maṣīr* pl. امصرة *amṣira*, مصران *muṣrān*, مصارين *maṣārīn*[2] gut; pl. bowels, intestines, guts, tripe; see also under صير

تمصير *tamṣīr* settling, settlement, colonization, civilization; Egyptianization

متمصر *mutamaṣṣir* Egyptianized, naturalized in Egypt

مصطكاء *maṣṭakā'*, *muṣṭakā'* and مصطكى *maṣṭakā* mastic, resin of the mastic tree (Pistacia lenticus); liquor distilled from mastic | شجرة المصطكاء *šajarat al-m.* mastic tree (Pistacia lenticus; *bot.*)

مصل *maṣala u* to curdle (milk); to strain, filter (ه s.th.)

مصل *maṣl* whey; (pl. مصول *muṣūl*) serum (*med.*) | علم المصول *'ilm al-m.* serology

مصلى *maṣlī* serous (*med.*)

مصمص *maṣmaṣa* to suck (ه s.th.); to suck up, soak up, absorb (ه s.th.); to sip and turn around in the mouth (ه a liquid) II *tamaṣmaṣa* to sip and turn around in the mouth (ه a liquid)

مض *maḍḍa u* (*maḍḍ*, مضيض *maḍīḍ*) to hurt, pain (ه s.o.); to burn, sting (ه s.o.); to torment, harass, trouble, molest (ه ب s.o. with); — (1st pers. perf. *maḍiḍtu*) *a* (مضض *maḍaḍ*, مضيض *maḍīḍ*, مضاضة *maḍāḍa*) to be in pain, feel pain, suffer; to be distressed, worried, troubled IV to cause pain (ه to s.o.), hurt (ه s.o.); to torment, torture, agonize (ه s.o.)

مض *maḍḍ* pain, torment, torture, anguish, agony; painful, burning, stinging, smarting

مضض *maḍaḍ* pain, suffering, torment, torture, anguish, agony, affliction, distress; sour milk | على مضض unwillingly, reluctantly, grudgingly

مضاض *muḍāḍ* brackish water, brine, salt water

مضاضة *maḍāḍa* agony, torture

ممض *mumiḍḍ* agonizing, tormenting

مضر *maḍara, maḍura u* and *maḍira a* (*maḍr*, *maḍar*, مضور *muḍūr*) to turn sour (milk)

مضر *maḍir* and ماضر *māḍir* sour (milk)

لغة مضر *luġat muḍara* the language of Muḍar, the Arabic language

مضغ *maḍaġa a u* (*maḍġ*) to chew (ه s.th.) | مضغ الكلام (*kalām*) to slur, speak indistinctly

مضغ *maḍġ* chewing, mastication

مضغة *muḍġa* pl. مضغ *muḍaġ* s.th. to be chewed; bite, bit, morsel; small chunk of meat; ○ embryo; ○ chewing gum | مضغة طيبة (*ṭayyiba*) titbit; جعله مضغة في الافواه (*ja'alahū muḍġatan*) to make s.o. the talk of the town, send tongues wagging about s.o.

مضاغة *muḍāġa* s.th. chewed, chew, quid

مضمض *maḍmaḍa* to rinse

مضى *maḍā i* (*muḍīy*) to go away, leave, depart; to make off, decamp, abscond; with ب: to take s.th. away, remove s.th.; to pass, elapse, go by, expire, run out (time); to advance, progress (في in); to proceed (في in or with s.th., also ب), continue (في, also ب, s.th., to do s.th.), go on (في doing s.th.); to pursue, practice, exercise (في s.th., also في مهنة *fī mihnatin* a profession); to penetrate deeper, enter deeper, go deeper (في into s.th.); to bring to an end, wind up, terminate, conclude, accomplish, carry out, execute, perform (على s.th.); (with imperf.) to set out to do s.th., proceed to do s.th.; — (مضاء *maḍā'*) to be sharp, cut (sword) | مضى سبيله (*sabīlahū*) to pass away, die; مضى لسبيله (*li-sabīlihī*) do.; مضى على البيع (*bai'*) to conclude a bargain; مضى على ذلك شهور (*šuhūrun*) months have passed since then; مضى فى كلامه (*kalāmihī*) to go on talking; مضى ما مضى let bygones be bygones! no more of that! فيما مضى (*fī-mā*) or فيما مضى من الزمان (*zamān*) formerly, previously, heretofore, once, before, in the past; لم يمض غير قليل حتى *lam yamḍi ġairu qalīlin ḥattā* it did not take long until ..., before long ...; من سنة مضت *min sanatin maḍat* one year ago; ومضى فقال and he went on to say, and he added **II** to make pass, cause to go by; to spend, pass (ه time, فى with s.th.) **IV** to spend, pass (ه time); to carry out, execute, perform, accomplish, conclude, terminate, wind up, bring to an end (ه s.th.); to pass, put behind o.s. (ه examination); to undersign, sign (ه s.th.) | امضى امره على (*amrahū*) to throw one's full support behind s.th., endorse s.th. wholeheartedly

مضى *muḍīy* departure, leave; passing; lapse, elapsing, expiration (of a period of time); continuation (فى of s.th.); deeper penetration, deeper insight (فى into); carrying out, execution, pursuit (فى of an intention, of a plan) | مضى المدة *m. al-mudda* lapse of time, superannuation; التملك بمضى المدة (*tamalluk*) usucapion, prescription (*jur.*); على مضى الزمن (*m. iz-zaman*) lastingly, for long, permanently; المضى فى الحرب (*ḥarb*) the continuation of the war

مضاء *maḍā'* sharpness, keenness; penetration, sagacity, acute discernment; energy | مضاء العزيمة strength of purpose, resolution, determination, energy, go

امضى *amḍā* sharper, more incisive, more effective

تمضية *tamḍiya* execution, performance, accomplishment, completion; spending, passing (of time) | تمضية الوقت *t. al-waqt* pastime

امضاء *imḍā'* realization, execution, accomplishment, completion; signing, signature | صاحب الامضاء the undersigned

ماض *māḍin* pl. مواض *mawāḍin* sharp, keen, cutting; acute, penetrating, incisive, effective; energetic; past, bygone; الماضى the past; past tense, perfect, preterit (*gram.*) | ماضى العزيمة resolute, determined; الشهر الماضى (*šahr*) last month

ممض *mumḍin* signer, signatory

ممضى *mumḍan* undersigned, signed

مط *maṭṭa u* (*maṭṭ*) to expand by pulling, stretch, draw out (ه s.th.); to draw tight, tighten, tauten (ه s.th.) **II** to expand, stretch (ه s.th.); to scold, revile, abuse (ه s.o.) **V** to expand; to stretch; to distend, widen, spread, lengthen; to be capable of extension or lengthening, be expandable, stretchable, elastic; to be rubberlike

مط *maṭṭ* expansion, extension, stretching, distention, lengthening, drawing out

مطاط *maṭṭāṭ* expandable, extensible, stretchable, elastic; dilatory; rubbery, rubberlike; rubber; caoutchouc

تمطط *tamaṭṭuṭ* expandability, extensibility, elasticity

مطر *maṭara u* to rain (مطرت السماء *maṭarat is-samā'u* it rained); to shower with rain (ه s.o.; of the sky); to pour out (ه ب over s.o. s.th.), shower, douse (ه ب s.o. with); to do, render (ه s.o., بخير *bi-ḵairin* a good turn, a favor); to run swiftly (horse), speed away **IV** to rain (of the sky); to cause (ه s.th.) to rain (على upon); to shower (ه ب s.o. with or ◦ على upon s.o. s.th.), heap (◦ ب or ◦ على upon s.o. s.th.) | امطر عليه وابلا من (*wābilan*) or امطره بوابل من (*bi-wābilin*) he showered him with a hail of (e.g., stones), with a rain of (e.g., blows), with a flood of (e.g., abuses, threats), etc. **X** to ask for rain; to ask (من or ◦ s.o.) a favor; to wish (◦ for s.th.), desire (◦ s.th.); to invoke, call down (◦ على upon s.o. s.th.)

مطر *maṭar* pl. امطار *amṭār* rain | محطة لرصد الامطار *maḥaṭṭa li-raṣd al-a.* pluviometrical station

مطرة *maṭra, maṭara* pl. *-āt* downpour, rain shower

مطر *maṭir* and مطير *maṭīr* rainy, abounding in rain

ممطر *mimṭar* and ممطرة *mimṭara* pl. مماطر *mamāṭir*² raincoat

ماطر *māṭir* rainy, abounding in rain

ممطر *mumṭir* rainy, abounding in rain | مواسم ممطرة rainy seasons, periods of rain

مطرن *maṭrana* to raise to the rank of metropolitan or archbishop, consecrate as metropolitan or archbishop (◦ s.o.) **II** *tamaṭrana* to be instated or consecrated as metropolitan (*Chr.*)

مطران *muṭrān, maṭrān, miṭrān* pl. مطارنة *maṭārina,* مطارين *maṭārīn*² metropolitan, archbishop (*Chr.*)

مطرنة *maṭrana* dignity or office of a metropolitan, metropolitanate, archiepiscopate (*Chr.*)

مطرنية *maṭraniya,* مطرانية *muṭrānīya* pl. *-āt* diocese of a metropolitan, archbishopric, archdiocese (*Chr.*)

مطق **V** to smack one's lips

مطل *maṭala u* (*maṭl*) to draw out, lengthen, extend, stretch (◦ s.th.); to stretch (◦ a rope); to hammer, forge, shape by hammering (◦ iron); to postpone, defer, delay; to put off (◦ ب s.o. with) **III** to tarry, temporize, take one's time; to put off (◦ ب s.o. with)

مطول *maṭūl* deferring, delaying, procrastinating, tardy, dilatory, slow

مطيلة *maṭīla* pl. مطائل *maṭā'il*² wrought iron

مماطلة *mumāṭala* postponement, deferment, procrastination, delay

(مطو) مطا *maṭā u* (*maṭw*) to quicken one's pace, hurry, walk fast **IV** to mount (◦ an animal); to ride (◦ on an animal) **V** to stretch o.s., loll; to stretch (ب s.th., one's body, one's limbs); to walk proudly, strut, swagger **VIII** to mount (◦ an animal); to board (◦ a vehicle), get in (◦), get aboard (◦); to ride (◦ on an animal, in a vehicle)

مطوة *maṭwa* hour, time, moment

مطية *maṭīya* pl. مطايا *maṭāyā,* مطى *maṭīy* mount, riding animal; expedient, means to an end, instrument, tool

مع *ma'a* (prep.) with, simultaneously with, together with, accompanied by, in the company of; in the estimation, eyes, or opinion of; in spite of, despite; toward, in relation to; معا *ma'an* together; at the same time, simultaneously; with one another | مع ان although; ومع ان — الا ان *wa-ma'a anna — illā anna* although — nevertheless ..., to be sure — but ..., it is true — but ...; مع ذلك or مع هذا in spite of it, nevertheless, notwithstanding, still; مع كل هذا in spite of all that; مع كونه غنيا (*kaunihī ġanīyan*) although he is rich, for all his being rich, rich as he is; ليس مع الحكومة (*laisa*) he is not for the government, he doesn't side with the government; مع الحائط along the wall; كان معه it was with him, he had it with him; ما معكم what do you have with you? what have you brought along? what's up your sleeve? الست معي في ان (*a-lasta*) don't you also think that ...? wouldn't you share my view that ...? استعمل وسائل القسوة معه *ista'mala wasā'ila l-qaswati ma'ahū* he brought harsh measures to bear on him

معية *ma'īya* company; escort; suite, retinue, entourage, attendants | بمعية فلان (في معية) in the company of so-and-so; بمعية هذا herein enclosed, herewith

معج V to wind, meander

معد pass. *mu'ida* to have a gastric ailment, suffer from dyspepsia, have a stomach-ache

معدة *ma'ida, mi'da* pl. معد *mi'ad* stomach

معدى *ma'idī, mi'dī* of or pertaining to the stomach, gastric, stomachic | امراض معدية gastric diseases; حمى معدية (*hummā*) gastric fever

ممعود *mam'ūd* suffering from a gastric disease, dispeptic

معر *ma'ira a* (*ma'ar*) to fall out (hair) IV to become poor, impoverished, be reduced to poverty V = I

معار *ma''ār* (*eg.*) braggart, braggadocio, swaggerer

معز *ma'z, ma'az* (coll.; n. un. ة) pl. امعز *am'uz*, معيز *ma'īz* goat

ماعز *mā'iz* pl. مواعز *mawā'iz*² goat

معاز *ma''āz* goatherd

معس *ma'asa a* (*ma's*) to rub (ه s.th.); to squash, crush (ه s.th.)

معض *ma'iḍa a* (*ma'ḍ*) and VIII to be annoyed (على by), be angry (من at), resent (من s.th.)

امتعاض *imti'āḍ* anger, resentment, annoyance, displeasure; excitement, agitation

ممتعض *mumta'iḍ* annoyed, vexed, angry; upset, excited

معط *ma'aṭa a* (*ma'ṭ*) to tear out, pull out, pluck out (ه hair, feathers)

معط *ma'iṭ* and امعط *am'aṭ*², f. معطاء *ma'ṭā'*², pl. معط *mu'ṭ* hairless, bald

معك *ma'aka a* (*ma'k*) to rub (ه s.th.)

معكرونه *ma'karūna* macaroni

¹معمعة *ma'ma'a* pl. معامع *ma'āmi'*² confusion, jumble, mess, tohubohu; tumult, uproar; turmoil; pl. wars, battles

معمعان *ma'ma'ān* raging, roar (of a storm), turmoil, thick (of a battle), height, climax (of heat and cold) | معمعان الصيف *m. aṣ-ṣaif* high summer; معمعان الشتاء deepest winter

²معمعي *ma'ma'ī* yes-man

معن IV to apply o.s. assiduously, devote all one's efforts (في to s.th.); to be keen, intent (في on), be eager (في for); to examine closely, study carefully, scrutinize (في s.th.); to go to extremes (في in s.th.), overdo, carry too far (في s.th.) | امعن النظر في (*naẓara*) to fix one's eyes on s.th., regard s.th. attentively, examine s.th. closely, scrutinize s.th. V to become engrossed or absorbed, bury o.s. (في in), regard attentively, examine carefully (في s.th.), look closely (في at s.o., at s.th.), scrutinize (في s.o., s.th.)

ماعون *mā'ūn* pl. مواعين *mawā'īn*² implement, utensil, instrument; vessel, receptacle, container; (coll.) implements, utensils, gear; (*syr.*) ream of paper

ماعونة *mā'ūna* pl. *-āt*, مواعين *mawā'īn*² (*eg.*) lighter, barge

امعان *im'ān* and امعان النظر *i. an-naẓar* close examination, careful study, scrutiny (في of s.th.); امعان devotion (في to s.th.), care, carefulness, assiduity, diligence, attentiveness, attention

تمعن *tama''un* close examination, careful study, scrutiny; care, carefulness | بتمعن carefully

(معو) معا *ma'ā u* (معاء *mu'ā'*) to mew, miaow (cat)

1 معى *mi'an, ma'y* and معاء *mi'ā'* pl. امعاء *am'ā'*, امعية *am'iya* gut; intestines, bowels, entrails | الامعاء الدقيقة the small intestine; المعى الغليظ the large intestine

معوى *mi'awī* of or pertaining to the intestines, intestinal; enteric | الحمى المعوية (*ḥummā*) typhoid fever, enteric fever, abdominal typhus

2 معية *ma'īya* see مع

مغاث *muġāṯ* (*eg.*) root of Glossostemon Bruguieri (*bot.*)

مغر *maġar* and مغرة *muġra* reddish, russet color

امغر *amġar*[2] reddish brown, russet

مغربة *maġraba* (*mor.*) Moroccanization

مغص *maġaṣa* to cause gripes; pass. *muġiṣa* (*maġṣ*) to have gripes or colic, suffer from colic

مغص *maġṣ, maġaṣ* and مغيص *maġīṣ* gripes; colic | مغص كلوى (*kulwī*) renal colic

ممغوص *mamġūṣ* suffering from colic; having gripes

مغط *maġaṭa a* (*maġṭ*) to stretch, extend, expand, draw out II do.

متمغط *mutamaġġiṭ* stretchable, elastic (rubber); tough, viscous, ropy, sticky

مغطس *maġṭasa* to magnetize, make magnetic, subject to magnetic induction (ه s.th.) II *tamaġṭasa* to be magnetized, become magnetic

مغطسة *maġṭasa* magnetism

ممغطس *mumaġṭas* magnetized, magnetic

خشب المغنة *kašab al-muġna*, خشب المغنى *k. al-muġnā* mahogany (wood)

مغنط *maġnaṭa* to magnetize, subject to magnetic induction (ه s.th.)

مغنطيس *miġnaṭīs, maġnaṭīs* magnet | ○ مغنطيس كهربائى (*kahrabā'ī*) electromagnet

مغناطيس *miġnāṭīs, maġnāṭīs* magnet; magnetism

مغنطيسى *miġnaṭīsī* magnetic; hypnotic

مغنطيسية *miġnaṭīsīya* and مغناطيسية magnetism

مغنيسيا *maġnīsiyā* magnesia

المغول *al-muġūl* the Mongols; the Moguls | بلاد المغول Mongolia

مغولى *muġūlī* Mongolian

مقت *maqata u* (*maqt*) to detest, abhor, loathe, hate (ه s.o., ه s.th.); — *maquta u* (مقاتة *maqāta*) to be abominable, detestable, loathsome, hated, odious II = *maqata*; to make (ه s.o.) hateful (الى to s.o.), make s.o. (الى) loathe (ه s.o.)

مقت *maqt* hate, hatred, detestation, loathing, aversion, disgust; hateful, odious

مقيت *maqīt* and ممقوت *mamqūt* hated, detested; hateful, odious; detestable, abominable, loathsome, repugnant, disgusting

مقدونس *maqdūnis* parsley

مقدونى *maqdūnī* Macedonian (adj. and n.)

مقع *maqa'a a* (*maq'*) to drink avidly, toss down (ه s.th.) VIII pass. *umtuqi'a* to turn pale

ممتقع *mumtaqa'* pale, pallid, wan, sallow

مقل *maqala u* (*maql*) to look (ه at s.o.), eye, regard (ه s.o.)

مقلة *muqla* pl. مقل *muqal* eye; eyeball | مقلة العين *m. al-'ain* eyeball

□ مقانق *maqāniq* (= نقانق) small mutton sausages (*syr.*)

مكة *makka*[2] (usually followed by the epithet المكرمة *al-mukarrama*) Mecca

مكى *makkī* Meccan (adj. and n.)

مكوك *makkūk* pl. مكاكيك *makākīk*[2] drinking cup; shuttle

ماكوك *mākūk* pl. مواكيك *mawākīk*[2] drinking cup; shuttle

مكث *makaṯa* u (*makṯ*, مكوث *mukūṯ*) to remain, abide, stay, live, dwell, reside (ب in a place)

مكث *makṯ* and مكوث *mukūṯ* remaining, staying, lingering, abiding; stay, sojourn

مكوجى see كوى

مكدام (Engl.) *makadām* macadam

مكدونى *makdūnī* Macedonian (adj. and n.)

مكدونيا *makdūniyā* Macedonia

مكر *makara* u (*makr*) to deceive, delude, cheat, dupe, gull, double-cross (ب s.o.) III to try to deceive (ه s.o.)

مكر *makr* cunning, craftiness, slyness, wiliness, double-dealing, deception, trickery

مكرة *makra* ruse, artifice, stratagem, wile, trick, dodge

مكار *makkār* and مكور *makūr* cunning, sly, crafty, wily, shrewd, artful; sly, crafty person, impostor, swindler

ماكر *mākir* pl. مكرة *makara* sly, cunning, wily

مكروب *mikrūb* pl. *-āt*, مكاريب *makārīb*[2] microbe

مكرونه *makarūna* macaroni

مكس *makasa* i (*maks*) and II to collect taxes III to haggle, bargain (ه with s.o.)

مكس *maks* pl. مكوس *mukūs* tax, specif., excise or sales tax; toll, custom, duty, impost; market dues | دار المكوس custom-house

مكاس *makkās* tax collector

المكسيك *al-maksīk* Mexico

المكلا Mukalla (seaport in Aden Protectorate, chief town of Hadhramaut)

مكن[1] *makuna* u (مكانة *makāna*) to be or become strong; to become influential, gain influence, have influence (عند with s.o.), have power II to make strong or firm, consolidate, strengthen, cement, establish firmly, deepen (ه s.th.); to lend weight (ه to s.th.); to put down or set down firmly (ه s.th.), give (ه s.th.) a firm stance; to put (ه s.o.) in a position (من to do s.th.), give (ه s.o.) the possibility (من to do s.th.), enable (ه من s.o. to do s.th.), make possible (ه من for s.o. s.th.); to place (من s.th.) in s.o.'s (ه) hands; to furnish, provide (ه من s.o. with); to give or lend a firm position (ل to s.o., to s.th.); to give power (ل ف to s.o. over) IV to enable (ه من s.o. to do s.th.); to be possible, feasible (ه for s.o.) | يمكنه *yumkinuhū* he can (ان do s.th.); يمكن ان it is possible that ...; it may be that ..., possibly ..., perhaps ..., maybe ...; اكثر ما يمكن (*akṯara*) as much as possible; لا يمكن it is impossible V to have or gain influence, weight, or prestige (عند with s.o.), have or gain power; to be native, indigenous, resident; to gain ground; to spread; to be consolidated, firmly established; to consolidate, strengthen, gain in strength; to seize (من on s.th.), possess o.s., take possession (من of s.th.); to have command or mastery (من of s.th.), command, master (من s.th.); to be in a position, be able (من to do s.th.), be capable (من of), have the power (من to do s.th.) X to consolidate, strengthen, deepen, become firmly established, establish itself; to seize (من on s.th.), possess o.s., take possession (من of); to have command or mastery (من of s.th.), command, master (من s.th.); to be able (من to do s.th.), be capable (من of)

مكنة *mukna, makina* power, ability, capacity, capability, faculty; possibility; strength, firmness, solidity, intensity, force, vigor

مكان pl. امكنة, اماكن and مكانة see كون

مكين *makīn* pl. مكناء *mukanā'*[2] strong, firm, solid; firmly established, unshakable; deep-seated, deep-rooted, deeply ingrained, inveterate (feeling); influential, distinguished, of note, of rank, respected; powerful, potent

امكن *amkan*[2] see متمكن

تمكين *tamkīn* strengthening, consolidation, cementation; deepening, intensification; fixation, establishment; enabling, enablement, capacitation; livery of seizin, investiture (*Isl. Law*)

امكان *imkān* power, capacity, capability; faculty, ability; possibility | بقدر الامكان *bi-qadri l-i.* or على قدر الامكان as much as possible, as far as possible; عدم الامكان *'adam al-i.* impossibility; عند الامكان when (if) possible, possibly; فى امكانه ان it is in his power, he is in a position to ...; هو فى الامكان it is in the realm of possibility; ليس فى الامكان it is impossible, unthinkable, inconceivable

امكانية *imkānīya* pl. *-āt* possibility; ○ potential (*phys.*)

تمكن *tamakkun* power, authority, control, mastery, command; ability, capability, faculty; restraint, self-control, self-possession (also تمكن من النفس)

ماكن *mākin* strong, firm, solid, lasting, enduring

ممكن *mumkin* possible; thinkable, conceivable | غير ممكن impossible; من الممكن ان possibly, perhaps, maybe

ممكنات *mumkināt* possibilities

متمكن *mutamakkin* an adept, a proficient, a master; strengthened, cemented; firmly established, firmly fixed; consolidated; deep-rooted, deep-seated, deeply ingrained, inveterate; lasting, enduring; declinable (*gram.*) | متمكن امكن (*amkan*[2]) declinable with nunnation, triptote (*gram.*); متمكن غير امكن (*ġairu amkana*) declinable in two cases, diptote (*gram.*); غير متمكن indeclinable (*gram.*); متمكن فى جلسته (*jalsatihi*) firmly seated

[2]مكنة *makina* and ماكينة *mākīna* pl. *-āt* and مكائن *makā'in*[2] machine

مكنى *makanī* mechanical

مكوجى see كوى

[1]مل *malla* (1st pers. perf. *maliltu*) *a* (ملل *malal*, ملال *malāl*, ملالة *malāla*) to be or become weary, tired, bored, impatient; to tire, become tired (ه of s.th.), become fed-up (ه with) | لا يمل indefatigable, untiring, unflagging **IV** to be tiresome, irksome, wearisome, boring, tedious, vexatious; to vex, annoy, irritate (على or ه s.o.); (= املى) to dictate (على ه s.th. to s.o.) **V** to be wearied, fed-up; to be bored; to be restless, fidgety; to embrace a religion (ملة *millatan*) **VIII** to embrace a religion (ملة *millatan*)

مل *mall* weary, tired, fed-up; bored

ملة *malla* hot ashes, live embers

ملة *milla* pl. ملل *milal* religious community; religion, creed, faith, confession, denomination

ملى *millī* religious, confessional, denominational | مجلس ملى (*majlis*) court of justice of a religious minority (in Egypt abolished since 1956)

ملة *mulla* pl. ملل *mulal* basting stitch, tacking stitch; spring mattress

ملل *malal* and ملال *malāl* tiredness, boredom, ennui; listlessness, weariness; annoyance, irritation, vexation

ملال *mulāl* morbid unrest, restlessness, fidgetiness, feverishness

ملالة *malāla* weariness, boredom; impatience; ennui, tedium

ملول *malūl* tired, wearied, bored; weary, fed-up, disgusted

ملى *mullā* bread baked in hot ashes

مملول *mamlūl* offensive, disgusting

ممل *mumill* tiresome, tedious, boring, wearisome, irksome, loathsome, disagreeable

²مل *mill* pl. *-āt* (formerly) the smallest monetary unit in Palestine and Jordan, $^1/_{1000}$ of a Palestinian pound

ملأ *mala'a* *a* (ملء *mal'*, ملأة *mal'a*, *mil'a*) to fill, fill up (ب or من or ه ه s.th. with); to fill out (ه a form, a blank); to take up, fill, occupy (ه space); to fill (ه a vacancy) | ملأ الدهر (*dahra*) his (its) fame spread far and wide; ملأ الساعه (*sā'ata*) to wind up a watch or clock; ملأ شدقيه بالهواء (*šidqaihi bi-l-hawā'*) to puff one's cheeks; ملأ العين (*'aina*) to satisfy completely, please; ملأ الفضاء بالشكوى (*faḍā'a bi-š-šakwā*) to fill the air with complaints, voice loud laments; ملأ فاه ب (*fāhu*) to talk big about ..., shoot off one's mouth about ...; — ملئ *mali'a* to be or become filled, filled up, full, replete III to help, assist, support, back up (على ه s.o. in), side (ه with s.o.); to make common cause, join forces (ه على with s.o. against) IV to fill (ه s.th., also a vacancy) V to fill, become full; to be filled (ه or من with), be full (ه or من of) VIII to fill, become full; to be filled (glass; pass.); to be filled (ه, من or ب with s.th., ه also with a feeling), be full (ه, من or ب of, ه also of a feeling); to fill (ه s.th.); to fill up (ه s.th.); to imbue, fill (ه s.o., ه with a feeling)

ملء *mal'* filling (also, e.g., of vacancies); filling out

ملء *mil'* pl. املاء *amlā'* filling, quantity which fills s.th., fill; quantity contained in s.th. | ملء اهابه الكبرياء *m. ihābihī l-kibriyā'u* he is all pride and arrogance; ملء بطنه *m. baṭnihī* as much as one can eat, one's fill; ملء قدح *m. qadaḥin* a cupful; ملء اليد *m. al-yad* a handful; ملء كسائه *m. kisā'ihī* corpulent fat; بملء الفم *bi-m. il-fam* in a loud voice; بملء فيه *bi-mil'i fīhi* with a ring of deep conviction (with verbs like "say", "declare", "exclaim", etc.); loudly, at the top of one's voice or one's lungs (with verbs like "shout", "cry", etc.); ضحك بملء (or ملء) شدقيه *ḍaḥika bi-mil'i* (or *mil'a*) *šidqaihi* to grin from ear to ear; قال بصوت ملؤه الشفقة (*bi-ṣautin mil'uhū š-šafaqatu*) he said in a voice full of mercy ...; لى ملء الحرية فى (*m. ul-ḥurrīya*) I have complete freedom to ..., I am completely at liberty to ...; وقف موقفا ملؤه الحزم (*mauqifan mil'uhū l-ḥazm*) he assumed a posture that was all determination; انت ملء حياتى (*ḥayātī*) you are all my life; ينام ملء جفنيه (*mil'a jafnaihi*) he is sound asleep, he sleeps the sleep of the just

ملأ *mala'* pl. املاء *amlā'* crowd, gathering, assembly, congregation; audience; (general) public; council of elders, notables, grandees | على الملأ publicly, in public; على ملأ العالم (*m. il-'ālam*) for everyone to see, before all the world; الملأ الاعلى (*a'lā*) the heavenly host, the angels

ملاءة *mulā'a*, □ ملاية *milāya* pl. *-āt* wrap worn by Egyptian women; sheet, bed sheet

ملىء, ملى *malī'* full (ب of), filled, replete (ب with); bulging, swelling (ب with); plump; stout, fat, corpulent, obese; rich, abounding (ب in); well-to-do, wealthy; solvent | ملىء البدن *m. al-badan* stout, fat, corpulent

ملآن *mal'ān*, f. ملأى *mal'ā* or ملآنة pl. ملاء *milā'* full, filled, replete; plump, fat

مُمالأة *mumāla'a* partiality, bias; collaboration (*pol.*)

املاء *imlā'* filling (also, e.g., of a vacancy)

امتلاء *imtilā'* repletion, fullness; full, round form, plumpness; bulkiness; fatness, stoutness, corpulence

مملوء *mamlū'* filled, filled up; imbued; loaded

ممالئ *mumāli'* partial, biased, prejudiced; collaborator (*pol.*)

ممتلئ *mumtali'* full, filled, filled up, replete | ممتلئ الجسم *m. al-jism* stout, fat, corpulent

ملاريا *malāriyā* malaria

ملايو *malāyū*, جزر الملايو *juzur al-m.* the Malayan Archipelago

ملج *malaja u* (*malj*) to suck (ه the mother's breast) VIII to suck

مالج *mālaj* pl. موالج *mawālij*² trowel

ملح *malaḥa u a* and *maluḥa u* (ملوح *mulūḥ*, ملوحة *mulūḥa*, ملاحة *malāḥa*) to be or become salt(y); — *maluḥa u* (ملاحة *malāḥa*, ملوحة *mulūḥa*) to be beautiful, handsome, pretty, comely, nice, elegant II to salt, season with salt (ه s.th.); to salt away, salt down, preserve with salt, corn, cure (ه s.th.) IV to be salt(y) X to find (ه s.th.) beautiful, pretty, nice, or witty

ملح *milḥ* m. and f., pl. املاح *amlāḥ*, ملاح *milāḥ* salt; gunpowder; witticism, wittiness, wit, esprit | ملح انكليزى bitter salt, Epsom salt; ملح البارود *m. al-bārūd* saltpeter; gunpowder; ملح النشادر *m. an-nušādir* sal ammoniac, ammonium chloride; املاح (*ma'dinīya*) معدنية mineral salts

ملحى *milḥī* salt, salty, saline

ملحة *milḥa* bond, obligation, commitment, covenant

ملحة *mulḥa* pl. ملح *mulaḥ* funny story, anecdote, bon mot, witticism

ملاح *mallāḥ* sailor, seaman, mariner; (*mor.*) ghetto of Moroccan cities

ملاحة *malāḥa* beauty, grace, gracefulness; elegance; kindness, kindliness, friendliness, amiability; saltiness, salt taste, saltness, salinity

ملاحة *mallāḥa* pl. *-āt* salina, saline spring; saltern, saltworks, salt mine; saltcellar

ملاحة *milāḥa* navigation, shipping | ملاحة تجارية (*tijārīya*) mercantile shipping, maritime transportation; ملاحة جوية (*jawwīya*) aviation; ملاحة داخلية (*dākilīya*) inland navigation; ملاحة نهرية (*nahrīya*) river traffic; صالح للملاحة navigable

ملاحى *milāḥī* navigational, shipping, marine, maritime; nautical

ملوحة *mulūḥa* saltiness, salt taste

مليح *malīḥ* pl. ملاح *milāḥ*, املاح *amlāḥ* salt, salty, briny, salted; pretty, handsome, comely; beautiful; nice, pleasant, agreeable; witty | (*eg.*) علقة مليحة (*'alqa*) a sound beating

املوحة *umlūḥa* pl. امالیح *amālīḥ*² joke, anecdote

مملحة *mamlaḥa* pl. ممالح *mamāliḥ*² salina; saltern, saltworks; saline spring; saltcellar

تمليح *tamlīḥ* salting, salting down, preservation in salt, corning, curing

مالح *māliḥ* salt, salty, briny

موالح *mawāliḥ*² (pl. of مالحة *māliḥa*, citrus fruits; (*syr.*) salted nuts, peanuts, almond

مملوح *mamlūḥ* salted, salty

مملّح *mumallaḥ* salted; salted down, corned, cured

مستملح *mustamlaḥ* brilliant, witty, bright, clever, interesting

[1]ملخ *malaka a* (*malk*) to pull out, tear out (ه s.th.); to wrench, dislocate, luxate (ه a joint) **VIII** to pull out, extract (ه s.th.)

مليخ *malīk* tasteless, insipid

[2]ملوخية *mulūkīya* Jew's mallow (Corchorus olitorius; *bot.*) cultivated as a pot herb; a thick soup made of this herb (*eg., syr.*)

ملد *malida a* (*malad*) to be tender (esp., twig)

أماليد *amālīd*[2] tender twigs

أملد *amlad*[2], f. ملداء *maldā'*[2] tender, flexible

ملس *malisa a* and *malusa u* (ملاسة *malāsa*, ملوسة *mulusa*) to be smooth, level, even **II** to make smooth, to smooth, level, even (ه s.th.); to make slippery (ه s.th.); to pass the hand, brush (with the hand) (على over), stroke, caress (على s.th.) **V** to become smooth; to glide, slide, slip; to grope; to slip away, escape **VII** (also املس *immalasa*) to become smooth; to glide, slide, slip; to slip away; to escape

ملس *malas* (*eg.*) a thin outer garment; silk fabric for women's dresses

ملس *malis* smooth, sleek

ملاسة *malāsa* smoothness

أملس *amlas*[2], f. ملساء *malsā'*[2], pl. ملس *muls* smooth, sleek

ملص *maliṣa a* (*malaṣ*) to glide, slide, slip; to slip away, escape; to disengage o.s., free o.s., (عن, من from an obligation), rid o.s. (عن, من of) **V** to rid o.s. (من of), shirk, dodge, evade (من s.th.)

ملص *maliṣ* smooth, sleek, slippery

مليص *malīṣ* smooth, sleek, slippery; miscarried fetus, stillborn child

تملص *tamalluṣ* slipping away, escaping, escape

[1]ملط *malaṭa u* (*malṭ*) to plaster with mud or mortar (ه a wall); to shave off (ه hair) **II** to mortar, plaster (ه a wall)

ملط *malṭ* (*eg.*) stark naked | عريان ملط (*'uryān*) stark naked

ملط *milṭ* pl. أملاط *amlāṭ*, ملوط *mulūṭ* dishonorable, discreditable; scoundrel | خلط ملط *kilṭ milṭ* or *kalṭ malṭ* pell-mell, in confusion

ملاط *milāṭ* pl. ملط *muluṭ* mortar

مليط *malīṭ* and أملط *amlaṭ*[2] pl. ملط *mulṭ* hairless

[2]مالطة *malṭa* Malta

مالطى *malṭī* Maltese (adj. and n.)

ملق *maliqa a* (*malaq*) to flatter (ه s.o.) **II** = **I**; to even, level, plane (ه s.th.) **III** = **I** **IV** to become poor, impoverished, be reduced to poverty **V** to flatter (الى, ل or ه s.o.)

ملق *maliq* and ملاق *mallāq* flatterer, adulator

ملقة *malaqa* pl. *-āt*, أملاق *amlāq* (*eg.*) Egyptian mile, league, the distance of approximately one hour's walk

مملقة *mimlaqa* planer, leveler; roller

تمليق *tamlīq* and تملق *tamalluq* flattery, adulation

ملك *malaka i* (*malk, mulk, milk*) to take in possession, take over, acquire (ه s.th.), seize, lay hands (ه on), possess o.s., take possession, lay hold (ه of); to possess, own, have (ه s.th.), be the owner (ه of); to dominate, control (ه s.th.); to be master (ه of); to rule, reign, exercise power or authority, hold sway, lord it (على or ه over); to be capable (ه of), be equal (ه to); to be able, be in a position (ان or ه to do s.th.) | ملكه الغيظ (ġaiẓ) anger overwhelmed him, got the better of him; ملك عليه جميع مشاعره (jamīʿa mašāʿirihī) to dominate s.o.'s every thought and deed, be uppermost in s.o.'s mind; ملك عليه حسه (ḥissahū) to take possession of s.o.'s feelings; ملك عليه لبه (lubbahū) to preoccupy s.o.'s heart; ملك عليه نفسه (nafsahū) to lay hold of s.o.'s soul, dominate s.o.'s thinking, affect s.o. deeply, stir up, arouse, excite s.o.; ملك على نفسه امرها (amrahā) to have o.s. under control, keep one's temper; ملك العينين من البكاء (ʿainain, bukāʾ) to hold back the tears; ملك نفسه (nafsahū) to control o.s., restrain o.s.; لم يملك ان he could not refrain from ..., he couldn't help it, he had to ...; ما ملكت (يملك) يمينه (yamīnuhū) his fortune, his property, his possessions **II** and **IV** to make (ه s.o.) the owner; to put (ه s.o.) in possession (ه of), transfer (ه to s.o.) ownership (ه of); to transfer, assign, make over, convey (ه ه to s.o. s.th.); to make (ه s.o.) king or sovereign (على over) **V** to take in possession, take over, appropriate, acquire (ه s.th.), take possession (ه of s.th., ه of s.o.), seize, lay hands (ه on s.th.), lay hold (ه of s.th.); to possess, own, have (ه s.th.), be in possession (ه of); to become king or sovereign (على over); to become prevalent, become fixed, take root (habit) **VI** to gain control (ه over a feeling, نفسه nafsahū over o.s.); to control o.s., restrain o.s., hold back; to refrain, keep (عن from s.th.) | ما تمالك عن he couldn't help (doing s.th.), he couldn't refrain from ... **VIII** to possess, own, have (ه s.th.); to gain, win (ه s.th.); to acquire (ه s.th.) | امتلك نواصى الشىء (nawāṣiya š-šaiʾ) to be master of s.th., rule over s.th. **X** to appropriate (ه s.th.), take possession (ه of); to dominate, control (ه s.th.); to possess, own, have (ه s.th.); to master (ه s.th.)

ملك **mulk** rule, reign, supreme authority, dominion, domination, dominance, sway, power; sovereignty, kingship, royalty; monarchy; tenure, holding, right of possession, possessory right, ownership

ملك **milk** pl. املاك **amlāk** property, possessions, goods and chattels, fortune, wealth; estate; landed property, real estate; pl. possessions (= colonies); lands, landed property, estates | املاك اميرية (amīrīya) or املاك الحكومة government lands; ملك ثابت landed property, real property, real estate, realty, immovables; ملك منقول personal estate, personal property, personalty, movables; املاك مبنية (mabnīya) developed lots, real estate developments; صاحب الاملاك, ذو الاملاك landowner; ملك اميرى (amīrī) government property; ملك مطلق (muṭlaq) general property, fee simple (absolute) (*Isl. Law*); ملك شائع joint property, joint tenancy, co-ownership

ملك **malik** pl. ملوك **mulūk**, املاك **amlāk** king, sovereign, monarch

ملكة **malika** pl. **-āt** queen | ملكة الجمال *m. al-jamāl* beauty queen

ملك **malak** (for ملأك) angel | ملك حارس guardian angel

ملكى **mulkī** possessory, possessive, proprietary; civilian, civil (as opposed to military) | بدلة ملكية (badla) civilian clothes; موظف ملكى (muwaẓẓaf) civil servant

ملكى **malakī** royal, kingly, regal; monarchic, sovereign; monarchist; angelic

ملكية **malakīya** monarchy, kingship, royalty

ملكية **milkīya** pl. **-āt** property; ownership (*jur.*) | الملكية الكبرى (kubrā) large landed property; نزع الملكية *nazʿ al-m.* expropriation, dispossession

ملكة *malaka* pl. *-āt* trait of character, natural disposition, aptitude, bent; gift, faculty, talent, knack

ملكوت *malakūt* realm, kingdom, empire; kingship, royalty, sovereignty | ملكوت السماوات *m. as-samāwāt* the Kingdom of Heaven (*Chr.*)

ملكوتى *malakūtī* divine, heavenly

ملاك *malāk, milāk* foundation, basis, fundament, essential prerequisite

ملاك *milāk* (*tun.*) betrothal, engagement; engagement present (of the fiancé to the prospective bride)

ملوكى *mulūkī* royal, kingly, regal; monarchic; monarchist

ملوكية *mulūkīya* monarchic rule, monarchism, kingship, royalty; monarchist leaning

ملاك *mallāk* pl. *-ūn* owner, proprietor; landowner, landholder, landed proprietor | كبار الملاكين *kibār al-m.* large landowners

ملاكى *mallākī* private

مليك *malīk* pl. ملكاء *mulakā'*[2] king; possessor, owner, proprietor

مليكة *malīka* queen

مملكة *mamlaka* pl. ممالك *mamālik*[2] kingdom, empire, state, country; royal power, sovereignty

تمليك *tamlīk* transfer of ownership, conveyance of property, alienation

تملك *tamalluk* taking possession, occupancy, seizure; possession; right of possession, possessory right, tenure, holding; domination, control, mastery

تمالك *tamāluk* self-control

امتلاك *imtilāk* taking possession, occupancy, seizure; possession; right of possession, possessory right, tenure, holding; domination, control, mastery | امتلاك النفس *imt. an-nafs* self-control

استملاك *istimlāk* pl. *-āt* acquisition; appropriation, taking possession, occupancy, seizure

مالك *mālik* pl. ملاك *mullāk*, ملك *mullak* reigning, ruling; owning, possessing, holding; owner, proprietor, master, possessor, holder | مالك الحزين heron (*zool.*)

مالكى *mālikī* Malikite, belonging to the Malikite school of theology; a Maliki

المالكية *al-mālikīya* the Malikite school of theology

مملوك *mamlūk* owned (ل by), in possession (ل of), belonging (ل to); (pl. مماليك *mamālīk*[2]) white slave, mameluke; Mameluke | غير مملوك incapable of individual possession, (res) extra commercium (*Isl. Law*)

مملك *mumallik* assignor, transferor, conveyer, alienator

ممتلك *mumtalak* owned, in possession; pl. ممتلكات *mumtalakāt* property; estates, landed property; possessions, dependencies, colonies | ممتلكات اميرية (*amīrīya*) government property; الممتلكات المستقلة (*mustaqilla*) the Dominions

ململ *malmala* to hurry, hasten; to make restless, make fidgety (ه s.o.) II *tamalmala* to murmur, to mumble, mumble into one's beard; to grumble, be disgruntled, be angry; to be restless, fidgety, nervous; to twitch nervously; to be or become wavering, uncertain

ململة *malmala* and تململ *tamalmul* unrest, restlessness, fidgetiness, nervousness

ملنخوليا *malankōliyā* melancholia

[1]ملا (ملو) *malā u* (*malw*) to walk briskly, run II to make (ه s.o.) enjoy (ه s.th.) for a long time (said of God) IV to dictate (ه على to s.o. s.th.) V to enjoy (ه ,ب ,من s.th.) X to take from dictation (ه s.th.)

ملا *malan* pl. املاء *amlā'* open country, open tract of land; steppe, desert

الملوان *al-malawān* day and night

ملوة *malwa* malouah, a dry measure (Eg. = 2 قدح = 4.125 l)

ملى *maliy* (relatively long) period of time; مليا *malīyan* for quite a while, for a long time

املاء *imlā'* dictation; ○ transmission (of a telephone message)

[2]□ ملاية *milāya* pl. *-āt* (< ملاءة *mulā'a*) wrap worn by Egyptian women; sheet, bed sheet

ملية *maliya* pl. ملايا *malāyā* (*tun.*) garment of Bedouin women

مليار (Fr.) *milyār* pl. *-āt* (U.S.) billion, (G.B.) milliard

مليجرام *milligrām* pl. *-āt* milligram

مليم (Fr. *millième*) *mallīm, malīm* pl. *-āt*, ملاليم *malālīm*[2] the smallest monetary unit in Egypt (= $^1/_{1000}$ pound); see also under لوم

مليمتر *millīmitr* pl. *-āt* millimeter

مليون *malyūn* pl. *-āt*, ملايين *malāyīn*[2] million | اصحاب الملايين millionaires

م *mm.* abbreviation of millimeter

مما *mimmā*, shortened form م *mimma* = *min mā*

ممن *mimman* = *min man*

[1]من *man* 1. (interr. pron.) who? which one? which ones? 2. (relative pron.) who; the one who; those who; one who; whoever, whosoever, everyone who, he who

[2]من *min* (prep.) 1. of; some, some of, (a) part of; belonging to, pertaining to, from among | كان من to belong or pertain to, be among ..., fall under ...; من ذلك ان (*anna*) among other things ...; منهم من (*man*) some of them; منهم من — ومنهم من some of them — others ..., there are (were) those who — and others who ...; رجل من قريش (*rajul*) a man of the Koreish tribe; يوم من الايام (*yaum, ayyām*) some day, some day or other; امر من الامور (*amr*) s.th. or other, some affair, some business; اكل من الطعام (*ṭa'ām*) he ate (a little, some) of the food; ما رأيته من الكتب *mā ra'aituhū min al-kutub* (what I have seen of the books =) the books I have seen; ما رأيته من كتب (what I have seen of books =) what(ever) books I have seen; ما لله من شريك God has no partner whatsoever; ما من احد يقدر (*aḥadin yaqdiru*) nobody can ...; ما من شخص (*šaḵṣin*) there is absolutely none who ...

consisting of, made of, of (material) | ثوب من حرير (*ṯaub*) a garment of silk, a silk dress

at, on (time) | من الليل (*lail*) at night; من يومه (*yaumihī*) on the very same day; من ساعته at that moment, at once, right away

at, on, by (place) | هزه من منكبه (*hazzahū, mankibihī*) he shook him by the shoulder

like, as, such as, as for instance; namely, to wit | صفات ازلية من العلم والقدرة والارادة (*ṣifāt azalīya, 'ilm, qudra, irāda*) eternal attributes such as knowledge, power, volition; اذا صح ما قالته الجرائد من ان (*ṣaḥḥa*) if what the newspapers say is true, namely that ...

in an exclamation: يا طولها من ليلة *yā ṭūlahā min lailatin* oh, the length of the night! what a long night it is! ما اخفه من حمل *mā aḵaffahū min ḥimlin* how light a burden it is! ويحه من مخبول (*wai-ḥahū*) woe to this fool!

in relation to, with respect to, toward | مقاصد المانيا من تركيا Germany's intentions as far as Turkey is concerned

substituting for an accusative (originally, in a partitive sense): اذكى ذلك من فضولها this kindled her curiosity

2. from, away from, out of, from the direction of | اخرج من هنا *uḵruj min hunā* get out of here! جاء من بغداد he came from Baghdad; من طرف (*ṭarafi*) and من قبل (*qibali*) on the part of, on the side of, from, by; من — الى from — (up) to; كان منه واليه (*wa-ilaihi*) to depend entirely on s.o., be inseparable from s.o., appertain to s.o.; ما كان منهم فى what share they had in ..., to what extent they were involved in ..., what part they played in ...

from, beginning ..., starting ..., since, for; after | من شهر (*šahr*) for a month (past), since one month ago; من مدة (*mudda*) for some time (in the past); بعد ايام من هذه الحوادث (*ba'da ayyāmin*) a few days after these events

of, by, at, about (denoting the source of one's fear, fright, alarm, apprehension, etc.), e.g., فزع من, خاف من, etc.

against, from (with verbs denoting protection, defense, warning, freeing, exemption), e.g., منعه من, حماه من, حرره من, اعفاه من, etc.

through, by, via (with verbs of motion to denote the way, route, or means) | دخل من الباب he entered through the gate; من طريق الراديو by radio

than (with the comparative) | اقوى من ان *aqwā min an* too strong as to ..., too strong for ...

due to, owing to, for, because of; at, about (with verbs denoting emotions; as, for instance, "be amazed", "be delighted", "be glad", etc.), e.g., تعجب من, دهش من, etc.

by, through (with the passive to indicate the doer, agent, perpetrator)

as to compounds such as من بعد, من حيث, من دون, من غير, من قبل see under the second word

³من *manna u* (*mann*) to be kind, kindly, benign, gracious, benevolent, obliging (على to or toward s.o.); to show, grant, or do s.o. (على) a favor, bestow blessings, benefits, favors (على upon s.o.); to grant, award, present, give (على ب to s.o. s.th.), confer, bestow graciously (على ب upon s.o. s.th.), bless (على ب s.o. with), inspire (على ب s.o. with; of God) **IV** to tire, fatigue, weaken (ه s.o.), sap the strength (ه of s.o.) **V** do. **VIII** to be kind, kindly, benign, gracious, benevolent, obliging (على to or toward s.o.), to show, grant, or do s.o. (على) a favor, bestow blessings, benefits, favors (على upon s.o.); to bestow or confer most graciously (على ب upon s.o. s.th.), kindly grant, award, or give (على ب to s.o. s.th.)

من *mann* gracious bestowal; favor; benefit, blessing, boon; gift, present, largess; honeydew; manna; (pl. امنان *amnān*) a weight of 2 رطل *raṭl* | بمنه تعالى by the grace of God

منة *minna* pl. منن *minan* grace; kindness, kindliness, good will, friendliness, amiability, graciousness, benevolence, benignity; favor, act of kindness, benefit, blessing, boon, gift, present

منة *munna* pl. منن *munan* strength, vigor, stamina | شديد المنة strong, vigorous, sturdy

منان *mannān* kind, kindly, benign, gracious; munificent, liberal, generous; benefactor; المنان (one of the attributes of God) the Benefactor

منون *manūn* fate, destiny; fate of death, death

امتنان *imtinān* grateful obligation, indebtedness, obligedness, gratitude

ممنون *mamnūn* indebted, obligated, obliged, grateful, thankful (ل to s.o.); weak, languid

ممنونية *mamnūnīya* grateful obligation, indebtedness, obligedness, gratitude

ممتن *mumtann* indebted, much obliged (ل to s.o.)

منتول *mintūl* menthol

منجنيق *manjanīq* f., pl. *-āt*, مجانق *majāniq*[2] mangonel, ballista, catapult

منجو *mangū* mango

منح *manaḥa a* (*manḥ*) to grant, give, accord, award (ه ه to s.o. s.th.), bestow, confer (ه ه upon s.o. s.th.) **III** to bestow favors (ه upon s.o.)

منح *manḥ* granting, giving, donation, bestowal, conferment, award(ing)

منحة *minḥa* pl. منح *minaḥ* act of kindness; privilege; gift, present, donation, grant, favor, benefit, benefaction; compensation; remuneration, allowance, indemnity (*jur.*); scholarship, stipend | منحة الاقامة *m. al-iqāma* living allowance; منحة جامعية (*jāmiʿīya*) academic scholarship; منحة السكنى *m. as-suknā* housing allowance, rent allowance

مانح *māniḥ* donor, giver, granter

[1]مندل *mandal* see ندل

[2]منديل *mandīl, mindīl* pl. مناديل *manādīl*[2] kerchief; handkerchief; head kerchief

منذ *mundu* and مذ *mud* 1. (prep.) since, for; ago | منذ شهر (*šahr*) for a month (past), since one month ago; a month ago; منذ ايام (*ayyām*) for the past few days; a few days ago; منذ عهد قريب (*ʿahd*) of late, lately, recently; منذ الآن (*āna*) from now on, henceforth; منذ اليوم (*yaum*) as of today, from this day on

2. (conj.) since, ever since, from the time when | منذ كنت طفلا صغيرا (*tiflan*) since I was a small child

بحر المنش *baḥr al-manš* the Sea of Le Manche, i.e., the English Channel

منشوبية *manšūbīya* (from Copt. *manšōpi*) cell, living quarters (*Copt.-Chr.*)

منشورى *manšūrī* Manchurian

منصون *manṣūn* monsoon

منطر *manṭara* to throw down, toss down

منطق *manṭaqa* to gird (ب ه s.th. with) **II** to gird o.s., swathe o.s. (ب with), wind around one's body (ب s.th.)

منطوفلة *manṭūfla* (*syr.*) slipper

منع *manaʿa a* (*manʿ*) to stop, detain, keep from entering or passing (ه s.o.); to hinder, prevent (ه s.th.; ه من or عن s.o. from), keep, restrain, hold back (ه s.o. من or عن from); to bar, block, obstruct (ه ه s.o.'s way or access to); to withdraw, take away (من or عن or ه ه from s.o. s.th.), deprive (من or عن or ه ه s.o. of); to forbid, interdict (من or عن or ه ه to s.o. s.th.), prohibit (من or عن or ه ه s.o. from); to decline to accept, declare impossible or out of the question (ان that); to refuse, deny (عن ه or ه ه s.th. to s.o.), withhold (عن ه or ه ه s.th. from s.o.); to stop, cease (ه doing s.th., عن with regard to s.o.), abstain, refrain (ه from doing s.th., عن with regard to s.o.); to ward off, avert, keep, keep away (عن ه s.th. from s.o.); to protect, guard (من ه s.o. from), defend (ه s.o., ه s.th., عن against); — *manuʿa u* (مناع *manāʿ*, مناعة *manāʿa*) to be strongly fortified, inaccessible, impregnable; to be unconquerable, invincible, insurmountable **II** to fortify, strengthen, make inaccessible (ه s.th.) **III** to put up resistance, act in opposition (ه to s.o.), oppose, counteract (ه s.o.), work against s.o. (ه); to stand up, rise (ه against s.o.); to resist, oppose (ف s.th.), offer resistance, object, raise objections (ف to s.th.), revolt, rebel (ف against s.th.); to refuse, deny (ه ه s.o. s.th.) **V** to refuse, decline (عن to do s.th.); to desist, refrain, abstain, keep (عن from s.th., from doing s.th.), forbear, leave off (عن s.th.), stop, cease (عن doing s.th.), avoid (عن s.th. or doing s.th.); to be or become inaccessible, unassailable, impregnable; to strengthen, grow in strength; to seek protection (ب with or in) **VIII** to refrain, abstain, keep (عن from doing s.th.), forbear (عن s.th.), stop, cease (عن doing s.th.); to be prevented (عن from); to be impossible (على for s.o.); to refuse (عن to do s.th.), decline, turn down (عن s.th.); to refuse to have anything to do (على with), keep aloof (على from)

منع *man'* hindering, impeding, obstruction; prevention, obviation, preclusion; prohibition, interdiction, ban, injunction; closure, stop, discontinuation, embargo; withdrawal, deprival, dispossession; withholding, detention

منعة *man'a* resistance, power, force, vigor, strength, stamina, insuperability, invincibility

منيع *manī'* pl. منعاء *muna'ā'*[2] unapproachable, inaccessible, impervious, impenetrable, forbidding; well-fortified; mighty, strong, powerful; impregnable, unconquerable; insurmountable, insuperable, invincible, immune | منيع الجانب strong, unassailable; حاجز منيع insurmountable barrier

مناعة *manā'a* inaccessibility; strength, impregnability; hardiness, sturdiness, power of resistance; immunity (to a disease, also *dipl.*); imperviousness, impermeability, impenetrability, forbiddingness

امنع *amna'*[2] harder to get at, more forbidding; offering greater resistance

ممانعة *mumāna'a* opposition; resistance, revolt, rebellion; ○ inductive resistance (*el.*)

تمنع *tamannu'* rejection, refusal

امتناع *imtinā'* refraining, abstention (عن from); refusal, denial; impossibility

مانع *māni'* hindering, forbidding, etc., see **I**; preventive; prohibitive; — (pl. موانع *mawāni'*[2]) hindrance, obstacle, obstruction; impediment; a preventive, preservative, prophylactic; objection; — (pl. *-āt*) ○ cutout, anti-interference device (*radio*) | ما رأى مانعا (*ra'ā*) to have no objections; لا مانع *lā māni'a* there is nothing in the way, nothing prevents me (you, etc.) from (عن)

ممنوع *mamnū'* forbidden, prohibited, banned, interdicted; indeclinable (*gram.*) | ممنوع التدخين no smoking! ممنوع الدخول no admittance! keep out! off limits!

ممنوعية *mamnū'īya* forbiddenness

ممتنع *mumtani'* refraining, abstaining, forbearing; rejecting, refusing; prevented; forbidden, interdicted, prohibited, banned; inaccessible (على to s.o.); forbidding, inscrutable, impenetrable, elusive; difficult to imitate; impossible

منغنيس *manġanīs* manganese

منغوليا *munġūliyā* Mongolia

منفيلا (It. *manovella*) *manafella* crank

منلوج *manalōg* see منولوج

منى) منا (منو and *manā u* (*manw*) and منى *manā i* (*many*) to put to the test, try, tempt, afflict (ب ه s.o. with; of God); pass. منى *muniya* to be afflicted (ب with), be sorely tried (ب by), suffer, sustain, undergo, experience (ب s.th.), be affected, hit, smitten, stricken (ب by); to find by good luck, be so fortunate as to find (ل s.th.) **II** to awaken the desire (ب or ه ه in s.o. for), make s.o. (ه) wish (ب or ه for); to make (ه s.o.) hope (ب or ه for), give (ه s.o.) reason to hope (ب or ه for), raise hopes (ب or ه of) in s.o. (ه); to promise (ه ب ,ان s.o. that) | منى نفسه ب (*nafsahū*) to indulge in the hope of ..., have every hope that ... **IV** to shed (ه blood); to emit, ejaculate (▲ sperm) **V** to desire (▲ s.th.), wish (▲ for s.th.; ▲ ل s.o. s.th.) **X** to practice onanism, masturbate

منى *manan* and منية *manīya* pl. منايا *manāyā* fate, destiny, lot; fate of death; death

منى *minan* semen, sperm

منوى *minawī* seminal, spermatic

منى *minan* m. and *minā* f. the valley of Mina near Mecca

منية *munya, minya* pl. منى *munan* wish, desire; object of desire

امنية *umnīya* pl. امان *amānin*, امانى *amānīy* wish, demand, claim, desire, longing, aspiration

تمنية *tamniya* and امناء *imnā'* emission, ejaculation of the sperm

تمن *tamannin* pl. *-āt* wish; desire; request

استمناء *istimnā'* self-pollution, masturbation, onanism

منولوج *manolōj, monolōg* pl. *-āt* monologue; (cabaret) act | منولوجات فكاهية (*fukāhīya*) skits, comic sketches, music-hall songs

منومتر *manūmitr* pl. *-āt* manometer, pressure gauge

المنيا *al-minyā* El Minya (city in central Egypt)

مهجة *muhja* pl. مهج *muhaj*, مهجات *muhajāt* lifeblood, heartblood; heart; innermost self, intrinsic nature, core; soul; life | طعنت الآمال فى مهجتها (*ṭu'inat*) hopes received the deathblow

مهد **II** to spread out evenly (▲ s.th.); to smooth, smoothen (▲ s.th.); to pave (▲ a road); to flatten, plane, make even or level (▲ s.th.); to arrange, settle, straighten, put in order (▲ s.th.); to free from obstacles, clear, pave (▲ s.th.; esp., the way, ل for or to); to make easy, facilitate, ease, make easily accessible (▲ ل to s.o. s.th.); to get ready, prepare (▲ s.th.), make (▲ a bed, etc.); to pass (الكرة *al-kurata* the ball, ل to s.o.); (verb alone, without qualifying direct object) to pave, open, clear, or prepare the way (ل ب for s.th. by or with), open, prepare, begin, start, initiate, bring about, set in motion (ل ب s.th. by or with) **V** to be paved, be clear or cleared, be or become open (way); to be or get settled or arranged; to go smoothly, go well, come off well; to be in order, be put in order, get straightened out

مهد *mahd* pl. مهود *muhūd* bed; cradle | من المهد الى اللحد (*laḥd*) from cradle to grave; قتله فى مهده to nip s.th. in the bud; كان فى مهده to be still in its beginnings or infancy, not have progressed beyond the early stages

مهاد *mihād* place of rest, resting place; bed; bosom, pale, fold (fig., in which s.th. rests)

تمهيد *tamhīd* smoothing, leveling, paving; facilitation, easing; preparation; foreword, preface, proem; introduction; preliminaries | تمهيدا ل in order to facilitate ...; in preparation of ..., as a preliminary step toward ..., for the purpose of ...

تمهيدى *tamhīdī* introductory, prefatory, preliminary, preparatory | اجراءات تمهيدية (*ijrā'āt*) preliminaries; preliminary proceedings (*jur.*); حكم تمهيدى (*ḥukm*) interlocutory decree, interlocutory judgment (*jur.*); قرار تمهيدى (*qarār*) provisional injunction, temporary restraining order (*jur.*); شرح تمهيدى (*šarḥ*) prefatory remarks

ممهد *mumahhad* leveled, smoothed, smooth, even, level; well-ordered, well-arranged, well-prepared; prepared, cleared, open (way); paved (road)

ممهد *mumāhad* paved, improved (road)

[1] مهر *mahara* *u* *a* (*mahr*, مهار *mahār*, مهارة *mahāra*, مهور *muhūr*) to be skillful, adroit, dexterous, skilled, adept, proficient, expert, experienced, seasoned; — *u* *a* (*mahr*) to give a dower (ها to the bride) **III** to vie in skill (ه with s.o.) **IV** to give a dower (ها to the bride)

مهر *mahr* pl. مهور *muhūr* dower, bridal money; price, stake; ransom

مهر *muhr*, pl. امهار *amhār*, مهارة *mihāra* foal, colt

مهرة *muhra* pl. مهر *muhar*, مهرات *muharāt* filly

مهارة *mahāra* skillfulness, adroitness, dexterity, skill, expertness, proficiency, adeptness

ماهر *māhir* pl. مهرة *mahara* skillful, adroit, dexterous, skilled, proficient, adept, expert, practiced, experienced, seasoned

[2] مهر *muhr* seal, signet; stamp

مهردار *muhrədār* keeper of the seal

مهرجان *mahrajān*, *mihrajān* pl. *-āt* festival, festivity, celebration | مهرجان بريطانيا Festival of Britain

مهك *mahaka* *a* (*mahk*) to grind, crush, bruise, pound

مهكة *makha*, *muhka* freshness of youth, bloom of youth

مهل *mahala* *a* (*mahl*, مهلة *muhla*) to tarry, dawdle, be slow, take one's time (ف in s.th.) **II** and **IV** to give (ه s.o.) time, grant (ه s.o.) a respite or delay **V** to be slow, proceed slowly and deliberately (ف in s.th.) | تمهل فى خطاه (*kuṭāhu*) to slacken one's pace; تمهل يقول he said slowly ... **VI** = **V**; **X** to ask (ه s.o.) for a respite; to ask (ه s.o.) to wait

مهل *mahl*, *mahal* slowness, leisureliness, ease; leisure; مهلا *mahlan* slowly, leisurely, in no hurry | على مهل slowly, leisurely, in no hurry; مهلك *mahlaka* easy does it! take it easy! على مهلك take it easy! take your time!

مهلة *muhla* respite, delay; time limit for a decision, time to think s.th. over

مهيلة *muhaila* large boat (*ir.*)

امهال *imhāl* grant of respite, concession of a delay

امهالى *imhālī* tending to delay, dilatory

تمهل *tamahhul* slowness, deliberateness | بتمهل slowly; gradually

متمهل *mutamahhil* slow, deliberate, leisurely, unhurried, easy

متماهل *mutamāhil* leisurely, comfortable, easy, unhurried, slow

مهما *mahmā* (conj.) whatever, whatsoever; no matter how much, however much, much as ...; whenever | مهما يكن من الامر (*yakun*, *amr*) whatever the case may be, be it as it may

مهن *mahana* *u* *a* (*mahn*, مهنة *mahna*) to serve (ه s.o.); to humble, degrade, treat in a humiliating manner (ه s.o.); to hackney, wear out in common service, wear out by use (ه s.th.); — *mahuna* *u* (مهانة *mahāna*) to be despicable, base, low, mean, menial **III** to practice (ه a profession) **VIII** to humble, degrade, treat in a humiliating manner (ه s.o.); to revile (ه s.o.); to despise (ه s.o.); to employ for menial services (ه s.o.); to hackney, wear out in common service, wear out by use (ه s.th.); to practice professionally, as a trade (ه s.th.)

مهنة *mihna* pl. مهن *mihan* work, job, occupation, calling, vocation, profession, trade, business

مهنى *mihnī* professional, vocational; gainfully employed | الارشاد المهنى (*iršād*) vocational guidance

مهين *mahīn* pl. مهناء *muhanā'*[2] despised, despicable, contemptible, vile

امتهان *imtihān* degradation, humiliation, contempt, disdain; abuse, misuse, improper treatment

ماهن *māhin* pl. مهان *muhhān* menial servant

مهاة *mahāh* pl. مهوات *mahawāt*, مهيات *mahayāt* wild cow

(موء)[1] ماء *mā'a u* (مواء *muwā'*) to mew, miaow

مواء *muwā'* mewing, miaow (of a cat)

ماه[2] and ماى see موه

موبيليات *mōbīliyāt* (pl.) furniture

(موت) مات *māta u* (*maut*) to die; to perish; to lose life, become dead; to abate, subside, die down, let up (wind, heat) **II** and **IV** to make (ه s.o.) die, let (ه s.o.) perish; to kill, put to death (ه s.o.); to be the death of s.o. (ه), cause the death of s.o. (ه) **IV** to mortify (نفسه o.s., one's flesh); to suppress, deaden (ه s.th.) **VI** to feign death, pretend to be dead; to feign weakness; to be sluggish, listless, slack (فى in s.th.) **X** to seek death; to defy death, sacrifice o.s., risk one's life; to strive desperately (فى for), make desperate efforts (فى in order to); to fight desperately

موت *maut* and موتة *mauta* death; decease, demise | موت ابيض (*abyaḍ*) natural death

موات *mawāt* that which is lifeless, an inanimate thing; barren, uncultivated land, wasteland

موتان *mautān*, *mūtān* dying, death; epidemic, plague

ميت *mayyit*, *mait* pl. اموات *amwāt*, موتى *mautā* lifeless, inanimate, dead, deceased

ميتة *maita* corpse, carcass, carrion; meat of an animal not slaughtered in accordance with ritual requirements (*Isl. Law*)

ميتة *mīta* manner of death | ميتة الابطال death of a hero, death in battle

ممات *mamāt* place where s.o. died; decease, death

اماتة *imāta* killing; mortification (of the flesh)

استماتة *istimāta* death defiance; desperate effort, desperate struggle (فى for)

مائت *mā'it* dying, moribund, mortal

مميت *mumīt* lethal, fatal, mortal, deadly | خطيئة مميتة (*kaṭī'a*) mortal sin

ممات *mumāt* antiquated, obsolete

مستميت *mustamīt* death-defying, reckless, heroic; martyr; suffering a martyr's death

موتوسيكل (Fr. *motocycle*) *mōtōsīkil* pl. *-āt* motorcycle

(موج) ماج *māja u* (*mauj*, موجان *mawajān*) to heave, swell, roll, surge (sea); to be excited, agitated (ب by) **II** to ripple (ه the surface of water, etc.); to wave (ه the hair) **V** = **I**; to rise in waves; to ripple, be rippled (as, the surface of water); to undulate, move in undulations; to sway, roll **VI** to be waved, be undulate; to form an undulating line (حول around); to flow, flood, swell, surge

موج *mauj* pl. امواج *amwāj* billows, surges, seas, breakers; waves; ripples; — (n. un. موجة *mauja* pl. *-āt*) billow, surge, sea, breaker; wave; ripple; oscillation, vibration, undulation | موج طويل long wave (*radio*); موج قصير short wave (*radio*); موج متوسط (*mutawassiṭ*) medium wave (*radio*); امواج صوتية (*ṣautīya*) sound waves; امواج مستمرة (*mustamirra*) continuous waves; امواج مضمحلة (*muḍmaḥilla*(

damped waves; امواج منعكسة (*mun'akisa*) reflected waves, indirect waves; امواج موجهة (*muwajjaha*) directional beams (*radio*); ○ موجة حارة (*ḥārra*) heat wave, hot spell; موجة الشباب *m. aš-šabāb* bloom of youth, freshness of youth; سعة الموجة *sa'at al-m.* amplitude; طول الموجة *ṭūl al-m.* wave length (*radio*); موجة استنكار a wave of disapproval

مواج *mawwāj* undulating, undulant; surging, rolling; waved, undulated, undulate; ○ (pl. *-āt*) transmitter (*radio*)

تمويج *tamwīj* waving (of the hair) | التمويج على البارد cold wave, permanent wave

تموج *tamawwuj* pl. *-āt* oscillation, vibration; undulation, undulant motion; swaying, rolling | تموجات صوتية (*ṣautīya*) sound waves; ○ تموج الهواء *t. al-hawā'* atmospheric vibrations

مائج *mā'ij* surging, swelling, rolling, tumultuous, stormy, high (sea)

ممو ج *mumawwaj* undulated, undulate, waved, wavy, wavelike, undulatory

متموج *mutamawwij* surging, rolling, undulating, undulant, wavelike, undulatory; wavy (hair) | الحمى المتموجة (*ḥummā*) undulant fever, Malta fever, brucellosis (*med.*)

متماوج *mutamāwij* undulate, waved, wavy, rippled; curled

مودة *mōda* pl. *-āt* fashion, style; fashionable; pl. hat fashions, millinery | على المودة of the latest fashion, fashionable, modish, stylish

مودل *mōdell* or موديل *mōdēl* pl. *-āt* model, pattern

¹(مور) مار *māra u* (*maur*) to move to and fro, move from side to side V do.

موار *mawwār* ○ pendulum

تمور *tamawwur* swaying, swinging motion; تمورا to and fro, back and forth

²مار look up alphabetically and under مر *marra*

³المورة *al-mōra* Morea, Poloponnesus

□ موراتزم *mūrātizm* (*eg.*) rheumatism

موراني *mūrānī* (*syr.*) = مارونى look up alphabetically

مورفين *murfīn* morphine

مورينة *mūrīna* pl. *-āt* wooden beam, rafter

موز *mauz* (coll.; n. un. ة) banana

¹ماس *mās* diamond (cf. الماس alphabetically)

ماسى *māsī* diamond (used attributively)

²موسى *mūsā* f., pl. مواس *mawāsin*, امواس *amwās* straight razor

³موسى *mūsā* Moses | سمك موسى *samak m.* plaice, flounder (*zool.*)

موسوى *mūsawī* Mosaic(al)

موسطردة (It. *mostarda*) *musṭarda* mustard

موسكو *moskū*, *moskō* Moscow

موسيقار *mūsīqār* musician

موسيقى *mūsīqā* (f.) music

موسيقى *mūsīqī* musician; musical | آلة موسيقية musical instrument

ماش *māš* (n. un. ة) leguminous plant with black edible grains, Indian pea (Phaseolus max. L.; *bot.*)

الموصل *al-mauṣil* Mosul (city in N Iraq)

موضه (= موده) *mōḍa* fashion, style

موق see ماق

¹مول II to make rich, enrich (ه s.o.); to finance (ه s.th.) V to be financed; to become rich, wealthy X to become rich, wealthy

مال *māl* pl. اموال *amwāl* property, possessions, chattels, goods; wealth, affluence; fortune, estate; money; income, revenue; assets, capital, stock, fund; (*eg.*) tax, esp., land tax; (*Isl. Law*) marketable title; pl. property, assets, chattels, goods; pecuniary resources, funds; taxes | ذو مال wealthy, rich; مال احتياطى (*iḥtiyāṭī*) reserve fund; مال الاطيان (*eg.*) land tax; مال الحرام *m. al-ḥarām* ill-gotten gain; مال الحكومة (*eg.*) taxes; اموال مقررة (*muqarrara*) direct taxes; مال نقلى (*naqlī*) or مال منقول movable property, movables (*Isl. Law*); مال ثابت landed property, real property, immovables; مال غير متقوم (*mutaqawwim*) thing without commercial value (*Isl. Law*); امين المال treasurer; بيت المال *bait al-m.* (public) treasury; رأس مال etc., see رأس

مالى *mālī* monetary, pecuniary, financial; finance (in compounds); fiscal; financier, capitalist | بيت مالى (*bait*) finance house, banking house; تضخم مالى (*taḍakkum*) inflation; سنة مالية (*sana*) fiscal year; غرامة مالية (*ġarāma*) or عقوبة مالية a fine

مالية *māliya* monetary affairs, finance, public revenue; finances, financial situation | وزارة المالية finance ministry, treasury department

موال *mawwāl* pl. *-ūn* (*ir.*) financier, capitalist

تمويل *tamwīl* financing; (*eg.*) taxpaying

ممول *mumawwil* pl. *-ūn* (*eg.*) taxpayer

ممول *mumawwal* propertied, wealthy, rich

متمول *mutamawwil* rich, wealthy, well-to-do; financier, capitalist

موال[2] *mawwāl* pl. مواويل *mawāwīl*[2] a poem in colloquial language, often sung to the accompaniment of a reed pipe

مواليا *mawāliyā* do.

موم *mūm* wax

مومياء *mūmiyā'*, مومية *mūmiya* pl. *-āt* mummy

(مون) مان *māna u* (*maun*, مؤنة *mu'na*) and II to provision, supply with provisions (ه s.o.); to provide, furnish, supply (ب ه or ه s.o. or s.th. with) V to store up provisions, lay in provisions, provision o.s.

مونة *mūna* provisions; (*eg.*) mortar

تموين *tamwīn* food supply, provisioning; supply; replenishment

مواني[2] pl. of مينا

مونيخ *mūnik̲* Munich

(موه) ماه *māha u* (*mauh*) to mix (ه ب s.th. with); — *u a* (*mauh*, مؤوه *mu'ūh*, ماهة *māha*) to abound in water II to abound in water; to pour water (ه into), admix water (ه to); to thin, dilute, water down, adulterate (ه s.th.); to falsify (ه, على s.th.), misrepresent (ه s.th.); to feign, affect (ب على s.th. toward s.o.); to camouflage (ه s.th.; *Syr., mil.*); to coat, overlay, plate (ه ب a base metal with gold or silver) IV to add water (ه to)

ماء *mā'* pl. مياه *miyah*, امواه *amwāh* water; liquid, fluid; juice | كالماء الجارى fluently, smoothly, like clockwork; ماء ابيض (*abyaḍ*[2]) cataract (eye disease); ماء الزهر *m. az-zahr* orange-blossom water; ماء الشباب *m. aš-šabāb* freshness of youth, prime of youth; ماء عذب (*'aḏb*) fresh water, potable water; ماء غازى pl. مياه غازية carbonated water, mineral water; ماء الكولونيا Eau de Cologne; ماء الوجه *m. al-wajh* honor, decency, modesty, self-respect; اراق ماء وجهه *arāqa mā'a wajhihī* to sacrifice one's honor, abase o.s.; to dishonor, disgrace s.o.; بذل ماء وجهه do.; ماء الورد *m. al-ward* rose water; مياه اقليمية (*iqlīmiya*) territorial waters; مياه الامطار *m. al-amṭār* rain water; مياه جوفية (*jaufiya*) ground water; مياه ساحلية (*sāḥilīya*) coastal waters; بنو ماء السماء *banū m. as-samā'* the Arabs

ماهى *māhī* and ماوى *māwī* watery, aqueous, aquatic

مائى *mā'ī* aquatic, water; liquid, fluid; hydraulic

ماهية look up alphabetically

ماوية *māwīya* and مائية *mā'īya* juice, sap

تمويه *tamwīh* coating, plating; clothing, attire, garb; overfilling; feigning, pretending, affectation; camouflage (*Syr., mil.*); distortion (of facts), misrepresentation, falsification | كأس التمويه *ka's at-t.* overfull cup

تمويهى *tamwīhī* feigned, sham, mock, make-believe | غارة تمويهية mock attack, feint

موه see ماوية

موت and see مبتة مست

(ميح) ماح *māḥa* **i** (*maiḥ*, ميحوحة *maiḥūḥa*) to strut, walk with affected dignity; to waddle **V** and **VI** to reel, totter, stagger; to swing **X** to ask (ه ه s.o. a favor), request (ه s.th.) | استماح عذرا من (*'uḏran*) to apologize for s.th.

(ميد) ماد *māda* **i** (*maid*, ميدان *mayadān*) to be moved, shaken, upset, shocked; to sway; to swing; to feel giddy, be dizzy; ماد ب to shake s.th. violently **VI** to sway back and forth, swing from side to side

ميدة *mīda* pl. ميد *miyad* (*eg.*) lintel, breastsummer (*arch.*)

ميداء *mīdā'* measure, amount, length, distance; *mīdā'a* (prep.) in front of, opposite, facing

ميدان *maidān, mīdān* pl. ميادين *mayādīn*[2] square, open place, open tract; field; arena; battleground, battlefield; combat area, fighting zone; race course, race track; playground (fig.); field, domain, line, sphere of activity | ميدان التدريب drill ground; military training center; ميدان الحرب *m. al-ḥarb* theater of war; ميدان السباق race course, race track; ميدان العمل *m. al 'amal* field of activity, scope of action; ميدان القتال battlefield; خرج من ميدان العمل to be put out of service or commission; ظهر فى الميدان to turn up, appear on the scene; فى ميدان الشرف *fī m. iš-šaraf* on the field of honor; مدافع الميدان fieldpieces, field guns, infantry howitzers

مائد *mā'id* pl. ميدى *maidā* dizzy, seasick

مائدة *mā'ida* pl. *-āt*, موائد *mawā'id*[2] table | مائدة التشريح operating table; مائدة الزينة *m. az-zīna* dressing table; مائدة السفرة *m. as-sufra* dining table

مداليون *madāliyōn* medallion

[1](مير) مار *māra* **i** (*mair*) and **IV** to provide (عياله *'iyālahū* for one's family)

ميرة *mīra* pl. مير *miyar* provisions, supplies, stores

ميار *mayyār* caterer, purveyor, supplier

[2]ميرى *mīrī* (= اميرى) public, governmental, government-, state- (in compounds); fiscal; الميرى the government, the fisc, the exchequer | مال الميرى government taxes; املاك الميرى government land

ميرآلاى *mīrālāy* (formerly, *Eg.*) colonel

ميرلواء *mīrliwā'* (*Ir.*) brigadier general

[3]مير (Fr. *maire*) *mēr* pl. اميار *amyār* (*maġr.*) mayor

ميرون *mairūn* chrism (*Chr.*)

(ميز) ماز *māza* **i** (*maiz*) to separate, keep apart (بين two things); to distinguish, honor, favor (ه s.o.) **II** to confer distinction (ه upon s.o.), distinguish, commend, honor, favor (ه s.o., عن above s.o. else, also على); to distinguish, set aside, cause to stand out (ه, ه s.o., s.th., عن from); to prefer (عن ه or ه s.o. or s.th. to); to separate, segregate, set apart, single out, select, choose, pick (ه, ه s.o., s.th.); to grant a special right or privilege (ه to s.o.), privilege (ه s.o.); to distinguish, differentiate, discriminate (عن ه, ه s.o., s.th. from, also بين; من between two things, one thing from another) **IV** to distinguish, mark (ه s.th.); to prefer (ه s.th.) **V** to be set apart, be separated or separate, be distinct, be distinguished, be differentiated; to distinguish o.s., be distinguished, be marked, stand out; to be marked out with distinction, be honored, be favored; to be preferred | تميز غيظا (*ġaiẓan*) to burst with anger **VI** to distinguish o.s. (في in); to differ **VIII** to distinguish o.s. (ب by, في in s.th., عن or على above s.o. or s.th., من as compared with s.o. or s.th.); to be distinguished, be marked (ب by); to be characterized, be signalized (ب by); to excel, surpass, outdo, outshine (عن or على s.o. or s.th.); to have the advantage, take preference (على over), be preferred (على to); to differ (من or على from s.o., في or ب in, in that ...)

ميز *maiz* distinction; favoring, preferment

ميزة *mīza* peculiarity, distinguishing feature, distinctive mark, essential property, characteristic; prerogative, priority right

اميز *amyaz*² preferable (على to)

تمييز *tamyīz* distinction; preference; preferment, favoring, favoritism, preferential treatment; privileging; partiality; separation, segregation, sifting, singling out; specification (*gram.*); differentiation; discrimination, judgment, discretion, common sense; realization, discernment, conscious perception; deliberate intention | سن التمييز *sinn at-t.* age of discretion (*jur.*); محكمة التمييز *maḥkamat at-t.* court of cassation (*Syr.*); من غير تمييز unwittingly, unintentionally, with no definite purpose in mind; اخرجه عن دائرة التمييز (*akrajahū*) to deprive s.o. of his clear judgment, rob s.o. of his senses

امتياز *imtiyāz* pl. *-āt* distinction, (mark of) honor; advantage, benefit, merit; difference, distinction, differentiation, discrimination; special right, privilege; concession, patent, permit, license, franchise; (oil) concession; prerogative, priority right | الامتيازات الاجنبية (*ajnabīya*) the capitulations (of Western powers in the Orient); الامتيازات الدبلوماسية diplomatic privileges; صاحب الامتياز holder of the concession, concessionaire, responsible publisher of a newspaper

مميز *mumayyiz* distinguishing, distinctive; characteristic, peculiar, proper; discriminating, discerning, reasonable, rational (*Isl. Law*)

مميزة *mumayyiza* pl. *-āt* distinguishing feature, distinctive mark, characteristic trait, peculiarity; distinction, (mark of) honor; advantage, merit

مميز *mumayyaz* distinguished, preferred, favored, privileged; distinct, separate, special

متميز *mutamayyiz* distinguished, distingué; marked, notable, prominent, outstanding, characterized by distinctive traits, characteristic

ممتاز *mumtāz* distinguished, differentiated; exquisite, select, choice, rare; outstanding, superior, first-rate, first-class, top-notch, exceptional, excellent; privileged; special, extra; (as an examination grade) passed with distinction, excellent | درجة ممتازة (*daraja*) special class; ديون ممتازة (*duyūn*) privileged debts, preferred debts; عدد ممتاز (*'adad*) special issue (of a periodical)

ميزانين (It. *mezzanino*) *mēzānīn* mezzanine

[1]ماس (ميس) *māsa i* (*mais*, ميسان *mayasān*) to move to and fro, swing from side to side; to walk with a proud, swinging gait V to walk with a proud, swinging gait

ميس *mais* proud gait; proud bearing

ميس *mīs* pl. امياس *amyās* (*eg.*) target

مياس *mayyās* walking with a lofty, proud gait, strutting

[2]ميس (Engl. *mess*), ميس الضباط *m. aḍ-ḍubbāṭ* officers mess

ماط (ميط) *māṭa i* (*maiṭ*, ميطان *mayaṭān*) to remove, pull away, draw back (ه s.th.) IV do. | اماط اللثام عن to disclose, uncover, reveal s.th., bring s.th. to light

ماع (ميع) *mā'a i* (*mai'*) to flow; to spread; to melt, dissolve (fat) II to soften, attenuate, dilute, liquefy (ه s.th.) IV to melt, liquefy (ه s.th.) V and VII to be melted, melt, dissolve

ميع *mai'* flowing, flow; liquidity, fluidity

ميعة *mai'a* storax, a kind of incense obtained from the storax tree, resin of the storax tree (Styrax officinalis); prime, bloom (of youth); indulgence, compliance; unstableness, unsteadiness

ميوعة *muyū'a* liquid state; unstableness, unsteadiness

اماعة *imā'a* melting, liquefaction

تميع *tamayyu'* liquescence, liquefaction

مائع *mā'i'* melting, liquid, fluid; liquescent, semiliquid; vague (expression); undecided, pending, in flux (situation)

ميكا (Engl.) mica

ميكانى *mīkānī* mechanical, mechanized

ميكانيكا *mīkānīkā* mechanics

ميكانيكى *mīkānīkī* mechanical, automatic, mechanized, mechanic; motorized; a mechanic

ميكروب *mikrūb* pl. *-āt* microbe

ميكروفون *mikrōfōn* pl. *-āt* microphone

[1]مال (ميل) *māla i* (*mail*, ميلان *mayalān*) to bend, bend down (الى to; على over); to bow down, lean over, turn (على to s.o.); to incline, slope, slant, tilt, tip, be inclined, slanting, oblique; to incline, tend, be favorably disposed (الى to), have a predilection, a liking, an inclination, a propensity (الى for), feel sympathy (الى for), sympathize (الى with), favor (الى s.o.); to take sides, to side (مع with), be partial, biased, prejudiced; to lean (على against); to revolt, rebel (على against), be hostile (على to s.o.); to be disinclined, be averse (عن to s.th.); to have an antipathy, a distaste, a dislike (عن for); to deviate, digress, turn away, depart (عن from); مال به الى to drag or take s.o. or s.th. along to ...; — (ميول *muyūl*) to prepare to set (sun); to decline, draw to its end (day, night); — ميل *mayila a* (*mayal*) to be bent, bowed, tilted, averted, turned aside II and IV to incline, tip, tilt, bend, bow (ه s.th.); to make (ه s.o.) inclined, sympathetic or favorably disposed (نحو or الى to s.o., to s.th.), incline, dispose (ه s.o.'s mind نحو or الى to), fill (ه s.o.) with sympathy (الى for); to make (ه s.o.) disinclined or averse (عن to), turn s.o.'s mind (ه) away from (عن), alienate (ه عن s.o. from) V and VI to reel, totter, stagger; to waver (tone); to sway, swing X to cause to incline, incline, tip, tilt (ه s.th., الى to or toward); to win (ه s.o., als القلوب the hearts), attract, win over, bring to one's side (ه s.o.), gain favor (ه with s.o.), win s.o.'s (ه) affection

ميل *mail* pl. ميول *muyūl*, اميال *amyāl* inclination, tilt; bend, turn, deflection; obliqueness, obliquity, slant; slope, incline, declivity; deviation, divergence, declination (*astron.*); affection (الى for), attachment (الى to); predilection, liking, sympathy (الى for); propensity, disposition, bent, leaning, inclination, taste, desire, wish, longing; tendency, trend, drift (الى to, toward)

ميال **mayyāl** inclined, favorably disposed (الى to), leaning (الى toward); in favor (الى of), biased (الى toward or for)

اميل **amyal**[2] more inclined, strongly inclined (الى to), more in favor (الى of)

امالة **imāla** pronunciation of *a* shaded toward *e* (*gram.*)

تمايل **tamāyul** reel(ing), swaying, tottering, stagger(ing), waver(ing); vibration

مائل **mā'il** inclining (الى to or toward); bending down, bowing down, leaning over; bent, tilted; sloping, declivitous (terrain); inclined, slanting, oblique | سطح مائل (*saṭḥ*) inclined plane (*math.*)

[2]ميل **mīl** pl. اميال **amyāl** mile (= 4000 ذراع); milestone | ميل بحرى (*baḥrī*) nautical mile, knot

[3]ميلى milli-, $^1/_{1000}$ (in measures)

مان (مين) **māna** *i* (*main*) to lie, tell a lie

مين **main** pl. ميون **muyūn** lie, falsehood, untruth

ميان **mayyān** and مائن **mā'in** liar

[1]مينا **mīnā** and ميناء **mīnā'** glaze, glazing; enamel (of the teeth; as a coating of metal, glass, or pottery); (pl. موانى **mawānī'**[2]) dial (of a watch or clock) | مطلى بالمينا (*maṭlīy*) enamel-coated, enameled

[2]ميناء **mīnā'** f. and مينة **mīna** pl. موان **mawānin**, مين **miyan** port, harbor, anchorage | ميناء جوية (*jawwīya*) airport

ن

نابلس *nābulus*[2] Nablus (town in W Jordan)

نابلى *nābulī* or نابولى *nābūlī* Napoli, Naples (seaport in S Italy)

نارجيل *nārajīl* coconut(s) (coll.)

نارجيلة *nārajīla* (n. un.) coconut; Persian water pipe, narghile

ناردين *nāradīn* nard, spikenard

نارنج *nāranj* bitter orange

نازى *nāzī* Nazi

نازية *nāzīya* Nazism

ناس *nās* men, people, folks (cf. انس)

ناسوت *nāsūt* human nature, humanity

[1]نأم *na'ama* *i* *a* to sound, resound, ring out; to groan, moan

نأمة *na'ma* noise, sound, tone

[2]نؤوم **na'ūm** see نوم

ناموس **nāmūs** pl. نواميس **nawāmīs**[2] law; rule; honor; see also نمس

[1]نأى **na'ā** *a* (*na'y*) to be far, far away, distant, remote (عن from), keep away, stay away, keep at a distance, remain aloof, go away, move away, depart, absent o.s. (عن from), leave (عن s.th., s.o.) **III** to keep far away, keep at a distance (عن ه or ه s.o. or s.th. from), keep a wide distance (ه, ه between s.o. or s.th., عن and) **IV** to remove, move away, take away, place at a distance (عن ه s.o. from) **VI** to move away, move apart, draw away from one another; to be away from one another, be at a distance, be separated, be apart; to keep away, stand aloof, be away, be at a distance (عن from) **VIII** to

be away, be at a distance (عن from); to go away, move away, draw away, depart, absent o.s. (عن from), leave (عن s.th., s.o.)

نأي *na'y* remoteness

نأي *na'y* and نؤى *nu'ā* pl. آناء *ānā'*, انآء *an'ā'* ditch

انأى *an'ā* farther away, remoter, more distant

منأى *man'an* distant place | كان بمنأى عن to keep away from, remain aloof from, keep out of, not get involved in, refuse to have anything to do with

تناء *tanā'in* great distance, remoteness

ناء *nā'in* far, far away, distant, remote; outlying, out-of-the-way, secluded

²ناى *nāy* pl. *-āt* nay, a flute without mouthpiece, made of bamboo, rarely of wood, in different sizes, which, when blown, is held in a slanting forward position (unlike a German flute)

انبوب *unbūb* and انبوبة *unbūba* pl. انابيب *anābīb*[2] joint (of a knotted stem), part between two nodes; tube, pipe, conduit, conduit pipe, main duct; tube (e.g., of toothpaste); light bulb | انبوب الرئة *u. ar-ri'a* windpipe, trachea (*anat.*); انبوب الطوربيد torpedo tube; انبوب مفرغ (*mufarraǥ*) vacuum tube (*radio*); خط الانابيب *ḵaṭṭ al-a.* pipeline

انبوبى *unbūbī* tubular, tube-shaped, fistulous; pipe- (in compounds)

نبأ *naba'a a* (نبء *nab'*, نبوء *nubū'*) to be high, raised, elevated, protruding, projecting, prominent; to overcome, overpower, overwhelm (على s.o.); to turn away, withdraw, shrink (عن from); to be repelled, repulsed, sickened, disgusted, shocked (عن by) II to inform, notify, tell, advise (عن or ب ه s.o. of s.th.), let (ه s.o.) know (عن or ب about), make known, announce, impart, communicate (عن or ب ه to s.o. s.th.); to be evidence (عن of), show, indicate, manifest, bespeak, reveal, disclose (عن s.th.) IV to inform, notify, tell, advise (ب ه s.o. of), let (ه s.o.) know (ب about), make known, announce, impart, communicate (ب ه to s.o. s.th.) V to predict, foretell, forecast, prognosticate, presage, prophesy (ب s.th.); to claim to be a prophet, pose as a prophet X to ask for news, for information (ه s.o.); to inquire (ه after), ask (ه about)

نبأ *naba'* pl. انباء *anbā'* news, tidings, information, intelligence; announcement; report, news item, dispatch | وكالة الانباء *wakālat al-a.* or مكتب الانباء *maktab al-a.* news agency, wire service

نبأة *nab'a* faint noise, low sound

نبوءة *nubū'a* pl. *-āt* prophecy

انباء *inbā'* pl. *-āt* notification, information, communication

تنبؤ *tanabbu'* pl. *-āt* prediction, forecast, prognostication, prophecy

نبت *nabata u* (*nabt*) to grow (esp., of plants, also, e.g., of teeth); to sprout, germinate; to produce plants, bring forth vegetation (soil) II to plant, sow, seed (ه s.th.) IV to germinate, cause to sprout (ه a seed); to make (ه s.th.) grow; to grow, plant, cultivate (ه s.th.) X to plant, cultivate, grow, raise (ه plants); to breed (ه plants), culture (ه e.g., bacteria)

نبت *nabt* germination, sprouting; growth; vegetable growth, vegetation, plants; herbage, herbs, grass; sprout, plant | قوة النبت *qūwat an-n.* germinability, germinative faculty

نبتة *nabta* plant, sprout, shoot, seedling

نبات *nabāt* (coll.) plants, vegetation; — (pl. *-āt*) plant, vegetable organism; herb | نبات اقتصادى (*iqtiṣādī*) economic plant; نبات الزينة *n. az-zīna* ornamental plant; نبات طبي (*ṭibbī*) medicinal plant; آكل النبات herbivorous animal; سكر النبات *sukkar an-n.* rock candy; علم النبات *'ilm an-n.* botany

نباتي *nabātī* vegetable, vegetal, plant- (in compounds); botanical; botanist; vegetarian (adj. and n.)

نبوت *nabbūt* pl. نبابيت *nabābīt²* (*eg.*) quarterstaff, cudgel, bludgeon, club, truncheon, night stick

منبت *manbat, manbit* pl. منابت *manābit²* plantation, plant nursery, arboretum; hotbed, birthplace, fountainhead, headspring, origin, source

تنبيت *tanbīt* planting, cultivation, seedbed planting

استنبات *istinbāt* planting, cultivation, growing

نابتة *nābita* generation

مستنبت *mustanbat* cultivated, grown, raised, bred; plantation, nursery, culture | ○ مستنبت البكتريا bacterial culture

نبح *nabaḥa a* (*nabḥ*, نباح *nubāḥ, nibāḥ*, نبيح *nabīḥ*) to bark (على at s.o.), bay (على s.o.) VI to bark at each other; to bark simultaneously, answer each other's barks (dogs, e.g., at night)

نبح *nabḥ*, نباح *nubāḥ, nibāḥ* and نبيح *nabīḥ* barking, bark, baying, yelp(ing)

نباح *nabbāḥ* barker, yelper

نبذ *nabaḏa i* (*nabḏ*) to hurl, fling, throw, or toss, away (ه s.th.); to reject, discard, spurn (ه s.th.); to cast out, cast off, ostracize, expel, banish, disown, repudiate, remove, eliminate, dismiss, abandon, forsake, give up, renounce (ه, ه s.o., s.th.); to withdraw, turn away (ه from), relinquish, forswear (ه s.th.); to break, violate, infringe (ه a contract, a treaty), default (الى against s.o.) | نبذه النواة (*nabaḏa n-nawāh*) to reject or dismiss s.th. or s.o. with disdain, spurn or scorn s.th. or s.o. II = I; to press (ه grapes) III to separate, secede, withdraw (ه from s.o.), oppose, resist (ه s.o.) | نابذه الحرب (*ḥarba*) to declare war on s.o. IV to press (ه grapes) VI to be feuding VIII to withdraw, retire, retreat | انتبذ ناحية (*nāḥiyatan*) to step aside, withdraw to one side; to retreat into a corner

نبذ *nabḏ* throwing away, discarding; rejection, repudiation, disavowal; renunciation, resignation; surrender, relinquishment, abandonment; (pl. انباذ *anbāḏ*) small amount, a little, a trifle, bagatelle | نبذ الطاعة insubordination

نبذة *nubḏa* pl. نبذ *nubaḏ* small piece, part, portion, fragment, fraction, section; (newspaper) article, story; tract, pamphlet, leaflet; small ad(vertisement)

نبيذ *nabīḏ* cast-off, discarded, rejected, disowned, repudiated, dismissed; (pl. انبذة *anbiḏa*) wine | روح النبيذ *rūḥ an-n.* spirits of wine, alcohol

نابذ *nābiḏ*: ○ القوة النابذة (*qūwa*) centrifugal force

منبوذ *manbūḏ* cast-off, discarded; cast-out, ostracized, banished, expelled, disowned, repudiated; abandoned; foundling, waif; neglected, disregarded; المنبوذون the untouchables (in India), the pariahs

نبر *nabara i* (*nabr*) to raise, elevate; to go up with the voice, sing in a high-pitched voice; to stress, emphasize, accentuate; to shout, yell, scream (ه at s.o.); to cry out VIII to swell, become swollen

نبر *nabr* accentuation, accent, stress, emphasis

نبر *nibr* and انبار *anbār* pl. انابر *anābir²*, انابير *anābīr²* barn, shed, granary, storeroom, storehouse, warehouse

نبرة *nabra* pl. *nabarāt* swelling, intumescence, protuberance; stress, accent, accentuation; tone (of the voice); pl. نبرات inflection of the voice, intonation, cadence

منبر *minbar* pl. منابر *manābir*[2] mimbar; pulpit; rostrum, platform, dais

منبار *minbār* pl. منابير *manābīr*[2] gut, intestine | منبار محشى (*maḥšīy*) sausage

نبراس *nibrās* pl. نباريس *nabārīs*[2] lamp, light, lantern | اتخذ منه نبراسا (*ittakaḏa*) to take s.o. for an example, model o.s. after s.o.

نبز *nabaza* i (*nabz*) to give a derisive or insulting name (ه to s.o.) II do.

نبز *nabaz* pl. انباز *anbāz* nickname, sobriquet

نبس *nabasa* i (*nabs*, نبسة *nubsa*), to utter, say, speak II do. | ما نبس بكلمة (*bi-kalima*) he did not say a word

نبش *nabaša* u (*nabš*) to excavate, dig up, dig out of the ground, unearth, exhume, disinter (ه s.th.); to uncover, lay open, unveil, disclose, reveal, bring to light, bring out into the open (ه s.th.) II to search, rummage, burrow (فى in s.th.), ransack, rifle (فى s.th.)

نبش *nabš* excavation, unearthing, digging up; examination, search, exploration; uncovering, disclosure, revelation | نبش القبور desecration of graves, body snatching

نباش *nabbāš* gravedigger; body snatcher

نبيش *nabīš* dug up, excavated

انبوش *unbūš* and انبوشة *unbūša* pl. انابيش *anābīš*[2] excavation, excavated object

نبض *nabaḍa* i (*nabḍ*, نبضان *nabaḍān*) to beat, throb, pulsate, palpitate (heart, pulse); — u (نبوض *nubūḍ*) to flow off, run off, drain (water)

نبض *nabḍ*, *nabaḍ* pl. انباض *anbāḍ* throbbing, throb, pulsation, palpitation; pulse

نبضة *nabḍa*, *nabaḍa* pulsation, pulse beat

نابض *nābiḍ* pulsating, pulsative, beating, throbbing, palpitating; spring, mainspring, coil spring, spiral spring | نابض بالحياة (*bi-l-ḥayāh*) vibrant with life

منبض *manbiḍ* spot where the pulse or heartbeat is felt

نبط *nabaṭa* u i (*nabṭ*, نبوط *nubūṭ*) to well out, gush out, spout, issue, stream forth (water) II (*eg.*) to find fault (على with s.o.), carp, scoff, gibe, sneer (على at s.o.) IV to cause (ه s.th.) to gush out or well forth, bring (ه s.th.) to the surface; to find, discover (ه water, oil, etc.), come upon (ه), open up, tap (ه a source, a well, etc.) X to find, discover (ه water, oil, etc.), come upon (ه), open up, tap (ه a source, a well, etc.); to invent, discover, think up, devise, design, contrive, find out (ه s.th.); to derive, extract, draw, take (ه من s.th. from)

نبط *nabaṭ* depth, deep, profundity; the innermost, inmost part, core, heart

النبط *an-nabaṭ* pl. الانباط *al-anbāṭ* the Nabateans

نبطى *nabaṭī* Nabatean (adj. and n.)

استنباط *istinbāṭ* discovery, invention

مستنبط *mustanbiṭ* discoverer, inventor

مستنبطات *mustanbaṭāt* discoveries, inventions

نبع *naba'a* u i a (*nab'*, نبوع *nubū'*, نبعان *naba'ān*) to well, well up, gush forth, flow, issue (من from); to rise, spring, originate (river) IV to cause (ه s.th.) to gush forth or flow out

نبع *nab'* a tree whose wood was used in arrow-making; spring, source | قرع

النبع بالنبع (*nab'a*) approx.: to cross swords with the opponent

منبع *manba'* pl. منابع *manābi'*[2] spring, well; fountainhead, springhead, source, origin | منبع زيت *m. zait* or منبع بترول oil well

ينبوع *yanbū'* pl. ينابيع *yanābī'*[2] spring, source, well

نبغ **nabağa** *a u i* (*nabğ*, نبوغ *nubūğ*) to arise, emerge (من from), come to the fore, come in sight, appear, show; to spread, diffuse, be diffused; to have superior or extraordinary qualities, stand out, distinguish o.s., be distinguished, be marked; to excel, be outstanding (في in); to be an outstanding, exceptional man, be a genius

نبوغ *nubūğ* eminence, distinction; superior or extraordinary qualities, exceptional faculties, giftedness, talent, genius; outstanding greatness, brilliancy, genius (of an artistic achievement)

نابغ *nābiğ* outstanding, distinguished; gifted, talented; man of genius, brilliant person

نابغة *nābiğa* pl. نوابغ *nawābiğ*[2] a distinguished, famous, or outstanding man, a poetic genius

نبق **nabq**, *nibq*, *nabaq*, *nabiq* (coll.; n. un. ة) nabk, a Christ's-thorn (Zizyphus spina-christi; *bot.*); lotus fruit; lotus blossom

انبيق *anbīq*, *inbīq* pl. انابيق *anābīq*[2] alembic, distilling flask

نبكة **nabka**, *nabaka* hill, hillock

نبل **nabala** *u* (*nabl*) to shoot arrows (ه at s.o.); — *nabula u* (نبالة *nabāla*) to be noble, noble-minded, generous, magnanimous, highborn, patrician; to be above s.th. (عن), be too high-minded to stoop to (عن)

نبل *nabl* (coll.; n. un. ة) pl. نبال *nibāl*, انبال *anbāl* arrows

نبل *nubl* and نبالة *nabāla* nobility, nobleness, exalted rank or station, eminence; noble-mindedness, high-mindedness, magnanimity, generosity

نبل *nabl* and نبيل *nabīl* pl. نبال *nibāl*, نبلاء *nubalā'*[2] noble; lofty, exalted, sublime, august; aristocratic, highborn, highbred, patrician, distinguished; noble-minded, high-minded, generous, magnanimous; excellent, outstanding, superior; magnificent, splendid, glorious; النبيل pl. النبلاء (formerly:) title of members of the Egyptian royal family

نبال *nabbāl* pl. نبالة *nabbāla* and نابل *nābil* pl. نبل *nubbal* archer, bowman

نبه **nabaha** *u*, *nabiha a* and *nabuha u* (نباهة *nabāha*) to be well-known, noted, renowned, famous; — *nabiha a* (*nabah*) to heed, mind, note, observe (ل s.th.), pay attention (ل to), take notice (ل of); to wake up, awaken **II** to call s.o.'s attention (ه) to (الى or على), point out, show, indicate (الى or على ه to s.o. s.th.); to inform, tell, apprise, notify (الى or على ه s.o. of); to remind (الى ه s.o. of); to inform, instruct, brief (على ه s.o. about); to warn, caution (ه s.o.); to wake, awaken, rouse (ه من النوم s.o. from sleep); to arouse, alert, stir up, excite, stimulate (ه s.o.) **IV** to awaken, rouse (ه s.o., ه s.th.) **V** to perceive, notice, note, realize (ل or الى s.th.), become aware, become conscious (ل or الى of); to be alerted, have one's attention drawn (ل or الى, على to), take notice (ل or الى, على of), pay attention (ل or الى, على to), be mindful, heedful (ل or الى, على of); to wake up, awaken; to come to, regain consciousness (with لنفسه *li-nafsihī*) **VIII** to be on one's guard, be wary, cautious, careful; to be awake, alert, wakeful; to awaken, wake up; to perceive, notice, note, observe (الى or ل s.th.); to understand, realize, grasp, comprehend (الى or ل s.th.); to be aware, be conscious (الى or ل of s.th.); to pay attention (الى or ل to); to come to, regain consciousness (with لنفسه li-nafsihī)

نبه nubh insight, discernment, perception, acumen, sagacity; understanding, attention; vigilance, alertness

نبه nabih and نبيه nabīh pl. نبهاء nubahā'[2] noble, highborn, patrician; outstanding, eminent, distinguished, excellent; famous, renowned, celebrated; understanding, sensible, discerning, judicious, perspicacious

نباهة nabāha fame, renown, celebrity; exalted rank or station, eminence, nobility; vigilance, alertness; intelligence

منبهة manbaha a call to draw s.o.'s attention to s.th. (على), rousing call, incitement, impetus, incentive (على to)

تنبيه tanbīh rousing, awakening; excitation, stimulation, incitement, arousing; warning, cautioning, alerting; notification, notice, information; admonition, exhortation, advice, counsel, briefing, instruction, direction; nota bene, note, remark, annotation (in books) | آلة التنبيه horn (of an automobile, etc.)

تنبه tanabbuh awakening, wakefulness, alertness

انتباه intibāh attention, attentiveness; vigilance, watchfulness, alertness; foresight, circumspection, prudence, care, carefulness; caution; heed, notice, observance | بانتباه attentively, carefully

نابه nābih noble, highborn, patrician; eminent; well-known, renowned, distinguished; famous, important

منبه munabbih awakening, rousing; warning, cautioning, alerting; excitant, stimulant; (pl. -āt) alarm clock; stimulus, stimulative agent, stimulant, excitant

متنبه mutanabbih awake, wakeful; alert, vigilant, watchful

منتبه muntabih awake, wakeful; alert, vigilant, watchful; attentive, heedful; careful, prudent, cautious, wary, guarded

(نبو) نبا nabā u (نبو nabw, nubūw) to be far off, distant, remote; to move away, withdraw in the distance; to miss (arrow, عن the target); to bounce off, rebound, bounce, bound (عن الى from—to; ball); to disagree (عن with); to be contradictory (عن to), to conflict, be in conflict, be inconsistent (عن with); to be offensive, repugnant (عن to s.o.); to dislike, find repugnant (عن s.th.) | نبا به المكان (makānu) he felt unable to remain in the place

نبي nabīy pl. -ūn, انبياء anbiyā'[2] prophet | خشب الانبياء guaiacum wood

نبوى nabawī prophetic, of or pertaining to a prophet or specifically to the Prophet Mohammed

نبوة nubūwa prophethood, prophecy

ناب nābin repugnant, distasteful, improper, ugly

نتأ nata'a a (نتء nat', نتوء nutū') to swell; to bulge, bulge out; to protrude, project, jut out, stand out, be prominent, protuberant, embossed, in relief

نتأة nat'a hill, hillock, elevation

نتوء nutū' swelling, intumescence, growth, tumor; outgrowth, excrescence; protrusion, projection, protuberance, prominence, bulge; hill, hillock, elevation | نتوء الجبهة n. al-jabha salient, bulge in the front line (mil.)

ناتئ nāti' pl. نواتئ nawāti'[2] swelling, swollen; protruding, projecting, jutting out, salient, protuberant, bulging; bulge, hump, protuberance | ناتئ كعبرى (ku'burī) wristbone

ناتئة nāti'a pl. نواتئ nawāti'[2] projection, protrusion, jut, prominence; outgrowth, excrescence, protuberance; hump, elevation

نتج **nataja** *i* (نتاج *nitāj*) to bear, bring forth, throw (ه a young one); to proceed, derive, arise, follow, ensue, result (من or عن from), be the result of (من or عن) **IV** to bear, throw (ه a young one); to bring forth, yield, generate, produce, make, manufacture, fabricate, create, originate, cause, provoke, bring about, occasion (ه s.th.), give rise (ه to) **X** to conclude, gather, infer, deduce, derive, trace (ه من s.th. from), draw a conclusion (من from)

نتاج ***nitāj*** (act or process of) bearing, throwing, littering (of animals); brood, litter, offspring, young ones, young animals | نتاج الخيل *n. al-kail* foal(s)

نتيجة ***natīja*** pl. نتائج *natā'ij*² result, upshot, issue, outcome, consequence; product, effect, immediate result, fruits, yield, proceeds, gain, profit; (*techn.*) output; conclusion, inference, deduction; almanac, calendar; *natījata* (prep.) because of, as a result of, due to, owing to | بالنتيجة consequently, hence, therefore; نتيجة الجيب *n. al-jaib* pocket calendar; نتيجة الحائط wall calendar

انتاج ***intāj*** generation; making, manufacture; production; rearing, raising, breeding, growing, cultivation; productivity; creating, creation, creative activity; output (of a machine; ○ in mining) | الانتاج الادبى (*adabī*) literary production; رسم الانتاج *rasm al-i.* excise tax

استنتاج ***istintāj*** pl. *-āt* inference, conclusion; deduction

ناتج ***nātij*** resultant, resulting, following, ensuing, proceeding, deriving, arising (عن from); result; maker, producer

منتوج ***mantūj*** pl. *-āt* product, creation, work, production

منتج ***muntij*** bearing, giving birth, producing; fruitful, productive; fertile, fecund, prolific; conclusive (evidence); maker, manufacturer, producer; film producer

منتجات ***muntajāt*** proceeds, returns, yields, products | منتجات زراعية (*zirā'īya*) agricultural products, farming products, produce

مستنتج ***mustantij*** maker, manufacturer, producer

نتحة **natḥa** exudation

¹نتر **natara** *u* (*natr*) to grab, grasp, wrest away, take away by force (ه s.th.)

²نترات **nitrāt** nitrate

نتروجين **nitrōjēn** nitrogen

نتش **nataša** *i* (*natš*) to pull out, extract (ه s.th.); to pluck out, tear out (ه s.th.); to snatch away; to beat, strike, hit

منتاش ***mintāš*** tweezers, pincette

نتع **nata'a** *u i* (نتوع *nutū'*) to well up, bubble up, trickle out, ooze out, dribble, trickle; — (*eg.*) to lift up, carry away (ه s.o.)

نتف **natafa** *i* (*natf*) to pluck out, pull out, tear out (ه hair, and the like) **II** do.

نتفة ***nutfa*** pl. نتف *nutaf* tuft of hair; a small amount, a little of s.th.

نتيف ***natīf*** pulled out, torn out; plucked

نتن **natana** *i*, **natina** *a* (*natn*) and **natuna** *u* (نتانة *natāna*, نتونة *nutūna*) to have an offensive smell, be malodorous, stink; to decompose, rot, decay, become putrid **II** to render putrid, putrefy (ه s.th.); to cause to decay or rot, decompose (ه s.th.) **IV** = **I**

نتن ***natn*** and نتانة *natāna* stench, evil smell, malodor; rotting, putrescence, putrefaction, decomposition; decay

نتن ***natin*** stinking, evil-smelling, malodorous; rotten, putrid, putrescent, putrefied, decayed, decomposed; (*eg.*) miserly, closefisted, stingy, niggardly

منتن *munattan* putrefied, putrescent, rotten, decayed, decomposed

منتن *muntin* stinking, evil-smelling, malodorous; rotting, putrescent, putrid, decayed

نثر **naṯara** *u* *i* (*naṯr*, نثار *niṯār*) to scatter, disperse, strew, sprinkle (ه على s.th. over or on); to write in prose (ه s.th.) **II** to scatter, disperse, strew about (ه s.th.) **VI** and **VIII** to be scattered about, be strewn about, be dispersed; to scatter, disperse; to fall off, fall out

نثر *naṯr* scattering, dispersal, dispersion; prose

نثرى *naṯrī* prose, prosaic, in prose; small, little, insignificant, trifling, petty; نثريات sundries, miscellany | مصاريف نثرية incidental expenses; petty expenses

نثار *nuṯār* scattered fragments; floating particles (dust); tiny pieces; ○ confetti

نثير *naṯīr* scattered, dispersed

تناثر *tanāṯur* dispersion (e.g., of a machine gun)

ناثر *nāṯir* prose writer, prosaist

منثور *manṯūr* scattered, dispersed, strewn about; prosaic, prose; wallflower, gillyflower (Cheiranthus cheiri; *bot.*); see also هباء *habā'*

متناثر *mutanāṯir* scattered

نجب **najuba** *u* (نجابة *najāba*) to be of noble birth, be highborn, aristocratic, patrician, noble, distinguished, excellent, high-minded, generous, magnanimous **IV** do.; to give birth (ه to a child), bear (ه a child); to beget, sire (ه s.o.) | انجب منها he had children by her **VIII** and **X** to choose, select, pick out (ه s.th.)

نجب *najb* and نجبة *nujaba* noble, high-minded, generous, magnanimous

نجابة *najāba* nobility, nobleness, noble descent, exalted rank or station, eminence; excellence, superiority, perfection

نجيب *najīb* pl. نجب *nujub*, نجباء *nujabā'*[2], انجاب *anjāb* of noble breed; highborn, highbred, of noble descent, noble, distinguished, aristocratic, patrician; excellent, superior, outstanding

نجاب *najjāb* dromedary rider, courier

انتجاب *intijāb* choice; selection

نجح **najaḥa** *a* (*najḥ*, *nujḥ*, نجاح *najāḥ*) to turn out well, come off well, succeed; to progress well, develop satisfactorily; to succeed, have success (ى in), be successful; to pass (ى الامتحان the examination) **II** and **IV** to give (ه s.o.) success, let (ه, ه s.o., s.th.) succeed, render successful (ه, ه s.o., s.th.), make (ه s.th.) a success

نجح *nujḥ* favorable, successful outcome, happy ending; success; satisfactory development, good progress

نجاح *najāḥ* favorable, successful outcome, happy ending; success; satisfactory development, good progress; passing (of an examination) | لقى نجاحا (*laqiya*) to have success, be successful, succeed, meet with success

نجيح *najīḥ* sound, good (advice, opinion)

انجاح *injāḥ* success

ناجح *nājiḥ* successful; passing, having passed (examination)

نجد **najada** *u* (*najd*) to help, aid, assist, support (ه s.o.), stand by s.o. (ه); — *najida* *a* (*najad*) to sweat, perspire **II** to furnish (ه s.th.); to upholster (ه s.th.); to comb, card, tease (القطن *al-quṭna* cotton) **III** = *najada* **IV** = *najada*; to travel in the highland (of Arabia) **X** to ask for help (ه s.o.), appeal for help (ب to s.o.), seek aid (ه or ب from s.o.); to take liberties, make bold (على with s.o.)

نجد najd pl. نجاد nijād highland, upland, tableland, plateau; the Arabian highland, Nejd

نجدى najdī Nejd, Nejdi, native of Nejd

نجدة najda pl. najadāt help, aid, succor, assistance, support; emergency, crisis, trouble, difficulty, distress, calamity; courage, bravery, intrepidity, undauntedness; pl. auxiliaries, reinforcements | بوليس النجدة help! help! النجدة! النجدة! approx.: riot squad (Eg.)

نجاد nijād sword belt | طويل النجاد tall, of tall stature

نجّاد najjād upholsterer; (pl. نجادة) a kind of boy scout (Syr.)

نجادة nijāda upholsterer's trade, upholstery

تنجيد tanjīd upholstering, upholstery work

نجذ najaḏa i (najḏ) to importune (٥ s.o.)

مناجذ manājiḏ² moles (zool.)

ناجذ nājiḏ pl. نواجذ nawājiḏ² molar | ابدى عن نواجذه (abdā) to show one's teeth, display a hostile, threatening attitude (ل toward s.o.); عض بالنواجذ ('aḍḍa) to grit one's teeth; عض على ناجذيه (nājiḏaihi) to have reached the age of manhood; عض بالنواجذ على to cling stubbornly to ..., stick doggedly to ...

نجر najara u (najr) to hew, carve, plane (٥ wood)

نجر najr heat, hot time of the day

نجّار najjār pl. -ūn carpenter, cabinetmaker, joiner

نجار nujār origin, descent, stock, root

نجارة nujāra wood shavings

نجارة nijāra woodworking, cabinetwork, joinery, carpentry

منجر minjar pl. مناجر manājir² plane (tool)

منجور manjūr pulley; sheave; waterwheel; woodwork, paneling, wainscoting

نجز najaza u (najz) to carry out, execute, implement, realize, accomplish, fulfill, complete (٥ s.th.); — najiza a (najaz) to be carried out, be executed, be implemented, be realized, be accomplished, be completed, be achieved II to carry out, execute, implement, realize, effect(uate), accomplish (٥ s.th.); to fulfill, grant, answer (٥ a wish, and the like) III to fight, battle, struggle (٥ against s.o.) IV to carry out, execute, implement, realize, effect(uate), accomplish, complete, consummate (٥ s.th.); to do (٥ work, a job); to perform (٥ an action, an operation); to fulfill (٥ a promise), discharge (٥ a duty); to finish (على s.o.) off, deal (على s.o.) the deathblow X to ask for the fulfillment (٥ of a promise)

نجز najz and نجاز najāz execution, implementation, realization, effectuation, completion, consummation, accomplishment, achievement, fulfillment, discharge

تنجيز tanjīz and انجاز injāz execution, implementation, realization, effectuation, accomplishment, achievement, completion, consummation; performance; fulfillment, discharge

مناجزة munājaza and تناجز tanājuz fight, struggle, contention, strife

ناجز nājiz completed; full, total, whole, entire, complete, consummate

نجس najusa u (نجاسة najāsa) and najisa a (najas) to be impure, unclean, soiled, dirty, sullied, stained, tainted II and IV to soil, sully, dirty, pollute, contaminate, defile, stain, taint (٥ s.th.) V to be or become impure, unclean, soiled, sullied, polluted, contaminated, defiled, stained, tainted; to sully o.s., contaminate o.s., defile o.s.

نجس *najas* and نجاسة *najāsa* impurity, uncleanness, uncleanliness, dirt, filth, squalor

نجس *najis* pl. انجاس *anjās* impure, unclean, defiled, polluted, contaminated, soiled, sullied, dirty, filthy, squalid

نجس *najis* and نجيس *najīs* incurable, fatal (disease)

تنجيس *tanjīs* soiling, sullying, defilement, contamination, pollution

نجاشى *najāšī, nijāšī* Negus, Emperor of Ethiopia

نجع *naja'a a* (*naj'*, نجوع *nujū'*) to be useful, beneficial, salutary, have a wholesome effect II and IV do. VIII to take refuge (ب with s.o.), resort, have recourse (ب to); to seek (ه rest, and the like) X to seek (ه pasture, rest, relaxation)

نجع *naj'* pl. نجوع *nujū'* hamlet, small village

نجعة *nuj'a* search for food

نجيع *najī'* useful, beneficial; wholesome, healthful, salubrious, salutary; — blood

ناجع *nāji'* useful, beneficial; wholesome, healthful, salubrious, salutary

منتجع *muntaja'* refuge, retreat; recreation center; health resort, rest center, convalescent home, sanatorium

نجف *najaf* pl. نجاف *nijāf* (sand) hill, dune; dam, dike, levee; النجف *an-najaf* An Najaf (town in central Iraq)

نجفة *najafa* pl. *-āt* chandelier, luster

نجل *najala u* (*najl*) to beget, sire, father (ه a son)

نجل *najl* pl. انجال *anjāl* offspring, descendant, scion, son; progeny, issue

نجيل *najīl* pl. نجل *nujul* a variety of orchard grass (Dactylis; *bot.*); herbage

انجل *anjal*², f. نجلاء *najlā'*² large-eyed; large, big, wide (eye); gaping (wound) | طعنة نجلاء (*ṭa'na*) a blow causing a gaping wound; heavy blow or thrust

منجل *minjal* pl. مناجل *manājil*² scythe, sickle

منجلة *manjala* vise

²انجيل look up alphabetically

نجم *najama u* (نجوم *nujūm*) to appear, come in sight, rise (star), begin, commence, set in; to result, follow, ensue, arise, proceed, derive, originate, spring (عن or من from) | نجم قرنه (*qarnuhū*) to begin to show II to observe the stars; to predict the future from the stars, practice astrology; to pay in installments V to observe the stars, predict the future from the stars

نجم *najm* pl. نجوم *nujūm* installment, partial payment; نجوما *nujūman* in installments

نجم *najm* pl. نجوم *nujūm*, انجم *anjum* celestial body; star; lucky star; constellation, asterism; (coll.) herbs, herbage, grass | نجم ذو ذنب (*ḏū ḏanab*) comet; نجوم السينما film stars, movie stars

نجمة *najma* pl. *najamāt* star; asterisk (*typ.*) | نجمة سينمائية film star, movie star; مرض النجمة *maraḍ an-n.* a disease afflicting horses

نجمى *najmī* star-shaped, stelliform, starlike, stellate, stellular, stellar, astral; — in installments, installment- (in compounds)

نجيمة *nujaima* small star, starlet

نجام *najjām* and منجم *munajjim* pl. *-ūn* astrologer

منجم *manjam* pl. مناجم *manājim*² source, origin; mine; pit

تنجيم *tanjīm* astrology

(نجو) نجا *najā u* (*najw*, نجاء *najā'*, نجاة *najāh*) to save o.s., be saved, be rescued, make for safety, get away (من from), escape (من s.th.), be delivered (من from) | نجا بنفسه (*bi-nafsihī*) or نجا بروحه (*bi-rūḥihī*) to save o.s. (من from); نجا بحياته (*bi-ḥayātihī*) to save one's life, save one's skin; — (*najw*, نجوى *najwan*) to entrust a secret (ه to s.o.) **II** and **IV** to deliver, save, rescue, bring to safety (ه s.o., من from) **III** to whisper (ه ب to s.o. s.th.), entrust (ه ب to s.o. s.th. secret), take into one's confidence (ه s.o.), confide (ه in s.o.) | ناجى نفسه (*nafsahū*) to soliloquize, talk to o.s., say to o.s. **VI** to whisper to each other, carry on a whispered conversation, converse intimately, confidentially, exchange secrets, exchange ideas **VIII** to whisper into each other's ear (ه s.th.) **X** to save o.s. (من from), escape (من s.th.); to be delivered (من from)

نجا *najan* deliverance, release, rescue

نجاة *najāh* escape, flight; deliverance, rescue; salvation, redemption; safety

نجو *najw* excrement

نجوة *najwa* pl. نجاء *nijā'* elevation, rising ground, upland | فى نجوة من free from, far from, a long way from

نجوى *najwā* pl. نجاوى *najāwā* confidential talk, secret conversation

نجى *najīy* pl. انجية *anjiya* secret; confidant, intimate friend, bosom friend

منجى *manjan* safety, security (من from)

منجاة *manjāh* pl. مناج *manājin* safe place, haven, refuge; safeguard, protection; rescue, salvation | كان بمنجاة من to be safe from, be secure from, be safeguarded against

تنجية *tanjiya* rescue, salvation, deliverance

مناجاة *munājāh* secret conversation; confidential talk | مناجاة الارواح spiritism, spiritualism

منج *munajjin* rescuer, savior, deliverer

نحب *naḥaba i a* (*naḥb*, نحيب *naḥīb*) and **VIII** to sob, weep, cry, wail, lament

نحب *naḥb* weeping, crying, sobbing, sighing, moaning, wail(ing), lamentation; time, period, term, span, interval; death | قضى نحبه *qaḍā naḥbahū* to fulfill one's vow, redeem one's pledge; to pass away, die, expire

نحيب *naḥīb* loud weeping, wail(ing), lamentation

نحت *naḥata i u* (*naḥt*) to hew, dress (ه stone or wood), plane, smooth, face; to carve, cut out, hew out, chisel, sculpture; to form, coin (ه s.th.)

نحت *naḥt* wood or stone dressing, woodwork, stonework; sculpturing, sculpture

نحات *naḥḥāt* stonemason, stonecutter, stone dresser; sculptor

نحاتة *nuḥāta* shavings, parings, chips, splinters, slivers

منحت *minḥat* pl. مناحت *manāḥit*[2] chisel

نحر *naḥara u* (*naḥr*) to cut the throat (ه of an animal), slaughter, butcher, kill (ه an animal) **VI** to fight; to kill each other, hack each other to pieces, engage in internecine fighting **VIII** to commit suicide; ○ to be scuttled (ship) | انتحر شنقا (*šanqan*) to hang o.s., commit suicide by hanging

نحر *naḥr* killing, slaughter(ing), butchering | يوم النحر *yaum an-n.* Day of Immolation (on the 10th of Zu'lhijja)

نحر *naḥr* pl. نحور *nuḥūr* upper portion of the chest, throat

نحر *niḥr* and نحرير *niḥrīr* pl. نحارير *naḥārīr*[2] skilled, adept, proficient, versed, experienced (في in)

نحير *naḥīr* and منحور *manḥūr* killed, slaughtered, butchered

منحر *manḥar* throat, neck

انتحار *intiḥār* suicide; ○ scuttling

منتحر *muntaḥir* suicide (person)

نحيزة *naḥīza* nature, natural disposition | طيب النحيزة *ṭayyib an-n.* good-natured, good-humored; كريم النحيزة high-minded, noble-minded, of generous disposition

نحس **naḥasa** *a* (*naḥs*) to make (ه s.o.) unhappy, bring (ه s.o.) bad luck; — *naḥusa u* (نحوسة *nuḥūsa*, نحاسة *naḥāsa*) and *naḥisa a* (*naḥas*) to be unlucky, ominous, ill-fated, calamitous, ill-boding, portend evil **II** to cover, coat, or sheathe with copper, to copper (ه s.th.)

نحس *naḥs* pl. نحوس *nuḥūs* misfortune, calamity, disaster

نحس *naḥs, naḥis* unlucky, luckless, ominous, calamitous, disastrous, ill-fated, ill-starred, sinister, ill-omened, ill-boding

نحاس *naḥḥās* coppersmith

نحاس *nuḥās* copper; (*tun.*) a small coin | نحاس اصفر (*aṣfar*[2]) brass

مناحس *manāḥis*[2] ominous events

منحوس *manḥūs* luckless, ill-fated, star-crossed

نحف **naḥufa** *u* (نحافة *naḥāfa*) to be thin, slim, slender, lean, skinny; to become thin, lose weight **IV** to make thin, weaken, debilitate, enervate, emaciate

نحافة *naḥāfa* leanness, thinness, slenderness, slimness; enervation, emaciation, wasting away

نحيف *naḥīf* pl. نحاف *niḥāf*, نحفاء *nuḥafā'*[2] thin, slim, slender, slight; delicate, of fragile build; lean, gaunt, enervated, debilitated, emaciated

منحف *manḥaf* dieting resort, weight-reducing resort

منحوف *manḥūf* thin, slim, slender, slight; lean, gaunt, enervated, debilitated, emaciated

نحل **naḥala** *u a*, *naḥula u* and *naḥila a* (نحول *nuḥūl*) to be emaciated; to waste away, lose weight, grow thin; — *naḥala a* (*nuḥl*) to make a donation, make a present (ه to s.o.); to ascribe, attribute, impute (wrongly, unduly) (ه ه to s.o. s.th.) **IV** to make thin, enervate, emaciate (ه s.o.); to weaken (ه s.th.) **V** and esp. **VIII** to ascribe to o.s., claim for o.s. (لنفسه), assume unduly, presume, arrogate to o.s. (ه s.th.); to embrace (ه a religion); to borrow, adopt, take over (ه foreign words); to take up (ه s.th.) | انتحل الاسلام to profess Islam; انتحل اسمه (*ismahū*) to assume s.o.'s name; انتحل الاعرابية (*a'rābīya*) to claim to be a Bedouin; انتحل الاعذار (*a'ḏār*) to think up excuses, make excuses, use pretexts or subterfuges; انتحل شخصية فلان (*šakṣīyata*) to pass o.s. off as s.o., purport to be ..., impersonate s.o.

نحل *naḥl* (coll.; n. un. ة) bee

نحلة *niḥla* pl. نحل *niḥal* present, gift, donation; creed, faith, sect

نحال *naḥḥāl* beekeeper, apiarist, apiculturist

نحالة *niḥāla* beekeeping, apiculture

نحول *nuḥūl* leanness, skinniness, thinness, slimness, slenderness; enervation, emaciation, wasting away

نحيل *naḥīl* and ناحل *nāḥil* pl. نحلى *naḥlā*, نحل *nuḥḥal* thin, slim, slender, lean, skinny; enervated, emaciated, gaunt

منحل *manḥal* pl. مناحل *manāḥil*[2] beehive; apiary, apicultural station

انتحال *intiḥāl* undue assumption, arrogation; literary theft, plagiarism

منتحل *muntaḥil* plagiarist

منتحل *muntaḥal*: اسم منتحل (*ism*) assumed name, alias, pseudonym, nom de guerre

نحم **naḥama** *i* (*naḥm*, نحيم *naḥīm*, نحمان *naḥamān*) to clear one's throat; to wheeze, pant, gasp

نحام *nuḥām* flamingo

نحن **naḥnu** we

نحنح **naḥnaḥa** and **II** *tanaḥnaḥa* to clear one's throat, to hem, say "ahem"

نحنحة *naḥnaḥa* hem, hawk, little cough

(نحو) نحا **naḥā** *a u* (*naḥw*) to wend one's way (ه, ه to), go, walk, move, turn (ه, ه to, toward), take the road (ه to), go in the direction (ه of) | نحا نحوه (*naḥwahū*) to follow s.o., follow s.o.'s example, be guided by s.o. or s.th.; to imitate s.o.; to be of the same nature, of the same kind, on the same line as ..., be like ...; نحا نحو الباب to walk toward the door; نحا به نحو الباب to show s.o. to the door **II** to put aside, push away, brush aside (ه s.th.); to remove, take away (ه من s.th. from) **IV** to turn away, avert (بصره عن *baṣarahū ʿan* one's eyes from); to turn (على against s.o.), assail, overcome (على ب s.o. with); to heap (على ب upon s.o. reproach, or the like), shower (على ب s.o. with); to turn, apply o.s., attend (على to s.th.) **V** to step aside, go away, withdraw, move away, fall back (عن or من from); to turn away; to forgo, renounce, waive (عن s.th.); to abandon, give up, surrender, yield, relinquish (عن s.th.); to retreat, retire (ه to a place); to lean, rest, support o.s. (ل on) **VIII** to turn (ه to, toward); to lean, support o.s. (ل on) | انتحى ناحية to turn aside; انتحى جانبا do., step back, withdraw, retire

نحو *naḥw* pl. انحاء *anḥā'* direction; side; section, part; way, course, method, manner, mode, fashion; (with foll. genit.) corresponding to, analogous to, similar to, like, somewhat like; (*gram.*) grammar; syntax | على نحو ما (*naḥwi*) in the manner of, as; على نحو ما (*naḥwin*) rather, pretty much; على هذا النحو in this manner, this way; in this respect; وعلى هذا النحو and so forth, and so on; فى نحو الساعة السابعة at about the seventh hour, at about 7 o'clock, around seven; من نحوى as far as I am concerned, as for me, for my part, I for one; نحوا من (*naḥwan*) approximately, roughly, about, circa (with foll. figure); فى انحاء الارض (*a. il-arḍ*) all over the earth; فى كل انحاء العالم (*ʿālam*) (or المعمورة) all over the world; النحو المقارن (*muqārin*) comparative grammar

نحو *naḥwa* (prep.) in the direction of, toward, to; according to, in analogy with, similar to, like, as, as for instance; approximately, roughly, about, around, circa

نحوى *naḥwī* syntactical; grammatical; grammarian; philologist

منحى *manḥan* pl. مناح *manāḥin* aim, goal, object, end, purpose; manner of acting, mode of conduct, behavior; direction; (rhetorical, literary) form; field, domain, realm, province, bailiwick, sphere (fig.) | مناحى الحياة *m. l-ḥayāh* walks of life

ناح *nāḥin* pl. نحاة *nuḥāh* grammarian; philologist

ناحية *nāḥiya* pl. نواح *nawāḥin* side; direction; viewpoint, standpoint, aspect; region, area, section; sphere, domain, field; district, canton; (*Ir.*) subdivision of a قضاء *qaḍā'*, roughly corresponding to a county; off side, secluded part, corner (e.g., of a room); *nāḥiyata* in the direction of, toward, to | من ناحية with regard to, in respect to, as to, as for, concerning, regarding, on the part of; من ناحية اخرى (*uḵrā*) on the other hand; من الناحية العسكرية (*ʿaskarīya*) from a military standpoint; من ناحية قانونية de jure; من ناحية واقعية (*wāqiʿīya*) de facto; سليم النواحى sound in body; متعدد النواحى *mutaʿaddid an-n.* many-sided; من جميع النواحى in every respect

نخ **naḵḵ** pl. انخاخ *anḵāḵ* mat; rug, carpet

نخب **naḵaba** *u* (*naḵb*) and VIII to select, pick, choose (ه s.th.); to choose, make one's choice; to vote, go to the polls; to elect (ه s.o.)

نخب **naḵb** selection, choice; a drink to s.o.'s health | شرب نخبه (*šariba*) to drink to s.o.'s health, toast s.o.

نخبة **nuḵba** pl. نخب *nuḵab* selected piece, selected item, selected passage; the pick, cream, elite, flower

انتخاب **intiḵāb** pl. *-āt* election (*pol.*); choice; selection

انتخابى **intiḵābī** of or pertaining to an election or elections, election (used attributively); elective; electoral | معركة انتخابية (*maʿraka*) election campaign

ناخب **nāḵib** and منتخب **muntaḵib** pl. *-ūn* elector (esp., *pol.*), voter, constituent

منخوب **manḵūb** lean, emaciated

منتخب **muntaḵab** chosen, elected, selected, hand-picked; elected candidate; (pl. *-āt*) team (in sports); منتخبات selected pieces, selected items, selected passages

نخر **naḵara** *u i* (*naḵr*, نخير *naḵīr*) to snort; to snore; to gnaw (فى on s.th.), bore, burrow, eat (فى into s.th.; worm); to eat away (ه at s.th.); to enervate, sap, ruin, decay (ه s.th.); — *naḵira* *a* (*naḵar*) to be eaten away, worm-eaten, rotten, decayed, full of holes; to spoil, rot, decay; to decompose, disintegrate, crumble

نخر **naḵr** snorting, snort; snoring, snore; decay, rot, rottenness; tooth decay, caries

نخر **naḵir** and ناخر *nāḵir* worm-eaten; rotting, decaying

نخير **naḵīr** snort(ing), snoring, snore; grunt(s)

منخر **manḵar**, *manḵir*, *minḵar* pl. مناخر *manāḵir*² nostril; nose

منخار **minḵār** pl. مناخير *manāḵīr*² nostril; nose

نخرب **naḵraba** to eat holes into s.th. (ه), eat away (ه at); to hollow out (ه s.th.)

نخروب **nuḵrūb** pl. نخاريب *naḵārīb*² hole; cavity, hollow; cell; honeycomb

نخز **naḵaza** *a* (*naḵz*) to bore into or through s.th. (ه; worm)

نخس **naḵasa** *a u* (*naḵs*) to prick, goad, prod, urge on, drive on (ه an animal)

نخاس **naḵḵās** drover; cattle dealer; slave trader; white slaver

نخاسة **niḵāsa** cattle trade; slave trade; white-slave traffic

منخس **minḵas** pl. مناخس *manāḵis*² spur, goad, prod (for driving cattle)

منخاس **minḵās** pl. مناخيس *manāḵīs*² spur, goad, prod (for driving cattle)

نخشوش **naḵšūš** pl. نخاشيش *naḵāšīš*² gill, branchia (respiratory organ of fish)

نخع V to clear one's throat, hawk, spit out, expectorate

نخاع **nuḵāʿ**, *niḵāʿ* pl. نخع *nuḵuʿ* spinal marrow, spinal cord; bone marrow, medulla; brain

نخاعة **nuḵāʿa** phlegm, mucus, sputum, expectoration

نخل **naḵala** *u* (*naḵl*) to sift, bolt, sieve out (ه s.th.); to strain (ه s.th.) V and VIII do.

نَخْل *nak̲l* (coll.; n. un. ة) and نَخِيل *nak̲īl* palm; date palm

نُخَالَة *nuk̲āla* residue left in a sieve; bran; waste, refuse | لا يساوى ملء اذنه نخالة *lā yusāwī mil'a udnihi nuk̲ālatan* he isn't worth a bent nickel

مُنْخَل *munk̲al, munk̲ul* pl. مناخل *manā-k̲il²* sieve

نخم *nak̲ima a (nak̲am)* and V to clear one's throat, hawk, spit out, expectorate

نُخَامَة *nuk̲āma* phlegm, mucus, sputum, expectoration

غدة نُخَامِيَّة *g̲udda nuk̲āmīya* hypophysis, pituitary body (anat.)

نَخَا (نخو) *nak̲ā u (نَخْوَة nak̲wa)* to be proud, haughty, supercilious (على toward s.o.) II and IV to inflame, incite, excite, stimulate, arouse, awaken (ه s.th.)

نَخْوَة *nak̲wa* haughtiness, arrogance; pride, dignity, sense of honor, self-respect; high-mindedness, generosity

ند *nadda i (nadd, ندد nadad, نداد nidād, ندود nudūd, ندید nadīd)* to run away, flee; to slip away; to slip out (exclamation); to escape (عن s.o.) II to expose, show up, compromise (ب s.o.); to criticize (ب s.o. or s.th.), find fault (ب with)

ند *nadd* high hill; — *nadd, nidd* incense (of aloeswood, with ambergris, musk and frankincense)

ند *nidd* pl. انداد *andād* equal, (a)like, same; an equal, a peer; partner; antagonist, rival

ندید *nadīd* pl. ندداء *nudadā'²* equal; rival

تندید *tandīd* pl. -āt criticism; revilement, abuse, disparagement, defamation

ندب *nadaba u (nadb)* to mourn, lament, bewail (ه the deceased); to appoint, assign (ل ه s.o. to an office), detail (ل ه

s.o. for a job, for a task); to send as a representative or delegate, to delegate, depute, deputize (ه s.o.); to commission, charge, entrust (ب ه s.o., with); — *nadiba a (nadab)* to scar over, cicatrize, heal IV = *nadiba* VIII to appoint, assign (ل ه s.o. to an office), detail (ل ه s.o. for a job, for a task); to commission, charge, empower, authorize (ل ه s.o. to do s.th., ب with), order (ل ه s.o. to do s.th.); to entrust (ل to s.o. a task); (mil.) to detach, detail, transfer (ل ه s.o. to); (with نفسه *nafsahū*) to apply o.s., devote o.s., dedicate o.s. (ل to s.th.); to give (ه a country) the mandate (على over); to comply readily (ل with an order or instruction), be willing, be prepared, stand ready (ل to); to present o.s. (الى to s.o.), turn (الى toward, to)

ندب *nadb* weeping, wailing, lamentation; lament, dirge, elegy; assignment, commissioning, delegation, deputation; appointment, authorization, mandation

ندب *nadab* pl. انداب *andāb,* ندوب *nudūb* scar, cicatrice

ندبة *nadba* pl. انداب *andāb,* ندوب *nudūb* scar, cicatrice; scabby wound

ندبة *nudba* lamentation for the dead; elegy; dirge, funeral song

ندابة *naddāba* pl. -āt hired female mourner

مندب *mandab* pl. منادب *manādib²* wail, lamentation | باب المندب *Bab el Mandeb* (strait between SW Arabia and Africa; geogr.)

انتداب *intidāb* deputation, appointment; commissioning, charging, authorization; detailing, detachment, assignment, mission; (pl. -āt) mandate (over a territory); mandatory rule | دولة الانتداب *daulat al-int.* mandatory power; لجنة الانتدابات *lajnat al-int.* Mandate Commission (of the League of Nations)

انتدابى *intidābī* mandatory | ادارة انتدابية (*idāra*) mandatory administration

نادبة *nādiba* pl. *-āt*, نوادب *nawādib*² hired female mourner

مندوب *mandūb* bewailed, bemoaned, mourned, lamented; regrettable, deplorable, lamentable; — (pl. *-ūn*) deputy, delegate, agent, functionary, commissioner; representative; representative of the press, correspondent, reporter (of a newspaper); plenipotentiary, authorized agent; (*Isl. Law*) recommended | مندوب التأمين insurance agent; مندوب خاص (*kāṣṣ*) special envoy; مندوب سام (*sāmin*) High Commissioner; مندوب فوق العادة ambassador extraordinary; مندوب مفوض (*mufawwaḍ*) plenipotentiary, authorized agent; (*dipl.*) minister; مندوب فوق العادة ووزير مفوض ambassador extraordinary and minister plenipotentiary (official title of ambassadors)

مندوبية *mandūbīya* delegation; High Commission

منتدب *muntadab* deputized, delegated; commissioned, charged; entrusted; appointed; assigned, detailed | دولة منتدبة (*daula*) mandatory power

ندح *nadaḥa a* (*nadḥ*) to extend, expand, enlarge (ه s.th.)

ندحة *nadḥa*, *nudḥa* wide, open space; freedom (of action) | لا ندحة عنه (*nadḥata*) it is indispensable, unavoidable, inevitable; لا اجد لى ندحة عن (*ajidu, nadḥatan*) I feel compelled to …

مندوحة *mandūḥa* pl. منادح *manādiḥ*² and منتدح *muntadaḥ* alternative, choice; freedom of action | لا مندوحة له عن (*mandūḥata*) it is indispensable, absolutely necessary, mandatory, imperative for him; لك عنه مندوحة (or منتدح) it is up to you, it is optional for you; لم ير مندوحة من (*lam yara mandūḥatan*) to feel obligated, feel compelled to …

ندر¹ *nadara u* (*nadr*, ندور *nudūr*) to be rare; to be uncommon, unusual; — *nadura u* (ندارة *nadāra*) to be strange, odd, queer, unusual, extraordinary **V** to make fun (ب or على of); to joke, jest **VI** to tell each other stories and jokes

ندر *nadr* rare; strange, odd

ندرة *nadra*, *nudra* and ندورة *nudūra* rarity, rareness; *nadratan* rarely, seldom | فى الندرة rarely, seldom

اندر *andar* pl. انادر *anādir*² (*tun.*) threshing floor

اندر *andar*² rarer

مندرة *mandara* pl. منادر *manādir*² (*tun.*) threshing floor; see also below

منادرات *munādarāt* causeries on amusing, witty topics

تندر *tanaddur* amusement, fun-making, joking

تنادر *tanādur* gay chat

نادر *nādir* rare; infrequent; strange, odd, unusual, uncommon; excellent, precious, priceless; an eccentric, a crank, an odd fellow; نادرا *nādiran* rarely, seldom | فى النادر rarely, seldom; نادر المثال unparalleled, singular, unique; عملة نادرة (*'umla*) specie, hard money

نادرة *nādira* pl. نوادر *nawādir*² rarity, rare thing, rare phenomenon; rare, uncommon word; phenomenon, prodigy, extraordinary person; funny, droll story, anecdote, joke; accident, incident

□² مندرة *mandara* (for منظرة, esp. *eg.*) pl. منادر *manādir*² reception parlor for male visitors; منادر (= مجالس) parties

ندس *nadasa u* to throw down, bring to the ground (ه s.o.); to revile, defame, discredit (ه s.o.)

ندف *nadafa i* (*nadf*) to tease, comb, or card cotton

ندف *nadf* teasing, combing, carding (of cotton) | جهاز الندف *jahāz an-n.* card, carding machine

ندفة *nudfa* pl. ندف *nudaf* flock (of wool); flake | ندفة الثلج *n. aṯ-ṯalj* snowflake

نديف *nadīf* and مندوف *mandūf* carded, teased (cotton)

نداف *naddāf* cotton carder, cotton teaser

مندف *mindaf* pl. منادف *manādif*[2] teasing bow (for carding cotton)

[1] ندل *nadala u* (*nadl*) to snatch away (ه s.th.)

□ ندل *nadl* = نذل

مندالة *mindāla* rammer

نادل *nādil* pl. ندل *nudul* waiter; servant who waits on table

[2]مندل *mandal*: ضرب المندل *ḍarb al-m.* (*eg.*) a magic practice in which a fortuneteller, or a medium, prophesies while contemplating a mirror-like surface

[3]منديل look up alphabetically

ندم *nadima a* (*nadam*, ندامة *nadāma*) to repent (على of), rue, regret (على s.th.) III to drink, carouse (ه with s.o.) V = I VI to drink together, carouse together

ندم *nadam*, ندامة *nadāma* remorse, repentance, regret

نديم *nadīm* pl. ندماء *nudamā'*[2], ندام *nidām* drinking companion; friend, intimate, confidant

ندمان *nadmān*[2] pl. ندامى *nadāmā* repenting, repentant, rueful, remorseful, regretful

مندم *mandam* remorse, repentance, regret

منادمة *munādama* drinking companionship, intimate friendship

تندم *tanaddum* remorse, repentance, regret

نادم *nādim* pl. ندام *nuddām* repenting, repentant, rueful, remorseful, regretful

منادم *munādim* drinking companion, boon companion, intimate

متندم *mutanaddim* repenting, repentant, rueful, remorseful, regretful

نده *nadaha a* (*nadh*) to drive, urge, spur on (ه s.o.); to drive away (ه s.o.)

ندا (ندو) *nadā u* (*nadw*) to call (ه s.o.); to invite; to call together, convoke, convene, summon (ه a meeting); to get together, meet, convene, assemble, gather; — ندى *nadiya a* (ندى *nadan*, نداوة *nadāwa*, ندوة *nudūwa*) to be moist, damp, dewy, wet | شيء يندى له الجبين an embarrassing or shocking thing, a disgraceful thing II to moisten, wet, bedew (ه s.th.) III to shout, call out, cry out, exclaim; to call (ب or ه s.o. or for s.o., also على), summon (ه s.o., also على); to call out, shout (ه to s.o.); to call for s.th. (ب), invite to s.th. (ب); to proclaim, announce (ب s.th.); to emphasize (ب s.th.); ○ to announce, act as announcer (*radio*); to cry one's wares, hawk (على s.th. to be sold) | نودي به رئيسا (*nūdiya*) to be proclaimed president IV = II; to be noble, generous, magnanimous V to be moistened, be bedewed; to show o.s. generous, liberal, openhanded VI and VIII to get together, meet, convene, gather, assemble, form a club

ندوة *nadwa* council; debating group, study group; club | دار الندوة city hall, town hall; parliament, house of representatives, chamber of deputies

ندوة *nudūwa* and نداوة *nadāwa* moistness, moisture, dampness

ندى *nadan* pl. انداء *andā'*, اندية *andiya* moistness, moisture, dampness, wetness; dew; generosity, liberality, magnanimity

ند *nadin* and نديان *nadyān*² moist, damp | ندى الكف *n. al-kaff* generous, liberal, openhanded

ندى *nadīy* moist, damp; tender, delicate | ندى الكف *n. al-kaff* generous, liberal, openhanded

نداء *nidā'* pl. *-āt* shout; call; exclamation; summons; public announcement; proclamation, appeal; address; vocative (*gram.*) | نداء الاستغاثة call for help, distress signal; حرف النداء *ḥarf an-n.* interjection (*gram.*); اصدر نداء ل (*aṣdara*) to issue a proclamation to

مناداة *munādāh* calling, shouting; call; vocative; public notice, announcement; proclamation | بيع المناداة *bai' al-m.* public sale, auction

ناد *nādin* pl. اندية *andiya*, نواد *nawādin* club; circle; association; clubhouse | ناد رياضى (*riyāḍī*) athletic club; دار النادى clubhouse

مندى *munaddan* wet, damp; bedewed, dewy; refreshing

مناد *munādin* caller; herald; town crier; auctioneer; ○ announcer (*radio*)

منادى *munādan* noun in the vocative (*gram.*)

مندية *mundiya* pl. *-āt* disgraceful, evil deed; insult, abuse, affront

منتدى *muntadan* pl. منتديات *muntadayāt* gathering place, assembly room; club

نذر *naḏara u i* (*naḏr*, نذور *nuḏūr*) to dedicate, consecrate (ه لله s.th. to God); to vow, make a vow | نذرت لله ان I vow to God that ..., I swear by God that ...; نذر على نفسه ه to vow to o.s., make the solemn pledge to ...; — *naḏira a* (*naḏar*) to have been warned, be on one's guard (ب against) **IV** to warn (ه ب s.o. of or against), caution (ه ب s.o. against), admonish (ه s.o.); to announce (ب ه to s.o. s.th.), give notice or warning (ه ب to s.o. of), notify in advance (ه s.o., ب of) | انذره بتسليم منزله (*bi-taslīmi manzilihī*) he gave him notice to vacate the premises

نذر *naḏr* pl. نذور *nuḏūr*, نذورات *nuḏūrāt* vow, solemn pledge; votive offering, ex-voto

نذير *naḏīr* pl. نذر *nuḏur* consecrated to God; vowed, solemnly pledged; warner; herald, harbinger, forerunner; warning; alarm | ○ نذير الخطر *n. al-ḵaṭar* air-raid warning

انذار *inḏār* pl. *-āt* warning; announcement, notice; admonition; air-raid warning, alarm | ○ انذار بوقوع غارات جوية (*bi-wuqū' ḡārāt jawwīya*) or انذار للاخطار (*li-l-aḵṭār*) air-raid warning; انذار نهائى (*nihā'ī*) ultimatum; ○ صفارة الانذار *ṣaffārat al-i.* warning siren

تناذر *tanāḏur* syndrome (*med.*)

ناذر *nāḏir* one who has made a vow

منذور *manḏūr* solemnly pledged, vowed, consecrated to God

منذر *munḏir* warner, cautioner

منذرة *munḏira* alarm signal; warning sign (ب against)

نذل *naḏula u* (نذالة *naḏāla*, نذولة *nuḏūla*) to be low, base, mean, vile, despicable, debased, depraved

نذل *naḏl* pl. انذال *anḏāl*, نذول *nuḏūl* low, base, mean, vile, despicable, debased, depraved; coward

نذيل *naḏīl* pl. نذلاء *nuḏalā'*², نذال *niḏāl* low, base, mean, vile, despicable, debased, depraved; coward

نذالة *naḏāla* depravity

نربيج *narbīj* pl. نرابيج *narābīj*² mouthpiece of a narghile

نربيش *narbīš* pl. نرابيش *narābīš*[2] mouthpiece of a narghile

نرجس *narjis, nirjis* narcissus (*bot.*)

نرد *nard* backgammon, tricktrack

نردين *nardīn* nard, spikenard

نرفزة *narfaza* nervousness

منرفز *munarfaz* (*pal.-syr.*) nervous

نرنج *naranj* bitter orange

نروج *nurūj, narūj* Norway

نرويج *nurwīj* Norway

نرويجى *nurwījī* Norwegian

نز *nazza i* (*nazz*, نزيز *nazīz*) to seep, trickle, ooze, or leak, through; to vibrate (string)

نز *nazz, nizz*, نزازة *nuzāza* pl. نزوز *nuzūz* seepage, leakage water

نز *nazz* swift, nimble, agile, lively, sprightly; changeable, inconstant, unsteady, fickle

نزة *nazza, nizza* (sensuous) passion, lust

نزيز *nazīz* unsteady, inconstant, unstable; sensuous, passionate

نزح *nazaḥa a i* (*nazḥ*, نزوح *nuzūḥ*) to be far off, be distant; to leave (من s.th.), depart, emigrate (عن from); to immigrate (الى to); to wander, migrate, rove, roam, range; ○ to march off, pull out (troops); pass. نزح به *nuziḥa bihi* to emigrate, be away from home, live abroad; — (*nazḥ*) and IV to scoop out, bail out, empty (ه s.th.); to drain, dry out (ه a well, a ditch, a latrine, and the like) VIII to emigrate

نزح *nazḥ* scooping out, emptying; draining, drainage

نزح *nazaḥ* pl. انزاح *anzāḥ* muddy water

نزوح *nuzūḥ* emigration

نزوح *nazūḥ* and نزيح *nazīḥ* far-off, faraway, distant, remote

نازح *nāziḥ* far-off, faraway, distant, remote; going away from home, moving to other lands, leaving for distant shores, emigrating; emigrant; one who scoops out, bails out or empties, a latrine cleaner

نزر *nazr* and نزير *nazīr* little; insignificant, trivial, petty; trifle, small amount, insignificant number, negligible portion | نزر الحديث taciturn, of few words; نزر قليل tiny amount

نزع *naza'a i* (*naz'*) to pull out, extract (ه s.th.); to remove, take, take away, strike, cross off (ه عن s.th. from); to take off, shed (ه a garment); to strip, divest, deprive, rob (ه من or عن s.o. of s.th.); to wrest, take away (ه من from s.o. s.th., possession, right, reputation, etc.); to remove (ه s.o. from a position), depose, dismiss, fire, cashier, demote, reduce in rank (ه s.o.); to adduce as proof or in refutation (ب s.th.); (intr.) to move, proceed, go, betake o.s., repair (الى to); to emigrate (الى to); — (نزوع *nuzū'*) to desire (الى s.th.), wish, long, yearn, pine (الى for); to incline, tend, have an inclination or a tendency (الى to); to take on, take over, adopt (الى s.th.), resort (الى to; e.g., to a method); to absent o.s., depart (عن from); to desist, abstain, refrain (عن from), keep clear (عن of), give up, avoid, eschew (عن s.th.); to be in the throes of death | نزع منه نازع الى (*nāzi'un*) he felt a desire for ..., discovered his inclination to ... II to remove, take away (ه s.th.) III to fight, struggle, contend, dispute (ه with s.o.), combat (ه s.th.); to contest, challenge (فى s.th.); to attempt to wrest (ه ه from s.o. s.th.), contest (ه ه s.o.'s right to s.th.); to be in the throes of death VI to contend with one another; to rival (ه for s.th.), contest each other's right (ه to), carry on a dispute, be at variance (ه over) **VIII** to pull out, extract, pluck out, tear out (ه s.th. من from); to snatch, wrest (ه من from s.o. s.th.), tear away, pull off (ه من s.th. from); to take, draw, borrow (ه s.th.); to be removed, be taken away

نزع *naz'* removal; withdrawal, elimination; deposition, removal from office; death struggle, agony of death | نزع السلاح disarming, disarmament; مؤتمر نزع السلاح *mu'tamar n. as-s.* disarmament conference; نزع الملكية *n. al-milkīya* expropriation

نزعة *naz'a* pl. *naza'āt* inclination, tendency, leaning; attitude, position, stand

نزوع *nuzū'* striving, endeavor, longing, wish, desire (ال for)

نزاع *nazzā'* tending, having an inclination (ال to), leaning (ال toward)

نزيع *nazī'* pl. نزاع *nuzzā'* stranger

منزع *manza'* pl. منازع *manāzi'*[2] intent, intention, purpose; aim, end, objective, goal; way, method; manner, behavior

منزع *minza'* arrow

نزاع *nizā'* fight, struggle, strife, contest, controversy; dispute; death struggle, agony of death | بلا نزاع (*bi-lā*) indisputably, incontestibly, incontrovertibly, indubitably, undeniably; عليه نزاع disputed, contested, debatable; لا نزاع فيه (*nizā'a*) undisputed, uncontested, unquestioned

منازعة *munāza'a* pl. *-āt* fight, struggle, strife, contention, controversy, quarrel, dissension, discord; dispute; matter in controversy, case at issue (before a court of justice)

تنازع *tanāzu'* fight, struggle, strife, contention, controversy | تنازع البقاء *t. al-baqā'* struggle for existence

انتزاع *intizā'* removal, withdrawal, elimination; dispossession, expropriation

نازعة *nāzi'a* pl. نوازع *nawāzi'*[2] tendency, inclination, leaning

منزوع *manzū'* removed, taken away | منطقة منزوعة السلاح (*minṭaqa*) demilitarized zone

منازع *munāzi'* struggling with death, being in the throes of death; contending, fighting, militant, litigious, renitent | ليس من منازع في no one will deny that ...

منازع عليه *munāza' 'alaihi* contested, disputed, debatable

متنازع *mutanāzi'* conflicting, clashing

متنازع عليه (*mutanāza'*) and متنازع فيه contested, disputed, debatable; litigated matter, matter in controversy, case at issue

منتزع *muntaza'* taken, drawn (من from)

نزغ *nazġ* and نزغة *nazġa* pl. *nazaġāt* incitement to evil | نزغ الشيطان *n. aš-šaiṭān* insinuations of the devil, satanic inspiration

نزف *nazafa* **i** (*nazf*) to drain, exhaust, empty (ه s.th.); to dry up (ه a well); to draw off (ه blood); to be drained, exhausted, spent; pass. نزف دمه *nuzifa damuhū* to lose much blood, bleed (to death) **IV** to drain, empty (ه a well); to be exhausted **X** to drain off, draw, extract (ه من s.th. from); to exhaust, consume, use up, swallow up, devour (ه s.th.)

نزف *nazf* exhaustion, draining, emptying; hemorrhage; loss of blood | ○ النزف الدموى (*damawī*) hemophilia (*med.*)

نزفة *nuzfa* small quantity, modicum (of a liquid)

نزيف *nazīf* weakened by loss of blood; bleeding, effusion of blood; hemorrhage, hemorrhea (*med.*)

منزوف *manzūf* exhausted through loss of blood

نزق **nazaqa** *i* (*nazq*) and *naziqa a* (*nazaq*, نزوق *nuzūq*) to storm ahead, rush forward; to be hasty, rash, precipitate, impetuous, lightheaded, frivolous, reckless, ruthless **II** to spur on, urge on (ه a horse)

نزق **nazaq** haste; rashness, precipitateness, impetuosity; lightheadedness, recklessness, thoughtlessness, frivolity

نزق **naziq** hasty; rash, precipitate, impetuous; thoughtless, heedless, careless, inattentive, lightheaded, frivolous, flighty, superficial

نزك **nazaka** *u* (*nazk*) to stab, pierce (ه s.o.)

نيزك **naizak** pl. نيازك *nayāzik*[2] short lance; shooting star, meteor

نزل **nazala** *i* (نزول *nuzūl*, to dismount, alight; to descend, go down, come down, move down, get down, step down, climb down; to get off (من, e.g., a train), get out, step out (من, e.g., of a car), debark, disembark (من from a vessel); to put down, land (airplane); to fall (rain); to descend from heaven, be revealed (esp., the Koran); to fall, sink, sag (prices), drop (water level); to subside, abate, let up, decrease; to stop, or halt, for a rest, to camp; to stop, stop over, put up, take up quarters, take lodgings, lodge, room, stay to live (على or ب at s.o.'s home, also عند), live, dwell (ه in a place), inhabit (ه a place); to step into the arena, take the field, meet an opposing team (sports); to give in, yield (على e.g., to s.o.'s pleas); to give up, renounce, resign (عن ل s.th. in s.o.'s favor), cede, waive, relinquish, abandon (عن s.th.); to resign (عن from); to refrain (عن from), forgo (عن s.th.); to descend, come (ب upon s.o.; misfortune, punishment, etc.), befall, hit, afflict (ب s.o.; misfortune), happen, occur (ب to s.o.); to fall (على upon s.o.), attack, assail, assault (على s.o.); to enter, embark (على upon s.th.), set out (على to do s.th.), tackle, attack (على s.th.), pounce (على on s.th.); (with ب:) to take, bring, lead, etc., s.o. or s.th. down (الى to); — *nazila a* (نزلة *nazla*) to have a cold | نزل الى البر (*barr*) to disembark, go ashore, land; نزل الى الميدان (*maidān*) to take the field; نزل دون منزلته (*manzilatihī*) to sink below one's level; نزل ضيفا على (*ḍaifan*) to avail o.s. of s.o.'s hospitality, stay as a guest with s.o.; نزل على حكمه (*ḥukmihī*) to defer, give in, yield, submit to s.o.; to comply with the standard of s.th.; نزل عند ارادته (*irādatihī*) to defer to s.o.'s will, do s.o.'s bidding; نزل عند رغبته or طلبه (*raġbatihī*, *ṭalabihī*) to comply with, or fulfill, s.o.'s wish or demand; نزل منزلا (*manzilan*) to occupy a place or position, get to a place or into a position; نزل منزله اللائق (*manzilahū*) to occupy one's due place; نزل منزلة فلان (*manzilata f.*) to hold the position of, serve as **II** to cause to come down; to make (ه s.o.) descend, dismount, or step down; to lower, let down (ه s.th., e.g., a bucket, a curtain, etc.); to send down (ه على a revelation to a prophet), reveal (ه s.th.); to take down, put down (ه s.th.); to lower, decrease, diminish, lessen, minimize, curtail, reduce (ه or من s.th.); to dip, tilt (ه s.th.); to lower, strike (ه a flag); to relieve, divest, discharge (ه عن s.o. of), depose, dethrone (ه عن العرش s.o.); to unload (ه s.th.); to grant hospitality (ه to s.o.), receive hospitably, take in, put up, lodge, accommodate (ه s.o.); to deduct, subtract (ه من s.th. from); to insert, inlay (ه في s.th. in, e.g., ivory in wood); (*Tun.*) to cede (ه s.th.) on the basis of *inzāl* (q.v.) | نزل درجته (*darajatahū*) to demote s.o., reduce s.o. in rank **III** to get into a fight, join issue, clash (ه with s.o.) **IV** to bring down, take down; to cause to descend, dismount, or step down; to send down, reveal (ه على

s.th. to s.o.; of God); to bestow, grant, give (ه s.th.; of God); to make (ه s.o.) alight, stop, halt, camp, put up, take up quarters, live, stay, abide (ه in a place); to unload (ه s.th.); to take ashore (ه الى البر *ilā l-barr* s.th. from a vessel); to land, put ashore, disembark, debark (ه troops); to lower, strike (ه a flag); to abase, degrade; to lower, decrease, diminish, reduce (ه الى number, price, etc., to); to cause (ه ب to s.o. loss), inflict (ه ب upon s.o. a loss); to compel, force, coerce (ه على s.o. to) | ما انزل الله به من سلطان (*sulṭān*) (lit.: God has given it no power, i.e.) futile, vain, fruitless, unavailing, unfounded, absurd, preposterous, completely arbitrary, random; انزل الى البحر (*baḥr*) to launch (ه a ship); انزلوهم ضيوفا عليهم (*ḍuyūfan*) they took them in as guests; انزل به خسارة فادحة (*ḵusāratan fādiḥatan*) to inflict a heavy loss on s.o.; انزله منزلة فلان (*manzilata f.*) he had him occupy the same position as, gave him the same status as, made him equal in rank with **V** to lower o.s., stoop, condescend (الى to s.th.); to abase o.s., humble o.s., demean o.s., eat crow; to give up, renounce, resign, waive, forgo (عن s.th.), refrain (عن from) **VI** to give up, renounce, resign, waive, forgo (عن ل s.th. in favor of), refrain (عن from), yield, surrender, abandon, relinquish (عن s.th.); to cede (عن ل s.th. to); to leave, assign, transfer, make over (عن ل s.th. to); to lower o.s., stoop, condescend; to deign; to dismount, or line up, for battle | تنازل (or تنزل) عن العرش ل (*'arš*) to abdicate in favor of; تنازل عن منصب (*manṣib*) to lay down an office, resign from office **X** to ask (ه s.o.) to step down; to call down, invoke (ه s.th.); to make (ه s.o.) descend; to call upon s.o. (ه) to waive or forgo (عن s.th.); to force (ه the beleaguered) to surrender; to deduct, subtract (ه من s.th. from)

نزل **nazl** pl. نزول **nuzūl**, نزل **nuzul** quarters, lodging; hotel, inn; — (pl. نزول *nuzūl*) small tribal unit (of Bedouins); camp, camp site (of nomads, gypsies)

نزل **nuzl** pl. انزال **anzāl** food served to a guest

نزلة **nazla** putting up, stopping, stop, stay, arrival | نزلة الحج *n. al-ḥajj* (*eg.*) festival of the return of the mahmal from Mecca (celebrated in the months of Safar or Rabia I)

نزلة **nazla** pl. **nazalāt** cold; catarrh | نزلة شعبية (*šu'abīya*) bronchial catarrh; نزلة صدرية (*ṣadrīya*) bronchitis; نزلة وافدة influenza (*med.*)

نزالة **nizāla** settlement, colony

نزول **nuzūl** descending, descent; dismounting, alighting; getting off or out (of a vehicle), disembarkation, debarkation; landing (of an airplane); arrival; putting up, stopping, stop, stopover, stay; cession, surrender, relinquishment, renunciation, resignation; falling, fall, drop; sinking; decline in prices, price slump | نزولا على according to, in accordance with, in deference to; نزولا عند رغبته (*raḡbatihī*) in compliance with his wish, in deference to his wish, at his request; نزولا عند طلبه (*ṭalabihī*) in compliance with his demand, in accordance with his request; نزول المطر *n. al-maṭar* rainfall

نزولى **nuzūlī** relative to decline (in prices and stocks), recessive, falling, sinking

نزيل **nazīl** pl. نزلاء **nuzalā'**[2] guest; stranger; lodger, boarder; inmate; occupant, tenant

منزل **manzil** pl. منازل **manāzil**[2] stopping place, way station, camp site; apartment, flat; house; lunar phase; see also under verb **I** | منزل الاستراحة resthouse; منازل اللهو واللعب *m. al-lahw wa-l-la'b* amusement centers; اهل المنزل *ahl al-m.* household, family; صاحب المنزل landlord

منزلى *manzilī* domestic, house (adj.); private; household (adj.)

منزلة *manzila* degree, grade, rank; position, status, standing; dignity; see also under verb I and IV

تنزيل *tanzīl* sending down, bringing down; revelation, inspiration; reduction, diminution, lowering, lessening, decrease; — (pl. *-āt*) reduction (of prices); subtraction (*arithm.*); deduction, discount; inlaying, inlay work | تنزيل الرتبة *t. ar-rutba* or تنزيل المقام *t. al-maqām* demotion, reduction in rank; تنزيل نقدى (*naqdī*) currency devaluation

نزال *nizāl* and منازلة *munāzala* lining up for battle; encounter, battle, fight

انزال *inzāl* bringing down, lowering; landing, debarkation, disembarkation; ejaculation of sperm; (pl. *-āt*) lease contract for life over a habous estate (*Tun.*) | انزال الى البحر (*baḥr*) launching (of a ship); انزال الى العمل (*'amal*) commissioning (of a ship)

تنازل *tanāzul* condescension; yielding, relenting; relinquishment, surrender, waiver, renunciation; transfer, assignment, cession; resignation, abdication; lining up for battle; struggle, fight, battle | عدم التنازل *'adam at-t.* relentlessness, intransigence; عقد التنازل *'aqd at-t.* deed of cession

استنزال *istinzāl* deduction, discount

نازل *nāzil* living, resident

نازلة *nāzila* pl. نوازل *nawāzil*[2] occurrence, event; mishap, accident, calamity, reverse, blow of fate; (*tun.*) (judicial) case, legal action | نازلة مدنية (*madanīya*; *tun.*) civil action; اوراق نازلة (*tun.*) records of a lawsuit; قسم النوازل *qism an-n.* (*tun.*) division for contentious matters (of a court of justice); قام بنازلة (*tun.*) to take legal action, commence a lawsuit

منزول ***manzūl*** **(*eg.*) a kind of narcotic**

منزولى ***manzūlī*** **(*eg.*) narcotics addict, dope addict**

منزل ***munazzal*** **inlaid (with ivory or a precious metal)**

منزل ***munzal*** **sent down (from heaven), revealed**

متنازل ***mutanāzil*** **abdicating, resigning; one who waives, cedes or assigns a right, assignor**

مستنزل ***mustanzil*** **lessee on the basis of *inzāl* (*Tun.*; see above)**

نزنز ***naznaza*** **to rock, dandle (a baby)**

نزه ***nazuha u*** **(نزاهة *nazāha*) to be far (عن from), be untouched, unblemished (عن by), be free (عن from); to steer clear (عن of), keep away, refrain (عن from, esp., from a base or dishonorable action); — *naziha a* to be respectable, honorable, decent II to deem or declare (ه s.o.) above s.th. (عن) V = *nazuha*; to be (far) above s.th. (عن); to go for a walk, take a walk, promenade, stroll about; to go out; to amuse o.s., enjoy o.s., have a good time**

نزه ***nazih*** **and نزيه *nazīh* pl. نزهاء *nuzahā'*[2], نزاه *nizāh* pure, chaste, blameless, above reproach, of unblemished record, decent, honorable, respectable; honest, upright, righteous; scrupulous, correct; impartial**

نزه ***nazah*** **and نزاهة *nazāha* purity, blamelessness, honesty; uprightness, righteousness, probity, integrity, respectability; impartiality**

نزهة ***nuzha*** **pl. نزه *nuzah*, *-āt* walk, stroll, promenade; pleasure ride; outing, excursion, pleasure trip; recreation; amusement, entertainment, diversion, fun; excursion spot, picnic ground, sightseeing spot, tourist attraction**

منزهة *manzaha* pl. منازه *manāzih*² recreation ground; park; garden

تنزيه *tanzīh* elimination of anthropomorphic elements from the conception of deity, deanthropomorphism (*theol.*)

تنزه *tanazzuh* pl. *-āt* walk, stroll, promenade

منزه *munazzah* infallible; free (عن from), (far) above s.th. (عن)

متنزه *mutanazzih* pl. *-ūn* walker, stroller, promenader; excursionist

متنزه *mutanazzah* promenade, walk, stroll; park

منتزه *muntazah* pl. *-āt* promenade, walk, stroll; recreation ground; park

¹(نزو) نزا *nazā u* (نزو *nazw*, *nuzūw*, نزوان *nazawān*) to spring, jump, leap, bound; — (نزوان *nazawān*) to escape (عن s.th.) | نزا به قلبه الى (*qalbuhū*) to long, yearn for **V** to spring, jump, leap, bound; to be in a state of great commotion, be violently agitated; to heave, tremble (breast)

نزوان *nazawān* sally, sortie; outburst, outbreak, eruption

نزوة *nazwa* pl. *nazawāt* (n. vic.) jump, leap, bound; sally, sortie; outburst, outbreak, eruption; surge, flare, flare-up; impetuosity, violence, vehemence; fit, attack, paroxysm; sudden mood, caprice, whim

²نازى and نازية look up alphabetically

نسأ *nasa'a a* (نسء *nas'*) to put off, postpone, delay, defer, procrastinate (ه s.th.); — (نساء *nasā'*) to allow (ه s.o.) time to pay, grant (ه s.o.) credit **IV** = **I**

نساء *nasā'* long life, longevity

نساء *nisā'* women, see نسو

نسيئة *nasī'a* credit, delay of payment; *nasī'atan* on credit

منسأة *minsa'a* stick, staff

نسب *nasaba u i* (*nasab*, نسبة *nisba*) to relate, refer (الى ه s.th. to), link, correlate, bring into relation (الى ه s.th. with); to trace (الى ه s.th. to s.o. as the originator, الى ه s.o.'s ancestry to); to ascribe, attribute, impute, lay (ل or الى ه s.th. to s.o.), charge (ل or الى ه with s.th. s.o.), accuse (ل or الى ه of s.th. s.o.) **III** to stand in the same relationship (ه to s.o.); to correspond (ه, ه to s.o., to s.th.), tally (ه with s.th.); to suit, fit (ه, ه s.o., s.th.), go (ه, ه with), become, befit, behoove (ه s.o.); to harmonize, agree, be in keeping, be compatible, consistent (ه with); to be similar (ه, ه to s.o., to s.th.), resemble (ه, ه s.o., s.th.), be like s.o. or s.th. (ه, ه); to be in agreement, in conformity, in accordance, to tally, check (ه with), be conformable (ه to); to be of the same family (ه as), be or become related by marriage (ه to) **VI** to be related to one another, be relatives; to be alike, be akin, be mutually corresponding, be interrelated, be in agreement or conformity, be in the right proportion, be proportionate, match, fit together, go together; to be in agreement, in conformity, in accordance, to tally, check (مع with), be conformable (مع to) **VIII** to be related (الى to s.o.); to derive one's origin (الى from), trace one's ancestry (الى to); to derive one's name (الى from), be named (الى after); to belong, pertain, be relative (الى to); to be associated (الى with), belong (الى to a clan, a party, a faction, etc.); to attach o.s. (الى to), associate, affiliate (الى with); to join (الى e.g., a political party); to be admitted (الى to a community), be affiliated (الى with, esp., as an extraordinary, not a full, member) **X** to trace back the ancestry (ه of s.o.); to deem proper (ه s.th.), approve (ه of), sanction, condone (ه s.th.)

نسب *nasab* pl. انساب *ansāb* lineage, descent; origin, extraction, derivation, provenience; kinship, relationship, affinity, relationship by marriage | سلسلة النسب *silsilat an-n.* family tree, pedigree, ancestral line, genealogy; علماء الانساب *'ulamā' al-a.* genealogists

نسبة *nisba* ascription, attribution, imputation; kinship, relationship, affinity, relationship by marriage; connection, link; agreement, conformity, affinity; — (pl. نسب *nisab*) relation, reference, bearing; ratio, rate; measure; proportion (*math.*); percentage; adjective denoting descent or origin, ending in ى - | نسبة الى (*nisbatan*) and (or ل) بالنسبة الى in respect to, with regard to, regarding, concerning, as to; as compared with, in comparison with; in relation to, with reference to; for, to; على نسبة in proportion to, in keeping with, in accordance with, according to, corresponding to, commensurate with; نسبة الموت *n. al-maut* death rate; نسبة مئوية (*mi'awiya*) percentage

نسبى *nisbī* relative, comparative; percentual, percentile; proportional; نسبيا *nisbīyan* relatively | ○ وزن نسبي (*wazn*) specific gravity

نسبية *nisbīya* relativity

نساب *nassāb* genealogist

نسيب *nasīb* erotic introduction of the ancient Arabic kasida; — (pl. انسباء *ansibā'*²) relative, kinsman (by marriage); brother-in-law; son-in-law; descending from a distinguished family, patrician, highborn, noble

انسب *ansab*² more adequate, more appropriate, more suitable, better qualified, fitter

مناسبة *munāsaba* suitability, suitableness, appropriateness, aptness, adequacy; fitness; correlation, analogy, correspondence; kinship, relationship, affinity; — (pl. *-āt*) relation, reference, bearing, relevancy, pertinence; link; connection; occasion, opportunity | في مناسبة or لمناسبة or بمناسبة on the occasion of; بهذه المناسبة in this connection; لهذه المناسبة due to these circumstances, for this reason, therefore, consequently, hence; في كل مناسبة whenever an opportunity arises, at every suitable occasion

تناسب *tanāsub* proportional relation, proportionality; proportionateness, balance, evenness; uniformity; regularity, symmetry; harmony; ○ proportion, mathematical equation; reciprocal relationship, interrelation; link, connection | عدم التناسب *'adam at-t.* disproportion

انتساب *intisāb* membership; affiliation | طالب بالانتساب student by affiliation

منسوب *mansūb* related, brought into relation; attributed, ascribed, imputed (الى to s.o.); belonging, pertaining (الى to); relative (to), concerning, regarding (s.o. or s.th.); — (pl. مناسيب *manāsīb*²) level, altitude; water level | منسوب البحر *m. al-baḥr* sea level; مناسيب عالية (*'āliya*) high water levels, high waters

منسوبية *mansūbīya* nepotism

مناسب *munāsib* suitable, fitting, appropriate, proper, adequate; corresponding, commensurate; correspondent, congruous, analogous, conformable; proportional (*math.*)

متناسب *mutanāsib* proportionate, properly proportioned; proportional; mutually corresponding, analogous | متناسب الاجزاء even, regular, symmetrical

منتسب *muntasib* member, affiliate | عضو منتسب (*'uḍw*) associate (e.g., of an academy)

ناسوت *nāsūt* human nature, humanity

نسج *nasaja* u i (*nasj*) to weave (ه s.th.); to knit | نسج على منواله (*minwālihī*) to imitate s.o., follow in s.o.'s tracks, walk in s.o.'s footsteps, act or proceed like s.o.; نسج نسجه (*nasjahū*) do. VIII to be woven

نسج *nasj* weaving; fabric, texture | نسج الخيال *n. al-kayāl* fabling, flight of fancy

نساج *nassāj* weaver

نساجة *nisāja* art of weaving; weaver's trade, textile industry

نسيج *nasīj* pl. نسج *nusuj*, انسجة *ansija*, انساج *ansāj* texture, web, tissue (also *anat.*); woven fabric, textile | نسيج خلوى (*kalawī*) cellular tissue (*anat.*); نسيج العنكبوت *n. al-'ankabūt* spider's web, cobweb; نسيج وحده *n. waḥdihī* unique in his (its) kind, singular, unparalleled; نسيج عصره *n. 'aṣrihī* unique in his (its) time

منسج *mansaj*, *mansij* pl. مناسج *manāsij*² weaver's shop, weaving mill

منسج *minsaj* loom

منسوج *mansūj* woven; woven fabric, textile; texture, tissue, web; pl. منسوجات woven goods, dry goods, textiles

نسخ *nasaka* a (*nask*) to delete (ه s.th.); to abolish (ه s.th.); to abrogate, invalidate (ه s.th.); to repeal, revoke, withdraw (ه s.th.); to cancel (ه a contract); to replace (ه ب s.th. by), substitute (ه ب for s.th. s.th. else); to transcribe, copy (ه s.th.) III to supersede, supplant, replace (ه s.th.), take the place (ه of s.th.) V to be deleted, abolished, abrogated, invalidated VI to succeed each other, follow successively; to pass from one body into another, transmigrate (soul) VIII to abolish, cancel, abrogate, invalidate (ه s.th.); to transcribe, copy (ه s.th.) X to demand the abolition (ه of s.th.); to transcribe, copy (ه s.th.)

نسخ *nask* abolition, abolishment, abrogation, cancellation, invalidation; copying, transcription | قلم النسخ *qalam an-n.* Neskhi ductus (see below); آلة النسخ duplicating machine, mimeograph; copying press

نسخى *naskī* Neskhi, the ordinary cursive Arabic script, the common calligraphic style

نسخة *nuska* pl. نسخ *nusak* transcript; copy (also, e.g., of a book, of a newspaper, etc.)

نساخ *nassāk* pl. نساخة *nassāka* copyist, transcriber; scribe, scrivener, clerk

تناسخ *tanāsuk* succession; transmigration of souls, metempsychosis

استنساخ *istinsāk* copying, transcription

ناسخ *nāsik* pl. نساخ *nussāk* abrogative, abolishing; copyist, transcriber | آية ناسخة Koranic verse which abrogates and supersedes another verse

منسوخ *mansūk* abrogated (Koranic verse)

نسر V to get torn; to break, snap X to become eagle-like

نسر *nasr* pl. نسور *nusūr*, نسورة *nusūra* eagle; vulture

نسارية *nusārīya* eagle

ناسور *nāsūr* pl. نواسير *nawāsīr*² fistula, tumor

منسر *minsar*, *mansir* pl. مناسر *manāsir*² beak (of predatory birds); band, gang, group, troop

نسطورى *nusṭūrī* pl. نساطرة *nasāṭira* Nestorian

نسغ *nusḡ* sap (of a plant)

نسف *nasafa* i (*nasf*) to pulverize, atomize, spray (ه s.th.); to carry away and scatter (wind — the dust); to blow up, blast (ه s.th.); ○ to torpedo (ه a ship) IV to scatter (esp., wind — the dust) VIII to raze (ه s.th.); to to blow up, blast (ه s.th.)

نسف *nasf* blowing up, blasting; destruction, demolition

نساف *nussāf* pl. نساسيف *nasāsif*² a variety of swallow; rhinoceros hornbill (*zool.*)

نسافة *nusāfa* chaff

نسافة *nassāfa* pl. *-āt* torpedo boat

منسف *minsaf* and منسفة *minsafa* pl. مناسف *manāsif*² winnow

ناسف *nāsif* and ناسفة *nāsifa* explosive, dynamite

نسق *nasaqa u* (*nasq*) and II to string (ه pearls); to put in proper order, arrange nicely, range, array, order, marshal, dispose (ه s.th.); to set up, line up (ه s.th.) V to be well-ordered, be in proper order, be nicely arranged; to be arranged, arrayed, disposed VI do.; to be geared to each other, be well-coordinated (weapons) VIII = V

نسق *nasq* ordering, successive arrangement, lining up, alignment

نسق *nasaq* order, array, layout, arrangement, disposition; connection, succession, sequence; manner, mode, system, method; symmetry; نسقا *nasaqan* in regular order, in rows | على نسق in the manner of; على نسق واحد in the same manner, equally, evenly, uniformly; حروف النسق conjunctions (*gram.*)

نسيق *nasīq* well-ordered, well-arranged, regular, even, uniform

تنسيق *tansīq* ordering, arraying; setting up, drawing up; distribution, disposition; arrangement; systematic arrangement; planned economy | تنسيق داخلى (*dāḵilī*) interior decoration

تنسق *tanassuq* uniformity

تناسق *tanāsuq* order; symmetry; harmony

منسق *munassaq* well-ordered, well-arranged; staggered (troop formation); harmonious

متناسق *mutanāsiq* well-ordered, well-arranged, regular, symmetrical

نسك *nasaka u* and *nasuka u* (نساكة *nasāka*) to lead a devout life; to live the life of an ascetic V do.; to be pious, devout, otherworldly

نسك *nask, nusk, nusuk* piety, devoutness; asceticism; reclusion

نسكى *nusukī* ascetic (adj.)

نسك *nusuk* sacrifice; ceremonies (of the pilgrimage)

ناسك *nāsik* pl. نساك *nussāk* hermit, recluse, penitent; ascetic; pious man, devotee

منسك *mansik* pl. مناسك *manāsik*² hermitage, cell of an ascetic; place of sacrifice; ceremony, ritual, esp., during the pilgrimage

نسل *nasala u* (*nasl*) to beget, procreate, sire, father (ه children); — *u* to pluck out (ه s.th.); to pluck (ه s.th.); to ravel out, unravel, untwist, fray (ه s.th.); to molt; (نسول *nusūl*) to fall out (hair, feathers) II to separate into fibers, to shred, ravel (ه rags); to unravel, undo (ه a woven or knitted fabric) IV to beget, procreate, sire, father (ه children); to molt; to fall out (hair, feathers) VI to propagate, breed, reproduce, multiply; to beget offspring; to descend, be descended (من from)

نسل *nasl* pl. انسال *ansāl* progeny, offspring, issue, descendants | تقليل النسل birth control; الحرث والنسل (*ḥarṯ*) the civilization of mankind

نسالة *nusāla* fibrous waste, thrums; ravelings; lint

○ نسالة *nassāla* raveling machine, willow

نسولة *nasūla* brood animal

○ نسيلة *nasīla* offprint, reprint

انسال *insāl* procreation, generation

تناسل *tanāsul* sexual propagation, procreation, generation, reproduction | اعضاء التناسل sexual organs, genitals; ضعف التناسل *ḍuʿf at-t.* sexual impotence

تناسلى *tanāsulī* procreative, propagative; genital, sexual | مرض تناسلى (*maraḍ*) venereal disease

تناسليات *tanāsulīyāt* sexual organs

نسم *nasama* i (*nasm*, نسمان *nasamān*) to blow gently II to commence, start, begin (فى s.th.) V to blow; to breathe; to inhale (ه s.th.); to exhale (ب a fragrant smell), smell pleasantly, be redolent (ب of), be fragrant (ب with) | تنسم الخبر (*ḵabara*) to nose around for news, sniff out the news

نسم *nasam* pl. انسام *ansām* breath; breath of life

نسمة *nasama* pl. *-āt* breath; whiff, waft; breeze; ○ aura; breathing, living creature; person, soul (e.g., in a census, as a numerative in statistics)

نسيم *nasīm* pl. نسام *nisām*, نسائم *nasāʾim*² breath of air, fresh air; wind, breeze | شم النسيم *šamm an-n.* Egyptian popular holiday celebrated on the Monday following Greek-Coptic Easter

منسم *mansim* pl. مناسم *manāsim*² foot sole, padded foot (of animals)

متنسم *mutanassam* (with foll. genit.) place where s.th. blows, is exhaled, emanates, or exudes

نسناس *nasnās*, *nisnās* pl. نسانس *nasānis*² a fabulous creature of the woods, having one leg and one arm; (*eg.*) monkey

نسوة *niswa*, نسوان *niswān* and نساء *nisāʾ* women (pl. of امرأة)

نسوى *niswī* and نسائى *nisāʾī* female, feminine, womanly, women's; نسائيات women's affairs, things belonging to a woman's world

نسائية *nisāʾīya* feminist movement

نسى *nasiya* a (*nasy*, نسيان *nisyān*) to forget (ه s.th.) | ما انس لا انس *mā ansa lā ansa* (lit.: whatever I may forget, I shall not forget, i.e.) I shall never forget; sometimes also: ما انس لا انسى (*ansā*) and ان انس فلا انسى (*in*) I shall never forget IV to make (ه s.o.) forget (ه s.th.) VI to pretend to have forgotten (ه s.th.); to forget, neglect, omit (ه s.th.), become oblivious (ه of)

نسى *nasy* oblivion, forgetfulness; s.th. one has forgotten | اصبح نسيا منسيا *aṣbaḥa nasyan mansīyan* to be completely forgotten, fall into utter oblivion

نسى *nasīy*, نساء *nassāʾ* and نسيان *nasyān*² forgetful, oblivious

نسيان *nisyān* oblivion, forgetfulness

منسى *mansīy* forgotten; pl. منسيات (as opposed to محفوظات) things once memorized and now forgotten

نش *našša* i (*našš*, نشيش *našīš*) to sizzle, simmer, bubble, boil up; to hiss; — to drive away flies

ورق نشاش *waraq naššāš* blotting paper

منشة *minašša* fly whisk

نشأ *našaʾa* a and نشؤ *našuʾa* u (نشء *našʾ*, نشوء *nušūʾ*, نشأة *našʾa*) to rise, rise aloft, emerge, appear, loom up; to come into being, come into existence, originate, form, arise, come about, crop up; to proceed, spring (من or عن from), grow out (من or عن of); to follow, ensue, result, derive (من or عن from); to grow, grow up; to develop, evolve | نشأ نشوءا ذاتيا (*ḏātīyan*) to start by itself, arise spontaneously, come about automatically

II to cause to grow; to bring up, raise (ه a child) IV to cause (ه s.th.) to rise; to create, bring into being (ه s.th., of God); to bring forth, produce, generate, engender (ه s.th.), give rise (ه to s.th.); to make, manufacture, fabricate (ه s.th.); to build, construct (ه s.th.); to call into existence, originate, start, found, establish, organize, institute (ه s.th.); to set up, erect (ه s.th.); to install (ه s.th.); to compose, draw up (ه a piece of writing), write (ه a book); to bring up, raise, rear (ه a child); to begin, start, commence, initiate (ه s.th.) V to grow, develop, spread, gain ground X to search, ask, look (ه for news)

نشء *naš'* youth; new generation | النشء الجديد the young generation

نشأة *naš'a* growing up, upgrowth, growth; early life, youth; rise, birth, formation, genesis; origin; youth, young generation; culture, refinement; upbringing, background (of a person) | نشأة مستأنفة (*musta'nafa*) rebirth, renaissance

نشوء *nušū'* growing, growth, development, evolution | ○ مذهب النشوء والترقى *maḏhab an-n. wa-t-taraqqī* theory of evolution, evolutionism

○ النشوئيون *an-nušū'īyūn* the evolutionists

منشأ *manša'* place of origin or upgrowth; birth place, home town, home; fatherland, homeland, native country; origin, rise, birth, formation, genesis; source, springhead, fountainhead; beginning, start, onset

تنشىء *tanši'* upbringing, education

تنشئة *tanši'a* upbringing, education

انشاء *inšā'* creation; origination; bringing about; setting up, establishment, organization, institution; formation; making, manufacture, production; erection; building, construction; founding, foundation; installation; composition, compilation, writing; letter writing; style, art of composition; essay, treatise | انشاءات عسكرية (*'askarīya*) military installations; اعادة الانشاء *i'ādat al-i.* reconstruction

انشائى *inšā'ī* creative; constructive; relating to composition or style; stylistic; editing, editorial | برنامج انشائى (*barnāmaj*) production program; قطعة انشائية (*qiṭ'a*) exercise in composition; موضوع انشائى theme, composition

ناشئ *nāši'* growing, growing up; arising, originating, proceeding, emanating, springing, resulting (عن from); beginner; (in sports) junior; youngster, youth

ناشئة *nāši'a* youth, rising generation

منشئ *munši'* creating; creative; creator; organizer, promoter, founder; author, writer

منشأة *munša'a* pl. *-āt* creation, product, work, opus; foundation, establishment; installation; institution, institute; pl. installations (e.g., industrial, military)

[1]نشب *našiba a* (*našb*, نشبة *nušba*, نشوب *nušūb*) to be fixed, be attached, cling, stick, adhere (فى to); to attend (ب s.th.), be incident (ب to); to get involved (فى in), meddle (فى with); to break out (war) | ما نشب or لم ينشب not to hesitate II and IV to stick on, paste on, attach, fix, insert (ه s.th.)

نشب *našab* property, possession

نشوب *nušūb* clinging, adherence (فى to); outbreak

نشاب *naššāb* arrow maker; archer, bowman

نشاب *nuššāb* (coll.; n. un. ة) pl. نشاشيب *našāšīb*[2] arrows

منتشب *muntašib* fierce, violent (battle)

[2]منشوبية look up alphabetically

نشج *našaja i* (نشيج *našīj*) to sob

نشد *našada u* (*našd*, نشدة *našda*, نشدان *nišdān*) to seek (ه s.th.), look, search (ه for); to adjure, implore (ه ه s.o. by, e.g., الله *allāha* by God) **III** to adjure, implore (ه ان يفعل or ه ه s.o. to do s.th., ه ه s.o. by, e.g., الله *allāha* by God) **IV** to seek (ه s.th.), look, search (ه for); to sing (ه s.th.); to recite (ه ه to s.o. verses) **VI** to recite verses to each other **X** to ask (ه s.o.) to recite verses

نشيد *našīd* and انشودة *unšūda* pl. نشائد *našā'id*[2], انشاد *anšād*, اناشيد *anāšīd*[2] song; hymn, anthem | نشيد الاناشيد or نشيد الانشاد the Song of Solomon, the Song of Songs; النشيد الأممى (*umamī*) the International; نشيد حماسى (*ḥamāsī*) rallying song; نشيد عسكرى (*'askarī*) soldier's song, marching song; military march; نشيد قومى (*qaumī*) or نشيد وطنى (*waṭanī*) national anthem; نشيد ليلى (*lailī*) serenade; نشيد ملكى (*malakī*) royal anthem

مناشدة *munāšada* urgent request, earnest appeal, adjuration

انشاد *inšād* recitation, recital

منشود *manšūd* sought, aspired, desired, pursued (aim, objective)

منشد *munšid* singer

نشادر *nušādir* and نوشادر *nūšādir* ammonia

نشر *našara u* (*našr*) to spread out (ه s.th.); to unfold, open (ه s.th.); to unroll (ه s.th.); to hoist (ه a flag); — *u i* to spread, diffuse, emit (ه e.g., a scent); to announce publicly, publicize (ه s.th.); to publish (ه a book, an advertisement, etc.); to propagate, spread (ه s.th.); — *u* (*našr*, نشور *nušūr*) to resurrect from the dead (ه s.o.); — to saw apart (ه s.th.) **II** to spread out, unfold (ه s.th.) **IV** to resurrect from the dead (ه s.o.) **V** to be spread out, be unfolded; to spread **VIII** to be spread out, be unfolded; to spread (news, a disease, etc.); to spread out, extend, expand; to be propagated, be conveyed (waves); to be diffused, be scattered, be dispersed, be thrown into disorder; ○ to fan out, extend (*mil.*)

نشر *našr* unfolding; spreading, diffusion; propagation; promulgation; publication; notification, announcement; resurrection | نشر الدعوة *n. ad-da'wa* propaganda; يوم النشر *yaum an-n.* Day of Resurrection; دار النشر publishing house

نشرة *našra* pl. *našarāt* (public) notice, proclamation; publication; report, account; announcement; advertisement; circular; leaflet, pamphlet, handbill; periodical; order, ordinance, decree, edict | نشرة الاخبار or نشرة اخبارية (*ikbārīya*) newscast, news (*radio*); نشرة دورية (*daurīya*) periodical publication; نشرة اسبوعية (*usbū'īya*) weekly publication, weekly paper; newsreel; نشرات جوية (*jawwīya*) weather report (*radio*); نشرة خاصة بالاسعار (*kāṣṣa*) prospectus, price list; نشرة رسمية (*rasmīya*) official publication, bulletin; نشرة شهرية (*šahrīya*) monthly publication; ○ نشرة يومية (*yaumīya*) order of the day (*mil.*)

نشار *naššār* sawyer

نشارة *nišāra* (activity of) sawing

نشارة *nušāra* sawdust

نشور *nušūr* resurrection | يوم النشور *yaum an-n.* Day of Resurrection

منشار *minšār* pl. مناشير *manāšīr*[2] saw

انتشار *intišār* spreading, spread, diffusion, diffusiveness

ناشر *nāšir* publisher

منشور *manšūr* spread abroad, propagated, made public, published; sawn (apart); — (pl. *-āt*, مناشير *manāšīr*[2]) leaflet, pamphlet, handbill; circular; prospectus; proclamation; order, ordinance, decree, edict; prism (*math.*)

منشورى look up alphabetically

منتشر *muntašir* spreading, spread out; widespread, current, rife; prevailing, prevalent, predominant

نشز **našaza** *u i* (*našz*) to be elevated, be located high above; to rise; — (نشوز *nušūz*) to be recalcitrant, disobedient (على, من, ب toward her husband; said of a woman); to treat (a wife) brutally (said of a man) **IV** to restore to life, revive, reanimate (ه s.th.)

نشز **našaz** pl. انشاز *anšāz* elevated place, high ground

نشاز **našāz** dissonance, discord

نشوز **nušūz** animosity, hostility; antipathy; dissonance, discord; (*Isl. Law*) violation of marital duties on the part of either husband or wife, specif., recalcitrance of the woman toward her husband, and brutal treatment of the wife by the husband

ناشز **nāšiz** protruding, elevated, raised; jarring, dissonant, discordant; recalcitrant

ناشزة **nāšiza** pl. نواشز *nawāšiz*[2] recalcitrant woman, shrew, termagant

نشط **našiṭa** *a* (نشاط *našāṭ*) to be lively, animated, brisk, sprightly, vivacious, spirited, active, eager, keen, zealous, brave, cheerful, gay; to display vim and energy (في in some work), be energetic and active, work energetically and actively (الى for, toward); to be in the mood (ل for), feel like doing s.th. (ل); to be glad, enthusiastic (ل about); to apply o.s. eagerly, attend actively (ل to some activity), embark briskly (ل upon s.th.) | نشط من عقاله (*ʻiqālihi*) to be freed from one's shackles, be unfettered, be unshackled; — *našaṭa* *u* (*našṭ*) to tie a knot (ه in a rope), knot (ه a rope) **II** and **IV** to incite, spur on, enliven, stimulate, activate, excite (ه, ه s.o., s.th.); to strengthen, invigorate, animate, inspirit, energize (ه s.o.), impart vim and energy (ه to s.o.), encourage, embolden (ه s.o., الى to do s.th.); to knot, tie up (ه s.th.) **V** to be lively, animated, brisk, sprightly, vivacious, spirited, active, eager, keen, zealous, brave, cheerful, gay; to display vim and energy (في in some work), be energetic and active, work energetically and actively (الى for, toward); to be in the mood (ل for), feel like doing s.th. (ل)

نشط **našiṭ** lively, animated, spirited, brisk, sprightly, vivacious, agile, nimble; stirring, bustling, busy, enterprising, energetic, active

نشطة **našṭa** energy; eagerness, ardor, zeal

نشاط **našāṭ** briskness, sprightliness, liveliness, animation, vivacity; agility, alacrity, eagerness, ardor, zeal, energy, vim, activeness; activity; lively activity, action, operation; strength, power (physical and mental); vigor, vital energy, vitality | نشاط جوى (*jawwī*) aerial activity; نشاط اشعاعى (*išʻāʻī*) radioactivity; ذو نشاط اشعاعى radioactive; مواد ذات نشاط اشعاعى (*mawādd*[2]) radioactive substances, radioactive matter; صاحب نشاط active; عديم النشاط inactive, dull, listless (stock market)

نشيط **našīṭ** pl. نشاط *nišāṭ* brisk, lively, spirited, animated, cheerful, gay; stirring, bustling, busy, active, energetic; glad, happy, enthusiastic (ل about), actively devoted (ل to) | الجنس النشيط (*jins*) the stronger sex

انشوطة **unšūṭa** pl. اناشيط *anāšīṭ*[2] knot, slipknot, bow, noose

منشط **manšaṭ** pleasant thing

تنشيط **tanšīṭ** encouragement, incitement; stimulation; enlivening, animation, activation

ناشط *nāšiṭ* brisk, lively, spirited, animated, cheerful, gay; stirring, bustling, busy, active, energetic

منشط *munšiṭ* spur, incentive, impetus, stimulus

نشع *naša'a a* (*naš'*) to tear out, tear off (ه s.th.) VIII do.

نشع *naš'* leakage water, seepage

منشع *munašša'* sodden, soggy, soaked, drenched, soaking wet

نشف *našafa u* (*našf*) to suck up, absorb (ه s.th.); — *našifa a* to dry, dry up, dry out, become dry II to dry, make dry (ه s.th.); to wipe (dry), rub dry (ه s.th.) | نشف ريقه (*rīqahū*) to exert o.s., toil hard; to pester, molest s.o. V = *našifa*; to wipe o.s. dry; to be wiped dry, be dried

نشف *našaf* desiccation, dryness

نشاف *naššāf* blotting paper

نشافة *naššāfa* sheet of blotting paper, blotting pad; blotter; towel

منشفة *minšafa* pl. مناشف *manāšif*[2] towel; cleaning rag; napkin

تنشيف *tanšīf* drying

ناشف *nāšif* desiccated, dried up, dry; hard, stiff, tough

نشق *našiqa a* (*našq* and *našaq*) to smell, sniff, inhale (ه s.th.); to snuff up the nostrils (ه s.th.) II and IV to give (ه ه s.o. s.th.) to smell, make (ه s.o.) inhale (ه s.th.) V and VIII to inhale, breathe in; to snuff up the nostrils (ه s.th.) | انتشق الهواء (*hawā'a*) to get some fresh air X = I; to nose around (ه for), sniff out (ه s.th.)

نشق *našq*, تنشق *tanaššuq* and استنشاق *istinšāq* inhaling, inhalation

نشوق *našūq*, *nušūq* snuff

تنشيقة *tanšīqa* pinch of snuff

نشل *našala u* (*našl*) to take away, snatch away, steal, pilfer (ه s.th.); to extricate (from dangers, difficulties, etc.), liberate, deliver, save (ه s.o.) VIII to extricate; to raise, raise aloft; to gather up, pick up (shipwrecked persons, etc.), save, rescue (ه s.o.)

نشل *našl* pickpocketing, pickpocketry

نشال *naššāl* pickpocket

نشان *nišān* and نيشان *nīšān* pl. نياشين *nayāšīn*[2] sign; mark; aim, goal; target; decoration, medal, order; (*eg.*) bridal attire

نشنجى *našanjī* and نشانجى *našānjī* marksman, good shot, sharpshooter

نشنكاه *nišankāh* sight (of a gun)

نشنش *našnaša* to be nimble, swift, brisk, adroit, dexterous, agile, active; to boil up, sizzle, simmer, bubble II *tanašnaša* to be nimble and dexterous; to revive, recover, pick up

نشو and (نشى) نشى *našiya a* (نشوة *našwa*, *nušwa*, *nišwa*) to be or become intoxicated, be or become drunk II to starch (ه clothes, linen) VIII to become intoxicated X to smell (ه a scent), to inhale (ه a breeze)

نشوة *našwa* fragrance, aroma, scent, perfume; intoxication, drunkenness; frenzy, delirium | نشوة الطرب *n. aṭ-ṭarab* rapture, elation, exultation, enthusiasm, ecstasy

نشا *našan* scent, perfume; starch, cornstarch

نشاء *našā'* starch, cornstarch

نشوى *našawī* starchy; pl. نشويات starchy foodstuffs

نشوان *našwān*[2], f. نشوى *našwā*, pl. نشاوى *našāwā* intoxicated, drunk; enraptured, elated, exultant, flushed

انتشاء *intišā'* intoxication

نص **naṣṣa** *u* (*naṣṣ*) to fix, lay down, appoint, stipulate (على s.th.), provide (على for), specify, determine (على or عن s.th.), define (على s.th.); to fix or determine the text (ه of s.th.), draw up, compose (ه a letter); to arrange, stack, pile up in layers (ه s.th.); to set up, line up (ه s.th.)

نص *naṣṣ* pl. نصوص *nuṣūṣ* text; wording, version; passage, word, phrase, sentence, clause; expression, manner of expression, language, phraseology, style; provision, term, stipulation, condition; arrangement; manifestation, evidence | بنصه verbatim, بنصه وفصه *bi-n. wa-faṣṣihī* in the very words, ipsissimis verbis, literally, precisely; نصا وروحا *naṣṣan wa-rūḥan* in letter and spirit

نصة *nuṣṣa* pl. نصص *nuṣaṣ* forelock

منصة *minaṣṣa* pl. *-āt*, مناص *manāṣṣ*[2] raised platform, dais, tribune, podium; bridal throne; easel | منصة الحكم *m. al-ḥukm* position of power; منصة الخطابة rostrum

تنصيص *tanṣīṣ* quotation | علامات التنصيص *'alāmāt at-t.* quotation marks

منصوص عليه *manṣūṣ 'alaihi* fixed, appointed, stipulated, provided for, specified; determined; laid down in writing

نصب **naṣaba** *u* (*naṣb*) to raise, rear, erect, set up, put up (ه s.th.); to prepare, get ready, fit up (ه s.th.); to pitch (ه a tent); to plant, raise (ه a standard, a flagstaff), hoist (ه a flag); to plant (ه a tree); ○ to level, aim (ه a cannon); to appoint to an office, install in an official position; to show, manifest, display (ل toward s.o., ه evil, enmity); to direct, aim (ه s.th., e.g., criticism, على against or at s.o.); (*eg.*) to cheat, swindle, dupe, gull, deceive (على s.o.); (*gram.*) to pronounce (a final consonant) with the vowel *a*; to put (a noun) in the accusative, put (a verb) in the subjunctive | نصب له الحرب (*ḥarba*) to declare war on s.o.; نصب له شركا (*šarakan*) or نصب له فخا (*fakkan*) to set a trap for s.o.; نصب له كمينا (*kamīnan*) to prepare an ambush for s.o.; نصب مكيدة (*makīdatan*) to devise a clever plan, hatch a plot; — **naṣaba** *u* (*naṣb*) to distress, trouble, fatigue, wear out, exhaust (disease or sorrow; ه s.o.); to jade (ه s.o.) | نصبوا انفسهم ل (*anfusahum*) they made every effort in order to ..., they struggled hard to ...; — **naṣiba** *a* (*naṣab*) to be tired, fatigued, jaded, worn out, exhausted; to exert o.s. to the utmost (في in) **II** to set up, set upright, rear, raise, lift up (ه s.th.); to install (ه ه s.o. as), appoint (ه ه s.o. to an office) | نصب اذنيه (*udnaihi*) to prick up one's ears **III** to be hostile (ه to s.o.), fight, combat, oppose (ه s.o.), display enmity | ناصبه الحرب (*ḥarba*) to declare war on s.o.; ناصبه الشر (*šarra*) to show o.s. openly hostile to s.o., open hostilities against s.o.; ناصبه العداء (*'adā'a*) to declare o.s. the enemy of s.o. **IV** to tire, fatigue, wear out, exhaust (ه s.o.); to fix a share or allotment (ه for s.o.) **VIII** to rise up, straighten up, draw o.s. up; to plant o.s.; to rise; to get up, stand up, get on one's feet; to stand upright, be in a vertical position; to be set up, be raised; to be appointed (ل to an office), hold an office (ل); (*gram.*) to be pronounced with *a* (final consonant), be in **naṣb** (accusative or subjunctive) | انتصب للحكم (*li-l-ḥukm*) to sit in judgment

نصب **naṣb** setting up, putting up, placing; erection; planting, raising (e.g., of a flagstaff); appointment, installation, investiture; pronunciation of a final consonant with *a*; the putting a noun in the accusative, or a verb in the subjunctive (*gram.*); disease, illness; (*eg.*) swindle, trickery, skulduggery, deception, fraud

نصب *naṣb* pl. انصاب *anṣāb* s.th. planted in the ground, set up, or erected; plants (coll.)

نصب *nuṣb, nuṣub* pl. انصاب *anṣāb* statue; idol, graven image; monument | نصب تذكارى (*taḏkārī*) monument, cenotaph

نصب *nuṣba* (prep.) in front of, opposite, facing | نصب عينى (*'ainayya*) before my eyes; جعل (وضع) ه نصب عينيه (*'ainaihi*) to direct one's attention to ..., have ... in view

نصب *naṣab* exertion, strain, hardship, fatigue; (pl. انصاب *anṣāb*) flag planted in the ground

نصبة *naṣba* pl. *-āt* plant

نصبة *nuṣba* post; pale, stake, pier, buttress, pillar; signpost, guidepost

نصاب *niṣāb* origin, beginning; (*Isl. Law*) minimum amount of property liable to payment of the *zakāh* tax; minimum number or amount; quorum; (pl. *-āt*, نصب *nuṣub*) sword hilt, knife handle, saber guard | فى نصابه in its proper place, in good order, perfectly all right; استقرت الامور فى نصابها (*istaqarrat*) things were straightened out, returned to normal; وضع الحق فى نصابه (*ḥaqqa*) to restore justice; وضع or رد (اعاد) امرا الى نصابه (*radda, a'āda amran*) to straighten s.th. out, set a matter right; عاد الهدوء الى نصابه (*hudū'u*) peace has been restored; اتماما للنصاب (*itmāman*) so as to complete the number, in order to round off the amount

نصاب *naṣṣāb* fraud, cheat, sharper, swindler, impostor; deceitful, fraudulent

نصيب *naṣīb* pl. نصب *nuṣub*, انصباء *anṣibā'²*, انصبة *anṣiba* share, participation (فى in); share of profits, dividend; luck, chance; fate, lot | كان من نصيبه to fall to s.o.'s share or lot; كان من نصيبه ان to be so fortunate as to ..., have the good fortune to ...; كان نصيبه من ذلك الاخفاق (*ikfāqu*) to have bad luck in s.th., draw a blank; هو على نصيب وافر من (*wāfirin*) to have an ample share in ...

يانصيب *yā-naṣīb* lottery

منصب *manṣib* pl. مناصب *manāṣib²* place where s.th. is planted, set up, or erected; office, dignity, rank, position, post | اصحاب المناصب or ارباب المناصب high dignitaries

منصب *minṣab* pl. مناصب *manāṣib²* kitchen range, cookstove

تنصيب *tanṣīb* appointment, nomination; installation, induction (in an official position)

انتصاب *intiṣāb* raising, rearing, righting; setting up, putting up; erection

ناصب *nāṣib* tiring, wearisome, exhausting; — (pl. نواصب *nawāṣib²*) word governing the subjunctive (*gram.*)

منصوب *manṣūb* erected; set-up, raised; planted in the ground; fixed, fastened, attached; installed in office; leveled, aimed (cannon; على at); (pl. *-āt*) word in the accusative or subjunctive

منتصب *muntaṣib* set upright, set-up, raised, planted in the ground; erected; upright, erect, straight, vertical, perpendicular

نصت *naṣata i* (*naṣt*) and **IV** to listen, hearken, give ear (الى or ل to s.o., ل to s.th.) **V** to try to hear; to eavesdrop, listen secretly

متنصت *mutanaṣṣit* eavesdropper

نصح *naṣaḥa a* (*naṣḥ, nuṣḥ*, نصاحة *naṣāḥa*, نصيحة *naṣīḥa*) to give (ه, ل s.o.) sincere advice, advise, counsel (ه, ل s.o., ب to do s.th.), admonish, exhort; — *a* (*naṣḥ*, نصوح *nuṣūḥ*) to be sincere; to mean well (ل with s.o.), wish s.o. (ل) well, be well-disposed, show good will (ل toward s.o.); to act in good faith (ل toward s.o.) **III** to give (ه s.o.) sincere advice; to be sincere in one's intentions (ه toward s.o.) **VI** to be loyal and sincere toward each other **VIII** to take good advice, follow an advice **X** to ask (ه s.o.) for advice, be advised (ه by s.o.), consult (ه s.o.)

نصح *naṣḥ, nuṣḥ* good advice; counseling, counsel; guidance

نصيح *naṣīḥ* sincere; faithful adviser

نصيحة *naṣīḥa* pl. نصائح *naṣā'iḥ*² sincere advice; friendly admonition, friendly reminder | بذل نصيحة to give a word of advice

نصوح *naṣūḥ* sincere, true, faithful, loyal

استنصاح *istinṣāḥ* consultation

ناصح *nāṣiḥ* pl. نصاح *nuṣṣāḥ*, نصح *nuṣṣaḥ* sincere; good counselor, sincere adviser

نصر *naṣara u* (*naṣr*, نصور *nuṣūr*) to help, aid, assist (ه على s.o. against); to render victorious, let triumph (ه على s.o. over; of God); to deliver (ه من s.o. from), keep, protect, save **II** to Christianize, convert to Christianity (ه s.o.) **III** to help, aid, assist, support, defend, protect (ه s.o.) **V** to try to help, seek to support (ل s.o.), stand up for s.o. (ل); to become a Christian **VI** to render mutual assistance, help each other **VIII** to come to s.o.'s (ل) aid, be on s.o.'s (ل) side, side with s.o. (ل); to be victorious; to gain a victory, to triumph (على over); to take revenge (من on) **X** to ask (ه s.o.) for assistance

نصر *naṣr* help, aid, assistance, support, backing; victory; triumph

نصرة *nuṣra* help, aid, assistance, support, backing

نصرانى *naṣrānī* pl. نصارى *naṣārā* Christian

نصرانية *naṣrānīya* Christianity

نصير *naṣīr* pl. نصراء *nuṣarā'*² helper; supporter, defender, protector; ally, confederate; adherent, follower, partisan; furtherer, promoter, patron

النصيرية *an-nuṣairīya* the Ansarie, a gnostic sect in Syria

ناصور *nāṣūr* pl. نواصير *nawāṣīr*² fistula

منصر *manṣar* pl. مناصر *manāṣir*² (*eg.*) band of robbers

تنصير *tanṣīr* Christianization; baptism

مناصرة *munāṣara* assistance, help, aid, support, backing, furtherance, promotion, patronage

انتصار *intiṣār* (pl. *-āt*) victory, triumph; revenge

ناصر *nāṣir* pl. *-ūn*, انصار *anṣār*, نصار *nuṣṣār* helper; protector; granting victory | اخذ بناصره to help s.o.

انصار *anṣār* (pl.) adherents, followers, partisans, sponsors, patrons, friends; الانصار the Medinan followers of Mohammed who granted him refuge after the Hegira

الناصرة *an-nāṣira* Nazareth

ناصرى *nāṣirī* of Nazareth; Nazarene

منصور *manṣūr* supported, aided (by God); victorious, triumphant; victor; المنصورة El Mansûra (city in N Egypt)

مناصر *munāṣir* helper, supporter, defender, protector

منتصر *muntaṣir* victorious, triumphant

نصع *naṣa'a a* (نصوع *nuṣū'*) to be clear, pure; to be plain, evident, obvious, manifest, patent; to recognize (ب s.th., esp., a claim or title) **IV** to recognize, acknowledge (ب s.th.)

نصوع *nuṣū'* whiteness; brightness (of a color)

نصيع *naṣī'* pure, clear; plain, evident, obvious, ostensible, manifest, patent

نصاعة *naṣā'a* purity; clearness, clarity (also, e.g., of argumentation, of expression)

ناصع *nāṣiʿ* pure, clear; plain, evident, obvious, ostensible, manifest, patent; white | ناصع البياض *n. al-bayāḍ* snow-white; حق ناصع (*ḥaqq*) plain truth; لهم جباه ناصعة approx.: they have a clean slate, their skirts are clean

نصف *naṣafa u i* (*naṣf*) to reach its midst (day), become noon **II** to divide in the middle, bisect, halve (ه s.th.) **III** to share (ه with s.o.) half of s.th. (ه), go halves (ه ه with s.o. in), share equally (ه ه with s.o. s.th.) **IV** to be just; to treat with justice (ه s.o.), be just (ه with s.o.); to see that justice is done (ه to s.o.), see that s.o. (ه) gets his right; to treat without discrimination (ه s.o.); to establish s.o.'s (ه) right (من in the face of a rival or oppressor); to serve (ه s.o.) **V** to submit, subordinate o.s. (ه to s.o.), serve (ه s.o.); to demand justice **VIII** to reach its midst, be in the middle, be midway, be half over (day, night, month, lifetime); to appeal for justice (من to), demand justice (من from); to do justice (ل to s.o.); to take vengeance, revenge o.s. (من on) **X** to demand justice

نصف *niṣf, nuṣf* pl. انصاف *anṣāf* half, moiety; middle | نصف الدائرة semicircle; نصف شهرى *n. šahrī* semimonthly; انصاف العذارى *a. al-ʿaḏārā* demi-vierges; نصف القرد *n. al-qird* lemur; نصف القطر *n. al-quṭr* radius; نصف الليل *n. al-lail* midnight; نصف النهار *n. an-nahār* midday, noon; القسط نصف السنوى *al-qisṭ n. as-sanawī* the semiannual installment

نصف *niṣf* (uninfl.) medium, middling; of medium size or quality; middle-aged

نصفى *niṣfī* half-, semi-, hemi-, demi- | تمثال نصفى (*timṯāl*) bust; شلل نصفى (*šalal*) hemiplegia; عمى نصفى (*ʿaman*) hemianopia

نصف *naṣaf* and نصفة *naṣafa* justice

نصيف *naṣīf* veil

تنصيف *tanṣīf* halving, bisection

مناصفة *munāṣafatan* half of it (of them), by halves, half and half, by equal shares, fifty-fifty

انصاف *inṣāf* justice, equity, fairness; just treatment

ناصف *nāṣif* pl. نصاف *nuṣṣāf*, نصف *naṣaf*, نصفة *naṣafa* servant

منصف *munaṣṣif* halving, bisecting, dividing into two equal parts

منصف *munṣif* a righteous, just man; equitable, fair, just

منتصف *muntaṣaf* middle | فى منتصف الطريق halfway, midway; منتصف الساعة العاشرة 9:30, half past nine; منتصف الليل *m. al-lail* midnight; منتصف النهار *m. an-nahār* midday, noon

نصل *naṣala a u* (نصول *nuṣūl*) to fall out, fall off, fall to the ground, drop; to fade (color); to get rid (من of), free o.s. (من from) **V** to free o.s. (من from), rid o.s. (من of); to renounce, disavow, shirk (من s.th.), withdraw (من from); to wash one's hands of s.th. (من), vindicate o.s., clear o.s., justify o.s. | تنصل من التبعة (*tabiʿa*) or تنصل من المسؤولية (*mas'ūlīya*) to refuse to take the responsibility, evade or shirk the responsibility

نصل *naṣl* (coll.; n. un. ة) pl. نصال *niṣāl*, انصل *anṣul*, نصول *nuṣūl* arrowhead, spearhead; blade of a knife or sword; ○ spread or surface of a leaf (*bot.*)

ناصل *nāṣil* falling, dropping; faded

نصمة *naṣama* icon, idol, graven image

ناصية *nāṣiya* pl. نواص *nawāṣin* forelock; fore part of the head; (street) corner | اخذ بناصيته to seize, take by the forelock, tackle properly (ه s.th.); ملك ناصيته to be or become master of s.th., have or get s.th. under control, master or control s.th.; امتلك نواصيه (*imtalaka*) do.; كل الآمال معقودة بناصيته all hopes are pinned on him; حجر الناصية *ḥajar an-n.* cornerstone, quoin

نض **naḍḍa** *i* (*naḍḍ*, نضيض *naḍīḍ*) to ripple, drip, percolate, ooze, leak, dribble, trickle **II** to move, shake (ه s.th.)

نض *naḍḍ* cash, hard money, specie, coin; نضا *naḍḍan* in (hard) cash

مال ناض *māl nāḍḍ* cash, hard money, specie, coin

نضب **naḍaba** *u* (نضوب *nuḍūb*) to seep away in the ground, be absorbed by the ground; to dry up, run dry, peter out; to be exhausted, be depleted, become less, diminish, decrease; to dwindle, decline; to die | لا ينضب inexhaustible, incessant **IV** to exhaust, drain, deplete, dry up (ه s.th.)

ناضب *nāḍib* pl. نضب *nuḍḍab* dried up, dry; arid, barren, sterile

نضج **naḍija** *a* (*naḍj*) to be or become ripe, ripen, mature (also fig., of an affair, of a personality, or the like); to be well-cooked, be or become well done (meat); to maturate (tumor) **IV** to bring to ripeness or maturity, make ripe, ripen (ه s.th.); to let (ه s.th.) ripen; to cook well, do well (ه s.th.)

نضج *naḍj*, *nuḍj* ripeness, maturity

نضوج *nuḍūj* ripeness, maturity

نضيج *naḍīj* ripe, mature; well-cooked, well done (food)

ناضج *nāḍij* ripe, mature; well-cooked, well done (food)

نضح **naḍaḥa** *i* (*naḍḥ*) to wet, moisten, sprinkle, spray, splash (ه ب s.th. with); to water (ه plants); to slake, quench (ه thirst); to defend, protect (عن s.th.); to justify, vindicate (عن s.th.), answer (عن for); — *a* (*naḍḥ*) to exude or ooze a fluid (ب); to sweat, perspire; to leak; to flow over (ب with); to shed, spill (ه s.th.); to effuse (ه s.th.)

نضاحة *naḍḍāḥa* sprinkler

منضح *minḍaḥ* shower, douche

منضحة *minḍaḥa* pl. مناضح *manāḍiḥ*² watering can; shower, douche

نضد **naḍada** *i* (*naḍd*) to pile up, stack, tier, arrange in layers (ه s.th.); to put in order, array, arrange (ه s.th.) **II** do.; to compose, set (ه s.th.; *typ.*)

نضد *naḍad* pl. انضاد *anḍād* bedstead; pile, stack, rows, tiers (e.g., of sacks)

نضد *nuḍud* tables

نضيد *naḍīd* arranged one above the other, tiered, in rows, in layers; orderly, tidy, regular

نضيدة *naḍīda* pl. نضائد *naḍā'id*² cushion, pillow, mattress

منضدة *minḍada* pl. *-āt*, مناضد *manāḍid*² table; worktable, desk; bedstead; framework, rack, stand

تنضيد *tanḍīd* typesetting, composition (*typ.*)

منضد *munaḍḍid* pl. *-ūn* typesetter, compositor (*typ.*)

منضد *munaḍḍad* forming a regular string, regularly set (esp., of teeth)

نضر **naḍara** *u*, **naḍira** *a* and **naḍura** *u* (نضرة *naḍra*, نضور *nuḍūr*, نضارة *naḍāra*) to be flourishing, blooming, verdant, fresh, beautiful; to be bright, brilliant, luminous, radiant **II** to make (ه s.th.) shine; to make (ه s.th.) bloom **V** to be verdant, blooming, in blossom

نضر *naḍir* flourishing, blooming, verdant, fresh, radiant, glowing

نضرة *naḍra* bloom, flower, freshness; glamor, splendor; beauty; health, vigor; opulence, wealth

نضار *nuḍār* (pure) gold

نضارة *naḍāra* bloom, flower, freshness; youthfulness; gracefulness, grace; health, vigor

نضير *naḍīr* flourishing, blooming, verdant, fresh, radiant, glowing; gold

ناضر *nāḍir* flourishing, blooming, verdant, fresh, radiant, glowing, beautiful

نضف *naḍaf* wild marjoram

نضف *naḍif* dirty, unclean

نضيف *naḍīf* dirty, unclean

نضل *naḍala u* (*naḍl*) to surpass, beat, defeat (ه s.o.) **III** to try to surpass (ه s.o.), vie, compete, contend, dispute (ه with s.o.); to defend (عن s.o.), stand up for s.o. (عن) **VI** to vie with one another

نضال *niḍāl* struggle, strife, dispute, controversy, fight, battle; contest, competition; defense, defensive battle

نضالى *niḍālī* combative, pugnacious

مناضلة *munāḍala* struggle, strife, dispute, controversy, fight, battle; contest, competition; defense, defensive battle

مناضل *munāḍil* fighter, combatant, defender

نضناض *naḍnāḍ* hissing viciously, flicking its tongue menacingly (snake)

(نضو) نضا *naḍā u* (*naḍw*) to take off (ه a garment, one's clothes); to undress (عن s.o.), نضا عن نفسه to get undressed; (*naḍw, nuḍūw*) to dwindle, wane, decline; to fade (esp., color) **II** to take off (ه a garment), strip (عن s.o.) of a garment (ه) **IV** to exhaust, jade, make lean (ه a riding animal); to wear out, wear thin (ه s.th.) **VIII** to unsheathe (ه a sword)

نضو *naḍw* pl. انضاء *anḍā'* a worn, tattered garment

نضو *niḍw* pl. انضاء *anḍā'* lean

نط *naṭṭa u* (*naṭṭ*) to spring, jump, leap; to skip, hop

نط *naṭṭ* jumping, jump | نط الحبل *n. al-ḥabl* skipping the rope (children's game); نط طولى (*ṭūlī*) broad jump

نطة *naṭṭa* (n. vic.) jump, leap

نطاط *naṭṭāṭ* jumper; a variety of grasshopper; restless, flighty, lightheaded

نطح *naṭaḥa a* (*naṭḥ*) to push, thrust (with the head or horns), butt **III** to bump (ه on or against s.th.), ram (ه s.th.); to touch (ه s.th.) **VI** and **VIII** to thrust or butt one another; to struggle (with one another)

نطح *naṭḥ* push(ing), thrust(ing), butting; el Nath, a star in the horn of Aries, α Arietis (*astron.*)

نطحة *naṭḥa* (n. vic.) push, thrust, butt

نطاح *naṭṭāḥ* given to butting, a butter

نطيح *naṭīḥ* butted

مناطحة *munāṭaḥa* bullfight

ناطح *nāṭiḥ*: ناطحة السحاب *n. as-saḥāb* pl. نواطح السحاب *nawāṭiḥ as-s.* skyscraper

نطر *naṭara u* (*naṭr*, نطارة *niṭāra*) to watch, guard (ه s.th.)

نطر *naṭr* watch, guard, protection

نطارة *niṭāra* watch, guard, protection

نطار *nuṭṭār* scarecrow

ناطر *nāṭir* pl. نطار *nuṭṭār*, نطراء *nuṭarā'*[2], نطرة *naṭara*, نواطر *nawāṭir*[2] guard, keeper, warden (esp., of plantations and vineyards), rural warden; lookout in a ship's crow's-nest

ناطور *nāṭūr* pl. نواطير *nawāṭīr*[2] guard, keeper, warden (esp., of plantations and vineyards), rural warden; lookout in a ship's crow's-nest

ناطورة *nāṭūra* (*syr.*) (woman) chaperon

نطرون *naṭrūn* natron, esp., the native product of Egypt which is extracted from the salt lakes of Wādī Naṭrūn northwest of Cairo

نطس **V** to examine thoroughly, investigate carefully, scrutinize (عن s.th.); to possess or employ much skill, be proficient (ب in s.th.)

نطس *naṭs, naṭus* well-informed, knowledgeable, experienced, seasoned, skilled

نطاسى *naṭāsī, niṭāsī* well-informed, knowledgeable, experienced, seasoned, skilled; (pl. نطس *nuṭus*) a skilled, experienced physician

نطع pass. *nuṭiʿa* to change color, turn pale V to be pigheaded, obstinate

نطع *naṭʿ, niṭʿ* pl. انطاع *anṭāʿ*, نطوع *nuṭūʿ* leather mat used as a tablecloth and gaming board, in former times also during executions

نطع *niṭʿ, niṭaʿ* pl. نطوع *nuṭūʿ* hard palate

الحروف النطعية *al-ḥurūf an-niṭʿiya* the sounds ت, د and ط (*phon.*)

نطف *naṭafa u i* (*naṭf*, تنطاف *tanṭāf*, نطفان *naṭafān*, نطافة *niṭāfa*) to dribble, trickle

نطفة *nuṭfa* pl. نطف *nuṭaf* drop; sperm

نطق *naṭaqa u* (*nuṭq*, نطوق *nuṭūq*, منطق *manṭiq*) to articulate; to talk, speak, utter (ب s.th.); to pronounce (ب s.th.) | نطق بكلمة (*bi-kalima*) to say a word II to make (ه s.o.) speak or pronounce; to gird, girdle (ه s.o.) IV to make (ه s.o.) speak or talk V to gird o.s.; to be surrounded X to question (ه s.o.); to interrogate, examine, cross-examine (ه s.o.)

نطق *nuṭq* articulated speech; pronunciation; word, saying, utterance; order, ordinance, decree | صدر النطق السامى ب it was decreed by order of His Majesty that ...; نطق بالحكم (*ḥukm*) pronouncement of sentence; فاقد النطق dumfounded, speechless

نطقى *nuṭqī* phonetic(al)

نطاق *niṭāq* pl. نطق *nuṭuq* girth, girdle, belt; ○ garrison belt; circle, ring, enclosure; limit, boundary; range, extent, scope, compass, sphere, domain, purview; cordon | نطاق الجوزاء *n. al-jauzāʾ* Orion's Belt (*astron.*); نطاق الحصار blockade ring; واسع النطاق comprehensive; extensive, far-reaching; large-scale

منطق *manṭiq* (faculty of) speech; manner of speaking, diction, enunciation; eloquence; logic | ليس من المنطق ان it is illogical to ...; علم المنطق *ʿilm al-m.* logic

منطقى *manṭiqī* logical; dialectic(al); — (pl. مناطقة *manāṭiqa*) logician; dialectician

منطق *minṭaq* pl. مناطق *manāṭiq*[2] belt, girdle

منطقة *minṭaqa* pl. مناطق *manāṭiq*[2] belt, girdle; zone; vicinity, range, sphere, district, area, territory; ○ (*mil.*) sector | ○ منطقة الاحتلال occupied territory; المنطقة الحارة (*ḥārra*) the Torrid Zone, the tropics; ○ منطقة البترول oil area, oil fields; منطقة البروج the zodiac (*astron.*); منطقة الجوزاء *m. al-jauzāʾ* Orion's Belt (*astron.*); ○ منطقة حرام (*ḥarām*) or منطقة ممنوعة prohibited area; منطقة الحرب *m. al-ḥarb* war zone; ○ منطقة حرة (*ḥurra*) free zone; ○ منطقة صماء (*ṣammāʾ*) dead zone (of radio waves); منطقة صناعية (*ṣināʿiya*) industrial area; ○ منطقة الضرب *m. aḍ-ḍarb* field of fire; ○ منطقة كروية (*kurawīya*) spherical zone; المنطقتان المعتدلتان (*muʿtadilatān*) the two Temperate Zones; ○ منطقة مجردة من التجهيزات الحربية (*mujarrada, ḥarbīya*) demilitarized zone; منطقة النفوذ sphere of influence

منطقى *minṭaqī* zonal

منطيق *minṭīq* very eloquent

استنطاق *istinṭāq* examination, interrogation, hearing; questioning

ناطق *nāṭiq* talking, speaking; endowed with the faculty of speech; eloquent; plain, distinct, clear; endowed with reason, reasonable, rational (being); speaker (also, e.g., in parliament); spokesman | الناطقون بالضاد the Arabic-speaking portion of mankind (lit.: those who pronounce the *ḍād*); حيوان ناطق (*ḥaya-*

wān) rational being; دليل ناطق conclusive evidence; شريط ناطق sound film; جريدة ناطقة newsreel

منطوق *manṭūq* pronounced, uttered, expressed; wording; text; statement; formulation | بالمنطوق according to the text; expressly, explicitly, unequivocally; منطوق الحكم *m. al-ḥukm* dispositive portion of the judgment (*jur.*); منطوق العقد *m. al-ʿaqd* the exact terms of the contract; منطوق القانون text of the law, legal text; منطوق الكلمة *m. al-kalima* literal meaning of a word

مستنطق *mustanṭiq* examining magistrate

نطل **naṭala** u (*naṭl*) to squeeze out; to apply warm compresses (ه to), foment, bathe with warm water or medicated liquid (ه s.th.)

نطول *naṭūl* warm compress; fomentation, lavation or bath in a medicated liquid

نطنط **naṭnaṭa** to hop up and down, skip

نظر **naẓara** u (*naẓar*, منظر *manẓar*) to perceive with the eyes, see, view, eye, regard (ه, ه or الى s.o., s.th.), look, gaze, glance (ه, ه or الى at), watch, observe, notice (ه, ه or الى s.o., s.th.), pay attention (ه, ه or الى to); to expect (ه s.th.); to envisage, consider, contemplate, purpose (ه or فى s.th.); to have in mind, have in view (الى s.th.), put one's mind, direct one's attention (الى to s.th.); to take up, try, hear (فى a case; court), look into a case (فى), examine (ه or فى a case); to judge, rule, decide (بين between two litigant parties); to take care (ل of s.o.), help (ل s.o.), stand by s.o. (ل), look after s.o. (ل) | نظر اليه شزرا (*šazran*) to give s.o. a sidelong glance, look askance at s.o.; فى القضية or نظر القضية (*qaḍīya*) to try a case (*jur.*); نظر فى طلب فلان (*ṭalabi f.*) to process s.o.'s application, take care of s.o.'s application; نظر من فرجة المفتاح or فوهة المفتاح (*furjati l-miftāḥ*, *fūhati l-m.*) to peep through the keyhole; انظر بعده *unẓur baʿdahū* see below! انظر ظهره (*ẓahrahū*) see reverse! please turn over! II to make comparisons, draw parallels (بين between) III to equal (ه, ه s.o., s.th.), be equal (ه, ه to s.o., to s.th.); to equalize, put on an equal footing (ب ه, ه s.o., s.th. with), equate, liken, compare (ب ه, ه s.o., s.th. to); to vie, compete, be in competition (ه with s.o.), rival (ه s.o.); to argue, debate, dispute (ه with s.o.), point out (ه ب to s.o. s.th.) by way of argument or objection, confront (ه ب s.o. with); to superintend, supervise (ه s.th.) IV to grant (ه s.o.) a delay or respite V to regard, watch or observe attentively (ه, ه s.o., s.th.), look closely (ه, ه at s.o., at s.th.), scrutinize (ه, ه s.o., s.th.); to bide one's time, wait VI to face each other, lie opposite; to be symmetrical (*math.*); to dispute, argue (with one another); to quarrel (على about), fight (على over s.th.); to contend (with each other) (على for s.th.), contest each other's right (على to s.th.) VIII to wait (ه for s.o.), expect (ه, ه s.o., s.th.), await, anticipate (ه s.th.); to look closely (ه at s.o.); to look on expectantly, bide one's time, wait | انتظر الشىء الكبير من to expect much of ...; انتظر من ورائه كل خير (*warāʾihī kulla ḵairin*) to set the greatest expectations in s.th. X to wait, await, expect; to have patience, be patient; to request a delay or respite; to ask (ه s.o.) to wait, keep (ه s.o.) waiting

نظر *naẓar* pl. انظار *anẓār* seeing, eyesight, vision; look, glance, gaze; sight; outlook, prospect; view; aspect; appearance, evidence; insight, discernment, penetration; perception; contemplation; examination (فى of); inspection, study, perusal; consideration, reflection; philosophical speculation; theory; handling (فى of a matter); trial, hearing (في of a case, in court); supervision, control, surveillance; competence, jurisdiction; attention, heed, regard, notice, observance, respect, consideration, care | نظرا الى (or ل) in view of, with a view to, in regard to, with respect to, in consideration of, on the basis of, due to, because of, for; بالنظر ل do.; بصرف النظر عن (*bi-ṣarfi n-n.*) or بقطع النظر عن (*bi-qaṭ'i n-n.*) regardless of, irrespective of; تحت النظر under consideration, being studied, being dealt with; دون نظر الى irrespective of, regardless of; في نظرى in my eyes, in my opinion; للنظر في for the study of, for consideration, for further examination of, for handling ..., for action on ...; ○ النظر الى الحياة (*ḥayāh*) weltanschauung; اعادة النظر *i'ādat an-n.* re-examination, reconsideration, resumption, retrial, revision; اهل النظر *ahl an-n.* speculative thinkers; theoreticians, theorists; بعيد النظر or طويل النظر farsighted; قصر النظر *qiṣar an-n.* shortsightedness; قصير النظر shortsighted; المحكمة ذات النظر (*maḥkama*) the court of competent jurisdiction; مسألة فيها نظر (*mas'ala*) an unsettled, open question, an unsolved problem; من له نظر (*man*) s.o. noteworthy, a distinguished man; the responsible, or authorized, person; اخذ بالنظر to catch the eye; ادار نظره في (*adāra*) to let one's eyes roam over ...; تابع (راجع) بالنظر ل falling to the responsibility of, under the jurisdiction of, subject to the authority of; سارق النظر اليه or سارقه النظر or استرق النظر اليه (*nāẓara*) to glance furtively at s.o., give s.o. a surreptitious look; في هذا الامر نظر this matter calls for careful study, will have to be considered; قطع النظر عن to take no account of, disregard s.th.; هو تحت نظر فلان he is under the protection of so-and-so, he is patronized by so-and-so

نظر *niẓr* similar, like; equal | عديم النظر unparalleled, unequaled, matchless, unique of his (its) kind

نظرة *naẓra* pl. *naẓarāt* look, glance; sight, view; viewing, contemplation (الى of s.th.); pl. نظرات (philosophical) reflections

نظرة *naẓira* delay, postponement, deferment (of an obligation)

نظرى *naẓarī* optic(al); visual; theoretic(al); speculative

نظرية *naẓarīya* theory; theorem; reflection, meditation, contemplation

نظير *naẓīr* pl. نظراء *nuẓarā'*[2], f. pl. نظائر *naẓā'ir*[2] similar, like, same, equal, matching, corresponding, comparable; an equivalent; facing, opposite, parallel; (with foll. genit.) in the manner of, in the same manner as, just like, just as; transcript, copy | نظير *naẓīra* (prep.) as a compensation for, in consideration of, in return for, in exchange for, for, on, e.g., نظير دفع خمسين مليما (*daf' k. malīman*) on paying 50 millièmes; نظراؤه people of his kind, people like him; نظير السمت *n. as-samt* or النظير nadir (*astron.*); مقطوع (or منقطع) (*munqaṭi'*) النظير incomparable; ليس له نظير unparalleled, unequaled, matchless, unique of his (its) kind

نظيرة *naẓīra* head, foremost rank | في نظيرة (with foll. genit.) at the head of

نظار *naẓẓār* keen-eyed; (pl. نظارة *naẓẓāra*) spectator, onlooker

نظارة *naẓẓāra* pl. *-āt* field glass, binocular; telescope, spyglass; (pair of) eyeglasses, spectacles (occasionally also pl. نظارات with singular meaning: a pair of eyeglasses); (pair of) goggles | نظارة فردية (*fardīya*) or نظارة واحدة eyeglass, monocle; ○ نظارة معظمة (*mu'aẓẓima*) magnifying glass; نظارة الميدان *n. al-maidān* field glass

نظاراتى *naẓẓārātī* optometrist; optician

نظارة *niẓāra* supervision, control, inspection, management, administration, direction; ministry (now obsolete)

ناظور *nāẓūr* field glass

منظر *manẓar* pl. مناظر *manāẓir*² sight; view, panorama; look(s), appearance, aspect; prospect, outlook, perspective; an object seen or viewed, photographic object; scene (of a play); spectacle; stage setting, set, scenery; place commanding a sweeping view; lookout, watchtower | منظر عام (*ʿāmm*) general view, panorama, landscape, scenery; ○ مناظر خارجية (*ḵārijīya*) shots on location (in motion-picture making); مناظر طبيعية (*ṭabīʿīya*) scenic views, scenery, landscapes

منظرة *manẓara* pl. مناظر *manāẓir*² place commanding a scenic view; view, scenery, landscape, panorama; watchtower, observatory; guestroom, reception room, drawing room, parlor

○ منظر *minẓar* (pair of) eyeglasses, spectacles; telescope, spyglass

منظار *minẓār* pl. مناظير *manāẓīr*² telescope, spyglass; magnifying glass; mirror, speculum, -scope (e.g., laryngoscope) | منظار معظم (*muʿaẓẓim*) magnifying glass; رقب بمنظار اسود (*aswada*) to have a pessimistic outlook, look on the dark side of everything

مناظرة *munāẓara* emulation, rivalry, competition; quarrel, argument, altercation, debate, dispute, discussion, controversy; supervision, control, inspection

تناظر *tanāẓur* difference of opinion, squabble, wrangle, altercation; symmetry (*math.*)

انتظار *intiẓār* waiting, wait; expectation | على غير انتظار unexpectedly

ناظر *nāẓir* pl. نظار *nuẓẓār* observer, viewer, spectator, onlooker; overseer, supervisor; inspector; manager, director, superintendent, administrator, principal, chief; (cabinet) minister (now obsolete) | ناظر الوقف *n. al-waqf* trustee of a wakf, administrator of a religious endowment

ناظرة *nāẓira* administratress, directress, manageress, headmistress, matron

ناظر *nāẓir* and ناظرة *nāẓira* pl. نواظر *nawāẓir*² eye; look, glance | بين ناظريه (*nāẓiraihi*) before his eyes

منظور *manẓūr* seen; visible; foreseen, anticipated, expected; supervised, under supervision, controlled; envied, regarded with the evil eye; under consideration (case), pending (complaint, lawsuit; امام in a court) | منظور اليه one under supervision, subordinate, underling, protégé, charge, ward, pupil; غير منظور invisible; unforeseen, unexpected; أدوات منظورة (*adawāt*) visual training aids; دعوى منظورة (*daʿwā*) pending lawsuit; الشخص المنظور فى امره (*šaḵṣ*) person whose case is under consideration

مناظر *munāẓir* similar, like, equal; competitor, rival, adversary, opponent (esp., in a discussion); interlocutor

نظف **naẓufa** *u* (نظافة *naẓāfa*) to be clean, cleanly, neat, tidy **II** to clean, cleanse, polish (ه s.th.) **V** to clean o.s., become clean

نظافة *naẓāfa* cleanness, cleanliness, neatness, tidiness

نظيف *naẓīf* pl. نظفاء *nuẓafāʾ*², نظاف *niẓāf* clean, neat, tidy; well-groomed, well-tended

انظف *anẓaf*² cleaner, neater

تنظيف *tanẓīf* pl. *-āt* cleaning, cleansing | تنظيف الاظفار manicure

نظلى **nazlī** (*eg.*) delicate, feminine

نظم **naẓama** *i* (*naẓm*, نظام *niẓām*) and **II** to string (ه pearls); to put in order, to order (ه s.th.); to array, arrange, classify, file (ه s.th.); to adjust (ه s.th.); to set, regulate (ه s.th.); to tune (ه an instrument); to lay out, get ready, prepare (ه s.th.); to set right, rectify, correct (ه s.th.); to put together, group, make up, assemble (ه s.th.); to organize (ه s.th.); to stage (ه s.th.); to compose (one's words) metrically, poetize, versify, write poetry **V** and **VI** to be strung; to be ordered, be in good order, be well-arranged, be well-organized **VIII** do.; to be classified; to affiliate (ف with); to enter, join (ف an organization, a corporation); to permeate, pervade (ه s.o., ه s.th.); to come over s.o. (ه), seize, befall, overcome (ه s.o., ه s.o.'s limbs, s.o.'s body; of a sentiment, tremor, shudder, etc.)

نظم *naẓm* order; arrangement; system; institution, organization; string of pearls; verse, poetry

نظام *niẓām* pl. *-āt*, نظم *nuẓum*, انظمة *anẓima* proper arrangement, regularity; conformity, congruity; methodical, organic structure; organization; order; method; system; rule, statute, law; system of regulations | على هذا النظام along this line, in this manner; نظام الاجانب alien status; alien act; نظام الاحوال الشخصية (*šakṣīya*) personal statute (*jur.*); نظام اساسى (*asāsī*) (basic) constitutional law, statutes, constitution; نظام اقتصادى (*iqtiṣādī*) economic system; نظام البادية *n. al-bādiya* agricultural system; نظام البوليس والادارة *n. al-būlīs wa-l-idāra* police and administrative system; نظام جوازات السفر *n. jawāzāt as-safar* passport system; نظام الحياة *n. al-ḥayāh* (way of) life; النظام الرأسمالى (*ra'smālī*) the capitalistic economic system; النظام العام (*'āmm*) public order; نظام المرور traffic laws

نظامى *niẓāmī* orderly, regular, normal; methodical, systematic; regular (army)

تنظيم *tanẓīm* arrangement; readjustment, reorganization, reform; control, regulation, adjustment; organization; tactics; road construction (*Eg.*) | تنظيم المرور traffic control; اعادة التنظيم *i'ādat at-t.* reorganization

انتظام *intiẓām* order, regularity; methodicalness, systematic arrangement | بانتظام regularly, accurately; فى انتظام regular, fixed, ordered, methodical, systematic, orderly, normal

ناظم *nāẓim* arranger; organizer, adjuster; regulator; versifier, poet; (pl. نواظم *nawāẓim*²) weir, barrage (*Ir.*)

منظوم *manẓūm* ordered, orderly, tidy; metrical, poetical; poem; pl. *-āt* poetries, poetical works

منظومة *manẓūma* treatise in verse, didactic poem; row, rank

منظم *munaẓẓim* arranger, organizer; promoter, sponsor

منظم *munaẓẓam* arranged, ordered, kept in order, orderly, tidy; neat, well-tended, well-kept; systematically arranged, systematized; regular | جيش منظم (*jaiš*) regular army; غير منظم irregular

منظمة *munaẓẓama* pl. *-āt* organization | منظمة التغذية والزراعة (*m. at-taḡḏiya*) Food and Agriculture Organization, F.A.O.

منتظم *muntaẓim* regular; even, uniform, steady, orderly; methodical; systematic | ○ موجات منتظمة (*maujāt*) uniform waves (*radio*)

نعب *na'aba a i* (*na'b*, نعيب *na'īb*) to croak, caw (raven); — *a* (*na'b*) to speed along

نعاب *nu'āb* croak(ing), caw (of a raven)

نعاب *na''āb* croaking, cawing; ominous, ill-boding

نعت *na'ata a* (*na't*) to describe, characterize (ه, ه s.o., s.th.), qualify (ه s.th.)

نعت *na't* description, qualification, characterization; — (pl. نعوت *nu'ūt*) quality, property, attribute, characteristic; descriptive, qualifying word, qualifier; attribute (*gram.*); epithet

نعتى *na'tī* descriptive, qualifying, qualificative

منعوت *man'ūt* substantive accompanied by an attribute

نعجة **na'ja** pl. **na'ajāt**, نعاج **ni'āj** female sheep, ewe

نعر **na'ara a i** (نعير **na'īr**, نعار **nu'ār**) to grunt; to cry, scream, roar, bellow; to spurt, gush forth (blood from a wound)

نعرة *na'ra* noise, din, clamor, roar

نعرة *nu'ra, nu'ara* nose

نعرة *nu'ara* pl. *-āt*, نعر *nu'ar* horsefly, gadfly

نعرة *na'ara, nu'ara* pl. *-āt* haughtiness, arrogance, pride | نعرة اقليمية (*iqlīmīya*) jingoism, chauvinism

نعار *nu''ār* noisy, uproarious, vociferous, clamoring, shouting; agitator, rabble rouser

نعير *na'īr* noise, din, clamor, shouting; bellowing, mooing, lowing (esp., of cattle)

نعارة *na'āra, na''āra* earthen jug (sometimes with two handles), pot

ناعور *nā'ūr* ○ hemophilia

ناعورة *nā'ūra* pl. نواعير *nawā'īr*[2] noria, Persian wheel

نعس **na'asa a u** (**na's**) to be sleepy, drowsy; to take a nap, to doze, slumber; to be dull, listless, slack, stagnant (market, trade) **II** and **IV** to make sleepy, put to sleep (ه s.o.) **VI** to pretend to be sleepy or asleep; to doze, be sleepy, feel drowsy

نعسة *na'sa* doze, nap, slumber

نعاس *nu'ās* sleepiness, drowsiness; lethargy

نعسان *na'sān*[2] sleepy, drowsy

ناعس *nā'is* pl. نعس *nu's* sleepy, drowsy; dozing, slumbering

نعش **na'aša a** (**na'š**), **II** and **IV** to raise, lift up; to revive, reanimate; to refresh, invigorate, animate, arouse, stimulate, enliven, inspirit (ه s.o.) **VIII** to rise from a fall; to recover, recuperate from illness; to be animated, be refreshed, be stimulated, be invigorated, be strengthened, revive, come to new life

نعش *na'š* bier | بنات نعش الصغرى *banāt n. aṣ-ṣuḡrā* Ursa Minor (*astron.*); بنات نعش الكبرى *b. n. al-kubrā* Ursa Major (*astron.*)

نعشة *na'ša*: نعشة الموت *n. al-maut* euphoria; swan song, death song

انعاش *in'āš* animation, reanimation, resuscitation, restoration to life; refreshment; reconstruction, restoration | ○ انعاش اقتصادى (*iqtiṣādī*) economic boost

انتعاش *inti'āš* resurgence, revival; animation, invigoration, stimulation, refreshment, recreation

منعش *mun'iš* animating, refreshing, invigorating, restorative

نعظ **na'aẓa a** (**na'ẓ, na'aẓ**, نعوظ **nu'ūẓ**) to be erect (penis) **IV** to be sexually excited

ناعوظ *nā'ūẓ* exciting sexual desire, sexually stimulating, aphrodisiac

نعق **na'aqa a i** (**na'q**, نعيق **na'īq**) to croak, caw (raven); to bleat (sheep); to cry, scream, screech

ناعق *nā'iq*: كل ناعق وناعر all that is alive and astir, everybody and his brother, every Tom, Dick and Harry

نعل **na'ala a** (**na'l**), **II** and **IV** to furnish with shoes (ه s.o.), shoe (ه s.o., ‌ه a horse); — **na'ila a** (**na'al**) to be shod **V** = **na'ila** **VIII** to wear sandals; to wear shoes, be shod

نعل *na'l* pl. نعال *ni'āl*, انعل *an'ul* sandal; shoe; horseshoe

ناعل *nā'il* shod; soled

نعم *na'ama u a* and *na'ima a* (نعمة *na'ma*, منعم *man'am*) to live in comfort and luxury, lead a life of ease, lead a comfortable and carefree life; to be delighted (ب by), be happy, be glad (ب about, at), be pleased (ب with), delight, take pleasure (ب in); to enjoy, savor, taste, experience (ب s.th.) | نعم بالا ب (*na'ima bālan*) to feel serene and confident about ...; — *na'ima a* (*na'am*) to be green and tender (twig), to be or become fine, powdery; — *na'uma u* (نعومة *nu'ūma*) to be soft, tender, smooth **II** to smooth, soften (ه s.th.); to pulverize, powder (ه s.th.); to accustom to luxury (ه s.o.); to pamper, coddle, effeminate, provide with a life of ease (ه s.o.) **IV** to make good, nice, comfortable, pleasant (ه or ب s.th.); to give (ب على s.o. s.th.), bestow, confer (ب على upon s.o. s.th.); to bestow favors (على upon s.o.), be graciously disposed (على toward s.o.); to apply o.s., devote o.s. (فى to s.th.), take great pains (فى with s.th.) | انعم الله صباحك (*ṣabāḥaka*) good morning! انعم النظر فى (*naẓara*) to look closely at, scrutinize s.th., regard s.th. attentively, pore over s.th., become engrossed in, ponder s.th. **V** to live in luxury, lead a life of ease and comfort; to enjoy (ب s.th.)

نعم *ni'ma* with foll. indeclinable noun with article and nominative ending. what a perfect ..., wonderful ...! truly, an excellent ... | نعم الرجل زيد *n. r-rajulu zaidun* what an excellent man Zaid is! نعم الشباب شبابهم *n. š-šabābu šabābuhum* what a wonderful youth they have! انه نعم الخليل *innahū n. l-ḵalīlu* he is a wonderful friend indeed! فبها ونعمت *fa-bihā wa-ni'mat* in that case it's all right; نعم ما فعلت (*fa'alta*) well done!

نعم *na'am* yes! yes indeed! certainly! surely! (introducing a verbal clause:) to be sure ...; *na'am?* (*colloq.*) I beg your pardon? what did you say?

نعم *na'am* pl. انعام *an'ām* grazing livestock (sheep, camels, cattle, goats)

نعمة *na'ma* life of ease, good living; amenity, comfort; prosperity; happiness; enjoyment, pleasure, delight

نعمة *ni'ma* pl. نعم *ni'am*, انعم *an'um*, نعمات *ni'māt*, *ni'imāt* benefit, blessing, boon, benefaction, favor, grace, kindness | بنعمة الله by the grace of God; واسع النعمة very well off, wealthy, rich; النعم الثلاث the Three Graces; ولى نعمته (نعمه) *walīy ni'matihī* (*ni'amihī*) his benefactor

نعمى *nu'mā* happiness

نعماء *na'mā'* favor, good will, grace | فى النعماء والبأساء (*wa-l-ba'sā'*) in good and bad days

نعمان *nu'mān* blood | شقائق النعمان anemone (*bot.*)

نعام *na'ām* (coll.; n. un. ة) pl. نعائم *na'ā'im*[2] ostrich (*zool.*)

نعيم *na'īm* amenity, comfort, ease, happiness, felicity; gentle, tranquil, peaceful | نعيم الله the grace of God, the blessings of God

النعائم *an-na'ā'im* name of several stars in Sagitta (*astron.*)

نعومة *nu'ūma* softness, smoothness, tenderness, delicacy, fineness; finely ground state, powdery consistency | من (منذ) نعومة اظفاره from his earliest youth, since his tender age

انعم *an'am*[2] softer

منعام *min'ām* munificent benefactor

مناعم *manā'im*[2] favors, blessings, boons; amenities, comforts, pleasures, delights

تنعيم *tan'īm* pampering, coddling, effemination

انعام *in'ām* act of kindness, favor, benefaction; gift, donation, grant, distinction, bestowal, award | انعام النظر *i. an-naẓar* careful examination, serious consideration

ناعم *nāʿim* soft; smooth; tender; fine, powdery | ناعم الظفر *n. aẓ-ẓufr* young, youthful, tender; سكر ناعم (*sukkar*) powdered sugar

منعم *munʿim* donor, benefactor

نعنع *naʿnaʿ* and نعناع *naʿnāʿ* mint (*bot.*); peppermint

نعناعى *naʿnāʿī* peppermint (adj.)

نعى *naʿā a* (*naʿy, naʿīy,* نعيان *naʿyān*) to announce the death (ه of s.o., الى to s.o.); to hold s.th. (ه) against s.o. (على), reproach, blame (ه على s.o. for); — *naʿā i* to lament, wail; to deplore (ه s.th.)

نعى *naʿīy* one who announces s.o.'s death; blame, reproach

نعية *naʿya* pl. *naʿayāt* news of s.o.'s death, death notice

منعى *manʿan* and منعاة *manʿāh* pl. مناع *manāʿin* news of s.o.'s death

نغبة *naḡba, nuḡba* swallow, gulp, draught

نغبشة *naḡbaša* noise

نغز *naḡaza a* (*naḡz*) to tickle (ه s.o.); to prick (ه s.o., with a needle, or the like); to sow dissension, stir up enmity (بين between)

نغش *naḡaša a* (*naḡš,* نغشان *naḡašān*) to be agitated, be shaken III to play (ه with s.o.), tease (ه s.o.), dally, flirt (ه with s.o.) V = I

نغشة *naḡša* pl. *naḡašāt* motion; shaking

نغاش *nuḡāš* and نغاشى *nuḡāšī* very small; midget, dwarf

نغاشة *naḡāša* banter, raillery, teasing, playfulness; elegance

نغص II and IV to disturb, ruffle, spoil (على s.o.'s ه pleasure, joy, life, or the like), make loathsome (ه على to s.o. s.th.) V to be disturbed, be ruffled, be spoiled, become loathsome

منغص *munaḡḡiṣ* exciting

نغل *naḡila a* (*naḡal*) to fester, suppurate (wound) | نغل قلبه على (*qalbuhū*) to harbor resentment against, hold a grudge against

نغل *naḡl, naḡil* illegitimate child; bastard

نغيل *naḡīl* illegitimate child; bastard

نغولة *nuḡūla* illegitimacy, bastardy

نغم *naḡama u i* and *naḡima a* (*naḡm, naḡam*) to hum a tune; to sing II and V do.

نغم *naḡm* and *naḡam* pl. انغام *anḡām* tune, air, melody; voice, part (*mus.*, of a contrapuntal composition); timbre, tone color; sound, tone

نغمة *naḡma, naḡama* pl. *naḡamāt* tone; sound; musical note, tone (of the gamut; *mus.*); inflection, intonation, melody; song, chant

تناغم *tanāḡum* symphonia, concord (of sounds)

منغوم *manḡūm* melodious (voice)

(نغو) نغا *naḡā u* (*naḡw*) and نغى *naḡā i* (*naḡy*) to speak (الى to s.o.) III to whisper (ه in s.o.'s ear); to talk gently, kindly, tenderly (ه to s.o., esp., to a child); to flatter, court (ه s.o.); to twitter (bird); (*eg.*) to babble (child)

نف *naffa i* to blow one's nose; to snuff

نفة *naffa* (*tun.*) pinch of snuff; snuff

نفاف *naffāf* snuffer

نفث *nafaṯa u i* (*nafṯ*) to spit, spit out, expectorate, discharge, cough out (ه s.th.); to squirt out (ه its venom; of a snake); to exhale, puff out (ه the smoke; of a smoker); to utter, voice (ه s.th.); to exude and inspire (ه في with s.th. s.o.), transfuse (ه في s.th. into s.o.)

نفث *nafṯ* expectoration; saliva, spittle | نفث الشيطان *n. aš-šaiṭān* erotic poetry

نفثة *nafṯa* pl. *nafaṯāt* expectoration; saliva, spittle; pl. expectorated or ejected matter, expectorations, discharge, outpourings, emissions, effusions; invectives, accusations | نفثات الاقلام literary productions

نفاثة *nufāṯa* saliva, spittle

(طائرة) نفاثة *naffāṯa* jet plane

نفاثى *naffāṯī* jet- (in compounds) | تسيير نفاثى jet propulsion

نفاثة *naffāṯa* pl. *-āt* woman who spits on the knots (in exercising a form of Arabian witchcraft in which women tie knots in a cord and spit upon them with an imprecation; Kor. 113,4); sorceress

نفج *nafaja u* (*nafj*, نفجان *nafajān*, نفوج *nufūj*) to spring up and take to flight (game); to jump, leap, bound; to vaunt, brag, boast **V** to brag, boast **VIII** = **I**

نفج *nafj* bragging, boasting

نفاج *naffāj* braggart, show-off; snob

نافجة *nāfija* pl. نوافج *nawāfij*[2] musk bag; container for musk

نفح *nafaḥa a* (*nafḥ*, نفحان *nafaḥān*, نفاح *nufāḥ*) to spread, be diffused (fragrance), exhale a pleasant smell, be fragrant; to blow (wind); to make s.o. (ه) a present of (ب), present (ب ه s.o. with); to treat (ه ه s.o. to s.th.) **III** to protect, defend (عن s.th.)

نفحة *nafḥa* pl. *nafaḥāt* breeze, gust; breath; diffusing odor; fragrance, perfume scent; gift, present

منفحة *minfaḥa* rennet

نفخ *nafaḵa u* (*nafḵ*) to blow, puff; to breathe; to blow up, inflate, fill with air (ه or فى s.th.); ○ to pump up, fill (a tire); ○ to fill with gas (balloon); to blow (ه tunes, فى on an instrument); to breathe s.th. (ه) into s.o. (فى), inspire (ه فى s.o. with); to inflate, puff up, elate, flush with success, fill with pride (ه s.o.) | نفخ فى البوق (*būq*) to blow the trumpet; نفخ فى روحه (*rūḥihī*) to animate, inspirit s.o.; نفخ فى صورته (*ṣūratihī*) to bring s.th. into being, give birth to s.th.; نفخ فى زمارة روحه (*zammārati rūḥihī*) to rouse s.o.'s temper; نفخ الشمعة (*šam'a*) to blow out a candle; نفخ شدقيه (*šidqaihi*) to be puffed up, become inflated **VIII** to be blown up, inflated, filled with air; to swell; to puff up, become inflated | انتفخ سحره (*saḥruhū*) and انتفخت مساحره (*masāḥiruhū*) his lungs became inflated (out of fear or pride)

نفخ *nafḵ* blowing, blowing up, inflation, pumping up, filling with air

نفخة *nafḵa* (n. vic.) blow, puff; breath; gust; distention, inflation, swelling; conceit, overweeningness, haughtiness | نفخة كذابة (كاذبة) (*kaḏḏāba*) self-conceit, vainglory, bumptiousness

نفاخ *naffāḵ* flatulent

نفاخ *nuffāḵ* swelling

نفاخة *nuffāḵa* bladder; bubble

منفخ *minfaḵ* pl. منافخ *manāfiḵ*[2] bellows

منفاخ *minfāḵ* pl. منافيخ *manāfīḵ*[2] bellows; air pump, tire pump; blowpipe

تنفخ *tanaffuḵ* inflatedness, inflation; bumptiousness, bumptious behavior

انتفاخ *intifāḵ* process of being inflated; distention, inflation, swelling, protuberance; flatulence, meteorism (*med.*) | انتفاخ الرئة *int. ar-ri'a* pulmonic emphysema

نافخ *nāfiḵ* blowing; blower; flatulent | ما بالدار نافخ ضرمة (*n. ḍarmatin*) there is not a soul in the house

منفوخ *manfūḵ* blown up, puffed up, inflated; swollen; pumped up, inflated;

paunchy, obese, fat; conceited, self-conceited, overweening, snobbish

منتفخ *muntafiḵ* blown up, puffed up, inflated; swollen

نفد **nafida** *a* (*nafad*, نفاد *nafād*) to be exhausted, depleted, used up; to run out, come to an end, dwindle away; to be out of print | نفد لديه معين الصبر (*ma'īn aṣ-ṣabr*) to be at the end of one's patience **IV** and **X** to use up, consume, spend, exhaust, drain, deplete (ه s.th.); to taste thoroughly, enjoy to the full (ه s.th.) | استنفد كل وسع (*kulla wus'in*) to exhaust, or avail o.s. of, every possibility

نفدة *nafda* pl. *nafadāt* entry (in an account book), booked item

نفاد *nafād* exhaustion, consumption, depletion (of stores), dwindling, wastage, waste

النفود *an-nafūd* Nafud (desert in N Nejd)

نافد *nāfid*: نافد الصبر *n. aṣ-ṣabr* impatient

نافدة *nāfida* void, vacuum

نفذ **nafaḏa** *u* (نفاذ *nafāḏ*, نفوذ *nufūḏ*) to pierce, bore (ه s.th. or من through s.th.), penetrate (ه, من s.th.), go or pass (ه, ب through s.th.); to penetrate (الى into), get through, pass through (الى to); ○ (*mil.*) to break through, fight one's way through the enemy (من or فى); to get (الى to s.o.), arrive (الى at s.o.'s place), reach (الى s.o.); to lead (الى to), give, open (الى on; of a door or window); to communicate, be connected (الى with; of a building, lot, premises), join; to be carried out, be executed, be legally valid, be effective, be operative, be enforceable, be executable, be executory; to do well or skillfully (فى s.th.) **II** and **IV** to cause (ه s.th.) to pierce or penetrate; to carry out, execute, accomplish, effect (ه s.th., also, an idea), do, perform, fulfill, discharge (ه a duty); to realize, implement, carry into effect (ه a plan, a project, ideas); to enforce (ه a resolution); to carry through (ه a program); to execute, carry out (ه a sentence; فى against s.o.); to transmit, convey, send, dispatch, forward (ه s.th. الى to s.o.) **V** to be executed, be carried out

نفذ *nafaḏ* pl. انفاذ *anfāḏ* opening, aperture, orifice, hole, vent, outlet, escape, way out

نفاذ *nafāḏ* penetration, permeation; implementation, realization, effectuation; effectiveness; execution | نفاذ البصيرة perspicacity, acute discernment, penetration

نفاذ *naffāḏ* piercing, penetrating; effective, effectual; permeable, pervious

نفوذ *nufūḏ* penetration, permeation; effectiveness, effect, action; influence, prestige, authority | نفوذ مطلق (*muṭlaq*) full powers, free hand, unlimited authority; ذو نفوذ influential; نطاق النفوذ sphere of influence

منفذ *manfaḏ*, *manfiḏ* pl. منافذ *manāfiḏ*[2] opening in a wall, air hole, window; passage, passageway, exit; outlet; way out, escape; entrance, access; gateway, gate; loophole, dodge; ○ electrode (*el.*) | ○ منفذ المياه *m. al-miyāh* flood gate, lock gate, sluice gate; المنفذ البحرى (*baḥrī*) access to the sea

تنفيذ *tanfīḏ* carrying out, implementation, effectuation, realization; discharge, accomplishment, fulfillment, performance, execution; distraint, legal execution (*jur.*) | دخل فى طور (دور) التنفيذ (*ṭauri*, *dauri t-t.*) to become effective, come into force; عون التنفيذ *'aun at-t.* minor executory officer, bailiff (*tun.*); قسم التنفيذ *qism at-t.* executive division (of a court); احكام قابلة للتنفيذ executory decisions, precepts, executions, writs of fieri facias (*jur.*)

تنفيذى *tanfīḏī* executory, executive | لجنة تنفيذية (*lajna*) executive committee

انفاذ *infāḏ* sending, dispatch, conveyance, delivery, transmission; carrying out, execution, discharge, performance

نافذ *nāfiḏ* piercing, penetrating; effective, operative, effectual; legally valid | اصبح نافذا (*aṣbaḥa*) to become operative, become effective, come into force (law); الحكم نافذ فيه (*ḥukmu*) the sentence will be carried out, has legal force; نافذ الكلمة *n. al-kalima* influential, powerful; نافذ المفعول valid, effective, in force; امر نافذ (*amr*) strict order

نافذة *nāfiḏa* pl. نوافذ *nawāfiḏ*[2] opening in a wall, air hole; window; ○ wicket | ○ نافذة الاطلاق *n. al-iṭlāq* loophole, embrasure

منفذ *munaffiḏ* executant, executer, executioner | منفذ الوصية *m. al-waṣīya* executor (*jur.*); عون منفذ (*ʿaun*) minor executory officer, bailiff (*tun.*)

متنفذ *mutanaffiḏ* influential

نفر *nafara u i* (نفور *nufūr*, نفار *nifār*) to shy, bolt, stampede (animal); — *i* (*nafar*) to flee, run away; to have an aversion (من to), have a distaste (من for); to avoid, shun, eschew (عن or من s.th.), keep clear (عن or من of), turn away, flee (عن or من from); to hurry, rush, hasten (ل or الى to); — *i* (نفور *nufūr*) to swell, bulge out, protrude, jut out, stick out **II** to startle, frighten, scare away, chase away, drive away (ه s.th.); to fill (ه s.o.) with an aversion (من to), arouse a distaste (ه من in s.o. for), make loathsome (ه من to s.o. s.th.), alienate, estrange, deter (ه من s.o. from), spoil s.o.'s (ه) pleasure (من in), make (ه s.o.) dissatisfied (من with) **III** to avoid (ه, ه s.o., s.th.), keep away (ه from s.o.), have an aversion (ه to s.o.); to contradict (ه s.th.), be incompatible (ه with) **VI** to avoid each other; to conflict, clash; to disagree, be incongruous, incompatible, mutually repellent **X** to be frightened away; to call upon s.o. (ه) to fight (على against), call out (ه s.o.) to go to war (على against)

نفر *nafar* pl. انفار *anfār* band, party, group, troop; troops; person, individual; (*mil.*) soldier, private; man (as a numerative)

نفرة *nafra* aversion, distaste, dislike, antipathy

نفور *nufūr* shying, flight; bolting, stampede (of an animal); aversion, distaste, dislike, displeasure, alienation, estrangement

نفور *nafūr* shy, easily frightened, scary, fearful, timid; reticent, diffident, bashful, coy, reserved

نفير *nafīr* pl. انفار *anfār*, انفرة *anfira* band, party, group, troop; departure into battle; trumpet | نفير عام (*ʿāmm*) general call to arms, levy en masse; general alarm

نافورة *nāfūra* pl. نوافير *nawāfīr*[2] fountain

نوفرة *naufara* pl. نوافر *nawāfir*[2] fountain

تنفير *tanfīr* estrangement, alienation, repulsion, deterrence

تنافر *tanāfur* mutual aversion or repulsion, disagreement, disunion, dissension, conflict, strife, incongruity, discord

نافر *nāfir* pl. نفر *nafr*, *nuffar* fleeing, fugitive, shy, fearful, timid; having an aversion (من to) or a distaste (من for); swelling, protuberant, bulging, protruding, projecting, jutting out; relief-like, in relief; three-dimensional, 3-D (film)

منفر *munaffir*, *munfir* repulsive, repellent

نفس *nafusa u* (*nafas*, نفاس *nifās*, نفاسة *nafāsa*) to be precious, valuable, priceless; — *nafisa a* (*nafas*) to be sparing, niggardly

(ب with s.th.); — (نفاسة *nafāsa*) to envy, begrudge (ه على s.o. s.th.); — *nafisa a* and pass. *nufisa* (نفاس *nifās*) to be in childbed **II** to cheer up, comfort, appease, reassure (ه s.o.); to relieve (عن s.o. ه of s.th., esp., of sorrow, cares), dispel, banish (عن s.o.'s ه worries, anxieties); to air (عن one's secret feelings), give vent (عن to one's emotions), uncover, reveal, voice, get off one's chest, get out of one's system, abreact (عن one's suppressed desires, frustrations, fears, etc.); to desist (عن from), cease (عن doing s.th.); pass. *nuffisa* to get lost (عن to s.o.); to let out air, leak; to be in childbed **III** to compete, vie (ه عن with s.o. in); to compete, fight, struggle (على for), seek, try to obtain, desire (على s.th.), strive, be out (على for), aspire (على to) **V** to breathe, inhale and exhale; to take breath, pause for breath, have a breather, have a break, take a rest | تنفس الحسرات المؤلمة (*al-ḥasarāti l-mu'lima*) to heave painful sighs; تنفس الصعداء (*ṣuʿadāʾa*) to sigh deeply; to breathe a sigh of relief, breathe again; تنفس النفس الاخير (*nafasa*) to be at one's last gasp, be dying; تنفس عن الحياة (*ḥayāh*) to breathe one's last, die **VI** to rival, compete, vie, contend (على for, فى in s.th.)

نفس *nafs* f., pl. نفوس *nufūs*, انفس *anfus* soul; psyche; spirit, mind; life; animate being, living creature, human being, person, individual (in this sense, masc.); essence, nature; inclination, liking, appetite, desire; personal identity, self (used to paraphrase the reflexive pronoun; see examples below) | بنفسه he himself; personally, in person; نحن بنفوسنا we ourselves; فى نفس الامر (*n. il-amr*) in reality, actually, in fact; فى نفس الواقع do.; عند انفسهم in their own opinion; جاءنى هو نفسه (بنفسه) he himself came to me, he came personally to see me; جاء من نفسه he came of his own accord; ما وعدت به فيما بينى وبين نفسى what I had promised myself; نفس الامر *n. al-amr* the essence of the matter, the nature of the affair; نفس الشىء the thing itself; the same thing, the very thing; الثقة بالنفس and الاعتماد على النفس (*ṯiqa*) self-confidence, self-reliance; بشق النفس *bi-šiqqi n-n.* or بشق الانفس (following لا ... الا) with (the greatest) difficulty, barely; صغير النفس base-minded, low-minded; عفيف النفس unselfish, selfless, altruistic; علم النفس *ʿilm an-n.* psychology; كبير النفس high-minded, proud; محبة النفس *maḥabbat an-n.* amour propre, selfishness; بذل النفس والنفيس to make every conceivable sacrifice, sacrifice all, give up all one's possessions

نفسى *nafsī* spiritual, mental, psychic(al); (pl. *-ūn*) psychologist | التحليل النفسى psychoanalysis; حالة نفسية state of mind, mood

نفسية *nafsīya* mental life, inner life, psyche; frame of mind; mentality, mental attitude, disposition; psychology

نفس *nafas* pl. انفاس *anfās* breath; whiff; puff (from a smoking pipe, from a cigarette); swallow, gulp, draught; style of an author; freedom, liberty, convenience, discretion | حتى النفس الاخير to the last breath; ذو نفس enough to slake the thirst; refreshing (drink); ضيق النفس *ḍīq an-n.* labored breathing, asthma; هو فى نفس من اموره he acts according to his own desires; انت فى نفس من امرك (*amrika*) you can do as you please! امسك انفاسه (*anfāsahū*) to hold one's breath; فاضت انفاسه (*anfāsuhū*) to give up the ghost

نفسة *nufsa* respite, delay

نفساء *nafsāʾ*[2] pl. نوافس *nawāfis*[2] confined, in childbed; a woman in childbed

نفسانى *nafsānī* psychic(al), mental | طب نفسانى (*ṭibb*) psychiatry; طبيب نفسانى psychiatrist; عالم نفسانى psychologist

○ نفسانية *nafsānīya* psychology

نفاس *nifās* parturition, delivery, childbirth, confinement, accouchement; childbed, puerperium; see also below | حمى النفاس *ḥummā n-n.* or حمى نفاسية puerperal fever, childbed fever

نفاسة *nafāsa* preciousness, costliness

نفيس *nafīs* precious, costly, valuable, priceless

نفيسة *nafīsa* pl. نفائس *nafā'is²* gem, object of value, precious thing

منفس *manfas* pl. منافس *manāfis²* breathing hole, air hole, valve

تنفيس *tanfīs* airing, ventilation

منافسة *munāfasa* pl. *-āt* emulation; competition (also *com.*); rivalry; athletic event, contest, match

نفاس *nifās* emulation; competition (also *com.*); rivalry; athletic event, contest, match

تنفس *tanaffus* respiration

تنفسى *tanaffusī*: جهاز تنفسى (*jahāz*) respiratory system

تنافس *tanāfus* mutual competition, rivalry; fight, struggle (على for) | تنافس حيوى (*ḥayawī*) struggle for existence

منافس *munāfis* competitor; rival

متنفس *mutanaffas* place to breathe freely; breathing space, free scope (for s.th.), free atmosphere; relief, escape, way out

نفش *nafaša u* (*nafš*) to tease (ه wool); to swell out, puff up; to swell, become swollen; to ruffle its feathers (bird) **II** to comb or card (ه cotton) **V** to puff up, become inflated; to ruffle the feathers, bristle the hair **VIII** do.

نفش *nafaš* wool

نفاش *naffāš* a variety of large lemon

منفوش *manfūš* puffed up, inflated; ruffled, bristling; disheveled (hair); fluffy (hair, wool)

نفض *nafaḍa u* (*nafḍ*) to shake (ه s.th.), shake off (ه عن s.th. from), shake out, dust, dust off (ه s.th.); to knock the ashes from a cigarette (ه); to make (ه s.o.) shiver (fever); — *u* (نفوض *nufūḍ*) to recover, recuperate (من from) | نفض عنه الكسل (*kasala*) or نفض غبار كسله (*ġubāra kasalihī*) to shake off one's laziness; نفض غباره (*ġubārahū*) lit.: to shake off its dust, i.e., to have reached the end of, be finished with; نفض عنه الهم (*hamma*) to shake off one's sorrows, shed one's anxiety; نفض فى لعب الاوراق (*la'ibi l-aurāq*) to gamble away at cards; نفض يده من الامر (*yadahū, amr*) to chuck s.th., shake off s.th., rid o.s. of, refuse to have anything to do with; نفض يده من يد فلان to break with s.o., dissociate o.s. from, go back on s.o. **II** to shake violently, shake out, dust off (ه s.th.) **IV** to use up completely, exhaust (ه provisions, stores); to be devoid of all means, be reduced to poverty, be impoverished, be depleted; to shake off (ه عن s.o. from); to remove, dismiss (ه عن s.o. from) **VIII** to be shaken off, be dusted off; to shake; to shudder, shiver, tremble (من with) | انتفض واقفا (*wāqifan*) to jump up, jump to one's feet

نفض *nafaḍ* that which is shaken off or falls off

نفضى *nafaḍī*: ○ غابة نفضية deciduous forest, leafy forest

نفضة *nafaḍa* scouting party, reconnaissance patrol

نفضة *nufaḍa* ague fit, feverish shiver

نفاض *nafāḍ* ague fit, feverish shiver

نفاضة *nufāḍa* that which is shaken off or falls off

نفيضة *nafīḍa* pl. نفائض *nafā'iḍ²* scouting party, reconnaissance patrol

منفض *minfaḍ* sieve; winnow

منفضة *minfaḍa* pl. منافض *manāfiḍ²* ashtray; feather duster; ○ vacuum cleaner

انتفاض *intifāḍ* shaking, shiver, shudder, tremor

انتفاضة *intifāḍa* (n. vic.) shiver, shudder, tremor

نفط *nafṭ* naphtha, petroleum

نفطى *nafṭī* of naphtha, soaked in naphtha; oil-, petroleum- (in compounds) | مصباح نفطى (*miṣbāḥ*) oil lamp

نفطة *nafṭa* blister

نفطة *nufaṭa* irritable, touchy, thin-skinned; hot-tempered

منفط *munaffiṭ* blistering, vesicatory

نفع *nafa'a a* (*naf'*) to be useful, beneficial, advantageous, be of use (ه to s.o.), avail, help (ه s.o.); to be usable, to do, serve (ل for) | لا ينفع useless, of no use II to utilize, turn to use, put to use (ه s.th.); to use (ه s.th.), make use (ه of) VIII to turn to advantage, turn to good account, put to use, utilize, use (من or ب s.th.), take advantage, avail o.s., make use (من or ب of); to profit, gain, benefit (من or ب by s.th.); to enjoy (من or ب s.th.) X = II

نفع *naf'* use, avail, benefit, advantage, profit, gain; good, welfare

نفعى *naf'ī* out for one's own advantage, self-interested, selfish; profiteer

نفاع *naffā'* very useful, of good use

نفوع *nafū'* pl. نفع *nufu'* very useful, of good use

منفعة *manfa'a* pl. منافع *manāfi'²* use, avail, benefit; beneficial use, useful service; advantage, profit, gain; (*Isl. Law*) yield of a utilizable thing or of a right, produce; interest; public establishment, public-service facility | منافع عامة (عمومية) (*'āmma, 'umūmīya*) public-service facilities, specif., property set aside, or available, for public use; منافع صحية (*ṣiḥḥīya*) sanitary facilities

انتفاع *intifā'* use, employment, utilization, exploitation, usufruct; benefit, advantage, profit, gain

نافع *nāfi'* useful, beneficial, advantageous, profitable, usable, serviceable; wholesome, salutary

نافعة *nāfi'a* public works | وزير النافعة minister of public works

منتفع *muntafi'* beneficiary, usufructuary

نفق *nafaqa u* (نفاق *nafāq*) to sell well, find a ready market (merchandise); to be brisk, active (market); — *nafaqa* and *nafiqa a* (*nafaq*) to be used up, be spent, run out (stores, provisions, money), be exhausted; — *nafaqa u* (نفوق *nufūq*) to die, perish (esp., of an animal) II to sell III to dissemble, dissimulate, play the hypocrite | نافق ضميره (*ḍamīrahū*) to act contrary to the dictates of one's conscience IV to spend, expend, lay out, disburse (ه على money for); to use up, consume, spend, exhaust, waste, squander, dissipate (ه s.th.); to spend, pass (ه time); to provide (على for s.o., esp., for s.o.'s means of support), support (على s.o.), bear the cost of s.o.'s (على) maintenance V تنفق بكذبة على (*bi-kiḏbatin*) to tell s.o. a fib X to spend, waste (ه على money for)

نفق *nafaq* pl. انفاق *anfāq* tunnel, underground passageway

نفقة *nafaqa* pl. -*āt*, نفاق *nifāq* expense; cost; outlay, expenditure, disbursement; cost of living, maintenance, support; (*Isl. Law*) adequate support, esp., of the wife; charitable gift, handout (to the poor) | على نفقته at s.o.'s expense; قليل النفقات inexpensive, cheap

نفاق *nafāq* brisk trade, good business; salability (of a commodity)

منفاق *minfāq* squanderer, wastrel, spendthrift, profligate

منافقة *munāfaqa* hypocrisy, dissimulation, dissemblance

نفاق *nifāq* hypocrisy, dissimulation, dissemblance

انفاق *infāq* spending, expenses, outlay, expenditure, disbursement

نافق *nāfiq* selling well, easily marketable, in demand (commodity)

منافق *munāfiq* hypocrite, dissembler

نفل V and VIII to do more than is required by duty or obligation, to supererogate (specif., prayers, charity, or the like)

نفل *nafl* supererogatory performance, specif., a work of supererogation

نفل *nafal* pl. انفال *anfāl*, نفول *nufūl*, نفال *nifāl* booty, loot, spoil; present

نفل *nafal* clover

نافلة *nāfila* pl. نوافل *nawāfil*[2] supererogatory performance; work of supererogation; gift, present; booty, loot, spoil | من نافلة القول ان (*n. il-qaul*) it goes without saying that ...

نفنف *nafnaf* pl. نفانف *nafānif*[2] air, atmosphere; steep hillside, precipitous cliff

نفنوف *nafnūf* (*ir.*) a woman's dress

نفو and (نفى) نفا *nafā u* (*nafw*) and نفى *nafā i* (*nafy*) to expel, eject, oust, ostracize, exclude (عن or من ه s.o. from), remove, evict, banish, exile, expatriate (ه s.o.); to deport (ه s.o.); to refute, disprove, rebut, controvert, repudiate (ه s.th.); to deny (ه s.th.); to reject, dismiss, discard, disclaim, disavow, decline, refuse, disallow (ه s.th.); to exclude, preclude (ه s.th.); to negate (*gram.*) **III** to hunt, chase, pursue, track down (ه s.o.); to exclude, preclude (ه s.th.); to contradict (ه s.th.), be contrary (ه to); to be incompatible, be inconsistent (ه with) **VI** to be mutually exclusive or contradicting, cancel each other out, be incompatible **VIII** to be banished, be exiled, be expelled; to be refuted, be disproved, be controverted, be contradicted, be denied; to fall off, fall away, be dropped, be omitted, be absent, be nonexistent **X** to reject as worthless, useless, unacceptable (ه s.th.)

نفى *nafy* expulsion; banishment, exile, expatriation; ejection, ousting, eviction, ostracism; deportation; denial, disclaimer, disavowal, repudiation, disproof, refutation, rebuttal; refusal, rejection, disallowance, prohibition, ban; negation (*gram.*) | حرف النفى *ḥarf an-n.* particle of negation (*gram.*); شاهد نفى witness for the defense (as opposed to شاهد اثبات *š. iṯbāt*)

نفيى *nafyī* negative

نفى *nafīy* denied; rejected, discarded

نفاء *nafā'*, نفاة *nafāh* and نفاوة *nafāwa* s.th. discarded as worthless or useless; dross, refuse, waste, scrap, offal, sweepings, garbage

نفاية *nufāya* pl. -*āt* s.th. discarded as worthless or useless; remnant, remains; discard, castoff; reject, throwout; dross, refuse, waste, scrap, offal, sweepings, garbage; ○ نفايات excretions (*biol.*)

منفى *manfan* pl. مناف *manāfin* place of exile; banishment, exile

منافاة *munāfāh* contradiction, incompatibility, inconsistency

تناف *tanāfin* mutual incompatibility

انتفاء *intifā'* absence, lack

منفى *manfīy* turned down, denied, rejected, discarded; negated, negative; banished, exiled, expatriated; deported

مناف *munāfin* incompatible

نق **naqqa** *i* (نقيق *naqīq*) to croak (frog); to cackle, cluck (hen)

نقاق *naqqāq* surly person, gruff man, grumbler; griper, carper, faultfinder

نقاقة *naqqāqa* frog

نقيق *naqīq* croaking, croak; cackling, cackle

[1]نقب **naqaba** *u* (*naqb*) to bore, pierce, perforate, breach (ه s.th.), make a hole or breach (ه in), punch or drill a hole (ه through); to dig, dig up, dig out, excavate, hollow out (ه s.th.); to traverse (ه a country), pass, travel (ﻓﻰ through); to inquire, ask, look, search (عن for), examine thoroughly, investigate, explore, search into, delve into; — *naqiba a* (*naqab*) to be perforated, be full of holes **II** to drill (عن for, e.g., for oil); to examine thoroughly, study, investigate (عن s.th.), penetrate, delve, search (عن into), look, search (عن for); to travel (ﻓﻰ through) **III** to vie in virtues (ه with s.o.) **V** to examine, study, investigate (عن s.th.), look, search (عن for); to veil her face (woman); to be perforated, be full of holes **VIII** to put on a veil, veil one's face

نقب *naqb* digging, excavation; piercing, perforation; — (pl. انقاب *anqāb*, نقاب *niqāb*) hole, opening, breach; boring, bore; tunnel

نقاب *naqqāb* punch

نقاب *niqāb* pl. نقب *nuqub*, انقبة *anqiba* veil | كشف النقاب عن to uncover, reveal, disclose s.th.

نقابة *niqāba* pl. *-āt* cooperative society; union, association, guild; corporation; syndicate; trade-union, labor union | نقابة العمال *n. al-ʿummāl* trade-union, labor union

نقابى *niqābī* cooperative; syndicalistic; syndicalist; trade-unionist

نقابية *niqābīya* syndicalism; trade-unionism

نقيب *naqīb* pl. نقباء *nuqabāʾ*[2] leader, head, headman; director, principal, chief; chairman of a guild; president; syndic, corporation lawyer; (*mil.*) captain (army), lieutenant (navy) (*Eg.* 1939 and *U.A.R.*); tongue of a balance | نقيب الاشراف head of the Alids, head of the descendants of the Prophet

نقيبة *naqība* pl. نقائب *naqāʾib*[2] soul, spirit, mind, intellect; natural disposition, nature, temper, character

منقب *manqib*, *minqab* and منقبة *manqaba* pl. مناقب *manāqib*[2] mountain trail, defile, pass

منقب *minqab* and منقبة *minqaba* punch, perforator, drill; lancet

مناقب *manāqib*[2] virtues, outstanding traits; glorious deeds, feats, exploits

تنقيب *tanqīb* pl. *-āt* drilling (esp., for oil); digging, excavation; investigation, examination, inquiry, search, exploration, research

منقب *munaqqib* investigator, researcher, scholar, explorer

[2]النقب *an-naqab* Negev (desert region in S Israel)

نقح **naqaḥa** *a* (*naqḥ*) to prune, lop (ه a tree), trim, clip (ه s.th.) **II** do.; to review, revise, read over carefully, correct (ه a writing), improve, polish, refine (the style) **IV** to check, go over, re-examine, revise, correct (ه s.th.)

تنقيح *tanqīḥ* checking, (re-)examination; revision; correction

نقد *naqada* u (*naqd*) to pay in cash (ه ، to s.o. s.th.); to peck (ه at); to examine critically (ه s.th.); to criticize (ه على s.o. for) **III** to call to account (ه s.o.) **IV** to pay (ه ، to s.o. s.th.) **VIII** to criticize (ه s.th.), find fault (ه with), take exception (ه to), disapprove (ه of); to show up the shortcomings (على of s.o.), criticize (على s.o.); to receive payment in cash

نقد *naqd* criticism; — (pl. نقود *nuqūd*) cash, ready money; pl. specie, coins, change; نقدا in cash; for cash, cash down | بالنقد in cash; for cash, cash down; ورق النقد *waraq an-n.* banknotes, paper money; حافظة النقود change purse

نقدى *naqdī* monetary, pecuniary; numismatic, of coin; cash (adj.) | تضخم نقدى (*taḍakḳum*) inflation; جزاء نقدى (*jazā'*) a monetary fine

نقدية *naqdīya* ready money, cash

نقاد *naqqād* critic; reviewer

نقادة *naqqāda* captious critic, caviler, carper

منقد *manqad* (*eg.*) brazier

منقاد *minqād* pl. مناقيد *manāqīd*[2] beak, bill (of a bird)

انتقاد *intiqād* pl. *-āt* objection, exception; criticism, censure, reproof, disapproval; review, critique

ناقد *nāqid* pl. *-ūn*, نقاد *nuqqād*, نقدة *naqada* critic

منتقد *muntaqid* critic

منتقد *muntaqad* blameworthy, reprehensible, objectionable, exceptionable

نقذ *naqaḏa* u (*naqḏ*) to deliver, save, rescue (ه من s.o. from); — *naqiḏa* a (*naqaḏ*) to be saved, be rescued, save o.s., escape **IV** to deliver, save, rescue (ه من s.o. from); to salvage, recover (ه s.th.) **X** = **IV**

انقاذ *inqāḏ* deliverance, salvation, saving, rescue; salvaging, recovery; relief

استنقاذ *istinqāḏ* deliverance, salvation, saving, rescue; salvaging, recovery; relief

منقذ *munqiḏ* rescuer, savior, deliverer

نقر *naqara* u (*naqr*) to dig; to pierce, bore, hollow out, excavate (ه s.th.), make a cavity or hole (ه in); to cut, carve (ه s.th., esp., stone or wood); to engrave, inscribe (ى in); to peck up (ه a grain; of a bird); to peck (ه at s.o.); to strike, bang, knock, rap (على at, on); to drum (ه on s.th.); to snap one's fingers; to offend, annoy, vex, hurt, insult, revile, malign, defame (ه s.o.), cast a slur (ه on s.o.), make insinuations (ه against s.o.); to investigate, examine (عن s.th.); — *naqira* a (*naqar*) to be offended, annoyed, miffed (على at) **II** to peck, peck up (ه s.th.); to investigate, examine (عن s.th.) **III** to have an argument, to quarrel, wrangle, bicker (ه with s.o.)

نقر *naqr* excavation, hollowing out, carving out, engraving; hollow, cavity, hole; snap(ping) of the fingers

نقر *naqir* annoyed, offended, hurt, miffed

نقرة *naqra* pl. *naqarāt* blow, knock, bang, rap; drumbeat; pluck(ing) (of strings)

نقرة *nuqra* pl. نقر *nuqar*, نقار *niqār* pit, hollow, cavity, hole; depression; orbit, eye socket; neck furrow, nape

نقرة *niqra* bickering, wrangle, argument, quarrel

نقار *naqqār* carver, engraver | نقار الخشب *n. al-ḳašab* woodpecker (*zool.*)

نقارية *nuqqārīya* pl. *-āt* (*eg.*) a percussion instrument resembling a kettledrum

نقير *naqīr* tiny spot on a date pit; an utterly worthless thing | لا يجدى شروى نقير

lā yujdī šarwā n. it won't help the least bit, it won't get you anywhere at all; لا يملك شروى نقير he has absolutely nothing, he hasn't got a red cent to his name; لا فتيل ولا نقير nothing at all, not the least little bit

نقيرة *naqīra* pl. نقائر *naqā'ir*² corvette

نقارة *naqqāra* small drum having a hemispheric body of copper or wood

ناقور *nāqūr* pl. نواقير *nawāqīr*² (Koranic) a wind instrument

نقورة *naqūra* (*eg.*) prattle, idle talk, rigmarole

منقار *minqār* pl. مناقير *manāqīr*² beak, bill (of a bird); pickax

مناقرة *munāqara* bickering, wrangle, argument, quarrel

ناقرة *nāqira* pl. نواقر *nawāqir*² bickering, wrangle, argument, quarrel; misfortune, calamity

نقرزان *naqrazān* (*eg.*) small drum; drummer

نقرس *niqris* gout; skilled and experienced (physician)

نقريس *niqrīs* skilled and experienced (physician)

نقز *naqaza u i* (*naqz*, نقاز *niqāz*, نقزان *naqazān*) to bound, leap, skip, hop II to rock, dandle (ه a child)

نقزة *naqza* jump, leap, start

ناقوس *nāqūs* pl. نواقيس *nawāqīs*² (church)bell; gong; hand bell (used, e.g., in Coptic liturgy); bell jar, globe

نقش *naqaša u* (*naqš*) to variegate, dapple, make many-colored, daub with various colors, bedaub (ه s.th.); to paint; to chisel, sculpture, carve out; to engrave (ه s.th., على on, in) II to paint; to engrave; to sculpture III to argue, dispute (ه with s.o.); to discuss (ه s.th.); to debate (ه a question); to criticize (ه s.th.), object, raise an objection (ه to), raise a protest (ه against); to hear, examine, interrogate (ه s.o.; *jur.*) VI to carry on a dispute, to debate (في about) VIII to extract, pull out (ه a prick or thorn)

نقش *naqš* pl. نقوش *nuqūš* painting, picture, drawing; engraving; inscription; sculpture, figure

نقاش *naqqāš* painter; house painter; artist; sculptor

نقاشة *niqāša* (art of) painting or sculpture

منقش *minqaš* pl. مناقش *manāqiš*² chisel

منقاش *minqāš* pl. مناقيش *manāqīš*² chisel

مناقشة *munāqaša* argument, controversy, dispute, debate, discussion; contestation, opposition, objection, protest

نقاش *niqāš* argument, controversy, dispute, debate, discussion

منقوش *manqūš* colored, dappled, variegated; painted; engraved; sculptured; inscribed

مناقش *munāqiš* opponent in a dispute; disputant

نقص *naqaṣa u* (*naqṣ*, نقصان *nuqṣān*) to decrease, become less, diminish, be diminished, be reduced (ه by an amount; of a number); to decrease, diminish, lessen, reduce, impair (ه s.th.), prejudice (ه, ه s.o., s.th.), be prejudicial (ه, ه to), detract (ه, ه from); to lower, peg down (ه s.th.); to be deficient, lacking, incomplete, insufficient, inadequate, defective, faulty, imperfect; نقصه الشيء (*šai'u*) he lacked, needed the thing, was in want of the thing; to fall short (عن of), be less, be lower (عن than) | ١٣ عاما تنقص شهرا واحدا (*'āman, šahran*) 13 years minus one month II and IV to decrease, diminish, lessen (ه s.th.); to reduce, lower, peg down (ه s.th.); to curtail, cut (ه s.th.) III to invite bids (ه for a project, etc., so as to determine the lowest bidder) **VI** to decrease gradually, diminish slowly, grow less or smaller by degrees **VIII** to decrease, diminish, become less; to wane; to impair, diminish, lessen (▲ s.th.) | انتقص من قدره (*qadrihī*) to disparage s.o., detract from s.o., degrade s.o. **X** to ask for a reduction (▲ of s.th.); to find (▲ s.th.) decreased, deficient, short, defective, imperfect, inferior; to discover the absence (▲ of), miss (▲ s.th.)

نقص *naqṣ* decrease, diminution; deficit, loss, damage; wantage, lack, want, shortage (في of); gap, blank, omission; defect, shortcoming, failing, fault, blemish; deficiency, imperfection, inferiority | نقص المواليد falling birth rate; مركب نقص *murakkab n.* inferiority complex

نقصان *nuqṣān* = نقص *naqṣ*

نقيصة *naqīṣa* pl. نقائص *naqā'iṣ*[2] shortcoming, failing, fault, defect

تنقيص *tanqīṣ* diminution, lessening, decrease, reduction, lowering

مناقصة *munāqaṣa* pl. *-āt* competition to determine the lowest bidder, public invitation to submit bids (for public works), notice to bidders; award of contract to the lowest bidder

انقاص *inqāṣ* diminution, lessening, decrease, reduction, lowering, curtailment

تناقص *tanāquṣ* decrease, diminution, decrement

انتقاص *intiqāṣ* impairment, lessening

ناقص *nāqiṣ* pl. نقص *nuqqaṣ* decreasing, diminishing; diminished, lowered, decreased, reduced; faulty, defective; deficient, lacking, imperfect, incomplete; short of supply, scarce; less (عن than); growing lighter; defective (*gram.*)

منقوص *manqūṣ* deficient, incomplete; insufficient, inadequate

نقض *naqaḍa u* (*naqḍ*) to destroy, demolish, tear down, wreck, raze (▲ s.th.); to tear apart, take apart, undo (▲ s.th.); to break, violate, infringe (▲ s.th., esp., a contract or similar legal obligation); to cancel, abolish, repeal, abrogate, revoke, nullify, declare void, annul (▲ s.th.); to invalidate, refute (▲ a suspicion); to quash, rescind, reverse (▲ a sentence) | نقض الولاء (*walā'a*) to renounce allegiance, to revolt; لا ينقض *lā yunqaḍu* irrefutable; incontestable, irrevocable **III** to be in disagreement (▲ with), be contradictory, contrary, opposite (▲ to), contradict (▲ s.th.), be incompatible, inconsistent (▲ with) **V** to be destroyed, be demolished, be torn down, be wrecked, be razed; to be broken, be violated; to be undone; to disintegrate, decay, fall down, break down, collapse; to disappear, wear off, fade away, die away **VI** to contradict each other; to be mutually exclusive **VIII** = **V**; to rise, mutiny, rebel, revolt (على against); to attack (على s.o.), take the field, go to war (على against s.o.)

نقض *naqḍ* destruction, demolition; breach, violation, infringement; infraction, offense; refutation, invalidation; veto (*pol.*); contradiction, logical incompatibility | نقض الحكم *n. al-ḥukm* reversal of a sentence; نقض السلام *n. as-salām* breach of the peace; محكمة النقض والابرام *maḥkamat an-n. wa-l-ibrām* Court of Cassation (*Eg.*); لا يجوز نقضه (*yajūzu*) (it is) no longer open to an appeal, incapable of revision, irrevisable, legally valid, final (sentence); حق النقض *ḥaqq an-n.* right of veto

انقاض *anqāḍ* (pl. of نقض *nuqḍ*) debris; rubble

نقيض *naqīḍ* opposed, opposite, contrary, antithetical, contradictory; antithesis, opposition, contrast, opposite | على نقيض contrary to, in opposition to, in contradistinction to, unlike; على النقيض on the contrary; انتقل من النقيض الى نقيضه (*intaqala*) to go from one extreme to the other, move in extremes

نقيضة *naqīḍa* pl. نقائض *naqā'iḍ²* polemic poem; contrast

مناقضة *munāqaḍa* sharp contrast, contradiction; opposition; contestation of a right

تناقض *tanāquḍ* mutual contradiction, incompatibility; inconsistency, contrariety

انتقاض *intiqāḍ* collapse, breakdown; uprising, revolt, rebellion

منقوض *manqūḍ* destroyed, demolished, wrecked; broken, violated; undone, repealed, abrogated, annulled; refutable, disprovable

مناقض *munāqiḍ* contradictory, contrary, incompatible, inconsistent | مناقض ذاته (*ḏātahū*) self-contradictory

متناقض *mutanāqiḍ* mutually contradicting, contradictory, conflicting, mutually incompatible; pl. متناقضات contrasts, contrarieties, contradictions, oppositions

نقط **naqaṭa** *u* (*naqṭ*) to point, provide with diacritical points (ه a letter) **II** do.; to spot, dot, dab, stain, speckle (ه s.th.); to fall in drops, drip; to cause (ه s.th.) to drip, let (ه s.th.) fall in drops, drop (ه s.th.); to distribute (ب or ه s.th.) as a present (على to s.o.); to give a wedding present (ها to the bride)

نقطة *nuqṭa* pl. نقط *nuqaṭ*, نقاط *niqāṭ* point, dot; diacritical point; period, full stop; drop; jot, tittle, speck; trifle, tiny piece; part (esp., of motors, of machines); matter, affair, subject, point; detail, particular; item; spot, location, site; place, village, hamlet, market town (*geogr.*); branch, post (*adm.*); base, position, outpost (*mil.*); (*eg.*) wedding present; النقطتان colon (*typ.*) | نقطة الاتصال *n. al-ittiṣāl* junction (of traffic lanes); ◯ نقطة الارتكاز fortified position, pocket of resistance (*mil.*); ◯ نقطة اساسية (*asāsīya*) key position; نقطة الاستفهام interrogation mark; نقطة الاطفاء *n. al-iṭfā'* or نقطة المطافئ fire station; نقطة البوليس police station, station house; نقطة التحول *n. at-taḥawwul* turning point, turn of events, turn of the tide; نقط التشحيم grease nipples (of motors); نقطة جمركية (*gumrukīya*) customs station, customhouse; ◯ نقطة خارجية (*kārijīya*) outpost; نقطة الذنب *n. aḏ-ḏanab* aphelion (*astron.*); نقطة الرأس *n. ar-ra's* perihelion (*astron.*); نقطة العنبر *n. al-'anbar* mole; beauty spot; نقطة العين *n. al-'ain* leucoma (*med.*); ◯ نقطة القتال combat area, zone of action; داء النقطة epilepsy; فوز بالنقط (*fauz*) victory on points (in sports)

نقوط *nuqūṭ* (*syr.*, *eg.*) wedding present to the bride

نقيطة *nuqaiṭa* droplet

نقاطة *naqqāṭa* dropping tube, dropper, pipette

منقوط *manqūṭ* having one (diacritical) point; pointed, having (diacritical) points; spotted, dotted, speckled | فصلة منقوطة (*faṣla*) semicolon

منقط *munaqqaṭ* pointed, having (diacritical) points; spotted, dotted, speckled

نقع **naqa'a** *a* (*naq'*) to soak, steep (ه في s.th. in); to infuse, brew (ه tea, etc.); to slake, quench (ه thirst); to stagnate, be stagnant, gather in a pool (water) **IV** to soak, macerate (ه s.th. in a liquid); to slake, quench (ه thirst) **X** to stagnate, be stagnant; to become impure and foul by stagnation (water); to be swampy (ground)

نقع *naq'* maceration, soaking, steeping; infusion; (pl. انقع *anqu'*) stagnant water, quagmire, swamp, bog; (pl. نقاع *niqā'*, نقوع *nuqū'*) dust

نقاعة *nuqāʿa* infusion

○ نقاعيات *nuqāʿīyāt* infusoria

نقيع *naqīʿ* infusion; that with which s.th. is soaked or permeated; (*eg.*) juice obtained from dried fruits soaked in water

نقوع *naqūʿ* dried fruit, dried apricots

منقع *manqaʿ* pl. مناقع *manāqiʿ*[2] quagmire, swamp, bog; sump, place where water gathers | منقع الدم *m. ad-dam* place of execution

منقوع *manqūʿ* macerated, soaked; infusion

مستنقع *mustanqaʿ* pl. *-āt* quagmire, swamp, bog; moor, morass, marsh, fen | حمى المستنقعات *ḥummā l-m.* swamp fever, malaria

نقف *naqf*, *niqf* chick

نقل **naqala** *u* (*naql*) to move from its place, move away, displace (ه s.th.); to remove, take away, carry away, carry, transport (ه الى s.th. to); to transfer, transplant, shift, translocate, relocate (ه، ه من ... الى s.o., s.th. from ... to); to transmit, convey, communicate, bring, deliver, make over, pass on, hand over (ه الى s.th. to s.o.); to remove, dismiss (ه s.o.); to move, remove (الى to); to copy (من from); to translate (من ... الى from one language into the other); to hand down, pass on, report, relate (ه الى s.th. to s.o., عن from, or based on, s.o. or a source); to quote (عن an author or a literary work); to render (ه a text); to enter, post (ه an item; in bookkeeping); to communicate, spread (ه الى a disease to s.o.), infect (ه الى s.o. with); to transfer, assign, convey, cede (ه الى s.th., esp. a right, to s.o.) **II** to move, move away, displace, move on, move forward, advance, transport, move about, let wander, let roam (ه s.th., esp., a great deal of s.th. or a great number of things, s.th. successively, one thing after the other) | نقل خطاه (*kuṭāhu*) to stride along, move along **III** to exchange (ه ه with s.o. words); to cast, shoot (ه ه at s.o. glances); to report (ه ه to s.o, s.th.), inform (ه ه s.o. of); to hand, pass (ه ه to s.o. s.th.) **V** to be carried, be carried away, be removed, be transported; to be transferred, be conveyed, be assigned; ○ to be transmitted (by radio); to shift, change its locality; to change one's residence, remove, go elsewhere; to change position (*mil.*); to move about; to walk about; to rove, roam, migrate, wander, travel about | تنقل فى منازل البلاغة (*m. al-balāḡa*) to be versed in rhetoric **VI** to carry, transport (ه s.th.); to report to one another, relate or tell each other (ه s.th.); to exchange (ه s.th.); to spread, report, relate (ه a story, etc.), pass on, hand down (ه s.th.); to spread by word of mouth (ه s.th.) | تناقلته الالسن (*alsun*) to pass from mouth to mouth, be on everybody's lips, be the talk of the town; تناقلته الايدى (*aidī*) to pass from hand to hand, change hands; تناقلت الجرائد الخبر (*kabara*) the report was taken up by the entire press; تناقل الكلام (*kalāma*) to talk with one another, have a talk **VIII** to be carried, be carried away, be removed, be transported; to be transferred, be conveyed, be assigned; ○ to be transmitted (by radio); to shift, change its locality; to change one's residence, remove, go elsewhere; to change position (*mil.*); to walk about; to rove, roam, migrate, wander, travel about; to be transferred (official); to be turned over, be delivered, be transferred (ship); to be communicated (disease), spread (الى to); to be spread, circulate, make the rounds (rumor); to be transplanted (الى into or to); to move, move along, travel;

to betake o.s., proceed, go, take the road (الى to), head (الى for), turn (الى to); to apply o.s., turn (الى to a field of interest); to turn, make a turn (الى into another street; of an automobile); to pass (من from one owner الى to the other); ○ to be propagated, spread (waves, etc.; الى to, occasionally also فى); ○ to jump across (el. spark); to shift (from attack to defense); to go away, depart (من and عن from), leave a place (من and عن); to go around (فى in or among), make the round (فى of), visit (one after the other) | انتقل به الى to shift, translocate, relocate s.th. to; انتقل الى رحمة الله (*raḥmati llāh*) lit.: to pass away into God's mercy, i.e., to die; انتقل الى جوار ربه (*j. rabbihī*) lit.: to be transferred into the presence of the Lord, i.e., to die, pass away

نقل **naql** carrying, carriage; conveyance, transportation, transport; removal; translocation, relocation, transplantation; transfer (also, e.g., of an official); change of residence, move, remove; transmission (also by radio); translation; transcription, transcript, copy; tradition; report, account; entry, posting (in an account book); conveyance, transfer, assignment, cession | نقلا عن based on, according to; نقل الدم *n. ad-dam* and نقل الدماء blood transfusion; ○ نقل الصور باللاسلكى *n. aṣ-ṣuwar bi-l-lāsilkī* radiophotography; نقل ميكانيكى motor transport (of passengers and cargoes); اجرة النقل *ujrat an-n.* cartage, carriage, freight; سيارة النقل *sayyārat an-n.* truck, lorry; معاليم النقل transfer fees, assignment fees; وسائل النقل means of transportation, conveyances

نقلى **naqlī** traditionary, traditional; of or pertaining to transportation, transport- (in compounds) | سيارة نقلية (*sayyāra*) truck, lorry

نقليات **naqlīyāt** transport services, transportation system, transportation; transports | نقليات عسكرية (*'askarīya*) troop transports

نقل **naql, nuql** pl. نقول **nuqūl** candied almonds or nuts, candy, sweets, dried fruits, etc., as a dessert

نقل **naqal** rubble, debris

نقلة **nuqla** migration

نقلة **nuqla** pl. نقل **nuqal** gossip; pattern, model

نقال **naqqāl** portable, transportable

نقالة **naqqāla** pl. *-āt* stretcher; ambulance; transport, transport vessel; truck, lorry

نقيل **naqīl** (*yem.*) mountain trail, defile, pass

منقل **manqal** and منقلة **manqala** pl. مناقل **manāqil**[2] brazier

منقلة **manqala** a day's march; way station, stopping place; ○ protractor

تنقل **tanaqqul** change of locality; change of residence; (*mil.*) change of position, station or garrison; traveling, roving, roaming, wandering, migration; conveyance, transportation, transport; transmission (*radio*); transfer; reshuffle, shake-up, reorganization, change of personnel; regrouping, shifting, rearrangement

انتقال **intiqāl** change of locality; locomotion; change of residence, move, remove, removal; translocation, relocation; transfer; conveyance, transportation, transport; transition (من — الى from — to); transmission; communication, infection; transit, passage (of the sun through the zodiac); demise, death | طور الانتقال *ṭaur al-int.* transition period; فترة الانتقال *fatrat al-int.* interim period, interim stage, stage of transition; عيد انتقال العذراء *'īd int. al-'adrā'* Day of the Assumption of the Virgin (*Chr.*)

انتقالى *intiqālī*: عهد انتقالى (*'ahd*) transition period

ناقل *nāqil* pl. *-ūn*, نقلة *naqala*, نقال *nuqqāl* carrying; carrier; bearer; translator; copyist; — conductor (*el.*) | ناقل السرعة *n. as-sur'a* gear-shift lever (of an automobile)

ناقلة *nāqila* pl. *-āt* transport, transport vessel | ناقلة البترول *n. al-betrōl* and ناقلة الزيت *n. az-zait* tanker; ناقلة الجنود troopship, transport; ناقلة الطائرات aircraft carrier

ناقلية *nāqilīya* conductivity (*el.*)

منقول *manqūl* carried, conveyed, transported; transferred; transmitted; translated; copied, transcribed; movable, mobile, portable; handed down, traditional; traditional stock; (pl. *-āt*) a movable thing | منقولات or اموال (املاك) منقولة movable property, movables, effects, personal property; منقولات المنزل *m. al-manzil* household furniture, household effects

متنقل *mutanaqqil* movable, mobile; portable; ambulant, itinerant, migrant, roving, roaming; nomad; inconstant, changing | مستشفى متنقل (*mustašfan*) temporary field hospital, ambulance

منتقل *muntaqil* ambulatory; movable, mobile; contagious, infectious, communicable | الاعياد المنتقلة the movable feasts; علة منتقلة (*'illa*) contagious disease

نقم *naqama i* (*naqm*) and *naqima a* (*naqam*) to revenge o.s., avenge o.s., take revenge (من on s.o.), take vengeance; to be hostile (على to), be full of rancor or vindictiveness, have a spite, be resentful (على against s.o.), be mad, angry (على at s.o., ه for, because of); to hate, loathe, detest (على s.o.); to hold s.th. (ه) against s.o. (على) VIII to revenge o.s., avenge o.s., take revenge (من on); to take vengeance (ل for)

نقمة *naqma* revenge, vengeance; rancor, spite, grudge, resentment; misfortune, adversity, punishment, trial, affliction, heavy blow; retribution

نقمة *niqma*, *naqima* pl. نقم *niqam*, نقمات *niqamāt* revenge, vengeance; rancor, spite, grudge, resentment; misfortune, adversity, punishment, trial, affliction, heavy blow

انتقام *intiqām* revenge, vengeance

ناقم *nāqim* avenger; hostile (على to); indignant, angry (على at or about)

منتقم *muntaqim* avenger; vindictive, revengeful

نقنق[1] *naqnaqa* to croak (frog); to cackle, cluck (hen); to gnaw, nibble

نقانق[2] *naqāniq*[2] small mutton sausages (*syr.*)

نقه *naqaha a* (نقوه *nuqūh*) and *naqiha a* (*naqah*) to be on the road to recovery, to convalesce; to recover, recuperate (من from) VIII do.

نقه *naqah* and نقهة *naqha* recovery, convalescence

نقه *naqih* recovering, convalescent

نقاهة *naqāha* recovery, convalescence | دار النقاهة rest center, convalescent home

ناقه *nāqih* a convalescent

نقو and نقى (نقى) *naqiya a* (نقاء *naqā'*, نقاوة *naqāwa*, *nuqāwa*) to be pure II to purify, clean, cleanse (ه s.th.); to rid of extraneous matter (ه s.th.); to select, pick out, cull, sift, sort (ه s.th.); to hand-pick (ه s.th.) IV to purify, clean, cleanse (ه s.th.) VIII to pick out, select (ه s.th.)

نقاء *naqā'* purity

نقاوة *naqāwa*, *nuqāwa* purity; ◯ fineness (of a precious metal); selection, culling; elite; pick, best

نقاية *nuqāya* selection, elite, pick

نقي **naqīy** pl. نقاء **niqā'**, انقياء **anqiyā'**[2] pure, clean, immaculate, unstained; clear, limpid, free of dirt or extraneous matter

تنقية **tanqiya** cleaning, cleansing, purification; sifting, sorting

انتقاء **intiqā'** selection | ○ قدرة على الانتقاء (*qudra*) selectivity (*radio*)

منتق **muntaqan** selected; select

نكأ **naka'a** *a* (نكء **nak'**) to scrape the scab (▲ off a wound)

نكب **nakaba** *u* (**nakb**, **nakab**) to make unhappy, miserable, afflict, distress (• s.o.; of fate); to drop (▲ s.th.); to put (• s.o.) out of favor; — (نكوب **nukūb**) to blow sideways; to veer, shift (wind); — (*nakb*, *nukūb*) to deviate, swerve (عن from, esp., from a path, road, route, course) **II** to avert, divert, deflect, turn away, remove (▲ s.th.) **V** to deviate, swerve (▲ or عن from); to avoid, shun, eschew (▲ or عن s.th.); to refrain (عن from), steer clear (عن of); to take upon one's shoulders, to shoulder, take upon o.s., assume (▲ s.th.) | تنكب به عن to make s.o. deviate or swerve from

نكب **nakb** pl. نكوب **nukūb** and نكبة **nakba** pl. **nakabāt** misfortune, calamity; disaster, catastrophe

منكب **mankib** pl. مناكب **manākib**[2] shoulder; side, flank; highland, upland | دفع بمنكبيه الهواء (*mankibaihi*, *hawā'*) approx.: to race along, dash along

منكوب **mankūb** fate-stricken, afflicted with disaster; unhappy, unfortunate, ill-fated, miserable; victim (of a catastrophe)

نكت **nakata** *u* (**nakt**) to scratch up (▲ the ground) **II** to crack jokes (على about s.o.), poke fun (على at), ridicule (على s.o.)

نكتة **nukta** pl. نكت **nukat**, نكات **nikāt** jot, tittle, speck, spot; witty remark, witticism, wisecrack, joke; anecdote; pun, play on words; the point of a joke | حاضر النكتة quick-witted, quick at repartee

نكات **nakkāt** witty; humorous, piquant; mocker, scoffer

تنكيت **tankīt** chaffing, legpulling; teasing, banter, raillery, mockery; joking, jesting, funmaking

منكت **munakkit** mocker, scoffer

نكث **nakaṯa** *u i* (**nakṯ**) to break, violate, infringe (▲ a contract or similar legal obligation) **VIII** to be broken, be violated

نكث **nakṯ** breach, violation (of a contract, etc.)

ناكث **nākiṯ** perfidious, faithless, false, disloyal

نكح **nakaḥa** *u i a* (نكاح **nikāḥ**) to marry (ها a woman), get married (ها with) **III** to become related by marriage (• to s.o.) **IV** to give in marriage (ها • to s.o. a girl)

نكاح **nikāḥ** marriage; marriage contract; matrimony, wedlock

مناكح **manākiḥ**[2] (pl.) women

نكد **nakida** *a* (**nakad**) to be hard, harsh, difficult; to be unhappy, miserable; — **nakada** *u* (**nakd**) to give little (• to s.o.); to torment, pester, molest (• s.o.) **II** to make life hard, difficult, miserable (• for s.o.), embitter s.o.'s (•) life **III** to torment, harass, pester, molest (• s.o.) **V** to be made miserable, be embittered (life)

نكد **nakd** pl. انكاد **ankād** misfortune; hardship, adversity; molestation, trouble, nuisance; worry, concern | نكد الطالع misfortune

نكد **nakid** pl. انكاد **ankād**, مناكيد **manākīd**[2] hard, troublesome, laborious; unhappy; peevish, cross, bad-tempered

انكد **ankad**[2] troublesome, painful, excruciating

مناكدة *munākada* pl. *-āt* inconvenience, discomfort, trouble, burden

منكود *mankūd* unhappy, unfortunate; ill-fated | منكود الحظ *m. al-ḥaẓẓ* pl. مناكيد الحظ *manākīd al-ḥ.* ill-starred, unlucky, unfortunate

نكر **nakira** *u* (*nakar, nukr,* نكور *nukūr,* نكير *nakīr*) not to know (ه, ‎ ه s.o., s.th.), have no knowledge, be ignorant (ه of s.th.); to deny, disown, disavow, renege (ه s.th.) **II** to disguise, mask (ه s.o.); to use in its indefinite form (ه a noun; *gram.*) **III** to disapprove (ه of s.o.), reject (ه s.o.) **IV** to pretend not to know (ه s.o.), refuse to have anything to do (ه, ‎ ه with s.o., with s.th.); to refuse to acknowledge, disown, disavow, disclaim, deny (ه s.th.); to renounce, renege (ه s.th.); to refuse, deny (ه على s.th. to s.o.), dispute, contest (ه على s.th. of s.o.); to reject (ه على s.th. with regard to s.o.), disapprove (ه على of s.th. with regard to s.o.); to censure, blame, rebuke (ه على s.o. for), criticize (ه من s.th. in s.o.); to hold s.th. (ه) against s.o. (على), reproach (ه على s.o. for) | انكر ذاته (*ḏātahū*) to deny o.s.; انكر نفسه (*nafsahū*) to harbor self-doubts; انكرت انى اراه I pretended not to see him **V** to be in disguise, be disguised, disguise o.s.; to change for the worse, change beyond recognition; to become estranged, be alienated (ل from s.th.); to snub (ل s.o.), treat (ل s.o.) with hostility, deal ungraciously (ل with s.o.); to deny o.s. (ل, e.g., a feeling), shut out from one's heart (ل s.th.) **VI** to have no knowledge, be ignorant (ه of s.th.); to pretend not to know (ه s.th.), feign ignorance, make as if one doesn't know; to refuse to have anything to do (ه with), snub, cut, ignore, pretend not to know (ه s.o.) **X** not to know (ه, ‎ ه s.o., s.th.), have no knowledge, be ignorant (ه of s.th.); to disapprove (ه of s.th.), reject (ه s.th.); to detest, loathe (ه s.th.)

نكر *nukr* denial, disavowal

نكر *nakir* unknown, little known

نكرة *nakira* indefinite noun (*gram.*); unknown person

نكران *nukrān* denial | لا نكران *lā nukrāna* it is incontestable; نكران الجميل ingratitude; نكران الذات self-denial

نكير *nakīr* denial, disavowal; disapproval, rejection; negation; reprehensible, repugnant, disgusting, vile, revolting, loathsome, abominable, atrocious; one of the Angels of Death (see منكر) | شد عليه النكير (*šadda*) to reproach s.o. severely

انكر *ankar*[2], f. نكراء *nakrā'*[2] reprehensible, abominable, disgusting, vile, revolting, loathsome | ابتسامة نكراء a vicious smile

انكار *inkār* denial, disavowal, negation, contestation; refusal, rejection, nonacceptance | انكار الذات self-denial, selflessness, unselfishness; انكار لجميله (*li-jamīlihī*) ingratitude toward s.o.

انكارى *inkārī* denying, disaffirmative; negative

تنكر *tanakkur* disguise, masquerade | محفل التنكر *mahfil at-t.* fancy-dress party, costume ball

تنكرى *tanakkurī*: حفل تنكرى (*ḥafl*) masked ball, costume ball

استنكار *istinkār* disapproval; horror, aversion, loathing

ناكر *nākir* denying, disavowing; unfriendly, hostile, forbidding | ناكر الجميل ungrateful

منكر *munakkar* indeterminate; indefinite (*gram.*)

منكر *munkar* denied; not recognized, unacknowledged, disowned, disavowed, disclaimed; disagreeable, shocking, detestable, abominable; abomination, atrocity; pl. منكرات objectionable, forbidden, or reprehensible, actions | منكر ونكير the two angels who examine the dead in their graves as to their faith

متنكر **mutanakkir** disguised, in disguise; incognito | رقص متنكر (*raqṣ*) masked ball, costume ball

مستنكر **mustankar** objectionable, reprehensible; odd, strange

نكز **nakaza** *u* (*nakz*) to prick; to goad, egg on (ه s.o.)

نكس **nakasa** *u* (*naks*) to turn around, turn over, invert, reverse, turn upside down (ه s.th.); to lower, withdraw, retract, pull in (ه s.th.); to bow, bend, tilt (رأسه *ra'sahū* or برأسه one's head); to cause a relapse (ه of an illness); pass. *nukisa*: to suffer a relapse **II** = **I**; to hang at half-mast (ه a flag) **VIII** to be turned over, be inverted, be reversed; to sink, drop forward (head), to relapse, suffer a relapse

نكس **nuks** and نكسة **naksa** relapse; degeneration, degeneracy; decadence

تنكس **tanakkus** degeneration (*biol.*)

انتكاس **intikās** relapse

منكوس **mankūs** inverted, reversed; relapsing, suffering a relapse

منكس **munakkas** inverted, reversed | منكس الرأس *m. ar-ra's* with bowed head

منتكس **muntakis** relapsing, suffering a relapse

نكش **nakaša** *i a* (*nakš*) to clear out, dredge, clean (ه s.th., esp., a well); to stir up, rout up, turn up, hoe up, rake up, dig up, break (ه the ground); to rummage, ransack, search (ه s.th.); to disorder, ruffle, tousle, dishevel (ه s.th.); to shake (ه trees)

منكش **minkaš** pl. مناكش **manākiš**[2] hoe, mattock; rake

منكاش **minkāš** pl. مناكيش **manākīš**[2] ○ dredger; poker, fire iron; (*eg.*) pickax

نكص **nakaṣa** *i u* (*nakṣ*, نكوص *nukūṣ*, منكص *mankaṣ*) to withdraw, turn away (عن from); to recoil, shrink (عن from) | نكص على عقبيه (*'aqibaihi*) to retreat, climb down, give up one's intention **II** to cause (ه s.o.) to retreat **VIII** to fall back, recoil, retreat

نكف **nakafa** *u* (*nakf*) to stop, arrest (ه s.th.); to disdain, scorn, spurn (عن s.th.); to reject (عن s.th.) | لا ينكف (*yunkafu*) irresistible, resistless; immeasurable, unfathomable **III** to vex, annoy, trouble, pester, harass, torment (ه s.o., ه with) **X** to be proud, haughty; to disdain, scorn, spurn, reject (عن or من s.th.), look down upon (عن or من), have an aversion (عن or من to), loathe, detest (عن or من s.th., also ه); to refrain (ان from doing s.th.)

نكفة **nakafa** parotid gland

نكفي **nakafī** parotid (adj.) | التهاب الغدة النكفية (*ḡudda*) inflammation of the parotid gland, parotitis, mumps (*med.*)

نكاف **nukāf** ○ parotitis, mumps (*med.*)

[1]نكل **nakala** *i u* (نكول *nukūl*) and **nakila** *a* (*nakal*) to recoil, shrink (من or عن from), flinch, shirk (من or عن s.th.), desist, refrain, abstain, draw back, withdraw (من or عن from); — *nakala* (نكلة *nakla*) and **II** to make an example (ب of s.o.), punish severely (ب s.o.), teach s.o. (ب) a lesson; to maltreat, torture (ب s.o.) **II** and **IV** to repel, force back, drive back, hold off, deter (ه عن s.o. from)

نكل **nikl** pl. انكال **ankāl**, نكول **nukūl** fetter, shackle, chain; bit (of a bridle)

نكال **nakāl** exemplary punishment, warning example, warning

نكول **nukūl** refusal to testify in court (*Isl. Law*)

تنكيل **tankīl** exemplary punishment; forcing back, driving back, containment; maltreatment, torture

[2]نكل *nikl* nickel

نكه *nakaha* *i a* (*nakh*) to blow, breathe (على or ل in s.o.'s face)

نكهة *nakha* smell of the breath; fragrance, smell, scent, aroma

نكى *nakā* *i* (نكاية *nikāya*) to cause damage, to harm; to hurt, injure (في or ه s.o.); to vex, annoy, offend (ب s.o.)

نكاية *nikāya* wrong, harm, damage, prejudice; vexation, annoyance, grievance, offense, outrage, chicanery | نكاية فيه *nikāyatan fīhi* in defiance of him, to spite him; اغلظ فيه النكاية (*aḡlaẓa, nikāyata*) to beset s.o. grievously, ride roughshod over s.o.

انكى *ankā* worse; causing more damage, more harmful, hurting or offending more grievously

[1]نم *namma* *u i* (*namm*) to betray, reveal, disclose, bespeak, indicate, show (على or عن s.th.); to give evidence (عن of s.th.); to report in a libelous manner (ه على s.th. about s.o.), sow dissension (بين among or between)

نم *namm* slander, calumniation, calumny; (pl. *-ūn*, انماء *animmā'*[2]) talebearer, scandalmonger, slanderer, calumniator

نمة *nimma* louse

نمام *nammām* (*eg.*) a variety of mint (Mentha sativa L.; *bot.*)

نمام *nammām* slanderer, calumniator

نميمة *namīma* pl. نمائم *namā'im*[2] slander, defamation, calumny

نامة *nāmma* stir, bustle, life

[2]نمى *nummī* pl. *-āt* coin | علم النميات *'ilm an-n.* numismatics

نموذج look up alphabetically

[1]نمر V to become angry, furious (ل with s.o.), turn into a tiger; to bluster, swagger

نمر *namir* pl. نمر *numur*, انمار *anmār* leopard; tiger

نمر *namir* clean, pure, healthy, wholesome (esp., water)

نمرة *namira* leopardess; tigress

نمرة *numra* pl. نمر *numar* speck, spot

انمر *anmar*[2], f. نمراء *namrā'*[2], pl. نمر *numr* spotted, striped, brindled

منمر *munammar* spotted, striped, brindled

[2]نمر II to mark with numbers, to number, provide with a number (ه s.th.)

نمرة *numra, nimra* pl. نمر *numar, nimar* number, numero; figure | نمرة واحد *nimrat w.* first-class, first-rate, A-1, excellent

نمارة *nammāra* pl. *-āt* numberer, numbering machine, date stamp

تنمير *tanmīr* numbering, numeration, count

منمر *munammar* numbered, counted

نمرسى *numrusī* pl. نمارسة *namārisa* (*eg.*) chinaware dealer

نمرق *numruq* and نمرقة *numruqa* pl. نمارق *namāriq*[2] cushion, pad; pillow; panel, saddle pad

نمس *namasa* *i* (*nams*) to keep secret, hide, conceal (ه s.th.); to confide a secret (ه to s.o.), confide in s.o. (ه), let (ه s.o.) in on a secret, make (ه s.o.) one's confidant III to confide a secret (ه to s.o.)

نمس *nims* (coll.; n. un. ة) pl. نموس *numūs* ichneumon, mongoose; ferret, marten, weasel

ناموس *nāmūs* pl. نواميس *nawāmīs*[2] sly, cunning, wily; confidant; (coll.; n. un. ة) mosquito(es); see also alphabetically | الناموس الاكبر the Archangel Gabriel

ناموسية *nāmūsīya* mosquito net

نمسا *nimsā*, النمسا *an-nimsā* Austria

نمساوى *nimsāwī* Austrian (adj. and n.)

نمش *namiša a* (*namaš*) to be freckled, have freckles

نمش *namaš* (coll.; n. un. ة) freckles; discolored spots on the skin

نمش *namiš* freckled

انمش *anmaš*[2], f. نمشاء *namšā'*[2], pl. نمش *numš* freckled

نمط *namaṭ* pl. نماط *nimāṭ*, انماط *anmāṭ* way, manner, mode, fashion; form, shape; sort, kind | على نمط in the manner of; على هذا النمط in this manner, this way, after this fashion; حديث النمط new-fashioned, modern; عتيق النمط old-fashioned, outmoded; هم على نمط واحد they are of the same stamp, they are all alike

نمطى *namaṭī* formal, rigid, stiff

نمق **II** to embellish, decorate, ornament, adorn (ه s.th.); to write in an elegant, lofty style (ه s.th.); to compose (ه a text)

تنميق *tanmīq* ornamentation, embellishment; glorification, exaltation, aggrandizement; elaborate embellishment (with figures of speech); composition (of a text, in elegant style)

منمق *munammaq* adorned, embellished; elegant, in good style, ornate, flowery (text, language)

نمل *namila a* (*namal*) to tingle, prickle, be numb, be benumbed (a limb)

نمل *naml* (coll.; n. un. ة) pl. نمال *nimāl* ant

نملى *namlī* antlike; ant- (in compounds); formic

نملية *namlīya* meat safe, food safe

نمل *namal* itching, tickling sensation; tingle, prickle, pricking sensation

نمل *namil* creeping, crawling; teeming with ants; nimble, deft

انملة *unmula* pl. انامل *anāmil*[2] fingertip

تنميل *tanmīl* itching, tickling sensation; tingle, prickle, pricking sensation

منمول *manmūl* teeming with ants

نمنم *namnama* to stripe, streak (ه s.th.); to adorn, embellish, ornament (ه s.th.)

نمنم *nimnim* streaks or ripples in the sand (caused by the wind)

نمنمة *namnama*, *nimnima* wren (*zool.*)

O منمنمة *munamnama* miniature

نما (نمو) *namā u* (نمو *numūw*) to grow; to increase; to rise

نمو *numūw* growth; progress

نموذج *namūdaj*, *numūdaj* pl. *-āt* and نماذج *namādij*[2] model; type; pattern; sample, specimen; exemplar, example; blank, form

نموذجى *namūdajī* exemplary, model

نمى *namā i* (*namy*, نماء *namā'*, نمية *namīya*) to grow; to increase, augment, multiply; to rise; to progress, make progress, advance; to thrive, prosper, flourish; to be ascribed, be attributed (الى to s.o.); to ascribe, attribute (الى ه s.th. to s.o.); to be told, be reported (الى to s.o.; of an event), reach (الى s.o.; news), come to s.o.'s knowledge **II** and **IV** to make grow, increase, augment, promote, further, advance (ه s.th.) **VIII** to trace one's origin (الى to s.o.), descend, be descended (الى from), be related (الى to); to be affiliated, be associated, have connections (الى with); to depend, be dependent (الى on); to belong (الى to, esp., to an organization), be a member (الى of an organization)

نماء *namā'* growth, expansion, increase, augmentation, increment, accretion

نمى *namīy* growth, expansion, increase, augmentation, increment, accretion

نماة *namāh* pl. نمى *naman* small louse

تنمية *tanmiya* expansion, promotion, furtherance, advancement; increase, augmentation; raising, stepping up, intensification, boost

انماء *inmā'* expansion, promotion, furtherance, advancement, increase, augmentation; raising, stepping up, intensification, boost; cultivation, breeding (of plants)

انتماء *intimā'* membership

نامية *nāmiya* pl. نوام *nawāmin* growth; morbid growth, morbid formation, excrescence, tumor (*med.*) | النوامى السرطانية (*saraṭānīya*) cancerous formations (*med.*)

منتم *muntamin* belonging, pertaining

منتمى *muntaman* descent, origin, relationship, affiliation, membership

نهب **nahaba** *a u* and **nahiba** *a* (*nahb*) to plunder, rifle, take by force (ه s.th.) | نهب الارض *nahaba l-arḍa* and نهب الطريق (*ṭarīqa*) to cover the distance (الى to) quickly or at tremendous speed **IV** to let (ه s.o.) rifle (ه s.th.); to leave, surrender as booty (ه ه to s.o. s.th.) **VI** to grip, seize (ه the soul, the heart) | تناهب الارض عدوا (*arḍa 'adwan*) to race along at a tearing pace **VIII** to grip, seize (ه the soul, the heart); to rifle, snatch away (ه s.th.); to take in eagerly, devour (ه s.th.; said of the eyes) | انتهب الطريق (*ṭarīqa*) to cover the distance (الى to) quickly or at tremendous speed

نهب *nahb* robbery, plundering, pillage, looting, spoliation; gallop; (pl. نهاب *nihāb*) plunder, spoils, booty, loot; نهبا *nahban* by robbery

نهبة *nuhba* booty, plunder, spoils, loot

نهبى *nuhbā* booty, plunder, spoils, loot

نهاب *nahhāb* robber; plunderer, marauder, looter

نهبرة *nuhbura* abyss; hell

نهج **nahaja** *a* (*nahj*) to proceed, act; to enter (ه upon a road), take (ه a route or course), follow, pursue (ه a way, a road); to make clear, clarify (ه s.th.); to be open, plain, distinct; — **nahaja** *i* and **nahija** *a* (*nahaj*) to be out of breath, gasp for breath, pant | نهج خطة (*kiṭṭatan*) to pursue a plan; to assume an attitude; نهج على منواله (*minwālihī*) to follow s.o.'s example **II** to put out of breath, make breathless, cause to pant (ه s.o.) **IV** do.; to be clear (matter, affair); to make clear, clarify, explain (ه s.th.) **VIII** to enter (ه upon a road), take (ه a route or course), follow, pursue (ه a way, a road) | انتهج سبيله (*sabīlahū*) and **X** استنهج سبيله to follow s.o.'s example, follow s.o.'s footsteps, imitate s.o.

نهج *nahj* pl. نهوج *nuhūj* open way; road; method, procedure, manner | نهج نهجه (*nahjahū*) to follow s.o.'s method; النهج القويم the straight path, the right way, the proper manner

نهج *nahaj* quick breathing, panting; breathlessness

نهيج *nahīj* quick breathing, panting; breathlessness

ناهج *nāhij* open, plain road

منهج *manhaj*, *minhaj* pl. مناهج *manāhij*[2] open, plain, easy road; manner, procedure, method; program; course | منهج التعليم curriculum; مناهج البحث *m. al-baḥṯ* methodology of research, research methods

منهاج *minhāj* pl. مناهيج *manāhīj*[2] way, road; method; program

نهد **nahada** *a u* (نهود *nuhūd*) to become round and full, swell (breasts); to be buxom, have round, swelling breasts **V** to sigh **VI** to share the expenses; to distribute among each other in equal shares (ه s.th.)

نهد *nahd* pl. نهود *nuhūd* female breast, bosom; elevation, rise, hump, bump

تنهد *tanahhud* pl. *-āt* sigh

ناهد *nāhid* full, round, swelling (breast); in the bloom of youth; buxom

نهر *nahara a* (*nahr*) to flow copiously, stream forth, gush forth; to chide, scold, reproach (ه s.o.); to turn away with angry words, brush off, rebuff, reject, repulse, drive away, chase away (ه s.o.) VIII to chide, scold (ه s.o.); to drive away, chase away (ه s.o.)

نهر *nahr* pl. انهر *anhur*, انهار *anhār*, نهور *nuhūr* stream, river; — (pl. *anhur* and *anhār*) column (of a newspaper) | ما بين النهرين (*nahrain*) Mesopotamia; ما وراء النهر Transoxiana; نهر اردن Eridanus (*astron.*); *n. urdunn* the Jordan river; نهر السلام *n. as-salām* the Tigris; نهر الشريعة the Jordan river

نهرى *nahrī* river- (in compounds), riverine, fluvial, fluviatile

نهار *nahār* pl. انهر *anhur*, نهر *nuhur* daytime, day (from dawn to dusk, as distinguished from يوم *yaum* = day of 24 hours) | نهارا وليلا *nahāran wa-lailan* by day and by night; ليل نهار *laila nahāra* day and night; نهار انهر (*anhar*) a wonderful day

نهارى *nahārī* relating to day or daytime, diurnal; نهاريات news of the day, miscellany (heading of a newspaper column)

انهر *anhar*[2] see *nahār*

نهير *nahīr* copious, ample, abundant, plentiful, much

نهير *nuhair* pl. *-āt* little river, creek, brook; a tributary, an affluent

انتهار *intihār* rebuke, scolding, reprimand, reproof; rejection, rebuff, repulse, repulsion

نهز *nahaza a* (*nahz*) to push, thrust, shove (ه s.o.); to drive, urge on (ه s.o.); to repulse, hold off, ward off (ه s.o.) III to be near s.th. (ه, esp., fig.), approach, attain, reach (ه s.th.); to seize (ه s.th.) | ناهز البلوغ to attain (the age of) majority; ناهز الخمسين he was close to fifty, he was pushing fifty VIII انتهز الفرصة (*al-furṣata*) to seize or take the opportunity, take advantage or avail o.s. of the opportunity; انتهز ه فرصة ل (*furṣatan*) to use s.th. as an opportunity for

نهزة *nuhza* opportunity, occasion

نهاز *nahhāz*: نهاز الفرص *n. al-furaṣ* quick to seize an opportunity, an opportunist

انتهاز *intihāz*: انتهاز الفرص *int. al-furaṣ* exploitation of opportunities, opportunism

انتهازى *intihāzī* timeserver, opportunist

انتهازية *intihāzīya* opportunism

نهش *nahaša i* (*nahš*) to bite, snap, grab with the teeth (ه s.th.); to tear to pieces, mangle (ه s.o.)

نهاش *nahhāš* snappish, biting, mordacious, sharp

نهض *nahaḍa a* (*nahḍ*, نهوض *nuhūḍ*) to rise, get up (عن from a seat, from bed); to take off, start (airplane); to pounce (الى on s.o., on s.th.); to raise, lift, hoist, heave, carry (ب s.o., s.th.); to carry on, practice, pursue, attack resolutely, tackle, handle, take in one's hands, further, promote, encourage (ب s.th.), give a boost, give impetus (ب to s.th.), bring new life (ب into s.th.), bring about an upswing (ب of s.th.); to stand up (ب for), take up the cause of (ب), espouse, support, endorse, champion (ب s.th.); to rise, revolt, rebel (على against s.o.); to get ready, prepare (ل for a piece of work, a task, or the like), begin, start, undertake (ل s.th.), enter, embark (ل upon); to be apposite, pertinent, apropos (argument) | نهض قائما (*qā'iman*) he got on his feet, he got up; نهض بالامر (*bi-l-amr*) to assume power, take the command; نهضت الحجة ب (*ḥujja*) proof has been established for ...; نهض بالخسائر والضحايا (*ḍaḥāyā*) to take losses and sacrifices readily upon o.s. **III** to offer resistance (ه to), resist, oppose, defy (ه s.o.); to argue, dispute (ه with s.o.) **IV** to tell (ه s.o.) to rise, lift up, raise, help up (ه s.o.), awaken, (a)rouse, stir up, animate, inspire, stimulate, excite, incite (ه s.o.) **VI** to get up, stand up, rise, draw o.s. up **VIII** do. **X** to awaken, (a)rouse, stimulate, animate, encourage, incite, instigate, egg on (ه s.o., الى to)

نهض **nahḍ** awakening, rise, growth, boom, upswing, advancement, progress

نهضة **nahḍa** pl. *-āt* getting up, rising; awakening (esp., national), rise, growth, boom, upswing, advancement, progress; resurgence, revival, rebirth, renaissance; (spiritual) movement; ability, capability, power | عيد النهضة *ʿīd an-n.* Day of National Awakening (of Iraq, celebrated on the 9th of Shaban)

نهوض **nuhūḍ** raising, boosting, revival, restoration, promotion, advancement, furtherance, encouragement, activation (ب of s.th.)

مناهضة **munāhaḍa** resistance, opposition

انهاض **inhāḍ** awakening, arousing, stimulation, animation; promotion, advancement, encouragement, initiation of an upswing, of a boom

استنهاض **istinhāḍ** awakening, arousing, stimulation, animation; promotion, advancement, encouragement, initiation of an upswing, of a boom

ناهض **nāhiḍ** rising, getting up; active, diligent, energetic | دليل ناهض conclusive proof, cogent evidence

نهق **nahaqa**, **nahiqa** *a* (*nahq*, نهاق *nuhāq*, نهيق *nahīq*) to bray (donkey)

نهك **nahaka** *a* (نهاكة *nahāka*) to wear off, wear out, use up, consume (ه s.th.); to grind down, crush (ه s.th.); — (*nahk*) and **nahika** *a* (*nahk*, نهكة *nahka*) to exhaust, weaken, enfeeble, debilitate, sap the strength of, wear out, wear down, enervate, unnerve, waste, emaciate (ه s.o.); **nahika** and pass. **nuhika** to be worn off, worn out, run down, used up, spent, exhausted, enervated, gaunt, emaciated | نهك عرضه (*ʿirḍahū*) to injure s.o.'s honor **IV** to exhaust, wear out, enervate, ruin (ه s.o.) **VIII** to waste, emaciate, enervate, exhaust (ه s.o.); to violate, abuse, defile, profane, desecrate (ه s.th.); to infringe, violate (ه a law), offend against (ه); to rape, ravish (ها a woman); to insult, defame, malign, slander, abuse, brutalize (ه a man) | لا ينتهك *lā yuntahaku* inviolable, sacrosanct, sacred, consecrated

نهك **nahk** weakening, exhaustion, enervation, attrition; consumption, depletion, exhaustion; abuse, misuse; infraction, violation; profanation, desecration; sacrilege

نهكة **nahka** exhaustion; emaciation, wasting away

انهاك **inhāk** exhaustion

انتهاك **intihāk** weakening, exhaustion, enervation, attrition; consumption, depletion, exhaustion; abuse, misuse; infraction, violation; profanation, desecration; sacrilege; rape | انتهاك الحرمة *int. al-ḥurma* sacrilege; انتهاك العورة *int. al-ʿaura* offense involving moral turpitude

منهك **munhik** grueling, exhausting

نهل **nahila** *a* (*nahal*, منهل *manhal*) to drink

نهلة **nahla** pl. *nahalāt* drink, draught, gulp, swallow

منهل **manhal** pl. مناهل *manāhil*[2] watering place, spring, pool

نهم **nahima** *a* (*naham*, نهامة *nahāma*) to have a ravenous appetite, be insatiable; to be greedy, covetous (ف of)

نهم **naham** ravenous appetite, voracity; greed, greediness, avidity

نهمة **nahma** burning desire, craving, greed, avidity

نهم **nahim** greedy, avid; insatiable, voracious; glutton, gourmand

نهيم **nahīm** greedy, avid; insatiable, voracious; glutton, gourmand

منهوم **manhūm** greedy, avid; insatiable; covetous, desirous (ب of s.th.)

نهنه **nahnaha** to restrain, hold back, keep, prevent (عن ، s.o. from); to sob

(نهو) and (نهى) نها **nahā** *u* (*nuhw*) and نهى **nahā** *a* (*nahy*) to forbid (عن ، s.o. s.th., to do s.th.), prohibit, ban (عن ، s.o. from doing s.th.), interdict, proscribe (عن ، to s.o. s.th.); to restrain, hold back, keep, prevent (عن ، s.o. from); pass. نهى *nuhiya* to come, get (الى to s.o.; of news), reach (الى s.o.), come to s.o.'s knowledge **IV** to get (الى ، s.th. to s.o.), make s.th. (،) reach s.o. (الى); to communicate, transmit, make known (الى ، s.th. to s.o.), bring (، s.th.) to s.o.'s (الى) knowledge, inform, apprise (، الى s.o. of s.th.); to bring to an end, terminate, finish, end, wind up, conclude, complete (، s.th.); to put an end to s.th. (،), settle, decide (، s.th.) **VI** to come to an end, run out, expire (period of time); to attain a high degree; to come, get (الى to s.o.), reach (الى s.o.); to desist, refrain, abstain (عن from), give up, renounce, forgo, abandon (عن s.th.), cease, stop (عن doing s.th.) | تناهى الى اسماعهم (*asmā'ihim*) to come to s.o.'s hearing, to s.o.'s knowledge **VIII** to be concluded, terminated, finished, done with, settled, decided, be over; to run out, expire, come to an end (appointed time); to end, end up, wind up (ب by, in or with); to finish, terminate, conclude, wind up (عن s.th.), be or become finished, done, be through (من with s.th.); to wind up, land eventually (الى at), get ultimately (الى to); (with الى ان) to come or lead to the point where ..., end at the point where ..., get eventually so that ..., result in ...; to come to s.o.'s (الى) knowledge; to lead, lead up, bring (ب الى s.o. to); to desist, refrain, abstain (عن from s.th.), give up, renounce, forgo, abandon (عن s.th.), cease, stop (عن doing s.th.) | انتهى الامر الى ان the upshot was that ..., the long and short of it was that ...; انتهى به الامر الى ان he got to the point where ...

نهى **nahy** prohibition, ban, interdiction, proscription | النهى والامر (*amr*) unlimited, absolute authority, dictatorial power, command

نهيى **nahyī** prohibitory, prohibitive, prohibitionary

نهى **nuhan** intelligence, understanding, reason, mind, intellect

نهية **nuhya** mind, intellect

نهاء **nihā'** utmost degree, limit

نهاية **nihāya** pl. *-āt* end; termination, conclusion; outcome, result, upshot; the utmost; limit, utmost degree, extreme, extremity; *nihāyatan* in the end, at last, finally, ultimately, eventually | فى النهاية in the end, at last, finally, ultimately, eventually; الى النهاية to the end; بلا نهاية (*bi-lā*) unending(ly); الى غير نهاية or الى ما لا نهاية له (*lā nihāyata*) unendingly, to infinity, ad infinitum; للنهاية to the greatest extent, extremely; نهاية الارب *n. al-arab* the ultimate goal; النهاية الصغرى (*ṣuḡrā*) minimum; النهاية الكبرى (العظمى) (*kubrā, 'uẓmā*) maximum; النهاية العليا (*'ulyā*) the best grade, the highest rating (in a system of school marks); اعلى درجة فى النهاية الكبرى (*a'lā darajatin*) absolute maximum (of temperature);

اقل درجة فى النهاية الصغرى (*aqallu d.*) absolute minimum; حد النهاية *ḥadd an-n.* utmost limit, last step; كان نهاية فى الحذق (*nihāyatan, ḥiḏq*) to be the ne plus ultra of skill, be extremely skillful

نهائى *nihā'ī* extreme, utmost, last, final; ultimate, eventual; final, decisive, conclusive, definitive; نهائيا *nihā'iyan* at last, finally | انذار نهائى (*inḏār*) or بلاغ نهائى (*balāḡ*) ultimatum; حكم نهائى (*ḥukm*) final decision, final judgment (*jur.*); علاج نهائى extreme remedy, last resource; فوز نهائى (*fauz*) ultimate triumph, eventual success; مباراة نهائى a final match, final (in sports)

لا نهائى *lā-nihā'ī* infinite, unending

لا نهائية *lā-nihā'iya* infinity

انهاء *inhā'* finishing, termination, completion, conclusion; settlement; suspension, stop

تناه *tanāhin* finity, finitude, limitedness; expiration (of a period of time)

انتهاء *intihā'* end, termination, completion, conclusion, close; expiration | انتهاء الاجل *int. al-ajal* end of life, death

ناه *nāhin* interdictory, prohibitory, prohibitive | هذا رجل ناهيك من رجل (*rajulun nāhīka*) here is a man to fill any man's shoes; ناهيك من (also عن or ب) how excellent is ...! how remarkable is ...! suffice it to ...! let it be enough to ...! to say nothing of ..., not to mention ..., let alone ...; above all, in the first place, primarily; take, for instance, ...! ناهيك ب it is enough to mention ...; ناهيك بأن (*bi-an*) let it be enough to ...; let it suffice you to know that ...; not to mention the fact that ...; to say nothing of the fact that ...; aside from the fact that ...

ناهية *nāhiya* pl. نواه *nawāhin* ban, prohibition, proscription

منهى *manhīy* forbidden, prohibited, interdicted, illicit

متناه *mutanāhin* finished, terminated, expired; limited, bounded, finite; utmost, extreme; excessive, exaggerated | غير متناه unlimited, boundless, infinite, unending, endless; متناه فى الدقة (*diqqa*) extremely thin, of the greatest fineness; متناه فى الصغر (*ṣiḡar*) extremely tiny, minute

منته *muntahin* ceasing, running out; finished, done; expired (validity)

منتهى *muntahan* finished, terminated; end; the utmost, extreme; highest degree, utmost limit | بمنتهى الشدة *bi-m. š-šidda* with extreme force; فى منتهى الدقة (*m. d-diqqa*) extremely thin; بلغ منتهاه to reach its highest degree

ناء (نوء) *nā'a u* (*nau'*) to fall down, sink down, break down, collapse, succumb (ب under a burden); to weigh heavily (ب upon s.o.) | ناء بالحمل (*ḥiml*) to bear a burden with difficulty; to be weighed down by a burden; ناء بكلكله (*bi-kalkalihī*) to oppress s.o. grievously, weigh heavily upon s.o. III to offer resistance (ه to s.o.), resist, oppose, withstand, defy (ه s.o.); to vie, compete (ه with s.o.); to fight, struggle, contend (ه with s.o.) | ناوأه العداء (*'adā'a*) to be hostile to s.o., treat s.o. with hostility IV to weigh down, crush (ه s.o.)

نوء *nau'* pl. انواء *anwā'*, نوآن *nū'ān*, tempest, storm; gale, hurricane

مناوأة *munāwa'a* resistance, opposition, recalcitrance, insubordination; struggle, contention, strife

[1]ناب (نوب) *nāba u* (*naub*, مناب *manāb*, نيابة *niyāba*) to represent (عن s.o.), act as representative (عن of s.o.), deputize, substitute (عن for s.o.), act as deputy, substitute, or proxy (عن of s.o.), take s.o.'s (عن) place, replace (عن s.o.), perform s.o.'s (عن) office, act in s.o.'s (عن) behalf; to return from time to time (الى to s.o.), visit periodically (الى s.o.),

frequent (الى s.o.'s place); — (*naub*, نوبة *nauba*) to afflict, hit, strike, befall (ه s.o.; of misfortune), happen, occur (ه to s.o.), fall to s.o.'s (ه) lot or share, descend (ه upon s.o.) **II** to appoint (ه s.o.) as deputy or agent (عن of), commission, depute, or delegate (ه s.o.) to act in behalf of (عن) **III** to take turns, alternate (ه with s.o.) **IV** to depute, deputize (ه s.o.), commission or delegate (ه s.o.) to act in behalf of (عن), in s.o.'s (عن) place; to empower, authorize (ه s.o.) to act in behalf of (عن); to come from time to time (الى to s.o.), visit frequently (الى s.o.), frequent (الى s.o.'s place) | اناب الى الله to turn repentantly to God **VI** to take turns, alternate (فى or على in, also ه in some activity), do s.th. (فى or على, also ه) by turns; to visit, befall or afflict (ه s.o.) successively or alternately | تناوبته الخطوب he has suffered one misfortune after the other **VIII** to befall, beset, afflict (ه s.o.), happen, occur (ه to s.o.)

نوبة *nauba* pl. نوب *nuwab* change, alternation, shift, rotation; (one's) turn; time, instance (= مرة *marra*); case, instance, occasion; — (pl. *-āt*) fit, attack, paroxysm (*path.*); crisis; change (or relief) of the guard, guard duty, guard; bugle call; (*syr.*) troupe of musicians, small orchestra of native instruments | بالنوبة alternately, in rotation, by turns, successively, one by one, one after the other; نوبة عصبية (*'aṣabīya*) nervous crisis; نوبات غضبه *n. ġaḍabihī* his fits of rage; نوبة قلبية (*qalbīya*) heart attack; نوبات المطر *n. al-maṭar* rainy spells, periods of rain; جاءت نوبته it was his turn

نوبتجى *naubatjī* on duty; commander of the guard, officer on duty

نوبة *nūba* pl. نوب *nuwab* misfortune, calamity, mishap, misadventure, accident, reverse, heavy blow

نيابة *niyāba* representation, replacement, substitution, proxy, deputyship; branch office, branch, agency; delegation; prosecution, office of the district attorney | نيابة عن *niyābatan 'an* in place of, instead of, in lieu of; بالنيابة acting, deputy, by proxy; مدير المصلحة بالنيابة (*mudīr al-maṣlaḥa*) the deputy director of the department; بالنيابة عن in the name of, in behalf of; نيابة عمومية (*'umūmīya*) prosecution, office of the district attorney; رئيس النيابة chief prosecutor; وكيل النيابة representative of the prosecution, prosecuting attorney; النيابات المالية (*mālīya*) the financial delegations (in Algeria)

نيابى *niyābī* vicarious, deputed, delegated; representative; parliamentary | حكومة نيابية representative (parliamentary) government; مجلس نيابى (*majlis*) parliament

مناب *manāb* replacement, substitution, proxy, deputyship; substitute; office performed by proxy, place taken as deputy; share, portion, allotment | ناب منابه to represent s.o., substitute for s.o., act in s.o.'s behalf

مناوبة *munāwaba* alternation, rotation; *munāwabatan* alternately, in rotation, by turns, successively, one by one, one after the other | بالمناوبة do.; مناوبة الرى *m. ar-rīy* (*Eg.*) periodic rotation in irrigation

انابة *ināba* authorization; deputation, delegation, appointment as authorized agent or deputy | انابات قضائية (*qaḍā'īya*) requests for legal assistance (from court to court)

تناوب *tanāwub* alternation, rotation, periodic change; ○ alternation (*el.*) | بالتناوب successively, one after the other, one by one, by turns, alternately, in rotation

نائب *nā'ib* pl. نواب *nuwwāb* representative, agent, proxy, substitute, alternate; delegate; deputy; (with foll. genit.) vice-; authorized agent; sergeant (formerly, *Syr.*; *mil.*); authorized representative of a cadi, assistant magistrate (*Isl. Law*), also نائب شرعى (*šar'ī*) | نائب الرئيس vice-president; vice-chairman; نائب عام (*'āmm*) or نائب عمومى (*'umūmī*) public prosecutor; نائب العريف corporal (*Ir.*); نائب القنصل *n. al-qunṣul* vice-consul; نائب الملك *n. al-malik* viceroy; نائب مالى (*mālī*) financial delegate (*Alg.*); مجلس النواب *majlis an-n.* house of representatives, parliament

نائب *nā'ib* share, portion; allotment; contingent, quota; distributive share in estate, statutory portion

نائبة *nā'iba* pl. *-āt,* نوائب *nawā'ib*[2] vicissitudes, ups and downs (of luck, of a battle, etc.); heavy blow, disaster, calamity, misfortune

منوب *munawwib* mandator (*jur.*); constituent, voter

منوب *munawwab*: ضابط منوب officer on duty, commander of the guard

مناوب *munāwib* on duty (esp. officer)

منيب *munīb* repentant

متناوب *mutanāwib* alternating, alternate, rotating, successive | تيار متناوب (*tayyār*) alternating current (*el.*)

[2]بلاد النوبة *bilād an-nūba* Nubia

نوبى *nūbī* Nubian (adj. and n.)

[1](نوت) نات *nāta u* (*naut*) to sway, reel, totter, stagger

[2]نوت *nōt* and نوتة *nōta* notes (*mus.*), also نوت الموسيقى *n. al-mūsīqā*

نوتة *nōta* note, remark

[3]نوتى *nūtī* pl. نواتى *nawātīy,* نوتية *nūtīya* seaman, mariner, sailor; skipper | نوتى اول seaman apprentice, نوتى ممتاز (*mumtāz*) seaman (*mil.*; *Eg.* 1939); نواتى السفينة ship's crew

[1]نوح *nūḥ* Noah

[2](نوح) ناح *nāḥa u* (*nauḥ,* نواح *nuwāḥ,* نياح *niyāḥ,* نياحة *niyāḥa,* مناح *manāḥ*) to wail, weep, lament; to mourn, bemoan, bewail (على s.o.); to coo (pigeon) **III** to be opposite s.th. (ه), lie face to face (ه with), face (ه s.th.) **V** to swing; to pendulate, dangle; to sway **VI** to howl, whine (wind)

نوح *nauḥ* and نواح *nuwāḥ* loud weeping, wailing, lamentation (for the dead)

نواح *nawwāḥ* mourner

نواحة *nawwāḥa* hired female mourner

نائحة *nā'iḥa* pl. نوائح *nawā'iḥ*[2], نائحات *nā'iḥāt* hired female mourner

مناحة *manāḥa* lamentation, wailing, mourning

نوخ **II** to halt for a rest; to take up residence **IV** to make (ه a camel) kneel down; to stay, remain (ب at a place) | اناخ عليه البؤس بكلكله (*bu'su bi-kalkalihī*) to be in great distress, be in a grave plight **X** to kneel down

مناخ *munāḵ* pl. *-āt* halting place, way station; residence, abode; — *munāḵ, manāḵ* climate

مناخى *munāḵī, manāḵī* climatic

(نود) ناد *nāda u* (*naud,* نواد *nuwād,* نودان *nawadān*) and **V** to sway; to swing back and forth; to pendulate

[1]نور **II** to flower, blossom, be in bloom; to put forth or bear (ه blossoms); to light, illuminate, fill with light, furnish with lights (ل or ه s.th.); to shed light (ل or ه on s.th.); to enlighten (ل or ه s.o.); to light (ه a lamp) **IV** انار *anāra* to light, illuminate, fill with light, furnish with

lights (ه s.th.); to throw light (ه on a problem), elucidate, explain, clarify (ه a problem); انور *anwara* to come to light, show, appear, be uncovered, be disclosed, be revealed **V** to be lighted, be lit, be illuminated; to receive enlightenment, be enlightened **X** to seek enlightenment, insight, or an explanation; to receive light, be lighted, be lit, be illuminated; to obtain enlightenment, gain insight, get an explanation, receive information

نار ***nār*** f., pl. نيران *nīrān* fire; rifle fire, gunfire; conflagration; النار Hell | جبل النار *jabal an-n.* volcano; شريط النار slow match, fuse; شيخ النار *šaik an-n.* the Devil; اشهر من نار على علم (*'alam*) very famous; كان على نار to be on pins and needles; نيران حامية (*ḥāmiya*) heavy fire, drumfire (*mil.*)

نارى ***nārī*** fiery, igneous, fire- (in compounds); burning, blazing, red-hot | آلة نارية (in popular usage) motor, any motor-driven device; دراجة نارية (*darrāja*) motorcycle; سلاح نارى firearm; سهم نارى (*sahm*) rocket; طلق نارى (*ṭalaq*) shot (from a firearm), rifleshot, gunshot; العاب نارية fireworks; مقذوف نارى projectile (of a firearm), bullet, shell

نور ***naur*** (coll.; n. un. ة) pl. انوار *anwār* blossom(s), flower(s)

نور ***nūr*** pl. انوار *anwār* light; ray of light, light beam; brightness, gleam, glow; illumination; light, lamp; ○ headlight (of an automobile); lantern | ○ نور براق (*barrāq*) blinker, flashing light; ○ نور ثابت steady light; نور الدلالة *n. ad-dalāla* leading light (*naut.*); نور كشاف (*kuššāf*) or نور كاشف searchlight (*mil.*); ○ انوار خفية (*ḵafiya*) indirect lighting; ام النور *umm an-n.* the Virgin Mary; سبت النور *sabt an-n.* Easter Saturday (*Chr.*); عليك نور bravo! excellent! well done! رأى النور to come into being, come into the world, be born

نورى ***nūrī*** luminary, luminous, like light; light-, lighting- (in compounds); bright, shining, brilliant, radiant

نورانى ***nūrānī*** luminous

نورانية ***nurānīya*** luminosity, brilliance

نور ***nawar*** (coll.) gypsies; vagabonds, tramps

نورى ***nawarī*** gypsy; vagabond, tramp

نورة ***nūra*** lime; depilatory agent

نير ***nayyir*** luminous; shining, brilliant; lighted, illuminated, brightly lit, full of light; clear, plain, distinct; النيران sun and moon

نوار ***nuwwār*** (coll.; n. un. ة) pl. نواوير *nawāwīr*² blossom(s), flower(s)

منار ***manār*** and منارة ***manāra*** pl. مناور *manāwir*², منائر *manā'ir*² lighthouse; minaret

منور ***manwar*** pl. مناور *manāwir*² light hole (in a wall); skylight

تنوير ***tanwīr*** flowering, blossoming, bloom, efflorescence; lighting, illumination; enlightenment; التنوير and تنوير العقول the Enlightenment

مناورة see below

انارة ***ināra*** lighting, illumination; enlightenment

نائرة ***nā'ira*** hatred, flame of war

منور ***munawwar*** lighted, illuminated; enlightened; shining, brilliant; bright | المنورة epithet of Medina

منير ***munīr*** luminous, radiant, brilliant, shining; enlightening, illuminative | جسم منير (*jism*) luminous body, luminary, illuminant

متنور ***mutanawwir*** lighted, illuminated

مستنير ***mustanīr*** lighted, illuminated; enlightened; educated; an educated person

[2]مناورة *munāwara* maneuver; trick; shunting (railroad); مناورات military maneuvers | مناورات جوية (*jawwīya*) air maneuvers; مناورة دبلوماسية diplomatic maneuver; عامل المناورة shunter

نورج *nauraj* pl. نوارج *nawārij*[2] threshing machine, thresher

نورز *nauraz* (coll.; n. un. ة) sea gull(s) (*zool.*)

نورستانيا *nūrastāniyā* neurasthenia

نوروز *naurūz* Persian New Year's Day

[1](نوس) ناس *nāsa u* (*naus*, نوسان *nawasān*) to dangle, swing back and forth, bob

نواس *nawwās* dangling, bobbing, swinging; ○ pendulum (*Syr.*)

[2]ناووس *nāwūs*, ناءوس *nā'ūs* pl. نواويس *nawāwīs*[2] sarcophagus

[3]ناس *nās* people, see انس

نوسر *nausara* to form a fistula (ناسور)

نوش III to skirmish, engage in a skirmish (ه with s.o.); to brush (ه against s.th.), play (ه around or about s.th.)

نوشة *nauša* (*eg.*) typhoid fever

مناوشة *munāwaša* skirmish, engagement, encounter | مناوشة حربية (*ḥarbīya*) engagement, armed clash; pl. hostilities

مناويش *manāwīš*[2] and مناويشى *manāwīšī* (*eg.*) bluish purple

نوشادر *nūšādir* ammonia

(نوص) ناص *nāṣa u* (*nauṣ*, مناص *manāṣ*, منيص *manīṣ*) to avoid, shirk, evade, dodge (عن s.th.), flee, draw back (عن from) VIII to grow dim, die down (light, lamp)

نوص *nauṣ* wild ass, onager

مناص *manāṣ* and منيص *manīṣ* avoidance, shirking, evasion; escape, way out | لا مناص منه (*manāṣa*) inevitable, unavoidable

(نوط) ناط *nāṭa u* (*nauṭ*, نياط *niyāṭ*) to hang, suspend (ه ب s.th. on); to entrust (ه ب s.th. to s.o., ه ب s.o. with), commission (ه ب s.o. to do s.th.), charge (ه ب s.o. with); to make dependent, conditional (ب or على ه s.th. on); pass. نيط *nīṭa* to depend, be dependent, be conditional (ب on), be linked (ب to), be connected (ب with), belong (ب to); to be entrusted (ب to s.o.); to hang, be suspended (على on) II and IV = I | اناطه بشرط (*bi-šarṭin*) to make s.th. dependent on (or subject to) a condition, make s.th. conditional; اناطه بعهدته (*bi-'uhdatihī*) to entrust s.o. with the responsibility for s.th., make s.o. responsible for s.th.

نوط *nauṭ* pl. انواط *anwāṭ*, نياط *niyāṭ* s.th. suspended, hanging, or attached; decoration, medal, order, badge of honor | نوط الجدارة *n. al-jadāra* order of merit

نيط *naiṭ* pl. نياط *niyāṭ* aorta | منظر يشق له نياط القلوب (*manẓarun yušaqqu*) a heart-rending sight; قطع نياط القلوب to break the heart

مناط *manāṭ* place where s.th. is suspended; object, butt (e.g., of mockery); anchor (of hope) | مناط الثريا *m. aṯ-ṯurayyā* or مناط الجوزاء *m. al-jauzā'* the highest heavens, as high, or as far, as the Pleiades (or Gemini, respectively)

تنوط *tanawwuṭ*, *tunawwiṭ* weaverbird

منوط *manūṭ* dependent, conditional (ب on)

منوط *munawwaṭ* entrusted, commissioned (ب with), in charge of (ب)

مناط *munāṭ* entrusted, commissioned (ب with), in charge of (ب)

نوع II to divide into various kinds, classify (ه s.th.); to make different, diversify, vary, variegate (ه s.th.), give variety (ه to); to change, alter, vary, modify, alter in its outward appearance (ه s.th.), change the appearance (ه of) V to be of various kinds or forms; to be manifold, diverse, varying, variegated, multiform, complex

نوع **nau'** pl. انواع **anwā'** kind, sort, type, species; variety; way, manner, mode, fashion; form; nature, character, quality, grade; نوعا **nau'an** somewhat, a little; to a certain extent, in some measure, in a certain way, so to speak, as it were | نوعا ما somehow or other, in a way, after a fashion, somewhat; نوعا وكية (*wa-kammīyatan*) in nature and quantity, qualitatively and quantitatively; بنوع خاص (*ḵāṣṣ*) in particular, especially; الاول من نوعه the first of his (its) kind; ظالمون على انواعهم oppressors of all kinds, all sorts of oppressors; نوع الانسان *n. al-insān* or النوع الانسانى the human race

نوعى **nau'ī** relative to the nature or type; characteristic, peculiar, proper; essential; specific | ثقل (وزن or) نوعى (*ṯiql, wazn*) specific gravity

تنويع **tanwī'** change, alteration, modification

تنوع **tanawwu'** diversity, variety, multiplicity; change, change-over, readjustment

منوع **munawwa'** different, diverse, various, miscellaneous, sundry, manifold, multifarious, complex

متنوع **mutanawwi'** different, diverse, various, miscellaneous, sundry, manifold, multifarious, complex; متنوعات miscellany (heading of a newspaper column)

[1](نوف and نيف) **nāfa u** (*nauf*) to be high, lofty, exalted, sublime; to exceed (عن or على s.th., esp., a number), be above (عن or على), be more than (عن or على), go beyond (عن or على) | ما ينوف على الخمسين more than fifty II نيف **nayyafa** and IV to go beyond (عن or على), be more than (عن or على), exceed (عن or على s.th.) | ما ينيف عن ثلاث سنوات (*ṯalāṯi sanawātin*) more than three years, over three years

ناف **nāf** yoke

نوف **nauf** pl. انواف **anwāf** that which exceeds a number or measure, excess, overplus, surplus

نيف **nayyif** excess, overplus, surplus | نيف و or ونيف together with round figures: some ..., ... and some, ... odd, e.g., نيف وعشرون some twenty, twenty and some, twenty odd

نيافة **niyāfa** Excellency, Eminence (*Copt.-Chr.*; title of cardinals and bishops)

منيف **munīf** high, tall, lofty; exalted, sublime; outstanding, excellent

[2]منوفى **manūfī** a brand of Egyptian cotton

نوفبر **nūfimbir, novembir** November

نوق V تنوق **tanawwaqa** and تنيق **tanayyaqa** to be squeamish, fastidious, finical, dainty, choosy (فى in) X استنوق **istanwaqa**: استنوق الجمل (*jamala*) he mistook the he-camel for a she-camel (proverbially of a mistake)

ناقة **nāqa** pl. نوق **nūq**, نياق **niyāq**, ناقات **nāqāt** she-camel | لا ناقة لى فى الامر ولا جمل (*nāqata, jamala*) I have no hand in this matter, I have nothing to do with it

نيق **nayyiq** squeamish, finical, fastidious, choosy, dainty, overnice

انوك **anwak**[2] foolish, silly, stupid

(نول) نال **nāla u** (*naul*) to give, donate, present, offer, hold out, grant, award (ه ل or ب to s.o. s.th.), confer, bestow (ه ل or ب upon s.o. s.th.) II to let (ه s.o.) obtain (ه s.th.), give, afford, bring, yield (ه ه to s.o. s.th.) III to give, hand, pass, present, offer, extend, serve, hand over, deliver (ه ل or ه to s.o. s.th.) | ناوله القربان (*qurbāna*) to administer the Communion to s.o. (*Chr.*) **VI** to reach (ه for s.th.), take (ه s.th.); to accept (ه s.th.); to receive, get, obtain (ه s.th.); to take, eat (ه food), have (ه a meal, tea, coffee, etc.); to take s.th. (ه) out of (من), derive, draw, obtain (ه من s.th. from); to take in, grasp, comprehend (ه the meaning of s.th.); to take up, treat, discuss (ه a subject), deal with (ه); to extend (ه to), include, encompass (ه s.th.); to reach (ه s.o.; of a glance); to partake of the Communion, communicate (*Chr.*)

نول *naul* pl. انوال *anwāl* gift; way, manner, mode, fashion; loom; freightage, freight

نوال *nawāl* gift, s.th. received; favor, benefit; that which is proper, right, incumbent, a duty | نوالك ان تفعل كذا you must do this; ليس ذلك بنوال that's improper, that isn't right

منول *minwal* and منوال *minwāl* loom

منوال *minwāl* way, manner, mode, fashion; method, procedure; form | على هذا المنوال in this manner, this way; هم على منوال واحد they are of one stamp, they are all alike; منوالك ان تفعل كذا you must do it this way

مناولة *munāwala* presentation, offering, handing over, delivery; Communion (*Chr.*)

تناول *tanāwul* taking of food, eating, drinking; comprehension, grasp, receptivity; Communion (*Chr.*)

متناول *mutanāwil* reaching out, taking, seizing, grabbing; partaking of the Lord's Supper, communicating; communicant

متناول *mutanāwal* attainable, available, within reach; attainableness, availability; reach, range | أعسر متناولا difficult to reach, hard to get at; تحت (فى) متناول يده (*m. yadihī*) available, at s.o.'s disposal, within reach, handy, on hand; فى متناوله attainable to s.o., within s.o.'s reach; فى متناول الجميع within everybody's means; فى متناول كل الافهام comprehensible to all, understood by all; جعل ه فى متناوله to bring s.th. within s.o.'s reach, make s.th. attainable, available to s.o.

نولون *naulūn* and ناولون *nāwulūn* pl. نوالين *nawālīn*[2] freightage, freight

نام (نوم) *nāma* (1st pers. perf. *nimtu*) *a* (*naum*, نيام *niyām*) to sleep, slumber; to go to bed; to go to sleep; to abate, subside, let up, calm down, be calm (wind, sea, etc.); to be inactive, dull, listless (market); to be benumbed, be numb (limb); to neglect, omit, overlook (عن s.th.), forget (عن about s.th.), fail to think of (عن); to be reassured (الى by s.th.), accept (الى s.th.), assent (الى to), acquiesce (الى in); to place confidence (الى in s.o.), trust (الى s.th.) | ينام ملء جفنه (*mil'a jafnihī*) he sleeps the sleep of the just **II** to lull (ه s.o.) to sleep, make (ه s.o.) sleep, put to bed (ه, esp., a child); to anesthetize, narcotize, put to sleep (ه s.o.) **IV** = **II**; **VI** to pretend to be asleep; to place confidence, put trust (الى in s.o.) **X** to let o.s. be lulled to sleep or narcotized (ل by s.th.); to accede (ل to s.th.), comply (ل with); to trust (الى s.o.), have confidence (الى in s.o.), rely, depend (الى on s.o.); to entrust (الى ب s.th. to s.o.); to be reassured (الى by s.th.), accept tacitly (الى s.th.), acquiesce (الى in s.th.), content o.s., be content (الى with)

نوم *naum* sleep, slumber | غرفة النوم *ġurfat an-n.* bedroom; قميص النوم nightgown, nightshirt

نومى *naumī* of or pertaining to sleep, somn(i)-, sleeping- (in compounds)

نومة *nauma* sleep, nap

نومة *nuwama* one who sleeps much, sleeper

نوام *nawwām* one given to sleep, sleeper

نؤوم *na'ūm* sound asleep; one given to sleep, sleeper; late riser, slugabed

منام *manām* sleep; (pl. *-āt*) dream

منام *manām* place to sleep; bedroom, dormitory

منامة *manāma* place to sleep; bedroom, dormitory; nightwear, nightgown, nightshirt; — المنامة Manama (capital of Bahrein Islands)

تنويم *tanwīm* lulling to sleep; narcotization, anesthetization; hypnotism, hypnosis

نائم *nā'im* pl. نيام *niyām*, نوم *nuwwam*, نيم *nuyyam*, نوام *nuwwām*, نيام *nuyyām* sleeping; asleep; numb, benumbed (limb); calm, tranquil, peaceful (night)

منوم *munawwim* sleep-inducing, somniferous, soporific; narcotic; hypnotist; (pl. *-āt*) a soporific, somnifacient | جرعة منومة (*jur'a*) soporific potion, sleeping draught, nightcap; دواء منوم (*dawā'*) a soporific, somnifacient

نون II to add a final *nūn* (ه to a noun), provide with the nunnation (ه a noun; *gram.*)

نون *nūn* pl. *-āt* name of the letter ن; — (pl. نينان *nīnān*, انوان *anwān*) large fish, whale | ذو النون the Prophet Jonah

نونى *nūnī* shaped like a ن, crescent-shaped

نونة *nūna* dimple in the chin

تنوين *tanwīn* nunnation (*gram.*) | هما كالتنوين والاضافة (*iḍāfa*) they are like day and night, they are diametrically opposed, they are as unlike as they could be

نوه II to raise, elevate (ه s.th.); to praise, laud, extol, acclaim (ب s.o.), speak highly (ب of); to commend, cite (ب s.o. or s.th.); to stress, emphasize (ب s.th.); to make mention, speak (ب of s.o. or s.th.), refer (ب to, also عن to s.th.), name, mention (عن s.th.); to hint (عن or ب or الى at), allude (عن or ب or الى to), intimate, imply (عن or ب or الى s.th.)

تنويه *tanwīh* encomium, tribute, praise; mentioning, mention; reference; hint, allusion

نوى *nawā i* (نية *nīya*, نواة *nawāh*) to intend, propose, purpose, plan, have in mind, make up one's mind (ه to do s.th.), resolve, determine (ه on s.th. or to do s.th.); — *i* (نوى *nawan*) to absent o.s., go away (عن or من from) II to miaow (cat) III to make an enemy of s.o. (ه), fall out with s.o. (ه), be hostile, antagonistic (ه to), declare o.s. the enemy (ه of) VIII to propose, purpose, intend (ه to do s.th.)

نوى *nawan* remoteness, distance; destination

نوى *nawan* (coll.) date pits; fruit kernels, stones

نواة *nawāh* (n. un.) pl. نويات *nawayāt* date pit; fruit kernel, stone; core; center; atomic nucleus; nucleus (fig., from which s.th. will grow), central point, starting point | نواة الذرة *n. ad-ḏarra* atomic nucleus

نووى *nawawī* nuclear, nucleal, nuclei-, nucleo- (in compounds); of or pertaining to nuclear physics, nuclear, atomic | اسلحة نووية (*asliḥa*) nuclear weapons

نى *nayy* fat; see also under نىء

نية *nīya* pl. *-āt*, نوايا *nawāyā* intention, intent, design, purpose, plan, scheme; determination, will, volition, direction of will; tendency, inclination, desire | على نية with the intention to ...; فى النية ان it is intended to ...; حسن النية *ḥusn an-n.* good intention, good will, sincerity, honesty; سلامة النية *salāmat an-n.* guilelessness, innocence, sincerity; bona fides, good faith (*jur.*); سليم النية undesigning, guileless, artless, sincere; simplehearted, ingenuous, simple-minded; سوء النية *sū' an-n.* evil intent, insincerity, malice, cunning, deceit; (*jur.*) bad faith, mala fides, dolus malus; بسوء النية against one's better judgment; (*jur.*) in bad faith, mala fide; صافى النية *ṣāfī n-n.* sincere, candid, frank, openhearted; اخلص له النية (*nīyata*) to be loyally attached to s.o. or s.th.; اخلص نيته ل or حسنت نيته فى *ḥasunat nīyatuhū fī* do.; to have good intentions, be well-intentioned toward ...; اصلح نيته (*nīyatahū*) to evoke the right intention in one's heart (ethical and religious); عقد النية على to determine on s.th., resolve to do s.th., direct one's intention to

مناو *munāwin* hostile, unfriendly

(نىء) ناء *nā'a* *i* (نىء *nay'*, نيوء *nuyū'*, نيوءة *nuyū'a*) to be raw, uncooked (esp., meat)

نىء *nī'*, نى *nīy* raw; unripe; gross (weight); see also under نوى

ناب *nāb* pl. انياب *anyāb*, نيوب *nuyūb*, انايب *anāyib*[2] canine tooth, eyetooth; tusk; fang | كشر عن انيابه (*kaššara*) to bare one's teeth

ناب *nāb* pl. انياب *anyāb*, نيوب *nuyūb*, نيب *nīb* old she-camel

نيتروجين *nitrōžēn* nitrogen

متنيح *mutanayyaḥ* late lamented, deceased (*Chr.*; *eg.*)

[1]نير *nayyir* see نور

[2]نير *nīr* pl. انيار *anyār*, نيران *nīrān* yoke

نيرة *nīra* gums (of the teeth)

نيروز *nairūz* New Year's Day (*Chr.-Copt.*)

نيزك *naizak* pl. نيازك *nayāzik*[2] short lance; shooting star, meteor

نيس *nīs* Nice (seaport in S France)

نيسان *nīsān*[2] April (*Syr.*, *Leb.*, *Jord.*, *Ir.*)

نيشان *nīšān* see نشان (نشن)

نيص *nīṣ* porcupine

نوط ,نياط see نيط

نوف see نيف

نوق see نيق

نيقوسيا *nīqōsiyā* Nicosia (capital of Cyprus)

(نيك) ناك *nāka* *i* to have sexual intercourse (ها with a woman)

نيكل *nikl* nickel

[1](نيل) نال *nāla* (1st pers. perf. *niltu*) *a* (*nail*, منال *manāl*) to obtain, attain, achieve (ه s.th.), get hold, get possession (ه of); to win, gain, acquire, earn (ه s.th.); to get, obtain, procure (ه ل s.th. for s.o.); to accomplish (ه من s.th. with s.o.), succeed (ه من in s.th. with s.o.), get s.th. (ه) from s.o. (من); to affect, influence (من s.o., s.th.), bear upon s.th. (من); to cause damage, do harm (من to s.o., to s.th.), prejudice, impair, harm (من s.th.) | نال من عرضه (*'irḍihī*) to decry, depreciate, discredit, defame, malign, slander s.o.; نال منه اوفر منال (*aufara manālin*) to do s.o. untold damage, harm s.o. most grievously; ناله بسوء (*bi-sū'in*) to harm s.o. or s.th.; ناله بضر (*bi-ḍurrin*) do.; نال من نفسه ابلغ منال see منال below IV to make or let (ل or ه s.o.) obtain (ه s.th.), procure, get (ه ل or ه ه s.th. for s.o.)

نيل *nail* obtainment, attainment, acquisition; a favor received

منال *manāl* obtainment, attainment, achievement, acquisition | بعيد المنال unattainable; intangible, impalpable, far from reality; صعب المنال *ṣa'b al-m.* unattainable; قريب (or سهل) المنال (*sahl*) easy to get, attainable; ممكن المنال *mumkin al-m.* attainable; نال من نفسه ابلغ منال (*ablaġa manālin*) it made the deepest impression on him

نائل *nā'il* acquirer, earner, obtainer, gainer, winner; a favor received, a boon, benefit, gain

نيل[2] II to dye with indigo (ه s.th.)

نيل *nīl*, نيلة *nīla* indigo plant, indigo

منيل *munayyal* dyed with indigo

نيل[3] II (*eg.*) to channel Nile water onto the fields for the purpose of alluviating the soil

النيل *an-nīl* the Nile | زمن النيل *zaman an-n.* time of the Nile inundation; عرائس النيل flowers of the European white water lily (nenuphar)

نيلي *nīlī* of the Nile, Nile (adj.), Nilotic

منيل *manyal* Nilometer

تنييل **tanyīl** (*eg.*) **alluviation of the soil by irrigation or inundation**

نيلج **nīlaj indigo**

نيلوفر **nīlūfar European white water lily, nenuphar**

نيلون **nailōn, nīlòn nylon**

نينه **nīna mother**

نية **see** نوى

نيورالجيا **niyūraljiyā neuralgia**

نيوزيلاندا **niyūzīlandā New Zealand**

ضوء نيوني **ḍau' niyūnī neon light**

ه

ها *hā* ha! look! there! ها هو *hā huwa* look, there he is! ها انتم *hā antum* you there! as a prefix (mostly written defectively): هذا *hāḏā*, f. هذه *hāḏihi*, هذى *hāḏī*, pl. هؤلاء *hā'ulā'i*, dual m. هذان *hāḏāni*, f. هاتان *hātāni* this one, this; see also alphabetically; — هذاك *hāḏāka*, f. هاتيك *hātīka* pl. هؤلائك *hā'ulā'ika* that one, that; — هكذا *hākaḏā* so, thus; وهكذا *wa-hākaḏā* and so forth; — هاهنا *hāhunā* here; — هاءنذا ,هأنذا *hā'anaḏā*, ها انت ذا, هأنتذا *hā'antaḏā*, ها هو ذا, ها نحن اولاء I (emphatic form); you there; this one, that one, that; we here, etc.; here I am! there you are! etc.; — with suffix: هاك *hāka* pl. هاكم *hākum* here, take it! there you are! there you have ...! following (below) is (are) ...; هاكه *hākahū* there he is

هاء *hā'* pl. *-āt* name of the letter ه

هابيل *hābīl*[2] Abel

هات *hāti* pl. هاتوا *hātū* give me (us) ...! bring me (us) ...! let me (us) have ...!

هاتان **see under** ها

هاتور **hātōr Hator, the third month of the Coptic calendar**

هارب **(Engl.) harb harp (musical instrument)**

هاشمى **see** هشم

الهافر **al-hāvir Le Havre (seaport in N France)**

هاك, هاكم **and** هاكه **see** ها

هؤلاء **see** ها

هأنذا, هأنتذا **see** ها

هانم **hānum pl.** هوانم **hawānim**[2] **lady, woman**

هوانمى **hawānimī ladylike, womanlike, feminine**

هأهأ **ha'ha'a to burst into laughter**

هاهنا **see** ها

هاواى **hāwāy Hawaii**

هاون **hāwun,** هاوون **hāwūn pl.** هواوين **hawāwīn**[2], اهوان **ahwān mortar (vessel) |** مدفع الهاون **midfa' al-h. mortar (*mil.*)**

هايتى *haitī* Haiti

[1]هب *hab* imperative of وهب

[2]هب *habba u* (*habb*) to get in motion, start moving; to approach, attack, tackle (الى or ل s.th.), embark (الى or ل upon), begin (الى or ل with), start doing s.th. (الى or ل); (with foll. imperf.) to proceed abruptly to do s.th., set out to do s.th.; to rush, fly (الى at s.o.); to wake up; to rise, get up (من from, esp., from sleep); to revolt, rebel, rise (على against s.o.); — (*habb*, هبوب *hubūb*, هبيب *habīb*) to blow (wind); to rage (storm); to break out (fire); to waft, drift (على in s.o.'s direction; of a scent), meet (على s.o.; of a pleasant smell) | هب للحرب (*ḥarb*) to take up arms, enter the war; هب للمقاومة (*muqāwama*) to take up arms in opposition, rise in arms; هب واقفا (*wāqifan*) to plant o.s., station o.s., stand; هبت ريحه (*rīḥuhū*) he is in clover, he is in luck's way, he has a lucky hand with everything; هب فيه الكلب (*kalb*) the dog attacked him, fell upon him; كل من هب ودب (*man, dabba*) everybody and his brother, every Tom, Dick and Harry **II** to tear, rend (ه s.th.); to blacken with soot (ه s.th.); to besmut (ه s.th.); to botch, bungle, do in slipshod manner (ه s.th.) **IV** to wake up, awaken, rouse (ه من s.o. from sleep) **V** to be torn

هبة *habba* gust, squall

هبة *hiba* see وهب

هباب *habāb* fine dust

هباب *hibāb* soot, smut

هبوب *habūb* strong wind, gale

هبوب *hubūb* blowing (of the wind)

مهب *mahabb* pl. مهاب *mahābb*[2] place where or from which the wind blows; windy side, weather side, direction of the wind; blowing of the wind; draft | فى مهب الرياح storm-swept, exposed to storms, threatened by storms

هبت *habata i* (*habt*) to knock out, fell, throw to the ground (ه s.o.); pass. *hubita* to be despondent, faint-hearted; to be dim-witted

هبيت *habīt* despondent, faint-hearted, cowardly; dim-witted

هبر *habara u* (*habr*) to mangle (with the teeth; ه s.o.); to carve into large pieces (ه meat)

هبر *habr* boned meat

هبرة *habra* piece or slice of meat

هبيرة *hubaira* hyena | ابو هبيرة *abū h.* frog

هبش *habaša i* (*habš*) to gather up, gather, collect (ه s.th.); to seize, grab, clutch (ب with the hand or with the claws)

هبط *habaṭa u i* (هبوط *hubūṭ*) to descend, go down, come down; to fall down, drop; to settle down; to sink; to dip, slope down; to fall to the ground; to fall in, come down, collapse (roof); to set down, land, alight (airplane, travelers, ه in a country); to lose weight, become lean (body); to abate, subside, let up, stop, die down (wind, fire, etc.); to fall, drop, slump (prices); to go, come (ه to a place); — *u* (*habṭ*) and **IV** to cause to sink or descend, lower, let down, bring down, take down, send down, fling down, throw down (ه, ه s.o., s.th.); to lower, cut down, reduce (ه the price); to come (ه to a place)

هبط *habṭ* reduction, lowering; decrease, diminution

هبطة *habṭa* descent, decline, fall, drop; depression (*geogr.*)

هبوط *hubūṭ* sinking; fall, drop, decline, descent; diminution, lessening, lowering, reduction (of the price); decrease; weakness, feebleness; slump (on the stock market); (airborne) landing | هبوط

اضطرارى (*iḍṭirārī*) emergency landing; هبوط الرحم *h. ar-raḥim* prolapse of the uterus, hysteroptosis

هبوط *habūṭ* slope, declivity, drop, cliff, bluff

هبيط *habīṭ* emaciated, skinny, enervated, worn out

○ اهبوطة *uhbūṭa* pl. اهابيط *ahābīṭ*² parachute

مهبط *mahbiṭ* pl. مهابط *mahābiṭ*² place of a fall, of descent; landing place, airstrip, runway; falling, fall, drop; place of origin, birth place, cradle (fig.); ○ cathode (*el.*) | مهبط الوحى *m. al-waḥy* the cradle of Islam; فى مهبط الغروب at (the time of) sunset

هابط *hābiṭ* descending, falling, dropping, sinking | ○ هابط بالمظلة الواقية (*miẓalla, wāqiya*) paratrooper

مهبوط *mahbūṭ* emaciated, skinny, enervated, worn out

هبل **habila** *a* (*habal*) to be bereaved of her son (mother) **V** to take a vapor bath **VIII** to avail o.s., take advantage (ه of an opportunity); to intrigue, scheme | اهتبل هبلك *ihtabil habalaka* watch out for your own interests! take care of your own affairs! mind your own business!

هبل *hiball* a tall, husky man

هبيل *habīl* dolt, fool

اهبل *ahbal*², f. هبلاء *hablā'*², pl. هبل *hubl* dim-witted, weak-minded, imbecilic, idiotic

مهبل *mahbal, mahbil* pl. مهابل *mahābil*² vagina

مهبلى *mahbalī* vaginal

مهبل *mihbal* nimble

مهبول *mahbūl* stupid, imbecilic, idiotic; dolt, dunce, fool

هبهب **habhaba** to bark, bay

هبهاب *habhāb* mirage, fata morgana; swift, nimble

(هبو) هبا **habā** *u* (هبو *hubūw*) to rise in the air (dust, smoke); to run away, bolt, take to flight

هبوة *habwa* pl. *habawāt* swirl of dust

هباء *habā'* pl. أهباء *ahbā'* fine dust; dust particles floating in the air | هباء منثور atoms scattered in all directions; ذهب هباء (*habā'an*) to vanish, dissolve into nothing, end in smoke; ذهب هباء منثورا (*habā'an*) or ضاع هباء منثورا (*ḍā'a*) to go up in smoke, fall through, come to nought, dissolve into nothing; ذهب به هباء (*habā'an*) to ruin, thwart s.th.; to scatter s.th. in all directions

هباءة *habā'a* (n. un.) dust particle; mote

¹هتر **hatara** *i* (*hatr*) to tear to pieces (ه s.th.) **III** to abuse, revile, insult, call names (ه s.o.) **IV** (also pass. *uhtira*) to become feeble-minded, childish (old man) **VI** to revile each other, fling accusations at each other; to be contradictory, conflicting (testimonies; *Isl. Law*) **X** to be negligent and careless; to act in a reckless, irresponsible manner; to make light (ب of s.th.), attach little importance (ب to), slight, disdain, despise (ب s.th.); to jeer, scoff (ب at s.o.), deride, ridicule, mock (ب s.o.); pass. *ustuhtira* to be infatuated (ب with), dote (ب on)

هتر *hitr* pl. اهتار *ahtār* drivel, twaddle, childish talk; lie, untruth, falsity, falsehood

هتر *hutr* feeble-mindedness, dotage

مهاترة *muhātara* abuse, revilement, vituperation, insult; pl. *-āt* wrangle, bickering

تهاتر *tahātur* confrontation of similar evidence (*Isl. Law*)

استهتار *istihtār* recklessness, thoughtlessness; wantonness, unrestraint, licentiousness; disdain, scorn

مهتر *muhtar* driveling, twaddling, raving; childish old man

مستهتر *mustahtir* heedless, careless; reckless, thoughtless, irresponsible; wanton, unrestrained, uninhibited

مستهتر *mustahtar* blindly devoted (ب to), infatuated (ب with), doting (ب on)

هاتور[2] look up alphabetically

هتف **hatafa** *i* (*hatf*) to coo (pigeons); — (هتاف *hutāf*) to shout; to rejoice, shout with joy; to acclaim, hail, cheer, applaud (ل or ب s.o.); to jeer, boo (ضد s.o.); to praise highly, extol (ب s.th.) | هتف به to call out to s.o.; هتف به هاتف (*hātifun*) a voice called out to him, an invisible force told him, made him (do s.th.); هتف بحياته (*bi-ḥayātihī*) to cheer s.o.; هتف ثلاثا (*ṯalāṯan*) to give (ل s.o.) three cheers VI to shout encouragement to one another, encourage one another (على to do s.th.)

هتفة *hatfa* shout, cry, call

هتاف *hutāf* pl. *-āt* shout, cry, call; exclamation of joy; hurrah; acclamation, acclaim, applause; cheer (ل to s.o.) | هتاف الحرب *h. al-ḥarb* battle cry, war cry; عاصفة من الهتاف storm of applause, thundering applause

هاتف *hātif* shouting, calling loudly; (in earlier Sufism) invisible caller, voice; (pl. هواتف *hawātif*[2]) telephone; ○ loudspeaker; pl. هواتف exclamations, shouts, cries, calls | هاتف القلب *h. al-qalb* inner voice; بالهاتف by telephone

هاتفى *hātifī* telephonic, telephone- (in compounds)

هتك **hataka** *i* (*hatk*) to tear apart, rip apart (ه s.th., esp., a curtain, a veil); to unveil, uncover, discover, disclose, reveal (ه s.th.); to disgrace, rape, ravish (ها a woman) | هتك عرضه (*'irḍahū*) to disgrace s.o. II to tear to shreds, rip to pieces, tatter (ه s.th.) V to get torn; to be exposed, shown up, discredited, disgraced, dishonored, ravished, raped; to give o.s. over (فى to s.th. disgraceful); to be disgraceful, dishonorable, shameless, impudent VIII pass. of *hataka*

هتك *hatk* tearing, rending, ripping apart; disclosure, exposure, exposé; dishonoring, disgracing, degradation, debasement, rape, ravishing | هتك الاستار disclosure, uncovering of s.th. hidden

هتكة *hutka* dishonoring, disgracing, degradation, debasement

هتيكة *hatīka* disgrace, scandal

تهتك *tahattuk* shamelessness, immorality; impudence, insolence

متهتك *mutahattik* insolent, impudent; shameless, dishonorable

مستهتك *mustahtik* insolent, impudent; shameless, dishonorable

هتامة *hutāma* s.th. broken off, fragment, breakage

اهتم *ahtam*[2], f. هتماء *hatmā'*[2], pl. هتم *hutm* having no front teeth; toothless

هتن **hatana** *i* (*hatn*, هتون *hutūn*) to discharge a pouring rain (sky)

هتون *hatūn* rain-fraught, heavy with rain (cloud)

هج **hajja** *u* (هجيج *hajīj*) to burn, be on fire, be aflame; to flame, blaze, be ablaze II to set ablaze, stir up, stoke (ه the fire)

هجأ **haja'a** *a* (هجء *haj'*, هجوء *hujū'*) to be appeased (hunger) IV اهجأ جوعه (*jū'ahū*) to appease s.o.'s hunger

هجد **hajada** *u* (هجود *hujūd*) and V to stay awake at night, keep a night vigil; to spend the night in prayer

هجر **hajara** u (*hajr*, هجران *hijrān*) to emigrate; to dissociate o.s., separate, part, secede, keep away (ه, ه from), part company (ه with); to give up, renounce, forgo, avoid (ه s.th.); to abandon, surrender, leave behind (ه الى s.th. to s.o.), relinquish, leave, give up, vacate (ه s.th., الى in favor of s.o.) II to induce (ه s.o.) to emigrate III to emigrate IV to leave, abandon, give up (ه s.th.); to talk nonsense, talk through one's hat VI to desert one another, part company, separate, break up

هجر *hajr* abandonment, forsaking, leaving, separation; avoidance, abstention; separation from the beloved one; hottest time of the day

هجر *hujr* obscene language

هجرة *hijra* departure, exit; emigration, exodus; immigration (الى to); الهجرة the Hegira, the emigration of the Prophet Mohammed from Mecca to Medina in 622 A.D. | دار الهجرة Medina

هجرى *hijrī* of the Hegira, pertaining to Mohammed's emigration | سنة هجرية (*sana*) a year of the Hegira, a year of the Muslim era (beginning with Mohammed's emigration)

هجرة *hujra, hijra* pl. هجر *hujar, hijar* agricultural settlement of the Wahabi Ikhwan in Nejd

هجراء *hajrā'*[2] obscene language

هجير *hajīr* midday heat

هجيرة *hajīra* midday heat, midday, noon

مهجر *mahjar* pl. مهاجر *mahājir*[2] place of emigration, retreat, refuge, sanctuary; emigration; settlement, colony

مهاجر *mahājir*[2] obscenities

مهاجرة *muhājara* emigration

هاجرة *hājira* pl. هواجر *hawājir*[2] midday heat, midday, noon; — (pl. *-āt*, هواجر *hawājir*[2]) obscene language, obscenity

هاجرى *hājirī* midday (adj.); excellent, outstanding

مهجور *mahjūr* abandoned, forsaken, deserted; lonely, lonesome; in disuse, out of use, obsolete, antiquated, archaic

مهاجر *muhājir* emigrant, émigré; المهاجرون those Meccans who emigrated to Medina in the early period of Islam

هجس **hajasa** u i (*hajs*) to occur all of a sudden (فى نفسه to s.o.), come to s.o.'s mind (فى نفسه); to mumble, mutter, talk to o.s.

هجس *hajs* idea, thought; foolish talk

هجسة *hajsa* pl. *hajasāt* idea, thought; notion, concept; fear, apprehension, anxiety, concern, misgiving, scruple; pl. fixed ideas, apprehensions, misgivings

هجاس *hajjās* braggart, boaster, show-off

هاجس *hājis* pl. هواجس *hawājis*[2] idea, thought; notion, concept; fear, apprehension, anxiety, concern, misgiving, scruple; pl. fixed ideas, apprehensions, misgivings

هجص (*eg.*) **hagaṣ** mischief, nuisance, horseplay

هجع **haja'a** a (هجوع *hujū'*) to sleep peacefully, to be or become calm, quiet, still; to be silenced, calm down, subside (uproar, excitement, and the like); — (*haj'*) to appease (ه the hunger) IV to allay, appease (ه the hunger)

هجعة *haj'a* slumber

هجوع *hujū'* slumber; lull, calming down; subsidence, abatement, letup, remission, ebbing (e.g., of a disease)

مهجع *mahja'* pl. مهاجع *mahāji'*[2] bedchamber; quarters, barracks room (*Syr., mil.*) | رئيس المهجع approx.: barracks orderly, barracks sergeant (*Syr., mil.*)

هجل **hajala** *u* (*hajl*) to cast amorous glances, make sheep's eyes

هجم **hajama** *u* (هجوم *hujūm*) to make for s.o. (على), rush, pounce (على upon s.o.); to attack, assail, charge (على s.o., s.th.); to raid (على s.th.); to take by surprise, capture in a surprise attack, storm (على s.th.); to enter without permission (على s.th.), force one's way (على into), intrude, trespass (على on), invade (على s.th.); to keep quiet **II** to make (ه s.o.) attack, order s.o. (ه) to attack **III** to attack, assail, charge (ه, ه s.o., s.th.); to launch an attack (ه on); to make for s.th. (ه), rush, pounce (ه upon); to raid (ه s.th.); to assault (ه s.o.), fall upon s.o. (ه); to intrude, trespass (ه on), invade (ه s.th.) **IV** = **II**; **V** to fall upon (على) **VI** to attack one another **VII** to fall down, collapse (house); to be in poor health, be frail; to flow down (tears); to shed tears (eye)

هجمة **hajma** pl. *hajamāt* attack, charge; assault, onset, onslaught, raid, surprise attack, coup de main; severity (of winter) | ○ هجمة معاكسة (*muʻākisa*) counterattack

هجمى **hajmī** aggressive, violent, outrageous, brutal

هجوم **hajūm** violent wind

هجوم **hujūm** attack, charge, assault, onset, onslaught, raid; offensive; fit, attack, paroxysm (of a disease); forward line, forwards (in soccer, and the like) | هجوم جانبي (*jānibī*) flank attack; هجوم جوى (*jawwī*) air raid; هجوم مضاد (*muḍādd*) or هجوم معاكس (*muʻākis*) counterattack; خط الهجوم *ḳaṭṭ al-h.* forward line (in soccer, and the like); قلب الهجوم *qalb al-h.* the center forward (in soccer, and the like)

هجومى **hujūmī** aggressive, offensive

مهاجمة **muhājama** attack, charge; assault, onset, onslaught, raid; ○ police raid, police roundup

تهجم **tahajjum** pl. *-āt* assault, attack, raid

مهاجم **muhājim** attacker, assailant, aggressor; forward (in soccer, and the like)

هجن **hajuna** *u* (هجنة *hujna*, هجانة *hajāna*, هجونة *hujūna*) to be incorrect or faulty **II** to excoriate, flay, censure scathingly, run down, disparage (ه s.o.) **X** to consider (ه s.th.) bad, wrong or improper; to disapprove (ه of s.th.), condemn, reject (ه s.th.)

هجنة **hujna** fault, defect, shortcoming; meanness, baseness

هجان **hajjān** pl. هجانة *hajjāna* camel rider

هجين **hajīn** pl. هجن *hujun*, هجناء *hujanāʼ*[2], مهاجين *mahājīn*[2], مهاجنة *mahājina* low, lowly, base, ignoble, mean; — (pl. هجن *hujun*) racing camel, dromedary

هجينة **hajīna** pl. هجائن *hajāʼin*[2] racing camel, dromedary

استهجان **istihjān** disapproval, disapprobation

هجا (هجو) **hajā** *u* (*hajw*, هجاء *hijāʼ*) to ridicule, mock, satirize, disparage, run down (ه s.o.); to lampoon (ه s.o.) **II** and **V** to spell (ه s.th.) **III** to compose defamatory or satiric poems (ه against s.o.), defame, satirize, lampoon, ridicule, mock (ه s.o.) **VI** to ridicule each other in satiric verse

هجو **hajw** ridiculing, scoffing; defamation, disparagement; lampoonery, mockery, ridicule, irony; satiric poem, satire

هجوى **hajwī** defamatory, denigrating, disparaging, satiric

هجاء **hijāʼ** derision, ridiculing, scoffing; satire; defamatory poem; (pl. اهجية *ahjiya*) spelling, successive order of letters; alphabet

هجائى **hijāʼī** alphabetical; satiric

اهجوة *uhjūwa* and اهجية *uhjīya* pl. اهاجى *ahājīy* satiric poem, lampoon

تهجية *tahjiya* and تهج *tahajjin* spelling

هاج *hājin* spelling; defamatory, denigrating; mocker, scoffer, derider; satirist

هد *hadda u* (*hadd*, هدود *hudūd*) to break, crush, break off, pull down, tear down, raze, demolish, wreck, destroy (ه s.th.); to undermine, sap, weaken, ruin (ه, ه or من s.o., s.th.); — *i* (هديد *hadīd*) to crash down, fall down, collapse; — *a i* (*hadd*) to be weak and decrepit II to threaten, menace (ه ب s.o. with), scare, frighten, terrify, daunt, cow, intimidate, browbeat (ه s.o.) V do. VII to be or get torn down, demolished, razed, wrecked; to fall down, collapse, break down; to be broken down, be dilapidated, be in ruins, be a wreck

هد *hadd* razing, pulling down, wrecking; demolition, destruction

هدة *hadda* and هديد *hadīd* heavy, thudding fall; thud, crash (of s.th. collapsing)

هداد *hadād* slowness, gentleness; هداديك *hadādaika* gently! slowly! take it easy!

مهدة *mihadda* rock crusher, jawbreaker

تهديد *tahdīd* pl. *-āt* threat, menace; intimidation | تهديد بالتشهير extortion by threats of public exposure, blackmail (*jur.*)

تهديدى *tahdīdī* threatening, menacing

تهدد *tahaddud* threat, menace; intimidation

مهدود *mahdūd* destroyed, demolished, wrecked | مهدود القوى *m. al-quwā* weakened, debilitated, exhausted

مهدد *muhaddid* menacing, threatening; threatener, menacer

مهدد *muhaddad* threatened, menaced

هدأ *hada'a a* (هدء *had'*, هدوء *hudū'*) to be calm, still, quiet, tranquil; to become calm, calm down; to subside, abate, let up, die down (storm, etc.); to stop, halt, linger, rest, remain, stay (ب at a place); to stop (عن s.th., doing s.th.), cease (عن to do s.th.) | هدأ روعه (*rau'uhū*) to become composed, calm down II to calm, quiet, pacify, tranquilize, appease, soothe, placate, temper, assuage, allay (من or ه s.th., ه s.o.); ○ to slow down, drive slowly | هدأ اعصابه (*a'ṣābahū*) to soothe the nerves; هدأ من روعه (*rau'ihī*) to reassure s.o., set s.o.'s mind at rest; هدئ روعك *haddi' rau'aka* calm down! take it easy! don't worry! don't be afraid! هدئ من روعك (*rau'ika*) calm down! take it easy! IV = II; to lull (ه a baby) to sleep

هدء *had'* calm(ness), quiet(ness), peace, tranquillity, stillness

هدأة *hud'a* calm, quiet, peace, tranquillity, stillness

هدوء *hudū'* calm(ness), quiet(ness), peace, tranquillity, stillness | بهدوء calmly, quietly

تهدئة *tahdi'a* calming, quieting, pacification, tranquilization, appeasement, reassurance; ○ slowing down, slow driving

هادئ *hādi'* calm, quiet, peaceful, tranquil, still | هادئ القلب *h. al-qalb* calm(ly), confident(ly); هادئ البال composed(ly), with one's mind at ease; المحيط الهادئ (*muhīṭ*) the Pacific Ocean

هدب *hadiba a* (*hadab*) to have long lashes (eye); to have long, drooping branches (tree) II to fringe, trim with fringes (ه a garment)

هدب *hudb*, *hudub* (coll.; n.un. ة) pl. اهداب *ahdāb* eyelashes; fringes | باهداب trimmed with fringes, fringed; تمسك باهدابه (*bi-ahdābihī*) to be most devoted to s.o., be at s.o.'s beck and call, be under s.o.'s thumb; تمسك (or تعلق) باهداب الشيء to adhere, cling to s.th.; اخذ باهداب الشيء to apply o.s. to, attend to, engage in, cultivate, practice s.th.

هدب **hadib** having long lashes

اهدب **ahdab**², f. هدباء **hadbā'**² having long lashes

هداب **huddāb** (coll.; n. un. ة) fringes; edging, border

هدج **hadaja** *i* (**hadj**, هدجان **hadajān**, هداج **hudāj**) to shamble, shuffle along, walk with unsteady, tottering or tremulous steps (old man), totter, hobble, limp **II** to make (ه s.th.) tremble **V** to tremble, quaver, shake (voice)

هودج **haudaj** pl. هوادج **hawādij**² camel litter, howdah; sedan chair, litter

هدر **hadara** *i* (**hadr**, هدير **hadīr**) to peal, rumble, roll (thunder); to surge (sea); to roar (lion); to bray (donkey, camel); to clamor, raise a din, be noisy; to storm, rage, rant, shout, bawl, bellow (person); to snarl (in a fury); to bubble, boil, simmer; (with ب) to blare s.th. out; — *u i* (**hadr**, **hadar**) to be in vain, be made to no avail (effort); to be spent uselessly (money); to be shed in vain or with impunity (blood); — (**hadr**) to shed in vain or with impunity (ه blood); to spend uselessly, squander, waste (ه effort or money); to ruin (ه the health) **IV** to regard as nonexistent (ه s.th.); to consider invalid (ه s.th.); to invalidate, void (ه s.th.); to thwart, foil, ruin (ه s.th.)

هدرا **hadran** uselessly, to no avail; in vain, for nothing, futilely | ذهب هدرا to melt away uselessly, futilely, be spent in vain, be wasted

هدر **hudr** fall, tumble

هدار **haddār** swirling, rushing, torrential, roaring, raging; surging (sea); weir; spillway, millrace

هدارة **haddāra** waterfall

هدير **hadīr** roaring, roar; surge, raging, storming, uproar

مهدر **muhdar** invalid, void

هدف **hadafa** *u* (**hadf**) to approach (الى s.o. or s.th.), draw or be near s.o. or s.th. (الى); to aim (الى at) **IV** to approach (الى s.o. or s.th.), draw or be near s.o. or s.th. (الى) **V** to strut **X** to be exposed, be open (ل or الى to a danger); to be susceptible or sensitive (ل to); to make (ه s.th.) one's goal or object, aim (ه at), have before one's eyes, have in mind (ه s.th.)

هدف **hadaf** pl. اهداف **ahdāf** target; aim, end, object, objective, purpose, design, intention; goal (in sports) | جعله هدفا ل to make s.o. the target or object of ..., expose s.o. to s.th; كان هدفا ل to be exposed, be open to ...; ○ اهداف حربية (**ḥarbīya**) military targets

هداف **haddāf** sharpshooter, marksman

هدفان **hadafān** (practice) target

مستهدف **mustahdif** exposed, open (ل to s.th.)

هدل **hadala** *i* (هديل **hadīl**) to coo (pigeon); — *i* (**hadl**) to let down, let hang, dangle (ه s.th.); — **hadila** *a* (**hadal**) and **V** to hang loosely, dangle; to flow, be wide and loose (garment)

اهدل **ahdal**², f. هدلاء **hadlā'**², pl. هدل **hudl** hanging down loosely, flowing

مهدل **muhaddal** hanging down loosely, flowing

هدم **hadama** *i* (**hadm**) to tear down, pull down, raze, wreck, demolish, destroy (ه s.th.); to tear up (ه s.th.) **II** to tear down, pull down, raze, wreck, demolish, destroy (ه s.th.); to tear up, blast, blow up (ه s.th.) **V** to be torn down, be razed, be demolished, be destroyed, be wiped out; to be dilapidated; to fall down, break down, collapse **VII** do.

هدم *hadm* razing, pulling down, wrecking (of a building); demolition, destruction

هدم *hidm* pl. اهدام *ahdām*, هدم *hidam* old, worn garment; pl. هدوم *hudūm* clothes, clothing

هدام *haddām* destructive

هدام *hudām* seasickness

تهديم *tahdīm* wrecking, demolition, destruction, annihilation

تهدم *tahaddum* fall, downfall, crash, collapse, breakdown

هادم *hādim* crushing, devastating, annihilating, destructive; destroyer, demolisher

مهدوم *mahdūm* torn down, razed, demolished, wrecked, destroyed

مهدم *muhaddam* and متهدم *mutahaddim* torn down, razed, demolished, wrecked, destroyed, in ruins, dilapidated, ramshackle, tumble-down

مستهدم *mustahdim* dilapidated, tumbledown (walls)

هدن **hadana** *i* (هدون *hudūn*) to be or become quiet; to calm down, quiet down **III** to conclude a truce (ه with s.o.)

هدنة *hudna* pl. *-āt* calm(ness), quietness, peace, tranquillity, stillness; pause, intermission, cessation; truce, armistice

هدانة *hidāna* truce, armistice; peace

هدون *hudūn* calm(ness), quiet(ness), peace, tranquillity, stillness

مهادنة *muhādana* conclusion of a truce, truce negotiations

هدهد **hadhada** to rock, dandle (ه a child)

هدهد *hudhud* pl. هداهد *hadāhid*[2] hoopoe (*zool.*)

هدى **hadā** *i* (*hady*, هدى *hudan*, هداية *hidāya*) to lead (ه s.o.) on the right way, guide (ه s.o., ‌ه on a course); to guide, show, direct (الى ه s.o. to), show (ه s.o.) the way (الى to); to lead (ه s.o., to the true faith); to supply, bring, procure (ه s.th.); — *i* (هداء *hidā'*) to bring, lead, conduct (ها الى the bride to the bridegroom) **III** to exchange presents (ه with s.o.) **IV** to bring, lead, conduct (ها الى the bride to the bridegroom); to give as a present (الى or ل ه s.th. to s.o.), present (الى or ل s.o., ه with), make s.o. (الى or ل) a present of (ه); to dedicate (الى or ل ه s.th. to s.o.), confer, bestow, award (ه e.g., an order); to send, convey, transmit (ه ه to s.o. s.th.) **V** to be rightly guided, be led well; to get (الى to), reach (الى a place, s.th.) **VI** to make each other presents, exchange presents; to exchange among each other (ه s.th., also التحية *at-taḥīya* to exchange greetings, greet or salute each other); to guide, lead, conduct, take, bring (ه s.o.); to sway to and fro, swing rhythmically (in walking); to walk with a swinging gait; to stride; to move forward, move on, advance; to get (الى to), reach (الى a place); to get as far as (الى), penetrate (الى to); to flock (الى to s.o.), rally (الى around s.o.) **VIII** to be rightly guided, be led on the right way; to be led, be shown, be taken (الى, ل to); to find the way (الى to); to find, detect, discover (الى s.th.), come upon s.th. (الى); to hit upon s.th. (الى or ل, e.g., an idea), be made aware, think (الى or ل of), arrive (الى or ل at); to be led back, find one's way back (الى to the true faith, من away from evil); to be guided (ب by s.o.), take (ب s.o. or s.th.) as an example or model, follow s.o.'s (ب) lead **X** to ask to be rightly guided, pray for divine guidance, seek the right way

هدى *hady* guidance, direction; way, road, course, direction; manner, mode, fashion

هدى *hudan* right guidance (esp., in a religious sense); guiding, leading (of s.o.); right way, true religion | كان على هدى to be on the right way; to embrace the true religion; على غير هدى aimlessly, at random; سار على غير هدى to wander aimlessly

حدية *hadya, hidya* (line of) conduct, procedure, policy, course, way, direction; manner, mode, fashion

هدية *hadīya* pl. هدايا *hadāyā* gift, present, donation; offering, sacrifice

هداية *hidāya* guidance | على غير هداية without divine guidance, aimlessly, at random

اهدى *ahdā* better guided; more correct, more proper, better

اهداء *ihdā'* presentation; donation, grant(ing); award, bestowal, conferment; dedication (of a book)

هاد *hādin* pl. *-ūn,* هداة *hudāh* leading, guiding; leader, guide

مهدى *mahdīy* rightly guided; Mahdi

مهتد *muhtadin* rightly guided

هذا *hāḏā* (dem. pron.), f. هذه *hāḏihī,* هذى *hāḏī,* pl. هؤلاء *hā'ulā'i,* dual m. هذان *hāḏāni,* f. هاتان *hātāni* this one, this | بهذا *bi-hāḏā* hereby, herewith; لهذا *li-hāḏā* therefore, for this reason; مع هذا herewith; in spite of it, nevertheless; هذا الى ان (*ilā an*) besides, moreover, furthermore, what's more; هذا و besides, moreover, furthermore, what's more; on the other hand; هذا ويوجد (*yūjadu*) besides, there is ...

هذب *haḏaba* i (*haḏb*) to prune, trim (ه s.th.); to clean, purify, cleanse, smooth (ه s.th.), polish (ه s.th., also fig., e.g., the style) II do.; to improve, refine (ه s.th.); to rectify, set right, correct (ه s.th.); to check, revise (ه s.th.); to bring up (ه a child); to educate, instruct (ه s.o.) V pass. of II

تهذيب *tahḏīb* expurgation, emendation, correction; rectification; revision; training; instruction; education, upbringing; culture, refinement

تهذيبى *tahḏībī* of or pertaining to education, educational, educative; instructive, didactic

تهذب *tahaḏḏub* upbringing, manners, education

مهذب *muhaḏḏib* teacher, educator

مهذب *muhaḏḏab* well-mannered, well-bred, refined, polished, urbane, cultured, educated, well-behaved, polite, courteous

متهذب *mutahaḏḏib* well-mannered, well-bred, refined, polished, urbane, cultured, educated, well-behaved, polite, courteous

هذر *haḏara* u i (*haḏr*) to prattle, babble, prate, talk nonsense; to blurt out, blab (ب s.th.) II to joke, make fun, jest

هذر *haḏr* prattle, babble, idle talk; raillery, taunting words

هذر *haḏar* prattle, babble, idle talk; mockery, scoffing

هذر *haḏir* prattling, garrulous

هذرم *haḏrama* to babble, jabber, prattle, prate

هذلول *huḏlūl* pl. هذاليل *haḏālīl*[2] elevation, hillock; little river, small stream

خط هذلولى *ḵaṭṭ huḏlūlī* hyperbola (*math.*)

هذى *haḏā* i (*haḏy,* هذيان *haḏayān*) to talk irrationally, rave, be delirious

هذاء *huḏā'* raving, irrational talk, delirium

هذيان *haḏayān* senseless jabber, rigmarole, raving, drivel, delirium; state of absent-mindedness; folly; madness, insanity, mania, craze; hallucination

هاذ *hāḏin* delirious, raving

هر *harra* i (هرير *harīr*) to growl; to whimper, whine

هر *hirr* pl. هررة *hirara* tomcat; cat

هرة *hirra* pl. هرر *hirar* cat

هرير *harīr* growling, growl; yelping, whining, whimper(ing); spitting (of a cat)

هريرة *huraira* kitten

هرأ *hara'a* a to tear, lacerate (ه s.th.); to wear out, wear off (ه a garment); to affect strongly, beset grievously, try, wear out, harm, hurt (ه s.o.); to irritate (ه the skin); to be bitingly cold (wind) II to cook too much, overdo (ه meat) IV = II; V to be overdone (meat); to be torn, lacerated VIII to be torn, lacerated, mangled, torn to pieces; to be worn out, shabby

هراء *hurā'* prattle, idle talk

مهترئ *muhtari'* overdone, boiled to shreds; torn, lacerated, mangled; worn out, shabby

هرب *haraba* u (هرب *harab*, هروب *hurūb*, مهرب *mahrab*, هربان *harabān*) to flee (الى to); to escape (من a danger); to desert; to run away, elope (مع with) II to help (ه s.o.) to escape; to force to flee, put to flight (ه s.o.); to liberate, free (ه a prisoner); to rescue (ه a distrained or impounded thing; *jur.*); to engage in illicit trade, to traffic; to smuggle V to escape, elude (من s.th.); to shirk, dodge, evade (من a duty, or the like)

هرب *harab* flight, escape, getaway; desertion; elopement

هروب *hurūb* flight

هربان *harbān* fugitive, runaway, on the run; a runaway, a fugitive, a refugee

هراب *harrāb* coward

مهرب *mahrab* pl. مهارب *mahārib*[2] (place of) refuge, retreat, sanctuary; flight, escape, getaway | لا مهرب منه (*mahraba*) inescapable, unavoidable

تهريب *tahrīb* illicit trade, trafficking; smuggling, smuggle, contrabandism

هارب *hārib* fugitive, runaway, on the run; a runaway, a fugitive, a refugee; deserter; see also alphabetically

مهرب *muharrib* illicit dealer, trafficker; smuggler

مهرب *muharrab* pl. *-āt* smuggled goods, contraband

هرج *haraja* i (*harj*) to be excited, agitated, in commotion II to make (ه s.o.) drunk, befuddle, cloud, fog, blur (ه s.o.'s mind or perceptions); to joke, make fun, jest (في in conversation)

هرج *harj* excitement, agitation, commotion; disorder, muddle, confusion | هرج ومرج (*wa-marj*) turmoil, confusion, chaos

مهرج *muharrij* jester, clown, buffoon

هرجلة *harjala* chaos, muddle, confusion

هردبشت *hardabašt* buncombe, nonsense; trash, rubbish, junk

هرس *harasa* u (*hars*) to crush, mash, squash, bruise, pound (ه s.th.); to tenderize by beating, pound until tender (ه meat)

هريسة *harīsa* a dish of meat and bulgur; (*eg.*) a sweet pastry made of flour, melted butter and sugar

هراس *harrās* pl. *-āt* steamroller

آلة هراسة *āla harrāsa* steamroller ○

مهراس *mihrās* pl. مهاريس *mahāris*[2] mortar

هرش II to sow dissension (بين between, among) III to quarrel, wrangle (ه with); to dally, joke, banter (ه with)

هرش *harš* scratching; wear and tear, attrition, depreciation (of tools, machinery, etc.)

هراش *hirāš* quarrel, wrangle

مهروش *mahrūš* worn out, battered

هرطق *harṭaqa* to become a heretic

هرطقة *harṭaqa* heresy

هرطوقى *harṭūqī* pl. هراطقة *harāṭiqa* heretic (*Chr.*)

هراطقى *harāṭiqī* heretic (*Chr.*)

هرطمان *hurṭumān* a brand of oats

هرع *hara'a* a (*hara'*) and pass. *huri'a* to hurry, hasten, rush (الى to) II pass. *hurri'a* and IV *ahra'a* do.

هرع *hara'* hurry, haste, rush

هراع *hurā'* hurry, haste, rush

هرف *harafa* i (*harf*) to praise excessively, shower with extravagant praise (ب s.th. or s.o.)

هرق *haraqa* a (*harq*) to shed, spill (ه s.th.) IV do.; to sacrifice (ه s.th.)

مهراق *muhrāq* poured out, spilled

مهرقان *mahraqān*, *muhraqān*, *muhruqān* shore, coast; ocean

اهراق *ihrāq* shedding, spilling | اهراق الدماء *i. ad-dimā'* bloodshed

مهرق *muhraq* spilled, shed; — (pl. مهارق *mahāriq*[2]) parchment; ○ wax paper

هرقل *hiraql*[2], *hirqil*[2] Heraclius (Byzantine emperor); Hercules

هرم *harima* a (*haram*, مهرم *mahram*, مهرمة *mahrama*) to become senile and decrepit II to mince, chop (ه s.th.)

هرم *haram* decrepitude, senility; old age

هرم *haram* pl. اهرام *ahrām*, اهرامات *ahrāmāt* pyramid | ○ هرم ناقص frustum of pyramid, truncated pyramid (*math.*)

هرمى *haramī* pyramidlike, pyramidical, pyramidal

اهرامى *ahrāmī* pyramidlike, pyramidical, pyramidal

هرم *harim* decrepit, senile; advanced in years, aged, old; old man

هرمس *harmasa* to be grave, stern, gloomy (face)

هرمون *hormōn* pl. *-āt* hormone

هرهر *harhara* to move, shake (ه s.th.); to attack (على s.o.)

هرا[1] (هرو) *harā* u (*harw*) to cane, thrash, wallop (ه s.o.)

هراوة *hirāwa* pl. هراوى *harāwā* stick, cane; cudgel, truncheon, club

هراة[2] *harāh*[2] Herat (city in NW Afghanistan)

هروى *harawī* of Herat

هرول *harwala* to walk fast; to hurry, hasten, rush (الى to)

هرولة *harwala* quick pace, haste, hurry

مهرول *muharwil* hurrying, speeding; in a hurry

هرى *hury* pl. اهراء *ahrā'* granary

هار *hārin* reeling, tottering, unsteady

هز *hazza* u (*hazz*) to shake (ب or ه s.th.); to swing, brandish, wave (ه a lance or sword); to jolt to and fro, jog, rock (ه s.o.); to make (ه s.o.) tremble; to convulse, shake, rock, upset, sway (ه s.th.) | هز كتفيه (*katifaihi*) to shrug (one's shoulders); هز رأسه (*ra'sahū*) to nod, shake one's head; هز ذيله (*ḏailahū*) to wag its tail II to shake, swing, brandish, wave (ه s.th.) V to be moved, agitated, shaken, jolted, upset, convulsed, receive a shock; to move, stir, shake, sway, swing, vibrate, oscillate VIII do.; to tremble, quake, quiver; to be moved, touched, deeply affected (ل by); to rock (rider on a camel) | لا نهتز له كثيرا this won't affect us greatly, this is not likely to disconcert us, this will hardly cause us any headache; اهتز فرحا (*faraḥan*) to tremble with joy; اهتز اليه قلبه (*qalbuhu*) to be elated by s.th.

هزة *hazza* (n. vic.) pl. *-āt* motion, movement, stir, commotion, agitation; convulsion; jolt, jog, push; ○ (electric) shock; vibration, oscillation; tremor, shake | هزة ارضية (*arḍīya*) seismic shock, earthquake; هزة السرور (الطرب ,الفرح) (*ṭarab, faraḥ*) joyous excitement, delight, rapture

هزة *hizza* liveliness, vivacity, high spirits

هزاز *hazzāz* shaking, jolting; rocking; rolling, swinging; shaker (in concrete construction, for coal, and the like)

هزيز *hazīz* bluster(ing), sough (of the wind); rumbling, roll (of thunder)

مهزة *mahazza* excitement, agitation

تهزيز *tahzīz* movement, agitation, shaking

اهتزاز *ihtizāz* convulsion, shock; trembling, shaking, tremor; swinging, oscillation, vibration; excitement, agitation, commotion, emotion

اهتزازه *ihtizāza* (n. vic.) tremor, vibration

مهتز *muhtazz* trembling, tremulous, shaking, quivering

هزأ *haza'a*, هزئ *hazi'a a* (هزء *haz'*, *huz'*, هزؤ *huzu'*, هزوء *huzū'*, مهزأة *mahza'a*) to scoff, jeer, sneer, laugh (من or ب at), make fun (من or ب of), deride, ridicule, mock (من or ب s.o.) **V** and **X** to deride, mock (من or ب s.o., s.th., also على)

هزء *haz'*, *huz'* and هزؤ *huzu'* derision, scorn, disdain, contempt; mockery

هزئى *huz'ī* mocking, derisive

هزأة *huz'a* object of ridicule, butt of derision, laughingstock

هزأة *huza'a* mocker, sarcast; scorner, disdainer, despiser

مهزأة *mahza'a* derision, scorn, disdain, contempt; mockery; scornful laughter, sneer

استهزاء *istihzā'* mockery, ridicule, derision, scorn | باستهزاء mockingly, derisively

هازئ *hāzi'* mocker, scoffer

مستهزئ *mustahzi'* mocker, scoffer

هزبر *hizabr, hizbar* pl. هزابر *hazābir*[2] lion

هزج *hazija a* to sing

هزج *hazaj* name of a poetic meter

اهزوجة *uhzūja* pl. اهازيج *ahāzīj*[2] song

[1]هزر *hazara i* (*hazr*) to laugh **II** (*eg.*) to joke, make fun, jest

هزار *hizār* (*eg.*) joking, jesting, funmaking

[2]هزار *hazār* pl. *-āt* nightingale

هزع *haza'a a* (*haz'*) to hurry, be quick **V** do.

هزيع *hazī'* part of the night

هزل *hazala i* (*hazl, huzl*), *hazila a* (*hazal*) and pass. *huzila* to be emaciated, lean, skinny; to lose weight, become lean, skinny, emaciated; — *hazala i* (*hazl*) to joke, talk lightly, jokingly; to cause to lose weight, make lean, emaciate, enervate (ه s.o.) **II** to emaciate, waste away, enervate (ه s.o.) **III** to joke, make fun, jest (ه with s.o.) **IV** to emaciate, waste away, enervate (ه s.o.) **VII** to be or become lean

هزل *hazl* joking, jesting, fun

هزلى *hazlī* jocular, funny, amusing, droll, humorous; humoristic; comical

هزلية *hazlīya* or رواية هزلية comedy (*theat.*)

هزل *hazil* joker, jester, funnyman, wag, wit

هزال *huzāl* emaciation; leanness, skinniness

هزال *hazzāl* joker, jester, funnyman, wag, wit

هزيل *hazīl* pl. هزلى *hazlā* lean, skinny, emaciated

مهزلة *mahzala* pl. -*āt*, مهازل *mahāzil*² comedy

هازل *hāzil* joking, jocose, jocular, funny, humorous, amusing; joker, wag, wit | صحف هازلة (*ṣuḥuf*) funnies, comics

مهزول *mahzūl* pl. مهازيل *mahāzīl*² emaciated, wasted, haggard, gaunt; weak, feeble

هزم *hazama* **i** (*hazm*) to put to flight, rout, vanquish, defeat (ه the enemy); to put out of action, neutralize (ه an opponent) **VII** to be defeated, be routed, be put to flight

هزم *hazm* vanquishing, routing; defeat

هزيم *hazīm* roll of thunder, rumbling, rumble, thunder; fleeing, fugitive, in flight, on the run

هزيمة *hazīma* pl. هزائم *hazā'im*² defeat, rout | ○ روح الهزيمة *rūḥ al-h.* defeatism

انهزام *inhizām* (suffering of) defeat, frustration; rout, (disorganized) flight

انهزامى *inhizāmī* pl. -*ūn* defeatist

انهزامية *inhizāmīya* defeatism

هزهز *hazhaza* to move, agitate, shake, jolt, shock, convulse, upset (ه, ه s.o., s.th.) **II** *tahazhaza* to be moved, agitated, shaken, convulsed, upset, receive a shock

هزهزة *hazhaza* pl. هزاهز *hazāhiz*² movement, agitation, shock, convulsion, commotion, disturbance

هس *hassa* **i** (*hass*) to whisper

هس *hass* whisper, whispering; soliloquy

هس *huss* hush! quiet! silence!

هسيس *hasīs* whisper, whispering sound

هستولوجيا *histōlōjiyā* histology

هستريا and هيستريا *histēriyā* hysteria

هسترى *histērī* hysteric(al)

[1] هش *hašša* **i** (هشوشة *hušūša*) to be crisp (bread) — **u i** (هشاش *hašāš*, هشاشة *hašāša*) to be in good spirits, display a cheerful mien, wear a smile; to smile (ل or ب at s.o.), meet s.o. (ل or ب) in a courteous, amiable manner, receive s.o. kindly; to cheer up (ل over or because of), be delighted (ل by); — **u** to drive away, chase away (ه flies, and the like); — **u i** (*hašš*) to chop off (ه على leaves for the cattle) **II** to cheer up, enliven (ه s.o.), raise s.o.'s (ه) spirits

هش *hašš* delicate, fragile; crisp, brittle, crumbly, friable; fresh and soft; gay, cheerful, happy, lively, brisk

هشاش *hašāš* soft, crumbly, friable

هشيش *hašīš* soft

هشاشة *hašāša* gaiety, cheerfulness, happiness

هاش *hāšš* crisp; blithe, cheerful, bright-faced | هاش باش (*bāšš*) gay and happy

[2] هش *hušš* hush! quiet! silence!

هشم *hašama* **i** (*hašm*) and **II** to destroy (ه s.th.); to smash (ه s.th.); to crush (ه s.th.) **V** and **VII** to be or get smashed, destroyed

هشيم *hašīm* frail, fragile; dry stalks, straw, chaff

هاشمى *hāšimī* Hashemite

مهشم *muhaššam* destroyed (city); crushed

هصر *haṣara* i (*haṣr*) to pull toward o.s., bend down (ه s.th., e.g., a branch); to produce a crack or break (ه in), crack, break (ه s.th.)

هصور *haṣūr* epithet of the lion

هضّ *haḍḍa* u (*haḍḍ*) to walk fast, move briskly, advance, progress, get on

هضب *haḍaba* i (*haḍb*) to be long-winded, verbose

هضبة *haḍba* pl. هضاب *hiḍāb* hill, elevation, mountain

هضم *haḍama* i (*haḍm*) to digest (ه the food; of the stomach); to oppress, terrorize, outrage, wrong, treat with injustice (ه s.o.); to stand, bear, endure (ه s.o.); to stomach (ه s.th.), put up with s.th. (ه) VII to be digested VIII to oppress, wrong (ه s.o.), do (ه s.o.) an injustice

هضم *haḍm* digestion; patience, long-suffering | هضم الجانب forbearance, compliance, indulgence; سهل الهضم *sahl al-h.* easily digestible, light

هضمى *haḍmī* digestive, alimentary

هضوم *haḍūm* digestible, agreeing, wholesome

هضيم *haḍīm* digested; digestible; oppressed, terrorized, outraged; slender, slim

هضيمة *haḍīma* encroachment, inroad, injustice, wrong, outrage, oppression

انهضام *inhiḍām* digestion; digestibility

مهضوم *mahḍūm* digested; digestible; oppressed, terrorized, outraged

هطع IV to protrude the neck (in walking) | اهطع فى العدو (*ʿadw*) to run fast

هطل *haṭala* i (*haṭl*, هطلان *haṭalān*, تهطال *tahṭāl*) to flow in torrents, fall heavily, pour down (rain) VI do.

هطل *hiṭl* wolf

هطول *huṭūl*: هطول الامطار *h. al-amṭār* downpour, heavy rain

هيطل *haiṭal* pl. هياطلة *hayāṭila*, هياطل *hayāṭil*[2] fox

هفّ *haffa* i (هفيف *hafīf*) to pass swiftly, flit past; to flash; to brush, touch lightly; — i (*haff*, *hafīf*) to blow, whiffle, sough (wind); to spread, waft (fragrance) | هفت نفسه الى (*nafsuhū*) he yearned for ...; هف على باله it occurred to him all of a sudden, it flashed across his mind

هفّ *hiff* empty; light, light-headed, thoughtless, frivolous

هفاف *haffāf* flashing, sparkling, shining; blowing (wind); light, fleeting; thin and transparent, diaphanous

الهفوف *al-hufūf* Hofuf (chief town of al-Hasa district in E Saudi Arabia)

مهفة *mihaffa* fan; feather duster

مهفوف *mahfūf* light headed, irresponsible, reckless, unscrupulous

هفت *hafata* i (*haft*, هفات *hufāt*) to fall down, collapse; to be nonsensical, absurd; to talk nonsense VI to pounce, rush, fall, plunge (على on or into); to crowd in (على on), throng, flock (على to), tumble one over the other, fall all over themselves; to suffer a breakdown; to cave in, collapse, break down; to be broken, wrecked, ruined (nerves)

هفتان *haftān* (*eg.*) weak, exhausted, spent, weakened

تهافت *tahāfut* collapse, breakdown | تهافت الاعصاب nervous breakdown

هافت *hāfit* wrong, erroneous (opinion)

مهفوت *mahfūt* baffled, startled, perplexed

الهافر look up alphabetically

هفهف *hafhafa* to be slender, slim; to float in the air II *tahafhafa* to be slender, slim

هفهفة *hafhafa* sough, whispering of the wind

هفهاف *hafhāf* slender, slim, svelte; slight, frail, delicate; thin, sparse (e.g., beard); diaphanous, transparent, gossamery; light, weightless, defying gravity; flowing, waving, fluttering

مهفهف *muhafhaf* slender, slim, svelte; thin

هفا (هفو) *hafā* u (*hafw*, هفوة *hafwa*, هفوان *hafawān*) to slip, commit a lapse, make a mistake; to err; to be weak with hunger, famished, starved; to hurry, rush (الى to); to reach quickly (الى for s.th.), snatch (الى at s.th.); with ب: to induce s.o. (الى to), tempt s.o. to do s.th. (الى); (هفو *hafw*, *hufūw*) to flutter, fly, float in the air; to throb violently, beat feverishly, flutter, be passionately excited, be impassioned (heart; esp., with love); to feel a desire, yearn (الى for)

هفوة *hafwa* pl. *hafawāt* slip, lapse, error, mistake, fault, offense, sin

هاف *hāfin* famished, starved

هكتار *hiktār* pl. *-āt* hectare

هكذا *hākaḏā* so, thus, this way, in this manner

هيكل look up alphabetically

هكم V to be dilapidated, ramshackle, tumbledown; to fall down, collapse; to mock, scoff; to make fun (ب or على or ه of s.o.), ridicule, deride, jeer (ب, على, ه s.o.); to be annoyed (على by), regret (على s.th.)

اهكومة *uhkūma* derision, mockery, taunt, gibe

تهكم *tahakkum* mockery, derision, scorn, irony, sarcasm

تهكمى *tahakkumī* mocking, derisive, sarcastic, scornful

متهكم *mutahakkim* mocking, ironical

هل[1] *hal* interrogative particle introducing direct and indirect question; also preceding the first part of an alternative question: هل — ام *hal — am* whether — or

هلا *hallā* = هل لا is (or does) not ...? why not?

هل[2] *halla* i (*hall*) to appear, come up, show (new moon); to begin, set in (month) II to say the words *lā ilāha illā llāh*; to shout with joy, rejoice, exult, jubilate; to applaud, acclaim, cheer (ل s.o.) IV to appear (new moon); to cheer, exult; to offer up (ب ل an animal to a deity) V to shine, gleam, glow, be radiant; to beam with joy (face); to be delighted, jubilant; to cheer, rejoice, exult, jubilate VII to fall heavily, pour down (rain); to begin (ف with), take up, undertake tackle, attack (ف s.th.), embark (ف upon) X to begin, set in (new month); to raise one's voice; to intone, strike up (ه a tune); to begin, start (ه a task); to open, begin, introduce, initiate (ه ب s.th. with or by)

هلال *hilāl* pl. اهلة *ahilla*, اهاليل *ahālīl*[2] new moon; half-moon, crescent; parenthesis; any crescent-shaped object

هلالى *hilālī* lunar; crescent-shaped, lunate, sickle-shaped

هلل *halal* fright, terror, dismay

تهليل *tahlīl* pl. تهاليل *tahālīl*[2] utterance of the formula *lā ilāha illā llāh*; rejoicing, exultation, jubilation; applause, acclamation, acclaim, cheering, cheers

تهلل *tahallul* joy, jubilation, exultation

استهلال *istihlāl* beginning, opening, introduction, initiation

استهلالى *istihlālī* incipient, initial, starting, opening, introductory, initiative

مهلل *muhallal* crescent-shaped, lunate

متهلل *mutahallil* jubilant, rejoicing, exultant; radiant, beaming

مستهل *mustahall* beginning, start, outset

هلب *haliba a* (*halab*) to be hairy, covered with hair

هلب *halib* hairy, covered with hair; shaggy, hirsute

هلب *hulb* (coll.; n. un. ة) hair, bristles

هلب *hilb* pl. اهلاب *ahlāb* anchor, grapnel, grappling iron, boat hook

اهلب *ahlab*², f. هلباء *halbā'*², pl. هلب *hulb* hairy, hirsute, shaggy

هلابة *hulāba* lochia (*med.*)

مهلبية *muhallabīya* a dessert resembling blancmange, made of rice flour, milk and sugar

هليلج *halīlaj* and اهليلج *ihlīlaj* myrobalan, emblic (fruit of Phyllanthus emblica L.; *bot.*); ellipse (*geom.*)

اهليلجى *ihlīlajī* elliptic(al)

¹هلس *halasa i* (*hals*) to emaciate, consume, waste away (ه s.o.; of a disease); pass. *hulisa* to be consumptive, suffer from pulmonary tuberculosis **II** to waste away, become lean, emaciated, haggard; to talk nonsense **IV** to smile

هلس *hals* emaciation, wasting away; pulmonary tuberculosis, consumption, phthisis; nonsense, bosh, silly talk

²هلوسة look up alphabetically

هلسنكى *helsinkī* Helsinki (capital of Finland)

هلع *hali'a a* (*hala'*) to be impatient or restless, be anxious, be in despair

هلع *hala'* impatience, restlessness, uneasiness; fear, burning anxiety; alarm, dismay

هلع *hali'* impatient, restless, uneasy, anxious; dismayed, appalled

هلوع ***halū'*** **impatient, restless, uneasy, anxious; dismayed, appalled**

هلوف ***hillauf*** **bearded; bristly**

هلقم ***halqama*** **to gulp down, devour (ه s.th.)**

هلك ***halaka i*** **(*halk, hulk,* هلاك *halāk,* تهلكة *tahluka*) to perish; to die; to be annihilated, wiped out, destroyed II and IV to ruin, destroy (ه s.th.) | اهلك الحرث والنسل (*ḥarṯ, nasl*) to destroy lock, stock and barrel VI to exert o.s., do one's utmost (فى in); to pounce, fall, throw o.s. (على upon); to fight desperately (على for); to covet, crave (على s.th.); to feel enthusiasm (على for), devote o.s. eagerly (على to), go all out (على for); to become languid, tired, weak; to drop in utter exhaustion (على on); to break down, collapse VII and VIII to risk danger, imperil o.s., act desperately X to exert o.s., do one's utmost (فى in); to waste, squander, spend, exhaust, use up, consume (ه s.th.); to discharge, pay off, amortize (ه a debt); pass. *ustuhlika* to perish, die**

هلك ***hulk*** **death; destruction, ruin**

هلكة ***halka, halaka*** **total loss, ruin, destruction; disaster; jeopardy, perilous situation, danger**

هلاك *halāk* total loss, ruin, destruction; perdition, eternal damnation

مهلكة ***mahlaka, mahluka, mahlika*** **pl. مهالك *mahālik*² dangerous place, danger spot; dangerous situation; danger, peril**

تهلكة ***tahluka*** **ruin; jeopardy, perilous situation, danger**

تهالك ***tahāluk*** **enthusiasm, zeal, ardor (على for), (vivid) interest (على in); weakness, fatigue, languor**

استهلاك *istihlāk* consumption; attrition, wear and tear; discharge, amortization

استهلاكى *istihlākī* consumer- (in compounds; e.g., goods, prices, etc.)

هالك *hālik* pl. هلكى *halkā*, هلك *hullak*, هلاك *hullāk*, هوالك *hawālik*² perishing, dying; dead; mortal, destructible, perishable; doomed to perdition, damned; irretrievably lost, irredeemable

مهلك *muhlik* destructive, devastating, annihilating, scathing, withering; pernicious, ruinous, dangerous, perilous, deadly, lethal; medium of destruction or extermination

متهالك *mutahālik* broken down, down-and-out; exhausted

مستهلك *mustahlik* consumer

مستهلك *mustahlak* consumption

هللويا *hallilūyā* hallelujah

¹هلم *halumma* up! get up! come! now then! come on! onward! forward! (with acc.) out with ...! bring ...! give me (us) ...! | هلمى اليه (*halummī*) now then, go (f.) quickly to him! هلم بنا (*bi-nā*) come on! let's go! وهلم جرا (*jarran*) and so on, etc.

²هلم *hillam* languid, listless, slack, limp

هلام *hulām* jelly, gelatin

هلامى *hulāmī* jellylike, gelatinous

تهلين *tahlīn* Hellenization

هلهل *halhala* to weave finely (ه s.th., also a poem), weave flimsily (ه s.th.); to wear out (ه a garment), let it become shabby, threadbare, thin

هلهل *halhal* fine; thin, flimsy; delicate

هلاهل *hulāhil* fine; thin, flimsy; delicate

هلهولة *halhūla* pl. هلاهيل *halāhīl*² (*eg.*) worn dress, old rag, tatters

مهلهل *muhalhal* thin, flimsy, gauzelike, diaphanous; finely woven (also, of a poem), worn, shabby, threadbare, tattered, ragged

هلوسة *halwasa* hallucination; vision

هليكوبتر *helikoptar* helicopter

هليلج *halīlaj* and اهليلج *ihlīlaj* myrobalan, emblic (fruit of Phyllanthus emblica L.; *bot.*); ellipse (*geom.*)

اهليلجى *ihlīlajī* elliptic(al)

هليون *hilyaun* asparagus

¹هم *hum* they (3rd pers. m. pl. of the pers. pron.)

²هم *hamma* u (*hamm*, مهمة *mahamma*) to disquiet, make uneasy, fill with anxiety, distress, grieve (ه s.o.); to preoccupy, interest, regard, concern, affect (ه s.o.), be of interest (ه to s.o.); to be on s.o.'s (ه) mind, be s.o.'s (ه) concern; to worry, trouble (ه s.o.); to be important, be of importance or consequence (ه to s.o.); — (*hamm*) to worry, be concerned (ب about); to have in mind, intend, plan (ب s.th., to do s.th.); to consider (ه doing s.th.), think of doing s.th. (ه); to be about, be going (ب, بأن to do s.th.), be on the point of doing s.th. (ب, بأن), begin to, start doing s.th. (ب, بأن); to rise, get up **IV** to grieve, distress, concern, preoccupy, affect, regard (ه s.o.); to be on s.o.'s (ه) mind, be s.o.'s (ه) concern; to worry, trouble (ه s.o.); to be of interest (ه to s.o.), interest (ه s.o.); to be important, be of consequence, to matter **VIII** to be distressed, grieved, worried (ب by); to worry, be concerned (ب about); to concern o.s. (ب, occasionally also ل, with); to feel concern (ب for), take an interest (ب in); to attach importance (ب to); to be interested (ب in); to look (ب after); to pay attention (ب to), take notice (ب of), bear in mind (ب s.th.); to go to trouble, go to great lengths (ل ب on behalf of or for s.o. about s.th.); to take care (ب of s.o.), take s.o. (ب) under one's wing, help, assist (ب s.o.); to provide (ب for); to be anxious or solicitous (ل about)

هم *hamm* pl. هموم *humūm* anxiety, concern, solicitude; worry, care; sorrow, grief, affliction, distress; interest; intention, design, plan; important matter; weight, moment, importance, significance, consequence

هم *himm* pl. اهمام *ahmām*, f. همة *himma*, pl. *-āt*, همائم *hamā'im*[2] decrepit, senile; old man

همة *himma* pl. همم *himam* endeavor, ambition, intention, design; resolution, determination; zeal, ardor, eagerness; high-mindedness, high-aiming ambition | بعيد الهمة and عالى الهمة high-aspiring, having far-reaching aims; high-minded

همام *hammām* careworn, worried; anxious, solicitous; eager, active, energetic

همام *humām* pl. همام *himām* high-minded; generous, magnanimous; heroic, gallant

اهم *ahamm*[2] more important, of greater importance

اهمية *ahammīya* importance, significance, consequence; interest | عديم الاهمية unimportant; علق اهمية على (*'allaqa*) to attach importance to; كان من الاهمية بمكان عظيم (*makānin*) to be of the greatest importance

مهمة *mahamma* pl. مهام *mahāmm*[2] important matter; task, function, duty; commission, assignment, mission | مهام الامور important matters; مهام المنصب *m. al-manṣib* official duties, official functions

تهميم *tahmīm* lulling a baby to sleep by singing

تهميمة *tahmīma* lullaby

اهتمام *ihtimām* pl. *-āt* concern, interest; anxiety; solicitude; care; attention; endeavor, ambition

هام *hāmm* important, significant, momentous, weighty, ponderous, grave, serious; interesting

هامة *hāmma* pl. هوام *hawāmm*[2] vermin; pest; reptile; see also under هوم

مهموم *mahmūm* concerned, worried, anxious, distressed, grieved, sorrowful; preoccupied; interested

مهم *muhimm* important, significant, momentous, weighty, ponderous, grave, serious; interesting

مهمة *muhimma* pl. *-āt* important matter; pl. requirements, exigencies; equipment, material(s); stores, supplies, provisions | مهمات حربية (*ḥarbīya*) war material; ○ مهمات متحركة (*mutaḥarrika*) rolling stock

مهتم *muhtamm* interested (ب in); concerned, anxious, solicitous (ب about); attentive (ب to), mindful (ب of)

مهتمات *muhtammāt* tasks, functions, duties

هما *humā* both of them (3rd pers. dual of the pers. pron.); see also همو

همايونى *humāyūnī* imperial

همج *hamija a* (*hamaj*) to be hungry

همج *hamaj* (coll.; n. un. ة) pl. اهماج *ahmāj* small flies, gnats; riffraff, rabble, ragtag; savages, barbarians

همج *hamaj* hunger | همج هامج ravenous hunger, voracious appetite

همجى *hamajī* uncivilized, savage; rude; barbaric, barbarous; a savage, barbarian

همجية *hamajīya* savageness, savagery; rudeness; barbarism

همد *hamada u* (همود *humūd*) to abate, subside, let up, calm down, die away, fade away, die down, cool off; to become smaller, shrink **II** and **IV** to quiet, calm, still, appease, placate, soothe, mitigate, alleviate, allay, stifle, quell, suppress, put out, extinguish (ه s.th.)

همود *humūd* extinction; cooling off (of a passion, and the like); lull; fatigue, exhaustion, tiredness; motionlessness, torpor; stiffness, rigidity, rigor; death

هامد *hāmid* calm, quiet, still, extinct; lifeless; rigid, stiff (corpse)

همر **hamara u i** (*hamr*) to pour out, shed (ه s.th., water, tears) **VII** to be poured out, be shed; to pour down (rain), flow (tears)

همرة *hamra* shower of rain; growl(ing), snarl(ing)

همز **hamaza u i** (*hamz*) to prick; to drive, urge on, prod, goad on (ه, ه s.o., s.th.); to spur (ه one's horse); (*gram.*) to provide with *hamza* (ه a letter or word)

همز *hamz* spurring, goading, prodding, urging, pressing; beating, striking, kicking; backbiting, slander | همز ولمز (*lamz*) innuendoes, defamatory insinuations; taunts, gibes, sneers

همز *hamz* glottal stop before or after a vowel (*phon.*)

همزة *hamza* pl. *hamazāt* hamza, the character designating the glottal stop: ء (*gram.*) | همزة القطع *h. al-qaṭ'* disjunctive hamza (*gram.*); همزة الوصل *h. al-waṣl* conjunctive hamza (*gram.*); همزة الوصل بين the (connecting) link between ...

هماز *hammāz* slanderer, backbiter

مهمز *mihmaz* pl. مهامز *mahāmiz*² spur; goad

مهماز *mihmāz* pl. مهاميز *mahāmīz*² spur; goad

همس **hamasa i** (*hams*) to mumble, mutter; to whisper (ب s.th., الى to s.o.) | همس فى اذنه (*fī uḏnihī*) to whisper in s.o.'s ear **VI** to whisper together, exchange whispered remarks

همس *hams* mutter(ing), mumble; whisper(ing)

همسة *hamsa* pianissimo of a singer; whisper; pl. همسات *hamasāt* whispering, whispers

هوامس *hawāmis*² mumbled or whispered words

همش **hamaša u** (*hamš*) to bite (ه s.o.)

هامش *hāmiš* margin (of a book, page, etc.) | ... على هامش on the periphery of ..., on the side lines of ..., aside from, in connection with ..., on the occasion of ..., apropos of | على هامش الاخبار sidenotes of the news (title of a BBC news commentary)

هامشى *hāmišī* marginal

همع **hama'a a u** to shed tears (eye); to stream, flow, well

همك **hamaka u** (*hamk*) to urge, press (ه فى s.o. to do s.th.) **VII** to be engrossed, be completely engaged (فى in s.th.), be dedicated (فى to), give o.s. up, abandon o.s. wholeheartedly (فى to, also على), be lost, become absorbed (فى in), be completely taken up, be preoccupied (فى with)

انهماك *inhimāk* wholehearted dedication, abandon, engrossment, exclusive occupation, absorption; preoccupation

منهمك *munhamik* engrossed, absorbed, lost (فى in), taken up, preoccupied (فى with); given, addicted (فى to); dedicated (فى to)

همل **hamala u i** (*haml*, هملان *hamalān*, همول *humūl*) to be bathed in tears, shed tears (eye) **IV** to neglect (ه s.th.); to omit, leave out (ه s.th.); to disregard, fail to consider or notice, overlook, forget (ه s.th.); to cease to use, disuse (ه s.th.); to leave unpointed, provide with no diacritical points (ه a consonant; *gram.*) **VI** to be careless, negligent, remiss, lazy **VII** to be bathed in tears, shed tears (eye); to pour down (rain)

همل *hamal* left to o.s., to one's own devices, left alone; left untended (cattle); neglected, disregarded

اهمال *ihmāl* negligence; neglect; dereliction of duty; carelessness, heedlessness, inattention; nonobservance, disregard, nonconsideration

هامل *hāmil* pl. همل *hummal* roving, roaming; vagabond, tramp

مهمل *muhmil* negligent, neglectful, remiss; careless, heedless, inattentive, slovenly

مهمل *muhmal* neglected; omitted; disregarded, not taken into account; obsolete, antiquated; lacking, devoid of, not provided with; without diacritical points, unpointed (*gram.*); المهملات deadletter office | مهمل الامضاء without signature, unsigned; رسالة مهملة dead (i.e., undeliverable) letter; سلة المهملات *sallat al-m.* wastebasket; كمية مهملة (*kammīya*) negligible quantity

هملج *hamlaja* to amble (horse)

هملاج *himlāj* pl. هماليج *hamālīj*[2] ambler, ambling horse

همهم *hamhama* to say "hmm"; to mumble, mutter; to grumble; to growl, snarl; to hum, buzz, drone

همهمة *hamhama* pl. *-āt*, هماهم *hamāhim*[2] an inarticulate utterance ("hmm, hmm"), e.g., to express astonishment, and the like; mumble, mutter(ing); hum, buzz, drone (also, e.g., of an airplane); growl, snarl

(همو) هما *hamā u* (*hamw*) to flow; to pour forth; see also alphabetically

[1]هن *hanna i* to weep, sigh; to long, yearn (الى for)

[2]هن *hunna* they (3rd pers. f. pl. of the pers. pron.)

[3]هنة *hana* see under هنو

[1]هنا *hunā* and ههنا *hāhunā* here, over here, in this place; *hunā* (with foll. verb) there, then, now, by now, at this point | الى هنا or لهنا here, over here, to this place; up to here, so far, up to this point, up to this amount; من هنا from here; of this, hereof, from this, hence; for this reason, therefore; by this, hereby; هنا وهناك here and there

هناك *hunāka* and هنالك *hunālika* there, over there, in that place; there is (are) | هناك قول مأثور (*qaul*) there is a proverb; الى هناك there, over there, to that place; من هناك from there, from that place; ماذا هنالك what's up? what's the matter?

[2]هنأ *hana'a u a i* (هنء *han'*, *hin'*, هناء *hanā'*) to be beneficial, wholesome, healthful, salutary, salubrious (ل or ه to s.o.), do s.o. (ل or ه) good; — هنئ *hani'a a* (هنأ *hana'*) to be delighted (ب with), take pleasure (ب in) enjoy (ب s.th.) II to congratulate, felicitate (ه ب or على s.o. on or on the occasion of); to make happy, gladden, delight (ه s.o.) V to enjoy, savor (ب s.th.), take pleasure (ب in)

هناء *hanā'* and هناءة *hanā'a* happiness, bliss; good health, well-being; congratulation, felicitation

هناء *hinā'* tar

هنیء *hanī'* healthful, salutary, salubrious, wholesome, beneficial; pleasant, agreeable; easy, smooth, comfortable | هنيئا مريئا or هنيئا لك *hanī'an marī'an* approx.: may it do you much good! I hope you will enjoy it (i.e., food)!

تهنئة *tahni'a* pl. تهانئ *tahāni'*[2] congratulation, felicitation

هانئ *hāni'* happy, delighted, glad; servant; هانئة *hāni'a* servant girl, maid

مهنئ *muhanni'* congratulator, wellwisher

الهند *al-hind* India; the (East) Indians | الهند البريطانية British India; الهند الصينية (*ṣīnīya*)

Indochina; الهند الشرقية (*šarqīya*) East India; جزر الهند الغربية *juzur al-h. al-ġarbīya* the Caribbean Islands, the West Indies

هندى *hindī* Indian; (pl. هنود *hunūd*) an Indian | المحيط الهندى (*muḥīṭ*) the Indian Ocean; الهنود الحمر (*ḥumr*) the American Indians

مهند *muhannad* sword made of Indian steel

هندب *hindab*, هندباء *hindibā'* wild chicory, endive (*bot.*)

هنداز *hindāz* measure

هندازة *hindāza* cubit (*Eg.*, = 65.6 cm)

هندسة *handasa* engineering; mechanical engineering; architecture, architectural engineering; army engineering; geometry; geodesy, surveying | علم الهندسة *'ilm al-h.* geometry; هندسة الرى *h. ar-riyy* irrigation engineering; الهندسة الزراعية (*zirā'īya*) agronomy; الهندسة السطحية (*saṭḥīya*) plane geometry, planimetry; الهندسة الفراغية (*farāġīya*) solid geometry, stereometry; هندسة المدن *h. al-mudun* town planning; الهندسة المعمارية (*mi'mārīya*) architecture; هندسة الميدان *h. al-maidān* combat engineering; الهندسة الكهربائية (*kahrabā'īya*) electrotechnics, electrical engineering; هندسة اللاسلكى *h. al-lā-silkī* radio engineering; الهندسة المدنية (*madanīya*) civil engineering; الهندسة الميكانيكية mechanical engineering

هندسى *handasī* technical, technological; geometrical; of or relative to mechanical engineering; engineering, industrial | فرقة هندسية (*firqa*) corps of engineers; القوات الهندسية (*qūwāt*) corps of engineers; the engineers (*mil.*)

هنداسة *hindāsa* = هندازة, see above

مهندس *muhandis* architect; engineer; technician | مهندس زراعى (*zirā'ī*) agricultural engineer; مهندس عسكرى (*'askarī*) army engineer; مهندس كهربائى (*kahrabā'ī*) electrotechnician, electrical engineer; مهندس معمارى (*mi'mārī*) architect

هندم *handama* to order, array, adjust (ه s.th.); to make smart, neat, trim; to dress up, spruce up (ه s.o.)

هندمة *handama* harmony; orderliness, tidiness, neatness, trimness

هندام *hindām* harmony; orderliness, tidiness, neatness, trimness; attire, dress, garb | اصلح هندامه to adjust one's clothes; to dress, dress up

مهندم *muhandam* well-ordered, well-arrayed; orderly, tidy, neat; trim, smart; well-dressed; made to measure, tailor-made (suit)

هنشير *hanšīr* pl. هناشير *hanāšīr*[2] (*tun.*) country estate

هنغارى *hunġārī* Hungarian (adj. and n.)

هنف II to hurry, hasten, rush III and VI to laugh contemptuously, sneer; to sob, whimper

هناك and هنالك see [1]هنا

[1]هنم *hanam* dried dates

[2]هانم look up alphabetically

هنيهة *hunaiha* a little while; *hunaihatan* for a little while

هنهن *hanhana* to lull to sleep with a song (ل a baby)

هنهونة *hanhūna* lullaby

هنة *hana* pl. *-āt*, هنوات *hanawāt* thing; s.th. unimportant, trifle, bagatelle; blemish, defect, fault, flaw

هنو *hinw* time

هنى *hanīy* (= هنىء) wholesome, delicious

هه *hih* (interj.) oh! alas! woe! (also derogatorily) oh, come now!

هنا[1] see هِهُنا

[1]هو *huwa* he; it (3rd pers. m. sing. of the pers. pron.); God; ذا see هوذا

هوية *huwīya* essence, nature; coessentiality, consubstantiality; identity; identity card (= بطاقة الهوية, تذكرة الهوية) | اوراق الهوية *aurāq al-h.* identification papers, credentials; تذكرة الهوية *taḏkirat al-h.* (*ir., syr.*) identity card; عرف هويته (*'urifa*) to be identified

[2]هوة *hūwa* see هوى

هوتة *hauta, hūta* pl. هوت *huwat* depression in the ground; chasm, abyss

هوج *hawaj* folly, light-headedness, rashness, thoughtlessness

اهوج *ahwaj*[2], f. هوجاء *haujā'*[2], pl. هوج *hūj* reckless; impatient, rash, thoughtless, narebrained, precipitate, hasty, foolhardy, violent, vehement, frantic

هوجاء *haujā'*[2] pl. هوج *hūj* hurricane, tornado, cyclone

(هود) هاد *hāda u* (*haud*) to be a Jew **II** to proceed slowly; to intoxicate, inebriate (ه s.o.; of wine); to make Jewish (ه s.o.) **III** to be indulgent, forbearing, conciliatory, considerate, complaisant, obliging (ه to s.o.), to avoid, shun (ه s.o.), stay out of s.o.'s (ه) way **V** to become a Jew or Jewish

الهود *al-hūd* the Jews, the Jewry

هوادة *hawāda* forbearance, indulgence' consideration, complaisance, obligingness; clemency, leniency, gentle-heartedness; relaxation, mitigation (of laws)

تهويد *tahwīd* Judaization

مهاودة *muhāwada* complaisance, obligingness, indulgence, consideration | مهاودة الاسعار low pricing

متهود *mutahawwid* Judaized, under Jewish influence or control

متهاود *mutahāwid* moderate (price)

هدج see هودج

ذا see هوذا

(هور) هار *hāra u* (*haur*, هؤور *hu'ūr*) to be destroyed, crash down, fall down, collapse; — (*haur*) to pull down, topple, wreck, demolish, destroy (ه s.th., esp., a building); to bring down, throw to the ground (ه s.o.) **II** to endanger, imperil, jeopardize, expose to danger (ه s.o.); to bring down, throw to the ground (ه s.o.) **V** to be destroyed, crash down, fall down, collapse; to rush headlong into danger; to be light-headed, careless, irresponsible; to elapse, pass, go by (time) **VII** to be demolished or torn down; to crash down, fall down, collapse; to fall apart (line of argument)

هور *haur* pl. اهوار *ahwār* lake

هورة *haura* pl. *-āt* danger, peril

هوارى *hawwārī* pl. هوارة *hawwāra* volunteer; ○ short-term soldier, irregular; الهوارة irregular troops

هير *hayyir* rash, precipitate, thoughtless, ill-considered, imprudent

تهور *tahawwur* light-headedness, carelessness, irresponsibility; hastiness, rashness, precipitance

انهيار *inhiyār* crash, fall, downfall; collapse, breakdown

متهور *mutahawwir* rash, hasty, precipitate; frivolous, thoughtless; light-headed, careless, irresponsible, reckless; foolhardy, daredevil

هورمون *hormōn* hormone

[1]هوس *hawisa a* (*hawas*) to be baffled, startled, perplexed; to be utterly confused, be at a complete loss, be at one's wit's end **II** to baffle, startle, perplex, confuse, bewilder, confound (ه s.o.); to delude, beguile, befool, infatuate, dazzle blind (ه s.o.); to craze, drive crazy, render

insane (ه s.o.) V to be beguiled, befooled, infatuated, dazzled, lose one's head; to abandon o.s. completely; to be a fantast, a visionary VII to be beguiled, befooled, infatuated, dazzled

هوس *hawas* foolishness, folly, craze, madness; dreaminess, visionariness, rapture, ecstasy; wild fancy, fantasy; raving madness, frenzy; infatuation, blindness, delusion

هويس *hawīs* thought, idea, concept, notion

هويس *hawīs* and هاويس *hāwīs* pl. اهوسة *ahwisa* (eg.) lock, canal lock

اهوس *ahwas*[2] foolish, crazy, mad; dazzled, blind, infatuated

مهووس *mahwūs* (religious) visionary

مهوس *muhawwas* foolish, crazy, mad; dazzled, blind, infatuated

متهوس *mutahawwis* pl. *-ūn* fantast, visionary

[2]هوسة *hausa* clamor, shouting, uproar

هوش *hawiša a* (*hawaš*) and هاش *hāša u* (*hauš*) to be excited, be in a state of commotion II to excite, agitate, unsettle (ه ,ه s.o., s.th.); to rouse, incite, stir up, inflame (ه the mob); to sick (ه على a dog on), set, incite (ه على s.o. against); to exert a disturbing influence (على on) III to annoy by its barking (ه s.o.; of a dog) V to get tumultuous, get excited, run riot

هوشة *hauša* excitement, agitation, commotion, riot, uproar, ruckus, rumpus, row, fracas; turmoil, tumult

تهويش *tahwīš* excitation, agitation; incitement, instigation

مهوش *muhawwiš* exciting; troublemaker, agitator, rabble rouser

(هوع) هاع *hā'a u a* (*hau'*) to vomit, throw up; to retch II to make (ه s.o.) vomit V = I

[1]هاك *hāka* see ها

[2]هوكى *hokī* hockey | هوكى الازلاق ice hockey

(هول) هال *hāla u* (*haul*) to frighten, scare, terrify, appall, horrify, strike with terror (ه s.o.) II to alarm, dismay, frighten, terrify, horrify, fill with horror (ه s.o.); to threaten, menace, scare (على ب s.o. with); to wield menacingly (ب a stick); to picture (ه s.th.) as a terrible thing, make (ه s.th.) appear terrible; to exaggerate, overemphasize (ه or من s.th.), make much ado, make a great fuss (من about) X to deem significant (ه s.th.); to consider terrific, appalling, tremendous (ه s.th.); to be horrified (ه at), be appalled, be staggered (ه by)

هول *haul* pl. اهوال *ahwāl*, هؤول *hu'ūl* terror, fright, alarm, shock, horror, dismay; power | ابو الهول *abū l-h.* the Sphinx; يا للهول *yā la-l-haul* oh, how terrible!

هولة *haula* a terrifying thing, a fright; object of fear or terror

هال *hāl* mirage, fata morgana; cardamom (spice)

هالة *hāla* pl. *-āt* halo (around moon or sun, also, e.g., of a saint); ring around the eye; nimbus, aureole, glory

تهويل *tahwīl* pl. *-āt*, تهاويل *tahāwīl*[2] frightening, scaring, alarming, intimidation, cowing, browbeating; exaggeration; nightmare, phantom, bugbear, bogey, bugaboo; pl. تهاويل embellishments, ornamental flourishes; pleasant visions

هائل *hā'il* dreadful, frightful, terrible, horrible, appalling, ghastly, awful; huge, vast, formidable, gigantic, prodigious, tremendous, stupendous; extraordinary, enormous, fabulous, amazing, astonishing, surprising; grim, hard, fierce (battle, fight)

مهول *muhawwil* terrible, dreadful

هولاندا *holandā* or هولانده *holanda* Holland

هولاندى *holandī* Dutch, Hollandish; (pl. *-ūn*) Dutchman, Hollander

هوليوود Hollywood

هوم II to nod drowsily (head of s.o. falling asleep); to doze off, fall asleep; to doze, nap V to doze off, fall asleep; to doze, nap

هامة *hāma* pl. *-āt*, هام *hām* head; crown, vertex; top, summit; see also under همّ

[1]هان (هون) *hāna u* (*haun*) to be or become easy (على for s.o.), be of little importance (على to); هان عليه ان to attach no importance to the fact that..., care little that...; — (*hūn*, هوان *hawān*, مهانة *mahāna*) to be or become despicable, contemptible II to make easy, ease, facilitate (ه على s.th. for s.o.); to represent or picture (ه s.th., على to s.o.) as easy or as of little importance; to make light (ه or من of), belittle, minimize, deride, flout, disparage (ه or من s.th.) | هون عليك (*hawwin*) take it easy! don't get excited! never mind! IV to despise (ه, ه s.o., s.th.); to humble, humiliate, abase, demean, scorn, disdain, slight, treat with contempt or disdain (ه s.o.); to insult (ه s.o.) VI to consider easy (ب s.th.); to think little, make little (ب of), attach little importance (ب to), disdain, despise (ب s.th.); to be negligent, remiss, lax, careless (فى or ب in s.th.), neglect (فى or ب s.th.); (with negation) not to fail (فى to do s.th.), not to tire (فى of doing s.th.) X استهان *istahāna* and استهون *istahwana* to consider easy (ب s.th.); to make little (ب of), esteem lightly, disesteem, underrate, undervalue (ب s.th.); to disdain, despise (ب s.th.); to misunderstand, misjudge (ب s.th.) | لا يستهان به (*yustahānu*) not to be sneezed at, not to be overlooked

هون *haun* ease, leisure, convenience, comfort; easiness, facility; هونا *haunan* slowly, gently, leisurely, imperceptibly | على هون slowly, gently, leisurely, imperceptibly; على هونك at your convenience

هون *hūn* disgrace, shame, degradation, abasement

هوان *hawān* despicableness, lowly, contemptible position; insignificance, negligibleness; degradation, abasement; disgrace, shame, ignominy

هين *hayyin*, *hain* pl. *-ūn*, اهوناء *ahwinā'*[2] easy; insignificant, negligible, of little value; inconsiderable; unimportant; plain, simple, homely, modest | هين لين *hain lain* simple and nice

هينة *hīna* easiness, facility; convenience, comfort, ease; leisure

هوينا *huwainā* gentleness, mildness, kindliness; slowness, leisureliness, leisure, ease; الهوينا slowly, gently, leisurely, unhurriedly

اهون *ahwan*[2], f. هوناء *haunā'*[2] easy; comfortable; — (elative) easier; smaller, less, lesser; of less value, more worthless | ما اهونه (*ahwanahū*) how small, how worthless it is! اهون الشرين *a. aš-šarrain* the lesser evil

مهانة *mahāna* contempt, despicableness; degradation, abasement, humiliation, disgrace, shame

اهانة *ihāna* insult; affront, contumely, abuse

تهاون *tahāwun* disesteem, disdain, scorn, neglect; indifference (ب to s.th.)

استهانة *istihāna* disesteem, disdain, scorn, neglect; contempt

مهين *muhīn* insulting, abusive, offending; contemptuous, humiliating, disgraceful, ignominious, outrageous

متهاون *mutahāwin* negligent, remiss, lax, indifferent

مستهين *mustahīn* disdainer, scorner, despiser

²هاون look up alphabetically

¹هوى *hawā i* (*huwīy*) to drop, fall, tumble, fall down, come down, sink; to topple, tumble down, be upset; to swoop down (predatory bird); to pounce, fall (على upon); to blow (wind); to overthrow (ب s.o. or s.th.) | هوى على رقبتها (*raqabatihā*) he fell in her arms, he embraced her; هوى بمقامه (*maqāmihī*) to degrade s.o.; — *hawiya a* (هوى *hawan*) to love (ه, ه s.o., s.th.); to become fond (ه, ه of); to like (ه, ه s.o., s.th.); to go in (ه for a hobby), take up as a hobby (ه s.th.) **II** to air, ventilate (ه a room), expose to the wind or to fresh air (ه s.th.); to fan the air **III** to show o.s. complaisant (ه to s.o.), humor (ه s.o.); to flatter (ه s.o.) **IV** to fall down, drop; to drop (ب s.th.); to pounce, fall (على upon s.o., ب with); to lean, bend (على over); to reach (الى for), grab, grasp (الى at), make for s.th. (الى); to strive (الى for), aspire (الى to), desire (الى s.th.) | اهوى بيده الى (*bi-yadihī*) to stretch out one's hand for, reach out for **V** to be aired, be ventilated **VI** to break down, collapse; to plunge down, throw o.s. down **VII** to fall down, drop; to be thrust down **X** to attract (ه s.o.); to seduce, tempt (ه s.o.); to entice, lure (ه s.o.); to charm, enchant, fascinate, enrapture, delight, entrance, carry away (ه s.o.)

هوى *hawan* pl. اهواء *ahwā'*, هوايا *hawāyā* love; affection; passion; inclination, liking, bent, wish; desire, longing, craving; fancy, whim, caprice, pleasure; اهواء sects, heretic tendencies | على هواه to be convenient to s.o., please s.o.; فى الهوى in love; اصحاب الاهواء sectarians, dissenters

هوة *hūwa* pl. *-āt*, هوى *huwan* abyss, chasm; cave, cavern; pit, hole, ditch, trench; (fig.) gulf

هواء *hawā'* pl. اهوية *ahwiya*, اهواء *ahwā'* air; atmosphere; wind, draft; weather, climate | الهواء الاصفر (*aṣfar*) the plague; هواء طلق (*ṭalq*) open air; fresh air; فى الهواء الطلق outdoors, in the open, in fresh air; هواء مضغوط compressed air; سلك الهواء *salk al-h.* aviation; طلمبة الهواء *ṭulumbat al-h.* air pump

هوائى *hawā'ī* airy, breezy; aerial, air- (in compounds), atmospheric(al); pneumatic; ○ inside (diameter, width); antenna, aerial, also سلك هوائى (*silk*); flighty, whimsical, capricious; ethereal; fantastic | دولاب هوائى wind wheel; ○ هوائى اطارى (*iṭārī*) frame antenna; ○ هوائى طوقى (*ṭauqī*) loop antenna; ○ هوائى مرتفع (*murtafi'*) elevated antenna; ○ هوائى مرسل (*mursil*) transmitting antenna; ○ هوائى مزدوج (*muzdawij*) two-wire antenna; ○ هوائى مستقبل (*mustaqbil*) receiving antenna; ○ هوائى مفرد (*mufrad*) single-wire antenna

هواء *hawwā'* amateur

هواية *hawāya* pl. *-āt* hobby, sport or art cultivated as an amateur; amateurism, amateurship

هواية *hawwāya* fan; ventilator

اهوى *ahwā* more desirable, preferable

اهوية *uhwīya* abyss, chasm, deep, depth

مهوى *mahwan*, مهواة *mahwāh* pl. مهاو *mahāwin*[2] abyss, chasm, gulf; place of one's longing, object of desire; atmosphere

مهواة *mihwāh* ventilator

تهوية *tahwiya* airing, ventilation

استهواء *istihwā'* fascination, captivation; enchantment; seducement, enticement, temptation; suggestion

هاو *hāwin* pl. هواة *huwāh* falling, dropping, sinking; loving, in love; lover; fancier, fan, amateur; dabbler, dilettante

هاوية *hāwiya* chasm, gulf, abyss, infernal depth, bottomless pit, hell

²هوية *huwīya* see ¹هو

هى *hiya* she (3rd pers. sing. f. of the pers. pron.)

هيا *hayyā* (interj.) up! come on! let's go! now then!

(هيء) هاء *hā'a i a* and هيؤ *hayu'a u* (هيأة *hai'a*, هياءة *hayā'a*) to be shapely, well-formed, beautiful to look at, present a handsome appearance; — *a* (هيئة *hī'a*) to desire, crave (الى s.th.) **II** to make ready, get ready, put in readiness (ه s.th.); to prepare (ه s.th.); to fix up, fit up, set up (ه s.th.); to pave the way (ل for s.o., for s.th.); to arm, mobilize, get in fighting condition (*mil.*); to put in order, to order, array, arrange (ه s.th.); to incline, dispose, make inclined (ه ل s.o. to), influence (ه ل s.o. in favor of) | هيأ الاسباب ل (*asbāba*) to pave the way for ...; هيأ ذاته ل (*ḏātahū*) to prepare o.s. (at heart) for ...; هيأ فرصة ملائمة ل (*furṣatan mulā'imatan*) to offer a good opportunity for ... **III** to agree, come to an agreement (ه في with s.o. about); to concur (ه في with s.o. in); to adapt o.s., adjust o.s. (ه to s.o.) **V** to be prepared, be in readiness, be ready, stand ready (ل for); to be armed, be prepared for war, be in fighting condition (*mil.*); to prepare o.s., get ready (ل for); to be possible (ل to s.o.); to be well-dressed | تهيأ *tahayya'* make ready! (mil. command) **VI** to adapt themselves to one another, make mutual adjustment; to be in agreement, be agreed

هيئة *hai'a* pl. *-āt* form, shape; exterior, appearance, guise, aspect, bearing; air, mien, physiognomy; attitude, position; situation, condition, state; group, (social) class; society, association; body, corporation; organization; board, commission, committee; corps; cadre, skeleton organization | هيئة الامم المتحدة *h. al-umam al-muttaḥida* and الهيئة الامية (*umamīya*) the United Nations Organization; الهيئة الاجتماعية (*ijtimā'īya*) human society; هيئة الاذاعة اللاسلكية *h. al-iḏā'a al-lā-silkīya* broadcasting corporation; هيئة اركان الحرب *h. arkān al-ḥarb* general staff; هيئة اركان حرب الاسطول (*usṭūl*) naval staff; هيئة برلمانية (*barlamānīya*) parliamentary group; هيئة التحكيم board of arbitration; jury, committee of judges, committee of umpires (in sports), the referees (in military maneuvers); هيئة التدريس teaching staff; faculty, professoriate (of an academic institution); هيئة حاكمة or حكومية (*hukūmīya*) governmental agency, authority; هيئة دبلوماسية diplomatic corps; الهيئة السعدية (*sa'dīya*) the Sa'dist Union (formerly, a political group in Egypt); هيئة طبية (*ṭibbīya*) ambulance corps; هيئة نيابية (*niyābīya*) representative body, parliamentary body; علم الهيئة *'ilm al-h.* astronomy

هيّئ *hayyi'*, هيء *hayi'* good-looking, handsome; shapely

تهيئة *tahyi'a* preparation; training; adaptation, adjustment, accommodation

مهايأة *muhāya'a* joint usufruct, use or profit sharing (*Isl. Law*)

○ تهيؤ *tahayyu'* military preparations

تهايؤ *tahāyu'* (mutual) adaptation, (mutual) adjustment

مهيأ *muhayya'* prepared; ready

(هيب) هاب *hāba* (1st pers. perf. *hibtu*) *a* (هيبة *haiba*, مهابة *mahāba*) to fear, dread (ه, ه s.o., s.th.), be afraid (ه, ه of); to stand in awe (ه, ه of), be awed (ه, ه by); to honor, respect, revere, venerate (ه s.o.) **II** to make (ه s.th.) be dreaded (الى by s.o.), make it dreadful to s.o., inspire s.o. (الى) with awe (ه of); to make s.th. (ه) appear dreadful or awesome (الى to s.o.); to threaten, frighten, intimidate, cow, daunt (على s.o.) **IV** to call out, shout (ب to s.o.);

to call upon s.o. (ب), appeal (ب to s.o.); to drive, urge, rouse, egg on, encourage (ب الى s.o. to) V = I; to awe, frighten, scare, threaten (ه s.o.) VIII = I

هيبة *haiba* fear, dread, awe; reverence, veneration, esteem, respect; awe-inspiring appearance, venerableness, gravity, dignity; standing, prestige

هياب *hayyāb* timid, timorous, shy, diffident; respectful

هيوب *hayūb* timid, timorous, shy, diffident; respectful; awful, fearful, dreadful; awe-inspiring, awesome, venerable

مهاب *mahāb* object of reverence and respect

مهابة *mahāba* dignity

تهيب *tahayyub* fear, dread; awe

مهوب *mahūb* and مهيب *mahīb* dreaded, dreadful, awful

مهيب *muhīb* awe-inspiring, awesome, venerable; grave, solemn, dignified

متهيب *mutahayyib* respectful, reverential

هيت II to call (ب s.o.)

هيت *haita*, هيت لك (*luka*) come here!

(هيج) هاج *hāja* i (*haij*, هيجان *hayajān*, هياج *hiyāj*) to be astir or stirred up, be or get excited, agitated; to rise; to awaken, be awakened, spring up (desire); to be in great excitement, be very upset, be furious, indignant (على about, at); to run high, be rough, stormy (sea); — هاج and II to move, stir, agitate (ه s.th.); to stir up, excite (ه s.th.); to disturb, trouble, perturb, disquiet (ه s.th.); to provoke, incite, stimulate (ه s.th.); to kindle, ignite, inflame, incense (ه s.th.); to make (ه the blood) boil; to awaken, arouse, evoke (ه e.g., a desire); to bring to light (ه s.th.); to irritate, inflame (ه an organ); to drive, urge on, spur on (ه, ه s.o., s.th., على to); to rouse, start, scare up (ه a bird) IV = II; V and VIII to be astir, be restive, be in a state of commotion, be disturbed, be excited, be agitated; to be awakened, be (a)roused, be scared up

هيج *haij* excitement; agitation; commotion, disturbance, turmoil; dissension, strife; combat, battle

هيجا *haijā* and هيجاء *haijā'* fight, combat, battle, war

هيجان *hayajān* excitement; agitation; commotion, disturbance, turmoil, tumult; outburst of rage, fury, irritation, indignation, bitterness

هياج *hiyāj* excitement; agitation; commotion, disturbance, turmoil, tumult; outburst of rage, fury, irritation, indignation, bitterness; raging, uproar (of the elements)

تهييج *tahyīj* excitation, agitation, stimulation; provocation, incitement; instigation; stirring up, fanning; incensement, inflammation; ○ induction (*el.*)

تهيج *tahayyuj* disturbance, commotion, turmoil; excitement, agitation; emotional disturbance; affect (*jur.*)

هائج *hā'ij* stirring, astir, agitated, in commotion; rough, heaving (sea, waves); excited, impassioned; angry, furious, enraged | هاج هائجه he became angry, he flew into a rage

مهيج *muhayyij* exciting, stirring, rousing, stimulating; provocative, inciting; incendiary, inflammatory; agitator, troublemaker, incendiary, seditionary, rabble rouser; (pl. *-āt*) a stimulant, an excitant

متهيج *mutahayyij* and مهتاج *muhtāj* agitated, upset, excited, impassioned

هيدروجين *hidrōžēn* hydrogen

هير II to hurl down, topple, tear down, destroy, demolish (ه s.th.)

هير *hayyir* see هور

هيراطيقى *hīrāṭīqī* hieratic (writing)

هيروغليفى *hīroğlīfī* hieroglyphic

هيروين *hīruwīn* heroin (*chem.*)

(هيش) هاش *hāša i* (*haiš*) to be agitated, excited

هيش *hīš* thicket, brush, scrub

هيشة *haiša* excitement; commotion, turmoil, tumult, riot

(هيض) هاض *hāḍa i*: هيض جناحه *hīḍa janāḥuhū* his wing was broken, he was powerless

هيضة *haiḍa* summer cholera, cholera morbus; Asiatic cholera

مهيض *mahīḍ* broken, shattered | مهيض الجناح *m. al-janāḥ* broken-winged, helpless, feeble, sapless

(هيط) هاط *hāṭa i* (*haiṭ*) to shout, clamor, raise a din, be tumultuous

هيط *haiṭ* shouting, clamor, din, uproar, ruckus

هياط *hiyāṭ* shouting, clamor | هياط مياط (*miyāṭ*) tumultuous uproar, ruckus, wild shouting, tumult

هطل see هيطل

مهيع *mahya'* pl. مهايع *mahāyi'²* broad, paved road

(هيف) هاف *hāfa i* (*haif*) to be parched, thirsty; — *a* (*haif*) to run away (slave); — هيف *hayifa* and *hāfa a* (*haif*, *hayaf*) to be slim, slender, slight, frail

هيف *haif* parching wind

هيف *hayaf* slenderness, slimness

هيوف *hayūf* burned up with thirst

هيفان *haifān²* parched; thirsty

اهيف *ahyaf²*, f. هيفاء *haifā'²*, pl. هيف *hīf* slender, slim; slight, frail, wispy

هيكل *haikal* pl. هياكل *hayākil²* temple; large building, edifice; altar; skeleton; framework (of a structure), frame; chassis (of an automobile); colossal, gigantic, huge

هيكلى *haikalī*: مناورة هيكلية (*munāwara*) cadre maneuver, skeleton exercise (*mil.*)

¹(هيل) هال *hāla i* (*hail*) to pour, strew, sprinkle (ه s.th. on على) II and IV do.; to pile up (ه sand, earth; said of the wind) VII to be heaped up, be poured in a heap, fall in a heap; to rain down (bombs); to shower (على ب s.o. with), assail (على s.o., على ب s.o. with; instead of ب also accusative of a verbal noun) | انهال عليها ضربا وشتما (*ḍarban wa-šatman*) he fell upon her with blows and abusive language

هيل *hail* piled-up sand | الهيل والهيلمان (*hailamān*) heaps of money, enormous sums

هيلان *hayalān* sand heap

انهيال *inhiyāl*, انهيال الارض *inh. al-arḍ* landslide

²هيول *hayūl* mote, atom

³هيولى *hayūlā*, *hayyūlā* primordial matter; matter; substance

هيولى *hayūlī* material (adj.)

هيولانى *hayūlānī* material (adj.)

(هيم) هام *hāma i* (*haim*, هيمان *hayamān*) to fall in love (ب with); to be in love (ب with); to be enthusiastic, ecstatic, frantic, beside o.s.; to be in raptures, be crazy (ب about), be gone on (ب); to roam, rove, wander | هام على وجهه (*wajhihī*) to wander aimlessly about; هام فى وديان (*widyān*) approx.: he was no longer himself, he was floating in higher regions, he was beside himself, he was out of his senses; هام بانظاره to let one's eyes wander; — (هيام *huyām*, *hiyām*) to thirst (ب for)

II to confuse, bewilder, puzzle, mystify, mislead (ه s.o.); to infatuate, enchant, captivate, carry away, rob of his senses (ه s.o.; of love) X pass. استهيم *ustuhyima* to be infatuated, enchanted, captivated, carried away; to be passionately in love

هيام *huyām, hiyām* passionate love; burning thirst

هيوم *hayūm* confused, puzzled, baffled, mystified, perplexed

هيمان *haimān*[2], f. هيمى *haimā*, pl. هيام *hiyām* madly in love; very thirsty

هائم *hā'im* pl. هيم *huyyam*, هيام *huyyām* perplexed, mystified, baffled, puzzled, confused; out of one's senses, beside o.s.; in love, mad with love

مستهام *mustahām* in love, mad with love

هيمن *haimana* to say "amen"; to guard (على s.o.), watch (على over s.o.), watch narrowly (على s.o.), keep an eye on (على); to control (على s.th.)

هيمنة *haimana* supervision, superintendence, surveillance; control; suzerainty, supremacy, ascendancy, hegemony

مهيمن *muhaimin* supervising, superintending, controlling; guardian; protector; master (على of s.th., also, e.g., of a situation)

هين and هينة see [1]هون

هينم *hainama* to murmur softly

هيه *hīh* (interj.) hey! let's go! step lively! look alive!

هيهات *haihātu, haihāta, haihāti* but oh! far from the mark! wrong! what an idea! how preposterous! | هيهات ان it is absolutely out of the question that ...; هيهات ان يفعل كذا how far he is from doing so! هيهات بين هذا وذاك what a difference between them! how different they are! وهيهات لك ذلك and how impossible is this to you!

و

wa 1. and; and also, and ... too | ولا واحد not one, not a single one; — 2. (with foll. acc.) with | واياه *wa-iyyāhu* with him; لا يتفق ومبادئهم (*yattafiqu, mabādi'ahum*) it is not in agreement with their principles; — 3. introducing circumstantial (*ḥāl*) clauses: while, as, when, whereas | قال وهو يبتسم (he said while he smiled) he said with a smile; جاء والشمس طالعة (*šamsu*) he arrived at sunrise; — 4. (with foll. genit.) by (in oaths) | والله by God! — 5. (with foll. genit.) many a, how many | وكأس شربت (*ka'sin*) many a cup have I emptied! how many cups I have drunk! — أو *a-wa* see أ

والا *wa-illā* (and if not), otherwise, else

وان *wa-in* even if, even though, although

ولو *wa-lau* even if, even though, even in case that

ولكن *wa-lākin, wa-lakinna* (the latter with foll. acc. or pers. suffix) but, however, yet

وا *wā* (with the foll. noun ending in *-āh*) oh | وا اسفاه *wā asafāh*! oh grief! alas!

وابور (Fr. *vapeur*; *colloq.*) *wābūr* pl. *-āt* steam engine; steamer, steamship; locomotive, railroad train; factory, mill; machine, engine, apparatus; hot plate, heater, stove | وابور اكسبريس express train; وابور البضاعة freight train, goods train;

وابور الركاب *w. ar-rukkāb* passenger train; وابور الرى *w. ar-riyy* irrigation pump; وابور الزلط *w. az-zalaṭ* (*eg.*) steamroller; وابور طارة *w. ṭāra* paddle steamer; وابور العادة *w. al-ʿāda* local train, accommodation train, way train

وات *wāt* watt (*el.*)

واحة *wāḥa* pl. *-āt* oasis

وأد *waʾada* يئد *yaʾidu* to bury alive (ها a newborn girl) **V** and **VIII** اتأد *ittaʾada* to be slow, act or proceed deliberately, tarry, hesitate, temporize (فى in s.th.) | اتأد فى مشيته (*mišyatihī*) to walk slowly, unhurriedly, saunter

وئيد *waʾīd* deliberate, unhurried, slow; deliberateness; وئيدا *waʾīdan* slowly; gradually

تؤدة *tuʾada* deliberateness, slowness | على تؤدة slowly, deliberately, unhurriedly

متئد *muttaʾid* slow

وأر *waʾara* يئر *yaʾiru* (*waʾr*) to frighten (ه s.o.) **X** to be frightened, be struck with terror

وارسو *warsō* Warsaw (capital of Poland)

واشنطون *wāšinṭōn* Washington

واط *wāṭ* watt (*el.*)

واق واق *wāqwāq* in the descriptions of Arab geographers, name of two different groups of islands (one east of China, the other located in the Indian Ocean)

موئل *mauʾil* refuge, asylum

وأم **III** to agree, be in agreement (ه, ه with); to suit (ه, ه s.o., s.th.), be suited (ه, ه to), harmonize (ه, ه with) **VI** to agree, tally, harmonize

وئام *wiʾām* agreement; unity, concord, harmony

مواءمة *muwāʾama* agreement; unity, concord, harmony

واه *wāha*, واها *wāhā* (interj.) with ل or ب to express admiration: how wonderful is (are) ...! with على to express regret: alas ...! too bad for ...!

واو *wāw* name of the letter و

وئية *waʾīya* kettle

وبئ *wabiʾa* يوبأ *yaubaʾu* (وبأ *wabaʾ*), وبؤ *wabuʾa u* (وباء *wabāʾ*, وباءة *wabāʾa*) and pass. وبئ *wubiʾa* to be plague-stricken, infected, infested, poisoned, contaminated

وبأ *wabaʾ* pl. اوباء *aubāʾ* infectious disease; epidemic

وباء *wabāʾ* pl. اوبئة *aubiʾa* infectious disease; epidemic

وبائى *wabāʾī* infectious, contagious; epidemic(al); pestilential

وبئ *wabiʾ* and وبىء *wabīʾ* infected, poisoned, contaminated, infected; plague stricken, plague-ridden, plague-infected

موبوء *maubūʾ* poisoned, contaminated, infested; infected, stricken (ب by), affected (ب with)

وبخ **II** to reprimand, rebuke, censure, reprove, scold, chide (ه على s.o. for)

توبيخ *taubīḵ* reproach, reproof, censure; reprimand, rebuke

وبر *wabira* يوبر *yaubaru* (*wabar*) to have abundant hair or wool, be covered with thick hair, be hirsute, hairy

وبر *wabr* pl. وبور *wubūr*, وبار *wibār*, وبارة *wibāra* daman (Hyrax syriaca; *zool.*)

وبر *wabar* pl. اوبار *aubār* hair, fur of camels and goats (furnishing the material for tents) | اهل الوبر *ahl al-w.* the Bedouins (as distinguished from اهل المدر)

وبر *wabir* covered with hair, hairy, hirsute

اوبر *aubar*², f. وبراء *wabrā'*² covered with hair, hairy, hirsute

موبر *muwabbar* hairy, woolly

وبش *wabaš* trash, rubbish, bosh; pl. اوباش *aubāš* rabble, riffraff

وبق *wabaqa* يبق *yabiqu* and *wabiqa* يوبق *yaubaqu* (*wabaq*, وبوق *wubūq*, موبق *maubiq*) to perish, go to ruin, be destroyed **IV** to ruin (ه s.o.); to debase, humiliate, mortify (ه s.o.)

موبق *maubiq* place of destruction, of perdition; prison, jail

موبقة *mūbiqa* pl. *-āt* grave offense; act of violence, crime; mortal sin

وبل *wabala* يبل *yabilu* (*wabl*) to shed heavy rain (sky); — *wabula* يوبل *yaubulu* (*wabal*, وبال *wabāl*, وبالة *wabāla*, وبول *wubūl*) to be unhealthy, unwholesome, noxious (climate, air)

وبل *wabl* downpour

وبال *wabāl* unhealthiness of the air or climate; evil consequences of a deed; harm, evil, curse

وبيل *wabīl* unhealthy, unwholesome (climate, food); of evil consequences, hurtful, noxious, calamitous, disastrous, pernicious

وابل *wābil* heavy downpour; (fig.) hail, shower | امطره وابلا من الرصاص (*raṣāṣ*) to shower s.o. with a hail of bullets; امطر عليه وابلا من الشتم (*šatm*) to shower s.o. with a flood of abuse

وبه *wabaha*, *wabiha* يوبه *yaubahu* (*wabh*) and **IV** to heed, mind (ل or ب s.o.), pay attention (ل or ب to), take notice (ل or ب of)

وتد **II** to drive or ram in firmly (ه a peg or stake); to fix, fasten, secure (ه s.th.) | وتد فى بيته (*baitihī*) to stay at home

وتد *watad*, *watid* pl. اوتاد *autād* peg, pin; tent pin, tent peg; stake, pole

وتر *watara* يتر *yatiru* (*watr*) to string, provide with a string (ه the bow); to wrong, harm (ه s.o.), cheat, dupe (ه s.o., ه out of, with regard to) **II** to stretch, strain, draw tight, tighten, pull taut (ه a rope, a muscial string, and the like) **III** to do or perform (ه s.th.) at intervals, intermittently, with interruptions **IV** to string, provide with a string (ه the bow) **V** to be or become strained, stretched, tight, taut | توترت العلاقات (*'alāqāt*) relations were strained **VI** to follow in uninterrupted succession; to repeat itself, recur

وتر *watr*, *witr* uneven, odd (number); وترا singly, one by one, separately

وترى *watrī*, *witrī* uneven, odd (number)

وتر *watar* pl. اوتار *autār* string (of a bow, of a musical instrument); sinew, tendon (*anat.*); chord (*geom.*); hypotenuse (*geom.*) | ضرب على الوتر الحساس (*ḥassās*) to touch on a sensitive spot, get to the heart of a matter; وتر صوتى (*ṣautī*) vocal cord

وترى *watarī* stringed, string- (in compounds)

وتيرة *watīra* pl. وتائر *watā'ir*² manner, way, mode, fashion; procedure, method; style; tone | على هذه الوتيرة in this manner, this way; على وتيرة واحدة in the same manner; uniformly, in unison; استمر على هذه الوتيرة he continued in this tone

تترى *tatrā* one after the other, one by one, in succession, successively

توتر *tawattur* tension (also *el.* = voltage); strain | توتر الاعصاب nervousness, nervous tension; توتر سياسى (*siyāsī*) political tension

تواتر *tawātur* succession; repetition, recurrence; frequency, constancy, incessancy, continuance; persistence; frequency (*el.*) | على تواتر successively, one after the other, in succession

موتور *mautūr* one who has been wronged by the murder of a relative, but to whom blood revenge is still denied

متوتر *mutawattir* stretched, strained, taut, tense, rigid, firm, tight

متواتر *mutawātir* successive

وتين *watīn* pl. وتن *wutun* اوتنة *autina* aorta

وتى III to come (ه to, upon; of s.th. pleasant), befall (ه s.o.; s.th. pleasant); to be complaisant, obliging (ه toward s.o.), oblige (ه s.o.); to be favorable, propitious (ه to s.o.); to be convenient (ه to s.o.), suit (ه s.o.); to turn out successful, be a success (ه for s.o.); to be suited, suitable (ه to s.o.), become, befit (ه s.o.), go well with (ه); to agree (ه with; of food)

موات *muwātin* pleasant, agreeable, pleasing, appealing, engaging, winning, becoming; favorable, propitious

وثأ *waṯa'a* يثأ *yaṯa'u* (وثء *waṯ'*) to bruise, contuse (ه a limb); to wrench, sprain (ه a limb); — وثئ *waṯi'a* يثأ *yaṯa'u* (وثأ *waṯa'*, وثوء *wuṯū'*) and pass. وثئ *wuṯi'a* to get bruised, be wrenched, be sprained IV = I *waṯa'a*

وثء *waṯ'* contusion, bruise; sprain, wrench

وثاءة *waṯā'a* contusion, bruise; sprain, wrench

وثب *waṯaba* يثب *yaṯibu* (*waṯb*, وثوب *wuṯūb*, وثيب *waṯīb*, وثبان *waṯabān*) to jump, leap, spring, bound; to skip, hop, caper; to jump up, start; to jump up and run (الى to); to rush (الى to), make a rush (الى for); to jump, dash (على at s.o.), pounce, fall (على upon s.o.) II and IV to make (ه, ه s.o., s.th.) jump, bounce (ه s.th.) III to pounce, fall (ه upon s.th.) V to jump up, start; to rush, dash (الى to, at); to hop, skip, bound, leap, jump; to approach eagerly, with enthusiasm, tackle energetically (الى s.th.); to pounce (على, فى upon); to awaken, recover, rise VI to jump, leap, spring, bound, make a jump; to be fast, short, come pantingly (breathing)

وثب *waṯb* jump(ing), leap(ing) | وثب بالزانة (*zāna*) pole vault(ing); وثب طويل broad jump; وثب عال (*'ālin*) high jump; تخطى وثبا من فوق to hurdle over ...

وثبة *waṯba* (n. vic.) pl. *waṯabāt* jump, leap, bound; attack; daring enterprise, bold undertaking; rise; awakening | وثبة احساسية (*iḥsāsīya*) impulsive motion

وثاب *waṯṯāb* given to jumping, bouncy, full of bounce; fiery, hotheaded, impetuous; dashing, daring, enterprising

مواثبة *muwāṯaba* prompt assertion of a claim in the presence of witnesses (*Isl. Law*)

متوثب *mutawaṯṯib* awakening, rising; vigorous, energetic

وثر *waṯura* يوثر *yauṯuru* (وثارة *waṯāra*) to be soft (bed); — *waṯara* يثر *yaṯiru* (*waṯr*) to make soft, make smooth (ه s.th., esp., the bed)

وثر *waṯir* soft, snug, cozy, comfortable (bed, seat); smooth (cloth)

وثير *waṯīr* soft, snug, cozy, comfortable (bed, seat); smooth (cloth)

وثار *wiṯār* soft bed

ميثرة *mīṯara* pl. مواثر *mawāṯir*[2], مياثر *mayāṯir*[2] saddlecloth, blanket, drape

وثق *waṯiqa* يثق *yaṯiqu* (ثقة *ṯiqa*, وثوق *wuṯūq*) to place one's confidence, put faith (ب in), rely, depend (ب on), trust (ب in; من ان that), be confident (ب of; من ان that) | يوثق به (*yūṯaqu*) trustworthy, reliable; وثق من النفس to have self-confidence; — *waṯuqa* يوثق *yauṯuqu* (وثاقة *waṯāqa*) to be firm, solid; to be sure, be certain (من of) II to make firm or solid, strengthen, cement, consolidate (ه s.th.); to document, authenticate, confirm, certify (ه s.th.), attest (ه to), notarize (ه s.th.), draw up a notarial deed (ه over); to link firmly, bind closely (بين — وبين s.o. to) **III** to enter into an agreement, make a treaty (ه with s.o.) | واثق نفسه على (*nafsahū*) to make a firm resolution on, intend firmly to (do s.th.) **IV** to tie, fasten (ه ب s.th. to); to bind, tie up, fetter (ه ب s.o. with) **V** to be firm, consolidated, firmly established; to proceed with confidence, act trustfully (في in s.th.) **X** to make sure, make certain (من of), check, verify (من s.th.); to have confidence (ه in s.o.), trust (ه s.o.)

ثقة *ṯiqa* trust, confidence, faith, reliance | على ثقة trusting (من in), relying (من on), confident, certain, sure (من of); هو على ثقة من انه he is certain that he ...; ثقة بالنصر (*naṣr*) confidence in victory; ثقة بالنفس or ثقة بنفسه self-confidence, self-reliance; اخو ثقة *akū ṯ.* trustworthy; عدم الثقة *'adam aṯ-ṯ.* distrust, mistrust; طلب عدم الثقة (*ṭalab*) motion of "no confidence" (*parl.*); — *ṯiqa* pl. -*āt* trustworthy, reliable; trustworthy person, trusted agent, informant, reliable authority or source; pl. authorities | ○ ثقة عسكرى (*'askarī*) military expert

وثاق *waṯāq, wiṯāq* pl. وثق *wuṯuq* tie, bond, fetter, shackle, chain (also fig.) | شد وثاقه (*šadda*) to tie s.o. up, fetter, shackle s.o.

وثاقة *waṯāqa* firmness, solidity, strength

وثيق *waṯīq* pl. وثاق *wiṯāq* firm, strong, solid; safe, secure, dependable, reliable

وثيقة *waṯīqa* pl. وثائق *waṯā'iq*[2] document, deed, writ, instrument, paper, record, voucher, certificate, receipt, policy; diplomatic note | الوثيقة العظمى (*'uẓmā*) the Magna Charta; وثيقة التفويض warrant of attorney (*jur.*)

اوثق *auṯaq*[2], f. وثقى *wuṯqā* firmer, stronger

موثق *mauṯiq* pl. مواثق *mawāṯiq*[2] covenant, agreement, contract, treaty, pact

ميثاق *mīṯāq* pl. مواثيق *mawāṯīq*[2] covenant, agreement, contract, treaty, pact, alliance; charter | ميثاق هيئة الامم المتحدة *m. hai'at al-umam al-muttaḥida* the Charter of the United Nations; ميثاق عدم الاعتداء *m. 'adam al-i'tidā'* nonaggression pact

توثيق *tauṯīq* consolidation, strengthening, cementation; documentation, authentication, attestation, notarization; functions of a notary public, notariate | توثيق الديون consolidation of debts, specif., consolidation of several government loans into an overall public debt

توثقة *tauṯiqa* security, surety, guaranty

وثاق *wiṯāq* see *waṯāq* above

واثق *wāṯiq* trusting, confident, certain, sure

موثوق *mauṯūq*: موثوق به trustworthy, reliable, dependable; من مصدر موثوق به (*maṣdar*) from a reliable source

موثق *muwaṯṯiq* pl. -*ūn* notary public

وثل *waṯal* palm-fiber rope, manila rope, hemp rope

وثيل *waṯīl* palm-fiber rope, manila rope, hemp rope

وثن *waṯan* pl. وثن *wuṯun*, اوثان *auṯān* graven image, idol

وثنى *waṯanī* idolater, pagan, heathen; pagan, idolatrous

وثنية *waṯanīya* paganism

وجب *wajaba* يجب *yajibu* (وجوب *wujūb*) to be necessary, requisite, obligatory, indispensable; to be incumbent, imposed, enjoined (على on), be s.o.'s (على) duty | وجب عليه ان it is his duty to ..., he is in duty bound to ..., he has to ..., he must ...; كما يجب as it should be, as it must be, comme il faut; — (*wajb*, وجيب *wajīb*, وجبان *wajabān*) to throb, beat, palpitate (heart) **II** to make s.th. (ه) s.o.'s (على) duty, make s.th. (ه) incumbent (على on s.o.), impose, enjoin (ه على s.th. on s.o.), obligate (ه على s.o. to) **IV** to make s.th. (ه) s.o.'s (على) duty, make s.th. (ه) incumbent (على on), impose, enjoin (ه على s.th. on s.o.), make necessary, obligatory, binding (ه على s.th. for s.o.), obligate (على s.o., ه to); to decide positively (ه ل s.th. in favor of s.o.), adjudge, adjudicate, award, grant (ه ل s.th. to s.o.) **X** to deserve, merit (ه s.th.), be worthy (ه of); to be entitled, have a title (ه to), have a claim (ه on); to deem necessary or obligatory (ه s.th.) | عمل يستوجب الشكر (*šukra*) an act deserving of thanks, a meritorious undertaking

وجبة *wajba* pl. *wajabāt* meal, repast; menu (*syr.*) | وجبة الطعام *w. aṭ-ṭa'ām* meal, repast; وجبة ناشفة dry rations, emergency ration (approx.: D ration; *mil.*)

ايجاب *ījāb* obligation, liability, commitment; affirmation; confirmation, assertion; consent, assent; positive reaction, compliance; offer of contract, offer (*jur.*) | ايجابا ل in conformity with, in accordance with, according to, in pursuance of; محل الايجاب *maḥall al-ī.* competent authority; مراجع الايجاب the competent authorities; رد (اجاب or) بالايجاب to answer in the affirmative, say yes

ايجابى *ījābī* positive; affirmative; active (defense)

ايجابية *ījābīya* positivism

واجب *wājib* necessary, requisite, essential, indispensable, inevitable, unavoidable, inescapable; incumbent, imperative, binding, obligatory; proper, adequate, fair; — (pl. *-āt*, وجائب *wajā'ib*[2]) duty, obligation; incumbency; requirement, exigency, necessity; task, assignment | واجب عليك it is your duty; يرى من واجبه he considers it his duty; بالواجب obligatorily; dutifully, duly; deservedly; واجب العرض *w. al-'arḍ* suitable for presentation (petition, application); واجبات منزلية (*manzilīya*) homework (of a student)

موجوب *maujūb* moral obligation, dictate, injunction

موجب *mūjib* obligating, necessitating, requiring, inducing, motivating, causing; (pl. *-āt*) cause, reason, motive; need, exigency, requirement, necessity; matter of decorum, formality | على موجب or بموجب according to, in accordance with; on the basis of, on account of; by virtue of, on the strength of; لا موجب ل (*mūjiba*) there is no reason for ..., one need not ...

موجبة *mūjiba* cause, reason, motive, deed entailing certain inevitable consequences

موجب *mūjab* necessary, requisite, obligatory, made binding; effect, consequence; affirmative (*gram.*); positive (also, e.g., *el.*)

موجبة *mūjaba* affirmative sentence

مستوجب *mustaujib* deserving, worthy

وجد *wajada* يجد *yajidu* (وجود *wujūd*) to find (ه s.th.); to hit upon s.th. (ه), come across s.th. (ه), meet with s.th. (ه); to get, obtain (ه s.th.); to invent, make up (ه ه s.th. as); to find (good, bad) (ه s.th.); pass. *wujida* (وجود *wujūd*): to be found, be there, exist; to be; يوجد *yūjadu* there is (are); — (*wajd*) to experience, feel, sense (ه affections, afflictions); to suffer, be in a state of painful agitation; to love (ب s.o.), be impassioned (ب by), long ardently, languish (ب for); — *i u* (*wajd*) to be angry (على with), have a grudge (على against) **IV** to produce, evoke, provoke, engender, bring into being, originate, cause, bring about (ه s.th.); to create, make (ه s.th.); to achieve, accomplish, effect (ه s.th.); to invent (ه s.th.); to let (ه s.o.) find or obtain (ه s.th.), get, procure (ه ه for s.o. s.th.), furnish, supply (ه ه to s.o. s.th.); to force, compel (على ه s.o. to) **V** to be passionately in love (ب with); to grieve (ل or ب for) **VI** to show up, turn up, come; to exist, be existent, be there, be available; to affect passion

وجد *wajd* strong emotion, emotional upset; passion, ardor; ecstasy of love

وجدان *wijdān* passionate excitement; ecstasy; emotional life, psychic forces; feeling, sentiment

وجدانى *wijdānī* emotional; psychic, mental; sentimental

وجود *wujūd* finding, discovery; being; existence; presence; whereabouts; stay, visit

وجودى *wujūdī* existential; existentialist | الفلسفة الوجودية (*falsafa*) existentialism

موجدة *maujida* feeling, emotion, passion, excitement; anger, grudge, resentment, ill will

ايجاد *ījād* creation, procreation, production, origination; procuring, procurement, furnishing, supply; calculation, computation, evaluation

واجد *wājid* finding; finder; agitated, excited, upset, worried (على about); in love (ب with)

موجود *maujūd* found; available, on hand, existing, existent; present; living being, creature; stock, store, supply; pl. *-āt* everything in existence, the creation; (*com.*) assets, stocks

موجد *mūjid* originator, author, creator

وجر *wajr* pl. اوجار *aujār* cave, cavern, grotto; den, lair, habitation

وجرة *wajra*, *wajara* pitfall

وجار *wijār* pl. اوجرة *aujira* cave (of wild animals), den, lair, burrow

ميجار *mījār* pl. مواجير *mawājīr*[2] bat; racket; earthen kneading trough

وجز *wajaza* يجز *yajizu* and *wajuza* يوجز *yaujuzu* (*wajz*, وجازة *wajāza*, وجوز *wujūz*) to be brief, succinct, terse, concise, summary **IV** to be concise, terse; to be brief, succinct (فى or ه in); to abridge, summarize, epitomize (ه s.th.), make it short

وجز *wajz* short, brief, succinct; terse, concise, summary, compendious

وجيز *wajīz* short, brief, succinct; terse, concise, summary, compendious | بوجيز العبارة briefly stated, in a few words, reduced to its essentials, in a nutshell

ايجاز *ījāz* shortness, brevity, succinctness; conciseness, terseness; abridgment | ايجازا or بالايجاز in short, briefly, concisely; واليكها بالايجاز (*ilaikahā*) the matter is, briefly, as follows

موجز *mūjaz* summarized; concise, terse; abstract, epitome; outline, brief sketch; summary, résumé

وجس *wajasa* يجس *yajisu* (*wajs*, وجسان *wajasān*) to be apprehensive, be afraid, be worried, be seized with fear **IV** to have presentiments, forebodings, apprehensions; to have a presentiment (ه of), fear (ه s.th.), be afraid, apprehensive, in dread (ه of); to feel, sense, realize (ه s.th.), be aware (ه of) | اوجس خيفة (*ḵīfatan*) to have a sensation of fear; اوجس فيه الملل (*malala*) to feel that s.o. is bored, sense s.o.'s boredom **V** = **IV**; to listen anxiously, apprehensively (ه to); to taste, nibble, sip (ه of s.th.) | توجس شرا من (*šarran*) to regard s.th. as an evil omen

وجس *wajs* fear, apprehension, anxiety, concern, uneasiness

توجس *tawajjus* timorousness, timidity, apprehensiveness

واجس *wājis* disquieting thought, foreboding, evil premonition

وجع **waji'a** يوجع *yauja'u* (*waja'*) to feel pain, be in pain; to hurt, pain (ه s.o.) **IV** to cause pain (ه to s.o.); to pain, hurt (ه s.o.) **V** to suffer pain, be in pain; to voice one's pain, give vent to one's pain, to lament; to feel grief, sorrow or pity, feel sorry, feel compassion (ل for s.o.), commiserate (ل with), pity (ل s.o.)

وجع **waja'** pl. اوجاع *aujā'*, وجاع *wijā'* pain, ache; ailment | وجع السن *w. as-sinn* toothache; الوجع بكبدك (*bi-kabidika*) an imprecation (lit.: may pain strike your liver!)

وجيع **wajī'** painful; grievous, sad

توجع **tawajju'** pain, ache; lament

موجوع **maujū'** feeling pain, in pain, aching; ailing; suffering

وجف **wajafa** يجف *yajifu* (*wajf*, وجوف *wujūf*, وجيف *wajīf*) to be agitated, excited, troubled, in commotion; — (*wajīf*) to throb, beat (heart) **IV** to agitate, excite, trouble, disturb (ه s.th.); to make (ه s.th.) tremble **X** to set (ه the heart) aflutter

واجف **wājif** beating, throbbing (heart) | في صوت واجف (*ṣaut*) in a tremulous voice

وجق **wujaq** (*tun.*) the "Oudjak" (Tunisian gendarmery)

وجاق **wujāq**, اوجاق *ūjāq* pl. وجاقات *wujāqāt* range, cooking stove; (heating) stove; kitchen, galley; caboose; Janizary corps

وجل **wajila** يوجل *yaujalu* (*wajal*, موجل *maujal*) to be afraid, be scared; to be a coward, be craven **IV** to fill with fear, frighten (ه s.o.)

وجل **wajal** pl. اوجال *aujāl* fear, dread

وجل **wajil** pl. *-ūn*, وجال *wijāl* fearful, apprehensive, timorous; cowardly, craven

وجم **wajama** يجم *yajimu* (*wajm*, وجوم *wujūm*) to be silent; to be speechless, dumfounded (with fear, rage, and the like); to be shy; to be despondent, dejected, depressed

وجم **wajim** silent, speechless, dumfounded; despondent, dejected, depressed

وجوم **wujūm** silence; anxious, apprehensive silence; speechlessness from indignation, speechless indignation; despondency; shyness; anxiety, concern, sorrow

واجم **wājim** silent, speechless, dumfounded; despondent, dejected, depressed

وجنة **wajna** pl. *wajanāt* cheek

وجه **wajuha** يوجه *yaujuhu* (وجاهة *wajāha*) to be a man of distinction, belong to the notables **II** to raise to eminence, distinguish, honor (ه s.o.); to turn one's face, turn, go (الى to), head (الى for); to send, dispatch (ه الى s.o. to); to aim, level (ل or الى ه s.th. at), direct, steer, guide, channel (ل or الى ه s.th. to); to turn (ه s.th., e.g., one's face, one's attention, etc., ل or الى to); to address (ه الى a request, a question, a letter, etc., to) | وجه عليه تهمة (*tuhmatan*) to raise an accusation, bring a charge against s.o.; وجه النظر الى (*naẓara*) to turn one's eyes to **III** to be opposite s.th. (ه), be in front (ه of); to face, front (ه a locality or toward); to meet face to face, encounter (ه s.o.); to see personally (ه s.o.), speak personally (ه to s.o.), have an interview or audience (ه with); to face (ه e.g., a problem), be faced (ه with), find o.s. in the face of (ه); to meet, counter, obviate, withstand, defy (ه a danger); to stand up (ه to s.o.), oppose (ه s.o.); to hold one's own (ه against s.th.); to envisage, have in mind, consider (ه s.th.); to declare openly, say frankly (ه بأن to s.o. that); to bring face to face, confront (ه ب s.o. with s.o. else or with s.th.) **IV** to distinguish, honor (ه s.o.) **V** to betake o.s., repair, go, wend one's way (نحو or الى to), head (نحو or الى for), bend one's steps (نحو or الى toward); to turn one's face, turn (ل or الى to s.o.), face (ل or الى s.o.); to turn, apply (ب الى to s.o. for) **VI** to face each other, meet face to face **VIII** اتجه *ittajaha* to tend, be directed, be oriented (نحو or الى to, toward), be aimed, aim (نحو or الى at); to head, make (الى for), face, turn one's face (الى toward); to turn, be turned (نحو or الى to s.o., to s.th.); to lead, go (نحو or الى to, toward; of a road); to point (نحو or الى to; of a signpost); to come to s.o.'s (ل) mind, occur (ل to s.o.; of an idea)

جهة *jiha* pl. *-āt* side; direction; region, part, section, area; district, precinct, city quarter; agency, authority; administrative agency; (*tun.*) administrative district; الجهات the outskirts, the outlying districts, the provinces | الى جهة in the direction of, toward; من جهة from the direction of, from, on the part of, concerning, regarding, as to, with respect or regard to; من جهة الشمال (*šamāl*) from the north; من جهة ... ومن جهة اخرى (ثانية or) (*ukrā, tāniya*) on the one hand ... on the other hand; من كل جهة from all sides, on all sides; من جهتي for my part, as for me, I for one; من هذه الجهة as seen from this angle, under this aspect, from this viewpoint; جهة الاختصاص or الجهة المختصة (*muktaṣṣa*) the competent authority; جهة اليسار *jihata l-yasār* at left, to the left, on the left side

مجلس جهوى *majlis jihawī* council of an administrative district (*Tun.*)

وجه *wajh* pl. وجوه *wujūh* face, countenance; front, face, façade; outside; surface; right side of a fabric; dial (of a clock or watch); face, obverse (of a coin); prominent personality; exterior, look(s), appearance, guise, semblance; side; direction; intention, intent, design, purpose, aim, goal, objective, end; course, policy, guiding principle, precept; way, manner, mode, procedure, method; reason, cause; sense, meaning, signification, purport; beginning, start, outset, first part of a given period of time; — (pl. وجوه *wujūh* and اوجه *aujuh*) aspect; approach, point of view; viewpoint, standpoint; — (pl. اوجه *aujuh*) phase (of the moon; also *el.*) | 1. Adverbial phrases: وجها apparently; وجها بوجه (or لوجه) face to face, in private, personally, directly; وجها من الوجوه (with preceding negation) in no way (whatsoever); بوجه الاجمال *bi-w. il-ijmāl* on the whole, by and large, in general; بوجه (or على وجه) التقريب approximately, roughly, nearly; بوجه خاص or على وجه خاص (*kāṣṣ*) especially, in particular; بوجه (or على وجه) عام (*ʿāmm*) generally, in general; بوجه ما some way or other, somehow; in a certain way, to a certain extent; بدون وجه حق (*w. ḥaqqin*) without any legitimate claim, without being in the least entitled, in an entirely unlawful manner; على وجه in the manner of, in the form of, in the shape of; with regard to, concerning, about; على وجهه in his own way; in the right manner, correctly, properly, as it should be; على غير وجهه improperly, incorrectly, wrongly; مضى على وجهه and ذهب على وجهه to go one's own way, go one's way; على هذا الوجه in this manner, this way, thus; على وجه الاجمال (*w. al-ijmāl*) on the whole, by and large, in general; altogether, in the aggregate; على الوجه التالى in the following manner, as follows; على وجه التفصيل at great length, in detail, elaborately; على وجه الحصر (*w. il-ḥaṣr*) in a condensed form, briefly stated, in a nutshell; على وجه العموم in general, generally; على وجه اليقين with certainty; فى وجهه before him, in his presence; counter to him; before his (very) eyes; لوجه الله for the sake of God, regardless of any reward in this life; for nothing, gratis; من كل وجه in every respect, from every point of view, on all grounds; من وجوه كثيرة from many points of view, in many respects; من بعض الوجوه in some ways; من كل الوجوه in every respect, in every way, all the way through, completely; — 2. Verbal phrases: ابيض وجهه *ibyaḍḍa wajhuhū* to enjoy an excellent reputation, stand in good repute; اسود وجهه *iswadda wajhuhū* to fall into discredit, be discredited, be in disgrace; اخذ وجها to win respect, gain prestige; اخذ وجه العروسة (*wajha l-ʿarūsa*) to consummate marriage; اهانه فى وجهه to insult s.o. to his face; بيض وجهه *bayyaḍa wajhahū* to make s.o. appear blameless, in a favorable light, to whitewash, exculpate, vindicate, justify s.o., play s.o. up, make much of s.o.; to honor s.o., show honor to s.o.; خلا له وجه الطريق (*kalā, wajhu ṭ-ṭ.*) his way was unobstructed, he had clear sailing; سفه وجهه *saffaha wajhahū* or سود وجهه (*sawwada*) to expose s.o., show s.o. up, make a fool of s.o., bring s.o. into discredit, disgrace s.o., dishonor s.o.; شوه وجه الحقيقة *šawwaha wajha l-ḥ.* to distort the truth; شوه وجه الوظيفة to disgrace one's profession or office; ضرب وجه الامر وعينه (*wajha l-amri wa-ʿainahū*) to touch on the very essence of a matter, hit the mark; قام فى وجه فلان to stand up to s.o., take a stand against s.o.; هرب من وجه فلان to flee from s.o.; — 3. Nominal phrases: الوجه البحرى (*baḥrī*) Lower Egypt; الوجه القبلى (*qiblī*) Upper Egypt; وجه الحال the circumstances, the state of affairs, the factual situation; وجه الشبه *w. aš-šibh* point of resemblance; وجه النهار *wajha n-nahār* during the daytime; كلام ذو وجهين (*kalām*) equivocal statement, ambiguous words; اوجه القمر *a. al-qamar* the lunar phases; وجوه الناس prominent people, leading personalities; — 4. لا وجه ل (*wajha*) there is no reason for; لا وجه له من الصحة (*ṣiḥḥa*) it has no validity at all

وجهى *wajhī* facial, of the face

وجهة *wijha, wujha* pl. *-āt* direction, trend, drift; course (of a ship); intention, design, aim, goal, objective; respect, regard; (= وجهة النظر *w. an-naẓar*) angle, point of view, viewpoint, standpoint | من هذه الوجهة in this respect; from this point of view; من وجهة اخرى (*ukrā*) from a different standpoint, from another point of view; وجهته باريس he is on his way to Paris

وجاهة *wajāha* esteem, credit, repute, prestige, influence, standing, rank, distinction, notability; acceptability; well-foundedness, soundness, solidity, validity | ذو وجاهة person of rank; notable, noted, eminent, distinguished; اهل الوجاهة *ahl al-w.* the notables

وجاهى *wijāhī* contradictory (*jur.*)

وجيه *wajīh* pl. وجهاء *wujahāʾ*[2] notable, noted, eminent, distinguished; eminent man, person of note, notable; leader; excellent, outstanding; acceptable, well-founded, sound; الوجهاء the notables | سبب وجيه (*sabab*) sound reason

وجيهة *wajīha* pl. *-āt* lady of high social standing; lady of society, socialite

تجاه *tujāha* (prep.) in front of, facing, opposite

توجيه *taujīh* aiming, leveling, directing; orientation; guidance, direction; controlling, steering, channeling, leading, guiding; (methodical) instruction; (pl. *-āt*) directive, instruction; allocation; transfer, conveyance, assignment | توجيه خطاه *t. kuṭāhu* directives that one receives

توجيهى *taujīhī*: السنة التوجيهية (*sana*) fifth grade of a secondary school, the completion of which is prerequisite before admittance to a university (*Eg.*); شهادة توجيهية diploma conferred after the successful completion of the fifth grade of a secondary school, entitling the holder to admittance to a university (*Eg.*); طلبة التوجيهى *ṭalabat at-t.* fifth graders of a secondary school (*Eg.*)

مواجهة *muwājaha* opposite position, opposition; meeting; facing, anticipation, countering, obviation; encounter; confrontation; talk from person to person, personal talk; audience; interview; *muwājahatan* face to face, (from) person to person | بمواجهته in his presence

توجه *tawajjuh* attention; favoritism, patronage

اتجاه *ittijāh* pl. *-āt* direction; inclination, bent, trend, drift; tendency; orientation; course (e.g., of a ship) | طريق ذو اتجاه واحد one-way street; اتجاه واحد One Way Only (traffic sign)

واجهة *wājiha* pl. *-āt* face, front; outside; façade; show window | واجهة القتال front line, fighting front

موجه *muwajjih* mate (naval rank; *Eg.* 1939)

موجه *muwajjah* remote-controlled, guided

متجه *muttajih* directed, tending, aiming (فى in a direction)

متجه *muttajah* direction | فى كل متجه in all directions; in all fields, in every respect

وحد *waḥada* يحد *yaḥidu* (وحدة *waḥda*, حدة *ḥida*) and *waḥuda* to be alone, unique, singular, unmatched, without equal, incomparable **II** to make into one, unite, unify, standardize, regularize (ه s.th.); to connect, join, link, unite, bring together, fit together, combine, consolidate, amalgamate, merge (بينهم different parts) | وحد الله to declare God to be one; to profess belief in the unity of God, be a monotheist; وحد الديون to consolidate, or fund, debts **V** to be one, alone, by o.s., the only one, singular, unique; to be lonely, solitary, live in solitude, lead a secluded life; to do alone, perform or carry out by o.s. (ب s.th.); to be reduced to one; to be united, be combined, be unified, be standardized, be concerted, be consolidated; to become one, form a unity | توحد برأيه (*bi-ra'yihī*) to stand alone with one's opinion; توحده بعنايته (*bi-ʿināyatihī*) to single s.o. out for one's special care, give s.o. particular attention **VIII** اتحد *ittaḥada* to be one, form a unity; to be united, be combined, be consolidated, be amalgamated, merge, form, or join in, a union; to unite, combine (ب with); to be agreed, be unanimous; to agree, concur; to act jointly

حدة *ḥida* solitude, solitariness | على حدة alone, by o.s., apart from others, detached, isolated, secluded; separate(ly); كل على حدة everyone by himself, each by himself (itself), each separately, each individually

وحده *waḥdahū*, f. وحدها *waḥdahā* or على وحده *ʿalā waḥdihī* etc., he alone, he by himself | جاء وحده he came alone; لا ... وحده بل not only ... but

وحدة *waḥda* oneness, singleness, unity; solitariness, isolation, seclusion, privacy, solitude, loneliness; self-containment, independence; union; — (pl. *-āt*) military unit; crew; single group, grouping; plant unit, installation; (subsidiary) unit (of an industrial plant); branch office, suboffice (of an administrative agency) | ○ وحدات الاشارة *w. al-išāra* communications units (*mil.*); وحدة الزمن *w. az-zaman* time unit; وحدة طائفية denominational group, religious minority; الوحدة العربية (*ʿarabīya*) Arab unity, the Arab Union

وحدانى *waḥdānī* single, solitary, separate, individual; sole, only, exclusive;

singular, unique; matchless, unequaled, incomparable; single, unmarried

وحدانية *waḥdānīya* soleness, solitariness; isolation, seclusion, privacy; solitude, loneliness; oneness, singleness, unity (esp. of God); singularity, uniqueness, incomparableness

وحيد *waḥīd* alone; solitary, lonely; single, separate, individual, sporadic, isolated; sole, only, exclusive; singular, unique; matchless, unequaled, incomparable | وحيدة ابويها *w. abawaihā* her parents' only daughter

اوحد *auḥad*[2] singular, unique

توحيد *tauḥīd* unification, union, combination, fusion; standardization, regularization; consolidation, amalgamation, merger; belief in the unity of God; profession of the unity of God; monotheism; (*myst.*) mergence in the unity of the universe | توحيد الديون consolidation of debts; توحيد الزوجة *t. az-zauja* monogamy; توحيد الكلمة *t. al-kalima* unification, union, joining of forces, unanimity; توحيد المنتوجات standardization of industrial products; علم التوحيد *'ilm at-t.* (Islamic) theology

توحد *tawaḥḥud* soleness, singleness, solitariness; isolation, seclusion, privacy; solitude, loneliness

اتحاد *ittiḥād* oneness, singleness, unity; concord, accord, unison, harmony, unanimity, agreement; combination; consolidation, amalgamation, merger, fusion; alliance, confederacy; association; federation; union; ○ chemical compound | باتحاد in unison, with combined efforts, together, jointly; اتحاد الآراء unanimity; باتحاد الآراء unanimously; اتحاد البريد العام (*'āmm*) Universal Postal Union; اتحاد جنوب افريقية *itt. janūb ifrīqiya* the Union of South Africa; اتحاد الدول العربية *itt. ad-duwal al-'arabīya* the United Arab States (i.e., the United Arab Republic and Yemen); الاتحاد السوفييتى or اتحاد السوفيت (السوفيتى) the Soviet Union

اتحادى *ittiḥādī* unionist; unionistic; federal | حكومة اتحادية federal government

واحد *wāḥid* one (numeral); someone, somebody, a certain person, a certain ...; sole, only; (pl. وحدان *wuḥdān*) single, solitary, separate, individual, sporadic, isolated | واحدا فواحدا or واحدا واحدا or واحد بعد الآخر or واحد بعد واحد one by one, single, separately, one after the other, one at a time, successively; الواحد the One (attribute of God); الواحد منهم each of them, every one of them; واحد كهذا such a one, such a man, (any)one like that; كل واحد *kullu wāḥidin* everyone, everybody; فى موضع واحد (*mauḍi'in*) in one and the same place; ولا واحد not a single one, not one; زرافات ووحدانا *zarāfātin wa-wuḥdānan* in groups and alone

موحد *muwaḥḥid* professor of the unity of God; الموحدون the Almohades

موحد *muwaḥḥad* combined, consolidated, amalgamated; united; unified; standardized, regularized; ○ unipolar (*el.*); having one diacritical point (letter)

متوحد *mutawaḥḥid* solitary, rare, sporadic, isolated; recluse, hermit

متحد *muttaḥid* united, combined, consolidated, amalgamated; uniform, standardized; harmonious, united, unanimous, in agreement, concordant | الولايات المتحدة (*wilāyāt*) the United States; الامم المتحدة (*umam*) the United Nations

مستوحد *mustauḥid* solitary, lonely, isolated

وحش IV to be deserted, desolate (region); to oppress, make uneasy, fill with anxiety (ه s.o.); to make (ه s.o.) feel lonely, make lonesome (ه s.o.); to grieve by one's absence (ه s.o.) **V** to be desolate, deserted, waste; to be or become wild, savage, brutal; to brutalize, become brutish **X** to be desolate, deserted, waste; to feel lonely; to be distressed, saddened by the separation (ل from s.o.), miss badly (ل s.o.); to have an aversion (من to), feel a distaste (من for), feel repelled (من by); to be unable to warm or reconcile o.s. (من to), feel no particular liking (من for); to be alienated, become estranged; to be afraid

وحش *waḥš* waste, deserted, lonely, dreary, desolate; wild, untamed (animal); — (pl. وحوش *wuḥūš*, وحشان *wuḥšān*) wild animal, wild beast; game; monster | الوحوش الضارية (*ḍāriya*) the predatory animals, the beasts of prey

وحشة *waḥša* loneliness, forlornness, desolation, cheerlessness, dreariness; (fig.) chilliness, frostiness, frigidity, coldness (e.g., of relations); gloom, melancholy, weird feeling; strangeness, estrangement, alienation

وحشى *waḥšī* untamed, wild; brutish, savage, uncivilized, barbarous; brutal; cruel; ugly; repulsive, disgusting; directed outward, outer, external (esp., of anatomical parts) | الكعب الوحشى (*ka'b*) outer anklebone

وحشية *waḥšīya* wildness, savageness, ferocity, brutality, savagery; barbarity, barbarism

ايحاش *īḥāš* loneliness, forlornness

توحش *tawaḥḥuš* return to a wild or savage state, wildness, savageness, barbarity, brutalization; brutality

استيحاش *istīḥāš* strangeness, estrangement, alienation, unsociability; weirdness, uncanniness, eeriness

موحش *mūḥiš* desolate, dreary, deserted, forlorn, lonely, waste; oppressed, uneasy, anxious; weird, eerie, uncanny

متوحش *mutawaḥḥiš* wild (animal), savage; barbarous, barbaric; brutal, cruel; a savage; a barbarian

مستوحش *mustauḥiš* wild, savage; a savage; lonesome, lonely; melancholic, gloomy, sad, unhappy

وحف *waḥf* luxuriant and black (hair)

وحل *waḥila* يوحل *yauḥalu* to sink in mire, get stuck in the mud; to be stuck, be stranded, come to a deadlock, be in a fix **II** to soil with mud, muddy (ه s.th.); to become slimy, muddy or mucky (the ground) **IV** to mire (ه s.o.), make (ه s.o.) stick fast in the mud, get s.o. into a quagmire, throw s.o. in the mud **V** to be or become dirty, muddy, miry **X** = **V**

وحل *waḥl*, *waḥal* pl. وحول *wuḥūl*, اوحال *auḥāl* mud, mire, slough, morass

وحل *waḥil* muddy, dirty, miry

موحل *mauḥil* muddy ground, slough; fix, predicament

موحل *muwaḥḥal* muddy, miry; mud-covered, mud-spattered; dirty

وحم *waḥima* يحم *yaḥimu*, يوحم *yauḥamu* (*waḥam*) to feel appetite, have a longing, a craving (ه for), desire (ه s.th.)

وحم *waḥam* a craving for certain food during pregnancy; appetite, craving, longing, ardent desire

وحام *waḥām*, *wiḥām* a craving for certain food during pregnancy; appetite, craving, longing, ardent desire

وحمى *waḥmā* pl. وحام *wiḥām*, وحامى *waḥāmā* craving for certain food (pregnant woman)

وحوح *waḥwaḥa* to tremble, shiver, shudder (من from, with)

وحى *waḥā* يحى *yaḥī* (*waḥy*) to inspire (ل ب s.o. with); to reveal (الى ب to s.o. s.th.) **IV** to inspire (الى ب s.o. with); to reveal

(الى ب to s.o. s.th.; of God); to give an idea, give an impression (من of); to suggest, give rise to the idea (ان that), create the impression (ان that, as if); pass. اوحى الى *ūḥiya ilayya* it occurred to me, the idea suggested itself, I came to think, I was inspired X to ask s.o.'s (ه) advice, seek s.o.'s (ه) counsel, consult (ه s.o.); to let o.s. be inspired (ه ▲ with s.th. by s.o.), seek inspiration (ه ▲ in s.th. from s.o.); to derive, deduce (من ▲ s.th. from) | استوحى الفكرة (*fikrata*) to let o.s. be guided by the thought; استوحى موعظة من (*mau'iẓatan*) to draw a lesson from

وحى *waḥy* inspiration; revelation (*theol.*)

ايحاء *īḥā'* suggestion | ايحاء ذاتى (*ḏātī*) autosuggestion

○ واح *wāḥin* radio transmitter; ○ الواحى radio

موح *mūḥin* inspiring; revealing; dispenser of revelations

موحى *mūḥan* pl. موحيات *mūḥayāt* inspiration, revelation

مستوحى *mustauḥan* influenced, advised, guided, inspired (من by); derived, deduced (من from)

وخز **wakaza** يخز *yakizu* (*wakz*) to sting, prick, twinge (ه s.o.); to pierce, transfix, stab to death (ه s.o.); to vex, pester, harass, beset, irritate, torment (ه s.o.)

وخز *wakz* stinging, pricking; sharp, local pain, twinges | وخز الضمير compunctions, pangs of remorse

وخزة *wakza* (n. vic.) sting, prick, twinge

وخزان *wakazān* needling, nagging

وخاز *wakkāz* stinging, pricking; biting, sharp, pungent, smarting, fierce, violent

واخز *wākiz* stinging, pricking; biting, sharp, pungent, smarting, fierce, violent

وخط **wakaṭa** يخط *yakiṭu* (*wakṭ*) to turn gray, make gray-haired (ه s.o.; of age)

وخم (see also تخم [1]) *wakuma* يوخم *yaukumu* (وخامة *wakāma*) to be unhealthy (e.g., air, climate); to be unwholesome, heavy, indigestible; — *wakima* يوخم *yaukumu* (*wakam*) to suffer from indigestion VIII اتخم *ittakama* to suffer from indigestion

تخمة *tukama* pl. *-āt*, تخم *tukam* surfeit; indigestion; upset stomach

وخم *wakam* unhealthy air; dirt, filth, squalor

وخم *wakim* unhealthy; unwholesome, heavy, indigestible; dirty, filthy, squalid

وخيم *wakīm* unhealthy; indigestible; bad, evil, dangerous, fatal, disastrous | وخيم العاقبة of evil consequences

وخامة *wakāma* unhealthiness, unwholesomeness; evil nature

اوخم *aukam*[2] unhealthier; worse

مستوخم *mustaukam* indigestible; unwholesome | مجاز مستوخم (*majāz*) tasteless metaphor (*rhet.*)

وخى **wakā** يخى *yakī* (*waky*) to intend, purpose (▲ s.th., to do s.th.), have in mind, have in view (▲ s.th.), aim (▲ at), aspire (▲ to), be out for (▲) II do.; to lead, guide (ه s.o.) V to intend, purpose (▲ s.th., to do s.th.), have in mind, have in view (▲ s.th.), aim (▲ at), aspire (▲ to), strive (▲ for), be out for (▲), put one's mind (▲ to), set one's mind, be intent (▲ on) | توخى طريقة to follow a method, proceed methodically, systematically; توخى غاية to pursue an object, have an aim in mind

وخى *waky* pl. وخى *wukīy*, *wikīy* intention, aim, plan

توخ *tawakkin* design, intent

ود **wadda** (1st. pers. perf. *wadidtu*) *a* (*wadd*, *wudd*, *widd*, وداد *wadād*, *wudād*, مودة *mawadda*) to love, like (▲, ه s.o., s.th.), be fond (▲, ه of); to want, wish (▲ s.th., ان or لو or لوان that s.th. be) | اود ان يفعل ذلك لو

I should like him to do this; كما يود as he likes; وددت لو كان غنيا (lau, ğanīyan) I wish he were rich; ود نفسه بعيدا عن (nafsahū) to wish o.s. far away from III to make friends, become friends (ه with s.o.) V to show love or affection (ل or الى to s.o.); to try to gain favor (الى with), seek s.o.'s (الى) friendship; to curry favor, ingratiate o.s. (الى with), flatter one's way (الى into); to attract, captivate (ه s.o.), win s.o.'s (ه) love or friendship VI to love each other, be on friendly terms, be friends

ود wadd, widd, wudd love, affection, amity, friendship; wish, desire | كان بودنا لو (bi-waddinā) we should be pleased if

ود wadd, widd, wudd pl. اوداد audād, اود awudd, awidd loving; affectionate, tender; fond, attached, devoted; lover

ودى waddī, widdī, wuddī friendly, amicable

وداد wadād, widād, wudād love, friendship

ودادى wadādī amicable, friendly, of a friend

ودود wadūd favorably disposed, attached, devoted, fond, friendly

وديد wadīd favorably disposed, attached, devoted, fond, friendly

مودة mawadda love; friendship

تواد tawādd friendly relations, good terms

ودج wadaj pl. اوداج audāj jugular vein | انتفخت اوداجه (his jugular veins swelled, i.e.) he flew into a rage, he became furious; (also used in the sense of:) to become inflated with pride, swagger, bluster

وداج widāj jugular vein

ودر II to endanger, imperil (ه s.o.); to waste (ه s.th.)

ودع wada'a يدع yada'u (wad') to put down, lodge, deposit (ه s.th.); (usually only in imperf. and imp.) to let, leave; to leave off, stop, cease; to give up, omit, skip (ه s.th., الى in order to turn to s.th. else) | دع عنك da' 'anka desist! stop! دع عنك or دعك من da'ku min not to speak of ..., let alone ...; دعك من هذا (da'ka) stop that! cut it out! دعنا من هذا (da'nā) let's not talk about it! enough of that! دعنا نذهب let us go! يدع محلا (maḥallan) to leave room; — wadu'a يودع yaudu'u (وداعة wadā'a) to be gentle, mild-tempered, meek, peaceable II to see off, bid farewell (ه s.o.); to take leave (ه of), say farewell (ه to s.o.) IV to put down, lay down (ه ه, ه s.o., s.th. in a place, also fig., s.th. in a book), lodge, deposit (ه ه s.th. in a place); to entrust (ه ه to s.o. s.th.); to leave (ه ه with s.o. s.th.), give (ه ه s.o. s.th.) for safekeeping, give s.th. (ه) in charge of s.o. (ه), consign (ه ه to s.o. s.th.) | اودعه السجن (sijna) to throw s.o. in prison X to lay down, put down, place, lodge, deposit (ه ه s.th. in a place); to entrust, consign, commit (ه ه to s.o. s.th.), leave (ه ه s.th. with s.o.), give (ه ه s.o. s.th.) for safekeeping, give s.th. (ه) in charge of s.o. (ه); to put on half pay, transfer to provisional retirement (ه an official); to store, warehouse (ه s.th.) | استودعه الله (llāha) to commend s.o. to God's protection; استودعك الله farewell! God with you! good-by! adieu!

دعة da'a mild-temperedness, meekness, gentleness, gentle-heartedness; calm, composure, equanimity

ودع wad' lodging, depositing, deposition

ودع wad', wada' (coll.; n. un. ة) seashells

وداع wadā' farewell, leave-taking, adieu, valediction; الوداع and وداعا farewell! adieu! God with you! good-by!

وداعة wadā'a gentle-heartedness, gentleness, mild-temperedness, meekness, peaceableness

وديع *wadīʿ* calm, peaceable, gentle-hearted, mild-tempered, meek

وديعة *wadīʿa* pl. ودائع *wadāʾiʿ*[2] s.th. entrusted to s.o.'s custody, trust, charge; deposited amount; deposit

ميدعة *mīdaʿa* apron; (doctor's) smock

توديع *taudīʿ* farewell, adieu, leave-taking; valediction

ايداع *īdāʿ* lodging, consigning, depositing, deposition | بطاقة الايداع deposit slip, certificate of deposit; warrant of arrest; محضر الايداع *maḥḍar al-ī.* official record of deposit (*jur.*)

استيداع *istīdāʿ* lodging, consigning, depositing, deposition; reserve; transfer to provisional retirement (of an official); putting on half pay (*mil.*) | فى الاستيداع in provisional retirement; unattached, on half pay; ○ مخزن الاستيداع *makzan al-ist.* depot

وادع *wādiʿ* consignor, depositor, deponent, lodger; gentle, mild, meek; peaceable, composed, calm; moderate; low, deep

مودع *mūdiʿ* consignor, lodger, depositor; gentle, mild, meek; moderate; low, deep

مودع *mūdaʿ* lodged, consigned; deposited; deposit; المودع لديه (*ladaihi*) keeper, consignee, depository

مستودع *mustaudiʿ* depositor

مستودع *mustaudaʿ* lodged, consigned; deposited; stored; in provisional retirement; unattached, on half pay, in reserve; — (pl. *-āt*) depository, repository; storehouse; warehouse, depot; ○ hangar; ○ container, reservoir, (storage) tank | ○ مستودع التدريب training center (*mil.*)

وديقة *wadīqa* pl. ودائق *wadāʾiq*[2] lawn, meadow

ودك *wadak* fat

ودك *wadik*, ودوك *wadūk*, وديك *wadīk* and وادك *wādik* fat (adj.)

ودى *wadā* يدى *yadī* to pay blood money (ه for s.o. killed) IV to perish, die; to cut off (ب s.o.; of death); to kill, destroy (ب s.o., s.th.) | اودى بحياته (*bi-ḥayātihī*) to destroy s.o.'s life; اودى بصحته (*bi-ṣiḥḥatihī*) to ruin s.o.'s health, sap s.o.'s strength

دية *diya* pl. *-āt* blood money, wergild; indemnity for bodily injury

واد *wādin* pl. اودية *audiya*, وديان *widyān* valley; river valley, river bed, ravine, gorge, wadi; river; (newspaper) column | اسال اودية من الحبر (*ḥibr*) to pour forth floods of ink; نحن فى واد وانتم فى واد we belong to different camps; there is a deep gulf between us, we stand worlds apart; حوم به الفكر فى اودية شتى (*ḥawwama, fikru, šattā*) approx.: his thoughts trailed off, he was thinking of s.th. else, he was absent-minded; ذهب صيحة فى واد (*ṣaiḥatan*) to die unheard (call); هام فى وديان approx.: he was no longer himself, he was floating in higher realms, he was beside himself, he was out of his senses; فى كل واد everywhere, on all sides; وادى حلفا *w. ḥalfā* Wadi Halfa (town in N Sudan, on Egyptian border)

ذر (وذر) only imperf. يذر *yaḏaru* and imp. *ḏar* to let, leave; to let alone, leave alone; to let be, stop, cease; to leave behind

ورب II to equivocate, express o.s. in equivocal terms (عن about) III to double-cross, dupe, outfox, outsmart (ه s.o.)

ورب *warb* pl. اوراب *aurāb* obliqueness, obliquity, slantingness; oblique direction, inclination, slope, slant, diagonal | بالورب obliquely, slantingly, aslant; diagonally, transversely

وراب *wirāb* obliqueness, obliquity

مواربة *muwāraba* equivocation, ambiguity | فى غير مواربة or بدون مواربة unequivocally, in no uncertain terms

موروب *maurūb* oblique, inclined, slanting, sloping; diagonal, transverse; partly open, ajar (door)

موارب *muwārab* ajar (door)

ورث *wariṯa* يرث *yariṯu* (*wirṯ*, ارث *irṯ*, ارثة *irṯa*, وراثة *wirāṯa*, رثة *riṯa*, تراث *turāṯ*) to be heir (ه to s.o.), be s.o.'s (ه) heir; to inherit (ه or عن or من ▲ s.th. from s.o.) **II** to appoint as heir (ه s.o.); to transfer by will, leave, bequeath, make over (▲ ه to s.o. s.th.) **IV** = **II**; to draw down, bring down (▲ ه on s.o. s.th.), cause (▲ ه s.o. s.th.) **VI** to have inherited (▲ s.th.); to possess as an inheritance (▲ s.th.)

ارث *irṯ* heritage, inheritance, legacy; estate (of inheritance)

ورث *wirṯ* inheritance, legacy

وراثة *wirāṯa* inheritance, legacy; hereditariness, hereditary transmission, heredity

وراثى *wirāṯī* hereditary | امراض وراثية hereditary diseases

وريث *warīṯ* pl. ورثاء *wuraṯā'*[2] heir, inheritor

تراث *turāṯ* inheritance, legacy

ميراث *mīrāṯ* pl. مواريث *mawāriṯ*[2] heritage, inheritance, legacy, estate

توارث *tawāruṯ* transmission by inheritance; heredity

وارث *wāriṯ* pl. ورثة *waraṯa*, وراث *wurrāṯ* inheriting; heir, inheritor

موروث *maurūṯ* inherited; handed down, transmitted, traditional; hereditary

مورث *muwarriṯ* and *mūriṯ* testator, legator

متوارث *mutawāraṯ* inherited

ورد[1] *warada* يرد *yaridu* (ورود *wurūd*) to come, arrive; to appear, show up; to be found, be met with, be said (فى in a book, letter, etc.), be mentioned (فى in); to reach (الى or ▲ a place), arrive (الى or ▲ at), come to, get to, travel to; to be received (على by s.o.; letter, money, or the like), come to s.o.'s (على) hands; to accrue, come (على to s.o.; revenue, proceeds, etc.) **II** to make (▲ s.th.) reach (ب s.th. else or s.o.), get s.th. (▲) to (ب); to bring in, import (▲ s.th.); to supply, furnish, feed (ب ▲ s.th. to); to deposit (ب ▲ s.th. in), pay (ب ▲ s.th. into) **IV** to make or have (▲, ه s.o., s.th.) come (▲ or على to), bring, take (الى or على ▲, ه s.o., s.th. to); to transfer, convey, transport, move (الى ▲ s.th. to a place); to import (▲ s.th.); to deposit, pay in (▲ an amount); to produce, present (▲ s.th.); to supply, furnish (▲ s.th.); to mention, state, set forth, bring up, allege, adduce, cite, quote (▲ s.th.), interpose, introduce, mention casually, drop in passing, throw in (▲ s.th., ب in one's speech) **VI** to arrive successively, come one after the other; to succeed one another, be successive, consecutive; to arrive, come in, come to hand (news, dispatches); to coincide, happen to be identical (ideas, thoughts) **X** to have (▲ s.th.) supplied or furnished (من by or from), buy, draw, get, procure (من ▲ s.th. from); to import (من ▲ s.th. from)

ورد *wird* watering place; animals coming to the water; — (pl. اوراد *aurād*) specified time of day or night devoted to private worship (in addition to the five prescribed prayers); a section of the Koran recited on this occasion | الورد الذى طالما التسبيح به (*ṭālamā*) and الورد الذى يتلى فى الغدو والآصال (*yutlā fī l-ġudūw wa-l-āṣāl*) approx.: always the same old story

بنت وردان *bint wardāna* pl. بنات وردان *banāt w.* cockroach

وريد *warīd* pl. اوردة *aurida*, ورد *wurud*, ورود *wurūd* vein; jugular vein | حبل الوريد *ḥabl al-w.* jugular vein

ورود *wurūd* coming, arrival, advent; receipt; appearance

مورد *maurid* pl. موارد *mawārid*[2] place of arrival, (place of) destination; access to the water, to a watering place; watering place; spring, well; resource, resort, expedient; place of origin, of provenience; source of income; income, revenue; supply; importation | موارد الدولة *m. ad-daula* government revenues; موارد الزيت *m. az-zait* oil wells; موارد المعيشة *m. al-ma'īša* food-supply lines

موردة *maurida* watering place; landing place, quay, wharf

توريد *taurīd* pl. *-āt* furnishing, provision, purveyance; importation, import; supply; feed | توريد البضائع supply of goods

ايراد *īrād* adduction, allegation, bringing up, mention(ing), citation, quotation; — (pl. *-āt*) importation, import; supply; revenue, income; returns, proceeds, takings, receipts; yield, gain, profit

توارد *tawārud* successive arrival; accidental identity of ideas

استيراد *istīrād* importation, import(s)

وارد *wārid* pl. وراد *wurrād* arriving; found, mentioned; newcomer, arrival; pl. *-āt* imports; receipts, incomings, returns, proceeds, takings | واردات وصادرات imports and exports

مورد *muwarrid* supplier, furnisher, purveyor, contractor

مستورد *mustaurid* importer

مستوردات *mustauradāt* imported goods, imports

ورد[2] II to blossom, be in bloom (tree); to apply rouge (ه to), rouge, make up (ه s.th.); to dye or color red (ه s.th.) V to be or become red; to take on a rosy color, glow, be aglow, be flushed (cheek) VI = V

ورد *ward* (coll.; n. un. ة) pl. ورود *wurūd* rose(s); blossoms, flowers, bloom

وردة *warda* (n. un.) rose; rosette; cockade; rosebush; (*eg.*) washer; (*eg.*) packing ring (of a piston)

وردى *wardī* roseate, rose-colored, rosy; pink

وردية *wardīya* rosary

وردة *wurda* reddish color

تورد *tawarrud* a reddening, red coloration

مورد *muwarrad* rosy, ruddy, red

متورد *mutawarrid* rosy

جبال الاوراس *jibāl al-aurās* the Aurès Mountains (in E Algeria)

ورش[1] *waraša* يرش *yarišu* (*warš*) to interfere with s.o.'s (على) plans, thrust o.s. on s.o. (على) II to disturb the peace, make trouble

ورش *wariš* lively, brisk; restless, restive

وارش *wāriš* obtrusive; intruder, parasite

ورشة[2] *warša* pl. *-āt*, ورش *wiraš* workshop | ورشة الاصلاح *w. al-iṣlāḥ* repair shop, service station; ورشة غسيل laundry

ورط II and IV to entangle, embroil, involve (ه s.o. in difficulties), put s.o. (ه) in an unpleasant situation, get s.o. in a bad fix V to let o.s. in for difficulties, get o.s. into trouble; to be entangled, be embroiled, become involved (في in) X to be entangled, be embroiled, become involved (في in)

ورطة *warṭa* pl. *waraṭāt*, وراط *wirāṭ* difficult or critical situation, difficulty, trouble, plight, predicament, awkward position, dilemma, fix, jam; embroilment, bad entanglement

تورط *tawarruṭ* entanglement, involvement (في in)

مورّوط *maurūṭ* in a plight, in a bad fix, in a dilemma

مورّط *muwarraṭ* in a plight, in a bad fix, in a dilemma

ورع *wariʻa* يرع *yariʻu* (*waraʻ*) and *waruʻa* (وراعة *warāʻa*) to be pious and godfearing V to pause (عن before), be cautious, hesitate (عن about), refrain, abstain (عن, من from)

ورع *waraʻ* piety, piousness, godliness, godfearingness; caution, cautiousness, carefulness; timorousness, timidity, shyness, reserve

ورع *wariʻ* pl. اوراع *aurāʻ* pious, godly, godfearing; cautious, careful; reticent, reserved

ورف *warafa* يرف *yarifu* (*warf*, وريف *warīf*, وروف *wurūf*) to stretch, extend, become long (shadow); to sprout, be green, verdant, in bloom (plant) II and IV to stretch, extend, become long (shadow)

وارف *wārif* extending, stretching (shadow); green, verdant, blooming; luxuriant

ورق II to leaf, burst into leaf, put forth leaves, sprout; to leaf, thumb (ه a book); to paper (ه a wall) IV to leaf, burst into leaf, put forth leaves, sprout

ورق *waraq* (coll.; n. un. ة) pl. اوراق *aurāq* foliage, leafage, leaves; paper; paper money, banknotes; thin sheet metal, laminated metal | ورق تمغة *w. tamġa* stamped paper; ورق الرسم *w. ar-rasm* drawing paper; ورق مزركش *w. muzarkaš* wallpaper, paper hangings; ورق السنفرة *w. as-sanfara* emery paper, glass paper, sandpaper; ورق شفاف (*šaffāf*) tracing paper; ورق الشاهدة carbon paper; ورق مطبوع (*tun.*) stamped paper; ورق عادم wastepaper; ورق مقوى (*muqawwan*) cardboard, pasteboard; ورق الكتابة writing paper; ورق اللعب *w. al-laʻib* playing cards; ورق اللف *w. al-laff* wrapping paper; ورق نشاف (or نشاش) (*naššāf*, *naššāš*) blotting paper; ورق نقدى paper money; ورق اليانصيب *w. al-yā-naṣib* lottery tickets; اوراق الاشغال business papers, commercial papers; اوراق الاعتماد credentials; اوراق الحكومة government bonds; اوراق القضية *a. al-qaḍīya* court records; اوراق مالية securities, bonds; banknotes, paper money; اوراق الموسيقى *a. al-mūsīqā* sheet music; اوراق نقدية (*naqdīya*), ورق النقد *w. an-naqd* banknotes, paper money; حبر على ورق (*ḥibr*) mere ink on paper, of no effect (e.g., treaty, agreement); طرح الاوراق على المائدة to lay the cards on the table; to show one's hand

ورقة *waraqa* (n. un.) leaf; petal; sheet of paper; piece of paper, slip; note; card, ticket; document, record, paper; thin metal plate, leaf of sheet metal | ورقة البريد postcard; ورقة البنك banknote; ورقة مدموغة (*madmūġa*) stamped sheet; ورقة لعب *w. laʻib* playing card; ورقة مالية banknote; bond, security; ورقة الاتهام *w. al-ittihām* bill of indictment

ورقى *waraqī*: نقود ورقية paper money

ورق *wariq* leafy, green, verdant

وراق *warrāq* pl. *-ūn* paper manufacturer, papermaker; stationer; wastepaper dealer; copyist (of manuscripts)

وراقة *wirāqa* papermaking, paper manufacture; stationery business, stationer's trade

وارق *wāriq* leafy, green, verdant

مورق *muwarriq* stationer

مورق *mūriq* leafy

ورك *wark*, *wirk*, *warik* f., pl. اوراك *aurāk* hip, haunch; thigh

ورل *waral* pl. ورلان *wirlān*, اورال *aurāl* varan, monitor lizard (*zool.*)

ورم *warima* يرم *yarimu* (*waram*) to be swollen; to swell, become swollen II to cause to swell, inflate (ه s.th.) | ورم انفه (*anfahū*) to annoy, vex, irritate, infuriate s.o.; ورم بانفه (*bi-anfihī*) to be puffed up, conceited, stuck-up **V** = **I**

ورم *waram* pl. اورام *aurām* swelling, intumescence, tumor | فى انفه ورم (*anfihī*) he is stuck-up

تورم *tawarrum* swelling, rising, intumescence

وارم *wārim* swollen

مورم *muwarram* swollen

ورن *waran* varan, monitor lizard (*zool.*)

ورنش *warnaša* to varnish, lacquer, japan (ه s.th.)

ورنيش *warnīš* varnish, lacquer, japan; shoe polish | ورنيش الارضية *w. al-arḍīya* floor wax

اوره *aurah*², f. ورهاء *warhā'*² stupid, dumb; cheeky, brazenfaced, impudent

وروار *warwār* bee eater (Merops; *zool.*)

¹ورى *warā* يرى *yarī* (*wary*) to kindle, fire, take fire (lighter) **II** do.; to strike fire; to hide, conceal, keep secret, secrete (ه s.th.); to allude (عن ب to s.th. with); to pretend, feign, affect, simulate (ب s.th.) **III** to try to keep secret (ه s.th.); to hide, conceal (ه ه s.th. in); to disguise, mask (ه s.th.) | واراه التراب (*turāba*) to inhume, bury s.o. **IV** = **I**; to strike fire **V** to hide, conceal o.s. (من or عن from) **VI** do.; to disappear from the sight (عن of s.o., also عن الانظار)

الورى *al-warā* the mortals, mankind | خير الورى *ḵair al-w.* the best of all men, the Prophet Mohammed

وراء *warā'a* (prep.) behind, in the rear of, at the back of; after; beyond, past; over and above, beside, in addition to; (adv.) *warā'u* behind, in the rear, at the back | الى الوراء to the rear; backward; كان وراءه to be favorably disposed to s.o., stand behind s.o., support, back s.o.; ما وراء الاردن (*urdunn*) Transjordan; ما وراء الاكمة (*akama*) what is at the bottom of it, what's behind it; وراء الاكمة ما وراءها there is more in it than meets the eye, there is s.th. wrong; ما وراء البحر (*baḥr*) overseas; ما وراء الطبيعة the supernatural, the transcendental; metaphysics; ما وراء النهر (*nahr*) Transoxiana; من وراء *min warā'i* (with foll. genit.) behind, from behind; beyond, past; over and above; by means of, through, by; التكسب من وراء الدعارة (*takassub, di'āra*) professional prostitution; كان من وراء مقدرة العقل البشرى (*maqdurati l-'aqli l-bašarī*) to be beyond the power of human comprehension

ورائى *warā'ī* hind, rear, back, located at the back, directed backward

اورى *aurā* (elative) better concealing (ل s.th.)

تورية *tauriya* hiding, concealment; dissemblance, dissimulation, hypocrisy; equivocation, ambiguity, double-entendre, allusion

²توراة look up alphabetically

¹وز *wazza u* (*wazz*) to incite, set (ه على s.o. against)

²وز *wazz* = اوز *iwazz* (see up alphabetically)

وزب *wazaba* يزب *yazibu* (وزوب *wuzūb*) to flow (water)

ميزاب *mīzāb* pl. ميازيب *mayāzīb*² drain pipe, drain; gutter, sewer; roof gutter | انفتحت ميازيب السماء *infataḥat m. us-samā'* the heavens opened their gates

¹وزر *wazara* يزر *yaziru* (*wizr*) to take upon o.s., carry (ه a burden); — *wazara yaziru* and *wazira* يوزر *yauzaru* (*wizr, wazr,* زرة *zira*) to commit a sin **III** to help, assist, aid, support (ه على s.o. in) **IV** to support,

back up (ه s.o.), strengthen s.o.'s (ه) arm VI to help each other VIII اتزر *ittazara* to wear a loincloth; to put on (ه a garment); to commit a sin

وزر **wizr** pl. اوزار *auzār* heavy load, burden, encumbrance; sin, crime; responsibleness, responsibility | حمله وزره (*ḥammalahū*) to make s.o. bear the responsibility for s.th., make s.o. answerable for s.th.; وضعت الحرب اوزارها *waḍaʻat il-ḥarbu auzārahā* the war has come to an end

وزرة **wizra** pl. *wizarāt* loincloth

وزرة **wazara** pl. *-āt* skirt, skirting (*arch.*)

²وزر V to become a (cabinet) minister X to appoint as (cabinet) minister (ه s.o.); to be appointed as (cabinet) minister

وزير **wazīr** pl. وزراء *wuzarā'*² (cabinet) minister; vizier; queen (in chess) | وزير بلا وزارة (*bi-lā*) minister without portfolio; وزير مفوض (*mufawwaḍ*) minister plenipotentiary (*dipl.*); وزير مقيم (*muqīm*) minister resident (*Tun.*); الوزير الاكبر the Prime Minister (*Tun.*); مجلس الوزراء *majlis al-w.* cabinet, council of ministers; for the various departments see under وزارة

وزارة **wizāra** pl. *-āt* ministry; (rarer, also) cabinet, government | وزارة الارشاد القومى *w. al-iršād al-qaumī* Ministry of National Guidance (*Eg.*); وزارة الاستعلامات ministry of information; وزارة الاشغال العمومية (*ʻumūmīya*) ministry of public works; وزارة الاوقاف ministry of religious endowments, wakf ministry; وزارة البحرية *w. al-baḥrīya* naval department, ministry of the navy; وزارة التجارة ministry of commerce; وزارة التربية والتعليم (*w. at-tarbiya*) ministry of education; وزارة الحربية *w. al-ḥarbīya* war ministry; وزارة الحقانية *w. al-ḥaqqānīya* ministry of justice; وزارة الخارجية *w. al-ḵārijīya* foreign ministry; وزارة الداخلية *w. ad-dāḵilīya* ministry of the interior; وزارة الزراعة ministry of agriculture; وزارة الشؤون الاجتماعية *w. aš-šu'ūn al-ijtimāʻīya* ministry of social affairs; وزارة الشؤون البلدية والقروية (*baladīya, qarawīya*) Ministry of Municipal and Rural Affairs (*Eg.*); وزارة الصحة العمومية *w. aṣ-ṣiḥḥa al-ʻumūmīya* ministry of public health; وزارة الطيران *w. aṭ-ṭayarān* air ministry; وزارة العدل (or العدلية) *w. al-ʻadl* (*al-ʻadlīya*) ministry of justice; وزارة المالية *w. al-mālīya* finance ministry; وزارة المعارف ministry of education; وزارة المواصلات *w. al-muwāṣalāt* ministry of communications

وزارى **wizārī** ministerial

وزع **wazaʻa** يزع *yazaʻu* (*wazʻ*) to curb, restrain (ه s.o.) II to distribute (ه على s.th. among or to, ه بين s.th. among), allot, apportion, deal out (ه على, ه الى s.th. to s.o.); to deliver (ه the mail); pass. *wuzziʻa* to be distributed, be divided (بين among) V to be distributed; to be divided; to divide among themselves, (successively, alternately) beset and torment (ه s.o.; e.g., anxieties, sorrows, thoughts)

اوزاع **auzāʻ** groups or crowds of people

وزيعة **wazīʻa** pl. وزائع *wazā'iʻ*² share, portion, allotment

توزيع **tauzīʻ** distribution (also, e.g., in motion-picture industry); division, apportionment, allotment; delivery; sale, market | توزيع الثروة *t. aṯ-ṯarwa* distribution of (public) wealth; توزيع العمل *t. al-ʻamal* division of labor; توزيع الجوائز distribution of prizes, award of prizes; توزيع الارباح distribution (or payment) of dividends; توزيع مستعجل (*mustaʻjil*) special delivery, express delivery (mail)

وازع **wāziʻ** obstruction, obstacle, impediment

موزع **muwazziʻ** distributing; distributor | موزع البريد postman, mailman

موزع *muwazza'* distributed; scattered, dispersed | موزع الفكر and موزع الخواطر *m. al-fikr* absent-minded; unconcentrated, distraught, scatterbrained

وزال *wazzāl* genista, broom (*bot.*)

وزن *wazana* يزن *yazinu* (*wazn*, زنة *zina*) to weigh (ه s.th.); to balance, equilibrate, equalize, even up (ه s.th.); to weigh out, sell by weight (ه ل s.th. to s.o.) **III** to equal in weight (ه s.th.), be of the same weight as (ه), be balanced (ه with), equilibrate, counterbalance (ه s.th.); to outweigh (ه s.th.), compensate, make up (ه for); to balance, equilibrate, poise (بين two things); to compare (بين — و s.th. with), weigh one thing against the other; to make a comparison, draw a parallel (بين — وبين between — and); to distribute equally (ه s.th.) **VI** to be balanced, be in equilibrium, be counterpoised, be in equipoise

زنة *zina* weighing; weight

وزن *wazn* pl. اوزان *auzān* weight; (poetic) measure, meter; noun or verb pattern, form (*gram.*); tonnage of a vessel); weight, weight class (in boxing, etc.) | لا وزن له (*wazna*) or عديم الوزن imponderable; insignificant, of no consequence, negligible; اقام وزنا كبيرا ل to attach great importance to, set great store by; مصلحة الوزن والكيل *maṣlaḥat al-w. wa-l-kail* bureau of standards; وزن الديك *w. ad-dīk* bantamweight (boxing); الوزن الفارغ dead weight

وزنة *wazna* pl. *wazanāt* weight; gold or silver talent; (*Ir.*) weight of about 100 kg (varying; officially 108.835 kg) | وزنة اضافية (*iḍāfīya*) additional weight, overweight

وزنى *wazni* weight- (in compounds), of weight; ponderable, appreciable; weighty, ponderous, grave

وزان *wizāna* (prep.) commensurate with, corresponding to, in conformity with, in analogy to, following the model or pattern of

وزين *wazīn* weighty, ponderous | وزين الرأى of sound judgment, judicious

ميزان *mīzān* pl. موازين *mawāzīn*[2] balance, scales; weight; measure; poetic measure, meter; rule, method; justice, equity, fairness, impartiality; الميزان Libra, Balance (*astron.*) | ميزان الحرارة *m. al-ḥarāra* thermometer; ميزان راصد self-registering scales; ميزان طبلى (*ṭablī*) weighing machine, platform scale; weighbridge; ميزان الماء spirit level, level

ميزانية *mīzānīya* balance, equilibrium, equipoise; balance (*com.*); budget | ميزانية ملحقة (*mulḥaqa*) supplementary budget

موازنة *muwāzana* equality of weight, balance, equilibrium, equipoise; outweighing; counterbalance, counterpoise, counterweight, compensation; stabilizing effect; comparing, weighing; comparison, parallel (بين between); budget; (*tun.*) timetable, schedule

توازن *tawāzun* balance, equilibrium, equipoise; poise, balance; balancing, poising | توازن سياسى (*siyāsī*) political balance; توازن القوى *t. al-quwā* balance of power; اعاد التوازن بين to restore the balance between

اتزان *ittizān* balance, equilibrium, equipoise; mental health; harmony; impartiality

وازن *wāzin* weighing; of full weight; drunk, tight

موزون *mauzūn* weighed; of full weight; balanced, in equilibrium, evenly poised; well-considered, well-advised, deliberate; well-balanced, well-proportioned, well-measured; rhythmically balanced; of sound judgment, judicious

موازن *muwāzin* outweighing, counterbalancing, equal, equivalent

متوازن *mutawāzin* balanced, in equilibrium

متزن *muttazin* balanced, measured, regular; well-balanced, harmonious (in color, and the like)

وزى III to be parallel (ه to s.th.); to be opposite s.th. (ه), be the counterpart (ه of); to correspond, amount, be equal or equivalent (ه to), equal (ه s.th.) VI to be parallel, run side by side; to be mutually corresponding, be equivalent

موازاة *muwāzāh* equal distance; parallelism; equivalence

تواز *tawāzin* equal distance; parallelism; equivalence | على التوازى side by side, parallel

مواز *muwāzin* parallel; equivalent

متواز *mutawāzin* parallel; similar | متوازى الاضلاع ○ parallelogram; ○ متوازى السطوح parallelepiped

وسخ *wasiḵa* يوسخ *yausaḵu* (*wasaḵ*) to be or become dirty II and IV to dirty, soil, sully, stain, foul (ه s.th.) V and VIII اتسخ *ittasaḵa* = I

وسخ *wasaḵ* pl. اوساخ *ausāḵ* dirt; filth, squalor

وسخ *wasiḵ* dirty, filthy, soiled, sullied, unclean

وساخة *wasāḵa* dirtiness, filthiness, uncleanness, dirt, filth, squalor

وسد II to put under s.o.'s (ه) head (ه a pillow), rest, lay (ه ه s.o.'s head on), bed (ه ه s.o. on) | وسده التراب (*turāba*) to lay s.o. or s.th. to rest in the ground; وسده صدره (*ṣadrahū*) to take s.o. to one's breast, hug s.o. V to lay one's head on a pillow (ه); to rest or recline on a pillow or cushion (ه)

وساد *wasād, wusād, wisād* pl. وسد *wusud* pillow, cushion | لزم الوساد *lazima l-wasāda* to be confined to bed

وسادة *wisāda* pl. *-āt,* وسائد *wasā'id*[2] pillow, cushion

موسد *muwassad* easy, smooth, paved (way)

موسر see يسر

وسط II to place, put, or set in the middle (ه s.th.); to choose or appoint as mediator (ه بين s.o. between) V to be in the middle or center (ه of); to stand in the middle, keep to the middle, hold the middle between two extremes, steer a middle course; to mediate (ب ل for s.o. s.th.; بين between), act as mediator or go-between (ق in)

وسط *wasaṭ, wasṭ* pl. اوساط *ausāṭ* middle; center, heart; waist; milieu, environment, surroundings, sphere; means, instrument, agent, medium; mediocrity, medium quality, average; pl. circles, quarters, classes, strata (of the population); — *wasaṭ* pl. اوساط *ausāṭ* median, medial, middle, central; in the middle, middle-of-the-road, moderate; intermediate (between two extremes); middling, mediocre, average, mean, medium; — *wasṭa* (prep.) in the middle, heart, or center of, in the midst of, amid, among | ق وسط من (*wasaṭin*) in the middle or midst of, within; ق الوسط in the very center; midway; of medium quality; ق وسطنا in our midst, among us; وسط الصيف *w. aṣ-ṣaif* midsummer; حجم وسط (*ḥajm*) medium size; حل وسط (*ḥall*) middle solution, middle course, compromise; السيرة الوسط (*saira*) medium pace; a moderate, neutral attitude; الاوساط الدبلوماسية diplomatic circles; الاوساط العامة (*'āmma*) the general public, the public at large; اوساط الناس the middle classes

وسطى *wasaṭī, wasṭī* of or relative to the milieu or environment

وسطانى *wasṭānī* middle, central, medial, median; intermediate; middling, medium, mediocre

وسطية *wasṭīya* pl. *-āt* patio, inner courtyard

وساطة *wisāṭa* mediation, intervention; good offices, recommendation, intercession | بوساطة by means of, through, by, per; عن وساطة فلان through the good offices of s.o.; قدم وساطته ل to offer one's good offices for

وسيط *wasīṭ* pl. وسطاء *wusaṭā'*[2] middle, intermediary, intermediate, medial, median; mediator, intercessor; intermediary; agent, go-between, broker, middleman; medium (occultism) | العصر الوسيط (*'aṣr*) the Middle Ages

وسيطة *wasīṭa* pl. وسائط *wasā'iṭ*[2] means, medium | وسائط المواصلات والنقل *w. al-muwāṣalāt wa-n-naql* means of communication and transportation

اوسط *ausaṭ*[2] pl. اواسط *awāsiṭ*[2], f. وسطى *wusṭā* pl. وسط *wusaṭ* middle, central; الوسطى the middle finger | فى اواسط هذا الاسبوع (*usbū'*) in the middle of this week; اواسط الشهر *a. aš-šahr* the middle of the month; اواسط افريقية Central Africa; اوروبا الوسطى (*urubbā*) Central Europe; الشرق الاوسط (*šarq*) the Middle East; الطبقات الوسطى (*ṭabaqāt*) the middle classes; القرون (or العصور) الوسطى the Middle Ages; نتيجة وسطى mean result, average

توسط *tawassuṭ* mediation, intervention; situation or position in the middle, intermediateness, intermediacy; mediocrity

واسطة *wāsiṭa* pl. وسائط *wasā'iṭ*[2] mediator, mediatress, intermediary; mediacy, agency, instrumentality, agent, device, means, medium; expedient | بواسطة by means of, through, by, per; on the part of, by; بالواسطة indirectly, mediately; بهذه الواسطة by this means or device, by that; بواسطة ذلك by means of that, by that; واسطة الاتصال *w. al-ittiṣāl* link

متوسط *mutawassiṭ* middle, medium; medial, median, intermediate; centrally located, central; mediating, intermediary; mediator, go-between; mean, average | متوسطو الحال those of average means; متوسط الحجم *m. al-ḥajm* middle-sized, of medium size; متوسط العمر *m. al-'umr* middle-aged; متوسط القامة of medium height, middle-sized; متوسط النوع *m. an-nau'* middling, of medium quality; البحر الابيض المتوسط (*baḥr, abyaḍ*) the Mediterranean; موجات متوسطة (*maujāt*) medium waves (*radio*); متوسط الهجوم center forward (soccer)

وسع *wasu'a* يوسع *yausu'u* (وساعة *wasā'a*) to be wide, roomy, spacious, vast, extensive; — *wusi'u* يسع *yasa'u* (سعة *sa'a*) to be wide, roomy, spacious; to be well-to-do, be well off; to hold, accommodate, house, seat, etc. (ه, ه s.o., s.th.), have room, have capacity (ه, ه for); to contain, comprise, comprehend, encompass, include (ه s.th.); to be large enough, suffice, be sufficient, adequate, enough (ه, ه for); — *wasi'a yasa'u* (وسع *wus'*, سعة *sa'a*) esp. with negation: to be possible (ه for s.o.), be permitted, be allowed (ه to s.o.), be in s.o.'s (ه) power, be up to s.o. (ه); to be able (ه to do s.th.), be capable (ه of); to be allowed (ه to do s.th.) | لا يسعنى أن اقول I cannot say; ما اسع ذلك I can't do that
II to make wider, roomier, more spacious (ه s.th.); to extend, expand (ه s.th.); to widen, enlarge (ه or من s.th.); to broaden (ه s.th.); to be generous, liberal, openhanded (على toward s.o., ه ه toward s.o. with s.th.); to make rich, enrich (على s.o.) | وسع خطاه (*kuṭāhu*) to take longer strides, stride out, quicken one's pace; وسع المكان ل (*makāna*) to make room for **IV** = **II**; to be or become rich | اوسعه برا (*birran*) to

treat s.o. with the greatest reverence, bestow ample favors upon s.o.: اوسعه شتما (*šatman*) to heap abuse on s.o.; اوسعه ضربا (*ḍarban*) to give s.o. a sound beating, wallop s.o.; اوسع النفقة (*nafaqata*) to incur great expenses **V** to be extended, be expanded, be widened; to spread (out), extend, widen, expand; to have enough room, sit comfortably; to make o.s. comfortable, make o.s. at home (ف in); to enlarge, expatiate (ف on), talk or write at great length (ف about); to proceed (ف in); to continue (ف s.th., in s.th.) | توسع فى النفقة (*nafaqa*) to incur great expenses **VIII** اتسع ***ittasaʿa*** to be extended, be expanded, be widened, be enlarged; to expand, widen, grow, increase; to stretch far and wide, be vast; to extend, range; to become rich; to be large or wide enough, suffice, be sufficient, adequate, enough (ل for); to hold, accommodate, house, seat, etc. (ل s.o., s.th.), have room (ل for); to be at s.o.'s (ل) disposal; to be susceptible (ل of); to be able (ه to do s.th.), be capable (ه of) | بكل ما تتسع له الكلمة من معنى (*kalimatu, maʿnan*) in the widest sense of the word **X** to widen, expand, become wider; to become larger, increase in size; to find wide or large (ه s.th.)

سعة ***saʿa*** wideness, roominess, spaciousness; extent, range, compass; volume, holding capacity, capacity; capability, faculty, power, ability; comfortableness, comfort; plenty, abundance, profusion; luxury, affluence, wealth | ذو سعة well-to-do, wealthy; عن سعة or بسعة amply, abundantly; على الرحب والسعة (*ruḥb*) welcome! على قدر سعتى (*qadri saʿatī*) to the best of my abilities; كان فى سعة من رزقه (*rizqihī*) to be wealthy, live in luxury; سعة الصدر *s. aṣ-ṣadr* patience, long-suffering; سعة كهربائية (*kahrabāʾīya*) electric capacity; ○ سعة الموجة *s. al-mauja* amplitude (*el.*)

وسع ***wusʿ*** ability, capability, faculty; capacity; power, strength; holding capacity | وسعه *wusʿuhū* what he can do, what is in his power; فى وسعه ان it is in his power to ..., he can ...; فى وسعى ان اقول I can, or I may, say; ليس فى وسعه الا (*illā*) he has no other possibility but ..., he cannot but ...; بذل وسعه to go to great pains, do one's best or utmost

وسع ***wasaʿ*** vastness, vast space

وسعة ***wusʿa*** wideness, roominess, spaciousness; extent, range, compass; plenty, abundance, profusion (من of)

وسيع ***wasīʿ*** pl. وساع ***wisāʿ*** wide, vast; roomy, spacious, large; capacious

اوسع ***ausaʿ***[2] wider, larger, roomier, more spacious | أوسع صدرا (*ṣadran*) more patient; اوسع مدى (*madan*) broader, wider

توسيع ***tausīʿ*** widening, expansion; broadening, extension; enlargement, increase

توسعة ***tausiʿa***: اجل التوسعة *ajal at-t.* reprieve, respite (*jur.*)

توسع ***tawassuʿ*** extending, extension, widening, increase, enlargement; expansion | مع التوسع in a wider sense, by extension; توسع استعمارى (*istiʿmārī*) imperialistic expansion; ○ توسع الحرب *t. al-ḥarb* extension of the (theater of) war; سياسة التوسع *siyāsat at-t.* policy of expansion

توسعى ***tawassuʿī*** expansionist (adj.) | سياسة توسعية (*siyāsa*) policy of expansion, expansionist policy

اتساع ***ittisāʿ*** extending, extension, extensiveness, wideness, spaciousness, vastness, expanse, range, scope, compass, extent; ○ amplitude (*el.*); ○ gauge (of railroad tracks); sufficiency, adequacy | اتساع فى الكلام (*kalām*) vagueness of expression; عدم الاتساع ل *ʿadam al-itt.* insufficiency, inadequacy for

واسع *wāsiʿ* wide; broad; large, roomy, spacious, vast, sweeping, extensive; far-reaching | واسع الانتشار widespread; واسع الرحمة (العدل) *w. ar-raḥma* (*al-ʿadl*) abounding in mercy (in justice); واسع الصدر *w. aṣ-ṣadr* patient; forbearing, indulgent, generous, magnanimous; واسع النطاق far-reaching, extensive; comprehensive; large-scale; رجل واسع الحيلة (*rajul, ḥīla*) a resourceful, ingenious man; ثوب واسع (*ṯaub*) wide or loose garment; سهل واسع (*sahl*) vast (sweeping) plain; شارع واسع broad street

موسوعة *mausūʿa* pl. *-āt* comprehensive work; encyclopedia; thesaurus

موسوعى *mausūʿī* encyclopedic

موسع *mūsiʿ* rich, wealthy

متسع *muttasiʿ* wide, extensive, vast, spacious, roomy, large; ample, abundant, sufficient

متسع *muttasaʿ* space; room | لم يجد متسعا من الوقت ل (*yajid, waqt*) or لم يكن فى الوقت متسع ل (*yakun*) not to have enough time for; ○ متسع حيوى (*ḥayawī*) lebensraum

وسق *wasaqa* يسق *yasiqu* (*wasq*) to load, freight (ه ه a ship with) **IV** do. **VIII** اتسق *ittasaqa* to be in good order, be well-ordered; to harmonize, be in keeping (مع with) **X** to be or become possible (ل for s.o.)

وسق *wasq* pl. وسوق *wusūq*, اوساق *ausāq* load, freight, cargo

اتساق *ittisāq* harmony

متسق *muttasiq* in good order, well-ordered; balanced, harmonious

وسكى *wiskī* whiskey

وسل **V** to ingratiate o.s., curry favor (الى with), seek to gain access (الى to), seek or solicit s.o.'s (الى) favor; to implore, beseech, entreat (الى s.o.), plead (الى with s.o.); to ask s.o.'s (ب) help, turn with a request (ب to s.o.); to use as a means (ب s.th.), make use (ب of a means)

وسيلة *wasīla* pl. وسائل *wasāʾil*² means, medium; device, expedient, instrument, tool, agent; measure, step | وسائل الاحتياط precautionary measures, precautions; وسائل التعليم educational aids, training aids, material of instruction; وسائل التكييف air-conditioning installation; وسائل المواصلات *w. al-muwāṣalāt* means of communication; وسائل النقل *w. an-naql* means of transportation; ابتغى الوسيلة to try to ingratiate o.s. (الى ب with s.o. by s.th.); اتخذ منه وسيلة ل (*ittakaḏa*) to regard s.th. as an expedient for ...

توسل *tawassul* request, entreaty, fervent plea; petition, application | توسلا الى *tawassulan ilā* so as to succeed by this means in ..., in order to get to the point where ...

وسم *wasama* يسم *yasimu* (*wasm*, سمة *sima*) to brand (ه cattle); to stamp, mark, brand (ه ,ه ب s.o., s.th. as) | وسمه بالعار to brand s.o. as infamous, stigmatize s.o.; وسم جبينه ب (*wusima jabīnuhū*) to be written in s.o.'s face **II** to distinguish (ه s.o.), confer distinction (ه upon s.o.), award a decoration or order (ه to) **V** to scrutinize, regard attentively, watch closely (ه s.th.); to examine carefully (ه s.th.); to regard (ه s.o.), look at (ه); to be marked, characterized (ب by) | توسم فيه خيرا (*kairan*) to see promising signs in s.o., expect a lot of good of s.o., set great hopes on s.o. **VIII** اتسم *ittasama* to be branded; to be marked, characterized (ب by); to bear the stamp of (ب)

سمة *sima* pl. *-āt* sign, mark, characteristic; outward characteristic, feature, trait; stamp, impress, character (of s.th.); visa (*Saudi Ar.*); pl. *-āt* also: features, facial expression, mien, bearing

وسم *wasm* pl. وسوم *wusūm* brand; tribal mark, tribal brand; characteristic, mark; coat of arms

وسام *wisām* pl. اوسمة *ausima* badge; decoration, medal; order; badge of honor | وسام الاستحقاق order of merit; وسام ربطة الساق *w. rabṭat as-sāq* Order of the Garter; وسام الشرف (جوقة الشرف) *w. aš-šaraf* (*jauqat aš-š.*) Legion of Honor; الوسام العلوى (*ʿalawī*) the Moroccan "Ouissam alaouite"

وسامة *wasāma* grace, gracefulness, charm, beauty

وسيم *wasīm* pl. وسماء *wusamāʾ*[2], وسام *wisām* graceful, comely, pretty, good-looking; beautiful (face)

موسم *mausim* pl. مواسم *mawāsim*[2] time of the year, season; festive season (الموسم specif., the Muslim hadj festival); festival, feast day, holiday; fair; fixed date, deadline; harvest | المواسم والاعياد the feasts and holidays; موسم الاصطياف summer season (of a health resort); موسم تمثيلى (*tamṯīlī*) or موسم مسرحى (*masraḥī*) theater season; موسم الحج *m. al-ḥajj* season of the Pilgrimage; موسم القطن *m. al-quṭn* cotton harvest, cotton season

موسمى *mausimī*: الريح الموسمية (*rīḥ*) the monsoon

ميسم *mīsam* pl. مواسم *mawāsim*[2], مياسم *mayāsim*[2] branding iron; brand; stigma

موسوم *mausūm* branded; stigmatized; marked, characterized (ب with)

وسن *wasina* يوسن *yausanu* (*wasan*, سنة *sina*) to sleep, slumber

وسن *wasan* slumber, doze

سنة *sina* slumber, doze | سنة من النوم (*naum*) a short nap

وسن *wasin* sleepy, drowsy, somnolent

وسنان *wasnān*[2], f. وسنى *wasnā* sleepy, drowsy, somnolent

وسوس *waswasa* to speak under one's breath, whisper (ل or الى to s.o.); to instill evil (ل or الى in s.o.; passion, devil), prompt or tempt s.o. (ل or الى) with wicked suggestions; to awaken doubts, arouse scruples (ل or الى in s.o.'s mind; conscience) **II** *tawaswasa* to feel uneasy, have scruples, be anxious, worried, full of apprehensions; to be in doubt, have misgivings, be suspicious

وسوسة *waswasa* pl. وساوس *wasāwis*[2] devilish insinuation, temptation; disturbance; scruple; misgiving, suspicion; rustling, rustle, whisper (of leaves, and the like)

وسواس *waswās* pl. وساوس *wasāwis*[2] devilish insinuation, temptation; wicked thoughts; doubt, misgiving, suspicion; delusion, fixed idea; uneasiness, anxiety, concern; melancholy; الوسواس the Tempter, Satan | وسواس القطن *w. al-quṭn* cotton buds

موسوس *muwaswas* obsessed with delusions

[1]**وسى** **IV** to shave (ه the head)

موسى *mūsā* f., pl. مواس *mawāsin*, امواس *amwās* straight razor; see also alphabetically

[2]**وسى** **III** (variant of اسى **III**) and مواساة see اسى

وشب *wišb* pl. اوشاب *aušāb* horde, mob, crowd

وشيج *wašīj*: وشيج الاتصال *w. al-ittiṣāl* closely connected

وشيجة *wašīja* pl. وشائج *wašāʾij*[2] close tie

متواشج *mutawāšij* connected, interrelated

وشح **II** to adorn or dress (ه s.o., with the *wišāḥ*, q.v.) **V** and **VIII** اتشح *ittašaḥa* to put on, don (ب a belt, sash, and the like); to throw on loosely (ب a cloak or

68

similar garment); to garb o.s. (ب with); to assume (ب a name), go by a name (ب)

وشاح *wišāḥ*, *wušāḥ* pl. وشح *wušuḥ*, اوشحة *auśiḥa*, وشائح *wašā'iḥ*² ornamented belt worn by women (in older times, a double band worn sashlike over the shoulder); sash, scarf, cummerbund; band (esp., of an order); tie, bond (fig.); swordbelt; military sash

وشاحة *wišāḥa* sword

توشيح *taušīḥ* pl. تواشيح *tawāšīḥ*² composition (*mus.*); postclassical form of Arab poetry, arranged in stanzas

موشح *muwaššaḥ*, موشحة *muwaššaḥa* pl. -*āt* postclassical form of Arab poetry, arranged in stanzas

متشح *muttašiḥ* clad, garbed, attired (ب in)

وشر *wašara* يشر *yaširu* (*wašr*) to saw, saw apart (ه s.th.)

موشور *maušūr* pl. مواشير *mawāšīr*² prism

موشوري *maušūrī* prismatic(al)

وشع II to reel, spool (ه cotton)

وشيع *wašī'* hedge

وشيعة *wašī'a* pl. وشائع *wašā'i'*² reel, spool, bobbin | وشيعة التحريض induction coil (*el.*)

وشق *wašaq* lynx (*zool.*)

وشك *wašuka* يوشك *yaušuku* (*wašk*, وشاكة *wašāka*) and II to be quick, hurry IV to be on the point or verge (أن of doing s.th.), be about to do s.th. (على or ان), be close (على to) | يوشك أن he almost ..., he all but ...

وشك *wašk*, *wušk* speed, swiftness, hurry | على وشك ان on the point or verge of (doing s.th.), about to (do s.th.), على وشك الخروج about to go out, just going out

وشكان *waškān*, *wuškān* speed, swiftness

وشيك *wašīk* imminent, impending, near, forthcoming | وشيك الزوال *w. az-zawāl* doomed to early ruin; وشيك الحل *w. al-ḥall* close to a solution, almost solved (problem)

وشل *wašal* pl. اوشال *aušāl* dripping water, tears

وشم *wašama* يشم *yašimu* (*wašm*) and II to tattoo (ه s.th.)

وشم *wašm* pl. وشام *wišām*, وشوم *wušūm* tattoo, tattoo mark

وشيمة *wašīma* enmity, hostility, malice

وشنة *wašna*, *wišna* (*eg.*) morello, mahaleb cherry

وشوش *wašwaša* to whisper in s.o.'s (ه) ear II *tawašwaša* to whisper

وشوشة *wašwaša* whispering, whisper

وشى *wašā* يشى *yašī* (*wašy*) to embellish, ornament with many colors, embroider (ه a fabric); — (*wašy*, وشاية *wišāya*) to slander, defame (ب ال s.o. with); to inform (ب against), denounce, betray (ب s.o.) II to embellish, ornament with many colors, embroider (ه a fabric)

شية *šiya* pl. -*āt* blotch, spot; blemish, flaw, fault, defect; mark, sign

وشى *wašy* pl. وشاء *wišā'* many-colored ornamentation, embroidery; embroidered or painted fabric

وشاء *waššā'* vendor of embroidered or painted fabrics

وشاية *wišāya* defamation, slander

توشية *taušiya* embellishment, ornamentation; embroidery

واش *wāšin* pl. واشون *wāšūn*, وشاة *wušāh* traitor; slanderer, calumniator; informer, denunciator

وصب **waṣaba** يصب *yaṣibu* (وصوب *wuṣūb*) to last; — *waṣiba* يوصب *yauṣabu* (*waṣab*) and **V** to be (chronically) ill

وصب *waṣab* pl. اوصاب *auṣāb* illness; discomfort, hardship, suffering

واصب *wāṣib* lasting, permanent

وصد **waṣada** يصد *yaṣidu* (*waṣad*) to be firm, stand firmly **IV** to close, shut (ه a door) | اوصد الباب فى وجهه (*wajhihī*) to block s.o.'s way, deny s.o. access

وصيد *waṣīd* pl. وصد *wuṣud* threshold, doorstep

وصف **waṣafa** يصف *yaṣifu* (*waṣf*) to describe, depict, portray, picture (ه, ه s.o., s.th.); to characterize (ه, ه s.o., s.th.); to praise, laud, extol (ه s.o.); to attribute, ascribe (ه ب to s.o. a quality), credit (ه ب s.o. with), praise (ه ب s.o. for), say s.th. (ب) to s.o.'s (ه) credit; to prescribe (ه ل a medicine to s.o.) | لا يوصف (*yūṣafu*) indescribable; nondescript **VI** to describe to one another, tell one another (ه s.th.) **VIII** اتصف *ittaṣafa* to be described; to possess as a characteristic (ب a quality or peculiarity); to be distinguished, known, characterized, marked (ب by a quality, property, peculiarity) **X** to consult (ه a doctor)

صفة *ṣifa* pl. *-āt* quality, property; attribute; characteristic, distinguishing mark, peculiarity; adjective (*gram.*); asyndetic relative clause (without relative pronoun; *gram.*); way, manner | بصفة as, in the capacity of; بصفته وزيرا in his capacity of minister, as a minister; بصفة خاصة (*ḵāṣṣa*) in particular, especially, specifically; بصفة غير رسمية (*ġairi rasmīyatin*) unofficially

وصف *waṣf* description, depiction, portrayal, characterization; — (pl. اوصاف *auṣāf*) quality, property; characteristic, distinguishing mark, peculiarity; adjective (*gram.*); pl. اوصاف description of a person | شىء يفوق الوصف (*yafūqu l-waṣfa*) a thing beyond description, an indescribable thing; اخذ اوصافه to take down s.o.'s personal description

وصفة *waṣfa* description, depiction, portrayal; medical prescription

وصفى *waṣfī* descriptive, depictive

وصاف *waṣṣāf* describer, depicter

وصيف *waṣīf* pl. وصفاء *wuṣafā'*[2] servant; page

وصيفة *waṣīfa* pl. وصائف *waṣā'if*[2] maid, servant girl; maid of honor, lady in waiting

مواصفة *muwāṣafa* detailed description; explanation, interpretation; specification; pl. *-āt* specifications | مواصفة العلاج directions for treatment

موصوف *mauṣūf* described, depicted, portrayed, pictured; characterized (ب by), having as an attribute (ب s.th.); noun followed by an attribute or asyndetic relative clause (*gram.*); prescribed

متصف *muttaṣif* characterized (ب by), possessing as a property or an attribute (ب s.th.)

مستوصف *mustauṣaf* pl. *-āt* clinic

وصل **waṣala** يصل *yaṣilu* (*waṣl*, صلة *ṣila*) to connect, join, unite, combine, link, interlock (ب ه s.th. with), attach (ب ه s.th. to); to establish (صلة *ṣilatan* a contact, a connection; a relation بين — و between — and); to bring into relation (بين — و s.th. with s.th. else); to give (ب ه s.o. s.th.), bestow, confer (ب ه upon s.o. s.th.), award (ب ه to s.o. s.th.); — (وصول *wuṣūl*) to arrive (الى or ه at a place); to come to s.o.'s (الى or ه) hands; to reach (الى or ه, ه s.o., s.th.); to come, get (الى or ه, ه to); to reach (الى or ه an amount), amount to (الى or ه); to enter (الى a phase); to get (ب الى s.o. to or to the point where) | وصلنى خطاب I have received a letter; وصله

يصل هذا الخبر (*kabar*) he received the news; يصل هذا الى حد كذا (*ḥaddi k.*) this gets to the point where ...; وصل الى الصفحة الحاسمة (*ṣafḥa*) to enter the decisive phase **II** to connect, join, unite, combine (ه ب s.th. with); to make (ه, ه s.o., s.th.) get (الى to), see that s.o. or s.th. (ه, ه) gets to (ه); to get, take, bring, move, lead, show, conduct, convey, channel (ه الى, ه s.o., s.th. to); to give (ه s.o.) a ride, a lift; to carry, transport, transfer, convey (ه الى s.th. to); to deliver, transmit, communicate (ه الى s.th. to); to conduct, act as a conductor (*el.*); to accompany, escort (ه الى s.o. to); to connect (ه الى s.th. to an electric circuit, ه ب one apparatus with another, an electric device with the main line), plug in (ه s.th.); to turn on, switch on (ه s.th.; *el.*) **III** to continue (في or ه s.th.), proceed (في or ه in or with); to persist, persevere (في or ه in); to be connected (ه with), bear (ه on), belong, pertain (ه to); to be close friends, maintain close relations (ه with s.o.); to have sexual intercourse (ها with a woman) | واصل الليل بالنهار (*laila, nahāri*) to work day and night; واصل جهده (or سعيه) في (*jahdahū, sa'yahū*) to make untiring efforts for **IV** = **II**; ○ to put through (a long-distance call) | اوصل كل ذى حق بحقه (*kulla dī ḥaqqin bi-ḥaqqihī*) to give everyone his due **V** to obtain access (الى to); to gain access by certain means (الى to), get (الى into) in some way or other; to attain (الى to), arrive (الى at), reach (الى s.th.), come by s.th. (الى) **VI** to be interconnected; to form an uninterrupted sequence **VIII** اتصل *ittaṣala* to be joined (ب to), be connected (ب with); to combine, unite (ب with); to get in touch (ب with s.o., also, e.g., by telephone); to contact (ب s.o.); to have relation (ب to), bear (ب on), be connected, have to do (ب with); to join (ب s.o. or s.th.); to be attached (ب to); to be near s.o. or a place (ب), be adjacent, continuous (ب to), adjoin (ب s.th.), border, abut (ب on), belong (ب to); to come to s.o.'s (ب) knowledge; to be continued, continue, go on; to be continuous, form a continuous chain; to be related (الى to); to trace one's descent (الى to); to come, get (الى to), arrive (الى at), reach (الى s.th.) | قد اتصل بنا ان it has come to our knowledge that ...; اتصل به تلفونيا to get in touch with s.o. by telephone, have o.s. connected with; اتصلت به النار to catch fire

صلة *ṣila* pl. *-āt* junction, juncture; relation; connection; link, tie, bond; relationship, kinship; present, gift, grant; syndetic relative clause (*gram.*); ○ leadin, lead-in wire (*radio*) | صلة الوصل *ṣ. al-waṣl* connecting link

وصل *waṣl* junction, juncture, connection; union, combination; linkage, nexus; synopsis, summary; reunion of lovers; (pl. اوصال *auṣāl*) relation, link, tie, connection; contact (*el.*); (pl. وصولات *wuṣūlāt*) voucher, receipt | وصل الفائت synopsis of the previous chapters of a newspaper serial; ليلة الوصل *lailat al-w.* last night of a lunar month

وصل *wuṣl*, *wiṣl* pl. اوصال *auṣāl* limb, member (of the body); pl. articulations, joints | حل اوصاله (*ḥalla*) or قطع اوصاله to dismember, dissect s.th.

وصلة *waṣla* a character (ٱ) over silent alif (*gram.*)

وصلة *wuṣla* pl. *-āt*, وصل *wuṣal* junction, juncture; connection; contact (*el.*); attachment, fastening, fixture; tie, link; joint (also *arch.*); hinge; connecting piece, coupling; inset, insertion; overlap (*arch.*); line of communication; hyphen | وصلة التمدد *w. at-tamaddud* expansion joint (*arch.*)

وصلية *wuṣlīya* connecting road, side road; feeder road

وصول *wuṣūl* arrival; attainment, obtainment, achievement; receipt; (pl. *-āt*) receipt, voucher

وصولى *wuṣūlī* upstart, parvenu

وصيل *waṣīl* inseparable friend, intimate, chum

الموصل *al-mauṣil* Mosul (city in N Iraq)

توصيل *tauṣīl* uniting, joining, connecting; supply, feed; connection, junction; electric contact, feed wire, feeder; electric circuit, connection layout, connection; conductivity (*el.*); communication, transmission, transfer, conveyance; delivery; execution, dispatch, discharge; (pl. تواصيل *tawāṣīl*²) receipt, voucher | ○ توصيل الى الارض (*arḍ*) ground connection, ground (*radio*); ○ توصيل على التضاعف (*taḍā'uf*) multiple connection, series parallel (*el.*); ○ توصيل على التوازى (*tawāzī*) parallel connection (*el.*); ○ توصيل على التوالى series connection (*el.*); جيد التوصيل *jayyid at-t.* of good conductivity, good conductor (*el.*); ○ سداد التوصيل *saddād at-t.* (male) plug (*el.*)

توصيلة *tauṣīla* connection, contact (*el.*) | توصيلة الارض *t. al-arḍ* ground connection (*radio*)

وصال *wiṣāl* reunion, being together (of lovers); communion (in love)

مواصلة *muwāṣala* connection; continuation, continuance; continuity; pl. *-āt* lines of communication, communications | مواصلة حديدية (*ḥadīdīya*) rail communication; مواصلة سلكية (*silkīya*) wire communication; أسباب المواصلة means of communication, communications; طرق المواصلات *ṭuruq al-m.* traffic routes; وزارة المواصلات ministry of communications

ايصال *īṣāl* pl. *-āt* joining, connecting, junction; uniting, union; connection; communication; conveyance; transport, transportation; passage; transmission; putting through (of a long-distance call); receipt, voucher

توصل *tawaṣṣul* attainment (الى of an objective), achievement (الى of a purpose); arrival; reunion

تواصل *tawāṣul* continuance; continuity | بتواصل continually, persistently

اتصال *ittiṣāl* connectedness, unitedness, union; juncture, conjunction, link; connection; contact; liaison; establishment of contacts; tuning in (of a radio); contacting (ب of), getting in touch (ب with); junction, intersection (of two roads); continuance, continuation; continuity | على اتصال ب in touch with; استمر فى اتصاله به (*istamarra*) to keep in touch with s.o.; نقط الاتصال *nuqaṭ al-itt.* points of contact; اتصال تليفونى telephone connection

موصول *mauṣūl* bound, tied; glued, riveted (ب to), fixed (ب on; of the eyes); relative pronoun (*gram.*) | اياما موصولة (*ayyāman*) for several (or many) consecutive days, for some time

موصل *muwaṣṣil* pl. *-āt* conductor (*el.*) | ○ موصل ارضى (*arḍī*) ground wire (*radio*); ○ موصل سلكى (*silkī*) wire, wiring (*el.*)

متواصل *mutawāṣil* persistent, continued, continuous, continual, unceasing, incessant, uninterrupted

متصل *muttaṣil* persistent, continued, continuous, continual, unceasing, incessant, uninterrupted; adjoining, adjacent, contiguous | ضمير متصل pronominal suffix (*gram.*); متصل الحلقات *m. al-ḥalaqāt* closely interlinked, closely connected

وصم *waṣama* يصم *yaṣimu* to disgrace, tarnish, blemish (ه name, honor); to afflict with the blemish (ب of s.th.; ه s.o.), put the blame for s.th. (ب) on s.o. (ه) **V** to be tarnished, sullied (honor)

وصم *waṣm* disgrace

وصمة *waṣma* disgrace; mark of disgrace, stain, blot, blemish; fault, flaw, shortcoming, defect; ailing condition, malaise

توصيم *tauṣīm* ailing condition, malaise

وصوص *waṣwaṣa* to peep through a hole or crack; (also = وسوس) to whisper

وصوص *waṣwaṣ* and وصواص *waṣwāṣ* pl. وصاوص *waṣāwiṣ*[2] peephole

وصوصة *waṣwaṣa* furtive glance, peep, peek

وصى II and IV to entrust, commend, commit (ه ب to s.o.'s charge or care s.o.); to direct, bid, advise, counsel (ه ب s.o. to do s.th.), recommend (ه ب to s.o. s.th.), impress (ه ب on s.o. s.th.); to order (ه s.o., ب to do s.th.), charge, commission (ه ب s.o. with), enjoin (ه ب on s.o. s.th.), make s.th. (ب) incumbent (ه on s.o.); to order (ه ب from s.o. s.th.), give s.o. (ه) an order for (ب), place an order (ه ب with s.o. for); to decree (ب s.th.); to make one's will; to will, determine or decree by will (ان that); to bequeath, make over, transfer by will (ل ب to s.o. s.th.); to appoint as executor (الى s.o.) | اوصاه خيرا ب (*ḵairan*) he urged him to take care of X استوصى به خيرا (*ḵairan*) to make s.th. one's concern (or one's business), make a point of s.th. (in deference to another's recommendation); to mean well, have the best intentions with; استوصى بالاجر خيرا (*bi-l-ajri ḵairan*) to fix a moderate or low price

وصى *waṣīy* pl. اوصياء *auṣiyā'*[2] plenipotentiary, mandatory, authorized agent, commissioner; executor; legal guardian, curator, tutor; administrator, caretaker, trustee; regent; testator; client, principal, mandator | وصى على العرش (*'arš*) regent, prince regent

وصية *waṣīya* pl. وصايا *waṣāyā* direction, directive, instruction, injunction, order, command, commandment; recommendation, advice, counsel, admonition, exhortation; will, testament, testamentary disposition; bequest, legacy | الوصايا العشر (*'ašr*) the Ten Commandments

وصاة *waṣāh* and وصاية *waṣāya* prescription; order, ordinance, regulation, decree; instruction, direction, advice, counsel

وصاية *wiṣāya* guardianship, curatorship, tutorship; executorship; tutelage; mandate (*pol.*); trusteeship | مجلس الوصاية *majlis al-w.* regency council

توصية *tauṣiya* pl. *-āt*, تواص *tawāṣin* recommendation; admonition, exhortation, advice, counsel; proposal, suggestion; order, instruction, direction, commission, mandate; (commercial) order, commission | بالتوصية to order, on commission; خطاب توصية letter of recommendation; شركة توصية *širkat t.* limited partnership

ايصاء *īṣā'* = توصية; appointment of an executor (*Isl. Law*)

موص *muwaṣṣin* and *mūṣin* client, principal; mandator, testator | شريك موص silent partner

موصى به *mūṣan bihī* that which has been disposed of; bequeathed, willed; bequest, legacy; decreed, ordered; recommended; موصى عليه registered (letter); الموصى له legatee; heir; الموصى اليه executor

وضؤ *waḍu'a* يوضؤ *yaḍu'u* (وضوء *wuḍū'*, وضاءة *waḍā'a*) to be pure, clean V to perform the ritual ablution before prayer

وضاء *wuḍḍā'* brilliant, radiant, bright

وضاءة *waḍā'a* purity, cleanness, cleanliness

وضوء *wuḍū'* purity, cleanness, cleanliness; ritual ablution before prayer

وضوء *waḍū'* water for the ritual ablution

وضىء *waḍī'* pl. وضاء *wiḍā'* pure, clean

تَوَضُّؤ *tawaḍḍu'* ritual ablution

مِيضَأَة *mīḍa'a* and مِيضَاءَة *mīḍā'a* fountain or basin for the ritual ablution

توضيب *tauḍīb* arrangement; preparation; dressing, processing (mining industry)

وضح *waḍaḥa* يضح *yaḍiḥu* (وضوح *wuḍūḥ*) to be or become clear, plain, patent, manifest, evident; to appear, show, come out, come to light, become visible **II** and **IV** to make clear, make plain (ه s.th.); to explain, explicate, clear up, clarify, expound, elucidate, illustrate (ه s.th.); to set forth, propound (ه s.th.); to make visible, make manifest, show (ه s.th.); to indicate, designate, denote, express (ه s.th.) **V** = **I**; to be made clear, be clarified, be cleared up; to be shown, be indicated; to be obvious **VIII** اتضح *ittaḍaḥa* = **I** and **V**; to follow clearly (من from), be explained (من by) **X** to ask (ه s.o.) for an explanation, for clarification (ه of s.th.); to examine, investigate, explore (ه or عن s.th.), inquire, search (ه or عن into); to try to see clear (ه in), seek to understand clearly (ه s.th.)

وضح *waḍaḥ* pl. اوضاح *auḍāḥ* light, brilliance, luminosity, brightness | فى وضح النهار (*w. in-nahār*) in broad daylight

وضاح *waḍḍāḥ* bright, clear, brilliant, shining, luminous

وضوح *wuḍūḥ* clarity, clearness, plainness, distinctness; visibleness; obviousness; appearance | بوضوح clearly, plainly, distinctly

اوضح *auḍaḥ*[2] clearer

توضيح *tauḍīḥ* elucidation; showing, visualization; explanation; clarification; explication, illustration

ايضاح *īḍāḥ* pl. *-āt* elucidation; showing, visualization; explanation; clarification; explication, illustration

ايضاحى *īḍāḥī* clarifying, explanatory, explicatory, illustrative, elucidative

اتضاح *ittiḍāḥ* clarity, clearness; plainness, distinctness; visibleness, manifestness

استيضاح *istīḍāḥ* pl. *-āt* request for clarification, inquiry, formal question, interpellation

واضح *wāḍiḥ* clear, lucid; plain, distinct; obvious, patent, manifest; visible, conspicuous; evident, apparent, ostensible | واضح بذاته (*bi-ḏātihī*) self-evident; self-explanatory; من الواضح ان it is obvious that ...; الامر واضح وضوح الشمس فى رابعة النهار (*wuḍūḥa š-šamsi fī rābi'ati n-nahār*) the matter is clear as daylight

متضح *muttaḍiḥ* plain, distinct; clear; obvious, patent, manifest

وضر *waḍar* pl. اوضار *auḍār* dirt, filth

وضع *waḍa'a* يضع *yaḍa'u* (*waḍ'*) to lay, lay off, lay on, lay down, put down (ه s.th.); to set down (ه s.th.); to place (ه s.th.); to set up, erect (ه s.th.); to fix, attach, affix (ه فى s.th. to, on, in); to lay, put (ه فى s.th. into); to impose (ه على s.th. on s.o.); to take (ه عن s.th. from s.o.), rid of a burden, unburden (عن s.o.), unsaddle (عن a horse); to bear (ه a child), give birth to (ه); to invent, contrive, devise, originate, produce (ه s.th.); to found, establish, set up, start (ه s.th.); to write down, put down in writing, set down, lay down (ه s.th.); to write, compile, compose (ه a book or similar work of the mind), create (ه s.th.); to coin (ه a new word, a new term, or the like); to humble, humiliate, disparage (من or ه s.o.), derogate, detract (من or ه from); — (*waḍ'*, وضوع *wuḍū'*, ضعة *ḍa'a*, *ḍi'a*) with نفسه *nafsahū*: to abase o.s., humble o.s.; — *waḍu'a* يوضع *yauḍu'u* (وضاعة *waḍā'a*) to be low, lowly, humble | وضع اساسا (*asāsan*) to lay a foundation, lay a cornerstone; وضع ثقته فى (*tiqatahū*) to place one's confidence in; (على جانب or) وضعه جانبا (*jāniban*) to lay, or put, s.th. aside; وضعه فى جيبه (*jaibihī*) to put s.th. in one's pocket; وضع حدا ل (*ḥaddan*) to put an end to s.th.; وضع ختما على (*ḵatman*) to place a seal on; وضع السلاح to lay down arms; وضعت السلسلة فى عنقه *wuḍiʿat is-silsilatu fī ʿunuqihī* approx.: to have a millstone about one's neck, be seriously handicapped; وضع مشروعا to make or form a plan; وضع من قدره (*qadrihī*) to depreciate s.th., lower the value of s.th.; وضع تقريرا to write or make a report; وضع اقتراحات to draw up proposals, make suggestions; وضعه فى مقدمة اهتمامه (*muqaddamati htimāmihī*) to devote particular attention to s.th., make s.th. one's foremost concern, give priority to s.th.; وضع لفظا ل (*lafẓan*) to coin a word for; وضع للفظ معنى خاصا به (*li-l-lafẓi maʿnan ḵāṣṣan bihī*) to give a special meaning to an expression, place a particular construction on an expression; وضعه نصب عينيه (*nuṣba ʿainaihi*) to point out, demonstrate s.th. to s.o.; وضع نظارته على عينيه (*naẓẓāratahū*) to put on one's glasses; وضع نظما (*nuẓuman*) to lay down rules; وضعه على حدة (*ḥidatin*) to set s.th. apart, single out s.th.; وضعه موضعه (*mauḍiʿahū*) to put s.th. in the place of s.th. else; وضعه موضع التنفيذ (*mauḍiʿa t-t.*) to put s.th. into force, make s.th. effective or operative; to implement s.th.; وضعه موضع الشك (*mauḍiʿa š-šakk*) to doubt s.th., question s.th.; وضعه موضع العمل (*mauḍiʿa l-ʿamal*) to put s.th. into action, translate s.th. into deeds; وضع الفكرة موضع الفعل (*fikrata mauḍiʿa l-fiʿl*) to translate the idea into action; وضع نفسه موضع فلان to put o.s. in s.o.'s position; وضعه فى غير موضعه to mislay, misplace s.th.; وضع يده على (*yadahū*) to take possession of, lay hold of; وضع يده على الف اسير to take 1,000 prisoners; وضع يده على صديره to lay one's hand over one's heart; وضعه من يده (*yadihī*) to lay s.th. aside, toss s.th. aside; وضعه تحت يده to put s.th. in s.o.'s power **IV** to hurry; to take an active part, participate actively (فى in); pass. *ūḍiʿa* to suffer losses (فى in) **VI** to behave humbly and modestly; to abase o.s., humble o.s.; to agree, come to an agreement (على on) **VIII** اتضع *ittaḍaʿa* to humble o.s., abase o.s.

ضعة *ḍaʿa*, *ḍiʿa* lowness, lowliness, humbleness; scantiness, poorness, inferiority

وضع *waḍʿ* pl. اوضاع *auḍāʿ* laying down; putting down; laying on; fixing, attaching; setting up; placing; writing down, record(ing); drawing up, execution (of a document, deed, etc.); composition (of a printed work); writing, compilation (of a book); creation; invention; coining (of a word); coinage; conclusion (of a treaty); parturition, delivery, childbirth; regulation, rule; sketch, draft; attitude, bearing, carriage; posture, pose (of the body, e.g., in dancing, before a camera); position, location; situation; statement (*math.*); foundation, establishment; — humiliation; — pl. اوضاع circumstances, conditions; statutes; rules, principles; manner; mores, practices, usages, customs; conventions, conventional rules | وضعا وقولا *waḍʿan wa-qaulan* in words and deeds; الوضع الحالى the present situation; وضع اليد *w. al-yad* laying on of the hand; occupation, occupancy, seizure; آلام الوضع labor pains

وضعة *waḍʿa*, *wiḍʿa* situation; position

وضعى *waḍʿī* relating to situation or position, situational, positional; positive; positivistic; positivist (*philos.*); man-made; based on convention, conventional | قانون وضعى positive law (*jur.*); القيم الوضعية (*qiyam*) decimals (*math.*)

وضعية *waḍʿīya* situation; positivism (*philos.*)

وضاعة *waḍāʻa* lowness, lowliness, humbleness

وضيع *waḍīʻ* pl. وضعاء *wuḍaʻāʼ*² lowly, humble, base, vulgar, common; plebeian; low; inferior | الطبقة الوضيعة (*ṭabaqa*) the lowest class; الوضيع والرفيع low and high, the lowly and the great

وضيعة *waḍīʻa* pl. وضائع *waḍāʼiʻ*² s.th. put down, laid down or deposited; s.th. entrusted to s.o.'s custody, trust, charge, deposit; (*Isl. Law*) resale with a loss; price reduction, rebate

موضع *mauḍiʻ* pl. مواضع *mawāḍiʻ*² place, spot, site, locality; passage (in a book); object (of s.th.); position, situation, location; rank; occasion | فى موضعه in the right place, at the right time, timely, convenient, opportune; فى غير موضعه in the wrong place, out of place; فى موضع الحال in the present case; كان موضع حفاوة (*mauḍiʻa ḥafāwatin*) he was the object of a (festive) reception; موضع الاعجاب *m. al-iʻjāb* object of admiration; موضع الحنان *m. al-ḥanān* object of sympathy; see also *waḍaʻa* I; موضع قدم *m. qadamin* a foot (of ground)

موضعى *mauḍiʻī* local

تواضع *tawāḍuʻ* humility, modesty; lowness, lowliness, humbleness

اتضاع *ittiḍāʻ* humility, modesty; lowness, lowliness, humbleness

واضع *wāḍiʻ* writer, author; creator; inventor; originator; in childbed; unveiled (woman) | واضع اليد *w. al-yad* occupier, occupant; holder of actual possession, possessor (*jur.*)

موضوع *mauḍūʻ* pl. -*āt*, مواضيع *mawāḍīʻ*² object; theme, subject, topic; question, problem, issue; subject matter, matter; treatise, essay, article, paper; axiom; postulate (*math.*) | فهرس الموضوعات *fihris al-m.* table of contents, index; ادرك الموضوع *adraka l-mauḍūʻa* he got the point; غير ذى موضوع not topical, not timely

موضوعى *mauḍūʻī* objective; concerning the subject matter, the subject itself (not the form)

موضوعية *mauḍūʻīya* objectivism (*philos.*)

مواضعات *muwāḍaʻāt* analogous (word) coinings

متواضع *mutawāḍiʻ* humble; modest, unpretentious, unassuming, simple; small, little, insignificant

وضم **waḍam** pl. أوضام *auḍām* meat counter, meat block, butcher's block

وطئ **waṭiʼa** يطأ *yaṭaʼu* (وطء *waṭʼ*) to tread underfoot (ه s.th.), tread, step, walk (ه on); to set foot (ه on); to walk (ه over); to mount (ه a horse); to trample down, trample underfoot (ه s.th.); to have sexual intercourse (ها with a woman) **II** to pave, level, make smooth or even (ه s.th., esp., the way); to make smooth and soft, prepare, fix up, make comfortable (ه a seat, the bed, or the like, ل for s.o.); to make ready, prepare (ه s.th.); to reduce, slash (ه s.th.); to force down, press down (ه s.th.); to lower (ه s.th.) | وطأ صوته (*ṣautahū*) to lower the voice **III** to agree, be in agreement (ه على with s.o. on) **IV** to make (ه s.o.) step or tread (ه on); to make (ه s.o.) trample down (ه s.th.) **VI** to agree, be in agreement, cooperate, work hand in hand, act in concert, play into each other's hands, act in collusion (على in s.th., in order to carry out s.th.)

وطء *waṭʼ* and وطاء *waṭāʼ* low ground, depression

وطأة *waṭʼa* pressure; oppression, coercion, compulsion, force; gravity; violence, vehemence | شديد الوطأة cruel (على to), having a deadly effect (على on), of fatal consequences (على for); اشتدت وطأة الشىء

(*ištaddat*) to aggravate, become grave, trying, grueling (distress); لاشتداد وطأة المرض *li-št. w. il-maraḍ*) because of the violence with which the disease struck

وطىء *waṭī'* low; flat, level

اوطأ *auṭa'*[2] lower

موطأ *mauṭa'* and موطىء *mauṭi'* pl. مواطىء *mawāṭi'*[2] place where the foot is set down, footing, foothold; footprint, footstep, track; footstool | موطىء الاقدام *m. al-aqdām* a foot (of ground); مواطىء الاقدام the ground

توطئة *tauṭi'a* introduction, initiation; preparation; reduction, lowering | لتوطئة in preparation of ..., for the purpose of ...; توطئة الصوت *t. aṣ-ṣaut* lowering of the voice

مواطأة *muwāṭa'a* agreement; secret understanding, connivance, collusion

تواطؤ *tawāṭu'* agreement; secret understanding, connivance, collusion

واطىء *wāṭi'* low; muffled, subdued, soft (voice) | الاراضى الواطئة the Netherlands

وطب *waṭb* pl. وطاب *wiṭāb*, اوطاب *auṭāb*, اواطب *awāṭib*[2] milkskin | مملوء الوطاب ب amply provided with; خالى الوطاب empty-handed

وطد *waṭada* يطد *yaṭidu* (*waṭd*) and II to make firm, strong or stable, strengthen, brace, reinforce, cement, consolidate, stabilize (ه s.th.); to stamp down, ram, tamp (ه earth, etc.); to pave (ه ل the way for s.o.), prepare (ه ل the ground for) | وطد ثقته فى (*ṯiqatahū*) to rely firmly on, put one's faith in; وطد العزم أن (*'azma*) to resolve firmly to ..., come to the firm decision to ...; وطد عرى المحبة (*'urā l-maḥabba*) to strengthen the bonds of friendship; وطد اقدامه فى (*aqdāmahū*) to gain a footing in

وطيد *waṭīd* firm; strong; solid, sturdy; unshakable | وطيد الامل ب (*w. al-amal*) having strong hopes of, confident of

اوطاد *auṭād* mountains

ميطدة *mīṭada* rammer, tamper

توطيد *tauṭīd* strengthening, bracing, reinforcement, cementation; consolidation, stabilization | توطيد السلم *t. as-silm* safeguarding, or maintenance, of peace; توطيد سعر الفرنك *t. si'r al-f.* stabilization of the franc

موطد *muwaṭṭad* firm, strong; solid, sturdy | موطد الاركان firmly established, resting on firm foundations

وطر *waṭar* pl. اوطار *auṭār* wish, desire; aim, end, object, purpose

وطيس *waṭīs* furnace | حمى الوطيس (*ḥamiya*) there was fierce fighting; حامى الوطيس fierce, grim, bitter (fighting)

وطش *waṭaša* يطش *yaṭišu* (*waṭš*) to strike, hit, slap (ه s.o.)

وطف *waṭifa* يوطف *yauṭafu* (*waṭaf*) to have bushy eyebrows

اوطف *auṭaf*[2], f. وطفاء *waṭfā'*[2] bushy-browed; وطفاء rain-heavy and low-hanging (cloud)

وطن *waṭana* يطن *yaṭinu* (*waṭn*) to dwell, live, reside, stay (ب in a place) II to choose for residence (ه a place), settle down, get settled, take up one's residence (ه in a place) | وطن نفسه على (*nafsahū*) to get used to, adjust o.s. to, reconcile o.s. to, put up with; to prepare o.s. mentally for; to make up one's mind to (do s.th.) V to settle down (ه or ب in a place) | توطنت نفسه على (*nafsuhū*) = وطن نفسه على (see above) X to choose for residence (ه a place); to settle (ه a country); to settle down, get settled, take up one's residence (ه in); to live permanently (ه in a place); to take root, become naturalized, acclimated (ه in)

وطن *waṭan* pl. اوطان *auṭān* homeland, home country, fatherland; home | الوطن القبلى (*qiblī*) Cape Bon (*tun.*); الوطن القومى الاسرائيلى (*qaumī, isrā'īlī*) the Jewish

National Home; اهل وطنه *ahl w.* his countrymen, his compatriots; حب الوطن *ḥubb al-w.* patriotism; ○ شائع الوطن cosmopolitan

وطنى *waṭanī* home, native; indigenous, domestic; patriotic; national; nationalistic; (pl. *-ūn*) nationalist, patriot | مصنوعات وطنية domestic products, products of the country

وطنية *waṭanīya* nationalism; national sentiment, patriotism

موطن *mauṭin* pl. مواطن *mawāṭin*[2] residence, domicile; habitat; native place, home town, home; native country, home country, fatherland; place, locality, area, region, section, district, zone; point, spot; right place; right time | موطن الضعف *m. aḍ-ḍuʿf* soft or sore spot; weak spot, weakness; وضع يده على موطن العلة (*yadahū, m. il-ʿilla*) to lay one's finger on an open sore, touch a sore spot; الموطن الوضيع the lowest point, the low mark, the bottom

استيطان *istīṭān* immigration; settling down; settling, settlement, colonization; "istitan", a special impost in Tunisia

مواطن *muwāṭin* countryman, compatriot, fellow citizen | مواطن عالمى (*ʿālamī*) world citizen

متوطن *mutawaṭṭin* native, indigenous, domestic; resident; deep-rooted; endemic (*med.*)

مستوطن *mustauṭin* native, indigenous, domestic; resident; deep-rooted

وطواط *waṭwāṭ* pl. وطاوط *waṭāwiṭ*[2], وطاويط *waṭāwīṭ*[2] bat (*zool.*)

□ وطى II for وطأ II

واط *wāṭin* low; soft; see alphabetically

وظب *waẓaba* يظب *yaẓibu* (وظوب *wuẓūb*) to do persistently, regularly, keep doing, practice constantly (على or ه s.th.), continue to do s.th. III do.; to persevere, persist (على in), take pains (على with), devote o.s. assiduously, apply o.s. with perseverance or steadily (على to s.th.)

مواظبة *muwāẓaba* diligence, assiduity, perseverance, persistence

مواظب *muwāẓib* diligent, assiduous, persevering, persistent

وظف II to assign (ه على s.th. to s.o.); to impose (ه على s.th., esp. a tax, on s.o.), burden, encumber (ه على with s.th. s.o.); to assign an office (ه to s.o.), appoint to an office, employ, hire (ه s.o.); to invest (ه money) V to be appointed to an office, obtain a position, get a job; to hold an office, work in a position, have a job | توظف فى الحكومة to work as an official with the government

وظيفة *waẓīfa* pl. وظائف *waẓāʾif*[2] daily ration; pay; office, position, post, job; officialship, officialdom; duty, task, assignment; (school) assignment, lesson, homework; employ, service; work; function | ادى وظيفة (*addā*) to fill a post, attend to an office, exercise a function; وظائف خالية (*ḵāliya*) vacancies; want ads (in a newspaper); علم الوظائف *ʿilm al-w.* or علم وظائف الاعضاء *ʿi. w. al-aʿḍāʾ* physiology

وظيفى *waẓīfī* functional

توظيف *tauẓīf* employment, appointment (to an office) | توظيف المال investment

موظف *muwaẓẓaf* fixed (salary); employed, appointed; — (pl. *-ūn*) employee; official, officer, civil servant; functionary | موظف الحكومة government official; موظف عمومى (*ʿumūmī*) public functionary; اكبر الموظفين senior official

وعب *waʿaba* يعب *yaʿibu* (*waʿb*) to take the whole, all (ه of s.th.) IV do.; to insert (ه فى s.th. in) X = I; to uproot, root out, extirpate, exterminate (ه s.th.); to embrace, enclose, encircle (ه s.o., بين ذراعيه with the arms); to contain, hold

(ه s.th.); to be able to take in (ه s.th.), have room (ه for); to comprehend, understand, grasp, take in (ه s.th.)

استيعاب *isti'āb* capacity; study; full comprehension, grasp

وعث *wa't, wa'it* difficult, hard, troublesome, tiresome, laborious, arduous

وعثاء *wa'tā'*[2] difficulty, trouble, hardship, inconvenience, discomfort

وعد *wa'ada* يعد *ya'idu* (*wa'd*) to make a promise; to give one's word; to promise (ه ب or ه ه s.o. s.th.); to threaten (ه ب s.o. with) | وعد نفسه بأن to promise o.s. to ..., intend firmly to ...; وعد بشرفه (*bi-šarafihī*) to pledge o.s. on one's honor, give one's word of honor **III** to make an arrangement; to arrange for a meeting or rendezvous, make an appointment (ه ه with s.o. for a given time or at a certain place) **IV** = **I**; **V** to threaten, to menace (ه s.o.) **VI** to make an appointment **VIII** اتعد *itta'ada* to come to an understanding, agree among each other, make arrangements (أن that)

عدة *'ida* promise

وعد *wa'd* pl. وعود *wu'ūd* promise

وعيد *wa'īd* threats; promises

وعيدى *wa'īdī* threatening, menacing, minatory

موعد *mau'id*, موعدة *mau'ida* pl. مواعد *mawā'id*[2] promise; pledge, engagement, commitment; rendezvous, date, appointment; time and place of an appointment; appointed time; time, date, deadline; anniversary | كان على موعد معه (or منه) to have an appointment with s.o.

ميعاد *mī'ād* pl. مواعيد *mawā'īd*[2] promise; appointment, date, rendezvous; appointed time; time agreed on, time fixed by appointment; deadline, date (esp. also due date for repaying a debt); consulting hour, office hour(s) (of a doctor, etc.); visiting hours (in museums, etc.); (time of) departure (of trains, buses, etc.) | فى الميعاد or فى ميعاده on time, punctually; على غير ميعاد (*ġairi m.*) untimely, unpunctually; من غير ميعاد *min ġairi m.* quite unexpectedly, all of a sudden, suddenly; كان على ميعاد مع to have an appointment with; بيان المواعيد *bayān al-m.* railroad timetable; ميعاد الاكل *m. al-akl* mealtime, eating time; ميعاد التسليم date of delivery; ميعاد المرأة *m. al-mar'a* menses; مواعيد عرقوبية (*'urqūbīya*) deceptive promises; ارض الميعاد *arḍ al-m.* the Land of Promise

مواعدة *muwā'ada* arrangement, agreement; appointment, rendezvous, date

ايعاد *ī'ād* threat

توعد *tawa''ud* threat

توعدى *tawa''udī* threatening, menacing, minatory

موعود *mau'ūd* promised; fixed, appointed, stipulated (time); موعود and موعودة *mau'ūda* pl. مواعيد *mawā'īd*[2] promise

وعر *wa'ara* يعر *ya'iru* (*wa'r* and وعور *wu'ūr*) and *wa'ira* يوعر *yau'aru* (*wa'ar*), *wa'ura* *yau'uru* (وعارة *wa'āra*, وعورة *wu'ūra*) to be rough, rugged, difficult (terrain) **V** = **I**

وعر *wa'r* rock debris; rugged, roadless terrain

وعر *wa'r* pl. وعور *wu'ūr*, اوعار *au'ār* covered with rock debris; cleft, riven, rugged, wild; rough, uneven; roadless, pathless; hard, difficult

وعير *wa'ir* covered with rock debris; cleft, riven, cragged, rugged, wild; rough, uneven; roadless, pathless; hard, difficult

وعورة *wu'ūra* unevenness, roughness; difficulty | وعورة الارض *w. al-arḍ* difficult terrain

اوعر *au'ar*[2] rougher, more rugged, harder

وعز IV to give to understand, intimate, insinuate (ب or ف s.th., الى to s.o.), point out by a sign or motion (ب or الى ب to s.o. s.th.); to suggest (ب or الى ب to s.o. s.th.); to inspire (ب or الى ب s.o. with, s.o. to do s.th.); to advise, counsel, recommend (ب or الى ب to s.o. s.th.); to induce (الى ب s.o. to); to instruct, direct, order (الى s.o., ب to do s.th.)

ايعاز *īʿāz* advice, counsel, recommendation; suggestion, intimation, hint

ايعازى *īʿāzī* advisory, recommendatory, inspiring, inspiratory

موعز به *mūʿaz bihī* inspired, suggested by a higher authority

وعس *waʿasa* يعس *yaʿisu* (*waʿs*) to make experienced, make wise (ه s.o.; of fate)

وعس *waʿs* pl. اوعاس *auʿās* quicksand

ميعاس *mīʿās* quicksand

وعظ *waʿaẓa* يعظ *yaʿiẓu* (*waʿẓ*, عظة *ʿiẓa*) to preach (ه to s.o.), appeal to s.o.'s (ه) conscience; to admonish, exhort (ه s.o.); to warn (ه عن s.o. of), caution (ه عن s.o. against) **VIII** اتعظ *ittaʿaẓa* to let o.s. be admonished or warned; to accede to an admonition, take advice; to learn a lesson, take a warning (ب from), let s.th. (ب) be a warning

عظة *ʿiẓa* pl. *-āt* sermon; lesson, moral; warning; admonition

وعظ *waʿẓ* and وعظة *waʿẓa* admonition; warning; sermon; paraenesis

موعظة *mauʿiẓa* pl. مواعظ *mawāʿiẓ*[2] religious exhortation, spiritual counsel; exhortatory talk, exhortation; stern lecture, severe reprimand

واعظ *wāʿiẓ* pl. وعاظ *wuʿʿāẓ* preacher

وعق *waʿq*, *waʿiq* surly, grumpy, cross; ill-tempered, irritable, peevish, cantankerous, petulant

وعك **V** to be indisposed, unwell

وعك *waʿik* indisposed, unwell

وعكة *waʿka* indisposition, illness; sultriness

توعك *tawaʿʿuk* indisposition

موعوك *mauʿūk* indisposed, unwell; ill

متوعك *mutawaʿʿik* indisposed, unwell; ill

وعل *waʿl*, *waʿil* pl. اوعال *auʿāl*, وعول *wuʿūl* mountain goat

وعوع *waʿwaʿa* to howl, yelp, bark, bay

وعى *waʿā* يعى *yaʿī* (*waʿy*) to hold (ه s.th.); to comprise (ه s.th.); to contain (ه s.th.); to retain in one's memory, remember, know by heart, know (ه s.th.); to pay attention (الى or ه to), heed, bear in mind (الى or ه s.th.); to perceive, hear (ه s.th.); to become aware (الى of) | وعى على نفسه (*nafsihī*) to dawn on s.o., become clear to s.o.; لا يعى (he is) unconscious; لا يكاد يعى (he is) almost unconscious; لا يعى ما يقول he doesn't know what he is saying **II** to warn, caution (ه من s.o. against) **IV** to put (ه s.th. into a vessel or container) **V** to act with caution, with prudence; to be on one's guard (من against), beware (من of)

وعى *waʿy* attention, attentiveness, heedfulness, carefulness, advertence; consciousness; awareness; feeling, sentiment, sense; wakefulness, alertness | فى غير وعى unnoticed, without being noticed; وعى قومى (*qaumī*) national consciousness, nationalism; ما وراء الوعى the subconscious; استرجع وعيه and عاد الى وعيه to regain consciousness, come to; فقد وعيه to lose consciousness, faint, pass out; دون وعى unconscious(ly)

وعاء *wiʿāʾ* pl. اوعية *auʿiya*, اواع *awāʿin* vessel (also *anat.*), container, receptacle | اوعية دموية (*damawīya*) blood vessels

واع *wāʿin* attentive, heedful, careful; conscious, in one's senses, wide awake

وغد **wağd** pl. اوغاد **auğād,** وغدان **wuğdān** miserable, wretched; scoundrel

وغر **wağara** يغر **yağiru, wağira** يوغر **yauğaru** (*wağr, wağar*) to be hot, be angry | وغر صدره على (*ṣadruhū*) to boil with anger against s.o., harbor malice against s.o., feel hatred for s.o. IV اوغر صدره على (*ṣadrahū*) to arouse s.o.'s anger against, stir up s.o. against, arouse bitter feelings in s.o. against V to be furious, burn with rage

وغر *wağr, wağar* anger, wrath, ire, rancor, spite, malice, hatred

وغل *wağala* يغل *yağilu* (وغول *wuğūl*) to penetrate deeply (في into); — (*wağl, wuğūl,* وغلان *wağalān*) to intrude (على on s.o.), come uninvited (على to) IV to penetrate deeply (في into); to apply o.s. intensively (في to an activity); to push, press (في ه s.o. into); to hurry | اوغل في السير (*sair*) to walk briskly, advance quickly; اوغل في الكلام (*kalām*) to exaggerate, draw a longbow V to penetrate deeply (في into); to advance further and further

وغل *wağl* intruder, parasite

توغل *tawağğul* penetration, absorption, preoccupation

واغل *wāğil* intruder, parasite; extraneous, irrelevant; deep, deep-rooted, deep-seated, inveterate (feeling)

موغل *mūğil* deep-reaching, deep-rooted

وغى *wağy, wağan* din, clamor, tumult, uproar

وفد *wafada* يفد *yafidu* (*wafd,* وفود *wufūd,* وفادة *wifāda*) to come, travel (على or الى to s.o., esp. as an envoy); to arrive (على or الى before s.o., in s.o.'s presence); to visit, come to see (على s.o.), call on s.o. (على) II and IV to send, dispatch (على or الى ه s.o. to, also ه a delegation); to delegate, depute (على or الى ه s.o. to, also ه a group) III to come or arrive together (ه with s.o.) VI to arrive together; to throng, flock (على to)

وفد *wafd* arrival, coming; — (pl. وفود *wufūd,* اوفاد *aufād*) a delegation, a deputation; الوفد (formerly, *Eg.*) the Wafd party

وفدى *wafdī* of or relative to the Wafd; Wafdist, a member or adherent of the Wafd

وفادة *wifāda* arrival | اكرم (or احسن) وفادته (*wifādatahū*) to receive s.o. hospitably, receive s.o. with kindness, treat s.o. with deference

وفود *wufūd* arrival

ايفاد *īfād* delegation, deputation, dispatch

وافد *wāfid* pl. وفود *wufūd,* اوفاد *aufād,* وفاد *wuffād* arriving; (new)comer, arrival; envoy; epidemic(al) (disease); pouring in, coming (ideas, memories)

وافدة *wāfida* an epidemic

موفد *mūfad* appointed or nominated for a special assignment; delegate | الموفد البابوى apostolic delegate

وفر *wafara* يفر *yafiru* (*wafr,* وفور *wufūr*) and *wafura* يوفر *yaufuru* (وفارة *wafāra*) to abound, be ample, abundant, numerous, plentiful; to increase, augment, grow, become more II to increase, augment, make abundant (ه s.th.); to give abundantly (ه ل of s.th. to s.o.); to furnish (ه evidence, proof); to save (ه s.th.), be sparing, be economical, hold back, economize (ه with); to lay by, put by (ه s.th., esp., money); to save (ه على s.o. s.th.) | وفر عليه مصاريف كثيرة to save s.o. a lot of expenses IV to increase, augment (ه s.th.) V to abound, be ample, abundant, plentiful; to suffice, be sufficient, be enough; to be fulfilled (condition); to be of full value, sterling, up to standard, unexceptionable, valid; to prosper, thrive, be successful; to spare no trouble, go to any length (على in an undertaking or activity), give all one's attention, devote o.s. intensively, dedicate o.s. (على to); to be saved | توفرت فيه الصفات اللازمة he has the necessary qualities; توفرت فيه الشروط he fulfills the conditions **VI** to be numerous; to abound, be ample, abundant, plentiful; to increase, multiply, grow in number; to be fulfilled (conditions); to fall amply to s.o.'s (ل) share (e.g., qualities) | توافر فيه الشباب والجمال (*šabāb, jamāl*) he is richly endowed with youth and good looks

وفر ***wafr*** abundance, wealth; profusion, superabundance; (pl. وفور *wufūr*, *-āt*) excess, surplus, overplus; economy; saving

وفرة ***wafra*** plenty, abundance, profusion

وفير ***wafīr*** abundant, ample

اوفر ***aufar***[2] more abounding (ه in); more amply provided or endowed (ه with); thriftier, more economical | اوفر حظا (*ḥazzan*) luckier, more fortunate

توفير ***taufīr*** increase, augmentation; raising, raise, rise; economizing, economy; saving | صندوق التوفير *ṣundūq at-t.* savings bank

توفر ***tawaffur*** abundance, profusion, wealth; superabundance; increase, rise, augmentation, spread, expansion; fulfillment | عند توفر الشروط as soon as the conditions are fulfilled

وافر ***wāfir*** ample, abundant, plentiful; numerous, profuse, superabundant; (with foll. genit.) abounding in; overlong (year); الوافر name of a poetic meter

موفور ***maufūr*** ample, abundant, plentiful; loaded, swamped; wealthy, moneyed, rich; complete, perfectly intact | موفور المطالب *m. al-maṭālib* having many wishes

متوفر ***mutawaffir*** ample, abundant; thrifty, economical; savings yield or interest

متوافر ***mutawāfir*** ample, abundant, plentiful, profuse

وفز **V** to be roused, be alerted **X** to lie in wait; to be in suspense; to be prepared, be in a state of alertness

وفز ***wafz, wafaz*** pl. اوفاز *aufāz* hurry, haste | كان على اوفاز to be on one's toes, be on the alert

مستوفز ***mustaufiz*** alert, quick, vivid, lively (e.g., mind); excited

وفض ***wafaḍa*** يفض *yafiḍu* (*wafḍ*) to run; to hurry, rush

وفضة ***wafḍa*** pl. وفاض *wifāḍ* leather bag, traveling bag | خالى الوفاض empty, vacant, free; empty-handed

وفيعة ***wafīʿa*** penwiper

وفق ***wafiqa*** يفق *yafiqu* (*wafq*) to be right, proper, suitable, fit, appropriate **II** to make fit, make suitable, adapt, fit, adjust, accommodate (ه s.th.); to make consistent, bring to agreement, reconcile (بين different things; بين — وبين s.th. with); to reconcile (بين two parties), make peace, re-establish normal relations (بين between); to give s.o. (ه) success (ل or الى in achieving s.th.; of God); pass. *wuffiqa* to have success, be successful (ل or الى in or with), have the good fortune, be lucky enough (الى to), succeed (الى in) | وفق كل التوفيق الى (*wuffiqa kulla t-t.*) to succeed completely in, have every success in or with **III** to befit, become (ه s.o.); to suit (ه s.o.), be suitable, acceptable, agreeable, favorable, convenient (ه to s.o.), be consistent with s.o.'s (ه) wishes or interests; to fit, suit (ه s.o.; garment); to agree (ه with s.th., ه with s.o., في or على in s.th.); to be agreed, unanimous, of the same opinion, concur (ه في or على with s.o. in s.th.); to fit (ه s.th.), be consistent, be in keeping, be in line (ه with s.th.); to correspond, be analogous (ه to s.th.); to be in agreement, be in accordance, be in conformity, be in harmony, go, harmonize (ه with); to fall in, tally, coincide (ه with); to agree (ه with; of food, climate, etc.), be wholesome, beneficial (ه for); to be conducive (ه to); to agree, consent, assent, subscribe (على to), grant, confirm, approve, sanction, license, authorize, ratify (على s.th.); to adapt, fit (بين one thing to the other), make consistent, compatible, bring to agreement, reconcile, balance, equilibrate (بين two things) **V** to be aided, assisted, favored (by God); to have success, be successful, prosper, succeed **VIII** اتفق *ittafaqa* to agree, come to an agreement, reach an agreement; to agree, be in agreement, in accordance, in conformity, in keeping, in line, in harmony, be consistent, be compatible, coincide, tally, square, fall in line (مع or و with acc.: with); to be agreed, be unanimous; to make a contract, conclude an agreement, a treaty, agree on an arrangement; to agree (على on s.th.), arrange (على s.th.), come to terms (على about s.th., مع with s.o.); to chance, happen accidentally, come to pass, occur, happen (ل to s.o., e.g., an oversight); to fall unexpectedly (ل to s.o.), turn out successfully (ل for s.o.) contrary to his expectations; to be given, be destined (ل to s.o.) | كما اتفق (*ka-mā*) as chance would have it, at random, haphazardly, carelessly; كيفما اتفق (*kaifa-mā*) however it may turn out, whatever may come; no matter how, anyway; at any rate, in any case

وفق *wafq* sufficient amount; sufficiency; agreement, accordance, conformity; harmony, concord; *wafqa* or وفقا ل or من وفق in accordance with, in conformity with, conformable to, according to, commensurate with; in pursuance of, pursuant to, on the strength of, on the basis of | وفق الاصل *wafqa l-aṣl* true, accurate, exact (copy)

وفقة *wafqa*: اجر بالوفقة *ajr bi-l-w.* piece wage, task wage, wage for piecework

اوفق *aufaq*[2] more suitable, fitter, more appropriate

توفيق *taufīq* conformation, adaptation, accommodation; balancing, adjustment, settlement; reconciliation, mediation, arbitration, peacemaking, re-establishment of normal relations; success (granted by God), happy outcome, good fortune, good luck, prosperity, successfulness, succeeding | لجنة التوفيق *lajnat at-t.* board of arbitration

وفاق *wifāq* accordance, conformity, conformance; unity, concord, harmony; consent, assent; agreement, covenant; وفاقا ل in accordance with, in conformity with, conformable to, according to, commensurate with; in pursuance of, pursuant to, on the strength of, on the basis of

موافقة *muwāfaqa* agreement, conformity, conformance; accordance; correspondence, analogy; suitability, fitness; approval, consent, assent, authorization, sanction

توافق *tawāfuq* coincidence, congruence, congruity; agreement, conformity, conformance

اتفاق *ittifāq* coincidence, congruence, congruity; agreement, conformity, conformance; accident, chance; (pl. *-āt*) covenant, compact, convention, contract; understanding, arrangement, entente; agreement, treaty, pact | اتفاقا accidentally, by chance, by coincidence; بالاتفاق by (mutual) agreement, by appointment; اتفاق الآراء unanimity; باتفاق الآراء unanimously; اتفاق بحرى (*baḥrī*) naval agreement; اتفاق تجارى (*tijārī*) commercial agreement, trade agreement; اتفاق عدم الاعتداء *itt. ʿadam al-iʿtidāʾ* nonaggression pact; دول الاتفاق الصغير *duwal al-itt.* the countries of the Little Entente

اتفاقى *ittifāqī* accidental, fortuitous, chance; based on convention, conventional

اتفاقية *ittifāqīya* pl. *-āt* agreement, treaty; convention, concordat

موفق *muwaffaq* successful, prospering, fortunate, lucky

موافق *muwāfiq* accordant, conformable, congruous, consistent, concordant, corresponding, analogous; suitable, fit, appropriate; agreeable, acceptable, convenient, favorable, propitious, wholesome, beneficial, conducive

متوفق *mutawaffiq* successful, prospering, fortunate, lucky

متفق عليه *muttafaq ʿalaihi* agreed upon

وفى **wafā** يفى *yafī* to be perfect, integral, complete, unabridged; — (وفاء *wafā'*) to live up (ب or ه to a promise, an agreement, a vow, or the like), redeem, fulfill, carry out, keep (ب or ه s.th.); to satisfy, gratify (ب a wish, a desire), supply (ب a need); to serve (ب a purpose); to meet, fulfill, discharge (ب an obligation, an engagement); to pay (a debt); to redeem (a pledge); to cover (costs, expenses); to be sufficient, be enough, suffice (ب for), be adequate (ب to); to make up, compensate fully (ب for), counterbalance (ب s.th.); to be equivalent (ب to s.th.), fulfill the function (ب of s.th.), substitute (ب for); to realize or carry out (fully, completely; ب s.th.) **II** to bring up to standard, complete, round out (ه s.th.); to give (ه ه s.o. s.th.) to the full extent, let s.o. (ه) have his full share of s.th. (ه); to present, set forth, or treat exhaustively (a topic) **III** to come (ه to s.o.), appear, show up (ه before s.o., in s.o.'s presence); to bring, take, deliver (ب ه to s.o. s.th.), supply, provide, furnish (ب ه s.o. with); to fulfill (ه s.o.'s wish), comply (ه with s.o.'s request) | وافاه اجله (*ajaluhū*) his fate overtook him **IV** to give to the full; to fullfill, keep (ب or ه s.th.), live up (ب or ه to); to come or draw near s.th. (على), approach (على s.th.); to exceed, transcend (على s.th.), go beyond (على) | اوفى على الانتهاء to draw to a close; عمره الآن قد اوفى على التاسعة (*ʿumruhū*) he is already past nine years of age **V** to exact fully (ه s.th.), take one's full share (ه of), receive in full (ه s.th.); توفاه الله God has taken him unto Him; pass. *tuwuffiya* to die **VI** to be complete; to decide unanimously (على for, in favor of) **X** to receive in full, exact (fully) (ه s.th.); to give (fully) (ه ل to s.o s.th.), let s.o. have his full share of; to complete, bring to a finish (ه s.th.), go through with s.th. (ه); to sit out, hear to the end (ه a program); to bring to its full value (ه s.th.); to treat exhaustively (ه a topic); to exhaust (ه s.th.); to present in detail, at great length (ه s.th.); to fulfill (ه the condition); to receive full compensation or indemnity

وفاء *wafā'* keeping, fulfillment, redemption (e.g., of a promise); meeting, discharge (of an obligation); payment (of a debt); counterbalance, setoff, compensation; faithfulness, fidelity; good faith; loyalty, allegiance; fulfillment, accomplishment, realization, completion | وفاء ل *wafā'an li* in fulfillment of, in discharge of; as an offset to; as a compensation for; يوم وفاء النيل *yaum w. an-nīl* the Day of the Nile Inundation (popular holiday; *Eg.*); احتفظ بالوفاء ل to remain loyal to s.o.

وفاة *wafāh* pl. وفيات *wafayāt* decease, demise; death; death certificate | كثرة الوفيات *kaṯrat al-w.* high mortality, high death rate

وفى *wafīy* pl. اوفياء *aufiyā'*[2] true to one's word; faithful (lover); reliable, trustworthy; entire, whole, total, full, complete, integral, perfect

اوفى *aufā* more faithful, more loyal; more complete, of greater perfection; serving better (ب a purpose), fulfilling better (ب a wish, etc.)

توفية *taufiya* satisfaction; fulfillment, discharge

موافاة *muwāfāh* arrival; communication (ب of a message)

ايفاء *īfā'* fulfillment, discharge; payment | قادر على الايفاء solvent

استيفاء *istīfā'* acceptance by the creditor of the performance or payment due (*Isl. Law*); fulfillment; exhaustive treatment; performance, discharge, accomplishment, execution, consummation, completion; payment

واف *wāfin* faithful, loyal; full, complete, perfect; quite sufficient, enough; ample, abundant; adequate

موف *muwaffin* completing, rounding out (a number) | فى الموفى عشرين (ثلاثين) من الشهر (*šahr*) on the 20th (30th) day of the month

متوفى *mutawaffan* deceased, dead

وقة *wuqqa, wiqqa* pl. *-āt*, وقق *wiqaq* oka, a weight, see اقة

وقب *waqaba* يقب *yaqibu* (*waqb*) to be sunken, hollow (eye); to become dark, gloomy

وقب *waqb* pl. اوقاب *auqāb* cavity; hollow, hole; eye socket, orbit

وقبة *waqba* cavity

وقت II to appoint, fix, or set a time (ه for), schedule (ه s.th.) for a given time; to time (ه s.th.); to set a time limit (ه for)

وقت *waqt* pl. اوقات *auqāt* time; period of time, time span; moment, instant | وقتا *waqtan* once, at one time, one day; بوقته at once, right away, immediately; فى وقته on time; at the right time, in good time, timely; فى غير وقته at the wrong time, untimely; فى نفس الوقت or فى الوقت نفسه at the same time, simultaneously; فى اول وقت *fī awwali waqtin* one of these days, at the first opportunity; للوقت or لوقته at once, right away, immediately; لهذا الوقت at this time; مع الوقت in (due) time, in the course of time, by and by, gradually; من وقت لآخر (*li-āḵara*) from time to time; اوقاتا اوقاتا do.; فى بعض الاوقات at times, sometimes; فى كثير من الاوقات often, frequently; وقت الفراغ *w. al-farāġ* leisure, sparetime, free time; الوقت المدنى (*madanī*) civil time; وقت اوربا الوسطى *w. urubbā l-wusṭā* Central European time; اشارة الوقت *išārat al-w.* time signal (*radio*)

وقتئذ *waqta'iḏin* then, at that time, by then

وقتذاك *waqtaḏāka* then, at that time, by then

وقتما *waqtamā* (conj.) while, as

وقتى *waqtī* temporal, of time; time- (in compounds); temporary; passing, transient, transitory; provisional, interim; momentary; وقتيا for some time, for a short time | تصوير وقتى time exposure (*phot.*)

موقت *mauqit* pl. مواقت *mawāqit*[2] appointed time; appointment, date

ميقات *mīqāt* pl. مواقيت *mawāqīt*[2] appointed time; date, deadline; time; season, time of the year; meeting point, rendezvous; pl. times of departure and arrival, timetable | مواقيت الاقلام business hours; مواقيت الحج *m. al-ḥajj* rendezvous points and times of the Mecca pilgrims

توقيت *tauqīt* timing; reckoning of tim'e time | توقيت صيفى (*ṣaifī*) daylight-saving time; توقيت محلى (*maḥallī*) local time; فى الساعة العاشرة حسب توقيت جرينتش (*ḥasaba t. g.*) at 10.00 hours Greenwich mean time

موقوت *mauqūt* appointed, fixed, set (time); temporary; limited in time, scheduled for a given time; provided with a time fuse (bomb)

موقت *muwaqqit* timing, determining the time; timekeeper, timetaker; controller

موقت *muwaqqat* and مؤقت *mu'aqqat* scheduled for a given time or hour; appointed, fixed, set (time); effective for a certain time, for a time only, temporal, temporary, passing, transient, transitory, provisional, interim | موقتا temporarily, provisionally, for the time being; بصورة موقتة (*bi-ṣūra*) do.; حكومة موقتة provisional government

وقح *waqaḥa* يقح *yaqiḥu* (قحة *qiḥa*, *qaḥa*), *waquḥa* يوقح *yauquḥu* (وقاحة, وقوحة *waqāḥa*, *wuqūḥa*) and *waqiḥa yauqaḥu* (*waqaḥ*) to be shameless, impudent, insolent **V** do.; to behave impudently (على toward s.o.), display insolent manners **VI** to display impudence, behave in an insolent manner

قحة *qiḥa* impudence, shamelessness, insolence, impertinence, sauciness

وقح *waqiḥ* impudent, shameless, insolent, impertinent, saucy, cheeky, forward

وقاح *waqāḥ* (m. and f.) pl. وقح *wuquḥ* impudent, shameless, insolent, impertinent, saucy, cheeky, forward

وقيح *waqiḥ* impudent, shameless, insolent, impertinent, saucy, cheeky, forward

وقاحة *waqāḥa* impudence, insolence, impertinence, sauciness, cheek, nerve

وقوحة *wuqūḥa* impudence, insolence, impertinence, sauciness, cheek, nerve

وقد *waqada* يقد *yaqidu* (*waqd*, *waqad*, وقود *wuqūd*) to take fire, ignite, burn **II** and **IV** to kindle, ignite, light (▲ s.th.) | اوقد فيه النار (*nāra*) to set s.th. on fire **V** = I; to kindle, light, ignite (▲ s.th.) **VIII** اتقد *ittaqada* = I; to break forth (anger), be aroused (zeal) | اتقد غيرة (حماسا) على (*ġairatan*, *ḥamāsan*) to burn with zeal (enthusiasm) for **X** to kindle, light, ignite (▲ s.th.)

وقد *waqd*, *waqad* burning, combustion; fire; fuel

وقدة *waqda* fire; blaze

وقاد *wiqād* fuel

وقاد *waqqād* burning, fiery; lively, heated; bright, brilliant, radiant (star); (pl. *-ūn*) stoker

وقود *waqūd* fuel (also for motors) | مخزن الوقود *makzan al-w.* coal cellar, coal storeroom

وقيد *waqīd* fuel

موقد *mauqid* pl. مواقد *mawāqid*[2] fireplace; hearth; stove; ○ boiler of a locomotive | موقد الغاز kerosene stove

ايقاد *īqād* kindling, lighting, setting on fire, ignition

توقد *tawaqqud* burning, combustion

اتقاد *ittiqād* burning, combustion

موقود *mauqūd* kindled, lit, ignited, burning

متوقد *mutawaqqid* burning, flaming, blazing | متوقد الذهن *m. aḏ-ḏihn* fiery, impulsive, having a lively mind

متقد *muttaqid* aflame, burning

مستوقد *mustauqad* hearth, fireplace; ○ bath heater, geyser

وقذ *waqaḏa* يقذ *yaqiḏu* (*waqḏ*) to hit fatally, hit hard, throw down, fell (٥ s.o.)

وقيذ *waqīḏ* and موقوذ *mauqūḏ* fatally ill

وقر *waqara* يقر *yaqiru* (*waqr*) to break, fracture, crack (▲ s.th., esp. a bone); — to be settled, certain, an established fact; to stay, remain | وقر فى نفسه ان to him it was an established fact that ...; وقر فى خلده (*kaladihī*) do.; وقرت الصورة فى نفسه (*ṣūratu*) the picture stood vividly before his mental eye; — *waqura* يوقر *yauquru* (وقار *waqār*, وقارة *waqāra*) to be dignified, sedate, staid, grave **II** to respect, honor, revere, reverence (ه s.o.); to render grave or sedate (ه s.o.) **IV** to load, burden, overload (ه a beast of burden); to oppress (ه s.o.), weigh heavily (ه upon); to be overladen with fruit (tree)

وقر *waqr* pl. وقور *wuqūr* cavity, hollow

وقرة *waqra* cavity, hollow

وقر *wiqr* pl. اوقار *auqār* heavy load, burden

وقار *waqār* gravity, sobriety, dignity, deportment commanding respect; sedateness, dignified bearing

وقور *waqūr* grave, sedate; dignified; venerable, reverend

توقر *tawaqqur* dignified bearing

موقر *muwaqqar* respected, held in respect; venerable, reverend

وقص **waqaṣa** يقص *yaqiṣu* to break s.o.'s neck (ه)

وقظ **waqaẓa** يقظ *yaqiẓu* (*waqẓ*) to beat brutally (ه s.o.) **II** to arouse, incite, inflame, whip up (ه s.th., e.g., passions)

وقع **waqa'a** يقع *yaqa'u* (وقوع *wuqū'*) to fall; to fall down, drop; to tumble; to come to pass, take place, occur; to happen (ل to s.o.), befall (ل s.o.); to get (ف in a situation, also, e.g., in a fix); to get (الى to), arrive (الى at); to come, run (على across), meet (على with); to fall (على to s.o., to s.o.'s lot or share); to alight, settle down (على on; bird); to have sexual intercourse (على with a woman); to be divided (ف into), consist (ف of); to be located, be situated, lie (*geogr.*); — (وقيعة *waqī'a*) to slander, backbite, defame, disparage (ف or ب s.o.); — (*waq'*) to rush, pounce, fall (ب upon s.o.) | وقعوا ف بعضهم they fell to quarreling, they fell out with one another; وقع بايديهم (*bi-aidīhim*) he fell into their hands; وقع تحت حواسه (*hawāssihī*) to enter s.o.'s range of perception, become palpable, tangible for s.o.; وقعت ف حبه (*ḥubbihī*) she fell in love with him; وقعت حرب (*ḥarb*) war broke out; وقع الحق (*ḥaqq*) the law has been determined; وقع الحق عليه he was found guilty; وقع ف الفخ (*fakk*) to walk into the trap, get caught in the snare; وقع فريسته (*farīsatahū*) to fall victim to s.o., become a prey of s.o.; وقع من قلبه ف مكان (*min qalbihī fī makānin*) to take s.th. to heart; to make s.th. one's business, attend to s.th.; وقع القول عليه (*qaul*) he was called upon to speak, he was given the floor; وقع ف نفسه أن it came to his mind, it occured to him to ...; وقع الكلام ف نفسه (*kalām*) the words impressed him, went to his heart, touched him; وقعت ف نفسه (or من) she has made an impression on him, she has bewitched him; وقع ف هواها (*hawāhā*) he fell in love with her; وقع موقعه (*mauqi'ahū*) to stand in place of, stand for; وقع ف غير موقعه (*fī ğairi mauqi'ihī*) to be misplaced, stand in the wrong place, be used in the wrong context (word); وقع الكلام منه موقعا (*kalāmu, mauqi'an*) the words moved or impressed him; وقع الامر منه موقعا حسنا (*mauqi'an ḥasanan*) the matter pleased him very much, was most welcome to him; وقع عنده موقع الرضى (*mauqi'a r-riḍā*) it met his approval; وقع ف النفوس موقعا جليلا to leave a strong, splendid impression; وقع موقع الاستغراب to cause raised eyebrows, cause astonishment **II** to let fall, drop (ه, ه s.o., s.th.); to cause to fall, bring down, throw down, overthrow (ه, ه s.o., s.th.); to perform, carry out, execute (ه s.th.); to enter, record, register (على or ف ه s.th. in or on); to sign (ه s.th.); to inflict (ه على a punishment on s.o.); to play (على on a musical instrument); to sow dissension (بين between, among) | وقع حجزا على (ḥajzan) to seize, confiscate, impound or distrain s.th.; وقعه بالاحرف الاولى (bi-l-aḥrufi l-ūlā) to initial s.th.; وقع نفسه (nafsahū) to give o.s. up; وقع على الوتر الحساس (al-watar al-ḥassās) to touch the sensitive spot **III** to attack (ه s.o.), fight (ه with); to have sexual intercourse (ها with a woman) **IV** to let fall, drop (ه, ه s.o., s.th.); to cause to fall, bring down, throw down, overthrow (ه, ه s.o., s.th.); to plunge (ه في s.o. into s.th., esp. fig.), get, land (ه في s.o. in a situation); to fall (ب upon s.o.), attack, assault (ب s.o.); to score a hit (ب on); to sow the seeds of discord, drive a wedge (بين — وبين between — and); to project (ه s.th.) | اوقع الرعب في قلبه (ar-ruʿba fī qalbihī) to strike terror to s.o.'s heart, frighten or scare s.o.; اوقع عقوبة على to inflict a punishment on; اوقعه في كمين to let s.o. walk into an ambush **V** to expect, anticipate (ه s.th.); to prepare o.s., wait (ه for); to dread (ه s.th.); to be inflicted (على on s.o.; punishment), be passed (على against s.o.; judgment) **X** to expect, anticipate, dread (ه s.th.), feel uneasy, be concerned (ه about), look forward with apprehension (ه to)

وقع *waqʿ* falling, dropping, tumbling; fall, drop, tumble; thump, thud, blow; happening, occurrence, incidence; impression (s.th. makes), effect; impact | وقع اقدام footfall, footsteps; وقع الاقدام ثقيلة heavy footfall; كان له احسن وقع في النفوس (aḥsanu waqʿin) to make the best impression on everyone

وقعة *waqʿa* pl. *waqaʿāt* fall, drop, tumble; thump, thud, blow; shock, jolt; incident, occurrence; encounter, combat, battle; meal, repast

وقاع *waqqāʿ* and وقاعة *waqqāʿa* talebearer, scandalmonger, slanderer

وقوع *wuqūʿ* falling, fall, tumble; setting in, incidence (of an event), occurence, happening

وقيعة *waqīʿa* pl. وقائع *waqāʾiʿ*[2] incident, event, occurrence, happening; encounter, battle; — pl. وقائع happenings, goings on, developments; factual findings, factual evidence, facts (of a legal case); proceedings (of an assembly); facts | دفتر الوقائع *daftar al-w.* minute book; الوقائع المصرية (*miṣrīya*) the Egyptian Official Gazette (the oldest Arab newspaper)

موقع *mauqiʿ* pl. مواقع *mawāqiʿ*[2] place where s.th. drops or falls down; place, site, locality, spot; position (of a ship and *mil.*); scene; situation, location, position; impression; time or date on which s.th. falls | مواقع الاطلال (sites of) ruins; مواقع النظر *m. an-naẓar* field (or range) of vision; موقع متقدم (*mutaqaddim*) advanced position (*mil.*); مواقع النجوم the orbits of the stars; لم يكن يعرف موقع وقته ذاك من الليل (*mauqiʿa waqtihī*) he did not know what time of the night it was at that moment; see also *waqaʿa* (at end of illustrative phrases)

موقعة *mauqaʿa* pl. مواقع *mawāqiʿ*[2] battlefield; fighting, combat, battle

ميقعة *mīqaʿa* device for sharpening or honing; grindstone, whetstone

توقيع *tauqīʿ* dropping; performance, consummation, execution; discharge, undertaking (of an act or action); infliction (of a punishment); entering, recording, registration; (pl. *-āt*) signature | بتوقيع فلان (or تحت توقيع) signed by, from the pen of; مهمل التوقيع (*muhmal*) without signature, unsigned

توقيعي *tauqīʿī* rhythmic(al)

وقاع *wiqāʿ* coition, sexual intercourse

ايقاع *īqāʿ* pl. *-āt* rhythm; projection

ايقاعي *īqāʿī* rhythmic(al)

توقع *tawaqqu'* expectation; anticipation

واقع *wāqi'* falling, dropping, tumbling; occurring, happening; actual, real, factual; material, corporeal, tangible; event, fact, matter of fact; factual findings, factual evidence, facts; located, situated (*geogr.*); transitive (*gram.*); الواقع reality, the real, material world | واقعا *wāqi'an* or في واقع الامر or في الواقع in effect, indeed, as a matter of fact, actually, really, in reality; بواقع *bi-wāqi'i* to the amount of (with foll. figure); غير واقع untrue, unreal; intransitive (*gram.*); الامر الواقع the accomplished fact; واقع الحال factual findings, factual evidence, facts; الواقع أن (*anna*) it is a fact that ..., as a matter of fact ..., actually ...; دون الواقع بكثير (*dūna, bi-kaṯīrin*) far from being true; من واقع هذه السجلات (*sijillāt*) according to the data contained in these registers

واقعة *wāqi'a* incident, occurrence, event; happening, development; fact; accident, mishap; fighting, combat, battle

واقعي *wāqi'ī* actual, real; de facto; realistic; positive; positivistic (*philos.*)

واقعية *wāqi'īya* reality

موقع *muwaqqi'* signing; signer, signatory

موقع *muwaqqa'* entered, recorded, registered; signed

متوقع *mutawaqqa'* expected, anticipated; supposed, presumable, probable, likely | من المتوقع ان it is expected that ...

وقف *waqafa* يقف *yaqifu* (*waqf*, وقوف *wuqūf*) to come to a standstill, come to a stop; to stand still; to place o.s., post o.s., station o.s., take one's stand, step (فوق on s.th.), stand (فوق on, دون in the way of s.th.); to stop (عند or على at; الى at, short of, = to reach, extend to, go as far as); to halt; to pause; to hesitate, waver, have doubts or scruples (في in s.th.); to use the pausal form, pronounce a word without *i'rāb* ending (*gram.*); to rise, get up, stand up, get on one's feet; to plant o.s., station o.s., stand erect, hold o.s. erect; to stand; to stand on end (hair); to withstand, resist, oppose; to take up position (على at); to stand (مع by s.o.), stick (مع to s.o.), side (مع with s.o.), support, back (مع s.o.); with foll. participle: to continue to do s.th., keep doing s.th.; — (*wuqūf*) to occupy o.s. (على with), attend (على to), go in for (على); to read (على s.th.); to apply o.s., devote o.s. (على to); to take an interest, be interested (على in); to inquire, seek information, inform o.s. (على about); to learn, be informed (على of); to understand, comprehend, grasp, learn (على s.th.); to come to know (على s.th.), become acquainted (على with); to know (على s.th.); — (*waqf*) to bring to a standstill, to a stop, arrest, halt, stop (ه, ه s.o., s.th.), put an end (ه to s.th.); to hinder, prevent, hold back (ه, ه or ب s.o., s.th., دون or عن from); to make dependent, conditional (ه على s.th. on), pass. *wuqifa* to depend, be conditional (على on); to apprise, inform, notify (ه على s.o. of), acquaint (ه على s.o. with), let s.o. (ه) know (على about); to tell, advise, instruct (ه على s.o. about), call s.o.'s (ه) attention (على to); to donate, grant, create, institute (ه على s.th. for a pious or charitable purpose), bequeath as a religious endowment or wakf (ه على s.th. to); to make over, bequeath, transfer (ه على s.th. to); to dedicate, consecrate, devote (ه على s.th. to a purpose); to assign, appoint (ه s.th., ل to, to a purpose), designate, set apart (ه s.th., ل for s.th., for a purpose); to apply, devote (نفسه *nafsahū* o.s., ل to s.th., to a task) | قف *qif* halt! (command); stop! (e.g., on a traffic sign); وقف امامه (*amāmahū*) to resist, oppose, stop s.th., put an end to s.th.; وقف الى جانبه to be on s.o.'s side;

وقف الى يساره (yasārihī) to stand at his left; وقف سدا دون (saddan) to rise as an obstacle in the way to s.th., stand in the way to s.th.; لا يقف دونه شيء nothing will stand in his (or its) way, nothing can stop him (or it); وقف حائرا to be in a quandary, at a loss what to do; وقف على الحياد (ḥiyād) to remain neutral, observe strict neutrality; وقف على ساق الجد ل (sāqi l-jidd) to throw o.s. into s.th., identify o.s. with s.th., go to great lengths, make every effort in order to ...; وقف على شفير الهلاك (šafīri l-halāk) to be on the brink of ruin, be about to perish; وقف عند حد ... (ḥaddi) to stop at or short of ..., go as far as ...; وقف في وجه فلان (wajhi f.) to offer s.o. resistance, stand up against s.o.; وقف موقفا من (mauqifan) to assume an attitude, take a stand toward or with regard to; وقف موقفا ملؤه الحزم (mil'uhū l-ḥazm) to assume an attitude of utmost determination; وقف وقفا (waqfan) to assume a posture; وقف وقفة (waqfatan) to stand still; to assume an attitude; وقفه عن العمل ('amal) to suspend s.o. from duty **II** to bring to a standstill, to a stop, arrest, halt, stop, hold up, check, stunt, obstruct, trammel, hamper, slow down (ه, ه s.o., s.th.); to park (ه an automobile); to raise, erect, set up, set upright, place in an upright position (ه s.th.); to arrest, seize (ه s.o.); to hold back, restrain, keep, prevent (ه عن s.o. from); to acquaint (ه على s.o. with); to institute a religious endowment or wakf (على for the benefit of, in favor of) | وقفه عند حده (ḥaddihī) to put s.o. in his proper place **IV** to make (ه s.th.) stand, set up (ه s.th.); to bring to a standstill, to a stop, arrest, halt, stop, hold up, check, stunt, obstruct, trammel, hamper, slow down (ه, ه s.o., s.th.); to stop, suspend, stay, discontinue, interrupt (ه s.th.); to break off, sever (ه relations); to postpone, put off, delay, defer (ه an activity); to arrest, seize, apprehend, capture (ه s.o.); to suppress, ban (ه a newspaper); to acquaint (ه على s.o. with), inform, notify, apprise (ه على s.o. of), let s.o. (ه) know (على about); to tell, advise, instruct (ه على s.o. about), call s.o.'s (ه) attention (على to); to donate, grant, create, institute (ه على s.th. for a pious or charitable purpose), bequeath as a religious endowment or wakf (ه على s.th. to); to bequeath, make over, transfer (ه على s.th. to); to assign, appoint (ه على s.th. to), designate, set apart (ه على s.th. for); to devote (ه على s.th. to a purpose); to spend (ه efforts, على for) | اوقف اهتمامه على (htimāmahū) to concentrate on; اوقف تنفيذ الحكم (tanfīḏa l-ḥukm) to stay the execution of a sentence, grant a reprieve; to stay the execution (of a judgment in a civil case), arrest a judgment (jur.); اوقف حركة المرور (ḥarakata l-murūr) to obstruct traffic; اوقفه عن العمل ('amal) to relieve s.o. of his post, remove s.o. from office **V** to stop, halt, come to a stop, put in a stop, stop over; to come to a standstill; to stand still; to reach a deadlock (fig., of negotiations, and the like); to pause (عن in an activity), suspend, interrupt (عن s.th.); to stop, quit (عن s.th., doing s.th.), discontinue (عن s.th.); to desist, refrain, abstain (عن from); to waver, be undecided, hesitate (في in s.th.); to depend, be dependent, conditional (على on); to rest, be based (على on), be due (على to); to consist (على in) **VI** to fight each other; to meet in battle **X** to ask (ه s.o.) to stop; to bring to a stop, to stop, halt, hold up, detain, check, impede, obstruct, trammel, hamper, slow down (ه, ه s.o., s.th.), stunt, arrest (ه s.th.); to give s.o. (ه) pause; to call on a vessel (ه) to stop; to try to hold or retain; to hold (ه s.th.; fig.) | استوقف نظره (naẓarahū) to catch s.o.'s eye, arouse s.o.'s attention; استوقف الانتباه to arrest the attention

وقف *waqf* stopping, stop; halting, halt; discontinuation, suspension, stay, standstill; pausing, resting; stagnation, dullness, listlessness (of the market); pause (*gram.*); checking, restraining, prevention; interruption, hitch, impediment, obstacle, obstruction; suspension from duty, removal from office, discharge, dismissal; blocking (of an account), stoppage (of salaries); — (pl. اوقاف *auqāf*) religious endowment, wakf, "habous" (*Isl. Law*); endowment (in general), endowment fund; unalienable property | كان وقفا على (*waqfan*) to be completely dependent on; وقفا على restricted to; وقف اهلى (*ahlī*), وقف خاص (*ḵāṣṣ*) or (*ir.*) وقف ذرية *w. ḏurrīya* family endowment, private wakf, estate in mortmain entailed in such a manner that its proceeds will accrue to the members of the donor's family, and, after the death of its last descendant, go to a charitable purpose; وقف خيرى (*ḵairī*), (*tun.*) وقف عام (*ʿāmm*) public endowment, endowment set apart for a charitable or religious purpose, public wakf; ناظر الوقف *nāẓir al-w.* administrator of an endowment, trustee, curator; الاوقاف the wakf system, estates in mortmain; وزارة الاوقاف the ministry entrusted with government supervision of estates in mortmain, wakf ministry; وقف اطلاق النار *w. iṭlāq an-nār* cease-fire (*mil.*); وقف التنفيذ stay of execution (*jur.*); اكل خبز الوقف (*ḵubza l-w.*) to have independent means of subsistence, have a sinecure

وقفى *waqfī* of or pertaining to endowments or the wakf system, wakf- (in compounds)

وقفية *waqfīya* wakf system, endowment system; list of religious endowments, of the estates in mortmain; original charter of a wakf

وقفة *waqfa* (n. vic.) pl. *-āt* standing, stand, stance; position, posture; halt, stop; pause; ○ period, full stop (punctuation mark); station, way station, specif. that on Mount ʿArafāt during the Pilgrimage; attitude, stand, policy; eve of a religious festival, also يوم الوقفة | وقفة العيد الصغير *w. al-ʿīd aṣ-ṣaḡīr* the day preceding *ʿīd al-fiṭr*, the Feast of Breaking the Ramadan Fast on the 1st day of Shawwal; وقفة العيد الكبير (*kabīr*) the day preceding *ʿīd al-aḍḥā*, the Feast of Immolation on the 10th day of Zu'lhijja

وقاف *waqqāf* overseer, supervisor, warden, keeper

وقوف *wuqūf* stopping, stop; halting, halt; standing; stand, stance; (with على:) study, pursuit, occupation (with), search, inquiry (into), investigation, cognizance, knowledge, understanding, comprehension; (*Isl. Law*) abeyance of rights; pl. of واقف *wāqif* standing

موقف *mauqif* pl. مواقف *mawāqif*² stopping place; station; (cab, etc.) stand; (bus, train, etc.) stop; parking lot, parking place; stopover, stop; place, site; scene, scenery; position, posture; situation; attitude; stand, position, opinion | موقف حربى (*ḥarbī*) strategic situation; موقف سياسى (*siyāsī*) political situation; موقف عدائى (*ʿadāʾī*) hostile attitude; مهيمن الموقف *muhaimin al-m.* master of the situation; موقفه من his attitude toward, his stand with regard to

توقيف *tauqīf* raising, setting up, erection; apprehension, detention, seizure, arrest; parking

ايقاف *īqāf* raising, setting up, erection; apprehension, detention, seizure, arrest; stopping, halting, checking, arresting, stunting, trammeling, hampering, impeding, obstruction; stoppage, suspension (e.g., of work); interruption, discontinuation; postponement, deferment, delay, stay, arrest; removal from office, suspension from duty; notice, notification |

ايقاف التنفيذ stay of execution (*jur.*); ايقاف الحكم *ī. al-ḥukm* arrest of judgment (*jur.*); ايقاف الدعوى *ī. ad-daʿwā* stay of proceedings (*jur.*); ايقاف الدفع *ī. ad-dafʿ* delay of payment, respite, moratorium; ايقاف العمل *ī. al-ʿamal* suspension of work

توقف *tawaqquf* halt, cessation, standstill; pause; stopover, stop (also, of an airplane); hesitation, wavering; dependence (على on) | التوقف عن الدفع (*dafʿ*) suspension of payment (*jur.*)

واقف *wāqif* stopping, halting, coming to a stop; standing still, motionless, at rest; standing; upright, erect; acquainted, familiar (على with s.th.); bystander, spectator, onlooker (during a street scene); wakif, donor of a wakf | على الواقف instantly, on the spot, right away, at once; هب واقفا *habba wāqifan* to get on one's feet, get up, stand up, rise

موقوف *mauqūf* arrested, stopped; suspended; interrupted, discontinued; delayed, postponed, deferred; apprehended, detained, arrested; person under arrest, prisoner; suspended from duty, removed from office; entailed through an endowment, established as a wakf; unalienable, in mortmain; donated, granted, instituted; dedicated, devoted; designated, set apart, reserved (على for); dependent, conditional (على on); based, resting (على on); abeyant, in abeyance (rights; *Isl. Law*) | الموقوف عليه beneficiary or usufructuary of a wakf; الاراضى الموقوفة (*arāḍī*) the estates in mortmain; لاعب موقوف disqualified player (*athlet.*); موقوف قيد المحاكمة (*qaida l-muḥākama*) detained pending investigation, committed for trial

متوقف *mutawaqqif* dependent, conditional (على on)

وقل V to climb, mount

[1]**وقواق** *waqwāq* and واقواق *wāqwāq* in the descriptions of Arab geographers, name of two different groups of islands (one east of China, the other located in the Indian Ocean)

[2]**وقوق** *waqwaq* cuckoo

[1]**وقى** *waqā* يقى *yaqī* (*waqy*, وقاية *wiqāya*) to guard, preserve (ه s.th.), take good care (ه of); to safeguard, shield, shelter, preserve, protect, keep (ه ه s.o. from), guard (ه ه s.o. against); to protect, offer or afford protection (ه against); to prevent, obviate (ه a danger) **V** and **VIII** اتقى *ittaqā* to beware, be wary (ه of), guard, be on one's guard, protect o.s., make sure (ه against) | اتقى الله to fear God; اتقى الله فى حق الشىء (*ḥaqqi*) (lit.: to fear God with regard to s.th., i.e.) to spare s.th. or deal mercifully with s.th. for fear of God, show regard for s.th. for God's sake, make s.th. a matter of conscience

وقى *waqy* protection; safeguard

وقاء *waqāʾ*, *wiqāʾ* protection; prevention

وقاية *wiqāya* protection; prevention; precaution; obviation, averting; defense (من against); prophylaxis (*med.*) | الوقاية من الغارات الجوية (*jawwīya*) anti-aircraft defense; معدات الوقاية *muʿaddāt al-w.* safety device

وقاية *waqqāya* protective covering

وقائى *wiqāʾī* preventive | الطب الوقائى (*ṭibb*) preventive medicine, prophylaxis

وقى *waqīy* protecting; protector, preserver, guardian

تقوى *taqwā* godliness, devoutness, piety

تقى *tuqan* godliness, devoutness, piety

تقى *taqīy* pl. اتقياء *atqiyāʾ*[2] godfearing, godly, devout, pious

تقية *taqīya* fear, caution, prudence; (in Shiitic Islam) dissimulation of one's religion (under duress or in the face of threatening damage)

واق *wāqin* preserving, guarding, protecting; preventive, preservative, prophylactic; protective; guardian, protector | واق من الريح (*rīḥ*) protecting from the wind; درع واق (*dir'*) protective armor; صفحة واقية (*ṣafḥa*) flyleaf; dust cover, jacket, wrapper; مظلة واقية (*miẓalla*) parachute; معطف واق (*mi'ṭaf*) raincoat; قناع واق gas mask

واقية *wāqiya* protection, shelter, shield; a preventive, a preservative

متق *muttaqin* godfearing, godly, devout, pious

[2] □ وقية *wiqīya* (*eg.*), *wuqīye* (*syr.*) a weight, in Eg. = $^1/_{12}$ *raṭl* = 37 g; in Aleppo = 320 g, in Beirut = 213.39 g, in Jerusalem = 240 g

وكأ V and VIII اتكأ *ittaka'a* to support one's weight (على on), lean (على against, on); to recline (على in a chair, and the like)

تكأة *tuka'a* staff; support, prop, stay; back (of a chair, etc.); idler, lazybones

توكؤ *tawakku'* resting, leaning, reclining

اتكاء *ittikā'* resting, leaning, reclining

متكأ *muttaka'* pl. *-āt* support, prop, stay; cushion, pad; sofa; couch

وكب *wakaba* يكب *yakibu* (*wakb*, وكوب *wukūb*, وكبان *wakabān*) to walk slowly, proceed or advance slowly III to accompany (ه s.o.), escort (ه s.o., ه s.th.); to convoy, accompany as military escort (ه s.th.)

موكب *maukib* pl. مواكب *mawākib*² parade, pageant; procession; mounted escort, retinue, cortege; triumph | موكب المشاعيل torchlight procession; موكب الجنازة *m. al-janāza* funeral procession

مواكبة *muwākaba* military escort, convoying, convoy duty

وكد II to make fast, fasten (ه s.th.); to corroborate, substantiate (ه s.th.); to confirm, affirm (ه s.th.); to give assurance (ه of), assert (ه s.th.) V to be corroborated, substantiated, asserted, affirmed, confirmed; to ascertain (من a fact), make sure, convince o.s. (من of)

وكد *wakd* wish, desire, intention, aim, goal, end, purpose, object, aspiration, endeavor, effort, attempt

وكيد *wakīd* corroborated, substantiated, confirmed; sure, certain; positive

توكيد *taukīd* pl. *-āt*, تواكيد *tawākīd*² confirmation; affirmation, assurance; assertion; emphasis, stress; (*gram.*) intensifying apposition; pleonasm

موكد *muwakkad* sure, certain, definite

متوكد *mutawakkid* sure, certain, positive, convinced

وكر *wakr* pl. اوكار *aukār*, وكور *wukūr* nest, bird's nest; aerie; habitation, abode, retreat; ○ aircraft hangar | وكر اللصوص den of robbers

وكرة *wakra* pl. وكر *wukar* bird's nest

وكز *wakaza* يكز *yakizu* (*wakz*) to strike with the fist (ه s.o.); to thrust, push, hit; to spur (ه a horse); to pierce, transfix (ه ب s.o. with)

وكس *wakasa* يكس *yakisu* (*waks*) to decline in value, depreciate; to decrease, diminish, reduce, lower (ه the value or price of); pass. *wukisa* to suffer losses (in business) II to decrease, diminish, reduce, lower (ه the value of)

وكس *waks* decline, drop (of value or price); depreciation; loss | باع بالوكس to sell at a loss

وكع *waku'a* يوكع *yauku'u* (وكاعة *wakā'a*) to be hard, strong, sturdy

ميكعة *mīka'a* plowshare

وكف **wakafa** يكف **yakifu** (**wakf**, وكفان **wakafān**) to drip, trickle; to be defective and leak

وكف **wakf** leaking, leak (of a ship)

وكل **wakala** يكل **yakilu** (**wakl** and وكول **wukūl**) to entrust (الى ه s.th. to s.o., with s.th. s.o.), assign (الى ه s.th. to s.o.), commission, charge (ه الى s.o. with), put s.o. (الى) in charge (ه of) **II** to authorize, empower, appoint as representative or agent (ه s.o.); to put s.o. (ه) in charge (ب of), engage as legal counsel (ه an attorney, عن or ب in a matter in dispute); to invest s.o. (ه) with full power, give s.o. power of attorney (فى in); to entrust (ب ه to s.o. s.th.) **III** to be on a confidential basis (ه with s.o.), be in a position of mutual trust (ه with s.o.); to trust (ه s.o.) **IV** to entrust, assign (الى ه s.th., a task, to s.o.) **V** to be appointed as representative or agent, take over or act as (legal) representative; to act as commissioner, as agent, or by proxy (فى in s.th.); to take upon o.s., assume (ب s.th.); to be responsible, answerable, answer, vouch (ب for), guarantee, warrant (ب s.th.); to rely, depend (على on), place one's confidence (على in), trust (على in) | توكل كل الله to trust in God, put o.s. in God's hands **VI** to trust each other; to react with indifference, be noncommital, indifferent **VIII** اتكل **ittakala** to rely, depend (على on), trust (على in)

وكيل **wakīl** pl. وكلاء **wukalā'**[2] authorized representative, attorney in fact, proxy; (business) manager; head clerk; deputy, vice-; agent; trustee; mandatary, defense counsel; attorney, lawyer; (*Syr.*, *mil.*) approx.: technical sergeant | وكيل الاحباس in Tunis, commissioner for estates in mortmain; الوكيل البابوى (*bābawī*) papal legate; وكيل بلوك امين *w. bulūk amīn* (1939 وكيل امين) approx.: quartermaster corporal (*mil.*; *Eg.*); وكيل اونباشى *w. onbāšī* (1939 وكيل محارب *w. muḥārib*) private first class (*Eg.*); وكيل باشجاويش staff sergeant (*Eg.*); وكيل شاويش ,وكيل جاويش (1939 وكيل ضابط مجاهد *w. mujāhid*) sergeant; noncommissioned officer (*Tun.*); company sergeant-major, master sergeant (*Syr.*, *mil.*); وكيل الحق العام *w. al-ḥaqq al-ʿāmm* government commissioner at Tunisian courts (*Tun.*); وكيل قنصل *w. qunṣul* vice-consul; وكيل مدير *w. mudīr* deputy director; وكيل الوزارة undersecretary of state

تكلة **tukala** one who relies on others, who is incapable of attending to his own affairs

وكالة **wakāla** pl. *-āt* representation, deputyship, proxy; full power, power of attorney; management; agency; (*Eg.*) inn, caravansary, resthouse, khan | وكالة الانباء *w. al-anbā'* news agency, wire service; وكالة الاشهار *w. al-išhār* advertising agency

توكيل **taukīl** appointment as representative, agent, deputy, or proxy, delegation of authority; authorization; power of attorney, full power; warrant of attorney

توكل **tawakkul** trust, confidence; trust in God; passivity of living (of the early ascetics and mystics)

تواكل **tawākul** mutual confidence or trust; indifference

اتكال **ittikāl** trust, confidence, reliance

موكل **muwakkil** constituent, principle, mandator

موكل **muwakkal** commissioned, charged (ب with), in charge (ب of), responsible, answerable (ب for)

متوكلى **mutawakkilī**: المملكة المتوكلية اليمنية (*mamlaka*, *yamanīya*) the Yemenite Kingdom (official designation)

موكم **mūkim** offensive, hurting (word)

وكن **wakana** يكن **yakinu** (wakn, وكون **wukūn**) to brood, sit on its eggs (bird); to hatch, incubate (على or ه eggs)

وكن **wakn** pl. وكون **wukūn** bird's nest, aerie

وكنة **wakna, wukna** pl. **wukunāt** nest

وكى **wakā** يكى **yakī** to tie up (ه a waterskin, or the like)

وكاء **wikā'** pl. اوكية **aukiya** thong or string for tying up a waterskin or bag

ولج **walaja** يلج **yaliju** (لجة **lija**, ولوج **wulūj**) to enter (الى or ه s.th., into s.th.), penetrate (الى or ه into) | ولج الباب to go in by the door **IV** to make (ه s.th.) enter (فى s.th. else); to introduce, insert, interpose, intromit, interpolate, thrust (ه فى s.th. into) **V** = **I**; to engage (ه in), take upon o.s. (ه s.th.)

ولوج **wulūj** penetration, entering, entry

وليجة **walīja** intimate friend, confidant; secret depth (of the heart)

ايلاج **īlāj** insertion, intromission, interposition, interpolation, intercalation

مولج **maulij** pl. موالج **mawālij**[2] entrance

موالج see ملح

ولد **walada** يلد **yalidu** (ولادة **wilāda**, لدة **lida**, مولد **maulid**) to bear (ه a child), give birth (ه to); to beget, generate, procreate; to bring forth, produce (ه s.th.) | ولدت منه to have a child by s.o. (woman) **II** to assist in childbirth (ها a woman; of a midwife); to generate, produce (ه من s.th. from); to engender, breed, cause, occasion, (ه s.th.); to bring up, raise (ه a child) **IV** to make (ها a woman) bear children | اولدها طفلا (*tiflan*) he got her with child **V** to be born; to be descended (من from s.o.); to be generated, produced (من from), be brought forth, be engendered, bred, caused, occasioned (من by); to originate, grow, develop, arise, proceed, follow, result (من from) **VI** to propagate, reproduce, multiply by generation **X** to want children; to want the generation (ه من of s.th. from), want to produce (ه من s.th. from)

ولد **walad** pl. اولاد **aulād**, ولد **wuld** descendant, offspring, scion; child; son; boy; young animal, young one; (coll.) progeny, offspring, children | ولد الزناء *w. az-zinā'* illegitimate child, bastard; ولد الملاعنة *w. al-mulā'ana* child whose paternity is contested by لعان *li'ān* (q.v.) (*Isl. Law*)

ولدة **walda** childbirth, birth | ولدت اثنين فى ولدة she gave birth to two at a time

لدة **lida** childbirth, birth; (pl. لدون **lidūn**, لدات **lidāt**) person of the same age, contemporary; coetaneous

ولادة **wilāda** parturition, childbearing, childbirth, birth, confinement, delivery | ولادة معجلة (*mu'ajjala*) premature birth; حديث الولادة newborn; علم الولادة *'ilm al-w.* obstetrics (*med.*)

ولادة **wallāda** frequently producing offspring, bearing many children; fertile, prolific, fruitful

ولود **walūd** frequently producing offspring, bearing many children; fertile, prolific, fruitful; littering, having young

ولودية **wulūdīya** childishness, puerility

وليد **walīd** pl. ولدان **wildān** newborn child, baby; boy, son; young, new; (with foll. genit.) the product of, the result of, occasioned by, engendered by, sprung from | وليد ساعته *w. sā'atihī* conceived on the spur of the moment (idea, plan, etc.)

وليدة **walīda** pl. ولائد **walā'id**[2] newborn girl; girl; product

وليد **wulaid** little child

مولد **maulid** pl. موالد **mawālid**[2] birthplace; birthday; anniversary, birthday of a saint (also *Chr.*) | المولد النبوى (*nabawī*), مولد النبي *m. an-nabīy* the Prophet's birthday; لغة المولد *luġat al-m.* mother tongue, native language

ميلاد *milād* pl. مواليد *mawālīd*² birth; time of birth, nativity; birthday; pl. مواليد age classes, age groups (recruitment, etc.) | عيد الميلاد *ʿīd al-m.* Christmas (*Chr.*); قبل ميلاد السيد المسيح (*sayyid*) or only قبل الميلاد before Christ, B.C.; نقصان المواليد *nuqṣān al-m.* falling birth rate

ميلادى *mīlādī* birthday- (in compounds); relating to the birth of Christ; after Christ, A.D. | سنة ميلادية (*sana*) year of the Christian era

توليد *taulīd* procreation, begetting; generation, producing, production; midwifery, assistance at childbirth, delivery | دار التوليد and مصحة للتوليد (*maṣaḥḥa*) maternity home; فن التوليد *fann at-t.* obstetrics, midwifery; معمل (or محطة) توليد القوة الكهربائية *maʿmal* (*maḥaṭṭat*) *t. al-qūwa al-kahrabāʾiya* electric power station; توليد الهلال "generation of the crescent", the first appearance of the new moon on the first day of the month

تولد *tawallud* generation, production

استيلاد *istīlād* generation, production

والد *wālid* procreator, progenitor; father, parent; الوالدان the parents, father and mother

والدة *wālida* pl. *-āt* mother; parturient woman, woman in childbed

والدى *wālidī* paternal

مولود *maulūd* produced, born, come into the world; birth; birthday; — (pl. مواليد *mawālīd*²) newborn baby, infant; child, son; pl. مواليد creations, novelties, nouveautés | المواليد الثلاثة the three kingdoms of nature

مولد *muwallid* generating, producing, procreative, generative; procreator, progenitor; obstetrician, accoucheur; — (pl. *-āt*) generator (*techn.*) | ○ مولد التيار *m. at-tayyār* or مولد كهربائى (*kahrabāʾī*) generator, dynamo; ○ مولد التيار المتناوب *m. at-t. al-mutanāwib* alternating-current generator, alternator; مولد الحموضة oxygen; مولد الماء hydrogen; مولد ذرى (*ḏarrī*) atomic reactor

مولدة *muwallida* pl. *-āt* midwife

مولد *muwallad* born, begotten, produced, generated; brought up, raised; born and raised among Arabs (but not of pure Arab blood); not truly old Arabic, introduced later into the language, postclassical (esp. of words); half-breed, half-caste, half-blood; (pl. *-āt*) product; pl. المولدون the postclassical (also, recent) Arab authors

ولدنة *waldana* childhood; childish trick, puerility

ولس *walasa* يلس *yalisu* (*wals*) to deceive, cheat, dupe (ه s.o.) **III** to play the hypocrite; to double-cross (ه s.o.); to misrepresent, distort (ب s.th.) **IV** to misrepresent, distort (ب s.th.)

ولس *wals* fraud, deceit, deception; cunning, craft, double-dealing, duplicity

موالسة *muwālasa* fraud, deceit, deception; cunning, craft, double-dealing, duplicity

ولط *walṭ* volt (*el.*)

ولع *waliʿa* يولع *yaulaʿu* (*walaʿ*, ولوع *walūʿ*) to catch fire, burn; to be dead set (ب on), be mad (ب after), be crazy (ب about), be passionately fond (ب of), be madly in love (ب with); to glow with enthusiasm (ب for), be enthusiastic (ب about) **II** to kindle, light (ه s.th.), set fire (ه to); to make (ه s.o.) crave (ب s.th.), inflame s.o.'s (ه) desire (ب for), enamor (ب ه s.o. of) **IV** = **II**; pass. *ūliʿa* to be fond, enamored (ب of s.th.), be very devoted, be given (ب to); to be dead set, be hell-beńt (ب on); to be in love (ب with) V = I

ولع *wala'* passionate love; ardent desire, craving; passion

ولع *wali'* madly in love

ولوع *walū'* greed, craving, eager desire; love

ولاعة *wallā'a* (cigarette) lighter

تولع *tawallu'* passionate love; ardent desire, craving; passion

مولع *mūla'* in love (ب with); dead set, hell-bent (ب on), mad (ب after), crazy (ب about); passionately fond, enamored (ب of s.th.); enthusiastic (ب about), full of enthusiasm (ب for)

ولغ **walağa** يلغ **yalağu** (*walğ*, ولوغ *wulūğ*) to lick, lap (esp., of a dog); to defile (ق s.o.'s honor) | ولغ ق الدم (*dam*) to taste blood, become bloodthirsty

ولكن **wa-lākin**, **wa-lākinna** (the latter with foll. acc. or pers. suffix) but, however, yet

ولم **IV** to give a banquet

ولم *walm, walam* saddle girth, cinch

وليمة *walīma* pl. ولائم *walā'im*[2] banquet

وله **walaha**, يله **yalihu**, **waliha** يوله **yaulahu** (*walah*) to lose one's head, become mad (with love, grief, or the like), be thrown off one's balance, go off the deep end **II** and **IV** to make crazy, throw into utter confusion (ه s.o.), drive (ه s.o.) out of his wits **V** = **I**; to be infatuated (ب with)

وله *walah* distraction, utter confusion, giddiness, hare-brainedness; painful agitation; passionate love, amorous rapture

ولهان *walhān*[2] distracted, confused, bewildered, out of one's wits, giddy, hare-brained; passionately in love

توله *tawalluh* distraction, utter confusion, giddiness, hare-brainedness; infatuation

واله *wālih* distracted, confused, bewildered, out of one's wits, giddy, hare-brained; grief-stricken, deeply afflicted

متوله *mutawallih* distracted, confused, bewildered, out of one's wits, giddy, hare-brained

ولو see و

ولول **walwala** to cry "woe"; to lament, wail, howl, break into loud wails

ولولة *walwala* pl. ولاول *walāwil*[2] wailing, wails

ولى **waliya** يلى **yalī** to be near s.o. or s.th. (ه, ه), be close (ه, ه to), lie next (ه to); to adjoin (ه s.th.), be adjacent (ه to); to follow (ه, ه s.o., s.th.); to border (ه on); — (ولاء *walā'*, ولاية *walāya*) to be a friend (ه of s.o.), be friends (ه with); — (ولاية *walāya, wilāya*) to be in charge (على or ه of s.th.), manage, run, administer, govern, rule (على or ه s.th.), have power, authority, or the command (على or ه over) | ما يلى the following, what follows; كما يلى as follows, like this; فيما يلى in what follows, in the following, in the sequel; ما يلى البدن من الملابس (*badana*) the underwear, the underclothes; غرفة تلى السقف (*ğurfa, saqf*) a chamber under the roof; ولى الحكم (*ḥukma*) to take over the government, come into power **II** to turn (ه ه to or toward s.o. s.th., e.g., the back, the face of s.th.); to turn away (عن or ه from s.th.), avoid, shun (عن or ه s.th.); to turn around, turn back, wheel around; to flee (عن or ه from s.th.); to pass, go by, glide away (days, years); to appoint as manager, director, administrator, governor, or ruler (ه s.o.); to put (ه s.o.) in charge (ه of), make s.o. (ه) the head of (ه); to entrust (ه ه s.o. with, to s.o. s.th.), commission, charge (ه ه

s.o. with), assign (ه ه to s.o. s.th.) | ولاه دبره (*duburahū*) or ولاه ظهره (*ẓahrahū*) to turn one's back on s.o. or s.th.; ولوا عنه الادبار they turned their backs on him, they turned away from him; ولى هاربا (*hāriban*) to take to flight, run away; ولى وجهه (*wajhahū*) to turn, face (ه toward) **III** to be a friend, a helper, a supporter, a patron, a protector; to help, aid, assist (ه s.o.); to do constantly, incessantly (ه s.th.); to continue without interruption (ه s.th., to do s.th.), go about s.th. (ه) successively, systematically; to pursue, practice, cultivate (ه s.th., e.g., arts); to follow immediately (ه s.th.; time), be subsequent (ه to) **IV** to bring close (ه ه to s.o. s.th.); to turn (ه ه toward s.o. one's back, or the like); to commit (ه ه to s.o. the care or responsibility for), entrust, commission, charge (ه ه s.o. with); to do, render (ه ه s.o. a favor); to do (ه ه to s.o. s.th. harmful), bring (ه ه upon s.o. s.th.); to display, evince (ه ه toward s.o. s.th., e.g., indifference) | اولاه ثقته (*tiqatahū*) to have confidence in s.o.; اولاه معروفا to do s.o. a favor **V** to occupy, fill, hold (ه an office), be entrusted (ه with), be in charge (ه of); to take possession, take charge (ه of), take over, take upon o.s., undertake, take in hand (ه an affair), attend (ه to); to take care (ه of), see (ه to s.th.), arrange (ه for s.th.); to assume the responsibility (ه for), seize control (ه of); to take over the government, come into power; to turn away, desist, refrain (عن from), forgo (عن s.th.) | تولى الحكم (*ḥukma*) to be in power, hold supreme power; to seize power; تولاه اليأس (*ya'su*) he was seized (or overcome) by despair **VI** to follow in succession, without interruption; to come continually (على to), arrive constantly (على at); to progress, continue (e.g., an advance, a march) **X** to possess o.s., take possession (على of), seize (على s.th.), make o.s. master of (على); to receive as one's own, take over, capture, confiscate, requisition, occupy (على s.th.); to overpower, overwhelm, overcome (على s.o.); to take prisoner, capture (على s.o.)

ولى *walīy* near, nearby; neighboring, adjacent; close; — (pl. اولياء *auliyā'*[2]) helper, supporter, benefactor, sponsor; friend, close associate; relative; patron, protector; legal guardian, curator, tutor; a man close to God, holy man, saint (in the popular religion of Islam); master; proprietor, possessor, owner | ولى الله the friend of God; ولى الامر *w. al-amr* the responsible manager, the man in charge; ruler; tutor, legal guardian; ولى الدم *w. ad-dam* avenger of blood, executor of a blood feud; ولى السجادة *w. as-sajjāda* title of the leader of a Sufi order in his capacity of inheritor of the founder's prayer rug; ولى العهد *w. al-ʿahd* successor to the throne, heir apparent, crown prince; ولى النعمة *w. an-niʿma* benefactor

ولية *walīya* holy woman, saint; woman, lady

ولاء *walā'* friendship, amity; benevolence, good will; fidelity, fealty, allegiance; devotion, loyalty; clientage (*Isl. Law*) | معاهدة ولاء *muʿāhadat w.* treaty of friendship

ولائى *walā'ī* friendly, amicable, of friendship

ولاية *wilāya* sovereign power, sovereignty; rule, government; — (pl. *-āt*) administrative district headed by a vali, vilayet (formerly, under the Ottoman Empire), province; state | الولايات المتحدة (*muttaḥida*) the United States; ولاية العهد *w. al-ʿahd* succession to the throne; — *walāya* guardianship, curatorship; legal power; friendship | هم على ولاية واحدة they stick together, they assist each other

اولى *aulā* more entitled (ب to); worthier, more deserving; more appropriate, better suited (ب for), more suitable, more adequate (ب to); see also under اول | بالاولى or من باب اولى with greater reason, all the more reason, the more so; هى اولى به منه it is more natural for her than for him, it is for her rather than for him, she is more entitled to it than he is

اولوية *aulawīya* priority; precedence

مولى *maulan* pl. موال *mawālin* master, lord; protector, patron; client; charge; friend, companion, associate; المولى the Lord, God; مولاى *maulāya* and مولانا *maulānā* form of address to a sovereign

مولاة *maulāh* mistress, lady

مولوى *maulawī* pl. *-īya* a dervish of the order of Maula Jalal-ud-din Rumi

مواليا *mawāliyā* see [2]موال *mawwāl*

تولية *tauliya* appointment (as vali, to an executive position, as successor); resale at cost price (*Isl. Law*)

ولاء *wilā'* succession, sequence, series, continuation; ولاء *wilā'an* or على ولاء successively, uninterruptedly

موالاة *muwālāh* friendship; contract of clientage (*Isl. Law*); constancy, incessancy, continuance (of an action)

ايلاء *īlā'* annulment of a marriage after the husband's sworn testimony to have refrained from marital intercourse for a period of at least four months (*Isl. Law*)

تول *tawallin* entrance office, taking over of an office to management, direction, administration, government

توال *tawālin* continuous succession, uninterrupted sequence, continuation | على التوالى continuously, without interruption; successively, consecutively, one after the other, one by one; على توالى الايام (*t. l-ayyām*) in the course of time; بتوالى السنين *bi-t. s-sinīn* with the years, in time, as time goes on

استيلاء *istīlā'* appropriation; seizure, taking possession; capture, conquest

وال *wālin* pl. ولاة *wulāh* leading, managing, executive, administrative; ruler; governor, vali; prefect (administrative officer, *Mor.*) | ولاة الامور the leading personalities, the leaders

موال *muwālin* friend, helper, supporter; client, feudal tenant, vassal, dependent, partisan, follower, adherent

موالية *muwāliya* clientage, clientele, following, adherence

متول *mutawallin* entrusted, commissioned, in charge | متولى الاعمال (*ir.*) chargé d'affaires

متوال *mutawālin* successive, consecutive, uninterrupted, incessant; — (pl. متاولة *matāwila*) member of the Shiite sect of Metualis in Syria

ومأ IV to motion, signal, beckon, make a sign; to point out, indicate (الى s.th.), point (الى to); to make a gesture

ايماء *īmā'* mimic action, gestures, gesticulations | فن الايماء *fann al-ī.* pantomime, dumb show (as an art); ايماء الى *īmā'an ilā* with reference to

ايماءة *īmā'a* pl. *-āt* gesture; nod

مومأ *mūma'*: المومأ اليه the one referred to, the above-mentioned

ومد *wamid* sultry, muggy

ومس *wamasa* يمس *yamisu* (*wams*) to rub off; to smooth, polish (ه ب s.th. with)

مومس *mūmis* and مومسة *mūmisa* pl. *-āt* prostitute

ومض *wamaḍa* يمض *yamiḍu* (*wamḍ*, وميض *wamīḍ*, ومضان *wamaḍān*) to flash IV to glance furtively; to wink (ه at s.o.)

ومضة *wamḍa* (n. vic.) pl. *-āt* blink, blinking; gleam of light; reflection of light

وميض *wamīḍ* blinking, sparkle, twinkle

ومق **wamiqa** يمق *yamiqu* (*wamq*) to love tenderly (ه s.o.)

موماة *maumāh*, موماء *maumā'* pl. موام *mawāmin* desert

ون **wanna** *i* (*wann*) to buzz, hum (bee)

الوندل *al-wandal* the Vandals

ونش (Engl. *winch*) *winš* pl. *-āt*, اوناش *aunāš* winch; crane, derrick | ونش دوار (*dawwār*) derrick crane; ونش عائم floating crane; ونش باليد (*yad*) hand winch

ونى **wanā** ينى *yanī*, **wanīya** يونى *yaunā* (ونى *wany*, *wanan*, *wanīy*, وناء *winā'*) to be or become faint, weak, tired, dispirited, despondent, sapless, effete, lose vigor, flag, languish | لا ينى (with foll. imperf.) not to tire (of doing s.th.); بهمة لا تنى *bi-himmatin lā tanī* with unflagging zeal **II** to be slow, slack, lax, negligent, remiss (فى in some work) **VI** to flag, languish, relax, slacken; to be or become slack, limp, flabby; to hesitate, waver, temporize (فى in), wait (فى with)

ونى *wanan* slackening, relaxation; slackness; weakness, languor, lassitude

وناء *wanā'* slackening, relaxation; slackness; weakness, languor, lassitude

توان *tawānin* tiring, flagging; slowness; flabbiness, limpness; negligence, indifference

وان *wānin* weak, feeble, spent, exhausted | غير وان unremitting, untiring, unflagging

متوان *mutawānin* weak, languid, slack, limp, flabby; negligent, remiss, slow, tardy

وهب **wahaba** يهب *yahabu* (*wahb*) to give, donate (ل or ه ه s.th. to s.o.); to grant, accord (ل or ه ه s.th. to s.o.); to present (ل or ه ه with s.th. s.o.); to endow (ل or ه s.o., ه with) | وهبته من ذات نفسها she gave herself unreservedly to him; هب *hab* suppose that ..., assuming that ...; هبنى فعلت *habnī fa'altu* suppose I had done it; هبنى — هبنى (with foll. acc.) suppose I were — or I were; ولنهب ان (*wal-nahab*) let us suppose that ...

هبة *hiba* pl. *-āt* gift, present, donation, grant | عقد الهبة *'aqd al-h.* deed of gift

وهبة *wahba* tip, gratuity

وهابى *wahhābī* Wahabite; Wahabi

الوهابية *al-wahhābīya* Wahabiism

موهبة *mauhiba* pl. مواهب *mawāhib*[2] gift; talent

ايهاب *ihāb* donation, grant(ing)

واهب *wāhib* giver, donor

موهوب *mauhūb* given, granted; gifted; talented; موهوب له recipient of a gift or grant, donee

وهج **wahaja** يهج *yahiju* (*wahj*, وهجان *wahajān*) to glow, burn, blaze, flame; to be incandescent; to gleam, glitter, glisten **IV** to light, kindle (ه the fire) **V** to glow, burn, blaze, flame; to be incandescent; to gleam, glitter, glisten; to flicker (eyes)

وهج *wahaj* blaze, fire; white heat, incandescence; glare of the sun

وهاج *wahhāj* glowing; white-hot, incandescent; blazing; sparkling, flashing; brilliant, radiant | نور وهاج (*nūr*) glaring light; ذهب وهاج (*ḏahab*) glittering gold

وهيج *wahīj* blaze, fire; white heat, incandescence; glare of the sun

وهجان *wahajān* fire, blaze; glow

وهد **II** to level, even, prepare (ل ه s.th. for)

وهد *wahd* lowland, low ground, depression

وهدة *wahda* pl. وهاد *wihād*, وهد *wuhad* depression, lowland; abyss, precipice, chasm, deep pit, gorge, ravine; lowness, low level (of morals)

اوهد *auhad*[2] low, depressed, low-lying (land)

وهر *wahara* يهر *yahiru* (*wahr*) to involve in difficulties (ه s.o.); to frighten, scare (ه s.o.) II do.; to put out, disconcert, confuse (ه s.o.)

وهرة *wahra* terror, fright, fear, alarm, dismay, consternation

وهران *wahrān*[2] Oran (seaport in NW Algeria)

وهق *wahq*, *wahaq* pl. اوهاق *auhāq* lasso

وهل *wahila* يوهل *yauhalu* (*wahal*) to be frightened, appalled, dismayed; to take alarm II to frighten, scare, intimidate, cow (ه s.o.), strike terror to s.o.'s heart (ه)

وهل *wahal* terror, fright, fear, alarm, dismay, consternation

وهلة *wahla* fright, terror; moment, instant | لاول وهلة *li-awwali wahlatin* at first sight; right away, at once; فى الوهلة الاولى (*ūlā*) at first, first off

وهم *wahama* يهم *yahimu* (*wahm*) to imagine, fancy, think, believe, suppose, presume, guess, surmise; to misconstrue, misinterpret (فى s.th.), have a wrong idea or notion (فى of); — *wahima* يوهم *yauhamu* (*waham*) to make a mistake, be mistaken (فى in, about) II and IV to instill a delusion, a prejudice, a groundless fear (ه in s.o.); to make (ه s.o.) believe (أن that), make as if V to have a presentiment (ه of), suspect, presume, imagine (ه the existence of), be under the delusion (ه of); to think, believe (ه ه s.th. to be s.th. else), regard (ه ه s.th. as), take (ه ه s.th. for) VIII اتهم *ittahama* to suspect (ه s.o.); to question, doubt (ه a fact), have doubts (ه about); to charge (ه ب s.o. with), impute (ه ب to s.o. s.th.), suspect, accuse (ه ب s.o. of), indict (ه ب s.o. for)

تهمة *tuhma* accusation, charge; suspicion; insinuation

وهم *wahm* pl. اوهام *auhām* delusive imagination, erroneous impression, fancy, delusion; belief, guess, surmise, conjecture; imagination; bias, prejudice; error; self-deception, self-delusion; illusion; suspicion, misgiving, doubt; foreboding, evil presentiment

وهمى *wahmī* thought, believed, imagined, fancied; imaginary; seeming, apparent; presumed, supposed, hypothetical; delusive | امراض نفسية ووهمية (*nafsīya, wahmīya*) emotional disturbances, psychic disorders

وهمية *wahmīya* chimera, phantom, delusion; guess, surmise, conjecture, supposition, belief; imaginative power, imagination

ايهام *īhām* pl. *-āt* deception, deceit, fraud, imposition; misleading, delusion; suggestion | رفع الايهام *raf' al-ī.* rectification, correction

توهم *tawahhum* suspicion; imaginative power; imagination

اتهام *ittihām* suspecting; accusation, charge; indictment | دائرة الاتهام the prosecuting authority, the prosecution; قرار الاتهام *qarār al-itt.* information (*jur.*); ورقة الاتهام *waraqat al-itt.* bill of indictment

اتهامية *ittihāmīya* (*tun.*) indictment | هيئة الاتهامية *hai'at al-itt.* the prosecuting authority, the prosecution

واهمة *wāhima* phantasy, imagination, imaginative power

موهوم *mauhūm* fancied, imagined, imaginary; fantastic

متهم *muttahim* accuser; indictor; prosecutor

متهم *muttaham* suspected, suspicious; accused, charged; indicted; defendant | متهم المنظر *m. al manẓar* suspicious-looking

وهن *wahana, wahina* يهن *yahinu, wahuna* يوهن *yauhunu* (*wahn, wahan*) to be weak, feeble, lack the strength (فى for), be incapable (فى of); to grow feeble, languish, flag; to lose vigor or courage | لا يهن untiring, unflagging, inexhaustible **II** to weaken, enfeeble (ه s.o.), sap the strength (ه of s.o.); to discourage, dishearten, wear down, unnerve (ه s.o.); to deem or declare (ه s.th.) weak **IV** to weaken (ه s.o.); to discourage (ه s.o.)

وهن *wahn* weak, feeble

وهن *wahn, wahan* weakness, feebleness, saplessness

وهين *wahīn* foreman, overseer

موهن *mauhin* deep of the night

واهن *wāhin* pl. وهن *wuhun* weak, feeble; weakened, debilitated; enervated, unnerved; sapless, effete, spent, dispirited, despondent

[1] وهى *wahā* يهى *yahī* (*wahy*), *wahiya* (*wahan*) to be weak, feeble, frail, fragile **IV** to weaken, sap (ه, من s.th.)

واه *wāhin* pl. وهاة *wuhāh* weak, feeble; thin; frail, fragile, brittle, friable; flimsy; unsubstantial, inessential, insignificant, trivial; untenable, unfounded, baseless, groundless (excuse, argument)

[2] واه, واها look up alphabetically

وى *wai* woe! shame!

ويبة *waiba* pl. *-āt* whiba, a dry measure (*Eg.* = 33 l)

[1] ويح *waiḥa* (with foll. genit. or pers. suffix) alas ...! woe unto ...! (expressing regret, disapproval); ويحك *waiḥaka* woe unto you! ويحا ل *waiḥan li* woe to ...!

[2] واحة *wāḥa* pl. *-āt* oasis

ويركو (Turk. *vergi*) *wērkō* tribute formerly paid by Egypt to the Sultan; excise tax; (*Pal.*) real-estate tax

ويسكى *wiskī* whiskey

[1] ويك *waika* (= *wailaka*) woe unto you!

[2] ويكة (*eg.*) *wēka* = باميا *bāmiyā* okra, gumbo (Abelmoschus esculentus; *bot.*)

ويل *wail* affliction, distress, woe; (with ل or ويل *waila* with pers. suffix) woe! ويل لك *wailun laka* or ويلك *wailaka* woe unto you!

ويلة *waila* pl. *-āt* calamity, disaster, distress, affliction, woe, misfortune, adversity

ى

يا *yā* (vocative and exclamatory particle) O, oh | يا حسرتى (*ḥasratī*) oh, my misfortune! يا سلام (*salām*) good Lord! good heavens! oh dear! يا طالما (*ṭālamā*) how often ...; how many times ...! يا للتعس ويا للشقاء *yā la-t-ta'si wa-yā la-š-šaqā'* oh, what a calamity! يا له من رجل (*rajulin*) oh, what a man! يا ما how much! how many! how often! how many times! ... يا لله من (*li-llāhi*) what a calamity is ...! how unfortunate is ...! رأى see يا ترى

ياء *yā'* name of the letter ى

اليابان *al-yābān* Japan

يابانى *yābānī* Japanese; (pl. *-ūn*) a Japanese

ياردة *yarda* pl. *-āt* yard (measure of length)

يازرجة *yāzirja* astrology

يازرجى *yāzirjī* pl. *-īya* astrologer

يئس *ya'isa a i* (يأس *ya's*, يآسة *ya'āsa*) to renounce, forgo (من s.th.); to give up all hope (من of) IV to make (ه s.o.) renounce or forgo; to deprive of hope (ه s.o.) X = I

يأس *ya's* renunciation, resignation; hopelessness, desperation | سن اليأس *sinn al-y.* the climacteric

يؤوس *ya'ūs* in despair, despairing; hopeless, desperate

يائس *yā'is* hopeless, desperate (person)

ميؤوس *mai'ūs*: ميؤوس منه lost, desperate (cause)

مستيئس *mustai'is* hopeless, desperate (person)

ياسمين *yāsamīn* jasmine (*bot.*)

ياسنت *yāsint* hyacinth (*bot.*)

ياطاش *yāṭāš*: خدمة بالياطاش *kidma bi-l-y.* (*tun.*) piecework, jobwork

يافا *yāfā* Jaffa (seaport in SW Palestine)

يافطة *yafṭa*, *yāfiṭa* sign, signboard, plaque, name plate, doorplate

ياقة *yāqa* pl. *-āt* collar

ياقوت *yāqūt* (coll.; n. un. ة) pl. يواقيت *yawāqīt*[2] hyacinth (*bot.*); hyacinth, sapphire | ياقوت احمر (*aḥmar*) ruby; ياقوت اخضر (*akḍar*) green corundum; ياقوت جمرى (*jamrī*) carbuncle

ياميش *yāmīš* dried fruits

يانسون *yānisūn* anise, aniseed

ياور *yāwir* pl. *-īya* adjutant, aide-de-camp

ياى *yāy* pl. *-āt* spring, spiral spring

يباب *yabāb* devastated, waste

يبس *yabisa a* (*yabs*, *yubs*) to be or become dry, to dry II and IV to make dry, to dry (ه s.th.)

يبس *yabs*, *yubs*, *yabas* dryness

يبس *yabs*, *yabis* dried, dried out, desiccated, arid; اليبس *al-yabs* the dry land, land, terra firma

يبوسة *yubūsa* dryness (also fig., e.g., of writing or speech style)

يابس *yābis* dry, dried out, desiccated, arid; rigid, hard, firm, compact; اليابسة *al-yābisa* land, terra firma

يتم *yatama i*, *yatuma u* and *yatima a* to be or become an orphan, be bereaved of one's parents IV to orphan, deprive of his parents (ه s.o.) V = I

يتم *yatm*, *yutm*, *yatam* orphanhood

يتيم *yatīm* pl. ايتام *aitām*, يتامى *yatāmā* orphan; unique of its kind, unequaled, unmatched, incomparable; — *yatīm* f. ة single, sole, one only, isolated | ملجأ الايتام *malja' al-a.* and دار الايتام orphanage

ميتم *maitam* pl. مياتم *mayātim*[2] orphanage

ميتم *muyattam* orphaned, parentless; orphan

يثرب *yaṯrib*[2] original name of Medina

يحبور see حبر

ميحار *miḥār* mace, scepter; crosier; bat, mallet

يحمور *yaḥmūr* see حمر

يحيى *yaḥyā* John

يخت *yakt* pl. يخوت *yukūt* yacht

يخضور see خضر

يخنة *yakna* and يخنى *yaknī* a kind of ragout

يد *yad* f., pl. ايد *aidin*, اياد *ayādin* hand; foreleg; handle; power, control, influence, authority; assistance, help, aid; (*Isl. Law*) (personal) possession, actual control; benefit; favor | 1. With prepositions: يدا بيد *yadan bi-yadin* personal(ly), from hand to hand; ... بين يدى (*yadai*) in front of; بين يديه in front of him; in his presence; in his power; بايدينا *bi-aidīnā* or بين ايدينا at our disposal; الكلام بين ايديكم (*kalāmu*) you have the floor, you may speak; ما بين ايدينا من what ... are before us or present themselves to us; تحت اليد on hand, handy, available; تحت يده under his authority, in his power; على يد pl. على ايدى (with foll. genit.) at the hand(s) of; على يده or عن يده with his help, through his good offices; على ايدى الناس with the help of other people; at the hands of other people; فى اليد in hand, on hand, available; — 2. Construct forms: يد الجوزاء *y. al-jauzā'* a bright star in Orion; لا افعله يد الدهر (*yada d-dahr*) I shall never do it; يد المظلة *y. al-miẓalla* umbrella handle; يد النكاح conjugal authority (*Isl. Law*); ذو اليد powerful, influential; holder of actual control, possessor (*Isl. Law*); ساعة اليد wrist watch; سبط اليدين *sabiṭ al-y.* liberal, openhanded, generous; شنطة اليد *šanṭat al-y.* handbag; شغل اليد *šuġl al-y.* or عمل اليد *'amal al-y.* manual work; handwork; صفاد اليد handcuff; صفر اليدين *ṣifr al-y.* empty-handed; عربة اليد *'arabat al-y.* handcart; قنبلة اليد *qunbulat al-y.* hand grenade; — 3. Other phrases: يد بيضاء (*baiḍā'*) pl. اياد بيضاء benefit, favor; skill, competence, capability, qualification, achievement; له يد بيضاء فى to be skilled, versed, experienced in; to have the upper hand in; يد مبطلة (*mubṭila*) unrightful possession (*Isl. Law*); يد محقة (*muḥiqqa*) rightful possession (*Isl. Law*); بقى مكتوف الايدى امام (*baqiya*) to stand helpless before ...; دق يدا بيد (*daqqa*) to clap one's hands; ذهبوا ايدى (or ايادى) سبا *ḏahabū aidiya* (*ayādiya*) *sabā* to be scattered in all directions; اسدى اليه يدا (*asdā*) to do s.o. a favor; سقط فى يده (*suqiṭa*) to stand aghast, be embarrassed, be bewildered; اسقط فى يده (*usqiṭa*) do.; شد يده على (*šadda yadahū*) to cling to s.th.; مصنوع باليد or مشغول باليد handmade; طلب يد المرأة (*yada l-mar'a*) to propose to a woman, ask her hand in marriage; اعطاه شيئا عن ظهر يد *a'ṭāhu 'an ẓahri yadin* to give s.o. s.th. for nothing, give s.o. s.th. as a present; اليد العاملة labor force, labor; الايدى العاملة man power, labor, workmen, hands; قدمه باليد (*qaddamahū*) to hand s.th. over personally, deliver s.th. in person; له عندى يد I am obliged to him for a favor; له يد فى he has a hand in ...; له اليد الطولى فى (*ṭūlā*) to be powerful in, have decisive influence on; له عند الناس يد he has great influence on other people, he can accomplish a great deal with other people; ما لى بذلك يدان that is not in my power; مد يد المساعدة (المعونة or العون) *madda yada l-musā'ada* (*l-ma'ūna, l'-aun*) to extend one's help, lend a helping hand; هم يد واحدة على (*'alayya*) they are in league against me; وضع يده على (*yadahū*) to take possession of; يده قصيرة he is incapable, his powers are limited

يدوى *yadawī* manual; hand- (in compounds) | شغل يدوى (*šuġl*) or عمل يدوى (*'amal*) manual work; handwork; صناعة يدوية handicraft; طراز يدوى hand-operated model (of an apparatus); العملة اليدويون (*'amala*) the manual workers, labor

يربوع *yarbū'* pl. يرابيع *yarābī'*[2] jerboa (*zool.*)

ياردة look up alphabetically

يرع *yari'a a* (*yara'*) to be a coward, be chickenhearted

يراع *yarā'* cowardly; — (coll.; n. un. ة) glowworm, firefly; cane, reed; reed pen

يرقان *yaraqān* a plant disease, mildew; jaundice; (coll.; n. un. ة) larvae (*zool.*) | يرقان الضفادع tadpoles

ميروق *mairūq* affected by mildew, mildewy; jaundiced

اليرموك *al-yarmūk* Yarmuk river (in NW Jordan)

يزيدى *yazīdī* Yezidi, belonging to the Yezidi sect

اليزيدية *al-yazīdīya* the religion of the Yezidis; the Yezidis or Devil Worshipers (of Kurdistan)

يزرجه *yazarja* astrology

يزكى *yazakī* pl. يزك *yazak* guard, sentry

يازول *yāzūl* a variety of wild garlic (Allium roseum L., *bot.*)

يسر *yasira a* (*yasar*) to be or become easy; — *yasura u* (*yusr*) to be small, little, insignificant; to be or become easy **II** to level, smoothen, pave, prepare (على ه for s.o. s.th.); to ease, make easy, facilitate (على ه for s.o. s.th.) | يسر السبيل امامه ل to pave the way for s.o. to ..., enable s.o. to (do s.th.) **III** to be lenient, indulgent, obliging, complaisant (ه with s.o.), humor (ه s.o.) **IV** to live in easy circumstances; to be or become rich; to be lucky, fortunate; to have an easy confinement (woman) **V** to become easy; to be made easy, be facilitated; to succeed, turn out successful; to thrive, prosper; to be made possible, be possible (ل for s.o.) **X** to be easy; to succeed, be successful

يسر *yusr* ease, easiness, facility; easy, pleasant circumstances; prosperity, affluence, wealth, abundance, luxury

يسرة *yasra* left side

يسار *yasār* ease, easiness, facility; comfort; prosperity, affluence, wealth, abundance, luxury; left hand; left side | يسارا or عن اليسار to (at, on) the left

يسارى *yasārī* leftist, left-wing (*pol.*)

يسرى *yusrā* pl. يسريات *yusrayāt* left side; اليسرى the left hand

يسير *yasīr* easy (على for); small, little, slight, insignificant, (of time) short; plain, homely; simple, uncomplicated

ايسر *aisar*[2] easier; smaller, lesser, slighter, more insignificant; more prosperous, wealthier; left; left-handed; left-sided

ميسر *maisir* an ancient Arabian game of chance (forbidden by the Koran) played with arrows without heads and feathering, for stakes of slaughtered and quartered camels

ميسرة *maisara* pl. مياسر *mayāsir*[2] left side; left wing (of an army)

ميسرة *maisara*, *maisura*, *maisira* ease, comfort; prosperity, affluence, wealth, abundance, luxury

تيسير *taisīr* facilitation

ميسور *maisūr* pl. مياسير *mayāsīr*[2] easily done, easily accomplished, within easy reach, easy to carry out, feasible without difficulty; easy; successful, fortunate, lucky; prosperous, well-to-do, in easy circumstances

ميسر *muyassar* facilitated, made easy, within easy reach; successful, fortunate, lucky; prosperous, well-to-do, wealthy, rich

موسر *mūsir* pl. *-ūn*, مياسير *mayāsīr*[2] prosperous, well-to-do, wealthy, rich

متيسر *mutayassir* facilitated, made easy; easy; within easy reach; on hand, available; taking a smooth and successful course, going smoothly; successful, fortunate, prosperous, well-to-do | متيسر الحال well off, in easy circumstances

يسقجى *yasaqjī* kavass, consular guard, armed attendant

يسمين **yasmīn** jasmine

يسوع **yasū'**[2] Jesus

يسوعى **yasū'ī** Jesuitic(al); (pl. *-ūn*) Jesuit

يشب **yašb** jasper

يشم **yašm** jade

يشمق **yašmaq** and يشمك **yašmak** (Turk. *yaşmak*) face veil worn by women

يصب **yaṣb** and يصف **yaṣf** jasper

ياطاش look up alphabetically

يعبوب **ya'būb** see عب

يعسوب **ya'sūb** see عسب

يعقوب **ya'qūb**[2] Jacob, James; see also عقب

يعقوبى **ya'qūbī** pl. يعاقبة **ya'āqiba** Jacobite; Jacobitic (*Chr.*)

يافوخ **yāfūḵ** pl. يوافيخ **yawāfīḵ**[2] vertex, crown of the head

يفطة **yafṭa** (= يافطة) sign, signboard, plaque, name plate, doorplate

يفع **yafa'a** *a* (*yaf'*) to reach adolescence; to be at the age of puberty **IV** and **V** do.

يفع **yaf'** adolescence; puberty

يفع **yafa'** hill, range, highland; — (pl. ايفاع **aifā'**) boy at the age of puberty, adolescent, youth, teen-ager, juvenile

يفاع **yafā'** hill

يافع **yāfi'** adolescent, grown-up; boy at the age of puberty, adolescent, youth, teen-ager, juvenile

ياقوت look up alphabetically

يقطين see قطن

يقظ **yaqiẓa** *a* (*yaqaẓ*) and **yaquẓa** *u* (يقاظة *yaqāẓa*) to be awake; to wake; to be on one's guard, be wary, watchful, alert, vigilant **II** and **IV** to wake up (ه s.o.); to awaken, arouse, stir up, provoke (ه s.th.); to warn, alert, put on his guard (ه s.o.) **V** to be awake; to be vigilant, watchful, alert, on one's guard **X** to wake up, awaken, be awakened, be roused from sleep (على by); to have o.s. awakened, ask to be wakened; to be awake; to be watchful, vigilant, alert

يقظ **yaquẓ, yaqiẓ** pl. ايقاظ **aiqāẓ** awake; watchful, vigilant, alert, wary, cautious

يقظة **yaqẓa, yaqaẓa** waking, wakefulness; sleeplessness, insomnia; watchfulness, vigilance; wariness, caution; alertness, keenness of the mind

يقظان **yaqẓān**[2], f. يقظى **yaqẓā**, pl. يقاظى **yaqāẓā** awake; attentive, alert; wary, cautious; watchful, vigilant | ابو اليقظان rooster, cock

ايقاظ **īqāẓ** awaking, reveille

تيقظ **tayaqquẓ** wakefulness; watchfulness, vigilance, alertness, wariness, caution

متيقظ **mutayaqqiẓ** awake; watchful, vigilant, wary, cautious; alert, attentive

مستيقظ **mustaiqiẓ** awake

يقن **yaqina** *a* (*yaqn, yaqan*) to be sure, certain; to know for certain (ب or ه s.th.), be sure, be certain, be convinced (ب or ه of) **IV**, **V** and **X** to ascertain (ب or ه s.th.), make sure (ب or ه of s.th.); to know for certain (ب or ه s.th.), be sure, be certain, be convinced (ب or ه of)

يقن **yaqn, yaqan** certainty, certitude

يقن **yaqan, yaqun, yaqin** and يقنة **yaqana** credulous, ingenuous, unsuspecting

يقين **yaqīn** certainty, certitude (ب about), conviction (ب of) | يقينا certainly, surely, positively; انا على يقين من ان or انا على يقين ان I am convinced, I am positive, I am certain that ...; كونوا على يقين you can be sure; حق اليقين *ḥaqq al-y.* absolute certainty

يقينى *yaqīnī* definitely laid down, positive, absolute, indisputable; يقينيات *yaqīnīyāt* established truths, axioms

ميقان *mīqān* credulous

موقن *mūqin* convinced (ب of); certain, sure (ب of)

متيقن *mutayaqqin* convinced, positive, sure, certain

اليكون see كون

يمّ **II** to betake o.s., repair, resort, go, turn, wend one's way (ه or صوب *ṣauba*, نحو *naḥwa* or شطر *šaṭra* to or toward a place), set out, head, be headed (ه, صوب, نحو, شطر for); to direct, turn (ه s.th.) | يمم فى فم البركان (*fami l-burkān*) to venture into the lion's den; يمم وجهه شطر (*wajhahū šaṭra*) to turn or face toward **V** to betake o.s., repair, resort, turn (ه to), make, head (ه for); to aim (ه at), intend (ه s.th.)

يمّ *yamm* pl. يموم *yumūm* open sea; (*syr.*) side | من يمى from my side, on my part

يمام *yamām* (coll.; n. un. ة) pl. *-āt*, يمائم *yamā'im*² pigeon, dove

يمن *yamana u*, *yamina a*, *yamuna u* (*yumn*, ميمنة *maimana*) to be lucky, fortunate **II** to go to the right **V** to see a good omen (ب in) **X** do.

يمن *yumn* good luck, good fortune, prosperity, success

يمن *yaman* and يمنة *yamna* right side or hand; يمنا to (at, on) the right; يمنة *yamnatan* do. | شاما ويمنا to the north and south; يمنة ويسرة (*yasratan*) to the right and left

اليمن *al-yaman* Yemen

يمنى *yamanī* from Yemen, Yemenite

يمين *yamīn* f., pl. ايمان *aimān* right side; right hand | يمينا or عن اليمين to (at, on) the right; يمينا وشمالا to the right and left; ما ملكت (تملك) يمينه *mā malakat* (*tamliku*) *yamīnuhū* his possessions

يمين *yamīn* f., pl. ايمن *aimun*, ايمان *aimān* oath | يمين الامانة *y. al-amāna* oath of allegiance; يمين الصبر *y. aṣ-ṣabr* perjury; يمين قانونية (*qānūnīya*) oath of office, official oath; يمين كاذبة perjury; يمين الولاء والاخلاص *y. al-walā' wa-l-iḵlāṣ* oath of allegiance; ايمن الله *aimunu llāhi* and ايم الله *aimu llāhi* I swear by God!

يمينى *yamīnī* of or pertaining to the right side, right-hand, right; ○ اليمينيون the right-wing parties

يمنى *yumnā* pl. يمنيات *yumnayāt* right hand; right side

ايمن *aiman*², f. يمنى *yumnā* right-hand, right, on the right; lucky

ميمنة *maimana* pl. ميامن *mayāmin*² right side; right wing (of an army)

تيمن *tayammun* auspiciousness, good augury, good omen

ميمون *maimūn* pl. ميامين *mayāmīn*² fortunate, lucky; blessed; monkey | ميمون الطائر favorable, auspicious; على الطائر الميمون happy journey! Godspeed!

ميمن *muyamman* lucky, auspicious

ينايرِ *yanāyir*², ينائر *yanā'ir*² January

ينبوع *yanbū'* see نبع

ينسون *yansūn* (= يانسون) anise, aniseed

ينع *yana'a a i* (*yan'*, *yun'*, ينوع *yunū'*) to become ripe, ripen, mellow **IV** do.

ينيع *yanī'* ripe, mellow

ايناع *īnā'* ripening, mellowing

يانع *yāni'* pl. ينع *yan'* ripe, mellow

اليهود *al-yahūd* the Jews, Jewry

يهودى *yahūdī* Jewish; Jew

يهودية *yahūdīya* Judaism

يوبيل *yūbīl* jubilee

يوحنا *yūḥannā* John | يوحنا الصابغ John the Baptist

يود *yūd* iodine

ياور look up alphabetically

يورانيوم *yurāniyum* uranium

يوزباشى *yuzbāšī* pl. *-īya* captain, battery commander; (as a naval rank) lieutenant (formerly, *Eg.*)

يوسف *yūsuf*[2] Joseph; (*eg.*, *syr.*) يوسف افندى *y. afandī* (coll.) tangerines

يوسفى *yūsufī* (*eg.*) tangerines

يوطنة (from Fr. *lieutenant; tun.*) *yūṭana* lieutenant

يوغسلافيا *yūgoslāviyā* Yugoslavia

يوغسلافى *yūgoslāvī* Yugoslavian

ياقة look up alphabetically

يوليو *yūliyō* and يوليه *yūliya* July

يوم III to hire by the day (ه s.o.)

يوم *yaum* pl. ايام *ayyām* day; pl. also: age, era, time | اليوم *al-yauma* today; يوم *yauma* on the day when ...; ايام *ayyāma* in the days of, during; اياما *ayyāman* for a few days; ايامه *ayyāmuhū* his lifetime, his life; يومها *yaumahā* then, at that time, that day; يوما or يوما ما sometime, some day, one of these days; ذات يوم *ḏāta yaumin* one day, once; يوما يوما or يوما فيوما or يوما بعد يوم or يوما عن يوم day by day, day after day, from day to day; بعد اليوم from today on, starting today; فى يومنا هذا nowadays, these days; فى يوم وليلة (*laila*) overnight, from one day to the other; كل يوم *kulla yaumin* daily, every day; من يوم الى يوم or من يوم ليوم from one day to the other, from day to day; من يومه from that time on, henceforth; right away; منذ اليوم from now on, as of now, henceforth; من ايام a few days ago; for the past few days; بعد ذلك بايام a few days after that; — يوم الاحد *y. al-aḥad* Sunday; يوم الاثنين *y. al-iṯnain* Monday; يوم الثلاثاء *y. aṯ-ṯalāṯā'* Tuesday; يوم الاربعاء *y. al-arbi'ā'* Wednesday; يوم الخميس *y. al-ḵamīs* Thursday; يوم الجمعة *y. al-jum'a* Friday; يوم السبت *y. as-sabt* Saturday; — يوم اسود black day, unlucky day; يوم الاشتغال workday; يوم ايوم (*aiwam*) a bad day; يوم الدين *y. ad-dīn* the Day of Judgment; يوم رأس السنة *y. ra's as-sana* New Year's Day; يوم عطلة *y. 'uṭla* day off, free day, holiday; ابن اليوم *ibn al-y.* man of today, modern man; ابن يومه of one day, short-lived, passing, ephemeral; ابن الايام a man of the world, a sophisticated man; على توالى الايام (*tawālī l-a.*) in the course of time, in time

يومئذ *yauma'iḏin* (on) that day, then, at that time

يومذاك *yaumaḏāka* (on) that day, then

يومى *yaumī* daily; by the day; يوميا daily, every day; يوميات everyday events; everyday chronicle; daily news | جريدة يومية daily newspaper

يومية *yaumīya* daily wages, a day's wages; daily ration; a day's work, daily task; diary, journal; daybook; calendar

مياومة *muyāwama* work by the day, day labor; *muyāwamatan* daily, by the day, per day, per diem | عامل مياومة day laborer, hired man

اليونان *al-yūnān* the Greeks; Greece

يونانى *yūnānī* Greek; (pl. *-ūn*) a Greek

يونانية *yūnānīya* Grecism; Greek language

يونس *yūnus*[2] Jonah

اليونسكو *al-yūneskō*, هيئة اليونسكو *hai'at al-y.* UNESCO, the United Nations Educational, Scientific and Cultural Organization

يونوسفير *yonosfēr* ionosphere (*radio*)

يونيو *yūniyō* and يونيه *yūniya* June

PRINTED IN INDIA